CHALLENGE AND EXTEND provides suggestions for additional research, writing assignments, and projects that allow students to further explore section content.

RETEACH offers you suggestions for presenting section material in different ways to help students having difficulty.

ASSESS alerts you to the standard assessment materials available for each lesson.

REVIEW offers strategies to help students prepare for assessment.

ANSWERS to all of the questions in the *Pupil's Edition* are provided at point-of-use.

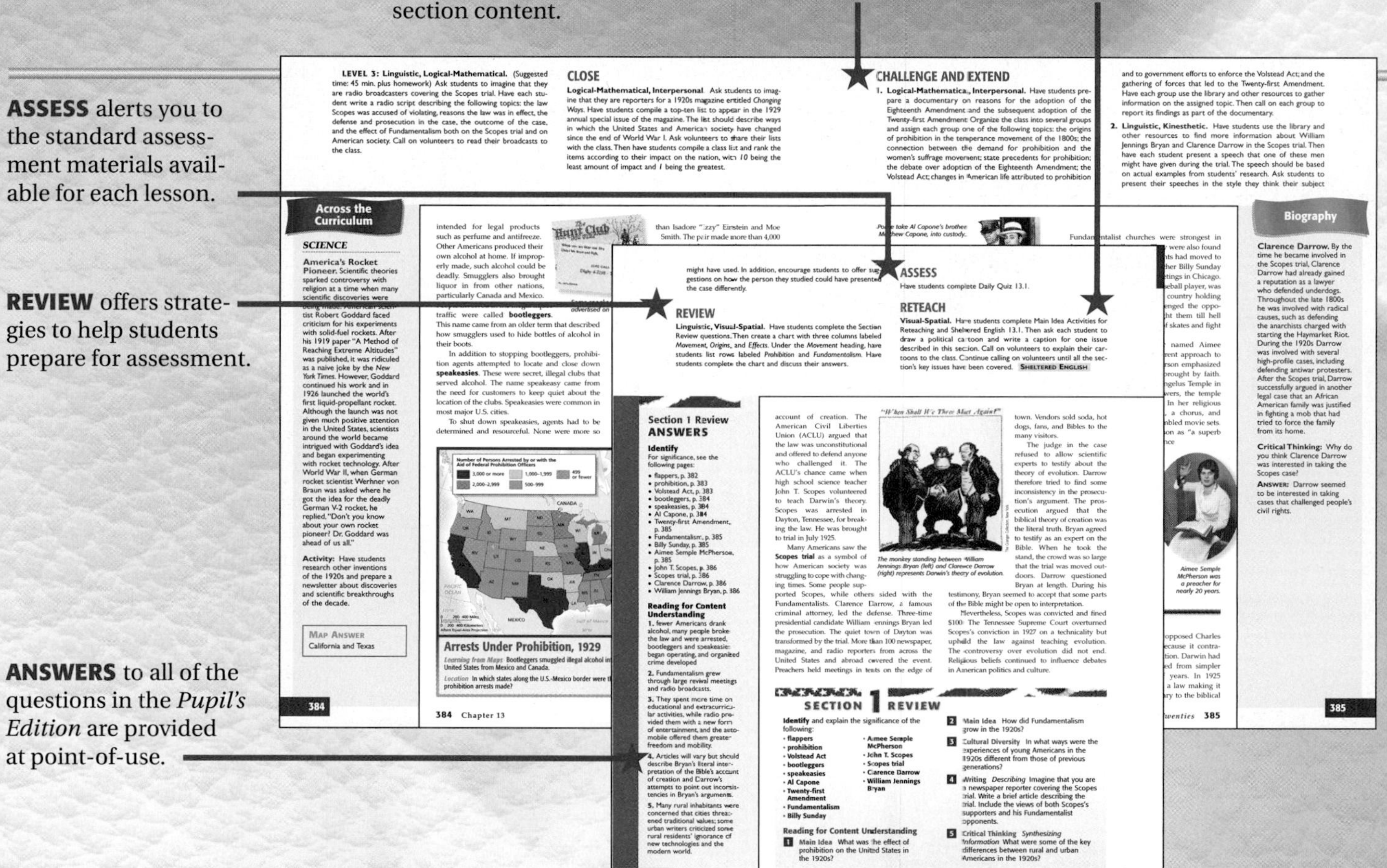

Teaching Resources CD–ROM

No need to lug home dozens of teaching resource booklets to plan your lessons. Planning and managing lessons has never been easier than with the *Teaching Resources CD–ROM*. This convenient, all-in-one planning tool includes all the teaching resources for ***Call to Freedom,*** as well as valuable planning and assessment tools.

EDITABLE LESSON PLANS

With the *Teaching Resources CD–ROM*, you can take the lesson plans designed for ***Call to Freedom*** and tailor them to your personal preferences and your classroom's specific needs. They're easy to edit in several word-processing formats.

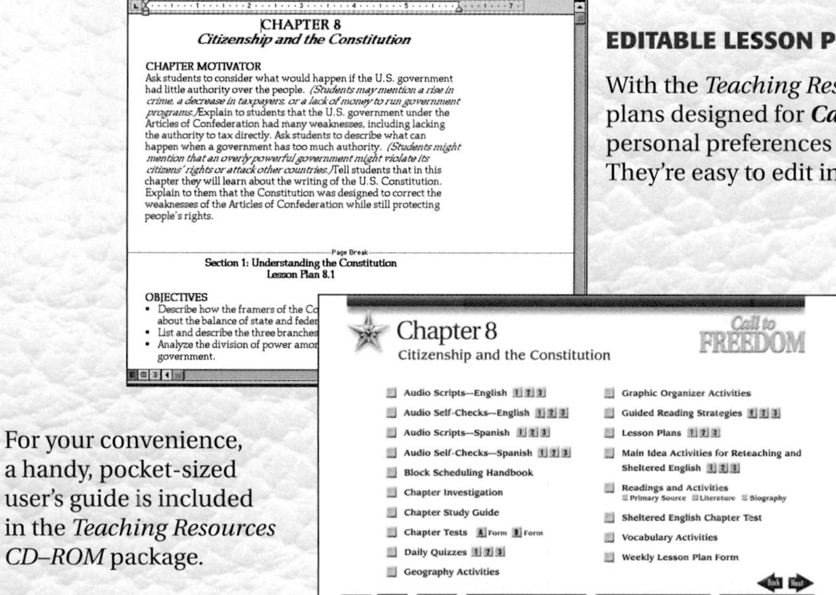

RESOURCES AT YOUR FINGERTIPS

All teaching resources are presented in easy-to-understand, point-and-click menu formats. Conveniently organized by chapter, all teaching resources are right at your fingertips. Whether you want to preview a quiz, print out activity sheets, or access transcripts from the *Audio CD Program*, all you have to do is make your selection and click your mouse.

For your convenience, a handy, pocket-sized user's guide is included in the *Teaching Resources CD–ROM* package.

Strategies to help your students master course material

The *Call to Freedom Pupil's Edition* provides you with a variety of ways to help you review content with your students and assess their comprehension.

CHAPTER 13 REVIEW

Chapter Summary

The 1920s were a time of great social change and economic prosperity in the United States. Social movements such as Fundamentalism, nativism, and prohibition sparked heated debates about education, immigration, and alcohol consumption. New forms of mass media and mass entertainment—including movies and radio—also strongly influenced American culture. In addition, actors, musicians, painters, and writers made many contributions to the arts in America.

On a separate sheet of paper, complete the following activities.

Identifying People and Ideas

Describe the historical significance of the following:

1. prohibition
2. Fundamentalism
3. John T. Scopes
4. National Origins Act
5. Marcus Garvey
6. talkies
7. Charles Lindbergh
8. Harlem Renaissance
9. Bessie Smith
10. Ernest Hemingway

Internet Activity go.hrw.com SB1 Silent Movies

Search the Internet through the HRW Web site to find information about movies and movie stars of the silent screen. Use the information to create a movie poster advertising a popular 1920s film. Include the names of the film's stars.

Understanding Main Ideas

1. Why was prohibition difficult to enforce?
2. What were some reasons why Fundamentalism spread in the 1920s?
3. How did Marcus Garvey promote black nationalism?
4. What political and economic advances did women achieve during the 1920s?
5. What forms of mass entertainment developed during the 1920s?
6. What were the major literary movements of the 1920s?

Reviewing Themes

1. **Citizenship and Democracy** Why did U.S. immigration policy change during the 1920s?
2. **Technology and Society** How did the development of radio and movies affect the lives of Americans?
3. **Cultural Diversity** How did African Americans contribute to the cultural changes in the United States during the 1920s?

Using the Time Line

Number your paper from 1 to 6. Match the letters on the time line below with the following events.

1. The teaching of the theory of evolution is challenged in court.
2. The United States passes an emergency quota on immigration.
3. The first American radio station broadcasts the results of the 1920 presidential election.
4. Prohibition goes into effect.
5. American Indians gain citizenship.
6. The first motion picture with sound is made.

1920 1921 1922 1923 1924 1925 1926 1927 1928

a b c d e f

Building Your Portfolio

Complete the following activities individually or in groups.

1. **Coming to America** Imagine that you are a European visitor to the United States during the 1920s. Choose one or several areas of the country to visit. Create a journal describing your travels to share with your friends back home. Along with your journal entry, you may wish to include maps of your travels, illustrations of the things you saw, and descriptions of the people you met and their activities.
2. **Radio Program** Imagine that you are the writer of a radio show about the rise of celebrities during the 1920s. Select one or more famous people from the decade to discuss on your show and write a script for your radio program. You may wish to interview someone, describe his or her accomplishments, or broadcast one of the person's games or performances. You may also discuss what makes someone a celebrity in the United States during the 1920s. When you have finished, present your radio show for the class.

History Skills Workshop

Using Visual Resources Study the image to the right, which is a painting by Jacob Lawrence. Then answer the following questions: (a) Where do you think the people in the painting are going? (b) What ideas or emotions do you think the artist is trying to communicate in the painting? (c) Draw a picture or write a description about what these people encountered upon reaching their destinations.

406 Chapter 13

Chapter Reviews offer a variety of projects and activities to help your students retain content. Activities include questions for reviewing chapter themes, main ideas, and the time line; critical-thinking and geography questions; history skills and writing activities; and Internet and portfolio projects.

History Skills WORKSHOP

Organizing Information

Whenever you write an essay or report or are working on a portfolio project, one of the biggest challenges you face is how to organize your information. While researching a topic, you usually record many details, but not necessarily in any type of order. You will have to decide on the best way to organize specific details around central ideas. A good method for doing this is to create a visual representation.

Cluster Diagram A cluster diagram is used to organize specific details around more general concepts. The diagram is a group of ovals with connecting lines between them. A cluster diagram is a great way to make sense of ideas when you are brainstorming a topic with others.

Example Suppose you are asked to come up with important events of the American Revolution. Your list might include:

Treaty of Paris of 1783 negotiations
Battle of Trenton
battles
First Continental Congress
meetings
Battle of Camden
Second Continental Congress

Your cluster diagram might look like this:

Sequencing Flowchart A sequencing flowchart is a series of boxes with arrows showing their connections. Use sequencing flowcharts when you are trying to determine the order in which certain events occurred.

Example Suppose you were asked to explain how the colonists declared their independence from Great Britain. You might come up with some ideas like:

- Parliament taxed the colonists without their agreement.
- The Second Continental Congress drafted the Declaration of Independence.
- British troops clashed with colonists at Lexington and Concord.
- Colonists staged protests, such as the Boston Tea Party.

You could then turn this list into a clear sequence of events:

Parliament taxed the colonists without their agreement. → Colonists staged protests, such as the Boston Tea Party. → British troops clashed with colonists at Lexington and Concord. → The Second Continental Congress drafted the Declaration of Independence.

Practicing the Skill

1. Brainstorm some important events from the French and Indian War, and write the list on your paper.
2. Create a cluster diagram showing rough groupings of your ideas.
3. Select one category from your cluster diagram and use a sequencing flowchart to organize the information.

218 History Skills Workshop

History in Action UNIT 3 PORTFOLIO

The Road to Independence Board Game

Complete the following activity in small cooperative groups.

You and your associates have been hired by W & H Entertainment, Inc. to create a new board game called "The Road to Independence" for ages 12 to adult. The executives at W & H were not very specific on what the game should look like or exactly how it should be played. They have left these decisions up to you. They do want the game to require players to correctly answer historical questions about Americans' struggle for independence from Great Britain. If players answer the game's questions correctly, they get to move around the game board. The first player to cross the finish line is the winner. Your job is to design all the components of this new game, including question cards, the game board, game pieces, and the rule book.

Materials To complete the activity, you will need index cards, posterboard, scissors, pens, pencils, markers, and your textbook.

Parts of the Project Before you turn in your portfolio project, make sure you have included the following components:

1. **Question Cards** Choose five categories from American history between 1763 and 1783 that relate to the colonists' struggle for independence. Possible categories include famous leaders, significant battles, and important meetings. For each category, come up with at least 10 questions and answers. Write this information on one side of the index cards. Color code the other side of each index card according to category. Use the skills you learned in the History Skills Workshop to help you organize your information while thinking of questions.
2. **Game Board and Pieces** Design and illustrate a board for your game that will allow players to move forward as they correctly answer questions. Design game pieces for the different players, and provide some way to move (dice, spinner, number cards). Make your board and game pieces as attractive as possible. Remember, you want to impress the executives at W & H.
3. **Rule Book** Write a set of rules to accompany your game. The rules should be clear and thorough.

When you have finished creating your game, play a practice round to make sure it works properly. Go back and make any revisions to the rules or design if necessary. Be prepared to present your game to W & H (the class).

Students playing a board game

The **History Skills Workshop** reinforces vital social studies skills, while **History in Action** asks students to work together to create portfolio projects that apply the skills they have learned in the workshop.

Strategies for review and assessment

Daily Quizzes **provide an objective assessment for each section of the chapter.**

Chapter Study Guides **contain exercises that help students master chapter content and review material for tests.**

Strategies for students who need extra attention

Call to Freedom **provides activities and reteaching approaches specifically designed for students having difficulty comprehending content and for those who are acquiring English.**

Main Idea Activities for Reteaching and Sheltered English help English language learners, special education students, and students having difficulty mastering content. Activities review each section's core concepts using different formats, such as graphic organizers, visual cues, and extra vocabulary aids.

Sheltered English Chapter and Unit Tests provide alternative tests for English language learners. These tests are also great for special education students and others who need a more focused approach to content assessment.

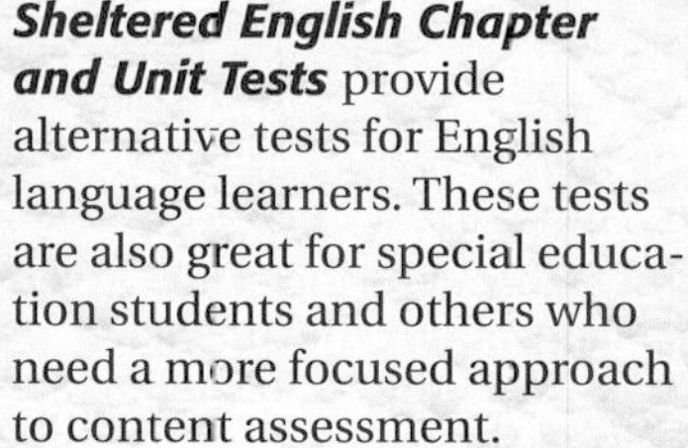

The ***Audio CD Program*** presents in-depth audio section summaries and self-check activity sheets for students who respond to auditory learning. Available in English and Spanish. Transcripts can be printed from the ***Teaching Resources CD–ROM*** to allow students to read along as they listen.

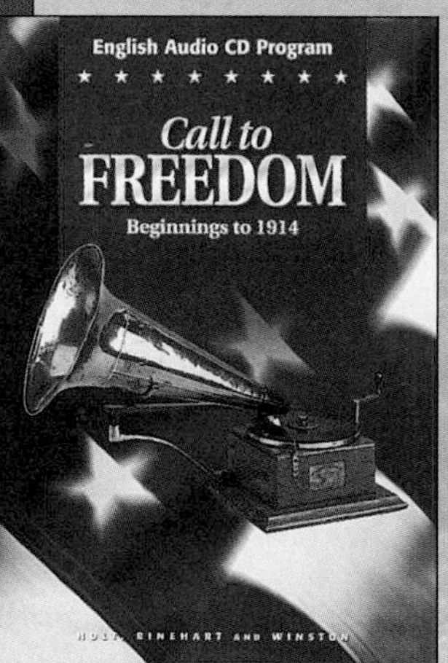

Standardized Test Practice Handbook **takes your students through Reading Comprehension, Reading Vocabulary, Language, and Social Studies Skills lessons designed to prepare them for success on your state's or district's standardized tests. Students practice valuable test-taking skills with lessons that are tied directly to the content they are studying in their American history classroom.**

Chapter and Unit Tests **help evaluate students' understanding of chapter and unit content.**

Test Generator CD–ROM **provides a database of questions correlated to each chapter for the course, allowing you to create customized tests.**

Experience high-tech

User-Friendly Online and Multimedia Resources

Call to Freedom **offers intriguing online activities to challenge your students to explore history, while strengthening their computer and research skills.**

Holt, Rinehart and Winston makes it easy for your students to enrich their knowledge of American history by exploring the Internet. The go.hrw.com site links students to a vast collection of educational online materials. With just a click of the mouse, students can complete structured, Web-based activities related to content in *Call to Freedom.*

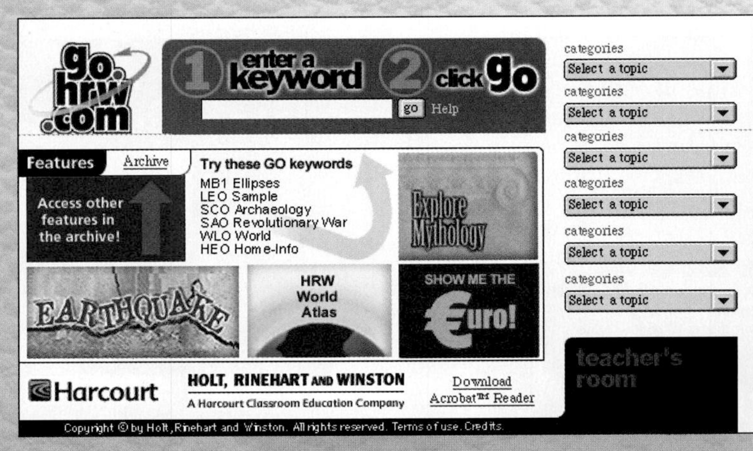

ALWAYS SAFE AND SECURE

All sites are pre-screened and monitored, so you can be sure the links always contain appropriate, non-commercial, and valuable information that enhances student learning.

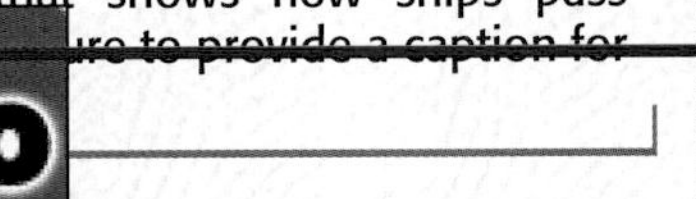

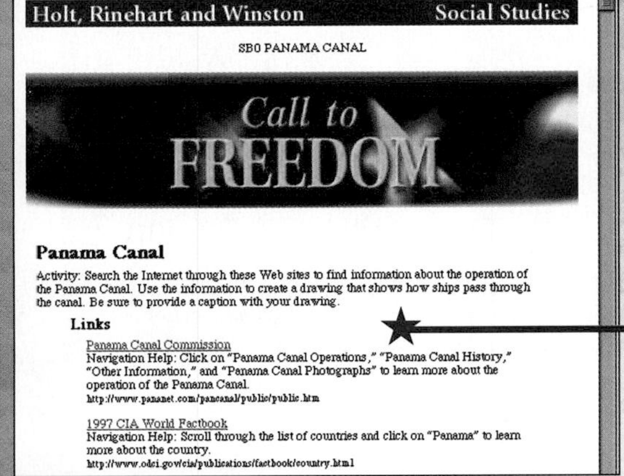

HERE'S HOW IT WORKS:

1. Simply type the address found in the *Pupil's* and *Teacher's Editions*—**go.hrw.com**.

2. On the **go.hrw.com** home page, type the keyword—such as **SBØ Panama Canal**—that's provided in the textbook.

3. On the activity page, students can read about each site's contents and follow navigation tips to complete the activity.

Try it out for yourself. Visit **go.hrw.com** and type in these sample keywords for examples of the excellent activities and links available to you and your students:

SBO Veterans

SBO Cold War

SBO Panama Canal

Online resources at your fingertips

Internet Resources for Social Studies **explains how to navigate and conduct social studies research on the Internet.**

Reading Strategies for Social Studies **reinforce reading skills while teaching historical concepts.**

history

Experience hands-on learning at the Smithsonian Institution

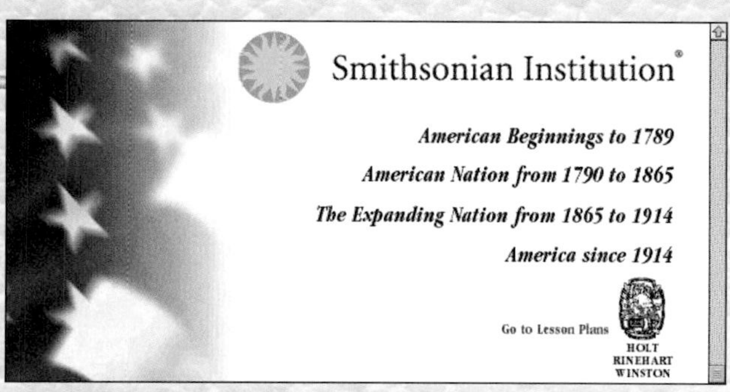

Holt, Rinehart and Winston provides access to selected Smithsonian Institution Web sites, giving you and your students unparalleled entry into a range of primary source materials, virtual tours, and online exhibits.

Just think: Your students can listen to America's earliest music in **Creation's Journey: Native American Music.** Or gaze upon presidential portraits in the **National Portrait Gallery. You Be the Historian** presents students with a historical case study and asks them to analyze evidence and draw conclusions. All tours through the Smithsonian come fully supported by teacher and student material to make using them a snap.

HERE'S HOW IT WORKS:

1. Simply type the address found in the teacher's edition—**www.si.edu/hrw**
2. Choose a time period.
3. Select one or more exhibits.

Smithsonian Institution®

CNN/Turner Learning guides your students through the past

Holt, Rinehart and Winston and CNN have joined forces to provide you and your students with exceptional current and historical news content, adding depth and relevance to your daily instruction.

CNN Presents America: Yesterday and Today makes American history meaningful to students. Your students can experience first-hand heartfelt reactions to the Vietnam War Memorial or watch the refitting of the *USS Constitution* by Annapolis midshipmen. A *Teacher's Guide* offers background information, a description of each segment, and teaching suggestions. It also contains thought-provoking before- and while-viewing questions that ask students to think critically about the topics on the video. After-viewing activities offer suggestions for hands-on research, writing, and portfolio assignments.

Portfolio and Performance Assessment for Social Studies **includes a set of customizable scoring rubrics for all product- and performance-based assessments, such as oral presentations, journals, artwork, debates, and writing assignments. Located on the *Teaching Resources CD–ROM.***

Fun, interactive technology keeps your students engaged

Your class will love working together in groups to solve interesting problems and make important decisions while exploring our two interactive CD–ROM programs!

American History Simulations CD–ROM makes history come alive. These activities challenge your students to experience the past in ways they never thought possible. By role-playing important decision-makers in history, students learn history while they hone important analytical, interpretive, and problem-solving skills. Intriguing simulations include investigating turn-of-the-century political machines, serving on a community task force during the Great Depression, deciding the best course for winning the space race, and consulting on an urban plan.

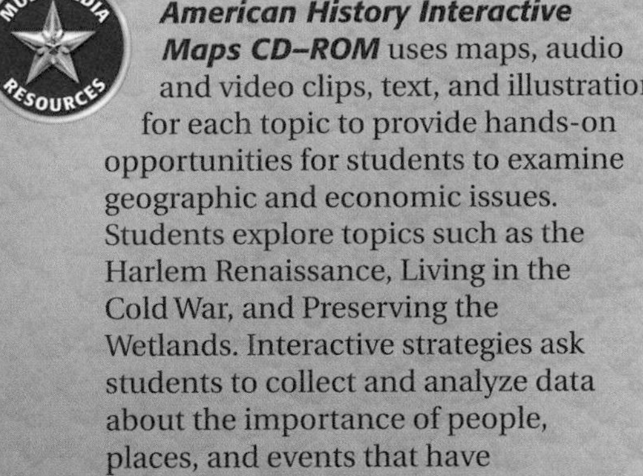

American History Interactive Maps CD–ROM uses maps, audio and video clips, text, and illustrations for each topic to provide hands-on opportunities for students to examine geographic and economic issues. Students explore topics such as the Harlem Renaissance, Living in the Cold War, and Preserving the Wetlands. Interactive strategies ask students to collect and analyze data about the importance of people, places, and events that have affected our nation's past. Online reviews make assessment simple.

More resources to interest and engage your students

Appeal to your students' sense of curiosity by providing visual references from *American History Visual Resources.* This transparency and worksheet directory includes *Linking History and Geography* and *Everyday Life in America,* plus *Art in American History.*

More multimedia resources that grab your students' attention

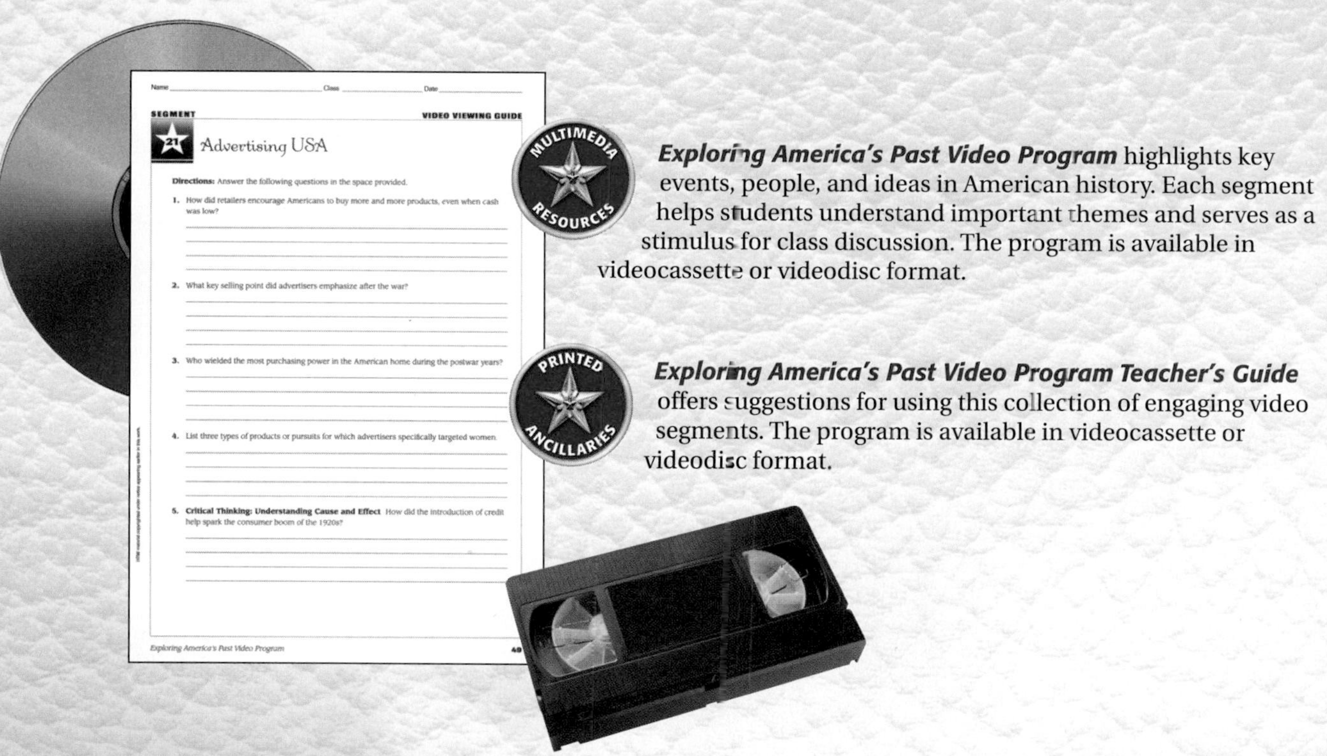

Name ____ Class ____ Date ____

SEGMENT 21 VIDEO VIEWING GUIDE

Advertising USA

Directions: Answer the following questions in the space provided.

1. How did retailers encourage Americans to buy more and more products, even when cash was low?
2. What key selling point did advertisers emphasize after the war?
3. Who wielded the most purchasing power in the American home during the postwar years?
4. List three types of products or pursuits for which advertisers specifically targeted women.
5. **Critical Thinking: Understanding Cause and Effect** How did the introduction of credit help spark the consumer boom of the 1920s?

Exploring America's Past Video Program 49

Exploring America's Past Video Program highlights key events, people, and ideas in American history. Each segment helps students understand important themes and serves as a stimulus for class discussion. The program is available in videocassette or videodisc format.

Exploring America's Past Video Program Teacher's Guide offers suggestions for using this collection of engaging video segments. The program is available in videocassette or videodisc format.

The ***American Music Audio CD Program*** contains songs chosen for their relevance to crucial moments and themes throughout American history. Your students can compare and contrast the musical styles of jazz, blues, and ragtime, or feel the plight of the slaves with a moving song of freedom. The program includes teaching strategies for listening, interpreting lyrics, and examining the role that music has played in shaping our nation.

The *Global Skill Builder CD–ROM* is a comprehensive program containing interactive lessons that motivate students to strengthen their map, graph, and computer skills. A *User's Guide and Teacher's Manual* containing technology instructions and project sheets for each lesson is included.

Call to FREEDOM

Teaching Resources

- Chapter Investigations
- Block Scheduling Handbook with Team Teaching Strategies
- Geography Activities
- Guided Reading Strategies
- Vocabulary Activities
- Readings and Activities
- Graphic Organizer Activities
- American History Outline Maps
- American History Political Cartoons
- Writing About American History
- Citizenship Simulations and Case Studies
- The Constitution: Past, Present, and Future

Multimedia and Online Resources

- Teaching Resources CD–ROM
- American History Simulations CD–ROM
- American History Interactive Maps CD–ROM
- American Music Audio CD Program
- HRW Internet Resources for Social Studies
- CNN Presents America: Yesterday and Today Video Program
- Exploring America's Past Video Program
- Exploring America's Past Video Program Teacher's Guide
- Global Skill Builder CD–ROM
- American History Visual Resources
- Art in American History
- HRW Reading Strategies for Social Studies

Review and Assessment Resources

- Chapter Study Guides
- Social Studies Skills Review
- Daily Quizzes
- Chapter and Unit Tests
- Test Generator CD–ROM and Test Item Listing
- HRW Portfolio and Performance Assessment for Social Studies
- Standardized Test Practice Handbook

Reteaching, Sheltered English, and Spanish Resources

- Main Idea Activities for Reteaching and Sheltered English
- Spanish Glossary
- Sheltered English Chapter and Unit Tests
- English Audio CD Program
- Spanish Audio CD Program

Photo credits: Background image on all pages, videotape image, page IX and XIX, Image ©1997 Photodisc, Inc.; artifacts on pages III, V, VII, IX, XV, and XIX, Christie's Images; page XVII, ship and Vietnam War Memorial, CNN Video; page XVIII, HRW Photo by Sam Dudgeon; page XX, train image, Ernest H. Robl; all other images, Christie's Images.

HRW Located at www.hrw.com

Content Reviewers

Dr. Richard Abbott
Eastern Michigan University
Reconstruction

Dr. Armando C. Alonzo
Texas A&M
Mexican American, Texas

Dr. Charles Bussey
Western Kentucky
American Studies, U.S. History Since 1945

Dr. Dennis Downey
Millersville University
American social history; Gilded Age and Progressive Era

Dr. Selika Ducksworth
University of Wisconsin at Eau Claire
20th-century U.S., military history, African American

Dr. Jeronima Echeverria
California State University at Fresno
Modern U.S., social studies education

Dr. Bruce Fehn
University of Iowa
Social Studies Education

Dr. Paul A. Gilje
University of Oklahoma
U.S., 1492–1865

Dr. David Hamilton
University of Kentucky
Modern U.S.

Dr. Raymond Hyser
James Madison University
Gilded Age and Progressive Era

Dr. Elizabeth Jameson
University of New Mexico
American West and U.S. social

Dr. John R. Jameson
Kent State University
Public, 20th-century U.S.

Dr. Beverly Jones
North Carolina Central University
Reconstruction

Dr. Yasuhide Kawashima
University of Texas at El Paso
Colonial and revolutionary America, American legal

Dr. Robin Kilson
University of Texas at Austin
African American

Dr. Burton Kirkwood
University of Evansville
Recent U.S.

Dr. Joyce Peterson
Florida International University
U.S. social

Dr. Jack Rakove
Stanford University
American Revolution, early American political

Dr. Janann Sherman
University of Memphis
20th-century U.S., women

Dr. James Smallwood
Oklahoma State
U.S. South, African American

Dr. Mark C. Smith
University of Texas at Austin
20th-century U.S. cultural history

Dr. Richard Ugland
The Ohio State University
U.S. History–20th Century; WWII

Dr. John R. Wunder
University of Nebraska
American West

Dr. Gerald Zahavi
State University of New York at Albany
20th-century U.S. labor and social

Educational Reviewers

Anastacio Asuncion
Piedmont Middle School
San Jose, California

David Burns
Thomas A. Edison High School
Alexandria, Virginia

Larry Couser
Richard King High School
Corpus Christi, Texas

Anne Edwards
Place Middle School
Denver, Colorado

Nancy Hammond
Fred Lynn Middle School
Woodbridge, Virginia

Valerie Hill
Gaston Middle School
Dallas, Texas

Marilyn Kretzer
Johnston Middle School
Houston, Texas

Dwane Martinson
Hamilton Middle School
Seattle, Washington

Rudy Martinez
Thomas A. Edison High School
San Antonio, Texas

Lotty Repp
W. T. White High School
Dallas, Texas

Ron Tripp
Shepherd High School
Shepherd, Michigan

Helen Webb
Wayne Seale Middle School
Corpus Christi, Texas

George Wood
Gregory-Portland Junior High School
Portland, Texas

Field Test Teachers

Sandra Poe Borowiecki
New Hartford Perry Junior High School
New Hartford, New York

Mary Beth Breshears
Wood Middle School
Fort Leonard Wood, Missouri

Richard J. Giannicchi
West Seneca Junior High School
West Seneca, New York

Kim Gravell
Dripping Springs Middle School
Dripping Springs, Texas

Debora K. Lofton
Charles F. Blackstock Junior High School
Port Hueneme, California

Stan Mendenhall
Broadmoor Junior High School
Pekin, Illinois

Daniel Murray
Hackett Middle School
Albany, New York

Martha Potter
John Jay Middle School
Katonah, New York

Linda Rothrock
Harlandale Middle School
San Antonio, Texas

Amy Thompson
Union Middle School
San Jose, California

Call to FREEDOM

1865 to the Present

CONTENTS

Themes in American History xvi
Geography Themes xvii
Critical Thinking and the Study of History xviii
Atlas xx

UNIT 1
American Beginnings
(Beginnings–1750) 1
American Teens in History
Young Pioneers 1
Time Line 2

PLANNING GUIDE 3a
CHAPTER 1
The Founding of the Nation
(Beginnings–1791) 4
1 The World Before the Opening of the Atlantic 5
2 The Age of Exploration 10
3 The English Colonies 14
Biography *John Smith* 15
American Literature *"To My Dear and Loving Husband" by Anne Bradstreet* 17
4 The American Revolution 21
Historical Documents
The Declaration of Independence 26
5 Forming a Nation 30

U.S. symbol, the bald eagle

PLANNING GUIDE 35a
CHAPTER 2
Citizenship and the Constitution
(1787–Present) 36
1 Understanding the Constitution 37
American Literature Federalist Paper *"No. 51" by James Madison* 39
Biography *Sandra Day O'Connor* 42
Historical Documents
The Constitution 44
2 The Bill of Rights 64
Biography *James Madison* 65
Linking Past to Present
Freedom of Assembly 67
3 Rights and Responsibilities of Citizenship 70
Geography and History
The Living Constitution 78

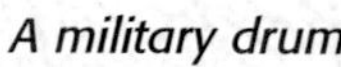

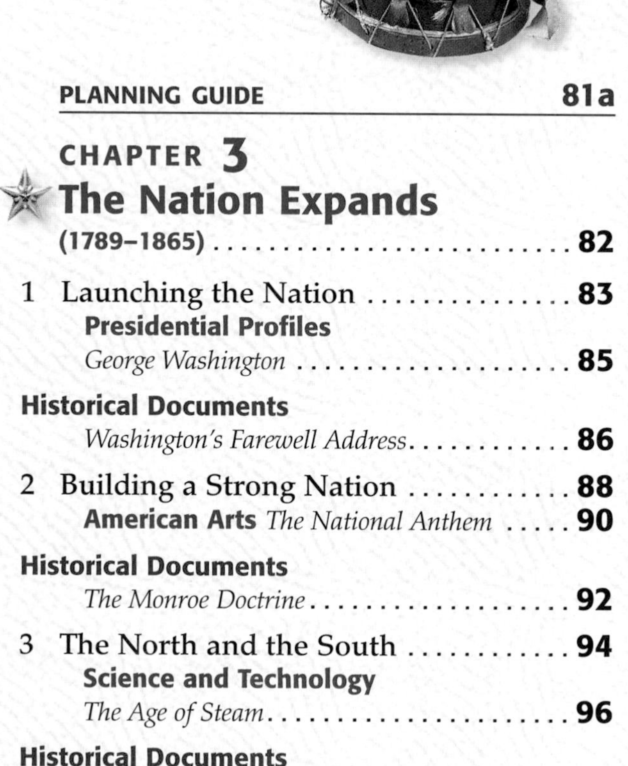

A military drum

PLANNING GUIDE 81a

CHAPTER 3

The Nation Expands
(1789–1865) 82

1 Launching the Nation 83
Presidential Profiles
George Washington 85

Historical Documents
Washington's Farewell Address 86

2 Building a Strong Nation 88
American Arts *The National Anthem* 90

Historical Documents
The Monroe Doctrine 92

3 The North and the South 94
Science and Technology
The Age of Steam 96

Historical Documents
The Seneca Falls Declaration of Sentiments 99

4 Expanding West 101
Linking Past to Present
Water Usage in the West 104

5 The Civil War 106

Historical Documents
The Emancipation Proclamation and The Gettysburg Address 112

History Skills Workshop
Reading Maps 116

History in Action Unit 1 Portfolio
The United States: The Diorama 117

A school for freedpeople

UNIT 2

Industrial America
(1850–1900) 118

American Teens in History
Young Immigrants 119

Time Line 120

PLANNING GUIDE 121a

CHAPTER 4

Reconstruction
(1865–1877) 122

1 Rebuilding the South 123

Historical Documents
Lincoln's Second Inaugural Address 125
Linking Past to Present *Historically Black Colleges and Universities* 127
Presidential Profiles *Andrew Johnson* 128

2 The Fight over Reconstruction 130
3 Reconstruction in the South 136
4 The New South 142
American Literature *"The Wife of His Youth" by Charles W. Chesnutt* 146

PLANNING GUIDE 149a

CHAPTER 5

The West
(1850–1890) 150

1 The Wars for the West 151
American Literature *"I Will Fight No More Forever" by Chief Joseph* 155
Biography *Geronimo* 156

2 Miners and Railroads 158
Global Connections
The Railroads of India 161

3 The Cattle Kingdom 164
4 Farming the Great Plains 170

Geography and History
The Economy of the West 178

PLANNING GUIDE 181a

CHAPTER 6
An Industrial Nation
(1876–1900) 182

1 The Second Industrial Revolution . . 183
Science and Technology
The Wizard of Menlo Park 186

2 Big Business 189
Biography *Andrew Carnegie* 191

Historical Documents
Andrew Carnegie's Gospel of Wealth 192
American Literature The House of Mirth *by Edith Wharton* 193

3 Industrial Workers 195

4 Populism 200
Linking Past to Present
Third Political Parties 204

Song about Ellis Island

PLANNING GUIDE 207a

CHAPTER 7
Immigrants and Cities
(1870–1900) 208

1 A New Wave of Immigration 209
Global Connections
Coming to America 212

2 City Life 215
American Arts *Frederick Law Olmsted* . . . 218
Biography *Jane Addams* 220

3 Society and Culture 222

History Skills Workshop
Reading Charts and Graphs 230

History in Action Unit 2 Portfolio
Journey Across the World: The Travel Agency . . 231

UNIT 3
A Growing America
(1865–1920) 232

American Teens in History
Young Workers 233

Time Line 234

PLANNING GUIDE 235a

CHAPTER 8
The Spirit of Reform
(1868–1920) 236

1 The Gilded Age 237

2 Progressive Ideals 241

3 Reforming the Workplace 247
Global Connections *Worker Reforms* . . . 250

4 Women's Suffrage and Temperance 252
American Arts *Mary Cassatt* 253
Biography *Frances Willard* 254

Historical Documents
Women's Right to the Suffrage *by Susan B. Anthony* 256

5 Minorities Fight for Change 258

Children working in a cannery

The Granger Collection, New York

Theodore Roosevelt campaign items

PLANNING GUIDE 263a

CHAPTER 9
The Progressive Presidents
(1900–1920) . . . 264

1 Roosevelt Becomes President . . . 265
Presidential Profiles
Theodore Roosevelt . . . 267
American Literature
The Jungle *by Upton Sinclair* . . . 269
2 The Taft Administration . . . 272
3 Woodrow Wilson's Reforms . . . 278
Linking Past to Present
Income Tax . . . 280

PLANNING GUIDE 285a

CHAPTER 10
America As a World Power
(1865–1914) . . . 286

1 The United States Gains Overseas Territories . . . 287
Biography *Queen Liliuokalani* . . . 290
Global Connections
Japanese Immigrants in Hawaii . . . 291
2 The Spanish-American War . . . 294
American Literature
The War Dispatches of Stephen Crane . . . 298
3 The United States and Latin America . . . 301
Science and Technology
The Panama Canal . . . 303
4 The United States and Mexico . . . 308

Geography and History
The United States in the Modern Age . . . 314
History Skills Workshop
Identifying Cause and Effect . . . 318
History in Action Unit 3 Portfolio
Muckraker Magazine . . . 319

UNIT 4
The Changing Nation
(1914–1929) . . . 320

American Teens in History
Young War Supporters . . . 321
Time Line . . . 322

PLANNING GUIDE 323a

CHAPTER 11
World War I
(1914–1919) . . . 324

1 The Road to War . . . 325
2 Wilson and Neutrality . . . 329
Science and Technology
The Airplane in World War I . . . 331
Presidential Profiles *Woodrow Wilson* . . 333
3 Americans Prepare for War . . . 335
4 Americans "Over There" . . . 339
American Arts *John Philip Sousa* . . . 341
5 Establishing Peace . . . 344
Linking Past to Present
The League of Nations and the UN . . . 346

Historical Documents
The Fourteen Points . . . 350

Trench warfare during World War I

PLANNING GUIDE 353a

CHAPTER 12
The 1920s: An Unsettled Decade (1919–1929) 354

1 Returning to "Normalcy" 355
Global Connections
The Influenza Epidemic of 1918–1919 357
2 Republicans in Power 362
3 "The Business of America Is Business" 367
Biography *Henry Ford* 368
4 The U.S. Economy 373
American Literature
The Great Gatsby *by F. Scott Fitzgerald* 375

The Granger Collection, New York

The good times of the 1920s came to a screeching halt when the stock market crashed in October 1929.

PLANNING GUIDE 379a

CHAPTER 13
The Roaring Twenties (1920–1929) 380

1 Prohibition America 381
2 A Changing Population 387
3 Americans at Play 393
Linking Past to Present
Movie Special Effects 395
Biography *Mary Pickford* 396
4 The Arts 399
American Arts *Georgia O'Keeffe* 404

Geography and History
American Migrations, 1865–1930 408
History Skills Workshop
Using Visual Resources 412
History in Action Unit 4 Portfolio
Life in the Twenties: *The Play* 413

Flappers during the 1920s

UNIT 5
A World in Crisis (1929–1945) 414

American Teens in History
Young Relief Workers 415
Time Line 416

PLANNING GUIDE 417a

CHAPTER 14
The Great Depression (1929–1939) 418

1 The End of Prosperity 419
2 Hoover and the Depression 425
American Literature
Their Eyes Were Watching God *by Zora Neale Hurston* 427
3 Roosevelt and the New Deal 431
Historical Documents
Roosevelt's First Inaugural Address 433
Presidential Profiles
Franklin D. Roosevelt 434
4 The Second New Deal 437
Linking Past to Present
Social Security 439

PLANNING GUIDE 445a

CHAPTER 15
The Depression at Home and Abroad
(1929–1939) . . . 446

1 Workers and Farmers in the New Deal . . . 447
American Literature The Grapes of Wrath *by John Steinbeck* . . . 451
2 Americans Face Hard Times . . . 453
Biography *Frances Perkins* . . . 454
3 Arts and Entertainment . . . 457
4 The Depression Abroad . . . 462
Global Connections *The Spanish Civil War* . . . 465

Geography and History *The Global Depression* . . . 470

PLANNING GUIDE 473a

CHAPTER 16
World War II
(1938–1945) . . . 474

1 World War II Begins . . . 475
2 Mobilizing for War . . . 480
American Arts Oklahoma! . . . 482
3 The War in North Africa and Europe . . . 484
Biography *Daniel Inouye* . . . 485
Global Connections *The Eastern Front* . . 488
4 War in the Pacific . . . 490
5 Final Victory and Consequences . . . 495
Science and Technology *Antibiotics* . . . 497

Victorious Allied troops liberate Paris.

History Skills Workshop
Distinguishing Fact from Opinion and Identifying Bias . . . 502
History in Action Unit 5 Portfolio
The New Deal Game Show . . . 503

UNIT 6
Postwar America
(1945–1960) . . . 504

American Teens in History
Young Musicians . . . 505
Time Line . . . 506

PLANNING GUIDE 507a

CHAPTER 17
The Cold War Begins
(1945–1955) . . . 508

1 The World After War . . . 509
2 The Roots of the Cold War . . . 513
Historical Documents
The Truman Doctrine . . . 514
Linking Past to Present
American Military Bases Abroad . . . 516
3 The Truman Era . . . 518
Presidential Profiles *Harry S Truman* . . . 519
4 The Korean War . . . 522
5 Cold War Fears . . . 527
American Literature
The Crucible *by Arthur Miller* . . . 530

Geography and History *The Cold War* . . . 534

PLANNING GUIDE 537a

CHAPTER 18
Peace and Prosperity
(1945–1960) . . . 538

1 Eisenhower's Foreign Policy . . . 539
Global Connections
The Eisenhower Doctrine . . . 542

A suburban family takes to the open road in the 1950s.

2 A Prosperous Nation **544**
Science and Technology *Television* **545**

3 A Changing Culture. **550**
American Arts *Jackson Pollock* **552**

4 The Early Civil Rights Movement . . . **554**
Biography *Rosa Parks*. **558**

History Skills Workshop
Using Primary and Secondary Sources. **562**

History in Action Unit 6 Portfolio
A Cold War Scrapbook **563**

UNIT 7
Searching for Solutions
(1945–1978). **564**

American Teens in History
Young Politicians **565**

Time Line **566**

PLANNING GUIDE **567a**

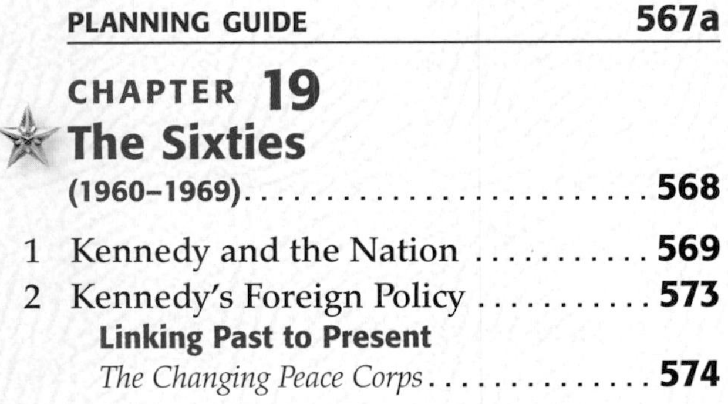

CHAPTER 19
The Sixties
(1960–1969). **568**

1 Kennedy and the Nation **569**

2 Kennedy's Foreign Policy **573**
Linking Past to Present
The Changing Peace Corps. **574**

3 The Johnson Administration **578**
Presidential Profiles
Lyndon B. Johnson **579**

4 New Movements in America **583**
American Arts *Andy Warhol* **585**

5 Science in the 1960s **588**
Science and Technology
The Apollo Program. **590**

PLANNING GUIDE **593a**

CHAPTER 20
The Search for Equal Rights
(1960–1978). **594**

1 The Civil Rights Movement. **595**
Biography *Martin Luther King Jr.* **598**

Historical Documents
Martin Luther King Jr.'s I Have a Dream. . . **602**

2 Rights for Hispanics. **604**
Biography *César Chávez*. **605**
American Literature
Poetry of Angela de Hoyos **607**

3 The Women's Rights Movement **610**
Linking Past to Present
Women in the Workplace Today **613**

4 Rights for All **616**

Martin Luther King Jr.

The Vietnam Veterans Memorial

PLANNING GUIDE 621a

CHAPTER 21
War in Vietnam
(1945–1975) 622

1 Early Conflicts in Vietnam 623
2 The Escalation of the War 627
Linking Past to Present
The United States and Vietnam Today 629
3 A Divided Nation 631
4 The War Under Nixon 636
Presidential Profiles
Richard Nixon 637
American Arts
The Vietnam Veterans Memorial 640

Geography and History
The Struggle for Vietnam 644
History Skills Workshop
Doing Research and Making an Outline 648
History in Action Unit 7 Portfolio
Vietnam War Documentary 649

UNIT 8
Modern America
(1968–Present) 650
American Teens in History
Young Volunteers 651
Time Line 652

PLANNING GUIDE 653a

CHAPTER 22
A Search for Order
(1968–1980) 654

1 The Nixon Presidency 655
2 Watergate and Beyond 660
3 The Carter Administration 666
Presidential Profiles *Jimmy Carter* 667
Linking Past to Present
The Changing Automobile 668
4 American Society in the 1970s 672
American Arts *Twyla Tharp* 675

PLANNING GUIDE 679a

CHAPTER 23
The Republican Years
(1980–1992) 680

1 The Reagan Years 681
Presidential Profiles *Ronald Reagan* 683
2 Reagan's Foreign Policy 687
3 George Bush's Presidency 692
Global Connections
The Fall of the Berlin Wall 694
4 Technology and Culture 699
American Literature
"Mother Tongue" by Amy Tan 701

President Reagan and Soviet leader Gorbachev

PLANNING GUIDE 705a

CHAPTER 24
The United States Looks to the Future
(1992–Present) 706

1 The Clinton Administration 707
Presidential Profiles *Bill Clinton* 709

2 Clinton's Foreign Policy. 713
American Arts *Worldbeat Music* 714

3 Americans in the 1990s 718
Science and Technology *Computers* 721

4 Preparing for the Twenty-first Century 723
Linking Past to Present *Careers in the Twenty-first Century* 726

Geography and History *The World's Energy* 730

History Skills Workshop *Writing a Paper* 734

History in Action Unit 8 Portfolio *Textbook Final Chapter* 735

NATO celebrates its 50th anniversary.

REFERENCE SECTION

Presidents of the United States 738
Facts About the States 743
Important Supreme Court Cases 744
Gazetteer 748
Glossary 757
Index 772
Acknowledgments 796

MAPS

United States of America: Political xx
United States of America: Physical xxii
World: Political xxiv
North America: Political xxvi
South America: Political xxvii
Europe: Political xxviii
Asia: Political xxix
Africa: Political xxx
Pacific Islands: Political xxxi
Native American Culture Areas 7
Columbus's Voyages, 1492–1504 11
The Thirteen Colonies 16
The Fight for Independence, 1776–1781 23
Early European Settlements 35
The Northwest Ordinance: Becoming a State 78
Joining the Union 79
The Louisiana Purchase 89
Major Overland Routes to the West by 1860 103
The War in the West 109
The War in the East 109
The United States in 1860 115
Aid for Freedpeople 126
Reconstruction in the South 134
The South After the Civil War 138
African American Colleges Before 1900 149
Indian Reservations and Battles to 1890 153
Cattle Trails and Western Railroads to 1890 168
Populating the West 172
The Mining Boom 178
The West Around 1870 180
The West Around 1900 181
Labor Strikes, 1870–1900 198
Agricultural Regions, 1900 202
Growth of Cities, 1880–1900 216
Dry States, 1890–1919 255
Women and Suffrage, 1890–1920 257
National Parks and Conservation 270
The Election of 1912 277
U.S. Territories in the Pacific 292
The Spanish-American War in 1898 297
U.S. Interests in Latin America 305
Global Possessions in 1914 316
World War I, 1914–1917 332
The Western Front in 1918 342
Europe After the Treaty of Versailles, 1919–1920 347
American Advances During World War I, Sept.–Nov. 1918 353
Arrests Under Prohibition, 1929 384
Harlem Renaissance, 1920s and 1930s 401
Mexican American Population in 1930 409

Discrimination Against African Americans in 1930 411
The Tennessee Valley Authority, 1933–1945 436
The Dust Bowl, 1930s 450
Japanese Expansion, 1931–1938 466
Effects of the Depression 471
World War II in Europe, 1939–1941 477
World War II in Europe, 1942–1945 487
World War II in the Pacific, 1941–1945 493
The Bataan Death March 501
The Marshall Plan, 1948–1951 515
The Election of 1948 520
The Korean War, 1950–1953 524
The Height of the Cold War, 1960 534
Cold War Defenses 537
The Cold War in Europe in 1955 541
America on the Move, 1950–1960 547
Alaska and Hawaii 561
The Election of 1960 570
The 1962 Cuban Missile Crisis 576
The 1961 Freedom Rides 597
African American Voter Registration, 1965 621
French Indochina 624
The Vietnam War 628
The Ho Chi Minh Trail 644
OPEC Member Nations in the Middle East and Northern Africa 657
Central America and the Caribbean in the 1980s 688
Breakup of the Soviet Sphere, 1989–1992 695
The 1991 Persian Gulf War 697
Energy Sources in the United States 732

CHARTS

Causes and Effects of the Revolution 25
The Articles of Confederation and the Constitution 32
The Executive Departments 41
Separation of Power and Checks and Balances 63
Amending the U.S. Constitution 68
Requirements for Federal Office 80
The Expanding Electorate 81
U.S. Cotton Production, 1790–1860 97
Representatives in the House 107
African American Property Owners in the South, 1860 and 1870 143

Cotton Production and Cotton Prices 144
Population of Omaha 163
Causes and Effects of Increased Western Settlement 174
Estimated Bison Population 177
U.S. Land in Farms 179
Steel Production, 1865–1895 184
Vertical and Horizontal Integration 190
Shifting Patterns of Immigration 210
Total Immigration to the United States, 1860–1900 229
Causes and Effects of the Progressive Movement 242
Labor and Wages, 1900–1910 248
Labor Union Membership, 1900–1920 251
Progressive Presidential Reforms, 1906–1914 282
U.S. Trade with Cuba, 1891–1900 295
Estimated U.S. Investments in Mexico, 1897–1919 310
U.S. Overseas Expansion, 1898–1899 314
U.S. Exports and Imports, 1865–1915 315
Causes and Effects of World War I 348
A Consumer Culture 371
Persons Working in the U.S. Private Sector 377
Households with Radios, 1922–1930 379
Female Labor Force, 1890–1930 392
Population Shift: Rural to Urban, 1880–1930 408
African American Migration, 1910–1930 410
The Typical Business Cycle 423
Unemployment During the Depression 426
Select New Deal Programs 441
The Crash 445
Decline in Gross National Product, 1929–1932 470
Average Income per Person, 1929–1940 472
Growth in Federal Spending, 1928–1940 473
Causes and Effects of World War II 498

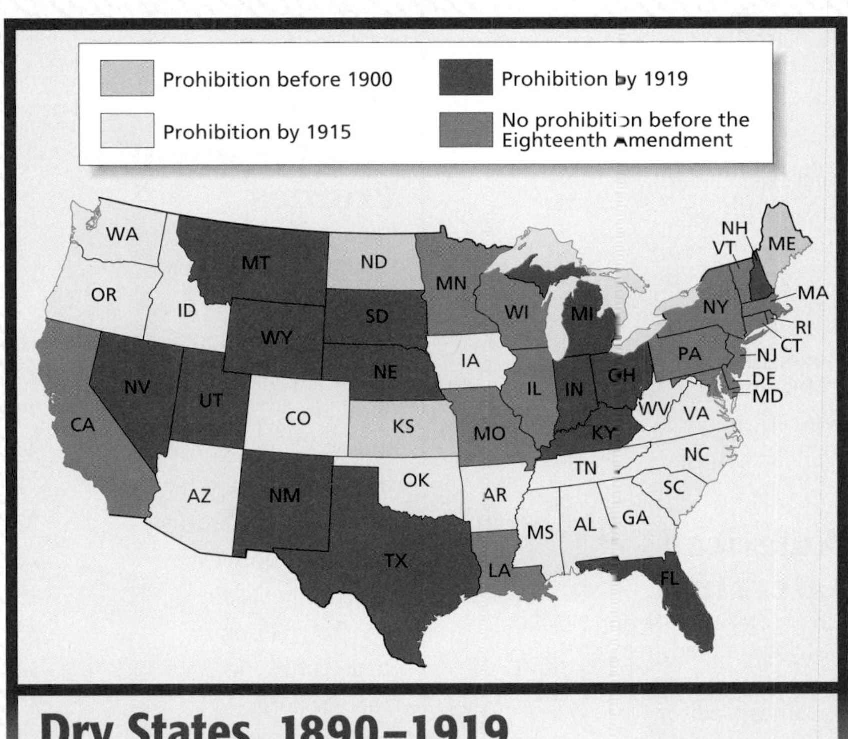

Dry States, 1890–1919

Causes and Effects of World War II

Long-Term Causes

Treaty of Versailles

Debts from World War I

Global and local economic problems

Totalitarian governments

Repeated acts of aggression

Immediate Causes

Germany's invasion of Poland

Japanese aggression in Asia

Japanese attack on Pearl Harbor

World War II

Effects

Millions of deaths and widespread destruction in Europe and Asia

The Holocaust

The emergence of the United States as a superpower

Defense Spending As Part of Total U.S. Budget, 1945–1995 536

The Growth of Suburbs, 1910–1960 549

Women in the Labor Force 614

U.S. Troops in Vietnam, 1964–1972 633

Causes and Effects of the Vietnam War 639

U.S. Armed Forces Serving During Wartime 646

American Opinions on the Vietnam War, 1965–1971 647

Causes and Effects of the Energy Crisis 658

The Impeachment Process 662

U.S. Defense Spending, 1945–1995 684

Total Federal Debt, 1981–1995 711

U.S. Immigration, 1996 719

U.S. Employment 725

Top World Consumers of Energy, 1994 730

Leading Energy Producers, 1990–1992 731

U.S. Energy Use, 1970–1995 733

FEATURES

American Arts

The National Anthem 90

Frederick Law Olmsted 218

Mary Cassatt 253

John Philip Sousa 341

Georgia O'Keeffe 404

Oklahoma! 482

Jackson Pollock 552

Andy Warhol 585

The Vietnam Veterans Memorial 640

Twyla Tharp 675

Worldbeat Music 714

American Literature

"To My Dear and Loving Husband" by Anne Bradstreet 17

Federalist Paper "No. 51" by James Madison 39

"The Wife of His Youth" by Charles W. Chesnutt 146

"I Will Fight No More Forever" by Chief Joseph 155

The House of Mirth by Edith Wharton 193

The Jungle by Upton Sinclair 269

The War Dispatches of Stephen Crane 298

The Great Gatsby by F. Scott Fitzgerald 375

Their Eyes Were Watching God by Zora Neale Hurston 427

The Grapes of Wrath by John Steinbeck 451

The Crucible by Arthur Miller 530

Poetry of Angela de Hoyos 607

"Mother Tongue" by Amy Tan 701

American Teens in History

Young Pioneers 1

Young Immigrants 119

Young Workers 233

Young War Supporters 321

Young Relief Workers 415

Young Musicians 505

Young Politicians 565

Young Volunteers 651

Biographies and Presidential Profiles

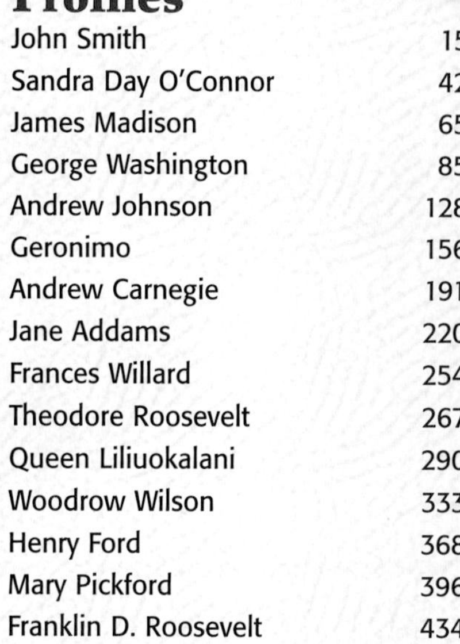

John Smith 15

Sandra Day O'Connor 42

James Madison 65

George Washington 85

Andrew Johnson 128

Geronimo 156

Andrew Carnegie 191

Jane Addams 220

Frances Willard 254

Theodore Roosevelt 267

Queen Liliuokalani 290

Woodrow Wilson 333

Henry Ford 368

Mary Pickford 396

Franklin D. Roosevelt 434

Frances Perkins 454

Daniel Inouye 485
Harry S Truman 519
Rosa Parks 558
Lyndon B. Johnson 579
Martin Luther King Jr. 598
César Chávez 605
Richard Nixon 637
Jimmy Carter 667
Ronald Reagan 683
Bill Clinton 709

Geography and History

The Living Constitution 78
The Economy of the West 178
The United States in the Modern Age 314
American Migrations, 1865–1930 408
The Global Depression 470
The Cold War 534
The Struggle for Vietnam 644
The World's Energy 730

Global Connections

The Railroads of India 161
Coming to America 212
Worker Reforms 250
Japanese Immigrants in Hawaii 291
The Influenza Epidemic of 1918–1919 357
The Spanish Civil War 465
The Eastern Front 488
The Eisenhower Doctrine 542
The Fall of the Berlin Wall 694

Historical Documents

The Declaration of Independence 26
The Constitution 44
Washington's Farewell Address 86
The Monroe Doctrine 92
The Seneca Falls Declaration of Sentiments 99
The Emancipation Proclamation and The Gettysburg Address 112
Lincoln's Second Inaugural Address 125
Andrew Carnegie's *Gospel of Wealth* 192
Women's Right to the Suffrage by Susan B. Anthony 256
The Fourteen Points 350
Roosevelt's First Inaugural Address 433
The Truman Doctrine 514
Martin Luther King Jr.'s *I Have a Dream* 602

History in Action Unit Portfolios

The United States: The Diorama 117
Journey Across the World: The Travel Agency 231
Muckraker Magazine 319
Life in the Twenties: The Play 413
The New Deal Game Show 503
A Cold War Scrapbook 563
Vietnam War Documentary 649
Textbook Final Chapter 735

History Skills Workshop

Reading Maps 116
Reading Charts and Graphs 230
Identifying Cause and Effect 318
Using Visual Resources 412
Distinguishing Fact from Opinion and Identifying Bias 502
Using Primary and Secondary Sources 562
Doing Research and Making an Outline 648
Writing a Paper 734

Linking Past to Present

Freedom of Assembly 67
Water Usage in the West 104
Historically Black Colleges and Universities 127
Third Political Parties 204
Income Tax 280
The League of Nations and the UN 346
Movie Special Effects 395
Social Security 439
American Military Bases Abroad 516
The Changing Peace Corps 574
Women in the Workplace Today 613
The United States and Vietnam Today 629
The Changing Automobile 668
Careers in the Twenty-first Century 726

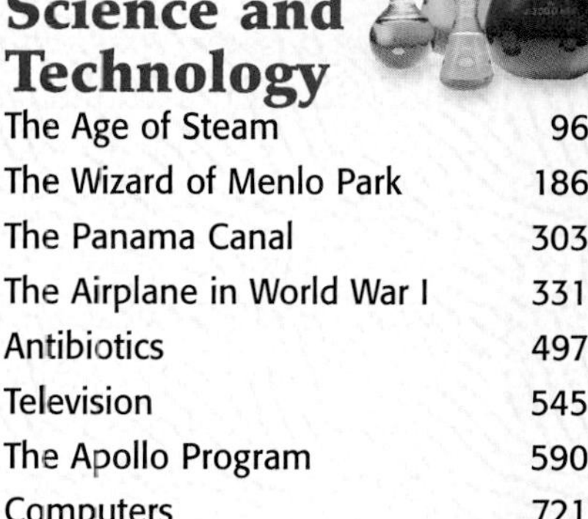

Science and Technology

The Age of Steam 96
The Wizard of Menlo Park 186
The Panama Canal 303
The Airplane in World War I 331
Antibiotics 497
Television 545
The Apollo Program 590
Computers 721

The Granger Collection, New York

Time Lines

American Beginnings (Beginnings–1865) 2
Industrial America (1850–1900) 120
A Growing America (1865–1920) 234
The Changing Nation (1914–1929) 322
A World in Crisis (1929–1945) 416
Postwar America (1945–1960) 506
Searching for Solutions (1945–1978) 566
Modern America (1968–Present) 652

Themes in American History

Call to Freedom begins every chapter with a set of theme questions. These questions are drawn from seven broad themes central to American history: Global Relations, Constitutional Heritage, Citizenship and Democracy, Technology and Society, Cultural Diversity, Geographic Diversity, and Economic Development. These themes provide a framework for the historical events in each chapter. This framework will help you understand the connections between historical events and see how past events relate to the social, political, and economic challenges our nation faces today.

As you begin each chapter, examine the theme questions and answer them based on your own experiences or prior knowledge. As you read the chapter, explore how the theme questions relate to the issues and events discussed. By tracing the themes through the book, you will be able to see how each theme has developed over time.

An Inca knife

Global Relations

Since the first Asian nomads crossed a land bridge to the continent thousands of years ago, America has been involved in global events. The Global Relations theme invites you to trace ways in which our nation's political, social, and economic development has affected—and been affected by—other countries and their people.

Constitutional Heritage

No study of American history would be complete without examining the U.S. Constitution, the document that provides the legal framework for our democratic government. The Constitutional Heritage theme will help you understand the Constitution's origins and how it has evolved through constitutional amendments, Supreme Court rulings, and congressional actions. This theme also explores how individuals and different groups in the nation's history have influenced the Constitution and have been affected by it. Finally, this theme asks you to consider how the relationship between Americans and their government has changed over time.

Citizenship and Democracy

The seal of the U.S. Congress

Throughout our history, Americans have struggled to define, possess, and protect individual rights and personal freedoms, such as the freedom of speech and religion, the right to vote, and the right to privacy. Americans have also worked to uphold the responsibilities of citizenship that accompany membership in our democracy. The Citizenship and Democracy theme explores how changing social, economic, and political conditions have influenced the theory and practices of these rights, freedoms, and responsibilities. This theme also examines the many conflicts that have arisen over these democratic values, and Americans' attempts to resolve these conflicts.

Technology and Society

From the building of the transcontinental railroad and the construction of skyscrapers during the Second Industrial Revolution to the computers that help you with your school assignments and personal projects today, technology has influenced every aspect of our culture and society. The Technology and Society theme explores technological developments and their influence on the U.S. economy and life.

Cultural Diversity

Our nation's rich and unique culture comes from its many ethnic, racial, and religious groups. The Cultural Diversity theme examines America's experience in dealing with diverse culture groups from the time of the Spanish explorers to recent immigration from around the world.

Geographic Diversity

The Geographic Diversity theme explores ways in which the nation's vast and diverse geography has played an important role in American history. The theme examines how the development of the nation's resources has helped shape its economy, society, and politics. In addition, the Geographic Diversity theme traces how public and government attitudes about resources and the environment have changed over time.

Economic Development

President Calvin Coolidge said in 1925 that "the business of America is business." The Economic Development theme asks you to explore the relationship between history and economics in the United States. The theme traces the changing relationship between government, business, and labor in America. It examines how the growth of a strong national economy has influenced the country's domestic and global politics, as well as individual lives and American society.

The Granger Collection, New York

Advertisement for barbed wire

Geography Themes

History and geography share many elements. History describes important events that have taken place from ancient times until the present day. Geography describes how physical environments affect human events. It also examines how people's actions influence the environment around them. To describe a series of events without placing them in their physical settings is to tell only part of the story. Geography themes include:

Location describes a site's position. It is the spot on the earth where something is found, often expressed in terms of its position in relation to other places.

Place refers to the physical features and the human influences that define a site and make it different from other sites. Physical features include landscape, climate, and vegetation. Human influences include land use, architecture, and population size.

Region is the common cultural or physical features of an area that distinguish it from other areas. One region may be different from another area because of physical characteristics, such as landforms or climate, or because of cultural features, such as dominant languages or religions.

Movement describes the way people interact as they travel, communicate, and trade goods and services. Movement includes human migration as well as the exchange of goods and ideas.

Human-Environment Interaction deals with the ways in which people interact with their natural environments, such as clearing forests, irrigating the land, and building cities. This theme is particularly important to the study of history in that it shows how people shape and are shaped by their surroundings.

Critical Thinking and the Study of History

Throughout *Call to Freedom*, you are asked to think critically about the events and issues that have shaped U.S. history. Critical thinking is the reasoned judgment of information and ideas. People who think critically study information to determine its accuracy. They evaluate arguments and analyze conclusions before accepting them. Critical thinkers are able to recognize and define problems and develop strategies for resolving them.

The development of critical thinking skills is essential to effective citizenship. Such skills empower you to exercise your civic rights and responsibilities. For example, critical thinking skills equip you to judge the messages of candidates for office and to evaluate news reports.

Helping you develop critical thinking skills is an important goal of *Call to Freedom*. The following eight critical thinking skills appear in the section reviews and chapter reviews.

Identifying Cause and Effect is part of interpreting the relationships between historical events. A cause is any action that leads to an event; the outcome of that action is an effect. Historians often point out multiple causes and effects for historical events. For example, economic and political problems caused the Soviet Union to break apart. This break-up ended the Cold War between the United States and the Soviet Union. This event in turn had many far-reaching effects.

A piece of the Berlin Wall

Evaluating is assessing the significance or overall importance of something, such as the success of a reform movement, the actions of a president, or the results of a major conflict. You should base your judgment on standards that others will understand and are likely to share. For example, you might consider the outcome of the Vietnam War and evaluate its effect on U.S. foreign policy. You could also evaluate the way in which debate over the war shaped domestic events in the United States.

Vietnam Service Medal

Synthesizing Information involves combining information and ideas from several sources or points in time to gain a new understanding of a topic or event. Much of the narrative writing in *Call to Freedom* is a synthesis. It pulls together historical data from many sources and perspectives from many people into a chronological story about our nation. Synthesizing information is important to understanding how many individual stories add up to create the big picture of events. Synthesizing the history of the Second Industrial Revolution, for example, might involve studying descriptions or images of factories and cities from the late 1800s, together with population and economic statistics. You could

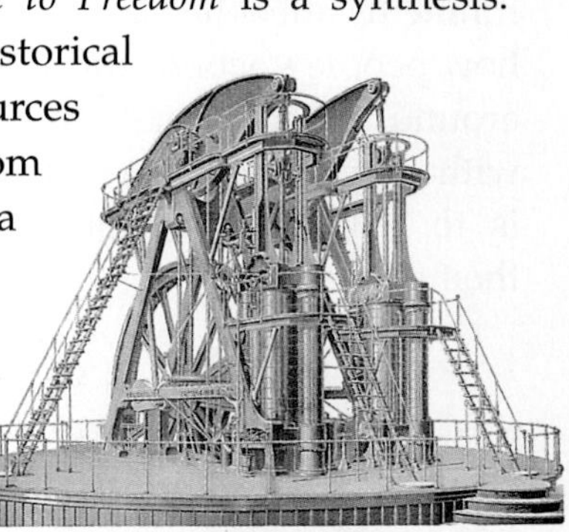

Corliss engine

also examine the writings of industrial workers, business owners, immigrants, inventors, and others who lived during the period.

Drawing Conclusions is forming a possible explanation for an event, a situation, or a problem. This explanation should be an educated guess based on available evidence. Often you must be prepared to test your conclusions against new evidence or arguments. For example, a historian might conclude that the gains African Americans made because of the civil rights movement in the 1950s and 1960s inspired other groups to struggle for their rights. The historian would then organize the evidence needed to support this conclusion and challenge other explanations of the origins.

Determining the Strength of an Argument involves understanding the main points of an argument and determining if the argument is logical, well organized, and based on factual information. You should look for flaws in reasoning as well as possible errors in the conclusions of an argument. In addition, you need to consider whether the statements that the argument uses to support its points are accurate. For example, a historian might examine the Truman Doctrine and ask whether President Truman had a strong justification for telling the nations of the world that the United States would oppose the spread of communism.

Making Comparisons is examining events, situations, or points of view for their similarities and differences. *Comparing* focuses on both the similarities and the differences. *Contrasting* focuses only on the differences. For example, a comparison between the years immediately following World Wars I and II would note that both postwar economies had to adjust to decreased defense spending and the job requirements of returning veterans. In contrast, the United States was more involved in international politics after World War II. Other factors to compare and contrast could include domestic reactions to communism following each war.

Identifying Generalizations and Stereotypes means viewing historical events and situations in ways that are fair to all cultural groups affected. Determining whether statements about a given group are consistent with each other and with the available facts helps you identify bias and unfair generalizations. Understanding how individuals and groups are sometimes inaccurately stereotyped by factors such as age, gender, religion, race, political views, and economic status broadens your knowledge of American history. For example, learning about American Indian cultures in the West before the arrival of American settlers helps you understand that settlers did not move into an empty western landscape. They encountered a land already settled by people with rich cultures.

Supporting a Point of View involves choosing a viewpoint on a particular event or issue and persuasively arguing for that position. Your argument should be well organized and based on specific evidence that supports the point of view you have chosen. Supporting a point of view often involves working with controversial or emotional issues. For example, you might consider the points of view surrounding the New Deal legislation of the 1930s. Whether you choose a position in favor of the agencies and programs created by the New Deal or against them, you would state your opinion clearly and give reasons to defend it.

The Granger Collection, New York

New Deal poster

ATLAS

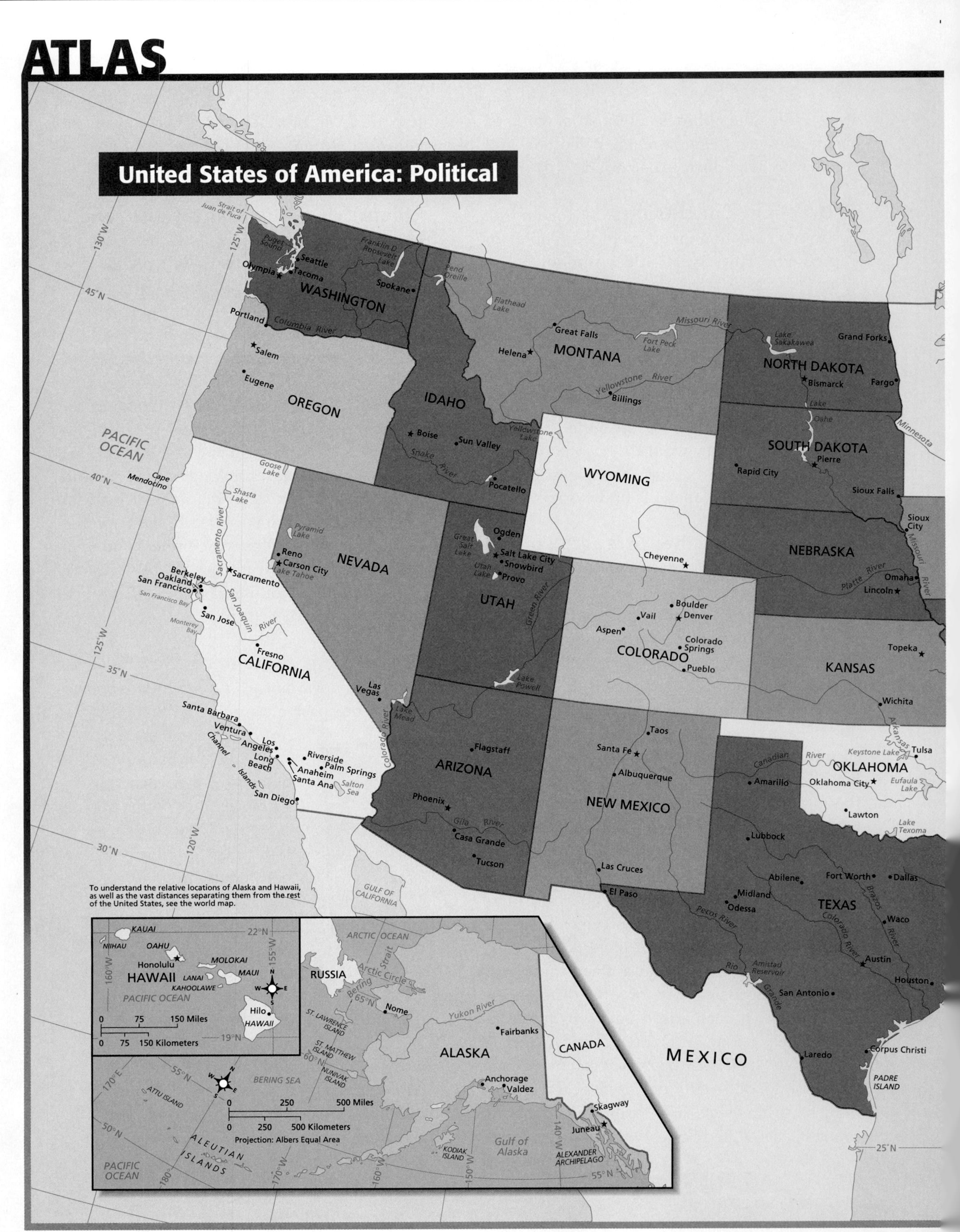

United States of America: Political
WASHINGTON
OREGON
CALIFORNIA
NEVADA
IDAHO
MONTANA
WYOMING
UTAH
COLORADO
ARIZONA
NEW MEXICO
NORTH DAKOTA
SOUTH DAKOTA
NEBRASKA
KANSAS
OKLAHOMA
TEXAS
MEXICO
CANADA
RUSSIA
ALASKA
HAWAII
PACIFIC OCEAN
Seattle
Tacoma
Olympia
Spokane
Portland
Salem
Eugene
Boise
Sun Valley
Pocatello
Great Falls
Helena
Billings
Bismarck
Grand Forks
Fargo
Pierre
Rapid City
Sioux Falls
Sioux City
Omaha
Lincoln
Cheyenne
Ogden
Salt Lake City
Snowbird
Provo
Reno
Carson City
Sacramento
Berkeley
Oakland
San Francisco
San Jose
Fresno
Las Vegas
Santa Barbara
Ventura
Los Angeles
Long Beach
Riverside
Palm Springs
Anaheim
Santa Ana
San Diego
Boulder
Denver
Vail
Aspen
Colorado Springs
Pueblo
Topeka
Wichita
Taos
Santa Fe
Albuquerque
Las Cruces
Flagstaff
Phoenix
Casa Grande
Tucson
Tulsa
Oklahoma City
Lawton
Amarillo
Lubbock
El Paso
Abilene
Midland
Odessa
Fort Worth
Dallas
Waco
Austin
Houston
San Antonio
Laredo
Corpus Christi
PADRE ISLAND
Strait of Juan de Fuca
Puget Sound
Franklin D. Roosevelt Lake
Pend Oreille
Flathead Lake
Missouri River
Fort Peck Lake
Lake Sakakawea
Lake Oahe
Yellowstone River
Yellowstone Lake
Snake River
Columbia River
Minnesota
Goose Lake
Shasta Lake
Sacramento River
San Joaquin River
Pyramid Lake
Lake Tahoe
San Francisco Bay
Monterey Bay
Great Salt Lake
Utah Lake
Green River
Lake Powell
Lake Mead
Colorado River
Salton Sea
Channel Islands
Gila River
Platte River
Arkansas River
Canadian River
Keystone Lake
Eufaula Lake
Lake Texoma
Pecos River
Brazos River
Amistad Reservoir
Rio Grande
Cape Mendocino
GULF OF CALIFORNIA
130°W
125°W
120°W
45°N
40°N
35°N
30°N
25°N
To understand the relative locations of Alaska and Hawaii, as well as the vast distances separating them from the rest of the United States, see the world map.
KAUAI
NIIHAU
OAHU
Honolulu
MOLOKAI
LANAI
MAUI
KAHOOLAWE
Hilo
HAWAII
22°N
19°N
160°W
155°W
0 75 150 Miles
0 75 150 Kilometers
ARCTIC OCEAN
Arctic Circle
Bering Strait
Nome
Yukon River
Fairbanks
ST. LAWRENCE ISLAND
ST. MATTHEW ISLAND
NUNIVAK ISLAND
BERING SEA
Anchorage
Valdez
Skagway
Juneau
Gulf of Alaska
KODIAK ISLAND
ALEXANDER ARCHIPELAGO
ATTU ISLAND
ALEUTIAN ISLANDS
PACIFIC OCEAN
0 250 500 Miles
0 250 500 Kilometers
Projection: Albers Equal Area
65°N
60°N
55°N
50°N
170°E
180°
170°W
160°W
150°W
140°W

CANADA
MAINE
NEW YORK
PENNSYLVANIA
OHIO
INDIANA
ILLINOIS
MICHIGAN
WISCONSIN
MINNESOTA
IOWA
MISSOURI
KENTUCKY
TENNESSEE
WEST VIRGINIA
VIRGINIA
NORTH CAROLINA
SOUTH CAROLINA
GEORGIA
ALABAMA
MISSISSIPPI
ARKANSAS
LOUISIANA
FLORIDA
VT
NH
MA
CT
RI
NJ
DE
MD
ATLANTIC OCEAN
GULF OF MEXICO
THE BAHAMAS
CUBA
National capital
State capitals
Other cities
0
250
500 Miles
0
250
500 Kilometers
Projection: Albers Equal Area
Robinson Projection

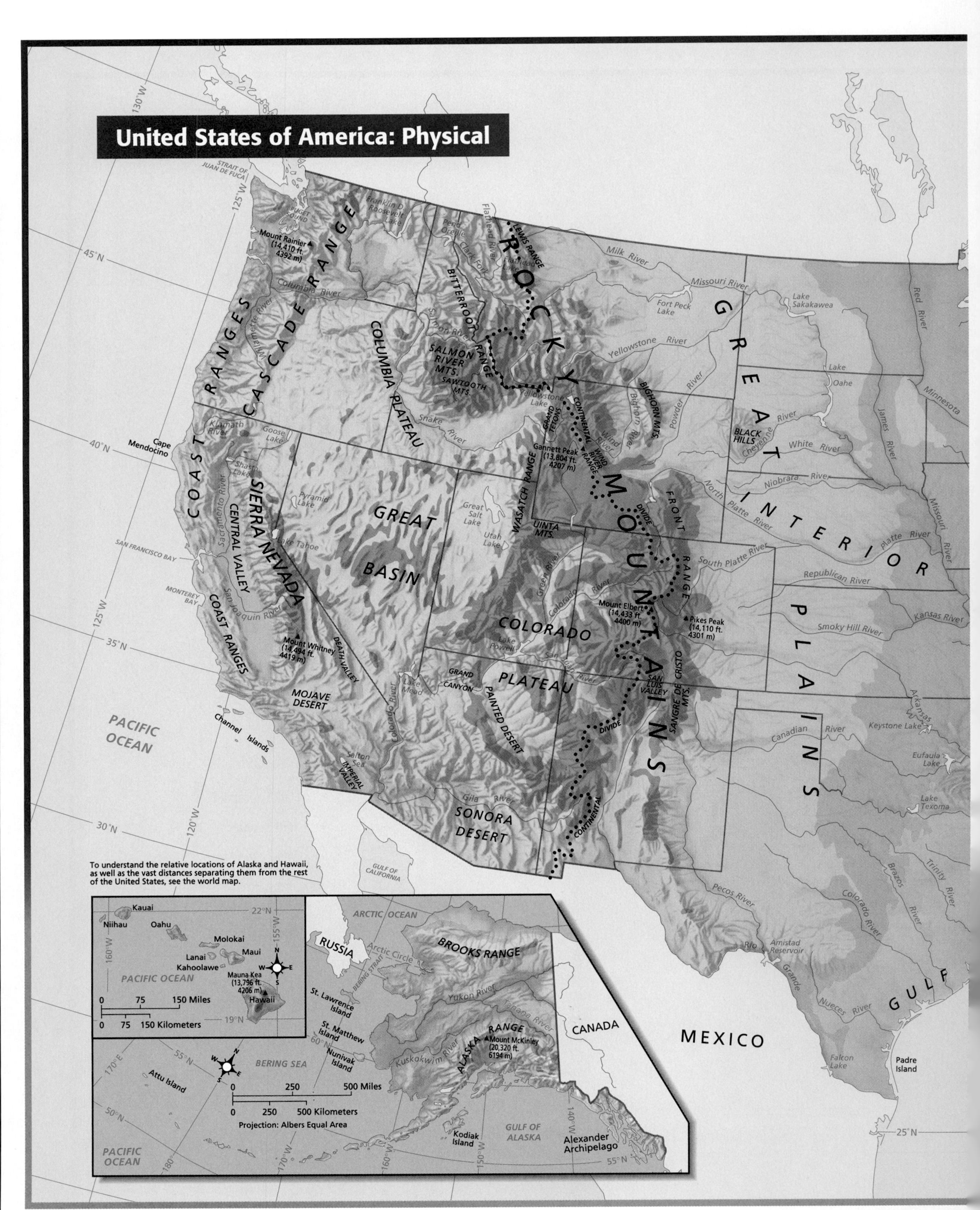
United States of America: Physical
To understand the relative locations of Alaska and Hawaii, as well as the vast distances separating them from the rest of the United States, see the world map.
PACIFIC OCEAN
MEXICO
CANADA
ROCKY MOUNTAINS
GREAT INTERIOR PLAINS
GREAT BASIN
COLORADO PLATEAU
COLUMBIA PLATEAU
CASCADE RANGE
COAST RANGES
SIERRA NEVADA
CENTRAL VALLEY
MOJAVE DESERT
SONORA DESERT
Mount Rainier (14,410 ft. 4392 m)
Mount Whitney (14,494 ft. 4419 m)
Mount Elbert (14,433 ft. 4400 m)
Pikes Peak (14,110 ft. 4301 m)
Gannett Peak (13,804 ft. 4207 m)
Mount McKinley (20,320 ft. 6194 m)
Mauna Kea (13,796 ft. 4206 m)
Projection: Albers Equal Area

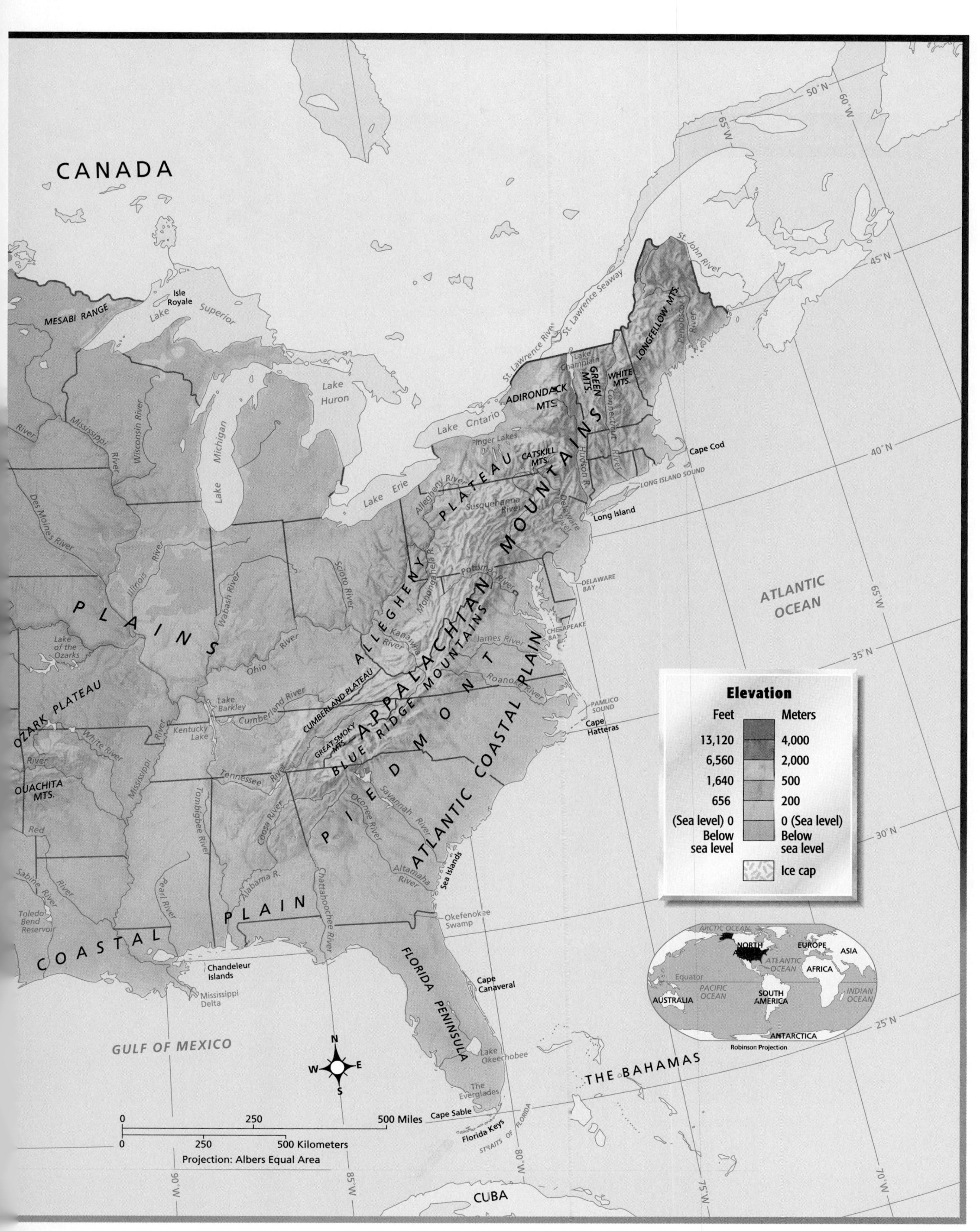

CANADA
ATLANTIC OCEAN
GULF OF MEXICO
THE BAHAMAS
CUBA
PLAINS
COASTAL PLAIN
ATLANTIC COASTAL PLAIN
PIEDMONT
APPALACHIAN MOUNTAINS
ALLEGHENY PLATEAU
BLUE RIDGE MOUNTAINS
CUMBERLAND PLATEAU
GREAT SMOKY MTS.
OZARK PLATEAU
OUACHITA MTS.
ADIRONDACK MTS.
CATSKILL MTS.
GREEN MTS.
WHITE MTS.
LONGFELLOW MTS.
MESABI RANGE
FLORIDA PENINSULA
Isle Royale
Lake Superior
Lake Michigan
Lake Huron
Lake Erie
Lake Ontario
Lake Champlain
Finger Lakes
St. Lawrence River
St. Lawrence Seaway
St. John River
Penobscot River
Connecticut River
Hudson R.
Delaware River
Susquehanna River
Allegheny River
Monongahela R.
Potomac River
James River
Kanawha River
Roanoke River
Savannah River
Oconee River
Altamaha River
Chattahoochee River
Coosa River
Alabama R.
Tombigbee River
Pearl River
Tennessee River
Cumberland River
Ohio River
Scioto River
Wabash River
Illinois River
Wisconsin River
Mississippi River
Des Moines River
White River
Red River
Sabine River
Toledo Bend Reservoir
Lake of the Ozarks
Lake Barkley
Kentucky Lake
Cape Cod
LONG ISLAND SOUND
Long Island
DELAWARE BAY
CHESAPEAKE BAY
PAMLICO SOUND
Cape Hatteras
Sea Islands
Okefenokee Swamp
Cape Canaveral
Lake Okeechobee
The Everglades
Cape Sable
Florida Keys
STRAITS OF FLORIDA
Chandeleur Islands
Mississippi Delta
50° N
45° N
40° N
35° N
30° N
25° N
60° W
65° W
70° W
75° W
80° W
85° W
90° W
Elevation
Feet
Meters
13,120
4,000
6,560
2,000
1,640
500
656
200
(Sea level) 0
0 (Sea level)
Below sea level
Below sea level
Ice cap
ARCTIC OCEAN
NORTH AMERICA
EUROPE
ASIA
ATLANTIC OCEAN
AFRICA
Equator
PACIFIC OCEAN
SOUTH AMERICA
AUSTRALIA
INDIAN OCEAN
ANTARCTICA
Robinson Projection
N
S
E
W
0
250
500 Miles
0
250
500 Kilometers
Projection: Albers Equal Area

World: Political

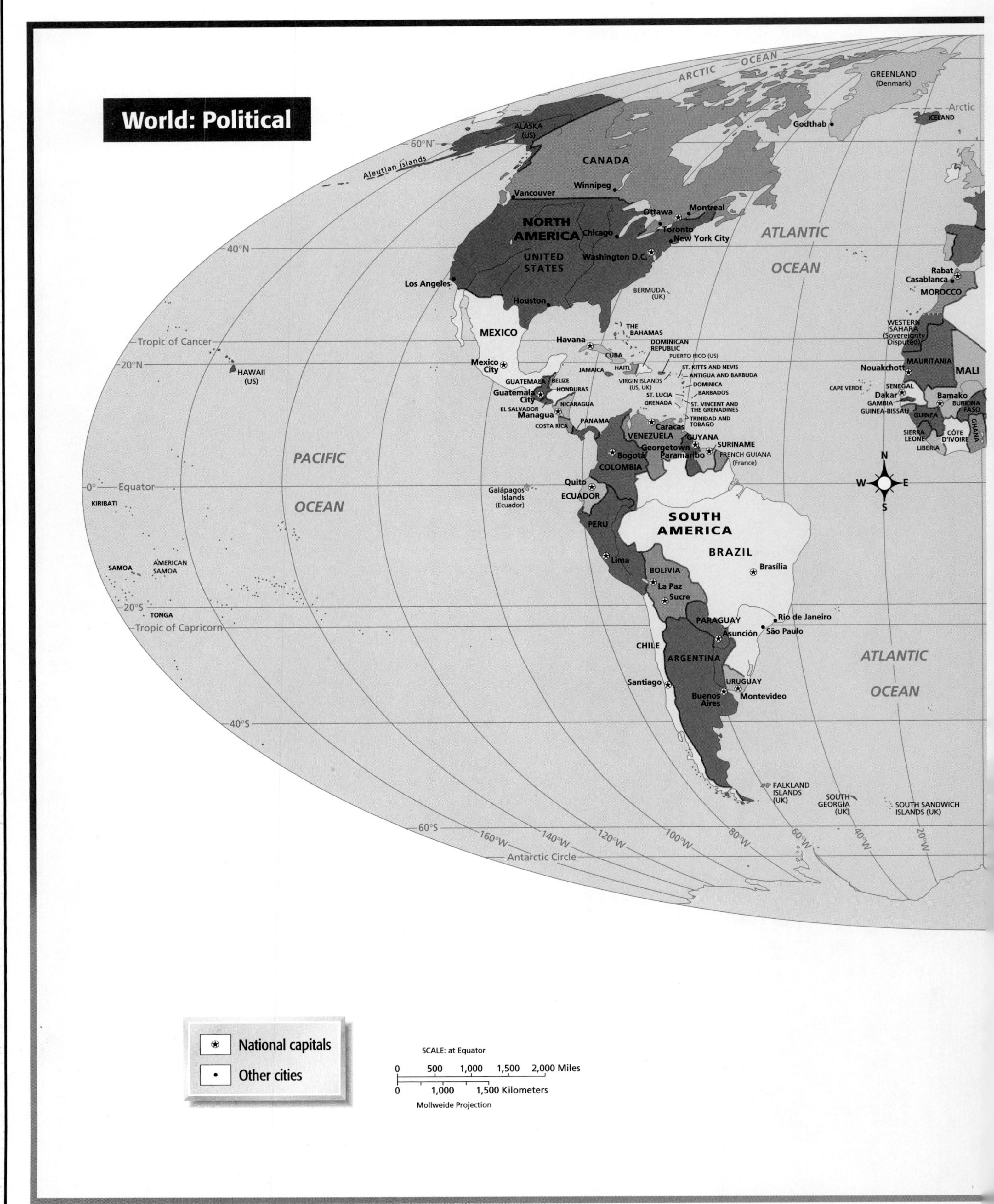

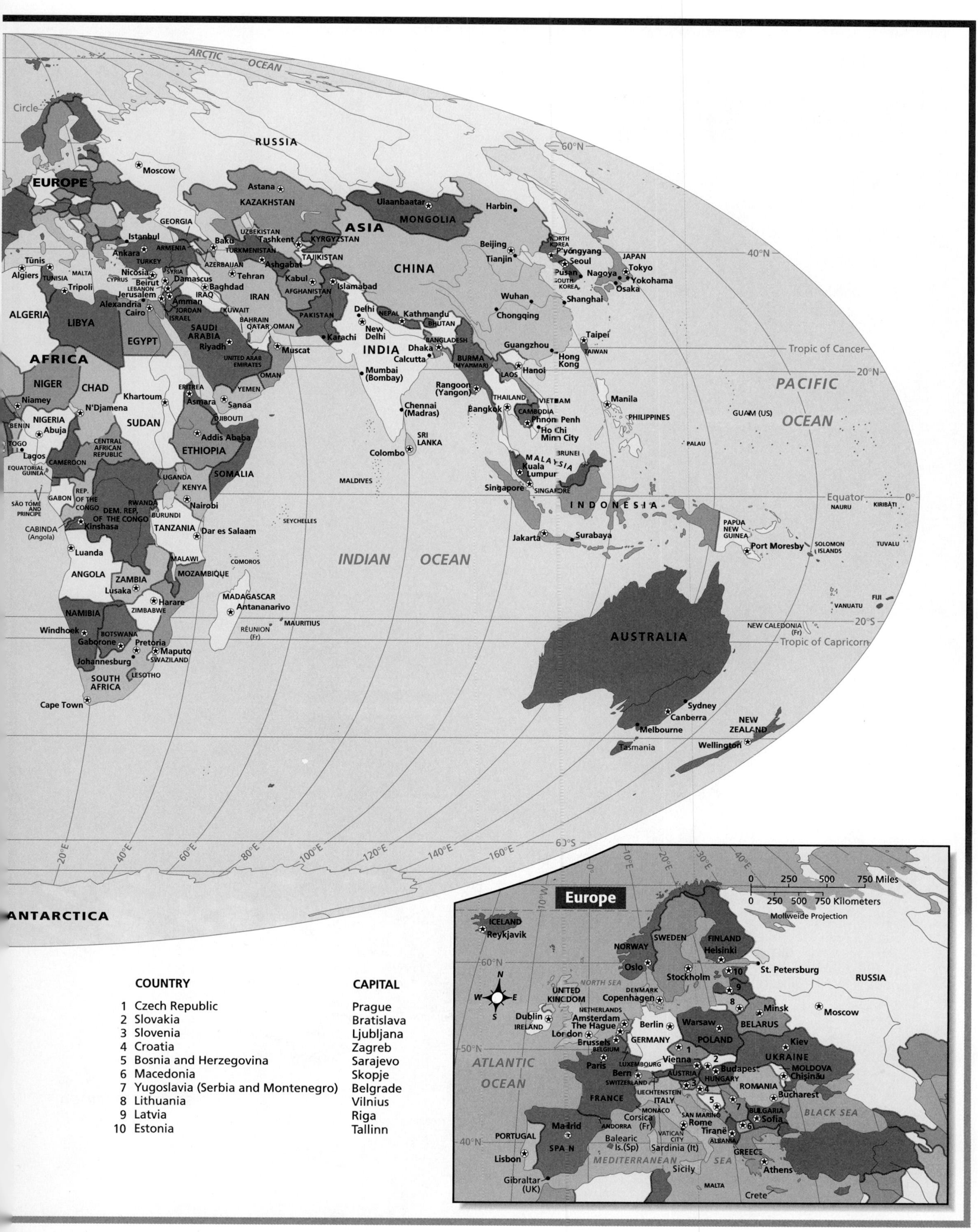

ARCTIC OCEAN
Circle
RUSSIA
Moscow
EUROPE
Astana
KAZAKHSTAN
Ulaanbaatar
MONGOLIA
Harbin
ASIA
GEORGIA
Istanbul
ARMENIA
Baku
UZBEKISTAN
Tashkent
KYRGYZSTAN
TURKMENISTAN
TAJIKISTAN
Ankara
TURKEY
AZERBAIJAN
Ashgabat
Tunis
Algiers
TUNISIA
MALTA
CYPRUS
Nicosia
Beirut
LEBANON
SYRIA
Damascus
Tehran
Baghdad
IRAQ
Kabul
AFGHANISTAN
Islamabad
CHINA
Beijing
Tianjin
NORTH KOREA
P'yongyang
Seoul
SOUTH KOREA
Pusan
JAPAN
Tokyo
Nagoya
Yokohama
Osaka
Tripoli
Jerusalem
Amman
ISRAEL
JORDAN
Alexandria
Cairo
IRAN
KUWAIT
BAHRAIN
QATAR
OMAN
PAKISTAN
Delhi
New Delhi
NEPAL
Kathmandu
BHUTAN
Wuhan
Chongqing
Shanghai
ALGERIA
LIBYA
EGYPT
SAUDI ARABIA
Riyadh
UNITED ARAB EMIRATES
Muscat
Karachi
INDIA
BANGLADESH
Dhaka
Calcutta
BURMA (MYANMAR)
Guangzhou
Hong Kong
Taipei
TAIWAN
Tropic of Cancer
AFRICA
NIGER
CHAD
Niamey
N'Djamena
Khartoum
SUDAN
ERITREA
Asmara
YEMEN
Sanaa
DJIBOUTI
Mumbai (Bombay)
LAOS
Hanoi
Rangoon (Yangon)
THAILAND
Bangkok
VIETNAM
CAMBODIA
Phnom Penh
Ho Chi Minh City
Manila
PHILIPPINES
PACIFIC OCEAN
GUAM (US)
NIGERIA
Abuja
BENIN
TOGO
Lagos
CENTRAL AFRICAN REPUBLIC
Addis Ababa
ETHIOPIA
Chennai (Madras)
SRI LANKA
Colombo
PALAU
EQUATORIAL GUINEA
CAMEROON
SOMALIA
UGANDA
KENYA
MALDIVES
BRUNEI
MALAYSIA
Kuala Lumpur
Singapore
SINGAPORE
GABON
SÃO TOMÉ AND PRÍNCIPE
REP. OF THE CONGO
DEM. REP. OF THE CONGO
RWANDA
BURUNDI
Kinshasa
Nairobi
SEYCHELLES
INDONESIA
Equator
NAURU
KIRIBATI
CABINDA (Angola)
TANZANIA
Dar es Salaam
Jakarta
Surabaya
PAPUA NEW GUINEA
Port Moresby
SOLOMON ISLANDS
TUVALU
Luanda
ANGOLA
MALAWI
COMOROS
MOZAMBIQUE
INDIAN OCEAN
ZAMBIA
Lusaka
Harare
ZIMBABWE
MADAGASCAR
Antananarivo
VANUATU
FIJI
NAMIBIA
Windhoek
BOTSWANA
Gaborone
Pretoria
Maputo
SWAZILAND
RÉUNION (Fr)
MAURITIUS
NEW CALEDONIA (Fr)
AUSTRALIA
Tropic of Capricorn
Johannesburg
LESOTHO
SOUTH AFRICA
Cape Town
Sydney
Canberra
Melbourne
NEW ZEALAND
Wellington
Tasmania
60°N
40°N
20°N
0°
20°S
60°S
20°E
40°E
60°E
80°E
100°E
120°E
140°E
160°E
ANTARCTICA
COUNTRY
1 Czech Republic
2 Slovakia
3 Slovenia
4 Croatia
5 Bosnia and Herzegovina
6 Macedonia
7 Yugoslavia (Serbia and Montenegro)
8 Lithuania
9 Latvia
10 Estonia
CAPITAL
Prague
Bratislava
Ljubljana
Zagreb
Sarajevo
Skopje
Belgrade
Vilnius
Riga
Tallinn
Europe
0 250 500 750 Miles
0 250 500 750 Kilometers
Mollweide Projection
ICELAND
Reykjavik
NORWAY
SWEDEN
FINLAND
Helsinki
Oslo
Stockholm
St. Petersburg
RUSSIA
NORTH SEA
DENMARK
Copenhagen
UNITED KINGDOM
Dublin
IRELAND
NETHERLANDS
Amsterdam
The Hague
London
Brussels
BELGIUM
Berlin
GERMANY
Warsaw
POLAND
Minsk
BELARUS
Moscow
Kiev
UKRAINE
ATLANTIC OCEAN
LUXEMBOURG
Paris
Vienna
AUSTRIA
Bern
SWITZERLAND
LIECHTENSTEIN
Budapest
HUNGARY
MOLDOVA
Chişinău
ROMANIA
Bucharest
FRANCE
ITALY
MONACO
Corsica (Fr)
SAN MARINO
Rome
BULGARIA
Sofia
BLACK SEA
PORTUGAL
Madrid
ANDORRA
SPAIN
Balearic Is.(Sp)
VATICAN CITY
Sardinia (It)
Tiranë
ALBANIA
GREECE
Lisbon
MEDITERRANEAN SEA
Sicily
Athens
Gibraltar (UK)
MALTA
Crete

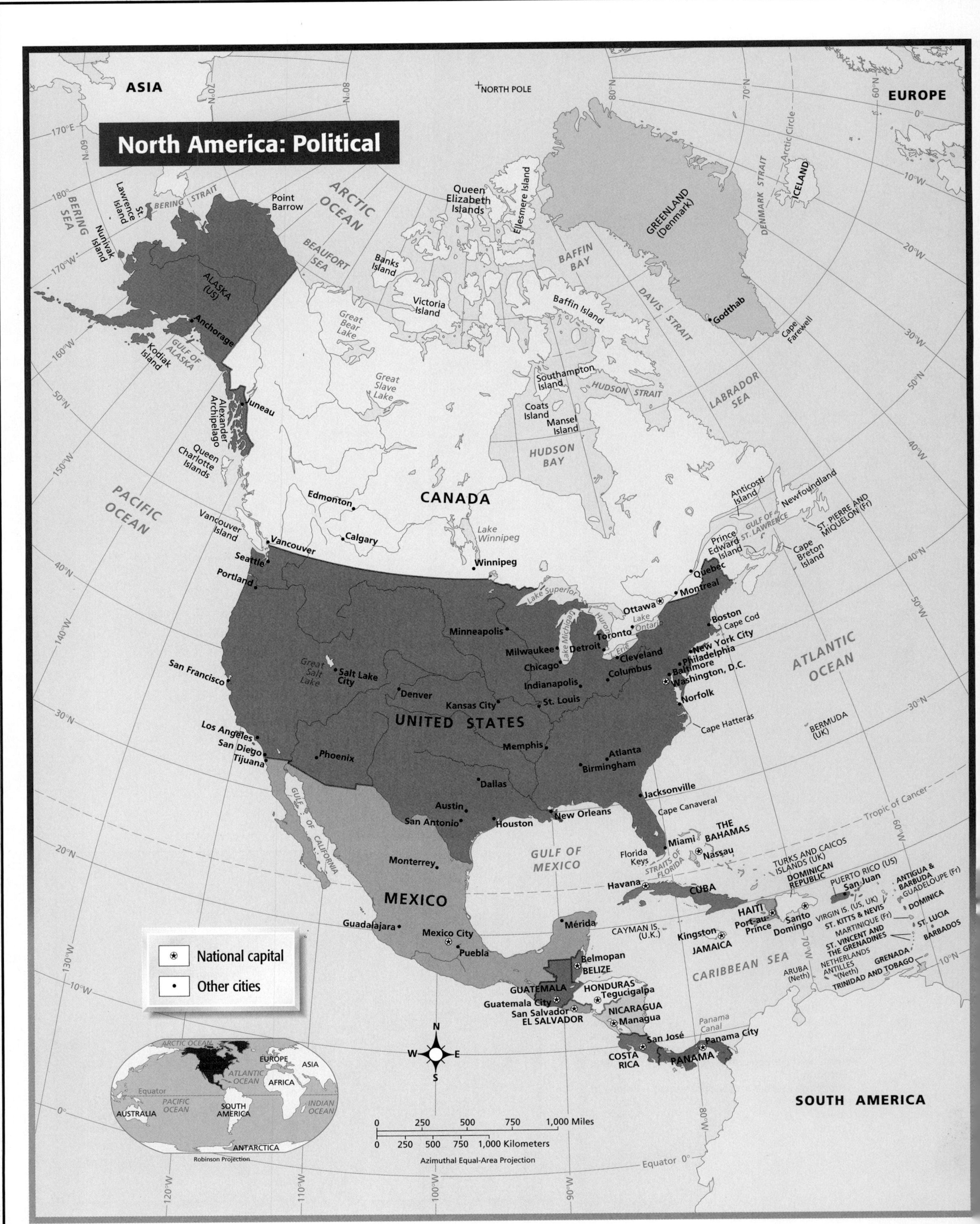
North America: Political
ASIA
NORTH POLE
EUROPE
ARCTIC OCEAN
BERING SEA
BERING STRAIT
St. Lawrence Island
Nunivak Island
Point Barrow
BEAUFORT SEA
Banks Island
Victoria Island
Queen Elizabeth Islands
Ellesmere Island
GREENLAND (Denmark)
ICELAND
DENMARK STRAIT
Arctic Circle
BAFFIN BAY
Baffin Island
DAVIS STRAIT
Godthab
Cape Farewell
ALASKA (US)
Anchorage
GULF OF ALASKA
Kodiak Island
Juneau
Alexander Archipelago
Queen Charlotte Islands
Great Bear Lake
Great Slave Lake
Southampton Island
HUDSON STRAIT
Coats Island
Mansel Island
LABRADOR SEA
HUDSON BAY
PACIFIC OCEAN
Vancouver Island
Edmonton
CANADA
Calgary
Vancouver
Lake Winnipeg
Winnipeg
Anticosti Island
Newfoundland
GULF OF ST. LAWRENCE
ST. PIERRE AND MIQUELON (Fr)
Prince Edward Island
Cape Breton Island
Quebec
Montreal
Ottawa
Lake Superior
Lake Huron
Lake Michigan
Lake Ontario
Lake Erie
Seattle
Portland
Boston
Cape Cod
Minneapolis
Toronto
Milwaukee
Detroit
New York City
Philadelphia
Cleveland
Baltimore
Chicago
Washington, D.C.
Columbus
ATLANTIC OCEAN
San Francisco
Great Salt Lake
Salt Lake City
Indianapolis
Denver
Kansas City
St. Louis
Norfolk
UNITED STATES
Cape Hatteras
Los Angeles
San Diego
Tijuana
Phoenix
Memphis
Atlanta
Birmingham
BERMUDA (UK)
Dallas
Jacksonville
Cape Canaveral
GULF OF CALIFORNIA
Austin
San Antonio
Houston
New Orleans
Tropic of Cancer
Miami
THE BAHAMAS
Nassau
Florida Keys
STRAITS OF FLORIDA
GULF OF MEXICO
Monterrey
TURKS AND CAICOS ISLANDS (UK)
DOMINICAN REPUBLIC
PUERTO RICO (US)
San Juan
ANTIGUA & BARBUDA
GUADELOUPE (Fr)
Havana
CUBA
MEXICO
HAITI
Port-au-Prince
Santo Domingo
VIRGIN IS. (US, UK)
ST. KITTS & NEVIS
MARTINIQUE (Fr)
DOMINICA
ST. LUCIA
BARBADOS
ST. VINCENT AND THE GRENADINES
Guadalajara
Mexico City
Mérida
CAYMAN IS. (U.K.)
Kingston
JAMAICA
Puebla
Belmopan
BELIZE
CARIBBEAN SEA
ARUBA (Neth)
NETHERLANDS ANTILLES (Neth)
GRENADA
TRINIDAD AND TOBAGO
GUATEMALA
Guatemala City
HONDURAS
Tegucigalpa
San Salvador
EL SALVADOR
NICARAGUA
Managua
San José
Panama Canal
Panama City
COSTA RICA
PANAMA
SOUTH AMERICA
National capital
Other cities
ARCTIC OCEAN
EUROPE
ASIA
ATLANTIC OCEAN
AFRICA
Equator
PACIFIC OCEAN
SOUTH AMERICA
INDIAN OCEAN
AUSTRALIA
ANTARCTICA
Robinson Projection
N
S
E
W
0 250 500 750 1,000 Miles
0 250 500 750 1,000 Kilometers
Azimuthal Equal-Area Projection
Equator 0°
170°E
180°
170°W
160°W
150°W
140°W
130°W
120°W
110°W
100°W
90°W
80°W
70°W
60°W
50°W
40°W
30°W
20°W
10°W
0°
70°N
80°N
60°N
50°N
40°N
30°N
20°N
10°N

South America: Political
CENTRAL AMERICA
CARIBBEAN SEA
Barranquilla
Cartagena
Caracas
Lake Maracaibo
VENEZUELA
Orinoco River
Georgetown
GUYANA
Paramaribo
SURINAME
Cayenne
FRENCH GUIANA (Fr.)
ATLANTIC OCEAN
Medellín
Bogotá
COLOMBIA
Cali
Malpelo Island (Colombia)
Rio Negro
Quito
ECUADOR
Equator
Guayaquil
Galápagos Islands (Ecuador)
Amazon River
Belém
BRAZIL
PERU
Marañón River
Ucayali River
Trujillo
Callao
Lima
Recife
São Francisco River
Salvador
PACIFIC OCEAN
Lake Titicaca
BOLIVIA
La Paz
Arequipa
Brasília
Lake Poopó
Sucre
Belo Horizonte
PARAGUAY
Paraguay River
Asunción
Campinas
São Paulo
Rio de Janeiro
Curitiba
Tropic of Capricorn
San Ambrosio Island (Chile)
San Félix Island (Chile)
CHILE
Paraná River
Uruguay River
Pôrto Alegre
Córdoba
Juan Fernández Islands (Chile)
Valparaíso
Santiago
Rosario
URUGUAY
Buenos Aires
Morón
San Justo
Lomas de Zamora
Montevideo
RÍO DE LA PLATA
ARGENTINA
ATLANTIC OCEAN
National capital
Other cities
STRAIT OF MAGELLAN
FALKLAND ISLANDS (UK)
Tierra del Fuego
SOUTH GEORGIA ISLAND (UK)
0 250 500 750 1,000 Miles
0 250 500 750 1,000 Kilometers
Azimuthal Equal-Area Projection
ARCTIC OCEAN
NORTH AMERICA
EUROPE
ASIA
ATLANTIC OCEAN
AFRICA
PACIFIC OCEAN
SOUTH AMERICA
AUSTRALIA
INDIAN OCEAN
ANTARCTICA
Robinson Projection
N
S
E
W
20°N
10°N
0°
10°S
20°S
30°S
40°S
50°S
110°W
100°W
90°W
80°W
70°W
60°W
50°W
40°W
30°W
20°W

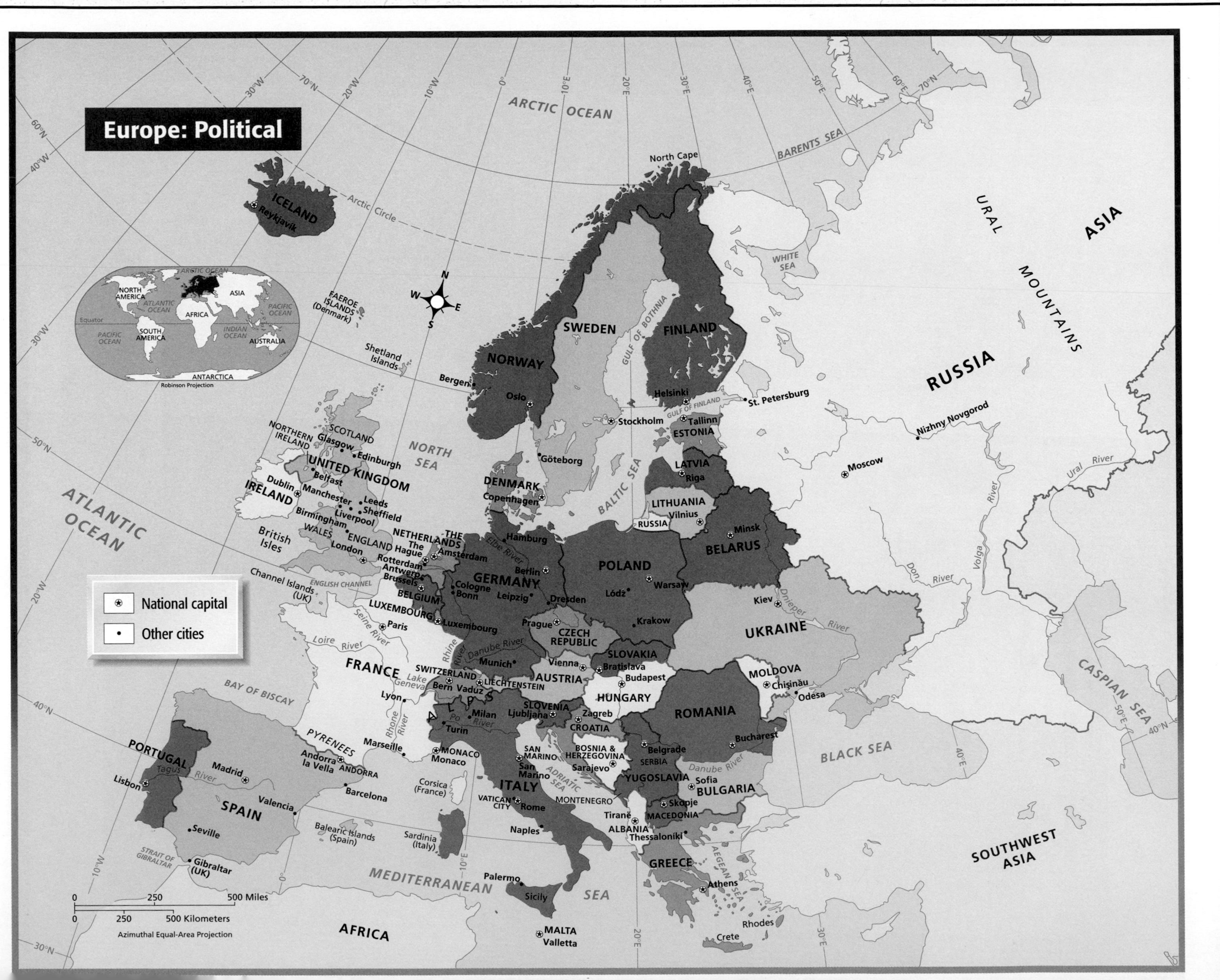
Europe: Political
National capital
Other cities
ARCTIC OCEAN
ATLANTIC OCEAN
NORTH SEA
BARENTS SEA
WHITE SEA
BALTIC SEA
GULF OF BOTHNIA
GULF OF FINLAND
BAY OF BISCAY
MEDITERRANEAN SEA
ADRIATIC SEA
AEGEAN SEA
BLACK SEA
CASPIAN SEA
ENGLISH CHANNEL
STRAIT OF GIBRALTAR
ASIA
AFRICA
SOUTHWEST ASIA
URAL MOUNTAINS
ALPS
PYRENEES
Arctic Circle
ICELAND
Reykjavik
FAEROE ISLANDS (Denmark)
Shetland Islands
British Isles
IRELAND
Dublin
NORTHERN IRELAND
UNITED KINGDOM
SCOTLAND
Glasgow
Edinburgh
Belfast
Manchester
Leeds
Sheffield
Liverpool
Birmingham
WALES
ENGLAND
London
Channel Islands (UK)
NORWAY
Oslo
Bergen
North Cape
SWEDEN
Stockholm
Göteborg
FINLAND
Helsinki
DENMARK
Copenhagen
ESTONIA
Tallinn
LATVIA
Riga
LITHUANIA
Vilnius
RUSSIA
BELARUS
Minsk
POLAND
Warsaw
Lódz
Krakow
GERMANY
Berlin
Hamburg
Dresden
Leipzig
Cologne
Bonn
Munich
THE NETHERLANDS
Amsterdam
The Hague
Rotterdam
BELGIUM
Antwerp
Brussels
LUXEMBOURG
Luxembourg
FRANCE
Paris
Lyon
Marseille
CZECH REPUBLIC
Prague
SLOVAKIA
Bratislava
AUSTRIA
Vienna
HUNGARY
Budapest
SWITZERLAND
Bern
LIECHTENSTEIN
Vaduz
SLOVENIA
Ljubljana
CROATIA
Zagreb
BOSNIA & HERZEGOVINA
Sarajevo
YUGOSLAVIA
SERBIA
MONTENEGRO
Belgrade
MACEDONIA
Skopje
ALBANIA
Tiranë
GREECE
Athens
Thessaloníki
Crete
Rhodes
BULGARIA
Sofia
ROMANIA
Bucharest
MOLDOVA
Chişinău
UKRAINE
Kiev
Odesa
Moscow
St. Petersburg
Nizhny Novgorod
ITALY
Rome
Milan
Turin
Naples
Palermo
Sicily
Sardinia (Italy)
Corsica (France)
SAN MARINO
San Marino
VATICAN CITY
MONACO
Monaco
MALTA
Valletta
SPAIN
Madrid
Barcelona
Valencia
Seville
Gibraltar (UK)
Balearic Islands (Spain)
ANDORRA
Andorra la Vella
PORTUGAL
Lisbon
Volga River
Don River
Dnieper River
Ural River
Danube River
Rhine River
Elbe River
Po River
Rhone River
Seine River
Loire River
Tagus River
Lake Geneva
0 250 500 Miles
0 250 500 Kilometers
Azimuthal Equal-Area Projection
Robinson Projection
Equator

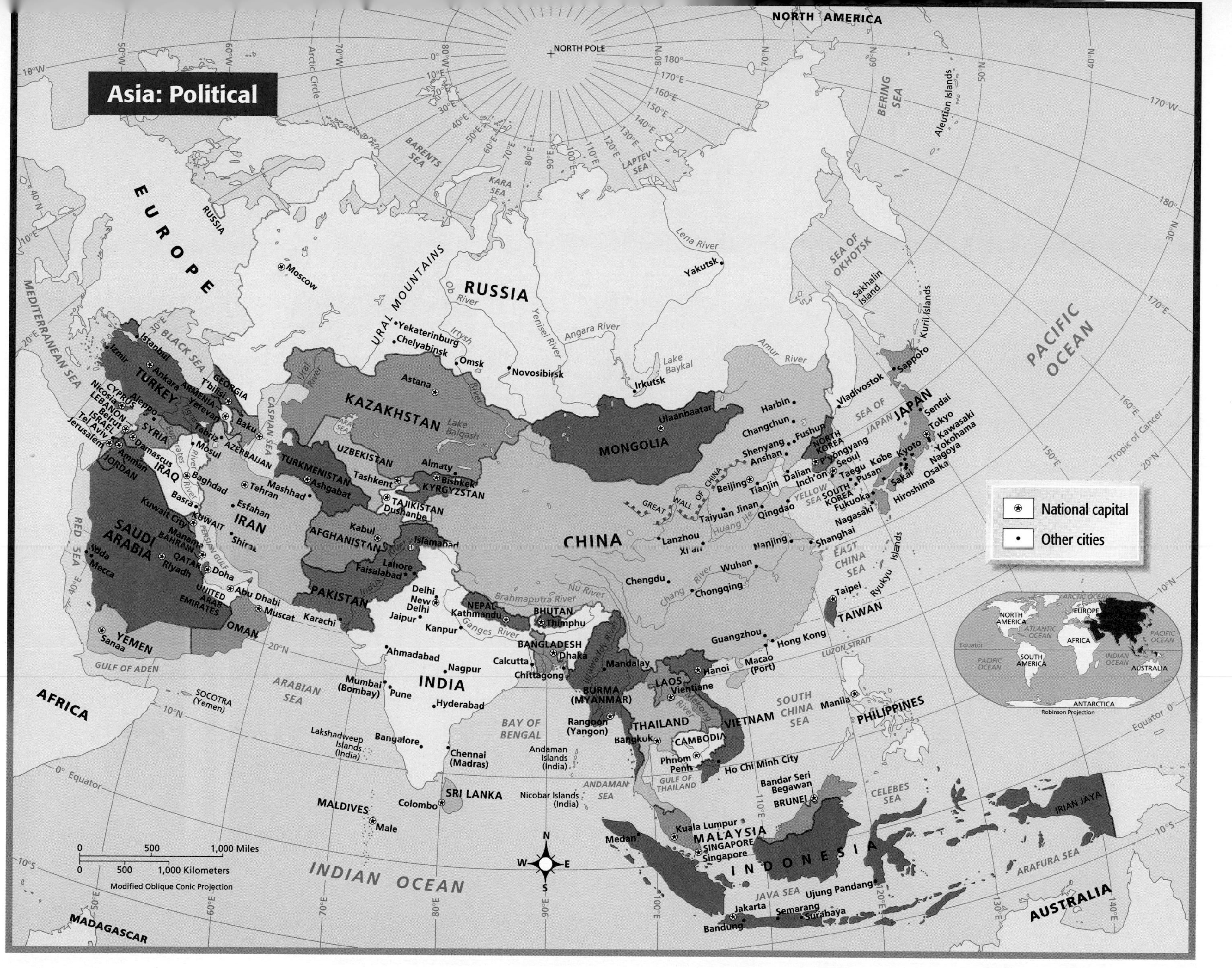

Asia: Political
National capital
Other cities
0 500 1,000 Miles
0 500 1,000 Kilometers
Modified Oblique Conic Projection
Robinson Projection
NORTH POLE
Arctic Circle
Tropic of Cancer
Equator
NORTH AMERICA
EUROPE
AFRICA
AUSTRALIA
MADAGASCAR
PACIFIC OCEAN
INDIAN OCEAN
ARABIAN SEA
BAY OF BENGAL
ANDAMAN SEA
GULF OF THAILAND
SOUTH CHINA SEA
EAST CHINA SEA
YELLOW SEA
SEA OF JAPAN
SEA OF OKHOTSK
BERING SEA
BARENTS SEA
KARA SEA
LAPTEV SEA
CASPIAN SEA
ARAL SEA
BLACK SEA
MEDITERRANEAN SEA
RED SEA
PERSIAN GULF
GULF OF ADEN
CELEBES SEA
JAVA SEA
ARAFURA SEA
LUZON STRAIT
URAL MOUNTAINS
GREAT WALL OF CHINA
Lena River
Ob River
Irtysh River
Yenisei River
Angara River
Amur River
Ural River
Lake Baykal
Lake Balqash
Huang He
Chang River
Nu River
Brahmaputra River
Ganges River
Indus River
Irrawaddy River
Mekong River
Tigris River
Euphrates River
Aleutian Islands
Kuril Islands
Sakhalin Island
Ryukyu Islands
Andaman Islands (India)
Nicobar Islands (India)
Lakshadweep Islands (India)
SOCOTRA (Yemen)
RUSSIA
KAZAKHSTAN
UZBEKISTAN
TURKMENISTAN
KYRGYZSTAN
TAJIKISTAN
AFGHANISTAN
PAKISTAN
INDIA
NEPAL
BHUTAN
BANGLADESH
SRI LANKA
MALDIVES
CHINA
MONGOLIA
NORTH KOREA
SOUTH KOREA
JAPAN
TAIWAN
PHILIPPINES
BURMA (MYANMAR)
THAILAND
LAOS
CAMBODIA
VIETNAM
MALAYSIA
SINGAPORE
BRUNEI
INDONESIA
IRIAN JAYA
IRAN
IRAQ
SYRIA
TURKEY
GEORGIA
ARMENIA
AZERBAIJAN
CYPRUS
LEBANON
ISRAEL
JORDAN
SAUDI ARABIA
KUWAIT
BAHRAIN
QATAR
UNITED ARAB EMIRATES
OMAN
YEMEN
Moscow
Yekaterinburg
Chelyabinsk
Omsk
Novosibirsk
Irkutsk
Yakutsk
Vladivostok
Astana
Almaty
Bishkek
Tashkent
Dushanbe
Ashgabat
Kabul
Islamabad
Lahore
Faisalabad
Karachi
Delhi
New Delhi
Jaipur
Kanpur
Kathmandu
Thimphu
Dhaka
Calcutta
Chittagong
Ahmadabad
Nagpur
Mumbai (Bombay)
Pune
Hyderabad
Bangalore
Chennai (Madras)
Colombo
Male
Ulaanbaatar
Harbin
Changchun
Shenyang
Anshan
Fushun
Beijing
Tianjin
Dalian
Taiyuan
Jinan
Qingdao
Lanzhou
Xi'an
Nanjing
Shanghai
Wuhan
Chengdu
Chongqing
Guangzhou
Hong Kong
Macao (Port)
P'yongyang
Seoul
Inch'on
Taegu
Pusan
Sapporo
Sendai
Tokyo
Kawasaki
Yokohama
Nagoya
Kyoto
Osaka
Kobe
Sakai
Hiroshima
Fukuoka
Nagasaki
Taipei
Manila
Mandalay
Rangoon (Yangon)
Bangkok
Hanoi
Vientiane
Phnom Penh
Ho Chi Minh City
Bandar Seri Begawan
Kuala Lumpur
Singapore
Medan
Jakarta
Bandung
Semarang
Surabaya
Ujung Pandang
Istanbul
Ankara
Izmir
Nicosia
Beirut
Tel Aviv
Jerusalem
Amman
Damascus
Aleppo
Mosul
Baghdad
Basra
Kuwait City
Manama
Doha
Riyadh
Abu Dhabi
Muscat
Jidda
Mecca
Sanaa
T'bilisi
Yerevan
Baku
Tabriz
Tehran
Mashhad
Esfahan
Shiraz
ANTARCTICA
ARCTIC OCEAN
ATLANTIC OCEAN
SOUTH AMERICA

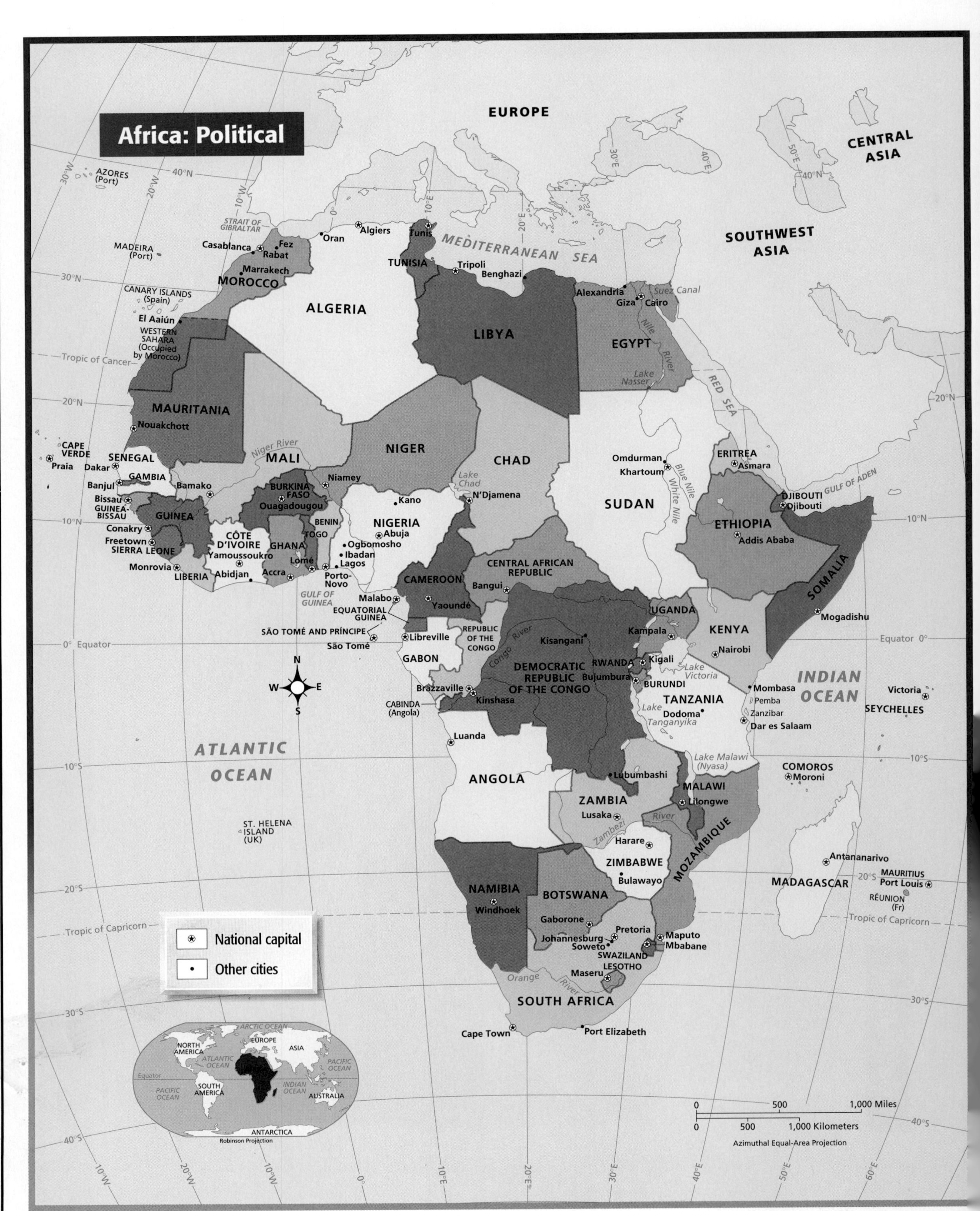

Africa: Political
EUROPE
CENTRAL ASIA
SOUTHWEST ASIA
AZORES (Port)
MADEIRA (Port)
STRAIT OF GIBRALTAR
CANARY ISLANDS (Spain)
MEDITERRANEAN SEA
Casablanca
Fez
Rabat
Marrakech
MOROCCO
Oran
Algiers
Tunis
TUNISIA
Tripoli
Benghazi
Alexandria
Giza
Cairo
Suez Canal
ALGERIA
LIBYA
EGYPT
El Aaiún
WESTERN SAHARA (Occupied by Morocco)
Tropic of Cancer
Lake Nasser
Nile River
RED SEA
MAURITANIA
Nouakchott
CAPE VERDE
Praia
SENEGAL
Dakar
GAMBIA
Banjul
Bissau
GUINEA-BISSAU
GUINEA
Conakry
Freetown
SIERRA LEONE
Monrovia
LIBERIA
MALI
Niger River
Bamako
BURKINA FASO
Ouagadougou
NIGER
Niamey
CHAD
Lake Chad
N'Djamena
SUDAN
Omdurman
Khartoum
Blue Nile
White Nile
ERITREA
Asmara
DJIBOUTI
Djibouti
GULF OF ADEN
ETHIOPIA
Addis Ababa
SOMALIA
Mogadishu
CÔTE D'IVOIRE
Yamoussoukro
Abidjan
GHANA
Accra
TOGO
Lomé
BENIN
Porto-Novo
NIGERIA
Kano
Abuja
Ogbomosho
Ibadan
Lagos
GULF OF GUINEA
CAMEROON
Yaoundé
Malabo
EQUATORIAL GUINEA
SÃO TOMÉ AND PRÍNCIPE
São Tomé
CENTRAL AFRICAN REPUBLIC
Bangui
Libreville
GABON
REPUBLIC OF THE CONGO
Congo River
Brazzaville
Kinshasa
CABINDA (Angola)
DEMOCRATIC REPUBLIC OF THE CONGO
Kisangani
UGANDA
Kampala
KENYA
Nairobi
RWANDA
Kigali
Bujumbura
BURUNDI
Lake Victoria
TANZANIA
Dodoma
Lake Tanganyika
Mombasa
Pemba
Zanzibar
Dar es Salaam
Equator
INDIAN OCEAN
Victoria
SEYCHELLES
ATLANTIC OCEAN
Luanda
ANGOLA
Lubumbashi
Lake Malawi (Nyasa)
MALAWI
Lilongwe
ZAMBIA
Lusaka
Zambezi River
Harare
ZIMBABWE
Bulawayo
MOZAMBIQUE
COMOROS
Moroni
ST. HELENA ISLAND (UK)
NAMIBIA
Windhoek
BOTSWANA
Gaborone
Pretoria
Johannesburg
Soweto
Maputo
Mbabane
SWAZILAND
LESOTHO
Maseru
Orange River
SOUTH AFRICA
Cape Town
Port Elizabeth
Antananarivo
MADAGASCAR
MAURITIUS
Port Louis
RÉUNION (Fr)
Tropic of Capricorn
National capital
Other cities
ARCTIC OCEAN
NORTH AMERICA
EUROPE
ASIA
ATLANTIC OCEAN
PACIFIC OCEAN
SOUTH AMERICA
INDIAN OCEAN
AUSTRALIA
ANTARCTICA
Robinson Projection
0 500 1,000 Miles
0 500 1,000 Kilometers
Azimuthal Equal-Area Projection

Pacific Islands: Political

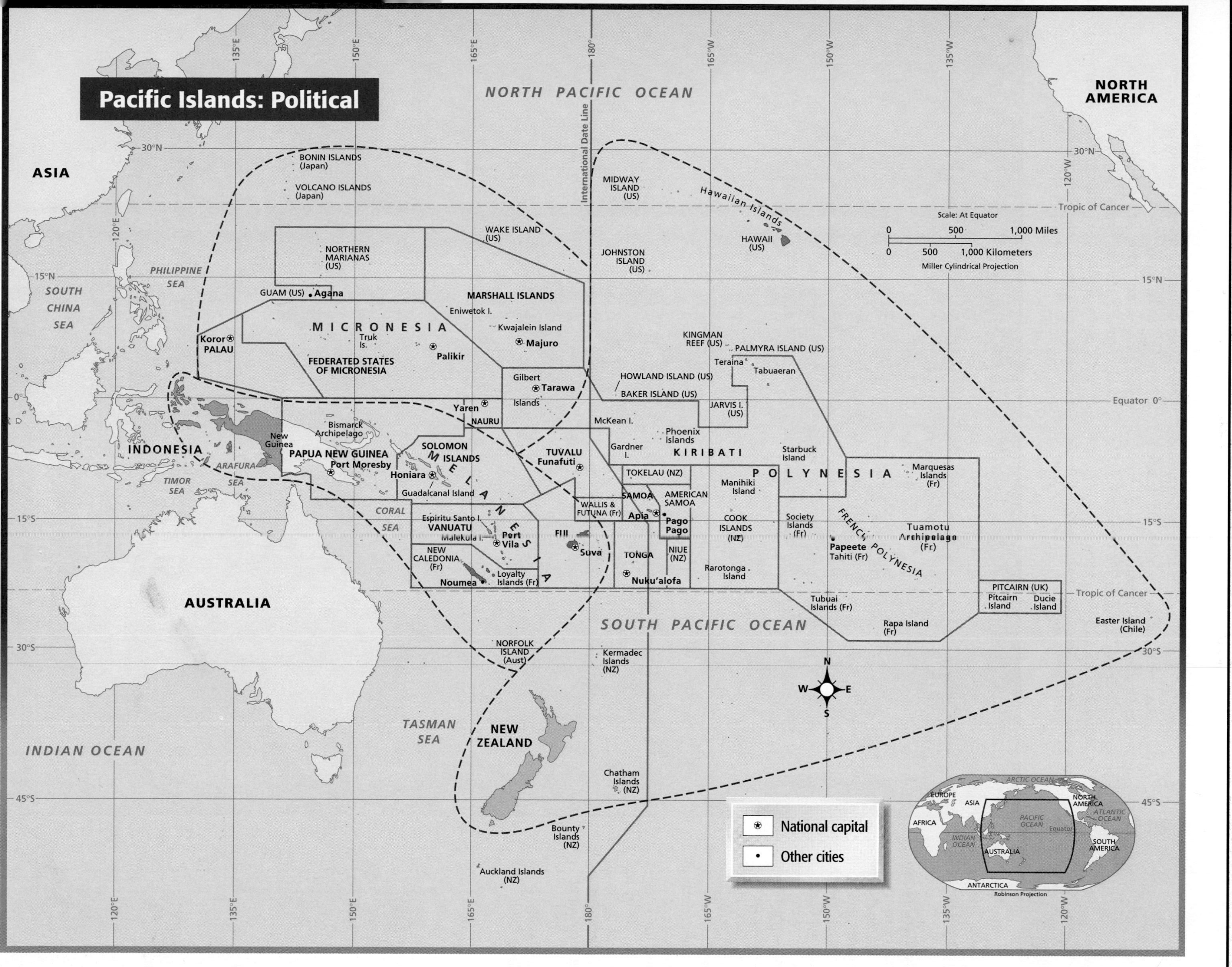

Introducing UNIT 1

CHAPTER 1
The Founding of the Nation

The first Americans probably crossed a land bridge to migrate from Asia to North America. Europeans explored and settled in the Americas as an outgrowth of their search for a sea route to Asia. Contact with Europeans often had devastating results for American Indians. Growing tensions between the British colonists and Great Britain led the colonies to declare independence in 1776 and form the United States of America. The colonies won the Revolutionary War in 1783 and formed a government under the U.S. Constitution in 1788.

CHAPTER 2
Citizenship and the Constitution

The framers of the Constitution developed a system of checks and balances that divides power among the legislative, executive, and judicial branches of government. To address concerns about individual rights, Congress added 10 amendments—known as the Bill of Rights—to the Constitution in 1791.

Internet Activity

Early American Maps. Have students search the Internet through the HRW Web site for maps of North America created between 1800 and 1840. Have students compare the maps they find. Then explain that much of the Americas was unmapped during this period. Next, have students write down the differences among the maps. Then, as students work through the unit, have them account for these differences. Finally, use the maps to discuss the geographic challenges that people settling the United States faced.

go.hrw.com
SB1 Maps

UNIT 1 American Beginnings
(Beginnings–1865)

CHAPTER 1 **The Founding of the Nation** (BEGINNINGS–1791)

CHAPTER 2 **Citizenship and the Constitution** (1787–PRESENT)

CHAPTER 3 **The Nation Expands** (1789–1865)

The Constitution specifies the rights of U.S. citizens and the responsibilities of the federal and state governments.

CHAPTER 3
The Nation Expands

George Washington served as the first president and set the new government on a firm footing. The nation grew greatly with the Louisiana Purchase. The United States fought Great Britain in the War of 1812. American Indians were forced west of the Mississippi River by President Jackson's Indian removal policy. The Industrial and Transportation Revolutions dramatically affected the nation. The South based its economy on cotton and slave labor. More Americans moved west, and the United States expanded with the annexation of Texas and the Mexican Cession following the Mexican War. Continuing conflict over slavery led to the Civil War.

UNIT MOTIVATOR

Ask students to recall a time when they were in unfamiliar surroundings. *(Examples might include the first day at a new school or moving to a new neighborhood.)* Encourage them to try to remember their experiences on that day and then to write about them in a journal entry. Tell students that in this unit they will learn about the experiences of people who moved to new lands in the Americas and how the United States and other nations developed.

American Teens
IN HISTORY
Young Pioneers

Early colonists saw America as the land of opportunity, a place to succeed and build a better future. As settlers struggled to build towns and start farms, they often relied on contributions from family members. By the mid-1800s, good farming land along the Atlantic coast was scarce. Many families headed west, looking for land to cultivate.

Once the pioneers reached their destination, children and teenagers spent countless hours doing much of the essential work of western settlement. Children aged 7 to 12 helped feed their families. They gathered edible wild plants, which they called "vegetables out of place."

Typically, teenage boys did the hard work of plowing the fields.

Teenagers had different responsibilities. Both boys and girls hunted wild animals. Boys worked in the fields with their fathers. Girls usually worked in the home and garden beside their mothers. Teenage girls might work in the fields if the farm was new or if there were no boys in the family. One teenager, Susie Crocket, helped plant the fields and trap animals on her family's farm in Oklahoma. Crocket recalled, "I hated to see Ma come in with a big batch of sewing, for I knew it meant many long hours sitting by her side sewing seams." Crocket believed that as a girl she was treated differently. "I could help the boys with the plowing or trapping, but they would never help me with sewing."

Edna Matthews Clifton grew up on a Texas frontier farm. She attended family celebrations and had good times at play and school. What she remembered most, however, was the work. Clifton cut wood, gardened, gathered, harvested, hunted, made soap, mopped, washed, and weeded. She particularly dreaded picking time. On summer mornings with the sun shining brightly, she saw the fields standing "like a monster." She wrote, "Sometimes I would lie down on my sack. . . . Sometimes they would pour water over my head to relieve me." Clifton understood "that *work was necessary.* Everybody worked; it was a part of life, for there was no life without it."

In this unit you will learn more about the people who helped create and expand the United States. The young nation faced many challenges, but it also offered its citizens many new opportunities.

LEFT PAGE: *George Caleb Bingham's painting* Daniel Boone Escorting Pioneers

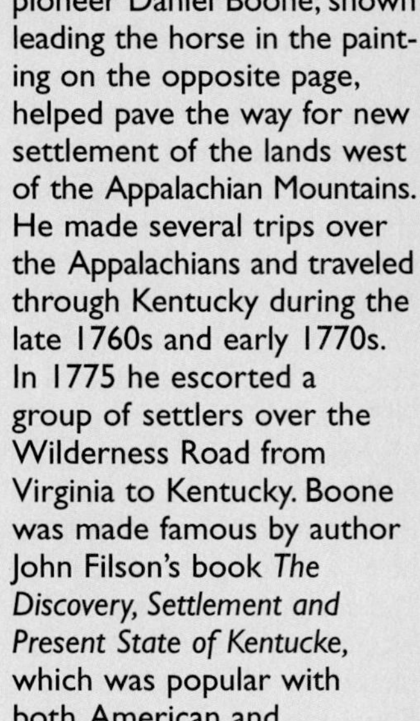

Using Visual Resources

Daniel Boone and the Frontier. Explorer and pioneer Daniel Boone, shown leading the horse in the painting on the opposite page, helped pave the way for new settlement of the lands west of the Appalachian Mountains. He made several trips over the Appalachians and traveled through Kentucky during the late 1760s and early 1770s. In 1775 he escorted a group of settlers over the Wilderness Road from Virginia to Kentucky. Boone was made famous by author John Filson's book *The Discovery, Settlement and Present State of Kentucke,* which was popular with both American and European readers.

Critical Thinking: Do you think that George Caleb Bingham, the artist who made the painting shown on the opposite page, approved or disapproved of Daniel Boone and his role in leading settlers west?

ANSWER: Bingham probably approved. His painting shows Boone as a heroic, confident leader. The settlers following him have calm expressions that suggest they feel safe even though they are surrounded by dark trees and mountains.

TEACH

ALL LEVELS: Visual-Spatial. (Suggested time: 30 min.) Instruct students to choose one of the U.S.-related events from the time line that does not have an image associated with it. Have students create an illustration for that event. Ask volunteers to share their work with the class. After students read the unit, have them evaluate how well their illustration depicts the event they chose.

ALL LEVELS: Logical-Mathematical, Visual-Spatial, Interpersonal. (Suggested time: 30 min.) Organize the class into small groups. Provide each group with a world map. Have students find the appropriate locations on the map for at least 10 of the events on the time line. Instruct students to label the events on the map and to write an annotation for each that includes the date and a brief description. In addition, students should mark each event with a symbol to indicate if it relates to arts and architecture, exploration and settlement, or war and politics. Remind students to include a key describing the symbols they use.

Cultural Diversity

Michelangelo. Artist Michelangelo originally resisted Pope Julius II's order to paint the ceiling of the Sistine Chapel. The artist protested that he was a sculptor, not a painter. However, the pope insisted, and Michelangelo began work on the ceiling in 1508. Although he started the enormous project with assistants, he was not satisfied with their work. As a result, Michelangelo completed the brilliant masterpiece over the next four years with little help. A gifted painter, poet, and sculptor, Michelangelo was one of the most influential artists of the Italian Renaissance.

Activity: Have students hold above their heads a sheet of paper taped to a piece of cardboard. Instruct students to draw a picture while in this position. When they are finished, ask students to write a brief description of some of the physical difficulties that Michelangelo might have encountered while painting the ceiling of the Sistine Chapel.

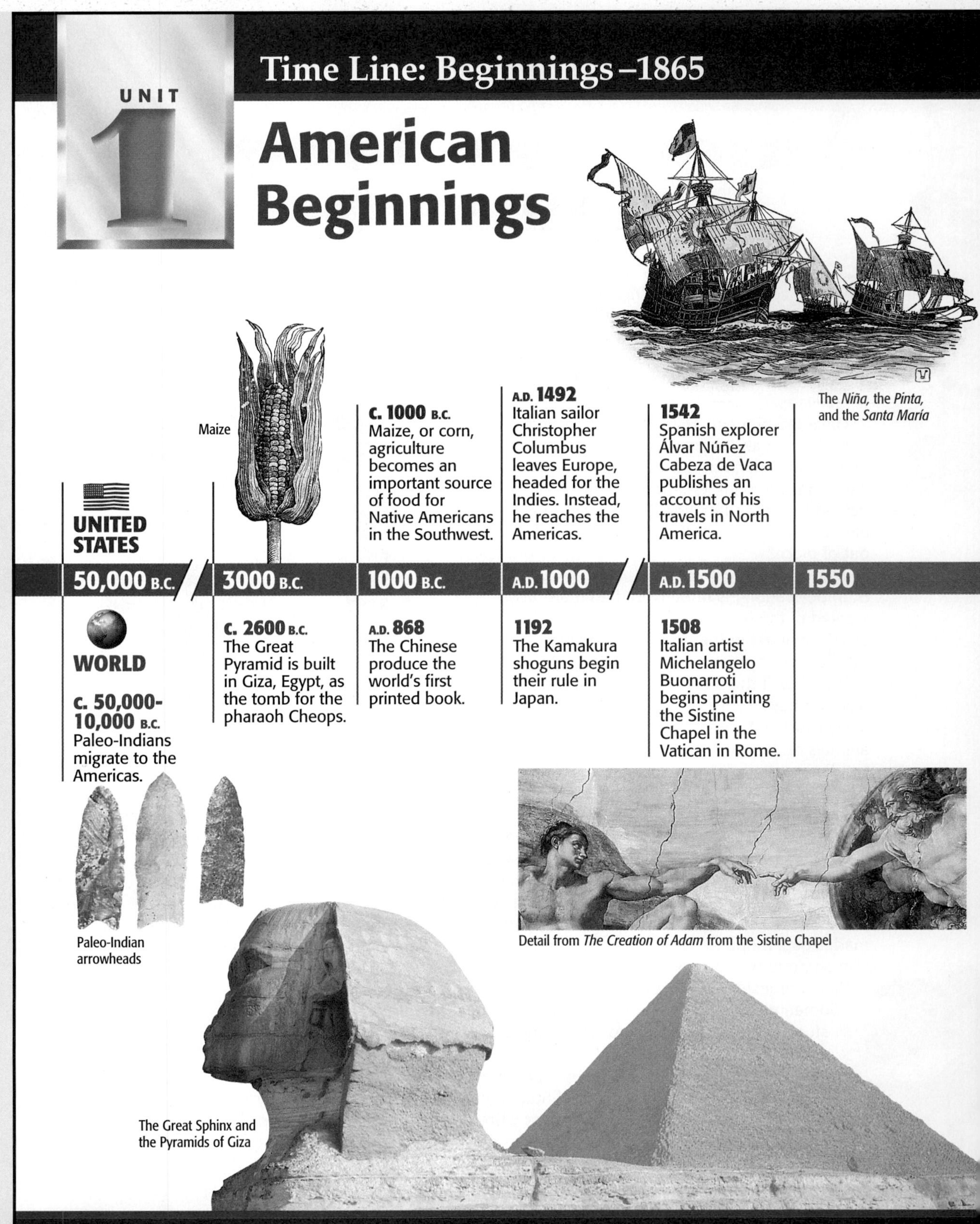

Time Line: Beginnings–1865

UNIT 1

American Beginnings

UNITED STATES

c. 1000 B.C. Maize, or corn, agriculture becomes an important source of food for Native Americans in the Southwest.

A.D. 1492 Italian sailor Christopher Columbus leaves Europe, headed for the Indies. Instead, he reaches the Americas.

1542 Spanish explorer Álvar Núñez Cabeza de Vaca publishes an account of his travels in North America.

Maize

The *Niña*, the *Pinta*, and the *Santa María*

50,000 B.C. | 3000 B.C. | 1000 B.C. | A.D. 1000 | A.D. 1500 | 1550

WORLD

c. 50,000–10,000 B.C. Paleo-Indians migrate to the Americas.

c. 2600 B.C. The Great Pyramid is built in Giza, Egypt, as the tomb for the pharaoh Cheops.

A.D. 868 The Chinese produce the world's first printed book.

1192 The Kamakura shoguns begin their rule in Japan.

1508 Italian artist Michelangelo Buonarroti begins painting the Sistine Chapel in the Vatican in Rome.

Paleo-Indian arrowheads

Detail from *The Creation of Adam* from the Sistine Chapel

The Great Sphinx and the Pyramids of Giza

CHALLENGE AND EXTEND

1. **Logical-Mathematical, Visual-Spatial.** Ask each student to choose one of the events from the time line. Then have students use the library or other resources to find additional information about the event. Have students use the research to create a time line that details the period leading up to the event. Encourage students to include images in their time lines. Have volunteers present their time lines to the class. After the presentations, display students' work in chronological order around the classroom.

2. **Linguistic.** Have students choose two of the cultures described in events on the time line. Instruct students to use the library or other resources to find information about each of these cultures at the time the events occurred. Then ask students to write a report that compares and contrasts the two cultures. Students should include in their reports information about each culture, such as aspects of daily life, major achievements, and physical environment. Encourage students to be creative in the way that they present the information in their reports.

A colonial bed

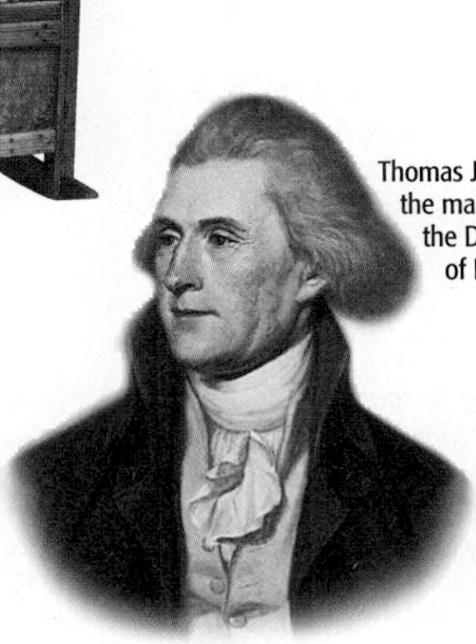

Thomas Jefferson is the main author of the Declaration of Independence.

A Civil War uniform and sword

1607 English colonists establish a settlement at Jamestown in Virginia.

1776 The thirteen colonies issue the Declaration of Independence and break away from Great Britain.

1804 Lewis and Clark begin their journey to explore the American West.

1865 General Lee surrenders at Appomattox Courthouse, ending the Civil War.

1600 | 1650 | 1700 | 1750 | 1800 | 1850

1608 Samuel de Champlain founds Quebec in present-day Canada.

1652 The Dutch establish a colony near the Cape of Good Hope in Africa.

1703 Peter the Great of Russia lays the foundation stone for the city of St. Petersburg.

1811 Simón Bolívar leads an independence movement in Venezuela.

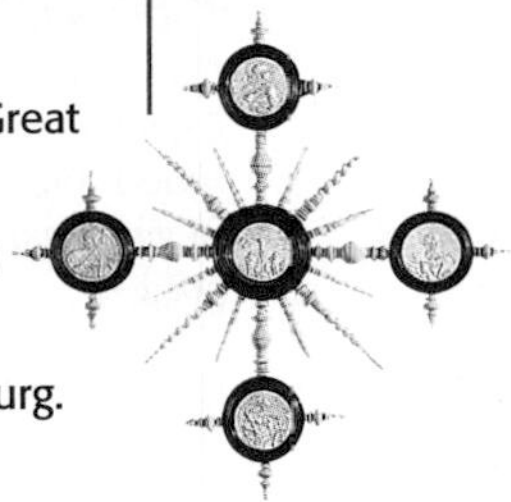

Altar cross created for Peter the Great

An African mask from the 1600s

Painting of Simón Bolívar on a jewel box

USING THE TIME LINE

1. Which events shown on the time line have to do with the founding of the United States?
2. How many years passed between Columbus's arrival in the Americas and the independence of the thirteen colonies?
3. Where did Europeans establish colonies in the 1600s?

Activity Identify the time line entries that relate to exploration. Create a chart of these journeys. Provide information on who led the explorations and where and when they took place. You might need to do some research using the library, your textbook, or other sources to find some additional information for your chart.

Citizenship and Democracy

Writing the Declaration of Independence.

In June 1776 Thomas Jefferson became chairman of the committee chosen to prepare one of the most important documents in U.S. history. As chairman, it was Jefferson's responsibility to write the original draft of the Declaration of Independence. Then Jefferson and his committee made more than 30 changes to the draft before presenting it to the Continental Congress for approval. The Congress spent several days making further additions and deletions before the final version was completed and approved on July 4, 1776.

Critical Thinking: Why might the Congress have taken so much time to develop a final version of the Declaration of Independence?

ANSWER: to consider the various opinions of members of the Congress and to ensure that such an important document was accurate and properly worded

USING THE TIME LINE ANSWERS

1. the establishment of the Jamestown settlement; American colonies declaring independence
2. 284 years
3. the Cape of Good Hope, Jamestown, Quebec

CHAPTER PLANNING GUIDE
The Founding of the Nation

	SECTION LESSON OBJECTIVES	PRINT RESOURCES	MULTIMEDIA RESOURCES	SHELTERED ENGLISH RESOURCES
Section 1: The World Before the Opening of the Atlantic (pp. 5–9)	★ Identify where the first Americans came from, and examine the influence of the environment on Native Americans. ★ Explain what Europe was like during the Middle Ages. ★ Analyze the effects of trade on different regions of Africa, Asia, and the Mediterranean.	★ Guided Reading Strategies 1.1 ★ Primary Source Reading 1: Iroquois Creation Legend ★ Section 1 Review, p. 9 ★ Daily Quiz 1.1	★ *Teaching Resources CD–ROM*, Lesson 1.1 ★ Linking Geography and History Transparency 3: Native American Culture Areas ★ Art in American History Transparency 1: Mesa Verde ★ Everyday Life in America Transparency 1: Influence of the Roman Catholic Church, Middle Ages	★ Main Idea Activities for Reteaching and Sheltered English 1.1
Section 2: The Age of Exploration (pp. 10–13)	★ Examine the reasons for Europeans' voyages of exploration. ★ Describe the effects of the Protestant Reformation on Europe and the Americas. ★ Explore the reasons Europeans were interested in colonizing North America.	★ Guided Reading Strategies 1.2 ★ Geography Activity 1: Crossing the Atlantic ★ Section 2 Review, p. 13 ★ Daily Quiz 1.2	★ *Teaching Resources CD–ROM*, Lesson 1.2 ★ *American History Interactive Maps CD–ROM*: The Columbian Exchange ★ *American Music Audio CD Program*: "Alabado" ★ HRW Web site	★ Main Idea Activities for Reteaching and Sheltered English 1.2
Section 3: The English Colonies (pp. 14–20)	★ Analyze the role of religion in colonial life. ★ Examine the economic ties between the colonies and England. ★ Describe the economic and political differences between the colonies.	★ Guided Reading Strategies 1.3 ★ Literature Reading 1: Narrative of the Life of Olaudah Equiano ★ Section 3 Review, p. 20 ★ Daily Quiz 1.3	★ *Teaching Resources CD–ROM*, Lesson 1.3 ★ *American History Simulations CD–ROM*: Building a Colony ★ HRW Web site	★ Main Idea Activities for Reteaching and Sheltered English 1.3
Section 4: The American Revolution (pp. 21–25)	★ Explain why Britain imposed new taxes on the colonies, and examine the colonists' response. ★ Describe the events that led the First Continental Congress to break free from Britain. ★ Analyze the events that finally ended the American Revolution.	★ Guided Reading Strategies 1.4 ★ Biography Reading 1: Paul Revere ★ American History Political Cartoon 1: Defeating the British ★ Section 4 Review, p. 25 ★ Daily Quiz 1.4	★ *Teaching Resources CD–ROM*, Lesson 1.4 ★ *Exploring America's Past* Video Segment: American Beginnings; *Teacher's Guide*, pp. 2–3	★ Main Idea Activities for Reteaching and Sheltered English 1.4
Section 5: Forming a Nation (pp. 30–33)	★ Examine the problems that arose under the Articles of Confederation. ★ Explore some of the main issues debated at the Constitutional Convention. ★ Analyze opposition to the new Constitution, and explain how concerns were addressed.	★ Guided Reading Strategies 1.5 ★ Graphic Organizer 1: The Settlement of North America ★ American History Political Cartoon 2: Ratifying the Constitution ★ Section 5 Review, p. 33 ★ Daily Quiz 1.5	★ *Teaching Resources CD–ROM*, Lesson 1.5 ★ *American History Simulations CD–ROM*: The Democracy Project	★ Main Idea Activities for Reteaching and Sheltered English 1.5
Chapter Review and Assessment (pp. 34–35)		★ Chapter 1 Review, pp. 34–35 ★ Vocabulary Activity 1 ★ Chapter 1 Study Guide ★ Chapter 1 Test (Form A or B)	★ Audio Program, Ch. 1 (English and Spanish) ★ *Global Skill Builder CD–ROM* ★ Chapter 1 Test Generator ★ HRW Web site	★ Spanish Glossary ★ Sheltered English Chapter 1 Test

CHAPTER OVERVIEW

Looking for direct western trade routes to Asia, Europeans found the lands that later became known as North and South America. The resulting Columbian Exchange provided Europe with important new crops, including corn and tomatoes, but European diseases such as smallpox had devastating effects on many Native Americans.

In 1607 a group of colonists established Jamestown, the first permanent English settlement in North America. Settlers of the 13 English colonies, however, eventually grew to resent the restrictions and taxes imposed by Great Britain. After fighting broke out between Patriot and British troops in Lexington, Concord, and near Boston in 1775, the colonists issued the Declaration of Independence the following year. The United States won its independence from Britain with the surrender of Cornwallis at Yorktown.

The first national government, established under the Articles of Confederation, had only a weak central authority that proved insufficient to address many of the challenges facing the new nation. In 1787 delegates met in Philadelphia and drafted the Constitution of the United States, based on the ideas of federalism and a balance of power between three branches of government. The Constitution took effect in June 1788, and the Bill of Rights, guaranteeing the rights of individual citizens, was added in 1791.

CHAPTER INVESTIGATION

The Chapter Investigation is an extended, multipart activity designed for students to work cooperatively and apply the chapter content in the creation of a project. You may choose to use the Chapter 1 Investigation, Series of Informational Booklets, either as a substitute for teaching the section lessons or as an alternate assessment.

BLOCK SCHEDULING 

The teacher lesson plans for each section offer a variety of activity choices to help you present the material in a block scheduling format. For further suggestions on block scheduling, see the *Block Scheduling Handbook with Team Teaching Strategies,* pp. 1–6.

Meeting Individual Needs

ABILITY LEVELS

LEVEL 1 Basic level activities designed for all students encountering new material.

LEVEL 2 Intermediate level activities designed for average students.

LEVEL 3 Challenging activities designed for above-average students.

SHELTERED ENGLISH These activities address the needs of students with Limited English Proficiency.

Smithsonian Institution®

Internet Connections and Lesson 1
www.si.edu/hrw

CNN Presents America:
Yesterday and Today 1850 to the Present
Segment: Native Americans Keep Their Culture Alive

Additional Resources

Books for Teachers

Commager, Henry Steele and Richard Morris. *The Spirit of the Story of the American Revolution as Told by Participants.* De Capo, 1995. Reprint. Lets original sources tell the story of the founding of America.

Josephy, Alvin M., Jr., ed. *America in 1492.* Newberry, 1991. Examines Native American civilizations before the arrival of Columbus.

Nash, Gary B. *Red, White, and Black: The Peoples of Early North America,* 3rd ed. Prentice-Hall, 1991. Discusses race relations in colonial America.

Books for Students

Katz, William Loren. *Breaking the Chains: African American Slave Resistance.* Atheneum, 1990. Examines slave resistance and escape during the Middle Passage and in America.

McPhillips, Martin. *The Constitutional Convention.* Silver, 1986. Focuses on the Constitutional Convention and the views of Jefferson, Madison, Franklin, and Hamilton (for students reading below grade level).

Scott, John Anthony. *Settlers on the Eastern Shore: The British Colonies in North America, 1607–1750.* Facts on File, 1991. Uses primary sources to show what life was like for settlers.

Multimedia Materials

Age of Discovery: English, French, and Dutch Explorations. Video, 12 min. Coronet. Looks at Cartier, Drake, and other explorers.

Inventing a Nation. Video, 52 min. Time Life Distribution Center. Focuses on the decade in which the Constitution was written. Describes debates involving Mason, Madison, and Hamilton.

Making of Revolution. Video, 26 min. Time Life Distribution Center. Traces the development of the colonies' unified effort against England.

The Founding of the Nation

CHAPTER MOTIVATOR

Write the word *America* on the chalkboard. Under it write the words *Who, What, Where, When,* and *Why.* Ask students to list words they think of when they are asked these questions in relation to America. Have students share their words with the class. Lead a discussion about why there may be such variety in students' answers. Focus the discussion on the many different people, countries, customs, and beliefs that have helped shape the present-day United States. Ask students to explore the *"Why"* question: What were the different reasons that people came to the Americas? What did the Americas offer that other countries did not? Engage students in a discussion about whether the United States still offers its inhabitants these same opportunities today.

Presenting Themes

- **Geographic Diversity**
  Students might suggest that settlements would be established to protect trade routes, to increase the nation's wealth, or to locate and control natural resources.
- **Citizenship and Democracy**
  Students might say it means that a government was established with the conviction that citizens have certain rights that the government cannot violate.
- **Constitutional Heritage**
  Students might say that a nation could establish a set of laws, such as a constitution, to help define the powers of its government.

Using the Time Line

Have students write headlines for the events listed on the time line. After they have finished reading the chapter, ask them to sketch a cartoon about one of the events.

The Granger Collection, New York

CHAPTER 1

The Founding of the Nation

(Beginnings–1791)

"The land of Liberty! how sweet the sound!" declared Eliza Wilkinson in 1782. Just a few years earlier Wilkinson—a young widow from Charleston, South Carolina—had shown little interest in politics. Soon, however, she was swept up in a movement against British rule. By 1782 Wilkinson—the once loyal British subject—was among many people proudly calling themselves Americans.

Geographic Diversity
Why would nations establish settlements in other regions?

Citizenship and Democracy
What does it mean for a country to be founded on the idea of liberty?

Constitutional Heritage
What might a nation do to prevent its government from misusing power?

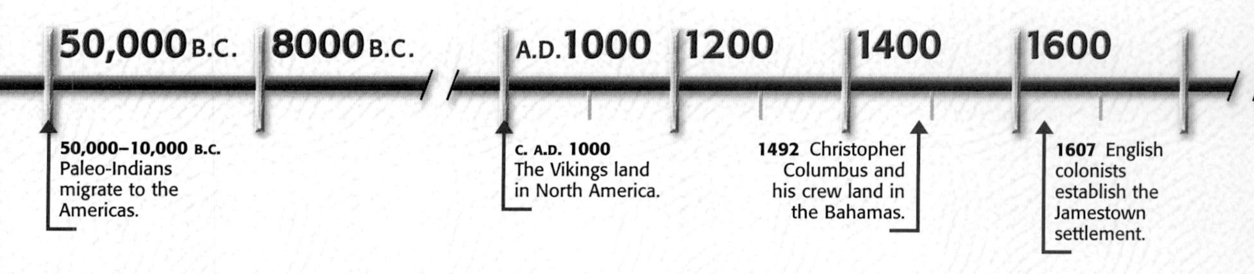

OBJECTIVES

- **Identify where the first Americans came from, and examine the influence of the environment on Native Americans.**
- **Explain what Europe was like during the Middle Ages.**
- **Analyze the effects of trade on different regions of Africa, Asia, and the Mediterranean.**

FOCUS

Motivate Before Reading

Have students write a few sentences about something they remember doing for the first time. Lead a discussion on some of the mental and physical attributes necessary to accomplish something for the first time. Ask students why it seemed so difficult the first time compared to later trials. Tell students that in this section they will

SECTION 1

The World Before the Opening of the Atlantic

Reading Focus

Where did the first Americans come from, and how did the environment influence Native Americans?

What was Europe like during the Middle Ages?

How did trade affect different regions of Africa, Asia, and the Mediterranean?

Key Terms

artifacts
Paleo-Indians
migration
societies
culture
Iroquois League
Middle Ages
feudalism
Crusades
Silk Road

ACCORDING TO SOME northwestern Native American tribes, when the world was young there were only "the trees, the moon, the sun, water, and a few animals." In this emptiness, the lonely Raven walked along the beach and wished for companions. To Raven's surprise, a clam emerged from the sand and released a crowd of tiny people. Raven "sang a beautiful song of great joy," say the northwestern storytellers, for "he had brought the first people to the world." This story represents one of the many different ways that people explain how the first humans arrived in the Americas.

The character of the Raven appears in many Native American stories.

IMAGE ON LEFT PAGE: *The Battle of Lexington*

1760 | 1765 | 1770 | 1775 | 1780 | 1785 | 1790

1763 Pontiac's Rebellion starts.

1775 Fighting at Lexington and Concord marks the beginning of the Revolutionary War.

1776 The Declaration of Independence is approved.

1781 The British surrender at Yorktown.

1787 Delegates sign the U.S. Constitution.

1791 The Bill of Rights becomes part of the Constitution.

Section 1 RESOURCES

PRINT

- ★ Guided Reading Strategies 1.1
- ★ Primary Source Reading 1: Iroquois Creation Legend
- ★ Section 1 Review, p. 9
- ★ Daily Quiz 1.1

MULTIMEDIA

- ★ *Teaching Resources CD–ROM*, Lesson 1.1
- ★ Linking Geography and History Transparency 3: Native American Culture Areas
- ★ Art in American History Transparency 1: Mesa Verde
- ★ Everyday Life in America Transparency 1: Influence of the Roman Catholic Church, Middle Ages

SHELTERED ENGLISH

- ★ Main Idea Activities for Reteaching and Sheltered English 1.1

learn about the first inhabitants of the Americas, their struggles for survival, and the various cultures that influenced their lifestyle.

Introduce Key Terms

Linguistic, Logical-Mathematical, Interpersonal. Review this section's key terms with students. Have students use their textbooks to create a crossword puzzle using each of the section's key terms. Ask students to use definitions of each term as clues. When students have finished, have them exchange puzzles, complete them, and return them to their creators for grading.
SHELTERED ENGLISH

TEACH

Have students read Section 1 and complete Guided Reading Strategies 1.1. Choose one or more of the following activities to explore the section content with students. For further suggestions on block scheduling or team teaching, see the *Block Scheduling Handbook.*

LEVEL 1: Linguistic. (Suggested time: 15 min.) As a class, go over students' Guided Reading Strategies. Then use the Reading Focus questions to highlight the main ideas of the section.
SHELTERED ENGLISH

Across the Curriculum

SCIENCE

Dating Migrations. Scientists have used a variety of methods to determine the dates of migrations across Beringia. They have tried to date the tools found at archaeological sites in present-day Alaska. They have examined pollen residue from the Ice Age to determine when there was enough plant life to sustain the animal herds that migrants would have been likely to follow. Some biologists who have studied the dental traits (teeth formations) of Native Americans argue that three separate major migrations took place, a theory that studies of blood types appear to confirm. However, scientists have not reached agreement on any of these issues.

Critical Thinking: Why is it important for scientists to accurately date the migrations across Beringia?

ANSWER: Doing so would provide a key to establishing a timetable for the prehistory of the Western Hemisphere.

Multimedia Resources

Linking Geography and History Transparency 3: Native American Culture Areas, and Art in American History Transparency 1: Mesa Verde

The First Americans

Many scientists believe that people first arrived in North America during the last Ice Age, when glaciers covered much of Earth's surface. As the ocean levels dropped, a land bridge called Beringia was exposed between northeastern Asia and present-day Alaska. **Artifacts**, or remains of objects made by humans, indicate that **Paleo-Indians**, or the first Americans, crossed Beringia into Alaska sometime between 50,000 and 10,000 B.C. This **migration**, or movement of people from one region to another, occurred over a long time. Most Paleo-Indians traveled through Alaska and migrated south.

Paleo-Indians were hunter-gatherers, people who hunt animals and gather wild plants to provide for their needs. In time, these Native Americans began practicing agriculture, which provided stability and allowed complex **societies** to develop. A society is a group that has a common **culture**—shared values and traditions, such as language, government, and family relationships.

The earliest civilizations in the Americas developed in Mesoamerica—present-day Mexico and portions of Central America—and South America. The largest civilizations in Mesoamerica were the Olmec, Maya, Toltec, and Aztec. In South America the Inca civilization was the largest. Its empire stretched from present-day Colombia to central Chile.

Southwestern Native American tribes built cliff dwellings, like this one in Mesa Verde, Colorado, to protect themselves from weather and attacks.

An Inca knife

North America produced several complex farming cultures. The Mogollon and Hohokam were two of the first groups in the present-day southwestern United States to develop agriculture. Another southwestern group, the Anasazi (ahn-uh-SAHZ-ee), built large pueblos and developed irrigation systems in mesas and canyons. The Mississippian culture, Adena, and Hopewell developed in the Mississippi, Missouri, and Ohio River valleys. These cultures built large burial and religious mounds. The Adena were primarily hunter-gatherers, while the Hopewell and the Mississippian culture supported their large populations with agriculture and trade.

North American Culture Areas

In North America many different Native American culture areas developed. In the far North, the Inuit and the Aleut hunted large mammals and fished in the frozen Arctic, using dogsleds and kayaks for transportation. The Inuit sometimes used blocks of ice to build igloos for housing. In the Subarctic, Native Americans were nomadic, following the seasonal migrations of the caribou.

The Northwest Coast culture area stretched along the 2,000-mile shoreline from southern Alaska to northern California. A mild climate and rich food supplies allowed large, nonagricultural populations to develop. People in the Northwest fished for salmon and hunted whale. They also used trees to build houses and to carve images of totems—ancestor or animal spirits—on tall poles.

Farther south the California region included deserts, forests, and river-filled valleys. Native Americans there lived in isolated family groups or small villages. In the Columbia Plateau, Native Americans lived in permanent villages near rivers. They fished for salmon, hunted small game, and gathered plants. In the desertlike Great Basin, most people lived in small hunter-gatherer groups.

Native Americans of the Southwest also lived in a dry environment. They practiced irrigation to

ALL LEVELS: Logical-Mathematical, Visual-Spatial. (Suggested time: 30 min.) Have students create a collage or mural depicting how trade in the 1200s influenced Africa, Asia, and the Mediterranean. Encourage students to include images of the goods that were traded most frequently. **SHELTERED ENGLISH**

LEVEL 2: Visual-Spatial, Kinesthetic, Interpersonal. (Suggested time: 40 min.) Organize the class into several small groups. Assign each group one of the Native American cultures discussed in this section. Have each group act out a way that the group was influenced by its environment. *(One example may include the Native Americans of the Arctic building an igloo or using a dogsled.)* As each group acts out an activity, have the other groups identify which Native American culture is being depicted. Finally, lead a discussion on where the first Americans came from.

LEVEL 3: Linguistic, Logical-Mathematical. (Suggested time: 40 min. plus homework) Give each student a slip of paper with one of the following words written on it: *noble, vassal,* or *peasant.* Then ask them whether they felt they had any control over the paper, and thus the role, they chose. Remind students that in the feudal system people did not have a voice in their economic or social position—it was determined at birth. Have students write a one-page essay on what life was like for the social class they each picked. Ask volunteers to share their essays with the class.

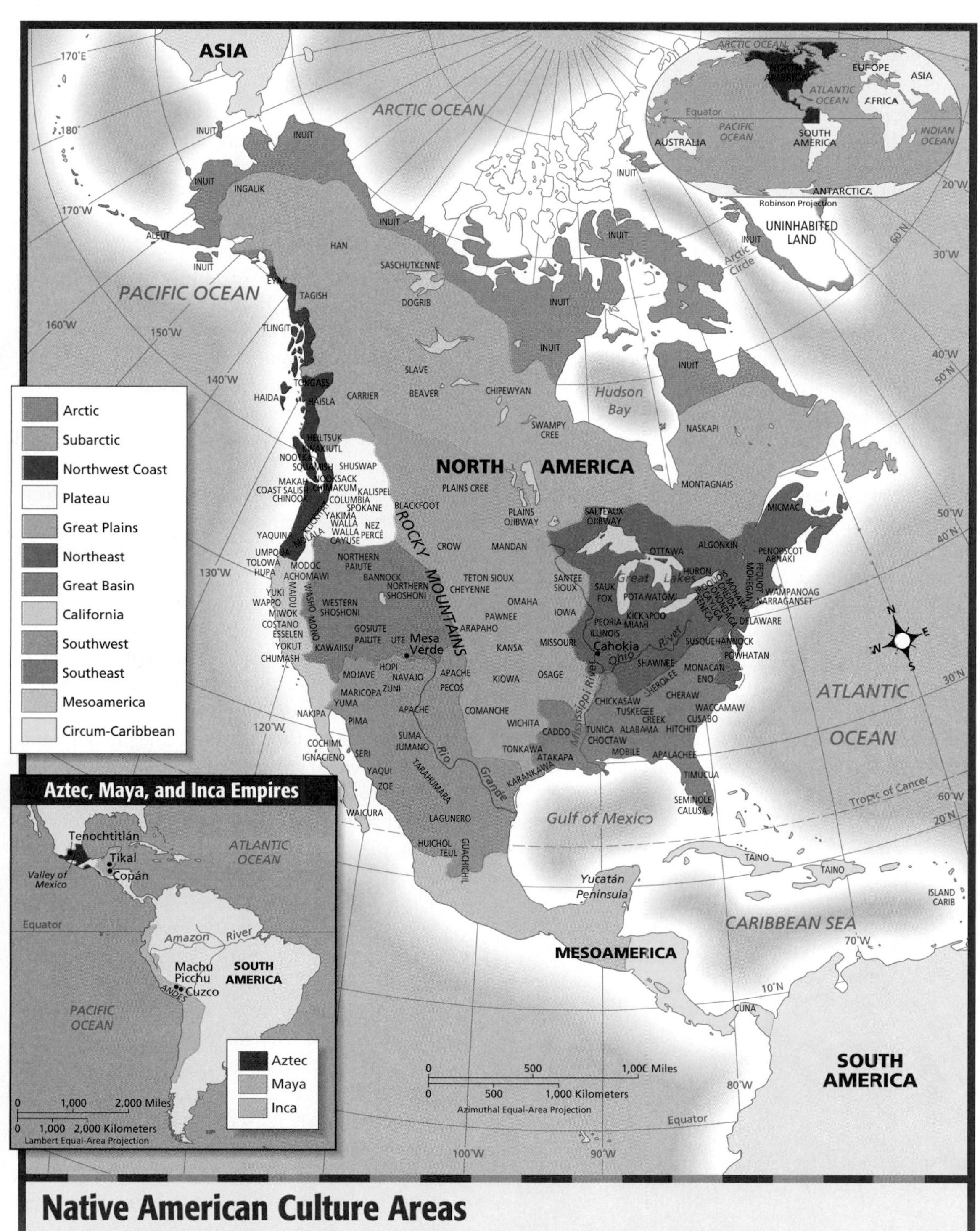

Native American Culture Areas

Learning from Maps Various Native American cultures inhabited the Americas. These cultures adapted to a wide range of climatic and geographic regions.

Human-Environment Interaction How might the geography and climate of an area influence the culture that develops there?

Geographic Diversity

Life on the Great Plains. Archaeologists have discovered evidence that humans hunted on the Great Plains in modern-day Nebraska almost 10,000 years ago. These early hunters pursued large bison that are extinct today. Sometime around A.D. 200, Native Americans who might have been from the Hopewell culture brought maize and beans into the region, thus introducing agriculture. However, it was not until sometime after A.D. 1000 that Native Americans on the Great Plains engaged in more extensive farming and grouped individual houses into small communities. These Native Americans may have been the ancestors of the Pawnee, who later inhabited the region.

Critical Thinking: What evidence would you look for to prove that the Pawnee were descendants of the earlier people who built houses and farmed the Great Plains?

ANSWER: Students might mention that they would investigate the types of tools or artwork to establish a link between the two groups.

MAP ANSWER

Cultures must adapt their ways of gathering food, establishing communities, and designing shelter for the environment in which they live.

CLOSE

Visual-Spatial. Provide students with a blank world map and colored pencils. Have them locate the following regions from this section: continental North America, Newfoundland, the Mediterranean Sea, Jerusalem, Rome, the Black Sea, China, the Sahara Desert, and Mali (Africa). Ask students to use different colors to identify the different regions of the world and to state why the area was important. Tell students that these maps will be used in a future activity. **SHELTERED ENGLISH**

CHALLENGE AND EXTEND

Linguistic, Logical-Mathematical, Interpersonal. Have students use the library and other resources to research one North American culture discussed in this section. Ask students to gather information about the selected culture's population, the territory it occupied, and its lifestyle. Have each student create a brochure of important facts about the selected culture.

Global Relations

The Silk Road. By the first century A.D., one large caravan left western China every month to travel west on the Silk Road. The great Roman Empire eagerly bought Chinese silk, a rare fabric in the West. Merchants sent other items as well, such as furs, ivory, ceramics, jade, and cinnamon. Caravans returning to China carried valuables like gold, glass, and wool and linen fabrics. Historians have noted, however, that more than trade goods traveled on the Silk Road. Technologies involving weaving and agriculture were also transported between China and the rest of the world on the Silk Road. Moreover, the East and the West exchanged philosophical ideas and religious beliefs via this route, including Buddhism, Islam, and Christianity. Finally, local environments were changed when fruits and vegetables transported on the road were planted.

Critical Thinking: What routes for the transfer of ideas and technologies are currently in use?

ANSWER: Students might mention the Internet, e-mail, television, telephones, fax machines, newspapers, and magazines.

Multimedia Resources

Everyday Life in America Transparency 1: Influence of the Roman Catholic Church

grow crops such as maize. Some tribes, including the Navajo and Apache, hunted game, gathered food plants, and raided the villages of agricultural groups such as the Pueblo.

Millions of buffalo grazed on the grassland of the Great Plains, which stretch from Canada to the Rio Grande and lie between the Mississippi River and the Rocky Mountains. Native Americans in the Plains grew crops, gathered plants, and hunted buffalo on foot.

The East was primarily wooded and rich in resources. Southeastern tribes lived and farmed in villages along river valleys. Northeastern tribes lived in an area stretching west from the Atlantic to the Mississippi Valley and south from the Great Lakes to present-day Virginia and North Carolina. The Algonquian in the colder north were seminomadic, while tribes living farther south farmed and built permanent villages. The Iroquois were an agricultural people. They developed the **Iroquois League**, a political confederation of the Cayuga, Mohawk, Oneida, Onondaga, and Seneca tribes.

The Middle Ages

The first Europeans known to have had contact with Native Americans were the Vikings from Scandinavia. These seafaring people had settled Iceland and Greenland. Around the year A.D. 1000 Leif Eriksson sailed farther west. He eventually landed in Labrador and Newfoundland, Canada. The Vikings explored along the coast and established a colony that lasted for a few years.

Peasants like these tended the manor fields.

Feudal Europe

The Vikings were the only Europeans to explore the Americas during Europe's **Middle Ages**. This era started with the collapse of the Roman Empire in the late A.D. 400s and began to end around 1350. During this time Europe experienced political disorder, and many trade networks broke down. Some city populations declined as people moved to the countryside.

The early Middle Ages saw the rise of **feudalism**—a system of government in which people pledge loyalty to a lord in exchange for protection. A person's birth often determined his or her economic and social position in the feudal system. Monarchs and nobles defended their kingdoms and manors, or large estates, with the help of vassals. Vassals were knights and lords who gave their services in exchange for land. Peasant tenants, serfs, and slaves farmed the manor land. Manors provided most of the necessities for their inhabitants. Nobles ruled their manors without interference because there was little central government. The Catholic Church was the center of most social and religious life.

Nobles gradually lost power as monarchs expanded their control over vast areas. These growing kingdoms were called nations and included England and France. In 1215 English nobles forced King John to accept Magna Carta, or the Great Charter. The charter gave certain rights to the nobles and established that English monarchs must observe the law.

Trade also increased in the early 1200s. Merchants in Italian coastal cities traded regularly with countries around the Mediterranean Sea. As trade increased, Europeans built new towns and expanded existing cities. Towns and populations grew even faster as improved farming methods led to increased food production. Such changes in technology, trade, and political power marked the decline of Europe's Middle Ages.

REVIEW

Logical-Mathematical, Visual-Spatial. Have students complete the Section Review questions. Then ask them to go through the section and write the title of each subsection in their notebooks. Under each title, have students write one or two sentences that convey the subsection's main idea. Ask volunteers to share their examples with the class.

ASSESS

Have students complete Daily Quiz 1.1.

RETEACH

Linguistic, Logical-Mathematical. Have students complete Main Idea Activities for Reteaching and Sheltered English 1.1. Ask students to identify the goods exchanged and any significant movements of groups of people on the maps they created during the Close activity. Remind students to create a new legend for their maps. Have students write a sentence explaining each event's significance. SHELTERED ENGLISH

Trade Across Continents

During the Middle Ages, Muslims made military conquests and built trade networks around the Mediterranean. Along with Christians and Jews, Muslims proved their religious devotion by visiting the Holy Land, which included the city of Jerusalem. Fearing that Muslim rulers would forbid Christians to enter Jerusalem, Pope Urban II called on Christians to fight a crusade, or holy war:

> **"Jerusalem . . . is now held captive by the enemies of Christ. . . . When an armed attack is made upon the enemy, let this one cry be raised by all the soldiers of God: it is the will of God!"**

With these words, Christians launched the **Crusades**, five wars fought between 1096 and 1221 for possession of the Holy Land. The Crusades brought Europeans into closer contact with the East and increased their interest in trade with Asia and Africa.

Meanwhile, Genghis Khan was leading the Mongols, nomadic warriors from Central Asia, in an invasion of China. By 1279 his grandson Kublai Khan (KOO-bluh KAHN) ruled an empire that stretched 4,000 miles across Asia's central plains.

Statue of a trader in the Middle Ages

Kublai Khan used his powerful navy to open vast trading networks with present-day southern India, Sri Lanka, and Sumatra. Merchants also used the **Silk Road**, an overland trade route that stretched several thousand miles from China to the Black Sea.

In 1368 the Ming dynasty overthrew the Mongol Empire. In the early 1400s China sponsored several long ocean voyages.

Some Chinese merchants traveled to East African kingdoms, where thriving port cities traded goods such as ivory and gold. Berbers—nomads from North Africa—used camels to carry goods across the Sahara Desert. They brought salt south and gold north. People used salt to prevent food from spoiling too quickly.

In West Africa, Ghana (GAHN-uh) gained wealth trading gold, which Arab merchants carried to the Mediterranean. Mali emerged in the early 1200s after Ghana's collapse. In the late 1200s North African traders brought Islam to Mali and parts of Sudan. The Songhay (SAWNG-hy) Empire also had great influence in the area. Songhay's Muslim rulers helped spread Islamic culture throughout their vast territory.

SECTION 1 REVIEW

Identify and explain the significance of the following:

- **artifacts**
- **Paleo-Indians**
- **migration**
- **societies**
- **culture**
- **Iroquois League**
- **Leif Eriksson**
- **Middle Ages**
- **feudalism**
- **Crusades**
- **Kublai Khan**
- **Silk Road**

Reading for Content Understanding

1. **Main Idea** How were European societies organized during the Middle Ages?
2. **Main Idea** What influence did trade have within different empires in Africa, Asia, and the Mediterranean?
3. **Geographic Diversity** *Human-Environment Interaction* From where did the first people to reach North America come, and how did the environment affect Native American cultures?
4. **Writing** *Classifying* Write a paragraph explaining both the positive and the negative aspects of trade among various peoples or kingdoms during the Middle Ages.
5. **Critical Thinking** *Drawing Conclusions* Why do you think that Native Americans who practiced agriculture were more likely than hunter-gatherers to establish permanent settlements?

Section 1 Review ANSWERS

Identify
For significance, see the following pages:

- artifacts, p. 6
- Paleo-Indians, p. 6
- migration, p. 6
- societies, p. 6
- culture, p. 6
- Iroquois League, p. 8
- Leif Eriksson, p. 8
- Middle Ages, p. 8
- feudalism, p. 8
- Crusades, p. 9
- Kublai Khan, p. 9
- Silk Road, p. 9

Reading for Content Understanding

1. European societies were organized on the basis of feudalism.
2. Trade introduced new goods and ideas to the different empires.
3. They crossed Beringia; it influenced housing, transportation, settlement patterns, diet, and culture.
4. Paragraphs will vary but students should mention both advantages and disadvantages of such trade.
5. Hunter-gatherers had to follow migrating animals and look for fresh sources of plants.

SECTION 2 LESSON PLAN

OBJECTIVES

- Examine the reasons for Europeans' voyages of exploration.
- Describe the effects of the Protestant Reformation on Europe and the Americas.
- Explore the reasons Europeans were interested in colonizing North America.

FOCUS

Motivate Before Reading

Ask each student to list three reasons to settle an unknown area. Allow time for students to share their answers. Then ask students to identify ways that settlement might affect the area. Have students share these answers. Then tell students that in this section they will learn why Europeans began to colonize the Americas.

Section 2 RESOURCES

PRINT

★ Guided Reading Strategies 1.2

★ Geography Activity 1: Crossing the Atlantic

★ Section 2 Review, p. 13

★ Daily Quiz 1.2

MULTIMEDIA

★ *Teaching Resources CD–ROM,* Lesson 1.2

★ *American History Interactive Maps CD–ROM:* The Columbian Exchange

★ *American Music Audio CD Program:* "Alabado"

★ HRW Web site

SHELTERED ENGLISH

★ Main Idea Activities for Reteaching and Sheltered English 1.2

The Age of Exploration

Reading Focus

Why did Europeans set out on voyages of exploration?

How did the Protestant Reformation affect Europe and the Americas?

Why were Europeans interested in colonizing North America?

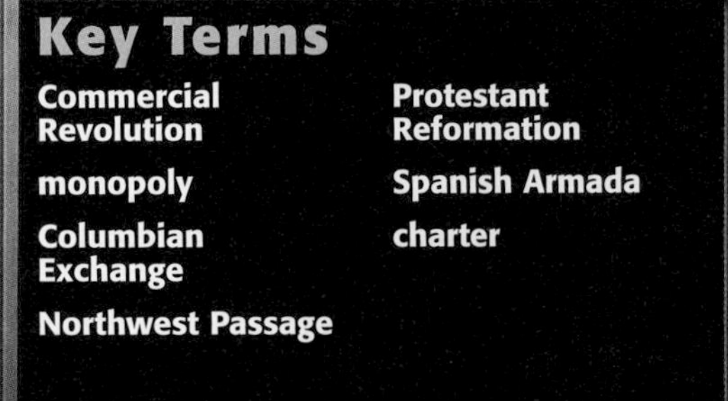

IN 1299 THE CITY OF ARRAS *in present-day France was famous for its wealthy merchants. The local Crespin family was so rich that it loaned money to cities, bishops, and even monarchs. The rise to power of the Crespins and other merchants worried some Europeans. "Money is too much worshipped here," wrote poet Adam de la Halle. Others, however, welcomed the changing economy because it provided opportunities for workers to make money and improve their social status.*

European moneylenders and borrowers in the 1300s

Economic Growth

In the 1400s Europe experienced the **Commercial Revolution**, a period of economic development that improved business practices. During this time a network of merchants, bankers, and traders brought prized goods to Europe's markets. Gold, ivory, slaves, and salt came from Africa, while silk and spices came from Asia. Traders used long and difficult overland routes, such as the Silk Road, to reach the Mediterranean Sea. From there, goods were shipped to Europe. Italian city-states, particularly Venice, had a **monopoly**, or economic control, in Europe of this profitable trade. Some European countries looked for a sea route to Africa and Asia so they could establish direct trade.

Portugal became one of the leaders in exploration. Hoping to gain wealth and territory and to spread Christianity, Prince Henry the Navigator paid for expeditions to explore the west coast of Africa. In his 1487–88 voyage, Bartolomeu Dias sailed past the southern tip of Africa, which he called the Cape of Good Hope "for the promise it gave of the finding of India." Dias then returned home. Portugal built posts along Africa's coast, trading with local rulers for gold, ivory, and slaves. Enslaved Africans in Portugal's colonies endured hard labor and harsh living conditions.

Introduce Key Terms

Linguistic, Musical-Rhythmic. Review this section's key terms with students. Ask students to use their textbooks to determine the meaning of each term. When students are finished, have them each write a brief poem or song that incorporates all the terms. **SHELTERED ENGLISH**

TEACH

Have students read Section 2 and complete Guided Reading Strategies 1.2. Choose one or more of the following activities to explore the section content with students. For further suggestions on block scheduling or team teaching, see the *Block Scheduling Handbook*.

LEVEL 1: Linguistic. (Suggested time: 15 min.) As a class, go over students' Guided Reading Strategies. Then use the Reading Focus questions to highlight the main ideas of the section. **SHELTERED ENGLISH**

ALL LEVELS: Visual-Spatial, Logical-Mathematical. (Suggested time: 30 min.) Give each student a blank world map. Then have them review the section and determine the areas with which Europeans wanted to trade. Have students identify the trading routes that Europeans established and goods they sought. Then

Columbus's Bold Idea

Christopher Columbus, an Italian sailor from Genoa, hoped to find a sea route to Asia by sailing west across the Atlantic Ocean. King Ferdinand and Queen Isabella of Spain funded Columbus's fleet. The *Niña*, the *Pinta*, and the *Santa María* set sail on August 3, 1492. The crew became uneasy as time passed with no sight of land. Then on October 12, 1492, a lookout cried "Land! Land!" Columbus had reached one of the islands in the Bahamas. When Columbus explored other islands, he met the Taino (TY-noh). He called them Indians, believing that he was in the Indies, or Asia.

When the *Santa María* struck a coral reef and sank, Columbus built a small colony for its crew called *La Navidad*. He then set sail for Spain. After a stormy voyage he arrived before Ferdinand and Isabella with gold nuggets, exotic treasures, and some Taino captives. The monarchs appointed Columbus a royal admiral and governor of the new Spanish territories.

Christopher Columbus

When he returned to *La Navidad*, Columbus found that the colony had been destroyed. He created new settlements. On his next voyage he became the first European to see South America. Soon, poor conditions in the Caribbean colonies led to rebellion. Ferdinand and Isabella removed Columbus as governor.

First voyage, 1492–1493
Second voyage, 1493–1496
Third voyage, 1498
Fourth voyage, 1502–1504
Land seen by Columbus or crew members

NORTH AMERICA · ATLANTIC OCEAN · Gulf of Mexico · Yucatán Peninsula · SAN SALVADOR · BAHAMA ISLANDS · CUBA · JAMAICA · HISPANIOLA · PUERTO RICO · CARIBBEAN SEA · PACIFIC OCEAN · MESOAMERICA · TRINIDAD · SOUTH AMERICA · 80°W · 70°W · 60°W · 30°N · 20°N · 10°N

NORTH AMERICA · EUROPE · AZORES · PORTUGAL · SPAIN · CANARY ISLANDS · AFRICA · ATLANTIC OCEAN · SOUTH AMERICA

0 250 500 Miles
0 250 500 Kilometers
Modified Azimuthal Equal-Area Projection

Columbus's Voyages, 1492–1504

Learning from Maps Christopher Columbus made four trips to the Americas over a 12-year period. During these voyages, Columbus learned much about the lands and waters of the Caribbean Sea.

Location On which voyage did Columbus reach the southwest edge of Cuba?

Linking Past to Present

Remembering Columbus. While many Americans regard Columbus as a hero for his achievements, many American Indians consider Columbus Day a day of mourning. On October 11, 1992, to mark the eve of the 500th anniversary of Columbus's arrival in North America, members of the National Congress of American Indians held a rally on the lawn of the U.S. Capitol. In Oklahoma, Cherokee chief Wilma Mankiller reminded Americans that Columbus's arrival marked the beginning of centuries of problems for American Indians.

Activity: Have students use the library or search the Internet through the HRW Web site to find information on Columbus and the impact of Europeans on the Americas. Have students write an obituary for Columbus describing his place in history.

go.hrw.com
SB1 Columbus and Indians

MAP ANSWER
second

Multimedia Resources

American History Interactive Maps CD–ROM: The Columbian Exchange lead a discussion on the reasons for and results of their voyages to Asia and the Americas. **SHELTERED ENGLISH**

LEVEL 3: Linguistic, Logical-Mathematical. (Suggested time: 30 min. plus homework.) Have students use information from the text and class notes to write an encyclopedia entry about the Protestant Reformation. Ask students to focus on the effects of the Protestant Reformation in Europe and Africa. During the next class, call on volunteers to read their entries to the class.

CLOSE

Logical-Mathematical, Interpersonal. Organize the class into two groups. Ask one side to write down everything negative they can think of that resulted from European explorations of the Americas. Have the other side list all the positive aspects of these explorations. Then have each group present its list.

CHALLENGE AND EXTEND

Linguistic, Logical-Mathematical. Have students use the library and other resources to find when Columbus Day officially

Across the Curriculum

LITERATURE

The Conquest.
Historians have access to three very different accounts of Cortés's attack on the Aztec Empire. Bernal Díaz, who accompanied Cortés to Mexico, was angered by the inaccuracies he found in official accounts of the expedition, so at age 76 he wrote his own work , *The Conquest of New Spain.* The Aztec also left accounts in their own language, some written within 10 years of the events. Some of these writings, which are kept in libraries in Paris, Mexico City, and elsewhere, were translated into English and published in 1962 as *The Broken Spears: The Aztec Account of the Conquest of Mexico.*

Activity: Have each student write an essay explaining how these accounts might vary.

Multimedia Resources

American Music Audio CD Program: "Alabado"

Columbus's fourth voyage to the Americas ended in shipwreck. After being rescued, Columbus returned to Spain a broken man. He died in 1506, still believing that he had found a route to Asia.

Some Europeans who doubted that Columbus had reached the Indies continued to search for a water route to Asia. Sponsored by England, Italian sailor John Cabot reached the North American coast in 1497. Following Bartolomeu Dias's general route, Vasco da Gama sailed around the Cape of Good Hope and across the Indian Ocean. He arrived in India in 1498, thus winning for Portugal the race to Asia. In 1501 Italian Amerigo Vespucci (ve-SPOO-chee) sailed to South America. He noted, "We arrived at a new land which . . . we observed to be a continent." Europeans began calling the continents North and South America in his honor.

Spanish America

Spain continued to search for a western route to Asia. In 1513 Vasco Núñez de Balboa crossed present-day Panama on foot and reached the Pacific Ocean. Spain hoped to sail to Asia by way of this ocean. Ferdinand Magellan (muh-JEL-uhn) set sail with five ships in 1519 to find a waterway to the Pacific. Near the southern tip of South America, Magellan found a narrow sea passage to the Pacific. He crossed the ocean and reached islands off the coast of Asia, where he was killed. Juan Sebastián de Elcano captained the one ship that returned to Spain in 1522. The 18 surviving sailors were the first people to circumnavigate, or sail completely around, Earth.

This map from the 1540s shows French explorations and settlements in North America. This map was drawn upside-down, so Canada is at the bottom and Florida is in the upper-right corner.

In the process of exploration, plants, animals, and diseases were transferred between the "Old World"—Europe, Asia, and Africa—and the "New World" of the Americas. This transfer has become known as the **Columbian Exchange**. Explorers brought American plants, such as corn, tomatoes, and potatoes, to Europe. They took wheat, horses, and cattle to the Americas. Explorers also carried diseases such as smallpox, measles, and typhus.

With no resistance to these diseases, American Indians died in huge numbers. The remaining Indians were thus vulnerable to conquest. In 1519 Hernán Cortés began his conquest of the Aztec Empire. In the 1530s Francisco Pizarro (puh-ZAHR-oh) conquered the Inca Empire.

Juan Ponce de León, Pánfilo de Narváez, and Hernando de Soto each led expeditions to Florida, looking for gold. All failed to find riches. Francisco Vásquez de Coronado's expedition reached the Grand Canyon, while Juan Rodríguez Cabrillo (kah-BREE-yoh) sailed up the California coast. These explorations gave Spain vast territories that had great mineral wealth. Using the labor of American Indians and enslaved Africans, Spain mined the wealth of the Americas to fill the royal treasury.

Spain created the Council of the Indies to oversee its American empire. Pueblos, or towns, served as trading posts and as centers of local government. Presidios, or military bases, protected towns in remote frontier areas. Priests established missions to convert local Indians to Catholicism. King Philip II of Spain issued an order stating that

> **"preaching the holy gospel . . . is the principal purpose for which we order new discoveries and settlements to be made."**

The Race for Empires

While Spain built its empire, other European nations searched for a **Northwest Passage**—a waterway in North America that would connect became recognized as a national holiday and why it is celebrated when it is. In addition, ask students to research local Columbus Day customs. Finally, call on volunteers to present their findings in an oral report to the class.

REVIEW

Logical-Mathematical, Visual-Spatial. Have students complete the Section Review questions. Then ask students to make a chart organizing the section's material about European explorations in the Americas. Encourage students to use their charts as study guides.

ASSESS

Have students complete Daily Quiz 1.2.

RETEACH

Logical-Mathematical, Visual-Spatial. Have students complete Main Idea Activities for Reteaching and Sheltered English 1.2. Then have students create a time line that highlights significant events or voyages of exploration in the Americas from 1450 to 1650. **SHELTERED ENGLISH**

the Atlantic to the Pacific. In the 1530s Jacques Cartier sailed to Canada and claimed land for France. Around 75 years later Samuel de Champlain explored the Great Lakes region and founded the French colony of Quebec. He noted that by exploring:

> **"we gain knowledge of different countries, regions and kingdoms; through it we attract and bring into our countries all kinds of riches; through it . . . Christianity [is spread] in all parts of the earth."**

In 1609 English captain Henry Hudson sailed for the Dutch to present-day New York. The next year, while sailing for England, he reached present-day Hudson Bay. Although explorers failed to find a Northwest Passage, their voyages were the basis for European land claims in North America.

The Reformation

While Europeans explored the Americas, events in Europe were challenging Spain's power. In 1517 a priest named Martin Luther started the **Protestant Reformation**, a religious movement that began as an effort to reform the Catholic Church. Luther and other reformers became known as Protestants because they protested some of the church's practices. Throughout Europe fighting broke out between Catholics and Protestants. King Philip II of Spain assembled a huge naval fleet—the **Spanish Armada**—to invade England and overthrow its Protestant queen, Elizabeth I. In 1588 the smaller English fleet defeated the Armada.

Queen Elizabeth I

New Colonies in North America

With the Spanish navy weakened, other nations challenged Spain's power overseas. France established trading posts and fishing villages in Canada. In the late 1600s René-Robert de La Salle explored the Mississippi River valley. France called its North American territory New France.

In 1624 about 30 Dutch families settled in New Netherland. In 1638 the Swedish founded New Sweden near the Dutch colony. The Dutch seized New Sweden in 1655, claiming that it intruded upon their lands and fur trade.

England's Queen Elizabeth gave Sir Walter Raleigh a **charter**, a document granting permission to establish a colony. In 1585 he sent an expedition to Roanoke Island, part of present-day North Carolina. John White resettled Roanoke in 1587 and then went back to England. In 1590 he returned to find the colony deserted. Despite search efforts, White noted, "never any of them [were] found, nor seen to this day."

SECTION 2 REVIEW

Identify and explain the significance of the following:

- **Commercial Revolution**
- **monopoly**
- **Christopher Columbus**
- **Columbian Exchange**
- **Northwest Passage**
- **Martin Luther**
- **Protestant Reformation**
- **Spanish Armada**
- **Queen Elizabeth I**
- **charter**

Reading for Content Understanding

1. **Main Idea** What motivated Europeans to explore?
2. **Main Idea** How did the Protestant Reformation affect political power in Europe and North America?
3. **Economic Development** How did European countries benefit from establishing colonies in North America?
4. **Writing** *Describing* Imagine that you are an explorer. Write a journal entry describing the people you encounter.
5. **Critical Thinking** *Drawing Conclusions* Do you think Columbus's voyages were a success or a failure? Explain your answer.

Section 2 Review ANSWERS

Identify

For significance, see the following pages:

- Commercial Revolution, p. 10
- monopoly, p. 10
- Christopher Columbus, p. 11
- Columbian Exchange, p. 12
- Northwest Passage, p. 12
- Martin Luther, p. 13
- Protestant Reformation, p. 13
- Spanish Armada, p. 13
- Queen Elizabeth I, p. 13
- charter, p. 13

Reading for Content Understanding

1. Europeans wanted to establish direct trade routes to Asia and Africa, gain wealth, and spread Christianity.

2. Spain was weakened by the loss of the Armada it had sent to fight Protestant England. As a result, other European nations began to challenge Spain's power in the Americas.

3. European countries gained access to wealth and natural resources by establishing colonies in the Americas.

4. Answers will vary based on the voyage students choose, but students should describe the peoples encountered as if they are seeing them for the first time.

5. Answers will vary but students should state their opinions and offer logical support for them.

Section 3 Lesson Plan

OBJECTIVES

- Analyze the role of religion in colonial life.
- Examine the economic ties between the colonies and England.
- Describe the economic and political differences between the colonies.

FOCUS

Motivate Before Reading

Write the following phrase on the chalkboard: *move to another part of the country.* Ask students to write down three positive and three negative experiences they might have if they had to do this. After students have written their responses, ask volunteers to share their ideas. Then lead a discussion about what it would be like to move to another state or country. Explain to students that in this

Section 3 RESOURCES

PRINT
- ★ Guided Reading Strategies 1.3
- ★ Literature Reading 1: Narrative of the Life of Olaudah Equiano
- ★ Section 3 Review, p. 20
- ★ Daily Quiz 1.3

MULTIMEDIA
- ★ *Teaching Resources CD–ROM,* Lesson 1.3
- ★ *American History Simulations CD–ROM:* Building a Colony
- ★ HRW Web site

SHELTERED ENGLISH
- ★ Main Idea Activities for Reteaching and Sheltered English 1.3

The English Colonies

Reading Focus

What role did religion play in colonial life?

What was the economic relationship between the colonies and England?

How did the colonies differ from one another economically and politically?

Key Terms

Bacon's Rebellion
Mayflower Compact
town meetings
House of Burgesses
Parliament
bicameral legislature
Dominion of New England
imports
exports
Navigation Acts
Middle Passage
Great Awakening

IN 1605 A GROUP of English merchants asked the Crown for a charter to found a settlement and search for gold in North America. The area they wanted to settle was part of the region called Virginia, which at the time extended from present-day Maine to South Carolina. King James I granted the request, promising the London Company the rights to "all the lands, woods, soils, grounds, . . . ports, rivers, mines, minerals, . . . [and] commodities" along a section of the Virginia coast. The company's efforts, wrote King James, "may in time bring . . . a settled and quiet government."

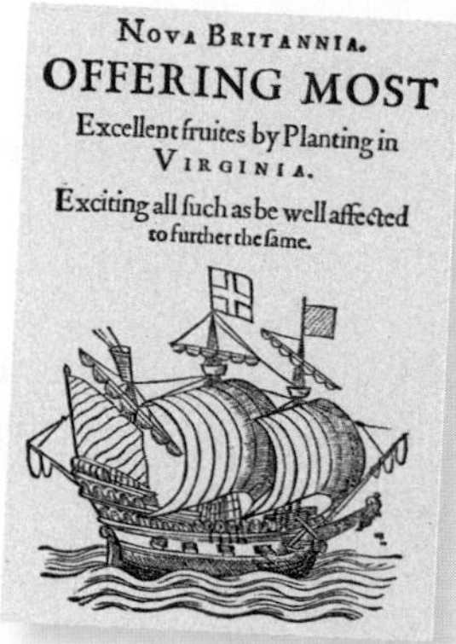

London Company advertisement

 The Settlement of Virginia

The failure of Roanoke led the London Company to take a different approach to settlement. Instead of relying on the wealth of one person, investors formed a joint-stock company, so that several people shared the costs and risks.

On April 26, 1607, the first three ships sent by the London Company arrived in Virginia. The 105 male colonists established Jamestown, named after the king. Instead of building sturdy shelters or planting crops, they searched for gold. By the time winter arrived, two thirds of the colonists were dead, and the rest were starving and sick. In 1608 Captain John Smith gained control of the colony. He forced the settlers to plant crops and build better housing. About 400 more colonists arrived the next year. Smith returned to England, and that winter, disease and starvation struck the colony. By the summer of 1610, only 60 colonists were still alive.

The Powhatan Confederacy—a powerful alliance of Algonquian Indians—taught the colonists how to grow North American crops such section they will learn about the settlers that came to the Americas, their relationship with their homeland, and how colonial life differed depending on which colony one called home.

Introduce Key Terms

Linguistic, Logical-Mathematical. Review this section's key terms with students. Ask students to use their textbooks to find the meaning of each term. Then have students create a brief quiz using definitions as questions and the terms as answers. When students have finished the task, collect the quizzes and inform them that they will be used in a future activity. **SHELTERED ENGLISH**

TEACH

Have students read Section 3 and complete Guided Reading Strategies 1.3. Choose one or more of the following activities to explore the section content with students. For further suggestions on block scheduling or team teaching, see the *Block Scheduling Handbook.*

LEVEL 1: Linguistic. (Suggested time: 15 min.) As a class, go over students' Guided Reading Strategies. Then use the Reading Focus questions to highlight the main ideas of the section. **SHELTERED ENGLISH**

as corn. However, the relationship between the two groups was rarely peaceful. In 1622 fighting broke out between the colonists and the Powhatan, beginning a war that lasted for the next 20 years. In one attack, the Powhatan killed about 350 colonists. In 1624 the colony's problems convinced England to cancel the London Company's charter and to make Virginia a royal colony.

The colony encouraged immigration because the high death rate had led to labor shortages. Many poor colonists signed an indenture, or contract, to work for several years for those who paid their ship fare to Virginia. Large numbers of these indentured servants died because of poor living conditions and disease. Some Africans came to Virginia as indentured servants, but by the late 1600s many were being kept in slavery. Slaves worked on the developing tobacco plantations.

Indentured servants often struggled to make a living after their contracts ended. They sometimes built farms on American Indian land. In 1676 Nathaniel Bacon led a group of poor colonists in an attack against some Indians. Bacon and his followers then attacked and burned Jamestown during **Bacon's Rebellion**. After Bacon died, the rebellion ended. Fearing another revolt by former indentured servants, many farmers began to use more slave labor in the Virginia colony.

Biography

The Granger Collection, New York

John Smith

Captain John Smith was a man of great physical and mental strength. Smith was born in 1580 in England to a farming family. At the age of 17, he entered the military, serving with English troops in the Netherlands. He fought in many military campaigns across Europe. These experiences helped prepare Smith for the difficulties he and the other colonists faced in Virginia.

After helping save Jamestown, Smith explored and mapped the Chesapeake Bay region. He also led an expedition exploring New England, from which he returned with a cargo of fish and furs. Smith later published books about his adventures in North America, including *The Generall Historie of Virginia* and *A Description of New England.*

The Founding of Plymouth

While Jamestown was being settled, religious tension was increasing in England. A Protestant group called the Puritans wanted to reform, or purify, the Church of England. One sect, or religious group, of Puritans wanted to separate from the Church of England entirely. English authorities often persecuted these Separatists.

One Separatist sect that emigrated to escape such persecution became known as the Pilgrims. On September 16, 1620, the *Mayflower* sailed from England with more than 100 men, women, and children as passengers. The Pilgrims drew up a basic agreement to govern their colony in the **Mayflower Compact**, creating

"such just and equal laws . . . as shall be thought most meet [fitting] and convenient for the general good of the colony."

The Pilgrims chose to land in present-day Massachusetts, where they established the colony of Plymouth. Nearly half the Pilgrims died from sickness during the first winter. For some time, the Pilgrims met no American Indians. However, in the spring the Pilgrims met two English-speaking Indians, Samoset and Squanto. William Bradford, the Pilgrim leader, noted that Squanto showed

Biography

John Smith and Algonquian Indians. Captain John Smith was captured by Algonquian Indians. They brought him to the Powhatan capital, Werowocomoco. Smith later wrote in *The Generall Historie of Virginia* that they had set him before an altar stone to be killed when the 13-year-old Pocahontas, daughter of the leader of the Powhatan Confederacy, threw herself over his body, saving his life.

Critical Thinking: Why do you think some historians doubt Smith's story about Pocahontas?

ANSWER: Answers will vary but students might suggest that it is unlikely that Pocahontas would have gone to such lengths to save the life of a stranger.

Geographic Diversity

American Forests. English forests had been depleted in the 1500s. Sailors to America returned home with stories of woods so dense they could smell the pine trees before they saw land. The English hoped that by settling the area they could exploit its resources.

Critical Thinking: How might this attitude toward use of colonial resources be detrimental in the long run?

ANSWER: English settlers might not conserve resources.

ALL LEVELS: Logical-Mathematical, Visual-Spatial. (Suggested time: 25 min.) Have each student create a political cartoon showing the political or economic ties between the colonies and England. Some possible topics include Bacon's Rebellion and the Navigation Acts. Remind students to include a caption that helps explain the political or economic link that the cartoon is attempting to portray. Encourage students to share their cartoons with the class, then lead a discussion on the ties that England maintained with the colonies. **SHELTERED ENGLISH**

ALL LEVELS: Linguistic, Logical-Mathematical. (Suggested time: 25 min. plus homework) Have students select one of the original thirteen colonies and prepare an advertisement that its founder might have written in order to attract new settlers. Remind students to focus on the secular and religious opportunities the colony offered in comparison to some of the other colonies. (One example would be religious toleration in Rhode Island.) During the next class ask volunteers to present their advertisements. Finally, lead a discussion on the different opportunities available in each colony. **SHELTERED ENGLISH**

LEVEL 2: Linguistic, Interpersonal, Intrapersonal. (Suggested time: 45 min.) Inform the class that they will be conducting a panel discussion with some important New England colonists as guests. Assign a student to act as moderator for the discussion. Assign three other students the roles of John Smith, Roger

Daily Life

Early Housing. Jamestown colonists described their first homes as wigwams, although they were modeled after English shacks, not American Indian huts. Their homes were so flimsy that in bad weather the colonists sought protection under a rotten old tent. Early visitors to the colony were shocked by the houses. One person wrote that they were worse than the shacks on which they were modeled.

Activity: Have students use the library or search the Internet through the HRW Web site to find more information on housing in the early colonies. Ask each student to make a model of a colonial home.

go.hrw.com
SB1 Colonial Housing

MAP ANSWER
the Southern colonies

Multimedia Resources

American History Simulations CD–ROM: Building a Colony

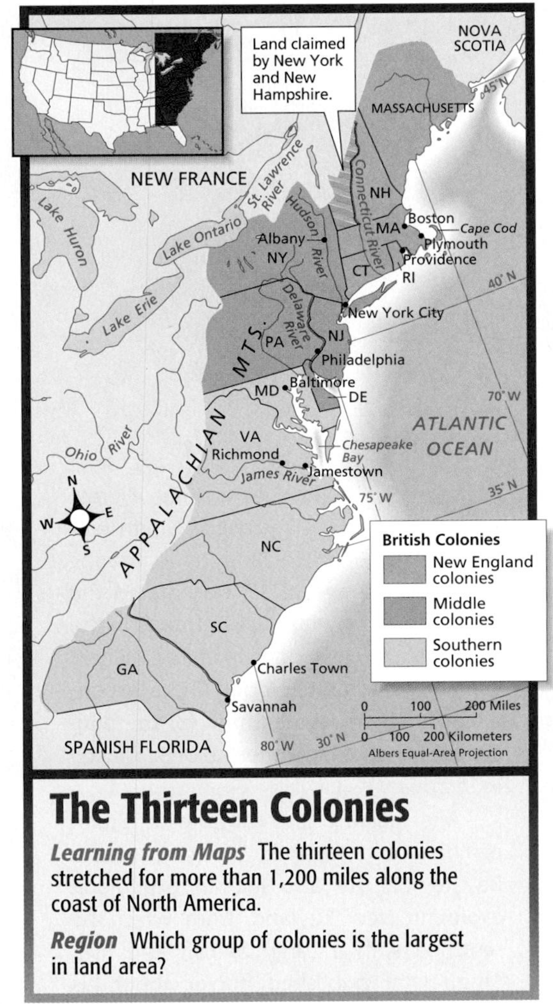

The Thirteen Colonies

Learning from Maps The thirteen colonies stretched for more than 1,200 miles along the coast of North America.

Region Which group of colonies is the largest in land area?

them "how to set [plant] their corn, [and] where to take [catch] fish." He also helped the Pilgrims establish peaceful relations with the Wampanoag Indians. To celebrate their harvest and their first year at Plymouth, the Pilgrims invited about 90 Wampanoag as guests to what became known as the first Thanksgiving.

A Pilgrim boy's leather shoes

Courtesy Peabody Essex Museum, Salem, Massachusetts

The New England Colonies

In England, Puritans were persecuted for being dissenters—people who disagree with official religious or political opinions. In 1629 King Charles I granted some Puritans a charter to establish a colony in New England. The next year a fleet set sail. These Puritans believed that they had a covenant, or sacred agreement, with God to build an ideal Christian community. Aboard the *Arbella,* John Winthrop, the colony's governor, wrote that "we must consider that we shall be like a City upon a Hill; the eyes of all people are on us." By the end of 1630, about 1,000 more colonists had come to the Massachusetts Bay Colony.

While most colonists in Virginia were men, Puritan colonists tended to come in family groups that usually had some money and skills. The Puritans established several towns, including Boston, the colony's capital. Colonists also settled to the north, in present-day New Hampshire, which became a royal colony in 1680.

In its charter, Massachusetts had the right to govern itself, giving it more independence than Virginia, a royal colony. The Massachusetts General Court, which had representatives from each town, elected the governor. Settlements decided local issues in gatherings known as **town meetings**. Politics and religion were closely linked in Massachusetts—only church members could vote.

Ministers were highly respected members of the community. Religion also shaped everyday life. On most Sundays, colonists heard a morning and an afternoon sermon. In 1636 Harvard College was founded to teach ministers. In 1647 Massachusetts passed a law requiring towns with 50 or more households to appoint someone to teach children to read and write so they could read the Bible. This was one of the first public education laws in Europe or the Americas.

In the 1630s several important Puritans left Massachusetts because of their dissenting views. In 1636 minister Thomas Hooker left and helped found Connecticut. Roger Williams, another minister, said that the General Court had no authority in spiritual matters and should pay for American Indian land that it took. In response, Puritan authorities banished Williams. In 1636 he moved

Williams, and William Penn. Allow these students time to prepare for their roles. Have the audience prepare a list of questions for the guests. Ask students to prepare questions that reflect different attitudes toward the roles of government and religion in colonial life. Then conduct the panel discussion. Allow time at the end of class to discuss the shifting role religion played in the founding of the various colonies and in their inhabitants' daily lives.

LEVEL 2: Linguistic, Logical-Mathematical, Interpersonal. (Suggested time: 45 min.) Organize the class into three groups and inform students that they will debate whether governments in the early English colonies were democratic. Before beginning the debate, briefly review the appropriate format and procedures of a debate and assign the roles of timekeeper and referee. Have one group use the text and their notes to support the claim that governments were democratic, while the second group uses the sources to argue that the governments were undemocratic. Ask the third group of students to act as judges. Allow time at the end of the debate to discuss the similarities and differences between the colonial system of government and our current system.

N Noah did view
The old world & now

O Young Obadias,
David, Josias
All were pious.

P Peter deny'd
His Lord and cry'd.

Q Queen Esther sues
And saves the *Jews*.

R Young pious Ruth.
Left all for Truth.

S Young Sam'l dear
The Lord did fear.

A page from the New England Primer, *an early schoolbook*

south and established a settlement called Providence, which later became part of Rhode Island. Williams tried to establish fair dealings with the local Indians and supported religious tolerance. Anne Hutchinson also questioned Puritan authority. She was put on trial for her beliefs and banished from Massachusetts.

Community and religious conflicts peaked in New England with the Salem witch trials of 1692. More than 100 colonists were accused of witchcraft, and 19 people were executed. By the next year, some of the officials and clergymen involved in the witchcraft trials had come to regret their participation.

New Southern Colonies

The Puritans were not the only religious group to come to America to escape persecution. Maryland was founded as a haven for Catholics. It was a proprietary colony, which meant that the proprietor, or owner, controlled the government. Proprietor Cecilius Calvert, the second Lord Baltimore, sent 200 colonists to Maryland in 1634, most of whom were men. Having learned from the Jamestown experience, settlers in Maryland planted food crops before starting to grow tobacco for profit. When religious conflicts arose as Protestants began moving to the colony, Maryland passed the Toleration Act of 1649, which stated:

> **"No person . . . professing [claiming] to believe in Jesus Christ shall . . . be . . . molested [persecuted], or . . . any way compelled [forced] to the belief or exercise of any other religion."**

American Literature

"To My Dear and Loving Husband"
Anne Bradstreet

When John Winthrop's flagship, the Arbella, *set sail for Boston in 1630, the Bradstreet family was on board. Twenty years later, Anne Bradstreet became the first published American poet with her collection* The Tenth Muse Lately Sprung Up in America. *Despite the demands of living in a new settlement and raising eight children, she continued writing and producing some of her finest poetry, including the following poem to her husband, Simon Bradstreet.*

If ever two were one, then surely we.
If ever man were loved by wife, then thee;
If ever wife was happy in a man,
Compare with me, ye women, if you can.
I prize thy love more than whole
mines of gold
Or all the riches the East doth hold.
My love is such that rivers cannot quench,
Nor ought but love from thee,
give recompense.
Thy love is such I can no way repay,
The heavens reward thee manifold I pray.
Then while we live, in love let's so
persevere
That when we live no more, we may
live ever.

Understanding Literature

1. What value does Anne Bradstreet place on her marriage?
2. What words in the poem hint at Bradstreet's feelings toward her husband?

Across the Curriculum

LITERATURE

Anne Bradstreet. *The Tenth Muse Lately Sprung Up in America* was published without Anne Bradstreet's knowledge. Although she was embarrassed to see her work in print, she did not stop writing. Her poems show her initial difficulties with life in Massachusetts, but they also demonstrate her religious faith and her faith in her new home. Today she is most admired for the poems that portray domestic life, describing her feelings for her husband and children.

Activity: Have students find one of the works of an early colonial writer, such as Bradstreet, Nathaniel Morton, William Hubbard, Edward Taylor, or Cotton Mather. Ask each student to read one and write a review on it.

American Literature Answers

1. more than any amount of wealth
2. words such as loved, happy, and prize

TEACHER TO TEACHER

LEVEL 3: Linguistic, Logical-Mathematical, Intrapersonal. (Suggested time: 35 min.) Scott Meek of Chicago, Illinois, suggested the following activity: Ask students to imagine that they are living in the decade of the 1660s and England has recently passed the Navigation Acts. Inform students that they must first decide whether they support or oppose these new laws. Have students who support the Navigation Acts, write an editorial that might have appeared in an English newspaper that supported this legislation. Have students who oppose these acts write an editorial that may have appeared in an American newspaper that opposed the restrictions. Remind students to discuss both the purpose and effects of the Navigation Acts.

CLOSE

Logical-Mathematical, Visual-Spatial, Interpersonal. Organize the class into three groups. Provide each group with a large piece of butcher paper or posterboard and markers. Assign each group one of the three colonial regions—New England, middle, or southern colonies. Have each group create a poster that

Economic Development

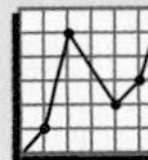

Slavery in the Early 1600s. Initially farmers in Virginia did not use much slave labor, in part because England did not take part in the African slave trade. In the early 1600s obtaining slaves was difficult because the Dutch, Spanish, and Portuguese controlled the so-called Slave Coast of West Africa.

Critical Thinking: Why might Virginia planters have difficulty purchasing slaves in the early 1600s?

ANSWER: Their primary trading networks were linked to England, which did not take part in the slave trade.

In 1663 Charles II gave land south of Virginia to eight of his supporters. This land, called Carolina, had two areas of settlement, each with its own governor. In 1729 the English government purchased Carolina and divided it into two separate royal colonies—North and South Carolina.

Most colonists in North Carolina were poor farmers from Virginia, and there were few towns until the early 1700s. Settlement in South Carolina began in 1700, when about 100 colonists arrived. They founded Charles Town, which was later called Charleston. The colony attracted many settlers, and wealthy people received large land grants. Records suggest that African laborers taught the colonists how to raise rice in the 1690s. Plantation owners used slaves to do the hard work involved in rice production.

In 1732 King George II granted a charter to found a colony for poor English people, such as those who had been jailed for debt. The king also hoped that this new colony—Georgia—would be a buffer between South Carolina and Spanish Florida. In 1733 James Oglethorpe founded the town of Savannah. The settlers there became unhappy with Oglethorpe's rules, which limited the size of land grants and outlawed slavery. Eventually, the colony eliminated these rules. In 1752 the trustees gave up their charter, and Georgia became a royal colony. Rice plantations worked by slaves soon dotted Georgia's fertile coast, while inland farmers struggled to survive.

 The Middle Colonies

In 1664 the English challenged the Dutch claim to the territory occupied by New Netherland. Charles II's brother, the Duke of York, organized an English fleet that arrived in the harbor of New Amsterdam, the capital of New Netherland. The colony surrendered without any shots being fired. When New Netherland became the English colony of New York, most Dutch settlers remained there.

Shortly after the conquest of New Netherland, the Duke of York granted lands between the Hudson and Delaware Rivers to Sir George Carteret and Lord John Berkeley. These proprietors divided the land into East and West Jersey, which were made into the single royal colony of New Jersey in 1702. The Society of Friends, or the Quakers, made up one of the largest groups in New Jersey. The Quakers were a Protestant sect that believed in the equality of the sexes before God, religious tolerance for all peoples, and nonviolence. The Quakers were often persecuted for their beliefs.

One proprietor of the East Jersey colony was a Quaker named William Penn, whose father had loaned money to King Charles II. In 1681 the king paid his debts by granting Penn a charter for a colony that became known as Pennsylvania. Penn advertised throughout Europe for colonists, offering land grants and religious freedom to all Christians. Many of these settlers became farmers.

Penn visited his colony and treated local American Indians with respect. He also designed the colony's capital, which he named Philadelphia, or City of Brotherly Love. In 1682 he acquired a region that was called Delaware. Pennsylvania and Delaware shared the same governor until Delaware became a separate colony in 1776.

The Granger Collection, New York

Colonial Quakers in Pennsylvania attend a meeting.

accurately portrays the assigned region's history, culture, and economy. Encourage students to include the colonies that made up the region, the dates of settlement, the founding fathers, the major religions, the form of government, and the principle occupations. Students may wish to include pictures or illustrations to accompany their written text.

CHALLENGE AND EXTEND

1. **Logical-Mathematical, Interpersonal.** To help students learn more about the religions that shaped colonial life, have students conduct research on one of the religious groups discussed in the section—Catholics, Puritans, or Quakers. Have students gather additional information about the history of the religion, including its founder, place of origin, basic tenets, and current worldwide membership. Encourage students to interview individuals (if possible) who practice the religion they have chosen in order to gain a better understanding of the traditions, customs, and fundamental beliefs.
2. **Linguistic.** Have students use the library and other resources to research the Salem witchcraft trials of the late 1600s. Encourage students to gather excerpts from the trials and statistics about them. Allow students to choose the formats for presenting their findings.

Life in the Thirteen Colonies

State Capital, Commonwealth of Virginia, Courtesy Library of Virginia, image altered.

Beginning in 1619, two representatives from every town in the Virginia colony met in Jamestown as the House of Burgesses.

In England the Privy Council, a group of royal advisers, set policy for all thirteen colonies. Each colony had either an appointed or an elected governor, who served as the head of government. There were also colonial courts. In some cases, colonists elected representatives to an assembly that made laws. Virginia's **House of Burgesses** was the first colonial assembly. The assemblies were modeled on England's **Parliament**, or legislature. Parliament consists of a **bicameral legislature**—a lawmaking body that is made up of two houses, or groups.

When the Duke of York became King James II, he began suspending colonial charters and united the New England colonies under the **Dominion of New England** in 1686. A royal council and Governor Sir Edmund Andros ruled the Dominion. The king's attempts to centralize power made him unpopular in both England and the colonies. Parliament asked James's daughter Mary and her Dutch husband, William, to jointly rule England. When William landed in England with his army in the fall of 1688, James fled the country. When the colonists learned of this Glorious Revolution, they removed Andros and formed new assemblies. In time, the monarchs issued new colonial charters.

The Navigation Acts

One of England's main interests in its colonies was economic profit. Like other European nations, England practiced mercantilism—creating and maintaining wealth by controlling trade. England wanted to establish a favorable balance of trade by decreasing its **imports**, items purchased from other countries, and increasing its **exports**, items sold to other countries.

Between 1650 and 1696, Parliament passed a series of **Navigation Acts** to control colonial trade. The acts required colonists to use English ships to transport goods. All trade goods had to pass through English ports, where duties, or import taxes, were added to the items. Parliament also forbade colonists from trading "enumerated articles," or specified items, with any country other than England. These goods included sugar, tobacco, and cotton. However, customs officials often failed to enforce such regulations, and colonial trade networks developed.

One important part of the trade networks was the slave trade, which involved the transportation of more than 10 million Africans across the Atlantic Ocean to be sold as slaves in the Americas. This often deadly voyage was called the **Middle Passage**. Olaudah Equiano described his experiences in the Middle Passage: "The shrieks of the women, and the groans of the dying, rendered [made] the whole a scene of horror almost inconceivable [unbelievable]." Despite the human cost, the slave trade and slave labor became an important part of the colonial economy.

The Granger Collection, New York

Charlestown, July 24th, 1769.
TO BE SOLD,
On THURSDAY the third Day of AUGUST next,
A CARGO OF NINETY-FOUR PRIME, HEALTHY
NEGROES,
CONSISTING OF
Thirty-nine MEN, Fifteen BOYS, Twenty-four WOMEN, and Sixteen GIRLS.
JUST ARRIVED,
In the Brigantine DEMBIA, *Francis Bare*, Master, from SIERRA-LEON, by
DAVID & JOHN DEAS.

Slave auction poster

The Colonial Economies

The colonial economies varied from region to region. The South relied on agriculture and raw materials, such as timber and furs, for its economic base. With a warm climate and long growing season, the South produced cash crops—crops grown

Constitutional Heritage

Separation of Church and State. The years following the Great Awakening brought a new trend toward the separation of church and state. This movement for religious freedom gained momentum in the years leading up to and following the American Revolution. Eventually, the Constitution would guarantee the separation of church and state.

Critical Thinking: How did the Great Awakening's ideas contribute to the movement for the separation of church and state?

ANSWER: The Great Awakening's promotion of religious independence and its strong support of religious freedom might have convinced people that religion must function separately from government to ensure the freedom of its practice.

REVIEW

Linguistic, Interpersonal. Have students complete the Section Review questions. Then organize the class into pairs. Provide each student with the quiz he or she created in the Introduce Key Terms activity. Ask students to exchange quizzes with their partners. After students have answered the questions, have them return the quizzes to their partners for grading. **SHELTERED ENGLISH**

ASSESS

Have students complete Daily Quiz 1.3.

RETEACH

Linguistic, Musical-Rhythmic. Have students complete Main Idea Activities for Reteaching and Sheltered English 1.3. Then organize the class into small groups. Ask each group to develop a mnemonic device (such as a rhyme or an acrostic) that will help its members remember which colonies were included in the different regions—New England, middle, and southern. When groups have finished this task, ask them to share their memory strategies with the rest of the class. **SHELTERED ENGLISH**

Section 3 Review ANSWERS

Identify

For significance, see the following pages:

- Bacon's Rebellion, p. 15
- Mayflower Compact, p. 15
- town meetings, p. 16
- House of Burgesses, p. 19
- Parliament, p. 19
- bicameral legislature, p. 19
- Dominion of New England, p. 19
- imports, p. 19
- exports, p. 19
- Navigation Acts, p. 19
- Middle Passage, p. 20
- Great Awakening, p. 20

Reading for Content Understanding

1. motivated Pilgrims and Puritans to immigrate; Maryland founded as a haven for Catholics; Pennsylvania founded on the basis of religious freedom for all Christians; shaped daily life and government in New England

2. England established and controlled a favorable balance of trade between itself and the colonies.

3. New England's climate would not support cash crops, so the economy was based on fishing, shipbuilding, and trade; the long growing season and fertile land of the middle colonies allowed significant agricultural yield to export food and livestock; the warm climate and long growing season let the South base its economy on agriculture and raw materials.

4. Answers will vary depending on which colonies students choose.

5. Both groups of settlers had difficulty establishing their colonies and both received help from American Indians.

mainly to be sold for profit. The main cash crops—tobacco, rice, and indigo—required a large labor force. By the 1700s enslaved Africans did most of the work on plantations. To control slaves, most colonies passed slave codes, or laws.

New England had a more diverse economy. With a harsh climate and rocky soil, few New England farms could grow cash crops. Most families used their own labor, and not slave labor, to farm. Rich fishing waters and abundant lumber made fishing and shipbuilding two leading industries in New England, while Boston was a leader in colonial commerce.

With a good growing season and plenty of fertile land, the middle colonies produced surpluses of foodstuffs and livestock for export. Indentured servants performed much of the labor. Merchants in Philadelphia and New York City exported colonial goods to Europe and the West Indies. These cities became two of the largest and most important colonial cities.

A Revival of Faith

While the colonies had different economies, they shared some experiences. During the 1730s and 1740s, many colonists from New England to Georgia experienced what historians have called a "great awakening" in their religious lives. This **Great Awakening** was an unorganized but widespread movement of evangelical Christian revivals, or large church gatherings. Jonathan Edwards, George Whitefield, and other ministers preached that all people, regardless of their social status, were born sinners. They also said that everyone had an equal chance to be saved. Such messages of spiritual equality may have eventually encouraged some colonists to demand greater political equality.

Courtesy of the Free Library of Philadelphia

Colonial woman spinning wool for local use

SECTION 3 REVIEW

Identify and explain the significance of the following:

- **Bacon's Rebellion**
- **Mayflower Compact**
- **town meetings**
- **House of Burgesses**
- **Parliament**
- **bicameral legislature**
- **Dominion of New England**
- **imports**
- **exports**
- **Navigation Acts**
- **Middle Passage**
- **Great Awakening**

Reading for Content Understanding

1 **Main Idea** How did religion affect the colonies and colonial life?

2 **Main Idea** What economic ties existed between England and the colonies?

3 **Geographic Diversity** *Region* What effect did the environment have on the economies that developed in the New England, middle, and southern colonies?

4 **Writing** *Classifying* Imagine that you are a colonist in the late 1600s. Write a letter to a cousin in England telling him or her how the colonies differ from each other economically and politically.

5 **Critical Thinking** *Making Comparisons* How were the experiences of the Pilgrims similar to those of the Jamestown settlers?

OBJECTIVES

- **Explain why Britain imposed new taxes on the colonies, and examine the colonists' response.**
- **Describe the events that led the First Continental Congress to break free from Britain.**
- **Analyze the events that finally ended the American Revolution.**

FOCUS

Motivate Before Reading

Write the word *independence* on the chalkboard. Ask students to come up with a definition for it. Ask students why people long for independence. After students have shared ideas, ask them to imagine that they are parents of a young teenager. Then ask students whether they would want to give their children independence. Lead a discussion about why a parent might not want to

The American Revolution

Reading Focus

Why did Britain impose new taxes on the colonies, and how did the colonists respond?

What events led the First Continental Congress to break away from Britain?

What events ended the American Revolution?

Key Terms

Pontiac's Rebellion
Stamp Act
Townshend Acts
Boston Massacre
Intolerable Acts
Battle of Bunker Hill
Declaration of Independence
Battle of Saratoga
Battle of Yorktown
Treaty of Paris of 1783

IN 1748 SWEDISH SCIENTIST Peter Kalm traveled through the British colonies, which he said "have increased so much in their number of inhabitants, and in their riches, that they almost vie [compete] with Old England." Kalm also noted that the colonists were very independent, and that British trade laws caused them "to grow less tender for their mother country." The tensions that Kalm saw increased as the colonies and Great Britain grew further apart.

The Granger Collection, New York

King George III

Conflicts in the Colonies

From 1689 to 1763, France and England fought a series of wars to become the world's most powerful nation. The fighting ended with the British victory in the French and Indian War. As a result, France lost its lands in North America. Britain gained Canada, French lands east of the Mississippi River, and Florida. Spain, which had allied with Britain, received French Louisiana.

As the fighting ended, more settlers crossed the Appalachian Mountains onto American Indian land. In 1763 Chief Pontiac led Indians in **Pontiac's Rebellion**. They destroyed many British forts before Pontiac surrendered. To prevent more conflict, Britain issued the Proclamation of 1763, banning settlement west of the Appalachians.

Colonial conflicts were costly. To raise money, in 1764 Parliament passed the Sugar Act, which set duties on molasses and sugar. Some colonists argued that Britain did not have the right to tax them because there were no colonial representatives in Parliament. The colonists protested, "No taxation without representation." Samuel Adams of Boston voiced his opposition to the tax:

> **"For if our trade may be taxed, why not our lands? Why not the produce of our lands and, in short, everything we possess or make use of?"**

Section 4
RESOURCES

PRINT

- ★ Guided Reading Strategies 1.4
- ★ Biography Reading 1: Paul Revere
- ★ American History Political Cartoon 1: Defeating the British
- ★ Section 4 Review, p. 25
- ★ Daily Quiz 1.4

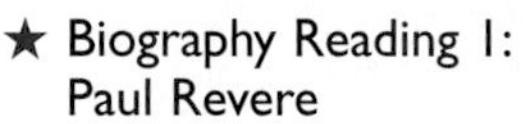

MULTIMEDIA

- ★ *Teaching Resources CD–ROM*, Lesson 1.4
- ★ *Exploring America's Past* Video Segment: American Beginnings; *Teacher's Guide*, pp. 2–3

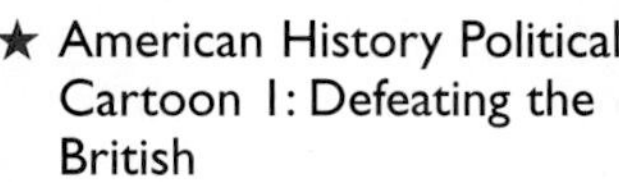

SHELTERED ENGLISH

- ★ Main Idea Activities for Reteaching and Sheltered English 1.4

grant independence to a young teenager. Tell students that in this section they will learn what happened when the colonists asked for independence.

Introduce Key Terms

Linguistic, Logical-Mathematical, Interpersonal. Review this section's key terms with students. Organize the class into pairs and provide each pair with note cards. Have students write a key term on one side of a card and clues about it on the reverse side. Ask students to take turns reading clues and definitions while partners attempt to identify the key terms. **SHELTERED ENGLISH**

TEACH

Have students read Section 4 and complete Guided Reading Strategies 1.4. Choose one or more of the following activities to explore the section content with students. For further suggestions on block scheduling or team teaching, see the *Block Scheduling Handbook*.

LEVEL 1: Linguistic. (Suggested time: 15 min.) As a class, go over students' Guided Reading Strategies. Then use the Reading Focus questions to highlight the main ideas of the section. **SHELTERED ENGLISH**

Using Visual Resources

Paul Revere.
Craftspeople and artisans formed the backbone of the revolutionary movement. Engraver and silversmith Paul Revere used all of his skills to promote the cause of American independence. His engravings, such as this one of the Boston Massacre, were produced for documentary and propaganda purposes rather than for artistic enjoyment. In cartoons of the Boston Tea Party, Revere included a key to help readers identify each ship. Although the figures in his artwork were somewhat crude, they depicted incidents of importance to a colonial audience.

Critical Thinking: Why might colonists appreciate artwork that had political significance?

ANSWER: It reflected events that were critical to their daily lives.

Merchants in Massachusetts and New York agreed to boycott, or not buy, certain British goods until Parliament removed the duties.

In response, Prime Minister George Grenville proposed the **Stamp Act** in 1765. This act required colonists to pay for an official stamp, or seal, when they bought paper items such as newspapers and legal documents. Many colonists protested this tax on everyday items produced in the colonies. Some colonists formed secret societies called the Sons of Liberty, which sometimes used violence to frighten tax collectors. In October, delegates from nine colonies met and issued a declaration that the Stamp Act violated their rights and liberties. They asked Parliament to repeal, or abolish, the act. Parliament repealed the act in 1766, but asserted its authority to make laws for the colonies.

In 1767 Parliament passed the **Townshend Acts**, which required new import duties. The colonists responded with another boycott. When the Massachusetts legislature protested the acts, the British governor disbanded it. British soldiers arrived in Boston in 1768. On March 5, 1770, British troops fired into a mob, killing five people in the **Boston Massacre**.

Paul Revere's engraving of the Boston Massacre

Parliament repealed the Townshend duties but left the tax on tea. Colonists were further angered when Parliament passed the Tea Act in 1773. On December 16, a group of colonists crept onto three ships in Boston Harbor and dumped chests of tea overboard. To punish Massachusetts for this Boston Tea Party, Parliament passed four laws in 1774 that colonists called the **Intolerable Acts**. These acts included closing Boston Harbor and canceling the colony's charter.

The Revolutionary War Begins

In September 1774, colonial delegates met in Philadelphia for the First Continental Congress. The delegates discussed the crisis and recommended boycotting British goods and arming colonial militias. They also sent King George III a list of their rights. In response, British leaders ordered the colonists' weapons seized. General Thomas Gage targeted the militia weapons stored in Concord, about 20 miles from Boston. On April 18, 1775, colonists Paul Revere and William Dawes rode across the countryside warning, "The British are coming!"

The next morning, the militia met a large force of British troops at Lexington, near Concord. The colonial leader shouted to his men, "Don't fire unless fired upon. But if they mean to have a war, let it begin here!" Suddenly, a shot rang out. To this day, no one knows who fired this "shot heard round the world." The short battle that followed resulted in 18 colonial casualties. The British next marched to Concord, where they met more militia. After some British troops set fire to a few buildings, they retreated back to Boston. The militia fired upon them, inflicting many casualties.

Word of the fighting spread, and representatives from the colonies met in Philadelphia in May for the Second Continental Congress. The delegates organized the Continental Army and chose Virginian George Washington, a well-respected veteran of the French and Indian War, as commander. The Congress also sent the king a petition asking for a peaceful resolution.

After the battle at Concord, the colonial forces held Boston under siege—a military blockade of a

ALL LEVELS: Linguistic, Logical-Mathematical. (Suggested time: 25 min.) Assign each student one event that led to the end of the war. Ask each student to come up with a newspaper headline about the assigned event. Once students have finished their headlines, organize the class into small groups and have them list relevant information that might have been included in a story about each group member's event. **SHELTERED ENGLISH**

LEVEL 2: Linguistic, Logical-Mathematical, Visual-Spatial. (Suggested time: 30 min.) Ask students to create a chart or other type of graphic organizer that will include information about the various pieces of legislation that Britain's Parliament passed that negatively affected the colonies. Ask students to include three columns titled *Act, Purpose,* and *Response*. Under *Act*, have students list *Sugar, Stamp, Townshend,* and *Tea*. Students may use their textbooks and notes to fill in the purpose of and response to each act.

LEVEL 3: Linguistic, Logical-Mathematical. (Suggested time: 40 min. plus homework) Have students write an essay about one of the following events: the First Continental Congress, fighting at Lexington, or fighting at Concord. Ask students to focus on how the assigned event affected the conflict.

A soldier in the Continental Army

city or fort. Warned of a British plan to secure Charlestown, which overlooks Boston, colonial soldiers took up defensive positions atop nearby Bunker Hill and Breed's Hill. By the next morning, June 17, the colonial forces had secured the hills. The British then mounted a frontal assault. The colonial commander ordered his troops, who were low on gunpowder, not to fire on the British soldiers "until you see the whites of their eyes." The colonists finally retreated after running out of ammunition during the **Battle of Bunker Hill**.

In March 1776 General Washington's army positioned cannons on a hill overlooking Boston and fired on the British troops. On March 7 General William Howe ordered the British to retreat. Boston, the birthplace of the Revolution, was back in colonial hands.

Fighting for Independence

In January 1776 Thomas Paine published *Common Sense,* a pamphlet in which he argued that countries should be ruled by laws created by the people instead of by a monarchy. Many colonists agreed with Paine's ideas. In June the Continental Congress decided to break away from Britain. Thomas Jefferson, a delegate from Virginia, was the main author of the **Declaration of Independence**. This document defined the colonists' rights, listed their complaints against Britain, and declared the colonies free and independent. On July 4, 1776, the Continental Congress approved the Declaration of Independence, creating the United States of America.

The signers of the Declaration of Independence drew inspiration from the Enlightenment, an intellectual movement that applied reason and logic to political behavior. Enlightenment philosophers believed that government was a social contract between people and their ruler. English philosopher John Locke agreed and added that people had a natural right to overthrow a corrupt government.

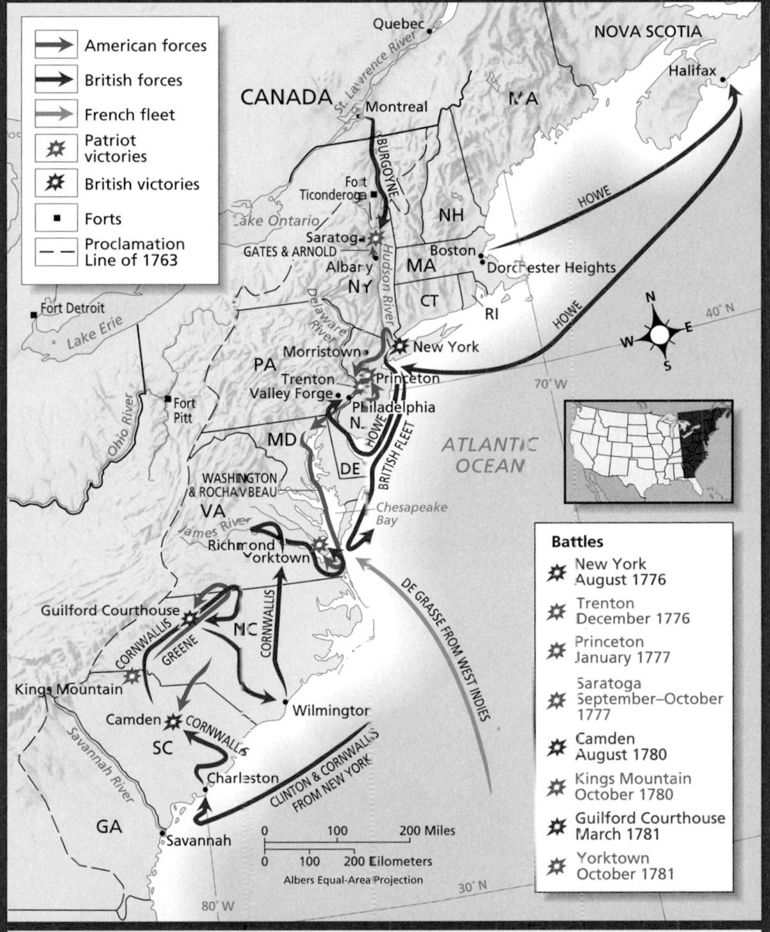

The Fight for Independence, 1776–1781

Learning from Maps The Revolutionary War was fought across the vast area of the thirteen colonies. British troops could be transported on ships of the British fleet, while the American army had to move on foot.

Region Where did most of the later battles of the war take place?

Citizenship and Democracy

Women and the Armies. As many as 20,000 women are believed to have worked for the British and American armies, although more women are thought to have served with the British than with the Patriots. Women during the Revolution served in many capacities. For example, they served as cooks, nurses, doctors, laundresses, guides, and seamstresses. Some traveled with their husbands; others were single women who earned a living by working for the army.

Critical Thinking: Why do you think more women worked for the British armies?

ANSWER: Students might mention that Britain had a large military force in North America and needed a great deal of support for its troops.

MAP ANSWER

in the Southern colonies

CLOSE

Logical-Mathematical, Interpersonal. Organize the class into two groups. Provide each group with a large piece of butcher paper and markers. Have one group list the grievances the colonists had with the British Parliament, while the second group lists Britain's grievances toward the colonies. Allow 20 minutes for each group to brainstorm ideas. Encourage students to refer to their notes and text for help. After the brainstorming session, have each group select a spokesperson to present the grievances to the class. Then lead a discussion on how these issues led to war between Britain and the colonies.

CHALLENGE AND EXTEND

Logical-Mathematical, Musical-Rhythmic. Have students use the library or other resources to locate the lyrics to a song about the Revolutionary War. Ask students to analyze the lyrics to determine which side the songwriter supported. If the song mentions any significant battles, have students research each battle. Encourage students to play a recorded version or read the lyrics of their songs when they present their findings.

Across the Curriculum

MATH

Pay and Rations.
Each soldier in the Second Regiment was paid $6.67 monthly. Rations consisted of a pound of beef or pork, a pound of bread or flour a day, a few vegetables when available, four ounces or rum or whiskey a day, and a small quantity of vinegar, salt, soap, and candles a week.

Activity: Have students use the library or other resources to find the monthly salary and rations of a soldier in the U.S. Army today. Then ask students to figure the percentage increase in pay and rations from then to today.

Multimedia Resources

Exploring America's Past Video Segment: American Beginnings; *Teacher's Guide,* pp. 2–3

Search 17721, Play To 35419
Videodisc White Side B

Play Pause

See *Teacher's Guide* for Spanish barcode.

Early Battles

The colonists were now in revolt against Britain, which had a large army and the world's most powerful navy. In contrast, the colonists had poorly trained local militias. However, the colonists were fighting for a cause they supported, while the British army faced a largely hostile civilian population. Colonists known as Patriots supported independence. Loyalists, or Tories, were loyal to Britain. More than 50,000 Loyalists fled the colonies during the Revolution.

Some Patriots wanted to fight a defensive war, while other military leaders wanted to invade Canada. The Patriots had taken Fort Ticonderoga, which controlled access to Lake Champlain, a waterway into Canada. In November 1775, Patriot troops captured Montreal. When the Patriots advanced on the city of Quebec on New Year's Eve, they suffered a crushing defeat.

Farther south, General Washington had moved his troops to New York. On June 29, 1776, Patriots spotted British ships approaching New York Bay. Led by General Howe, the British battered the Patriots until late August. Washington's troops retreated to avoid complete destruction.

Patriot Victories

General Howe sent troops to secure New Jersey in November 1776. Deciding to establish a winter base for his troops, Howe settled in New York City. Washington decided to attack some British forces left in Trenton, New Jersey. On Christmas night, Washington's forces crossed the icy Delaware River. On December 26, the Patriots launched a surprise attack. The battle at Trenton lasted less than an hour before the British surrendered. Washington next attacked nearby Princeton, driving back the British forces. These victories boosted the spirits of the colonial troops.

 Hard Times and Victory

In the spring of 1777, British military leaders proposed a campaign to cut New England off from the rest of the colonies. The plan called for General John Burgoyne's troops in Canada to retake Fort Ticonderoga, then march south. Meanwhile, a second British force would march east from western New York, and General Howe's troops in New York City would move north. All three forces would combine near Albany, New York.

Burgoyne took Fort Ticonderoga by early July and began marching south. However, Howe moved to attack Philadelphia, instead of marching to Albany as planned. On September 11, 1777, his forces battled General Washington's troops at Brandywine Creek. The Patriots suffered heavy losses and retreated. Meanwhile, Burgoyne's troops were badly outnumbered when they clashed with Patriot soldiers at the **Battle of Saratoga**. On October 17, 1777, Burgoyne surrendered, marking the Patriots' greatest victory in the war up to that point.

After Saratoga, the French formally declared their support for the Patriots. The Marquis de Lafayette, who had already been fighting for the Patriots, believed that "the welfare of America is closely bound up with the welfare of mankind." Spain also helped the Patriots.

The entry of foreign allies into the war came at a critical time. After the victory at Saratoga, Washington settled his troops at Valley Forge,

Washington Crossing the Delaware, *by German-born American Emanuel Leutze*

REVIEW

Linguistic, Logical-Mathematical, Interpersonal. Have students complete the Section Review questions. Then have each student create a study guide for this section. Have students replace each key term or person's name in their study guides with a blank space. Then have students exchange guides, fill in the blanks, and return them to their authors for grading.

ASSESS

Have students complete Daily Quiz 1.4.

RETEACH

Logical-Mathematical, Visual-Spatial. Have students complete Main Idea Activities for Reteaching and Sheltered English 1.4. Then provide students with blank maps of the original thirteen colonies, along with colored pencils or markers. Have students locate the major battles discussed in this section. Next to each location, have students provide the date of the battle and a brief description of the outcome. **SHELTERED ENGLISH**

Pennsylvania. Over the harsh winter of 1777–78, about one fourth of the soldiers stationed there died of disease and malnutrition. The troops grew restless and frustrated. In February 1778 an experienced Prussian army officer named Baron Friedrich von Steuben came to Washington's aid. He began training the troops and soon turned the Continental Army into a stronger fighting force.

By early 1781 British forces were in control of most of the South. British general Charles Cornwallis then moved his troops into Yorktown, Virginia.

Washington and the Comte de Rochambeau (raw-shahm-boh), a French general, moved their troops south. They surrounded the British and lay siege to Yorktown in September. The French fleet kept British ships from providing aid. Badly outnumbered, Cornwallis surrendered on October 19, 1781. A witness to the **Battle of Yorktown** described the surrender:

> **"The British officers rode right on before the army, who marched out beating and playing a melancholy [sad] tune, their drums covered with black handkerchiefs."**

The **Treaty of Paris of 1783** formally ended the war. Washington disbanded the army, noting, "The citizens of America are . . . acknowledged to be possessed of absolute freedom and independency."

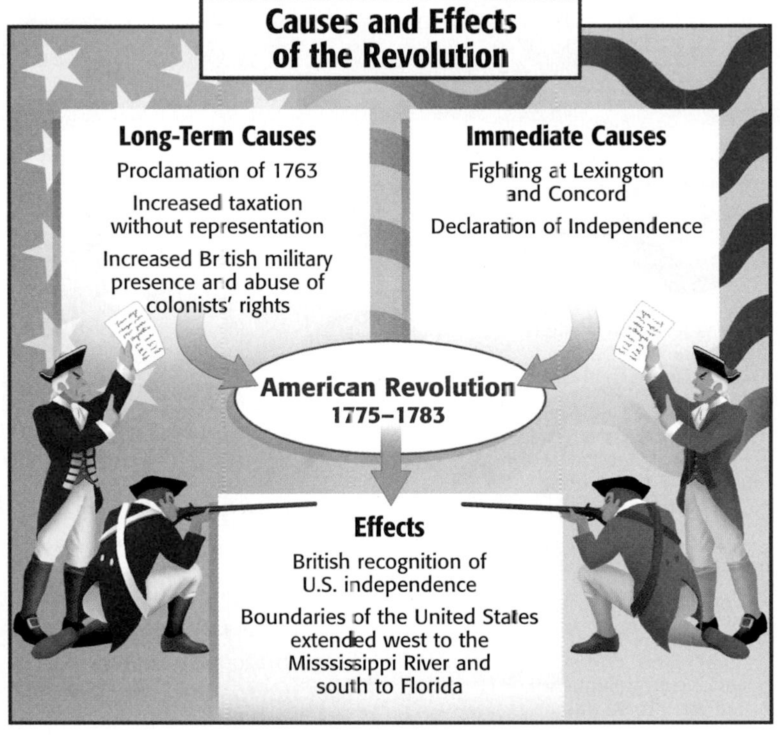

SECTION 4 REVIEW

Identify and explain the significance of the following:

- **Pontiac's Rebellion**
- **Stamp Act**
- **Townshend Acts**
- **Boston Massacre**
- **Intolerable Acts**
- **Battle of Bunker Hill**
- **Declaration of Independence**
- **Battle of Saratoga**
- **Battle of Yorktown**
- **Treaty of Paris of 1783**

Reading for Content Understanding

1. **Main Idea** Why did Britain attempt to raise money from the colonies, and how did the colonists respond to new taxes?
2. **Main Idea** What events marked the beginning of the Revolutionary War?
3. **Citizenship and Democracy** How did Enlightenment ideas influence the signers of the Declaration of Independence?
4. **Writing** *Creating* Make a pamphlet listing the events leading to the war's end and the signing of the Treaty of Paris of 1783.
5. **Critical Thinking** *Determining the Strength of an Argument* Do you think the British were justified in their taxation policies? Explain your answer.

Section 4 Review ANSWERS

Identify

For significance, see the following pages:

- Pontiac's Rebellion, p. 21
- Stamp Act, p. 22
- Townshend Acts, p. 22
- Boston Massacre, p. 22
- Intolerable Acts, p. 22
- Battle of Bunker Hill, p. 23
- Declaration of Independence, p. 23
- Battle of Saratoga, p. 24
- Battle of Yorktown, p. 25
- Treaty of Paris of 1783, p. 25

Reading for Content Understanding

1. To pay for colonial conflicts; colonists protested the taxes with boycotts, violence, and protests such as the Boston Tea Party.

2. The First Continental Congress recommended arming colonial militias, and Patriot troops fought the British at Lexington and Concord to keep the British from seizing Patriot weapons.

3. The concept of a social contract between people and their ruler and John Locke's theory of the natural right of people to overthrow a corrupt government were influences on the Declaration of Independence.

4. Pamphlets will vary but should describe the end of the war at Yorktown and outline the terms of the peace treaty.

5. Answers will vary but students should state their opinions and explain their reasoning

Historical Sidelight

Drafting the Declaration. Thomas Jefferson asked John Adams to draw up the first draft of the Declaration of Independence. Adams refused, saying, "Reason first—You are a Virginian, and a Virginian ought to appear at the head of this business. Reason second—I am obnoxious, suspected, and unpopular. You are very much otherwise. Reason third—You can write ten times better than I can."

Critical Thinking: What do John Adams's comments say about his character?

ANSWER: Answers will vary but students should suggest that Adams was an honest and determined person and that he put the good of the nation above his own ambitions.

PRIMARY SOURCE ▶

The primary source on pupil's pages 26–29 has been given in its entirety.

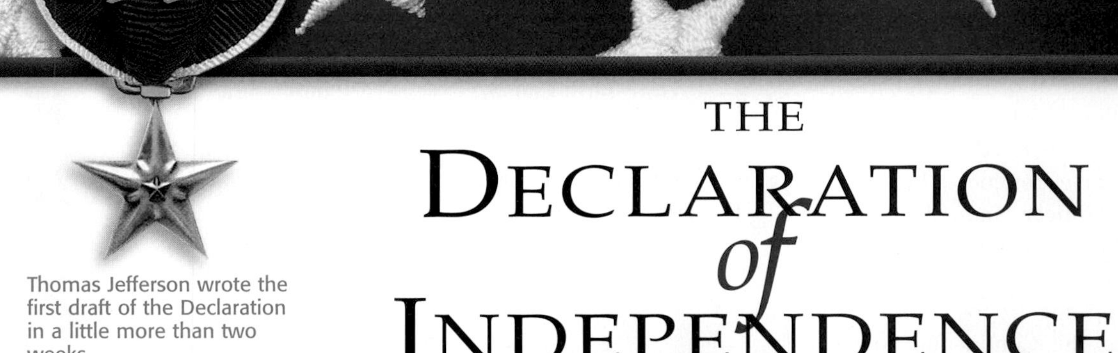

Thomas Jefferson wrote the first draft of the Declaration in a little more than two weeks.

In the first paragraph, the signers state that it is important to justify why the colonists must break their political ties with Britain.

impel: force

endowed: provided

"Laws of Nature" and "Nature's God" refer to the belief common during the Scientific Revolution that certain patterns are constant and predictable and that they come from a supreme being. Natural or "unalienable" rights (the rights to life, liberty, and the pursuit of happiness) cannot be taken away. English philosopher John Locke had argued that people created governments to protect their natural rights. If a government abuses its powers, it is the right as well as the duty of the people to do away with that government.

usurpations: wrongful seizures of power

despotism: unlimited power

THE DECLARATION of INDEPENDENCE

In Congress, July 4, 1776

The unanimous Declaration of the thirteen united States of America,

When in the Course of human events, it becomes necessary for one people to dissolve the political bands which have connected them with another, and to assume among the Powers of the earth, the separate and equal station to which the Laws of Nature and of Nature's God entitle them, a decent respect to the opinions of mankind requires that they should declare the causes which impel them to the separation.

Natural Rights

We hold these truths to be self-evident, that all men are created equal, that they are endowed by their Creator with certain unalienable Rights, that among these are Life, Liberty, and the pursuit of Happiness. That to secure these rights, Governments are instituted among Men, deriving their just powers from the consent of the governed,

That whenever any Form of Government becomes destructive of these ends, it is the Right of the People to alter or to abolish it, and to institute new Government, laying its foundation on such principles and organizing its powers in such form, as to them shall seem most likely to effect their Safety and Happiness. Prudence, indeed, will dictate that Governments long established should not be changed for light and transient causes; and accordingly all experience hath shown, that mankind are more disposed to suffer, while evils are sufferable, than to right themselves by abolishing the forms to which they are accustomed. But when a long train of abuses and usurpations, pursuing invariably the same Object evinces a design to reduce them under absolute Despotism, it is their right, it is their duty, to throw off such Government, and to provide new Guards for their future security.—

LEFT: *Revolutionary War hero Paul Revere*

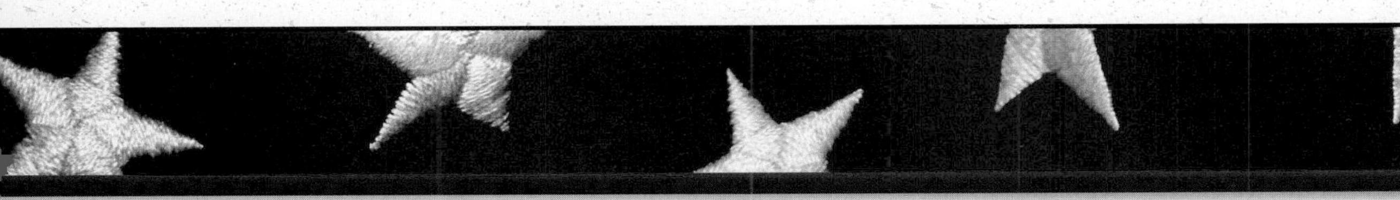

Colonists' Complaints Against the King

Such has been the patient sufferance of these Colonies; and such is now the necessity which constrains them to alter their former Systems of Government. The history of the present King of Great Britain is a history of repeated injuries and usurpations, all having in direct object the establishment of an absolute Tyranny over these States. To prove this, let Facts be submitted to a candid world.

He has refused his Assent to Laws, the most wholesome and necessary for the public good.

He has forbidden his Governors to pass Laws of immediate and pressing importance, unless suspended in their operation till his Assent should be obtained; and when so suspended, he has utterly neglected to attend to them.

He has refused to pass other Laws for the accommodation of large districts of people, unless those people would relinquish the right of Representation in the Legislature, a right inestimable to them and formidable to tyrants only.

He has called together legislative bodies at places unusual, uncomfortable, and distant from the depository of their Public Records, for the sole purpose of fatiguing them into compliance with his measures.

He has dissolved Representative Houses repeatedly, for opposing with manly firmness his invasions on the rights of the people.

He has refused for a long time, after such dissolutions, to cause others to be elected; whereby the Legislative Powers, incapable of Annihilation, have returned to the People at large for their exercise; the State remaining in the mean time exposed to all the dangers of invasion from without, and convulsions within.

He has endeavored to prevent the population of these States; for that purpose obstructing the Laws of Naturalization of Foreigners; refusing to pass others to encourage their migration hither, and raising the conditions of new Appropriations of Lands.

He has obstructed the Administration of Justice, by refusing his Assent to Laws for establishing Judiciary Powers.

He has made Judges dependent on his Will alone, for the tenure of their offices, and the amount and payment of their salaries.

He has erected a multitude of New Offices, and sent hither swarms of Officers to harass our people, and eat out their substance.

He has kept among us, in times of peace, Standing Armies without the Consent of our legislature.

He has affected to render the Military independent of and superior to the Civil Power.

He has combined with others to subject us to a jurisdiction foreign to our constitution, and unacknowledged by our laws; giving his Assent to their Acts of pretended legislation:

tyranny: oppressive power exerted by a government or ruler

candid: fair

Here the Declaration lists the charges that the colonists had against King George III. How might the language in the list appeal to people's emotions?

relinquish: release, yield

inestimable: priceless

formidable: causing dread

Why do you think the king had his colonial legislatures meet in places that were hard to reach?

annihilation: destruction

convulsions: violent disturbances

naturalization of foreigners: the process by which foreign-born persons become citizens

appropriations of land: setting aside land for settlement

tenure: term

a multitude of: many

Name five acts that the Declaration states have been committed by the king and the British Parliament.

Daily Life

Independence Day. In a letter, John Adams declared that July 2, the day that the Continental Congress voted for independence, should be celebrated with "pomp and parade, with shows, games, sports, guns, bells, bonfires, and illuminations." However, Independence Day is actually celebrated on July 4, the day that the Continental Congress approved the final draft of the Declaration. Most members did not sign the document until August 2.

Activity: Have students research the origins of other national holidays, such as Thanksgiving, and share their findings with the class.

Side-Column Answer

Answers may vary but students should point to words such as *absolute despotism, repeated injuries and usurpations,* and *tyranny* and mention that these words convey a sense of injustice.

Side-Column Answer

If few colonists could reach these places, they would not be able to protest policies.

Side-Column Answer

Answers will vary but should list five acts from the Declaration.

Citizenship and Democracy

The Signers. The 56 signers of the Declaration of Independence shared many characteristics—almost all were Protestant white males and were fairly wealthy. Forty-eight of the signers were born in America.

Critical Thinking: What might have happened to the signers of the Declaration if the Revolution had failed?

ANSWER: They might have been charged with treason against Great Britain.

SIDE-COLUMN ANSWER
no taxation without representation

SIDE-COLUMN ANSWER
It emphasizes the kings role in wrongdoings against the colonists.

quartering: lodging, housing

What was the colonists' rallying cry to protest the king's tax policies?

The "neighboring Province" that is referred to here is Canada.

arbitrary: not based on law

render: make

abdicated: given up

foreign mercenaries: soldiers hired to fight for a country not their own

perfidy: violation of trust

insurrections: rebellions

petitioned for redress: asked formally for a correction of wrongs

Notice that the Declaration has 18 paragraphs beginning with "He has" or "He is." What is the effect of this repetition?

unwarrantable jurisdiction: unjustified authority

magnanimity: generous spirit

conjured: urgently called upon

consanguinity: common ancestry

acquiesce: consent to

For quartering large bodies of armed troops among us:

For protecting them, by a mock Trial, from Punishment for any Murders which they should commit on the Inhabitants of these States:

For cutting off our Trade with all parts of the world:

For imposing taxes on us without our Consent:

For depriving us in many cases, of the benefits of Trial by Jury:

For transporting us beyond Seas to be tried for pretended offences:

For abolishing the free System of English Laws in a neighboring Province, establishing therein an Arbitrary government, and enlarging its Boundaries so as to render it at once an example and fit instrument for introducing the same absolute rule into these Colonies:

For taking away our Charters, abolishing our most valuable Laws, and altering fundamentally the Forms of our Governments:

For suspending our own Legislature, and declaring themselves invested with Power to legislate for us in all cases whatsoever.

He has abdicated Government here, by declaring us out of his Protection and waging War against us.

He has plundered our seas, ravaged our Coasts, burnt our towns, and destroyed the lives of our people.

He is at this time transporting large armies of foreign mercenaries to complete the works of death, desolation and tyranny, already begun with circumstances of Cruelty & perfidy scarcely paralleled in the most barbarous ages, and totally unworthy the Head of a civilized nation.

He has constrained our fellow Citizens taken Captive on the high Seas to bear Arms against their Country, to become the executioners of their friends and Brethren, or to fall themselves by their Hands.

He has excited domestic insurrections amongst us, and has endeavored to bring on the inhabitants of our frontiers, the merciless Indian Savages, whose known rule of warfare, is an undistinguished destruction of all ages, sexes and conditions.

In every stage of these Oppressions We have Petitioned for Redress in the most humble terms: Our repeated Petitions have been answered only by repeated injury. A Prince, whose character is thus marked by every act which may define a Tyrant, is unfit to be the ruler of a free People.

Nor have We been wanting in attention to our British brethren. We have warned them from time to time of attempts by their legislature to extend an unwarrantable jurisdiction over us. We have reminded them of the circumstances of our emigration and settlement here. We have appealed to their native justice and magnanimity, and we have conjured them by the ties of our common kindred to disavow these usurpations, which, would inevitably interrupt our connections and correspondence. They too have been deaf to the voice of justice and of consanguinity. We must, therefore, acquiesce in the necessity, which denounces our

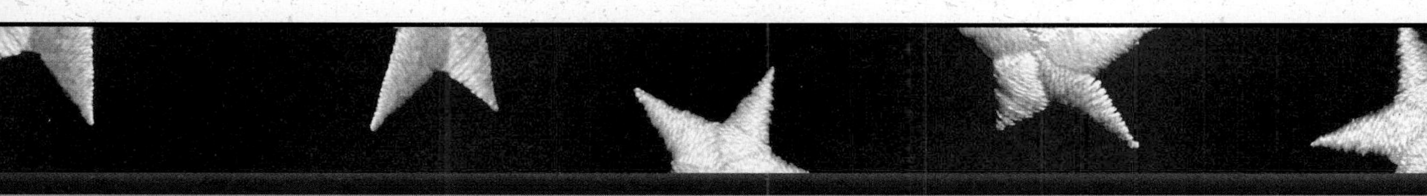

Separation, and hold them, as we hold the rest of mankind, Enemies in War, in Peace Friends.

An Independent United States

We, therefore, the Representatives of the united States of America, in General Congress, Assembled, appealing to the Supreme Judge of the world for the rectitude of our intentions, do, in the Name, and by Authority of the good People of these Colonies, solemnly publish and declare, That these United Colonies are, and of Right ought to be Free and Independent States; that they are Absolved from all Allegiance to the British Crown, and that all political connection between them and the State of Great Britain, is and ought to be totally dissolved; and that as Free and Independent States, they have full Power to levy War, conclude Peace, contract Alliances, establish Commerce, and to do all other Acts and Things which Independent States may of right do. And for the support of this Declaration, with a firm reliance on the Protection of Divine Providence, we mutually pledge to each other our Lives, our Fortunes and our sacred Honor.

rectitude: rightness

In this paragraph, the signers state their actual declaration of independence. What rights would the new United States of America now have as an independent nation?

John Hancock
President of Massachusetts

GEORGIA
Button Gwinnett
Lyman Hall
George Walton

NORTH CAROLINA
William Hooper
Joseph Hewes
John Penn

SOUTH CAROLINA
Edward Rutledge
Thomas Heyward, Jr.
Thomas Lynch, Jr.
Arthur Middleton

MARYLAND
Samuel Chase
William Paca
Thomas Stone
Charles Carroll of Carrollton

VIRGINIA
George Wythe
Richard Henry Lee
Thomas Jefferson
Benjamin Harrison
Thomas Nelson, Jr.
Francis Lightfoot Lee
Carter Braxton

PENNSYLVANIA
Robert Morris
Benjamin Rush
Benjamin Franklin
John Morton
George Clymer
James Smith
George Taylor
James Wilson
George Ross

DELAWARE
Caesar Rodney
George Read
Thomas McKean

NEW YORK
William Floyd
Phillip Livingston
Francis Lewis
Lewis Morris

NEW JERSEY
Richard Stockton
John Witherspoon
Francis Hopkinson
John Hart
Abraham Clark

NEW HAMPSHIRE
Josiah Bartlett
William Whipple
Matthew Thornton

MASSACHUSETTS
Samuel Adams
John Adams
Robert Treat Paine
Elbridge Gerry

RHODE ISLAND
Stephen Hopkins
William Ellery

CONNECTICUT
Roger Sherman
Samuel Huntington
William Williams
Oliver Wolcott

Congress adopted the final draft of the Declaration of Independence on July 4, 1776. A formal copy, written on parchment paper, was signed on August 2, 1776.

The following is part of a passage that the Congress took out of Jefferson's original draft: "He has waged cruel war against human nature itself, violating its most sacred rights of life and liberty in the persons of a distant people who never offended him, captivating and carrying them into slavery in another hemisphere, or to incur miserable death in their transportation thither." Why do you think the Congress might have wanted to delete this passage?

Daily Life

American Soldiers. After the Continental Congress adopted the Declaration of Independence, some of its members requested that copies be made for the commanders of the troops who were fighting the war. Official word of the Declaration reached General George Washington in New York on July 9, 1776, and he ordered that all troops be gathered for a reading of the document. General Washington hoped that reading the document aloud to the troops would help boost their morale.

Critical Thinking: Why would the Declaration boost soldiers' morale?

ANSWER: It would strengthen their resolve for fighting.

SIDE-COLUMN ANSWER

power to levy war, secure peace, contract alliances, establish commerce, and do all the other things that independent states do

SIDE-COLUMN ANSWER

Slavery was extremely controversial, as many states, mostly southern ones, did not wish to abolish it. Delegates from states wishing to continue slavery would not have agreed to sign the Declaration if the passage had remained.

Section 5 Lesson Plan

OBJECTIVES

- **Examine the problems that arose under the Articles of Confederation.**
- **Explore some of the main issues debated at the Constitutional Convention.**
- **Analyze opposition to the new Constitution, and explain how concerns were addressed.**

FOCUS

Motivate Before Reading

Ask students to imagine that they are forming a new history club for the school. Then give students 15–20 minutes to create rules for the club. Have students take notes on any difficulties they had setting these rules. Tell students that in this section they will learn how delegates to the Constitutional Convention faced similar problems in Philadelphia in 1787.

Section 5 RESOURCES

PRINT

- ★ Guided Reading Strategies 1.5
- ★ Graphic Organizer 1: The Settlement of North America
- ★ American History Political Cartoon 2: Ratifying the Constitution
- ★ Section 5 Review, p. 33
- ★ Daily Quiz 1.5

MULTIMEDIA

- ★ *Teaching Resources CD–ROM,* Lesson 1.5
- ★ *American History Simulations CD–ROM:* The Democracy Project

SHELTERED ENGLISH

- ★ Main Idea Activities for Reteaching and Sheltered English 1.5

Forming a Nation

Reading Focus

What problems arose under the Articles of Confederation?

What were some of the main issues debated at the Constitutional Convention?

Why did some people oppose the new Constitution, and how were their concerns addressed?

Key Terms

Articles of Confederation
Constitutional Convention
Great Compromise
Three-Fifths Compromise
federalism
legislative branch
executive branch
judicial branch
checks and balances
amendments
Bill of Rights

IN THE FIRST YEAR of the Revolutionary War, a young professor moved to New Hampshire, where he began teaching at Dartmouth College. Soon after, without revealing his name, he published a short essay calling for the newly independent states to establish representative governments. However, he warned that the American people needed to take great care when building their new governments. "They [the people] are now planting a seed, which will arise" with tree branches "extended to shelter the liberty of succeeding ages," he stated.

The bald eagle, symbol of the United States

Forming a New Government

Many states created their own constitution—a set of basic principles and laws that determines the powers and duties of the government. Most state constitutions began with a bill of rights—a document describing the civil liberties, or individual rights, that a government promises its citizens.

The Articles of Confederation

On November 15, 1777, the Second Continental Congress approved the **Articles of Confederation**, which created a national government with limited powers. In March 1781 the last state ratified, or formally approved, the Articles. The first permanent national government of the United States was thus in effect.

This new national government consisted of the Confederation Congress, in which each state had one vote. The Congress could coin and borrow money, negotiate treaties, and resolve conflicts between states. The Congress could not force states to contribute money or soldiers. There was no federal executive, such as a president, or a national court system.

Introduce Key Terms

Linguistic. Review this section's key terms with students. As each term is introduced, ask students to write anything they know about the term. Have students leave three lines of space after each response. Tell students that they will use these responses later in the section. **SHELTERED ENGLISH**

TEACH

Have students read Section 5 and complete Guided Reading Strategies 1.5. Choose one or more of the following activities to explore the section content with students. For further suggestions on block scheduling or team teaching, see the *Block Scheduling Handbook*.

LEVEL 1: Linguistic. (Suggested time: 15 min.) As a class, go over students' Guided Reading Strategies. Then use the Reading Focus questions to highlight the main ideas of the section. **SHELTERED ENGLISH**

ALL LEVELS: Visual-Spatial, Logical-Mathematical. (Suggested time: 25 min. plus homework) Have students create a graphic organizer with two columns. The first column should be labeled *Articles of Confederation* and should identify problems that occurred under the document. The second column should be

Problems with the Articles

The new Congress had several issues to address, such as raising money to pay its war debts. Because Congress's ability to obtain money from the states was limited, it decided to raise revenue by selling its western lands. Congress passed the Land Ordinance of 1785 to organize surveys and division of these public lands. Congress also passed the Northwest Ordinance of 1787 to establish a political structure for the Northwest Territory. This region included present-day Illinois, Indiana, Michigan, Ohio, and Wisconsin.

The nation's economic problems worsened when Spain closed the lower Mississippi River to U.S. shipping in 1784. This action cut off western farmers' only effective way to transport goods to and from the East. Attempts to negotiate a treaty with Spain failed. In 1783 Britain closed many of its ports to U.S. ships and forced American merchants to pay tariffs—taxes on imports or exports—on goods sent to Britain. While U.S. exports declined, British goods flowed freely into the United States. This trade imbalance created serious economic problems.

Congress was powerless to fix the problem. It had no authority to establish tariffs or to regulate interstate commerce—trade conducted between two or more states. States adopted trade policies that were beneficial to their own interests rather than cooperating to improve the nation's trade position. In 1785 a British magazine playfully referred to the new nation as the "Dis-United States."

The states had other economic problems. Massachusetts was in a depression—a steep drop in economic activity. Many farmers who could not pay their land taxes had their property taken away. Daniel Shays, a poor farmer and veteran of the Revolutionary War, led a farmers' uprising in September 1786 known as Shays's Rebellion. The farmers hoped to stop the foreclosures on their farms, but state militia troops soon defeated the rebels. The national government, however, proved powerless to help put down the rebellion.

The Constitutional Convention

Alarmed by the nation's problems, Congress invited each of the 13 states to send delegates to a **Constitutional Convention** to be held in Philadelphia in May 1787. The invitation noted that the delegates were to revise the Articles of Confederation and

> **"to render [make] the federal constitution adequate to the exigencies [needs] of government, and the preservation of the Union."**

Rhode Island refused to attend, but the other 12 states sent a total of 55 delegates.

Several issues divided the delegates. The smaller states objected to the larger states' plan for a national legislature with representatives chosen in proportion to state populations. After deadlocking over the issue, delegates formed a special committee, which proposed the **Great Compromise**. It proposed that every state, regardless of its size, would receive two votes in the upper house of the legislature. In the lower house, each state would have representation according to its population.

Southerners wanted slaves to be counted as part of their state populations so that they would have more representatives. Northerners wanted slaves to be counted in deciding a state's taxes but

The delegates elected George Washington president of the Constitutional Convention. Virginian James Madison also played a crucial role.

Constitutional Heritage

Limits of the Articles of Confederation. Under the Articles of Confederation the states did not always respond to the requests of Congress. The legislative body did not even meet on a regular basis, and between 1783 and 1785 it met in four different cities. Members also did not attend every meeting. It took a great deal of effort to gather enough members to ratify the Treaty of Paris.

Critical Thinking: Why would such organizational problems make it difficult to run a country?

ANSWER: It would be difficult to make quick and important decisions with such loose organization.

Multimedia Resources

American History Simulations CD–ROM: The Democracy Project

labeled *Constitution* and should examine how the Constitution addressed the problems found in the Articles. Once students have finished, discuss the major issues that were debated at the Constitutional Convention. For homework, have students create a flowchart showing the compromises reached at the convention.

LEVEL 3: Linguistic, Intrapersonal. (Suggested time: 40 min.) Have each student write an essay persuading states to vote for or against ratification of the Constitution. Those arguing against the Constitution should point out their objections to it, and those arguing for it should explain how the delegates at the convention addressed the concerns of those opposed to the document.

CLOSE

Linguistic, Interpersonal. Organize the class into three groups. Assign each group one of the three branches of the federal government. Have each group create a presentation that explains the components of the assigned branch and its responsibilities.

CHALLENGE AND EXTEND

Linguistic, Visual-Spatial. Have students create a brochure describing the three branches of the federal government and the way each branch "checks" the other branches. Encourage students

Section 5 Review ANSWERS

Identify

For significance, see the following pages:

- Articles of Confederation, p. 30
- Constitutional Convention, p. 31
- Great Compromise, p. 31
- Three-Fifths Compromise, p. 32
- federalism, p. 32
- legislative branch, p. 32
- executive branch, p. 32
- judicial branch, p. 32
- checks and balances, p. 32
- amendments, p. 33
- Bill of Rights, p. 33

Reading for Content Understanding

1. debt, trade restrictions, lack of cooperation between the states, Shays's Rebellion, Congress had no power to establish tariffs or regulate interstate commerce

2. They debated the proportion of slaves to be counted toward taxation and representation and the method for determining how many representatives each state would have in Congress.

3. They wanted to protect personal liberties and states rights.

4. Paragraphs should mention that each of the three branches of government has certain responsibilities and that each branch's power is in some way balanced by that of the other two branches.

5. Answers will vary but students should state their opinions and explain their reasoning.

The Articles of Confederation and the Constitution

ARTICLES	CONSTITUTION
EXECUTIVE BRANCH	
No executive to administer and enforce legislation; Congress has sole authority to govern. Executive committee to oversee government when Congress is out of session	President administers and enforces federal laws.
LEGISLATIVE BRANCH	
A unicameral (one-house) legislature Each state had one vote, regardless of population. Nine votes (of the original 13) to enact legislation	A bicameral (two-house) legislature Each state has equal representation in the Senate; each state is represented according to population in the House of Representatives. Simple majority to enact legislation
JUDICIAL BRANCH	
No national court system Congress to establish temporary courts to hear cases of piracy	National court system, headed by the Supreme Court Courts to hear cases involving national laws, treaties, and the Constitution as well as cases between states, between citizens of different states, or between a state and citizen of another state
OTHER MATTERS	
Admission to the Confederation by 9 votes (of 13) Amendment of the Articles by unanimous vote The states retained independence.	Congress to admit new states; all must have a republican form of government Amendment of the Constitution by two-thirds vote of both houses of Congress or by national convention, followed by ratification by three fourths of the states The states accept the Constitution as the supreme law of the land.

not its representatives. The delegates accepted the **Three-Fifths Compromise**. It provided that three fifths of the slaves in each state be counted as part of that state's population when allotting representatives to the lower house.

The Living Constitution

The delegates to the Constitutional Convention created a balanced government based on the idea of **federalism**. Federalism is the distribution of governmental power within a nation between a central authority and the states or provinces that make up the nation.

The federal government is organized under three branches. The **legislative branch**, or Congress, is responsible for proposing bills and passing them into laws. Congress is made up of two houses. The Senate, or upper house, is composed of two members from each state. In the House of Representatives, or lower house, each state is represented according to its population. The **executive branch** includes the president and the administrative departments of the government. The **judicial branch** is made up of all the national courts. This branch is responsible for interpreting laws, punishing criminals, and settling disputes between states. (For the full text of the Constitution, see page 44.)

The framers of the Constitution established **checks and balances**, a system to prevent any branch of government from becoming too powerful. For example, the framers gave Congress the to make their pamphlets illustrate the balance of power the Constitution.

REVIEW

Linguistic, Logical-Mathematical. Have students complete the Section Review questions. Then ask students to review the definitions they created in the Introduce Key Terms activity. Have students use the spaces provided in their notebooks to write what they have learned about each of the key terms as they studied the section's material.

ASSESS

Have students complete Daily Quiz 1.5.

RETEACH

Visual-Spatial, Logical-Mathematical. Have students complete Main Idea Activities for Reteaching and Sheltered English 1.5. Then provide students with newspapers, magazines, butcher paper, and any other art materials they may need in order to create a collage showing the protections found in the Bill of Rights. Encourage volunteers to explain their collages to the class.

SHELTERED ENGLISH

power to propose and pass bills into law, but also gave the president the power to veto congressional legislation. In later years, the Supreme Court established that it had the power to determine whether laws passed by Congress are unconstitutional.

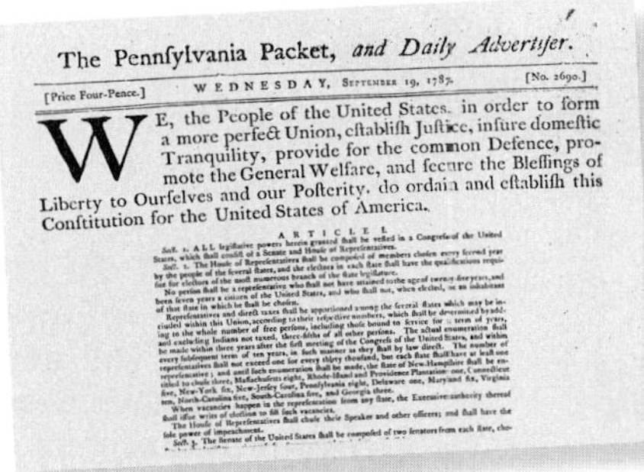

The Pennſylvania Packet, and Daily Advertiſer.

[Price Four-Pence.] WEDNESDAY, September 19, 1787. [No. 2690.]

WE, the People of the United States, in order to form a more perfect Union, eſtabliſh Juſtice, inſure domeſtic Tranquility, provide for the common Defence, promote the General Welfare, and ſecure the Bleſſings of Liberty to Ourſelves and our Poſterity, do ordain and eſtabliſh this Conſtitution for the United States of America.

An early printed copy of the Constitution

According to the Constitution, the laws of the federal government have authority over state laws. The federal government can enforce its laws through the use of troops under the president's command. However, the Constitution also allows states to keep control over many functions, such as local government and education.

In September 1787, after 16 weeks of debate, delegates signed a final draft of the Constitution and sent it to Congress. Congress then sent the document to the states for ratification. The Constitution would go into effect as soon as nine states ratified it.

The Ratification Fight

When the Constitution was made public, it sparked a heated debate. Some Americans feared that the new national government would take too much power away from the states and would not protect the rights of individual citizens. People who opposed the Constitution were called Antifederalists. Supporters of the Constitution, called Federalists, believed that it provided a good balance of power. One of the strongest defenses of the Constitution appeared in the *Federalist Papers*, a series of essays written by Alexander Hamilton, James Madison, and John Jay.

In December 1787 Delaware became the first state to ratify the Constitution. The Constitution went into effect in June 1788, after New Hampshire became the ninth state to ratify it. The next month, Congress declared the Constitution ratified and arranged for the first presidential and congressional elections under the new government of the United States.

Several states had ratified the Constitution only after the assurance that a bill of rights would be added as **amendments**—official changes, corrections, or additions. By December 1791 the states had ratified the first 10 amendments to the Constitution, known as the **Bill of Rights**. (For a full discussion of the Bill of Rights, see Chapter 2.) The Bill of Rights has helped the U.S. Constitution to survive as the oldest functioning written national constitution in the world.

SECTION 5 REVIEW

Identify and explain the significance of the following:

- **Articles of Confederation**
- **Constitutional Convention**
- **Great Compromise**
- **Three-Fifths Compromise**
- **federalism**
- **legislative branch**
- **executive branch**
- **judicial branch**
- **checks and balances**
- **amendments**
- **Bill of Rights**

Reading for Content Understanding

1 **Main Idea** What problems plagued the new nation under the Articles of Confederation?

2 **Main Idea** What issues did delegates debate at the Constitutional Convention?

3 **Constitutional Heritage** Why did some people insist that a bill of rights be added to the Constitution?

4 **Writing** *Describing* Write a paragraph describing how the federal government is organized.

5 **Critical Thinking** *Determining the Strength of an Argument* If you had been a citizen during the ratification process, would you have been a Federalist or an Antifederalist? Explain your answer.

Chapter 1 Review ANSWERS

Identifying People and Ideas

1. economic control

2. official changes, corrections, or additions to the Constitution

3. thought he could reach Asia by traveling west across the Atlantic Ocean; reached the Bahamas

4. the elected assembly of colonial Virginia; the first colonial assembly

5. a legislative body with two houses

6. called delegates to meet to revise the Articles of Confederation; actually created the Constitution

7. terrifying and often deadly voyage by slaves across the Atlantic Ocean

8. movement of people from one region to another

9. where British surrendered to Americans, ending the American Revolution

10. the first 10 amendments to the Constitution

Using the Time Line

1. b
2. a
3. f
4. c
5. e
6. d

Review and Assessment RESOURCES

PRINT
★ Chapter 1 Review, pp. 34–35
★ Vocabulary Activity 1
★ Chapter 1 Study Guide
★ Chapter 1 Test (Form A or B)

MULTIMEDIA
★ Audio Program, Ch. 1 (English and Spanish)
★ *Global Skill Builder CD–ROM*
★ Chapter 1 Test Generator
★ HRW Web site

SHELTERED ENGLISH
★ Spanish Glossary
★ Sheltered English Chapter 1 Test

ASSESS

Have students complete one of the Chapter 1 Tests. As an alternate assessment, assign the Chapter 1 Investigation.

Understanding Main Ideas

1. It influenced transportation, diet, culture, housing, agriculture, and settlement patterns.

2. Italian city-states had a monopoly on overland trade, and the overland routes to Asia were long and difficult

3. differences—the Jamestown colonists were seeking wealth, while the Plymouth colonists were seeking religious freedom; similarities—both groups had to learn to deal with the local American Indians and the rugged climate

4. The Privy Council in England set colonial policy, each colony had a governor, colonial courts existed, and some colonies had elected assemblies.

5. increasing tensions over taxation, the Boston Massacre, the Boston Tea Party, and the Intolerable Acts

6. Every state would get two votes in the upper house of the legislature, while in the lower house, each state would receive representatives based on its population.

7. The federal government is divided into three branches. Each branch has its own responsibilities and ways of checking the other branches' powers.

Reviewing Themes

1. the need for a sea route to Asia, the desire to exploit rich natural resources, the search for religious freedom

2. Colonists declared independence because they agreed with Thomas Paine's idea that countries should be ruled by laws created by the people rather than a monarchy; it stated that government is a social contract between the people and their ruler;

CHAPTER 1 REVIEW

Chapter Summary

Trade with Africa and Asia motivated Europeans to explore the world. After Columbus's voyages, Europeans colonized the Americas–often with devastating results for American Indians. English colonists protested when Britain imposed new taxes, and in 1776 the colonies declared their independence. The Revolutionary War lasted from 1775 to 1783. The U.S. Constitution was signed in 1787, and the Bill of Rights was added later.

On a separate sheet of paper, complete the following activities.

Identifying People and Ideas

Describe the historical significance of the following:

1. monopoly
2. amendments
3. Christopher Columbus
4. House of Burgesses
5. bicameral legislature
6. Constitutional Convention
7. Middle Passage
8. migration
9. Battle of Yorktown
10. Bill of Rights

Internet Activity

go.hrw.com
SB1 Revolutionary War

Imagine that you are a travel agent planning an educational tour. Search the Internet through the HRW Web site for information on important battlefields of the Revolutionary War. Put together a one-page travel brochure describing the sites that your clients could visit on their tour.

Understanding Main Ideas

1. How did the environment influence the development of Native American culture groups?
2. Why were Europeans interested in finding a sea route to Asia?
3. What were the differences and similarities between the Jamestown and Plymouth settlements?
4. How were the thirteen colonies governed before King James II came to power?
5. What events led to the outbreak of the Revolutionary War?
6. What were the terms of the Great Compromise?
7. How is the federal government organized under the Constitution?

Reviewing Themes

1. **Geographic Diversity** What motivated Europeans to explore and colonize the Americas?

Using the Time Line

Number your paper from 1 to 6. Match the letters on the time line below with the following events.

1. **Leif Eriksson lands in North America.**
2. **Paleo-Indians cross Beringia into Alaska.**
3. **Delegates sign a final draft of the Constitution.**
4. **Christopher Columbus and his crew land in the Americas.**
5. **Thomas Jefferson drafts the Declaration of Independence.**
6. **A small group of English settlers establishes the Jamestown colony.**

50,000 B.C. | A.D. 1000 | 1300 | 1600 | 1700 | 1730 | 1760 | 1790

a b c d e f

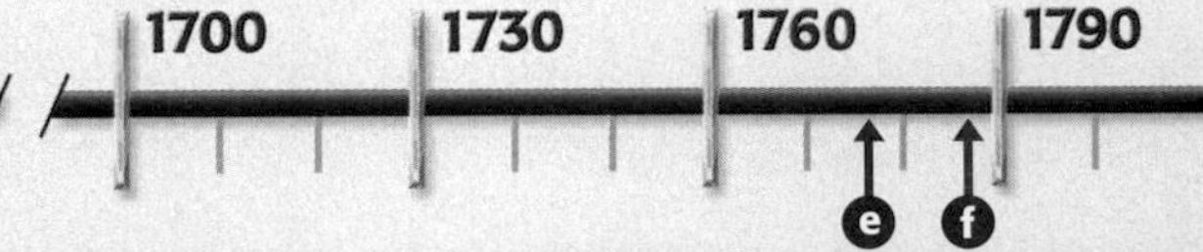

RETEACH

Linguistic, Logical-Mathematical, Visual-Spatial. Organize students into five groups. Assign each group one section from the chapter. Have students create maps, charts, or diagrams illustrating the major events in the assigned section. Encourage each group to include relevant dates and a brief description of each significant event. **SHELTERED ENGLISH**

Using the Internet

Have students continue their research to find additional information about the sites of Revolutionary War battles. Encourage students to provide pictures of the uniforms worn by soldiers on both sides, as well as information regarding the number of soldiers who were killed on each side, how long the battle lasted, and the leading generals on each side.

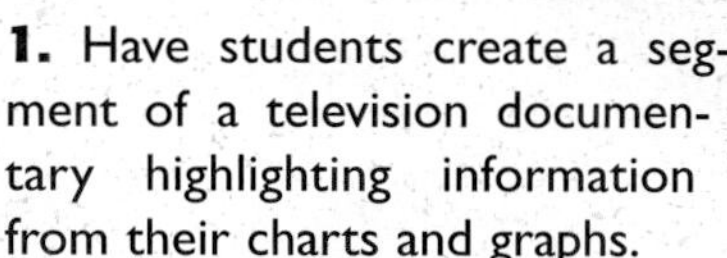

Portfolio Extensions

1. Have students create a segment of a television documentary highlighting information from their charts and graphs.

2. For each play presented, have students write reviews on how accurately the play portrays colonial life.

2. **Citizenship and Democracy** Why did the colonists declare their independence from Britain, and what are some important ideas in the Declaration of Independence?
3. **Constitutional Heritage** How does the Constitution guard against the misuse of power?

Thinking Critically

1. **Drawing Conclusions** How did the Protestant Reformation affect European colonization of North America?
2. **Making Comparisons** Compare and contrast the New England, middle, and southern colonies.

Writing About History

1. **Creating** Make a poster supporting or opposing the ratification of the Constitution. Include specific reasons for your position.
2. **Expressing** Imagine that you are a Loyalist or a Patriot. Write a letter to a friend explaining your choice.

Linking Geography and History

1. **Human-Environment Interaction** How did the Columbian Exchange affect American Indians and Europeans?
2. **Region** How did geography and climate influence the economic development of the New England, middle, and southern colonies?

Building Your Portfolio

Complete the following activities individually or in groups.

1. **Trade Today** Use the textbook or your library to research and compile a list of 10 goods that the United States imports and 10 goods that it exports. Then prepare a map of the world that shows trade patterns between the United States and other countries. Draw symbols on the map to show the goods that the United States imports and exports.
2. **Settling a New Land** The first Jamestown settlers—many of whom were goldsmiths and jewelers—lacked the skills necessary for survival. Imagine that you are putting together a group of colonists to settle in North America. Decide how many people to take with you, what kinds of occupations they should have, and where to settle. Make sure you explain the reasons for each choice. Then write a short play about your first month in the colony. You may wish to perform your play for the class.

History Skills Workshop

Reading Maps Study the map below, which shows early settlements in North America. Then answer the following questions: (a) In what present-day state was New Amsterdam located? (b) What river connected Fort Orange and the New Amsterdam settlement? (c) How far was Quebec from Montreal?

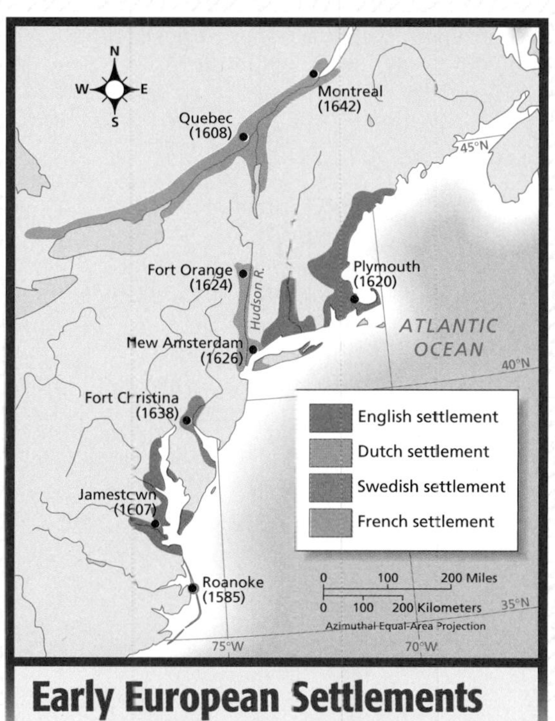

Early European Settlements

that Britain had violated this contract; and that the colonies were declaring their independence.

3. It distributes power between the states and the national government and balances power among the three branches of the federal government.

Thinking Critically

1. A number of Protestant nations, including England, challenged Catholic Spain's weakened power by establishing colonies in North America.

2. They all had settlers from England; their climates and economies varied.

Writing About History

1. Posters will vary but might include the separation of powers between central and state governments, the central government's authority over the states, fear of new taxes, or the need for a bill of rights.

2. Students supporting the patriots might say that they did not believe Great Britain had a right to rule the colonies. Students supporting the Loyalists might say British rule would promote peace and prosperity.

Linking Geography and History

1. Both groups benefited from the exchange of plants and animals, but American Indians were hurt by European diseases, such as smallpox, measles, and typhus.

2. by affecting the types of industry and agriculture that developed and the kinds of labor people performed

History Skills Workshop

(a) New York; (b) the Hudson River; (c) about 150 miles

CHAPTER PLANNING GUIDE

Citizenship and the Constitution

	SECTION LESSON OBJECTIVES	PRINT RESOURCES	MULTIMEDIA RESOURCES	SHELTERED ENGLISH RESOURCES
Section 1: Understanding the Constitution (pp. 37–43)	★ Describe how the framers of the Constitution addressed concerns about the balance of state and federal powers. ★ List and describe the three branches of the federal government. ★ Analyze the division of power among the three branches of government.	★ Guided Reading Strategies 2.1 ★ Biography Reading 2: John Jay ★ Primary Source Reading 2: Antifederalists ★ Section 1 Review, p. 43 ★ Daily Quiz 2.1	★ *Teaching Resources CD–ROM*, Lesson 2.1 ★ *Exploring America's Past Civics and Citizenship Skills* Video Segment: Who Has the Power? *Teacher's Guide*, pp. 53–56 ★ HRW Web site	★ Main Idea Activities for Reteaching and Sheltered English 2.1
Section 2: The Bill of Rights (pp. 64–69)	★ Discuss freedoms listed in the First Amendment. ★ Identify the amendments that reflect issues with pre–Revolutionary War British officials, and describe how each addresses one of these concerns. ★ Examine the rights that the amendments provide to people accused of crimes.	★ Guided Reading Strategies 2.2 ★ Graphic Organizer 2: The Bill of Rights ★ Section 2 Review, p. 69 ★ Daily Quiz 2.2	★ *Teaching Resources CD–ROM*, Lesson 2.2 ★ *Exploring America's Past Civics and Citizenship Skills* Video Segment: The Roles of a Citizen; *Teacher's Guide*, pp. 49–52	★ Main Idea Activities for Reteaching and Sheltered English 2.2
Section 3: Rights and Responsibilities of Citizenship (pp. 70–75)	★ Describe how a person can become a U.S. citizen. ★ Identify the important responsibilities of citizenship. ★ Evaluate why it is important for citizens to be involved with their community and government.	★ Guided Reading Strategies 2.3 ★ Literature Reading 2: *The Free Citizen* ★ Geography Activity 2: Changes in Electoral Votes ★ Section 3 Review, p. 75 ★ Daily Quiz 2.3	★ *Teaching Resources CD–ROM*, Lesson 2.3 ★ *Exploring America's Past Civics and Citizenship Skills* Video Segment: On the Campaign Trail; *Teacher's Guide*, pp. 61–64 ★ HRW Web site	★ Main Idea Activities for Reteaching and Sheltered English 2.3
Chapter Review and Assessment (pp. 76–77)		★ Chapter 2 Review, pp. 76–77 ★ Vocabulary Activity 2 ★ Chapter 2 Study Guide ★ Chapter 2 Test (Form A or B)	★ Audio Program, Ch. 2 (English and Spanish) ★ *Global Skill Builder CD–ROM* ★ Chapter 2 Test Generator ★ HRW Web site	★ Spanish Glossary ★ Sheltered English Chapter 2 Test

CHAPTER OVERVIEW

The Constitution signed in 1787 created a unique and lasting government. The conflicts between the Federalists, who wanted a strong central government, and the Antifederalists, who wanted to limit the power of the central government, led the framers of the Constitution to develop a system of checks and balances. This system divides power among the legislative, executive and judicial branches of government.

Although the checks and balances system promised that no one group would become too strong in the central government, many people remained concerned about individual rights. For this reason, the first Congress added 10 amendments—known as the Bill of Rights—to the Constitution. These amendments guaranteed the basic rights of U.S. citizens, including the right to free speech, freedom of religion, and freedom of assembly.

The Constitution also specifies how a person can become a citizen of the United States and lists the responsibilities of citizenship. These responsibilities include obeying authority, paying taxes, serving on juries, and serving in the military. The most crucial duties of a citizen involve the electoral process, which allows citizens to vote and become politically involved in other ways, such as campaigning for a candidate. Finally, rather than handing over power to the government, U.S. citizens are expected to become involved in their communities.

CHAPTER INVESTIGATION

The Chapter Investigation is an extended, multipart activity designed for students to work cooperatively and apply the chapter content in the creation of a project. You may choose to use the Chapter 2 Investigation, Citizenship How-To Booklets, either as a substitute for teaching the section lessons or as an alternate assessment.

BLOCK SCHEDULING 

The teacher lesson plans for each section offer a variety of activity choices to help you present the material in a block scheduling format. For further suggestions on block scheduling, see the *Block Scheduling Handbook with Team Teaching Strategies*, pp. 7–12.

Meeting Individual Needs

ABILITY LEVELS

LEVEL 1 Basic level activities designed for all students encountering new material.

LEVEL 2 Intermediate level activities designed for average students.

LEVEL 3 Challenging activities designed for above-average students.

SHELTERED ENGLISH These activities address the needs of students with Limited English Proficiency.

Smithsonian Institution®

Internet Connections and Lesson 2
www.si.edu/hrw

CNN Presents America:
Yesterday and Today 1850 to the Present
Segment: The Right to Vote

Additional Resources

Books for Teachers

Barber, Soritors A. *On What the Constitution Means.* Johns Hopkins University Press, 1984. Discusses the intent of the framers.

Berns, Walter. *Taking the Constitution Seriously.* Simon and Schuster, 1987. Describes the responsibilities of citizenship as outlined in the Constitution.

Kirk, Russell. *The Conservative Constitution.* Regnery Gateway, 1990. A reassessment of the meaning of the Constitution.

Books for Students

Adler, Mortimer J. *We Hold These Truths: Understanding the Ideas and Ideals of the Constitution.* Macmillan, 1987. An introduction to constitutional concepts.

Faber, Doris, and Harold Faber. *We the People: The Story of the United States Constitution Since 1787.* Macmillan, 1987. Recounts the history of the Constitution to the present (for students reading below grade level).

Holder, Angela R. *The Meaning of the Constitution,* 2nd ed. Barron, 1987. Clause-by-clause explanation of the Constitution.

Multimedia Materials

The Constitution: Relevant for Today? Video, 57 min. Close-Up Foundation/SSSS. Students discuss the Constitution's relevance today.

The Constitution—Foundations of Our Government. Video, Associated Press. Discusses federalism, the separation of powers, and checks and balances.

The Constitution—A History of Our Future. Video, 21 min. Coronet/MTI Films and Video. Uses humor, drama, and music to illustrate the realities of citizen-based government.

Citizenship and the Constitution

CHAPTER MOTIVATOR

Ask students to consider what would happen if the U.S. government had little authority over the people. *(Students may mention a rise in crime, a decrease in taxpayers, or a lack of money to run government programs.)* Explain to students that the U.S. government under the Articles of Confederation had many weaknesses, including lacking the authority to tax directly. Ask students to describe what can happen when a government has too much authority. *(Students might mention that an overly powerful government might violate its citizens' rights or attack other countries.)* Tell students that in this chapter they will learn about the writing of the U.S. Constitution. Explain to them that the Constitution was designed to correct the weaknesses of the Articles of Confederation while still protecting people's rights.

Presenting Themes

- **Citizenship and Democracy**
  Students might mention efforts to increase voter participation through education. Students could also discuss the ways in which the government protects the right to vote.
- **Constitutional Heritage**
  Students could point out that the organization of government determines the ways in which power and authority are exercised. Students might also say that in a democracy, power comes from the people, and that the government should be organized so that it represents the will of the people.
- **Cultural Diversity**
  Students might mention well-known Americans from different groups who are currently in positions of authority or who contributed to the formation of the United States.

Using the Time Line

Have students place the dates and descriptions listed on the time line in chronological order on a large sheet of white paper. Have them write a question about each event and answer it as they read and discuss the chapter.

CHAPTER 2

Citizenship and the Constitution

(1787–Present)

Thomas Jefferson admired the ideas of ancient Greek philosophers such as Aristotle. "Liberty and equality," wrote Aristotle, "will be best attained [reached] when all persons alike share in the government." Some 2,000 years after Aristotle, U.S. leaders began the process of creating a democratic system of government. Today most Americans can participate in the political process.

Citizenship and Democracy
How can a nation ensure that every citizen has a voice in the government?

Constitutional Heritage
How does a government's organization affect the distribution of power?

Cultural Diversity
What contributions have different groups and individuals made to the nation's formation and government?

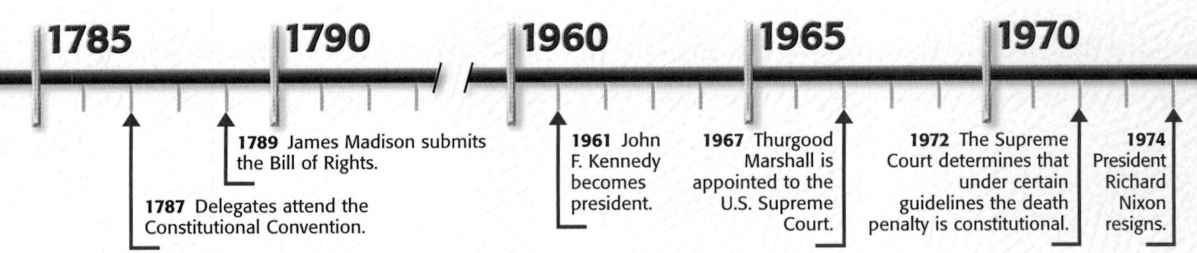

OBJECTIVES

- **Describe how the framers of the Constitution addressed concerns about the balance of state and federal powers.**
- **List and describe the three branches of the federal government.**
- **Analyze the division of power among the three branches of government.**

FOCUS

Motivate Before Reading

Ask students what might happen if no one but the president made, enforced, and interpreted the nation's laws. *(Students may mention that the president would be able to make laws that benefited his or her best interests.)* Explain that to prevent any one person from obtaining too much power, the framers of the Constitution created a government that has three branches. Tell them that each branch

Understanding the Constitution

Reading Focus

How did the framers of the Constitution address concerns about the balance of state and federal powers?

What are the three branches of the federal government?

How is power divided among the three branches of government?

Key Terms

delegated powers
elastic clause
reserved powers
concurrent powers
representative democracy
apportionment
impeach
veto
executive orders
pardons
cabinet

TODAY A SIGN on the Justice Department building in Washington, D.C., reads, "No Free Government Can Survive That Is Not Based on the Supremacy of Law." This idea is central to the U.S. Constitution. Antifederalists opposed the Constitution for fear that the government it created would be too powerful and thus endanger the rights of the people. Federalists such as James Madison assured them that a system grounded in law was the best safeguard of the people.

The Constitution

The Granger Collection, New York

IMAGE ON LEFT PAGE: *Students view historic artwork in Washington, D.C.*

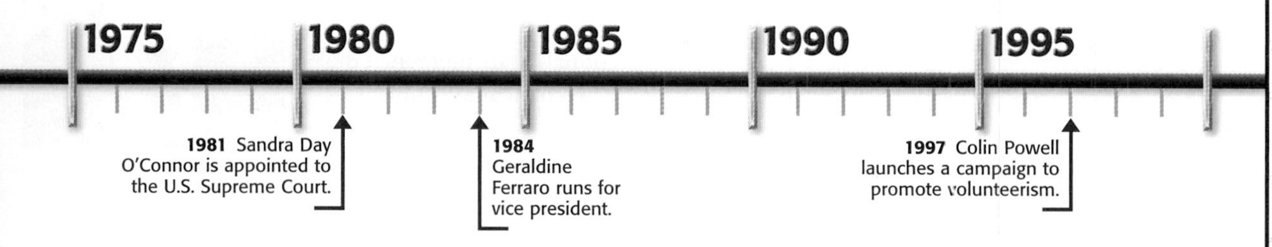

Section 1 RESOURCES

PRINT

- ★ Guided Reading Strategies 2.1
- ★ Biography Reading 2: John Jay
- ★ Primary Source Reading 2: Antifederalists
- ★ Section 1 Review, p. 43
- ★ Daily Quiz 2.1

MULTIMEDIA

- ★ *Teaching Resources CD–ROM,* Lesson 2.1
- ★ *Exploring America's Past Civics and Citizenship Skills* Video Segment: Who Has the Power? *Teacher's Guide,* pp. 53–56
- ★ HRW Web site

SHELTERED ENGLISH

- ★ Main Idea Activities for Reteaching and Sheltered English 2.1

has its own responsibilities yet is still responsible to the other two. Tell students that in this section they will learn about how the framers of the Constitution addressed the concerns of the Antifederalists, the role of each branch, and how power is divided among the branches.

Introduce Key Terms

Linguistic. Review this section's key terms with students. Pair students with a partner. Tell students to write each term on one side of an index card and its definition on the other. Have pairs take turns quizzing one another about the definitions.
SHELTERED ENGLISH

TEACH

Have students read Section 1 and complete Guided Reading Strategies 2.1. Choose one or more of the following activities to explore the section content with students. For further suggestions on block scheduling or team teaching, see the *Block Scheduling Handbook.*

LEVEL 1: Linguistic. (Suggested time: 15 min.) As a class, go over students' Guided Reading Strategies. Then use the Reading Focus questions to highlight the main ideas of the section.
SHELTERED ENGLISH

Geographic Diversity

Reapportionment. The reapportionment of congressional seats after the 1990 census benefited some states, while others lost seats. For example, California gained seven additional seats, Florida received four, and Texas gained three. New York, Pennsylvania, Ohio, Michigan, and Illinois all lost more than one seat.

Critical Thinking: What does the 1990 reapportionment reveal about population growth in different regions of the country?

ANSWER: The South and the West experienced greater population growth than the North and the East.

Multimedia Resources

Exploring America's Past Civics and Citizenship Skills Video Segment: Who Has the Power? *Teacher's Guide*, pp. 53–56

Search 15359, Play to 30879
Videodisc Gold Side A

Play Pause

See *Teacher's Guide* for Spanish barcode.

The Federal System

The Antifederalists opposed the Constitution because they wanted a limited national government—one that would not have too much power. To address Antifederalist concerns, in 1787 the writers of the Constitution established the separation of powers between the states and the federal government.

Delegated powers, those granted to the federal government, include coining money, running the country's postal system, regulating interstate and international trade, providing for the nation's defense, declaring war, and conducting diplomacy. These powers allow the national government to protect citizens and to assure a more uniform economic system throughout the country.

The seal of the U. S. Congress

The **elastic clause** of the Constitution, found in Article I, Section 8, allows Congress to stretch its delegated powers to address issues that the nation's founders could not have foreseen. For example, the Constitution gives the federal government the power to run the postal system, which was the main form of long-distance communication when the Constitution was written. Today the government also regulates modern forms of long-distance communication technology, such as telephones and computers.

The powers retained by the state governments or by citizens are **reserved powers**. These powers include conducting elections, regulating trade within each state, establishing local governments, and regulating education. The federal and state governments also share powers. These **concurrent powers** include taxing, borrowing money, enforcing laws, and providing for citizens' welfare.

The Legislative Branch

The legislative branch makes the nation's laws. "Members of Congress are the human connection between the citizen and . . . government," noted one member of Congress. The founders discussed the legislative branch in Article I of the Constitution to emphasize that the United States would be a **representative democracy**, or government by representatives of the people.

The House and Senate

The House of Representatives is the larger of the two houses of Congress. Currently it has 435 members (originally it had 65). To maintain the current total, Congress decided that no state can gain a representative unless another state loses one. The number of representatives for each state is based on the U.S. census, a population count taken every 10 years. Congress examines changes in the population to determine the **apportionment**, or distribution, of representatives. After the 1990 census, for example, Texas gained three additional seats in the House while New York lost three.

House members represent a particular district of voters in a state. House members must be at least 25 years old, U.S. citizens for seven or more years, and residents of the state from which they are elected. They do not have to live in the district they represent, however.

Senators represent their entire state. They must be at least 30 years old, U.S. citizens for nine or more years, and residents of the state they represent. Each state has two senators. The one who has served longer is the state's senior senator.

The term for a House member is two years and for a Senate member is six years. No law limits the number of times someone may be elected to Congress. However, in recent years many Americans have supported imposing term limits to restrict the number of terms a member can serve.

Organization

Congress holds regular sessions, or meetings, every year beginning on January 3. During a time of national emergency the president may call a congressional meeting after the regular session has already ended. For example, President Abraham

Newt Gingrich became Speaker of the House in 1995.

ALL LEVELS: Linguistic, Logical-Mathematical, Interpersonal. (Suggested time: 30 min.) Discuss with students an imaginary situation in which the school has decided to create a council to deal with curriculum development for its U.S. history classes. Explain to students that school officials are still unsure about how best to represent students' interests: Should each class receive the same number of representatives on the council, or should representation be based on the number of students in each class? Organize the class into two groups. Ask one group to create a list of arguments in support of equal representation, and the other group to create a list of arguments favoring representation based on class size. Then have both groups debate the merits of both sides of the argument and vote to see which method they would prefer. Tell students that the same situation occurred during the writing of the U.S. Constitution. Describe the compromise that was reached to create both the House of Representatives, in which states are represented by population, and the Senate, in which states have equal representation.

SHELTERED ENGLISH

ALL LEVELS: Visual-Spatial, Kinesthetic. (Suggested time: 45 min. plus homework) As a class, discuss the concept of federalism and the division of powers between the federal and state governments. Have students read this section of the text to find examples of the use of delegated powers, the elastic clause,

American Literature

Federalist Paper "No. 51"

James Madison

During the debates over the ratification of the Constitution, New York newspapers printed a series of essays supporting ratification and countering Antifederalist arguments. The Federalist Papers *were written by Alexander Hamilton, John Jay, and James Madison. In this excerpt from essay "No. 51," Madison discusses the means by which the separation of powers among the various branches of government would be preserved.*

In order to lay a due [proper] foundation for . . . the different powers of government, . . . it is evident that each department should have a will of its own; and should be so constituted [set up] that the members of each should have as little agency [power] as possible in the appointment of the members of the others. Were this principle rigorously adhered to [strictly followed], it would require that all the appointments for the supreme executive, legislative, and judiciary magistracies [offices] should be drawn from the same fountain of authority, the people, through channels having no communication . . . with one another. . . . But the great security against a gradual concentration of the several powers in the same department consists in giving to those who administer each department the necessary constitutional means and personal motives to resist encroachments [advances] of the others. The provision for defense must . . . be made commensurate [equal] to the danger of attack. . . . It may be a reflection on human nature that such devices should be necessary to control the abuses of government. But what is government itself but the greatest of all reflections on human nature? If men were angels, no government would be necessary. If angels were to govern men, neither external nor internal controls on government would be necessary. In framing a government which is to be administered by men over men, the great difficulty lies in this: you must first enable the government to control the governed; and in the next place oblige [force] it to control itself.

Understanding Literature

1. What is the "fountain of authority"?
2. According to the excerpt, who should the government govern?

Constitutional Heritage

Concurrent Powers. In *Federalist Paper* "No. 32," Alexander Hamilton explained that state governments retained any powers they had before the drafting of the Constitution. The only exceptions, he said, were those powers listed in the Constitution as belonging to the federal government or as forbidden to the states. Hamilton also noted that in cases where "similar authority in the States would be absolutely and totally contradictory" to the operations of the federal government, the federal government would retain that power. Thus, in a conflict between the concurrent powers of the states and the federal government, the federal government is always considered superior.

Critical Thinking: Why is it important that the federal government have ultimate authority?

ANSWER: Students might respond that there must be one overriding source of authority to maintain unity among the 50 states.

AMERICAN LITERATURE ANSWERS

1. the people
2. the people and itself

Lincoln called Congress into a special session during the Civil War.

The political party with the most members in each house of Congress is called the majority party. The party with fewer members is the minority party of that house. The leader of the House of Representatives is the Speaker of the House. House members select the Speaker, who is usually from the majority party. The vice president of the United States serves as the president of the Senate. The vice president does not join in Senate debates and can cast a vote only if there is a tie. When the vice president is absent, the president *pro tempore,* usually the longest-serving senator of the majority party, leads the Senate.

Congress carries out most of its work in committees that examine every proposed bill. Currently the Senate has 16 standing, or permanent, committees and the House has 19. Each committee specializes in certain types of legislation.

reserved powers, and concurrent powers. For homework, have each student create a collage showing the use of one of these types of powers. **SHELTERED ENGLISH**

ALL LEVELS: Visual-Spatial, Interpersonal. (Suggested time: 45 min.) Tell students that they have been assigned to describe the U.S. government to citizens of another country who are considering changing their nation's constitution. Have students work in small groups to create posters that show the role of each of the three branches of the federal government and the interactions among the branches. After groups have finished, have each group explain its poster to the country seeking the information (the class). **SHELTERED ENGLISH**

TEACHER TO TEACHER

LEVEL 3: Linguistic, Logical-Mathematical. (Suggested time: 45 min. plus homework) Valerie Hill of Dallas, Texas, suggested the following activity: Explain to students that some decisions of the courts, especially the Supreme Court, have far-reaching implications. Assign students significant Supreme Court decisions to research. Have students write a report that includes a description of both sides of the argument in the case, a summary of the Court's decision, and their own opinions about

Citizenship and Democracy

Exercising the Veto. The president's ability to veto legislation is an important check on Congress's power. Between 1789 and 1990, presidents vetoed 2,492 bills, with 2,433 of these vetoes taking place after 1865. The vetoes were overridden by Congress only 103 times.

Critical Thinking: Why is the veto power important?

ANSWER: because it prevents Congress from having absolute authority in lawmaking

Using Visual Resources

Herblock. Cartoonist Herbert Block, who drew the cartoon on this page, signs his cartoons "Herblock." He has been awarded the Pulitzer Prize three times for his work. Block begins work on a cartoon as soon as the previous day's newspaper comes out—about two hours after he finished his cartoon for that day. He reads the paper about three times before he begins doodling.

Critical Thinking: What does the cartoon on this page say about the relationship between the executive and the legislative branches?

ANSWER: It shows that the executive branch can pressure the legislative branch to get what it wants.

For example, all bills relating to taxes originate in the House Ways and Means Committee.

The Executive Branch

Article II of the Constitution specifies the powers of the executive branch, which is responsible for enforcing the laws approved by Congress. The president, as head of the executive branch, is the most powerful elected official in the country.

Becoming President

To become president, one must be a native-born U.S. citizen, at least 35 years old, and have been a resident of the United States for at least 14 years. All presidents have been white men. In recent years, candidates have become more diverse, with African Americans such as Jesse Jackson seeking the presidency. Geraldine Ferraro became the first woman on the ticket of a major party when she was the Democratic nominee for vice president in 1984. No non-Christian has yet been president. When John F. Kennedy took office in 1961, he became the first Roman Catholic president.

Americans elect a president and vice president every four years. The president determines the vice president's responsibilities, which often include representing the president at official functions. Franklin D. Roosevelt, who won four presidential elections, has been the only president to serve more than two terms. The Twenty-second Amendment, ratified in 1951, prevents anyone from serving more than two terms as president. If the president dies, resigns, or is removed from office, the vice president becomes president.

The House of Representatives has the authority to **impeach**, or bring charges against, a president suspected of committing a crime or violating the essential presidential duties. The Senate tries all impeachment cases. If a president is found guilty, Congress can remove him or her from office. In 1868 Andrew Johnson became the first president to be impeached. President Bill Clinton was impeached in 1998. In each case the Senate tried the president and found him not guilty. In 1974 President Richard Nixon resigned to avoid possible impeachment.

Presidential Duties

The president has many duties, which involve overseeing all aspects of the government. The system of checks and balances often sets the president against Congress, particularly when the president's party is different from that of the majority party in Congress. First Lady Eleanor Roosevelt once noted, "It isn't really possible under our system, I fear, for the Executive and the Legislative to get along well."

Despite their differences, the executive and legislative branches must cooperate for the system to work. As President Lyndon Johnson observed:

> **"What a President says and thinks is not worth five cents unless he has the people and Congress behind him. Without the Congress I'm just a six-feet-four Texan. With Congress I'm President of the United States in the fullest sense."**

Although Congress passes laws, the president can influence legislation by encouraging members to approve or reject certain bills. The president also has the power to **veto**, or cancel, legislation. Congress can override a president's veto, but doing so is very difficult because it requires a two-thirds majority vote.

"Thanks—Thanks a lot—Thanks again—can I lean back now?"

The Herblock Gallery (Simon & Schuster, 1968)

President Lyndon Johnson was famous for praising members of Congress, or patting them on the back, so that they would pass his legislation.

the significance of the case and decision. Have students place their finished reports in a binder so that other students can find out more information about these important decisions.

LEVEL 3: Linguistic, Kinesthetic, Interpersonal. (Suggested time: 45 min. plus homework) Explain to students that part of the reason the framers of the Constitution delegated some powers directly to the federal government—rather than to state governments—was to avoid creating situations that would make interactions between the states difficult. Organize the class into three groups. Have each group create a three-minute comedic skit that highlights the confusion that could occur if a specific power that is now delegated to the national government were held by state governments. For example, students could describe a construction project in which suppliers from one state kept shipping materials that were the wrong size to another state because states had been given the power to establish their own standards of weights and measures. Have each group act out its skit for the class. Finally, discuss the importance of the division of powers in the Constitution.

CLOSE

Linguistic, Logical-Mathematical, Intrapersonal. To conclude the lesson, ask students to write a letter pretending to be a

The Executive Departments

DEPARTMENT OF STATE
- conducts foreign relations
- protects U.S. citizens abroad
- issues passports and visas

DEPARTMENT OF THE TREASURY
- mints coins and issues money
- collects taxes and pays bills
- manages government funds

DEPARTMENT OF JUSTICE
- investigates violations of federal laws
- prosecutes cases before courts
- administers naturalization laws
- enforces immigration laws

DEPARTMENT OF THE INTERIOR
- controls public lands
- maintains public parks
- supervises American Indian reservations
- controls water resources

DEPARTMENT OF AGRICULTURE
- conducts studies to help farmers
- manages food stamp and school lunch programs
- helps farmers raise and market crops
- directs soil conservation programs

DEPARTMENT OF COMMERCE
- sets standards for weights and measures
- encourages and regulates foreign trade
- publishes reports on business and trade

DEPARTMENT OF LABOR
- determines standards of labor
- publishes employment information
- directs public employment services

DEPARTMENT OF DEFENSE
- maintains U.S. armed services
- conducts military studies
- operates military bases

DEPARTMENT OF HEALTH AND HUMAN SERVICES
- directs public health services
- sees that foods and medicines are safe

DEPARTMENT OF HOUSING AND URBAN DEVELOPMENT
- helps urban-housing programs
- helps cities plan traffic control
- helps cities plan mass transportation
- cooperates with metropolitan-area planners

DEPARTMENT OF TRANSPORTATION
- helps develop the nation's transportation policy
- supervises federal-aid highway programs
- promotes transportation safety

DEPARTMENT OF ENERGY
- helps develop the nation's energy policy
- promotes conservation of energy
- regulates energy resources

DEPARTMENT OF EDUCATION
- sets guidelines for granting financial aid to schools
- conducts research on educational subjects
- administers federally sponsored educational programs

DEPARTMENT OF VETERANS AFFAIRS
- administers medical and disability benefits to veterans and their families
- provides pensions and death benefits for veterans

After Congress passes a law, federal agencies and departments usually determine how to put it into effect. To carry out laws that affect administrative matters or executive policy, the president sometimes issues **executive orders**, nonlegislative directives that have the force of law. In an emergency the president may issue an executive order that stretches the definition of laws enacted by Congress.

The president, although a civilian, is also commander in chief of the armed forces. Although the president can send U.S. troops into emergency situations, only Congress can declare war. The president's many other responsibilities include carrying out foreign relations through both diplomatic ties and the negotiation of treaties. The president also has the power to grant **pardons**, or freedom from punishment, for persons convicted of federal crimes or who are facing criminal charges.

Executive Departments

Numerous departments carry out most of the work of the executive branch. Currently there are 14 executive departments. The heads of these departments make up the **cabinet**, which advises

Constitutional Heritage

The Nixon Pardon. Perhaps the most famous pardon in presidential history took place on September 8, 1974, when President Gerald R. Ford granted an "absolute pardon unto Richard Nixon for all offenses against the United States which he, Richard Nixon, has committed or may have committed or taken part in." President Nixon had resigned from office after he had been accused of involvement in illegal actions while president. Ford said that he granted the pardon because prosecuting the former president would be too difficult and disturbing for the nation.

Critical Thinking: Do you think it was a good idea for President Ford to pardon President Nixon?

ANSWER: Some students might say that Nixon should have been tried for his alleged crimes; others may agree with President Ford's reasoning.

member of the Constitutional Convention who wants to update the people of his or her state about the Convention. Letters should describe the reasons for the division of power between the federal government and state governments. Then have students identify and describe how power was divided. You might wish to have them examine the Constitution starting on page 44 to find examples.

CHALLENGE AND EXTEND

1. **Visual-Spatial, Kinesthetic.** Assign students a specific state or states to research. Then have them create a chart with 10-year intervals (from 1950 to the present) on the horizontal axis, and the state's population and number of representatives in the House of Representatives on the vertical axis. Ask them to compare the changes in representation and population growth among the various states since 1950.
2. **Visual-Spatial, Logical-Mathematical, Kinesthetic.** Lead a class discussion that covers the differences between delegated, reserved, and concurrent powers. Have students review old newspapers and magazines to find examples of the use of each of these types of powers. Then hang three large pieces of butcher paper around the classroom. Label each paper with the name of one of the types of powers. Have students tape copies of articles they have found onto the appropriate piece of paper.

Biography

Sandra Day O'Connor. Supreme Court Justice Sandra Day O'Connor has achieved several "firsts" in her legal career. By 1965 she had become the first female assistant attorney general in Arizona. In the Arizona senate, she served as majority leader for two years—the first woman to hold such a position in any U.S. state. When Ronald Reagan appointed O'Connor to the Supreme Court, she was the first woman to hold this important post in government.

Activity: Have students use the library or search the Internet through the HRW Web site to find more information on Sandra Day O'Connor. Then ask them to write brief biographies that expand on the information included in the text.

go.hrw.com
SB1 O'Connor

Biography

Sandra Day O'Connor

Sandra Day O'Connor was born in El Paso, Texas, in 1930. She attended college and law school at Stanford University in California. She began her legal career working as a deputy county attorney in California. Later she moved to Arizona, where she served as the assistant state attorney general and then as a state legislator. In 1973 she became the majority leader for the Arizona state senate before being appointed a judge on the state's second-highest court.

In 1981 President Ronald Reagan appointed O'Connor to the Supreme Court. Although she was appointed by a Republican president, O'Connor has at times opposed Republican policies when deciding cases. Her decisions illustrate how Supreme Court justices often can be free from party politics once appointed. When asked how she hoped to be remembered, O'Connor replied that she would like her tombstone to read simply, "Here lies a good judge."

the president. Some departments, such as the State Department, handle foreign-policy issues. Others, such as the Department of Education, focus on domestic issues.

The Judicial Branch

The third branch of the government is the judicial branch, which consists of a series of federal courts headed by the U.S. Supreme Court. Article III of the Constitution defines the duties of the courts.

The Federal Court System

The president appoints all judges on each level of the federal court system for life. Each of these judges receives the appointment for life to ensure that he or she will make decisions free from the influence of a particular party. Federal judge Shirley Wohl Kram explains her duties, "It is the judge's role to resolve grievances and the role of the legislature to supply the answers for the social and economic problems facing the community."

The lower courts in the federal system are divided according to the types of cases over which they have jurisdiction, or authority. Each state has at least one district court to handle federal cases. States with large populations usually have more than one district court. Currently there are 94 U.S. district courts.

Above the lower courts are 13 courts of appeals, which make sure that cases are tried properly in the lower courts. Someone convicted of a crime who believes that his or her rights were violated in the original trial can appeal the case to the higher court.

The courts of appeals do not use juries. Instead, a panel of judges decides whether the lower court handled the original case properly. If the judges uphold, or accept, the lower court's decision, then the case's original outcome remains. If they believe that the case was handled improperly, they usually send it back to the lower court for a new trial. The courts of appeals have the final say in most of the cases they review. Sometimes, however, the U.S. Supreme Court chooses to review decisions of the courts of appeals.

The Supreme Court

Most cases presented to the Supreme Court originate in lower courts. However, some cases—such as those that involve international diplomats or disputes between states—go directly to the Supreme Court.

Once students have finished, carry on a class discussion explaining why students classified the articles the way they did.

REVIEW

Linguistic, Logical-Mathematical. Have students complete the Section Review questions. Then have them write a paragraph describing why it was important to clearly define the roles of the three branches of the U.S. government. Encourage students to consider why it was important for each branch to have some way of limiting the other two branches' power when necessary.

ASSESS

Have students complete Daily Quiz 2.1.

RETEACH

Linguistic, Interpersonal. Have students complete Main Idea Activities for Reteaching and Sheltered English 2.1. Then ask them to create a study guide for this section. Have students exchange guides with each other and complete the guides.

SHELTERED ENGLISH

Congress determines how many justices sit on the Court; typically that number is fixed at nine. The chief justice of the United States leads the Supreme Court. Unlike for the president and members of Congress, the Constitution sets no specific requirements for being a Court justice. So far, however, every justice has been an attorney. William Howard Taft is the only person to have been both president (1909–13) and a Supreme Court chief justice (1921–30).

Supreme Court Justice Ruth Bader Ginsburg speaks to a group of students.

In the past 50 years the Supreme Court has become more diverse. In 1967 Thurgood Marshall became the first African American justice; the second was Clarence Thomas in 1991. Currently two women sit on the high court—Ruth Bader Ginsburg and Sandra Day O'Connor, who became the first female Court justice after her 1981 appointment by President Ronald Reagan. Each justice contributes greatly to the Court. As O'Connor explained:

> **"The Court benefits from broad and diverse experiences of its members. My own experience in all three branches of state government gave me a background which differed from a majority of my colleagues. It undoubtedly has helped me understand and appreciate the importance and value of the federal system designed by the Framers of the Constitution."**

O'Connor and other Supreme Court justices have time to review around 100 of the thousands of cases appealed to them each year. The justices carefully choose which cases to hear. Generally, cases heard by the Court must involve an important constitutional or public interest issue. If the Court refuses to hear a case, the decision of the court of appeals is final. If the Court finds a law unconstitutional and Congress disagrees with the ruling, lawmakers can begin the process of amending the Constitution.

SECTION 1 REVIEW

Identify and explain the significance of the following:

- **delegated powers**
- **elastic clause**
- **reserved powers**
- **concurrent powers**
- **representative democracy**
- **apportionment**
- **impeach**
- **veto**
- **executive orders**
- **pardons**
- **cabinet**
- **Sandra Day O'Connor**

Reading for Content Understanding

1. **Main Idea** How are the state and federal powers balanced in the Constitution?
2. **Main Idea** List the three branches of the federal government, and explain how power is divided among them.
3. **Citizenship and Democracy** How does a state's population affect that state's representation in the House and Senate?
4. **Writing** *Describing* Write a two-paragraph essay that explains how the judicial system is structured.
5. **Critical Thinking** *Synthesizing Information* Do you think the three branches of government share power equally? If not, which branch do you think has the most power, and why?

Section 1 Review ANSWERS

Identify

For significance, see the following pages:

- delegated powers, p. 38
- elastic clause, p. 38
- reserved powers, p. 38
- concurrent powers, p. 38
- representative democracy, p. 38
- apportionment, p. 38
- impeach, p. 40
- veto, p. 40
- executive orders, p. 41
- pardons, p. 41
- cabinet, p. 41
- Sandra Day O'Connor, p. 43

Reading for Content Understanding

1. Some powers are delegated to the federal government, some are reserved to the states, and others are shared.

2. legislative—makes laws; executive—enforces laws; judicial—determines if the laws are constitutional and whether they are being applied correctly

3. The number of representatives in the house is based on population, but each state has two senators.

4. Paragraphs will vary but should include the hierarchical nature of the court system and the different jurisdictions of the lower and upper courts.

5. Answers will vary but students should explain their reasoning.

Constitutional Heritage

The Preamble. Although short, the Preamble was hotly debated in the state ratifying conventions. The phrase "We the People" was particularly contentious, since the delegates to the conventions had been appointed by states, rather than elected by the people. Patrick Henry challenged this phrase during the ratifying process in Virginia, saying, "The people gave them [the delegates to the Constitutional Convention] no power to use their name. That they exceeded their power is perfectly clear."

Critical Thinking: How might someone have countered Henry's argument?

ANSWER: The people gave the states the right to appoint the delegates, so the people actually did give them power.

PRIMARY SOURCE ▶

The primary source on pupil's pages 44–63 has been given in its entirety.

THE CONSTITUTION

"WE THE PEOPLE OF THE UNITED STATES, IN ORDER TO FORM A MORE PERFECT UNION, ESTABLISH JUSTICE, INSURE DOMESTIC TRANQUILITY, PROVIDE FOR THE COMMON DEFENCE, PROMOTE THE GENERAL WELFARE, AND SECURE THE BLESSINGS OF LIBERTY TO OURSELVES AND OUR POSTERITY, DO ORDAIN AND ESTABLISH THIS CONSTITUTION FOR THE UNITED STATES OF AMERICA."

Parts of the Constitution that have been ruled through are no longer in force or no longer apply because of later amendments.

Preamble
The short and dignified Preamble explains the goals of the new government under the Constitution.

LEFT: Independence Hall, Philadelphia

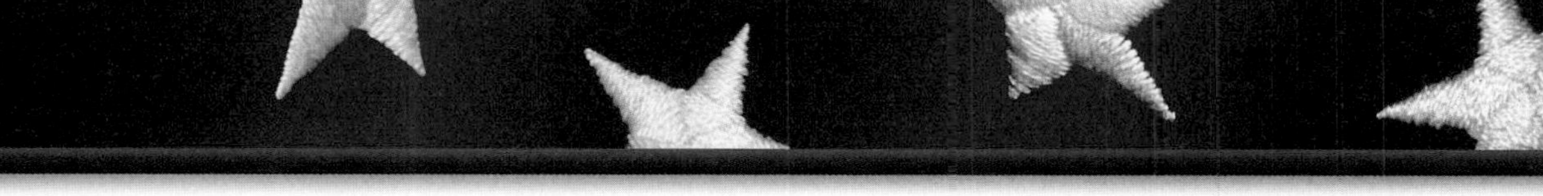

ARTICLE I

Section 1. All legislative Powers herein granted shall be vested in a Congress of the United States, which shall consist of a Senate and House of Representatives.

Section 2. The House of Representatives shall be composed of Members chosen every second Year by the People of the several States, and the Electors in each State shall have the Qualifications requisite for Electors of the most numerous Branch of the State Legislature.

No Person shall be a Representative who shall not have attained to the Age of twenty five Years, and been seven Years a Citizen of the United States, and who shall not, when elected, be an Inhabitant of that State in which he shall be chosen.

Representatives and direct Taxes shall be apportioned among the several States which may be included within this Union, according to their respective Numbers~~, which shall be determined by adding to the whole Number of free Persons, including those bound to Service for a Term of Years, and excluding Indians not taxed, three fifths of all other Persons~~. The actual Enumeration shall be made within three Years after the first Meeting of the Congress of the United States, and within every subsequent Term of ten Years, in such Manner as they shall by Law direct. The Number of Representatives shall not exceed one for every thirty Thousand, but each State shall have at Least one Representative~~; and until such enumeration shall be made, the State of New Hampshire shall be entitled to chuse three; Massachusetts eight; Rhode Island and Providence Plantations one; Connecticut five; New York six; New Jersey four; Pennsylvania eight; Delaware one; Maryland six; Virginia ten; North Carolina five; South Carolina five; and Georgia three~~.

When vacancies happen in the Representation from any State, the Executive Authority thereof shall issue Writs of Election to fill such Vacancies.

The House of Representatives shall chuse their Speaker and other Officers; and shall have the sole Power of Impeachment.

Section 3. The Senate of the United States shall be composed of two Senators from each State~~, chosen by the Legislature thereof~~, for six Years; and each Senator shall have one Vote.

Immediately after they shall be assembled in Consequence of the first Election, they shall be divided as equally as may be into three Classes. The Seats of the Senators of the first Class shall be vacated at the Expiration of the second Year, of the second Class at the Expiration of the fourth Year, and of the third Class at the Expiration of the sixth Year, so that one third may be chosen every second Year~~; and if Vacancies happen by~~

Legislative Branch

Article I explains how the legislative branch, called Congress, is organized. The chief purpose of the legislative branch is to make the laws. Congress is made up of the Senate and the House of Representatives. The decision to have two bodies of government solved a difficult problem during the Constitutional Convention. The large states wanted the membership of Congress to be based entirely on population. The small states wanted every state to have an equal vote. The solution to the problem of how the states were to be represented in Congress became known as the Great Compromise.

The number of members each state has in the House is based on the population of the individual state. Each state has at least one representative. In 1929 Congress permanently fixed the size of the House at 435 members. Today, if each member of the House were to represent only 30,000 Americans, the House would have more than 8,600 members.

Every state has two senators. Senators serve a six-year term. Every two years, one third of the senators reach the end of their terms. In any election, at least two thirds of the senators stay in office. This system ensures that there are experienced senators in office at all times.

Linking Past to Present

Income Tax. Although the Constitution gave Congress the right to raise revenue through taxes, the Constitution stood in the way of an income tax until the passage of the Sixteenth Amendment in 1913. The Union passed the first income tax during the Civil War to pay for maintaining the army. The minimum rate of this tax was 3 percent on income above $600, and the maximum was 5 percent on income over $10,000. This tax remained in effect until 1872. However, when Congress enacted an income tax in 1894, the Supreme Court ruled it unconstitutional for failing to apportion the tax burden fairly "among the several States." Once the Sixteenth Amendment was passed, however, the personal income tax became an increasingly important source of federal revenue. In the 1998 federal budget, it accounted for an estimated 41 percent of federal revenue—a little less than $50 billion.

Activity: Tell students to use the library or other resources to find information about the U.S. income tax. Have them create a chart that shows the percentage of federal revenues from income tax at three points during the past 50 years.

Technology and Society

Availability of Information. For many years, the best way for the public to learn about congressional proceedings was through the *Congressional Record*, a bulky set of printed volumes. With the wide availability of the Internet, tracking a congressperson's votes has become easier. The Library of Congress supports a Web site that covers every aspect of the government. In addition, independent organizations, such as Project Vote Smart, provide links to help track congressional votes.

Activity: Have students use the library or search the Internet through the HRW Web site to track a current piece of legislation. Ask them to find out how their congressperson voted.

go.hrw.com
SB1 Library of Congress

~~Resignation, or otherwise, during the Recess of the Legislature of any State, the Executive thereof may make temporary Appointments until the next Meeting of the Legislature, which shall then fill such Vacancies.~~

No Person shall be a Senator who shall not have attained to the Age of thirty Years, and been nine Years a Citizen of the United States, and who shall not, when elected, be an Inhabitant of that State for which he shall be chosen.

The only duty that the Constitution assigns to the vice president is to preside over meetings of the Senate. Modern presidents have usually given their vice presidents more responsibilities.

The Vice President of the United States shall be President of the Senate, but shall have no Vote, unless they be equally divided.

The Senate shall chuse their other Officers, and also a President pro tempore, in the Absence of the Vice President, or when he shall exercise the Office of President of the United States.

The Senate shall have the sole Power to try all Impeachments. When sitting for that Purpose, they shall be on Oath or Affirmation. When the President of the United States is tried, the Chief Justice shall preside: And no Person shall be convicted without the Concurrence of two thirds of the Members present.

The House charges a government official with wrongdoing, and the Senate acts as a court to decide if the official is guilty.

Judgment in Cases of Impeachment shall not extend further than to removal from Office, and disqualification to hold and enjoy any Office of honor, Trust or Profit under the United States: but the Party convicted shall nevertheless be liable and subject to Indictment, Trial, Judgment and Punishment, according to Law.

Congress decided that elections will be held on the Tuesday following the first Monday in November of even-numbered years. The Twentieth Amendment states that Congress shall meet in regular session on January 3 of each year. The president may call a special session of Congress whenever it is necessary.

Section 4. The Times, Places and Manner of holding Elections for Senators and Representatives, shall be prescribed in each State by the Legislature thereof; but the Congress may at any time by Law make or alter such Regulations, except as to the Places of chusing Senators.

~~The Congress shall assemble at least once in every Year, and such Meeting shall be on the first Monday in December, unless they shall by Law appoint a different Day.~~

Congress makes most of its own rules of conduct. The Senate and the House each have a code of ethics that members must follow. It is the task of each house of Congress to discipline its own members. Each house keeps a journal, and a daily, unofficial publication called the *Congressional Record* details what happens in congressional sessions. The general public can learn how their representatives voted on bills by reading the *Congressional Record.*

Section 5. Each House shall be the Judge of the Elections, Returns and Qualifications of its own Members, and a Majority of each shall constitute a Quorum to do Business; but a smaller Number may adjourn from day to day, and may be authorized to compel the Attendance of absent Members, in such Manner, and under such Penalties as each House may provide.

Each House may determine the Rules of its Proceedings, punish its Members for disorderly Behaviour, and, with the Concurrence of two thirds, expel a Member.

Each House shall keep a Journal of its Proceedings, and from time to time publish the same, excepting such Parts as may in their Judgment require Secrecy; and the Yeas and Nays of the Members of either House on any question shall, at the Desire of one fifth of those Present, be entered on the Journal.

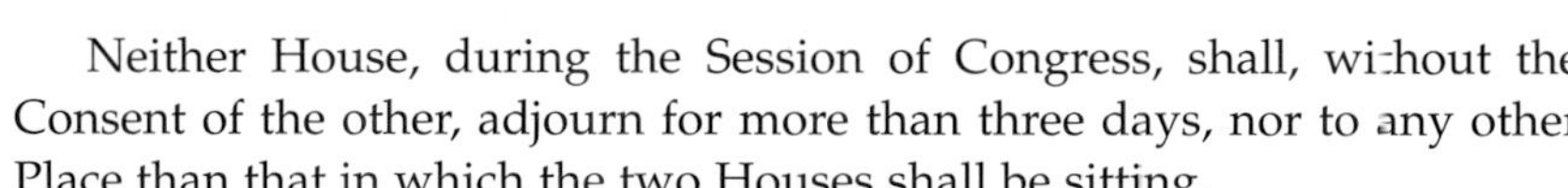

Neither House, during the Session of Congress, shall, without the Consent of the other, adjourn for more than three days, nor to any other Place than that in which the two Houses shall be sitting.

Section 6. The Senators and Representatives shall receive a Compensation for their Services, to be ascertained by Law, and paid out of the Treasury of the United States. They shall in all Cases, except Treason, Felony and Breach of the Peace, be privileged from Arrest during their Attendance at the Session of their respective Houses, and in going to and returning from the same; and for any Speech or Debate in either House, they shall not be questioned in any other Place.

No Senator or Representative shall, during the Time for which he was elected, be appointed to any civil Office under the Authority of the United States, which shall have been created, or the Emoluments whereof shall have been encreased during such time; and no Person holding any Office under the United States, shall be a Member of either House during his Continuance in Office.

The framers of the Constitution wanted to protect members of Congress from being arrested on false charges by political enemies who did not want them to attend important meetings. The framers also wanted to protect members of Congress from being taken to court for something they said in a speech or in a debate.

Section 7. All Bills for raising Revenue shall originate in the House of Representatives; but the Senate may propose or concur with Amendments as on other Bills.

Every Bill which shall have passed the House of Representatives and the Senate, shall, before it become a Law, be presented to the President of the United States; If he approve he shall sign it, but if not he shall return it, with his Objections to that House in which it shall have originated, who shall enter the Objections at large on their Journal, and proceed to reconsider it. If after such Reconsideration two thirds of that House shall agree to pass the Bill, it shall be sent, together with the Objections, to the other House, by which it shall likewise be reconsidered, and if approved by two thirds of that House, it shall become a Law. But in all such Cases the Votes of both Houses shall be determined by yeas and Nays, and the Names of the Persons voting for and against the Bill shall be entered on the Journal of each House respectively. If any Bill shall not be returned by the President within ten Days (Sundays excepted) after it shall have been presented to him, the Same shall be a Law, in like Manner as if he had signed it, unless the Congress by their Adjournment prevent its Return, in which Case it shall not be a Law.

Every Order, Resolution, or Vote to which the Concurrence of the Senate and House of Representatives may be necessary (except on a question of Adjournment) shall be presented to the President of the United States; and before the Same shall take Effect, shall be approved by him, or being disapproved by him, shall be repassed by two thirds of the Senate and House of Representatives, according to the Rules and Limitations prescribed in the Case of a Bill.

The power of taxing is the responsibility of the House of Representatives. The framers felt that because members of the House are elected every two years, representatives would listen to the public and seek its approval before passing taxes.

The veto power of the president and the ability of Congress to override a presidential veto are two of the important checks and balances in the Constitution.

Linking Past to Present

Veto Power. In 1996 Congress passed the line-item veto, which gave the president the power to cancel specific items in spending bills. Proponents of the law hoped that it would help stop wasteful spending by allowing the president to prevent unnecessary spending. However, almost immediately a group of lawmakers challenged the line-item veto on constitutional grounds. A federal court decided that the law was unconstitutional because it upset the system of checks and balances built into the Constitution. The judge claimed that the power to revoke spending appropriations once they are passed is a congressional power and "according to the [Constitution's] Framers' careful design, may not be delegated at all."

Critical Thinking: Do you think the line-item veto would significantly change the system of checks and balances that the framers built into the Constitution?

Answer: Students' answers will vary. Some may say yes, the veto would give the president too much power. Others may say no, it would be a useful way for the president to help Congress control spending.

Historical Sidelight

The First Postal Service. Before the Constitution was ratified, Congress had established a postal service under the Articles of Confederation. Benjamin Franklin served as the postmaster general. The postal service expanded rapidly, with revenue increasing from $37,935 in 1790 to $1,707,000 by 1829. By the early 1800s the government considered the post office so important that the postmaster general was made a cabinet member.

Activity: Have students use the school library to research the history of the postal service. Ask them to prepare a time line describing changes in postal services.

The framers of the Constitution wanted a national government that was strong enough to be effective. This section lists the powers given to Congress. The last sentence in Section 8 contains the famous "elastic clause"—so called because it has been stretched (like elastic) to fit many different circumstances. The clause was first disputed when Alexander Hamilton proposed a national bank. Thomas Jefferson said that because the Constitution did not specifically give Congress the power to establish a bank, it could not do so. Hamilton argued that the bank was "necessary and proper" in order to carry out other powers of Congress, such as borrowing money and regulating currency. This argument was tested in the courts in 1819 in the case of *McCulloch* v. *Maryland,* when Chief Justice Marshall ruled in favor of the federal government. Powers given to the government by the elastic clause are called implied powers.

Section 8. The Congress shall have Power To lay and collect Taxes, Duties, Imposts and Excises, to pay the Debts and provide for the common Defence and general Welfare of the United States; but all Duties, Imposts and Excises shall be uniform throughout the United States;

To borrow Money on the credit of the United States;

To regulate Commerce with foreign Nations, and among the several States, and with the Indian Tribes;

To establish an uniform Rule of Naturalization, and uniform Laws on the subject of Bankruptcies throughout the United States;

To coin Money, regulate the Value thereof, and of foreign Coin, and fix the Standard of Weights and Measures;

To provide for the Punishment of counterfeiting the Securities and current Coin of the United States;

To establish Post Offices and post Roads;

To promote the Progress of Science and useful Arts, by securing for limited Times to Authors and Inventors the exclusive Right to their respective Writings and Discoveries;

To constitute Tribunals inferior to the supreme Court;

To define and punish Piracies and Felonies committed on the high Seas, and Offences against the Law of Nations;

To declare War, grant Letters of Marque and Reprisal, and make Rules concerning Captures on Land and Water;

To raise and support Armies, but no Appropriation of Money to that Use shall be for a longer Term than two Years;

To provide and maintain a Navy;

To make Rules for the Government and Regulation of the land and naval Forces;

To provide for calling forth the Militia to execute the Laws of the Union, suppress Insurrections and repel Invasions;

To provide for organizing, arming, and disciplining, the Militia, and for governing such Part of them as may be employed in the Service of the United States, reserving to the States respectively, the Appointment of the Officers, and the Authority of training the Militia according to the discipline prescribed by Congress;

To exercise exclusive Legislation in all Cases whatsoever, over such District (not exceeding ten Miles square) as may, by Cession of particular States, and the Acceptance of Congress, become the Seat of the Government of the United States, and to exercise like Authority over all Places purchased by the Consent of the Legislature of the State in which the Same shall be, for the Erection of Forts, Magazines, Arsenals, dock-Yards, and other needful Buildings;—And

To make all Laws which shall be necessary and proper for carrying into Execution the foregoing Powers, and all other Powers vested by this

Constitution in the Government of the United States, or in any Department or Officer thereof.

Section 9. ~~The Migration or Importation of such Persons as any of the States now existing shall think proper to admit, shall not be prohibited by the Congress prior to the Year one thousand eight hundred and eight, but a Tax or duty may be imposed on such Importation, not exceeding ten dollars for each Person~~.

The Privilege of the Writ of Habeas Corpus shall not be suspended, unless when in Cases of Rebellion or Invasion the public Safety may require it.

No Bill of Attainder or ex post facto Law shall be passed.

No Capitation, or other direct, Tax shall be laid, unless in Proportion to the Census or Enumeration herein before directed to be taken.

No Tax or Duty shall be laid on Articles exported from any State.

No Preference shall be given by any Regulation of Commerce or Revenue to the Ports of one State over those of another: nor shall Vessels bound to, or from, one State, be obliged to enter, clear, or pay Duties in another.

No Money shall be drawn from the Treasury, but in Consequence of Appropriations made by Law; and a regular Statement and Account of the Receipts and Expenditures of all public Money shall be published from time to time.

No Title of Nobility shall be granted by the United States: And no Person holding any Office of Profit or Trust under them, shall, without the Consent of the Congress, accept of any present, Emolument, Office, or Title, of any kind whatever, from any King, Prince, or foreign State.

Although Congress has implied powers, there are also limits to its powers. Section 9 lists powers that are denied to the federal government. Several of the clauses protect the people of the United States from unjust treatment. For example, Section 9 guarantees the writ of *habeas corpus* and prohibits bills of attainder and *ex post facto* laws.

Section 10. No State shall enter into any Treaty, Alliance, or Confederation; grant Letters of Marque and Reprisal; coin Money; emit Bills of Credit; make any Thing but gold and silver Coin a Tender in Payment of Debts; pass any Bill of Attainder, ex post facto Law, or law impairing the Obligation of Contracts, or grant any Title of Nobility.

No State shall, without the Consent of the Congress, lay any Imposts or Duties on Imports or Exports, except what may be absolutely necessary for executing its inspection Laws: and the net Produce of all Duties and Imposts, laid by any State on Imports or Exports, shall be for the Use of the Treasury of the United States; and all such Laws shall be subject to the Revision and Controul of the Congress.

No State shall, without the Consent of Congress, lay any Duty of Tonnage, keep Troops, or Ships of War in time of Peace, enter into any Agreement or Compact with another State, or with a foreign Power, or engage in War, unless actually invaded, or in such imminent Danger as will not admit of delay.

Section 10 lists the powers that are denied to the states. In our system of federalism, the state and federal governments have separate powers, share some powers, and are each denied other powers.

Citizenship and Democracy

***Gibbons* v. *Ogden*.** The power to regulate interstate commerce was first tested in the Supreme Court case *Gibbons* v. *Ogden* (1824). Ogden and Gibbons operated two rival steamboat companies between New York and New Jersey. Ogden had a monopoly granted by the state of New York, but Gibbons had a federally granted license to operate a steamboat company. The Supreme Court held that Gibbons's license was valid because the federal government had jurisdiction over all interstate commerce. In the Court's decision, Chief Justice John Marshall explained that if the states' powers were interpreted broadly and the federal government's were interpreted narrowly, the Constitution would be "a magnificent structure, indeed, to look at, but totally unfit for use."

Critical Thinking: Why might *Gibbons* v. *Ogden* be considered a landmark Supreme Court case?

ANSWER: It not only established that federal law supersedes state law but also set a precedent for interpreting federal powers broadly.

Constitutional Heritage

The President. Initially, the writers of the Constitution agreed that the president would be chosen by the national legislature for a single, seven-year term. Since many delegates opposed a strong executive branch, the president was to remain subordinate to the legislature. However, when the Constitution was turned over to the Committee on Style, Gouverneur Morris, who wanted a stronger executive, reworded the article outlining the role of the president. He changed the length of the president's term, allowed the president to run for more than one term, and altered the method by which the president would be elected. These changes passed with little debate, partly because the delegates were ready to go home and partly because many members believed that George Washington would be the first president and felt that his virtues would check any abuse of power made possible by a strong executive.

Critical Thinking: Why might many of the delegates to the Convention have opposed a one-person executive?

ANSWER: Having just fought for independence from the British king, they feared that they might create another monarchy.

ARTICLE II

Section 1. The executive Power shall be vested in a President of the United States of America. He shall hold his Office during the Term of four Years, and, together with the Vice President, chosen for the same Term, be elected, as follows.

Each State shall appoint, in such Manner as the Legislature thereof may direct, a Number of Electors, equal to the whole Number of Senators and Representatives to which the State may be entitled in the Congress: but no Senator or Representative, or Person holding an Office of Trust or Profit under the United States, shall be appointed an Elector.

~~The Electors shall meet in their respective States, and vote by Ballot for two Persons, of whom one at least shall not be an Inhabitant of the same State with themselves. And they shall make a List of all the Persons voted for, and of the Number of Votes for each; which List they shall sign and certify, and transmit sealed to the Seat of the Government of the United States, directed to the President of the Senate. The President of the Senate shall, in the Presence of the Senate and House of Representatives, open all the Certificates, and the Votes shall then be counted. The Person having the greatest Number of Votes shall be the President, if such Number be a Majority of the whole Number of Electors appointed; and if there be more than one who have such Majority, and have an equal Number of Votes, then the House of Representatives shall immediately chuse by Ballot one of them for President; and if no Person have a Majority, then from the five highest on the List the said House shall in like Manner chuse the President. But in chusing the President, the Votes shall be taken by States, the Representation from each State having one Vote; A quorum for this Purpose shall consist of a Member or Members from two thirds of the States, and a Majority of all the States shall be necessary to a Choice. In every Case, after the Choice of the President, the Person having the greatest Number of Votes of the Electors shall be the Vice President. But if there should remain two or more who have equal Votes, the Senate shall chuse from them by Ballot the Vice President~~.

The Congress may determine the Time of chusing the Electors, and the Day on which they shall give their Votes; which Day shall be the same throughout the United States.

No Person except a natural born Citizen~~, or a Citizen of the United States, at the time of the Adoption of this Constitution~~, shall be eligible to the Office of President; neither shall any Person be eligible to that Office who shall not have attained to the Age of thirty five Years, and been fourteen Years a Resident within the United States.

In Case of the Removal of the President from Office, or of his Death, Resignation, or Inability to discharge the Powers and Duties of the said Office, the Same shall devolve on the Vice President, and the Congress

Executive Branch
The president is the chief of the executive branch. It is the job of the president to enforce the laws. The framers wanted the president's and vice president's term of office and manner of selection to be different from those of members of Congress. They decided on four-year terms, but they had a difficult time agreeing on how to select the president and vice president. The framers finally set up an electoral system, which varies greatly from our electoral process today. The Twelfth Amendment changed the process by requiring that separate ballots be cast for president and vice president. The rise of political parties has since changed the process even more.

In 1845 Congress set the Tuesday following the first Monday in November of every fourth year as the general election date for selecting presidential electors.

The youngest elected president was John F. Kennedy; he was 43 years old when he was inaugurated. (Theodore Roosevelt was 42 when he assumed office after the assassination of McKinley.) The oldest elected president was Ronald Reagan; he was 69 years old when he was inaugurated.

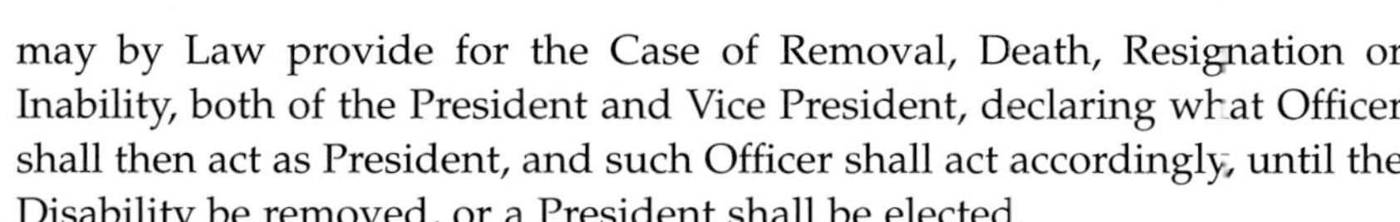

may by Law provide for the Case of Removal, Death, Resignation or Inability, both of the President and Vice President, declaring what Officer shall then act as President, and such Officer shall act accordingly, until the Disability be removed, or a President shall be elected.

The President shall, at stated Times, receive for his Services, a Compensation, which shall neither be increased nor diminished during the period for which he shall have been elected, and he shall not receive within that Period any other Emolument from the United States, or any of them.

Before he enter on the Execution of his Office, he shall take the following Oath or Affirmation:—"I do solemnly swear (or affirm) that I will faithfully execute the Office of President of the United States, and will to the best of my Ability, preserve, protect and defend the Constitution of the United States."

Section 2. The President shall be Commander in Chief of the Army and Navy of the United States, and of the Militia of the several States, when called into the actual Service of the United States; he may require the Opinion, in writing, of the principal Officer in each of the executive Departments, upon any Subject relating to the Duties of their respective Offices, and he shall have Power to grant Reprieves and Pardons for Offenses against the United States, except in Cases of Impeachment.

He shall have Power, by and with the Advice and Consent of the Senate, to make Treaties, provided two thirds of the Senators present concur; and he shall nominate, and by and with the Advice and Consent of the Senate, shall appoint Ambassadors, other public Ministers and Consuls, Judges of the supreme Court, and all other Officers of the United States, whose Appointments are not herein otherwise provided for, and which shall be established by Law: but the Congress may by Law vest the Appointment of such inferior Officers, as they think proper, in the President alone, in the Courts of Law, or in the Heads of Departments.

The President shall have Power to fill up all Vacancies that may happen during the Recess of the Senate, by granting Commissions which shall expire at the End of their next Session.

Section 3. He shall from time to time give to the Congress Information of the State of the Union, and recommend to their Consideration such Measures as he shall judge necessary and expedient; he may, on extraordinary Occasions, convene both Houses, or either of them, and in Case of Disagreement between them, with Respect to the Time of Adjournment, he may adjourn them to such Time as he shall think proper; he shall receive Ambassadors and other public Ministers; he shall take Care that the Laws be faithfully executed, and shall Commission all the Officers of the United States.

Emolument means "salary, or payment." In 1969 Congress set the president's salary at $200,000 per year. The president also receives an expense account of $50,000 per year. The president must pay taxes on both.

The oath of office is administered to the president by the chief justice of the U.S. Supreme Court. Washington added "So help me, God." All succeeding presidents have followed this practice.

The framers wanted to make sure that an elected representative of the people controlled the nation's military. Today, the president is in charge of the army, navy, air force, marines, and coast guard. Only Congress, however, can decide if the United States will declare war. This section also contains the basis for the formation of the president's cabinet. Every president, starting with George Washington, has appointed a cabinet.

Most of the president's appointments to office must be approved by the Senate.

Every year the president presents to Congress a State of the Union message. In this message, the president introduces and explains a legislative plan for the coming year. This clause states that one of the president's duties is to enforce the laws.

Cultural Diversity

First Ladies. The term *first lady* became common after the Civil War, but before then presidents' wives were referred to as Mrs. President and presidentress. Although first ladies are not mentioned in the Constitution, almost all presidents—even unmarried ones—have found someone to fill that role. For example, Dolley Madison served as first lady for widower Thomas Jefferson, before assuming that role for her own husband. Recent first ladies have done more than serve as their husband's hostesses, and some—such as Betty Ford and Rosalynn Carter—have suggested that the government should pay the first lady a salary.

Activity: Ask students to use the library or search the Internet through the HRW Web site to write a short biography of one first lady. They should pay particular attention to the role the first lady played in her husband's presidency. Have students present their biographies to the class, and lead a class discussion comparing the roles of the first lady over time.

go.hrw.com
SB1 First Ladies

Biography

John Marshall. During its early years, the Supreme Court was considered a fairly unimportant institution. When John Marshall was appointed chief justice in 1801, he and his colleagues had to meet in the basement of the Capitol because there was no Supreme Court building. Having served in the Revolutionary War, Marshall was a committed nationalist, who eventually established the Supreme Court as the final interpreter of the Constitution and made it into an important check on the power of Congress and the president.

Critical Thinking: How might Marshall's war experiences have shaped his ideas about the Constitution?

ANSWER: Having fought to gain independence, he would be committed to making sure that the constitutional system worked fairly. In particular, he might have wanted to ensure that no one branch of government could establish total control.

Section 4. The President, Vice President and all civil Officers of the United States, shall be removed from Office on Impeachment for, and Conviction of, Treason, Bribery, or other high Crimes and Misdemeanors.

ARTICLE III

Judicial Branch
The Articles of Confederation did not set up a federal court system. One of the first things that the framers of the Constitution agreed upon was to set up a national judiciary. With all the laws that Congress would be enacting, there would be a great need for a branch of government to interpret the laws. In the Judiciary Act of 1789, Congress provided for the establishment of lower courts, such as district courts, circuit courts of appeals, and various other federal courts. The judicial system provides a check on the legislative branch; it can declare a law unconstitutional.

Section 1. The judicial Power of the United States, shall be vested in one supreme Court, and in such inferior Courts as the Congress may from time to time ordain and establish. The Judges, both of the supreme and inferior Courts, shall hold their Offices during good Behaviour, and shall, at stated Times, receive for their Services, a Compensation, which shall not be diminished during their Continuance in Office.

Section 2. The judicial Power shall extend to all Cases, in Law and Equity, arising under this Constitution, the Laws of the United States, and Treaties made, or which shall be made, under their Authority;—to all Cases affecting Ambassadors, other public Ministers and Consuls;—to all Cases of admiralty and maritime Jurisdiction;—to Controversies to which the United States shall be a Party;—to Controversies between two or more States;— ~~between a State and Citizens of another State~~;— between Citizens of different States;—between Citizens of the same State claiming Lands under Grants of different States~~, and between a State, or the Citizens thereof, and foreign States, Citizens or Subjects~~.

In all Cases affecting Ambassadors, other public Ministers and Consuls, and those in which a State shall be Party, the supreme Court shall have original Jurisdiction. In all the other Cases before mentioned, the supreme Court shall have appellate Jurisdiction, both as to Law and fact, with such Exceptions, and under such Regulations as the Congress shall make.

The Trial of all Crimes, except in Cases of Impeachment, shall be by Jury; and such Trial shall be held in the State where the said Crimes shall have been committed; but when not committed within any State, the Trial shall be at such Place or Places as the Congress may by Law have directed.

Congress has the power to decide the punishment for treason, but it can punish only the guilty person. "Corruption of Blood" means punishing the family of a person who has committed treason. It is expressly forbidden by the Constitution.

Section 3. Treason against the United States, shall consist only in levying War against them, or in adhering to their Enemies, giving them Aid and Comfort. No Person shall be convicted of Treason unless on the Testimony of two Witnesses to the same overt Act, or on Confession in open Court.

The Congress shall have Power to declare the Punishment of Treason, but no Attainder of Treason shall work Corruption of Blood, or Forfeiture except during the Life of the Person attainted.

ARTICLE IV

Section 1. Full Faith and Credit shall be given in each State to the public Acts, Records, and judicial Proceedings of every other State. And the

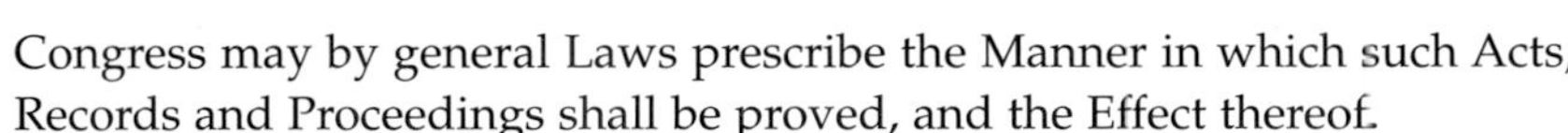

Congress may by general Laws prescribe the Manner in which such Acts, Records and Proceedings shall be proved, and the Effect thereof.

Section 2. The Citizens of each State shall be entitled to all Privileges and Immunities of Citizens in the several States.

A Person charged in any State with Treason, Felony, or other Crime, who shall flee from Justice, and be found in another State, shall on Demand of the executive Authority of the State from which he fled, be delivered up, to be removed to the State having Jurisdiction of the Crime.

~~No Person held to Service of Labour in one State, under the Laws thereof, escaping into another, shall, in Consequence of any Law or Regulation therein, be discharged from such Service or Labour, but shall be delivered up on Claim of the Party to whom such Service or Labour may be due~~.

The States
States must honor the laws, records, and court decisions of other states. A person cannot escape a legal obligation by moving from one state to another.

Section 3. New States may be admitted by the Congress into this Union; but no new State shall be formed or erected within the Jurisdiction of any other State; nor any State be formed by the Junction of two or more States, or Parts of States, without the Consent of the Legislatures of the States concerned as well as of the Congress.

The Congress shall have Power to dispose of and make all needful Rules and Regulations respecting the Territory or other Property belonging to the United States; and nothing in this Constitution shall be so construed as to Prejudice any Claims of the United States, or of any particular State.

Section 4. The United States shall guarantee to every State in this Union a Republican Form of Government, and shall protect each of them against Invasion; and on Application of the Legislature, or of the Executive (when the Legislature cannot be convened) against domestic Violence.

Section 3 permits Congress to admit new states to the Union. When a group of people living in an area that is not part of an existing state wishes to form a new state, it asks Congress for permission to do so. The people then write a state constitution and offer it to Congress for approval. The state constitution must set up a representative form of government and must not in any way contradict the federal Constitution. If a majority of Congress approves of the state constitution, the state is admitted as a member of the United States of America.

ARTICLE V

The Congress, whenever two thirds of both Houses shall deem it necessary, shall propose Amendments to this Constitution, or, on the Application of the Legislatures of two thirds of the several States, shall call a Convention for proposing Amendments, which, in either Case, shall be valid to all Intents and Purposes, as Part of this Constitution, when ratified by the Legislatures of three fourths of the several States, or by Conventions in three fourths thereof, as the one or the other Mode of Ratification may be proposed by the Congress; Provided that ~~no Amendment which may be made prior to the Year One thousand eight hundred and eight shall in any Manner affect the first and fourth Clauses in the Ninth Section of the first Article; and that~~ no State, without its Consent, shall be deprived of its equal Suffrage in the Senate.

The Amendment Process
America's founders may not have realized just how enduring the Constitution would be, but they did set up a system for changing or adding to it. They did not want to make it easy to change the Constitution. There are two ways in which changes can be proposed to the states and two ways in which states can approve the changes and make them part of the Constitution.

Constitutional Heritage

Admission of New States. Although the framers of the Constitution wanted to allow new states to be admitted, many also wanted to preserve the power of the original states. One delegate suggested that the total number of representatives in the lower house from the new states should never exceed the total from the original states.

Critical Thinking: If this plan had become part of the Constitution, how might it have affected current U.S. government?

ANSWER: States along the Atlantic would have a disproportionate amount of power.

Geographic Diversity

Texas. The admission of Texas to the Union was extremely controversial, and eventually passed by only one vote. Many people felt that at least four additional states could be formed out of the large territory of Texas. However, Texas retains the same physical size as when it was admitted.

Critical Thinking: What obstacles does the Constitution provide to dividing up a state once it is admitted to the Union?

ANSWER: The state legislature and the Congress have to consent.

Historical Sidelight

Amendments. Since the ratification of the Constitution, more than 10,000 amendments have been proposed, many with little hope of passing. For example, one amendment proposed changing the country's name to the United States of Earth because it was possible to admit new states until "every nation on earth has become part of [the United States]."

Critical Thinking: Why might someone propose an amendment with little chance of passage?

ANSWER: Proposing an amendment might bring public attention to an issue.

Cultural Diversity

The Signers. At age 26, Jonathan Dayton was the youngest person to sign the Constitution. Benjamin Franklin, at 81, was the oldest. Franklin's signature was particularly important. As one of the most renowned men in America, he gave respectability to the new document.

Critical Thinking: Why might having such age diversity be important to developing a lasting Constitution?

ANSWER: The age diversity brought different perspectives and experiences to the framers' efforts.

National Supremacy
One of the biggest problems facing the delegates to the Constitutional Convention was the question of what would happen if a state law and a federal law conflicted. Which law would be followed? Who would decide? The second clause of Article VI answers those questions. When a federal law and a state law disagree, the federal law overrides the state law. The Constitution and other federal laws are the "supreme Law of the Land." This clause is often called the supremacy clause.

ARTICLE VI

All Debts contracted and Engagements entered into, before the Adoption of this Constitution, shall be as valid against the United States under this Constitution, as under the Confederation.

This Constitution, and the Laws of the United States which shall be made in Pursuance thereof; and all Treaties made, or which shall be made, under the Authority of the United States, shall be the supreme Law of the Land; and the Judges in every State shall be bound thereby, any Thing in the Constitution or Laws of any State to the Contrary notwithstanding.

The Senators and Representatives before mentioned, and the Members of the several State Legislatures, and all executive and judicial Officers, both of the United States and of the several States, shall be bound by Oath or Affirmation, to support this Constitution; but no religious Test shall ever be required as a Qualification to any Office or public Trust under the United States.

Ratification
The Articles of Confederation called for all 13 states to approve any revision to the Articles. The Constitution required that 9 out of the 13 states would be needed to ratify the Constitution. The first state to ratify was Delaware, on December 7, 1787. Almost two and a half years later, on May 29, 1790, Rhode Island became the last state to ratify the Constitution.

ARTICLE VII

The Ratification of the Conventions of nine States, shall be sufficient for the Establishment of this Constitution between the States so ratifying the Same.

Done in Convention by the Unanimous Consent of the States present the Seventeenth Day of September in the Year of our Lord one thousand seven hundred and Eighty seven and of the Independence of the United States of America the Twelfth. In witness whereof We have hereunto subscribed our Names,

George Washington—
President and deputy from Virginia

NEW HAMPSHIRE
John Langdon
Nicholas Gilman

DELAWARE
George Read
Gunning Bedford, Jr.
John Dickinson
Richard Bassett
Jacob Broom

MASSACHUSETTS
Nathaniel Gorham
Rufus King

MARYLAND
James McHenry
Daniel of St. Thomas Jenifer
Daniel Carroll

CONNECTICUT
William Samuel Johnson
Roger Sherman

NEW YORK
Alexander Hamilton

VIRGINIA
John Blair
James Madison, Jr.

NEW JERSEY
William Livingston
David Brearley
William Paterson
Jonathan Dayton

NORTH CAROLINA
William Blount
Richard Dobbs Spaight
Hugh Williamson

PENNSYLVANIA
Benjamin Franklin
Thomas Mifflin
Robert Morris
George Clymer
Thomas FitzSimons
Jared Ingersoll
James Wilson
Gouverneur Morris

SOUTH CAROLINA
John Rutledge
Charles Cotesworth Pinckney
Charles Pinckney
Pierce Butler

GEORGIA
William Few
Abraham Baldwin

Attest:
William Jackson, Secretary

THE AMENDMENTS

Articles in addition to, and Amendment of the Constitution of the United States of America, proposed by Congress, and ratified by the Legislatures of the several States, pursuant to the fifth Article of the original Constitution.

[The First through Tenth Amendments, now known as the Bill of Rights, were proposed to the states for ratification on September 25, 1789, and declared in force on December 15, 1791.]

First Amendment

Congress shall make no law respecting an establishment of religion, or prohibiting the free exercise thereof; or abridging the freedom of speech, or of the press; or the right of the people peaceably to assemble, and to petition the Government for a redress of grievances.

Second Amendment

A well regulated Militia, being necessary to the security of a free State, the right of the people to keep and bear Arms, shall not be infringed.

Third Amendment

No Soldier shall, in time of peace, be quartered in any house, without the consent of the Owner, nor in time of war, but in a manner to be prescribed by law.

Fourth Amendment

The right of the people to be secure in their persons, houses, papers, and effects, against unreasonable searches and seizures, shall not be violated, and no Warrants shall issue, but upon probable cause, supported by Oath or affirmation, and particularly describing the place to be searched, and the persons or things to be seized.

Fifth Amendment

No person shall be held to answer for a capital, or otherwise infamous crime, unless on a presentment or indictment of a Grand Jury, except in cases arising in the land or naval forces, or in the Militia, when in actual service in time of War or public danger; nor shall any person be subject for the same offence to be twice put in jeopardy of life or limb; nor shall be compelled in any criminal case to be a witness against himself, nor be deprived of life, liberty, or property, without due process of law; nor shall private property be taken for public use, without just compensation.

Sixth Amendment

In all criminal prosecutions, the accused shall enjoy the right to a speedy and public trial, by an impartial jury of the State and district wherein the

Bill of Rights
One of the conditions set by several states for ratifying the Constitution was the inclusion of a bill of rights. Many people feared that a stronger central government might take away basic rights of the people that had been guaranteed in state constitutions. If the three words that begin the preamble—"We the people"—were truly meant, then the rights of the people needed to be protected.

The First Amendment protects—among other freedoms—freedom of speech—and forbids Congress to make any "law respecting an establishment of religion" or restraining the freedom to practice religion as one chooses.

A law enforcement official may enter a person's home with a search warrant, which allows the law official to look for evidence that could convict someone of committing a crime.

The Fifth, Sixth, and Seventh Amendments describe the procedures that courts must follow when trying people accused of crimes. The Fifth Amendment guarantees that no one can be put on trial for a serious crime unless a grand jury agrees that the evidence justifies doing so. It also says that a person cannot be tried twice for the same crime.

The Sixth Amendment makes several guarantees, including a prompt trial and a trial by a jury chosen from the state and

Global Relations

Thomas Jefferson. At the time of the Constitutional Convention, Thomas Jefferson was in Paris as part of a diplomatic mission to France. Jefferson became increasingly convinced of the evils of monarchy as he saw the violations of civil liberties that the French people had to tolerate. For example, the king could issue a *lettre du cachet*, which could order someone exiled or imprisoned without recourse. In addition, the aristocracy could destroy land without having to reimburse the owner for the damage. In his correspondence to delegates to the Constitutional Convention, Jefferson strongly advocated the inclusion of a bill of rights.

Critical Thinking: How might Jefferson's experiences in France have made him insist on including a bill of rights in the Constitution?

ANSWER: Having witnessed what could happen if individual rights were violated, Thomas Jefferson would probably have been more convinced than many other American lawmakers of the importance of protecting those rights.

Linking Past to Present

Civil Liberties. Throughout the 1900s the Supreme Court has extended the coverage of the civil liberties in the Bill of Rights. For some time, justices ruled that the Bill of Rights did not override state laws. Although the Fourteenth Amendment stated that the states could not deprive citizens of their constitutional rights, few justices changed their interpretations. In the mid-1900s, Justice Hugo Black began to reinterpret the Fourteenth Amendment, believing that the guarantees in the Bill of Rights were absolute. Most justices have tempered this position, believing that these guarantees are restrained by competing social interests.

Activity: Have students bring in newspaper articles that deal with the exercise of civil liberties. Using these articles to start discussion, have students describe what they think are proper and improper limitations of civil liberties.

district in which the crime was committed. The Sixth Amendment also states that an accused person must be told why he or she is being tried and promises that an accused person has the right to be defended by a lawyer.

crime shall have been committed, which district shall have been previously ascertained by law, and to be informed of the nature and cause of the accusation; to be confronted with the witnesses against him; to have compulsory process for obtaining witnesses in his favor, and to have the Assistance of Counsel for his defence.

The Seventh Amendment guarantees a trial by jury in cases that involve more than $20, but in modern times, usually much more money is at stake before a case is heard in federal court.

Seventh Amendment

In Suits at common law, where the value in controversy shall exceed twenty dollars, the right of trial by jury shall be preserved, and no fact tried by a jury, shall be otherwise re-examined in any Court of the United States, than according to the rules of the common law.

Eighth Amendment

Excessive bail shall not be required, nor excessive fines imposed, nor cruel and unusual punishments inflicted.

The Ninth and Tenth Amendments were added because not every right of the people or of the states could be listed in the Constitution.

Ninth Amendment

The enumeration in the Constitution, of certain rights, shall not be construed to deny or disparage others retained by the people.

Tenth Amendment

The powers not delegated to the United States by the Constitution, nor prohibited by it to the States, are reserved to the States respectively, or to the people.

Eleventh Amendment

[Proposed March 5, 1794; declared ratified January 8, 1798]

The Judicial power of the United States shall not be construed to extend to any suit in law or equity, commenced or prosecuted against one of the United States by Citizens of another State, or by Citizens or Subjects of any Foreign State.

The Twelfth Amendment changed the election procedure for president and vice president. This amendment became necessary because of the growth of political parties. Before this amendment, electors voted without distinguishing between president and vice president. Whoever received the most votes became president, and whoever received the next highest number of votes became vice president.

Twelfth Amendment

[Proposed December 9, 1803; declared ratified September 25, 1804]

The Electors shall meet in their respective states, and vote by ballot for President and Vice-President, one of whom, at least, shall not be an inhabitant of the same state with themselves; they shall name in their ballots the person voted for as President, and in distinct ballots the person voted for as Vice-President, and they shall make distinct lists of all persons voted for as President, and of all persons voted for as Vice-President, and of the number of votes for each, which lists they shall sign and certify, and transmit sealed to the seat of the government of the United States, directed to the President of the Senate;—The President of the Senate shall, in the presence of the Senate and House of Representatives, open all the certificates and the votes

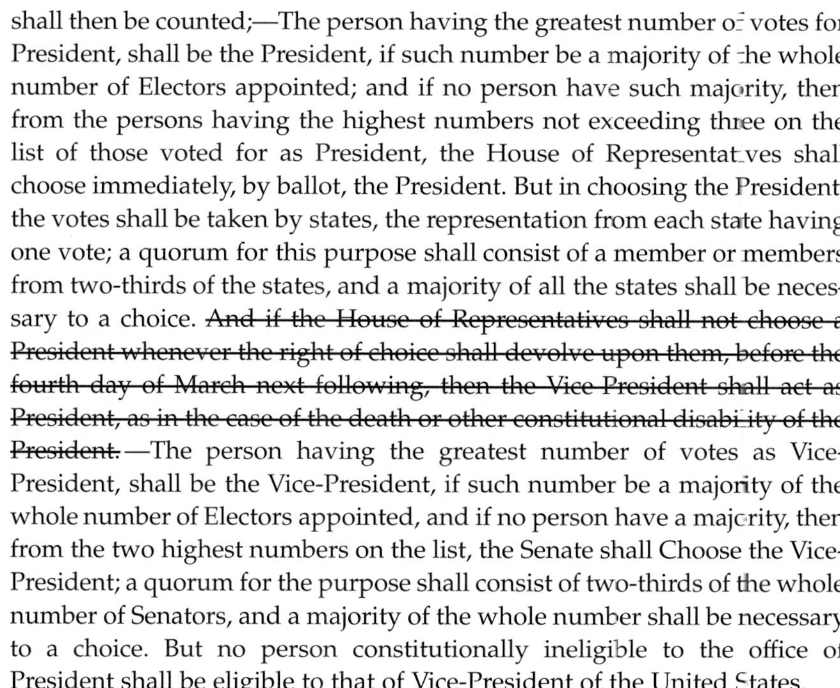

shall then be counted;—The person having the greatest number of votes for President, shall be the President, if such number be a majority of the whole number of Electors appointed; and if no person have such majority, then from the persons having the highest numbers not exceeding three on the list of those voted for as President, the House of Representatives shall choose immediately, by ballot, the President. But in choosing the President, the votes shall be taken by states, the representation from each state having one vote; a quorum for this purpose shall consist of a member or members from two-thirds of the states, and a majority of all the states shall be necessary to a choice. ~~And if the House of Representatives shall not choose a President whenever the right of choice shall devolve upon them, before the fourth day of March next following, then the Vice President shall act as President, as in the case of the death or other constitutional disability of the President.~~—The person having the greatest number of votes as Vice-President, shall be the Vice-President, if such number be a majority of the whole number of Electors appointed, and if no person have a majority, then from the two highest numbers on the list, the Senate shall Choose the Vice-President; a quorum for the purpose shall consist of two-thirds of the whole number of Senators, and a majority of the whole number shall be necessary to a choice. But no person constitutionally ineligible to the office of President shall be eligible to that of Vice-President of the United States.

Thirteenth Amendment

[Proposed January 31, 1865; declared ratified December 18, 1865]

Section 1. Neither slavery nor involuntary servitude, except as a punishment for crime whereof the party shall have been duly convicted, shall exist within the United States, or any place subject to their jurisdiction.

Section 2. Congress shall have power to enforce this article by appropriate legislation.

Although some slaves had been freed during the Civil War, slavery was not abolished until the Thirteenth Amendment took effect.

Fourteenth Amendment

[Proposed June 16, 1866; declared ratified July 28, 1868]

Section 1. All persons born or naturalized in the United States, and subject to the jurisdiction thereof, are citizens of the United States and of the State wherein they reside. No State shall make or enforce any law which shall abridge the privileges or immunities of citizens of the United States; nor shall any State deprive any person of life, liberty, or property, without due process of law; nor deny to any person within its jurisdiction the equal protection of the laws.

Section 2. Representatives shall be apportioned among the several States according to their respective numbers, counting the whole number of per-

In 1833 the Supreme Court ruled that the Bill of Rights limited the federal government but not the state governments. This ruling was interpreted to mean that states were able to keep African Americans from becoming state citizens: if African Americans were not citizens, they were not protected by the Bill of Rights. The Fourteenth Amendment defines citizenship and prevents states from interfering in the rights of citizens of the United States.

Citizenship and Democracy

Postwar Amendments. Three amendments—the Thirteenth, Fourteenth, and Fifteenth—were initially meant to respond to changes demanded by the northern victory in the Civil War. Many sections in these amendments deal exclusively with wartime issues. At the time it was passed, many southerners interpreted the Fourteenth Amendment as a way for the North to punish them for their "rebellion" by making the South maintain African American civil rights. However, scholars have argued that the Fourteenth Amendment remains the most important addition to the Constitution since the Bill of Rights because of the due process and equal protection clauses that it included.

Critical Thinking: Why might scholars believe the Fourteenth Amendment is so important?

ANSWER: The Fourteenth Amendment redefined citizenship and for the first time appeared to guarantee African Americans their civil rights. However, it also made amendments apply to state law.

Daily Life

Suffrage. The passage of the Fourteenth and Fifteenth Amendments dramatically increased African Americans' political participation. Strikes broke out among African American workers throughout the South. The workers staged sit-ins on segregated carriages in Richmond, Virginia, and when police tried to stop their protests, angry crowds formed, demanding, "Let's have our rights." Almost every institution of black life, particularly the church, worked to mobilize the African American vote and to educate new voters. So many African American laborers attended the Republican state convention in Virginia that Richmond's tobacco factories had to close. African Americans' enthusiasm for their new rights could be summed up by one African American who wrote, "You can teach me the law, but you cannot [teach] me what justice is."

Critical Thinking: Why might African Americans after the Civil War have found the vote to be so important?

ANSWER: Since African Americans had been denied any form of political participation, they hoped that the vote would help them become full citizens of the United States and accepted members of their community.

sons in each State~~, excluding Indians not taxed~~. But when the right to vote at any election for the choice of electors for President and Vice President of the United States, Representatives in Congress, the Executive and Judicial officers of a State, or the members of the Legislature thereof, is denied to any of the ~~male~~ inhabitants of such State, ~~being twenty one years of age,~~ and citizens of the United States, or in any way abridged, except for participation in rebellion, or other crime, the basis of representation therein shall be reduced in the proportion which the number of such ~~male~~ citizens shall bear to the whole number of ~~male~~ citizens ~~twenty one years of age~~ in such State.

Section 3. No person shall be a Senator or Representative in Congress, or elector of President and Vice President, or hold any office, civil or military, under the United States, or under any State, who, having previously taken an oath, as a member of Congress, or as an officer of the United States, or as a member of any State legislature, or as an executive or judicial officer of any State, to support the Constitution of the United States, shall have engaged in insurrection or rebellion against the same, or given aid or comfort to the enemies thereof. But Congress may by a vote of two-thirds of each House, remove such disability.

Section 4. The validity of the public debt of the United States, authorized by law, including debts incurred for payment of pensions and bounties for services in suppressing insurrection or rebellion, shall not be questioned. But neither the United States nor any State shall assume or pay any debt or obligation incurred in aid of insurrection or rebellion against the United States~~, or any claim for the loss of emancipation of any slave~~; but all such debts, obligations and claims shall be held illegal and void.

Section 5. The Congress shall have power to enforce, by appropriate legislation, the provisions of this article.

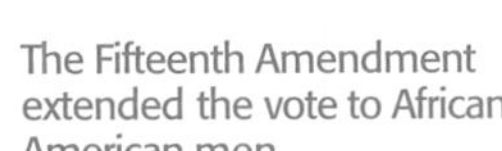
The Fifteenth Amendment extended the vote to African American men.

Fifteenth Amendment

[Proposed February 27, 1869; declared ratified March 30, 1870]

Section 1. The right of citizens of the United States to vote shall not be denied or abridged by the United States or by any State on account of race, color, or previous condition of servitude.

Section 2. The Congress shall have power to enforce this article by appropriate legislation.

Sixteenth Amendment

[Proposed July 12, 1909; declared ratified February 25, 1913]

The Congress shall have power to lay and collect taxes on incomes, from whatever source derived, without apportionment among the several States, and without regard to any census or enumeration.

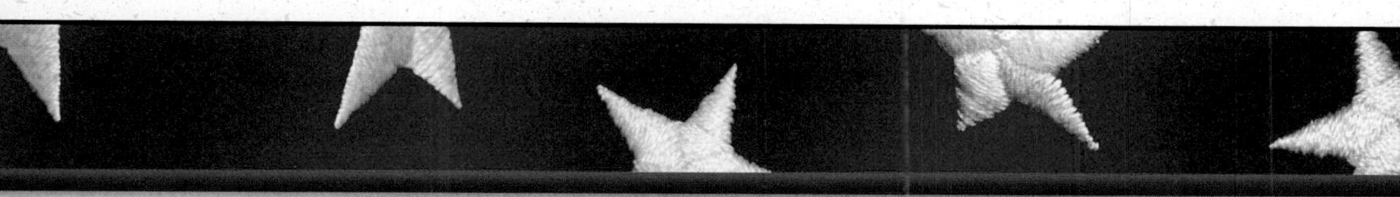

Seventeenth Amendment

[Proposed May 13, 1912; declared ratified May 31, 1913]

The Senate of the United States shall be composed of two Senators from each State, elected by the people thereof, for six years; and each Senator shall have one vote. The electors in each State shall have the qualifications requisite for electors of the most numerous branch of the State legislatures.

When vacancies happen in the representation of any State in the Senate, the executive authority of such State shall issue writs of election to fill such vacancies: *Provided,* That the legislature of any State may empower the executive thereof to make temporary appointments until the people fill the vacancies by election as the legislature may direct.

~~This amendment shall not be so construed as to affect the election or term of any Senator chosen before it becomes valid as part of the Constitution.~~

The Seventeenth Amendment requires that senators be elected directly by the people instead of by the state legislature.

Eighteenth Amendment

[Proposed December 18, 1917; declared ratified January 29, 1919; repealed by the Twenty-first Amendment December 5, 1933]

~~**Section 1.** After one year from the ratification of this article the manufacture, sale, or transportation of intoxicating liquors within, the importation thereof into, or the exportation thereof from the United States and all territory subject to the jurisdiction thereof for beverage purposes is hereby prohibited.~~

~~**Section 2.** The Congress and the several States shall have concurrent power to enforce this article by appropriate legislation.~~

~~**Section 3.** This article shall be inoperative unless it shall have been ratified as an amendment to the Constitution by the legislatures of the several States, as provided in the Constitution, within seven years from the date of the submission hereof to the States by the Congress.~~

Although many people felt that the Eighteenth Amendment was good for the health and welfare of the American people, it was repealed 14 years later.

Nineteenth Amendment

[Proposed June 4, 1919; declared ratified August 26, 1920]

The right of citizens of the United States to vote shall not be denied or abridged by the United States or by any State on account of sex.

Congress shall have power to enforce this article by appropriate legislation.

Abigail Adams was disappointed that the Declaration of Independence and the Constitution did not specifically include women. It took almost 150 years and much campaigning by groups for women's suffrage to finally achieve voting privileges.

Twentieth Amendment

[Proposed March 2, 1932; declared ratified February 6, 1933]

Section 1. The terms of the President and Vice-President shall end at noon on the 20th day of January, and the terms of Senators and Representatives

Biography

Elizabeth Cady Stanton. The efforts of Elizabeth Cady Stanton, a tireless crusader for women's rights, contributed to the passage of the Nineteenth Amendment in 1920. Although she was active in the antislavery cause, she opposed passage of the Fourteenth and Fifteenth Amendments—which gave citizenship and the right to vote to African American men—because these laws did not include women. At her urging, in 1878 Senator Aaron A. Sargent of California introduced a women's suffrage amendment to the Constitution. This amendment was introduced and defeated repeatedly throughout Stanton's lifetime. She died in 1902, eighteen years before the passage of the amendment for which she had worked so hard.

Critical Thinking: Do you think that Stanton was right to oppose the Fourteenth and Fifteenth Amendments? Explain your answer.

ANSWER: Students' answers will vary. Some may say that she was right to say that women deserved the vote as much as African American men; however, some may say that she was wrong to oppose voting rights for African American men simply because women would not also get the vote.

Biography

George W. Norris. During his long congressional career, George W. Norris not only created and worked to pass the Twentieth Amendment but also worked for the introduction of presidential primaries and for the direct election of senators. Although he was always a Republican, Norris rarely voted along party lines. In defense of his independence, he claimed he "would rather be right than regular."

Activity: Have students find examples of recent political reforms. Then have them draft bills or constitutional amendments that could be used to enact the reforms.

In the original Constitution, a newly elected president and Congress did not take office until March 4, which was four months after the November election. The officials who were leaving office were called lame ducks because they had little influence during those four months. The Twentieth Amendment changed the date that the new president and Congress take office. Members of Congress now take office on January 3, and the president takes office on January 20.

at noon on the 3d day of January, of the years in which such terms would have ended if this article had not been ratified; and the terms of their successors shall then begin.

Section 2. The Congress shall assemble at least once in every year, and such meeting shall begin at noon on the 3d day of January, unless they shall by law appoint a different day.

Section 3. If, at the time fixed for the beginning of the term of the President, the President elect shall have died, the Vice-President elect shall become President. If a President shall not have been chosen before the time fixed for the beginning of his term, or if the President elect shall have failed to qualify, then the Vice-President elect shall act as President until a President shall have qualified; and the Congress may by law provide for the case wherein neither a President elect nor a Vice-President elect shall have qualified, declaring who shall then act as President, or the manner in which one who is to act shall be selected, and such person shall act accordingly until a President or Vice-President shall have qualified.

Section 4. The Congress may by law provide for the case of the death of any of the persons from whom the House of Representatives may choose a President whenever the right of choice shall have devolved upon them, and for the case of the death of any of the persons from whom the Senate may choose a Vice-President whenever the right of choice shall have devolved upon them.

~~**Section 5.** Sections 1 and 2 shall take effect on the 15th day of October following the ratification of this article.~~

~~**Section 6.** This article shall be inoperative unless it shall have been ratified as an amendment to the Constitution by the legislatures of three-fourths of the several States within seven years from the date of its submission.~~

The Twenty-first Amendment is the only amendment that has been ratified by state conventions rather than by state legislatures.

Twenty-first Amendment

[Proposed February 20, 1933; declared ratified December 5, 1933]

Section 1. The eighteenth article of amendment to the Constitution of the United States is hereby repealed.

Section 2. The transportation or importation into any State, Territory, or possession of the United States for delivery or use therein of intoxicating liquors, in violation of the laws thereof, is hereby prohibited.

~~**Section 3.** This article shall be inoperative unless it shall have been ratified as an amendment to the Constitution by conventions in the several States, as provided in the Constitution, within seven years from the date of the submission hereof to the States by the Congress.~~

Twenty-second Amendment

[Proposed March 21, 1947; declared ratified February 26, 1951]

Section 1. No person shall be elected to the office of the President more than twice, and no person who has held the office of President, or acted as President, for more than two years of a term to which some other person was elected President shall be elected to the office of the President more than once. ~~But this Article shall not apply to any person holding the office of President when this Article was proposed by the Congress, and shall not prevent any person who may be holding the office of President, or acting as President, during the term within which this Article becomes operative from holding the office of President or acting as President during the remainder of such term.~~

~~**Section 2.** This article shall be inoperative unless it shall have been ratified as an amendment to the Constitution by the legislatures of three-fourths of the several States within seven years from the date of its submission to the States by the Congress.~~

From the time of President Washington's administration, it was a custom for presidents to serve no more than two terms of office. Franklin D. Roosevelt, however, was elected to four terms. The Twenty-second Amendment made into law the old custom of limiting a president to no more than two terms.

Twenty-third Amendment

[Proposed June 16, 1960; declared ratified March 29, 1961]

Section 1. The District constituting the seat of Government of the United States shall appoint in such manner as the Congress may direct:

A number of electors of President and Vice-President equal to the whole number of Senators and Representatives in Congress to which the District would be entitled if it were a State, but in no event more than the least populous state; they shall be in addition to those appointed by the States, but they shall be considered, for the purposes of the election of President and Vice-President, to be electors appointed by a State; and they shall meet in the District and perform such duties as provided by the twelfth article of amendment.

Section 2. The Congress shall have power to enforce this article by appropriate legislation.

Until the ratification of the Twenty-third Amendment, the people of Washington, D.C., could not vote in presidential elections.

Twenty-fourth Amendment

[Proposed August 27, 1962; declared ratified January 23, 1964]

Section 1. The right of citizens of the United States to vote in any primary or other election for President or Vice-President, for electors for President or Vice-President, or for Senator or Representative in Congress, shall not be denied or abridged by the United States or any State by reason of failure to pay any poll tax or other tax.

Citizenship and Democracy

Poll Tax. Congress started trying to end the poll tax in 1939. After Reconstruction, 11 southern states imposed the tax, 5 of which still levied it in 1964. The poll tax was often explicitly adopted to discriminate against African American voters. For example, when the poll tax was passed in Virginia in 1902, one representative said, "Discrimination! Why, that is precisely what we propose."

Critical Thinking: Why might an amendment be necessary for ending the poll tax?

ANSWER: because Congress has no power over state election policies

Historical Sidelight

Woodrow Wilson. Realization of the need for the Twenty-fifth Amendment began during Woodrow Wilson's term. In 1919 Wilson suffered a stroke and could not meet with the cabinet for seven months. While the president was ill, his vice president, Thomas Marshall, made it clear that he did not want to serve as president. Instead, the seriously ill Wilson conducted government affairs through his wife, Edith.

Critical Thinking: How can the U.S. government continue to run even when the head of state is ill?

ANSWER: The system of checks and balances provides a framework for the government to continue.

Constitutional Heritage

Presidential Succession. The rules for determining presidential succession have been amended several times, but the line of succession has never been tested past the vice president. Of the nine vice presidents who have succeeded presidents who have died or resigned, only four have been re-elected to a full term.

Activity: Have students research and draw a chart of the line of succession for the current presidency.

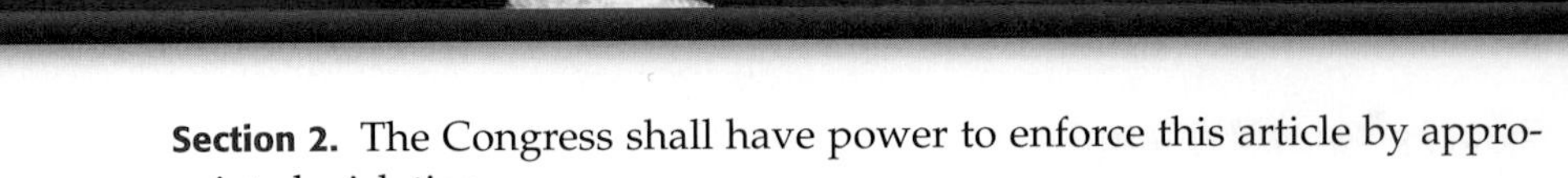

Section 2. The Congress shall have power to enforce this article by appropriate legislation.

The illness of President Eisenhower in the 1950s and the assassination of President Kennedy in 1963 were the events behind the Twenty-fifth Amendment. The Constitution did not provide a clear-cut method for a vice president to take over for a disabled president or upon the death of a president. This amendment provides for filling the office of the vice president if a vacancy occurs, and it provides a way for the vice president—or someone else in the line of succession—to take over if the president is unable to perform the duties of that office.

Twenty-fifth Amendment

[Proposed July 6, 1965; declared ratified February 10, 1967]

Section 1. In case of the removal of the President from office or of his death or resignation, the Vice-President shall become President.

Section 2. Whenever there is a vacancy in the office of the Vice-President, the President shall nominate a Vice-President who shall take office upon confirmation by a majority vote of both Houses of Congress.

Section 3. Whenever the President transmits to the President pro tempore of the Senate and the Speaker of the House of Representatives his written declaration that he is unable to discharge the powers and duties of his office, and until he transmits to them a written declaration to the contrary, such powers and duties shall be discharged by the Vice-President as Acting President.

Section 4. Whenever the Vice-President and a majority of either the principal officers of the executive departments or of such other body as Congress may by law provide, transmit to the President pro tempore of the Senate and the Speaker of the House of Representatives their written declaration that the President is unable to discharge the powers and duties of his office, the Vice-President shall immediately assume the powers and duties of the office as Acting President.

Thereafter, when the President transmits to the President pro tempore of the Senate and the Speaker of the House of Representatives his written declaration that no inability exists, he shall resume the powers and duties of his office unless the Vice-President and a majority of either the principal officers of the executive department or of such other body as Congress may by law provide, transmit within four days to the President pro tempore of the Senate and the Speaker of the House of Representatives their written declaration that the President is unable to discharge the powers and duties of his office. Thereupon Congress shall decide the issue, assembling within forty-eight hours for that purpose if not in session. If the Congress, within twenty-one days after receipt of the latter written declaration, or, if Congress is not in session, within twenty-one days after Congress is required to assemble, determines by two-thirds vote of both Houses that the President is unable to discharge the powers and duties of his office, the Vice-President shall continue to discharge the same as Acting President; otherwise, the President shall resume the powers and duties of his office.

Twenty-sixth Amendment

[Proposed March 10, 1971; declared ratified July 5, 1971]

Section 1. The right of citizens of the United States, who are eighteen years of age or older, to vote shall not be denied or abridged by the United States or by any State on account of age.

Section 2. The Congress shall have power to enforce this article by appropriate legislation.

Twenty-seventh Amendment

[Proposed September 25, 1789; declared ratified May 7, 1992]

No law, varying the compensation for the services of the Senators and Representatives, shall take effect, until an election of Representatives shall have intervened.

The Voting Act of 1970 tried to set the voting age at 18. However, the Supreme Court ruled that the act set the voting age for national elections only, not state or local elections. This ruling would make necessary several different ballots at elections. The Twenty-sixth Amendment gave 18-year-old citizens the right to vote in all elections.

Separation of Power and Checks and Balances

LEGISLATIVE BRANCH (Congress)	writes the laws; confirms presidential appointments; ratifies treaties; grants money; declares war
EXECUTIVE BRANCH (President)	proposes laws; administers the laws; commands armed forces; appoints ambassadors and other officials; conducts foreign policy; negotiates treaties
JUDICIAL BRANCH (Supreme Court)	interprets the Constitution and other laws; reviews lower-court decisions

Legislative → Executive: may reject appointments; may reject treaties; may withhold funding for presidential initiatives; may impeach president; may override a veto

Executive → Legislative: may adjourn Congress in certain situations; may veto bills

Legislative → Judicial: may propose constitutional amendments to overrule judicial decisions; may impeach Supreme Court justices; may reject appointments to the Supreme Court

Judicial → Legislative: may declare laws unconstitutional

Judicial → Executive: may declare executive actions unconstitutional

Executive → Judicial: appoints judges

Constitutional Heritage

Congressional Pay Raises. Ironically, one of the latest constitutional amendments to pass was proposed by framer James Madison. Although amendments that have been passed in recent decades have included a deadline for passage, Madison never included one for what became the Twenty-seventh Amendment. The amendment states that congressional pay raises cannot take effect until a new Congress meets. After more than 200 years, Michigan became the required 38th state to approve the amendment. Madison had suggested the amendment in 1789, along with the other amendments that eventually made up the Bill of Rights. However, only 6 states ratified the amendment—out of the 11 needed to pass it—and it was largely forgotten until the 1980s, when an aide to a Texas legislator began a crusade to get it passed.

Critical Thinking: Do you think the issue of congressional pay raises is more important now than it was in 1789?

ANSWER: Students' answers will vary. Some may say it is more important now because of budgetary concerns. Others may think that it was more important in 1789, when legislators may have needed guidance in allocating pay raises.

Section 2 Lesson Plan

OBJECTIVES

- **Discuss freedoms listed in the First Amendment.**
- **Identify the amendments that reflect issues with pre–Revolutionary War British officials, and describe how each addresses one of these concerns.**
- **Examine the rights that the amendments provide to people accused of crimes.**

FOCUS

Motivate Before Reading

Ask students to identify the rights they possess as U.S. citizens. *(Students may identify freedom of speech, religion, or the press.)* Ask students what protects these rights. Explain to students that these rights are protected in the Bill of Rights of the U.S. Constitution. Tell them that in this section they will learn about some protections provided by the Bill of Rights.

Section 2 RESOURCES

PRINT

- ★ Guided Reading Strategies 2.2
- ★ Graphic Organizer 2: The Bill of Rights
- ★ Section 2 Review, p. 69
- ★ Daily Quiz 2.2

MULTIMEDIA

- ★ *Teaching Resources CD–ROM*, Lesson 2.2
- ★ *Exploring America's Past Civics and Citizenship Skills* Video Segment: The Roles of a Citizen; *Teacher's Guide*, pp. 49–52

SHELTERED ENGLISH

- ★ Main Idea Activities for Reteaching and Sheltered English 2.2

The Bill of Rights

Reading Focus

What are the main freedoms of the First Amendment, and why are they important?

Which constitutional amendments reflect issues with pre-Revolutionary War British officials, and how do the amendments address those concerns?

What rights do the amendments give to people accused of crimes?

Key Terms

petition
search warrant
due process
indict
double jeopardy
eminent domain

JAMES MADISON WAS WORRIED. It looked as if the Constitution might not be ratified. The Antifederalists were waging a strong campaign. Even Madison's home state of Virginia was hesitating. Forceful speaker Patrick Henry proposed that Virginia ratify the Constitution only if it included 40 amendments he had written. The Virginia legislature rejected Henry's list, but approved the Constitution with the understanding that it would be amended somehow. Madison had originally opposed amending the Constitution. However, to assure its ratification, he put together its first set of amendments.

Madison's quill pen

 The First Amendment

James Madison helped secure the Constitution's ratification with the promise that a bill of rights would be added to it. In 1789 Madison began narrowing down the huge list of more than 200 proposed amendments. He then submitted the shortened list of amendments to the House of Representatives. Of those, the House approved 12 amendments, and the states ratified 10. Those 10 amendments, called the Bill of Rights, represent the essential protection of individual liberties for citizens of the United States. As Madison explained:

> **"The safety and happiness of society are the objects at which all political institutions aim and to which all such institutions must be sacrificed."**

The ideas spelled out in the First Amendment form the most basic rights of all U.S. citizens. Sometimes called the five freedoms, these rights include freedom of religion, speech, the press, assembly, and petition.

Introduce Key Terms

Visual-Spatial, Kinesthetic. Review this section's key terms with students. Have them create a crossword puzzle using the key terms for this section. When they have completed their puzzles, ask students to exchange them with a neighbor and answer the questions. **SHELTERED ENGLISH**

TEACH

Have students read Section 2 and complete Guided Reading Strategies 2.2. Choose one or more of the following activities to explore the section content with students. For further suggestions on block scheduling or team teaching, see the *Block Scheduling Handbook*.

LEVEL 1: Linguistic. (Suggested time: 15 min.) As a class, go over students' Guided Reading Strategies. Then use the Reading Focus questions to highlight the main ideas of the section. **SHELTERED ENGLISH**

LEVEL 1: Visual-Spatial, Kinesthetic. (Suggested time: 45 min.) Tell students that the Second, Third, and Fourth Amendments were designed to address specific problems that colonists had with British officials prior to the Revolutionary War. Have each student create a diorama that illustrates a problem

Freedom of Religion

The First Amendment begins by declaring that "Congress shall make no law respecting an establishment of religion, or prohibiting the free exercise thereof." This means that the government cannot support a religion or interfere with any American's decision to practice a religion or not.

At the time the Constitution was written, most nations had a state religion, a system of religious beliefs supported by the government. For example, the Church of England was the state religion of Great Britain. After the Revolution, some Americans supported the separation of church and state, which would keep the government from establishing an official religion and from favoring any religion over others.

Freedom of Speech and of the Press

The importance of the second and third freedoms in the First Amendment is reflected in an idea expressed by former congresswoman Margaret Chase Smith. "The key to security," she once said, "is public information." Everyone in the United States is guaranteed the freedom of speech. Americans have the right to express their own ideas and opinions and to hear the ideas and opinions of others.

Freedom of speech does not mean that people can say anything they want to, however. The Supreme Court has ruled that speech presenting a serious threat to public safety, such as falsely shouting "Fire!" in a crowded theater, is not protected by the First Amendment. Justice Oliver Wendell Holmes explained:

> **"The question in every case is whether the words used are used in such circumstances and are of such a nature to create a clear and present danger that . . . Congress has a right to prevent."**

Another kind of unprotected speech is slander, or the intentional telling of lies that damages someone's reputation.

Intentionally writing a lie that harms another person is called libel. In protecting Americans' freedom of the press, the founders recalled the case of John Peter Zenger. The publisher of *New York Weekly Journal*, Zenger had gone on trial in 1735 for printing a factual article that criticized New York's royal governor. The jury found Zenger not guilty, establishing that "the truth is a defense against libel."

Freedom of Assembly and Petition

Another freedom Americans have is that of assembly, or of holding meetings. Anyone may gather with anyone else to discuss issues or to conduct

Biography

The Granger Collection, New York

James Madison

James Madison was born in Virginia in 1751. He attended the College of New Jersey, now Princeton University, before entering Virginia politics. Early in his career Madison became a strong supporter of religious freedom.

Madison served in Congress until 1797. He continued to influence politics from his family plantation, where he remained a slaveholder despite his belief in individual liberty. In 1801 Madison became secretary of state. He served as president from 1809 to 1817 and continued to be active in politics up until his death in 1836. Madison is often called the Father of the Constitution because of his central role in framing the document and adding the Bill of Rights.

Biography

James Madison. The delegates to the 1787 Constitutional Convention agreed to keep their proceedings secret, but James Madison took meticulous notes, recording the debates and the speeches. These notes were not published until 1840, four years after Madison's death, and they remain the most detailed account of the Constitutional Convention.

Critical Thinking: What useful purpose might the notes Madison took have served at the Convention?

ANSWER: The notes could provide a record so that delegates could review important details.

addressed by one of these amendments. For example, students can create a scene in which British soldiers are staying in a colonist's home. Have students label the diorama so that it indicates which amendment addressed the problem depicted. Ask students to display their dioramas in the classroom and explain their significance. After students have finished, discuss why it was important to include these protections in the Bill of Rights. **SHELTERED ENGLISH**

ALL LEVELS: Linguistic, Interpersonal. (Suggested time: 45 min.) Tell students that the Supreme Court wants to know how young people interpret the Constitution. Divide the class into several small groups. Assign each group one or more amendments to review. Have each group use the text and material from class discussion to create a description of the freedoms that are protected by the amendment or amendments. After each group has finished its list, have one member present the information to the entire class. Discuss the importance of each amendment and any limitations that may apply to it. **SHELTERED ENGLISH**

LEVEL 3: Linguistic, Logical-Mathematical, Interpersonal. (Suggested time: 45 min.) Have students develop a list of guidelines for class discussions. Tell students that the purpose for creating the guidelines is to make sure that class discussions are conducted effectively. After students have finished, have them share

Global Relations

Quartering Troops. In 1689 Parliament passed an act that protected British citizens from having to house troops in their homes. The British law did not apply to America, and during the French and Indian War (1754–63), colonists discovered that they had no legal protection against the practice of quartering.

Critical Thinking: Why did the colonists come to resent the practice of quartering?

ANSWER: Quartering troops was an invasion of their privacy, and feeding the British soldiers cost money.

Multimedia Resources

Exploring America's Past Civics and Citizenship Skills Video Segment: The Roles of a Citizen; *Teacher's Guide*, pp. 49–52

Search 558, Play to 15357
Videodisc Gold Side A

Play Pause

See *Teacher's Guide* for Spanish barcode.

These students express their freedom of speech and of assembly by organizing an Earth Day celebration.

business. As long as those people gather peacefully and are not involved in any illegal activity, the government cannot interfere.

The right to **petition**, or make a request of, the government is another right of the American people. Any American can present a petition, or formal request, to a government official. The right of petition enables Americans to express their dissatisfaction with current laws or to suggest new ones.

Protecting Citizens

The Second, Third, and Fourth Amendments all relate to concerns that grew out of the colonists' disputes with British officials before the Revolution. These amendments continue to affect American life today.

Militias

The Second Amendment deals with state militias. As the conflict with Great Britain increased before the Revolution began, colonial militias prepared for war. The "shot heard round the world" that started the Revolutionary War came when British troops tried to seize the weapons of the Massachusetts militia.

The founders believed that the states needed to continue to maintain militias for emergencies. Today the National Guard has replaced state militias. National Guard members can be called to serve in wars and to help restore order during crises, such as in the event of a natural disaster.

Many people have debated the Second Amendment's intent regarding firearms. Some people argue that gun control laws violate the Second Amendment's declaration that "the right of the people to keep and bear arms shall not be infringed [violated]." In 1939 the Supreme Court approved restrictions for nonmilitary firearms. Years later, a U.S. court of appeals ruled that gun control laws do not violate the Second Amendment. The Supreme Court let that ruling stand in 1983.

Quartering and Search and Seizure

The Third Amendment prohibits the military from forcing citizens to provide housing for soldiers, an idea that may seem odd today. Before the Revolution, however, the British government pressured the colonies to provide food and shelter for British soldiers.

British authorities also issued writs of assistance, which empowered law officials to search colonists' property for illegal goods without first establishing a probable cause of illegal activity. Anger over such actions resulted in the Fourth Amendment's restriction against "unreasonable

These members of the National Guard are helping local citizens prevent a river from flooding.

their ideas with the rest of the class, and then vote to determine which ideas to include in the guidelines. Then lead a discussion about the difficulties encountered when creating the guidelines. Finally, explain to students that the process used to write the classroom guidelines was similar to the process used to establish the Bill of Rights.

CLOSE

Linguistic, Musical-Rhythmic. Have students write a poem or song about the importance of the Bill of Rights. Students should be sure to describe the protections provided by each amendment and the reasons why the colonists wanted to include each amendment in the Bill of Rights. Encourage students to share their songs or poems with the rest of the class.

CHALLENGE AND EXTEND

1. **Linguistic, Logical-Mathematical, Intrapersonal.** Encourage students to search newspapers and magazines to find examples of court cases that involve issues dealing with the freedoms protected by the Bill of Rights. An example might be a criminal case in which the defense claims that the evidence against the accused was gained through an illegal search. Have

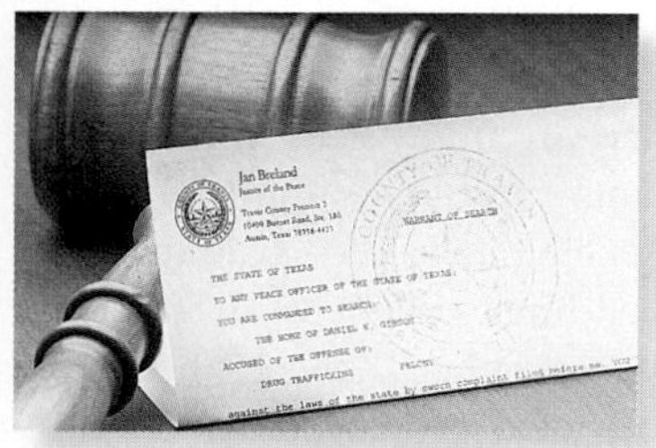

Judges issue search warrants like this one to allow law enforcement officials to search a suspected criminal's home.

searches and seizures." To conduct a search reasonably, authorities usually must first obtain a **search warrant**. This warrant is a judge's order that authorizes the search because the property in question seems likely to contain evidence relating to a crime.

Authorities do not always need a warrant to conduct a search. Under certain circumstances, such as when a suspect is trying to destroy evidence or conceal a weapon, police can conduct an emergency search. This helps to protect both the officers and any evidence necessary to prove illegal activity.

Protection of the Accused

The Fifth, Sixth, Seventh, and Eighth Amendments establish guidelines for trying people accused of a crime. The goal of these amendments is to protect the rights of the accused. No one may be punished for a crime without **due process**, or the fair application, of the law.

Due Process

According to the Fifth Amendment, a court cannot try someone for a serious crime unless a grand jury decides that enough evidence exists to **indict**, or formally accuse, the person. The Fifth Amendment also protects people from being forced to testify in their own trial in a criminal case. To refrain from testifying, the defendant "pleads the Fifth." Anyone found not guilty in a criminal trial cannot face **double jeopardy**, or be tried again for the same crime.

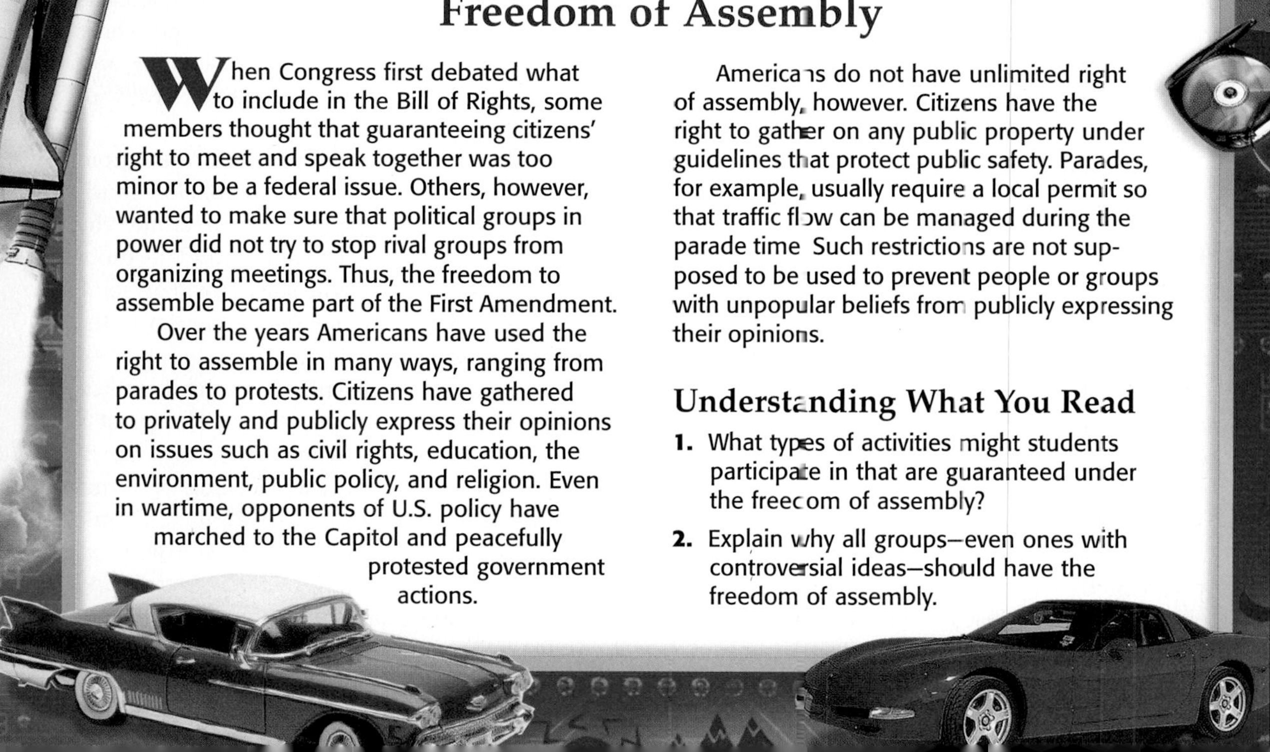

Linking Past to Present

Freedom of Assembly

When Congress first debated what to include in the Bill of Rights, some members thought that guaranteeing citizens' right to meet and speak together was too minor to be a federal issue. Others, however, wanted to make sure that political groups in power did not try to stop rival groups from organizing meetings. Thus, the freedom to assemble became part of the First Amendment.

Over the years Americans have used the right to assemble in many ways, ranging from parades to protests. Citizens have gathered to privately and publicly express their opinions on issues such as civil rights, education, the environment, public policy, and religion. Even in wartime, opponents of U.S. policy have marched to the Capitol and peacefully protested government actions.

Americans do not have unlimited right of assembly, however. Citizens have the right to gather on any public property under guidelines that protect public safety. Parades, for example, usually require a local permit so that traffic flow can be managed during the parade time Such restrictions are not supposed to be used to prevent people or groups with unpopular beliefs from publicly expressing their opinions.

Understanding What You Read

1. What types of activities might students participate in that are guaranteed under the freedom of assembly?
2. Explain why all groups—even ones with controversial ideas—should have the freedom of assembly.

Citizenship and Democracy

Double Jeopardy. While the Fifth Amendment prohibits double jeopardy, in some circumstances an individual can be tried twice with the same evidence. Officials have used federal civil rights laws to prosecute individuals found not guilty in criminal court cases. Because the second trials are civil trials, they do not violate the double jeopardy provision of the Fifth Amendment. Prosecutors used this strategy in 1994 to secure a conviction against a man accused of murdering civil rights workers in Mississippi in 1964.

Critical Thinking: Why might the government use civil rights laws to prosecute someone found not guilty in a criminal trial?

ANSWER: Answers will vary but students might suggest that there was not enough evidence to obtain a criminal conviction in the first trial.

LINKING PAST TO PRESENT ANSWERS

1. Answers will vary according to students' experiences.
2. Students' opinions will vary.

students write a summary of the case that describes the issue in question, states the amendment that applies to the case, tells whether the right was upheld or denied, and gives their opinion about the issue in question.

2. **Linguistic, Interpersonal, Intrapersonal.** Explain to students that the right to petition is guaranteed by the First Amendment. As a class, have students identify problems in their community or in the nation that they feel are not being adequately addressed. Tell students to briefly discuss these problems. Then have them choose one problem that they think they can solve. Ask students to brainstorm on appropriate solutions to this problem. Have them vote to see which solution they support. Then have them develop a petition that asks for government action on the topic and states the proposed solution. Ask students in the class who agree with the idea to sign the petition.

REVIEW

Visual-Spatial, Kinesthetic, Interpersonal. Have students complete the Section Review questions. Then ask them to work with a partner to make a chart that describes the protections

Constitutional Heritage

Cruel and Unusual Punishment. The Supreme Court's 1972 ruling that the death penalty violated the constitutional guarantee against cruel and unusual punishment was based on the process for determining death-penalty sentencing in most states. The courts found the sentencing process unfair because it varied a great deal from state to state. Most states immediately began setting new guidelines for death-penalty sentences. In 1976 a Georgia man convicted of murder was sentenced to death. The Supreme Court ruled that the new Georgia standards were not unfair and that the death penalty in this case was constitutional.

Critical Thinking: Why did the Supreme Court require states to set strict guidelines for death-penalty sentences?

Answer: The Supreme Court wanted to make the application of the death penalty as uniform as possible across the country.

Amending the U.S. Constitution

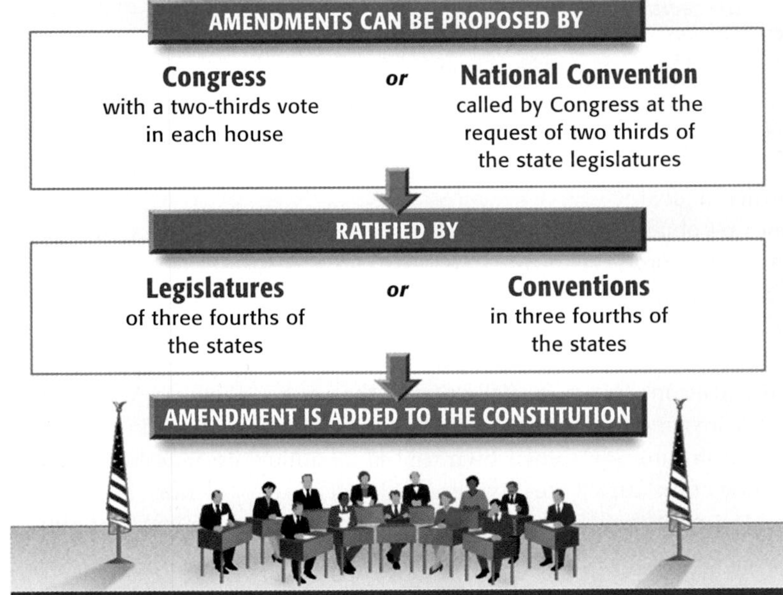

The final clause of the Fifth Amendment states that no one will be deprived of property "without due process of law." The one exception involves the government's power of **eminent domain**, or the right to take personal property to further the public's interest. This would include, for example, the seizing of private lands to build a public road. However, the government must pay the owners a fair amount of money for the property unless the citizens obtained it through illegal activities, such as selling illegal drugs.

Trials

The Sixth Amendment states that someone who is indicted for a crime must have a prompt, public trial by a jury. The accused has the right to know what crime he or she is charged with and to hear and to question the prosecution witnesses. The accused also has the right to an attorney. Today the government pays for the attorney if the person cannot afford legal services.

The accused has the right to refuse any of his or her Sixth Amendment rights. For example, some defendants refuse the services of an attorney, while others choose to have a trial in front of a judge alone instead of before a jury. In many cases, defendants can bypass the trial by agreeing to a plea bargain—pleading guilty to a lesser charge rather than risk being convicted of a crime that may carry a greater sentence.

The Seventh Amendment establishes that juries can decide civil cases. These cases usually involve disputes over money or property. If a person harms another person without breaking the law—for example, by refusing to pay back a debt—the injured party may sue in civil court.

Bail and Punishment

The Eighth Amendment establishes that people accused of a crime have a method of getting out of jail until their trial is over. Defendants gain their release in exchange for bail, money paid to the court to guarantee that they will show up for trial. Whoever pays the bail gets his or her money back at the end of the trial only if the defendant has attended court. If the defendant does not show up for trial, the court keeps all the bail money and issues a warrant for the immediate arrest of the defendant.

The Eighth Amendment prevents courts from setting bail amounts that are too high. How much bail is "too high" depends on the crime, the accused person's financial resources, and the probability that the person will show up. For some people accused of extremely serious crimes, the judge may refuse to grant bail.

The Eighth Amendment also prohibits inflicting "cruel and unusual punishments" against a person convicted of a crime. For many years, Americans have debated the meaning of "cruel and unusual punishments." In 1972 the Supreme Court ruled that the death penalty, as it was carried out by most states at the time, was cruel and unusual. The Court also found that the processes by which many states sentenced people to death provided by each amendment and the reasons for including these protections in the Bill of Rights. Once each set of partners has finished creating its chart, have students take turns quizzing one another about the Bill of Rights.

ASSESS

Have students complete Daily Quiz 2.2.

RETEACH

Visual-Spatial, Kinesthetic, Logical-Mathematical. Have students complete Main Idea Activities for Reteaching and Sheltered English 2.2. Then ask students to draw a political cartoon about one of the amendments. Cartoons should focus on what could happen without the protection provided by that amendment. Encourage students to explain their cartoons to the class. **SHELTERED ENGLISH**

were unfair. However, the Court did not rule that all executions are cruel and unusual. All states that use the death penalty must follow guidelines spelled out by the Supreme Court.

Other Rights of the People

The final two amendments in the Bill of Rights provide a general protection for other individual rights and reserve some governmental powers for the states and for the people. The Ninth Amendment states that listing specific rights in the Constitution does not mean that citizens do not have additional rights. This amendment gives the courts and Congress the ability to determine other fundamental rights of citizens.

Education is one right that was not included in the Constitution but which most Americans consider a fundamental right. "Education is not just another consumer item. It is the bedrock [foundation] of our democracy," explained educational leader Mary Hatwood Futrell. Today state governments provide free education—from elementary to high school—to all citizens.

The Tenth Amendment grants to the states and the people any powers that the Constitution does not specifically give to Congress or prohibit from the states. Recently a group of governors used this amendment to challenge a federal law that required states to pay for and carry out a federal information program. The courts agreed, stating that this requirement interfered with the states' rights, implied under the Tenth Amendment, to determine their own budget priorities. Thus, the last amendment in the Bill of Rights continues to protect the rights of citizens and to balance power between the federal and state governments.

These students benefit from free public education, which many people now consider a right of citizenship.

SECTION 2 REVIEW

Identify and explain the significance of the following:

- **James Madison**
- **petition**
- **search warrant**
- **due process**
- **indict**
- **double jeopardy**
- **eminent domain**

Reading for Content Understanding

1 **Main Idea** What are the five main freedoms guaranteed to U.S. citizens under the First Amendment, and why are they important?

2 **Main Idea** How do the Second, Third, and Fourth Amendments address concerns from the Revolutionary period?

3 **Citizenship and Democracy** How does the Ninth Amendment protect people's rights and individual freedoms?

4 **Writing** *Expressing* What rights of the accused are protected by the Constitution? Do you agree or disagree with protecting these rights? Explain your answer in one or two paragraphs.

5 **Critical Thinking** *Evaluating* What do you think are the three most important ways that the Bill of Rights influences our lives today? Explain your answers.

Section 2 Review ANSWERS

Identify

For significance, see the following pages:

- James Madison, p. 64
- petition, p. 66
- search warrant, p. 67
- due process, p. 67
- indict, p. 67
- double jeopardy, p. 67
- eminent domain, p. 68

Reading for Content Understanding

1. They protect the right to freedom of religion, speech, the press, assembly, and petition; they are considered the most basic rights of U.S. citizens.

2. Second—militias provided a defense against the British army; Third—a response to British quartering of troops; Fourth—a reaction to the writs of assistance

3. It allows for rights that are not specifically mentioned in the Constitution.

4. The Constitution states that the accused must have due process; prohibits double jeopardy; calls for a prompt, public trial; and requires appropriate bail and punishment. Students should offer their opinion and discuss amendments that protect persons accused of a crime and offer arguments for or against those amendments.

5. Students' opinions will vary but they should take a stance and explain their reasoning.

OBJECTIVES

- **Describe how a person can become a U.S. citizen.**
- **Identify the important responsibilities of citizenship.**
- **Evaluate why it is important for citizens to be involved with their community and government.**

FOCUS

Motivate Before Reading

Organize the class into several small groups. Ask members of each group to consider what it means to be a U.S. citizen. *(Students will probably give many answers. However, they should point out that U.S. citizens have certain rights that are not necessarily protected in other countries.)* Have a representative from each group present the group's answer to the rest of the class. Explain to students that

Section 3 RESOURCES

PRINT

- ★ Guided Reading Strategies 2.3
- ★ Literature Reading 2: *The Free Citizen*
- ★ Geography Activity 2: Changes in Electoral Votes
- ★ Section 3 Review, p. 75
- ★ Daily Quiz 2.3

MULTIMEDIA

- ★ *Teaching Resources CD–ROM*, Lesson 2.3
- ★ *Exploring America's Past Civics and Citizenship Skills* Video Segment: On the Campaign Trail; *Teacher's Guide*, pp. 61–64
- ★ HRW Web site

SHELTERED ENGLISH

- ★ Main Idea Activities for Reteaching and Sheltered English 2.3

Rights and Responsibilities of Citizenship

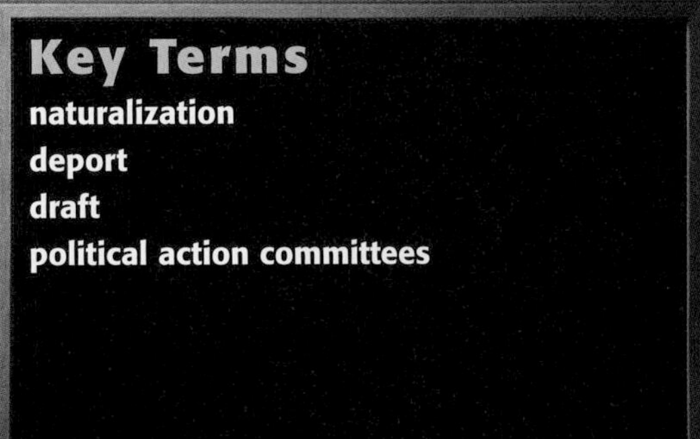

Reading Focus

How can a person become a U.S. citizen?

What are some of the most important responsibilities of citizenship?

Why is it important for citizens to be involved with their community and government?

Key Terms

naturalization
deport
draft
political action committees

PATRICK HENRY ARGUED that the United States should be open for all people who wanted to become citizens. "Let . . . Liberty stretch forth her fair hand toward the people of the old world," he said "—tell them to come, and bid them welcome." Many people desiring liberty have become U.S. citizens. Jozef Patyna immigrated to the United States in the early 1980s to flee an unjust government in Poland. "The idea of freedom and democracy is what the people have an instinctive need for," explained Patyna.

The Statue of Liberty

 Becoming a Citizen

The Constitution protects the rights of all U.S. citizens. People can become U.S. citizens in many ways. Anyone born in the United States or a territory it controls is a citizen. People born in Puerto Rico, for example, are citizens because that island is a commonwealth that remains a U.S. territory.

People born in a foreign country can become U.S. citizens if one of their parents is a citizen. People born in a foreign country whose parents are not U.S. citizens can become citizens only if they move to the United States and undergo a long process in gaining citizenship called **naturalization**. The U.S. Immigration and Naturalization Service (INS) oversees this process.

Foreign-born people who permanently move to a new country are called immigrants. In the United States, legal immigrants have many of the same rights and responsibilities as citizens. They cannot vote or hold public office, however. In some states they cannot hold some government there is no correct answer, but that many people associate U.S. citizenship with choices and rights. Tell students that along with the rights that one is guaranteed as a U.S. citizen, there are certain responsibilities. Then tell them that in this section they will learn about how a person can become a U.S. citizen and the responsibilities that go along with citizenship.

Introduce Key Terms

Linguistic. Review this section's key terms with students. Have students use context cues to create definitions for the terms. Then ask them to write the definitions in their notebooks and write sentences correctly using each term. **SHELTERED ENGLISH**

TEACH

Have students read Section 3 and complete Guided Reading Strategies 2.3. Choose one or more of the following activities to explore the section content with students. For further suggestions on block scheduling or team teaching, see the *Block Scheduling Handbook.*

LEVEL 1: Linguistic. (Suggested time: 15 min.) As a class, go over students' Guided Reading Strategies. Then use the Reading Focus questions to highlight the main ideas of the section. **SHELTERED ENGLISH**

jobs either. The U.S. government also has the right to **deport**, or send back to the country of origin, any immigrant who breaks the law or who is in the country illegally.

Only legal immigrants can begin the process of naturalization. All legal immigrants have to be able to support themselves financially or have someone sponsor them and assume that financial responsibility. After living in the United States for five years, legal immigrants over the age of 18 may petition for naturalization. At that point the INS sets a hearing to test the immigrants' qualifications. The immigrants must prove that they are law-abiding and that they support the U.S. Constitution. They must also take a series of tests to prove that they can read, write, and speak English, and that they have a basic understanding of U.S. history and government.

This Asian immigrant is taking the oath of allegiance to become a U.S. citizen.

After the immigrants pass this hearing, the INS conducts a background check on them to make sure they have not hidden any information about themselves. Finally, they go before a naturalization court, where they take an oath of allegiance to the United States and then receive their certificate of naturalization. At that point all young children of the newly naturalized citizens also become citizens.

Becoming a naturalized citizen takes dedication and effort. An elderly Japanese immigrant wrote a poem to celebrate her naturalization:

> **"Going steadily to study English,**
> **Even through the rain at night,**
> **I thus attain [acquire],**
> **Late in life,**
> **American citizenship."**

Naturalized citizens and resident immigrants contribute a great deal to the United States. Many famous Americans, such as scientist Albert Einstein and Secretary of State Madeleine Albright, have been naturalized citizens. The only distinctions between naturalized and native-born citizens are that naturalized citizens can lose their citizenship and they cannot become president or vice president.

Duties of Citizens

In addition to having certain rights, American citizens have responsibilities to themselves, their government, and other citizens. For the system of representative democracy to work, Americans need to fulfill their civic responsibilities. "The stakes . . . are too high for government to be a spectator sport," explained former Texas congresswoman Barbara Jordan.

Obeying Authority

Citizens elect officials to make laws for them. In turn, citizens must obey the laws passed by those officials. If citizens disagree with a law, they can try to get it changed in a variety of ways, such as by speaking with their local representative, challenging the law in court, petitioning, or voting for elected officials who oppose the law.

Obeying the law includes knowing what the laws are. Thus, citizens need to stay informed of and be aware of changes to laws that affect them. Ignorance of a particular law will not prevent a person from being punished for breaking it.

Citizens also have an obligation to respect the rights of others and to respect people in authority. These people, including parents, teachers, and police officers, have been entrusted with looking out for the welfare of others. Parents, for example, have a responsibility to provide for their children's basic needs, including food, clothing, shelter, and education. In return, children have a responsibility

Across the Curriculum

MATH

Immigration. The peak year for immigration to the United States was 1907, when 1,285,349 people arrived on U.S. shores. The lowest was 1933, with only 23,068 immigrants arriving.

Activity: Have students use the library or search the Internet through the HRW Web site or reference works to determine the current annual immigration level for the United States. Then have them determine the percentage increase from the lowest immigration figure in the twentieth century to now. *(Take the current figure, subtract the change since 1933, and divide by the number in 1933 to get the percentage.)*

go.hrw.com
SB1 Immigration

LEVEL 1: Visual-Spatial, Kinesthetic. (Suggested time: 30 min.) Have students use the text and notes from class discussion to create a chart depicting the three ways that a person can become a U.S. citizen. Remind students to highlight the steps a person must take to gain citizenship if he or she is not born a U.S. citizen. Discuss these methods with the class. Then create various scenarios describing a person's background. Ask students to explain if the person in each scenario is automatically a U.S. citizen because of his or her circumstances of birth, if the person became a naturalized citizen, or if the person is not a U.S. citizen. **SHELTERED ENGLISH**

ALL LEVELS: Logical-Mathematical, Interpersonal, Intrapersonal. (Suggested time: 45 min.) Ask students to identify groups that help to make their community a better place to live. *(Students may mention groups such as the YMCA, Girl Scouts, MADD, SADD, Neighborhood Watch, Little League, and other organizations.)* Discuss the variety of ways that these groups and others like them affect the community. Tell students that these organizations frequently rely on volunteers from the community. Have students create an advertisement for an organization in their community that encourages citizens to volunteer. **SHELTERED ENGLISH**

Across the Curriculum

MATH

The Flat Tax. Some critics have argued that a flat income tax (one that charges every U.S. worker the same percentage of income) would benefit the U.S. economy. They maintain that the current income tax system is expensive to operate. In addition, they claim that many people invest their money in order to receive tax breaks rather than seek out sound investments that would promote economic growth. In 1996 Jack Kemp, who would later be a Republican vice presidential candidate, claimed that a flat tax would double the growth of the U.S. economy. Opponents argue that the flat tax would benefit the wealthy at the expense of middle-class Americans.

Activity: Have students calculate what a person with an annual salary of $26,000 and a person whose salary is $140,000 would have to pay if the flat tax was set at 7 percent. *($1,820; $9,800)* Use these calculations to begin a discussion about the fairness of the flat tax.

Consumers like this teenager pay sales tax when they buy goods.

to obey their parents. Government authorities may step in to protect any children whose parents do not take proper care of them.

Paying Taxes

Benjamin Franklin once claimed, "In this world, nothing is certain but death and taxes." Paying taxes is a necessary part of being a good citizen. The government relies on taxes to pay for the many services it provides. If Americans did not pay taxes, the government might be unable to provide public roads, police and fire departments, or even public schools.

People pay many kinds of taxes, such as sales taxes, excise taxes, and tariffs. For example, consumers often pay sales taxes when buying items at a store. Sales tax rates vary from place to place because most sales taxes are set and collected by state and local governments.

Property taxes are taxes people pay based on the value of the property they own. The tax amount owed is a certain percentage of the value of the property. Most school funding comes from property taxes.

April 15 of every year is income tax day. By that day all Americans who earned money the year before must give a certain percentage of their income from that year to the federal, and sometimes the state, government. The amount of income tax that a person has to pay depends on the level of his or her income.

Income taxes and property taxes are progressive—they collect a higher percentage of money from those with higher incomes and greater wealth. Regressive taxes, such as sales taxes, are taxes that apply equally to all Americans. If a person buys a product, he or she pays the same amount of sales tax on the item regardless of his or her individual income.

Serving in the Military

Citizens also have the duty to protect and defend the nation from harm. This means that if a war breaks out, citizens should try to help in the war effort. U.S. citizens have had to go to war a number of times in the nation's history. In some war situations the federal government has issued a **draft**, or requirement of military service, to raise the needed number of soldiers.

Upon turning 18, every male U.S. citizen must fill out a card like this one to register for a potential draft.

The United States has maintained all-volunteer armed forces since 1973. However, young men are required to register with the government when they turn 18. This registration provides the government with a record of potential draftees in case a war breaks out. Women are not required to register for the draft, although many women serve in the armed forces.

Serving on Juries

All citizens can be called for jury duty, which involves listening to a court case and reaching a verdict on it. It is important for citizens to serve when called for jury duty, otherwise fulfilling each person's Sixth Amendment right to a trial by jury would be difficult.

LEVEL 2: Linguistic, Logical-Mathematical, Interpersonal. (Suggested time: 45 min.) Organize the class into groups and assign each group one of the following responsibilities of U.S. citizens: obeying U.S. laws, paying taxes, serving in the military, participating in elections, or being involved in the community. Have students discuss the importance of citizens fulfilling these responsibilities. Tell them to write a short story about what might happen if U.S. citizens did not fulfill these responsibilities. For instance, students can create a humorous scenario in which nobody votes in an election except the two candidates and therefore nobody wins the election. Encourage volunteers to read their stories to the class.

CLOSE

Linguistic, Logical-Mathematical. Review the differences between rights and responsibilities with the class. Create a three-column chart on the chalkboard. The first column should randomly list the rights and responsibilities of U.S. citizens. Label the second column *Rights* and the third column *Responsibilities*. For each right or responsibility listed in the first column, have students identify under which category or categories it falls and put a check mark in the appropriate column or columns. Have students explain why they classified each item as they did. **SHELTERED ENGLISH**

Americans also have a duty to testify in court if needed. If a person were to witness a crime, for example, he or she should be willing to testify about the event. Judges may issue subpoenas, or orders to appear in court, to force people to testify.

Citizens and Elections

Elections form the basis of representative democracy in the United States. Voting in elections is crucial to maintaining the country's democratic system. Through free elections, U.S. citizens choose who will lead the government. Not all countries allow their citizens to participate in elections.

An active voter should be an informed voter. Citizens should try to find out as much as they can about the issues and candidates before voting. Much of this information is available through newspapers, television, and other forms of media. However, informed voters should watch out for propaganda, or material that is slanted deliberately to support or harm a cause.

Voting is not the only way that Americans participate in elections. Many become involved by campaigning for a particular candidate or issue. Anyone can help campaign, even if he or she is not eligible to vote. Citizens can also contribute money to a candidate directly or through **political action committees** (PACs), organizations that collect money to distribute to candidates who support the same issues as the contributors.

Voters in the United States must be at least 18 years old. Many people younger than 18 can help campaigns by handing out pamphlets, making signs, or otherwise encouraging citizens to vote. Some schools have clubs, such as the Teen-Age Republicans and the Young Democrats, that allow teenagers to get involved in party politics.

High school student Janet Benson's active participation in the Teen-Age Republicans shaped her career goals. "Some people want a career in science or sports," she noted. "For me, it's politics. I love it." Many active members of political clubs get to know political leaders well. Some continue to be active in politics as adults.

Citizens and Government

Being involved in elections is just one of the many ways in which citizens can participate in their government. Even after an election, people can influence officials by letting them know what the citizens want done.

Some citizens join interest groups, organizations designed to lobby politicians on behalf of particular issues. People form many kinds of interest groups, and most groups represent the views of a particular segment of society. The American Farm Bureau Federation, for example, is an interest group made up of farmers. It lobbies to get aid for farms—for example, financial assistance to help when a natural disaster destroys crops or to maintain prices of farm products.

Other groups, called public interest groups, lobby for issues that affect all Americans. Mothers Against Drunk Driving (MADD) and Students Against Drunk Driving (SADD) are two public interest groups that work to end drunk driving, which kills thousands of Americans each year. MADD began in 1980 after a drunk driver killed 13-year-old Cari Lightner.

These students are helping run a candidate's campaign during a local election.

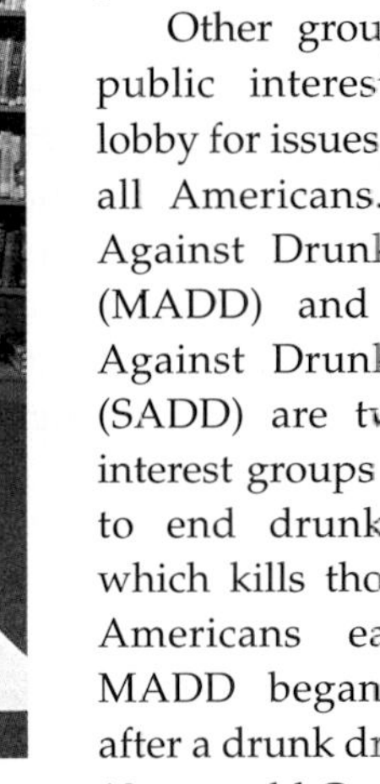

Global Relations

Voter Participation. Political scientists compiled information regarding voter participation in several nations during the 1980s and discovered that the United States ranked among the lowest in voter turnout. In a survey of 20 democracies, the United States ranked 19th in voter participation, with only 52 percent of the electorate actually voting.

Critical Thinking: Why do you think U.S. voter turnout is low?

ANSWER: Students might respond that many people are not interested in politics or believe that their vote does not matter.

Multimedia Resources

Exploring America's Past Civics and Citizenship Skills Video Segment: On the Campaign Trail; *Teacher's Guide*, pp. 61–64

Search 558, Play to 15439
Videodisc Gold Side B

Play Pause

See *Teacher's Guide* for Spanish barcode.

CHALLENGE AND EXTEND

1. **Linguistic, Visual-Spatial, Interpersonal.** Have students write to one or more of the community organizations discussed in this section of the text to obtain more information about the services it provides. Students should also inquire about volunteer opportunities with that organization. Have students use information from replies to their letters to create a bulletin-board display that not only describes the various organizations' functions but also advertises actual volunteer opportunities.

2. **Visual-Spatial, Kinesthetic, Interpersonal.** Remind students about the importance of U.S. citizens fulfilling their responsibilities to the government. Tell them that the purpose of this activity is to see if people are actually fulfilling these responsibilities. Have students create a survey that lists each responsibility identified in this section and asks the person completing the survey how often he or she fulfills each of these responsibilities. Tell students to use these four headings on their surveys: *Almost Never, Sometimes, Regularly,* and *Always.* Have students survey 10 adults by asking them to circle the choice that best applies to them. Once everyone has finished,

Section 3 Review ANSWERS

Identify

For significance, see the following pages:

- naturalization, p. 70
- deport, p. 71
- draft, p. 72
- political action committees, p. 73

Reading for Content Understanding

1. by being born in the United States or in a U.S. territory, having a parent who is a U.S. citizen, or going through the naturalization process

2. obeying authority, paying taxes, serving in the military, performing jury duty, community service

3. Immigrants cannot vote, hold public office, or, in some states, have government-supported jobs.

4. Poems will vary but should promote volunteerism.

5. Paragraphs will vary but should describe a community problem and possible solutions for it.

These members of Students Against Drunk Driving visited Washington, D.C., to speak out against drinking and driving.

Her mother, Candy Lightner, found out that under her state's law, drunk driving was not a serious crime and that the driver would probably not spend any time in prison. Lightner founded MADD to change that policy. In explaining her motivation, she said:

> **"I believe that for every problem there is a solution. . . . I believe in the rights of victims. And I do feel that if you believe in something badly enough, you can make a difference."**

MADD began to lobby for tougher laws against drunk drivers. As a result, every state strengthened its laws against drunk driving. MADD and SADD also work to educate people about the dangers of drunk driving. "We are changing the way people think about drinking and driving," said Lightner. "But more than that, we have caused people to change their behavior, and that is saving lives."

Citizens do not have to join a group to influence political leaders. Individuals can and should let officials know how they feel about certain issues by writing letters and by going to public meetings. Attending city council meetings is a good way to learn about and influence local issues. If public officials do not know how citizens feel about an issue, they cannot represent them effectively.

 Citizens and Their Communities

Being part of a representative democracy does not mean that citizens hand over all the responsibility for society to their elected leaders and government. Indeed, a successful democratic society requires the involvement of all citizens in improving the communities in which they live.

Just as there are many interest groups that help U.S. citizens lobby for new legislation, there are numerous groups that organize citizens for community service. Some small communities whose local governments have limited budgets rely on volunteers to provide many public services, such as fire protection. Other volunteer groups assist

These volunteers are helping their neighbor by repainting a fence.

have students create bar graphs for each category that identify how often people are fulfilling their responsibilities. Discuss the results of the survey as a class.

REVIEW

Linguistic, Kinesthetic. Have students complete the Section Review questions. Then ask them to write an editorial encouraging people to take part in their community or government. Discuss the importance of citizen involvement in a representative democracy, and review the responsibilities that accompany being a U.S. citizen.

ASSESS

Have students complete Daily Quiz 2.3.

RETEACH

Linguistic, Interpersonal. Have students complete Main Idea Activities for Reteaching and Sheltered English 2.3. Then ask them to take one key term from this section and write a few sentences detailing important information they learned about it. As a class, review each of the terms by having students read their descriptions. **SHELTERED ENGLISH**

Colin Powell launches an effort to increase volunteerism throughout the country.

government-sponsored agencies, including police departments. For example, Citizens on Patrol and the Neighborhood Watch organize volunteers to walk their neighborhoods and inform police of any possible criminal activity they observe in the area. Neighborhoods with citizen patrols usually have lower crime rates than those that do not.

Other groups help do jobs in place of the government. The American Red Cross helps citizens in times of natural disasters or other emergencies. Habitat for Humanity helps to build houses for lower-income families. The Boy Scouts and Girl Scouts organize numerous projects to improve the environment, such as planting trees.

The country's leaders expect all citizens to try to do something to serve others in their communities. Service projects do not have to be big to have an effect. They can include simple acts to improve the appearance of a community, such as picking up trash or painting over graffiti. They may also help individuals—perhaps by volunteering to serve food in a homeless shelter or by visiting an elderly person in a retirement home.

Every day many people in the community need assistance. The nation is strengthened when all citizens do their part to help the country and their fellow citizens. As retired general Colin Powell declared when he launched a campaign to promote volunteerism in 1997:

> **"This is the time for each and every one of us . . . to look into our own community, to find someone who is in need . . . to lift up a fellow American and put him on the road to success in this wonderful country of ours."**

SECTION 3 REVIEW

Identify and explain the significance of the following:
- **naturalization**
- **deport**
- **draft**
- **political action committees**

Reading for Content Understanding

1 **Main Idea** How can someone become a U.S. citizen?

2 **Main Idea** What responsibilities do citizens have to their country?

3 **Cultural Diversity** What rights do citizens have that immigrants do not?

4 **Writing** *Creating* Write a short poem that might be used to encourage people to volunteer in their communities or to become involved in the government.

5 **Critical Thinking** *Identifying Cause and Effect* Write about a problem within your community—its causes and effects—and give examples of possible ways to get people more involved in correcting the problem.

Chapter 2 Review ANSWERS

Identifying People and Ideas

1. government by representatives of the people

2. bring charges against a government official

3. first woman to serve on the U.S. Supreme Court

4. the "Father of the Constitution" and a U.S. president

5. order issued by a judge authorizing a search based on probable cause

6. fair application of the law

7. to be tried again for the same crime

8. process by which people born in foreign countries become U.S. citizens

9. requirement of military service

10. organizations that collect money to support certain issues and political candidates who favor those issues

Using the Time Line

1. a
2. g
3. e
4. f
5. c
6. d
7. b

Understanding Main Ideas

1. Legislative branch creates laws; executive branch enforces laws; judicial branch determines if the laws are constitutional and whether they are being applied correctly.

2. Delegated powers are specifically granted to the federal government; reserved powers belong to the state governments or to citizens; concurrent powers are granted to both the state and federal governments.

Review and Assessment RESOURCES

PRINT
- ★ Chapter 2 Review, pp. 76–77
- ★ Vocabulary Activity 2
- ★ Chapter 2 Study Guide
- ★ Chapter 2 Test (Form A or B)

MULTIMEDIA
- ★ Audio Program, Ch. 2 (English and Spanish)
- ★ *Global Skill Builder CD–ROM*
- ★ Chapter 2 Test Generator
- ★ HRW Web site

SHELTERED ENGLISH
- ★ Spanish Glossary
- ★ Sheltered English Chapter 2 Test

ASSESS

Have students complete one of the Chapter 2 Tests. As an alternate assessment, assign the Chapter 2 Investigation.

3. to answer the objections of the Antifederalists and protect individual rights

4. Fifth Amendment—provides grand jury indictment for felonies, protects against self-incrimination, and prohibits double jeopardy; Sixth Amendment—ensures the right to a prompt public trial, right to hear and question prosecution witnesses, right to an attorney; Seventh Amendment—ensures the right to a jury in civil cases; Eighth Amendment—ensures right to a fair bail, prohibits cruel and unusual punishment

5. Naturalized citizens can lose their citizenship, and they cannot become president or vice president.

6. obeying authority, paying taxes, military service, jury duty, community service

Reviewing Themes

1. Voting allows citizens to elect representatives who will serve their interests.

2. by dividing the powers of government among different branches

3. Most Americans are descendants of immigrants to the United States.

Thinking Critically

1. Students might claim that the qualifications ensure that only mature citizens acquainted with what is happening in the nation are elected to the presidency.

CHAPTER 2 REVIEW

Chapter Summary

To ensure a system of checks and balances, the framers of the Constitution divided the government into three branches–legislative, executive, and judicial. Leaders later added the Bill of Rights to protect individual liberties. Citizens have certain rights and responsibilities that must be carried out for representative democracy to work.

On a separate sheet of paper, complete the following activities.

Identifying People and Ideas

Describe the significance of the following:

1. representative democracy
2. impeach
3. Sandra Day O'Connor
4. James Madison
5. search warrant
6. due process
7. double jeopardy
8. naturalization
9. draft
10. political action committees

Internet Activity

go.hrw.com
SB1 Supreme Court

Search the Internet through the HRW Web site for more information on Supreme Court justices. Choose one justice who served on the Court during the 1800s. Write a detailed biography of his life, including a summary of the major court cases he helped to decide.

Understanding Main Ideas

1. What are the three branches of the federal government, and what are their primary responsibilities?
2. What are delegated powers, reserved powers, and concurrent powers?
3. Why did the founders add the Bill of Rights to the Constitution?
4. Which amendments focus on the rights of people accused of crimes? What rights do these amendments guarantee?
5. What are the only differences between the rights of naturalized citizens and the rights of native-born citizens?
6. What are the duties and responsibilities of citizenship?

Using the Time Line

Number your paper from 1 to 7. Match the letters on the time line below with the following events.

1. **Delegates from 12 of the 13 states meet to create a new system of government.**
2. **Geraldine Ferraro becomes the first woman to run for vice president on a major-party ticket.**
3. **Richard Nixon becomes the first president to resign rather than risk impeachment.**
4. **President Ronald Reagan appoints Sandra Day O'Connor as the first female justice on the Supreme Court.**
5. **Thurgood Marshall becomes the first African American justice appointed to serve on the Supreme Court.**
6. **The Supreme Court rules that the death penalty is not cruel and unusual.**
7. **John F. Kennedy becomes the first Catholic U.S. president.**

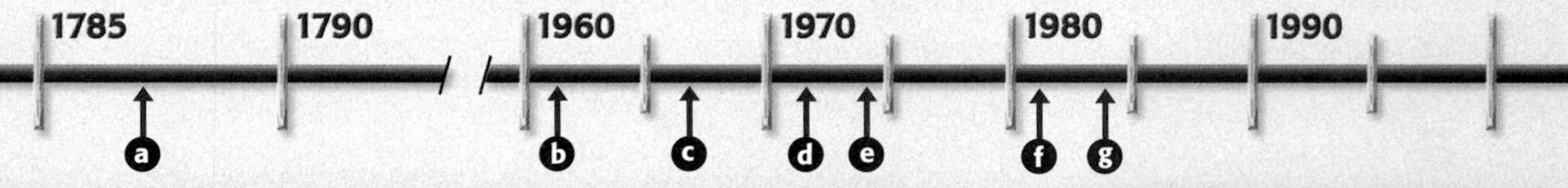

RETEACH

Linguistic, Kinesthetic, Interpersonal. Organize the class into several small teams to play "The Chapter Review Game." Each team should create 10 questions about the chapter. Have students write the questions on note cards, then place the note cards in a large box. Take turns reading a question to each team and allowing it to answer. The team with the most correct responses is the winner.

Using the Internet

Have students continue their research to find information about a current Supreme Court justice. Have students write a biographical report similar to the one they wrote in the Chapter Review Internet Activity.

Portfolio Extensions

1. Have students assemble their campaign information into a presentation designed to sway the city council to act on their issue.

2. Ask students to continue their library research by picking a specific case to research and showing in a chart how each justice voted.

Reviewing Themes

1. **Citizenship and Democracy** Why is voting an important responsibility in a representative democracy?
2. **Constitutional Heritage** How does the Constitution prevent any one branch of the federal government from becoming too powerful?
3. **Cultural Diversity** Why might it be said that the United States is a nation of immigrants?

Thinking Critically

1. **Determining the Strength of an Argument** Recall the qualifications for becoming president. Why do you think the framers of the Constitution put these in place?
2. **Synthesizing Information** How were some amendments to the Bill of Rights influenced by Americans' experiences before and during the Revolution?
3. **Identifying Cause and Effect** Serving on juries is required by law and is an important responsibility of citizenship. What problems might arise if people were unwilling to fulfill this responsibility?

Writing About History

1. **Expressing** Imagine that you have immigrated to the United States. Write a letter to a friend back home explaining why you have done so.
2. **Informing** Write a two-paragraph essay explaining how the Constitution guarantees that the federal government considers minority rights while honoring majority rule.

Linking Geography and History

1. **Movement** How might movements of large numbers of people from one part of the country to another affect states' representation in Congress?
2. **Human-Environment Interaction** What actions can people take to physically improve their communities?

Building Your Portfolio

Complete the following activities individually or in groups.

1. **Freedom of Petition** Think about something in your community that is important to you, such as the existence of crosswalks, parks, or holiday parades. Write a letter to a local official about this element of your community. Make sure the letter explains to the official why you are writing and what you want to be done. Then organize a campaign to get others to sign your letter. Support your campaign by creating signs, letters, flyers, and other items.
2. **The Supreme Court** Use your library or other resources to find out information about the nine Supreme Court justices sitting on the bench today. Then create a detailed time line showing the names of each justice, what year he or she was confirmed, and which president nominated him or her. In addition, include some brief biographical information on each justice.

History Skills Workshop

Using Primary Sources On February 28, 1963, President John F. Kennedy gave a speech to Congress in support of a civil rights bill. He also took the opportunity to discuss the importance of voting rights for African Americans. Read the following excerpt of his speech. Then explain in a paragraph what Kennedy meant by this passage.

> "The right to vote in a free American election is the most powerful and precious right in the world—and it must not be denied on the grounds of race or color. It is a potent [powerful] key to achieving other rights of citizenship."

2. The Second Amendment was a response to British occupation. The Third Amendment was a response to British quartering of troops. The Fourth Amendment was a reaction to the writs of assistance.

3. Refusing jury duty would obstruct the constitutional guarantee to a jury trial in civil cases.

Writing About History

1. Letters might discuss political freedom or educational and economic opportunities.

2. Paragraphs will vary but should mention that the Constitution guarantees specific rights, such as freedom of religion, that cannot be overturned by a simple majority vote, but can be altered through a constitutional amendment that requires a two-thirds majority.

Linking Geography and History

1. Some states would gain House seats, others would lose seats.

2. Students might mention volunteer efforts such as highway clean-up days.

History Skills Workshop

Paragraphs will vary but should suggest that voting is a key part of active citizenship and that no one should be prevented from voting based on race or color.

FOCUS

Ask students to identify a document that is more than 200 years old and that governs the lives of more than 260 million people of widely varying racial, ethnic, and cultural backgrounds. *(Students should identify the U.S. Constitution.)* Tell students that in this lesson they will learn more about the Constitution and the growth of the United States.

TEACH

Have students read the Geography and History lesson. Choose one or more of the following activities to explore the Geography and History content with students.

ALL LEVELS: Logical-Mathematical, Interpersonal. (Suggested time: 30 min.) Have students create flash cards containing the information about the requirements of, term of, and method

Constitutional Heritage

Rights in the Northwest Ordinance. The Northwest Ordinance included a bill of rights that applied to Americans who lived in the Northwest Territory. Among the protections included in the ordinance were the right to a trial by jury, a ban on cruel or unusual punishment, and a guarantee that government in the area would be representative. The ordinance also included a provision that protected private contracts from government interference. This contract clause appeared later in the U.S. Constitution.

Critical Thinking: In what ways might the Northwest Ordinance have influenced the drafting of the U.S. Constitution?

ANSWER: The ordinance included a bill of rights and provisions such as the contract clause that later appeared in the Constitution.

SKILLS ANSWERS

1. 60,000

2. Congress

3. Ohio, Indiana, Illinois, Michigan, Wisconsin

Geography & History

The Living Constitution

The present government of the United States began operation in 1789 and is based on a written Constitution that was adopted by the 13 original states. The United States has remained strong through many crises because its Constitution established a government in which the people choose their leaders to make their laws. The Constitution's principles and methods of governing have been firm enough to enforce its authority, but flexible enough to adapt to great changes over more than 200 years.

Today the original nation of 13 states—which housed fewer than 4 million people—has grown to 50 states and some 270 million people. The United States now stretches across North America, from the Atlantic Ocean to the shores of the Pacific, and includes Alaska in the Northwest and the faraway islands of Hawaii in the Pacific. ■

The Union

The Northwest Ordinance was adopted by Congress in 1787 under the Articles of Confederation, before the Constitution was written. It set out a method for admitting new states to the Union that remains in place today. The last states admitted to the Union were Alaska and Hawaii in 1959.

The Northwest Ordinance: Becoming a State

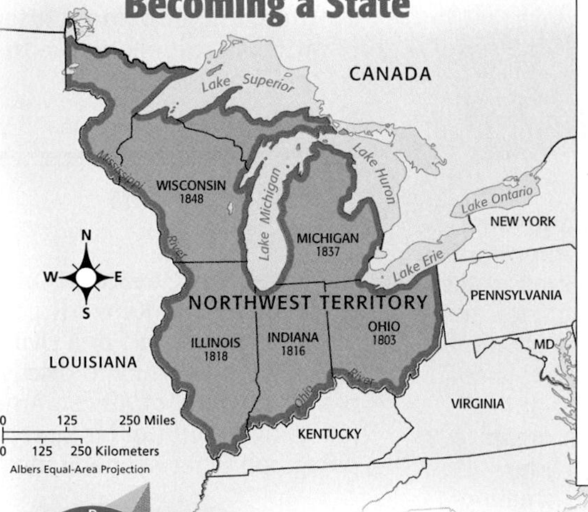

STEPS TO STATEHOOD

Congress specifies that three to five territories will be carved out of the Northwest Territory.

For each territory, Congress appoints a governor, a secretary, and three judges.

When a territory's population reaches 5,000 free male inhabitants of voting age, it elects a territorial legislature and sends a nonvoting delegate to Congress.

Once a territory's population increases to 60,000 free inhabitants, it becomes eligible for statehood and can draft a state constitution.

Congress approves the state constitution, and the territory becomes a state.

Sources: *Record of America; The Oxford Companion to American History*

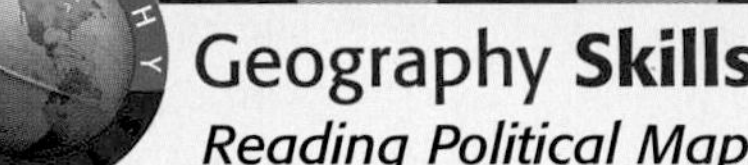

Geography Skills
Reading Political Maps

1. How many people have to be living in a territory for it to be eligible for statehood?

2. Who, or what, has to approve a territory's proposed constitution before the territory becomes a state?

3. In what order did the states of the Northwest Territory join the Union?

78

of selection for the federal offices included in the chart on page 80. Then have students take turns quizzing one another on the information found in the chart. **SHELTERED ENGLISH**

LEVEL 3: Linguistic. (Suggested time: 45 min. plus homework) Tell the class that the process of becoming a state has not changed since 1787. Ask students if they believe today's American public would be willing to admit a new state based on these requirements. Have students prepare an opinion survey using the steps outlined in the Northwest Ordinance for applying for statehood (page 78). Their questions should be phrased to require a yes or no answer. Once students have created their surveys, instruct them to pose the questions to 10 adults. Tabulate the responses to each question and discuss the overall results with the class.

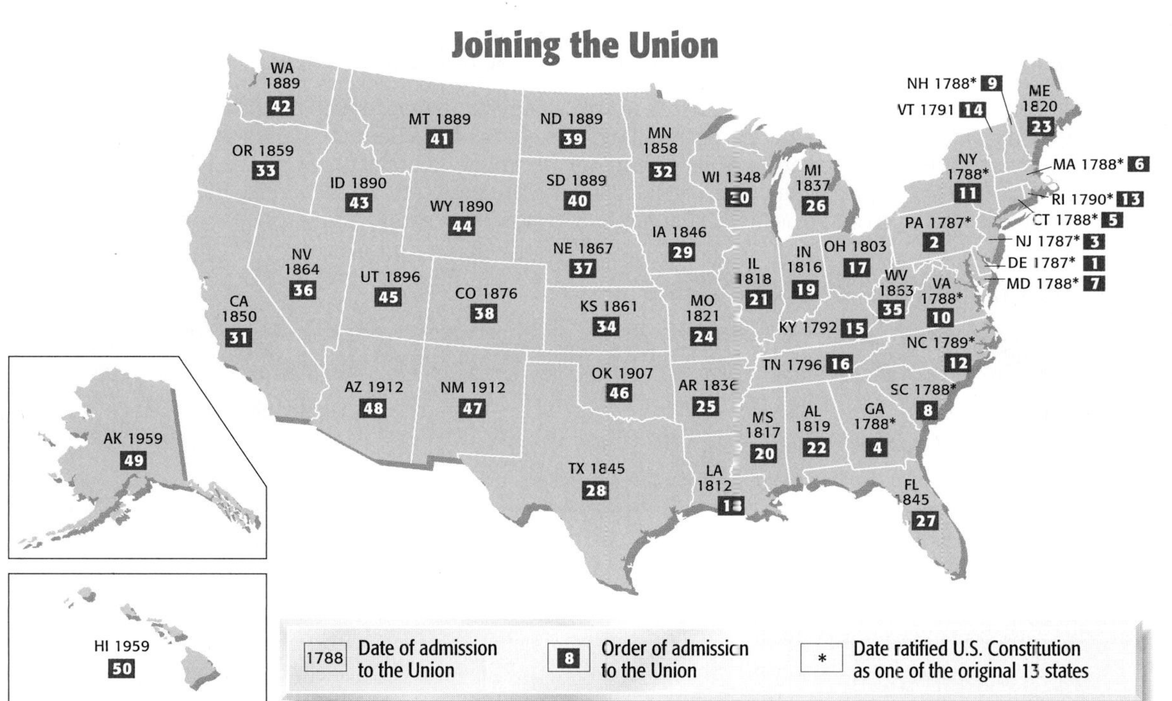

Geography **Skills**

Reading Special-Purpose Maps

1. Which three states ratified the Constitution first?
2. What were the original 13 states?
3. What states were admitted to the Union in the 1900s?

History Note 1

Congress established the method for admission of new states to the Union in the Northwest Ordinance of 1787. Before that, however, people in the northeastern portion of present-day Tennessee made the first attempt to create a new state. This proposed state of "Franklin," named after Benjamin Franklin, appealed to Congress for statehood. Franklin's application for statehood came in 1784 after North Carolina turned over the Tennessee territory to the new United States government. Before Congress acted on Franklin's statehood, North Carolina decided to reclaim the region. For a brief time both the state of North Carolina and the proposed state of Franklin tried to enforce laws in the region. Finally, in 1790 North Carolina again turned over control of the region to the national government. Six years later the proposed state of Franklin became part of the new state of Tennessee.

History Note 2

Not all states went through the territory stage before admission to the Union. Texas was an independent country before it became a state. California went directly to statehood because of its rapidly growing population. Kentucky, Maine, Vermont, and West Virginia started out as parts of other states.

Rocky Mount, capitol for the first territorial government of Tennessee

Geographic Diversity

West Virginia and Statehood. The state of West Virginia was formed when 27 counties in western Virginia refused to secede from the Union in 1861. Slaves made up only 4 percent of the population of the region, and the people of the area were not strongly dedicated to preserving the institution of slavery. All but one of these counties organized to create a separate state. Congress approved the request for statehood, and President Abraham Lincoln signed the statehood bill into law on June 20, 1863, recognizing West Virginia as the 35th state.

Critical Thinking: How did cultural differences within Virginia lead to the formation of a new state?

ANSWER: Attitudes toward slavery divided Virginia when the Civil War began.

SKILLS ANSWERS

1. Delaware, New Jersey, Pennsylvania

2. Connecticut, Delaware, Georgia, Maryland, Massachusetts, New Hampshire, New Jersey, New York, North Carolina, Pennsylvania, Rhode Island, South Carolina, Virginia

3. Alaska, Arizona, Hawaii, New Mexico, Oklahoma

CLOSE

Linguistic, Logical-Mathematical. Give students a list consisting of imaginary people that gives information about each person's age, the number of years he or she has lived in the United States, and his or her citizenship status. For each person on the list, have students identify whether he or she meets the requirements for any of the following offices: president, Supreme Court justice, senator, or representative. For each person who does not meet a requirement, have students write an explanation of why he or she is not qualified for the position in question.

CHALLENGE AND EXTEND

Linguistic, Logical-Mathematical. Ask students to choose one of the 50 states from the map on page 79. Using the library or other resources have them conduct research about the population growth of the state they have chosen since its admittance to the Union. Students should create a bar graph illustrating the state's population growth in regular intervals from its admission date to today. Have them prepare a report that highlights periods of significant growth, or decline, and provides an historical explanation of these changes.

Constitutional Heritage

Presidential Qualifications. Contemporary political concerns determined many of the qualifications for the presidency included in the U.S. Constitution. In an attempt to squelch the rumor that delegates to the Constitutional Convention intended to invite a foreign king to rule the country, the delegates themselves included the constitutional provision requiring the president to be a natural-born citizen. They chose a 14-year residency requirement to disqualify British Loyalists who had left during the American Revolution and later returned to the United States.

Critical Thinking: What does the reasoning behind the presidential qualifications reveal about the drafting of the Constitution?

ANSWER: The delegates hoped to solve pressing political issues as well as to create a design for operating the country in the future.

SKILLS ANSWERS

1. president and vice president—35; Supreme Court justice—none; senator—30; representative—25

2. yes

Representatives and Citizens

The Constitution sets the requirements for federal officials, including the president and vice president, Supreme Court justices, and members of the Senate and House of Representatives. House members represent congressional districts that are distributed among the states based on a census count of the population. The average population size of each congressional district has grown remarkably since 1789.

Requirements for Federal Office

OFFICE	REQUIREMENTS	TERM	SELECTION
President Vice President	• 35 years old • Natural-born citizen • Live in United States 14 years	4 years	Elected by electoral college
Supreme Court Justice	• None	Life	Appointed by president and approved by Senate
Senator	• 30 years old • U.S. citizen 9 years • Live in state where elected	6 years	Originally chosen by state legislature (per Constitution) Currently elected by voters (per Seventeenth Amendment)
Representative	• 25 years old • U.S. citizen 7 years • Live in state where elected	2 years	Elected by voters of district

Geography Skills
Reading Charts

1. What are the age requirements for federal officials?
2. Are members of Congress required to live in the states they represent?

President Franklin D. Roosevelt gave many radio speeches.

History Note 3

Franklin D. Roosevelt, the only president elected to more than two terms, was elected four times. In 1951 the Twenty-second Amendment was ratified, limiting any one president to two terms. In 1995 the U.S. Supreme Court ruled that neither the states nor Congress could pass laws limiting congressmembers' terms. A constitutional amendment that limits the terms of congressmembers has failed to pass Congress.

REVIEW

Linguistic, Logical-Mathematical. Refer students to the map on page 81 and remind them that during the 1900s the percentage of eligible voters in the United States has increased from 25 percent to nearly 75 percent of the population. Then explain that voter turnout has decreased during this same period from about 70 percent to around 50 percent of eligible voters. As a class, have students brainstorm why they think voter turnout is so low and suggest a list of possible solutions to change the current trend.

ASSESS

Have the students complete Geography and History Quiz 1.

RETEACH

Logical-Mathematical, Visual-Spatial. Organize the class into groups. Provide each group with a piece of butcher paper and any necessary art supplies. Assign each group a map, chart, or graph from this lesson. Have each group create a poster that explains their assigned map, chart, or graph and highlights its important facts. **SHELTERED ENGLISH**

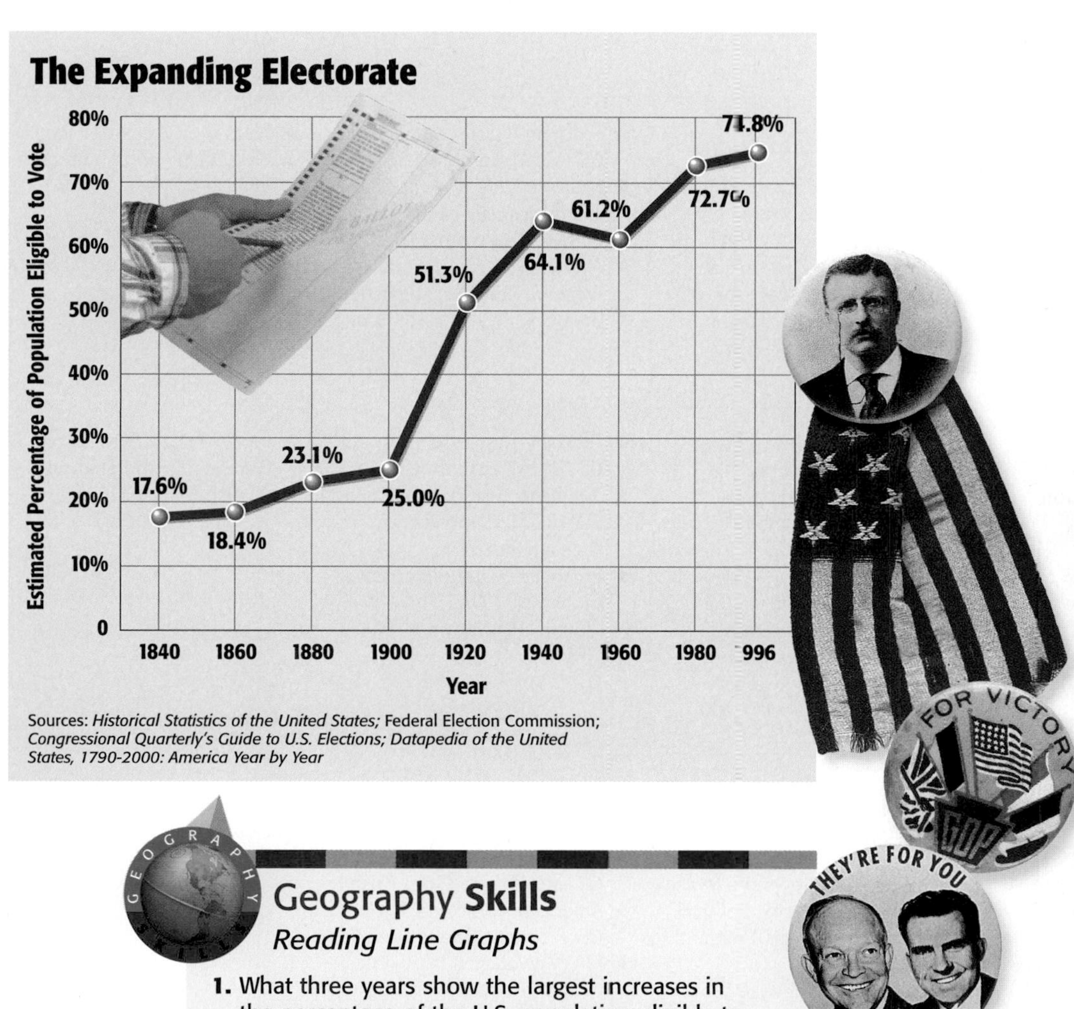

Sources: *Historical Statistics of the United States;* Federal Election Commission; *Congressional Quarterly's Guide to U.S. Elections; Datapedia of the United States, 1790-2000: America Year by Year*

Geography **Skills**

Reading Line Graphs

1. What three years show the largest increases in the percentage of the U.S. population eligible to vote?
2. What amendments to the Constitution help explain the changes in 1920 and 1980?

History Note 4

The Constitution generally gives states the right to decide who is eligible to vote in elections. Over the years however, constitutional amendments have extended the right to vote to more and more people. The Fifteenth Amendment, ratified in 1870, protects the right of people of any race to vote. The Nineteenth Amendment, passed in 1920, gives women the right to vote in all states. The Twenty-sixth Amendment, passed in 1971, lowered the minimum voting age from 21 to 18.

Across the Curriculum

MATH

Voter Turnout. In 1932 an estimated 75,768,000 Americans were of voting age. That year, 39,758,759 people voted in the presidential election, while 37,657,000 cast ballots for Congress. As of 1960, the number of eligible voters had reached 109,672,000. Some 68,838,219 people voted in that year's presidential election, and 64,133,000 voted in the congressional election. By 1992 the number of Americans eligible to vote had reached 189,044,000. Of that number, 104,425,014 voted in that year's presidential election, while 96,239,000 voted for a member of Congress.

Activity: Have students determine which year had the highest percentage of eligible voters cast a ballot for a presidential candidate. *(1960)* Then ask them to determine which year had the lowest percentage of voters turn out for the presidential election. *(1932)* Then have students write a paragraph offering possible explanations for the differences.

SKILLS ANSWERS

1. 1920, 1940, and 1980

2. The Nineteenth Amendment, ratified in 1920, gave women the right to vote, and the Twenty-sixth Amendment, ratified in 1971, lowered the voting age to 18 years.

CHAPTER PLANNING GUIDE
The Nation Expands

	SECTION LESSON OBJECTIVES	PRINT RESOURCES	MULTIMEDIA RESOURCES	SHELTERED ENGLISH RESOURCES
Section 1: Launching the Nation (pp. 83–87)	★ Identify the problems President Washington faced at home and abroad. ★ Analyze ways in which Alexander Hamilton helped solve the nation's economic problems. ★ Explain the challenges John Adams faced during his presidency.	★ Guided Reading Strategies 3.1 ★ American History Political Cartoon 3: Party Politics ★ Section 1 Review, p. 87 ★ Daily Quiz 3.1	★ *Teaching Resources CD–ROM*, Lesson 3.1 ★ Everyday Life in America Transparency 6: *Frakturs:* Folk Art in Federalist America	★ Main Idea Activities for Reteaching and Sheltered English 3.1
Section 2: Building a Strong Nation (pp. 88–93)	★ Evaluate the significance of the Lewis and Clark expedition. ★ Explain why the United States fought the War of 1812, and describe its outcome. ★ Analyze how Andrew Jackson responded to domestic issues.	★ Guided Reading Strategies 3.2 ★ Geography Activity 3: The Seminole Wars ★ American History Political Cartoon 4: The Louisiana Purchase, and Cartoon 6: Jackson and the Bank ★ Section 2 Review, p. 93 ★ Daily Quiz 3.2	★ *Teaching Resources CD–ROM*, Lesson 3.2 ★ Everyday Life in America Transparency 7: Portrait of Native Americans, 1833 ★ *American Music Audio CD Program:* "The Star-Spangled Banner"	★ Main Idea Activities for Reteaching and Sheltered English 3.2
Section 3: The North and the South (pp. 94–100)	★ Describe how the Industrial Revolution and the Transportation Revolution changed American life. ★ Analyze the effect of the cotton boom on the South and slavery. ★ Explain what some of the major reform movements hoped to achieve.	★ Guided Reading Strategies 3.3 ★ Literature Reading 3: Encouraging Women's Rights ★ American History Political Cartoon 5: Temperance Reform, and Cartoon 7: Slavery in America and England ★ Section 3 Review, p. 100 ★ Daily Quiz 3.3	★ *Teaching Resources CD–ROM*, Lesson 3.3 ★ *American History Simulations CD–ROM:* Choosing a Factory Site ★ *American History Interactive Maps CD–ROM:* The Cotton Plantation ★ HRW Web site	★ Main Idea Activities for Reteaching and Sheltered English 3.3
Section 4: Expanding West (pp. 101–05)	★ Explain the events that led Texas to win its independence from Mexico. ★ Describe the challenges travelers faced on the journey west. ★ Identify the events that led to the Mexican War, and examine the outcome of the conflict.	★ Guided Reading Strategies 3.4 ★ Primary Source Reading 3: A Mexican Views the War ★ American History Political Cartoon 8: James Polk and Foreign Policy ★ Section 4 Review, p. 105 ★ Daily Quiz 3.4	★ *Teaching Resources CD–ROM*, Lesson 3.4 ★ *American History Simulations CD–ROM:* The Gold Rush ★ *American Music Audio CD Program:* "Joe Bowers" ★ HRW Web site	★ Main Idea Activities for Reteaching and Sheltered English 3.4
Section 5: The Civil War (pp. 106–11)	★ Discuss the events that demonstrated growing sectional conflict over slavery. ★ Identify events that led to the Civil War. ★ Describe the battles that occurred in the eastern and western theaters of the war.	★ Guided Reading Strategies 3.5 ★ Biography Reading 3: Clara Barton ★ Graphic Organizer 3: Maintaining a Balance ★ Section 5 Review, p. 111 ★ Daily Quiz 3.5	★ *Teaching Resources CD–ROM*, Lesson 3.5 ★ *Exploring America's Past* Video Segment: A Divided Vision; *Teacher's Guide*, pp. 4–6 ★ *American History Simulations CD–ROM:* Global Politics and the Civil War	★ Main Idea Activities for Reteaching and Sheltered English 3.5
Chapter Review and Assessment (pp. 114–15)		★ Chapter 3 Review, pp. 114–15 ★ Vocabulary Activity 3 ★ Chapter 3 Study Guide ★ Chapter 3 Test (Form A or B)	★ Audio Program, Ch. 3 (English and Spanish) ★ *Global Skill Builder CD–ROM* ★ Chapter 3 Test Generator ★ HRW Web site	★ Spanish Glossary ★ Sheltered English Chapter 3 Test

CHAPTER OVERVIEW

After the ratification of the U.S. Constitution, the early U.S. presidents worked hard to put the country on a firm footing. To do so, the nation had to deal with domestic problems, such as the Whiskey Rebellion and how to repay the war debt, and foreign problems, such as how to react to the XYZ affair.

In 1803 the Senate approved the Louisiana Purchase, more than doubling the nation's territory. Once the United States proved it could defend itself in the War of 1812, it began to gain respect as a nation.

In the years following the War of 1812, the nation underwent many changes. The Industrial and Transportation Revolutions altered the economy and the way Americans worked. Reformers worked to improve American society. The nation's territory expanded again with the fixing of Oregon's boundaries, the annexation of Texas, the Mexican Cession, and the Gadsden Purchase.

These changes, however, could not mask the underlying problems caused by the nation's division over slavery. Despite numerous attempts at compromise, tensions continued to rise between the North and the South. Following Abraham Lincoln's victory in the 1860 presidential election, several southern states seceded from the Union, thus leading to the Civil War.

CHAPTER INVESTIGATION

The Chapter Investigation is an extended, multipart activity designed for students to work cooperatively and apply the chapter content in the creation of a project. You may choose to use the Chapter 3 Investigation, Creative Consultants for Feature Films, either as a substitute for teaching the section lessons or as an alternate assessment.

BLOCK SCHEDULING 

The teacher lesson plans for each section offer a variety of activity choices to help you present the material in a block scheduling format. For further suggestions on block scheduling, see the *Block Scheduling Handbook with Team Teaching Strategies,* pp. 13–18.

Meeting Individual Needs

ABILITY LEVELS

LEVEL 1 Basic level activities designed for all students encountering new material.

LEVEL 2 Intermediate level activities designed for average students.

LEVEL 3 Challenging activities designed for above-average students.

SHELTERED ENGLISH These activities address the needs of students with Limited English Proficiency.

Smithsonian Institution®

Internet Connections and Lesson 3
www.si.edu/hrw

CNN Presents America:
Yesterday and Today 1850 to the Present
Segment: John Brown's Legacy

Additional Resources

Books for Teachers

Ambrose, Stephen F. *Undaunted Courage: Meriwether Lewis, Thomas Jefferson, and the Opening of the American West.* Knopf, 1996. Biography of Lewis that recounts the Lewis and Clark expedition and Lewis's life before and after the expedition.

Flexner, James T. *Washington: The Indispensable Man.* NAL-Dutton, 1984. Distillation of the author's award-winning biography.

McLoughlin, W. G. *Cherokee Renascence in the New Republic.* Princeton University Press, 1987. History of the Cherokee and their relationship with the U.S. government.

Books for Students

Hamilton, Virginia. *Many Thousand Gone: African Americans from Slavery to Freedom.* Random House, 1992. General history of slavery, including biographies of famous and unknown slaves and personal narratives.

Levine, Ellen. *If Your Name Was Changed at Ellis Island.* Scholastic, 1993. Introduction to the history of U.S. immigration.

Van Steenwyk, Elizabeth. *California Gold Rush: West with the Forty-Niners.* Watts, 1991. Recounts the gold rush in California (for students reading below grade level).

Multimedia Materials

Hearts and Hands. Video, 63 min. Hearts and Hands Media Arts/SSSS. Documentary on American women during the 1800s.

Thomas Hart Benton. Video, 51 min. SSSS. Dramatization of Missouri senator Thomas Hart Benton's opposition to slavery and his role in keeping Missouri from seceding.

A Nation Asunder. Two videos, 55 min. each. SSSS. Traces Civil War from Fort Sumter to surrender at Appomattox.

The Nation Expands

CHAPTER MOTIVATOR

Ask students to imagine someone who currently is 75 years old. Ask students about the era in which the person was born. Have them brainstorm the political and social changes in American life that this person would have witnessed. Remind students that in its first 75 years, the United States added over 1 million square miles of new territory, fought in three major wars, and experienced dramatic societal changes, such as the end of slavery. Tell students that in this chapter they will learn about these changes and how the U.S. Constitution was both strong enough and flexible enough to govern such a rapidly changing country.

Presenting Themes

- **Global Relations**
  Students might mention disputes over borders, clashes between cultures, or attempts by powerful nations to control weaker ones.
- **Citizenship and Democracy**
  Students might mention that citizens can work for legislation that ensures equality and promotes equal access to educational and employment opportunities.
- **Technology and Society**
  Students might mention that new technology can change the ways people work, open new business opportunities, and close others.

Using the Time Line

Give each student some note cards. Have students write one time line event on each card. As they come across each event in the chapter, have them write the significance of the event on the opposite side of the appropriate note card. As a review of the chapter, ask students to take turns quizzing each other on the time line events.

Albert Bierstadt, *Emigrants Crossing the Plains*, 1867, Oil on Canvas, A011.IT; National Cowboy Hall of Fame, Oklahoma City, OK

CHAPTER 3

The Nation Expands

(1789–1865)

As the 1800s began, the United States was a young country with limitless opportunities for the future. In his first inaugural address, President Thomas Jefferson described the United States as "a rising nation, spread over a wide and fruitful land, traversing [crossing] all the seas with the rich productions of their industry."

Global Relations
Why might nations go to war?

Citizenship and Democracy
How might citizens try to extend equal rights to all people?

Technology and Society
How might changes in technology affect a nation's economy and society?

1790 | 1800 | 1810 | 1820

1789 George Washington is elected president.

1804 Lewis and Clark set out on their journey west.

1814 Britain and the United States sign the Treaty of Ghent, ending the War of 1812.

OBJECTIVES

- **Identify the problems President Washington faced at home and abroad.**
- **Analyze ways in which Alexander Hamilton helped solve the nation's economic problems.**
- **Explain the challenges John Adams faced during his presidency.**

FOCUS

Motivate Before Reading

Define the word *precedent.* Tell students that George Washington chose to serve only two terms as president. This set a precedent for future presidents. Then describe how Franklin Roosevelt chose to break with precedent. Ask students to write a brief paragraph in which they discuss why precedents are useful and when it might be worthwhile to break with precedent. Ask volunteers to share

Launching the Nation

Reading Focus

- What problems did President Washington face at home and abroad?
- How did Alexander Hamilton help solve the nation's economic problems?
- What challenges did John Adams face during his presidency?

Key Terms

- Judiciary Act
- strict construction
- loose construction
- Whiskey Rebellion
- political parties
- XYZ affair
- Alien and Sedition Acts
- Twelfth Amendment

*O*NCE THE STATES HAD *ratified the U.S. Constitution, George Washington looked forward to retiring from public life and living quietly on his Virginia farm. However, his friends soon drew him into politics as a presidential candidate. When Washington hesitated to run, fellow politician Gouverneur Morris told him, "Should the idea prevail [become known] that you would not accept the presidency, it should prove fatal . . . to the new government." Morris concluded confidently, "Of all men, you are the best fitted to fill that office."*

Courtesy of the John Carter Brown Library at Brown University

1788 print of George Washington with state seals

IMAGE ON LEFT PAGE: *Albert Bierstadt's painting* Emigrants Crossing the Plains *shows settlers moving west in the mid-1800s.*

1830 **1840** **1850** **1860**

1830 Congress passes the Indian Removal Act.

1836 Texas wins its independence from Mexico.

1846 Congress declares war on Mexico.

1857 The Supreme Court issues the *Dred Scott* decision.

1865 General Lee surrenders at Appomattox Courthouse, ending the Civil War.

Section 1 RESOURCES

PRINT

- ★ Guided Reading Strategies 3.1
- ★ American History Political Cartoon 3: Party Politics
- ★ Section 1 Review, p. 87
- ★ Daily Quiz 3.1

MULTIMEDIA

- ★ *Teaching Resources CD–ROM,* Lesson 3.1
- ★ Everyday Life in America Transparency 6: *Frakturs:* Folk Art in Federalist America

SHELTERED ENGLISH

- ★ Main Idea Activities for Reteaching and Sheltered English 3.1

their ideas with the class. Tell students that in this section they will learn about the first decade of the new federal government under the Constitution, the precedents set by Presidents Washington and Adams, and how those precedents influenced the development of economic policy, foreign relations, and political parties.

Introduce Key Terms

Linguistic, Logical-Mathematical. Review this section's key terms with students. Have them use their textbooks to find the meaning of each term. Ask students to identify a person associated with each term and to explain the person's connection to the term. **SHELTERED ENGLISH**

TEACH

Have students read Section 1 and complete Guided Reading Strategies 3.1. Choose one or more of the following activities to explore the section content with students. For further suggestions on block scheduling or team teaching, see the *Block Scheduling Handbook*.

LEVEL 1: Linguistic. (Suggested time: 15 min.) As a class, go over students' Guided Reading Strategies. Then use the Reading Focus questions to highlight the main ideas of the section. **SHELTERED ENGLISH**

Economic Development

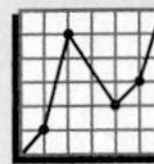

The Confusing Debt. When he accepted the position of treasury secretary, Alexander Hamilton faced a large and confusing national debt involving several different creditors. The debt included IOUs written by the quartermaster, the officer in charge of army supplies; winning tickets from lotteries that the government had held to raise money but had not repaid; certificates that soldiers had received when the government had been unable to pay them for their military service; and payment owed to foreigners who had loaned the nation money. It was Hamilton's task to sort through this mass of paperwork in an attempt to reduce the debt.

Critical Thinking: How did the various types of government debt make Hamilton's job difficult?

ANSWER: He had to determine the size of the debt and to whom it was owed before he could make plans to reduce it.

Washington Sets Precedents

In February 1789 the electoral college unanimously elected George Washington president, with John Adams as vice president. After taking office, President Washington wrote, "The first of everything in our situation will serve to establish a precedent." A precedent is an action or decision that later serves as an example.

Congress organized the executive branch, creating departments that specialized in different areas of national policy. Washington appointed Alexander Hamilton as secretary of the treasury, Thomas Jefferson as secretary of state, Henry Knox as secretary of war, and Samuel Osgood as postmaster general. Washington began to meet with the department heads as a group, which became known as the cabinet.

In September 1789 Congress passed the **Judiciary Act**, creating the federal court system. Washington appointed John Jay as the first chief justice of the United States and Edmund Randolph as attorney general. Washington wrote to the Supreme Court justices:

> **"The happiness of the people of the United States . . . depend[s] in a considerable degree on the interpretation and execution of its laws."**

President Washington with some of his key advisers (left to right): Washington, Henry Knox, Alexander Hamilton, Thomas Jefferson, and Edmund Randolph

Hamilton and National Finances

As secretary of the treasury, Alexander Hamilton had to deal with the national debt—the amount of money the United States owed to various lenders. The U.S. government had raised some money by selling bonds, or certificates that represent money owed, to citizens. It promised to buy the bonds back later at a higher price. To maintain the trust of lenders, Hamilton proposed that the federal government pay its debt to foreign nations and repay citizens the full value of all bonds. Despite opposition from Thomas Jefferson and Representative James Madison, Congress approved Hamilton's plan.

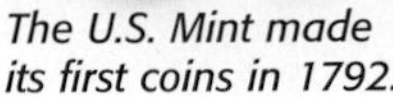

The U.S. Mint made its first coins in 1792.

Hamilton also wanted the federal government to assume, or pay, most of the debts owed by the states for Revolutionary War expenses. The southern states, which had few war debts, did not want their citizens to be taxed to help pay the debts of other states. However, they did want to move the nation's capital. They believed that having the capital in New York gave the northern states too much influence. As a compromise, Congress approved the debt assumption plan and chose the site of present-day Washington, D.C., as the new national capital.

Hamilton wanted to create a national bank to provide a safe place to deposit government funds and to serve as a source of loans for the government and businesses. Madison and Jefferson opposed the bank because they believed in **strict construction**—that the federal government could do only what the Constitution specifically said it could do. Hamilton argued for **loose construction**, meaning that the federal government could take reasonable actions that the Constitution did not specifically forbid it from taking. In his opinion, the clause in Article I, Section 8, stating that Congress has the right "to make all laws . . . necessary and proper" was "elastic," or intended to be flexible. President Washington and Congress supported Hamilton. In 1791 Congress chartered the Bank of the United States for 20 years.

ALL LEVELS: Logical-Mathematical, Interpersonal. (Suggested time: 45 min.) Ask students to imagine that they are organizing a panel discussion, members of which will include Republicans Thomas Jefferson and James Madison and Federalists John Adams and Alexander Hamilton. Have each student prepare a list of topics for conversation and questions to ask each guest. (Conversation topics and questions should be based on challenges facing the Adams administration.) After students have finished preparing, have them exchange their lists of topics and questions with other students. Instruct class members to write out what they think each guest would have said about each topic or question. Encourage volunteers to share their ideas with the class. **SHELTERED ENGLISH**

LEVEL 2: Linguistic, Logical-Mathematical, Interpersonal. (Suggested time: 45 min.) Have students write a one-page memo from Alexander Hamilton to George Washington, outlining Hamilton's financial plans for the United States. Have volunteers present their memos and explain why Thomas Jefferson disagreed with some of Hamilton's ideas.

LEVEL 3: Linguistic, Logical-Mathematical. (Suggested time: 45 min. plus homework) Ask students to imagine that they

George Washington

George Washington entered the presidency with a tremendous sense of responsibility to the country. He wanted to be both a proper, dignified leader and a president who listened to the needs of the people. Washington was sometimes trapped between the importance of his office and his wish to be treated like an ordinary citizen. At his inauguration, for example, Washington told his military guard, "The affection of my fellow citizens is all the guard I want." However, he decided that the escort was necessary to maintain the dignity of the presidency.

The pressure to live up to the country's expectations often made life difficult for Washington. He was very sensitive to attacks made against him in the press, leading Thomas Jefferson to write, "I think he feels those things [criticisms] more than any person I ever met." Washington did not run for re-election in 1796. He had little time to enjoy his retirement from politics, however, because he died in 1799.

New Conflicts

In 1793 France declared war on Britain. On April 22, President Washington issued the Neutrality Proclamation, which stated that the United States would remain neutral toward all nations at war in Europe. However, both Britain and France violated U.S. neutrality. Some French agents tried to recruit American ships to attack the British. Britain seized hundreds of American merchant ships trading with the French West Indies. Rumors spread that the British were also encouraging American Indians to fight against American settlers on the frontier. Washington sent John Jay to London to negotiate a peaceful resolution. The Senate ratified Jay's Treaty in 1795. That same year, diplomat Thomas Pinckney arranged a treaty with Spain, which had closed the port of New Orleans to U.S. trade. In Pinckney's Treaty, Spain agreed to reopen New Orleans to American shipping.

Washington also faced domestic issues. As settlers moved to the Northwest Territory, they forced American Indians off their lands. An Indian confederation led by Chief Little Turtle of the Miami defeated U.S. forces in 1790 and 1791. Then on August 20, 1794, General Anthony Wayne defeated the confederation in the Battle of Fallen Timbers. In 1795 Indian leaders signed the Treaty of Greenville, giving Americans access to Indian lands in most of present-day Ohio.

More conflict broke out after Congress passed a tax on U.S.-made whiskey to help pay off the national debt. Some protesters in rural western Pennsylvania reacted violently. Washington ordered several states to call out their militias and led more than 10,000 soldiers toward the area. Most of the rebels fled as the troops approached, thus ending the **Whiskey Rebellion** in November 1794 without a real battle.

Having faithfully served as president for two terms, Washington decided not to run again. In his Farewell Address, he warned that the greatest threats to America were public debt, foreign alliances, and political divisions at home.

The Granger Collection, New York

Pennsylvanians opposed to the whiskey tax tar and feather a tax collector.

Presidential Profiles

George Washington. President Washington wrote the first draft of his Farewell Address, but he feared that it contained too many "egoisms." He asked Alexander Hamilton to revise this first draft. Although Washington liked the new document, he revised Hamilton's draft himself before releasing it. Thus, Hamilton and Washington both deserve credit for writing the Farewell Address.

Activity: Have students write a brief paragraph on Washington's views and allow a fellow student to edit the paragraph. Have students compare the original paragraph and the revision.

Multimedia Resources

Everyday Life in America Transparency 6: *Frakturs:* Folk Art in Federalist America

are neutral observers in the Northwest Territory. Have each student write a report that answers the following questions: What conflicts existed between settlers and American Indians? Why did the Indians form a confederation? Why did the two groups go to war? What happened at the Battle of Fallen Timbers? What were the terms of the Treaty of Greenville?

CLOSE

Linguistic, Visual-Spatial. Ask students to create a book cover jacket for a book about the 1790s. Have students write their title on the cover and create an illustration to accompany it. On the left inside cover, have students create a mock table of contents, and on the right have them write a brief summary of what a book on the 1790s might discuss. Have volunteers share their book cover jackets with the class.

CHALLENGE AND EXTEND

Linguistic, Musical-Rhythmic. Have students develop political campaigns for the election of 1800. Organize the class into two groups, one for Adams and one for Jefferson. Ask each group to select a campaign manager. Have each group prepare political speeches on the issues; slogans and campaign songs that emphasize

Linking Past to Present

Presidential Communications. President Washington sent the draft of his Farewell Address to David Claypoole, publisher of a Philadelphia newspaper called the *American Daily Advertiser.* Because Claypoole reserved the front page for advertisements, he ran the address on the second and third pages. Other newspapers copied the story from the *Advertiser,* and Americans slowly learned about their president's farewell message. With the advent of modern communications devices, such as radio and television, people around the world now learn about presidential messages immediately, instead of waiting weeks or months for word to spread.

Critical Thinking: What problems might poor communications have caused for presidents in the late 1700s and early 1800s?

ANSWER: Response time to a national emergency would be slow, and secondhand information could be incomplete or erroneous.

HISTORICAL DOCUMENTS ANSWERS

1. He advised against political parties.

2. Answers will vary but students should state their opinions and offer support for them.

HISTORICAL DOCUMENTS

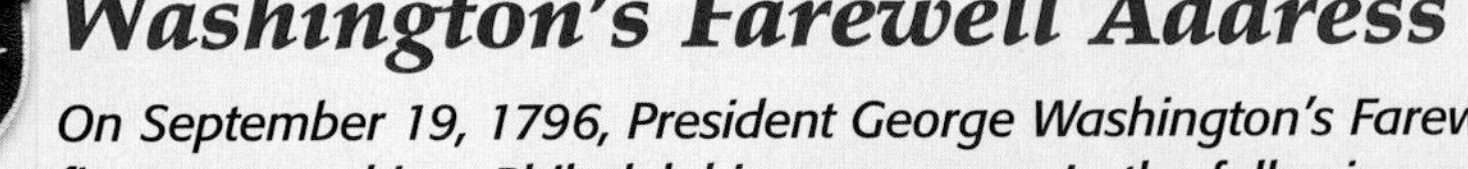

1796

Washington's Farewell Address

On September 19, 1796, President George Washington's Farewell Address first appeared in a Philadelphia newspaper. In the following excerpt he advised the nation on its economy, political parties, and foreign policy.

In contemplating [considering] the causes which may disturb our Union, it occurs as matter of serious concern that any ground should have been furnished for characterizing parties by geographical discriminations: Northern and Southern; Atlantic and Western. . . .

Let me now . . . warn you in the most solemn manner against the baneful [destructive] effects of the spirit of party generally. . . .

Of all the dispositions and habits which lead to political prosperity, religion and morality are indispensable [necessary] supports. . . .

Promote, then, as an object of primary importance, institutions for the general diffusion [spreading] of knowledge. In proportion as the structure of a government gives force to public opinion, it is essential that public opinion should be enlightened.

As a very important source of strength and security, cherish public credit. One method of preserving it is to use it as sparingly as possible, . . . avoiding likewise the accumulation of debt, . . . not ungenerously throwing upon posterity [future generations] the burden which we ourselves ought to bear. . . .

Observe good faith and justice toward all nations. Cultivate [seek] peace and harmony with all. . . .

The great rule of conduct for us, in regard to foreign nations, is in extending our commercial relations to have with them as little political connection as possible. . . .

It is our true policy to steer clear of permanent alliances with any portion of the foreign world.

Understanding Primary Sources

1. What was President Washington's most important advice?
2. Do you think his advice is still important today? Explain your answer.

President John Adams

Despite George Washington's warning, **political parties**—groups that help elect government officials and influence government policies—played an important role in the 1796 presidential election. Alexander Hamilton helped shape the Federalist Party's policies, which included strengthening the federal government and promoting trade and industry. The Federalists, who were most popular in New England, nominated former vice president John Adams and Thomas Pinckney.

Thomas Jefferson and James Madison started the Democratic-Republican Party, or Republicans, which wanted to limit the power of the federal government. The party was most popular in the South and the West. The Republicans chose Thomas Jefferson and Aaron Burr as their candidates. Adams received 71 electoral votes, and Jefferson came in second with 68. Under the Constitution at that time, the second-place finisher became vice president, even if that person was from a different political party than the president. Thus, Adams and Jefferson served together.

the merits of the candidate; press releases to cast the candidate in a positive light; and advertisements to spread the candidate's message to the public. Hold a rally in which each group presents its campaign to the rest of the class.

REVIEW

Linguistic, Logical-Mathematical. Have students complete the Section Review questions. Then ask students to write a brief essay describing whether they think Washington and Adams were successful presidents. Students should use events from the section to support their opinions.

ASSESS

Have students complete Daily Quiz 3.1.

RETEACH

Linguistic, Visual-Spatial, Logical-Mathematical. Have students complete Main Idea Activities for Reteaching and Sheltered English 3.1. Then ask each student to draw two coins, one to represent the Federalists and the other to represent the Democratic-Republicans. Each coin should have a symbol and an inscription that conveys the student's understanding of the depicted party. **SHELTERED ENGLISH**

The XYZ Affair

One of Adams's first actions as president was to send a diplomatic team to Paris to improve relations with France. Three French agents informed the U.S. diplomats that negotiations would not begin without a $250,000 bribe. The furious diplomats refused to meet this demand and told Adams that their mission was a failure. On hearing the news of the so-called **XYZ affair**, Federalists called for war with France, crying, "Millions for defense, but not one cent for tribute [forced payment]!" At Adams's urging, Congress strengthened the army and the navy. However, Adams stunned many Federalists by not asking Congress to declare war on France. In 1800 the United States and France signed a treaty that ended the undeclared war that was being fought on the seas.

Republicans criticized Federalist support for war with France. To quiet the criticism, the Federalist-controlled Congress passed the **Alien and Sedition Acts** in 1798. The Alien Act allowed the president to deport, or expel, foreign citizens from the United States on suspicion of anti-government activities. The Sedition Act made it illegal to "write, print, utter or publish" any false or hostile words against the U.S. government or the administration's policies.

In response, Jefferson and Madison wrote the Virginia and Kentucky Resolutions. They argued that the Alien and Sedition Acts were unconstitutional because they went beyond the powers granted to the federal government and interfered with the powers of the state governments. Future politicians used the resolutions to argue that the states could declare laws or actions of the federal government to be illegal.

John Adams campaign button

The Election of 1800

In the 1800 presidential election, Thomas Jefferson and Aaron Burr defeated John Adams and Charles Pinckney. Jefferson and Burr received 73 electoral votes each. Voters could not vote separately for president and vice president, so the House of Representatives broke the tie, electing Jefferson president. In 1804 the states ratified the **Twelfth Amendment**, which required a separate ballot for president and vice president. The election of 1800 proved that the nation could transfer power peacefully from one party to another. Jefferson later wrote that the election was

> **"as real a revolution in the principles of our government as that of 1776 was in its form; . . . [caused] by the rational and peaceable instrument of reform, the suffrage [vote] of the people."**

SECTION 1 REVIEW

Identify and explain the significance of the following:

- **George Washington**
- **Judiciary Act**
- **strict construction**
- **loose construction**
- **Whiskey Rebellion**
- **political parties**
- **John Adams**
- **XYZ affair**
- **Alien and Sedition Acts**
- **Thomas Jefferson**
- **Twelfth Amendment**

Reading for Content Understanding

1 **Main Idea** What foreign and domestic difficulties did President Washington face?

2 **Main Idea** What issues did John Adams face as president?

3 **Economic Development** What were Alexander Hamilton's plans for improving the U.S. economy?

4 **Writing** *Creating* Write an editorial commenting on the rise of political parties.

5 **Critical Thinking** *Supporting a Point of View* Do you think that the founding of the national bank was constitutional? Explain your answer.

Section 1 Review ANSWERS

Identify

For significance, see the following pages:

- George Washington, p. 83
- Judiciary Act, p. 84
- strict construction, p. 84
- loose construction, p. 84
- Whiskey Rebellion, p. 85
- political parties, p. 86
- John Adams, p. 86
- XYZ affair, p. 87
- Alien and Sedition Acts, p. 87
- Thomas Jefferson, p. 87
- Twelfth Amendment, p. 87

Reading for Content Understanding

1. the national debt, British and French infringements on U.S. neutrality, conflict with British-supported American Indians, conflict with Spain over closing the port of New Orleans, and the Whiskey Rebellion

2. Adams had a vice president from another political party, had to deal with the XYZ affair and the resulting undeclared war, and faced Republicans' response to the Alien and Sedition Acts.

3. Hamilton wanted to pay foreign debts, pay the full value of bonds, have the federal government assume most of the debt owed by states, and create a national bank.

4. Editorials will vary but students should state their opinions about the rise of political parties and offer explanations for them.

5. Students should state their opinions about the constitutionality of the national bank and support their reasoning with arguments from the section.

SECTION 2 LESSON PLAN

OBJECTIVES

- Evaluate the significance of the Lewis and Clark expedition.
- Explain why the United States fought the War of 1812, and describe its outcome.
- Analyze how Andrew Jackson responded to domestic issues.

FOCUS

Motivate Before Reading

Tell students the story of Meriwether Lewis and Thomas Jefferson, on their knees in the president's White House office, examining maps of the Louisiana Territory and the Pacific Northwest that were spread out on the floor before them. Ask students to imagine what the two men talked about as they examined the maps and write brief examples of what might have been said in their

Section 2 RESOURCES

PRINT

- ★ Guided Reading Strategies 3.2
- ★ Geography Activity 3: The Seminole Wars
- ★ American History Political Cartoons 4: The Louisiana Purchase, and Cartoon 6: Jackson and the Bank
- ★ Section 2 Review, p. 93
- ★ Daily Quiz 3.2

MULTIMEDIA

- ★ *Teaching Resources CD–ROM,* Lesson 3.2
- ★ *American Music Audio CD Program:* "The Star-Spangled Banner"

SHELTERED ENGLISH

- ★ Main Idea Activities for Reteaching and Sheltered English 3.2

Building a Strong Nation

Reading Focus

What was the significance of the Lewis and Clark expedition?

What led to the War of 1812, and what was the outcome?

How did Andrew Jackson respond to domestic issues during his presidency?

Key Terms

judicial review
Louisiana Purchase
Battle of New Orleans
Treaty of Ghent
Monroe Doctrine
Missouri Compromise
Democratic Party
states' rights
Indian Removal Act

THE DAY WAS MARCH 4, 1801, and Thomas Jefferson was about to be sworn in as president of the United States in the new capital city of Washington. While George Washington and John Adams had worn splendid outfits and ridden in carriages to their inaugurations, Jefferson chose to walk the few blocks from his boardinghouse to the Capitol Building. A reporter observed, "His dress was, as usual, that of a plain citizen, without any distinctive badge of office." Known by some Republicans as "The People's Friend," Jefferson demonstrated his views on government by not wearing fancy clothes to the inauguration.

Coin celebrating Jefferson's inauguration

Collection of the American Numismatic Society, New York

Jefferson in Office

President Jefferson kept some Federalist policies and institutions, such as the Bank of the United States. However, he decreased military spending and repealed domestic taxes. He also told Secretary of State James Madison to withhold some commissions of judges that President Adams had appointed late in the evening before he left office.

One such "midnight judge," William Marbury, argued that under the Judiciary Act of 1789, the Supreme Court had the authority to force the executive branch to hand over his commission. In *Marbury* v. *Madison* the Court ruled against Marbury, saying that some powers Congress had given the Court in the Judiciary Act were unconstitutional. Chief Justice John Marshall's ruling established the principle of **judicial review**, which means that the Supreme Court has the right to declare an act of Congress to be unconstitutional. The Court gained great power with this ruling. Although the Court's decision supported the actions of Jefferson's administration, the president would face many challenges ahead.

conversation. Have volunteers read segments of their mock conversations to the class. Then tell students that in this section they will learn how the United States expanded westward and study conflicts that this expansion created.

Introduce Key Terms

Linguistic, Logical-Mathematical. Review this section's key terms with students. Have them use context cues to write a definition for each term. Then ask them to write a sentence using each term. **SHELTERED ENGLISH**

TEACH

Have students read Section 2 and complete Guided Reading Strategies 3.2. Choose one or more of the following activities to explore the section content with students. For further suggestions on block scheduling or team teaching, see the *Block Scheduling Handbook.*

LEVEL 1: Linguistic. (Suggested time: 15 min.) As a class, go over students' Guided Reading Strategies. Then use the Reading Focus questions to highlight the main ideas of the section. **SHELTERED ENGLISH**

The Louisiana Purchase

President Jefferson was greatly concerned that France once again owned Louisiana:

> **"There is on the globe one single spot, the possessor of which is our natural and habitual enemy. It is New Orleans, through which the produce of three-eighths of our territory must pass to market."**

In response to a U.S. attempt to buy New Orleans, France offered to sell all of Louisiana for $15 million. On October 20, 1803, the Senate approved the **Louisiana Purchase**, which stretched west from the Mississippi River to the Rocky Mountains.

Jefferson sent a small expedition led by Meriwether Lewis and William Clark to explore the West. In May 1804 the Lewis and Clark expedition began its journey by going up the Missouri River. A Shoshoni woman named Sacagawea (sak-uh-juh-WEE-uh) helped the group cross the Great Plains. Other Shoshoni Indians led Lewis and Clark across the Rocky Mountains. After the difficult journey, the explorers followed the Columbia River to the Pacific Ocean.

An illustrated page from William Clark's journal

Lewis and Clark explored the Pacific Northwest during the winter. In March 1806 the expedition started its long trek home, reaching St. Louis in September. In their reports and journals, Lewis and Clark described the West's lands and people. They also provided scientific information on the region's plants and animals.

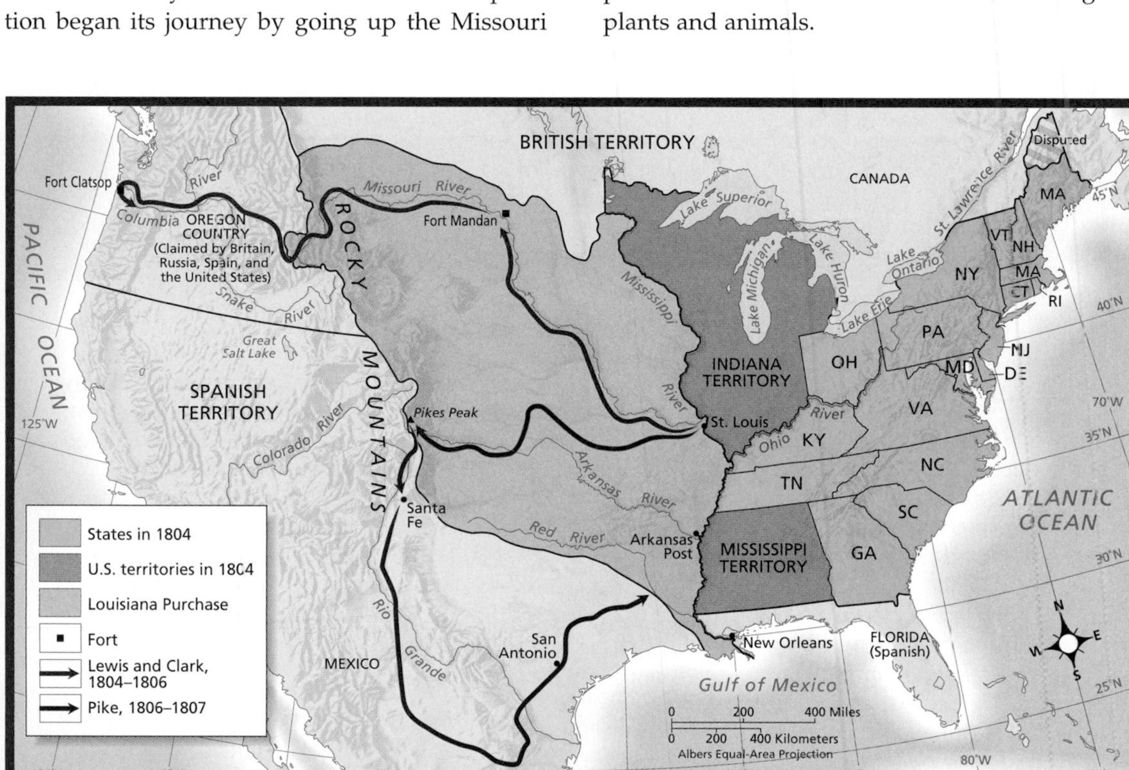

The Louisiana Purchase

Learning from Maps Meriwether Lewis and William Clark, and later Zebulon Pike, led expeditions to explore the vast Louisiana Territory.

Place From which city did both the Lewis and Clark and the Pike explorations begin?

Constitutional Heritage

The Constitution and the Louisiana Purchase. Like his colleagues James Madison and James Monroe, Thomas Jefferson believed in a strict constructionist interpretation of the Constitution. Yet all three supported the Louisiana Purchase because they saw the opportunity to expand the United States as more important than strict construction of the Constitution. Treasury Secretary Albert Gallatin offered Jefferson the particularly persuasive argument that the United States had "an inherent right to acquire territory."

Activity: Ask students to write to Thomas Jefferson to convince him to go ahead with or turn away from the Louisiana Purchase.

MAP ANSWER

St. Louis

ALL LEVELS: Linguistic, Visual-Spatial. (Suggested time: 45 min. plus homework) Organize students into small groups and assign each group one of the following topics: causes of the War of 1812; the Battle of Tippecanoe; the Battle of Horseshoe Bend; the Battle of New Orleans; or the Treaty of Ghent. Ask students to imagine that they are running a museum dedicated to the War of 1812. Have each group create an exhibit based on the assigned topic. Ask a member of each group to explain its exhibit to the class. **SHELTERED ENGLISH**

ALL LEVELS: Visual-Spatial, Logical-Mathematical. (Suggested time: 45 min.) Have students create a graphic organizer, labeling the columns as follows: *the Second Bank of the United States, the Nullification Controversy,* and *Indian Policy.* Have students label the rows as follows: *Response of the Jackson Administration, Response of the President's Adversaries,* and *Impact of Jackson's Policies on Future Administrations.* Ask students to complete the organizer by filling in the appropriate information. Finally, have volunteers explain their organizers to the class. **SHELTERED ENGLISH**

Historical Sidelight

"The Star-Spangled Banner." The flag that inspired Francis Scott Key to write the national anthem has 15 stars and 15 stripes (8 red and 7 white). In 1814 the United States had 18 states, but variation in the number of stars and stripes displayed on U.S. flags was common at that time. Congress finally passed a law in 1818 mandating 13 stripes. The number and arrangement of the stars was not standardized until 1912, by executive order of President Taft. The flag that inspired Francis Scott Key was donated to the Smithsonian Institution about 100 years after the bombardment of Fort McHenry.

Activity: Have students use the library and other resources to conduct research on the U.S. flag. Have students create time lines showing the changes to the flag over the years.

American Arts Answers

1. He saw the American flag still flying.

2. It celebrated the bravery and freedom of the American people.

Multimedia Resources

American Music Audio CD Program: "The Star-Spangled Banner"

Trouble with Britain

France had agreed to sell Louisiana in part because it was at war with Britain. Neither Britain nor France wanted the United States to supply war materials to its enemy. The British and French navies stopped and searched hundreds of American merchant ships. The British also searched the ships for deserters from the British navy. In a practice called impressment, the British forced these people and others to serve in their navy. British officials even impressed U.S. citizens, despite the protests of the U.S. government.

In 1807 Congress passed the Embargo Act, which in effect prohibited trade with all foreign nations. Northern economies, which relied heavily on trade, suffered, but the act did little to hurt Britain or France. In 1809 Congress repealed the unpopular law and passed the Non-Intercourse Act, which banned trade only with Britain and France. This act went into effect just before James Madison, the newly elected president, took office.

The War of 1812

Britain also angered many Americans by providing military aid to American Indians in the Northwest Territory. Tecumseh, a Shawnee chief, was trying to unite Indian nations into a confederation to oppose settlers. On November 7, 1811, Indiana Territory governor William Henry Harrison fought a group of Indians in the Battle of Tippecanoe. Harrison's soldiers forced the Indians to retreat and destroyed their village near the Tippecanoe River. Tecumseh thus lost the support he needed to create a great Indian confederacy.

Some members of Congress, the War Hawks, wanted to declare war on Britain. Federalists in New England, who preferred to renew friendly business ties with Britain, opposed them. Speaking to Congress on June 1, 1812, President Madison said that Britain was in "a state of war against the United States." In response, Congress declared war. A few months later, Madison was re-elected.

American Arts

The National Anthem

American Francis Scott Key was aboard a British warship when the British attacked Fort McHenry. When the battle ended, Key saw the U.S. flag still flying above the fort. The Americans had won. Key later explained his joy:

> *"Through the clouds of the war the stars of that banner still shone in my view. . . . My heart spoke; and 'Does not such a country and such defenders of their country deserve a song?' was its question."*

Key wrote a poem to express his feelings and set the verses to the melody of a popular song, which became quite popular. Soon Key's composition was published as "The Star-Spangled Banner." A few months later, Americans played the new piece at the Battle of New Orleans. In 1931 "The Star-Spangled Banner" became the official national anthem of the United States.

The Granger Collection, New York

Sheet music for "The Star-Spangled Banner"

Understanding the Arts

1. How did Francis Scott Key know the Americans had won the battle?
2. Why do you think "The Star-Spangled Banner" became popular?

LEVEL 2: Linguistic, Logical-Mathematical, Interpersonal. (Suggested time: 45 min. plus homework) Ask students to imagine that they are accompanying Lewis and Clark on their expedition. Have them write journal entries describing the people, plants, and animals encountered; the land traveled; the dangers faced; and the travel conditions experienced by the explorers. Ask volunteers to read portions of their journal entries to the class. Finally, discuss the significance of Lewis and Clark's expedition with the class.

LEVEL 3: Linguistic, Logical-Mathematical, Intrapersonal. (Suggested time: 45 min.) Ask students to imagine that President Monroe has asked for their advice before issuing the Monroe Doctrine. Read the excerpt from the doctrine on page 92 as a class. Then ask each student to prepare a memo for the president advising him to do one of the following: issue the proposed message "as is"; modify it in particular ways; or not issue the message. Ask each student to offer support for the option he or she chose. Each memo should also attempt to show the president whether his proposed message fits well with the foreign relations precedents dating back to President Washington in the 1790s. To conclude, call on the advisers to vote whether to recommend that the message be issued.

British forces set fire to many government buildings in Washington during the War of 1812.

Early in the war, a U.S. invasion of Canada failed, giving Britain control of the strategic Great Lakes region. On September 10, 1813, U.S. captain Oliver Hazard Perry's fleet won a battle on Lake Erie. Perry sent General William Henry Harrison a message: "We have met the enemy and they are ours." Harrison defeated the British and their American Indian allies in early October near the Thames River in Canada. Tecumseh's death in the battle ended the threat of the British–American Indian alliance in the Great Lakes area.

Farther south, Creek forces led by Red Eagle destroyed Fort Mims in present-day Alabama. Andrew Jackson, a general in the Tennessee militia, led his soldiers in a decisive victory over the Creek at Horseshoe Bend in 1814. Red Eagle surrendered days later, ending the Creek War.

Meanwhile, the British navy was blockading and attacking U.S. seaports. In 1814 the British captured Washington, setting fire to the White House and other buildings. The British then attacked Baltimore, Maryland, which was guarded by Fort McHenry. The Americans refused to surrender, and the British retreated. The British next attacked New Orleans on January 8, 1815. At the **Battle of New Orleans**, General Jackson won a great victory. Meanwhile, a peace treaty ending the war had been signed two weeks earlier.

The peace agreement that Jackson had yet to hear about was the **Treaty of Ghent**, signed on December 24, 1814, in Belgium. Following months of negotiations, the treaty ended the War of 1812 and restored all conquered territory. However, the diplomats found no solutions to the problems of impressment or trade embargoes.

American flag from 1818

Peace and Prosperity

After the War of 1812, the United States entered "the Era of Good Feelings" with the election of James Monroe in 1816. He served two terms. During Monroe's presidency, the Convention of 1818 set the U.S.-Canada border at the 49th parallel and established the joint British and U.S. occupation of Oregon. In the 1819 Adams-Onís Treaty, Spain ceded, or gave up, Florida to the United States. At the time, Spain was involved in struggles with its Latin American colonies. In response, Monroe issued the **Monroe Doctrine** in 1823. The doctrine warned European nations not to colonize or interfere in the Americas.

Monroe faced a domestic crisis in 1819 when Missouri applied for statehood. At that time there were 11 free states and 11 slave states in the Union. Representative Henry Clay of Kentucky proposed the **Missouri Compromise**, which would let Missouri enter the Union as a slave state while Maine joined as a free state. The compromise would also prohibit slavery in any new territories or states formed north of the 36°30' line. Congress approved the compromise in 1820.

To unify the nation economically, Clay proposed the American System, a plan to use protective tariffs to boost domestic industries and to pay for internal improvements. Congress approved a protective tariff, and the first federal road project was the Cumberland, or National, Road. The road eventually ran from Maryland to Illinois. In the Northeast, canals were built because water transportation was usually quicker, easier, and cheaper than overland travel. New Yorkers paid about $7 million to build the Erie Canal, which ran from Buffalo to Albany. When it was completed in 1825, the canal opened up transportation between the Great Lakes region and New York City.

Citizenship and Democracy

Politics and the Monroe Doctrine. The Monroe Doctrine is remembered as an important foreign-policy declaration, but it also played a role in the presidential ambitions of John Quincy Adams. Adams hoped to succeed Monroe in the White House, but he knew that many Americans were suspicious of him because he desired close relations with Great Britain. So when the British wanted to issue a joint declaration opposing European influence in the Americas, Adams persuaded Monroe to issue the doctrine without British participation. Strongly nationalistic Americans approved of this decision, and Adams was not attacked as pro-British in the 1824 election.

Critical Thinking: How can domestic political issues influence foreign affairs?

ANSWER: Domestic political issues can lead a country to begin or end negotiations with a foreign country or can lead to war.

CLOSE

Visual-Spatial, Logical-Mathematical. Ask students to imagine that this section, Building a Strong Nation, is a book of its own. Have each student draw a picture for its front cover. Call on volunteers to explain their illustrations and invite comment from other members of the class.

CHALLENGE AND EXTEND

Linguistic, Logical-Mathematical, Intrapersonal. Ask the class to generate a list of options available to the federal government in the 1830s for dealing with the Indian population in the southeastern United States. Assign one of these options to each group. Then have each group use the library or other resources to analyze the strengths and weaknesses of the assigned option. Hold a policy conference in which each group reports its findings. Conclude by discussing the problems of the Jackson administration's Indian Removal policy. Call on volunteers to express their points of view on what the government could have done differently, allow ample time for them to elaborate, and allow others to argue the point.

Cultural Diversity

Cherokee Society. Many Cherokee believed that they could avoid conflict with settlers by adopting practices similar to those of white society. For example, in the early 1800s, the Cherokee invited missionary societies to establish schools in their towns. In these schools, Cherokee children learned how to read and write English. In 1821 a Cherokee named Sequoyah produced a writing system that used 85 characters to represent Cherokee syllables. Up to that time there were no written American Indian languages. In 1828 the Cherokee began publishing a newspaper, the *Cherokee Phoenix*, in both English and Cherokee. The Cherokee also created a system of government modeled on the U.S. Constitution. They established an electoral system, a bicameral council, and a court system, all headed by a principal chief.

Activity: Using the library or other resources, have students find more information on the *Cherokee Phoenix* and write a summary of some of its recurring themes.

Historical Documents Answers

1. He warned not to become involved in the politics of countries in the Western Hemisphere.

2. It limited Europeans' opportunities for political and economic expansion in the Western Hemisphere.

HISTORICAL DOCUMENTS

1823

The Monroe Doctrine

On December 2, 1823, President James Monroe issued what became known as the Monroe Doctrine. The following is an excerpt from the doctrine, which has had a significant effect on U.S. foreign policy.

We . . . declare that we should consider any attempt on their [European powers'] part to extend their [political] system to any portion of this hemisphere as dangerous to our peace and safety.

With the existing colonies or dependencies of any European power we have not interfered and shall not interfere. But with the governments who have declared their independence and maintained it, and whose independence we have . . . acknowledged, we could not view any interposition [interference] for the purpose of oppressing [unjustly ruling] them, or controlling in any other manner their destiny, by any European power in any other light than as the manifestation [realization] of an unfriendly disposition toward the United States. . . .

Our policy in regard to Europe . . . remains the same, which is, not to interfere in the internal concerns of any of its powers. . . . But in regard to those continents [the Americas], circumstances are . . . different. It is impossible that the allied powers should extend their political system to any portion of either continent without endangering our peace and happiness. . . .

It is equally impossible, therefore, that we should behold such interposition in any form with indifference.

Understanding Primary Sources

1. What warning did Monroe give to the European powers in the Monroe Doctrine?
2. What do you think is the most important part of this document?

The Age of Jackson

John Quincy Adams won the 1824 presidential election by defeating Andrew Jackson, who had campaigned as a representative of the common people. Jackson's supporters became known as the **Democratic Party**. Many supporters of President Adams began calling themselves National Republicans. Jackson and John C. Calhoun, his running mate, won the 1828 election.

Many white men voted for the first time in 1828. They had gained suffrage when states eliminated property ownership as a voting qualification. Political parties began holding nominating conventions—public meetings to select the party's presidential and vice presidential candidates. This democratic expansion is referred to as Jacksonian Democracy. President Jackson rewarded some of his supporters with government jobs—a practice known as the spoils system.

A national crisis arose before the 1828 election when Congress passed a high protective tariff. Southerners opposed it because the South relied heavily on imported goods. Calhoun, who was from South Carolina, supported **states' rights**, or the belief that state power should be greater than federal power. He wrote that states had the right to nullify, or cancel, federal laws. When Congress passed a new tariff in 1832, Calhoun resigned as vice president. South Carolina's legislature

REVIEW

Linguistic, Logical-Mathematical, Interpersonal. Have students complete the Section Review questions. Then organize the class into several groups. Have each group write a short quiz on the important events described in this section. Have groups exchange quizzes and answer the questions. Discuss any questions that students find problematic.

ASSESS

Have students complete Daily Quiz 3.2.

RETEACH

Visual-Spatial, Logical-Mathematical, Interpersonal. Have students complete Main Idea Activities for Reteaching and Sheltered English 3.2. Then organize the class into three groups and assign each group one of the Reading Focus questions. Have each group create a poster that answers the question and identifies important events, ideas, and people related to the answer. Have groups explain their posters to the class. **SHELTERED ENGLISH**

declared the tariffs to be "null, void . . . nor binding upon this State." Jackson threatened to send troops into South Carolina to enforce the law. The nullification crisis ended after Congress agreed to gradually lower the tariffs and South Carolina agreed to enforce the law.

Andrew Jackson

Also in 1832, Jackson vetoed a bill to renew the charter of the Second Bank of the United States. In *McCulloch* v. *Maryland*, the Supreme Court had ruled that the Constitution gave Congress implied powers, such as the right to establish the Bank. However, Jackson disagreed. In spite of his conflicts with Congress and the Court, he remained popular with voters and easily won re-election with Martin Van Buren as his running mate. He then moved most of the Bank's funds to state banks.

Van Buren won the 1836 presidential election. Soon after he took office, a financial crisis, known as the Panic of 1837, struck the nation. The resulting economic depression hurt his re-election campaign in 1840. William Henry Harrison, the hero of the Battle of Tippecanoe, won the election.

 Indian Removal

With President Jackson's support, Congress had passed the **Indian Removal Act** in 1830. This act authorized the removal of American Indians living east of the Mississippi River to Indian Territory. This newly created region contained most of present-day Oklahoma. To oversee federal Indian policy, Congress had created the Bureau of Indian Affairs. In the 1840s Indian removal in the former Northwest Territory was completed. In the Southeast, many of the Choctaw, Creek, and Chickasaw were removed in the 1830s.

In Georgia, the Cherokee sued the state, arguing that the tribe was an independent nation. In 1831 the Supreme Court disagreed, saying that tribes were "domestic dependent nations." Later, in *Worcester* v. *Georgia,* the Court ruled that only the federal government had authority over American Indians, but Georgia defied the ruling. The Cherokee were removed to Indian Territory in 1838. Almost one fourth of the 18,000 Cherokee died on this 800-mile walk known as the Trail of Tears.

In present-day Florida, Seminole leader Osceola called for armed resistance to removal:

> **"When the Great Spirit tells me to go with the white man, I go, but he tells me not to go. I have a rifle. . . . I say, we must not leave our homes and lands."**

Despite resistance, the U.S. Army removed some 3,000 Seminole and killed many others by 1842.

SECTION 2 REVIEW

Identify and explain the significance of the following:

- **judicial review**
- **Louisiana Purchase**
- **Andrew Jackson**
- **Battle of New Orleans**
- **Treaty of Ghent**
- **Monroe Doctrine**
- **Missouri Compromise**
- **Democratic Party**
- **states' rights**
- **Indian Removal Act**

Reading for Content Understanding

1. **Main Idea** What caused the War of 1812, and how did it end?
2. **Main Idea** How did President Jackson react to domestic crises?
3. **Constitutional Heritage** How did the Cherokee use the courts to resist removal?
4. **Writing** *Expressing* Write a one-paragraph report on the Lewis and Clark expedition explaining why the mission was important.
5. **Critical Thinking** *Evaluating* Why did the nation spend money on internal improvements in the early 1800s?

Section 2 Review ANSWERS

Identify

For significance, see the following pages:

- judicial review, p. 88
- Louisiana Purchase, p. 89
- Andrew Jackson, p. 91
- Battle of New Orleans, p. 91
- Treaty of Ghent, p. 91
- Monroe Doctrine, p. 91
- Missouri Compromise, p. 91
- Democratic Party, p. 92
- states' rights, p. 92
- Indian Removal Act, p. 93

Reading for Content Understanding

1. The British refused to stop searching U.S. ships, practiced impressment of U.S. citizens, and provided military aid to American Indians in the Northwest Territory, thus leading to war; it ended with the signing of the Treaty of Ghent, which restored all conquered territory but failed to address impressment or trade embargoes.

2. Jackson threatened to send U.S. troops to South Carolina to enforce a new 1832 tariff and vetoed the renewal of the charter for the Second Bank of the United States.

3. They sued the state of Georgia in 1831, arguing that they were an independent nation and not subject to Georgia law.

4. Paragraphs will vary but should mention that the expedition was important because it provided scientific information on the lands obtained from the Louisiana Purchase.

5. Answers will vary but students should state their opinions and offer support for them.

OBJECTIVES

- Describe how the Industrial Revolution and the Transportation Revolution changed American life.
- Analyze the effect of the cotton boom on the South and slavery.
- Explain what some of the major reform movements hoped to achieve.

FOCUS

Motivate Before Reading

Ask students to list five examples of modern technology and to describe how each example has changed life in the United States. Call on volunteers to offer examples from their lists. Tell students that in this section they will learn how technology fundamentally changed American life before the Civil War and how some Americans responded to those changes.

Section 3 RESOURCES

PRINT

★ Guided Reading Strategies 3.3

★ Literature Reading 3: Encouraging Women's Rights

★ American History Political Cartoon 5: Temperance Reform, and Cartoon 7: Slavery in America and England

★ Section 3 Review, p. 100

★ Daily Quiz 3.3

MULTIMEDIA

★ *Teaching Resources CD–ROM,* Lesson 3.3

★ *American History Simulations CD–ROM:* Choosing a Factory Site

★ *American History Interactive Maps CD–ROM:* The Cotton Plantation

★ HRW Web site

SHELTERED ENGLISH

★ Main Idea Activities for Reteaching and Sheltered English 3.3

The North and the South

Reading Focus

How did the Industrial Revolution and the Transportation Revolution change life in the United States?

What effect did the cotton boom have on the South and slavery?

What did some of the major reform movements hope to achieve?

Key Terms

Industrial Revolution
nativists
Transportation Revolution
cotton gin
Nat Turner's Rebellion
abolition
Second Great Awakening
emancipation
Seneca Falls Convention
temperance movement

IN THE 1800S NEW IDEAS and inventions transformed the way people lived and worked in the northern United States. Massachusetts senator Daniel Webster wrote enthusiastically in 1847 about advances in science and technology, "It is an extraordinary era in which we live. It is altogether new. The world has seen nothing like it before." What most impressed Webster was "the application of this scientific research to the pursuits of life."

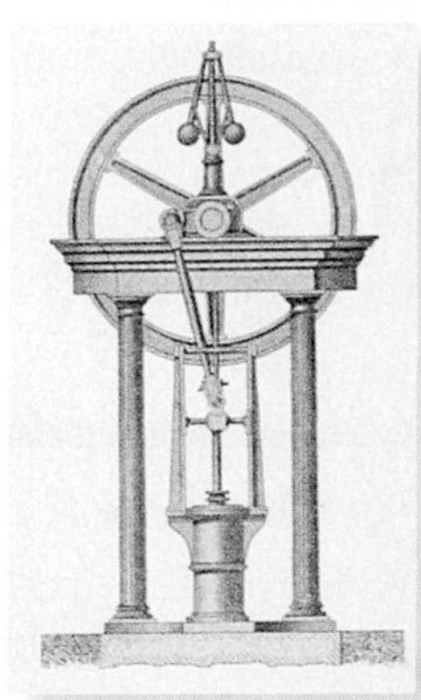

A steam engine design

 The Industrial Revolution

In the mid-1700s Britain underwent the **Industrial Revolution**, a period of rapid growth in the use of machines in manufacturing and production. The first factories were textile mills that used water-powered machinery. With the help of Englishman Samuel Slater, American merchants built their first textile mill in Rhode Island in 1793. Most mills were in the Northeast because as one mill owner noted, "Our thousand rivers and streams afford [provide] an inexhaustible supply of . . . power."

Under the Rhode Island system, mill owners hired entire families and divided factory work into simple tasks. In 1813 businessman Francis Cabot Lowell built his first textile mill in Waltham, Massachusetts. His idea of combining spinning and weaving cloth in one mill and employing single women to work in his factories became known as the Lowell system. When he needed more waterpower to expand, he built more mills in a town later named Lowell. The female workers, mostly from local farms, were known as Lowell girls. Visitors were dazzled by the machinery, clean factories, and workers' boardinghouses.

Changes in Working Life

As factory machines increased in size and speed, employees had to work faster to keep up with the

Introduce Key Terms

Linguistic, Logical-Mathematical. Review this section's key terms with students. Then ask students to pair terms according to some linking idea, common denominator, or event and use both terms in a sentence. For example, a student might write, the *Second Great Awakening* encouraged people to call for *abolition.* Students may need to use some terms more than once.

SHELTERED ENGLISH

TEACH

Have students read Section 3 and complete Guided Reading Strategies 3.3. Choose one or more of the following activities to explore the section content with students. For further suggestions on block scheduling or team teaching, see the *Block Scheduling Handbook.*

LEVEL 1: Linguistic. (Suggested time: 15 min.) As a class, go over students' Guided Reading Strategies. Then use the Reading Focus questions to highlight the main ideas of the section.

SHELTERED ENGLISH

equipment. Mill machinery was also dangerous, with many moving parts. A reporter described the working conditions at Lowell in 1846:

> **"Each girl usually attends three looms. Doing so requires constant attention. . . . The room is full of cotton filaments [fibers] and dust, which we were told are very harmful to the lungs."**

As conditions worsened, immigrants replaced the Lowell girls. Between 1840 and 1860, more than 4 million immigrants, mostly from Ireland and Germany, came to the United States. These immigrants filled the need for cheap labor in the Industrial Revolution. However, many native-born citizens felt threatened by the immigrants' different backgrounds and the economic competition they presented. Americans who opposed immigration were called **nativists**. In 1850 a group of nativists founded what became known as the Know-Nothing Party, whose candidates won several state elections.

Low wages, long hours, and the fear of losing their jobs led many workers to form trade unions—organizations created to improve working conditions. Unions sometimes staged strikes, in which members refused to work in an attempt to force employers to meet union demands. Most early strikes failed because courts and police usually supported companies. To get laws changed, many unions became politically active.

In 1840 President Martin Van Buren granted federal employees a 10-hour workday. Union leaders wanted to extend this protection to employees of private businesses, who often put in 12 hours a day, six days a week. Although some states passed 10-hour-day laws, many companies avoided such laws by requiring workers to sign special contracts. Despite such setbacks, unions continued to fight for workplace reforms.

Changing Factories

As the Industrial Revolution progressed, more factory owners turned to steam instead of waterpower to run their machinery. The use of steam engines allowed factories to be built in places that did not have suitable waterpower. Building factories closer to cities and transportation centers lowered the price of labor and shipping costs.

Some businesses also relied on mass production, or the efficient production of large numbers of identical goods. In the 1790s inventor Eli Whitney had tried to mass-produce rifles using a concept called interchangeable parts. This meant that each vital part that went into making a product would be made exactly the same. By the 1840s interchangeable parts allowed some factories to mass-produce goods.

The Transportation Revolution

The Industrial Revolution was fueled by the **Transportation Revolution**—a rapid growth in the speed and convenience of transportation. One new transportation method was the steamboat. The first successful commercial steamboat was Robert Fulton's *Clermont*, which sailed up the Hudson River on August 9, 1807. Steamboats were well suited to river travel because they could move quickly against the current and did not rely on uncertain winds. Steamboats shaved months off the travel time from New Orleans to Pittsburgh and lowered shipping prices more than 75 percent. These savings created a boom in trade and encouraged more settlers to move to the Midwest.

What the steamboat did for water travel, the train did for land travel. First developed in Britain,

This scene from an early New England textile mill shows the growing use of machinery in industry.

Linking Past to Present

Modern Life in Lowell. When the textile mills in Lowell began to close in 1926, the city went into an economic depression. The demand for textiles during World War II revived the town's economy, but when the war ended, the industry slumped, and by the 1960s the mills had almost disappeared from Lowell. Many people living in the town were bitter and viewed the old mill's buildings as ugly reminders of hard times. However, some residents recognized the historical value of the mills and saw them as potential tourist attractions. In 1974 the Lowell Heritage State Park opened, and in 1978 the Lowell National Historical Park was created. Although the city still faces economic difficulties, it has used its past to improve its present economy.

Activity: Have students use the library or other resources to research and report on efforts to preserve local historical sites.

Multimedia Resources

American History Simulations CD–ROM: Choosing a Factory Site

ALL LEVELS: Linguistic, Visual-Spatial, Logical-Mathematical. (Suggested time: 30 min.) Have students read about the Industrial and Transportation Revolutions on pages 94–97. Then have them write a detailed outline of the material. Students should use *The Industrial Revolution, Changes in Working Life, Workers Organize, Changing Factories,* and *The Transportation Revolution* as roman numerals one through four. As students write supporting details, encourage them to use complete sentences with correct grammar, punctuation, and spelling. Remind students of the proper guidelines for creating subheads and for listing supporting details.

ALL LEVELS: Linguistic, Logical-Mathematical. (Suggested time: 45 min.) Ask students to imagine that they are reporters for *Reform* magazine and have been sent to interview one of the reformers from this section. Ask students to prepare three to five questions and question another student about them. Have each student answer the questions based on the responses they think the reformer being questioned would give. When students have finished their interviews, lead a discussion on the reformers covered in this section.

Biography

Robert Fulton. Before achieving fame as the inventor of the *Clermont,* the first successful steamboat, Robert Fulton tried other inventions, including a naval torpedo, a diving vessel similar to a submarine, and a machine to help transport ships through canals. His first attempt at building a steamboat ended in failure. The weight of the machinery caused the ship to break in two and sink. This experience taught Fulton to build his ships with stronger hulls. The *Clermont* was 133 feet long and 18 feet wide. Two 15-foot paddle wheels were attached to its sides. On its maiden voyage, the ship averaged nearly 5 miles per hour.

Activity: Have students draw or locate a picture of the *Clermont* and a picture of a modern vessel. Then have students write a summary describing the differences between the two vessels.

Science and Technology Answers

1. Fuel held in the boiler was used to heat water to produce steam; steam then entered the cylinder, thus pushing the piston; and the condenser pulled steam out of the cylinder to speed up the piston.

2. Answers will vary but students might mention that steam engines made work and transportation easier.

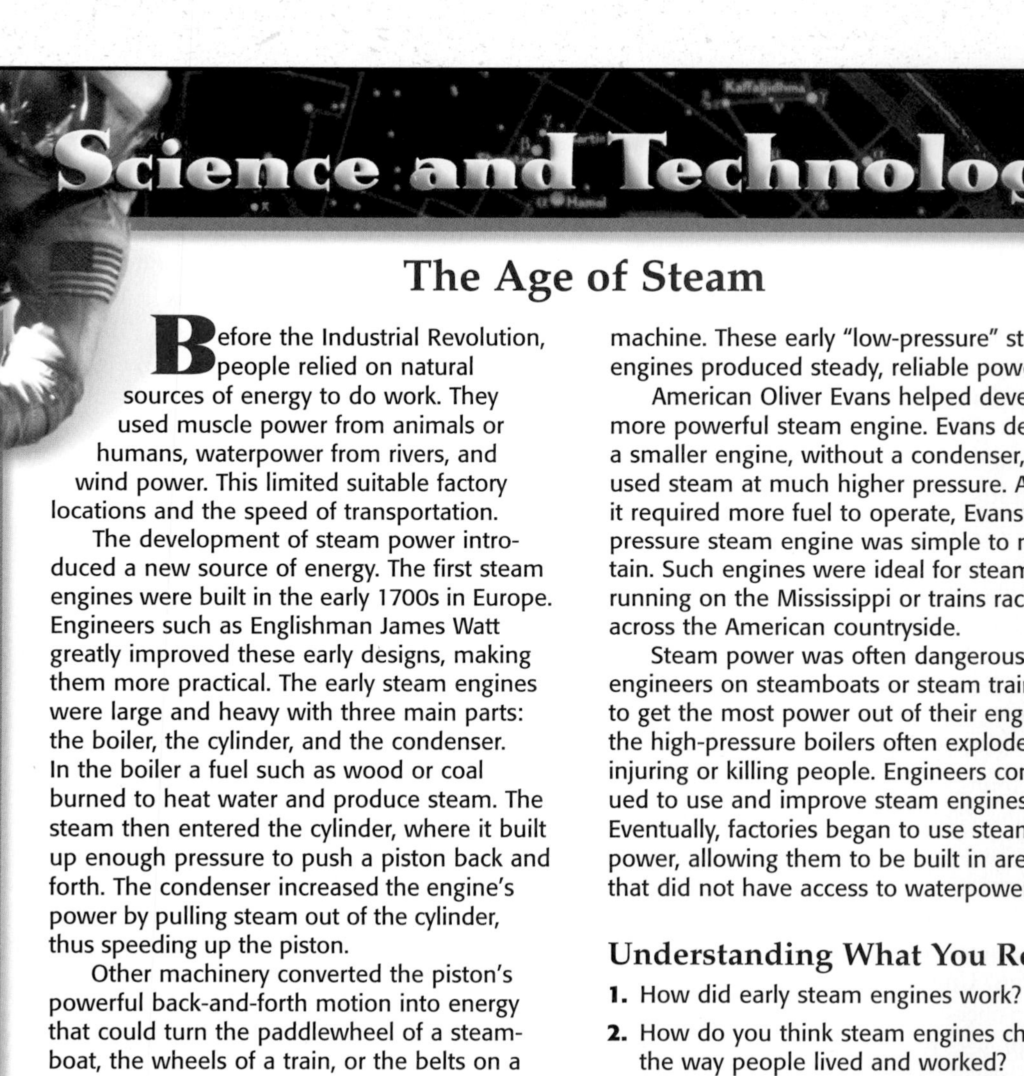

Science and Technology

The Age of Steam

Before the Industrial Revolution, people relied on natural sources of energy to do work. They used muscle power from animals or humans, waterpower from rivers, and wind power. This limited suitable factory locations and the speed of transportation.

The development of steam power introduced a new source of energy. The first steam engines were built in the early 1700s in Europe. Engineers such as Englishman James Watt greatly improved these early designs, making them more practical. The early steam engines were large and heavy with three main parts: the boiler, the cylinder, and the condenser. In the boiler a fuel such as wood or coal burned to heat water and produce steam. The steam then entered the cylinder, where it built up enough pressure to push a piston back and forth. The condenser increased the engine's power by pulling steam out of the cylinder, thus speeding up the piston.

Other machinery converted the piston's powerful back-and-forth motion into energy that could turn the paddlewheel of a steamboat, the wheels of a train, or the belts on a machine. These early "low-pressure" steam engines produced steady, reliable power.

American Oliver Evans helped develop a more powerful steam engine. Evans designed a smaller engine, without a condenser, that used steam at much higher pressure. Although it required more fuel to operate, Evans's high-pressure steam engine was simple to maintain. Such engines were ideal for steamboats running on the Mississippi or trains racing across the American countryside.

Steam power was often dangerous. As engineers on steamboats or steam trains tried to get the most power out of their engines, the high-pressure boilers often exploded, injuring or killing people. Engineers continued to use and improve steam engines. Eventually, factories began to use steam power, allowing them to be built in areas that did not have access to waterpower.

Understanding What You Read

1. How did early steam engines work?
2. How do you think steam engines changed the way people lived and worked?

LEVEL 2: Visual-Spatial, Logical-Mathematical. (Suggested time: 45 min.) Have each student prepare a flowchart to illustrate the origins of the cotton boom, events that promoted its growth, and effects of the cotton gin in particular on the growth of slavery, southern agriculture, and northern industry, especially textiles. Display students' work around the classroom and allow time for students to observe and comment on the work of others. **SHELTERED ENGLISH**

LEVEL 3: Linguistic, Intrapersonal, Interpersonal. (Suggested time: 30 min. plus homework) For homework, have students read the excerpt from the Declaration of Sentiments issued by the Seneca Falls Convention in 1848 that is found in this section. Ask students to write a letter from one of the convention delegates to a friend back home. The letter should describe how the delegate feels about the convention and outline the grievances the delegates have decided to include in the Declaration of Sentiments. Invite volunteers to share their letters with the class. Use the occasion to clarify terms and the conditions in which women lived at the time.

steam-powered trains became popular in the United States in the 1830s. By 1860 there were about 30,000 miles of railroad track linking almost every major city in the eastern United States. Senator Daniel Webster declared in 1847 that the railroad "towers above all other inventions of this or the preceding [previous] age."

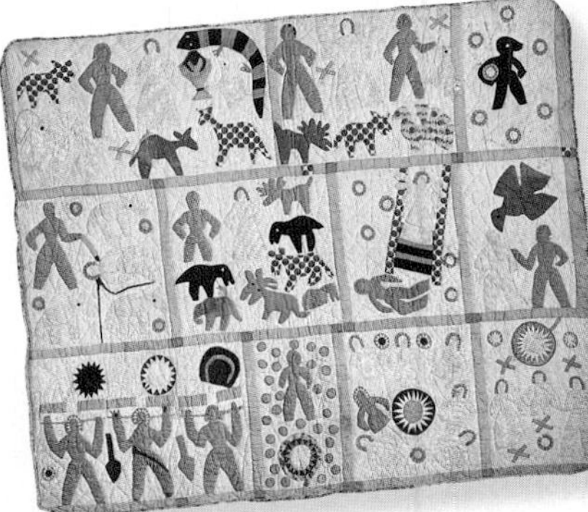

Slaves made crafts, such as this quilt, that reflected their culture.

Around the same time, Samuel Morse invented the telegraph. Telegraph companies strung telegraph lines on poles alongside railroads and opened telegraph offices in many train stations. By 1854 more than 15,000 miles of telegraph cable connected cities throughout the United States.

 The South and Slavery

The textile boom increased the demand for cotton. At the same time, the South's major cash crops—tobacco, rice, and indigo—were greatly decreasing in price. Growing cotton became more profitable in the 1790s when inventor Eli Whitney developed the **cotton gin**. This machine removed the seeds from cotton much faster than workers could by hand. By 1860 cotton accounted for more than half of all U.S. exports. Most of the South—from South Carolina to east Texas—formed what is known as the Cotton Kingdom, or cotton belt. This region grew most of the country's cotton crop.

Growing and harvesting cotton required many field hands, as did other southern crops such as rice and Louisiana sugarcane. Rather than hiring workers through a wage-labor system, the South relied heavily on slaves. In the first half of the 1800s, about one third of white southern families owned slaves. A smaller percentage were planters, large-scale farmers who owned more than 20 slaves. Despite their small numbers, planters held a lot of political power. To a smaller degree, slavery was also practiced in the North, but it had much less economic importance than in the South.

By 1860 more than half of all free African Americans lived in the South. To many white southerners, free African Americans threatened the institution of slavery because they proved that African Americans could live outside the slave system. Many cities and states passed laws limiting the rights of free African Americans, such as the right to vote, travel freely, or hold certain jobs.

Most southern communities also passed strict slave codes prohibiting slaves from traveling or learning to read or write. Slaveholders often relied on harsh punishments and threats to ensure slaves' obedience. On large plantations, the majority of slaves were assigned specific jobs. They usually worked in the fields from sunrise to sunset.

Despite the harsh realities of daily life, many slaves found comfort in their community and culture. The most important unit of slave communities was the family. Slaves feared being sold to another plantation and separated from their families. To

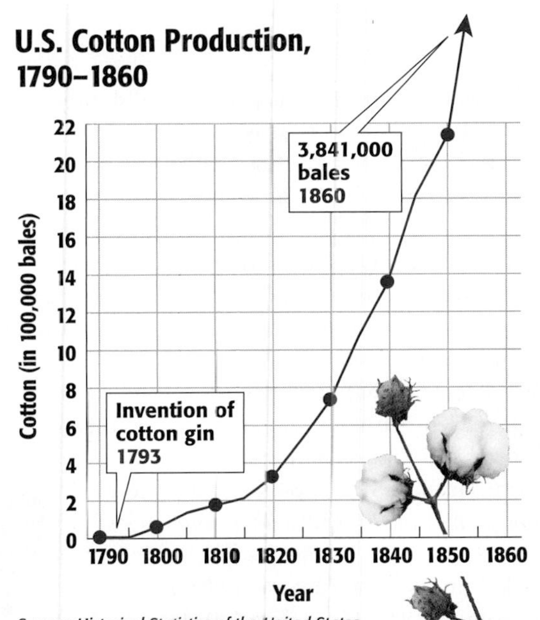

King Cotton The cotton gin led to dramatic increases in southern cotton production, which exceeded 1 million bales by 1835. During what decades did cotton production nearly double?

Biography

Eli Whitney. As a student, Eli Whitney showed little interest in subjects other than mathematics. Although he did not enjoy working on the family farm, he loved to spend time in his father's workshop. As a teenager, he started a successful business producing nails. When the demand for nails declined, Whitney made hat pins. After deciding that a college education would be useful, he taught school for a few years to save money. To make ends meet while attending Yale, he repaired equipment for the school. By the time he was 27 years old, Whitney had invented the cotton gin, which revolutionized the cotton industry in the United States.

Activity: Have students use the library or search the Internet through the HRW Web site to find information on the life of Eli Whitney. Have each student write a brief biography showing significant events in his life.

go.hrw.com
SB1 Eli Whitney

CHART ANSWER

between 1800 and 1810, 1820 and 1830, and 1830 and 1840

CLOSE

Linguistic, Logical-Mathematical, Intrapersonal. Direct students' attention to the quotation from Daniel Webster on the first page of the section. Ask each student to write a brief essay explaining how technology turned Webster's time into "an extraordinary era." Remind students to use correct grammar, punctuation, and spelling. Allow time for students to work on their essays in class and have them finish for homework. During the next class, have volunteers share their essays with the class.

CHALLENGE AND EXTEND

1. **Logical-Mathematical, Interpersonal, Intrapersonal.** Have each student use the library or other resources to prepare a brief outline of the life, career, and beliefs of a particular abolitionist during the 1830s. Then organize the class into an abolitionist convention from this era. Have the assembled delegates prepare an agenda, speak to the convention, and write a statement describing actions to be taken after the convention. Encourage students to speak from the perspective of the particular abolitionist they have researched. For example,

Across the Curriculum

MATH

Slaves' Daily Lives. Some supporters of slavery attempted to justify the institution by arguing that the "wages" that slaves earned in food and shelter were roughly equivalent to the wages that factory workers earned in the North. One slavery supporter wrote that "a slave consumes in meat two hundred pounds of bacon or pork, cost . . . $8; thirteen bushels of Indian corn, costing $2; this makes up his food. Now for salt and medicines add $1, and it runs thus: a year's food is $11. Their clothing . . . $7.50." These figures were probably exaggerated by slave owners to help justify slavery.

Activity: Have students use the slavery supporters' figures to determine the daily rate of pay a slave earned for his or her "wages," given a work week of six days *(six cents a day).*

Multimedia Resources

American History Interactive Maps CD–ROM: The Cotton Plantation

Slave auctions like this one often resulted in the breakup of slave families.

make sure that the children never forgot their heritage, enslaved parents told them stories passed down from earlier generations. Slaves also told folktales that taught lessons about how to survive under slavery.

Another important aspect of slave culture was religion. Some slaves expressed their religious beliefs through spirituals. These emotional Christian songs blended African and European traditions. Many spirituals, such as "The Heavenly Road," reflected slaves' belief in their equality before God:

> **"Come, my brother, if you never did pray,**
> **I hope you may pray tonight;**
> **For I really believe I'm a child of God**
> **As I walk in the heavenly road."**

In small ways, slaves tried to gain a measure of control over their lives. Some slaves ran away. Others worked slowly to protest work conditions. While violent slave revolts were rare, planters lived in fear that such revolts would occur. Nat Turner led the most violent slave revolt in the United States. A well-educated slave from Virginia, Turner believed that God had called on him to overthrow slavery. Almost 60 white people were killed during **Nat Turner's Rebellion** in August 1831. More than 100 slaves were killed in putting down the rebellion, and Turner was tried and executed. As a result of the rebellion, many states strengthened their slave codes.

 The Abolition Movement

During the 1830s Americans organized a movement to support **abolition**, or a complete end to slavery, in the United States. The **Second Great Awakening**, a period of evangelism that began in the 1790s and had become widespread by the 1830s, helped further the abolition movement. Many ministers, in particular Charles Grandison Finney, believed that slavery was morally wrong. These ministers inspired followers to become abolitionists. The ideal of the Declaration of Independence, that all men are created equal, inspired other abolitionists.

Abolitionists furthered their cause with speaking tours, newspapers, and pamphlets. Leading abolitionist William Lloyd Garrison published the *Liberator,* an antislavery newspaper. He also helped found the American Anti-Slavery Society in 1833. This group wanted immediate **emancipation**, or freedom from slavery, as well as equality for African Americans. Two white southerners, sisters Angelina and Sarah Grimké, also became well-known antislavery activists. Angelina Grimké asked southern women to "persuade your husband, father, brothers and sons that slavery is a crime *against God and man.*"

Many former slaves were active in the antislavery movement. Some, like Frederick Douglass, shared powerful stories of their lives in captivity through written slave narratives and speeches. Douglass published a newspaper called the *North Star* and became one of the most important African American leaders of the 1800s. Former slaves Henry Highland Garnet and Sojourner Truth also fought for the abolitionist cause.

Frederick Douglass

By the 1830s a loosely organized group of abolitionists had begun helping slaves escape to the North and to Canada. They created the Underground Railroad, a network of people who arranged transportation and hiding places for fugitives, or escaped slaves. Escaped slave Harriet

William Lloyd Garrison and Frederick Douglass would demand an immediate end to slavery; others might argue that the abolitionist movement ought to spread the word in the North about the evils of slavery or help slaves escape.

2. **Linguistic, Visual-Spatial, Musical-Rhythmic.** Have groups of students use the library or other resources to prepare reports on various aspects of slavery and slave culture in antebellum America. Start by having the class generate suitable topics to be researched in detail. Encourage students to include art, charts, graphs, songs, and other materials in their reports.

REVIEW

Linguistic, Logical-Mathematical. Have students complete the Section Review questions. Write one of the section's key people or events on a note card and give one card to each student. Have each student write on the card two clues about the person or event. Then have students return their cards to you. Read the clues aloud and have students write down the person or event to which the clues refer. Read the answers to students and then discuss any items that are unclear.

Tubman returned to the South and led hundreds of slaves to freedom during her lifetime.

Reforming Society

Women who had to defend their role in the antislavery movement, such as Sojourner Truth and the Grimké sisters, also began to fight for women's rights. Elizabeth Cady Stanton and Lucretia Mott organized the **Seneca Falls Convention**, held in Seneca Falls, New York, in July 1848. At the convention, 100 people signed the Declaration of Sentiments, which listed the injustices that women suffered in society.

The convention launched the organized women's rights movement in the United States. Susan B. Anthony, Elizabeth Cady Stanton, and Lucy Stone emerged as its major leaders. Thousands of women participated in the struggle. They demanded equal pay for equal work, equal educational opportunities, property rights for married women, and the right to vote. These women had some success, such as property rights for married women, but did not gain other major reforms, such as the right to vote, for many years.

HISTORICAL DOCUMENTS

1848

The Seneca Falls

Declaration of Sentiments

Elizabeth Cady Stanton and Lucretia Mott helped write the Declaration of Sentiments. This excerpt shows how it was modeled on the Declaration of Independence.

We hold these truths to be self-evident: that all men and women are created equal; that they are endowed [provided] by their Creator with certain inalienable [permanent] rights; that among these are life, liberty, and the pursuit of happiness. . . .

The history of mankind is a history of repeated injuries and usurpations [seizures] on the part of man toward woman, having in direct object the establishment of an absolute tyranny [unjust rule] over her. To prove this, let facts be submitted to a candid [fair] world.

He has never permitted her to exercise her inalienable right to [vote]. . . .

He has taken from her all right in property, even to the wages she earns. . . .

He has monopolized nearly all the profitable employments, and from those she is permitted to follow, she receives but a scanty remuneration [payment]. He closes against her all the avenues to wealth and distinction which he considers most honorable to himself. . . .

He has denied her the facilities for obtaining a thorough education, all colleges being closed against her. . . .

He has endeavored [tried], in every way that he could, to destroy her confidence in her own powers, to lessen her self-respect, and to make her willing to lead a dependent and abject [hopeless] life. . . .

Resolved, That woman is man's equal—was intended to be so by the Creator, and the highest good of the race demands that she should be recognized as such.

Understanding Primary Sources

1. What are some of the injustices that the declaration describes?
2. How is the Declaration of Sentiments modeled after the Declaration of Independence?

Biography

Stanton and Anthony. Elizabeth Cady Stanton and Susan B. Anthony formed a close friendship and worked together as leaders in the women's rights movement. Stanton gave Anthony encouragement and moral support, and Anthony kept Stanton—who was raising seven children—up to date on developments in the movement. As a single woman, Anthony sometimes became frustrated with Stanton's family duties. "Those of you who have the talent to do honor to poor womanhood," Anthony wrote to Stanton, "have all given yourselves over to baby-making."

Critical Thinking: What might be the advantages of close friends leading a movement together?

ANSWER: Answers may include flexibility, understanding, and the contribution of everyone's strengths.

HISTORICAL DOCUMENTS ANSWERS

1. Answers may include the inabilities to vote or own property, enjoy equal employment and pay, obtain an equal education, and achieve self-confidence.
2. The language and the organization of the documents are similar.

ASSESS

Have students complete Daily Quiz 3.3.

RETEACH

Linguistic, Interpersonal. Have students complete Main Idea Activities for Reteaching and Sheltered English 3.3. Organize the class into small groups and assign each group one of the following topics: Industrial Revolution, Transportation Revolution, cotton boom, slave culture, social reform, abolition, and women's rights. Have each group write a newspaper headline that captures this section's main point about the assigned topic. Have each group read its headline to the class, then call on members of other groups to identify the significance of the events described by each headline. If students have difficulty identifying the significance of a particular headline, review material on that subject with the class. **SHELTERED ENGLISH**

Section 3 Review ANSWERS

Identify

For significance, see the following pages:

- Industrial Revolution, p. 94
- nativists, p. 95
- Transportation Revolution, p. 95
- cotton gin, p. 97
- Nat Turner's Rebellion, p. 98
- abolition, p. 98
- Second Great Awakening, p. 98
- emancipation, p. 98
- Seneca Falls Convention, p. 99
- temperance movement, p. 100

Reading for Content Understanding

1. It made growing cotton more profitable and increased the demand for slaves.

2. The women's rights movement sought equal pay for equal work, equal educational opportunities, property rights for married women, and the right to vote.

3. The Industrial Revolution changed the way Americans worked, spurring both immigration and nativism. The Transportation Revolution shortened travel time and lowered shipping costs, which led to increased trade and more settlers moving to the Midwest.

4. Posters might mention abolition, women's education, the common-school movement, African American education, or special needs education.

5. Answers might mention groups such as Mothers Against Drunk Driving or literacy projects and compare them to the temperance movement and efforts to expand education during the mid-1800s.

100

Reformers also tried to improve social conditions in the United States. Cities faced many challenges as a result of the rapid growth that occurred when immigrants and rural inhabitants moved to urban areas in search of jobs. Many urban residents, particularly immigrants, lived in overcrowded and poorly built apartments. Epidemics were fairly common because cities lacked clean water, public health regulations, or sanitary ways to dispose of garbage and human waste. Reformers hoped to improve these urban living conditions.

A temperance poster

Reformers also targeted alcohol abuse, which they believed contributed to crime, family violence, and poverty. This **temperance movement** urged people to give up or to limit alcohol consumption. By 1855 thirteen states had banned or restricted alcohol sales.

Dorothea Dix helped reform prisons after finding terrible conditions and poor treatment of people with mental illnesses in Massachusetts jails. Her efforts also led to the establishment of state hospitals where people with mental illnesses could receive professional treatment.

One of the most important reform efforts was the movement to improve children's education. As the immigrant population grew, reformers argued that the nation needed a better education system to help people acquire the skills needed to become responsible citizens. The common-school movement argued that all children, regardless of their economic background, should be educated in a common place. Reformer Horace Mann led this movement during the mid-1800s.

Educational opportunities improved for women when Emma Willard opened the first college-level institution for female students in the United States. Oberlin College became the first coeducational college, admitting both men and women, and the first college to accept African Americans. Educational opportunities expanded for African Americans when black colleges were founded. Efforts to improve education also extended to people with special needs, such as those with hearing or visual impairments. Thus, the efforts of school reformers reached many parts of American society.

SECTION 3 REVIEW

Identify and explain the significance of the following:

- **Industrial Revolution**
- **nativists**
- **Transportation Revolution**
- **cotton gin**
- **Nat Turner's Rebellion**
- **abolition**
- **Second Great Awakening**
- **emancipation**
- **Seneca Falls Convention**
- **temperance movement**

Reading for Content Understanding

1 **Main Idea** How did the cotton boom affect the South and slavery?

2 **Main Idea** What were the main goals of the women's rights movement?

3 **Economic Development** How did the Industrial Revolution and the Transportation Revolution affect Americans?

4 **Writing** *Creating* Imagine that you are a member of a society for reform, such as abolition or education. Create a poster outlining the goals of your movement.

5 **Critical Thinking** *Making Comparisons* How do you think some of the reform movements of the mid-1800s are similar to or different from reform efforts today?

Section 4 Lesson Plan

OBJECTIVES

- Explain the events that led Texas to win its independence from Mexico.
- Describe the challenges travelers faced on the journey west.
- Identify the events that led to the Mexican War, and examine the outcome of the conflict.

FOCUS

Motivate Before Reading

Define *manifest destiny.* Organize the class into six groups and assign each an identity: a northern senator, a southern farmer, a slave, an American Indian, an American living in the Republic of Texas, or a Mexican citizen. Have the group decide how a person of the assigned identity might respond to the idea of manifest destiny.

Expanding West

Reading Focus

- What events led Texas to win its independence from Mexico?
- What challenges did travelers face on the journey west?
- What events led to the Mexican War, and what was its outcome?

Key Terms

- Republic of Texas
- Oregon Trail
- manifest destiny
- Treaty of Guadalupe Hidalgo
- Mexican Cession
- Gadsden Purchase
- forty-niners
- California Gold Rush

IN THE EARLY 1800S American settlers and traders continued to push west. Pioneer Moses Austin recalled a typical conversation with hopeful early settlers: "Have you any [land]? No, but I expect I can get it. . . . Did you ever see the country? No, but everybody says it is good land." The settlers' quest for land brought them into contact with American Indians and Mexican citizens already living in the West.

Alamo defender Davy Crockett's rifle

Alamo Collection, photograph courtesy the Daughters of the Republic of Texas Library

Section 4 RESOURCES

PRINT

- ★ Guided Reading Strategies 3.4
- ★ Primary Source Reading 3: A Mexican Views the War
- ★ American History Political Cartoon 8: James Polk and Foreign Policy
- ★ Section 4 Review, p. 105
- ★ Daily Quiz 3.4

MULTIMEDIA

- ★ *Teaching Resources CD–ROM,* Lesson 3.4
- ★ *American History Simulations CD–ROM:* The Gold Rush
- ★ *American Music Audio CD Program:* "Joe Bowers"
- ★ HRW Web site

SHELTERED ENGLISH

- ★ Main Idea Activities for Reteaching and Sheltered English 3.4

American Settlers in Texas

In 1810 Father Miguel Hidalgo y Costilla led Mexicans in a rebellion against Spain. This revolt failed, but in 1821 Mexico became an independent nation. The Mexican government soon changed old Spanish policies. In California, it ended the mission system. In Texas, officials recruited settlers to increase its small population.

In 1821 Stephen F. Austin, the son of Moses Austin, brought 300 American families to Texas. These settlers agreed to become Mexican citizens, obey Mexican laws, and be loyal to the Catholic Church. By 1834 more than 20,000 Americans had moved to Texas. They greatly outnumbered Tejanos, settlers of Spanish descent living in Texas. After American settlers ignored Mexico's laws, the government restricted U.S. immigration and enforced an existing ban on slavery. People who had brought slaves to Texas were upset. Other Texans believed that Texas was not fairly represented in the Mexican government.

These tensions led some Texans to revolt. The first battle of the Texas Revolution took place near the town of Gonzales in October 1835. In San Antonio, Texans led by William Travis and Jim Bowie occupied the Alamo, an old mission. Some Tennessee volunteers, including frontiersman Davy Crockett, joined them. As Mexican general Antonio López de Santa Anna marched his army

Tell students that in this section they will learn how the United States expanded westward and what resulted from that growth.

Introduce Key Terms

Visual-Spatial, Logical-Mathematical. Review this section's key terms with students. Give each student a blank outline map of the continental United States. Ask students to identify the location of each key term and explain its historical importance. For example, students would match the term *California Gold Rush* with the location of Sutter's Fort. For the terms that do not apply to a specific location, have students use context cues to write a definition. **SHELTERED ENGLISH**

TEACH

Have students read Section 4 and complete Guided Reading Strategies 3.4. Choose one or more of the following activities to explore the section content with students. For further suggestions on block scheduling or team teaching, see the *Block Scheduling Handbook*.

LEVEL 1: Linguistic. (Suggested time: 15 min.) As a class, go over students' Guided Reading Strategies. Then use the Reading Focus questions to highlight the main ideas of the section. **SHELTERED ENGLISH**

Biography

Juan Seguín. After fighting in the Texas Revolution, Juan Seguín served in the new republic's senate and as mayor of San Antonio. However, racial and political conflicts in Texas and Mexico caused him to suffer. His attempts to keep the peace between Anglos and Tejanos brought harsh criticism from some Texans. Seguín moved to Mexico in 1842, but when he arrived President Santa Anna told him he could either go to prison or serve in the military. Seguín chose military service because he had to provide for his family. He fought against the United States during the Mexican War. When the war ended he received permission to live in Texas, where he stayed on a ranch near San Antonio. In 1867 he returned to Mexico to live with family members. Seguín died in Mexico in 1890.

Critical Thinking: Why do you think Juan Seguín moved back and forth between Texas and Mexico so much?

ANSWER: He was probably seen as an outsider by both Anglo Texans and Mexicans, particularly since he fought for both sides during his life.

Multimedia Resources

American Music Audio CD
Program: "Joe Bowers"

toward San Antonio, Travis ignored orders to retreat. When Santa Anna arrived with about 3,000 soldiers, some 150 Texan soldiers were at the Alamo.

Santa Anna's army surrounded the Alamo for 13 days. Travis sent officer Juan Seguín and others to get reinforcements. About 30 arrived before the Mexican army attacked on March 6, 1836. The Mexicans suffered heavy losses, but soon overwhelmed the Texans and killed all the defenders. After the battle, Mexican forces attacked Texas troops near Goliad. Severely outnumbered, the Texans surrendered. Santa Anna charged them with treason and had them executed.

These losses failed to break the spirit of the Texas rebels. Sam Houston, the commander in chief of the new Texas army, decided to make a stand at San Jacinto, near present-day Houston. On April 21, 1836, the Texans attacked, yelling, "Remember the Alamo! Remember Goliad!" Caught by surprise, the Mexican army was destroyed. The Texans captured Santa Anna and forced him to recognize Texas independence. Voters elected Sam Houston as president of the **Republic of Texas**, which had become an independent nation.

The Journey West

As some Americans moved to Texas, others headed farther west. Mountain men went to the Rocky Mountains and beyond, trapping animals and selling their furs. The era of fur trading lasted only a few decades. By the 1840s settlers had begun to follow the mountain men to the West. Many Americans traveled to the Pacific Northwest. First missionaries such as Marcus and Narcissa Whitman and then settlers followed the **Oregon Trail**. This route stretched some 2,000 miles across the northern Great Plains and the Rocky Mountains. Most pioneers traveled in wagon trains. Their journey usually began in late spring and lasted about six months. The pioneers kept up a tiring pace from dawn until dusk. American Indians often helped them on their journey.

A mountain man

The Oregon Trail split into two branches. Most settlers followed the trail north to Oregon Country, which had fertile valleys for farming. Others took the southern route, the California Trail. These travelers were interested in trade, not settlement. In 1839 Swiss immigrant John Sutter built a colony known as Sutter's Fort, near the Sacramento River. It became a popular destination for traders. American merchants also traveled on the Santa Fe Trail, which ran from Independence, Missouri, to Santa Fe, New Mexico. The long trip across the desert and mountains was dangerous, but the lure of high profits drew the traders.

Some pioneers who headed west were Mormons, or members of the Church of Jesus Christ of Latter-Day Saints, founded in New York by Joseph Smith in 1830. Mormons were often persecuted for their beliefs and practices. In 1844 an anti-Mormon mob murdered Smith. The Mormons then decided to move west to present-day Utah. Brigham Young, the new head of the Mormon Church, organized the trek along the Mormon Trail. Upon seeing the Great Salt Lake in 1847, Young said, "This is the place whereon we will plant our feet." By 1860 about 40,000 Mormons lived in Utah.

Santa Anna surrenders to the wounded Sam Houston after the Battle of San Jacinto.

ALL LEVELS: Linguistic, Visual-Spatial, Logical-Mathematical. (Suggested time: 30 min.) Organize the class into groups. Assign each group one of the following territories: California, New Mexico, Oregon, or Utah. Have each group prepare a pamphlet encouraging American immigrants to settle in the assigned territory. The pamphlets should be set in the 1840s and explain how to travel to the territory and what life will be like once the settlers arrive. Have each group explain its pamphlet, then invite comment on the unique features of each, as well as common themes.

LEVEL 3: Linguistic, Visual-Spatial, Intrapersonal. (Suggested time: 45 min. plus homework) Have students write a series of letters from an American settler in Texas to family members back in the United States. The postcards should describe the following topics: the requirements to become a settler in Texas; the settlers' grievances with the Mexican government; the battles of the Texas Revolution; the events that led to the Mexican War; and the outcome of the conflict. Encourage volunteers to read segments of their letters to the class.

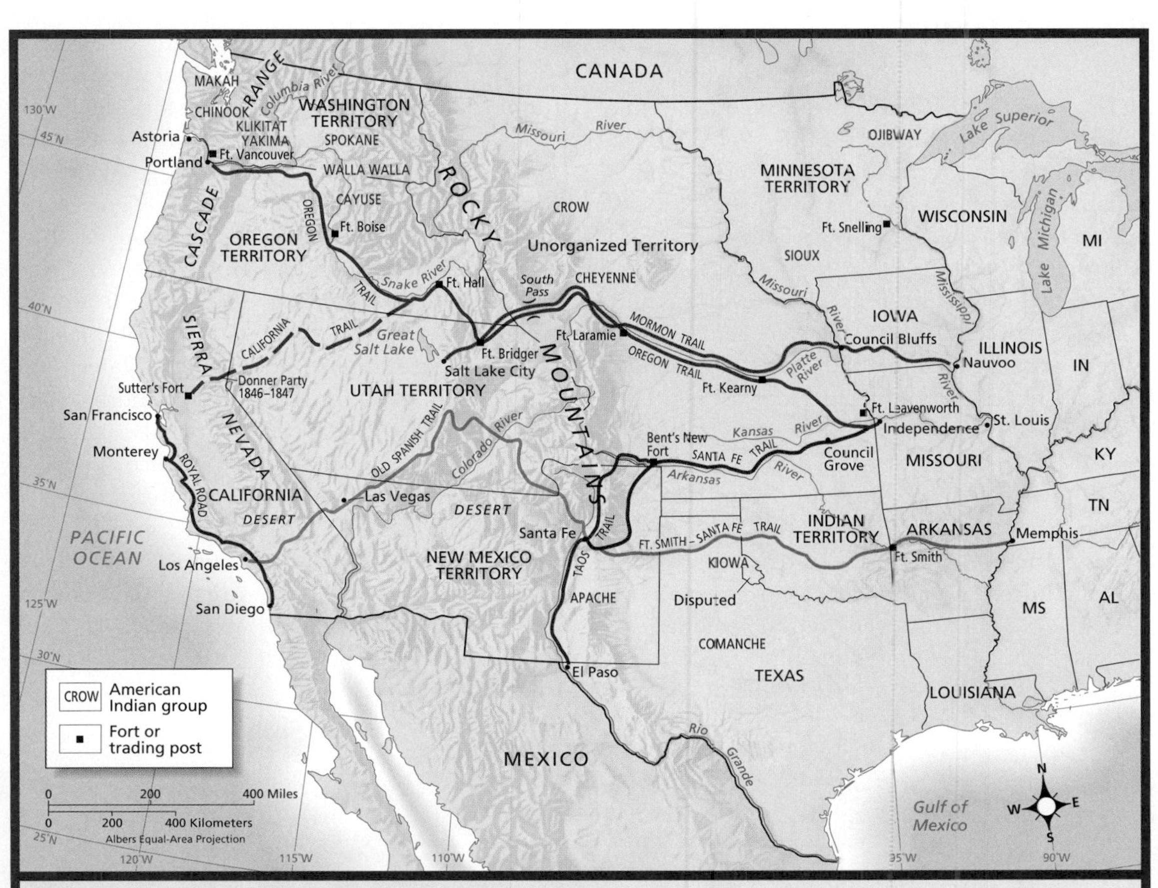

Major Overland Routes to the West by 1860

Learning from Maps The rough terrain and a lack of constant water supply made travel on many of the overland routes extremely dangerous.

Movement What trails led between Fort Laramie and Fort Bridger? What pass allowed settlers to cut through the Rocky Mountains?

 Manifest Destiny

By the 1840s many Americans believed in **manifest destiny**, the idea that the United States was meant to expand across the continent to the Pacific Ocean. Democrat James K. Polk won the 1844 presidential election on a platform supporting westward expansion. In 1846 Britain agreed to give the United States all Oregon Country land south of the 49th parallel. This treaty established the final portion of the present-day U.S.-Canada border. Oregon became a U.S. territory in 1848.

After Congress voted to annex Texas in March 1845, Mexico cut off diplomatic relations with the United States. In addition, Mexico rejected the U.S. claim that the Rio Grande marked the southern border of Texas. President Polk ordered General Zachary Taylor to take about 3,500 soldiers into the disputed border region. After Polk learned that Mexican troops had crossed the river and attacked U.S. soldiers, he gave this message to Congress:

> **"Mexico has passed the boundary of the United States, has invaded our territory, and shed American blood upon the American soil. . . . The two nations are now at war."**

Two days later, on May 13, 1846, Congress declared war on Mexico.

Presidential Profiles

James K. Polk. The oldest of 10 children, James Polk lived far from a school, so his parents taught him math and reading at home. He proved to be a good student, and he later graduated with honors from the University of North Carolina. After studying law, he began his political career, first serving in the Tennessee legislature, then in the U.S. House of Representatives, where he became Speaker of the House after just 10 years. He left the House to become governor of Tennessee in 1839. When Polk was elected president in 1844, he promised that he would not run for a second term. He was a hard worker, rarely taking time off from his duties as president. Polk died less than four months after leaving office, leading some historians to argue that his hard work in the White House had ruined his health and cost him his life.

Activity: Have students use the library or search the Internet through the HRW Web site to find information on James Polk. Ask them to use the information to write a brief biography of his life.

go.hrw.com
SB1 James Polk

MAP ANSWER

the Mormon Trail and the Oregon Trail; South Pass

CLOSE

Linguistic, Logical-Mathematical, Interpersonal. Organize the class into small groups. Ask each group to conclude how life in the United States changed as a result of the events described in this section. Have each group create two lists; one describing life in the United States before settlement expanded west of the Mississippi and one describing the United States after westward expansion. Post each group's list in the classroom to promote easy comparison.

TEACHER TO TEACHER

CHALLENGE AND EXTEND

Linguistic, Visual-Spatial, Interpersonal. Denny Schillings of Homewood, Illinois, suggested the following activity: Have students use the library or other resources to gather information about the terms of the Treaty of Guadalupe Hidalgo. Organize students into groups, assigning each group to represent opposition to or support for the treaty. Have each group produce a set of historical documents that includes the following items: a map showing the

Economic Development

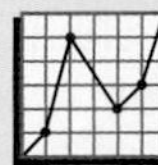

The Desert Land Act. As people began to dream of claiming land in the West, the U.S. government decided to promote irrigation for farming through the Desert Land Act. This act allowed individuals to buy up to 640 acres at $1.25 an acre. However, when they bought the land, they had to pay only 25 cents an acre. After three years, buyers had to show that they were irrigating the land and also had to pay off the rest of the debt. Thus, buyers who appeared to be improving their lands were given interest-free loans.

Critical Thinking: Why might the government want to encourage individuals to irrigate their land?

ANSWER: to help make the new U.S. territories productive

The Mexican War

General Taylor's soldiers had already driven the Mexican troops back across the Rio Grande. While Taylor waited for reinforcements, Polk ordered General Stephen Kearny to attack Santa Fe. Kearny took the city without a fight in August 1846. After securing New Mexico, Kearny headed to southern California.

Meanwhile, in the Bear Flag Revolt in June 1846 a small group of American settlers near Sutter's Fort declared that California was an independent republic. Commodore John Drake Sloat seized California's capital at Monterey. Farther south, Commodore Robert Stockton planned a naval invasion. With support from Kearny's forces, Stockton captured Mexican-held Los Angeles, San Diego, and San Gabriel. By early 1847 Mexican forces in California had surrendered.

Once Taylor received reinforcements, he pushed the Mexican army farther into the Mexican interior. President Polk then sent General Winfield Scott to the port of Veracruz, the strongest fortress in Mexico. Scott's naval forces laid siege to the city until it fell on March 29. Scott next pushed more than 250 miles inland toward Mexico City. By August, U.S. troops were at the edge of the city. Mexican soldiers and civilians fought fierce battles on the outskirts of the capital. U.S. troops captured Mexico City on September 14, 1847.

Signed in February 1848, the **Treaty of Guadalupe Hidalgo** ceded much of Mexico's northern territory to the United States. This **Mexican Cession** included the present-day states of California, Nevada, and Utah. It also contained most of Arizona and New Mexico, parts of Colorado and Wyoming, and the area claimed by Texas north of the Rio Grande. Five years later, the United States acquired additional land in the **Gadsden Purchase** that included the southern parts of Arizona and New Mexico. The Gadsden Purchase fixed the southern boundaries of the continental United States.

Linking Past to Present

Water Usage in the West

When the Mormons arrived in Utah, they dammed a mountain stream, flooded the soil, and planted their first crops. Because resources were scarce, Brigham Young told settlers:

> "*There shall be no private ownership of the streams that come out of the canyons, nor the timber that grows on the hills. These belong to the people: all the people.*"

As more settlers moved west, the U.S. government helped them adapt to the harsh environment. In the late 1800s U.S. Department of Agriculture agents taught Great Plains farmers how to find water and conserve water resources. In 1902 the government created the Bureau of Reclamation to construct irrigation works. The bureau built dams, reservoirs, and canals to bring more water to dry places.

Today the bureau manages water projects in 17 states west of the Mississippi River. It delivers water to about 10 million acres of land and provides flood control and community assistance during droughts. One of the agency's most important goals is to increase water availability to the millions of people who live in the West.

Understanding What You Read

1. Why was cooperation so important to the Mormon settlement in Utah?
2. How might states cooperate to share water?

LINKING PAST TO PRESENT ANSWERS

1. Cooperation helped them conserve resources so they could build a thriving agricultural community.
2. Answers will vary but students might suggest building dams together and sharing irrigation systems.

Multimedia Resources

American History Simulations CD–ROM: The Gold Rush

land acquisitions; a summary outlining the provisions of the treaty; and a position statement clarifying the group's view on the terms of the treaty.

REVIEW

Visual-Spatial, Logical-Mathematical. Have students complete the Section Review questions. Then ask them to create an annotated time line that features events covered in this section.

ASSESS

Have students complete Daily Quiz 3.4.

RETEACH

Visual-Spatial, Logical-Mathematical, Kinesthetic. Have students complete Main Idea Activities for Reteaching and Sheltered English 3.4. Then supply each student with a blank outline map of the United States and a list with landmarks, cities, rivers, mountains, battles, and trails discussed in this section. Have students label their maps to identify the location of each item on the list. Then have students write a sentence next to each item on the list that explains its importance. **SHELTERED ENGLISH**

The California Gold Rush

On January 24, 1848, James Marshall was building a sawmill near Sutter's Fort when he glanced down:

> **"My eye was caught with the glimpse of something shining in the bottom of the ditch. . . . I reached my hand down and picked it up; it made my heart thump, for I was certain it was gold."**

Gold-mining tools

In 1849 nearly 100,000 gold-seekers, known as **forty-niners**, traveled to California hoping to become rich. This event became known as the **California Gold Rush**. Some forty-niners took wagon trains across the country, while others traveled by sea. Most of these trips lasted three months or longer.

Few of the forty-niners had any previous gold-mining experience. The forty-niners would prospect, or search for gold, along the banks of streams or in shallow surface mines. The first prospector to arrive at a site would "stake a claim." Arguments and violent disputes often broke out over claims. There were few authorities to provide law and order in the mining communities. Mining camps and boom towns grew quickly when claims opened up and then disappeared just as quickly when claims died out.

In 1853 California's gold production peaked at more than $60 million. Few gold-rush miners became rich, however. Many settlers found that they could make a good living supplying miners with food, equipment, and services. Miners paid high prices for basic necessities because the large amounts of gold in circulation caused severe inflation in California.

The lure of gold in California attracted miners from around the world. Some 24,000 young Chinese men immigrated to California between 1849 and 1853. Prospectors also came from Mexico, South America, and Europe. More than 10,000 immigrants arrived in 1849 alone. Most forty-niners came to San Francisco.

California's economy was transformed by gold mining, trade, and business growth. Without the gold rush, California's population probably would have continued to grow slowly instead of increasing rapidly. The territory became eligible for statehood only two years after it was acquired by the United States.

SECTION 4 REVIEW

Identify and explain the significance of the following:
- **Republic of Texas**
- **Oregon Trail**
- **manifest destiny**
- **Treaty of Guadalupe Hidalgo**
- **Mexican Cession**
- **Gadsden Purchase**
- **forty-niners**
- **California Gold Rush**

Locate and explain the importance of the following:
- **Santa Fe**
- **San Francisco**

Reading for Content Understanding

1. **Main Idea** What difficulties did settlers have as they traveled west?
2. **Main Idea** What events caused the Mexican War, and what was the result?
3. **Geographic Diversity** *Movement* What effect did the gold rush have on California?
4. **Writing** *Informing* Write an article for a newspaper in Texas or Mexico explaining how Texas won its independence from Mexico. Include in your article an account of the fighting at the Alamo and the Battles of Goliad and San Jacinto.
5. **Critical Thinking** *Evaluating* Do you think the United States was justified in declaring war against Mexico? Explain your answer.

Section 4 Review ANSWERS

Identify
For significance, see the following pages:
- Republic of Texas, p. 102
- Oregon Trail, p. 102
- manifest destiny, p. 103
- Treaty of Guadalupe Hidalgo, p. 104
- Mexican Cession, p. 104
- Gadsden purchase, p. 104
- forty-niners, p. 105
- California Gold Rush, p. 105

Locate
For locations, see the map on page 103.

Reading for Content Understanding
1. Settlers traveling west had to maintain a tiring pace and faced rough terrain, such as deserts and mountains.
2. Belief in Manifest Destiny encouraged the United States to annex Texas, which led to the border dispute that started the war; as a result of the war, Mexico ceded much of its northern territory to the United States.
3. People flocked to California, which altered the territory's economy and helped it to become a state.
4. Articles will vary but should take either a Texan or Mexican perspective on the fighting and present issues from that viewpoint.
5. Answers will vary but students should choose a point of view and defend it.

OBJECTIVES

- Discuss the events that demonstrated growing sectional conflict over slavery.
- Identify events that led to the Civil War.
- Describe the battles that occurred in the eastern and western theaters of the war.

FOCUS

Motivate Before Reading

Read Lincoln's *Gettysburg Address* to the class. Then ask students to read it themselves, the speech is found just after this section of the text. Taking suggestions from the class, translate the speech into modern English and discuss its meaning. Tell students that in this section they will learn about the regional conflicts of the 1850s,

Section 5 RESOURCES

PRINT
- ★ Guided Reading Strategies 3.5
- ★ Biography Reading 3: Clara Barton
- ★ Graphic Organizer 3: Maintaining a Balance
- ★ Section 5 Review, p. 111
- ★ Daily Quiz 3.5

MULTIMEDIA
- ★ *Teaching Resources CD–ROM,* Lesson 3.5
- ★ *Exploring America's Past* Video Segment: A Divided Vision; *Teacher's Guide* pp. 4–6
- ★ *American History Simulations CD–ROM:* Global Politics and the Civil War

SHELTERED ENGLISH
- ★ Main Idea Activities for Reteaching and Sheltered English 3.5

The Civil War

Reading Focus

What events demonstrated the growing sectional conflict over slavery?

What events led to the Civil War?

What battles occurred in the eastern and western theaters of war?

Key Terms

- Compromise of 1850
- Republican Party
- Kansas-Nebraska Act
- *Dred Scott* decision
- Confederate States of America
- Battle of Antietam
- Emancipation Proclamation
- Battle of Gettysburg
- Gettysburg Address
- Appomattox Courthouse

IN 1858 ABRAHAM LINCOLN said, "'A house divided against itself cannot stand.'. . . I believe this government cannot endure, permanently half slave *and half* free.*" Lincoln stated that he did not expect the house to fall—nor did he think the Union would be dissolved. "But I* do *expect it will cease to be divided," he said. "It will become* all *one thing, or* all *the other." For many Americans in the mid-1800s, the issue of slavery was threatening national unity.*

The Granger Collection, New York

Abraham Lincoln

Conflict over Slavery

California's application for statehood in 1850 threatened the balance between free and slave states that had been maintained since the Missouri Compromise. Senator Henry Clay proposed the **Compromise of 1850**, which let California enter the Union as a free state. The rest of the Mexican Cession was divided into two territories—Utah and New Mexico. Local voters would decide the issue of slavery in these territories. The voters would elect representatives to their legislatures, which would pass laws on slavery. The compromise also abolished the slave trade in the nation's capital and included the Fugitive Slave Act. This act made it a crime to assist runaway slaves and allowed them to be arrested even in areas where slavery was illegal. It increased support for the abolition movement.

Harriet Beecher Stowe's *Uncle Tom's Cabin,* published in 1852, also increased antislavery sentiment. Within a decade, the novel sold more than 2 million copies in the United States. In 1854 the **Republican Party** was formed mainly to prevent the spread of slavery to the West. That same year the **Kansas-Nebraska Act** was passed. It created two new territories, Kansas and Nebraska, where voters would decide the slavery issue. The act also ended the Missouri Compromise's restriction on slavery north of the 36°30' line.

the secession of southern states and the formation of the Confederacy, and the devastating Civil War that followed.

Introduce Key Terms

Linguistic, Logical-Mathematical. Review this section's key terms with students. Then have them write each term in the appropriate location on a time line. For each term, have students write a sentence explaining how it led to or played a part in the Civil War. **SHELTERED ENGLISH**

TEACH

Have students read Section 5 and complete Guided Reading Strategies 3.5. Choose one or more of the following activities to explore the section content with students. For further suggestions on block scheduling or team teaching, see the *Block Scheduling Handbook*.

LEVEL 1: Linguistic. (Suggested time: 15 min.) As a class, go over students' Guided Reading Strategies. Then use the Reading Focus questions to highlight the main ideas of the section. **SHELTERED ENGLISH**

Violence Breaks Out

Antislavery and pro-slavery groups rushed people to Kansas to vote in the election that would determine the issue of slavery there. When the results produced a pro-slavery territorial legislature, antislavery Kansans created their own legislature. Pro-slavery forces destroyed property and killed one man in the town of Lawrence in 1856. Abolitionist John Brown led a group to avenge the attack and killed five pro-slavery men. About 200 people died in the continuing violence, which newspapers called Bleeding Kansas.

In 1857 the U.S. Supreme Court dealt abolitionists a blow with the ***Dred Scott* decision**. Scott was a slave who sued for his freedom, saying that he had become free by living in free territory. The Court ruled that African Americans were not citizens under the Constitution. Therefore, they did not have the right to file suit in federal court. The Court also ruled that the Missouri Compromise's restriction on slavery was unconstitutional. This ruling meant that Congress had no right to ban slavery in any federal territory.

Sectional tensions increased in 1859 when John Brown seized the federal arsenal in Harpers Ferry, Virginia. U.S. Marines soon defeated Brown and his men, ending John Brown's raid. Brown was hanged for his acts on December 2, 1859. Southerners, however, were angered that many abolitionists called John Brown a hero.

Secession

The Granger Collection, New York

Jefferson Davis

Many southerners associated the Republican Party with abolitionists and John Brown. They were also concerned about the South's loss of power in Congress. They warned that a Republican victory in the 1860 presidential election would mean disunion. Republican Abraham Lincoln won the election. Four days later, South Carolina's legislature called a convention to consider secession, or withdrawing from the Union. On December 20, 1860, the delegates unanimously voted for secession. Mississippi, Florida, Alabama, Georgia, Louisiana, and Texas soon followed.

Representatives in the House

YEAR	SLAVE STATES	FREE STATES
1840	88	135
1860	85	155

On February 4, delegates from the seceding states met in Montgomery, Alabama. They formed a new nation—the **Confederate States of America**, or the Confederacy. The delegates wrote a constitution and elected Jefferson Davis of Mississippi president of the Confederacy. Alexander Stephens of Georgia became vice president.

The Civil War Begins

Hoping to prevent more southern states from seceding, President Lincoln pledged in his inaugural address that he would not try to abolish slavery in the South. He promised the South that the federal "government will not assail [attack] you. You can have no conflict without being yourselves the aggressors." However, Lincoln also stated his intention to preserve the Union:

> **"No State, upon its own mere motion, can lawfully get out of the Union. . . . Acts of violence, within any State or States, against the authority of the United States, are revolutionary."**

The Confederacy was already seizing federal property and military bases in the South. On April 12, 1861, Confederate soldiers opened fire on Fort Sumter, which controlled the entrance to Charleston Harbor in South Carolina. After more than 30 hours of bombardment, Major Robert Anderson surrendered the fort. Lincoln declared that a state of rebellion existed in the South and called on the states to provide a total of 75,000 militiamen to put down the rebellion. Thousands of volunteers responded to Lincoln's call.

Biography

Dred Scott. Dred Scott is thought to have been born into slavery around 1795 in Virginia. Scott moved to Missouri with his owner, Peter Blow, in 1827. When Blow died, his daughter sold Scott to John Emerson. Scott was later owned by both Emerson's widow and his brother-in-law, John Sanford. In 1857, after the famous Supreme Court case involving his status as a slave, Scott and his family were purchased by Henry Blow, the son of Scott's first owner, who promptly emancipated them. Scott worked as a hotel porter in St. Louis until his death from tuberculosis in 1858.

Critical Thinking: What does the fact that Scott had so many owners during his life reveal about the security of a slave's personal and family life?

ANSWER: Slaves could have their lives turned upside down at any time by being sold to another owner.

Multimedia Resources

Exploring America's Past Video Segment: A Divided Vision; *Teacher's Guide*, pp. 4–6

Search 1821, Play to 7543
Videodisc White Side A

Play

Pause

See *Teacher's Guide* for Spanish barcode.

ALL LEVELS: Visual-Spatial, Logical-Mathematical. (Suggested time: 45 min. plus homework) Have each student design a Web site covering events that demonstrated growing sectional conflict over slavery, thus leading to the Civil War. The design should include links between related people and events. For example, a page about the Kansas-Nebraska Act should have a link to a page about John Brown. Encourage students to add appropriate illustrations to their pages. Remind students that all pages should include correct grammar, spelling, and punctuation.
SHELTERED ENGLISH

LEVEL 2: Linguistic, Logical-Mathematical, Musical-Rhythmic. (Suggested time: 45 min. plus homework) Organize students into two groups to create presentations on the battles of the Civil War. One group will cover the eastern theater, and the other will cover the western theater. The presentations should describe the major battles, the generals involved, and the significance of each battle to the outcome of the war. Instruct each group to use storyboards, posters, or other visual aids in their presentations.

Across the Curriculum

MATH

Tredegar Iron Works. Richmond, Virginia, was the site of the Tredegar Iron Works, the South's only major mill equipped to produce cannons and railroad tracks. After Virginia seceded, Tredegar's 900 employees set to work producing guns for Confederate soldiers. Tredegar also produced the iron plates that protected the frigate *Merrimack*. By 1863 the number of workers employed by the mill had risen to 2,500.

Critical Thinking: By what percentage did the number of people employed at the Tredegar Iron Works increase from 1861 to 1863?

ANSWER: around 178 percent *(Subtract 900 from 2,500, divide by 900, and convert the decimal to a percentage by multiplying by 100.)*

Multimedia Resources

American History Simulations CD–ROM: Global Politics and the Civil War

Virginia, North Carolina, Tennessee, and Arkansas joined the Confederacy shortly after Lincoln's request for troops. The largely pro-Union population of western Virginia broke away from the Confederacy. This led to the creation of West Virginia, which joined the Union in 1863. Four slave states—Delaware, Kentucky, Maryland, and Missouri—bordered the North. These border states remained in the Union.

Union army drum

The North had several key advantages over the South. With a much larger population, the North could recruit more soldiers. Most of the nation's factories—particularly those that could produce military supplies—were in the North. The region's network of railways allowed for more efficient movement of troops and supplies to the war front. The Union was also able to raise more money to spend on the war effort.

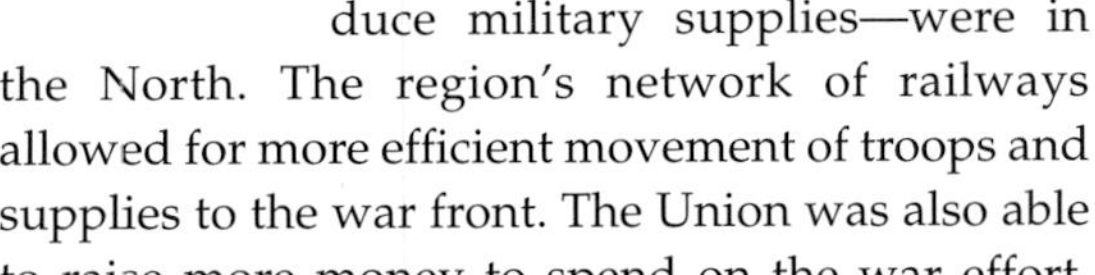

Union general Winfield Scott developed a two-part military strategy to defeat the South. He wanted to use a naval blockade to cut off southern seaports and strangle the South's economy. Scott also emphasized the need to gain control of the Mississippi River, which would separate Arkansas, Louisiana, and Texas from the Confederacy. Other northern leaders called for an attack on Richmond, Virginia, the Confederate capital.

The Confederacy's strategy was to defend itself against northern attacks and wear down the Union's will to fight. The South also hoped that Britain would support the Confederacy because of southern cotton's importance to Britain's textile industry. However, the South failed to gain any official foreign allies.

The War in the East

President Lincoln soon ordered General Irvin McDowell to push toward Richmond. In July 1861, Union soldiers met the Confederates about 25 miles southwest of Washington, along a creek called Bull Run. The Union troops drove the Confederate line back. Then a southern officer cried out, "Look! There is [Confederate general] Jackson standing like a stone wall! Rally behind the Virginians!" The Confederates responded and rallied behind "Stonewall" Jackson. When southern reinforcements arrived, the Union army retreated to Washington. As a result of this First Battle of Bull Run, the Union lost its hopes of quickly winning the war.

In the spring of 1862 Lincoln sent Union forces under the command of General George B. McClellan back into Virginia. By April 1862 McClellan had 100,000 troops near Richmond. He faced General Robert E. Lee. In 1861 Lee had refused Lincoln's request to take command of Union forces. After Virginia seceded, Lee resigned from the U.S. Army and joined the Confederates.

On June 26, 1862, Lee attacked McClellan in what became known as the Seven Days Battles. The Confederates suffered more than 20,000 casualties but inflicted nearly 16,000 on the Union and forced McClellan to retreat. Lincoln then ordered General John Pope to advance on Richmond from Washington. Caught off guard by Lee, Pope's army fell apart at the Second Battle of Bull Run. By the end of August 1862, Lee had pushed most of the Union forces out of Virginia.

Confederate leaders hoped that a major victory on Union soil would break northern morale and secure European aid. On September 17, 1862, the Union army met the Confederates along Antietam Creek in Maryland. The **Battle of Antietam** was the bloodiest single-day battle of the war—and in U.S. history. The Confederacy suffered more than 13,700 casualties and the Union

General Robert E. Lee was widely respected in the North and the South for his leadership.

LEVEL 3: Linguistic, Logical-Mathematical, Interpersonal. (Suggested time: 45 min.) Have each student read the Emancipation Proclamation, found just after this section of the text. Then organize the class into groups to represent each of these areas: Kentucky, Alabama, New Orleans, California, and West Virginia. Have group members analyze the effect of the Proclamation on the status of slaves in its area and cite selected passages from the document to support their reasoning. Have each group report its findings to the class.

CLOSE

Linguistic, Logical-Mathematical. Direct students' attention to the quotation from Abraham Lincoln at the beginning of the section. Then point out the quotation from General Grant at the end of the section. Ask students to decide how accurate Lincoln's prediction was and to cite evidence from the chapter to support their points of view. Also have students decide whether they agree with Grant's criticism of the Confederate cause, then have them support their opinions. Call on volunteers to present their conclusions.

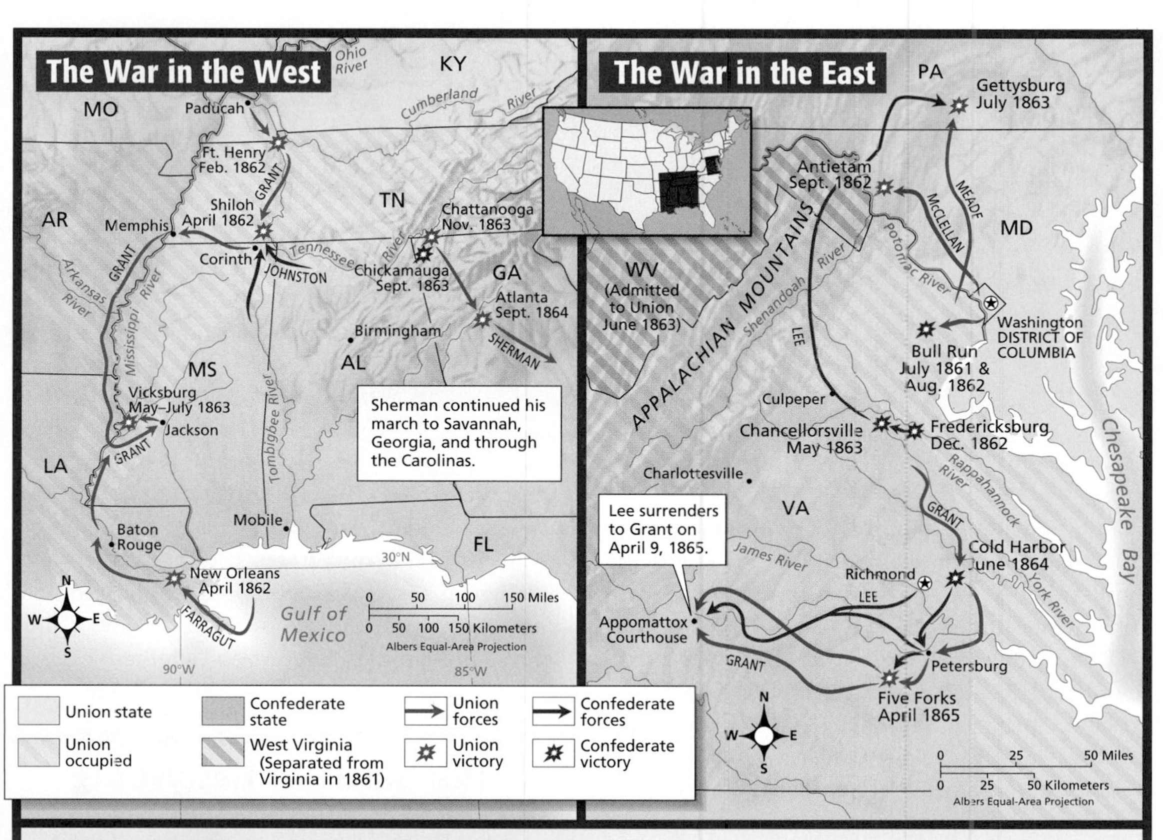

Major Battles of the Civil War

Learning from Maps In the West, Union forces tried to split the Confederacy by capturing the Mississippi River and by dividing the Upper and Lower South. In the East, the opposing sides threatened each other's capitals while trying to win a decisive victory.

Location What two battles took place in July 1863? What battles took place in Union states?

about 12,500. The battle was an important victory for the Union. Lee lost nearly a third of his troops, and his advance was stopped. However, McClellan refused to pursue Lee's retreating troops. This led Lincoln to later relieve McClellan of his command.

On September 22, 1862, after the victory at Antietam, Lincoln issued the **Emancipation Proclamation**. This proclamation called for all slaves in nonoccupied areas rebelling against the Union to be freed. It went into effect on January 1, 1863. Abolitionist Frederick Douglass wrote, "We shout for joy that we live to record this righteous decree [order]." Congress then authorized African Americans to enlist in the army. During the war, about 180,000 African Americans served with the Union Army.

The War in the West

Union strategy in the West focused on controlling the Mississippi River. The most important figure in the western theater of war was General Ulysses S. Grant. When the Civil War broke out, Grant volunteered for service with the Union army. His aggressiveness in battle set him apart from Union leaders such as General McClellan.

In early 1862 Grant led Union troops into Tennessee. With help from Union navy gunboats, Grant took Fort Henry and Fort Donelson. He continued his advance south. On April 6 the Confederates caught Grant by surprise and pushed the Union army back at the Battle of Shiloh. Grant ordered his troops to hold their

Geographic Diversity

The Caves of Vicksburg.

Vicksburg was built on the side of a hill that was easy to dig, yet firm enough for solid excavation. During the siege of Vicksburg, the city's residents burrowed a system of more than 500 caves in the side of the hill. Women and children took shelter in these caves when Union soldiers launched their artillery attacks. The people of Vicksburg brought furniture, rugs, and stoves into the caves, which they staffed with their slaves.

Activity: Have students use the library and other resources to find information on how people in other cities during the war protected women and children. Ask students to write a report or draw a diagram based on their findings.

MAP ANSWER

Vicksburg and Gettysburg; Antietam and Gettysburg

CHALLENGE AND EXTEND

1. **Linguistic, Logical-Mathematical.** Assign each student a border state or a Confederate state. Then have them use the library or other resources to find information on the secession movement in the assigned state. Ask students to determine the significant issues and to find out how the decision regarding secession was made. Then organize a meeting in which students act as representatives of the states they researched and explain the states' reasons for remaining in the Union or seceding.

2. **Linguistic, Visual-Spatial, Logical-Mathematical.** Organize the class into groups to weigh the advantages and disadvantages of each side in the Civil War. Have students use the library and other resources to investigate such subjects as industrial resources, agricultural production, financial resources, military leadership, troop strength, naval strength, and population. Have each group prepare a chart to illustrate the results of its investigations. Display the charts around the room and allow time for students to observe the various findings. To conclude, hold a discussion in which students identify the strengths and weaknesses of the North and the South.

Using Visual Resources

Surrender at Appomattox. The painting on the next page depicts the Confederate surrender at Appomattox Courthouse. General Robert E. Lee is seated to the left wearing his gray Confederate uniform. Lt. Col. Charles Marshall stands over Lee's shoulder as he officially agrees to the Confederate surrender. General Grant is depicted calmly sitting to the right in his blue Union uniform. He is surrounded by several other Union officers who seem to wait in anticipation. It has been suggested that the Union soldiers' lack of jubilation at the signing helped ease General Lee's pain as he signed the official surrender papers.

Activity: Have students use the library and other resources to find more information on the events at Appomattox. Have students write a newspaper article reporting on the surrender.

Confederate general George Pickett led thousands of troops in a costly charge against Union forces at the Battle of Gettysburg.

ground, whatever the cost. During the night, Union reinforcements arrived. Grant mounted a counterattack the next day and forced the Confederates to retreat.

The Union army next focused on capturing key southern positions along the Mississippi River. In late April, Union naval officer David G. Farragut captured New Orleans. He then proceeded up the Mississippi, taking Baton Rouge, Louisiana, as well as Natchez, Mississippi. Only Vicksburg, Mississippi, stood in the way of total Union dominance of the river. Previous attempts to take Vicksburg had failed. Vicksburg's high river bluffs allowed Confederate general John C. Pemberton's forces to cover the surrounding area with heavy guns. General Grant began a siege of Vicksburg in mid-May. As supplies ran out, the city's residents resorted to eating horses, dogs, and rats. Pemberton surrendered on July 4, 1863. Grant later said, "The fate of the Confederacy was sealed when Vicksburg fell."

Life During Wartime

The war effort affected the lives of most Americans. Women replaced farmers and industrial workers who had left for war. Led by Dorothea Dix, more than 3,000 women served as paid nurses in the Union army. Clara Barton provided medical aid to Union troops and later founded the American Red Cross. Despite such efforts, about twice as many soldiers died of disease than died in combat.

In the North, Peace Democrats, or Copperheads, opposed the war. To silence such critics, President Lincoln suspended *habeas corpus*—the constitutional protection against unlawful imprisonment. Many antiwar activists were arrested. In 1863 antidraft riots occurred after Congress passed a law that allowed the draft of men into the army. Many southerners resented the Confederate draft, passed in 1862. This draft excluded those who owned a large number of slaves. Some southerners said the conflict was a "rich man's war, [a] poor man's fight." In 1863 food shortages—caused in part by the Union blockade—led to riots in several southern cities.

 The Battle of Gettysburg

After winning a battle at Chancellorsville, Virginia, General Lee hoped to destroy northern morale with an attack into Union territory. He advanced into southern Pennsylvania. At the town of Gettysburg, Confederate and Union troops clashed, triggering the **Battle of Gettysburg**.

On July 1, 1863, the Confederates pushed the Union line back to Cemetery Ridge. The next day, the Union turned back a major Confederate assault. As General George Meade reinforced the Union line, Lee ordered General George Pickett to attack on July 3. Most of the nearly 15,000 men who took part in Pickett's Charge up Cemetery Ridge were killed or captured. One Union lieutenant wrote, "The battle was now over, but nobody knew it." The Confederacy's casualties were more than 28,000, and the Union's were more than 23,000.

Gettysburg was a turning point in the war. The Union victory there and Grant's capture of Vicksburg on the same day renewed northern support for the war effort. President Lincoln dedicated the Union to winning the war in the **Gettysburg Address**. His speech became one of the most famous in U.S. history.

REVIEW

Linguistic, Logical-Mathematical, Interpersonal. Have students complete the Section Review questions. Ask students to create crossword puzzles based on any 10 of the key terms or names listed in the Section Review. Have students exchange their puzzles and complete them. Then, have each student pass the completed puzzle to a third student for grading.

ASSESS

Have students complete Daily Quiz 3.5.

RETEACH

Linguistic, Logical-Mathematical, Intrapersonal. Have students complete Main Idea Activities for Reteaching and Sheltered English 3.5. Have students refer to the text to create a preview for an upcoming movie about the events in this section. Previews should be designed to generate interest in the movie by highlighting significant information. Remind students to give the movie a title. Ask volunteers to share their previews with the rest of the class. **SHELTERED ENGLISH**

The War's End

Impressed with General Grant's successes, President Lincoln made him supreme commander of the Union armies. In early 1864 Grant advanced into eastern Virginia. There he engaged General Lee in battles that stretched Confederate soldiers and supplies to their limits. Although Union forces suffered massive casualties, Grant pressed forward. In June 1864 he reached Petersburg, just south of Richmond, and laid siege to the city.

Meanwhile, General William Tecumseh Sherman marched south from Tennessee with 100,000 troops. On September 2, 1864, he captured Atlanta, Georgia, a vital railroad junction. The capture of Atlanta showed that progress was being made toward victory and helped Lincoln win a landslide re-election in 1864. Shortly after the election, Sherman marched toward Savannah, Georgia. On Sherman's march, he engaged in total war—targeting military and civilian resources to destroy an opponent's ability to fight. Hoping to speed the war's end, he ordered his troops to destroy bridges, railways, crops, and livestock. When Sherman finally reached Savannah on December 10, 1864, his army had left a path of destruction 60 miles wide and almost 300 miles long. Sherman then marched toward the Carolinas.

In April 1865 Grant broke through Lee's defenses at Petersburg. Lee realized the situation was hopeless. He noted, "There is nothing left for me to do but go and see General Grant, and I would rather die a thousand deaths."

Lee surrenders to Grant at Appomattox Courthouse on April 9, 1865.

The two generals met in the town of **Appomattox Courthouse** on April 9, 1865. Lee signed the surrender documents ending the war. Grant later wrote:

> **"I felt . . . sad and depressed at the downfall of a foe who had fought so long and valiantly [bravely], . . . for a cause, though that cause was, I believe, one of the worst for which a people ever fought."**

Some 620,000 Americans had lost their lives in the four years of bloody fighting, making the Civil War the most deadly conflict in U.S. history.

SECTION 5 REVIEW

Identify and explain the significance of the following:

- **Compromise of 1850**
- **Republican Party**
- **Kansas-Nebraska Act**
- ***Dred Scott* decision**
- **Abraham Lincoln**
- **Confederate States of America**
- **Jefferson Davis**
- **Robert E. Lee**
- **Battle of Antietam**
- **Emancipation Proclamation**
- **Ulysses S. Grant**
- **Battle of Gettysburg**
- **Gettysburg Address**
- **Appomattox Courthouse**

Reading for Content Understanding

1. **Main Idea** What events showed the regional tensions over slavery?
2. **Main Idea** Make a time line listing some of the major battles of the Civil War. Be sure to include which side won each battle.
3. **Geographic Diversity** *Region* What was the Union's strategy for winning the war?
4. **Writing** *Informing* Imagine that you are a foreign journalist touring the United States in early 1861. Write an article on the events that were the immediate cause of the Civil War.
5. **Critical Thinking** *Determining the Strength of an Argument* Do you think that President Lincoln was justified in suspending *habeas corpus*? Explain your answer.

Section 5 Review ANSWERS

Identify

- Compromise of 1850, p. 106
- Republican Party, p. 106
- Kansas-Nebraska Act, p. 106
- *Dred Scott* decision, p. 107
- Abraham Lincoln, p. 107
- Confederate States of America, p. 107
- Jefferson Davis, p. 107
- Robert E. Lee, p. 108
- Battle of Antietam, p. 108
- Emancipation Proclamation, p. 109
- Ulysses S. Grant, p. 109
- *habeas corpus*, p. 110
- Battle of Gettysburg, p. 110
- Gettysburg Address, p. 110
- Appomattox Courthouse, p. 111

Reading for Content Understanding

1. Compromise of 1850, reaction to *Uncle Tom's Cabin*, formation of the Republican Party, the Kansas-Nebraska Act and Bleeding Kansas, the *Dred Scott* decision, and John Brown's raid

2. Time lines will vary but should include the significant battles and state which side won.

3. The Union wanted to break the southern economy with a naval blockade, control the Mississippi River to split the Confederacy, and attack Richmond.

4. Articles will vary but should mention the secession of southern states and the formation of the Confederate States of America.

5. Answers will vary but students should state their opinions and offer logical support for them.

HISTORICAL DOCUMENTS ANSWERS

The Emancipation Proclamation

1. He claimed that military and naval authority allowed him to issue the Emancipation Proclamation.

2. He freed slaves in the areas that were in rebellion against the United States.

3. He needed the support of the North, and not all northerners believed that the Civil War was fought over slavery.

Gettysburg Address

1. It has already been consecrated by the soldiers who fought at Gettysburg.

2. to reunite the Union; many Americans were getting tired of the war after years of fighting and the deaths of so many soldiers.

PRIMARY SOURCE ▶

The primary source on pupil's pages 112–13 have been given in their entirety.

Chapter 3 Review ANSWERS

Identifying People and Ideas

1. president of the United States who issued the Emancipation Proclamation

2. area purchased from France that stretched from the Mississippi River to the Rocky Mountains

HISTORICAL DOCUMENTS

The Emancipation Proclamation

When the Union army won the Battle of Antietam, President Lincoln felt that the timing was right for a bold move. In late September 1862 he issued a preliminary Emancipation Proclamation. On January 1, 1863, the following official Proclamation went into effect.

A Proclamation by the President of the United States of America

Whereas on the twenty-second day of September, A.D. 1862, a proclamation was issued by the President of the United States, containing, among other things, the following, to wit [namely]:

"That on the first day of January, A.D. 1863, all persons held as slaves within any state or designated part of a state, the people whereof shall then be in rebellion against the United States, shall be then, thenceforward [afterward], and forever free; and the executive government of the United States, including the military and naval authority thereof, will recognize and maintain the freedom of such persons and will do no act or acts to repress [keep down] such persons or any of them, in any efforts they may make for their actual freedom.

"That the Executive will on the first day of January aforesaid, by proclamation, designate the states and parts of states, if any, in which the people thereof, . . . shall then be in rebellion against the United States; and the fact that any state or the people thereof shall on that day be in good faith represented in the Congress of the United States by members chosen thereto at elections wherein a majority of the qualified voters of such states shall have participated shall, in the absence of strong countervailing [opposing] testimony, be deemed [declared] conclusive evidence that such state and the people thereof are not then in rebellion against the United States."

Now, therefore, I, Abraham Lincoln, President of the United States, by virtue of the power in me vested [empowered] as Commander-in-Chief of the Army and Navy of the United States in time of actual armed rebellion against the authority and government of the United States, and as a fit and necessary war measure for suppressing said rebellion, do, on this first day of January, A.D. 1863, and in accordance with my purpose so to do, publicly proclaimed for the full period of one hundred days from the first day above mentioned, order and designate as the states and parts of states wherein the people thereof, . . . are in this day in rebellion against the United States the following, to wit:

Arkansas, Texas, Louisiana (except the parishes of St. Bernard, Plaquemines, Jefferson, St. John, St. Charles, St. James, Ascension, Assumption, Terrebonne, Lafourche, St. Mary, St. Martin, and Orleans, including the city of New Orleans), Mississippi, Alabama, Florida, Georgia, South Carolina, North Carolina, and Virginia (except the forty-eight counties designated as West Virginia, and also the counties of Berkeley, Accomac, Northampton, Elizabeth City, York, Princess Anne, and Norfolk, including the cities of Norfolk and Portsmouth), and which excepted parts are for the present left precisely as if this proclamation were not issued.

And by virtue of the power and for the purpose aforesaid, I do order and declare that all persons held as slaves within said designated states and parts of states are, and henceforward shall be, free; and that the executive government of the United States, including the military and naval authorities thereof, will recognize and maintain the freedom of said persons.

And I hereby enjoin upon [order] the people so declared to be free to abstain [hold back] from all violence, unless in necessary self-defense; and I recommend to them that, in all cases when allowed, they labor faithfully for reasonable wages.

And I further declare and make known that such persons of suitable condition will be received into the armed service of the United States to garrison [defend] forts, positions, stations, and other places, and to man vessels of all sorts in said service.

And upon this act, sincerely believed to be an act of justice, warranted by the Constitution upon military necessity, I invoke [call upon] the considerate judgment of mankind and the gracious favor of Almighty God.

Understanding Primary Sources

1. What authority did Lincoln claim allowed him to issue the Emancipation Proclamation?
2. In what places does Lincoln free slaves?
3. Why do you think Lincoln did not free all slaves?

Abraham Lincoln's *Gettysburg Address*

On November 19, 1863, Abraham Lincoln addressed a crowd gathered to dedicate a cemetery at the Gettysburg battlefield. His short speech reminded Americans of the ideals on which the republic was founded.

Four score and seven years ago our fathers brought forth on this continent, a new nation, conceived [created] in Liberty, and dedicated to the proposition that all men are created equal.

Now we are engaged in a great civil war, testing whether that nation, or any nation so conceived and so dedicated, can long endure. We are met on a great battlefield of that war. We have come to dedicate a portion of that field, as a final resting place for those who here gave their lives that that nation might live. It is altogether fitting and proper that we should do this.

But, in a larger sense, we can not dedicate—we can not consecrate [make holy]—we cannot hallow—this ground. The brave men, living and dead, who struggled here, have consecrated it, far above our poor power to add or detract. The world will little note nor long remember what we say here, but it can never forget what they did here. It is for us the living, rather, to be dedicated here to the unfinished work which they who fought here have thus far so nobly advanced. It is rather for us to be here dedicated to the great task remaining before us—that from these honored dead we take increased devotion to that cause for which they gave the last full measure of devotion—that we here highly resolve that these dead shall not have died in vain—that this nation, under God, shall have a new birth of freedom—and that government of the people, by the people, for the people, shall not perish from the earth.

Understanding Primary Sources

1. Why does Lincoln say that he and the other members of the crowd cannot consecrate the battlefield?
2. For what cause does Lincoln say the soldiers at Gettysburg died? Why–at this particular point in the war–do you think that Lincoln decided to remind Americans of this cause and its importance?

3. president of the United States from 1797–1801

4. called for all slaves in nonoccupied areas rebelling against the United States to be freed

5. period of rapid growth in the use of machines for manufacturing and production

6. invention that spurred the growth of the U.S. cotton industry and of slavery

7. warned European nations not to colonize or interfere in the Americas

8. independent nation formed after Texas won its independence from Mexico in 1836, annexed by the United States in 1845

9. president who agreed to the Louisiana Purchase

10. idea that the United States was meant to expand across the continent to the Pacific Ocean

Using the Time Line

1. c
2. b
3. e
4. a
5. d

Understanding Main Ideas

1. The United States faced violations of American neutrality at sea by Britain and France, attacks by Native Americans on settlers that were encouraged by Britain, and the closing of the Port of New Orleans by Spain; Britain refused to stop violating American neutrality at sea and provided military aid to Native Americans, thus resulting in the War of 1812.

2. Settlement resulted in violent conflicts, such as the Battle of Fallen Timbers, and forced relocations.

Review and Assessment **RESOURCES**

PRINT
- ★ Chapter 3 Review, pp. 114–15
- ★ Vocabulary Activity 3
- ★ Chapter 3 Study Guide
- ★ Chapter 3 Test (Form A or B)

MULTIMEDIA
- ★ Audio Program, Ch. 3 (English and Spanish)
- ★ *Global Skill Builder CD–ROM*
- ★ Chapter 3 Test Generator
- ★ HRW Web site

SHELTERED ENGLISH
- ★ Spanish Glossary
- ★ Sheltered English Chapter 3 Test

ASSESS

Have students complete one of the Chapter 3 Tests. As an alternate assessment, assign the Chapter 3 Investigation.

3. In trying to maintain a balance between slave and free states, the United States reached the Missouri Compromise, and in deciding whether slavery would be allowed in the Mexican Cession, the nation reached the Compromise of 1850.

4. Results included cheap labor for the Industrial Revolution and rising nativism.

5. Americans worked for abolition, women's rights, improved urban living conditions, temperance, prison reform, better treatment for the mentally ill, the common-school movement, and educational opportunity for women, African Americans, and those with special needs.

6. Slaves generally lived in poor conditions, and the work they performed was usually long and strenuous.

7. The results included conflict with Mexico over government regulations, which led Texans to fight for independence.

8. It brought many people there, changed its economy, and helped it become a state.

Reviewing Themes

1. The United States annexed Texas, Mexico and the United States disagreed over the southern border of Texas, President Polk sent U.S. troops into the disputed area, Mexican soldiers crossed the Rio Grande and attacked the U.S. troops; Mexico ceded much of its northern territory in the Treaty of Guadalupe Hidalgo.

2. They publicized the injustices against women in the Seneca Falls Declaration, and they expanded educational opportunities for women.

CHAPTER 3 REVIEW

Chapter Summary

The United States expanded its borders with the Louisiana Purchase and fought the War of 1812. Conflict with American Indians broke out as more settlers moved west. The Industrial and Transportation Revolutions changed American life. The South's economy depended on cotton and slavery. The U.S. victory in the Mexican War greatly increased the nation's size. Rising tensions over the issue of slavery led to the Civil War.

On a separate sheet of paper, complete the following activities.

Identifying People and Ideas

Describe the historical significance of the following:

1. Abraham Lincoln
2. Louisiana Purchase
3. John Adams
4. Emancipation Proclamation
5. Industrial Revolution
6. cotton gin
7. Monroe Doctrine
8. Republic of Texas
9. Thomas Jefferson
10. manifest destiny

Internet Activity

go.hrw.com
SB1 Cabinet

Search the Internet through the HRW Web site for information about the president's cabinet, including what departments there are and who heads each one. Then compare the number of cabinet positions today with the number in the first cabinet. Write two short paragraphs discussing what the cabinet reflects about our government today and how that contrasts with government during George Washington's presidency.

Understanding Main Ideas

1. What foreign policy challenges did the young nation face, and how did these tensions lead to the War of 1812?
2. How did western settlement affect American Indians in the early and mid-1800s?
3. Why was the United States divided over slavery, and what compromises were reached on slavery?
4. What were some of the results of increased immigration in the mid-1800s?
5. What reform movements did Americans participate in during the mid-1800s?
6. What was life like for slaves in the South in the 1800s?
7. What were the results of increased American migration to Texas?
8. How did the gold rush affect California?

Using the Time Line

Number your paper from 1 to 5. Match the letters on the time line below with the following events.

1. **The Indian Removal Act is passed.**
2. **Lewis and Clark begin their journey west.**
3. **General Lee surrenders, ending the Civil War.**
4. **George Washington is elected the first president of the United States.**
5. **The United States and Mexico go to war.**

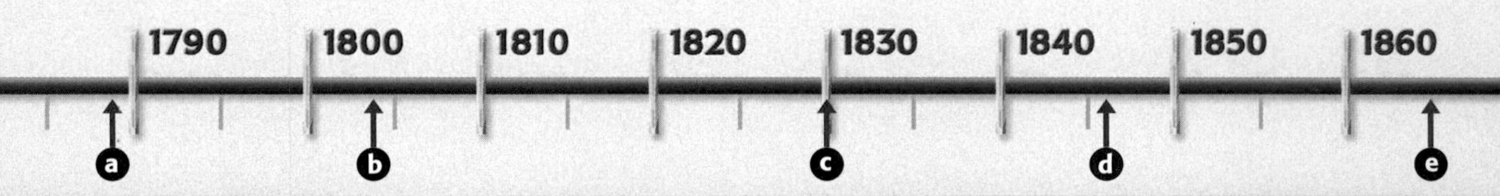

RETEACH

Visual-Spatial, Logical-Mathematical. Organize the class into five groups and assign each group one of the chapter's sections. Have each group create a series of detailed cartoons or drawings representing the major events of its assigned section. Display the cartoons and drawings around the classroom and have each group explain the significance of its work.

Using the Internet

Have students continue their research to find information about current cabinet members. Tell students to write a transcript of a mock interview with one of the current members of the cabinet. Students should ask about the member's background and responsibilities in the cabinet.

Portfolio Extensions

1. Have students choose one of the three areas and imagine that they are immigrants to that area. Instruct students to make a list of items that, based on the brochure, they think will be useful in their new home.

2. Have students write a brief article that might have appeared in one of the abolitionist newspapers.

Reviewing Themes

1. **Global Relations** What events led to the Mexican War, and what were the consequences of this war?
2. **Citizenship and Democracy** How did women try to achieve greater rights?
3. **Technology and Society** In what ways did the Industrial and Transportation Revolutions change American society?

Thinking Critically

1. **Evaluating** Do you think Thomas Jefferson's actions as president benefitted the nation? Explain your answer.
2. **Identifying Cause and Effect** What effect did Abraham Lincoln's election as president have on the country?
3. **Drawing Conclusions** Why might reformers think it important that all members of society receive an education?

Building Your Portfolio

Complete the following activities individually or in groups.

1. **Regional Differences** Select a region of the country (either the South, the Northeast, or the West). Then create a brochure that might be used to attract settlers or immigrants to that region in the 1850s. Your brochure should focus on the region's economy, culture, and historical points of interest.
2. **Abolitionist Literature** Imagine that you have been hired to promote one of the abolitionist newspapers published in the 1800s in the northern United States. Create a poster to advertise one of these works, either William Lloyd Garrison's the *Liberator*, or Frederick Douglass's *North Star.* Be sure that your poster clearly states what these newspapers are about. Your poster should give a brief biography of either publisher and should also discuss the history of the abolition movement.

Writing About History

1. **Expressing** Write a note to George Washington thanking him for his years of service to the United States. Include Washington's accomplishments in the Revolutionary War and his later political life.
2. **Informing** Write a newspaper article explaining the resources and strategies of the North and the South during the Civil War. Include information about the final outcome of the war.

Linking Geography and History

1. **Region** Why did protective tariffs hurt southerners more than northerners?
2. **Movement** What trails did Americans take to reach California and the Southwest?

History Skills Workshop

Reading Maps Study the map below. Then answer the following questions: (a) How many slave states were there in 1860? (b) How many free states were there in 1860? (c) What was the total number of senators for the free and slave states in 1860?

The United States in 1860

3. The Industrial Revolution changed the way Americans worked and spurred both immigration and its resulting nativism. The Transportation Revolution shortened travel time and lowered shipping costs, which led to increased trade and more settlers moving to the Midwest.

Thinking Critically

1. Answers will vary but students should consider the growth of the nation that occurred during his presidency.

2. Answers will vary but students should mention the secession of southern states as a result of his election, which led to the Civil War.

3. Answers will vary but students might mention that reformers thought it was important for all citizens in a democratic society to have the skills necessary for success.

Writing About History

1. Thank-you notes will vary but should mention incidents from Washington's military career and his presidency.

2. Articles will vary but should discuss the North's superiority in resources and the differences in military strategy.

Linking Geography and History

1. Southerners relied heavily on imported goods.

2. They took the Oregon, California, Santa Fe, and Mormon Trails.

History Skills Workshop

(a) slave—15; (b) free—18; (c) free—36; slave—30

TEACH

ALL LEVELS: Visual-Spatial. (Suggested time: 45 min.) Ask students to make a special-purpose map showing a route with which they are very familiar. They might want to map their route from home to school or to a relative's house. Have them create a title, legend, labels, and a compass rose for their map. Then instruct them to create five questions that a person could answer by using their map. Tell students to look at the information under the How to Read a Map section of this activity for clues about how to design their questions. Then have students exchange maps and complete the questions on the map they are given. Remind students that knowing how to read maps will help them understand how geographic factors have influenced history.

SKILLS ANSWERS

1. an ocean
2. political

Reading Maps. Have students bring road maps to class. Ask students to choose a city on their maps. Direct students to use the scale on their maps to draw a circle with a 50-mile radius from the center of their chosen city. Then instruct students to make a list of the physical features and cities, counties, and states within that 50-mile radius. Have volunteers present their maps and lists to the class.

History Skills

WORKSHOP

Reading Maps

Maps provide a wealth of historical and geographical information. To read maps, you must understand their terms and symbols.

Types of Maps Types of maps include *physical maps, political maps,* and *special-purpose maps.* Physical maps show the landforms that mark Earth's surface. Political maps illustrate political units such as states and nations. Special-purpose maps present specific information, such as the routes of explorers or the outcome of an election.

Map Features A map's legend, or key, explains any special symbols, colors, or shading used on the map. Labels designate political and geographic place-names as well as physical features.

Most maps in this textbook have a *compass rose,* or directional indicator. The compass rose indicates the four cardinal points: north, south, east, and west. Many maps also include a scale, showing both miles and kilometers, to help you find the distance between two points on the map.

The *absolute location* of any place on Earth is given in terms of latitude and longitude. Latitude is the number of degrees north or south of the equator, an imaginary line that runs around Earth halfway between the North and South Poles. Longitude is the number of degrees east or west of the prime meridian, an imaginary line that runs from the North Pole to the South Pole through western Europe and Africa.

How to Read A Map

1. **Study the title and the legend** Read the map's title and legend to determine the map's subject and the geographic area it covers. Familiarize yourself with any symbols, lines, colors, and shading used.
2. **Study the map** Study the map's basic features and details. If it is a special-purpose map, study the specific information given.
3. **Check directions and distances** Use the compass rose and scale to determine direction, location, and distance.

Practicing the Skill

Study the map below. Then answer the following questions.

1. Near what type of geographic feature are most of the cities located?
2. What type of map is shown here?

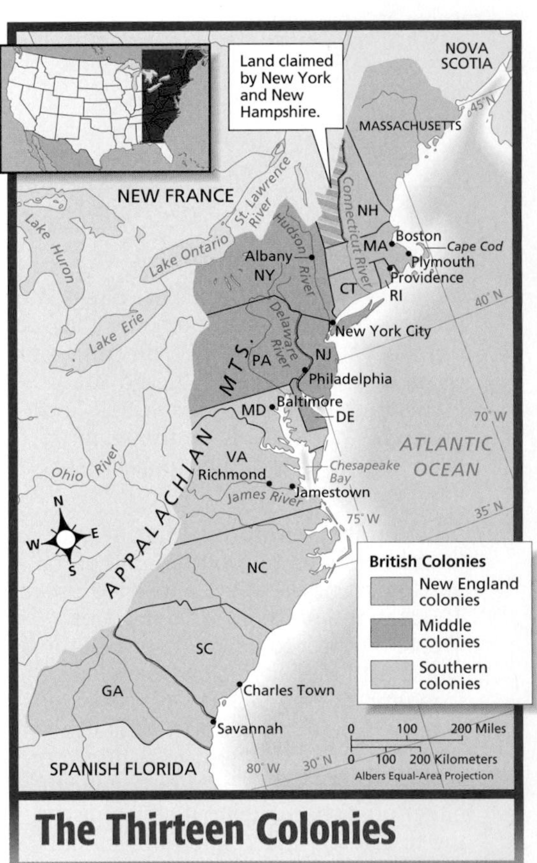

The Thirteen Colonies

ALL LEVELS: Linguistic, Musical-Rhythmic, Interpersonal. (Suggested time: 45 min.) Instruct each student to write a song that can be added to the presentation of his or her narrative. Students' lyrics may describe their historical figure or their figure's time period. Suggest to students that they either make up their own tune or use a familiar one. During their presentations students should perform their songs or read the lyrics for the class. Each group should include the lyrics to its songs in the brochure that accompanies its diorama. Encourage students to use language, musical styles, and instruments that are appropriate to their historical figure's time period.

History in Action

UNIT 1 PORTFOLIO

The United States: The Diorama

Complete the following activity in small, cooperative groups.

Your group will create a diorama showing the history of the United States from the first people to arrive in North America to the Civil War. This three-dimensional exhibit will include a backdrop map of the United States with historical figures in front of it. Each group member will make one figure. Each figure will be from a different time period. Use symbols, colors, or shading on the map to relate to each historical figure. Pay close attention to the clothing your figure wears and the objects he or she carries.

Materials To complete this activity, you will need large sheets of paper for creating the background and cardboard or sticks for making your people stand up. You will also need various art supplies, such as cloth, construction paper, glue, markers, paints, and paper.

Parts of the Project To make your diorama, complete the following tasks:

1. **Overview** You and the members of your group will create figures for your diorama. The group as a whole will decide on the time periods to represent. You should have as many time periods as group members. The time span is from the beginning of North American settlement to the Civil War.

2. **Roles** Here are the different roles that each group member will need to perform in order to make your project a success:
   - **Researchers:** All group members will gather information and images for the time periods and the map. Each group member will also research his or her specific time period to decide on the figure to create and how to relate that figure to the background map.
   - **Artists:** The group as a whole will create the map. Each group member will create his or her figure and provide its clothing and objects.
   - **Writers:** Each group member will write a paragraph explaining the significance of his or her historical figure. All paragraphs should be written from the figure's point of view. Be sure to include information on what daily life would have been like for your figure. Gather the narratives together as a brochure to accompany the diorama.

3. **Presentation** Once you have completed your diorama, present it to the class. Each group member will read the narrative for his or her figure.

Once all groups have made their presentations, the class as a whole will compare the different time periods represented. The class will then come up with one time line that best identifies the unit.

Teenagers prepare an exhibit.

Resources. Suggest to students that they look at art or photographs of their historical figure or from their figure's time period. Instruct students to pay particular attention to their figure's clothes and hair, as well as to any objects he or she might carry. Autobiographies or published letters, if available, will help students write their narratives from the historical figure's point of view.

Presentations. You may want to teach or remind students about good presentation skills. Students can practice speaking clearly, making eye contact with their audience, and avoiding expressions such as "you know."

Brochures. Have students create brochures that are visually appealing, free from spelling and grammatical errors, and relatively easy to read. Encourage them to add a brief bibliography to each narrative.

Introducing UNIT

CHAPTER 4

Reconstruction

Following the Civil War, the government had to reunite the nation and define the rights of African Americans. After President Lincoln's assassination, these decisions fell to President Andrew Johnson. The Fourteenth Amendment was passed to protect former slaves and bring reforms to the South. These reforms did not last, however. By 1877 a New South had emerged in which white southerners dominated.

CHAPTER 5

The West

Settlers moving west in the mid-1800s came into conflict with American Indians, who were eventually forced onto reservations. More people were motivated to move west by discoveries of gold, the building of the transcontinental railroad, and government offers of free land. Settlement and farming in this region led the Great Plains to become the breadbasket of the world.

Internet Activity

Buffalo Soldiers. The buffalo soldiers served in African American cavalry and infantry regiments in the U.S. Army on the western frontier. Have students search the Internet through the HRW Web site to find more information about the buffalo soldiers. Tell students to imagine that they are traveling reporters preparing an article about the buffalo soldiers for a popular magazine. Instruct students to make a list of five interview questions and then write the soldiers' "answers" based on the information they gather from the Web sites. Students should then write their articles, in which they should include information about the history of the buffalo soldiers and "quotations" from their interviews. In addition, encourage students to include images in their articles if possible.

go.hrw.com
SB1 Buffalo Soldiers

UNIT 2 Industrial America (1850–1900)

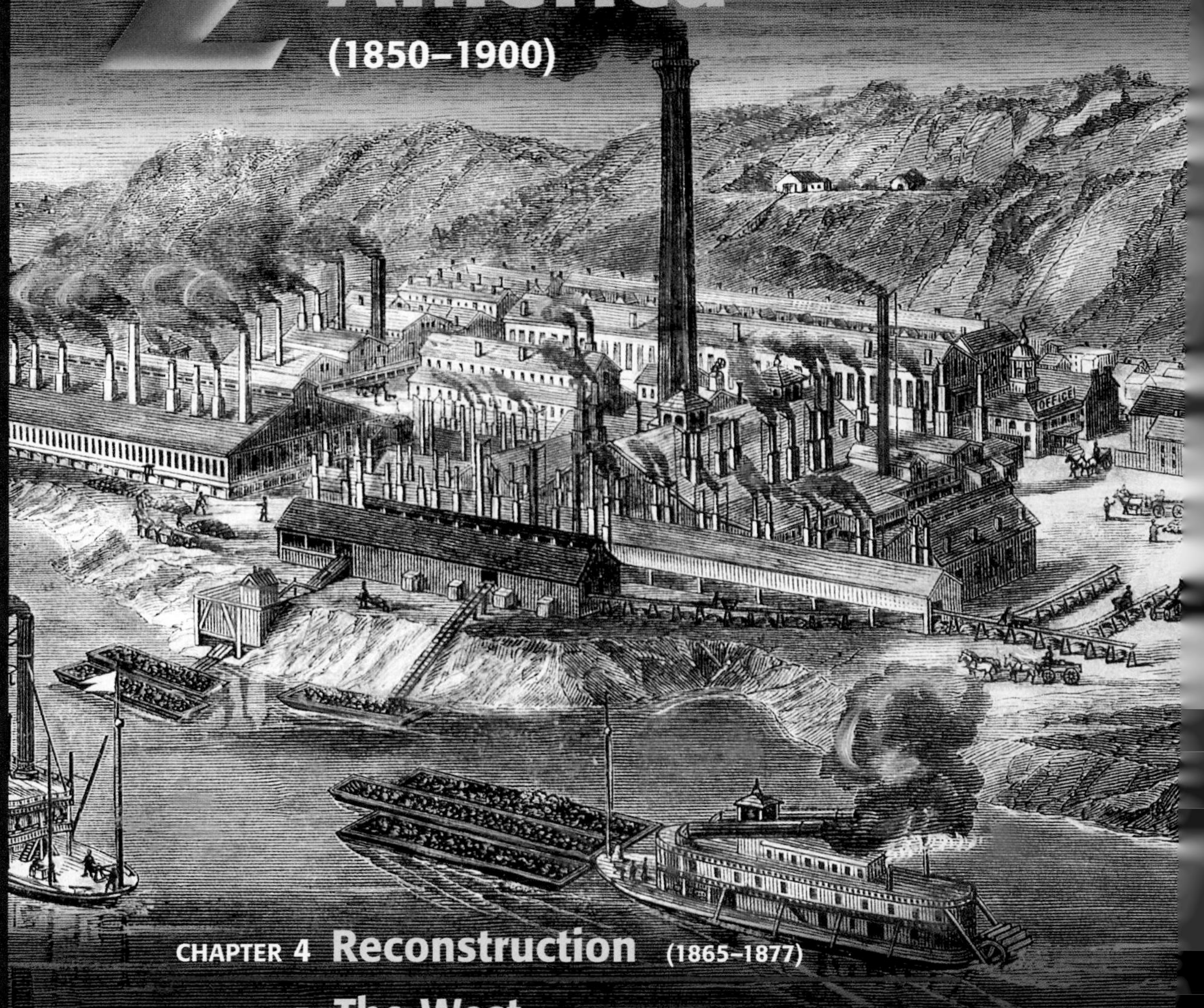

CHAPTER 4 **Reconstruction** (1865–1877)

CHAPTER 5 **The West** (1850–1890)

CHAPTER 6 **An Industrial Nation** (1876–1900)

CHAPTER 7 **Immigrants and Cities** (1880–1900)

CHAPTER 6

An Industrial Nation

The Second Industrial Revolution brought the development of new industries, inventions, and power sources. The organization of business also changed. Laborers formed unions to improve working conditions. Groups such as the Populist Party tried to improve farmers' economic problems and increase their political influence.

CHAPTER 7

Immigrants and Cities

After 1880 immigration from eastern and southern Europe greatly increased. The population of U.S. cities such as Chicago swelled with both immigrants and migrants from rural America. Skyscrapers and mass transit also changed cities. The late 1800s saw the rise of mass culture, a publishing boom, and new trends in literature, painting, and photography.

UNIT MOTIVATOR

Create a display of common objects that are made of steel. *(Objects might include cutlery, staples, or tools.)* Ask students to suggest what the objects might have in common. As a class, discuss the answer and the effects of the Second Industrial Revolution on the United States. Tell students that in this unit they will learn about the many changes in the United States between 1850 and 1900.

American Teens

IN HISTORY

Young Immigrants

During the 1880s and 1890s about 9 million immigrants poured into the United States. Most were farmers from Austria-Hungary, Italy, Poland, and Russia who brought their families with them. Immigrant children and teenagers found life in the United States both difficult and exciting. Many immigrant teens worked outside the home. Some immigrants came from communities that had a tradition of family labor. For example, many Italian immigrant families operated according to the expression, the "door [of a house] is open to he who contributes—otherwise you stay outside." Italian boys were thus more likely to work than attend school. Other immigrant groups, such as Jews from eastern Europe, tried to keep their children out of the full-time labor force and in school during their teen years.

In the late 1800s and early 1900s most European immigrants arrived at Ellis Island, New York.

The Granger Collection, New York

The rapid increase in the number of immigrant children often led to overcrowded schools. Some schools had students attend in two shifts. Each group received instruction for only half of the school day. Some students also had to share resources. One student remembered sharing a desk with another girl and having to "put an arm around her waist so I shouldn't fall off."

School administrators placed immigrant children in classrooms according to their ability to speak, read, or write English. Many immigrants were put in classrooms with students three to four years younger than they were. One goal of public school instruction was to "Americanize" immigrant students. One student from Serbia recalled that "at school I went as Tomas . . . because the teacher would not pronounce or spell my own [name]." However, many immigrant youths found teachers that provided wonderful instruction. A student named Dora said that her teacher "changed the course of my life. . . . Because of her I was introduced to everything that was good in the United States."

In this unit you will learn more about the immigrants who came to the United States in the late 1800s. You will also learn about Reconstruction and the West, as well as an industrializing America.

LEFT PAGE: *In the late 1800s Pittsburgh, Pennsylvania, became a leading iron and steel producer.*

The Granger Collection, New York

Using Visual Resources

The Iron and Steel Industry. The engraving on the opposite page shows an ironworks in Pittsburgh, Pennsylvania. Iron ore and coal deposits located in the Midwest led to the development of important iron and steel manufacturing centers, such as Pittsburgh. In the years before the Civil War, U.S. iron production quickly increased to meet the demand for items such as railroad tracks. Steel, although it was superior to iron, was too expensive to manufacture for common applications. The development of the Bessemer process and the Siemens-Martin open-hearth method in the 1850s, however, made it possible to profitably produce large amounts of steel. After the Civil War the demand for steel for construction, railroads, and other uses led to rapid growth of the American steel industry.

Critical Thinking: Why might an artist want to make an engraving of an ironworks?

ANSWER: It might have been at the request of the owner, or the artist may have wanted to show something that was very important to the city.

TEACH

ALL LEVELS: Kinesthetic, Visual-Spatial. (Suggested time: 30 min.) Ask students to choose one of the events from the time line. Have students imagine that they are public relations officials for the place where the event occurred. Provide students with the necessary art supplies and instruct them to create a poster that encourages people to visit the site of the event. For example, a student could make a poster inviting people to visit the Brooklyn Bridge on its opening day. Posters should include the year of the events, an illustration of the event, and a written caption describing the illustration.

ALL LEVELS: Linguistic, Logical-Mathematical, Visual-Spatial. (Suggested time: 30 min.) Have students make a list of the significant terms and names from the time line. Ask volunteers to share their lists with the class. Write a master list on the chalkboard. Instruct students to create a crossword puzzle using at least 10 terms or names from the master list as the answers. Tell students to use information from the descriptions of the time line events to write the clues. After creating the puzzles, students should exchange them, solve them, and then return them to their authors for grading.

Historical Sidelight

Ford's Theater. In 1861 John Thomson Ford purchased the building that had formerly housed the First Baptist Church of Washington. Many residents of the city were upset at the idea of a church being converted into a theater. One person who had attended services at the church declared that the enterprise would surely meet with disaster. The prediction came true when, in its first year of operation, the theater burned down in a fire caused by a defective gas meter. Ford, however, rebuilt his theater. The new Ford's Theater was quite popular and hosted almost 500 performances before it was shut down following the assassination of President Lincoln.

Critical Thinking: Why might the theater have been shut down after the assassination of Lincoln?

ANSWER: Students' answers will vary but might suggest that it was done out of respect for the Lincoln family and for Lincoln himself.

Time Line: 1850–1900

UNIT 2

Industrial America

A Pony Express rider

Thomas Watson, Alexander Graham Bell's assistant, holds the first telephone.

UNITED STATES

1860 The Pony Express begins delivering mail in the West.

1865 John Wilkes Booth assassinates President Abraham Lincoln while the president attends a play at Ford's Theater.

1866 Cowboys drive cattle north from Texas on the Chisholm Trail for the first time.

1872 P. T. Barnum opens the "Greatest Show on Earth," his circus in Brooklyn, New York.

1876 Alexander Graham Bell develops the first telephone.

1850	1854	1858	1862	1866	1870	1874

WORLD

1865 Lewis Carroll publishes *Alice's Adventures in Wonderland.*

1869 The Suez Canal in Egypt opens. It connects the Mediterranean and Red Seas.

1874 Painters stage the first impressionist art exhibition in Paris, France.

In one of her adventures in "Wonderland," Alice grew tall.

Claude Monet's *Impression: Sunrise*

Clipper ships like *Royal Charter* traveled through the Suez Canal.

CHALLENGE AND EXTEND

1. Logical-Mathematical, Visual-Spatial. Have students create a time line similar to the one in the unit opener, where U.S. events are on top and world events are on the bottom. Ask students to research the U.S. population and the world population during the time period from 1850–1900. For each four-year interval on the time line, students should provide the populations for both the United States and the world. Encourage students to make note of any significant population changes and to speculate as to why these changes occurred.

2. Linguistic, Logical-Mathematical. Have students imagine that it is 1896 and they are sports reporters for their local newspaper. Using the library or other resources, students should write an article that highlights the important information about the first modern Olympic Games. Students should include information about the various athletic events held, any U.S. athletes who won medals, any participants from their home state, and some facts about the city of Athens. Encourage students to include an illustration of an event as well. Ask volunteers to share their articles with the class.

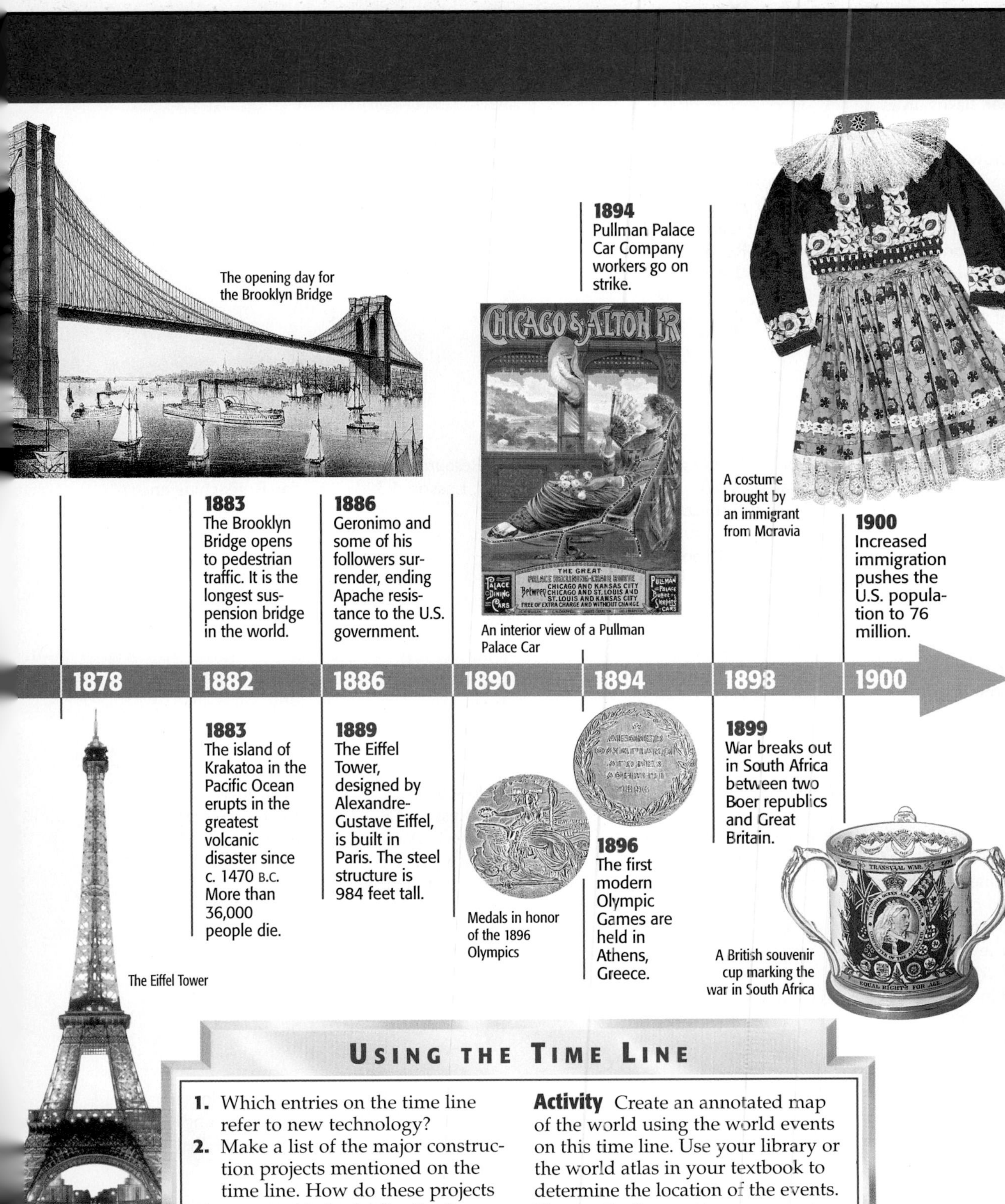

USING THE TIME LINE

1. Which entries on the time line refer to new technology?
2. Make a list of the major construction projects mentioned on the time line. How do these projects represent industrialization?
3. Which time line entries refer to "firsts": actions, events, or things?

Activity Create an annotated map of the world using the world events on this time line. Use your library or the world atlas in your textbook to determine the location of the events. Then write the events on your map with brief explanations of what happened. You may also wish to illustrate your map.

Technology and Society

The Eiffel Tower. Engineer Alexandre-Gustave Eiffel built the Eiffel Tower in Paris for the Centennial Exposition of 1889, which marked the 100th anniversary of the French Revolution. The Paris landmark was built in less than a year. Special elevators that could rise along the tower's curved path were designed by the Otis Elevator Company in the United States. When completed, the Eiffel Tower was twice as tall as the Great Pyramid of Giza. Plans were made to tear down the tower in 1909, but its usefulness as a radio antenna saved the structure. The Eiffel Tower stood as the world's tallest building until 1930, when the Chrysler Building was erected in New York City.

Activity: Have students use the library or other resources to find more information about the Eiffel Tower. Then have them write a paragraph about what it might have been like to have been one of the workers who built the tower.

USING THE TIME LINE ANSWERS

1. Bell's telephone
2. Suez Canal, Brooklyn Bridge, Eiffel Tower; they used the materials and technologies of industrialization.
3. Pony Express run, Chisholm Trail cattle drive, invention of the telephone, impressionist art exhibition, modern Olympics

CHAPTER PLANNING GUIDE
Reconstruction

	SECTION LESSON OBJECTIVES	PRINT RESOURCES	MULTIMEDIA RESOURCES	SHELTERED ENGLISH RESOURCES
Section 1: Rebuilding the South (pp. 123–29)	★ Analyze the effect of the end of the Civil War on southern life. ★ Compare and contrast the views of Lincoln, Congress, and Johnson about Reconstruction. ★ Evaluate the impact of the Freedmen's Bureau on former slaves' lives.	★ Guided Reading Strategies 4.1 ★ Section 1 Review, p. 129 ★ Daily Quiz 4.1	★ *Teaching Resources CD–ROM,* Lesson 4.1 ★ *Exploring America's Past* Video Segment: A Play of Fate; *Teacher's Guide,* pp. 9–11	★ Main Idea Activities for Reteaching and Sheltered English 4.1
Section 2: The Fight over Reconstruction (pp. 130–35)	★ Explain how Black Codes restricted the freedoms of African Americans. ★ Analyze reasons why Radical Republicans wanted to impeach President Johnson. ★ Describe Republicans' efforts to protect the civil rights of African Americans.	★ Guided Reading Strategies 4.2 ★ American History Political Cartoon 13: Radical Reconstruction ★ Section 2 Review, p. 135 ★ Daily Quiz 4.2	★ *Teaching Resources CD–ROM,* Lesson 4.2 ★ HRW Web site	★ Main Idea Activities for Reteaching and Sheltered English 4.2
Section 3: Reconstruction in the South (pp. 136–41)	★ Describe the roles played by African Americans, northerners, and southern white Republicans in rebuilding the South. ★ Explain how the Ku Klux Klan attempted to disrupt the process of Reconstruction. ★ Analyze the factors that led to the end of Reconstruction.	★ Guided Reading Strategies 4.3 ★ Primary Source Reading 4: *Plessy* v. *Ferguson* ★ Literature Reading 4: "Jim Crow Cars" ★ Graphic Organizer 4: Congress and Reconstruction ★ Section 3 Review, p. 141 ★ Daily Quiz 4.3	★ *Teaching Resources CD–ROM,* Lesson 4.3	★ Main Idea Activities for Reteaching and Sheltered English 4.3
Section 4: The New South (pp. 142–47)	★ Describe the problems southern farmers faced after the Civil War. ★ Explain reasons why some business leaders wanted to create a "New South." ★ Identify the various forms of culture that emerged in the South during and after Reconstruction.	★ Guided Reading Strategies 4.4 ★ Biography Reading 4: George Washington Carver ★ Geography Activity 4: Tenant Farming and Sharecropping ★ Section 4 Review, p. 147 ★ Daily Quiz 4.4	★ *Teaching Resources CD–ROM,* Lesson 4.4 ★ Everyday Life in America Transparency 13: Life During Reconstruction ★ *American Music Audio CD Program:* "When Johnny Comes Marching Home"	★ Main Idea Activities for Reteaching and Sheltered English 4.4
Chapter Review and Assessment (pp. 148–49)		★ Chapter 4 Review, pp. 148–49 ★ Vocabulary Activity 4 ★ Chapter 4 Study Guide ★ Chapter 4 Test (Form A or B)	★ Audio Program, Ch. 4 (English and Spanish) ★ *Global Skill Builder CD–ROM* ★ Chapter 4 Test Generator ★ HRW Web site	★ Spanish Glossary ★ Sheltered English Chapter 4 Test

CHAPTER OVERVIEW

As the Civil War ended, many Confederate soldiers returned home to find their cities destroyed. Meanwhile, former slaves celebrated their freedom but were often uncertain about their rights and how they would make a living. This was partly because of the Black Codes, laws that served to limit the freedoms of African Americans. On the other hand, the Fourteenth and Fifteenth Amendments were passed to bolster African Americans' rights.

Many white southerners opposed Reconstruction because they thought it costly, corrupt, and unjust. Organizations such as the Ku Klux Klan used violence to terrorize African Americans, white Republicans, and public officials. Racially motivated riots occurred in some southern cities.

The South's economy and society underwent some changes as a result of Reconstruction. For example, many poor whites and African Americans turned to sharecropping to make a living. The South also began to develop industries such as textile manufacturing. Southern culture flourished in the works of writers and composers who celebrated and often criticized the rich cultural traditions of the region.

CHAPTER INVESTIGATION

The Chapter Investigation is an extended, multipart activity designed for students to work cooperatively and apply the chapter content in the creation of a project. You may choose to use the Chapter 4 Investigation, Reconstruction Multimedia Presentations, either as a substitute for teaching the section lessons or as an alternate assessment.

BLOCK SCHEDULING 

The teacher lesson plans for each section offer a variety of activity choices to help you present the material in a block scheduling format. For further suggestions on block scheduling, see the *Block Scheduling Handbook with Team Teaching Strategies*, pp. 19–24.

Meeting Individual Needs

ABILITY LEVELS

LEVEL 1 Basic level activities designed for all students encountering new material.

LEVEL 2 Intermediate level activities designed for average students.

LEVEL 3 Challenging activities designed for above-average students.

SHELTERED ENGLISH These activities address the needs of students with Limited English Proficiency.

Smithsonian Institution®

Internet Connections and Lesson 4
www.si.edu/hrw

CNN Presents America:
Yesterday and Today Impeaching Andrew Johnson
Segment: The Life of Lincoln

Additional Resources

Books for Teachers

Foner, Eric. *Short History of Reconstruction.* HarperCollins, 1990. Provides modern analysis of Reconstruction.

Joynes, Gerald David. *Branches Without Roots: Genesis of the Black Working Class in the American South, 1862–1882.* Oxford University Press, 1986. Explores what emancipation meant for former slaves in economic terms.

Mellon, James, ed. *Bullwhip Days: The Slaves Remember.* Avon, 1992. Former slaves recall life in the South from slavery through Reconstruction.

Books for Students

Franklin, John Hope. *Reconstruction After the Civil War.* University of Chicago Press, 1962. Classic account of American life during Reconstruction.

McKissack, Patricia, and Fredrick McKissack. *Sojourner Truth: "Ain't I a Woman?"* Scholastic, 1992. Biography of a woman born into slavery who later became a leading advocate for women's rights.

Mettger, Zak. *Reconstruction: America After the Civil War.* Lodestar Books, 1994. Explains and examines the post–Civil War era. Details Ku Klux Klan activities and corrupt governments.

Multimedia Materials

Ku Klux Klan—The Invisible Empire. Video, 47 min. Carousel Film and Video. Uses interviews and newsreel footage to discuss the activities of this group.

Reconstructing the South. Video, 30 min. PBS Video. Examines Andrew Johnson's early efforts and Reconstruction in general. Discusses the significance of the Thirteenth, Fourteenth, and Fifteenth Amendments to the Constitution.

"Separate But Equal." Video, 8 min. Britannica. Describes how Jim Crow laws, the KKK, and *Plessy* v. *Ferguson* maintained inequality.

Reconstruction

CHAPTER MOTIVATOR

Ask the class to imagine a house that has been knocked down by a powerful storm. Have students consider whether they would rebuild the house to look exactly like the original or revise the design in some ways. Discuss the advantages of each with the class. Explain to students that after the Civil War ended, the United States was faced with a similar situation—how to rebuild a nation after it had been torn apart by war. Conclude by telling students that as they read this chapter they will learn how this task was achieved and how the war changed the relationships between the federal and state governments and among various social groups.

Presenting Themes

- **Constitutional Heritage** Students could point out that many businesses, homes, and transportation facilities must be rebuilt to restore the country's economy and infrastructure.
- **Citizenship and Democracy** Students might mention that a nation's definition of a democratic society might change in response to political events, changes in society, and new ways of thinking.
- **Cultural Diversity** Students could mention that the newly freed people might be able to contribute more fully to a nation's culture through their cultural and professional talents.

Using the Time Line

Organize the class into small groups and assign each group an event from the time line. Ask members of each group to draw a rough illustration of their assigned event. Hang the illustrations around the room in chronological order and refer to them as they come up during the lesson. After completing the lesson, have students determine whether each event helped or hurt the nation's efforts to rebuild after the Civil War.

CHAPTER 4

Reconstruction

(1865–1877)

The Civil War was over, but two major issues remained unresolved. First, the federal government had to decide the conditions by which the South could rejoin the Union. Second, the government had to define the rights of the 4 million African Americans freed by the Emancipation Proclamation. As abolitionist Frederick Douglass explained, "The work does not end with the abolition of slavery, but only begins."

Constitutional Heritage
How might a nation attempt to rebuild itself following a civil war?

Citizenship and Democracy
Why might a nation's definition of a democratic society change over time?

Cultural Diversity
How might the experiences of a newly freed group affect a nation?

JAN. 1865 Congress proposes the Thirteenth Amendment.

JULY 1866 Race riots erupt in New Orleans.

MAR. 1867 Congress passes the first federal Reconstruction Act.

NOV. 1868 Ulysses S. Grant is elected president.

FEB. 1869 Congress proposes the Fifteenth Amendment.

FEB. 1870 Hiram Revels is elected to the U.S. Senate.

OBJECTIVES

- **Analyze the effect of the end of the Civil War on southern life.**
- **Compare and contrast the views of Lincoln, Congress, and Johnson about Reconstruction.**
- **Evaluate the impact of the Freedmen's Bureau on former slaves' lives.**

FOCUS

Motivate Before Reading

Have students create lists of all the steps that are necessary to make a peanut butter and jelly sandwich. Once the lists are finished, have volunteers write the steps they included on the chalkboard. Point out the differences that exist between the lists. Tell students that in this section they will learn about the different plans people created for Reconstruction.

SECTION 1

Rebuilding the South

Reading Focus

What effect did the end of the Civil War have on southern life?

How did Lincoln, Congress, and Johnson differ in their views on Reconstruction?

In what ways did the Freedmen's Bureau aid newly freed slaves?

Key Terms

Reconstruction
amnesty
Thirteenth Amendment
Freedmen's Bureau

A SOUTHERNER WHO KEPT A *diary while traveling through Georgia after the Civil War recorded the destruction he saw: "Every village and station we stopped at presented an array [group] of ruined walls and chimneys standing useless." When he reached the once prosperous city of Columbia, South Carolina, burnt and empty buildings greeted him. The war had dramatically changed the landscape of the South and the lives of southerners.*

A Georgia newspaper with news of Robert E. Lee's surrender

The Museum of the Confederacy, Richmond, Virginia, Katherine Wetzel, Photographer

IMAGE ON LEFT PAGE: *A school for freedpeople in Vicksburg, Mississippi*

1871 — 1873 — 1875 — 1877

MAY 1872 Fisk Jubilee Singers introduce much of the country to African American spirituals.

NOV. 1874 Republicans lose control of the House of Representatives.

MAR. 1875 Congress passes the Civil Rights Act of 1875.

MAR. 1877 The Compromise of 1877 ends Reconstruction.

Section 1 RESOURCES

PRINT
- ★ Guided Reading Strategies 4.1
- ★ Section 1 Review, p. 129
- ★ Daily Quiz 4.1

MULTIMEDIA
- ★ *Teaching Resources CD–ROM,* Lesson 4.1
- ★ *Exploring America's Past* Video Segment: A Play of Fate; *Teacher's Guide,* pp. 9–11

SHELTERED ENGLISH
- ★ Main Idea Activities for Reteaching and Sheltered English 4.1

Introduce Key Terms

Linguistic. Review this section's key terms with students. Have them write a definition for each term. Then ask students to write sentences using the terms. **SHELTERED ENGLISH**

TEACH

Have students read Section 1 and complete Guided Reading Strategies 4.1. Choose one or more of the following activities to explore the section content with students. For further suggestions on block scheduling or team teaching, see the *Block Scheduling Handbook.*

LEVEL 1: Linguistic. (Suggested time: 15 min.) As a class, go over students' Guided Reading Strategies. Then use the Reading Focus questions to highlight the main ideas of the section. **SHELTERED ENGLISH**

ALL LEVELS: Linguistic, Interpersonal. (Suggested time: 30 min.) George Wood of Portland, Texas, suggested the following activity: Have students create charts that compare and contrast

Geographic Diversity

African Americans in the Cities.

Emancipation changed the face of southern cities. Before the war, not many African Americans lived in southern cities. The few who did often lived in the same neighborhoods as whites. After the war, the black population doubled in the 10 largest southern cities. Newly freed slaves moved from the country to the city looking for better jobs and safer living conditions. They settled on the edges of cities, in poor neighborhoods that were segregated from white residents.

Critical Thinking: What other aspects of city life do you think attracted African Americans after the war?

ANSWER: Students could mention that newly freed people might have more freedom to build their own lives in a city. For example, they might have more opportunities to attend churches, join organizations, and take part in a wide variety of cultural events.

The South After the Civil War

After the South's surrender, weary southern soldiers—many permanently disabled—returned home to find their farms destroyed and their cities in ruins. However, the damage went beyond crops and buildings. Former Confederate Josiah Reams reached his home in Tennessee to find:

> **"My father and stepmother . . . [had] died. My only brother was killed . . . and a half-brother on the Union side . . . died. So our home was broken up and I was penniless."**

Many southerners faced the threat of starvation. The Shenandoah Valley in Virginia, once full of rich farmland, was now battle-scarred and barren. Across the South, harvests of cotton, rice, corn, and other crops were well below normal. Many farm animals had been killed or had run away. Food prices, already high because of wartime shortages, remained high.

When food was available, distributing it was difficult. The widespread destruction of railroads by Union troops had disabled transportation and communications throughout the South. Living in Richmond, Virginia, Mary Chesnut wrote in her diary about the isolation: "We are shut in here. . . . All RR's [railroads] destroyed—bridges gone. We are cut off from the world."

Much of Richmond, Virginia, burned in the last days of the war.

In addition, financial institutions, which had begun to collapse during the war, continued to struggle. Banks failed and merchants went bankrupt because few southerners could repay their debts. The Confederate currency they held was now worthless. Former Confederate general Braxton Bragg found that "*all, all* was lost, except my debts."

The Meaning of Freedom

Despite having to suffer through the postwar difficulties, freedpeople, or newly freed slaves, had reason to celebrate as word of emancipation spread slowly through the South. Freedom meant important changes for families. Numerous couples held ceremonies to legalize marriages that had not been recognized under slavery. Many freedpeople searched for relatives who had been sold away from their families years earlier. One man walked 600 miles through Georgia and North Carolina looking for his wife and children. Other freedpeople placed newspaper ads seeking information about their children. Many women began to work at home rather than in the fields.

Now that they could travel without a pass, many freedpeople moved from mostly white counties to places with more African Americans. Some freedpeople in the Upper South tried to find work in Lower South states such as Texas, Florida, and Mississippi, where expanding farms needed new workers. Other freedpeople traveled simply to test their new freedom of movement. A South Carolina woman explained, "I must go, if I stay here I'll never know I'm free."

For most former slaves, freedom to travel was just the first step on a long road toward equal rights and a new way of life. Adults took new last names and began to insist on being called Mr. or Mrs., rather than by their first name or by nicknames. Most freedpeople, such as Henry Adams, wanted the same rights as whites. Adams said, "If I cannot do like a white man I am not free."

Many African Americans left white-controlled churches and created their own congregations. These new churches became the first large the different Reconstruction plans suggested by Lincoln, Republicans in Congress, and Johnson. Charts should include categories that describe (a) how the plan will bring the South back into the Union, (b) what consequences southern states will face as a result of withdrawing from the Union, and (c) how the plan will help freedpeople. You may wish to draw an incomplete chart on the chalkboard and have students fill in the missing material, or hand out copies of a completed chart and have students answer questions about it. Once students have finished, review the charts or questions with the class. Call on volunteers to share their answers for each category with the class. **SHELTERED ENGLISH**

LEVEL 2: Linguistic, Intrapersonal. (Suggested time: 45 min. plus homework) Discuss with the class the overall destruction that occurred in some areas of the South during the Civil War. Then ask students to imagine that they are reporters for a northern magazine who have been sent to the South to write about the effects of the war. Have each student write an article that reports the physical changes in the South along with the emotional responses to these changes. Students may wish to refer to the text for details pertaining to the destruction. Ask volunteers to share their articles with the class.

After the Civil War, African Americans bought and filled out family records such as this one.

organizations run by African Americans. Church members established voluntary associations and mutual aid societies to help those in need.

Many freedpeople wanted their own land to farm. At the end of the Civil War, General William Tecumseh Sherman had issued an order to break up plantations in coastal South Carolina and Georgia. He wanted to divide the land into 40-acre plots and give them to freedpeople as compensation for their forced labor during slavery. Many white planters, however, refused to surrender their land. Some freedpeople pointed out that it was only fair that they receive some of this land, because the labor they had performed as slaves had made the plantations prosper. At this time, many freedpeople were unsure about where they would live, what kind of work they would do, and what rights they had.

Planning Reconstruction

The U.S. government soon stepped in to help freedpeople in the South. The government also faced the task of bringing the defeated southern states back into the Union. **Reconstruction**—the process of reuniting the nation and rebuilding the southern states in the absence of slavery—lasted from 1865 to 1877.

Lincoln's Plan

President Lincoln wanted to reunite the nation as quickly and painlessly as possible. Before the war ended, he proposed a plan for readmitting the southern states. He wanted to offer southerners **amnesty**, or an official pardon, for all illegal acts supporting the rebellion. Those southerners who pledged an oath of loyalty to the United States and accepted a ban on slavery would receive amnesty. Any southern state with at least 10 percent of its voters making this pledge could establish a new state government and be readmitted to the Union. Louisiana and other southern states that had been occupied by Union troops before the war's end quickly elected new state legislatures under this Ten-Percent Plan.

The Wade-Davis Bill

Some politicians believed that Congress had the constitutional authority to admit new states. Thus,

HISTORICAL DOCUMENTS

1865 *Lincoln's Second Inaugural Address*

On March 4, 1865, President Lincoln laid out his approach to Reconstruction in his second inaugural address. As this excerpt shows, Lincoln hoped to reunite the nation and its people.

"With malice [hatred] toward none, with charity for all, with firmness in the right, as God gives us to see the right, let us strive on to finish the work we are in, to bind up the nation's wounds, to care for him who shall have borne the battle, and for his widow, and his orphan—to do all which may achieve and cherish a just, and a lasting peace."

Understanding Primary Sources

1. What is Lincoln asking of the nation?
2. What issues might have prevented Lincoln's request from being fulfilled?

Citizenship and Democracy

The Ten-Percent Plan in Louisiana. In Louisiana, pro-Union politicians from the wealthy port city of New Orleans led the movement to re-enter the Union. In 1864, delegates organized a convention to write a new constitution so that Louisiana could rejoin the Union. No plantation owners or African Americans were present at the convention. The new constitution abolished slavery and gave New Orleans the leading role in state politics by making it the state capital. New Orleans served as Louisiana's seat of government until 1882, when the capital was returned to Baton Rouge.

Critical Thinking: Why might the pro-Union politicians have wanted to keep the plantation owners out of the convention?

ANSWER: Students might answer that the plantation owners were strong advocates of the Confederacy.

HISTORICAL DOCUMENTS ANSWERS

1. to heal the nation from the effects of war, care for those who served in the war and for the families of casualties, and to achieve a permanent peace

2. disagreements in Congress and lasting animosity between southern and northern states

LEVEL 3: Linguistic, Logical-Mathematical, Intrapersonal. (Suggested time: 45 min.) Assign each student the role of a Confederate soldier, a freedperson, or an agent of the Freedmen's Bureau. Have students assume their roles and then write to the editor of a newspaper stating which Reconstruction plan they favor and why they support it. (If students do not agree with any of the plans, have them create a list of ideas they would have included in their own plan.) After students have written their letters, organize the class into small groups. Have students read their letters to the other members of their group. Using their letters as guides, students in each group should then create a graphic organizer identifying the strengths and weaknesses of each plan.

CLOSE

Logical-Mathematical, Interpersonal. Organize the class so that every student has a partner. You may want to have students who are having difficulty with the material work with peer tutors. Have one student in the pair state everything he or she knows about one of the following topics: the conditions affecting former Confederate soldiers and freedpeople at the end of the war; the elements of the three Reconstruction plans described in this section; or the impact of the Freedmen's Bureau on freedpeople. The second student should take notes on what the first student says. When finished, the person taking notes should add information

Citizenship and Democracy

Pocket Veto. Members of Congress approved the Wade-Davis Bill just before Congress adjourned. The end of the congressional session made it possible for President Lincoln to use a "pocket" veto to kill the measure. In effect, the president put the bill in his pocket and refused to sign it. If a president does not sign a bill within 10 days while Congress is in session, the bill automatically becomes a law without the president's signature. However, if Congress is adjourned, the bill dies if the president does not sign it. A pocket veto cannot be overturned by congressional vote.

Activity: Ask students to imagine that it is 1864, and they are members of Congress. Have them work in committees to write a plan that they think President Lincoln would have accepted for readmitting the southern states. Encourage students to consider what rules they would set to ensure that ex-Confederates would support the Union and end slavery.

MAP ANSWER
Mississippi, North Carolina, South Carolina

they argued, Congress should handle the southern states' return to the Union. Many Republican members of Congress simply disagreed with Lincoln's plan for Reconstruction. They shared the views of one senator who said,

> **"The people of the North are not such fools as to . . . turn around and say to the traitors, 'all you have to do [to return] is . . . take an oath that henceforth you will be true to the Government.'"**

Two Republicans—Senator Benjamin Wade and Representative Henry Davis—proposed a stricter alternative to Lincoln's plan. Under the Wade-Davis Bill, a state had to meet two conditions before it could rejoin the Union. First, it had to ban slavery. Second, a majority of adult males in the state had to take the loyalty oath. Furthermore, only southerners who swore that they had never supported the Confederacy would be allowed to vote or to hold office. President Lincoln refused to sign this bill into law, because few southerners could fulfill its requirements.

The Thirteenth Amendment

One thing Republicans agreed on was abolishing slavery. The Emancipation Proclamation had freed slaves only in the Confederate states that had been unoccupied by Union forces. The proclamation allowed slavery to continue in the border states. In addition, many people feared that the federal courts might someday declare the Emancipation Proclamation unconstitutional. On January 31, 1865, at Lincoln's urging, Congress proposed the **Thirteenth Amendment** to the Constitution, which made slavery illegal throughout the United States. The amendment then went into effect on December 18, 1865. Abolitionist William Lloyd Garrison declared that his work was now finished and called for the American Anti-Slavery Society to disband. Frederick Douglass, however, insisted that "Slavery is not abolished until the black man has the ballot [vote]."

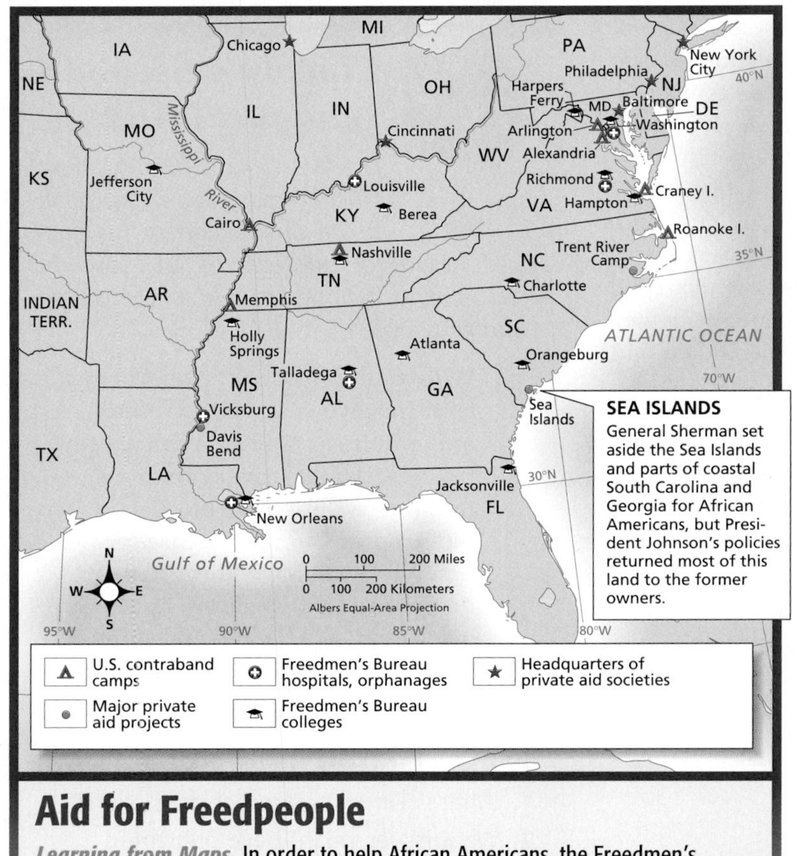

Aid for Freedpeople

Learning from Maps In order to help African Americans, the Freedmen's Bureau and several private aid societies distributed food and clothing, set up hospitals, and operated schools.

Location According to the map, which states had major private aid projects?

The Freedmen's Bureau

In addition, in 1865 Congress established the **Freedmen's Bureau** to provide relief for all poor people—black and white—in the South. The bureau had a difficult job. At its high point about 900 agents served the entire South. Bureau commissioner that may have been overlooked by his or her partner. Then students should switch tasks with their partners and repeat the process until each topic has been covered. Encourage students to ask questions about any of the material that they are having difficulty understanding.

CHALLENGE AND EXTEND

1. **Linguistic, Intrapersonal.** Remind students that the events described in this section took place in 1865–66. Draw their attention to Mary Chesnut's observation that the South had been isolated. Ask each student to write an entry in Chesnut's diary that predicts the future of the South based on the events of the first year after the war. Encourage students to try to capture some of the emotions that Chesnut may have felt as a result of these events.
2. **Musical-Rhythmic, Intrapersonal.** Remind students of the loss that was felt by many soldiers who returned home after the war to find their homes destroyed or their families gone. Have students write poems or songs that depict these feelings. Encourage students who can play a musical instrument to put their lyrics to music. Have students share their work with the rest of the class.

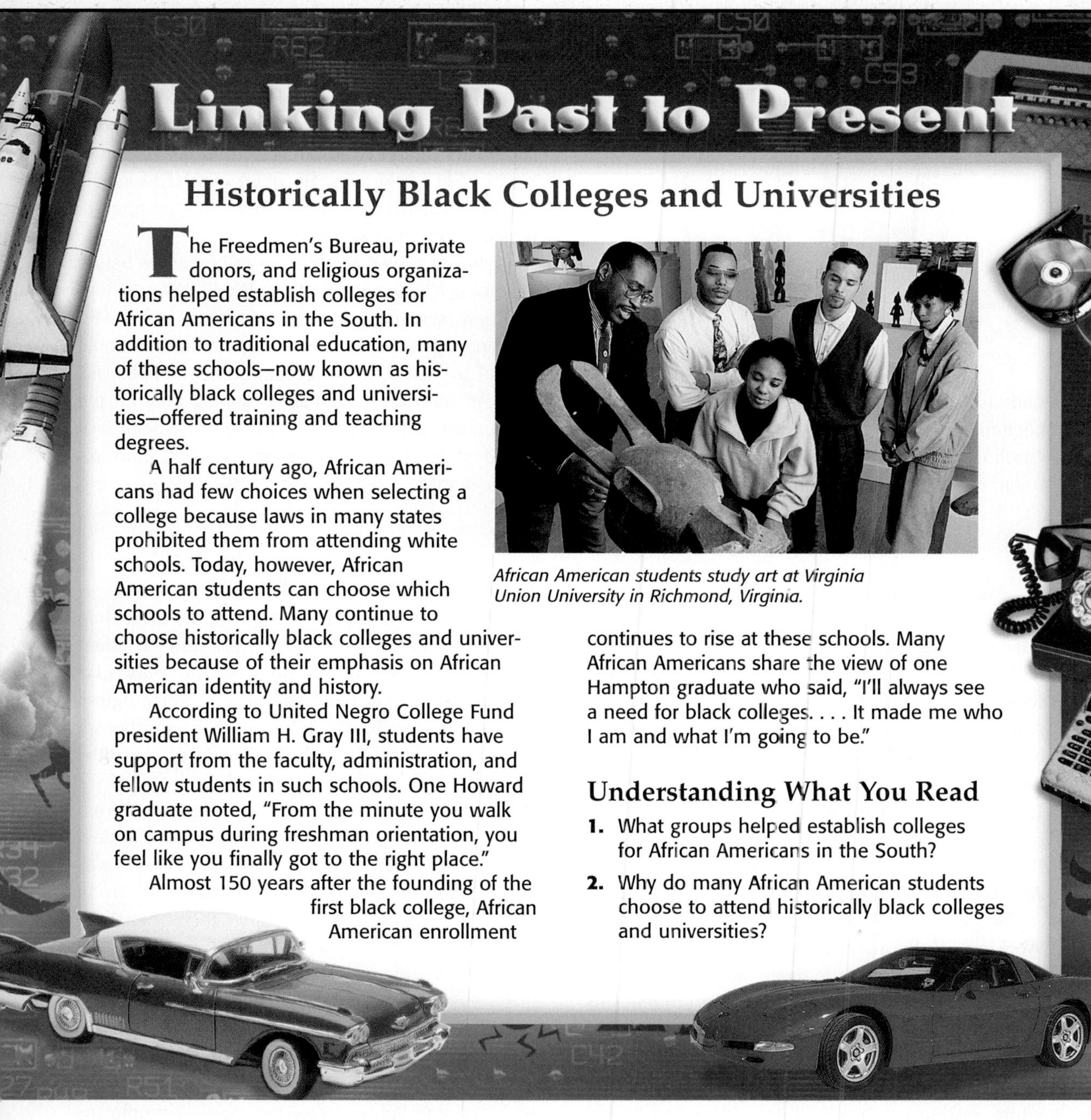

Linking Past to Present

Historically Black Colleges and Universities

The Freedmen's Bureau, private donors, and religious organizations helped establish colleges for African Americans in the South. In addition to traditional education, many of these schools—now known as historically black colleges and universities—offered training and teaching degrees.

A half century ago, African Americans had few choices when selecting a college because laws in many states prohibited them from attending white schools. Today, however, African American students can choose which schools to attend. Many continue to choose historically black colleges and universities because of their emphasis on African American identity and history.

African American students study art at Virginia Union University in Richmond, Virginia.

According to United Negro College Fund president William H. Gray III, students have support from the faculty, administration, and fellow students in such schools. One Howard graduate noted, "From the minute you walk on campus during freshman orientation, you feel like you finally got to the right place."

Almost 150 years after the founding of the first black college, African American enrollment continues to rise at these schools. Many African Americans share the view of one Hampton graduate who said, "I'll always see a need for black colleges. . . . It made me who I am and what I'm going to be."

Understanding What You Read

1. What groups helped establish colleges for African Americans in the South?
2. Why do many African American students choose to attend historically black colleges and universities?

Oliver O. Howard eventually decided to use the bureau's limited budget to distribute food to the poor and to provide education and legal help for freedpeople. The bureau also assisted African American war veterans.

The Freedmen's Bureau played an important role in establishing more schools in the South. Laws against educating slaves meant that most freedpeople had never learned to read or write. Before the war ended, however, northern groups such as the American Missionary Society began providing books and teachers. The teachers were mostly women who were committed to helping freedpeople. One teacher said of her students:

> **"I never before saw children so eager to learn. . . . It is wonderful how [they] . . . can have so great a desire for knowledge, and such a capacity for attaining [reaching] it."**

Biography

Charlotte Forten. Charlotte Forten was born in Philadelphia to a prosperous free black family in 1837. She was active in the antislavery movement. Forten attended a teacher-training school, and in 1862 she became the first African American teacher hired to teach freedpeople in the Sea Islands. Her long teaching day began at noon, when she and two other teachers taught about 100 children. In the evening, she tutored adults in reading and spelling. Forten wrote about her two years in the Sea Islands for *Atlantic Monthly* magazine. Her essays convinced many northerners that freedpeople were capable and enthusiastic citizens.

Critical Thinking: Why do you think Forten's essays were important?

ANSWER: Students might mention that the essays may have helped convince northerners that it was important to support education for freedpeople.

Linking Past to Present Answers

1. Freedmen's Bureau, private donors, religious organizations
2. Students might mention that black colleges and universities emphasize African American identity and history, and students feel they get the support from the faculty and administration that they want.

3. **Linguistic, Logical-Mathematical.** Have students use the library to find information about one of the abolitionists mentioned in this chapter. Have them use this information to create a resumé for the abolitionist. Remind students to include a purpose statement describing the abolitionist's goal, an education summary, a previous work experience list, and professional references for the abolitionist. After students have finished creating the resumés, call on volunteers to present their information to the class.

REVIEW

Kinesthetic, Interpersonal. Have students complete the Section Review questions. Then ask students to think of five questions about the section and write each one on a note card. Organize the class into two teams. Have students play a few innings of Review Baseball. Have each team establish an order in which its members will answer questions. Remind students that this order cannot be changed. Determine which team will "bat" first. Ask the first student a question. If he or she answers the question

Presidential Profiles

Andrew Johnson. Had it not been for an incompetent assassin, Andrew Johnson might have been killed or wounded on the same day as President Lincoln. John Wilkes Booth's plot included an attack on Secretary of State William Seward and Vice President Johnson as well as President Lincoln. Seward was injured but not killed by one of Booth's accomplices. Johnson, however, escaped harm. The man assigned to kill him had checked into the vice president's hotel, taking a room right above his. The would-be assassin had stored his weapons in the hotel room and gone downstairs to ask questions about the vice president and his guards. He then left before carrying out his part of the plot, apparently having lost his nerve.

Activity: Have students conduct research and write newspaper articles on the assassination plot.

Multimedia Resources

Exploring America's Past Video Segment: A Play of Fate; *Teacher's Guide*, pp. 9–11

Search 17571, Play to 26353
Videodisc White Side A

Play

Pause

See *Teacher's Guide* for Spanish barcode.

PRESIDENTIAL PROFILES

Andrew Johnson

Andrew Johnson had a long political career before becoming president. Born to a poor family in North Carolina, Johnson became a tailor's apprentice. Unhappy with this arrangement, Johnson ran away to Tennessee, where he started his own tailoring business. Eventually, he became a prosperous landowner and entered politics, but he never forgot his humble beginnings. He often criticized wealthy southern planters, calling them a "pampered, bloated, corrupted aristocracy."

Johnson served as governor of Tennessee before becoming a U.S. senator. During the Civil War, he was the only senator from a Confederate state who remained loyal to the Union. Hoping that he would appeal to voters in the border states, Republicans selected Johnson as Lincoln's running mate in the presidential campaign of 1864. He had been vice president for less than six weeks when Lincoln's death elevated Johnson to the presidency.

After the war, some freedpeople organized their own education efforts. For example, Freedmen's Bureau agents found that some African Americans had opened schools in abandoned buildings. Many white southerners continued to believe that African Americans should not be educated. Some whites burned down schools and attacked teachers and students. Despite such opposition, by 1869 more than 150,000 students attended the more than 3,000 schools that had been established. The Freedmen's Bureau also helped establish several colleges for African Americans, including Howard and Fisk.

Students quickly filled the new classrooms. Working adults attended classes in the evening. African Americans made these sacrifices for many reasons, including their desire to learn to read the Bible. They also hoped that education would help them to understand and protect their rights and to enable them to find better jobs. Both black and white southerners benefited from the effort to provide greater access to education in the South.

A New President

While the Freedmen's Bureau was helping African Americans in the South, the issue of how the southern states would rejoin the Union remained unresolved. Soon, however, a tragic event ended Lincoln's dream of reuniting the country.

Lincoln's Assassination

On the evening of April 14, 1865, a little more than a month after his second inauguration, President Lincoln and his wife attended the play *Our American Cousin* at Ford's Theater in Washington. During the play, John Wilkes Booth—a southerner hostile to Lincoln's policies—sneaked into the president's theater box and shot him.

Lincoln was rushed to a boardinghouse across the street, where he died at about 7:30 the next morning. Secretary of the Navy Gideon Welles was by the president's side. He later wrote that "strong and brave men wept when I met them" with the news of Lincoln's death.

Vice President Andrew Johnson was sworn into office that morning. Reconstruction was now his responsibility. Republicans approved of President Johnson because he seemed to favor a tougher approach to Reconstruction than Lincoln had. Senator Wade spoke for many Republicans when he told the new president, "Johnson, we have faith in you."

Johnson's Reconstruction Plan

Despite his tough talk, Johnson's plan for the reentry of the southern states into the Union was similar to Lincoln's Ten-Percent Plan. Johnson gave amnesty to all southerners who pledged an oath of loyalty and who promised to support the correctly, it counts as a hit. Then have the student walk to first base. Have students that reach base advance one base each time a teammate correctly answers a question. Runs are scored when a person crosses home plate. Incorrect answers count as an out. Once a team has three outs, allow the other team to take a turn answering questions. Repeat this process as many times as you wish. Be sure to allow teams an equal number of turns. Before you play, you may want to determine the difficulty of each question and assign it an appropriate hit value. (During this time, students can review the section's material.) For example, the easiest questions can count as singles, while the hardest questions can count as home runs.

ASSESS

Have students complete Daily Quiz 4.1.

RETEACH

Linguistic, Logical-Mathematical. Have students complete Main Idea Activities for Reteaching and Sheltered English 4.1. Then ask students to imagine that they work for the Freedmen's Bureau and are in charge of obtaining contributions to help run the organization. Have students create flyers explaining its goals and asking for contributions to help run programs. **SHELTERED ENGLISH**

abolition of slavery. He also returned all property except slaves to southerners who received amnesty. Johnson did add some special restrictions to his plan. Wealthy southerners and former Confederate officials could not receive amnesty without a presidential pardon. In the end, however, this was not as restrictive as it might seem. Johnson shocked Republicans by eventually pardoning almost 7,000 people.

Johnson established a system for setting up new southern state governments. First, he appointed a temporary governor for each state. Then in each state, southerners who had taken the loyalty oath elected delegates to a convention that would revise their state constitution. Voters then elected state officials and representatives to the U.S. Congress. Once a state government was in place, it had to declare that secession was illegal and refuse to pay Confederate debts before the state could be readmitted to the Union. Virginia and three states that had already set up governments using Lincoln's Ten-Percent Plan—Arkansas, Louisiana, and Tennessee—were allowed to keep their governments in place.

By the end of 1865 all the southern states except Texas had created new governments. Johnson approved all these governments and declared that the United States was restored. When the new representatives from each state came to the capital, he asked Congress to allow them to take their seats in the House and Senate.

Lincoln's funeral procession passes through Springfield, Illinois, in April 1865. A month later, Andrew Johnson issued his plan of Reconstruction.

However, Republicans did not approve of the new representatives, many of whom had been military officers and political leaders in the Confederacy. For example, Alexander Stephens, the former vice president of the Confederacy, was elected a U.S. senator from Georgia. Most Republicans did not believe that people like Stephens were loyal to the United States.

Congress therefore refused either to seat the new representatives or to readmit the southern states into the Union. Clearly, the nation was still divided over who should control Reconstruction and what direction it should take.

SECTION 1 REVIEW

Identify and explain the significance of the following:

- **Reconstruction**
- **amnesty**
- **Thirteenth Amendment**
- **Freedmen's Bureau**
- **John Wilkes Booth**
- **Andrew Johnson**

Reading for Content Understanding

1 **Main Idea** How did life in the South change after the Civil War?

2 **Main Idea** What were the various Reconstruction plans, and how did they differ?

3 **Citizenship and Democracy** How did freedpeople express their new freedom?

4 **Writing** *Persuading* Write a one-paragraph editorial that explains the importance of the Freedmen's Bureau for both black and white southerners.

5 **Critical Thinking** *Evaluating* Why might owning farmland have been important for freedpeople?

Section 1 Review ANSWERS

Identify

For significance, see the following pages:

- Reconstruction, p. 125
- amnesty, p. 125
- Thirteenth Amendment, p. 126
- Freedmen's Bureau, p. 126
- John Wilkes Booth, p. 128
- Andrew Johnson, p. 128

Reading for Content Understanding

1. Property had been destroyed, southerners faced starvation, banks failed, and newly freed slaves tried to gain land and mobility.

2. Lincoln's Ten-Percent Plan, the Wade-Davis Bill, Johnson's plan; they differed based on the percentage of people required to pledge loyalty to the Union. For more differences, see pages 125–26 and page 128.

3. They worked their own land, formed their own churches, formalized marriages, looked for lost family members, and moved to new areas.

4. Editorials might mention the bureau's role in providing urgent food, legal help, and educational opportunities to poor black and white southerners.

5. It was important because it meant economic security, the freedom to control their own lives, and a place to raise their families.

OBJECTIVES

- **Explain how Black Codes restricted the freedoms of African Americans.**
- **Analyze reasons why Radical Republicans wanted to impeach President Johnson.**
- **Describe Republicans' efforts to protect the civil rights of African Americans.**

FOCUS

Motivate Before Reading

Ask students to identify good reasons to remove a president from office. List their replies on the chalkboard. Read Article II, Sections 1 and 4, of the Constitution to the class. These deal with the presidential oath of office and the reasons why a president may be impeached. Ask students to compare their reasons with those listed in the Constitution. Then tell students that they will learn

Section 2
RESOURCES

PRINT

★ Guided Reading Strategies 4.2

★ American History Political Cartoon 13: Radical Reconstruction

★ Section 2 Review, p. 135

★ Daily Quiz 4.2

MULTIMEDIA

★ *Teaching Resources CD–ROM*, Lesson 4.2

★ HRW Web site

SHELTERED ENGLISH

★ Main Idea Activities for Reteaching and Sheltered English 4.2

The Fight over Reconstruction

Reading Focus

How did Black Codes restrict African Americans' freedoms?

Why did Radical Republicans try to impeach President Johnson?

How did Republicans try to protect the civil rights of African Americans?

Key Terms

Black Codes
Radical Republicans
Civil Rights Act of 1866
Fourteenth Amendment
Reconstruction Acts
Fifteenth Amendment

TO TEST HIS NEWFOUND FREEDOM, in 1865 Henry Adams left the plantation where he had been enslaved. A group of white men stopped Adams on the road and asked who owned him. When Adams replied that he was free, the men beat him. Such incidents of violence were not unusual in the post–Civil War South. Many white southerners opposed African Americans' freedom and feared the consequences of that freedom. This resentment and fear also affected local authorities and state governments.

A federal soldier protects an African American man from violence.

The Black Codes

While Congress debated the rules for restoring the Union, in 1866 the new state legislatures approved by President Johnson began passing laws to deny African Americans' civil rights. "This is a white man's government, and intended for white men only," declared Governor Benjamin F. Perry of South Carolina. Soon every southern state passed **Black Codes**—laws that greatly limited the freedom of African Americans.

Each state had a set of Black Codes, which were usually designed to help white southerners economically. Black Codes forced African Americans to work on farms or as servants and required them to sign labor contracts that re-created conditions similar to those under slavery. One of South Carolina's Black Codes, for example, stated:

> **"All persons of color who make contracts for service or labor, shall be known as servants, and those with whom they contract shall be known as masters."**

In most southern states, any African American who could not prove he or she was employed more about the attempted impeachment of President Andrew Johnson in this section.

Introduce Key Terms

Linguistic, Logical-Mathematical. Review this section's key terms with students. Have them use context cues to write definitions in their notebooks for each term. Then ask students to decide what all of the terms have in common. Explain to them that each of these key terms has something to do with Reconstruction. SHELTERED ENGLISH

TEACH

Have students read Section 2 and complete Guided Reading Strategies 4.2. Choose one or more of the following activities to explore the section content with students. For further suggestions on block scheduling or team teaching, see the *Block Scheduling Handbook.*

LEVEL 1: Linguistic. (Suggested time: 15 min.) As a class, go over students' Guided Reading Strategies. Then use the Reading Focus questions to highlight the main ideas of the section. SHELTERED ENGLISH

The Granger Collection, New York

Under the Black Codes, white southerners could arrest unemployed African Americans and auction off their labor to the highest bidder.

could be arrested and punished with one year of work without pay. Other Black Codes prevented African Americans from owning guns, holding public meetings, or renting property in cities.

African Americans were alarmed by the Black Codes. As one Civil War veteran declared, "If you call this Freedom, what do you call Slavery?" African Americans organized and took action to oppose the codes. One group sent a petition to officials in South Carolina, which had one of the strictest Black Codes:

> **"We simply ask . . . that the same laws which govern *white men* shall govern *black men*; that we have the right of trial by a jury of our peers; that schools be established for the education of *colored children* as well as white . . . that, in short, we be dealt with as others are—in equity [equality] and justice."**

Such calls for equality had little effect on the new state governments, however.

The Radical Republicans

The Black Codes angered many Republicans who felt the South was returning to its old ways. Most Republicans were moderates who wanted the South to have loyal state governments but also believed that African Americans should receive their rights as citizens. Most moderates hoped that the South would not have to be forced to follow the laws passed by the U.S. government.

Another group in Congress, called the **Radical Republicans**, wanted the South to change much more than it had before it could return to the Union. Like the moderates, they considered the Black Codes to be undemocratic and cruel. The Radical Republicans, however, wanted the federal government to be much more involved in Reconstruction, fearing that too many southern leaders remained loyal to the former Confederacy. Thaddeus Stevens of Pennsylvania and Charles Sumner of Massachusetts led the Radical Republicans.

A harsh critic of President Johnson, Stevens was known for his honesty, his sharp tongue, and his interest in economic justice for both African Americans and poor white southerners. Sumner had been a strong opponent of slavery before the Civil War and continued to argue tirelessly for African Americans' civil rights. These included the right to vote and the right to fair laws. Stevens and Sumner both felt that President Johnson's Reconstruction plan was a failure. Although the Radical Republicans did not control Congress, they began to gain support among moderates when President Johnson ignored criticism of the Black Codes. "The same national authority that destroyed slavery must see that this other pretension [the Black Codes] is not permitted to survive," said Sumner.

Thaddeus Stevens

Johnson Versus Congress

In early 1866 Congress proposed a bill to increase the powers of the Freedmen's Bureau by allowing it to use military courts to try individuals accused of violating African Americans' rights. Supporters of the bill hoped that these courts would be more

Daily Life

Apprenticeships. The Black Codes included laws that affected African American children as well as adults. In many states, the Black Codes forced orphans and poor children into apprenticeships. These apprenticeships kept black children working as unpaid laborers on plantations. Many of the children had been separated from their parents during slavery. For a child whose parents were poor, a judge could declare that the child be apprenticed without the parents' consent. Former slave owners usually had first choice of apprenticeship. In some cases, the apprentices had to continue to work unpaid, even beyond the age of 16.

Critical Thinking: What effect do you think these apprenticeships had on the futures of freed children?

ANSWER: Students might suggest that the apprenticeships most likely kept black children tied to their former plantations. Students might also note that apprenticeships probably prevented children from attending school and learning skilled trades or other professions.

ALL LEVELS: Visual-Spatial, Logical-Mathematical, Interpersonal. (Suggested time: 30 min.) Discuss with students the significance of African Americans becoming more involved in the political system of the South. Have students create campaign posters encouraging voters to elect African Americans to public office in the South. Have volunteers show their posters and explain how their work appeals to a wide range of southern voters. Suggest that for extra credit students come up with ideas to increase the number of African American voters. Encourage students to think not only of ideas that would encourage African Americans to vote but also ideas that would make the process more accessible to them. **SHELTERED ENGLISH**

LEVEL 2: Logical-Mathematical, Interpersonal. (Suggested time: 45 min.) Tell students that they are going to serve as members of a congressional committee that is investigating the effects of the Black Codes on the freedoms of African Americans. Have students create lists describing the injustices caused by the Black Codes. Then ask them to develop testimonials to present to Congress (the class) describing how the Civil Rights Act of 1866, the Fourteenth Amendment, and the Fifteenth Amendment will bring an end to the restrictions imposed by the Black Codes. Encourage students to use logical reasoning to support their opinions.

Citizenship and Democracy

The Civil Rights Act. With the Civil Rights Act of 1866, Republicans outlawed the southern states' Black Codes. Northern laws that discriminated against African Americans were also overturned. The act spelled out African Americans' basic rights as citizens, such as the rights to make contracts, sue in courts of law, and own property.

Critical Thinking: Why do you think the Civil Rights Act of 1866 was so important?

ANSWER: Students could argue that the act was the next logical step after the Thirteenth Amendment formally freed enslaved people. It spelled out African Americans' rights as citizens for the first time. Students could also argue that this act laid the groundwork for the Fourteenth Amendment.

fair than local courts in the South. To the surprise of many members of Congress, Johnson vetoed the bill and insisted that Congress could not pass any new laws until the southern states again were represented in Congress. He also argued that the Freedmen's Bureau was unnecessary because he believed that African Americans did not need any special assistance.

Republicans responded with the **Civil Rights Act of 1866**. This act provided African Americans with the same legal rights as white Americans. Republicans believed that without rights for African Americans, the South would never have a strong economy or democracy.

President Johnson once again used his veto, arguing that the act gave too much power to the federal government. He also rejected the principle of equal rights for African Americans, insisting that they did not understand "the nature and character of our institutions." The Republicans overrode Johnson's veto.

The Fourteenth Amendment

Many Republicans were concerned that the Civil Rights Act might be overturned by Congress once the southern states were readmitted. To protect the new civil rights laws from hostile presidents or legislators, Republicans proposed an amendment to the Constitution in the summer of 1866.

Equal Protection

The **Fourteenth Amendment** guaranteed citizenship and equal protection under the law to all people born or naturalized within the United States with the exception of American Indians. It said that state governments could not "deprive any person of life, liberty, or property, without due process of law."

The amendment also banned many former Confederate officials from holding state or federal offices. In addition, the amendment made state laws subject to federal court review. The final section of the amendment gave Congress the power to pass any laws needed to enforce any part of the amendment. The editors of one black newspaper wrote, "We are entering upon the greatest political contest that has ever agitated [upset] the people of the country."

The 1866 Elections

President Johnson and most Democrats opposed the Fourteenth Amendment. As a result, civil rights for African Americans became a key issue in the 1866 congressional elections. Republican candidates asked Americans to support civil rights by voting for the Republican Party. To help the Democrats, Johnson traveled around the country defending his Reconstruction plan.

Johnson's speaking tour was a disaster and did little to help win votes for the Democratic Party. He got into arguments with spectators and often seemed to wander from the subject. When a spectator at one of his speeches cried out, "Hang Jeff Davis!" Johnson replied angrily, "Why don't you hang Thad Stevens? . . . I can tell you, my countrymen, I have been fighting traitors in the south, and . . . I am prepared to fight traitors at the north, . . . with your help." Such outbursts did not impress many voters.

The Granger Collection, New York

President Johnson traveled to cities such as Philadelphia, Cleveland, and St. Louis when he campaigned for Democratic candidates in 1866.

LEVEL 3: Logical-Mathematical, Interpersonal. (Suggested time: 60 min. plus homework) As a class, conduct a mock impeachment trial for President Andrew Johnson. Organize the class into four groups. Have one group act as attorneys for the House of Representatives and present the case against the president. Have the second prepare a defense of the president. Have the third group act as the Senate and prepare questions to ask the attorneys for both sides and vote at the end of the trial whether or not to convict. Have the fourth act as reporters observing the trial who are preparing a news story describing the events. After the trial, discuss with students what happened during each aspect of the case.

CLOSE

Linguistic, Logical-Mathematical, Intrapersonal. To conclude the lesson, review the main ideas of the Thirteenth, Fourteenth, and Fifteenth Amendments with the class. Then ask students to write a journal entry describing whether they think the rights of freedpeople were adequately protected by the passage of these amendments. Encourage students to consider the events discussed in this section when explaining their opinions.

Southern whites fire on African American demonstrators during the New Orleans riot of 1866.

Violence in the South

Two major riots in the South also hurt Johnson's campaign. On May 1, 1866, a dispute in Memphis, Tennessee, between local police and black Union soldiers turned into a three-day wave of violence against African Americans. To make things worse, police officers joined in the attacks on freedpeople. By the time federal troops restored peace, 46 African Americans were dead.

Three months later, another riot took place in New Orleans when African Americans attempted to hold a peaceful political demonstration. This time 34 African Americans and 3 white Radical Republicans were killed. Again, the local police participated in the violence, and federal troops had to restore order. These widely publicized events convinced many voters that Johnson's Reconstruction plan was failing.

Congress Takes Charge

The 1866 elections gave the Republican Party a commanding two-thirds majority in both the House and the Senate. This gave the Republicans the power to override any presidential veto. In addition, the Republicans became united as the moderates joined with the Radicals. Together they called for a new form of Reconstruction.

The Reconstruction Acts

In March 1867 Congress passed the first of several **Reconstruction Acts**. These acts divided the South into five districts that were controlled by military commanders. The acts also required all southern states to create new state constitutions supporting the Fourteenth Amendment before they could be readmitted to the Union. In addition, the states would be required to give African American men the right to vote.

Thaddeus Stevens was one of the new Reconstruction Acts' most enthusiastic supporters. Defending them before Congress, he argued:

> **"Have not loyal blacks quite as good a right to choose rulers and make laws as rebel whites? Every man, no matter what his race or color . . . has an equal right to justice, honesty, and fair play with every other man; and the law should secure him those rights."**

President Johnson disagreed strongly with Stevens, arguing that African Americans did not deserve the same treatment as white people. He also insisted that the Reconstruction Acts used "powers not granted to the federal government or any one of its branches."

Impeachment

Congress knew that Johnson did not support its Reconstruction policies. To limit his power, Congress passed an act preventing the president from removing cabinet officials without the approval of the U.S. Senate. Johnson defied the new law soon after by firing Secretary of War Edwin Stanton.

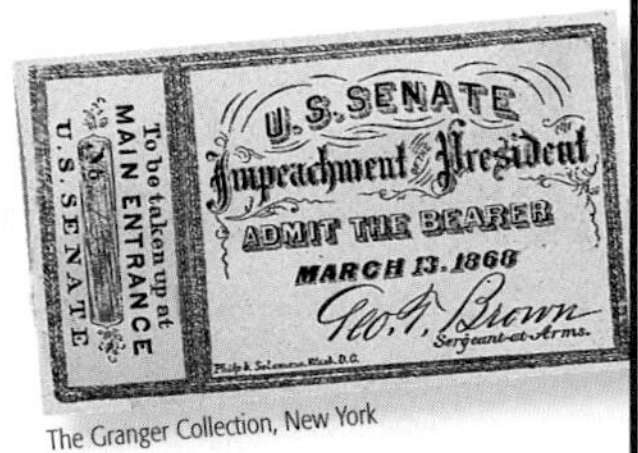

A ticket to President Andrew Johnson's 1868 trial in the Senate

The Granger Collection, New York

Citizenship and Democracy

The Firing of Stanton. President Lincoln had appointed Edwin Stanton secretary of war shortly after the Civil War began. Stanton's able leadership contributed to the Union victory. Although he continued as secretary of war under Johnson, Stanton did not agree with Johnson's Reconstruction policies. The secretary called for more severe punishment of the southern states. He also supported the Republicans' act that created the Freedmen's Bureau and the Civil Rights Act of 1866. Shortly before Johnson fired Stanton, the secretary of war was helping congressional Republicans come up with new Reconstruction laws. It was Stanton's support for Johnson's Republican opponents that caused Johnson to fire Stanton.

Activity: Ask students to use the library or search the Internet through the HRW Web site to find information about Edwin Stanton and his political beliefs. Then have students draw up a letter that Stanton might have written in defense of himself and his beliefs. Ask volunteers to read their letters to the class.

go.hrw.com
SB1 Stanton

CHALLENGE AND EXTEND

1. **Linguistic, Visual-Spatial.** Have students conduct research using the library or other resources to find out more about laws that made up the Black Codes. Ask each student to imagine being a northern journalist who has been assigned to expose unfair southern laws. Have students write articles on one of these laws. Combine these articles into a newsletter that is designed to promote justice for African Americans. You may wish to have some students work on the layout and design of the newsletter.

2. **Linguistic, Logical-Mathematical.** Explain to students that the impact of the Fifteenth Amendment was realized shortly after ratification. Explain to them that the 1870 presidential election was one of the first tests of the amendment's impact. Have students conduct research to examine the 1870 election. Tell them to write reports to Congress that describe the amendment's effect on the 1870 election. Have students describe attempts that were made to keep African Americans from voting, as well as analyze African Americans' influence on the outcome of the election.

Daily Life

Going to the Polls. "The Great Epoch in the history of our race has at last arrived," wrote African American Robert Fitzgerald about the election of 1868. He was talking about southern African Americans exercising their right to vote. African American voters took part in election parades and attended Republican meetings during the campaign. In many parts of the South, however, they faced intimidation and violence when they took part in political events. In some towns, whites closed down polls on election day or blocked African Americans from voting. In Louisiana, government officials refused to protect African American voters from white violence and even advised them to stay away from the polls.

Critical Thinking: How do you think violence against black voters affected the election of 1868?

ANSWER: Students could mention that violence most likely resulted in fewer votes for Grant and other Republican candidates, since many African Americans were kept from voting.

MAP ANSWER
Tennessee

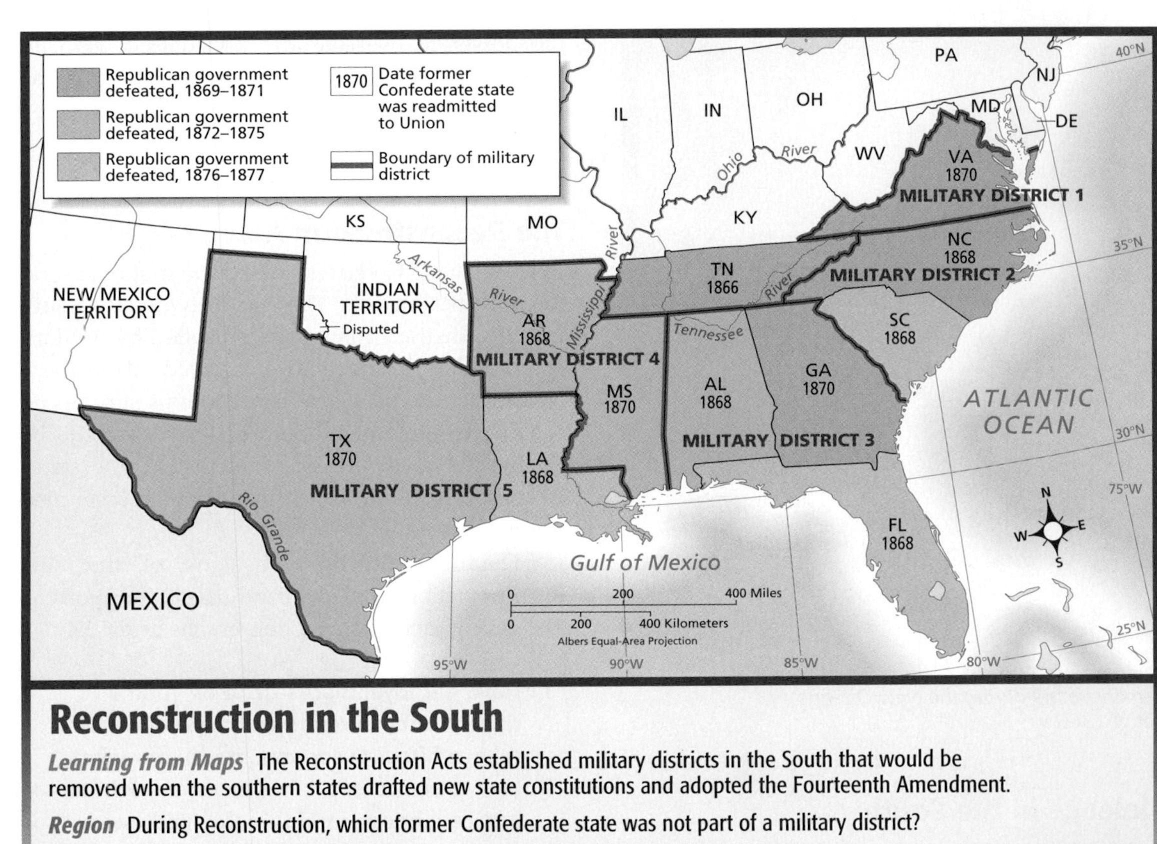

Reconstruction in the South

Learning from Maps The Reconstruction Acts established military districts in the South that would be removed when the southern states drafted new state constitutions and adopted the Fourteenth Amendment.

Region During Reconstruction, which former Confederate state was not part of a military district?

The House of Representatives responded by voting for presidential impeachment for the first time in U.S. history. Impeachment is the process of bringing charges of wrongdoing against a public official. The next step, under Article I of the Constitution, was a trial in the Senate. A two-thirds majority was required to find Johnson guilty and remove him from office.

Although Johnson was unpopular with Republicans, some of them believed he was being judged unfairly. Others did not want to disrupt the balance of powers by interfering with presidential authority over the cabinet. By a single vote, Senate Republicans failed to convict Johnson. Even so, the trial broke his power as president.

The Election of 1868

The Democratic Party chose former New York governor Horatio Seymour as its 1868 presidential candidate. The Republican Party chose Ulysses S. Grant. As a war hero, Grant appealed to many northern voters. He had no political experience but supported the congressional Reconstruction plan. He ran under the slogan "Let Us Have Peace."

Shortly after Grant was nominated, Congress readmitted seven southern states: Alabama, Arkansas, Florida, Georgia, Louisiana, North Carolina, and South Carolina. (Tennessee already had been readmitted in 1866.) Under the terms of readmission, these seven states approved the Fourteenth Amendment and agreed to let African American men have the vote. During the election, however, white southerners used violence to keep African Americans from the polls in many states.

The Granger Collection, New York

Ulysses S. Grant

REVIEW

Visual-Spatial, Logical-Mathematical. Have students complete the Section Review questions. Then ask them to create a flowchart that shows the relationships between the key terms for this section. Ask volunteers to display their flowcharts and explain them to the class. **SHELTERED ENGLISH**

RETEACH

Linguistic, Logical-Mathematical. Have students complete Main Idea Activities for Reteaching and Sheltered English 4.2. Then ask students to make a bulleted list of all of the key terms from this section along with their definitions. Assist students with terms that they are having difficulty defining. **SHELTERED ENGLISH**

ASSESS

Have students complete Daily Quiz 4.2.

Despite such tactics, thousands of African Americans voted for Grant and the "party of Lincoln." One black newspaper reported that many freedpeople "see clearly enough that the Republican party [is] their political life boat." African American votes helped Grant win a narrow victory.

This poster—which includes images of African American preachers, soldiers, and students—celebrated the passage of the Fifteenth Amendment.

The Fifteenth Amendment

Congressional Republicans wanted to protect their Reconstruction plan, which they believed most African American voters would support. Some Radical Republicans argued that it was not fair that only eight northern states allowed African Americans to vote while all southern states were required to grant suffrage to African American men.

In 1869 Congress proposed the **Fifteenth Amendment**, which gave African American men throughout the United States the right to vote. Abolitionist William Lloyd Garrison praised "this wonderful, quiet, sudden transformation of four millions of human beings from . . . the auction block to the ballot-box." The amendment, which went into effect in 1870, was one of the last important pieces of Reconstruction legislation passed at the federal level.

The Fifteenth Amendment did not please every reformer, however. Women's rights activists were angry because the amendment did not also grant women the right to vote.

SECTION 2 REVIEW

Identify and explain the significance of the following:

- **Black Codes**
- **Radical Republicans**
- **Thaddeus Stevens**
- **Civil Rights Act of 1866**
- **Fourteenth Amendment**
- **Reconstruction Acts**
- **Fifteenth Amendment**

Reading for Content Understanding

1. **Main Idea** What was the purpose of the Black Codes?
2. **Main Idea** Why did Radical Republicans want to remove President Johnson from office?
3. **Constitutional Heritage** What did Congress do to guarantee the civil rights of African Americans?
4. **Writing** *Creating* Write a slogan that might have been used by the Republican or the Democratic Party to appeal to voters in either the 1866 congressional election or the 1868 presidential election.
5. **Critical Thinking** *Making Comparisons* How might a conservative white southerner have viewed the Fourteenth and the Fifteenth Amendments? How might a Radical Republican or an African American have viewed these amendments?

Section 2 Review ANSWERS

Identify

For significance, see the following pages:

- Black Codes, p. 130
- Radical Republicans, p. 131
- Thaddeus Stevens, p. 131
- Civil Rights Act of 1866, p. 132
- Fourteenth Amendment, p. 132
- Reconstruction Acts, p. 133
- Fifteenth Amendment, p. 135

Reading for Content Understanding

1. The Black Codes were designed to limit the freedom of African Americans.

2. President Johnson opposed their Reconstruction policies and had violated a law preventing the president from removing cabinet officials.

3. Congress passed the Civil Rights Act of 1866 and overrode Johnson's veto, proposed the Fourteenth and Fifteenth Amendments, and passed the Reconstruction Acts.

4. Slogans should summarize the Reconstruction policies of Republicans and Democrats and explain the parties' stances on the major issues of each election year.

5. Conservative white southerners most likely opposed the Fourteenth and Fifteenth Amendments. Radical Republicans and African Americans would probably have supported these amendments.

OBJECTIVES

- Describe the roles played by African Americans, northerners, and southern white Republicans in rebuilding the South.
- Explain how the Ku Klux Klan attempted to disrupt the process of Reconstruction.
- Analyze the factors that led to the end of Reconstruction.

FOCUS

Motivate Before Reading

Ask students to discuss how a nation's government might respond if a region of that nation was rebelling or not abiding by the nation's laws. *(Students might say that a government might send troops to occupy the region and force its occupants to follow the laws.)* Explain to them that Reconstruction was basically an occupation of the South. Tell the class that in this section they will learn about the changes that

Section 3 RESOURCES

PRINT

- ★ Guided Reading Strategies 4.3
- ★ Primary Source Reading 4: *Plessy* v. *Ferguson*
- ★ Literature Reading 4: "Jim Crow Cars"
- ★ Graphic Organizer 4: Congress and Reconstruction
- ★ Section 3 Review, p. 141
- ★ Daily Quiz 4.3

MULTIMEDIA

- ★ *Teaching Resources CD–ROM,* Lesson 4.3

SHELTERED ENGLISH

- ★ Main Idea Activities for Reteaching and Sheltered English 4.3

Reconstruction in the South

Reading Focus

What roles did African Americans, northerners, and southern white Republicans play in rebuilding the South?

How did the Ku Klux Klan try to stop Reconstruction?

What factors led to the end of Reconstruction?

Key Terms

carpetbaggers
scalawags
Ku Klux Klan
Panic of 1873
Civil Rights Act of 1875
General Amnesty Act of 1872
Compromise of 1877
Redeemers
poll tax
segregation
Jim Crow laws
Plessy v. *Ferguson*

GOVERNMENTS ELECTED with the support of African American votes took control of most southern states. This led planter William Henry Ravenel to express concerns about the future in his daily journal: "The experiment [Reconstruction] is now to be tried. . . . It produces a financial, political, and social revolution [in] the South." Ravenel feared how the actions of the new governments would affect southern society, but he still hoped that God would "bless the effort and make it successful."

William Henry Ravenel

Reconstruction Governments

The Republican Party controlled most southern governments partly because the Fourteenth Amendment banned a large number of former Confederates from holding office. Most of these Republican officeholders were unpopular with the majority of white southerners.

Carpetbaggers and Scalawags

Many white southerners called northern-born Republicans **carpetbaggers**. Most of these northerners had come South after the war, carrying all their possessions in a bag made from carpeting. Many southerners resented "carpetbaggers," believing that they had moved south to profit from Reconstruction. Southern Democrats were no more fond of white southern Republicans. They referred to them as **scalawags**, which means liars and cheats. Democrats believed that "scalawags" had betrayed the South by voting for the Republican Party.

Despite southern resentment, northerners and white southern Republicans had many reasons for taking part in Reconstruction. Some northerners shared the view of one reformer who strongly believed he "had a Mission with a large M" to help

Reconstruction brought to the South and about opposition to those changes.

Introduce Key Terms

Linguistic. Review this section's key terms with students. Have them write definitions for the terms in their notebooks. After students have read the section, review the terms with the class by stating clues and having students decide which term your clues describe. Encourage students to develop questions about each of the terms that they think may be answered in the section.
SHELTERED ENGLISH

TEACH

Have students read Section 3 and complete Guided Reading Strategies 4.3. Choose one or more of the following activities to explore the section content with students. For further suggestions on block scheduling or team teaching, see the *Block Scheduling Handbook*.

LEVEL 1: Linguistic. (Suggested time: 15 min.) As a class, go over students' Guided Reading Strategies. Then use the Reading Focus questions to highlight the main ideas of the section.
SHELTERED ENGLISH

The Granger Collection, New York

In this cartoon, the South bears the heavy burden imposed by President Grant, federal troops, and carpetbaggers during Reconstruction.

freedpeople. Others hoped to make money while rebuilding the southern economy. An Illinois man who had moved to Texas explained, "I am going to introduce new ideas here in the farming line." Many southern Republicans were small farmers who had supported the Union during the war. Others, like Mississippi governor James Alcorn, were former members of the Whig Party who preferred to become Republicans rather than join the Democrats. By 1872, about 25 percent of southern whites were Republicans.

African Americans in Politics

African Americans seeking equality overwhelmingly supported Reconstruction and were the largest group of southern Republican voters. During Reconstruction, voters elected more than 600 African American representatives to state legislatures and sent 16 to Congress. Other African Americans held important state offices such as lieutenant governor, treasurer, and secretary of state. Many more held local offices in counties throughout the South. Apart from their regular duties, these politicians helped enforce civil rights laws that white officials often ignored. In Georgia, for example, Justice of the Peace Tunis Campbell arrested some white overseers who mistreated black workers. One African American called Campbell "the champion of their rights and the bearer of their burden."

African American politicians came from many different backgrounds. Hiram Revels was born a free man in North Carolina. He went to college in Illinois and became a Methodist minister. During the Civil War, he served as a chaplain in the Union army. In 1870 Revels became the first African American in the U.S. Senate when he took over the seat previously held by Jefferson Davis. Blanche K. Bruce was another important African American leader. Bruce grew up in slavery in Virginia and later became a prominent Republican politician in Mississippi. He served one term as a U.S. senator and was active in politics for many years.

Reconstruction Reforms

The Reconstruction governments provided money for many new programs and organizations. These governments helped to establish the first state-funded public school systems in the South and built new hospitals, prisons, and orphanages. Republican governments also passed laws prohibiting discrimination against African Americans.

During this period, southern states spent large amounts of money building or repairing railroads, bridges, and public buildings—improvements intended to help the southern economy recover

The Granger Collection, New York

The first African American members of Congress: (left to right) Hiram Revels, Benjamin Turner, Robert DeLarge, Josiah Wells, Jefferson Long, Joseph Rainey, and Robert Elliott

Using Visual Resources

Carpetbaggers. Contrary to their appearance in most cartoons of the day—including the one on this page by American cartoonist James Wales—most carpetbaggers were well-educated professionals, such as lawyers, journalists, and business leaders. Many were members of the Union army who decided to remain in the South after the war. The carpetbaggers who won political office during Reconstruction generally supported equal rights for African Americans. Some were even asked to run for office by freedpeople. In economic matters, however, the carpetbaggers were more moderate. They hoped to build railroads and modernize the southern economy, but few supported land grants for freedpeople.

Critical Thinking: How do you think the carpetbaggers wanted to change the southern economy?

ANSWER: Students could mention that the carpetbaggers probably wanted to reform the southern economy so that it was more like that of the North.

ALL LEVELS: Linguistic, Musical-Rhythmic. (Suggested time: 35 min.) Explain to students that many northern Republicans moved to the South shortly after the war. Tell students that their presence was frequently frowned upon by southerners. Have students write songs or poems that describe life for a northern Republican who moved south after the war. Encourage students to include the reasons many southerners were upset by northern Republicans' presence and to include explanations of the terms *carpetbaggers* and *scalawags* in their works. Ask volunteers to read their poems or sing their songs to the class.

LEVEL 2: Logical-Mathematical, Interpersonal. (Suggested time: 45 min.) Organize the class into three groups. The first group will represent white southern Republicans, the second will represent African Americans, and the third will represent northerners. Each group should review this section of the text and class notes to identify the Reconstruction contributions of the group it represents. Then have each group prepare a narrated presentation that highlights the efforts of the group it represents. Encourage students to create visual aids to help emphasize the key points of their presentations. Finally, have each group give its presentation to the rest of the class.

Daily Life

White Leagues. In addition to the Ku Klux Klan, some white southerners also formed groups called white leagues that were designed to deny southern African Americans their rights. The goal of the white leagues was to use violence to restore white rule in the South. Instead of operating secretly like the Klan, the white leagues resorted to open violence against African Americans and Radical Republicans. The leagues assaulted Republican politicians, broke up court sessions, and terrorized African Americans. In 1874, members of the white league of Louisiana even took over government buildings in New Orleans, including the city hall, state legislature, and a weapons-supply depot. President Grant ordered federal troops to put down the rebellion.

Critical Thinking: What effect do you think the activities of the white leagues had on Republican power in the South?

ANSWER: Students could mention that the white leagues most likely weakened support for the Republicans in the South.

MAP ANSWER
four

from the war. To get the money for these projects, the Reconstruction governments raised taxes and issued bonds.

Opposition to Reconstruction

Despite all of these efforts to rebuild the South, the majority of white southerners opposed Reconstruction. Democrats claimed that the Reconstruction governments were unjust and illegal. They also disliked having the federal soldiers stationed in their states. Many white southerners disapproved of African American officeholders. One Democrat noted, "'A white man's government' [is] the most popular rallying cry we have."

In 1866 a group of white southerners in Tennessee created the **Ku Klux Klan**. This secret society opposed African Americans obtaining civil rights, particularly suffrage, and used violence and terror to frighten and discourage them. The Klan's membership grew rapidly as it spread throughout the South. Klan members wore robes and hoods to hide their identities as they attacked—and even murdered—African Americans, white Republican voters, and public officials, usually at night. Charlotte Fowler described her husband's murder by the Klan:

> **"We still had a little grandchild living with me. . . . I heard somebody by the door. . . . The little child followed its grandfather to the door. . . and just then I heard the report [shot] of a pistol, and they shot him down. And this little child ran back to me before I could get out and says, 'Oh grandma, they have killed my poor grandpappy.'"**

Local governments did little to stop the violence because many officials feared the Klan or

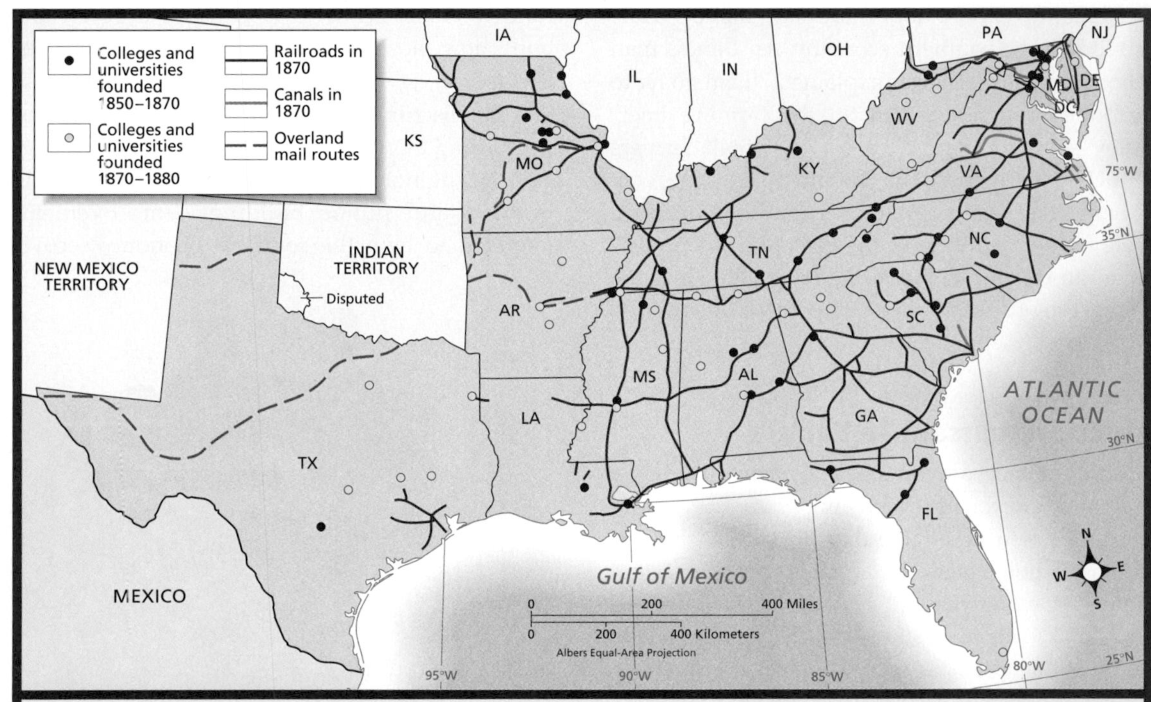

The South After the Civil War

Learning from Maps After the Civil War many Reconstruction programs contributed to the rapid growth in transportation and education in the South.

Place How many colleges and universities were founded in Alabama from 1850 to 1870?

LEVEL 3: Linguistic, Intrapersonal. (Suggested time: 45 min.) Tell students that in spite of efforts to rebuild and reform southern society, there were many groups that attempted to keep African Americans from achieving equality. Ask students to imagine that they are southern Republicans who have been assigned to write editorials for a local newspaper shortly after the Civil War. Editorials should identify the local groups and actions that kept African Americans from enjoying full equality. Have students explain why they believe these activities are unconstitutional and counterproductive to the overall process of Reconstruction. Encourage volunteers to share their ideas with the class.

CLOSE

Linguistic, Intrapersonal. Arrange a panel of students to discuss who was responsible for Reconstruction's failure to reform southern society. (You may wish to organize the class into small groups to allow each student ample opportunity to participate. If you do, assign a moderator to each group.) Have students take turns participating in the discussion and offering their opinions. After some discussion, tell students that no single group can take all of the blame for Reconstruction's failure. Explain to them that there were many factors that contributed to its failure.

were sympathetic to its activities. In Kentucky a committee of African Americans presented a list of at least 70 murder victims and a formal complaint to the state legislature about the lack of action against the Klu Klux Klan. "We regard them [the Klan] as now being licensed to continue their dark and bloody deeds under cover of the dark night," they wrote.

In 1870 and 1871 the federal government passed a series of laws that made it a federal crime to interfere with elections or deny citizens equal protection under the law. Thus, by the mid-1870s the Klan was no longer an organized threat, although it would re-emerge later. Even with the decline of the Klan, white mobs continued to assault African Americans and Republicans throughout the 1870s. Such actions made federal action and protection necessary for Reconstruction's success.

African American men—one of them a soldier—voting in the South

The Election of 1876

The violence that took place throughout the South was not the only challenge to Reconstruction. Northerners also grew more critical of the Reconstruction policies during the early 1870s.

Republican Support Fades

Although President Grant was re-elected in 1872, his administration suffered many scandals that upset voters. The financial **Panic of 1873**, which helped cause a severe economic downturn, also hurt the Republican Party. In 1874 the Republicans lost control of the House of Representatives to the Democrats. Nevertheless, Republicans managed to pass one last act—the **Civil Rights Act of 1875**, which allowed African Americans to sue private businesses for discrimination.

Southern and national politics had also changed with the passage of the **General Amnesty Act of 1872**. This act repealed Section III of the Fourteenth Amendment and allowed former Confederates, with the exception of those of high rank, to hold public office. Many of these former Confederates were Democrats. As a result, southern state governments gradually became controlled by the Democratic Party.

Republicans could tell that support for Reconstruction was also fading in the North, where people were growing concerned about economic problems and government corruption. Thus, the Republicans selected for their 1876 presidential candidate Ohio governor Rutherford B. Hayes, who believed the time had come to end federal support of the Reconstruction governments. The Democrats nominated New York governor Samuel J. Tilden.

The Compromise of 1877

During the election, Democrats in the South again used violence at the polls. Senator Blanche K. Bruce of Mississippi described the problem:

> **"In many parts of the State corrupt and violent influences were brought to bear [used] . . . changing the number of votes cast; . . . threats and violence were practiced directly upon the masses of voters . . . to deter [prevent] them from [voting]."**

The election between Hayes and Tilden was very close. When the votes from the electoral college came in, Tilden appeared to have won, but Republicans questioned the election returns in three southern states.

Across the Curriculum

MATH

The Popular Vote. The votes in the presidential election of 1876 broke down along regional lines. Hayes won the majority of nonsouthern states, while Tilden dominated the South.

Activity: Copy the following chart onto the chalkboard and have students use it to determine what percentage of the ex-Confederate states Tilden won by popular vote *(73%)* and what percentage Hayes won *(27%)*. *(If students are having trouble, you may want to review the steps for determining percentages—divide the total number of states won by the total number of ex-Confederate states and move the decimal point two places to the right.)*

Popular Vote, Election of 1876

State	Rutherford Hayes	Samuel Tilden
AL	68,708	102,989
AR	38,649	58,086
FL	23,849	22,927
GA	50,533	130,157
LA	75,315	70,508
MS	52,603	112,173
NC	108,484	125,427
SC	91,786	90,897
TN	89,566	133,177
TX	45,013	106,372
VA	95,518	140,770

CHALLENGE AND EXTEND

1. **Linguistic, Interpersonal.** Assign each student one of the key terms, people, or events depicted in this section. Have students use their textbooks or the library to find information about the term, person, or event. Have students write brief summaries, similar to an encyclopedia entry, of their assigned items' meaning and significance. Once students have finished their summaries, call the terms out in alphabetical order, and have students go to the front of the class and read their summaries.

2. **Linguistic, Logical-Mathematical, Intrapersonal.** Ask students to read about the Supreme Court's decision in the case of *Plessy* v. *Ferguson*. Have students research the arguments presented in the case. Then tell students to imagine that they are John Marshall Harlan, the only Supreme Court justice who disagreed with the Court's decision. Have students write dissenting opinions that argue against the Court's decision. Have students point out the constitutional grounds on which their opinions are based and also describe the negative effects that they think will result from the decision.

Section 3 Review ANSWERS

Identify

For significance, see the following pages:

- carpetbaggers, p. 136
- scalawags, p. 136
- Hiram Revels, p. 137
- Blanche K. Bruce, p. 137
- Ku Klux Klan, p. 138
- Panic of 1873, p. 139
- Civil Rights Act of 1875, p. 139
- General Amnesty Act of 1872, p. 139
- Rutherford B. Hayes, p. 139
- Compromise of 1877, p. 140
- Redeemers, p. 140
- poll tax, p. 140
- segregation, p. 140
- Jim Crow laws, p. 140
- *Plessy* v. *Ferguson*, p. 141
- John Marshall Harlan, p. 141

Reading for Content Understanding

1. African Americans—took advantage of employment and education opportunities; northern whites—tried to reform southern society and rebuild the economy; white southern Republicans—small pro-Union farmers made efforts to hinder wealthy planters.

The Election Commission hears testimony on disputed returns from the presidential election of 1876.

A special commission of 10 members of Congress and five Supreme Court justices settled the issue. The commission narrowly decided to give all the disputed votes to Hayes. Hayes thus won the election by one electoral vote. In the **Compromise of 1877**, the Democrats agreed to accept Hayes's victory if all remaining federal troops were removed from the South. They also asked for funding for internal improvements in the South and the appointment of a southern Democrat to the president's cabinet. Shortly after he took office in 1877, President Hayes removed the last of the federal troops from the South.

Turning Back the Clock

Reconstruction ended at different times in southern states, depending on when the Democrats regained control of a particular state government. In general, their first order of business was to eliminate the Reconstruction reforms.

The Redeemers

The individuals behind the Democratic Party's return to power in the South were known as the **Redeemers**. The Redeemers included people from many different backgrounds, such as U.S. senator John T. Morgan of Alabama—a former general in the Confederate army—and newspaper editor Henry Grady of Georgia, who was interested in promoting southern industry. "Never was nobler duty confided [given] to human hands than the uplifting and upbuilding of the... South," said Grady. The Redeemers wanted to reduce the size of state government and limit the rights of African Americans. They lowered state budgets and got rid of social programs. They cut property taxes and reduced public funding for schools. The Redeemers also succeeded in limiting African Americans' civil rights.

In an effort to deny the vote to African Americans, the Redeemers set up the **poll tax**, which required individuals to pay a special tax before they could vote. The poll tax, however, often stopped not only African American men but also some white men from voting. To bypass this result, some states more carefully targeted African American voters by requiring them to pass literacy tests. A "grandfather clause" was usually written into law as well, allowing any man whose father or grandfather could vote before 1867 to avoid poll taxes and literacy tests. This meant that almost every white man could benefit from the clause, but few black men could.

Segregation and Jim Crow

Another change made by the Democratic governments was the introduction of legal **segregation**—the forced separation of whites and African Americans in public places. **Jim Crow laws**—laws that enforced segregation—began appearing in southern states in 1881. African Americans had to stay in different hotels than whites, sit in separate theater sections, and ride in separate railcars. One white southerner described segregated areas as "in every instance . . . the most uncomfortable, uncleanest, and unsafest place[s]."

The Granger Collection, New York

An African American man is ordered to leave a "whites only" railroad car.

African Americans challenged these laws in

REVIEW

Linguistic, Visual-Spatial, Interpersonal. Have students complete the Section Review questions. Then draw their attention to the terms in the Identify section. Ask them to create a list of definitions by using a brief phrase to describe each term. Then have students scramble the list to create an activity involving matching the terms in each list to the definitions. Have each student exchange his or her activity with a classmate and answer the questions.

RETEACH

Linguistic, Logical-Mathematical. Have students complete Main Idea Activities for Reteaching and Sheltered English 17.3. Explain to students that the government wants them to evaluate Reconstruction's success. Have students review material from this section and from class notes to determine their opinions on the subject. Students should write short summaries of their findings. SHELTERED ENGLISH

ASSESS

Have students complete Daily Quiz 17.3.

court. In 1883, however, the U.S. Supreme Court ruled that the Civil Rights Act of 1875 was unconstitutional. The Court also ruled that the Fourteenth Amendment applied only to the actions of state governments. This allowed private individuals and businesses to practice segregation.

Plessy v. *Ferguson*

In 1896 the U.S. Supreme Court returned to the issue of segregation in the case ***Plessy* v. *Ferguson***. Homer Plessy was an African American who had purchased a first-class ticket on a Louisiana train. When he tried to sit in the first-class car, he was arrested because Louisiana's Jim Crow laws did not allow African Americans to ride in first class with whites. Plessy and his lawyers argued that this violated the Fourteenth Amendment's guarantee of equal legal treatment.

The Court ruled against Plessy, arguing that it was legal to force African Americans and whites to use separate facilities as long as the facilities were of equal quality. According to the Court, this was fair so long as "separate-but-equal" facilities were provided for African Americans.

The only justice who disagreed with the Court's decision was John Marshall Harlan. Justice Harlan explained his concerns in a dissenting, or disagreeing, opinion:

> **"In the eye of the law, there is in this country no superior, dominant [controlling], ruling class of citizens. . . . Our Constitution is color-blind, and neither knows nor tolerates classes among citizens. In respect of civil rights, all citizens are equal before the law."**

Few white Americans agreed with Justice Harlan in 1896, however. Segregation continued to be widespread both in the South and in the North. In addition, the public schools, libraries, parks, and other areas open to African Americans were usually inferior in quality to those created for whites. Thus, in practice, the "separate-but-equal" facilities usually were "separate-and-unequal."

A judge's gavel

SECTION 3 REVIEW

Identify and explain the significance of the following:

- **carpetbaggers**
- **scalawags**
- **Hiram Revels**
- **Blanche K. Bruce**
- **Ku Klux Klan**
- **Panic of 1873**
- **Civil Rights Act of 1875**
- **General Amnesty Act of 1872**
- **Rutherford B. Hayes**
- **Compromise of 1877**
- **Redeemers**
- **poll tax**
- **segregation**
- **Jim Crow laws**
- ***Plessy* v. *Ferguson***
- **John Marshall Harlan**

Reading for Content Understanding

1 **Main Idea** What contributions did African Americans, northern whites, and white southern Republicans make to the Reconstruction process?

2 **Main Idea** Why did some white southerners oppose Reconstruction? Why did some of them form the Ku Klux Klan?

3 **Citizenship and Democracy** What was the Compromise of 1877, and how did it lead to the end of Reconstruction?

4 **Writing** *Persuading* Imagine that you are a newspaper editor who opposes the *Plessy* v. *Ferguson* ruling. Write an editorial to convince your readers that the ruling is wrong.

5 **Critical Thinking** *Evaluating* Do you think the civil rights aspects of Reconstruction were a short-term failure but a long-term success? Explain your answer.

2. They disliked having federal soldiers in their states, believed Reconstruction governments were unjust and illegal, and resented civil rights gains by African Americans. The Klan was formed to destroy Republican governments and deny rights to African Americans.

3. This agreement gave disputed electoral votes to Hayes. It ended Reconstruction by agreeing to withdraw federal troops from the South, providing greater federal funding for southern internal improvements, and allowing the appointment of a southern Democrat to the president's cabinet.

4. Editorials might argue that the decision violated the rights of African Americans because separate facilities were often poorly maintained and not equal in quality to white facilities.

5. Students might argue that after Reconstruction, African Americans lost civil rights, but the amendments passed during Reconstruction would later ensure these same rights.

SECTION 4 LESSON PLAN

OBJECTIVES

- Describe the problems southern farmers faced after the Civil War.
- Explain reasons why some business leaders wanted to create a "New South."
- Identify the various forms of culture that emerged in the South during and after Reconstruction.

FOCUS

Motivate Before Reading

Ask students to identify the resources they would need in order to be successful farmers. *(Students' answers should include land, a barn, seeds, farm machinery, and a source of water.)* List their answers on the chalkboard. Tell students that during and after Reconstruction, poor African Americans and whites often lacked land and the money to buy it. Explain to them that because of this lack

Section 4
RESOURCES

PRINT

★ Guided Reading Strategies 4.4

★ Biography Reading 4: George Washington Carver

★ Geography Activity 4: Tenant Farming and Sharecropping

★ Section 4 Review, p. 147

★ Daily Quiz 4.4

MULTIMEDIA

★ *Teaching Resources CD–ROM*, Lesson 4.4

★ Everyday Life in America Transparency 13: Life During Reconstruction

★ *American Music Audio CD Program:* "When Johnny Comes Marching Home"

SHELTERED ENGLISH

★ Main Idea Activities for Reteaching and Sheltered English 4.4

The New South

Reading Focus

What problems did some southern farmers face at the end of the Civil War?

Why did some business leaders hope to create a "New South"?

What were some popular forms of southern culture during and after Reconstruction?

Key Terms

sharecropping

AFTER RENTING LAND FOR YEARS, Charley White and his wife, Lucille, saved enough money to buy their own farm in Texas. Reflecting back on the purchase, Charley White said, "The house wasn't much more than a shack." The fact that it belonged to them made all the difference. "It just set us on fire. We didn't seem to get half as tired, or if we did we didn't notice it." Lucille White told her husband that "even the rocks look pretty." Many other African American farmers, however, were not fortunate enough to share the Whites' accomplishment.

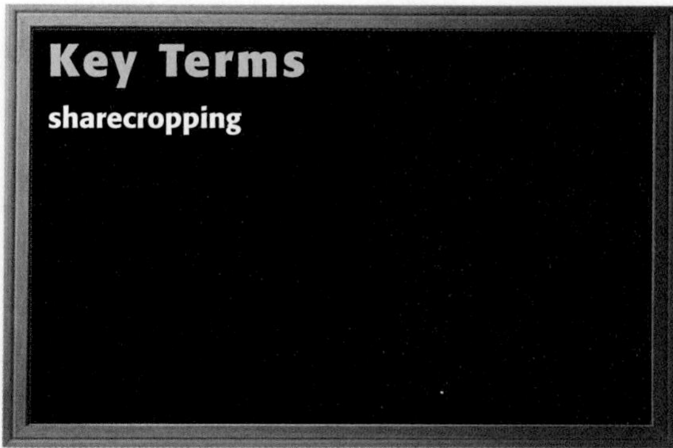

Farmers used harrows such as this one to smooth their soil.

Farming in the South

Throughout most of the South, few African Americans could afford to buy or even rent their own farms and the necessary farm supplies. Moving west also was costly. Thus, many African Americans remained on plantations, while others tried to make a living in the cities.

The Growth of Sharecropping

Those African Americans who stayed on plantations often became part of a system known as **sharecropping**, or sharing the crop. Landowners provided the land, tools, and supplies, and sharecroppers provided the labor. At harvest time, the sharecropper gave most of the crop to the owner. Whatever remained belonged to the sharecropper.

The sharecropping system allowed poor African Americans and poor whites to farm land that they could not afford to rent or buy. The system also enabled small farmers to hire people to work on their land. Many sharecroppers hoped to save enough money from selling their share of the crops to buy a farm. Only a few were able to achieve this dream, however.

of resources they often turned to new ways of earning a living. Tell students that in this section they will learn about changes in the labor system of the South following the Civil War, the goals of the "New South" business movement, and the various forms of culture that emerged in the South during and after Reconstruction.

Introduce Key Terms

Linguistic. Review this section's key terms with students. Have students use context cues to write a definition for each term in the section. Then have students write a sentence using each term.
SHELTERED ENGLISH

TEACH

Have students read Section 4 and complete Guided Reading Strategies 4.4. Choose one or more of the following activities to explore the section content with students. For further suggestions on block scheduling or team teaching, see the *Block Scheduling Handbook.*

LEVEL 1: Linguistic. (Suggested time: 15 min.) As a class, go over students' Guided Reading Strategies. Then use the Reading Focus questions to highlight the main ideas of the section.
SHELTERED ENGLISH

A Cycle of Debt

When sharecropping families needed food, clothing, or supplies, they went to the general store. Most families bought goods on credit because they had little money. When the harvest came, sharecroppers hoped to sell their crops and pay off their debt to the store. However, bad weather or low crop prices often prevented them from making as much money as they had hoped.

Many merchants cheated sharecroppers by charging them for items they did not purchase. Some landowners also cheated sharecroppers by taking more than their fair share of the crop. Abolitionist Frederick Douglass complained about the treatment of sharecroppers:

> **"The merchant puts him [the sharecropper] off with his poorest commodities [goods] at highest prices, and can say to him take these or nothing. . . . By this means the laborer is brought into debt, and hence is kept always in the power of the land-owner. . . . On such a system of fraud and wrong one might well invoke [request] a bolt from heaven."**

As a result of such practices, most sharecroppers found themselves deeper in debt at the end of the harvest than they had been when they planted their crops.

African American Property Owners in the South, 1860 and 1870

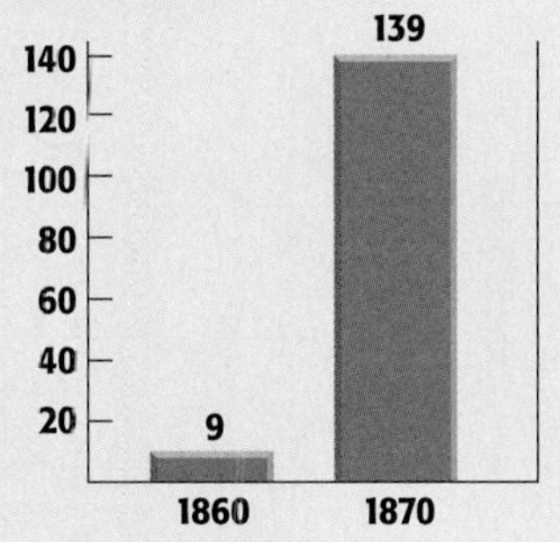

Figures are for owners in former Confederate states.
Source: *The Facts of Reconstruction*

Owning Property The number of African American property owners in the South dramatically increased in the years following the Civil War. How much did this number increase from 1860 to 1870?

Too Much Cotton

Many farmers saw planting cotton as a sure way to make money. Cotton was one of the South's most important cash crops—crops that farmers grow to sell to others rather than to use themselves. Cotton had a worldwide market and could be sold or stored easily. As a result, numerous landowners and sharecroppers grew cotton, hoping to pay their debts or save money. When too many farmers planted cotton, however, the supply became too great and the price per bale dropped. One man wrote his father about a drop in the price of cotton: "It nearly ruined us. . . . The farmers are very blue here. But getting ready to plant cotton again."

The Granger Collection, New York

Children in the South often had to help their parents pick cotton at harvest time.

Even though many farmers understood the drawbacks of planting cotton, they felt too much pressure from banks or landlords to change their ways. "Cotton raising has grown to be a necessity more than a choice," a farmer in Alabama said. Another southern man explained,

> **"Cotton is the thing to get credit on in this country. . . . You can always sell cotton. You leave home with a wagon load of cotton and you will go home that night with money in your pocket; you load up your wagon with wheat or corn . . . and I doubt some days whether you could sell it."**

Daily Life

The General Store. General stores grew in importance after the Civil War because of the need for farm credit. The general stores that dotted the South served many functions: grocery store, department store, and hardware store. General stores also served as banks, pharmacies, and meeting places. Both black and white customers traveled over bad roads to buy clothing, food, medicines, and other staple goods that they could not grow or make themselves. Store owners extended credit—at interest rates as high as 40 percent—for these purchases, as well as for seed and equipment to plant crops. Local farmers gathered to hold meetings of fraternal societies at general stores. Community members gathered at the store to hear local gossip and political news.

Critical Thinking: Why was the general store such an important institution in the South?

ANSWER: Students might mention that it provided services that were critical to everyday life.

CHART ANSWER
130,000

ALL LEVELS: Visual-Spatial, Logical-Mathematical, Interpersonal. (Suggested time: 40 min.) Discuss with the class the rise of sharecropping and the textile industry in the South. Tell students to imagine that they are African Americans who have recently gained their freedom and need to explore career opportunities. Have them create graphic organizers that compare the advantages and disadvantages of sharecropping with those of wage labor in southern textile mills. After completing their organizers, have students decide which system they would choose. Encourage students to decide whether they would give different advice to people with different lifestyles or personalities.
SHELTERED ENGLISH

LEVEL 2: Linguistic, Musical-Rhythmic, Interpersonal. (Suggested time: 45 min. plus homework) Describe to the class the various forms of southern entertainment or culture discussed in this section. Have students create either literature or folk ballads that are similar to those created during that era. Have students include references to southern culture during the Reconstruction Era in their work.

LEVEL 3: Linguistic, Logical-Mathematical, Intrapersonal. (Suggested time: 45 min. plus homework) Ask each student to write a short story that describes the experiences of a poor southerner trying to improve his or her life in the New South. The story should include references to the labor system,

Economic Development

Railroads. From 1877 to 1900 the South built railroad lines at a faster rate than the nation as a whole. In 1860 the South had only about 10,000 miles of railroads. By 1900 some 60,000 miles of railroads—one third of the country's lines—connected southern towns and cities to the rest of the nation. Railroad-building had an immediate effect on the southern economy. Farmers profited by cutting railroad ties from their land and selling them to the rail companies. Farm families also made money by selling chickens, eggs, meat, and other farm products to the railroad workers.

Critical Thinking: How do you think the railroads helped the southern economy in the long term?

ANSWER: Students might mention that railroads would help the southern economy by shipping more crops and other goods to more areas.

CHART ANSWER
Prices dropped.

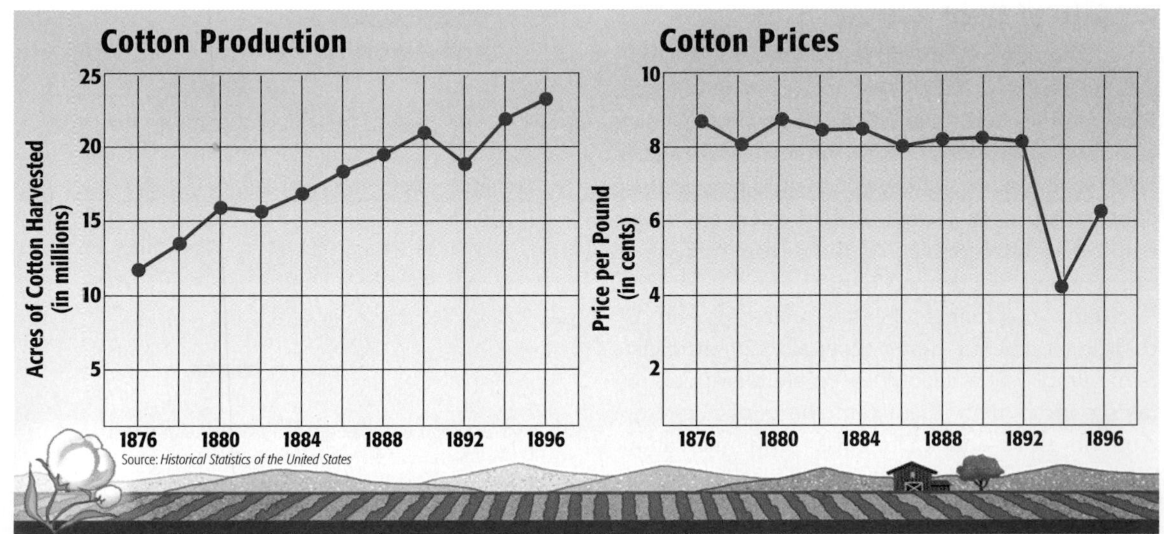

King Cotton During the late 1800s cotton remained a primary crop for many farmers. According to the graphs, what generally happened as cotton production increased?

The "New South" Movement

The southern economy, like the southern farmer, relied on cash crops such as cotton. This created cycles of good and bad years as prices went up or down. Tired of watching the southern economy suffer, some business leaders wanted to create a "New South" that had an industrial base in addition to its agricultural one. They hoped industry would strengthen the southern economy.

Southern Industry

Henry Grady, a newspaper editor in Atlanta, was one of the leaders of the New South movement. "The new South presents a perfect democracy," he wrote, "and a diversified [varied] industry that meets the complex needs of this complex age." Grady and his supporters wanted to take advantage of the South's resources—such as its cotton production and cheap and abundant labor—to build textile mills and other factories. They hoped their plans for development would interest investors.

Grant Hamilton's From Darkness to Light *(1895) shows the New South rising from the destruction of the Civil War.*

New industries developed in the South, though not as quickly or in as many areas as Grady hoped. One of the great changes after the Civil War was the repair of the old railroads and the growth of new lines as workers laid thousands of miles of railroad track throughout the South. The new railroads allowed companies to ship goods faster and farther than ever before. The telegraph lines that accompanied the railroads also helped bring news to small southern towns.

The most successful industrial development in the South involved textile production. Businesspeople built textile mills that produced cotton fabric in many small towns, drawing hundreds of people from the countryside to work in the mills. While this industry pumped new life into the southern economy, the New South was far from the "perfect democracy" that Grady had claimed. The most important example of this lack of democracy was the cotton mills' refusal to hire African Americans.

economic changes, and cultural traditions that are depicted in this section. Ask for volunteers to read their stories to the class and invite other students to comment on them.

CLOSE

Visual-Spatial, Logical-Mathematical, Interpersonal. Ask students to list the ways that life in the New South differed from life in the Old South. Then organize the class into small groups and have members share their lists with one another and create a chart comparing and contrasting the two. **SHELTERED ENGLISH**

CHALLENGE AND EXTEND

1. **Linguistic, Logical-Mathematical.** Ask students to locate a short story by an author discussed in this section or lyrics from an African American spiritual. Tell students to imagine that they are entertainment critics assigned to write reviews of the chosen works. Reviews should explain how the stories or spirituals reflect the lives and values of southerners during this period, as well as the changes in society that occurred after the Civil War. Have students rate the works based on political commentary using a four-star rating system. Ask volunteers to read their reviews to the class.

Southern Mill Life

Work in the cotton mills appealed to farm families that had trouble making ends meet. As one mill worker explained, "It was a necessity to move and get a job, rather than depend on the farm." Recruiters sent out by the mills promised good wages and steady work.

Entire families often worked in the same mill. One company in South Carolina asked for "whole families with at least three workers for the mill in each family." Mills employed large numbers of women and children. Many children started working around the age of 12; some started earlier than that. Women did most of the spinning and were valued workers, although few women had the opportunity to advance within the company.

Many mill workers were proud of the skills they used, but they did not enjoy their work. One unhappy worker described it as "the same thing over and over again. . . . The more you do, the more they want done." Workers often labored six days a week, 12 hours a day. Cotton dust and lint filled the air, causing asthma and an illness known as brown-lung disease. Fast-moving machinery caused many injuries and some deaths. Despite the long hours and dangerous working conditions, wages were low. However, mill work did offer an alternative to farming.

Southern Literature

While the New South movement sought to modernize the South, many southerners looked to the arts to reinforce their traditions. Southern literature, an important element of southern culture, gained national popularity in the late 1800s. The most famous writer about the South at the end of Reconstruction was probably Mark Twain. Twain, whose real name was Samuel Clemens, wrote *The Adventures of Tom Sawyer* in 1876. Although Twain wrote about many subjects, his novels and stories about the South were among his most admired.

Part of the reason that southern literature gained national attention was that many of these stories involved people and places in the South that seemed exotic to northerners. The popular writer Mary Noailles Murfree, for example, wrote short stories and novels about the people who lived in the mountains of eastern Tennessee. Another writer, George Washington Cable, wrote novels about the African American community in New Orleans. Cable used his writing as an opportunity to protest racial prejudice in the South.

Mary Noailles Murfree began her writing career by producing short stories, which she read to her family.

Joel Chandler Harris was one of the most popular southern writers. He wrote short stories about a fictional plantation slave named Uncle Remus, a wise old storyteller who taught lessons by reciting folktales. Another author, William J. Faulkner, brought together many more African American folktales in his book *The Days When the Animals Talked*. Both Harris and Faulkner based their work on stories they were first told by enslaved African Americans and later by freedpeople.

Many white southern writers set their stories in a pre–Civil War South full of beautiful plantations and happy slaves. Unlike these authors who presented romantic images of life on southern plantations, African American writer Charles W. Chesnutt wrote plantation stories that showed the greed and cruelty of the slavery system. Chesnutt was born in Ohio but raised in North Carolina. Many of his short stories are in a book called *The Conjure Woman*.

A southern dancing party

Across the Curriculum

LANGUAGE ARTS

Frances Ellen Harper. Another African American who won praise for writing about black life was Frances Ellen Harper. Before the Civil War, Harper was most recognized for her poetry and speeches in support of abolition. After the Civil War, she experimented with new literary forms. Her book *Sketches of Southern Life* (1872), a series of poems in black dialect, describes African American experiences during slavery and Reconstruction. It is considered by some critics to be her finest work.

Activity: Have students read a selection from Harper's *Sketches of Southern Life* and write an essay that compares and contrasts the writing and subject matter with one of Charles Chesnutt's short stories.

Multimedia Resources

Everyday Life in America Transparency 13: Life During Reconstruction

AMERICAN LITERATURE ANSWERS

(page 146)

1. He escaped and was told that his wife had been sold.
2. He wanted to prepare them for what was about to take place.

2. **Linguistic, Logical-Mathematical.** Explain to students that the agreements made between landowners and sharecroppers were generally created in a way that was profitable for the landowner but kept the sharecropper in a cycle of debt. Have students write sample contracts between a landowner and a sharecropper. Tell them that the contracts should specify the amount of land and types of supplies the landowner would provide, as well as how much of the final crop yield the sharecropper would give in return. Remind students that a contract should contain the dates on which the agreement will begin and end, the terms of the agreement, the signatures of both parties involved, and a witness's signature.

3. **Linguistic, Logical-Mathematical, Intrapersonal.** Have students use the library and other resources to find accounts of southern mill workers describing the working conditions in the mills. Have each student write a campaign speech for a southern reformer who is seeking to improve the conditions in the mills. Encourage students to be as descriptive as possible when explaining the working conditions and to offer suggestions for changes in the mills. Encourage volunteers to share their speeches with the rest of the class.

Section 4 Review ANSWERS

Identify

For significance, see the following pages:

- sharecropping, p. 142
- Henry Grady, p. 144
- Mark Twain, p. 145
- Mary Noailles Murfree, p. 145
- Joel Chandler Harris, p. 145
- Charles W. Chesnutt, p. 145
- Fisk Jubilee Singers, p. 147

Reading for Content Understanding

1. Sharecroppers did not own the land they farmed, were often in debt to landowners and store owners, and were forced to grow cotton.

2. Business leaders wanted to strengthen and protect the southern economy by diversifying from a strictly agricultural-based economic system.

3. Southern literature and spirituals were popular throughout the country.

4. Paragraphs will vary but might describe families working in the mills, female spinners, the repetitive nature of work, long hours, dusty conditions, and dangerous machines.

5. Black and white sharecroppers may have both faced heavy debts and hard work in the fields; black sharecroppers faced the additional burdens of racism, segregation, and Jim Crow laws.

American Literature

"The Wife of His Youth"

Charles W. Chesnutt

African American Charles W. Chesnutt wrote about slavery and racial prejudice. In "The Wife of His Youth," the main character, Mr. Ryder, is courting a young widow, Mrs. Dixon. Ryder has been apart from his wife for 25 years. He must choose between his first wife, a woman he married when he was a slave, and the widow. In the following excerpt, Mr. Ryder tells his friends about his wife.

Charles W. Chesnutt

The Granger Collection, New York

"Suppose that this husband, soon after his escape, had learned that his wife had been sold away, and that such inquiries [investigations] as he could make brought no information of her whereabouts. . . . Suppose, too, that he made his way to the North . . . and there, where he had larger opportunities, had improved [himself]. . . . And then suppose that accident should bring to his knowledge the fact that the wife of his youth, . . . was alive and seeking him, but that he was absolutely safe from recognition or discovery, unless he chose to reveal himself. My friends, what would the man do? . . ."

There was something in Mr. Ryder's voice that stirred the hearts of those who sat around him. . . . It was observed, too, that his look rested more especially upon Mrs. Dixon. . . .

She was the first to speak: "He should have acknowledged her." "Yes," they all echoed, "he should have acknowledged her."

"My friends and companions," responded Mr. Ryder, "I thank you, one and all. It is the answer I expected, for I knew your hearts."

He turned and walked toward the closed door of an adjoining room. . . . He came back in a momemt, leading by the hand his visitor of the afternoon. . . .

"Ladies and gentlemen," he said, "this is the woman, and I am the man, whose story I have told you. Permit me to introduce to you the wife of my youth."

Understanding Literature

1. How does Mr. Ryder become separated from his wife?
2. Why do you think Mr. Ryder chooses to tell his friends about his wife?

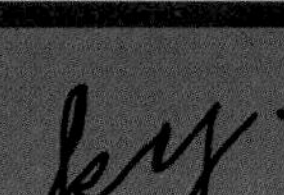

Southern Music

Southern music also grew in popularity after the Civil War. Popular musical instruments in the South included the violin, the banjo, and the guitar. Fiddle players provided the music for square dancing, a popular pastime. Mary Noailles Murfree described a country dance in "The Dancin' Party at Harrison's Cove":

"Now and then a guffaw [laugh] mingled with the violin's resonant [loud] strains and the dancers' well-marked pace; the women talked to each other with somewhat more animation [cheerfulness] than was their wont [typical practice], under the stress of the unusual excitement of a dancing party."

REVIEW

Linguistic, Logical-Mathematical. Have students complete the Section Review questions. Tell them to make lists of important people, places, and ideas found in the section. Then have students create lists that contain explanations of each term. Have each student exchange his or her list with another student and then match terms to the definitions. Finally, tell students to return the finished lists for grading.

ASSESS

Have students complete Daily Quiz 4.4.

RETEACH

Logical-Mathematical. Have students complete Main Idea Activities for Reteaching and Sheltered English 4.4. Then write two lists on the chalkboard. One list should identify changes that occurred in the South after the Civil War. The other should identify the causes of these events. For example, the first list could contain the term *sharecropping* and the second could contain the description *lacked money to buy land.* Some of the terms from the first list may have more than one cause. Have students match each term with its cause or causes. Then review students' answers.
SHELTERED ENGLISH

One of the most important musical styles of the period was the spiritual. These songs were based on Christian hymns and African music sung in the days of slavery. In these songs the lead singer often called out a verse that the rest of the singers would repeat. Although the lead singer might change the words slightly to reflect current events, the lyrics usually described the sorrows of slavery and the hope for freedom. One of the best-known spirituals, "Swing Low Sweet Chariot," expressed African Americans' longing for "the promised land," where they would be free from slavery:

Jubilee Singers, Courtesy of Fisk University

Many of the original Fisk Jubilee Singers were recently emancipated slaves.

> **"Swing low sweet chariot,**
> **Comin' for to carry me home,**
> **Swing low sweet chariot,**
> **Comin' for to carry me home,**
> **I look'd over Jordan, an' what did I see,**
> **Comin' for to carry me home,**
> **A band of angels comin' after me,**
> **Comin' for to carry me home,**
> **If you get-a there befo' I do,**
> **Tell all of my friends I'm comin' too."**

During Reconstruction, the Fisk Jubilee Singers—a group of students from Fisk University in Nashville, Tennessee—traveled widely to earn money for their school. They brought African American music to a national audience. This singing group entertained people with spirituals, touring the United States in 1871 and 1872 and performing in Europe in 1873. Their tours made Fisk University famous and also raised enough money to save the college from financial ruin and build a new campus. Other African American colleges, such as Hampton University in Virginia, formed similar singing groups, which increased the popularity of spirituals.

SECTION 4 REVIEW

Identify and explain the significance of the following:

- **sharecropping**
- **Henry Grady**
- **Mark Twain**
- **Mary Noailles Murfree**
- **Joel Chandler Harris**
- **Charles W. Chesnutt**

Reading for Content Understanding

1. **Main Idea** What were some of the drawbacks of being a sharecropper in the years after the Civil War?
2. **Main Idea** Why did some business leaders want to develop southern industry?
3. **Cultural Diversity** What types of southern culture were popular throughout the United States?
4. **Writing** *Describing* Write a paragraph describing what life might have been like in a southern mill.
5. **Critical Thinking** *Making Comparisons* How were the lives of black and white sharecroppers similar? How were they different?

Multimedia Resources

American Music Audio CD
Program: "When Johnny Comes Marching Home"

Chapter 4 Review ANSWERS

Identifying People and Ideas

1. made slavery illegal
2. provided relief for poor blacks and whites in the South
3. laws that limited the freedom of African Americans
4. Lincoln's vice president; became president in 1865
5. the first African American in the U.S. Senate
6. guaranteed citizenship and equal protection to all people born or naturalized in the United States, except American Indians
7. Civil War hero who was elected president in 1868
8. a secret society that tried to drive Republicans out of the South and deny African Americans equal rights
9. Supreme Court decision that ruled that segregated facilities were legal as long as they were of equal quality
10. agricultural labor system in which people farmed a piece of land owned by someone else

Using the Time Line

1. c
2. e
3. d
4. a
5. b

CHAPTER 4 REVIEW

Review and Assessment RESOURCES

PRINT
★ Chapter 4 Review, pp. 148–49
★ Vocabulary Activity 4
★ Chapter 4 Study Guide
★ Chapter 4 Test (Form A or B)

MULTIMEDIA
★ Audio Program, Ch. 4 (English and Spanish)
★ *Global Skill Builder CD–ROM*
★ Chapter 4 Test Generator
★ HRW Web site

SHELTERED ENGLISH
★ Spanish Glossary
★ Sheltered English Chapter 4 Test

ASSESS

Have students complete one of the Chapter 4 Tests. As an alternate assessment, assign the Chapter 4 Investigation.

Understanding Main Ideas

1. They differed based on the percentage of people required to pledge loyalty to the Union. For other differences, see pages 125–26 and page 128.

2. It provided African Americans with the same legal rights as whites. Johnson vetoed it because he thought it gave the federal government too much power and discriminated against whites; Congress overrode his veto.

3. The acts forced southern states to approve the Fourteenth Amendment, gave African Americans the right to vote, and divided the South into military districts.

4. African Americans—tried to rebuild their lives after the Civil War by taking advantage of new freedoms, including educational and job opportunities; northerners—wanted to reform southern society and make money while rebuilding the southern economy; white southern Democrats—tried to eliminate the Reconstruction reforms, limit African Americans' rights, lower state budgets, and cut state programs

5. They resented Republican attempts to give freedoms to African Americans.

6. disputed and close race, involving violence and fraud, between presidential candidates Hayes and Tilden; Hayes chosen president in exchange for withdrawal of federal troops from South and appointment of southern Democrat to the cabinet

7. dance music, folk ballads, and religious music, including hymns and spirituals

CHAPTER 4 REVIEW

Chapter Summary

After the Civil War, the United States struggled with restoring the southern states to the Union and dealing with the rights of former slaves. Americans differed in their approach to Reconstruction. At the end of Reconstruction, the Union was restored, but African Americans continued to be denied their full citizenship rights.

On a separate sheet of paper, complete the following activities.

Identifying People and Ideas

Describe the historical significance of the following:

1. Thirteenth Amendment
2. Freedmen's Bureau
3. Black Codes
4. Andrew Johnson
5. Hiram Revels
6. Fourteenth Amendment
7. Ulysses S. Grant
8. Ku Klux Klan
9. *Plessy* v. *Ferguson*
10. sharecropping

Internet Activity 

go.hrw.com
SB1 Colleges

Search the Internet through the HRW Web site to find information on one of the historically black colleges or universities that was founded during Reconstruction. Then use the information to create a one-page brochure about that school.

Understanding Main Ideas

1. How did the Reconstruction plans of Lincoln, the Radical Republicans, and Johnson differ?
2. What was the Civil Rights Act of 1866? Why did President Johnson veto it, and how did Congress react to his veto?
3. How did the Reconstruction Acts of 1867 protect the rights of African Americans in the South?
4. What roles did African Americans, northerners, and white southern Democrats play in Reconstruction?
5. Why were most white southerners loyal to the Democratic Party?
6. What crisis was resolved by the Compromise of 1877? What were the elements of this compromise?
7. What musical styles were popular in the South after the Civil War?

Using the Time Line

Number your paper from 1 to 5. Match the letters on the time line below with the following events.

1. **Congress proposes the Fifteenth Amendment, giving African American men the right to vote.**
2. **Democrats take control of the House of Representatives.**
3. **Hiram Revels becomes the first African American senator.**
4. **Congress proposes an amendment to make slavery illegal throughout the United States.**
5. **Americans elect Ulysses S. Grant, a Civil War hero, president.**

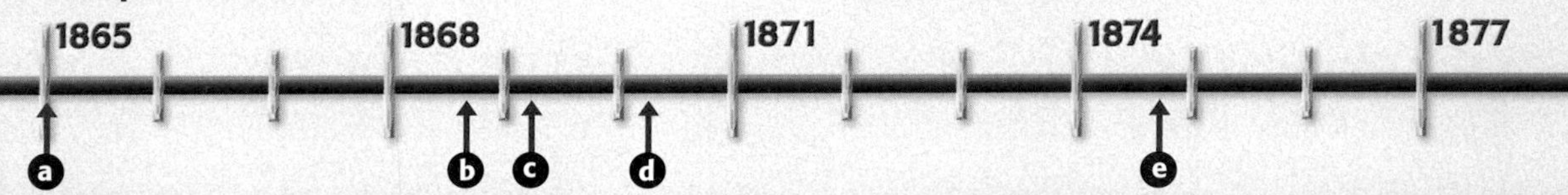

RETEACH

Visual-Spatial, Interpersonal. Organize students into four groups. Assign a group to cover material from each section of the chapter. Give each group a large sheet of butcher paper, markers, and other materials, and ask them to develop a collage depicting the main points of the section. Then have each group develop an oral presentation that explains its collage.

Using the Internet

Ask students to continue their research to find additional information about the locations of historically black colleges that were built during Reconstruction. Then have students create a map that identifies the city and state where each of these colleges is located.

Portfolio Extensions

1. Have students read one another's journal entries and identify the differences in lifestyle based on people's job choices and locations.

2. Have students expand on the poems or songs they wrote by writing short stories similar to those of the post–Civil War period.

Reviewing Themes

1. **Constitutional Heritage** Which three amendments to the Constitution attempted to protect the rights of African Americans? How did these amendments protect those rights?
2. **Citizenship and Democracy** How did democracy expand during Reconstruction?
3. **Cultural Diversity** What contributions did African Americans make to southern society, government, and culture?

Thinking Critically

1. **Drawing Conclusions** Why might southern culture have increased in popularity during the late 1800s?
2. **Synthesizing Information** If you were a freedperson living in the South in 1870, how would your life have changed after emancipation?
3. **Evaluating** How might the Redeemers' efforts to limit the rights of African Americans affect poor whites?

Writing About History

1. **Informing** Imagine that you are a foreign newspaper reporter in Washington. Write a one-paragraph news article on either the assassination of President Lincoln or President Johnson's impeachment trial.
2. **Describing** Imagine that you are a teacher from the North who moved to the South to teach African Americans after the Civil War. Write a letter to your family telling them about your experiences.

Linking Geography and History

1. **Movement** Why did many freedpeople leave their homes and towns?
2. **Place** Explain why the Civil War left the South a poor region.

Building Your Portfolio

Complete the following activities individually or in groups.

1. **Travel Journal** Imagine that you are traveling through the South during Reconstruction. Create a journal describing what you see. You may wish to include maps of the places you have visited and descriptions of the people you have met.
2. **Freedom** Write a poem or song about an African American who was set free at the end of the Civil War. If you create a poem, find an image to illustrate it. If you write a song, select a musical style in which it would be performed.

History Skills Workshop

Reading Maps Study the map below, which shows historically black colleges and universities, and answer the following questions: (a) According to the map, which state had the most African American colleges and universities? (b) Which states located outside the former Confederacy had African American colleges and universities? (c) Why might most African American colleges and universities have been located in the South?

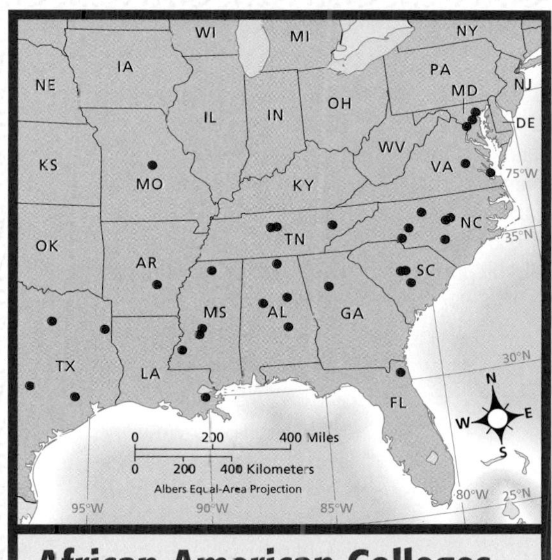

African American Colleges Before 1900

Reviewing Themes

1. Thirteenth—freed the slaves; Fourteenth—extended equal protection under the law to African Americans; Fifteenth—granted the right to vote to African American men

2. by including equal rights for African Americans

3. They wrote about southern society, popularized spirituals, and began to vote and run for office.

Thinking Critically

1. Answers will vary but students may suggest that southern culture became more popular because African Americans were finally allowed to be educated and to speak out about slavery.

2. You would gain freedom and rights to vote, travel, and learn to read and write.

3. Poll taxes may have stopped poor whites from voting, and cutting public funding would have taken money from schools.

Writing About History

1. News article should summarize the main people, facts, reasons, and consequences of either news event.

2. Letters could detail the enthusiasm of the freedpeople for learning to read and also the conditions teachers faced.

Linking Geography and History

1. to test their freedom and to find loved ones

2. War destroyed farms, banks, railroads, and other major parts of the southern economy.

History Skills Workshop

(a) North Carolina;
(b) Missouri, Maryland; (c) The South was where many African Americans still lived.

CHAPTER PLANNING GUIDE
The West

	SECTION LESSON OBJECTIVES	PRINT RESOURCES	MULTIMEDIA RESOURCES	SHELTERED ENGLISH RESOURCES
Section 1: The Wars for the West (pp. 151–57)	★ Describe what life was like for American Indians living on the Great Plains. ★ Explain the causes and results of the conflict between American Indians and U.S. settlers in the West. ★ Evaluate the effect that the Dawes Act and the reservation system had on American Indians.	★ Guided Reading Strategies 5.1 ★ Biography Reading 5: Sarah Winnemucca ★ Graphic Organizer 5: Settling the West ★ Section 1 Review, p. 157 ★ Daily Quiz 5.1	★ *Teaching Resources CD–ROM*, Lesson 5.1 ★ Linking Geography and History Transparency 12A: Native American Resistance, 1830–1890 ★ *Exploring America's Past* Video Segment: The Last Generation; *Teacher's Guide*, pp. 12–13 ★ Art in American History Transparency 15: Navajo Eye Dazzler Blanket ★ HRW Web site	★ Main Idea Activities for Reteaching and Sheltered English 5.1
Section 2: Miners and Railroads (pp. 158–63)	★ Describe the challenges associated with early mining in the West. ★ Examine the problems associated with building the transcontinental railroad. ★ Evaluate the railroads' impact on western settlement and development.	★ Guided Reading Strategies 5.2 ★ Section 2 Review, p. 163 ★ Daily Quiz 5.2	★ *Teaching Resources CD–ROM*, Lesson 5.2 ★ *American History Simulations CD–ROM:* The Gold Rush ★ Everyday Life in America Transparency 14: Currier and Ives View of the West, 1868 ★ Linking Geography and History Transparency 10A: Growth of Transportation, 1840–1890	★ Main Idea Activities for Reteaching and Sheltered English 5.2
Section 3: The Cattle Kingdom (pp. 164–69)	★ Identify the factors that led to the growth of the cattle industry during the 1870s. ★ Describe the life of a cowboy during the cattle boom days of the 1870s. ★ Analyze the decline of the Cattle Kingdom.	★ Guided Reading Strategies 5.3 ★ Primary Source Reading 5: Cowhands and Cattle Drives ★ Section 3 Review, p. 169 ★ Daily Quiz 5.3	★ *Teaching Resources CD–ROM*, Lesson 5.3 ★ *American Music Audio CD Program:* "O Bury Me Not"	★ Main Idea Activities for Reteaching and Sheltered English 5.3
Section 4: Farming the Great Plains (pp. 170–75)	★ Examine the reasons why settlers moved to the Great Plains. ★ Discuss the various challenges that farming families faced on the Plains. ★ Describe daily life on the Plains.	★ Guided Reading Strategies 5.4 ★ Geography Activity 5: The Oklahoma Land Rush ★ Literature Reading 5: *The Life of an Ordinary Woman* ★ Section 4 Review, p. 175 ★ Daily Quiz 5.4	★ *Teaching Resources CD–ROM*, Lesson 5.4 ★ Everyday Life in America Transparency 16: Farming Technology, Late 1800s	★ Main Idea Activities for Reteaching and Sheltered English 5.4
Chapter Review and Assessment (pp. 176–77)		★ Chapter 5 Review, pp. 176–77 ★ Vocabulary Activity 5 ★ Chapter 5 Study Guide ★ Chapter 5 Test (Form A or B)	★ Audio Program, Ch. 5 (English and Spanish) ★ *Global Skill Builder CD–ROM* ★ Chapter 5 Test Generator ★ HRW Web site	★ Spanish Glossary ★ Sheltered English Chapter 5 Test

CHAPTER OVERVIEW

The Great Plains encompass more than one third of the entire United States and were home to the Plains Indians. In the mid-1800s white settlers began moving into the Great Plains. To ensure peace, U.S. officials initially negotiated treaties with the Plains Indians, but later fighting led to the U.S. government's policy of confining Indians to reservations.

After gold was discovered in 1859 near Denver, Colorado, thousands of eastern prospectors began to travel to the West. Many settled there to work in mines owned by large companies. As settlement increased, so did the need for goods and information. After the Civil War, the building of railroads further increased the rate of growth in the West.

Large-scale cattle ranching began in the West after the Civil War, when railroads made it possible to transport cattle to processing plants. Cattle ranching became an extremely profitable business.

The 1880s brought challenges for ranchers. Farmers moving west often bought the land where cattle once roamed. Competition for land led to range wars, and natural catastrophes led to the Cattle Kingdom's decline.

With the adoption of the Homestead Act in 1862, large numbers of settlers began to move west. Although life on the Plains was filled with hard work and loneliness, population growth brought improvements.

CHAPTER INVESTIGATION

The Chapter Investigation is an extended, multipart activity designed for students to work cooperatively and apply the chapter content in the creation of a project. You may choose to use the Chapter 5 Investigation, Cause-and-Effect Time Line, either as a substitute for teaching the section lessons or as an alternate assessment.

BLOCK SCHEDULING 

The teacher lesson plans for each section offer a variety of activity choices to help you present the material in a block scheduling format. For further suggestions on block scheduling, see the *Block Scheduling Handbook with Team Teaching Strategies*, pp. 25–30.

Meeting Individual Needs

ABILITY LEVELS

LEVEL 1 Basic level activities designed for all students encountering new material.

LEVEL 2 Intermediate level activities designed for average students.

LEVEL 3 Challenging activities designed for above-average students.

SHELTERED ENGLISH These activities address the needs of students with Limited English Proficiency.

Smithsonian Institution®

Internet Connections and Lesson 5
www.si.edu/hrw

CNN Presents America:
Yesterday and Today 1850 to the Present
Segment: The Oldest Levis

Additional Resources

Books for Teachers

Brown, Dee. *Bury My Heart At Wounded Knee: An Indian History of the American West.* Holt, 1971. Classic text that gives frontier history from the point of view of American Indians.

Love, Nat. *The Life and Adventures of Nat Love.* University of Nebraska Press, 1995. A memoir by one of the most famous African American cowboys. Originally published in 1907, the memoir covers Love's childhood as a slave and his life as a cowboy.

White, Richard. *"It's Your Misfortune and None of My Own": A History of the American West.* University of Oklahoma Press, 1991. Scholarly history of the West.

Books for Students

Editors of Time-Life Books. *The Wild West.* Warner, 1993. Illustrated general history of the settlement of the West.

Freedman, Russell. *Buffalo Hunt.* Holiday, 1988. A history of how the buffalo were hunted. Examines both the American Indians' way of hunting and the slaughter by whites that brought the buffalo to the brink of extinction.

Wilder, Laura Ingalls. *On the Way Home: The Diary of a Trip From South Dakota to Mansfield, Missouri in 1894.* Harper, 1996. The diary of the writer of the Little House books. Describes her journey to Mansfield, where she would live and write her books. Includes 24 pages of rare photographs.

Multimedia Materials

The Black West. Video, 28 min. Beacon Films. Examines the role of African Americans in westward expansion.

Ghost Town Hunters. Video, 50 min. SSSS. Debunks television and movie myths about the West.

Nez Percé: Portrait of a People. Video, 23 min. National Park Service/SSSS. History of the Nez Percé.

The West

CHAPTER MOTIVATOR

Write the following terms on the chalkboard: *the West, American Indians, cowboys, cattle ranches, settlers, farmers, miners,* and *railroads*. Call on volunteers to provide words that they associate with each of these terms. Under each term, write the words that students provide and discuss why they made the association. Then ask students to identify relationships between the main terms you listed. Conclude by telling students that in this chapter they will learn more about how these terms are interconnected. They will also study the reasons people settled on the Great Plains, the problems that settlement caused for American Indians, the changes that settlement brought to the United States, and what daily life was like in the West.

Presenting Themes

- **Economic Development** Students should mention that the government might provide economic incentives for people to move to that region as well as provide funding for improved transportation and communication in that region.
- **Cultural Diversity** Students might say that the group may impose its beliefs and customs on another, or even invade the other group's territory.
- **Geographic Diversity** Students could suggest that people might adjust to a new environment by forming communities and planting crops.

Using the Time Line

Have students write down several questions about one of the entries on the time line. Their questions should focus on the *who, what, when, where,* and *why* of the event they chose. After students have read the chapter, call on volunteers to answer the questions for each event.

CHAPTER 5

The West

(1850–1890)

After the Civil War, Americans witnessed the rapid growth of the U.S. population and the spread of settlements throughout the West. This flood of miners, ranchers, and farmers transformed the western landscape, as did the railroads that carried them westward. Civil War veteran Ely Parker, who was an American Indian, watched this change with concern. "The Indian [tribes]," he wrote, "are more seriously threatened . . . than ever before."

Economic Development
In what ways might a government promote economic development in a new region?

Cultural Diversity
How might the actions of one group affect the culture of another?

Geographic Diversity
How might people adjust to living in a different environment?

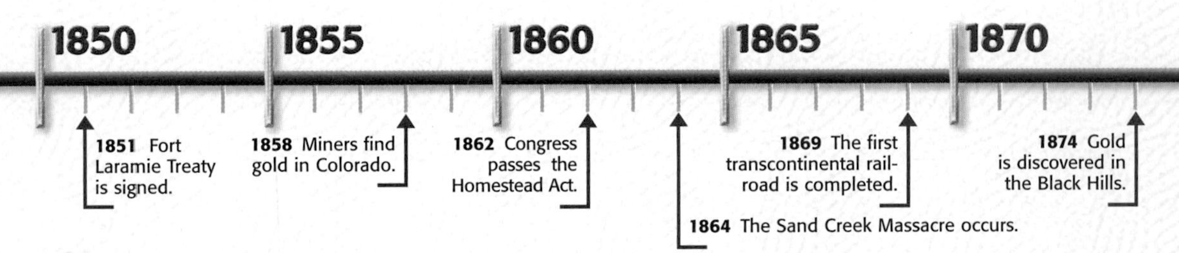

OBJECTIVES

- **Describe what life was like for American Indians living on the Great Plains.**
- **Explain the causes and results of the conflict between American Indians and U.S. settlers in the West.**
- **Evaluate the effect that the Dawes Act and the reservation system had on American Indians.**

FOCUS

Motivate Before Reading

Ask if anyone in the class has ever had to move to another city or state because of a parent's job and have them identify how their lives have changed as a result of the move. Explain to students that in this section they will learn how the U.S. government forced the Plains Indians to leave their lands and how their lives changed as a result.

The Wars for the West

Reading Focus

What was life like for American Indians on the Great Plains?

What were the causes and results of conflict between American Indians and U.S. settlers in the West?

How did the reservation system and the Dawes Act affect American Indians?

Key Terms

Fort Laramie Treaty

reservations

Sand Creek Massacre

Bozeman Trail

Treaty of Medicine Lodge

Battle of the Little Bighorn

Long Walk

Ghost Dance

Massacre at Wounded Knee

Dawes General Allotment Act

LIKE MANY SIOUX BEFORE HIM, Standing Bear was eager for his first buffalo hunt. "Watch the buffalo closely. . . . They are very quick and powerful," warned his father. "They can get their horns under your horse and toss him high in the air." When he got close to the buffalo herd, Standing Bear recalled, "I realized how small I was." He brought down a buffalo and rode proudly back to camp to give his mother the buffalo skin. Buffalo hunts were important to American Indians' way of life on the Great Plains.

The Granger Collection, New York

Cheyenne warrior's shield

Section 1 RESOURCES

PRINT

- ★ Guided Reading Strategies 5.1
- ★ Biography Reading 5: Sarah Winnemucca
- ★ Graphic Organizer 5: Settling the West
- ★ Section 1 Review, p. 157
- ★ Daily Quiz 5.1

MULTIMEDIA

- ★ *Teaching Resources CD–ROM,* Lesson 5.1
- ★ Linking Geography and History Transparency 12A: Native American Resistance, 1830–1890
- ★ *Exploring America's Past* Video Segment: The Last Generation; *Teacher's Guide,* pp. 12–13
- ★ Art in American History Transparency 15: Navajo Eye Dazzler Blanket
- ★ HRW Web site

SHELTERED ENGLISH

- ★ Main Idea Activities for Reteaching and Sheltered English 5.1

IMAGE ON LEFT PAGE: *Plains Indians observe the westward movement of settlers and the railroad in the late 1800s.*

1875 | **1880** | **1885** | **1890**

1876 The Sioux defeat the U.S. Army in the Battle of the Little Bighorn.

1881 Helen Hunt Jackson's *A Century of Dishonor* is published.

1887 Congress approves the Dawes General Allotment Act.

1890 The Massacre at Wounded Knee ends the war between the U.S. Army and Plains Indians.

Introduce Key Terms

Linguistic. Review this section's key terms with students. Work with students to develop a definition for each and ask volunteers to use each term in a sentence. **SHELTERED ENGLISH**

TEACH

Have students read Section 1 and complete Guided Reading Strategies 5.1. Choose one or more of the following activities to explore the section content with students. For further suggestions on block scheduling or team teaching, see the *Block Scheduling Handbook.*

LEVEL 1: Linguistic. (Suggested time: 15 min.) As a class, go over students' Guided Reading Strategies. Then use the Reading Focus questions to highlight the main ideas of the section. **SHELTERED ENGLISH**

ALL LEVELS: Logical-Mathematical, Intrapersonal. (60 min. plus homework) Have students imagine how Cheyenne chief Black Kettle must have felt as he escaped from the Sand Creek Massacre. Tell students to use information from the text to develop an oral history of the events that occurred at Sand Creek. Have students include descriptions of the agreement the Cheyenne had negotiated with the Bureau of Indian Affairs, Cheyenne attempts to show they were peaceful, Colonel

Using Visual Resources

Buffalo Soldiers. The buffalo soldiers, shown in the photograph on this page, were critical in protecting the settlers who moved onto the Plains. Four regiments—two cavalry and two infantry—served for 25 years on the western frontier, fighting American Indians and outlaws in nearly 200 battles. Between 1870 and 1890, fourteen African American soldiers in these regiments were awarded the Medal of Honor for their outstanding service.

Activity: Have students conduct research on the buffalo soldiers and then work in groups to put together a bulletin-board display about the soldiers' 25 years of service.

The Great Plains

The Great Plains lie between the Mississippi River and the Rocky Mountains, stretching north into Canada and south into Texas. Early explorers such as Stephen Long thought that the Great Plains, which were dry and barren except for grasslands, were no better than a desert.

Despite their harshness, the Great Plains were home to the Plains Indians. Groups such as the Apache and the Comanche lived on the southern Plains around Texas and present-day Oklahoma. The Cheyenne and Arapaho roamed across the central Plains. The Pawnee occupied parts of Nebraska, while the Sioux spread north across Minnesota to Montana. Plains Indians spoke many languages and used a common sign language to communicate with each other.

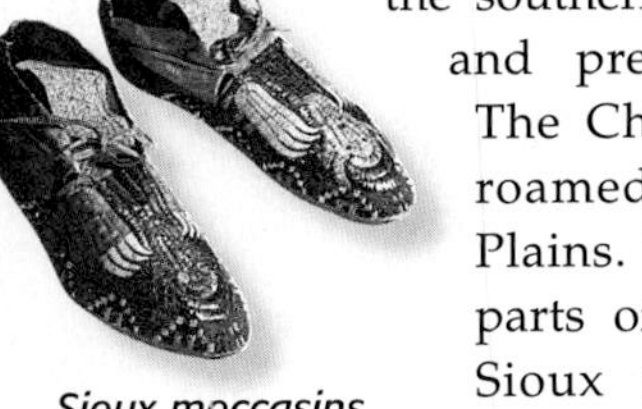
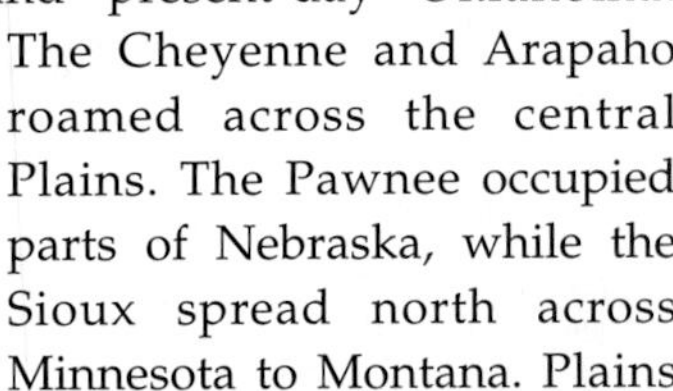

Sioux moccasins

For survival, Plains Indians depended on two animals—the horse and the buffalo. After the Spanish brought horses to America in the 1500s, Plains Indians traveled on horseback and became highly mobile. Indian hunters were able to move onto the Plains year-round, following the herds of buffalo that roamed the land.

Most hunters used a short bow and arrows to shoot the buffalo at close range from horseback. Plains Indians used the buffalo for food, shelter, and tools. Women dried buffalo meat to make jerky. They also made clothing and tepees from buffalo hides and cups and tools from buffalo horns. As one Sioux explained, "When our people killed a buffalo, all of the animal was utilized [used] in some manner; nothing was wasted." With the buffalo providing many of their needs, the Plains Indians prospered. By 1850 some 75,000 American Indians lived on the Plains.

Negotiations and Conflicts

When miners and settlers began crossing the Great Plains in the mid-1800s, U.S. officials sent agents to negotiate treaties with the Plains Indians. The first major agreement was the **Fort Laramie Treaty**, signed with northern Plains tribes in Wyoming in 1851. Two years later, several southern Plains tribes signed a treaty at Fort Atkinson in Kansas.

These treaties accepted Indian claims to most of the Great Plains and allowed the United States to build forts and roads and to travel across Indian homelands. The U.S. government promised to pay for any damages to Indian land. The treaties, however, did not keep the peace for long. After the discovery of gold in present-day Colorado in 1858, thousands of miners came into conflict with the Cheyenne and Arapaho.

In 1861 the U.S. government negotiated new treaties that created **reservations**, areas of federal land set aside for Indians. The Bureau of Indian Affairs operated the reservations. The government expected Indians to stay on the reservations, which made hunting buffalo almost impossible. Many Indians refused to live on reservations. Some continued to fight, while others shared the view of Cheyenne chief Black Kettle. "It is not my intention or wish to fight the whites," he declared. "I want to be friendly and peaceable and keep my tribe so."

He did not get his wish. In November 1864 U.S. Army colonel John M. Chivington led a surprise attack on Black Kettle's camp on Sand Creek

Several African American cavalry regiments served in the western U.S. Army. American Indians nicknamed these African American troops "buffalo soldiers."

Chivington's attacks, and Chief Black Kettle's emotions regarding seeing so many of his people killed. Once students have finished creating their oral histories, have them discuss the significance of the events that occurred at Sand Creek.

ALL LEVELS: Kinesthetic, Visual-Spatial. (Suggested time: 45 min.) On an outline map of the United States, have students highlight the Great Plains. Ask them to locate and identify the area that was home to the major tribes discussed in this section. Finally, have students draw arrows to indicate the location of the reservations where these tribes were forced to relocate. **SHELTERED ENGLISH**

TEACHER TO TEACHER

LEVEL 2: Linguistic, Kinesthetic, Interpersonal. (Suggested time: 45 min. plus homework) Helen Webb of Corpus Christi, Texas, suggested the following activity: Organize the class into small groups and have them use the library to further explore the importance of the buffalo to American Indian culture. You may wish to give the various groups different subtopics to investigate, such as the buffalo's usefulness to American Indians as a source of

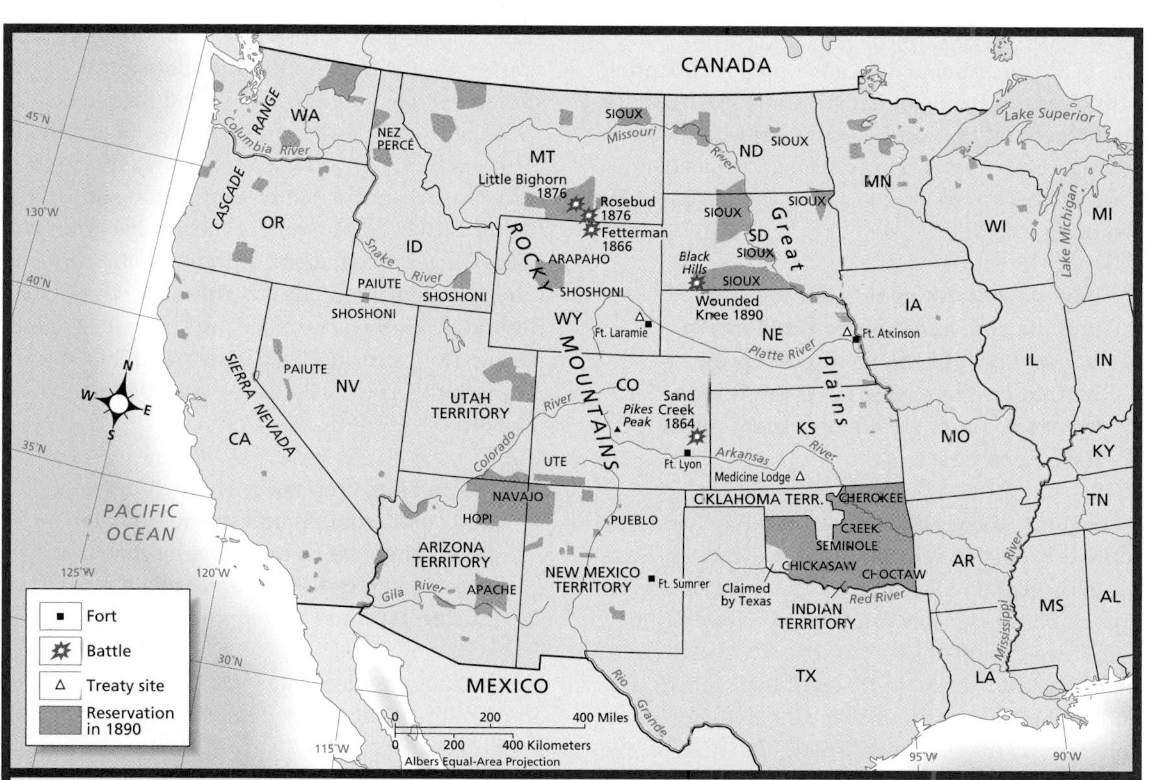

Indian Reservations and Battles to 1890

Learning from Maps As settlers moved to the West, American Indians were forced to accept treaties that placed them on reservations.

Location Which present-day state contained the most reservation lands?

in southeastern Colorado. The Cheyenne raised a white flag and a U.S. flag to show that they were peaceful. Chivington ignored the flags. "Kill and scalp all, big and little," he ordered. The soldiers killed around 200 men, women, and children. Black Kettle was among the Cheyenne who escaped the **Sand Creek Massacre**.

Fighting on the Plains

News of the Sand Creek Massacre spread across the Great Plains. Along with the news came more pioneers, miners, and conflicts.

The Bozeman Trail

Many miners used the **Bozeman Trail**, a route named after pioneer John M. Bozeman that ran from Wyoming to Montana. To protect the miners, the U.S. Army built forts along the trail, which went through Sioux hunting grounds. Sioux chief Red Cloud responded to the army's actions with war. In late 1866 warrior Crazy Horse and a group of Sioux lured 82 cavalry troops to their deaths in an ambush.

William Tecumseh Sherman, the famous Civil War general, had been placed in charge of the western armies. He threatened the "extermination [of the Sioux], men, women, and children." The U.S. Army had little success in this effort, however, and asked Red Cloud to negotiate. He replied, "When we see the soldiers moving away and the forts abandoned, then I will come down and talk." In 1868 the U.S. Army closed the Bozeman Trail and abandoned the forts along it. Many Sioux then moved to the Black Hills Reservation in Dakota Territory.

Historical Sidelight

The Comanche. The Spanish were the first to use the term *Comanche*, but according to anthropologist Marvin K. Opler, the term actually came from the Ute word *Komantcia*, which means "anyone who wants to fight me all the time." To the Spanish, *Komantcia* sounded like *Comanche*.

Critical Thinking: What might the definition of the term *Komantcia* tell us about the relationship between the Comanche and other tribes on the Great Plains?

ANSWER: The term implies that the Comanche were a warring tribe that fought with other tribes of the Great Plains.

Multimedia Resources

Linking Geography and History Transparency 12A: Native American Resistance, 1830–1890

MAP ANSWER

Oklahoma

food and materials for creating shelter and tools. Have each group create a visual display on butcher paper that highlights the uses of the buffalo in the area it studied. Each group should then present its findings to the rest of the class. Finally, have students create a list of all of the ways that American Indians used the buffalo.

LEVEL 3: Logical-Mathematical, Interpersonal, Visual-Spatial. (Suggested time: 90 min.) Organize the class into small groups, and have students use their textbooks to review one of the following: the Battle of the Little Bighorn, the Long Walk, or the Massacre at Wounded Knee. Ask each group to create a one-act play depicting the incident. Have a narrator explain the events that occurred and describe their significance.

LEVEL 3: Visual-Spatial, Interpersonal. (Suggested time: 45 min.) Have students create a graphic organizer (resembling a grid) that compares and contrasts the treatment of the American Indian nations discussed in this chapter. On the vertical axis, have students list the Indian nations. On the horizontal axis, have students identify possible interactions each nation had with the U.S. government, such as signing a treaty, moving to a reservation, and going to war. Have students place a check mark in each box that corresponds to the Indian nation mentioned and the interactions that occurred. Once students have finished, discuss the similarities and differences that existed between the interactions that each nation had with the U.S. government.

Using Visual Resources

The Battle of the Little Bighorn. The Battle of the Little Bighorn, shown on this page in an 1889 lithograph by Kurz and Allison, is one of the most commonly depicted images in Western art. As with much of the art that depicts life in the old West, the paintings of the battle are more romantic than they are historically accurate. They portray Custer and his troops bravely fighting the Indians in the face of defeat.

Critical Thinking: If you were living in the East and saw this picture in your newspaper, what would you think about life in the West?

ANSWER: Answers will vary but may include the belief that life in the West was dangerous yet heroic.

Multimedia Resources

Exploring America's Past Video Segment: The Last Generation; *Teacher's Guide*, pp. 12–13

Search 26361, Play to 32607
Videodisc White Side A

Play

Pause

See *Teacher's Guide* for Spanish barcode.

The Comanche

The U.S. government was also busy negotiating with southern Plains Indians. In the 1867 **Treaty of Medicine Lodge**, most of these tribes agreed to live on reservations. Many Comanche leaders in Texas disapproved of the treaty, however. Chief Ten Bears asked:

> **"Why do you ask us to leave the rivers, and the sun, and the wind, and live in houses? Do not ask us to give up the buffalo for the sheep. . . . If the Texans had kept out of my country, there might have been peace."**

Fighting soon broke out between the Comanche and the Texans. When the U.S. Army and the Texas Rangers were unable to defeat the Comanche warriors in battle, the U.S. forces tried a new strategy. The army cut off the Comanche's access to food and water and captured many of their horses. The Comanche could not survive under these conditions. In 1875 Quanah Parker, the last of the Comanche war leaders, surrendered.

The U.S. War with the Sioux

While fighting on the southern Plains was ending, new trouble was starting to the north. In 1874 Lieutenant Colonel George Armstrong Custer's soldiers discovered gold in the Black Hills. The U.S. government responded by insisting that the Sioux who lived in the area sell their reservation land in the Black Hills. Sitting Bull, a Sioux shaman, or spiritual leader, protested these new demands:

> **"What treaty that the whites have kept has the red man broken? Not one. What treaty that the white man ever made with us have they kept? Not one."**

Other Sioux leaders listened to Sitting Bull and refused to give up the Black Hills. Fighting soon started between the U.S. Army and the Sioux.

Custer, a Civil War veteran, was in command of the U.S. Army 7th Cavalry. On June 25, 1876, his scouts found a Sioux camp along the Little Bighorn River in Montana. Leading 264 of his soldiers, Custer raced ahead without waiting for any reinforcements. In the **Battle of the Little Bighorn**, Sioux warriors led by Crazy Horse and Sitting Bull surrounded Custer and his troops. Sitting Bull's cousin Pte-San-Waste-Win described the battle that followed:

> **"The soldiers fired many shots, but the Sioux shot straight and the soldiers fell dead. When we came to the hill there were no soldiers living and Long Hair [Custer] lay dead among the rest."**

Newspapers called the battle "Custer's Last Stand." It was the worst defeat the U.S. Army suffered in the West.

The Battle of the Little Bighorn was also the Sioux's last major victory. In late 1877 Crazy Horse was killed after surrendering to the U.S. Army. Sitting Bull fled to Canada with a few of his followers. With two of their most important leaders gone, the northern Plains Indians soon surrendered to the U.S. Army.

At the Battle of the Little Bighorn, a troop of the 7th Cavalry suffered a devastating defeat at the hands of Sioux warriors. None of the cavalry troops survived the battle.

CLOSE

Logical-Mathematical, Visual-Spatial. To conclude the lesson, ask students to make a chart with three columns. In the first two columns, have students list the names of Plains Indian tribes and the treaties they signed. For the third column, ask students to summarize in one or two sentences how the treaty affected the tribe's way of life.

CHALLENGE AND EXTEND

1. **Linguistic, Logical-Mathematical, Interpersonal.** Organize the class into small groups. Pair each group with another group. Have one group represent white settlers' interests, and the other American Indians' interests. Groups should work together to formulate a compromise between the white settlers and the Plains Indians that satisfies both groups and then explain the compromise to the class.
2. **Linguistic, Logical-Mathematical, Interpersonal.** Have students use the library to locate information on non-Plains Indian tribes and any treaties these tribes may have made with the U.S. government. Ask students to compare the Plains Indians' treaties to the other treaties that they researched. Finally, have students report their findings to the class.

Indians in the Southwest and Far West

Far from the Great Plains, other American Indians fought against their relocation to reservations. Their struggles were rarely successful.

The Long Walk

In 1863 the U.S. government ordered the Navajo of present-day Arizona and New Mexico to settle on a reservation. The Navajo refused. Kit Carson, a former scout, led U.S. troops in raids on the Navajo's fields, homes, and livestock. Then he lay siege to the Navajo warriors, who were in a well-defended canyon in northeastern Arizona.

When the Navajo ran out of food and shelter, they started surrendering to the U.S. Army. In 1864 the army led Navajo captives on the **Long Walk**, a 300-mile march across the desert to a reservation at Bosque Redondo, New Mexico. Along the way, hundreds of Navajo died. At Bosque Redondo the Navajo suffered harsh conditions until 1868, when they negotiated for a new reservation located in Arizona and New Mexico.

The Nez Percé

While the Navajo were moving to their new reservation, the U.S. government was promising to let the peaceful Nez Percé keep their homelands in northeastern Oregon. Within a few years, however, settlers persuaded the government to move the Nez Percé to a reservation in present-day Idaho.

Nez Percé leader Chief Joseph reluctantly agreed to move. Before leaving, a few angry Nez Percé killed some settlers. Fearing revenge, the Nez Percé fled. The U.S. Army chased this band of around 700 Indians across Idaho, Wyoming, and Montana. Although outnumbered, the band defeated or avoided the army for weeks before trying to escape to Canada. Less than 40 miles

Biography

Chief Joseph. Chief Joseph is said to have been a brave and peace-loving man who recommended complying with the U.S. government's policies. His followers, however, did not wish to do so. After he was taken prisoner, he was sent to Oklahoma. He was later sent to Colville Reservation in Washington State, where he died in 1904.

Critical Thinking: What do you think the government should have done in response to Chief Joseph's request? Why?

ANSWER: Students will likely say that they think that Joseph and his people should have been allowed to return to their homeland.

American Literature

"I Will Fight No More Forever"

Chief Joseph

Chief Joseph led the Nez Percé from 1871 to 1877. He gave the following speech to the U.S. Army officers who took him prisoner on October 5, 1877.

Tell General Howard I know his heart. What he told me before, I have in my heart. I am tired of fighting. Our chiefs are killed. . . . The old men are all dead. It is the young men who say yes and no. He who led on the young men [Joseph's brother, Alokut] is dead. It is cold and we have no blankets. The little children are freezing to death. My people, some of them, have run away to the hills, and have no blankets, no food; no one knows where they are perhaps freezing to death. I want to have time to look for my children and see how many I can find. Maybe I shall find them among the dead. Hear me, my chiefs. I am tired; my heart is sick and sad. From where the sun now stands I will fight no more forever.

Chief Joseph

Understanding Literature

1. How does Chief Joseph express his grief for the condition of his people?
2. Why does Chief Joseph want to "fight no more forever"?

Multimedia Resources

Art in American History Transparency 15: Navajo Eye Dazzler Blanket

AMERICAN LITERATURE ANSWERS

1. by pointing out how they have been treated
2. He says he is tired, sick, and sad from seeing his people die.

3. **Linguistic, Logical-Mathematical.** Have students use the library to find out more information about the Battle of the Little Bighorn, the Massacre at Wounded Knee, and the rise of the religious movement known as the Ghost Dance. Explain to students that the U.S. government and the Sioux viewed these events in very different ways. Have students use their research to create two descriptions of each of these events. The first description should be from the point of view of the U.S. government, while the second description should be based on Sioux interpretations of the events. Encourage volunteers to share their descriptions with the rest of the class.

4. **Linguistic, Intrapersonal.** Have students use the library to find information about one of the American Indian leaders discussed in this section. Tell students to write a paper about the leader that contains the following elements: a description of the leader's tribe and where he originally lived and was forced to move; the interactions (if any) the leader had with the U.S. government; and an evaluation of how the leader's actions affected his tribe. Ask for volunteers to share information with the class about the leaders they studied. Then place all of the reports in a binder so that other classes can view them.

Biography

Geronimo. Geronimo, whose Apache name, Goyathlay, means "one who yawns," is one of the few Indian leaders during the wars for the West to have died from natural causes. After his final surrender, Geronimo was sentenced to perform hard labor in a Florida work camp. In 1894 he was sent to Fort Still, Oklahoma, where he died on February 17, 1909. According to those who worked with him in Oklahoma, Geronimo never lost his fighting spirit and volatile disposition. When General George Crook visited the Oklahoma reservation in 1890, he found Geronimo in the schoolhouse threatening with a stick any children who misbehaved.

Activity: Have students conduct an Internet search through the HRW Web site for information on Geronimo. Then ask them to write a diary entry that Geronimo might have written during his lifetime.

go.hrw.com
SB1 Geronimo

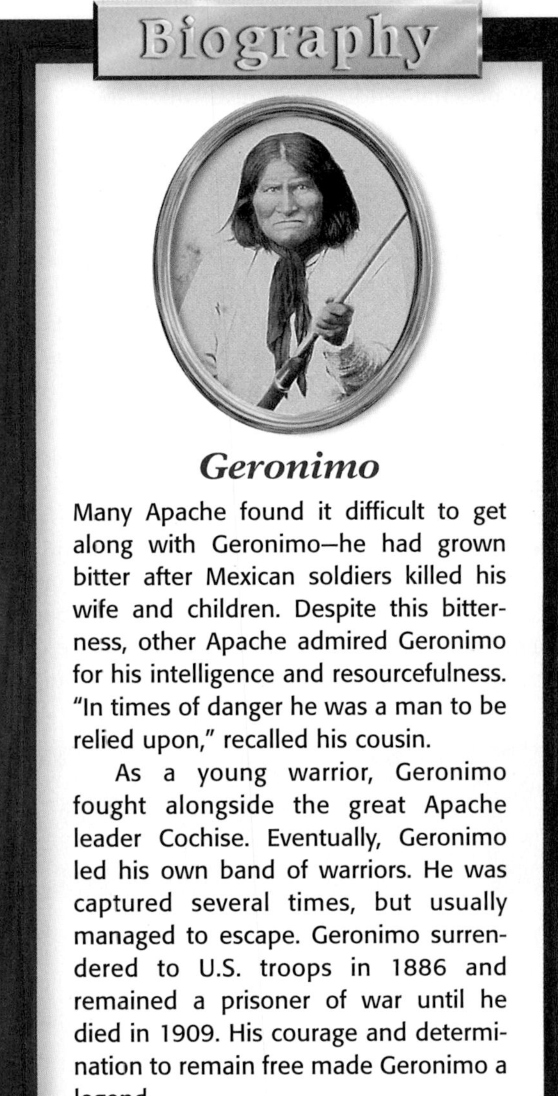

Geronimo

Many Apache found it difficult to get along with Geronimo—he had grown bitter after Mexican soldiers killed his wife and children. Despite this bitterness, other Apache admired Geronimo for his intelligence and resourcefulness. "In times of danger he was a man to be relied upon," recalled his cousin.

As a young warrior, Geronimo fought alongside the great Apache leader Cochise. Eventually, Geronimo led his own band of warriors. He was captured several times, but usually managed to escape. Geronimo surrendered to U.S. troops in 1886 and remained a prisoner of war until he died in 1909. His courage and determination to remain free made Geronimo a legend.

from the border, U.S. troops overtook and surrounded the Nez Percé. Chief Joseph surrendered on October 5, 1877, and the U.S. government sent the Nez Percé to a reservation in present-day Oklahoma.

The End of Armed Resistance

By the 1880s most American Indians had stopped fighting. The Apache of the Southwest, however, continued to battle the U.S. Army. The Apache were fierce raiders, known for their ability to survive in the desert. Settlers living illegally on Apache lands feared them. In the 1870s the U.S. Army gathered some Apache on a reservation in San Carlos, Arizona. One Apache called the reservation "nothing but cactus, rattlesnakes, heat, rocks, and insects."

A Chiricahua Apache named Geronimo and his small band of warriors left the reservation and resisted capture until 1884. The next year Geronimo escaped again. When the U.S. Army caught him, he broke free once more on the way to the reservation. "I feared treachery [dishonesty]," he said. This time the army sent 5,000 soldiers to capture Geronimo and 24 of his followers. Finally, in September 1886, he surrendered, ending the Apache armed resistance. The U.S. government sent Geronimo and all Chiricahua Apache to Florida as prisoners of war.

The Ghost Dance and Wounded Knee

Meanwhile, in 1881 Sitting Bull and his Sioux followers returned from Canada after running out of food during the hard winter. "I wish it to be remembered," Sitting Bull said, "that I was the last man of my tribe to surrender my rifle." He joined most of the Sioux on Standing Rock Reservation in Dakota Territory. Black Elk, a Sioux shaman, described the difficulties of reservation life: "All our people now were settling down in square gray houses . . . around them the [whites] had drawn a line to keep them in. . . . The people were in despair."

At this time a religious movement known as the **Ghost Dance** began. Wovoka, a Paiute Indian, predicted the arrival of a paradise in which Indians would live freely and at peace. The buffalo herds would return and the settlers would disappear. This paradise was for those Indians who performed the sacred Ghost Dance.

When the Ghost Dance spread across the Plains, U.S. officials did not understand its meaning. They did, however, fear that it would inspire the Sioux to rebel. While following orders to arrest Sioux leaders, reservation police killed Sitting Bull in 1890. In response, many Sioux left the reservations. Later that year, the U.S. Army found a camp of Sioux near Wounded Knee Creek in South Dakota. When the two groups faced one another,

REVIEW

Linguistic, Logical-Mathematical, Intrapersonal. Have students complete the Section Review questions. Then ask them to analyze how they think the Dawes General Allotment Act and the reservation system changed American Indians' ways of life. Students should then write one journal entry from the point of view of a Plains Indian that explains what life was like before the Dawes Act and the reservation system, and another entry that describes what life was like afterward.

ASSESS

Have students complete Daily Quiz 5.1.

RETEACH

Linguistic, Logical-Mathematical. Have students complete Main Idea Activities for Reteaching and Sheltered English 5.1. Then ask them to read the Reading Focus questions at the beginning of the section and summarize their understanding of each topic in three sentences or less. **SHELTERED ENGLISH**

a shot rang out. The U.S. troops began firing and killed at least 150 Indians. This **Massacre at Wounded Knee** marked the end of more than 25 years of war on the Great Plains.

Policy and Protest

By the 1870s many American Indian tribes were living on reservations. Indian leaders spoke out against the reservation system, complaining that Bureau agents stole government food and money meant for Indians. In addition, reservation land was usually not suitable for farming or buffalo hunting. As a result, many Indians were starving.

In the late 1870s a Paiute Indian named Sarah Winnemucca became one of the first Indians to call for reform. "Day after day my people were begging me to go east to talk for them," she explained. She eventually pleaded her case in Washington. She also gave lectures on the need to reform the reservation system. After listening to her, "many people were moved to tears," according to one spectator.

Another person pushing for reservation reform was writer Helen Hunt Jackson. In 1881 she published *A Century of Dishonor*, which criticized the federal government's treatment of Indians. She wrote that "it makes little difference where one opens the record of the history of the Indians; every page and every year has its dark stain." The popularity of Jackson's writings helped spread the reform message.

Once the major wars for the West had ended, many reformers believed that Indians would be better off if they adopted the ways of white people. Congress passed the **Dawes General Allotment Act** in 1887 to lessen the tribal influence on Indian society by making land ownership private rather than shared. The Dawes Act split up reservation lands and divided them among individual Indians. Families were supposed to receive 160 acres, single adults 80 acres. The act also promised U.S. citizenship to American Indians.

The Granger Collection, New York

Sarah Winnemucca

After it split up the reservations, the government sold the land that remained unassigned. As a result, Indians lost much of the land that they occupied before the Dawes Act. Despite the hopes of reformers, the Dawes Act claimed more land from American Indians than all the wars combined, did not grant them citizenship as promised, and failed to improve their lives.

SECTION 1 REVIEW

Identify and explain the significance of the following:

- **Fort Laramie Treaty**
- **reservations**
- **Sand Creek Massacre**
- **Bozeman Trail**
- **Treaty of Medicine Lodge**
- **George Armstrong Custer**
- **Sitting Bull**
- **Battle of the Little Bighorn**
- **Long Walk**
- **Geronimo**
- **Ghost Dance**
- **Massacre at Wounded Knee**
- **Sarah Winnemucca**
- **Dawes General Allotment Act**

Reading for Content Understanding

1. **Main Idea** What events started the wars in the West?
2. **Main Idea** What were the consequences of the wars in the West?
3. **Geographic Diversity** *Region* Why were the horse and buffalo important for the Plains Indians?
4. **Writing** *Describing* Imagine that you are an American Indian who will be affected by the Dawes Act. Write a letter to a member of Congress describing how your life has changed since living on the reservation and how the Dawes Act will affect you.
5. **Critical Thinking** *Evaluating* Why do you think the Ghost Dance was important to American Indians in the West?

Section 1 Review ANSWERS

Identify

For significance, see the following pages:

- Fort Laramie Treaty, p. 152
- reservations, p. 152
- Sand Creek Massacre, p. 153
- Bozeman Trail, p. 153
- Treaty of Medicine Lodge, p. 154
- George Armstrong Custer, p. 154
- Sitting Bull, p. 154
- Battle of the Little Bighorn, p.154
- Long Walk, p. 155
- Geronimo, p. 156
- Ghost Dance, p. 156
- Massacre at Wounded Knee, p. 157
- Sarah Winnemucca, p. 157
- Dawes General Allotment Act, p. 157

Reading for Content Understanding

1. Incidents include territorial disputes, discovery of gold, and relocation programs.

2. The U.S. government divided reservations and gave land to American Indian families and individuals, then sold the rest of the land.

3. Horses provided mobility, and buffalo provided food, shelter, and tools.

4. Letters should mention that reservations deprived Indians of many cultural traditions and that owning land would be preferable to living on a reservation.

5. It inspired hope among the Indians that their native way of life would return.

Section 2 Lesson Plan

OBJECTIVES

- Describe the challenges associated with early mining in the West.
- Examine the problems associated with building the transcontinental railroad.
- Evaluate the railroads' impact on western settlement and development.

FOCUS

Motivate Before Reading

Ask students to discuss the possible dangers and other problems of working in a mine or laying a railroad line. *(Students might mention dangerous conditions such as mines emitting poisonous gases or collapsing, or poor working conditions such as long hours, hard work, or low pay.)* Then tell students that despite these problems, mining and the building of railroads helped to settle the West.

Section 2 RESOURCES

PRINT
- ★ Guided Reading Strategies 5.2
- ★ Section 2 Review, p. 163
- ★ Daily Quiz 5.2

MULTIMEDIA
- ★ *Teaching Resources CD–ROM,* Lesson 5.2
- ★ *American History Simulations CD–ROM:* The Gold Rush
- ★ Everyday Life in America Transparency 14: Currier and Ives View of the West, 1868
- ★ Linking Geography and History Transparency 10A: Growth of Transportation, 1840–1890

SHELTERED ENGLISH
- ★ Main Idea Activities for Reteaching and Sheltered English 5.2

Miners and Railroads

Reading Focus

What were some of the challenges of mining in the West?

What obstacles did the builders of the transcontinental railroad face?

How did the transcontinental railroad affect the settlement and development of the West?

Key Terms

Comstock Lode
bonanza
boom towns
Pony Express
transcontinental railroad
Pacific Railway Acts

IN 1859 GREAT EXCITEMENT swept the United States when news reached the East of a Colorado gold strike in 1858. Traveling west to examine this find, New York Tribune *editor Horace Greeley announced that the "discovery is . . . the richest and greatest [gold mine] in America." Thousands of prospectors in wagons labeled "Pikes Peak or Bust" raced west to the mining region around Pikes Peak. Most of these "fifty-niners," as they were called, traveled hundreds of miles only to find that the early prospectors had started the rush by filling part of their mine with extra gold.*

Gold ore

The Mining Booms

Many fifty-niners, still full of excitement created by the California Gold Rush, continued to search for strikes. Some miners found gold in other parts of Colorado. Gold rushes also occurred in Idaho in 1862 and two years later in Montana.

The Comstock Lode

The same year that miners rushed to Pikes Peak, prospectors Peter O'Riley and Patrick McLaughlin struck gold and silver in western Nevada. Their good fortune attracted the attention of miner Henry Comstock, who convinced the partners that he owned the water source they were using at the mine. O'Riley and McLaughlin gave Comstock a share in their find to avoid legal trouble. Comstock bragged that he had found the mine, and the discovery became known as the **Comstock Lode**.

Within a year, thousands of California miners arrived, and Virginia City sprang up almost overnight. The Comstock Lode was a **bonanza**—a large deposit of precious ore. In the next 20 years, the Lode produced nearly $400 million worth of gold and silver.

Introduce Key Terms

Linguistic. Review this section's key terms with students. Show as many pictures as possible that illustrate the terms. Then explain the connection between the pictures and the terms and discuss what students think each term means and how it applies to the mines and railroads. **SHELTERED ENGLISH**

TEACH

Have students read Section 2 and complete Guided Reading Strategies 5.2. Choose one or more of the following activities to explore the section content with students. For further suggestions on block scheduling or team teaching, see the *Block Scheduling Handbook*.

LEVEL 1: Linguistic. (Suggested time: 15 min.) As a class, go over students' Guided Reading Strategies. Then use the Reading Focus questions to highlight the main ideas of the section. **SHELTERED ENGLISH**

LEVEL 1: Linguistic. (Suggested time: 20 min.) Discuss with students the significant gold discoveries that led people west in search of gold. Explain to students that many prospectors had signs on their wagons declaring where they were going. For example, many prospectors' wagons held signs reading "Pikes Peak

These miners are bringing ore out of a mine shaft along the Comstock Lode in the 1860s.

Mining Companies

Comstock sold his share of the mine to a big corporation for $11,000. Large companies had the funds needed to remove the silver and gold trapped within the quartz rock. To get this quartz, miners dug and blasted tunnels hundreds of feet long into the mountain. Then they loaded the ore onto mining carts and brought it to the surface. The ore was usually shipped by train to a refining center, where powerful stamping mills crushed the ore, and large machines called smelters melted the pieces so that the metal could be separated. Mining became a big business as large companies bought up mining claims from miners who could not afford such expensive equipment.

 A Miner's Life

As companies dug bigger and deeper mines in the West, the work became more dangerous. Miners risked their lives every day that they went underground.

Working in the Mines

To ride down into the mines, miners squeezed together on elevator platforms just a few feet wide. These "cages" had no walls, and a careless move or an accident could pin a miner between the wall and the moving cage with deadly results. Down in the poorly lit tunnels, miners used picks, drills, and explosives to get to the gold- and silver-rich rock. In the 1860s miners began using power drills, which produced dust that caused serious lung problems. Unexpected explosions killed or injured many miners. In addition, dynamite explosions sometimes created poisonous gases.

In the deeper tunnels, temperatures often rose above 130°F. An Idaho miner recalled that in the cold winters, "I came off work soaked to the skin, and before reaching home all my clothes were frozen fast on me and I couldn't take them off myself." The hot, stuffy air was often filled with toxic gases. Some tunnels had so little oxygen that candles would not burn. Cave-ins and floods from underground springs sometimes killed miners or trapped them below ground. The threat of fire in the mines was also a great concern. With all these hazards, mining was one of the most dangerous jobs in the country. In the West, concerns about safety and wages led to the creation of several miners' unions in the 1860s.

The Miners

In addition to the dangerous work, miners faced other difficulties. Many Mexican immigrants and Mexican Americans were experienced miners, skilled in assaying, or testing, the contents of valuable ore. Despite their skill, they were often denied the better-paying mining jobs. Chinese immigrants faced similar job discrimination.

People from all over the world worked in the western mines. Some miners came from the eastern United States, while others immigrated from Europe, Central and South America, Asia, and Australia. Some miners hoped to get rich and return to their native countries, but most hoped to stay in the United States.

Mining Towns

Mining booms also produced **boom towns**, communities that grew suddenly when a mine opened and disappeared just as quickly when the mine closed down. Most boom towns had general stores, saloons, and boardinghouses. Business owners charged high prices for goods and services. This was partly to make a big profit and partly because most merchandise had to be shipped west and then transported to the remote mining communities. "The sociable [friendly] man is lost in the money making," admitted one store

Economic Development

Mining Unions. In response to the harsh working conditions associated with mining, in 1864 the Miners' Protective Association (MPA) organized the first strike of miners in the Comstock Lode. The demands of the MPA—increased wages, improved working conditions, and shorter hours—spread throughout the mining industry. In 1893 the labor movement expanded to the city of Butte, Montana. There, the Western Federation of Miners (WFM) organized other labor groups in the hope of preventing the U.S. military from intervening in labor disputes. By 1903 the WFM had more than 50,000 members.

Critical Thinking: What purpose do unions serve?

ANSWER: Unions provide a central agency that promotes the well-being of a specific group of workers.

Multimedia Resources

American History Simulations CD–ROM: The Gold Rush

or Bust." Have students choose one of the locations where gold was discovered and create a sign for a wagon that describes the destination. Encourage students to create brief but catchy signs that people can read at a glance and easily remember. Ask volunteers to explain their signs to the rest of the class.
SHELTERED ENGLISH

LEVEL 2: Linguistic, Visual-Spatial, Logical-Mathematical. (Suggested time: 45 min.) Explain to students that although many individuals traveled west to get rich quick, mining soon became a company business. Tell students that running a mine was very expensive. Have students review material from this section about mining companies to create a flowchart describing the mining process. Then have students write a paragraph underneath their flowcharts that explains how this process forced individual miners out and allowed mining companies to buy their claims.

ALL LEVELS: Visual-Spatial, Interpersonal. (Suggested time: 45 min.) Organize the class into two groups. Assign one group the task of using the text to review the difficulties associated with mining in the West, and have the other group review the problems associated with western railroad building. Each group should prepare a short television news documentary that describes these difficulties. After both groups have made their presentations, have students create a chart comparing the problems faced during these two tasks.

Biography

Clara Brown. Clara Brown, a former slave, was one of the "fifty-niners" to arrive in Colorado looking for a better life. Following the gold miners, she moved to Central City, Colorado, where she set up a laundry in the mining camp. Brown later expanded her services to include nursing care, a Sunday school, and a shelter for the less-fortunate people in the camp. Those who could not afford to pay were not turned away, and "Aunt Clara" became legendary throughout Colorado for her good deeds. After saving $10,000, she returned to Virginia and Kentucky to find relatives she had left behind. She returned to Colorado with 34 of them and lived there until her death at age 82.

Critical Thinking: What types of services do you think the mining camps needed?

ANSWER: In addition to laundry, services might include boot repair, sewing, and cooking.

Multimedia Resources

Everyday Life in America Transparency 14: Currier and Ives View of the West, 1868

Families faced many hardships in the early mining camps.

owner. In his autobiographical work *Roughing It*, Mark Twain described Virginia City during its boom years:

> **"[It] had grown to be the 'livest' town . . . that America had ever produced. The sidewalks swarmed with people. . . . The streets themselves were just as crowded. . . . Money-getting schemes . . . were . . . in every brain."**

Boom towns were dangerous places that lacked basic law and order. "To be raised in a mining camp," as one man put it, "means an experience as full of thrills and wounds and scars as going to the war." There were few women or families in most boom towns. In 1860, for example, there were more than 75 men for every woman in Virginia City. Most women who lived in mining towns faced a life of hard work and few friends. "I was never so lonely and homesick in all my life," wrote one young woman.

Women contributed to the local economy by washing, cooking, making clothes, chopping wood, and growing food for the miners. Women also helped turn some mining camps into successful permanent communities by raising families, teaching in schools, and writing for local papers. Such efforts drew more Americans to the West.

Crossing the Continent

More Americans began moving west, increasing the need to send goods and information between the East and West. The **Pony Express**, established in 1860, used a system of messengers on horseback to carry mail from one relay station to another along a 2,000-mile route. Telegraph lines, which sent messages faster, quickly put the Pony Express out of business.

Some Americans hoped to improve communication and travel across the country by building a **transcontinental railroad** to connect the East to the West. Many businesspeople and politicians were confident that such a railroad could be built despite the many geographic obstacles and the expensive labor and resources needed.

Poster advertising the Pony Express

To help railroad companies overcome these difficulties, the federal government passed the **Pacific Railway Acts** in 1862 and in 1864. These acts gave railroad companies loans and large land grants, which could be sold to pay for construction costs. By 1872 Congress had granted more than 125 million acres of public land to railroad companies. In exchange, the government required the railroads to carry U.S. mail and troops at reduced rates. These acts inspired many companies to begin laying tracks.

 The Great Race

Two companies, the Central Pacific and the Union Pacific, took the lead in the great race to complete the transcontinental railroad. In February 1863 the Central Pacific began building east from Sacramento, California. At the end of the year, the Union Pacific started in Omaha, Nebraska, and headed west.

Working on the Railroad

To build its railroad, the Union Pacific hired thousands of workers, particularly Irish immigrants.

LEVEL 3: Linguistic, Logical-Mathematical. (Suggested time: 45 min. plus homework) Tell students that they have been selected to be advertising executives for P&T Railroad. Their job is to increase public awareness of the company's influence on immigration to the West and the speed of travel to the West, as well as improvements in communications and the growth of western businesses. Have students use the text and notes from class to determine the effect of railroad development on each of these topics. Then have students design posters with at least two paragraphs of advertising copy and illustrations that promote the railroad.

CLOSE

Logical-Mathematical, Intrapersonal. To conclude the lesson, ask students to name the western states located in the Great Plains. Write their responses on the chalkboard and have students brainstorm as many facts as they can about each of the states (main cities, goods produced, and main attractions). Finally, discuss with students whether they believe mining, the railroad, or both were responsible for the current development of the western states.

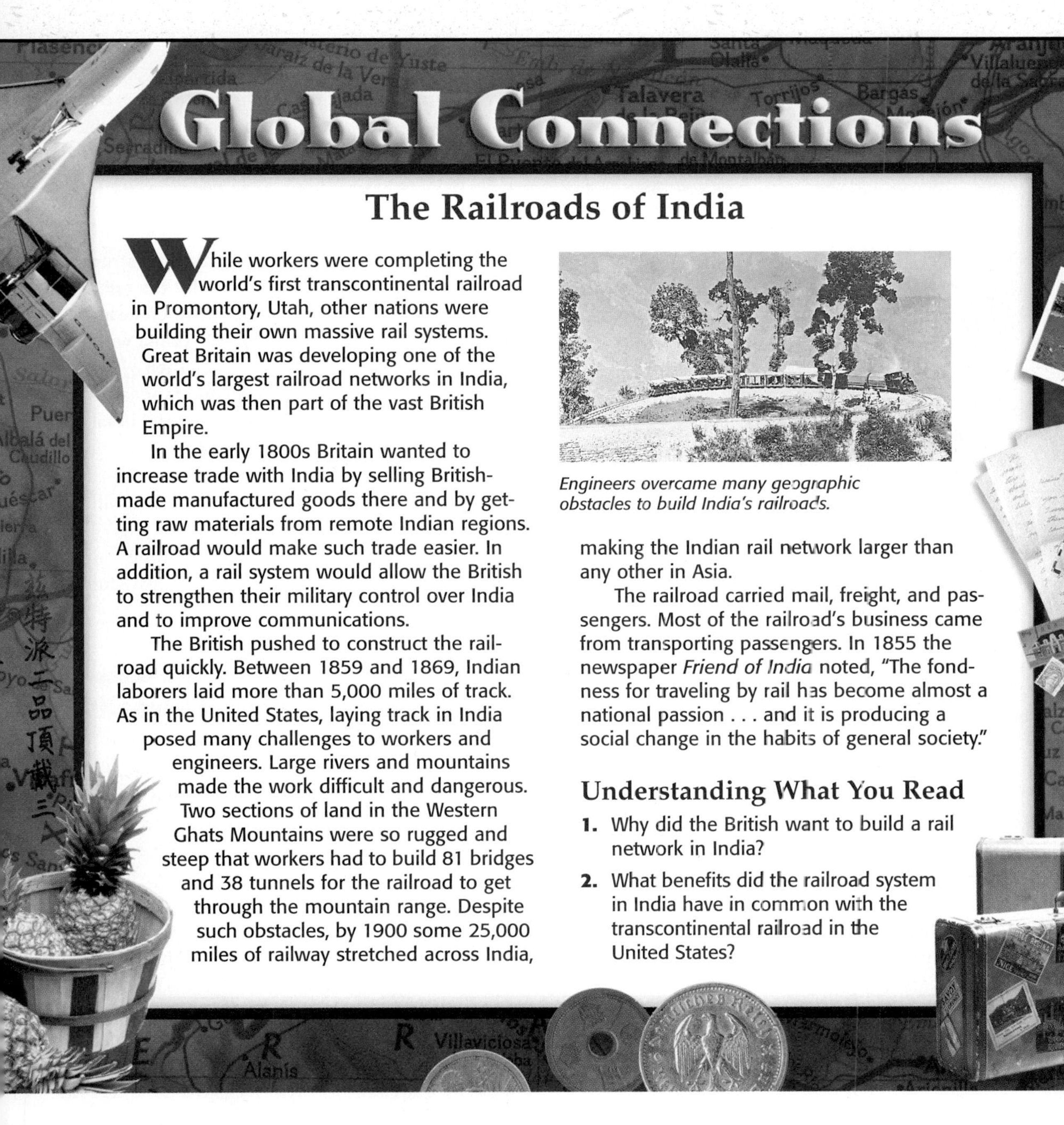

Global Connections

The Railroads of India

While workers were completing the world's first transcontinental railroad in Promontory, Utah, other nations were building their own massive rail systems. Great Britain was developing one of the world's largest railroad networks in India, which was then part of the vast British Empire.

In the early 1800s Britain wanted to increase trade with India by selling British-made manufactured goods there and by getting raw materials from remote Indian regions. A railroad would make such trade easier. In addition, a rail system would allow the British to strengthen their military control over India and to improve communications.

The British pushed to construct the railroad quickly. Between 1859 and 1869, Indian laborers laid more than 5,000 miles of track. As in the United States, laying track in India posed many challenges to workers and engineers. Large rivers and mountains made the work difficult and dangerous. Two sections of land in the Western Ghats Mountains were so rugged and steep that workers had to build 81 bridges and 38 tunnels for the railroad to get through the mountain range. Despite such obstacles, by 1900 some 25,000 miles of railway stretched across India, making the Indian rail network larger than any other in Asia.

Engineers overcame many geographic obstacles to build India's railroads.

The railroad carried mail, freight, and passengers. Most of the railroad's business came from transporting passengers. In 1855 the newspaper *Friend of India* noted, "The fondness for traveling by rail has become almost a national passion . . . and it is producing a social change in the habits of general society."

Understanding What You Read

1. Why did the British want to build a rail network in India?
2. What benefits did the railroad system in India have in common with the transcontinental railroad in the United States?

Economic Development

Asa Whitney. In 1845 New York merchant and trader Asa Whitney proposed that Congress grant land to an independent firm to build a railroad extending from Lake Superior to the Pacific Ocean. When Congress did not respond, Whitney launched a propaganda campaign. Other powerful people around the nation joined his campaign, as they too hoped to profit from expanded East-West trade. Their efforts did not pay off until the need to ship California gold to East Coast banks forced Congress to respond. In 1853 the U.S. Army began surveying routes for a transcontinental railroad.

Critical Thinking: Why do you think Whitney was so interested in the construction of an East-West railway?

ANSWER: Such a railway would open up trade between the East and the West and thus provide a larger market for Whitney to sell his goods.

GLOBAL CONNECTIONS ANSWERS

1. Britain wanted to increase trade with India, strengthen and extend its military control over India, and improve communications.
2. Answers will vary but may include that both railroads carried mail, freight, and passengers.

Some laborers were Civil War veterans. Under former brigadier general Jack Casement, "the Casement Army" worked long, hard days laying rails across the Great Plains.

Chinese immigrants made up some 85 percent of the Central Pacific workforce. The railroad's part-owner Leland Stanford praised these Chinese workers as "quiet, peaceful, [and] industrious" but paid them less than white laborers. Chinese crews were also given the most dangerous jobs and were required to work longer hours than other railroad laborers. Nonetheless, Chinese workers took on the job because the $30 a month that the Central Pacific paid was in some cases 10 times as high as wages in China.

Geographic Obstacles

The Central Pacific workers struggled to cross the Sierra Nevada range in California. Breaking apart

CHALLENGE AND EXTEND

1. **Linguistic, Visual-Spatial, Kinesthetic.** Have half of the class research the Union Pacific Railroad, and the other half the Central Pacific Railroad. Students should then make a map showing the company's major routes and the large cities along that route. Then have each student create an example of a Web page or another visual display that outlines the history of the railroad and incorporates the map that he or she created.
2. **Linguistic, Interpersonal, Intrapersonal.** Have students review the text and use outside resources to find descriptions of the conditions that miners encountered on the job. Ask students to work in pairs, with one student acting as a newspaper reporter and the other as a mine worker. Have the reporters conduct interviews with the miners based on the working conditions found in the mines. Remind students who are acting as reporters to ask questions that facilitate a description of the working conditions in the mines. Have the interviewer take notes during the interview. Encourage groups to share their information with the class.

REVIEW

Linguistic, Logical-Mathematical, Intrapersonal. Have students complete the Section Review questions. Then ask them to

Geographic Diversity

Standard Time Zones. By the 1880s increased communication and travel between the East and the West necessitated the introduction of a standard time system. Proposed by William F. Allen at a Chicago meeting of railroad owners in 1883, the new system of four equal time zones replaced the previous system of telling time based on the position of the sun. Although the new system was adopted almost immediately, it was not formally recognized as a system until Congress passed the Standard Time Zone Act of 1918.

Critical Thinking: What problems might occur without a standard system of time zones in effect?

ANSWER: Communication would be difficult, and things like travel schedules would be impossible to coordinate.

Multimedia Resources

Linking Geography and History Transparency 10A: Growth of Transportation, 1840–1890

The success of the transcontinental railroad led to the creation of other railroad lines linking the East and the West. Here workers on the Northern Pacific pose for an 1886 photograph.

its rock formations required large amounts of blasting powder and the explosive nitroglycerin. In the winter of 1866, many workers were trapped and killed in snow drifts over 60 feet high. "Many of them we did not find until . . . the snow melted," reported a company official.

Meanwhile, the Union Pacific workers faced harsh weather on the Great Plains. In addition, the company pressured them to work at a rapid pace—at times laying 250 miles of track in six months. Faced with greater geographic obstacles, the Central Pacific took four years to lay the first 115 miles of track. For both lines, providing food and supplies for their workers became more difficult as they pushed into remote areas. The railroad companies often relied on local resources. Professional hunters such as "Buffalo Bill" Cody shot thousands of buffalo to feed workers on the Union Pacific as it crossed the Plains.

The Golden Spike

When the two railroads neared completion, Congress required them to connect at Promontory, Utah. On May 10, 1869, workers and reporters watched the two lines meet for the first time. In a dramatic ceremony, a golden spike was used to connect the railroad tie joining the two tracks. Alexander Toponce witnessed the event:

> **"Governor Stanford, president of the Central Pacific, took the sledge [hammer], and the first time he struck he missed the spike and hit the rail. What a howl went up! Irish, Chinese, Mexicans, and everybody yelled with delight. 'He missed it.' . . . Then Stanford tried it again and tapped the spike. . . . The tap was reported in all the offices east and west."**

The transcontinental railroad had finally united the East and the West. Following its completion, companies continued building railroads until the West was crisscrossed with shining rails.

The Impact of the Railroads

The transcontinental railroad increased both economic growth and the population in the West. The railroad companies encouraged settlement by providing better transportation for people and goods and by selling land to settlers.

Time and Cargo

Another benefit of railroads was that they saved time. The Union Pacific advertised that a trip from Omaha, Nebraska, to San Francisco, California,

Workers from the Central Pacific and the Union Pacific celebrate the completion of the transcontinental railroad at Promontory, Utah.

list the geographic characteristics of their state or region. Discuss the problems or advantages these characteristics might raise when building a railroad or digging mines. Finally, have students compare the problems/advantages in their area to those faced when building the transcontinental railroad or when mining in the West.

ASSESS

Have students complete Daily Quiz 5.2.

RETEACH

Linguistic, Logical-Mathematical, Intrapersonal. Have students complete Main Idea Activities for Reteaching and Sheltered English 5.2. Then ask them to think about the difficult conditions that miners and railroad workers endured in the West. Students should imagine that they work in the mines or for one of the railroad companies and then make a list of these conditions, as well as safety standards that they would like to see established, to send to Congress. Ask volunteers to share their lists with the class. **SHELTERED ENGLISH**

Advertisement for the Union Pacific Railroad

would take four days—instead of a month by wagon. The Union Pacific also promised greater safety: "Travelers for pleasure, health or business will find a trip over the Rocky Mountains healthy and pleasant."

The new railroads also helped businesses. In time, telegraph lines ran alongside railroads, opening up the West to faster and more convenient communication. Western timber companies, miners, cattle ranchers, and farmers used railroads to ship items to the East. Wood, metals, beef, and grain traveled east in exchange for manufactured products that were shipped west.

Railroad Booms and Busts

Railroad companies encouraged people to invest money in the railroads, sometimes unwisely. Railroad speculation and the collapse of railroad owner Jay Cooke's banking firm helped start the Panic of 1873 and the depression that followed. By the 1880s many of the smaller western railroads were deep in debt.

Despite such setbacks, Americans remained interested in railroad investments. By 1890 there were around 199,000 miles of railroad track in operation compared to only about 35,000 miles in 1865. Almost 750,000 Americans worked for railroad companies. Railroads had become one of the biggest industries in the United States and one of the most important in the West.

City on the Rise In 1865 the Union Pacific Railroad laid its tracks through the city of Omaha, Nebraska, causing the population to soar. How much did Omaha's population increase between 1860 and 1900?

SECTION 2 REVIEW

Identify and explain the significance of the following:

- **Comstock Lode**
- **bonanza**
- **boom towns**
- **Pony Express**
- **transcontinental railroad**
- **Pacific Railway Acts**
- **Leland Stanford**

Reading for Content Understanding

1. **Main Idea** Why was mining one of the most dangerous jobs in the West?
2. **Main Idea** What were some of the difficulties in building a transcontinental railroad?
3. **Cultural Diversity** Why do you think so few women lived in mining towns?
4. **Writing** *Creating* Write a short song that might have been sung at the celebration of the connection of the Union Pacific and Central Pacific Railroads. Your song should focus on how the railroad will change life in the West or improve communication between family members.
5. **Critical Thinking** *Drawing Conclusions* Why do you think the railroad is still one of the most effective ways of transporting goods across the country, even though faster forms of transportation have been developed?

CHART ANSWER
100,722 people

Section 2 Review ANSWERS

Identify
For significance, see the following pages:

- Comstock Lode, p. 158
- bonanza, p. 158
- boom towns, p. 159
- Pony Express, p. 160
- transcontinental railroad, p. 160
- Pacific Railway Acts, p. 160
- Leland Stanford, p. 161

Reading for Content Understanding

1. The heat was almost unbearable, the air was often toxic and lacked oxygen, floods and cave-ins were a constant threat, and mechanisms such as elevators were unsafe.
2. Difficulties included discrimination against immigrant workers, harsh terrain, hostile Indians, rough weather, and a lack of food and supplies.
3. Answers will vary but students should point out that mining towns were volatile places to live.
4. Songs will vary but might mention the economic opportunities associated with connecting the East and the West.
5. Railroads are less expensive than other modes of transportation and are not as adversely affected by weather problems.

SECTION 3 LESSON PLAN

OBJECTIVES

- Identify the factors that led to the growth of the cattle industry during the 1870s.
- Describe the life of a cowboy during the cattle boom days of the 1870s.
- Analyze the decline of the Cattle Kingdom.

FOCUS

Motivate Before Reading

Ask students to describe what a cowboy's life was like, based on their impressions from watching television and movies. Explain to students that while some of what they see in the media about cowboys is accurate, much of it is overglorified. Tell the class that in this section they will learn about the contributions of cowboys and ranchers to the growth of the West.

Section 3 RESOURCES

PRINT

★ Guided Reading Strategies 5.3

★ Primary Source Reading 5: Cowhands and Cattle Drives

★ Section 3 Review, p. 169

★ Daily Quiz 5.3

MULTIMEDIA

★ *Teaching Resources CD–ROM,* Lesson 5.3

★ *American Music Audio CD Program:* "O Bury Me Not"

SHELTERED ENGLISH

★ Main Idea Activities for Reteaching and Sheltered English 5.3

The Cattle Kingdom

Reading Focus

What factors led to a cattle boom in the 1870s?

What was life like for cowboys?

What caused the decline of the Cattle Kingdom?

Key Terms

Texas longhorn
Cattle Kingdom
open range
range rights
vaqueros
roundup
cattle drive
Chisholm Trail
range wars

IN THE MID-1800s Texas ranchers began gathering up huge herds of wild cattle. Describing these herds, one rancher wrote, "Cattle are permitted to range . . . over a large surface of country, thirty, forty, and even fifty miles in extent [size]." Keeping track of these roaming cattle required great skill. Although the ranch hands who did this work faced many hardships, a rancher wrote that "the young men that follow this 'Cow-Boy' life . . . generally become attached to it." These cowboys and ranchers helped start the cattle-ranching industry in the West.

A wealthy rancher bought this golden bull clock.

The Roots of Ranching

Spanish settlers brought their cattle to California and Texas in the 1700s. These cattle later mixed with English breeds to create the **Texas longhorn**, which spread rapidly throughout western Texas. Longhorn cattle were lean and tough, with horns up to five feet across. Many butchers said the longhorn had too little meat, calling it "8 pounds of hamburger on 800 pounds of bone and horn." Nonetheless, settlers preferred to raise longhorns because the animals needed very little water and could survive harsh weather.

The new breed was also resistant to a terrible disease commonly called Texas fever. This sickness, which was transmitted by ticks that infested the cattle, was usually deadly. Unfortunately, healthy longhorns were often carriers, which meant they could endanger other cattle breeds and oxen by giving them the ticks.

In the 1850s ranchers rounded up Texas longhorns and sold them to miners, U.S. soldiers, railroad workers, and American Indians living on reservations. During the Civil War, the cattle herds grew because Texas was isolated from its markets and unable to sell cattle for much of the war.

Introduce Key Terms

Linguistic. Review this section's key terms with students. Ask students to write a short story about the old West that includes all of the key terms from this section. If they do not know a term, they should use the text or a dictionary to find its meaning.
SHELTERED ENGLISH

TEACH

Have students read Section 3 and complete Guided Reading Strategies 5.3. Choose one or more of the following activities to explore the section content with students. For further suggestions on block scheduling or team teaching, see the *Block Scheduling Handbook.*

LEVEL 1: Linguistic. (Suggested time: 15 min.) As a class, go over students' Guided Reading Strategies. Then use the Reading Focus questions to highlight the main ideas of the section.
SHELTERED ENGLISH

ALL LEVELS: Linguistic, Visual-Spatial. (Suggested time: 45 min.) Discuss the events that led to the rise and decline of the Cattle Kingdom. Have each student create a comic book that highlights the major events and changes that took place in the cattle industry during the mid-1800s. Comic books should contain these

Ranchers brought their cattle to railroad towns to sell them to buyers, who then shipped the cattle to meatpacking plants farther east.

Open-Range Ranching

Following the Civil War, the demand for beef in the East increased as the economy and the population expanded. A cow worth $3 to $6 in Texas could be sold for $38 in Kansas or $80 in New York. Nobody drove the longhorns to eastern markets, however, because of the distance and the danger of transmitting Texas fever to other farm animals.

The Cattle Boom

In 1867 businessman Joseph McCoy had the idea "to establish a market whereat the southern . . . [rancher] and the northern buyer would meet." The creation of new western railroads made this possible. McCoy built pens for cattle in the small town of Abilene, Kansas, which was located on the Kansas Pacific Railroad line. Cattle could be shipped by rail from Abilene straight to processing plants in St. Louis, Missouri. The idea was a great success. When rancher J. F. Ellison sold his cattle in Abilene, his son recalled, "This trip proved to be a profitable one. . . . Father had $9,000 cash, which was a lot of money in those days." Soon many Texas ranchers were making the trip north to sell their herds of cattle.

Around the same time, cattle ranching began to expand onto the Great Plains. Ranchers found that the tough longhorns did well on the Plains and were free of disease. In 1890 it was discovered that the cold winters killed the ticks that carried the Texas fever. Ranchers began taking many of their cattle north to Colorado, Wyoming, Nebraska, and Montana. In 1871 more than 600,000 cattle had been moved from Texas onto the Plains. The many ranches in the land stretching from Texas north to Canada formed the **Cattle Kingdom**. Many ranchers grazed their huge herds on the **open range**, or public land. The U.S. government did not charge ranchers for using this public land that was once occupied by Plains Indians and buffalo herds.

The Ranches

One of the people who saw the profits of ranching was Elizabeth Collins. When she and her husband had trouble mining gold, Collins decided "to discontinue the business of mining and engage in that of cattle raising." She moved to the Teton Valley in Montana and started ranching. She was so successful she earned the name "Cattle Queen of Montana."

Collins was just one of many ranchers who became prosperous during the cattle boom. Charles Goodnight started the first ranch in the Texas Panhandle, more than 250 miles from any town or railroad. Speculators in the East and in Europe invested money in ranches the same way that they did in railroads. Some of the resulting ranches were huge, such as the XIT Ranch, which covered more than 3 million acres.

Elizabeth Collins

Most ranchers did not own this much land. Instead, they concentrated on buying the **range rights**, or water rights, to ponds and rivers. This gave them access to scarce water as well as ownership of the land around it. With range rights, ranchers could eliminate competition by stopping farmers and other ranchers from using the water.

Historical Sidelight

Cattle's Impact on Native Animals. The introduction and subsequent breeding of cattle in the West had a detrimental effect on animals native to the region. In a campaign to kill all animals that might prey on their livestock, ranchers poisoned the carcasses of dead animals that predators would later eat, killing huge numbers of bears, mountain lions, coyotes, ground squirrels, and prairie dogs. In some cases, ranchers eliminated these animals from the region entirely. To protect the grazing lands for their livestock, ranchers also killed any native animals that might eat the grass intended for the cattle or sheep. In one case in Colorado, a ranching family killed 1,080 antelope that had been grazing on the grasslands that the ranchers had claimed for their cattle.

Critical Thinking: Why did ranchers at times kill native species?

ANSWER: The ranchers were motivated by the economic need to protect their livestock investment.

significant events: the breeding of Texas longhorn cattle, the building of holding pens and processing plants for cattle along railroad lines, the use of the open range and the buying of range rights, the growth of cattle towns, range wars, and the end of the open range. **SHELTERED ENGLISH**

LEVEL 2: Linguistic, Logical-Mathematical. (Suggested time: 30 min.) Have students create a job description for a cowboy. They should include an overall description of the job's responsibilities, as well as descriptions of a cowboy's specific duties. Once students have finished, lead a class discussion about cowboy life during the 1870s.

LEVEL 3: Logical-Mathematical, Interpersonal. (Suggested time: 45 min.) Tell students that they will take part in an imaginary lawsuit in which a rancher is suing a farmer because the barbed-wire fence the farmer put up has made it impossible for the rancher's cattle to walk to the river to drink water. Assign students the roles of the defendant, the plaintiff, attorneys for both sides, the judge, and the jury. Students should use information from the text to create arguments for both the farmer and the rancher. After all the testimony has been heard, have the jury decide whether the rancher has a legitimate claim.

Across the Curriculum

LANGUAGE ARTS

Vaqueros. In addition to acquiring herding techniques and protective clothing from the vaqueros, American cowboys adopted many of the vaqueros' ranching vocabulary. For example, the word *lariat* comes from the Spanish *la reata*, *stampede* from *estampida*, and *lasso* from *lazo*.

Activity: Ask students to use a dictionary to find other common words that came from another language. Students should complement their examples with the matching origins.

Cowboys borrowed many of their methods and equipment from the vaqueros who worked on ranches in California and the Southwest.

The remote locations of many ranches meant that some ranchers were the local authority. Joseph McCoy noted that the cattle rancher considered himself "an independent sovereign [ruler] . . . capable of conducting his affairs in his own way." Isolated ranchers needed to be self-reliant and capable of solving their own problems. Mary Jaques, who lived on a Texas ranch for two years, explained:

> **"The ideal ranchman must be butcher, baker, carpenter, . . . blacksmith, plain cook, milker. . . . It is a fact that each of these trades will have to be practiced to some extent sooner or later."**

The Cowboys

The workers who took care of a rancher's cattle were known as cowhands or cowboys. They became symbols of the American West for many people around the world. Cowboys borrowed many of their techniques from the Mexican **vaqueros** (vah-KER-ohs), ranch hands who tended cattle and horses. From the vaqueros came the western saddle, the lariat—a rope used for lassoing cattle—and the leather chaps that cowboys wore over their pants for protection against the thorny brush. The cowboys borrowed the vaqueros' broad felt hat and changed it into the familiar high-peaked cowboy hat. Cowboys also adopted the bandanna, a cloth that covered the face to protect it from dust and served as a handkerchief or bandage.

Many cowboys were Mexican Americans or African Americans. African American cowboy Nat Love wrote an autobiography in which he described daily ranch life:

> **"When we were not on the trail taking large herds of cattle or horses to market to be delivered to other ranches, we were engaged in range riding, moving large numbers of cattle from one grazing range to another, keeping them together, and hunting up strays."**

Although most cowhands were men, some women worked alongside cowboys. One female rancher explained, "I love to work with my cattle, and have spent a good deal of my time on the range."

Gathering the cattle together was known as the **roundup**. At the spring roundups, cowboys branded young calves and horses. Branding involved burning a ranch's unique mark onto an animal to prevent thieves from stealing horses and cattle and selling them as their own.

Riding the range involved a great deal of hard work as well as danger from cattle thieves, bad weather, and unpredictable livestock. The words to one western song warned potential cowboys,

> **"Some boys go up the trail for pleasure,**
> **But that's where you get it most**
> **awfully wrong.**
> **For you haven't any idea of the trouble**
> **they [the cattle] give us**
> **While we go driving them along."**

Cowboys worked for low wages, and few were able to make enough money to start their own ranches. Despite these factors, many agreed with Love, who said he enjoyed his days as a cowboy because he had "a genuine love of the free and wild life of the range."

Cowboy Nat Love

CLOSE

Linguistic, Logical-Mathematical. Ask students to brainstorm a list of the factors that might cause a cattle ranch to fail. Write their answers on the chalkboard. Then ask students why, with so many risks, cattle ranchers would have wanted to continue in the business and how they might have overcome its difficulties. Have students imagine that they are ranchers, and ask them to write a letter to a friend that describes how their ranch overcame these difficulties.

CHALLENGE AND EXTEND

1. **Linguistic, Interpersonal.** Have students use the library or other available resources to research famous American cowboys. After compiling a list, have students choose a cowboy and write a brief biographical sketch of the person. Ask volunteers to share their biography with the class. Finally, have students combine their descriptions into an *Encyclopedia of American Cowboys*.

Cattle Drives and Cattle Towns

One of the most important and dangerous duties of the cowboy was the **cattle drive**. On these long journeys, cowboys herded cattle to the market or to the northern Plains for grazing. These trips usually lasted several months and covered hundreds of miles.

Riding the Trail

The **Chisholm Trail** was one of the earliest and most popular routes for cattle drives. Blazed by Texas cowboy Jesse Chisholm in 1867, this trail ran from San Antonio, Texas, to the cattle town of Abilene, Kansas. Charles Goodnight blazed a trail leading from Texas to New Mexico Territory that became known as the Goodnight-Loving Trail. The most heavily used route, the Western Trail, headed north from San Antonio, Texas, to Dodge City, Kansas.

Cattle drives usually started in the spring. Some cowboys specialized in cattle drives and took other ranchers' cattle to market for them. These cowboys made several of the long, difficult trips in one year. Cattle driving was rugged and dangerous work. Cowboy James H. Cook described life on the trail:

> **"There was plenty of rough country, with creeks and steep-banked rivers to be crossed. We had no tents or shelter of any sort other than our blankets."**

The cattle were as difficult to deal with as the geographical challenges. During storms they would stampede. Then cowboys would have to track down the strays and round them up again. At night, cowboys had to stand watch over the cattle herds. Cowboy "Teddy Blue" Abbott complained, "There was never enough sleep. . . . I have often sat in my saddle sound asleep." Most cowboys were happy to reach the end of the cattle drive.

Cowboy's spur

The Cattle Towns

A large cattle town such as Dodge City or Abilene was usually at the end of the trail. Small businesses sprang up as more cowboys passed through town. Many of these businesses were owned or operated by women such as Malinda Jenkins, who ran a boardinghouse in Fort Worth, Texas. To get her business started, she traded her sewing machine for the first month's rent and bought a cookstove on credit. Eventually, she paid off her debts and had a successful business.

Boardinghouses, hotels, saloons, and restaurants in cattle towns counted on tired cowboys spending money during the few days they were in town. Most ranchers paid the cowboys in cash when the drive ended. Cowboys spent their money on food, hot baths, and comfortable beds after long weeks on the trail. John Baumann described his cowboy friends in Dodge City:

> **"The boys have received their wages; $200 or $300 perhaps, in a lump, and are turning themselves loose. . . . Clean-shaven and [wearing] new store clothes from head to foot, we scarcely recognize each other."**

During the cattle drive season the large number of rowdy cowboys could make life in cattle towns rough and violent. While there were rarely shoot-outs in the streets, there were often fights and disorderly behavior. Law officials such as Wyatt Earp made their reputations while keeping the peace in cattle towns.

Colt revolver

The End of the Open Range

In the early 1880s cattle ranching became increasingly profitable. In 1882 Gustavus Swift used the newly invented refrigerator railroad car to carry beef from packing plants to the big eastern cities. This increased the national demand for beef and made cities such as Chicago, Illinois, famous for their meatpacking factories.

Daily Life

The Chuck Wagon. Trail crews were often led by an older cowboy who could no longer withstand the long, harsh days on horseback. Serving as cook, doctor, dentist, and entertainer, he rode on the chuck wagon. This vehicle was a sturdy wagon with iron axles and wide tires. Carrying the entire crew's food, bedrolls, firewood, tools, and personal possessions, the trail boss would ride ahead of the crew to set up the next night's camp, start a fire, and prepare coffee and meals.

Activity: Have students draw pictures of what they think the inside of a chuck wagon might have looked like. Have students label each item and explain its purpose.

Multimedia Resources

American Music Audio CD Program: "O Bury Me Not"

2. **Visual-Spatial, Logical-Mathematical, Kinesthetic.** Have students use the library to find information about the towns or regions that were significant to the cattle industry. Then ask them to create a map identifying these towns or regions that includes a legend showing whether the area was known for cattle ranching, its holding pens, its meat processing, or its consumer market. Ask students to label key railroad routes and the cities along them that were used to transport cattle. Have students indicate what function each stop along the route served.

3. **Linguistic, Logical-Mathematical.** Ask students to identify how the typical cowboy dressed and the items a cowboy carried. *(Students should identify cowboy hats, lassos, chaps, bandannas, and saddles.)* Explain to students that many of these items, traditionally associated with cowboys of the West, were introduced by Mexican vaqueros. Have students use the library to find out more information about vaqueros. Have students write a two-page report identifying the contributions of Mexican vaqueros to cowboys in the United States. Encourage volunteers to share the information they find with the rest of the class.

Economic Development

Cowboys to Cattle Ranchers. During the early days of the cattle industry, the economic rewards of the cattle drive often extended to the cowboys as well as to the ranch owners. In many instances, a cowboy's payment would come in the form of a portion of the cattle he had helped brand. Cowboys could also take and raise motherless calves, or mavericks, whose ownership could not be determined. Large cattle corporations eventually put an end to these practices, however, as the price of cattle rose and available land became scarce.

Critical Thinking: How would ranchers benefit from allowing cowboys to own their own cattle?

Answer: Cowboys could learn the importance of ownership and heighten their sense of responsibility. Ranchers would also not have to come up with so much cash at one time.

Map Answer
the Rocky Mountains

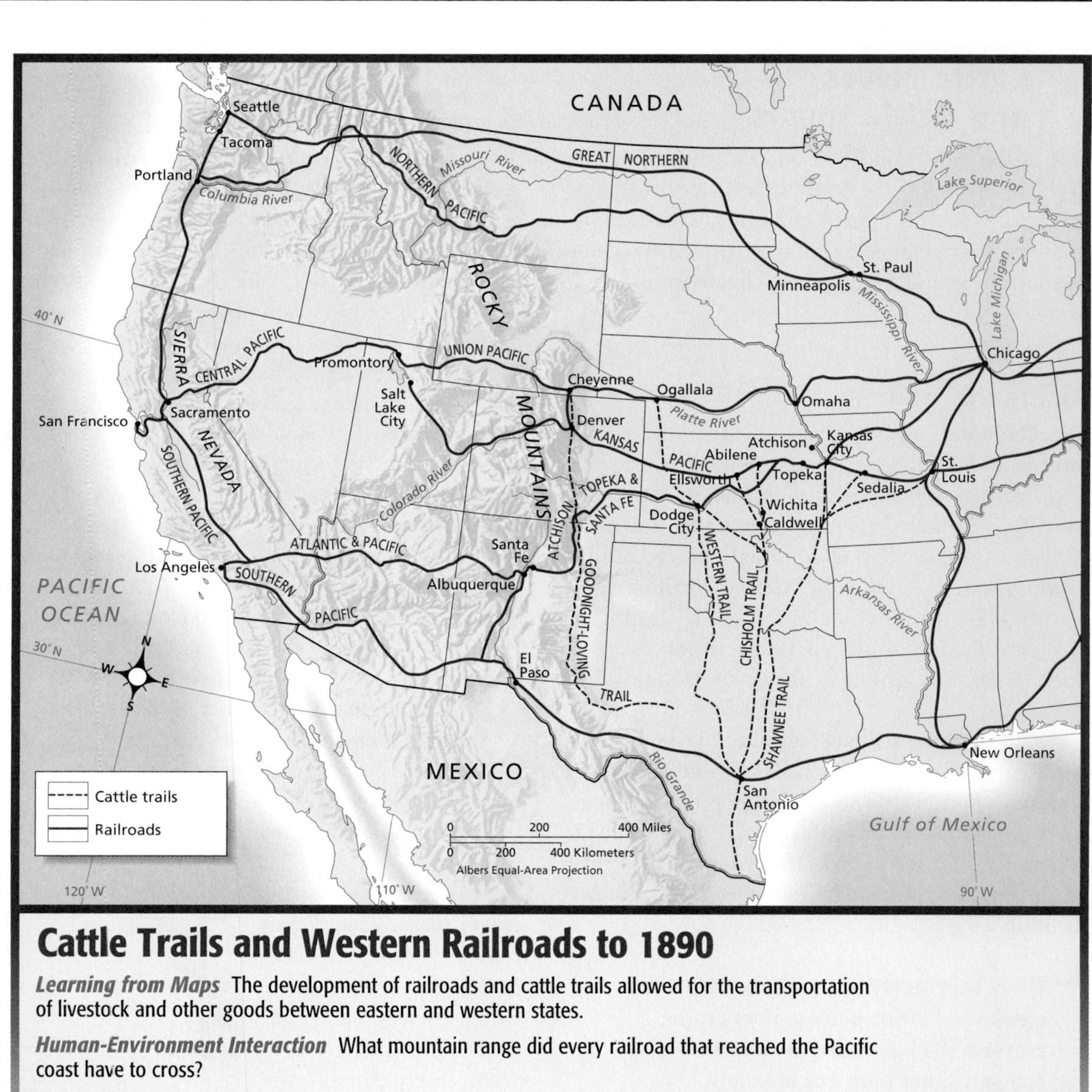

Cattle Trails and Western Railroads to 1890

Learning from Maps The development of railroads and cattle trails allowed for the transportation of livestock and other goods between eastern and western states.

Human-Environment Interaction What mountain range did every railroad that reached the Pacific coast have to cross?

Range Wars

While the cattle business boomed, ranchers faced increased competition for use of the open range. As more settlers came to the Great Plains, farmers began to buy range land where cattle had once grazed. Smaller ranchers also began competing with the large ranches for land. Then in 1873 Joseph Glidden invented barbed wire, which allowed westerners to fence off large amounts of land at a low cost. Westerners had been unable to do this because traditional fencing material, such as stones and lumber, was scarce on the Great Plains.

Large ranchers moved quickly to fence in the open range to keep out farmers and smaller ranchers. Some farmers and small ranchers responded by cutting fences and moving onto the land or stealing cattle. This competition led to **range wars** between large ranchers, small ranchers, and farmers. Although the large ranchers often won these battles, few ranchers could continue to count on letting their cattle roam free on public land.

Cattle ranchers also fought with sheep owners. As the number of sheep increased in the 1880s, so did the competition for grasslands. Sheep chewed the grass down so far that there was nothing left

REVIEW

Linguistic. Have students complete the Section Review questions. Ask them to create a crossword puzzle using the key terms from this section. Students should exchange their puzzle with another student in the class. After completing the other's puzzle, have students check each other's work. **SHELTERED ENGLISH**

ASSESS

Have students complete Daily Quiz 5.3.

RETEACH

Interpersonal. Have students complete Main Idea Activities for Reteaching and Sheltered English 5.3. Then assign each student a partner and ask the pairs to write each key term from this section on a small piece of paper and place the pieces of paper inside a hat or box. Partners should take turns choosing a slip of paper and making a statement about the word written on it (the same statement may not be repeated). Students should continue until each pair has covered all the terms. **SHELTERED ENGLISH**

for the cattle. Despite threats and violence against them, sheep ranchers continued to prosper in the West.

The Decline of the Cattle Kingdom

By the 1880s an estimated 7 million cattle roamed the Great Plains. These large numbers drove down cattle prices. To improve prices, ranchers began introducing eastern cattle to the western range. These cattle produced larger amounts of tastier beef than the Texas longhorns but were not well adapted to the conditions on the Plains.

In 1885 and 1886 disaster struck the Cattle Kingdom. The huge cattle herds on the Plains had eaten much of the prairie grass that ranchers depended on for feed. Unusually severe winters in both years made the ranching situation even worse. Thousands of cattle died, particularly the new eastern breeds. Most ranches lost 30 percent of their herd, and some ranchers lost as many as 9 out of 10 cattle. "The prairies were seen thickly dotted with the dead bodies of famished [starved] and frozen animals," according to Elizabeth Collins. Rancher Granville Stuart saw the damage to his herd and vowed, "I never wanted to own again an animal that I could not feed and shelter."

Many ranchers were ruined financially. To pay their debts, ranchers rushed to sell their cattle, even though the prices were low. Cattle towns were also hard hit. While cattle ranching continued, it became more costly. Ranchers were forced to buy winter feed for their cattle and to raise smaller herds. Low prices, harsh weather, and greater competition for grazing land brought an end to the reign of the Cattle Kingdom.

The Granger Collection, New York

Joseph Glidden's barbed wire made it easier and more affordable to build fences around western ranches and farms, helping lead to the end of the open range.

SECTION 3 REVIEW

Identify and explain the significance of the following:

- **Texas longhorn**
- **Joseph McCoy**
- **Cattle Kingdom**
- **open range**
- **Elizabeth Collins**
- **range rights**
- **vaqueros**
- **Nat Love**
- **roundup**
- **cattle drive**
- **Chisholm Trail**
- **range wars**

Reading for Content Understanding

1. **Main Idea** Why did cattle ranching become profitable in the 1870s?
2. **Main Idea** What factors led to the end of the Cattle Kingdom?
3. **Economic Development** How did ranching and cattle trails help western economic development?
4. **Writing** *Describing* Imagine that you are a cowboy during the late 1800s. Write a paragraph explaining what your daily life is like. Include some of the problems or mishaps you might face.
5. **Critical Thinking** *Drawing Conclusions* Why might American Indians have become cowboys?

Section 3 Review ANSWERS

Identify

For significance, see the following pages:

- Texas longhorn, p. 164
- Joseph McCoy, p. 165
- Cattle Kingdom, p. 165
- open range, p. 165
- Elizabeth Collins, p. 165
- range rights, p. 165
- vaqueros, p. 166
- Nat Love, p. 166
- roundup, p. 166
- cattle drive, p. 167
- Chisholm Trail, p. 167
- range wars, p. 168

Reading for Content Understanding

1. Reasons include large demand for cattle in the East, new cattle breeds that needed little water to survive, inexpensive railroad transportation, and range rights.
2. Factors included low prices, competition for grazing lands, and harsh weather.
3. Cattle drives brought money to local towns, provided jobs for cowboys, and led to the creation of meatpacking plants.
4. Paragraphs will vary but students might describe hard work for low pay, problems with cattle thieves, and bad weather.
5. American Indians were accomplished riders who were familiar with the terrain and adept at handling animals.

SECTION 4 LESSON PLAN

OBJECTIVES

- **Examine the reasons why settlers moved to the Great Plains.**
- **Discuss the various challenges that farming families faced on the Plains.**
- **Describe daily life on the Plains.**

FOCUS

Motivate Before Reading

Ask students to imagine that the local newspaper has announced this morning that the U.S. government is giving away 160-acre plots of government-owned land to any U.S. citizen who is willing to pay a small registration fee and move to where the land is located. Ask students if they think many people will want the land. *(Students should respond that demand would probably be high.)* Explain to

Section 4
RESOURCES

PRINT

★ Guided Reading Strategies 5.4

★ Geography Activity 5: The Oklahoma Land Rush

★ Literature Reading 5: *The Life of an Ordinary Woman*

★ Section 4 Review, p. 175

★ Daily Quiz 5.4

MULTIMEDIA

★ *Teaching Resources CD–ROM,* Lesson 5.4

★ Everyday Life in America Transparency 16: Farming Technology, Late 1800s

SHELTERED ENGLISH

★ Main Idea Activities for Reteaching and Sheltered English 5.4

Farming the Great Plains

Reading Focus

Why did settlers move to the Great Plains?

What challenges did farming families face on the Plains?

What was daily life like on the Plains?

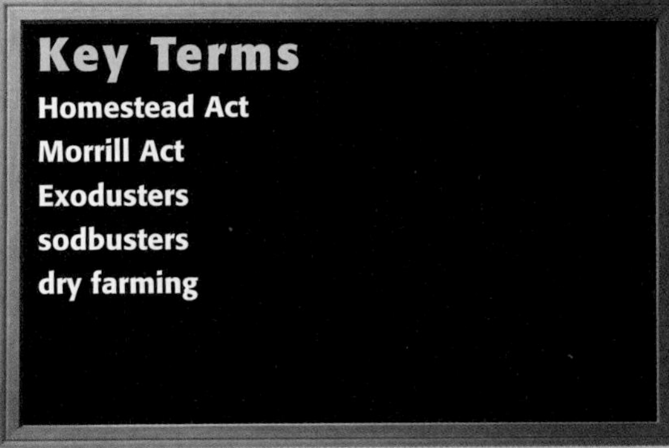

Key Terms

Homestead Act
Morrill Act
Exodusters
sodbusters
dry farming

In 1879 Scottish writer Robert Louis Stevenson took the transcontinental railroad across the United States. Most of the other passengers were settlers moving to the West. When a passenger began to play the song "Home Sweet Home," all conversation stoppped, "and the faces began to lengthen," noted Stevenson. Then "an elderly, hard-looking man . . . [asked] the performer [to] stop. 'I've heard about enough of that,' he [said]. 'Give us something about the good country we're going to.'" The passengers cheered, and the performer began to play music for dancing. Despite being homesick, most settlers hoped to build a better life in the West.

Pioneer rail ticket

 Settling the Plains

In 1862 Congress passed two important land grant acts that helped open the West to settlers. The **Homestead Act** gave government-owned land to small farmers. Any adult who was a U.S. citizen or planned to become one could receive 160 acres of land in exchange for a small registration fee and a promise to live on the land for five years. The **Morrill Act** granted more than 17 million acres of federal land to the states. The act required each state to sell this land and use the money to build colleges to teach agriculture and engineering.

The federal government also offered land in the present-day state of Oklahoma that had formerly belonged to Creek and Seminole Indians. In March 1889 officials announced that homesteaders could file claims on these lands starting at noon on April 22. Within a month of the announcement, some 50,000 people had rushed to Oklahoma to stake their claim. In all, the settlers claimed more than 11 million acres of former Indian land in the Oklahoma land rush.

Federal land grants encouraged settlers to move west. At first, settlers made this journey in wagons as earlier pioneers had done on the students that although the government is not currently giving away land, it did follow this policy in the 1860s.

Introduce Key Terms

Linguistic. Review this section's key terms with students. Write the terms from this section on the chalkboard and ask volunteers to write a sentence using each term. Then have the class use the terms to write a short dialogue between two people. If students are not familiar with a term, have them use the text or a dictionary to find its meaning. **SHELTERED ENGLISH**

TEACH

Have students read Section 4 and complete Guided Reading Strategies 5.4. Choose one or more of the following activities to explore the section content with students. For further suggestions on block scheduling or team teaching, see the *Block Scheduling Handbook.*

LEVEL 1: Linguistic. (Suggested time: 15 min.) As a class, go over students' Guided Reading Strategies. Then use the Reading Focus questions to highlight the main ideas of the section. **SHELTERED ENGLISH**

Before the completion of the transcontinental railroad, pioneers moving west had to travel alone or as part of massive wagon trains that rolled across the Plains.

Oregon Trail. These trips were filled with hard work, boredom, and danger. "I am getting impatient for our journey to come to an end," wrote one pioneer woman. There were dangerous obstacles such as rivers, valleys, and mountains to cross. Rough weather and sickness could also make the trip risky.

The trip west on the railroads was safer and faster. As railroads stretched across the Great Plains, many settlers chose to travel by train. The railroad companies encouraged people to move west by printing posters and pamphlets advertising fertile and inexpensive land. The Union Pacific even promised free houses to settlers on its land in Nebraska. Many railroads also offered lower fares to pioneers.

The Homesteaders

The great stretches of land drew pioneers to the Great Plains. The Plains offered pioneers the chance to make a fresh start.

Moving West

People from all over the country chose to move west. One train traveler noted that "they came from almost every quarter. From Virginia, from Pennsylvania, from New York, from far western Iowa and Kansas." People who had already moved to the Great Plains often chose to move again after a few years. All of these settlers hoped to find prosperity on the Plains, usually by starting their own farms. Many farming families moved from areas where farmland was becoming scarce or expensive, such as New England. Others were the descendants of earlier pioneers to the Midwest. Many single women moved west because the Homestead Act granted land to unmarried women, which was unusual for the time.

The promise of land also drew a large group of African Americans west. In 1879 Benjamin Singleton led 20,000 to 40,000 southern African Americans to Kansas. These settlers became known as **Exodusters** because of their exodus, or mass departure, from the South. Many of these Exodusters were sharecroppers such as John Solomon Lewis, who explained his reasons for moving his family:

> **"I one day said to the man I rented [land] from: 'It's no use, I works hard and raises big crops and you sells it and keeps the money, and brings me more and more in debt, so I will go somewhere else.'"**

Soon black communities, such as Nicodemus, Kansas, developed, having drawn many African Americans west with land advertisements. Other Exodusters moved west, seeking not only more economic opportunity but also equal rights, which they were denied in the South after Reconstruction.

Many African American families, such as the Shores, moved to the Great Plains.

Linking Past to Present

The Morrill Act. The Morrill Act of 1862 granted each state loyal to the Union during the Civil War 30,000 acres of land for each representative and senator the state had in Congress. The land was to be sold and the money used to establish at least one college in the state dedicated to teaching agriculture and engineering. Under the Morrill Act, 70 land-grant universities were established. These include Rutgers University and Pennsylvania State University.

Critical Thinking: What benefits could the nation have received from granting public lands for the establishment of agricultural and engineering colleges?

ANSWER: The grants would encourage people to move west, and by teaching agriculture and engineering, the universities could prepare people to cultivate the lands and build cities.

ALL LEVELS: Linguistic, Interpersonal. (Suggested time: 45 min.) Organize the class into small groups. Have each group develop a weather report describing a natural disaster that hit farming communities on the Great Plains during the span of this section (e.g., grasshoppers, drought, extreme heat or cold). Have a representative from each group act as a meteorologist and discuss the disaster with the class. Other group members can serve as reporters on location or create a weather map or drawing of the area hit by the disaster to illustrate the disaster's effects. Finally, as a class, discuss the overall difficulties that extreme weather conditions have posed for farmers on the Great Plains. **SHELTERED ENGLISH**

LEVEL 2: Visual-Spatial, Kinesthetic, Interpersonal. (Suggested time: 45 min.) Have students use the textbook to review information about daily life on the Plains and make a poster depicting a day in the life of a settler. *(Students might show activities such as plowing, cutting hay, building houses, preparing meals, or washing clothing.)* Display students' posters in the classroom and ask volunteers to explain the activity they have depicted in their work. **SHELTERED ENGLISH**

LEVEL 3: (Suggested time: 45 min.) **Linguistic, Intrapersonal.** Discuss with the class reasons why settlers were willing to move to the Great Plains. Then ask students to imagine that they are railroad executives from the 1860s offering free land or houses to settlers. Ask them

Cultural Diversity

Number of Farms and Diversity of Farmers. From 1860 to 1920 the number of farms in the United States increased by approximately 4.4 million. In 1800 there were some 450,000 European-American farmers. By 1850 the number had climbed to almost 1.5 million and by 1910 the number had reached 6.4 million.

Critical Thinking: Why do you think so many Europeans became farmers in the western United States?

ANSWER: Immigrants poured into the western states to join their families who had already settled and established farms there. They also searched for new economic opportunities outside of crowded eastern cities.

MAP ANSWER

railroads, trails, and cattle trails

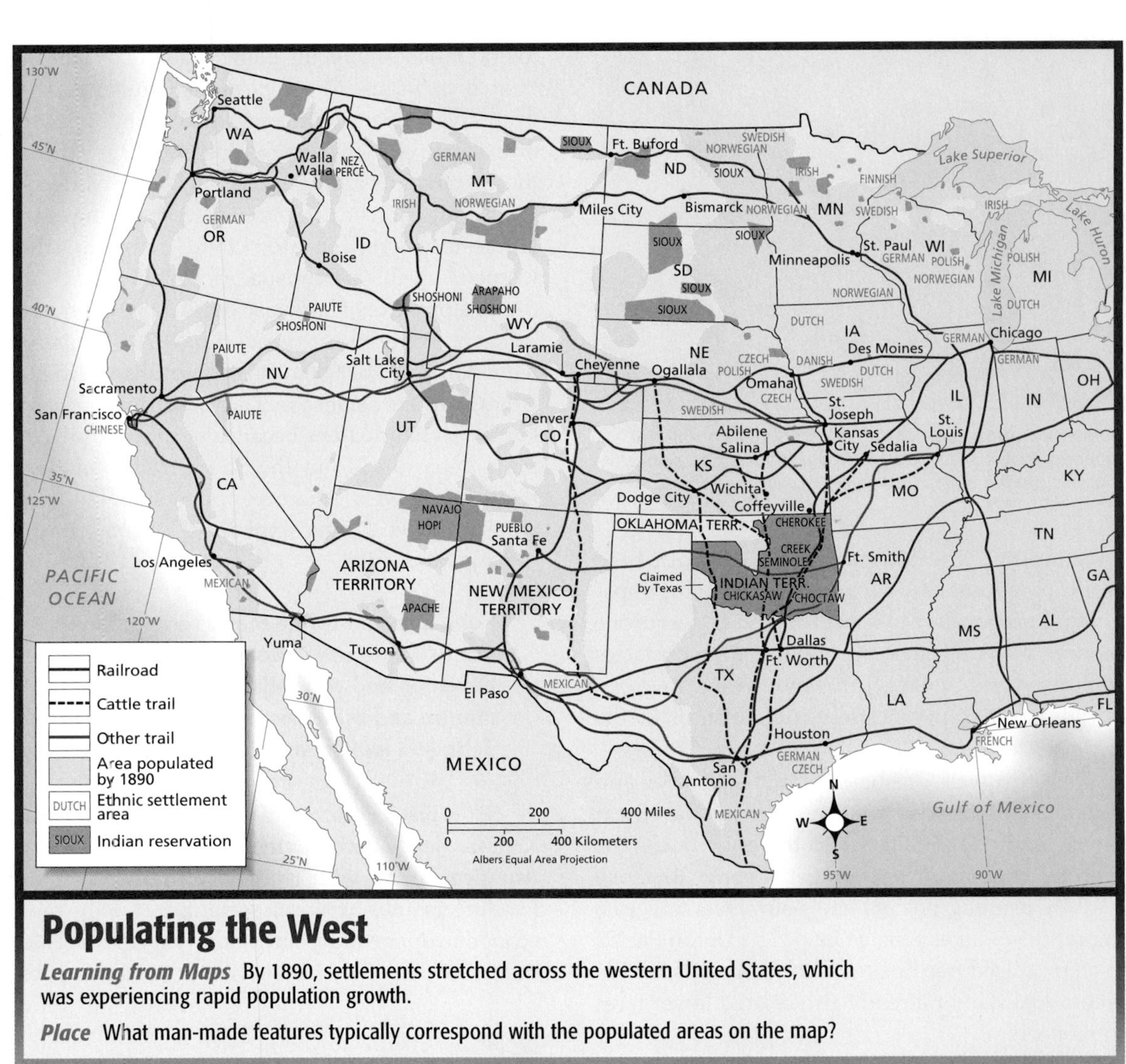

Populating the West

Learning from Maps By 1890, settlements stretched across the western United States, which was experiencing rapid population growth.

Place What man-made features typically correspond with the populated areas on the map?

Immigrants

Western homesteads also appealed to immigrants, who could receive land grants under the Homestead Act if they promised to stay in the United States. Norwegian, Swedish, Danish, German, and Czech immigrants created many small communities on the Great Plains. These groups were looking for economic opportunity. Usually, a relative made the journey to America first and then wrote letters home encouraging family members to come. One immigrant described his good economic prospects to his family, writing "that a farm had been given to him by the government. It was 60 acres of land, [with] good soil."

In addition, thousands of Mennonites, a religious group from Russia, came to the Great Plains. They were some of the first to begin large-scale farming and introduced American farmers to a type of red wheat that grew very well on the Plains.

Farming on the Plains

Although the inexpensive land and rich soil appealed to settlers, the Great Plains presented unique challenges to farmers. "Whatever I had learned of farming in the East, had to be . . . learned over again here," wrote one pioneer.

to write two newspaper advertisements, one designed to attract eastern farmers and one to attract new immigrants. The advertisements should emphasize the benefits of moving to the Great Plains.

CLOSE

Linguistic, Logical-Mathematical, Intrapersonal. Tell students to imagine that they live on a small farm in Virginia and want to move west. Have students write a letter to a family member or friend explaining why they want to move to the Plains and what they expect life will be like there.

CHALLENGE AND EXTEND

1. **Kinesthetic, Interpersonal.** Organize the class into small groups. Have students use the library to find accounts of everyday life on the Great Plains. Tell each group to create an act of a play based on the accounts they have read. Have each group assign specific roles to each student. Tell group members to include a narrator, who will discuss the general conditions encountered on the Plains. Have each group present its act to the class, and then lead a class discussion about life on the Plains.

The Environment

When settlers came to the Plains, they found a mostly flat landscape covered with grass. On the eastern half of the Great Plains, the prairie grass grew up to eight feet tall. In contrast, the grass in the western part of the Plains was just a few inches tall.

Settlers found that the seasons were extreme on the Plains. In the winter, temperatures on the northern Plains could fall to 40° below zero Fahrenheit, while the scorching summer temperatures could reach 110°. Farmers could not raise the same crops that they had grown in the East because the climate of the Plains was much drier. Settlers also faced the threat of blizzards and tornadoes. The dangerous and unpredictable weather made life difficult for the pioneers.

Mechanical farming equipment such as the reaper made it easier for western farmers to harvest huge fields of wheat.

A Storm of Grasshoppers

In the summer of 1874, many farmers in Kansas and nearby states were expecting a very good harvest. Then one day they saw something startling on the horizon—millions of grasshoppers were swarming toward the fields. Settler Mary Lyon described the strange scene: "They began, toward night, dropping to earth, and it seemed as if we were in a big snowstorm where the air was filled with enormous-size flakes." Mary Roberts, another pioneer woman, said "When they came down, they struck the ground so hard it sounded almost like hail."

The grasshoppers covered the fields in a carpet up to four inches thick. They ate settlers' crops from the fields, the food in their houses, and even their clothing. Lyon recalled that by the time the grasshoppers left, "They [had] devoured every green thing but the prairie grass." The huge swarms returned each year, then suddenly stopped. Swarms occasionally returned in later years but never as dramatically as in the 1870s.

New Ways of Farming

Farmers learned to cope with the challenges of the Great Plains by developing new farming equipment and methods. The root-filled sod beneath the grass was very tough and could actually break the plows that many farmers had brought with them to the Plains. Inventor John Deere's deep steel plow made it possible to break through the sod, allowing the farmers to plant crops in the tough soil. The farmers on the Plains, along with the plows they used, were nicknamed **sodbusters** for the hard work they had in breaking up the sod.

In the 1890s a farmer named Hardy Campbell began to teach farmers on the western Plains a new method called **dry farming**. This method shifted the focus from water-dependent crops such as corn to more hardy crops like red wheat. In addition, farmers left part of their fields unplanted each year so that the soil preserved water. Even on the eastern Plains, which received more rain, farmers discovered that the soil required special care. As one observer noted, they "learned that their lands needed feeding as well as their cattle and hogs." Although imperfect, these dry-farming methods helped farmers make it through drought years.

By the 1880s mechanical farming was becoming increasingly common. Cyrus McCormick made his fortune designing, building, and selling farm equipment to thousands of eager customers. Horse-drawn machines such as McCormick reapers collected wheat stalks, and threshing machines separated the grain from the husk. By using machinery, farmers could work much more quickly on large fields with fewer workers.

Corporate farmers who could afford to invest in the needed land and machinery created huge bonanza farms where they grew thousands of bushels of wheat. Farmer Oliver Dalrymple used "eighty horses, twenty-six breaking plows, forty

Daily Life

Blizzards on the Plains. Winter weather was said to be particularly harrowing on the Great Plains. Settlers were often struck by blizzards more severe than those in other parts of the country. A driving wind carried fine ice particles through the air with such force that no person or animal could stand to be exposed to it for very long. When these storms hit, settlers placed ropes along the perimeters of their houses to serve as guides to keep them from getting lost in the blinding snow and freezing to death in the cold.

Critical Thinking: What technological advancements probably make the Great Plains' winters more bearable today?

ANSWER: Improvements include heating, electric street lights, improved communications, and equipment for clearing roads.

Multimedia Resources

Everyday Life in America Transparency 16: Farming Technology, Late 1800s

2. **Visual-Spatial, Logical-Mathematical, Kinesthetic.** Discuss with the class some of the inventions that made farming more efficient on the Great Plains. Students should choose one of these inventions to research. Then have them create an advertisement for the invention that contains a description of the problem the invention was meant to overcome.

3. **Linguistic, Logical-Mathematical.** Have students use the library to find information about the influence of the Homestead Act on the settlement of the Great Plains. Ask students to focus on information about mass movements to the area, such as the migration of the Exodusters or the Mennonites. Have students write a paper explaining each group's reasons for moving to the Great Plains and describing how each influenced Great Plains culture. Encourage students to share their ideas with the rest of the class.

4. **Linguistic, Visual-Spatial.** Give students a blank outline map of the United States and ask them to fill in the map to show the states that currently make up the Great Plains. Then have students number the states in the order that they were admitted to the United States. Students should also identify the year in which each state received statehood. Ask students to write a few paragraphs explaining the reason for the rapid growth of this area of the United States.

Section 4 Review ANSWERS

Identify

For significance, see the following pages:

- Homestead Act, p. 170
- Morrill Act, p. 170
- Exodusters, p. 171
- sodbusters, p. 173
- dry farming, p. 173
- Cyrus McCormick, p. 173

Reading for Content Understanding

1. Land grants and the opportunity to make a fresh start motivated settlers.

2. Harsh weather, unfamiliar terrain, and new crops made farming difficult. Children had to work long hours and did not receive adequate education; women had to work the farms, mind the homes, and often teach school for little pay.

3. Farmers used new techniques such as dry farming and new equipment, including plows, reapers, and threshing machines. This led the Great Plains to become known as the breadbasket of the world.

4. Letters should discuss a day spent in a cramped schoolroom with few books, followed by an afternoon of working on the farm.

5. Answers will vary but should compare the difficulties discussed in question 4 with those faced by today's teens.

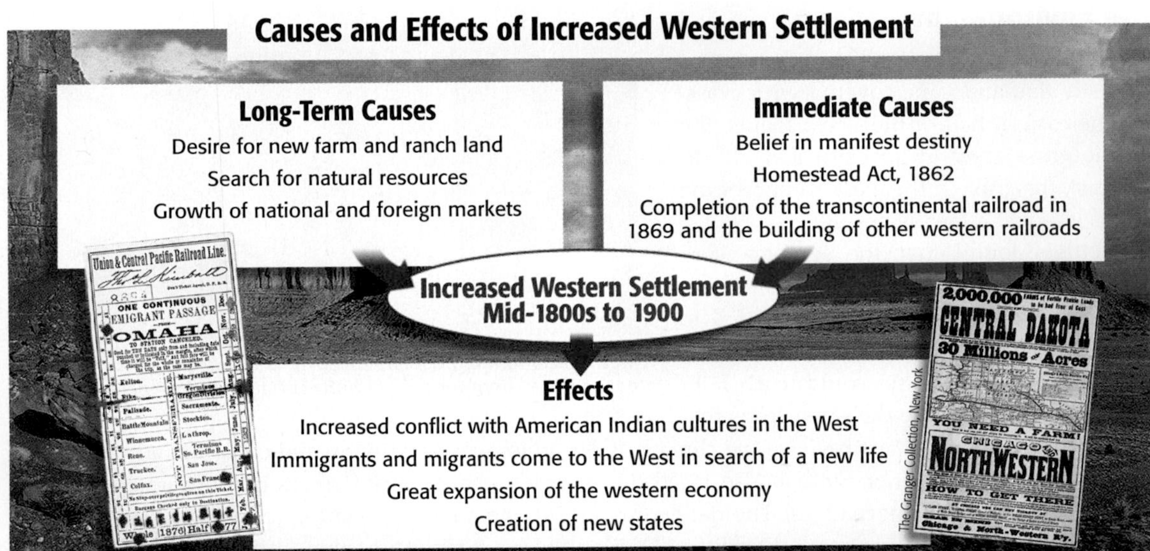

cross plows, twenty-one seeders, [and] sixty harrows [spiked farming tools]" to plant crops on 7,000 acres of a North Dakota farm.

Once they harvested their crops, farmers shipped their harvest east by train. From there, crops were shipped overseas. As farming technology improved, the Great Plains became known as the breadbasket of the world because of all of the grains that the region's farmers produced.

Daily Life on the Plains

Settler Gro Svendsen described the challenges of Plains life, "When one begins to farm, it takes a great deal to get started—especially when one must begin with nothing." Building a house was one of the first challenges that settlers faced. With very little wood available, many families built houses from bricks of sod cut out of the ground. Although cheap to build, these sod homes were typically very small and uncomfortable. Pioneer May Avery explained a few of the common problems. "The roof leaked something awful [and inside] we killed a snake or two . . . and several centipedes." For all their faults, however, the small homes did provide necessary shelter.

Once a home was built, daily chores kept pioneer families busy. For example, settlers had to make and mend their own clothes. Without machines to do the work, washing clothes was a tremendous chore that usually took an entire day to complete. Pioneers usually made their wash soap from lye and animal fat. One pioneer woman's list of 11 washday chores started with "build fire in back yard to heat kettle of rain water," and ended with "brew cup of tea, set and rest and rock a spell and count blessings." Women also prepared meals and often grew vegetables, raised chickens, or made butter to earn money for the family.

Farming families raised livestock and worked hard in the fields, plowing and planting. Harvesting a crop such as wheat required reaping, binding, and stacking. In addition, pioneers often had to build or repair most of their farm buildings and machinery.

Children helped with many chores around the farm. Farm families were often large, and everyone had a task. Author Laura Ingalls Wilder was one of four children in a pioneer family that plowed its own fields, built its own homes, and made many of its own clothes. In *The Long Winter,* Wilder described harvesting hay:

> **"While Pa tossed the hay from the wagon she [Laura] spread it as well as she**

Windmills were used to pump water in the West.

REVIEW

Visual-Spatial, Kinesthetic. Have students complete the Section Review questions. Then ask them to create a graphic organizer that shows reasons why a family should or should not move to the Plains. **SHELTERED ENGLISH**

ASSESS

Have students complete Daily Quiz 5.4.

RETEACH

Visual-Spatial, Intrapersonal. Have students complete Main Idea Activities for Reteaching and Sheltered English 5.4. Write each Reading Focus question from this section on a separate sheet of butcher paper. Organize the class into three groups and assign one question per group. Have students make drawings that represent the answer to their question. Groups should present their work to the class and describe what is depicted in each drawing. **SHELTERED ENGLISH**

could, walking around and around on the stack to pack it tightly. . . . Laura was proud. Her arms ached and her back ached and her legs ached . . . but she did not tell anyone.”

Wilder's books about settlers' lives on the prairie gained a large readership and are still popular today.

Nebraska State Historical Society

This group of students in Hecla, Montana, posed with their teacher in October 1893.

Building Communities

Communities were an important part of life on the Plains. Many early settlers found life on their remote farms to be extremely difficult. About her mother's life as a pioneer, Esther Clark explained: “It took [courage] to live twenty-four hours at a time, month in and out, on the lonely and lovely prairie.” Farmers developed communities so that they could assist one another in times of need.

One of the first things that many pioneer communities did was establish a local church and a school. Churches served as gathering places for pioneer families. Even small communities made an effort to get schools started. Many communities raised money and ran the schools themselves. One woman recalled proudly, “They [the school board] and the pupils and I built that school house with our own hands.”

Pioneer schools were usually small one-room buildings where children of all ages learned together in one class. Few children had schoolbooks, and many children went to school only part of the year because they had to help with farmwork. Most teachers in these pioneer schools were young women who made little money.

Frontier families worked very hard to provide a community for themselves and for their children. Through these efforts, more people found the West an appealing place to live and raise a family.

SECTION 4 REVIEW

Identify and explain the significance of the following:
- **Homestead Act**
- **Morrill Act**
- **Exodusters**
- **sodbusters**
- **dry farming**
- **Cyrus McCormick**

Reading for Content Understanding

1. **Main Idea** What motivated settlers to move west?
2. **Main Idea** Why was farming on the Plains difficult, and how did that affect pioneers' lives?
3. **Economic Development** What technology helped Plains farmers, and how did it affect the region's economic development?
4. **Writing** *Expressing* Imagine that you are a student on the Plains in the late 1800s. Write a letter to a friend discussing a typical day at your school and on the farm.
5. **Critical Thinking** *Making Comparisons* Do you think it would be easier to be a teenager today or in the West in the 1890s? Explain your answer in a paragraph, using information from the chapter and your personal experiences.

Chapter 5 Review ANSWERS

Identifying People and Ideas

1. areas of federal land set aside for Indians by treaties
2. rancher who was so successful she earned the name “Cattle Queen of Montana”
3. a Sioux shaman who refused to give up the Black Hills and led the defeat of the U.S. Army
4. a bonanza discovery of gold and silver that drew thousands of miners to Virginia City, Nevada
5. acts passed in 1862 and 1864 that gave railroad companies loans and large land grants
6. African American cowboy who wrote an autobiography describing ranch life
7. one of the earliest and most popular routes for cattle drives; ran from San Antonio, Texas, to the cattle town of Abilene, Kansas
8. southern African Americans who moved west in a mass departure, or exodus, to Kansas
9. businessman who built holding pens in Abilene, Kansas
10. gave government-owned land to small farmers

Using the Time Line

1. c
2. a
3. b
4. e
5. d

Review and Assessment RESOURCES

PRINT
- ★ Chapter 5 Review, pp. 176–77
- ★ Vocabulary Activity 5
- ★ Chapter 5 Study Guide
- ★ Chapter 5 Test (Form A or B)

MULTIMEDIA
- ★ Audio Program, Ch. 5 (English and Spanish)
- ★ *Global Skill Builder CD–ROM*
- ★ Chapter 5 Test Generator
- ★ HRW Web site

SHELTERED ENGLISH
- ★ Spanish Glossary
- ★ Sheltered English Chapter 5 Test

ASSESS

Have students complete one of the Chapter 5 Tests. As an alternate assessment, assign the Chapter 5 Investigation.

Understanding Main Ideas

1. The Plains Indians hunted buffalo to support all of their needs, communicated with different tribes with a common sign language, and were highly mobile. Women did much of the hard work to turn the buffalo into food and supplies.

2. The Indians were persecuted and forced to live on reservations.

3. Frequent cave-ins, toxic air, extreme heat, and unsafe equipment made mining dangerous.

4. Dangers include cattle thieves, hostile Indians, bad weather, and stampedes.

5. The cattle boom resulted from the linking of markets by the railroads and the success of breeding longhorn cattle.

6. It increased growth in the West, improved communication, and depleted buffalo herds.

7. Immigrants moved west to find economic success and to take advantage of land grants.

Reviewing Themes

1. Factors include extension of the railroad, discovery of mine deposits, and distribution of land grants.

2. Reservation life precluded Indians from hunting buffalo, leaving them without their primary source of food, tools, and supplies and depriving them of their cultural traditions.

3. Droughts, tornadoes, and snowstorms destroyed crops, and breaking through tough sod required new plowing techniques.

CHAPTER 5 REVIEW

Chapter Summary

When settlers and miners moved west in the mid-1800s, conflicts arose with American Indians. The U.S. government sent Indians to reservations. The discovery of gold, the transcontinental railroad, and offers of free land encouraged more western settlement. The 1870s saw the rise of the Cattle Kingdom. With new farming techniques and inventions, the Great Plains became the breadbasket of the world.

On a separate sheet of paper, complete the following activities.

Identifying People and Ideas

Describe the historical significance of the following:

1. reservations
2. Elizabeth Collins
3. Sitting Bull
4. Comstock Lode
5. Pacific Railway Acts
6. Nat Love
7. Chisholm Trail
8. Exodusters
9. Joseph McCoy
10. Homestead Act

Internet Activity

go.hrw.com
SB1 Western Paintings

Imagine that you are putting together a documentary guide to western artists. Search the Internet through the HRW Web site to find at least three paintings about the West. For each image, write a few sentences explaining how the image does, or does not, accurately show life in the West in the late 1800s.

Understanding Main Ideas

1. What was life like for the Plains Indians?
2. How did the wars for the West affect American Indians?
3. What factors made mining in the West such a dangerous job?
4. What dangers did cowboys face?
5. Why was there a cattle boom in the 1870s?
6. What effect did the transcontinental railroad have on western settlement?
7. Why did many immigrants move to the West?

Reviewing Themes

1. **Economic Development** What factors led to the expansion of the economy in the West in the late 1800s?
2. **Cultural Diversity** What effect did the movement of American Indians to reservations have on their social and economic life?

Using the Time Line

Number your paper from 1 to 5. Match the letters on the time line below with the following events.

1. **A golden spike connects the last railroad tie of the transcontinental railroad.**
2. **The northern Plains Indians sign the Fort Laramie Treaty.**
3. **The Homestead Act grants 160-acre plots of land to people who can pay a small fee and will live on the land for five years.**
4. **Congress passes the Dawes General Allotment Act, which splits up reservation lands.**
5. **Helen Hunt Jackson publishes *A Century of Dishonor*, criticizing the treatment of American Indians.**

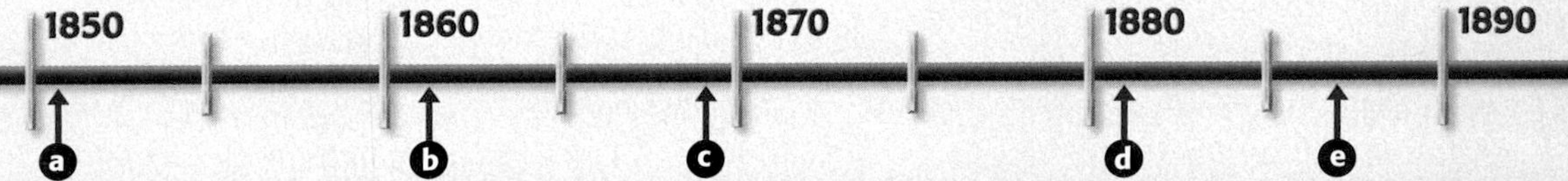

RETEACH

Logical-Mathematical, Interpersonal, Visual-Spatial. Organize students into four groups and assign one of the chapter's sections to each group. Have students review their assigned section and highlight its main points in a presentation for the class. Schedule a time for each group to make its presentation.

SHELTERED ENGLISH

Using the Internet

Have students choose one of the paintings they described in the Internet Activity in the pupil's edition. Have them continue their research for information about the artist who painted the piece. Then have students create a resumé for the artist that highlights his or her significant achievements.

Portfolio Extensions

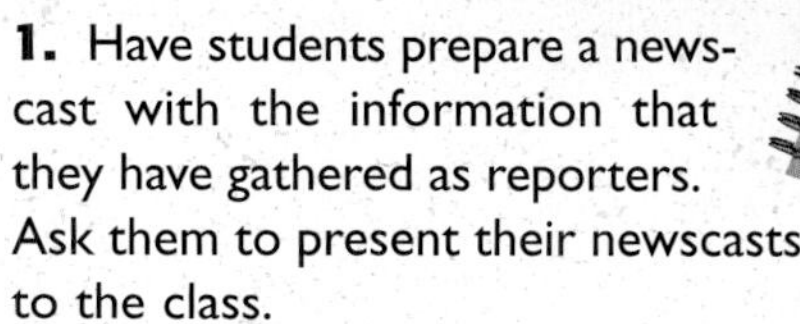

1. Have students prepare a newscast with the information that they have gathered as reporters. Ask them to present their newscasts to the class.

2. Have students write several journal entries about the trip west with their families. Tell them to mention some of the items on their lists and describe how they were used.

3. **Geographic Diversity** In what ways did the environment affect the crops that farmers planted and the farming methods they used?

Thinking Critically

1. **Identifying Cause and Effect** What effect do you think the invention of cars, trucks, and airplanes has had on the railroad industry?
2. **Evaluating** List two positive and two negative consequences of economic development in the West.
3. **Making Comparisons** What similarities and differences were there among mining towns, cattle towns, and farming communities?

Writing About History

1. **Describing** Imagine that you are in one of the mining boom towns of the late 1860s. Write a two-paragraph letter home to your family back East telling about your life in the West. Describe your work as a miner or a boardinghouse keeper.
2. **Creating** Write a four-line stanza for a cowboy song that might have been sung on one of the long cattle drives to the North.

Linking Geography and History

1. **Movement** Most of the Exodusters came from Kentucky, Tennessee, and Mississippi. Why do you think they moved to Kansas and other parts of the West instead of to the North or the Northeast?
2. **Place** Describe the physical environment of the Great Plains.

Building Your Portfolio

Complete the following activities individually or in groups.

1. **Battle of the Little Bighorn** Imagine that you are a newspaper reporter from the East who has been assigned to cover the Battle of the Little Bighorn. To help your readers understand more about the event, either write a biographical sketch of two key figures in the battle, prepare a relief map of the battle site, or create an illustration of the battle.
2. **Heading West** Imagine that your family has decided to move west in 1870. You are in charge of making sure you are prepared for the challenges that lie ahead. Make a list of 10 things you will take with you. Then imagine that you have arrived in your new home. Write a journal entry about how each item on your list has helped you on the frontier. Note if there are items you wish you had chosen to bring, and explain why.

History Skills Workshop

Reading Graphs Study the graph below and then answer the following questions. (a) How many buffalo (bison) were there in the United States in 1800? (b) How many buffalo were there in the United States in 1889? (c) What was the estimated buffalo population in 1994? (d) What factors led to the decline of the buffalo population?

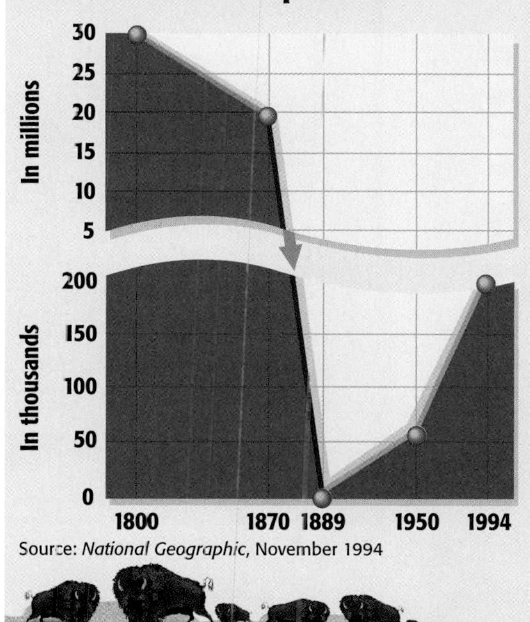

Thinking Critically

1. The railroad is used less frequently for personal travel but has remained an efficient means of moving cargo.

2. positive effects—economic prosperity for thousands, establishment of colleges, development of the frontier; negative effects—destruction of animal species and mistreatment of American Indians

3. similarities—hard work and poor education; differences—mining and cattle towns had less of a sense of community and, unlike farming communities, were short-lived.

Writing About History

1. Letters might describe the harsh working environment, the good pay, or the cultural groups living in the town.

2. Songs will vary but might describe the harshness of the trail and the dangers faced.

Linking Geography and History

1. Reasons may include the promise of land grants and the desire to start anew in an area not directly involved in the Civil War.

2. Answers may describe vast expanses of flat grasslands between the Mississippi River and the Rocky Mountains that were unusually dry.

History Skills Workshop

(a) around 30 million; (b) less than 1,000; (c) around 200,000; (d) destruction of their lands and overhunting

FOCUS

Ask students to suggest reasons why many Americans moved to the West during the late 1800s. Explain that the availability and affordability of land were big attractions to settlers. Mention that another factor was the possibility of mining gold and silver. Tell students that in this activity they will study westward expansion as people sought opportunities in farming, mining, and ranching.

TEACH

Have students read the Geography and History lesson. Choose one or more of the following activities to explore the Geography and History content with students.

Technology and Society

Hydraulic Mining. One mining technique used in the late 1800s involved aiming high-pressure water cannons at hills to rip away the soil to get at the precious metals within. The soil washed into rivers and streams, filling many of them with rocks and gravel. In the spring the clogged waterways flooded the fields of neighboring farms, often ruining the crops. The farmers protested, and the state of California began to regulate hydraulic mining in the 1890s.

Critical Thinking: How might government regulation of hydraulic mining affect miners' work?

ANSWER: It probably made mining much more difficult, in some cases impossible.

SKILLS ANSWERS

1. Virginia City and Carson City, in Nevada; Leadville, Colorado; Virginia City, Montana; Tucson, Arizona; Salt Lake City, Utah
2. Nome, Fairbanks, and Juneau in Alaska; Sacramento, California; Boise and Coeur d'Alene in Idaho; Helena, Montana; Boulder, Denver, and Cripple Creek in Colorado; Deadwood, South Dakota
3. mountainous terrain

Geography & History

The Economy of the West

In the last half of the 1800s, great numbers of settlers followed the trails of earlier pioneers westward across North America. People moved west for new economic opportunities in farming, mining, and ranching. Prospectors and miners staked claims throughout the West, hoping to strike it rich. Ranchers bought cattle from Texas to the northern Great Plains. Farmers planted vast wheat fields where once only buffalo had roamed.

Networks of railroads brought more settlers west and connected the West with eastern markets. By 1890 settlement was so extensive throughout the West that the U.S. Census Bureau reported the official end of the frontier. ■

Western Mining and Farming

A mining boom in the late 1800s brought thousands of prospectors to the West. Successful strikes in western mines contributed to a huge increase in the amount of gold and silver produced in the United States. Farmers also moved west in increasing numbers during the late 1800s, looking for fertile land to settle.

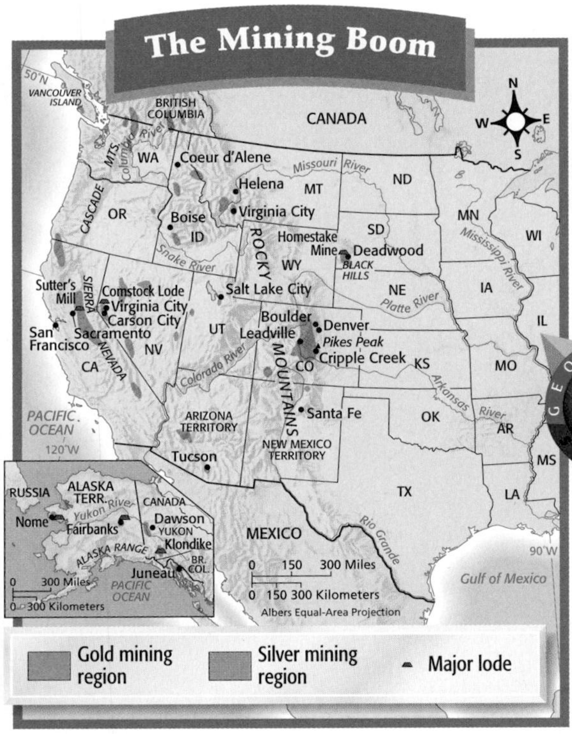

The Mining Boom

Gold mining region — Silver mining region — Major lode

Mining equipment

Geography Skills

Reading Special-Purpose Maps

1. What U.S. cities were located near silver mining regions in the West?
2. What U.S. cities developed near gold mining regions?
3. In what kind of terrain were most of the gold and silver strikes made?

178

ALL LEVELS: Visual-Spatial, Logical-Mathematical. (Suggested time: 30 min.) Tell students that facts that are presented in pie graphs can also be shown in bar graphs. Refer students to the pie graphs shown on page 179 that compare the total acreage of U.S. farmland east of the Mississippi River to the acreage west of the river. Have students transfer the data from the pie graphs to a bar graph, remembering to label both axes. **SHELTERED ENGLISH**

LEVEL 3: Linguistic, Intrapersonal. (Suggested time: 40 min.) Explain to students that the westward expansion in the latter half of the 1800s had an effect on the people already living west of the Mississippi River. Ask students to write journal entries for the years 1870 and 1900 from the perspective of someone living in the West.

U.S. Land in Farms

States east of the Mississippi River

States west of the Mississippi River

1870:
407,735,000 total acres

24.8%

75.2%

1900:
841,202,000 total acres

56.3%

43.7%

1995:
972,000,000 total acres

21.4%

78.6%

Sources: *Historical Statistics of the United States; 1997 World Almanac and Book of Facts*

History Note 1

Before Americans began to move west in the late 1800s, many people called the region between the Mississippi River and the Rocky Mountains the Great American Desert. Scarce water and often violent weather encouraged this belief. Today irrigation and modern farming techniques have helped turn parts of the West into some of the world's richest farming regions.

History Note 2

The rich farmlands of the western United States have helped make this country one of the world's largest exporters of farm products such as wheat and corn. Today farming makes up less than 2 percent of the total annual U.S. gross national product. Manufacturing and service industries currently account for the largest portions of the gross national product.

Geography **Skills**

Reading Pie Graphs

1. What percentage of total U.S. farmland was located west of the Mississippi in 1870? in 1995?
2. How has the geographical distribution of total farmland in the United States changed between 1870 and 1995?
3. How many acres of farmland were in the United States in 1995?

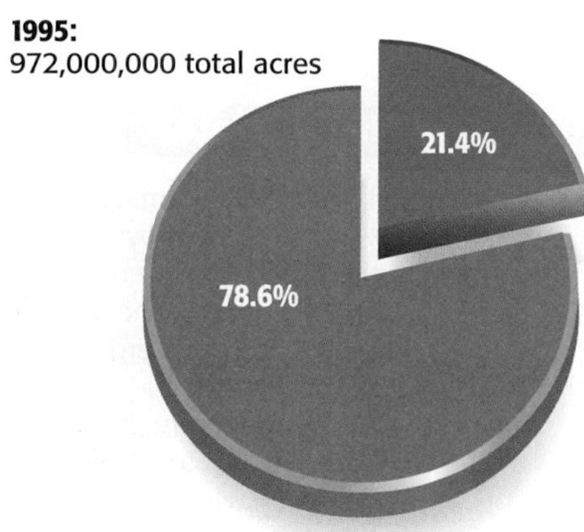

Barns and grain silo

Daily Life

Farming. Farmers on the Great Plains led difficult lives. Many families lived in dugouts or houses made from carved blocks of sod. These dwellings were cheap, easy to build, and fireproof, but they were also dirty, damp, and insect- and snake-ridden. The climate was harsh, with freezing winters and scorching summers. In 1893, for example, the citizens of Glendive, Montana, experienced a low temperature of –47(F in the winter and a summer high of 117°F.

Critical Thinking: Why might people have moved to the Great Plains in spite of these conditions?

ANSWER: They were hoping to escape the crowded East Coast and make a success at farming.

SKILLS ANSWERS

1. 24.8 percent; 78.6 percent
2. The eastern United States once had the vast majority of U.S. farmland. Today the situation is reversed, with more than three fourths of the total U.S. farmland being found west of the Mississippi River.
3. 972,000,000

CLOSE

Linguistic, Visual-Spatial. Refer students to the maps on pages 178, 180, and 181. Ask them to create a chart that compares the resources of the western states in 1870 and 1900, assuming that western states are those lying on or between the Rocky Mountains and the Pacific Ocean. Have students include in their charts whether each state possessed the following: grazing land for cattle or sheep, railroads, farmland, and gold or silver mines.

CHALLENGE AND EXTEND

Linguistic, Intrapersonal. Have students choose one of the major railroad systems—the Union Pacific, the Kansas Pacific, or the Central Pacific—from the map on page 180. Then have them use the library or other resources to write a travelogue that might be written by someone traveling that route today. Ask students to include information about the climate, culture, geography, agriculture, industries, and cities that currently exist along the old railroad line.

Daily Life

Sheepherding. The life of a sheepherder in the West during the 1800s was very similar to that of sheepherders 200 years earlier. The sheepherders, often known by the Spanish name *pastores,* spent much of their time alone, tending flocks that usually averaged about 1,500 sheep. Sheepherders traveled on foot, often accompanied by dogs that helped them control the flocks.

Critical Thinking: How did the lives of the *pastores* differ from those of cowboys who tended cattle?

ANSWER: Students might mention that the cowboys relied upon horses, while *pastores* generally traveled on foot.

SKILLS ANSWERS

1. Cheyenne, Salt Lake City, San Francisco
2. South Texas
3. From these towns, railroads helped transport beef to markets around the country.

The Changing West

In the 1860s the U.S. government passed the Homestead Act, which sold government-owned western lands at a very low cost. The federal government also passed the Pacific Railway Acts, giving railroad companies land for every mile of track they laid. By 1900 a network of railroad lines crisscrossed the mountains and farmlands of the increasingly populated West.

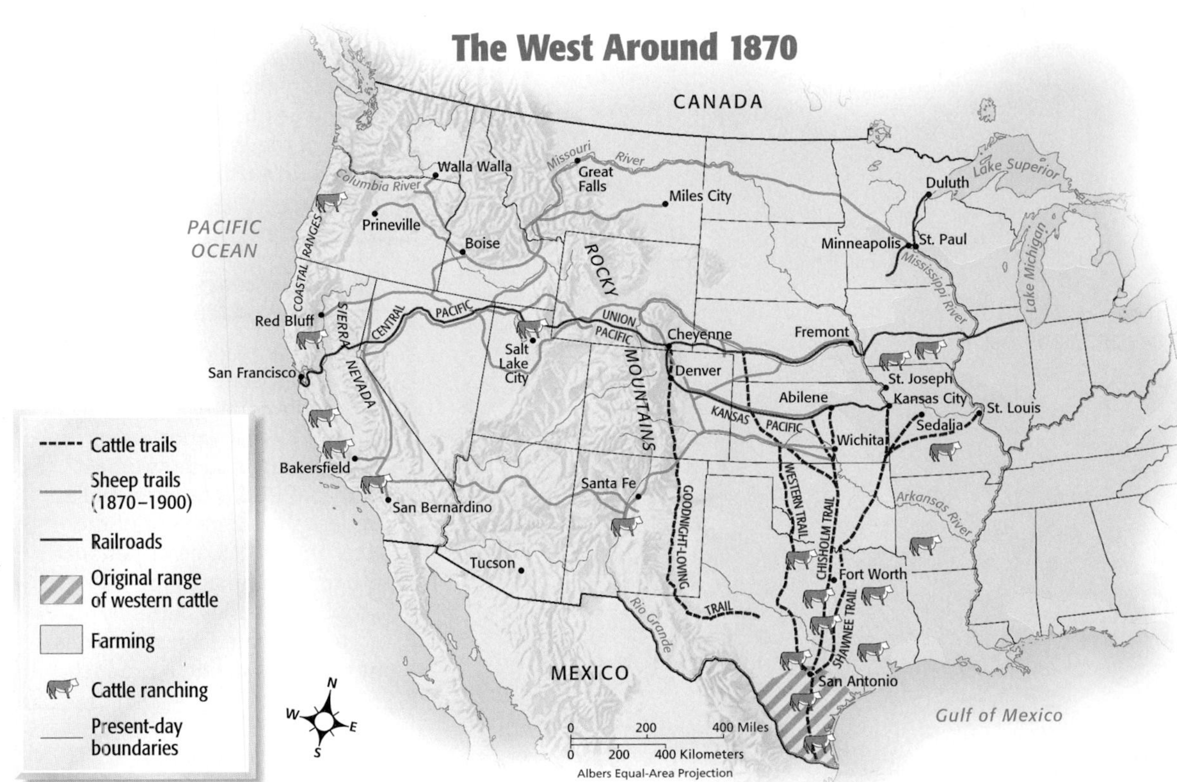

Geography Skills

Reading Special-Purpose Maps

1. What towns and cities were served by the Union Pacific and Central Pacific railroad lines by 1870?
2. Where did the cattle trails that ran north to the railroads begin?
3. Why do you think cattle trails ended at towns along railroad lines?

History Note 3

Although many of our images of the West are of cowboys and cattle drives, sheepherders also moved millions of sheep along a network of western trails. Experienced sheepherders were often immigrants from places like France, Mexico, and Spain. They helped move large western herds with as many as 7,000 sheep. One of the first great sheep drives in the United States provided food for hungry miners during the California Gold Rush.

REVIEW

Logical-Mathematical, Interpersonal. Have students create flash cards covering the information about western states on pages 178–81. On the front of each card, students should write a question related to the information about land resources, the railroads, or economic development from this lesson. Then ask students to write the answer to each question on the back of the card. Finally have students use the cards to quiz each other about westward expansion.

ASSESS

Have students complete Geography and History Quiz 2.

RETEACH

Linguistic, Logical-Mathematical. Have students imagine that they are traveling to the western states discussed in this activity. Then have them create a postcard from one of the states to send back home. The postcard should identify the state the student is visiting and should include a brief description of the resources found there. **SHELTERED ENGLISH**

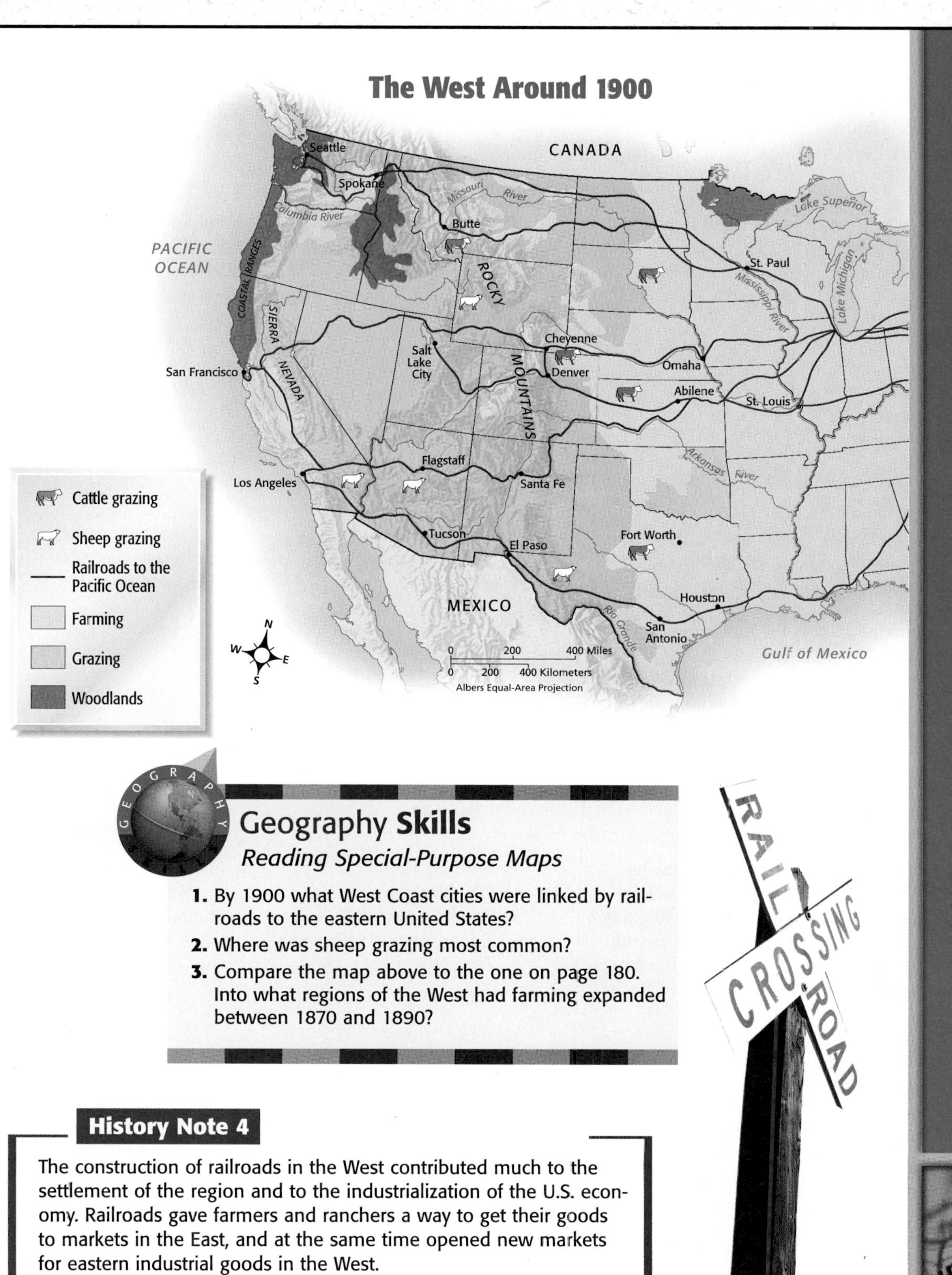

Geography **Skills**

Reading Special-Purpose Maps

1. By 1900 what West Coast cities were linked by railroads to the eastern United States?
2. Where was sheep grazing most common?
3. Compare the map above to the one on page 180. Into what regions of the West had farming expanded between 1870 and 1890?

History Note 4

The construction of railroads in the West contributed much to the settlement of the region and to the industrialization of the U.S. economy. Railroads gave farmers and ranchers a way to get their goods to markets in the East, and at the same time opened new markets for eastern industrial goods in the West.

Economic Development

Building Railroads. Because building railroads was expensive, Congress and many states passed measures to help businesses construct railroads in the West. Railroad companies received and used 188 million acres of free land in the form of grants from the federal and state governments. One company, the Northern Pacific, received nearly 40 million acres of land. In addition, Congress loaned the railroads from $16,000 to $48,000 per mile of track.

Critical Thinking: Why did Congress give land to the railroads?

ANSWER: to encourage the rapid development of a useful, high-speed transportation network

SKILLS ANSWERS

1. Los Angeles, Seattle, San Francisco
2. in the Southwest
3. Farming had expanded to the Rocky Mountains, the northern states, and along the West Coast.

CHAPTER PLANNING GUIDE
An Industrial Nation

	SECTION LESSON OBJECTIVES	PRINT RESOURCES	MULTIMEDIA RESOURCES	SHELTERED ENGLISH RESOURCES
Section 1: The Second Industrial Revolution (pp. 183–88)	★ Describe how the Second Industrial Revolution affected the U.S. economy. ★ Identify the key inventions of the Second Industrial Revolution. ★ Explain how the inventions of the late 1800s changed people's lives.	★ Guided Reading Strategies 6.1 ★ Graphic Organizer 6: Inventions and Ideas ★ Section 1 Review, p. 188 ★ Daily Quiz 6.1	★ *Teaching Resources CD–ROM*, Lesson 6.1 ★ *Exploring America's Past* Video Segment: New and Improved; *Teacher's Guide*, pp. 14–15 ★ HRW Web site	★ Main Idea Activities for Reteaching and Sheltered English 6.1
Section 2: Big Business (pp. 189–94)	★ Identify changes in the way that businesses of the late 1800s were organized. ★ Describe how some business leaders explained their success. ★ Explain why some Americans opposed monopolies and how they fought them.	★ Guided Reading Strategies 6.2 ★ Section 2 Review, p. 194 ★ Daily Quiz 6.2	★ *Teaching Resources CD–ROM*, Lesson 6.2	★ Main Idea Activities for Reteaching and Sheltered English 6.2
Section 3: Industrial Workers (pp. 195–99)	★ Explain how the Second Industrial Revolution affected U.S. workers. ★ Describe why workers formed labor unions and how these unions were organized. ★ Examine how major strikes affected workers.	★ Guided Reading Strategies 6.3 ★ Primary Source Reading 6: Autobiography of Mother Jones ★ Biography Reading 6: Frederick W. Taylor ★ Geography Activity 6: Pullman's Company Town ★ Section 3 Review, p. 199 ★ Daily Quiz 6.3	★ *Teaching Resources CD–ROM*, Lesson 6.3 ★ HRW Web site	★ Main Idea Activities for Reteaching and Sheltered English 6.3
Section 4: Populism (pp. 200–05)	★ Examine the effects of industrialization on farmers and actions they took to fight for change. ★ Explain how farmers wanted to change the money supply. ★ Describe the issues supported by the Populists.	★ Guided Reading Strategies 6.4 ★ Literature Reading 6: *Struggling Upwards* ★ Section 4 Review, p. 205 ★ Daily Quiz 6.4	★ *Teaching Resources CD–ROM*, Lesson 6.4 ★ Everyday Life in America Transparency 16: Farming Technology, Late 1800s	★ Main Idea Activities for Reteaching and Sheltered English 6.4
Chapter Review and Assessment (pp. 206–07)		★ Chapter 6 Review, pp. 206–07 ★ Vocabulary Activity 6 ★ Chapter 6 Study Guide ★ Chapter 6 Test (Form A or B)	★ Audio Program, Ch. 6 (English and Spanish) ★ *Global Skill Builder CD–ROM* ★ Chapter 6 Test Generator ★ HRW Web site	★ Spanish Glossary ★ Sheltered English Chapter 6 Test

CHAPTER OVERVIEW

During the mid- to late 1800s, new sources of power and other technological advances led to the Second Industrial Revolution. As a result of this revolution, the United States was able to make steel faster and cheaper; the railroad industry grew at unprecedented rates; oil became a big business; and electrical power was used in homes and factories.

Taking advantage of these new technologies, entrepreneurs established corporations. Many of these corporations began to combine to create monopolies over their industries. Concern over a few companies controlling so much of particular markets eventually led some citizens to oppose monopolies and to encourage Congress to pass legislation regulating them.

During the Second Industrial Revolution, machines began to replace craftsworkers. Factories became more mechanized, and working conditions deteriorated, spurring workers to form labor unions. Workers grew increasingly discontented, and violent strikes often occurred.

With improved technology, farmers were able to increase crop production, which lowered produce prices. Many farmers had a difficult time paying their bills. Farmers organized to fight for their causes and eventually helped form the Populist Party. Although the party enjoyed some success, the Republicans won the presidential election of 1896.

CHAPTER INVESTIGATION

The Chapter Investigation is an extended, multipart activity designed for students to work cooperatively and apply the chapter content in the creation of a project. You may choose to use the Chapter 6 Investigation, Industrial Graphic Novels, either as a substitute for teaching the section lessons or as an alternate assessment.

BLOCK SCHEDULING 

The teacher lesson plans for each section offer a variety of activity choices to help you present the material in a block scheduling format. For further suggestions on block scheduling, see the *Block Scheduling Handbook with Team Teaching Strategies*, pp. 31–36.

Meeting Individual Needs

ABILITY LEVELS

LEVEL 1	Basic level activities designed for all students encountering new material.
LEVEL 2	Intermediate level activities designed for average students.
LEVEL 3	Challenging activities designed for above-average students.
SHELTERED ENGLISH	These activities address the needs of students with Limited English Proficiency.

Smithsonian Institution®

Internet Connections and Lesson 6
www.si.edu/hrw

CNN Presents America:
Yesterday and Today 1850 to the Present
Segment: Endangered Edison

Additional Resources

Books for Teachers

Avrich, Paul. *The Haymarket Tragedy.* Princeton University Press, 1984. Detailed account of the 1886 Haymarket Riot in Chicago.

McMath, Robert C. *American Populism: A Social History, 1877–1898.* Hill & Wang, 1993. Social history of the agrarian revolt of the late 1800s.

Schlereth, Thomas J. *Victorian America: Transformation of Everyday Life, 1876–1915.* HarperCollins, 1992. Surveys U.S. social history of the late nineteenth century.

Books for Students

Hughes, Thomas P. *American Genesis.* Viking Penguin, 1990. Focuses on technology as the driving force behind U.S. economic development.

James, Portia. *The Real McCoy.* Smithsonian Institution Press, 1990. Examines African American innovations and inventions (for students reading below grade level).

Meltzer, Milton. *Bread & Roses: The Struggle of American Labor, 1865–1915.* Facts on File, 1990. Discusses the formative years of the American labor movement.

Multimedia Materials

An Industrial Revolution in Pittsburgh—1865–1890. Video, 20 min. Agency for Instructional Technology. Uses the steel industry to explore the impact of the Industrial Revolution on cities. Profiles Andrew Carnegie.

The Industrial North. Video, 15 min. Agency for Instructional Technology. Examines northern industry and the way it differed from that of the South.

The Pullman Strike. Video, 20 min. Multi-Media Productions/SSSS. Describes major events in labor conflict.

An Industrial Nation

CHAPTER MOTIVATOR

Ask students to recall advances in technology, discussed in earlier chapters, that occurred during the Industrial Revolution. *(Answers will vary but students might mention trains, steam engines, the telegraph, or the cotton gin.)* Then ask students how those advances affected everyday life. *(Students might say that they made some activities more efficient.)* Inform students that there was a Second Industrial Revolution during the late 1800s. Have students list inventions they think may be attributed to this period. Then ask students to check items off on their lists as they read the chapter, so they can see how many inventions they identified correctly. Tell students that in this chapter they will learn how new inventions made life easier for some people but caused problems for others.

Presenting Themes

- **Technology and Society** Students might say that new sources of energy and advances in manufacturing can lead a country to produce new items that other countries need, or to improve on products already being made, thus stimulating the economy.
- **Economic Development** Students might say that a government could pass new laws to encourage continued economic growth or to regulate growing industries.
- **Citizenship and Democracy** Students might say that citizens could support specific economic policies by voting for candidates backing policies they favor. People opposed to economic policies might hold protests or form organizations that work to change those policies.

Using the Time Line

Have students choose three events from the time line. As they read the chapter, have them create a newsreel report about each event they chose. Call on volunteers to present their newsreels to the class.

The Granger Collection, New York

CHAPTER 6
An Industrial Nation
(1876–1900)

To celebrate the nation's 100th birthday, the Centennial Exposition opened in Philadelphia on May 10, 1876. The Chicago *Tribune* urged Americans to come even "if you have to live six months on bread and water to make up for the expense." During the next six months some 10 million visitors viewed "the results . . . of the best brains of all lands." The new technology on exhibit was bringing U.S. agriculture and industry into a new era.

Technology and Society
How might new sources of energy and advances in manufacturing transform a country's economy?

Economic Development
How might a government respond to economic and industrial expansion?

Citizenship and Democracy
What political action might citizens take in response to economic changes?

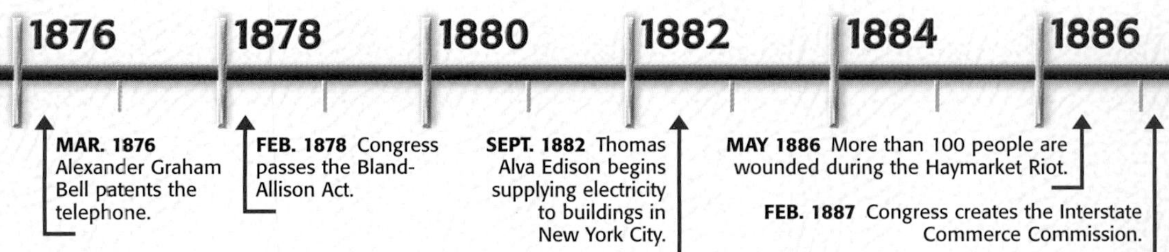

MAR. 1876 Alexander Graham Bell patents the telephone.

FEB. 1878 Congress passes the Bland-Allison Act.

SEPT. 1882 Thomas Alva Edison begins supplying electricity to buildings in New York City.

MAY 1886 More than 100 people are wounded during the Haymarket Riot.

FEB. 1887 Congress creates the Interstate Commerce Commission.

OBJECTIVES

- **Describe how the Second Industrial Revolution affected the U.S. economy.**
- **Identify the key inventions of the Second Industrial Revolution.**
- **Explain how the inventions of the late 1800s changed people's lives.**

FOCUS

Motivate Before Reading

Write the following names on the chalkboard as headings: *Thomas Alva Edison, George Westinghouse, Alexander Graham Bell, Orville and Wilbur Wright,* and *Cornelius Vanderbilt.* Ask students to identify the inventions or businesses associated with the people listed. Write correct responses under each name. Then ask students what each person has in common with others on the list. Explain to the class

The Second Industrial Revolution

Reading Focus

How did the Second Industrial Revolution affect the U.S. economy?

What were the key inventions of the Second Industrial Revolution?

How did the inventions of the late 1800s change people's lives?

Key Terms

Second Industrial Revolution

Bessemer process

patent

THE MOST POPULAR EXHIBIT at the 1876 Centennial Exposition in Philadelphia was the massive Corliss steam engine. Weighing 700 tons and standing 40 feet tall, the engine drew large crowds of spectators as it powered the equipment in the exhibition's Machinery Hall. One exhibition guidebook declared, "The first thing to do is to see the tremendous iron heart." Atlantic Monthly *editor William Dean Howells wrote that machinery such as the Corliss engine demonstrated "the national genius" of the United States. For Howells and many others at the fair, the exhibits in Machinery Hall represented "the glorious triumphs of skill and invention."*

The Corliss Engine ran all the equipment in the exhibition's Machinery Hall.

IMAGE ON LEFT PAGE: *Centennial Exposition in Philadelphia, 1876*

1888 | 1890 | 1892 | 1894 | 1896 | 1898

JULY 1890 Congress passes the Sherman Antitrust Act.

JUNE 1892 The Homestead Strike begins.

MAY 1894 The Pullman Strike begins, eventually halting midwestern railroad traffic.

Section 1 RESOURCES

PRINT

- ★ Guided Reading Strategies 6.1
- ★ Graphic Organizer 6: Inventions and Ideas
- ★ Section 1 Review, p. 188
- ★ Daily Quiz 6.1

MULTIMEDIA

- ★ *Teaching Resources CD–ROM,* Lesson 6.1
- ★ *Exploring America's Past* Video Segment: New and Improved; *Teacher's Guide,* pp. 14–15
- ★ HRW Web site

SHELTERED ENGLISH

- ★ Main Idea Activities for Reteaching and Sheltered English 6.1

that each name is associated with an invention or a business that was created during the Second Industrial Revolution and that in this section they will learn more about these individuals and their inventions.

Introduce Key Terms

Linguistic. Review this section's key terms with students. Have students write a definition for each term. Call on volunteers to write a sentence on the chalkboard using one of the terms. Then have students write sentences in their notebooks using each of the terms. **SHELTERED ENGLISH**

TEACH

Have students read Section 1 and complete Guided Reading Strategies 6.1. Choose one or more of the following activities to explore the section content with students. For further suggestions on block scheduling or team teaching, see the *Block Scheduling Handbook.*

LEVEL 1: Linguistic. (Suggested time: 15 min.) As a class, go over students' Guided Reading Strategies. Then use the Reading Focus questions to highlight the main ideas of the section. **SHELTERED ENGLISH**

Technology and Society

The Bessemer Process. Two men—American William Kelly and Englishman Henry Bessemer—simultaneously developed ideas for improving steel manufacturing. Kelly and Bessemer both discovered that forcing air into molten iron would generate intense heat. This heat would burn the impurities out of the iron and create high-quality steel. Bessemer actually built the machine that made possible the process bearing his name. The Bessemer process was first used in the United States in November 1864. A factory in Wyandotte, Michigan, used the process in a furnace that weighed more than two tons.

Activity: Have students use the library or search the Internet through the HRW Web site to find information on ways that technology has changed people's lives. Ask students to use the information to write several paragraphs explaining whether technology has had a positive or negative impact.

go.hrw.com
SB1 Technology

CHART ANSWER
almost 5 million tons

Railroads and Steel

Technological advances such as those displayed at the 1876 Centennial Exposition were vital to the **Second Industrial Revolution**. It was a period of explosive growth in U.S. manufacturing in the late 1800s. By the mid-1890s, the United States had become the world's industrial leader.

An Age of Steel

Some of the most significant advances in technology occurred in the steel industry. Steel is iron that has been strengthened considerably by heating it and combining it with other metals. Skilled workers originally produced steel in small batches, but it was difficult and expensive to make. In the 1850s British inventor Henry Bessemer discovered an easier and less expensive way to make steel. Bessemer found that by blasting hot air through melted iron he could remove the iron's impurities quickly. The **Bessemer process** allowed several tons of iron to be made into steel in only 10 or 20 minutes instead of taking a day or more.

The Bessemer process helped U.S. steel production skyrocket from 77,000 tons in 1870 to more than 1 million tons in 1879. At first the demand for steel rails for railroads fed this growth, but soon steel mills were also making girders for tall buildings and cable for suspension bridges. As production climbed, steel prices dropped from more than $100 per ton in 1873 to $17 per ton by 1900. This made it affordable to use steel for items such as nails, wire, and pipes.

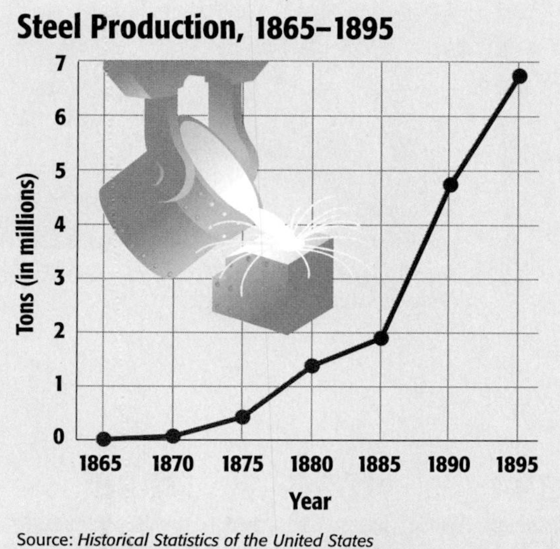

Built of Steel Steel had many uses, which caused its production to skyrocket in the late 1800s. About how much steel was produced in 1890?

A Railroad Boom

As steel dropped in price, so did the cost of constructing railroads. Companies built thousands of miles of new steel track. Railroad mileage grew from some 30,000 miles in 1860 to 199,000 miles by 1900. These stronger, longer-lasting rails could carry heavier loads. A network of railroad lines soon carried heavy freight traffic across the nation.

New technology also made railroad travel both faster and safer. Steel locomotive boilers could withstand greater steam pressure, making trains more powerful. Improved air brakes designed by George Westinghouse and Granville T. Woods made travel on these new trains safer than on earlier models. In addition, elegant passenger and sleeping cars designed by George Pullman made long-distance travel more comfortable. One group of businessmen heading west called their Pullman car a "beautiful . . . moving hotel."

Other developments also improved railroad service. Cornelius Vanderbilt and other powerful railroad owners began consolidating, or buying smaller companies to form one large company. Consolidation of the many smaller rail lines into a few large networks improved efficiency and decreased travel time. In 1860 it had taken two days and 17 line changes to travel from New York City to Chicago. By 1870 passengers could make the trip in 24 hours without changing trains or rail-road lines. Vanderbilt also improved the efficiency of railroad services in urban areas. One newspaper called Vanderbilt "the great railway king of the country."

The railroads had a huge impact on the economy and development of the United States. Manufacturers and farmers could get their products to market more rapidly than ever by rail. Cities such as Chicago and Kansas City grew rapidly where major rail lines crossed. Railroads also promoted western development by offering

ALL LEVELS: Linguistic, Visual-Spatial. (Suggested time: 45 min.) Assign each student one of the inventions or processes discussed in this section, such as the invention of electric power or the Bessemer process. Ask students to illustrate a poster identifying machines that use the assigned technology or items that are made with that technology. Have each student refer to the section to write a caption identifying the inventor of the technology or process, its common uses, and its influence on U.S. industry. Encourage volunteers to show their posters to the class and to explain the significance of the technology illustrated. Finally, lead a discussion on the ways that these and other inventions influenced the U.S. economy. **SHELTERED ENGLISH**

LEVEL 2: Linguistic, Visual-Spatial. (Suggested time: 25 min. plus homework) Have each student develop a graphic organizer with the following column titles: *Steel, Railroads, Oil, Electric Power, Communications, Automobiles,* and *Airplanes.* Ask students to use the following titles for rows: *Year of Invention or Change, Inventor or Business Pioneer,* and *Changes to American Culture or Economy.* Ask students to fill in the relevant information on the graphic organizer. Once students have finished creating their organizers, have volunteers share their answers with the class.

LEVEL 3: Linguistic, Interpersonal. (Suggested time: 30 min. plus presentation) Ask students to imagine that they have the ability to send a letter back in time. Have each student write a letter

The Illinois Central Railroad connected many towns across the Midwest.

free tickets to settlers. Rail travel made the journey west faster and safer for settlers. As rail travel and shipping increased, railroads and their related industries became some of the largest employers in the United States.

Striking Oil

Another important technological breakthrough in the late 1800s was the development of petroleum, or oil, as a power source. People had known about oil for many years but had few ways to use it. This changed in the 1850s, when Dr. Benjamin Silliman Jr. discovered how to refine crude oil into a fuel called kerosene. Kerosene could be used for cooking and heating, but one of its most popular uses was for home lighting. The development of kerosene and other refined fuels greatly increased the demand for oil.

As the demand for oil increased, people began searching for a reliable petroleum source. In 1859 retired railroad conductor Edwin L. Drake proved that it was possible to pump crude oil from the ground. People mockingly referred to his oil well as "Drake's Folly," but they stopped laughing when the well began producing 20 barrels per day. Wildcatters, or oil prospectors, drilled for oil in Ohio, Pennsylvania, and West Virginia. Oil became a big business as these states began producing millions of barrels annually. Companies also built oil refineries to turn the crude oil into finished products, such as kerosene. One superintendent in the industry referred to oil workers as "men who are supplying light for the world."

Electric Light and Power

Electricity emerged as another source of light and power during the Second Industrial Revolution. The invention of the electric generator in the mid-1880s allowed electricity to be used in greater quantities and more reliably than ever before.

The possible uses of electricity drew the interest of inventors like Thomas Alva Edison, who began his career as a telegraph operator. He soon started designing improvements to the telegraph equipment, receiving his first **patent** at age 22. A patent is an exclusive right to manufacture or sell an invention. Edison's inventions soon earned him enough money to start his own research laboratory in 1876 in Menlo Park, New Jersey.

Researchers at Menlo Park wanted to create practical items that they could patent. As Edison explained:

> **"I do not regard myself as a pure scientist. . . . I am only a professional inventor . . . with the object of inventing that which will have commercial utility."**

Edison's name eventually appeared on more than 1,000 patents.

In 1878 Edison viewed an experimental light display powered by electricity. He recalled that "this electric light idea took possession of me." Edison announced in the national press that he would soon invent a practical electric light, even though he had not yet started any experiments. Working feverishly, by the end of 1879 Edison and his team of inventors had succeeded in creating the lightbulb.

Although the electric lightbulb received great publicity, Edison was faced with a problem—very few homes or businesses had access to electricity. To address this problem, Edison built a power plant that began

Inventor Thomas Edison and his original electric lightbulb

Daily Life

Lighting. Before the use of electricity, Americans relied on a number of sources for light. Lamps that burned animal fat or vegetable grease were widely used. Superior to these were lamps that burned whale oil. However, by the mid-1800s whale oil had become expensive. Gas derived from coal oil, another source for light, was also costly. Other materials used to light lamps, such as camphene, were fire hazards. Kerosene, however, provided a cheap source of illumination, particularly after the invention of special lamps that eliminated the smoke and odor caused by the burning oil.

Critical Thinking: How might the invention of kerosene have improved Americans' daily lives?

ANSWER: Answers will vary but students could mention improvements in lighting and increased safety after dark.

Multimedia Resources

Exploring America's Past Video Segment: New and Improved; *Teacher's Guide*, pp. 14–15

Search 32611, Play to 38767
Videodisc White Side A

Play

Pause

See *Teacher's Guide* for Spanish barcode.

to one of the inventors discussed in this section. Letters should focus on how the invention changed people's lives and influenced the U.S. economy. Allow students time in class to write their letters. Then call on volunteers to read their letters to the class. Finally, review the significance of each invention with the class.

CLOSE

Logical-Mathematical, Visual-Spatial. To conclude the lesson, create a three-column chart on the chalkboard. Label the columns: *Invention, Inventor,* and *Effect on Life in the United States.* Organize the class into two teams and have each team decide on an order for members to answer questions. Then fill in one of the squares of the chart on the chalkboard and call on a member of one team to identify a corresponding piece of information for that row of the chart. A correct answer equals one point and allows the team that came up with it to continue answering. Incorrect answers cause a team to lose its turn. At the end of the game, the team with the most points is the winner.

Technology and Society

Electric Lighting. Charles Brush, an inventor who had grown up on a farm in Ohio, designed an electric generator that produced enough current to power an electric light. Soon thereafter, he created an arc lamp that gave off an intense blue illumination. In 1877 Brush's generator won a contest in Philadelphia, thus drawing attention to his arc lamp. In its earliest uses, Brush's device lit downtown Cleveland and the courthouse dome in Wabash, Indiana.

Critical Thinking: Why was Edison's lightbulb an improvement over Brush's arc lamp?

Answer: Before Edison developed the lightbulb, electricity had been used mostly for outdoor lighting.

Science and Technology Answers

1. the carbon telephone transmitter, the phonograph, the electric lightbulb
2. The telephone transmitter made it possible to send stronger telephone signals and greatly improved sound quality; the phonograph allowed for the direct recording of sound and allowed people to hear recorded music; the lightbulb essentially added hours to people's day.

Science and Technology

The Wizard of Menlo Park

Before he turned 30, Thomas Alva Edison was already a talented inventor. In 1876 he used funding from his inventions to build a new laboratory in Menlo Park, New Jersey. There he was given the nickname "The Wizard of Menlo Park."

Edison designed Menlo Park as an "invention factory." He had a team of skilled specialists to help him. Edison also employed young people who wanted to learn about technology firsthand. Many of them began by working for free. In fewer than six years at Menlo Park, Edison patented more than 400 devices or ideas created by his team. Three of their most important inventions were the carbon telephone transmitter, the phonograph, and the electric lightbulb.

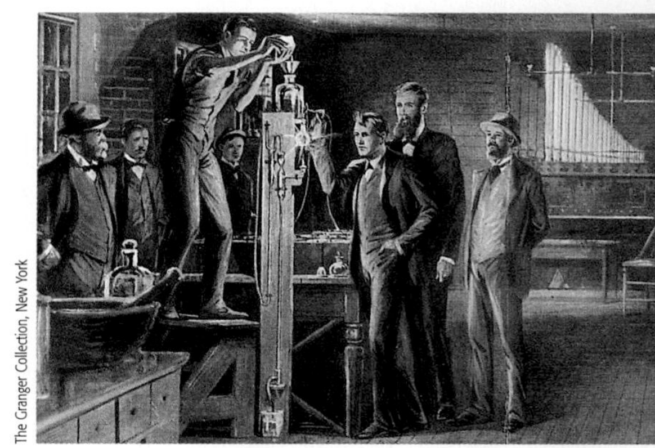
The Granger Collection, New York

Thomas Edison's team of inventors at Menlo Park work on creating a lightbulb.

The telephone transmitter came first. Edison improved Alexander Graham Bell's original design in several ways that made it possible to send stronger telephone signals. This greatly improved the sound quality of telephone messages. Today many telephones are still based on Edison's ideas.

His success with the telephone encouraged Edison's team to try recording the human voice. Their experiments resulted in the first phonograph. A person operated this device by speaking into a tube and turning a crank. The vibrations caused by the voice moved a small needle up and down on a tin cylinder. This created a pattern of tiny indentations that formed a groove around the cylinder. The pattern was a record of the person's voice. To play the phonograph, a person touched another needle to the groove and turned the crank again. The indentations caused the needle to vibrate and re-created the sound of the voice through a small speaker.

This invention thrilled Americans. Edison even demonstrated the device to President Rutherford B. Hayes and his wife, Lucy. Eventually, other inventors improved the phonograph and used it to play music.

One of Edison's greatest achievements at Menlo Park was the creation of the electric lightbulb. After many failures, Edison's team succeeded in using electricity to heat a filament placed inside a glass bulb with no air in it. The material would glow brightly and provide a steady source of light.

In the 1880s few buildings had electricity, so Edison tackled the problem of providing it. In 1882 he left Menlo Park and started an electric power plant in New York City that provided electric lighting for more than 80 buildings. Edison eventually formed an electric power company and built a new, larger laboratory in West Orange, New Jersey. In 1929 a full-scale re-creation of Menlo Park was built in Greenfield Village, Michigan. It remains a popular tourist attraction.

Understanding What You Read

1. What were some of the inventions created at Menlo Park?
2. How did these inventions change people's lives?

CHALLENGE AND EXTEND

1. **Linguistic, Logical-Mathematical.** Have students use the library or other resources to find additional information on the life of one inventor or business pioneer discussed in the section. Then have students create an encyclopedia entry about the person. Instruct students to discuss the individual's upbringing and invention. Also ask students to describe how success changed the inventor's or business pioneer's life. Encourage students to read their entries to the class.

2. **Visual-Spatial, Interpersonal.** Mary Beth Breshars of Fort Leonard Wood, Missouri, suggested the following activity: Assign each student one invention or business discussed in the section and have them use the text to research its significance. Then have students create drawings representing their assigned topics. Have students take turns showing their drawings to the class and having their classmates identify what is pictured.

supplying electricity to dozens of buildings in New York City in September 1882. The *New York Times* reported that with electric lighting in the newspaper offices, "it seemed almost like writing by daylight."

Edison's power company used direct current (DC) to transmit electricity to the homes and offices of consumers. While safe and relatively powerful, DC is difficult to transmit over long distances. This led Edison's power company to concentrate on providing electricity in heavily populated cities, where there were many customers nearby.

The Granger Collection, New York

The typewriter was also invented in the late 1800s.

In the late 1880s George Westinghouse bought a patent for an alternating current (AC) generator designed by Serbian immigrant Nikola Tesla. Unlike DC, AC could be transmitted easily over long distances. Tesla's generator design allowed Westinghouse to build an AC-based electrical network that competed with Edison Electric. Electric use spread rapidly, and electric utilities became a growing business. Electricity was used to light urban homes and businesses and to power factories. Electricity also powered hundreds of streetcars in cities across the nation, allowing urban residents to travel quickly and cheaply.

Advances in Communications

There were also great advances in communication technology in the late 1800s. Thomas Edison and other inventors continued to improve the telegraph. By 1861 telegraph wires connected the East and West coasts. Five years later, a cable on the Atlantic Ocean's floor successfully connected the United States and Britain.

The telegraph had some disadvantages. It carried only written messages and was difficult for untrained people to use. These problems were solved in March 1876 when inventor Alexander Graham Bell patented the telephone, or "talking telegraph." A Scottish-born speech teacher who also worked with hearing-impaired people, Bell studied the science of sound. His telephone made long-distance communication easier than ever before. Bell soon demonstrated the telephone at the Centennial Exposition, where judges called it a "marvel."

Like electric lighting, the telephone depended on a large network of wires. Telephone companies raced to lay thousands of miles of phone lines. By 1884 Boston and New York City were linked by phone. The number of telephones in American homes and businesses increased rapidly, from around 55,000 in 1880 to almost 1.5 million by 1900. Bell became very wealthy as a result of his company's success. He founded a scientific journal and continued to invent a wide range of devices. Eventually, his Bell Telephone Company became American Telephone and Telegraph, one of the nation's largest and longest lasting monopolies.

Automobiles and Planes

The Second Industrial Revolution produced breakthroughs in transportation as well as communications. In 1876 German engineer Nikolaus A. Otto invented an engine powered by gasoline, another fuel produced from oil. Gasoline motors typically were much lighter than steam engines and more efficient than electric motors, which relied on heavy batteries that ran down quickly. Gasoline

The Granger Collection, New York

Switchboard operators run one of the many telephone systems created after Alexander Graham Bell (right) invented the telephone.

The Granger Collection, New York

Economic Development

Telephone Companies. At first, the telephone was considered so unusual that Western Union called it a toy and refused to buy the rights from Alexander Graham Bell. However, the potential of the telephone quickly became apparent, and many companies tried to start their own phone services. In 1879 the Bell Telephone Company successfully sued Western Union after it started the American Speaking Telephone Company. Bell himself faced 587 lawsuits contesting his exclusive patent to the telephone. Some 125 companies operated phone services while the courts deliberated these lawsuits, but Bell won every case, including 13 that went all the way to the Supreme Court.

Critical Thinking: Why did so many companies want to operate a telephone service?

ANSWER: They realized that telephone service would be popular and could produce great profits.

REVIEW

Linguistic, Logical-Mathematical. Have students complete the Section Review questions. Then assign each student one invention or process discussed in this section. Have each student write a paragraph describing the industry before the invention and another paragraph describing the industry after the invention. Have volunteers read their paragraphs to the class.

ASSESS

Have students complete Daily Quiz 6.1

RETEACH

Linguistic, Visual-Spatial, Logical-Mathematical. Have students complete Main Ideas for Reteaching and Sheltered English 6.1. Then ask them to create crossword puzzles using the definitions of the section's key terms and the terms listed in the Identify portion of the Section Review as clues and the terms themselves as answers. Once the puzzles are created, have students exchange puzzles and fill in the answers. Finally, have students return the puzzles to their authors for grading. **SHELTERED ENGLISH**

Section 1 Review ANSWERS

Identify

For significance, see the following pages:

- Second Industrial Revolution, p. 184
- Bessemer process, p. 184
- Thomas Alva Edison, p. 185
- patent, p. 185
- Alexander Graham Bell, p. 187
- Orville and Wilbur Wright, p. 188

Reading for Content Understanding

1. Answers will vary but students should produce an organizer that correctly identifies five inventions, their inventors, and the date each was created.

2. Answers will vary but should mention that the inventions of the late 1800s allowed people to travel farther distances in shorter amounts of time, to communicate over longer distances more quickly, and to power their homes and businesses.

3. The U.S. economy changed from a rural, small-scale economy to the world's industrial leader.

4. Answers will vary but students should choose one invention and explain why it was the most important one.

5. Through the use of patents, inventors gain exclusive rights to manufacture or sell their inventions. Answers regarding whether patents encourage people to develop new technologies will vary but students should state their opinions and explain their reasoning.

soon competed with steam and electricity as a power source for a new type of transportation, the automobile.

In 1893 Charles and James Duryea used a gasoline engine to build the first practical motorcar in the United States. By the early 1900s thousands of cars were being built in the United States by many different manufacturers. Most of these early cars were too expensive for anyone but the wealthy to afford. As automobiles became more common, states began improving roads, passing traffic laws, and requiring car owners to take driving tests.

New engine technology also helped make another transportation breakthrough possible. Orville and Wilbur Wright were bicycle makers who began experimenting with airplane designs in the 1890s. Fascinated by flight, the brothers used the Smithsonian Institution to research previous flying attempts. They applied this research and their own theories to create a lightweight airplane with a small gas-powered engine.

In Kitty Hawk, North Carolina, Orville Wright made the first piloted flight in a powered plane on December 17, 1903. He later wrote:

> **"I got on the machine [airplane] at 10:35 for the first trial. . . . The machine lifted from the truck. . . . [It] would rise suddenly . . . and then as suddenly, on turning the rudder, dart for the ground. A sudden dart when out about 100 feet from the end of the tracks ended the flight. Time about 12 seconds."**

The Wright brothers' first airplane had to be steered while lying down. The plane was so light that a strong gust of wind could knock it over.

Those few seconds led to fame for the Wright brothers, who eventually achieved a flight of about 24 miles. They patented their airplane in 1906. Few planes were built in the United States before 1914, in part because early planes had limited range and cargo capacity.

Inventions such as the motorcar and the airplane resulted in great public excitement. However, they were not widely used at first, partly because of their cost. They eventually joined many other inventions of the late 1800s in changing the way that Americans worked, traveled, and lived.

SECTION 1 REVIEW

Identify and explain the significance of the following:

- **Second Industrial Revolution**
- **Bessemer process**
- **Thomas Alva Edison**
- **patent**
- **Alexander Graham Bell**
- **Orville and Wilbur Wright**

Reading for Content Understanding

1 **Main Idea** Create a graphic organizer listing at least five important inventions of the Second Industrial Revolution, their inventors, and the year that they were invented.

2 **Main Idea** How did inventions affect people's lives in the late 1800s?

3 **Technology and Society** How did the Second Industrial Revolution transform the U.S. economy?

4 **Writing** *Informing* Imagine that you are an editor of a magazine in the 1880s. Write a short editorial about what you think the most important invention of the period is and why.

5 **Critical Thinking** *Drawing Conclusions* What advantages do inventors gain from patenting an invention? Do you think this encourages inventors to develop new technologies? Explain your answer.

OBJECTIVES

- Identify changes in the way that businesses of the late 1800s were organized.
- Describe how some business leaders explained their success.
- Explain why some Americans opposed monopolies and how they fought them.

FOCUS

Motivate Before Reading

Write the title of this section, *Big Business*, on the chalkboard. Ask each student to list modern companies that they would associate with big business. Call on volunteers to read the names of the companies they identified and state what each one produces. Point out to the class any companies that are listed on more than one student's list. Explain to the class that they have probably learned

Section 2 RESOURCES

PRINT

★ Guided Reading Strategies 6.2

★ Section 2 Review, p. 194

★ Daily Quiz 6.2

MULTIMEDIA

★ *Teaching Resources CD–ROM*, Lesson 6.2

SHELTERED ENGLISH

★ Main Idea Activities for Reteaching and Sheltered English 6.2

Big Business

Reading Focus

What changes occurred in the way that businesses were organized in the late 1800s?

How did some business leaders explain the reasons for their success?

Why did some Americans oppose monopolies, and what action was taken?

Key Terms

free enterprise
entrepreneurs
corporations
vertical integration
horizontal integration
trust
Sherman Antitrust Act

IN HIS LECTURE TITLED "Acres of Diamonds," minister Russell H. Conwell declared, "I say that you ought to get rich. . . . It is all wrong to be poor." Conwell traveled the United States giving his speech throughout the late 1800s, presenting it some 6,000 times to an estimated 13 million people. He stressed the same theme repeatedly, "that in this country of ours every man has the opportunity to make more of himself." Conwell's audiences shared the fascination of many Americans for the wealth and power generated by big business.

A flyer announcing a Russell H. Conwell speech

 The Growth of Big Business

In the late 1800s the U.S. government generally promoted **free enterprise**—business that is free from government involvement. In 1883 Yale professor William Graham Sumner described free enterprise, also known as laissez-faire:

> **"Let us translate it into blunt English, and it will read, Mind your own business. It is nothing but the doctrine [idea] of liberty. Let every man be happy in his own way."**

The government did, however, promote the interests of business by giving such aid as protective tariffs for manufacturers and land grants to railroad companies. This assistance and the government's laissez-faire policies benefited **entrepreneurs**—people who start new businesses.

In the late 1800s, many entrepreneurs organized their businesses as **corporations**—companies that sell shares of ownership called stocks. Corporations must be approved and chartered by state governments. Stockholders in a corporation typically receive a dividend, or a percentage of company profits, that is based on how much stock about the modern companies they identified through television, magazines, or newspapers and that big business has become ingrained in American culture. Tell students that in this section they will learn about the birth and growth of big business in the United States.

Introduce Key Terms

Linguistic, Logical-Mathematical. Review this section's key terms with students. Then have them match each term with at least one other term and write a sentence identifying the relationship between them. Have students repeat this process until they have used each term at least once. For example, students can link *entrepreneurs* with *free enterprise* and point out that the goal of *entrepreneurs* in a *free enterprise* system is to make money. As students study this section, have them add information to explain the relationships. **SHELTERED ENGLISH**

TEACH

Have students read Section 2 and complete Guided Reading Strategies 6.2. Choose one or more of the following activities to explore the section content with students. For further suggestions on block scheduling or team teaching, see the *Block Scheduling Handbook.*

Economic Development

The Effects of Mergers. A wave of mergers that occurred in the United States during the late 1890s and early 1900s changed the structure of U.S. industry. Prior to this movement, very few companies controlled their industries on the national level. By 1904, however, more than half of the output in 78 industries was controlled by one or two competitors in each industry. These companies generally resulted from mergers. Mergers created companies that were worth huge amounts of money. In 1896, before the merger wave, less than 10 companies (excluding railroads) were worth more than $10 million each. Eight years later, 300 firms were worth that much.

Activity: Have students use the library or other resources to investigate the worth of companies that were formed as the result of mergers in the late 1890s or early 1900s and that still exist today. Have students determine the change in each company's worth since it merged.

CHART ANSWER

Both vertical and horizontal integration can be used as a way to cut down on production costs.

they own. Although the stockholders actually own the corporation, they do not run its day-to-day affairs. Instead, they elect a board of directors. The board in turn appoints the main officials of the corporation, such as the president and vice president.

Stock certificate

Corporations provided several important advantages over previous methods of organizing companies. Unlike business partners or members of joint-stock companies, the stockholders in a corporation are not personally responsible for the debts of the business. This means that if a corporation fails, the stockholders lose only the money that they invested. Stockholders are also usually free to sell their shares to whomever they want whenever they want. These factors made investing less risky than it had been previously and thus encouraged more investment in businesses. By 1900 more than 100 million shares a year were being traded on the New York Stock Exchange.

For entrepreneurs, stock sales provided a way to raise large amounts of money to pay for modern factories and to expand businesses. One corporate leader explained that shares of stock represented "nothing more than good will and prospective [expected] profits." These profits did not always appear, however.

Throughout the late 1800s, the economy followed a cycle of boom and bust, with businesses succeeding during the boom periods and failing during the busts. During the Panic of 1873, the New York Stock Exchange shut down for 10 days. The depression in 1893 had an even greater effect on the economy, causing unemployment and business failures across the nation. One businessman described his life in such bust times as being "work by day and worry by night, week in and week out, month after month." Despite these bust periods, American businesses continued to grow.

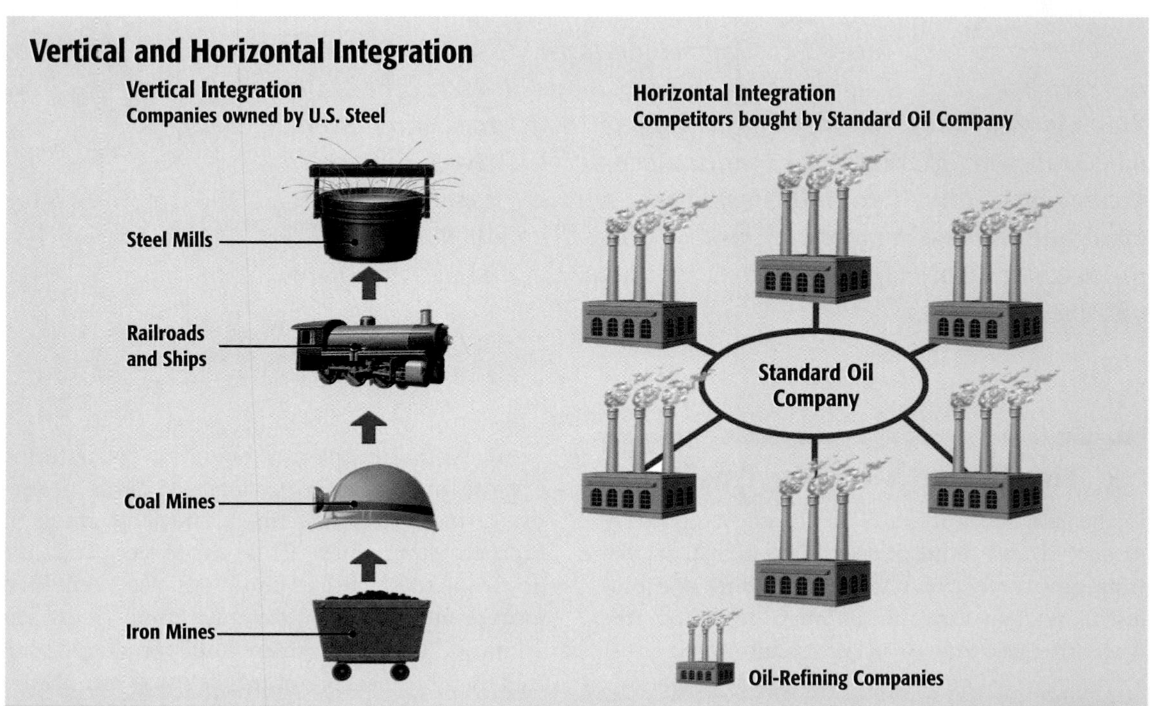

Big Business Corporations in the late 1800s used methods such as horizontal and vertical integration to increase tremendously in size. U.S. Steel owned companies associated with each step in the steel-making process. Standard Oil bought out most of its competitors. Why would horizontal or vertical integration help a company?

LEVEL 1: Linguistic. (Suggested time: 15 min.) As a class, go over students' Guided Reading Strategies. Then use the Reading Focus questions to highlight the main ideas of the section.

SHELTERED ENGLISH

ALL LEVELS: Linguistic, Logical-Mathematical. (Suggested time: 45 min.) Review the actions that led the U.S. government to try to control monopolies. Ask students to imagine that it is 1890 and the Sherman Antitrust Act is being debated in Congress. Have students send a telegram to a congressmember, either supporting or opposing the act. Ask students to use the text to support their individual positions and to design telegrams that are less than 50 words. (To help make the assignment historically realistic, you may want to provide students with a list of the Morse code symbols and have them translate their messages into the code. Such lists can be found in many dictionaries and encyclopedias.)

LEVEL 2: Linguistic, Logical-Mathematical, Intrapersonal. (Suggested time: 25 min. plus presentation) Ask students to imagine that they are key figures in the Second Industrial Revolution. Choices may include Andrew Carnegie, J. P. Morgan, John D. Rockefeller, Herbert Spencer, or any other individual mentioned in this section. Have each student develop a brief oral presentation explaining the individual's significance to the Second Industrial Revolution and how he became successful. Encourage volunteers to share their work with the class.

Business Leaders

Entrepreneurs and business leaders were some of the most widely respected members of American society in the late 1800s. Political leaders praised successful businesspeople as fine examples of American individuality and talent.

Carnegie and Steel

Andrew Carnegie was one of the most admired business leaders of the late 1800s. While working as an executive for the Pennsylvania Railroad, Carnegie used personal connections to borrow money that he then invested in iron mills and bridge-building businesses. These investments were so successful that in 1865 Carnegie left the railroad company. "I was no longer merely an official working for others . . . ," he wrote, "but a full-fledged business man."

Inspired by the Bessemer process, in 1873 Carnegie focused his efforts on steelmaking. He expanded by buying out his competitors when steel prices were low. Although he never held a monopoly on steel production in the United States, by 1900 Carnegie's mills were producing more steel than all of Britain's steel mills combined. Carnegie's businesses succeeded in part through his use of **vertical integration**—owning businesses involved in each step of a manufacturing process. To lower his cost of production, Carnegie purchased the iron ore mines, coal fields, and railroads needed to supply and support his steel mills.

Rockefeller and Oil

John D. Rockefeller was also extremely successful in business consolidation. He began his rise to wealth and power as a bookkeeper. By age 21 he was a partner in a wholesale business and soon decided to start an oil-refining company. By 1870 Rockefeller's Standard Oil Company, which started in Cleveland, Ohio, was the nation's largest oil refiner. Like Carnegie, Rockefeller used vertical integration. Standard Oil made its own barrels and cans and controlled most of the pipelines, tank cars, and storage facilities it used. Many railroads that wanted Standard Oil's valuable shipping business offered Rockefeller lower rates and rebates—partial returns of payment. At times he even got railroads to agree not to provide service to his competitors.

Rockefeller's company was also organized through **horizontal integration**—owning all the businesses in a particular field. By 1879 his companies controlled more than 90 percent of the U.S. oil-refining business, making them a monopoly. Rockefeller used consolidation as a means of cutting costs. He also formed a **trust**—a legal arrangement grouping together a number of companies under a single board of directors. To earn higher

Biography

Andrew Carnegie

Andrew Carnegie was born in Scotland in 1835 and immigrated to Pennsylvania at age 13. As a teenager, Carnegie worked at a textile mill, then as a machine cleaner in a factory. His big break came when he got a job as a railroad messenger, which led to his becoming a telegraph operator and then an assistant to a railroad manager.

Carnegie constantly impressed his employers with his hard work and ability to learn quickly. One employer, Thomas Scott, loaned Carnegie $600 to make his first investment in a company. Carnegie soon became wealthy by making wise investment choices. Unlike many other successful businesspeople of his era, Carnegie continued to live very simply, warning that "the amassing of wealth is one of the worst species of idolatry [worship of false images]."

Biography

Andrew Carnegie. Although committed to philanthropy, Andrew Carnegie did not feel guilty about amassing a great fortune. Carnegie believed that the best way to help humanity was to allow individuals to make large amounts of money that they could distribute to society's needy. In *"The Gospel of Wealth,"* Carnegie claimed that "even the poorest can be made to see this, and to agree that great sums gathered by some of their fellow citizens and spent for public purposes, from which the masses reap the principal benefit, are more valuable to them than if scattered among themselves in trifling amounts."

Critical Thinking: Explain why you agree or disagree with Carnegie's claims.

ANSWER: Answers will vary. Some students may argue that philanthropists who have experience with money will best know how to spend it. Others may point out that each individual knows what he or she needs most.

LEVEL 3: Linguistic, Logical-Mathematical. (Suggested time: 45 min. plus homework) Explain to students that the way businesses were organized and run changed during the Second Industrial Revolution. Have students write a short report describing business changes mentioned in this section. Ask students to include the following topics in their reports: formation of corporations, introduction of vertical integration, use of horizontal integration, and establishment of trusts. Have students describe how each of these business practices altered the way industries were organized and operated. Finally, lead a discussion on the changes in business practices that occurred during this period.

CLOSE

Linguistic, Visual-Spatial. Organize students into groups of three and assign each member one of the following topics dealing with business organization: vertical integration, horizontal integration, or trusts. Ask group members to imagine that they are presidents of major corporations at the turn of the century. Tell them that they are each to appear before their corporation's board of directors (the rest of the class) to explain changes in organizational structure that they would like to introduce to the business. Encourage students to develop simple visual aids to help clarify the

Historical Sidelight

The Sherman Antitrust Act. Although the Sherman Antitrust Act was ratified in 1890 by both houses of Congress, with only one dissenting vote, it did not immediately bring about significant change. Many business leaders ignored it, which is evidenced by the merger movement that took place shortly after the act was passed. This lack of change was due in part to the Supreme Court's narrow interpretation of the act in cases such as *United States* v. *E.C. Knight Co.* In this 1895 case the Court ruled that the mergers involving American Sugar Refining Company—which controlled more than 98 percent of the nation's sugar refining—did not fall under the realm of the Sherman Antitrust Act because the mergers dealt with manufacturing rather than interstate commerce.

Activity: Have students use the library and other resources to find information on *United States* v. *E.C. Knight Co.* and write a summary of the Court's ruling.

Historical Documents Answers

1. He believes individualism, private property, the law of accumulation of wealth, and the law of competition are humanity's highest accomplishments.

2. These laws are sometimes unequal, unjust and imperfect.

profits, trusts often tried to eliminate competition and to regulate production, raising prices for consumers in the process. Rockefeller stated, "The day of combination [trusts] is here to stay. Individualism has gone, never to return."

Social Darwinism and Philanthropy

Many individuals who supported laissez-faire capitalism also believed in social Darwinism. This was a view of society based loosely on scientist Charles Darwin's theory of natural selection.

Darwin argued that over long periods of time species evolved by adapting to their environments. Social Darwinists argued that a similar process took place in human societies, and that

John D. Rockefeller founded several philanthropic organizations.

"survival of the fittest" determined who would succeed. Important social Darwinists such as sociologist Herbert Spencer also claimed that government regulation of businesses harmed the "natural" economic order.

Business leaders such as Andrew Carnegie and John D. Rockefeller supported Spencer's theories. Rockefeller once told a Sunday school class that

> **"the growth of large business is merely a survival of the fittest. . . . This is not an evil tendency in business. It is merely the working-out of a law of nature and a law of God."**

Some business leaders used social Darwinism to justify their accumulation of great wealth while their companies supported child labor, low wages, and unsafe working conditions. If poor people wanted to improve their situation, these leaders argued, it was their own responsibility to work hard and rise above the rest of society. Other business leaders claimed that the wealthy had a duty to aid the poor because nature predetermined who was poor and who was rich. These leaders tried to help the poor through philanthropy, or giving money to charities.

Such beliefs led Carnegie to give away most of his fortune. During his lifetime he donated more than $350 million to charity. About $60 million of this money went to found public libraries, in order to expand access to books. Other business leaders, including Rockefeller, also gave large amounts of money to various causes. By the late 1800s, charities had received millions of dollars from philanthropists.

HISTORICAL DOCUMENTS

1889

Andrew Carnegie's *The Gospel of Wealth*

The following excerpt is from an article written by Andrew Carnegie in 1889. Later called "The Gospel of Wealth," it explains his views on capitalism.

> "Individualism, private property, the law of accumulation of wealth, and the law of competition . . . these are the highest results of human experience, the soil in which society so far has produced the best fruit. Unequally or unjustly, perhaps, as these laws sometimes operate, and imperfect as they appear to the idealist, they are, nevertheless, . . . the best and most valuable of all that humanity has yet accomplished."

Understanding Primary Sources

1. What laws does Andrew Carnegie believe are humanity's highest accomplishments?
2. What flaws does Carnegie note in these laws?

changes they would like to make. Also, ask them to refer to other successful corporations that have adopted the practices.

CHALLENGE AND EXTEND

1. **Linguistic, Logical-Mathematical.** Have students use the library or other resources to find information on businesses that came under scrutiny as a result of the Sherman Antitrust Act. Have each student write a summary of why the practices of a specific business were called into question and how the new law affected the business. Call on volunteers to share their work with the rest of the class.

2. **Logical-Mathematical, Visual-Spatial.** Remind students that corporations sell stocks. Show students how to track stocks using a newspaper. Have each student choose at least two stocks to track. (You may wish to have them track corporations that were in existence during the time frame of this chapter, such as Western Union or Ford Motor Company.) Have students check the value of the companies' stock for an entire month and create a line graph depicting changes in value over the period. Once students have finished tracking their stocks, discuss the differences between the values of each corporation's stocks and ask students to hypothesize on reasons for the changes.

American Literature

The House of Mirth
Edith Wharton

The House of Mirth *was written by Edith Wharton in 1905. It established her as a popular and critically successful author. The novel is the story of Lily Bart, a young woman trying first to advance and then to preserve her place in New York City high society. The novel describes the resentment faced by newly rich families attempting to join this restricted social circle. It also explores the power of money and the changing world of the city. In the following excerpt, the season of dinner parties, entertaining, and theater-going has begun under the watchful eye of the wealthy Mrs. Peniston.*

Fifth Avenue had become a nightly torrent [flood] of carriages surging upward to the fashionable quarters about the [Central] Park, where illuminated windows and outspread awnings betokened [showed] the usual routine of hospitality. . . .

This particular season Mrs. Peniston would have characterized as that in which everybody "felt poor" except the Welly Brys and Mr. Simon Rosedale. It had been a bad autumn in Wall Street. . . . Even fortunes supposed to be independent of the market either betrayed a secret dependence on it, or suffered from a sympathetic affection [connection]: fashion sulked in its countryhouses, or came to town incognito [disguised], general entertainments were discountenanced [disapproved], and informality and short dinners became the fashion. . . .

The Granger Collection, New York

Edith Wharton won a Pulitzer Prize in 1920 for her novel The Age of Innocence.

The mere fact of growing richer at a time when most people's investments are shrinking, is calculated to attract envious attention; and according to Wall Street rumours, Welly Bry and Rosedale had found the secret of performing this miracle.

Rosedale, in particular, was said to have doubled his fortune, and there was talk of his buying the newly-finished house of one of the victims of the crash, who, in the space of twelve short months, had made the same number of millions, built a house on Fifth Avenue, filled a picture-gallery with old masters [valuable paintings], entertained all New York in it, and [then] been smuggled out of the country between a trained nurse and a doctor, while his creditors mounted guard over the old masters, and his guests explained to each other that they had dined with him only because they wanted to see the pictures. Mr. Rosedale meant to have a less meteoric [fast-rising and fast-falling] career.

Understanding Literature

1. What has caused many members of New York's upper class to "feel poor"?
2. How does Simon Rosedale attract the attention of high society?
3. What does the story of the "victim of the crash" suggest about the attitudes of some members of New York's upper class?

Biography

Edith Wharton. During Edith Wharton's life, the United States went from being an isolationist nation to one of the world's major powers. Although a business boom was occurring around her, Wharton chose instead to focus her stories on less obvious changes in American society. Her first major novel, *The House of Mirth,* dealt with the social scene in New York at the beginning of the 1900s and one woman's struggle between middle-class morals and her search for wealth. It was a tremendous critical success, as was Wharton's Pulitzer Prize–winning novel, *The Age of Innocence.*

Activity: Read other sections of *The House of Mirth* to students and ask them to consider how these selections compare to the excerpt on this page. Have students create book jackets containing information on the book and the author.

American Literature Answers

1. trouble in the stock market
2. by buying the luxurious, well-decorated house on Fifth Avenue that had once belonged to another investor in the stock market
3. It suggests that people are important when they have money, and do not really exist or matter once they lose money.

REVIEW

Linguistic, Interpersonal. Have students complete the Section Review questions. Then organize the class into two groups—one supporting business monopolies, and the other opposing them. Have students in each group refer to the text to support their position. After groups have gathered information, have them debate the following question: Is the Sherman Antitrust Act an overall benefit to the United States? Then review the arguments for and against the act.

ASSESS

Have students complete Daily Quiz 6.2.

RETEACH

Visual-Spatial, Logical-Mathematical. Have students complete Main Idea Activities for Reteaching and Sheltered English 6.2. Review the concepts of vertical and horizontal integration with the class. Have students create political cartoons showing the benefits of either vertical or horizontal integration.

SHELTERED ENGLISH

Section 2 Review ANSWERS

Identify
For significance, see the following pages:

- free enterprise, p. 189
- entrepreneurs, p. 189
- corporations, p. 189
- Andrew Carnegie, p. 191
- vertical integration, p. 191
- John D. Rockefeller, p. 191
- horizontal integration, p. 191
- trust, p. 191
- Sherman Antitrust Act, p. 194

Reading for Content Understanding

1. Social Darwinists argued that "survival of the fittest" would determine who would succeed and that government interference in business would upset the natural order.

2. They demanded government intervention to control the growth and actions of monopolies and trusts. These people did so because they believed that competition was needed to keep prices low and the quality of goods and services high.

3. corporations, vertical integration, horizontal integration, trusts

4. Answers will vary but students should state whether they would support the legislation and explain why.

5. Answers will vary but students should state whether they agree with Carnegie and other business leaders and explain their reasoning.

The Antitrust Movement

Critics of big business argued that many entrepreneurs earned their fortunes not through natural selection but by using unfair business practices. These criticisms grew stronger in the 1880s as corporations became more powerful. Large corporations often used their size and power to drive smaller competitors out of business. Andrew Carnegie and John D. Rockefeller pressured railroads to charge their companies lower shipping rates. Powerful trusts also arranged to sell goods and services at prices below market value. After smaller competitors went bankrupt trying to match these prices, the trusts would raise them again.

Opponents became concerned when trusts gained a monopoly on a product such as oil or a service such as telephone communication. Critics argued that such monopolies reduced the competition that was needed to keep prices low and the quality of goods and services high. Members of monopolistic trusts regularly agreed to match each other's prices to avoid the risks of competition. Other companies merged with their rivals to dominate an industry or a service. Powerful businessman and banker J. P. Morgan once said, "I like a little competition, but I like combination better." Some Americans were also concerned about the political influence of wealthy trusts. Union leader John W. Hayes called trusts "the common enemy of society."

Monopolies and trusts pick Uncle Sam's pockets in this cartoon.

Many citizens and small businesses demanded government action to help control monopolies and trusts. Supporters of trusts responded that they were more efficient and gave the consumer a reliable product. One newspaper editor declared that "the right to cooperate is as unquestionable as the right to compete."

Although many in Congress were supportive of big business, they could not ignore the concerns of voters. As Senator John Sherman explained, "You must heed their appeal. . . . Society is now disturbed by forces never felt before." In July 1890 Congress passed the **Sherman Antitrust Act**, which stated that any "attempt to monopolize . . . any part of the trade or commerce among the several States" was a crime. However, the act did not clearly define just what a trust was in legal terms. The antitrust laws were thus difficult to enforce, and corporations and trusts continued to grow in size and power.

SECTION 2 REVIEW

Identify and explain the significance of the following:

- **free enterprise**
- **entrepreneurs**
- **corporations**
- **Andrew Carnegie**
- **vertical integration**
- **John D. Rockefeller**
- **horizontal integration**
- **trust**
- **Sherman Antitrust Act**

Reading for Content Understanding

1 **Main Idea** What did social Darwinists argue about society?

2 **Main Idea** How and why did some people try to protect business competition?

3 **Economic Development** What new forms of business ownership and organization developed in the late 1800s?

4 **Writing** *Persuading* Imagine that you are a member of Congress debating antitrust legislation. Write a short speech arguing why trusts and monopolies should or should not be controlled by law.

5 **Critical Thinking** *Supporting a Point of View* Do you agree with the ideas expressed by business leaders such as Andrew Carnegie about the importance of competition, individualism, and philanthropy? Explain your answer.

OBJECTIVES

- **Explain how the Second Industrial Revolution affected U.S. workers.**
- **Describe why workers formed labor unions and how these unions were organized.**
- **Examine how major strikes affected workers.**

FOCUS

Motivate Before Reading

Ask students to imagine playing a team game or sport for school in which the rules suddenly became much more rigid and hard to follow. Then ask students what difficulties might be involved in convincing everyone to refuse to play until the rules were changed. *(Students might mention that some might not wish to sit out of the game for fear that they would not be allowed to play in the future.)*

Industrial Workers

Reading Focus

How did the Second Industrial Revolution affect U.S. workers?

Why did workers form labor unions, and how were they organized?

How did major labor strikes affect workers?

Key Terms

collective bargaining
Knights of Labor
Haymarket Riot
American Federation of Labor
Homestead Strike
Pullman Strike

AT THE BEGINNING OF the Second Industrial Revolution, skilled workers called puddlers turned hot, liquid iron into steel. One puddler said he felt "like some frantic baker in the inferno kneading a batch of iron bread." Puddlers' skills made them valuable to employers and difficult to replace. However, over time, factory owners began replacing puddlers with machines. Like many other skilled workers, puddlers began losing their jobs as well as their bargaining power with employers.

Labor union announcement

The New Workplace

During the Second Industrial Revolution, machines run by unskilled workers replaced many skilled craftspeople. Because these low-paid workers required little training, they usually could be replaced easily. Therefore, they feared that complaining about wages or working conditions would cause them to lose their jobs.

As machines became more widely used in industries, factories focused on specialization—having workers repeatedly perform a single step in the production process. Specialization lowered costs and increased production. This focus on reducing costs caused managers to value efficiency.

In the early 1880s Frederick W. Taylor, an efficiency engineer with the Midvale Steel Company, performed time-and-motion studies to standardize worker activity. Taylor examined the steps that workers performed to do their jobs and measured the time each step took. He then found ways to do these tasks more efficiently, in order to lower labor costs and make them a measurable, predictable part of production. Taylor explained that "in the past the man has been first; in the future the system must be first."

Section 3
RESOURCES

PRINT

- ★ Guided Reading Strategies 6.3
- ★ Primary Source Reading 6: Autobiography of Mother Jones
- ★ Biography Reading 6: Frederick W. Taylor
- ★ Geography Activity 6: Pullman's Company Town
- ★ Section 3 Review, p. 199
- ★ Daily Quiz 6.3

MULTIMEDIA

- ★ *Teaching Resources CD–ROM*, Lesson 6.3
- ★ HRW Web site

SHELTERED ENGLISH

- ★ Main Idea Activities for Reteaching and Sheltered English 6.3

Tell students that in this section they will learn how industrial workers dealt with similar difficulties and about problems associated with forming unions.

Introduce Key Terms

Linguistic, Interpersonal. Review this section's key terms with students. Then ask them to write at least one question about each term. Have students choose partners, exchange papers, and attempt to answer the questions. Instruct students to keep the questions they answered to use during the Reteach activity.
SHELTERED ENGLISH

TEACH

Have students read Section 3 and complete Guided Reading Strategies 6.3. Choose one or more of the following activities to explore the section content with students. For further suggestions on block scheduling or team teaching, see the *Block Scheduling Handbook*.

LEVEL 1: Linguistic. (Suggested time: 15 min.) As a class, go over students' Guided Reading Strategies. Then use the Reading Focus questions to highlight the main ideas of the section.
SHELTERED ENGLISH

Across the Curriculum

LITERATURE

Out of This Furnace. In 1941 Thomas Bell published the novel *Out of This Furnace*, the story of an immigrant family living in Pennsylvania. Bell described the exhausting routine of mill work when he explained that "Kracha worked from six to six, seven days a week, one week on day turn, one week on night. . . . At the end of each day-turn week came the long turn of twenty-four hours, when he went into the mill Sunday morning at six and worked continuously until Monday morning." Bell noted that this "constant shifting of turns made settlement into an energy-saving routine impossible; just when he was getting used to sleeping at night he had to learn to sleep during the day."

Activity: Have students use the library or search the Internet through the HRW Web site to find information on the lives of steelworkers. Ask students to write a short fictional account from the perspective of a steelworker.

go.hrw.com
SB1 Steelworkers

The Granger Collection, New York

Scientific management encouraged the creation of factories like this one, where each worker performed a few specific tasks.

Taylor's ideas became so popular that he left Midvale and became a well-known and successful consultant to many businesses. In 1911 he published *The Principles of Scientific Management* and established efficiency studies as a standard part of U.S. industry.

By focusing on how to reduce the cost of labor, scientific management encouraged managers to see workers as parts of the production process, not as individuals. In factories, managers increasingly ignored working conditions. Managers strictly regulated workers' activities, such as taking a break to get a drink of water. Injuries increased as workers used more machines and were pushed to work at a rapid pace. Companies rarely took responsibility for work-related injuries. As conditions grew worse, workers sought ways to bring about change.

 Labor Unions

To improve working conditions, workers formed labor unions, usually in spite of their employers' objections. Unions increased workers' power because an entire workforce of a business was not as easily replaced as one individual worker. When all workers acted collectively, or together, they had a much greater chance of success. Unions tried to use **collective bargaining**—in which union leaders negotiated for better wages and working conditions on behalf of all workers in a particular factory or industry. Most employers opposed collective bargaining, sharing the feelings of one company president who said, "I shall never give in. I would rather go out of business."

The Knights of Labor

Founded by Uriah Stephens, the **Knights of Labor** was a union originally organized like a secret society. During a depression in the 1870s, the union built a network of local assemblies. It sought to, as Stephens said, "include men and women of every creed and color." In 1879 Terence V. Powderly became the leader of the Knights. He eliminated the secrecy surrounding the organization and turned it into the first truly national labor union in the United States. Under Powderly's leadership, the Knights worked for goals such as an eight-hour workday, equal pay for equal work, regulation of trusts, and an end to child labor. Unlike most unions at the time, the Knights welcomed both skilled and unskilled workers as members.

Women not only joined the union but also took an active role in it. Union organizer Mary Harris Jones was called Mother Jones by the workers whose rights she fought to protect. Jones organized

The Knights of Labor was one of the few unions to accept African Americans like Frank J. Farrell (left), shown here introducing Terence V. Powderly (center).

The Granger Collection, New York

ALL LEVELS: Linguistic, Logical-Mathematical, Intrapersonal. (Suggested time: 30 min. plus presentation) Have students review the section to determine the reasons that workers formed unions. Ask them to imagine that they are union representatives attempting to convince a group of workers to join the union. Then have each student write a speech convincing the workers to join. Encourage students to include emotional and logical appeals to workers. Ask volunteers to share their speeches with the class.

LEVEL 3: Linguistic. (Suggested time: 45 min. plus homework) Explain to students that early labor strikes often resulted in violence and that the government usually sided with businesses when determining ways to end disputes. Assign students one of the following topics: the Haymarket Riot, the Homestead Strike, or the Pullman Strike. Ask students to write a newspaper article describing the assigned event, why violence occurred (if it did), and how the strike affected workers. Then ask students to write editorials in response to the articles, offering their opinions about the events, workers' actions, the company's actions, and any government involvement.

LEVEL 3: Visual-Spatial, Logical-Mathematical. (Suggested time: 45 min.) Explain to students that a series of interrelated issues led to growing unrest among workers during the late 1800s. Have students create flowcharts identifying the relationships

many strikes among workers, such as a group of poorly paid Virginia miners whose lives were very difficult. She described their condition:

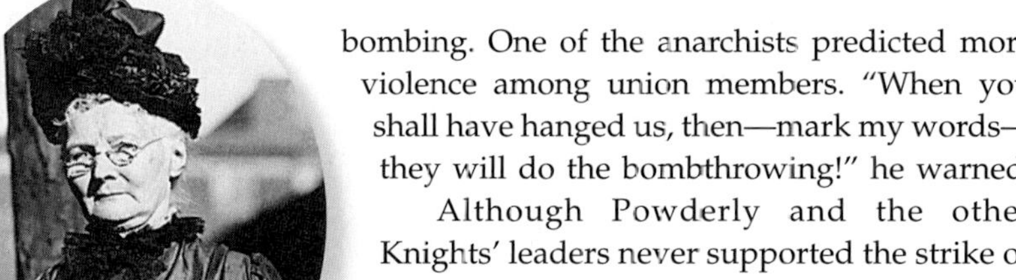

Mary Harris "Mother" Jones

> **"In some of these [company] camps the miners are forced to pay as much as $9 a barrel for sugar, 18 cents a pound for fat pork, and $8 to $10 a month rent for a company shack, the roof of which is so poor that when it rains the bed is moved from place to place in the attempt to find a dry spot. Many a miner works his whole life and never handles a cent of money."**

Even though workers faced such problems, Powderly was reluctant to support strikes. Local Knights of Labor chapters, however, supported the great railroad strike of 1877 that affected the nation from coast to coast. Such strikes led the Knights to their greatest strength in the mid-1880s. By 1886 the Knights' membership had increased to 700,000.

The Haymarket Riot

By 1886 other unions were gaining strength. In May thousands of union members in Chicago, Illinois, went on strike to support an eight-hour workday. Two strikers were killed in a clash with police. The next night, workers met at Haymarket Square to protest the killings. When police arrived to break up the crowd, someone threw a bomb that wounded more than 60 officers and killed 8 of them. The police responded by firing into the crowd, killing several people and wounding 100 others. The Chicago *Herald* described the event that became known as the **Haymarket Riot** as "wild carnage [slaughter]."

Eight anarchists—people who oppose all forms of government—were arrested and convicted of conspiracy, although there was no hard evidence directly linking them to the bombing. One of the anarchists predicted more violence among union members. "When you shall have hanged us, then—mark my words—they will do the bombthrowing!" he warned.

Although Powderly and the other Knights' leaders never supported the strike or the Haymarket demonstration, several local chapters of the Knights did. One of the convicted anarchists, Albert Parsons, held a Knights of Labor membership card. Public opinion linked the Knights to the Haymarket Riot and its violence. As a result, membership in the Knights declined rapidly.

The AFL

Another union, the **American Federation of Labor** (AFL), fared better than the Knights. Unlike the Knights, the AFL organized individual national unions, such as the mineworkers and the steelworkers unions, into a loose association. Led by Samuel Gompers, the AFL limited its membership to skilled workers, which gave the union great bargaining power but excluded the majority of workers.

Gompers said that the AFL tried to "accomplish the best results in improving the conditions of the working people . . . today and tomorrow" by negotiating for better wages, hours, and working conditions. By 1890 the AFL's membership was larger than that of the Knights and by 1904 it had more than 1.5 million members.

The bombing at Haymarket Square resulted in the deaths of several police officers and a decline in union support.

Using Visual Resources

Mother Jones. Mary Harris Jones began her work organizing coal miners living in Pennsylvania during the 1890s. In 1900, when she was leading a strike of hard-coal workers, newspapers published photographs showing her as a grandmotherly figure—as in the photograph on this page—leading miners to protest poor working conditions. Her grandmotherly appearance did not detract from her militant views or her sharp wit, however. Having a flair for the dramatic in all of her endeavors, in the strike of 1900 Harris organized the wives of the miners to march over the mountains late at night, while banging tin pans. The women then blocked any workers who attempted to break the strike the following morning.

Activity: Have students use the library or search the Internet through the HRW Web site to find information on Mother Jones. Then have students write a letter of recognition, citing her achievements as a labor organizer.

go.hrw.com
SB1 Mother Jones

among the following occurrences: managers began to focus on efficiency; unskilled workers began running machines; on-the-job injuries increased; workers kept silent about low wages and poor conditions for fear of being fired; machines began to replace skilled workers; production increased while production costs decreased; machines became more widely used; managers ignored working conditions; and factories focused on specialization.

CLOSE

Logical-Mathematical. Write the following Reading Focus question on the chalkboard: *How did the Second Industrial Revolution affect U.S. workers?* Then have each student make a two-column chart listing the impact of the Second Industrial Revolution on workers. Ask them to list positive effects in one column and negative effects in the other. Ask volunteers to share their charts with the class. **SHELTERED ENGLISH**

CHALLENGE AND EXTEND

Musical-Rhythmic, Interpersonal. Provide students with sample lyrics from songs dealing with the labor movement of the late 1800s. (Philip Foner's *American Labor Songs of the Nineteenth Century* is a good source.) Have students examine the lyrics to

Citizenship and Democracy

Labor and Anarchists. Organized labor discovered that assistance from anarchists did not help their cause. Anarchists—particularly those who used violence—were unpopular with the public. Moreover, when anarchists became involved in labor activities, the public often blamed labor unions for the resulting violence. After anarchist Alexander Berkman shot Henry Frick during the Homestead Strike, Berkman was surprised that the workers denounced him for using violence. One striker told him that the workers respected the law and opposed violence. Berkman spent 14 years in prison for his crime.

Critical Thinking: Why did the workers reject anarchism?

ANSWER: Workers were striking to receive more benefits from the U.S. economic and political system, not to destroy that system. In addition, anarchists turned the public against unions.

MAP ANSWER
Nevada

Strikes Against the Entrepreneurs

Unions continued to use strikes to improve conditions. Sometimes workers went on strike for the right to create a union or establish a chapter of a national union. Sometimes business owners pushed unions into striking in hopes of gaining government support in breaking the union. One such conflict occurred in 1892 at one of Andrew Carnegie's steel plants.

The Homestead Strike

Previously, workers had gotten along well with managers at the Carnegie Steel Company in the mill town of Homestead, Pennsylvania. This changed in 1889 when Henry Frick became chairman of the company. In 1892, union members protested Frick's plan to introduce new machinery to the plant. New machines would reduce the number of workers. When an agreement with the union could not be reached, Frick set out to break the union and cut costs. He announced that the company would negotiate only with individual workers, not the union.

On June 29 the **Homestead Strike** began while Carnegie was out of the country. Frick locked workers out of the plant. He refused to negotiate with the union or allow union members back to work. The workers responded by seizing control of the town of Homestead. Frick then hired private detectives from the Pinkerton agency to break the power of the union by force.

The striking workers were prepared, however. Gunfire erupted on July 6, when the Pinkerton detectives tried to enter the steelworks from barges on the Monongahela River. Nine workers and seven Pinkertons were killed in the battle that followed. After a long standoff, the outnumbered and trapped Pinkertons surrendered. They were then marched through the streets and insulted by crowds. Pennsylvania's governor called out the state militia to restore order. Although the strike continued for four more months, the union was eventually defeated. Frick sent a message to

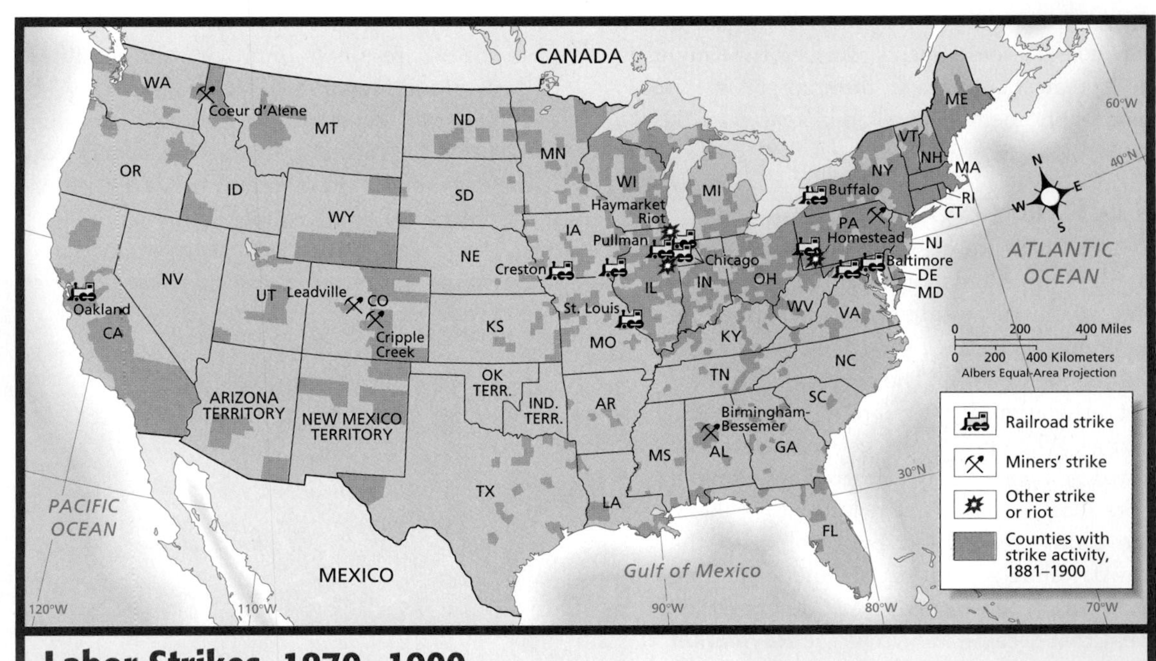

Labor Strikes, 1870–1900

Learning from Maps Workers went on strike to improve wages and working conditions. Many strikes cost lives and accomplished little for the workers.

Place Which state had no strikes or riots from 1881 to 1900?

songs that express themes that are discussed in the text. Ask students to use these themes to write their own labor song.

REVIEW

Linguistic, Interpersonal. Have students complete the Section Review questions. Then ask them to imagine that the Haymarket Riot occurred in modern times. Have students work in groups to write a script for a five-minute news report on the riot. Have each group present its report to the class. Encourage students to offer feedback on other groups' reports.

ASSESS

Have students complete Daily Quiz 6.3.

RETEACH

Linguistic. Have students complete Main Idea Activities for Reteaching and Sheltered English 6.3. Then ask them to write what they learned about each of the key terms. Refer students to the questions they answered in the Introduce Key Terms activity. Ask them to see if they can now answer the questions. Lead a discussion on any topic that students still find difficult.
SHELTERED ENGLISH

Carnegie, "Our victory is now complete."

The Pullman Strike

Another major strike occurred among the workers at George Pullman's company. The Pullman Palace Car Company had established the company town of Pullman, Illinois, where most of its workers lived. Workers had to pay higher rents and utility costs than in nearby towns.

The Granger Collection, New York

Pinkertons confront workers during the Homestead Strike.

During a depression that began in 1893, Pullman laid off nearly half of the company's workers and cut the wages of those who remained by 25–40 percent without lowering rents. On May 11, 1894, workers protesting the wage cuts began the **Pullman Strike**. Support for the strike quickly spread throughout the railroad industry. The American Railway Union, headed by Eugene V. Debs, supported the strikers by refusing to work on trains carrying Pullman cars. By July, traffic on most midwestern rail lines was halted because almost all trains carried Pullman cars. The railroad officials then ordered the Pullman cars to be attached to U.S. mail cars, so that workers who stopped Pullman cars could be charged with the federal offense of interfering with the U.S. mail.

The federal government backed the railroad companies. Despite the protest of the Illinois governor, President Grover Cleveland sent federal troops to Chicago, the heart of the strike. Cleveland vowed:

> **"If it takes every dollar in the Treasury and every soldier in the United States to deliver a postal card in Chicago, that postal card should be delivered."**

The U.S. attorney general broke the strike by securing a court order demanding that the workers stop their strike because they were acting in restraint of trade. He used the Sherman Antitrust Act—originally intended to curb big business, not labor—to get the court order and keep the trains rolling. Debs was arrested and later sentenced to six months in jail for violating the court order. Strikes continued, but defeats like the Pullman Strike and the government's continued support of big business over the unions set the industrial labor movement back for several decades to come.

SECTION 3 REVIEW

Identify and explain the significance of the following:

- **Frederick W. Taylor**
- **collective bargaining**
- **Knights of Labor**
- **Terence V. Powderly**
- **Mary Harris Jones**
- **Haymarket Riot**
- **American Federation of Labor**
- **Samuel Gompers**
- **Henry Frick**
- **Homestead Strike**
- **Pullman Strike**

Reading for Content Understanding

1 Main Idea Why were the Knights of Labor and the American Federation of Labor formed, and how were they organized?

2 Main Idea How did the major strikes of the late 1800s affect American workers?

3 Technology and Society What impact did changes in industry and new technology have on the workplace?

4 Writing *Describing* Imagine that you are a newspaper journalist during the Haymarket Riot. Write a short article describing the events and outcome of the riot.

5 Critical Thinking *Making Comparisons* Compare the Knights of Labor with the American Federation of Labor. How were the unions similar? How were they different?

Section 3 Review ANSWERS

Identify

For significance, see the following pages:

- Frederick W. Taylor, p. 195
- collective bargaining, p. 196
- Knights of Labor, p. 196
- Terence V. Powderly, p. 196
- Mary Harris Jones, p. 196
- Haymarket Riot, p. 197
- American Federation of Labor, p. 197
- Samuel Gompers, p. 197
- Henry Frick, p. 198
- Homestead Strike, p. 198
- Pullman Strike, p. 199

Reading for Content Understanding

1. to gain better wages and working conditions; the Knights of Labor had a network of local assemblies that accepted skilled and unskilled workers of any race or sex. The American Federation of Labor was a loosely organized group of national unions that was made up of skilled laborers.

2. Workers benefited little from the strikes because business leaders and the government were not willing to negotiate.

3. New changes in industry and technology often eliminated the jobs of skilled workers, who could be replaced by low-wage, unskilled workers.

4. Articles should define anarchism and describe the impact of the riot on organized labor.

5. Answers will vary according to students' opinions but should explain that the Knights of Labor accepted skilled and unskilled workers, while the AFL allowed only skilled workers.

OBJECTIVES

- Examine the effects of industrialization on farmers and actions they took to fight for change.
- Explain how farmers wanted to change the money supply.
- Describe the issues supported by the Populists.

FOCUS

Motivate Before Reading

Ask students to define the term *inflation.* If they have difficulty, explain its meaning. Then tell students that during the late 1800s and early 1900s, many farmers supported using inflation as an economic tool to help them pay their debts. Ask students what kind of debts farmers might incur and how inflation could help remedy

Section 4 RESOURCES

PRINT

★ Guided Reading Strategies 6.4

★ Literature Reading 6: *Struggling Upwards*

★ Section 4 Review, p. 205

★ Daily Quiz 6.4

MULTIMEDIA

★ *Teaching Resources CD–ROM,* Lesson 6.4

★ Everyday Life in America Transparency 16: Farming Technology, Late 1800s

SHELTERED ENGLISH

★ Main Idea Activities for Reteaching and Sheltered English 6.4

SECTION 4

Populism

Reading Focus

What effects did industrialization have on farmers, and what actions did farmers take to fight for change?

How did farmers want to change the money supply?

What issues did the Populist Party support?

Key Terms

National Grange
Interstate Commerce Act
Interstate Commerce Commission
free coinage
gold standard
Sherman Silver Purchase Act
Farmers' Alliances
Populist Party

IN THE LATE 1800S many western farmers blamed their economic hardships on the railroads. Frank Norris's 1901 novel, The Octopus, *shows the farmers' point of view. The octopus in the story is the railroads, which threaten farmers' livelihoods by charging high rates. When farmer Dyke asks a railroad official on what basis the company raised shipping rates, the response is: "All—the—traffic—will—bear." However, the rate increase will leave Dyke with no profit from his harvest. Unless Dyke pays back the money he borrowed to raise his crops, the bank will foreclose on his home. Dyke realizes that "not only would the Railroad devour every morsel of his profits, but also it would take from him his home."*

Farm family

 Rural Unrest

From 1860 to 1900, the U.S. population more than doubled, from 31.5 million to 76 million. To feed the growing population, the number of farms tripled, from 2 million to 6 million. Many farmers borrowed money to buy land and machinery, as farming became more mechanized. With modern machines, farmers in 1900 could produce a bushel of wheat almost 20 times faster than in 1830. However, the combination of more farms and greater productivity led to overproduction and lower prices for crops. Many farmers responded to lower prices by increasing crop production, which eventually pushed prices even lower.

As their income decreased, many farmers found it more difficult to pay their bills. Those who could not make their mortgage payments lost their farms and homes. Many became tenant farmers. By 1880 one fourth of all farms were rented by tenants, and the number kept growing. Many Americans could not even afford to rent land and thus became farm laborers. By 1900 there were 4.5 million farm laborers in the United States.

their problems. Finally, tell students that they will learn how inflation and government intervention were used to help farmers.

Introduce Key Terms

Linguistic, Logical-Mathematical. Review this section's key terms with students. Remind the class that sometimes definitions for terms made up of more than one word can be deduced by combining the definitions of each word. Have students try to explain each term based on their knowledge of each word. Then ask them to use context cues from the text to determine whether their definitions are correct. **SHELTERED ENGLISH**

TEACH

Have students read Section 4 and complete Guided Reading Strategies 6.4. Choose one or more of the following activities to explore the section content with students. For further suggestions on block scheduling or team teaching, see the *Block Scheduling Handbook.*

LEVEL 1: Linguistic. (Suggested time: 15 min.) As a class, go over students' Guided Reading Strategies. Then use the Reading Focus questions to highlight the main ideas of the section. **SHELTERED ENGLISH**

Many farmers blamed businesspeople—wholesalers, brokers, grain buyers, grain elevator operators, and particularly railroad owners—for profiting at their expense. Leonidas Polk, an editor of a North Carolina farm journal, expressed this view when he wrote,

> **"There is something radically wrong. . . . The railroads have never been so prosperous. . . . The banks have never done a better . . . business. . . . Manufacturing enterprises have never made more money. . . . Towns and cities flourish and 'boom,' . . . and yet agriculture languishes [declines]."**

As economic conditions grew worse for farmers, they began to organize associations—like workers had done—to further their interests.

The Granger Collection, New York

This Granger poster shows the group's ideal image of farm life.

The National Grange

In 1866 clerical worker Oliver Kelley toured the South for the U.S. Department of Agriculture. Kelley saw firsthand how the nation's farmers suffered. After that tour, Kelley and several government clerks founded the National Grange of the Patrons of Husbandry in 1867. The **National Grange** was a social and educational organization for farmers. The Grange wanted to ease the isolation of farm life and improve farmers' living standards. Local granges, or chapters, were quickly established, and membership grew rapidly, to more than 1.5 million by 1874.

Granges formed organizations called cooperatives to buy goods in bulk at lower prices, increasing farmers' buying power. Farmers also formed cooperative societies to sell their crops, hoping that by joining together they could demand higher prices. Unfortunately for farmers, these cooperatives were often run by people who were inexperienced in business. In addition, banks, merchants, and railroads usually organized to oppose these cooperatives. As a result, most of the cooperatives fared poorly.

The Grange then shifted its focus to politics. It campaigned for political candidates who supported farmers' goals and demanded legislation to regulate rates for the use of railroads and grain elevators. In a few states, the Grange managed to enact laws regulating railroads, which farmers relied on to ship their crops.

The issue of railroad regulation came before the U.S. Supreme Court in 1877 in the case of *Munn* v. *Illinois.* The Court ruled that the government did have the right to regulate the railroads and other businesses that affected the public interest. In the 1886 case of *Wabash* v. *Illinois,* the Court clarified that the federal government could only regulate companies that did business across state lines. Regulation of rates for railroad lines within states fell to the state governments.

Congress also tried to exert its authority. In February 1887 it passed the **Interstate Commerce Act** to provide some uniform national regulations over trade between the states. This act created the **Interstate Commerce Commission** (ICC) to ensure that railroads charged fair rates and did not discriminate in favor of big shippers. However, the commission lacked any real power to enforce its regulations, and the courts gave the agency little help when it appealed to them.

Daily Life

Farming Debt. The accounts of Matt Brown, a Mississippi farmer, reveal the financial difficulties that farmers faced during the late 1800s. In 1892 Brown owed the local store more than $200. One year later, the debt totaled $452.41, and his purchases for the year far exceeded the $171 worth of work he had done for the store owner in an effort to pay off his debt. His purchases included clothing, food, plow tools, land rental, and miscellaneous supplies. Brown was never able to pay off his debt. His 1905 bill included charges for his coffin.

Critical Thinking: What do Brown's accounts reveal about his life?

ANSWER: The money he earned as a farmer never paid for the cost of running his farm and household.

Multimedia Resources

Everyday Life in America Transparency 16: Farming Technology, Late 1800s

ALL LEVELS: Linguistic, Visual-Spatial. (Suggested time: 45 min.) Have students make charts showing problems that industrialization created for farmers and how various pro-farm organizations proposed to solve those problems. Have students place the following headings on the horizontal axis: *Debt Incurred From Equipment Purchases, Overproduction and Corresponding Drops in Prices, Inability to Pay Back Debts,* and *High Storage and Railroad Fees.* On the vertical axis, have students place the following headings: *The National Grange, The Farmers' Alliances,* and *The Populist Party.* Have students use information from the text to write descriptions of what each organization attempted to do about the farmers' problems. Finally, call on volunteers to share their charts and review them with the class. **SHELTERED ENGLISH**

LEVEL 2: Linguistic, Visual-Spatial. (Suggested time: 45 min. plus homework) Have each student write a story for a news magazine and design a cover that goes with the story. Ask students to have their stories explain at least four major points of the Populist Party's platform and whether these policies were adopted. Have students create magazine covers that offer some insight into the story. Encourage students to share their stories and covers with the class. Finally, lead a discussion on the issues that Populists supported.

Constitutional Heritage

Regulating Railroads. One railroad practice that states hoped to regulate was known as long haul–short haul discrimination. Railroads often charged higher rates for carrying goods short distances than they did for long distances. The state of Illinois attempted to outlaw the practice and sued the Wabash, St. Louis & Pacific Railway Company to prevent it from charging more for short hauls. The Supreme Court ruled against Illinois, however, claiming that the state did not have the power to regulate interstate commerce. It also rejected federal efforts to end the practice—including a section in the Interstate Commerce Act—on technical grounds. It was not until 1910 that the federal government passed a law banning long haul–short haul discrimination.

Critical Thinking: Why might the state of Illinois have objected to long haul–short haul discrimination?

ANSWER: It saw the practice as an attempt to make additional profits without providing additional services.

MAP ANSWER

grapes, wheat, hay, vegetables, barley, strawberries

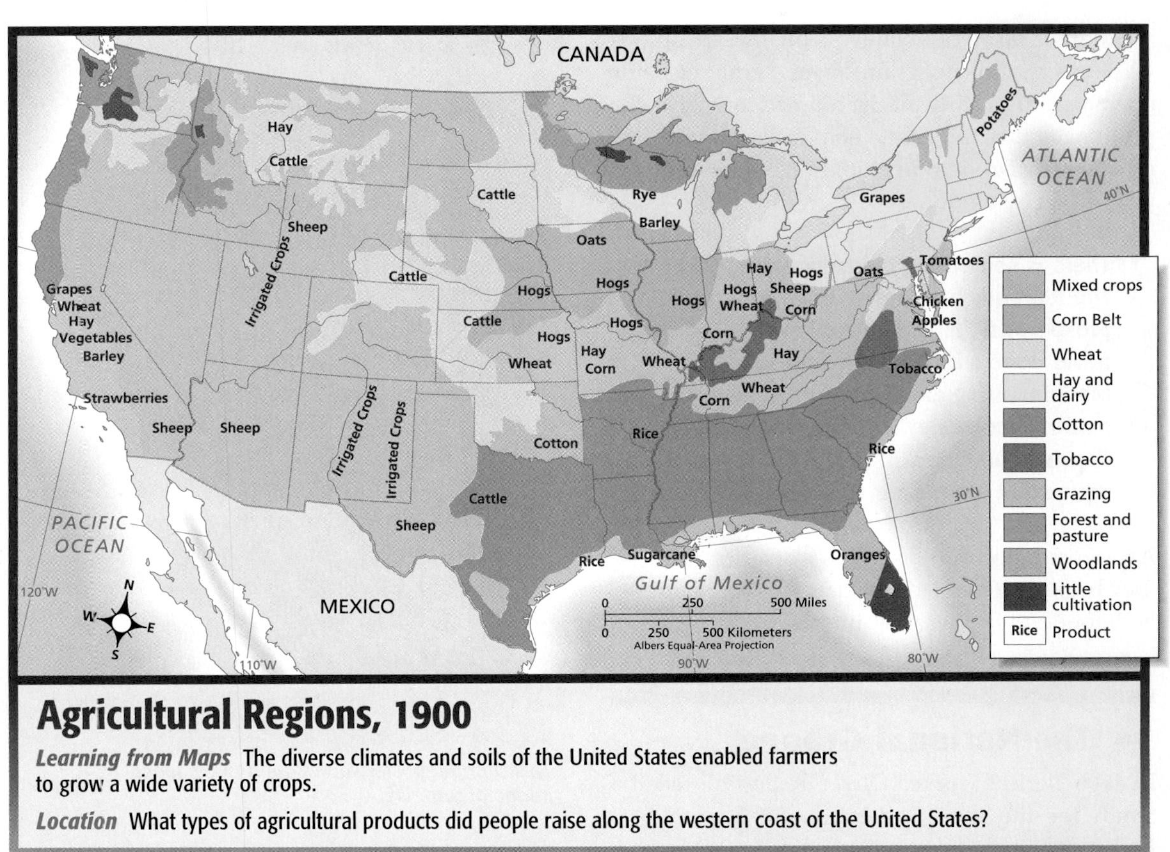

Agricultural Regions, 1900

Learning from Maps The diverse climates and soils of the United States enabled farmers to grow a wide variety of crops.

Location What types of agricultural products did people raise along the western coast of the United States?

Money Issues

Railroad rates were not the only concern facing farmers. Farmers' problems most often involved money issues, such as debt, credit, and low crop prices. Many farmers thought that assistance would come only from national legislation that affected the money supply.

Farmers for Silver

Since 1792, the United States had allowed free and unlimited coinage. **Free coinage** meant that gold and silver were coined and that paper money was worth a specific amount of gold or silver. The Coinage Act of 1873 placed the United States strictly on a **gold standard**—meaning that only gold could back U.S. currency.

Tied to the gold standard, the money supply tended to grow more slowly than the nation's population. This meant that there were fewer dollars in circulation for each citizen, which resulted in deflation—a shrinking of the money supply and a general lowering of prices. Farmers supported coining silver to create inflation—an increase in the money supply and a rise in prices. With inflation, farmers hoped that prices for farm products would rise, thus increasing their income and allowing them to pay their debts more easily.

1863 silver half dollar

Silver Politics

During the late 1870s there was considerable support for free coinage of silver. Many farmers began backing political candidates who supported free silver coinage. One such politician was William Jennings Bryan of Nebraska, who claimed that with

LEVEL 3: Linguistic, Logical-Mathematical, Intrapersonal. (Suggested time: 45 min.) Explain to students that in the case of *Munn* v. *Illinois*, the Supreme Court ruled that the federal government did have the power to regulate railroads and other businesses that affected the public interest. Then point out that in the case of *Wabash* v. *Illinois*, the Court ruled that the federal government could only regulate businesses that crossed state lines. Ask students to imagine that they are lawyers for the federal government who are seeking appeals to the latter decision so that the government can have more control over railroads. Have students use information from the text to write a request to the Supreme Court for an appeal of *Wabash* v. *Illinois*. Encourage students to include logical reasons why the U.S. government should be allowed more control over this industry.

CLOSE

Visual-Spatial, Logical-Mathematical. To conclude the lesson, ask students to draw political cartoons depicting the issues related to farmers' struggles and free coinage. Have students include captions that highlight the issue being presented. Ask volunteers to explain their cartoons. **SHELTERED ENGLISH**

Grover Cleveland

the free coinage of silver all "necessary reforms will be possible." In February 1878 Congress passed the Bland-Allison Act, allowing limited silver coinage, over President Hayes's veto.

A new political party, the Greenback Party, favored inflating the money supply with paper dollars not backed by gold or silver. In the presidential election of 1880 the Greenback Party nominated Iowa congressman James B. Weaver as its candidate. The two major parties, however, largely ignored the money issue.

The Republicans finally made continued coinage of silver an issue in the presidential election of 1888. President Cleveland, a Democrat, lost the election to Republican Benjamin Harrison, grandson of former president William Henry Harrison. After the election, the Republican Congress passed the **Sherman Silver Purchase Act** to increase the amount of silver purchased for coinage. However, this act did not help farmers economically as much as they had hoped.

Farmers' Alliances

Many farmers formed their own political organizations to increase their power. First locally, then regionally, they organized to elect candidates and to achieve policies favorable to them. These political organizations became known as the **Farmers' Alliances**.

The Texas alliance started as a frontier farmers' association in 1877 and quickly grew to become the Grand State Alliance in 1879. Other alliances joined, and membership soared, topping 1.5 million in 1890. The Colored Farmers' Alliance had more than 1 million members of its own.

The Farmers' Alliances were more politically active than the Grange had been. Their goals and proposals put more emphasis on government legislation to help farmers. The Alliances called for increased railroad regulation and lower interest rates.

In the 1890 elections the Alliances ran candidates who emerged as a serious political force, particularly in the West and in the South. These candidates won the governorships of Texas and Georgia and gained control of both houses of the Georgia legislature. Alliance supporters also won more than 35 seats in the U.S. Congress.

The Populist Party

Following their state and local successes, farmers raised their political sights and hopes. At a conference in Cincinnati, Ohio, in 1891, Alliance leaders met with representatives from labor and reform organizations. They agreed to organize a new national political party, the People's Party. This organization, better known as the **Populist Party**, represented the high point of farmers' political activity.

The Election of 1892

In 1892 the Populist Party held its first national convention in Omaha, Nebraska, where the group decided on a platform of far-reaching reforms. The Populists' goal was to remove the influence of big

The Colored Farmers' Alliance fought for the rights of African American farmers like this family from Virginia.

Citizenship and Democracy

The Colored Farmers' Alliance. African Americans organized the first black Farmers' Alliance in Texas in 1886. Two years later, several black farmers' alliances agreed to merge. They called the new group the Colored Farmers' National Alliance and Co-operative Union. The Colored Farmers' Alliance worked closely with the Farmers' Alliances and had many of the same goals, but white farmers did not agree to unite with African Americans until 1892, when members of both groups joined the Populist Party.

Critical Thinking: How might white farmers' refusal to join African American farmers have hurt the cause of farmers in the 1880s?

ANSWER: Because many whites would not work with African Americans, farmers were not united in their struggle to achieve their common goals.

LINKING PAST TO PRESENT ANSWERS

(for page 204)

1. because they did not feel that the major parties represented their interests

2. Answers will vary but students might say that third parties bring attention to important issues that the major parties ignore.

CHALLENGE AND EXTEND

1. **Linguistic, Visual-Spatial, Interpersonal.** Organize the class into two groups. Assign one group the presidential election of 1892, and the other the election of 1896. Then organize each group into smaller groups to represent all the significant parties running for election. Have members of each group research the party platforms and prepare campaign speeches, placards, and a campaign song for their assigned party. Encourage groups to highlight significant events of the campaign. Have each group present its speech, placard, and song to the class.

2. **Visual-Spatial, Interpersonal.** Assign each student one of the presidential elections from 1876 through 1896. Have students use the library or other resources to research their assigned election. Then ask students to prepare wall charts listing issues and each party's approach to them. Once students have completed their charts, have the entire class create a composite chart listing recurring issues and outcomes. Finally, discuss the recurring issues and how they affected each election.

Section 4 Review ANSWERS

Identify

For significance, see the following pages:

- Oliver Kelley, p. 201
- National Grange, p. 201
- Interstate Commerce Act, p. 201
- Interstate Commerce Commission, p. 201
- free coinage, p. 202
- gold standard, p. 202
- Benjamin Harrison, p. 203
- Sherman Silver Purchase Act, p. 203
- Farmers' Alliances, p. 203
- Populist Party, p. 203
- James B. Weaver, p. 204
- William Jennings Bryan, p. 205

Reading for Content Understanding

1. falling prices for their goods, which meant that they faced debt and the loss of their property; they organized cooperatives and political parties to pressure politicians to respond to their problems.

2. the regulation and government ownership of railroads, telephone and telegraph systems; the free coinage of silver; removal of big business's influence on government; the eight-hour work day; immigration restrictions

3. to cause inflation and bring up crop prices

4. Paragraphs should discuss reforms that the Populists advocated and their difficulties in the 1896 election.

5. Answers should mention that the Populists aimed at the common people, supporting issues such as free coinage of silver and a shorter workday.

business on government and to provide all Americans with greater democracy and voice in the government. Populist Mary Lease expressed their sentiments:

> **"Wall Street owns the country. It is no longer a government of the people, by the people, and for the people, but a government of Wall Street, by Wall Street, and for Wall Street."**

To restore the political power of the common people, the Populist platform called for government ownership of railroads and the telephone and telegraph systems, and it supported the "free and unlimited coinage of silver and gold." To attract votes from industrial workers, the Populists supported the eight-hour workday and immigration restrictions.

In the 1892 presidential election the Democrats nominated Grover Cleveland, and the Republicans nominated Benjamin Harrison. The significant issue of the campaign was the Republicans' support for high tariffs. This time Cleveland won. James B. Weaver, the Populist candidate, won an impressive 1 million votes, about 8.5 percent of the total popular vote.

The Panic of 1893

Shortly after Grover Cleveland took office, the Philadelphia and Reading Railroad failed, causing a stock market panic. This triggered the worst economic downturn that Americans had yet experienced. By 1894 millions of Americans

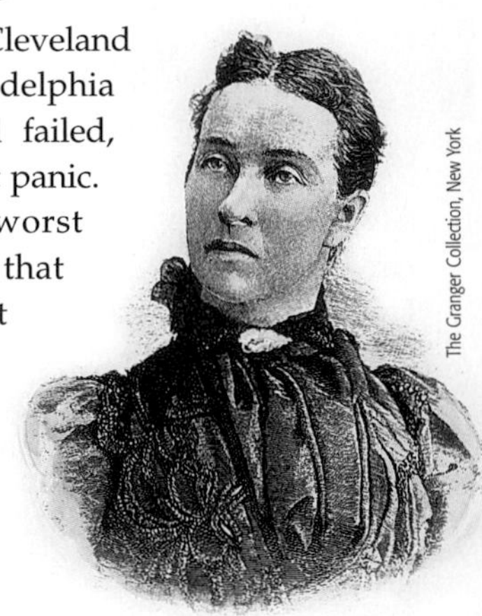

The Granger Collection, New York

In 1895 Mary Lease published her views on populism in a well-known book.

Linking Past to Present

Third Political Parties

Ever since the presidential election of 1796, the United States has had a two-party system. However, at times some Americans have felt that the two major parties did not adequately represent their views. Thus, many Americans formed or joined third political parties, such as the Populist Party.

Dissatisfied with the Democratic and Republican presidential candidates for the 1992 and 1996 elections, Americans supported several new political parties. Ross Perot ran as an independent candidate in 1992. Perot then founded the Reform Party and ran as its candidate in 1996. Each time he campaigned on a platform of government reform. Ralph Nader ran in 1996 for the Green Party, which was formed in 1984. This party had an environmental platform. In 1996 Perot was on the ballot in all 50 states, and Nader was on the ballot in 18 states.

While running as an independent candidate in the 1992 presidential campaign, Perot joined the Republican and Democratic candidates in televised debates. Perot received almost 20 million votes in the election, about 19 percent of the total. Although a third-party candidate has yet to win a presidential election, third parties remain an important part of the democratic process.

Understanding What You Read

1. Why have Americans formed political parties in the past?
2. What role do you think third parties play in the democratic process?

REVIEW

Visual-Spatial, Logical-Mathematical. Have students complete the Section Review questions. Then ask them to analyze how industrialization was only one cause of farmers' troubles. Have each student create a list of problems that farmers faced and another list identifying Populist solutions to those problems.

ASSESS

Have students complete Daily Quiz 6.4.

RETEACH

Linguistic, Logical-Mathematical. Have students complete Main Idea Activities for Reteaching and Sheltered English 6.4. Then have them review the principles supported by the National Grange, the farmers' alliances, and the Populists. Have each student work with a partner to write a dialog summarizing the main political issues that the nation faced in the late 1800s.

SHELTERED ENGLISH

were unemployed and some 690,000 workers went on strike to protest reduced wages.

The depression had multiple causes, but some Americans blamed the money system. Many investors reacted to the downturn by selling their investments in exchange for gold, causing a gold drain. Bank depositors feared a further downturn and exchanged their paper money and silver coins for gold at federal banks. The result was a serious shortage of U.S. gold reserves, which forced the government to sell bonds to increase the gold supply.

Democrat William Jennings Bryan supported many Populist ideas.

The Election of 1896

With the economic panic, many voters began to agree with the Populists' call for reform. In 1896 the Republicans nominated William McKinley for president, and he came out firmly against free coinage of silver. Many Democrats saw this platform as a chance to win Populist and some Republican votes.

At the Democrats' nominating convention their nominee, William Jennings Bryan, swept the crowd with an emotional speech. In support of free coinage of silver he said, "You shall not press down upon the brow of labor this crown of thorns. You will not crucify mankind upon a cross of gold."

The Democrats had put the Populists in a difficult position by adopting their strongest issue. The Populists had to decide between running their own candidate, and thus splitting the silver vote, or supporting Bryan and possibly being absorbed by the Democrats. The Populists decided to nominate Bryan but chose their own vice president.

The Democrats carried the South and the West. However the Republicans won the election with the strong support of the more heavily populated Midwest and Northeast. The well-financed Republican campaign had convinced many industrial workers in large urban areas that free silver coinage would create high unemployment. McKinley's victory in the election of 1896 marked the end of both the Populist Party and the organized farmers' parties.

SECTION 4 REVIEW

Identify and explain the significance of the following:

- **Oliver Kelley**
- **National Grange**
- **Interstate Commerce Act**
- **Interstate Commerce Commission**
- **free coinage**
- **gold standard**
- **Benjamin Harrison**
- **Sherman Silver Purchase Act**
- **Farmers' Alliances**
- **Populist Party**
- **James B. Weaver**
- **William Jennings Bryan**

Reading for Content Understanding

1 **Main Idea** What problems did farmers face during the late 1800s, and how did they respond?

2 **Main Idea** What issues did farmers support in the National Grange and the Populist Party?

3 **Economic Development** Why did many farmers support the free coinage of silver?

4 **Writing** *Informing* Write a paragraph explaining the goals of the Populist Party and why it did not win the 1896 presidential election.

5 **Critical Thinking** *Making Comparisons* In what ways was the Populist Party different from the Democratic and Republican Parties?

Chapter 6 Review ANSWERS

Identifying People and Ideas

1. dramatically sped up the process of making steel

2. created a practical electric light bulb, a power plant to supply electricity to New York City, and held more than 1,000 patents

3. business that is free from government involvement

4. steel baron from the late 1800s; major philanthropist and believer in "The Gospel of Wealth"

5. owning all the businesses in a particular industry

6. strike led by Pullman workers when their wages were cut; eventually halted traffic on most midwestern rail lines; federal troops were called in to end the strike.

7. Knights of Labor leader who turned the group into the first national labor union

8. organized various national unions of skilled workers into a loose association

9. union organizer who fought to protect workers' rights

10. basing the worth of each dollar or coin on a specific amount of gold

Using the Time Line

1. c **4.** e

2. d **5.** f

3. b **6.** a

Understanding Main Ideas

1. Technological breakthroughs increased production rates, decreased costs, and allowed products to be produced and shipped by means never before possible.

Review and Assessment RESOURCES

PRINT
- ★ Chapter 6 Review, pp. 206–07
- ★ Vocabulary Activity 6
- ★ Chapter 6 Study Guide
- ★ Chapter 6 Test (Form A or B)

MULTIMEDIA
- ★ Audio Program, Ch. 6 (English and Spanish)
- ★ *Global Skill Builder CD–ROM*
- ★ Chapter 6 Test Generator
- ★ HRW Web site

SHELTERED ENGLISH
- ★ Spanish Glossary
- ★ Sheltered English Chapter 6 Test

ASSESS

Have students complete one of the Chapter 6 tests. As an alternate assessment, assign the Chapter 6 Investigation.

2. corporations—allowed many people to invest their money in one place with limited investment risk; vertical integration—allowed business owners to control each step of the manufacturing process; horizontal integration—allowed for the ownership of all the businesses in one industry.

3. To lower the cost of production, Carnegie purchased the companies that provided goods and services to his steel industry, thus decreasing the end cost of his products.

4. Henry Frick refused to negotiate with the union. The Pennsylvania state militia intervened, and the workers did not receive any gains.

5. Overproduction led to lower prices and lower profits for farmers.

6. Congress passed the act to increase the amount of silver used for coinage, which was supposed to lead to higher inflation and, thus, higher prices for farm goods.

Reviewing Themes

1. It catapulted the country into a period of unprecedented economic growth, making the United States one of the world's industrial leaders.

2. help—protective tariffs for manufacturers and land grants to railroads; control—passed Sherman Antitrust Act to control monopolies and Interstate Commerce Act to increase control over railroads.

3. Industrial workers formed unions to fight for better working conditions and wages; Farmers formed Farmers' Alliances, which helped them organize to elect politicians who supported policies favorable to farmers.

CHAPTER 6 REVIEW

Chapter Summary

The Second Industrial Revolution resulted in the growth of new industries such as steel and new inventions such as the lightbulb. This revolution also changed the way that businesses were organized and how people worked. Industrial workers created unions to gain better working conditions. Farmers formed the National Grange and the Populist Party in an effort to reverse their hard times and increase their political influence.

On a separate sheet of paper, complete the following activities.

Identifying People and Ideas

Describe the historical significance of the following:

1. Bessemer process
2. Thomas Alva Edison
3. free enterprise
4. Andrew Carnegie
5. horizontal integration
6. Pullman Strike
7. Terence V. Powderly
8. American Federation of Labor
9. Mary Harris Jones
10. gold standard

Internet Activity 

go.hrw.com
SB1 Inventions

Search the Internet through the HRW Web site to find information about the inventions of the late 1800s. Create a chart showing some of the inventions that are still used today. Include when they were invented, who invented them, and a caption explaining their importance both at the time they were invented and today. You may include drawings of the inventions as well.

Understanding Main Ideas

1. How did technological breakthroughs help bring about the Second Industrial Revolution?
2. What changes took place in the way that American businesses were organized?
3. How did Andrew Carnegie use the method of vertical integration to gain control of the steel industry?
4. What were the causes and outcome of the strike at Carnegie's Homestead plant?
5. Why were the years 1860 to 1900 difficult for American farmers?
6. Why did Congress pass the Sherman Silver Purchase Act?

Reviewing Themes

1. **Technology and Society** What effect did the Second Industrial Revolution have on the U.S. economy?

Using the Time Line

Number your paper from 1 to 6. Match the letters on the time line below with the following events.

1. **More than 100 people are wounded in the Haymarket Riot in Chicago.**
2. **Congress creates the Interstate Commerce Commission to regulate trusts.**
3. **Thomas Edison begins supplying New York City buildings with electrical power.**
4. **Congress passes the Sherman Antitrust Act to stop the growing power of the trusts.**
5. **The Pullman Strike shuts down railroad traffic across the Midwest.**
6. **Congress passes the Bland-Allison Act, allowing some silver coinage.**

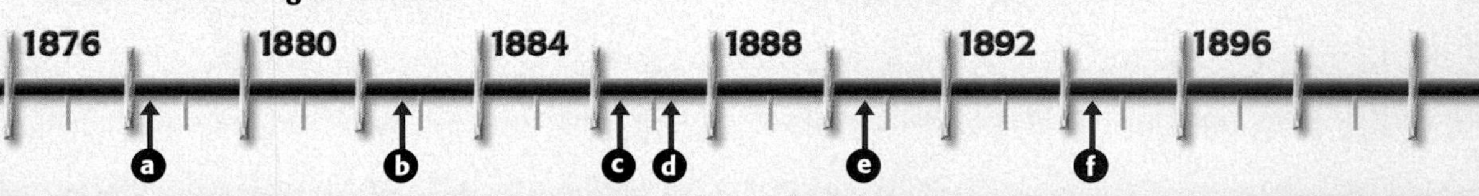

RETEACH

Visual-Spatial, Logical-Mathematical, Interpersonal. Organize the class into four groups and assign each group one of the four sections of the chapter. Have each group review its section to identify the main ideas. Instruct each group to create a storyboard that illustrates one or more of the main ideas. To conclude the lesson, ask each of the groups to present its storyboard to the rest of the class.

SHELTERED ENGLISH

Using the Internet

Have students continue their research to find information specifically on Thomas Edison. Then ask students to imagine that they are Thomas Edison writing his autobiography. Have each student write a paragraph for the autobiography explaining which invention Edison would most want to be remembered for today and why.

Portfolio Extensions

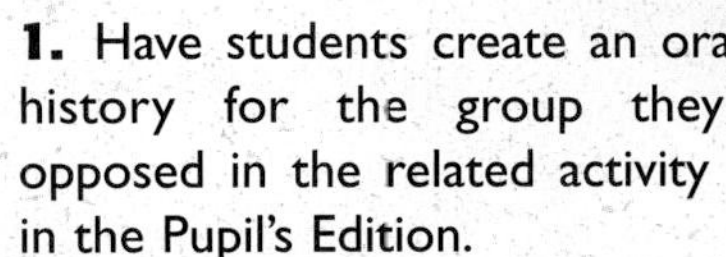

1. Have students create an oral history for the group they opposed in the related activity in the Pupil's Edition.

2. Ask students to write a brief report on which candidate they would have supported in one of the elections and why they would have chosen that candidate.

2. **Economic Development** What actions did government take to help big business? What steps did government take to control big business?
3. **Citizenship and Democracy** How did many industrial workers and farmers react to the economic changes of the Second Industrial Revolution?

Thinking Critically

1. **Supporting a Point of View** Many business leaders opposed attempts by politicians, unions, and competitors to regulate businesses. Do you agree or disagree with these business leaders? Explain your answer.
2. **Drawing Conclusions** Why do you think the Knights of Labor sought such a wide range of members, including African Americans, unskilled workers, and women?
3. **Evaluating** Although the Populist Party lost the presidential election of 1892, several reforms in the party's platform were later put into effect. Which reform do you think was the most important? Explain your answer.

Building Your Portfolio

Complete the following activities individually or in groups.

1. **Oral History** Create an oral history that might have been told about the Homestead Strike. First, research the events that took place during the strike. Then choose a perspective based on the views of a group of participants in the strike, such as the strikers or the mill management. When you have finished your oral history, relate your account to the rest of the class.
2. **Presidential Elections** Research and create a campaign poster for a candidate in either the 1892 or the 1896 presidential election. (Remember that in 1892, the third-party candidate made a strong showing.) Make sure that your poster includes the important issues of that election and states the candidate's position on those issues.

Writing About History

1. **Classifying** Which new invention of the Second Industrial Revolution do you think most changed Americans' lives? What is a modern invention that has had a similar impact on your life? Explain your answers in a paragraph.
2. **Persuading** Write a newspaper editorial supporting one of the candidates in the 1896 presidential election. Be sure to identify the main issue or issues supported by this candidate.

Linking Geography and History

1. **Location** Why do you think that most factories were built along major railroads or waterways?
2. **Region** Why do you think the Populist Party was more popular in the South than it was in the North?

History Skills Workshop

Using Visual Resources Study the image below, which is an artist's sketch of federal troops firing on Pullman Company workers. Write one paragraph describing this scene from the point of view of the troops and another paragraph from the point of view of the Pullman Company strikers.

The Granger Collection, New York

Thinking Critically

1. Answers will vary but students should support their points of view with examples of why they think their positions are correct.

2. Answers will vary but students might mention that labor was an issue that was common to all people. Therefore, the Knights of Labor wanted a wide range of members.

3. Answers will vary but students should chose a reform and explain why they consider it to be most important.

Writing About History

1. Answers will vary but students should name an invention from the Second Industrial Revolution as well as a modern one and explain why they chose them.

2. Editorials will vary but students should identify either William McKinley (against free silver) or William Jennings Bryan (for free silver) and state why they would have supported him.

Linking Geography and History

1. Such locations made it easier and cheaper to bring in raw materials and easier to ship out finished goods.

2. Answers will vary but students should point out that the Populist Party was created for farmers and that there were more farmers in the South than in the North.

History Skills Workshop

Paragraphs will vary but in one, students should state reasons why the government was needed to settle the strike. In the other paragraph, students should argue against government intervention in the strike.

CHAPTER PLANNING GUIDE
Immigrants and Cities

	SECTION LESSON OBJECTIVES	PRINT RESOURCES	MULTIMEDIA RESOURCES	SHELTERED ENGLISH RESOURCES
Section 1: A New Wave of Immigration (pp. 209–14)	★ Explain the reasons for immigration to the United States in the late 1800s, and identify the countries from which immigrants came. ★ Describe immigrant life in the United States during the late 1800s. ★ Analyze ways that Americans tried to limit immigration.	★ Guided Reading Strategies 7.1 ★ American History Political Cartoon 14: Attitudes Toward Immigration ★ Literature Reading 7: *My Ántonia* ★ Section 1 Review, p. 214 ★ Daily Quiz 7.1	★ *Teaching Resources CD–ROM,* Lesson 7.1 ★ Linking Geography and History Transparency 13A: Sources of Immigration, 1891–1910 ★ HRW Web site	★ Main Idea Activities for Reteaching and Sheltered English 7.1
Section 2: City Life (pp. 215–21)	★ Identify reasons for mass immigration to cities, and discuss problems that resulted from this rapid urban growth. ★ Describe technological developments that made larger cities possible. ★ Analyze ways that city residents organized to deal with the challenges of urban life.	★ Guided Reading Strategies 7.2 ★ Geography Activity 7: The Growth of Cities ★ Primary Source Reading 7: *How the Other Half Lives* ★ American History Political Cartoon 15: Urban Life ★ Section 2 Review, p. 221 ★ Daily Quiz 7.2	★ *Teaching Resources CD–ROM,* Lesson 7.2 ★ Linking Geography and History Transparency 11: Growth of Cities, 1840, and Transparency 11A: Growth of Cities, 1840–1900 ★ *American History Interactive Maps CD–ROM:* Development of a Modern City ★ *American Music Audio CD Program:* "Twilight Rag" ★ HRW Web site	★ Main Idea Activities for Reteaching and Sheltered English 7.2
Section 3: Society and Culture (pp. 222–27)	★ Examine new forms of popular entertainment that developed in the late 1800s. ★ Describe changes in American literature and publishing in the late 1800s. ★ Identify new styles of art and methods of photog-raphy that developed in the late 1800s.	★ Guided Reading Strategies 7.3 ★ Graphic Organizer 7: Social and Artistic Responses to a Growing Nation ★ Biography Reading 7: P. T. Barnum ★ Section 3 Review, p. 227 ★ Daily Quiz 7.3	★ *Teaching Resources CD–ROM,* Lesson 7.3	★ Main Idea Activities for Reteaching and Sheltered English 7.3
Chapter Review and Assessment (pp. 228–29)		★ Chapter 7 Review, pp. 228–29 ★ Vocabulary Activity 7 ★ Chapter 7 Study Guide ★ Chapter 7 Test (Form A or B)	★ Audio Program, Ch. 7 (English and Spanish) ★ *Global Skill Builder CD–ROM* ★ Chapter 7 Test Generator ★ HRW Web site	★ Spanish Glossary ★ Sheltered English Chapter 7 Test

CHAPTER OVERVIEW

During the late 1800s immigrants flooded into the United States. These people were different from immigrants from previous generations in that many came from different countries, spoke different languages, practiced different religions, moved to different areas, and worked primarily as unskilled laborers rather than as skilled artisans. They were often discriminated against, both privately and through such legislation as the Chinese Exclusion Act of 1882.

Many immigrants, as well as large numbers of the nation's rural dwellers, moved to big cities. This growth of cities led to new problems, such as poor sanitation and overcrowding. New technologies, such as elevators and improved plumbing, and new social philosophies of the era, such as settlement houses and local police, were used to correct these problems and thus to enable cities to begin to grow into today's modern urban areas.

The late 1800s also witnessed the rise of a uniquely American mass culture. This culture included the rise of spectator sports, such as baseball and football. There was also a growth in the number and type of publications being read throughout the country; a shift in the focus of arts and literature, from romanticism to realism; and the rise of new art forms such as photography.

CHAPTER INVESTIGATION

The Chapter Investigation is an extended, multipart activity designed for students to work cooperatively and apply the chapter content in the creation of a project. You may choose to use the Chapter 7 Investigation, Talk Show: The Changing Face of America, either as a substitute for teaching the section lessons or as an alternate assessment.

BLOCK SCHEDULING 

The teacher lesson plans for each section offer a variety of activity choices to help you present the material in a block scheduling format. For further suggestions on block scheduling, see the *Block Scheduling Handbook with Team Teaching Strategies,* pp. 37–42.

Meeting Individual Needs

ABILITY LEVELS

LEVEL 1 Basic level activities designed for all students encountering new material.

LEVEL 2 Intermediate level activities designed for average students.

LEVEL 3 Challenging activities designed for above-average students.

SHELTERED ENGLISH These activities address the needs of students with Limited English Proficiency.

Smithsonian Institution®

Internet Connections and Lesson 7
www.si.edu/hrw

CNN Presents America:
Yesterday and Today 1850 to the Present
Segment: The "Ellis Island" of Texas

Additional Resources

Books for Teachers

Daniels, Roger. *Coming to America.* HarperCollins, 1991. Study of late nineteenth century immigration to the United States.

Maltby, Marc S. *The Origins and Early Development of Professional Football.* Garland Publishing, 1997. Provides a general overview of the birth of professional football as well as describes how the game became part of the nation's social fabric.

Sclereth, Thomas J. *Victorian America: Transformations of Everyday Life, 1876–1915.* HarperCollins, 1992. Surveys U.S. social history in the late nineteenth century.

Books for Students

Brown, Gene. *The Struggle to Grow: Expansionism and Industrialization (1880–1913).* 21st Century Books, 1993. Primary sources provide a presentation of life during this period. Covers urbanization, immigration, social reformers, and new technology.

Clark, Judith Freeman. *America's Gilded Age: An Eyewitness History.* Facts on File, 1992. Firsthand accounts of major events of the 1880s.

Kirkland, Wallace. *The Many Faces of Hull House: The Photographs of Wallace Kirkland.* University of Illinois Press, 1989. Provides a pictorial history of the best known settlement house in the United States.

Multimedia Materials

The Golden Door: Our Nation of Immigrants. Video, 19 min. Knowledge Unlimited/SSSS. Shows the immigrant experience.

The American Diary—New Beginnings (1895–1904). Video, 25 min. Aims Media Inc. Highlights American history between the years 1895 and 1904.

The 1880s. Video, 32 min. Kaw Valley/SSSS. Describes developments in politics and popular culture during the 1880s.

Immigrants and Cities

CHAPTER MOTIVATOR

Ask students to write a few sentences discussing the people, communities, and cultures found in a typical major city. Call on volunteers to read their descriptions to the class. As students read their sentences, list on the chalkboard various ethnic groups, types of communities (i.e., upper class, middle class, etc.), or any cultural aspects (i.e., museums, theaters, etc.) that might be mentioned. Point out to students that most major modern cities contain a variety of ethnic groups, varying types of neighborhoods, and many different cultural opportunities. Tell students that in this chapter they will learn about the wave of immigrants that came to the United States in the late 1800s, the challenges they faced, and the culture that developed as a result.

Presenting Themes

- **Cultural Diversity**
  Students might mention negative effects of increased immigration, such as tension over jobs or racial tension, or students can mention positive effects such as bringing skilled workers to a particular industry or creating more ethnically diverse neighborhoods.
- **Technology and Society**
  Students might mention that new technology could affect daily life by creating new ways to carry out familiar activities and by lowering the cost of goods or services.
- **Geographic Diversity**
  Students might mention that such growth could mean that cities are becoming more important than farms or that new industrial centers are being created.

Using the Time Line

Have students transfer the time line to their notebooks, leaving gaps between events. At the end of each entry, have students list the major events related to the growth of cities. Then ask students to list possible advantages and disadvantages associated with each event.

CHAPTER 7

Immigrants and Cities

(1870–1900)

In 1870 landscape architect Frederick Law Olmsted spoke to a Boston crowd about the rapid growth of U.S. cities. "There will," he predicted, "soon be larger towns than any the world has yet known." Urban areas were being filled both with immigrants and with migrants from rural areas. These new city residents struggled to adjust to factory work and different lifestyles. They also helped create a distinctive urban culture.

Cultural Diversity
In what ways might increased immigration affect a nation?

Technology and Society
How might technology affect people's daily lives?

Geographic Diversity
What effect might the growth of large urban areas have on a nation?

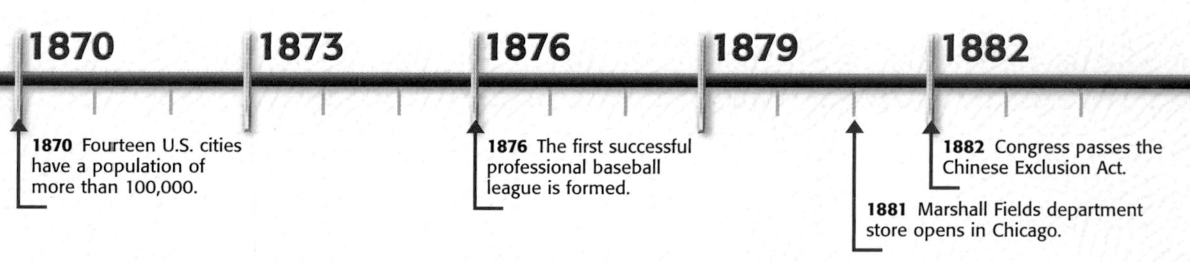

OBJECTIVES

- Explain the reasons for immigration to the United States in the late 1800s, and identify the countries from which immigrants came.
- Describe immigrant life in the United States during the late 1800s.
- Analyze ways that Americans tried to limit immigration.

FOCUS

Motivate Before Reading

Review with students the definition of the word *immigrant.* Then ask them to identify immigrant groups that arrived during the nation's early years. Discuss why these groups came to America. Explain to students that during the late 1800s and early 1900s, immigrants began pouring into urban areas of the United States. Tell students that in this section they will learn about the immigrant

A New Wave of Immigration

Reading Focus

Why did immigrants come to the United States, and where did they emigrate from during the late 1800s?

What was life in the United States like for immigrants in the late 1800s?

How did some Americans try to limit immigration?

Key Terms

old immigrants
new immigrants
steerage
tenements
benevolent societies
Chinese Exclusion Act
Immigration Restriction League

LEE CHEW LIVED IN CHINA as a poor peasant working on his father's farm. He had little hope of ever owning his own land. When Chew saw a man from his village who had "returned with unlimited wealth, which he had obtained in the country of the American wizards," Chew decided to leave China. Like millions of other immigrants to the United States, he left behind everything and everyone he knew and traveled to a strange land carrying little but the hope of opportunity.

The Granger Collection, New York

Asian immigrants in the 1800s

IMAGE ON LEFT PAGE: *City streets grew more crowded in the late 1800s as urban populations increased.*

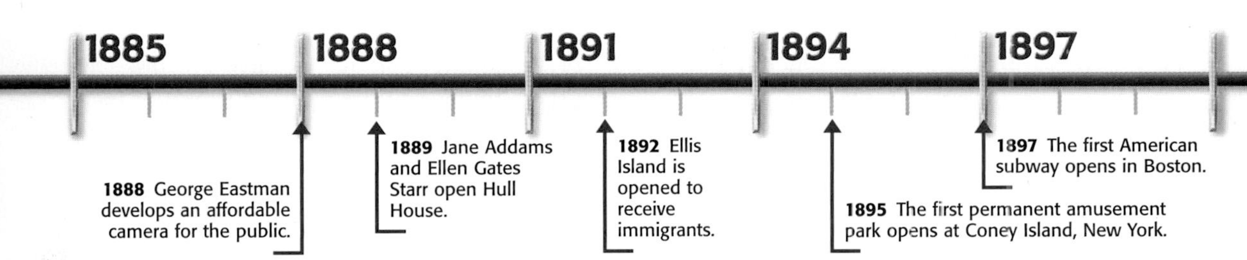

Section 1 RESOURCES

PRINT

- ★ Guided Reading Strategies 7.1
- ★ American History Political Cartoon 14: Attitudes Toward Immigration
- ★ Literature Reading 7: *My Ántonia*
- ★ Section 1 Review, p. 214
- ★ Daily Quiz 7.1

MULTIMEDIA

- ★ *Teaching Resources CD–ROM,* Lesson 7.1
- ★ Linking Geography and History Transparency 13A: Sources of Immigration, 1891–1910
- ★ HRW Web site

SHELTERED ENGLISH

- ★ Main Idea Activities for Reteaching and Sheltered English 7.1

groups that arrived in the United States around 1900 and how these groups' expectations were similar to, and different from, those of earlier immigrants.

Introduce Key Terms

Logical-Mathematical. Review this section's key terms with students. Then have them match each term with at least two others and identify the relationship between them. Have students repeat this process until they have used each term at least once. For example, students can match the term *new immigrants* with *old immigrants* and make the connection that both groups moved to the United States; then link the term to *steerage* and note that many new immigrants traveled in this section of a ship. As students study this section, have them add information that helps explain the relationship between the terms they connected.
SHELTERED ENGLISH

TEACH

Have students read Section 1 and complete Guided Reading Strategies 7.1. Choose one or more of the following activities to explore the section content with students. For further suggestions on block scheduling or team teaching, see the *Block Scheduling Handbook.*

Geographic Diversity

Immigrant Destinations. Although most immigrants settled in cities, a significant number moved to rural areas. About 20 percent were Czechoslovakian immigrants, who settled in the Great Plains states; many of them worked on farms while the others started small businesses or became artisans. Another group known as the Volga Germans also moved in large numbers to the Plains region. These Germans had first settled in Russia but left after they suffered economic difficulties and political oppression. Many Volga Germans moved to Kansas and Nebraska, and approximately half of these immigrants started their own farms.

Critical Thinking: Why might some immigrants have moved to rural areas?

ANSWER: Many immigrants probably came from rural areas in Europe and sought jobs they knew how to do well.

CHART ANSWER
northern and western Europeans; eastern and southern Europeans

Multimedia Resources

Linking Geography and History Transparency 13A: Sources of Immigration, 1891–1910

New Immigrants

Many immigrants shared Lee Chew's vision of America as a land of opportunity and wealth. While immigrants continued to come to the United States by the millions, immigration patterns began to change in the late 1800s. Immigrants who had come to the United States before the 1880s were often called **old immigrants**. They were mostly from Britain, Germany, Ireland, and Scandinavia. Many were skilled workers who spoke English. Most of the old immigrants were also Protestants, except for the Irish and some Germans.

After 1880 many more immigrants came to the United States, often from different countries than previous immigrants. As many immigrants arrived during the 1880s as had come between 1800 and 1860. By 1910 more than 70 percent of these immigrants to the United States were so-called **new immigrants** from southern and eastern Europe. Thousands of Czechs, Greeks, Hungarians, Italians, Poles, Russians, and Slovaks came to the United States looking for a better life. For example, immigrant Miriam Zunser hoped "for all manner of miracles [in] a strange, wonderful land!"

Many of these new immigrants sought economic opportunities while others, including Armenians and Jews, were escaping political and religious persecution. The immigrants who arrived in the late 1800s brought many new cultural practices with them. They also held a variety of religious beliefs, including Eastern Orthodoxy, Roman Catholicism, and Judaism.

Coming to America

The industrial boom of the late 1800s created job opportunities that attracted many immigrants. Immigrants often wrote to family members and friends back home, urging them to come to America. They also sent money for the journey. To attract immigrants, railroad and steamship companies hired business agents. These agents tended to paint unrealistic pictures of easy success in the United States.

Shoes worn by an Ellis Island immigrant

Immigrants usually had to endure a difficult journey. Most immigrants bought the cheapest fares and traveled in **steerage**, an area on a ship's lower levels near where the steering mechanisms were located. In cramped conditions with poor ventilation and no privacy, passengers experienced seasickness, and some died from disease. A journalist emigrating from Naples, Italy, wondered,

> **"How can a steerage passenger remember that he is a human being when he must first pick the worms from his food . . . and eat in his stuffy, stinking bunk, or in the hot and fetid [foul] atmosphere where 150 men sleep, or . . . [next] to a seasick man?"**

Despite the hardships, some immigrants held on to their dreams. One immigrant wrote that a group of them "peered through the portholes into the blackness at night . . . and forgot our seasickness in anticipation of the wonders we were to behold."

Shifting Patterns of Immigration

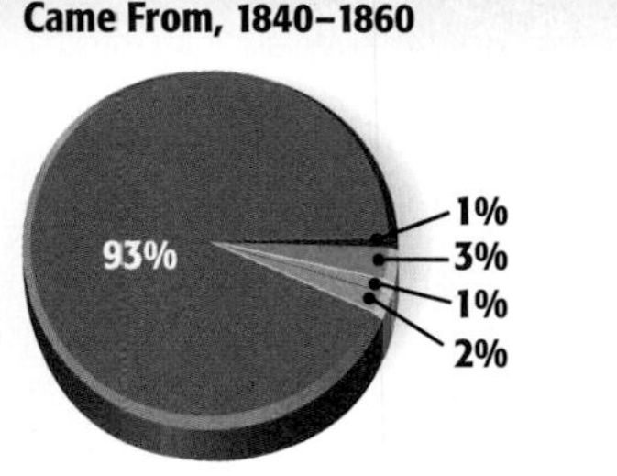

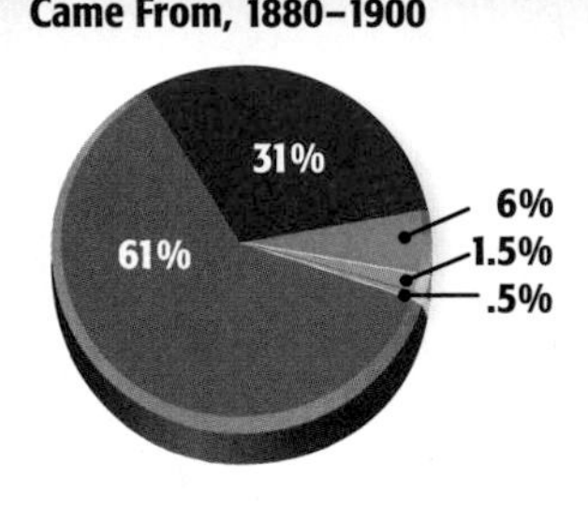

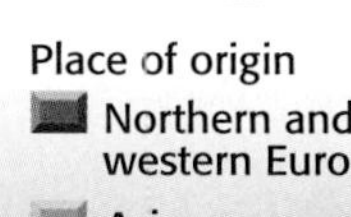

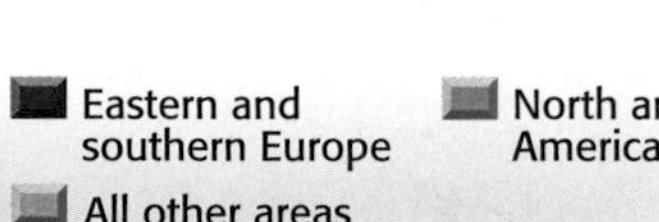

Source: *Historical Statistics of the United States*

America's Newcomers The pattern of immigration to the United States changed dramatically toward the end of the 1800s. What group experienced the greatest increase in immigration between 1840–1860 and 1880–1900?

LEVEL 1: Linguistic. (Suggested time: 15 min.) As a class, go over students' Guided Reading Strategies. Then use the Reading Focus questions to highlight the main ideas of the section. **SHELTERED ENGLISH**

ALL LEVELS: Visual-Spatial, Kinesthetic. (Suggested time: 45 min. plus homework) Provide students with blank outline maps of the world. Ask each student to develop a key, differentiating between new and old immigrants. Then have students identify which countries new immigrants came from and which countries old immigrants came from. Have students create two lists on the back of their maps. The first should identify the reasons old immigrants came to the United States, and the second should list the reasons new immigrants came. Finally, discuss the similarities and differences between where new and old immigrants came from and their reasons for coming to the United States. **SHELTERED ENGLISH**

LEVEL 3: Linguistic, Intrapersonal. (Suggested time: 45 min.) Explain to the class that many immigrants came to the United States with unrealistic expectations and when they arrived in America, life was often different than they had expected. Have students refer to the text to write journal entries describing the conditions immigrants faced after they arrived in the United States. Ask them to include the following information: the areas in which immigrants settled, the job opportunities that were available

Ellis Island

Once immigrants reached the United States, they went first to immigration processing centers. For many years, these centers were poorly run by state and local governments. In 1890 the federal government began assuming control of the immigration centers. Two years later the U.S. government opened a new receiving office on Ellis Island in New York Harbor. Millions of immigrants came through Ellis Island over the next 40 years. Italian immigrant Edward Corsi described the approach to Ellis Island:

Ellis Island became so well known that songs were written about it.

> **"The Statue of Liberty . . . looming shadowy through the mist . . . brought silence. . . . This symbol of America . . . inspired awe in the hopeful immigrants."**

Most Asian immigrants entered the country through West Coast stations such as Angel Island in San Francisco Bay. In the processing centers, officials interviewed immigrants to decide whether to let them enter the country. Officials also conducted physical examinations, deporting any person who carried an infectious disease such as tuberculosis. The majority of immigrants were admitted, however. After admission, they entered the United States in search of work and a new life.

Immigrant Life

Once they arrived in the United States, the majority of new immigrants settled in large cities, where they hoped to find work and other people from their homeland. Because life in their new country was often very different from what they were used to, many immigrants lived in neighborhoods with others who shared their nationality.

In these neighborhoods, immigrants could hear their own language, eat familiar foods, and preserve their customs. Many immigrant groups published newspapers in their own languages and founded schools, churches, synagogues, and other organizations to preserve their beliefs and customs. In New York City, for example, Jewish immigrants founded a thriving theater that gave performances in the Yiddish language.

Immigrants often opened local shops and small neighborhood banks. Business owners helped new arrivals by extending store credit for food purchases and by giving small loans. Such financial aid was important for newcomers because there were few commercial banks in most immigrant neighborhoods. In 1904 Italian immigrant Amadeo Pietro Giannini started the Bank of Italy in San Francisco, which later became the Bank of America.

Even with neighborhood support, immigrants often found urban life difficult. Many of them lived in **tenements**—poorly built, overcrowded apartments—and worked under exhausting conditions. One girl described the difference between her hopes and reality:

> **"[I dreamed] of the golden stairs leading to the top of the American palace where father was supposed to live. [I] went 'home' to . . . an ugly old tenement in the heart of the Lower East Side. There were stairs to climb but they were not golden."**

New immigrants often shopped at stores that carried foods from their homeland, like this Italian grocery in New York City.

Daily Life

Life in Steerage. European immigrants usually spent the 8 to 14 days needed to cross the Atlantic jammed together in steerage compartments. Steerage usually did not have portholes and had few ventilators to provide fresh air. In some cases, up to 47 passengers shared each toilet.

Critical Thinking: Why might disease have been a problem in steerage?

ANSWER: Diseases were easily spread in the confined quarters of steerage.

Across the Curriculum

MATH

Ellis Island. Immigrants arriving at Ellis Island could be detained for a variety of reasons, including illness, suspected criminal background, or lack of money. In 1907 the number of immigrants arriving at Ellis Island who were admitted to the United States was 1,004,576, while another 195,450 were detained; of those, 121,737 were temporarily detained; 9,203 were hospitalized; and the remaining 64,510 were held for other reasons.

Activity: Have students determine the total number of immigrants who arrived at Ellis Island in 1907 (1,200,026) and the percentage of those who were admitted (83.7 percent).

to them, ways that immigrants tried to help each other, and ways that Americans tried to limit immigration. Encourage volunteers to read their entries to the class. As students describe the conditions faced, write them on the chalkboard. Ask students to search the section to find out how immigrants dealt with the conditions they encountered. Write students' responses next to the appropriate term on the chalkboard.

LEVEL 3: Visual-Spatial, Logical-Mathematical. (Suggested time: 40 min. plus homework) Have students complete the Section Review questions. Then have them work individually or in groups to create a scrapbook similar to one that an immigrant might have made after a journey to the United States. Scrapbooks should describe the voyage, where the immigrant lived and worked, any forms of prejudice an immigrant could have faced, and forms of help he or she might have received from the community. Ask students to include letters, newspaper articles, illustrations, photographs, ticket stubs, maps, song lyrics, or any other items that might be found in someone's scrapbook. Encourage students to explain their scrapbooks to the class. Finally, review the conditions immigrants faced and how the scrapbooks reflect immigrants' lives.

Economic Development

"Birds of Passage." Many of the immigrants who arrived in the United States were young, single men who had no intention of settling. They worked for several months, saved their earnings, and then returned to their homelands. Immigration officials referred to these men as "birds of passage" because, like birds, they migrated every year. While exact figures are impossible to determine, it is estimated that one third of the immigrants to the United States did not remain here.

Activity: Ask students to imagine that they are immigrants returning to Italy after 3 years in the United States. Have students search the Internet through the HRW Web site to find information on "birds of passage." Have students write letters to their family members explaining why they are returning home.

go.hrw.com
SB1 Birds of Passage

Global Connections Answers

1. They dealt with poverty and persecution in their homelands.

2. They hoped for better lives and a change of pace.

Immigrant parents emphasized education as a key to their children's success. Students here participate in a physical fitness program.

Some immigrant communities formed **benevolent societies**—aid organizations founded to provide help in cases of sickness, unemployment, and death. At that time, there were few national government agencies to provide such aid.

Despite the challenges, immigrants often found opportunities in the United States that they would not have had at home. Many immigrants tried to adjust to their new country by eagerly embracing American culture. New immigrants encouraged their children to learn English and to become familiar with American customs. Some parents stressed education to their children as a way of improving their future chances for success. Russian immigrant Mashke Antin recalled that free public schools were her father's "chief hope for us children, the essence of American opportunity." Many immigrants successfully met the challenges of living in a new country and were able to build a future for their families in the United States.

Immigrant Workers

Although many of the new immigrants had been agricultural workers in their homelands, few could afford to buy land in the United States. Instead, they found work in the cities, where about 90 percent of all manufacturing in the United States took place by 1900.

Global Connections

Coming to America

For many immigrants, the decision to leave their homes was difficult. However, poverty and persecution helped convince millions of Europeans from countries such as Greece, Italy, and Poland to immigrate to the United States in search of a better life.

Many of these immigrants hoped to return home wealthy after earning money overseas. Other immigrants, such as Jews and Armenians, saw the United States as a place to settle to escape religious and ethnic persecution. In Russia, many Jewish mothers sang a lullaby to their children:

> *"America is for everyone*
> *They say, it's the greatest piece*
> *of luck*
> *For Jews, it's a garden of Eden*
> *A rare and precious place."*

The political freedom found in the United States also appealed to many immigrants.

These various factors helped attract large numbers of immigrants in the late 1800s and early 1900s. In spite of the cultural and language differences between the United States and their homelands, millions of eastern and southern Europeans came to the United States during this period. Others immigrated to Canada or South American nations such as Argentina and Brazil.

Understanding What You Read

1. What factors encouraged people to emigrate from their homelands in Europe?
2. Why do you think so many European immigrants chose to settle in the Americas?

CLOSE

TEACHER TO TEACHER

Linguistic, Visual-Spatial. Lotty Repp of Dallas, Texas, suggested the following activity: Have each student create a graphic organizer comparing new immigrants to old immigrants. Have students answer the following questions: Where did they come from? Why did they come? Where did they settle? What problems did they face?

CHALLENGE AND EXTEND

Linguistic, Logical-Mathematical, Intrapersonal. Have students use the library or other resources to find more information about a government receiving office, such as Ellis Island or Angel Island, that operated in the late 1800s and early 1900s. Have students write an essay describing what happened at these receiving stations as immigrants arrived in the United States. Encourage students to consider immigrants' first impressions of the United States compared to their overall expectations.

Because the majority of immigrants came from rural areas, few had any skills in manufacturing or industrial work. With little money and limited knowledge of English, most of these immigrants were forced to take low-paying, unskilled industrial jobs. Many of these jobs were in the construction, garment, or steel industries. "Wherever the heat is most . . . scorching, the smoke and soot most choking," wrote one Hungarian immigrant, "there we are certain to find compatriots [people from the same homeland] bent . . . with toil."

Immigrant families like this one often worked together in sweatshops making garments.

The typical workweek for industrial laborers in the late 1800s consisted of six 10-hour days, but longer hours were also common. Employers offered immigrants relatively low wages, which were nevertheless often higher than they could have earned in their home countries. Women and children earned even less, and many families depended on their wages for survival.

Not all industrial labor took place in large factories. Some immigrants worked long hours for little pay in small shops or factories located in or near working-class neighborhoods. Usually associated with the garment industry, these workplaces were called sweatshops because of the workers' long hours and often unhealthy working conditions. In small rooms, workers crowded around tables and sewing machines. Writer Joseph Kirkland described a sweatshop in New York:

> **"In one such place there were fifteen men and women in one room, which contained also a pile of mattresses on which some of the men sleep at night."**

A large number of garment workers were paid by the week, but some earned wages based on the number of garment pieces they completed. These so-called piece workers had to work quickly.

Immigrant women also commonly worked as maids and cooks for middle- or upper-class families. Other women ran boardinghouses in their homes. They cooked for their boarders and laundered their clothes. Women in these occupations worked long hours from dawn until dusk.

Immigrants with the appropriate skills sometimes found work in a wide range of occupations. Some worked as bakers, carpenters, masons, metalworkers, or skilled machinists. Other immigrants saved, shared resources, or borrowed money to open small businesses, such as barbershops, candy stores, laundries, restaurants, or street vending carts. New immigrants tended to open the same types of businesses in which earlier immigrants from the same country were already successful.

Many immigrants traveled back and forth between Europe and the United States before returning permanently to Europe. For example, it was common for Italian male immigrants to eventually return to Italy. The immigrants who stayed in the United States often paved the way for the success of future generations.

Opposition to Immigration

The rise in immigration in the late 1800s increased anti-immigrant feeling among some Americans. Nativists argued that U.S. immigration policies allowed in too many new immigrants. Nativists also claimed that the new immigrants' poverty and lack of education would harm American society. Many nativists also held racial and ethnic prejudices against immigrants from Asia, southern Europe, and eastern Europe. Nativists argued that the different languages and cultural backgrounds of these immigrants would prevent them from becoming good U.S. citizens.

Labor unions, particularly in the West, also opposed immigration. They feared that immigrants

Historical Sidelight

The Parochial School. Catholics from Ireland, Germany, Italy, and Poland all came to the United States at the end of the 1800s. They clung to church traditions, forming parishes that were Irish Catholic, German Catholic, or Italian Catholic. These new churches troubled nativists. To many native-born, Protestant U.S. citizens, the Catholic Church was considered foreign, and they wanted immigrants to abandon it. Anti-Catholic sentiments surfaced more and more frequently, particularly in urban areas and in the new public schools that were required almost everywhere in the country by the end of the century. In response, Catholic immigrants formed their own parochial schools.

Critical Thinking: Why might Catholic parents have sent their children to parish schools?

Answer: They might have wanted their children to be educated by and in school with people who shared their beliefs.

REVIEW

Linguistic, Visual-Spatial, Logical-Mathematical. Have students complete the Section Review questions. Then provide students with butcher paper. Have each student draw a Venn diagram on the paper and title the left circle *Old Immigrants* and the right circle *New Immigrants.* Ask students to refer to the text to find ways the two groups were alike and different. Have students list similarities within the inner circle and differences in the respective outer circles. Ask students to report their findings to the class.

ASSESS

Have students complete Daily Quiz 7.1.

RETEACH

Logical-Mathematical. Have students complete Main Idea Activities for Reteaching and Sheltered English 7.1. Then ask them to review the section and list reasons that immigrants may or may not have wanted to move to the United States during the late 1800s or early 1900s. Finally, have students consider the reasons they identified and state whether they would have recommended immigration to a friend or family member. **SHELTERED ENGLISH**

Section 1 Review ANSWERS

Identify

For significance, see the following pages:

- old immigrants, p. 210
- new immigrants, p. 210
- steerage, p. 210
- tenements, p. 211
- benevolent societies, p. 212
- Henry Cabot Lodge, p. 214
- Chinese Exclusion Act, p. 214
- Immigration Restriction League, p. 214

Reading for Content Understanding

1. Many immigrants lived in crowded apartments and faced dangerous and exhausting working conditions.

2. They limited immigration through legislation such as the Chinese Exclusion Act and through organizations such as the Immigration Restriction League.

3. Many immigrants came to the United States seeking a better life. Some wanted better economic conditions, while others wanted to escape political and religious persecution; during the late 1800s, most immigrants were Czechs, Greeks, Hungarians, Italians, Poles, Russians, or Slovaks.

4. Letters will vary but should include examples of good and bad living conditions and encourage family members to come to the United States.

5. Answers will vary but students may refer to racial and ethnic biases, fears that immigrants would take away jobs, and the belief that new immigrants would not be good citizens.

willing to work for low wages would take jobs away from union members. Some politicians agreed. Senator Henry Cabot Lodge of Massachusetts declared, "If we have any regard for the welfare, the wages, or the standard of life of American workingmen, we should take immediate steps to restrict foreign immigration." Some business leaders, however, favored immigration. They wanted a large supply of workers to keep labor costs down. One businessman said, "Their home countries have borne [paid] the expense of rearing them . . . and then America . . . reaps whatever profits there are" from their work.

The Granger Collection, New York

This cartoon shows the attitude of nativists who looked down on many new immigrants during the late 1800s.

In some places, nativists committed violence against immigrants. Other nativists worked to stop or limit immigration by lobbying for anti-immigration legislation. For example, about 105,000 people of Chinese descent lived in the United States in 1880. Two years later, Congress passed the **Chinese Exclusion Act**, which prohibited Chinese people from immigrating to the United States for 10 years. This act marked the first time a nationality was prohibited from entering the country. As a result, the Chinese American population suffered a steady decline in the late 1800s. Congress extended the ban into the early 1900s.

To further reduce the number of immigrants, nativists founded the **Immigration Restriction League** in 1894. The league demanded that all immigrants prove that they could read and write before being allowed into the country. Supporters of the league argued that this measure would reduce immigration from eastern and southern Europe while preserving immigration from western and northern Europe. Congress passed a law requiring a literacy test for immigrants in 1897, but President Cleveland vetoed it, saying that the bill was "narrow, and un-American."

Despite the opposition from nativists, immigrants continued to arrive in large numbers and played an essential role in industrial growth in the late 1800s. Immigrants constructed many of the nation's buildings, roads, and railroads. They also performed much of the low-wage factory work that drove the rapid economic growth of the United States.

SECTION 1 REVIEW

Identify and explain the significance of the following:

- **old immigrants**
- **new immigrants**
- **steerage**
- **tenements**
- **benevolent societies**
- **Henry Cabot Lodge**
- **Chinese Exclusion Act**
- **Immigration Restriction League**

Reading for Content Understanding

1 **Main Idea** What were living conditions like for many immigrants?

2 **Main Idea** What steps did some Americans take to change U.S. immigration policies?

3 **Geographic Diversity** *Movement* Why did immigrants come to the United States, and what countries did they emigrate from in the late 1800s?

4 **Writing** *Persuading* Imagine that you are an immigrant to the United States in 1885. Write a letter to your family back home, telling them about your good and bad experiences, and try to persuade them to join you.

5 **Critical Thinking** *Identifying Generalizations and Stereotypes* Why did some Americans oppose immigration in the late 1800s?

OBJECTIVES

- **Identify reasons for mass immigration to cities, and discuss problems resulting from this rapid urban growth.**
- **Describe technological developments that made larger cities possible.**
- **Analyze ways that city residents organized to deal with the challenges of urban life.**

FOCUS

Motivate Before Reading

Ask students to identify the advantages of living in a city as opposed to a rural area. Write their responses on the chalkboard. Then ask them to imagine themselves living in a city with the advantages that they described after its population has doubled in a short period of time. Ask them to describe how their lives might change and what problems they might expect. Tell students that in

City Life

Reading Focus

Why did so many people move to cities, and what problems resulted from the rapid urban growth?

What technological developments made larger cities possible?

How did city residents organize to deal with the challenges of urban life?

Key Terms

mass transit
suburbs
department stores
settlement houses
Hull House

IN THE 1880S, Kate Richards O'Hare and her family lived on a Kansas ranch. "Those were wonderful days," she recalled. An economic depression brought hard times to her family, however. O'Hare wrote sadly, "The [live]stock was sold, the home dismantled. . . . Then came the day when we left the ranch and went to the city." There the young girl was shocked by the masses of people and the fierce struggle to find work. The O'Hare family was one of thousands of migrant and immigrant families that moved to U.S. cities in the late 1800s, where they faced new challenges as city-dwellers and industrial workers.

Train schedules for Boston and Chicago

The Growth of Cities

During the late 1800s immigrants and native-born Americans moved to cities in record numbers, causing rapid urban growth. In 1850 there were only six cities in the United States with a population greater than 100,000. By 1870 this number had grown to 14, and by 1900 there were more than 35 such cities. In particular, the urban population of midwestern cities grew dramatically during those years. Chicago's population rose from 30,000 in 1850 to 1.7 million in 1900.

Although some city residents were businesspeople and skilled workers, many more were poor laborers. Agricultural hardships drove large numbers of rural residents to the cities. One writer described Chicago's new residents as having "come for the common avowed object [declared goal] of making money." Hoping to escape discrimination and find better economic opportunities, African Americans from the rural South began moving to northern cities in the 1890s. These native-born Americans joined thousands of immigrants also seeking jobs.

Section 2 RESOURCES

PRINT

- ★ Guided Reading Strategies 7.2
- ★ Geography Activity 7: The Growth of Cities
- ★ Primary Source Reading 7: *How the Other Half Lives*
- ★ American History Political Cartoon 15: Urban Life
- ★ Section 2 Review, p. 221
- ★ Daily Quiz 7.2

MULTIMEDIA

- ★ *Teaching Resources CD–ROM,* Lesson 7.2
- ★ Linking Geography and History Transparency 11: Growth of Cities, 1840, and Transparency 11A: Growth of Cities, 1840–1900
- ★ *American History Interactive Maps CD–ROM:* Development of a Modern City
- ★ *American Music Audio CD Program:* "Twilight Rag"
- ★ HRW Web site

SHELTERED ENGLISH

- ★ Main Idea Activities for Reteaching and Sheltered English 7.2

this section they will learn about a period in U.S. history when cities were faced with the changes that were just described. Advise the class that as they read this section they should look for the reasons such growth took place and the impact that it had.

Introduce Key Terms

Linguistic, Logical-Mathematical. Review this section's key terms with students. Then have students scan the section and use context cues to write a definition for each key term. Ask volunteers to read their definitions to the class. Then discuss with students the urban problem that each key term addresses. SHELTERED ENGLISH

TEACH

Have students read Section 2 and complete Guided Reading Strategies 7.2. Choose one or more of the following activities to explore the section content with students. For further suggestions on block scheduling or team teaching, see the *Block Scheduling Handbook.*

LEVEL 1: Linguistic. (Suggested time: 15 min.) As a class, go over students' Guided Reading Strategies. Then use the Reading Focus questions to highlight the main ideas of the section. SHELTERED ENGLISH

Technology and Society

The Introduction of Skyscrapers. A group of architects led by engineer William Le Baron Jenney used iron or steel girders for the frames of their innovative skyscraper designs. Called the Chicago School, these architects' first triumph, the Home Insurance Company Building of Chicago, was finished in 1884. Their buildings, some of which were only eight stories high, towered above neighboring structures. Moreover, they caught on largely because of other new inventions such as elevators and electric lights.

Activity: Have students use the library and other resources to find information on modern innovations that are used in skyscrapers. Ask each student to draw the design of an 1880s skyscraper and label the innovations contained in a typical structure. Call on volunteers to report their findings to the class.

MAP ANSWER
the Northeast

People from the country were often amazed by the noise and the crowds in the city. One woman who arrived in New York City in 1901 noted:

> **"I never saw so many people on the streets, shouting, going in all directions. Having come from a little bit of a village with a few houses, it was to say the least disturbing."**

By the turn of the century about 40 percent of Americans lived in urban areas, and the percentage kept climbing in the early 1900s.

The Changing Look of the City

Increased size was not the only change affecting cities in the late 1800s. New technology made living in a large city more convenient, thus encouraging continued urban expansion.

Skyscrapers

In the mid-1800s typical downtown city buildings were five stories tall. Architects were limited to designing buildings of this size for reasons of safety and practicality. Construction materials at that time, such as brick, stone, and wood, were either too weak or too heavy to be used in very tall buildings. Taller buildings also required residents to walk up many flights of stairs. Another inconvenience was that water could not reliably be pumped higher than the fifth floor.

The rapid growth of cities placed a great strain on the available downtown space. Architects, particularly Louis Sullivan of Chicago, and engineers responded by designing skyscrapers—multistory buildings with metal frames. The availability of stronger and lower-cost steel helped make the skyscraper possible. The steam-powered safety elevator, patented by Elisha Otis in 1861, solved the problem of carrying people up and down these towering buildings. Other breakthroughs, such as improved plumbing and ventilation, helped architects create even taller buildings. By 1900 the tallest building in the United States was the 435-foot-tall Park Row Building in New York City—some four times taller than the early skyscrapers.

Public Transportation

Skyscrapers allowed developers to use limited city space more efficiently. As more tall buildings were constructed, city centers became more densely

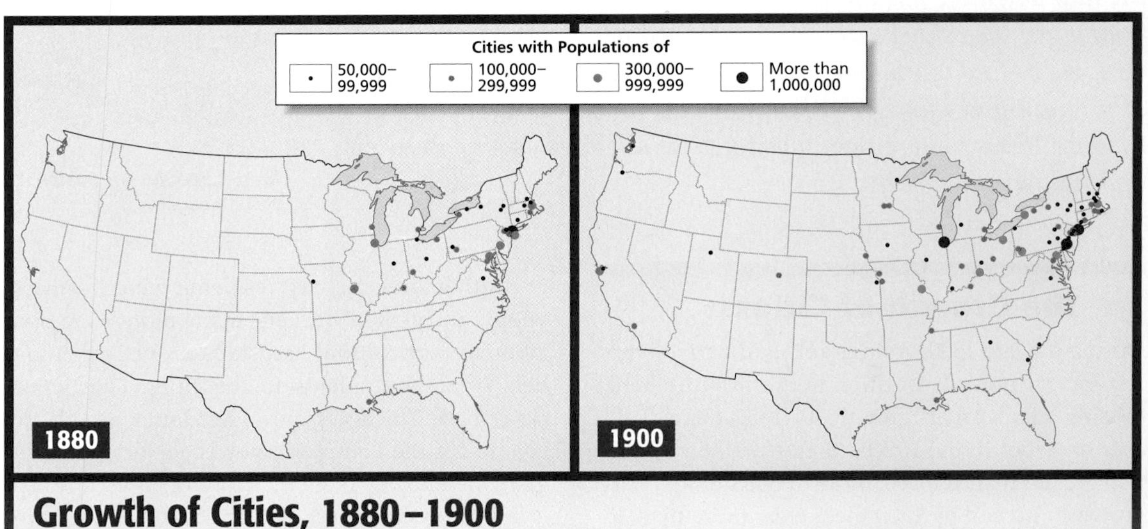

Growth of Cities, 1880–1900

Learning from Maps The introduction of mass transit systems and continued increases in manufacturing helped many cities grow between 1880 and 1900.

Region Which region had the most large cities in both 1880 and 1900?

ALL LEVELS: Visual-Spatial, Logical-Mathematical. (Suggested time: 45 min.) As a class, discuss some of the problems that resulted from rapid urban growth. Then organize the class into a few groups of about six students each. Have members of each group determine who will depict the problem that each of the following innovations sought to improve or solve: skyscrapers, elevators, central air ventilation systems, mass transit systems, public parks, and suburbs. Ask each student to illustrate the assigned item, determine what problem it addresses, and identify how it addresses that problem. After students complete their work, have them show their illustrations and explain how they allowed urban areas to grow larger. **SHELTERED ENGLISH**

ALL LEVELS: Visual-Spatial, Kinesthetic. (Suggested time: 90 min.) Discuss with students the ways that cities changed as a result of immigration in the late 1800s and early 1900s. Organize the class into four groups. Have two groups depict cities prior to the wave of immigration, and the other two groups depict cities after the influx of immigrants. Provide groups with the necessary art supplies to create a diorama portraying a typical urban area. Have each group design its diorama to reflect elements that were incorporated in cities during their assigned era. Finally, have groups present their dioramas to the class and discuss the urban changes that resulted from the influx of immigrants.

The Granger Collection, New York

Chicago city streets crowded with people, buildings, and public transportation

populated. Pedestrians and horse-drawn carts crowded city streets that were often poorly paved or not paved at all.

City planners tried to ease the congestion by creating several forms of **mass transit**, or public transportation. By the 1890s cities like New York and Chicago had elevated railroads that ran on tracks above the streets. A more complicated and expensive option was to build underground railroads known as subways. The first American subway opened in Boston in 1897, followed in 1904 by the much larger New York City subway. Cable cars, first used in the 1860s, were also common. Electric trolleys became popular in the 1890s. These streetcars carried people to and from work cheaply and quickly.

If they could afford it, many middle-class Americans chose to live outside the city, in quieter areas where they could buy their own homes. They moved to **suburbs**—residential neighborhoods outside of downtown areas. The new mass transit networks of trolleys, subways, and commuter trains made it possible for people to live in the suburbs and work in the cities.

New Places for the Public

In addition to places for people to live and work, urban leaders in the late 1800s wanted to create public places to enhance a city's image and improve the quality of city life. Not all city residents could afford to move to the suburbs in search of quiet. As cities grew larger, public areas began to disappear. Although town commons and greens had existed in the United States since the 1600s, the public park—a space specially designed for recreation—was unknown until the mid-1800s. About that time New York City began setting aside land for public use to provide residents with quiet, green spaces. The city hired landscape architect Frederick Law Olmsted to design Central Park. The idea of preserving green areas in cities for recreation caught on, and many cities began building parks.

In the 1870s a group of Chicago leaders founded a public library, declaring that "every person in the community, however humble, . . . has a right to be supplied with books." During the late 1800s cities and towns across the country established public libraries to educate and serve their residents. Many communities benefited from the philanthropy of Andrew Carnegie, who donated millions of dollars for library construction.

Philanthropists in several large U.S. cities also began creating museums where the public could see displays of art, natural history, and science. These museums, such as the Metropolitan Museum of Art in New York and the Art Institute of Chicago, were intended to educate the public and to create beautiful city centers. The founders of the Boston Museum of Fine Arts stated that the museum "ought to be a popular institution, in the widest sense of the term."

Giant retail shops known as **department stores** also appeared in some city centers in the late 1800s. These stores provided a great variety of

Streetcars transported people from suburbs to their jobs in the city.

Across the Curriculum

LITERATURE

How the Other Half Lives. Jacob Riis's *How the Other Half Lives* proved influential. His work inspired many reformers, including Theodore Roosevelt, who was then the police commissioner of New York. Roosevelt declared, "*How the Other Half Lives* had been to me both an enlightenment and an inspiration for which I felt I never could be too grateful."

Activity: Have students obtain a copy of Riis's book. Discuss some of the passages describing the lives of immigrants in New York City during the 1880s.

Multimedia Resources

American' History Interactive Maps CD–ROM: Development of a Modern City

American Arts Answers

(page 218)

1. He wanted to create a rural retreat for city dwellers.

2. a place for parents to bring children, particularly during the summer

3. It provided a place to relax, explore, exercise, mingle, and take the children.

LEVEL 2: Linguistic, Intrapersonal. (Suggested time: 45 min.) Ask students to imagine that they are living in an urban area in the United States during the early 1900s. Have each student write to a friend living in a rural area, describing the following topics: reasons for urban population growth; problems that have accompanied growth; attempts to solve these problems; and key individuals who tried to improve urban living conditions. Encourage students to include their own ideas for improving the quality of urban life. Ask volunteers to read their letters to the class. Finally, lead a discussion on the problems related to urban growth.

LEVEL 3: Visual-Spatial, Logical-Mathematical, Linguistic. (Suggested time: 45 min.) As a class, discuss difficulties that immigrants faced in cities. Ask each student to create a brochure designed to attract new immigrants to a major city. Brochures should focus on organizations that were created to address immigrants' problems, such as benevolent societies, churches, unions, lodges, political clubs, and settlement houses. Have students identify the problem or problems that each type of organization addressed. Finally, ask volunteers to explain their brochures to the class.

Across the Curriculum

HEALTH

Drinking Water. As U.S. cities began to grow rapidly during the late 1800s, supplying residents with healthy drinking water became very important. Up until this time, many people lived in rural areas and took water from wells, cisterns, or springs. By 1880 most large cities had begun to pipe water into their central areas, but the availability of water for individual use varied depending on wealth. People in tenements could get water from hall taps or street hydrants but had no access to water inside their personal residences. Wealthier families connected their houses' pipes to their city's new main lines. Disposing of wastewater, however, remained a major health hazard in most urban areas.

Question: Why might disposing of waste water present a problem?

ANSWER: It can lead to unsanitary conditions or pollute a clean water supply.

Multimedia Resources

Linking Geography and History Transparency 11: Growth of Cities, 1840

American Arts

Frederick Law Olmsted

Frederick Law Olmsted, who was one of the first designers to call himself a landscape architect, is best known as the chief architect of New York City's Central Park. In addition to designing Central Park, Olmsted planned Prospect Park in Brooklyn; South Park in Chicago; the Stanford University grounds in California; the grounds of the U.S. Capitol in Washington, D.C.; and the Boston park system.

In 1857 Olmsted was appointed superintendent of Central Park, the first major public park in the United States. He created new plans for the park with designer Calvert Vaux. Olmsted planned Central Park to serve as a rural retreat for city-dwellers. He hoped that it would be a place where they could relax while they explored the park's natural landscape. For this reason, he carefully planned every square foot of the park's surface, including every tree and bush, as well as every arch. Olmsted also hoped that the park would offer a place for people to exercise. He wanted to create a setting where people of all social classes might gather outdoors.

This 1870 image shows Frederick Law Olmsted's plan for Central Park.

The Granger Collection, New York

Olmsted's designs for Central Park called for three main bodies of water—the Lake, the Meer, and the Pond. To make the Pond area more attractive to visitors, Olmsted planted trees along its edge and lined its path with benches. He purposely placed the Pond near busy streets, hoping that it would attract walkers, if only for a brief period of rest.

South of the Lake is the Children's District. It was designed as a place where parents could bring their children during the hot summer months. Because infant and child deaths in the city sharply increased during hot weather, staying cool was important. "For them," Olmsted said, "the best that can be done is to spend an occasional day or part of a day in the Park."

In additon, Central Park offered other leisure activities, such as horseback riding, ice skating, boating, and baseball. Central Park proved extremely popular, attracting an average of 30,000 visitors a day for a total of 10 million in 1871. It remains a popular destination today for New York City's residents as well as its tourists.

Understanding the Arts

1. What did Frederick Law Olmsted hope to achieve with the Pond area of Central Park?
2. What is the Children's District?
3. Why do you think Central Park became such a popular attraction?

CLOSE

Linguistic, Logical-Mathematical, Intrapersonal. Have students scan material from this section and select what they think was the most important improvement in city life in the early 1900s. Have each student write a paragraph explaining the selected improvements. Each student's paragraph should discuss the problems the improvement was designed to address, how it solved the problem, and why the student thinks it was the most important one. Allow time for volunteers to explain their choices to the class.

CHALLENGE AND EXTEND

1. **Linguistic, Intrapersonal.** Lead a discussion on the concept of settlement houses and provide students with background information on Hull House. Have students use the library or other resources to find information on Jane Addams and her efforts to help immigrant families. Pair students and have each pair write a mock interview. Have one student be the interviewer and write questions about how Jane Addams has helped immigrants. Have the second student pose as an immigrant and write the responses. Encourage students to include information

goods all in one location. New department stores included Jordan Marsh in Boston and Marshall Fields, which opened in 1881 in Chicago. These grew increasingly popular, relying on low prices, high sales volumes, and newspaper advertising to attract customers. In 1896 one writer described the great success of a department store owned by John Wanamaker:

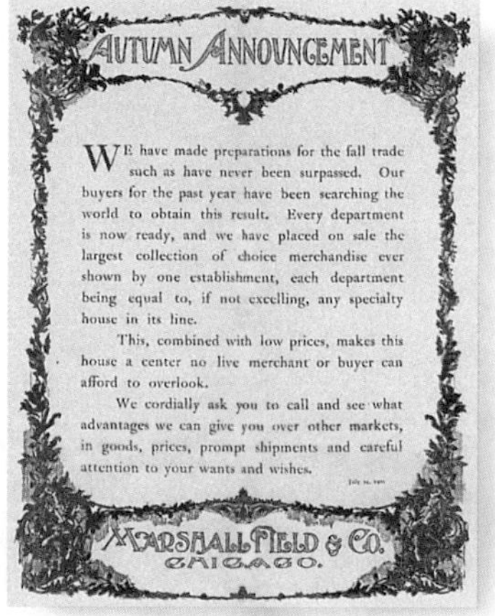
AUTUMN ANNOUNCEMENT

WE have made preparations for the fall trade such as have never been surpassed. Our buyers for the past year have been searching the world to obtain this result. Every department is now ready, and we have placed on sale the largest collection of choice merchandise ever shown by one establishment, each department being equal to, if not excelling, any specialty house in its line.

This, combined with low prices, makes this house a center no live merchant or buyer can afford to overlook.

We cordially ask you to call and see what advantages we can give you over other markets, in goods, prices, prompt shipments and careful attention to your wants and wishes.

MARSHALL FIELD & CO.
CHICAGO.

A Marshall Fields advertising brochure

> **"In Philadelphia everybody goes to Wanamaker's. . . . He tells you each morning in the newspapers what he has got today, and if you want it you had better go and get it: the chances are it will be gone tomorrow."**

Although department stores were designed to sell goods, they were also elaborate buildings designed to awe and impress the public. Many had vaulted ceilings, elegant displays, huge plate glass windows, and bright lighting. As one New Yorker noted in 1899, window-shopping along the street in front of the "gleaming store-windows" provided many people with "a cheap form of social entertainment." Department stores and skyscrapers helped create new "downtown" business sections in the centers of many U.S. cities.

Urban Problems

Despite the new public parks, skyscrapers, and streetcars, U.S. cities in the late 1800s suffered from a wide range of problems. Many urban areas were unprepared for the tremendous population growth that they experienced. City leaders worked to meet the many challenges that arose during this time. However, they often lacked the laws, organizations, and resources necessary to protect citizens' health and well-being.

Housing Problems

Cities' rapid population growth often resulted in shortages of affordable housing. Consequently, many families found themselves packed into tiny apartments in overcrowded tenement buildings. Journalist and photographer Jacob Riis described the conditions faced by poor urban residents in his book *How the Other Half Lives:*

> **"Nine lived in two rooms, one about ten feet square that served as parlor, bedroom, and eating room, the other a small hall room made into a kitchen. The rent was . . . more than a week's wages for the husband."**

Overcrowding and lack of sanitation frequently led to disease and health problems. The poor suffered the most. Many tenement buildings were packed together in areas close to city factories. Rooms in these buildings were often dark, with few windows to let in light or to allow air to circulate. Families in many buildings had to walk down to the streets to draw their water from public sidewalk pumps. In most cities, landlords were not required by law to repair their buildings or to maintain safety standards.

Fire and crime were also common problems in urban neighborhoods. By the late 1800s this had

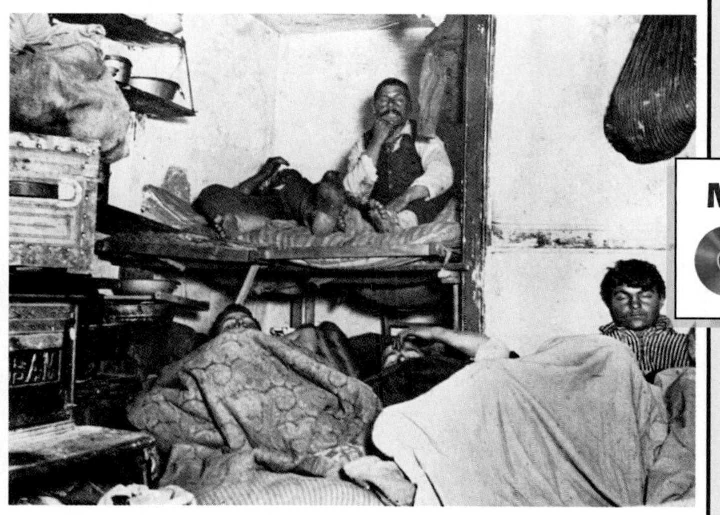
In the late 1880s Jacob Riis photographed crowded living conditions like this room in New York City.

Global Relations

European Parks. The parks of European cities provided inspiration for New York City's Central Park. In 1848 Andrew Jackson Downing, an early proponent of a large park in New York City, wrote an essay in which an unidentified traveler describes the beauties of parks in Germany. Later, when visiting Britain in 1850, Downing expressed amazement at the size and charm of city parks in London. Inspired by his visit, Downing determined that New York possessed the funds and the land to build its own great park. Downing's vision was realized by others, including architect Frederick Law Olmsted.

Activity: Have students search the Internet through the HRW Web site to find information about Central Park today. Ask them to find out how many visitors enjoy the park in a given year and write a paragraph about some of its attractions.

go.hrw.com
SB1 Central Park

Multimedia Resources

Linking Geography and History Transparency 11A: Growth of Cities, 1840–1900 from their research about specific actions that Addams took to improve her community and help immigrants.

2. **Visual-Spatial, Logical-Mathematical.** Have students choose a major city in the United States or assign them each a specific city to research. Have students use the library or other resources to obtain population statistics for the selected city. Encourage students to obtain data covering 1850 to the present. Then ask each student to make a bar graph depicting population changes at 10-year intervals. For each major population increase or decrease, have students hypothesize about its cause. Finally, display several students' bar graphs on the chalkboard and discuss similarities and differences in population changes among the various cities, along with possible reasons for them.

3. **Linguistic, Logical-Mathematical, Intrapersonal.** Have students use the library or other resources to find reasons for and consequences of the Chinese Exclusion Act. Ask each student to write an essay providing this information and addressing the following question: Would legislation similar to the Chinese Exclusion Act be tolerated in the United States today?

Linking Past to Present

Hull House Association. The goals and work of Jane Addams live on in the form of the Jane Addams Hull House Association. The Chicago-based organization currently serves approximately 225,000 people and operates more than 35 facilities throughout Chicago. The association, which operates close to 100 programs, has maintained Jane Addams's goal of improving people's self-reliance. Some of these programs include job training, child care, foster care, counseling, literacy, and home delivery of meals.

Activity: Have students use the library or other resources to find information about local social service organizations that focus on assisting children. Then have students work together to create a guide to social services in your community or state.

Multimedia Resources

American Music Audio CD Program: "Twilight Rag"

Biography

Jane Addams

Jane Addams was born into a prosperous midwestern family in 1860. She graduated from college at the head of her class, but illness and injury prevented her from becoming a doctor as she had originally planned. After visiting the Toynbee Hall community center in London, Addams was inspired to found Hull House in Chicago.

Addams was a compassionate and practical leader who responded to the needs of her community. When Chicago failed to clear trash off of the neighborhood streets, Addams became a city garbage inspector and forced the garbage collectors to do their jobs. As a reformer, lecturer, and writer, she reached beyond Chicago to touch many lives for many years. She was a co-winner of the Nobel Peace Prize in 1931 for her work with the Woman's International League for Peace and Freedom. Addams once wrote that democracy must be "a rule of living as well as a test of faith."

led many major cities to hire full-time firefighters and establish permanent police forces. Police officers also provided public services, such as helping lost children and enforcing health and traffic codes. In spite of these improvements, the reform efforts of most city governments were limited by internal corruption or a lack of funds.

Urban Organizations

City residents often established their own organizations to make life easier. Many immigrant communities created benevolent societies. Workers from a variety of backgrounds established associations that assisted injured or unemployed members and provided places to meet socially. Others formed lodges for recreation or political clubs to discuss local and national issues.

In the late 1800s African American religious groups emerged as a powerful force to organize and aid their urban communities. African American ministers often served as political as well as spiritual leaders in black neighborhoods. One report from a Baptist organization described black ministers as "a class of men who . . . have won the confidence, love, and respect of their people."

African American women, who made up the majority of church members and volunteer leaders, often helped these ministers with their work. Through the churches, black women held power and influence in their communities. One woman noted that the typical man in her community believed that men should be the leaders in society. She said, "But whenever it comes to church affairs, he quietly puts his hands in his pockets and steps aside leaving it for the women to do."

The Granger Collection, New York

African Americans used their own churches in the late 1800s to help address urban problems.

REVIEW

Visual-Spatial, Logical-Mathematical. Have students complete the Section Review questions. Then have each student outline the section. Using the subsection titles as main ideas, tell students to write two to four supporting details under each heading. When students have finished their outlines, call on volunteers to identify supporting details for each heading.

ASSESS

Have students complete Daily Quiz 7.2.

RETEACH

Logical-Mathematical, Interpersonal. Have students complete Main Idea Activities for Reteaching and Sheltered English 7.2. Then have students take on the role of urban planners for the fictitious city of Quimbly. Advise students that the city has recently experienced an immense population growth because of immigration to the area and that this growth is expected to continue for some years. Tell students that their task is to create a list of problems the city can expect and offer plans for solving those problems. Encourage students to refer to the section for ideas on problems and solutions. **SHELTERED ENGLISH**

The Settlement Houses

Many private aid organizations offered assistance to poor people in the late 1800s. In addition to benevolent societies, there were **settlement houses**—neighborhood centers in poor areas, staffed by professionals and volunteers, that offered education, recreation, and social activities.

Settlement houses began in Britain but also became common in the United States. Janie Porter Barrett established an African American settlement house in Norfolk, Virginia. The most famous settlement house was **Hull House**, founded by Jane Addams and Ellen Gates Starr in 1889. Addams and Starr were among the many upper-class women of their era who received a college education but found few job opportunities open to them. Addams wanted to do work that would help the poor. "I was quite settled in my mind that I should study medicine and 'live with the poor,'" she once recalled. Addams and Starr moved into a run-down building in a poor neighborhood in Chicago and turned it into Hull House. The work at Hull House focused most on the needs of immigrant families.

Addams brought in many other women like herself who sought a career that they felt was useful. These female social workers lived at the settlement house. Addams believed that it was best for the workers to live among the people they hoped to help. As she later explained:

Reformer Florence Kelley began her career at Hull House.

> **"I gradually became convinced that it would be a good thing to rent a house in a part of the city where many . . . needs are found, in which young women who have been given over too exclusively to study might . . . learn of life from life itself; where they might try out some of the things they have been taught."**

Addams and her staff participated in a variety of activities. They established a kindergarten and a public playground. They taught classes in English and U.S. government to help immigrants become citizens. The staff also worked for reforms such as child labor laws and the eight-hour workday for women. Hull House served as a model for other settlement houses. By 1900 there were more than 100 settlement houses in the United States. Many of the women involved in running Hull House later became active in a variety of national reform movements.

SECTION 2 REVIEW

Identify and explain the significance of the following:
- **mass transit**
- **suburbs**
- **Frederick Law Olmsted**
- **department stores**
- **settlement houses**
- **Hull House**
- **Jane Addams**

Reading for Content Understanding

1. **Main Idea** Make a chart listing technological developments in the 1800s and how they helped cities deal with rapid growth.
2. **Main Idea** What organizations did citizens form to help solve some of the urban problems?
3. **Geographic Diversity** Why did so many Americans choose to move from the country to the cities?
4. **Writing** *Describing* Imagine that you are a journalist in New York City in 1900. Write a newspaper article about the positive and negative changes that have taken place in the city over the last few decades.
5. **Critical Thinking** *Drawing Conclusions* What steps do you think a city government could have taken to solve some of the urban problems that developed in the late 1800s?

Section 2 Review ANSWERS

Identify
For significance, see the following pages:
- mass transit, p. 217
- suburbs, p. 217
- Frederick Law Olmsted, p. 217
- department stores, p. 217
- settlement houses, p. 221
- Hull House, p. 221
- Jane Addams, p. 221

Reading for Content Understanding

1. Charts will vary but should include descriptions of skyscrapers, elevators, and advances in plumbing as well as explain how these developments enabled cities to deal with rapid growth.

2. Organizations formed to help solve urban problems included benevolent societies, religious groups, unions, lodges, and political clubs.

3. People moved to cities to enjoy economic and educational advantages, libraries, parks, theaters, museums, and hospitals.

4. Articles will vary but should identify changes such as immigration, skyscrapers, or mass transit, and explain why each is considered to be positive or negative.

5. Answers will vary but students should demonstrate an understanding of the problems that cities faced and provide examples of possible solutions to them.

OBJECTIVES

- Examine the new forms of popular entertainment that developed in the late 1800s.
- Describe changes in American literature and publishing in the late 1800s.
- Identify new styles of art and methods of photography that developed in the late 1800s.

FOCUS

Motivate Before Reading

Organize students into small groups and have them list recreational or cultural activities—such as watching television or listening to the radio—that interest all members of the group. When students have finished their lists, have groups write their findings on the chalkboard. Ask students to identify any items that were on all the groups' lists. Point out to the class that such lists would

Section 3 RESOURCES

PRINT

★ Guided Reading Strategies 7.3

★ Graphic Organizer 7: Social and Artistic Responses to a Growing Nation

★ Biography Reading 7: P. T. Barnum

★ Section 3 Review, p. 227

★ Daily Quiz 7.3

MULTIMEDIA

★ *Teaching Resources CD–ROM*, Lesson 7.3

SHELTERED ENGLISH

★ Main Idea Activities for Reteaching and Sheltered English 7.3

Society and Culture

Reading Focus

What new forms of popular entertainment developed in the late 1800s?

How did American literature and publishing change in the late 1800s?

In the late 1800s, what new styles of art and methods of photography developed?

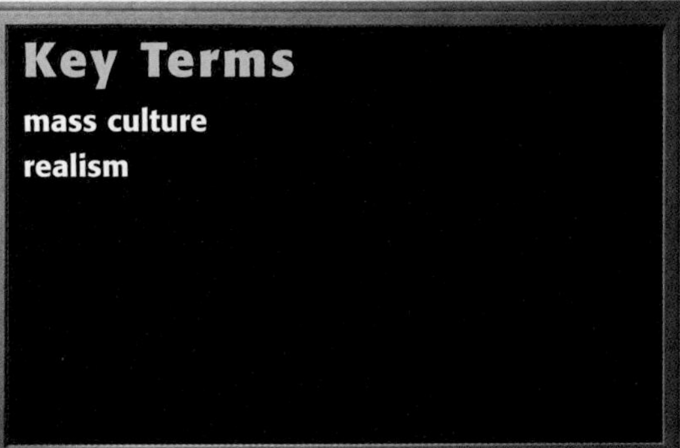

Key Terms

mass culture

realism

IN FEBRUARY 1872 the partners of "P. T. Barnum's Museum, Menagerie and Circus" held an emergency meeting. The other partners told Barnum that the circus had become too big and expensive and that they needed to cut costs. Barnum replied that he was going to make the circus even bigger and travel from town to town by train instead of by wagons, "so as to hit good-sized towns every day in the season." His gamble paid off, and that year Barnum's circus, billed as the "Greatest Show on Earth," earned record profits as it toured the country.

Poster for P. T. Barnum's popular circus

Mass Culture

P. T. Barnum's success reflected changes in American society in the late 1800s. Increased population, improved transportation, growing cities, and a boom in publishing all contributed to the rise of **mass culture**—leisure and cultural activities shared by large numbers of people.

Early examples of mass culture included world's fairs—international expositions featuring exhibits and participants from all over the world. These fairs grew more popular in the United States after the great success of the Philadelphia Centennial Exposition in 1876. The exposition combined displays of the latest technological inventions with exhibits of world cultures. Fair organizers hoped to attract and educate huge crowds by appealing to people's curiosity.

Millions of visitors came to the world's fairs to see the amazing exhibits. Others saw the fairs as a chance to relax and enjoy themselves during their time off. Beginning with the Chicago Exposition in 1893, fair organizers tried to fill this need for relaxation by providing places for pure entertainment.

probably be similar in other parts of the United States, and that combined, the activities that are shared by many U.S. citizens make up what is known as mass culture. Tell students that in this section they will learn how a mass culture developed in the United States.

Introduce Key Terms

Linguistic, Logical-Mathematical. Review this section's key terms with students. Ask students to use the text to write a definition for each term. Then have each student write a sentence using each key term. **SHELTERED ENGLISH**

TEACH

Have students read Section 3 and complete guided Reading Strategies 7.3. Choose one or more of the following activities to explore the section content with students. For further suggestions on block scheduling or team teaching, see the *Block Scheduling Handbook.*

LEVEL 1: Linguistic. (Suggested time: 15 min.) As a class, go over students' Guided Reading Strategies. Then use the Reading Focus questions to highlight the main ideas of the section. **SHELTERED ENGLISH**

Thousands of visitors relaxed and enjoyed themselves at Luna Park on Coney Island.

For example, outside of the main exhibit area known as the White City, the Chicago fair featured an attraction called the Midway. This was a mile-long strip of displays, restaurants, shops, and theaters. Rides such as the Ferris wheel were also located in the Midway, which proved to be the most popular site at the exposition.

The demand for public entertainment soon led to the creation of amusement parks, most notably on New York City's Coney Island. The first permanent amusement park, Sea Lion Park, was built in 1895 on the island. Other parks soon followed, and by 1905 thousands of people visited Coney Island to enjoy rides and displays at places such as Luna Park and Dreamland. In 1904 the *New York Times* reported on the opening day of the summer season at Coney Island:

> **"They took the lid off Coney Island last night, and a quarter of a million men and women got a glimpse of a swaying, rocking, glittering magic city by the sea."**

Part of the appeal of amusement parks was the technology used in them. Mechanical rides such as Shoot-the-Chutes, the Barrel of Fun, and the Ferris wheel offered visitors thrills and new experiences. The parks also gave visitors a chance to relax in an informal setting with people from different backgrounds. "It was a world removed," noted one journalist, "shut away from the . . . clatter and turmoil of the streets." Inexpensive train fares from New York City and affordable admission tickets attracted many low-wage workers to the amusement parks. People from all walks of life made trips to Coney Island each year, enjoying the sights and sounds.

 The Rise of Sports

Athletic events also began drawing large crowds of spectators. In 1896 the first modern Olympics—held in Athens, Greece—led to an increased worldwide interest in track and field events.

Spectator Sports

In addition to track and field, other popular spectator sports included baseball and football. Baseball began as an amateur sport that grew in popularity after the Civil War. Early baseball players did not wear gloves, and pitchers tossed the ball underhand toward the batter. Gradually, padded gloves, catcher's masks, and new pitching styles were introduced, making the game safer for players and more exciting for fans. Players were organized into a national professional league in 1876. The professional baseball teams—such as the Philadelphia Athletics, New York Mutuals, and Chicago White Stockings—were located in large cities where they could draw crowds of a few thousand people per game.

An early baseball and glove, now preserved in the Baseball Hall of Fame

Football became an increasingly popular amateur sport on college campuses. Crowds gathered to watch teams such as Harvard and Yale. These early games were very rough, and few players wore helmets. Yale football player and future coach Alonzo Stagg explained that "injuries

Daily Life

The Amusement Park. Although amusement parks are designed to entertain people, their beginnings are linked to the streetcar, railway, and subway companies. These new forms of public transportation relied on electricity and were charged a fixed rate by the electric company. So when few people rode the trains at night or on the weekends, the transit companies still had to pay. Thus, they were not making money. The solution was to build pleasure parks at the ends of the lines. These parks started off simply enough, with a few picnic tables, usually near some water. Soon there were sports fields, restaurants, boat rides, and new treats like the Ferris wheel.

Critical Thinking: Why would transit companies want to build public amusement parks?

ANSWER: If transit companies could get passengers on their cars during evenings and weekends, they could make more money.

ALL LEVELS: Visual-Spatial, Kinesthetic. (Suggested time: 45 min.) Explain to students that in the late 1800s several different forms of popular entertainment came into vogue. Provide students with art supplies and have each student make a mobile depicting some of the new forms of entertainment. Each segment of the mobile should represent a different form of entertainment that became popular, such as amusement parks or baseball. Once students have finished, call on volunteers to show them to the class. Finally, lead a discussion on how each of these forms of entertainment has changed. **SHELTERED ENGLISH**

LEVEL 2: Linguistic, Logical-Mathematical. (Suggested time: 30 min. plus homework) Ask students to imagine that they are art critics from the late 1800s and they have been assigned to write articles describing new trends in art and photography. Have students identify each change that took place; state how it differed from the method or subject matter that had been used earlier; and state their opinion regarding whether the change is a positive one. Once students finish writing their articles, have volunteers read them to the class. Then, as a class, review the changes.

LEVEL 3: Linguistic, Logical-Mathematical, Interpersonal. (Suggested time: 45 min.) Have students review the section and list all of the changes they can find that took place in

Linking Past to Present

Football. Football as we know it was created by Ivy League schools in the 1870s. McGill and Harvard played the first intercollegiate game in May 1874. It was played using Rugby Union rules, which allow 15 players on each side with scrums causing constant changes in possession. In the late 1870s the number of players was reduced to 11 per side and scrums were replaced with the line of scrimmage, which allowed one team to control the ball for a series of plays. Around the same time, universities began to focus on increasing their enrollment. Schools soon realized that a winning football team attracted new students. Winning teams also attracted alumni dollars. Even people who had not gone to a school began to associate themselves with a successful team. Football evolved from a game played by students to one played for spectators. The game has changed with the introduction of the forward pass and various types of padding worn by players, and is more ingrained in American mass culture than ever.

Critical Thinking: What role has the media played in the growth of pastimes like football?

ANSWER: Generally, the more coverage the media provide to new pastimes, the more popular they become.

were disregarded. . . . Two or three dependable substitutes were all that a team thought of needing."

For many people, spectator sports became a way to forget the concerns of their daily lives while watching their local team play. Fans from a wide variety of cultural, social, and economic backgrounds could unite in supporting a team. African Americans, however, were excluded from playing in early professional sports leagues. This led to the creation of independent African American sports leagues in the 1900s.

Exercise and Health

In addition to enjoying organized sports, many Americans became interested in outdoor exercise for fun and health. Popular activities included boating, hiking, and swimming. More Americans also began playing golf and tennis.

In the late 1800s the first modern bicycle was developed. It had two equal-sized wheels and air-filled rubber tires. These safer, more comfortable vehicles led to a boom in bike sales, what New York writer Henry Brown called "the great bicycle craze of the Nineties." Brown wrote, "It was . . . the Bicycle that created the present enormous vogue for [popularity of] athletics amongst women."

Early bicycles had one large wheel and one smaller one. In the 1890s people found bicycles much easier to ride when both wheels were made the same size.

Many young women defied tradition when they wore short pants called bloomers—named after women's rights activist Amelia Bloomer—while riding bicycles. Women also began to participate in increasing numbers in college sports such as field hockey or games such as lawn tennis.

The Growth of Publishing

To meet the growing interest in athletics, newspapers began running sports sections to report the latest game scores and team news. People interested in reading about sports or other events found more newspapers to read in the late 1800s. The invention in 1884 of the linotype, an automatic typesetting machine, greatly reduced the time and cost of printing. As printed material became less expensive to produce, more newspapers and magazines were published. In 1850 there were fewer than 300 daily newspapers in the United States. By 1900 there were more than 2,000.

Advertisement for the January 1898 issue of Harper's *magazine*

Big cities often produced many newspapers, some printed in foreign languages for immigrant readers. Newspaper advertisers began running pictures and full-page ads for the first time. Many of these advertisements were for department stores. An editor for the New York *Herald* boasted in 1872, "What a picture of the metropolis [city] one day's advertisements in the *Herald* presents to mankind!"

Competition for readers pushed newspapers into making other changes. In the late 1890s newspaper publishers Joseph Pulitzer and William Randolph Hearst began using color printing for the first time. They also began featuring Sunday comic strips, such as the Yellow Kid and the Katzenjammer Kids.

Magazines also flourished during the late 1800s. They tended to be more focused on specific subjects than newspapers. Popular magazines included the *Delineator* and *Ladies' Home Journal* for

American literature and publishing in the late 1800s. For each change, have students identify events that led to it and what resulted from it. Some changes will have more than one cause or result. For example, students can identify a rise in the number of newspapers and magazines as one of the changes that took place; point out the invention of the linotype as a cause; and state that one result was that with the increase in the number of publications, some American newspapers began printing their materials in foreign languages. Have volunteers identify their cause-and-effect relationships for the class.

CLOSE

Linguistic, Logical-Mathematical. Have students review the section and choose the five changes or developments that they think had the most influence on mass culture in the United States. Ask students to write a headline for each change or development. Remind students to make their headlines short, interesting, and informative. When students have finished, ask them to choose a partner, exchange papers, and write two supporting pieces of information under each headline.

women's issues, the political magazine *The Nation*, and literary magazines such as *Scribner's Magazine*. Reduced prices, better printing quality, and improved writing helped such magazines expand their readership.

By 1900 the daily newspaper had become a powerful cultural force in people's everyday lives. It provided news of local, national, and world events, advertisements for the latest products, and information on sports and entertainment. Weekly and monthly magazines carried articles, essays, and short stories on a wide range of topics. Together, magazines and newspapers played an important role in informing Americans and shaping their views of the world.

Popular American Literature

The printing revolution also made books more affordable. Authors experimented with new story locations and writing styles to interest an expanding audience. Some of the best-known authors in the late 1800s used a style known as local color in their writing. Their stories focused on common local scenes and described the landscape and customs of regional America. For example, Samuel Clemens, who wrote under the name Mark Twain, set many of his stories in the Mississippi River region and the Far West. Twain often used exaggerated characters for comic effect.

George Washington Cable was one of several authors who became well known for writing novels and short stories set in the South before the Civil War. The Northeast was represented by the work of writers such as Sarah Orne Jewett. She believed that her writing should inform readers about rural New Englanders and their way of life. "I wanted the world to know their grand, simple lives," Jewett explained.

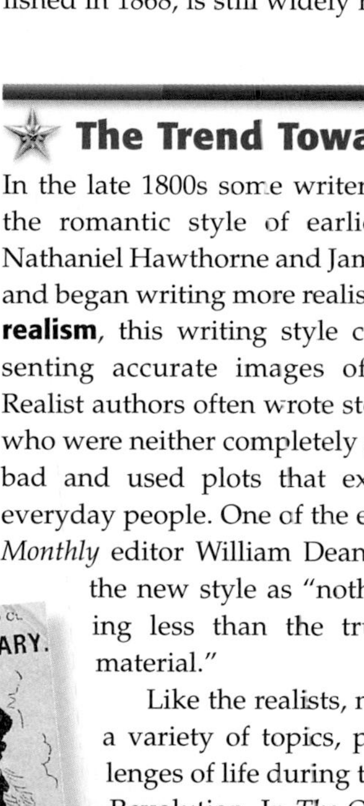

Dime novels like this one were popular in the late 1800s.

Many authors of the late 1800s wrote novels that offered advice to young people on how to prepare for the future. These stories often reinforced society's ideas about success for men and women. Horatio Alger Jr. wrote a popular series of "rags-to-riches" novels about fictional young men who rose from humble beginnings to achieve great wealth. Alger wrote more than 100 such books, including *Work and Win* and *Risen from the Ranks*. For many people, Alger's books told the story of the American dream—that all Americans could achieve financial success by being honest and hardworking.

Louisa May Alcott's stories about young women and domestic life were very popular even though her characters sometimes challenged the traditional roles of women. *Little Women*, published in 1868, is still widely read today.

The Trend Toward Realism

In the late 1800s some writers turned away from the romantic style of earlier authors such as Nathaniel Hawthorne and James Fenimore Cooper and began writing more realistic stories. Known as **realism**, this writing style concentrated on presenting accurate images of American society. Realist authors often wrote stories with characters who were neither completely good nor completely bad and used plots that explored the lives of everyday people. One of the early realists, *Atlantic Monthly* editor William Dean Howells, described the new style as "nothing more and nothing less than the truthful treatment of material."

Like the realists, naturalists dealt with a variety of topics, particularly the challenges of life during the Second Industrial Revolution. In *The Octopus*, Frank Norris describes the fights over land between farmers and railroad companies. Stephen Crane wrote about people's struggles to survive in stories like "The Open Boat." In 1900 Theodore Dreiser wrote *Sister Carrie*, a novel that describes the experiences of a young woman who moves to Chicago from the country and experiences life in the big city. In one passage

Historical Sidelight

The Dime Novel. Along with technological changes in the publishing world in the late 1800s, there came a new product known as the dime novel. New printing methods had cut the costs of production, and book publishers were finally able to take advantage by flooding the market with cheap reading material. In 1860 the firm of Beadle and Adams decided to sell the first "Dollar Book for a Dime," and the response was better than expected. The firm's first dime novel, *Malaeska* by Ann Sophia Stephens, sold 500,000 copies. Sales continued to soar into the next century. A few themes were particularly popular: the rags-to-riches stories of Horatio Alger, working girl romances, and tales of the Wild West. "Buffalo Bill" Cody became famous partially because of the many novels that made him an American folk legend.

Critical Thinking: Why were dime novels so popular?

ANSWER: They were cheap and entertaining.

CHALLENGE AND EXTEND

1. **Visual-Spatial Kinesthetic, Intrapersonal.** Review the concept of mass culture with the class. Have students use the library and other resources to investigate changes in the current mass culture of the United States. Then ask students to create a collage displaying the significant changes that occurred. For example, students can depict use of the Internet and cellular phones or changes in recreational habits, such as the rise of extreme sports. Have volunteers present their collages and explain their choices to the class. Finally, have students work together to create a comprehensive list of elements that distinguish current mass culture in the United States from that of the past. **SHELTERED ENGLISH**

2. **Linguistic, Visual-Spatial, Kinesthetic.** Assign each student one artist discussed in the section. Have students use the library and other resources to find examples of the assigned artist's work. Ask each student to write a summary describing the assigned artist's style and comparing it to other artists of the period. Then have each student choose a favorite work by the assigned artist and bring a book containing a picture of it or a photocopy from the book to class. Have each student make a brief presentation on the assigned artist, using the copy of the favorite work to illustrate the artist's style.

Section 3 Review ANSWERS

Identify

For significance, see the following pages:

- mass culture, p. 222
- Louisa May Alcott, p. 225
- realism, p. 225
- William Dean Howells, p. 225
- Henry James, p. 226
- Winslow Homer, p. 226
- Mary Cassat, p. 226
- George Eastman, p. 227

Reading for Content Understanding

1. Many people enjoyed activities such as amusement parks, spectator sports, newspapers, bicycling, magazines, and popular novels.

2. Better-quality printed material became less expensive to produce. As a result, many more novels, newspapers, and magazines were printed. These cheap publications informed and entertained a greater number of Americans than ever before.

3. There were trends toward local color, realism, and naturalism in literature and the introduction of more convenient film and cheaper cameras in photography.

4. Answers will vary but should include specific examples of activities (e.g., going to amusement parks or museums) and reasons the student enjoys them.

5. Answers will vary but should demonstrate a clear understanding of what topics realist authors chose—in general presenting an accurate image of American society—and how they reflected society.

Dreiser describes Carrie's thoughts after she passes by fancy stores for the rich while searching for a job to pay her rent:

> **"As for Carrie, her understanding of the moral significance of money was the popular understanding, nothing more. The old definition: 'Money: something everybody else has and I must get,' would have expressed her understanding of it thoroughly."**

Other authors of the time, such as Edith Wharton, showed the behavior and attitudes of the American upper class. Henry James wrote several such manners novels, including *Portrait of a Lady*. Both James and Wharton spent many years traveling and living in Europe, as many wealthy Americans did. James preferred to live quietly in England, writing about American life from a distance.

American Painters

In the mid-1800s members of the Hudson River school, also called the American Romantics, had helped create a distinctly American style of painting that celebrated westward expansion. Some artists, such as Albert Bierstadt and George Inness, were strongly influenced by the American Romantic painters. "A work of art does not appeal to the intellect," Inness once stated. "Its aim is . . . to awaken an emotion." His bold landscapes were widely admired in Europe.

James McNeill Whistler used his mother as his model in this painting.

Artist Winslow Homer became famous for his watercolor paintings like The Blue Boat.

Other American painters turned away from romantic art. Winslow Homer developed a distinctive style of watercolor painting as he created seascapes and scenes of New England rural life. His images were unsentimental, showing people struggling against the power of nature. In the 1880s he moved to the coast of Maine and painted landscapes and seascapes there until his death. Describing his isolation, he once wrote, "I am four miles from telegram & P.O. [post office] & under a snow bank most of the time." Homer liked living in the country, telling his brother, "The life I have chosen gives me full hours of enjoyment."

Some other respected American painters worked mainly in Europe, where there were better art schools and many wealthy supporters of the arts. John Singer Sargent became particularly admired for his detailed and realistic portraits. He was hired to paint many of the notable figures in European society. Mary Cassatt was the first American to join the impressionist movement in France. The impressionists painted scenes of everyday life, concentrating on representing light and color accurately. Cassatt usually painted women, particularly

REVIEW

Linguistic, Logical-Mathematical. Have students complete the Section Review questions. Then ask students to imagine that they are writers who have been asked to write a chapter for a book about American culture during the early 1900s. Encourage students to include material on each of the following topics: popular entertainment, literature, publishing, art, and photography. When students finish their chapters, have them exchange their work with another student, read it, and discuss the similarities and differences in perceptions of American culture during the early 1900s.

ASSESS

Have students complete Daily Quiz 7.3.

RETEACH

Have students complete Main Idea Activities for Reteaching and Sheltered English 7.3. Organize the class into three small groups. Have each group respond to one of the three Reading Focus questions by creating a magazine cover page that illustrates major changes of the late 1800s. Have each group explain its cover to the rest of the class. **SHELTERED ENGLISH**

mothers with their children. Another artist fascinated by color was James McNeill Whistler. He painted many scenes in watercolor while living in Russia, France, and Britain. To create a certain mood, Whistler often emphasized color in his paintings rather than details of his subjects. "As music is the poetry of sound, so painting is the poetry of sight," Whistler wrote.

Kodak's first camera could take 100 images. For $10 customers could return the camera and film to Kodak for development.

The Granger Collection, New York

A New Art Form

Photography offered another way of creating realistic images of the world. In 1880 the wet-plates used by early photographers were replaced by a more convenient type of camera film. George Eastman made further improvements, leading to cheaper cameras and the box camera in 1888. His company, Kodak, sold cameras that people simply mailed back to Kodak when they wanted the pictures developed. Kodak's slogan was "You Press the Button—We Do the Rest."

Advances in photography and printing enabled newspapers to use black and white photos more widely in the 1890s. One of the best-known news photographers in the United States was New Yorker Jacob Riis, who specialized in realistic pictures of urban life and the city's slums.

Art photographers also emerged in the 1890s. Led by Alfred Stieglitz, these photographers used the camera in much the same way as a painter used a brush and canvas. Many people admired the photographs taken by Stieglitz and others. However, many art critics insisted that photography was not a true art form because it relied on machines. Despite these criticisms, photography continued to grow in popularity. In the process, photographers captured many images of work, play, and daily life in the rapidly changing United States.

SECTION 3 REVIEW

Identify and explain the significance of the following:

- **mass culture**
- **Louisa May Alcott**
- **realism**
- **William Dean Howells**
- **Henry James**
- **Winslow Homer**
- **Mary Cassatt**
- **George Eastman**

Reading for Content Understanding

1 **Main Idea** What activities did many Americans enjoy in the late 1800s?

2 **Main Idea** What changes occurred in American literature and publishing during the late 1800s?

3 **Cultural Diversity** What new styles of art and photography tried to capture American life?

4 **Writing** *Informing* Imagine that you are a city resident writing to a friend in the country about the many kinds of public activities that you have in the city. Explain what your favorite activities are and why.

5 **Critical Thinking** *Synthesizing Information* Why do you think that realist authors chose the story topics that they did? How did these topics reflect society in the late 1800s?

Chapter 7 Review ANSWERS

Identifying People and Ideas

1. people who came to America between 1880 and 1900, from Asia, and southern and eastern Europe

2. organizations that helped new immigrants

3. founded in 1894 in opposition to the wave of new immigrants, pushed legislation to require all immigrants to prove they could read and write before being allowed into the country

4. residential neighborhoods outside of downtown areas, established when people moved out of the cities to live in quieter areas

5. founder of Hull House in Chicago, one of the main activists in the settlement house movement

6. neighborhood centers in poor areas of large cities staffed by professionals and volunteers that offered education, recreation, and social activities

7. a school of writing that concentrated on presenting accurate images of American society

8. local color writer whose subject was life in the northeastern United States

9. painted unsentimental images of the struggle of life in rural New England

10. leisure and cultural activities shared by a large number of people

Using the Time Line

1. d
2. c
3. b
4. a
5. e

Review and Assessment RESOURCES

PRINT
- ★ Chapter 7 Review, pp. 228–29
- ★ Vocabulary Activity 7
- ★ Chapter 7 Study Guide
- ★ Chapter 7 Test (Form A or B)

MULTIMEDIA
- ★ Audio Program, Ch. 7 (English and Spanish)
- ★ *Global Skill Builder CD–ROM*
- ★ Chapter 7 Test Generator
- ★ HRW Web site

SHELTERED ENGLISH
- ★ Spanish Glossary
- ★ Sheltered English Chapter 7 Test

ASSESS

Have students complete one of the Chapter 7 Tests. As an alternate assessment, assign the Chapter 7 Investigation.

Understanding Main Ideas

1. old immigrants—mostly from Britain, Germany, and Scandinavia; skilled workers; generally Protestant; usually settled outside cities; new immigrants—from Asia as well as southern and eastern Europe; usually unskilled workers; held a variety of religious beliefs; settled in cities.

2. They usually lived in crowded apartments and faced dangerous and exhausting working conditions.

3. Immigrants and native-born Americans alike moved to cities because they hoped to make more money and sought the conveniences offered in urban areas.

4. Answers will vary but should refer to several of the following: disease and health problems, rampant crime, housing problems, lack of sanitation fresh air, clean water, and fire protection.

5. New forms of entertainment became popular, such as spectator sports, exercise, and amusement parks. Old forms of entertainment such as newspapers and magazines began selling at cheaper prices to many more customers.

6. American literature began to focus on presenting a more accurate picture of the way everyday people lived.

Reviewing Themes

1. Answers will vary but should refer to input from new immigrants as well as bringing together anti-immigrant forces.

2. Answers will vary but should mention that technological changes allowed large numbers of people to live and work in cities, as well as to travel farther and faster.

CHAPTER 7 REVIEW

Chapter Summary

Immigration from eastern and southern European countries increased after the Civil War. Many of these immigrants moved to cities, where they joined large numbers of migrants from rural America. Rapidly growing cities faced a variety of problems such as overcrowding and poverty. A new mass culture developed, and Americans began exploring new styles in literature, painting, and photography.

On a separate sheet of paper, complete the following activities.

Identifying People and Ideas

Describe the historical significance of the following:

1. new immigrants
2. benevolent societies
3. Immigration Restriction League
4. suburbs
5. Jane Addams
6. settlement houses
7. realism
8. Louisa May Alcott
9. Winslow Homer
10. mass culture

Internet Activity 

go.hrw.com
SB1 Ellis Island

Search the Internet through the HRW Web site to find information about Ellis Island in the late 1800s and early 1900s. Use this information to create a two-page journal describing an immigrant's trip to and arrival in the United States. You may include pictures with your journal.

Understanding Main Ideas

1. How were new immigrants different from old immigrants?
2. What were daily life and work like for immigrants in the late 1800s?
3. Why did cities grow so rapidly?
4. What problems resulted from urban growth?
5. How did popular entertainment begin to change in the late 1800s?
6. What changes took place in American literature in the late 1800s?

Reviewing Themes

1. **Cultural Diversity** What effect did increased immigration have on the United States?
2. **Technology and Society** How did the technological changes of the late 1800s affect Americans?
3. **Geographic Diversity** How did the growth of large cities affect American society?

Using the Time Line

Number your paper from 1 to 5. Match the letters on the time line below with the following events.

1. **The first permanent amusement park opens for business in New York.**
2. **Ellis Island begins receiving immigrants.**
3. **Jane Addams and Ellen Gates Starr found Hull House, a settlement house to help immigrants and the poor.**
4. **Congress bans Chinese immigrants from entering the United States for 10 years.**
5. **Boston opens the first subway in the United States.**

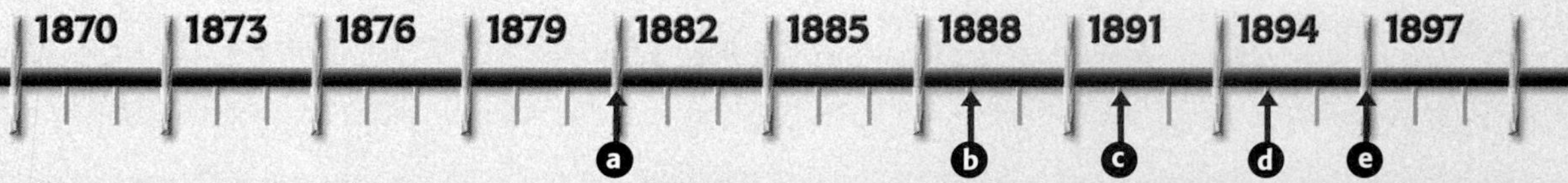

RETEACH

Visual-Spatial, Interpersonal. Organize the class into three groups and assign each group one of the chapter's sections. Have each group create a storyboard describing the cultural changes covered in the section along with a brief oral presentation describing the changes depicted. Have each group present and explain its storyboard to the class.

SHELTERED ENGLISH

Using the Internet

Ask students to expand their search to include information about Asian immigrants arriving at Angel Island. Have them write a paragraph comparing and contrasting the experiences of European and Asian immigrants.

Portfolio Extensions

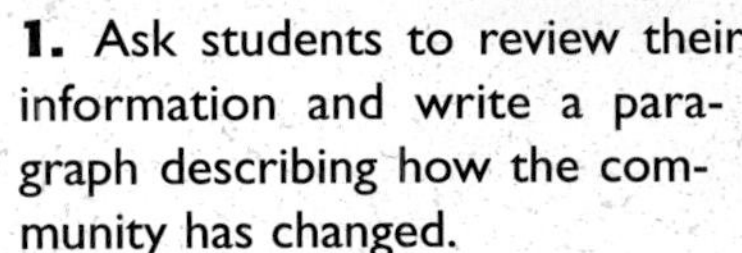

1. Ask students to review their information and write a paragraph describing how the community has changed.

2. Have students use the writing style of the author researched to write their own stories reflecting life in the early 21st century.

Thinking Critically

1. **Identifying Generalizations and Stereotypes** Why did some people oppose the arrival of new immigrants to the United States?
2. **Identifying Cause and Effect** What factors do you think contributed to the development of mass culture?
3. **Evaluating** Why do you think city officials felt that libraries, museums, and parks would improve a city's image?

Writing About History

1. **Informing** Imagine that you are a museum official in the 1890s preparing an exhibit of American art. Write a brief essay discussing the major painters of the period and their artistic styles.
2. **Creating** Write a short poem or song that expresses the feelings of an immigrant seeing a U.S. city for the first time.

Linking Geography and History

1. **Movement** Why did many immigrants come to the United States?
2. **Human-Environment Interaction** How was technology used to help manage the increasing size of cities?

Building Your Portfolio

Complete the following activities individually or in groups.

1. **Immigrant Communities** Many immigrant communities established during the 1800s, such as Boston's North End and Chinatown in San Francisco and New York, are still thriving parts of U.S. cities today. Research a modern immigrant community and create a tourist brochure to attract visitors to that community. Your brochure should include some historical information about the community as well as descriptions and images of current attractions.
2. **Authors of the Second Industrial Revolution** Select an American author who began his or her work in the late 1800s or the early 1900s. Authors may include, but are not limited to, the following: Mark Twain, William Dean Howells, Stephen Crane, Frank Norris, Theodore Dreiser, Henry James, Edith Wharton, and Horatio Alger Jr. Use the library or other resources to research your author. Create a script with questions and answers for an interview with the author on his or her life. Include information on one of the author's stories explaining how the story reflects life during the late 1800s. Perform the interview for the class.

History Skills Workshop

Reading Charts Study the chart below, which shows the number of immigrants arriving in the United States from 1860 to 1900, and answer the following questions: (a) During what period was the growth in immigration the greatest? (b) During what two decades was immigration the highest? (c) Why do you think this was the case?

Total Immigration to the United States, 1860–1900

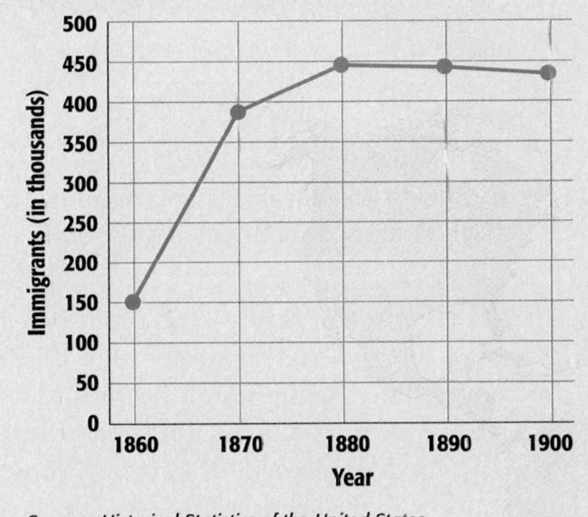

Source: *Historical Statistics of the United States*

3. Answers will vary but should discuss some of the era's new problems, along with new solutions to deal with those problems.

Thinking Critically

1. Some people feared that new immigrants' poverty and lack of education would hurt the nation.

2. increased population, improved transportation, growing cities, and a boom in publishing

3. They might have thought these items would attract people from areas that did not offer them.

Writing About History

1. Answers will vary but will probably include a brief discussion of turning away from earlier styles of romantic art in favor of new styles. For many painters, the new focus was now American subjects painted in American settings.

2. Answers will vary but will probably express optimism regarding coming to the land of opportunity and fear that expectations might not be met.

Linking Geography and History

1. Many came in the hope of prosperity, as well as to escape religious and political persecution in their own countries.

2. It was used to build taller buildings, improve public transportation, bring water to buildings, and provide electricity.

History Skills Workshop

(a) from 1860 to 1870;
(b) the 1880s and 1890s;
(c) The nation's economy was booming.

TEACH

ALL LEVELS: Linguistic, Logical-Mathematical, Visual-Spatial. (Suggested time: 45 min.) Tell students that charts and graphs can often convey information more efficiently and clearly than detailed written explanations. Have each student create two questions that can be answered from the pie graphs titled "Shifting Patterns of Immigration," on this page. Collect the students' questions. Then ask students to write a description of all the information presented on the two pie graphs. Have students exchange their written description with a classmate. Read aloud five of the questions submitted by students, then have them use only the description they have been given to answer the questions. Next, have students open their books and answer the same five questions using the pie graphs. Finally, discuss with students which source was easier to use.

SKILLS ANSWERS

1. northern and western Europe

2. nothing, because you don't know the total number of immigrants arriving

3. The vast majority of immigrants to the United States in both periods came from Europe.

Understanding Charts. Ask students to create a chart presenting the same information as the pie graphs on this page. Students should use the geographic areas as row headings. Remind students to label and title their charts. Have volunteers present their final products to the class.

History Skills WORKSHOP

Reading Charts and Graphs

Charts and graphs categorize and display data in a variety of ways. The type of chart or graph depends on the subject matter and the information being represented.

Charts There are many different kinds of charts. *Flowcharts* show a sequence of events or the steps involved in a process. They are useful in showing cause-and-effect relationships. *Organizational charts* show the structure of an organization. They generally identify the rank and function of an organization's parts and the relationships among them. *Tables* are charts that present categories of data in columns.

How to Read a Chart

1. **Read the title** Read the title to identify the chart's purpose.
2. **Study the chart's parts** Read the chart's heading, subheadings, and labels to identify the categories used.
3. **Analyze the data** When reading quantities, note increases or decreases in amounts presented in the chart. When reading dates, note intervals of time. With flowcharts and organizational charts, follow directional arrows or lines.

Graphs There are several different types of graphs. A *line graph* often plots changes in quantities over time. A line graph has a horizontal axis and a vertical axis. A *bar graph* displays changes in quantities over time or compare quantities within categories. A *pie graph*, or *circle graph*, displays proportions by showing sections of a whole as if they were slices of a pie. All sections of the circular image add up to an entire pie, or 100 percent.

How to Read a Graph

1. **Read the title** Read the title to identify the subject and purpose of the graph.
2. **Study the labels** Read the labels that define each section of the graph's axes, bars, or sections.
3. **Analyze the data** Note increases or decreases in quantities. Look for trends, relationships, and changes in the data.

Shifting Patterns of Immigration

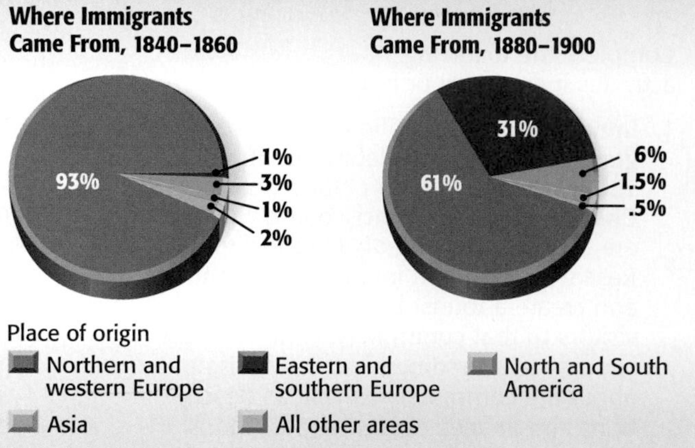

Source: *Historical Statistics of the United States*

Practicing the Skill

Study the graphs above. Then answer the following questions.

1. Which group experienced the greatest percent decrease in immigration between 1840–1860 and 1880–1900?
2. What do these graphs tell you about the actual number of immigrants arriving?
3. What generalizations or conclusions about immigration can you draw based on the information in these graphs?

ALL LEVELS: Linguistic, Intrapersonal. Tell students to choose one of the other four groups. Have them imagine that they are a member of that group and have taken the trip described in the brochure. Instruct students to write a letter to the travel agent who planned their trip. The letter should mention some of the highlights or difficulties of their trip. Students should also include a sketch that accurately reflects their new home or trip. Remind students to use correct grammar, spelling, punctuation, and sentence structure in their letters. Have volunteers share their letters and sketches with the class.

History in Action

UNIT 2 PORTFOLIO

Journey Across the World: The Travel Agency

Complete the following activity in small, cooperative groups.

Imagine that your class has been transported back in time to the second half of the 1800s. Your group operates a travel agency and is in charge of the travel plans for four groups of people: old immigrants coming to the United States, new immigrants arriving in the United States, cowboys on a cattle drive, and pioneers heading to the West. Your group's job is to provide a complete itinerary, or travel plan, for your customers. A number of travel agencies are competing for the business. You want the travelers to select your company as their travel agency.

Materials To complete this activity, you will need some U.S. and world maps and some blank outline maps to chart the journey for your customers. You will also need some art supplies such as construction paper, markers, pens, and glue to create your brochure.

Parts of the Project To create your itinerary and brochure, complete the following tasks:

1. **Research** Use the library and your textbook to research the journey of each customer group. Your itinerary needs to include point of origin, means of travel, length of travel, arrival time, and cost. You will also need to research the travelers' destinations. Find information on what your customers need to bring with them and what housing and job opportunities they can expect once they reach their destination.

2. **Creating the Itinerary** Graph the course your customers will take on one of the blank maps. Also, provide a detailed travel schedule in the form of a chart or a graph. Include as much information as possible on travel time, meals, weather conditions, and places to stay during the journey.

3. **Writing the Brochure** Organize the information you have gathered into a brochure. The brochure should welcome your travelers to their new home and include information on housing, jobs, schools, and potential difficulties and opportunities. You may want to illustrate your brochure with images or photographs.

4. **Presentation** Present your itinerary and brochure to your customers (the class). This is your last chance to present any information that might influence your customers to select your travel agency.

Continue this activity by having your customers select the travel agency they want to use for their journey. Customers should evaluate your agency's itinerary in terms of detail, historical accuracy, and overall appeal of the brochure.

Students locating places on a map

Travelers' Tales. Encourage students to use the library or other resources to research first-person accounts of the journeys of immigrants, cowboys, and pioneers. These travelers' tales can provide a wealth of details for the brochures and sales pitches.

Sightseeing. Students may want to include in their brochures information on interesting places to visit, historic landmarks, or special geographic features that their customers will encounter on their trip.

Bridging Cultures. In brochures for immigrants, students should consider including a list of useful English phrases. In brochures for cowboys and pioneers, students might include information on the customs of the American Indians they may encounter or some useful Spanish phrases.

Introducing

UNIT

3

CHAPTER 8
The Spirit of Reform

In the Progressive Era, reformers tried to address the economic, political, and social problems caused by rapid urban growth and the Second Industrial Revolution. Their efforts resulted in new laws regulating working conditions, civil-service reform, expanded political participation, and temperance laws. Labor unions also worked to improve conditions for workers. In addition, women fought for and gained suffrage, while African Americans and other groups sought their civil rights.

CHAPTER 9
The Progressive Presidents

Presidents Theodore Roosevelt, William Howard Taft, and Woodrow Wilson supported various progressive reforms. Roosevelt tried to control trusts and supported the Pure Food and Drug Act and the conservation movement. Taft initiated 90 antitrust lawsuits but alienated many progressives with his positions on tariffs and conservation. Wilson supported tariff and banking reform and the regulation of big business.

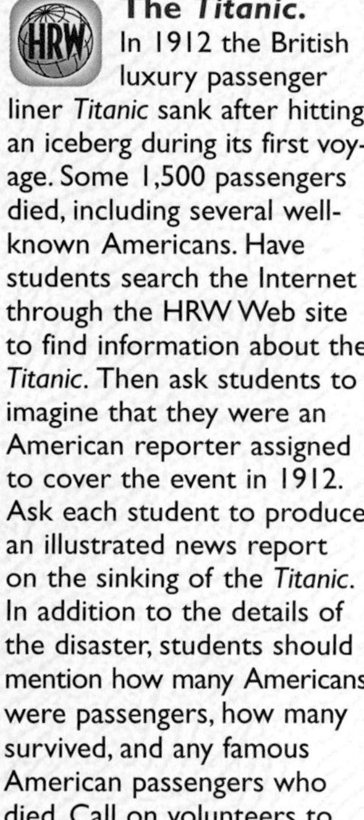

Internet Activity

The *Titanic*. In 1912 the British luxury passenger liner *Titanic* sank after hitting an iceberg during its first voyage. Some 1,500 passengers died, including several well-known Americans. Have students search the Internet through the HRW Web site to find information about the *Titanic*. Then ask students to imagine that they were an American reporter assigned to cover the event in 1912. Ask each student to produce an illustrated news report on the sinking of the *Titanic*. In addition to the details of the disaster, students should mention how many Americans were passengers, how many survived, and any famous American passengers who died. Call on volunteers to share their articles with the class.

go.hrw.com
SB1 Titanic

UNIT 3

A Growing America
(1865–1920)

CHAPTER 8 **The Spirit of Reform** (1868–1920)

CHAPTER 9 **The Progressive Presidents** (1900–1920)

CHAPTER 10 **America As a World Power** (1865–1914)

CHAPTER 10

America As a World Power

The desire for new markets, raw materials, and national prestige drove the United States to expand its territory and influence. The nation acquired Alaska and Hawaii and traded with China and Japan. Victory in the Spanish-American War brought Cuba, Guam, Puerto Rico, and the Philippines under U.S. influence. The United States became more involved in Latin America. The government built the Panama Canal and intervened in the affairs of the Dominican Republic, Haiti, Mexico, and Nicaragua.

UNIT MOTIVATOR

Share the information in the chapter overviews with students. Ask students to write a paragraph in which they speculate on what it means for the United States to be a world leader. Have students answer the following questions in their paragraphs: What are the responsibilities of world leadership? Are there any rights or privileges? Are there any disadvantages? When you have finished the unit, ask students to look at their paragraphs again and decide what changes or additions they would make to their concept of world leadership.

American Teens IN HISTORY

Young Workers

During the late 1800s the United States became a leading industrial nation. Many people left their farms and moved to the cities. With the increased number of factories, teenagers' employment opportunities began to change. Cotton textile mills in the Northeast and the South became some of the largest industrial employers of children and teenagers. In 1850 some 9,000 children who were 14 years old or younger worked in southern cotton mills. By 1900 that number had increased to 25,000. Almost half of these children were younger than 12 years old. For southern girls younger than 14 years old, no job paid better than mill work.

Winslow Homer's painting Cotton Pickers *shows African American girls working in cotton fields in the late 1800s.*

Mill owners tried to attract entire families to work in the mills. One-parent families, usually headed by women, found mill work particularly attractive. Because mill owners usually paid adult men low wages, the entire family was often forced to work to meet expenses. Young mill worker Marie Proulx remembered:

> "*My father was never able to support a family of eight children on $1.10 per day. . . . Oh, were we miserable! . . . So I had to go work somewhere, and all there was were the mills.*"

Teenagers working full-time in the mills often labored 12 hours a day, six days a week.

Coal mines in western Pennsylvania also hired many child laborers. Almost always boys, these workers were sent underground into the mines at the age of 12 or 13. By the age of 17 or 18, these boys had become miners' helpers. Boys were also more likely than girls to sell newspapers on city streets. These positions became more important with the growth of publishing and big cities. Standing wherever people commuted, newsboys could earn more money selling newspapers than any other product.

In this unit you will learn more about the reform movements to limit child labor. You will also learn more about the Progressive Era and the United States as an international power.

Left Page: *A Currier and Ives print of Broadway in New York City in the late 1800s*

Using Visual Resources

Urban Growth. The Currier and Ives print on the opposite page shows Broadway in New York City. The scene reflects several important trends in the United States in the late 1800s and early 1900s. Increased immigration, particularly from southern and eastern Europe, swelled the urban population of the United States. According to the census of 1920, more people were living in cities than in the countryside. The print also illustrates the taller buildings that were constructed during this time and the mass transit systems, such as streetcars, that made it possible for cities to expand outward.

Critical Thinking: Based on the scene in this print, what potential problems do you think were affecting U.S. cities during this era? What reforms to these problems would you suggest?

Answer: Students' answers will vary but may suggest overcrowding, disorganized traffic, or dangerous conditions for pedestrians. Students might suggest reforms such as traffic signals or crosswalks.

TEACH

ALL LEVELS: Linguistic, Logical-Mathematical. (Suggested time: 45 min.) Ask students to write a list ranking each event on the time line in order of significance, from most important to least important. Collect students' papers. On the chalkboard tally how many students ranked each event as the most significant. Have students choose one of the top three events and write a brief essay explaining why it was chosen as the most important event on the time line. Remind students to use proper grammar, spelling, punctuation, and sentence structure.

ALL LEVELS: Kinesthetic, Interpersonal. (Suggested time: 45 min.) Write the names of five events from the time line on slips of paper. Avoid violent events such as the killings in Amritsar, India. Organize the class into five groups and tell them that they will be playing charades. You may need to explain the rules of the game. Have each group choose a slip of paper and then prepare a brief silent skit that describes the event chosen. Allow five minutes for groups to prepare. As each group performs, have the other groups try to identify which event the performers are describing. Students may use the time line to help them identify the events. **SHELTERED ENGLISH**

Global Relations

The Statue of Liberty. The Statue of Liberty has greeted millions of immigrants at their arrival in New York Harbor. The monument was designed by French sculptor Frédéric-Auguste Bartholdi. The statue was constructed by applying sheets of copper over a very detailed wooden, supporting frame. This technique kept the cost and weight of the statue manageable. The frame was created by Alexandre-Gustave Eiffel, who later built the Eiffel Tower in Paris. A gift from France to the United States, the Statue of Liberty was formally installed on Bedloe's Island—now called Liberty Island—in New York Harbor in 1886.

Activity: Ask students to design a second Statue of Liberty. Have students draw or build a model of their design. Students should also choose a location for their statue and an inscription for its base. *(You may want to read Emma Lazarus's poem "The New Colossus" to the class to help inspire students.)* Ask volunteers to share their work with the class.

CHALLENGE AND EXTEND

1. **Linguistic.** A number of important people are mentioned in the time line. Have students choose one of these people and use the library or other resources to find more information about his or her life. Instruct students to create a resumé for their chosen person. Remind students that a resumé usually includes a statement of goals or objectives, a list of past positions held and achievements, and the names of several personal or professional references. You may want to show students several examples of resumés.

2. **Linguistic, Logical-Mathematical.** Have students choose one of the scientific or technological events from the time line, such as the discovery of the Cro-Magnon man or the invention of the first practical fountain pen. Tell students to use the library or other resources to research their chosen development. Then have students write an article for the journal *Science and Technology Monthly* from the perspective of the scientist or inventor. In the articles the scientists or inventors should describe their work and speculate on its potential impact on society. Encourage volunteers to share their articles with the class.

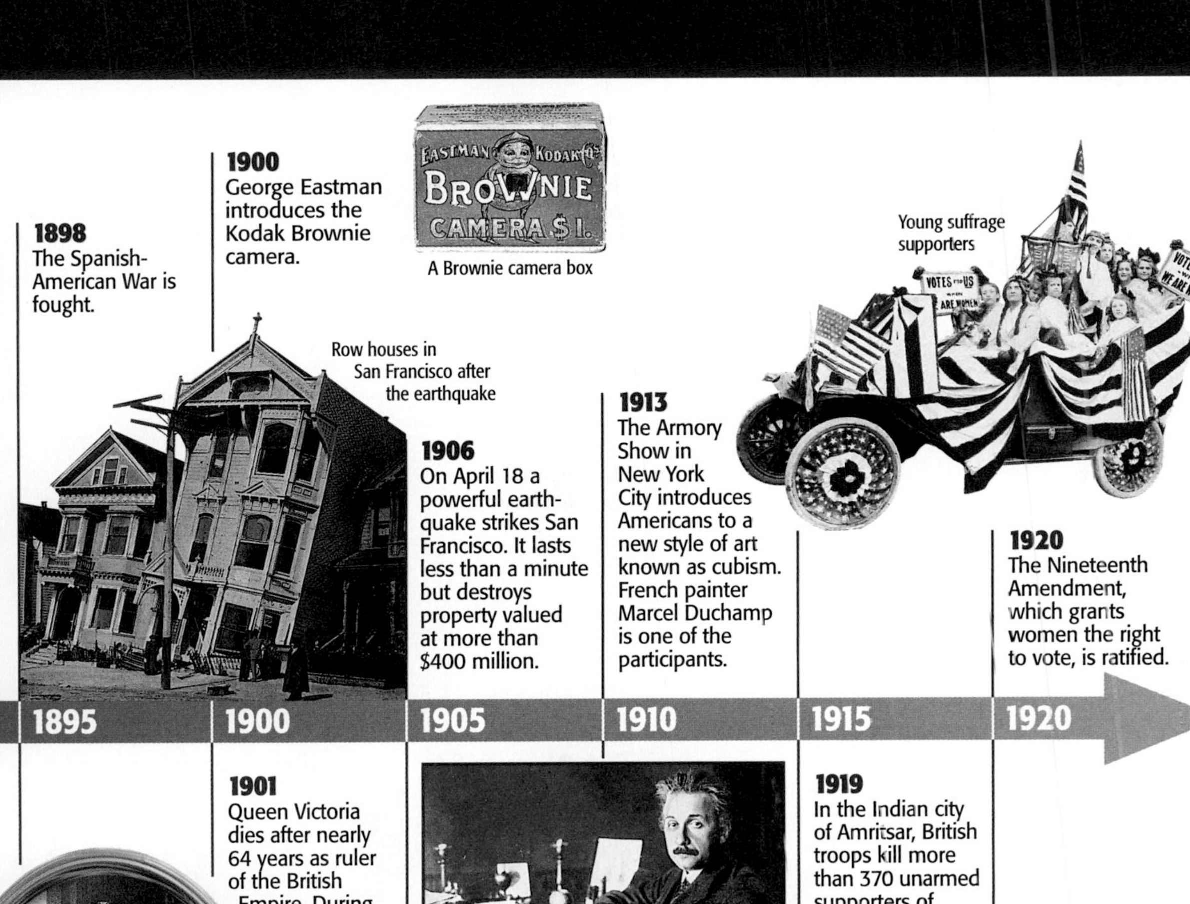

Biography

Albert Einstein. The physicist Albert Einstein is now viewed as one of the greatest minds in history. This was not always the case. As a child he did not learn to speak until much later than most children and was sometimes even considered to have learning problems. However, while still in his twenties he developed some important scientific ideas, including his famous equation, $E = mc^2$, relating energy to the speed of light. Einstein's ideas about electromagnetism, light, gravity, and motion dramatically altered the way scientists viewed the universe.

Activity: Have students use the library or other resources to create a time line of important events in the life of Albert Einstein.

USING THE TIME LINE ANSWERS

1. the Armory Show, the Nineteenth Amendment

2. Entries from 1868 to 1900.

USING THE TIME LINE

1. Which entries represent change in American society?
2. Compare the entries on this time line to those on the Unit 2 Time Line. Which entries are from the same time period? Use this information to create a new time line combining the Unit 2 and Unit 3 Time Lines.

Activity Use the information on this time line to create a chart that classifies these entries according to their subject. Your chart should have the dates on one side and the subject headings on the other. Subject headings for the chart might include culture, environment, politics, and science and technology.

CHAPTER PLANNING GUIDE
The Spirit of Reform

	SECTION LESSON OBJECTIVES	PRINT RESOURCES	MULTIMEDIA RESOURCES	SHELTERED ENGLISH RESOURCES
Section 1: The Gilded Age (pp. 237–40)	★ Explain how bosses controlled city politics. ★ Discuss some problems associated with the federal government during the Gilded Age. ★ Explain how the appointment of federal officials changed during the late 1800s.	★ Guided Reading Strategies 8.1 ★ American History Political Cartoon 16: Tammany Hall ★ Section 1 Review, p. 240 ★ Daily Quiz 8.1	★ *Teaching Resources CD–ROM*, Lesson 8.1 ★ *American History Simulations CD–ROM:* The Political Machine ★ HRW Web site	★ Main Idea Activities for Reteaching and Sheltered English 8.1
Section 2: Progressive Ideals (pp. 241–46)	★ Evaluate the contributions of middle-class reformers and muckrakers in the progressive movement. ★ Describe ways that progressives changed government. ★ Explain how progressives addressed the nation's social problems.	★ Guided Reading Strategies 8.2 ★ Literature Reading 8: *The Shame of the Cities* ★ Section 2 Review, p. 246 ★ Daily Quiz 8.2	★ *Teaching Resources CD–ROM*, Lesson 8.2 ★ *Exploring America's Past* Video Segment: A New Beginning; *Teacher's Guide*, pp. 16–17 ★ Everyday Life in America Transparency 17: Muckraker Photography, 1911 ★ HRW Web site	★ Main Idea Activities for Reteaching and Sheltered English 8.2
Section 3: Reforming the Workplace (pp. 247–51)	★ Identify ways that progressives attempted to change labor laws. ★ Examine the courts' reaction to labor legislation. ★ Explain how labor organized to improve working conditions.	★ Guided Reading Strategies 8.3 ★ Geography Activity 8: Limiting the Workday ★ Primary Source Reading 8: Reform Efforts ★ Section 3 Review, p. 251 ★ Daily Quiz 8.3	★ *Teaching Resources CD–ROM*, Lesson 8.3	★ Main Idea Activities for Reteaching and Sheltered English 8.3
Section 4: Women's Suffrage and Temperance (pp. 252–57)	★ Describe how higher education and women's social clubs led to reform efforts in the late 1800s and early 1900s. ★ Explain how women participated in the temperance movement. ★ Identify the methods women used to gain the vote.	★ Guided Reading Strategies 8.4 ★ Section 4 Review, p.257 ★ Daily Quiz 8.4	★ *Teaching Resources CD–ROM*, Lesson 8.4 ★ Art in American History Transparency 19: *Summertime: Woman and Child in a Rowboat*	★ Main Idea Activities for Reteaching and Sheltered English 8.4
Section 5: Minorities Fight for Change (pp. 258–61)	★ Describe reforms African Americans sought during the Progressive Era. ★ Identify the difficulties that American Indians faced during the Progressive Era. ★ Analyze major changes for Chinese Americans and Mexican Americans during the Progressive Era.	★ Guided Reading Strategies 8.5 ★ Biography Reading 8: Ida B. Wells-Barnett ★ Graphic Organizer 8: Reform Movements ★ Section 5 Review, p. 261 ★ Daily Quiz 8.5	★ *Teaching Resources CD–ROM*, Lesson 8.5	★ Main Idea Activities for Reteaching and Sheltered English 8.5
Chapter Review and Assessment (pp. 262–63)		★ Chapter 8 Review, pp. 262–63 ★ Vocabulary Activity 8 ★ Chapter 8 Study Guide ★ Chapter 8 Test (Form A or B)	★ Audio Program, Ch. 8 (English and Spanish) ★ *Global Skill Builder CD–ROM* ★ Chapter 8 Test Generator ★ HRW Web site	★ Spanish Glossary ★ Sheltered English Chapter 8 Test

CHAPTER OVERVIEW

The late 1800s, often called the Gilded Age, were marked by political corruption on both the local and the national level. After several scandals involving powerful politicians, Americans began to distrust government and call for change. Reforms included civil service examinations for government officials.

Hoping to address the problems of rapid industrialization, a group of reformers known as progressives began to push for improvements in society. Focusing mainly on urban problems, these largely middle-class reformers worked to raise the standard of living in U.S. cities, worked to decrease corruption in politics, and struggled to improve public education.

Progressives also tried to improve conditions for working people, paying particular attention to the abuses of child labor. Other reformers worked with labor unions to increase wages, improve safety, and shorten working hours.

Women and minorities—who often faced discrimination—began to seek changes in society. Educated women advocated temperance, women's suffrage, and job opportunities. African Americans, Mexican Americans, American Indians, and Chinese Americans also attempted to overcome racial discrimination and assert their rights.

CHAPTER INVESTIGATION

The Chapter Investigation is an extended, multipart activity designed for students to work cooperatively and apply the chapter content in the creation of a project. You may choose to use the Chapter 8 Investigation, Gilded Age Children's Book, either as a substitute for teaching the section lessons or as an alternate assessment.

BLOCK SCHEDULING 

The teacher lesson plans for each section offer a variety of activity choices to help you present the material in a block scheduling format. For further suggestions on block scheduling, see the *Block Scheduling Handbook with Team Teaching Strategies*, pp. 43–48.

Meeting Individual Needs

ABILITY LEVELS

LEVEL 1 Basic level activities designed for all students encountering new material.

LEVEL 2 Intermediate level activities designed for average students.

LEVEL 3 Challenging activities designed for above-average students.

SHELTERED ENGLISH These activities address the needs of students with Limited English Proficiency.

Smithsonian Institution®

Internet Connections and Lesson 8
www.si.edu/hrw

CNN Presents America:
Yesterday and Today 1850 to the Present
Segment: Women in the Rotunda

Additional Resources

Books for Teachers

Brasch, Walter M. *Forerunners of Revolution: Muckrakers & the American Social Conscience.* University Press of America, 1990. Examines the role of muckrakers.

Davis, Allen F. *Spearheads for Reform: The Social Settlements & the Progressive Movement, 1890–1914.* Rutgers University Press, 1985. Scholarly history of the progressive movement.

Rosenberg, Rosalind. *Divided Lives: American Women in the Twentieth Century.* Hill and Wang, 1992. History of the twentieth-century women's movement.

Books for Students

Brady, Kathleen. *Ida Tarbell: Portrait of a Muckraker.* University of Pittsburgh Press, 1989. Describes Tarbell's life and work.

Leavell, Perry. *Woodrow Wilson.* Chelsea House, 1987. Biography of Wilson's private and public life.

McKissack, Patricia C. *W. E. B. Du Bois.* Watts, 1990. Biography of the African American civil rights leader.

Multimedia Materials

The American Diary—New Beginnings (1895–1904). Video, 25 min. Aims Media Inc. Highlights American history between the years 1895 and 1904.

The Progressive Era: Reform Works in America. Video, 23 min. Britannica. Examines the Progressive Era.

Progressives, Populists, and Reform in America (1890–1917). Video, 32 min. Guidance Associates/SSSS. Primary sources show reformers' work.

The Spirit of Reform

CHAPTER MOTIVATOR

Ask students to remember what they have learned so far about industrialization in the United States. *(Students may mention growing output, increasing sources of transportation, or rising wages.)* Have students list the problems caused by industrialization. *(Students might mention dangerous working conditions, inadequate housing, poor public services, child labor, lack of representation for workers, and misuse of natural resources.)* Discuss how similar problems have been handled recently. Conclude by telling students that in this chapter they will learn about efforts to deal with the problems of industrialization and about the people who led reform efforts.

Presenting Themes

- **Constitutional Heritage** Students might suggest that a Supreme Court ruling could expand, protect, or limit workers' rights.
- **Citizenship and Democracy** Students might mention that reformers could use the media to draw public attention to an issue, try to get legislation passed, or attempt to apply their own solution to a problem.
- **Cultural Diversity** Students might point out that people might establish organizations, publish information, make speeches, and propose new laws and constitutional amendments to fight for the guarantee of equal rights.

Using the Time Line

Have each student choose an event from the time line. Then ask them to write three questions about the event. Have students answer their questions as they read the chapter.

The Granger Collection, New York

■ CHAPTER 8 ■

The Spirit of Reform

(1868–1920)

New York politician George W. Plunkitt described the questionable practices that led to his success. "I've made a big fortune out of the game, and I'm gettin' richer every day . . . ," he boasted. "I seen my opportunities and I took 'em." A growing number of people in the late 1800s were becoming angry with the actions of politicians such as Plunkitt. They soon called for economic, political, and social reform across the nation.

Constitutional Heritage
What effect might a Supreme Court ruling have on workers' rights?

Citizenship and Democracy
How might reformers try to address political inequalities in a democracy?

Cultural Diversity
How might a group fight for equal rights?

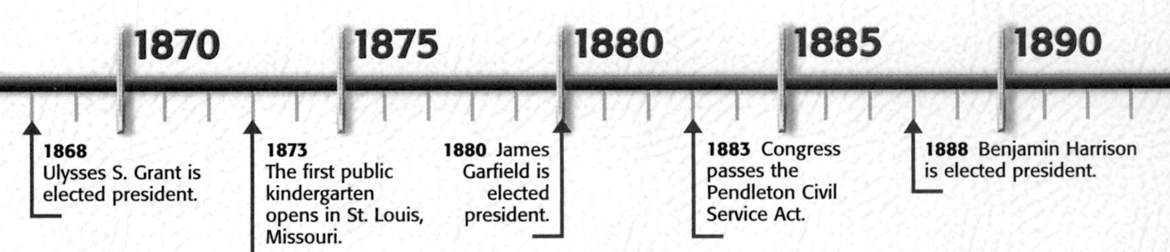

OBJECTIVES

- Explain how bosses controlled city politics.
- Discuss some problems associated with the federal government during the Gilded Age.
- Explain how the appointment of federal officials changed during the late 1800s.

FOCUS

Motivate Before Reading

Ask students to look up the term *gilded.* Explain to students that *gilded* can apply to almost anything that seems good on the outside but really is not. Ask them to give examples of something that might be considered gilded. Finally, tell students that in this section they will learn why the term was applied to society at the turn of the century.

SECTION 1

The Gilded Age

Reading Focus

In what ways did bosses control city politics?

What were some of the problems in federal government during the Gilded Age?

How did the appointment of federal officials change during the late 1800s?

Key Terms

bosses

political machines

mugwumps

Pendleton Civil Service Act

WHEN MAGAZINE EDITOR Lincoln Steffens visited St. Louis, Missouri, he noted the citizens' pride in their city. "The visitor is told of the wealth of the residents, of the financial strength of the banks, and of the growing importance of the industries," Steffens wrote. However, Steffens also witnessed a different aspect of the city. It had poorly paved streets littered with garbage. The crumbling City Hospital was crowded with the sick. Even in the hotel, muddy water ran out of the taps of his bath. Steffens's experience highlighted the contrasts that caused people to refer to the late 1800s as the Gilded Age.

THE GILDED AGE

A TALE OF TO-DAY

BY MARK TWAIN

CHARLES DUDLEY WARNER

FULLY ILLUSTRATED FROM NEW DESIGNS

SOLD BY SUBSCRIPTION ONLY.

HARTFORD: AMERICAN PUBLISHING COMPANY. W. E. BLISS & CO., TOLEDO, OHIO. 1874.

The novel The Gilded Age

IMAGE ON LEFT PAGE: *A suffrage parade in 1912 in New York City*

1895 | 1900 | 1905 | 1910 | 1915

1895 Booker T. Washington gives his Atlanta Compromise speech.

1901 The New York State Tenement House Law is passed.

1909 The National Association for the Advancement of Colored People is formed.

1913 The Seventeenth Amendment is ratified.

1919 The states ratify the Eighteenth Amendment.

1920 The Nineteenth Amendment gives women the vote.

Section 1 RESOURCES

PRINT

- ★ Guided Reading Strategies 8.1
- ★ American History Political Cartoon 16: Tammany Hall
- ★ Section 1 Review, p. 240
- ★ Daily Quiz 8.1

MULTIMEDIA

- ★ *Teaching Resources CD–ROM,* Lesson 8.1
- ★ *American History Simulations CD–ROM:* The Political Machine
- ★ HRW Web site

SHELTERED ENGLISH

- ★ Main Idea Activities for Reteaching and Sheltered English 8.1

Introduce Key Terms

Linguistic. Review this section's key terms with students. Then ask volunteers to write sentences on the chalkboard using one of the terms, until all terms have been covered.
SHELTERED ENGLISH

TEACH

Have students read Section 1 and complete Guided Reading Strategies 8.1. Choose one or more of the following activities to explore the section content with students. For further suggestions on block scheduling or team teaching, see the *Block Scheduling Handbook.*

LEVEL 1: Linguistic. (Suggested time: 15 min.) As a class, go over students' Guided Reading Strategies. Then use the Reading Focus questions to highlight the main ideas of the section.
SHELTERED ENGLISH

LEVEL 1: Visual-Spatial, Logical-Mathematical. (Suggested time: 30 min.) Work with students to create a chart on the chalkboard that lists the major political problems of the Gilded Age. One column should describe who benefited from political

Historical Sidelight

William Plunkitt. Tammany Hall party boss William Plunkitt became a millionaire through his political activities. At one point in 1870, he held four posts in New York state and city government—assemblyman, alderman, police magistrate, and county supervisor—earning salaries for three of these positions. He once explained how Tammany Hall worked, saying that the moment he knew where the party planned to make public improvements, he invested money in those areas. When the plans became public knowledge, Plunkitt sold his holdings at a profit, a process that he called honest graft. His political philosophy was, "I seen my opportunities and I took 'em."

Activity: Have students use the library or search the Internet through the HRW Web site to find information about prominent Tammany Hall politicians. Then have them use the information they found to write biographies of the politicians.

go.hrw.com
SB1 Tammany Hall

Corruption in Politics

In 1873 Mark Twain and Charles Dudley Warner published the best-selling novel *The Gilded Age.* Twain believed that American society looked golden from a distance but was merely gilded, or coated with cheap gold paint, on the outside. This meant that society, despite its positive appearance, was ugly and corrupt on the inside. Twain argued that the country lived by the motto "Get rich; dishonestly if we can, honestly if we must."

Machine Politics

State and local politics suffered from corruption during the Gilded Age. Powerful organizations used illegal methods to control government and grow rich from it. The rapid growth of cities in the late 1800s made possible the rise of **bosses**, political leaders who controlled elections through bribery and payoffs. For example, in return for votes and money, a boss might provide jobs, order neighborhood improvements, or allow an illegal business to stay in operation. Author James Bryce explained that the boss

> **"rewards the loyal, punishes the mutinous [disloyal], . . . negotiates treaties. He generally avoids publicity . . . and is all the more dangerous because he sits, like a spider, hidden in the midst of his web."**

The bosses drew much of their support from immigrants. "There's got to be . . . somebody that any bloke [man] can come to—no matter what he's done—and get help," explained one Boston politician. The boss system offered immigrants both jobs and social mobility—opportunities often denied to them in the larger society.

Members of Tammany Hall blame each other for stealing public money.

The Granger Collection, New York

City bosses developed **political machines**—organizations that guaranteed votes at election time through both legal and illegal methods. Political machines usually printed election ballots listing only their party's candidates. These were often printed on colored paper, so the bosses would know how individuals voted. Party organizers also paid citizens for their votes and hired the people who counted the votes. New York City boss William Marcy Tweed declared, "The ballots made no result; the counters made the result." Through their political machines, bosses protected their political positions and controlled the spending of public money. Thus, bosses personally profited from their own dishonesty.

Tammany Hall

New York City's political machine, Tammany Hall, became widely known throughout the country. Through corrupt practices, Boss Tweed may have succeeded in stealing nearly $200 million from the city treasury. He was eventually convicted of another crime, however, and died in jail.

Some politicians thought that the political machines were a fair exchange of money, influence, and jobs for working-class votes. For example, after winning city elections in 1888, Tammany Hall members provided some 12,000 jobs to supporters, particularly Irish immigrants.

National Scandals

In the late 1800s political scandals were also common on the national level. The administration of Republican Ulysses S. Grant—who was elected in 1868 and re-elected in 1872—was widely regarded as corrupt. During his second term, for example, government revenue officials were jailed for their part in the Whiskey Ring. They took bribes from whiskey distillers seeking to avoid paying taxes.

Members of Congress also participated in corrupt activities. In 1872 the *New York Sun* broke the story of a new scandal. The major owners of the corruption, while the other column should describe who was hurt by this corruption. **SHELTERED ENGLISH**

ALL LEVELS: Visual-Spatial, Logical-Mathematical. (Suggested time: 30 min.) Organize the class into two groups. Have each member of one group create a political cartoon showing how federal officials were appointed prior to the Pendleton Civil Service Act, while members of the other group depict how officials were appointed after the act. Have members of each group explain their work to the class. **SHELTERED ENGLISH**

LEVEL 3: Linguistic, Interpersonal. (Suggested time: 45 min. plus homework) Organize the class into two teams, and have them hold a debate between city bosses and reformers. Have each group prepare questions for the other group regarding reforms. Then ask them to trade questions with the other side, prepare answers, and hold the debate.

CLOSE

Linguistic, Logical-Mathematical. To conclude the lesson, have students write a newspaper article that explains to contemporary readers the concept of the use of the name Gilded Age for the late 1800s. Ask them to come up with an attention-grabbing headline and an article that explains good and bad aspects of the period.

Union Pacific Railroad had created a construction company called Crédit Mobilier of America. The owners gave or sold shares in this company to the members of Congress responsible for awarding federal land grants to the railroads. The congressmen then gave large federal land grants to Crédit Mobilier. These grants increased the value of the company's stock. The congressmen who received shares and the railroad owners profited at the public's expense.

The Granger Collection, New York

In this cartoon corrupt officials weigh down the Grant administration.

The Crédit Mobilier scandal damaged the careers of several Gilded Age politicians, including Schuyler Colfax, Grant's vice president. This political corruption led many Americans to angrily question the honesty of those running the federal government.

Gilded Age Presidents

During the 1876 presidential campaign, Democrats called for government reform. The Democratic candidate, Samuel J. Tilden, had already attacked corruption in his own party. He promised to establish an honest administration in Washington, D.C. The Republicans nominated Rutherford B. Hayes, a moderate reformer who promised "thorough, radical, and complete" changes in government. He was a war hero who had a reputation for honesty. The House of Representatives declared him the winner by a slim margin over Tilden in a disputed election.

Republicans won another close victory in 1880 with the election of reformer James Garfield and his vice president, Chester Arthur. On July 2, 1881, frustrated federal job-seeker Charles Guiteau confronted President Garfield at a Washington railroad station. He shouted "Arthur [is] President now," and shot Garfield twice. The president died from his wounds in September, and Vice President Arthur became president.

In the 1884 election, Republicans chose James G. Blaine as their nominee rather than another reform candidate. Blaine's record of association with corruption upset many Republican reformers, who came to be known as **mugwumps** (the Algonquian Indian word for big chiefs). Dissatisfied mugwumps left the Republican Party and threw their support behind the Democratic nominee, Grover Cleveland, who had a reputation for political honesty. In a campaign full of personal attacks, American voters chose Cleveland over Blaine as president. Cleveland involved himself in all the day-to-day details of the presidency. He worked hard to hire and fire government employees based on their merit rather than their party loyalty.

Four years later in 1888, Cleveland again won the popular vote. This time, however, he lost the electoral vote and thus the presidential election, to Republican Benjamin Harrison. Harrison controlled inflation and helped pass the Sherman Antitrust Act, which regulated monopolies. Nevertheless, Cleveland remained popular, and in 1892, crowds sang:

> **"Grover, Grover, four more**
> **years of Grover—**
> **Out they go and in we come**
> **and we'll be in the clover."**

The Granger Collection, New York

In 1881 Charles Guiteau shot President James Garfield at a railroad station.

Using Visual Resources

Political Cartoons. The mugwumps tended to be elite, university-educated leaders who personally had difficulty getting the masses interested in their political causes. However, political cartoons, such as the one at the left, which appeared in the comic magazine *Puck*, had far more success. In fact, *Puck* became the most effective weapon the mugwumps had for swaying opinion among middle-class voters. *Puck* had a circulation of 85,000 by 1880, a low price (10 cents an issue), and was printed using the latest technology, so that the cartoons were colorful and eye-catching. The cartoon on this page was part of the magazine's effort to prevent Ulysses S. Grant from winning a third term. Featuring Grant balancing on rings labeled "whiskey ring" and "navy ring" while he uses his teeth to support major figures from those scandals, the cartoon's caption read, "Puck Wants a Strong Man at the Head of Government—But Not *This* Kind."

Critical Thinking: Why might this cartoon have hurt Grant's re-election chances?

ANSWER: It reminded readers of the major scandals in which Grant had been involved and the types of people with whom he associated.

Multimedia Resources

American History Simulations CD–ROM: The Political Machine

CHALLENGE AND EXTEND

Visual-Spatial. Have students use the library or other resources to find information on one of the presidential candidates mentioned in this section. Then ask them to create a political advertisement supporting the person they chose.

REVIEW

Linguistic, Intrapersonal. Have students complete the Section Review questions. Then have them write a paragraph arguing in favor of civil service reform. Ask students to cite examples of corruption covered in the section to support their arguments.

ASSESS

Have students complete Daily Quiz 8.1.

RETEACH

Logical-Mathematical, Visual-Spatial. Have students complete Main Idea Activities for Reteaching and Sheltered English 8.1. Then ask them to work individually or in groups to create a political cartoon or newspaper ad that illustrates the need for political reform during the Gilded Age. SHELTERED ENGLISH

Section 1 Review ANSWERS

Identify

For significance, see the following pages:

- bosses, p. 238
- political machines, p. 238
- William Marcy Tweed, p. 238
- Rutherford B. Hayes, p. 239
- James Garfield, p. 239
- Chester Arthur, p. 239
- mugwumps, p. 239
- Grover Cleveland, p. 239
- Benjamin Harrison, p. 239
- Pendleton Civil Service Act, p. 240

Reading for Content Understanding

1. Scandals ruined many political careers, caused many people in the United States to question the honesty of the government, and led to calls for reform.

2. It established a merit system for awarding jobs. This system was under the control of the Civil Service Commission.

3. They used illegal methods to control elections, and in return for support, gave working-class voters jobs, improved their neighborhoods, and let illegal businesses continue operating.

4. Charts should include: Grant—Republican (1868, 1872); Hayes—Republican (1876); Garfield—Republican (1880); Arthur—Republican (1881); Cleveland—Democrat (1884, 1892); Harrison—Republican (1888); McKinley—Republican (1896).

5. Answers will vary but students should offer their opinions and explain their reasoning.

Winning both the popular and electoral vote in 1892, Cleveland defeated Harrison and returned to the White House. During Cleveland's second term the country faced a recession. Cleveland angered many fellow Democrats with his economic policies. In 1896 the Democrats nominated William Jennings Bryan. He lost to Republican William McKinley. The practical, friendly McKinley worked well with Congress and was re-elected in 1900. During his two terms, he helped restore public confidence in the presidency by avoiding the corruption and scandals that had plagued the federal government in the Gilded Age.

Civil Service Reform

Many Americans reacted to the widespread corruption of the Gilded Age by demanding changes in the civil service, or government jobs. The party in control of the government had long taken advantage of the spoils system to award jobs to loyal members, whether they were qualified or not. Every time a new party took power, many current government employees were replaced. This resulted in ruined careers and inefficient administrations. Henry Adams, author and grandson of former president John Quincy Adams, commented on this practice in 1870. He said that "all my friends have been or are on the point of being driven out of the government."

A fellow official congratulates Senator George Pendleton on his plan for civil service reform.

Reformers wanted a system that used competitive exams to award civil service jobs based on merit. They argued that this system would keep out incompetent and corrupt workers. President Hayes had promoted some reform efforts during his administration in the 1870s. Some Americans also believed that the spoils system had been responsible for President Garfield's assassination. *The Nation*, a weekly newspaper, noted that "the crime seems to have acted on public opinion . . . like a spark on a powder-magazine [gunpowder storage]." This reaction led to a movement to pass stronger civil service reform legislation.

President Chester Arthur responded to the public's demands by supporting the **Pendleton Civil Service Act**. This act established a merit system controlled by the Civil Service Commission. Passed in January 1883, the act initially only affected about 14,000 out of 130,000 federal jobs. President Cleveland doubled the number of positions covered by the legislation. The act has since been expanded so that it now affects almost 90 percent of government jobs.

SECTION 1 REVIEW

Identify and explain the significance of the following:

- **bosses**
- **political machines**
- **William Marcy Tweed**
- **Rutherford B. Hayes**
- **James Garfield**
- **Chester Arthur**
- **mugwumps**
- **Grover Cleveland**
- **Benjamin Harrison**
- **Pendleton Civil Service Act**

Reading for Content Understanding

1 Main Idea How did scandals affect national politics in the Gilded Age?

2 Main Idea How did civil service reform affect the appointment of federal officials?

3 Citizenship and Democracy How did bosses and political machines control city governments?

4 Writing *Classifying* Make a chart that shows the presidents during the Gilded Age, their political party, and the year they were elected or became president.

5 Critical Thinking *Evaluating* Do you agree that civil service jobs should be merit based? Explain your answer.

OBJECTIVES

- Evaluate the contributions of middle-class reformers and muckrakers in the progressive movement.
- Describe ways that progressives changed government.
- Explain how progressives addressed the nation's social problems.

FOCUS

Motivate Before Reading

Ask students what they think of when they hear the word *progress.* Write students' responses on the chalkboard. Tell students that as they read this section they will learn how the word applied to many aspects of everyday life, including politics, education, and medicine, during the late 1800s.

Progressive Ideals

Reading Focus

What role did middle-class reformers and muckrakers play in the progressive movement?

How did progressives change government?

How did progressives address the nation's social problems?

Key Terms

progressives
muckrakers
direct primary
Seventeenth Amendment
recall
initiative
referendum
Wisconsin Idea

ONE COLD, SNOWY MORNING in late December 1891, Florence Kelley and her three children arrived on the front steps of Hull House in Chicago. When she knocked on the door, Jane Addams answered. "We were welcomed as though we had been invited," Kelley later wrote. "We stayed." At Hull House, Kelley not only found refuge but also joined the increasingly popular movement for reform. She went on to become one of the nation's leading social reformers.

Hull House in Chicago

The Progressive Movement

In the late 1800s a group of reformers who became known as the **progressives** began working to improve American society. Progressives wanted to address the social and political problems caused by rapid industrial expansion and urban growth. Progressives believed that by studying these issues, they could develop plans that would correct the root causes of the problems. For example, many progressives sought to change the environments that contributed to crime, disease, and poverty.

A large number of progressives were members of the growing middle class. The industrial and urban growth that caused many problems in the late 1800s also contributed to an increase in the number of professionals and small-business owners. These individuals formed an educated group that wanted to improve the quality of life throughout society. They often had leisure time and training, both of which were helpful in organizing reform movements. Although many people in the progressive movement came from middle-class backgrounds, some working-class and wealthy Americans also sought reforms.

Section 2 RESOURCES

PRINT

- ★ Guided Reading Strategies 8.2
- ★ Literature Reading 8: *The Shame of the Cities*
- ★ Section 2 Review, p. 246
- ★ Daily Quiz 8.2

MULTIMEDIA

- ★ *Teaching Resources CD–ROM*, Lesson 8.2
- ★ *Exploring America's Past* Video Segment: A New Beginning; *Teacher's Guide*, pp. 16–17
- ★ Everyday Life in America Transparency 17: Muckraker Photography, 1911
- ★ HRW Web site

SHELTERED ENGLISH

- ★ Main Idea Activities for Reteaching and Sheltered English 8.2

Introduce Key Terms

Linguistic. Review this section's key terms with students. Have them use context cues from the section to create definitions for each of the terms. Then organize students into groups and have each group create a brief presentation explaining one of the terms. When groups have finished preparing, have a member or members of each group make the presentations to the class.
SHELTERED ENGLISH

TEACH

Have students read Section 2 and complete Guided Reading Strategies 8.2. Choose one or more of the following activities to explore the section content with students. For further suggestions on block scheduling or team teaching, see the *Block Scheduling Handbook*.

LEVEL 1: Linguistic. (Suggested time: 15 min.) As a class, go over students' Guided Reading Strategies. Then use the Reading Focus questions to highlight the main ideas of the section.
SHELTERED ENGLISH

Across the Curriculum

LANGUAGE ARTS

Journalism. Muckraking journalists were generally more educated than the previous generation of newspaper and magazine writers. Earlier journalists had often written dramatic and one-sided stories, while muckrakers distanced themselves from this practice by following the scientific method. They gathered facts about an issue and then wrote about it more objectively.

Critical Thinking: Why would muckrakers be concerned with reporting stories based on facts rather than on dramatic depictions?

ANSWER: They probably thought that the truth, supported by facts, would be more shocking to most people than sensational stories.

Multimedia Resources

Exploring America's Past Video Segment: A New Beginning; *Teacher's Guide*, pp. 16–17

Search 38771, Play to 45857
Videodisc White Side A

Play

Pause

See *Teacher's Guide* for Spanish barcode.

Causes and Effects of the Progressive Movement

Long-Term Causes
Urbanization
Growth of the middle class
Industrial working conditions

Immediate Causes
Scandals about political corruption
Rise of powerful corporations
Changes in immigration

Progressive Movement

Effects
Expanded democracy
Antitrust legislation
Business reforms
Social reforms
Urban reforms

Progressive leaders did not always agree on which social problems were the most important or how these problems should be solved. As a result, the progressives focused their efforts in a variety of areas. These actions included promoting health and education in poor neighborhoods, reforming government, and improving working conditions. Many progressives believed that to achieve all of these goals, the federal government needed to step in and regulate business, health, and safety issues. Progressives wanted greater cooperation between the government and the public to solve social problems.

Muckrakers

Journalists also became involved in the progressive movement. Reporters began writing about corruption in business and politics. They hoped that their articles would lead to greater public awareness of problems and eventually to reform measures. These journalists were soon nicknamed "**muckrakers**" because they "raked up" and exposed the muck, or filth, of society.

Some muckrakers such as Ida Tarbell became well known for articles attacking unfair business practices. Tarbell wrote a series of articles criticizing John D. Rockefeller's Standard Oil Company:

> **"Very often people who admit the facts, who are willing to see that Mr. Rockefeller has employed force and fraud to secure his ends, justify him by declaring, 'It's business.' That is, 'it's business' has come to be a legitimate [acceptable] excuse for hard dealing, sly tricks, [and] special privileges."**

Tarbell argued that companies had to follow fair business practices to protect competition.

Reporter Lincoln Steffens exposed scandals in city politics in some of the first muckraking articles. They were published in 1902 in *McClure's Magazine*. These articles were later collected in a book called *The Shame of the Cities*. Although the urban corruption that he exposed shocked some readers, Steffens later claimed that "every one of those articles was an understatement."

Ida Tarbell wrote many muckraking articles for McClure's Magazine.

The Granger Collection, New York

ALL LEVELS: Logical-Mathematical, Visual-Spatial. (Suggested time: 45 min.) Organize the class into groups and assign each group one of the following topics dealing with how progressives changed government: direct primary, recall, initiative, or referendum. Provide students with butcher paper and markers. Then ask them to make a poster that defines the term, contains an illustration, and explains how and when the term is used.
SHELTERED ENGLISH

LEVEL 2: Logical-Mathematical. (Suggested time: 30 min.) Organize students into two groups; one to focus on middle-class reformers and the other on muckrakers. Have members of each group list steps taken to achieve reform by people and organizations representing its assigned progressive group. Ask a member of each group to read its list to the class. Then, as a class, discuss similarities and differences between the ways that middle-class reformers and muckrakers attempted to achieve progressive goals.

Muckrakers often focused on the plight of poor people, such as this Jewish immigrant, who lived in a coal cellar.

Muckrakers also investigated issues such as slum housing, the use of child labor, and racial discrimination. Their articles angered many city politicians and business leaders. They also helped unite the progressive movement by influencing voters to challenge corrupt practices and by encouraging some politicians to call for reforms.

 Expanding Democracy

Concern about political corruption convinced some progressives to reform state and local governments. They helped pass reform measures that gave voters more power in selecting political candidates and in getting laws passed.

Election Reforms

Progressives passed a number of election reforms that reduced political machines' ability to influence the voting process. Reformers in many cities and states introduced ballots that listed all candidates, regardless of their party. Many states also adopted a secret ballot to ensure that a person's vote was confidential. Progressives patterned these ballot changes on methods used in Australia.

Reformers also broadened political participation by introducing the **direct primary**. This allowed voters to choose candidates for public office directly rather than relying on party leaders to select the candidates. In addition, the ratification of the **Seventeenth Amendment** in 1913 allowed Americans to vote directly for U.S. senators. They had previously been elected by state legislatures.

Petitioning for Change

Other reform measures allowed voters to petition for action on political issues even if there was no regular election or vote scheduled. For example, some states like Oregon, as well as cities like Los Angeles, passed a measure known as the **recall**. Voters who are dissatisfied with an elected official can sign a petition asking for a special vote to recall, or remove, that official before the end of his or her term. If enough voters sign the petition, the vote takes place and the official must abide by its results.

Reformers in Oregon and the Midwest also pushed for two reforms that gave voters the power to affect new legislation directly. The **initiative** gives voters the ability to propose a new law by collecting signatures on a petition supporting that law. If enough signatures are collected, the proposed law is placed on the ballot for the public to vote on at the next election. A similar measure, the **referendum**, allows voters to approve or disapprove legislation that has already been proposed or passed by a state or local government. This gives voters the opportunity to overrule laws with which they disagree.

 Reforming City and State Governments

In addition to broadening political participation, progressives worked to change the structure of city government and state politics. Many Americans were upset by the corruption and waste in public services that resulted from political machines like the one run by New York's Boss Tweed. Samuel M. "Golden Rule" Jones, a business leader who became mayor of Toledo, Ohio, argued that government should not be used "for the purpose of plundering [stealing from] the poor."

Businesspeople and other professionals often led the effort to make local government more efficient and more responsive to citizens' needs.

Citizenship and Democracy

Muckraking. The January 1903 issue of *McClure's Magazine* provides evidence that muckraking had become firmly entrenched as a popular form of American literature. It featured three articles that showed that corruption could be found almost everywhere in American society, including businesspeople, politicians, and ordinary citizens. In the issue, Lincoln Steffens described widespread political corruption in Minneapolis; Ida Tarbell reported that Standard Oil head John D. Rockefeller conspired with railroad companies to set rates that favored his large refineries; and Ray Stannard Baker analyzed the difficulties of workers who crossed picket lines during the 1902 United Mine Workers strike.

Critical Thinking: How does the variety of subjects covered in the January 1903 issue of *McClure's* suggest a need for widespread change?

ANSWER: The variety shows that many different aspects of American society faced corruption and, therefore, widespread change was needed.

Multimedia Resources

Everyday Life in America Transparency 17: Muckraker Photography, 1911

LEVEL 3: Linguistic, Intrapersonal. (Suggested time: 30 min. plus homework) Ask students to imagine that they are considering joining the progressive movement. Have each student write to a friend about what aspects of society need reforming, what reforms they want to become involved with, and why. Then ask volunteers to read their letters to the class.

LEVEL 3: Linguistic, Interpersonal. (Suggested time: 45 min.) Ask students to write a dialog that they might have had with Robert La Follette. Have them express support for or opposition to his ideas. Encourage students to include La Follette's ideas as well as their own reasons for support or opposition.

CLOSE

Visual-Spatial. To conclude the lesson, have students draw a political cartoon depicting an issue taken up by the progressive reformers. Have students write a caption of at least three sentences describing their cartoons. Ask volunteers to explain their work to the class. Then ask other students to provide their classmates with feedback about the cartoons.

Geographic Diversity

The White City. Many of the ideas about city planning came together in the White City—a model city constructed for the World's Columbian Exposition in 1893. Designed by Frederick Law Olmsted, who led the construction of New York's Central Park, and Chicago architect Daniel Burnham, the White City spurred a flurry of new development plans in cities nationwide during the early 1900s.

Activity: Have students search the Internet through the HRW Web site to find more information about city planning during the late 1800s and early 1900s. Ask them to explain in a short report the problems city planners were facing and what kinds of solutions these planners offered.

go.hrw.com
SB1 City Planning

Some reformers wanted to replace elected officials with professionals who would run city government more like a business. Several cities changed to a council-manager government, which put power in the hands of professional administrators. Under this system, voters elect a city council that appoints a professional manager to run the city. The system is modeled on a corporation, where a board of directors chooses a chief executive to run the business. By 1914 there was a professional City Managers' Association.

The commission form of city government was first introduced in 1900 in Galveston, Texas, after a severe hurricane destroyed much of the city. The commission made rebuilding efforts more efficient.

Many other cities took a similar business-influenced approach, called the commission government. This form of city government is headed by a group of elected officials. Each official manages a major city agency, such as housing, sanitation, or transportation.

These new forms of city administration became popular during the Progressive Era. However, many urban residents found that these systems created a city government that was less responsive to their needs. The council-manager and commission forms of government were most popular in small to medium-sized cities, which dealt with fewer problems than large cities.

State governments faced some of the same problems as cities. Corrupt urban officials such as city bosses were often part of a statewide political machine that influenced all party decisions. Some reformers challenged these political machines. In Wisconsin, Republican Robert La Follette opposed the power of the party bosses, arguing that government should be directly responsive to the people. La Follette supported the direct primary, tax reform, new state commissions, and the use of professionals to manage social problems.

Robert La Follette created a popular model for reforming government.

As one political writer described La Follette's appeal to voters, "He is eager to be the people's champion; his mind is aglow with visions of great enactments [laws] for the public welfare."

La Follette failed to win his party's nomination for governor in 1896 and in 1898. He finally won the governor's seat in 1900. As governor, La Follette developed the **Wisconsin Idea**—a program of reforms to reduce the influence of political machines and to professionalize state government. This idea became a model for progressive reformers in other states. La Follette later served in the U.S. Senate until he died in 1925.

City Planning

Political corruption was just one of many problems faced by growing U.S. cities. Progressive minister Josiah Strong declared that

> **"the city is the nerve center of our civilization. It is also the storm center. . . . The city has become a serious menace [threat] to our civilization."**

As many native-born Americans and immigrants moved to U.S. cities looking for work, city officials found themselves unable to keep up

CHALLENGE AND EXTEND

1. **Kinesthetic, Logical-Mathematical, Visual-Spatial.** Have students work in groups to create a model of an ideal progressive city. Ask each group to include housing, parks, public transportation, and other features of a well-planned community. Each group should lay out its city on butcher paper or make a three-dimensional model. Have each group present its model to the class. Then lead a discussion on the elements common to all of the examples. **SHELTERED ENGLISH**

2. **Linguistic, Visual-Spatial.** Have students use the library or other resources to find photographs of urban life during the Progressive Era and to find more information about the reforms that were enacted. Have students write short stories or poems about some aspect of urban life in the late 1800s and early 1900s. Students should use the photos they found and their research to create the setting and to help with the writing. When they are finished, have students present their stories or poems to the class.

with demands for housing and social services. The results were unsanitary and unsafe conditions for thousands of families living in poverty. Many people crowded into tenements, whose owners failed to make needed improvements in living conditions. Progressive Lawrence Veiller described the effects of tenement living on children and society:

> **"A child living its early years in dark rooms, without sunlight or fresh air, does not grow up to be a normal, healthy person. . . . It is not of such material that strong nations are made."**

The Granger Collection, New York

An artist's version of an ideal progressive city—attractive, clean, and safe

Progressives addressed these problems in a variety of ways. Veiller successfully campaigned for the 1901 New York State Tenement House Law, which made the construction of dark and airless tenements illegal. The law required new buildings to have better ventilation, toilets, and running water. New York's law became a model for other states' housing reform. Many progressives also established settlement houses patterned after Jane Addams's Hull House in Chicago. These organizations worked in immigrant and poverty-stricken communities to improve education, sanitation, and housing conditions.

Urban reforms led to the creation of new professions such as city planning and civil engineering. City planners worked with local officials to control and regulate city growth by establishing zoning laws, creating safer building codes, and developing public park lands. Civil engineers improved city transportation by paving streets and building bridges. Sanitation engineers tried to solve the problems of water supply, waste disposal, and pollution. Cities that addressed these problems experienced a dramatic drop in death rates by the end of the century. The many improvements carried out during the Progressive Era gave urban Americans some of the highest standards of public services in the world.

Social Reforms

Progressive leaders were interested in using scientific principles and new organizations to deal with political problems. Progressive leaders also applied this approach to reforming public and professional education.

Public Education

Many progressives believed that by improving public education, they could cure social ills and fulfill the demand from business and industry for better-educated managers. To meet the changing needs of students, high school courses were broadened to include areas such as health, citizenship, and job training. School enrollment increased greatly in the late 1800s. This was largely because the reformers' push for education had led to the creation of new public high schools and to the introduction of public kindergartens. In addition, many states passed laws requiring children to attend school.

Many progressives started kindergarten programs to serve the needs of poor city residents, particularly immigrants. Kindergartens taught basic social skills to children between the ages of three and seven. In 1873 reformer Susan Blow opened the first American public kindergarten in

Biography

Robert M. La Follette. In 1924 Robert La Follette ran for president. His party, the League of Progressive Political Action, supported government ownership of public utilities, collective bargaining for labor, relief measures for farmers, and lower taxes for people with moderate incomes.

Critical Thinking: In what ways was La Follette's party platform similar to his Wisconsin Idea?

ANSWER: In both cases, La Follette supported reforms that would help the working class and the poor.

REVIEW

Linguistic, Logical-Mathematical. Have students complete the Section Review questions. Ask students to imagine that they are government officials, each writing a report on what is being done to improve democracy. Have them include the following concepts in their reports: direct primaries, the Seventeenth Amendment, recalls, initiatives, and referendums.

ASSESS

Have students complete Daily Quiz 8.2.

RETEACH

Linguistic, Logical-Mathematical, Visual-Spatial. Have students complete Main Idea Activities for Reteaching and Sheltered English 8.2. To review the section's material, have students make two bulleted lists: one of social problems during the late 1800s, and another of the progressives' goals. Then have students use examples from American society today to discuss the progressives' successes. **SHELTERED ENGLISH**

Section 2 Review ANSWERS

Identify

For significance, see the following pages:

- progressives, p. 241
- muckrakers, p. 242
- Lincoln Steffens, p. 242
- Ida Tarbell, p. 242
- direct primary, p. 243
- Seventeenth Amendment, p. 243
- recall, p. 243
- initiative, p. 243
- referendum, p. 243
- Robert La Follette, p. 244
- Wisconsin Idea, p. 244
- John Dewey, p. 246
- Joseph McCormack, p. 246

Reading for Content Understanding

1. middle-class reformers—promoted health and education in poor neighborhoods, government reforms, and improved working conditions; muckrakers—raised public awareness of problems and reform measures

2. They tried to improve living conditions, establish settlement houses, broaden the high school curriculum, create new public schools, introduce kindergartens, and get laws passed that required children to attend school.

3. They introduced election reforms and created the initiative, referendum, and recall.

4. Articles will vary but should mention that progressives influenced laws that improved living conditions and established settlement houses.

5. Dewey's methods focused on developing critical-thinking and problem-solving skills; answers will vary.

High school students study science in 1900.

St. Louis, Missouri. By 1898 more than 4,000 kindergartens had opened in the United States.

One supporter of early childhood education, John Dewey, was an important philosopher and educator. As the director of the University of Chicago's Laboratory School, Dewey tried to develop teaching methods suited to the interests and needs of students. Two teachers at the school described the classes as based on "the idea of the school-house as a home." The goal was to nurture children and to give them critical-thinking skills to help them in everyday life. For example, Dewey wanted to teach children problem-solving skills rather than have them simply memorize their lessons. Dewey's teaching methods became the model for progressive education throughout the country.

Progressivism in Medicine

Progressives also tried to improve the education of medical professionals. In the late 1800s the United States suffered from a lack of well-trained and professionally organized doctors. For example, researchers had identified the causes of infectious diseases such as malaria, pneumonia, tuberculosis, and yellow fever. However, there were few medical organizations to help spread this knowledge.

Under the leadership of Joseph McCormack, the American Medical Association (AMA), which brought together local medical organizations, was reorganized in 1901. The AMA supported laws protecting public health. Its reform efforts reflected the progressives' ability to unite professionals to better help society.

Doctors struggled to control contagious diseases.

SECTION 2 REVIEW

Identify and explain the significance of the following:

- **progressives**
- **muckrakers**
- **Lincoln Steffens**
- **Ida Tarbell**
- **direct primary**
- **Seventeenth Amendment**
- **recall**
- **initiative**
- **referendum**
- **Robert La Follette**
- **Wisconsin Idea**
- **John Dewey**
- **Joseph McCormack**

Reading for Content Understanding

1 **Main Idea** What contributions did middle-class reformers and muckrakers make to the progressive movement?

2 **Main Idea** What social reforms did progressives try to make?

3 **Citizenship and Democracy** How did progressives work to fight corruption in local and state governments?

4 **Writing** *Informing* Imagine that you are a muckraker journalist for *McClure's Magazine.* Write a short article explaining how progressives have addressed problems in U.S. cities in the early 1900s.

5 **Critical Thinking** *Drawing Conclusions* Describe John Dewey's teaching methods. What do you think are the advantages of Dewey's approach?

OBJECTIVES

- **Identify ways that progressives attempted to change labor laws.**
- **Examine the courts' reaction to labor legislation.**
- **Explain how labor organized to improve working conditions.**

FOCUS

Motivate Before Reading

Have students discuss the reasons people hold jobs today. *(Answers could include the need to earn a living or the desire to make a contribution to society.)* After listing the reasons on the chalkboard, explain to students that in the 1800s, having a job could be dangerous and was not always very profitable. Tell students that in this section they will learn about economic changes in the 1800s and

Reforming the Workplace

Reading Focus

How did progressives attempt to change labor laws?

How did the courts react to labor legislation?

How did labor organize to improve working conditions?

Key Terms

Triangle Shirtwaist Factory Fire
capitalism
socialism
Industrial Workers of the World

EVERY DAY AT 7:00 A.M. 15-year-old Sadie Frowne sat down at her machine in a garment factory in Brooklyn, New York. "The machines go like mad all day, because the faster you work the more money you get," she wrote. "Sometimes in my haste I get my finger caught and the needle goes right through it." When her workday ended at 6:00 P.M., she felt exhausted. One of the progressives' main goals was to establish better working conditions for children like Frowne.

The Granger Collection, New York

Labor union booklet

Child Labor Reform

Low wages for unskilled workers in the late 1800s meant that many more children had to work to help support their families. Girls often cooked and cleaned for boarders, and boys sold newspapers or shined shoes on the streets. Girls also worked with their mothers at home, sewing garments or making artificial flowers and costume jewelry.

Many children also worked in industrial areas. In 1900 more than 1.75 million children aged 15 and under worked in mines, mills, and factories. The terrible situation of these children moved many progressives to action. One wealthy reformer, Marie Van Vorst, posed as a poor woman to investigate conditions in a South Carolina textile mill. She saw children as young as five years old working in the mills. She described one young girl:

> **"Through the looms I catch sight of . . . my landlord's little child. She is seven; so small that they have a box for her to stand on. . . . I can see only her fingers as they clutch at the flying spools; her head is not high enough, even with the box, to be visible."**

Section 3 RESOURCES

PRINT

- ★ Guided Reading Strategies 8.3
- ★ Geography Activity 8: Limiting the Workday
- ★ Primary Source Reading 8: Reform Efforts
- ★ Section 3 Review, p. 251
- ★ Daily Quiz 8.3

MULTIMEDIA

- ★ *Teaching Resources CD–ROM,* Lesson 8.3

SHELTERED ENGLISH

- ★ Main Idea Activities for Reteaching and Sheltered English 8.3

their positive and negative effects on workers, and how organized labor and reformers tried to balance the interests of both workers and business owners.

Introduce Key Terms

Linguistic, Logical-Mathematical. Review this section's key terms with students. Have students discuss any words they associate with these terms and write them on the chalkboard. Then have students find definitions of the terms in the textbook and write them down. Ask them to compare the definitions with the lists on the chalkboard to determine if their associations were correct. **SHELTERED ENGLISH**

TEACH

Have students read Section 3 and complete Guided Reading Strategies 8.3. Choose one or more of the following activities to explore the section content with students. For further suggestions on block scheduling or team teaching, see the *Block Scheduling Handbook*.

LEVEL 1: Linguistic. (Suggested time: 15 min.) As a class, go over students' Guided Reading Strategies. Then use the Reading Focus questions to highlight the main ideas of the section. **SHELTERED ENGLISH**

Citizenship and Democracy

Child Labor. Activist Mary "Mother" Jones crusaded for the rights of child workers as well as adults. In 1897 she organized children during a textile strike in Kensington, Pennsylvania. She marched on Washington, D.C., with 10,000 children who worked in the mills. According to Jones, many of these children had lost fingers—or even whole hands—in the mills. Most of the children were thin and sickly looking. They carried banners that read, "We Want Time to Play."

Critical Thinking: Why might this march have been an effective protest?

ANSWER: Having members of Congress see the children might underscore the need for child labor laws. In addition, the children's demands might have seemed reasonable.

CHART ANSWER
between 16 and 17 cents per hour

"Tired?" Van Vorst asked the child, who nodded without stopping. The girl received 40 cents a day for her work, providing cheap labor for the manufacturer, and $2.40 a week for her parents.

Florence Kelley, who had raised her three children at Chicago's Hull House, led the progressive crusade against child labor. Her strategy was to "investigate, educate, legislate, and enforce." Beginning her career as a social reformer at Hull House, Kelley traveled throughout the United States lobbying for labor laws to protect women and children. As a boardmember of the National Consumers' League—the major lobbying group for women's and children's labor issues—Kelley established about 60 local consumer leagues throughout the United States.

Progressives wanted to keep companies from using the labor of children, like this young coal miner.

The National Child Labor Committee worked with labor committees to pass laws restricting child labor in many states. Although Congress passed federal child labor laws in 1916 and 1919, the Supreme Court declared them unconstitutional. A later attempt to pass a constitutional amendment restricting child labor failed to be ratified.

Earning a Living In the early 1900s employees worked fewer hours than before but earned a higher hourly wage. What was the average hourly wage in 1902?

Safety in the Workplace

Child labor reform was only part of the progressive effort to help American workers. Some progressives cooperated with labor unions to get legislation passed that addressed the low wages, long hours, and unsafe working conditions faced by millions of adult workers. Many progressives supported the eight-hour workday. The National Consumers' League led efforts to establish laws to guarantee a minimum wage and limit working hours. As a result, many states passed minimum-wage laws and maximum-hour laws for women.

Tragic accidents also led reformers to call for safety regulations in the workplace. In 1900 some 35,000 people were killed by industrial accidents, and about 500,000 suffered injuries. In 1911 the Triangle Shirtwaist Company in New York City was the site of a shocking accident. As some 500 immigrant women prepared to leave the clothing factory one day, a fire broke out in the 10-story building. The women tried to escape through exit doors but found that the managers had locked them. Other workers crammed into elevators or leaped into the elevator shafts as the fire and smoke spread around them. Some women jumped hand-in-hand from the top of the burning building, falling to their deaths. By the time firefighters finally brought the **Triangle Shirtwaist Factory Fire** under control, 146 workers had died.

The factory owners, insurance company, city building inspectors, and fire departments were all blamed in the investigation. No one was convicted on criminal charges, however. At a memorial service for the victims of the fire, union organizer

ALL LEVELS: Linguistic, Logical-Mathematical, Visual-Spatial. (Suggested time: 45 min.) Have students make a poster encouraging workers, including children, to join a union. Ask them to include in their posters the kinds of reforms that a union might have supported. **SHELTERED ENGLISH**

LEVEL 2: Linguistic, Logical-Mathematical, Intrapersonal. (Suggested time: 45 min.) Ask students to imagine that they are union leaders responding to progressive reforms. Have each student write a letter to a progressive leader describing a specific organization or law that progressives fought for labor reform. Encourage students to focus on reasons the union leader might object to the organization or law.

LEVEL 3: Linguistic, Logical-Mathematical. (Suggested time: 45 min. plus homework) Have students imagine that they have been working as reformers who support legislation to reduce working hours and that they have just read the Court's decision in *Lochner* v. *New York* or *Muller* v. *Oregon*. Have them write a speech describing to others in their movement the decision's impact on their reform efforts and how they might oppose decisions with which they disagree.

Rose Schneiderman appealed to other workers for action:

> **"This is not the first time girls have been burned alive in the city. Each week I must learn of the untimely death of one of my sister workers. . . . The life of men and women is so cheap and property is so sacred. . . . It is up to the working people to save themselves."**

The Granger Collection, New York

The loss of life in the Triangle Shirtwaist Factory Fire shocked the country.

Accidents such as the Triangle Shirtwaist Factory Fire encouraged legislation that increased factory safety standards and improved working conditions. State legislatures passed some mine and factory safety laws and new inspection regulations.

Labor leaders and progressive reformers also fought for workers' compensation laws, which would provide money to individuals who were injured on the job. Previously, employers had held workers responsible for any injuries received on the job. In 1902 Maryland became the first of many states to adopt a workers' compensation law. However, the workplace laws were not always strictly enforced, so working conditions remained difficult in many places.

The Courts and Labor

Some business leaders opposed workforce regulations and believed that the economy should operate without government interference. State and federal courts often upheld these views. The courts argued that the Fourteenth Amendment protected businesses against regulations that deprived them of property without due process of law.

Lochner v. *New York*

In an 1898 decision the Supreme Court ruled that states could limit the hours worked by people in particularly dangerous jobs such as mining. Under the same principle, the state of New York later passed a law that limited bakers to a 10-hour workday because of the unhealthy working conditions in bakeries. A bakery owner named Joseph Lochner challenged the 10-hour law, claiming that it interfered with his right to run his business. The case eventually went to the U.S. Supreme Court.

In *Lochner* v. *New York* the Court ruled that states could not restrict ordinary workers' hours and that the New York law was unconstitutional. Justice Rufus Peckham's opinion stated:

> **"The freedom of master and employee to contract with each other . . . cannot be prohibited or interfered with without violating the Fourteenth Amendment's guarantee of liberty."**

Muller v. *Oregon*

The Supreme Court did uphold some laws that limited the hours that women and children worked. In the 1908 case *Muller* v. *Oregon*, the Court upheld laws limiting women's hours. Defense attorney Louis Brandeis enlisted the help of progressive reformers Florence Kelley and Josephine Goldmark. Together they collected medical and labor study data to support their legal argument. After hearing this evidence, the Court ruled that pregnancy and other health factors distinguished female workers from male workers. The justices wrote that a woman's health

Constitutional Heritage

Oliver Wendell Holmes. In his dissent from the *Lochner* decision, Supreme Court Justice Oliver Wendell Holmes criticized the Court for basing its decision on an economic theory—that government should not interfere in business—rather than on the Constitution. Holmes claimed that the Constitution exists "for people of fundamentally differing views," and that cases ought to be decided without considering economics.

Critical Thinking: Who might Justice Holmes have meant when he mentioned "people of fundamentally differing views"?

ANSWER: He might have been referring to both business owners and workers.

CLOSE

Linguistic, Visual-Spatial. To conclude the lesson, have students work individually or in groups to create a two-column chart. The first column will list the working conditions created by industrialization, and the second will show the ways progressives tried to better those conditions. Ask students to have their charts cover the issues of child labor, unions in the reform movement, and significant pieces of legislation. Ask volunteers to share their charts with the class.

CHALLENGE AND EXTEND

Linguistic, Visual-Spatial. Refer students to the Global Connections feature on this page. Then point out that workers in many other nations, including Great Britain and Germany, experienced poor working conditions during the late 1800s and early 1900s. Have students use the library or other resources to construct a bulletin board showing examples of working conditions and statistics on job safety in different countries during this period. Make sure they include the United States in their displays.

Across the Curriculum

MATH

Women in Unions. The number of female workers increased from 4 million in 1890 to 8 million in 1910. At that time, women made up 20 percent of the labor force. However, only 1 in every 100 women were union members, while 1 in every 14 men belonged to a labor union.

Activity: Have students calculate the size of the workforce in 1910. *(Since women made up 20 percent, or one fifth, of the labor force, have students multiply 8 million by 5 to get 40 million.)* Also have students calculate the number of women who belonged to unions at the time. *(Since only 1 in every 100 women joined a union, have students divide 8 million by 100 to get 80,000.)* Finally, discuss how the low numbers of female union members might have affected their working conditions.

Global Connections Answers

1. European unions used strikes and collective bargaining.

2. They won retirement pensions, and some won the eight-hour workday and received insurance against unemployment.

is a matter of public concern and that this public interest allowed the government to regulate women's working hours.

For the progressives, this was an important decision because *Muller* v. *Oregon* was the first case successfully argued from economic, scientific, and social evidence rather than prior legal principle. Progressives and union leaders continued using such evidence in their efforts to win similar legal protection for male workers.

Josephine Goldmark fought to protect the rights of female workers.

Labor Organizations

While progressives used the nation's courts and legislatures to try to change labor laws, unions continued to negotiate with employers for improved working conditions. A major union goal was gaining higher wages. In 1910 millions of working men and women lived in poverty. Union membership increased from more than 800,000 in 1900 to about 5 million in 1920. Most unions discouraged women from joining, so some female workers organized their own unions. For example, reformers started the national Women's Trade Union League (WTUL) in 1903.

The American Federation of Labor (AFL) continued to be one of the most powerful labor unions, with some 4 million members by 1920. The AFL concentrated on organizing workers in skilled trades. Its goals were higher wages, better working conditions, and union recognition. These goals followed AFL president Samuel Gompers's idea of "pure and simple unionism."

Global Connections

Worker Reforms

Like American laborers, European workers formed unions and often went on strike for better wages, hours, and working conditions. European unions proved more successful at organizing and winning their demands. By the mid-1880s strikes had been legalized in industrialized European countries and were a standard union tactic.

National general strikes, in which all of the workers in a country go on strike at the same time, occurred in Belgium, the Netherlands, and Sweden. Some strikes resulted in violence, but most of the thousands of strikes that occurred annually in Europe were peaceful. Collective bargaining between workers and employers also resolved many disputes.

The labor movement was strongest in Britain, where there were about 4 million union members in 1913. As their standard of living declined in the early 1900s, British workers staged several major labor protests. A series of transportation strikes paralyzed the nation in 1911. Riots broke out in Liverpool, requiring some 50,000 troops to restore order.

In the early 1900s, British workers won retirement pensions. British miners gained an eight-hour workday. In 1911 Parliament passed the British National Insurance Act, which provided some workers with insurance against unemployment.

Understanding What You Read

1. How did European unions try to bring about changes in the workplace?
2. What gains did British workers make?

REVIEW

Linguistic, Logical-Mathematical, Visual-Spatial. Have students complete the Section Review questions. Then have each student make a time line showing the passage of labor reform laws and major court rulings that affected laborers. Ask students to explain on their time lines why the reforms were needed and why the Court ruled the way it did.

ASSESS

Have students complete Daily Quiz 8.3.

RETEACH

Visual-Spatial, Logical-Mathematical. Have students complete Main Idea Activities for Reteaching and Sheltered English 8.3. Assign students one of the Reading Focus questions at the beginning of the section. Then have them work individually or in groups to create a graphic organizer showing how the text responds to the question. After they finish the graphic organizers, have students exchange their work with others until they have had a chance to examine graphic organizers dealing with each of the questions. **SHELTERED ENGLISH**

Gompers and others like him supported the system called **capitalism**, in which private businesses run most industries, and competition determines how much goods cost and how much workers are paid.

Some union members embraced more radical ideas than those supported by the AFL. These workers claimed that capitalism was unfair. Instead, they supported **socialism**, a system in which the government or the workers own and operate a nation's means of production. Socialists hoped that if the government ran industries and manufacturing, it would be more sympathetic to workers' concerns.

Some socialists and union leaders founded the **Industrial Workers of the World** (IWW) in 1905. Led by William D. "Big Bill" Haywood, the IWW worked to bring all laborers together into one large industrial union that would try to overthrow capitalism. The IWW unionized many workers who were unwelcome in the AFL, including unskilled laborers, immigrants, women, African Americans, and migrant workers.

Haywood said that workers and capitalists were engaged in a bitter "class struggle." As part of this struggle, the IWW organized many strikes across the country. The IWW gained supporters in 1912 after its successful textile mill strike in Lawrence, Massachusetts. The next year, however, the union lost a major silkworkers' strike in Paterson, New Jersey.

Labor Union Membership, 1900–1920

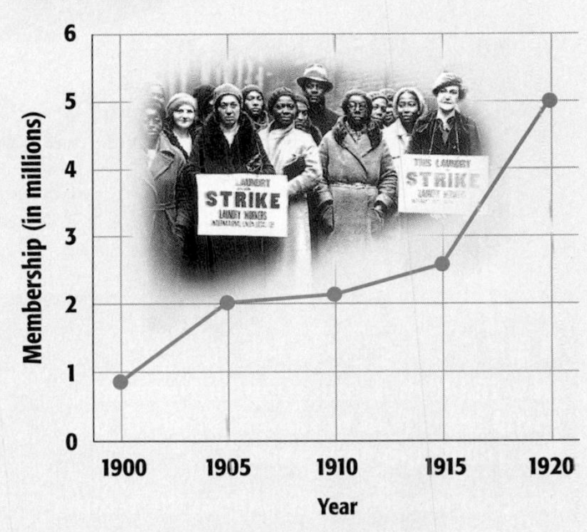

Source: *Historical Statistics of the United States*

The Growing Unions The nation's industrial growth and the efforts of progressive reformers helped labor unions' membership grow. During which five-year period was union membership the highest?

The beliefs and actions of the IWW frightened many Americans, particularly wealthy and powerful leaders of big business. Political opposition, arrests of union leaders, and government investigations weakened the IWW. By 1920 the union had practically disappeared.

SECTION 3 REVIEW

Identify and explain the significance of the following:

- **Florence Kelley**
- **Triangle Shirtwaist Factory Fire**
- **capitalism**
- **socialism**
- **Industrial Workers of the World**
- **William D. Haywood**

Reading for Content Understanding

1 **Main Idea** How did many progressives try to reform labor practices?

2 **Main Idea** How did labor unions try to address workplace issues?

3 **Constitutional Heritage** What did the Supreme Court decide in *Muller* v. *Oregon* and *Lochner* v. *New York*? What reasons did the Court give in its rulings?

4 **Writing** *Describing* Write a half-page news article about the Triangle Shirtwaist Factory Fire in 1911.

5 **Critical Thinking** *Determining the Strength of an Argument* Do you think that the courts should or should not have attempted to regulate the workplace? Explain your answer.

CHART ANSWER
1915 to 1920

Section 3 Review ANSWERS

Identify
For significance, see the following pages:

- Florence Kelley, p. 248
- Triangle Shirtwaist Factory Fire, p. 248
- capitalism, p. 251
- socialism, p. 251
- Industrial Workers of the World, p. 251
- William D. Haywood, p. 251

Reading for Content Understanding

1. Many progressives pushed for child labor laws, worked with unions, and encouraged legislation addressing low wages, long hours, and unsafe working conditions.

2. Some unions pushed for capitalism or socialism to address workplace issues. Other unions held strikes.

3. *Muller* v. *Oregon*—the Court ruled that women's health was a matter of public concern and therefore allowed the government to regulate women's work hours; *Lochner* v. *New York*—the Supreme Court ruled that the state could not limit the number of hours worked by ordinary workers.

4. Articles will vary but should discuss the tragedy and how it could have been avoided, as well as how it led to increased factory safety standards and improved working conditions.

5. Answers will vary but students should state their opinions and offer logical arguments to support them.

OBJECTIVES

- **Describe how higher education and women's social clubs led to reform efforts in the late 1800s and early 1900s.**
- **Explain how women participated in the temperance movement.**
- **Identify the methods women used to gain the vote.**

FOCUS

Motivate Before Reading

Ask each student to write a few sentences explaining why the right to vote is important. Ask volunteers to share their explanations with the class. After students explain their reasoning, ask them who had the right to vote during the Progressive Era. *(Students should mention that only male citizens over the age of 21 had the right to vote.)*

Section 4 RESOURCES

PRINT

★ Guided Reading Strategies 8.4

★ Section 4 Review, p.257

★ Daily Quiz 8.4

MULTIMEDIA

★ *Teaching Resources CD–ROM,* Lesson 8.4

★ Art in American History Transparency 19: *Summertime: Woman and Child in a Rowboat*

SHELTERED ENGLISH

★ Main Idea Activities for Reteaching and Sheltered English 8.4

Multimedia Resources

Art in American History Transparency 19: *Summertime: Woman and Child in a Rowboat*

SECTION 4

Women's Suffrage and Temperance

Reading Focus

How did higher education and women's social clubs lead to reform efforts in the late 1800s and early 1900s?

How did women participate in the temperance movement?

What methods did women's rights activists use to gain the vote?

Key Terms

Woman's Christian Temperance Union

Anti-Saloon League

Eighteenth Amendment

National American Woman Suffrage Association

National Woman's Party

Nineteenth Amendment

DURING THE SUMMER OF 1910, a campaign tour for women's right to vote stopped in Warren, Illinois. The local crowd greeted the female activists with colorful banners and enthusiasm. The activists told Warren's residents that their state representative had opposed the Woman Suffrage bill. The crowd brought the representative forward and demanded to know if he would change his vote and support the bill the next time. "It looks as if I would have to," he responded. To the delight of the crowd, he shouted, "I can't fight against a woman's campaign. I'm for you."

Suffrage supporter

Progressive Women

In the years following the Seneca Falls Convention of 1848, women's rights activists had achieved some important breakthroughs. These included property rights for married women and increased access to higher education.

In the late 1800s women began attending college in record numbers. Several women's colleges had been founded in the mid-1800s, including Vassar, Smith, and Wellesley. Women's colleges were designed "to develop as fully as may be the powers of womanhood," said Sophia Smith, founder of Smith College. In addition, many of the new state universities admitted both men and women. Some educators opposed women's higher education, however. For example, in 1874 a professor at Harvard Medical School argued that the physical and mental strain of too much thinking would harm a woman's health.

Finally, tell students that in this section they will learn how women fought for and gained the right to vote.

Introduce Key Terms

Linguistic, Logical-Mathematical. Review this section's key terms with students. Then have students write one sentence on each reform organization or amendment, explaining its purpose. Ask volunteers to share their sentences with the class.
SHELTERED ENGLISH

TEACH

Have students read Section 4 and complete Guided Reading Strategies 8.4. Choose one or more of the following activities to explore the section content with students. For further suggestions on block scheduling or team teaching, see the *Block Scheduling Handbook*.

American Arts

Mary Cassatt

Mary Cassatt was born into a wealthy Pennsylvania family in 1844. From an early age she was interested in the arts, but she found the American art school she attended dull. She moved to Europe, where she studied painting for years, developing her own vivid, colorful style. Her successful career showed the increased opportunities available to women in the late 1800s.

French painter Edgar Degas saw one of Cassatt's paintings in the 1870s. He remarked, "There is a person who feels as I do." Degas invited Cassatt to become the only American to exhibit with the impressionists, a school of painters who created richly colored scenes of everyday life. Cassatt later became the first impressionist to exhibit in the United States.

While many impressionists painted public scenes, Cassatt often chose mothers and young children as her subjects, creating sensitive portraits. Her work helped to increase American interest in impressionist painting. In the early 1890s she painted a large mural, titled *Modern Woman,* for the Women's Building at the World's Columbian Exposition in Chicago. The mural was lost after the exposition ended.

Mary Cassatt's paintings, such as Young Mother Sewing, *often showed mothers and daughters sharing daily activities.*

Cassatt was also influenced by Japanese prints displayed in Paris, France. Inspired by the exhibition, Cassatt created some prints in her own style. She was uninterested, however, in most of the styles of modern art that were introduced during the early 1900s.

Cassatt was a precise and outspoken person who painted only who and what she wanted. She never taught any students because she believed that each artist had to develop his or her own personal style. When Cassatt died in 1926, she was regarded as one of the finest American artists of her time.

Understanding the Arts

1. Why did Mary Cassatt go to Europe to study art?
2. How was Cassatt's work similar to and different from that of the other impressionists? Why do you think this was the case?
3. What do you think Cassatt is trying to show in the above painting?

Using Visual Resources

Young Mother Sewing. The painting by Mary Cassatt, entitled *Young Mother Sewing,* utilizes the rich use of color that typified impressionists' work. The rich color in the background seems to combine with the soft hues of both subjects' skin to create a feeling of closeness between the mother and daughter.

Activity: Have students use the library and other resources to find examples of works by Cassatt. Then ask each student to write a review of how one work uses color to create an emotional effect.

AMERICAN ARTS ANSWERS

1. She found American art schools dull and wanted to learn new styles in Europe.
2. Her work was similar to that of other impressionists in that it used richly colored scenes of everyday life. It was different in that most impressionists painted public scenes while Cassatt often painted young children and women; answers will vary but students should explain their reasoning.
3. Answers will vary but students may mention that Cassatt was trying to show the close relationship between a modern woman and her child or that women often had to perform many tasks at the same time.

LEVEL 1: Linguistic. (Suggested time: 15 min.) As a class, go over students' Guided Reading Strategies. Then use the Reading Focus questions to highlight the main ideas of the section. **SHELTERED ENGLISH**

ALL LEVELS: Linguistic, Logical-Mathematical, Interpersonal. (Suggested time: 45 min.) Organize the class into pairs. Then have each student write two headlines for each of the following topics: women's social clubs or women's education in the late 1800s, the temperance movement, and women's struggle for suffrage. Once students have finished writing their headlines, have them work with their partners to list facts that might accompany an article on each headline. Have volunteers share their headlines and supporting information with the class.

LEVEL 2: Linguistic, Interpersonal. (Suggested time: 45 min.) Have students list questions about the progressive movement that they might want to ask a female reformer mentioned in this section. Then pair students and have one person play the reformer while the other asks questions. Then have students reverse roles. Once students have had a chance to play both roles, have volunteers re-create their interviews for the class. Then lead a discussion on female reformers and the issues that concerned them.

Biography

Frances Willard. One of the most important reform activists in the United States during the late 1800s was Frances Willard. Her organizational skills and firm belief in women's rights led her to mold the Woman's Christian Temperance Union (WCTU) into an organization that supported numerous reforms. She called the sum of her ideas the Do-Everything Policy, arguing that in order to reduce the problems of alcohol abuse, the WCTU had to reform all areas of society. Most importantly, women should be given the vote so that they could support laws to protect the family and prevent alcohol abuse. Although her ideas were radical for the time, Willard always couched her calls to action in language that appealed to traditional feminine values, explaining that women needed to vote on issues related to "home protection" and urging women to become more active "for God and home and native land."

Activity: Have students imagine that they are living in the late 1800s. Ask them to write a letter supporting or criticizing Willard's Do-Everything Policy.

Biography

Frances Willard

Frances Willard was born in Churchville, New York, in 1839. She attended North Western Female College in Illinois and graduated in 1859. After graduating, she supported herself as an educator and travel writer.

Willard later became involved in the Woman's Christian Temperance Union (WCTU). Her fiery speeches and effective organizing skills led to her election as WCTU president in 1879, a position she held for the next 20 years.

Willard was interested in a wide range of women's rights issues. She expanded the work of the WCTU beyond temperance drives. She supported the ballot for women as a "weapon for the protection of the home." In addition, she helped the WCTU create departments dealing with issues such as public health, education, and prison reform. When Willard died in 1898, the WCTU had expanded its membership worldwide.

Despite such views, many women seized the opportunity to expand their education. More than 20 percent of college students were women in 1870. That number rose to about 40 percent in 1910. After graduation, however, most of these women found that there were few jobs available for them. Jane Addams explained the frustration this caused her and other women. She stated that she could "not understand this apparent waste of herself, this elaborate [complex] preparation, if no work is provided for her." Many female graduates entered fields such as teaching, social work, and library management. However, they found it harder to join male-dominated professions such as law and medicine.

Women who were denied access to such careers often played a central role in progressive reform movements. Many middle-class women became active as members of local women's social clubs. The General Federation of Women's Clubs (GFWC) was founded in 1890 with more than 200 member organizations. It grew steadily throughout the Progressive Era and had almost 1 million members by 1910. Middle-class African American women formed their own clubs when they were denied membership in most clubs established by white women. One African American women's club adopted the motto "Lifting As We Climb."

In addition to providing places for women to meet and discuss social and political issues, these clubs often supported community improvements. Locally, club members raised money and provided volunteers for projects such as improved libraries, better schools, and scholarship fund-raising. National clubs helped organize local club efforts and schedule lecturers to speak to club members on a wide range of topics. Charlotte Perkins Gilman, a writer and women's rights activist, praised the positive influence of clubs on women's participation in reform movements:

> **"The woman's clubs reached almost everyone and brought her out of the sacred selfishness of the home and into the broader contact and relationship so essential to social progress. . . . The clubs are united and federating [organizing] by towns, states, nations."**

The Temperance Movement

Another area in which female progressives were vital participants was the temperance movement. Temperance reformers had been arguing since the 1840s that alcohol was to blame for many of

LEVEL 2: Visual-Spatial, Logical-Mathematical. (Suggested time: 30 min.) Explain to students that the fight for temperance was a long, drawn-out battle. Have students create a flowchart that shows the progression of the fight against alcohol. Next to each stage they identify, have students list what was accomplished and how it differed from the previous stage. Be sure to have students include the 1840s, the 1870s, the Woman's Christian Temperance Union, the Anti-Saloon League, and the Eighteenth Amendment. Ask volunteers to share their flowcharts with the class. As students identify the various stages of the struggle, identify the significant roles played by such women as Carry Nation and Frances Willard.

LEVEL 3: Linguistic, Logical-Mathematical. (Suggested time: 30 min. plus homework) Ask students to imagine that they are writers for a Progressive Era women's magazine. Have students write an article explaining how women tried to improve society in the late 1800s. Encourage students to discuss education, women's clubs, and the fight for and the adoption of the Nineteenth Amendment. Have volunteers read their articles to the class, then discuss reasons for the adoption of the Nineteenth Amendment, its historical development, and how it expanded the democratic process.

society's problems. They claimed that alcohol abuse disrupted the family and led to crime and poverty. In the 1870s many reformers renewed the fight against alcohol.

One of the first temperance crusades of this period began in Hillsboro, Ohio. Women demanded that liquor dealers give up their trade

> **"in the name of our . . . ruined lives . . . for the good of the town, in the name of God who will judge you and us, [and] for the sake of our souls."**

During the 1870s the movement spread to hundreds of small towns as reformers shut down more than 1,000 saloons. A few women even followed the example of temperance leader Carry Nation, who stormed into saloons with a hatchet, chopping bars and smashing liquor bottles and glasses.

In 1874, reformers created the **Woman's Christian Temperance Union** (WCTU). This organization united women from many different backgrounds in the fight against alcohol abuse. Frances Willard served as president of the WCTU from 1879 to 1898. She created a highly effective organization with 10,000 local branches that represented every state, territory, and major city in the nation. Under Willard's leadership, the WCTU began addressing issues beyond temperance, including the fight for women's suffrage.

The size and success of the WCTU inspired other temperance organizations. The **Anti-Saloon League** was founded in 1893 and became particularly active in the early 1900s. As a result of such widespread temperance efforts, by 1916 the sale of alcohol was illegal in 23 states, primarily in the rural West and South. In 1919, temperance efforts eventually led to the passage of the **Eighteenth Amendment**, which outlawed the "manufacture, sale, or transportation" of alcoholic beverages in the United States.

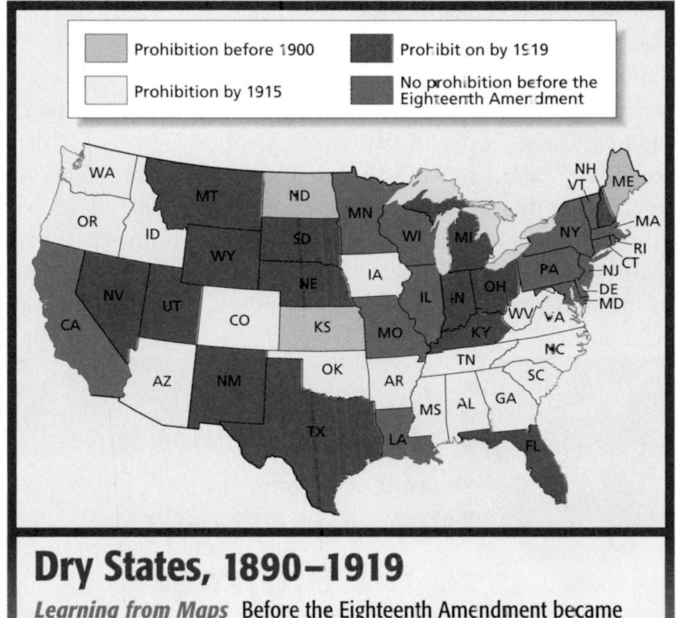

Dry States, 1890–1919

Learning from Maps Before the Eighteenth Amendment became law, many states had taken steps to ban alcohol.

Place Which states had prohibited the sale of alcohol before 1900?

Cartoons often showed temperance leader Carry Nation as a warrior attacking alcohol.

Women's Suffrage

In addition to focusing on reform projects such as the temperance movement and settlement houses, women during the Progressive Era also organized in a renewed effort to gain suffrage. Although progressives supported other women's reform efforts, some progressive leaders still considered the suffrage issue controversial. Many Americans shared their opinion.

Historical Sidelight

Opposition to Women's Suffrage. Women fighting for the right to vote not only had to change the minds of individuals who objected to women's suffrage but also had to battle the efforts of highly funded opponents. The liquor lobby opposed women's suffrage because it feared that the vote for women would mean prohibition and the end of profits made from the sale of alcohol. Industrialists also opposed women's suffrage because they feared the labor reforms that women would support. In 1919 the Eighteenth Amendment was passed, ending the liquor lobby's fight against women's suffrage. In addition, public recognition of women's contributions to the U.S. effort in World War I helped end industrialists' opposition to women's suffrage, thus paving the way for the passage of the Nineteenth Amendment.

Activity: Have students use the library and other resources to research the struggle for women's suffrage. Then have each student create a time line showing significant events in the struggle.

MAP ANSWER

Kansas, Maine, and North Dakota

CLOSE

Linguistic, Logical-Mathematical, Visual-Spatial. Ask students to list the accomplishments and failures of female progressives. Then have students list events that led to each success or defeat. Ask volunteers to share their lists with the class. As students list events, ask how each one affected the overall movement and to identify other events that resulted from it.

CHALLENGE AND EXTEND

Linguistic, Logical-Mathematical. Ask each student to choose a woman discussed in this section to research, such as Carry Nation, Frances Willard, Susan B. Anthony, or Carrie Chapman Catt, and use the library or other resources to find information on that individual. Have each student use the findings to write an encyclopedia entry explaining the contribution of the woman to either the women's suffrage or temperance movement. Ask volunteers to read their entries to the class.

Biography

Stanton and Anthony. Elizabeth Cady Stanton and Susan B. Anthony formed a close friendship and became an excellent team for leading the women's rights movement. Stanton gave Anthony encouragement and moral support, and Anthony kept Stanton—who was raising seven children—up to date on developments in the movement. As a single woman, Anthony sometimes became frustrated with Stanton's family duties. "Those of you who have the talent to do honor to poor womanhood," Anthony wrote to Stanton, "have all given yourselves over to baby-making."

Critical Thinking: What might be the advantage of close friends leading a movement together?

ANSWER: Answers may include flexibility, understanding, and the contribution of everyone's strengths.

HISTORICAL DOCUMENTS ANSWERS

1. She was charged with voting in a presidential election.

2. She believed women should have the right to vote because it was both men and women who formed the Union and secured liberty for everyone.

Resistance to Suffrage

The suffrage movement had many opponents. Some people feared that the vote would give women too much political power. For example, political bosses worried that women would fight corruption. Many businessmen were also opposed to reforms that a large number of women supported, such as child labor laws and the minimum wage. Other people argued that women belonged in the home as homemakers and mothers, rather than in the world of politics. This argument was also accepted by many women's club members, who believed that women should lead efforts for social change but avoid politics.

Carrie Chapman Catt waves to supporters.

Suffragists strongly challenged such claims. One suffragist leader responded to her opponents by arguing that women

> **"must go beyond the house. No longer is home compassed [contained] by four walls. Many of its most important duties lie now involved in the bigger family of the city and state."**

HISTORICAL DOCUMENTS

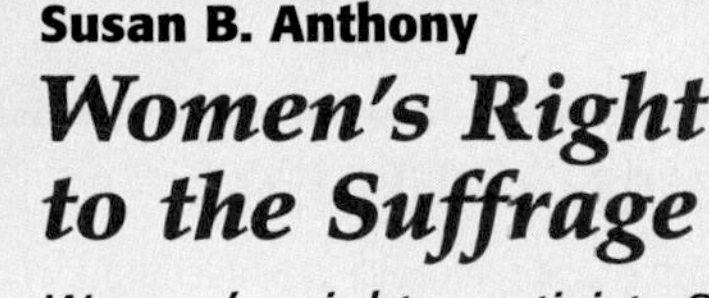

Susan B. Anthony

1873

Women's Right to the Suffrage

Women's rights activist Susan B. Anthony defended herself before a New York state court in 1873 after she was arrested for voting. The following is an excerpt from her speech.

> "Friends and fellow citizens: I stand before you to-night under indictment for the alleged crime [accusation] of having voted at the last presidential election, without having a lawful right to vote. It shall be my work this evening to prove to you that in thus voting, I not only committed no crime, but, instead, simply exercised my citizen's rights, guaranteed to me and all United States citizens by the National Constitution. . . . It was we, the people, not we, the white male citizens; nor yet we, the male citizens; but we, the whole people, who formed the Union. And we formed it, not to give the blessings of liberty, but to secure them; not to the half of ourselves and the half of our posterity, but to the whole people—women as well as men."

Understanding Primary Sources

1. What crime was Susan B. Anthony accused of committing?
2. Why does Anthony believe that women should have the vote?

Suffrage Organizations

In 1890 Elizabeth Cady Stanton and Susan B. Anthony began the **National American Woman Suffrage Association** (NAWSA) to focus on getting the vote for women. That same year, women gained full suffrage in the state of Wyoming. Colorado, Idaho, and Utah followed in the 1890s. Despite these early successes, the NAWSA faced great challenges as it tried to lobby for suffrage across the nation.

Carrie Chapman Catt, who had fought successfully for women's suffrage in the West, became the president of the NAWSA in 1900. Catt mobilized more than 1 million volunteers for the movement. She promoted the NAWSA's goals through campaigns and speeches. Catt argued that female voters were needed to help bring about progressive reforms. She also pointed out that women deserved to have a voice in creating the laws that affected them.

Some women believed that the efforts of the NAWSA did not go far

REVIEW

Linguistic, Logical-Mathematical, Visual-Spatial. Have students complete the Section Review questions. Then have students create a crossword puzzle using the terms and names from the Identify portion of the Section 4 Review. Have students exchange their puzzles, answer the questions, and return them to their authors for grading.

ASSESS

Have students complete Daily Quiz 8.4.

RETEACH

Linguistic, Logical-Mathematical, Visual-Spatial. Have students complete Main Idea Activities for Reteaching and Sheltered English 8.4. Then ask them to review the principles supported by the organizations listed in the key terms. Lead the class in creating a chart that summarizes what each organization supported and how it differed from other groups interested in the same issues. **SHELTERED ENGLISH**

enough. In 1913 former NAWSA member Alice Paul founded what would become the **National Woman's Party** (NWP). The NWP used methods such as parades and public demonstrations to draw attention to its cause, as well as more controversial activities such as pickets, hunger strikes, and civil disobedience. Paul and other NWP leaders were jailed on several occasions for such actions.

The NWP and the NAWSA campaigned for a constitutional amendment to grant women the vote. The success of other progressive reforms encouraged these groups. In 1916 both the Democratic and Republican Parties supported women's suffrage. In 1920 the combined efforts of the NAWSA and the NWP resulted in the passage of the **Nineteenth Amendment**. This amendment gave women in the United States the vote.

The NWP continued to push for women's rights by supporting an equal rights amendment. The NAWSA helped create the League of Women Voters, an organization that encouraged women to educate themselves on public issues, to vote regularly, and to support additional social reform measures.

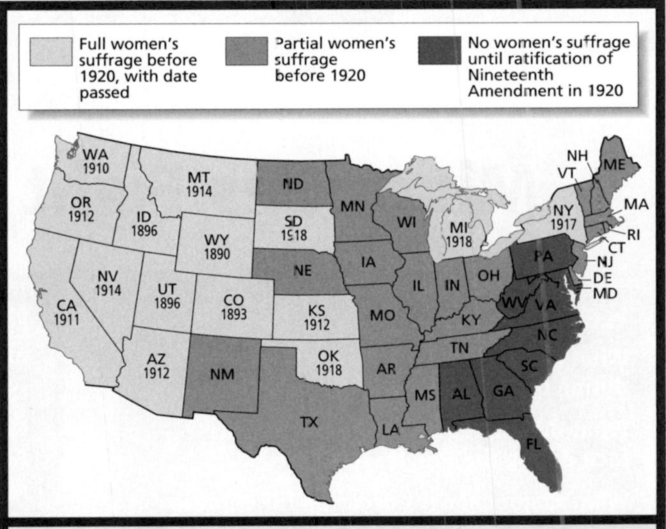

Women and Suffrage, 1890–1920

Learning from Maps The National American Woman Suffrage Association and the National Woman's Party successfully led the fight for women's suffrage.

Place Which states had no women's suffrage before the ratification of the Nineteenth Amendment?

MAP ANSWER

the states of the Southeast and mid-Atlantic coast

SECTION 4 REVIEW

Identify and explain the significance of the following:

- **Woman's Christian Temperance Union**
- **Frances Willard**
- **Anti-Saloon League**
- **Eighteenth Amendment**
- **Susan B. Anthony**
- **National American Woman Suffrage Association**
- **Carrie Chapman Catt**
- **Alice Paul**
- **National Woman's Party**
- **Nineteenth Amendment**

Reading for Content Understanding

1 **Main Idea** What role did higher education and women's social clubs play in reform efforts during the late 1800s and early 1900s?

2 **Main Idea** In what ways did women contribute to the temperance movement?

3 **Constitutional Heritage** How did some women fight for suffrage? What legislation was passed as a result of their efforts?

4 **Writing** *Creating* Imagine that you have just joined the NAWSA. Write a brief paragraph and a slogan for a poster supporting the women's suffrage movement.

5 **Critical Thinking** *Evaluating* What do you think were the most important contributions made by women to the progressive movement? Explain your answer.

Section 4 Review ANSWERS

Identify

For significance, see the following pages:

- Woman's Christian Temperance Union, p. 255
- Frances Willard, p. 255
- Anti-Saloon League, p. 255
- Eighteenth Amendment, p. 255
- Susan B. Anthony, p. 256
- National American Woman Suffrage Association, p. 256
- Carrie Chapman Catt, p. 256
- Alice Paul, p. 257
- National Woman's Party, p. 257
- Nineteenth Amendment, p. 257

Reading for Content Understanding

1. Many women became educated but found few jobs open to them, so many joined social clubs to push for reforms.

2. destroyed saloons, formed the Woman's Christian Temperance Union and Anti-Saloon League

3. National American Women Suffrage Association campaigned for suffrage, National Woman's Party held parades and demonstrations; Nineteenth Amendment

4. Work will vary but students should explain why female citizens should be allowed to vote.

5. Answers will vary but students should state which contributions they found most important and why.

OBJECTIVES

- **Describe reforms African Americans sought during the Progressive Era.**
- **Identify the difficulties that American Indians faced during the Progressive Era.**
- **Analyze major changes for Chinese Americans and Mexican Americans during the Progressive Era.**

FOCUS

Motivate Before Reading

Ask students to define the term *discrimination.* Then ask them if they know of any legislation that has been passed to end discrimination. *(Students might mention the Fourteenth and Fifteenth Amendments.)* Tell students that in this section they will learn about the struggles in the late 1800s to end discrimination against women and minorities.

Section 5
RESOURCES

PRINT

★ Guided Reading Strategies 8.5
★ Biography Reading 8: Ida B. Wells-Barnett
★ Graphic Organizer 8: Reform Movements
★ Section 5 Review, p. 261
★ Daily Quiz 8.5

MULTIMEDIA

★ *Teaching Resources CD–ROM,* Lesson 8.5

SHELTERED ENGLISH

★ Main Idea Activities for Reteaching and Sheltered English 8.5

Minorities Fight for Change

Reading Focus

What reforms did African Americans seek during the Progressive Era?

What difficulties did American Indians face during the Progressive Era?

What major changes occurred for Chinese Americans and Mexican Americans during the Progressive Era?

Key Terms

Atlanta Compromise
Niagara Movement
National Association for the Advancement of Colored People
National Association of Colored Women
Society of American Indians

On July 25, 1900, African American professor and writer W. E. B. Du Bois stepped up to a podium in London's Westminster Town Hall. Before him sat reporters and delegates from around the world, gathered for the first Pan-African Conference. In solemn tones, Du Bois asked his audience to consider the key question facing the world. That problem, he declared, was how and why racial differences were used as "the basis of denying to over half the world the right of sharing . . . the opportunities and privileges of modern civilization."

W. E. B. Du Bois

African Americans Fight for Change

White reformers in the progressive movement often ignored issues such as racial discrimination. While other areas of life were improving during the late 1800s, discrimination and segregation increased throughout the nation.

Booker T. Washington

Some African American leaders, particularly Booker T. Washington, promoted efforts to improve the economic conditions of African Americans. Born a slave in 1856, Washington became a respected educator while in his twenties. In 1881 he founded the Tuskegee Institute in Alabama to educate and train black schoolteachers. Washington explained the practical goals of Tuskegee in his autobiography *Up from Slavery.* "The student shall be so educated that he shall be enabled to meet conditions as they exist *now.*" Tuskegee also drew African American teachers such as scientist George Washington Carver. Carver's agricultural research addressed many farming problems in the South.

Introduce Key Terms

Linguistic, Logical-Mathematical. Review this section's key terms with students. Ask students to define each term and write a sentence using it. **SHELTERED ENGLISH**

TEACH

Have students read Section 5 and complete Guided Reading Strategies 8.5. Choose one or more of the following activities to explore the section content with students. For further suggestions on block scheduling or team teaching, see the *Block Scheduling Handbook*.

LEVEL 1: Linguistic. (Suggested time: 15 min.) As a class, go over students' Guided Reading Strategies. Then use the Reading Focus questions to highlight the main ideas of the section. **SHELTERED ENGLISH**

ALL LEVELS: Linguistic, Logical-Mathematical. (Suggested time: 30 min.) Have each student create a two-column chart. The first column should identify each minority group mentioned in the section. The second should describe what life was like for each group in the late 1800s and early 1900s. Then discuss any organizations or legislation that helped progressives address the concerns of these groups. **SHELTERED ENGLISH**

Booker T. Washington, founder of the Tuskegee Institute

In addition to his administrative duties at Tuskegee, Washington was an influential writer and public speaker. He argued that African Americans should not spend their time fighting discrimination and segregation but instead should focus on improving their own educational and economic well-being. Washington explained his philosophy in 1895 before a group at the Cotton States Expo in Atlanta, Georgia. In his **Atlanta Compromise** speech he noted:

> **"In all things that are purely social we [whites and African Americans] can be as separate as the fingers, yet one as the hand in all things essential to mutual [shared] progress."**

Other African American leaders believed that economic progress alone was not enough.

Ida B. Wells-Barnett

One such leader was journalist Ida B. Wells-Barnett. She was a suffragist and an outspoken opponent of violence against African Americans. After three of her friends were lynched, or killed by a mob, Wells-Barnett began writing antilynching editorials in her Memphis newspaper, *Free Speech.* These courageous articles drew national attention to the lynching of black men in the South. She also helped organize an international crusade against lynching.

In 1895 Wells-Barnett published the book *Red Record,* which reported lynching statistics for a three-year period. Although repeated death threats forced Wells-Barnett to move to the North, she continued her antilynching campaign.

The Granger Collection, New York

Ida B. Wells-Barnett was orphaned as a teenager and raised her five brothers and sisters.

W. E. B. Du Bois

The approach of W. E. B. Du Bois also contrasted with that of Booker T. Washington. Born in Massachusetts in 1868, Du Bois went to Fisk University and later earned a doctoral degree from Harvard. He criticized Washington for holding African Americans responsible for correcting racial injustice. Du Bois also disagreed with Washington's emphasis on job training rather than liberal arts education.

Du Bois challenged Washington's arguments in a collection of essays published in 1903 called *The Souls of Black Folk.* "The problem of the twentieth century," wrote Du Bois, "is the problem of the color-line." Du Bois explained that his goal was "to make it possible for a man to be both a Negro and an American . . . without having the doors of Opportunity closed roughly in his face." Du Bois brought attention to cases of racial prejudice and wrote dozens of articles, speeches, and influential books on African American history.

African American Organizations

In 1905 W. E. B. Du Bois and other African Americans who shared his views met at Niagara Falls, Canada. Calling themselves the **Niagara Movement**, they demanded economic and educational equality, as well as an end to segregation and discrimination. Their platform insisted that "to ignore, overlook, or apologize for these wrongs is to prove ourselves unworthy of freedom."

To help further the goals of the Niagara Movement, Du Bois joined with reformers such as Mary White Ovington to found the **National Association for the Advancement of Colored People** (NAACP) in 1909. The new organization included many well-known leaders in the progressive movement, such as Jane Addams and John Dewey. These progressives were appalled by the lynchings and recent tide of race riots against African Americans in northern and southern cities. Du Bois acted as director of publicity and research and also as the editor of the NAACP journal, *The Crisis.*

Biography

James Weldon Johnson. In 1916 James Weldon Johnson became the NAACP's first black field secretary. He effectively began to expand the organization's membership, particularly in the South. By 1920 half of the association's 90,000 members were southerners. He went on to become a professor of literature at Fisk University as well as an author. Some of his famous works include the following: *The Autobiography of an Ex-Colored Man, The Book of American Negro Spirituals,* and *Negro Americans, What Now.* His efforts eventually won him the Spingarn medal.

Critical Thinking: Why might the NAACP have increased its membership in the southern states?

ANSWER: The fight for civil rights was most difficult in the South.

LEVEL 3: Linguistic, Interpersonal. (Suggested time: 30 min. plus homework) Organize the class into several small groups and assign each one of the reform organizations discussed in this section. Have each group use material from the section to create a brief presentation about the organization's efforts.

CLOSE

Logical-Mathematical, Interpersonal. Organize the class into small groups. Have each group create a brief oral presentation on minorities' fight for change during the Progressive Era.

CHALLENGE AND EXTEND

TEACHER TO TEACHER

Linguistic, Kinesthetic, Intrapersonal. (Suggested time: 45 min. plus homework) Mary Beth Breshears of Fort Leonard Wood, Missouri, suggested the following activity: Have students debate the ideas of Booker T. Washington and W. E. B. Du Bois. Ask students to prepare by writing a short speech outlining the assigned leader's goals and plans. Then lead a debate by asking each group questions that reveal the differences between these leaders.

Section 5 Review ANSWERS

Identify

For significance, see the following pages:

- Booker T. Washington, p. 258
- Atlanta Compromise, p. 259
- Ida B. Wells-Barnett, p. 259
- W. E. B. Du Bois, p. 259
- Niagara Movement, p. 259
- National Association for the Advancement of Colored People, p. 259
- National Association of Colored Women, p. 260
- Society of American Indians, p. 260

Reading for Content Understanding

1. by obeying the Dawes Act and adopting the beliefs and practices of American society to gain U.S. citizenship

2. Chinese immigration slowed because of laws restricting the number of Chinese allowed to enter the United States, while Mexican immigration rose because Mexicans could freely enter the United States.

3. by promoting efforts to improve African Americans' economic conditions through education and training; by protesting violence against African Americans; by bringing attention to cases of racial prejudice; and by forming organizations to work against racial discrimination

4. Essays will vary but should identify some challenges minority groups faced.

5. Washington—believed that African Americans should focus on improving their own educational and economic opportunities; Du Bois—disagreed with Washington's emphasis on job training and downplaying of liberal arts education and brought attention to cases of racial prejudice.

The NAACP worked to bring racial inequality to the attention of white Americans and attacked racial discrimination through the court system. In *Guinn* v. *United States* in 1915, the NAACP won the first of several important Supreme Court decisions. This ruling outlawed the grandfather clause, which had been widely used in southern states to prevent African Americans from voting.

The National Urban League was an influential black organization founded in 1911. This group helped many African Americans—particularly those moving from the South to northern cities—find jobs and housing and adjust to a new life in an urban environment. The **National Association of Colored Women** (NACW), led by antilynching activist Mary Church Terrell, supported political reforms for African Americans. These reforms included women's suffrage and protecting the voting rights of black men in the South.

Gertrude S. Bonin helped found the Society of American Indians.

 American Indians

Progressive reforms did not address the many problems—such as widespread poverty and a shrinking population—that the majority of American Indians faced. Most Indians lived on reservations, where living conditions were often hard, housing was poor, and medical care was limited. Many Indian children were sent away from the reservations to boarding schools that taught little or nothing about traditional Indian culture. These schools provided basic or vocational education, but students found few jobs available when they returned home.

Several American Indians founded the **Society of American Indians** in 1911 to assist those living on the reservations. Members believed that the Dawes Act, which authorized the breakup of the reservation system, was the best solution to Indians' poverty and unemployment. The group also argued that Indians should adopt the beliefs and practices of the larger American society in an effort to gain U.S. citizenship.

Most of the Society's members, however, did not understand the views of Indians who lived on the reservations and who wanted to preserve traditional Indian culture. A large number of Indians saw the breakup of reservations under the Dawes Act not as a benefit but as the end of the traditional Indian way of life. The importance of traditional beliefs was stressed in advice given by Sioux chief Sitting Bull: "Take the best of the old Indian ways—always keep them. They have been proven for thousands of years. Do not let them die."

Some American Indians protested the policies of the Dawes Act by refusing their government land allotments. Other Indians wanted to slow down the allotment process and allow people to remain on reservations. These efforts met strong resistance from the federal government.

Chinese Americans

Asian immigrants also faced barriers. Many Chinese immigrants who came to the United States were men who mined gold and built railroads. Although most had planned to return home, many later decided to stay.

The Chinese American population grew slowly as a result of laws passed in the 1880s that severely restricted Chinese immigration. In 1900 the Chinese American population was less than 90,000. Chinese Americans also faced other forms of discrimination. Ing Weh-teh wrote his friend in China that in America he had "to labor, to suffer, floating from one place to another, persecuted by the whites, for more than twenty years."

Chinese Americans often formed their own neighborhoods in cities such as San Francisco.

The first Chinese telegraph operator in San Francisco

REVIEW

Linguistic, Interpersonal. Have students complete the Section Review questions. Have each student create a study guide based on minorities' fight for change during the Progressive Era. Ask students to leave blank spaces in their study guides wherever they would use a key term or the name of an individual mentioned in the section. Have students exchange guides, fill in the blanks, and return them for grading.

RETEACH

Linguistic, Visual-Spatial. Have students complete Main Idea Activities for Reteaching and Sheltered English 8.5. Organize the class into several small groups. Assign each group one of the organizations mentioned in this section. Have students work together to create a flyer that lists two or three goals the organization supported. Have a member of each group read its flyer to the class. **SHELTERED ENGLISH**

ASSESS

Have students complete Daily Quiz 8.5.

One man recalled how he and his friends tried to preserve a sense of community by gathering at neighborhood shops:

> **"They all just like to get together. . . . Sometimes they even get some idea [news] from China. . . . We communicate, see, otherwise you're alone. You know nothing."**

Even with such efforts to maintain their cultural ties, life was often difficult for many Chinese Americans.

Many Mexican immigrants were agricultural workers, like these laborers knocking walnuts out of trees in an orchard.

Mexican Americans

While Chinese immigration declined during the early 1900s, immigration from Mexico increased greatly. Between 1900 and 1930 nearly 1 million Mexicans crossed the border into the United States. Immigrants could move freely across the U.S. borders with Mexico and Canada during this time. The lyrics to one Mexican song from the period tells of the sadness many immigrants felt and explains why many made the journey:

> **"For I am not to blame**
> **That I leave my country thus;**
> **The fault lies in the poverty,**
> **Which keeps us all in want."**

Most Mexican immigrants moved into areas that had previously been part of Mexico, such as Texas or California. Cities with existing Hispanic communities—such as San Antonio and El Paso, Texas, and Los Angeles, California—grew in size as a result. The majority of Mexican immigrants took agricultural jobs, although large numbers also worked in factories or meatpacking plants.

Although Mexican immigrants and Mexican Americans played an important role in the economy of the Southwest, many faced discrimination and harsh labor conditions. Despite these challenges, immigrants often returned to Mexico to encourage other family members and friends to move to the United States.

SECTION 5 REVIEW

Identify and explain the significance of the following:

- **Booker T. Washington**
- **Atlanta Compromise**
- **Ida B. Wells-Barnett**
- **W. E. B. Du Bois**
- **Niagara Movement**
- **National Association for the Advancement of Colored People**
- **National Association of Colored Women**
- **Society of American Indians**

Reading for Content Understanding

1. **Main Idea** How did the Society of American Indians try to overcome the hardships faced by American Indians?
2. **Main Idea** What changes in immigration took place for Chinese Americans and Mexican Americans in the late 1800s and early 1900s?
3. **Cultural Diversity** How did some African Americans work to end racial injustice?
4. **Writing** *Informing* Write a short essay explaining the challenges faced by minority groups in the Progressive Era.
5. **Critical Thinking** *Making Comparisons* Compare and contrast the approaches of Booker T. Washington and W. E. B. Du Bois to improving life for African Americans.

Chapter 8 Review ANSWERS

Identifying People and Ideas

1. organizations that guaranteed votes at election time

2. emphasized problem solving and became the progressive educational model

3. system in which private businesses run most industries, and competition determines the cost of goods and how much workers are paid

4. worked to bring all laborers together to overthrow capitalism

5. served as president of the Woman's Christian Temperance Union from 1879 to 1898

6. president of the National American Woman Suffrage Association who mobilized more than 1 million volunteers

7. gave women in the United States the vote

8. speech in which Booker T. Washington noted that whites and African Americans needed to work together for progress

9. African American leader who founded the Tuskegee Institute and promoted efforts to improve economic conditions and educational opportunities for African Americans

10. African American leader who published *The Souls of Black Folk* and brought attention to cases of racial prejudice

Using the Time Line

1. c
2. a
3. e
4. d
5. b
6. f

Review and Assessment **RESOURCES**

PRINT
- ★ Chapter 8 Review, pp. 262–63
- ★ Vocabulary Activity 8
- ★ Chapter 8 Study Guide
- ★ Chapter 8 Test (Form A or B)

MULTIMEDIA
- ★ Audio Program, Ch. 8 (English and Spanish)
- ★ *Global Skill Builder CD–ROM*
- ★ Chapter 8 Test Generator
- ★ HRW Web site

SHELTERED ENGLISH
- ★ Spanish Glossary
- ★ Sheltered English Chapter 8 Test

ASSESS

Have students complete one of the Chapter 8 Tests. As an alternate assessment, assign the Chapter 8 Investigation.

Understanding Main Ideas

1. Bosses used political machines to ensure votes at election time.

2. Progressive reforms provided more choices by listing the names of all candidates, adopting secret ballots, and allowing for direct primaries and election of U.S. senators.

3. It was La Follette's program of reform to decrease the influence of political machines and professionalize government.

4. Working conditions were often unsanitary, unsafe, and required people to work extremely long hours.

5. to unite women from many different backgrounds in the struggle against alcohol

6. Washington believed that African Americans needed to work to improve their own educational and economic opportunities; Du Bois disagreed with Washington's emphasis on job training and downplaying of liberal arts education.

Reviewing Themes

1. *Lochner* v. *New York* ruled that the state could not limit the number of hours worked by the ordinary laborer. In *Muller* v. *Oregon*, the Court determined that women's health was a matter of public safety, and therefore limits on the number of working hours could be established for them.

2. to focus on getting the vote for women

3. Answers will vary but may mention that African Americans gave speeches, published written materials, opened schools, and formed organizations to attempt to gain equal rights.

CHAPTER 8 REVIEW

Chapter Summary

The Progressive Era was a time when many concerned Americans attempted to reform society. They worked to reform such areas as politics, government, the workplace, public schools, and cities. Other Americans tried to improve the lives of women, African Americans, American Indians, immigrants, and other groups.

On a separate sheet of paper, complete the following activities.

Identifying People and Ideas

Describe the historical significance of the following:

1. political machines
2. John Dewey
3. capitalism
4. Industrial Workers of the World
5. Frances Willard
6. Carrie Chapman Catt
7. Nineteenth Amendment
8. Atlanta Compromise
9. Booker T. Washington
10. W. E. B. Du Bois

Internet Activity 

go.hrw.com
SB1 Suffrage Movement

Search the Internet through the HRW Web site to find information about the women's suffrage movement. Create a time line of at least 10 important events in the women's suffrage movement, ending with the Nineteenth Amendment. Briefly explain in a caption why each event was important.

Understanding Main Ideas

1. How did bosses use political machines to control local and city governments?
2. How did reforms give voters more choice in selecting their candidates for public office?
3. What was the Wisconsin Idea?
4. What were working conditions like for child laborers and other factory workers in the late 1800s?
5. Why did some women form the Woman's Christian Temperance Union?
6. How did Booker T. Washington and W. E. B. Du Bois differ in their approaches to fighting for equal rights?

Reviewing Themes

1. **Constitutional Heritage** What was the significance of the ruling in *Lochner* v. *New York*? How did the Supreme Court's decision in

Using the Time Line

Number your paper from 1 to 6. Match the letters on the time line below with the following events.

1. **Grover Cleveland loses the presidency to Benjamin Harrison.**
2. **The first public kindergarten opens in St. Louis, Missouri.**
3. **Leaders of the progressive movement form the National Association for the Advancement of Colored People.**
4. **The New York State Tenement Law outlaws the construction of dark and airless tenements.**
5. **The Pendleton Civil Service Act establishes a merit system for federal jobs.**
6. **The Nineteenth Amendment is passed.**

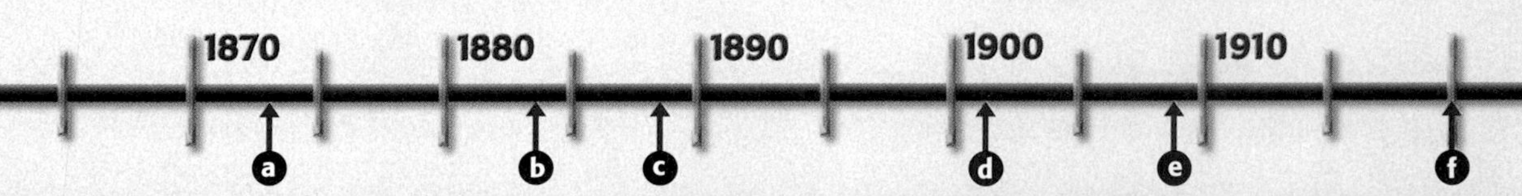

RETEACH

Interpersonal, Visual-Spatial. Organize students into groups and assign each group one of the chapter's sections. Have students create annotated time lines on butcher paper illustrating the main topics of the section. Ask students to include hand-drawn pictures, photographs, or cartoons to illustrate their time lines. Then ask them to share their time lines with the class. **SHELTERED ENGLISH**

Using the Internet

Have students continue their research to find information on support for the ratification of the Nineteenth Amendment. Then ask students to design pamphlets to persuade people to support the adoption of the Nineteenth Amendment.

Portfolio Extensions

1. Have students choose one of the five problems and develop a solution. Have volunteers present their solutions to the class.

2. Ask students to write a newspaper article about the Supreme Court decision they studied. Have students include a description of the case, the Court's decision, and how that decision might affect reform efforts.

Muller v. *Oregon* partially reverse its earlier ruling?

2. **Citizenship and Democracy** Why did women form the National American Woman Suffrage Association?
3. **Cultural Diversity** How did African American leaders try to gain equal rights during the late 1800s and early 1900s?

Thinking Critically

1. **Identifying Cause and Effect** What events led the public to call for civil service reform during the Gilded Age? What was the result of this public outcry?
2. **Making Comparisons** How were progressives similar to and different from previous reformers?
3. **Evaluating** Which of the progressive reform efforts do you think was the most significant? Explain your answer.

Writing About History

1. **Informing** Imagine that you are writing a section of a history book that explores women's participation in various reform efforts during the Progressive Era. Write a half-page feature on this topic.
2. **Expressing** Write a letter to Booker T. Washington telling him whether you agree with his Atlanta Compromise speech. Include reasons to support your position.

Linking Geography and History

1. **Region** What problems did residents of urban areas in the United States face that rural residents did not?
2. **Human-Environment Interaction** Why did many American Indians object to the breakup of reservation lands and tribal society?

Building Your Portfolio

Complete the following activities individually or in groups.

1. **Muckrakers** If muckrakers were investigating problems in American society today, what do you think would be the top five problems they would address? Find newspaper and magazine articles and images on these topics. Use this information to create a bulletin-board display titled Reforming Society Today.
2. **The Supreme Court** Use your textbook or the library to find information about an important Supreme Court reform case of the late 1800s. Create arguments for the defending and prosecuting attorneys, as well as for the justices' ruling. Present your case to the class. Include whether you think the decision supported progressive reform.

History Skills Workshop

Using Primary Sources In his book *How the Other Half Lives,* reformer Jacob Riis described the living conditions of many poor urban people. Read the excerpt to the right, which is Riis's description of a New York City tenement house, and answer the following questions: (a) What connection is Riis making between tenement houses and the child's illness? (b) Why do you think Riis chose this example to illustrate poor people's living conditions? (c) How do you think readers might have responded to these descriptions?

> "Suppose we look into [a tenement] on Cherry Street. . . . Here is a door. Listen! that short hacking cough, that tiny helpless cry—what do they mean? . . . The child is dying of measles. With half a chance it might have lived. But it had none. That dark bedroom killed it."

Thinking Critically

1. scandals such as those involving the Whiskey Ring and Crédit Mobilier, combined with corrupt political machines such as Tammany Hall; civil service reform legislation such as the Pendleton Civil Service Act

2. Progressives fought for changes just as previous reformers had, but they formed social and political organizations that had a significant impact on society.

3. Answers will vary but students should choose a reform movement and explain their reasoning.

Writing About History

1. Features will vary but students should mention women's involvement in the temperance movement as well as their struggle for suffrage.

2. Letters will vary but should explain why students think unity between the races is or is not needed to work on problems that are essential to human progress.

Linking Geography and History

1. sanitation and overcrowding problems

2. They feared that the breakup of the reservation system would end their traditional way of life.

History Skills Workshop

(a) that the tenement house caused the illness; (b) Answers will vary but students may point out that by using a child as the example, Riis is trying to gain sympathy for the situation; (c) Answers will vary but students might point out that the reader would want to improve life in the tenements.

CHAPTER PLANNING GUIDE
The Progressive Presidents

	SECTION LESSON OBJECTIVES	PRINT RESOURCES	MULTIMEDIA RESOURCES	SHELTERED ENGLISH RESOURCES
Section 1: Roosevelt Becomes President (pp. 265–71)	★ Identify ways that President Roosevelt attempted to balance the needs of both business and labor. ★ Analyze Roosevelt's attempts to regulate businesses and railroads. ★ Describe why Roosevelt and others promoted the conservation movement.	★ Guided Reading Strategies 9.1 ★ Literature Reading 9: *Sister Carrie* ★ American History Political Cartoon 17: The Power of Trusts ★ Section 1 Review, p. 271 ★ Daily Quiz 9.1	★ *Teaching Resources CD–ROM*, Lesson 9.1 ★ Everyday Life in America Transparency 18: Progressives and Children, Early 1900s ★ HRW Web site	★ Main Idea Activities for Reteaching and Sheltered English 9.1
Section 2: The Taft Administration (pp. 272–77)	★ Identify how William Howard Taft's administration was similar to and different from Roosevelt's administration. ★ Analyze the progressives' reasons for turning against President Taft. ★ Describe events that took place during the 1912 election.	★ Guided Reading Strategies 9.2 ★ Primary Source Reading 9: 1912 Election ★ Biography Reading 9: William Jennings Bryan ★ Geography Activity 9: The 1904 and 1912 Presidential Elections ★ Section 2 Review, p. 277 ★ Daily Quiz 9.2	★ *Teaching Resources CD–ROM*, Lesson 9.2	★ Main Idea Activities for Reteaching and Sheltered English 9.2
Section 3: Woodrow Wilson's Reforms (pp. 278–83)	★ Describe some characteristics of Woodrow Wilson's administration. ★ Identify economic reforms that President Wilson pursued. ★ Summarize ways that President Wilson tried to regulate corporations.	★ Guided Reading Strategies 9.3 ★ Graphic Organizer 9: Presidential Reforms ★ Section 3 Review, p. 283 ★ Daily Quiz 9.3	★ *Teaching Resources CD–ROM*, Lesson 9.3 ★ HRW Web site	★ Main Idea Activities for Reteaching and Sheltered English 9.3
Chapter Review and Assessment (pp. 284–85)		★ Chapter 9 Review, pp. 284–85 ★ Vocabulary Activity 9 ★ Chapter 9 Study Guide ★ Chapter 9 Test (Form A or B)	★ Audio Program, Ch. 9 (English and Spanish) ★ *Global Skill Builder CD–ROM* ★ Chapter 9 Test Generator ★ HRW Web site	★ Spanish Glossary ★ Sheltered English Chapter 9 Test

CHAPTER OVERVIEW

Theodore Roosevelt's Square Deal was designed to treat all Americans fairly. Roosevelt was a bold and forceful leader who was willing to push his agenda through Congress to satisfy citizens' calls for change. He took on big business by pushing for antitrust legislation and by prosecuting "bad trusts." His administration also set aside large amounts of land for conservation.

Roosevelt's hand-picked successor, William Howard Taft, won the election of 1908. Taft was expected to carry on Roosevelt's policies, and for the most part he did. However, Taft's support for lowering tariffs; his firing of Roosevelt's Chief of Forestry, Gifford Pinchot; and his unwillingness to use his presidential power to push his agenda through caused him to lose Roosevelt's support.

Having lost the 1912 Republican nomination to Taft, Roosevelt ran as a third-party candidate. This split the Republican vote and allowed the Democratic candidate, Woodrow Wilson, to win the election. Wilson convinced Congress to pass legislation that helped small businesses, reformed the banking system, and established some regulation of working hours.

CHAPTER INVESTIGATION

The Chapter Investigation is an extended, multipart activity designed for students to work cooperatively and apply the chapter content in the creation of a project. You may choose to use the Chapter 9 Investigation, Progressive Presidents Triptychs, either as a substitute for teaching the section lessons or as an alternate assessment.

BLOCK SCHEDULING 

The teacher lesson plans for each section offer a variety of activity choices to help you present the material in a block scheduling format. For further suggestions on block scheduling, see the *Block Scheduling Handbook with Team Teaching Strategies*, pp. 49–54.

Meeting Individual Needs

ABILITY LEVELS

LEVEL 1 Basic level activities designed for all students encountering new material.

LEVEL 2 Intermediate level activities designed for average students.

LEVEL 3 Challenging activities designed for above-average students.

SHELTERED ENGLISH These activities address the needs of students with Limited English Proficiency.

Internet Connections and Lesson 9
www.si.edu/hrw

CNN Presents America:
Yesterday and Today 1850 to the Present
Segment: FDA on the Lookout

Additional Resources

Books for Teachers

Broderick, Francis L. *Progressivism at Risk: Electing a President in 1912.* Greenwood Press, 1989. Addresses issues surrounding the 1912 presidential election.

Cashman, Sean D. *America in the Age of the Titans.* New York University, 1988. Provides a thorough account of the Progressive Era.

Giese, James R. *The Progressive Era: The Limits of Reform.* 2nd ed. Social Studies Consortium, 1989. Provides a review of progressive reforms.

Books for Students

Cooper, John Milton, Jr. *Pivotal Decades.* Norton, 1990. Reviews historical developments from 1900 to 1920.

Fritz, Jean. *Bully for You, Teddy Roosevelt!* Putnam, 1991. Explores the life of Theodore Roosevelt (for students reading below grade level).

Leavell, Perry. *Woodrow Wilson.* Chelsea House, 1987. Examines Wilson's private and public life.

Multimedia Materials

Theodore Roosevelt. Video, 27 min. Coronet/MTI Films and Video. Photographs and film footage capture scenes from Theodore Roosevelt's life.

The United States in the 20th Century: 1900–1912. Video, 12 min. Coronet Instructional Films. Focuses on the administrations of Roosevelt and Taft.

The United States in the 20th Century: 1912–1920. Video, 12 min. Coronet Instructional Films. Examines the presidency of Woodrow Wilson.

The Progressive Presidents

CHAPTER MOTIVATOR

Ask students to speculate on when and in what circumstances the United States might benefit from a president who allows the nation to follow its own course without government intervention rather than attempting to master, or control, its course through government intervention. Ask students to list whether each president between 1865 and 1900 actively sought government intervention to guide the nation. Tell students that in this chapter they will learn about activist presidents in the early 1900s, their responses to public demand for mastery of the problems arising from rapid industrialization, and their disagreements over government's role in managing change.

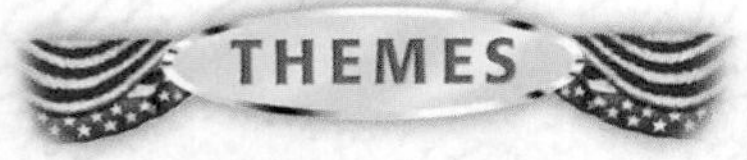

Presenting Themes

- **Economic Development** Students might mention that the government can keep business from getting too powerful by passing laws. Students might also discuss how laws regulating businesses may be designed to protect the health and safety of the nation's citizens.
- **Geographic Diversity** Students might mention that the government can pass laws to protect natural resources, animals, and wilderness areas. For instance, it can set aside land for parks, prohibit businesses from exploiting natural resources in certain areas, or force businesses to clean up after themselves.
- **Citizenship and Democracy** Students might discuss ways that political parties and leaders determine what voters want. For instance, parties and leaders can hold public meetings, take public opinion polls, and read letters sent by voters. Once they have determined what voter's want, politicians can respond by passing laws addressing voters' concerns.

Using the Time Line

Have students use the time line to create an organizational chart. The chart should categorize each law on the time line according to whether it was passed during the Roosevelt, Taft, or Wilson administration.

The Granger Collection, New York

CHAPTER 9

The Progressive Presidents

(1900–1920)

Activist Jane Addams joined other reformers in 1912 at the Progressive Party's national convention in Chicago. She described the mix of social workers, religious leaders, scholars, and politicians: "Suddenly, as if by magic, the city of Chicago became filled with men and women from every state in the Union who [had] . . . like [similar] hopes." These people hoped to create democratic reforms on the national level.

Economic Development
In what ways might a government try to reform business?

Geographic Diversity
How might a nation try to protect the natural environment?

Citizenship and Democracy
How might political parties and political leaders respond to voters' concerns?

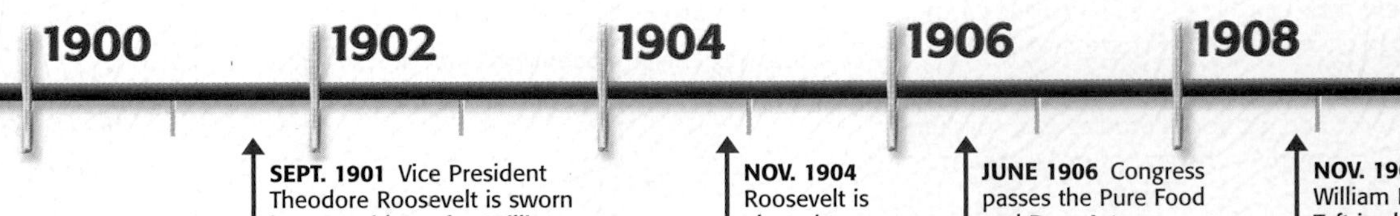

SEPT. 1901 Vice President Theodore Roosevelt is sworn in as president after William McKinley's assassination.

NOV. 1904 Roosevelt is elected to a second term as president.

JUNE 1906 Congress passes the Pure Food and Drug Act.

NOV. 1908 William Howard Taft is elected president.

OBJECTIVES

- **Identify ways that President Roosevelt attempted to balance the needs of both business and labor.**
- **Analyze Roosevelt's attempts to regulate businesses and railroads.**
- **Describe why Roosevelt and others promoted the conservation movement.**

FOCUS

Motivate Before Reading

Ask students to raise their hands if they have ever visited a state or national park. Then, ask them to identify activities that people can participate in when visiting a state or national park. *(Answers will vary but students should identify at least some of the following: hiking, biking, swimming, canoeing, fishing, or picnicking.)* Explain to students that although Theodore Roosevelt did not come up with the

Roosevelt Becomes President

Reading Focus

How did President Roosevelt try to balance the needs of both business and labor?

What did Roosevelt do to regulate businesses and railroads?

Why did Roosevelt and others promote the conservation movement?

Key Terms

arbitration
Square Deal
Pure Food and Drug Act
conservation
National Park Service

THE SUMMER TOUR following President William McKinley's second inauguration in 1901 was filled with friendly crowds eager to shake the president's hand. In September McKinley greeted a group of well-wishers in Buffalo, New York. The event turned to tragedy, however, when anarchist Leon Czolgosz (CHAWL-gawsh) pulled out a pistol and shot the president at point-blank range. As he lay fatally wounded, the president whispered, "My wife, be careful how you tell her—oh be careful!" A little more than a week later, McKinley was dead.

President McKinley is assassinated in 1901.

IMAGE ON LEFT PAGE: *Theodore Roosevelt campaigning for the Progressive Party in 1912*

1910 | 1912 | 1914 | 1916 | 1918

NOV. 1912 Woodrow Wilson is elected president.

FEB. 1913 The Sixteenth Amendment is ratified.

DEC. 1913 The Federal Reserve Act becomes law.

OCT. 1914 Congress passes the Clayton Antitrust Act.

SEPT. 1916 The Keating-Owen Child Labor Act is passed.

Section 1 RESOURCES

PRINT

- ★ Guided Reading Strategies 9.1
- ★ Literature Reading 9: *Sister Carrie*
- ★ American History Political Cartoon 17: The Power of Trusts
- ★ Section 1 Review, p. 271
- ★ Daily Quiz 9.1

MULTIMEDIA

- ★ *Teaching Resources CD–ROM,* Lesson 9.1
- ★ Everyday Life in America Transparency 18: Progressives and Children, Early 1900s
- ★ HRW Web site

SHELTERED ENGLISH

- ★ Main Idea Activities for Reteaching and Sheltered English 9.1

idea of national or state parks, it was under his leadership that millions of acres of public land came under control of the forest service. Tell students that in this section they will learn about this and other achievements that were accomplished under Roosevelt's administration.

Introduce Key Terms

Linguistic, Logical-Mathematical. Review this section's key terms with students. Have students use context cues to determine the significance of each term. Then ask students to write sentences using each of the terms. Call on volunteers to read their sentences to the class. **SHELTERED ENGLISH**

TEACH

Have students read Section 1 and complete Guided Reading Strategies 9.1. Choose one or more of the following activities to explore the section content with students. For further suggestions on block scheduling or team teaching, see the *Block Scheduling Handbook.*

LEVEL 1: Linguistic. (Suggested time: 15 min.) As a class, go over students' Guided Reading Strategies. Then use the Reading Focus questions to highlight the main ideas of the section. **SHELTERED ENGLISH**

Linking Past to Present

The PATCO Strike. In 1981 members of the Professional Air Traffic Controllers Organization (PATCO) went on strike. The air traffic controllers, whose job it was to direct airline traffic, claimed that they were overworked and underpaid. Two days after PATCO went on strike, President Ronald Reagan fired all the striking air traffic controllers and replaced them. To justify his actions, the president pointed to a federal statute that outlawed strikes by federal employees such as air traffic controllers. Union members nationwide protested the president's actions and accused him of being antiunion. The president responded by saying that although he supported unions, the law was the law, and he would not allow it to be broken, even though past presidents had ignored it.

Critical Thinking: Why might President Reagan's reaction to the PATCO strike have differed from President Roosevelt's reaction to the UMW strike?

ANSWER: President Reagan was responding to a strike dealing with federal workers prohibited from striking, while Roosevelt was dealing with a private union. The Air Traffic Controllers strike put Americans in immediate danger, while the United Mine Workers strike only would have been a problem if it had lasted a long time.

Roosevelt's Path to the Presidency

After President McKinley's assassination in early September 1901, Vice President Theodore Roosevelt took the oath of office. At age 42 he was the youngest man ever to become president.

Roosevelt was greatly influenced by his father, who taught him to be hardworking and fair-minded. Although Roosevelt came from a wealthy family, he was sympathetic to the problems of the less fortunate. After graduating from Harvard University, Roosevelt became a politician, serving in the New York state legislature. He earned a reputation for being a moderate reformer with a stubborn streak. During an early dispute with other members of the Republican Party, Roosevelt once declared:

> **"I would rather go out of politics having the feeling that I had done what was right than stay in . . . knowing in my heart that I had acted as I ought not to."**

Roosevelt's early political career was successful, but the death of his first wife, Alice Lee, in 1884 was a great blow to him. "The light has gone out of my life," he wrote. Leaving politics, he moved west to the Dakotas, where he ran a ranch for several years. While there, he transformed himself into a rugged outdoorsman. Roosevelt then returned to politics, eventually serving as governor of New York. He was chosen to run as McKinley's vice presidential candidate in 1900. He also remarried, this time to childhood friend Edith Carow.

Theodore Roosevelt served as assistant secretary of the navy in 1897 and 1898.

The Granger Collection, New York

Although he promised Republican leaders that he would "continue, absolutely unbroken, the policy of President McKinley," Roosevelt quickly made his own mark on the nation. Unlike most of the Gilded Age presidents, who had seen themselves more as administrators, Roosevelt believed the president should be an active leader. He pushed for his legislation to be passed and aggressively used his executive powers. He also tried to be responsive to public opinion.

A 1902 cartoon that showed Roosevelt saving a bear cub inspired the first Teddy Bear.

 Labor and Business

President Roosevelt believed that the interests of business, labor, and consumers should be balanced in order to protect the public good. In his opinion, if any one group gained too much power, it might take unfair advantage of the others.

Coal Miners Strike

President Roosevelt demonstrated his beliefs in his response to a Pennsylvania coal miners' strike in 1902. Coal mine operators had refused to meet the demands of the United Mine Workers for better pay, an eight-hour workday, and acceptance of their union. In May more than 150,000 miners went on strike in protest throughout Pennsylvania's vast coalfields.

The strike lasted several months, leading to coal shortages and rising prices. Roosevelt declared that the strike had "become a matter of vital concern to the whole nation" because it threatened to leave the country without heating fuel in the coming winter. He argued that as president it was his responsibility to become involved in the dispute.

Many of the mine owners believed that Roosevelt would send the U.S. Army into Pennsylvania to force the strikers back to work. Instead, Roosevelt brought the strikers and managers together for **arbitration**, a formal meeting to discuss and settle disagreements.

ALL LEVELS: Visual-Spatial, Intrapersonal. (Suggested time: 45 min.) Discuss early conservation efforts with the class. Then have each student create a poster that illustrates the impact of President Roosevelt's conservation policies. Ask students to design their posters to express support either for preservationists, such as John Muir, or conservationists, such as Gifford Pinchot. Call on volunteers to explain their work to the class. **SHELTERED ENGLISH**

ALL LEVELS: Linguistic, Logical-Mathematical. (Suggested time: 30 min.) Have students list disputes between business and labor that occurred during President Roosevelt's administration. For each instance, have students describe the actions that President Roosevelt took and state whether his actions favored business or labor or were neutral. Call on volunteers to describe incidents, explain President Roosevelt's actions, and state whether they favored either party. Allow other students to offer feedback on their classmates' statements. **SHELTERED ENGLISH**

To get both sides to agree to arbitration, Roosevelt threatened to have the federal government take over the mines if the two groups did not cooperate. As a result of the negotiations, the strike was settled and the crisis ended in time to supply coal to the nation for the winter.

The Square Deal

President Roosevelt's actions broke with the traditional presidential approach to labor disputes. In the past, presidents had either refused to become involved or had sided against labor. Roosevelt's actions helped the efforts of labor unions to bargain with management. In 1903 Roosevelt described his approach during the strike as part of a program to treat every citizen fairly, a plan he called the **Square Deal**. He promised:

> **"The labor unions shall have a square deal, and the corporations shall have a square deal, and in addition all private citizens shall have a square deal."**

When some critics questioned whether Roosevelt's Square Deal was going to interfere with competition, he explained, "I do not mean . . . it is possible to give every man the best hand. . . . All I mean is that there shall not be any crookedness in the dealing." The Square Deal soon became a key part of Roosevelt's political program.

Roosevelt Takes on the Trusts

President Roosevelt made regulating trusts one of the most important goals of his administration. He later recalled, "The absolutely vital question was whether the government had power to control them at all." He believed that it did.

Roosevelt accepted that the economic changes that occurred during the Second Industrial Revolution had encouraged the growth of large corporations and trusts. While many progressives believed that all trusts were threats to fair competition, Roosevelt argued instead that there were "good" trusts and "bad" trusts. According to Roosevelt, a good trust was efficient and provided consumers with needed products and services at reasonable prices. A bad trust, however, restricted trade unfairly and used its influence to charge high prices. Roosevelt's goal was to shut down the bad trusts but to allow the good ones to stay in business.

The first bad trust that Roosevelt tackled was the Northern Securities Company, an enormous corporation that had a monopoly on the major railroad lines in the Northwest. In 1902 he ordered the Justice Department to prosecute this powerful trust under the Sherman Antitrust Act. The influential businessman J. P. Morgan, an executive of

Theodore Roosevelt

Theodore Roosevelt was born into a wealthy family in New York City in 1858. Despite his privileged upbringing, Roosevelt believed that his success came as a result of his hard work. As a boy, he suffered from severe asthma and poor eyesight. "I was nervous and timid," Roosevelt remembered.

At the age of 11, however, he began improving his health through exercise and outdoor activities. His asthma got better and he became a strong and confident young man. Roosevelt was very energetic and always seemed to be rushing from one task to the next. He was impatient with anyone who could not keep up with his rapid pace. Reporter Lincoln Steffens once wrote about Roosevelt, "He took joy in everything he did, in hunting, camping, in ranching, in politics, in reforming the police or the civil service."

At the age of 55 Roosevelt still had an adventurous spirit. As he explained about a trip to the jungles of Brazil, "I had just one more chance to be a boy, and I took it!"

Presidential Profiles

Theodore Roosevelt and the American West. In 1884 Theodore Roosevelt headed west to live on a ranch in the Dakota Territory. Following the deaths of his wife and mother and a failed run for the presidency in the election of 1884, Roosevelt told a friend that his political career was over. He had decided to head west to become a cowboy. Roosevelt spent three years in the Badlands of Dakota, one of the roughest parts of the country. His western experience changed his life. Living in the West contributed to his love of nature. Roosevelt believed that, like physical exercise, living close to nature made him a better person. As one of Roosevelt's guides noted of the transformation, "He was a Westerner at heart." The influence of his western experience can be seen throughout his later political career.

Activity: Have students review the section to find aspects of Theodore Roosevelt's presidency that were most likely influenced by his years in the Badlands.

LEVEL 2: Linguistic, Logical-Mathematical, Interpersonal. (Suggested time: 45 min.) Organize the class into small groups and assign each group one of the following topics: the United Mine Workers strike, the *Northern Securities* case, conservation, or Roosevelt and the muckrakers. Have each group create a newspaper headline for its assigned topic. Then ask groups to exchange headlines. Have each group list details that might be included in a newspaper article covering the topic. Then ask each group to exchange the headlines a second time. This time, have groups write stories incorporating the details supplied by the previous groups. After a third and final exchange between groups, ask the receiving group to critique the accuracy of the story itself.

LEVEL 3: Logical-Mathematical, Interpersonal. (Suggested time: 30 min. plus homework) For homework, have students work in pairs to construct a dialog between President Roosevelt and J. P. Morgan on the president's intention to prosecute the Northern Securities Company for violating the Sherman Antitrust Act. The dialog should reveal these historical figures' differing points of view regarding the Sherman Antitrust Act and the role of the federal government in regulating the conduct of giant business combinations. Have two students act out their dialog for the class, then invite students to compare and contrast it with their own dialogs.

Economic Development

J. P. Morgan. By the time of the *Northern Securities* case, J. P. Morgan had already proved to be one of the most influential business leaders in the United States. He had shown his willingness to help the U.S. economy develop. In the 1870s he used his connections to become a leading source of government financing and to provide the nation's businesses with the capital they needed to grow. Following the Panic of 1893, when the U.S. government's gold reserve was running low, Morgan helped organize an effort to resupply the gold reserve with $62 million in gold.

Critical Thinking: Given J. P. Morgan's contributions to the U.S. economy, why do you think he was outraged by the Supreme Court's decision in the *Northern Securities* case?

ANSWER: He had done so much to help the economy that he probably believed that the U.S. government should not interfere in his business.

Multimedia Resources

Everyday Life in America Transparency 18: Progressives and Children, Early 1900s

THE LION-TAMER

President Roosevelt, the trustbuster, taming powerful businesses

Northern Securities, was shocked at Roosevelt's action. He visited the White House and told the president, "If we have done anything wrong, send your man to my man and they can fix it up."

Roosevelt refused Morgan's offer, insisting that every citizen, rich or poor, had to obey the law. In 1904 the U.S. Supreme Court narrowly upheld the Sherman Antitrust Act and then dissolved Northern Securities. The Court's decision sent a warning to large corporations. Roosevelt followed this victory by supporting legislation that regulated the railroads and their shipping rates. Such actions gained Roosevelt a reputation as a trustbuster, even though his administration did not actually attack a large number of trusts.

The 1904 Election

Roosevelt faced the 1904 presidential election with some concern. Although he had strong public support, his antitrust efforts had angered powerful business leaders. Some Americans also feared his expansion of the federal government's powers and disapproved of government interference in the economic system. The Democrats chose former New York judge Alton Parker to run against Roosevelt. Parker accused Roosevelt of being a radical. Former president Grover Cleveland declared that the Democrats were filled with "hope and confidence" at their chances of winning the election.

The Republicans began a well-organized campaign to promote their candidate across the country. Roosevelt was already an expert at dealing with the press because he had met regularly with reporters throughout his first term. His witty and direct manner of speaking charmed the public and helped him become a widely recognized figure. By contrast, Parker was neither well known nor a gifted speaker. The result was a huge victory in November 1904 for Roosevelt and his Square Deal platform of equal opportunity and reform.

Roosevelt and the Muckrakers

In some cases, public pressure forced President Roosevelt to seek reform. Newspaper and magazine articles by muckraking journalists helped raise public awareness of problems within the food and drug industries. The American Medical Association also called for better food standards and proper labeling. Nevertheless, Congress resisted the pressure to pass reforms.

The turning point came in 1906 when muckraker Upton Sinclair published *The Jungle*, a novel that exposed the practices of the meatpacking industry. The book's vivid descriptions of spoiled meat being packed and sold to consumers shocked readers, including Roosevelt.

He responded to the public outcry by launching a federal investigation. His report concluded that

> **"the stockyards and packing houses are not kept even reasonably clean, and . . . the method of handling and preparing food products is uncleanly and dangerous to health."**

Although he did not get the strict regulation that he wanted, Roosevelt persuaded Congress to pass the **Pure Food and Drug Act** in June 1906.

CLOSE

Visual-Spatial, Logical-Mathematical, Intrapersonal. Have each student design a commemorative medal to be awarded to future citizens whose public conduct exemplifies the attitudes and values exhibited by Theodore Roosevelt. Ask students to create a brief speech to accompany the award. Encourage students to use examples from the section to describe President Roosevelt's actions. Call on volunteers to display their designs and explain the symbolism of their medals to the class. Display students' work around the classroom.

CHALLENGE AND EXTEND

1. **Logical-Mathematical, Interpersonal.** Organize the class into four groups. Have them use the library and other resources to investigate the early twentieth-century dispute over a proposed dam and reservoir in the Hetch Hetchy Valley, designed to provide San Francisco with a new water supply. Have students investigate the circumstances in which the dispute arose, various options that were considered, the conflict between conservationists and others, and the conflict among conservationists. Then ask students to imagine that they are involved in a meeting of a congressional committee. The question

American Literature

The Jungle

Upton Sinclair

Upton Sinclair wrote The Jungle *to create sympathy for the conditions under which immigrants lived and worked. Readers were shocked by his descriptions of the unsanitary practices in the meatpacking industry. Sinclair later said about Americans' reaction, "I aimed at the public's heart, and by accident I hit it in the stomach." In the following excerpt from* The Jungle, *the Rudkus family describes conditions at a Chicago meat plant.*

Meat sales dropped after The Jungle *was published.*

The family had a first-hand knowledge of the great majority of Packingtown swindles. For it was the custom, as they found, whenever meat was so spoiled that it could not be used for anything else, either to can it or else to chop it up into sausage. . . .

Jonas had told them how the meat that was taken out of pickle [vinegar solution] would often be found sour, and how they would rub it up with soda to take away the smell, and sell it to be eaten on free-lunch counters; also of all the miracles of chemistry which they performed, giving to any sort of meat, fresh or salted, whole or chopped, any color and any flavor and any odor they chose. . . .

It was only when the whole ham was spoiled that it came into the department of Elzbieta. . . . Mixed with half a ton of other meat, no odor that ever was in a ham could make any difference. There was never the least attention paid to what was cut up for sausage; there would come all the way back from Europe old sausage that had been rejected. . . . There would be meat that had tumbled out on the floor, in the dirt and sawdust, where the workers had tramped and spit uncounted billions of . . . germs. There would be meat stored in great piles in rooms; and the water from leaky roofs would drip over it, and thousands of rats would race about on it. This is no fairy story.

Understanding Literature

1. What happened to spoiled meat?
2. Why do you think *The Jungle* led to new health laws?

This act prohibited the manufacture, sale, or transportation of mislabeled or contaminated food and drugs sold in interstate commerce. Congress also passed the Meat Inspection Act, which required inspections of meat plants.

Roosevelt was not always in favor of the muckrakers' work. "Men with the muck rake are often indispensable [vital] to the well-being of society, but only if they know when to stop raking the muck," he once commented. Nonetheless, the articles written by muckrakers helped generate public support for Roosevelt's expansion of the federal government's regulatory powers. His activism set a standard for later progressive presidents. At the same time, though, Roosevelt's reform efforts increased the tension within the Republican Party between progressive and traditional Republicans.

Across the Curriculum

LITERATURE

Upton Sinclair. On assignment for *The Appeal to Reason,* a socialist weekly, Upton Sinclair went undercover as a laborer in the slaughterhouses of Chicago. His task was to expose the horrific working conditions of the meatpacking industry. After seven weeks, Sinclair returned to New Jersey to write about what he had seen. He presented his exposé in the form of a fictional story about a Slavic immigrant family. The story appeared serially in the weekly, and gained wide acclaim. Nonetheless, five book publishers rejected the novel as too controversial. Only after some 12,000 readers of the serial sent in orders for advance copies of the book, was it published.

Activity: Have students use the library and other resources to write a biography of Upton Sinclair. Call on a volunteer to read his or her biography to the class.

American Literature Answers

1. It was either canned or chopped up for sausage.
2. Answers will vary but students might mention that most people had been unaware of conditions in the meatpacking industry and thus demanded reform once they found out.

before the committee is whether to recommend adoption or rejection of a proposed bill to permit construction of the reservoir on land protected as part of Yosemite National Park. Have two groups of students provide expert testimony (including charts, maps, statistics, and other visual evidence) to the committee. Have one group attempt to push for construction, and the other against it. Ask a third group to serve as committee members who obtain facts from individuals giving testimony, clarify issues, and finally vote whether to recommend passage of the bill. The fourth group will work as reporters to prepare newspaper articles that detail the debate and explain the committee's vote to the public.

2. Linguistic, Visual-Spatial, Interpersonal. Larry Couser of Corpus Christi, Texas, suggested the following activity: Organize the class into four groups. Assign each group a block of time. You can limit the activity to this section or extend it to span the entire chapter. Provide students with markers, felt tip pens, and butcher paper. Ask the groups to use the textbook to create a time line of the important events and issues for their assigned block of time. Each group should then fill the

Geographic Diversity

The Sierra Club. In 1892 John Muir helped organize the Sierra Club. During his 22 years as its president, Muir watched the Sierra Club grow into one of the most influential environmental organizations in the United States. At first, the Sierra Club focused on organizing camping trips. However, the club became increasingly involved in efforts to preserve America's wilderness. One of its earliest efforts involved a campaign to stop the construction of a dam in Yosemite's Hetch Hetchy Valley. While the club failed to stop construction of the dam, the campaign inspired members to devote more time to preserving national parks and wilderness areas. Over the years, the Sierra Club has helped save many wilderness areas. Its efforts continue to protect our country's environment.

Activity: Have students use the library or search the Internet through the HRW Web site to find more information on the National Park Service. Then ask them to write a paragraph on a national park they would like to visit or have already visited.

go.hrw.com
SB1 National Parks

MAP ANSWER

Olympic, Mt. Rainier, and North Cascades National Parks

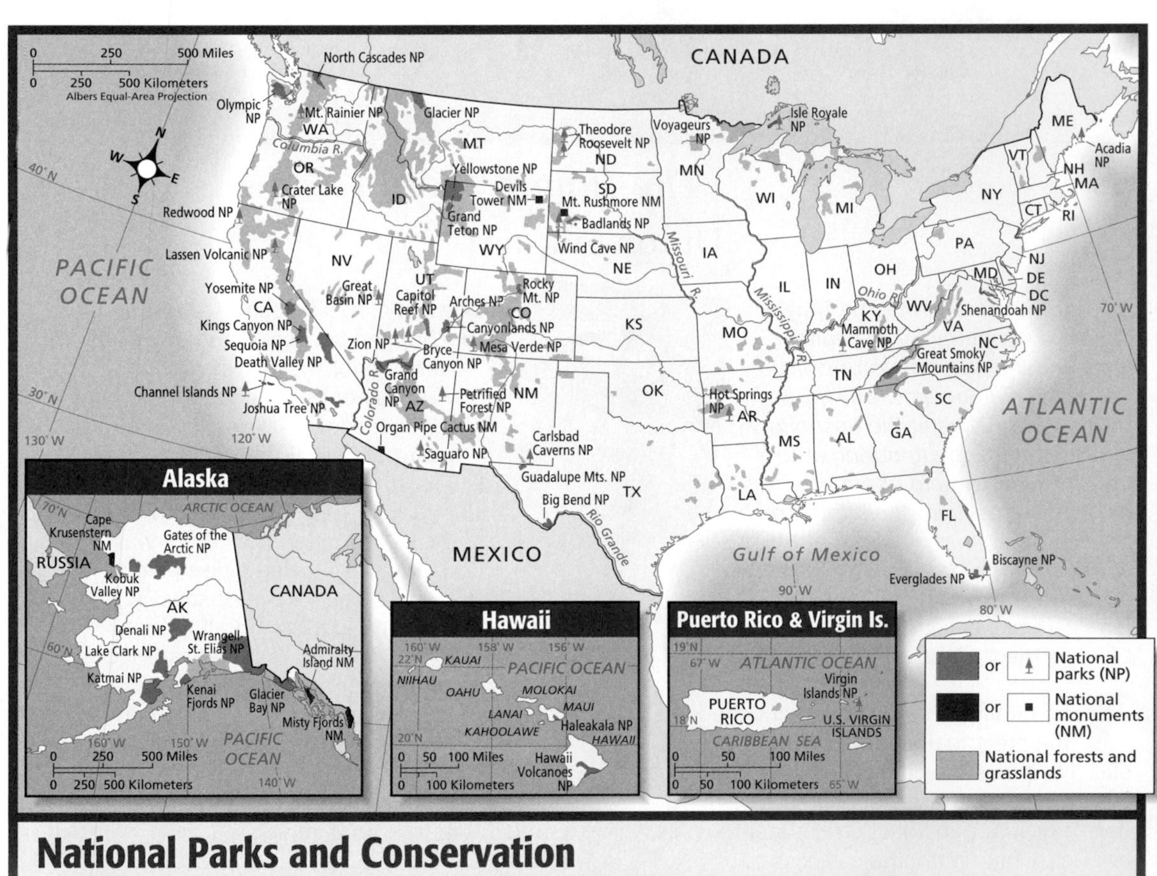

National Parks and Conservation

Learning from Maps In 1872 Yellowstone National Park became the first national park in the United States. Since that time 54 national parks have been added to the system.

Location What national parks are located in Washington State?

Conservation

One reform effort of great personal importance to President Roosevelt was the **conservation** movement, or the effort to protect nature and its resources. Roosevelt had been interested in nature for many years. As a boy he read many books on birds and wildlife and often spent hours in the American Museum of Natural History, which his father had helped found. Later in life he became an eager hunter and birdwatcher. Roosevelt's love of the outdoors made him the first president to consider conservation an important issue.

There were two different points of view among the members of the conservation movement. Those calling themselves preservationists believed that nature should be preserved because of its beauty. Many preservationists, such as John Muir and Charles Sargent, argued that the remaining ancient forests of the West should be completely protected from logging and enjoyed as an unspoiled part of nature. Muir wrote:

> **"Thousands of tired, nerve-shaken, over-civilized people are beginning to find out that going to the mountains is going home; that wildness is a necessity; and that mountain parks and reservations are useful not only as fountains of timber and irrigating rivers, but as fountains of life."**

Muir became a widely respected forest expert and a leader of the conservation movement.

remaining space with other details about its time period. When students are through, combine the sections to form a class time line.

REVIEW

Linguistic, Logical-Mathematical. Have students complete the Section Review questions. Ask each student to write a one-page outline explaining how President Roosevelt's actions support his concept of a square deal. Call on volunteers to use their outlines to explain their findings to the class. Invite comments from others regarding the accuracy and insight of the outlines.

ASSESS

Have students complete Daily Quiz 9.1.

RETEACH

Visual-Spatial, Interpersonal. Have students complete Main Idea Activities for Reteaching and Sheltered English 9.1. Then organize the class into groups and have each judge the success or failure of President Roosevelt in meeting the needs of business and labor, regulating businesses and railroads, or promoting conservation. Have each group prepare a visual organizer to report its conclusion to the rest of the class. **SHELTERED ENGLISH**

Other members of the conservation movement were more concerned with conserving the natural resources of the United States. Known as conservationists, this group wanted to manage the use of these natural resources more efficiently. "Forestry is the art of using a forest without destroying it," Chief of Forestry Gifford Pinchot (PIN-shoh) declared. He argued that forests should not be preserved simply "because they are beautiful," but more importantly because they produced the materials necessary to build "prosperous homes."

President Roosevelt meets with preservationist John Muir at Yosemite Valley, California, site of the first national park.

Despite their different opinions on how people should interact with nature, preservationists and conservationists fought together to establish national and state parks on public lands. They also pushed for the foundation of wildlife refuges to protect endangered animals. Roosevelt supported these measures, stating, "We are not building this country of ours for a day." He hoped that parks could provide "rest, health, and recreation" for the American people for many years to come.

By 1870 millions of acres of federal lands had already been sold or given to private mining, logging, and railroad companies. These companies opposed the efforts made during the Progressive Era to conserve federal land. When Roosevelt took office, only 46 million acres of land had been set aside as national reserves.

Roosevelt took advantage of a federal law that allowed the president to set aside forest land. During his administration nearly 150 million acres of public land moved under the control of the Forest Service. These lands were equal in size to Great Britain and France combined. Roosevelt also doubled the number of national parks, created 16 national monuments, and established 51 wildlife refuges. This newly protected territory included the Grand Canyon and the Petrified Forest in Arizona and Zion in Utah. To help supervise the growing number of parks and monuments, the **National Park Service** was created in 1916. The National Park system has continued to expand with the addition of new land and services, as well as the establishment of urban parks.

SECTION 1 REVIEW

Identify and explain the significance of the following:

- **Theodore Roosevelt**
- **arbitration**
- **Square Deal**
- **Pure Food and Drug Act**
- **conservation**
- **National Park Service**

Locate and explain the importance of the following:

- **Grand Canyon**
- **Zion**

Reading for Content Understanding

1. **Main Idea** How did President Theodore Roosevelt try to help business and labor?
2. **Main Idea** What actions did Roosevelt take against corporations and railroads?
3. **Geographic Diversity** *Human-Environment Interaction* Why did supporters of the conservation movement want to protect America's natural resources?
4. **Writing** *Persuading* Imagine that you are a Republican Party leader. Write a brief essay arguing for or against Roosevelt's reform efforts. Give examples to support your argument.
5. **Critical Thinking** *Evaluating* Why might people have called Theodore Roosevelt an "activist president"?

Section 1 Review ANSWERS

Identify

For significance, see the following pages:

- Theodore Roosevelt, p. 266
- arbitration, p. 266
- Square Deal, p. 267
- Pure Food and Drug Act, p. 268
- conservation, p. 270
- National Park Service, p. 271

Locate

For locations, see the map on page 270.

Reading for Content Understanding

1. His Square Deal aimed to treat both business and labor fairly, and he threatened that the federal government would take over the mines if strikers and managers in the United Mine Workers strike did not agree to arbitration.

2. He ordered the Justice Department to prosecute trusts that restricted trade unfairly and supported legislation designed to regulate railroads.

3. Preservationists wanted to preserve nature's beauty, while other members of the movement sought to conserve resources.

4. Answers will vary but students should take a position regarding Roosevelt's policies and give examples from the section to support their arguments.

5. Unlike most presidents of the era, he believed that presidential power should be used aggressively, a belief he practiced when he promoted legislation such as the Pure Food and Drug Act and pushed for arbitration during the UMW strike.

OBJECTIVES

- Identify how William Howard Taft's administration was similar to and different from Roosevelt's administration.
- Analyze the progressives' reasons for turning against President Taft.
- Describe events that took place during the 1912 election.

FOCUS

Motivate Before Reading

Explain to students that Theodore Roosevelt decided not to seek re-election in 1908, and instead persuaded the Republican Party to nominate Secretary of War William Howard Taft. Ask students to imagine that they are President Roosevelt and write a letter to William Howard Taft, explaining what the former president expects of his successor. When they have finished the letters, tell

Section 2
RESOURCES

PRINT

- ★ Guided Reading Strategies 9.2
- ★ Primary Source Reading 9: 1912 Election
- ★ Biography Reading 9: William Jennings Bryan
- ★ Geography Activity 9: The 1904 and 1912 Presidential Elections
- ★ Section 2 Review, p. 277
- ★ Daily Quiz 9.2

MULTIMEDIA

- ★ *Teaching Resources CD–ROM*, Lesson 9.2

SHELTERED ENGLISH

- ★ Main Idea Activities for Reteaching and Sheltered English 9.2

The Taft Administration

Reading Focus

How was William Howard Taft's administration similar to and different from Roosevelt's administration?

Why did progressives turn against President Taft?

What events took place during the election of 1912?

Key Terms

Payne-Aldrich Tariff
New Nationalism
Bull Moose Party
New Freedom

THEODORE ROOSEVELT DECLARED in 1904 that he would not run for a third term in 1908. Many people doubted him, however, and Roosevelt grew upset with the rumors that he would run again for president. In early 1908 he told his press secretary that a new candidate needed to be chosen, saying, "We had better turn to Taft." William Howard Taft was secretary of war and a good friend of Roosevelt. When the press secretary brought him the news, Taft said in surprise, "I must go over and thank Theodore." When Taft arrived, Roosevelt encouraged him, saying, "Yes, Will, it's the thing to do."

The Granger Collection, New York

President William Howard Taft

William Howard Taft

President Roosevelt was confident that Taft was a responsible leader and the best choice to continue the Square Deal. "There will be no backward step under Taft," he assured one supporter during the 1908 election.

The Reluctant President

Taft was born in Ohio in 1857. His family was moderately wealthy and his parents pushed him to pursue a legal career. After graduating second in his class at Yale, Taft completed law school and went on to hold a variety of appointed government offices. He spent eight years serving as a U.S. Circuit Court judge and found the judiciary to be his true calling. "I love judges, and I love courts," he said on one occasion. His greatest ambition was not to become president but to be appointed to the U.S. Supreme Court and serve as chief justice.

Taft disliked political campaigns, and only Roosevelt's encouragement persuaded him to run students that in this section they will learn about Taft's presidential years, the growing split between Taft and Roosevelt, and the presidential election of 1912.

Introduce Key Terms

Linguistic, Logical-Mathematical. Review this section's key terms with students. Have them use context cues to write a definition for each term. Then ask students to decide which term least fits with the others and to explain why. *(Students should conclude that the Payne-Aldrich Tariff is the only term that does not directly pertain to the election of 1912.)* **SHELTERED ENGLISH**

TEACH

Have students read Section 2 and complete Guided Reading Strategies 9.2. Choose one or more of the following activities to explore the section content with students. For further suggestions on block scheduling or team teaching, see the *Block Scheduling Handbook.*

LEVEL 1: Linguistic. (Suggested time: 15 min.) As a class, go over students' Guided Reading Strategies. Then use the Reading Focus questions to highlight the main ideas of the section. **SHELTERED ENGLISH**

for president. "A national campaign for the presidency is to me a nightmare," he once admitted. With Roosevelt's support and advice, however, Taft overcame his lack of campaign experience. He then easily defeated progressive Democrat William Jennings Bryan in the November 1908 election. Many pro-business Republicans were pleased with the election results because they believed Taft would be easier to work with than Roosevelt.

Taft and Roosevelt

Despite their friendship, Taft and Roosevelt had different personalities and different ideas about the role of the president. While Roosevelt was a skilled public speaker who enjoyed public attention, Taft often gave his speeches without enthusiasm. Unlike Roosevelt, Taft avoided the press and did not like to be interviewed by reporters. Although he was a friendly and polite man, Taft often seemed stiff and awkward in public.

Politically, Taft supported the regulation of big business and promised to continue Roosevelt's reform policies. Whereas Roosevelt had often acted swiftly in response to public concerns, however, Taft was more cautious. Most importantly, Taft thought that Roosevelt had claimed too much presidential power and had too often gone beyond the letter of the law. Taft felt strongly that the law, not personal beliefs or public opinion, should control the actions of the government and the president. For these reasons he was opposed to progressive reforms such as the recall, which he felt gave the voters too much power. Taft also believed that the government should not interfere too much in society. He explained his views:

> **"There is a line beyond which government cannot go with any good practical results in seeking to make men and society better."**

William Howard Taft and his wife, Helen, traveling to his inauguration

Taft Angers the Progressives

Supporters hoped that Taft's honesty and sense of duty would overcome his lack of experience in holding an elected office. Just before Taft took office, Roosevelt told one reporter, "He's [Taft is] all right, he means well, and he'll do his best." Even so, President Taft soon disappointed the progressive Republicans who had been so loyal to Roosevelt.

Reforms Under Taft

Taft replaced many of the members of Roosevelt's cabinet with corporate lawyers. Progressives claimed that these new cabinet members would be too pro-business to support reform. Taft argued that he needed their business experience and legal advice.

Taft started 90 antitrust lawsuits—more than double the number initiated by Roosevelt. These included lawsuits against the corporate giants U.S. Steel and International Harvester. Such court battles were lengthy and there was no guarantee that the government would win its cases against the trusts. One of the biggest antitrust victories for the Taft administration was the case against Standard Oil, which had begun during Roosevelt's administration.

Despite this victory, many progressives wanted bolder action from Taft. Some progressives, such as William Jennings Bryan and Robert La Follette, wanted new laws that would eliminate the trusts entirely.

Using Visual Resources

Taft's Inauguration. Helen Taft—seen on this page escorting her husband to the inauguration—was eager to replace Edith Roosevelt as first lady. The night before the inauguration, the capital was hit by an ice and snowstorm, which helped pave the way for a first in women's history. As part of the inaugural ceremonies, the outgoing president had traditionally rode along with the newly elected president on the ride from the Capitol Rotunda to the reviewing stand. However, weather conditions were so bad that Roosevelt decided not to accompany Taft on the ride. Taking Roosevelt's place, the new first lady accompanied her husband on the ride. She later recalled, "Perhaps I had a little secret elation in thinking that I was doing something which no woman had ever done before."

Activity: Have students use the library and other resources to find information on firsts in the history of first ladies. Have each student choose a first and write a brief article on the event.

ALL LEVELS: Linguistic, Logical-Mathematical, Visual-Spatial. (Suggested time: 30 min.) Ask each student to design a bumper sticker for one of the parties in the election of 1912. You may wish to assign each student a specific party to represent. Each sticker should support a major issue supported by the party. Then have students create a bulletin board display of all of their bumper stickers. Finally, lead a class discussion on the similarities and differences between the platforms and have students vote to determine which candidate they would have supported.
SHELTERED ENGLISH

LEVEL 2: Linguistic, Logical-Mathematical. (Suggested time: 45 min. plus homework) Ask students to imagine that they are political analysts covering the 1912 presidential election. Have them create headlines along with one-paragraph articles that describe each significant event and issue that served to divide the Republican Party. Then have students write an editorial explaining how they think the Republican split will affect the 1912 presidential election. Call on volunteers to share their articles with the class. Finally, lead a discussion on the actual results of the election.

Economic Development

The Payne-Aldrich Tariff. During the debate over the Payne-Aldrich Tariff, many Americans supported Taft's attempts to lower tariffs, largely because the cost of living was at the second-highest level in the nation's history. However, after the bill passed, many people felt that the new tariff did nothing to help lower duties, in part because regional economic differences hurt the president's efforts to lower them. For instance, Taft was unable to lower duties on wool, cotton, and industrial products because senators from eastern and western states banded together to defeat the proposed decrease.

Critical Thinking: Why might people from a specific region oppose lower tariffs on certain products?

ANSWER: High tariffs might prevent lower-priced foreign goods from outselling a region's main products.

Senator Nelson Aldrich and his tariff are defeated by public opinion as President Taft watches in concern.

Taft's inability to push such laws through Congress disappointed them. Business leaders, who had been some of Taft's strongest supporters, were also angry at the administration's prosecution of their companies. Taft believed that he was doing his duty by following the existing antitrust laws. He therefore ignored complaints from both sides on the issue.

Roosevelt watched Taft's actions with concern. He claimed that Taft was failing to distinguish between good and bad trusts and was hurting the U.S. economy in the process. Roosevelt wanted a special commission created to help regulate big business without filing so many lawsuits.

The Tariff

Another major issue that separated Taft from the progressives was the tariff. Many Republicans favored the existing high tariff rates. These made imported goods more expensive and thus helped protect American industries from foreign competition. Progressives and many Democrats believed that the high tariff made the cost of living too expensive for most Americans. Some people also argued that the tariff hurt the ability of American businesses to sell goods overseas. Roosevelt had avoided dealing with the tariff question during his terms in office because it was so complicated. Taft, however, had promised during his campaign that he would lead a fight to lower the tariff rates.

Taft's inexperience in dealing with Congress hurt his efforts to push for any significant tariff reduction. The **Payne-Aldrich Tariff**, passed in 1909, reduced many tariffs but raised others. It was criticized by progressive Republicans and by Democrats.

In a speech Taft responded to his critics by insisting that the Payne-Aldrich Tariff was "the best tariff bill that the Republican Party ever passed." This claim quickly drew an angry reaction from many people in the Midwest. The new tariff had hurt local industries there while providing little relief on the price of goods.

A Conservation Controversy

President Taft often felt misunderstood by the public. Perhaps the greatest public relations disaster of Taft's administration occurred in his battle with Roosevelt's close friend and ally, Chief of Forestry Gifford Pinchot. In 1909 Pinchot accused Secretary of the Interior Richard Ballinger of hurting conservation efforts by siding with the interests of big business and by leasing public lands. Taft tried without success to get the two officials to settle their differences quietly. Pinchot continued to attack Ballinger, and the issue began to attract national attention.

The Ballinger-Pinchot controversy soon turned into a public debate over whether Taft truly supported conservation as strongly as Roosevelt had. Taft was embarrassed by the situation and convinced that the charges made against Ballinger were unfounded. Taft finally decided to fire Pinchot. This act outraged conservationists and many other progressives, including Roosevelt. Taft defended himself, saying:

The Granger Collection, New York
Gifford Pinchot

> **"If I were to turn Ballinger out, in view of his innocence and in view of the conspiracy against him, I should be a white-livered skunk."**

LEVEL 3: Linguistic, Interpersonal. (Suggested time: 30 min. plus homework) Ask students to imagine that they voted for Taft out of allegiance to Roosevelt but are now unhappy with Taft's presidency. Have students write letters to President Taft telling him why they are displeased with his policies and describing actions they think Roosevelt would have taken if he were still president. Ask students to identify specific policies and actions mentioned in the section as examples of what displeases them. Call on students to read their letters to the class and explain why they objected to Taft's policies and actions. Finally, lead a discussion on the similarities and differences between the Roosevelt and Taft administrations and the reasons many progressives turned against Taft.

CLOSE

Visual-Spatial, Logical-Mathematical. Have each student create a flowchart that illustrates the sequence of events that led to Woodrow Wilson's victory in the 1912 presidential election. Have students begin with Roosevelt's recommendation of Taft in the 1908 election. Ask students to include events that caused the break between Roosevelt and Taft, led to the creation of the Bull Moose Party, and resulted in Wilson's victory. Have volunteers explain their flowcharts to the class.

President Taft balances awkwardly as he tries to satisfy both sides during the Ballinger-Pinchot affair.

Congress launched an investigation of Ballinger that resulted in no official charges but which made Taft's administration look worse to many conservationists. Taft was unable to win back progressive support, even though he expanded many of Roosevelt's conservation policies. He also transferred almost as much land into government reserves as Roosevelt had.

Roosevelt and the Progressive Party

As the election of 1912 neared, President Taft seemed to be losing much public support. The Republicans had already lost control of the House of Representatives in 1910, which shocked many party leaders.

The New Nationalism

Roosevelt had remained politically active and continued to develop his political philosophy. He expressed his views in a plan for government called the **New Nationalism**. This program called for a strong executive, more active business regulation, and the passage of additional social welfare measures. In 1910 Roosevelt described his new plan for government:

> **"The New Nationalism puts the national need before sectional or personal advantage. This New Nationalism regards the executive power [the president] as the steward of the public welfare. It demands of the judiciary that it shall be interested primarily in human welfare rather than property, just as it demands that the representative body [Congress] shall represent all the people rather than any one class of or section of the people."**

Taft was greatly angered by Roosevelt's speech, which he felt insulted the judiciary system and Taft's own antitrust efforts. He began working to reduce Roosevelt's influence in the Republican Party by seeking support from traditional Republicans. Many of these Republicans agreed that Roosevelt had gone too far with his support of government involvement in business and society.

The division between Taft and Roosevelt grew wider. Roosevelt told his oldest son that Taft "has not the slightest idea of what is necessary if this country is to make social and industrial progress." Many progressives agreed with Roosevelt. In 1912, nine Republican governors sent him a letter asking him to run for an unprecedented third term. Roosevelt knew that if he ran again he would be criticized but he agreed anyway. A reporter asked Roosevelt if the rumors about his candidacy were true. "My hat is in the ring!" Roosevelt replied. "The fight is on."

The Bull Moose Party

Roosevelt and his supporters rapidly put together a campaign

A button and bull moose pendant from the presidential campaign

Geographic Diversity

President Taft's Conservation Policies. After firing Gifford Pinchot, President Taft lost the support of many conservationists. However, during his administration, more than 80 million acres of land were set aside for conservation, and he received congressional approval for $20 million worth of conservation projects that had already been started. President Taft believed that Roosevelt had claimed too much presidential power and insisted on getting congressional approval before reserving land for conservation. Taft's conservation policies also differed from Roosevelt's because he believed that the federal government should avoid interfering with society whenever possible. This led him to emphasize cooperation with private business interests and to push state governments to take part in conservation reforms.

Activity: Have students use the library or other resources to research how much public land was set aside for conservation during each presidential administration since Taft. Have students create bar graphs depicting the information.

CHALLENGE AND EXTEND

1. **Linguistic, Logical-Mathematical.** Have students use the library or other resources to find information on the effects of third parties (Bull Moose or the Socialist Party, for example) and third-party candidates (such as Theodore Roosevelt or Eugene V. Debs in 1912) on presidential elections. Encourage students to consider the influence of such parties or candidates on what is generally a two-party system. Have each student write an essay evaluating this impact. Encourage students to discuss specifics of the 1912 election as well as the overall influence of third parties. Ask volunteers to read their essays to the class.

2. **Linguistic, Intrapersonal.** Have students use the library or other resources to find information on Theodore Roosevelt. Have students use their research to create a segment of a documentary on him. Ask students to discuss his preparation for becoming president, his policies as president, the split that developed between him and Taft, and how his policies changed throughout his career. Encourage students to create appropriate visual aids to accompany their documentaries. Call on volunteers to present their documentaries to the class.

Citizenship and Democracy

Third Parties and the Election of 1912. The participation of third parties in presidential elections is often connected with the rise of new social movements, such as the progressive movement. In the election of 1912, both Theodore Roosevelt and Eugene V. Debs entered the race as third-party candidates—Roosevelt for the Progressive Party and Debs for the Socialist Party. They both believed that the major parties were too slow in responding to widespread calls for reform. The Democratic Party responded by nominating a progressive candidate, Woodrow Wilson, who won the election. The split between Roosevelt and Taft, Debs's candidacy, and Wilson's support for progressive reforms drew voters away from the Republicans. The election of 1912 showed that while third parties rarely win elections, they help keep the major parties in touch with public concerns.

Critical Thinking: How do third parties help promote democracy?

ANSWER: Third parties help keep the major parties in touch with the people.

MAP ANSWER
(for page 277)
California

staff. The former president began traveling around the country to challenge Taft for the Republican nomination. In states with direct primaries, Roosevelt was the clear winner, receiving almost twice as many popular votes and many more delegates than Taft. Roosevelt lost the Republican nomination to Taft, however, in a party convention controlled by Taft's supporters.

In response, Roosevelt and his followers formed the Progressive Party. It was nicknamed the **Bull Moose Party** after Roosevelt told a crowd that he was "as strong as a bull moose." The party built its platform around Roosevelt's New Nationalism, promising to give more political power to the American people. Roosevelt declared, "We must drive the special interests out of politics. . . . For every special interest is entitled to justice, but not one is entitled to a vote in Congress."

The Election of 1912

Three major political opponents ran for the presidency in 1912: Theodore Roosevelt, William Howard Taft, and Democratic Party candidate Woodrow Wilson. In addition, Socialist Party candidate Eugene V. Debs ran for the fourth time.

The Republicans Split

The Progressive Party faced a great challenge, for it had to organize itself quickly to get on the ballot in every state in time for the November election. The young party also had to compete with the powerful Democratic and Republican political machines. Roosevelt's party did receive support from many progressive leaders. For example, Hull House founder Jane Addams stated that "the Progressive Platform contains all I have been fighting for for a decade."

Roosevelt threw himself into the campaign. During one frightening moment in Milwaukee, Wisconsin, Roosevelt was shot by a would-be assassin just before a scheduled speech. Bleeding from the wound, Roosevelt insisted on giving the speech anyway. Roosevelt told the stunned crowd, "I have just been shot, but it takes more than that to kill a Bull Moose." Despite Roosevelt's energetic campaign efforts, Taft trusted that voters would respect his record and reject Roosevelt's calls for reform.

The Granger Collection, New York

A cartoon showing Socialist candidate Eugene V. Debs as the king of the labor unions

Woodrow Wilson

The Democratic Party decided to challenge Taft by running pro-reform candidate Woodrow Wilson. Born in Virginia, Wilson earned a doctoral degree in history from the Johns Hopkins University and became a professor in 1890. Beginning in 1902 he served as president of Princeton University until he accepted the Democratic nomination to run for governor of New Jersey in 1910. Wilson's reforms while governor received national attention.

Wilson based his presidential campaign on a program called the **New Freedom**. This program called for government action against monopolies to ensure free competition. In his speeches, Wilson challenged the influence of

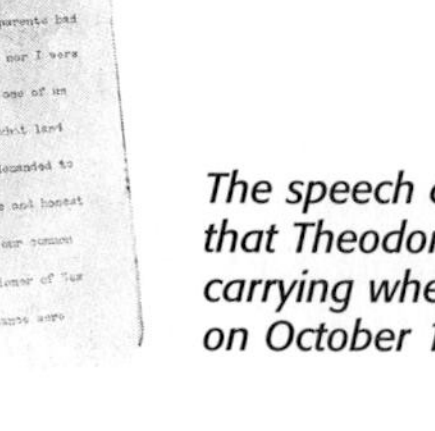

The speech and eyeglass case that Theodore Roosevelt was carrying when he was shot on October 14, 1912

REVIEW

Linguistic, Logical-Mathematical, Interpersonal. Have students complete the Section Review questions. Then, using the section's key terms and names from the Identify segment of the Section Review, assign one term to each student. Have students create questions about their assigned terms. Then ask students to exchange their questions. Have the receiving student create a set of multiple-choice answers for the questions. Then have students pass the questions and multiple-choice answers to different students. Finally, have students answer the multiple-choice questions they received.

ASSESS

Have students complete Daily Quiz 9.2.

RETEACH

Linguistic, Interpersonal. Have students complete Main Idea Activities for Reteaching and Sheltered English 9.2. Organize the class into three groups. Tell each group to create a title and a subtitle for a book on one of the following topics: the Taft presidency, Taft's conflict with Roosevelt and the progressives, or the 1912 presidential election. Then have each group create a possible table of contents for the book. **SHELTERED ENGLISH**

big business, encouraged small businesses, and supported reducing the tariff rate.

Wilson began his campaign without much political experience and without support from the Democratic Party. After struggling to gain the Democratic nomination, he won approval as he toured the nation. Wilson impressed voters with his intelligence, bold ideas, and independence from traditional machine politics.

Although Wilson did not receive a majority of the popular vote, he won a majority of electoral votes and thus the presidency. The November 1912 election results showed how damaging the split between Taft and Roosevelt had been for the Republican Party. Together their votes might have been enough to win the election. The number of votes won by Debs, Roosevelt, and Wilson—all reform candidates—also demonstrated the degree to which Americans favored progressive efforts to change society.

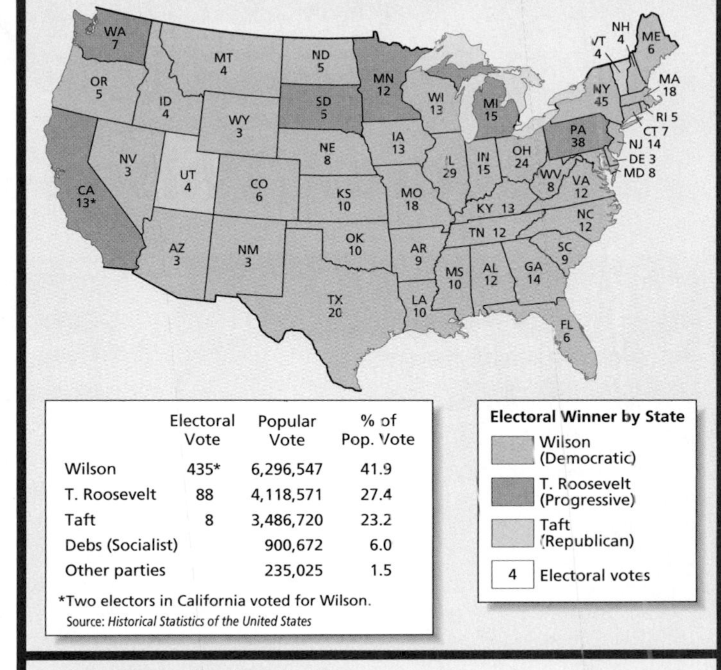

	Electoral Vote	Popular Vote	% of Pop. Vote
Wilson	435*	6,296,547	41.9
T. Roosevelt	88	4,118,571	27.4
Taft	8	3,486,720	23.2
Debs (Socialist)		900,672	6.0
Other parties		235,025	1.5

*Two electors in California voted for Wilson.

Source: *Historical Statistics of the United States*

The Election of 1912

Learning from Maps Wilson's strength was in the South. Although he won the electoral vote by a landslide, the only states outside the former Confederacy where he won at least half the popular votes were Kentucky, Maryland, and Oklahoma.

Location Which state split its electoral vote?

SECTION 2 REVIEW

Identify and explain the significance of the following:

- **William Howard Taft**
- **Payne-Aldrich Tariff**
- **Gifford Pinchot**
- **Richard Ballinger**
- **New Nationalism**
- **Bull Moose Party**
- **Woodrow Wilson**
- **New Freedom**

Reading for Content Understanding

1 **Main Idea** What were the similarities and the differences between Taft's and Roosevelt's views of the presidency?

2 **Main Idea** Why did President Taft's policies upset many progressives?

3 **Citizenship and Democracy** Why and by whom was the Progressive Party created in 1912? What effect did the Progressive Party have on the outcome of the 1912 presidential election?

4 **Writing** *Classifying* Write one or two paragraphs comparing the goals of Roosevelt's New Nationalism program with the goals of Wilson's New Freedom program.

5 **Critical Thinking** *Supporting a Point of View* Do you think that third political parties, such as the Progressive Party, help or hurt the democratic process? Explain your answer.

Section 2 Review ANSWERS

Identify

For significance, see the following pages:

- William Howard Taft, p. 272
- Payne-Aldrich Tariff, p. 274
- Gifford Pinchot, p. 274
- Richard Ballinger, p. 274
- New Nationalism, p. 275
- Bull Moose Party, p. 276
- Woodrow Wilson, p. 276
- New Freedom, p. 276

Reading For Content Understanding

1. Taft believed that the president should stick to the letter of the law, while Roosevelt believed in a powerful president. Taft believed in addressing public concerns slowly and cautiously, while Roosevelt pushed for swift responses.

2. Many feared that Taft's policies were too pro-business to support bold reforms.

3. An argument between Roosevelt and Taft caused a split in the Republican party. After Taft received the party's support, Roosevelt formed the Progressive Party and ran as its candidate. This split contributed to the election of the Democratic Party's candidate, Woodrow Wilson.

4. Paragraphs will vary but should point out that Roosevelt sought to increase presidential influence and to push for more active business regulations and the passage of additional social welfare reform, while Wilson sought government action against monopolies to encourage small businesses and to reduce the tariff rate.

5. Answers will vary but students should state their opinions and explain their reasoning.

OBJECTIVES

- Describe some characteristics of Woodrow Wilson's administration.
- Identify economic reforms that President Wilson pursued.
- Summarize ways that President Wilson tried to regulate corporations.

FOCUS

Motivate Before Reading

Explain to students the concept of an income tax. Have students work in small groups to list positive and negative effects of such a tax. Call on each group to report its list to the class. As groups identify various positives and negatives, write them under the appropriate heading on the chalkboard. Tell students that in this section they will learn how and why the income tax was established,

Section 3 RESOURCES

PRINT

- ★ Guided Reading Strategies 9.3
- ★ Graphic Organizer 9: Presidential Reforms
- ★ Section 3 Review, p. 283
- ★ Daily Quiz 9.3

MULTIMEDIA

- ★ *Teaching Resources CD–ROM*, Lesson 9.3
- ★ HRW Web site

SHELTERED ENGLISH

- ★ Main Idea Activities for Reteaching and Sheltered English 9.3

Woodrow Wilson's Reforms

Reading Focus

What were some characteristics of President Wilson's administration?

What economic reforms did Wilson pursue?

How did Wilson try to regulate corporations?

Key Terms

Underwood Tariff Act
Sixteenth Amendment
Federal Reserve Act
Clayton Antitrust Act
Federal Trade Commission
Keating-Owen Child Labor Act
Adamson Act
Federal Farm Loan Act

At his inauguration, Woodrow Wilson looked formal and serious as he stood next to a smiling William Howard Taft. While Taft seemed relieved to be leaving office, Wilson concentrated on the responsibility now facing him. In his brief inaugural address, Wilson emphasized the challenges that faced the United States. "This is not a day of triumph, it is a day of dedication," he declared in a calm voice. Wilson asked the crowd before him to look beyond their party loyalties and to consider the work that needed to be done to improve the nation.

Woodrow Wilson and his family

 Wilson in Office

Unlike Taft, who had served in the shadow of Theodore Roosevelt, President Wilson established himself as the clear leader of his administration. As one journalist observed, "[T]his administration is Woodrow Wilson's, and none other's. He is the top, the middle, and the bottom of it."

Many people were puzzled by Woodrow Wilson. He was a capable manager and a good public speaker, but he sometimes seemed cold and proud. While he had strong moral beliefs, he was also willing to be practical about political issues. Wilson was also very private about his ideas. He wrote many official papers on his own, typing them himself late at night. He established regular press meetings at the White House, but he very rarely answered questions directly and refused to be directly quoted in the newspapers.

Wilson was the first Democrat to be elected president in 20 years. In addition, the Democratic Party controlled both houses of Congress. Wilson also appointed many Democrats to government positions. He filled his cabinet with influential how it illustrated progressives' desire to spread the benefits of industrial growth, and how other progressive reforms expanded the reach of the U.S. government.

Introduce Key Terms

Linguistic, Visual-Spatial. Review this section's key terms with students. Have them prepare a three-column chart based on the key terms. Ask students to list each term in the left column, write a brief description of it in the middle column, and list the year it became law in the right column. Students will have to infer the dates of two of the terms. **SHELTERED ENGLISH**

TEACH

Have students read Section 3 and complete Guided Reading Strategies 9.3. Choose one or more of the following activities to explore the section content with students. For further suggestions on block scheduling or team teaching, see the *Block Scheduling Handbook*.

LEVEL 1: Linguistic. (Suggested time: 15 min.) As a class, go over students' Guided Reading Strategies. Then use the Reading Focus questions to highlight the main ideas of the section. **SHELTERED ENGLISH**

Woodrow Wilson entered the presidency with many new ideas and goals for reform.

party leaders such as William Jennings Bryan, who became secretary of state. Wilson also brought many southern politicians into his administration.

Democrats were eager to prove that they were ready to take charge of the country after so many years of Republican control. They united behind Wilson and his new policies. Wilson convinced congressional leaders to pass his reform measures. In addition, he became the first president since Thomas Jefferson to promote legislation in person before Congress.

Economic Reforms

During his presidential campaign, Wilson had supported two key economic reform measures: tariff reduction and banking reform. Once in office he moved quickly to push these reforms into law.

A New Tariff

President Wilson made tariff reduction the first part of his economic reform plan because he believed that lower tariff rates would help consumers. He therefore threw his support behind the **Underwood Tariff Act** of 1913, overcoming initial resistance from industries that had lobbied to keep rates high. The passage of the Underwood Tariff Act resulted in the lowest tariff rates in many years.

To help make up for the lost tariff revenue, the act also introduced a version of the modern-day income tax on personal earnings. Progressives had fought for years to pass a federal income tax, but the U.S. Supreme Court ruled that such taxes were unconstitutional. The **Sixteenth Amendment**, ratified by the states in February 1913, amended the Constitution and allowed the federal government to pass direct taxes, such as the income tax. Although it was a significant step in government policy, the new tax was quite low and did not affect most Americans.

Reforming the Banking Industry

After the Underwood Tariff Act was passed, Wilson turned his attention to improving the banking system. There were no national regulations governing banks, which resulted in great confusion and an unreliable money supply. Wilson knew banking reform would be much more difficult to pass than the tariff legislation. However, he told his friends confidently, "There is nothing that succeeds in life like boldness, provided you believe you are on the right side."

The Federal Reserve Building in Washington, D.C.

Historical Sidelight

Edith Bolling Wilson. President Wilson's wife, Ellen Wilson, died in the summer of 1914. The president was stricken by her death and grieved deeply. Concerned, some friends invited Edith Bolling Galt, a widow, to tea at the White House. Wilson and Galt soon were spending much time together, attending baseball games and taking drives. In May 1915 the smitten Wilson proposed to Galt. She refused, however, the expected response for ladies to first proposals at the time. He then began writing her long, romantic letters each day. He also discussed affairs of state and foreign policy secrets with her. In December 1915 the two married. Galt soon served as Wilson's closest advisor and ally. After his stroke in the fall of 1919, she assumed many duties of the presidency for the remainder of his term.

Critical Thinking: What problems might a president face when trying to combine an active social life, such as dating, with the duties of office?

ANSWER: Answers will vary but students might say that some people may condemn the president for taking too much time away from official duties, and political rivals might use the situation to spread scandalous rumors about the president to undermine his support.

ALL LEVELS: Visual-Spatial, Logical-Mathematical. (Suggested time: 45 min.) Point out to students that Woodrow Wilson's administration differed in many ways from that of other progressive presidents. Have each student create a political cartoon that highlights one of the characteristics of the Wilson administration. Encourage students to include a caption that helps clarify what the cartoon depicts. For example, students can draw a cartoon with President Wilson answering reporters' questions. The caption can read *But do not quote me on that.* Call on volunteers to share their cartoons with the class. Finally, discuss the characteristics that distinguished Wilson's administration from other progressive administrations and have students list these characteristics in their notebooks. **SHELTERED ENGLISH**

LEVEL 2: Linguistic, Logical-Mathematical. (Suggested time: 45 min.) Direct students' attention to W. E. B. Du Bois's criticism of President Wilson that is found in this section. Have each student assume the role of President Wilson and write a letter to Du Bois in which Wilson defends the reform record of his first administration, explains why he favored economic reforms over social reforms, and cites examples of legislation that promoted economic reform. Then have students exchange their letters. Ask students to write rebuttals from Du Bois to the letters they

Economic Development

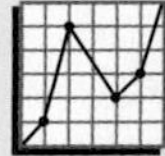

The Roots of the Federal Income Tax. With the coming of the Civil War, both the Union and the Confederacy were forced to raise money for military funding. In 1862 the Union turned to a federal income tax. The tax was a great help in paying for the war effort. Meanwhile, the Confederacy relied mainly on a tax collected through the states, but it failed to bring in enough money. After the war, the income tax was repealed. From that time until 1913 there existed an ongoing debate over the need for an income tax.

Activity: Have students use the library or search the Internet through the HRW Web site to help write a brief explanation of how income tax money is used.

go.hrw.com
SB1 Income Tax

LINKING PAST TO PRESENT ANSWERS

1. to raise revenue

2. Answers will vary but students should point out that rates often change during wars and national emergencies.

Linking Past to Present

Income Tax

Before the creation of an income tax in 1913, the federal government raised its money primarily from duties and tariffs, which became increasingly unpopular. In the late 1800s, even millionaires such as Andrew Carnegie and John D. Rockefeller paid no tax on their personal earnings.

The IRS Data Processing Center in Austin, Texas

The new income tax was a progressive tax. This meant that it took a larger percentage from someone with a high income than from someone with a low income. The tax was quite small, with a maximum rate of 7 percent. The income tax applied to about 4 percent of wage earners because yearly income below $4,000 was exempt, or free, from taxes. This was at a time when the average annual income was about $900.

Despite these modest beginnings, the income tax quickly became an important way for the federal government to raise money, particularly during wartime. Just a few years after the tax law was passed, for example, the maximum tax rate was temporarily raised to 77 percent to help fund national defense.

Many states also began collecting personal income tax in the early 1900s to help pay the cost of running state governments and of establishing new urban reforms.

As late as 1939, most Americans still did not have to pay federal taxes. This changed during the 1940s, when the minimum taxable income was lowered. As the federal government has received more tax money, it has greatly increased the number of benefits and services it provides to the public.

Today, the majority of Americans who earn wages must pay federal income taxes. In 1994 the federal government received more than 115 million personal income tax returns and collected almost $600 billion in income tax. The Internal Revenue Service (IRS) employs thousands of people to process these returns, which represent the government's single largest source of revenue.

Understanding What You Read

1. Why do the federal and state governments tax personal income?
2. What might motivate a government to raise or lower taxes?

One obstacle to banking reform was the lack of agreement on this issue among Wilson's fellow Democrats in Congress. Some wanted a central banking system controlled by the government. Others favored a decentralized system run by private bankers. Banking reform also met strong opposition from Republican leaders. Senator Henry Cabot Lodge, for example, called the president's economic reforms "dreadful assaults on business." In spite of these challenges, Wilson stayed firm. He insisted that the banking system had to be changed and that it needed to be run by the government to ensure fairness.

The result was a compromise called the **Federal Reserve Act**. Passed in December 1913, the act created a banking system called the Federal Reserve. This system is made up of 12 regional Federal Reserve banks as well as privately owned received. Call on volunteers to read their letters from Wilson to Du Bois, and ask others to read their rebuttals from Du Bois.

LEVEL 3: Linguistic, Logical-Mathematical, Intrapersonal. (Suggested time: 45 min. plus homework) Explain to students that President Wilson often backed legislation that regulated businesses. Have students create journal entries similar to ones that President Wilson might have written about his attempts to regulate businesses. Have each student create an entry about each of the following topics: the Clayton Antitrust Act, the Federal Trade Commission, the Keating-Owen Child Labor Act, and the Adamson Act. Once students have finished writing their entries, have volunteers read them to the class.

CLOSE

Linguistic, Musical-Rhythmic. Have each student prepare a poem or song that addresses the most significant policies of the Wilson administration. Once students have finished writing, have volunteers read or sing their songs or poems to the class. Finally, have the class determine the three most significant policies of the Wilson administration.

CHALLENGE AND EXTEND

1. **Logical-Mathematical, Interpersonal.** Have students use the library and other resources to research the controversy

banks. The Federal Reserve is overseen by an independent decision-making body that controls banking policy. The passage of the Federal Reserve Act gave stability to the national banking system. Over time, the Federal Reserve has also become responsible for regulating bank deposits and interest rates. This gives the federal government a way to try to minimize sudden changes between boom and bust cycles in the economy.

Regulating Big Business

Having created what he felt was a sound economic foundation for the country, President Wilson pushed for additional legislation regulating big business. Like Taft, Wilson distrusted the power of monopolies and trusts. "If there are men in this country big enough to own the government of the United States, they are going to [try to] own it," he warned. Wilson wanted a more powerful version of the Sherman Antitrust Act that could be used to break up these trusts.

The **Clayton Antitrust Act**, passed in October 1914, strengthened federal laws against business monopolies. The act also specifically stated that labor unions had the right to bargain collectively and go on strike. This prevented the new law from being used against organized labor as the Sherman Antitrust Act had been. Union leaders such as AFL president Samuel Gompers praised the Clayton Antitrust Act as a breakthrough for organized labor. However, state and federal courts often continued to favor business interests when interpreting the new law.

To further regulate corporations, Congress established the **Federal Trade Commission** (FTC) in 1914. The five-person commission was given broad powers to examine company records and investigate business practices. The commission passed along this information to the president and Congress. The FTC was also able to issue restraining orders to stop "unfair trade practices" from continuing. Over time, the FTC's role has expanded. Today, it also enforces business regulations and establishes standards for advertising and product labeling.

Wilson hoped that his antitrust efforts would provide open and fair competition while allowing

President Wilson using antitrust laws to challenge the power of greedy trusts

business to prosper. He predicted that the legislation he helped pass would be "the final step in setting the business of this country free." However, Republicans rejected Wilson's claim that his economic reforms had helped business. One Republican politician declared that business leaders were convinced Wilson had "put through a dangerous and destructive legislative program in which he has ignored every protest made by them."

Changes in Policy

Wilson believed that many social issues, such as women's rights, were best addressed by state governments rather than by the federal government. He also wanted to keep the support of business leaders and of southern Democrats. For these reasons he was at first reluctant to support laws intended to help organized labor or to support women's suffrage.

Wilson was also hesitant to reach out to minority groups. Although he had pledged during his campaign to support greater opportunities for

Across the Curriculum

SCIENCE

Food Labels. One of the Federal Trade Commission's main purposes is to prevent unfair trade practices that may deceive consumers. Thus, the FTC is one of several federal agencies involved in enforcing the 1990 Nutrition Labeling and Education Act (NLEA). The law requires food manufacturers to provide information on the nutritional value of their products and gives the FTC the power to punish food manufacturers who make deceptive claims on the labels of their products. For example, a cookie manufacturer cannot claim that its cookies are low fat unless they truly are low in fat.

Activity: Have students choose two food items from home. Then have each student read the items' nutritional information and write a paragraph comparing the products. Finally, ask students to decide if the items they chose are healthy.

surrounding President Wilson's appointment of Louis Brandeis to the U.S. Supreme Court. Then have the class hold a mock meeting of the Senate Judiciary Committee to decide whether to recommend to the Senate that Brandeis's appointment be ratified or rejected. Appoint a chair for the committee. Then have the committee call witnesses, ask questions, clarify the issues, and inquire into Brandeis's career and reputation. Conclude by having the committee vote on whether to recommend the ratification of Brandeis's appointment.

2. **Linguistic, Logical-Mathematical.** Have students use the library and other resources to find information on the reasons for the adoption of the Sixteenth Amendment and the effects of its passage. Ask each student to write an essay based on his or her research. Encourage students to include arguments that were made for and against the passage of the Sixteenth Amendment, as well as to show statistics regarding how much the United States collects annually from income tax. Call on volunteers to share their essays with the class.

REVIEW

Linguistic, Interpersonal. Have students complete the Section Review questions. Then have students write each key term and person from the Identify portion of the Section Review on one

Section 3 Review ANSWERS

Identify

For significance, see the following pages:

- Underwood Tariff Act, p. 279
- Sixteenth Amendment, p. 279
- Federal Reserve Act, p. 280
- Clayton Antitrust Act, p. 281
- Federal Trade Commission, p. 281
- Louis Brandeis, p. 282
- Keating-Owen Child Labor Act, p. 283
- Adamson Act, p. 283
- Federal Farm Loan Act, p. 283

Reading For Content Understanding

1. He was a strong leader and speaker, but very private about his ideas.

2. Wilson pushed for legislation, such as the Clayton Antitrust Act, and for new government bodies, such as the Federal Trade Commission.

3. The Underwood Tariff Act lowered tariff rates; the Sixteenth Amendment allowed the federal government to pass direct taxes; and the Federal Reserve Act created the Federal Reserve.

4. Answers will vary but students should mention that the party gained power by having a strong Democratic president as the nation's leader, a Democrat-controlled Congress to pass the nation's laws, and by appointing Democrats to other important positions.

5. Answers will vary but students might mention that Wilson's policies changed based on what the people wanted, and he needed to ensure the support of progressives to win the 1916 election.

Progressive Presidential Reforms, 1906–1914

REFORM LAWS	PASSED UNDER PRESIDENT	RESULTS
The **National Monuments Act** (1906) allowed the president to declare certain areas on federal lands to be protected historic or scientific landmarks.	T. Roosevelt	Roosevelt created national monuments that later became national parks, including the Grand Canyon in Arizona and Zion in Utah. Later presidents have added to this list.
The **Pure Food and Drug Act** (1906) prohibited the manufacture, sale, or transportation of mislabeled or contaminated food and drugs sold in interstate commerce.	T. Roosevelt	The law was a breakthrough in public health reform. It also increased Roosevelt's public support.
The **Payne-Aldrich Tariff** (1909) lowered tariffs on raw materials such as coal, iron, and lumber.	Taft	Progressives opposed the law, which left many tariff rates unchanged and raised some others.
The **Underwood Tariff Act** (1913) reduced tariffs on many goods by one third and created the first federal income tax.	Wilson	The public applauded the lower tariff rates, and the income tax became an important source of federal revenue.
The **Federal Reserve Act** (1913) created a special board to regulate the banking industry.	Wilson	The Federal Reserve provided stability to the banking industry and now influences the economy by setting the prime interest rate.
The **Clayton Antitrust Act** (1914) greatly strengthened antimonopoly laws and recognized organized labor's right to collective bargaining and to strike.	Wilson	For many years the law was limited by Supreme Court rulings. It is still in effect today.
The **Federal Trade Commission Act** (1914) created an independent commission to investigate businesses and issue complaints about unfair practices.	Wilson	The Federal Trade Commission still investigates business practices and helps enforce laws such as the Clayton Antitrust Act.

African Americans, he did not keep this promise. In "An Open Letter to Woodrow Wilson," W. E. B. Du Bois wrote:

> **"Not a single act and not a single word of yours since election has given anyone reason to infer [believe] that you have the slightest interest in the colored people or desire to alleviate [make easier] their intolerable position."**

In order to satisfy the demand of southern politicians, Wilson agreed to the racial segregation of federal facilities in Washington, D.C. This action was met by protests from African American leaders and caused Wilson to lose support among some progressives.

As the presidential race of 1916 approached, Wilson increased his support for progressive reforms by focusing on the needs of farmers and wage earners. He appointed Louis Brandeis, a progressive lawyer, to the U.S. Supreme Court. Brandeis was known nationally as "the people's attorney" for taking cases free of charge on behalf of consumers and laborers. The appointment sparked controversy. Nevertheless, after a fierce four-month battle between progressive supporters and conservative opponents, Brandeis was confirmed, becoming the first Jewish American to sit on the U.S. Supreme Court.

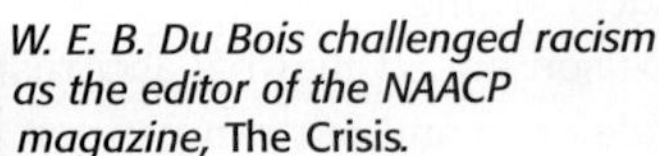

W. E. B. Du Bois challenged racism as the editor of the NAACP magazine, The Crisis.

side of a notecard. On the other side of the card, have students write a description of the term or person's importance. Organize students into pairs and have them take turns quizzing one another on the terms and people. If students are having difficulty understanding the importance of any of the terms or people, have them search the text for more information.

ASSESS

Have students complete Daily Quiz 9.3.

RETEACH

Logical-Mathematical, Interpersonal. Have students complete Main Idea Activities for Reteaching and Sheltered English 9.3. Ask students to determine the most important success of Wilson's first term. Then have them determine Wilson's most important defeat or weakness. Pair students and have each pair discuss their conclusions. Then call on volunteers to explain their thinking and to cite examples supporting their conclusions.

SHELTERED ENGLISH

In September 1916 Wilson helped pass the **Keating-Owen Child Labor Act**. This legislation prohibited companies from shipping their products across state lines if they employed children under the age of 14. In 1918, however, the Supreme Court overturned the act by ruling that only the states could regulate child labor.

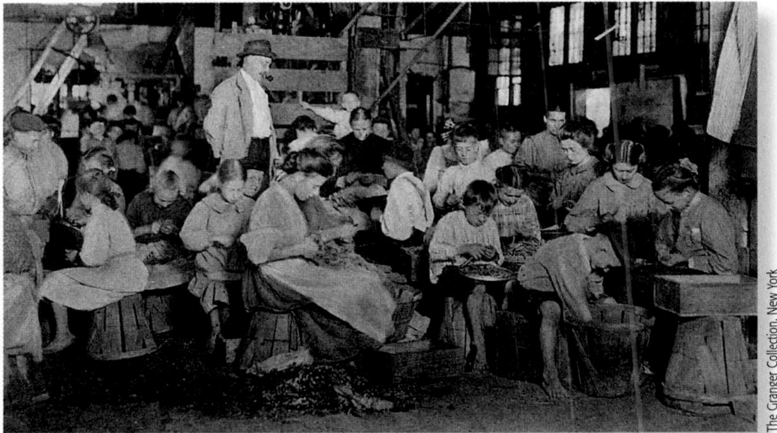

The Granger Collection, New York

The Keating-Owen Child Labor Act was an effort to address the situation of children such as these cannery workers.

Other progressive reforms backed by Wilson included a law requiring workers' compensation for federal employees. He also supported the **Adamson Act**, which limited the workday on the nation's railroads to eight hours. Finally, to help farmers, he supported the **Federal Farm Loan Act**. This act made it easier for farmers to obtain credit.

Although Republicans attacked these measures, many progressives and some socialists approved of Wilson's new reform efforts. As a result, they began to rally around the president. At the start of his 1916 presidential campaign, Wilson announced proudly:

> **"We have in four years come very near to carrying out the platform of the Progressive Party as well as our own; for we are also progressives."**

In the campaign Wilson faced Republican Charles Evans Hughes, a former U.S. Supreme Court justice. Both Wilson and Hughes received support from former members of the Progressive Party. Wilson won a narrow victory, receiving 277 electoral votes to Hughes's 254.

Wilson displayed great skill and determination at guiding his reform programs through Congress. His work helped unite a Democratic Party that included members with very different views. Wilson explained to a friend that he had a talent for putting his mind "at the service of others for the accomplishment of a common purpose." His impressive legislative record reflects the many progressive reforms put into place by 1920.

SECTION 3 REVIEW

Identify and explain the significance of the following:

- **Underwood Tariff Act**
- **Sixteenth Amendment**
- **Federal Reserve Act**
- **Clayton Antitrust Act**
- **Federal Trade Commission**
- **Louis Brandeis**
- **Keating-Owen Child Labor Act**
- **Adamson Act**
- **Federal Farm Loan Act**

Reading for Content Understanding

1 **Main Idea** What was the style of President Wilson's administration?

2 **Main Idea** What steps did Wilson take to regulate big business?

3 **Economic Development** What economic reforms did Wilson achieve in his first term?

4 **Writing** *Informing* Imagine that you are a member of the Democratic Party in 1912. Explain how your party gained influence following the presidential election.

5 **Critical Thinking** *Drawing Conclusions* Why do you think Wilson's reform policies changed during his presidency? Give several reasons to support your answer.

Chapter 9 Review ANSWERS

Identifying People and Ideas

1. two-term Republican president, supported progressive reforms and a powerful presidency, unsuccessful Progressive Party presidential candidate in 1912

2. a formal meeting to discuss disagreements

3. law prohibiting the manufacture, sale, or transportation of mislabled or contaminated food and drugs sold in interstate commerce

4. reform effort directed at protecting natural resources and preserving wilderness

5. Republican president who followed Roosevelt; supported Roosevelt's reforms but rejected his activism

6. nickname for the Progressive Party

7. Democratic president after Taft; advocated New Freedom reform program

8. constitutional amendment ratified in 1913 that allowed the federal government to pass direct taxes

9. banking industry reform that established the Federal Reserve system

10. law passed during the Wilson administration; strengthened federal antimonopoly laws and guaranteed the right to collective bargaining

Using the Time Line

1. a
2. c
3. d
4. b
5. e

Review and Assessment RESOURCES

PRINT
★ Chapter 9 Review, pp. 284–85
★ Vocabulary Activity 9
★ Chapter 9 Study Guide
★ Chapter 9 Test (Form A or B)

MULTIMEDIA
★ Audio Program, Ch. 9 (English and Spanish)
★ *Global Skill Builder CD–ROM*
★ Chapter 9 Test Generator
★ HRW Web site

SHELTERED ENGLISH
★ Spanish Glossary
★ Sheltered English Chapter 9 Test

ASSESS

Have students complete one of the Chapter 9 Tests. As an alternate assessment, assign the Chapter 9 Investigation.

Understanding Main Ideas

1. It was a program aimed at treating labor, business, and private citizens fairly.

2. He was so outraged that he persuaded Congress to pass the Meat Inspection Act and the Pure Food and Drug Act.

3. Taft supported the regulation of corporations, started 90 antitrust suits, and pushed for tariff reductions.

4. his support for lowering tariffs, his handling of the Ballinger-Pinchot controversy, and his unwillingness to use presidential power forcefully

5. Wilson insisted that the banking system had to be run by the government, which led to the passage of the Federal Reserve Act and the creation of the Federal Reserve.

6. Reforms included the Keating-Owen Child Labor Act, the Adamson Act, a law requiring workers' compensation for federal employees, and the Federal Farm Loan Act.

Reviewing Themes

1. Roosevelt started antitrust suits against "bad trusts"; Taft started twice as many antitrust suits; and Wilson pushed for the Clayton Antitrust Act and the Federal Trade Commission.

2. a movement with two separate goals—to preserve and protect nature and to manage and conserve natural resources; Important leaders include Gifford Pinchot, John Muir, Theodore Roosevelt, and Charles Sargent .

3. It was formed as a result of President Taft receiving the Republican nomination in the 1912 presidential election by people who wanted to see Theodore Roosevelt receive the nomination.

CHAPTER 9 REVIEW

Chapter Summary

The progressive movement gained supporters in both the Democratic and Republican Parties. In 1912 the Progressive Party was formed. Presidents Theodore Roosevelt, William Howard Taft, and Woodrow Wilson each helped pass a series of progressive reforms. These included efforts to control big business, improve the economy, build relations between labor and management, and conserve the environment.

On a separate sheet of paper, complete the following activities.

Identifying People and Ideas

Describe the historical significance of the following:

1. Theodore Roosevelt
2. arbitration
3. Pure Food and Drug Act
4. conservation
5. William Howard Taft
6. Bull Moose Party
7. Woodrow Wilson
8. Sixteenth Amendment
9. Federal Reserve Act
10. Clayton Antitrust Act

Internet Activity

go.hrw.com
SB1 Federal Reserve

Search the Internet through the HRW Web site to find information about how the Federal Reserve system works today. Use this information to create a graphic organizer that shows how the Federal Reserve's actions affect the economy.

Understanding Main Ideas

1. What was President Roosevelt's Square Deal?
2. How did Roosevelt respond to Upton Sinclair's *The Jungle*?
3. What were President Taft's business and economic reform policies?
4. Why did Taft lose the support of Roosevelt and many other progressives?
5. How did President Wilson help reform the banking industry?
6. What labor reforms were passed during Wilson's presidency?

Reviewing Themes

1. **Economic Development** What actions did Presidents Roosevelt, Taft, and Wilson take to regulate large corporations?
2. **Geographic Diversity** What was the conservation movement? Who were some of its leaders?
3. **Citizenship and Democracy** Why was the Progressive Party created?

Using the Time Line

Number your paper from 1 to 5. Match the letters on the time line below with the following events.

1. **President McKinley is assassinated.**
2. **William Howard Taft is elected president of the United States.**
3. **The Sixteenth Amendment is ratified, allowing a personal income tax.**
4. **Public concern over food safety leads to the passage of the Pure Food and Drug Act.**
5. **The Clayton Antitrust Act is passed.**

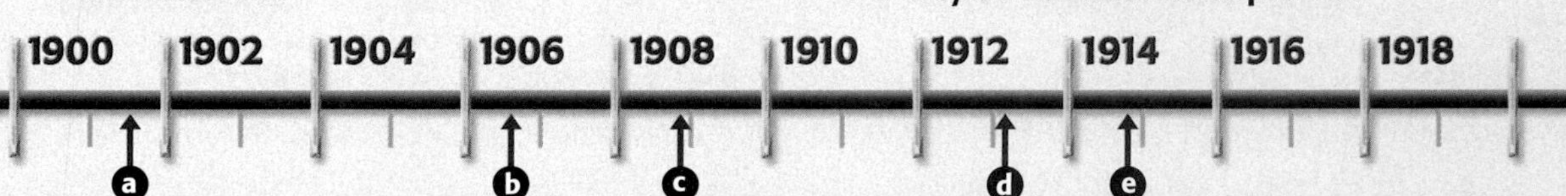

RETEACH

Logical-Mathematical, Interpersonal. Organize the class into two groups. Have one group list the similarities between the progressive presidents, and the other group list their differences. Have a member of each group read its list to the class. Then have students debate whether the progressive presidents were more similar to or different from one another.
SHELTERED ENGLISH

Using the Internet

HRW Have students continue their research to find more information on how the Federal Reserve currently functions. Ask each student to write a one-paragraph article on the role of the Federal Reserve in today's economy.

Portfolio Extensions

American History

1. Have students write a biography about one of the other progressive presidents. Then have students compare and contrast his life to Roosevelt's life.

2. Assign each student a specific national park, forest, or monument to research. Ask each student to write a one-page summary about the park's attractions.

Thinking Critically

1. **Making Comparisons** How did Roosevelt's view of the presidency differ from that of previous presidents? Use examples from his administration to explain your answer.
2. **Evaluating** Which of the progressive presidents do you think was most successful in reforming American society? Explain your answer.
3. **Identifying Cause and Effect** What effect did the formation of the Progressive Party have on the presidential election of 1912?

Writing About History

1. **Informing** Write a short newspaper article comparing Roosevelt's New Nationalism program with Wilson's New Freedom platform.
2. **Expressing** Write a letter to the editor stating your view on whether Roosevelt was right to choose Taft as his successor to the presidency.

Linking Geography and History

1. **Region** In what region of the country were most of the national parks and natural forests created? Why do you think this was the case?
2. **Human-Environment Interaction** What issue divided some members of the conservation movement?

Building Your Portfolio

American History

Complete the following activities individually or in groups.

1. **Theodore Roosevelt** Use your textbook or the library to find information about the life of Theodore Roosevelt. Focus on the following topics: Roosevelt the Conservationist, Roosevelt the Rancher, Roosevelt the Trustbuster, Roosevelt the Family Man, or Roosevelt the President. Use this information to write a biography about several aspects of Roosevelt's life. You should include some quotations by Roosevelt himself, as well as by other people talking about Roosevelt.
2. **National Parks** Use the library or other resources to find information about the national parks, monuments, wildlife refuges, or forests nearest you. Choose one of these locations and create a small brochure describing the area and explaining when and why it was founded. You should include pictures or a map with the brochure.

History Skills Workshop

Using Visual Resources Study the image to the right, which is a political cartoon of Theodore Roosevelt during the presidential campaign of 1912. The box behind Roosevelt is labeled *Vox Populi Vox Mei,* which in Latin means "The voice of the public is my voice." (a) Why do you think the artist drew Roosevelt as a king? (b) What message do you think the cartoon is trying to communicate to the public about Roosevelt's campaign? (c) What is the cartoon suggesting about Roosevelt's personality?

Thinking Critically

1. Previous presidents had been administrators while Roosevelt was an active president. Examples of his activism include the Square Deal, suits against bad trusts, and his strong support of conservation.

2. Answers will vary but students should state their opinions and explain their reasoning.

3. It split the Republican Party, which enabled Woodrow Wilson to win the election.

Writing About History

1. Paragraphs will vary but students should mention that New Nationalism called for a strong executive, more active regulation, and the passage of social welfare measures; while New Freedom called for government action against monopolies, increased support for small business, and reductions in tariffs.

2. Answers will vary but students should state their opinions and offer support for them.

Linking Geography and History

1. Most were in the western states; probably because the West was less developed and still had undisturbed land

2. The movement was divided over whether its goal should be conservation or preservation.

History Skills Workshop

(a) Roosevelt was very popular and a very active leader, similar to a king;
(b) Roosevelt is suited to lead the United States;
(c) Roosevelt is strong and forceful and loves being the center of attention.

CHAPTER PLANNING GUIDE
America As a World Power

	SECTION LESSON OBJECTIVES	PRINT RESOURCES	MULTIMEDIA RESOURCES	SHELTERED ENGLISH RESOURCES
Section 1: The United States Gains Overseas Territories (pp. 287–93)	★ Explain why some Americans favored expansion over isolationism. ★ Describe the events that led to the U.S. annexation of Hawaii. ★ Identify the goal of U.S. foreign policy in Japan and China.	★ Guided Reading Strategies 10.1 ★ Primary Source Reading 10: Japan and the West ★ Section 1 Review, p. 293 ★ Daily Quiz 10.1	★ *Teaching Resources CD–ROM*, Lesson 10.1 ★ Linking Geography and History Transparency 15: The American Empire	★ Main Idea Activities for Reteaching and Sheltered English 10.1
Section 2: The Spanish-American War (pp. 294–300)	★ Explain the effect of the press on U.S. involvement in the conflict in Cuba. ★ Describe what enabled the United States to win the war with Spain. ★ Analyze the effect of the Spanish-American War on the Philippines, Cuba, and Puerto Rico.	★ Guided Reading Strategies 10.2 ★ Biography Reading 10: William Randolph Hearst ★ Literature Reading 10: Fighting Spanish Imperialism ★ Geography Activity 10: The Philippine War ★ Section 2 Review, p. 300 ★ Daily Quiz 10.2	★ *Teaching Resources CD–ROM*, Lesson 10.2 ★ Everyday Life in America Transparency 19: Photojournalism in the Spanish-American War ★ HRW Web site	★ Main Idea Activities for Reteaching and Sheltered English 10.2
Section 3: The United States and Latin America (pp. 301–07)	★ Identify the steps that the United States took to build a canal across Panama. ★ Analyze the change in U.S. involvement in Latin America under President Theodore Roosevelt. ★ Describe how Presidents Taft and Wilson enforced the Monroe Doctrine.	★ Guided Reading Strategies 10.3 ★ American History Political Cartoon 19: Theodore Roosevelt and the Panama Canal ★ Section 3 Review, p. 307 ★ Daily Quiz 10.3	★ *Teaching Resources CD–ROM*, Lesson 10.3 ★ *Exploring America's Past* Video Segment: A Struggle Against Nature; *Teacher's Guide*, pp. 18–20 ★ HRW Web site	★ Main Idea Activities for Reteaching and Sheltered English 10.3
Section 4: The United States and Mexico (pp. 308–11)	★ Explain why the Mexican people revolted against their government in 1911. ★ Analyze President Woodrow Wilson's reasons for intervening in the Mexican Revolution. ★ Discuss reasons for the increase in Mexican immigration to the United States in the early 1900s.	★ Guided Reading Strategies 10.4 ★ Graphic Organizer 10: U.S. Involvement Overseas ★ Section 4 Review, p. 311 ★ Daily Quiz 10.4	★ *Teaching Resources CD–ROM*, Lesson 10.4 ★ *American History Interactive Maps CD–ROM*: U.S. Imperialism in Latin America	★ Main Idea Activities for Reteaching and Sheltered English 10.4
Chapter Review and Assessment (pp. 312–13)		★ Chapter 10 Review, pp. 312–13 ★ Vocabulary Activity 10 ★ Chapter 10 Study Guide ★ Chapter 10 Test (Form A or B)	★ Audio Program, Ch. 10 (English and Spanish) ★ *Global Skill Builder CD–ROM* ★ Chapter 10 Test Generator ★ HRW Web site	★ Spanish Glossary ★ Sheltered English Chapter 10 Test

CHAPTER OVERVIEW

As European countries established colonies around the world, U.S. leaders feared that the United States would be left out of the lucrative scramble for colonial resources and markets. Many also argued that expansion would help the United States protect its interests. In keeping with this concern for expansion, the United States added such territories as Alaska and Hawaii and became involved in opening trade with China and Japan.

The United States also supported Cuba's revolt against Spanish rule. This led to the Spanish-American War. After defeating Spain, the United States claimed the Philippines and Puerto Rico as territories and maintained its right to intervene in Cuban affairs.

The war convinced the U.S. government that a more efficient route was needed between the Pacific and Atlantic Oceans. After a revolution in Panama, the U.S. government began construction on a canal across the isthmus. The need to protect the canal and U.S. investment in Latin America led to growing U.S. interference with Latin American nations.

In Mexico the authoritarian rule of Porfirio Díaz led people to revolt. The political unrest that followed threatened U.S. investments. Eventually, the United States attacked Mexico. Although the dispute was resolved through negotiations, the Mexican government remained unstable.

CHAPTER INVESTIGATION

The Chapter Investigation is an extended, multipart activity designed for students to work cooperatively and apply the chapter content in the creation of a project. You may choose to use the Chapter 10 Investigation, Congressional Debate, either as a substitute for teaching the section lessons or as an alternate assessment.

BLOCK SCHEDULING 

The teacher lesson plans for each section offer a variety of activity choices to help you present the material in a block scheduling format. For further suggestions on block scheduling, see the *Block Scheduling Handbook with Team Teaching Strategies*, pp. 55–60.

Meeting Individual Needs

ABILITY LEVELS

LEVEL 1 Basic level activities designed for all students encountering new material.

LEVEL 2 Intermediate level activities designed for average students.

LEVEL 3 Challenging activities designed for above-average students.

SHELTERED ENGLISH These activities address the needs of students with Limited English Proficiency.

Smithsonian Institution®

Internet Connections and Lesson 10
www.si.edu/hrw

CNN Presents America:
Yesterday and Today 1850 to the Present
Segment: "Remember the *Maine!*"

Additional Resources

Books for Teachers

Hall, Linda B, and Don M. Coerver. *Revolution on the Border: The United States and Mexico, 1910–1920.* University of New Mexico Press, 1988. Account of the Mexican Revolution in the U.S.-Mexico borderlands.

LaFeber, Walter. *Panama Canal: The Crisis in Historical Perspective.* Oxford University Press, 1990. Historical perspective on the Panama Canal.

O'Toole, G.J. *The Spanish War: An American Epic, 1898.* Norton, 1986. History of the war and its impact on U.S. foreign policy.

Books for Students

Dolan, Edward F. *Panama & the United States: Their Canal, Their Stormy Years.* Watts, 1990. History of Panama and U.S.-Panama relations.

Marrin, Albert. *The Spanish-American War.* Atheneum, 1991. Explores causes and consequences of war, yellow journalism, and Teddy Roosevelt's role (for students reading below grade level).

Paterson, Thomas G., and Stephen G. Rabe, eds. *Imperial Surge: The United States Abroad, the 1890s-Early 1900s.* Heath, 1992. Explores U.S. expansion in the 1890s and early 1900s.

Multimedia Materials

Becoming a Modern Nation. Video, 28 min. Video Knowledge. Traces U.S. history from the Spanish-American War to World War I.

The Lure of Empire: America Debates Imperialism. Video, 27 min. Learning Corporation of America. Dramatizes the debate over the Spanish-American War and U.S. foreign policy in the Pacific.

The Splendid Little War. Video, 55 min. Belle Grove. Uses newsreels, reenactments, and period music to tell the story of the Spanish-American War.

America As a World Power

CHAPTER MOTIVATOR

Bring to class several newspaper articles describing U.S. involvement with other countries. Have students read the articles and discuss different countries with which the United States is involved. Then ask students to list the countries and whether U.S. concerns are economic, military, or political. Write on the chalkboard *Expansionism vs. Isolationism.* Briefly define both terms for the class and point out how citizens of the United States have been and continue to be divided over the level of U.S. involvement in world affairs. Conclude by telling students that in this chapter they will examine the roots of this controversy as well as the U.S. acquisition of new lands and its emergence as a world power.

THEMES

Presenting Themes

- **Geographic Diversity** Students might suggest that a nation might expand its boundaries to gain access to new markets or new sources of raw materials.
- **Economic Development** Students might say that a country could want to increase international trade to find new places to sell its goods or to acquire new goods to sell. It might also want to ensure that other nations do not develop a monopoly on trade.
- **Global Relations** Students could mention that nations might come into conflict if they hope to acquire the same territories. Students might also suggest that nations may feel threatened by countries with overseas territories in their areas or may come into conflict when one nation seems to be becoming too powerful.

Using the Time Line

Have students locate on a map areas that each of the events on the time line affected. After they have completed the chapter, have students write a newspaper article about one of the events.

CHAPTER 10

America As a World Power

(1865–1914)

While campaigning for the Senate in 1898, Albert J. Beveridge declared, "If England can govern foreign lands, so can America." Previously the United States had expanded only across the North American continent. However, as the 1800s came to a close, many Americans began to look overseas for a source of new lands. Beveridge summed up this attitude by saying that "the ocean does not separate us from lands of our duty and desire."

THEMES

Geographic Diversity
Why might a nation attempt to expand its boundaries?

Economic Development
For what reasons might a nation want to increase international trade?

Global Relations
How might a nation's overseas territories bring it into conflict with another nation?

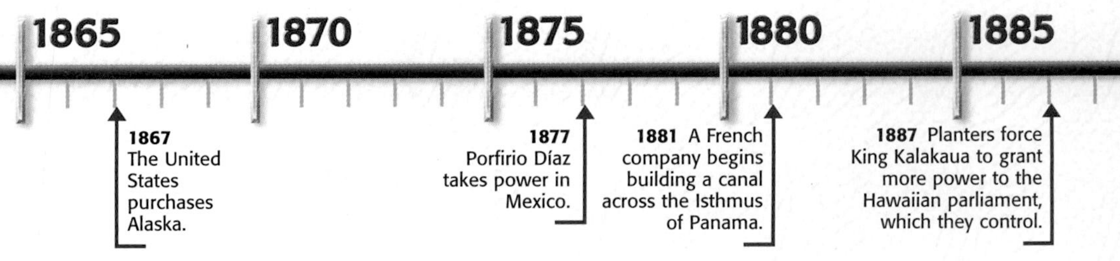

OBJECTIVES

- Explain why some Americans favored expansion over isolationism.
- Describe the events that led to the U.S. annexation of Hawaii.
- Identify the goal of U.S. foreign policy in Japan and China.

FOCUS

Motivate Before Reading

On the chalkboard, create two columns labeled *inside* and *outside*. Ask students to name sports facilities inside the school and outside the school. Record responses under the appropriate heading. Ask members of the class to describe how they would feel if some other classrooms began claiming the *outside* items, such as the baseball field, as their own and did not allow other classes to use

SECTION 1

The United States Gains Overseas Territories

Reading Focus

Why did some people favor expansion over isolationism?

What events led to the U.S. annexation of Hawaii?

What was the goal of U.S. foreign policy in Japan and China?

Key Terms

imperialism
isolationism
McKinley Tariff
subsidy
spheres of influence
Open Door Policy
Boxer Rebellion

ON THE MORNING OF MARCH 16, 1889, the crews of one British, three German, and three U.S. warships prepared for a possible battle. At any moment the peace of Apia Harbor—a port in the Pacific island-nation of Samoa—might erupt with blasts of heavy guns. The United States, Germany, and Britain had each sent their ships to gain control of the Samoa Islands. Before the warships could do battle, however, a sudden typhoon swept into the harbor, destroying all the ships except the British vessel. Although the typhoon had prevented hostilities that day, it did not end Western nations' competition for territories around the world.

Cartoon showing the United States and European nations struggling for power over the Samoans

IMAGE ON LEFT PAGE: *Battle of Manila Bay during the Spanish-American War*

1890 **1895** **1900** **1905** **1910**

1890 Congress passes the McKinley Tariff.

1895 Cuba revolts against Spain.

1898 The USS *Maine* explodes and sinks.

1900 Hawaii becomes a U.S. territory.

1904 President Theodore Roosevelt presents his corollary to the Monroe Doctrine.

1910 The Mexican Revolution begins.

1914 The Panama Canal is opened.

Section 1
RESOURCES

PRINT

★ Guided Reading Strategies 10.1

★ Primary Source Reading 10: Japan and the West

★ Section 1 Review, p. 293

★ Daily Quiz 10.1

MULTIMEDIA

★ *Teaching Resources CD–ROM*, Lesson 10.1

★ Linking Geography and History Transparency 15: The American Empire

SHELTERED ENGLISH

★ Main Idea Activities for Reteaching and Sheltered English 10.1

them. Explain to students that in this section they will learn how the United States was faced with a similar problem as other countries divided up the world into colonies and attempted to control colonial trade.

Introduce Key Terms

Linguistic, Logical-Mathematical. Review this section's key terms with students. As a class, define each term. Then discuss ways to refine the definitions. Write the clarified meanings on the chalkboard. Have students copy them and use each in a sentence. **SHELTERED ENGLISH**

TEACH

Have students read Section 1 and complete Guided Reading Strategies 10.1. Choose one or more of the following activities to explore the section content with students. For further suggestions on block scheduling or team teaching, see the *Block Scheduling Handbook*.

LEVEL 1: Linguistic. (Suggested time: 15 min.) As a class, go over students' Guided Reading Strategies. Then use the Reading Focus questions to highlight the main ideas of the section. **SHELTERED ENGLISH**

Economic Development

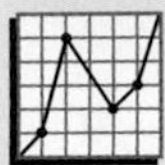

Mahan's Ideas. Alfred Mahan saw Britain as the model of a country relying on a strong navy to build a trading empire. He pointed out that Britain commanded sea lanes to the East through the Mediterranean and the Suez Canal and to the West through the Atlantic. Mahan hoped that the United States could develop an equally important sea route through a canal across Central America.

Critical Thinking: Why would control of the seas help trade?

ANSWER: In the 1800s most trade with foreign countries was accomplished through shipping.

Multimedia Resources

Linking Geography and History Transparency 15: The American Empire

Imperialism and Isolationism

Powerful Western nations were willing to risk war in such far-off places as Samoa to establish a naval base and to protect shipping routes in the Pacific. By the late 1800s the nations of Europe had become engaged in **imperialism**—the practice of extending a nation's power by gaining territories for a colonial empire. Between 1870 and 1914, Europeans built vast colonial empires, seizing control of most of Africa and much of Southeast Asia.

Several forces drove this wave of imperialism. Nations wanted new and plentiful sources of raw materials, such as copper, tin, and rubber, to maintain their industrial growth. At the same time, businesspeople needed new markets in which to sell their goods. Many people also saw colonies as a source of power and national pride.

The United States, however, had not built an overseas colonial empire like many European nations had. Americans were pursuing a limited policy of **isolationism**—avoiding involvement in the affairs of other nations. In his Farewell Address, President George Washington had advised the United States "to steer clear of permanent alliances" with other nations, particularly in Europe. U.S. leaders had tried to follow this advice by avoiding involvement in conflicts overseas.

The Granger Collection, New York

Uncle Sam begins to reap the harvest of imperialism.

Washington's advice had been fairly easy to follow partly because the United States enjoyed the security of a wide ocean separating it from Europe. Good relations with Britain meant that the powerful British navy stood between the United States and possible European enemies. Despite their support of isolationism, many Americans favored expanding the U.S. economy through foreign trade and building a strong military to protect U.S. interests.

Expansion

Many Americans thought that the United States needed to expand its lands to maintain its economic strength. One well-known supporter of expansion was Alfred T. Mahan. In his book *The Influence of Sea Power upon History*, Mahan argued that the United States needed a strong navy to protect its economic interests. Mahan also explained that a strong navy required overseas bases and coaling stations—places where steamships could take on coal for fuel. Senator Henry Cabot Lodge echoed the call for economic expansion through naval power. "Commerce follows the flag," Lodge declared, "and we should build up a navy strong enough to give protection to Americans in every quarter of the globe."

In 1867 the United States greatly expanded its territory when Secretary of State William Seward arranged the purchase of Alaska from Russia for \$7.2 million, less than two cents per acre. People laughed at the purchase, calling it "Seward's Folly" and the "Alaskan Icebox." Despite such criticism, Alaska added some 600,000 square miles to the United States—an area more than twice the size of Texas. Alaska contained natural resources such as furs, timber, and mineral wealth. The 1896 Klondike Gold Rush in Canada's Yukon Territory brought many miners to the region. Around 1900, miners found gold in Alaska, bringing more settlers to the region.

Seward believed that the United States "must continue to move on westward," and in 1867 the nation annexed the Midway Islands. The islands' location, about halfway between the U.S. West

LEVEL 1: Visual-Spatial, Logical-Mathematical, Kinesthetic. (Suggested time: 30 min. plus homework) Explain to the class that Hawaii was not always part of the United States and that it took a series of events to occur before it was annexed. Have students skim this section and take notes on the events leading to the annexation. Then ask them to use magazines, newspapers, their own artwork, and other sources to create a pictorial time line of the events that led to the annexation of Hawaii. Have students display their completed projects to the class and ask for volunteers to explain the relevance of each picture on their time line. **SHELTERED ENGLISH**

ALL LEVELS: Visual-Spatial, Logical-Mathematical. (Suggested time: 30 min.) Joe Kurpiewski of Arlington Heights, Illinois, suggested the following activity: Have each student create a chart titled *U.S. Territories*. The columns should be labeled *Alaska, Hawaii, Midway Islands,* and *Samoa*. The rows of the chart should be labeled *Name of Territory, Year Obtained, How Obtained,* and *Present Status of Territory*. Have students fill in the missing information on the chart.

Alaska's beautiful scenery and natural resources made it a valuable addition to the United States in the long run.

Coast and Japan, made Midway an excellent base and coaling station for the U.S. Navy. The United States also wanted the island group of Samoa for similar reasons, and in 1899 Germany and the United States agreed to divide the Samoa Islands. Britain, interested in territories elsewhere, had given up its part of Samoa to Germany.

Hawaii

Even more appealing than Samoa were the Hawaiian Islands. The Hawaiian people had first come in contact with Europeans in 1778, when British explorer Captain James Cook arrived in the islands.

Economic Interests

Soon after Cook's arrival, Pacific trading and whaling ships from the United States and other countries began stopping in Hawaii for supplies. After the sailors' arrival, American missionaries came to convert the Hawaiians to Christianity. Many of these missionaries remained in the islands, establishing businesses and raising crops such as sugarcane. Some missionary families eventually became wealthy sugar planters.

In 1795 Chief Kamehameha (kuh-may-uh-MAY-huh) had created a monarchy that united Hawaii's eight major islands. In 1839 Hawaii adopted written laws and a constitution based on U.S. and British models.

By the 1840s some 80 percent of the ships arriving in Hawaii were American owned, as were most shops, warehouses, and shipyards. By this time, sugar had become a leading export of the Hawaiian economy. Thousands of workers, particularly Chinese and Japanese, arrived to work on the sugar plantations. An 1875 treaty allowed Hawaiian sugar to be shipped duty-free to the United States. In exchange, Hawaii agreed not to grant territory or special privileges to any nation other than the United States. Hawaiian sugar production boomed, and the planters' influence grew. In 1887 they forced King Kalakaua (kah-LAH-KAH-ooh-ah) to sign a new constitution granting more power to the Hawaiian parliament, which the planters controlled. Many Hawaiians worried that foreigners were becoming too powerful.

Political Control

Sugar planters in Hawaii suffered a severe economic setback when Congress passed the **McKinley Tariff** in 1890. This law allowed all countries to ship sugar duty-free to the United

Pineapple plantations like this one were among the most profitable businesses on the Hawaiian Islands.

Across the Curriculum

LITERATURE

Jack London. Author Jack London spent a year at the Klondike gold rush, near the Alaskan frontier. Although he did not strike gold, his experiences provided valuable writing material. Some of his best short stories pit humans and animals against the harsh Alaskan environment.

Activity: Ask students to read a novel by Jack London and write a book report on it.

Cultural Diversity

Religion in Hawaii. Traditional Hawaiian religion was based on a belief in many gods who existed in all forces and objects. The religion also included a system of taboos, known as a *kapu* system, that maintained political and social order. King Kamehameha II had forbidden the practice of the Hawaiian religion shortly before he let Protestant missionaries come to the islands in 1820.

Critical Thinking: Why do you think Kamehameha forbade Hawaiians from practicing their traditional religion?

ANSWER: He may have wanted to westernize Hawaii.

LEVEL 2: Linguistic, Visual-Spatial, Intrapersonal. (Suggested time: 45 min. plus homework) Assign half the class the position of isolationism, and the other half the position of expansionism. Have each student imagine that the year is 1910 and write a persuasive report to Congress that states why the United States should pursue a policy of isolationism or expansion. Presentations should include at least one illustration (map, graph, chart, etc.) that supports the assigned position. Encourage volunteers to read their reports to the class. Finally, lead a discussion about the debate over isolationism.

LEVEL 3: Linguistic, Interpersonal. (Suggested time: 30 min.) Organize students into two groups and have one represent U.S. trade negotiators in Japan, and one represent U.S. trade negotiators in China. Have each group prepare a report that will introduce new members of their negotiating team to the situation in their assigned country. Their reports should discuss what the United States hopes to gain, strengths and weaknesses of the country's rulers, internal and external issues that will affect negotiations, and any potential problems that might arise. Pair students from the different groups and have them list differences and similarities of U.S. policy in Japan and China.

Biography

Queen Liliuokalani. In 1895 royalists who wanted to return Liliuokalani to power rebelled against Sanford B. Dole. They were defeated, and Liliuokalani was placed under house arrest. Eventually, she abdicated and pledged her loyalty to the new Republic of Hawaii. Liliuokalani wrote a song about Hawaii, "Aloha Oe," which means "Farewell to Thee."

Critical Thinking: Why might Liliuokalani have written "Aloha Oe"?

ANSWER: She may have wanted to remember Hawaii before her abdication.

Across the Curriculum

MATH

Hawaii's Ethnic Groups. According to the 1990 census, Hawaii's population totals about 1,108,000. More than 60 percent of the state's population is of Asian descent and includes Japanese, Filipinos, Chinese, part-Hawaiians, and full Hawaiians. Around one third of the Hawaiian population is white. African Americans make up around 2.5 percent of the population, and Hispanics more than 7 percent.

Activity: Have students calculate the number of Hawaiians who are of Asian descent *(664,000)*.

Biography

Queen Liliuokalani

Liliuokalani was born in Honolulu in 1838 and was educated by American missionaries. In 1887 she traveled across the United States and visited with President Grover Cleveland in Washington.

Liliuokalani became queen in 1891. After the revolt that ended her short reign, Liliuokalani continued to work to reclaim her throne. In her autobiography, *Hawaii's Story,* she wrote that "the United States could become a successful rival of the European nations in the race for conquest, and could create a vast military and naval power." She asked, "But is such an ambition laudable [admirable]?" Until her death in 1917 Liliuokalani served as a symbol of Hawaiian pride and a link to the islands' history.

States but gave U.S. sugar producers a **subsidy**, or bonus payment, of two cents per pound. Prices for Hawaiian sugar dropped, and the islands' economy collapsed.

In 1893 Queen Liliuokalani (li-lee-uh-woh-kuh-LAHN-ee), who had taken the throne in 1891, announced a new constitution that returned power to the monarchy. The planters revolted. John L. Stevens, U.S. ambassador to Hawaii, called 150 marines ashore to support the revolt. The revolt succeeded without any shots being fired. The planters established a new government with lawyer Sanford B. Dole as president. Acting without authority from the state department, Stevens recognized the new government and declared Hawaii to be under U.S. control on February 1, 1893. He wrote to the U.S. State Department that "the Hawaiian pear is now fully ripe, and this is the golden hour for the United States to pluck it." On a U.S. speaking tour at the time, Liliuokalani's 17-year-old niece, Princess Kaiulani, asked Americans to oppose annexation:

> **"I am strong . . . in the strength of seventy million people who in this free land will hear my cry, and will refuse to let their flag . . . dishonor . . . mine."**

President Grover Cleveland disapproved of the revolt and refused to annex Hawaii. However, he took little effective action to help restore the monarchy. The islands remained an independent republic until July 7, 1898, when Congress annexed them. Hawaii became a U.S. territory in 1900 and the 50th state in 1959.

The Opening of Japan

By the mid-1800s some European powers had established strong trade ties to much of East Asia—with the notable exception of Japan. The island-nation of Japan had isolated itself from the rest of the world for centuries. In the 1500s Japan was ruled by several competing family groups, some led by warrior-lords called shoguns. After an extended period of civil war, the leader of the Tokugawa family unified the country.

Suspicious of outsiders, the Tokugawa shoguns had expelled all westerners in the early 1600s. Only the Dutch East India Company was allowed to trade, and only at one port. The Tokugawa had also forbidden travel abroad.

Perry in Japan

The United States looked upon Japan as a trade market it could open before Europeans got there. The *Democratic Review* expressed the feelings of many Americans when it wrote that "the opening of commerce with Japan is demanded by reason,

CLOSE

Linguistic, Logical-Mathematical, Interpersonal. Summarize this section's events by organizing students into small groups and having them list reasons for and examples of the U.S. emergence from isolation to expansion. Ask groups to select one member to record their lists on the chalkboard. Review the lists and add reasons or examples, if necessary. Finally, have students write a complete list in their notebooks.

CHALLENGE AND EXTEND

1. **Linguistic, Logical-Mathematical.** Review Senator Henry Cabot Lodge's declaration on textbook page 288 that the United States needed greater naval power to support economic expansion. Have students use the library or other sources to research the establishment and growth of the U.S. Navy. Make sure they include figures on the size of the navy today. Have students report their findings to the class.

civilization, progress and religion." Eager to overcome Japan's isolationism, President Millard Fillmore sent Commodore Matthew Perry to secure "friendship, commerce, a supply of coal and provisions."

On July 8, 1853, an astonished Japanese crowd watched a fleet of four U.S. warships move into Edo (now called Tokyo) Harbor. Perry delivered a letter from President Fillmore suggesting a peaceful trade relationship. Perry's fleet then sailed off, and he returned in February 1854 with seven warships. To show some of the technological gains that trade with the United States would offer, Perry presented Japanese leaders with gifts of a telegraph transmitter and a model train. However, it was mostly the U.S. show of force that persuaded Japanese leaders to sign a treaty opening trade with the United States. Many Japanese leaders also pushed for trade because they believed that their country needed to industrialize.

In 1856 Townsend Harris arrived in Japan as the first U.S. consul general, or chief diplomat. His instructions were to secure a treaty that would open Japan to further trade. This was difficult because, as Harris wrote, "the absence of a man-of-war [warship] . . . tends to weaken my influence with the Japanese." He eventually overcame Japanese opposition and in 1858 negotiated a commercial treaty.

Japan Expands

In 1868, supporters of industrialization came to power in Japan and began a period of modernization known as the Meiji [MAY-jee] Restoration. Over the next 40 years, Japanese leaders invested heavily in industry and in strengthening the nation's military. The government sent Japanese students to Western schools to learn about modern science and technology and Western government. One such student, Yukichi Fukuzawa, realized

"what policy Japan must take to preserve herself among the powers of the

Global Relations

Japan's Changing Society. After the commercial treaty of 1858, which allowed people from the United States and several European countries to enter Japan, members of the samurai, or warrior class, made many attacks on westerners. They soon realized, however, that they could not keep foreigners out of the country. So the samurai began to push for reforms within Japan, and soon they forced the Tokugawa Shogunate to give up power.

Critical Thinking: Why might the samurai have resented westerners?

ANSWER: Answers will vary but students might say that they disliked or distrusted Western culture and influence.

Global Connections

Japanese Immigrants in Hawaii

Japanese immigrants began arriving in Hawaii in the 1860s but did not immigrate in large numbers until later in the 1800s. By 1923 they made up almost 43 percent of the population. Many Japanese were recruited and signed labor contracts to work on the islands' many sugar plantations. They came in search of more opportunities.

Japanese fieldworkers in Hawaii

Life on the plantations was difficult. The workday began at sunrise and ended at sundown. The working conditions were harsh, as workers planted, weeded, fertilized, watered, harvested, and hauled the sugarcane.

Many Japanese immigrants remained in Hawaii once their contracts expired because they could not afford to return to Japan. Some, believing there was a potential market for Japanese products, started their own businesses, such as importing food, clothing, and hardware.

Today people of Japanese descent make up about one fourth of Hawaii's population. They live on all the major islands and work in all occupations, including government, law, and education.

Understanding What You Read

1. Describe the working conditions on Hawaii's sugar plantations.
2. How have Japanese immigrants contributed to Hawaiian society?

GLOBAL CONNECTIONS ANSWERS

1. Working conditions were harsh, and the workday was long.
2. They have begun new businesses and taken part in all occupations.

2. **Visual-Spatial, Logical-Mathematical, Kinesthetic.** Alaska's size is difficult to comprehend. Have students, either individually or in teams of two, use an atlas or other resource to research the size of Alaska as well as the size (square miles) of the states that comprised the United States at the time of Alaska's purchase. Have students create a visual display that compares their findings. Encourage them to use charts, maps, or tables to present the information. When students have finished their displays, have them make a classroom bulletin board of their work.

3. **Linguistic, Logical-Mathematical.** Have students use the library or other available resources to find information on the Boxer Rebellion. Ask students to create a series of newspaper articles dealing with the causes of the rebellion, the actual events that took place, and the effects the rebellion had on U.S.-Chinese relations. Ask volunteers to share information from their reports with the class. When students have completed their articles, have them work in small groups to combine some of the articles into a newspaper.

Economic Development

Trade with China. In the 1800s American traders, hoping to find new markets, looked to Asian countries, particularly China. During the 1890s China imported many goods from the United States, including cotton textiles, kerosene, flour, iron, and steel. Nonetheless, China made up only 1.1 percent of all American exports for that decade.

Critical Thinking: Why might China have held so much allure for traders?

ANSWER: China's large population made it an attractive market.

MAP ANSWER

Howland Island, Baker Island, Jarvis Island

world. . . . The final purpose of all my work was to create in Japan a civilized nation as well equipped in the arts of war and peace as those of the Western world.”

By the end of the century, Japan was emerging as a major imperial power. Japan's invasion and defeat of China in 1894-95 gave the Japanese the same trade privileges in China as European nations had.

Japan dealt a similar blow to Russia. In 1904 the Japanese attacked Russian forces stationed in China. The Japanese won early victories over the Russians in the Russo-Japanese War. Japan sank an entire Russian fleet in a single battle. In 1905 U.S. president Theodore Roosevelt helped negotiate a peace treaty to end the war. Japan had won the respect it desired and had gained Korea, as well as a lease on Port Arthur in China, and other rights. In less than 50 years Japan had gone from an isolated nonindustrial country to a major world power. Hilary Herbert, U.S. secretary of the navy, said that “Japan has leaped, almost at one bound, to a place among the great nations of the earth.”

Asian goods like this fan were popular trade items.

Peabody Essex Museum, Salem, Massachusetts

Foreign Powers in China

Economic interests drew the United States not only to Hawaii and Japan but also to China. There the United States and many European nations engaged in a profitable trade.

Spheres of Influence

Japan's 1894 invasion of China with a modern, well-equipped army had resulted in a swift and surprisingly easy victory. In its defeat, China granted Japan trade privileges and formally accepted Japan's control of Korea. China surrendered Taiwan and other territories to Japan.

Other nations quickly took advantage of China's weakness to seize **spheres of influence**—areas where foreign nations control trade and natural resources. Many nations joined in what was called “the carving up of the Chinese melon.” Germany took control of a harbor in Shandong Province in November 1897. Other nations followed suit—Russia in the north, Great Britain on the coast opposite Hong Kong Island, and France and Japan in the southern provinces.

U.S. Territories in the Pacific

Learning from Maps Between 1850 and 1900 Alaska and many Pacific islands, including Hawaii, became U.S. territories.

Location Which U.S. territories were located along the equator?

The Open Door

The United States feared that it would be closed out of Chinese markets. Some of President William McKinley's advisers called for a U.S.

REVIEW

Visual-Spatial, Interpersonal. Have students complete the Section Review questions. Then organize students into several groups and assign each group one of the following areas: Alaska, Hawaii, Japan, or China. Give each group a piece of butcher paper and have students create a cause-and-effect chart describing how the United States gained land or influence in the area.

RETEACH

Linguistic, Visual-Spatial. Have students complete Main Idea Activities for Reteaching and Sheltered English 10.1. Ask them to create a crossword puzzle using the terms and people listed in the Identify section of the Section Review. Have students exchange puzzles, complete them, and return them to their authors for grading. **SHELTERED ENGLISH**

ASSESS

Have students complete Daily Quiz 10.1.

sphere of influence, but the nation lacked the naval power to accomplish this. Instead, the United States turned to diplomacy.

In 1899 Secretary of State John Hay sent a series of notes to Japan and most European nations outlining what became known as the **Open Door Policy**—that all nations should have equal access to trade with China. The goal of this policy was to protect U.S. trade interests. Japan and the European powers neither accepted nor rejected the Open Door Policy. Hay took advantage of this situation to announce that the policy had been accepted.

Participants in the Boxer Rebellion

The Boxer Rebellion

Within China, there was strong resentment of the power and control held by foreign nations. In 1900 this antiforeign hostility boiled over, producing the **Boxer Rebellion**. The Boxers were Chinese nationalists who were members of the "Fists of Righteous Harmony." The Boxers were angered by foreign involvement in Chinese affairs, mismanagement by the Chinese government, and the hunger and homelessness caused by a series of natural disasters.

In June 1900 the Boxers took to the streets of Beijing, China's capital, and murdered two foreign diplomats. They then laid siege to the walled settlement in which foreigners lived, killing more than 200 people. Knowing the attack was doomed, the Chinese government did not support the Boxers.

The siege continued for two months until military forces including U.S. Marines fought their way from the port of Tianjin to Beijing. The Boxers were soon defeated. Afterward, China was forced to accept a harsh settlement that included a $333 million cash payment, $25 million of which went to the United States. Secretary of State Hay then sent another Open Door note to Japan and the European nations, restating the U.S. position that all nations should have equal access to Chinese markets. Hay wanted to prevent any European colonization of China that would limit U.S. influence there. The Open Door Policy remained in effect long after the Boxer Rebellion.

SECTION 1 REVIEW

Identify and explain the significance of the following:

- **imperialism**
- **isolationism**
- **William Seward**
- **McKinley Tariff**
- **subsidy**
- **Liliuokalani**
- **Matthew Perry**
- **spheres of influence**
- **Open Door Policy**
- **Boxer Rebellion**

Reading for Content Understanding

1 **Main Idea** What arguments did people make for isolationism and for expansion in the 1800s?

2 **Main Idea** How did Hawaii become a part of the United States?

3 **Global Relations** What did U.S. leaders hope to accomplish in relations with Japan and China?

4 **Writing** *Persuading* Imagine that you are a member of Congress at the time William Seward proposes the purchase of Alaska from Russia. Write a short speech you might give to Congress, explaining why you are voting for or against the proposed purchase.

5 **Critical Thinking** *Making Comparisons* How were China's and Japan's reactions to foreign trade similar? How were they different?

Section 1 Review ANSWERS

Identify

For significance, see the following pages:

- imperialism, p. 288
- isolationism, p. 288
- William Seward, p. 288
- McKinley Tariff, p. 289
- subsidy, p. 290
- Liliuokalani, p. 290
- Matthew Perry, p. 291
- spheres of influence, p. 292
- Open Door Policy, p. 293
- Boxer Rebellion, p. 293

Reading for Content Understanding

1. isolationism—could keep United States from entanglement in outside affairs; expansionism—could improve the U.S. economy through foreign trade, some people believed that economic strength came from developing new lands

2. Americans took control of Hawaii from its royal rulers in 1893 and made it an independent country. In 1898, the United States annexed the islands, but did not make Hawaii a state until 1959.

3. They wanted to open new trading markets.

4. for—low price for such a large territory, desire to expand United States, and wealth in fur, timber, and minerals; against—Alaska's climate and distance from the United States made it unlikely many Americans would want to move there.

5. similar—both countries resisted trade; different—Japan improved its own industry and technology and became an imperial power, while China fought unsuccessfully against Western influence.

OBJECTIVES

- **Explain the effect of the press on U.S. involvement in the conflict in Cuba.**
- **Describe what enabled the United States to win the war with Spain.**
- **Analyze the effect of the Spanish-American War on the Philippines, Cuba, and Puerto Rico.**

FOCUS

Motivate Before Reading

Ask students to imagine what life was like for American colonists under British rule. *(The people had no say in the laws made by the monarch and Parliament, they paid taxes to a government over which they had no control, and the monarch could restrict or take away their rights whenever he or she wanted.)* Now ask students how willing they might be to assist another country that is controlled by a

Section 2 RESOURCES

PRINT

- ★ Guided Reading Strategies 10.2
- ★ Biography Reading 10: William Randolph Hearst
- ★ Literature Reading 10: Fighting Spanish Imperialism
- ★ Geography Activity 10: The Philippine War
- ★ Section 2 Review, p. 300
- ★ Daily Quiz 10.2

MULTIMEDIA

- ★ *Teaching Resources CD–ROM,* Lesson 10.2
- ★ Everyday Life in America Transparency 19: Photojournalism in the Spanish-American War
- ★ HRW Web site

SHELTERED ENGLISH

- ★ Main Idea Activities for Reteaching and Sheltered English 10.2

The Spanish-American War

Reading Focus

How did the press affect U.S. involvement in the conflict in Cuba?

What enabled the United States to win the war with Spain?

How did the Spanish-American War affect the Philippines, Cuba, and Puerto Rico?

Key Terms

yellow journalism
Teller Amendment
Anti-Imperialist League
Platt Amendment

JOSÉ MARTÍ WAS BORN in Havana, Cuba, on January 28, 1853. At the age of 15, Martí joined in a revolt against Cuba's Spanish rulers. For his actions, Martí was banished to Spain, where he earned a university degree. He later worked in Mexico as a journalist and in Guatemala as a teacher. Martí returned to Cuba in 1878 but was banished again for his actions. This time, he moved to New York City, where he continued to work tirelessly for Cuban independence. While anxiously watching events in his homeland, Martí waited for the day when he could return to fight the Spanish once again.

José Martí

 Revolts Against Spain

In the late 1800s only Cuba and Puerto Rico remained of Spain's once-great American empire. In 1868, Cubans revolted, beginning a decade-long struggle for freedom. Spain eventually regained control and forced many members of the Cuban independence movement, like José Martí, to leave the country.

After the revolt, U.S. trade with Cuba grew, and the United States invested some $50 million in Cuba, mostly in sugar and mining. However, in 1894 the Wilson-Gorman Tariff removed Cuban sugar from the list of duty-free products. This made Cuban sugar more expensive in the United States and harmed the Cuban economy.

In 1895 Cuba again erupted in revolt, further damaging its trade with the United States. Martí returned to Cuba to fight the Spanish but was killed soon after. He quickly became a Cuban hero. Spain decided to crack down harshly on Cuba, and sent General Valeriano Weyler to crush the rebellion. Because so many civilians supported the rebels, Weyler gathered several hundred thousand Cubans into barbed-wire camps, called *reconcentrados,* or reconcentration camps. He similarly autocratic government. Explain that in this section students will read about Spain's control of Cuba, why and how the United States became involved in a war with Spain to win Cuba's independence, and what effect this war had on Spain and its colonies.

Introduce Key Terms

Linguistic, Logical-Mathematical. Review this section's key terms with students. Write a sentence on the chalkboard for each of the key terms to provide a contextual cue to the term's meaning. Have students guess which key term each sentence identifies. Have them write their answers in their notebooks. Finally, have students use the textbook to write a definition for each term next to their initial responses. **SHELTERED ENGLISH**

TEACH

Have students read Section 2 and complete Guided Reading Strategies 10.2. Choose one or more of the following activities to explore the section content with students. For further suggestions on block scheduling or team teaching, see the *Block Scheduling Handbook*.

reasoned that anyone not in the camps was a rebel. More than 100,000 Cubans died in the camps because of bad and inadequate food and lack of sanitation. Weyler's harsh measures led many Americans to support the rebels.

The Road to War

Many Americans sympathized with the rebels, believing that the Cubans' struggle for liberation was similar to that of the United States in 1776. The conflict was widely reported, even exaggerated, in the American press, further increasing support for the Cubans.

The Press

Two newspapers—Joseph Pulitzer's New York *World* and William Randolph Hearst's *New York Journal*—were particularly critical of the Spanish. Their harsh words and stories were part of a competition between Pulitzer and Hearst to sell the most newspapers. This use of sensational, often exaggerated stories to attract readers is known as **yellow journalism**.

Pulitzer was the first to engage in yellow journalism, but Hearst soon outdid Pulitzer at his own game. Describing General Weyler as "pitiless, cold, an exterminator of men," the *New York Journal* went so far as to create the stories that Hearst wanted. To increase support for U.S. action in Cuba and to sell papers, Hearst hired artist and illustrator Frederic Remington to provide pictures of the conditions on the island. Remington supposedly telegraphed Hearst from Cuba, saying, "Everything is quiet. There is no trouble here. There will be no war." Hearst is said to have replied, "You furnish the pictures and I'll furnish the war."

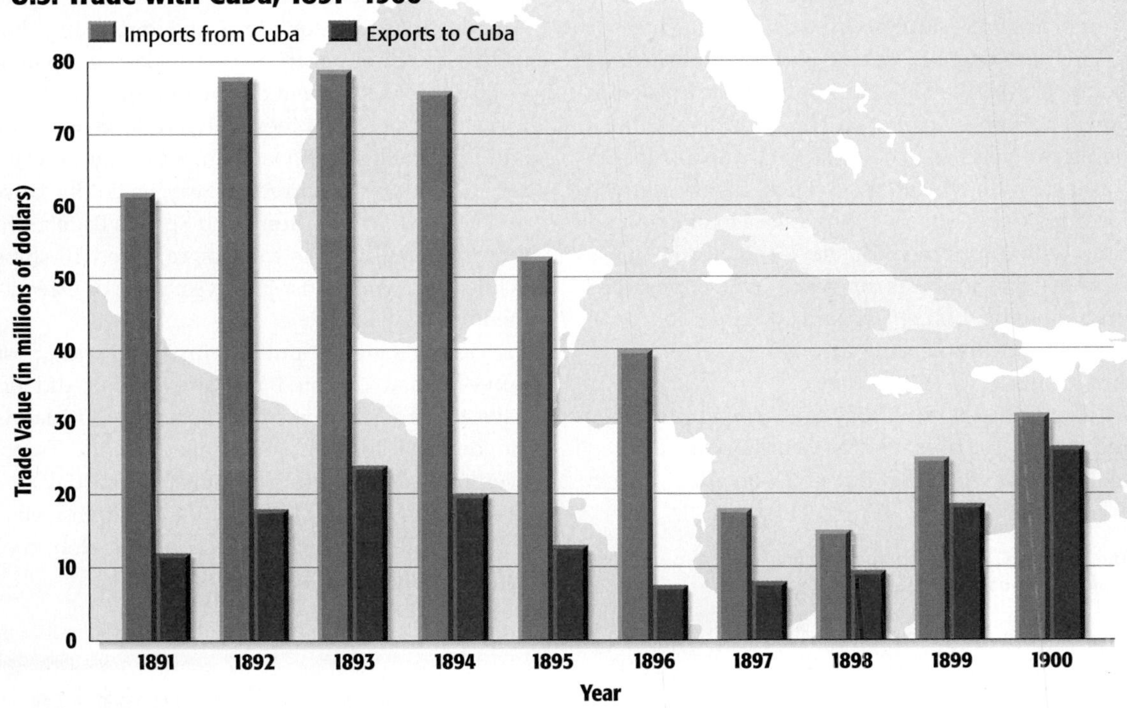

The Value of Trade The valuable trade with Cuba was a factor in the U.S. decision to go to war with Spain. What was the value of imports from Cuba in 1896?

Daily Life

Hearst's Papers. Comic strip artist R. F. Outcault helped coin the term *yellow journalism.* Newspapers in 1896 were just starting to use color printing. Outcault's "The Yellow Kid," which ran in William Randolph Hearst's *New York Journal*, displayed the new yellow ink. The color was so prominent, that it came to be associated with Hearst and the way he ran his paper.

Activity: Have students use material from the textbook to create headlines that Hearst may have run in his newspaper during the Spanish-American War. Remind them to reflect Hearst's biases.

Multimedia Resources

Everyday Life in America Transparency 19: Photojournalism in the Spanish-American War

CHART ANSWER
$40 million

LEVEL 1: Linguistic. (Suggested time: 15 min.) As a class, go over students' Guided Reading Strategies. Then use the Reading Focus questions to highlight the main ideas of the section. **SHELTERED ENGLISH**

LEVEL 1: Linguistic, Visual-Spatial. (Suggested time: 10 min.) Ask students to return to the *U.S. Territories* chart they created in the Teacher to Teacher activity. Have them add the Philippines, Puerto Rico, and Guam as new columns to their charts. Ask them to use their textbooks to find the information for the related rows on the chart. **SHELTERED ENGLISH**

ALL LEVELS: Visual-Spatial, Kinesthetic, Interpersonal. (Suggested time: 45 min. plus homework) Organize the class into groups of three or four students and have the groups prepare a television news report on one of the following events: the sinking of the *Maine*, the declaration of war, the Battle of Manila Bay, the Rough Riders, the Battle of Santiago de Cuba, and the invasion of Puerto Rico. Advise students that their news reports should be no more than one minute long. They are to present their information in present-day, television-news fashion, using maps, charts, or interviews in their reports. Have groups present their reports to the class in the order in which events occurred.

Across the Curriculum

ART

Frederic Remington. By the time Hearst sent him to Cuba to draw battle scenes, Remington had already established a reputation for himself as an artist depicting the West. He had toured the western United States in 1881, even working as a cowboy for a time. Traveling with the U.S. cavalry, he had witnessed fighting between U.S. soldiers and American Indians—struggles he later captured in illustrations and paintings.

Critical Thinking: Why might Hearst have considered Remington the right illustrator for the Spanish-American War?

ANSWER: Remington had experience with battlefield scenes in the West.

Political Pressure

Despite growing support for military action, President Cleveland remained strongly opposed to involvement in Cuba. In 1896, however, William McKinley, who supported Cuban independence, was elected president.

Growing international protest over the treatment of Cubans led the Spanish government to recall General Weyler in October 1897. Attempting to end the rebellion, Spain offered to grant Cubans autonomy—self-government without independence. However, Cuban rebels were committed to independence and refused the offer.

"Remember the *Maine*"

Several events led to war in Cuba. On February 9, 1898, Hearst published a letter that Dupuy de Lôme, the Spanish minister to the United States, had written to a friend. In it, de Lôme called President McKinley "weak and a bidder for the admiration of the crowd." The Spanish government was embarrassed by the letter, but many Americans were outraged.

On January 25, before Hearst published de Lôme's letter, the U.S. battleship *Maine* arrived in Havana Harbor to protect U.S. citizens and economic interests. Senator Mark Hanna compared this action to "waving a match in an oil well for fun." On February 15 the *Maine* exploded and sank with a loss of 260 men. Although the cause of the explosion was unclear, many Americans immediately blamed Spain. "Remember the *Maine*!" quickly became a rallying cry for angry Americans.

Congress approved $50 million that McKinley requested to prepare for war. Spain offered to negotiate but would not consider Cuban independence. Even though Cuba was not a U.S. territory, on April 20 Congress issued a resolution that declared Cuba independent. That same resolution also gave Spain three days to leave the island. Attached to the resolution was the **Teller Amendment**, which declared that the United States had no intention of taking over Cuba. In response to the U.S. resolution, Spain declared war on April 24. The next day, Congress passed and McKinley signed a declaration of war.

The Granger Collection, New York

President William McKinley

The New York Journal *announces the explosion aboard the* Maine.

$50,000 REWARD.—WHO DESTROYED THE MAINE?—$50,000 REWARD.

EDITION FOR GREATER NEW YORK

NEW YORK JOURNAL

AND ADVERTISER.

PRICE ONE CENT

NEW YORK, THURSDAY, FEBRUARY 17, 1898.—16 PAGES.

DESTRUCTION OF THE WAR SHIP MAINE WAS THE WORK OF AN ENEMY.

$50,000!

$50,000 REWARD! For the Detection of the Perpetrator of the Maine Outrage!

Assistant Secretary Roosevelt Convinced the Explosion of the War Ship Was Not an Accident.

The Journal Offers $50,000 Reward for the Conviction of the Criminals Who Sent 258 American Sailors to Their Death. Naval Officers Unanimous That the Ship Was Destroyed on Purpose.

$50,000!

$50,000 REWARD! For the Detection of the Perpetrator of the Maine Outrage!

Fighting in the Pacific

While attention was focused on Cuba, the U.S. Navy won a quick and spectacular victory nearly halfway around the world in the Pacific Ocean. Commodore George Dewey, commander of the American Asiatic squadron at Hong Kong, had orders to be prepared to attack the Spanish Philippines in the event of war. On April 30 Dewey arrived at the Philippines with four large warships and two smaller gunboats. The next day, ignoring reports that mines barred his way, he boldly sailed into Manila Bay and destroyed Spain's Pacific fleet there. Dewey's forces sank or captured 10 ships. While the Spanish lost 381 lives, none of Dewey's men were killed.

Dewey's victory put him in an awkward position—he had defeated the Spanish but did not have the troops necessary to occupy the islands. He decided to wait for reinforcements. Troops eventually arrived and on August 13, one day after the war had ended, U.S. troops and Filipino rebels led by Emilio Aguinaldo (ahg-ee-NAHL-doh) took control of the Philippine capital, Manila.

The War in the Caribbean

Many people expected victory in Cuba to come as quickly as it had in the Philippines. However, training and supplying thousands of volunteer troops took longer than getting the navy under way.

LEVEL 2: Linguistic, Intrapersonal. (Suggested time: 45 min.) Review the role that the American press played in stirring up citizens' feelings about war with Spain. Ask students to imagine that they are regular readers of the New York *World*. Have them write a letter to the editor supporting or criticizing the methods the *World* is using to encourage Americans' support for a declaration of war with Spain.

LEVEL 3: Linguistic, Interpersonal. (Suggested time: 45 min. plus homework) Organize the class into three groups and assign each group one of the following former Spanish territories: Cuba, the Philippines, or Puerto Rico. Tell members of each group that they have been asked by leaders in the former territory to create a plan for the future, particularly for policy toward the United States. The territories can either remain under U.S. control, pursue statehood, or attempt to gain their independence. Students must decide which of these options to pursue, why they think it is best for their territory, and what steps the territory's leaders ought to take. Have groups write short position papers outlining their ideas. Finally, have each group present its recommendation to the class.

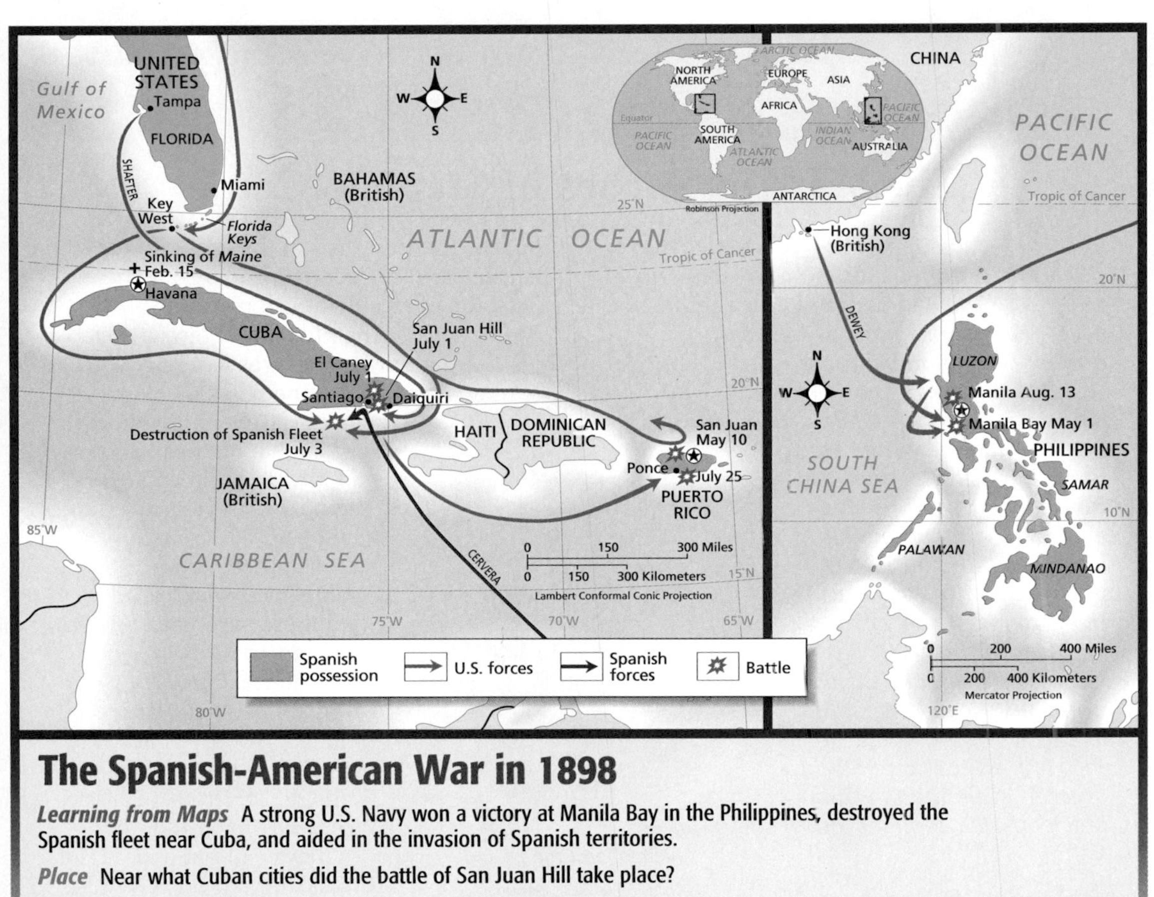

The Spanish-American War in 1898

Learning from Maps A strong U.S. Navy won a victory at Manila Bay in the Philippines, destroyed the Spanish fleet near Cuba, and aided in the invasion of Spanish territories.

Place Near what Cuban cities did the battle of San Juan Hill take place?

The Soldiers

At the start of the war, only about 28,000 soldiers were serving in the regular U.S. Army. The army was unprepared to train and supply the more than 280,000 soldiers who would see active duty. There were shortages of bullets and rifles, and soldiers received warm woolen uniforms to wear in the tropical heat. Once in Cuba, many soldiers were struck by deadly diseases such as yellow fever. For food the army purchased canned meat that one general called "embalmed beef." Of the few thousand U.S. forces who died during the war, only a small percentage died in battle. The rest died from food poisoning, disease, and other causes.

The most colorful group of soldiers in the war were the Rough Riders, the First Volunteer Cavalry commanded by General Leonard Wood. Second in command was Lieutenant Colonel Theodore Roosevelt. Anxious to join the fighting, Roosevelt organized a group of volunteers to fight in Cuba. The Rough Riders came from many walks of life. They included college athletes, miners, American Indians, ranchers, and cowboys.

Newspaper accounts of Roosevelt's charm and the Rough Riders' heroic achievements in battle earned the group the admiration of the American public. Many other U.S. soldiers also served bravely. Four privates of the African American 10th Cavalry rowed through heavy gunfire to rescue 15 members of a U.S. landing party. All four received the Congressional Medal of Honor for their actions.

The Battles

On June 1, 1898, U.S. ships caught the Spanish Caribbean fleet in the harbor of Santiago de Cuba. The more numerous and powerful U.S. Navy blockaded the harbor and made it safe for U.S. troops to land nearby. Set ashore on June 22 and

Daily Life

Conditions in the American Camps in Cuba. Lieutenant Colonel Alfred A. Woodhull served as a surgeon in the army. He observed many health problems at Camp Thomas, where more than 425 soldiers died. The most serious danger of infection came from the pileup of garbage. Woodhull noted that some regiments attempted to burn their kitchen garbage in furnaces, but no one had taken steps to build large enough furnaces to dispose of the refuse properly. This lack of hygiene led to pollution and the spread of illness and disease.

Critical Thinking: What might have prevented the army from taking steps to deal with the hygiene problem?

ANSWER: By the time the army realized the problem, leaders might have felt it was too late to correct it.

MAP ANSWER
Daiquiri, Santiago

CLOSE

Linguistic, Logical-Mathematical. Ask students to imagine that the U.S. Post Office has found a way to send letters back to 1898. Have students write letters of advice to President McKinley about the Spanish-American War. Ask them to advise the president on how to handle one or more of the following: yellow journalism, the de Lôme letter, the explosion of the USS *Maine*, the Teller Amendment, the Anti-Imperialist League, and the Platt Amendment.

CHALLENGE AND EXTEND

1. **Linguistic, Visual-Spatial, Interpersonal.** Organize the class into three groups. Assign each group one of the following areas of research: the Philippines before 1898, the Philippines under U.S. control, or the Philippines as an independent nation. Have each group report its findings to the class. Encourage students to use charts, graphs, and maps to highlight important information.

Historical Sidelight

Stephen Crane. Writer Stephen Crane got his first taste of journalism in his teens, working for an older brother at a news agency in Asbury Park, New Jersey. Later, Crane interrupted his college coursework to earn money as a reporter in New York. Newspaper editors often criticized his reporting because they thought he gave too much attention to his impressions and ignored the facts of events.

Activity: Have students conduct an Internet search through the HRW Web site to find more information on Stephen Crane. Ask them to write a brief report with the information they find.

go.hrw.com
SB1 Stephen Crane

American Literature Answers

1. exhausted
2. They broke through the Spanish guerrillas.
3. They wanted to rescue their fellow soldiers.
4. It may have made them realize the difficulties that soldiers faced and the heroism of their efforts.

American Literature

The War Dispatches of Stephen Crane

Although more readers know of Stephen Crane for his novel The Red Badge of Courage, *he also worked as a journalist during the Spanish-American War. He published many gripping war reports. While in his twenties, Crane was already such a popular reporter that his editors made a point of putting his name in their front-page headlines to attract more readers. The following war dispatch, "Night Attacks on the Marines and a Brave Rescue," appeared in the New York* World *on July 16, 1898. It reports an account of fighting in Cuba between U.S. Marines and Spanish soldiers.*

Stephen Crane

The Granger Collection, New York

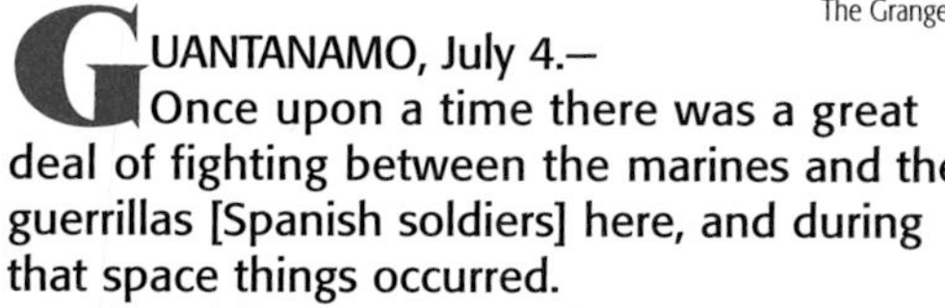

GUANTANAMO, July 4.—Once upon a time there was a great deal of fighting between the marines and the guerrillas [Spanish soldiers] here, and during that space things occurred.

The night attacks were heart-breaking affairs, from which the men emerged in the morning exhausted to a final degree, like people who had been swimming for miles. From colonel to smallest trumpeter went a great thrill when the dawn broke slowly in the eastern sky, and the weary band quite cheerfully ate breakfast. . . . Afterward the men slept, sunk upon the ground in an abandon [physical exhaustion] that was almost a stupor [daze].

Lieut. Neville, with his picket [forward group] of about twenty men, was entirely cut off from camp one night, and another night Neville's picket and the picket of Lieut. Shaw were cut off, fighting hard in the thickets [forests] for their lives. At the break of day the beleaguered [surrounded] camp could hear still the rifles of their lost pickets.

The problem of rescue added anxiety to the already tremendous anxiety of the fine old colonel. . . . The guerrillas were still lurking [sneaking] in the near woods, and it was unsafe enough in camp without venturing into the bush.

Volunteers from Company C were called for, and these seventeen privates volunteered:

Boniface, Conway, Fitzgerald, Heilner, Harmson, Hemerle, Lewin, Mann, Mills, Monahan, Nolan, O'Donnell, Ryan, Riddle, Sinclair, Sullivan, W. A., and Smith, J. H.

They went out under Lieut. Lucas. They arrived in Neville's vicinity just as he and his men, together with Shaw and his men, were being finally surrounded at close range. Lucas and his seventeen men broke through the guerrillas and saved the pickets, and the whole body then fell back to Crest Hill. That is all there is to it.

Understanding Literature

1. How did the soldiers feel after the night attacks?
2. How did Lieutenant Lucas and his men save the pickets?
3. Why do you think the U.S. soldiers from Company C volunteered to help in the rescue of the pickets that were cut off from camp?
4. What effect do you think this war dispatch had on readers in the United States?

2. **Linguistic, Interpersonal.** Have students use the library or other sources to find modern-day interpretations of the explosion of the USS *Maine*. Have students use their research to write a short story or play describing what may have happened. Encourage students to include background information about the controversy, present a theory of what caused the explosion, and offer information to support their theory. Have students read one other student's story or play and compare that theory to their own.

3. **Linguistic, Kinesthetic, Intrapersonal.** Ask students to imagine that they are U.S. senators in 1898. The USS *Maine* has just exploded, and the public is calling for war with Spain. Ask them to write a speech for or against the war. Tell them to consider the following information when deciding whether to support the war: the possibility that the sinking of the *Maine* was an accident, the overall risks and possible benefits of fighting Spain, and the mood of U.S. citizens. Encourage volunteers to present their speeches to the class.

aided by Cuban rebels, the U.S. troops moved to capture the hills around the main Spanish forces at Santiago. At the village of El Caney on July 1, some 7,000 U.S. soldiers overwhelmed about 600 Spanish defenders. The main U.S. force under General Hamilton Hawkins then attacked and captured San Juan Hill. A smaller force, including the Rough Riders and the African American 9th and 10th Cavalries, captured nearby Kettle Hill. A journalist on the scene described their charge:

> **"It was a miracle of self-sacrifice, a triumph of bulldog courage. . . . The fire of the Spanish riflemen . . . doubled and trebled [tripled] in fierceness, the crests of the hills crackled and burst in amazed roars and rippled with waves of tiny flame. But the blue line [of U.S. soldiers] crept steadily up and on."**

On July 3 the U.S. artillery was within range of the Spanish fleet, so the Spanish commander decided to try breaking through the U.S. blockade. Every Spanish ship was destroyed in the battle, with 474 Spaniards killed and 1,750 others captured. American forces suffered only two casualties. Santiago surrendered on July 17. A few days later, U.S. troops commanded by Nelson Miles invaded Puerto Rico, where they met little resistance. Puerto Rico soon surrendered. Spain asked for peace and signed a cease-fire on August 12, 1898.

 The Peace Treaty

The peace treaty between Spain and the United States placed Puerto Rico, Guam, Cuba, and the Philippines under U.S. control. Groups like the **Anti-Imperialist League**, made up of Americans who opposed the treaty, accused the United States of building a colonial empire. Despite such protests, the treaty was ratified by a vote of 57 to 27, one vote more than the two-thirds majority needed.

The Philippines

Spain had surrendered the Philippines in return for a $20 million payment from the United States. Many Americans wondered why their nation

The Rough Riders and the 9th and 10th Cavalries fight to help secure Santiago.

wanted the islands. Some believed that it would be wrong to annex the islands without the consent of the Filipinos. Other people agreed with President McKinley, who said that the United States would benefit from the islands' naval and commercial value, and that annexing the islands would keep Europeans from seizing them.

Filipino rebels, however, had helped U.S. forces capture Manila, and expected to gain their independence after the war. When the United States decided to keep the islands, the rebels began a guerrilla war against the U.S. forces. Some 70,000 U.S. soldiers fought in the Philippines, and hundreds of thousands of Filipinos died, before the war ended more than three years later in 1902.

On July 1, 1902, the U.S. Congress passed the Philippine Government Act. This act provided that the Philippines would be ruled by an appointed governor and a two-house legislature, the lower house of which was elected. In 1946 the United States granted full independence to the Philippines.

Cuba

Although the Teller Amendment had stated that the United States would not annex Cuba, President McKinley established a military government there. McKinley wanted to create stability and increase U.S. trade and influence in the region. He appointed General Leonard Wood as governor, and Wood quickly began building schools and a sanitation system. To combat disease, Dr. Walter

Using Visual Resources

African American Regiments. The image on this page shows the bravery of African American soldiers during the Spanish-American war. Both Theodore Roosevelt and Lieutenant John J. Pershing commanded African American regiments and testified to the courage and determination that these soldiers showed.

Critical Thinking: Why do you think the officers of the African American regiments were not African American?

ANSWER: Because of racial discrimination, African Americans were denied leadership positions in the army.

Economic Development

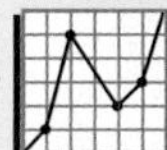

The Philippines. When Commodore George Dewey first took the Philippines, President McKinley declared that his main priority was not to take the territory from Spain. He assured European countries that he only wanted to maintain the Open Door Policy. By the time Spain surrendered, however, McKinley's attitude had changed.

Critical Thinking: Why would the United States want to keep European nations out of the Philippines?

ANSWER: The United States hoped to profit from a monopoly on trade with the Philippines.

REVIEW

Linguistic. Have students complete the Section Review questions. Ask students to adopt the perspective of a member of the Anti-Imperialist League and write a paragraph describing an event in this section. Link students' paragraphs to form the anti-imperialist story of the war. Lead a discussion on how the relating of historical events can change depending on point of view.

ASSESS

Have students complete Daily Quiz 10.2.

RETEACH

Logical-Mathematical. Have students complete Main Idea Activities for Reteaching and Sheltered English 10.2. Ask students to create an outline using these main ideas: causes of the Spanish-American War, events of the Spanish-American War, and the results of the Spanish-American War. Have students provide at least four supporting details for each main idea.

SHELTERED ENGLISH

Section 2 Review ANSWERS

Identify

For significance, see the following pages:

- José Martí, p. 294
- Joseph Pulitzer, p. 295
- William Randolph Hearst, p. 295
- yellow journalism, p. 295
- Teller Amendment, p. 296
- Emilio Aguinaldo, p. 296
- Theodore Roosevelt, p. 297
- Anti-Imperialist League, p. 299
- Platt Amendment, p. 300

Reading for Content Understanding

1. Newspaper reports of the conflict, which often included exaggerations, increased support for the Cubans.

2. The U.S. Navy was more numerous and powerful and destroyed the Spanish fleet.

3. They came under U.S. control.

4. Journal entries will vary but should include accurate descriptions of the battles and the poor conditions in the camps.

5. Answers will vary but might include yes—Cubans, like the American colonies, were fighting for their independence; or no—the United States should maintain its policy of isolation.

Reed, head of the Army Yellow Fever Commission, was sent to Cuba in 1900. He and his volunteers proved that yellow fever was transmitted by mosquitoes. Getting rid of standing water reduced the mosquito population, which in turn helped health officials to effectively control the disease.

Wood also oversaw the drafting of a Cuban constitution, which also included the **Platt Amendment**. The amendment limited Cuba's right to make treaties, required Cuba to sell or lease land to the United States for naval stations, and authorized the United States to intervene in Cuban affairs. Cuban leaders compared this to

> **"handing over the keys to our house so that they [the Americans] can enter it at any time, whenever the desire seizes them, day or night, whether with good or evil design [intentions]."**

The Cubans reluctantly accepted the Platt Amendment, and U.S. troops withdrew. The amendment remained in force until 1934.

Puerto Rico

Like Cuba, Puerto Rico had hoped for independence after the war. Instead, the U.S. government made the island a territory like the Philippines. On April 12, 1900, the Foraker Act established a civil

After the United States acquired Puerto Rico, the government built many new schools.

government that was headed by a governor and included a two-house legislature.

A debate soon arose over the citizenship status of the people of the new territories. Residents of Puerto Rico were considered citizens of the island but not of the United States. In 1917 the Jones Act granted Puerto Ricans U.S. citizenship and made both houses of the legislature elective. However, another 30 years passed before Puerto Ricans could elect their own governor. In 1952 Puerto Rico became a commonwealth. This unique status means that the island has its own constitution and elected officials. As with the 50 states, Puerto Rico can change its constitution as long as it does not conflict with that of the United States.

SECTION 2 REVIEW

Identify and explain the significance of the following:

- **José Martí**
- **Joseph Pulitzer**
- **William Randolph Hearst**
- **yellow journalism**
- **Teller Amendment**
- **Emilio Aguinaldo**
- **Theodore Roosevelt**
- **Anti-Imperialist League**
- **Platt Amendment**

Reading for Content Understanding

1. **Main Idea** How did the American press influence relations between the United States and Spain?
2. **Main Idea** What led to U.S. victory in the Spanish-American War?
3. **Global Relations** How did the war affect the Philippines, Cuba, and Puerto Rico?
4. **Writing** *Expressing* Imagine that you are a soldier during the Spanish-American War. Write a journal entry describing the war and the dangers you face.
5. **Critical Thinking** *Supporting a Point of View* If you had been a U.S. diplomat in Cuba in the 1890s, would you have supported going to war? Explain your answer.

OBJECTIVES

- Identify the steps that the United States took to build a canal across Panama.
- Analyze the change in U.S. involvement in Latin America under President Theodore Roosevelt.
- Describe how Presidents Taft and Wilson enforced the Monroe Doctrine.

FOCUS

Motivate Before Reading

Ask members of the class if they would take a job that required them digging a ditch 51 miles long, 300–500 feet wide, and up to 300 feet deep in an area infested with insects, poisonous snakes, rats, malaria, and yellow fever. Tell the class that to build the Panama Canal, the United States did just that. Tell students that in this section they will examine why and how the United States built

The United States and Latin America

Reading Focus

What steps did the United States take to build a canal across Panama?

How did U.S. involvement in Latin America change under President Theodore Roosevelt?

How did Presidents Taft and Wilson enforce the Monroe Doctrine?

Key Terms

Hay-Herrán Treaty
Hay-Bunau-Varilla Treaty
Panama Canal
Roosevelt Corollary
dollar diplomacy

WHEN THE SPANISH-AMERICAN WAR began in 1898, the U.S. battleship Oregon *was stationed at Puget Sound in Washington State. After receiving its orders, the* Oregon *set out at top speed on a 12,000-mile voyage. It traveled around the southern tip of South America to join the fighting in Cuba. Newspapers charted the* Oregon's *daily progress while the American public "breathlessly pushed her along." The trip lasted from March 19 to May 24, 1898—67 days!*

The USS Oregon

The Panama Canal

Despite the best efforts of the *Oregon*'s crew, the ship barely arrived in time to take part in the major battle around Cuba. The delay concerned many people. The United States needed to be able to quickly transfer key naval forces between the Caribbean and the Pacific. However, travel around the southern tip of South America took weeks.

Spanish explorer Vasco Núñez de Balboa had crossed the narrow Isthmus of Panama in Central America in the early 1500s. Since then, many people had dreamed of building a canal there to link the Pacific and Atlantic Oceans. In the late 1800s some U.S. leaders began to explore ways to dig a canal across the narrow neck of Central America. Such a canal would cut 8,000 miles off the voyage and join the Atlantic and Pacific naval fleets.

Negotiations

In 1850 the United States and Great Britain had signed the Clayton-Bulwer Treaty, which called for them to jointly build and maintain a canal. Despite

Section 3 RESOURCES

PRINT

- ★ Guided Reading Strategies 10.3
- ★ American History Political Cartoon 19: Theodore Roosevelt and the Panama Canal
- ★ Section 3 Review, p. 307
- ★ Daily Quiz 10.3

MULTIMEDIA

- ★ *Teaching Resources CD–ROM,* Lesson 10.3
- ★ *Exploring America's Past* Video Segment: A Struggle Against Nature; *Teacher's Guide,* pp. 18–20
- ★ HRW Web site

SHELTERED ENGLISH

- ★ Main Idea Activities for Reteaching and Sheltered English 10.3

the Panama Canal as well as the effects it had on U.S. relations with Latin America.

Introduce Key Terms

Linguistic, Visual-Spatial. Review this section's key terms with students. Have students create a five-column chart in their notebooks and head each column with a key term. Ask students to label the rows as follows: *date occurred, countries involved,* and *what it accomplished.* Have students use their textbooks to complete their charts. When students finish, ask for volunteers to reproduce their chart on the chalkboard. **SHELTERED ENGLISH**

TEACH

Have students read Section 3 and complete Guided Reading Strategies 10.3. Choose one or more of the following activities to explore the section content with students. For further suggestions on block scheduling or team teaching, see the *Block Scheduling Handbook.*

LEVEL 1: Linguistic. (Suggested time: 15 min.) As a class, go over students' Guided Reading Strategies. Then use the Reading Focus questions to highlight the main ideas of the section. **SHELTERED ENGLISH**

Geographic Diversity

Nicaragua. Many U.S. congressmembers believed the canal should cut through Nicaragua, but Philippe Bunau-Varilla wanted Congress to choose the Panama Canal route. Then a volcano erupted on an island in the Caribbean, destroying a city and killing nearly 30,000 people. Bunau-Varilla sent each senator a postage stamp picturing one of Nicaragua's many active volcanoes, one of which was located within 100 miles of the proposed canal. Congress soon came to the decision that Panama was the better location.

Critical Thinking: Why would a stamp of a volcano in Nicaragua affect U.S. opinion of the area as a canal site?

ANSWER: The stamp called attention to the dangers posed by Nicaragua's active volcanoes to a canal in the region.

Multimedia Resources

Exploring America's Past Video Segment: A Struggle Against Nature; *Teacher's Guide,* pp. 18–20

Search 9401, Play to 17713
Videodisc White Side B

Play

Pause

See *Teacher's Guide* for Spanish barcode.

the treaty, the countries never built a canal. In 1881 a French company headed by Ferdinand de Lesseps, who had engineered the Suez Canal in Egypt, began work. After spending nearly $300 million and losing some 20,000 lives, the company went bankrupt in 1887. At that time, less than one third of the planned 51-mile canal had been dug.

No one was a stronger supporter of a Central American canal than Theodore Roosevelt, who had become president in 1901 after the assassination of William McKinley. Influenced by the ideas of Alfred Mahan, Roosevelt believed that naval power was essential to U.S. strength and security. Earlier, Roosevelt had written to Mahan, "I believe we should build the [Central American] canal at once, and, in the meantime, . . . we should build a dozen new battleships." In 1901 Secretary of State John Hay completed negotiations with the British for the Hay-Pauncefote Treaty. Britain surrendered its interest in building and operating a Central American canal in exchange for a U.S. agreement to keep the canal open to all vessels at all times.

With this agreement settled, Secretary Hay began negotiating with Colombia, because the Isthmus of Panama was part of that country. Hay and the Colombian minister Thomas Herrán soon reached an agreement. The United States would pay $10 million plus $250,000 a year for a 99-year lease on a five-mile wide strip of land across the isthmus.

The U.S. Senate ratified the **Hay-Herrán Treaty** in March 1903, but the Colombian senate rejected it in hopes of better terms. President Roosevelt refused to pay more money to Colombia. He considered other ways of gaining the Isthmus of Panama, such as seizing it by force.

A New Nation

Philippe Bunau-Varilla, chief engineer with the French Canal Company, offered an alternative plan. In a meeting with Hay and Roosevelt, Bunau-Varilla informed them about the possibility of a revolt in the Colombian province of Panama. Bunau-Varilla knew about the effort, as he himself was organizing the plot. Bunau-Varilla came away from the gathering with the assumption that the United States would support—or at least not strongly discourage—the Panamanian revolt.

On November 2, 1903, a U.S. warship arrived in Colón, Panama. The next day the revolution broke out. Although Colombian forces tried to stop the rebellion, dense jungles blocked the land routes and the U.S. warship blocked the sea lanes to Panama. On November 4 Panama declared itself an independent nation. The United States recognized, or formally acknowledged, the new nation almost immediately. On November 13, Bunau-Varilla arrived in Washington, D.C., as the Panamanian minister to the United States. He met with the Roosevelt administration and five days later signed the **Hay–Bunau-Varilla Treaty**. The terms of this treaty were identical to the Hay-Herrán Treaty, except that the canal zone was widened to 10 miles. The United States was ready to build the canal.

This cartoon shows President Roosevelt digging the Panama Canal and throwing the dirt on Colombia, which had rejected an earlier canal plan.

The Granger Collection, New York

Building the Canal

Building the canal proved to be very difficult. The first obstacle to overcome was tropical disease, particularly yellow fever, which had been a serious problem for the earlier French effort. The canal route ran about 51 miles through jungles and

LEVEL 1: Logical-Mathematical, Linguistic, Visual-Spatial. (Suggested time: 30 min.) Have students list events in Latin America that led President Roosevelt to issue the Roosevelt Corollary. Discuss these events and ask each student to decide which were the most important. Then have each student create a graph, table, or other visual representation of the steps that led to the Roosevelt Corollary. Once students are finished, call on volunteers to share their work with the class. Finally, have students vote on which presentation best illustrates the sequence of events that led to the Roosevelt Corollary. **SHELTERED ENGLISH**

ALL LEVELS: Visual-Spatial, Logical-Mathematical. (Suggested time: 15 min. plus homework) Discuss the main events of this section with students. Then for homework, provide each student with an outline map of Latin America and have them label their maps with important places and events from this section. Ask students to label at least five points on the map, identifying the event, dates, causes, and implications for U.S. foreign policy. Display the maps around the classroom. **SHELTERED ENGLISH**

Science and Technology

The Panama Canal

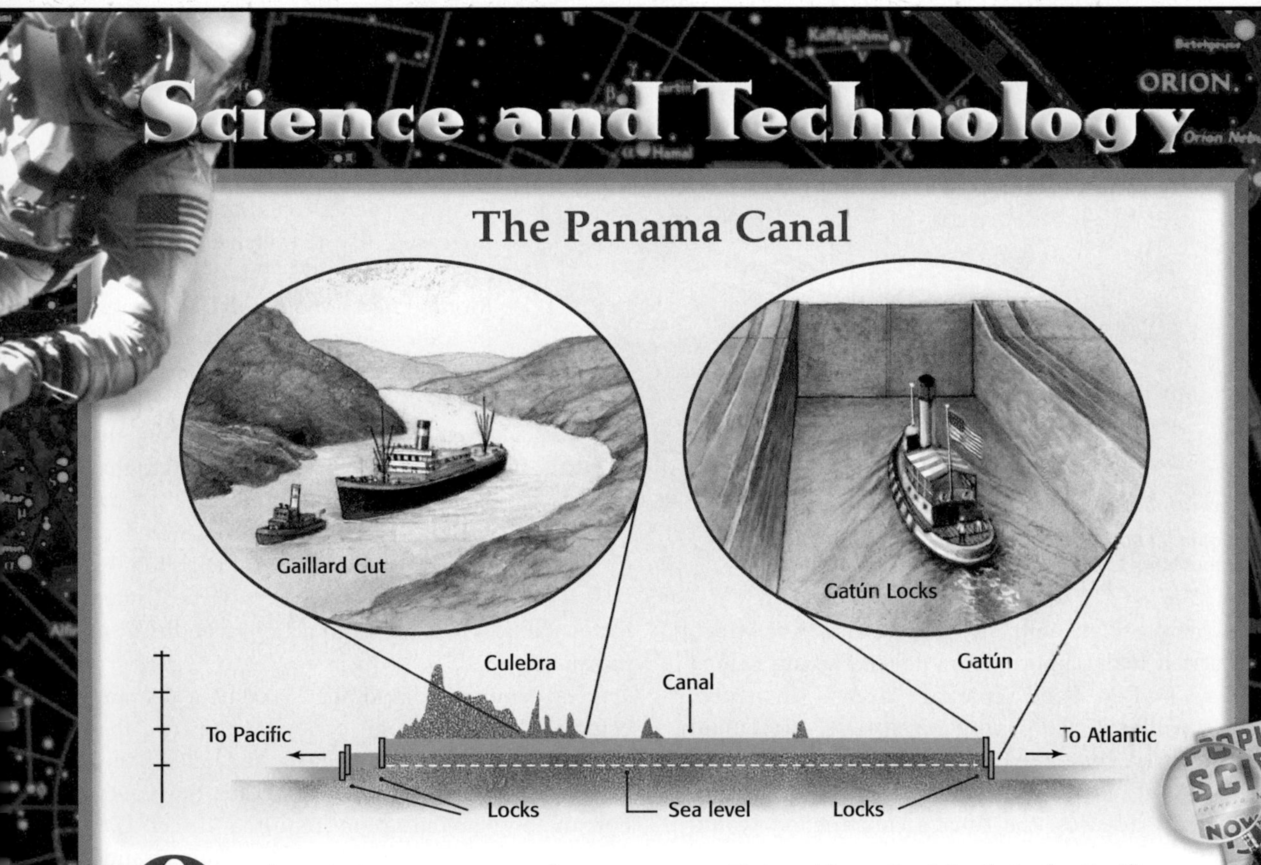

Once the U.S. Congress approved construction of a canal across the Isthmus of Panama, the massive undertaking began. The project faced many obstacles, including disease, floods, mountains, and swamps.

A big hurdle in the project was completing the Gaillard Cut through a mountain range. Even with dozens of huge shovels, removing all the rock and mud took workers years. Engineers built a large railroad to carry away the debris. It took workers 10 years to dig a path eight miles long and about 40 feet deep. Then engineers built a dam to control flooding from the nearby Chagres River. This dam created the great Gatún Lake.

Engineers then designed and built six enormous locks. A lock is a section of a canal with large gates at either end. Each of the six locks is eight stories tall and longer than three football fields. When a ship enters a lock, operators close the gates and raise or lower the water level inside the lock. When the water is at the desired height, the gates are opened and the ship continues on its way.

To travel from the Atlantic to the Pacific Ocean, a ship enters the Panama Canal near the town of Colón. The ship travels through the Gatún Locks, where the water level and therefore the ship is raised 85 feet. Then the ship travels down a long channel in Gatún Lake until it passes through the Gaillard Cut in the mountains. There the vessel is lowered 31 feet. The ship is eventually lowered to sea level by another series of locks, after which it follows another channel out to the ocean. The entire Panama Canal is about 51 miles long. A typical trip takes about nine hours. The canal reduces the distance a ship has to travel from one coast of the United States to another by about 8,000 miles. Completed in 1914, the Panama Canal remains one of the greatest engineering feats of the 1900s.

Understanding What You Read

1. What were some construction challenges in building the Panama Canal?
2. How do ships travel through the Panama Canal?

Economic Development

Compensation. It took nearly 20 years for Columbia to forgive the United States for the way it took over the Panama Canal. During the 1910s oil was discovered in Columbia, and the United States hoped to gain oil concessions from the country. In 1921, to regain Columbia's friendship, the United States agreed to pay $25 million in compensation for the canal.

Critical Thinking: Why might the United States have wanted Columbian oil?

ANSWER: The United States wanted the oil to run its industries.

SCIENCE AND TECHNOLOGY ANSWERS

1. Obstacles such as disease, floods, mountains, and swamps presented challenges to the construction of the canal.
2. Going from the Atlantic to the Pacific Ocean, ships enter near Colón; travel through the Gatún Locks, thus rising 85 feet; continue down a long channel to the Gaillard Cut, thus lowering 31 feet; pass through a series of locks, which lower the ships to sea level; and follow another channel out to the ocean.

LEVEL 2: Kinesthetic, Linguistic, Interpersonal. (Suggested time: 45 min. plus presentation) Have students consider the barriers that the United States overcame to build the Panama Canal. Have students work in groups to write skits in which people such as engineers, doctors, and diplomats talk about what they had to do to overcome obstacles. Have each character discuss both the drawbacks and benefits of building the canal. Have groups present their skits to the class.

LEVEL 3: Linguistic, Intrapersonal. (Suggested time: 30 min. plus presentation) Organize the class into four groups and tell them to prepare a panel discussion on the Monroe Doctrine. Have three of the groups prepare short speeches (about three minutes) on the Monroe Doctrine under Roosevelt, Taft, or Wilson. Ask the fourth group to prepare questions about each of these presidents' policies and their implications for the future of the Western Hemisphere. Moderate a discussion in which the representatives of the three presidents give their speeches and the fourth group asks them questions.

Across the Curriculum

SCIENCE

Studying Yellow Fever. Working in Cuba, Dr. Walter Reed had theorized that yellow fever was transmitted by mosquito bites. Proving this theory was difficult, however, because at the time, no animals were known to acquire the disease. So Reed and other doctors on his commission let mosquitoes bite them. When some came down with yellow fever, the experience proved Reed's point.

Activity: Have students search the Internet through the HRW Web site to find out the following: what actually causes yellow fever, its symptoms, and who developed the vaccine for the disease and when. Then have students create posters that illustrate some of the main events in yellow fever research leading up to the discovery of a vaccine.

go.hrw.com
SB1 Yellow Fever

The Granger Collection, New York

Some 43,000 workers dug through jungles and mountains to complete the Panama Canal.

swamps filled with mosquitoes, many of which carried malaria and yellow fever. Having helped Dr. Walter Reed combat disease in Cuba, Dr. William C. Gorgas organized a vast effort to rid the canal route of disease-carrying mosquitoes. Without his success in slowing the spread of deadly diseases, the canal's construction would have taken much longer. It also would have cost much more, in terms of lives and money.

Even with the reduced risk of disease, the work was very dangerous. Much of the canal had to be blasted out of solid rock. On one occasion, a bolt of lightning struck a 12-ton explosive charge, setting it off prematurely and killing seven workers. In several other incidents, workers died when their shovels struck the cap of an unexploded charge. One West Indian worker recalled, "The flesh of men flew in the air like birds many days."

The high mountain range of central Panama also stood as a challenge to the canal-building effort. To overcome this obstacle, chief engineers John Stevens and George W. Goethals directed workers to cut a narrow, eight-mile-long channel through solid rock using dozens of steam shovels.

Some 6,000 lives were lost building the **Panama Canal**, which finally opened to traffic on August 15, 1914. The cost was $367 million on top of the nearly $300 million spent in the failed French effort. In the end, however, the world had its "highway between the oceans."

Roosevelt and Latin America

With the construction of the Panama Canal, the United States had increased its involvement in Latin America. In 1823 President James Monroe had announced U.S. interest in Latin America when he warned European nations not to interfere in either Central or South America. In what became known as the Monroe Doctrine, he declared that "the American continents . . . are henceforth not to be considered as subjects for future colonization by any European powers." The United States would view any such actions as a threat to its safety.

The Monroe Doctrine had become a defining principle of U.S. foreign policy. At the time that Monroe announced it, however, the United States lacked the military power to enforce the policy. Fortunately, no situation required direct U.S. involvement. President Monroe's administration relied on Britain's large navy as well as British interest in keeping the area free of other European powers to enforce the Monroe Doctrine. This situation changed as the United States grew stronger and expanded its influence, particularly after the Spanish-American War.

George W. Goethals (center) directed the building of the Panama Canal. Dr. William C. Gorgas is second from the right.

CLOSE

Linguistic, Visual-Spatial. Draw a Venn diagram on the chalkboard. Label the left outer circle *Before Roosevelt* and the right outer circle *During Roosevelt.* Title the diagram *U.S. Relations with Latin America.* Have members of the class list policies that were different before Roosevelt became president and policies that changed when he became president in the appropriate circles on the chalkboard. Policies that stayed the same should be listed in the intersection of the circles. Finally, ask students to suggest possible reasons for the changes that occurred in U.S. policies dealing with Latin America.

CHALLENGE AND EXTEND

1. **Linguistic, Interpersonal.** Ask students to write a play about Teddy Roosevelt and his role in enabling the United States to obtain land for the Panama Canal. Major characters should include Roosevelt, Secretary of State John Hay, Thomas Herrán, and Philippe Bunau-Varilla. Have students use the library or other resources to find background information to include in the play. Encourage students to point out how the revolt in Panama helped the United States gain the land for the canal. Finally, have students present their plays to the class.

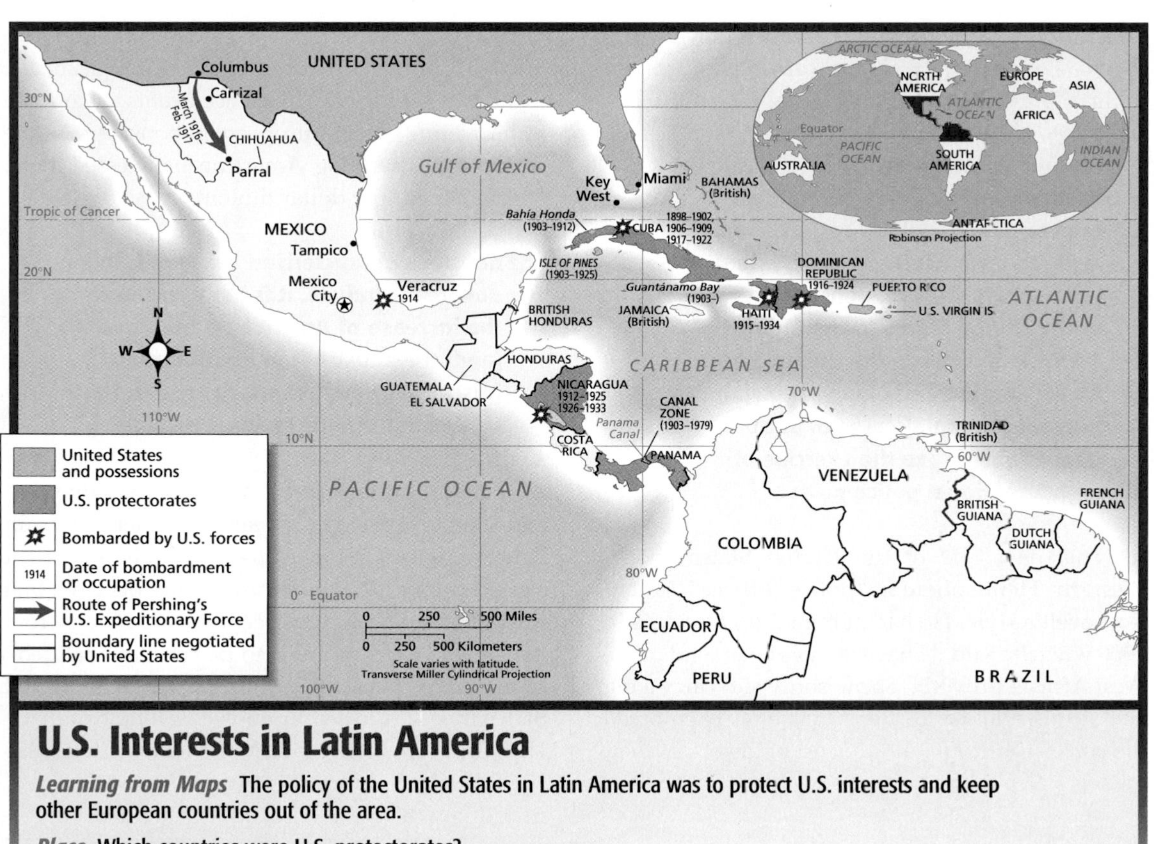

U.S. Interests in Latin America

Learning from Maps **The policy of the United States in Latin America was to protect U.S. interests and keep other European countries out of the area.**

Place **Which countries were U.S. protectorates?**

A Larger Role

During the late 1800s many European banks had invested in, and made loans to, a number of Latin American countries. When some of these nations had difficulty repaying their loans, European nations used force to collect their debts. Venezuela, under the rule of dictator Cipriano Castro, fell deeply in debt to British and German investors. In 1902 the Venezuelan government refused to repay these debts or to have the claims settled by a neutral third party.

European leaders wanted to act but were concerned about the Monroe Doctrine. In 1901, however, President Roosevelt had declared that the United States did "not guarantee any State against punishment if it misconducts itself." The only condition Roosevelt set was "that punishment does not take the form of acquisition [taking] of territory by any non-American power." The European nations interpreted this to mean that they could collect their debts—by force if necessary. Britain and Germany sent ships to blockade Venezuela. The Venezuelan dictator then asked Roosevelt to propose having the matter settled by a third party, which the Europeans accepted.

A similar situation developed in the Caribbean nation of the Dominican Republic in 1904. Again, European nations considered using force to collect their debts. This time Roosevelt worried that the foreign forces might not leave afterward. The presence of European forces in the Caribbean would not only have violated the Monroe Doctrine but also could have threatened U.S. power in the region and control of the Panama Canal.

The Roosevelt Corollary

President Roosevelt realized that if the United States prevented European creditors from collecting what was owed them, U.S. officials would need to intervene. The United States would have to force the debtor nations to repay their loans. In

Global Relations

Europe and the Western Hemisphere. European economic power in Central America remained a problem for later U.S. presidents. Woodrow Wilson's secretary of state, William Jennings Bryan, suggested that the U.S. government guarantee loans to Central America so that these countries would not turn to Europe for money. However, Wilson rejected this idea, saying that it was too radical.

Critical Thinking: Why did Central American nations rely on outside economic influence?

ANSWER: These nations needed money to industrialize and develop.

MAP ANSWER

Cuba, Dominican Republic, Haiti, Nicaragua, Panama

2. **Visual-Spatial, Logical-Mathematical, Kinesthetic.** Have students create a three-dimensional, scale model of the Panama Canal. Have them research the engineering decisions that led to the building of the canal and illustrate these decisions on their models. Encourage students to include an appropriate background around the canal that shows people working to complete it. Backgrounds should highlight the jungle, swamp, and mountains around the canal. Display the projects around the room. Have students vote on which model best depicts the canal.

3. **Linguistic, Logical-Mathematical.** Have students use the library and other resources to find information on the history of the Panama Canal. Ask students to use their research to create a chapter of a book dealing with the canal's history. Encourage students to include information such as changes in which country controlled the canal and information about the amount of goods that pass through the canal annually. Call on volunteers to share information from their chapters with the class.

Global Relations

Canal Zone Diplomacy. After work had begun on the Panama Canal, President Roosevelt declared to his secretary of war that if the United States wanted to tell European powers "hands off" in Latin America, it must be able to keep order there. The secretary agreed, noting that the inevitable effect of building the canal was the need for a U.S. "police" force in Central America. The secretary said that with trade and control came the obligation to keep order.

Activity: Have students write newspaper editorials for or against the Roosevelt Corollary. Ask them to consider whether this addition to the Monroe Doctrine gave the U.S. government too much power in the Western Hemisphere or was necessary to vital U.S. interests.

December 1904 the president outlined his thinking in what became known as the **Roosevelt Corollary** to the Monroe Doctrine:

> **"Chronic wrongdoing . . . may in America, as elsewhere, ultimately require intervention [involvement] by some civilized nation, and in the Western Hemisphere the adherence [observance] of the United States to the Monroe Doctrine may force the United States, however reluctantly [unwillingly], in flagrant [extreme] cases of such wrongdoing . . . to the exercise of an international police power."**

This new role of the United States as the Western Hemisphere's "police officer" suited Roosevelt's style. He had summed up his ideas in 1900 when he said, "I have always been fond of the West African proverb: 'Speak softly and carry a big stick, you will go far.'" Roosevelt actively enforced the corollary throughout the rest of his presidency.

Dollar Diplomacy

When William Howard Taft became president in 1909, he also acted to protect U.S. interests in Latin America. Instead of Roosevelt's "big-stick" approach of using military force, Taft used a policy known as **dollar diplomacy**, which emphasized using U.S. economic power and business investment to influence Latin American governments. Taft believed he could influence events, encourage stability, and keep European nations out of the region by expanding American businesses there. He explained that dollar diplomacy

> **"has been characterized as substituting dollars for bullets. It is . . . directed to the increase of American trade . . . [and] the substitution of arbitration [discussion] and reason for war in the settlement of international disputes."**

Taft supported American businesses overseas and tried to replace European investments in Latin America with U.S. investments. In an agreement signed in June 1911, the United States declared that it would help Nicaragua secure private loans from American banks in order to pay its national debt. In exchange, Nicaraguan officials gave the United States the right to send troops into their country if U.S. leaders felt it necessary. The United States also signed a similar agreement with Honduras.

Although the U.S. Senate rejected both agreements, the Taft administration informally observed the treaty terms anyway. In July, Nicaragua failed to repay a large loan from British investors. Secretary of State Chase Knox helped secure a $1.5 billion loan for Nicaragua from American bankers. In exchange, the bankers received control of the National Bank of Nicaragua and the government-owned railway. Local dissatisfaction over this agreement soon led to a revolt in Nicaragua. Taft sent in U.S. Marines to protect American interests. The marines remained until 1925, returned the next year, and finally left in 1933.

The Granger Collection, New York

Many Americans thought that President Taft struggled with issues that Theodore Roosevelt had handled with ease.

Wilson's Foreign Policies

President Woodrow Wilson, who took office in 1913, rejected the dollar diplomacy of the Taft administration. Wilson disapproved of the role of big business in foreign affairs and said he would not act to support any "special group or interests." Instead, he believed the United States had a moral obligation to

REVIEW

Linguistic, Logical-Mathematical. Have students complete the Section Review questions. Then have students write a short essay using specific events from the section to describe how the Panama Canal changed U.S. relations with Latin America. Have volunteers share their essays with the class.

ASSESS

Have students complete Daily Quiz 10.3.

RETEACH

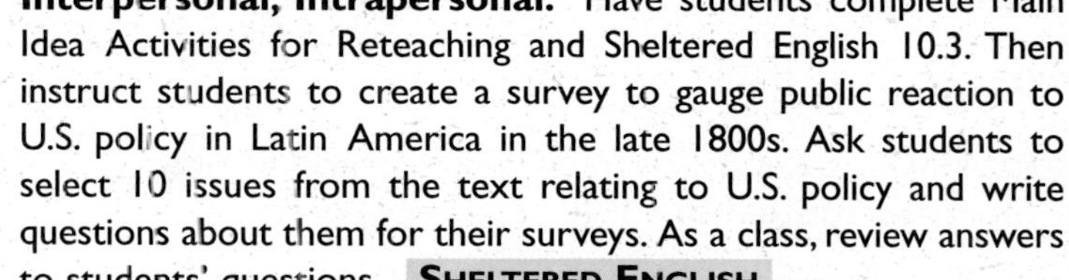

Interpersonal, Intrapersonal. Have students complete Main Idea Activities for Reteaching and Sheltered English 10.3. Then instruct students to create a survey to gauge public reaction to U.S. policy in Latin America in the late 1800s. Ask students to select 10 issues from the text relating to U.S. policy and write questions about them for their surveys. As a class, review answers to students' questions. **SHELTERED ENGLISH**

promote democracy in Latin America. He sought to protect U.S. interests in the region by encouraging the growth of state government. One newspaper responded to Wilson's policy by writing, "There is . . . not a word [here] to stir the greed of a dictator."

Wilson tended to oppose imperialist ideas. Nevertheless, he eventually sent more troops into Latin America than any previous president in an attempt to bring democracy to the region. For example, the Caribbean nation of Haiti had long been in financial disorder. The country also suffered a series of political revolutions that threatened people's lives and safety. In 1915 Haitian president Guillaume Sam ordered 167 political prisoners executed. As a result, he was overthrown and assassinated in another revolt. Previously, Germany and France had temporarily sent troops to Haiti to protect their interests. Wilson feared that those countries might try to seize control of Haiti during the violence. To prevent this, U.S. Marines landed in Haiti on July 29, 1915, and quickly restored peace. The United States took control of collecting customs taxes to pay Haiti's debts and installed a new government there.

Similar events occurred in the Dominican Republic. The customs arrangements established by President Roosevelt in 1905 had brought a

These U.S. Marines were among the many that President Wilson sent to restore order in Haiti.

stable government to this nation. In 1911, however, the Dominican president was assassinated and instability returned. By threatening to withhold customs revenue, Secretary of State Knox forced the Dominicans to accept a U.S.-supported government.

In 1913 William Jennings Bryan, the new secretary of state, began to oversee the Dominican Republic's finances. After Bryan resigned in 1916, however, the Dominican president opposed the appointment of a new financial adviser. Fearing more political unrest, Wilson declared martial law on the island and established a government run by the U.S. Navy. Wilson, like Roosevelt and Taft before him, refused to let internal political unrest in Latin America threaten U.S. interests there.

SECTION 3 REVIEW

Identify and explain the significance of the following:

- **Hay-Herrán Treaty**
- **Philippe Bunau-Varilla**
- **Hay–Bunau-Varilla Treaty**
- **William C. Gorgas**
- **Panama Canal**
- **Roosevelt Corollary**
- **dollar diplomacy**

Reading for Content Understanding

1 **Main Idea** What was President Theodore Roosevelt's foreign policy in Latin America?

2 **Main Idea** In what ways did Presidents Taft and Wilson differ from Roosevelt in enforcing the Monroe Doctrine?

3 **Technology and Society** Describe the steps that led to the completion of the Panama Canal.

4 **Writing** *Describing* Imagine that you are a worker helping to build the Panama Canal. Write a letter home to your family, describing the difficulties you have encountered during your time in Panama.

5 **Critical Thinking** *Determining the Strength of an Argument* President Roosevelt believed that the United States needed to serve as the international police officer of the Western Hemisphere. Do you agree? Explain your answer.

Section 3 Review ANSWERS

Identify

For significance, see the following pages:

- Hay-Herrán Treaty, p. 302
- Philippe Bunau-Varilla, p. 302
- Hay–Bunau-Varilla Treaty, p. 302
- William C. Gorgas, p. 304
- Panama Canal, p. 304
- Roosevelt Corollary, p. 306
- dollar diplomacy, p. 306

Reading for Content Understanding

1. Roosevelt believed the United States should serve as a police force to keep order in Latin America.

2. President Taft also continued involvement in Latin America, but he emphasized economic power and investment instead of military force. President Wilson opposed imperialism but enforced the Monroe Doctrine as part of his moral obligation to bring democracy to Latin America.

3. negotiations with Britain over control of a canal; failed negotiations with Columbia over leasing land for a canal; recognizing the government of Panama and signing a canal treaty with it; overcoming disease and other obstacles

4. Letters will vary but might mention the disease-carrying mosquitoes, the dangerous construction work, and excavation of the Gaillard Cut.

5. Answers will vary but students might say yes—the United States has an obligation to its neighbors to help with political difficulties as well as an obligation to protect U.S. investment in the area; or no—the United States should not interfere with other countries.

SECTION 4 LESSON PLAN

OBJECTIVES

- Explain why the Mexican people revolted against their government in 1911.
- Analyze President Woodrow Wilson's reasons for intervening in the Mexican Revolution.
- Discuss reasons for the increase in Mexican immigration to the United States in the early 1900s.

FOCUS

Motivate Before Reading

Ask students to brainstorm a list of reasons why people in a country might want to stage a revolution. *(Answers will vary but students might mention an unjust government or the desire for a democratic government.)* Explain to students that in this section they will study the causes and effects of the political, social, and economic unrest that affected Mexico at the turn of the century.

Section 4 RESOURCES

PRINT

★ Guided Reading Strategies 10.4

★ Graphic Organizer 10: U.S. Involvement Overseas

★ Section 4 Review, p. 311

★ Daily Quiz 10.4

MULTIMEDIA

★ *Teaching Resources CD–ROM,* Lesson 10.4

★ *American History Interactive Maps CD–ROM:* U.S. Imperialism in Latin America

SHELTERED ENGLISH

★ Main Idea Activities for Reteaching and Sheltered English 10.4

The United States and Mexico

Reading Focus

Why did the Mexican people revolt against their government in 1911?

Why did President Woodrow Wilson intervene in the Mexican Revolution?

Why did Mexican immigration to the United States increase in the early 1900s?

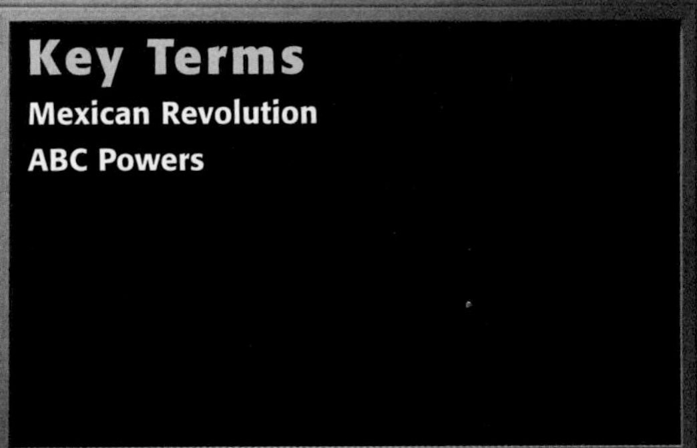

IN 1910 MEXICO CELEBRATED *the 100th anniversary of Father Miguel Hidalgo's call for revolution, known as the* Grito de Dolores. *Mexican president Porfirio Díaz treated guests from around the world to entertainment and fine food and toasted Mexico's successful revolt against Spain. Francisco Madero, another Mexican leader, celebrated the* Grito *in a different way. He published a pamphlet demanding that Díaz resign and calling for free elections. When Díaz refused, Madero began another revolution.*

Porfirio Díaz

★ The Mexican Revolution

For 34 years, from 1877 to 1911, Porfirio Díaz ruled Mexico and eagerly welcomed foreign investment. The United States became the biggest investor in Mexico, and by 1913 had invested more than $1 billion in Mexican land, mining, oil, railways, and manufacturing. More than 500,000 U.S. citizens lived and worked in Mexico. To open Mexico to foreign investors, Díaz had ruled the Mexican people harshly. He imprisoned his opponents and rewarded his supporters. Most of Mexico's 15 million people were landless and poor.

Many Mexicans found a new leader in democratic reformer Francisco Madero, who began the **Mexican Revolution** in 1910. After capturing Ciudad Juárez and gaining support throughout the country, Madero forced Díaz to resign in May. Madero was elected president. The Taft administration wanted a stable government in Mexico and quickly recognized Madero as president.

Despite Madero's victory, a struggle for power continued in Mexico. In February 1913 General Victoriano Huerta seized power and had Madero killed. The violence angered Woodrow Wilson, who was about to take office as U.S. president.

Introduce Key Terms

Linguistic. Review this section's key terms with students. Instruct them to write a short poem or story using all the key terms. **SHELTERED ENGLISH**

TEACH

Have students read Section 4 and complete Guided Reading Strategies 10.4. Choose one or more of the following activities to explore the section content with students. For further suggestions on block scheduling or team teaching, see the *Block Scheduling Handbook.*

LEVEL 1: Linguistic. (Suggested time: 15 min.) As a class, go over students' Guided Reading Strategies. Then use the Reading Focus questions to highlight the main ideas of the section. **SHELTERED ENGLISH**

ALL LEVELS: Visual-Spatial. (Suggested time: 15 min.) Have students reread the quotation on textbook page 309 from President Wilson regarding Victoriano Huerta's rise to power and discuss its meaning. Then have students imagine how one of the revolutionary figures discussed in this section might have responded to Wilson's quote and use this response to create a political cartoon. **SHELTERED ENGLISH**

These women were among the many people who fought in the Mexican Revolution.

Wilson refused to recognize the new Mexican government, saying:

> **"We hold, as I am sure all thoughtful leaders of republican government everywhere hold, that just government rests upon the consent of the governed."**

When a revolt led by Venustiano Carranza began gathering force, Wilson proposed that the two sides cease fighting and agree to a free election. If they agreed, Wilson said he would help the new elected Mexican government secure loans from U.S. banks. However, Wilson insisted that Huerta could not be a candidate in the election because he had seized power by force. Not surprisingly, Huerta refused.

Wilson then lifted the U.S. restrictions against selling arms in Mexico so that weapons could be supplied to the forces opposing Huerta. Wilson also stationed U.S. warships near Veracruz, Mexico, to block any foreign aid to Huerta. In addition to Carranza, two other major revolutionaries—Francisco "Pancho" Villa in the north and Emiliano Zapata in the south—led movements to overthrow Huerta. Like Carranza, both Villa and Zapata had supported Madero against Díaz. Both were heroes to Mexico's poor.

Although Carranza, Villa, and Zapata had a common goal in hoping to overthrow Huerta, they were not close allies. Their relationship was best described by the saying, "The enemy of my enemy is my friend." Each wanted to replace Huerta as Mexico's leader, leading to a strong rivalry among them.

The United States Reacts

The fighting in Mexico weakened its economy, leading a number of American business leaders to fear that they would lose their investments there. They wanted Huerta out of office, by force, if necessary. President Wilson, however, refused their demands.

The public pressure to intervene continued to grow. Many members of Congress demanded military action. The press at home and abroad also criticized Wilson's policy, but he refused to be swayed by such attacks. Wilson explained to his secretary, "I have to pause and remind myself that I am President of the United States and not of a small group of Americans with vested interests [investments] in Mexico."

President Wilson adopted a policy of "watchful waiting" toward the unrest in Mexico. At the same time, he looked for an opportunity to act against Huerta.

Tampico

In 1914 an incident finally gave Wilson the opportunity to act. The U.S. ship *Dolphin* was patrolling

The Granger Collection, New York

Pancho Villa (left) and Emiliano Zapata (right) led revolutionaries against Victoriano Huerta's government.

Cultural Diversity

Mexico's Class System. Porfirio Díaz had allowed his friends and associates to gain communal village lands for private use. Díaz thought this policy would improve agricultural production. However, this policy gave land ownership to very few Mexicans and divided rural Mexicans into two classes: the hacendados, or rich owners of estates, and peons, or landless workers.

Critical Thinking: Do you think Díaz's system would help or hurt agricultural production?

ANSWER: Students' answers will vary. Some may say that it would help because the farms would be run efficiently. Others may say that it would hurt because people would not work as hard for outside owners as they would for themselves.

Multimedia Resources

American History Interactive Maps CD–ROM: U.S. Imperialism in Latin America

LEVEL 3: Linguistic, Interpersonal, Intrapersonal. (Suggested time: 30 min. plus homework) Pair students and ask one member of the pair to imagine that he or she is a Mexican immigrant to the United States in the early 1900s; ask the other to imagine that he or she is writing a newspaper story on Mexicans who have come to the United States. Have the newspaper writer interview the immigrant. Then for homework have students write a newspaper article that might have appeared at the time.

CLOSE

Linguistic, Logical-Mathematical, Interpersonal. Have students prepare an outline describing President Wilson's political and military responses to the Mexican Revolution. Encourage them to include at least two supporting details under each heading. Then ask students to review their outlines with a partner and discuss the supporting details they included.

CHALLENGE AND EXTEND

Linguistic, Logical-Mathematical, Visual-Spatial. Have students use the library or other sources to research the Mexican Revolution. Then have students create annotated flowcharts describing significant events surrounding the revolution.

CHART ANSWER

Investments in oil increased the most.

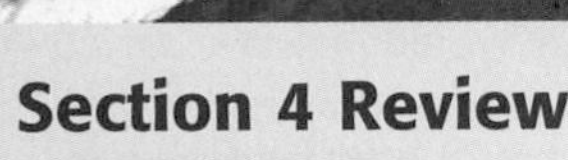

Section 4 Review ANSWERS

Identify

For significance, see the following pages:

- Porfirio Díaz, p. 308
- Francisco Madero, p. 308
- Mexican Revolution, p. 308
- Victoriano Huerta, p. 308
- Venustiano Carranza, p. 309
- Francisco "Pancho" Villa, p. 309
- Emiliano Zapata, p. 309
- ABC Powers, p. 310
- John J. Pershing, p. 311

Reading for Content Understanding

1. He wanted to bring political and economic reform to Mexico, which was ruled harshly by a dictator who refused to allow free elections.

2. to protect American economic interests and to install a democratic government in Mexico

3. during—to flee the violence and destruction of the war, to escape political persecution, to find industrial jobs; after—to escape poor economic conditions in Mexico, to fill jobs

4. Articles will vary but should mention Villa's background, his role as a leader of Mexico's poor, his role in the revolution, and his conflict with the United States.

5. Answers will vary but might mention that businesspeople were afraid their holdings and money might be seized by revolutionaries.

in Mexican waters. A group of its sailors went ashore at Tampico, Mexico, which was under military rule. When these soldiers accidentally entered a restricted area, Huerta's troops arrested them.

The sailors were soon released, and the local commander in Tampico apologized to Admiral Mayo, who was commanding the U.S. fleet. Mayo, however, was not satisfied with the apology. Even though he lacked the proper authorization, he wrote to the Mexican general in charge of Tampico:

> **"I must require that you send me . . . [an] apology for the act, together with your assurance that the officer responsible for it will receive severe punishment. Also that you publicly hoist the American flag in a prominent [important] position on shore and salute it with twenty-one guns."**

Wilson supported Mayo's demands. The Mexican general delivered the written apology, and Huerta expressed regret over the incident. The salute, however, was not delivered. On April 20, 1914, Wilson asked Congress for approval to use the armed forces "to obtain from General Huerta . . . the fullest recognition of the rights and dignity of the United States."

Estimated U.S. Investments in Mexico, 1897–1919

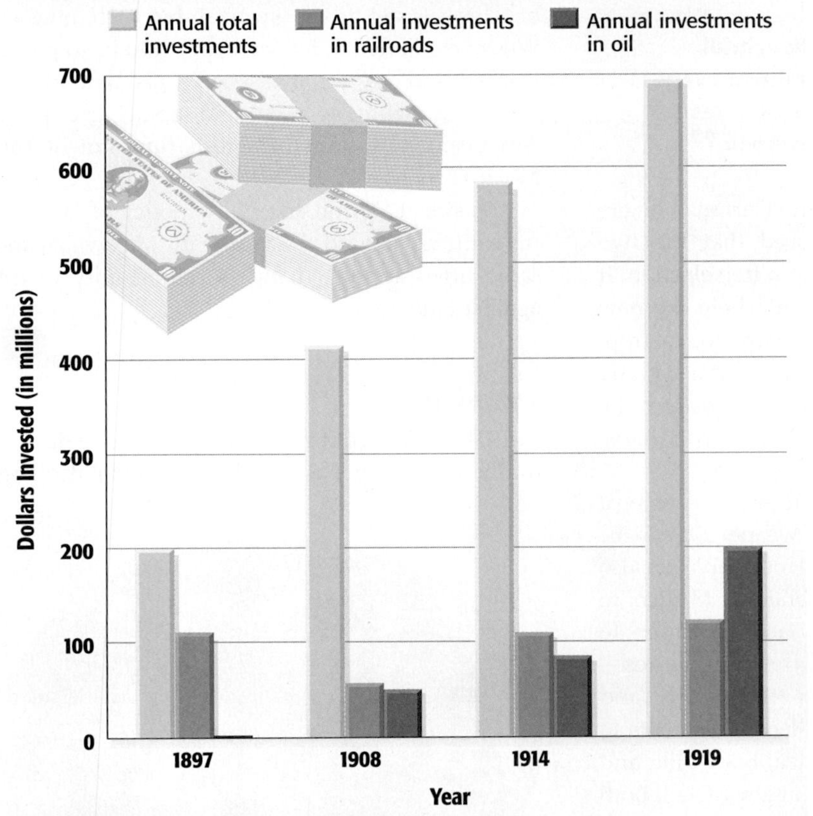

Source: Cleona Lewis, *America's Stake in International Investments*

Investment Concerns The disorder of the Mexican Revolution gave many Americans concern about money they had invested in Mexico's economy. In which category–railroads or oil–had U.S. investment increased the most by 1919?

Veracruz

Before the Tampico crisis could be resolved, Wilson learned that a German ship carrying a large supply of arms was cruising toward the port city of Veracruz, Mexico. Wilson did not want Huerta to receive these weapons, so the president ordered U.S. Marines to seize Veracruz. In late April 1914, U.S. forces captured the city. This action took the lives of 19 Americans and wounded 47 others. Some 200 Mexicans were killed and 300 more were wounded in the fighting.

The quick assault on Veracruz united Mexicans against the United States. Huerta broke off diplomatic relations, and the two nations stood on the brink of war. Then the **ABC Powers**—Argentina, Brazil, and Chile—offered to negotiate the dispute. Wilson accepted but Huerta rejected the proposed settlement. However, Huerta was soon forced to leave office. In

REVIEW

Logical-Mathematical. Have students complete the Section Review questions. Then organize the class into small groups. Prepare a set of questions and give each question a point value depending on its level of difficulty. Hold a quiz game in which groups compete for points by answering the questions correctly.

ASSESS

Have students complete Daily Quiz 10.4.

RETEACH

Linguistic, Visual-Spatial. Have students complete Main Idea Activities for Reteaching and Sheltered English 10.4. Next, have students find photos of the major figures of the Mexican Revolution or create their own portraits. Have students use the photos to create a picture web about the Mexican Revolution. Ask students to create a brief caption below each picture.

SHELTERED ENGLISH

August, Carranza and his forces occupied Mexico City and established a new government. The United States and several Latin American nations recognized Carranza as president of Mexico, and the U.S. troops withdrew from Veracruz.

Pursuing Pancho Villa

Despite Huerta's overthrow, Pancho Villa and Emiliano Zapata continued their revolts. Villa hoped to destroy the Carranza government and win the support of the Mexican people by attacking the United States. In January, Villa and his troops stopped a train at Santa Ysabel, Mexico, and killed 18 American mining engineers on board.

On March 9, 1916, Villa and his troops attacked Columbus, New Mexico, burning the town and killing 17 U.S. citizens. In response, President Wilson sent General John J. Pershing and 15,000 soldiers into Mexico. Pershing's forces chased Villa more than 300 miles but failed to capture him. Mexicans greatly resented having U.S. troops in their country. Wilson eventually agreed to Carranza's demands for withdrawal and recalled the troops.

In 1917 Carranza approved a liberal constitution to bring orderly rule to Mexico. However, in 1920 the forces of Álvaro Obregón revolted and killed Carranza. After 1920, peace gradually returned to Mexico.

The Granger Collection, New York

General John J. "Black Jack" Pershing led the failed effort to capture Pancho Villa.

The Mexican Revolution resulted in a large-scale Mexican migration to the United States. Many Mexicans fled the destruction of the war. Others fled to escape political persecution. These immigrants included upper- and middle-class refugees, as well as farmers and urban poor. Many hoped to find industrial jobs in the United States.

Between 1905 and 1909 more than 28,000 Mexicans immigrated to the United States. By 1915 about three times that number had arrived. Since then, economic and political factors have continued to draw many Mexican immigrants to the United States.

SECTION 4 REVIEW

Identify and explain the significance of the following:

- **Porfirio Díaz**
- **Francisco Madero**
- **Mexican Revolution**
- **Victoriano Huerta**
- **Venustiano Carranza**
- **Francisco "Pancho" Villa**
- **Emiliano Zapata**
- **ABC Powers**
- **John J. Pershing**

Reading for Content Understanding

1. **Main Idea** Why did Francisco Madero begin the Mexican Revolution?
2. **Main Idea** Why did the United States become involved in the Mexican Revolution?
3. **Cultural Diversity** Why did Mexican immigration to the United States increase during and after the Mexican Revolution?
4. **Writing** *Informing* Write an article that might have appeared in a Mexican newspaper in 1920 about the role Pancho Villa played in the Mexican Revolution.
5. **Critical Thinking** *Identifying Cause and Effect* Why did the revolution in Mexico make U.S. businesspeople uneasy?

Chapter 10 Review ANSWERS

Identifying People and Ideas

1. the practice of extending a nation's power by gaining territories for a colonial empire
2. ruler of Hawaii who was deposed when Americans took over the island
3. a rebellion led by nationalists in China to fight against foreign control
4. Cuban revolutionary who was banned from Cuba
5. American resolution declaring that it did not intend to take over Cuba
6. an amendment to the Cuban constitution that gave the United States broad powers over Cuba
7. an extension of the Monroe Doctrine stating that the United States should act to police the Western Hemisphere
8. reformer who began the Mexican Revolution
9. Argentina, Brazil, and Chile; powers that negotiated talks between the United States and Huerta
10. U.S. general who failed to capture Pancho Villa

Using the Time Line

1. a
2. e
3. b
4. c
5. d

Review and Assessment RESOURCES

PRINT
★ Chapter 10 Review, pp. 312–13
★ Vocabulary Activity 10
★ Chapter 10 Study Guide
★ Chapter 10 Test (Form A or B)

MULTIMEDIA
★ Audio Program, Ch. 10 (English and Spanish)
★ *Global Skill Builder CD–ROM*
★ Chapter 10 Test Generator
★ HRW Web site

SHELTERED ENGLISH
★ Spanish Glossary
★ Sheltered English Chapter 10 Test

ASSESS

Have students complete one of the Chapter 10 Tests. As an alternate assessment, assign the Chapter 10 Investigation.

Understanding Main Ideas

1. U.S. policy that all nations would have equal access to trade with China

2. exaggerated events that happened in Cuba

3. United States—gained territories; Spain—lost territories; Cuba—came under U.S. military control

4. negotiated with Britain, Columbia, and Panama; overcame tropical disease, the danger of construction work, and crossing the mountains; declared the Roosevelt Corollary

5. Huerta's government was not democratic and it had siezed power by force.

6. to prevent Mexico from getting arms from Germany

Reviewing Themes

1. to obtain new sources of raw materials, to develop new markets to sell goods, to gain prestige and power

2. Japan—sent Commodore Perry to deliver a letter of friendship, presented Japanese leaders with gifts, showed force through warships, negotiated a commercial treaty; China—established the Open Door Policy

3. Under pressure from public opinion, the U.S. government wanted to encourage the growth of an independent, democratic government in Cuba.

CHAPTER 10 REVIEW

Chapter Summary

As the U.S. economy grew, so did the desire to secure new foreign markets for American products. In the mid- and late 1800s the United States purchased Alaska from Russia, annexed the islands of Hawaii, and tried to open markets in Asia. Victory in the Spanish-American War gave the United States additional territories. Afterward, the United States became more involved in events in Latin America, including a revolution in Mexico.

On a separate sheet of paper, complete the following activities.

Identifying People and Ideas

Describe the historical significance of the following:

1. imperialism
2. Liliuokalani
3. Boxer Rebellion
4. José Martí
5. Teller Amendment
6. Platt Amendment
7. Roosevelt Corollary
8. Francisco Madero
9. ABC Powers
10. John J. Pershing

Internet Activity

go.hrw.com
SB1 Panama Canal

Search the Internet through the HRW Web site to find information about the operation of the Panama Canal. Use the information to create a drawing that shows how ships pass through the canal. Be sure to provide a caption for your drawing.

Understanding Main Ideas

1. What was the Open Door Policy?
2. How did the press help spark U.S. involvement in the conflict in Cuba?
3. How did the outcome of the Spanish-American War affect the United States, Spain, and Cuba?
4. Explain the steps that the United States took to build and control the Panama Canal.
5. Why did President Wilson refuse to recognize General Huerta's government in Mexico?
6. Why did President Wilson order U.S. troops into Mexico?

Reviewing Themes

1. **Geographic Diversity** Why did the United States want control of certain Pacific islands?
2. **Economic Development** What steps did the United States take to expand trade with China and Japan?

Using the Time Line

Number your paper from 1 to 5. Match the letters on the time line below with the following events.

1. **Secretary of State William Seward negotiates the purchase of Alaska from Russia.**
2. **Revolution breaks out in Mexico.**
3. **Congress passes the McKinley Tariff, allowing all countries to ship sugar duty-free to the United States.**
4. **The USS *Maine* explodes and sinks, killing 260 people.**
5. **Despite most Hawaiians' opposition, Hawaii becomes a U.S. territory.**

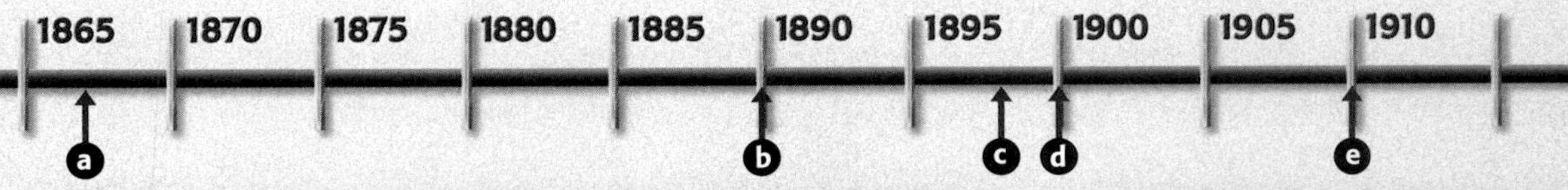

RETEACH

Visual-Spatial, Interpersonal. Organize students into four groups and assign each group a section of the text. Have groups create a collage that represents the assigned section. Ask students to use pictures or original illustrations to complete their projects. Schedule a time for each group to present its collage to the class. SHELTERED ENGLISH

Using the Internet

Have students continue their research on the Panama Canal. Ask students to create a poster that incorporates their drawing from the Chapter Review Internet activity with at least five statistics about the construction and operation of the canal.

Portfolio Extensions

1. Have students write a report on another one of the countries. Then have them compare the relationships of both countries with the United States.

2. Have students write a response to the pair of articles; ask them to discuss which article would most convince them to take action on the event presented.

3. **Global Relations** Why did the United States defend Cuba against Spain?

Thinking Critically

1. **Supporting a Point of View** Do you think the United States had good reasons for purchasing Alaska? Explain your answer.
2. **Synthesizing Information** Why did many Americans want to gain more overseas territory?
3. **Identifying Cause and Effect** What effect did the Mexican Revolution have on the people of Mexico?

Writing About History

1. **Creating** Imagine that you are a member of the Anti-Imperialist League. Create a pamphlet explaining your group's position and encouraging people to join your organization.
2. **Informing** Imagine that you are a journalist covering the Mexican Revolution. Write a half-page news story explaining the events leading to the revolution, as well as describing the involvement of the United States and the revolution's outcome.

Linking Geography and History

1. **Human-Environment Interaction** What physical obstacles stood in the way of building a canal across Panama?
2. **Location** Why did the United States want to acquire the Philippines?

History Skills Workshop

Using Visual Resources Study the image to the right, which is a 1904 cartoon by Joseph Keppler. In this cartoon an eagle symbolizing America stretches all the way from the United States to the Philippines. Then answer the following questions: (a) What message do you think Keppler was trying to get across to the viewer? (b) Do you agree with his message? Explain your answer.

Building Your Portfolio

Complete the following activities individually or in groups.

1. **Latin America** Choose one of the following Latin American nations: Argentina, Cuba, the Dominican Republic, Haiti, Mexico, Nicaragua, Panama, or Venezuela. Present a short report in class on the country's historical and present-day relationship with the United States. Your report should include appropriate images and a map of the country.
2. **Yellow Journalism** Select an event you have studied recently in class or one that is in the news. Then write two half-page newspaper articles, with headlines, on that topic. One article should report the facts as accurately as possible, and the other should be written in the style of yellow journalism. Finally, share your news articles with the class. Have the class vote for which articles they think best represent each style of journalism.

The Granger Collection, New York

Thinking Critically

1. Answers will vary but students might say yes—Alaska would greatly expand the United States and offered mineral wealth and other resources, or no—Alaska is too distant and too cold for American settlement.

2. They thought that economic strength came from developing new lands, and that expansion would help the United States recover from a recession in the 1890s.

3. It brought chaos, violence, and political persecution to some Mexicans; at the same time, it gave Mexicans a greater say in their government.

Writing About History

1. Pamphlets will vary but should express concern that the United States is building a colonial empire and support for isolationism.

2. News stories will vary but might include unfair distribution of wealth, lack of democracy, the Tampico crisis, the Veracruz incident, U.S. soldiers in Mexico, and the overthrow of Carranza.

Linking Geography and History

1. tropical forests, mountains, and rock

2. The Philippines had great naval and commercial value, in part because of its location.

History Skills Workshop

(a) Keppler's cartoon suggests that U.S. influence spanned much of the globe; (b) answers will vary but students should explain their reasoning.

FOCUS

Ask students to suggest benefits and costs of acquiring foreign territory. List students' answers under the headings *Benefits* and *Costs* on the chalkboard. Explain that in this activity they will learn about how the United States had to weigh these same pros and cons as it acquired foreign territory in the late 1800s.

TEACH

Have students read the Geography and History lesson. Choose one or more of the following activities to explore the Geography and History content with students.

ALL LEVELS: Logical-Mathematical, Visual-Spatial. (Suggested time: 35 min.) Refer students to the map on pages 316–17 that shows the various possessions countries had around the world

Citizenship and Democracy

Opposition to Hawaiian Statehood. Hawaii became the 50th state in 1959 despite the opposition of some members of Congress. Congressional opponents of Hawaiian statehood had various objections. Some felt it was unwise to add a state that did not border the existing United States. At a time when the struggle for civil rights was a volatile political issue, some southern members of Congress worried that Hawaiian congressional representatives would likely favor civil rights legislation. Cold War fears of communism concerned still others, who pointed to the unionized Hawaiian longshoremen and plantation workers. In the 1950s reports had surfaced suggesting that unions were pro-socialist or even communist.

Critical Thinking: What difficulties might have come up in 1959 because Hawaii was so far away from the rest of the United States?

ANSWER: Information might be slow to reach the islands and the islands might be harder to defend. Also, traveling or shipping goods over such a long distance could be expensive.

SKILLS ANSWERS

1. Cuba, the Philippines, Puerto Rico
2. Hawaii, American Samoa
3. 1898

Geography & History

The United States in the Modern Age

During the late 1800s many powerful nations, particularly European powers, tried to create global empires through conquest and political influence. The United States began acquiring overseas territories in the 1890s. Despite this expansion, the scope of U.S. possessions around the world remained much smaller than that of nations such as France, Germany, and Great Britain.

The expansion of U.S. power overseas helped develop U.S. foreign trade. American merchants exported increasing amounts of goods to consumers in global markets. American consumers were also able to buy more imported goods. ■

Latin America and the Pacific

As a result of the Spanish-American War, the United States took control of Spanish colonies in the Pacific and the Caribbean. These new possessions helped the United States protect its growing trade with those regions.

U.S. Overseas Expansion, 1898–1899

COLONY/COUNTRY	U.S. INVOLVEMENT	CURRENT STATUS
Cuba	Occupied by U.S. forces during Spanish-American War in 1898	Independent nation; the United States gave up right to intervene in Cuban affairs in 1934
Hawaii	Annexed by the United States in 1898	Became 50th U.S. state in 1959
Philippines	Ceded by Spain to the United States in 1898	Independent nation since 1946
Puerto Rico	Ceded by Spain to the United States in 1898	U.S. commonwealth since 1952
Samoa	Agreement in 1899 divided islands between the United States and Germany	Western Samoa independent since 1962; American Samoa still under U.S. control

Pineapples and sugar-cane were some of the Pacific crops prized by Americans.

Geography Skills
Reading Charts

1. What Spanish colonies did the United States gain as a result of the Spanish-American War?
2. What other territories came under U.S. control by the end of the 1800s?
3. When did the United States annex Hawaii?

314

in 1914. Provide students with outline maps and art supplies to create a map illustrating political boundaries today. (You may wish to divide the class into several groups and assign each group one of the continents.) Ask students to compare maps and discuss what changes have occurred since 1914. **SHELTERED ENGLISH**

LEVEL 3: Linguistic, Logical-Mathematical. (Suggested time: 40 min. plus homework) Have students create a log for a hypothetical trading voyage around the world. Tell them that they will start in North America and embark upon an expedition in which they will spend time on each of the different continents on the world map on pages 316–17. Students should make log entries about their visit to each continent, writing about the goods they will try to trade in each area and the trade routes they will use. Have volunteers share their logs with the class.

The flag of the commonwealth of Puerto Rico (top), the national flag of the Philippines (center), and the state flag of Hawaii (bottom)

U.S. Exports and Imports, 1865–1915

- Exports to Latin America (including the Caribbean)
- Imports from Latin America (including the Caribbean)
- Exports to Asia and the Pacific
- Imports from Asia and the Pacific

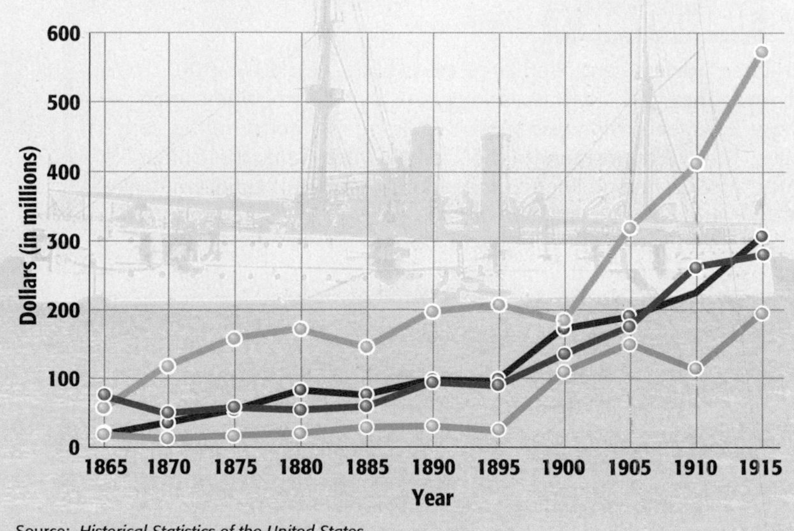

Source: *Historical Statistics of the United States*

History Note 1

Taking possession of Hawaii, the Philippines, and Puerto Rico helped the United States expand trade in the Pacific, Asia, and Latin America. "We want new markets," President William McKinley declared in 1898, "and as trade follows the flag, it looks very much as if we are going to have new markets."

Geography Skills

Reading Line Graphs

1. During which five-year period did the value of U.S. exports to Latin America grow the most?
2. By which year had the value of exports to Asia and the Pacific grown to more than $100 million?
3. During which five-year periods did imports from Latin America decline?

History Note 2

By the late 1800s the United States exported more goods to Europe than it imported from European nations. U.S. exports to Europe soared even higher after World War I began in 1914. American businesses provided money and supplies needed by the huge European armies. The war also caused a decline in exports from Europe. Americans responded by purchasing more goods from Asia and Latin America.

Global Relations

Keeping the Philippines. After Commodore George Dewey first captured the Philippines, President McKinley declared that taking the islands from Spain was not his main priority. He assured Europe that he only wanted to maintain the Open Door Policy throughout Asia. He also claimed that the United States had not attacked the Philippines to acquire territory but to enlarge American "commercial opportunity." By the time of Spain's surrender, however, McKinley had changed his mind.

Critical Thinking: Why might McKinley have changed his mind?

ANSWER: Students might mention that because the Philippines are close to China and Japan, they would provide a good base from which to protect U.S. trading interests with those countries. Students might also mention that McKinley may have worried that the United States was being left behind in the race for colonies and spheres of influence.

SKILLS ANSWERS

1. 1905–10
2. 1900
3. 1880–85, 1895–1900

CLOSE

Logical-Mathematical. Have students create a chart of areas and resources controlled in 1914. They should make a two-column chart with the headings *Continents* and *Resources,* then label the seven row headings *France, Germany, Great Britain, Japan, Portugal, Netherlands,* and *United States.* For example, in the row *Japan,* under *Continents* students would list Asia, and under *Resources* they would list silk.

CHALLENGE AND EXTEND

Linguistic, Logical-Mathematical. Have students imagine that they are business consultants in 1915. They have been hired to advise a U.S. corporation that is planning to start importing goods from Latin America and the Caribbean. Have students use the library or other resources to research the dramatic increase in U.S. imports from these areas from 1900 to 1915. In their reports to the corporation's president, students should answer questions such as: Why are imports increasing? What goods are being imported? and What countries are the leading exporters?

Geographic Diversity

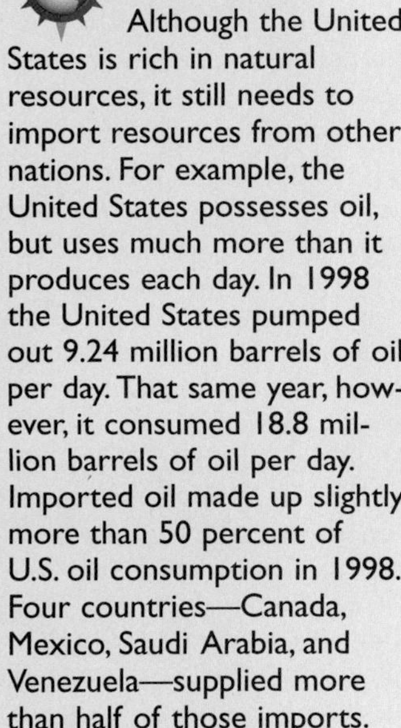

Natural Resources. Although the United States is rich in natural resources, it still needs to import resources from other nations. For example, the United States possesses oil, but uses much more than it produces each day. In 1998 the United States pumped out 9.24 million barrels of oil per day. That same year, however, it consumed 18.8 million barrels of oil per day. Imported oil made up slightly more than 50 percent of U.S. oil consumption in 1998. Four countries—Canada, Mexico, Saudi Arabia, and Venezuela—supplied more than half of those imports. As of May 1999 the United States kept 561 million barrels of oil in the U.S. Strategic Petroleum Reserve.

Critical Thinking: Why might the United States maintain an oil reserve?

ANSWER: Answers will vary but students might mention the need to cover a sudden, dramatic increase in demand or replace imports if one or more major supplier nations is unable or unwilling to deliver oil.

Global Expansion

Nations such as France, Germany, Great Britain, and Japan competed fiercely to establish overseas colonies and control foreign markets. This competition left regions such as Africa and southern Asia with only a few independent nations.

History Note 3

European powers controlled large areas of the world by 1900. However, they had few possessions in Latin America, where many former European colonies had won their independence in the early 1800s. The announcement of the Monroe Doctrine by the United States in 1823 helped keep European powers out of Latin America.

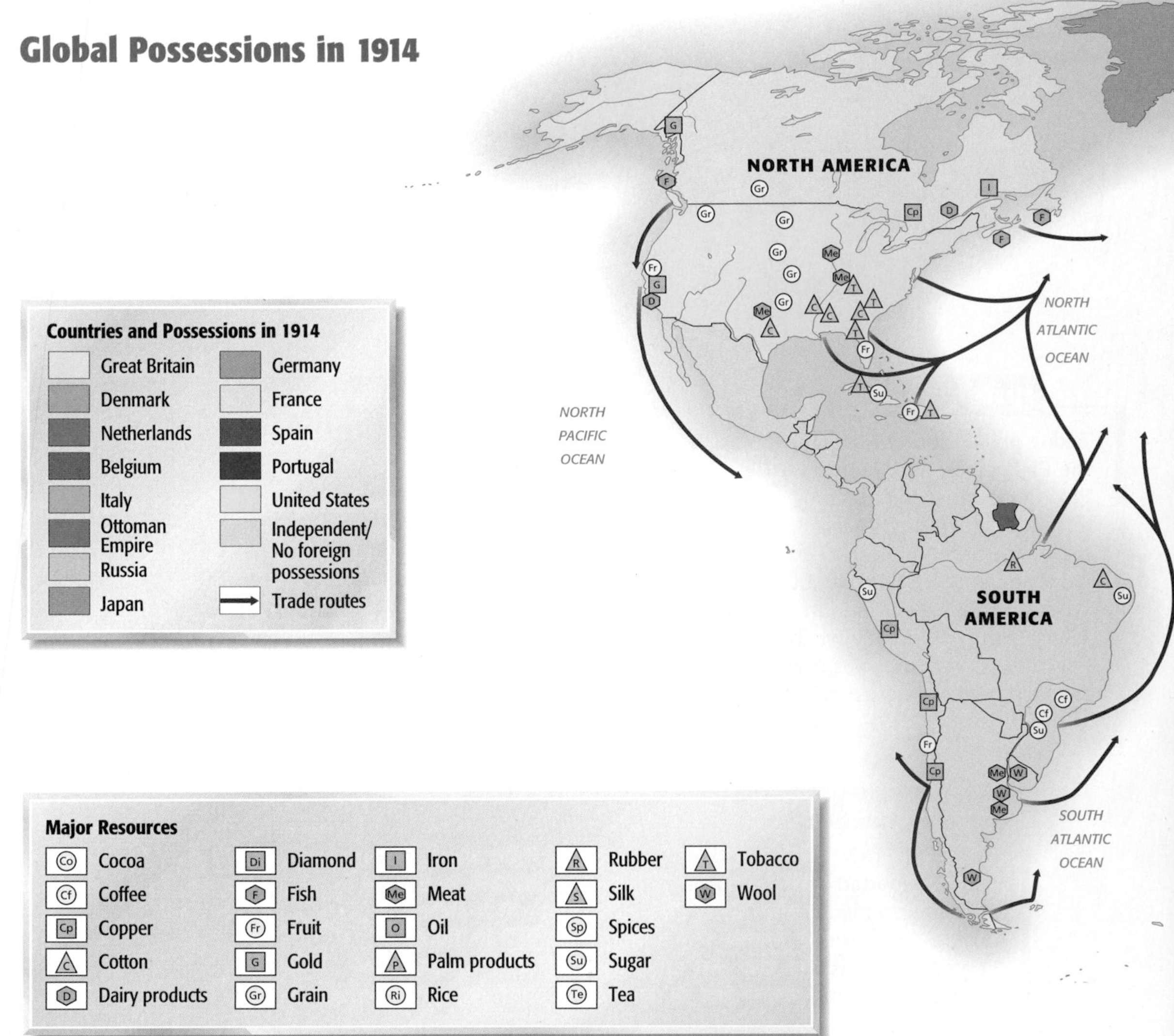

REVIEW

Logical-Mathematical, Visual-Spatial. Have students create a chart that lists the six continents pictured on pages 316–17. For each continent, ask students to provide the three most important available resources. Upon completion of the charts, lead a discussion comparing the available resources of the different regions of the world.

ASSESS

Have students complete Geography and History Quiz 3.

RETEACH

Logical-Mathematical, Visual-Spatial, Interpersonal. Have students use the information from the chart, graph, map, and history notes on pages 314–17 to create a time line that illustrates the expansion of the United States, Japan, and European nations from 1898 to 1914. Have volunteers present their time lines to the class. **SHELTERED ENGLISH**

History Note 4

During the late 1800s and early 1900s, several nations tried to gain control of China's huge economic market. Although China kept its own government, countries such as Britain, Germany, Japan, and the United States gained great influence over Chinese affairs. Japan in particular concentrated on expanding its power in Asia. By 1905 Japan had established control over Korea and Formosa (modern-day Taiwan) and was threatening to expand into northern China.

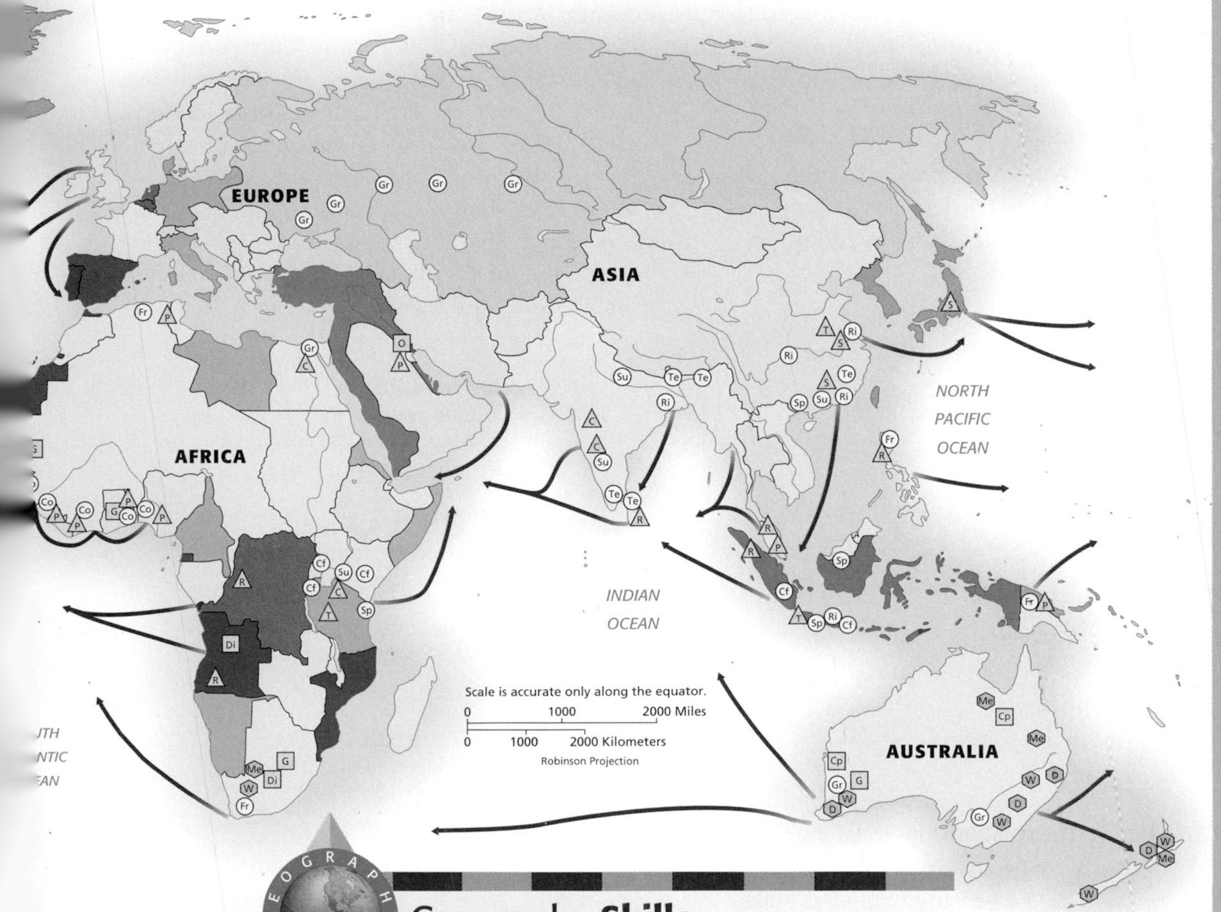

Geography Skills

Reading Special-Purpose Maps

1. What were Australia's major resources?
2. What nations had colonies in South America?
3. What Asian country had foreign colonies in 1914?

Geographic Diversity

Gold Rush in Australia. California was not the only place in the world to experience a gold rush. In 1851 gold was discovered in the area of Ballarat in Victoria, which was then a British colony in southeastern Australia. More than 2,000 miners rushed to Ballarat in the first few weeks following the strike, and within three years 50,000 had arrived. Rather than finding only gold dust or very fine grains of gold, as was often the case in California, miners in Australia regularly discovered gold nuggets, the largest of which weighed more than 200 pounds. By the late 1850s, single miners were no longer striking it rich in Ballarat. However, mining companies continued working the area until recessions in the 1870s and 1890s closed many mines.

Activity: Have students use the library or other resources to create a map identifying the locations of other gold rushes. Encourage students to note important information such as the date each rush began, the amount of gold that was found, and the value of that gold.

SKILLS ANSWERS

1. copper, dairy, gold, grain, meat, wool
2. France, Great Britain, Netherlands
3. Japan

TEACH

ALL LEVELS: Linguistic, Logical-Mathematical, Visual-Spatial. (Suggested time: 45 min.) Explain to students that flowcharts can be useful for showing cause-and-effect relationships because they illustrate a sequence of events. Show students some examples of simple flowcharts. Then instruct students to create a flowchart showing the causes and effects of an event that has been in the newspaper in the last month. You may want to start by having the class work together to create a list of events and their causes and effects. Remind students that many events have more than one cause and more than one effect. Next to each arrow connecting two boxes on their flowcharts, students should write an appropriate clue word or phrase to clarify the cause-and-effect relationship. Students should also include a title for their flowcharts. Ask volunteers to share their work with the class.

SKILLS ANSWERS

Students' answers will vary but they should include Díaz's method of ruling Mexico, Madero's pamphlet calling for free elections, and the economic conditions of much of the Mexican population.

Understanding Cause and Effect. For further practice, have students brainstorm a list of recent events that have taken place at school. *(Examples might include the addition of portable classrooms or a school team winning a championship.)* Write these events on the chalkboard. Then ask students to choose one of the events and to write a paragraph describing its causes and effects. Remind students to use clue words and phrases to signal cause-and-effect relationships.

History Skills

WORKSHOP

Identifying Cause and Effect

Identifying and understanding cause-and-effect relationships is crucial to the study of history. To investigate why an event took place and what happened as a result of that event, historians ask questions. These questions include: What were the immediate actions that triggered the event? What was the background of the event? Who was involved?

How to Identify Cause and Effect

1. **Look for clues** Certain words and phrases are clues to the existence of a cause-and-effect relationship. Note the following examples.

Clue Words and Phrases

Cause	Effect
because	aftermath
brought about	as a consequence
gave rise to	as a result of
inspired	depended on
led to	originating from
produced	outcome
provoked	outgrowth
spurred	proceeded from
the reason	resulting in

2. **Identify the relationship** Read carefully to identify how historical events may be related. Writers do not always state clearly the link between cause and effect. Sometimes a reader of history has to infer, or draw a conclusion about, the cause or the effect of a particular event or action.
3. **Check for complex connections** Beyond the immediate cause and effect, check for other, more complex connections. Note, for example, whether (1) there were additional causes of a given effect, (2) a cause had multiple effects, and (3) these effects themselves caused further events.

Example The following diagram presents important cause-and-effect relationships on the events leading up to the Spanish-American War. In the late 1800s some Cubans rebelled against Spanish rule. They wanted independence. To protect American interests in Cuba, the United States sent the battleship *Maine* to Havana Harbor. The *Maine* exploded, killing 260 people. Many Americans thought that Spain was responsible for the explosion. Responding to President William McKinley's request, Congress declared war on Spain in 1898.

Cause
Some Cubans wanted independence and rebelled against Spanish rule.

Effect/Cause
The U.S. government sent the battleship *Maine* to Cuba to protect American interests there. The *Maine* exploded, killing 260 people. Many Americans suspected that Spain was responsible.

Effect
Congress declared war on Spain in 1898.

Practicing the Skill

Reread Chapter 10, Section 4, in your textbook, which discusses the causes of the Mexican Revolution. Draw a diagram like the one above, showing the relationships between the actions and the outcomes of important events leading up to the Mexican Revolution.

ALL LEVELS: Linguistic, Logical-Mathematical. (Suggested time: 30 min.) Instruct each student to create a crossword puzzle using the clue words and phrases signifying cause and effect as well as any other important terms from his or her magazine article. Have students create a version of their article in which they substitute blanks for the important terms and clue words and phrases. Students should indicate in each blank where the corresponding term, word, or phrase should be written in the crossword puzzle. Then have students exchange their articles and use context cues to help them figure out the term, word, or phrase for each blank. Finally, have students return the completed puzzles to their creators for grading.

History in Action

UNIT 3 PORTFOLIO

Muckraker Magazine

Complete the following activity in small, cooperative groups.

Imagine that you are a journalist working for the fictitious news publication *Muckraker Magazine* during the early 1900s. Your editor has asked you to prepare a special issue examining the causes, effects, problems, and reforms of the Progressive Era. Five teams of reporters will work to put this special issue together. Each team will create one section of the magazine that focuses on a specific topic.

Materials To complete this activity, you will need posterboard, construction paper, or typing paper. You may wish to write your article on a computer. In addition, you will need markers, pens, pencils, and glue, tape, or rubber cement.

Parts of the Project To create your magazine, complete the following tasks:

1. **Planning and Writing** You will work on one of the following topics: urban living conditions; working conditions; politics and government; monopolies, trusts and big business; or social reform. As a group decide on the articles to include in your section of the magazine. Then decide who will research and write each article. Remember to identify the causes and effects of Progressive Era problems and reforms.

2. **Editing** When you have completed your article(s), pair off with another member of your group and exchange articles. Edit your partner's article(s) and offer constructive comments. Revise your own article(s) and prepare a final typed draft.

3. **Designing** Meet in your group to plan the design and layout for your magazine section. Decide how to organize the articles, and discuss images, charts, and maps that you might use to improve the layout.

4. **Laying out the Magazine** Next, decide who will be news editors and who will be photographers. News editors will begin laying out the magazine and writing headlines. The photographers will be selecting or creating images and writing captions. When these tasks have been completed, paste your section together. Combine it with other groups to make a complete issue of *Muckraker Magazine*.

Elect someone in the class to design the cover and table of contents for the magazine. Display the finished magazine in your classroom or in another area of your school.

Students prepare their school newspaper.

Planning and Writing. After students have done their research, encourage them to create cause-and-effect diagrams covering the topics of their articles. This will help them organize their articles before they begin to write.

Editing. Explain to students that the best criticism both points out what is good about a person's writing and provides concrete suggestions to revise what needs improvement. Encourage students to make as many constructive suggestions as they can to improve their partner's writing.

Laying Out the Magazine. Have students outline where they think articles and pictures should go before they start to cut and paste. Their outlines could be small pencil sketches or full-size pages, but the entire group should agree on where things will go before the editors place them.

Introducing UNIT

CHAPTER 11
World War I

Following a long period of increasing tensions, World War I began in Europe in 1914. The United States initially chose to remain neutral in the conflict, but the deaths of Americans in German U-boat attacks and the publication of the Zimmerman Note led the United States to declare war in 1917. After the Allied victory, Germany was forced to give up part of its territory and pay large war reparations, although President Wilson argued for less harsh peace terms.

CHAPTER 12
The 1920s: An Unsettled Decade

At the end of World War I the United States struggled through demobilization. Racial tensions increased, and race riots occurred in a number of U.S. cities. Labor strikes and fears of Communists and other radicals led to a Red Scare and rising xenophobia. Many Americans favored a policy of isolationism. Presidents Harding and Coolidge worked to promote American business. The stock market and automobile industry did extremely well. Many Americans enjoyed increased prosperity

Internet Activity

Edna St. Vincent Millay. Have students search the Internet through the HRW Web site to find information about the life and poetry of Edna St. Vincent Millay. Then ask students to write a biography that discusses her life, viewpoints on issues of her time, and one or more of her poems.

go.hrw.com
SB1 Millay

UNIT 4 The Changing Nation

(1914–1929)

CHAPTER 11 **World War I** (1914–1919)

CHAPTER 12 **The 1920s: An Unsettled Decade** (1919–1929)

CHAPTER 13 **The Roaring Twenties** (1920–1929)

during the 1920s, although some groups, such as farmers, did not share in it.

CHAPTER 13
The Roaring Twenties

During the 1920s the differences between urban and rural Americans became more pronounced. Nativism was strong and led to severe restrictions on immigration. For many people, particularly youth, the 1920s were a time of fun and new ideas, however. Jazz and the blues swept the nation, new fashions bucked tradition, and new types of entertainment became available. Mass media grew in influence as Americans could follow the same sports teams, listen to the same radio programs, see the same movies, and participate in the same fads. American culture flowered and strongly influenced American society. The Harlem Renaissance was an important period of African American artistic achievement.

UNIT MOTIVATOR

Have students write each of the chapter titles in their notebooks. Share the information in the chapter overviews with students. Then tell students to write under each title five questions that they have about the chapter. As students read the chapters, they should answer the questions. At the end of the unit, discuss students' questions and answers.

American Teens
IN HISTORY
Young War Supporters

Young people across the United States supported the nation's fight in World War I. These teenagers performed essential services and helped the Allies win.

Boy Scouts and Girl Scouts, who took an oath to serve their country when they joined their troops, fulfilled their duty with enthusiasm during the war. Under the slogan "Every Scout to Save a Soldier," Scouts sold almost half a billion dollars in Liberty Bonds and War Savings Stamps.

Some young people donated their own money to the war effort. Sunday school pupils in Cleveland, Ohio, each gave a dime toward the cost of a new warship. Victory Boys and Girls also pledged money, up to $10 a child, toward the war effort. They worked at odd jobs to earn money. These jobs included raising and selling guinea pigs, gathering nuts, and polishing shoes.

Other young people volunteered their labor. Girls joined knitting parties to make scarves and gloves for soldiers. Boys on vacation from school signed up with the U.S. Boy's Working Reserve "agricultural army" to help farmers grow food for soldiers overseas. One writer credited the Reserve workers "with saving the sugar-beet crop in Michigan, the apple crop in Georgia, [and] the berry crop in Oregon."

Some young people even left school to help boost agricultural production. The New York legislature, for example, proposed laws to allow 12-year-olds to stay out of school seven months out of the year to work on farms. After the war, however, the government urged these young people to return to school. One poster read:

> *"Boys and Girls*
> *The School Is Your Training Camp*
> *Uncle Sam Says*
> *ENLIST TODAY."*

Young war supporters often found that their work offered unexpected benefits. One teen who served as a machine operator earned $3.50 a day—several times what he could have earned before the war. Other young adults got the chance to travel. All had the satisfaction of serving their country.

In this unit you will learn about how Americans responded to World War I. You will also learn about American life during the 1920s—the exciting Jazz Age.

The Granger Collection, New York

The U.S. government created posters to encourage young people to join in the war effort.

LEFT PAGE: *U.S. soldiers prepare to "ship out" for service in World War I.*

Using Visual Resources

World War I Soldiers. The photograph on the opposite page shows U.S. soldiers on their way to serve in World War I. Many Americans had opposed the entry of the United States into World War I. However, the continued sinking of American ships by German U-boats and the publication of the Zimmerman Note forced President Wilson to ask Congress to declare war in April 1917. To build the necessary military strength, Congress passed the Selective Service Act of 1917. As a result, almost 24 million American men registered with the Selective Service, and nearly 3 million of them were drafted. Overall, nearly three out of every four soldiers serving in the U.S. wartime army were draftees.

Critical Thinking: Why might the facial expressions of the U.S. soldiers in the picture vary among individuals?

ANSWER: Some soldiers might feel pride and excitement about fighting for their country, while others might feel nervous or scared about the dangers of war.

TEACH

ALL LEVELS: Linguistic, Logical-Mathematical. (Suggested time: 35 min.) Ask students to categorize each event on the time line as either political or cultural in nature. Then have them determine whether each event had an impact on the United States, the international community, or both. Ask volunteers to share their classification of the events. In addition, have students choose three events from the time line and write in their notebooks one question about each. Students should answer these questions as they read the unit.

ALL LEVELS: Logical-Mathematical, Visual-Spatial. (Suggested time: 30 min.) Have students study the images that accompany the time line events. Tell students to choose five of the images and write several sentences providing any additional information about the events that can be inferred from the images. For example, students might deduce that Tutankhamen was wealthy because his burial mask is made of gold. Allow time in class for volunteers to share their insights into the time line images.

Global Relations

U.S. Neutrality. President Wilson originally wanted the United States to remain neutral in World War I. To this end he supported the neutrality of American merchant ships to trade freely. However, Germany blockaded Great Britain, and Britain blockaded the North Sea. American shipping was caught in the middle. The value of U.S. trade with Germany and Austria plummeted more than $165 million between 1914 and 1916. At the same time U.S. trade with the Allied countries rose dramatically, to about $3 billion. The United States developed a strong economic interest in seeing the Allies defeat the Central Powers, because most of the Allied purchases had been made with credit.

Critical Thinking: Why might Britain have established a blockade that prevented neutral nations from trading with other countries?

ANSWER: Britain might have wanted to prevent any country from selling food, weapons, or other supplies to the Central Powers or to a neutral nation trading with the Central Powers.

UNIT 4

Time Line: 1914–1929

The Changing Nation

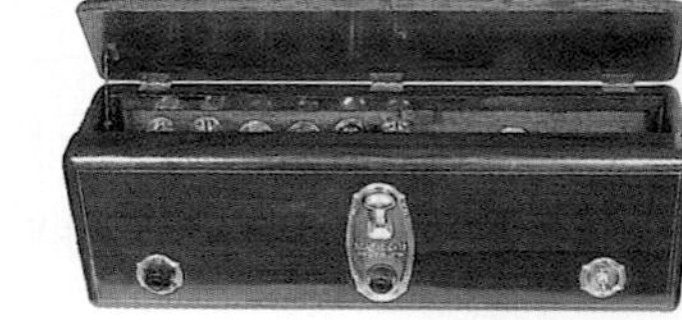
A radio with speaker from the 1920s

A World War I recruiting poster

UNITED STATES

1917 The U.S. Congress declares war on Germany after the German navy resumes unrestricted submarine warfare.

1918 President Woodrow Wilson proposes his Fourteen Points for a lasting peace after World War I.

1920 WWJ in Detroit becomes the first radio station to air regular commercial broadcasts.

1921 Langston Hughes's poem "The Negro Speaks of Rivers" appears in *The Crisis* magazine.

1914 | 1915 | 1916 | 1917 | 1918 | 1919 | 1920 | 1921

WORLD

1914 World War I begins after Austria-Hungary declares war on Serbia.

1915 A German submarine sinks the *Lusitania,* a British passenger liner. About 1,200 people, including 128 Americans, die.

1916 Determined Turkish resistance fighters battle the Allies in Gallipoli.

1917 The Bolshevik Revolution sweeps Russia and ends the rule of the czars.

1919 Leaders of the nations involved in World War I sign the Treaty of Versailles.

1921 Leading naval powers meet at the Washington Conference and agree to limit the size of their navies.

St. Basil Cathedral in Moscow

The Detroit News SECOND EXTRA

LUSITANIA IS TORPEDOED; ALL RESCUED

LLOYDS SAYS LINER HAS BEEN BEACHED

PASSENGERS WARNED BY MESSAGES BEFORE SHIP LEFT NEW YORK

An early newspaper headline reports inaccurate information.

CHALLENGE AND EXTEND

1. **Linguistic, Logical-Mathematical.** Have students choose one of the events from the time line. Ask students to use the library or other resources to find more information on the event they have chosen. Tell students to imagine that they are local journalists who have been sent to cover that event at the time it occurred. They should prepare a radio news broadcast that describes the event and highlights its significance for their local community. Ask for volunteers to share their broadcasts with the class.

2. **Linguistic, Logical-Mathematical.** Organize the class into small groups. Assign each group one of the events from the time line. Remind students that there are historical events that led up to each time line event, as well as events that resulted from each time line event. With this knowledge in mind, each group should create a museum exhibit that chronicles their event within a broader historical context. For example, an exhibit on Charles Lindbergh's flight could also include mentions of the Wright brothers' airplane experiments and the space shuttle. Have the groups display their exhibits around the classroom.

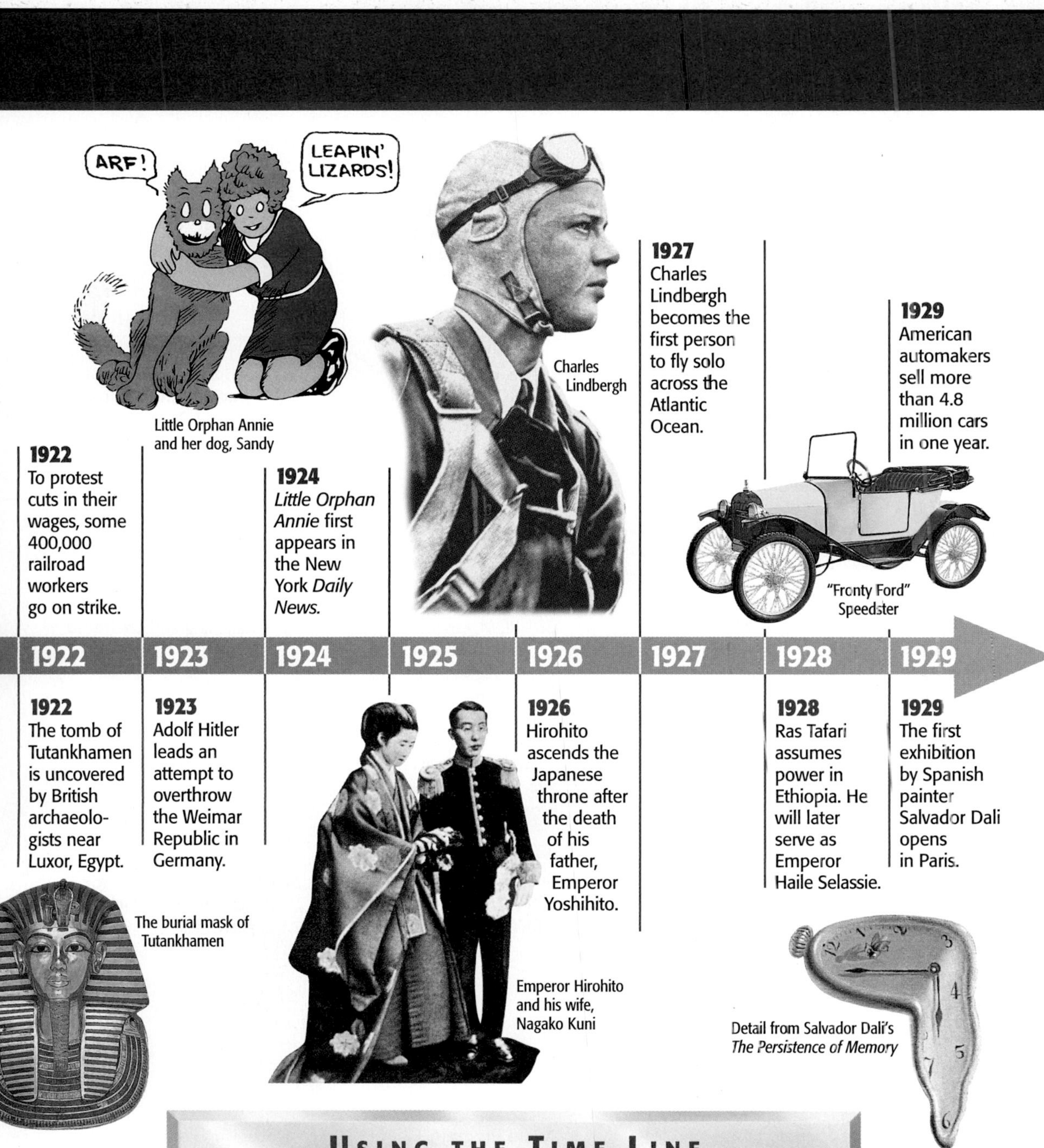

Little Orphan Annie and her dog, Sandy

Charles Lindbergh

"Fronty Ford" Speedster

The burial mask of Tutankhamen

Emperor Hirohito and his wife, Nagako Kuni

Detail from Salvador Dali's *The Persistence of Memory*

USING THE TIME LINE

1. Which entries shown on the time line relate to World War I?
2. In what order did the major international agreements occur?

Activity Choose one of the entries shown on the time line. Use your library or your textbook to find some additional information and events related to this entry. Be sure to note when these events occurred and their significance. Create a new time line focusing on this entry. (Your new time line might only include the months of one year.) Place the events and information for this entry in correct chronological order. You may also wish to illustrate your time line.

Using Visual Resources

Salvador Dali and Surrealism. The Spanish-born Salvador Dali was a well-known artist who lived during the 1900s. Some of his most famous works are examples of surrealist paintings. These types of paintings use images that seem to be taken from dreams or fantasies. The surrealist movement was particularly strong during the 1920s and 1930s. In addition to his paintings, Dali also worked on ballets, films, and plays during his artistic career.

Activity: Show students appropriate paintings by Dali or other surrealists, such as René Magritte or Joan Miró. Then have students write a paragraph interpreting one of the paintings. Students should include a description of the way that the artist has distorted traditional images.

Using the Time Line Answers

1. Austria-Hungary declares war on Serbia; sinking of the *Lusitania;* Congress declares war on Germany; Wilson proposes the Fourteen Points; leaders of the nations involved in World War I sign the Treaty of Versailles

2. 1919—Treaty of Versailles; 1921—Washington Conference

CHAPTER PLANNING GUIDE
World War I

	SECTION LESSON OBJECTIVES	PRINT RESOURCES	MULTIMEDIA RESOURCES	SHELTERED ENGLISH RESOURCES
Section 1: The Road to War (pp. 325–28)	★ Analyze the major causes of World War I. ★ Identify events that led most of Europe to become involved in the war. ★ Describe how the war's early battles proceeded and where they were fought.	★ Guided Reading Strategies 11.1 ★ American History Political Cartoon 20: Conflict in the Balkans ★ Section 1 Review, p. 328 ★ Daily Quiz 11.1	★ *Teaching Resources CD–ROM*, Lesson 11.1	★ Main Idea Activities for Reteaching and Sheltered English 11.1
Section 2: Wilson and Neutrality (pp. 329–34)	★ Describe trench warfare. ★ Analyze the effects of new weapons in World War I. ★ Explain how the United States tried to remain neutral, and identify events that forced the nation to enter the war.	★ Guided Reading Strategies 11.2 ★ Section 2 Review, p. 334 ★ Daily Quiz 11.2	★ *Teaching Resources CD–ROM*, Lesson 11.2 ★ Everyday Life in America Transparency 20: In the Trenches: Battle Sketches of World War I ★ HRW Web site	★ Main Idea Activities for Reteaching and Sheltered English 11.2
Section 3: Americans Prepare for War (pp. 335–38)	★ Explain how the U.S. government prepared the military for war. ★ Analyze the contributions of women and African Americans in the war. ★ Describe the effects of the war on industry and labor.	★ Guided Reading Strategies 11.3 ★ Section 3 Review, p. 338 ★ Daily Quiz 11.3	★ *Teaching Resources CD–ROM*, Lesson 11.3	★ Main Idea Activities for Reteaching and Sheltered English 11.3
Section 4: Americans "Over There" (pp. 339–43)	★ Describe the experiences of U.S. soldiers in World War I. ★ Analyze the progress of the final battles of the war. ★ Explain why Germany finally agreed to an armistice.	★ Guided Reading Strategies 11.4 ★ Biography Reading 11: Alvin C. "Sergeant" York ★ Primary Source Reading 11: A Journal of the Great War ★ Geography Activity 11: World War I ★ Section 4 Review, p. 343 ★ Daily Quiz 11.4	★ *Teaching Resources CD–ROM*, Lesson 11.4 ★ *Exploring America's Past* Video Segment: Letters from Home; *Teacher's Guide*, pp. 21–23 ★ Linking Geography and History Transparency 16: World War I: The Western Front, 1917–1918	★ Main Idea Activities for Reteaching and Sheltered English 11.4
Section 5: Establishing Peace (pp. 344–49)	★ Analyze the human and economic costs of the war. ★ Explain the terms of the Treaty of Versailles. ★ Describe Americans' reactions to the Treaty of Versailles.	★ Guided Reading Strategies 11.5 ★ Literature Reading 11: Battlefield Prose ★ Graphic Organizer 11: Major Moments of World War I ★ Section 5 Review, p. 349 ★ Daily Quiz 11.5	★ *Teaching Resources CD–ROM*, Lesson 11.5 ★ HRW Web site	★ Main Idea Activities for Reteaching and Sheltered English 11.5
Chapter Review and Assessment (pp. 352–53)		★ Chapter 11 Review, pp. 352–53 ★ Vocabulary Activity 11 ★ Chapter 11 Study Guide ★ Chapter 11 Test (Form A or B)	★ Audio Program, Ch. 11 (English and Spanish) ★ *Global Skill Builder CD–ROM* ★ Chapter 11 Test Generator ★ HRW Web site	★ Spanish Glossary ★ Sheltered English Chapter 11 Test

CHAPTER OVERVIEW

As a series of alliances drew European nations into World War I, the United States declared its neutrality. New war technologies such as airplanes, machine guns, and poison gases combined with trench warfare to create a virtual stalemate along the western front.

A series of incidents involving Germany's practice of unrestricted submarine warfare and the discovery of the Zimmerman Note led the United States to enter the war. However, the nation needed to prepare for battle. It did so by instituting a draft, using propaganda to promote the war effort, and overseeing the production of war goods. Americans at home stepped into the workforce to fill the positions left by soldiers and helped raise money for the war effort.

As Russia withdrew from fighting on the eastern front, Germany made a concerted effort to win the war on the western front. The Germans had almost reached Paris when the American Expeditionary Force entered the war. The addition of U.S. troops, along with problems resulting from Germany's lack of supplies and low morale, helped lead to the end of the war.

Although the Allies accepted many of President Wilson's Fourteen Points as a basis for negotiations, they drew up a very different peace settlement in the Treaty of Versailles. Opposition in the Senate meant that the United States never officially recognized the treaty, leaving the country to negotiate separate treaties with Austria, Germany, and Hungary.

CHAPTER INVESTIGATION

The Chapter Investigation is an extended, multipart activity designed for students to work cooperatively and apply the chapter content in the creation of a project. You may choose to use the Chapter 11 Investigation, Comic Book, either as a substitute for the lessons or as an alternate assessment.

BLOCK SCHEDULING 

The teacher lesson plans for each section offer a variety of activity choices to help you present the material in a block scheduling format. For further suggestions on block scheduling, see *the Block Scheduling Handbook with Team Teaching Strategies,* pp. 61–66.

Meeting Individual Needs

ABILITY LEVELS

LEVEL 1 Basic level activities designed for all students encountering new material.

LEVEL 2 Intermediate level activities designed for average students.

LEVEL 3 Challenging activities designed for above-average students.

SHELTERED ENGLISH These activities address the needs of students with Limited English Proficiency.

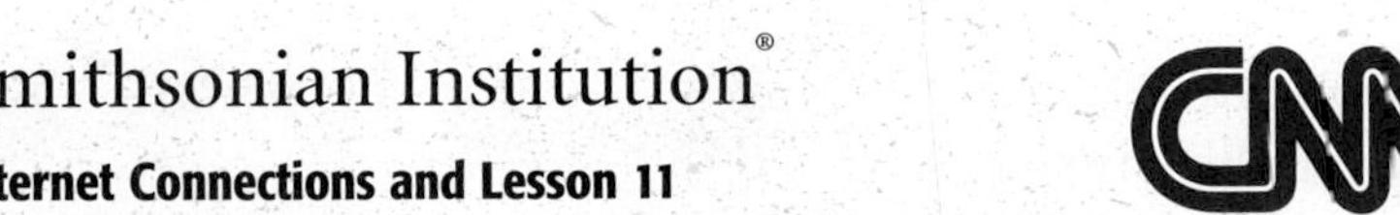

Smithsonian Institution®

Internet Connections and Lesson 11
www.si.edu/hrw

CNN Presents America:
Yesterday and Today 1850 to the Present
Segment: In the Trenches

Additional Resources

Books for Teachers

Bruce, Anthony. *An Illustrated Companion to the First World War.* Viking Penguin, 1990. Provides an illustrated overview of World War I.

Schneider, Dorothy, and Carl J. Schneider. *Into the Breach: American Women Overseas in World War I.* Viking Penguin, 1991. Story of the American women who took part in World War I.

Speed, R. B. *Prisoners, Diplomats, and the Great War: A Study in the Diplomacy of Captivity.* Greenwood Press, 1990. Looks at how POWs on both sides were treated during World War I.

Books for Students

Coffman, Edward M. *The War to End All Wars: Military Experience in World War I.* University of Wisconsin Press, 1996. A general history of World War I.

Hoehling, A. A. *The Last Voyage of the* Lusitania. Outlet Book Co., 1991. Account of the incident that helped lead to U.S. involvement in World War I.

McGowen, Tom. *World War I.* Watts, 1993. Gives an overview of political changes and military battles during World War I. Includes maps and dramatic photographs.

Multimedia Materials

The American Diary—The Price of Peace. Video, 24 min. Aims Media. Reviews U.S. role in the Great War and the struggle for a lasting peace.

Men of Bronze. Video, 58 min. Films Incorporated. Reviews the role of African American soldiers in World War I.

World War I—A Documentary on the Role of the USA. Video, 28 min. Aims Media. Describes events that led the United States into the war, the war itself, and Wilson's role at the Paris Peace Conference.

World War I

CHAPTER MOTIVATOR

Ask students to imagine a situation in which a European country asked Mexico to declare war on the United States and promised to help it regain New Mexico, Texas, and Arizona. Have students write a few sentences explaining how they would feel about such an event and how they think the United States would react. Ask volunteers to share their answers with the class. *(Most students will probably identify feelings of anger and point out that the United States would most likely declare war on the other country.)* Explain to students that the situation you described is in fact real and that Germany was the country that made the offer to Mexico. Tell students that in this chapter they will learn about the causes of World War I, the steps the United States took to prepare, and the outcome of the war.

Presenting Themes

- **Citizenship and Democracy** Students might mention that a government could appeal to patriotic feelings, urging citizens to support their nation in a time of national emergency. Students may also mention that the government might portray the enemy as a threat to the nation's security and well-being.
- **Global Relations** Students might mention that other nations may come to the defense of one side in a local conflict, thus expanding the fighting. Students might also mention that a nation depending on goods from the area in conflict may intervene to protect its own economic interests.
- **Technology and Society** Students might mention that new forms of technology can help the nations that developed them achieve victory. Students may also point out that new technology can make war more dangerous and influence offensive and defensive strategies.

Using the Time Line

Have each student select one event from the time line and write a brief paragraph on how it might have changed Americans' lives. After completing the chapter, have students evaluate their paragraphs based on what they have learned.

CHAPTER 11
World War I
(1914–1919)

On the afternoon of June 28, 1914, Gavrilo Princip walked the streets of Sarajevo (sahr-uh-YAY-voh), the capital of Bosnia. That morning, his accomplices had failed to complete their deadly mission—to kill Archduke Franz Ferdinand, the heir to the throne of Austria-Hungary. Suddenly, the archduke's car appeared. Stepping forward, Princip fired two shots, killing the archduke and his wife. With them died years of peace in Europe.

Citizenship and Democracy
How might a government encourage citizens to support a war effort?

Global Relations
How might a local conflict expand into a world war?

Technology and Society
How might new forms of technology change warfare?

1914 | **1915** | **1916**

JUNE 1914 A Serb nationalist assassinates Archduke Franz Ferdinand and his wife.

JULY 1914 Austria-Hungary declares war on Serbia, beginning World War I.

SEPT. 1914 The First Battle of the Marne occurs.

MAY 1915 A German U-boat sinks the *Lusitania.*

NOV. 1916 Woodrow Wilson is re-elected president.

OBJECTIVES

- Analyze the major causes of World War I.
- Identify events that led most of Europe to become involved in the war.
- Describe how the war's early battles proceeded and where they were fought.

FOCUS

Motivate Before Reading

Read students a description of the events that led to the assassination of Archduke Franz Ferdinand. Ask students to list possible reactions to suggest how such an event might have sparked a war. Call on volunteers to explain their ideas. Tell students that in this section they will learn about the causes of the war and how the assassination quickly led to global conflict.

The Road to War

Reading Focus

What were the main causes of World War I?

How did most of Europe become involved in the war?

Where was the early fighting in the war, and what were the results?

Key Terms

nationalism
militarism
balance of power
Triple Alliance
Triple Entente
mobilize
Central Powers
Allied Powers
First Battle of the Marne

IN THE EARLY 1900S Europe seemed to be at peace. There had not been a major war in the region since 1871. Political tensions were building, however, and most nations had continued to strengthen their armed forces. In 1888 German chancellor Otto von Bismarck had introduced a bill to the German parliament that added 750,000 soldiers to the German army. In his address he exclaimed, "We no longer ask for love, either from France or Russia. We run after nobody. We Germans fear God and nothing else on earth!" Before long the political tensions would explode into war on the European continent.

German citizens listen to an official announce the beginning of World War I.

IMAGE ON LEFT PAGE: *During World War I, millions of soldiers fought and died in trenches like this one.*

1917 | **1918** | **1919**

MAR. 1917 U.S. newspapers publish the Zimmerman Note.

APR. 1917 The United States declares war on Germany.

JAN. 1918 President Wilson announces the Fourteen Points.

NOV. 1918 Germany agrees to an armistice, ending World War I.

NOV. 1919 The U.S. Senate refuses to approve the Treaty of Versailles.

Section 1 RESOURCES

PRINT

- ★ Guided Reading Strategies 11.1
- ★ American History Political Cartoon 20: Conflict in the Balkans
- ★ Section 1 Review, p. 328
- ★ Daily Quiz 11.1

MULTIMEDIA

- ★ *Teaching Resources CD–ROM*, Lesson 11.1

SHELTERED ENGLISH

- ★ Main Idea Activities for Reteaching and Sheltered English 11.1

Introduce Key Terms

Linguistic, Logical-Mathematical. Review this section's key terms with students. Ask students to create graphic organizers, with lines linking each term to at least one other term. Then have students write sentences using each pair of terms.
SHELTERED ENGLISH

TEACH

Have students read Section 1 and complete Guided Reading Strategies 11.1. Choose one or more of the following activities to explore the section content with students. For further suggestions on block scheduling or team teaching, see the *Block Scheduling Handbook.*

LEVEL 1: Linguistic. (Suggested time: 15 min.) As a class, go over students' Guided Reading Strategies. Then use the Reading Focus questions to highlight the main ideas of the section.
SHELTERED ENGLISH

ALL LEVELS: Linguistic, Logical-Mathematical. (Suggested time: 45 min.) Ask students to write newspaper headlines covering the early battles of the war. Have volunteers share their headlines with the class. Then help students outline the topic of each headline by calling on volunteers to identify significant events

Economic Development

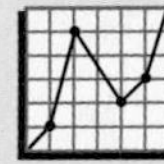

Tensions in Europe. One source of the growing tensions in Europe during the late 1800s and early 1900s was increased economic competition. During the 1800s and early 1900s, Britain had led Europe in industrial production. However, by 1914 Germany's production had surpassed that of Britain. The rapid growth of the German economy caused concern throughout Europe. The British experienced a decline in their share of foreign markets as Germans sought to expand their trade networks. The French—whose 1914 industrial output was only 40 percent of Germany's—realized that Germany could produce more weapons than they could.

Critical Thinking: Why did many other European nations fear German economic development?

ANSWER: It might hurt their own economies and it could make Germany a military power in the region.

 Causes of War

Despite the peace in Europe, relationships among nations were filled with fear and distrust. In this unstable political environment, even a minor incident could destroy the calm.

Nationalism

During the 1800s **nationalism**—the feeling that a specific nation, language, or culture is superior to all others—had become a force for unification. In 1871 Kaiser Wilhelm I unified a number of German states into the German Empire. Later the Pan-German movement sought to unite most of the other German-speaking people in Europe under Germany.

Although nationalism helped to create and enlarge Germany, it threatened the stability of some nations. Austria-Hungary included people of many nationalities and languages. One of these groups, the Slavs, wanted to create a nation of their own. Serbia was already an independent Slavic country on the Balkan Peninsula. The Serbs encouraged Slavs within Austria-Hungary to break free and join them in creating an independent, united Slavic empire in the Balkans. Russia, itself largely Slavic, supported Serbia's goal.

Austro-Hungarian leaders saw this movement as a threat to their authority. One Austrian official predicted that Slavic nationalism was "one of the powerful national movements which can neither be ignored nor kept down." The hostilities in the Balkan region became so intense that many people referred to the Balkans as a "powder keg." The Balkan region seemed a likely place to ignite a major European war.

BALKAN TROUBLES

THE BOILING POINT

In this 1912 British cartoon, European leaders try to keep trouble in the Balkans from boiling over.

Imperialism

Tensions also grew as many European nations competed to gain territories and build overseas empires. By the late 1800s Britain was the world's largest imperial power. France, Germany, Italy, and Russia wanted to create similar empires. These countries also struggled over territory in Europe. France, for example, wanted to recover Alsace-Lorraine (al-sas law-rayn), an area it had lost in a war with Germany in 1871.

As relationships grew more strained, some nations turned to **militarism**, a policy of aggressive military preparedness. European nations built larger militaries than ever before. Germany created the most powerful army in Europe. In 1912 and 1913 alone, Germany increased the size of its army by more than 20 percent. Germany also built a navy to rival Britain's, the world's most powerful.

 New Alliances

In the late 1800s European nations began to form alliances to try to create a **balance of power**—a situation in which the strength of rival alliances is nearly equal. European leaders thought that no country would start a war without a real advantage in military strength. In 1879 Germany allied with Austria-Hungary. Three years later Italy joined the union, making it the **Triple Alliance**. Austria-Hungary, Germany, and Italy pledged to support each other in case of attack.

Concerned by Germany's growing power, France formed a military alliance with Russia in 1893. Britain feared Germany's growing naval force and signed an entente, or understanding, with France. In 1907 Russia and Britain reached a similar agreement. The **Triple Entente** alliance united Britain, France, and Russia.

The Triple Alliance and the Triple Entente created a balance of power in Europe that was complicated and fragile. Many people, like Helmuth von Moltke, a German general, felt that "a European war is bound to come sooner or later."

 The Spark

In 1878 the Balkan province of Bosnia and Herzegovina had gained independence from Turkish rule. In 1908 Austria-Hungary annexed the province. This annexation angered many pertaining to each headline. Write the outlines on the chalkboard and have students copy them in their notebooks. **SHELTERED ENGLISH**

LEVEL 3. Linguistic, Logical-Mathematical. (Suggested time: 45 min.) Assign each student a nation that became involved in World War I at its inception. Ask students to imagine that they are ambassadors from their assigned nations. Have each student compose a diplomatic memorandum to one of the nations in their alliance explaining the overall causes of the war and how the assigned nation became involved. Have volunteers read their memorandums to the class.

CLOSE

Visual-Spatial, Logical-Mathematical. Help students understand nationalism, militarism, and balance of power by having them note the attributes of each and devise a symbol to express their understanding of the essential characteristics of each concept.

CHALLENGE AND EXTEND

Logical-Mathematical, Interpersonal. Organize the class into teams, each representing a nation at a peace conference in the aftermath of the archduke's assassination. Have students use the library and other resources to investigate the economic and political

The Granger Collection, New York

Felix Schwarmstadt's painting captures the 1914 assassination of Archduke Franz Ferdinand and his wife, Sophie.

Slavic nationalists who wanted the region allied with Serbia. Many of these nationalists belonged to a secret group known as the Black Hand, which used violence to achieve its goals.

On June 28, 1914, Archduke Franz Ferdinand, the heir to the throne of Austria-Hungary, visited Sarajevo with his wife, Sophie. As the visitors rode through the streets, Gavrilo Princip, a 19-year-old Serb nationalist and member of the Black Hand, stepped out from the crowd and shot them to death.

The archduke's assassination lit the fuse on the "powder keg" of Europe. The president of France advised an Austro-Hungarian official:

> **"With a little good will, this Serbian business is easy to settle. But it can just as easily become acute [severe]. Serbia has some very warm friends in the Russian people. And Russia has an ally, France."**

Austro-Hungarian leaders disregarded his advice. They wanted an excuse to crush Serbia and the Serbian-led Slavic nationalist movements. On July 28, 1914, Austria-Hungary declared war on Serbia.

Europe Goes to War

The next day Austria-Hungary began shelling the Serbian city of Belgrade. An earlier promise of support required Russia to defend Serbia. Initially, however, Russian czar Nicholas II hesitated to **mobilize**, or prepare his military for war. According to his foreign minister:

> **"The Tsar was silent. Then he said to me, in a voice full of deep feeling: 'This would mean sending hundreds of thousands of Russian people to their death. How can one help hesitating to take such a step?'"**

The czar decided to keep his earlier promise of support, however. Russia's mobilization led other countries to fulfill their own alliance obligations. In support of Austria-Hungary, Germany declared war on Russia on August 1, and on France, Russia's ally, two days later.

German troops invaded Belgium on August 3 to begin their march toward France. Britain, which had pledged to defend Belgian neutrality, then declared war on Germany. On August 5 Austria-Hungary declared war on Russia. The Great War—which later generations would know as World War I—had begun.

The alliance of Austria-Hungary and Germany became known as the **Central Powers**. Bulgaria and the Ottoman Empire would later join the

Russia mobilized its enormous army in response to Austria-Hungary's attack on Serbia.

Global Relations

Alliances. Many of the European alliances were designed to protect assets in other parts of the world. The British sought security for India, which was at that time a British colony. Their alliance with Russia was intended in part to clarify the status of Persia, Afghanistan, and Tibet, all of which could pose a threat to India if controlled by a foreign power. In the settlement, Russia and Britain agreed to the following terms: to recognize British control of Afghanistan; to allow Tibet to remain outside the control of any nation; and to divide Persia into three zones, one Russian, one British, and one neutral. Nonetheless, a primary reason for the alliance with Russia was British concern about German military expansion.

Critical Thinking: Why might the Germans view an alliance between western European nations and Russia with alarm?

ANSWER: The Germans believed they were being surrounded by potential enemies.

interests of the nations they represent. Then hold the conference, allowing each group to present its position. Finally, ask students to identify any compromises that could have prevented the war.

REVIEW

Logical-Mathematical, Interpersonal. Have students complete the Section Review questions. Have each student prepare a crossword puzzle using definitions of the terms in the Identify portion of the Section Review as clues and the terms as answers. Have students exchange puzzles, answer the questions, and return them to their authors for grading.

ASSESS

Have students complete Daily Quiz 11.1.

RETEACH

Visual-Spatial. Have students complete Main Idea Activities for Reteaching and Sheltered English 11.1. Give each student an outline map of Europe and ask them to locate and label the member nations of the Triple Alliance, Triple Entente, Allied Powers, and Central Powers. Call on volunteers to explain the significance of the alliances. **SHELTERED ENGLISH**

Section 1 Review ANSWERS

Identify

For significance, see the following pages:

- nationalism, p. 326
- militarism, p. 326
- balance of power, p. 326
- Triple Alliance, p. 326
- Triple Entente, p. 326
- Franz Ferdinand, p. 327
- Nicholas II, p. 327
- mobilize, p. 327
- Central Powers, p. 327
- Allied Powers, p. 328
- Wilhelm II, p. 328
- First Battle of the Marne, p. 328

Reading for Content Understanding

1. Nationalism led groups to try to form independent nations, thus threatening the stability of existing nations; imperialism increased conflicts as nations competed for territory; militarism made nations more fearful of their neighbors.

2. Early fighting left Germany facing France and Britain on the western front and Russia on the eastern front. On both fronts, fighting went back and forth.

3. Britain—defended Belgian neutrality after the German invasion; France—attacked by Germany because of its alliance with Russia; Germany—supported Austria-Hungary after Russia declared war; Russia—fulfilled its alliance obligations to Serbia by declaring war on Austria-Hungary

4. Memos will vary but should discuss the two-pronged attack's failure.

5. Answers will vary but students should defend their opinions.

Resistance by Belgian soldiers, such as these defending Antwerp, slowed the German army and prevented a quick victory over France.

Central Powers. Britain, France, and Russia fought together as the **Allied Powers**, or the Allies. Despite its alliance with Austria-Hungary and Germany, Italy joined the Allies in 1915. Eventually, 30 nations would fight in World War I.

Many Europeans expected the war to last no more than six months. Kaiser Wilhelm II told departing German troops, "You will be home before the leaves have fallen from the trees." Wilhelm's confidence came from the Schlieffen Plan, the military strategy by which Germany hoped to quickly defeat France before Russia had a chance to fully mobilize its army. The Schlieffen Plan called for a rapid two-pronged attack on France—one in the north through Belgium and one in the south—and a later attack on Russia.

The Belgians fiercely resisted the German army, upsetting the timetable of the Schlieffen Plan. The Belgian effort gave France and Britain valuable time to mobilize their troops.

The Battle of the Marne

Belgian resistance slowed German troops but did not stop them. By early September 1914 the Germans were 25 miles from Paris, the capital of France. The military governor warned, "I have received the order to defend Paris against the invader. This order I shall fulfill to the end." In the **First Battle of the Marne**, French troops launched a daring counterattack against the Germans. The French rushed to stop them along the Marne River east of Paris. After a few days of fighting, the Germans retreated. By mid-September the armies faced each other across the western front, a battle line extending from Switzerland to the North Sea.

Meanwhile, the Russians attacked the Central Powers in mid-August on the eastern front, which extended from the Black Sea to the Baltic Sea. The Russians quickly advanced into East Prussia, but Germany counterattacked and crushed the Russian forces. By late September 1914 the Central and Allied Powers both realized that the war would not be a short one.

SECTION 1 REVIEW

Identify and explain the significance of the following:

- **nationalism**
- **militarism**
- **balance of power**
- **Triple Alliance**
- **Triple Entente**
- **Franz Ferdinand**
- **Nicholas II**
- **mobilize**
- **Central Powers**
- **Allied Powers**
- **Wilhelm II**
- **First Battle of the Marne**

Reading for Content Understanding

1 **Main Idea** How did nationalism, imperialism, and militarism help cause World War I?

2 **Main Idea** Describe the early fighting in the war.

3 **Global Relations** Explain how Britain, France, Germany, and Russia became involved in the war.

4 **Writing** *Informing* Imagine that you are a German army officer in September 1914. Write a memo to the kaiser explaining the outcome of the Schlieffen Plan. Describe the plan in your memo.

5 **Critical Thinking** *Supporting a Point of View* Do you think that other European nations should have entered a war that originally started between Austria-Hungary and Serbia? Support your answer.

OBJECTIVES

- **Describe trench warfare.**
- **Analyze the effects of new weapons in World War I.**
- **Explain how the United States tried to remain neutral, and identify events that forced the nation to enter the war.**

FOCUS

Motivate Before Reading

Use the time line at the beginning of the chapter to identify events that occurred from the beginning of World War I to U.S. entry into the war in April 1917. Ask students to draw inferences about events on the time line and to explain their reasoning. For example, students might infer that the United States had no vital interests at stake in 1914; that circumstances affecting the nation had

Wilson and Neutrality

Reading Focus

What was trench warfare like?

How did new weapons affect the fighting in World War I?

How did the United States try to remain neutral in the war, and what events forced the United States to enter the war?

Key Terms

trench warfare
no-man's-land
stalemate
U-boats
Lusitania
***Sussex* pledge**
Zimmerman Note

THE DAY'S FIGHTING seemed over. Two Allied officers sat on a hill in southwestern Belgium. As they looked out over fields and villages, a dog barked at some sheep, and a girl sang as she walked. Soldiers laughed as they cooked their evening meal. Darkness fell. Then, as one officer remembered, "without a moment's warning, . . . we saw the whole horizon burst into flame." The Germans had begun to bombard the area. Stunned, the officers soon concluded that World War I had "a merciless, ruthless aspect [part] that we had not realized till then."

Soldiers from the 8th Battalion eating lunch

Section 2 RESOURCES

PRINT
- ★ Guided Reading Strategies 11.2
- ★ Section 2 Review, p. 334
- ★ Daily Quiz 11.2

MULTIMEDIA
- ★ *Teaching Resources CD–ROM*, Lesson 11.2
- ★ Everyday Life in America Transparency 20: In the Trenches: Battle Sketches of World War I
- ★ HRW Web site

SHELTERED ENGLISH
- ★ Main Idea Activities for Reteaching and Sheltered English 11.2

 The War in Europe

Soon after World War I began, military leaders began to revise old battle plans. The new war strategies—along with new weapons—made the Great War a conflict unlike any other.

Trench Warfare

After French troops stopped the enemy advance in the First Battle of the Marne, the Germans dug in and prepared to hold their ground. Both armies soon turned to **trench warfare**—the strategy of defending a position by fighting from the protection of deep ditches. Two massive systems of opposing trenches stretched for 400 miles across the western front. Trenches ranged from simple holes to complex networks that were six to eight feet deep with rooms for sleeping and eating.

The trenches were typically cold, wet, and dirty. A reporter described one very uncomfortable aspect of trench warfare:

> **"Men standing in slime for days and nights in field boots . . . lost all sense of feeling in their feet. These feet of theirs,**

changed dramatically between 1914 and 1917; or that despite efforts to avoid involvement, events finally drew the United States into the war. Tell students that in this section they will learn how the United States, despite its official neutrality, was drawn into the war.

Introduce Key Terms

Linguistic, Logical-Mathematical. Review this section's key terms with students. Have students use context cues to write a definition for each term. Then have students write at least one question they would like answered for each term. As students read the chapter, have them answer their own questions.

SHELTERED ENGLISH

TEACH

Have students read Section 2 and complete Guided Reading Strategies 11.2. Choose one or more of the following activities to explore the section content with students. For further suggestions on block scheduling or team teaching, see the *Block Scheduling Handbook*.

LEVEL 1: Linguistic. (Suggested time: 15 min.) As a class, go over students' Guided Reading Strategies. Then use the Reading Focus questions to highlight the main ideas of the section.

SHELTERED ENGLISH

Across the Curriculum

LITERATURE

All Quiet on the Western Front. One of the most influential novels that examined life in the trenches was Erich Maria Remarque's *All Quiet on the Western Front,* which was published in 1929. During World War I, Remarque had served in the German army. On at least two occasions he carried wounded soldiers out of combat. Remarque was wounded by grenade splinters in 1917. Because Remarque's novel offered a negative view of warfare, he was strongly criticized by the Nazis. Fearing for his life, Remarque fled Germany in 1931.

Activity: Have students obtain a copy of Remarque's novel and read passages that describe a soldier's life during the war. Then ask students to imagine that they are soldiers in the trenches during World War I. Have students write journal entries describing their experiences.

Multimedia Resources

Everyday Life in America Transparency 20: In the Trenches: Battle Sketches of World War I

so cold and wet, began to swell, and then go 'dead' and then suddenly to burn as though touched by red hot pokers.''

Trench warfare brought many health problems. In the trench environment, disease spread rapidly.

The area between opposing trenches, called **no-man's-land**, varied in width from about 200 to 1,000 yards. Much of the fighting took place in no-man's-land, which, according to a British soldier, was "littered with the bodies of men."

New Technology

New weapons made the war even more dangerous. In the trenches, soldiers set up groups of machine guns that fired 400 to 600 rounds of ammunition per minute. In addition, huge guns launched artillery shells, which exploded into deadly metal fragments over enemy positions.

Some shells contained poison gases, such as chlorine gas and mustard gas. These gases destroyed soldiers' lungs, killing the men slowly. Gas masks were effective, but soldiers had to either wear them all the time or be ready to slip them on in seconds.

Exposure to the elements, disease, and unsanitary conditions made trenches nearly as dangerous to soldiers as enemy fire.

The armies also used tanks and airplanes in the war. British and French forces developed tanks to support infantry attacks on trenches. Tanks were hard to destroy and could cause very heavy damage. Pilots used airplanes to gather information, shoot down enemy planes, and fire on trenches.

The Battle for Verdun

By late 1914 the war had become a **stalemate**—a situation in which neither side can win a decisive victory. In December 1915 German general Erich von Falkenhayn decided to capture the fortified French city of Verdun, located near the southern end of the trench line. The French, however, had other plans. When the Germans attacked in February 1916, French general Philippe Pétain (PAY-tan) vowed: "They shall not pass." The German advance stalled outside the city, but the battle for Verdun raged for months.

To relieve the pressure on Verdun, in July Allied forces launched an offensive along the Somme River, in northeastern France. Almost 20,000 Allied troops were killed the first day of fighting. When the battle ended in November, the Allies had forced the Germans to retreat only a few miles. However, the attack did succeed in drawing some German forces away from Verdun.

The fighting at Verdun dragged on for 10 months, making it the longest battle of the war. Although France held the city, both armies suffered great losses. The death total at the Somme and Verdun reached almost 1 million. On average, more than 138 soldiers died every single hour.

The War in the Atlantic

The stalemate on land made the battle in the North Sea and the Atlantic Ocean even more important. Britain used its large navy to cut off German supplies by blockading ports and placing mines in the North Sea. The British searched neutral ships for war materials before guiding them through the minefields.

German **U-boats**, or submarines, attacked British shipping to prevent supplies from reaching

Months of fierce fighting and intense bombing reduced Verdun and many other European cities to rubble.

ALL LEVELS: Linguistic, Visual-Spatial. (Suggested time: 30 min.) Assign each student a new weapon or strategy employed in World War I. Have students draw their assigned weapons or strategies. Ask each student to write a brief caption explaining the weapon's or strategy's effects on the war. Ask volunteers to present their illustrations to the class. **SHELTERED ENGLISH**

LEVEL 2: Logical-Mathematical, Interpersonal. (Suggested time: 45 min.) Have students read President Wilson's congressional message of April 1917, part of which is found on the last page of this section. Then review with students the constitutional procedure for declaring war. Organize the class into two groups, one to act as members of Congress arguing for remaining neutral, and one to act as members of Congress supporting a declaration of war. Have both groups prepare arguments supporting their positions and questions to ask the other group. Then have members of each group present their arguments to Congress (the entire class). Encourage members of the opposing congressional group to ask questions. Then have Congress (the class) vote on whether to declare war. Finally, discuss U.S. attempts to remain neutral and the events that led to its involvement in the war.

LEVEL 3: Visual-Spatial, Logical-Mathematical, Linguistic. (Suggested time: 25 min. plus homework and presentation) Lead a discussion on trench warfare. Then ask students to write a segment of a chapter on trench warfare to be added to a

Science and Technology

The Airplane in World War I

On December 17, 1903, brothers Orville and Wilbur Wright made history at Kitty Hawk, North Carolina. Orville made the first piloted flight in a powered airplane. Wilbur made the longest flight that day, remaining aloft for 59 seconds.

The Wrights wanted to sell flying machines to the U.S. government, but officials were not interested. The Wrights then took their invention to Europe. After countries there showed interest, the U.S. Army finally tested the airplane. In 1909 the army began supporting the Wrights' efforts to manufacture their machines.

Early airplanes were fragile. Most were biplanes, which meant that they had two wings, one above the other. Biplanes were made mostly of wood and fabric, light materials that sometimes broke apart if the planes climbed or dove too quickly. Most planes had a single propeller, usually in the front, and could not fly very fast.

At first, the Allies and the Central Powers used airplanes only for scouting. While pilots flew high over the battlefield, observers onboard took pictures of enemy troops and equipment. The pictures provided valuable information for military commanders. These scout planes did not carry weapons. Opposing pilots sometimes waved when flying by each other.

This friendliness changed, however. To prevent spying, both sides' armies installed machine guns on fighter planes and shot down enemy scouts. Engineers improved fighter planes' speed and maneuverability. Both the Allies and the Central Powers also built large bombers and developed planes that could take off from ships. Thousands of planes were built during the war.

Improvements in airplane design led to new uses after the war. Airmail service began in the United States in 1918, with World War I veterans serving as pilots. Regular airline travel began on a limited basis in the 1920s. The Wright brothers' dream of flying had become part of everyday life.

Understanding What You Read

1. How were airplanes used in World War I?
2. How were airplanes used in civilian life after the war?

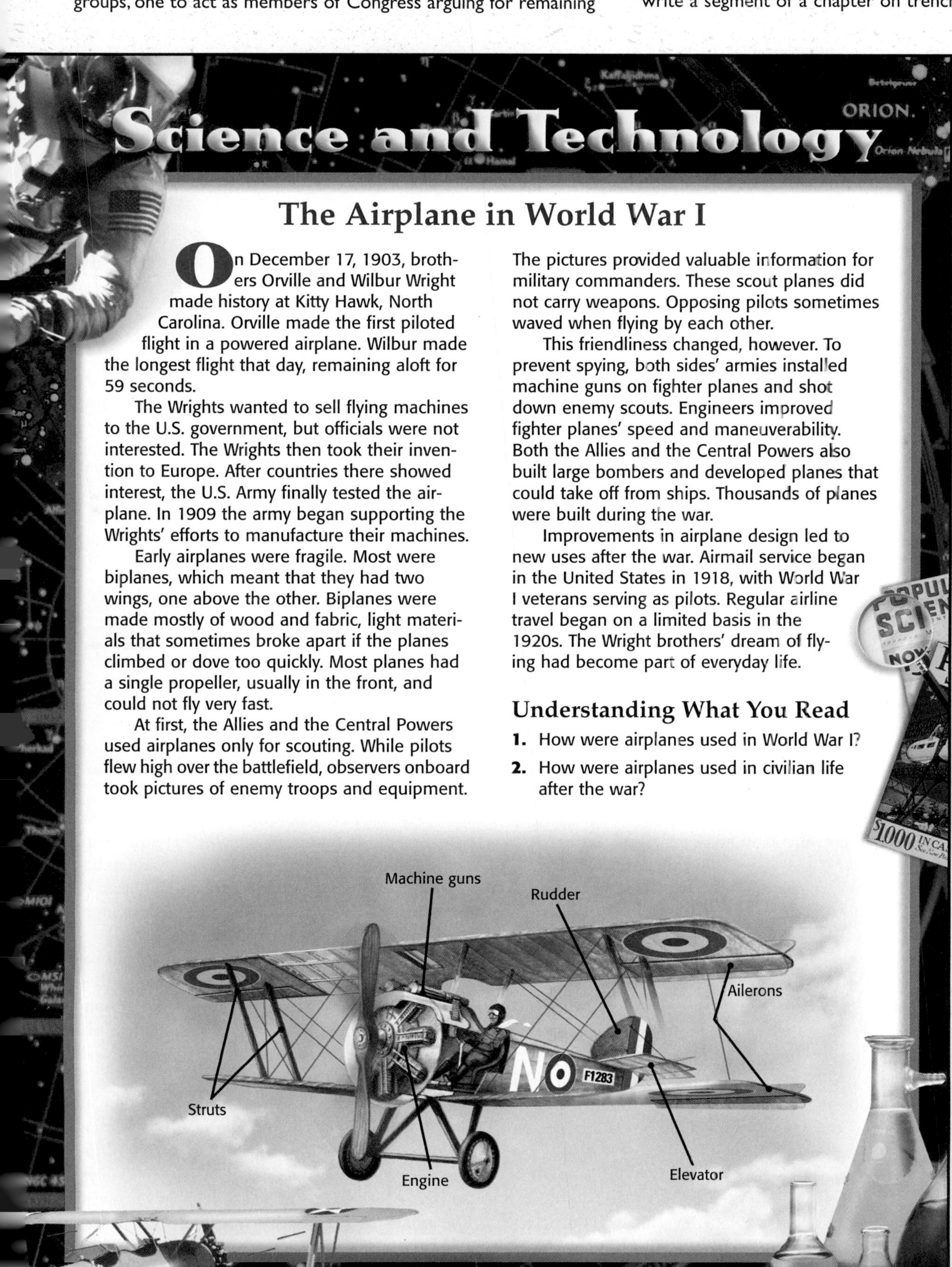

Technology and Society

Gas Warfare. At first, the Allies denounced gas warfare as barbaric. They pointed to the German use of gas as evidence that Germany posed a threat to civilization. However, as the Allies began to develop their own chemical weapons, official announcements regarding gas changed. The Allies claimed that their use of gas was a fair response to the Germans, who had used it first. In 1917 Britain and France imposed a news blackout on gas warfare because they did not want Americans to become alarmed as they prepared to send troops to Europe. By 1918 Allied governments praised the production of gas in America as proof that the United States played an important role in fighting the Germans.

Critical Thinking: How can propaganda be used to influence public opinion?

ANSWER: Students should note that propaganda can be used to point negatively to a rival's actions, while at the same time being used to justify similar actions in another country.

SCIENCE AND TECHNOLOGY ANSWERS

1. Planes were used for scouting, to attack enemy planes, and as bombers.

2. After the war, planes were used for airmail and passenger service.

book about World War I. Have students include information about the following topics: conditions in the trenches, size and shape of trenches, and the area between trenches known as no-man's-land. Encourage students to include drawings or photocopies of pictures to include in their chapter segments. Have students begin work in class and finish it for homework. During the next class, ask volunteers to present their segments to the class.

CLOSE

Linguistic, Logical-Mathematical, Intrapersonal. Organize the class into several small groups, assigning each member several of the terms in the Identify portion of the Section Review. Have each student determine how the assigned terms illustrate key aspects of the World War I experience. Have each group prepare a brief summary of the section by incorporating each student's explanations. Call on each group to read its summary to the class, and invite comment and evaluation by other students.

CHALLENGE AND EXTEND

1. **Linguistic, Logical-Mathematical.** Have students use the library or other resources to investigate the attitudes in their local community between 1914 and 1917 about U.S. neutrality

Global Relations

Neutral Rights. Woodrow Wilson's declaration of neutrality meant that the United States wanted to exercise its rights as a neutral nation. These rights allowed countries not involved in a war to continue trading, even with nations that were at war. International agreements from the 1600s and the 1700s permitted neutrals to trade, as long as they did not sell contraband or prohibited goods, such as war materials. In 1909 the United States and several other nations participated in a conference in London that produced a declaration of neutral rights, but the declaration was never ratified. When war broke out in 1914, the United States demanded that the 1909 declaration be recognized. However, Britain did not want Germany to receive U.S. goods and quickly changed its definition of items that were considered contraband.

Critical Thinking: Why would nations at war recognize the rights of neutral nations?

Answer: They might receive necessary goods, such as food, from neutral nations, or they might fear that these nations would join the struggle against them if their neutrality rights were not upheld.

Map Answer

Ypres, Somme, Marne, Verdun

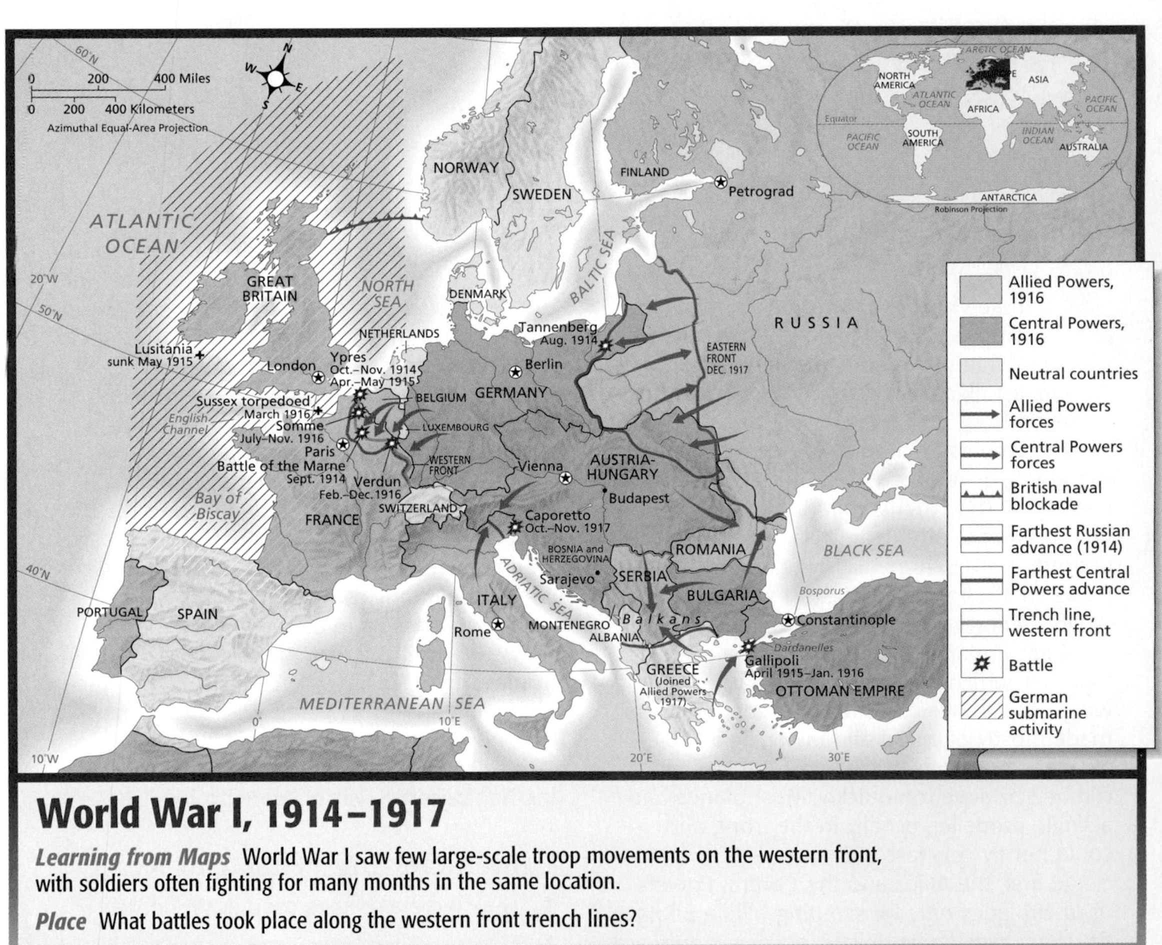

World War I, 1914–1917

Learning from Maps World War I saw few large-scale troop movements on the western front, with soldiers often fighting for many months in the same location.

Place What battles took place along the western front trench lines?

Britain and the Allies. Germany also began targeting neutral merchant ships suspected of carrying war supplies. Germany's submarine fleet, the world's largest and most advanced, caused heavy losses to Allied shipping.

Wilson Pursues Neutrality

Shortly after the war began in Europe, President Woodrow Wilson announced that the United States would remain neutral. Wilson's declaration of neutrality reflected the nation's policy of isolationism, or noninvolvement in foreign affairs.

American Opinion

Most Americans viewed the war as a European conflict. A popular American song title—"I Didn't Raise My Boy to Be a Soldier"—reflected this view. When forced to take a side, most Americans supported the Allies because of long-standing ties with Britain and France. However, millions of Americans had immigrated from and sympathized with the nations of the Central Powers.

Britain, France, and Germany used propaganda to influence public opinion in the United States. British propaganda represented Germany as cruel and inhumane. German propaganda pictured President Wilson as falsely claiming neutrality while actively favoring the Allies.

U.S. neutrality did not prevent American merchants from trading with the warring European nations. U.S. ships carried most of the supplies, including war materials, to the Allies. American banks invested $2 billion in European war bonds, though only $20 million of that was invested in German bonds.

and the war in Europe. Encourage students to use local newspapers, magazines, newsletters, and, if possible, transcripts of local radio broadcasts. Remind students that different segments of their community may have had different opinions. Once students have done their research, have them write a radio editorial that is representative of one segment of local opinion.

2. **Linguistic, Logical-Mathematical.** Have students use the library or other resources to investigate the military tactics used in one of the battles discussed in this section. Ask students to write an analysis of the strategies used by both sides. Have students identify how strengths in one strategy contributed to victory, while weaknesses in the other led to defeat, or how a battle was won in spite of a poor decision. Encourage students to identify any of the new military technologies discussed in this chapter that were used in the battles they researched. Ask volunteers to discuss their findings with the class.

REVIEW

Linguistic, Logical-Mathematical, Intrapersonal. Have students complete the Section Review questions. Then ask students to imagine that it is April 6, 1917, and they have just heard the news that Congress has agreed to President Wilson's request to declare war on Germany. Have each student write an editorial for

Woodrow Wilson

To many people, President Woodrow Wilson seemed cold and distant. In private, however, Wilson could be warm and lively. He credited his wife, Ellen Axson Wilson, with freeing his true personality. In August 1914, after 29 years of marriage, Ellen died. Wilson threw himself into his work to cope with his grief.

Seven months later, while still mourning his wife's death, Wilson met Edith Bolling Galt. He took her horseback riding and sailing. Wilson discussed affairs of state with her and even had a private telephone line installed between the White House and Edith's home.

Wilson and Galt married in December 1915. Wilson adored his new wife, and often sang her the popular hit "Oh, You Beautiful Doll!" With the entry of the United States into the war, however, the president's attention turned to more serious matters.

Americans Under Fire

The United States moved closer to entering the war on the Allies' side when Germany violated the rules of neutrality in the Atlantic. The rules required German submarines to stop and search merchant ships. The Germans often simply attacked without warning, however, knowing that their submarines were defenseless above water.

In May 1915 a U-boat sank the British passenger liner ***Lusitania*** off the coast of Ireland, killing nearly 1,200 people, including 128 Americans. The *Lusitania* attack infuriated the American public. President Wilson condemned the attack as "a violation not only of international law but of the fundamental decencies of civilization." The German government argued that the *Lusitania* had been carrying war materials and that Americans had been warned against traveling through the war zone.

Even after the *Lusitania* incident, Wilson tried to keep the nation out of the war. When a U-boat torpedoed the French passenger ship *Sussex* on March 24, 1916, however, he threatened to end diplomatic relations with Germany. Germany then issued the ***Sussex* pledge**, which included a promise not to sink merchant vessels "without warning and without saving human lives."

Campaigning for Peace

As President Wilson campaigned for re-election during the fall of 1916, he pledged to keep the country neutral and to work for peace. Wilson's opponent was Republican Charles Evans Hughes, a Supreme Court justice and former governor of New York. Hughes attacked Wilson for not strongly defending American rights in Europe.

The race was surprisingly close. Many Americans opposed Wilson's foreign policy. Other voters were less certain that Wilson could maintain his

In the Lusitania's *1915 voyage announcement the German Embassy warned Americans about the danger of traveling across the Atlantic.*

Presidential Profiles

Woodrow Wilson. Born in Virginia in 1856, Woodrow Wilson did not attend school until he was nine years old, because of the Civil War. He proved to be an excellent student, earning both a law degree and a doctoral degree by age 30. He taught history and political science and coached football at Wesleyan University until 1890, when he took a teaching position at Princeton. After he became president of the university in 1902, he started several new educational programs. In 1910 leaders of the Democratic Party in New Jersey asked him to run for governor. They believed that the scholar would be a weak governor whom they could easily control, an assumption that Wilson disproved with his strong and decisive leadership.

Activity: Have students use the library or search the Internet through the HRW Web site to find information on the life and the presidency of Woodrow Wilson. Have students write a brief article on one of his accomplishments.

go.hrw.com
SB1 Woodrow Wilson

a local newspaper stating whether he or she support the president's decision to enter the war or opposes U.S. involvement. Ask students to consider the dangers posed by new weapons and Germany's actions prior to the declaration when forming their opinions. Call on volunteers to read their editorials to the class, and invite comment from other students.

ASSESS

Have students complete Daily Quiz 11.2.

RETEACH

Logical-Mathematical, Visual-Spatial. Have students complete Main Idea Activities for Reteaching and Sheltered English 11.2. Ask each student to select the one event, trend, or development from those discussed in this section that he or she considers to have been most important in explaining why the United States decided to enter the war. Then have each student create a flowchart that places that event in the middle and links other significant events to it. **SHELTERED ENGLISH**

Section 2 Review ANSWERS

Identify

For significance, see the following pages:

- trench warfare, p. 329
- no-man's-land, p. 330
- stalemate, p. 330
- U-boats, p. 330
- *Lusitania*, p. 333
- *Sussex* pledge, p. 333
- Charles Evans Hughes, p. 333
- Arthur Zimmermann, p. 334
- Zimmerman Note, p. 334

Locate

For locations, see the map on page 332.

Reading for Content Understanding

1. It was cold, wet, unhealthy, dirty, and dangerous.

2. He continually pressed Germany to respect America's neutrality rights; Germany declared unrestricted submarine warfare on February 1, 1917, leading the United States to declare war.

3. All these technologies served to increase the casualty rate.

4. Diary entries will vary but should mention that the Germans argued that the *Lusitania* was carrying war materials.

5. Answers will vary but students should state their opinions and offer support for them.

This 1917 U.S. Army Air Service recruiting poster asks Americans to join the fight in World War I.

campaign promise to keep the United States out of the war. In the end, however, Wilson won a narrow victory in November 1916 with 277 electoral votes to Hughes's 254.

Once re-elected, Wilson began work on a settlement to end the war. In a speech to the Senate on January 22, 1917, Wilson proposed "peace without victory," in which the Allies and the Central Powers would both declare peace, with neither side the winner. Wilson's speech angered the Allies, particularly Britain. The Allies blamed the Central Powers for the war and wanted them to pay for wartime destruction. The Allies wanted territory, money, or at the very least, a German admission of guilt.

Congress Declares War

All hopes for a peaceful settlement ended when the Germans violated the *Sussex* pledge and resumed unrestricted submarine warfare on February 1, 1917. President Wilson soon broke off diplomatic relations with Germany and ordered U.S. merchant ships to be fitted with guns. Tensions increased when American newspapers published a decoded German telegram in March. In the note, dated January 19, German foreign minister Arthur Zimmermann proposed an alliance between Germany and Mexico against the United States. He told the German minister in Mexico that for its part, Mexico would "reconquer the lost territory in New Mexico, Texas, and Arizona." The telegram, known as the **Zimmerman Note**, outraged the American public.

In early April President Wilson responded to the new threats by asking Congress to declare war on Germany. Saying that "the world must be made safe for democracy," Wilson called on Americans to

> **"fight for the things which we have always carried nearest our hearts, for democracy . . . [and to] bring peace and safety to all nations and make the world itself at last free."**

Congress approved Wilson's request, and on April 6, 1917, the United States declared war on Germany.

SECTION 2 REVIEW

Identify and explain the significance of the following:

- **trench warfare**
- **no-man's-land**
- **stalemate**
- **U-boats**
- ***Lusitania***
- ***Sussex* pledge**
- **Charles Evans Hughes**
- **Arthur Zimmermann**
- **Zimmerman Note**

Locate and explain the importance of the following:

- **Verdun**
- **North Sea**

Reading for Content Understanding

1 **Main Idea** What was World War I like for soldiers fighting in the trenches?

2 **Main Idea** What did President Wilson do to enforce neutrality? Why did the United States finally decide to declare war against Germany in 1917?

3 **Technology and Society** What effect did machine guns, poison gas, tanks, and airplanes have on the fighting in World War I?

4 **Writing** *Describing* Imagine that you are a member of a German U-boat crew, or a passenger aboard the *Lusitania.* Write a short diary entry describing the *Lusitania* incident. You might analyze how the Germans' submarine warfare contributed to the U.S. entry into World War I.

5 **Critical Thinking** *Determining the Strength of an Argument* Do you think Wilson had good reasons to ask Congress to declare war? Explain your answer.

OBJECTIVES

- Explain how the U.S. government prepared the military for war.
- Analyze the contributions of women and African Americans in the war.
- Describe the effects of the war on industry and labor.

FOCUS

Motivate Before Reading

Explain to students that advertising campaigns are often used to raise public support for a war. Based on what they have already read in this chapter, have each student create a poster designed to raise support for the war effort. Have volunteers explain their posters to the class. Then tell students that in this section they will

Americans Prepare for War

Reading Focus

How did the U.S. government prepare the military for war?

What contributions did women and African Americans make to the war effort?

How did the war affect industry and labor?

Key Terms

Committee on Public Information
Selective Service Act
Liberty bonds
War Industries Board
Food Administration
National War Labor Board

Section 3 RESOURCES

PRINT

★ Guided Reading Strategies 11.3

★ Section 3 Review, p. 338

★ Daily Quiz 11.3

MULTIMEDIA

★ *Teaching Resources CD–ROM*, Lesson 11.3

SHELTERED ENGLISH

★ Main Idea Activities for Reteaching and Sheltered English 11.3

SHORTLY AFTER CONGRESS declared war, Major Palmer E. Pierce, an aide to the secretary of war, appeared before the Senate Finance Committee. Pierce was there to answer questions about how the War Department planned to spend the $3 billion it had requested. He explained that the money would go for "clothing, cots, camps, food, pay. . . . And we may have to have an army in France." The chairman of the Senate Finance Committee exclaimed, "Good Lord! You're not going to send soldiers over there, are you?" Even though most people supported the declaration of war, few were ready to risk American lives.

Blindfolded, the U.S. secretary of war drew the first numbers for the military draft on June 5, 1917.

Rallying the Public

Two weeks after Congress declared war on Germany, President Wilson created a new agency, the **Committee on Public Information** (CPI), to increase public support for the war effort. George Creel, the head of the CPI, launched a nationwide publicity campaign. Creel used rallies, parades, posters, and pamphlets to persuade Americans to support the war. The committee recruited movie stars to entertain troops. Hollywood produced movies like *The Kaiser: The Beast of Berlin* that showed enemy leaders as evil people, even monsters. Some 75,000 "four-minute men" explained the importance of American involvement in the Great War. These speakers gave short patriotic speeches in movie theaters, churches, and schools.

The government also restricted some freedoms. The Espionage Act of 1917 and the Sedition Act of 1918 provided severe penalties for aiding the enemy, refusing military duty, or speaking disloyally about the U.S. government, Constitution, or flag. Some 900 opponents of the war—including some labor leaders and socialists such as learn how the United States mobilized its resources for World War I.

Introduce Key Terms

Linguistic, Interpersonal. Review this section's key terms with students. Supply each student with a set of note cards. On one side, have each student write a term, and on the other, its definition. Then pair students and have them take turns reading their definitions and matching the terms. **SHELTERED ENGLISH**

TEACH

Have students read Section 3 and complete Guided Reading Strategies 11.3. Choose one or more of the following activities to explore the section content with students. For further suggestions on block scheduling or team teaching, see the *Block Scheduling Handbook.*

LEVEL 1: Linguistic. (Suggested time: 15 min.) As a class, go over students' Guided Reading Strategies. Then use the Reading Focus questions to highlight the main ideas of the section. **SHELTERED ENGLISH**

Cultural Diversity

African American Officers. Many African Americans faced discrimination as they attempted to build military careers during World War I. Although 13 percent of the army's enlisted men were African Americans, they made up only 1 percent of the officer corps. When the war began, African Americans with college degrees hoped to receive commissions as officers; however, the army refused to integrate the officer candidate schools. A separate school was eventually established, and approximately 1,100 African Americans received commissions. Nevertheless, they still faced discrimination, and most were prevented from rising above the rank of captain, regardless of their performance.

Critical Thinking: How might racial discrimination have hurt the effectiveness of the armed forces?

ANSWER: It might have created divisions within the army, instead of focusing attention on defeating the enemy.

Eugene Debs and Bill Haywood—were jailed as a result of the laws.

Some Americans criticized religious groups that were committed to nonviolence, characterizing them as traitors. German Americans faced harassment and charges of disloyalty because of strong anti-German feelings. In order to show their dislike for German things, people renamed familiar items: hamburgers became liberty sandwiches, and dachshunds became liberty pups.

U.S. troops prepare at a New Jersey training camp to fight in the war.

 Mobilizing for War

Encouraged by the CPI's publicity, some 73,000 men enlisted in the army in the six weeks following the declaration of war. However, these new recruits and the 98,000 men already in the armed forces were not enough to fight a modern war.

Drafting Soldiers

On May 18, 1917, Congress passed the **Selective Service Act**, which required men between the ages of 21 and 30 to register to be drafted into the armed forces. Almost 3 million men who served during the war were draftees. Some Americans saw the draft as a violation of their civil liberties. Others, such as Quakers, refused to fight because of their religious beliefs. Many of these men served in noncombat roles.

To organize and train the soldiers, the army built dozens of training camps. Most were located in the South, where mild winters allowed year-round training. Soldiers learned to dig trenches, survive poison-gas attacks, string barbed wire, fire rifles and machine guns, and throw hand grenades.

African American Soldiers

After the U.S. declaration of war, the government trained African American soldiers to fill noncombat roles. Pressure from the National Association for the Advancement of Colored People (NAACP) led the military to create some combat units and one officer-training camp for African Americans.

The majority of the 400,000 African Americans who served in the armed forces, however, did so in segregated units commanded by white officers. Once in Europe, most African American troops fought with divisions of the French army. U.S. officials worried that conflict might erupt within their army if white and black soldiers fought together.

While black soldiers fought "to make the world safe for democracy," African Americans at home protested ongoing discrimination and racially motivated violence. On July 28, 1917, some 15,000 African Americans marched in silence down New York City's Fifth Avenue. They carried signs and passed out leaflets declaring their message. Their *Why We March* leaflet stated:

> **"We march because we are thoroughly opposed to Jim Crow cars, segregation, discrimination, and disfranchisement [denial of voting rights], lynching, and the host of evils that are forced on us. We march because we want our children to live in a better land and enjoy fairer conditions than have fallen to our lot."**

 Organizing for War

In addition to raising troops, the government needed to raise money and supplies. To do so, it expanded its involvement in the economy.

ALL LEVELS: Visual-Spatial, Kinesthetic. (Suggested time: 30 min. plus homework and presentations) Organize the class into three groups. Have each group prepare a newsreel presentation on one of the following aspects of government mobilization for war: the Selective Service Act, the Committee on Public Information, industry guidance, or freedom restrictions.

LEVEL 3: Linguistic, Intrapersonal. (Suggested time: 45 min.) Ask students to imagine that they are members of either an African American or a women's rights group during World War I. Have each student write a speech that a member of one of these groups may have given describing the group's contribution to the war effort.

CLOSE

Linguistic, Visual-Spatial. Have each student design a stamp to commemorate public support for the war effort. Ask students to write a caption explaining what their stamp depicts.

CHALLENGE AND EXTEND

Linguistic, Visual-Spatial. Have students use the library or other resources to investigate local war efforts during World War I. Then have each student create a special edition of a local newspaper highlighting the community's war efforts.

Supplying the Armies

Congress increased income taxes, imposed a tax on business profits, and, most importantly, authorized the issue of war bonds. Money from the sale of **Liberty bonds** provided loans to the Allies to allow them to purchase food and war supplies. Liberty bonds raised more than $20 billion.

To oversee the production and distribution of goods manufactured by the nation's war industries, President Wilson created the **War Industries Board** (WIB). According to Bernard Baruch, head of the WIB, "No steel, copper, cement, rubber, or other basic materials could be used without our [WIB] approval." Most producers eagerly cooperated with the WIB. The automobile and steel industries, however, hesitated to yield to government control. The automakers gave in only after Baruch threatened to stop railroad service into and out of their plants. Steel producers also agreed to cooperate when Baruch threatened to take over their factories.

Feeding the Troops

With the passage of the Lever Food and Fuel Control Act of 1917, the federal government gained even greater control over the war effort. The act gave Wilson the right to establish price and production controls over food and fuel. Herbert Hoover took control of the **Food Administration**, an agency created to increase food supplies for the troops by expanding agricultural production and decreasing domestic consumption.

Hoover motivated farmers to produce at high levels by guaranteeing them high prices for their food crops. Production, as well as prices, increased greatly. Announcing that "food will win the war," Hoover promoted "meatless Mondays" and "wheatless Wednesdays" and encouraged people to plant vegetables at home in "victory gardens."

Women's War Efforts

American women contributed to the war effort in many ways. Some 25,000 female volunteers served in France. They worked as nurses, signalers, typists, and interpreters. The "Hello Girls" of the U.S. Army Signal Corps handled military telephone service, including translating calls and sending battle orders. None of the women in the military received any pension for their service.

Although officially not allowed in combat, many female nurses and ambulance drivers worked at the front lines. One female driver remembered the dangers:

> **"We had our first air-raid work last night. I was the night-driver on duty. . . . Some bombs fell very near just as I got to the [evacuation hospital]. . . . I had just stopped . . . when shrapnel [metal fragments] whizzed past my head and there was a tremendous crash close beside. . . . Then an ambulance call came and I tore off."**

Many other women volunteered for the Red Cross and served at home and abroad. First Lady Edith Wilson regularly served coffee and

The U.S. government used posters like these to inspire patriotism and encourage support for the war effort.

Economic Development

Working Conditions. In order for manufacturers to obtain lucrative government contracts, they had to agree to regulations that governed the workplace. Minimum wages were established for many workers, and some industries had to limit the workday to eight hours. Companies were not allowed to use child labor. Some industries had to provide special working conditions for women, including seats with backs and lunch breaks.

Activity. Have students use the library and other resources to find other stipulations that have been required in order for businesses to obtain government contracts. Have students create a list of these regulations. Then organize students into several groups and ask them to imagine that they are the board of directors of the American Boot Company. American Boot is seeking a government contract to produce boots for the U.S. Army. Have each board of directors make a presentation to a government committee (the class) explaining how American Boot will meet workplace regulations.

REVIEW

Linguistic, Logical-Mathematical. Have students complete the Section Review questions. Then have students use the terms in the Section Review to write a one-page essay explaining how the United States mobilized its resources to fight in World War I and how this process affected women and African Americans.

ASSESS

Have students complete Daily Quiz 11.3.

RETEACH

Visual-Spatial, Logical-Mathematical. Have students complete Main Idea Activities for Reteaching and Sheltered English 11.3. Ask each student to prepare a two-column chart showing various organizations formed and laws passed to promote the war effort. The second column should describe each organization's or law's purpose and effects. Once students have finished creating their charts, review them as a class. **SHELTERED ENGLISH**

Section 3 Review ANSWERS

Identify
For significance, see the following pages:

- Committee on Public Information, p. 335
- George Creel, p. 335
- Selective Service Act, p. 336
- Liberty bonds, p. 337
- War Industries Board, p. 337
- Bernard Baruch, p. 337
- Food Administration, p. 337
- Jeannette Rankin, p. 338
- National War Labor Board, p. 338

Reading for Content Understanding

1. It drafted soldiers through the Selective Service Act and established training camps.

2. Industry had to submit to government control under the War Industries Board, but profited from increased production. The shortage of workers and the formation of the National War Labor Board helped unions bargain for better wages, hours, and conditions.

3. Many African Americans served in the military; women did volunteer work overseas and at home and worked in factories.

4. Posters will vary but should show reasons why Americans should support the war effort and suggest direct actions that people can take, such as buying war bonds or joining the Red Cross.

5. Answers will vary but students should state their opinions regarding punishment for opposing the war and offer support for their answers.

Women joined the war effort by serving as ambulance drivers, often transporting wounded soldiers directly from the front lines to hospitals.

sandwiches to soldiers in Washington, D.C. On the home front, women filled important industrial jobs. More than 1.5 million women worked in factory positions left vacant by departing soldiers.

Some women, including social reformer Jane Addams, opposed U.S. entry into the war and worked for peace. Jeannette Rankin of Montana, the first woman elected to the U.S. Congress, cast one of the few votes against President Wilson's war resolution. She stated, "I want to stand by my country but I cannot vote for war."

Labor and the War

The effort to supply the troops overseas benefited all workers. Three conditions combined to produce high wages and a favorable environment for labor. First, American products were essential to Allied troops fighting in Europe, so it was important to maintain full production. Second, the war created a serious labor shortage as production increased and workers left to join the armed forces. The new female workers could not fill all the empty positions. Third, immigration to the United States nearly stopped during the war.

The new and remaining workers took advantage of the labor shortage to press for higher wages and better working conditions. They formed and joined unions and sometimes went on strike. During the course of the war more than 4 million workers went on strike—the highest proportion of the workforce to do so before or since the war. Unable to replace striking workers and faced with steady production orders, most companies gave in to worker demands and agreed to pay higher wages.

In April 1918 President Wilson created the **National War Labor Board** to settle disputes between workers and management and prevent strikes. The board was sympathetic to workers and supported their right to collective bargaining. It also outlined minimum-wage and maximum-hour standards in the workplace, and required fair pay for female workers.

SECTION 3 REVIEW

Identify and explain the significance of the following:

- **Committee on Public Information**
- **George Creel**
- **Selective Service Act**
- **Liberty bonds**
- **War Industries Board**
- **Bernard Baruch**
- **Food Administration**
- **Jeannette Rankin**
- **National War Labor Board**

Reading for Content Understanding

1 **Main Idea** What changes did U.S. government officials make to organize an army to fight in Europe during World War I?

2 **Main Idea** How did the war affect industry and labor? How did this situation benefit each?

3 **Cultural Diversity** How did women and African Americans serve in the war effort?

4 **Writing** *Creating* Create a poster to encourage Americans to support the war effort. You might advise Americans why it is important to buy Liberty bonds or to join the Red Cross.

5 **Critical Thinking** *Determining the Strength of an Argument* Do you agree with the government's action in punishing some people who opposed the war? Explain your answer.

OBJECTIVES

- Describe the experiences of U.S. soldiers in World War I.
- Analyze the progress of the final battles of the war.
- Explain why Germany finally agreed to an armistice.

FOCUS

Motivate Before Reading

Explain to students that as U.S. troops arrived in France, they were greeted by the French Republican Guard band, playing "The Star-Spangled Banner." Ask students to imagine that they are U.S. soldiers arriving to this greeting. Have them write postcards home describing the scene and suggesting why their arrival may have led to renewed expressions of French patriotism. Tell students that in

Americans "Over There"

Reading Focus

What were the experiences of U.S. soldiers in World War I?

How did the final battles of the war progress?

Why did Germany finally agree to an armistice?

Key Terms

American Expeditionary Force
Communists
Treaty of Brest-Litovsk
Second Battle of the Marne
armistice

IN JUNE 1917 the first U.S. forces arrived in France. In Paris the French Republican Guard band greeted the soldiers with "The Star-Spangled Banner," followed by the French national anthem, "La Marseillaise" (mahr-suh-layz). The sidewalks overflowed with people welcoming the troops. An American journalist traveling with the soldiers reported, "From the crowded balconies and windows overlooking the route, women and children tossed down showers of flowers and bits of colored paper. . . . There came from the crowds a good old genuine American whoop-em-up yell."

The Granger Collection, New York

Sheet music cover of George M. Cohan's World War I song

Section 4 RESOURCES

PRINT

★ Guided Reading Strategies 11.4

★ Biography Reading 11: Alvin C. "Sergeant" York

★ Primary Source Reading 11: A Journal of the Great War

★ Geography Activity 11: World War I

★ Section 4 Review, p. 343

★ Daily Quiz 11.4

MULTIMEDIA

★ *Teaching Resources CD–ROM,* Lesson 11.4

★ *Exploring America's Past* Video Segment: Letters from Home; *Teacher's Guide,* pp. 21–23

★ Linking Geography and History Transparency 16: World War I: The Western Front, 1917–1918

SHELTERED ENGLISH

★ Main Idea Activities for Reteaching and Sheltered English 11.4

The Americans Arrive

By the time the first U.S. troops arrived, the Allies were in bad shape. German troops were occupying Belgium and part of France. The German navy was destroying Allied ships at an alarming rate. Russia was barely able to hold the Germans back.

Joining the Fight

The French and British armies wanted U.S. troops on the front lines immediately. However, General John J. "Black Jack" Pershing refused to send soldiers to join French and British units. He wanted U.S. troops, known as the **American Expeditionary Force** (AEF), to serve as individual units. He wanted the AEF to be a "distinct and separate component of the combined forces, the identity of which will be preserved." The AEF included the regular army, the National Guard, and the new larger force of volunteers and draftees.

Starting in the fall of 1917, Pershing hurried his troops through a three-month training program. The U.S. soldiers, called doughboys, trained in this section they will learn about the experience of U.S. soldiers in the war, the last battles of the conflict, and why Germany finally agreed to an armistice.

Introduce Key Terms

Linguistic, Logical-Mathematical, Interpersonal. Review this section's key terms with students. Have each student use context cues to develop questions and use the key terms for answers in preparing a multiple-choice quiz. Have students exchange quizzes, answer the questions, and return the quizzes to their authors for grading. **SHELTERED ENGLISH**

TEACH

Have students read Section 4 and complete Guided Reading Strategies 11.4. Choose one or more of the following activities to explore the section content with students. For further suggestions on block scheduling or team teaching, see the *Block Scheduling Handbook.*

LEVEL 1: Linguistic. (Suggested time: 15 min.) As a class, go over students' Guided Reading Strategies. Then use the Reading Focus questions to highlight the main ideas of the section. **SHELTERED ENGLISH**

Global Relations

America and Russia. Many Americans were embarrassed that Russia, a nation ruled by a monarch, was their ally in a war fought to preserve democracy. Their initial delight that revolutionaries had overthrown the Russian monarchy turned to dismay, however, when they learned that the Bolsheviks had no interest in democracy. Alarmed by Russia's decision to abandon the war effort, the Allies sent troops to defeat the Bolsheviks and draw Russia back into the conflict. At the least, the Allies hoped to keep supplies in Russia from falling into German hands. The United States sent a total of 14,000 troops into northern Russia, and another 7,500 to assist Japanese troops that controlled the western seaport of Vladivostok. However, the Allied intervention proved to be a failure, and Russia did not re-enter the war.

Critical Thinking: How might the Allied intervention have hurt relations with Russia?

ANSWER: The presence of Allied troops might have made Russians suspicious of the Allies' intentions.

Multimedia Resources

Linking Geography and History Transparency 16: World War I: The Western Front, 1917–1918

World War I soldiers carried all their necessary equipment on their backs. A condiment can (top right) had compartments for coffee, sugar, and salt. A bacon tin (bottom right) stored meat.

specially dug trenches and practiced with real shells and rifles. Pershing's plan was to train these troops for victory. The Allies, however, grew impatient for the soldiers to enter the war.

Russia Leaves the War

The Allies feared defeat as their situation worsened. In November 1917, the Bolsheviks seized control of the Russian government. The Bolsheviks were **Communists**, or people who favor the equal distribution of wealth and the end of all forms of private property. The new government, led by Vladimir Lenin, faced famine and civil war. Russia withdrew from the fighting in December. In March 1918 the Central Powers and Russia signed the **Treaty of Brest-Litovsk**, a peace agreement removing Russia from the war.

The Final Battles

With Russia out of the war and most U.S. troops not yet ready to fight, Germany saw its last chance to win the war and seized it. In the spring of 1918 Germany launched a series of major attacks to break the the stalemate on the western front.

During these weeks, the first U.S. troops experienced the grim realities of war. Unlike the practice trenches, the trenches at the front were filled with trash, lice, and rats, and sometimes the remains of long-dead soldiers. The troops' diet consisted of hard biscuits, bacon, dried beef, and canned emergency rations. Once in battle, however, these hardships seemed unimportant. One U.S. Marine remembered, "I had been so horrified at the death, destruction, and danger on all sides that I had forgotten about my stomach."

On March 21 the Germans attacked along the Somme River near St. Quentin in northern France. The battle began with a five-hour bombardment by more than 6,000 heavy guns. Two days later, German artillery bombarded Paris from 75 miles away. After pushing some 40 miles into Allied lines, the German advance stalled as troops advanced farther and faster than their supplies. The attack cost the German army 250,000 casualties. Combined British and French losses were 133,000.

In April the German army launched its second offensive against the British line in northwestern France, near Belgium. British field marshal Douglas Haig told his troops:

> **"There is no other course open to us but to fight it out! Every position must be held to the last man. . . . With our backs to the wall, and believing in the justice of our cause, each one of us must fight on to the end."**

They did just that and the Germans failed to reach their target—a major railway junction. In 20 days of combat, both sides suffered about 110,000 casualties.

Farther south, the Germans forced French troops across the Aisne River and back toward the Marne River. German forces reached the Marne River and were threatening to break through the thin French line toward Paris. Ferdinand Foch, French commander of the Allied forces, declared, "Lose not another meter of ground!" At this point,

ALL LEVELS: Visual-Spatial, Logical-Mathematical. (Suggested time: 45 min.) Have students create annotated time lines depicting the progression of the final battles of the war. Ask students to identify each battle and when it was fought. Next to each battle, have students write a brief summary of the events that occurred. When students have finished their time lines, have volunteers share the information they depicted with the class. Finally, lead a discussion on the circumstances that led to Germany's acceptance of the armistice. **SHELTERED ENGLISH**

LEVEL 2: Linguistic, Logical-Mathematical, Intrapersonal. (Suggested time: 45 min.) Have students imagine that they are members of the American Expeditionary Force and assign each student a specific time period during the war. Have each student write a letter to a friend or family member explaining what is going on in the war and describing combat experiences and life in the army. Call on volunteers from each time period to read their letters to the class. Once volunteers have finished reading their letters, discuss the progression of the war, how the Central Powers seemed to lose public support, and how morale dropped among their troops.

LEVEL 3: Linguistic, Logical-Mathematical, Interpersonal (Suggested time: 30 min. plus homework) Organize the class into several small groups. Ask members of each group to imagine that they are high-ranking German officials discussing the

These German sharpshooters are moving into position near the front lines during fighting near the Aisne River in France.

two divisions of the American Expeditionary Force joined French forces to strike back.

U.S. troops stopped the German advance at the town of Château-Thierry (sha-toh-te-ree), fewer than 50 miles from Paris. French and U.S. troops then attacked the Germans at Belleau Wood. The battle started poorly for the Allies. When an observer asked a U.S. officer about withdrawing, however, he responded: "Retreat[?] . . . We just got here." The Allies then gradually drove back this second German offensive.

By the beginning of July 1918, 1 million U.S. troops and military personnel were stationed in France. At midnight on July 14, the Germans launched their last, desperate offensive at the **Second Battle of the Marne**. During the fighting, the U.S. 3rd Division blew up every bridge that the Germans had built across the Marne River. Both sides suffered heavy casualties, but the German losses crippled their ability to launch another offensive. The turning point of the war had finally come.

Driving The Germans Back

With the last German offensive beaten, the Allies attacked. In September—in the first distinctly American assault—U.S. forces defeated German troops at Saint-Mihiel near Alsace-Lorraine, on the border of France and Germany. One wounded but

American Arts

John Philip Sousa

John Philip Sousa was born in 1854 in Washington, D.C. He earned a place in the world of music by writing more marches than anyone else in history. In all, Sousa wrote some 140 military marches, including "Semper Fidelis" and "The Stars and Stripes Forever." His marches were hugely popular and still inspire strong feelings of patriotism.

During World War I, Sousa joined the U.S. Naval Reserve at the age of 62 to organize its band units. He toured with a navy band of more than 300 sailors. In addition to entertaining the troops, Sousa's band also assisted in the Liberty Loan and Red Cross drives. He wrote his "Liberty Loan" march at the request of Secretary of the Treasury William McAdoo.

John Philip Sousa

Sousa wrote many marches during the war, including "The Chantyman's March" and "Sabre and Spurs." In 1918, when anti-German feelings were running high, the American Relief Legion asked Sousa to write a wedding march to replace the often-used music of German composers. Sousa's "Wedding March" was performed at many wedding ceremonies held during World War I.

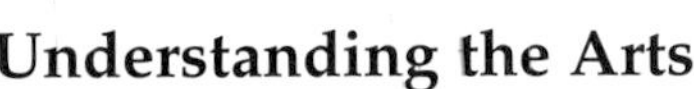

Understanding the Arts

1. How did John Philip Sousa serve in World War I?
2. Why do you think Sousa's music was so popular?

Biography

John Philip Sousa. At age six, John Philip Sousa was enrolled in a music conservatory, where he showed promise as a musician. When he was 13, Sousa was offered a job in a circus band, but his father persuaded him to join the U.S. Marine Band. He left the Marine Band in 1872, but returned in 1880 when he accepted the position of conductor. He left the Marine Corps 12 years later to form his own band, which proved to be very successful. During the Spanish-American War, he directed the music of the Sixth Army Corps. He then returned to civilian life, taking his band on a world tour during 1911–12. Sousa served in his third branch of the military when he took charge of the U.S. Navy's bands during World War I.

Activity: Have students listen to recordings of Sousa's music. Then have each student write a paragraph suggesting why Americans responded enthusiastically to this music during World War I.

AMERICAN ARTS ANSWERS

1. He organized the navy's bands, entertained troops, and helped raise money.
2. His marches inspired patriotic feelings as the nation prepared for war.

terms of the armistice. Have groups discuss why they should accept or reject the armistice. Ask students to consider the morale of the troops and the German people when weighing the evidence. Encourage students to take notes during this discussion. For homework, have each student write a communiqué to the German people explaining why Germany accepted the armistice.

CLOSE

Linguistic, Musical-Rhythmic. Have students write songs to commemorate the final battles of the war and Germany's acceptance of the armistice. Encourage students to include all the terms in the Identify portion of the Section Review in their songs. Ask volunteers to share their songs with the class. Finally, lead a discussion on the end of the war and the terms of the armistice.

CHALLENGE AND EXTEND

Visual-Spatial. Ask each student to prepare a map illustrating the engagements of the American Expeditionary Force during World War I. Have students use the library and other resources to find information about these battles. Then ask them to locate each battle and show which side won. Have students present their maps to the class and compare and contrast them for accuracy.

Cultural Diversity

The 369th. In September 1918, the 369th fought with the French 161st in some of the war's fiercest fighting. The 3rd Battalion captured 25 enemy machine guns and 125 prisoners. However, these victories came at great cost. The battalion, which started the campaign with 700 men, had 550 dead or wounded by the end of the first day of combat. The soldiers of the 369th continued to show their bravery, advancing nearly nine miles beyond the German lines.

Critical Thinking: What did the performance of the 369th reveal about these African American soldiers' dedication to the war effort?

ANSWER: They were willing to go to great lengths, perhaps even die, to help win the war.

MAP ANSWER

50 to 60 miles

Multimedia Resources

Exploring America's Past Video Segment: Letters from Home; *Teacher's Guide*, pp. 21–23

Search 1821, Play to 9603
Videodisc Blue Side A

Play

Pause

See *Teacher's Guide* for Spanish barcode.

The Western Front in 1918

Learning from Maps In 1918, after Russia withdrew from the war, Germany used its eastern forces to push into France.

Movement What was the farthest distance the German forces had to travel before retreating behind the armistice line?

proud soldier informed his parents, "Folks, we have them on the run." The Americans then joined the other Allies under the leadership of Ferdinand Foch to attack along the Meuse River and in the Argonne Forest.

Every available U.S. unit joined the fighting, including the African American soldiers of the 369th U.S. Infantry—the so-called Harlem Hell Fighters. The 369th spent more time in combat than any other U.S. unit and was the first Allied regiment to reach the Rhine River on the German border. The members of the 369th were awarded France's highest military honor—the Croix de Guerre (krwah-di-ger)—for their bravery.

By November 1918 General Pershing was able to report, "For the first time the enemy lines were completely broken through." One U.S. private recalled the scene after the fighting: "The roads and fields were strewn [covered] with dead Germans, horses, . . . helmets, [and] guns."

The Allies continued to advance toward the railway at Sedan on the Belgian border, which was the main supply line for German forces. Other Allied forces advanced all along the front. The German soldiers were so exhausted that a U.S. soldier with an empty pistol captured 300 of them simply by asking them to surrender.

Armistice

By the fall of 1918 the German people were as tired of the war as their soldiers. In October 1918, a German newspaper even dared to ask, "Do the people wish to continue war?" Many German civilians were without food or supplies. By 1918 an average of 800 Germans were dying daily from starvation, up from 240 per day in 1915. Food riots and strikes occurred in Germany and the other Central Powers nations.

German soldiers also rebelled. In October, when senior German naval officers planned a final suicide attack to break the British blockade, German sailors mutinied. They refused to sail on the mission and seized control of the naval station at Kiel, Germany. The Germans did not have enough soldiers to continue fighting. In the three months since the last Allied offensive began in August, the Allies had captured one quarter of all German soldiers in the field and one half of all German guns. By early November the commandant of Berlin sent a telegram that read, "All troops deserted."

Germany's allies in the Central Powers also began leaving the war. Bulgaria signed a truce on September 30, and a month later the Ottoman

REVIEW

Linguistic, Logical-Mathematical, Interpersonal. Have students complete the Section Review questions. Then ask students to outline this section. Have students exchange outlines, read them, and add supporting facts as needed. Then have students discuss the information they added.

ASSESS

Have students complete Daily Quiz 11.4.

RETEACH

Visual-Spatial, Logical-Mathematical. Have students complete Main Idea Activities for Reteaching and Sheltered English 11.4. Have each student draw a political cartoon to show how the American Expeditionary Force affected the course of World War I. You may wish to assign each student an individual or battle; have each student confine the cartoon to the item assigned. Ask students to create a caption for their cartoons. Call on volunteers to explain their work to the class. **SHELTERED ENGLISH**

© Dorling Kindersley Ltd./Courtesy of Spink & Son Ltd., London

These African American soldiers received the Croix de Guerre (right) from France for their bravery during the war.

Empire also quit the war. On November 4, 1918, the Allies reached a peace agreement with Austria-Hungary. Just four days later, German representatives traveled to the Allied headquarters at Compiègne (kohm-pyayn), France, to receive the terms of a cease-fire. As part of the agreement, Kaiser Wilhelm II abandoned the German throne and fled to the Netherlands. Germany became a republic.

The Allies demanded that Germany evacuate all occupied territory. German aircraft, tanks, and heavy artillery were to be destroyed, and Germany had to surrender its U-boats. Germany was also required to accept the possible occupation of German territory by Allied troops. The Germans had no choice but to agree to the Allies' terms. On the 11th hour of the 11th day of the 11th month, the **armistice**, or truce, went into effect. The Great War had ended. An Allied soldier described the troops' reaction to the news:

> **"There came a second of expectant silence, and then a curious rippling sound. . . . It was the sound of men cheering from the Vosges [a mountain range located in northeastern France] to the sea."**

In a different location, U.S. pilots yelled, "I've lived through the war!" and "We won't be shot at any more." However, the tragedy of the war took away from some of the celebration. When asked what the armistice meant, one British soldier replied, "Time to bury the dead."

SECTION 4 REVIEW

Identify and explain the significance of the following:

- **John J. Pershing**
- **American Expeditionary Force**
- **Communists**
- **Treaty of Brest-Litovsk**
- **Ferdinand Foch**
- **Second Battle of the Marne**
- **armistice**

Locate and explain the importance of the following:

- **Château-Thierry**
- **Argonne Forest**

Reading for Content Understanding

1 **Main Idea** What was World War I like for U.S. soldiers?

2 **Main Idea** Why, after so many early victories, did Germany finally surrender in World War I?

3 **Global Relations** What did the Allies demand of Germany following the armistice?

4 **Writing** *Informing* Imagine that you are a reporter for an American newspaper who has been assigned to cover the western front in 1918. In a one- or two-paragraph story, explain the condition of the German and Allied troops in the final battles, and describe the war's end.

5 **Critical Thinking** *Synthesizing Information* Do you think that the Allies could have won the war without the help of U.S. troops? Use information from the text to explain your answer.

Section 4 Review ANSWERS

Identify

For significance, see the following pages:

- John J. Pershing, p. 339
- American Expeditionary Force, p. 339
- Communists, p. 340
- Treaty of Brest-Litovsk, p. 340
- Ferdinand Foch, p. 340
- Second Battle of the Marne, p. 341
- armistice, p. 343

Locate

For locations, see the map on page 342.

Reading for Content Understanding

1. They endured bad food, the hardship of trench life, and the terrors of combat.

2. Many of Germany's civilians were dying of starvation, and its soldiers were deserting.

3. Germany was to become a republic; evacuate occupied territory; destroy aircraft, tanks, and heavy artillery; surrender U-boats; and agree to possible occupation of German territory.

4. Stories will vary but should discuss the exhaustion of the Germans and the excitement of the Allies.

5. Answers will vary but students should state their opinions and evaluate the American contribution to the war.

SECTION 5 LESSON PLAN

OBJECTIVES

- **Analyze the human and economic costs of the war.**
- **Explain the terms of the Treaty of Versailles.**
- **Describe Americans' reactions to the Treaty of Versailles.**

FOCUS

Motivate Before Reading

Using the Constitution, found in Chapter 2, have students prepare a graphic organizer to show the process by which treaties are ratified. Call on volunteers to explain their organizers to the class. Then discuss the process. Tell students that in this section they will learn about the human and economic costs of the war, the terms

Section 5
RESOURCES

PRINT

★ Guided Reading Strategies 11.5

★ Literature Reading 11: Battlefield Prose

★ Graphic Organizer 11: Major Moments of World War I

★ Section 5 Review, p. 349

★ Daily Quiz 11.5

MULTIMEDIA

★ *Teaching Resources CD–ROM,* Lesson 11.5

★ HRW Web site

SHELTERED ENGLISH

★ Main Idea Activities for Reteaching and Sheltered English 11.5

Establishing Peace

Reading Focus

What were the human and economic costs of the war?

What were the terms of the Treaty of Versailles?

How did Americans respond to the Treaty of Versailles?

Key Terms

Fourteen Points
self-determination
League of Nations
Big Four
reparations
Treaty of Versailles

ON NOVEMBER 7, 1918, an American reporter saw German officials arrive in France and mistakenly wired New York that the war was over. Celebrations erupted in hundreds of towns and cities. In New York City, thousands of men and women poured into the streets in a "wild, whooping dance of celebration." Famed Italian opera singer Enrico Caruso appeared at the window of his hotel and sang "The Star-Spangled Banner" to a joyous crowd below. Later, on November 11, when the armistice was actually signed, Americans celebrated all over again.

Two women sweep this marine off his feet after the armistice.

 Europe After The War

World War I carried a heavy human cost. The Allies lost more than 5 million soldiers as a result of the war. Some 116,000 U.S. troops died. More than half of them died of influenza, a viral infection. The Central Powers lost about 3.4 million soldiers. More than 20 million soldiers on both sides had been wounded. Thousands of civilians were also killed during the four years of fighting.

The economies of the nations involved in the war were ruined. The war also destroyed the land itself. A British visitor described the French countryside after the war:

> **"The horror . . . of war was made visible . . . on an extraordinary scale. . . . The completeness of the destruction was evident. For mile after mile nothing was left. No building was habitable [livable] and no field fit for the plow."**

The cost of the war has been estimated at more than $145 billion for the Allies and $63 billion for of the Treaty of Versailles, and the controversy that the treaty created in the United States.

Introduce Key Terms

Linguistic, Logical-Mathematical, Interpersonal. Review this section's key terms with students. Have students choose partners. Have one student in each pair select a term, and have the other use context cues from the section to write a sentence linking that term to another one. Then have students reverse roles and continue the process until all terms have been linked. Have students share their sentences with the class.

SHELTERED ENGLISH

TEACH

Have students read Section 5 and complete Guided Reading Strategies 11.5. Choose one or more of the following activities to explore the section content with students. For further suggestions on block scheduling or team teaching, see the *Block Scheduling Handbook*.

LEVEL 1: Linguistic. (Suggested time: 15 min.) As a class, go over students' Guided Reading Strategies. Then use the Reading Focus questions to highlight the main ideas of the section.

SHELTERED ENGLISH

the Central Powers. In addition, more than $30 billion in property had been destroyed and over $1 billion was spent on aid efforts. Industry and agriculture had nearly been wiped out in Belgium, France, and other parts of Europe.

France and Britain owed American banks billions of dollars for money borrowed during the war. Germany also faced debt and severe food shortages. Many people feared that these economic troubles would allow the communist revolution in Russia to expand to other nations.

Wilson's Fourteen Points

While Americans welcomed the armistice, President Wilson focused on making an enduring peace. Even before the United States entered the war, Wilson had been preparing for its end.

On January 8, 1918, Wilson outlined a vision for postwar Europe and a system to avoid future wars. This plan was called the **Fourteen Points**, because it contained 14 basic principles. (See pages 350–51.) The president believed that the peace terms must not be so hard on the Central Powers that the settlement would lead to another war.

Many of the Fourteen Points concerned the future of specific nations and regions. Some points called for freedom of ships on the seas, smaller armies and navies, and lower trade tariffs. Other points related to fair settlement of colonial claims of independence and an end to secret agreements between nations. Wilson also emphasized the right of people to decide their own political status—the right of **self-determination**. The last point called for the creation of the **League of Nations**—a congress of nations designed to settle international disputes and protect democracy.

Other Allied leaders, however, wanted a different kind of peace. An American journalist reported that Allied leaders wanted "a new world domination with themselves and ourselves dominating; what they decidedly do not want is a democratic peace." France and Britain also wanted to punish Germany for its role in the war and to ensure that Germany would never again be a world power. As one reporter wrote, Britain and France wanted Germany to "pay, pay, pay."

Many Americans agreed with these Europeans. A Montana rancher who had three sons fighting in France, however, wanted the government to do more than just punish Germany. The rancher knew that one or two of his sons could die in battle, and he accepted that possibility. As he explained in a letter to a member of Wilson's cabinet, the rancher wanted something in return:

> **"What I ask is that they do not give themselves in vain [for nothing]. . . . Take steps to see that there shall never be another tragedy like this. See that they do not die for anything less worthwhile. Fix the matter so that neither Germany nor any other nation can ruin the world."**

These members of the Disarmament Conference of the League of Nations are struggling with the problems of enforcing the peace.

The Paris Peace Conference

President Wilson arrived in Europe on December 13, 1918, ready to persuade the Allies to propose peace based on his Fourteen Points. He ignored his advisers, who feared that if he attended the peace conference, Allied leaders would force him to compromise. Wilson went because he felt "it is now my duty to play my full part in making good what [our soldiers] offered their lives to obtain."

Across the Curriculum

MATH

Mobilization. During the course of the war, Russia mobilized 12 million troops and suffered nearly 9.2 million casualties. The British Empire raised 8.9 million troops and had about 3 million casualties. France mobilized nearly as many troops as the British—8.4 million—but had 6 million casualties. The United States raised 4.3 million troops and had only 364,000 casualties. The Germans mobilized 11 million troops and suffered 7 million casualties, while Austria-Hungary reported an astounding 7 million casualties from the 7.8 million troops in its armed forces.

Activity: Have students prepare bar graphs comparing the levels of mobilization and the numbers of casualties for each nation.

ALL LEVELS: Linguistic, Logical-Mathematical. (Suggested time: 30 min.) Explain to students that President Wilson tried to rally the nation around the Treaty of Versailles, but that the two-thirds majority in the Senate needed to ratify the treaty was never obtained. Have students make two lists, one identifying objections made by the irreconcilables and another identifying objections made by reservationists. Have volunteers share their lists with the class and discuss the objections that were made. Finally, discuss the consequences of the Treaty of Versailles and the effects of the lack of formal U.S. recognition of the treaty.
SHELTERED ENGLISH

LEVEL 2: Linguistic, Logical-Mathematical. (Suggested time: 30 min.) Ask students to imagine that they are military advisers writing a report on the human and economic costs of World War I. Ask students to provide statistics distinguishing combat fatalities from deaths caused by illness, to cite figures regarding property damage, and to describe the extent of the destruction. Also encourage students to provide information on the economic effects of the war. Ask volunteers to read their reports to the class. Finally, lead a discussion on the human and economic costs of the war.

Global Relations

The League's Shortcomings. The League of Nations resolved minor disputes during the 1920s, but it had little success with conflicts involving major powers. For example, after the 1931 Japanese invasion of China, the League formed a commission to study the conflict. Rather than comply with the commission's recommendations, Japan left the League. Another failure occurred when many nations ignored the League's embargo against Italy, which was enacted following the Italian invasion of Ethiopia. Italy left the League in 1937 rather than face sanctions. In both cases, inability to enforce its decisions made the League ineffective in mediating conflicts among powerful nations.

Critical Thinking: Why do you think League members were unwilling to use stronger measures to stop international aggression?

ANSWER: Many nations had suffered terribly during World War I and wanted to avoid another war at all costs.

LINKING PAST TO PRESENT ANSWERS

1. Answers will vary but students should state their opinions and offer support for them.

2. conducts peacekeeping missions, provides famine relief, and delivers aid to refugees, developing countries, and children

Deciding Europe's Future

National leaders from around the world gathered in the Hall of Mirrors at Versailles on June 28, 1919, to sign the peace treaty.

Leaders of the Allied nations attended the peace conference at the palace of Versailles (ver-sy), outside of Paris. The new leaders of Russia refused to attend, and no representatives of the Central Powers were invited. The **Big Four**—President Woodrow Wilson of the United States, British prime minister David Lloyd George, French premier Georges Clemenceau (kle-mahn-soh), and Italian prime minister Vittorio Orlando—dominated the conference.

The peace conference was a clash between Wilson's ideals of peace and democracy and the European leaders' desire to reward their allies and punish their enemies. Lloyd George was most interested in keeping the British Empire together and protecting its long-term interests. Clemenceau wanted to punish Germany so severely that it could never again threaten France. Orlando was most concerned with ensuring that Italy received the territory that it had been promised when it entered the war on the Allies side.

Wilson was unable to persuade the other members of the Big Four to accept his goal of "peace without victory." The other leaders insisted that Germany accept the blame and pay the Allied Powers for the entire cost of the war. Forced to compromise, Wilson agreed that Germany would have to pay **reparations**—payments for damages

Linking Past to Present

The League of Nations and the UN

UN programs help many people, such as these Bosnian refugees.

Countries formed the League of Nations after World War I to maintain international peace. After World War II, nations formed the United Nations (UN) for similar reasons. The League of Nations failed partly because the United States and Germany were not members. The United States has been a UN member since its creation in 1945.

During the early years of its existence, fear of a U.S.-Soviet confrontation limited the UN's use of force to resolve conflicts. In the 1990s, however, increased international cooperation has strengthened the UN. The number of ongoing peacekeeping missions conducted by the UN increased from 5 in 1988 to 17 in 1998.

The UN also runs many humanitarian programs, including aid to refugees, developing countries, and children and famine relief. The UN has not always been able to keep the peace, but as its defenders have said, "If the UN did not exist, it would have to be invented."

Understanding What You Read

1. Do you think there is a need for the UN? Explain your answer.
2. What does the United Nations do today?

LEVEL 3: Linguistic, Intrapersonal. (Suggested time: 45 min.) Ask students to imagine that they are Woodrow Wilson and write two journal entries. The first, dated at the start of the peace talks, should discuss Wilson's plans for a peace treaty and his assessment of the motivations of Clemenceau, Orlando, and Lloyd George. The second, dated just after the Versailles Treaty is finalized, should discuss the treaty's provisions and Wilson's opinion of the treaty.

CLOSE

Linguistic, Visual-Spatial, Interpersonal. Assign each student one of the following topics: the signing of the Treaty of Versailles at the Paris Peace Conference, the debate over the treaty in the Senate, or the defeat of the treaty by a vote of the Senate. Have each student prepare a front page of a newspaper dealing with the assigned topic. Then organize the class into groups of three, one student for each topic. Have students read one another's work, and encourage them to offer feedback regarding accuracy.

and expenses brought on by war. The amount was eventually set at $33 billion. To provide France the defensive security that it desired, the president also agreed that Germany must return the border region of Alsace-Lorraine. Also, the Allies would gain control of the Rhineland and Saar Valley region in western Germany.

Wilson's Victories

The final peace settlement of World War I, the **Treaty of Versailles**, included a number of the Fourteen Points. The treaty partially incorporated the right of national self-determination. The people of some nations won the right to decide their own political situation, rather than have an outside empire decide it. Some new nations were formed and old ones were restored. Czechoslovakia and Yugoslavia were created and Poland was restored. Estonia, Finland, Latvia, and Lithuania became free nations. The Central Powers were also forced to surrender control of their colonies to the Allies.

However, the victorious Allies would not keep the Central Powers' colonies as their own. A system of mandate, or authority, gave the League of Nations control over these areas. The League assigned nations, such as France and Britain, to administer these areas until they were ready for independence.

Although the treaty was not everything that Wilson wanted, he felt that the League of Nations could resolve any problems that the treaty created or failed to solve. Wilson addressed the peace conference in February 1919. He said that although the war had caused many terrible things,

> **"some very beautiful things have come out of it. Wrong has been defeated, but the rest of the world has been more conscious than it was before of the majesty of right. People that were suspicious of one another can now live as friends . . . in a single family."**

Europe After the Treaty of Versailles, 1919–1920

Learning from Maps World War I led to the collapse of many empires and the formation of several new European countries.

Place How many new European countries were formed after World War I?

Global Relations

Treaty of Versailles. Woodrow Wilson hoped that the Treaty of Versailles would heal the wounds of war and guarantee world peace. However, the German people resented many provisions of the final treaty. The reparations agreement placed an almost impossible burden on their economy. Germany lost its colonies, whereas the Allies were permitted to keep theirs. Finally, the treaty contained provisions intended to humiliate the Germans, including an article that forced the German government to take responsibility for starting the war. In many ways, the Treaty of Versailles served as a source of continued international tension.

Activity: Have students use the library or search the Internet through the HRW Web site to find information on the Treaty of Versailles. Ask students to create a chart identifying points of the treaty that might cause future conflicts and speculating on what those conflicts might be.

go.hrw.com
SB1 Versailles

MAP ANSWER
seven

CHALLENGE AND EXTEND

1. **Logical-Mathematical, Interpersonal.** Organize the class into groups, each representing one of the Big Four at the Paris Peace Conference. Have students use the library and other resources to investigate the assigned nation's interests at Versailles. Ask each group to discuss the position its country took at the conference. Then have each group suggest items to include in the conference agenda. From the individual agendas, create a single plan for the conference. Then allow students to debate the issues and agree on terms for the treaty. Have the class compare its decisions with those made at Versailles.

2. **Linguistic, Logical-Mathematical.** Dwane Martinson of Seattle, Washington, suggested the following activity: As a class, reread Wilson's Fourteen Points and discuss their meaning. Then have students rewrite the Fourteen Points in their own words and create a world map. The map should illustrate the various issues involved, including any new nations—Alsace-Lorraine and the Dardanelles—and the European and U.S. possessions in Africa, Asia, the Pacific, and Latin America.

Citizenship and Democracy

The 1918 Congressional Elections. When President Wilson arrived in Paris in December 1918, he had just suffered a political setback in the United States. The Democratic Party had done poorly in the congressional elections of 1918, leaving Republicans in control of both houses of Congress. Before the election, Wilson had appealed to the American people to elect Democrats to guarantee the continuation of his policies. Wilson's political enemies used the election outcome to argue that the American people had lost confidence in the president.

Critical Thinking: Why would President Wilson want the Democrats to control Congress?

ANSWER: This would allow his policies, including the peace treaty, to pass easily.

All that remained was to persuade the U.S. Senate to ratify the treaty. Wilson was not prepared for the opposition he met there.

The League of Nations

For President Wilson, the most important part of the treaty was the creation of the League of Nations, which he believed would be "a definite guarantee of peace." In Wilson's plan, the League of Nations would include representatives from democratic nations. It would consist of a council, an assembly, and a permanent administrative staff. The League would promote peace by working cooperatively to settle disputes and to reduce armaments.

Each member nation would be represented in the assembly and would have one vote. The council would have four rotating members elected by the assembly, and five permanent members—Britain, France, Italy, Japan, and the United States. Eventually, all independent nations would be allowed to join, but the former Central Powers nations could not be members at first.

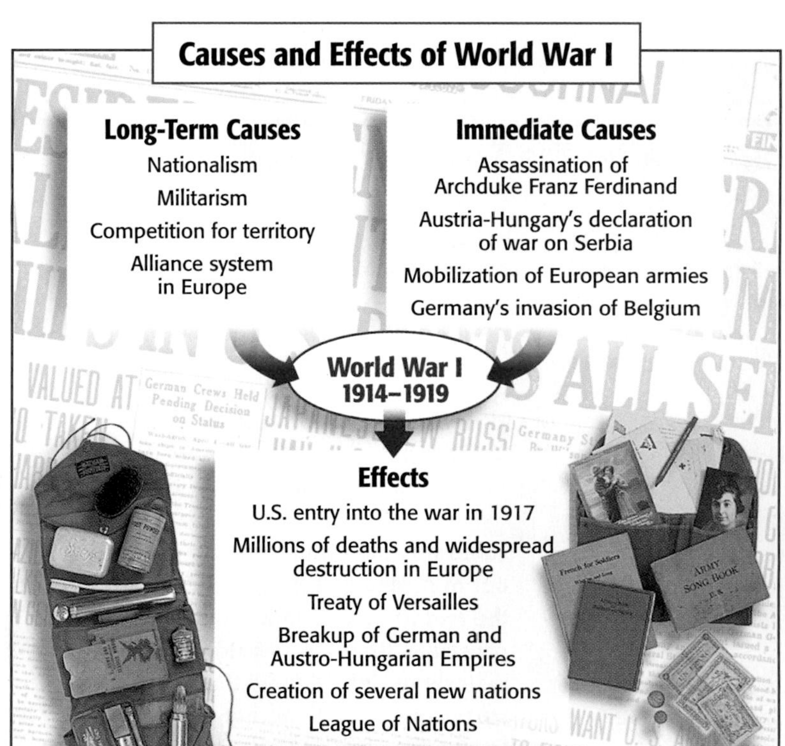

Causes and Effects of World War I

Long-Term Causes
- Nationalism
- Militarism
- Competition for territory
- Alliance system in Europe

Immediate Causes
- Assassination of Archduke Franz Ferdinand
- Austria-Hungary's declaration of war on Serbia
- Mobilization of European armies
- Germany's invasion of Belgium

World War I 1914–1919

Effects
- U.S. entry into the war in 1917
- Millions of deaths and widespread destruction in Europe
- Treaty of Versailles
- Breakup of German and Austro-Hungarian Empires
- Creation of several new nations
- League of Nations

Member nations would present disagreements to the Permanent Court of International Justice, or World Court. If a member nation did not obey the court's judgment, the League could impose penalties. They might include a ban on trade or even the use of military force.

Peace Without a Treaty

When President Wilson returned to the United States in July 1919, he found that Congress did not share his enthusiasm for the Treaty of Versailles or the League of Nations. Republican senator Henry Cabot Lodge, chairman of the Foreign Relations Committee, said:

> **"No peace that satisfied Germany in any degree can ever satisfy us. It can not be a negotiated peace. It must be a dictated peace, and we and our allies must dictate it."**

To secure the two-thirds majority needed to ratify the treaty, Wilson needed the support of the Republicans in Congress. They had won control of the House and the Senate in 1918. Wilson had offended some Republicans by not including them in the U.S. delegation to the peace conference. Although most Democratic senators supported the treaty, many Republican senators disagreed with certain parts of it and demanded changes. Wilson, expecting the treaty to pass without change, refused to negotiate.

A group of 14 Republican senators, called the irreconcilables, rejected the peace treaty outright. The remaining Republican senators were divided between mild reservationists, who wanted small changes, and strong reservationists, who demanded drastic revisions.

REVIEW

Linguistic, Logical-Mathematical, Intrapersonal. Have students complete the Section Review questions. Then ask students to write an epitaph for Woodrow Wilson summarizing his role as peacemaker. Call on volunteers to read their epitaphs and explain their meaning to the class. Invite students to evaluate the accuracy and insight of the epitaphs.

ASSESS

Have students complete Daily Quiz 11.5.

RETEACH

Linguistic, Visual-Spatial. Have students complete Main Idea Activities for Reteaching and Sheltered English 11.5. Ask students to create banners either supporting or opposing the Treaty of Versailles. Ask students to explain their banners to the class, pointing out who would have supported and who would have opposed the positions presented. Finally, discuss the results of the opposition to the treaty. **SHELTERED ENGLISH**

The Foreign Relations Committee, led by Senator Henry Cabot Lodge, demanded changes to the Treaty of Versailles.

Most of the Republicans' concerns focused on the extreme instances when the League of Nations could use military force to carry out its decisions. The Republicans were suspicious of European countries' motives. Many of them believed that membership in the League conflicted with Congress's constitutional power to declare war. Senator Lodge led the strong reservationists. In an attempt to force Wilson to compromise, Lodge delayed the treaty vote.

Wilson took his cause to the American public. He went on an extended speaking tour to defend the treaty and to get the public to pressure Republicans to pass it. As he traveled across the country, Wilson spoke to enthusiastic crowds. After a speech in Pueblo, Colorado, in September Wilson collapsed. He was rushed back to Washington, D.C., where he suffered a stroke in early October. Although he survived, Wilson never fully recovered. His wife, Edith Galt Wilson, took care of him and tried to persuade him to compromise on the treaty.

In November, Lodge presented the treaty for ratification with his list of reservations. He wanted to limit U.S. military involvement in the League, but otherwise his reservations did not change the treaty significantly. Wilson still refused any compromise on the League and ordered Democrats to vote against Lodge's version of the treaty.

In November 1919, the Senate defeated both versions—with and without reservations—of the Treaty of Versailles. Neither the Democrats nor the Republicans would vote for the other's version, but neither side had enough votes for the two-thirds majority. After further debate, the Senate again defeated the treaty in March 1920.

Congressional opposition and President Wilson's refusal to negotiate doomed the Treaty of Versailles to defeat in the Senate. Wilson's continued refusal to compromise cost him his goal of U.S. membership in the League of Nations. In the end, the United States negotiated separate peace treaties with Austria, Germany, and Hungary. The United States never joined the League of Nations, and the League's future as a world peace organization seemed uncertain.

SECTION 5 REVIEW

Identify and explain the significance of the following:
- **Fourteen Points**
- **self-determination**
- **League of Nations**
- **Big Four**
- **reparations**
- **Treaty of Versailles**
- **Henry Cabot Lodge**

Reading for Content Understanding

1. **Main Idea** How did the war affect the people and the economies of the nations involved?
2. **Main Idea** What were the conditions and requirements of the Treaty of Versailles?
3. **Geographic Diversity** *Human-Environment Interaction* How did World War I affect the European landscape?
4. **Writing** *Describing* Imagine that you are a visitor to the Capitol on the day that Senator Lodge presents his reservations about the Treaty of Versailles. In a letter to a friend, describe the different opinions expressed about the treaty.
5. **Critical Thinking** *Evaluating* If you had been a member of the Senate in 1919, what would your approach to a postwar peace have been?

Section 5 Review ANSWERS

Identify

For significance, see the following pages:
- Fourteen Points, p. 345
- self-determination, p. 345
- League of Nations, p. 345
- Big Four, p. 346
- reparations, p. 346
- Treaty of Versailles, p. 347
- Henry Cabot Lodge, p. 348

Reading for Content Understanding

1. There were 8.6 million battlefield deaths, 20 million more were wounded, and thousands of civilians died. The combatants spent an estimated $208 billion to wage war, more than $30 billion worth of property was destroyed, and over $1 billion was spent on relief efforts. Britain, France, and Germany were left with large debts.

2. partial incorporation of the right of self-determination; formation of Czechoslovakia and Yugoslavia; restoration of Poland; creation of a League of Nations; oversight of the Central Powers' colonies

3. It destroyed much of the landscape and caused over $30 billion in property damage.

4. Letters will vary but should present the views of the irreconcilables, the mild reservationists, and the strong reservationists.

5. Answers will vary but students should state their opinions and offer arguments to support them.

Global Relations

The Fourteen Points Speech. When Woodrow Wilson wrote the speech introducing the Fourteen Points in January 1918, he hoped that it would help bring an end to the war. In addition to the Fourteen Points, Wilson included some comments designed to gain support from moderates in Germany. The president declared that the United States did not "wish to injure her [Germany] or to block in any way her legitimate influence of power. . . . We wish her only to accept a place of equality among the peoples of the world—the new world in which we now live,—instead of a place of mastery."

Critical Thinking: Why did Wilson try to appeal to moderates in Germany?

ANSWER: He hoped that his promise of fair treatment would lead them to press for a negotiated peace.

HISTORICAL DOCUMENTS ANSWERS

(page 351)

1. freedom of ships on the seas and the removal of economic barriers

2. Belgium, Poland, France, Russia, and the occupied Balkan territories

3. Answers will vary but students should state their opinions and explain their reasoning.

Woodrow Wilson's

The Fourteen Points

President Wilson announced his specific proposals for a postwar peace—the Fourteen Points—in an address to Congress on January 8, 1918. An excerpt of the Fourteen Points appears below.

Gentlemen of the Congress:

It will be our wish and purpose that the processes of peace, when they are begun, shall be absolutely open and that they shall involve and permit henceforth no secret understandings of any kind. . . . The program of the world's peace, therefore, is our program; and that program, the only possible program, as we see it, is this:

I. Open covenants [agreements] of peace, openly arrived at, after which there shall be no private international understandings of any kind but diplomacy [negotiations] shall proceed always frankly and in the public view.

II. Absolute freedom of navigation upon the seas, outside territorial waters, alike in peace and in war, except as the seas may be closed in whole or in part by international action for the enforcement of international covenants.

III. The removal, so far as possible, of all economic barriers and the establishment of an equality of trade conditions among all the nations consenting to the peace and associating themselves for its maintenance.

IV. Adequate guarantees given and taken that national armaments [military equipment] will be reduced to the lowest point consistent [in agreement] with domestic safety.

V. A free, open-minded, and absolutely impartial [fair] adjustment of all colonial claims, based upon a strict observance of the principle that in determining all such questions of sovereignty [who should rule] the interests of the populations concerned must have equal weight with the equitable [just] claims of the government whose title is to be determined.

VI. The evacuation of all Russian territory and such a settlement of all questions affecting Russia as will secure the best and freest cooperation of the other nations of the world in obtaining for her an . . . opportunity for the independent determination of her own political development and national policy and assure her of a sincere welcome into the society of free nations under institutions of her own choosing; and more than a welcome, assistance also of every kind that she may need and may herself desire.

VII. Belgium, the whole world will agree, must be evacuated and restored, without any attempt to limit the sovereignty [self-rule] which she enjoys in common with all other free nations. No other single act will serve as this will serve to restore confidence among nations in the laws which they have themselves set and determined for the government of their relations with one another. Without this healing act the whole structure and validity [authority] of international law is forever impaired [damaged].

VIII. All French territory should be freed and the invaded portions restored, and the wrong done to France by Prussia in 1871 in the matter of Alsace-Lorraine, which has unsettled the peace of the world for nearly fifty years, should be righted, in order that peace may once more be made secure in the interest of all.

IX. A readjustment of the frontiers of Italy should be effected along clearly recognizable lines of nationality.

X. The peoples of Austria-Hungary, whose place among the nations we wish to see safeguarded and assured, should be accorded [given] the freest opportunity of autonomous [independent] development.

XI. Rumania, Serbia, and Montenegro should be evacuated; occupied territories restored; Serbia accorded free and secure access to the sea; and the relations of the several Balkan states to one another determined by friendly counsel [agreement] along historically established lines of allegiance and nationality; and international guarantees of the political and economic independence and territorial integrity [completeness] of the several Balkan states should be entered into.

XII. The Turkish portions of the present Ottoman Empire should be assured a secure sovereignty, but the other nationalities which are now under Turkish rule should be assured an undoubted [beyond dispute] security of life and an absolutely unmolested [unquestioned] opportunity of autonomous development, and the Dardanelles should be permanently opened as a free passage to the ships and commerce of all nations under international guarantees.

XIII. An independent Polish state should be erected which should include the territories inhabited by indisputably Polish populations, which should be assured a free and secure access to the sea, and whose political and economic independence and territorial integrity should be guaranteed by international covenant.

XIV. A general association of nations must be formed under specific covenants for the purpose of affording mutual guarantees of political independence and territorial integrity to great and small states alike.

Understanding Primary Sources

1. What freedoms does President Wilson want to guarantee?
2. What countries does Wilson want created or restored?
3. Do you think the Fourteen Points were fair to all the countries involved? Explain your answer.

The Granger Collection, New York

The Big Four; seated from left to right, Italian prime minister Vittorio Orlando, British prime minister David Lloyd George, French premier Georges Clemenceau, and U.S. president Woodrow Wilson

Chapter 11 Review ANSWERS

Identifying People and Ideas

1. heir to the throne of Austria-Hungary whose assassination led to World War I

2. prepare the military for war

3. a situation in which neither side can declare victory; the state of the war in late 1914

4. German promise not to sink merchant vessels "without warning and without saving human lives"

5. head of the Committee on Public Information, which used propaganda to build support in the United States for the war

6. settled disputes between workers and management in order to ensure that goods would be produced for the war effort

7. U.S. troops who served in Europe

8. commander of the American Expeditionary Force

9. payments for damages and expenses brought on by war

10. Republican senator who led opposition to the peace treaty

Using the Time Line

1. d
2. c
3. a
4. e
5. b

Understanding Main Ideas

1. Germany's repeated violation of American neutrality by sinking merchant ships, the discovery of the Zimmerman Note

2. wet, cold, dirty, unhealthy, and dangerous

Review and Assessment RESOURCES

PRINT
★ Chapter 11 Review, pp. 352–353
★ Vocabulary Activity 1
★ Chapter 11 Study Guide
★ Chapter 11 Test (Form A or B)

MULTIMEDIA
★ Audio Program, Ch. 11 (English and Spanish)
★ *Global Skill Builder CD–ROM*
★ Chapter 11 Test Generator
★ HRW Web site

SHELTERED ENGLISH
★ Spanish Glossary
★ Sheltered English Chapter 11 Test

ASSESS

Have students complete one of the Chapter 11 Tests. As an alternate assessment, assign the Chapter 11 Investigation.

3. Many African Americans served in the military; women volunteered in France as nurses, ambulance drivers, signalers, typists, interpreters, and telephone operators and took jobs in manufacturing.

4. They served as nurses, performed volunteer work, bought Liberty bonds, and grew more food.

5. After the destruction of bridges over the Marne and the loss of German soldiers, Germany lacked the ability to launch an offensive.

6. It was established to settle international disputes and protect democracy.

7. Students should discuss the opinions of Wilson and his Senate opponents.

Reviewing Themes

1. President Wilson created the Committee on Public Information to use publicity and propaganda to build support for the war.

2. After Franz Ferdinand was shot, nations fulfilled their commitments to other countries by joining the conflict between Serbia and Austria-Hungary.

3. Machine guns forced soldiers to huddle in trenches; airplanes provided information on enemy movements and performed limited bombing expeditions.

Thinking Critically

1. Answers will vary but students should state their opinions and explain their reasoning.

CHAPTER 11 REVIEW

Chapter Summary

Long-simmering tensions in Europe caused World War I to break out in 1914. The United States initially pursued a policy of neutrality. Then German U-boats killed Americans on neutral ships and newspapers published the Zimmerman Note. The United States entered the war in 1917 and helped the Allies win the conflict. Despite President Wilson's quest for "peace without victory," the Allies forced harsh postwar conditions on Germany.

On a separate sheet of paper, complete the following activities.

Identifying People and Ideas

Describe the historical significance of the following:

1. Franz Ferdinand
2. mobilize
3. stalemate
4. *Sussex* pledge
5. George Creel
6. National War Labor Board
7. American Expeditionary Force
8. John J. Pershing
9. reparations
10. Henry Cabot Lodge

Internet Activity 

go.hrw.com
SB1 Soldiers

Search the Internet through the HRW Web site to find information on U.S. soldiers who served in World War I. Create a profile of the regiments that fought together in a particular battle.

Understanding Main Ideas

1. What events led to U.S. entry into World War I?
2. What was war like in the trenches?
3. How did the war affect African Americans and women?
4. How did Americans at home contribute to the war effort?
5. Why was the Second Battle of the Marne the turning point of the war?
6. Why was the League of Nations part of the Treaty of Versailles?
7. How and why did American opinions differ on the League of Nations?

Reviewing Themes

1. **Citizenship and Democracy** How did the United States attempt to increase support for World War I at home?
2. **Global Relations** How did the assassination of Archduke Franz Ferdinand and his wife trigger a world conflict?
3. **Technology and Society** Explain how the machine gun and the airplane changed fighting in World War I.

Using the Time Line

Number your paper from 1 to 5. Match the letters on the time line below with the following events.

1. **President Wilson announces the Fourteen Points.**
2. **Woodrow Wilson is re-elected president.**
3. **Gavrilo Princip assassinates Archduke Franz Ferdinand and his wife, Sophie.**
4. **The U.S. Senate rejects the Treaty of Versailles.**
5. **A German U-boat attacks and sinks the *Lusitania.***

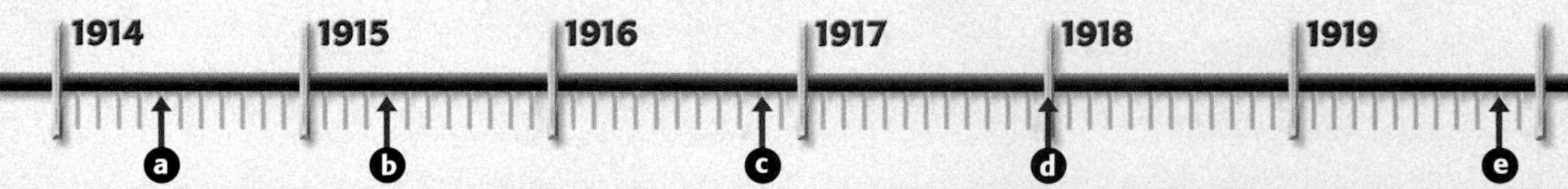

RETEACH

Visual-Spatial. Have students create annotated time lines based on the chapter. Ask students to trace the development of World War I, starting with the assassination of Franz Ferdinand and going through the congressional debate over the Treaty of Versailles and the subsequent treaties the United States signed. Have students write an explanation of the significance of each event.

Using the Internet

Have students continue their research to find information on the poetry written by soldiers during World War I. Ask students to choose one poem and write a brief summary explaining in their own words what they think the soldier-poet is trying to communicate.

Portfolio Extensions

1. After students have completed the posters, have them hold a contest to determine the best poster in each category.

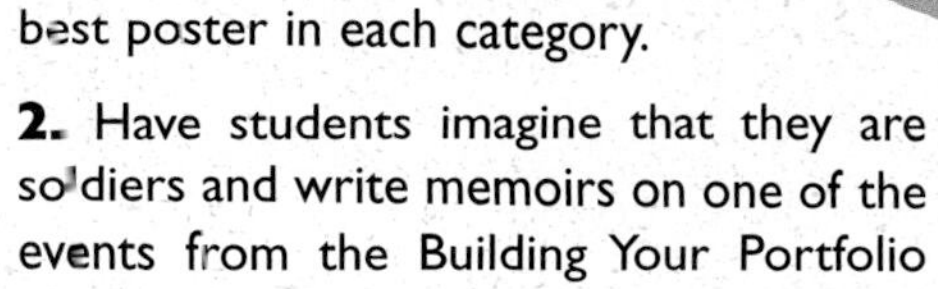

2. Have students imagine that they are soldiers and write memoirs on one of the events from the Building Your Portfolio activity.

Thinking Critically

1. **Evaluating** President Wilson thought that the last of his Fourteen Points was the most important. Of the points described in the chapter, which do you think is the most important? Explain your answer.
2. **Supporting a Point of View** Do you think that Germany should have been held totally responsible for the cost of World War I? Explain your answer.
3. **Identifying Cause and Effect** How did nationalism and imperialism contribute to tensions in Europe before World War I?

Writing About History

1. **Persuading** Imagine that you are preparing to vote in the 1916 presidential election. Make a campaign poster for the candidate of your choice. Be sure that your poster includes a slogan and the candidate's campaign pledges.
2. **Expressing** Imagine that you are a French soldier fighting with a unit of American soldiers. Write a letter home describing how they fought. Include your feelings on the benefits of having U.S. troops on your side.

Building Your Portfolio

Complete the following activities individually or in groups.

1. **The War on the Home Front** Create three posters to promote the war effort on the home front. You might develop posters for recruiting, for the war effort in the United States, or for the Food Administration. Write a paragraph that explains each poster. Then explain how each poster would have helped the war effort.
2. **Cataloging World War I** Imagine that you and your classmates are reporters. Each of you will write a story on one of the following: an airplane fight, trench warfare, the spotting of a U-boat, or the sinking of the *Lusitania.* Then combine this information with images and maps to create a booklet titled "Fighting in World War I."

Linking Geography and History

1. **Place** How did the borders of European nations change as a result of World War I? What nations lost territory and what new nations were formed?
2. **Human-Environment Interaction** How did trenches help soldiers survive the fighting in World War I? How did they expose soldiers to new dangers?

History Skills Workshop

Reading Maps Study the map below of the American advances during the fall of 1918. Then answer the following questions: (a) Which American advance covered more territory? (b) How did these advances relate to the armistice line?

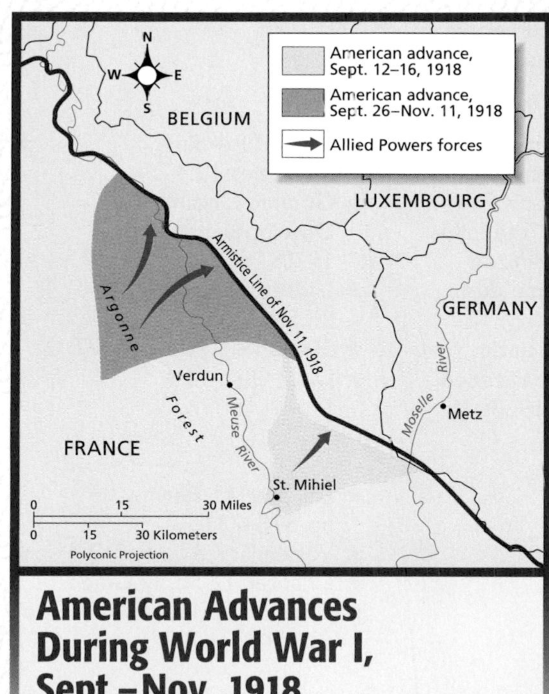

American Advances During World War I, Sept.–Nov. 1918

2. Answers will vary but those arguing for Germany's responsibility should point to its role as an aggressor, while those arguing against should point to the many tensions in Europe that led to the outbreak of the war.

3. Nationalism threatened the stability of existing nations; imperialism increased conflicts between nations as they competed for territory.

Writing About History

1. Posters will vary but those for Wilson should point to his stances on neutrality and working for peace, while those for Hughes should attack Wilson for his labor policies and his weak stance on defending American rights in Europe.

2. Answers will vary but students should mention the results of U.S. participation.

Linking Geography and History

1. Czechoslovakia and Yugoslavia were created; Poland had its borders restored; and Estonia, Finland, Latvia, and Lithuania became free nations. The Central Powers had to give up their colonies. Germany also lost Alsace-Lorraine, the Rhineland, and the Saar Valley.

2. Trenches protected soldiers from machine-gun and artillery fire; conditions in trenches led to illness and disease.

History Skills Workshop

(a) Sept. 26–Nov. 11, 1918; (b) Both advances brought U.S. troops closer to the armistice line.

CHAPTER PLANNING GUIDE
The 1920s: An Unsettled Decade

	SECTION LESSON OBJECTIVES	PRINT RESOURCES	MULTIMEDIA RESOURCES	SHELTERED ENGLISH RESOURCES
Section 1: Returning to "Normalcy" (pp. 355–61)	★ Analyze difficulties arising from the transition from war to a peacetime economy. ★ Explain the causes of the strikes and riots of 1919. ★ Explain how the Red Scare affected American society.	★ Guided Reading Strategies 12.1 ★ Primary Source Reading 12: Vanzetti's Last Statement ★ American History Political Cartoon 22: The Red Scare ★ Section 1 Review, p. 361 ★ Daily Quiz 12.1	★ *Teaching Resources CD–ROM*, Lesson 12.1 ★ HRW Web site	★ Main Idea Activities for Reteaching and Sheltered English 12.1
Section 2: Republicans in Power (pp. 362–66)	★ Analyze ways in which Presidents Harding and Coolidge strengthened the U.S. economy. ★ Discuss scandals that plagued President Harding and the Republicans. ★ Describe the goals of U.S. foreign policy during the 1920s.	★ Guided Reading Strategies 12.2 ★ American History Political Cartoon 21: Political Corruption in the 1920s ★ Biography Reading 12: Eugene Debs ★ Geography Activity 12: The Republican Decade ★ Section 2 Review, p. 366 ★ Daily Quiz 12.2	★ *Teaching Resources CD–ROM*, Lesson 12.2 ★ HRW Web site	★ Main Idea Activities for Reteaching and Sheltered English 12.2
Section 3: "The Business of America Is Business" (pp. 367–72)	★ Analyze the effects of the assembly line on manufacturing. ★ Describe how the automobile affected the economy and people's everyday lives. ★ Describe how advertising and the installment plan changed people's buying habits.	★ Guided Reading Strategies 12.3 ★ Section 3 Review, p. 372 ★ Daily Quiz 12.3	★ *Teaching Resources CD–ROM*, Lesson 12.3 ★ Art in American History Transparency 23: *Boomtown* ★ *Exploring America's Past* Video Segment: Advertising USA; *Teacher's Guide,* pp. 24–25	★ Main Idea Activities for Reteaching and Sheltered English 12.3
Section 4: The U.S. Economy (pp. 373–77)	★ Describe what caused the stock market boom in the 1920s. ★ Explain why the influence of organized labor declined during the 1920s. ★ Identify difficulties that farmers experienced during the 1920s.	★ Guided Reading Strategies 12.4 ★ Graphic Organizer 12: Developments of the 1920s ★ Literature Reading 12: "U.S.A." ★ Section 4 Review, p. 377 ★ Daily Quiz 12.4	★ *Teaching Resources CD–ROM*, Lesson 12.4	★ Main Idea Activities for Reteaching and Sheltered English 12.4
Chapter Review and Assessment (pp. 378–79)		★ Chapter 12 Review, pp. 378–79 ★ Vocabulary Activity 12 ★ Chapter 12 Study Guide ★ Chapter 12 Test (Form A or B)	★ Audio Program, Ch. 12 (English and Spanish) ★ *Global Skill Builder CD–ROM* ★ Chapter 12 Test Generator ★ HRW Web site	★ Spanish Glossary ★ Sheltered English Chapter 12 Test

CHAPTER OVERVIEW

The transition to a peacetime economy was difficult for the United States. The sudden loss of government contracts to produce war goods contributed to increased unemployment and a severe recession. At the same time, rising inflation increased the cost of living. Wages, however, did not rise. These problems led to labor disputes, racial violence, and fear of Communists.

The Republican Party benefited from these difficulties, and Warren G. Harding won the presidential election of 1920. Harding and his successor, Calvin Coolidge, based their economic policies on promoting the growth of business and otherwise leaving the economy alone. At the same time, they pursued a foreign policy based on isolationism and preventing further wars.

Henry Ford's Model T and the introduction of the moving assembly line helped to spur the growth of the U.S. automobile industry. This growth led to the expansion of related industries, such as oil. New methods of advertising, along with the advent of installment plans, encouraged people to spend even more money. Combined, these factors led to a boom for the U.S. economy.

This economic growth led to unprecedented investment in the stock market. Many people hoped to strike it rich by investing in the right stocks. However, industries such as coal, textiles, lumber, and agriculture faced difficult times, as did union labor.

CHAPTER INVESTIGATION

The Chapter Investigation is an extended, multipart activity designed for students to work cooperatively and apply the chapter content in the creation of a project. You may choose to use the Chapter 12 Investigation, 1920s Newspaper, either as a substitute for teaching the section lessons or as an alternate assessment.

BLOCK SCHEDULING 

The teacher lesson plans for each section offer a variety of activity choices to help you present the material in a block scheduling format. For further suggestions on block scheduling, see the *Block Scheduling Handbook with Team Teaching Strategies,* pp. 67–72.

Meeting Individual Needs

ABILITY LEVELS

LEVEL 1 Basic level activities designed for all students encountering new material.

LEVEL 2 Intermediate level activities designed for average students.

LEVEL 3 Challenging activities designed for above-average students.

SHELTERED ENGLISH These activities address the needs of students with Limited English Proficiency.

Smithsonian Institution®

Internet Connections and Lesson 12
www.si.edu/hrw

CNN Presents America:
Yesterday and Today 1850 to the Present
Segment: Americans and Their Automobiles

Additional Resources

Books for Teachers

Dumenil, Lynn. *The Modern Temper: American Culture and Society in the 1920s.* Hill and Wang, 1995. Surveys important events and ideas of the decade.

Haynes, John Earl, ed. *Calvin Coolidge and the Coolidge Era: Essays on the History of the 1920s.* Library of Congress, 1998. Includes 12 essays examining the presidency of Calvin Coolidge and American society during his administration.

Marchand, Roland. *Advertising the American Dream: Making Way for Modernity, 1920–1940.* University of California Press, 1985. Describes the interaction between advertising and American society.

Books for Students

Gourley, Catherine. *Wheels of Time: A Biography of Henry Ford.* Millbrook Press, 1997. Examines Henry Ford's life. Many photographs (for students reading below grade level).

Green, Harvey. *The Uncertainty of Everyday Life, 1915–1945.* HarperCollins, 1992. Examines life in the United States before, during, and after the 1920s.

Wade, Linda R. *Warren G. Harding.* Children's Press, 1989. Provides a biography of the 29th president (for students reading below grade level).

Multimedia Materials

The Age of Ballyhoo. Video, 52 min. Republic/SSSS. Cultural history of the 1920s. Includes newsreels of Sacco and Vanzetti.

The Big Red Scare of 1919–1920. Video, 10 min. Multimedia Productions/SSSS. Traces the origins of anticommunist and anti-immigrant hysteria in 1919 and 1920.

Henry Ford's American Dream. Video 30 min. Coronet/MTI Films. Discusses Ford's life and his introduction of a moving assembly line to mass-produce automobiles.

The 1920s: An Unsettled Decade

CHAPTER MOTIVATOR

Explain to students that in the presidential campaign of 1920, Warren G. Harding captured America's mood by saying that the people needed a return to "normalcy." Ask students to imagine that they live in the 1920s and have them write short paragraphs explaining what they think Harding meant and what the term *normalcy* might have meant to Americans. Have volunteers share their paragraphs with the class. Then discuss why people in the 1920s might have been attracted to a return to better times. Tell students that in this chapter they will learn how Americans responded to the social and economic changes of the 1920s, both by trying to return to normal procedures and by embracing these changes.

Presenting Themes

- **Citizenship and Democracy** Students might discuss how such fear could make the nation's citizens suspicious of all beliefs and values different from their own, which might then lead to attacks on freedom of speech and expression.
- **Economic Development** Students might discuss how economic priorities change and how the economy adjusts to new priorities. As the economy shifts away from producing military goods, new goods and new buyers must be found.
- **Technology and Society** Students might suggest that advances in technology generally make work easier and that depending on the nature of the new technology, jobs might be lost, gained, or require the use of new skills.

Using The Time Line

Have students classify each entry on the time line according to whether it appears to involve the economy, international relations, government and politics, or racial and ethnic relations.

CHAPTER 12

The 1920s: An Unsettled Decade

(1919–1929)

Florence Harriman was working for the Red Cross in Paris when World War I ended. She spent a joyous day wandering the streets with the crowds. To Harriman it seemed that "everything in the world were possible, and everything was new, and that peace was going to be what we had dreamed about." Peace, however, brought its own challenges, as Americans turned away from foreign affairs and concentrated on domestic concerns.

Citizenship and Democracy
How might fear of radical politics affect citizens?

Economic Development
In what ways might the end of a war affect economic growth?

Technology and Society
How might advances in manufacturing technology affect people's work environment?

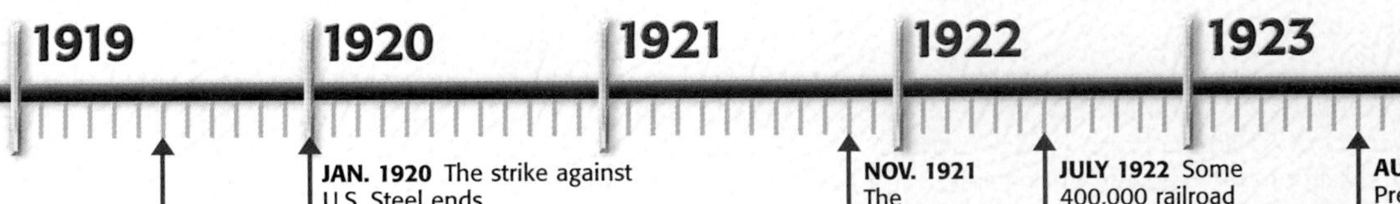

JULY 1919 A deadly race riot breaks out in Chicago, Illinois.

JAN. 1920 The strike against U.S. Steel ends.

NOV. 1921 The Washington Conference begins.

JULY 1922 Some 400,000 railroad workers go on strike to oppose wage cuts.

AUG. 1923 President Harding dies unexpectedly.

OBJECTIVES

- **Analyze difficulties arising from the transition from war to a peacetime economy.**
- **Explain the causes of the strikes and riots of 1919.**
- **Explain how the Red Scare affected American society.**

FOCUS

Motivate Before Reading

Ask students what they think the general mood of Americans was after World War I. As students identify correct responses, write them on the chalkboard and save them. *(Responses can be either positive, such as pride over the World War I victory; or negative, such as fear of communism or strikes.)* Tell students that although they might assume that citizens would be content since the nation had just

Returning to "Normalcy"

Reading Focus

What difficulties did the United States face in making the transition from war to peacetime?

What were some of the causes of the strikes and riots of 1919?

How did the Red Scare affect American society?

Key Terms

demobilization
Red Scare
anarchists
Palmer raids
xenophobia
American Civil Liberties Union

ONE AFTERNOON IN FEBRUARY 1919, teenager Bernard Katz headed up New York City's Fifth Avenue with a group of friends. Suddenly they saw a parade for the returning 369th U.S. Infantry, a heavily decorated African American unit. Caught up in the joy of the moment, Katz and his friends "stepped out into the middle of the street . . . and swung up Fifth Avenue behind the 369th and the fantastic sixty-piece band." When the parade ended, the participants, like the rest of the nation, had to face the challenges that accompanied the end of the war.

The U.S. government encouraged different groups, such as industrial workers and soldiers, to work together after World War I.

Section 1 RESOURCES

PRINT

- ★ Guided Reading Strategies 12.1
- ★ Primary Source Reading 12: Vanzetti's Last Statement
- ★ American History Political Cartoon 22: The Red Scare
- ★ Section 1 Review, p. 361
- ★ Daily Quiz 12.1

MULTIMEDIA

- ★ *Teaching Resources CD–ROM,* Lesson 12.1
- ★ HRW Web site

SHELTERED ENGLISH

- ★ Main Idea Activities for Reteaching and Sheltered English 12.1

IMAGE ON LEFT PAGE: *Howard Thain's painting* The Great White Way

1924 | **1925** | **1926** | **1927** | **1928**

NOV. 1924 Calvin Coolidge is elected president.

AUG. 1927 Nicola Sacco and Bartolomeo Vanzetti are executed.

AUG. 1928 The United States, France, and 13 other nations sign the Kellogg-Briand Pact.

won a war, in this section they will learn about some of the problems Americans faced after World War I.

Introduce Key Terms

Linguistic, Logical-Mathematical. Review this section's key terms with students. Then have students create a three-column graphic organizer. Ask students to label the first column *Key Terms* and list the section's terms below the heading. Have students label the other two columns *Problems Faced* and *Problems Addressed.* Ask students to determine if each key term describes a problem faced or a way of addressing a problem. Then have students write their answers in the appropriate squares of the organizer. Call on volunteers to share their answers with the class.
SHELTERED ENGLISH

TEACH

Have students read Section 1 and complete Guided Reading Strategies 12.1. Choose one or more of the following activities to explore the section content with students. For further suggestions on block scheduling or team teaching, see the *Block Scheduling Handbook.*

Economic Development

The Seattle General Strike. One strategy used by the Seattle strikers involved consumer organizing. Union members urged the entire community to boycott goods made in nonunion factories. Boycotts and other similar strategies got the community involved in the strike. These strategies also applied pressure on nonunion businesses. Every time a consumer bought a union-made good, nonunion businesses making the same product lost a potential sale.

Critical Thinking: Why would community involvement be important to the Seattle general strike?

ANSWER: It would show that the community supported the unions and was willing to make sacrifices to help them, thereby increasing the impact of the strike on business owners.

The Transition to Peace

Following World War I, the United States struggled through **demobilization**—the process of returning to a peacetime economy. Several challenges awaited the some 4.5 million soldiers who returned home after the war. Many soldiers found that the jobs they had left behind had been filled by others. Women had entered the industrial workforce in record numbers during wartime. When the war ended, government officials and union leaders asked women to give up these jobs. One American Federation of Labor (AFL) union insisted that women should quit work to make room for returning veterans:

> **"The same patriotism which induced [convinced] women to enter industry during the war should induce them to vacate their positions after the war."**

Many female workers disagreed with this point of view. "We stand now by your side. . . . We're equal, free at last," declared a group of female machinists. Despite their protests, many women were forced out of factory jobs. Some women found lower-paying work. However, by 1920 the percentage of women working outside the home had dropped below wartime levels.

The Granger Collection, New York

During World War I, large numbers of women took industrial jobs such as welding bomb casings.

While working women were being displaced and soldiers were returning to the job market, businesses began laying off employees. Billion-dollar military contracts had enabled many industries to expand during the war. During demobilization the government canceled these contracts. These cutbacks forced companies to slow production and reduce their workforce. As a result, unemployment soared from less than 2 percent in 1919 to almost 12 percent in 1921. The nation suffered a severe recession.

The recession hit American workers hard. Many people had been hoping for a bright economic future. During the war, wages had risen steadily, and unemployment had been extremely low. Some labor unions had enjoyed large increases in membership. However, prices had also risen during the war. The cost of living—the price of basic necessities such as food, shelter, and clothing—doubled between 1915 and 1920.

Immediately after the war, high inflation caused the cost of living to continue rising. Wages, however, remained about the same or declined. Unemployed Americans were particularly hard hit by rising prices. The weak economy created a tension between business and labor that worried many Americans.

Industrial Workers Strike

As economic conditions grew worse around the nation, thousands of industrial workers went on strike for better pay. In 1919 alone there were more than 3,600 strikes involving more than 4 million workers.

The Seattle General Strike

One of the strongest union towns in the United States in 1919 was Seattle, Washington. The wartime prosperity of the Seattle shipyards had encouraged workers in some 110 AFL-affiliated unions to organize a Central Labor Council. After the war, shipyard companies rejected union demands for

LEVEL 1: Linguistic. (Suggested time: 15 min.) As a class, go over students' Guided Reading Strategies. Then use the Reading Focus questions to highlight the main ideas of the section. **SHELTERED ENGLISH**

ALL LEVELS: Logical-Mathematical, Visual-Spatial. (Suggested time: 35 min.) Lead a discussion on the economic effects of World War I. Then have each student create a cause-and-effect chart that identifies the difficulties the United States faced as a result of its shift to a peacetime economy. Once students have finished their charts, ask volunteers to explain theirs to the class. Finally, ask students to suggest solutions to each problem they identified. **SHELTERED ENGLISH**

LEVEL 2: Linguistic, Logical-Mathematical. (Suggested time: 30 min. plus homework) Ask students to imagine that they are newspaper reporters. They have been asked to submit press releases chronicling significant events leading to and resulting from the Red Scare. Encourage students to include information on the following events: the strikes and riots of 1919, immigration of Communists and other radicals to the United States, the 1919 series of bombings, the Palmer raids, deportation of suspected Communists and other radicals, and the Sacco and Vanzetti trial. Remind students that a press release should have a title and should provide a brief summary of the event. When students have finished, call on volunteers to read their press releases to the class.

Global Connections

The Influenza Epidemic of 1918–1919

One of the most frightening events of World War I was a global epidemic of influenza, or flu. The epidemic had three major waves, the first beginning in Camp Funston, Kansas, in 1918. Soldiers from Camp Funston and other army bases are believed to have carried the epidemic to Europe as they went to fight in the war. Transmitted through the air, the flu spread rapidly among soldiers in the trenches, leading to an even deadlier second outbreak. Soldiers returning to the United States brought the flu to major cities. Other travelers soon spread the sickness around the world.

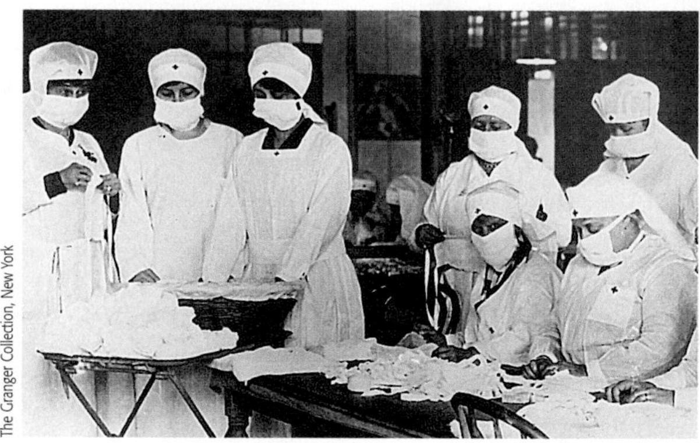

The Granger Collection, New York

Red Cross nurses make gauze masks to help prevent the spread of the flu.

The flu epidemic was different from most diseases because it struck otherwise healthy adults in large numbers. As quickly as an hour after exposure, victims developed raging fevers and severe headaches. Those with the worst cases literally suffocated as their lungs filled with fluid. A young woman at Camp Funston recalled the shock caused by the outbreak. "We'd be working with someone one day, and they'd go home because they didn't feel good, and the next day they were gone [dead]."

The epidemic killed more than half a million people in the United States, about 10 times the number of Americans killed in battle during World War I. Worldwide some 30 million people died from the flu. The epidemic of 1918–19 was one of the deadliest outbreaks of disease in recorded history.

Understanding What You Read

1. What were the symptoms of the flu, and whom did it affect?
2. Why did the flu spread so quickly?

higher wages. In response, the Metal Workers Union went on strike in January 1919.

The Metal Workers Union was one of the largest on the council. The metalworkers also had the sympathy of many other Seattle laborers. As a member of a local barbers' union explained, "We felt in duty bound to support those who support us." A plasterers' union member put the issue more bluntly: "We knew that if the metal trades were forced to their knees our turn would come next." In February the Central Labor Council called for a work stoppage in support of the metalworkers' strike. Some 60,000 union members went on a general strike—a strike involving all the union members in a community. "The eyes of the nation are fixed on Seattle," announced the council's secretary.

Business leaders and city officials viewed the strike as a dangerous challenge to their authority. Hoping to turn public opinion against the strikers,

Linking Past to Present

Studying the Epidemic. Scientists could do little to identify the virus that caused the flu epidemic of 1918–19. In recent years, researchers have considered examining the bodies of people who died from this flu and whose bodies remain frozen because they were buried near the North Pole. Scientists believe that they may be able to develop a vaccine against the flu if the virus has been preserved by the cold. Many scientists hope that a vaccine will prevent a similar virus from starting an epidemic. However, some people fear that thawing the bodies may result in another epidemic.

Critical Thinking: Should scientists study the virus in spite of the possible risks? Explain your answer.

ANSWER: Some students will argue that it is too risky, while others might argue that the benefits outweigh the risks.

GLOBAL CONNECTIONS ANSWERS

1. rapid development of a fever and severe headaches; the worst cases also involved the filling of the lungs with fluid; unlike most diseases, the flu epidemic attacked healthy adults.
2. It spread through the air, and soldiers lived in close proximity and traveled long distances.

TEACHER TO TEACHER

LEVEL 3: Linguistic, Logical-Mathematical, Interpersonal. (Suggested time: 45 min.) David Burns of Alexandria, Virginia, suggested the following activity: Organize students into groups that represent "management" and "unionized labor on strike" for a manufacturing plant in 1919. Have each group prepare a list of demands for a labor negotiation meeting. Then have representatives from each group present and explain their side's demands. After some negotiation, have each side regroup to discuss which demands it must have and what it might compromise on or drop. Then resume negotiations. After two or three rounds, have the labor group vote if it will accept management's latest offer or continue to strike. Finally, lead a discussion on the reasons for labor disputes following World War I and the problems in resolving these disputes.

CLOSE

Logical-Mathematical, Interpersonal. Ask students to use what they have learned in the section to revise their descriptions of the general mood of Americans following World War I, which

Historical Sidelight

The Russian Revolution. By 1917 many Russians were fed up with Czar Nicholas II because of his refusal to allow democratic political reforms and his mismanagement of the Russian army during World War I. In March 1917 the Russian people, along with members of the Russian army, overthrew the czar. By November, a group of Russian Communists known as Bolsheviks had seized control of the Russian government. This revolution is sometimes known as the October Revolution (for the month during which it occurred under the old Russian calendar).

Activity: Have students use the library or search the Internet through the HRW Web site to find more information on the Russian Revolution. Have students use the information they find to create time lines depicting the significant events of the revolution.

go.hrw.com
SB1 Russia

During the Seattle general strike, unions provided groceries to striking members.

many officials claimed that foreign radicals had started the strike. The press called the strikers "riffraff from Europe intent on terrorizing the community." Mayor Ole Hanson labeled the general strike "an attempted revolution." Hanson deputized 2,500 additional police. He also called in the state militia to patrol the streets. "Shoot on sight anyone causing disorder," he instructed.

Union leaders set up community kitchens and milk stations to feed the strikers and their families. Veterans among the strikers helped patrol the streets to keep order. Although the city remained peaceful, the majority of the public opposed the strike. After five days the strikers returned to work. None of their demands had been met.

The Steel Strike

The tension that led to the Seattle general strike was also present in the nation's largest industry—steel. The largest steel corporation, U.S. Steel, employed several hundred thousand workers. Such companies had great influence over their employees' lives. Steelworkers and their families typically lived in company-owned housing and shopped at company stores. In 1919 U.S. Steel chairman Elbert H. Gary said that this control benefited workers. He declared that his company wanted to "make the Steel Corporation a good place for the [workers] to work and live."

However, thousands of steelworkers were unhappy with their long hours and low pay. Steelworker Frank Smith was one of many who wondered "how a man is going to make a living for himself and his wife and . . . children" on such low wages. To improve their situation, steelworkers formed a union. They demanded eight-hour workdays, six-day workweeks, and wage increases to make up for the rising cost of living.

The leaders of the steel industry refused to recognize the union or meet with its representatives. On September 22, 1919, some 250,000 steelworkers walked off the job in Pittsburgh, Pennsylvania. They represented more than half of the industry's workforce. By week's end more than 350,000 workers were on strike. The steel industry was in danger of shutting down.

As in Seattle, the press accused the strike leaders, such as union organizer and communist William Z. Foster, of being revolutionaries. Company officials accused strikers of being anti-American radicals. Steel-mill owners hired armed guards. They also brought in so-called scabs—nonunion replacement workers—to run the mills. In addition, mill owners tried to divide strikers along ethnic lines. For example, owners in Chicago told Serb strikers that Italian strikers were going back to work to take the Serbs' jobs. By early January 1920, 20 strikers had been killed in violent confrontations. Some 100,000 union workers were

Heavily armed police officers patrolled the streets during a 1919 labor strike in New Jersey.

they created in the Motivate activity. Encourage students to reflect on both the causes and consequences of the social and political unrest that occurred after the war. Ask volunteers to read their revised descriptions to the class.

CHALLENGE AND EXTEND

1. **Linguistic, Visual-Spatial, Interpersonal.** Organize the class into three groups. Assign each group one of the following topics: the transition to a peacetime economy, labor unrest, or the Red Scare. Have each group prepare a section for a year-in-review issue of a magazine that covers the major events of 1919. Encourage groups to include pictures, interviews, and editorials. Once groups are finished, have a representative of each group make photocopies of the section and distribute them to another group. Have students take turns reading each group's section. Finally, combine the sections to create a magazine that the class can use for review.
2. **Linguistic, Visual-Spatial, Interpersonal.** Organize students into five groups. Have each group create a museum exhibit on one of the following topics: problems related to demobilization following World War I; the Seattle, Pittsburgh, and Boston strikes of 1919; the bombings and Palmer raids of 1919; the Sacco and Vanzetti trial; or the race riots of 1919.

still off the job and $112 million in wages had been lost. The unsuccessful struggle had broken the power of the union. Union bosses called off the strike. Labor leaders would wait years before trying to organize workers in heavy industries again.

The Boston Police Strike

In September 1919 a different type of strike drew national attention. Like the members of many other police departments, the Boston police were poorly paid. They wanted to form a union to negotiate for better wages and working conditions. Police Commissioner Edwin Curtis refused to allow police officers to unionize. After Curtis dismissed 19 police officers for trying to create a union, the police went on strike.

The actions of the police officers raised the question of whether government employees had the right to strike. Massachusetts governor Calvin Coolidge insisted that "the action of the police in leaving their posts is not a strike, it is desertion." President Wilson even declared the strike a "crime against civilization." With the police on strike, violence and looting broke out across the city. After two nights of disorder, two people were dead and nine others wounded. Coolidge called in the state militia to restore order.

The strike was broken, but Curtis refused to allow the officers to return to work. Coolidge backed Curtis, saying, "there is no right to strike against the public safety by anybody, anywhere, at any time." The entire police force was dismissed and replaced with a new one made up of unemployed veterans. These replacements received the higher wages and improved working conditions demanded by the strikers.

The Red Scare

The strikes and riots of 1919 led some Americans to worry that a communist revolution like the one in Russia might occur in the United States. In 1919 and 1920 these concerns led to a **Red Scare**. This was a widespread fear of Communists—also called Reds—and other radicals in the United States.

This Red Scare cartoon appeared in the Philadelphia Inquirer *in 1919.*

Political Threats

Some political groups wanted to bring enormous change to American society. They challenged democracy and the capitalist system. U.S. leaders feared the political goals of Communists, who wanted to share all property and wealth equally. Officials were also concerned about **anarchists**, who wanted to abolish all forms of government. Some Communists and anarchists were willing to use violence to accomplish their goals. Socialists made up a third political group that challenged the social structure of the United States. Some socialists supported revolution, but the majority wanted peaceful change through elections.

The most active Communists and anarchists were often recent immigrants from Europe. This led many Americans to stereotype most European immigrants as dangerous revolutionaries. In addition, major newspapers often reported labor strikes as the work of communist agents. However, in 1919 the communist parties in the United States had fewer than 40,000 members. Despite this fact, many Americans suspected that Reds were everywhere.

The Palmer Raids

Public concern increased following a series of bombings in 1919 aimed at business leaders and

Biography

A. Mitchell Palmer. In 1919 President Wilson appointed A. Mitchell Palmer, a lawyer and former congressmember from Pennsylvania, to the post of U.S. attorney general. During the remainder of World War I, Palmer used the Espionage Act to fight radicals and left-wing organizations. After the war, he relied on laws restricting free speech to clamp down on political radicals that he claimed were attempting to start a revolution. In June 1919 Palmer's house was bombed. That same night, bombs exploded in eight other U.S. cities. Several months later, Palmer launched the so-called Palmer raids.

Activity: Ask students to imagine that they are recent immigrants to the United States. Have each student write a letter to the editor of a newspaper explaining whether he or she thinks the Palmer raids were "un-American."

Have groups use the library and other resources to find photographs, newspaper headlines, posters, and other artifacts for their exhibits. Then ask students to create signs that describe the relevance of each exhibit item. When students are through, have them set up their exhibits in the classroom. Finally, have students tour each other's exhibits.

3. **Linguistic, Interpersonal.** Ask students to imagine that they are advisers to President Wilson and that they have been asked to help him prepare for his annual message to Congress for 1920. Organize the class into groups to investigate the causes of economic turmoil, social unrest, and political controversy in the nation over the past year. Have students use the library or other resources to prepare a report on such topics as unemployment resulting from demobilization, evidence of labor conflict, racial tension and violence, the fear of radicalism, and so on. Have each group write a briefing for the president. When all groups have finished writing, have a representative of each group read his or her group's briefing to the class.

REVIEW

Linguistic, Interpersonal. Have students complete the Section Review questions. Then give each student a note card with one of the terms from the Identify portion of the Section Review written

Citizenship and Democracy

The American Civil Liberties Union. The Civil Liberties Bureau was founded in 1917. Its members believed that laws restricting wartime protests violated the First Amendment. From the beginning, the organization fought a difficult battle. For instance, the government threatened the Bureau's free speech rights by barring its pamphlets from the U.S. mail. However, the group's efforts eventually helped convince the U.S. Supreme Court to take a greater role in protecting free speech. In 1920 the group changed its name to the American Civil Liberties Union, under which name it still exists today.

Activity: Have students read the Bill of Rights. Have each student pick one of the amendments and create a poster illustrating why the rights that amendment protects are important.

government officials. In June a bomb attack by an anarchist damaged the house of Attorney General A. Mitchell Palmer. He responded by ordering raids on suspected radical organizations, beginning in November 1919. The largest raids took place in January 1920. Federal agents in more than 30 cities arrested some 6,000 suspected radicals. These so-called **Palmer raids** often took place without warrants. In addition, there was little evidence against many of those arrested. Hundreds of immigrants were eventually deported as a result of the raids. Some were never officially charged with a crime.

Gradually, these violations of civil rights began to upset the public. When the New York state legislature expelled five representatives because they belonged to the Socialist Party, many people protested. Palmer then warned that radicals were planning a revolution on May 1, 1920, or May Day, an international labor holiday. When the revolution failed to take place, the public lost confidence in Palmer.

Sacco and Vanzetti

The Red Scare contributed to an atmosphere of **xenophobia**—fear and hatred of foreigners—that lingered long after the Palmer raids had ended. This xenophobia greatly influenced the trial of Italian immigrants Nicola Sacco and Bartolomeo Vanzetti. In May 1920 the two men were arrested and charged with robbing a Massachusetts shoe factory and murdering the paymaster and guard.

Sacco and Vanzetti were anarchists. They had lied to authorities about their political activities, fearing that they would be deported. This helped persuade some officials of their guilt. However, much of the evidence that the police had against the two anarchists was inconclusive. Sacco even had witnesses who said he was in another town on the day of the murders. Both men insisted that they were innocent and were being unjustly targeted because of their political beliefs.

Following a trial that many observers considered unfair, the two men were found guilty and sentenced to death in the electric chair. After the sentence was read, Vanzetti stood and gave a final statement:

> **"This is what I say: I would not wish to a dog or to a snake, to the most low and misfortunate creature of the earth—I would not wish to any of them what I have had to suffer for things that I am not guilty of. . . . I am suffering because I am a radical."**

Poet Edna St. Vincent Millay was one of many Americans who protested the trial of Sacco and Vanzetti.

Thousands of people protested the verdict. Leading the protests was the new **American Civil Liberties Union** (ACLU), an organization formed to protect people's constitutional rights. However, an official commission reviewed the case and found no grounds for retrial. Massachusetts governor Alvan T. Fuller refused to change the sentence. On August 23, 1927, Sacco and Vanzetti were executed. In 1977 Governor Michael Dukakis of Massachusetts issued a proclamation stating that Sacco and Vanzetti had been unjustly treated.

Ben Shahn, Bartolomeo Vanzetti and Nicola Sacco (1931–1932)

Immigrant artist Ben Shahn created this painting in the 1930s as part of a series showing the events of the Sacco and Vanzetti trial.

on it. Ask each student to write on the back side of the card a sentence that identifies the term without using it. Have students pass their cards around the room so other students can identify the terms they describe.

ASSESS

Have students complete Daily Quiz 12.1.

RETEACH

Logical-Mathematical, Visual-Spatial. Have students complete Main Idea Activities for Reteaching and Sheltered English 12.1. Organize the class into three groups and assign each group one of the section's Reading Focus questions. Have each group prepare a graphic organizer that answers its question. Ask a volunteer from each group to explain the group's organizer to the rest of the class. **SHELTERED ENGLISH**

Racial Violence

Foreigners and radicals were not the only targets of violence following World War I. The economic difficulties caused by demobilization also increased existing racial tensions, particularly in urban areas. Hundreds of thousands of African Americans had moved to northern cities during the war, often filling new factory jobs. African American communities grew in northern cities in formerly white neighborhoods. Many white northerners feared competition from the African American residents for housing and jobs. In the summer of 1919, called "Red Summer," these tensions exploded into urban race riots.

Many African Americans had to seek safe areas during the Chicago race riots of 1919.

The worst riot took place in Chicago, Illinois. After several violent race-related confrontations, antilynching activist Ida B. Wells-Barnett asked, "Will the legal, moral and civic forces of this town stand idly by?" Officials did nothing. Another incident soon occurred. In July 1919 a young African American named Eugene Williams went to a Lake Michigan beach near Chicago. Williams crossed into a whites-only area, where people began throwing rocks at him. He drowned. Fighting then broke out between white and African American bathers on the beach. The violence spread to the city. A week of rioting followed in which nearly 40 people were killed and more than 530 were injured.

Similar riots occurred in other cities, including Washington, D.C., and Tulsa, Oklahoma. By late 1919 there had been more than 25 race riots across the nation. Lynchings of African American men also took place, particularly in the South. The National Association for the Advancement of Colored People (NAACP) tried to stop these attacks. Despite such efforts, more than 70 African Americans were lynched in 1919.

SECTION 1 REVIEW

Identify and explain the significance of the following:

- **demobilization**
- **Red Scare**
- **anarchists**
- **A. Mitchell Palmer**
- **Palmer raids**
- **xenophobia**
- **Nicola Sacco and Bartolomeo Vanzetti**
- **American Civil Liberties Union**

Reading for Content Understanding

1. **Main Idea** Why did workers across the country go on strike in 1919?
2. **Main Idea** What began the Red Scare, and how did it affect Americans?
3. **Economic Development** What economic problems arose during demobilization, and why did these problems occur?
4. **Writing** *Creating* Make a pamphlet protesting either the guilty verdict in the Sacco and Vanzetti case or the race riots in Chicago in 1919. Be sure to include arguments to persuade others to join your protest.
5. **Critical Thinking** *Synthesizing Information* How might the economic troubles experienced during demobilization have affected race relations in northern cities?

Section 1 Review ANSWERS

Identify

For significance, see the following pages:

- demobilization, p. 356
- Red Scare, p. 359
- anarchists, p. 359
- A. Mitchell Palmer, p. 360
- Palmer raids, p. 360
- xenophobia, p. 360
- Nicola Sacco and Bartolomeo Vanzetti, p. 360
- American Civil Liberties Union, p. 360

Reading for Content Understanding

1. Postwar demobilization led to a rise in the cost of living and increased unemployment, thus leading workers to strike.

2. The Red Scare began when the strikes and riots of 1919 led many people to believe that communism and other radical political ideas were spreading to the United States. The Red Scare increased xenophobia and threatened civil liberties.

3. Businesses had to lay off workers, the cost of living increased, and prices rose more than wages; these problems occurred because veterans returned to work, many women and others lost their jobs, and businesses lost wartime government contracts.

4. Pamphlets will vary but each should include one or more examples supporting the student's opinion.

5. Rising unemployment may have led to competition between black and white workers for the same jobs, thus straining race relations.

SECTION 2 LESSON PLAN

OBJECTIVES

- **Analyze ways in which Presidents Harding and Coolidge strengthened the U.S. economy.**
- **Discuss scandals that plagued President Harding and the Republicans.**
- **Describe the goals of U.S. foreign policy during the 1920s.**

FOCUS

Motivate Before Reading

Organize the class into two groups—one to focus on foreign policy and the other on economics. Ask each group to make a list of Americans' attitudes today toward the issue they have been assigned. Discuss the lists with the class and then explain to students that in this section they will learn how Republican leaders of the 1920s helped to define American attitudes of the period toward the economy and foreign policy.

Section 2
RESOURCES

PRINT
- ★ Guided Reading Strategies 12.2
- ★ American History Political Cartoon 21: Political Corruption in the 1920s
- ★ Biography Reading 12: Eugene Debs
- ★ Geography Activity 12: The Republican Decade
- ★ Section 2 Review, p. 366
- ★ Daily Quiz 12.2

MULTIMEDIA
- ★ *Teaching Resources CD–ROM*, Lesson 12.2
- ★ HRW Web site

SHELTERED ENGLISH
- ★ Main Idea Activities for Reteaching and Sheltered English 12.2

SECTION 2

Republicans in Power

Reading Focus

How did the Harding and Coolidge administrations address economic issues?

What scandals plagued President Harding and the Republicans?

What was U.S. foreign policy during the 1920s?

Key Terms

Ohio Gang
Teapot Dome scandal
disarmament
Washington Conference
Five-Power Naval Treaty
Kellogg-Briand Pact

FOR THE PRESIDENTIAL ELECTION OF 1920, Republican candidate Warren G. Harding chose to campaign from his home in Marion, Ohio. In May, however, Harding traveled to Boston and gave a speech before a large crowd of supporters. He declared that "America's present need is not heroics but healing; not nostrums [fake remedies] but normalcy." When reporters asked him what he meant by normalcy, Harding replied, "I mean normal procedures, the natural way, without excess." Many Americans were troubled by the postwar problems. Harding's simple words promised a return to better times.

Harding campaign button

The Election of 1920

The Republicans were confident that they could win the presidency in 1920. Some Americans were angry with Democratic leaders for bringing the United States into World War I. Many people also blamed the Democratic Party for the economic troubles that followed the war. Republican leaders tried to appeal to voters by running a simple campaign that promised a return to prosperity.

The Republican Party nominated Ohio senator Warren G. Harding for president and Massachusetts governor Calvin Coolidge for vice president. Harding was chosen more for his charming and friendly nature than for his political talents. Coolidge had impressed voters by ending the Boston police strike. Together they campaigned on a pro-business platform. Harding also supported immigration restrictions and aid to farmers.

Republican leaders were careful to keep Harding, who was often not well informed on

Introduce Key Terms

Linguistic, Logical-Mathematical, Interpersonal. Review this section's key terms with students. Pair students and have one member of each pair select two terms that are in some way linked. Have the other member of each pair explain what the terms have in common. Ask students to take turns repeating this process until each term has been related to another. As a challenge, you may want to have students create links between three or more terms. **SHELTERED ENGLISH**

TEACH

Have students read Section 2 and complete Guided Reading Strategies 12.2. Choose one or more of the following activities to explore the section content with students. For further suggestions on block scheduling or team teaching, see the *Block Scheduling Handbook*.

LEVEL 1: Linguistic. (Suggested time: 15 min.) As a class, go over students' Guided Reading Strategies. Then use the Reading Focus questions to highlight the main ideas of the section. **SHELTERED ENGLISH**

issues, from making many public appearances. One politician told campaign organizers:

> **"Keep Warren at home. Don't let him make any speeches. If he goes out on a tour somebody's sure to ask him questions, and Warren's just the sort of . . . fool that will try to answer them."**

While Harding remained at his Ohio home during most of the campaign, his Democratic challengers traveled across the country. The Democrats chose Ohio governor James M. Cox to run for president and Assistant Secretary of the Navy Franklin D. Roosevelt to run for vice president. Both candidates tried to avoid domestic issues and emphasize foreign policy. They also supported the League of Nations.

Unfortunately for the Democrats, Americans cared little about the League. Most people wanted to avoid further involvement in European affairs. On election day, Harding took about 60 percent of the popular vote. A Democratic adviser declared, "It wasn't a landslide; it was an earthquake." A sizable number of voters were dissatisfied with both major parties, however. Socialist Party candidate Eugene V. Debs received some 900,000 votes despite still being in prison for his opposition to World War I.

Harding's Administration

Although he was popular with voters, President Harding was not a particularly gifted leader. He once told a journalist that he was often overwhelmed by the responsibilities of the presidency. Harding's main strengths were his party loyalty and ability to make political allies. Harding quickly assembled a talented cabinet. He appointed Charles Evans Hughes as secretary of state and Herbert Hoover as secretary of commerce. Hughes was a former governor of New York and associate justice of the Supreme Court. Hoover, a wealthy mining engineer, had been very successful in organizing wartime relief for millions of Belgians.

From the start, the Harding administration focused on strengthening the U.S. economy.

President Harding included several important business leaders in his cabinet.

Harding believed that government should promote the growth of business but otherwise leave the economy alone. He soon faced a tough decision over whether to raise or lower taxes. He admitted, "I can't make a . . . thing out of this tax problem. I listen to one side and they seem right, and then . . . I talk to the other side, and they seem just as right." To solve the dilemma, Harding turned to Secretary of the Treasury Andrew Mellon, a successful banker and business investor. He was also one of America's richest men.

Mellon declared, "The government is just a business and can and should be run on business principles." He proposed numerous tax cuts, many of which benefited businesses and wealthy Americans. Congress passed several of these tax cuts.

Mellon's critics questioned whether his tax cuts truly benefited most citizens. However, the public was generally pleased as business boomed and the post–World War I recession ended. The United States soon entered a period of rapid economic growth. Both unemployment and prices declined.

Political Scandals

Not all of President Harding's appointments were wise, however. He made a habit of choosing old friends to fill government posts, regardless of their qualifications. One group of officials in Harding's administration was known as the **Ohio Gang** because they had all been acquaintances of Harding in Ohio. Even Harding eventually recognized that

Presidential Profiles

Warren G. Harding. A friendly, popular man, Warren Harding won the presidency in 1920 largely because he had no enemies. His speeches—in a style he called "bloviating"—tended to be long-winded and full of clichés. One aide, aware of this tendency, advised Harding to give no speeches on the campaign trail.

Activity: Have students use the library or search the Internet through the HRW Web site to research Harding and write an encyclopedia entry for him.

go.hrw.com
SB1 Harding

Biography

Eugene V. Debs. Presidential candidate Eugene V. Debs had run for election many times on the socialist ticket before he ran in 1920. During the 1920 campaign, Debs gained the support of some Americans because of his willingness to go to jail for his beliefs. He ran on the slogan "From Prison to the White House" and included his convict number in his campaign advertisements.

Critical Thinking: Why would Debs include his convict number?

ANSWER: The number emphasized his imprisonment, which showed he was willing to go to jail for his beliefs.

ALL LEVELS: Logical-Mathematical, Visual-Spatial. (Suggested time: 45 min.) Ask students to imagine that they are members of Calvin Coolidge's campaign staff. They have been asked to create a poster to encourage people to vote for Coolidge. Tell students that they will need to address the scandals of the Harding administration while calling attention to Coolidge's talents and platform and the leadership of previous Republicans. Once students have finished, call on volunteers to explain their posters to the class. Have students vote on their favorite poster. **SHELTERED ENGLISH**

LEVEL 2: Linguistic, Logical-Mathematical, Visual-Spatial. (Suggested time: 20 min. plus homework) Discuss the strengths and weaknesses of the economic policies under Presidents Harding and Coolidge. Have each student create a political cartoon that either supports or challenges the two presidents' hands-off approaches to the economy. Encourage volunteers to explain their cartoons to the class.

LEVEL 3: Logical-Mathematical, Interpersonal. (Suggested time: 30 min.) Organize the class into a mock U.S. Senate session. Tell students that President Coolidge has submitted the Kellogg-Briand Pact to the Senate for approval. Have students debate the wisdom of ratifying the agreement. Encourage

Using Visual Resources

Teapot Dome. The political cartoon on this page uses symbolism to depict the public's outrage at the Teapot Dome scandal. The cartoon combines a teapot and an oil drum to resemble an advancing tank. Smoke billows out of the teapot's spout (the tank's gun). The tank with its smoking gun symbolizes the outraged public. In front of the tank, corrupt officials flee to the White House for protection.

Activity: Have students create their own political cartoons depicting the Teapot Dome scandal. Have volunteers explain their cartoons to the class.

The Teapot Dome scandal was a major threat to Harding's presidency.

most of these individuals were poorly qualified for their positions. He once declared to a reporter:

> **"I have no trouble with my enemies. I can take care of my enemies all right. But my . . . friends . . . [are] the ones that keep me walking the floor nights."**

Harding had reason to worry. For example, an investigation into the management of the Veterans Bureau discovered that its chief, Charles Forbes, had taken bribes. Forbes was fined $10,000 and sentenced to two years in prison.

The biggest scandal of the Harding administration involved Secretary of the Interior Albert Fall. Fall's heavy personal spending triggered a Senate investigation. This investigation revealed that Fall had transferred control of two naval oil reserves to his department. One of the reserves was at Teapot Dome, Wyoming. He then illegally leased the reserves to two oil companies. In return, he received cash and thousands of dollars in gifts and personal "loans." When caught, Fall claimed that he was acting in the nation's best interest. However, the **Teapot Dome scandal** led to his conviction for taking bribes. He was sentenced to a year in jail and fined $100,000.

Eventually, six members of Harding's administration resigned as a result of corruption charges. Harding never had to face these scandals publicly. On August 2, 1923, he died suddenly while on a western speaking tour. The scandals came to light shortly after his death. He was not directly involved in any of the corrupt activities. However, the trouble that his "friends" caused greatly damaged Harding's reputation.

Coolidge in Office

The scandals also hurt the reputation of the Republican Party. Vice President Calvin Coolidge, however, was not involved in the corruption. After he was sworn in as president, Coolidge fired those who were involved.

Coolidge was born on a Vermont farm and attended a one-room schoolhouse. To many people he symbolized old-fashioned values. Coolidge was a quiet man who once told a colleague, "If you don't say anything, you won't be called on to repeat it." His no-nonsense attitude comforted many Americans. His reputation for honesty helped the Republicans recover from the scandals.

Coolidge easily won the Republican presidential nomination in 1924. He ran on an even stronger pro-business platform than Harding had, stating that "the man who builds a factory builds a temple." Coolidge's conservative policies upset some progressive Republicans. They broke away to nominate Senator Robert La Follette of Wisconsin as the Progressive Party candidate. The Democrats were deeply divided between urban and rural interests. They finally nominated little-known lawyer John W. Davis.

Coolidge won a landslide victory in November 1924, receiving nearly 16 million votes. Davis received more than 8 million, while La Follette finished with nearly 5 million votes. The key to Coolidge's victory was his promise of continued economic prosperity. He retained several key members of Harding's cabinet to help plan his economic policies, which favored low taxes, low interest rates

Calvin Coolidge was often called Silent Cal by reporters.

them to focus on whether the pact continues the goals of U.S. foreign policy during the 1920s. Conclude by having students vote on whether to ratify or reject the pact.

CLOSE

Linguistic, Logical-Mathematical. Have students discuss reasons the economy needed strengthening after World War I. Then have them write newspaper headlines for a series of articles that describe how Presidents Harding and Coolidge attempted to strengthen the economy. After students have finished, call on volunteers to read their headlines to the class.

CHALLENGE AND EXTEND

Linguistic, Kinesthetic, Interpersonal. Have students research Albert Fall's participation in the Teapot Dome scandal. Have some students prepare charges against Fall, and ask other students to prepare his defense. Encourage students to consider several possible options for their defense or prosecution and try to anticipate the other side's strategies. Have each group select its best solution and use it in a mock trial.

on loans, and little economic regulation. He further reduced government spending and gave Treasury Secretary Mellon the freedom to propose more tax cuts. Tariffs were raised to increase the price of foreign goods and prevent them from competing with domestic goods.

Although these measures tended to benefit primarily those with higher incomes, the national economy steadily improved during Coolidge's administration. Coolidge firmly believed that the best government was one that rarely interfered in daily life. He once advised, "Never go out to meet trouble." For four years he kept government activity to a minimum. With a booming economy, he received few complaints from the public.

Coolidge was a pro-business presidential candidate.

Foreign Policy

During the 1920s the Republicans faced a difficult challenge in foreign policy. As a leading world power, the United States needed to protect its foreign interests. Many Americans, however, supported isolationism—the policy of avoiding involvement in other nations' affairs.

The Washington Conference

Republican leaders compromised by concentrating on foreign-policy issues that promoted economic growth and peace. Even most isolationists could accept these goals. Diplomats hoped that new treaties would prevent another world war and would strengthen the global economy. A healthy world economy would help the United States. During World War I, European allies had borrowed billions of dollars from the United States. To repay their loans, these countries needed peaceful conditions that would allow their economies to recover.

Many world leaders believed that the key to peace was **disarmament**—limiting or reducing military weapons. In November 1921 the United States invited other major nations to the **Washington Conference** to discuss naval disarmament and Asian affairs. During his opening speech, Secretary of State Charles Evans Hughes surprised the assembled foreign delegates. He challenged them to join the United States in destroying a total of 2 million tons of naval ships. Hughes also called for limits on the total naval strength of the major world powers. A journalist reported that the delegates reacted with a "mad chorus of approval."

The Washington Conference led to the **Five-Power Naval Treaty**. In addition to calling for reductions in naval strength, this treaty limited the maximum size of each nation's navy. The treaty allowed the United States and Great Britain to have the two largest navies, each of equal size and strength. Japan was allowed a navy three fifths that size. France and Italy were assigned navies roughly half the size of Japan's.

The conference also produced two treaties addressing Asian affairs. In the Four-Power Treaty, France, Great Britain, Japan, and the United States agreed to respect each other's rights in the Pacific. The Nine-Power Treaty pledged support for the Open Door policy. It also promised to respect "the independence, and the territorial and administrative integrity [organization] of China."

The Granger Collection, New York

After World War I some Americans called for an end to war and the destruction it caused.

Across the Curriculum

LANGUAGE ARTS

The Language of Politics. The creative use of the English language is a recurring theme in American politics. One example is the term *landslide*, which first came into use in politics in the 1800s. In nature, a landslide refers to a large amount of rocks and soil that suddenly tumble down a hill. In politics, however, the term is a metaphor for winning an election by a large number of votes. The term *landslide* is just one of many political metaphors. For example, the terms *avalanche* and *tidal wave* also are metaphors for winning an election by a large number of votes.

Activity: Have students use the library and other resources to find articles dealing with previous local, state, and national elections. Ask students to read the articles and identify, list, and define any other political metaphors they find.

REVIEW

Linguistic, Logical-Mathematical, Interpersonal. Have students complete the Section Review questions. Then have students use the words and names included in the Identify portion of the Section Review to write a narrative describing the 1920s. Ask students to include information on the economic policies, foreign-policy goals, and scandals of Presidents Harding and Coolidge. Allow students time to write their narratives during class or assign them as homework. Then organize the class into pairs and have students read their partners' work. Finally, encourage each pair to discuss the narratives.

ASSESS

Have students complete Daily Quiz 12.2.

RETEACH

Logical-Mathematical, Visual-Spatial. Have students complete Main Idea Activities for Reteaching and Sheltered English 12.2. Then list President Harding's and President Coolidge's major domestic and foreign policies on the chalkboard. Have each student create a Venn diagram for Harding and Coolidge that shows where their policies overlapped. **SHELTERED ENGLISH**

Section 2 Review ANSWERS

Identify

For significance, see the following pages:

- Warren G. Harding, p. 362
- Ohio Gang, p. 363
- Charles Forbes, p. 364
- Albert Fall, p. 364
- Teapot Dome scandal, p. 364
- Calvin Coolidge, p. 364
- disarmament, p. 365
- Washington Conference, p. 365
- Five-Power Naval Treaty, p. 365
- Kellogg-Briand Pact, p. 366
- Herbert Hoover, p. 366

Reading for Content Understanding

1. Both attempted to promote business but otherwise leave the economy alone.

2. pursued isolationism while promoting global peace, disarmament, and respect for nations' rights in China and the Pacific by signing treaties such as the Five-Power Naval Treaty and the Kellogg-Briand Pact

3. During the 1920 election, many Americans blamed the Democrats for the war and for the postwar economic troubles. During the 1928 election, the Republicans already controlled the presidency and the country was enjoying economic prosperity.

4. Articles will vary but should mention Charles Forbes, Albert Fall, and the Teapot Dome scandal.

5. Answers will vary but may mention that it was impossible for nations that signed the treaties to ensure that no nations broke the agreements they had made.

The Kellogg-Briand Pact

Diplomats took additional steps toward achieving world peace. France's foreign minister, Aristide Briand, and U.S. Secretary of State Frank Kellogg led efforts to create an agreement to end war. In August 1928 the United States and 14 other nations signed the **Kellogg-Briand Pact**. This pact tried to outlaw warfare. Eventually, most of the countries of the world signed the agreement.

There was no agreement on how to enforce the treaty, however. One U.S. senator remarked that the pact would be "as effective to keep down war as a carpet would be to smother an earthquake." Like the treaties signed at the Washington Conference, the Kellogg-Briand Pact was well intentioned but could not guarantee an end to military aggression. For American isolationists, this was a risk they were willing to take to avoid involvement in future foreign conflicts.

WHY WE SHOULD VOTE FOR HERBERT HOOVER TOLD IN TALKING MOTION PICTURES

Herbert Hoover used new technologies such as radio and film in his presidential campaign. This truck showed a Hoover campaign film to voters.

The Election of 1928

Foreign policy played only a small role in the 1928 presidential election. Each candidate concentrated on domestic issues, which interested the public more than international issues did. The Democratic candidate was Alfred E. Smith, the governor of New York. Smith represented urban interests. This concerned many rural Americans who distrusted big-city politicians. A large number of Protestants also opposed Smith because he was Catholic.

Calvin Coolidge decided not to run for re-election in 1928. Republicans nominated Secretary of Commerce Herbert Hoover. In contrast to Smith, Hoover seemed to represent traditional values. Hoover and the Republicans also benefited from the nation's economic prosperity.

Hoover's campaign platform consisted largely of promises of continued economic good times. His slogan "A Chicken for Every Pot and a Car in Every Garage" helped carry him to an easy victory. Hoover received more than 21 million votes to Smith's 15 million. Voters in the nation's 12 largest cities, however, supported Smith. The election results demonstrated the growing political differences between urban and rural America.

SECTION 2 REVIEW

Identify and explain the significance of the following:

- **Warren G. Harding**
- **Ohio Gang**
- **Charles Forbes**
- **Albert Fall**
- **Teapot Dome scandal**
- **Calvin Coolidge**
- **disarmament**
- **Washington Conference**
- **Five-Power Naval Treaty**
- **Kellogg-Briand Pact**
- **Herbert Hoover**

Reading for Content Understanding

1. **Main Idea** How did Presidents Harding and Coolidge attempt to strengthen the U.S. economy?
2. **Main Idea** What foreign policy did the leaders of the United States pursue during the 1920s?
3. **Citizenship and Democracy** Why did the Republicans have the advantage in the 1920 and 1928 elections?
4. **Writing** *Describing* Write a brief magazine article that details the scandals of the Harding administration.
5. **Critical Thinking** *Drawing Conclusions* Why do you think the international treaties of the 1920s were difficult to enforce?

OBJECTIVES

- **Analyze the effects of the assembly line on manufacturing.**
- **Describe how the automobile affected the economy and people's everyday lives.**
- **Describe how advertising and the installment plan changed people's buying habits.**

FOCUS

Motivate Before Reading

Ask students to write a few sentences on how their lives might change when they are old enough to drive an automobile. After students finish writing, call on volunteers to read their sentences to the class. Then ask students to come up with examples of routine activities that would not happen if the automobile had not been invented. *(Answers will vary but students might point out that*

"The Business of America Is Business"

Reading Focus

How did the assembly line affect manufacturing?

What effect did the automobile have on the economy and people's everyday lives?

How did advertising and the installment plan change people's buying habits?

Key Terms

Model T

assembly line

installment plan

THE MANUFACTURER'S CHALLENGE CUP, one of the first major automobile races, was held on October 25, 1902. One entry—Henry Ford's car—stood out from the rest. An observer said the car was "low, rakish [streamlined], and makes more noise than a freight train." Ford's 70-horsepower 999 was so fast that he feared for his driver's safety. However, the car turned out to be both fast and safe. The 999 led the race from the start and won by a large margin, covering five miles in five minutes and 20 seconds. The victory brought fame to Ford, who continued to experiment with car design.

Ford's 999 race car

The Model T

Henry Ford founded the Ford Motor Company in 1903. He wanted to create a vehicle "so low in price that no man making a good salary will be unable to buy one." Ford explained the basic principles of the car he wanted to build:

> **"It will be large enough for the family but small enough for the individual to run and care for. It will be constructed of the best materials, by the best men to be hired, after the simplest design that modern engineering can devise."**

After eight different models, Ford achieved his goal in 1908 with the **Model T**. Affectionately nicknamed the Tin Lizzie by the public, the Model T was easy to repair and maintain. It was not fancy or flashy. Ford had decided to produce the car only in black. It was, however, durable and reliable. It could be driven on any surface. This ability was

Section 3 RESOURCES

PRINT

- ★ Guided Reading Strategies 12.3
- ★ Section 3 Review, p. 372
- ★ Daily Quiz 12.3

MULTIMEDIA

- ★ *Teaching Resources CD–ROM*, Lesson 12.3
- ★ Art in American History Transparency 23: *Boomtown*
- ★ *Exploring America's Past* Video Segment: Advertising USA; *Teacher's Guide*, pp. 24–25

SHELTERED ENGLISH

- ★ Main Idea Activities for Reteaching and Sheltered English 12.3

they would not be able to take the bus to school or drive across country on vacation.) Tell students that in this section they will learn about the introduction of the Model T and other products and innovations that changed people's lives during the 1920s.

Introduce Key Terms

Linguistic. Review this section's key terms with students. Have students scan the section to locate the terms and use context cues to determine each term's meaning. Call on volunteers to share their definitions with the class. **SHELTERED ENGLISH**

TEACH

Have students read Section 3 and complete Guided Reading Strategies 12.3. Choose one or more of the following activities to explore the section content with students. For further suggestions on block scheduling or team teaching, see the *Block Scheduling Handbook.*

LEVEL 1: Linguistic. (Suggested time: 15 min.) As a class, go over students' Guided Reading Strategies. Then use the Reading Focus questions to highlight the main ideas of the section. **SHELTERED ENGLISH**

Biography

Henry Ford. Despite his wealth, Henry Ford was viewed as a man of the people. His simple, common-sense approach to problems impressed many Americans. They also loved his eccentricities. Throughout his life he was known to challenge children to footraces, jump onto tables, and enter his office through a window.

Critical Thinking: Why might Henry Ford's personality have attracted much public attention in the 1920s?

ANSWER: He was a wealthy and successful businessman. In addition, he seemed to embody common sense and a childlike sense of fun at a time when some people felt the world was growing more complex and unsettled.

Biography

Henry Ford

Henry Ford was born in 1863 on a farm near Dearborn, Michigan. From an early age he loved working with machines. "My toys were all tools," he later recalled, adding, "they still are." When he was a teenager, Ford left the family farm for Detroit and worked in a machine shop. He eventually became an engineer for the Edison Illuminating Company. In his free time he worked on designing and building a gasoline-powered automobile.

From the Collections of The Henry Ford Museum and Greenfield Village

Ford's success with the Model T made him wealthy and powerful. He even ran for the U.S. Senate in 1918, losing in a close race. Ford remained old-fashioned. In later years he often complained that the country was losing its traditional values. To encourage Americans to respect their past, he built Greenfield Village in Dearborn, Michigan. This historical town contains the original homes of famous Americans such as Orville and Wilbur Wright.

important because most roads in the 1920s were unpaved and filled with potholes and ruts.

Perhaps most importantly, the Model T was fairly inexpensive compared to previous automobiles. The low cost allowed many Americans to buy the Model T as their first car. As Ford and his engineers improved their manufacturing methods, prices dropped even lower. The cost of a Model T dropped from around $950 in 1909 to about $350 in 1920. By 1921 Ford controlled some 55 percent of the U.S. automobile market. He was selling more than 1 million cars annually.

The Model T, also called the Tin Lizzie

The Granger Collection, New York

Ford's Methods

To manufacture so many cars so cheaply, Henry Ford and his engineers developed a new assembly process. In the past, teams of workers built each car one at a time from start to finish. Ford's factories used a new, faster method.

The Assembly Line

This method was the moving **assembly line**. This system of chains, slides, and conveyor belts moved parts from one worker to another. Each car began on the assembly line as a simple chassis, or frame, with no parts attached. As it moved down the line, the chassis stopped at stations. At each stop one type of part, such as doors or seats, was quickly installed. When it reached the end of the line, the car was complete.

The assembly line controlled the pace of all the work in the factory. The key to the assembly line was that each worker performed only one simple task over and over again. Ford's engineers also introduced special machines to help workers perform their tasks more efficiently. In this way they divided the manufacturing process into many small steps. This approach was influenced by the

ALL LEVELS: Kinesthetic, Visual-Spatial. (Suggested time: 45 min.) Provide students with art supplies and copies of old magazines. Ask them to create collages that highlight the changes in U.S. industry and American consumer culture that are discussed in this section. Encourage students to focus on the introduction of the Model T, the moving assembly line, new advertising techniques, and Fordism. After students have finished, call on volunteers to explain their collages to the class. Finally, lead a discussion on the changes that occurred in U.S. industry and American consumer culture. **SHELTERED ENGLISH**

LEVEL 2: Linguistic, Logical-Mathematical. (Suggested time: 30 min. plus homework) Ask students to imagine that it is the 1920s and they are reviewing Henry Ford's Model T for a popular general magazine. Have each student write a review that emphasizes the bargain and opportunities the Model T provides Americans. Encourage students to include information on the new businesses that have begun appearing along roadsides throughout the United States. Call on volunteers to read their reviews to the class. Finally, lead a discussion on how the growth of the automobile industry affected American society during the 1920s.

theories of researcher Frederick W. Taylor. Taylor had described his ideas in the book *The Principles of Scientific Management.*

The benefits to production were tremendous. After the assembly line was introduced, the time needed to build a Model T fell from more than 12 hours to less than 2 hours. The assembly line also lowered manufacturing costs. In Michigan, Ford built several huge assembly lines at the River Rouge complex, the largest factory in America. This plant mass-produced hundreds of thousands of cars a year.

Assembly-line work was dull and tiring. Workers had to keep up with the line's speed at all times. The wife of one worker wrote to Ford, "The chain system [assembly line] you have is a *slave driver!*" Another worker explained why assembly-line work could be so tiring:

> **"The weight of a tack . . . is insignificant, but if you have to drive eight tacks in every Ford cushion that goes by your station within a certain time, and you know that if you fail to do it you are going to tie up the entire platform, and you continue to do this for four years, you are going to break under the strain."**

This stress caused assembly-line workers to quit on a regular basis.

Fordism

Constantly replacing these workers and training the new employees cost Ford's company a great deal of money. Unhappy autoworkers were also easy for unions to recruit. This troubled Ford, who was strongly antiunion.

To keep his workers from quitting their jobs or joining unions, Ford tried to create a better working environment. He offered an eight-hour workday and wages of up to $5 per day, a high amount for the time. Workers were encouraged to suggest ways to improve productivity. Ford also employed African Americans at a time when most auto plants hired only white workers. In addition, the company employed more than 9,000 people with disabilities. Visually impaired workers, for example, sorted parts.

Along with higher wages and other benefits, however, Ford placed strict requirements on his employees. Workers who drank alcohol, smoked tobacco, or joined unions could be fired. Ford also required immigrant employees to attend "Americanization" classes. Such classes taught civics and English to immigrant workers. These programs had been common in the early 1900s, and Ford continued them at his plants.

In the 1920s many people used the term "Fordism" to describe the assembly-line mass production of goods. Although not all owners agreed with Ford's higher salaries or his work policies, many companies began to imitate Fordism.

Mexican artist Diego Rivera painted this mural of a Ford assembly line in the 1930s.

Across the Curriculum

MATH

The Model T. In 1909–10 Ford Motor Company produced some 18,650 Model T automobiles. Ford doubled this production every year until the outbreak of World War I. As production rose, the price of the Model T fell.

Model T Prices

Year	Price
1910	$950
1912	$690
1914	$550
1916	$440
1918	$450
1920	$350

Activity: Have students prepare a bar graph showing the price changes for a Model T from 1910 to 1920. Then have students identify some reasons for the price fluctuations shown.

LEVEL 3: Linguistic, Kinesthetic. (Suggested time: 45 min. plus presentation) Ask students to imagine that they own a consulting firm in the 1920s. They have been asked to help raise funds for a new company that makes its product on an assembly line and offers consumers the option of buying the product on the installment plan. Have each student create a short presentation that will convince people to invest in the new company. Ask students to focus their presentations on the way that the assembly line is revolutionizing manufacturing and on how new advertising techniques and installment plans are changing consumer buying habits. After students have made their presentations, have them discuss the effects of these developments on consumer spending.

LEVEL 3: Logical-Mathematical, Visual-Spatial, Interpersonal. (Suggested time: 45 min.) Tell students that the class has the opportunity to host a pancake breakfast to raise money for a special field trip. Then organize the class into small groups. Have each group review material from this section (or from Chapter 6) on Frederick W. Taylor's ideas of scientific management. Then ask each group to use Taylor's principles to devise a plan for running the pancake breakfast. Allow groups about 20 to 25 minutes to devise their plans. Then have a representative from each group present its plan to the class. Finally, have students vote to determine which group's plan best utilizes the principles of scientific management.

Economic Development

Spindletop and the Oil Boom. In 1899 geologists and a group of investors began drilling for oil on Spindletop Hill near Beaumont, Texas. After nearly two years with no luck, they finally hit pay dirt. In January 1901 the well started bubbling. As workers fled, six tons of drilling pipe shot out of the hole. Things quieted down for a few minutes and then natural gas, followed by oil, began gushing out. The well blew oil more than 100 feet into the air. Nine days later, workers finally brought the well under control. The discovery of the Spindletop field led to the Texas oil boom and helped provide fuel for much of the nation's industrial growth.

Critical Thinking: What effect do you think the oil boom had on Texas?

ANSWER: Answers will vary but students might mention that it may have led to population growth, urbanization, and a stronger economy.

Multimedia Resources

Art in American History Transparency 23: *Boomtown*

 The Car Craze

Mass production transformed the U.S. auto industry. Instead of producing a few expensive luxury vehicles for the rich, mass production supplied inexpensive transportation to the public.

In 1929 nearly 5 million automobiles were manufactured in the United States. Automakers employed some 375,000 workers. Millions more workers held jobs that supported automobile manufacturing. For example, the automobile industry used large quantities of glass, paints, rubber, and steel. Oil and gas consumption in the United States also doubled from 1920 to 1929.

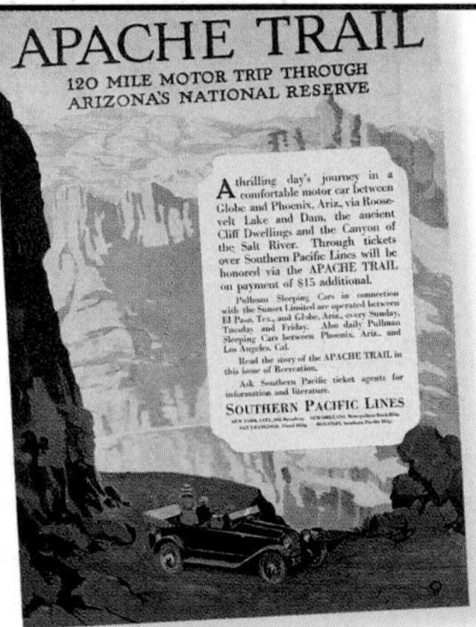

An advertisement for a driving vacation

Cars changed the landscape of America. New communites sprang up along country roads. Auto-industry towns boomed. For example, the population of Detroit, Michigan, jumped from around 285,000 in 1900 to about 1.5 million in 1930. The widespread use of trucks to ship goods was also important. Factories moved to the outskirts of cities, where real estate was cheaper. Most factories had previously been located in downtown areas that had access to central water and rail connections. The convenience of owning a car also allowed more people to move from city centers to suburbs. For the first time, millions of people commuted to work by car. As more people moved to the suburbs, construction companies built new communities.

Although there were many cars, there were few good roads. Soon federal and state governments were pouring millions of dollars into the construction of bridges, tunnels, and highways. By 1925 more than $200 million a year was being spent on roads. As traffic problems increased, automobile accidents multiplied. Some mechanics started body shops to repair the damage. As the number of accidents increased, drivers also needed insurance. The insurance industry expanded to meet this need.

Families began taking driving vacations. Responding to a survey, one woman declared, "I never feel as close to my family as when we are all together in the car." "Motor hotels," also known as motels, appeared throughout the country. Americans created auto clubs and magazines to encourage leisure travel. *Motor Car* magazine explained the joys of a driving vacation:

> **"You are your master, the road is ahead; you eat as you please . . . , sleeping when you will . . . , waking with the dawn. . . . Time and space at your beck and call; your freedom is complete."**

The increase in traffic led to the development of new roadside businesses. Service stations provided fuel for the millions of cars on the roads. Roadside restaurants fed hungry drivers and passengers. To catch the eyes of passing motorists, advertisers constructed billboards along highways across the nation. The automobile had transformed the economy and society of the United States.

 Business Booms

Many other industries also experienced economic growth in the 1920s. Electric utilities brightened

Electricity and new appliances made cooking and cleaning easier in the most modern homes of the 1920s.

The Granger Collection, New York

CLOSE

Linguistic, Logical-Mathematical. Assign each student one of the following topics: the automobile industry, advertising, the assembly line, or business growth. Then have each student write an encyclopedia entry on the assigned topic's effects on the United States in the 1920s. When students have finished writing, call on volunteers to read their entries to the class.

CHALLENGE AND EXTEND

1. **Logical-Mathematical, Visual-Spatial.** Have students use the library and other resources to research cars, other than Model Ts, that were available during the 1920s. Have each student create a model or illustration of one 1920s car and show how it differed from the Model T. Ask students also to provide a brief history about the car and its manufacturer. Encourage volunteers to share their projects with the class.
2. **Linguistic, Visual-Spatial.** Explain to students that even though the concept is still relatively the same, advertising has changed over the years. Have students use the library and other resources to find information on changes in the ways companies advertise. Have each student write a short summary of the changes that have taken place. The following are some topics that students may wish to include: celebrity

homes and streets. Telephone companies made instant communication possible. By the 1920s most homes in cities and suburbs had electricity. This led to the growing use of electrical household conveniences. People used small electrical appliances to iron their clothes, make their morning toast, or play their musical recordings.

Electricity also powered growing factories. The quantity of goods manufactured nearly doubled between 1921 and 1929. This growth was largely because of an increased production of durable consumer goods. These are large, long-lasting home appliances such as washing machines and refrigerators.

Food-processing plants produced large quantities of canned goods and packaged food products. Such foods were more convenient to prepare. Many goods were now sold on a national basis instead of only in smaller local markets. Trucks shipped these goods affordably across the country.

Chains of grocery and retail stores opened or expanded in the 1920s. They brought wider varieties of products to small towns at lower prices. Grocery stores such as A&P and Piggly Wiggly sold food at cheaper prices than many local stores. They did this by stocking and selling items in large quantities. Catalog retailers such as Sears, Roebuck, & Co. and F. W. Woolworth also began opening department stores across the country. These chains offered consumers a wide range of goods such as appliances, clothing, and home furnishings.

This growth in products and stores contributed to the rise of a consumer society. In a consumer society, people are continually encouraged to buy products to improve their lives and help the economy.

To make it easier to purchase goods, more companies offered the **installment plan**. This program allowed customers to buy goods by making a small initial down payment followed by additional monthly payments with interest. This increased the total cost of the item purchased, but the plan was convenient and popular. In the past many people delayed purchases until they had enough cash. These people were able to buy goods more quickly using the installment plan. During the 1920s, some 60 percent of all cars and furniture were purchased on credit.

A Consumer Culture

Households with Electricity

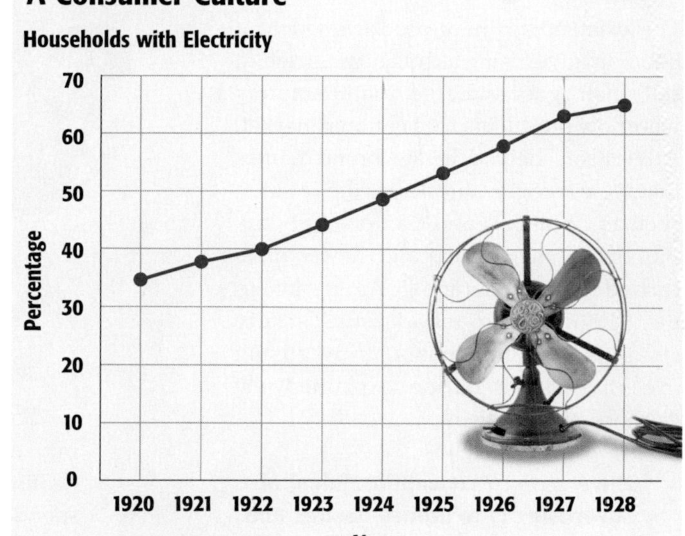

Automobile Sales

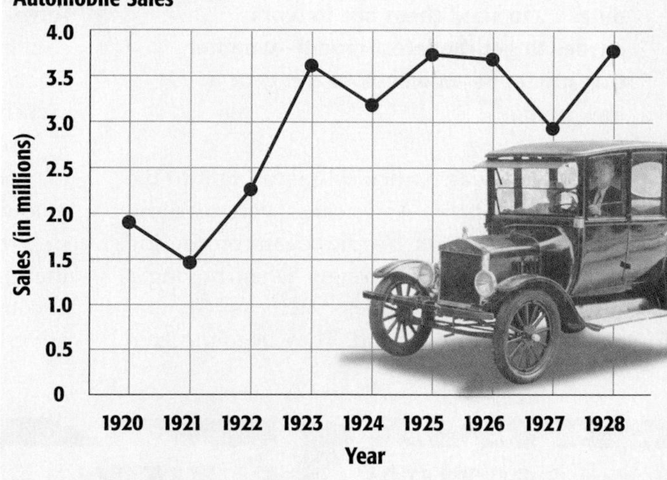

Source: *Historical Statistics of the United States*

The Granger Collection, New York

A Better Life During the 1920s the number of households with electricity increased, as did automobile sales. During what year were automobile sales the highest?

Daily Life

Advertising. During the 1920s advertising grew immensely. In 1919 total revenues for advertising companies were around $1.4 billion. By 1929 the total had soared to almost $3 billion. National brands increased their advertising by even greater percentages. One national brand-name producer of coffee spent less than $20,000 on magazine advertising in 1921. By 1927 this producer was spending more than $500,000. Nevertheless, in the early 1930s, studies revealed that only 37 percent of Americans believed the claims made in advertisements.

Critical Thinking: Why might people doubt the claims made in advertisements?

ANSWER: The claims made may have been too exaggerated.

CHART ANSWER
1928

Multimedia Resources

Exploring America's Past Video Segment: Advertising USA; *Teacher's Guide*, pp. 24–25

Search 9611, Play to 13343
Videodisc Blue Side A

Play

Pause

See *Teacher's Guide* for Spanish barcode.

endorsements, television commercials, subliminal advertising, Internet advertising, sponsoring of athletic events and stadiums, and promotional contests.

REVIEW

Linguistic, Musical-Rhythmic. Have students complete the Section Review questions. Then have each student create several radio jingles that capture the economic climate of the 1920s. Some possible topics include the growth of the automobile industry and the use of the assembly line and installment plans.

ASSESS

Have students complete Daily Quiz 12.3.

RETEACH

Visual-Spatial. Have students complete Main Idea Activities for Reteaching and Sheltered English 12.3. Assign each student a Reading Focus question from this section. Have each student draw a picture to illustrate the answer.
SHELTERED ENGLISH

Section 3 Review ANSWERS

Identify

For significance, see the following pages:

- Henry Ford, p. 367
- Model T, p. 367
- assembly line, p. 368
- installment plan, p. 371

Reading for Content Understanding

1. It enabled workers to focus on one specific task and led to the production of large quantities of goods at a cheaper cost and more efficient rate.

2. Americans purchased more consumer goods, which improved their daily lives and the economy. Advertising and installment plans encouraged Americans to buy even more goods and not to wait to make purchases until they could pay the full price.

3. Cars changed the way Americans vacationed, encouraged the growth of suburbs, contributed to an economic boom, led to the rise of new businesses and industries, and increased road construction.

4. benefits—shorter working hours, higher wages, the opportunity to work with management, and employment opportunities for African Americans and people with disabilities; drawbacks—dull and exhausting work, Ford's antiunion policies and strict rules regarding behavior, and Americanization classes (for immigrant workers).

5. Automobiles stimulated the growth of new and existing industries such as the food service, petroleum, and auto repair industries.

Selling to the People

The existence of new products led to a boom in advertising as businesses tried to sell their goods. Large manufacturers were now producing for a national market. Advertisers helped create brand names that were recognizable across the country, such as Coca-Cola and Campbell's Soup. Billboards, magazines, and newspapers carried ads encouraging Americans to buy. Radios also broadcast a steady stream of commercials. Advertising executive Bruce Barton explained the purpose of advertising:

> **"The American conception [idea] of advertising is to arouse desires and stimulate wants, to make people dissatisfied with the old and out-of-date . . . to send them out to work harder to get the latest model—whether that model be an icebox or a rug, or a new home."**

Advertising was particularly important to the automobile industry. Americans were earning more money. As a result, people began considering comfort and style more strongly when buying a car. Automobile companies such as General Motors recognized this trend. They began to gain rapidly on Ford Motor Company in the 1920s by advertising the variety of body styles and colors they offered. Most ads for home appliances were targeted at women. Many ads promised that new gadgets would allow consumers to enjoy more leisure time.

Advertisements often emphasized a product's advanced technology.

Some people accused advertisers of misleading consumers about products. Critics also claimed that advertisers urged consumers to spend more than they could afford. Home appliance ads tried to pressure wives into believing that they needed all the latest products to keep themselves and their families happy. "Why drown your soul in a greasy dishpan?" asked a dishwasher ad. Car ads suggested to men that they needed new, stylish cars to gain respect.

Ad writer Helen Woodward admitted that her job required "a passion for converting the other fellow, even if it is to something you don't believe in yourself." Advertising executives defended their agencies, however. They argued that by encouraging people to consume new products, advertisements stimulated the economy.

SECTION 3 REVIEW

Identify and explain the significance of the following:

- **Henry Ford**
- **Model T**
- **assembly line**
- **installment plan**

Reading for Content Understanding

1 **Main Idea** How did manufacturing change with the introduction of the assembly line?

2 **Main Idea** How did many Americans' lives change with the new prosperity of the 1920s? What role did advertising and installment plans play in these changes?

3 **Technology and Society** What effect did the Model T and other cars have on the economy and society of the United States?

4 **Writing** *Describing* Imagine that you work on the assembly line at Ford's River Rouge plant. Describe the benefits and drawbacks of your job.

5 **Critical Thinking** *Identifying Cause and Effect* How did automobiles affect other industries in the 1920s?

OBJECTIVES

- Describe what caused the stock market boom in the 1920s.
- Explain why the influence of organized labor declined during the 1920s.
- Identify difficulties that farmers experienced during the 1920s.

FOCUS

Motivate Before Reading

Show students a sample New York Stock Exchange listing from a newspaper. Ask students why people buy stocks. As students answer, write correct responses on the chalkboard. Tell students that in this section they will learn about the get-rich-quick atmosphere of the 1920s, which led to wild speculation and rapidly rising stock prices and lured countless Americans into the market.

The U.S. Economy

Reading Focus

What caused the stock market boom in the 1920s?

Why did organized labor's influence decline during the 1920s?

What difficulties did farmers experience during the 1920s?

Key Terms

synthetic

American Plan

Fordney-McCumber Tariff Act

ONE DAY IN WASHINGTON, D.C., Supreme Court Justice Louis Brandeis was going down the street when he saw an advertisement for tires that read, "Ride Now, Pay Later." The judge was outraged over the growth of consumerism in the nation. "I can't understand where all this . . . money comes from," he later told his brother. "We are certainly not earning it as a nation." Brandeis doubted that the U.S. economy was as strong as businesspeople believed it to be. However, he was one of a minority of Americans who openly questioned the prosperity of the 1920s.

Catalogs displayed hundreds of goods for consumers.

Prosperity and Growth

The U.S. economy grew rapidly for much of the 1920s. This prosperity led many Americans to dream of achieving great wealth. Some Americans thought that buying stocks was the easiest way to fulfill these dreams. The federal government's pro-business policies and the production boom of the 1920s led to increased profits for many companies. For example, in 1929 manufacturing profits tripled those made in 1920. As company profits rose, so did stock values and the dividends returned to the stockholders.

Thousands of Americans invested in the stock market. From 1923 to 1928, the amount of stock sold on the New York Stock Exchange on Wall Street increased by more than 400 percent. As author Frederick Lewis Allen observed:

> **"All sorts of people to whom the stock ticker had been a[n] . . . alien mystery were carrying [owned] a hundred shares of Studebaker . . . and whipping open the early editions of afternoon papers to catch the 1:30 quotations [on stock prices] from Wall Street."**

Section 4 RESOURCES

PRINT

- ★ Guided Reading Strategies 12.4
- ★ Graphic Organizer 12: Developments of the 1920s
- ★ Literature Reading 12: "U.S.A."
- ★ Section 4 Review, p. 377
- ★ Daily Quiz 12.4

MULTIMEDIA

- ★ *Teaching Resources CD–ROM*, Lesson 12.4

SHELTERED ENGLISH

- ★ Main Idea Activities for Reteaching and Sheltered English 12.4

Introduce Key Terms

Linguistic, Logical-Mathematical. Review this section's key terms with students. Ask students to use context clues to write a definition for each term. Then ask each student to write a sentence using each term. Finally, have students exchange sentences and compare them to their own. **SHELTERED ENGLISH**

TEACH

Have students read Section 4 and complete Guided Reading Strategies 12.4. Choose one or more of the following activities to explore the section content with students. For further suggestions on block scheduling or team teaching, see the *Block Scheduling Handbook.*

LEVEL 1: Linguistic. (Suggested time: 15 min.) As a class, go over students' Guided Reading Strategies. Then use the Reading Focus questions to highlight the main ideas of the section. **SHELTERED ENGLISH**

ALL LEVELS: Linguistic, Logical-Mathematical. (Suggested time: 30 min.) Have each student prepare a radio commercial similar to one that may have appeared in the 1920s and that encourages people to invest in the stock market. Have students use material from the section to convince listeners that the 1920s

Geographic Diversity

Rayon and the Southern Textile Industry. In the 1880s an economic revolution began along the edge of the Appalachian Mountains in the southeastern United States. Businesspeople in the region began a "cotton mill campaign." In North Carolina alone, an average of six mills per year were built between 1880 and 1900. The cotton mill became, along with the railroad, one of the region's main sources of economic growth. By the mid-1920s, however, cotton was going out of style. Americans, particularly young women, wanted clothes made from synthetics such as rayon. This trend was particularly true of rayon stockings. As one observer put it, "It was on the trim legs of post-war flappers . . . that rayon first stepped out into big business." Rayon revolutionized the southern textile industry. The first American rayon mill was built in North Carolina in 1925. Within 20 years, the region would produce more than 70 percent of the nation's rayon.

Critical Thinking: How did social change during the 1920s produce economic change in the South?

ANSWER: New fashion trends led to the decline of the cotton industry and the development of the rayon industry.

Allen reported stories of men and women who had made thousands of dollars by investing in companies about which they knew very little.

Many of these individuals borrowed money to invest in the stock market. They were confident that stock values would continue rising. Experts such as professor Irving Fischer of Yale University supported this view. Fischer predicted that the stock market growth would continue to be strong. He encouraged people to buy stocks. Some financial experts, however, were more cautious. They reminded Americans of the old proverb "What goes up must come down."

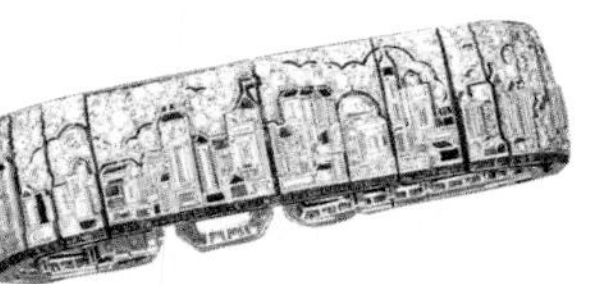

This 1920s bracelet shows the New York City skyline.

Despite the hopes of many investors, only a few Americans became extremely wealthy during the 1920s. Some earned their fortune outside the stock market by inventing new machines or creating successful businesses. Henry Ford, for example, went from tinkering in his garage to earning millions. J. C. Penney started as a general store clerk and went on to found a successful chain of department stores. He offered stock options to his managers so they could share in company profits. This profit sharing encouraged hard work. By 1929 the J. C. Penney Company had nearly 1,400 stores nationwide.

One of the most successful female entrepreneurs of the early 1900s was Madame C. J. Walker. Her "Walker System" of hair and skin care products for African Americans became the foundation for a thriving national business. Walker never forgot how she achieved her success. She often said, "I got my start by giving myself a start." She became a philanthropist and was also active in the NAACP. Although Walker died in 1919, her company continued to prosper. In the 1920s her daughter maintained the family tradition of supporting important African American causes.

The Granger Collection, New York

Madame C. J. Walker became a successful entrepreneur.

 The Limits of Prosperity

Certain "sick," or economically depressed, industries did not share in the nation's prosperity. Despite the economic boom, organized labor also suffered setbacks during the 1920s.

Sick Industries

Struggling industries included coal, textiles, and lumber. The coal industry suffered because coal was being replaced by oil, natural gas, and hydroelectric power as a source of energy. The introduction of **synthetic**, or artificial, fabrics such as rayon hurt the cotton textile industry. So did overproduction of cotton. The lumber industry faced a similar challenge as materials such as concrete replaced wood in many buildings. These industries were slow to adapt to changing technology and consumer demands. As a result, they did not share in the prosperity of the 1920s.

Many workers also faced financial difficulties. Skilled workers at large corporations generally received good pay and benefits. However, workers at smaller companies in service industries such as the retail or grocery trades were often less fortunate. In addition, unskilled factory and industrial workers usually received poor pay and few benefits. Several million unskilled workers were employed in these troubled industries.

During the 1920s the prices of many cotton fabrics dropped because of overproduction and competition with synthetic fibers.

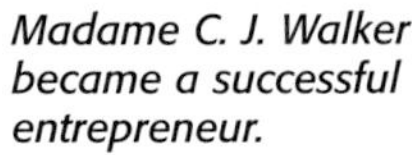

are a good time to invest. Call on volunteers to explain their commercials, and have students comment on the accuracy of each. Finally, lead a discussion on the conditions that encouraged investment and on the warning signs that the U.S. economy may not have been as strong as many Americans thought.

LEVEL 2: Linguistic, Logical-Mathematical, Interpersonal. (Suggested time: 30 min.) Organize students into pairs. Then have each pair write a dialogue between an advocate of the American Plan and a supporter of closed shops. Dialogues should focus on the relative advantages and disadvantages of each shop system from both a business owner's and a worker's perspective. Call on pairs of students to act out their dialogues for the class. Invite comparison and analysis from other students. Finally, discuss reasons for organized labor's decline in strength during the 1920s.

SHELTERED ENGLISH

LEVEL 3: Linguistic, Logical-Mathematical. (Suggested time: 45 min. plus homework) Ask students to imagine that they are congressional candidates from an agricultural district in their state during the 1920s. Have each student prepare a speech for or against the enactment of the Fordney-McCumber Tariff Act. The speech should explain why the proposed tariff will work to the advantage or disadvantage of the district's constituents. Have

American Literature

The Great Gatsby
F. Scott Fitzgerald

In 1925 F. Scott Fitzgerald published The Great Gatsby, *which many consider the novel that most represents the 1920s.* The Great Gatsby *is the story of the newly rich Jay Gatsby of Long Island, New York, and his tragic love for the beautiful Daisy Buchanan. Fitzgerald's novel describes an obsession with wealth and spending money that was true of some Americans in the 1920s. In the following excerpt, Nick Carraway—the novel's narrator and Gatsby's neighbor—describes the typical atmosphere of one of Gatsby's parties.*

There was music from my neighbor's house through the summer nights. . . . At high tide in the afternoon I watched his guests diving from the tower of his raft or taking the sun on the hot sand of his beach while his two motor boats slit the waters of the Sound. . . . On week-ends his Rolls-Royce became an omnibus [bus], bearing parties to and from the city, past nine in the morning and long after midnight, while his station wagon scampered like a brisk yellow bug to meet all trains. And on Mondays eight servants including an extra gardener toiled all day with mops and scrubbing-brushes and hammers and garden shears, repairing the ravages [damages] of the night before. . . .

At least once a fortnight [every two weeks] a corps [army] of caterers came down with several hundred feet of canvas and enough colored lights to make a Christmas tree of Gatsby's enormous garden. . . .

By seven o'clock the orchestra has arrived—no thin five piece affair but a whole pit full of oboes and trombones and saxophones . . . and cornets and piccolos and . . . drums. The last swimmers have come in from the beach now and are dressing upstairs; the cars from New York are parked five deep in the drive. . . .

I believe that on the first night I went to Gatsby's house I was one of the few guests who had actually been invited. People were not invited—they went there. They got into automobiles which bore [transported] them out to Long Island and somehow they ended up at Gatsby's door. Once there they were introduced by somebody who knew Gatsby and after that they conducted themselves according to the rules of behavior associated with amusement parks. Sometimes they came and went without having met Gatsby at all.

The Great Gatsby *was F. Scott Fitzgerald's most popular novel.*

Understanding Literature

1. What jobs were performed to prepare for the party and to entertain the guests once they had arrived?
2. Why do you think Gatsby spent so much money entertaining strangers?
3. How does F. Scott Fitzgerald's description of Gatsby's parties reflect the prosperity of the 1920s?

Across the Curriculum

LITERATURE

The Lost Generation. Author F. Scott Fitzgerald was one of a group of writers known as the Lost Generation. This group also included Ernest Hemingway, e. e. cummings, and T. S. Eliot. These authors tended to write about the United States in the 1920s with a sense of loss and disappointment. Their works often suggested that the growth of industry and urban society had changed America forever. They were also disappointed that the horrors of World War I had not resulted in a more permanent peace. Finally, they were frustrated by the country's growing obsession with wealth and consumption.

Critical Thinking: Why do you think the authors were called the Lost Generation?

ANSWER: They were lost in the sense that they disagreed with and felt they had no place in 1920s American society.

UNDERSTANDING LITERATURE ANSWERS

1. The garden was decorated with lights and canvas, and an orchestra entertained the guests.

2. He probably felt the need to prove his wealth and success to his guests.

3. The parties are described as extravagant, which reflects many people's tendency to live beyond their means in the 1920s.

volunteers deliver their speeches to the class. Finally, lead a discussion on the difficulties farmers faced during the 1920s and on the effects of the Fordney-McCumber Tariff Act.

CLOSE

Linguistic, Logical-Mathematical. Have each student create a title for a book on the 1920s that captures the decade's essence. Then ask students to create a table of contents for the book, which provides a glimpse into the topics that are covered. Students' table of contents should include the topics covered in this section.

CHALLENGE AND EXTEND

Linguistic, Logical-Mathematical. Have students use the library or other resources to find information on the various ways the U.S. government has provided assistance to farmers over the years. Ask students to write a report that discusses various methods and evaluates the effectiveness of each. Call on volunteers to share information from their reports with the class.

Section 4 Review ANSWERS

Identify

For significance, see the following pages:

- J. C. Penny, p. 374
- Madame C. J. Walker, p. 374
- synthetic, p. 374
- American Plan, p. 376
- Fordney-McCumber Tariff Act, p. 377

Reading for Content Understanding

1. the government's pro-business policies, increased profits resulting from the mass-production boom, the participation of thousands of individual investors

2. They faced a lack of government support, an increased labor supply that enabled businesses to avoid hiring union members, antiunion feelings resulting from the 1919 strikes and the Red Scare, the open-shop drive, and antilabor court decisions.

3. During the war, demand for crops had increased, and farmers had borrowed money to increase production. When the war ended, demand and prices for crops fell, which left farmers unable to pay their debts.

4. Paragraphs will vary but should mention that new materials such as concrete and synthetics and new power sources such as natural gas reduced the demand for goods such as coal, cotton textiles, and lumber.

5. Answers will vary but students should suggest possible actions and explain how they would have eased the crisis.

Labor in the 1920s

Organized labor also struggled to share in the decade's boom times. During World War I the federal government had feared work stoppages in war industries and thus supported union demands for higher wages. This led to increases in union membership. After the war ended, the government no longer supported labor. In addition, the labor supply increased. These changes allowed many businesses to avoid hiring union workers.

The violent strikes of 1919 had inspired strong antiunion feelings across the United States. Many Americans believed that unions were radical political organizations run by individuals who wanted to weaken American society. During the 1920s union membership declined sharply. It fell from a high of more than 5 million in 1920 to around 3.6 million just three years later.

At the same time, the courts often struck down pro-worker legislation and upheld companies' attempts to ban unions. Labor unions had worked to make industries into "closed shops" where only union members could be employed. The closed shop increased the power of unions. Union leaders could usually rely on the support of all the workers in a closed-shop industry. Business leaders responded by launching an open-shop campaign called the **American Plan**. In an open shop, union membership was not required and was sometimes even forbidden. Republicans openly supported the drive against unions. Attorney General Harry Daugherty said:

> **"So long and to the extent that I can speak for the government of the United States, I will use the power of the government to prevent the labor unions of the country from destroying the open shop."**

Unions fought the American Plan but with little success. One of the worst defeats suffered by labor occurred in July 1922. Some 400,000 railroad workers went on strike to oppose wage cuts. Daugherty secured a federal restraining order against the strikers in September. The strike collapsed. As union membership declined in the 1920s, business leaders no longer pushed for open shops.

Hard Times for Farmers

The postwar years were also difficult for farmers. Demobilization ended the prosperity that World War I had brought to American agriculture. Keeping the Allies supplied during the war had created high demand and high prices for agricultural products. In response, American farmers had increased their production. They often bought land and equipment on credit. When the war ended, so did the huge Allied demand for U.S. farm products.

Many farmers found themselves producing much more than they could sell. Food prices dropped dramatically. Nebraska corn, which had sold for $1.22 a bushel in 1919, sold for only 41 cents in 1920. When farm earnings dropped drastically, many farmers found it impossible to pay their debts. Nearly half a million farmers lost their land. To drive prices up, farmers needed to produce less. However, many farmers planted more in an attempt to recover their losses. Additional crops only made the problem worse by driving prices even lower.

To try to solve their problems, farmers in the Midwest elected a group of pro-agriculture

The drop in farm prices following World War I meant hard times for many farm families.

REVIEW

Linguistic, Interpersonal. Have students complete the Section Review questions. Then assign each student a topic from this section. Have students list details from the section that relate to their topics. Then ask students to exchange their lists and use the information they receive to write a brief paragraph on their new topic.

ASSESS

Have students complete Daily Quiz 12.4.

RETEACH

Logical-Mathematical. Have students complete Main Idea Activities for Reteaching and Sheltered English 12.4. Then have students create graphic organizers that have columns labeled as follows: *Segment of the Economy, Better/Worse,* and *Positive/Negative Changes*. In Column 1, have students list *Stock Market, Labor,* and *Farmers*. In Column 2, have students use an arrow to indicate whether the overall situation was better or worse at the end of the 1920s. In Column 3, have students list changes that occurred relating to the topic and use a plus or minus sign to indicate whether each change was positive or negative. **SHELTERED ENGLISH**

congressmen known as the Farm Bloc. The Farm Bloc helped pass legislation intended to ease the farm crisis. The **Fordney-McCumber Tariff Act** was designed to raise the demand and price for domestic crops by placing high taxes on imported farm products. The high tariff prevented many foreign farm goods from being sold in the United States. However, it also raised the cost of many consumer goods—which hurt everyone, including farmers.

Other suggestions included a government subsidy, or aid. One plan proposed that the government buy basic goods such as cattle, corn, cotton, and wheat. American farmers would receive more than market-value prices for these goods. The government would then sell the crops overseas at the lower world-market rates. Critics attacked this plan as unworkable. President Coolidge vetoed it.

Farmers kept pressing the federal government for assistance. Republican leaders, however, did not want to interfere with the free-enterprise system by regulating prices. Only large farms and ones with expensive, modern machinery prospered in the 1920s. Some of the biggest farms were run by agricultural corporations. These farms benefited from increased efficiency and large-scale operations.

Most farmers, however, were not so fortunate. In 1929 the average annual income of farmers was about a third of that of nonfarmers. Farm laborers, particularly migrant workers, fared even worse. They often received poor pay and worked under difficult conditions. A minister reported that in a settlement in California, "shelters were made of almost every conceivable [imaginable] thing—burlap, canvas, palm branches." The booming economy of the 1920s brought prosperity for many Americans, but did not bring good times for large numbers of farmers and union workers.

Persons Working in the U.S. Private Sector (in thousands)

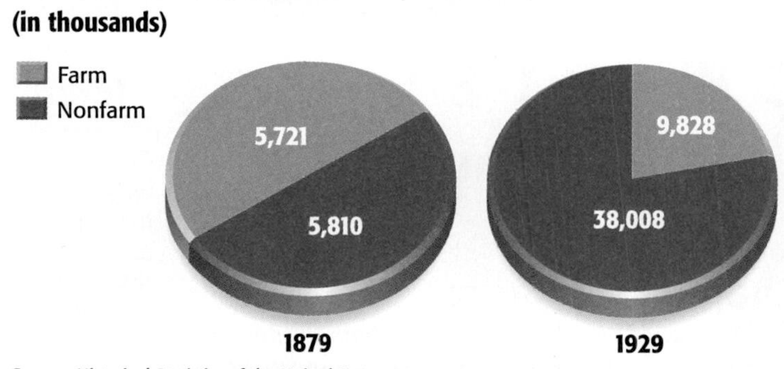

Source: *Historical Statistics of the United States*

Leaving the Farm Between 1880 and 1930, the increased use of farm machinery and the growth of industry contributed to a decrease in the number of farm jobs. How many more people worked in nonfarm jobs in 1929 than in 1879?

SECTION 4 REVIEW

Identify and explain the significance of the following:

- **J. C. Penney**
- **Madame C. J. Walker**
- **synthetic**
- **American Plan**
- **Fordney-McCumber Tariff Act**

Reading for Content Understanding

1. **Main Idea** What factors contributed to the stock market boom in the 1920s?
2. **Main Idea** What difficulties did unions face in the 1920s?
3. **Economic Development** How did the end of World War I affect farmers?
4. **Writing** *Informing* In a paragraph, explain why some industries struggled to compete during the 1920s.
5. **Critical Thinking** *Drawing Conclusions* What steps might farmers or the government have taken to ease the farm crisis?

CHART ANSWER
about 32,000

Chapter 12 Review ANSWERS

Identifying People and Ideas

1. the process of returning to a peacetime economy

2. widespread fear of Communists and political radicals after the war

3. fear of foreigners; was encouraged by the Red Scare

4. Republican whose presidency (1921–23) was plagued by scandal

5. scandal involving bribes accepted by the secretary of the interior in exchange for illegal oil leases

6. became president when Warren Harding died in 1923; served in office until 1929

7. founded the Ford Motor Company in 1903; helped establish the American automobile industry

8. manufacturing method in which each worker performs one simple task; makes production cheaper and more efficient

9. new method of buying products on credit, which made it easier to buy consumer goods

10. successful African American businesswoman; also active in civil rights causes

Using the Time Line

1. c **4.** e
2. b **5.** d
3. a

Review and Assessment RESOURCES

PRINT
★ Chapter 12 Review, pp. 378–79
★ Vocabulary Activity 12
★ Chapter 12 Study Guide
★ Chapter 12 Test (Form A or B)

MULTIMEDIA
★ Audio Program, Ch. 12 (English and Spanish)
★ *Global Skill Builder CD–ROM*
★ Chapter 12 Test Generator
★ HRW Web site

SHELTERED ENGLISH
★ Spanish Glossary
★ Sheltered English Chapter 12 Test

ASSESS

Have students complete one of the Chapter 12 Tests. As an alternate assessment, assign the Chapter 12 Investigation.

Understanding Main Ideas

1. increases in antiunion feelings, xenophobia, and calls for open shops; a decline in union participation

2. promoted policies that benefitted business, but otherwise avoided regulating the economy

3. to promote economic growth, disarmament, and world peace

4. The growth of the automobile industry spawned new industries, such as the petroleum industry, which contributed to a national economic boom.

5. Advertising encouraged people to consume, and installment plans provided credit so consumers could buy goods without having to pay fully for them.

6. The U.S. government's pro-business policies and the production boom increased stock values, which encouraged thousands of new investors.

7. Some stock market investors, inventors, and new businesses benefited the most. Industries dependent on old technologies, unions, and farmers benefited the least.

Reviewing Themes

1. It led to searches without warrants, convictions without sufficient evidence, deportations, and the labeling of many immigrants as Communists.

2. It led to higher unemployment, a cost-of-living increase, the displacement of female workers, competition between races for jobs, and tension between business and labor.

3. Work sped up and became more repetitive, boring, and stressful.

CHAPTER 12 REVIEW

Chapter Summary

The end of World War I brought both excitement and anxiety. Voters elected pro-business Republicans to the presidency. Fear of communism led to a Red Scare that swept the nation. Race riots also broke out in many U.S. cities. The automobile industry and the stock market boomed as Americans bought more goods. Although many Americans enjoyed prosperity, some groups—such as union members and farmers—faced hard times.

On a separate sheet of paper, complete the following activities.

Identifying People and Ideas

Describe the historical significance of the following:

1. demobilization
2. Red Scare
3. xenophobia
4. Warren G. Harding
5. Teapot Dome scandal
6. Calvin Coolidge
7. Henry Ford
8. assembly line
9. installment plan
10. Madame C. J. Walker

Internet Activity

go.hrw.com
SB1 The Twenties Abroad

Choose a country other than the United States that was involved in World War I. Search the Internet through the HRW Web site to find information about what happened in that country's economy during the 1920s. Then use this information to write a report.

Understanding Main Ideas

1. What was the overall outcome of the major labor strikes that took place in the United States following World War I?
2. What was the Republican Party's economic policy during the 1920s?
3. What were the goals of the Five-Power Naval Treaty, the Nine-Power Treaty, and the Kellogg-Briand Pact?
4. How did the automobile spark tremendous growth in the U.S. economy?
5. How did advertising and the installment plan contribute to the creation of a consumer society in the 1920s?
6. Why did the stock market expand greatly during the 1920s?
7. Which groups benefited the most and the least from the general economic prosperity of the 1920s?

Using the Time Line

Number your paper from 1 to 5. Match the letters on the time line below with the following events.

1. **President Harding dies suddenly while on a speaking tour.**
2. **Union leaders call off the unsuccessful strike against U.S. Steel.**
3. **Race riots break out in Chicago, Illinois, leaving nearly 40 people dead and more than 530 injured.**
4. **The United States and 14 other nations sign the Kellogg-Briand Pact, outlawing war.**
5. **Calvin Coolidge defeats Democrat John W. Davis and Progressive Party candidate Robert La Follette in the presidential election.**

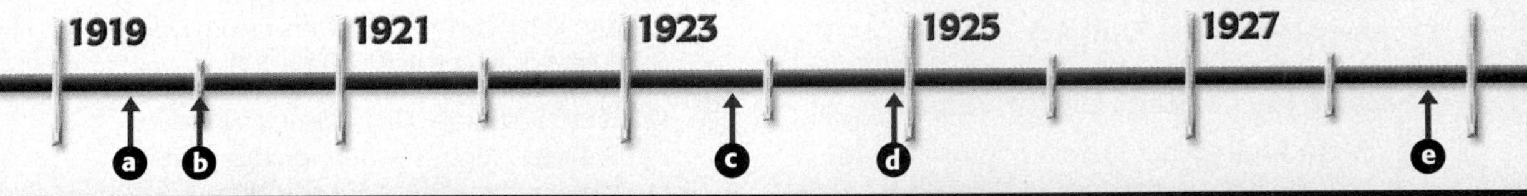

RETEACH

Logical-Mathematical, Interpersonal. Ask students to list 10 changes that took place in the United States from 1919 to 1929. Then have each student exchange papers with a partner. Have students identify at least one effect of each change and state whether it was positive or negative. **SHELTERED ENGLISH**

Using the Internet

Have students continue their research to add to their reports important political figures from the countries they investigated. Ask students to describe each individual's contribution to his or her country and explain how that person affected the country's history and economy during the 1920s.

Portfolio Extensions

1. Ask students to imagine that they are advertising executives for one of Ford's competitors. Have each student create a magazine and radio advertisement that will convince consumers to buy their company's car instead of a Model T.

2. Have each student create a radio advertisement for any candidate in the 1920, 1924, or 1928 presidential elections.

Reviewing Themes

1. **Citizenship and Democracy** In what ways did the Red Scare affect the civil rights of many Americans?
2. **Economic Development** What effects did demobilization have on the U.S. economy?
3. **Technology and Society** How did the development of the assembly line and mass production change Americans' working lives?

Thinking Critically

1. **Evaluating** Do you think advertising had a positive or negative effect on American society in the 1920s? Explain your answer.
2. **Identifying Generalizations and Stereotypes** What factors do you think contributed to the rise in lynchings and race riots following World War I?
3. **Identifying Cause and Effect** How did events in 1919 influence the outcome of the presidential election of 1920?

Writing About History

1. **Expressing** Imagine that you are a resident of Seattle, Washington, during the general strike of 1919. Write a brief diary entry on how the strike has affected you, your family, and your community.
2. **Informing** Imagine that you are a reporter for a local radio station in the Midwest during the 1920s. Write a news story on the economic situation facing midwestern farmers.

Building Your Portfolio

Complete the following activities individually or in groups.

1. **Advertising** Imagine that you are an advertising executive in the early 1920s and are in charge of a new ad campaign for Ford's Model T. Create two advertisements, one that might have appeared in a magazine and one that might have been broadcast on the radio.
2. **Campaigning for President** Create a campaign poster that might have appeared for a Democratic, Republican, or third-party candidate in the 1920, 1924, or 1928 presidential election. Make sure that your campaign poster contains a slogan and at least one of the party's platform issues.

Linking Geography and History

1. **Movement** How did the automobile affect Americans' travel habits?
2. **Human-Environment Interaction** How did the widespread use of the automobile change the American landscape?

History Skills Workshop

Reading Charts Radios were initially a luxury item. Their use increased dramatically during the 1920s as costs declined and people began to make purchases using the installment plan. Study the chart below. Then answer the following questions: (a) About how many households had radios in 1923? (b) Between what two years did the number of households with radios increase the most? (c) From 1925 to 1930, how many additional households bought radios?

Households with Radios, 1922–1930

U.S. Households (in millions): 0, 2, 4, 6, 8, 10, 12, 14

Year: 1922, 1923, 1924, 1925, 1926, 1927, 1928, 1929, 1930

Source: *Historical Statistics of the United States*

Thinking Critically

1. Answers will vary but should provide positive or negative effects to support the position stated.

2. Demobilization resulted in white and African American workers having to compete for scarce jobs and housing, particularly in northern cities where many African Americans had migrated during the war.

3. Many Americans blamed the Democrats for postwar problems, thus leading to a Republican victory.

Writing About History

1. Answers will vary but may discuss how the strike brought the laboring community together while business leaders and city officials tried to turn public opinion against it.

2. Answers will vary but should discuss the postwar fall in crop demand and prices, credit problems, and overproduction.

Linking Geography and History

1. led Americans to travel greater distances on trips and live farther from their jobs

2. led to the construction of highways, the growth of suburbs, the rise of new roadside businesses

History Skills Workshop

(a) about 1 million; (b) between 1929 and 1930; (c) about 11.75 million

CHAPTER PLANNING GUIDE
The Roaring Twenties

	SECTION LESSON OBJECTIVES	PRINT RESOURCES	MULTIMEDIA RESOURCES	SHELTERED ENGLISH RESOURCES
Section 1: Prohibition America (pp. 381–86)	★ Analyze the social changes for American teenagers after World War I. ★ Describe how prohibition affected the United States in the 1920s. ★ Explain how Fundamentalism developed and its role in the Scopes trial.	★ Guided Reading Strategies 13.1 ★ Geography Activity 13: The Prohibition Era ★ Section 1 Review, p. 386 ★ Daily Quiz 13.1	★ *Teaching Resources CD–ROM*, Lesson 13.1	★ Main Idea Activities for Reteaching and Sheltered English 13.1
Section 2: A Changing Population (pp. 387–92)	★ Explain how nativism affected immigration after World War I. ★ Analyze the challenges minority groups faced and the progress they made in the 1920s. ★ Describe how political and economic opportunities for women changed during the 1920s.	★ Guided Reading Strategies 13.2 ★ Primary Source Reading 13: Mexican Americans in the 1920s ★ Biography Reading 13: Marcus Garvey ★ Section 2 Review, p. 392 ★ Daily Quiz 13.2	★ *Teaching Resources CD–ROM*, Lesson 13.2 ★ Linking Geography and History Transparency 17: African American Population, 1920	★ Main Idea Activities for Reteaching and Sheltered English 13.2
Section 3: Americans at Play (pp. 393–98)	★ Explain what led to the rise of fads in the 1920s. ★ Analyze the effects of radio and the movies on American culture. ★ Describe Americans' attitudes toward actors and athletes in the 1920s.	★ Guided Reading Strategies 13.3 ★ Graphic Organizer 13: America's Popular Culture ★ Section 3 Review, p. 398 ★ Daily Quiz 13.3	★ *Teaching Resources CD–ROM*, Lesson 13.3 ★ HRW Web site	★ Main Idea Activities for Reteaching and Sheltered English 13.3
Section 4: The Arts (pp. 399–405)	★ Analyze the influence of the blues and jazz on American culture. ★ Explain the significance of the Harlem Renaissance and the Lost Generation. ★ Describe other major developments in American arts during the 1920s.	★ Guided Reading Strategies 13.4 ★ Literature Reading 13: Poetry of the Harlem Renaissance ★ Section 4 Review, p. 405 ★ Daily Quiz 13.4	★ *Teaching Resources CD–ROM*, Lesson 13.4 ★ Art in American History Transparency 28: *Falling Water (Kaufmann House)* ★ Everyday Life in America Transparency 22: Harlem Renaissance Art, 1920s ★ *American Music Audio CD Program:* "Harmonica Blues" ★ *American History Interactive Maps CD–ROM:* The Harlem Renaissance ★ HRW Web site	★ Main Idea Activities for Reteaching and Sheltered English 13.4
Chapter Review and Assessment (pp. 406–07)		★ Chapter 13 Review, pp. 406–07 ★ Vocabulary Activity 13 ★ Chapter 13 Study Guide ★ Chapter 13 Test (Form A or B)	★ Audio Program, Ch. 13 (English and Spanish) ★ *Global Skill Builder CD–ROM* ★ Chapter 13 Test Generator ★ HRW Web site	★ Spanish Glossary ★ Sheltered English Chapter 13 Test

CHAPTER OVERVIEW

During the early 1920s many Americans pushed for what they considered to be traditional American values. A prohibition amendment passed and the Fundamentalist movement grew. However, this push for traditional values lost some of its strength as people called for the repeal of prohibition and the Tennessee Supreme Court overturned the verdict in the Scopes trial.

As the number of people moving to the United States grew, many Americans became increasingly nativistic, leading Congress to pass laws restricting immigration. At the same time, the nation experienced internal migrations by African Americans and Mexican Americans, as well as the movement of many rural residents to the city.

Throughout the 1920s a national culture grew. Fueled by the growth of radio and movies, new fads swept the country, and public attention focused on celebrities such as movie stars and professional athletes. At the same time, the nation witnessed the development of two new styles of music that were rooted in African American culture: the blues and jazz. Accompanying this growth was the artistic movement known as the Harlem Renaissance, which along with the works of the Lost Generation, offered unique perspectives on culture and society.

CHAPTER INVESTIGATION

The Chapter Investigation is an extended, multipart activity designed for students to work cooperatively and apply the chapter content in the creation of a project. You may choose to use the Chapter 13 Investigation, 1920s Time Capsule, either as a substitute for teaching the section lessons or as an alternate assessment.

BLOCK SCHEDULING 

The teacher lesson plans for each section offer a variety of activity choices to help you present the material in a block scheduling format. For further suggestions on block scheduling, see the *Block Scheduling Handbook with Team Teaching Strategies*, pp. 73–78.

Meeting Individual Needs

ABILITY LEVELS

LEVEL 1 Basic level activities designed for all students encountering new material.

LEVEL 2 Intermediate level activities designed for average students.

LEVEL 3 Challenging activities designed for above-average students.

SHELTERED ENGLISH These activities address the needs of students with Limited English Proficiency.

Smithsonian Institution®

Internet Connections and Lesson 13
www.si.edu/hrw

CNN Presents America:
Yesterday and Today 1850 to the Present
Segment: The Negro Leagues

Additional Resources

Books for Teachers

Douglas, Ann. *Terrible Honesty: Mongrel Manhattan in the 1920s*. Farrar, Straus, and Giroux, 1995. Focuses on New York, skyscrapers, and racial issues.

Dumenil, Lynn. *The Modern Temper: American Culture and Society in the 1920s*. Hill and Wang, 1995. Surveys important events and ideas of the decade.

Vincent, Theodore G. *Voices of a Black Nation: Political Journalism in the Harlem Renaissance*. Africa World Press, 1991. Provides primary sources from the Harlem Renaissance.

Books for Students

Denenberg, Barry. *An American Hero: The True Story of Charles A. Lindbergh*. Scholastic, 1996. Covers Lindbergh's strengths and weaknesses in a biographical format.

Gardner, Robert, and Dennis Shortelle. *The Forgotten Players: The Story of Black Baseball in America*. Walker, 1993. Describes the role of the Negro Leagues in American culture (for students reading below grade level).

Lewis, David L. *When Harlem Was in Vogue*. Oxford University Press, 1989. Provides a narrative of major events, trends, and people of the Harlem Renaissance.

Multimedia Materials

The Big Red Scare of 1919–1920. Video, 10 min. Multi-Media Productions/SSSS. Traces the origins of anticommunist and anti-immigrant hysteria in 1919 and 1920.

History of the Twentieth Century, 1920–1929. Video, 60 min. ABC Video/SSSS. Expansive overview of Al Capone, prohibition, and other topics.

The Jazz Age, Part 2. Video, 26 min. McGraw Hill Films. Covers a wide range of Jazz-Age culture including sports and Lindbergh's flight.

The Roaring Twenties

CHAPTER MOTIVATOR

Ask students to identify trends or fads associated with their generation. For example, students might mention the rise of extreme sports or hip-hop music. As students identify these trends, write them on the chalkboard. Then ask students to organize the trends into categories. For instance, students can relate some trends to music and others to sports. Then ask students to think of life in the 1920s and try to identify fads of that era that would fall into the categories they created. Have students compare and contrast the trends of the two eras. Tell students that in this chapter they will learn about the American culture that developed in the 1920s. Ask students to consider the similarities and differences between trends of the 1920s and those of today as they read the chapter.

Presenting Themes

- **Citizenship and Democracy** Students might mention that prejudices and competition for jobs might cause citizens to demand immigration restrictions.
- **Technology and Society** Students might mention that people would be able to gather and send information faster and more easily.
- **Cultural Diversity** Students might mention that the cultural experiences of one group could influence the thought, artistic expression, and lifestyles of an entire country, particularly if the group's culture and ideas can be seen around the nation.

Using the Time Line

Have students record in their notes each event from the time line. Instruct students to leave gaps between events. Then ask students to consider each event as an action. As they read the chapter, have students find and list a reaction to each action.

CHAPTER 13

The Roaring Twenties

(1920–1929)

On July 2, 1921, the Radio Corporation of America (RCA) broadcast the Jack Dempsey–Georges Carpentier boxing match. Few Americans owned radios, so thousands gathered in clubs and theaters to hear the fight. Some 100,000 people in Manhattan stood outside the New York Times Building listening to loudspeakers. Radio broadcasting was one of the many developments that transformed American culture in the 1920s.

Citizenship and Democracy
Why might a nation attempt to restrict immigration?

Technology and Society
How might advances in communication technology affect people's lives?

Cultural Diversity
How might the experiences of a particular group affect the culture of an entire country?

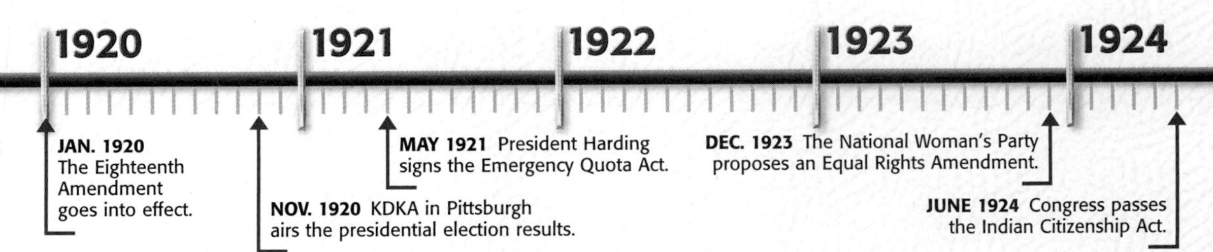

OBJECTIVES

- Analyze the social changes for American teenagers after World War I.
- Describe how prohibition affected the United States in the 1920s.
- Explain how Fundamentalism developed and its role in the Scopes trial.

FOCUS

Motivate Before Reading

Ask students to describe some of the clubs, extracurricular activities, and social functions they are involved in or attend at your school. List students' replies on the chalkboard. Then ask students to imagine how their life might be different if none of these activities were available. Call on students to share their thoughts. Explain that this situation was true for many young people until

Prohibition America

Reading Focus

What social changes took place among American teenagers after World War I?

How did prohibition affect the United States in the 1920s?

How did Fundamentalism develop, and what role did it play in the Scopes trial?

Key Terms

flappers
prohibition
Volstead Act
bootleggers
speakeasies
Twenty-first Amendment
Fundamentalism
Scopes trial

IN A 1924 INTERVIEW, an Indiana woman explained how her family and others had spent their leisure time in the past. "We were all much more together. People brought chairs and cushions out of the house and sat on the lawn. . . . We'd sit out so all evening." She went on to describe how neighbors would stop by, and how the young and the old would play games or music together. After World War I, however, this woman's family and many other American families began spending less of their leisure time together. This change was partly the result of young Americans, particularly teenagers, spending more of their free time with friends their own age.

Many Americans spent their leisure time listening to records played on phonographs.

IMAGE ON LEFT PAGE: *Magazine covers showing the changing fashions and music of the 1920s*

1925 | 1926 | 1927 | 1928 | 1929

JULY 1925 The Scopes trial takes place in Dayton, Tennessee.

MAY 1927 Charles Lindbergh completes the first solo flight across the Atlantic Ocean.

OCT. 1927 Warner Brothers releases the first talkie film, *The Jazz Singer*.

FEB. 1929 The St. Valentine's Day massacre occurs in Chicago.

Section 1 RESOURCES

PRINT

- ★ Guided Reading Strategies 13.1
- ★ Geography Activity 13: The Prohibition Era
- ★ Section 1 Review, p. 386
- ★ Daily Quiz 13.1

MULTIMEDIA

- ★ *Teaching Resources CD–ROM*, Lesson 13.1

SHELTERED ENGLISH

- ★ Main Idea Activities for Reteaching and Sheltered English 13.1

the early 1900s. Tell students that in this section they will learn how growing social and educational opportunities for youth, prohibition, and Fundamentalism changed American society during the 1920s.

Introduce Key Terms

Linguistic, Logical-Mathematical, Interpersonal. Review this section's key terms with students. Have students use the text to define each term. Then pair students and have one partner offer a single-word clue for one of the terms and the other partner guess which term it suggests. Once the term has been correctly identified, have the pair switch roles and repeat the process. Tell students to continue until they have reviewed all the section's key terms. **SHELTERED ENGLISH**

TEACH

Have students read Section 1 and complete Guided Reading Strategies 13.1. Choose one or more of the following activities to explore the section content with students. For further suggestions on block scheduling or team teaching, see the *Block Scheduling Handbook.*

Cultural Diversity

African American Education. Although the overall range of classes offered in public schools began to expand during the early 1900s, new classes generally were not offered in schools with predominately African American students. This occurrence may have been due to differences in the amount of money spent on educating white and black students. Between 1900 and 1930, the amount of money spent on schools increased in every southern state. However, the gap between the amount spent on white and black students also increased. While white students received an increasing variety of academic as well as vocational classes, African American students were offered fewer academic classes and mainly provided with classes on vocational training and character building.

Critical Thinking: In what other ways might differences in funding affect students?

ANSWER: Schools receiving less funding might not be able to offer as many extracurricular activities or afford as many teachers as better-funded schools.

A Changing Nation

After World War I, popular support for public education grew. The improved economy also enabled more children to attend school rather than having to work to help support their families. As a result, from 1915 to 1930, high school enrollment more than tripled.

American Youth

Changes in public education transformed the social lives of many young Americans. High schools began offering a wider range of classes, including job-training courses. Schools also offered extracurricular activities, which had been rare during the late 1800s. Organized sports and social clubs became widespread and popular. School-related activities such as sports events and dances took up an increasing amount of students' time each week.

Technology also changed the lives of young Americans. Radio broadcasts spread popular songs across the nation. The growing use of automobiles gave teenagers greater freedom, which worried some parents. Many teens preferred to go out with their friends rather than spend time with their families. "The two older children never go out when the family motors [drives]. They always have something else on," complained one mother.

A high school boys' basketball team

Straight dresses and short haircuts were popular among flappers.

Critics who did not approve of these changes in social activity accused American youth of being irresponsible. Journalist John Carter challenged these claims in a 1920 article in *Atlantic Monthly*:

> **"I would like to say a few things about my generation. . . . A keen interest in political and social problems, and a determination to face the facts of life, ugly or beautiful, characterizes us."**

Young Americans like Carter saw themselves as a new generation that was preparing for the challenges of a modern age.

Throughout the 1920s, many young Americans sought to break away from traditional standards of dress and behavior. For example, some young women stopped wearing long hair and uncomfortable clothing such as heavy corsets. Instead, they wore looser clothes, used cosmetics, and cut their hair short in a style called a bob. The *Ladies' Home Journal* called these women **flappers** because their style of loose clothing and unbuckled coats flapped when they walked. Being a flapper was not just about new fashions, however. As one observer noted, flappers pursued a wide variety of interests, "whether it were a marathon dancing contest, . . . a political campaign, or a social-service settlement."

Rural and Urban America

To many rural Americans, flappers and other new social trends reflected the growing division between the cultures of the city and country. During the 1920s the United States became an increasingly industrial and urban society. For the first time, more than half of the nation's population lived in cities or towns.

As cities grew, so did the number of industrial workers and the power of political machines. Big cities also often had large immigrant populations.

LEVEL 1: Linguistic. (Suggested time: 15 min.) As a class, go over students' Guided Reading Strategies. Then use the Reading Focus questions to highlight the main ideas of the section. **SHELTERED ENGLISH**

ALL LEVELS: Logical-Mathematical, Visual-Spatial, Interpersonal. (Suggested time: 45 min.) Organize the class into groups. Have each group create a graphic organizer that lists events that changed American teenagers' lives during the 1920s, and explains what these changes were. For example, students might identify increased high school enrollment as an event that caused change and explain that school attendance exposed students to more opportunities for social activities with peers. Have students list as many events as they can find in the section. Then have a representative of each group explain its organizer to the class. **SHELTERED ENGLISH**

LEVEL 2: Linguistic, Intrapersonal. (Suggested time: 30 min.) Ask students to imagine that they are 1920s police officers in charge of enforcing prohibition. Have each student prepare a brief statement for a reporter who wants an analysis of prohibition's goals and effectiveness. Tell students to focus on how prohibition affected police officers and public health. Ask for volunteers to present their statements to the class and encourage students to offer feedback.

These trends concerned many rural inhabitants. They felt that city life threatened traditional values.

At the same time, some popular urban writers criticized small-town America. These critics claimed that rural residents were ignorant of new technologies and unprepared to live in modern times.

 The Prohibition Debate

One of the key disagreements between urban and rural Americans involved **prohibition**—the banning of the manufacture, sale, and transportation of alcohol. The debate over alcohol use had gained national attention in the 1840s. At that time temperance reformers argued that Americans should limit their alcohol consumption. Later temperance supporters included political progressives, conservative Protestant Christian groups, and women's organizations such as the Woman's Christian Temperance Union. These groups believed that alcohol contributed to crime, poverty, and the breakup of families.

In the 1890s the temperance movement had gained new momentum with the founding of the national Anti-Saloon League. The league encouraged its members to vote only for pro-temperance candidates. By 1917 such political efforts had led 19 states to become "dry"—that is, places where liquor sales were banned.

Many prohibition supporters lived in rural areas. Prohibition opponents were concentrated in cities. They included large numbers of immigrants and industrial workers. Opponents of prohibition argued that it would give the government too much power over people's lives. Many Americans feared the law would make criminals out of ordinary people who drank moderately.

The outbreak of World War I tipped popular support in favor of prohibition. Public opinion turned against brewery owners partly because many brewers were of German descent and the United States was at war with Germany. Other Americans argued that all grain should be used for food in the war effort, not wasted in making alcohol. Congress responded by passing a prohibition amendment in December 1917. The states finally ratified the Eighteenth Amendment in 1919, and it went into effect in January 1920.

The Eighteenth Amendment did not actually specify how prohibition would be enforced. Congress passed the **Volstead Act** in October 1919. This act established federal penalties for the manufacture and sale of alcohol. It also made the Bureau of Internal Revenue responsible for enforcing prohibition.

 A Dry Nation

Supporters of prohibition expected little opposition once it was signed into law. John F. Kramer, the first prohibition commissioner, declared that liquor would not be "sold, nor given away, nor hauled in anything on the surface of the earth or under the earth or in the air." In areas that had already been dry before prohibition, Kramer was often able to fulfill this pledge.

Enforcing the Law

Police officers and prohibition agents arrested more than 500,000 people for violating prohibition. However, large quantities of illegal liquor remained readily available in cities and towns across the nation. Illegal alcohol came from a variety of sources. Some people stole industrial alcohol

Supporters of prohibition celebrated the ratification of the Eighteenth Amendment in 1919.

Daily Life

The Effectiveness of Prohibition. Some scholars argue that while prohibition did not end alcohol consumption in the United States, it may have caused as much as a 30 percent decrease in Americans' drinking. This decrease occurred largely because prohibition made drinking more expensive. For example, the price of whiskey rose 310 percent and the price of beer rose 600 percent during the 1920s.

Critical Thinking: Why else might prohibition have decreased alcohol consumption?

ANSWER: People might have been concerned about getting caught and going to jail.

LEVEL 3: Linguistic, Logical-Mathematical. (Suggested time: 45 min. plus homework) Ask students to imagine that they are radio broadcasters covering the Scopes trial. Have each student write a radio script describing the following topics: the law Scopes was accused of violating, reasons the law was in effect, the defense and prosecution in the case, the outcome of the case, and the effect of Fundamentalism both on the Scopes trial and on American society. Call on volunteers to read their broadcasts to the class.

CLOSE

Logical-Mathematical, Interpersonal. Ask students to imagine that they are reporters for a 1920s magazine entitled *Changing Ways*. Have students compile a top-ten list to appear in the 1929 annual special issue of the magazine. The list should describe ways in which the United States and American society have changed since the end of World War I. Ask volunteers to share their lists with the class. Then have students compile a class list and rank the items according to their impact on the nation, with *10* being the least amount of impact and *1* being the greatest.

Across the Curriculum

SCIENCE

America's Rocket Pioneer. Scientific theories sparked controversy with religion at a time when many scientific discoveries were being made. American scientist Robert Goddard faced criticism for his experiments with solid-fuel rockets. After his 1919 paper "A Method of Reaching Extreme Altitudes" was published, it was ridiculed as a naive joke by the *New York Times*. However, Goddard continued his work and in 1926 launched the world's first liquid-propellant rocket. Although the launch was not given much positive attention in the United States, scientists around the world became intrigued with Goddard's idea and began experimenting with rocket technology. After World War II, when German rocket scientist Werhner von Braun was asked where he got the idea for the deadly German V-2 rocket, he replied, "Don't you know about your own rocket pioneer? Dr. Goddard was ahead of us all."

Activity: Have students research other inventions of the 1920s and prepare a newsletter about discoveries and scientific breakthroughs of the decade.

MAP ANSWER
California and Texas

intended for legal products such as perfume and antifreeze. Other Americans produced their own alcohol at home. If improperly made, such alcohol could be deadly. Smugglers also brought liquor in from other nations, particularly Canada and Mexico. People involved in the illegal liquor traffic were called **bootleggers**. This name came from an older term that described how smugglers used to hide bottles of alcohol in their boots.

Some speakeasies advertised on cards.

In addition to stopping bootleggers, prohibition agents attempted to locate and close down **speakeasies**. These were secret, illegal clubs that served alcohol. The name speakeasy came from the need for customers to keep quiet about the location of the clubs. Speakeasies were common in most major U.S. cities.

To shut down speakeasies, agents had to be determined and resourceful. None were more so than Isadore "Izzy" Einstein and Moe Smith. The pair made more than 4,000 arrests in five years, often using outrageous disguises to gain entrance to the clubs. On one occasion, Einstein stood outside a speakeasy in light clothing in the bitter cold. Smith knocked on the door and shouted, "Give this man a drink! He's been frostbitten." The startled owner looked at the blue and shivering Einstein and quickly brought him a drink. The agents made their arrest.

Organized Crime

In major cities such as Chicago and New York, criminals organized powerful gangs to control the illegal liquor trade. Chicago was home to one of the nation's most famous and financially successful gangsters, Al "Scarface" Capone.

By 1927 Capone was making about $60 million a year. He dominated the bootlegging business through blackmail, bribery, and murder. Capone defended his actions by saying:

> **"I make my money by supplying a public demand. If I break the law, my customers, who number hundreds of the best people in Chicago, are as guilty as I am. Everybody calls me a racketeer. I call myself a businessman."**

Capone's business, however, was deadly. There were several hundred gang-related murders in Chicago alone during the 1920s. During a gang war in September 1926, eight carloads of gangsters sprayed Capone's headquarters with machine-gun fire in broad daylight. On February 14, 1929, Capone had his own gangsters—some disguised

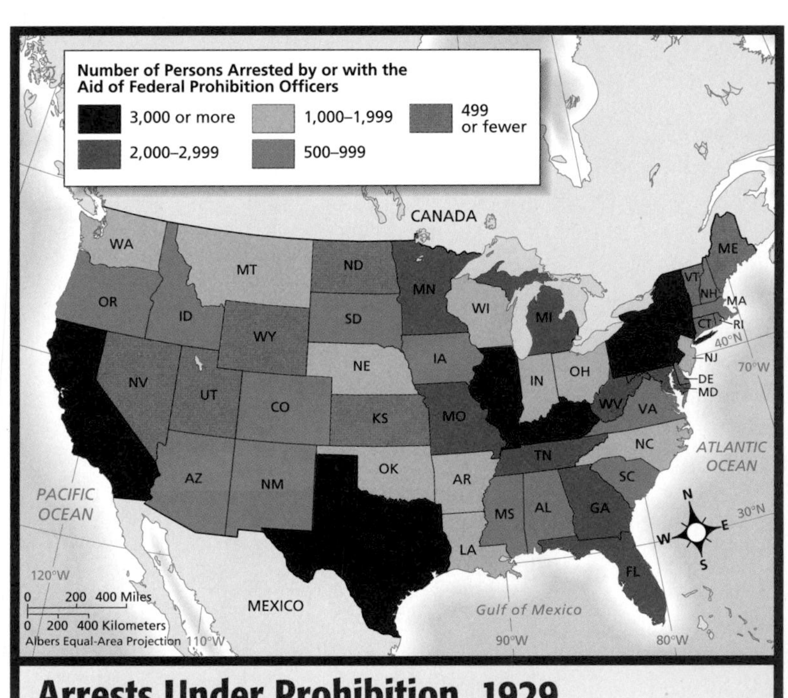

Arrests Under Prohibition, 1929

Learning from Maps Bootleggers smuggled illegal alcohol into the United States from Mexico and Canada.

Location In which states along the U.S.-Mexico border were the most prohibition arrests made?

CHALLENGE AND EXTEND

1. **Logical-Mathematical, Interpersonal.** Have students prepare a documentary on reasons for the adoption of the Eighteenth Amendment and the subsequent adoption of the Twenty-first Amendment. Organize the class into several groups and assign each group one of the following topics: the origins of prohibition in the temperance movement of the 1800s; the connection between the demand for prohibition and the women's suffrage movement; state precedents for prohibition; the debate over adoption of the Eighteenth Amendment; the Volstead Act; changes in American life attributed to prohibition and to government efforts to enforce the Volstead Act; and the gathering of forces that led to the Twenty-first Amendment. Have each group use the library and other resources to gather information on the assigned topic. Then call on each group to report its findings as part of the documentary.
2. **Linguistic, Kinesthetic.** Have students use the library and other resources to find more information about William Jennings Bryan and Clarence Darrow in the Scopes trial. Then have each student present a speech that one of these men might have given during the trial. The speech should be based on actual examples from students' research. Ask students to present their speeches in the style they think their subject

Police take Al Capone's brother, Matthew Capone, into custody.

as police officers—kill seven members of the rival gang. The attack was known as the St. Valentine's Day Massacre. Capone's career finally ended in 1931, when he was convicted for income tax evasion. He was ill when released from prison in 1939 and died eight years later.

The growth of organized crime greatly concerned many Americans. Alcohol consumption decreased during prohibition. However, it soon became clear that the law was very difficult to enforce nationwide. As a result, a movement to repeal prohibition began slowly gaining strength. On December 5, 1933, the **Twenty-first Amendment** ended national prohibition.

 Fundamentalism

Many Protestant groups were united by their support for prohibition but found themselves divided by other issues. One of the central debates involved how to interpret the Bible. Many Christians, often referred to as "modernists," believed that the Bible was divinely inspired but not literally true. An increasing number of Christians, however, joined a movement called **Fundamentalism**. Fundamentalists believe that the Bible is literally true and that it can be relied on as an unquestioned authority.

The movement's name came from a series of booklets, *The Fundamentals,* published between 1910 and 1915. These volumes set forth a series of conservative Protestant beliefs. Fundamentalism appealed to many people who were suspicious of modern industry and science. One Fundamentalist wondered what the value of scientific advances was. "While they are contributing to our material prosperity, they are more rapidly still undermining [destroying] our morals."

Fundamentalist churches were strongest in rural areas and small towns. They were also found in large cities where rural residents had moved to find work. Fundamentalist preacher Billy Sunday drew huge crowds to revival meetings in Chicago. Sunday, a former professional baseball player, was a fiery speaker. He traveled the country holding religious services. Sunday challenged the opponents of prohibition. "I will fight them till hell freezes over, then I'll buy a pair of skates and fight 'em on the ice."

A Canadian-born preacher named Aimee Semple McPherson used a different approach to spread Fundamentalism. McPherson emphasized the blessings and personal joy brought by faith. She preached in the immense Angelus Temple in Los Angeles. Built by her followers, the temple could hold some 5,000 people. In her religious services she used an orchestra, a chorus, and elaborate backgrounds that resembled movie sets. An observer described McPherson as "a superb actress. . . . She sweeps her audience as easily as the harpist beside her sweeps the wires."

McPherson broadcast her sermons over the radio with a transmitter so powerful that it frequently interfered with other stations. Using such new methods in addition to traditional revival meetings, Fundamentalist preachers like McPherson and Sunday carried their religious messages to millions of Americans.

Aimee Semple McPherson was a preacher for nearly 20 years.

The Scopes Trial

Many Fundamentalists strongly opposed Charles Darwin's theory of evolution because it contradicted the biblical account of creation. Darwin had argued that humans had evolved from simpler forms of life over millions of years. In 1925 the Tennessee legislature passed a law making it illegal to teach any theory contrary to the biblical

Biography

Clarence Darrow. By the time he became involved in the Scopes trial, Clarence Darrow had already gained a reputation as a lawyer who defended underdogs. Throughout the late 1800s he was involved with radical causes, such as defending the anarchists charged with starting the Haymarket Riot. During the 1920s Darrow was involved with several high-profile cases, including defending antiwar protesters. After the Scopes trial, Darrow successfully argued in another legal case that an African American family was justified in fighting a mob that had tried to force the family from its home.

Critical Thinking: Why do you think Clarence Darrow was interested in taking the Scopes case?

ANSWER: Darrow seemed to be interested in taking cases that challenged people's civil rights.

might have used. In addition, encourage students to offer suggestions on how the person they studied could have presented the case differently.

REVIEW

Linguistic, Visual-Spatial. Have students complete the Section Review questions. Then create a chart with three columns labeled *Movement, Origins,* and *Effects*. Under the *Movement* heading, have students list rows labeled *Prohibition* and *Fundamentalism.* Have students complete the chart and discuss their answers.

ASSESS

Have students complete Daily Quiz 13.1.

RETEACH

Visual-Spatial. Have students complete Main Idea Activities for Reteaching and Sheltered English 13.1. Then ask each student to draw a political cartoon and write a caption for one issue described in this section. Call on volunteers to explain their cartoons to the class. Continue calling on volunteers until all the section's key issues have been covered. **SHELTERED ENGLISH**

Section 1 Review ANSWERS

Identify

For significance, see the following pages:

- flappers, p. 382
- prohibition, p. 383
- Volstead Act, p. 383
- bootleggers, p. 384
- speakeasies, p. 384
- Al Capone, p. 384
- Twenty-first Amendment, p. 385
- Fundamentalism, p. 385
- Billy Sunday, p. 385
- Aimee Semple McPherson, p. 385
- John T. Scopes, p. 386
- Scopes trial, p. 386
- Clarence Darrow, p. 386
- William Jennings Bryan, p. 386

Reading for Content Understanding

1. fewer Americans drank alcohol, many people broke the law and were arrested, bootleggers and speakeasies began operating, and organized crime developed

2. Fundamentalism grew through large revival meetings and radio broadcasts.

3. They spent more time on educational and extracurricular activities, while radio provided them with a new form of entertainment, and the automobile offered them greater freedom and mobility.

4. Articles will vary but should describe Bryan's literal interpretation of the Bible's account of creation and Darrow's attempts to point out inconsistencies in Bryan's arguments.

5. Many rural inhabitants were concerned that cities threatened traditional values; some urban writers criticized some rural residents' ignorance of new technologies and the modern world.

account of creation. The American Civil Liberties Union (ACLU) argued that the law was unconstitutional and offered to defend anyone who challenged it. The ACLU's chance came when high school science teacher John T. Scopes volunteered to teach Darwin's theory. Scopes was arrested in Dayton, Tennessee, for breaking the law. He was brought to trial in July 1925.

Many Americans saw the **Scopes trial** as a symbol of how American society was struggling to cope with changing times. Some people supported Scopes, while others sided with the Fundamentalists. Clarence Darrow, a famous criminal attorney, led the defense. Three-time presidential candidate William Jennings Bryan led the prosecution. The quiet town of Dayton was transformed by the trial. More than 100 newspaper, magazine, and radio reporters from across the United States and abroad covered the event. Preachers held meetings in tents on the edge of town. Vendors sold soda, hot dogs, fans, and Bibles to the many visitors.

The monkey standing between William Jennings Bryan (left) and Clarence Darrow (right) represents Darwin's theory of evolution.

The judge in the case refused to allow scientific experts to testify about the theory of evolution. Darrow therefore tried to find some inconsistency in the prosecution's argument. The prosecution argued that the biblical theory of creation was the literal truth. Bryan agreed to testify as an expert on the Bible. When he took the stand, the crowd was so large that the trial was moved outdoors. Darrow questioned Bryan at length. During his testimony, Bryan seemed to accept that some parts of the Bible might be open to interpretation.

Nevertheless, Scopes was convicted and fined $100. The Tennessee Supreme Court overturned Scopes's conviction in 1927 on a technicality but upheld the law against teaching evolution. The controversy over evolution did not end. Religious beliefs continued to influence debates in American politics and culture.

SECTION 1 REVIEW

Identify and explain the significance of the following:

- **flappers**
- **prohibition**
- **Volstead Act**
- **bootleggers**
- **speakeasies**
- **Al Capone**
- **Twenty-first Amendment**
- **Fundamentalism**
- **Billy Sunday**
- **Aimee Semple McPherson**
- **John T. Scopes**
- **Scopes trial**
- **Clarence Darrow**
- **William Jennings Bryan**

Reading for Content Understanding

1 **Main Idea** What was the effect of prohibition on the United States in the 1920s?

2 **Main Idea** How did Fundamentalism grow in the 1920s?

3 **Cultural Diversity** In what ways were the experiences of young Americans in the 1920s different from those of previous generations?

4 **Writing** *Describing* Imagine that you are a newspaper reporter covering the Scopes trial. Write a brief article describing the trial. Include the views of both Scopes's supporters and his Fundamentalist opponents.

5 **Critical Thinking** *Synthesizing Information* What were some of the key differences between rural and urban Americans in the 1920s?

OBJECTIVES

- Explain how nativism affected immigration after World War I.
- Analyze the challenges minority groups faced and the progress they made in the 1920s.
- Describe how political and economic opportunities for women changed during the 1920s.

FOCUS

Motivate Before Reading

Have students read Henry Curran's observations of Ellis Island at the beginning of this section. Ask students to identify possible reasons for the situation and explain why the people involved were sad. Call on volunteers to share their opinions with the class. Then tell students that in this section they will learn about nativist attitudes that encouraged the U.S. government to limit immigration

A Changing Population

Reading Focus

How did nativism affect immigration after World War I?

What challenges did minority groups in the United States face during the 1920s, and what progress did they make?

How did women's political and economic opportunities change during the 1920s?

Key Terms

Emergency Quota Act
National Origins Act
Great Migration
Universal Negro Improvement Association
Indian Citizenship Act

IN JULY 1923 Henry Curran became commissioner of the immigration station on Ellis Island. In his first week of work Curran witnessed a scene that he later recorded in his memoirs. From his office window he watched hundreds of immigrants being forced to return home because of new laws restricting immigration. "They trooped aboard the big barges . . . some carrying little American flags, most of them quietly weeping." Such scenes, which Curran said "twisted something in my heart that hurts to this day," became increasingly common in the 1920s as Congress passed stricter immigration laws.

A coversheet for a 1923 song protesting immigration

Opposing Immigration

Immediately after World War I, the U.S. economy suffered a brief recession. Rapid demobilization led to layoffs and labor strikes. Many Americans blamed the hard times on the millions of immigrants living in the United States.

Nativism

A wave of nativism, or strong anti-immigrant feeling, swept the nation. Opponents of immigration claimed that immigrants took jobs away from U.S. citizens. Some Americans were also influenced by the Red Scare. They believed that immigrants introduced politically radical ideas—such as communism and anarchism—that were dangerous to American democracy. Alabama senator James Heflin claimed that:

> **"[immigrants] fill places that belong to the loyal wage-earning citizens of America. They preach a doctrine [belief] that is dangerous and deadly to our institutions. . . . They constitute a menace and danger to us every day."**

Section 2 RESOURCES

PRINT

- ★ Guided Reading Strategies 13.2
- ★ Primary Source Reading 13: Mexican Americans in the 1920s
- ★ Biography Reading 13: Marcus Garvey
- ★ Section 2 Review, p. 392
- ★ Daily Quiz 13.2

MULTIMEDIA

- ★ *Teaching Resources CD–ROM*, Lesson 13.2
- ★ Linking Geography and History Transparency 17: African American Population, 1920

SHELTERED ENGLISH

- ★ Main Idea Activities for Reteaching and Sheltered English 13.2

after World War I, as well as about challenges and opportunities that women and minority groups faced during the 1920s.

Introduce Key Terms

Linguistic, Logical-Mathematical. Review this section's key terms with students. Have students use context cues to define each term, summarize its meaning, or list its provisions. Then ask students to write a question about each term. As students read the section, have them answer their own questions.
SHELTERED ENGLISH

TEACH

Have students read Section 2 and complete Guided Reading Strategies 13.2. Choose one or more of the following activities to explore the section content with students. For further suggestions on block scheduling or team teaching, see the *Block Scheduling Handbook.*

LEVEL 1: Linguistic. (Suggested time: 15 min.) As a class, go over students' Guided Reading Strategies. Then use the Reading Focus questions to highlight the main ideas of the section.
SHELTERED ENGLISH

Linking Past to Present

Nativism. Nativism of the 1920s was not a new phenomenon. In the mid-1800s, the potato famine, political unrest, and poverty in Europe caused millions of immigrants to come to the United States. Nativists, alarmed by the growing foreign-born population, responded to this earlier wave of immigration by forming the American Party, also known as the Know-Nothing Party. It gained its nickname because members refused to discuss their political beliefs with outsiders. Rather than push for tough immigration restrictions, party members advocated extending to 21 years the time required for aliens to become U.S. citizens.

Critical Thinking: Why might nativists of the 1920s have pushed to restrict immigration while those of the 1850s did not?

ANSWER: Industrial expansion in the 1850s provided places for immigrants to work without displacing as many U.S. citizens. The recession following World War I, however, reduced employment opportunities. In addition, many immigrants in the 1920s were from eastern and southern Europe and stood out more in American society.

Nativists focused their criticism on immigrants from southern and eastern Europe. The languages, customs, and religious beliefs of these individuals were often different from those of earlier immigrants from northern and western Europe. Nativists considered these differences a threat to American culture. Arriving into this atmosphere of suspicion and hostility, one immigrant asked:

> **"Isn't it strange that here we are coming to a country where there is complete equality, but not quite so for the newly arrived immigrants?"**

Restricting Immigration

Even after the postwar recession ended, nativists were concerned by increasing immigration to the United States. More than 800,000 immigrants arrived in 1921 alone. In May 1921 President Harding signed the **Emergency Quota Act**. This law limited total immigration to the United States to 357,000 a year. It also restricted the number of immigrants from any European nation to only 3 percent of each nationality's U.S. population according to the 1910 U.S census.

Some pamphlets tried to help immigrants become U.S. citizens.

This law excluded many eastern and southern European immigrants because there were relatively small numbers of them living in the United States in 1910. The act set no limits, however, on immigration from nations in the Western Hemisphere. American farmers and business owners benefited from this policy because they hired many Canadian and Mexican immigrants.

Congress passed the **National Origins Act** in May 1924, further reducing total immigration. For example, this act completely banned Japanese immigration to the United States. In addition, the new law based the limits on European immigration on the 1890 U.S. census. As a result, the law gave even greater preference to immigrants from northern and western Europe. The act also made it much easier for the government to deport immigrants already living in the United States.

This 1920s cartoon argues that many new immigrants did not mix well into American society.

The Ku Klux Klan

The growing hostility toward immigrants also contributed to the rebirth of the Ku Klux Klan. Re-formed in 1915 by minister William J. Simmons in Stone Mountain, Georgia, the Klan grew slowly during World War I. Until 1920 the Klan had only a few thousand members. Its scope was confined to Alabama and Georgia. After 1920, however, the Klan began using recruiters and modern advertising to promote itself as a defender of "Americanism."

ALL LEVELS: Logical-Mathematical, Visual-Spatial. (Suggested time: 45 min.) Have each student prepare a cause-and-effect chart showing how nativism affected immigration to the United States after World War I. In the first column, have students point out arguments that were made against immigration. In the second column, have students identify actions that resulted from those arguments. For instance, in the first column, students could state that many Americans blamed immigrants for the economic difficulties they experienced after the war. In the second column, students can identify the Emergency Quota Act. Tell students that they should have more items in the first column than in the second. Call on volunteers to explain their charts to the class. **SHELTERED ENGLISH**

LEVEL 2: Logical-Mathematical, Visual-Spatial. (Suggested time: 20 min. plus homework) Have each student create a three-column graphic organizer showing the challenges African Americans, American Indians, Mexican Americans, and women faced during the 1920s, and the progress they made. In the first column, have students identify each group. In the second column, have them identify the challenges each group faced. In the third column, have students identify the progress each group made. Call on volunteers to explain their work to the class.

An anti-immigration Ku Klux Klan poster

Klan leaders pledged to protect the nation's white, Protestant society from threats of radical change and from people of different cultures and color. Members of the Klan not only were hostile toward African Americans but also targeted Catholics, Jews, and foreigners. The Klan used cross-burnings, beatings, kidnappings, and murders to terrorize its victims. Recruiters downplayed the Klan's racism and use of violence. Instead, they compared the Klan to the business and social clubs popular at the time. As a result, the Klan grew at an amazing rate. At its peak in the mid-1920s, the Ku Klux Klan claimed about 4 million members, including thousands of women and children.

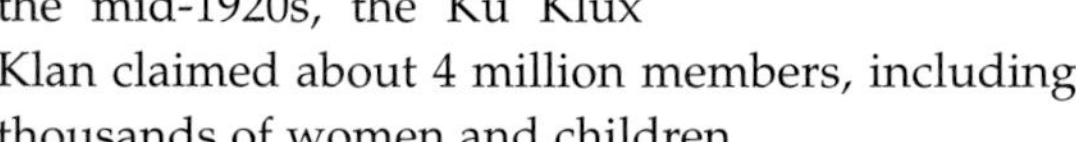

Soon the Klan became a strong force in local politics and influenced elections in states from Maine to Oregon. In Indiana, Klan leader David Stephenson virtually controlled local and state politics. He boasted, "I am the law." In 1925 Stephenson's career ended when he was convicted of second-degree murder. When his political allies abandoned him, he exposed widespread corruption within the Klan.

The news that Klan leaders, promoters, and recruiters were getting rich on membership dues greatly decreased the Klan's influence. The scandals and congressional investigations that followed further reduced the Klan's power nationwide.

Challenging Discrimination

Even before the expansion of the Klan, racism and poverty motivated many African Americans to leave the South. During the labor shortage of World War I, some 500,000 African Americans moved to midwestern and northern cities. They hoped to find better jobs and greater social opportunities. This mass movement was known as the **Great Migration**.

The NAACP and the UNIA

Even after they moved to northern communities, African Americans faced job discrimination and the threat of violence. Black leaders responded to these challenges in different ways. The National Association for the Advancement of Colored People (NAACP) fought segregation and racial inequality. It used the courts as well as writings to call attention to discrimination. W. E. B. Du Bois, a founding member of the NAACP, wrote that he expected change to come "through reason, human sympathy, and the education of children."

Marcus Garvey clashed with Du Bois and other NAACP leaders over integration. Garvey stated that he would not "waste time . . . waiting for white people to recognize me." He was born in Jamaica, where he first organized the **Universal Negro Improvement Association** (UNIA) in 1914. The UNIA's goals were to end imperialism in Africa and discrimination in the United States. In 1916 Garvey moved to the neighborhood of Harlem in New York City and founded a UNIA chapter. A powerful speaker, Garvey attracted an estimated 1 million members worldwide to the UNIA by 1921.

Garvey's Program

Garvey supported a movement called black nationalism, which encouraged African Americans to be economically independent and to take pride in their African heritage. As part of this effort he supported a "back to Africa" movement. This effort was intended to help African Americans resettle in Africa and rebuild its economy. Garvey also urged African Americans to start their own businesses in the United States. He personally

Marcus Garvey organized several international conventions of the UNIA.

Constitutional Heritage

Controversy over the Klan. In 1924 the Democratic Party was divided over a resolution condemning the Ku Klux Klan. Many southern and western Democrats tended to sympathize with the Klan, while party members from the North and the East, who represented many Catholics and immigrants, opposed the Klan bitterly. Fistfights broke out before party members finally voted down the resolution. As a result, the Democratic Party did not condemn the Klan by name but rather affirmed the party's allegiance to the U.S. Constitution.

Critical Thinking: Why might affirming allegiance to the Constitution be a way of criticizing the Ku Klux Klan?

ANSWER: The Klan's ideals contradicted the principles of equality laid out in the Constitution, and the Klan's methods violated basic constitutional freedoms as well as the laws of many states.

Multimedia Resources

Linking Geography and History Transparency 17: African American Population, 1920

LEVEL 3: Linguistic, Logical-Mathematical, Interpersonal. (Suggested time: 45 min.) Ask students to imagine that they are living in the 1920s. Organize the class into two groups and have them prepare for a debate on the following: *Resolved, the Nineteenth Amendment represents the beginning of women's campaign for political equality with men, not the final achievement of equality.* Have members of one group prepare arguments supporting the resolution and members of the other group prepare arguments refuting the resolution. Ask students to use information from the text to support their arguments. Then organize the class into groups of four, with two students representing each side of the debate. Finally, have each group conduct the debate.

CLOSE

Linguistic, Interpersonal. Organize students into small groups and have them discuss the responses of African Americans, American Indians, Mexican Americans, and immigrants to prejudice and discrimination in the 1920s. Have each student prepare an agenda for a meeting of community leaders who intend to deal with these issues. Agendas should suggest ways of easing tensions in the community and propose laws establishing consequences for acts of discrimination. Encourage volunteers to discuss their plans with the class.

Cultural Diversity

American Indians in World War I. Choctaw soldiers played an important role during World War I. The Germans had broken codes used by the U.S. Army, which made it unsafe to transmit plans and orders. Because the Germans could not interpret the Choctaw language, the U.S. Army asked several Choctaw to transmit battle plans in their native language. Their efforts led to the capture of 9 enemy officers, 185 enlisted personnel, and 31 machine guns.

Activity: Have students use the library and other sources to find information on American Indians' contributions to the war effort. Ask students to write an article summarizing their findings.

Mexican immigrants Lupe and Juan Salvador Villaseñor were married in 1929. In a traditional ceremony these coins, called arras, *are given by the groom to the bride to show that he will always provide for her.*

established several companies. In 1919 he founded the Black Star steamship line to provide trade and transportation between Africa and the Americas. In addition, the UNIA funded the *Negro World.* This publication quickly became the most widely read black newspaper in America.

In 1922, however, Black Star suspended operations. After the federal government investigated Black Star's finances, Garvey was convicted of mail fraud, fined $1,000, and sentenced to five years in jail. He served two years before being released in 1927 and deported to Jamaica. Despite his legal problems, the *Amsterdam News* described Garvey as having "made black people proud of their race. In a world where black is despised he taught them black is beautiful."

Mexican Americans

Like African Americans, many Mexican Americans had moved north to fill jobs during World War I. This migration continued during the 1920s as restrictions on European immigration and the expanding U.S. economy created a labor shortage. Thousands of Mexican American workers went to manufacturing centers such as Chicago, Detroit, and Pittsburgh.

In addition to this Mexican American migration north, between 500,000 and 1 million Mexicans immigrated to the United States during the 1920s. Some immigrants were searching for new economic opportunities. Others were escaping the problems caused by the Mexican Revolution. Most families of Mexican descent settled in the West and Southwest, particularly in California and Texas. There they worked mainly as agricultural laborers.

Life in their new country could be difficult for Mexican immigrants. They were usually poorly paid. The struggle to make ends meet often meant that young women had to work outside the home, which was a change from their traditional role. Immigrants often lived in temporary camps filled with shacks constructed of scrap wood. In some communities, Spanish-speaking residents formed barrios, or neighborhoods, where they shared a common culture. In the barrio, author and educator Ernesto Galarza recalled, "we heard Spanish on the streets and in the alleys." In contrast, when Galarza and his family left the barrio to go downtown they felt "like aliens in a foreign land."

American Indians

The thousands of American Indians living on reservations also faced hardships. Officials of the

A delegation of Pueblo Indians arrived in Washington, D.C., in 1923 to protest the mistreatment of tribal members and threats to tribal lands.

CHALLENGE AND EXTEND

1. **Linguistic, Logical-Mathematical, Intrapersonal.** Have students use the library and other resources to find information on the following topics: the life and career of Carrie Chapman Catt; the formation of the League of Women Voters; the life and career of Alice Paul; the National Woman's Party; and the proposed Equal Rights Amendment of 1923. Then have students use information about each of these topics to write an essay on the causes and effects of the changing role of women in the 1920s. Encourage students to read at least one other student's essay.

2. **Logical-Mathematical.** Have students use the library and other resources to find information on either the effects of changing demographic patterns resulting from the Great Migration or how people from various ethnic and religious groups expanded their economic opportunities and political rights in American society during the 1920s. Allow students to choose the format they would like to use to present the information they find to the class. Finally, have students make their presentations.

federal Bureau of Indian Affairs had hoped to address the problems of poverty and poor housing with the Dawes Act, passed in 1887. This act took reservation land away from American Indian tribes and allotted sections of it to individual Indians. Reservation land that was left over after this distribution was usually sold to non-Indians.

The breaking up of the reservations was intended to help establish independent Indian ranches and farms. Instead, the Dawes Act greatly disrupted tribal culture and removed millions of acres of land from Indian control. By 1934, American Indians owned only about a third of the land they had owned in 1887.

American Indians also faced political restrictions. Many Indians living within the United States were not recognized as U.S. citizens. Despite this restriction, during World War I around 10,000 American Indians served in the U.S. military. At home, American Indians purchased an estimated $25 million in war bonds. Indian leaders pointed to these patriotic acts and demanded U.S. citizenship. "Many of our young men . . . gave their lives for you," argued Deskaheh, a Cayuga chief. In response to these demands, Congress passed the **Indian Citizenship Act** in June 1924. This legislation granted all American Indians the legal protections and voting privileges of U.S. citizenship.

Indian leaders won another political victory in 1922 when the Pueblo tribes united to fight the Bursum Bill. This legislation would have taken away thousands of acres of Pueblo land. Receiving national support from groups such as the General Federation of Women's Clubs, the Pueblo successfully defended their ownership of tribal lands. Such political accomplishments gave some Indian leaders hope for future reforms. Many Indians, however, continued to suffer economic hardship and social discrimination during the 1920s.

Women in the 1920s

American women also made political gains during the decade. In 1920 they gained the vote with the ratification of the Nineteenth Amendment. Voting gave women the ability to influence national politics directly. It also increased women's opportunities to become political leaders.

After women gained the vote in 1920, suffragists encouraged them to go to the polls.

Women in Politics

In 1924 Nellie Tayloe Ross of Wyoming and Miriam "Ma" Wallace Ferguson of Texas became the first two female governors in the United States. By 1928, 145 women held seats in state legislatures, and 2 women had been elected to the U.S. House of Representatives.

The National Woman's Party (NWP), led by Alice Paul, sought broader social gains. The NWP called for the abolition of laws that regulated the type of work women could do, the pay they could receive, and the loans they could get. In December 1923 the NWP proposed an Equal Rights Amendment (ERA) to the U.S. Constitution.

Disagreements over the ERA divided the women's movement. The Women's Trade Union League had fought for labor legislation to protect women. It was concerned that the ERA would remove these legal safeguards. The League of Women Voters argued that the ERA was too broad and would interfere with women's roles in society. Paul disagreed with such arguments:

> **"If we get freedom for women, then they are probably going to do a lot of things that I wish they wouldn't do. But it seems to me that isn't our business to say what they should do with it. It is our business to see that they get it."**

The ERA failed to pass despite the efforts of the NWP and other supporters.

Historical Sidelight

Ma and Pa Ferguson. Had it not been for her husband's misconduct, Miriam "Ma" Wallace Ferguson may never have become governor of Texas in 1924. Jim Ferguson was elected as the state's governor in 1914. He soon was impeached, however, for appropriating state funds for personal use, depositing state funds in a bank in which he invested, and failing to repay a campaign loan from the liquor lobby. He was subsequently barred from holding public office in Texas. However, he still had widespread public support. This fact gave him the idea of having his wife run for governor so that he could remain involved in Texas politics. One popular campaign slogan that showed this connection stated, "Me for Ma, and I ain't got a dern thing against Pa!"

Activity: Have students use the library and other resources to find information on the governorships of both Ma and Pa Ferguson. Ask students to create campaign posters giving each governor's platform and providing some information on their earlier careers.

REVIEW

Logical-Mathematical, Interpersonal. Have students complete the Section Review questions. Then assign each student one Reading Focus question from this section. Have students use material from the section to create a practice quiz for the assigned question. Then organize students into groups of three—one member for each question. Have group members take each other's practice quizzes and review any incorrect answers.

RETEACH

Kinesthetic, Visual-Spatial. Have students complete Main Idea Activities for Reteaching and Sheltered English 13.2. Then ask students to discuss the challenges faced by the following groups in the United States during the 1920s: African Americans, American Indians, Mexican Americans, immigrants, and women. Finally, have students create a Venn diagram comparing and contrasting the challenges and successes of two of these groups during the 1920s. SHELTERED ENGLISH

ASSESS

Have students complete Daily Quiz 13.2.

Section 2 Review ANSWERS

Identify
For significance, see the following pages:

- Emergency Quota Act, p. 388
- National Origins Act, p. 388
- Great Migration, p. 389
- Marcus Garvey, p. 389
- Universal Negro Improvement Association, p. 389
- Indian Citizenship Act, p. 391
- Alice Paul, p. 391

Reading for Content Understanding

1. Congress passed the Emergency Quota Act and the National Origins Act, both of which restricted immigration.

2. violence, intimidation, and job discrimination; the NAACP fought racial inequality through the courts and by calling attention to discrimination, while the UNIA supported black nationalism

3. received the right to vote, held public offices, and entered the workplace in greater numbers

4. Articles will vary but students should point out that Mexican Americans were generally poorly paid, worked in northern manufacturing centers or as agricultural laborers in the West and Southwest, and faced poor living conditions.

5. Answers will vary but students might argue that since American Indians had proven their loyalty by fighting, they should receive the same rights as other Americans.

CHART ANSWER
1890—about 13 percent;
1930—almost 30 percent

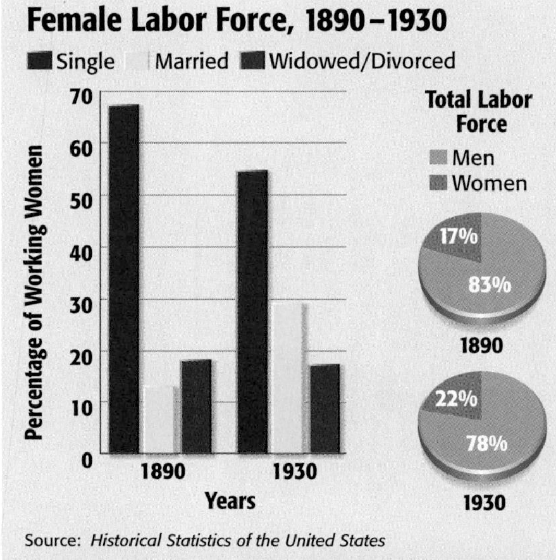

Women at Work By 1930 both the size and the distribution of the female labor force had changed significantly. What percentage of working women were married in 1890? in 1930?

Women at Work

Even without the passage of an Equal Rights Amendment, women's roles in the workplace were changing during the 1920s. World War I had provided thousands of women with the opportunity to enter industrial jobs traditionally held by men. As suffrage leader Harriot Stanton Blatch explained, "When men go a-warring, women go to work." After the war, business and union leaders asked women to give up these industrial jobs so that returning war veterans could go back to work.

Thousands of women sought other work because they were unwilling to surrender their economic and social independence. By the end of the 1920s the number of women working outside the home had risen by 2 million. Many of these women worked in offices as secretaries, telephone operators, or typists. The number of women in professional fields such as nursing and teaching also increased. Some professional women gained national recognition. For example, Dr. Florence R. Sabin became the first female member of the National Academy of Sciences.

In spite of these gains, women continued to face obstacles in the workforce. Most clerical, nursing, and teaching jobs paid relatively little for the skills required. In addition, employers often refused to hire minority women for such jobs. As a result, many African American and Hispanic women took lower-paying domestic or factory work. Women's rights activists continued to struggle throughout the 1920s to achieve greater social and economic equality.

SECTION 2 REVIEW

Identify and explain the significance of the following:

- **Emergency Quota Act**
- **National Origins Act**
- **Great Migration**
- **Marcus Garvey**
- **Universal Negro Improvement Association**
- **Indian Citizenship Act**
- **Alice Paul**

Reading for Content Understanding

1 **Main Idea** How did Congress respond to nativist concerns over immigration?

2 **Main Idea** What problems did African Americans face during the 1920s, and what solutions did black leaders seek?

3 **Citizenship and Democracy** What political and economic gains did women achieve during the 1920s?

4 **Writing** *Describing* Imagine that you are a journalist interviewing a Mexican immigrant family in the United States during the 1920s. Write a short article describing the family's experiences, including where its members live, their work, and any difficulties that they have encountered.

5 **Critical Thinking** *Identifying Cause and Effect* Why do you think that the participation of American Indians in World War I helped convince Congress to grant them U.S. citizenship?

OBJECTIVES

- Explain what led to the rise of fads in the 1920s.
- Analyze the effects of radio and the movies on American culture.
- Describe Americans' attitudes toward movie actors and professional athletes during the 1920s.

FOCUS

Motivate Before Reading

Ask students to identify some of the most famous people in the United States today. As students provide names, write them on the chalkboard. (You may need to guide students to identify some famous athletes and actors.) Then ask students to imagine an American culture in which athletes and actors were not considered important enough to obtain celebrity status. Have students

Americans at Play

Reading Focus

What led to the rise of fads in the 1920s?

How did radio and movies affect American culture?

What did Americans think of movie actors and professional athletes during the 1920s?

Key Terms

fads
nickelodeons
talkies

ONE DAY IN 1927 Alvin "Shipwreck" Kelly climbed onto a flagpole and did not come down. Day after day, he perched on top of the pole. When he was hungry or thirsty, Kelly hauled food and drink up in a bucket. At night he slept only briefly, fearing he would fall to his death. He never slept for more than 20 minutes at a time. After 23 days and seven hours on his flagpole, Kelly finally climbed down, having achieved his goal. Shipwreck Kelly was the new world-record holder in flagpole sitting. Some hotels actually hired him to attract business by sitting on flagpoles. Kelly sat on flagpoles for 145 days in 1929, earning $29,000.

Alvin "Shipwreck" Kelly sits on top of a flagpole in New York City.

Fads and Fun

Shipwreck Kelly's stunts were part of an adventurous spirit that led some Americans to nickname the decade the Roaring Twenties. The national economy enjoyed spectacular growth. Americans were encouraged to buy new consumer products and experiment with new leisure activities.

The 1920s were also a time of **fads**—interests followed with great enthusiasm by many people for a short time. Fads owed much of their existence to the increased influence of mass media in the 1920s. Across the nation people could watch the same movies and listen to the same radio broadcasts. They could also read the same articles and view the same advertisements. This ability allowed people throughout the country to share cultural activities such as fads.

Fads varied widely. In 1923 a Chinese game known as mah jongg

Mah jongg sets contain either 136 or 144 tiles.

Section 3 RESOURCES

PRINT

- ★ Guided Reading Strategies 13.3
- ★ Graphic Organizer 13: America's Popular Culture
- ★ Section 3 Review, p. 398
- ★ Daily Quiz 13.3

MULTIMEDIA

- ★ *Teaching Resources CD–ROM,* Lesson 13.3
- ★ HRW Web site

SHELTERED ENGLISH

- ★ Main Idea Activities for Reteaching and Sheltered English 13.3

describe how that would change life in the United States. After students have finished their descriptions, tell them that in this section they will learn about cultural developments of the 1920s, such as the rising popularity of professional athletes and movie actors.

Introduce Key Terms

Linguistic, Visual-Spatial. Review this section's key terms with students. Have them use the text to determine the meaning of each term. Then ask them to make sketches depicting each of the key terms. Call on volunteers to display their sketches and have other students identify the terms the drawings represent.
SHELTERED ENGLISH

TEACH

Have students read Section 3 and complete Guided Reading Strategies 13.3. Choose one or more of the following activities to explore the section content with students. For further suggestions on block scheduling or team teaching, see the *Block Scheduling Handbook.*

LEVEL 1: Linguistic. (Suggested time: 15 min.) As a class, go over students' Guided Reading Strategies. Then use the Reading Focus questions to highlight the main ideas of the section.
SHELTERED ENGLISH

Daily Life

Dance Marathons. New types of music that encouraged physical movement rather than passive listening led to a new fad in the 1920s: marathon dance contests. Couples competed to see who could dance continuously for the longest period of time. In one instance, a Houston, Texas, couple danced for 45 hours without stopping. A contest between eight couples in Baltimore, Maryland, eventually was stopped by police after 53 hours. Cash prizes and the thrill of winning motivated couples to continue dancing, even when they suffered swollen ankles and were near total exhaustion.

Critical Thinking: Why might parents in the 1920s have viewed this fad as dangerous?

ANSWER: Marathon dance contests could lead to physical injuries and illnesses. In addition, the contests often were held in roadhouses or speakeasies, both types of places of which many parents may have disapproved.

394

was particularly popular. Another widespread fad was the self-improvement program taught by Emile Coué, a French hypnotist. In 1923 millions of Americans were repeating Coué's simple self-help formula, "Every day, in every way, I'm growing better and better." Other popular new pastimes included crossword puzzles and miniature golf.

Radio

Listening to the radio was much more than a fad. Radio's popularity continued well beyond the 1920s. In 1920 WWJ in Detroit became the first radio station to air regular broadcasts. On November 2, 1920, KDKA in Pittsburgh reported the results of that year's presidential election.

Consumers had to buy magazines and newspapers to read the articles. Radio broadcasts, however, were free to anyone who had access to a radio. To make a profit, radio stations turned to advertising. The first radio advertisements were aired in 1922. Businesspeople loved radio advertising. Business sponsors brought in money that funded more powerful broadcasting equipment and additional radio programming.

Radio broadcasts fascinated many Americans and brought the larger world into individual homes. "We could pull unseen voices out of the air and into the living room from all over the world," remembered one man. Most radio airtime was devoted to live music. Major elections and special events also received live radio news coverage. WGN in Chicago, for example, captured its listeners' attention with live broadcasts of the Scopes trial. Broadcasts of sporting events also helped radio grow in popularity. Radio listeners cheered on their favorite teams during the 1921 World Series.

In 1926 the National Broadcasting Company (NBC) was created, followed the next year by the Columbia Broadcasting System (CBS). By gathering together many radio stations to broadcast their shows, NBC and CBS could reach large numbers of listeners. Soon the networks were broadcasting shows coast-to-coast. A woman working at home in rural Idaho, for example, could hear the daily news from New York City.

By 1929 some 10 million Americans owned radios. Families and friends often gathered to listen to their favorite shows. One woman remembered how her neighbor invited his friends

> **"to come listen to the 'Grand Old Opera' on [each] Saturday night. . . . We were thrilled and looked forward to this each week."**

Radio exposed people all around the country to the same programs, news stories, and advertisements. Live events in politics, sports, and entertainment could be shared by thousands. This common experience bridged cultural differences and helped to link American society.

The Majestic Theater in San Antonio, Texas, was one of many grand movie theaters built in the 1920s.

America Goes to the Movies

Movies were another form of entertainment that brought Americans together. Thomas Edison and others had invented moving pictures, also called movies, in the late 1800s.

The Film Industry

Early films were often short, silent scenes of trains or waterfalls. Many early theaters, which were

TEACHER TO TEACHER

ALL LEVELS: Linguistic, Kinesthetic, Interpersonal. (Suggested time: 45 min. plus homework) Ron Tripp of Shepherd, Michigan, suggested the following activity: Organize students into small groups and have each group develop a news show that might have been broadcast in the early days of radio. Have students include breaking news stories as well as sports and entertainment news. Remind each group to interrupt their broadcast for a commercial. Have students record their broadcasts and play them for the class.

ALL LEVELS: Linguistic, Visual-Spatial. (Suggested time: 30 min.) Have each student create a magazine advertisement for radio or motion pictures that shows how either medium is changing American culture. Ask students to include a slogan with their ads. Have volunteers share their advertisements and slogans with the class. **SHELTERED ENGLISH**

Linking Past to Present

Movie Special Effects

On April 14, 1894, the Holland brothers' amusement arcade opened in New York City. Inside the converted shoe store were 10 cabinets containing Thomas Edison's latest invention—the kinetoscope. For five cents these machines would display a 20-second film of moving images.

In 1896 special-effects pioneer Georges Méliès, a French magician, developed the technique of stop-action to film his magic tricks. Méliès discovered that by stopping and starting the camera, he could make objects seemingly appear, disappear, or change into other objects. His special effects in the 1902 film, *A Trip to the Moon,* influenced filmmakers everywhere.

Animators used computers to create the advanced three-dimensional insects in the film A Bug's Life.

The next year Edwin S. Porter thrilled audiences with *The Great Train Robbery.* Running about 10 minutes, the drama told the story of four bandits who robbed a train. By editing the film, Porter was able to cut backward in time and back and forth across space. These cuts allowed the audience to understand the entire story even though events were happening in different places at the same time.

In more recent years, technological breakthroughs have included color films, wide screens, and stereo. Other inventions were less successful. These included gimmicks such as three-dimensional movies, which required viewers to wear special paper eyeglasses. Smell-O-Vision, which tried to add smells to the movie experience, also flopped.

Movie special effects have come a long way. Today, moviemakers are using digital sound and computer-generated special effects in their films. In his 1990s films *Jurassic Park* and *The Lost World*, director Steven Spielberg used computer animation to draw the dinosaurs. He also used computers to make the dinosaurs' muscles appear to move naturally when they ran. Other new film technologies include interactive movies that allow the audience members to determine the outcome. There is even an updated version of three-dimensional movies without the glasses.

Movie theaters themselves are being redesigned to improve the moviegoing experience. Some of these new design features include gigantic screens and seats that move to allow audiences to feel the action taking place on screen.

Understanding What You Read

1. What special effect did Georges Méliès develop?
2. How did Edwin S. Porter influence the way that movies were directed?
3. Why do you think that many moviemakers use special effects in their films?

Technology and Society

Walt Disney and Animation. The prevailing animation process at the time Walt Disney made *Steamboat Willie* consisted of drawing a series of pictures of one or more characters onto pieces of celluloid. Also called a cel, celluloid had been invented in 1913. Each action picture was drawn to indicate slight movement. The cels were then placed over a background picture, and a camera shot the succession of drawings, one drawing per frame. When the film was shown at 24 frames per second, the characters appeared to move.

Critical Thinking: Why do you think Mickey Mouse was so popular during the 1920s and 1930s?

ANSWER: Answers will vary but students might say that audiences enjoyed the character and watching animated, humorous films.

LINKING PAST TO PRESENT ANSWERS

1. He developed stop-action filming that made objects seem to appear or disappear.
2. He edited his films to enable audiences to see events happening in different places at different times.
3. to create images that cannot be made in other ways and to enhance their films to attract moviegoers

LEVEL 2: Linguistic, Logical-Mathematical. (Suggested time: 45 min.) Have students list the celebrities discussed in this section and identify the field in which each achieved popularity. Then ask students to identify current celebrities in each field they identified. To conclude the activity, have each student write one paragraph analyzing the reasons individuals became celebrities in the 1920s and a second paragraph describing differences between celebrities then and now.

LEVEL 3: Linguistic, Logical-Mathematical. (Suggested time: 30 min. plus homework) Ask students to imagine that they are editors for an entertainment column in a 1920s magazine and that they have been assigned the task of writing an article on the decade's fads. Allow students time in class to begin their articles and have them finish them for homework. Encourage students to include information on what led to the rise of fads, the new fads of the decade, and people who became famous as a result of fads. During the next class, ask volunteers to share their columns with the class.

CLOSE

Visual-Spatial. Have each student create a poster advertising a movie about life in the 1920s. Ask them to provide the film's title, main setting, and a few characters. Have students focus on capturing

Biography

Mary Pickford. Born Gladys Mary Smith in 1893, in Toronto, Canada, Mary Pickford began acting in the theater at the age of five. She was touring by the age of eight, and by 18 was acting on Broadway and starring in early movies. She gave up the theater to focus on movies and soon rocketed to stardom. Audiences loved the innocent and girlish roles she often played. Actually an intelligent and shrewd businesswoman, Pickford became not only one of the most famous stars of the day but also one of the richest. She was the main force behind the founding of United Artists. Pickford retired in the early 1930s, and died in 1979, in Santa Monica, California.

Critical Thinking: Why do you think Pickford tired of playing innocent, little-girl roles when fans loved her so much in them?

Answer: Answers will vary but students might mention that as an intelligent woman she probably wanted to stretch her skills and take on more challenging and interesting roles.

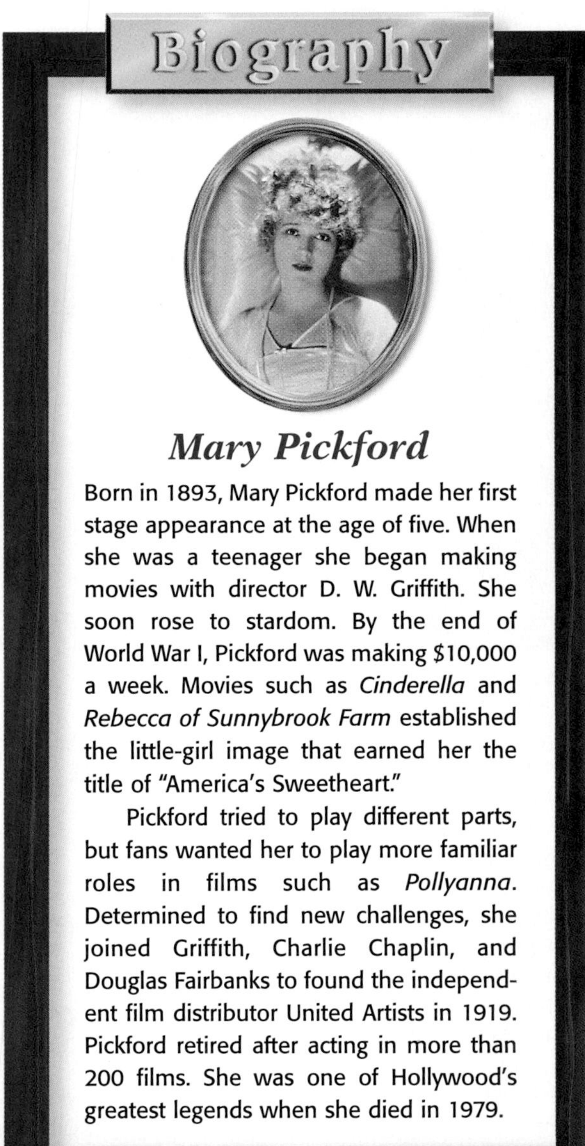

Biography

Mary Pickford

Born in 1893, Mary Pickford made her first stage appearance at the age of five. When she was a teenager she began making movies with director D. W. Griffith. She soon rose to stardom. By the end of World War I, Pickford was making $10,000 a week. Movies such as *Cinderella* and *Rebecca of Sunnybrook Farm* established the little-girl image that earned her the title of "America's Sweetheart."

Pickford tried to play different parts, but fans wanted her to play more familiar roles in films such as *Pollyanna*. Determined to find new challenges, she joined Griffith, Charlie Chaplin, and Douglas Fairbanks to found the independent film distributor United Artists in 1919. Pickford retired after acting in more than 200 films. She was one of Hollywood's greatest legends when she died in 1979.

called **nickelodeons** because admission was usually five cents, were stuffy, converted stores. After World War I, luxurious new theaters with balconies and enormous screens replaced the nickelodeons. Some of these "movie palaces" included orchestras to accompany the silent films. A New York woman described entering one of these theaters as "stepping into another world of fantasy."

By 1928 there were some 20,000 movie theaters in the United States. Millions of Americans went to the movies each year. Even people who lived in small towns made going to the movies a regular event. For example, on Saturdays one young girl's family would walk three miles from their farm in Massachusetts to the nearest town. "How we loved the serials [multipart movies] . . . and how we hoped never to miss a part," she remembered fondly.

In 1927 the first **talkies**—movies with sound or dialogue—thrilled American moviegoers. The first full-length feature talkie was Warner Brothers' *The Jazz Singer*, released in October 1927. Starring Al Jolson, it was an enormous box-office success. One theater owner described the film as "just about the most wonderful thing I had ever seen in my life." Other movie studios quickly adopted the new sound technology. In 1928 Walt Disney's talkie cartoon *Steamboat Willie* introduced audiences to Mickey Mouse.

Mickey Mouse became one of the country's most popular cartoon characters in the 1920s and 1930s.

The American film industry began its existence in New York and New Jersey. By the 1920s the industry was centered in Hollywood, California. Film companies began moving to Hollywood in 1911. They were attracted by sunny weather, cheap real estate, and beautiful natural scenery. Many studio founders were immigrants from eastern Europe. Their achievements were impressive during a time when nativism was strong. Samuel Goldwyn and the Warner Brothers—Harry, Sam, and Albert—emigrated from Poland. Louis B. Mayer arrived from Russia, and William Fox came from Hungary.

Movie Stars

American audiences were less interested in moviemakers than in movie stars. In the early 1920s, 40 million Americans went to the movies every week. By 1929 the number had increased to 80 million. These huge audiences turned their favorite actors and actresses into celebrities almost overnight. One teenager recalled how at the movies he and his friends would "stamp, whistle, holler, the spirit of the decade by identifying trends in radio, movies, sports, and aviation. Once students have finished their posters, call on volunteers to explain their work to the class.

CHALLENGE AND EXTEND

1. **Linguistic, Logical-Mathematical.** Have students use the library and other resources to find information on the growth of the entertainment business and its corresponding effect on the U.S. economy during the 1920s. Ask each student to assess the relationship between the growth of the industry and economic indicators such as increased consumer spending, production, and employment. Have each student write a one-page essay explaining the impact of the entertainment business, in its various manifestations, on the nation's economy.
2. **Linguistic, Musical-Rhythmic.** Have students select any cultural icon of the 1920s who is mentioned in this section, such as Charles Lindbergh, Babe Ruth, or Jim Thorpe. Ask students to use the library and other resources to find more information on their chosen subject. Have each student write a song or poem reflecting how the individual represents a major cultural trend of the 1920s. Call on volunteers to sing their songs or read their poems to the class and to explain the connection.

cheer, clap, and do everything possible to urge on our hero or heroine." Films also influenced national fashion and culture. Young Americans copied their idols' clothes, hairstyles, and ways of walking and talking.

Charlie Chaplin's lovable but pathetic character, the Tramp, may have been the best-known figure in America. Female moviegoers across the country packed theaters to watch heartthrob Rudolph Valentino ride across the desert in *The Sheik.* When Valentino died in 1926, tens of thousands of people, mostly women, lined up for blocks outside the funeral home. Other movie stars included Greta Garbo, Douglas Fairbanks, Clara Bow, and Mary Pickford. Many wealthy movie stars began to draw attention as much for their expensive lifestyles as for their film appearances.

Helen Wills was noted for her concentration on the court and her powerful serves.

 Sports Stars

As organized sports became increasingly popular, Americans also made celebrities out of star athletes. Perhaps the greatest athlete of the 1920s was Jim Thorpe, an American Indian of Sauk and Fox descent. Thorpe won gold medals at the 1912 Olympics in Stockholm, Sweden, in the pentathlon and decathlon. He later played professional baseball and football. In 1920 he became president of the newly formed National Football League. Thorpe played for and coached a number of teams before retiring in 1928.

Other outstanding athletes of the 1920s, such as swimmer Gertrude Ederle and tennis player Helen Wills, also became celebrities. At the 1924 Olympics, Ederle won a gold medal and two bronze medals. Two years later, she swam the English Channel in 14 hours and 31 minutes—nearly two hours faster than the men's record. Wills won four consecutive Wimbledon singles titles from 1927 to 1930. She won more than 30 Grand Slam events during her career.

Team sports were also popular. Thousands of fans packed college football stadiums to see powerful teams from such schools as Notre Dame and the University of Michigan. One of the greatest football players of the 1920s was Harold "Red" Grange, the "Galloping Ghost." He played halfback for the University of Illinois. After his spectacular senior year in 1925 Grange became the first athlete to appear on the cover of *Time* magazine.

As the 1920s began, professional baseball was stunned by a scandal. Players for the Chicago White Sox had accepted money to lose the 1919 World Series. Baseball recovered from the scandal with the help of an exciting young star named George "Babe" Ruth. He became one of baseball's greatest home-run hitters while playing for the New York Yankees. In 1920 he hit more home runs in one season than any previous player. The Yankees became the first team to draw more than 1 million fans in a season. Yankee Stadium was later called The House That Ruth Built. Ruth led the Yankees to four world championships and hit 714 home runs during his career, a record that stood for nearly 40 years.

African Americans were excluded from playing in the major leagues. In response, some black baseball players formed the Negro National League. Stars of these new teams included pitcher Satchel Paige, catcher and home-run hitter Josh Gibson, and outfielder "Cool Papa" Bell. These players were eventually included in baseball's Hall of Fame in Cooperstown, New York.

Home-run hitter Babe Ruth

Cultural Diversity

The Negro Leagues. In the late 1800s African American and white athletes played professional baseball on integrated teams. However, by the 1900s teams had become segregated. New black baseball leagues then formed. These leagues included teams in cities such as New York, Chicago, Detroit, and St. Louis. All these cities had growing African American populations because of the Great Migration. The Negro leagues began to decline in 1947, after Jackie Robinson was recruited to play for the Brooklyn Dodgers. This event ended the color barrier in major league baseball.

Activity: Have students use the library or search the Internet through the HRW Web site to learn more about Negro League players. Ask students to choose one player and design a baseball card for him. The card should include his picture, position, accomplishments, and a short biography.

go.hrw.com
SB1 Negro Leagues

REVIEW

Linguistic, Visual-Spatial. Have students complete the Section Review questions. Then ask students to create a graphic organizer that lists celebrities from the 1920s as column headings and their fields as headings for rows. To complete the organizer, have students fill in each person's accomplishments in his or her field.

ASSESS

Have students complete Daily Quiz 13.3.

RETEACH

Logical-Mathematical. Have students complete Main Idea Activities for Reteaching and Sheltered English 13.3. Have students draw a montage that illustrates American culture during the 1920s. Encourage students to include as many of the celebrities and popular pastimes mentioned in this section as possible. Display students' montages around the class. **SHELTERED ENGLISH**

Section 3 Review ANSWERS

Identify
For significance, see the following pages:

- fads, p. 393
- nickelodeons, p. 396
- talkies, p. 396
- Charlie Chaplin, p. 397
- Mary Pickford, p. 397
- Jim Thorpe, p. 397
- George "Babe" Ruth, p. 397
- Charles Lindbergh, p. 398
- Amelia Earhart, p. 398

Reading for Content Understanding

1. Fads escalated in part because of the increased influence of mass media, which enabled people throughout the country to share cultural activities and trends.

2. They treated movie and sports stars as celebrities and heroes.

3. Radio and movies exposed people around the country to the same influences, which led to fads and cultural trends.

4. Letters will vary but students should describe their amazement at the broadcast, the type of program they heard, where it originated, and whether they enjoyed it.

5. These individuals seemed to represent America's pioneering spirit, thus making them national heroes; students' answers will vary but should include an explanation of why they consider the individual to be a modern-day hero.

Daring Aviators

Pilot Charles Lindbergh was one of the biggest celebrities of the 1920s. Lindbergh took off from Long Island, New York, on the morning of May 20, 1927. His goal was to become the first person to fly solo across the Atlantic Ocean. Six expert pilots had already died while attempting this feat. By comparison, Lindbergh was a little known pilot without much financial backing. Few people thought that he could succeed where others had failed so tragically.

Lindbergh, who was called the Lone Eagle as well as Lucky Lindy, beat the odds. About 33 and a half hours after taking off, he landed his plane, the *Spirit of St. Louis,* in Paris. News of his arrival on the night of May 21 drew more than 100,000 French people to the airport to meet the daring pilot. Lindbergh later recalled:

> **"My name was called out over and over again. . . . I opened the door, and started to put my foot down onto ground. But dozens of hands took hold of me—my legs, my arms, my body. . . . I found myself lying . . . up on top of the crowd, in the center of an ocean of heads that extended as far out into the darkness as I could see."**

Back in the United States, Lindbergh's achievement captured the imagination of the American public. He was honored with parades, given multiple medals, and featured on a new postage stamp. Lindbergh's flight even helped boost investment in the aviation industry.

The Granger Collection, New York

Charles Lindbergh posing just before his historic flight across the Atlantic Ocean

Lindbergh inspired other daring aviators. In 1928 Amelia Earhart became the first woman to fly across the Atlantic. Earhart continued to thrill Americans with her long-distance journeys until she disappeared in 1937 while trying to fly around the world. In a time when many Americans felt that the frontier had disappeared, pilots such as Lindbergh and Earhart seemed to represent the return of the nation's old pioneering spirit.

SECTION 3 REVIEW

Identify and explain the significance of the following:

- **fads**
- **nickelodeons**
- **talkies**
- **Charlie Chaplin**
- **Mary Pickford**
- **Jim Thorpe**
- **George "Babe" Ruth**
- **Charles Lindbergh**
- **Amelia Earhart**

Reading for Content Understanding

1 **Main Idea** Why were fads so common during the 1920s?

2 **Main Idea** How did Americans treat movie and sports stars in the 1920s?

3 **Technology and Society** How did developments such as radio and movies affect American culture in the 1920s?

4 **Writing** *Expressing* Imagine that you have just heard a radio broadcast for the first time. Write a short letter about the experience of listening to the broadcast to a friend who has never heard a radio.

5 **Critical Thinking** *Drawing Conclusions* Why do you think many Americans considered individuals like Charles Lindbergh to be national heroes? Who do you consider to be a modern-day hero, and why?

OBJECTIVES

- **Analyze the influence of the blues and jazz on American culture.**
- **Explain the significance of the Harlem Renaissance and the Lost Generation.**
- **Describe other major developments in American arts during the 1920s.**

FOCUS

Motivate Before Reading

Locate and play recordings of 1920s blues and jazz music for the class. Ask students to describe the differences between the two musical forms. To explain the differences, encourage students to concentrate on each genre's instruments, tempo, and lyrics. Then ask students to describe similarities and differences between blues and jazz of the 1920s and today's popular music. Tell students that

The Arts

Reading Focus

How did the blues and jazz affect American culture?

Why were the Harlem Renaissance and the Lost Generation significant?

What were some of the other major developments in American arts in the 1920s?

Key Terms

Jazz Age
Harlem Renaissance
Lost Generation
expatriates
Armory Show

IN 1926, African American writer Langston Hughes published an influential essay in the magazine The Nation. *In it he declared that a new era of African American literature and art was beginning. "We young Negro artists who create now intend to express our individual dark-skinned selves without fear or shame," he announced. "We know we are beautiful." African American arts flourished during the 1920s and helped shape the cultural development of the decade.*

Poet Langston Hughes

The Jazz Age

One of the arts in which African Americans had the greatest influence during the 1920s was music. Two of the most popular musical styles were the blues and jazz. Both styles had deep roots in African American culture.

The Blues

The blues emerged from the countryside and small towns of the rural Mississippi Delta region in the South. The blues evolved from the spirituals and work chants that had been sung by enslaved African Americans. By the 1890s the blues had become a distinct musical style. Blues musicians often used instruments to imitate the singing voice. The most popular blues instruments were the guitar, harmonica, and piano. Blues performers sang lyrics dealing with a wide range of topics, including daily struggles, racism, and lost love.

Born in Alabama, musician W. C. Handy helped popularize the blues in the North. Known as the Father of the Blues, Handy wrote songs such as "St. Louis Blues." This hit song described life in a St. Louis neighborhood of the 1890s. The most

Section 4
RESOURCES

PRINT

★ Guided Reading Strategies 13.4

★ Literature Reading 13: Poetry of the Harlem Renaissance

★ Section 4 Review, p. 405

★ Daily Quiz 13.4

MULTIMEDIA

★ *Teaching Resources CD–ROM,* Lesson 13.4

★ Art in American History Transparency 28: *Falling Water (Kaufmann House)*

★ Everyday Life in America Transparency 22: Harlem Renaissance Art, 1920s

★ *American Music Audio CD Program:* "Harmonica Blues"

★ *American History Interactive Maps CD–ROM:* The Harlem Renaissance

★ HRW Web site

SHELTERED ENGLISH

★ Main Idea Activities for Reteaching and Sheltered English 13.4

in this section they will learn about a creative era in American arts that brought changes to music, literature, theater, photography, and architecture.

Introduce Key Terms

Linguistic, Logical-Mathematical. Review this section's key terms with students. Then point out that all but one of the terms have been created by combining two words. Have students use their knowledge of each separate word to determine the meaning of each key term. Then have students search the section to see how similar their definitions are to those found in the text. For the term that is not a combination of two words, have students use context cues from the text to determine the word's meaning. **SHELTERED ENGLISH**

TEACH

Have students read Section 4 and complete Guided Reading Strategies 13.4. Choose one or more of the following activities to explore the section content with students. For further suggestions on block scheduling or team teaching, see the *Block Scheduling Handbook.*

Geographic Diversity

Jazz Moves North. Like many other African Americans during the 1920s, black jazz musicians headed north in search of opportunity. Musicians such as Joseph "King" Oliver and Sidney Bechet were among the 400,000 African Americans who left the South between 1917 and 1922. Oliver and Bechet left New Orleans, and moved to Chicago. They and other black jazz musicians helped make Chicago an important center for the development of jazz.

Activity: Ask students to use the library and search the Internet through the HRW Web site to research jazz musicians of the 1920s and the Harlem Renaissance poet Langston Hughes. Have students write and record a script about popular and influential jazz musicians for a 1920s-era radio broadcast. Instruct students to include as part of the script an interview with Hughes, in which he explains his poetic technique and the influence of jazz in his work.

go.hrw.com
SB1 Jazz

Multimedia Resources

American Music Audio CD
Program: "Harmonica Blues"

Bessie Smith was known as the Empress of the Blues, while Louis Armstrong's fans nicknamed him "Satchmo."

successful blues recording artist of the 1920s was Bessie Smith. Jazz singer and trumpeter Louis (LOO-ee) Armstrong said that Smith had a "certain something in her voice no other blues singer could get. She had music in her soul." Other notable blues singers of the 1920s included Mamie Smith and Gertrude "Ma" Rainey.

Jazz

Like the blues, jazz music originated in the South, in cities such as New Orleans, Louisiana. Jazz was influenced by the blues as well as another African American music style—ragtime. Musician Scott Joplin helped create this lively piano music that was popular in the early 1900s. Other influences on jazz included West African folk music.

Important early jazz musicians included cornet player Joseph "King" Oliver, pianist Ferdinand "Jelly Roll" Morton, and Louis Armstrong. Armstrong was known for his deep singing voice as well as his trumpet-playing. He played with Oliver before forming the Louis Armstrong Hot Five. Armstrong developed performance techniques, such as stepping out from the group to play a solo, that are still popular with audiences today.

During the 1920s many musicians traveled from the South to northern cities like Chicago, bringing jazz music to urban African American audiences. In 1927 Edward "Duke" Ellington began appearing at jazz clubs in New York City. Ellington composed jazz classics such as "Black and Tan Fantasy." He used a large band and skillfully blended its many instruments. Ellington continued to compose and perform songs into his seventies. In addition to big-band hits, he wrote scores for movies, Broadway shows, and operas.

Brass horns such as the trumpet were popular with many jazz musicians.

Other bandleaders such as Benny Goodman and Paul Whiteman helped popularize jazz and bring it to an even wider audience. Whiteman paid composer George Gershwin to write a jazz symphony, "Rhapsody in Blue," that mixed elements of popular and classical music. People worldwide were soon enjoying this uniquely American style of music. Jazz became so popular in the 1920s that the decade is often called the **Jazz Age**.

The Harlem Renaissance

Jazz was one of many art forms that flourished in the New York City neighborhood of Harlem. As a result of the Great Migration, Harlem's population boomed, making the neighborhood the nation's largest African American community. Many African Americans involved in the arts—actors, musicians, painters, and writers—moved to Harlem. As a result, Harlem became a major center of African American cultural activity during the 1920s. As artist and writer Elton Fax said:

> **"Harlem epitomized [symbolized] a kind of freedom that we did not know: 'Once I get to Harlem, I won't need to worry about anything. Nobody's gonna bother me in Harlem.'"**

The **Harlem Renaissance**—a remarkable period of African American artistic achievement in the 1920s—took its name from the neighborhood. However, many artists who were identified with the Harlem Renaissance did not live in Harlem. Through their work, Harlem Renaissance artists expressed frustration and anger with racial inequality. They also showed

LEVEL 1: Linguistic. (Suggested time: 15 min.) As a class, go over students' Guided Reading Strategies. Then use the Reading Focus questions to highlight the main ideas of the section. **SHELTERED ENGLISH**

ALL LEVELS: Musical-Rhythmic, Visual-Spatial. (Suggested time: 30 min.) Have students prepare a graphic organizer showing the origins of the blues and jazz, the similarities between the two forms of music, and artists associated with each form during the 1920s. Allow students time to complete their organizers in class. Then ask volunteers to share their information. Finally, lead a discussion on the overall influence that the blues and jazz have had on American music and culture. **SHELTERED ENGLISH**

LEVEL 2: Linguistic, Visual-Spatial. (Suggested time: 45 min.) Explain to students that the 1920s brought many changes in photography and architecture. Have each student design a picture postcard depicting either the new subject matter of photographs or the new architecture and buildings being produced in the 1920s. On the back sides of the postcards, have students explain what they have depicted and how that type of photograph or architecture varies from those of previous generations.

their pride and hope for the future. This future was represented for many people by the ideal of the "New Negro". The New Negro was an independent African American proud of his or her artistic and intellectual achievements.

Literature

As editor of the magazine *The Crisis,* W. E. B. Du Bois published the works of many young African American writers. Scholar Alain Locke and NAACP leader and author James Weldon Johnson also published the works of other writers as well as their own material.

Much of the literature of the Harlem Renaissance showed the struggles of African American life. Poets Countee Cullen, Claude McKay, and Langston Hughes were each respected. McKay expressed his anger and resentment in poems such as "The Lynching" and "If We Must Die." Hughes was possibly the most famous of the Harlem Renaissance poets. He used his writing to explore the African heritage of black Americans. The poem "I, Too" expressed both his pride in being an African American and his optimism for the future:

"I, too, sing America.
I am the darker brother.
They send me to eat in the kitchen
When company comes,
But I laugh,
And eat well,
And grow strong.

Tomorrow,
I'll be at the table
When company comes.
Nobody'll dare
Say to me,
'Eat in the kitchen,'
Then.

Besides,
They'll see how beautiful I am
And be ashamed—

I, too, am America."

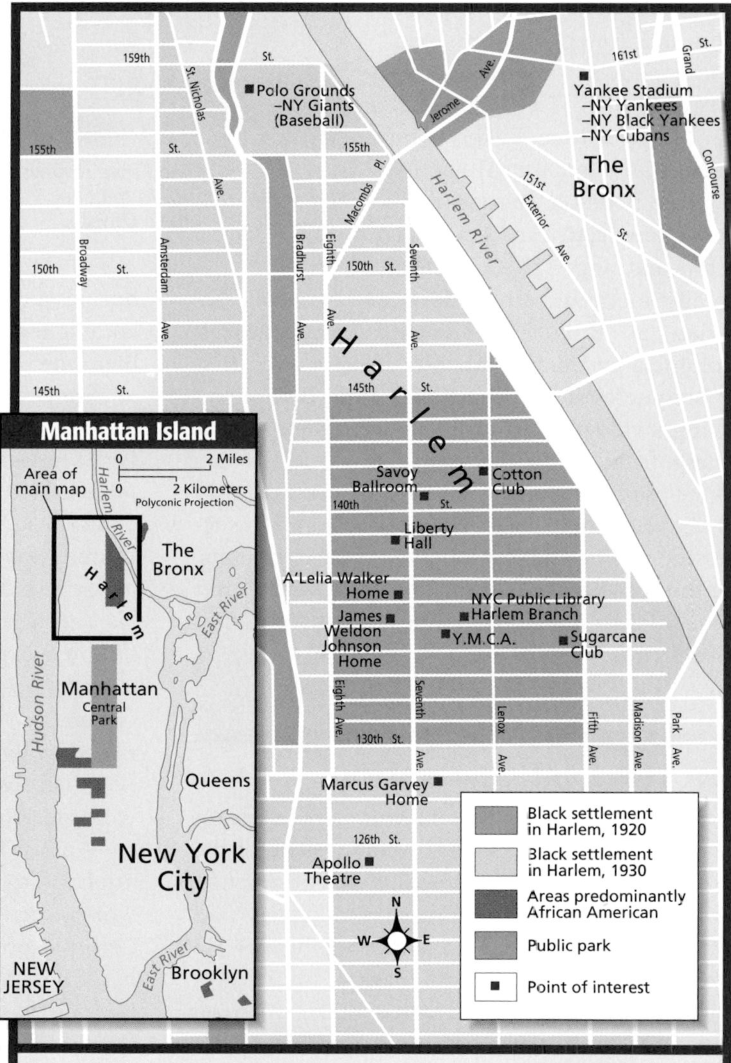

Harlem Renaissance, 1920s and 1930s

Learning from Maps The New York City neighborhood known as Harlem became an important center for African American art, literature, and music during the 1920s.

Movement What happened to the African American neighborhood in Harlem between 1920 and 1930?

Cultural Diversity

Duke Ellington. One way that jazz crossed the cultural line from an almost exclusively African American audience to a multicultural one was through Duke Ellington's appearances at the Cotton Club in Harlem. This nightclub could seat 500 people, many of whom were often Broadway stars or members of organized crime gangs. Good behavior was expected and required. Ellington's performances at the Cotton Club were also broadcast over radio throughout the United States, thus exposing audiences of many races to jazz.

Activity: Have students listen to recordings by Duke Ellington and explain how his music would appeal to people of all races.

MAP ANSWER

It greatly expanded in size.

Multimedia Resources

American History Interactive Maps CD–ROM: The Harlem Renaissance

Multimedia Resources

Everyday Life in America Transparency 22: Harlem Renaissance Art, 1920s

LEVEL 3: Linguistic, Logical-Mathematical. (Suggested time: 45 min. plus homework) Have each student write a short story or an act of a play expressing the significance of the Harlem Renaissance and the Lost Generation. Encourage students to focus on whether the two schools of artistic thought expressed essentially similar or different messages. In addition, encourage students as well to express how the Harlem Renaissance and the works of the Lost Generation reflected values and concerns of the 1920s. During the next class, call on volunteers to share their work. After each presentation, ask students to comment on how effectively the student presenter's work addressed issues at the heart of the Harlem Renaissance and the Lost Generation.

LEVEL 3: Linguistic, Intrapersonal. (Suggested time: 45 min.) Have students choose any combination of four artists, musicians, or writers of the 1920s and write a short script in which these individuals discuss trends in music, art, and literature that occurred during the decade. Encourage students to pick several different types of artists, such as jazz musicians, film actors, Harlem Renaissance artists, or members of the Lost Generation. Have students speculate on how each of these artists might have responded to one another's work.

Biography

Langston Hughes. Raised by his grandmother, Langston Hughes was a lonely child. He spent much of his time reading and writing. Hughes attended college for one year. He then worked at a variety of jobs, including busing tables and washing dishes. During that time, he wrote poetry for magazines published by organizations that championed rights for African Americans. Hughes experimented with combining his poetry with music such as jazz, a form that would gain broader popularity in the 1950s. A leader in the Harlem Renaissance, Hughes wrote a variety of material throughout his career, including poems, plays, children's books, short stories, novels, and a column in the *Chicago Defender,* a black weekly.

Critical Thinking: How might Hughes's life experiences have influenced his poetry?

ANSWER: His experiences exposed him to many examples of discrimination against African Americans as well as to other African American culture of the time.

Theater

The theater also thrived during the Harlem Renaissance. Leading roles in the theater had previously been off-limits to African Americans. In 1921, however, the black musical comedy *Shuffle Along* appeared on Broadway. Its success paved the way for other popular African American musicals. These shows introduced performers such as singer and dancer Josephine Baker, who became an international star.

Paul Robeson gained rave reviews for his performance in the title role of Shakespeare's Othello.

Paul Robeson was one of the best-known African American actors and singers. Robeson was an all-American football player and class valedictorian at Rutgers University. He attended Columbia University Law School before deciding to become an actor. His dynamic but disciplined acting style and powerful singing voice received praise from critics. Robeson starred in a wide range of productions, from the musical *Show Boat* to Shakespearean plays. He went on to make successful records and appeared in a variety of films. Performers such as Robeson, Charles Gilpin, and Rose McClendon helped open doors for other black actors.

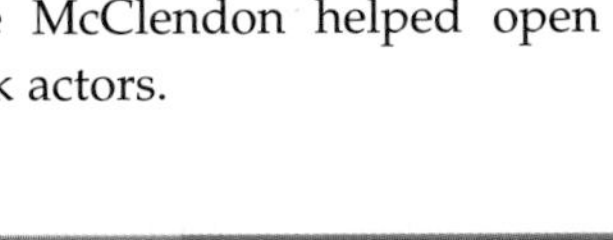

The Lost Generation

Harlem Renaissance writers were not alone in examining American society. Many writers of the 1920s were disgusted by the death and destruction of World War I. Author Ernest Hemingway had served as an ambulance driver during the war. He wrote that it was "the most colossal, murderous, mismanaged butchery that has ever taken place on earth. Any writer who said otherwise lied."

Some authors believed that the democratic ideals for which the war was fought had been abandoned when it ended. These writers also thought that American culture was too devoted to greed and money. Author Gertrude Stein called the writers who criticized postwar American society the **Lost Generation**.

After World War I many American writers moved to Europe to live as **expatriates**—people who leave their native country to live elsewhere. Other writers, including playwright Eugene O'Neill and poet Edna St. Vincent Millay, remained in the United States. Some expatriates who returned settled in New York City's Greenwich Village, which became a cultural center similar to Harlem.

Author Sinclair Lewis was a particularly harsh critic of big business and small-town America. One of Lewis's most popular novels, *Babbitt,* attacked businesspeople as narrow-minded. Lewis later became the first American to win a Nobel Prize in literature.

Some of the most influential members of the Lost Generation began writing in their early twenties. These authors included Ernest Hemingway, John Dos Passos, and F. Scott Fitzgerald. Many young Americans were drawn to their works. Hemingway developed a direct and simple writing style that inspired later authors. His novel *A Farewell to Arms* was a romantic tragedy based on his own experiences in World War I. The main character expressed a common attitude of the Lost Generation when he said, "I was always embarrassed by the words sacred, glorious, and sacrifice. . . . I had seen nothing sacred, and the things that were glorious had no glory."

Author F. Scott Fitzgerald also served in the armed forces during World War I. Fitzgerald's works, such as *This Side of Paradise* and *The Great Gatsby,* captured the spirit of the Jazz Age. He and his wife, Zelda, demonstrated the spirit of the Roaring Twenties. They were known for dancing until dawn and even jumping into a fountain at the end of a party. Fitzgerald struggled, however, to make enough money to maintain his lifestyle and still produce quality writing. In some ways, he and other members of the Lost Generation were like the main characters of *The Great Gatsby.* These characters seem to be successful but are unable to find happiness and satisfaction.

CLOSE

Linguistic, Logical-Mathematical, Interpersonal. Organize the class into small groups. Have each group create a series of five headlines highlighting changes in art and entertainment during the 1920s. When groups have finished creating the headlines, have them list three supporting details for each one that might be included in an article on the subject. Finally, have a member of each group read its headlines and supporting details to the class.

CHALLENGE AND EXTEND

1. **Linguistic, Kinesthetic, Visual-Spatial.** Have students find examples of the architecture of Louis Sullivan or Frank Lloyd Wright. Then have students read some of the two architects' writings. Ask students to indicate how Sullivan's and Wright's buildings reflect their ideas. Have students use the library and other resources to find examples of other buildings influenced by these architects. You may also want to have students construct a model of a building based on the architects' styles.

Edward Hopper's 1928 painting Manhattan Bridge Loop

New Directions in Art

The visual arts thrived in the 1920s. Leading artists broke away from traditional styles and explored new techniques and subjects.

The Armory Show

In the early 1900s Spanish artist Pablo Picasso helped create a new style of art, called cubism. This style combined images of a subject from multiple points of view into a single painting. Americans were introduced to cubism and other new painting styles at the **Armory Show**, an art exhibition held in New York City in 1913. The Armory Show inspired artists like Aaron Douglas to experiment with new cubist methods. Like other artists of the Harlem Renaissance, Douglas drew from the culture and history of African Americans in his work.

Other American painters were inspired by the Armory Show to paint nontraditional subjects. For example, artist Edward Hopper painted the urban landscape. Artist Georgia O'Keeffe probably best described the attitude of leading American artists in the 1920s. Explaining why she developed her own painting style, O'Keeffe said:

> **"I thought someone could tell me how to paint a landscape, but I never found that person. . . . They could tell you how they painted their landscape, but they couldn't tell me how to paint mine."**

Photography

By the 1920s photography had gained new popularity as an art form, due largely to the efforts of Alfred Stieglitz, the founder of modern art photography. Stieglitz promoted exhibitions and displayed modern art in his New York City gallery. He explained that the goal of his work was to use simple photography techniques "to hold a moment, to record something . . . completely." James Van Der Zee was another notable photographer of the 1920s who, like Stieglitz, was interested in recording scenes of daily life. Van Der Zee took hundreds of photographs of life in Harlem.

Although many artists of the 1920s focused on urban life, photographer Ansel Adams turned his camera to the drama of the wilderness. Adams became well known for his sharply

Photographer Ansel Adams took this picture of Vernal Fall in Yosemite National Park, California, in 1920.

Across the Curriculum

ART

American Reflections. Artists of the 1920s depicted changes in American life in a variety of ways. Thomas Hart Benton chose rural people of the Midwest and South as his favorite subjects. John Marin used variations in color, line, and geometry to make viewers almost hear the sounds of the city as they observed his work. Photographer Paul Strand used his camera to capture people unawares as they passed through New York City. He used buildings as the landscapes for his subjects.

Activity: Have students research the works of one of the artists mentioned in the text and write a review of one work that explains how the artist made use of color, shape, or light.

American Arts Answers

(page 404)

1. She wanted to make city people stop to look at them.
2. Answers will vary but students might suggest that the colors show patriotism and link the skull to the United States.

Multimedia Resources

Art in American History Transparency 28: *Falling Water (Kaufmann House)*

2. **Linguistic, Visual-Spatial.** Have students read a short story by Ernest Hemingway or another Lost Generation author. Then ask them to design a book jacket that might be appropriate for a collection of that author's work. Remind students that their book jackets should give an idea of the writer's message. Have volunteers share their book jackets with the class and explain why their design is appropriate.

3. **Logical-Mathematical, Musical-Rhythmic, Interpersonal.** Organize the class into small groups. Have each group create a segment for a decade-in-review television special on art and entertainment of the 1920s. Have students use the library and other resources to gather information and find examples to include in their segments. Encourage groups to include the blues and jazz, the Harlem Renaissance and the Lost Generation, photography, and architecture in the TV special. Have each group present its television segment to the class.

Section 4 Review ANSWERS

Identify

For significance, see the following pages:

- Bessie Smith, p. 400
- Louis Armstrong, p. 400
- Edward "Duke" Ellington, p. 400
- Jazz Age, p. 400
- Harlem Renaissance, p. 400
- Langston Hughes, p. 401
- Ernest Hemingway, p. 402
- Lost Generation, p. 402
- expatriates, p. 402
- F. Scott Fitzgerald, p. 402
- Armory Show, p. 403
- Georgia O'Keefe, p. 403
- Ansel Adams, p. 403

Locate

For locations, see the map on page 401.

Reading for Content Understanding

1. Its contributions in dance, literature, music, and theater influenced the artistic creations and culture of other Americans.

2. Charts should include the main architects, painters, and photographers discussed in this section.

3. They helped integrate African American culture with the national culture and created a uniquely American sound.

4. Reviews will vary but should describe how the writers reacted to the loss of idealism once the war ended, the emphasis on consumerism, and the illusion of success.

5. Both groups expressed discontent with social inequities and the status quo.

American Arts

Georgia O'Keeffe

Georgia O'Keeffe was born in Wisconsin in 1887. She saw the world from an artist's perspective at a very young age. "My first memory," she once recalled, "is of the brightness of light . . . light all around."

O'Keeffe studied art in Chicago and New York City and later taught in Amarillo, Texas. In Texas she often hiked into nearby Palo Duro Canyon, where the rock walls rose up to 1,000 feet and seemed to take on different colors in the light. There she first began to sketch the western landscapes that later became so important in her art. In 1916 a friend took a few of O'Keeffe's sketches to photographer Alfred Stieglitz in New York City. He loved her work and agreed to show it in his art gallery. It was the start of a brilliant career.

O'Keeffe moved to New York City and married Stieglitz. She began painting skyscrapers and other city buildings. She is best known, however, for her paintings of two other subjects—flowers and desert scenes. O'Keeffe painted single flowers at close range, showing tiny details. "Most people in the city rush around so, they have no time to look at a flower," she said. "I want them to see it whether they want to or not." O'Keeffe's flower paintings became very popular during the 1920s, often selling for more than $25,000 each.

After becoming a successful artist, O'Keeffe started to spend time in New Mexico, an area she called "the faraway" because of its lonely landscape. She began painting desert scenes—bleached bones, old churches, storms sweeping in over the mountains. O'Keeffe's work used rich color and complicated shapes. "I found that I could say things with color and shapes that I couldn't say in any other way—things that I had no words for," she explained.

Toward the end of her life, O'Keeffe remembered that "the men like to put me down as one of the best women painters. I think I'm one of the best painters." Many critics have agreed with her.

Georgia O'Keeffe's painting Cow's Skull: Red, White, and Blue

Understanding the Arts

1. What attracted Georgia O'Keeffe to both flowers and the desert as subjects for her paintings?
2. Why do you think O'Keeffe used red, white, and blue in this painting? How do these colors add different meaning to the skull?

REVIEW

Linguistic, Logical-Mathematical, Interpersonal. Have students complete the Section Review questions. Then have each student create a study guide on the arts in the 1920s. Ask students to include information on each term in the Identify portion of the Section Review, but to leave a blank space where the term would appear. When students have finished, have them exchange guides, fill in the blanks, and return the guides to their authors for grading.

ASSESS

Have students complete Daily Quiz 13.4.

RETEACH

Kinesthetic, Visual-Spatial, Interpersonal. Have students complete Main Idea Activities for Reteaching and Sheltered English 13.4. Then organize students into small groups. Ask each group to create a mobile showing changes in the arts during the 1920s and write a brief explanation of what is depicted in each segment of the mobile. When groups are through, have them present their mobiles to the class. **SHELTERED ENGLISH**

focused photographs of mountains in the Yosemite Valley. Adams tried to create images that communicated the emotions he felt as he saw the landscape. He believed that "to photograph truthfully and effectively is to see beneath the surfaces and record the qualities of nature and humanity which live . . . in all things."

 Architecture

Some of the most dramatic landscapes of the 1920s were built in big cities such as New York and Chicago. These cities were home to towering skyscrapers, which used the most advanced building materials. In the late 1800s technological advances had been combined with new artistic designs to create the first skyscrapers. In the 1890s architect Louis H. Sullivan had helped to make the design of tall buildings an art as well as a science. Sullivan's idea that "form follows function" greatly influenced the design of skyscrapers in the 1920s.

During the 1920s many American architects adopted what was known as the International style. They designed tall towers using modern materials such as reinforced concrete, glass, and steel. Architect Frank Lloyd Wright, a student of Sullivan's, had helped pioneer the use of these mass-produced materials in his designs during the early 1900s.

As a result of new building methods and great public interest, the construction of skyscrapers boomed. By 1929, skyscrapers had transformed the skylines of cities across the country. The Manhattan borough of New York City was well known for its skyline. Architects competed to build the tallest skyscraper. This competition led to the construction of the 102-story Empire State Building in Manhattan. Completed in 1931, it was the tallest building in the world at that time. To many Americans, the size and majesty of skyscrapers represented the limitless creative power of the 1920s.

The Chrysler Building was one of the best-known skyscrapers built in the 1920s.

SECTION 4 REVIEW

Identify and explain the significance of the following:

- **Bessie Smith**
- **Louis Armstrong**
- **Edward "Duke" Ellington**
- **Jazz Age**
- **Harlem Renaissance**
- **Langston Hughes**
- **Ernest Hemingway**
- **Lost Generation**
- **expatriates**
- **F. Scott Fitzgerald**
- **Armory Show**
- **Georgia O'Keeffe**
- **Ansel Adams**

Locate and identify the importance of the following:

- **Harlem**
- **Manhattan**

Reading for Content Understanding

1. **Main Idea** What were some of the accomplishments of the Harlem Renaissance?
2. **Main Idea** Make a chart listing some of the most significant American architects, painters, and photographers of the 1920s. Include a brief explanation of their major achievements.
3. **Cultural Diversity** In what ways did the blues and jazz influence American culture?
4. **Writing** *Informing* Imagine that you are writing a magazine review of the authors of the Lost Generation. Briefly describe their work and how it commented on life in the 1920s.
5. **Critical Thinking** *Making Comparisons* How were the writers of the Harlem Renaissance and the Lost Generation similar in their views of American society in the 1920s?

Chapter 13 Review ANSWERS

Identifying People and Ideas

1. the ban on the manufacture, sale, and transportation of alcohol

2. belief in the literal interpretation of the Bible

3. Tennessee science teacher convicted of teaching evolution; conviction was later overturned

4. law giving preference to western and northern European immigrants, banning Japanese immigrants, and making it easier to deport immigrants

5. leader of the black nationalist movement who organized the Universal Negro Improvement Association (UNIA)

6. name given to early movies that used sound

7. daring aviator who was the first to fly solo across the Atlantic Ocean

8. a remarkable period of African American artistic achievement

9. the most successful blues recording artist of the 1920s

10. novelist who personified the disillusion of the Lost Generation writers

Using the Time Line

1. e **4.** a
2. c **5.** d
3. b **6.** f

Understanding Main Ideas

1. It was not supported by many Americans and offered too much profit to those willing to violate it.

CHAPTER 13 REVIEW

Review and Assessment RESOURCES

PRINT
- ★ Chapter 13 Review, pp. 406–07
- ★ Vocabulary Activity 13
- ★ Chapter 13 Study Guide
- ★ Chapter 13 Test (Form A or B)

MULTIMEDIA
- ★ Audio Program, Ch. 13 (English and Spanish)
- ★ *Global Skill Builder CD–ROM*
- ★ Chapter 13 Test Generator
- ★ HRW Web site

SHELTERED ENGLISH
- ★ Spanish Glossary
- ★ Sheltered English Chapter 13 Test

ASSESS

Have students complete one of the Chapter 13 tests. As an alternate assessment, assign the Chapter 13 Investigation.

2. It appealed to many people who were suspicious of modern industry and science. Radio and revivals spread its message to many people.

3. He organized the Universal Negro Improvement Association, which worked to end imperialism in Africa and discrimination in America. It also published the *Negro World* to spread the ideas of black nationalism.

4. Women were granted the right to vote, began to get elected to public office, and had more employment opportunities.

5. radio and the movies

6. Harlem Renaissance and the Lost Generation

Reviewing Themes

1. Nativism led to passage of the Emergency Quota Act and the National Origins Act, both of which placed further restrictions on immigration.

2. Both affected Americans' lives by expanding their access to news and cultural influences from around the country, thus helping to create a national American culture.

3. Their contributions to dance, literature, music, and theater influenced the artistic creations and culture of other Americans.

Thinking Critically

1. The NAACP sought integration of African Americans into white society, while the UNIA supported black economic independence from white society and a "back to Africa" movement.

CHAPTER 13 REVIEW

Chapter Summary

The 1920s were a time of great social change and economic prosperity in the United States. Social movements such as Fundamentalism, nativism, and prohibition sparked heated debates about education, immigration, and alcohol consumption. New forms of mass media and mass entertainment—including movies and radio—also strongly influenced American culture. In addition, actors, musicians, painters, and writers made many contributions to the arts in America.

On a separate sheet of paper, complete the following activities.

Identifying People and Ideas

Describe the historical significance of the following:

1. prohibition
2. Fundamentalism
3. John T. Scopes
4. National Origins Act
5. Marcus Garvey
6. talkies
7. Charles Lindbergh
8. Harlem Renaissance
9. Bessie Smith
10. Ernest Hemingway

Internet Activity

go.hrw.com
SB1 Silent Movies

Search the Internet through the HRW Web site to find information about movies and movie stars of the silent screen. Use the information to create a movie poster advertising a popular 1920s film. Include the names of the film's stars.

Understanding Main Ideas

1. Why was prohibition difficult to enforce?
2. What were some reasons why Fundamentalism spread in the 1920s?
3. How did Marcus Garvey promote black nationalism?
4. What political and economic advances did women achieve during the 1920s?
5. What forms of mass entertainment developed during the 1920s?
6. What were the major literary movements of the 1920s?

Reviewing Themes

1. **Citizenship and Democracy** Why did U.S. immigration policy change during the 1920s?
2. **Technology and Society** How did the development of radio and movies affect the lives of Americans?
3. **Cultural Diversity** How did African Americans contribute to the cultural changes in the United States during the 1920s?

Using the Time Line

Number your paper from 1 to 6. Match the letters on the time line below with the following events.

1. **The teaching of the theory of evolution is challenged in court.**
2. **The United States passes an emergency quota on immigration.**
3. **The first American radio station broadcasts the results of the 1920 presidential election.**
4. **Prohibition goes into effect.**
5. **American Indians gain citizenship.**
6. **The first motion picture with sound is made.**

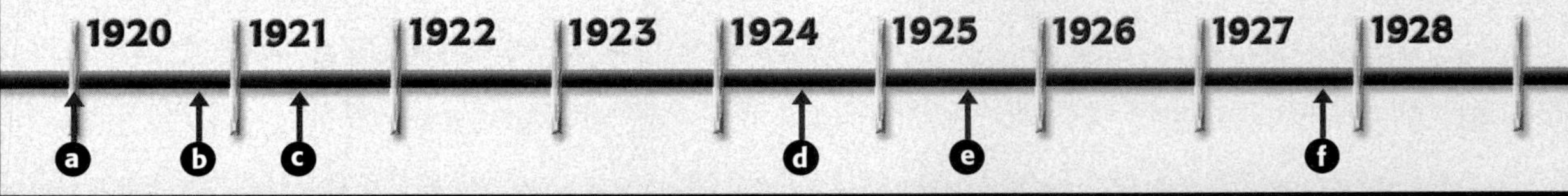

RETEACH

Kinesthetic, Visual-Spatial. Organize the class into four groups, one for each section of the chapter. Have each group create a skit that provides answers to each of the section's Reading Focus questions. Skits should feature major figures and developments from the section. Encourage students to be as creative as possible while maintaining historical accuracy. Have students perform their skits for the rest of the class. **SHELTERED ENGLISH**

Using the Internet

HRW Have students continue their research by writing a review of the movie as might have appeared in a 1920s entertainment magazine. Students should describe the film, critique it, and rate it for potential moviegoers.

Portfolio Extensions

1. Have student groups create travel brochures for each section of the country. Ask students to include economic and entertainment information on each region.

2. Have students create ads to encourage listeners to tune in to their broadcasts. Remind students that ads should be catchy and provide some information about their programs.

Thinking Critically

1. **Making Comparisons** How did the NAACP and the UNIA differ?
2. **Evaluating** Why do you think fads became common during the 1920s?
3. **Identifying Cause and Effect** How did prohibition contribute to a rise in organized crime?

Writing About History

1. **Expressing** Imagine that you are a supporter or opponent of national prohibition. Write a letter to the editor explaining your position.
2. **Describing** Imagine that you are the parent of a high school student during the 1920s. Describe how school life and social activities have changed since you went to school in the 1890s.

Linking Geography and History

1. **Movement** How did the Great Migration affect the spread of jazz music in the United States?
2. **Region** What social divisions developed between urban and rural communities during the 1920s?

Building Your Portfolio

Complete the following activities individually or in groups.

1. **Coming to America** Imagine that you are a European visitor to the United States during the 1920s. Choose one or several areas of the country to visit. Create a journal describing your travels to share with your friends back home. Along with your journal entry, you may wish to include maps of your travels, illustrations of the things you saw, and descriptions of the people you met and their activities.
2. **Radio Program** Imagine that you are the writer of a radio show about the rise of celebrities during the 1920s. Select one or more famous people from the decade to discuss on your show and write a script for your radio program. You may wish to interview someone, describe his or her accomplishments, or broadcast one of the person's games or performances. You may also discuss what makes someone a celebrity in the United States during the 1920s. When you have finished, present your radio show for the class.

History Skills Workshop

Using Visual Resources Study the image to the right, which is a painting by Jacob Lawrence. Then answer the following questions: (a) Where do you think the people in the painting are going? (b) What ideas or emotions do you think the artist is trying to communicate in the painting? (c) Draw a picture or write a description about what these people encountered upon reaching their destinations.

The Phillips Collection, Washington, D.C.

2. Answers will vary but should describe the role of radio and movies in promoting fads.

3. Answers will vary but students should note that the demand for alcohol led others to supply it for profit, thus contributing to the growth of organized crime.

Writing About History

1. Letters will vary but students should state their opinions and explain their reasoning.

2. Answers will vary but should mention the wider range of classes, extracurricular activities, and other school-related activities offered in the 1920s.

Linking Geography and History

1. As African Americans moved to urban areas in the North, northern clubs and radio stations began introducing jazz to all Americans.

2. Many rural inhabitants were concerned that the factory jobs, large immigrant populations, political machines, and the faster pace of urban life threatened traditional values. Some urbanites claimed that rural residents were ignorant of new technologies and unprepared to live in modern times.

History Skills Workshop

(a) to major northern cities; (b) that during the Great Migration many African Americans moved to large northern cities; (c) Pictures or descriptions will vary but might indicate competition for jobs, racial tension, and the existence of black communities like Harlem.

FOCUS

Ask students what the word *migration* means. As students respond, write phrases that relate to the definition on the chalkboard. Then have students combine the phrases to create their own definitions of migration. Tell students that in this lesson they will learn about migrations that took place within the United States.

TEACH

Have students read the Geography and History lesson. Choose one or more of the following activities to explore the Geography and History content with students.

ALL LEVELS: Visual-Spatial, Logical-Mathematical. (Suggested time: 30 min.) Have students examine the Mexican American Population in 1930 map on page 409. Ask them to

Across the Curriculum

MATH

Farms and Farmland. The growth in farm jobs between 1880 and 1930 was matched by an increase in the number of farms and in the total acreage devoted to farming. In 1880 there were slightly more than 4 million farms in the United States, totaling more than 536 million acres of land. Twenty years later, some 5.7 million farms covered more than 841 million acres of land. Between the turn of the century and 1920, the number of farms increased to almost 6.5 million, and the total farm acreage increased to about 959 million. In 1930 the number of farms had declined slightly, totaling just under 6.3 million, with over 991 million acres devoted to farming activities.

Activity: Have students create bar graphs showing the number of farms and total acreage devoted to farming between 1880 and 1930.

SKILLS ANSWERS

1. 1920

2. 1910s

3. 1920s

4. Answers will vary based on students' opinions but will probably mention a continued sharp increase in urban population and slow or no growth in rural population.

Geography & History

American Migrations, 1865–1930

The United States became increasingly industrialized from 1865 to 1930. Some of today's major U.S. cities, such as Chicago, Detroit, and St. Louis, grew rapidly as people moved there in search of better economic opportunities. Many Americans left rural areas, hoping to find industrial jobs in large towns and cities. For example, many African Americans relocated, first to southern mill towns, and later to northern cities.

Immigration also increased the urban population. Millions of immigrants came from all across Europe. Large numbers of immigrants also arrived from Mexico. Many European immigrants moved to cities in the Northeast and Midwest. Most Mexican immigrants settled in rural areas in the Southwest. Eventually, many Mexican Americans moved to cities, particularly in Texas and California. Gradually, all these different migrations reshaped U.S. cities. ■

Farms to Cities

Between 1880 and 1930, the United States shifted from being a largely rural nation to a mostly urban one. Many people moved to cities to find work.

Population Shift: Rural to Urban, 1880–1930

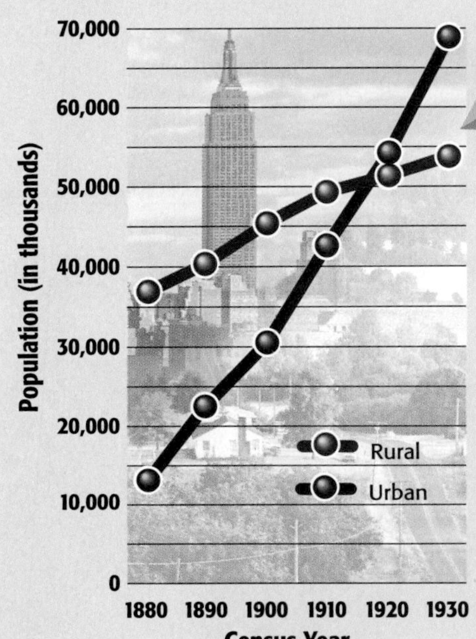

Source: *Historical Statistics of the United States*

Geography Skills
Reading Line Graphs

1. In what census year did the urban population of the United States become larger than the rural population?
2. In what decade did rural population experience the least growth?
3. In what decade did urban population experience the most growth?
4. What do you think the graph would show if it continued on to the present?

408

determine how many states fall into each of the categories listed in the map's key. Then have students create bar graphs depicting the number of states that fall into each of the categories. Ask volunteers to share their graphs with the class. Then have students discuss the similarities and differences in the information that can be deduced from their graphs and the map in the text (e.g., the map shows which states meet each category, while the graph only shows how many states fit each category). **SHELTERED ENGLISH**

LEVEL 3: Linguistic, Logical-Mathematical. (Suggested time: 45 min.) Have students write a summary describing the relationship between African American migration patterns and civil rights. Have students use information from the graph on page 410 and the map on page 411 to write their summaries. Students will most likely conclude that there was a strong relationship between civil rights and where African Americans moved. Finally, lead a discussion covering other possible explanations for this movement,

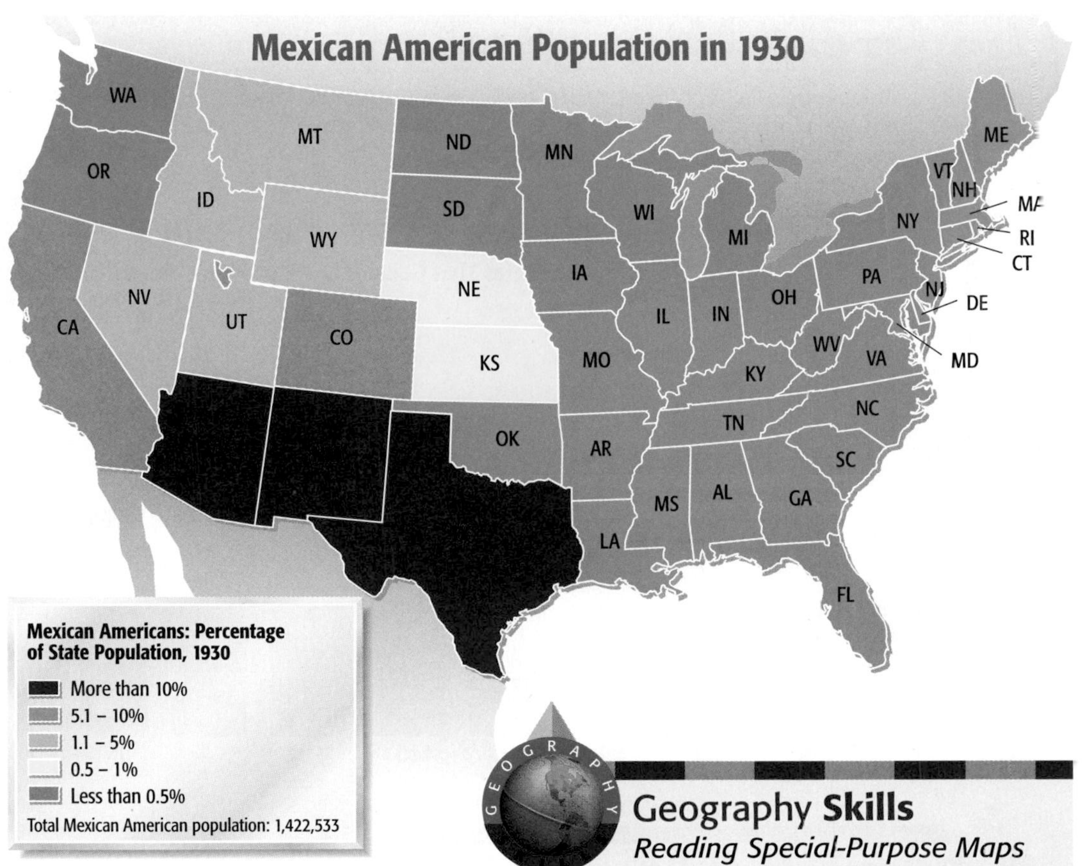

Geography Skills

Reading Special-Purpose Maps

1. How many states in 1930 had a Mexican American population that was 1.1 percent or more of the state's total population?
2. In which states did the highest percentage of Mexican Americans live?

History Note 1

In the early 1900s large numbers of Mexican immigrants began arriving in the United States. Between 1920 and 1930, nearly 500,000 Mexican immigrants settled in the United States, mostly in the West and the Southwest. In the first years after these new immigrants arrived, most lived in rural areas. By the 1930s, however, many Mexican Americans had migrated to large cities—such as Chicago, Los Angeles, and San Antonio—in search of higher-paying industrial jobs.

In 1937 this family of Mexican American migrant workers from Texas picked sugar beets in Minnesota.

Linking Past to Present

Mexican Immigration. The number of Mexican immigrants declined sharply after 1930, with only 1,560 Mexicans moving to the United States in 1935. The numbers increased again in the 1940s and 1950s. In 1960 some 32,708 Mexicans arrived in the United States. However, it was during the final decades of the 1900s that Mexican immigration dramatically increased. Between 1971 and 1979, some 637,200 immigrants left Mexico for the United States. During the 1980s that number rose to 974,200. In 1990 alone, an estimated 679,100 Mexicans immigrated to the United States.

Activity: Have students conduct research on possible reasons for the decrease in the number of Mexican immigrants to he United States during the 1930s. Ask volunteers to report their findings to the class.

Skills Answers

1. 10

2. Arizona, New Mexico, and Texas

such as the growth of northern cities and the availability of industrial jobs in the North.

CLOSE

Linguistic. Ask students to write headlines for each of the maps and graphs on pages 408–11. Tell students to assume that the headlines are for the last year depicted in each map or graph. For example, for the graph on page 410 students should assume that it is 1930 and could write a headline such as: *More African Americans Moving to New York Than to Any Other State.*

CHALLENGE AND EXTEND

Visual-Spatial, Logical-Mathematical. Have students use the library or other resources to research the percentage of Mexican Americans currently living in each U.S. state. Then have students create either a map similar to the map on page 409 or a bar graph similar to the one they made in the All Levels activity. Then ask students to discuss how the percentage of Mexican Americans living in each state has changed since 1930.

Geographic Diversity

Reasons for Migration. Some social scientists have suggested that migration requires both a "push" and a "pull." The "push" is the reason for leaving one's home, and the "pull" is the reason for choosing a particular place as one's new home. During the late 1800s, discrimination and lack of economic opportunity certainly provided African Americans in the South with "push." However, fewer than might be expected left the region. Some historians have argued that the North did not provide the "pull" during this era. When World War I and the immigration restrictions of the 1920s decreased the number of Europeans moving to the United States, however, African Americans began migrating to the North in large numbers.

Critical Thinking: How did the decline in the number of European immigrants provide a "pull" for African Americans in the South to move to the North?

Answer: Students might mention that jobs that formerly went to European immigrants became available to African Americans.

Skills Answers

1. New York; Illinois, Pennsylvania, Ohio, and Michigan

2. New York, Michigan, New Jersey, Florida, and California

The Great Migration

About 1910, thousands of African Americans began moving from the rural South to northern industrial cities in search of better jobs. This movement, known as the Great Migration, continued through World War I and the 1920s.

African American Migration, 1910–1930

States That Gained the Most African Americans (in thousands)

State	Total gain
NY	172.8
IL	119.3
PA	101.7
OH	90.7
MI	86.1
NJ	67
MO	35.9
FL	54.2 (3.2)
CA	36.4
IN	23.2

Legend: 1910–1920; 1920–1930

Geography Skills
Reading Bar Graphs

1. Which states' African American population increased by more than 200,000 between 1910 and 1930? by more than 100,000?
2. In which states was the gain in African American population between 1920 and 1930 more than double the gain between 1910 and 1920?

History Note 2

In 1930, three northern cities—Chicago, Detroit, and New York—had an African American population three times greater than it had been in 1910. The impact of this movement of African Americans, known as the Great Migration, can be seen in current population statistics. Today, around half of all African Americans in the United States live outside the South.

History Note 3

Even though racial discrimination was common in the South before 1900, few African Americans left the region in the late 1800s. As late as 1910, more than 80 percent of African Americans still lived in the South. Beginning in 1910, however, many African Americans began moving to northern and western cities. They were hoping to improve their lives with better jobs and opportunities.

In 1912 this African American family moved to Chicago from the rural South.

REVIEW

Linguistic, Logical-Mathematical. Have students use the information from pages 408–11 to write a newspaper article describing the overall changes that have resulted from American migrations between 1865 and 1930. Ask students to use information from the maps and graphs on these pages as evidence.

ASSESS

Have students complete Geography and History Quiz 4.

RETEACH

Logical-Mathematical, Interpersonal. Ask each student to write three questions based on the material presented on pages 408–11. Collect the questions and organize the class into two teams. Play a quiz game based on the questions. Allow students to look at the maps and graphs on these pages to answer the questions, but place a time limit on how long they have to answer. **SHELTERED ENGLISH**

Discrimination Against African Americans in 1930

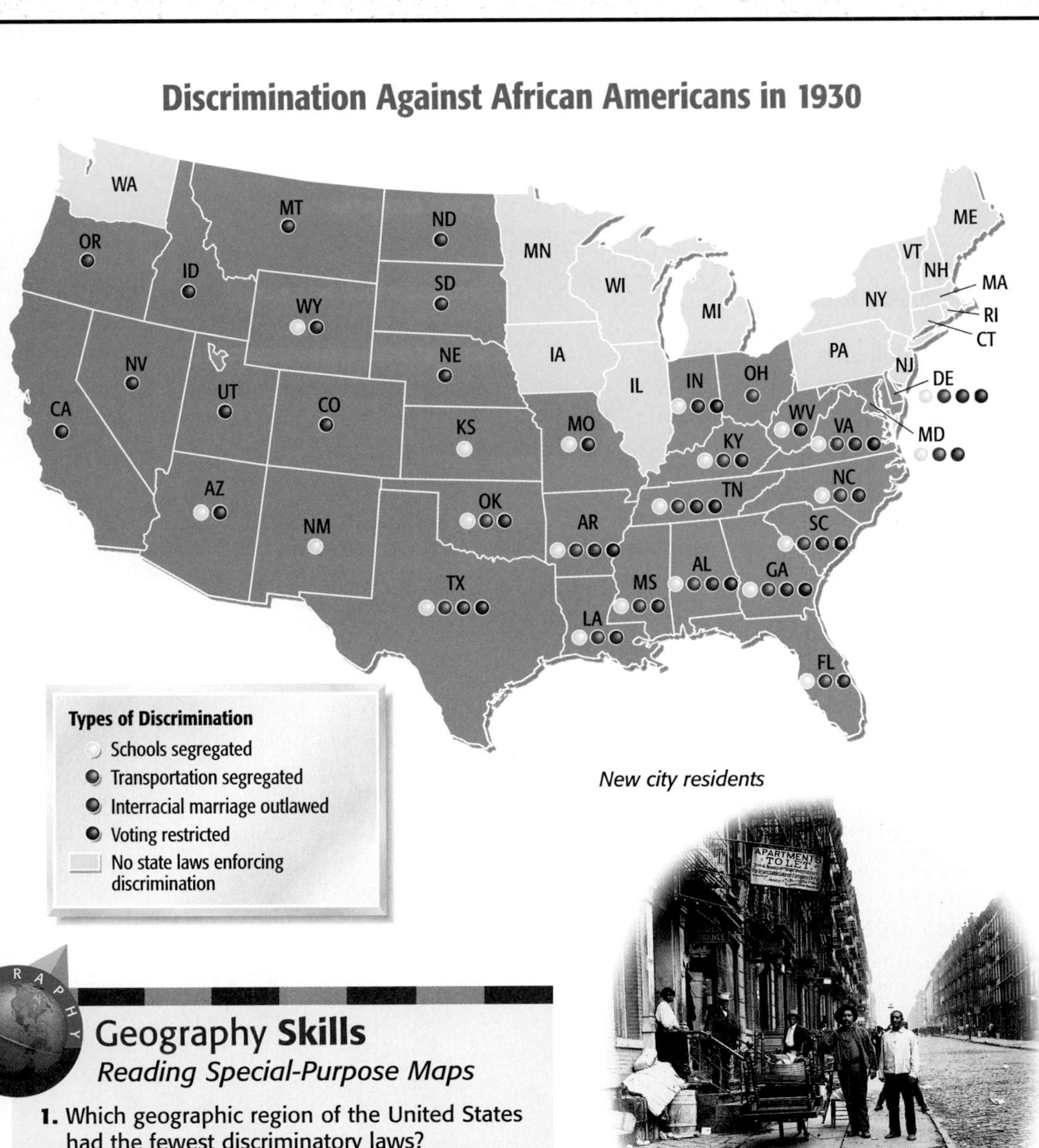

New city residents

Geography Skills
Reading Special-Purpose Maps

1. Which geographic region of the United States had the fewest discriminatory laws?
2. Which geographic region had the most discriminatory laws?
3. In which states did African Americans face the most discriminatory legislation? the least?

History Note 4

During the 1930s many African Americans moved north hoping to escape the economic hardships of the Great Depression. However, northern cities were experiencing high unemployment and poverty. During these hard times the National Association for the Advancement of Colored People fought to ensure equal treatment for African Americans.

Cultural Diversity

African Americans in Texas. Legal discrimination against African Americans in Texas increased significantly in the early 1900s. In the 1890s more than 100,000 African Americans voted in Texas elections. However, new laws including a poll tax reduced the number of black voters to only 5,000 in the 1906 elections. Many cities enacted laws segregating schools, public transportation, and housing. African Americans responded to the discrimination in some cities by forming their own transportation companies. They also brought lawsuits against segregation laws, efforts that usually did not result in success. Despite discrimination, African Americans in Texas created vibrant communities.

Critical Thinking: How did a poll tax limit African American voting?

ANSWER: A poll tax prevented poor people, many of whom were African Americans, from voting.

SKILLS ANSWERS

1. the Northeast
2. the Southeast
3. Alabama, Arkansas, Delaware, Georgia, South Carolina, Tennessee, Texas, and Virginia; Connecticut, Illinois, Iowa, Maine, Massachusetts, Michigan, Minnesota, New Hampshire, New Jersey, New York, Pennsylvania, Rhode Island, Vermont, Washington, Wisconsin

TEACH

ALL LEVELS: Linguistic, Visual-Spatial, Logical-Mathematical. (Suggested time: 45 min.) Have students turn back to page 320 and examine the image that opens this unit. Explain that images can be "read" the same way that one would read a story or a novel. Ask students to look for things like setting, characters, and story in the image. Begin discussing the image by talking about the depicted people as characters and asking students to suggest the response that each of the main figures in the image might have to the scene around them. Use students' ideas to discuss what these figures' personalities might be like. Have students base their assumptions on facial expressions, postures, and gestures. As the class discusses these ideas, encourage students to determine the image's main point. Finally, have students use this image as inspiration to write a dialogue between two of the people depicted.

SKILLS ANSWERS

1. immigrants–faceless hoard; government–inattentive Uncle Sam; United States–overflowing melting pot
2. those who have assimilated into American society; it is a familiar symbol of American society.
3. Immigrants are overwhelming American society and will not fit in; use of words "teeming," "flood," and "unassimilated," and image of immigrants overflowing the melting pot
4. Students' captions will vary but should express the artist's opinion that the U.S. government is not paying attention to the fact that millions of European and Asian immigrants are arriving and might not be able to assimilate into American society.

Understanding Political Cartoons. For further practice, have students bring to class political cartoons from newspapers or magazines that cover current events. Ask students to write a paragraph about how the cartoon expresses the artist's opinion. Students should point out any symbols the artist uses and what the symbols represent.

History Skills
WORKSHOP

Using Visual Resources

This textbook contains photographs as well as reproductions of famous paintings and other artwork. Gathering information from these sources is a key strategy to understanding history. Visual resources can provide a better understanding of how people in the past behaved, dressed, thought, and communicated with one another. Images can also provide an accurate record of historical events.

Gathering Information from Art

To effectively gather information from artwork, follow these steps.

1. **Determine the subject of the work** Study the people, objects, and actions in the artwork. Check the title or caption. In cartoons, artists often use familiar images to represent complex ideas.
2. **Examine the details** Study the background of the painting or drawing. Remember that *all* the visual evidence is important to understanding the historical event or period.
3. **Note the artist's point of view** If possible, determine whether the events are shown favorably or unfavorably. Ask yourself how the artwork might affect others.
4. **Use the information carefully** Remember that a work of art may be an artist's *interpretation* of an event. Try to determine how accurately the art shows the event before deciding how to use the information.

Using Cartoons as Primary Sources

Follow these steps to use cartoons as primary sources.

1. **Study the subject** Identify the people, events, or locations in the cartoon.
2. **Check for details** Note the expression, action, or setting. Look closely at the style of clothing and other details.
3. **Do not be misled** Remember that an artist uses images in a cartoon to represent people, ideas, and events. Because political cartoons are usually created shortly after an event occurs, the artist assumes that people have some familiarity with the subject.

The Granger Collection, New York

Practicing the Skill

Study the image above, which is a political cartoon from 1921 entitled *Spoiling the Broth*. The cartoon shows some Americans' fears about the number of immigrants arriving in the United States. Then answer the following questions.

1. How does the artist represent immigrants, the U.S. government, and the United States?
2. What does the melting pot represent? Why do you think the artist used this image?
3. What is the artist's opinion about immigration? How can you tell?
4. Write a three-sentence caption that might accompany the cartoon.

ALL LEVELS: Linguistic, Interpersonal. (Suggested time: 45 min.) Have each group write a script for an episode of a radio program called *Theater Today.* On the program several reviewers will critique the class performances of the other groups. Their reviews should consider the things that a review of a play might typically discuss, such as the writing, the performance, and the staging. However, in this case the reviewers should also discuss the historical aspects of each play: What things did each group present that the reviewers found interesting or surprising? Was there anything in the plays that was different from the information that the reviewers' group had gathered, and could those differences be explained? How well did performers, writers, and designers show the different aspects of society and culture during the 1920s? Have reviewers consider each play's visual aspects and the appropriateness of any costumes, music, or props used.

History in Action

UNIT 4 PORTFOLIO

Life in the Twenties: The Play

Complete the following activity in small, cooperative groups.

You and the members of your group are the writers, producers, directors, and actors of a play called *Life in the Twenties.* The play will include short segments on different aspects of society during the 1920s. You want to focus mainly on the arts and culture of the time, such as radio, movies, music, sports, and literature. You and your group need to decide what specific topics you will include.

Materials To complete this activity, you will need art supplies, costumes, and perhaps a cassette or compact disc player for the musical accompaniment.

Parts of the Project To create your play, complete the following tasks:

1. **Research** Use the library and your textbook to gather information. You will focus on the arts and culture of the 1920s, such as radio, movies, music, sports, and literature. Be sure to include information on some visual artists such as photographers and painters. As much as possible, you want to use the words of the people in the 1920s in your play. For example, find something Charles Lindbergh wrote about his trip across the Atlantic Ocean. Have someone play the role of Lindbergh and speak his words.
2. **Writing** Once you have gathered enough information, write your play. You might want to include some songs as well as spoken passages in your script. Your play will contain brief segments on different topics. Because your play does not have a plot, you will need to write some transitions between the different people or topics. Add stage directions to show how the characters will sing, speak, and move. You might want some characters to perform the different dances that were popular in the 1920s. In addition, you might want to play music from the 1920s.
3. **Rehearsal and Production** Once the play is written, decide who will direct it and who will play each of the characters. Prepare the necessary props and costumes. Finally, rehearse your play several times.

Perform your play after you have finished rehearsals. Provide the audience with an illustrated program, which includes some visual resources representing the subjects.

Students present a play to their class.

Research. Have students start by brainstorming a list of possible characters from people associated with literature, movies, music, painting, photography, radio, and sports during the 1920s. Students can then use the library and other resources to find quotations, music, or dances associated with their characters.

Writing. Have students outline each segment before they write it. Once the segments are written, students can write a draft of the complete script by adding the transitions to link the segments. Show students an example of a published script from a play as a model of how to write stage directions.

Rehearsal and Production. Tell students that it is important to rehearse their entire play at least once before performing it for the class. This dress rehearsal should continue even if the actors make mistakes. Students should also time their play so that you will know how much time to allow for the performances.

Introducing
UNIT
5

CHAPTER 14
The Great Depression

The U.S. stock market crash of October 29, 1929, started the Panic of 1929. The Great Depression followed. Banks failed, unemployment skyrocketed, and the gross national product plummeted. Many Americans disagreed with the Hoover administration's reluctance to provide direct federal relief. In 1932 Franklin D. Roosevelt was elected president in a landslide. His New Deal provided relief, jobs, and hope to many Americans.

CHAPTER 15
The Depression at Home and Abroad

Several New Deal programs supported unions. The Roosevelt administration also reached out to help farmers, who were hard hit by economic disaster and the devastation of the Dust Bowl. Although Roosevelt appointed many women and African Americans to federal positions and tried to end discrimination in some New Deal programs, the depression hit both groups particularly hard.

Internet Activity

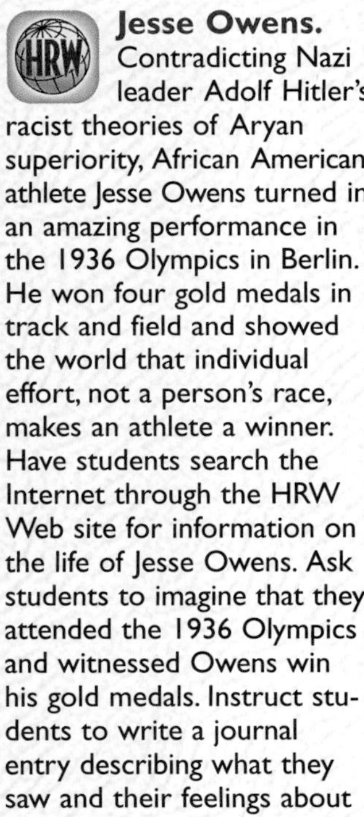

Jesse Owens. Contradicting Nazi leader Adolf Hitler's racist theories of Aryan superiority, African American athlete Jesse Owens turned in an amazing performance in the 1936 Olympics in Berlin. He won four gold medals in track and field and showed the world that individual effort, not a person's race, makes an athlete a winner. Have students search the Internet through the HRW Web site for information on the life of Jesse Owens. Ask students to imagine that they attended the 1936 Olympics and witnessed Owens win his gold medals. Instruct students to write a journal entry describing what they saw and their feelings about the event.

go.hrw.com
SB1 Owens

UNIT 5 A World in Crisis (1929–1945)

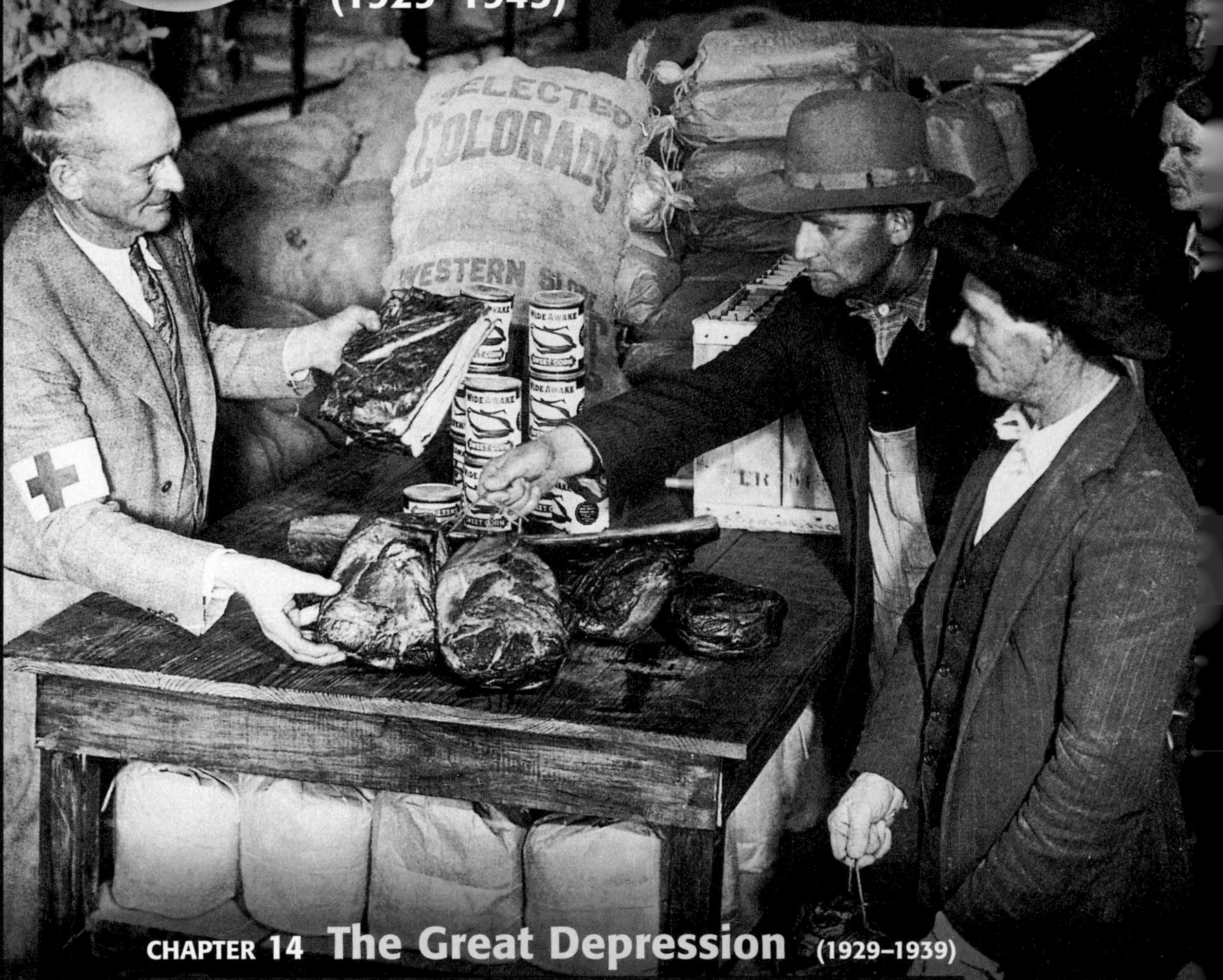

CHAPTER 14 **The Great Depression** (1929–1939)

CHAPTER 15 **The Depression at Home and Abroad** (1929–1939)

CHAPTER 16 **World War II** (1938–1945)

Entertainment and the arts during the depression helped people forget their troubles and realize that they were not alone in their suffering. The global depression also contributed to the rise of fascism and totalitarianism in some foreign nations.

CHAPTER 16
World War II

World War II began when Germany invaded Poland in 1939. At first the United States was officially neutral, although it did send aid to the British. Then, on December 7, 1941, the Japanese attacked Pearl Harbor, and the United States entered the war. After four years of intense fighting, the war in Europe ended when Germany surrendered. As Allied troops moved through Germany, the horror of the Holocaust slowly came to light. The war in the Pacific ended when the United States dropped atomic bombs on Hiroshima and Nagasaki, which led Japan to surrender.

UNIT MOTIVATOR

Share the information in the Chapter Overviews with students. Have students skim each chapter for as many place-names as they can find. Then make a list of the names on the chalkboard. Using a large sheet of butcher paper, have the class create a map showing each place on the list. Ask students to write in their notebooks one question about each place. Then, as they go through the unit, have students answer their questions.

American Teens
IN HISTORY
Young Relief Workers

When the Great Depression hit, it placed a significant burden on young Americans. Economic hardship forced many young people to drop out of school or college to look for work. However, jobs were scarce. By May 1935 more than 1 million Americans between the ages of 16 and 24 were unemployed.

In June 1935 President Franklin D. Roosevelt created the National Youth Administration (NYA), a special division of the Works Progress Administration. The NYA was one of many relief programs designed to help young people. It offered part-time jobs for young Americans still in school. For those no longer in school, the NYA provided jobs and work training.

High school students in campus work programs received jobs in or around their schools. They earned only about $6 a month, but the pay made a huge difference to the 1.5 million students enrolled in the program. The money allowed students to stay in school. These teenagers used the money to pay for their own schoolbooks, supplies, and bus fare. Other young people took part in out-of-school programs. Boys on the Onondaga Indian reservation in New York built a summer camp for children. Other young workers painted buildings, maintained city parks, performed carpentry tasks, and much more.

The Granger Collection, New York

The Civilian Conservation Corps was one of many relief programs. It provided jobs for young men 17 to 24 years old.

The NYA provided new opportunities for all its participants. Rural teenagers, for example, learned industrial skills. The NYA also attempted to integrate teenagers of different races. One boy recalled the program's meaning in his life:

> *"Maybe you don't know what it's like to come home and have everyone looking at you, and you know they're thinking, . . . 'He didn't find a job.' It gets terrible. You just don't want to come home. . . . I tell you, the first time I walked in the front door with my paycheck, I was somebody!"*

In this unit you will learn about the Great Depression and government efforts to help Americans. You will also learn about how World War II transformed the United States and the world.

LEFT PAGE: *Missouri residents wait for food at a Salvation Army center.*

Using Visual Resources

Photographing the Great Depression. During the Great Depression, the Farm Security Administration, one of Roosevelt's New Deal programs, assigned photographers to record life in rural America. The photograph on the opposite page is one of many that program produced. The photograph shows a worker for the American Red Cross distributing relief supplies during a drought in Arkansas in 1931. During the depression, areas of the country already struggling under the weight of economic hard times also had to deal with ecological disasters such as floods and droughts. The strained and burdened faces of the farmers in this photo reveal the extreme hardship that they were facing.

Critical Thinking: Why do you think the Roosevelt administration hired photographers to take pictures of rural life during the Great Depression?

ANSWER: Answers will vary but students might mention that the Roosevelt administration was trying to find work for everyone, and that government officials also wanted to have a historical record of events affecting farmers, an important segment of society.

TEACH

ALL LEVELS: Logical-Mathematical, Visual-Spatial. (Suggested time: 35 min.) Choose two colors of paper. Provide students with one sheet of paper of each color. Ask them to title one sheet *U.S. Events* and the other *World Events*. Have them fold each sheet into four sections and label the sections of each sheet *Arts and Entertainment, Economy and Society, Politics and War,* and *Science and Technology*. Ask students to place each of the events from the time line on the appropriate sheet and in the appropriate section. Have students highlight any events that could be considered both U.S. and world events. Call on volunteers to share with the class how they categorized the time line events.

ALL LEVELS: Linguistic, Logical-Mathematical. (Suggested time: 35 min.) Remind students that the title of this unit is *A World in Crisis*. Ask them to list on a sheet of paper each of the events on the time line that they think contributed to the atmosphere of crisis in the years from 1929 to 1945. For each event they list, ask students to write one to two sentences describing how they believe the event contributed to "a world in crisis." Ask volunteers to present their lists to the class.

Linking Past to Present

Man of the Year. *Time* magazine's first honoree as "Man of the Year" was pilot Charles Lindbergh in 1927. Subsequent winners have included many political leaders, including every U.S. president since Franklin D. Roosevelt, with the exception of Gerald Ford. As of 1998, Roosevelt is the only person to be named Man of the Year three times. In 1930 Mohandas Ghandi became the first person from outside the United States to be honored by the magazine. Six years later, Wallis Warfield Simpson was the first "Woman of the Year." As times continue to change, the face of the Man of the Year has changed, too. The Computer took home the prize in 1982, while Endangered Earth was honored in 1988.

Activity: Ask students to predict the next Man of the Year. Encourage them to consider the issues that society continues to face. Remind students that winners of the award do not have to be men or even human beings. Allow time in class for students to share their predictions. Have the class vote for their top three choices. You may want to have the class write a letter to the editor of *Time* magazine, in which they present their choices and the reasons for them.

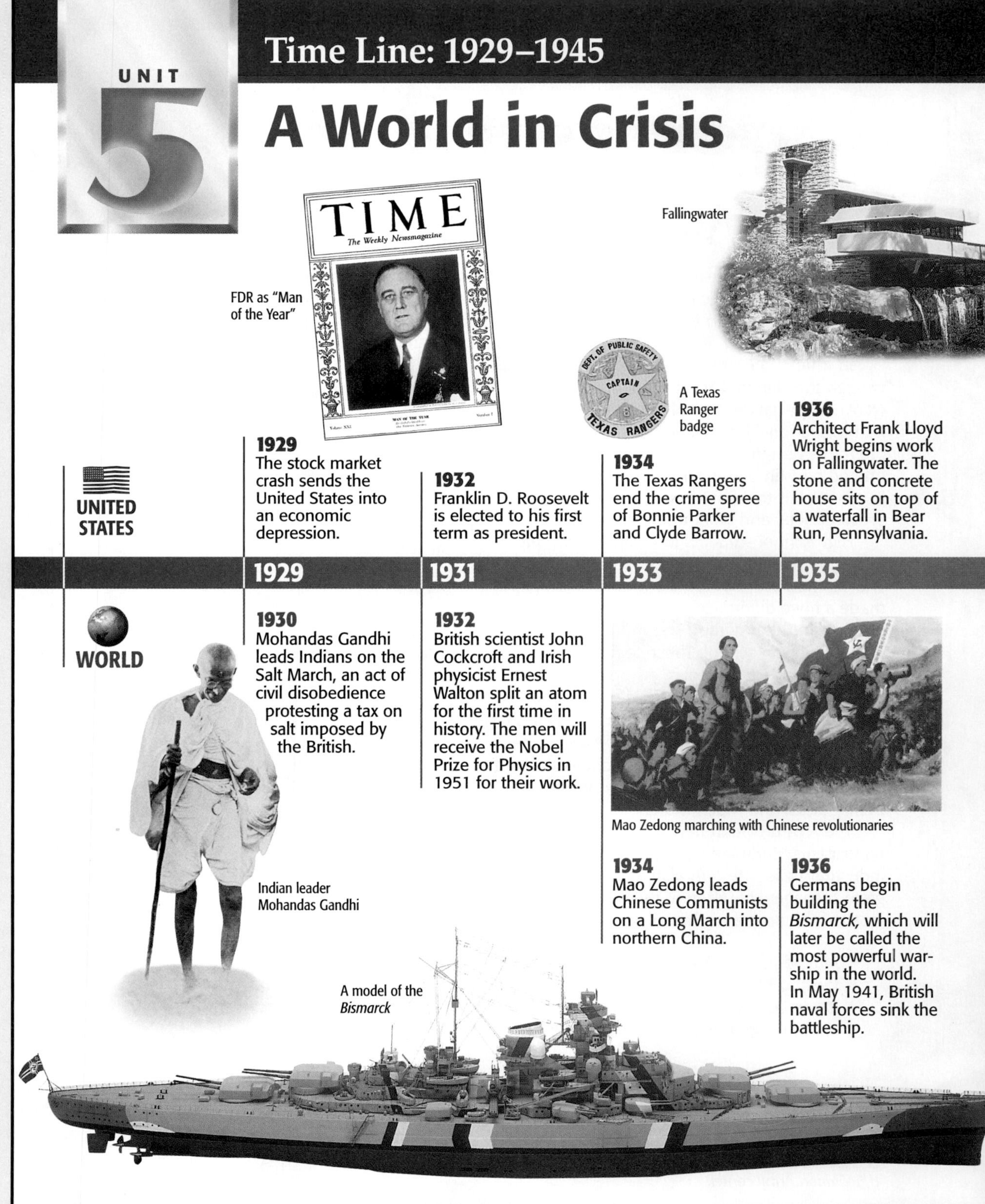

CHALLENGE AND EXTEND

1. **Linguistic, Interpersonal.** Organize the class into several groups. Have students use the library and other resources to find more information about the 1929 stock market crash. Then have each group create an October 2029 issue of a U.S. historical magazine for the 100th anniversary of Black Tuesday. Encourage students to include the following in their articles: causes of the crash, how the crash affected the nation, and attempts to get the economy back on track.

2. **Logical-Mathematical, Visual-Spatial.** Provide students with a large piece of butcher paper. Have them use the library or other resources to create a special purpose map that accurately portrays the years of global conflict from 1939 to 1945. Remind students to include any applicable events from the time line. Encourage students to provide a color-coded map key to help distinguish between the Allies and the Axis Powers. When students are finished, display their work in the classroom

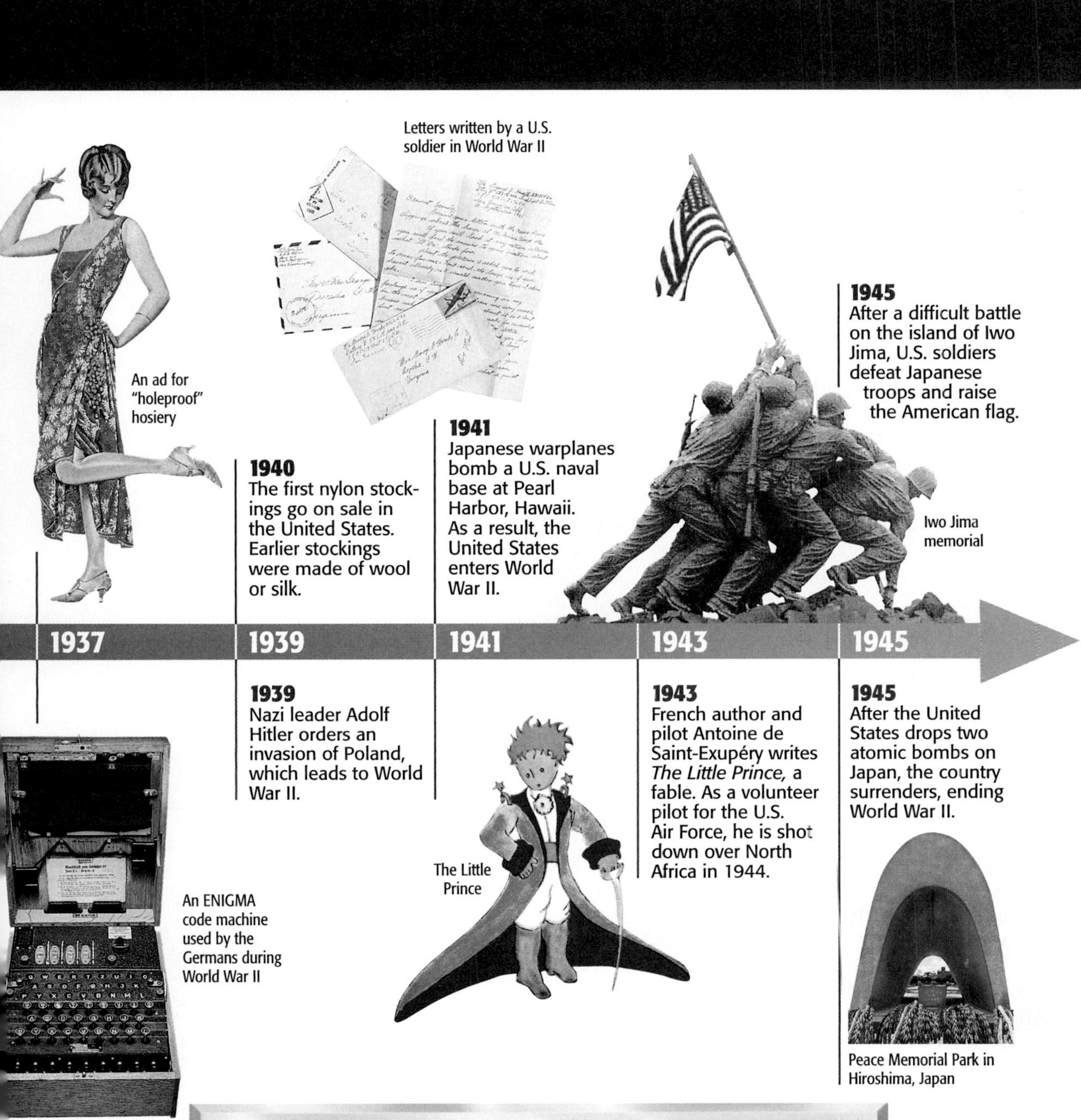

USING THE TIME LINE

1. Which entries on the time line are related to World War II?
2. Using only the time line, determine some of the countries that fought in World War II.

Activity Use the information on this time line and in your textbook to create a time line for World War II. Your time line should match the design of this time line, with U.S. events on the top and world events on the bottom. You will need to select the beginning and ending dates for your time line and divide the time line into intervals. You might want to include some images to illustrate your time line.

Technology and Society

Nylon Stockings. Japan was the largest source of the world's silk in the years before World War II. During the late 1930s, Japan raised the price of silk. As a result, the price of a pair of silk stockings in the United States nearly tripled by 1939. Besides their expense, silk stockings easily tore or ran, particularly when washed repeatedly. In 1940 DuPont introduced nylon, a synthetic fiber that was both sheer and strong. Nylon soon replaced silk in stockings. However, nylon stockings were available only for a short time. Soon after the United States declared war on Japan at the end of 1941, the U.S. government banned any civilian use of the synthetic fiber. All nylon was reserved for use in materials to support the war effort.

Activity: Have students use the library or other resources to make a list of the modern-day uses of nylon.

USING THE TIME LINE ANSWERS

1. splitting the atom (optional); sinking the *Bismarck;* Germany invades Poland; Japan bombs Pearl Harbor, and the United States enters the war; Antoine de Saint-Exupéry shot down; Iwo Jima; Japan surrenders

2. France, Germany, Great Britain, Japan, Poland, the United States

CHAPTER PLANNING GUIDE
The Great Depression

	SECTION LESSON OBJECTIVES	PRINT RESOURCES	MULTIMEDIA RESOURCES	SHELTERED ENGLISH RESOURCES
Section 1: The End of Prosperity (pp. 419–24)	★ Explain why many Americans invested in the stock market in the 1920s. ★ Describe events during the stock market crash and analyze how the crash affected the nation. ★ Identify the economic factors that led to the Great Depression.	★ Guided Reading Strategies 14.1 ★ Section 1 Review, p. 424 ★ Daily Quiz 14.1	★ *Teaching Resources CD–ROM,* Lesson 14.1	★ Main Idea Activities for Reteaching and Sheltered English 14.1
Section 2: Hoover and the Depression (pp. 425–30)	★ Explain how the Great Depression affected Americans' everyday lives. ★ Analyze President Hoover's actions to help Americans during the depression. ★ Describe how Hoover responded to the Bonus Army's demands.	★ Guided Reading Strategies 14.2 ★ American History Political Cartoon 23: Herbert Hoover and the Depression ★ Literature Reading 14: *Black Boy* ★ Primary Source Reading 14: Gordon Parks ★ Section 2 Review, p. 430 ★ Daily Quiz 14.2	★ *Teaching Resources CD–ROM,* Lesson 14.2 ★ *American Music Audio CD Program:* "Breadline Blues"	★ Main Idea Activities for Reteaching and Sheltered English 14.2
Section 3: Roosevelt and the New Deal (pp. 431–36)	★ Describe steps President Roosevelt took immediately after taking office to fight the depression. ★ Explain how New Deal programs addressed the problem of unemployment. ★ Identify programs that addressed the needs of industry and agriculture.	★ Guided Reading Strategies 14.3 ★ Geography Activity 14: The Public Works Administration ★ Section 3 Review, p. 436 ★ Daily Quiz 14.3	★ *Teaching Resources CD–ROM,* Lesson 14.3 ★ *Exploring America's Past* Video Segment: Rising from the Ashes; *Teacher's Guide,* pp. 26–28 ★ *American History Simulations:* A Plan for Prosperity ★ HRW Web site	★ Main Idea Activities for Reteaching and Sheltered English 14.3
Section 4: The Second New Deal (pp. 437–43)	★ Explain why some people were critical of the New Deal. ★ Identify programs passed during the Second New Deal. ★ Describe how President Roosevelt attempted to prevent the Supreme Court from overturning his New Deal programs.	★ Guided Reading Strategies 14.4 ★ American History Political Cartoon 24: FDR and the New Deal ★ Biography Reading 14: Mary McLeod Bethune ★ Graphic Organizer 14: Government Response to the Great Depression ★ Section 4 Review, p. 443 ★ Daily Quiz 14.4	★ *Teaching Resources CD–ROM,* Lesson 14.4 ★ HRW Web site	★ Main Idea Activities for Reteaching and Sheltered English 14.4
Chapter Review and Assessment (pp. 444–45)		★ Chapter 14 Review, pp. 444–45 ★ Vocabulary Activity 14 ★ Chapter 14 Study Guide ★ Chapter 14 Test (Form A or B)	★ Audio Program, Ch. 14 (English and Spanish) ★ *Global Skill Builder CD–ROM* ★ Chapter 14 Test Generator ★ HRW Web site	★ Spanish Glossary ★ Sheltered English Chapter 14 Test

CHAPTER OVERVIEW

In the fall of 1929, the stock market crashed. Banks and businesses failed throughout the United States, leaving thousands of Americans unemployed and without savings. President Hoover opposed direct aid. Instead, he encouraged businesses and private organizations to provide relief. Meanwhile, he focused on healing the nation's economy.

In the 1932 presidential election, Americans chose Democrat Franklin D. Roosevelt. Promising a New Deal, President Roosevelt pledged to do all he could to end the depression. He supported legislation to ease the banking crisis, provide relief to those in need, and help farmers. Despite some criticisms and adverse rulings by the Supreme Court, Roosevelt continued his efforts.

After winning re-election in 1936, Roosevelt tried to increase support for his programs. He asked Congress to expand the Supreme Court, but Congress rejected the idea. However, the Court began upholding more New Deal programs, and Roosevelt eventually filled seven Court vacancies.

Following a slight improvement in 1936 and early 1937, the economy began declining again. In 1938 the Republicans won back many seats in Congress. As the New Deal ended, critics charged that it had created a welfare state. Supporters argued that it had helped many people.

Meeting Individual Needs

ABILITY LEVELS

LEVEL 1 Basic level activities designed for all students encountering new material.

LEVEL 2 Intermediate level activities designed for average students.

LEVEL 3 Challenging activities designed for above-average students.

SHELTERED ENGLISH These activities address the needs of students with Limited English Proficiency.

CHAPTER INVESTIGATION

The Chapter Investigation is an extended, multipart activity designed for students to work cooperatively and apply the chapter content in the creation of a project. You may choose to use the Chapter 14 Investigation, A Documentary, either as a substitute for teaching the section lessons or as an alternate assessment.

BLOCK SCHEDULING 

The teacher lesson plans for each section offer a variety of activity choices to help you present the material in a block scheduling format. For further suggestions on block scheduling, see the *Block Scheduling Handbook with Team Teaching Strategies*, pp. 79–84.

Smithsonian Institution®

Internet Connections and Lesson 14

www.si.edu/hrw

CNN Presents America:

Yesterday and Today 1850 to the Present

Segment: Urban Youth Goes to Work

Additional Resources

Books for Teachers

Klingman, William K. *Nineteen Twenty-nine: The Year of the Great Crash.* HarperCollins, 1990. Traces the effects of the stock market crash.

Reiman, Richard A. *The New Deal & American Youth: Ideas in a Depression Decade.* University of Georgia Press, 1992. Examines the role of youth in the New Deal.

Rosenbaum, Herbert D., and Elizabeth Bartelme, eds. *Franklin D. Roosevelt: The Man, the Myth, the Era, 1882–1945.* Greenwood Press, 1987. Provides a biography of the president.

Books for Students

Daniel, Pete, et al. *Official Images: New Deal Photography.* Smithsonian, 1987. Provides dramatic images of New Deal photographs accompanied by essays analyzing propaganda techniques used by federal agencies.

Meltzer, Milton. *Brother, Can You Spare a Dime?* Facts on File, 1990. Discusses personal traumas experienced during the Great Depression.

Schraff, Anne E. *The Great Depression and the New Deal.* Watts, 1990. Explores effects of the stock market crash and FDR's programs (for students reading below grade level).

Multimedia Materials

Roll of Thunder, Hear My Cry. Video, 115 min. SSSS. Portrays the struggle of southern black landowners during the Great Depression.

The Great Depression: Witness to History. Video, 15 min. Guidance Associates/SSSS. Chronicles effects of the depression on everyday life.

You May Call Her Madam Secretary. Video, 57 min. Vineyard Video Productions/SSSS. Documents the life of Frances Perkins, the first female cabinet member.

The Great Depression

CHAPTER MOTIVATOR

Ask students to imagine a person who has a good job, money in the bank, a nice house, and a new car. Then ask them to imagine that this person's investments have suddenly become worthless and that his or her savings have been lost. In addition, the individual's place of employment has closed and the house and car have been taken away because the person can no longer make the payments. Have students draw before-and-after pictures to illustrate both situations. Then explain to students that people in the United States (and in much of the world) experienced similar situations during the Great Depression. Tell students that in this chapter they will investigate circumstances surrounding the depression and the impact it had on the government and people of the United States.

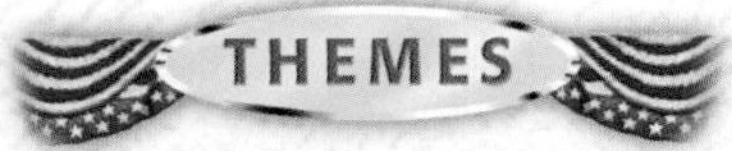

Presenting Themes

- **Economic Development** Students might mention that an economic depression could result from the loss of foreign markets, the overproduction of goods, sick industries, banking or investment crises, or other economic crises.
- **Constitutional Heritage** Students might mention that the Supreme Court might rule on the constitutionality of any measures taken by either other branch of the government to address the problems created by the crisis.
- **Citizenship and Democracy** Students might mention government responses such as providing direct aid to people suffering from the depression, creating programs that put people back to work, and assisting industries that are experiencing financial difficulties.

Using the Time Line

Discuss the time line with students and have them speculate on what people might have thought about each event when it occurred. Then have each student choose one event and write a journal entry from the perspective of someone at the time who has just read about the event in a newspaper. After students finish the chapter, have them revise their journal entries based on what they have learned.

The Granger Collection, New York

CHAPTER 14

The Great Depression

(1929–1939)

In May 1934, E. W. Bakke began another day of searching for work. He applied at many places, including a clock shop, an auto equipment factory, a rubber plant, and a candy factory. He received the same answer everywhere: "No help wanted." At one office a woman cut him off before he could begin, "No use—sorry." For millions of Americans like Bakke, the Great Depression brought unemployment, hard times, and worries about survival.

Economic Development
What factors might cause a nation to experience an economic depression?

Constitutional Heritage
What role might the Supreme Court play during times of economic crisis?

Citizenship and Democracy
How might the government respond to an economic depression?

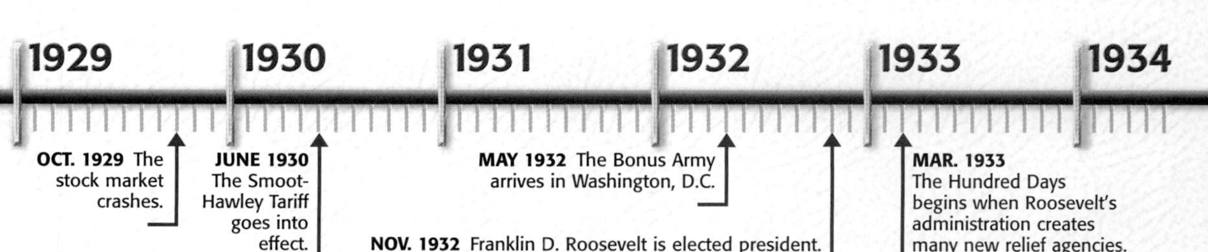

OBJECTIVES

- Explain why many Americans invested in the stock market in the 1920s.
- Describe events during the stock market crash and analyze how the crash affected the nation.
- Identify the economic factors that led to the Great Depression.

FOCUS

Motivate Before Reading

Have each student use a dictionary to write a definition of *speculation* as the word relates to investing. Then ask students if they would invest their entire savings in stocks if they thought they could double their investments within a month. After allowing students time to answer, ask them if they would go into debt to invest even more. Tell students that in this section they will study an era in

The End of Prosperity

Reading Focus

- Why did many Americans invest in the stock market in the 1920s?
- What took place during the stock market crash, and how did it affect the nation?
- What economic factors contributed to the Great Depression?

Key Terms

- bull market
- buying on margin
- speculation
- bear market
- Black Tuesday
- Panic of 1929
- Great Depression
- business cycle
- Smoot-Hawley Tariff

FOR MANY AMERICANS, the 1920s were a time of economic prosperity. That was the message of Republican presidential candidate Herbert Hoover in 1928. Hoover expressed his confidence in the economy in a speech at Stanford University. "We in America today," he stated proudly, "are nearer to the final triumph over poverty than ever before in the history of any land." Hoover promised that if elected president he would continue with the approach of Calvin Coolidge's administration. He would "go forward with the policies of the last eight years." Hoover and many others believed that there was no need for change.

Republicans Herbert Hoover and Charles Curtis ran for president and vice president in the 1928 election.

IMAGE ON LEFT PAGE: *The good times of the 1920s came to a screeching halt when the stock market crashed in October 1929.*

Section 1 RESOURCES

PRINT
- ★ Guided Reading Strategies 14.1
- ★ Section 1 Review, p. 424
- ★ Daily Quiz 14.1

MULTIMEDIA
- ★ *Teaching Resources CD–ROM,* Lesson 14.1

SHELTERED ENGLISH
- ★ Main Idea Activities for Reteaching and Sheltered English 14.1

1935 | 1936 | 1937 | 1938 | 1939

- **JAN. 1935** The Second New Deal begins.
- **AUG. 1935** Congress passes the Social Security Act.
- **NOV. 1936** President Roosevelt defeats Alfred Landon to win re-election.
- **FEB. 1937** Roosevelt presents his plan to change the Supreme Court.
- **MAR. 1938** The unemployment rate jumps as the U.S. economy continues to decline.

which some Americans invested all their money in stocks in hopes of making huge profits, only to lose their money when the stock market crashed and the nation entered an economic depression.

Introduce Key Terms

Linguistic, Logical-Mathematical. Review this section's key terms with students. Have students write sentences that each use at least two of the terms in a historically accurate way. Call on students to share their sentences. **SHELTERED ENGLISH**

TEACH

Have students read Section 1 and complete Guided Reading Strategies 14.1. Choose one or more of the following activities to explore the section content with students. For further suggestions on block scheduling or team teaching, see the *Block Scheduling Handbook*.

LEVEL 1: Linguistic. (Suggested time: 15 min.) As a class, go over students' Guided Reading Strategies. Then use the Reading Focus questions to highlight the main ideas of the section. **SHELTERED ENGLISH**

Across the Curriculum

MATH

Who Participated in the Stock Market?
Although everyone was said to be playing the stock market throughout the 1920s, in 1929 only 4 million Americans actually owned stock, out of a population of around 120 million. Yet throughout the decade, get-rich-quick stories circulated, such as those that told of scrubwomen and secretaries striking it rich and suddenly being able to ride to work in chauffeured limousines.

Activity: Have students determine the percentage of the American population that owned stock in 1929. *(Students should take the population that owned stock, 4 million, and divide it by the total population, 120 million, which roughly equals .033. Then students should multiply the result by 100 to convert it to a percentage, 3.3 percent.)*

The Stock Market Soars

American businesses boomed during the 1920s. Production and employment were high and on the rise. In 1921 about 1.5 million cars were sold. By 1929 that number reached some 4.5 million. More Americans than ever before owned houses, and about 80 million Americans per week were going to the movies.

A March 1929 Life *magazine cover highlighting the interest in the stock market*

Further evidence of the decade's prosperity was the increase in stock prices in the late 1920s. For example, RCA stock jumped from $85 a share to $420 during 1928. Many Americans, from homemakers to business executives, bought and sold stocks. The number of major investors totaled about half a million, but it seemed as though everyone were interested in the stock market. The increased demand for stocks led to higher share prices and more possibility of investment profits.

Many experts saw no end to this **bull market**, or continuing rise in stock market prices. Business leaders such as General Motors executive John J. Raskob encouraged the public to participate in the stock market boom. In a magazine article titled "Everyone Ought to Be Rich," Raskob stated that if a person invested $15 a week in stocks, "at the end of twenty years he will have at least $80,000. . . . He will be rich."

Many people who invested in the stock market were **buying on margin**—purchasing stocks on credit with a loan from a broker. Brokers borrowed this money from banks. This activity was **speculation**—the investing of money in a high-risk venture in hopes of making a profit. It was based on the belief that no matter how much a person paid for the stock, someone else would pay more. Few people predicted that a **bear market**, or a continuing drop in stock prices, would occur. At his inauguration in March 1929, President Herbert Hoover told Americans, "I have no fears for the future of our country. It is bright with hope."

 The Great Crash

On September 3, 1929, stock prices hit an all-time high. Shortly thereafter, prices began to slide downward. On Thursday morning, October 24, large-scale investors sold huge blocks of shares, causing prices to fall even more. However, the stock market rallied by the close of the business day.

President Hoover tried to reassure the American public, saying that "the fundamental business of the country . . . is on a sound and prosperous basis." Investors remained uneasy, however. *New York Times* reporter Elliott Bell recalled that around the New York Stock Exchange (NYSE) people were asking, "Who was in trouble? Who had gone under last? Where was it going to end?"

The stock market collapsed on October 29, 1929, which became known as **Black Tuesday**. As prices began to drop drastically, panicked investors began frantically selling their stocks. People who had bought on margin were forced to sell their stocks to try to raise money to pay their

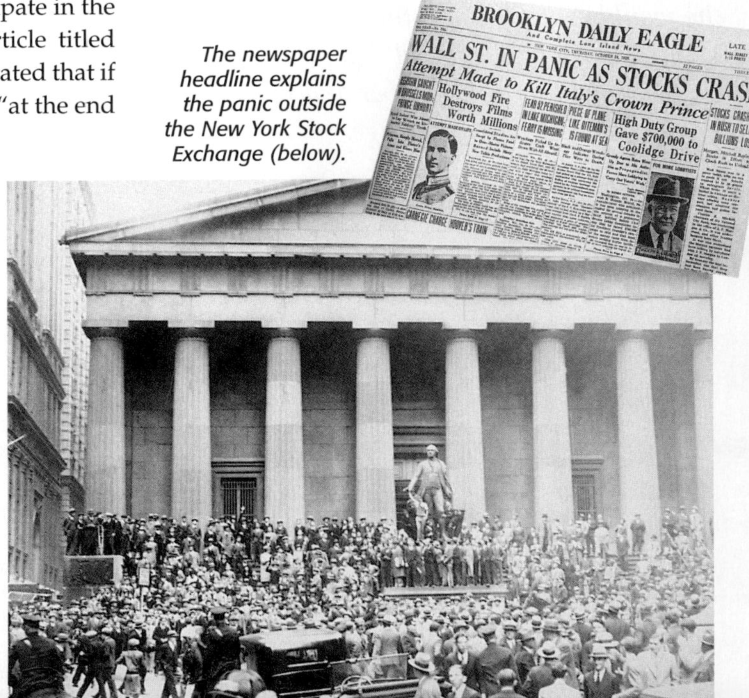
BROOKLYN DAILY EAGLE
WALL ST. IN PANIC AS STOCKS CRASH
Attempt Made to Kill Italy's Crown Prince
Hollywood Fire Destroys Films Worth Millions
High Duty Group Gave $700,000 to Coolidge Drive

The newspaper headline explains the panic outside the New York Stock Exchange (below).

ALL LEVELS: Logical-Mathematical, Visual-Spatial. (Suggested time: 30 min.) On a large piece of butcher paper and with the help of volunteers, create a cause-and-effect chart depicting conditions in the stock market that led to the crash. Then extend the cause-and-effect chart to show how the stock market crash combined with other events to cause the Great Depression. Have students discuss which factors they think were most important in bringing on the depression and highlight these causes on the chart. **SHELTERED ENGLISH**

LEVEL 2: Linguistic, Logical-Mathematical, Interpersonal. (Suggested time: 45 min.) Organize the class into several small groups and assign each group a type of media, such as newspapers, magazines, or radio. For the assigned medium, have each group develop an ad campaign that persuades people to invest in the stock market. Encourage students to use explanations and statistics from the text to convince their audience to invest in the market. Once the ad campaigns are finished, have a member of each group present its work to the class. Finally, have students provide feedback to other groups regarding the effectiveness of their campaigns and discuss reasons people invested in the stock market in the 1920s.

LEVEL 3: Linguistic, Logical-Mathematical. (Suggested time: 20 min. plus homework) Ask students to imagine that they are newspaper reporters covering the stock market crash of 1929.

loans. Other investors hoped to sell their stocks before the shares lost all value.

Fearful and confused investors mobbed Wall Street, where the NYSE is located. Telephone lines were jammed. Brokerages were filled with people trying to sell stock. Traders fought with each other on the floor of the exchange. Many people could not find any buyers for their stocks, causing the price of shares to continue falling. When no buyers could be found for the stock of the White Sewing Machine Company, a young messenger bid $1 per share and became a major stockholder in the company.

By the end of Black Tuesday more than 16 million shares had been traded, and some $15 billion in stock value had been lost. An investment banker recalled the mood on Wall Street. "It was like a thunderclap. Everybody was stunned. Nobody knew what it was all about." A journalist wrote, "When the closing bell rang, the great bull market was dead and buried."

The drop in stock prices continued, and the one-day stock market crash turned into the **Panic of 1929**. U.S. Steel stock fell from $261 to $150 a share, while General Electric stock dropped from $396 to $168 a share. By the end of November, losses had climbed to $50 billion. Many speculators who had bought on margin lost everything. They were forced to pay their brokers with savings or by pawning jewelry, china, and clothing to get cash. Even Americans who never invested in the market soon felt the lasting effects of the Great Crash. Author Frederick Lewis Allen wrote about how the crash affected people:

> **"Prosperity is more than an economic condition; it is a state of mind. . . . There was hardly a man or woman in the country whose attitude toward life had not been affected by it [the crash] in some degree and was not now affected by the sudden and brutal shattering of hope."**

The Economy Collapses

In the first months following the Panic of 1929, the nation's leaders played down its importance. Treasury Secretary Andrew Mellon even suggested to President Hoover that "a panic was not altogether a bad thing" because Americans had been living beyond their means in the 1920s.

The Granger Collection, New York

Just three weeks before the Great Crash, cartoonist Rollin Kirby warned investors that a bear market could quickly wipe out their profits.

Businesses Go Under

Mellon and many other leaders were slow to realize how serious a blow the stock market crash was to the economy. After the crash many businesses slowed production and laid off workers. As a result, these individuals found it difficult to buy new products or continue making payments on their installment plans. Frederick Lewis Allen noted, "Men and women were wondering how they could meet the next payment on the car or the radio or the furniture."

With fewer people buying goods, factories slowed their production even more and began laying off additional workers. This created a vicious cycle in which layoffs led to decreased consumer spending, which in turn led to more layoffs. These circumstances began affecting even prosperous companies. In Detroit in 1931, for example, the Ford Motor Company stopped producing its once successful Model A because demand slowed.

The nation became locked in a downward economic spiral known as the **Great Depression**. The gross national product (GNP), the total value of all

Economic Development

Warning Signs. Throughout 1928 the U.S. economy showed signs of trouble. Consumers stopped buying the manufactured goods, such as radios and cars, that had spurred the boom. As a result, the amount of manufactured goods that retailers had in stock increased threefold between 1928 and 1929. This surplus of goods caused prices to drop and also led manufacturers to decrease production. By July 1929 economic indicators, such as the amount of goods loaded onto freight cars and the number of contracts to build new homes, were showing an economic decline.

Critical Thinking: Why might Americans have chosen to ignore these economic warning signs?

ANSWER: They might not have wanted to believe that the prosperous times would ever end.

Have each student write an article that answers the following questions: What happened during the stock market crash? How has the stock market crash affected the nation? What can Americans do to recover economically? How will 1929 be a significant year in U.S. history? Call on volunteers to share their articles with the class.

CLOSE

Linguistic, Logical-Mathematical, Visual-Spatial. Have each student create a concept map of events surrounding the start of the Great Depression. Ask them to begin their maps by writing *Great Depression* in the center of their papers and circling it. Next, as they review the section have them list related events and connect them to the central circle. Have students extend each related event outward by adding at least one supporting idea. When students have completed the activity, have volunteers explain their concept maps to the class.

CHALLENGE AND EXTEND

1. **Logical-Mathematical.** Have students use the library and other resources to research a stock available in 1928 and that is still offered today. Have students find out the stock's price

Economic Development

Banking Problems. Perhaps nothing was more symbolic of the Great Depression than the lack of public confidence exhibited by bank runs. From the beginning of the crash in 1929 to 1932, almost one third of the nation's banks suspended payments and closed their doors. In 1932 alone more than 1,400 banks, with nearly $725 million in deposits, went under. With each bank failure, the discrepancy between how much the nation's banks had in cash reserves and how much they owed in deposits grew. By the time of Franklin D. Roosevelt's inauguration in 1933, the Department of the Treasury estimated that U.S. banks had a mere $7.37 billion in cash reserves, but owed $40.5 billion in liabilities.

Activity: Have students use the library and other resources to find information on bank failures in the United States that occurred at times other than the Great Depression. Ask students to compare the conditions leading to those bank failures to the ones that led to the bank failures of the Great Depression.

The Granger Collection, New York

The illustration Sold Out *expresses the feelings of many Americans in the Panic of 1929.*

goods and services produced in a given year, fell by almost 30 percent between 1929 and 1931. While the GNP fell, unemployment jumped. In 1932 the unemployment rate rose to more than 20 percent. Many people began to believe that the hard times were not going to end quickly.

The Banking Crisis

The Great Depression also affected the banking industry. Many banks were hard hit when customers were unable to repay their bank loans. These bankrupt customers included investors who had lost everything in the stock market crash and farmers who were suffering from a drastic drop in agricultural prices. Unable to collect the money they were owed, many local banks could not repay the money they had borrowed from larger banks. As a result, many of these smaller banks failed.

News of these bank failures triggered a panic among depositors because bank deposits were not insured. If a bank failed, depositors lost their entire savings. Fearing more bank failures, people across the country rushed to their banks to withdraw their money. However, banks usually kept on hand only a fraction of the total amount of money that people had deposited. The rest of the money was invested or loaned out to individuals and businesses. Therefore, few banks were able to pay all the depositors who tried to withdraw their money. These runs, or sudden demands, on banks had a devastating effect on the banking industry. Businesses that relied on bank loans to operate or expand could not function.

Unpaid loans, bad debts, and mass withdrawals by depositors led more than 9,700 American banks to fail between 1929 and 1933. These bank failures wiped out the savings that many people had counted on for their survival during hard times.

What Happened?

The Panic of 1929 did not cause the Great Depression. However, it revealed weaknesses in the economy that contributed to the depression.

The Business Cycle

Many economists argued that a recession in 1930 was a natural part of the **business cycle**—the pattern of alternating prosperity and recession in a free-enterprise economy. According to this cycle, people buy more goods during times of prosperity.

New York City bank customers stood in long lines to try to withdraw their money.

over the course of 1929 and, if possible, its price in 1940, 1950, and 1960. Then, ask students to imagine that they had bought 100 shares of the stock in January 1929. Ask them to calculate how much they would have lost or gained in the crash of 1929, and by 1940, 1950, and 1960. Finally, discuss the benefits and drawbacks of short-term speculation versus investing for the long-term.

2. **Logical-Mathematical, Visual-Spatial.** As this section notes, scholars disagree on exactly why the Great Depression occurred. Have students use the library and other resources to find information on possible causes of the depression. Encourage students to investigate the decline in world trade, the stock market crash, bank failures, and other possible causes. Then have students use their research to make a pie chart that explains the causes. The events that students determine to be most important should have the biggest pieces of the pie, while the least significant events should have the smallest pieces. Have students annotate their pie charts by writing a sentence or two next to each segment explaining its significance.

REVIEW

Linguistic, Logical-Mathematical, Interpersonal. Have students complete the Section Review questions. Then ask each

To meet this greater demand, businesses increase production and hire extra workers. Eventually, more goods are produced than sold, creating a surplus. To reduce the surplus, companies lower prices and therefore profits. Industries cut back production and lay off workers, which causes a recession. If a recession continues for an extended period of time, it becomes a depression. As factory output decreases, surpluses are gradually used up. Industries then increase production and rehire workers. These workers spend money, and the economy enters the recovery stage. Eventually, recovery leads to prosperity and the cycle repeats itself.

The Typical Business Cycle

Economic Trends At first, most Americans thought the stock market crash had caused only a temporary recession. What do you think a graph of the business cycle during the Great Depression would look like?

Predictions

Many economists in the late 1920s believed that a brief recession was bound to follow the prosperity. In 1928 housing construction slowed, consumer spending declined, and inventories began piling up. Before the Great Crash, some industries had reduced production and laid off workers. The decline in workers' incomes combined with the drop in bank deposits limited the money supply—the amount of money available for spending or investment.

Even as the economy worsened, leaders such as Treasury Secretary Mellon believed that the nation's economic problems were not serious. Mellon declared that prosperity would soon return. "People will work harder [and] . . . enterprising people will pick up the wrecks from less competent people," he said confidently. Instead, the recession turned into the most severe depression in U.S. history.

Industry and Agriculture

Overproduction, bank failures, and the stock market crash contributed to the Great Depression. Other causes included struggling industries, an unequal distribution of wealth, and unwise trade policies. Industries such as lumber, mining, and textiles had expanded during World War I. During peacetime these industries could not maintain this growth and became "sick."

Agriculture never recovered fully from the recession of 1920–21. Farmers had to pay high prices for farm equipment, labor, land, and transportation. At the same time, overproduction caused crop prices to fall. As a result, many farmers could not repay their bank loans. Farmers had to declare bankruptcy and lost their property through foreclosure. Lenders foreclose on, or take possession of, mortgages when borrowers can no longer make their loan payments. Lenders often sell the mortgaged properties to pay off the loan.

In the 1930s candy remained an affordable item. For 20 cents customers could buy one pound of candy.

Historical Sidelight

Tracking Stock Prices. Devices known as tickers, which were used to print the latest prices of stocks so that traders could keep track of changes in the market, also contributed to the stock market crash. At brokerage firms, workers posted signs indicating the prices reported on the tickers. During the final week of October 1929, stock prices were changing so rapidly that the stock tickers and the workers posting the signs could not keep pace. The prices reported on the tickers were often as much as 90 minutes old, which meant that stock brokers had no idea what the current prices actually were. This lack of accurate information contributed to the sense of panic that engulfed Wall Street.

Critical Thinking: Why did stock brokers need the current stock prices?

ANSWER: They needed to know if prices on particular stocks were rising or falling so that they could decide if they should buy or sell.

CHART ANSWER

It would be a longer and more severe period of depression with very little recovery or prosperity.

student to create an outline for an encyclopedia entry on the Great Depression. For each main heading, have students list at least two supporting details. As students create their outlines, have them replace any key terms or individual's names with blank spaces. Then have students exchange papers and fill in the missing terms and names in the appropriate locations. Finally, have students return the outlines to their authors for grading.

ASSESS

Have students complete Daily Quiz 14.1.

RETEACH

Linguistic, Visual-Spatial, Interpersonal. Have students complete Main Idea Activities for Reteaching and Sheltered English 14.1. On the chalkboard, list the major events surrounding the Great Depression. After reviewing the events, have students create a picture book that can explain the causes and impact of the Great Depression to next year's class. Have each student illustrate one event and include a brief caption. Then have students put their pages together to form the book. **SHELTERED ENGLISH**

Section 1 Review ANSWERS

Identify

For significance, see the following pages:

- bull market, p. 420
- buying on margin, p. 420
- speculation, p. 420
- bear market, p. 420
- Black Tuesday, p. 420
- Panic of 1929, p. 421
- Andrew Mellon, p. 421
- Great Depression, p. 421
- business cycle, p. 422
- Smoot-Hawley Tariff, p. 424

Reading for Content Understanding

1. because stock prices were soaring; business leaders were encouraging Americans to invest; people could buy on margin; and they believed no matter how much they paid for stock, someone else would pay more

2. Causes include overproduction, unsound banking practices, the stock market crash, sick industries, and the unequal distribution of wealth.

3. As stock prices plummeted, investors panicked and tried to sell their stocks. However, not enough buyers were available for all the stocks being sold, which forced prices to drop even more.

4. Answers will vary but students should describe the cyclical fluctuation between prosperity and recession and explain whether they think events following the stock market crash support the business cycle theory.

5. Answers will vary but students should mention some actions he might have taken and explain why they think these actions would or would not have ended the depression.

Wealth and Trade

Another economic weakness was the unequal distribution of wealth in the United States. In 1929 a mere 1 percent of the U.S. population held about one third of all personal wealth. At the same time, an estimated 60 percent of all American families earned less than the $2,000 a year needed to buy basic necessities. The result was that most people could not afford to buy the goods produced. In addition, many Americans had bought goods on credit. After the crash, they were not able to pay for these products.

In the 1930s the Ford Motor Company had to stop production of many of its cars, like the Model A Deluxe Phaeton.

A 1932 article in *Current History* described the frustration shared by many Americans:

> **"There is too much bread, too much wheat and corn, meat and oil. . . . We are not able to purchase the abundance that modern methods of agriculture, mining and manufacture make available. . . . Why is mankind being asked to go hungry and cold and poverty stricken in the midst of plenty?"**

In order to reverse the economic decline, people needed to be able to buy the surplus of available goods. During the early 1930s, most Americans had little money to spend. Wealthy Americans could not invest enough or buy enough items, like automobiles, to make up for the decline in purchases. As a result, the recovery did not occur.

President Hoover blamed world economic problems for the depression. In the late 1920s some European countries still struggled to make war reparations, while others tried to repay loans from World War I. Certain U.S. trade policies made matters worse. The June 1930 **Smoot-Hawley Tariff** raised U.S. duties on imports to all-time highs. Foreign governments responded by imposing their own trade restrictions. Higher foreign tariffs limited the markets in which American goods could be sold and made the worldwide depression worse. As the depression deepened, many Americans began to worry that a return to prosperity was unlikely anytime soon.

SECTION 1 REVIEW

Identify and explain the significance of the following:

- **bull market**
- **buying on margin**
- **speculation**
- **bear market**
- **Black Tuesday**
- **Panic of 1929**
- **Andrew Mellon**
- **Great Depression**
- **business cycle**
- **Smoot-Hawley Tariff**

Reading for Content Understanding

1 **Main Idea** Why did some people see the stock market as a way to get rich quickly?

2 **Main Idea** What were some of the causes of the Great Depression?

3 **Economic Development** What took place during the stock market crash, and what effect did it have on Wall Street and the U.S. economy?

4 **Writing** *Describing* Imagine that you are a business leader giving a magazine interview after October 29, 1929. Explain the business cycle and whether you think the events following the stock market crash support this pattern.

5 **Critical Thinking** *Drawing Conclusions* Do you think President Hoover could have taken any actions to prevent the Great Depression? Explain your answer.

OBJECTIVES

- **Explain how the Great Depression affected Americans' everyday lives.**
- **Analyze President Hoover's actions to help Americans during the depression.**
- **Describe how Hoover responded to the Bonus Army's demands.**

FOCUS

Motivate Before Reading

Ask students to number off from one to five. Then ask all students who called out a number five to stand up. Explain to students that at the height of the Great Depression, about one in every five people in the United States was unemployed. (You may want to compare this with the current unemployment rate.) Remind students that these unemployed people still had to provide for themselves

Hoover and the Depression

Reading Focus

In what ways did the Great Depression affect the everyday lives of Americans?

What actions did President Hoover take to help Americans during the depression?

How did Hoover respond to the Bonus Army's demands?

Key Terms

Hoovervilles
relief
Reconstruction Finance Corporation
public works
Agricultural Marketing Act
Federal Home Loan Bank Act
Bonus Army

IN LATE OCTOBER 1929, teenager Gordon Parks read a newspaper article describing the stock market crash. "I couldn't imagine financial disaster touching my small world; it surely concerned only the rich," he recalled. Parks was working part time, but soon felt the effect of the crash when his employer laid him off the next week. "Along with millions of others across the nation, I was without a job," he wrote. Unable to find a job that paid as well as his part-time job, Parks quit school to look for full-time work. He became one of the many Americans whose lives were suddenly changed by the Great Depression.

Unemployed workers gather in front of the White House to demand help.

The Depression Hits Home

Following the stock market crash in October 1929, production and investment slowed dramatically. Most construction ground to a halt. Across the nation, millions of Americans struggled to protect themselves and their families from economic ruin.

Out of a Job

In 1932 the U.S. unemployment rate was at more than 20 percent. In New Orleans, several hundred people answered an advertisement for a single position. In cities like New York, jobless people sold apples and pencils on the street. Several hundred thousand people, most of them men, left their homes in search of work. They traveled across the country on foot, by car, or by rail. One reporter called them "the nomads of the depression."

Although the depression affected all segments of society, African Americans, Mexican Americans, and recent immigrants were particularly hard hit. Members of minority groups were usually the first to be laid off from factory jobs so that white employees could keep their jobs. One African American steelworker whose factory laid him off

Section 2 RESOURCES

PRINT

- ★ Guided Reading Strategies 14.2
- ★ American History Political Cartoon 23: Herbert Hoover and the Depression
- ★ Literature Reading 14: *Black Boy*
- ★ Primary Source Reading 14: Gordon Parks
- ★ Section 2 Review, p. 430
- ★ Daily Quiz 14.2

MULTIMEDIA

- ★ *Teaching Resources CD–ROM,* Lesson 14.2
- ★ *American Music Audio CD Program:* "Breadline Blues"

SHELTERED ENGLISH

- ★ Main Idea Activities for Reteaching and Sheltered English 14.2

and their families. Tell students that in this section they will learn how the Great Depression affected Americans and how President Hoover responded to the crisis.

Introduce Key Terms

Linguistic, Logical-Mathematical, Interpersonal. Review this section's key terms with students. Provide each student with seven note cards. Ask students to write one key term on each note card and descriptive statements about the terms on the other sides. Then have each student choose a partner and take turns reading clues and identifying the terms.
SHELTERED ENGLISH

TEACH

Have students read Section 2 and complete Guided Reading Strategies 14.2. Choose one or more of the following activities to explore the section content with students. For further suggestions on block scheduling or team teaching, see the *Block Scheduling Handbook.*

LEVEL 1: Linguistic. (Suggested time: 15 min.) As a class, go over students' Guided Reading Strategies. Then use the Reading Focus questions to highlight the main ideas of the section.
SHELTERED ENGLISH

Economic Development

Economic Differences. The division between the wealthy and other Americans held firm throughout the depression. One writer in the 1930s noted that only 28 of the 86 theaters in New York remained open, but popular shows at these theaters had sold out even the most expensive seats. Likewise, some hotels had to cut their rates, but the Waldorf maintained its prices and remained fully occupied.

Critical Thinking: Why might the wealthy be less affected by the depression than the poor?

ANSWER: While wealthy people may have lost money in the stock market crash, they probably had other sources of income on which to fall back.

CHART ANSWER
1933

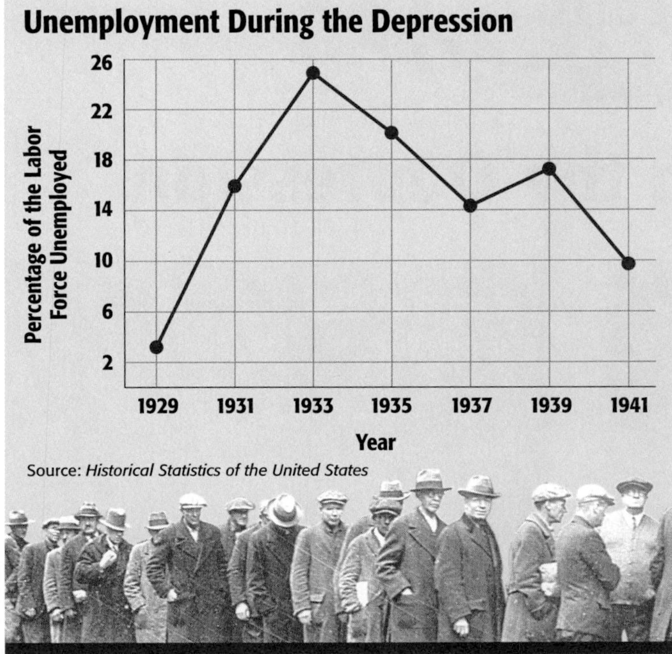

Work Wanted At the depth of the depression, about 25 percent of employable Americans did not have jobs. During what year was unemployment the highest?

was told "he needn't trouble looking for a job as long as there is so many white men out of work."

Women found it somewhat easier to get jobs during the depression. They found work primarily as clerks, maids, or waitresses—positions that survived the hard times better than factory jobs. However, these positions usually paid very low wages. Women who found jobs in other professions were generally paid less than men.

Hard Times All Over

The Great Depression affected Americans in every part of the country. Wages were so low that men and women who did have jobs often did not earn enough to support their families without making great sacrifices. Living conditions in urban areas became particularly difficult. Thousands of unemployed people competed for scarce jobs, food, and shelter. Louise Armstrong, author of *We, Too, Are the People,* wrote of a shocking scene in a large city:

> **"We saw a crowd of some fifty men fighting over a barrel of garbage which had been set outside the back door of a restaurant. American citizens fighting for scraps of food like animals!"**

Farm families were somewhat better equipped to provide themselves with basic necessities. However, poverty and drought made daily life a struggle for many rural residents. In one rural school in the Appalachian Mountains, a teacher told a sick-looking girl to go home and get something to eat. "I can't," the child replied. "It's my sister's turn to eat."

The depression also reached into the suburbs of the once prosperous middle class. The greatest fear among the middle class was the possibility of losing their homes.

Some people who lost their homes built clusters of shacks from cardboard boxes or old boards. They named these camps **Hoovervilles** because they blamed President Hoover for their situation. People in Hoovervilles typically camped outside of major cities. They used old newspapers, which they called "Hoover blankets," to keep warm. At times, desperate Americans begged for money or stole food. Some people eventually starved to death.

During the depression, some Americans slept where they found space to put down a mattress.

TEACHER TO TEACHER

ALL LEVELS: Linguistic, Visual-Spatial. (Suggested time: 25 min.) Nancy Hammond of Woodbridge, Virginia, suggested the following activity: Have students create political cartoons to depict President Hoover's response to the Great Depression. Students may want to convey a general sense of his response or depict a specific action. In either case, have them include an appropriate caption. When students have finished, call on volunteers to explain their cartoons to the class. Finally, lead a class discussion on actions that President Hoover took to help Americans during the Great Depression. SHELTERED ENGLISH

LEVEL 2: Linguistic, Intrapersonal. (Suggested time: 40 min.) Have students review the portion of this section on the Bonus Army. Then ask students to imagine that they are reporters assigned to interview President Hoover about the Bonus Army's protest in Washington, D.C. Have students write questions to ask Hoover and then the answers that they think he would have given. Students' questions should focus on the Bonus Army's demands, events leading up to the protest, and Hoover's response. Students should then add a brief closing describing public reaction to the event. When students have finished, call on volunteers to read

American Literature

Their Eyes Were Watching God
Zora Neale Hurston

Zora Neale Hurston's novel Their Eyes Were Watching God *was published in 1937. The novel centers around Janie Crawford's life story and her search for true love.* Their Eyes Were Watching God *also gives some insight into the lives of African Americans during the Great Depression. In order to find work, many African Americans traveled throughout the South. The following excerpt describes the arrival of migrant farmhands to a bean farm.*

Cover from Hurston's 1937 book, Their Eyes Were Watching God

Day by day now, the hordes [crowds] of workers poured in. Some came limping in with their shoes and sore feet from walking. It's hard trying to follow your shoe instead of your shoe following you. They came in wagons from way up in Georgia and they came in truck loads from east, west, north and south. Permanent transients [drifters] with no attachments and tired looking men with their families and dogs. . . . All night, all day, hurrying in to pick beans. Skillets, beds, patched up spare inner tubes all hanging and dangling from the ancient cars on the outside. . . .

People ugly from ignorance and broken from being poor. . . .

Finally no more sleeping places. Men made big fires and fifty or sixty men slept around each fire. But they had to pay the man whose land they slept on. He ran the fire just like his boarding place—for pay. But nobody cared. They made good money, even to the children. So they spent good money. Next month and next year were other times. No need to mix them up with the present.

Understanding Literature

1. Describe how the workers looked and felt as they came to work in the bean fields.
2. Why do you think they are only looking to the present?

Biography

Zora Neale Hurston. Zora Neale Hurston was one of the most prolific African American writers of the 1930s. During those years, she collected and published the stories and folk customs of poor African Americans living in Florida, Louisiana, Haiti, and Jamaica. Her lively style brought her praise from other folklorists and from anthropologists. Although she won acclaim in many circles for her work, several African American contemporaries criticized her books for being apolitical. Her works soon went out of print, and she died penniless and little known. Author Alice Walker almost single-handedly was responsible for reviving interest in Hurston's works when she discussed them in a 1971 article for *Ms.* magazine.

Activity: Have students read excerpts from some of Hurston's works and list themes that are common throughout them.

AMERICAN LITERATURE ANSWERS

1. They looked poverty-stricken and mentally and physically exhausted, and as if they felt emotionally beaten down. At the same time, they seemed eager and happy to have work and a chance to earn money.

2. because the future is too fearful and bleak to contemplate

Trying to Cope

The poverty caused by the Great Depression was a blow to the pride of many Americans. They resisted asking for assistance as long as they could. As the depression worsened, however, many people turned to traditional community support networks to help them. These networks included relatives, neighbors, and churches.

As the pressure on community networks increased, private organizations began providing direct **relief**—food, clothing, shelter, and money—to the needy. Organizations such as the Red Cross and the Salvation Army set up soup kitchens and breadlines. Hungry people could get free food there. People would often line up around the block for a piece of bread and a small cup of thin soup. Peggy Terry, who was a young girl during the their interviews. Finally, lead a class discussion on the appropriateness of the Bonus Army's demands and Hoover's response.

LEVEL 3: Linguistic, Logical-Mathematical. (Suggested time: 45 min.) Remind students of President Hoover's belief that government intervention during economic hard times would only destroy people's self-reliance and initiative. Assign half of the class to write a few paragraphs supporting Hoover's views and the other half to write a few paragraphs opposing them. Ask students to refer to the section to support their assigned positions. Allow time in class for volunteers to present their arguments.

LEVEL 3: Linguistic, Logical-Mathematical, Intrapersonal. (Suggested time: 20 min. plus homework) Review with students the effects of the Great Depression on Americans' everyday lives. Then ask students to imagine that they are volunteering in a soup kitchen during the depression. Have them write a letter to President Hoover describing the people who come to the soup kitchen and how the depression has hurt them. Encourage students to suggest ways that the president might help people at the soup kitchen. Finally, call on volunteers to read their letters to the class.

Economic Development

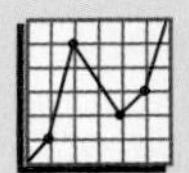

The Reconstruction Finance Corporation. Established in 1932, the Reconstruction Finance Corporation (RFC) was designed to lend money to financially troubled businesses and banks. Its financial assistance helped slow the rate of bank failures. However, a few large corporations received most of the money the RFC distributed.

Critical Thinking: What might be some of the benefits and drawbacks of the federal government helping private businesses?

ANSWER: Answers will vary but students might mention that benefits could include businesses being able to produce more, which could strengthen the economy; drawbacks might include businesses coming to depend on government aid.

Multimedia Resources

American Music Audio CD Program: "Breadline Blues"

depression, recalled going to the soup kitchen after school. "If you happened to be one of the first ones in line, you didn't get anything but water that was on top." The Red Cross and the Salvation Army also operated lodging houses where homeless men could spend the night.

As the depression worsened some desperate Americans took aggressive actions. In 1930 more than 1,000 New Yorkers standing in a Salvation Army breadline robbed two bakery trucks that were making a delivery at a nearby hotel. In Arkansas, hungry residents used guns to force Red Cross workers to give out food.

Few private relief organizations were prepared to cope with the severity of the depression. In Philadelphia, wealthy residents who contributed millions of dollars to local relief were stunned when the money ran out within months. Some business leaders were unsympathetic to the hardships faced by the unemployed. They were therefore reluctant to donate money to relief organizations. John Edgerton, president of the National Association of Manufacturers, accused the jobless of failing to save money or spend wisely. "[How] is our economic system, or government, or industry to blame?" he asked.

Many suffering Americans wondered when the government was going to get involved in fighting the depression. Some citizens wrote letters to the government in anger or desperation. They tried to convince leaders to change their hands-off policies. One New Jersey resident wrote to President Hoover in 1930:

> **"Our children have Schoolless days and Shoeless days and the land full of plenty and Banks bursting with money. Why does Every Thing have Exceptional Value. Except the Human being—why are we reduced to poverty and starving and anxiety and Sorrow. . . . Why not End the Depression have you not a Heart[?]"**

Hoover's Philosophy

Those looking for government assistance found little support from President Hoover or his advisers. For months Hoover insisted that the economic downturn was temporary. In 1930 he told a group of businesspeople, "The Depression is over."

In spite of what many Americans thought, Hoover was sympathetic to the troubles of the poor. For example, during World War I he had led efforts to help starving refugees in war-torn Europe. However, Hoover firmly opposed federal programs such as unemployment relief because he worried about destroying Americans' self-reliance. He was convinced that private charity, not federal aid, was the "American way." Hoover hoped that Americans would rise to the challenges posed by the Great Depression. He once wrote:

> **"The spread of government destroys initiative [independent action] and thus destroys character. Character is made in the community as well as in the individual by assuming responsibilities, not by escaping them."**

Hoover also believed that businesses should operate without interference from or involvement by the federal government. He asked business leaders to voluntarily maintain wage rates, keep up production, and cooperate with the government to build confidence in the economy. "We have passed the worst," he claimed in March 1930.

Hungry men hoped to find a good meal at a New York City soup kitchen in 1931.

CLOSE

Logical-Mathematical, Visual-Spatial. Have students create graphic organizers showing the causes of the Great Depression, the effects it had on Americans, and the actions Hoover took to deal with the economic crisis and help people. Have volunteers share their organizers with the class. Encourage students to use their organizers as study aids for the section. Then ask students whether, based on what they have learned, President Hoover was to blame for the suffering of Americans during the Great Depression and, if so, how much. Have students justify their answers.

CHALLENGE AND EXTEND

Logical-Mathematical, Visual-Spatial. Explain to students that many private organizations, such as the Red Cross or the Salvation Army, began providing direct relief to needy citizens during the Great Depression. Have students use the library and other resources to find information on a particular organization that provided relief. Ask students to create an informative poster that describes the type of relief available from the organization. Call on volunteers to describe the relief services provided by the organizations they studied.

Hoover's Aid Policies

When economic conditions did not improve, President Hoover was forced to act. He decided to try a program to stimulate the economy. However, he also wanted to preserve what he called "the principles of individual and local responsibility."

As this 1931 cartoon shows, many Americans blamed President Hoover for the depression.

Fixing the Economy

Hoover believed that providing money to American businesses was the best solution. In 1932 he established the **Reconstruction Finance Corporation** (RFC), which loaned money to businesses and banks to help keep them operating. The RFC saved many corporations, but the economy continued to decline. Hoover cut federal taxes and encouraged the federal government to spend about $150 million on **public works**. These building projects—such as hospitals, roads, and schools—would benefit the public. One public-works project was the construction of Boulder Dam along the Colorado River. The dam was later renamed Hoover Dam. The president hoped that programs like these would create jobs and thus help relieve the suffering of the poor and unemployed.

Helping Farmers

The agricultural industry also needed help. It had been depressed since the early 1920s. Most farmers reacted angrily to new hardships in the 1930s. Some people tried to stop bank agents and government officers from foreclosing on farms and evicting farmers from their homes. Other farmers protested the low prices paid for their products by publicly destroying crops.

Hoover was willing to assist farmers in obtaining loans to buy animal feed or farm equipment. However, he opposed giving farmers direct federal aid to pay for food, clothing, or shelter for their families. In 1929 Congress had passed the **Agricultural Marketing Act**. This act ended some farm subsidies and established the Federal Farm Board. As crop prices fell, Hoover instructed the board to help buy surplus wheat, cotton, and other farm products. By buying these commodities and taking them off the market, Hoover hoped to reduce the supply and generally boost prices. The federal government planned to store these crops and sell them later, when prices were higher.

This plan failed, however. The government did not purchase enough crops to make up for the huge supply. Farmers had also reacted to low market prices by growing more crops. The more they produced, the more prices fell, and the less money they made. Overall, the Federal Farm Board spent more than $180 million before it went out of existence in 1933.

Helping Homeowners

Hoover also tried to give indirect aid to homeowners. He supported the 1932 **Federal Home Loan Bank Act**. This act provided money to banks, financial institutions, and insurance companies so they could offer low-interest mortgages. Hoover believed that the act would reduce the number of foreclosures on homes. He also hoped that the act would encourage home construction, thus boosting employment and increasing the amount of money in the economy.

Despite such efforts, Hoover had little success in ending the depression. Many Americans believed that he had done too little, too late. One woman told her young nephew in 1932, "People were starving because of Herbert Hoover. My mother was out of work because of Herbert Hoover."

The Bonus Army

Veterans of World War I also suffered during the Great Depression. In 1924 Congress had passed the so-called bonus bill. This legislation

Technology and Society

The Hoover Dam. Herbert Hoover began working on plans for a dam on the Colorado River in the 1920s. Serving as secretary of commerce at the time, he used his engineering background to convince members of Congress to approve the project. As it was designed, the dam would not only control water flow but also generate a huge amount of electricity for the states of Arizona, California, Nevada, Utah, and Wyoming. To avoid conflicts over the amount of energy each state received, Hoover planned for each state to receive a set amount of the electricity the dam generated. Work on the dam began in 1931, and within five years residents of Los Angeles began receiving electricity from it.

Activity: Ask students to research the building of Hoover Dam. Have students draw one or more sketches showing some aspect of how the dam was built. Then have students write a paragraph summarizing how the dam generates electricity.

REVIEW

Linguistic, Visual-Spatial, Interpersonal. Have students complete the Section Review questions. Organize students into three groups. Have each group create a pamphlet describing either President Hoover's response to the depression, the overall effects of the depression on Americans, or events surrounding the Bonus Army. After students have finished, have each group share its pamphlet with the class.

ASSESS

Have students complete Daily Quiz 14.2.

RETEACH

Linguistic, Logical-Mathematical, Visual-Spatial. Ask students to create a three-column chart about the Great Depression. Have them label the columns *Causes, Effects,* and *Government Interventions.* Based on what students have learned about the era, have them complete the chart by listing as many items in each column as they can remember. Then have students review the text and add information that they forgot to include. Encourage students to use their charts as study guides.

SHELTERED ENGLISH

Section 2 Review ANSWERS

Identify

For significance, see the following pages:

- Hoovervilles, p. 426
- relief, p. 427
- Reconstruction Finance Corporation, p. 429
- public works, p. 429
- Agricultural Marketing Act, p. 429
- Federal Home Loan Bank Act, p. 429
- Bonus Army, p. 430

Reading for Content Understanding

1. It forced most Americans to struggle to protect themselves and their families from financial ruin.

2. Hoover ordered General MacArthur to disperse the veterans and restore order, which he did by leading troops using tear gas against the veterans.

3. businesses—supported the Reconstruction Finance Corporation and the Federal Home Loan Bank Act; workers—supported Federal Home Loan Bank Act, cut taxes, encouraged government spending on public works; farmers—supported the Agricultural Marketing Act, the Federal Home Loan Bank Act, and cut taxes

4. Answers will vary but students should point out that the incident was a blow to his popularity and might have cost him the election.

5. It shows he felt that government should play as small a role in the economy and in Americans' lives as possible.

Police clash with World War I veterans while trying to drive them from their camps in Washington, D.C.

authorized the payment of a bonus to all World War I veterans. The money would be put in a fund until 1945, when each veteran would receive an average of $1,000. Because the depression had left many veterans hungry and penniless, they wanted their money right away. In 1931 Congress passed a bill, over Hoover's veto, to loan veterans up to 50 percent of the bonus. Later that year Democrats in Congress proposed to pay the entire bonus in cash.

A group of veterans left Portland, Oregon, in the spring of 1932. They were headed to Washington, D.C., to pressure Congress to pay the bonus in cash. These veterans urged others to join them. They called themselves the Bonus Expeditionary Force but later became known as the **Bonus Army**. They arrived in May. By June about 15,000 other veterans had joined them in Washington. Some veterans carried signs that read, "Heroes in 1917—Bums in 1932." Their protest convinced the House of Representatives to pass a bill to immediately pay the bonus, but the Senate blocked the bill.

Most of the veterans went home, but some 2,000 marchers refused to obey a police order to leave. A small riot began. Two police officers and two veterans were killed. President Hoover ordered General Douglas MacArthur to restore order. MacArthur led a group of army troops against the veterans and their families. The troops threw tear gas, set the campgrounds on fire, and used bayonets to remove people from the area. A baby died from the tear gas. Reporter Thomas L. Stokes remembered walking through the demolished camp after the attack: "Some of the occupants watched their shacks burn quietly, standing beside piles of their few belongings. Then, one after another, they . . . wandered away."

Hoover and MacArthur defended their actions as necessary to protect the public. Photographs and news accounts of these unarmed and unemployed veterans of World War I being driven off by tear gas and bayonets outraged the public. One newspaper editor wrote, "If the Army must be called out to make war on unarmed citizens, this is no longer America." The public's reaction to the Bonus Army was another serious blow to Hoover's popularity. As the nation prepared for the 1932 presidential election, one observer declared, "If you put a rose in Hoover's hand it would wilt."

SECTION 2 REVIEW

Identify and explain the significance of the following:

- **Hoovervilles**
- **relief**
- **Reconstruction Finance Corporation**
- **public works**
- **Agricultural Marketing Act**
- **Federal Home Loan Bank Act**
- **Bonus Army**

Reading for Content Understanding

1 **Main Idea** How did the Great Depression affect most Americans?

2 **Main Idea** What was President Hoover's response to the Bonus Army?

3 **Citizenship and Democracy** In what ways did Hoover try to help businesses, workers, and farmers during the Great Depression?

4 **Writing** *Informing* Imagine that you are a political reporter. Write a short column on how you think Hoover's handling of the Bonus Army will affect the upcoming presidential election.

5 **Critical Thinking** *Evaluating* How does Hoover's quotation on page 428 reveal his philosophy about the role of government?

OBJECTIVES

- **Describe steps President Roosevelt took immediately after taking office to fight the depression.**
- **Explain how New Deal programs addressed the problem of unemployment.**
- **Identify programs that addressed the needs of industry and agriculture.**

FOCUS

Motivate Before Reading

Ask students what programs they think might help people today if the United States were experiencing a depression as serious as that of the 1930s. Record students' answers on the chalkboard. Then have each student write a short description of a program the government could follow if such a depression were to occur today.

Roosevelt and the New Deal

Reading Focus

What steps did President Roosevelt take to fight the depression immediately after taking office?

How did New Deal programs address the problem of unemployment?

What programs addressed the needs of industry and agriculture?

Key Terms

New Deal
Brain Trust
Hundred Days
fireside chats
Federal Deposit Insurance Corporation
Federal Emergency Relief Administration
National Industrial Recovery Act
Tennessee Valley Authority

AT THE DEMOCRATIC NATIONAL CONVENTION in Chicago, many party members believed they could defeat President Hoover in the 1932 election. The Democrats were less confident that anyone would be able to lead the nation out of the Great Depression. When Democrat Franklin D. Roosevelt found out that he had been nominated for the presidency, he hurried to Chicago to address the convention. He wanted to rally his supporters. "I pledge you, I pledge myself to a new deal for the American people . . . ," he declared. "This is more than a political campaign; it is a call to arms. Give me your help . . . to restore America to its own greatness."

The Granger Collection, New York

A 1932 campaign bumper plate

The Election of 1932

As the Great Depression worsened, it became clear that no Republican candidate was likely to win the presidency in 1932. Many voters had given Republicans credit for the prosperity of the 1920s. These voters now blamed Republicans for the economic collapse. President Hoover had little popular support. The Republicans lacked a better candidate, however, and decided to nominate him again.

Democrats nominated Franklin D. Roosevelt. He had served as assistant secretary of the navy in the Wilson administration and had run for vice president in 1920. Roosevelt won the New York governorship in 1928. While many viewed Hoover as a cold and uncaring man, Roosevelt appeared more concerned about people.

As the campaign progressed, Hoover continued to oppose any government takeover of relief efforts from communities and private charities. In contrast, Roosevelt promised that if elected, he would provide a **New Deal** to help the American people. He thought it was "common sense to take a method and try it. If it fails, . . . try another. But

Section 3 RESOURCES

PRINT

★ Guided Reading Strategies 14.3

★ Geography Activity 14: The Public Works Administration

★ Section 3 Review, p. 436

★ Daily Quiz 14.3

MULTIMEDIA

★ *Teaching Resources CD–ROM*, Lesson 14.3

★ *Exploring America's Past* Video Segment: Rising from the Ashes; *Teacher's Guide*, pp. 26–28

★ *American History Simulations:* A Plan for Prosperity

★ HRW Web site

SHELTERED ENGLISH

★ Main Idea Activities for Reteaching and Sheltered English 14.3

Multimedia Resources

Exploring America's Past Video Segment: Rising from the Ashes; *Teacher's Guide*, pp. 26–28

Search 13351, Play to 20085
Videodisc Blue Side A

Play

Pause

See *Teacher's Guide* for Spanish barcode.

Tell students that in this section they will look at new agendas the Roosevelt administration developed to fight the Great Depression.

Introduce Key Terms

Linguistic, Interpersonal. Review this section's key terms with students. Ask students to use context cues to write a definition for each term. Then write each key term on an index card and play a game in which each student draws a card and uses the key term in a sentence. Award students points for using the key terms correctly. Continue until every student has had an opportunity to create at least one sentence. **SHELTERED ENGLISH**

TEACH

Have students read Section 3 and complete Guided Reading Strategies 14.3. Choose one or more of the following activities to explore the section content with students. For further suggestions on block scheduling or team teaching, see the *Block Scheduling Handbook.*

LEVEL 1: Linguistic. (Suggested time: 15 min.) As a class, go over students' Guided Reading Strategies. Then use the Reading Focus questions to highlight the main ideas of the section. **SHELTERED ENGLISH**

Historical Sidelight

Dear Mr. President. Franklin D. Roosevelt's charm and fatherly appeal helped make him one of the most popular presidents in U.S. history. One sign of this popularity was the massive amount of letters Americans wrote to him. On average, Roosevelt received 5,000 letters a day, far more than any previous president. Whereas most earlier presidents had needed only one person to open their mail, Roosevelt had to hire a staff of more than 50. Americans wrote him about their lives, needs, and fears. They thanked him for his help. Many peoples' feelings for Roosevelt can be summed up by one unemployed man's closing line to his letter, "I've always thought of F.D.R. as my personal friend."

Activity: Have students use the library or the Internet through the HRW Web site to find out where to send a letter or e-mail message to the current U.S. president or first lady. Ask students to write a letter to either one. You may want to review the letters before they are sent.

go.hrw.com
SB1 President

Multimedia Resources

American History Simulations:
A Plan for Prosperity

above all, try something." Americans responded positively to Roosevelt's message. He won the November election in a landslide, receiving 472 electoral votes to Hoover's 59. Democrats also gained 90 seats in the House and 12 in the Senate, giving them large majorities in Congress.

The Brain Trust

Between Franklin Roosevelt's election as president and his inauguration in March 1933, the U.S. economy worsened. Industrial production dropped to its lowest point. As more banks failed, some states restricted banking operations. During these months, Roosevelt gathered together a group of experts for advice on policies and programs. Most members of this so-called **Brain Trust** were college professors, lawyers, labor leaders, and social workers. Key members included professors Rexford Tugwell and Raymond Moley.

Roosevelt also included some experienced reformers in his cabinet. The president appointed labor reformer Frances Perkins as secretary of labor, making her the nation's first female cabinet member. For secretary of the interior, Roosevelt chose Harold Ickes, a longtime leader of the urban reform movement in Chicago. Roosevelt also appointed many African Americans to government positions.

First Lady Eleanor Roosevelt also played an important role in the administration. Already an active member of several women's reform movements, as first lady she continued to fight for the underprivileged. During her husband's first term, she traveled some 50,000 miles to meet with political allies and reform leaders.

A 1933 magazine cover showing the differing personalities of Hoover and Roosevelt

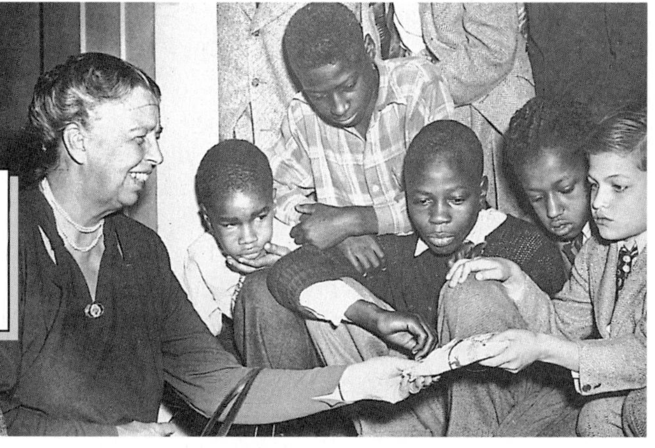

First Lady Roosevelt established a precedent when she was regularly photographed with African Americans.

Roosevelt's advisers disagreed on precisely how to fight the Great Depression. However, they agreed that ending the depression would require a new level of government involvement.

The Hundred Days

On March 4, 1933, millions of Americans crowded around their radios to hear President Roosevelt's inaugural address. Trying to lift people's spirits, he declared, "The people of the United States have not failed." Humorist Will Rogers wrote that the address inspired confidence in the new president:

> **"America hasn't been as happy in three years as they are today. No money, no banks, no work, no nothing, but they know they got a man in there who is wise to Congress, wise to our so-called big men. The whole country is with him."**

Instead of attending the Inaugural Ball, Roosevelt and his advisers met through the night. The next day Roosevelt called for a special session of Congress. This legislative session, which lasted from March 9 until mid-June, came to be called the **Hundred Days**. The bulk of the early New Deal programs was passed during this time.

Bank Reform

Roosevelt's first step was to save the nation's banks. On March 5, he announced that a four-day "bank holiday" would begin the next day. Every bank not already closed would be

LEVEL 1: Visual-Spatial. (Suggested time: 30 min.) Discuss with students three important problems that President Roosevelt addressed during the Hundred Days *(lack of confidence in the banks, unemployment, and low farm prices)*. Help students create charts that list why these three problems had to be addressed immediately and what programs Roosevelt created to address them during the first days of his administration. **SHELTERED ENGLISH**

ALL LEVELS: Logical-Mathematical, Visual-Spatial. (Suggested time: 30 min. plus homework) Ask students to create time lines covering the acts that resulted from the first legislative session of Roosevelt's presidency, known as the Hundred Days. Have students list the important pieces of legislation that were passed and, when possible, the dates of implementation. Under each piece of legislation, have students write a brief description of what the act was designed to accomplish. Encourage students to share their time lines with the class.

ALL LEVELS: Linguistic, Logical-Mathematical. (Suggested time: 30 min.) Ask students to imagine that they have been asked to publicize New Deal responses to the needs of American industry and agriculture and to the problem of unemployment. Assign each student at least one program or act that was designed to address one of the above-mentioned issues. Then ask students to create slogans to promote and explain the purpose of the assigned programs or acts. For example, to promote the TVA,

closed by federal order. On March 9, Congress passed the Emergency Banking Act. This act authorized the actions Roosevelt had already taken and allowed the government to examine bank records. Only stable banks were allowed to reopen.

On Sunday evening, March 12, some 60 million Americans sat around their radios. They heard the first of many **fireside chats**—radio broadcasts that Roosevelt made from the White House. The president assured Americans that it was safe to return their money to the banks. Most of the nation's banks reopened for business. Congress also created the **Federal Deposit Insurance Corporation** (FDIC) to protect bank accounts. During the depression the FDIC insured deposits up to $5,000 per account.

To protect investors and guard against stock fraud, Congress passed the Federal Securities Act and created the Securities and Exchange Commission (SEC). The SEC regulates companies that sell stocks or bonds.

Loan Assistance and Relief

Roosevelt's administration also moved quickly to help people who could not pay their mortgages. Some 250,000 families lost their homes in 1932 because they were unable to make loan payments. Congress created the Home Owners Loan Corporation (HOLC). The HOLC provided low-interest, long-term mortgage loans to many families. One woman who kept her home with the help of the HOLC wrote the president, "You have saved my life."

Roosevelt also reorganized all farm credit agencies into the Farm Credit Administration (FCA). Each day FCA loans typically saved 300 farms from foreclosure. In addition, the FCA refinanced about one fifth of all farm mortgages and kept thousands of rural banks from closing.

In May 1933 Congress authorized $500 million for the **Federal Emergency Relief Administration** (FERA). The president chose Harry L. Hopkins, a former relief supervisor in New York, as the FERA administrator. At least half of the FERA's relief money went to the states for direct distribution

HISTORICAL DOCUMENTS

Roosevelt's First Inaugural Address

President Roosevelt's first inaugural address was broadcast on the radio. In the following excerpt he tries to encourage the nation during its economic hard times:

"This great nation will endure as it has endured, will revive and will prosper. So, first of all, let me assert [state] my firm belief that the only thing we have to fear is fear itself. . . .

Our greatest primary task is to put people to work. This is no unsolvable problem if we face it wisely and courageously. It can be accomplished in part by direct recruiting by the government itself, treating the task as we would treat the emergency of a war, but, at the same time, through this employment, accomplishing greatly needed projects to stimulate and reorganize the use of our natural resources. . . .

I shall ask the Congress for the one remaining instrument to meet the crisis—broad executive power to wage a war against the emergency, as great as the power that would be given to me if we were in fact invaded by a foreign foe. For the trust reposed in [given to] me I will return the courage and the devotion that befit the time. I can do no less."

Understanding Primary Sources

1. What does President Roosevelt mean by "the only thing we have to fear is fear itself"?
2. Why do you think Roosevelt asks for broad executive power?

Economic Development

The Bank Holiday. During the nationwide bank holiday in March 1933, many Americans began to run out of cash. People at the time did not have credit and debit cards to use as alternatives to cash. As a result, some people began bartering as a way to pay for groceries or to make other purchases. At one boxing match in Madison Square Garden, people paid for their tickets with goods such as spark plugs and jigsaw puzzles.

Critical Thinking: If all the banks suddenly closed for four days and your family could not use any checks, credit cards, or debit cards, how do you think it would affect your lives?

ANSWER: Answers will vary but students might mention that it would make their lives very hard, particularly if they did not know about the bank closures in advance so as to prepare for the situation.

HISTORICAL DOCUMENTS ANSWERS

1. He was implying that Americans should show courage and not lose hope; that they can survive this depression.
2. Answers will vary but students might mention that he wanted to reduce interference with his New Deal programs because the crisis was urgent.

students could use the following slogan: "The Tennessee Valley Authority Will Make Sure You Have Electricity." After students complete their slogans, have volunteers share theirs with the class. Finally, discuss the types of assistance that helped Americans during the depression and explain how this assistance helped industry, agriculture, and the unemployed.

LEVEL 3: Linguistic, Logical-Mathematical. (Suggested time: 20 min. plus homework and presentation) Review with the class the idea of the fireside chat and the way Roosevelt used these chats to inform and reassure Americans about his new programs. For homework, ask students to imagine that they are one of President Roosevelt's speechwriters. Have them write a fireside chat describing several major New Deal programs. Have volunteers present their chats to the class.

CLOSE

Logical-Mathematical, Visual-Spatial. On the chalkboard, create a three-column chart with the headings *Program, Description,* and *Effectiveness.* Call on students to help you fill in the chart with the main New Deal programs covered in this section. Students should list, describe, and evaluate the effectiveness of each program. Make certain students identify which programs addressed the problem of unemployment and which addressed the needs of

Presidential Profiles

Franklin D. Roosevelt. Biographers of Roosevelt do not agree on how polio affected his personality and political career. Some argue that the experience transformed him from a pampered, unfocused young man into a serious person committed to helping others. Other biographers contend that Roosevelt already had these qualities and that this ordeal only strengthened his self-confidence and optimism.

Critical Thinking: How was Roosevelt's optimism an asset to Americans during the depression?

ANSWER: His optimism gave people faith that the economy would improve.

Daily Life

Women and the CWA. In 1933 First Lady Eleanor Roosevelt called the Conference on the Emergency Needs of Women. As a result of this meeting, 300,000 women—about half of those qualifying for relief—found work with the Civil Works Administration (CWA) doing jobs such as sewing and nursing.

Critical Thinking: Why do you think Eleanor Roosevelt called a conference to ensure that women received help?

ANSWER: Some people may have believed that only men, as the traditional providers, should receive benefits.

Franklin D. Roosevelt

Franklin D. Roosevelt was born in 1882 into a wealthy New York family. After attending Harvard University and Columbia University Law School, he practiced law. In 1911 Roosevelt won a seat in the New York legislature. He modeled his political career on that of his distant cousin Theodore Roosevelt, whose niece Eleanor he married in 1905. Although he was popular and intelligent, Franklin Roosevelt was not then considered a strong leader.

His life changed dramatically in 1921 when he suffered an attack of polio. The disease left him paralyzed in both legs. After extensive physical therapy, Roosevelt learned to move again with the help of leg braces.

He re-entered politics and enjoyed great success. Roosevelt's private battle with polio made him more compassionate and gave him the strength to lead the nation during great crisis. He once explained the source of his determination: "If you had spent two years in bed trying to wiggle your toe, after that anything would seem easy."

to families. By 1935 the FERA had spent some $3 billion helping Americans. However, many people disliked this kind of aid. They wanted jobs, not handouts. One aid recipient in Michigan told a FERA official: "It's very hard for me to ask for help. I don't want charity. I want work—any kind of work. I'll do road work, or anything."

The Civilian Conservation Corps (CCC) addressed this issue. The CCC provided government jobs for unmarried 17- to 24-year-old men. These men lived in U.S. Army camps while they planted trees, fought forest fires, and restored national historic sites and parks. During its lifetime, the CCC put nearly 3 million men to work. The Civil Works Administration (CWA) was a temporary work relief program in the winter of 1933. The CWA provided jobs for more than 4 million Americans in less than a year. "When I got that [CWA] card it was the biggest day in my whole life," a former insurance salesman in Alabama said. "At last I could say, 'I've got a job.'"

Reviving Business and Industry

President Roosevelt saw relief programs as a short-term solution. Economic recovery was his long-term goal. A key part of this plan was the **National Industrial Recovery Act** (NIRA), passed in 1933. The NIRA was an attempt to suspend antitrust laws, eliminate unfair competition, and prevent business failures. In a fireside chat Roosevelt explained the idea behind the NIRA:

> **"If all employers in each competitive group agree to pay their workers the same wages—reasonable wages—and require the same hours—reasonable hours—then higher wages and shorter hours will hurt no employer."**

The Civilian Conservation Corps hired single young men to conserve and develop natural resources.

industry and agriculture. Then have students evaluate the overall success of Roosevelt and the New Deal for the period covered.

CHALLENGE AND EXTEND

1. **Linguistic, Visual-Spatial.** Have each student use the library and other resources to find information on a state park or other public facility built by the Civilian Conservation Corps (CCC) or the Public Works Administration (PWA). Then have students use their research to create a brochure documenting the history of the state park or facility. Encourage students to include pictures or illustrations along with a written history. When students have finished, have volunteers share their work with the class.

2. **Linguistic, Logical-Mathematical.** Have students use the library and other resources to find information on one of the members of the Brain Trust. Ask each student to write a biographical sketch of the member they have chosen. The sketch should provide information about the person's life, academic pursuits, and professiona achievements. Encourage students to include a photograph or illustration to accompany their sketches if possible.

The NIRA created the Public Works Administration (PWA), a program to distribute government funds to help stimulate the economy. Headed by Secretary of the Interior Harold Ickes, the PWA provided some $3.3 billion for public works. Eventually, this figure rose to more than $6 billion.

Not all businesses that displayed the blue eagle followed the NRA's codes.

Although some people criticized Ickes for being slow to spend money, the PWA completed more than 34,000 projects. PWA workers completed work on Boulder Dam, built a new courthouse for Kalamazoo, Michigan, and created the Triborough Bridge in New York City. Between 1933 and 1939, the PWA helped build most of the country's new schools and many new courthouses, city halls, and sewage plants. The PWA also built thousands of miles of streets and highways.

The NIRA also addressed labor's concerns, guaranteeing workers the right to organize and bargain collectively. The NIRA created the National Recovery Administration (NRA) to develop codes that established prices, wages, and work hours for each industry. The NRA outlawed such practices as child labor and sweatshops. Merchants and manufacturers who supported NRA standards displayed a blue eagle with the slogan "We Do Our Part."

Although the NRA helped many people, it also had its problems. Some labor leaders referred to the NRA as the "National Run Around." Businesses that had agreed to NRA codes often found ways to avoid labor reforms and wage increases. When Secretary of Labor Frances Perkins was on a tour of major steel towns, local leaders in Homestead, Pennsylvania, tried to prevent her from meeting with unhappy workers. The workers wanted to discuss wages and working conditions. Perkins responded by holding a meeting at the local post office, which was federal property.

The limited achievements of the National Industrial Recovery Act did not last long. In May 1935 the Supreme Court unanimously declared the NIRA to be unconstitutional. The Court ruled that the federal government had no authority in peacetime to regulate interstate commerce so closely. The Court also ruled that the NIRA gave the president too much power.

Helping Rural America

In addition to helping workers and trying to revitalize business, the Roosevelt administration wanted to improve living conditions in rural America. A first step was to help farmers.

The AAA

New Deal officials encouraged farmers to grow fewer crops. The officials wanted this reduction to increase demand, raise prices, and increase farmers' earnings. Under the Agricultural Adjustment Act (AAA) of 1933, farmers received subsidies, or government payments, for not planting corn, cotton, rice, tobacco, and wheat. They were also paid not to raise hogs or produce dairy products. To raise money for the subsidies, the government taxed businesses that processed foods, such as wheat mills and meatpacking plants.

In 1933, for example, the government paid farmers to plow under 10 million acres of already planted cotton. Many farmers, and even some government officials, found these measures hard to accept. "To have to destroy a growing crop is a shocking commentary on our civilization," said Agriculture Secretary Henry Wallace.

The AAA helped stabilize farm prices, but critics complained that too many benefits were paid to large-scale farms. The AAA also often hurt the poorest farmers. Some landowners cut

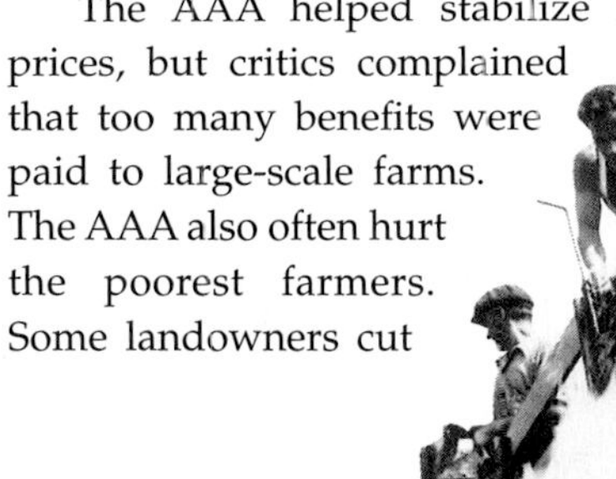

Dairy farmers dump milk from their trucks to protest low prices.

Geographic Diversity

The PWA in the West. The Public Works Administration (PWA) spent more that $2 billion to transform the landscape of the West—more money than was spent on any other region. The PWA constructed dams that harnessed the power of rivers to generate electricity and distribute water to dry lands. Within a seven-year span, from 1933 to 1940, the number of acres of irrigated, western farmland rose from less than 3 million to more than 4 million, and the number of projects to reclaim land for agriculture doubled.

Critical Thinking: Why do you think the PWA spent more money in the West than in any other region?

ANSWER: It may have spent more money there because the West had the greatest need for water and was an important agricultural region.

MAP ANSWER
(page 436)
Tennessee

REVIEW

Linguistic, Logical-Mathematical, Visual-Spatial. Have students complete the Section Review questions. Ask students to use the key terms from this section to create a crossword puzzle. Have students use definitions as clues and the terms as answers. When students are finished, ask them to exchange puzzles, complete them, and return them to their authors for grading.

ASSESS

Have students complete Daily Quiz 14.3.

RETEACH

Logical-Mathematical, Visual-Spatial. Have students complete Main Idea Activities for Reteaching and Sheltered English 14.3. Ask students to choose one of the New Deal organizations that affected Americans during the Great Depression. Have students create a poster describing the organization and its mission and encouraging citizens to take an active role in helping the country end the depression. Call on volunteers to explain their posters to the class and invite feedback from other students.

SHELTERED ENGLISH

Section 3 Review ANSWERS

Identify

For significance, see the following pages:

- Franklin D. Roosevelt, p. 431
- New Deal, p. 431
- Brain Trust, p. 432
- Eleanor Roosevelt, p. 432
- Hundred Days, p. 432
- fireside chats, p. 433
- Federal Deposit Insurance Corporation, p. 433
- Federal Emergency Relief Administration, p. 433
- Harry L. Hopkins, p. 433
- National Industrial Recovery Act, p. 434
- Tennessee Valley Authority, p. 436

Reading for Content Understanding

1. called a special session of Congress, which pushed through many New Deal programs

2. through work programs such as the CWA, CCC, PWA, and TVA

3. the NIRA, on the grounds that the federal government had no authority in peacetime to regulate interstate commerce so closely

4. business—NIRA; created the PWA and NRA; limited success; declared unconstitutional; rural residents—AAA; paid farmers to reduce production; helped stabilize farm prices; TVA; constructed a series of dams that controlled flooding and irrigation, and provided hydroelectric power

5. similar—both programs designed to help economy and businesses, both funded public works to create jobs; different—extent to which each intervened in the economy and gave direct relief

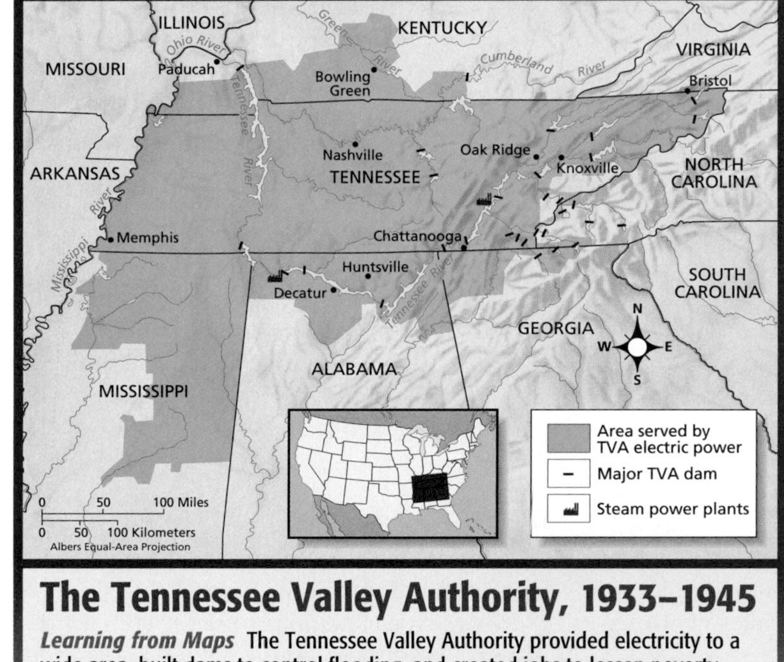

The Tennessee Valley Authority, 1933–1945

Learning from Maps The Tennessee Valley Authority provided electricity to a wide area, built dams to control flooding, and created jobs to lessen poverty.

Place In which state did the TVA build the most dams?

production by forcing renters and sharecroppers off their land. Because subsidies were based on the size of the farms, they were often not enough to help small-scale farmers.

In early 1936 the Supreme Court struck down the AAA. The Court ruled that the tax used to pay the subsidies was unconstitutional.

The TVA

In May 1933 Congress created the **Tennessee Valley Authority** (TVA). The TVA was a rural reform effort targeting the Tennessee Valley region. TVA workers constructed a series of dams in seven states along the Tennessee River basin. The dams controlled flooding, reduced soil erosion, and generated inexpensive hydroelectric power. Soon, thousands of rural families had electricity in their homes for the first time.

The TVA was perhaps the most ambitious and successful New Deal program. The TVA's long-term goal was to attract industry to the region and provide rural Americans with more dependable employment than farming. President Roosevelt hoped that the TVA and the many other pieces of legislation passed during the Hundred Days would put the nation on the road to recovery.

SECTION 3 REVIEW

Identify and explain the significance of the following:

- **Franklin D. Roosevelt**
- **New Deal**
- **Brain Trust**
- **Eleanor Roosevelt**
- **Hundred Days**
- **fireside chats**
- **Federal Deposit Insurance Corporation**
- **Federal Emergency Relief Administration**
- **Harry L. Hopkins**
- **National Industrial Recovery Act**
- **Tennessee Valley Authority**

Reading for Content Understanding

1 **Main Idea** What actions did President Roosevelt take after his inauguration?

2 **Main Idea** How did Roosevelt try to solve the unemployment problem during the Hundred Days?

3 **Constitutional Heritage** What New Deal legislation did the Supreme Court declare unconstitutional, and why?

4 **Writing** *Classifying* Identify the programs created to help businesses and rural residents. Briefly explain what each program did and whether it was successful.

5 **Critical Thinking** *Making Comparisons* Compare and contrast Herbert Hoover's and Franklin D. Roosevelt's solutions to the Great Depression.

OBJECTIVES

- Explain why some people were critical of the New Deal.
- Identify programs passed during the Second New Deal.
- Describe how President Roosevelt attempted to prevent the Supreme Court from overturning his New Deal programs.

FOCUS

Motivate Before Reading

Ask students to write a few sentences about how much they think the federal government should "take care of" the American people. Then have them give examples of how the government today cares for its citizens. Discuss students' responses. Then write *Social Security* on the chalkboard and ask students what they know about this program. Explain that it was first established in 1935 under

The Second New Deal

Reading Focus

- Why were some people critical of the New Deal?
- What programs were passed during the Second New Deal?
- How did President Roosevelt try to prevent the Supreme Court from overturning his New Deal programs?

Key Terms

- American Liberty League
- Share-Our-Wealth
- Second New Deal
- Social Security Act
- Rural Electrification Administration
- Emergency Relief Appropriation Act
- Works Progress Administration
- welfare state
- deficit spending

AFTER THE SUPREME COURT struck down the NIRA in May 1935, Justice Louis Brandeis walked back to his cloakroom. There he met with Thomas Corcoran, a young lawyer helping plan President Roosevelt's New Deal. Brandeis gave Corcoran a stern message. "I want you to go back and tell the President that we're not going to let this government centralize [take control of] everything. It's come to an end." Corcoran and the others who favored the New Deal chose to ignore this warning, but it revealed the strength of the opposition to the New Deal.

A cartoon showing the Supreme Court rejecting the AAA

New Deal Critics

Some opponents of the New Deal claimed that it discouraged free enterprise and was the beginning of socialism in the United States. These critics included leaders of powerful corporations such as Du Pont and General Motors. In 1934 a group of business leaders opposed to the New Deal created the **American Liberty League**.

Other critics argued that the New Deal had not done enough for the public. To help older Americans, Dr. Francis Townsend of California proposed the Old Age Revolving Pension (OARP). The plan would give citizens over 60 years old $200 a month and require them to spend the money within 30 days. Townsend hoped that the OARP would assist the elderly while putting more money into the economy. Thousands of Americans, particularly in the West, supported Townsend's plan.

Father Charles Coughlin, a Catholic priest in a Detroit suburb, was another critic of the New Deal. His radio show, *The Golden Hour of the Little Flower,* had millions of listeners nationwide. He often

Section 4 RESOURCES

PRINT

- ★ Guided Reading Strategies 14.4
- ★ American History Political Cartoon 24: FDR and the New Deal
- ★ Biography Reading 14: Mary McLeod Bethune
- ★ Graphic Organizer 14: Government Response to the Great Depression
- ★ Section 4 Review, p.443
- ★ Daily Quiz 14.4

MULTIMEDIA

- ★ *Teaching Resources CD–ROM,* Lesson 14.4
- ★ HRW Web site

SHELTERED ENGLISH

- ★ Main Idea Activities for Reteaching and Sheltered English 14.4

President Roosevelt's Second New Deal. Tell students that in this section they will learn about reform programs of the Second New Deal, why some people were critical of these reforms, and how President Roosevelt tried to save some of his reform programs.

Introduce Key Terms

Linguistic, Logical-Mathematical. Review this section's key terms with students. Ask each student to create a fill-in-the-blank quiz using the key terms of this section. Quizzes should contain enough questions to include all the terms. Have students list the key terms at the top of their papers. Then have students turn in their quizzes and explain that they will use them in a future activity. **SHELTERED ENGLISH**

TEACH

Have students read Section 4 and complete Guided Reading Strategies 14.4. Choose one or more of the following activities to explore the section content with students. For further suggestions on block scheduling or team teaching, see the *Block Scheduling Handbook*.

Biography

Huey Long. Huey Long was born in 1893 in Louisiana. Energetic, intelligent, and a gifted speaker, he entered politics after working first as a traveling salesman and then as a lawyer. He gained recognition when he took on the giant Standard Oil Company while serving as public service commissioner. In 1928 he was elected governor of Louisiana. While in office, Long achieved many positive results. He did so, however, by wielding ruthless and almost complete power. He controlled the state legislature and removed or threatened any officials who opposed him. In 1929 he was impeached for misconduct, but not convicted. Called by some the "dictator of Louisiana," Long successfully ran for the U.S. Senate in 1930. He did not take office until 1932, however, so that he could hand-pick his successor. As senator, the colorful Long continued to dominate the government of Louisiana until his assassination in 1935.

Critical Thinking: Do you think it is right for a politician to use unethical means to achieve worthwhile ends?

ANSWER: Answers will vary but some students might argue that the ends justify the means, while others may argue that unethical methods are never justifiable and although they may benefit some, they are bound to harm others.

discussed political and social issues on his program. At first, Coughlin supported President Roosevelt. Then Coughlin became impatient with the slow progress of the New Deal. He organized the National Union for Social Justice and the Union Party, as a challenge to the Democratic Party. The Union Party called for stronger government control over banking, business, and the money supply.

Huey Long was another critic who had supported Roosevelt's early New Deal programs. Known as the Kingfish, Long called himself a defender of the common people. As governor of Louisiana, Long had attacked corporations and built bridges and roads in the poorest sections of the state. He also gave free schoolbooks to children. His critics accused him of stealing state funds and ruthlessly using his political machine to crush all opponents.

As a U.S. senator in 1934, Long organized the **Share-Our-Wealth** plan. It had the slogan "Every Man a King." Long's plan seemed simple. He wanted the federal government to limit the size of all personal fortunes so that every family would be guaranteed a minimum income of $2,500 a year. Long declared that this would "break up the swollen fortunes of America and . . . spread the wealth among all our people." Many economists dismissed Long's program as far too expensive to work. Although New Deal critics like Long gained some popularity, Americans showed their support for Roosevelt in the 1934 congressional elections. Voters increased the Democrats' majorities in both houses of Congress.

Senator Huey Long was an exciting speaker and drew large crowds wherever he spoke.

New Reform Efforts

In response to New Deal critics and to the 1934 congressional elections, the Roosevelt administration proposed a new program of reforms in January 1935. Historians refer to this program as the **Second New Deal**.

Social Security

Congress passed the **Social Security Act** in August 1935. This act created Social Security, a pension plan for retired workers over age 65. The federal government would administer the plan. Its funds would come from a payroll tax on businesses and a tax on workers' wages. The Social Security Act also established unemployment insurance for workers. In addition, it provided financial aid for older Americans, people with disabilities, and families of deceased male workers.

The original law did not cover farmworkers or domestic workers. It also did not help people who lost their jobs because of illness. Nevertheless, the Social Security Act became one of the most far-reaching and long-lasting pieces of legislation from the Second New Deal. Over the years Social Security has been expanded to cover people who were previously excluded.

Other Reforms

Perhaps in response to Senator Long's Share-Our-Wealth campaign, Roosevelt supported the Revenue Act of 1935, better known as the Wealth Tax Act. This act raised taxes on the nation's wealthiest people and levied an "excess profits" tax on wealthy corporations. Congress wanted

LEVEL 1: Linguistic. (Suggested time: 15 min.) As a class, go over students' Guided Reading Strategies. Then use the Reading Focus questions to highlight the main ideas of the section. **SHELTERED ENGLISH**

LEVEL 1: Visual-Spatial, Intrapersonal. (Suggested time: 30 min.) Ask students to create political cartoons depicting President Roosevelt's attempt to increase the number of Supreme Court justices. Encourage students to include the reactions of the political community, including Roosevelt's opponents and members of his own party. Remind students to include a caption that helps explain their viewpoint. Have students share their work with classmates. Finally, lead a discussion on whether Roosevelt's attempt to increase the size of the Supreme Court fell within the realm of his constitutional powers. **SHELTERED ENGLISH**

ALL LEVELS: Linguistic, Logical-Mathematical. (Suggested time: 35 min.) Ask students to list cause-and-effect relationships for the main events in this section. For each event, have students provide at least one cause. For example, students can point out that opponents of the New Deal viewed it as the beginning of socialism in the United States; therefore, some business leaders created the American Liberty League. Encourage students to identify as many cause-and-effect relationships as they can. When they are finished writing, call on volunteers to share their answers with the class.

Most women employed by relief programs were given jobs such as cleaning or sewing.

to use the tax money to boost the U.S. economy. However, corporate leaders complained that the taxes actually discouraged business expansion by taking away funds that could be invested.

The government also improved utility services provided to rural areas. The **Rural Electrification Administration** (REA) soon extended electrical power lines into isolated rural areas. When the REA was established, only about 12 percent of American farms had electricity. By 1941 about 40 percent of the nation's farms did. Congress passed a law allowing a federal commission to regulate the interstate transmission and sale of electricity. Roosevelt also tried to lower the prices public utility companies charged for electricity and gas.

The WPA

Unemployment remained one of the biggest problems facing the Roosevelt administration. Even though the jobless rate had fallen, some 10 million Americans were still out of work. In April 1935 Congress passed one of the most important measures of the Second New Deal, the **Emergency Relief Appropriation Act**. This act provided close to $4.9 billion to help the unemployed. It also established a new federal public-works agency, the **Works Progress Administration** (WPA).

Social Security

When Congress passed the Social Security Act in 1935, critics complained that it ignored large segments of the population who needed assistance. Since that time, lawmakers have created numerous amendments to expand the act. By the late 1990s, Social Security programs covered 95 percent of the nation's workers.

The Social Security old-age pension program has proved expensive. By 1989 it accounted for one fourth of the federal budget. As the nation's population ages, many Americans worry that Social Security funds will run out. In the 1980s and 1990s, Congress began taking steps to protect Social Security funds. Congress increased the number of workers paying Social Security taxes and the amount of those taxes. In addition, Congress authorized a gradual increase in the retirement age from 65 to 67.

A local Social Security office

Understanding What You Read

1. How has the Social Security program expanded since 1935?
2. What have lawmakers done to ensure that there is enough money to fund Social Security?

Linking Past to Present

Problems with Social Security. Some financial experts estimate that even after government reforms, Social Security surplus funds will be depleted by 2029 and that at that time payroll taxes will meet only 75 percent of the benefits that must be paid. To confront this problem, the Clinton administration convened the Advisory Council on Social Security, which presented three possible solutions. One would increase Social Security revenues by investing in the stock market and increasing payroll taxes. A second would cut benefits and create individual accounts for all workers. A third would enable workers to invest some of the money themselves.

Activity: Have students search the Internet through the HRW Web site to find out about the benefits currently provided by Social Security. Then ask students to create a chart comparing the original benefits of Social Security to those of today.

go.hrw.com
SB1 Social Security

Linking Past to Present Answers

1. It now covers 95 percent of workers.
2. increased number of workers paying taxes and the amount of those taxes; authorized a raise in the retirement age

LEVEL 2: Linguistic, Logical-Mathematical, Visual-Spatial. (Suggested time: 45 min.) Remind students that some people were critical of Roosevelt's New Deal programs. Then ask students to create two print advertisements, one that criticizes the New Deal, and one that supports it. Students' ads should combine text and graphics to present the stated opinion. Critical advertisements also should offer an alternative to the New Deal. For example, students might create an ad that is sponsored by the National Union for Social Justice and that supports increased government control over the economy as the solution for ending the depression. Call on volunteers to share their advertisements with the class. Finally, lead students in a discussion on the reasons Americans criticized and supported the New Deal.

LEVEL 3: Linguistic, Visual-Spatial. (Suggested time: 45 min. plus homework) Have each student create an encyclopedia entry for the Second New Deal. Ask students to include information on each of the reforms that were passed, as well as arguments made for and against them. Encourage students to include visual aides to clarify what each reform program was designed to accomplish. Allow students time in class to begin writing and have them finish for homework. During the next class, call on volunteers to share their entries.

Across the Curriculum

LITERATURE

The Federal Theater. The Federal Theater Project (FTP) was formed both to give stage actors some way to make a living and to bring the world of theater to ordinary Americans. It succeeded in both aims. The FTP supported the efforts of some of the great writers and directors of the day, such as Arthur Miller, John Huston, and Orson Welles. They and other less famous participants toured the country on a quest to "democratize" theater. They presented Shakespeare, children's plays, radio dramas, and circuses. The program reached an estimated audience of 30 million Americans. It was discontinued in the late 1930s, after coming under attack by the House Un-American Activities Committee, which accused it of supporting communism.

Activity: Have students use the library and other resources to find information on FTP performances. Then ask students to create a poster advertising a theater opening for one of the performances they researched.

Headed by Harry L. Hopkins, the WPA employed more than 8.5 million Americans between 1935 and 1943. At the program's peak, more than 3 million people received a monthly WPA check. WPA workers built or repaired thousands of bridges, parks, public buildings, and roads. The WPA also had a special women's division. It provided work in fields such as bookbinding, home care for the elderly, nursing, sewing, and teaching.

The WPA Handicraft Project provided jobs for older Americans and people with disabilities.

Recognizing that creative artists also needed work, Hopkins launched Federal Project One. This program employed about 40,000 actors, artists, musicians, and writers in a variety of projects. The Federal Writers' Project paid writers to produce state and regional guidebooks and to record volumes of oral histories, including the narratives of former slaves. The Federal Theater Project produced plays such as *The Living Newspaper*. A popular all–African American version of William Shakespeare's *Macbeth* was set in Haiti instead of Scotland. The Federal Arts Project sponsored folk art, murals, and paintings. The Federal Music Project helped create new symphony orchestras and supported public performances. When asked why he was spending government money to support artists, Hopkins replied, "They've got to eat just like other people."

Some WPA relief money went to the newly formed National Youth Administration (NYA). The NYA gave part-time employment to more than 4.5 million high school and college-age students.

The Election of 1936

As the presidential election of 1936 drew near, Americans had to decide whether to vote for President Roosevelt and his New Deal programs. Despite the efforts of the Roosevelt administration, millions of Americans remained unemployed. Hundreds of factories were still closed.

The Republican Party chose Kansas governor Alfred M. Landon to run against Roosevelt. Landon had the support of many business interests, most major newspapers, and wealthier Americans. During the campaign, Landon criticized the inefficiency and expense of the New Deal. He called the Social Security Act "unjust, unworkable, stupidly drafted and wastefully financed." However, Republicans realized that many New Deal programs were popular. Therefore, Landon promised to continue helping the elderly and unemployed and to protect workers' rights.

WPA artists painted this mural inside Coit Tower in San Francisco to celebrate California agriculture.

Many Democrats were concerned that a third-party candidate would take votes away from Roosevelt and allow the Republicans to win the election. Huey Long had announced his entry into the presidential race, but the son-in-law of one of his political opponents assassinated the senator in September 1935.

The Democrats officially nominated Roosevelt for re-election in 1936. During the campaign, the president defended his New Deal programs. He told a crowd, "When Americans suffered, we refused to pass by on the other side. Humanity came first." A majority of Americans believed that Roosevelt had saved them from

CLOSE

Logical-Mathematical. Have students create a report card for President Roosevelt, based on his reform programs. Ask them to choose several important programs that were developed under the Second New Deal and give each a letter grade. Ask students to provide at least one comment for each program. Then have students share their report cards with their classmates and discuss the comments they provided.

CHALLENGE AND EXTEND

1. **Linguistic, Logical-Mathematical, Visual-Spatial.** Remind students that Roosevelt's victory in the 1936 election was helped by the support he received from organized labor, farmers, and African Americans. Have students use the library and other resources to research several of the presidential elections since 1936 to determine whether these groups had an impact on the final outcome of those races. Allow students to present their findings in a variety of ways, including charts, graphs, or oral or written reports.

economic disaster. Several million people were working again. Some large companies, such as General Motors, were also recovering.

Roosevelt won re-election in November 1936 with one of the largest majorities in U.S. history. He carried every state except Maine and Vermont. Roosevelt received more than 60 percent of the popular vote, and Landon just over 36 percent. Coughlin's Union Party received about 2 percent. The London magazine *The Economist* suggested that "on the whole, the poor won the election from the well-to-do."

The 1936 election marked the first time that one party had received a majority of votes from organized labor, farmers, and African Americans. Previously most African Americans had voted for the Republican Party because it had ended slavery under President Abraham Lincoln. In 1936, African Americans supported the Democratic Party because some New Deal programs had provided them with work and relief opportunities.

 The Supreme Court

President Roosevelt saw his landslide victory as approval for his New Deal programs. In his second inaugural address, Roosevelt described his goals for the term. He wanted to help the millions of Americans who

> **"at this very moment are denied the greater part of what the very lowest standards of today call the necessities of life. . . . I see one-third of a nation ill-housed, ill-clad [ill-clothed], ill-nourished."**

Roosevelt saw only one major roadblock standing in the way of greater reform—the Supreme Court. The Court had already struck down the NIRA and the AAA. With the constitutionality of the TVA and Social Security Act to be decided in upcoming Supreme Court cases, the whole future of the

Select New Deal Programs

FIRST NEW DEAL, 1933–1934	PROVISIONS
Emergency Banking Act	Gave the executive branch the right to regulate banks
Farm Credit Administration (FCA)	Refinanced loans to keep farmers from losing their land
Civilian Conservation Corps (CCC)	Employed young men on public-works projects
Federal Emergency Relief Administration (FERA)	Provided relief to the needy
Agricultural Adjustment Act (AAA) of 1933	Paid farmers to grow fewer crops; later declared unconstitutional
Tennessee Valley Authority (TVA)	Built dams and power plants in the Tennessee Valley region
Home Owners Loan Corporation (HOLC)	Lent money to homeowners to refinance their mortgages
Federal Deposit Insurance Corporation (FDIC)	Insured deposits in individual bank accounts
National Recovery Administration (NRA)	Regulated industry and raised wages and prices
Public Works Administration (PWA)	Set up public-works projects to increase employment
Civil Works Administration (CWA)	Provided federal jobs to the unemployed
Securities and Exchange Commission (SEC)	Regulated the securities market
Federal Housing Administration (FHA)	Insured bank loans for building and repairing homes
SECOND NEW DEAL, 1935–1938	**PROVISIONS**
Works Progress Administration (WPA)	Created jobs in public works, research, and the arts
Rural Electrification Administration (REA)	Provided electricity to rural areas lacking public utilities
National Youth Administration (NYA)	Provided job training and part-time jobs to students
National Labor Relations Act (NLRA)	Recognized labor's right to bargain collectively
Social Security Act	Provided unemployment benefits and retirement pensions
Farm Security Administration (FSA)	Provided loans to help tenant farmers buy land
Agricultural Adjustment Act (AAA) of 1938	Paid farmers to voluntarily limit crop production
Fair Labor Standards Act	Established a minimum wage and a 40-hour workweek

Economic Development

The Out-of-School Program. During the first year of the National Youth Administration (NYA), its out-of-school program helped young people find community jobs, such as painting public buildings and maintaining city parks. In later years the NYA also offered vocational guidance, job-placement programs, and job training. These efforts were often futile, however. Although young people might have gained specific job skills, there were few jobs to be had.

Activity: Have students research contemporary job programs for young people and prepare a report on how federal and local governments are helping young people find work and gain job skills.

2. **Linguistic, Logical-Mathematical.** Ask students to choose one of President Roosevelt's New Deal agencies or programs. Have them use the library and other resources to find out if the organization still operates today and, if so, how it compares to when it was first established. Have students report their findings and include information about major goals, the number of people affected, and annual budgets. For an agency or program that still exists, such as Social Security, have students analyze its effects on the lives of U.S. citizens.

3. **Linguistic, Logical-Mathematical.** Ask students to write a position paper on how the Roosevelt administration's New Deal programs affected the role of the federal government for the rest of the 1900s. Have students use the library and other resources to find ways that the New Deal changed the U.S. government. Encourage students to cite examples to support their position. Finally, ask volunteers to present their papers to the class.

Section 4 Review ANSWERS

Identify

For significance, see the following pages:

- American Liberty League, p. 437
- Francis Townsend, p. 437
- Charles Coughlin, p. 437
- Huey Long, p. 438
- Share-Our-Wealth, p. 438
- Second New Deal, p. 438
- Social Security Act, p. 438
- Rural Electrification Administration, p. 439
- Emergency Relief Appropriation Act, p. 439
- Works Progress Administration, p. 439
- welfare state, p. 443
- deficit spending, p. 443

Reading for Content Understanding

1. Some argued that they discouraged free enterprise and formed the beginning of socialism in the United States; others argued that the policies had not done enough for the public.

2. Organizers will vary but may include the Social Security Act, the Wealth Tax Act, the Rural Electrification Administration, the Emergency Relief Appropriation Act, the Works Progress Administration, the Federal Project One, and the National Youth Administration.

3. by submitting a bill to Congress to raise the number of justices from 9 to 15

4. Paragraphs will vary but students should point out that some New Deal programs still function and benefit society.

5. Answers will vary but students should use examples from this section to show whether New Deal policies helped, such as by lowering unemployment.

The Granger Collection, New York

President Roosevelt was willing to try a variety of remedies to help the ailing U.S. economy.

Democrats' New Deal legislation appeared to be in jeopardy.

In February 1937, two weeks after his second inauguration, Roosevelt stunned Congress and the nation. He submitted a bill to change the structure of the Supreme Court. He proposed to increase the maximum number of justices from 9 to 15. Because Roosevelt would appoint the additional judges, this plan would allow the president to establish a majority of justices that would be friendly to his reform programs.

Roosevelt's opponents quickly accused him of "court packing"—trying to pack, or fill, the Court with his own judges. The *Chicago Tribune* urged Congress to vote against the bill, declaring that "if Congress answers yes, the principle of an impartial and independent judiciary will be lost." Even some of Roosevelt's allies were uncomfortable with his plan. They believed it would upset the checks and balances of the federal government.

As the court-packing debate continued, the Supreme Court surprised observers by upholding several key pieces of New Deal legislation, including the Social Security Act. Many Americans wondered if Roosevelt's plan had influenced how the justices voted. One journalist noted that a "switch in time saved nine," meaning that the change in the justices' ruling kept their number at nine. Although Congress soon defeated the court-packing plan, Roosevelt filled seven Court vacancies, caused by death or retirement, within the following four years. Thus, Roosevelt got what he wanted. He appointed new justices and ensured that the Supreme Court contained a majority that supported his New Deal policies. However, the battle over Roosevelt's court-packing proposal had divided the Democratic Party. It also ended up costing Roosevelt valuable support within his party.

The End of the New Deal

During 1936 and early 1937 the economy seemed to be improving. To cut federal spending, President Roosevelt reduced the total number of people employed by WPA and other New Deal projects from more than 3 million to just under 2 million.

Recession

Unfortunately, private industries were not able to employ all of these workers. In August 1937 the economy began to decline again, and unemployment rose rapidly. The president's critics called this situation the "Roosevelt recession." In October the stock market dropped again. Unemployment greatly increased in March 1938. President Roosevelt and Congress responded by approving more than $3 billion to expand the WPA, restart the PWA, and fund other agencies.

The increase in federal spending reduced some unemployment and prevented the new recession from becoming much worse. The strain of the lengthy economic problem was beginning to show, however. During the congressional elections of 1938, the Democratic Party was divided between supporters of Roosevelt and those opposed to the New Deal. Republicans took advantage of this division and picked up 7 seats in the Senate and 75 in the House, as well as many governorships.

REVIEW

Logical-Mathematical, Interpersonal. Have students complete the Section Review questions. Organize the class into teams and assign each team one Second New Deal program. Then have each team list at least three facts that could help other students identify the program. Create a master list of all the Second New Deal programs on the chalkboard. Then have each team try to identify one or more programs from the clues provided. Award points based on the number of clues each team needs to identify the program—a correct guess after one clue is worth five points, after two clues is two points, and so on. The team with the most points at the end of the contest wins.

ASSESS

Have students complete Daily Quiz 14.4.

RETEACH

Linguistic, Logical-Mathematical. Have students complete Main Idea Activities for Reteaching and Sheltered English 14.4. Provide each student with one of the fill-in-the-blank quizzes created in the Introduce Key Terms activity. (Make sure students do not receive their own quizzes.) When students have completed the quizzes, have them return them to their authors for grading. **SHELTERED ENGLISH**

Evaluating the New Deal

By 1938 the New Deal was reaching the limits of what it could do for the economy. The federal budget had grown by several billion dollars. However, this spending increase was not enough to make up for lost private investment. Critics charged that the New Deal created a **welfare state**. This system of government institutions provides for basic needs of citizens. These needs might include health care and unemployment benefits. Critics also argued that the New Deal promoted **deficit spending**—having the government spend more money than it receives in revenue—for the first time during a period of peace.

Supporters of the New Deal argued that the federal government took on a necessary role. New Deal programs helped many people. Home loans, farm subsidies, bank deposit insurance, relief payments and jobs, pension programs, and unemployment insurance helped Americans survive the Great Depression. The New Deal also established minimum standards for working conditions and the protection of workers' rights. Many Americans believed that Roosevelt and the federal government were concerned with their well-being. One man recalled:

> **"My mother looks upon the President as someone so immediately concerned with her problems and difficulties that she would not be greatly surprised were he to come to her house some evening and stay to dinner."**

The Granger Collection, New York

President Roosevelt's fireside chats gave many people the feeling that the president cared for them personally.

The New Deal's effectiveness in fighting the depression remains a topic of much historical debate. Nonetheless, it has had lasting results, creating programs and agencies that still exist today. In addition, Roosevelt's leadership and popularity helped shift the balance of power in the federal government from the legislative branch to the executive branch.

SECTION 4 REVIEW

Identify and explain the significance of the following:

- **American Liberty League**
- **Francis Townsend**
- **Charles Coughlin**
- **Huey Long**
- **Share-Our-Wealth**
- **Second New Deal**
- **Social Security Act**
- **Rural Electrification Administration**
- **Emergency Relief Appropriation Act**
- **Works Progress Administration**
- **welfare state**
- **deficit spending**

Reading for Content Understanding

1. **Main Idea** Why did some Americans criticize President Roosevelt's New Deal policies?
2. **Main Idea** Make a graphic organizer that describes five important programs created during the Second New Deal.
3. **Constitutional Heritage** How did Roosevelt try to influence the Supreme Court's rulings on New Deal programs?
4. **Writing** *Informing* Write a paragraph on how New Deal programs might affect Americans today.
5. **Critical Thinking** *Synthesizing Information* Do you think the New Deal was successful in helping Americans and in ending the depression? Explain your answer.

Chapter 14 Review ANSWERS

Identifying People and Places

1. the high-risk investment of money in the hopes of making a profit

2. October 29, 1929, the day the stock market crashed

3. president (1933–45) whose New Deal programs expanded the role of government and provided relief during the depression

4. President Roosevelt's program for ending the depression

5. wife of President Roosevelt; active in women's reform movements and championed relief programs for women

6. radio broadcasts that President Roosevelt made from the White House

7. New Deal program designed to help businesses; was ruled unconstitutional by the Supreme Court

8. rural reform effort targeting the Tennessee Valley region; TVA workers constructed many dams

9. created unemployment insurance for workers and a pension plan for retirees

10. food, clothing, shelter, and money

Using the Time Line

1. e
2. c
3. d
4. b
5. a

Review and Assessment RESOURCES

PRINT
- ★ Chapter 14 Review, pp. 444–45
- ★ Vocabulary Activity 14
- ★ Chapter 14 Study Guide
- ★ Chapter 14 Test (Form A or B)

MULTIMEDIA
- ★ Audio Program, Ch 14 (English and Spanish)
- ★ *Global Skill Builder CD–ROM*
- ★ Chapter 14 Test Generator
- ★ HRW Web site

SHELTERED ENGLISH
- ★ Spanish Glossary
- ★ Sheltered English Chapter 14 Test

ASSESS

Have students complete one of the Chapter 14 tests. As an alternate assessment, assign the Chapter 14 Investigation.

Understanding Main Ideas

1. As stock prices plummeted, investors panicked and tried to sell their stocks. However, not enough buyers were available for all the stocks being sold, which led prices to drop even more.

2. They blamed the business cycle for the crash and thought that the depression was a short-term situation.

3. The Great Depression caused many Americans to lose their jobs and struggle against financial ruin.

4. banking—called a "bank holiday," pushed for the Emergency Banking Act of 1933, supported the creation of the FDIC; industry—supported the NIRA, which created the PWA

5. It paid farmers subsidies not to produce certain crops or goods and put rural residents to work on internal improvement projects.

6. Francis Townsend—proposed an old age pension program; Charles Coughlin—organized the National Union for Social Justice, which called for stronger government control over the economy; Huey Long—organized the Share-Our-Wealth plan

7. He tried passing the plan so that he could appoint judges who would not rule against his New Deal legislation; Congress defeated the idea.

Reviewing Themes

1. Overproduction, unsound banking practices, the stock market crash, and sick industries all contributed to the Great Depression.

CHAPTER 14 REVIEW

Chapter Summary

The stock market crash on October 29, 1929, marked the beginning of the Great Depression. The depression left millions of Americans unemployed. They became dissatisfied with President Hoover's efforts to help them. President Roosevelt introduced a wide range of New Deal programs to help businesses and individuals recover from the devastating effects of the depression.

On a separate sheet of paper, complete the following activities.

Identifying People and Ideas

Describe the historical significance of the following:

1. speculation
2. Black Tuesday
3. Franklin D. Roosevelt
4. New Deal
5. Eleanor Roosevelt
6. fireside chats
7. National Industrial Recovery Act
8. Tennessee Valley Authority
9. Social Security Act
10. relief

Internet Activity 

go.hrw.com
SB1 New Deal

Search the Internet through the HRW Web site for information about life histories that were collected as part of the Works Progress Administration. Then use this information to write a short biographical sketch of one of the people interviewed.

Understanding Main Ideas

1. What happened during the 1929 stock market crash?
2. How did President Hoover and many business leaders respond to the crash?
3. How did the Great Depression affect Americans' daily lives?
4. How did President Roosevelt try to revive banking and industry during the Hundred Days?
5. How did the New Deal try to help farmers and rural residents?
6. What alternatives to the New Deal did Francis Townsend, Charles Coughlin, and Huey Long propose?
7. Why did Roosevelt try to pass his court-packing plan, and what were the results?

Reviewing Themes

1. **Economic Development** What economic factors contributed to the Great Depression?

Using the Time Line

Number your paper from 1 to 5. Match the letters on the time line below with the following events.

1. **Roosevelt wins re-election by a record-breaking margin.**
2. **Angry veterans known as the Bonus Army arrive in Washington, D.C.**
3. **The Social Security Act is passed to provide security for older Americans and the unemployed.**
4. **The passage of the Smoot-Hawley Tariff raises tariffs on foreign goods and contributes to the global depression.**
5. **The stock market crashes on what becomes known as Black Tuesday.**

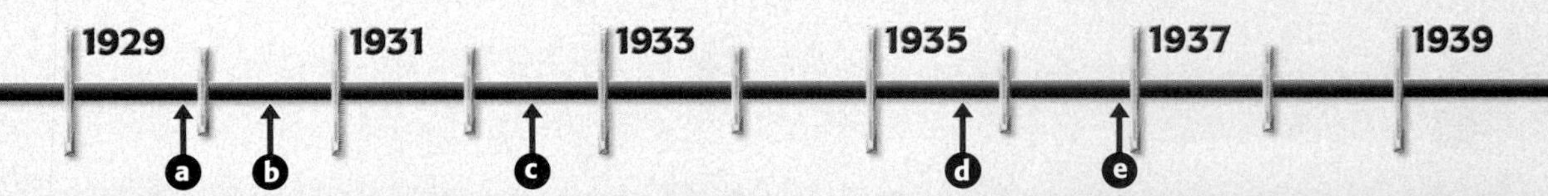

RETEACH

Logical-Mathematical, Visual-Spatial, Interpersonal. Organize the class into four groups and assign each group one of the chapter's sections. Have each group review its assigned section and record any specific effects of the Great Depression that it includes. Next to each effect, have students identify its cause.

SHELTERED ENGLISH

Using the Internet

Have students continue their research to find out more information about the Federal Writer's Project. Have students create a commemorative stamp illustrating the program's contributions to American history.

Portfolio Extensions

1. Have students view the presentations and attempt to determine which programs had the greatest effect on each individual.

2. After students have presented their reports, ask them to rank the stocks that were presented, from most profitable to least profitable.

2. **Constitutional Heritage** What role did the Supreme Court play in the New Deal?
3. **Citizenship and Democracy** How were some New Deal programs targeted to directly help the unemployed?

Thinking Critically

1. **Identifying Cause and Effect** Explain the cause of the banking crisis and its effect on the economy.
2. **Making Comparisons** Compare and contrast the programs that Hoover passed to help farmers during the depression with Roosevelt's New Deal programs.
3. **Evaluating** Do you think the New Deal was successful in fighting the effects of the Great Depression? Explain your answer.

Building Your Portfolio

Complete the following activities individually or in groups.

1. **Oral History Project** Interview at least three people in your community who were alive during the Great Depression. You may wish to ask them about how their family survived the depression, what they thought of Presidents Hoover and Roosevelt, or how the New Deal programs affected them. Combine your interviews into a brochure, audiotape, or videotape that you can present to your class.
2. **The Stock Market** Imagine that you are an investor in the stock market. Get a current copy of the financial section of the newspaper and select a company that you think will be successful in the future. Now imagine that you have 100 shares in this company and note the value of these shares. For the next month, keep track of how your stock is doing. At the end of the month, note the final value of your 100 shares. Then write a short report that details how your stock did and whether you made or lost money. Include a line graph that shows the gains and losses of your stock.

Writing About History

1. **Describing** Imagine that you are a teenager working for the CCC. Write a letter home describing the work you are doing and why it is important to other Americans.
2. **Creating** Imagine that you are an artist on Federal Project One. Create a flyer or song lyrics describing the effect of the WPA on life in your community.

Linking Geography and History

1. **Region** How did the TVA improve the lives of rural people in the Tennessee Valley?
2. **Human-Environment Interaction** How did agencies such as the CCC and PWA change the landscape of the United States?

History Skills Workshop

Reading Charts Study the chart below, which shows the collapse of share prices during the 1929 stock market crash. Then answer the following questions: (a) Which stock shown lost the most points between September 3 and November 13, 1929? (b) Which stock was worth the most on November 13, 1929? (c) Which stock lost the greatest percentage of its starting value?

The Crash

Company	High Price Sept. 3, 1929	Low Price Nov. 13, 1929
American Telephone and Telegraph	304	197 1/4
General Electric	396 1/4	168 1/8
General Motors	72 3/4	36
Montgomery Ward	137 7/8	49 1/4
U.S. Steel	261 3/4	150
Woolworth	100 3/8	52 1/4

Source: Frederick Lewis Allen, *Only Yesterday*

2. It ruled against the constitutionality of some New Deal programs, such as the NIRA.

3. They funded public works projects, which created jobs.

Thinking Critically

1. After the stock market crash, many people could not repay bank loans, so smaller banks could not repay loans from larger banks, thus causing larger banks to go into debt and close. This triggered panic, bank runs, and more bank closings.

2. Hoover's assisted farmers in buying feed and equipment but did not provide direct federal aid and ended some farm subsidies. Roosevelt's provided subsidies directly to farmers for not producing specific goods.

3. Answers will vary but students should provide specific examples of ways in which the New Deal did or did not alleviate the depression.

Writing About History

1. Letters will vary but should describe the type of work the CCC funded.

2. Flyers or song lyrics will vary but should mention how internal improvements will help the community.

Linking Geography and History

1. controlled flooding, reduced soil erosion, and generated hydroelectric power

2. CCC workers improved the environment, fought forest fires, and restored national historic sites; while WPA workers built dams, schools, and other public facilities.

History Skills Workshop

(a) General Electric; (b) American Telephone and Telegraph; (c) Montgomery Ward

CHAPTER PLANNING GUIDE
The Depression at Home and Abroad

	SECTION LESSON OBJECTIVES	PRINT RESOURCES	MULTIMEDIA RESOURCES	SHELTERED ENGLISH RESOURCES
Section 1: Workers and Farmers in the New Deal (pp. 447–52)	★ Describe how New Deal legislation helped organized labor. ★ Identify new labor unions formed and labor strategies used during the Great Depression. ★ Explain what happened to farmers and farmworkers during the Great Depression.	★ Guided Reading Strategies 15.1 ★ Biography Reading 15: Dorothea Lange ★ Geography Activity 15: Public Unrest During the Depression ★ Section 1 Review, p. 452 ★ Daily Quiz 15.1	★ *Teaching Resources CD–ROM,* Lesson 15.1 ★ *American Music Audio CD Program:* "Talkin' Dust Bowl" ★ Art in American History Transparency 31: Poster for *The Grapes of Wrath* ★ HRW Web site	★ Main Idea Activities for Reteaching and Sheltered English 15.1
Section 2: Americans Face Hard Times (pp. 453–56)	★ Describe the effects of the Great Depression on families and women. ★ Explain how the New Deal affected American Indians. ★ Identify New Deal efforts to help African Americans during the depression.	★ Guided Reading Strategies 15.2 ★ Primary Source Reading 15: American Indians and the Depression ★ Section 2 Review, p. 456 ★ Daily Quiz 15.2	★ *Teaching Resources CD–ROM,* Lesson 15.2 ★ *American Music Audio CD Program:* "He's Got the Whole World in His Hands"	★ Main Idea Activities for Reteaching and Sheltered English 15.2
Section 3: Arts and Entertainment (pp. 457–61)	★ Identify ways that the arts reflected Americans' experiences during the depression. ★ Explain how government programs helped support the arts during the Great Depression. ★ Describe how Americans entertained themselves during the depression.	★ Guided Reading Strategies 15.3 ★ Literature Reading 15: *Let Us Now Praise Famous Men* ★ Section 3 Review, p. 461 ★ Daily Quiz 15.3	★ *Teaching Resources CD–ROM,* Lesson 15.3 ★ Art in American History Transparency 30: *Parson Weems' Fable* and Transparency 32: *Sugaring Off* ★ Everyday Life in America Transparency 23: The 1936 Olympic Games and Transparency 24: America's Darling: Shirley Temple, 1930s	★ Main Idea Activities for Reteaching and Sheltered English 15.3
Section 4: The Depression Abroad (pp. 462–67)	★ Describe ways that the Good Neighbor policy differed from previous U.S. policies toward Latin America. ★ Explain the rise of dictators in European nations. ★ Identify ways the United States responded to events in Europe and Asia in the 1930s.	★ Guided Reading Strategies 15.4 ★ Graphic Organizer 15: The Great Depression Touches Everyone ★ Section 4 Review, p.467 ★ Daily Quiz 15.4	★ *Teaching Resources CD–ROM,* Lesson 15.4 ★ Everyday Life in America Transparency 25: The Rise of the Third Reich, 1930s ★ HRW Web site	★ Main Idea Activities for Reteaching and Sheltered English 15.4
Chapter Review and Assessment (pp. 468–69)		★ Chapter 15 Review, pp. 468–69 ★ Vocabulary Activity 15 ★ Chapter 15 Study Guide ★ Chapter 15 Test (Form A or B)	★ Audio Program, Ch. 15 (English and Spanish) ★ *Global Skill Builder CD–ROM* ★ Chapter 15 Test Generator ★ HRW Web site	★ Spanish Glossary ★ Sheltered English Chapter 15 Test

CHAPTER OVERVIEW

The Great Depression was a trying time for most Americans. Labor unrest was high, and workers held many strikes. At the same time, New Deal programs strengthened the position of organized labor. For farmers, the depression was particularly severe, especially for farmers in the Dust Bowl. Many families were forced to sell their farms or to move in search of work.

Other Americans also faced hardships. Families had trouble paying their bills, and many men left their families to look for jobs. African Americans received relief from the New Deal, but often faced discrimination and poverty. American Indians experienced the worst poverty. In response, the New Deal returned some lands to tribal ownership and gave some tribes self-government.

To forget their troubles, many Americans turned to the arts and entertainment, such as swing music, movies, radio shows, spectator sports, and art and literature with local themes. Government funding kept artists working.

On the international front, President Roosevelt worked to be a "Good Neighbor" in Latin America. In Europe and Asia, economic hardships led to the rise of several dictators. The United States remained neutral in conflicts abroad, but some people found it difficult to ignore the growing threats of war.

CHAPTER INVESTIGATION

The Chapter Investigation is an extended, multipart activity designed for students to work cooperatively and apply the chapter content in the creation of a project. You may choose to use the Chapter 15 Investigation, Great Depression Travelogues, either as a substitute for teaching the section lessons or as an alternate assessment.

BLOCK SCHEDULING 

The teacher lesson plans for each section offer a variety of activity choices to help you present the material in a block scheduling format. For further suggestions on block scheduling, see the *Block Scheduling Handbook with Team Teaching Strategies*, pp. 85–90.

Meeting Individual Needs

ABILITY LEVELS

LEVEL 1 Basic level activities designed for all students encountering new material.

LEVEL 2 Intermediate level activities designed for average students.

LEVEL 3 Challenging activities designed for above-average students.

SHELTERED ENGLISH These activities address the needs of students with Limited English Proficiency.

Internet Connections and Lesson 15
www.si.edu/hrw

CNN Presents America:
Yesterday and Today 1850 to the Present
Segment: Glimpses of the Depression

Additional Resources

Books for Teachers

Reiman, Richard A. *The New Deal & American Youth: Ideas & Ideals in a Depression Decade.* University of Georgia Press, 1992. Examines the role of youth in the New Deal.

Scott, William R. *The Sons of Sheba's Race.* Indiana University Press, 1992. Describes the role of African Americans in Italy's war with Ethiopia.

Watkins, T. H. *The Great Depression: America in the 1930s.* Little, Brown and Company, 1993. A noted historian's treatment of the Great Depression, from the late 1920s to the early 1940s.

Books for Students

Allen, Frederick L. *Since Yesterday.* HarperCollins, 1986. Reissue of a classic political and social history of the 1930s.

Freedman, Russell. *Franklin Delano Roosevelt.* Houghton Mifflin, 1992. An award-winning biography of Roosevelt by a distinguished writer of nonfiction for young adults.

Jenkins, Tony. *Nicaragua and the United States: Years of Conflict.* Watts, 1989. Traces the history of U.S. foreign policy in Nicaragua.

Multimedia Materials

Franklin D. Roosevelt: The Speeches Collection. Video, 40 min. MPI Home Video/SSSS. Includes a speech to CCC workers and a teacher's guide on Roosevelt.

Roll of Thunder, Hear My Cry. Video, 115 min. SSSS. Portrays the struggle of southern black landowners during the Great Depression.

Seeds of Discord: 1933–1936. Video, 25 min. Aims/SSSS. Covers the rise of Stalin, Hitler, and Mussolini.

The Depression at Home and Abroad

CHAPTER MOTIVATOR

Ask students to consider material from the previous chapter to determine how the Great Depression might have affected laborers and farmers as well as the arts and entertainment. Have each student create a list of possible effects for each category. Then have them determine how the depression may have affected other nations. For all the effects they list, have students explain why they think each would occur. Once students are finished, tell them that in this chapter they will learn how the Great Depression affected people in the United States and abroad. As students read the chapter, ask them to determine the accuracy of the lists they made.

Presenting Themes

- **Economic Development** Students might mention that the government may assist citizens by giving monetary aid to supplement their incomes, by distributing food or food stamps to cut down on living costs, or by providing job training.
- **Cultural Diversity** Students might mention that certain groups, such as investors, may suffer great financial losses, while other groups that have less money may lose their jobs and their homes. Some people may even die from starvation.
- **Global Relations** Students might mention that governments may take on more control of the economy and other aspects of citizens' lives. Some governments may even be overthrown and replaced by new leaders offering citizens more hope of economic recovery.

Using the Time Line

Ask each student to choose one event from the time line. Have students use the library and other resources to create an oral presentation about the event. As each topic is discussed during the lesson cycle, call on students to present information on the topics they researched.

Alexandre Hogue, *Drouth Stricken Area*, 1936, Oil on canvas, Dallas Museum of Art, Dallas Art Association Purchase, 1945.6

CHAPTER 15

The Depression at Home and Abroad

(1929–1939)

One day during the Great Depression young Clara Hancox found her piggy bank empty. Her mother told her that her father had taken the money. He needed it to look for work, and Clara was the only one in the family with any money. To Clara, it was not the missing money that was painful. Rather, "it was to see this happen to the man who in my eyes could do no wrong." In the 1930s, many people shared similar experiences.

Economic Development
In what ways might the government help citizens economically?

Cultural Diversity
How might different groups be affected by an economic downturn?

Global Relations
How might a nation's government change in response to economic difficulties?

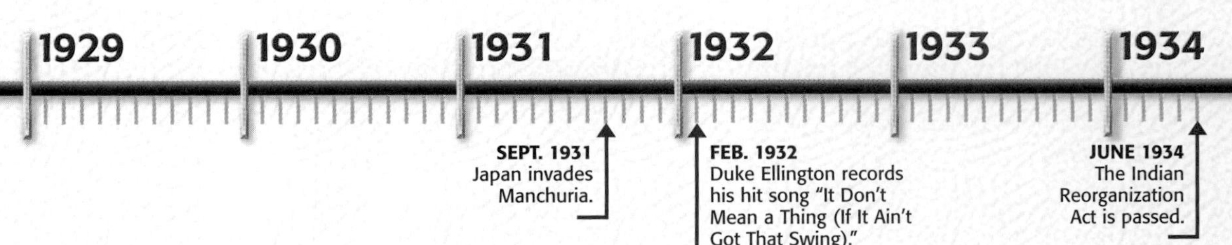

OBJECTIVES

- Describe how New Deal legislation helped organized labor.
- Identify new labor unions formed and labor strategies used during the Great Depression.
- Explain what happened to farmers and farmworkers during the Great Depression.

FOCUS

Motivate Before Reading

Ask students to list ways that an environmental disaster might affect farmers. *(Answers will vary but students might mention that an environmental disaster might ruin crops, cause farmers economic difficulties, and possibly even force them to quit farming.)* Then explain to students that in this section they will learn how the

Workers and Farmers in the New Deal

Reading Focus

How did New Deal legislation help organized labor?

What new labor unions were formed, and what new strategies did the unions use during the Great Depression?

What happened to farmers and farmworkers during the Great Depression?

Key Terms

National Labor Relations Act
Fair Labor Standards Act
Congress of Industrial Organizations
sit-down strike
Southern Tenant Farmers' Union
Dust Bowl
Farm Security Administration

IN THE WINTER OF 1931–32, newspaper editor Oscar Ameringer traveled the Midwest recording the stories of desperate and starving Americans. He offered a ride to one Arkansas family. The woman was hugging a dead chicken under her ragged coat. When asked where she had found the chicken, she said she had found it dead in the road. Then—referring to Herbert Hoover's 1928 campaign slogan—she added with grim humor, "They promised me a chicken in the pot, and now I got mine."

A child during the 1930s

IMAGE ON LEFT PAGE: *Alexandre Hogue's 1934 painting of the drought-stricken United States*

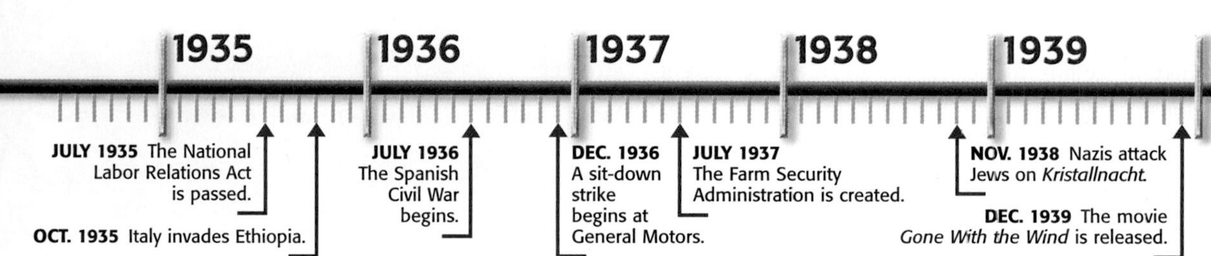

Section 1 RESOURCES

PRINT

- ★ Guided Reading Strategies 15.1
- ★ Biography Reading 15: Dorothea Lange
- ★ Geography Activity 15: Public Unrest During the Depression
- ★ Section 1 Review, p. 452
- ★ Daily Quiz 15.1

MULTIMEDIA

- ★ *Teaching Resources CD–ROM,* Lesson 15.1
- ★ *American Music Audio CD Program:* "Talkin' Dust Bowl"
- ★ Art in American History Transparency 31: Poster for *The Grapes of Wrath*
- ★ HRW Web site

SHELTERED ENGLISH

- ★ Main Idea Activities for Reteaching and Sheltered English 15.1

Great Depression, combined with an environmental disaster known as the Dust Bowl, affected American workers and farmers. Students also will learn how the depression affected organized labor.

Introduce Key Terms

Linguistic. Review this section's key terms with students. Work with students to help them develop a definition for each term. Then ask students to use each term in a sentence. When students have completed the assignment, ask volunteers to write their sentences on the chalkboard. **SHELTERED ENGLISH**

TEACH

Have students read Section 1 and complete Guided Reading Strategies 15.1. Choose one or more of the following activities to explore the section content with students. For further suggestions on block scheduling or team teaching, see the *Block Scheduling Handbook.*

LEVEL 1: Linguistic. (Suggested time: 15 min.) As a class, go over students' Guided Reading Strategies. Then use the Reading Focus questions to highlight the main ideas of the section. **SHELTERED ENGLISH**

Biography

John L. Lewis. Born in 1880 near Lucas, Iowa, John L. Lewis was the son of a miner. His father held a variety of jobs, and the family frequently had to move. After high school, Lewis spent several years in the West and Midwest working in a variety of jobs, including mining. After he and his family moved to Illinois, Lewis joined the local chapter of the United Mine Workers (UMW) union. He quickly began to rise among the ranks. In 1909 he was elected president of the local chapter of the UMW, and in 1920 he became president of the entire union. Lewis used his leadership position to fight to improve working conditions.

Activity: Have students use the library and other resources to find information on the leadership of John L. Lewis. Ask students to create a press release for the UMW that describes the significance of his leadership.

New Deal Labor Programs

In the mid-1930s the Roosevelt administration revised some of its New Deal labor programs, particularly after the Supreme Court struck down the National Industrial Recovery Act. In 1935 Senator Robert Wagner of New York sponsored legislation to strengthen and restore workers' rights. In July, Congress passed the **National Labor Relations Act** (NLRA), or Wagner-Connery Act. The NLRA gave workers the right to select their own unions by majority vote. Workers also gained the right to strike, boycott, and picket. The NLRA required employers to negotiate wages, hours, and working conditions with the workers' unions.

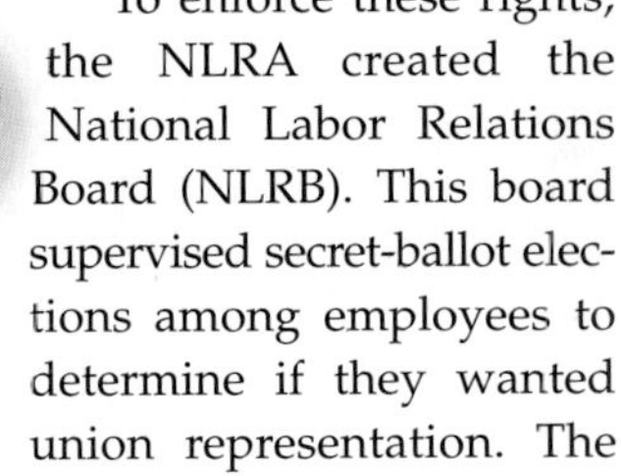

United Auto Workers buttons from the late 1930s

To enforce these rights, the NLRA created the National Labor Relations Board (NLRB). This board supervised secret-ballot elections among employees to determine if they wanted union representation. The NLRB also investigated charges of unfair labor practices and antiunion activities.

In 1938 Congress passed legislation on employee hours and wages. The **Fair Labor Standards Act** established a minimum wage of 40 cents an hour by 1940. The act also set a maximum standard workweek of 40 hours. In addition, the act banned the employment of children under 16 years of age.

Industrial Unions

With the passage of pro-labor laws, union membership increased. During the 1920s most workers had belonged to craft unions associated with the American Federation of Labor (AFL). Skilled workers who performed the same craft, or trade, belonged to these unions. Because industrial production required workers with many different skills, there were sometimes several different craft unions in one industry.

After the NLRA passed, some workers tried to organize industrial unions. These unions represent all skilled and unskilled workers in an industry. John L. Lewis, president of the United Mine Workers (UMW), and some other union leaders argued that industrial unions would give unions more power. Lewis failed to persuade the AFL leadership to abandon craft unions. He did, however, form the Committee for Industrial Organization. It brought together workers in the automobile, rubber, steel, and textile industries. In 1936 this group was organizing workers in mass-production industries. The committee became the **Congress of Industrial Organizations** (CIO) in 1938. The CIO joined together industrial unions. Lewis wanted the CIO to "organize the unorganized." The congress welcomed unions that had African Americans, immigrants, unskilled workers, and women as members. Industrial unions in the CIO included the International Ladies' Garment Workers Union, the United Auto Workers, and the United Mine Workers.

Union membership totals jumped from roughly 3 million in 1932 to more than 8 million in 1938. Unions used their influence to help elect pro-labor candidates and to lobby Congress.

With greater union strength came an increasing number of strikes. In early 1936, workers went on strike at the Goodyear Tire Factory in Akron, Ohio. Instead of leaving the factory to form a picket line, the striking workers sat on the production floor. They refused to leave until management met their demands. This was the first major **sit-down strike**, one in which workers remain in

Sit-down strikers at a General Motors plant established committees to provide for meals, education, and entertainment.

ALL LEVELS: Logical-Mathematical, Visual-Spatial. (Suggested time: 30 min.) Have each student create a political cartoon that shows at least one of the ways that New Deal legislation assisted organized labor. Ask students to include captions that explain what is taking place in the cartoon. Then ask students to create a second political cartoon, with caption, that shows one of the new strategies labor unions began using during the Great Depression. Once students are finished, have volunteers share their work with the class. **SHELTERED ENGLISH**

LEVEL 2: Linguistic, Logical-Mathematical, Visual-Spatial. (Suggested time: 45 min. plus homework) Organize students into groups and have them list problems that farmers and farmworkers faced during the Great Depression. Then have each group create an advertisement for a newspaper campaign urging Congress to support farm relief. Ads should contain information and images that illustrate students' points. When they are done, have groups explain their work to the class. For homework, have each student write a letter to President Roosevelt from the perspective of a farmer or farmworker. Students should use the lists their groups made to explain the hardships they are facing.

the factories but refuse to work. With workers occupying the plants, employers could not replace them. The sit-down strike forced factories to halt production until the conflict was resolved. The Akron workers won their demands and inspired others to stage similar strikes.

In late December 1936, autoworkers at a General Motors (GM) factory in Flint, Michigan, staged a sit-down strike. It soon spread to other company plants. Inside the Flint factory, striking workers prepared for a long strike. Outside, the wives of striking workers marched on picket lines, raised money, and mobilized support.

The autoworkers had no formal means to express their grievances to management. Their complaints ranged from the fast-paced speed of the work to frequent and lengthy layoffs. One woman said that the long, hard hours had turned her husband into

> **"a young man grown old from the speed-up. He has come home at night . . . so tired he couldn't eat. He was wakened the next morning with his hands so swollen he couldn't hold a fork."**

The strike lasted six weeks. It virtually halted GM's car production until the workers' demands were met. One autoworker recalled that "the inhuman high speed [was] *no more*." Within eight months of the strike, the membership of the United Auto Workers had increased to about 400,000—up from 30,000 one year earlier. Soon workers in other industries staged sit-down strikes. In 1937 more than 470 sit-down strikes occured. There had been less than 50 in 1936.

Farmers in the Depression

Organized labor gained strength with the New Deal, but farmers did not fare so well. During the 1920s, farmers had struggled with crop surpluses, low prices, and high costs. The stock market crash worsened their crisis. Many farmers found themselves unable to repay their loans. Banks took over ownership of many indebted farms. Between 1930 and 1935 as many as 750,000 farms were lost through bankruptcy or foreclosure.

The Southern Tenant Farmers' Union fought to protect the rights of sharecroppers and tenant farmers.

Farmers Take Action

Frustrated farmers often fought against foreclosures. When banks held auctions to sell animals, equipment, and farms, many people refused to bid market prices. They offered a few dollars for a barnyard of animals or for an entire farm. With no other offers, the banks accepted these low bids. The purchasers usually returned the items to their neighbors.

The Agricultural Adjustment Act (AAA) helped some farmers pay their mortgages. It hurt other farm families, however. Poor families, tenants, and sharecroppers often lost their jobs when farmers reduced production as the AAA required. In response, tenants, sharecroppers, and farm laborers joined forces in Arkansas. They organized the **Southern Tenant Farmers' Union** (STFU) in July 1934. STFU president J. R. Butler urged black and white farmworkers to join together. "The landlord is always betwixt us, beatin' us and starvin' us and makin' us fight each other," explained one farmer. The STFU had limited success, but it did bring attention to the problems that sharecroppers and tenant farmers faced.

The Dust Bowl

An environmental disaster also hurt farmers. In order to grow more crops, many Great Plains farmers had plowed up grazing land and the grasses that protected the topsoil. A severe drought and heat wave struck the Great Plains in the early 1930s. The land dried out. Soon heavy winds swept away the dried-out topsoil. These dust storms turned parts of the Great Plains into

Cultural Diversity

The Southern Tenant Farmers' Union. Although sharecropping and tenant farming had existed in the South for many years, they were not highly profitable livelihoods. During the Great Depression conditions for sharecroppers and tenant farmers worsened. Many were forced to give up their farms. In 1934 an integrated group of sharecroppers, tenant farmers, and farm laborers in Arkansas formed the Southern Tenant Farmers' Union. The union's membership grew quickly, reaching more than 25,000 members. The group received support from liberal clergy, reform organizations, and radicals across the country. However, in Arkansas, group members were subject to violence and other forms of harassment. By 1937 the union's influence had begun to decline.

Critical Thinking: Why might the union have faced violence and harassment?

ANSWER: because it opposed farm owners and integrated black and white farmworkers

LEVEL 3: Linguistic, Logical-Mathematical. (Suggested time: 20 min. plus homework) Ask students to imagine that they are labor leaders during the Great Depression. Have each student write a speech to encourage a group of workers to form a new labor union. (You may want to assign each student a specific union that was formed during the depression.) Ask students to include problems the union would address and strategies it would use to achieve its objectives. During the next class, call on volunteers to give their speeches. Finally, lead a discussion on the new types of labor unions formed during the depression and the effectiveness of the strategies they used.

CLOSE

Linguistic, Visual-Spatial. Ask students to make a list of significant events covered in this section. Have students create graphic organizers that show the causes and effects of these events. When students have finished, call on volunteers to share their organizers with the class.

Geographic Diversity

The Dust Bowl. One of the greatest environmental disasters in the United States was the severe drought that struck the Great Plains in the 1930s. In what became known as the Dust Bowl, winds picked up the dried earth, creating huge, dark clouds. During one three-day storm in 1934, about 350 million tons of topsoil were swept from the Great Plains as far east as Washington, D.C. and New York City. Many East Coast cities had to light their streetlights in the middle of the day because of the dust storm.

Activity: Have students use the library or search the Internet through the HRW Web site to find accounts of the Dust Bowl and then write a magazine article about it.

go.hrw.com
SB1 Dust Bowl

MAP ANSWER

Arizona, Nevada, and California

Multimedia Resources

American Music Audio CD Program: "Talkin' Dust Bowl"

Multimedia Resources

Art in American History Transparency 31: Poster for *The Grapes of Wrath*

the so-called **Dust Bowl**. One woman from Kansas remembered dust storms

> "**covering everything—including ourselves—in a thick, brownish gray blanket. . . . The door and windows were all shut tightly, yet those tiny particles seemed to seep through the very walls. It got into cupboards and clothes closets; our faces were as dirty as if we had rolled in the dirt; our hair was gray and stiff and we ground dirt between our teeth.**"

Many Americans were forced to leave their farms as drought turned their farmland to dust.

The dust came in all colors—brown, black, yellow, gray, and even red—depending on its source. A single dust storm could rage from one hour to three and a half days, often reducing visibility to zero.

The dust storms destroyed farm life in the area. Many farm families, often called "Okies" because they came from Oklahoma, abandoned their farms. They headed west to California looking for work. A documentary film created in the 1930s described these migrants:

> "**Nothing to stay for . . . nothing to hope for . . . homeless, penniless, and bewildered they joined the great army of the highways.**"

Migrant Workers

When Dust Bowl refugees arrived in California, they competed for jobs with migrant workers already there. By 1933 more than twice as many people were looking for work on California farms as there were jobs.

Many of these migrant workers were Mexican citizens. Because they were not U.S. citizens, some state and local governments did not allow them to participate in public-works projects. Other Mexican citizens were forced to leave the United States. Nearly 400,000 Mexican nationals were deported during the 1930s. Their American-born children, who were U.S. citizens, were also sent to Mexico.

Some Mexican migrant workers who remained in the United States organized for better working conditions. In 1933, for example, some 12,000 laborers in the San Joaquin Valley went on strike for higher wages for picking cotton. Migrant worker Lydia Ramos joined the strikers, explaining, "*We* were not going to break a strike." The strikers won a wage-rate increase. However, many migrant workers continued to experience hardship during the depression.

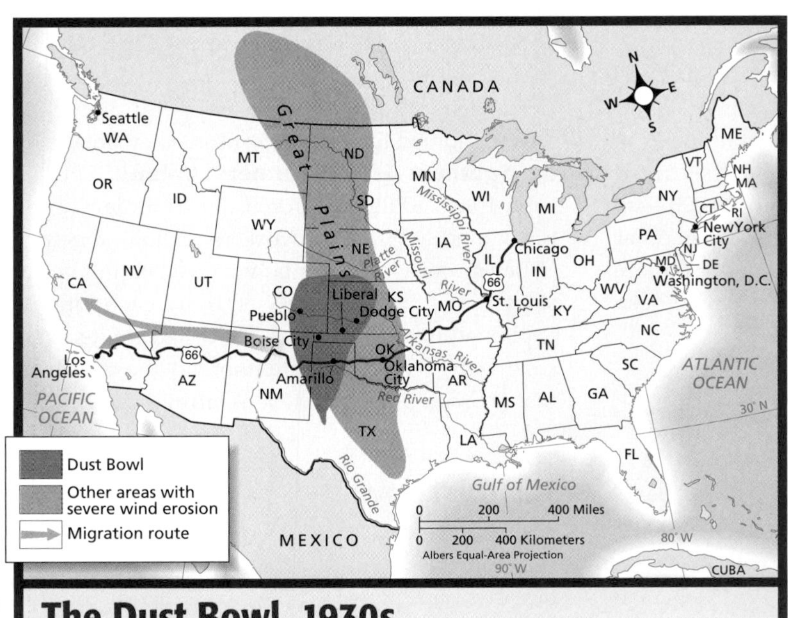

The Dust Bowl, 1930s

Learning from Maps Strong winds carried away dry topsoil in a vast region of the central United States, forming what became known as the Dust Bowl. Many farmers followed Route 66 west to escape the Dust Bowl.

Location From New Mexico, through which states did the typical migration route pass?

CHALLENGE AND EXTEND

1. **Linguistic, Intrapersonal.** Have students use the library and other resources to read about the experiences of farmers in the region of the Dust Bowl. Ask students to use the information they find to write a short story or play about the experiences of a teenager in a farming family living in the Dust Bowl during the 1930s. When students are finished, call on volunteers to read or present their work to the class.

TEACHER TO TEACHER

2. **Linguistic.** Valerie Hill of Dallas, Texas, suggested the following activity: Show students a copy of the 1984 movie *Country,* which follows a family's troubles during the farm foreclosures of the 1980s. Then have students write an essay comparing and contrasting the hardships shown to those farming families in the Dust Bowl experienced. *Country* is rated PG, but does contain some explicit language and violence. We recommend you prescreen it and get parents' permission before showing it.

American Literature

The Grapes of Wrath
John Steinbeck

John Steinbeck's The Grapes of Wrath *was published in 1939. The novel describes the Joad family's struggle during the Great Depression. After losing their farm in Oklahoma, the Joads travel to California. They find hard, miserable work as migrant farm laborers. In the following excerpt, the Joads prepare to leave their farm.*

For The Grapes of Wrath, *John Steinbeck won a Pulitzer Prize. The novel describes the hardships and suffering many Americans experienced during the 1930s.*

Now they were ready. Granma . . . saying, "What's all this? What you doin' now, so early?" But she was dressed and agreeable. And Ruthie and Winfield were awake, but quiet with the pressure of tiredness and still half dreaming. . . . And the movement of the family stopped. They stood about, reluctant [not wanting] to make the first active move to go. They were afraid, now that the time had come—afraid in the same way Grampa was afraid. . . .

And Tom shook himself free of the numbness. . . . "We got to get goin'." And the others came out of their numbness and moved toward the truck.

"Come on," Tom said. "Let's get Grampa on." Pa and Uncle John and Tom and Al went into the kitchen where Grampa slept. . . . They took him under the elbows and lifted him to his feet, and he grumbled and cursed thickly. . . . Out the door they boosted him, and when they came to the truck Tom and Al climbed up, . . . hooked their hands under his arms and lifted him gently up, and laid him on top of the load. . . .

They got into the cab, and then the rest swarmed up on top of the load. Connie and Rose of Sharon, Pa and Uncle John, Ruthie and Winfield, Tom and the preacher. Noah stood on the ground, looking up at the great load of them sitting on top of the truck. . . . Noah said, "How about the dogs, Pa?"

"I forgot the dogs," Pa said. He whistled shrilly, and one bouncing dog ran in, but only one. Noah caught him and threw him up on the top, where he sat rigid and shivering at the height. "Got to leave the other two," Pa called. "Muley, will you look after 'em some? See they don't starve?"

"Yeah," said Muley. "I'll like to have a couple dogs. Yeah! I'll take 'em."

"Take them chickens, too," Pa said.

Al got into the driver's seat. The starter whirred and caught. . . . And then the loose roar of the six cylinders and a blue smoke behind. "So long, Muley," Al called.

And the family called, "Good-by, Muley."

Understanding Literature

1. How do the Joads feel about leaving their farm?
2. How does John Steinbeck's *The Grapes of Wrath* reflect many people's everyday experiences during the Great Depression?

Across the Curriculum

LITERATURE

John Steinbeck. John Steinbeck grew up in rural California. This upbringing helped him relate to the hardships farmers faced during the Great Depression. He made this subject the focus of his Pulitzer Prize–winning novel *The Grapes of Wrath.* With the book's publication and the successful and popular movie version that followed, Steinbeck received far more critical praise and fame than he had ever expected or wanted. Partly in an effort to escape this scrutiny, he shifted his focus to marine biology for a time. He later returned to writing, but tried out other themes and styles, including travel pieces, a musical, and screenplays. Some of his other works include *Of Mice and Men, The Pearl,* and *East of Eden.*

Critical Thinking: Why do you think Steinbeck chose to write about farmers' struggles in the Great Depression?

ANSWER: Answers will vary but students might mention that his upbringing made him highly sensitive to the plight of farming people.

AMERICAN LITERATURE ANSWERS

1. They feel reluctant to leave and afraid.

2. It shows how many families were forced to relocate as a result of financial difficulties and natural disasters.

REVIEW

Linguistic, Logical-Mathematical. Have students complete the Section Review questions. Ask each student to outline the section. Have students replace each key term or person's name with a blank space. Then ask students to exchange papers, fill in the blanks, and return the outlines to their authors for grading.

ASSESS

Have students complete Daily Quiz 15.1.

RETEACH

Linguistic, Logical-Mathematical. Have students complete Main Idea Activities for Reteaching and Sheltered English 15.1. Ask each student to create two lists: one showing legislation or organizations that assisted labor, and another showing legislation or organizations that helped farmers. Then call on volunteers to explain how one of the laws or organizations that they listed helped either labor or farmers. SHELTERED ENGLISH

Section 1 Review ANSWERS

Identify
For significance, see the following pages:

- National Labor Relations Act, p. 448
- Fair Labor Standards Act, p. 448
- John L. Lewis, p. 448
- Congress of Industrial Organizations, p. 448
- sit-down strike, p. 448
- Southern Tenant Farmers' Union, p. 449
- Dust Bowl, p. 450
- Farm Security Administration, p. 452
- Dorothea Lange, p. 452

Locate
For locations, see the map on page 450.

Reading for Content Understanding

1. It gave workers the right to strike, boycott, picket, and choose their own unions.

2. a tenant farmers' union and industrial unions; sit-down strikes

3. By plowing up grazing land and the grasses protecting topsoil, they made the land more vulnerable to drought.

4. farmers—faced crop surpluses, low prices, high costs, and dust storms; many lost their farms and had to relocate; farmworkers—faced fierce competition for jobs, job loss, and even deportation

5. Answers will vary but students might mention that the image of the woman's tired, worn face and the sad children looking away from the camera would have created sympathy for farmers.

452

The Agricultural New Deal

In 1935 the federal government addressed some of the problems that migrant workers and tenant farmers faced. The Resettlement Administration (RA) helped farm laborers to resettle in areas with better land. In July 1937 the RA became part of the **Farm Security Administration** (FSA). The FSA was created to increase farm ownership. It issued long-term loans at low interest rates so tenants and sharecroppers could buy farms. The FSA also set up camps to provide shelter and medical care for migrant workers.

Dorothea Lange's Migrant Mother *captures this woman's determination to survive the depression.*

In addition, the FSA hired photographers and filmmakers to create a record of rural life. FSA photographer Dorothea Lange wanted to use her camera "to register the things about these people that were more important than how poor they were—their pride, their strength, their spirit." Lange's photograph *Migrant Mother* is one of the most famous images of the Great Depression. Other FSA photographers included Margaret Bourke-White and Gordon Parks. Pare Lorentz produced two documentary films, *The Plow That Broke the Plains* and *The River,* that showed the need for New Deal agricultural programs.

Other New Deal agricultural reforms focused more on the land than the people who worked it. The Soil Conservation Act of 1935 encouraged farmers to use new grasses and crops. It also established rain-conservation programs to protect the soil. A second Agricultural Adjustment Act (AAA) was passed in 1938. It allowed for payments to farmers who voluntarily restricted the number of acres in use. The AAA also placed limits on the amount of certain goods that could be marketed. It provided for storage of surpluses and for loans to farmers based on the value of stored crops. By the late 1930s, the aims of the first and second AAA and other New Deal agricultural programs had been partly met.

SECTION 1 REVIEW

Identify and explain the significance of the following:

- **National Labor Relations Act**
- **Fair Labor Standards Act**
- **John L. Lewis**
- **Congress of Industrial Organizations**
- **sit-down strike**
- **Southern Tenant Farmers' Union**
- **Dust Bowl**
- **Farm Security Administration**
- **Dorothea Lange**

Locate and explain the importance of the following:

- **Great Plains**
- **Oklahoma**

Reading for Content Understanding

1 **Main Idea** How did the NLRA help unions?

2 **Main Idea** What new unions and labor strategies were developed in the 1930s?

3 **Geographic Diversity** *Human-Environment Interaction* How did farmers' practices contribute to the Dust Bowl?

4 **Writing** *Classifying* Imagine that you are a federal official sent to investigate the problems of farmers and farmworkers during the Great Depression. Describe the different situations of each group.

5 **Critical Thinking** *Evaluating* Look at the photograph *Migrant Mother.* Do you think this image helped the FSA achieve its goal of gaining sympathy for farmers' difficulties? Explain your answer.

OBJECTIVES

- **Describe the effects of the Great Depression on families and women.**
- **Explain how the New Deal affected American Indians.**
- **Identify New Deal efforts to help African Americans during the depression.**

FOCUS

Motivate Before Reading

Ask students to imagine that their families are living in the 1930s. Given what they know about the Great Depression, have them write short diary entries explaining the depression's effects on family life. Then explain to students that in this section they will look at hardships that families, women, American Indians, and African Americans faced during the depression.

SECTION 2

Americans Face Hard Times

Reading Focus

How did the Great Depression affect families and women?

How did the New Deal affect American Indians?

What were the New Deal's efforts to help African Americans during the depression?

Key Terms

Indian Reorganization Act

Black Cabinet

IN THE DIFFICULT DAYS of the fall of 1931, Freda Stallings gave birth to her third child, a boy. Unfortunately, her husband, Odie, had lost his job. Freda and Odie Stallings did everything they could to take care of their two older children and their new baby. Odie Stallings walked miles looking for work. He insulated their shack with newspapers. Freda and Odie often slept with their baby in between them to keep him warm. After one cold night they woke to find their infant son dead. With no money for a coffin, they buried him in a cardboard box.

During the depression, homeless Americans took shelter wherever they could.

Family Life

During the Great Depression many Americans could not afford even the basic necessities of life—food, clothing, and shelter. For help, people often turned to their families. One person recalled that "the safety net was the big families. Even though you were unemployed, there was always somebody working, and the families somehow managed to hold together." Women tried to keep their households together with little income, often relying on the proverb "Use it up, wear it out, make it do, or do without."

Some men left their families and crisscrossed the country in search of jobs. Some never returned. Selma Hannish remembered that her father left home because he "didn't make seven dollars a month to pay the rent." Men who stayed with their families often found that their traditional role as the head of the household had changed. Some women replaced their husbands as their family's main economic support because they found it a little easier to get work. Many jobs traditionally held by women, such as clerical or service positions, were not as affected by the economic downturn as industrial jobs.

Section 2 RESOURCES

PRINT

- ★ Guided Reading Strategies 15.2
- ★ Primary Source Reading 15: American Indians and the Depression
- ★ Section 2 Review, p. 456
- ★ Daily Quiz 15.2

MULTIMEDIA

- ★ *Teaching Resources CD–ROM,* Lesson 15.2
- ★ *American Music Audio CD Program:* "He's Got the Whole World in His Hands"

SHELTERED ENGLISH

- ★ Main Idea Activities for Reteaching and Sheltered English 15.2

Introduce Key Terms

Linguistic, Logical-Mathematical. Review this section's key terms with students. Have students use context cues to define each term. Then ask students to write a question for each term that they think the section will answer. Have students answer their questions as they read the section. **SHELTERED ENGLISH**

TEACH

Have students read Section 2 and complete Guided Reading Strategies 15.2. Choose one or more of the following activities to explore the section content with students. For further suggestions on block scheduling or team teaching, see the *Block Scheduling Handbook.*

LEVEL 1: Linguistic. (Suggested time: 15 min.) As a class, go over students' Guided Reading Strategies. Then use the Reading Focus questions to highlight the main ideas of the section. **SHELTERED ENGLISH**

ALL LEVELS: Linguistic, Visual-Spatial. (Suggested time: 30 min.) Have students create a chart that has four columns and two rows. Tell students to label the columns *Families, Women, American Indians,* and *African Americans* and the rows *Problems* and *Solutions*. Have students complete the chart. In the *Solutions*

Biography

Frances Perkins. As secretary of labor, Perkins played a significant role in the New Deal. She helped write the Social Security Act and the Fair Labor Standards Act, among other laws. Although her antibusiness stance made her unpopular with Congress, industrialists, and the press, President Roosevelt relied strongly on her.

Activity: Have students use the library and other resources to find information on Frances Perkins and then write a brief biography of her life and accomplishments.

Cultural Diversity

Opposition to the Indian Reorganization Act. Although more than 70 percent of American Indian tribes voted to accept the Indian Reorganization Act, many people and groups objected to it. The Indian Rights Association objected to the act because it continued to segregate American Indian communities and eliminated the Bureau of Indian Affairs. Some members of Congress from western states objected to it because they feared land developers would buy up tribal lands.

Critical Thinking: Why might many American Indians have supported the act?

ANSWER: It returned some land to tribes.

Biography

Frances Perkins

Born in 1882 in Boston, Massachusetts, Frances Perkins grew up in a middle-class family. She earned a degree from Mount Holyoke College in chemistry and physics. In her senior year, she heard Florence Kelley of the National Consumers' League speak. Perkins later said that Kelley "first opened my mind to the necessity for and the possibility of work which became my vocation."

As a social worker, Perkins held a variety of positions, including one with the National Consumers' League and one as New York's industrial commissioner. When President Roosevelt offered to appoint her as his secretary of labor, she hesitated. Then she remembered her grandmother's advice: "If anybody opens a door, one should always go through." During her 12 years as secretary of labor, Perkins gained the respect of labor leaders.

Women in the Depression

Many married working women faced public hostility. One magazine editor's solution to end the depression was: "Simply fire the women, who shouldn't be working anyway, and hire the men. Presto! No unemployment. . . . No depression." In some cases, the government discriminated against women. For example, 26 states introduced legislation to prohibit married women from working. The U.S. government decided that only one member of a family could work in the federal civil service. As a result, thousands of women resigned from the civil service because they generally earned less than their husbands.

Many relief programs covered only men or families, so the depression hit single women particularly hard. For example, in 1934 there were some 75,000 homeless, single women in New York City. With no shelters available to them, these women often rode the subways all night.

African American and Hispanic women also faced hardships. Many who held domestic service jobs lost them to white women who were now looking for work. The percentage of African American women with jobs fell more than 12 percent during the 1930s.

Some New Deal programs offered relief to women. The Works Progress Administration (WPA) employed large numbers of women. Two WPA teachers in San Antonio, Texas, wrote First Lady Eleanor Roosevelt:

> **"Just when all seemed lost . . . this Adult Educational Program came, providing us with a means of livelihood, a ladder up which we could climb again to patriotism and self-respect."**

In addition to helping women through New Deal programs, President Roosevelt appointed many women to important positions at the federal level. He appointed Frances Perkins secretary of labor and made Florence Allen the first female federal court judge. In 1933 Ruth Bryan Owen became the first American woman appointed to an important diplomatic position. Mary Dewson, head of the Women's Division of the Democratic National Committee, used her position to encourage more federal appointments for women.

New Programs for American Indians

For American Indians, the New Deal brought programs designed to improve tribal life. Indians suffered from the deepest and most widespread poverty of any group in the United States in the early 1930s. They had a short life expectancy and squares, students also should state whether each solution was successful. When students have finished, call on volunteers to share their work. **SHELTERED ENGLISH**

LEVEL 3: Linguistic, Logical-Mathematical. (Suggested time: 30 min. plus homework) Ask students to imagine that they have been hired by a local group to recommend ways to help American Indians and African Americans during the depression. Ask students to create a pamphlet that identifies problems these groups faced, outlines possible solutions, and explains how these actions would help.

CLOSE

Linguistic, Musical-Rhythmic. Have students write their own versions of a blues song called *The Hard Times Blues.* Students' songs should consider how the Great Depression affected various segments of the U.S. population and how the government attempted to address each segment's problems. Encourage students who play instruments to put their songs to music. Call on volunteers to perform their songs for the class.

a death rate about twice that of the white population. Social worker and educator John Collier hoped to change these disturbing statistics.

Collier was appointed commissioner of the Bureau of Indian Affairs in 1933. He planned to reverse the Dawes Act and end what he called "a huge white land grab, . . . a blow, meant to be fatal, at Indian tribal existence." The **Indian Reorganization Act** (IRA) was passed in June 1934. It ended land allotment to individual Indians and allowed some lands to be returned to tribal ownership. The IRA also organized reservation tribes into self-governing bodies. The tribes had to write constitutions for their new governments and submit them to the federal government for approval.

Unlike previous treaties, the IRA required that Indian tribes vote to accept the act before it would go into effect. Many tribes rejected the legislation. The Navajo expressed a common sentiment: "We Indians don't think it is right for Collier to tell us we should govern ourselves, and then tell us how to do it." Other tribes felt differently:

> **"We have been led by the white people for 122 years since the white people came into this country. . . . We have no voice in anything. . . . Let us try a new deal. It can not be any worse than what it has been."**

More than 70 percent of the tribes voted to accept the IRA. This act restored some land to Indian tribes and generally improved the federal government's treatment of American Indians.

The signing of the Indian Reorganization Act

African Americans in the Depression

The Great Depression increased the economic problems of black workers. They typically had received lower wages than white workers. Poet Langston Hughes observed that "the depression brought everybody down a peg or two. And the Negroes had but a few pegs to fall."

New Deal Programs

Like women, African Americans were often the last ones hired and the first to be fired. African Americans worked in fields particularly hard hit by the depression. These industries included construction, lumber, unskilled manufacturing, and mining. Elmer Thomas, a black stockyard worker, argued that more African Americans lost their jobs because white laborers needed jobs. Thomas said, "They were hiring young, white boys, sixteen and eighteen years old, raw kids, didn't know a thing."

Hundreds of thousands of African Americans received relief and work from New Deal programs. In particular, the Federal Emergency Relief Administration and the Works Progress Administration offered aid. The Farm Security Administration began to employ some African Americans in supervisory positions. The aid many African Americans received from New Deal programs was more assistance than they had ever received from the federal government. Even the minimum WPA wages were much more than what many African Americans had been earning.

However, some African Americans said that the New Deal programs were discriminatory. Professor Ralph Bunche noted that for African Americans the New Deal meant "the same thing, but more of it." For example, black men in the Civilian Conservation Corps worked in units segregated from white men. The National Industrial Recovery Act (NIRA) established industrial codes that allowed employers to pay African Americans lower wages. In May 1935 President Roosevelt issued an executive order banning discrimination on WPA projects.

Economic Development

African Americans and the Depression. In 1932 an estimated one third of all African Americans were unemployed, and another third were underemployed. During the Great Depression, businesses in some urban centers, including more than 60 percent of Manhattan's hotels, refused to hire any African Americans. For those who could find jobs, the average pay for a day's work declined dramatically. In the North, for example, the income of African American skilled workers declined by nearly 50 percent. Many black men were forced to leave their homes and families to look for work.

Activity: Ask students to use the library and other resources to find employment figures for African Americans. Have students create a bar graph showing these figures in 10-year intervals from 1930 to the present.

CHALLENGE AND EXTEND

Linguistic, Logical-Mathematical. Have students use the library and other resources to research an organization or law discussed in this section. Ask students to write an evaluation of the organization or law they chose. Students should consider its purpose and overall impact on the group it was designed to assist.

REVIEW

Logical-Mathematical. Have students complete the Section Review questions. Then have students discuss the answers to each of the section's Reading Focus questions.

ASSESS

Have students complete Daily Quiz 15.2.

RETEACH

Logical-Mathematical, Visual-Spatial. Have students complete Main Idea Activities for Reteaching and Sheltered English 15.2. Organize the class into four groups. Assign each group one of the following: families, women, American Indians, or African Americans. Ask each group to create a poster showing problems the assigned group faced and attempts to solve them. Have each group explain its poster. **SHELTERED ENGLISH**

Section 2 Review ANSWERS

Identify:
For significance, see the following pages:

- Mary Dewson, p. 454
- Indian Reorganization Act, p. 455
- Black Cabinet, p.456
- Mary McLeod Bethune, p. 456
- Robert Weaver, p. 456
- Marian Anderson, p. 456

Reading for Content Understanding

1. Working women faced public hostility and often were fired and replaced with male workers; some states introduced legislation that prohibited married women from working; many families broke up when husbands left in search of work.

2. It returned some lands to tribal ownership, organized reservation tribes into self-governing bodies, and required tribes to write constitutions.

3. Hundreds of thousands of African Americans received relief and work as a result of New Deal legislation.

4. Answers will vary but students' articles should describe problems mentioned in this section.

5. Answers will vary but students might mention that achieving greater political power gave these groups a stronger political voice with which to fight discrimination and provided successful role models to others.

Multimedia Resources

American Music Audio CD Program: "He's Got the Whole World in His Hands"

Roosevelt's Record

Roosevelt sought the advice of African American leaders on matters ranging from economics to education. He appointed so many African Americans to significant government positions that they made up an unofficial **Black Cabinet**. Members of the Black Cabinet such as Mary McLeod Bethune and Robert Weaver met informally to discuss how the government could help African Americans. At the group's first meeting, Bethune urged all present to "think in terms as a 'whole' for the greatest service of our people." Many members also advised the Democratic Party on issues important to African Americans.

Despite his efforts to include African Americans in New Deal programs, Roosevelt did not support a federal antilynching law introduced in 1935. The president feared political backlash from white southern Democrats. Roosevelt needed their support in order to get his New Deal legislation passed. As he explained privately to NAACP supporters of the bill:

> **"I've got to get legislation passed by Congress to save America. . . . If I come out for the anti-lynching bill now, they [southern congressional leaders] will block every bill I ask Congress to pass to keep America from collapsing. I just can't take that risk."**

Mary McLeod Bethune urged the federal government to do more for African Americans during the depression.

Congress never passed the antilynching law. Nevertheless, Roosevelt received more than 75 percent of the African American vote in the 1936 presidential election. As one person explained, "It was not civil rights, it was jobs" that persuaded many African Americans to support Roosevelt.

First Lady Eleanor Roosevelt publicly supported minority rights. She and Bethune met regularly to discuss civil rights issues to bring to the president's attention. In 1939, members of the patriotic organization Daughters of the American Revolution (DAR) refused to allow Marian Anderson, a world-famous African American singer, to use their hall for a concert. The first lady resigned from the DAR in protest. With her support, Anderson performed at the Lincoln Memorial in March 1939 in front of 75,000 people. The concert was also broadcast nationwide. For many Americans, the event signified a bright spot. Bethune called it "a story of hope for tomorrow—a story of triumph—a story of pulling together—[a] story of splendor and real democracy."

SECTION 2 REVIEW

Identify and explain the significance of the following:

- **Mary Dewson**
- **Indian Reorganization Act**
- **Black Cabinet**
- **Mary McLeod Bethune**
- **Robert Weaver**
- **Marian Anderson**

Reading for Content Understanding

1 **Main Idea** What were the effects of the Great Depression on families and women?

2 **Main Idea** How did the Indian Reorganization Act change American Indian life?

3 **Cultural Diversity** How were African Americans affected by the New Deal?

4 **Writing** *Informing* Imagine that you are a reporter during the depression. Write an article noting how the depression and the New Deal changed living situations for a white farm family, an African American family, and an American Indian family.

5 **Critical Thinking** *Drawing Conclusions* Do you think President Roosevelt's appointment of women and African Americans to government positions helped them fight discrimination in society? Explain your answer.

OBJECTIVES

- Identify ways that the arts reflected Americans' experiences during the depression.
- Explain how government programs helped support the arts during the Great Depression.
- Describe how Americans entertained themselves during the depression.

FOCUS

Motivate Before Reading

Ask students to name some things they do to lift their spirits when they are down. Point out answers related to the arts and entertainment, such as going to see a movie or sports event. Explain that in this section students will learn how the arts and entertainment helped lift Americans' spirits and reflected their experiences during the Great Depression.

Arts and Entertainment

Reading Focus

How did the arts reflect Americans' experiences in the depression?

How did government programs help support the arts during the Great Depression?

How did Americans entertain themselves during the depression?

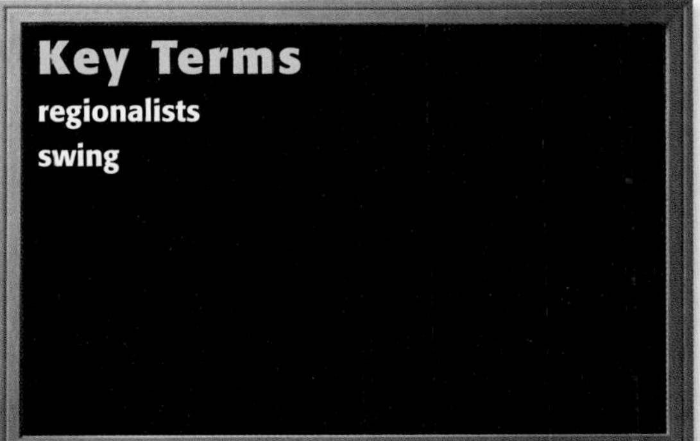

Key Terms

regionalists

swing

IN 1931 PRESIDENT HERBERT HOOVER was hoping to lift the spirits of Americans suffering through the Great Depression. "What the country needs is a good big laugh. There seems to be a condition of hysteria. If someone could get off a good joke every ten days I think our troubles would be over." Americans often turned to laughter during the depression to lighten their lives.

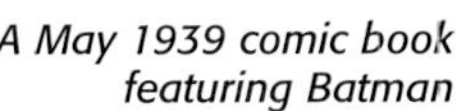

A May 1939 comic book featuring Batman

The Arts

Depression-era readers turned to detective stories and newly printed comic books to escape their woes. Superman, the Lone Ranger, Batman, and Wonder Woman all made their appearances in the 1930s. Popular magazines included *Family Circle*, *Life*, and *Time*.

Literature

Paperback books, designed to appeal to readers with limited budgets, were published in large quantities. The first ones cost 25 cents. One of the most popular books was Margaret Mitchell's novel *Gone With the Wind*. Many Americans left their own troubles behind and followed those of Scarlett O'Hara, the main character. In the best-seller, O'Hara, a once wealthy woman raised on a southern plantation, struggles to rebuild her family's fortune after the Civil War. Many readers identified with O'Hara's determination to triumph over hard times.

The pre–Civil War South was a popular setting for many other novels. William Faulkner created a mythical Mississippi county, Yoknapatawpha, to use as a setting for 14 novels and many short stories. From 1929 to 1942 Faulkner published

Section 3 RESOURCES

PRINT

- ★ Guided Reading Strategies 15.3
- ★ Literature Reading 15: *Let Us Now Praise Famous Men*
- ★ Section 3 Review, p. 461
- ★ Daily Quiz 15.3

MULTIMEDIA

- ★ *Teaching Resources CD–ROM*, Lesson 15.3
- ★ Art in American History Transparency 30: *Parson Weems' Fable* and Transparency 32: *Sugaring Off*
- ★ Everyday Life in America Transparency 23: The 1936 Olympic Games and Transparency 24: America's Darling: Shirley Temple, 1930s

SHELTERED ENGLISH

- ★ Main Idea Activities for Reteaching and Sheltered English 15.3

Introduce Key Terms

Linguistic, Logical-Mathematical. Review this section's key terms with students. Have them use context cues to determine the meaning of each key term. When students are finished, ask them to write a paragraph explaining how each term relates to the arts or entertainment. Finally, have students write in their notebooks definitions for each term. **SHELTERED ENGLISH**

TEACH

Have students read Section 3 and complete Guided Reading Strategies 15.3. Choose one or more of the following activities to explore the section content with students. For further suggestions on block scheduling or team teaching, see the *Block Scheduling Handbook.*

LEVEL 1: Linguistic. (Suggested time: 15 min.) As a class, go over students' Guided Reading Strategies. Then use the Reading Focus questions to highlight the main ideas of the section. **SHELTERED ENGLISH**

Using Visual Resources

American Gothic. Artist Grant Wood's realistic, and at times somewhat satirical, style in depicting American scenes is apparent in his painting *American Gothic,* seen on this page. Done in 1930, the painting captures the strength of personality of a proud, midwestern farm couple. Born and raised in Iowa, Wood knew his subject well. The couples' somber expressions reflect the seriousness and struggle of rural life. The man's deeply lined face shows the rigors of a life spent working the fields under a strong Iowa sun. At the same time, Wood surrounds the two hard-set faces with an idealistic farm scene. For the famous couple in the painting, Wood used his sister and his dentist.

Critical Thinking: Why do you think Wood has the man holding a pitchfork?

ANSWER: Answers will vary but students might mention that the man holds the tool as a symbol of his life and work and his pride in it.

Multimedia Resources

Art in American History Transparency 30: *Parson Weems' Fable* and Transparency 32: *Sugaring Off*

The Granger Collection, New York

William Faulkner

eight novels, including *The Sound and the Fury* and *Absalom, Absalom!* His characters confront issues of plantation life, slavery, and the Civil War. One character asks a southerner to "tell about the South. What's it like there. What do they do there. Why do they live there." In 1950 Faulkner received a Nobel Prize in literature.

Poet Robert Frost wrote about rural New England. He received the Pulitzer Prize four times for his poetry. Laura Ingalls Wilder also wrote about regional issues. Between 1932 and 1942 Wilder published a series of books about her childhood, including *Little House in the Big Woods* and *Little House on the Prairie.* Readers enjoyed her tales of surviving blizzards, grasshopper plagues, illness, and debt.

Other authors, such as James T. Farrell and John Dos Passos, wrote about the economic and social troubles of the Great Depression. Writer James Agee and Farm Security Administration photographer Walker Evans lived with sharecroppers in Alabama for about six weeks in 1936. From their experiences, they produced a nonfiction account of the lives of three families in *Let Us Now Praise Famous Men.* These books helped Americans realize that others shared in their economic difficulties.

Depression-Era Painting

Some visual artists helped Americans become more aware of the beauty of their nation. Painters who sought inspiration from regional customs and folk themes became known as the **regionalists**. They included Thomas Hart Benton, John Steuart Curry, and Grant Wood. Benton explained that art for the regionalists meant "American life as known and felt by ordinary Americans." Benton and Wood painted scenes of rural people at work. Curry's subjects were often American folk legends and history.

Other well-known artists of the 1930s included Edward Hopper, who painted realistic scenes of urban life. Anna "Grandma" Moses, in her seventies during the 1930s, became famous for painting images of what she called "old-timey" farm life.

Helping Artists

Unemployment hit actors, dancers, and other artists particularly hard. Critic Malcolm Cowley commented, "If we want to have poets in this country, we will have to keep them alive." One artist sent a plea to the government: "Kind of work: will accept any position. Salary: Enough to make a living on. At Present: Broke." The Roosevelt administration created several programs to help artists.

Federal arts projects, like the Works Progress Administration's Federal Project One, allowed many artists to continue practicing their craft. As writer Ralph Ellison noted, "Actually to be *paid* for writing . . . why that was a wonderful thing!" John Steinbeck wrote *The Grapes of Wrath* based on his Federal Writers' Project experiences. Richard Wright published an essay in a WPA collection of writings that provided the basis for his autobiographical work *Black Boy.* Painters, including Jacob Lawrence, used WPA-sponsored workshops and training to learn and improve their art. Lawrence later produced paintings of famous African Americans. The WPA's success guaranteed future generations of artists.

Grant Wood's painting American Gothic *reflects the hardworking spirit of many farm families.*

ALL LEVELS: Linguistic, Visual-Spatial, Interpersonal. (Suggested time: 45 min. plus homework) Organize students into groups. Have each group create a 2-page spread for a 1930s newspaper section covering the arts and entertainment. Groups should fill the section with small advertisements, announcements, and reviews for current and upcoming concerts, movies, art exhibits, book signings, and sports events. The spread also should include information for artists on government programs supporting the arts. Each student should create two or more items. Groups then should work together to design and lay out their spreads. When students are through, have them examine and comment on each others' work. **SHELTERED ENGLISH**

LEVEL 3: Linguistic, Interpersonal, Intrapersonal. (Suggested time: 45 min. plus homework) Ask students to imagine that they are writers in the 1930s. Have them write the script for a short story to be broadcast over the radio. The story should describe some events in the life of a typical American family of the 1930s. The story should reflect some common experiences of the time as well as being lighthearted enough to entertain a 1930s audience and help them forget some of their troubles. Have volunteers perform one story for the class. Finally, lead a discussion on how the arts reflected Americans' experiences in the depression.

 Moving Music

When many Americans wanted to be entertained, they listened to music. Jazz remained popular during the Great Depression. Count Basie, Duke Ellington, Benny Goodman, and other big-band leaders helped develop a new style of jazz called **swing**. Fletcher Henderson was an important composer and arranger of swing music. Swing musicians played in groups larger than most jazz groups in the 1920s. Swing also involved more written music than spontaneous compositions.

Bandleader Duke Ellington (front left) successfully blended the sounds and talents of his musicians.

The term *swing* became commonly used after Ellington's hit "It Don't Mean a Thing (If It Ain't Got That Swing)," recorded in February 1932. Millions of Americans forgot their troubles, at least briefly, while dancing to the fast-paced rhythms of swing music. Swing dancers became known as jitterbugs. Goodman, who was called the King of Swing, described the dancers as

> **"bugs, literally glued to the music, [who] would shake. . . . Their eyes popped, their heads pecked, their feet tapped out the time, arms jerked to the rhythm."**

At the height of the swing craze, many people seemed to be trying to dance their cares away.

Americans also drew inspiration and comfort from gospel, a traditional church-based form of African American music. Gospel developed from spirituals, jazz, and blues music. Singers Mahalia Jackson and Sister Rosetta Tharpe were among the best-known gospel artists of the time. They helped the music gain a wider group of listeners.

Folk music, particularly the work of singer and songwriter Woody Guthrie, was also very popular. Born in Oklahoma, Guthrie traveled and performed throughout the country during the depression. He often sang in migrant-worker camps in California. His songs were tales of loss and struggle. One song contained the line, "All along your green valley I'll work till I die"—a sad reality for some Americans.

 Movies and Radio

Many Americans also watched movies and listened to radio programs to escape the Great Depression. Despite the economic hard times, growing numbers of Americans found the money to buy movie tickets and radios. One theater owner explained that audiences wanted "the type of picture that lifts people into a happy world." They did not want "serious and sad pictures—they have too much of that at home!"

Movies

Moviegoers watched cartoons, comedies, gangster films, and westerns. The Marx Brothers' comedies made Americans laugh. Many others were amazed by Walt Disney's first full-length animated feature, *Snow White and the Seven Dwarfs.* Musicals also became popular as producers mastered the talkie. Dancers Fred Astaire and Ginger Rogers began their long-time association in the film *Flying Down to Rio.* Other popular movie stars included James Cagney, Marlene Dietrich, Greta Garbo, James Stewart, and John Wayne.

Fred Astaire and Ginger Rogers danced together in many movies.

The Granger Collection, New York

Linking Past to Present

Woody Guthrie's Music. More than 60 years after Woody Guthrie first became popular as a folk singer, his works are still being reinterpreted by modern musicians. In 1995 Guthrie's daughter, Nora, approached British musician Billy Bragg and asked him to write music to accompany the lyrics of some newly rediscovered Guthrie songs. Bragg teamed up with members of an American folk-rock band known as Wilco to rework some of the songs. The resulting compact disc, *Mermaid Avenue*, was released in 1998. It was named after the street where Guthrie lived in Brooklyn, New York, following World War II. After receiving much critical acclaim, the CD was nominated in 1998 as the year's best contemporary folk album.

Critical Thinking: Why might Woody Guthrie's lyrics still be popular today?

ANSWER: Answers will vary but students might mention that people still can relate to Guthrie's themes of loss and struggle.

CLOSE

Linguistic, Musical-Rhythmic, Visual-Spatial. Have students discuss how government programs helped support the arts during the Great Depression. Then ask students to imagine that they are artists in the 1930s. Have them either create a work of art, compose a song, or write a poem that expresses their gratitude to the government for helping them.

CHALLENGE AND EXTEND

Linguistic, Logical-Mathematical. Have students use the library and other resources to compare and contrast popular art, books, movies, music, and spectator sports of the depression era to those of today. Have students create a bulletin board that illustrates the popular arts and entertainment of each period. When students are finished, have them discuss their findings. Then have each student write an essay comparing and contrasting the arts and entertainment of the 1930s to those of today. Call on volunteers to share their essays with the class.

REVIEW

Linguistic, Visual-Spatial. Have students complete the Section Review questions. Then have students create graphic organizers

Across the Curriculum

LITERATURE

Gone With the Wind. Margaret Mitchell almost did not give her book *Gone With the Wind* to a publisher. Then one of her friends, on hearing that Mitchell had written a book, refused to believe it and claimed Mitchell did not take life seriously enough to have penned a novel. This claim motivated Mitchell to give her book to an agent. The novel became a publishing phenomenon, selling as many as 50,000 copies in one day and winning her a Pulitzer Prize. Mitchell sold the movie rights for $50,000—the most ever paid at the time. Although her novel focuses on the white South, Mitchell was involved in the African American community in Atlanta, where she volunteered in clinics and donated tuition money to medical students at Morehouse College.

Critical Thinking: Why might Mitchell have been hesitant to give her book to a publisher?

ANSWER: She may have felt that since it was her first novel it was not good enough.

Multimedia Resources

Everyday Life in America Transparency 23: The 1936 Olympic Games and Transparency 24: America's Darling: Shirley Temple, 1930s

Many Americans bought Shirley Temple dolls like this one made in the 1930s.

Katharine Hepburn also made her first movie appearance in the 1930s. She won an Academy Award for Best Actress in 1934 for her role in *Morning Glory*. She became one of the nation's greatest actors. She received a fourth Academy Award in 1982 at the age of 75.

Child actor Shirley Temple was the top box-office draw in Hollywood from 1935 to 1938. Most of her movies earned more than $5 million each. In 1934 she appeared in her first starring role, *Stand Up and Cheer.* She was only five years old. Temple danced and sang in many more movies.

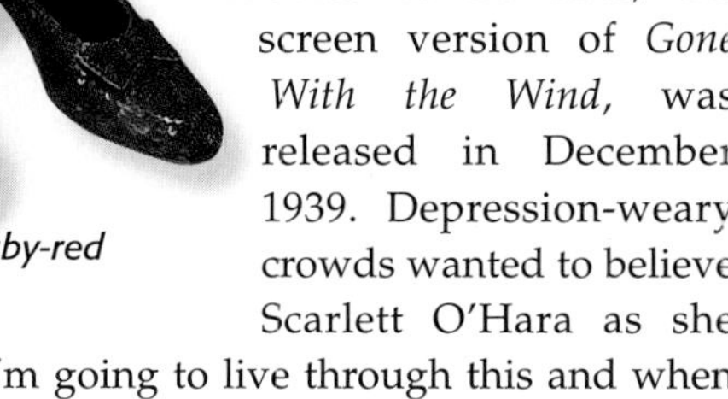

Dorothy's ruby-red slippers

One of the most popular movies of all time, the screen version of *Gone With the Wind*, was released in December 1939. Depression-weary crowds wanted to believe Scarlett O'Hara as she vowed, "I'm going to live through this and when it's all over, I'll never be hungry again!" The *Wizard of Oz* was another popular movie released that year. It told the story of Dorothy, a young girl swept away by a tornado from her home in Kansas. She ended up in the magical land of Oz, where she met many interesting characters.

Despite the great economic difficulties of the 1930s, each week an estimated 90 million Americans scraped together the 25 to 35 cents needed for a ticket to the movies. By September 1939 there were some 17,000 movie theaters in more than 9,000 towns. That meant there

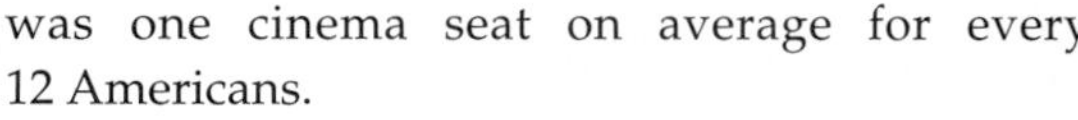

was one cinema seat on average for every 12 Americans.

Radio

Even more Americans listened to radio programs. As many as 97 million Americans, out of a population of almost 129 million, listened to a family-owned radio in 1938. By the 1930s there were many popular radio series, including comedies such as *The Jack Benny Show,* mysteries like *The Shadow,* and soap operas like *The Guiding Light.* Soap operas got their name from the fact that so many of the original advertising sponsors were soap companies.

Listeners also tuned in regularly to shows such as *Little Orphan Annie* and *The Lone Ranger.* Will Rogers hosted a popular radio show during the early days of the depression. On one program he joked about one cause of the depression—installment buying: "We'll show the world we are prosperous, even if we have to go broke to do it."

On the night of October 30, 1938, many radio listeners heard their program cut off by a special "news" bulletin. The "correspondent" sobbed,

> **"Ladies and gentleman, this is the most terrifying thing I have ever witnessed. . . . There, I can see the thing's body. It's large as a bear and it glistens like wet leather. . . . The eyes are black and gleam like a serpent."**

Listeners heard that strange vehicles were landing in New Jersey and that martians were coming out of them. CBS had said at the beginning of the program that the show was fictional. However, many listeners tuned in late and panicked. One man recalled, "I don't know what I did exactly, but I know I prayed harder and more earnest than ever before." The panic created by Orson Welles's *War of the Worlds* radio production was one demonstration of the influence of radio.

Gone With the Wind made Clark Gable and Vivien Leigh international movie stars.

listing the popular forms of the arts and entertainment in the 1930s; identifying some popular works or people associated with each form; and, where applicable, explaining how each form reflected Americans' experiences in the depression and how the government supported each form of entertainment. Call on volunteers to share their organizers with the class.

ASSESS

Have students complete Daily Quiz 15.3.

RETEACH

Logical-Mathematical, Visual-Spatial. Have students complete Main Idea Activities for Reteaching and Sheltered English 15.3. Have students list the popular arts and entertainment in the 1930s across the side of a piece of paper. Then ask students to write each term and name in the Identify portion of the Section Review under its associated form of entertainment. Finally, have students identify the specific type of the arts or entertainment associated with each name in the list. **SHELTERED ENGLISH**

Spectator Sports

The popularity of radio helped some spectator sports survive during the Great Depression. In the early 1930s attendance at sporting events fell. However, fans kept up with their favorite teams by listening to their games on the radio. When the economy improved, fans went back to the ball parks. Minor league and Negro League baseball attracted more people to their games by offering something new. They began to play games at night, when more people could attend.

New York Yankee manager Joe McCarthy (right) presents Lou Gehrig (left) with a trophy on "Lou Gehrig Day."

Baseball stars of the 1930s included Dizzy Dean, Lou Gehrig, and Satchel Paige. Gehrig, known as the Iron Horse, played in 2,130 consecutive games. His streak, which started in 1925, ended 14 years later. Two months after his retirement, the New York Yankees honored Gehrig. He was dying from a rare muscle disease. He told the crowd:

> **"Fans, for the past two weeks you have been reading about a bad break I got. Yet today I consider myself the luckiest man on the face of the earth."**

Many other athletes made their mark in the 1930s. Helen Wills continued to dominate women's tennis. Mildred "Babe" Didrikson Zaharias conquered almost all other women's sports. She played basketball and won Olympic medals in the javelin and hurdle events. Zaharias then turned to playing golf, where she was also successful. She said her childhood ambition "was to be the greatest athlete who ever lived."

African American track star Jesse Owens challenged Didrikson for that title. Owens was a sprinter and long jumper. On a single day in 1935, he broke five world records and tied one. The next year at the 1936 Olympic Games in Berlin, Germany, Owens won four gold medals. For many Americans, watching these athletes was a wonderful escape from their problems during the depression.

SECTION 3 REVIEW

Identify and explain the significance of the following:

- **Margaret Mitchell**
- **William Faulkner**
- **regionalists**
- **Thomas Hart Benton**
- **Duke Ellington**
- **Benny Goodman**
- **swing**
- **Woody Guthrie**
- **Shirley Temple**
- **Lou Gehrig**
- **Mildred Didrikson Zaharias**
- **Jesse Owens**

Reading for Content Understanding

1. **Main Idea** In what ways did artists focus on American life during the Great Depression?
2. **Main Idea** What forms of entertainment did Americans turn to in the 1930s?
3. **Economic Development** How did government programs support artists during the depression?
4. **Writing** *Expressing* Imagine that you are a folk singer like Woody Guthrie. Write the lyrics for a song that expresses how the depression has affected you.
5. **Critical Thinking** *Evaluating* What role do you think art and entertainment should play during a national economic crisis? Explain your answer in a brief paragraph.

Section 3 Review ANSWERS

Identify

For significance, see the following pages:

- Margaret Mitchell, p. 457
- William Faulkner, p. 457
- regionalists, p. 458
- Thomas Hart Benton, p. 458
- Duke Ellington, p. 459
- Benny Goodman, p. 459
- swing, p. 459
- Woody Guthrie, p. 459
- Shirley Temple, p. 460
- Lou Gehrig, p. 461
- Mildred Didrikson Zaharias, p. 461
- Jesse Owens, p. 461

Reading for Content Understanding

1. by showing people's struggles during the depression and by illustrating Americans' experiences and hardships in other periods

2. Americans turned to art, literature, movies, music, radio, and spectator sports.

3. The WPA's Federal Project One enabled many artists and writers to continue working and to get paid. It also sponsored workshops that helped artists develop their skills.

4. Lyrics will vary but students might mention difficulty getting work and how thankful they are for any work they can get.

5. Answers will vary. Some students may suggest that the arts and entertainment should be used to make people feel better, while others may argue that funds used to support the arts and entertainment should instead be used to revive businesses and provide relief.

SECTION 4 LESSON PLAN

OBJECTIVES

- Describe ways that the Good Neighbor policy differed from previous U.S. policies toward Latin America.
- Explain the rise of dictators in European nations.
- Identify ways the United States responded to events in Europe and Asia in the 1930s.

FOCUS

Motivate Before Reading

Ask students to list qualities that they would want in a leader during a time of crisis. Discuss these qualities with the class. Then tell students that in this section they will learn how strong leaders gained power in some European nations during the Great Depression, and how these leaders often ruled as dictators and ignored human rights.

Section 4
RESOURCES

PRINT
- ★ Guided Reading Strategies 15.4
- ★ Graphic Organizer 15: The Great Depression Touches Everyone
- ★ Section 4 Review, p.467
- ★ Daily Quiz 15.4

MULTIMEDIA
- ★ *Teaching Resources CD–ROM*, Lesson 15.4
- ★ Everyday Life in America Transparency 25: The Rise of the Third Reich, 1930s
- ★ HRW Web site

SHELTERED ENGLISH
- ★ Main Idea Activities for Reteaching and Sheltered English 15.4

The Depression Abroad

Reading Focus

How did the Good Neighbor policy differ from previous U.S. foreign policies toward Latin America?

Why did dictators rise to power in certain European nations?

How did the United States respond to events in Europe and Asia in the 1930s?

Key Terms

Good Neighbor policy
totalitarianism
Blackshirts
fascism
Nazis
Axis Powers
Kristallnacht
Neutrality Acts

IN 1930 MANY COFFEE FARMERS in the tiny Central American country of El Salvador decided not to pick their crop. According to one observer, "The country became permeated [filled] with the sick-sweet smell of rotting coffee fruits." There was nothing wrong with the crop. In fact, coffee was one of the country's main crops and sources of income. The berries were left to rot because the price of coffee was so low that harvesting the crop was not worth the farmers' time or money.

Coffee beans

The Depression in Latin America

The Great Depression took a heavy toll on the people and governments of Latin America. The situation in El Salvador was typical of many Latin American countries. As a U.S. diplomat explained:

> **"Roughly 90 percent of the wealth of the country is held by about one-half of one percent of the population. . . . The [rest of the] population has practically nothing."**

President Roosevelt's Latin American policy was to make the United States a "good neighbor—the neighbor who . . . respects the rights of others—the neighbor who respects his obligations and . . . his agreements." As part of his **Good Neighbor policy**, Roosevelt recognized that the United States "cannot merely take, but must also give." The Good Neighbor policy included a plan to increase economic aid to the nations of Latin America. The U.S. government also negotiated new trade agreements with many Latin American countries. For many of these countries, the United States was their most important trading partner.

INTRODUCE KEY TERMS

Linguistic, Logical-Mathematical. Review this section's key terms with students. Ask students to use the text to write a definition for each term. Then have each student create a crossword puzzle that has the definitions as clues and the terms as the answers. Once students have finished, have them exchange puzzles, complete them, and return them to the authors for grading. Finally, have students correct any incorrect answers.
SHELTERED ENGLISH

TEACH

Have students read Section 4 and complete Guided Reading Strategies 15.4. Choose one or more of the following activities to explore the section content with students. For further suggestions on block scheduling or team teaching, see the *Block Scheduling Handbook.*

LEVEL 1: Linguistic. (Suggested time: 15 min.) As a class, go over students' Guided Reading Strategies. Then use the Reading Focus questions to highlight the main ideas of the section.
SHELTERED ENGLISH

For Roosevelt, the Good Neighbor policy also meant respecting the borders of Latin American nations and following a course of nonintervention. In 1934 the Roosevelt administration nullified the Platt Amendment. The United States had used this law to intervene in Cuban affairs. Roosevelt also withdrew U.S. Marines who had been stationed in Haiti.

In 1938 Mexican president Lázaro Cárdenas put Mexico's oil industry under national control. The Roosevelt administration refused to intervene on behalf of U.S. companies. Roosevelt recognized that Mexico had the right to control its own resources. After negotiations, Mexico agreed to pay the oil companies for their property. Roosevelt's nonintervention policy, along with increased trade and cultural exchanges, improved U.S. relations with Latin America.

Soviet posters supporting Stalin and his policies

Dictators in Europe

Overseas, Europeans faced the enormous task of rebuilding their shattered nations. Debts from World War I still burdened European economies when the Great Depression struck. Nations took a variety of approaches to handling the economic disaster. For example, Great Britain raised tariffs and focused on increasing domestic production. Its government remained relatively stable. However, other nations experienced political turmoil. Several countries moved toward **totalitarianism**. In this political system, the government controls every aspect of citizens' lives.

The Soviet Union

The Soviet Union had experienced economic and political troubles for years. In the late 1920s, Soviet leader Joseph Stalin introduced a Five-Year Plan. It called for the rapid industrialization of the economy, particularly in heavy industries such as iron and steel and in machinery.

Stalin also forced farmers and peasants to give up their land to work on collectives—large government-owned farms. At the time, some 80 percent of the nation's people worked on farms. If farmers refused to give up their land, Soviet officials had them killed or deported to Siberia. Several million Soviets died as a result of the Soviet policy of forced collectivization. By 1935 more than 90 percent of the country's land was organized into collectives.

Stalin's totalitarian government increasingly controlled every aspect of people's lives. According to one young Communist, "All you heard about day and night was Stalin." Stalin closed churches and had his political opponents killed. Few people knew details of what Stalin and his supporters were doing. As a result, many foreigners were impressed by Stalin's economic plan. The Soviet Union industrialized while much of the rest of the Western world suffered from the depression. The U.S. government, which had withheld official recognition since 1917, formally recognized the Soviet Union in November 1933.

Italy

Elsewhere in Europe, many Italians were bitter that their country had not received new territory in return for its efforts during World War I. Suffering from economic difficulties after the war, many Italians began to look for strong leadership. They found it in former journalist and soldier Benito Mussolini.

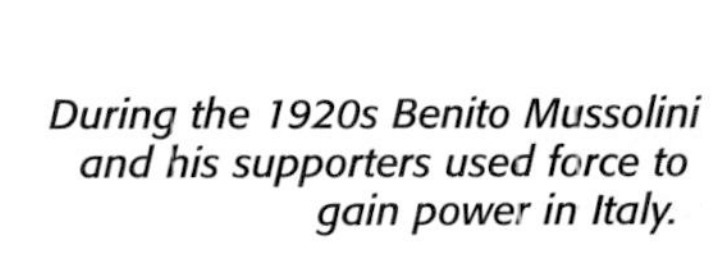
During the 1920s Benito Mussolini and his supporters used force to gain power in Italy.

Global Relations

Winning Over Latin America. President Roosevelt had a difficult time convincing Central and South American countries that the United States was willing to be a "good neighbor." In 1933 at the Pan-American Conference in Montevideo, Uruguay, the U.S. delegation found a hostile press and protesters with signs that attacked "yankee imperialism." U.S. diplomat Cordell Hull did everything he could to overcome the distrust of the diplomats from Latin America. He visited each delegation in its hotel to assure the members that the United States was committed to the Good Neighbor policy. Hull focused his efforts on one of the main opponents of the United States, Argentinean foreign minister Saavedra Lamas. To win his support, Hull incorporated Lamas's suggestions into his trade agreement. Hull achieved his goals, and thereafter U.S. relations with Latin America warmed considerably.

Critical Thinking: Why might the United States have sought to improve relations with Latin American countries during the Great Depression?

ANSWER: It needed trading partners and wanted stable international relations during economic hard times at home.

ALL LEVELS: Logical-Mathematical, Visual-Spatial. (Suggested time: 30 min.) Discuss with students President Roosevelt's Good Neighbor policy and the positive impact it had on relations with Latin America. Then have students draw a picture that explains the Good Neighbor policy to people in countries that speak other languages. **SHELTERED ENGLISH**

LEVEL 2: Linguistic, Logical-Mathematical, Intrapersonal. (Suggested time: 30 min. plus homework) Have students create headlines for significant events that took place in Europe and Asia during the 1930s. Then ask students to read their headlines to the class and discuss how the United States responded. For homework, have each student choose a headline and write an essay explaining how the United States responded to the event and stating whether he or she agrees with the response. If students disagree with how the United States responded, have them suggest alternate responses.

LEVEL 2: Linguistic, Logical-Mathematical, Visual-Spatial. (Suggested time: 45 min.) Assign each student one of the following historical figures: Adolf Hitler, Joseph Stalin, or Benito Mussolini. Ask students to create a historical comic strip illustrating their assigned individual's rise to power. Have students write short captions for each panel in their strips. Call on volunteers to explain their comic strips to the class.

Historical Sidelight

Politics as High Theater. Adolf Hitler approached politics as a form of theater. A master manipulator, he practiced his speeches before a mirror to test their visual power and drama. He photographed himself making various gestures and facial expressions to judge their impact. During speeches, he artfully lowered and raised his voice, moving from soft appeals to angry outbursts to hold his audience spellbound. Nazi rallies were designed like elaborate stage sets. Special lighting, banners, and music set the mood, and Hitler always arrived slightly late to build anticipation.

Critical Thinking: How did Hitler's knowledge of manipulation techniques help him gain power?

ANSWER: He knew how to deliver his message so as to win the German people's support.

Multimedia Resources

Everyday Life in America Transparency 25: The Rise of the Third Reich, 1930s

In 1922 Mussolini and his followers threatened to march on Rome. His supporters were known as **Blackshirts** after the color of their uniforms. Soon after, the Italian king gave Mussolini temporary dictatorial powers, which ended up lasting more than two decades. Mussolini's government was based on the political theory of **fascism**. This theory calls for a strong government headed by one individual. In fascist systems, the state—or government—is seen as more important than individuals. In accordance with this belief, the state has the duty to limit or destroy all opposition.

In October 1935 Mussolini expanded Italy's territory by invading the African nation of Ethiopia. Under Emperor Haile Selassie (HY-lee suh-LAS-ee), the Ethiopian forces fought bravely. However, they could not defend themselves against the modern weaponry of the Italian army. Italy quickly conquered Ethiopia and made it a colony. The League of Nations responded with penalties but lacked the authority to enforce them. The United States remained neutral during the conflict.

The Nazis used large, showy parades to encourage feelings of national pride and gain support.

Germany

Many Germans felt particularly bitter about the outcome of World War I. The Treaty of Versailles required Germany to pay war reparations, which crippled its economy. The Great Depression brought about its near collapse. Amid this suffering, war veteran and politician Adolf Hitler rose to power.

Hitler offered Germans a scapegoat, or someone to blame for problems. He had outlined his theories in *Mein Kampf (My Struggle)*. He wrote this book while in prison for attempting to overthrow the German government. In *Mein Kampf*, Hitler blamed intellectuals, Communists, and particularly Jews for Germany's defeat in World War I and its postwar problems. *Mein Kampf* also presented Hitler's plan for Germany's rise to regional and global power.

Hitler quickly gained a large following. In 1932 his National Socialist Party, or **Nazis**, won around 37 percent of the vote in national elections. The next year, Hitler became the chancellor of Germany. He soon seized absolute power and became a fascist dictator. He also established the Third Reich, an aggressive new German empire.

Hitler reduced Germany's unemployment and became more popular. Between March 1933 and March 1934, unemployment fell by more than 2 million. State spending helped many groups recover from the depression. German farmers, for example, received guaranteed prices for their produce. The government also funded housing and highway construction projects. One German woman who was a teenager during Hitler's rise to power explained his appeal:

> **"He promised us . . . that Germany would once again take its place in the world as a state worthy of respect. . . . So this man was not only admired but welcomed."**

Many Germans also found work in weapons factories. Hitler violated the Treaty of Versailles by rebuilding Germany's military and by moving to occupy the Rhineland, a border region in western Germany.

Hitler's plans included a campaign against Jews. The Nazis banned Jews and non-Nazis from government positions, and destroyed or seized their property. In September 1935 the government assigned Jews a lower class of citizenship. Despite these actions, Germany's capital city, Berlin, remained the site of the 1936 Olympic Games. During the Games, the German government tried to hide the evidence of its discrimination against Jews. Germany's economic accomplishments during a depression impressed many of the thousands of people in attendance at the Games.

LEVEL 3: Linguistic, Logical-Mathematical, Interpersonal. (Suggested time: 45 min.) Organize the class into two groups: one supporting U.S. intervention in Europe and Asia in the 1930s, and the other supporting a policy of isolationism. Allow groups 20 to 25 minutes to prepare their arguments by using information from the text to support their position. Then hold a debate on whether the United States should become involved in events in Europe and Asia. Make certain every student presents at least one argument. Follow up the debate with class discussion.

CLOSE

Logical-Mathematical, Interpersonal. Organize the class into two groups. Have each group create 20 questions about the section and place each one on a separate note card. When students are finished writing the questions, collect them and use them to play "Review Baseball." Start by having each team determine the order in which students wil answer questions. Then begin asking the questions. If a student answers correctly, he or she and any other base runners may advance one base. If a student answers incorrectly, it counts as an out. After three outs, have the other

After the Olympics, the German government returned to its plan for world domination. In October 1936 Germany and Italy formed a military alliance, the **Axis Powers**. In late 1936 Germany entered into a similar agreement with Japan.

The German government also revived many of its anti-Jewish activities, such as expelling Jews from all professions and from studying in universities. Jews faced increasing hardship and isolation, but the majority of them did not want to leave Germany. The Nazis, however, attempted to drive them out. On November 9, 1938, Nazis went on a rampage called ***Kristallnacht***, or the "night of broken glass." On *Kristallnacht*, Nazi mobs killed more than 90 Jews and seriously injured hundreds more. As one Jew remembered:

> **"Yesterday the synagogues burned. They burned in Germany. They burned in Austria. They burned in Czechoslovakia. . . . Most Jewish business was demolished. My synagogue was plundered [robbed]."**

The crowds demolished some 7,500 Jewish businesses and burned or destroyed nearly 200 synagogues. Violence against Jews spread throughout Germany and Austria. After *Kristallnacht* the Nazi persecution of Jews increased dramatically.

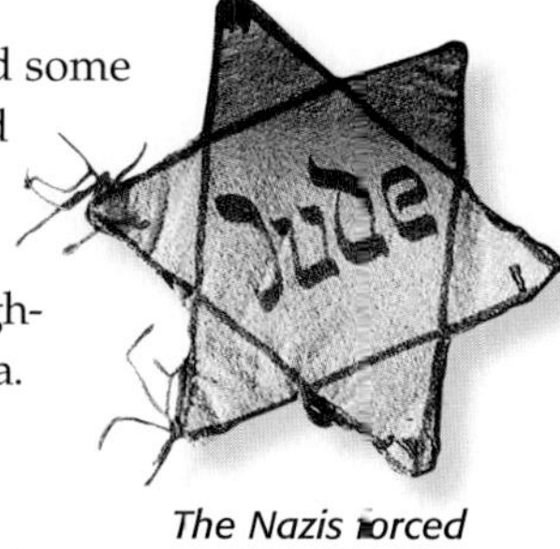

The Nazis forced Jews to wear identification patches on their clothing.

Civil War in Spain

As fascism spread through Italy and Germany, fascists also threatened to take over Spain's republican government. In July 1936 General Francisco Franco led a revolt that began three years of warfare. Germany and Italy provided Franco and his troops with military assistance. The Republicans received supplies from France, Mexico, and the Soviet Union.

Global Connections

The Spanish Civil War

The brutality of the Spanish Civil War attracted international attention. One particular event became representative of the war's viciousness. On April 26, 1937, a squadron of German aircraft flew over the tiny Spanish town of Guernica. The town hardly seemed an important strategic area. It had only one weapons plant and one bridge that might have been important for troop movement.

Nevertheless, German fighter planes bombed the town for three hours. It was market day in Guernica, so the town's population had swelled to around 10,000. More than 1,600 people were killed, and 800 others were wounded in the attack. About the only parts of the town left untouched by the bombing were the munitions plant and the bridge.

The horror of this event stunned people worldwide. The story of the town's slaughter became the focus of Spanish painter Pablo Picasso's *Guernica.* One of the most famous modern paintings, *Guernica* was displayed at the 1937 Paris World Exhibition. The painting hung in New York City's Museum of Modern Art until 1981. At Picasso's request, the museum returned the painting to Spain once democracy had been restored there.

Understanding What You Read

1. Why were so many people horrified by the events in Guernica?
2. Why do you think Pablo Picasso wanted his painting returned to Spain after democracy was restored?

Global Relations

The Spanish Civil War
President Franklin Roosevelt wanted the United States to stay out of the Spanish Civil War. By 1937 Congress had specifically outlawed selling arms to either side. Even so, some Americans still played a role in the fighting. Several large American corporations supported Franco because they feared that Communists might take over Spain if he lost. These companies sent over trucks and fuel, which had not been outlawed by Congress. Some Americans traveled to Spain to fight for the Republicans. These Americans included strong anti-Fascists, Communists, and socialists.

Activity: Have students use the library and search the Internet through the HRW Web site to find art about the Spanish Civil War. Then ask students to draw a picture for a children's book that shows the war's impact on children.

go.hrw.com
SB1 Spain

GLOBAL CONNECTIONS ANSWERS

1. because the bombing seemed to avoid military objectives and target civilians

2. perhaps to remind the Spanish people of the horrors of fascism team answer questions. At the end of the game, the team with the most runs wins.

CHALLENGE AND EXTEND

1. **Linguistic, Intrapersonal.** Have students use the library and other resources to find information about local reactions to events that occurred abroad during the Great Depression. Have each student search for an article that discusses one of the events and write a letter to an imaginary editor in response to that article. Encourage students to use reasons from the section and their research to support the positions they take in their letters. When students are finished, have volunteers read their letters to the class.

2. **Linguistic.** During the Spanish Civil War, American volunteers fought on the side of the Republicans. Have students prepare oral reports on the accomplishments of American volunteers who fought against fascism in Spain. Have each student deliver his or her report to the class.

MAP ANSWER

Beijing, Hangzhon, Lüshon, Nanjing, Shanghai, Shenyang, Tianjin

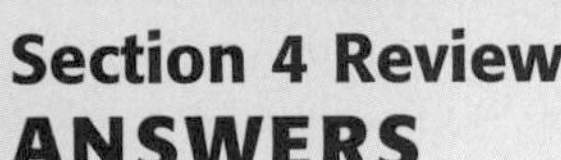

Section 4 Review ANSWERS

Identify

For significance, see the following pages:

- Good Neighbor policy, p. 462
- totalitarianism, p. 463
- Joseph Stalin, p. 463
- Benito Mussolini, p. 463
- Blackshirts, p. 464
- fascism, p. 464
- Adolf Hitler, p. 464
- Nazis, p. 464
- Axis Powers, p. 465
- *Kristallnacht,* p. 465
- Neutrality Acts, p. 467

Locate

For locations, see the map on page 466.

Reading for Content Understanding

1. He emphasized economic aid and trade agreements.

2. The United States adhered to its policy of neutrality.

3. the poor economy in many nations after World War I and the depression

4. Students in favor might argue that the United States should focus on its economy; those opposed might argue that the nation needs to act before events abroad get worse.

5. Stalin—eliminated opposition, wanted to industrialize; Mussolini—believed state was most important, wanted to gain land; Hitler—blamed problems on scapegoats, wanted to create a German empire

Many people saw the Spanish Civil War as part of a struggle to contain fascism. About 40,000 foreigners, including some 2,800 Americans, volunteered to fight with the Republicans against Franco. Novelist Ernest Hemingway drew on his experience there as a war correspondent to write *For Whom the Bell Tolls,* published in 1940. In this novel, an American character explained the importance of fighting in the war: "You believe in Life, Liberty, and the Pursuit of Happiness. . . . If this war is lost all of those things are lost."

In the spring of 1939, Republican forces disbanded. Franco's troops entered Madrid, Spain's capital, and Franco became dictator. An estimated 500,000 soldiers and civilians had died during the war.

Japan's Military Expansion

On the other side of the world, Japan also used military force to solve its economic problems. Japan's military leaders wanted to seize new territories to take control of their natural resources. They hoped to reduce Japan's reliance on foreign imports. In September 1931 Japan invaded Manchuria, in northern China. The League of Nations and the United States condemned the invasion, but neither wanted to fight a war to oppose it. By 1937 Japan occupied much of northern China.

Japan also began a massive naval buildup, which violated its pledge given at the Washington Conference in the early 1920s. The buildup upset the balance of power in the Pacific.

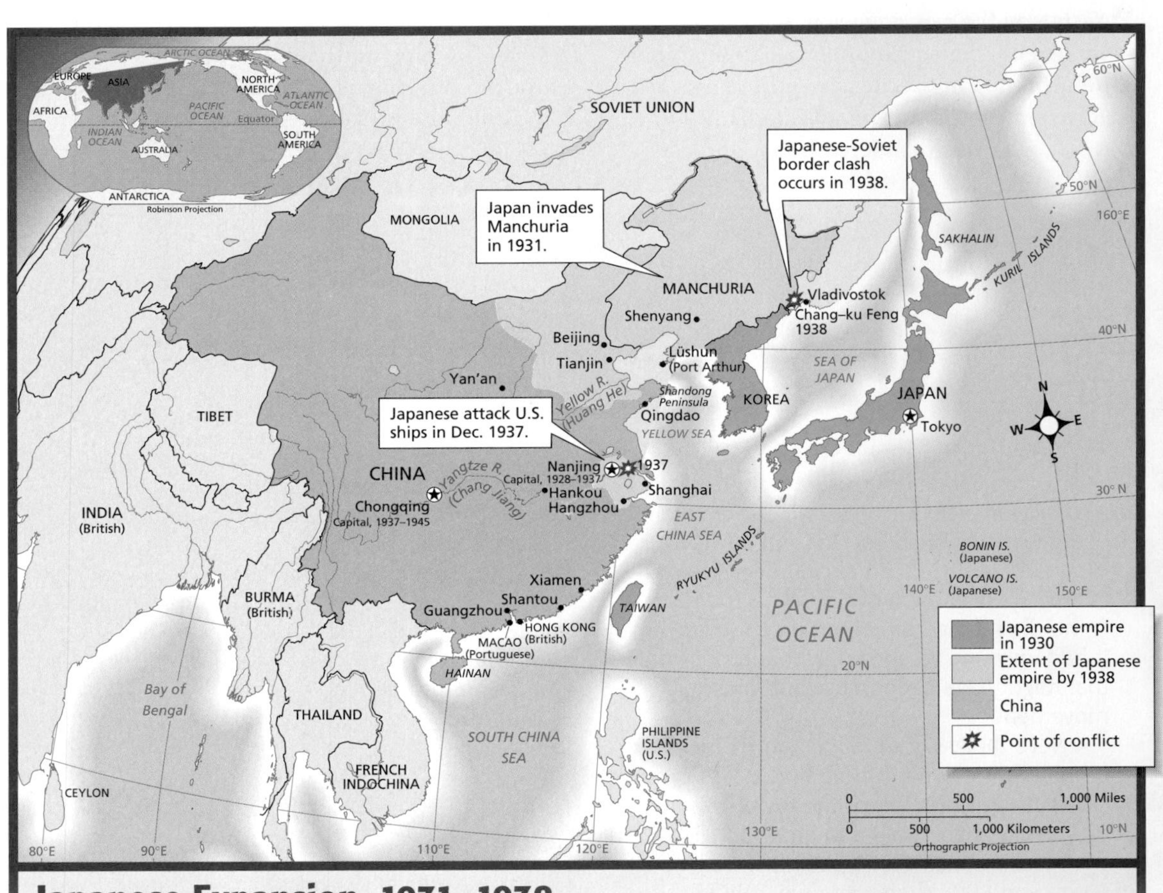

Japanese Expansion, 1931–1938

Learning from Maps Japan's military leaders believed that conquering neighboring lands would solve their country's economic problems.

Place What important Chinese cities had Japan captured by 1938?

REVIEW

Linguistic, Logical-Mathematical, Interpersonal. Have students complete the Section Review questions. Then organize students into five groups and assign each group one of the following: Latin America, the Soviet Union, Italy, Germany, or Japan. Have each group create a study guide for its assigned area that covers the events of the 1930s. Have groups share their study guides with the class.

ASSESS

Have students complete Da ly Quiz 15.4.

RETEACH

Logical-Mathematical. Have students complete Main Idea Activities for Reteaching and Sheltered English 15.4. Then have students refer to the text to find two related facts for each of the terms and names in the Identify portion of the Section Review. **SHELTERED ENGLISH**

On December 12, 1937, Japan tested the U.S. commitment to isolationism. Japanese planes destroyed the *Panay*, a U.S. gunboat, killing 2 people and wounding 30 others. President Roosevelt demanded an apology, payment for damages, and a guarantee against future incidents. In a letter dated December 16, Roosevelt wrote about the United States: "this nation wants peace." Japan's government agreed to the terms. The United States had avoided war for the moment.

Roosevelt's Response

President Roosevelt tried to maintain a balance between stopping aggression and keeping the United States out of war. Many Americans favored a policy of isolationism. They wanted the government to focus on domestic economic problems and not on international affairs. In the late 1930s Congress passed four **Neutrality Acts** to keep the nation out of international incidents. The first act, passed in 1935, prohibited the U.S. government from shipping arms to nations at war. Later neutrality acts extended the ban to include groups involved in civil wars.

Some Americans wanted to stop the expansion of Germany, Italy, and Japan. By October 1937,

Japan's aggression and refusal to honor its agreements are pictured in this 1931 cartoon.

Roosevelt had begun to believe that the growing aggression of these nations required action. He warned "that the epidemic of world lawlessness is spreading." Roosevelt saw war as a disease that must be contained to prevent further infection. Many Americans, however, still favored isolationism and were upset by Roosevelt's speech. They hoped that an isolationist policy would keep the government's focus on improving the U.S. economy.

SECTION 4 REVIEW

Identify and explain the significance of the following:

- **Good Neighbor policy**
- **totalitarianism**
- **Joseph Stalin**
- **Benito Mussolini**
- **Blackshirts**
- **fascism**
- **Adolf Hitler**
- **Nazis**
- **Axis Powers**
- ***Kristallnacht***
- **Neutrality Acts**

Locate and explain the importance of the following:

- **Japan**
- **Manchuria**

Reading for Content Understanding

1 **Main Idea** How did President Roosevelt change U.S. policy in Latin America?

2 **Main Idea** How did the United States respond to the territorial aggressions of Germany, Italy, and Japan?

3 **Global Relations** What brought dictators to power in Europe during the Great Depression?

4 **Writing** *Persuading* Imagine that you are an American living during the Great Depression. Write a letter to Congress persuading its members to pass the Neutrality Acts.

5 **Critical Thinking** *Making Comparisons* Compare the leadership styles and goals of Joseph Stalin, Benito Mussolini, and Adolf Hitler.

Chapter 15 Review ANSWERS

Identifying People and Ideas

1. president of the United Mine Workers who formed the Committee for Industrial Organization
2. strike in which workers remain in their factories but refuse to work
3. area of the Great Plains hit by tremendous dust storms
4. Farm Security Administration photographer known for photo *Migrant Mother*
5. ended individual land allotments, returned some lands to tribal ownership, organized reservation tribes into self-governing bodies
6. artists who were inspired by regional customs and folk themes
7. author who used a mythical Mississippi county as the setting of 14 novels
8. political system in which the government controls all aspects of life
9. Soviet leader who introduced a Five-Year Plan to industrialize the nation
10. followers of the National Socialist Party and Adolf Hitler

Using the Time Line

1. b
2. e
3. c
4. d
5. a

Understanding Main Ideas

1. by providing relief through programs such as FERA and the WPA
2. Union membership increased; skilled and unskilled workers formed industrial unions.

Review and Assessment RESOURCES

PRINT
★ Chapter 15 Review, pp. 468–69
★ Vocabulary Activity 15
★ Chapter 15 Study Guide
★ Chapter 15 Test (Form A or B)

MULTIMEDIA
★ Audio Program, Ch. 15 (English and Spanish)
★ *Global Skill Builder CD–ROM*
★ Chapter 15 Test Generator
★ HRW Web site

SHELTERED ENGLISH
★ Spanish Glossary
★ Sheltered English Chapter 15 Test

ASSESS

Have students complete one of the Chapter 15 Tests. As an alternate assessment, assign the Chapter 15 Investigation.

3. Americans enjoyed art, literature, movies, music, radio, and spectator sports.

4. Women tried to find jobs to make ends meet and many fathers left their families in search of work.

5. Many married, working women faced open hostility; some were fired and replaced by men; some states introduced legislation prohibiting married women from working; many single women became homeless.

6. The United States remained neutral as to events in Europe and Asia.

Reviewing Themes

1. farmers—the Agricultural Adjustment Act helped them pay their mortgages, while the Farm Security Administration gave long-term loans at low rates and set up shelters and medical care for migrant workers; artists—federal arts projects, such as the WPA's Federal Project One, helped artists continue working and sponsored workshops that helped artists develop their skills and talents.

2. American Indians—experienced the deepest and most widespread poverty of any group in addition to death rates nearly twice that of white Americans; Mexican migrant workers—many were not allowed to participate in public works projects and were deported

3. Fascist dictators gained control of the governments.

Thinking Critically

1. People suffering economically might be more willing to allow the government or dictators to control more aspects of their lives in hopes of improving the economic situation.

CHAPTER 15 REVIEW

Chapter Summary

The Great Depression was a period of tremendous suffering for Americans and others around the world. The New Deal strengthened the position of organized labor. For farmers, African Americans, American Indians, and women, the New Deal had a more mixed record. Americans turned to new and old forms of entertainment during the 1930s. In some foreign nations, the depression led to the rise of dictators.

On a separate sheet of paper, complete the following activities.

Identifying People and Ideas

Describe the historical significance of the following:

1. John L. Lewis
2. sit-down strike
3. Dust Bowl
4. Dorothea Lange
5. Indian Reorganization Act
6. regionalists
7. William Faulkner
8. totalitarianism
9. Joseph Stalin
10. Nazis

Internet Activity 

go.hrw.com
SB1 Great Depression

Search the Internet through the HRW Web site to find information about the Great Depression. Use the information to create a script for a play showing the difficulties one family might have faced.

Understanding Main Ideas

1. How did the New Deal respond to the needs of African Americans?
2. In what ways did organized labor change during the 1930s?
3. What forms of entertainment did Americans enjoy during the Great Depression?
4. How did families cope with the effects of the depression?
5. How did the lives of some women change during the 1930s?
6. In what ways did the United States respond to international events in the 1930s?

Reviewing Themes

1. **Economic Development** How did the New Deal help farmers and artists?
2. **Cultural Diversity** How did the Great Depression affect American Indians and Mexican migrant workers?
3. **Global Relations** How did the governments of Germany and Italy change in the 1930s?

Using the Time Line

Number your paper from 1 to 5. Match the letters on the time line below with the following events.

1. **Congress passes the Indian Reorganization Act.**
2. **Nazis attack Jews and Jewish properties in Germany on *Kristallnacht*.**
3. **Italian forces attack Ethiopia.**
4. **A sit-down strike begins that will virtually shut down General Motors.**
5. **Japanese troops attack the northern Chinese region of Manchuria.**

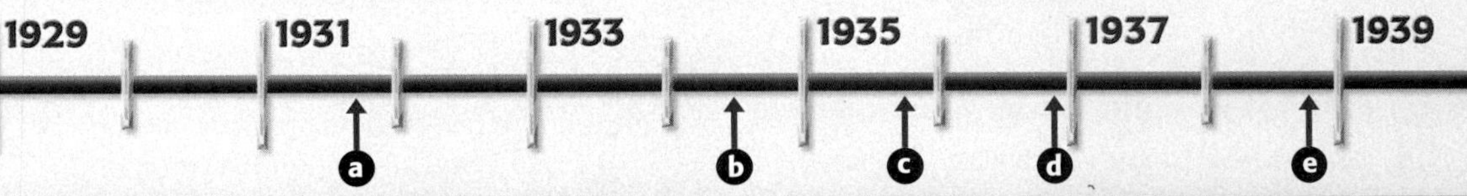

RETEACH

Logical-Mathematical, Visual-Spatial, Interpersonal. Organize the class into four groups and assign each group one of the four sections in this chapter. Have the groups review their assigned sections to locate and record specific effects of the Great Depression. Next to each effect, have students list its cause.

SHELTERED ENGLISH

Using the Internet

Have students continue their research to find information on the assistance that the U.S. government provided to Americans during the Great Depression. Have students use their findings to create another act or scene for the play they created in the Internet Activity.

Portfolio Extensions

1. Ask students to choose a partner and exchange proposals. Then have students evaluate the strengths and weaknesses of their partners' proposals.

2. Have students create an advertisement for the films they created. Remind students to consider, in creating their ads, what appealed to Americans during the Great Depression.

Thinking Critically

1. **Drawing Conclusions** How might poor economic conditions lead to dictatorship?
2. **Evaluating** Why did African Americans support the New Deal, even though some of its programs discriminated against them?
3. **Synthesizing Information** Was the New Deal successful? Explain your answer.

Writing About History

1. **Informing** Imagine that you are a radio announcer in the 1930s. Provide reviews to your listeners of the movies that are playing in theaters.
2. **Creating** Imagine that you are a WPA writer. Create a short story about your experiences during the depression.

Linking Geography and History

1. **Region** What was President Roosevelt's Latin American policy during the depression?
2. **Human-Environment Interaction** How did farmers' practices contribute to soil erosion in the Dust Bowl?

Building Your Portfolio

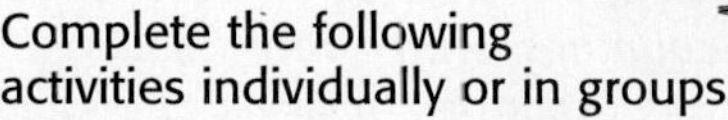

Complete the following activities individually or in groups.

1. **Feeding the Hungry** Imagine that you are a farmer during the Great Depression. You have crops to sell, but you cannot afford to ship them to market. People in cities need food but cannot afford to buy it. Propose a New Deal program that will get food to the hungry and income to the farmers. Create a proposal for Congress using visuals and an oral or written report.
2. **Movies and the Great Depression** Imagine that you are a movie producer in the 1930s who wants to create a short film that focuses on a well-known person from the era. Your subject can be from any field, such as government, sports, or entertainment. Your movie can be a documentary, a fictional account of his or her life, or a musical. Create a script and visuals for your film. You may want to perform or videotape your movie for the class.

History Skills Workshop

Using Primary Sources Mexican American César Chávez and his family were migrant workers during the Great Depression. Read the excerpt to the right, which is Chávez's recollection of his life during the depression. Then answer the following questions: (a) Why did Chávez sometimes miss school? (b) How did Chávez's family try to stay alive one winter? (c) How do you think their experiences compare to those of other families during the depression?

"We all of us climbed into an old Chevy that my dad had. And then we were in California, and [were] migratory workers. . . . Well, it was a strange life. . . . When we moved to California, we would work after school. Sometimes we wouldn't go [to school]. 'Following the crops,' we missed much school. Trying to get enough money to stay alive the following winter, the whole family picking apricots, walnuts, prunes. We were pretty new, we had never been migratory workers. We were taken advantage of quite a bit by the labor contractor."

2. Many African Americans supported the New Deal because they received relief and/or work from its programs; Roosevelt appointed a greater percentage of African Americans to supervisory positions than past presidents had; and African Americans received more assistance from the government than they ever had in the past.

3. Answers will vary but students should mention that the New Deal was successful in some ways but not in others.

Writing About History

1. Reviews will vary but should mention that cartoons, comedies, and gangster films were popular.

2. Stories will vary but should contain regional themes.

Linking Geography and History

1. He developed the Good Neighbor policy, which emphasized economic aid and trade agreements.

2. Farmers' plowing of grazing lands and grasses that protected topsoil combined with heavy winds to sweep the dried-out topsoil away.

History Skills Workshop

(a) because he had to work and his family had to follow the crops; (b) by picking apricots, walnuts, and prunes; (c) Answers will vary but students should point out that they suffered as many others did, but that their situation might have been rather extreme.

FOCUS

Ask students to identify effects of the Great Depression on the United States. Write their answers on the chalkboard. Then ask each student to sketch a flowchart showing how the depression may have affected other nations' economies. Have volunteers present their flowcharts. Tell students that in this lesson they will learn more about global effects of the Great Depression.

TEACH

Have students read the Geography and History lesson. Choose one or more of the following activities to explore the Geography and History content with students.

ALL LEVELS: Logical-Mathematical, Visual-Spatial. (Suggested time: 30 min.) Remind students that the information from a bar graph can also be presented as a line graph. Have students

Economic Development

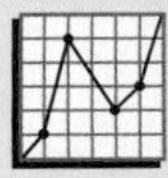

Unemployment Rates. Gross national product (GNP) is one way to measure a nation's economic health. Another is to measure the unemployment rate of the civilian labor force. During the 1920s, the highest unemployment rate occurred in 1921, when 11.7 percent of the civilian labor force aged 14 years and older was out of work. In 1929 only 3.2 percent of the workforce was unemployed. The following year, 8.7 percent was out of work. During the 1930s, the worst year of unemployment was 1933, when 24.9 percent of the workforce was unemployed. It was not until 1943, when only 1.9 percent of American workers was out of work, that the unemployment rate fell below that of 1929.

Activity: Have students present this information on unemployment rates in a line graph. Instruct students to place the dates along the horizontal axis and the percentages along the vertical axis.

SKILLS ANSWERS

1. Canada
2. Italy
3. 28.4 percent

Geography & History

The Global Depression

Although it began in the United States, the Great Depression soon became a global economic disaster. The economies of many countries were badly shaken. Industrial production fell, millions of people lost their jobs, and many people lost their entire life savings.

As the depression deepened, countries' economies continued to shrink. Unemployment rates skyrocketed, affecting nearly a fourth of the workforce in some industrial nations. In the United States, more than 20 percent of the labor force was out of work by 1932. The average amount of money people earned was cut nearly in half.

In the United States and other countries, governments increased spending to help the unemployed and the poor. Nevertheless, the depression did not end until World War II. Wartime production increased employment as people produced military supplies and other goods to support their country's war effort. ■

A World in Crisis

Many countries saw their gross national product (GNP)—the total value of all goods and services produced by a country in one year—fall dramatically during the depression. In addition, unemployment rates soared.

Decline in Gross National Product, 1929–1932

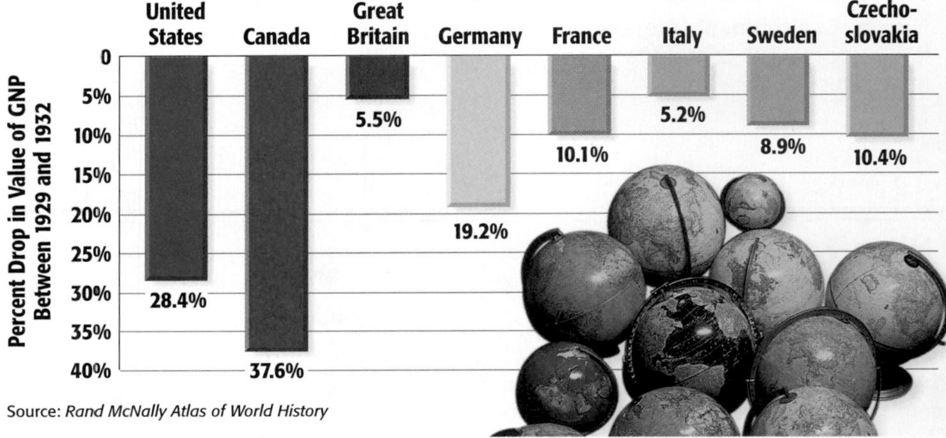

Source: *Rand McNally Atlas of World History*

Geography Skills
Reading Bar Graphs

1. Which country's GNP declined the most between 1929 and 1932?
2. Which country's GNP declined the least during that period?
3. How much did the U.S. GNP fall between 1929 and 1932?

470

create a line graph that illustrates the information from the bar graph on page 470, which is titled Decline in Gross National Product, 1929–1932. **SHELTERED ENGLISH**

LEVEL 3: Linguistic, Intrapersonal. (Suggested time: 45 min. plus homework) Ask students to imagine that they are Americans having financial difficulties between 1930 and 1939. Have them write telegrams to President Roosevelt requesting help from the federal government. Students should use information from History Notes 1 and 2 and the graph on page 472 when writing about the effects of the depression on their lives. Provide students with class time to write their telegrams. For homework, have students exchange telegrams and write the response they think the president would have given to the telegram they received. These responses should use information from the graph on page 473 to explain what the government is doing to meet the needs of Americans whose income has decreased.

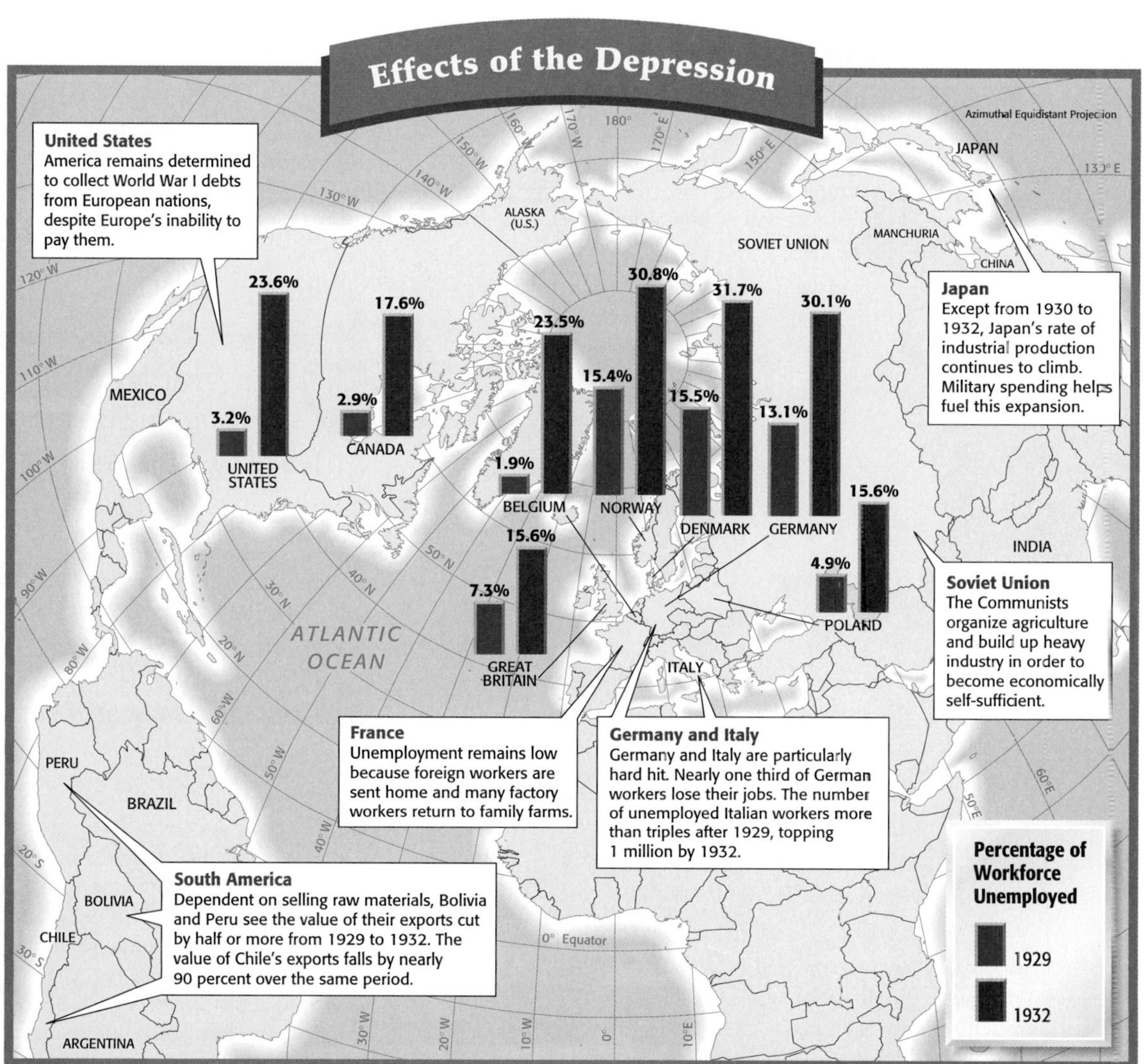

Geography Skills
Reading Special-Purpose Maps

1. In which three countries was more than 30 percent of the workforce jobless by 1932?
2. How were some South American countries affected by the depression?
3. Which country saw the greatest increase in its percentage of unemployed between 1929 and 1932?
4. How did Japan increase its rate of industrial production during the depression?

While traveling around Britain in search of work, this man lived in this mobile home he built.

Global Relations

Declining Global Imports. As the Great Depression worsened, global trade plummeted. The declining total dollar value of the imports of 75 countries revealed the extent of the economic crisis. In October 1929, global imports totaled almost $3 billion. After the U.S. stock market crash, however, imports steadily declined, dropping approximately $700 million over the next 12 months. The worst was yet to come. By October 1931, imports had fallen to $1.5 billion, only a little more than half of what they had been just two years earlier. In January 1933, two months before Franklin D. Roosevelt took office, import totals dropped below $1 billion.

Critical Thinking: How might internal economic conditions in one country affect other countries' economies?

ANSWER: If one country cannot afford to import goods, the countries selling the goods will also suffer economic hardships.

SKILLS ANSWERS

1. Denmark, Germany, and Norway
2. The total value of their exports dropped dramatically.
3. Belgium
4. partly through military spending

CLOSE

Linguistic, Logical-Mathematical. Have students prepare for the secretary-general of the League of Nations a brief memorandum, dated January 1, 1933, that summarizes the global effects of the Great Depression. Each memorandum should include at least one piece of information from the map and each of the graphs on pages 470–73.

CHALLENGE AND EXTEND

Linguistic, Logical-Mathematical, Visual-Spatial. Have students use the library or other resources to find out the average personal income in their city, county, or state for each year from 1929 to 1939. Students should then use this information to create a line graph showing the changes in the average personal income during this period. Instruct students to write a brief essay comparing and contrasting their graph with the one on page 472.

Citizenship and Democracy

Unemployed Leagues. The Unemployed Citizens' League of Seattle (UCL) was formed in 1931. Originally created as a cooperative group to obtain food and firewood, the UCL soon turned to politics and radical action, such as resisting evictions and restoring utility services that had been turned off for nonpayment. Similar groups organized in other parts of the country, and in 1933 a National Unemployed League was founded with 150,000 members. That year marked the high point of the unemployed leagues, however; and membership declined thereafter.

Critical Thinking: Why do you think Americans lost interest in the unemployed leagues after 1933?

Answer: Students might mention that the New Deal programs began to have an impact on employment levels after that year.

Skills Answers

1. 1929; 1933
2. It dropped slightly.
3. 1937

The Depression in the United States

In addition to increasing unemployment and lowering the GNP, the depression left people with less money to buy things. Increased government spending helped the economy recover, but it could not relieve all of the country's economic problems.

Average Income per Person, 1929–1940

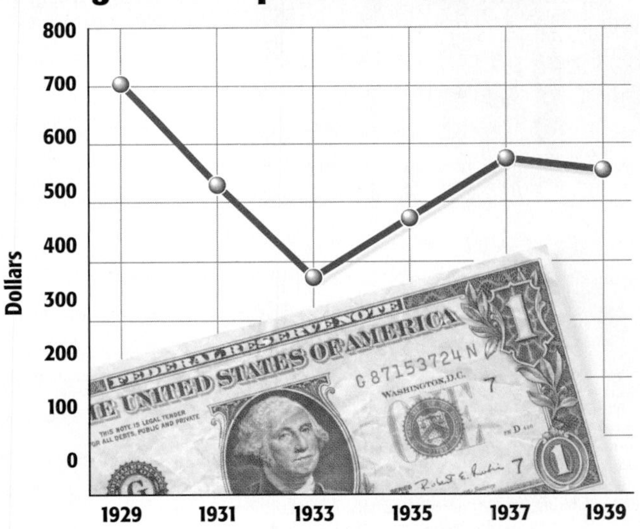

Source: *Datapedia of the United States, 1790–2000: America Year by Year*

Geography Skills
Reading Line Graphs

1. In which year shown on this graph was the average income per person highest? lowest?
2. What happened to the average income per person in 1939?
3. Between 1933 and 1939, in which year was income per person the highest?

History Note 1

How much Americans earned largely depended on where they lived. Workers in the Lower South, for example, generally earned far less than the national average in 1929. This remained true a decade later. On average, Mississippians earned about $216 each in 1940—about one third of the national average of $593 a year. The average worker in Alabama, Arkansas, and South Carolina earned about $300 or less in 1940. Those four states also had the lowest average personal income levels in 1929.

Some unemployed workers earned money selling apples on street corners.

History Note 2

About 1.5 million Americans were out of work in 1929. That number grew rapidly to about 12 million in 1932 and reached almost 13 million in 1933. Nearly 10 million Americans were still out of work when World War II broke out in Europe in 1939. During World War II, millions of American civilians found jobs in factories and plants producing war goods.

REVIEW

Linguistic, Interpersonal. Organize the class into groups and assign each group one of the graphs or the map from this lesson. Then ask each group to create a study guide with at least five questions and answers covering the assigned map or graph. Have each group present its guide to the class.

ASSESS

Have students complete Geography and History Quiz 5.

RETEACH

Logical-Mathematical. Have each student write four statements covering facts from this lesson. Each statement should contain a blank space that can be filled in by interpreting the map or graphs in this section. For example, *In 1933 the average income per person sank to about ________ per person, its lowest level during the Great Depression.* Have students exchange their statements, complete them, and return them to their authors for grading.
SHELTERED ENGLISH

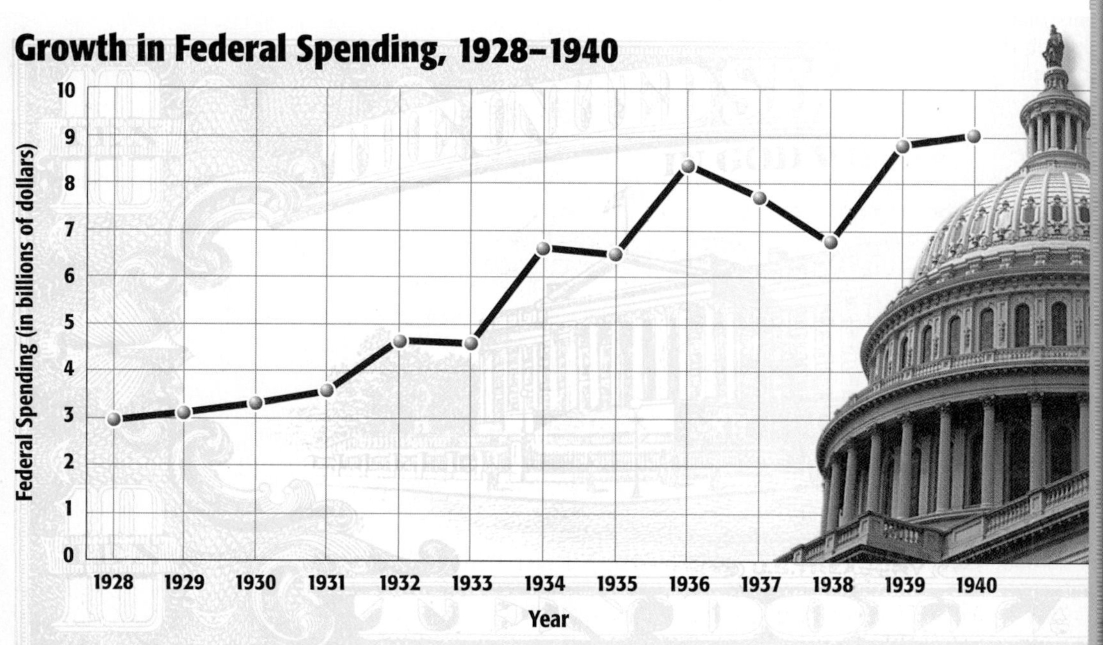

Source: *Historical Statistics of the United States*

Geography Skills
Reading Line Graphs

1. About how much more did the U.S. government spend in 1940 than it did in 1929?
2. What happened to U.S. government spending in 1937 and 1938? in 1939?

History Note 3

Under President Franklin D. Roosevelt's New Deal programs, the federal government gradually spent more money each year to pull the country out of the depression. The unemployment rate did drop—from about 25 percent in 1933 to some 14 percent in 1937—but not as much as was necessary to pull the nation out of the depression. The economy weakened again in 1937 and 1938, causing unemployment to rise and contributing to still higher federal spending.

The depression left many Americans struggling to find enough to eat.

Economic Development

The Recession of 1938. In 1937, when the U.S. government cut back its deficit spending, the economy worsened quickly and entered a recession. From September 1937 to June 1938, industrial production fell by a third, employment in manufacturing industries plummeted 23 percent, and national average income dropped 13 percent. The recession caused a crisis in the Roosevelt administration. Opponents of the New Deal argued that the recession was proof that the program should be abandoned. New Deal supporters tried to convince President Roosevelt to increase government spending again to save the economy. Roosevelt followed this latter advice, and the recession of 1938 came to an end.

Critical Thinking: How might increased government spending bring an end to a recession?

ANSWER: It could create new jobs, which enable people to work and make money, which in turn enables them to purchase more goods, thus improving business and leading to even more job growth.

SKILLS ANSWERS

1. $6 billion
2. declined; rose

CHAPTER PLANNING GUIDE
World War II

	SECTION LESSON OBJECTIVES	PRINT RESOURCES	MULTIMEDIA RESOURCES	SHELTERED ENGLISH RESOURCES
Section 1: World War II Begins (pp. 475–79)	★ List the parts of Europe that Germany conquered by mid-1940. ★ Describe how President Roosevelt aided Britain while preserving U.S. neutrality. ★ Describe the events that led to conflict between the United States and Japan.	★ Guided Reading Strategies 16.1 ★ American History Political Cartoon 25: The Nonaggression Pact ★ Section 1 Review, p. 479 ★ Daily Quiz 16.1	★ *Teaching Resources CD–ROM*, Lesson 16.1 ★ HRW Web site	★ Main Idea Activities for Reteaching and Sheltered English 16.1
Section 2: Mobilizing for War (pp. 480–83)	★ Explain how the United States mobilized for World War II. ★ Describe the effects of World War II on civilian women and minorities. ★ Analyze reasons for U.S. internment of Japanese Americans during World War II.	★ Guided Reading Strategies 16.2 ★ Biography Reading 16: Benjamin Oliver Davis Jr. ★ Section 2 Review, p. 483 ★ Daily Quiz 16.2	★ *Teaching Resources CD–ROM*, Lesson 16.2 ★ Everyday Life in America Transparency 26: Inside an Internment Camp, World War II ★ *Exploring America's Past* Video Segment: Prisoners of War; *Teacher's Guide*, pp. 29–30	★ Main Idea Activities for Reteaching and Sheltered English 16.2
Section 3: The War in North Africa and Europe (pp. 484–89)	★ Analyze the importance of the Allies' North Africa campaign. ★ Identify the major turning points of the war in Europe. ★ Describe how the Allies drove the Germans out of France.	★ Guided Reading Strategies 16.3 ★ Primary Source Reading 16: A Witness to the Normandy Invasion ★ Section 3 Review, p. 489 ★ Daily Quiz 16.3	★ *Teaching Resources CD–ROM*, Lesson 16.3 ★ Linking Geography and History Transparency 18: World War II in Europe, 1942–1945	★ Main Idea Activities for Reteaching and Sheltered English 16.3
Section 4: War in the Pacific (pp. 490–94)	★ Describe the path of Japanese forces after Pearl Harbor. ★ Identify the turning points of the war in the Pacific. ★ Analyze how the Allies advanced toward Japan.	★ Guided Reading Strategies 16.4 ★ Section 4 Review, p. 494 ★ Daily Quiz 16.4	★ *Teaching Resources CD–ROM*, Lesson 16.4 ★ Linking Geography and History Transparency 19: World War II in the Pacific, 1941–1945 ★ HRW Web site	★ Main Idea Activities for Reteaching and Sheltered English 16.4
Section 5: Final Victory and Consequences (pp. 495–99)	★ Explain how the Allies forced Germany and Japan to surrender. ★ Analyze the human and economic costs of World War II. ★ Describe events leading to the Holocaust.	★ Guided Reading Strategies 16.5 ★ Literature Reading 16: An Excerpt from *Night* ★ Graphic Organizer 16: A Time Line of War ★ Geography Activity 16: German Concentration Camps ★ Section 5 Review, p. 499 ★ Daily Quiz 16.5	★ *Teaching Resources CD–ROM*, Lesson 16.5 ★ *American Music Audio CD Program:* "Gee But I Want to Go Home"	★ Main Idea Activities for Reteaching and Sheltered English 16.5
Chapter Review and Assessment (pp. 500–01)		★ Chapter 16 Review, pp. 500–01 ★ Vocabulary Activity 16 ★ Chapter 16 Study Guide ★ Chapter 16 Test (Form A or B)	★ Audio Program, Ch. 16 (English and Spanish) ★ *Global Skill Builder CD–ROM* ★ Chapter 16 Test Generator ★ HRW Web site	★ Spanish Glossary ★ Sheltered English Chapter 16 Test

CHAPTER OVERVIEW

When World War II began, the United States maintained an official policy of neutrality. By relying on the Lend-Lease Act, the U.S. government was able to provide the Allies with needed war materials while maintaining a semblance of neutrality. After the Japanese attack on Pearl Harbor, however, the United States officially entered the war.

To prepare for the conflict, the U.S. government began helping industries convert to war production. With the increased output, many women and minorities were able to take industrial jobs.

The Axis Powers had conquered most of Europe by mid-1940. By mid-1944, however, the Allies had liberated both Italy and France. Hitler's earlier invasion of the Soviet Union meant that the Germans were fighting a war on two fronts.

In the Pacific, Japan won many early battles. To turn the tide of the war in the Pacific, the Allies relied on island-hopping tactics, which led to significant victories and served to cut off Japanese forces.

Through heavy bombing and ground assaults, the Allies forced a German surrender. In an attempt to force the Japanese to surrender, the United States dropped two atomic bombs on Japan. Shortly afterward, the Japanese surrendered, leaving the world to recover from the human and economic losses of another world war.

CHAPTER INVESTIGATION

The Chapter Investigation is an extended, multipart activity designed for students to work cooperatively and apply the chapter content in the creation of a project. You may choose to use the Chapter 16 Investigation, Reflections on World War II, either as a substitute for teaching the section lessons or as an alternate assessment.

BLOCK SCHEDULING 

The teacher lesson plans for each section offer a variety of activity choices to help you present the material in a block scheduling format. For further suggestions on block scheduling, see the *Block Scheduling Handbook with Team Teaching Strategies,* pp. 91–96.

Meeting Individual Needs

ABILITY LEVELS

LEVEL 1 Basic level activities designed for all students encountering new material.

LEVEL 2 Intermediate level activities designed for average students.

LEVEL 3 Challenging activities designed for above-average students.

SHELTERED ENGLISH These activities address the needs of students with Limited English Proficiency.

Smithsonian Institution®

Internet Connections and Lesson 16

www.si.edu/hrw

CNN Presents America:

Yesterday and Today 1850 to the Present

Segment: One Town Remembers

Additional Resources

Books for Teachers

Bernstein, Alison R. *American Indians and World War II.* University of Oklahoma Press, 1991. Surveys American Indians' contributions to the war effort and the effect of the war's aftermath on American Indian affairs.

Hilberg, Raul. *Perpetrators, Victims, Bystanders.* HarperCollins, 1993. A noted historian looks at Holocaust agents, victims, and collaborators and documents Allied inaction.

Overy, Richard. *Why the Allies Won.* Norton, 1996. Acclaimed scholar of modern history analyzes reasons for the Allied victory over the Axis Powers.

Books for Students

Cross, Robin. *Technology of War.* Thomson Learning, 1994. Traces the use of military technology. Advancements in radio communications, aviation, and electronics are included.

McGowen, Tom. *World War II.* Watts, 1993. Includes descriptions of major battles and an overview of political changes that occurred during the war.

Rosenberg, Maxine B. *Hiding to Survive: Stories of Jewish Children Rescued from the Holocaust.* Clarion Books, 1994. Fourteen Holocaust survivors, who were hidden from the Nazis as children, tell their stories. Photographs of the survivors today and as children are included.

Multimedia Materials

Dawn. Video, 60 min. WGBH/Boston. Focuses on development of the atomic bomb. Uses World War II as a backdrop to discuss scientists' work to perfect the atomic bomb.

The Home Front—1940 to 1945. 3 videos, 180 min. Reader's Digest/SSSS. Documents daily life on the American home front.

The World of Anne Frank. Video, 28 min. Ergo Media Inc. Interviews with Anne Frank's father and those who risked their lives to hide the Frank family during World War II. Parts of Anne Frank's diary are interwoven with the story.

World War II

CHAPTER MOTIVATOR

Have students write a paragraph in which they speculate on circumstances that might cause one nation to wage war against another. Call on volunteers to read their paragraphs to the class. Then list students' reasons on the chalkboard. Tell students that in this chapter they will learn how aggression by Germany, Italy, and Japan against their neighbors led to war; how the United States became involved in the conflict; how the war affected Americans at home; and how the United States and its allies devised a strategy for victory. As students read the chapter, encourage them to identify the reasons the United States entered World War II and have them compare these reasons to those on the chalkboard.

Presenting Themes

- **Citizenship and Democracy** Students might mention that a government might be tempted to sidestep citizens' civil rights in favor of wartime security issues.
- **Economic Development** Students might mention that war production might invigorate an economy or that destruction resulting from war could devastate a nation's economy.
- **Global Relations** Students might suggest that a nation could be allied with other countries that have become involved in a war; that it might have interests in defending other governments; or that it may want to keep an aggressive government in check.

Using the Time Line

Ask students to imagine that they are making a movie about World War II. Have each student write a brief scene for one of the events on the time line.

The Granger Collection, New York

CHAPTER 16

World War II

(1938–1945)

Just past 7:00 A.M. on Sunday, December 7, 1941, two U.S. soldiers were operating a radar station on the Hawaiian island of Oahu. They noticed "something completely out of the ordinary." A large formation of airplanes appeared to be headed their way. Within an hour, almost 200 Japanese warplanes attacked U.S. battleships anchored at Pearl Harbor. More than 2,300 U.S. soldiers and sailors were killed. Soon after, the United States entered World War II.

Citizenship and Democracy
How might involvement in a foreign war affect people's rights?

Economic Development
What effect might fighting a war have on a nation's economy?

Global Relations
Why might a nation become involved in a war on another continent?

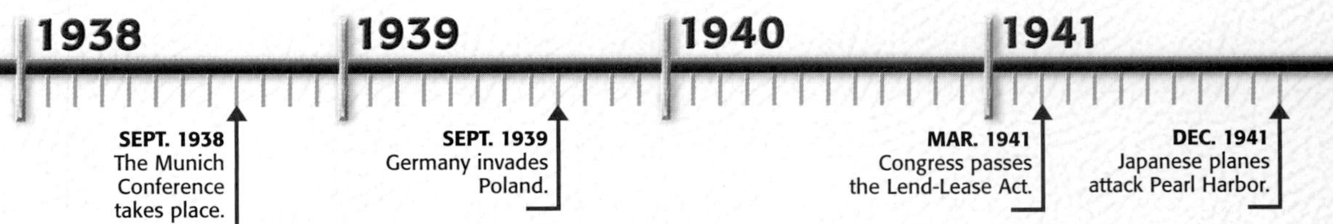

OBJECTIVES

- **List the parts of Europe that Germany conquered by mid-1940.**
- **Describe how President Roosevelt aided Britain while preserving U.S. neutrality.**
- **Describe the events that led to conflict between the United States and Japan.**

FOCUS

Motivate Before Reading

On the chalkboard, list the major nations that participated in World War II. Ask students to identify which nations fought on each side. As students answer, write their responses under the headings *Axis* and *Allies*. Tell students that in this section they will learn how World War II began and why the United States joined the Allies.

World War II Begins

Reading Focus

What parts of Europe did Germany conquer by mid-1940?

How did President Roosevelt aid Britain while preserving U.S. neutrality?

What events led to the conflict between the United States and Japan?

Key Terms

Munich Conference
appeasement
nonaggression pact
Allied Powers
Blitzkrieg
Maginot Line
Battle of Britain
Lend-Lease Act
Battle of the Atlantic
Atlantic Charter

ON THE NIGHT OF AUGUST 31, 1939, a group of special German troops attacked a radio station in the German town of Gleiwitz (GLY-vits) on the Polish border. Their mission was to stage an "incident" that the German government could use to justify an invasion of Poland. To make the Poles look responsible for the attack, the Germans dressed several convicted criminals in Polish military uniforms, shot them, and left the bodies at the station. Within hours, German forces began streaming across the Polish border in retaliation for the "attack." The incident at Gleiwitz helped trigger a war that would soon spread around the world.

German soldiers chop down a border gate between Germany and Poland on the first day of the invasion.

IMAGE ON LEFT PAGE: *The USS Shaw explodes in Pearl Harbor after being bombed by Japanese planes.*

Timeline: 1942 | 1943 | 1944 | 1945

FEB. 1942 The U.S. government decides to intern Japanese Americans.

JULY 1943 Allied forces invade Sicily.

JUNE 1944 The D-Day invasion takes place.

MAY 1945 Germany surrenders.

AUG. 1945 The United States drops atomic bombs on Japan.

SEPT. 1945 Japan surrenders.

Section 1 RESOURCES

PRINT

- ★ Guided Reading Strategies 16.1
- ★ American History Political Cartoon 25: The Nonaggression Pact
- ★ Section 1 Review, p. 479
- ★ Daily Quiz 16.1

MULTIMEDIA

- ★ *Teaching Resources CD–ROM,* Lesson 16.1
- ★ HRW Web site

SHELTERED ENGLISH

- ★ Main Idea Activities for Reteaching and Sheltered English 16.1

Introduce Key Terms

Linguistic, Logical-Mathematical. Review this section's key terms with students. Ask students to use context cues to define each term and have them write definitions in their notebooks. Then ask students to write sentences in which they use two or more of the terms accurately. For example, students might write the following: At the *Munich Conference*, Britain and France followed a policy of *appeasement* to avoid war with Germany. Call on volunteers to read their sentences until all the key terms have been used. **SHELTERED ENGLISH**

TEACH

Have students read Section 1 and complete Guided Reading Strategies 16.1. Choose one or more of the following activities to explore the section content with students. For further suggestions on block scheduling or team teaching, see *the Block Scheduling Handbook.*

LEVEL 1: Linguistic. (Suggested time: 15 min.) As a class, go over students' Guided Reading Strategies. Then use the Reading Focus questions to highlight the main ideas of the section. **SHELTERED ENGLISH**

Biography

Adolf Hitler. Adolf Hitler was born in 1889 in Bruneau, Austria. His father made a comfortable living as a customs official for the Austro-Hungarian Empire. Although Hitler was sent to good schools, he was a mediocre student and left school when he was just 16 years old. Hitler went to Vienna to become an artist. Vienna was a hotbed of anti-Semitic fervor, and Hitler quickly developed a hatred of Jews. In 1913, on the eve of World War I, he joined the Bavarian Reserve Infantry. Hitler served as a runner during World War I and received the Iron Cross for being shot in the leg. After Germany's defeat, Hitler developed another hatred, this one of democratic politicians.

Critical Thinking: How might Hitler's early life have shaped his later ideas and actions?

ANSWER: Students might answer that the anti-Semitism predominant in Vienna gave the angry, young Hitler an easy target for his hatred. Also, Hitler saw war as an opportunity to overcome what he felt were the injustices of his youth.

Hitler's War Machine

In 1935, two years after Adolf Hitler became chancellor of Germany, he launched a massive program to rebuild the country's military. Hitler had long dreamed of revenge for Germany's defeat in World War I. He began in 1936 by sending German troops to reoccupy the Rhineland, a demilitarized zone established by the Treaty of Versailles. Two years later, Hitler forced Austria to unite with Germany.

Many nations were still focused on their own economic problems from the Great Depression and ignored these actions. However, in 1938 Hitler drew the world's attention. He demanded that Czechoslovakia turn over the Sudetenland (soo-DAYT-uhn-land)—an area with many ethnic Germans—to Germany. The Czechs refused the demand, and Hitler threatened war. French and British leaders met with Hitler at the **Munich Conference**, held in September 1938. In an act of **appeasement**—giving in to an aggressor to preserve peace—they persuaded the Czechs to surrender the Sudetenland. Hitler promised this was "the last territorial claim I have to make in Europe." Upon hearing of the appeasement, British admiral Winston Churchill said, "The government had to choose between shame and war. They have chosen shame. They will get war."

Hitler seized the rest of Czechoslovakia in March 1939. He then demanded that Poland return the city of Danzig (present-day Gdańsk). It had been part of Germany until World War I.

The Fighting Begins

Britain and France responded to Hitler's demands by pledging to defend Poland if Germany attacked. To keep the Soviet Union out of the war, Hitler secretly negotiated an agreement with Soviet leader Joseph Stalin in August 1939. In this **nonaggression pact**, Hitler and Stalin agreed not to attack one another and to divide Poland between their countries.

Poland Falls

World War II began on September 1, 1939, when German forces invaded Poland. Two days later, Britain and France—who became known as the **Allied Powers**—declared war against Germany.

To hide its military buildup, Germany disguised warplanes like this one as mail planes.

German forces attacked Poland in a **Blitzkrieg**, a new kind of fast-moving "lightning war." The Blitzkrieg concentrated airplanes and tanks in strategic areas in order to break through enemy lines. German troops swept across Poland from the west, and soon after the Soviets invaded from the east. By the end of the month, the two armies occupied Poland and sent its government into exile.

Hitler Looks West

When Germany attacked Poland, Britain and France began to mobilize their armed forces. The French massed their troops behind the **Maginot Line**—a fortified wall that France had built along its border with Germany after World War I.

In April 1940, German troops occupied Denmark and invaded Norway. In May, Germany seized the Low Countries of Belgium, Luxembourg, and the Netherlands. In doing so, Germany moved north of the Maginot Line. From there, German troops rushed southward behind the fortified line into France. The Germans trapped Belgian, British, and French soldiers at the French port of Dunkirk. In a daring evacuation, British

Allied troops stream toward ships waiting to evacuate them from Dunkirk, France. Hundreds of ships of all sizes, including many privately owned boats, were used in the effort.

ALL LEVELS: Linguistic, Visual-Spatial. (Suggested time: 30 min.) Tell students that by mid-1940 Germany had conquered much of Europe. Have students create an annotated time line highlighting key events and policies that led to this conquest. Then ask what year Germany invaded each country, and the year that each of the other nations declared war on Germany. Finally, discuss reasons for Germany's expansion. **SHELTERED ENGLISH**

LEVEL 2: Logical-Mathematical, Visual-Spatial, Interpersonal. (Suggested time: 30 min.) Have students create a flowchart illustrating the events that led to war between the United States and Japan. Have students exchange flowcharts and make a list of questions about anything on the flowchart that is missing or that they do not understand. Students should then return the flowcharts to their authors for revision.

LEVEL 3: Linguistic, Logical-Mathematical. (Suggested time: 45 min. plus homework) Have students write a short essay on how the United States aided Britain while preserving U.S. neutrality. After students have completed their essays, have the class discuss aid to Britain. For homework, have students add to their essays by speculating on why the United States would want to help Britain and what might have happened if Britain had not received U.S. aid.

World War II in Europe, 1939–1941

Learning from Maps Within two years of unleashing its Blitzkrieg, or "lightning war," in 1939, Germany controlled most of Europe and North Africa.

Place What European countries remained free from Axis control?

ships carried hundreds of thousands of soldiers across the English Channel to safety between May 26 and June 3, 1940.

As Hitler's forces advanced on the French capital of Paris in June 1940, Italy joined Germany and declared war on the Allied Powers. Together, Italy and Germany were known as the Axis Powers. On June 22 France surrendered to Germany, which then took control of northern France. In central France a German-controlled French government was established in the city of Vichy. Many French soldiers who had escaped at Dunkirk continued to participate in the fight against Germany. Based in London, French general Charles de Gaulle (gohl) organized a "Free French" army to serve with other Allied troops.

Britain Stands Alone

With France defeated, Hitler prepared to invade Britain. To launch a successful invasion across the English Channel, Germany would first need to defeat the British Royal Airforce (RAF). In July 1940 the *Luftwaffe*—the German air force—began to attack RAF airfields and aircraft. For months the two sides fought for air supremacy in what is known as the **Battle of Britain**.

In late August, Hitler ordered the *Luftwaffe* to bomb civilian targets in hopes of destroying British morale. A new invention called radar helped the RAF detect incoming German aircraft. Without control of the skies, Hitler canceled his plans for a ground invasion of Britain in mid-September. Winston Churchill, now British prime minister,

Technology and Society

Blitzkrieg. The strategy behind the military tactic known as Blitzkrieg was a British rather than a German development. Two British military strategists, Major General John Frederick Charles Fuller and Captain Basil Liddell Hart, developed the strategy after the military tactics used in World War I resulted in a high death toll and limited territorial progress. Fuller and Hart theorized that a more effective strategy would be to attack weak spots in enemy defenses and penetrate deep behind enemy lines so that opposition forces would be cut off from each other. During World War II, German forces used high-speed military equipment such as Panzer tanks and Stuka dive-bombers to invade enemy territory. Then slower-moving German artillery and infantry attacked the isolated enemy troops.

Critical Thinking: Why might this method of warfare have been particularly effective?

ANSWER: Blitzkrieg tactics took defending nations by surprise and were difficult to counteract.

MAP ANSWER

Great Britain, Ireland, Portugal, Spain, Sweden, and Switzerland

CLOSE

Linguistic, Logical-Mathematical. Ask students to imagine that the date is December 8, 1941, and they are radio announcers who have just listened to President Roosevelt ask Congress to declare war on Japan. Have students create a special report for radio broadcast that reviews reasons for the declaration of war on Japan, explains that this will probably lead to war with Germany, and provides background information on German aggression in Europe. Have volunteers read their reports to the class.

CHALLENGE AND EXTEND

Linguistic, Logical-Mathematical, Intrapersonal. Assign each student one nation that Germany invaded in or before mid-1940. Have each student use the library and other resources to find more information on the invasion and occupation. Have students write a series of journal entries documenting events leading up to, during, and following the invasion. Ask volunteers to share their entries with the class. Lead a discussion on the similarities and differences between events in the various nations.

Linking Past to Present

Hawaii. The naval shipyard at Pearl Harbor is still used for repairing U.S. military vessels. It is also home to many U.S. Navy ships and military bases, and serves as a training base for submarine and antisubmarine warfare. Both the U.S. Pacific commander in chief and the Pacific Fleet Marine Force have their headquarters in Hawaii.

Critical Thinking: Why is Hawaii important to the U.S. military?

ANSWER: It's location enables the United States to protect its western coast and its interests in the Pacific.

Historical Sidelight

USS *Reuben James*. On October 31, 1941, the USS *Reuben James* was escorting a convoy of ships across the Atlantic when it was torpedoed and sunk by the German submarine *U-562*. About 115 American sailors died. The *Reuben James* was the first U.S. warship sunk by Germans in World War II.

Activity: Have students use the library or search the Internet through the HRW Web site to research the USS *Reuben James*. Ask students to imagine that they have just read about the incident. Tell them to write a letter to the editor opposing or supporting U.S. entry into the war.

go.hrw.com
SB1 Reuben James

expressed his nation's gratitude to the RAF pilots: "Never in the field of human conflict was so much owed by so many to so few."

U.S. Neutrality

The United States remained neutral in the early stages of the war. Although most Americans opposed Hitler, they did not want to fight in a European war. Many well-known Americans, such as pilot Charles Lindbergh, supported isolationism.

U.S. neutrality laws prevented President Franklin D. Roosevelt from providing war supplies to the Allies. In 1939 he asked Congress to adjust these laws. Congress later approved the "cash-and-carry" system. The Allies could purchase U.S. weapons, but they had to pay for the arms in cash and carry them back to Europe on their own ships. In another effort to supply the Allies, Roosevelt swapped 50 U.S. destroyers for 99-year leases on several of Britain's naval bases in the Caribbean. After France fell in 1940, Congress greatly increased the U.S. defense budget.

German bombing raids destroyed much of London, but St. Paul's Cathedral (right) survived.

With the war in Europe, Roosevelt broke with tradition in 1940 and ran for a third term as president. The Republicans chose lawyer Wendell Willkie as his opponent. Most Americans decided to stick with a leader they knew, and Roosevelt won an easy victory. During the election, Roosevelt had reassured Americans that "your boys are not going to be sent into any foreign wars." Even so, he was convinced that the United States would eventually have to enter the war. Roosevelt again asked Congress to expand U.S. aid to the Allies. He argued that if all of Europe fell to Hitler,

> **"it is no exaggeration to say that all of us in the Americas would be living at the point of a gun. . . . We must be the great arsenal [arms supplier] of democracy."**

Congress passed the **Lend-Lease Act** in March 1941. This act offered to loan $7 billion worth of weapons and other war supplies to cash-poor Britain. After Hitler broke the nonaggression pact and invaded the Soviet Union in June 1941, Roosevelt extended Lend-Lease to the Soviets.

The Battle of the Atlantic

As U.S. aid to Britain increased, Germany focused its submarine forces on stopping the transportation of weapons. The result was a long fight, called the **Battle of the Atlantic**, to control the ocean trade routes. German U-boats sank many Allied cargo ships and tried to cut Britain off from the United States, its main source of supplies. To reduce their losses, the Allies organized their cargo ships into protective groups called convoys. The U.S. Navy began escorting the convoys across the Atlantic as far as Iceland. The navy also tracked U-boats and notified the British of the submarines' locations.

In August 1941 President Roosevelt and Prime Minister Winston Churchill signed a document of cooperation known as the **Atlantic Charter**. In it they pledged not to acquire new territory as a result of war and to work for peace after the current conflict. Just a month after the signing, a German U-boat fired on a U.S. destroyer. When Roosevelt ordered U.S. forces to "shoot on sight," war between the United States and Germany seemed certain.

REVIEW

Linguistic, Logical-Mathematical. Have students complete the Section Review questions. Ask each student to develop a quiz based on the section. Then have students exchange quizzes, complete the questions, and return them to their authors for grading. Once the quizzes are graded, have students review the section to correct any questions they missed.

ASSESS

Have students complete Daily Quiz 16.1.

RETEACH

Logical-Mathematical, Interpersonal. Have students complete Main Idea Activities for Reteaching and Sheltered English 16.1. Then have them prepare a newspaper headline for each year discussed in this section. Headlines should identify a development that led to or was part of World War II. For each headline, ask students to list the subtopics they would include in a story on that subject. Call on volunteers to read their headlines. Invite other students to comment on the headlines and on the appropriateness of the items selected to accompany each story.
SHELTERED ENGLISH

Conflict with Japan

Like Germany and Italy, Japan had aggressively sought new territory. After conquering much of China during the 1930s, Japan set its sights on Southeast Asia and its valuable natural resources. Japan also allied itself with Germany and Italy in the late 1930s and became part of the Axis Powers in 1940. In July 1941 Japanese forces seized French Indochina. In response, President Roosevelt froze Japanese funds in the United States and blocked the sale of products critical to Japanese industry. Both actions deeply angered Japanese leaders. U.S. officials also demanded that Japan leave China and French Indochina.

Meanwhile, the Japanese military developed a plan to attack Hawaii. In late November 1941, aircraft carriers left Japan. Led by Admiral Isoroku Yamamoto, the Japanese fleet planned to destroy U.S. forces at Pearl Harbor and then complete the conquest of Southeast Asia.

On December 7, 1941, Japanese warplanes swept down out of the sky and attacked the base. One sailor aboard the USS *Oklahoma* remembered:

> **"Suddenly the ship lurched! . . . As she rolled over, I was . . . buffeted [knocked] and tossed about. Then the dark waters closed over me as the ship came to rest upside down on the bottom of the harbor."**

Naval destroyers protected ship convoys like this one.

The attack sank or damaged U.S. battleships in Pearl Harbor. That same day, Japanese forces attacked U.S. military bases in the Philippines and on Guam, Midway, and Wake Island.

The surprise attack on U.S. soil shocked many Americans. The next day Roosevelt asked Congress to declare war on Japan, calling December 7 "a date which will live in infamy [disgrace]." Germany then declared war on the United States. Less than 25 years after its entry into World War I, the United States joined the Allies in another global conflict.

SECTION 1 REVIEW

Identify and explain the significance of the following:

- **Munich Conference**
- **appeasement**
- **nonaggression pact**
- **Allied Powers**
- **Blitzkrieg**
- **Maginot Line**
- **Battle of Britain**
- **Winston Churchill**
- **Wendell Willkie**
- **Lend-Lease Act**
- **Battle of the Atlantic**
- **Atlantic Charter**

Locate and explain the importance of the following:

- **Munich**
- **Poland**
- **Danzig**
- **Belgium**
- **Dunkirk**
- **Vichy**

Reading for Content Understanding

1 **Main Idea** How did the United States aid the Allies while remaining neutral?

2 **Main Idea** Why did Japan attack Pearl Harbor?

3 **Geographic Diversity** *Movement* Make a graphic organizer describing and explaining Germany's early conquests in Europe.

4 **Writing** *Expressing* Imagine that it is June 1940 and France has just fallen to Germany. Create a script for a radio editorial expressing your support for or opposition to U.S. involvement in World War II

5 **Critical Thinking** *Determining the Strength of an Argument* Some historians have suggested that World War II might have been prevented if the Allies had refused Hitler's demands at the Munich Conference. Do you agree? Explain your answer.

Section 1 Review ANSWERS

Identify
For significance, see the following pages:

- Munich Conference, p. 476
- appeasement, p. 476
- nonaggression pact, p. 476
- Allied Powers, p. 476
- Blitzkrieg, p. 476
- Maginot Line, p. 476
- Battle of Britain, p. 477
- Winston Churchill, p. 477
- Wendell Willkie, p. 478
- Lend-Lease Act, p. 478
- Battle of the Atlantic, p. 478
- Atlantic Charter, p. 478

Locate
For locations, see the map on page 477.

Reading for Content Understanding

1. It used the "cash-and-carry" system, exchanged destroyers for leases on British Caribbean naval bases, and passed the Lend-Lease Act to loan the Allies weapons and other war supplies.

2. Japan wanted to destroy the U.S. fleet at Pearl Harbor to retaliate against U.S. economic actions against it and to complete its conquest of Southeast Asia.

3. Organizers will vary but should include information about the conquests of Poland, Austria, Czechoslovakia, Denmark, Norway, Belgium, Luxembourg, the Netherlands, and France.

4. Scripts will vary but each student should state a position and provide support for it.

5. Answers will vary but students should use material from the section to support their arguments.

OBJECTIVES

- **Explain how the United States mobilized for World War II.**
- **Describe the effects of World War II on civilian women and minorities.**
- **Analyze reasons for U.S. internment of Japanese Americans during World War II.**

FOCUS

Motivate Before Reading

Have students speculate on the ways that people living in a democracy might contribute to a war effort. Have students work together on a display illustrating some of these methods. Then discuss the methods depicted in the display. Tell students that in this section they will learn how the people of the United States mobilized for war and the effects the war had on them.

Section 2 RESOURCES

PRINT

★ Guided Reading Strategies 16.2

★ Biography Reading 16: Benjamin Oliver Davis Jr.

★ Section 2 Review, p. 483

★ Daily Quiz 16.2

MULTIMEDIA

★ *Teaching Resources CD–ROM*, Lesson 16.2

★ Everyday Life in America Transparency 26: Inside an Internment Camp, World War II

★ *Exploring America's Past* Video Segment: Prisoners of War; *Teacher's Guide*, pp. 29–30

SHELTERED ENGLISH

★ Main Idea Activities for Reteaching and Sheltered English 16.2

SECTION 2

Mobilizing for War

Reading Focus

How did the United States mobilize for World War II?

What effects did World War II have on civilian women and minorities?

Why did the U.S. government intern Japanese Americans during the war?

Key Terms

War Production Board
Selective Training and Service Act
Fair Employment Practices Committee
braceros
zoot-suit riots
internment

AFTER THE UNITED STATES entered World War II, the government called upon all U.S. citizens to join the war effort. Officials asked civilians to limit their use of canned foods, gasoline, tires, and other items needed to supply the troops. Most of Mary Speir's neighbors in Westminster, Maryland, flew American flags outside their homes, but she did not. She understood the great sacrifices that Americans would have to make to win the war. One day a man said to her, "You're not very patriotic, are you?" Speir—whose 20-year-old son had died in battle—answered, "It takes more than waving a flag to win a war."

The U.S. government used ration stamps to control the supply of materials important to the war effort.

Working for the War Effort

Still suffering from the Great Depression, the United States took on a huge and costly task when it entered World War II. However, the economy began to recover as the country mobilized to meet the demands of war.

Industry Gears Up for War

Production boomed as American factories turned out enormous quantities of tanks, jeeps, guns, and ammunition. Perhaps the most remarkable example of wartime production was the construction of Liberty ships—transport vessels designed to carry troops and supplies. Workers could build one of these ships in a matter of days, leading observers to joke that they were "built by the mile and chopped off by the yard."

Most workers were employed and earnings rose. Many Americans, including some rural residents, relocated to take high-paying factory jobs in the North and Midwest or shipyard jobs along the West Coast. Even so, U.S. agricultural production remained high. Farmers managed to feed Americans as well as the European Allies.

Introduce Key Terms

Linguistic. Review this section's key terms with students. Have students use context cues from the section to write a definition for each term. Pair students and have partners take turns reading their definitions. **SHELTERED ENGLISH**

TEACH

Have students read Section 2 and complete Guided Reading Strategies 16.2. Choose one or more of the following activities to explore the section content with students. For further suggestions on block scheduling or team teaching, see the *Block Scheduling Handbook.*

LEVEL 1: Linguistic. (Suggested time: 15 min.) As a class, go over students' Guided Reading Strategies. Then use the Reading Focus questions to highlight the main ideas of the section. **SHELTERED ENGLISH**

ALL LEVELS: Linguistic. (Suggested time: 15 min. plus homework) Assign each student one of the following topics: producing war materials, recruiting soldiers, or financing the war. Have each student create a public service announcement describing government preparations in their assigned area.

To prepare the nation for war, the government expanded its role and increased its regulation of the economy. The **War Production Board** (WPB) oversaw the conversion of factories to war production. In 1942, for example, the WPB banned the production of cars so that automotive plants could focus on producing military equipment. The WPB was later replaced by the Office of War Mobilization (OWM).

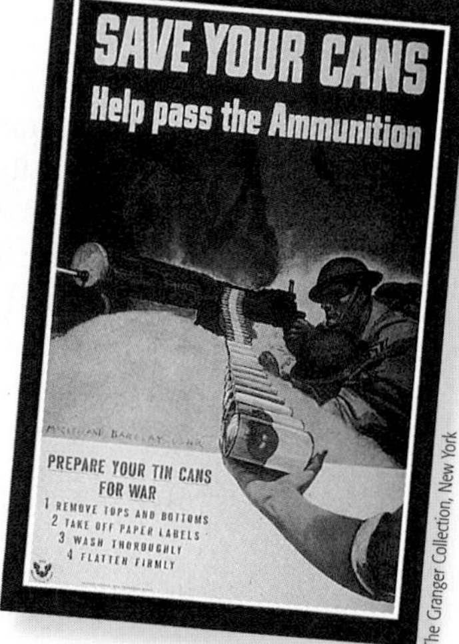

The Granger Collection, New York

A poster urging Americans to recycle

The Troops

In addition to reorganizing the economy, the U.S. government had to recruit and train millions of soldiers. Congress had prepared for this in 1940 when it passed the **Selective Training and Service Act**, the first peacetime draft in U.S. history. At first, the law required all men between the ages of 21 and 35 to register, but it later included men aged 18 to 38. Local draft boards granted deferments, or postponements of service, for medical or religious reasons. People who held jobs that were vital to the war effort were also excused from the draft.

More than 16 million Americans, including 1 million African Americans and some 300,000 Mexican Americans, served in the military. African American troops faced discrimination in the armed forces and generally served in segregated units. As the war went on, however, African Americans gradually won increased opportunities to serve in infantry, tank, and air force units and to train as officers.

Support and Sacrifice

After the attack on Pearl Harbor, the American people rallied together to support the war effort. The government worked hard to keep morale high, knowing that people had to endure shortages, hardships, and worse—the loss of loved ones.

To pay for the war effort, the government drastically increased taxes. For the first time, middle- and lower-income Americans had to pay income taxes. These tax increases paid only 40 percent of the war expenses, however. The government borrowed the difference, mostly by selling war bonds to the public.

Opportunities and Obstacles

The mobilization for war brought new opportunities to women and minorities. However, as they entered the workplace these groups still sometimes encountered unfair treatment.

Women

With the U.S. entry into the war, there were many new jobs and not enough workers. The government urged women to fill these new positions. As men left for war, women replaced them in factories and business offices. One female worker recalled her job at Rohr Aircraft:

> **"[I] learned how to use an electric drill, . . . how to rivet. . . . I was an eager learner, and I soon became an outstanding riveter. At Rohr I worked riveting the boom doors on P-38s [fighter planes]. . . The war really created opportunities for women. It was the first time we got a chance to show that we could do a lot of things that only men had done before."**

These men are signing up to join the 99th Pursuit Squadron—the first U.S. Army Air Corps unit to allow African Americans to enlist.

Daily Life

Children and the War. Many young people in the United States eagerly pitched in to support the war effort. They helped with scrap drives to collect essential materials, such as newspaper, metal, and rubber. They also purchased war stamps and bonds. In 1944 the U.S. armed forces bought 11,700 parachutes, 2,900 planes, and over 44,000 jeeps with money generated by school sales of war stamps and bonds.

Activity: Ask students to use the library or other resources to find information on how local children responded to the war. Have each student create a flyer promoting the activities of a local children's group.

Multimedia Resources

Exploring America's Past Video Segment: Prisoners of War; *Teacher's Guide*, pp. 29–30

Search 20091, Play to 27023
Videodisc Blue Side A

Play

Pause

See *Teacher's Guide* for Spanish barcode.

Multimedia Resources

Everyday Life in America Transparency 26: Inside an Internment Camp, World War II

TEACHER TO TEACHER

LEVEL 3: Logical-Mathematical. (Suggested time: 35 min.) Ron Tripp of Shepherd, Michigan, suggested the following activity: Have students create a two-column chart showing the war's impact on American women, African Americans, Mexican Americans, and Japanese Americans. The first column should identify what life was like for each group prior to the war. The second should identify wartime legislation or economic factors that changed life for each group and explain how.

CLOSE

Visual-Spatial. Have students create posters illustrating how the people of the United States mobilized for war and how the war changed their lives.

CHALLENGE AND EXTEND

Linguistic, Logical-Mathematical, Visual-Spatial. Have students use the library or other resources to research the use of movies to mobilize public opinion in favor of war. Have students report on ways that films defined American wartime culture.

Citizenship and Democracy

Broadway Supports the War. New York's Broadway theater district experienced a boom during World War II, both from troops on leave and from people on the home front looking for entertainment. Broadway showed its support for U.S. soldiers by performing benefit shows and offering soldiers the opportunity to appear in them. The cast of *Oklahoma!* put on 44 free performances for U.S. troops. Irving Berlin's musical spectacle *This Is the Army* boasted a cast of 300 soldiers.

Activity: Have students use the library and other resources to find more information on types of entertainment for soldiers during the war. Have students report on their findings.

American Arts Answers

1. *Oklahoma!* is about two cowboys trying to win the affections of two farm girls, and since many soldiers were separated from their loved ones it appealed to their hopes and dreams. The upbeat musical also lifted the spirits of many Americans.

2. because it was an extremely popular show, so many people would see war advertisements and notices presented at it

Although they did the same work as men, women often faced discrimination and received less pay.

Some 300,000 women worked in the armed forces. They joined organizations such as the Women's Auxiliary Army Corps (WAAC) and the Women's Airforce Service Pilots (WASP). Women performed a variety of military jobs. Some helped operate military communications systems. Others flew planes from factories to military units. Army and navy nurses served in combat areas.

African Americans

As during World War I, many African American civilians migrated from the South to cities in the North to join the industrial labor force. Despite their important contributions, African Americans often received less pay than white workers in similar jobs.

To protest this discrimination, African American labor leader A. Philip Randolph organized a march on Washington, D.C. Randolph agreed to cancel the march when President Roosevelt issued an executive order banning racial discrimination in defense industries. Roosevelt also created the **Fair Employment Practices Committee** (FEPC) to prevent discrimination in war industries and government jobs. African Americans gained new opportunities in some defense companies, earning better pay than before.

Mexican Americans

Many Mexican American civilians moved to the West Coast and the Midwest to take advantage of wartime job opportunities. In 1942, to meet a labor shortage in the Southwest, the U.S. government authorized Mexican workers called **braceros** to enter the United States. Some 200,000 braceros became a critical part of the agricultural economy in the West and the Southwest.

Mexican Americans faced discrimination during World War II despite supporting the war effort. Many young Mexican American men of the time

American Arts

Oklahoma!

In 1943 writer Richard Rodgers and composer Oscar Hammerstein II created *Oklahoma!*, one of the most popular musicals of all time. *Oklahoma!* is a simple, down-home story—the tale of two cowboys wooing two farm girls.

Oklahoma! opened on Broadway at the St. James Theatre on March 31, 1943. The musical was so popular that the theater often displayed the sign "We have no tickets for *Oklahoma!*" in the lobby. One night, a young couple showed up at the St. James box office hoping to get tickets, but the show was sold out. When the man mentioned that he was heading to Europe the next day to fight in the war, the ticket seller silently pushed over a pair of tickets. It might have been the man's last chance to see the show.

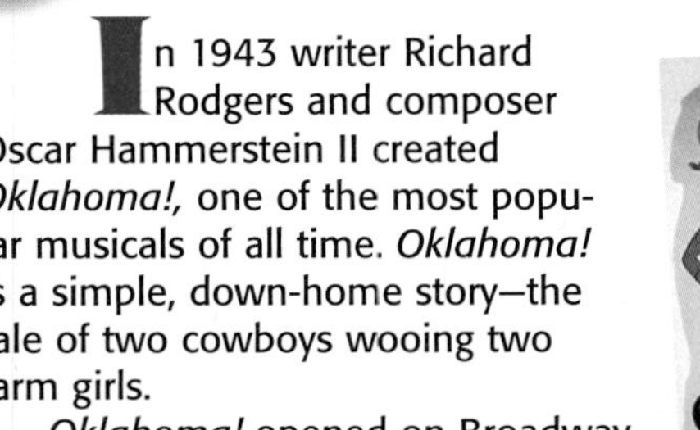

The upbeat musical Oklahoma! *lifted the spirits of many Americans during the war years.*

Oklahoma! was so popular that it was used to promote the war effort. Some *Oklahoma!* sheet-music covers contained a note in the left-hand corner urging people to buy U.S. War Savings Bonds. The musical ended its long run at the St. James in May 1949.

Understanding the Arts

1. Why did *Oklahoma!* appeal to wartime audiences?
2. Why do you think *Oklahoma!* was chosen to promote the war effort?

REVIEW

Linguistic. Have students complete the Section Review questions. Then ask students to write a page for a history book describing how government control over the economy changed during the war. Ask students to include a discussion of how these changes affected women and minority groups. Have students read one another's accounts.

ASSESS

Have students complete Daily Quiz 16.2.

RETEACH

Logical-Mathematical, Interpersonal. Have students complete Main Idea Activities for Reteaching and Sheltered English 16.2. Using red ink, create sets of index cards that identify changes in the United States that occurred during the war. Then use blue ink to create other sets that identify the causes of these changes. Have students work with a partner and take turns drawing a change card and matching the card with its appropriate cause card. As students create appropriate matches, have them discuss the relationship between each change and its cause. **SHELTERED ENGLISH**

wore zoot suits—outfits with oversized jackets, wide-brimmed hats, and baggy pants that fit tightly at the ankles. In Los Angeles in June 1943, groups of sailors attacked Mexican Americans wearing these outfits in the so-called **zoot-suit riots**. For 10 days, mobs roamed the city, assaulting Mexican Americans. Riots against Mexican Americans broke out in seven other cities. Nevertheless, many Mexican Americans made patriotic contributions.

These Japanese American women are standing outside the barber shop at the internment center in Malheur County, Oregon.

Japanese American Internment

Wartime anger after the Pearl Harbor attack led to widespread discrimination against Japanese Americans. In 1941 more than 125,000 people of Japanese descent lived in the United States, mostly on the West Coast. Some were issei, Japanese immigrants, but more were nisei, U.S. citizens born to Japanese immigrants.

After Pearl Harbor, many Americans questioned the loyalty of issei and nisei. Fearing the possibility of spying or sabotage, in February 1942 the U.S. government began a process of **internment**, or forced relocation and imprisonment. As part of this policy, the government moved most Japanese Americans to remote camps, which were largely located in the western United States. One woman remembered

> **"that sad morning when we realized suddenly that we wouldn't be free. . . . Suddenly you realized that human beings were being put behind fences just like on the farm where we had horses and pigs in corrals."**

Despite the internment policy, many Japanese Americans volunteered for military service. Many nisei served in the 442nd Regimental Combat Team, a highly distinguished unit that fought in Europe. Other Japanese Americans played a vital role in the Pacific campaign as interpreters and translators with military intelligence units.

SECTION 2 REVIEW

Identify and explain the significance of the following:

- **War Production Board**
- **Selective Training and Service Act**
- **A. Philip Randolph**
- **Fair Employment Practices Committee**
- **braceros**
- **zoot-suit riots**
- **internment**

Reading for Content Understanding

1 Main Idea What did the United States do to prepare for its entry into World War II?

2 Main Idea How did the war affect women, African Americans, and Mexican Americans?

3 Citizenship and Democracy Why did the U.S. government move Japanese Americans into internment camps during the war? How did some Japanese Americans show their patriotism despite this internment?

4 Writing *Describing* Imagine that you are a female defense worker during the war. Write several diary entries describing your new job.

5 Critical Thinking *Drawing Conclusions* Why do you think the U.S. government needed to regulate the economy during the war?

Section 2 Review ANSWERS

Identify

For significance, see the following pages:

- War Production Board, p. 481
- Selective Training and Service Act, p. 481
- A. Philip Randolph, p. 482
- Fair Employment Practices Committee, p. 482
- braceros, p. 482
- zoot-suit riots, p. 483
- internment, p. 483

Reading for Content Understanding

1. increased output and produced war materials, regulated what products were made, and required males between 21 and 35 (later between 18 and 38) to register for the draft

2. women—many took jobs in factories and business offices, while others joined the armed forces; African Americans—many moved to northern cities to take jobs, and the Fair Employment Practices Committee was established to investigate discrimination; Mexican Americans—many moved to take jobs on the West Coast and in the Midwest; braceros were allowed to enter the country and perform agricultural work

3. The U.S. government was worried about the threat of sabotage; they volunteered for military service.

4. Answers will vary but students should describe both positive and negative aspects of women's new jobs.

5. to organize resources and coordinate production for the war effort

Section 3 Lesson Plan

OBJECTIVES

- **Analyze the importance of the Allies' North Africa campaign.**
- **Identify the major turning points of the war in Europe.**
- **Describe how the Allies drove the Germans out of France.**

FOCUS

Motivate Before Reading

Ask students to list strategies and weapons used on land, at sea, and in the air during World War I. Have volunteers provide information about these strategies and weapons to the class. Tell students that in this section they will learn about the weapons and strategies used by Allied forces in North Africa and Europe

Section 3 RESOURCES

PRINT

★ Guided Reading Strategies 16.3

★ Primary Source Reading 16: A Witness to the Normandy Invasion

★ Section 3 Review, p. 489

★ Daily Quiz 16.3

MULTIMEDIA

★ *Teaching Resources CD–ROM*, Lesson 16.3

★ Linking Geography and History Transparency 18: World War II in Europe, 1942–1945

SHELTERED ENGLISH

★ Main Idea Activities for Reteaching and Sheltered English 16.3

The War in North Africa and Europe

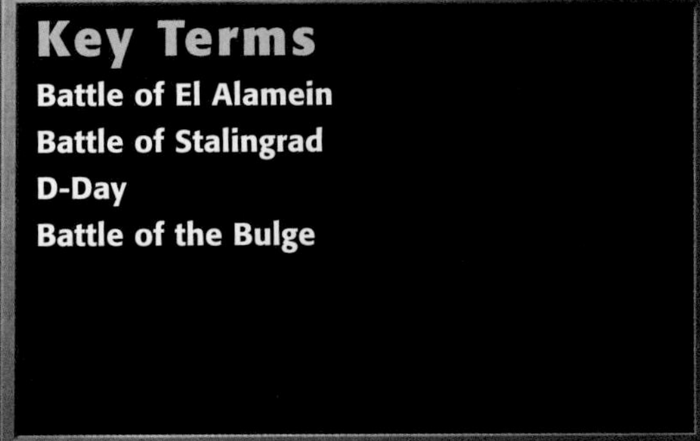

Reading Focus

Why was the Allies' North Africa campaign so important?

What were the major turning points of the war in Europe?

How did the Allies drive the Germans out of France?

Key Terms

Battle of El Alamein

Battle of Stalingrad

D-Day

Battle of the Bulge

AFTER THE DUNKIRK EVACUATION *in May and June 1940, British prime minister Winston Churchill declared, "We shall defend our Island, whatever the cost may be." His words inspired the nation. During the Battle of Britain, the RAF prevented a German invasion. However, the* Luftwaffe *continued to bomb London through the spring of 1941. Churchill had said, "We shall fight on the beaches. We shall fight in the fields and in the streets, . . . we shall never surrender." Despite widespread damage to their nation, the British people lived up to his words.*

Some of the Dunkirk evacuation boats

A Desperate Situation

In the fall of 1941, the Axis Powers pressed the Allies nearly to the breaking point. German submarine attacks were severely straining Britain's North Atlantic supply lines. Axis forces had occupied Greece and Yugoslavia and were steadily advancing in North Africa and the Soviet Union.

Two weeks after the attack on Pearl Harbor, President Roosevelt and Prime Minister Churchill met in Washington, D.C. They agreed to focus on defeating Germany first, rather than launching a full attack on Japan. The two leaders also discussed a possible attack on Axis positions in North Africa. In January 1942, China and the Soviet Union agreed to these war aims and pledged their resources to defeating the Axis Powers. They also agreed not to make a separate peace with any Axis nation.

In 1942 the war in the Atlantic looked more hopeful after the Allies introduced new sonar technology, which helped locate and track German submarines. New long-range patrol bombers also offered some protection to ships far out at sea.

during World War II. As students read the chapter, have them compare the strategies and weapons used during World War I to those used during World War II.

Introduce Key Terms

Linguistic, Visual-Spatial. Review this section's key terms with students. Then give students outline maps of Europe and North Africa and have them identify the location of each battle listed in the key terms. Next to each location, have students identify the significance of the battle. **SHELTERED ENGLISH**

TEACH

Have students read Section 3 and complete Guided Reading Strategies 16.3. Choose one or more of the following activities to explore the section content with students. For further suggestions on block scheduling or team teaching, see the *Block Scheduling Handbook*.

LEVEL 1: Linguistic. (Suggested time: 15 min.) As a class, go over students' Guided Reading Strategies. Then use the Reading Focus questions to highlight the main ideas of the section. **SHELTERED ENGLISH**

While Allied naval forces fought for command of the Atlantic, Allied air forces tried to destroy Germany's economic resources. Flying out of Britain, Allied bombers primarily targeted factories, railroads, and military centers, but they also hit many German cities. To improve the accuracy and effectiveness of their raids, U.S. bombers flew their missions in daylight. As a result, bomber crews suffered very high casualties but made large contributions to winning the war.

North Africa and Italy

In September 1940, Italian forces in Libya had attacked Egypt. They had hoped to capture the Suez Canal, a vital Allied supply route. The British counterattacked, however, and drove back the Italians. Adolf Hitler then sent the German *Afrika Korps*, commanded by General Erwin Rommel, to the region. For the next two years a back-and-forth battle raged over some 1,500 miles.

A master of warfare and surprise attacks, Rommel soon became known as the Desert Fox. By the summer of 1942, Rommel seemed ready to take Egypt, but a shortage of troops and supplies slowed his offensive. In November, British forces under General Bernard Montgomery stopped Rommel's advance in the **Battle of El Alamein**. About the same time, a combined British-American force under U.S. general Dwight D. Eisenhower landed west of Egypt in French North Africa. Eisenhower was an expert at organization and planning and soon had U.S. troops pushing back the German forces. Montgomery's and Eisenhower's troops trapped Rommel's retreating *Afrika Korps* between them. After a series of hard-fought battles in early 1943, the *Afrika Korps* surrendered.

Having driven the Axis troops from North Africa, the Allies decided to invade Italy, the place that Winston Churchill called the enemy's "soft underbelly." In July 1943, Allied forces landed on the island of Sicily. After winning control of the island, they began landing troops on the Italian mainland in September.

German sharpshooters search for enemy troops in North Africa. Wide-open spaces, dust, sand, heat, and disease all made desert fighting very difficult.

As the Allies advanced, the Italian government overthrew dictator Benito Mussolini in order to make peace. Hitler, however, was determined to stop the Allies in Italy. He stepped in to save Mussolini. German troops then took control of Italy and slowed the Allied advance with fierce fighting. In January 1944 the Allies tried to take the Germans by surprise by landing a force behind

Biography

Daniel Inouye

Daniel Inouye was born in Hawaii in 1924. After Japan attacked Pearl Harbor in 1941, he volunteered for military service and served in the famous 442nd Regimental Combat Team.

While in Italy, the 442nd captured Mount Folgorito, a heroic and spectacular accomplishment. Inouye recalled that while his unit was climbing the cliffs "some men had slipped and bounced as much as 100 feet down the steep slopes . . . but not one of them cried out and the soundless advance went on." They took the Germans by surprise and captured the mountain. In a later battle with the Germans, Inouye was wounded and lost his right arm.

After the war Inouye studied law and entered politics. He eventually became a U.S. representative and later a senator.

Biography

Daniel Inouye. At 18, Daniel Inouye left college to join the first nisei military outfit, the 442nd Regimental Combat Team. The outfit became the war's most decorated army unit. After the war, Inouye returned to college and earned a law degree in 1952. His real interest was politics, however. He ran for office and moved up the ranks. In 1959, when Hawaii gained statehood, Inouye won a seat in the U.S. House of Representatives to become the first Japanese-American to serve in the U.S. Congress. He was elected to the U.S. Senate in 1962. Senator Inouye has supported civil rights and minority causes. He also served on the Senate Watergate Committee and chaired the committee that investigated the Iran-contra affair.

Critical Thinking: How might Inouye's military service have helped his political career?

ANSWER: Students might mention that his service proved his patriotism and helped gain others' respect.

ALL LEVELS: Logical-Mathematical, Visual-Spatial. (Suggested time: 45 min.) Provide students with an outline map of Europe and North Africa or have them use the maps they worked on in the Introducing Key Terms activity. Ask students to review the section entitled "North Africa and Italy" and then label on the maps each location described in that section and calculate the distances between them. Then have students review material from Section 1 to identify areas that were under Axis occupation in December 1941. Finally, lead a question-and-answer discussion to help students deduce why the campaign in North Africa was so important to the Allies. **SHELTERED ENGLISH**

LEVEL 2: Linguistic, Logical-Mathematical. (Suggested time: 45 min.) Ask students to imagine that they are military advisers reporting on the progress of the war. Assign each student one of the following battles: Battle of El Alamein, Battle of Stalingrad, D-Day, or Battle of the Bulge. Have each student prepare a status report describing the outcome of the battle and explaining its importance. Ask volunteers to read their reports to the class. Then lead a discussion on why these battles are considered important. (A similar activity in Section 4 deals with the war in the Pacific; you may wish to combine the two activities.)

Using Visual Resources

Special Forces. The Rangers, pictured at the top of this page participating in the D-Day invasion, served in the U.S. Army's special forces during World War II. Modeled after the British commandos, the Rangers were specially trained to lead invasions into areas that were normally inaccessible, such as the steep cliffs pictured in this photograph. Timing also played an important role in the invasion. During the war, amphibious landings in Europe were usually conducted at night. However, with the complexities of the D-Day invasion, it was decided to attack just after dawn.

Critical Thinking: What factors made this invasion particularly dangerous?

ANSWER: Answers will vary but students should identify factors such as the surf, the exposure troops faced while on the beach and climbing the cliffs and hills, and the fact that Axis forces anticipated an invasion somewhere along France's coast.

German lines at the seaport of Anzio. The landing force failed to break through the German lines and remained trapped at Anzio for four months. Allied forces fighting their way up the Italian Peninsula eventually linked up with the Anzio force. Together they captured Rome, Italy's capital, in June. In late April 1945 the Allies drove the Germans out of Italy. That same month, Mussolini tried to flee the country but was instead captured and executed.

U.S. Rangers charged across the beach under heavy fire from German forces and then climbed these steep cliffs during the D-Day invasion.

Turning Points

In early 1943 the Allies had begun the final push to defeat the Axis Powers, and victories during the winter of 1942–43 brought the Allies closer to their goal. As British and U.S. troops advanced in North Africa and Italy, Soviet forces began driving the Axis Powers out of the Soviet Union. The turning point in the war between Germany and the Soviet Union came in the city of Stalingrad.

Stalingrad

After their initial invasion in June 1941, Axis forces had advanced deep into the Soviet Union. In mid-1942 a German army tried to capture the city of Stalingrad.

The **Battle of Stalingrad** was a fierce struggle. Soldiers fought hand-to-hand combat for each city block. As the harsh winter weather set in, Soviet reinforcements arrived and surrounded the German army. One German soldier described the scene:

> **"The men in field grey just slouched on, . . . filthy and . . . louse-ridden, their weary shoulders sagging. . . . Skin now loose-stretched over bone, so utter [complete] was the exhaustion, so utter the starvation. . . . And whenever any individual could do no more, when even the . . . fear of death ceased to have meaning, . . . the debilitated [weakened] body . . . came to a standstill. Soon . . . snow covered the object and only the toe of a jackboot or an arm frozen to stone could remind you that what was now an elongated [long] white hummock [small hill] had quite recently been a human being."**

Soviet soldiers scramble across a ditch that used to be a street in the city of Stalingrad. Most of the city was destroyed during the six months of fighting.

Finally, in late January 1943, with supplies running desperately low, the remaining German troops in Stalingrad surrendered. The Axis Powers had lost some 200,000 soldiers in the fighting.

Six months after the Battle of Stalingrad, the Soviets dealt another great blow to the Germans in a huge tank battle near the Soviet city of Kursk.

LEVEL 3: Linguistic, Intrapersonal. (Suggested time: 20 min. plus homework) Lead a discussion on the liberation of France. Then ask students to write a series of letters—similar to what a U.S. soldier might have sent home—describing how Allied forces drove the Germans out of France. Have students include descriptions of D-Day, the Allied advance through France, and the French uprising in Paris. Ask volunteers to read one of their letters to the class.

CLOSE

Visual-Spatial. Have each student prepare a series of commemorative stamps celebrating Allied efforts in North Africa and Europe during World War II. Encourage students to focus on heroes who led the troops to victory. Have students write a brief summary under each stamp. Call on volunteers to explain their stamps to the class. **SHELTERED ENGLISH**

The combined Soviet victories at Stalingrad and Kursk marked a turning point in the war. Hitler's attempt to conquer the Soviet Union was crushed. Axis troops retreated west toward Germany.

D-Day

President Roosevelt's top military adviser, General George C. Marshall, had long supported an Allied invasion of German-occupied France. General Eisenhower was put in charge of planning the invasion, called Operation Overlord. The plan called for a massive landing on the beaches of Normandy, in northern France. To mislead the Germans about the exact location of the attack, the Allies staged several decoy landings in other places.

On the morning of June 6, 1944—a date recorded in history as **D-Day**—some 150,000 Allied soldiers swarmed ashore in Normandy. Hundreds

World War II in Europe, 1942–1945

Learning from Maps In 1939 Germany began an aggressive attack, conquering most of Europe by 1942.

Place Which European countries remained neutral?

Biography

General George S. Patton. Known as Old Blood and Guts, General George S. Patton was one of America's most colorful commanders. Patton made his reputation leading successful tank campaigns. After the D-Day invasion, Patton led the Third Army on a dramatic sweep through France. In 1945 Patton's tank troops crossed the Rhine, advancing into Germany. Patton was relieved of his command in October 1945, after he publicly criticized the Allied policy of ridding Germany of all Nazi influences.

Critical Thinking: Why would Patton's criticisms of the U.S. government have cost him his job?

ANSWER: The army is under the control of the civilian government and must follow its orders.

MAP ANSWER

Ireland, Portugal, Spain, Sweden, and Switzerland

Multimedia Resources

Linking Geography and History Transparency 18: World War II in Europe, 1942–1945

CHALLENGE AND EXTEND

Linguistic. Have students use the library or other resources to find information on one of the following people: Omar Bradley, Dwight D. Eisenhower, George C. Marshall, Bernard Montgomery, George Patton, or Erwin Rommel. Have each student prepare a two- or three-page biography of the person. The biography should focus on the individual's early preparation for his role in the war as well as on his experience during the war. For example, a biography of Eisenhower might focus on his experience in organization along with his experience as a field commander, to point to his role as supreme commander of Allied troops.

REVIEW

Linguistic, Interpersonal. Have students complete the Section Review questions. Organize the class into four groups. Ask each group to prepare a brief presentation on the importance of each area of battle described in this section. Have each group give a presentation on one of the following areas: North Africa, Italy, western Europe, or the Soviet Union. Encourage other students to ask questions pertaining to the significance of the battles in each area.

Across the Curriculum

ART

Saving The Hermitage. In 1941 German troops pushed closer to Leningrad. Joseph Orbeli, curator of The Hermitage, Russia's great art museum, began putting into action a plan he had worked on since 1939. The plan was to transport all the art treasures of The Hermitage to a safer place. Over 500,000 priceless works, including paintings by Rembrandt and Leonardo da Vinci, were loaded into 31 train cars and shipped to a secret location. A month later, another 23 train cars were loaded with more art. However, the advancing German army cut off the last railroad out of Leningrad. The remaining art was stored in the cellar of The Hermitage.

Activity: Have students conduct research on how a local museum protects its collections against the threat of natural disasters and civil disturbances. If no plan is in place, encourage students to devise their own.

Global Connections Answers

1. About 1 million people died from starvation or exposure.

2. They killed many civilians and burned hundreds of villages.

3. The price of victory included the deaths of 14 million Soviet soldiers and 6 million civilians.

Global Connections

The Eastern Front

While the Allies fought the Axis Powers in western Europe, a fierce battle raged in the east. Millions of German and Soviet soldiers fought along the 4,000-mile eastern front. This front opened in June 1941, when some 13 million German soldiers invaded the Soviet Union. As the Germans swept eastward, they killed many civilians. Desperate to stop the Germans, the Soviets followed a scorched-earth policy, destroying anything the Germans might have found useful, such as factories and dams.

This poster encouraged Soviet citizens to help rebuild their country.

As part of their eastern-front strategy, the Germans tried to capture important Soviet cities. They blockaded Leningrad (present-day St. Petersburg), which soon ran out of fuel, running water, and food. The siege lasted around 900 days. By the time the Germans retreated, about 1 million people, or one third of Leningrad's population, had died. Many died from hunger and exposure to the extreme cold.

The Battle of Stalingrad (present-day Volgograd) began in September 1942. A Soviet soldier wrote, "Every street and house has turned into a battlefield." In January 1943, exhausted by both the fighting and the harsh winter weather, many of the German troops in Stalingrad surrendered.

As the German armies retreated westward, they burned hundreds of villages and killed thousands of people. "The enemy has destroyed everything," one Soviet soldier wrote.

The Allied victory on the eastern front came at a great price. German troops had pushed some 1,200 miles into Soviet territory, and 14 million Soviet soldiers had died defending their country. At least 6 million civilians also lost their lives, and thousands of children became orphans.

Understanding What You Read

1. How did the siege affect the people of Leningrad?
2. How did German troops treat Soviet civilians?
3. What was the cost of victory on the eastern front?

of warships off the coast attempted to protect them with a cover of gunfire. D-Day was the largest sea-and-land invasion in history.

The Allies faced fierce resistance during the invasion. One U.S. officer on the scene reported:

> **"[The assault units] were disorganized, had suffered heavy casualties and were handicapped by losses of valuable equipment. . . . They were pinned down by intense enemy fire. . . . Personnel and equipment were being piled up ashore . . . where congested [crowded] groups afforded good targets for the enemy."**

Nonetheless, the determined Allies continued their assault. By the end of D-Day, they had landed more than 155,000 troops in France.

Hundreds of thousands more Allied troops reinforced the D-Day forces during the summer.

ASSESS

Have students complete Daily Quiz 16.3.

RETEACH

Kinesthetic, Visual-Spatial. Have students complete Main Idea Activities for Reteaching and Sheltered English 16.3. Have students create a board game covering material from this section. The board should include squares representing battles and leaders, as well as ones that represent setbacks such as delays caused by supply problems. Students should also create index cards containing facts about the battles and leaders. Have players role a die to see how many squares to move. If they land on a square for a battle or leader, they should search the cards to find a fact pertaining to that square. If the match is correct, they can role again. If students land on a square with a setback, they should follow the instructions on the card, such as lose a turn. The winner is the first player to make it around the board **SHELTERED ENGLISH**

Victorious Allied troops move under Paris's Arc de Triomphe, *the largest triumphal arch in the world, and receive a warm welcome.*

With increased forces, U.S. general Omar Bradley led the breakout from the beaches and the Allied advance into France. Tank forces under General George Patton then broke through the German lines in July. Meanwhile, new Allied forces landed in southern France and began to advance northward. The liberation of France was at last in sight.

In August, fighting broke out in Paris as French citizens rose up against the German occupation forces. On August 24 a small unit of Free French troops entered the city. The next morning, Bradley arrived with his 12th Army Group. As one person described, "All Paris surged out to meet the Allied columns and welcome their liberators."

The Battle of the Bulge

After liberating Paris, the Allies began to push through Belgium and France toward Germany itself. Although defeat seemed certain, Hitler refused to surrender.

In December 1944 Hitler made a desperate attempt to split the advancing Allied armies by trying to recapture Antwerp, Belgium, the Allies' major supply port. The Germans' target was the Ardennes (ahr-den), a densely forested region defended by a few U.S. divisions. On December 16, some 25 divisions of the German army attacked in the heavy snow and almost broke the Allied lines. Surprised, outnumbered and without air support, the Americans fought bravely in the **Battle of the Bulge**. U.S. losses were heavy—some 77,000 casualties—but the American resistance had slowed the German counterattack.

As Allied reinforcements arrived, the German offensive stalled, then turned into a general retreat. The Battle of the Bulge ended Germany's ability to wage an offensive war. As 1945 began, the Soviets pushed toward Berlin, Germany's capital. U.S. and British troops prepared to cross the Rhine River into Germany from the west.

SECTION 3 REVIEW

Identify and explain the significance of the following:

- **Erwin Rommel**
- **Bernard Montgomery**
- **Battle of El Alamein**
- **Dwight D. Eisenhower**
- **Battle of Stalingrad**
- **George C. Marshall**
- **D-Day**
- **Omar Bradley**
- **George Patton**
- **Battle of the Bulge**

Reading for Content Understanding

1 **Main Idea** What military goals did the Allied forces achieve in their North Africa campaign?

2 **Main Idea** What battles were turning points for the war in Europe?

3 **Geographic Diversity** *Movement* Create a flow chart describing how the Allies pushed the Germans out of France.

4 **Writing** *Informing* Imagine that you are an American reporter during World War II. Write a brief article informing your readers about the Battle of the Bulge.

5 **Critical Thinking** *Synthesizing Information* How was cooperation among Allied nations important to the D-Day invasion?

Section 3 Review ANSWERS

Identify

For significance, see the following pages:

- Erwin Rommel, p. 485
- Bernard Montgomery, p. 485
- Battle of El Alamein, p. 485
- Dwight D. Eisenhower, p. 485
- Battle of Stalingrad, p. 486
- George C. Marshall, p. 487
- D-Day, p. 487
- Omar Bradley, p. 489
- George Patton, p. 489
- Battle of the Bulge, p. 489

Reading for Content Understanding

1. The Allied forces stopped Rommel's advance; retained control of the Suez Canal, a vital supply route; and secured a base in French North Africa, providing easier access to invade Italy.

2. the Battles of Stalingrad and Kursk and the D-Day invasion

3. Flowcharts will vary but should include the D-Day invasion and the efforts of Generals Bradley and Patton.

4. Articles will vary but should describe Germany's goals, the heavy U.S. casualties, and the results of Germany's loss.

5. Answers will vary but students should point out that large numbers of Allied troops and ships were used in the invasion, thus making cooperation essential to its success.

SECTION 4 LESSON PLAN

OBJECTIVES

- **Describe the path of Japanese forces after Pearl Harbor.**
- **Identify the turning points of the war in the Pacific.**
- **Analyze how the Allies advanced toward Japan.**

FOCUS

Motivate Before Reading

Show students pictures of the Marine Corps War Memorial (Iwo Jima Memorial). Ask students to write a description of the monument and to speculate about the significance of the battle. Tell students that in this section they will learn about U.S. involvement in the war in the Pacific.

Section 4 RESOURCES

PRINT

★ Guided Reading Strategies 16.4

★ Section 4 Review, p. 494

★ Daily Quiz 16.4

MULTIMEDIA

★ *Teaching Resources CD–ROM,* Lesson 16.4

★ Linking Geography and History Transparency 19: World War II in the Pacific, 1941–1945

★ HRW Web site

SHELTERED ENGLISH

★ Main Idea Activities for Reteaching and Sheltered English 16.4

War in the Pacific

Reading Focus

Where did Japan attack after its bombing of Pearl Harbor?

What three battles were the major turning points of the war in the Pacific?

How did the Allies advance toward Japan?

Key Terms

Bataan Death March
Battle of the Coral Sea
Battle of Midway
island-hopping
Battle of Leyte Gulf
kamikaze

ON NOVEMBER 20, 1943, U.S. Marines swarmed into the lagoon of Tarawa, one of the Gilbert Islands in the Pacific Ocean. Many flat-bottomed boats became stuck on reefs. As the marines waded ashore in chest-deep water, they came under a hail of Japanese machine-gun fire. "The water seemed never clear of . . . men," one witness recalled. "They kept falling, falling, falling . . . singly, in groups, and in rows." Yet the marines pressed on. Three days and 3,000 casualties later, they had overrun the island. Tarawa was just one of many difficult Allied landings in the Pacific.

U.S. Marines charge onto Tarawa and into Japanese machine-gun fire.

 Japan Advances Across the Pacific

In 1931, years before the battle at Tarawa, Japan had begun its wars of expansion in Asia by conquering Manchuria in China. Under General Hideki (hee-dek-ee) Tojo, Japan continued to expand across East Asia and the Pacific Ocean. Immediately after bombing Pearl Harbor, Japanese forces struck quickly to grab U.S. holdings in the Pacific and British and Dutch possessions in Southeast Asia.

By early 1942 Japan had seized the British colonies of Hong Kong and Singapore. Advancing through the independent country of Thailand, Japanese forces invaded Burma, a British colony. They then took control of the oil-rich Netherlands East Indies (present-day Indonesia) from the Dutch.

The Japanese also raced to strengthen their position against an expected U.S. counterattack in the Pacific. In December 1941 Japan had attacked and captured Guam and Wake Island, both U.S. territories. Farther north, Japanese forces landed on the U.S.-owned Aleutian islands of Kiska and

Introduce Key Terms

Linguistic, Interpersonal. Review this section's key terms with students. Have students use context cues to define each term and use it in a sentence. Pair students and ask them to share their sentences and definitions. **SHELTERED ENGLISH**

TEACH

Have students read Section 4 and complete Guided Reading Strategies 16.4. Choose one or more of the following activities to explore the section content with students. For further suggestions on block scheduling or team teaching, see the *Block Scheduling Handbook*.

LEVEL 1: Linguistic. (Suggested time: 15 min.) As a class, go over students' Guided Reading Strategies. Then use the Reading Focus questions to highlight the main ideas of the section. **SHELTERED ENGLISH**

ALL LEVELS: Visual-Spatial, Interpersonal. (Suggested time: 30 min. plus homework) Explain to students that during World War II many Americans found out about the progress of the war by watching newsreel footage shown before movies. Organize the class into groups and have each group develop a

These U.S. soldiers were among the thousands of prisoners who suffered brutal treatment on the Bataan Death March.

Attu, near Alaska. Japan also invaded the Philippines, another U.S. possession.

Under the direction of General Douglas MacArthur, U.S. and Filipino forces made a determined stand against the Japanese invasion. The capital of Manila fell quickly, however, and the islands' defenders retreated across Manila Bay to the Bataan Peninsula. Short of food, they held out on the fortified island of Corregidor as long as possible. In March 1942 President Roosevelt ordered MacArthur to go to Australia. "I shall return," he vowed before making his escape.

Weak and hungry, U.S. and Filipino units on the Bataan Peninsula and Corregidor surrendered soon afterward. The Japanese then made the more than 70,000 American and Filipino prisoners—many of whom were sick and wounded—march 65 miles up the peninsula to prison camps. In what became known as the **Bataan Death March**, the Japanese treated the prisoners harshly, killing many. More than 600 Americans and 10,000 Filipinos died on the Bataan Death March.

Halting Japan's Advance

In early 1942 Japan seemed unstoppable and ready to strike at India, Australia, Hawaii, and even the West Coast of the United States. Over the course of the year, however, Allied forces began to turn the tide of the war against Japan.

The Battle of the Coral Sea

To stop Japan's advance, the Allies had to defeat the Japanese navy. The U.S. Navy, commanded in the Pacific by Admiral Chester Nimitz, had a critical, top-secret advantage. Navy experts had cracked the Japanese communication code and could read secret Japanese messages. As a result, Nimitz learned that the Japanese planned to capture Port Moresby, in New Guinea.

To cut them off, Nimitz sent an Allied fleet to attack the Japanese invasion force in the Coral Sea northeast of Australia. In early May 1942, U.S. planes sank one Japanese carrier and damaged another in the **Battle of the Coral Sea**. The United States suffered losses as well. Japanese planes sank the U.S. carrier *Lexington* and damaged the *Yorktown*, but the Allies had stopped the Japanese advance for the first time.

The Battle of Midway

The secret work of the navy's code breakers contributed to a second important victory just weeks after the Battle of the Coral Sea. From intercepted messages, Nimitz learned that the Japanese planned to seize Midway, two islands located northwest of Hawaii. Nimitz ordered U.S. carriers to catch the Japanese by surprise.

The **Battle of Midway**, which took place between June 3 and 6, was a battle of carrier-based airplanes. Japanese and U.S. warplanes fought in

The Navajo Code Talkers used a special code in the Navajo language that the Japanese were never able to crack.

Cultural Diversity

Navajo Code Talkers. Critical to the success of the U.S. troops in the Pacific were the Navajo code talkers. The language of the Navajo is extremely complicated. It also is not a written language, and at the beginning of World War II experts estimated that fewer than 30 non-Navajos spoke the language fluently. In 1942 the U.S. Navy decided to use the Navajo language to transmit messages in code. Navajo code talkers could encode, transmit, and then decode a message faster than any communications machine of the time. Up to 420 Navajo served as code talkers for the marines during the war. Their services were used in such important battles as Guadalcanal and Iwo Jima.

Activity: Have students use the library or search the Internet through the HRW Web site to find more information on Navajo code talkers. Ask students to create a certificate of achievement that highlights the Navajo code talkers' accomplishments.

go.hrw.com
SB1 Code Talkers

simulation of a brief newsreel clip describing the Japanese advance after Pearl Harbor. Students can do this by taping several drawings depicting the events together, attaching the ends to sticks to create a scroll, and narrating the performance. Groups may wish to assign tasks such as script writers, scene illustrators, and announcers. Have each group present its newsreel to the class. **SHELTERED ENGLISH**

LEVEL 2: Linguistic, Logical-Mathematical. (Suggested time: 45 min.) Remind students of their roles in Section 3 as military advisers. Assign each student one of the following turning points in the Pacific: Battle of the Coral Sea, Battle of Midway, or Guadalcanal. Have each student prepare a status report describing the outcome of the battle and explaining why it marks a turning point in the war in the Pacific. Ask volunteers to read their reports to the class. Then lead a discussion explaining why these battles are considered turning points.

LEVEL 3: Linguistic, Logical-Mathematical, Intrapersonal. (Suggested time: 45 min.) Explain to students that as the United States attacked Okinawa, the Japanese relied on kamikaze tactics to win the battle. Ask students to write an essay analyzing the effectiveness of using kamikaze pilots at Okinawa. Encourage students to weigh the financial and human costs incurred by using such a strategy against the destruction and casualties it can cause the enemy. Ask volunteers to read their essays to the class.

Across the Curriculum

LITERATURE

Tales of the South Pacific. In 1944 Naval Reserve member James Michener was sent to the South Pacific, where he observed the activities and customs of civilians as well as U.S. military personnel. From this experience came his first book, *Tales of the South Pacific*, which won the Pulitzer Prize in 1948. This collection of short stories explored the emotions, boredom, and anxiety faced by U.S. troops as they waited for battle. In 1949 Michener's book was made into the popular Broadway musical *South Pacific*.

Critical Thinking: Why do you think the book and the musical were so popular?

ANSWER: People probably were interested in how U.S. troops lived so far away from home and how they fought the war.

the air trying to sink each others' aircraft carriers. When the battle was over, the United States had crippled the Japanese navy by sinking four of its carriers, while losing only one of its own. An officer on the Japanese carrier *Akagi* described his ship's fate:

> **"Within five minutes all her planes would be launched. Five minutes! Who would have dreamed that the tide of battle would shift completely in that brief interval of time? . . . The first Zero fighter [Japanese warplane] gathered speed and whizzed off the deck. At that instant a lookout screamed, 'Hell-divers!' I looked up to see three black enemy planes plummeting [diving] toward our ship. . . . Bombs! Down they came straight toward me!"**

After its defeat at Midway, the Japanese navy was on the defensive for the remainder of the war.

Guadalcanal

The Allies pressed the Japanese war effort even further on the island of Guadalcanal, one of the Solomon Islands in the Southwest Pacific. From Guadalcanal the Japanese air force could threaten the vital sea link between Australia and the United States. In August 1942 the United States began landing marines on the island to prevent Japanese troops from completing an airstrip there. The fighting on Guadalcanal was ferocious, but by early 1943 the Allies had won control of the island.

Taking the Offensive

In early 1943, despite their loss at Guadalcanal, the Japanese forces continued to advance through Burma toward India. They also were in firm control of China.

Yet with the victories in the Coral Sea, at Midway, and on Guadalcanal, the Allies finally had the chance to take the offensive in the Pacific. By 1943, U.S. submarines were attacking Japanese transport ships and cutting off the flow of raw materials to Japan. Allied commanders prepared to advance toward Japan itself.

Island-Hopping

The Allies planned to conquer one Pacific island after another, gradually moving closer to Japan. Allied forces would land only on the most important islands, thus isolating Japanese troops on bypassed islands. The Allies planned this strategy of **island-hopping** to gain bases from which they could bomb and later invade Japan. U.S. leaders used the strategy quite effectively.

The island-hopping began in late 1943. As forces under General MacArthur battled the Japanese on New Guinea in November, other troops attacked the Gilbert Islands. In the Gilberts the Japanese had heavily fortified the island of Tarawa. U.S. troops suffered a high casualty rate landing there, but the survivors fought hard and captured the island. Tarawa was just the beginning, and attacks followed on the Marshall, Mariana, Volcano, and Bonin Islands. With the capture of the islands of Saipan and Tinian in the Marianas, U.S. planes began bombing the main islands of Japan.

Massive landing craft, like these in the waters of the Philippines, delivered U.S. troops to enemy-held beaches. These vessels were crucial to the U.S. strategy of island-hopping in the Pacific.

CLOSE

Kinesthetic, Visual-Spatial, Interpersonal. Organize the class into small groups and assign each group one of the battles in this section. Have each group create the design for a museum exhibit on the assigned battle. To accompany their designs, have students write a brief summary providing information on the tactics used, commanding officers, and outcome of the battle. Have each group explain its design to the class.

CHALLENGE AND EXTEND

Linguistic, Logical-Mathematical. Have students use the library or other resources to conduct research on a major development in the war in the Pacific. For example, students might choose to research Admiral Chester Nimitz's use of the U.S. military intelligence's ability to crack the Japanese code or General MacArthur's island-hopping strategy in the Pacific. Have students write reports summarizing their findings. Encourage students to share information from their reports with the class.

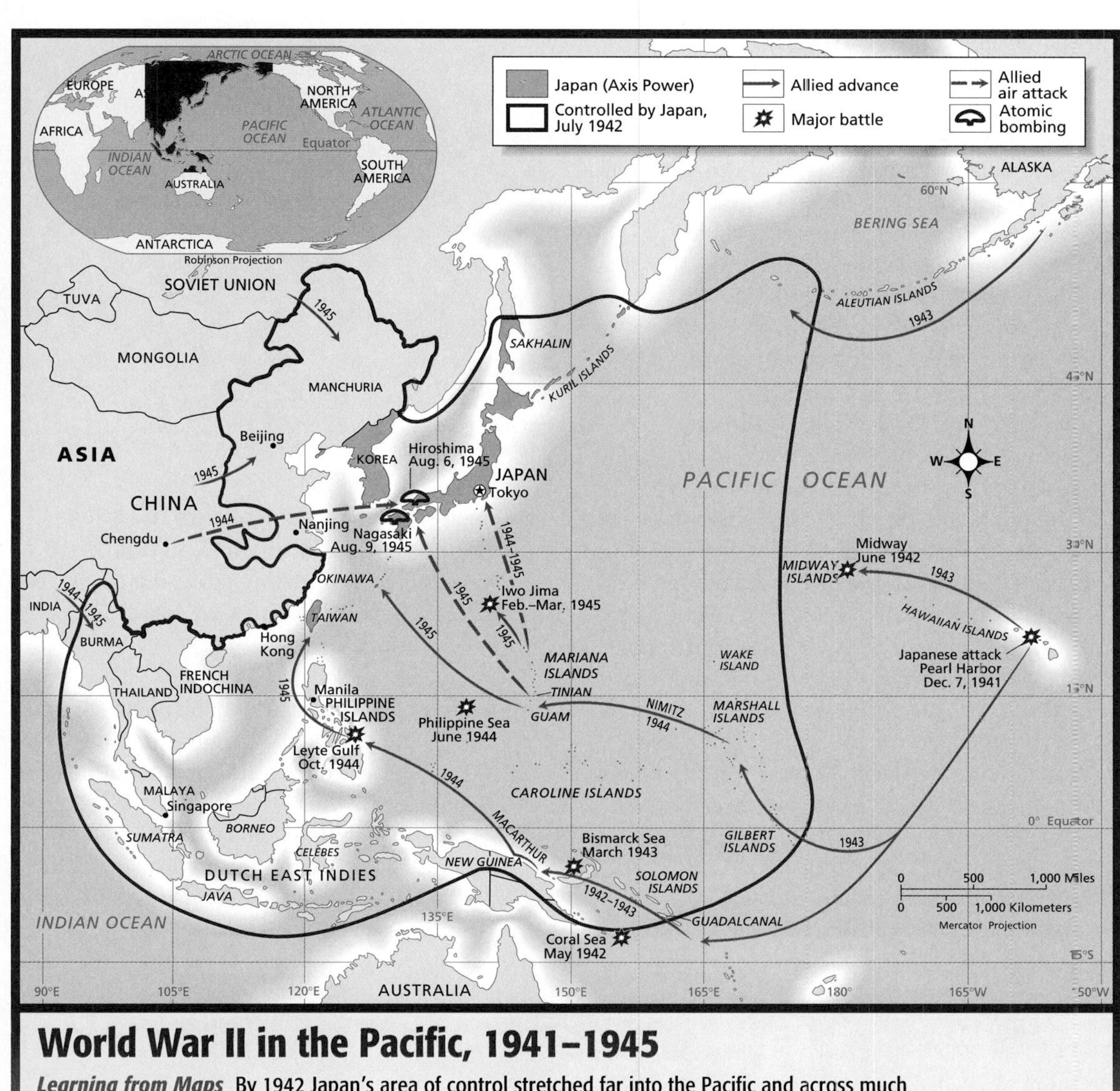

World War II in the Pacific, 1941–1945

Learning from Maps By 1942 Japan's area of control stretched far into the Pacific and across much of eastern Asia.

Movement What islands did the Allies attack after taking the Marshall Islands?

Liberating the Philippines

Having secured New Guinea, General MacArthur turned to the liberation of the Philippines in October 1944. The Japanese navy gathered to block the Allied invasion force and was decisively defeated in the **Battle of Leyte Gulf**—the largest naval engagement in history.

Shortly after the battle, MacArthur waded ashore on Leyte, keeping his promise to return to the Philippines. Aided by Filipino guerrillas, Allied forces began the advance toward Manila. In January 1945, Allied troops landed on the main island of Luzon. On March 3 they captured Manila. Fighting against fierce Japanese resistance, it was summer before all the main towns, roads, and airfields of the country were in Allied hands.

Final Battles

By spring 1945 the war against Japan had entered its final phase. U.S. bombers hit targets in Japan

Geographic Diversity

Advancements in Mapping. In 1940, about a year before the U.S. entry into World War II, the U.S. Army Air Corps determined that less than 10 percent of the world was mapped well enough for them to make even the most basic pilot charts. Thus, the air force developed a program of aerial photography and reconnaissance mapping. The program relied on a new photographic process known as the trimetrogon method. As a result of these efforts, huge areas that had previously gone unmapped were charted during the war years. Information from the World Aeronautical Charts, which were the result of the mapping program, are still used by countries all over the world.

Critical Thinking: How could the information in the World Aeronautical Charts be useful to people after the war?

ANSWER: Answers will vary but students might mention that airlines could use the information.

MAP ANSWER

Guam, Iwo Jima, Okinawa, the Philippines, and Tinian

Multimedia Resources

Linking Geography and History Transparency 19: World War II in the Pacific, 1941–1945

REVIEW

Linguistic, Visual-Spatial. Have students complete the Section Review questions. Ask them to create graphic organizers on the war in the Pacific. Columns should be labeled *Japan* and *United States*, and rows should be labeled with the locations discussed in this section. Have students write a description of each battle's significance in the column of the winning side.

ASSESS

Have students complete Daily Quiz 16.4.

RETEACH

Visual-Spatial. Have students complete Main Idea Activities for Reteaching and Sheltered English 16.4. Provide each student with an outline map of Asia and the Pacific. Ask students to develop a key identifying Japanese and U.S. victories, as well as turning points of the war in the Pacific. Have students label on their maps each battle discussed in this section and identify Japanese victories, U.S. victories, and turning points. To expand the activity, you may wish to have students write an annotation next to each significant battle that explains its importance. **SHELTERED ENGLISH**

Section 4 Review ANSWERS

Identify

For significance, see the following pages:

- Hideki Tojo, p. 490
- Douglas MacArthur, p. 491
- Bataan Death March, p. 491
- Chester Nimitz, p. 491
- Battle of the Coral Sea, p. 491
- Battle of Midway, p. 491
- island-hopping, p. 492
- Battle of Leyte Gulf, p. 493
- kamikaze, p. 494

Reading for Content Understanding

1. Hong Kong, the Philippines, Singapore, Thailand, Burma, the Netherlands East Indies, Guam, Wake Island, Manila, Kiska, and Attu; control of these areas was crucial to Japan's plan of expansion into East Asia and the Pacific.

2. These battles put the Japanese navy on the defensive and enabled Allied naval forces to take the offensive.

3. Because there were so many islands, Allied forces only attacked the key ones. This strategy served to cut off Japanese troops, while Allied forces moved closer to Japan.

4. Letters will vary but students should describe the goal of kamikaze missions and the damage that these pilots inflicted on U.S. ships.

5. Answers will vary but students should explain that with the loss of its aircraft carriers, the Japanese navy's ability to use planes launched from ships to bomb islands was diminished.

494

and caused enormous damage. A raid on Tokyo in March 1945 destroyed much of the Japanese capital. Despite the devastation and the heavy loss of life, the Japanese refused to surrender. In fact, Allied forces encountered some of the fiercest fighting of World War II as they got closer to Japan. The battle for the island of Iwo Jima (EE-woh JEE-mah) in February 1945, for example, cost the lives of almost 6,000 Americans and most of the 22,000 Japanese defenders.

On February 19, 1945, these U.S. Marines charged over the dunes of Iwo Jima and fought one of the deadliest battles in the war against Japan.

In the Battle of Okinawa in April 1945, the Japanese tried to stop Allied naval forces with the tactic of **kamikaze**—crashing piloted planes into Allied ships. In wave after wave, kamikaze pilots flew their aircraft filled with explosives straight at Allied ships off the island of Okinawa. Kamikaze planes were difficult to shoot down. Many struck their targets, causing heavy damage to Allied ships and killing more than 4,000 Allied sailors.

Despite the kamikaze attacks, U.S. soldiers remained committed to their goal—the complete defeat of Japan. One U.S. Marine officer recalled the hard fighting on Okinawa:

> **"We poured a tremendous amount of metal in on those positions. . . . It seemed nothing could possibly be living in that churning mass where the shells were falling and roaring but when we next advanced, [Japanese troops] would still be there."**

The losses during nearly three months of fighting on Okinawa were staggering. More than 110,000 Japanese troops—almost the entire force on Okinawa—died, as well as some 80,000 civilians. The Allies suffered more than 11,000 dead and some 33,000 wounded. With the fall of Okinawa, Allied leaders planned to attack Japan itself for a final victory.

SECTION 4 REVIEW

Identify and explain the significance of the following:

- **Hideki Tojo**
- **Douglas MacArthur**
- **Bataan Death March**
- **Chester Nimitz**
- **Battle of the Coral Sea**
- **Battle of Midway**
- **island-hopping**
- **Battle of Leyte Gulf**
- **kamikaze**

Reading for Content Understanding

1 **Main Idea** What areas did Japan conquer after bombing Pearl Harbor? Why did Japan want to control these areas?

2 **Main Idea** How did Guadalcanal and the Battles of the Coral Sea and Midway turn the tide of the war in the Pacific?

3 **Geographic Diversity** *Region* What role did geography play in the U.S. strategy to advance toward Japan itself?

4 **Writing** *Describing* Imagine that you are a sailor on a U.S. warship in the Pacific during World War II. Write a letter home describing a kamikaze attack.

5 **Critical Thinking** *Identifying Cause and Effect* Why did the destruction of its aircraft carriers at Midway destroy Japan's ability to wage an offensive war?

OBJECTIVES

- Explain how the Allies forced Germany and Japan to surrender.
- Analyze the human and economic costs of World War II.
- Describe events leading to the Holocaust.

FOCUS

Motivate Before Reading

Prior to class, ask students to talk to family members to see if they have any stories about a relative or friend who was affected by World War II. Then during the next class, have volunteers relate these stories to their peers. Once students have finished telling their stories, point out that World War II affected millions of

SECTION 5

Final Victory and Consequences

Reading Focus

How did the Allies force Germany and Japan to surrender?

What were the human and economic costs of World War II?

What events led to the Holocaust?

Key Terms

atomic bomb

Manhattan Project

Holocaust

genocide

TOWARD THE END of the war, the Allies mounted heavy bombing raids against the Axis Powers. In long flights over the Pacific Ocean, U.S. bombers battled Japanese fighter planes to drop tons of explosives on fortified enemy positions. One crew member described an attack on a Japanese airstrip in which "black puffs of ack-ack [antiaircraft fire] surround us, and some of the stuff hits. . . . The plane lurches and reels." The bomber survived, but that one mission to New Guinea lasted nine hours and covered more than 1,500 miles. The Allies would fight many more such battles before final victory.

Victory medal from World War II

Victory in Europe

As they did against Japan, the Allies bombed Germany heavily during the final months of World War II. The German cities of Berlin, Hamburg, and Leipzig sustained massive damage. In January 1945, Allied bombers destroyed the historic German city of Dresden. One U.S. soldier remembered, "Dresden was an inferno. . . . I have nightmares, even today, about the charred bodies." Bombing raids meant to destroy an enemy's ability to manufacture weapons killed many civilians, Allied and Axis alike.

During the early months of 1945, the Allies pushed the Germans back. British and U.S. forces raced toward the Rhine River to enter Germany from the west. These troops moved fast to capture bridges across the Rhine before the Germans destroyed them. Some Allied leaders—particularly Winston Churchill—thought it was important for the noncommunist Allies to occupy as much of Germany as possible to keep it out of Soviet hands.

Section 5
RESOURCES

PRINT

- ★ Guided Reading Strategies 16.5
- ★ Literature Reading 16: An Excerpt from *Night*
- ★ Graphic Organizer 16: A Time Line of War
- ★ Geography Activity 16: German Concentration Camps
- ★ Section 5 Review, p. 499
- ★ Daily Quiz 16.5

MULTIMEDIA

- ★ *Teaching Resources CD–ROM,* Lesson 16.5
- ★ *American Music Audio CD Program:* "Gee But I Want to Go Home"

SHELTERED ENGLISH

- ★ Main Idea Activities for Reteaching and Sheltered English 16.5

people throughout the world, some in drastic ways. Tell students that in this section they will learn about the end of the war and its human costs.

Introduce Key Terms

Linguistic, Logical-Mathematical. Review this section's key terms with students. Then have each student use context cues from the section to write a definition for each term. Instruct students to write a question about each term and answer the questions as they go through the section. **SHELTERED ENGLISH**

TEACH

Have students read Section 5 and complete Guided Reading Strategies 16.5. Choose one or more of the following activities to explore the section content with students. For further suggestions on block scheduling or team teaching, see the *Block Scheduling Handbook.*

LEVEL 1: Linguistic. (Suggested time: 15 min.) As a class, go over students' Guided Reading Strategies. Then use the Reading Focus questions to highlight the main ideas of the section. **SHELTERED ENGLISH**

Daily Life

Effects of the War. By the end of the war in Europe, an estimated 21 million Europeans were left homeless; over half of these had been deported from their own countries to work in labor camps. After the war, more than 5 million Soviet prisoners had to make their way back to the Soviet Union. The damage to homes in many countries was extensive. About 30 percent of the houses in Great Britain were destroyed or damaged. In France, Belgium, and the Netherlands, about 20 percent of the homes had been ravaged. Perhaps the hardest hit was Germany; almost 40 percent of houses in its major cities had been devastated.

Activity: Ask students to imagine being U.S. soldiers in Europe after the war. Have them write a letter to a friend or family member describing the destruction they see around them.

Multimedia Resources

American Music Audio CD Program: "Gee But I Want to Go Home"

Allied tanks roll through Berlin at the end of the war.

By mid-March 1945, British and U.S. forces had crossed the Rhine and were advancing east toward Berlin. Meanwhile, the Soviets pushed westward toward the city. With his enemies closing in, Hitler retreated to his underground bunker, or shelter, in the heart of the city. On April 30, as the Soviets advanced, Hitler committed suicide. Days later, on May 7, German officers surrendered unconditionally to the Allies. The next day—May 8, 1945—was declared V-E (Victory in Europe) Day. It marked the official end of World War II in Europe. For Americans, the joy was mixed with sorrow because only weeks before, on April 12, President Roosevelt had died of a stroke. Vice President Harry S Truman became president.

Victory in the Pacific

As Germany surrendered, the Allies were also near victory in the Pacific. Yet Allied leaders feared that a final invasion of Japan would result in enormous Allied loss of life.

The **atomic bomb**, a weapon that produced tremendous power by splitting atoms, offered an alternative to invasion. Since 1942, Allied scientists had been working on a secret program known as the **Manhattan Project** to develop an atomic bomb. In July 1945, they exploded the world's first atomic bomb in the desert near Alamogordo, New Mexico.

The bomb's destructive power was beyond all expectations. The explosion not only disintegrated the steel tower that held the bomb but also melted the desert sand into glass for 800 yards in all directions. President Truman called it "the most terrible thing ever discovered" and struggled with the decision to use such a deadly weapon. When Japan refused the Allies' demand for an unconditional surrender, Truman gave the order to use the bomb.

On August 6, 1945, the B-29 bomber *Enola Gay* dropped an atomic bomb on the Japanese city of Hiroshima. One survivor recalled:

> **"When I saw a very strong light, a flash, I put my arms over my face unconsciously. Almost instantly I felt my face was inflating. . . . I saw people looking for water and they died soon after they drank it. . . . The whole city was destroyed and burning. There was no place to go."**

In almost an instant, the atomic blast killed between 70,000 and 80,000 people. Thousands more died later from serious burns and radiation poisoning.

Despite the destruction, Japan refused to surrender. On August 9, U.S. forces dropped a second atomic bomb, this time on the city of Nagasaki. On September 2, 1945, Japan formally surrendered.

The atomic bomb dropped on Hiroshima destroyed everything within 1.5 miles of the spot where it exploded. This watch, found in the ruins, had stopped at the exact moment of the explosion—8:15 A.M.

ALL LEVELS: Linguistic, Musical-Rhythmic, Visual-Spatial. (Suggested time: 45 min.) Have each student prepare a poem, song, or work of art that expresses an understanding of the human or economic costs of the war. Call on volunteers to exhibit or perform their work for the class. Invite classmates to comment on these expressions of the costs of the war. Finally, lead a discussion on the human and economic costs of the war.

SHELTERED ENGLISH

LEVEL 3: Visual-Spatial, Intrapersonal. (Suggested time: 45 min. plus homework) Remind students that some 6 million Jews died at the hands of the Nazis. Have students create museum exhibits to illustrate the steps that led to the Holocaust and the enormity of this number of deaths. For example, students could calculate how large a jar would be needed to hold 6 million beans, how far around the earth 6 million feet of cloth would wrap, which cities or countries have populations of less than 6 million, or how many days are in 6 million hours.

LEVEL 3: Linguistic, Logical-Mathematical, Intrapersonal. (Suggested time: 30 min.) Ask students to imagine Harry S Truman writing his memoirs years after World War II. Have students describe his memoirs and the differences in how the Allies brought about an end to the wars in Europe and Asia. Encourage students to imagine and express President Truman's difficulty in deciding to drop the atomic bomb.

Science and Technology

Antibiotics

During World War I, wound infections killed some 15 percent of all soldiers who died. Infections were fast-moving and deadly—a scratch from barbed wire could kill a soldier in days if it became infected. By the end of World War II, such deaths were rare among Allied troops, thanks to a new drug called penicillin.

Sir Alexander Fleming discovered the lifesaving antibiotic penicillin.

British scientist Alexander Fleming discovered penicillin by accident in 1928. He noticed that a small dish of bacteria was covered with mold, which seemed to be killing the bacteria. This mold was penicillin, the first antibiotic ever discovered. Antibiotics prevent bacteria from growing, and in some cases, kill them. This allows the body's immune system to fight against disease and infection caused by bacteria.

It took years of work by researchers to refine the mold into a useful drug. By 1942, scientists were making small amounts of pure penicillin. The British could not produce enough penicillin to supply the military doctors. So in 1943 the U.S. government made penicillin production a top research priority, second only to the atomic bomb program. Scientists developed a method of growing a new type of mold in huge vats instead of small dishes or bottles. Scientists also used X rays to alter this penicillin mold so that it would produce even more penicillin.

By 1944 there was enough of the precious drug to treat thousands of wounded soldiers. After World War II, doctors began using penicillin to treat many different kinds of diseases and infections. Today, penicillin and other antibiotics are widely available and commonly prescribed by doctors. The drug that was such a lifesaver during the war is still saving lives.

Understanding What You Read

1. What is penicillin, and what does it do?
2. Why was penicillin important during World War II?
3. How might life be different today without antibiotics?

★ The Costs of the War

With Japan's surrender, World War II finally ended after six devastating years. Approximately 50 million people died—more than half of them civilians. Millions more were injured or left suffering from disease or malnutrition. China, Poland, and the Soviet Union were particularly hard hit. Both Germany and Japan lost many people as well.

In Europe, as in Asia, the war devastated national economies. Food production, industry, and transportation networks were destroyed in many areas. Millions of people found themselves homeless, lacking even the most basic necessities of food, fuel, water, and shelter. From London to Warsaw to Leningrad, large urban areas lay in ruins. Much of the world's great art and architecture was lost forever.

Across the Curriculum

LITERATURE

The Diary of Anne Frank. In July 1942 at the age of 14, Anne Frank, a Jewish girl living in Nazi-occupied Amsterdam, went into hiding with her family. For more than two years the Franks hid in the back of a warehouse. To help them survive, non-Jewish friends smuggled food to the Franks. However, in August 1944 an informer told the Nazi secret police of the hideout. The Franks were captured and sent to concentration camps, where every family member died except Anne's father. After the war, friends gave Anne's father the diary she had kept while in hiding. Published as a book, *The Diary of Anne Frank* is still one of the most widely read and moving accounts of life during the Holocaust.

Activity: Encourage students to read *The Diary of Anne Frank.* Have students write a book report on it.

SCIENCE AND TECHNOLOGY ANSWERS

1. Penicillin is an antibiotic; it kills bacteria or prevents their growth.

2. It was used to treat wounded soldiers who faced the risk of death from infection.

3. Answers will vary but students might mention that there might be more deaths from infection.

CLOSE

Logical-Mathematical, Interpersonal. Assign each student a Reading Focus question from this section and ask them to write three questions that relate to specific information about that topic. Have students search the text for answers to the questions they created. Then organize the class into groups of three so that each member has written questions about a different Reading Focus question. Have students present their questions to the other group members and have them discuss the answers.

CHALLENGE AND EXTEND

Linguistic, Logical-Mathematical. Have students use the library or other resources to find more information on the events leading to the atomic bomb's development. Ask students to use their research to create an encyclopedia entry describing the Manhattan Project. Encourage students to consider the following questions: Who worked on the project? Where was it developed? How long did it take to make the first bomb? Where and how were the first atomic bombs tested? What impact did the atomic bomb have on the position of the United States as a world power?

Section 5 Review ANSWERS

Identify

For significance, see the following pages:

- Harry S Truman, p. 496
- atomic bomb, p. 496
- Manhattan Project, p. 496
- Holocaust, p. 498
- genocide, p. 499

Reading for Content Understanding

1. Answers should mention that about 50 million people died and millions more were injured or suffered from malnutrition, and that many nations' economies were ruined and their food production diminished.

2. Time lines will vary but students should mention German laws that stripped Jews of their rights, jobs, and property; Nazi encouragement for Jews to leave Germany; imprisonment of those who stayed; and the use of ghettos and *Einsatzgruppen.*

3. Heavy bombing raids and the advance of Allied forces from the west and Soviet forces from the east forced Germany's surrender; the dropping of two atomic bombs on Japan led to its surrender.

4. Letters should include feelings of pride at defeating Germany and regret for the loss of so many lives.

5. Students who agree might cite the human and monetary costs of an Allied invasion. Those who disagree might refer to the civilian casualties and destruction in Hiroshima and Nagasaki.

The United States escaped almost all of the physical destruction that Europe and Asia suffered. In addition, U.S. government spending on war efforts finally lifted the nation out of the Great Depression. The U.S. economy emerged from the war more powerful than ever.

Prisoners were separated upon arrival at Auschwitz concentration camp. One survivor recalled that an SS officer sent prisoners to a line "on his right or his left, and this is the life or death of each of us."

The Holocaust

One of the most horrifying aspects of World War II was the **Holocaust**—Hitler and the Nazis' systematic attempt to kill the Jews of Europe. Soon after taking power in 1933, the Nazis wrote laws that stripped German Jews of their civil rights, jobs, and property. The Nazis tried to force German Jews to emigrate. The Nazis imprisoned those who remained in concentration camps, such as Dachau (DAH-kow) near Munich.

Early Measures

German expansion in Europe brought many more Jews under Hitler's control. Thousands of Jews lived in France, the Low Countries, and eastern Europe. Millions more lived in Poland and the Soviet Union. Hitler and other high-ranking Nazis found it impossible to force all these Jews to emigrate or to put them in concentration camps. Therefore, the Nazis took other steps.

In Poland, the Germans uprooted Jews from their homes in the countryside and forced them into isolated urban areas known as ghettos. Between April 1942 and April 1943, a ghetto in the Polish capital of Warsaw became the site of a brave but unsuccessful uprising against the Nazis.

The Germans also used special killing squads that were known as the *Einsatzgruppen* (YN-sahts-groo-puhn) to round up and shoot Jews. For three days in 1941, the *Einsatzgruppen* machine-gunned some 33,000 Jewish men, women, and children at Babi Yar near the Soviet city of Kiev. By the end of 1941, the *Einsatzgruppen* troops had killed around 600,000 Jews.

Causes and Effects of World War II

Long-Term Causes
- Treaty of Versailles
- Debts from World War I
- Global and local economic problems
- Totalitarian governments
- Repeated acts of aggression

Immediate Causes
- Germany's invasion of Poland
- Japanese aggression in Asia
- Japanese attack on Pearl Harbor

→ **World War II** →

Effects
- Millions of deaths and widespread destruction in Europe and Asia
- The Holocaust
- The emergence of the United States as a superpower

The Final Solution

In January 1942, senior Nazi officials met in a suburb of Berlin called Wannsee. At the Wannsee Conference these leaders agreed on a "final solution to the Jewish question." For the Nazis this "final solution"

REVIEW

Linguistic, Interpersonal. Have students complete the Section Review questions. Ask students to create study guides covering the significant events in this section. Have students replace each key term with a blank space. Then ask them to exchange guides with another student and answer the questions. Finally, have students return the guides to their authors for grading.

ASSESS

Have students complete Daily Quiz 16.5.

RETEACH

Logical-Mathematical, Visual-Spatial. Have students complete Main Idea Activities for Reteaching and Sheltered English 16.5. Then ask students to create an illustration of a scale (balance) weighing the costs and effects of an Allied victory against the possible effects of an Axis victory. For instance, as a cost of the Allied victory, students can identify the loss of lives of Allied troops in Europe, while listing the possible effect of an Axis victory as the extermination of all European Jews. Call on volunteers to explain their illustrations to the class and invite other students to comment on their insight and historical accuracy.

SHELTERED ENGLISH

was **genocide**—the deliberate murder of an entire people.

The Nazis planned to eliminate the Jews in specially built death camps. These camps were equipped with gas chambers to kill great numbers of people. The camps also had large furnaces to cremate the remains of the murdered people. By mid-1942 the Nazis had begun to ship Jews from throughout German-occupied Europe to the camps. People were packed shoulder-to-shoulder in railroad boxcars. Nazi officers sorted the Jews by age, sex, and health, often ripping families apart. Camp officers forced physically fit Jews to work in camp factories. The Nazis sent many other prisoners—mostly women and children, the elderly, the weak, and the sick—directly to the gas chambers for immediate execution.

Moritz Vegh, age 13, was sent from his home in the former Czechoslovakia to Auschwitz—the most notorious of the death camps. He recalled his terrifying arrival:

> **"When we got off the cattle truck, they ordered, 'Men, right; women, left.' . . . I went with my father. My little sister, Esther, she went with my mother. Esther was only eleven. She was holding my mother's hand. When they made a selection of the women, Esther clung to my mother. My mother wouldn't give her up. . . . They went straight to the gas chamber."**

The Nazis sent Moritz to work at Auschwitz for the rest of the war. As the Allies began to liberate the concentration camps in early 1945, many of the survivors were too weak or ill to move.

The Allied liberation revealed the horrifying magnitude of the Holocaust. Some 6 million Jews—about two thirds of all Jews living in Europe before the war—had perished in the Holocaust. The Nazis also sent thousands of other people—including gypsies, Slavs, political and religious radicals, and others—to be killed in the camps. Perhaps more than any other event, the Holocaust serves as a chilling reminder of the brutal, inhumane nature of Nazi thought and of the terrible cost of Nazi aggression.

Prisoners at this concentration camp in Evensee, Austria, were liberated by U.S. troops in 1945.

SECTION 5 REVIEW

Identify and explain the significance of the following:

- **Harry S Truman**
- **atomic bomb**
- **Manhattan Project**
- **Holocaust**
- **genocide**

Reading for Content Understanding

1. **Main Idea** What were the consequences of World War II in both human and economic terms?
2. **Main Idea** Create a time line of the events that led to the Holocaust.
3. **Global Relations** How did the Allies eventually force both Germany and Japan to surrender?
4. **Writing** *Expressing* Imagine that you are one of the Allied soldiers who helped defeat Germany. Write a letter to your hometown newspaper expressing your feelings on V-E Day.
5. **Critical Thinking** *Supporting a Point of View* Do you agree or disagree with the decision to drop atomic bombs on Japan? Explain your answer.

Chapter 16 Review ANSWERS

Identifying People and Ideas

1. policy of the French and British when they yielded to Hitler's aggression in an attempt to preserve peace

2. British prime minister during World War II

3. forced relocation and imprisonment of Japanese Americans by the U.S. government

4. U.S. general who led troops from the beaches into the interior of France following the D-Day invasion

5. U.S. Army general who became Allied supreme commander and led the Normandy invasion

6. battle between Allies and Germans in the Ardennes region of France; ended Germany's ability to wage an offensive war

7. forced march of American and Filipino prisoners of war during which Japanese killed many of the prisoners

8. important turning point for the war in the Pacific because it destroyed several Japanese aircraft carriers and put Japan on the defensive

9. top-secret project conducted in Los Alamos, New Mexico, that developed the atomic bomb

10. systematic extermination of Jews by the Nazis

Using the Time Line

1. e **4.** d
2. f **5.** b
3. a **6.** c

CHAPTER 16 REVIEW

Review and Assessment
RESOURCES

PRINT
- ★ Chapter 16 Review, pp. 500–01
- ★ Vocabulary Activity 16
- ★ Chapter 16 Study Guide
- ★ Chapter 16 Test (Form A or B)

MULTIMEDIA
- ★ Audio Program, Ch. 16 (English and Spanish)
- ★ *Global Skill Builder CD–ROM*
- ★ Chapter 16 Test Generator
- ★ HRW Web site

SHELTERED ENGLISH
- ★ Spanish Glossary
- ★ Sheltered English Chapter 16 Test

ASSESS

Have students complete one of the Chapter 16 Tests. As an alternate assessment, assign the Chapter 16 Investigation.

Understanding Main Ideas

1. The United States used the Lend-Lease Act to provide the Allies with war materials.

2. Women had greater opportunities for employment and served in various military capacities (WASP, WAAC, etc.).

3. It increased industrial production, and the resulting labor shortage created new job opportunities.

4. Europe—Battles of Stalingrad and Kursk, the D-Day invasion; Pacific—Guadalcanal and the Battles of the Coral Sea and Midway

5. The projected human and economic costs of an Allied invasion of Japan were too great, so the United States chose to drop atomic bombs.

Reviewing Themes

1. Many nisei were forced to relocate and were imprisoned, disregarding their rights as U.S. citizens.

2. The government exerted more control over the economy by determining what goods were needed and by guiding businesses into war production. The increased production spurred the economy.

3. Roosevelt realized that if the Axis Powers threatened democracy in Europe, they might also threaten it in the United States. Therefore, U.S. intervention was needed.

Thinking Critically

1. The strategy against Japan involved island-hopping, more battles at sea, and dropping atomic bombs. The strategy against Germany involved the invasion of Europe and bombing raids on German cities.

CHAPTER 16 REVIEW

Chapter Summary

In 1939 Germany's invasion of Poland began World War II. The United States aided Britain against Germany but remained neutral until Japan attacked Pearl Harbor in 1941. From 1941 to 1945, the United States and the other Allies waged war against the Axis Powers. After Germany surrendered, the horror of the Holocaust was revealed to the world. The war finally came to an end in September 1945 with the surrender of Japan.

On a separate sheet of paper, complete the following activities.

Identifying People and Ideas

Describe the historical significance of the following:

1. appeasement
2. Winston Churchill
3. internment
4. Omar Bradley
5. Dwight D. Eisenhower
6. Battle of the Bulge
7. Bataan Death March
8. Battle of Midway
9. Manhattan Project
10. Holocaust

Internet Activity

go.hrw.com
SB1 Veterans

Search the Internet through the HRW Web site to find more information about American veterans of World War II. Use the information to design a memorial to the veterans.

Understanding Main Ideas

1. How did the United States remain neutral during the early part of World War II while still helping the Allies?
2. How did World War II affect American women?
3. How did the war create new opportunities for African American civilians?
4. What were the turning points in the war in Europe and in the Pacific?
5. Why did the United States decide to drop atomic bombs on Japan?

Reviewing Themes

1. **Citizenship and Democracy** How did the war affect the rights of nisei?
2. **Economic Development** How did mobilizing for war change the U.S. economy?
3. **Global Relations** Why did President Franklin D. Roosevelt feel that the United States needed to serve as "the arsenal of democracy" for the world and become involved in World War II?

Using the Time Line

Number your paper from 1 to 6. Match the letters on the time line below with the following events.

1. **After Adolf Hitler commits suicide, German authorities surrender to the Allies.**
2. **The atomic bomb is dropped on Hiroshima.**
3. **The invasion of Poland begins.**
4. **Allied troops invade Normandy, France.**
5. **Pearl Harbor is bombed.**
6. **The Allies invade the Italian island of Sicily.**

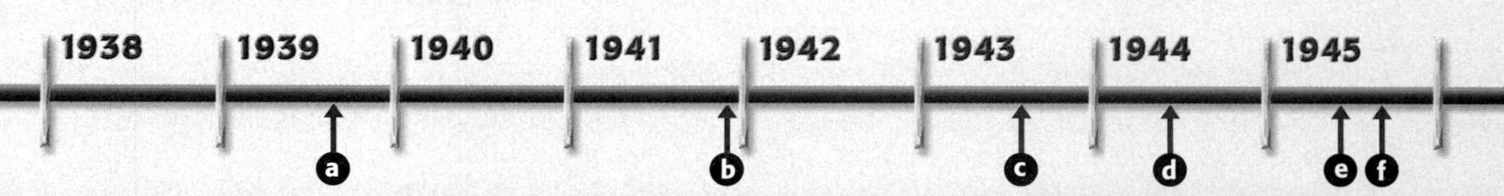

RETEACH

Logical-Mathematical, Visual-Spatial. Have students create a time line of significant events pertaining to World War II. Ask students to include events leading up to the war, turning points in the war, and events leading to the war's end. Have students write a brief annotation for each event. **SHELTERED ENGLISH**

Using the Internet

HRW Have students continue their research to find information about a soldier who received the Congressional Medal of Honor for his or her efforts in World War II. Have each student write a speech that describes why the soldier received the medal.

Portfolio Extensions

1. Have students write a letter to a relative or friend in another city explaining how individuals there can help the war effort.

2. Have students imagine that their scrapbooks are being published. Tell students to create a dust jacket for the book that includes the title, cover illustration, description of the book, and an "About the Author" blurb.

Thinking Critically

1. **Making Comparisons** How did Allied strategy differ in Germany and Japan?
2. **Evaluating** What were Adolf Hitler's reasons for starting World War II?
3. **Synthesizing Information** Why might fighting a war on multiple fronts be difficult?

Writing About History

1. **Informing** Imagine that you are a war correspondent covering D-Day. Write a newspaper article informing your readers about the event and the soldiers' reactions.
2. **Describing** Write a paragraph describing what might have happened if Britain had fallen to the Germans. Use examples from the chapter in your description.

Linking Geography and History

1. **Location** Look at the map of Europe on page xxviii and select several alternative locations to Normandy for the D-Day invasion. Why do you think Eisenhower selected Normandy?
2. **Movement** How was fighting in western Europe different from fighting along the western front during World War I?

Building Your Portfolio

Complete the following activities individually or in groups.

1. **Supporting the War Effort** Imagine that you work in the government's public relations office during World War II. Create an advertisement that would encourage people to make sacrifices for the war. Your advertisement might target a particular group—teenagers, for example—or appeal to all Americans. Then present the advertisement to your supervisor along with a short report explaining why the advertisement would be effective.
2. **Under Fire** Imagine that you were a soldier during World War II. You want to record your experiences before your memories fade with time. Choose either the war in Europe or in the Pacific and create a scrapbook of your experiences. Include descriptions of battles and sketches of some of the places you saw. Begin with the U.S. entry into the war and end with the final victory.

History Skills Workshop

Reading Maps In April 1942 the Allied forces in the Philippines surrendered to the Japanese. Some 70,000 Americans and Filipinos—both soldiers and civilians—were taken prisoner. The Japanese forced these starving survivors to march from Mariveles to San Fernando. The prisoners were loaded onto cargo trains at San Fernando and transported to prison camps farther north. Some 10,000 prisoners died during the Bataan Death March alone. Study the map of the Bataan Death March at the right. Then answer the following questions: (a) How far did the prisoners march before they were put on trains? (b) Where did their journey finally end?

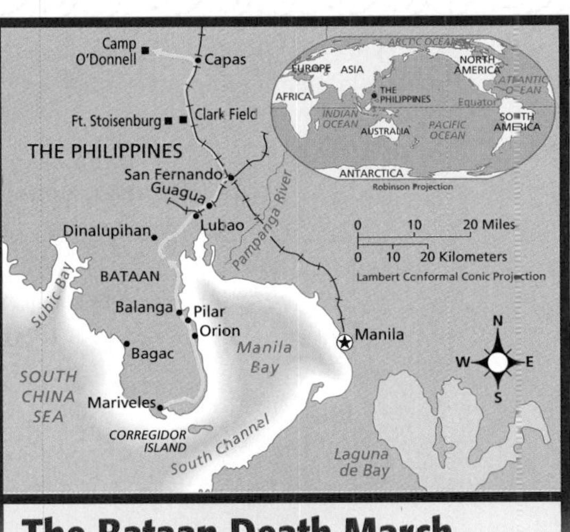

The Bataan Death March

2. Hitler wanted world domination and revenge for the German defeat in World War I.

3. Answers will vary but should mention that fighting a war on multiple fronts poses difficulties in manning, supplying, and defending all of the fronts.

Writing About History

1. Articles will vary but might mention bad weather during the invasion, confusion and disorganization during the battle, or success at landing more than 155,000 troops in France.

2. Answers will vary but students might mention the destruction of British cities or the deportation of British Jews to concentration camps.

Linking Geography and History

1. Answers will vary but students might suggest that Germany's defenses were weakest at Normandy, or that it is close to Paris.

2. Answers will vary but students might mention that advancements in airplanes, ships, submarines, tanks, amphibious vehicles, and other war machinery allowed Allied troops to move quickly and efficiently rather than being bogged down in trenches.

History Skills Workshop

(a) about 60 miles; (b) Camp O'Donnell

TEACH

ALL LEVELS: Linguistic, Logical-Mathematical. (Suggested time: 30 min.) Have students search the unit for quotations that are statements of fact and statements of opinion. Discuss why it might be important for a history book to include both. Identify the context cues that students should look for when searching for statements of fact and statements of opinion. Then have students speculate about opinions that the following people might have had about Franklin Roosevelt's first term in office: First Lady Eleanor Roosevelt, a member of the American Liberty League, a person employed by a public-works program, and a rural resident of the Tennessee Valley. Have students write several sentences that might express the opinions of each of these people. Then have students write a paragraph that might be appropriate for a history textbook. The paragraph should include all four opinions as well as cues to help the reader understand the difference between fact and opinion.

SKILLS ANSWERS

1. opinion; *I ask, I mean, Double-Crossing*

2. He is suggesting that Roosevelt is a Communist. Coughlin might hope that voters will believe him and elect him as president.

Identifying Bias. For further practice identifying bias, have students bring in political or issue-oriented advertisements from magazines or newspapers. Ask students to make a chart separating the provable facts in the advertisements from the statements of preference or opinion. Then have students write a brief paragraph describing any bias that they identified.

History Skills

WORKSHOP

Distinguishing Fact from Opinion and Identifying Bias

Historical sources may contain both facts and opinions. Sources such as diaries, letters, and speeches usually express personal views. The ability to distinguish fact from opinion is essential to judging the soundness of an argument or the reliability of a historical account.

When reading historical sources, try to identify a writer's *bias*—prejudices or strong feelings—that he or she might have about the subject. Many famous historical people had strong opinions that appear in their writings and speeches. Remember that just because a person is famous does not mean that you must agree with his or her opinions.

How to Distinguish Fact from Opinion

1. **Identify the facts** Ask yourself: Can the statement be proven? Determine whether the idea can be checked for accuracy in a source such as an almanac or encyclopedia. If so, it is probably factual. If not, it probably contains an opinion.
2. **Identify the opinions** Look for clues that signal a statement of opinion: phrases such as *I think* and *I believe,* comparative words like *greatest* and *more important,* and value-filled words like *extremely* and *ridiculous* imply a judgment, and thus an opinion.

How to Identify Bias

1. **Evaluate the information presented** What are the sources of information? How reliable are they? Why might a historical figure support one view over another? Be sure to distinguish between provable facts and someone's preferences or opinions.
2. **Make your own judgment** Remember that many of the historical documents you read are created by people who have their own opinions and points of view. It is up to you to read each document critically and to draw your own conclusions.

Practicing the Skill

Read the excerpt below, in which Father Charles Coughlin tells voters why they should not re-elect Franklin D. Roosevelt in 1936. Coughlin is running against the president. Then answer the questions that follow.

> "The hand of Moscow backs communist leaders in America . . . [and] aims to support FDR. . . . I ask you to purge [get rid of] the man who claims to be a Democrat from the Democratic Party, and I mean Franklin Double-Crossing Roosevelt."

1. Is this excerpt an example of a fact or an opinion? Which words let you know?
2. What bias, if any, does the author express about President Roosevelt? Why might Charles Coughlin be expressing bias?

ALL LEVELS: Linguistic, Logical-Mathematical, Kinesthetic. (Suggested time: 30 min.) Tell students that their game show will have a "bonus round" called Who Am I? Have students choose important people from Unit 5. Students will then make question cards for each person. On one side of these cards students should write the person's name. On the other side they should write the events, policies, or positions with which the person was associated. For example, students could write a question card for Marian Anderson. On the back of the card they might write: *African American singer who gave a famous performance at the Lincoln Memorial after the Daughters of the American Revolution refused to let her perform a concert in their hall.*

History in Action

UNIT 5 PORTFOLIO

The New Deal Game Show

Complete the following activity in small, cooperative groups.

You will be creating a game show called "The New Deal." The goal of the game is to help your classmates identify New Deal agencies and programs. Your group will come up with the specific format of the game. You will design all components of this new game.

Materials To complete this activity, you will need index cards, posterboard, scissors, pens, pencils, markers, and your textbook.

Parts of the Project To create your game, complete the following tasks:

1. **Question Cards** Choose eight New Deal programs or agencies discussed in Unit 5. Write the acronym, or abbreviation made by initials, of each program on an index card. For each program, create four additional cards. On one side of these cards, write one of the following categories: full name, date, description, or "Fact or Opinion." On the opposite side of the card include the information for that category. "Fact or Opinion" might include information such as who headed the organization or opinions about how helpful the program was. For this category, game players will identify the New Deal agency and identify whether the information is fact or opinion. You should be able to find most of this information in your textbook. You may also need to consult an encyclopedia or other library resources.
2. **Game Show Format** Once you have made the game cards, you will decide how to use them in your game show format. You will need to decide how players will win the game. You should also consider whether you want to have a game show host or allow the players to lead the show. You might also want to assign different point values to the categories based on their difficulty. Depending on the format you select, you might need to design some sort of signaling device for players.
3. **Rule Book** Write a set of rules for your game. The rules should be clear, easy to follow, and thorough.

When you have finished creating your game show, exchange it with another group. Have class members play the game. Select the best game show.

Students use index cards to record information.

Question Cards. Encourage students to choose programs from both the First and Second New Deal. A good variety would include public-works programs, programs for creative artists, rural electrification projects, and various forms of aid to farmers. Suggest to students that they also include some New Deal programs that were later overturned by the Supreme Court.

Game Show Format. Encourage students to consider various formats along which to organize their game shows. Players might draw cards at random or choose from categories. Competition may be among teams or individuals.

Rule Book. The rule book should state the object of the game. It should also cover topics such as how to choose the player or team that goes first, the scoring system, how to handle disputed answers, and tiebreakers. Remind students that they should use proper grammar, spelling, punctuation, and sentence structure when writing their rule books.

Introducing UNIT

CHAPTER 17
The Cold War Begins

After the end of World War II, the United States worked to prevent another world war and contain communism. To these ends, the United States helped form the United Nations and NATO, issued the Truman Doctrine, devised the Marshall Plan, and operated the Berlin Airlift. At home, the nation shifted to a peacetime economy. President Truman avoided a postwar recession, although rising inflation led to some labor unrest. As the Cold War deepened, a new Red Scare swept the United States. The House Un-American Activities Committee stepped up its investigations, and loyalty oaths became the order of the day. Abroad, communist North Korea invaded democratic South Korea. The United States led a UN effort to back South Korea, and the Korean War resulted. An armistice ended the fighting after three years.

Internet Activity

The United States and the Birth of Israel. After the horrors of the Holocaust became known, the United Nations decided to create a Jewish homeland. In 1947 the UN General Assembly divided Palestine, then under British control. Half the nation became an Arab state. The other half became the new nation of Israel, officially established in May 1948. Have students search the Internet through the HRW Web site to find more information about the role the United States played in the foundation of the independent state of Israel. Then have students write a journal entry from the point of view of President Truman, in which he explains why he supported the establishment of Israel.

go.hrw.com
SB1 Israel

UNIT 6 Postwar America

(1945–1960)

CHAPTER 17 **The Cold War Begins** (1945–1955)

CHAPTER 18 **Peace and Prosperity** (1945–1960)

CHAPTER 18
Peace and Prosperity

The 1950s was a decade of contrasts. Many Americans enjoyed newfound prosperity. The economy boomed and personal incomes soared. Millions of families moved to the suburbs. Technological advances improved life, and new types of entertainment, such as TV, enhanced people's leisure time. At the same time, not everyone enjoyed prosperity, and some people criticized suburban life for its conformity and materialism. While the nation enjoyed peace, many people also shared anxieties about the spread of communism and the growing nuclear arms race. A series of international conflicts also heightened Cold War tensions. Publicly, the United States pursued a policy of brinkmanship while covertly conducting operations against some communist governments. Conflicts also emerged domestically as an African American civil rights movement challenged segregation in public schools and elsewhere.

UNIT MOTIVATOR

Have students list what they think would be the top three priorities of a country after fighting a world war. *(Answers will vary but might include rebuilding, helping veterans find jobs, or working to prevent another war.)* Then ask students to predict what the United States focused on after World War II. After some discussion, tell students that in this unit they will learn about this period in U.S. history. At the unit's end, have them review their lists to see how accurate they were.

American Teens
IN HISTORY
Young Musicians

When he was just 14 years old, Buddy Holly saw what his future held. A friend played a Fats Domino record for him, and suddenly Holly knew he wanted to be a rock 'n' roll star. However, he had doubts about whether he could succeed. In 1953, after just a few years of practice, Holly and a friend won regular spots on a weekly radio show in their hometown of Lubbock, Texas. "You're destined to be a star," a manager at the radio station told Holly.

The manager's prediction came true. In 1957 Buddy Holly and the Crickets topped the charts with the hit single "That'll Be the Day." Later that year, after Holly performed on *The Ed Sullivan Show,* the host asked him about his rapid rise to stardom. Holly admitted, "Well, we've had a few rough times, I guess you'd say, but we've been real lucky, getting it this quick."

The Everly Brothers perform with Sam Cooke (center) on Shindig, *a popular television show.*

Holly was just one of many young musicians who became famous in the late 1950s. Following the great success of Elvis Presley—a huge star by the age of 19—many young people took up instruments and started bands. Excited teenagers crowded concert halls to listen to these new singing sensations.

One popular concert tour was called "America's Greatest Teenage Performing Stars." That show included the Everly Brothers—Don and Phil. This duo started in show business at a young age. They made radio appearances on the *Everly Family Show* when they were just eight and six. In 1955 the teenage brothers headed to Nashville to write songs for a country music publisher. Two years later they recorded their first #1 hit with "Bye Bye Love."

Some other young stars of the 1950s included Richie Valens and Frankie Lymon and the Teenagers. Valens died at age 17 in a plane crash that also killed Buddy Holly. Young musicians such as "Little" Stevie Wonder and the Jackson Five continued to top the charts throughout the 1960s and 1970s.

In this unit you will learn more about the cultural and social changes that swept the United States after World War II. You will also learn about the political challenges that faced the country, both at home and abroad.

LEFT PAGE: *Teenagers at a dance*

Using Visual Resources

Rock 'n' Roll Music. During the 1950s rock 'n' roll affected not only the music industry but also movies, radio, and the newly popular medium of television. Movies, such as *The Blackboard Jungle, Don't Knock the Rock,* and *Rock Around the Clock,* featured rock 'n' roll music. Sales of portable radios boomed, and the radio industry used rock 'n' roll music to help recover some of the business it was losing to the growing television industry. TV also developed its own share of rock 'n' roll programming, including the long-running show *American Bandstand,* which went on the air in 1952.

Critical Thinking: Do you think the teenagers in the photograph on the opposite page are dancing to rock 'n' roll music?

ANSWER: Students who say yes might point out that the teenagers appear to be dancing to fast-paced, enjoyable music, while students who say no may point out that the dancers are wearing suits and formal dresses, which could suggest that they are not listening to music that some people of the 1950s associated with teenage rebellion.

TEACH

ALL LEVELS: Linguistic, Logical-Mathematical. (Suggested time: 30 min.) Ask students to classify the events on the time line as either arts and sports, politics and war, or science and technology. Tell students that some events may fit in more than one category. Then ask students to choose one of these categories and have them write a headline for each event that falls into that category. Encourage volunteers to share their headlines with the class. You may want to have students include an illustration with one of their headlines.

ALL LEVELS: Logical-Mathematical, Visual-Spatial, Interpersonal. (Suggested time: 35 min.) Organize students into small groups. Provide each group with a world map and a map of the United States. Have students determine the approximate location where each time line event took place. Then ask students to label each event next to its related location on the appropriate map. Students also should include captions that give the date and a brief explanation of each event. Have each group present their maps to the class. Then display the maps around the classroom.

Technology and Society

ENIAC. British scientist Alan Turing developed the theory of digital logic and applied it to the invention of the Colossus computer, used during World War II. After the war, Turing's theory—combined with research by Dr. John Atanasoff—helped two American engineers, J. Presper Eckert Jr. and John Mauchly, develop the first general-purpose electronic digital computer. Their Electronic Numerical Integrator and Computer, known as ENIAC, was about the size of a railroad boxcar and weighed 30 tons. Working at the University of Pennsylvania, the two engineers had developed ENIAC for the U.S. Army.

Critical Thinking: Why might the military have wanted digital computers?

ANSWER: Answers will vary but students might mention that these devices could be useful in navigating planes and ships or in creating and breaking codes.

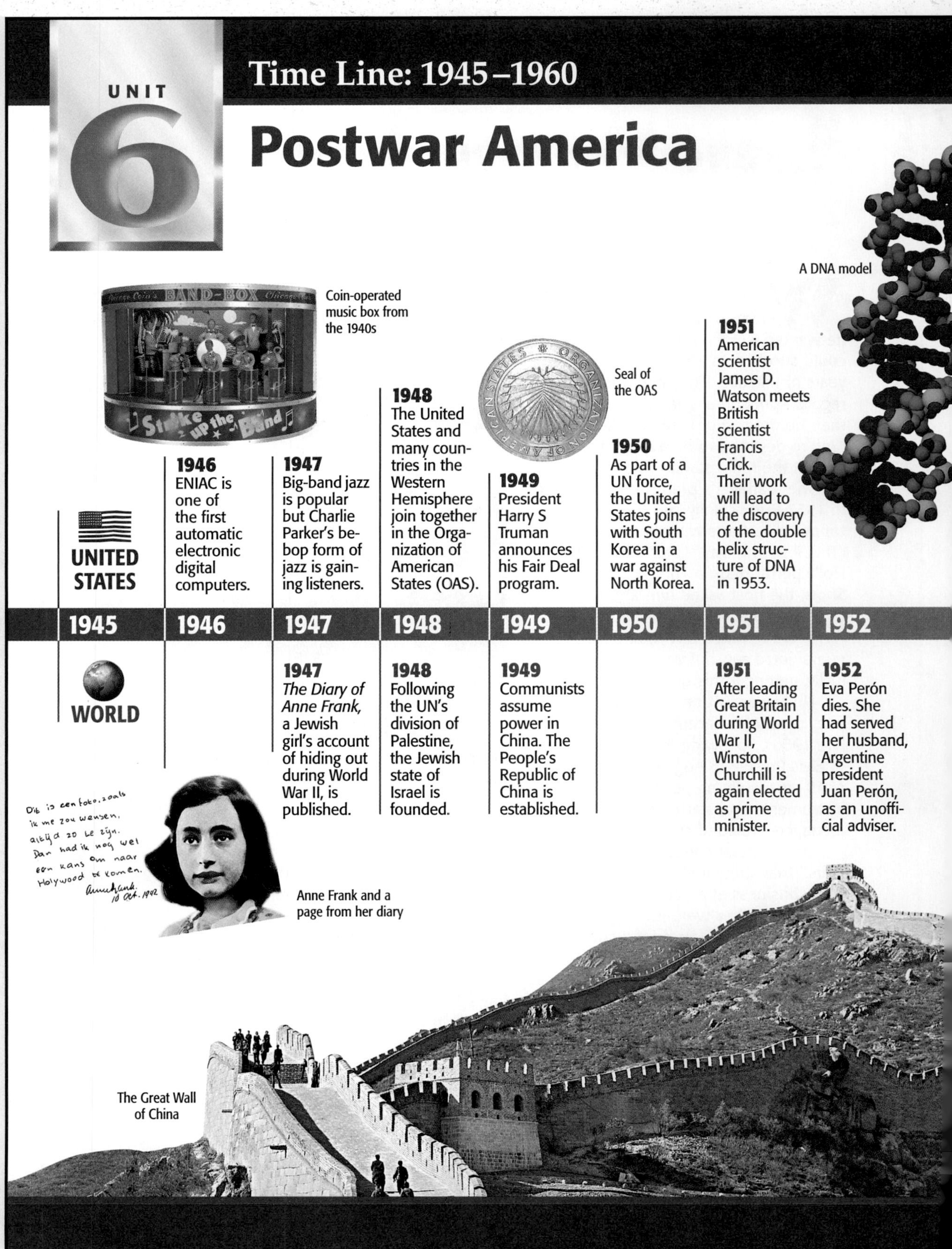

UNIT 6

Time Line: 1945–1960

Postwar America

Coin-operated music box from the 1940s

Seal of the OAS

A DNA model

UNITED STATES

1946 ENIAC is one of the first automatic electronic digital computers.

1947 Big-band jazz is popular but Charlie Parker's be-bop form of jazz is gaining listeners.

1948 The United States and many countries in the Western Hemisphere join together in the Organization of American States (OAS).

1949 President Harry S Truman announces his Fair Deal program.

1950 As part of a UN force, the United States joins with South Korea in a war against North Korea.

1951 American scientist James D. Watson meets British scientist Francis Crick. Their work will lead to the discovery of the double helix structure of DNA in 1953.

1945 | 1946 | 1947 | 1948 | 1949 | 1950 | 1951 | 1952

WORLD

1947 *The Diary of Anne Frank,* a Jewish girl's account of hiding out during World War II, is published.

1948 Following the UN's division of Palestine, the Jewish state of Israel is founded.

1949 Communists assume power in China. The People's Republic of China is established.

1951 After leading Great Britain during World War II, Winston Churchill is again elected as prime minister.

1952 Eva Perón dies. She had served her husband, Argentine president Juan Perón, as an unofficial adviser.

Anne Frank and a page from her diary

The Great Wall of China

CHALLENGE AND EXTEND

1. **Linguistic, Logical-Mathematical, Visual-Spatial.** Have students use the library or other resources to research the history of relations between Israel and its Arab neighbors since the nation was founded. Have students create an annotated time line that illustrates important events in this history. Encourage students to include peace agreements as well as conflicts. Have students display their time lines in the classroom.

2. **Linguistic, Logical-Mathematical.** Have students use the library or other resources to find out more about President Truman's Fair Dea plan. Ask students to prepare a summary that provides information on the objectives of the Fair Deal, the programs that were established under this plan, and the costs of the plan to taxpayers. Then ask students to create a report card for President Truman that grades him on the effectiveness of the Fair Deal. Allow time in class for students to share and discuss their findings.

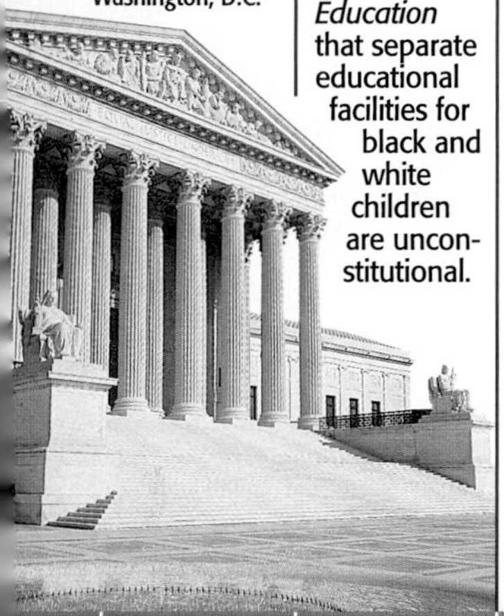

The Supreme Court Building in Washington, D.C.

1953 New Zealand explorer Edmund Hillary and Nepalese mountaineer Tenzing Norgay reach the summit of Mount Everest, the highest mountain in the world.

Hillary (left) and Norgay

1954 The Supreme Court rules in *Brown* v. *Board of Education* that separate educational facilities for black and white children are unconstitutional.

Elvis "The King" Presley

1956 Singer Elvis Presley performs live on *The Ed Sullivan Show.*

1956 Soviet troops crush anticommunist rebellions in Poland and Hungary.

The Jules Rimet World Cup trophy

1958 Two major credit cards, American Express and BankAmericard (later VISA), are introduced. They will change the spending habits of Americans.

1958 A seventeen-year-old player known as Pelé leads Brazil's soccer team to victory in the World Cup.

1959 The United States and other countries sign an agreement to preserve Antarctica for scientific interests.

King penguins in Antarctica

1959 The Dalai Lama, the spiritual leader of Tibetan Buddhists, is forced to flee China.

Buddhist Wheel of Life

1953 | 1954 | 1955 | 1956 | 1957 | 1958 | 1959 | 1960

USING THE TIME LINE

1. On what significant topic did the Supreme Court rule in the 1950s, and how did this decision reverse earlier practices?
2. What did James D. Watson and Francis Crick discover?
3. When did Communists assume power in China and establish the People's Republic?

Activity Use information from Unit 5 and Unit 6 Time Lines to identify a possible between the world time line entry in 1947 and the world time line entry in 1948. Explain why Anne Frank was in hiding during World War II. Write a diary entry for her. Identify events that might have helped lead to the creation of the Jewish state of Israel.

Geographic Diversity

Climbing Mount Everest. Located on the border between Nepal and Tibet, Mount Everest stands 29,028 feet above sea level, the highest point on Earth. In 1953 Sir Edmund Hillary and Tenzing Norgay became the first people to climb to the summit of Mount Everest. Their accomplishment is particularly remarkable considering they made the climb without the modern gear mountaineers use today. On the upper parts of Everest the temperature never rises above 32°F. At altitudes above 26,250 feet—well below the summit—the oxygen in the air is only one third the amount at sea level.

Activity: Have students use the library and other resources to research what type of gear modern-day mountaineers use to climb Mount Everest. Have students present their information in the form of a pamphlet.

USING THE TIME LINE ANSWERS

1. segregated educational facilities for white and black students; the ruling reversed the previous "separate but equal" practice in education and found segregated schools to be unconstitutional and unequal.
2. double helix structure of DNA
3. 1949

CHAPTER PLANNING GUIDE
The Cold War Begins

	SECTION LESSON OBJECTIVES	PRINT RESOURCES	MULTIMEDIA RESOURCES	SHELTERED ENGLISH RESOURCES
Section 1: The World After War (pp. 509–12)	★ Describe the agreements the Allies reached at Yalta and Potsdam. ★ Explain measures the Allies took to prevent another world war. ★ Identify postwar events that increased tensions between the Western Allies and the Soviet Union.	★ Guided Reading Strategies 17.1 ★ Primary Source Reading 17: The Path to the Atomic Bomb ★ Section 1 Review, p. 512 ★ Daily Quiz 17.1	★ *Teaching Resources CD–ROM*, Lesson 17.1 ★ Everyday Life in America Transparency 27: Postwar Painting, 1946	★ Main Idea Activities for Reteaching and Sheltered English 17.1
Section 2: The Roots of the Cold War (pp. 513–17)	★ Analyze major U.S. foreign-policy strategies after World War II. ★ Describe the purpose and result of the Marshall Plan. ★ Identify the major events in the Cold War between 1946 and 1950.	★ Guided Reading Strategies 17.2 ★ Geography Activity 17: Postwar Tensions in the Eastern Mediterranean ★ Section 2 Review, p. 517 ★ Daily Quiz 17.2	★ *Teaching Resources CD–ROM*, Lesson 17.2	★ Main Idea Activities for Reteaching and Sheltered English 17.2
Section 3: The Truman Era (pp. 518–21)	★ Explain how the U.S. government tried to ease the transition to peacetime. ★ Describe the issues and the outcome of the 1948 presidential election. ★ Describe what President Truman hoped to accomplish with his Fair Deal.	★ Guided Reading Strategies 17.3 ★ Section 3 Review, p. 521 ★ Daily Quiz 17.3	★ *Teaching Resources CD–ROM*, Lesson 17.3 ★ HRW Web site	★ Main Idea Activities for Reteaching and Sheltered English 17.3
Section 4: The Korean War (pp. 522–26)	★ Identify events that led to China becoming a communist nation. ★ Explain why the United States was involved in Korea and how the war ended. ★ Describe how the Korean War affected the 1952 presidential election.	★ Guided Reading Strategies 17.4 ★ Literature Reading 17: Fighting in Korea ★ Section 4 Review, p. 526 ★ Daily Quiz 17.4	★ *Teaching Resources CD–ROM*, Lesson 17.4 ★ HRW Web site	★ Main Idea Activities for Reteaching and Sheltered English 17.4
Section 5: Cold War Fears (pp. 527–31)	★ Analyze the causes of the new Red Scare. ★ Identify the role Senator Joseph McCarthy played in the new Red Scare. ★ Describe how post–World War II popular culture reflected Cold War fears.	★ Guided Reading Strategies 17.5 ★ Biography Reading 17: Margaret Chase Smith ★ Graphic Organizer 17: The United States Fights Communism ★ Section 5 Review, p. 531 ★ Daily Quiz 17.5	★ *Teaching Resources CD–ROM*, Lesson 17.5 ★ *American History Interactive Maps CD–ROM*: Living in the Cold War	★ Main Idea Activities for Reteaching and Sheltered English 17.5
Chapter Review and Assessment (pp. 532–33)		★ Chapter 17 Review, pp. 532–33 ★ Vocabulary Activity 17 ★ Chapter 17 Study Guide ★ Chapter 17 Test (Form A or B)	★ Audio Program, Ch. 17 (English and Spanish) ★ *Global Skill Builder CD–ROM* ★ Chapter 17 Test Generator ★ HRW Web site	★ Spanish Glossary ★ Sheltered English Chapter 17 Test

CHAPTER OVERVIEW

Following World War II, the United States and the Soviet Union returned to being enemies. The conflict was over Eastern Europe, but stopping the spread of communism became the focus of U.S. foreign policy.

After the war, the United States shifted to a peacetime economy. The government urged women to give up their jobs to returning veterans. The GI Bill of Rights provided educational opportunities and loans for veterans. However, the end of rationing increased inflation. Labor unions went on strike to demand wage increases. President Truman opposed the strikes, but later won the support of many labor unions when he vetoed the Taft-Hartley Act. Truman then worked to get his Fair Deal reforms passed, with moderate success.

Alarmed by North Korea's invasion of South Korea, the United Nations intervened in an attempt to halt the spread of communism. The Korean War resulted. After three years of fighting, an armistice was signed. This agreement left the two nations divided roughly along the 38th parallel.

Fears over the spread of communism led to a new Red Scare in America. The House Un-American Activities Committee (HUAC), along with Senator Joseph McCarthy, began a campaign against suspected Communists. However, the questionable tactics McCarthy used eventually were exposed during the Army-McCarthy hearings.

CHAPTER INVESTIGATION

The Chapter Investigation is an extended, multipart activity designed for students to work cooperatively and apply the chapter content in the creation of a project. You may choose to use the Chapter 17 Investigation, Post–World War II Puzzle, either as a substitute for teaching the section lessons or as an alternate assessment.

BLOCK SCHEDULING 

The teacher lesson plans for each section offer a variety of activity choices to help you present the material in a block scheduling format. For further suggestions on block scheduling, see the *Block Scheduling Handbook with Team Teaching Strategies*, pp. 97–102.

Meeting Individual Needs

ABILITY LEVELS

LEVEL 1 Basic level activities designed for all students encountering new material.

LEVEL 2 Intermediate level activities designed for average students.

LEVEL 3 Challenging activities designed for above-average students.

SHELTERED ENGLISH These activities address the needs of students with Limited English Proficiency.

Smithsonian Institution®

Internet Connections and Lesson 17
www.si.edu/hrw

CNN Presents America:
Yesterday and Today 1850 to the Present
Segment: A Helping Hand to Europe

Additional Resources

Books for Teachers

Blair, Clay. *The Forgotten War: America in Korea, 1950–1953.* Doubleday, 1989. Chronicles the international political history of the Korean War.

McCullough, David. *Truman.* Simon & Schuster, 1992. Prize-winning biography of Harry S Truman's political and private life.

Wallace, Patricia Ward. *The Politics of Conscience: A Biography of Margaret Chase Smith.* Praeger, 1995. Biography of Margaret Chase Smith, who was one of the first politicians to reject publicly Senator McCarthy's extremist views.

Books for Students

Halliday, Jon, and Bruce Cumings. *Korea: The Unknown War.* Pantheon, 1998. Examines the Korean War from the perspectives of both North and South Korea.

Leavell, Perry. *Harry S Truman.* Chelsea House, 1998. Part of World Leaders, Past and Present series (for students reading below grade level).

Steins, Richard. *The Postwar Years: The Cold War and the Atomic Age.* 21st Century Books, 1994. Overview of postwar peace and U.S. isolationism, including beginnings of the Cold War and realizations about the atomic age.

Multimedia Materials

Korea: MacArthur's War with Truman. Video, 40 min. Zenger/SSSS. Uses archival footage, maps, and contemporary images to document issues of the Korean War.

Truman and the Cold War. Video, 16 min. Learning Corporation of America. Looks at Truman's role in giving aid to European countries.

Truman and the Korean War. Video, 18 min. Learning Corporation of America. Examines events leading up to the Korean War, the war itself, and Truman's dismissal of General MacArthur.

The Cold War Begins

CHAPTER MOTIVATOR

Create a grid on the classroom floor representing Asia, Europe, and North America. Assign students to serve as ones, twos, or threes. The ones represent democracy, the twos communism, and the threes undecided nations. Assign the ones to stand primarily in North America and Western Europe; the twos in Eastern Europe; and the threes in Asia. Try to approximate the post–World War II political culture of each region by having students stand in an appropriate square. Have students roll a die to see how many squares to move. Tell students that any time a one or two moves into the space of a three, the three becomes the number of the person who landed in the space (to symbolize the expansion of democracy or communism).

Presenting Themes

- **Economic Development** Students might mention that a nation might give economic aid to gain the friendship of another nation and to help maintain or strengthen trade relations with a nation. Countries also may offer economic aid to allies and withhold aid from nations whose politics they oppose.
- **Global Relations** Students might mention that countries with political differences might compete for global superiority and power by supporting and spreading their political system to other countries; these goals can lead to conflict.
- **Citizenship and Democracy** Students might mention that nations may restrict certain civil rights, such as free speech, when involved in conflicts with other nations. Students also might note that a nation might improve its domestic policies, such as civil rights, to gain allies.

Using the Time Line

Have students make a chart with three columns headed *Cause, Event,* and *Effect.* Have students list in the center column the events from the time line. Then ask students to complete the chart as they read the chapter.

CHAPTER 17

The Cold War Begins

(1945–1955)

Cooperation during World War II had encouraged many Americans to trust the Soviet Union. President Franklin D. Roosevelt had even said, "I think the Russians are perfectly friendly; they aren't trying to gobble up all the rest of Europe or the world." Soon after the war ended, however, this view changed. The United States and the Soviet Union became locked in a struggle for world power.

Economic Development
Why might one country give economic aid to another?

Global Relations
How might political differences cause conflict and competition between two nations?

Citizenship and Democracy
How might global conflicts affect civil rights at home?

1945 **1946** **1947** **1948** **1949**

NOV. 1945 War crimes trials begin in Nuremberg, Germany.

MAR. 1947 President Truman announces the Truman Doctrine.

MAY 1948 The nation of Israel is founded.

JUNE 1948 The Soviet Union blockades the city of Berlin.

APR. 1949 NATO is created.

OBJECTIVES

- Describe the agreements the Allies reached at Yalta and Potsdam.
- Explain measures the Allies took to prevent another world war.
- Identify postwar events that increased tensions between the Western Allies and the Soviet Union.

FOCUS

Motivate Before Reading

Ask students to imagine that they live in a city that has been devastated by a global war. Many people have been killed, and many homes and businesses are destroyed. The war has ended, but they and many other people in the city fear another world war. Have students speculate on ways their leaders might prevent future world wars. Write the better ideas on the chalkboard. Then tell

The World After War

Reading Focus

What agreements did the Allies reach at the Yalta and Potsdam Conferences?

What measures did the Allies take to prevent another world war?

What postwar events led to increased tensions between the Western Allies and the Soviet Union?

Key Terms

Yalta Conference
Potsdam Conference
United Nations
Nuremberg Trials

At 5:47 P.M. on April 12, 1945, news announcers interrupted every radio and television program in the United States. They reported that President Roosevelt had died. Americans were shocked. The man who had led the United States through the Great Depression and most of World War II was gone. Harry S Truman became the new president. He told reporters, "When they told me yesterday what had happened, I felt like the moon, the stars, and all the planets had fallen on me." After just 82 days as vice president, Truman had to fill the great man's shoes.

The New York Times.

PRESIDENT ROOSEVELT IS DEAD; TRUMAN TO CONTINUE POLICIES; 9TH CROSSES ELBE, NEARS BERLIN

Roosevelt's death stunned many Americans.

Section 1 RESOURCES

PRINT

★ Guided Reading Strategies 17.1

★ Primary Source Reading 17: The Path to the Atomic Bomb

★ Section 1 Review, p. 512

★ Daily Quiz 17.1

MULTIMEDIA

★ *Teaching Resources CD–ROM,* Lesson 17.1

★ Everyday Life in America Transparency 27: Postwar Painting, 1946

SHELTERED ENGLISH

★ Main Idea Activities for Reteaching and Sheltered English 17.1

IMAGE ON LEFT PAGE: *Winston Churchill, Franklin D. Roosevelt, and Joseph Stalin (seated left to right) at Yalta*

1950 | 1951 | 1952 | 1953 | 1954

FEB. 1950 Senator Joseph McCarthy claims that Communists are working in the U.S. State Department.

JUNE 1950 The Korean War begins.

JUNE 1953 Julius and Ethel Rosenberg are executed for spying.

JULY 1953 A cease-fire ends the Korean War.

students that in this section they will learn about the steps the Allies took after World War II to prevent a third world war and about the rise in tensions between the Soviet Union and the United States.

Introduce Key Terms

Linguistic, Interpersonal. Review this section's key terms with students. Provide each student with note cards. Have students write one key term on each card. Then have them write clues about each term on the back of its card. Ask students to pair up and take turns reading the clues, while their partners try to identify the terms. **SHELTERED ENGLISH**

TEACH

Have students read Section 1 and complete Guided Reading Strategies 17.1. Choose one or more of the following activities to explore the section content with students. For further suggestions on block scheduling or team teaching, see the *Block Scheduling Handbook*.

LEVEL 1: Linguistic. (Suggested time: 15 min.) As a class, go over students' Guided Reading Strategies. Then use the Reading Focus questions to highlight the main ideas of the section. **SHELTERED ENGLISH**

Citizenship and Democracy

Supporting the United Nations. President Roosevelt realized that for the United Nations to be effective, it would require the support of the American people. In his January 1945 State of the Union Address, he declared, "In our disillusionment after the last war, we gave up the hope of achieving a better peace because we had not the courage to fulfill our responsibilities in an admittedly imperfect world. We must not let that happen again, or we shall follow the same tragic road again—the road to a third world war."

Critical Thinking: What historical event was Roosevelt referring to in his speech?

ANSWER: The U.S. decision not to enter the League of Nations after World War I.

Multimedia Resources

Everyday Life in America Transparency 27: Postwar Painting, 1946

Yalta and Potsdam

In February 1945 the Allies were close to victory in Europe. In the Soviet town of Yalta, a meeting took place between the "Big Three." These leaders were Franklin D. Roosevelt of the United States, Winston Churchill of Great Britain, and Joseph Stalin of the Soviet Union. At the **Yalta Conference**, they made plans for the postwar world. The resulting agreement would shape international affairs for years to come.

Clement Attlee, Harry S Truman, and Joseph Stalin (seated left to right) at the Potsdam Conference

The Yalta agreement called for the creation of a world peacekeeping organization. It also supported free elections and democratic governments in the nations being freed from Axis control. In addition, Stalin agreed to join the war against Japan after Germany surrendered. The agreement seemed to solve many problems. One of President Roosevelt's close advisers recalled, "We really believed in our hearts that this was the dawn of the new day we had all been praying for and talking about for so many years."

Stalin did not honor all of the agreements he had made at Yalta. For example, he did not want a democratic government established in Poland. Stalin saw Poland as a crucial buffer between Germany and his own country. After the Soviets liberated Poland from German control, they installed a pro-communist government in June 1945. This government later refused to allow free elections in Poland.

After Roosevelt's death in April, Harry S Truman had become president. Germany surrendered the following month. Soviet armies occupied most of Eastern Europe. In July, Truman traveled to Potsdam, Germany, to meet with Churchill and Stalin. At the **Potsdam Conference**, the three leaders divided Germany into four zones of occupation. Britain, France, the Soviet Union, and the United States would each control one zone. The former German capital of Berlin, located within the Soviet zone, was also divided into four sections.

Meanwhile, in the Pacific the Allies continued to fight Japan. The Allies demanded unconditional surrender from the Japanese government. Shortly before his arrival at Potsdam, Truman had learned of the successful atomic bomb test at Trinity Site, New Mexico. He decided to tell Churchill about the test, but not Stalin. Truman later approved the use of this new weapon against Japan. After the atomic bombing of Hiroshima and Nagasaki, Japan surrendered in September 1945.

Political Changes

While in Germany, President Truman visited Berlin. Shocked by the wartime devastation of the city, he and other political leaders looked for ways to prevent future wars.

The United Nations

The solution seemed to be an international organization that could resolve conflicts peacefully. In 1944, British, Chinese, Soviet, and U.S. representatives had met in Washington, D.C. They drafted a plan for a new organization to promote world peace—the **United Nations** (UN). The following year, representatives from 50 nations came together in San Francisco, California, to write the UN charter. The charter was unanimously approved and signed in June 1945. The first official UN session took place in January 1946.

The flags of member nations fly at the UN Building in New York City.

ALL LEVELS: Logical-Mathematical, Visual-Spatial. (Suggested time: 30 min.) Have each student prepare a graphic organizer that illustrates the agreements the Allies made at the Yalta and Potsdam Conferences. Students also should indicate which of the agreements was an attempt to prevent a third world war. Call on volunteers to explain their organizers to the class. **SHELTERED ENGLISH**

LEVEL 3: Linguistic, Logical-Mathematical. (Suggested time: 15 min. plus homework) Ask students to write an essay explaining the postwar events that led to increased tensions between the United States and the Soviet Union. Call on volunteers to read their essays. Encourage feedback and discussion.

CLOSE

Logical-Mathematical. Call on a student to read the quotation from Winston Churchill on textbook page 512. Ask students to explain what he meant. Then ask students to explain why U.S.-Soviet tensions increased after World War II despite steps the Allies had taken to prevent future world wars.

CHALLENGE AND EXTEND

Linguistic, Logical-Mathematical. Have students use the library and other resources to prepare an encyclopedia entry on the history of Israel. Encourage students to consider what events

The UN charter created two major bodies, the Security Council and the General Assembly. Fifteen member nations belong to the Security Council. Five nations—China, France, Great Britain, present-day Russia, and the United States—have permanent seats on the council. The other 10 nations are elected to the council for two-year terms. The Security Council authorizes diplomatic, economic, and military actions to settle disputes. The General Assembly is made up of all UN member nations. It meets annually to debate policy, vote on membership, and approve the budget. The UN charter also created the International Court of Justice, based in The Hague, Netherlands.

The War Crimes Trials

To discourage future acts of aggression, the Allies also held war crimes trials. These are trials of individuals accused of crimes against humanity and the international laws of warfare. Beginning in November 1945, the International Military Tribunal tried high-ranking Nazi officers. The trials were held in Nuremberg, Germany—the former site of huge Nazi rallies. The chief American attorney highlighted the importance of these **Nuremberg Trials**.

> **"The wrongs which we seek to condemn and punish have been so calculated, so malignant [harmful] and devastating, that civilization cannot tolerate their being ignored because it cannot survive their being repeated."**

The tribunal at Nuremberg found 21 Nazi leaders guilty of crimes against humanity and sentenced 12 of them to death. The tribunal also tried and convicted thousands of lesser officials. Many of the ex-Nazis were convicted for helping to run concentration camps during the Holocaust.

The International Military Tribunal for the Far East conducted similar war crimes trials in Japan. The tribunal convicted and executed former prime minister Hideki Tojo and six other Japanese leaders. It also convicted some 4,000 lesser Japanese war criminals.

During the trials soldiers could not use the defense that they had simply been following orders. The war crimes trials established that there is no defense for committing crimes against humanity. The trials also showed that nations could cooperate to prosecute war criminals.

These Nazi officials were the first of many charged with war crimes. Seated on the far left is Hermann Göring, head of Hitler's secret police.

The Birth of Israel

The Nuremberg Trials further exposed the horrors of the Holocaust. International support increased for the creation of a Jewish homeland. In 1947 the UN General Assembly divided Palestine, which Britain had occupied since World War I. Two states were to be formed—one Arab, one Jewish. In May 1948 the independent Jewish nation of Israel was established.

The United States immediately recognized Israel's independence. Just as swiftly, the armies of neighboring Arab states attacked the new nation. Israeli forces drove back the attackers and advanced to occupy Arab territory. After a bitter fight, the two sides signed an armistice in the spring of 1949. The Jews had a homeland. However, the war had created about 1 million Palestinian Arab refugees. Israel joined the United Nations in 1949.

Israel's national flag

A Divided Europe

Despite the efforts of Allied leaders to establish world peace after World War II, tensions in Europe

Global Relations

Recognition of Israel. Many State Department officials argued that the United States should not support an independent Israel. Instead, they called for international cooperation in governing the region. However, President Truman disagreed. The United States extended diplomatic recognition to Israel only 11 minutes after its first prime minister, David Ben-Gurion, announced the establishment of the new nation. Truman's decision rested in part on the fact that many Jewish Americans supported the new state. The president wanted to keep these voters satisfied with his administration's policies.

Critical Thinking: Why might many State Department officials have opposed U.S. support of an independent Israel?

ANSWER: They may have worried that the support might lead to conflicts between the United States and Arab countries.

have affected the development of the nation. Call on volunteers to share their entries with the class.

REVIEW

Logical-Mathematical, Visual-Spatial. Have students complete the Section Review questions. Ask students to prepare a chart with two columns labeled *Event* and *Results*. In the first column have students list the major events in the section. In the second column have students list the short- and long-term effects of each event. Ask volunteers to share their answers.

ASSESS

Have students complete Daily Quiz 17.1

RETEACH

Linguistic, Logical-Mathematical. Have students complete Main Idea Activities for Reteaching and Sheltered English 17.1. Then have students write headlines for the following topics: measures taken to prevent another world war, the Nuremberg Trials, the establishment of Israel, and conflicts between the United States and the Soviet Union. **SHELTERED ENGLISH**

Section 1 Review ANSWERS

Identify

For significance, see the following pages:

- Yalta Conference, p. 510
- Harry S Truman, p. 510
- Potsdam Conference, p. 510
- United Nations, p. 510
- Nuremberg Trials, p. 511

Reading for Content Understanding

1. Yalta—a world peacekeeping organization; free elections and democratic governments in nations being liberated from Axis control; that the Soviet Union would declare war on Japan after Germany's surrender; Potsdam—division of Germany and Berlin into four occupied zones; demand for Japan's unconditional surrender

2. Soviet installment of a pro-communist government and refusal to allow free elections in Poland; Soviet occupation of and expansion in Eastern Europe; American fears over spread of communism in Europe and at home; Stalin's use of terror and violence against fellow Soviets

3. They created a world peacekeeping organization, the United Nations.

4. Articles will vary but students may express relief that the world recognized what had occurred and had punished those responsible, or disappointment that more people were not punished.

5. Answers will vary but students might point out that World War II and the threat of another world war convinced the government that the United States needed to join to make a world peacekeeping organization effective.

remained high. Western diplomats were becoming very concerned about the plans of Stalin and the Soviet Union.

The United States and the Soviet Union disagreed strongly about the political future of Central and Eastern Europe. The status of Germany was a major issue. The United States wanted an independent and united Germany. The Soviets feared that if Germany united, it might once again invade their country—as it had in both world wars.

Editorial cartoon by Tom Little, 1948; courtesy of the *Nashville Tennessean*.

The Iron Curtain cut nations such as Czechoslovakia off from Western Europe.

The Soviet armies of occupation remained in Eastern Europe. They helped establish communist "satellite states" loyal to the Soviet Union. The Soviets argued that they were simply protecting their borders. Western diplomats viewed these actions differently. British prime minister Winston Churchill warned Americans about the threat posed by Soviet expansion in Europe:

> **"An Iron Curtain has descended across the [European] Continent. Behind that line lie all the capitals of the ancient states of Central and Eastern Europe. . . . All these famous cities and the populations around them lie in the Soviet sphere and all are subject . . . to a very high and increasing measure of control from Moscow."**

British and U.S. leaders feared that the Soviet Union's influence would continue to expand. This growth would threaten the democracies of Western Europe. Many observers were also troubled by stories of Stalin's use of terror and violence against Soviet citizens. These brutal acts suggested that Stalin would stop at nothing to protect and increase his power.

Some U.S. politicians were even concerned that Communists at home were cooperating with Soviet spies. Senator Arthur Vandenberg asked other members of Congress, "What is Russia up to? . . . We ask it in eastern Europe. . . . We ask it sometimes even in connection with events in our United States."

SECTION 1 REVIEW

Identify and explain the significance of the following:

- **Yalta Conference**
- **Harry S Truman**
- **Potsdam Conference**
- **United Nations**
- **Nuremberg Trials**

Reading for Content Understanding

1 **Main Idea** What plans did the Allies discuss at the Yalta and Potsdam Conferences?

2 **Main Idea** What created postwar tensions between the Soviet Union and the Western Allies?

3 **Global Relations** How did the Allies try to preserve world peace after World War II?

4 **Writing** *Expressing* Imagine that you are a Jew who lived through the Holocaust. Write a short article for an Israeli newspaper expressing your reaction to the Nuremberg Trials.

5 **Critical Thinking** *Drawing Conclusions* Why do you think the United States was willing to join the United Nations when it had not been willing to join the League of Nations after World War I?

OBJECTIVES

- Analyze major U.S. foreign-policy strategies after World War II.
- Describe the purpose and result of the Marshall Plan.
- Identify the major events in the Cold War between 1946 and 1950.

FOCUS

Motivate Before Reading

Ask students to imagine that they are an advisor to President Truman. The spread of communism poses a great threat to the nation. Have students discuss how the government might control the spread of communism. Then ask students what the results of some of their actions might be. Tell students that in this section

The Roots of the Cold War

Reading Focus

What were the major U.S. foreign-policy strategies after World War II?

What was the purpose and the result of the Marshall Plan?

What were the major events in the Cold War between the United States and the Soviet Union from 1946 to 1950?

Key Terms

Cold War
Truman Doctrine
Marshall Plan
containment
Berlin Airlift
North Atlantic Treaty Organization

ONE DAY IN THE SPRING OF 1945, U.S. and Soviet troops met each other at the Elbe River in Germany. The Soviets waited on the eastern shore of the river. Private Joseph Polowsky and a few other U.S. soldiers approached the Soviets cautiously. Through translators the two sides spoke to each other. "There were tears in the eyes of most of us . . . ," recalled Polowsky. They then pointed to the ruins around them, he remembered. "We embraced. We swore never to forget." Despite their shared relief at the end of the war, Polowsky felt "a sense of foreboding [uneasiness] that things might not be as perfect in the future as we anticipated."

A stamp showing the meeting at the Elbe River

Allies Become Enemies

The Soviet Union and the United States had allied against Germany in World War II. After the war they were the two most powerful nations in the world. Their alliance quickly turned into a bitter competition.

The so-called superpowers had little in common economically or politically. The United States was based on free enterprise and democracy. The Soviet Union was a communist country. Both governments wanted to spread their influence around the world. As a result, both countries became increasingly involved in the affairs of other nations. For example, the Soviet Union supported pro-communist independence movements in many colonized regions. The United States often opposed these efforts, fearing the spread of communism.

U.S. presidential adviser Bernard Baruch described U.S.-Soviet relations by saying, "Let us not be deceived—we are today in the midst of a cold war." Many people began using the term **Cold War** to describe the struggle between the

Section 2
RESOURCES

PRINT

★ Guided Reading Strategies 17.2

★ Geography Activity 17: Postwar Tensions in the Eastern Mediterranean

★ Section 2 Review, p. 517

★ Daily Quiz 17.2

MULTIMEDIA

★ *Teaching Resources CD–ROM,* Lesson 17.2

SHELTERED ENGLISH

★ Main Idea Activities for Reteaching and Sheltered English 17.2

they will learn about growing U.S.-Soviet tensions and the U.S. government's efforts to contain communism.

Introduce Key Terms

Linguistic, Logical-Mathematical. Review this section's key terms with students. Then ask them to write *Cold War* on a piece of paper. Next, have each student list the other terms chronologically to show the development of the Cold War over time. Call on volunteers to share their lists and have students discuss their accuracy. Finally, have students write a definition for each term. **SHELTERED ENGLISH**

TEACH

Have students read Section 2 and complete Guided Reading Strategies 17.2. Choose one or more of the following activities to explore the section content with students. For further suggestions on block scheduling or team teaching, see the *Block Scheduling Handbook*.

LEVEL 1: Linguistic. (Suggested time: 15 min.) As a class, go over students' Guided Reading Strategies. Then use the Reading Focus questions to highlight the main ideas of the section. **SHELTERED ENGLISH**

Economic Development

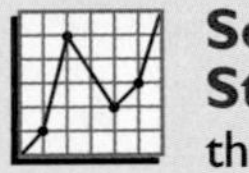

Soviet Strength. In 1947 the Soviet government published statistics on the devastation it suffered during World War II. Besides the cost in human lives—more than 20 million citizens were killed—the Soviet Union suffered catastrophic economic losses. Some 1,700 cities and 70,000 villages had been destroyed. Six million buildings, 90,000 bridges, and 56,000 miles of road were ruined. The Germans had killed or stolen millions of livestock animals. Despite these losses, the Soviet Union refused U.S. offers of economic aid.

Critical Thinking: Considering Soviet losses in World War II, why would U.S. officials still see the Soviet Union as a threat?

ANSWER: They saw Soviet control of Eastern Europe as proof that the Soviets could and would continue to expand communist influence.

Historical Documents Answers

1. democracy—based upon the will of the majority; supports freedoms, free institutions and representative government; communism—based upon the will of a minority; uses oppression to control the majority

2. the free peoples of the world; to safeguard their freedoms and world peace

United States and the Soviet Union for global power.

One of the first trouble spots was Greece. In August 1946, communist guerrillas revolted against the corrupt monarchy of Greece. The rebels were supported by the independent communist government of Yugoslavia. President Truman, however, believed the Soviets were behind the revolt. He decided to stop further Soviet expansion in Europe.

In March 1947 Truman announced that the United States would provide economic aid to help foreign countries fight communism. This policy became known as the **Truman Doctrine**. Congress approved $400 million in aid for Greece and its neighbor Turkey. This aid helped the Greek army defeat the rebels. The Truman Doctrine was successful in protecting the anti-communist governments of Greece and Turkey. However, it greatly angered Soviet leaders.

HISTORICAL DOCUMENTS

The Truman Doctrine

On March 12, 1947, President Truman presented Congress with his Cold War foreign policy. In the following excerpt from the Truman Doctrine, the president compares democracy and communism.

"At the present moment in world history nearly every nation must choose between alternative ways of life. . . . One way of life is based upon the will of the majority, and is distinguished by free institutions, representative government, free elections, and . . . freedom from political oppression. The second way of life is based upon the will of a minority forcibly imposed upon the majority. It relies upon terror and oppression . . . and the suppression of personal freedoms. I believe it must be the policy of the United States to support free peoples. . . .

The free peoples of the world look to us for support in maintaining their freedoms. If we falter in our leadership, we may endanger the peace of the world—and we shall surely endanger the welfare of our own nation."

Understanding Primary Sources

1. What distinguishes democracy from communism according to President Truman?
2. Who does Truman say the United States should support, and why?

The Marshall Plan

Some Europeans thought that communism would solve their economic troubles. The European economy had been severely damaged by World War II. Millions of people were unemployed and major industries were in ruin. Many people were homeless. Countless others were in danger of starvation.

General George C. Marshall had helped plan the D-Day invasion in World War II. He became U.S. secretary of state in 1947. Marshall argued that Europe's economic recovery was necessary to protect world peace. European recovery would also benefit the U.S. economy, which relied on trade with Europe. Marshall said:

> **"It is logical that the United States should do whatever it is able to do to assist in the return of normal economic health in the world, without which there can be no political stability and no assured peace."**

In what became known as the **Marshall Plan**, the United States offered "friendly aid" to help the nations of Europe rebuild. Some members of Congress thought the Marshall Plan would be too expensive. Others argued

ALL LEVELS: Logical-Mathematical, Visual-Spatial. (Suggested time: 30 min.) Ask students to choose a few events to include in a 1946–50 chapter of a pictorial history of the Cold War. For each event, have students create an illustration or political cartoon describing the event. Encourage students to include brief captions explaining the events depicted. Finally, call on volunteers to explain their illustrations or cartoons to the class. **SHELTERED ENGLISH**

ALL LEVELS: Linguistic, Logical-Mathematical, Visual-Spatial. (Suggested time: 45 min.) Ask students to create a chart with four columns and four rows. Have students label the columns *Truman Doctrine, Marshall Plan, Containment,* and *NATO.* Have them label the rows *When Developed, Countries Involved, Reasons for the Policy,* and *Goals of the Policy.* Then ask students to complete the charts. When students are done, lead a discussion about the success of each post–World War II foreign policy.

LEVEL 3: Logical-Mathematical, Interpersonal, Intrapersonal. (Suggested time: 20 min. plus homework) Ask students to imagine that they are going to testify before a congressional committee considering whether to continue funding for the Marshall Plan. Have each student prepare a brief explaining the purpose of the plan and its results. Suggest to students that they try to show how economic aid from the Marshall Plan has or has not helped the United States achieve the goals of the Truman

Tons of goods helped Europeans recover after the war.

that Communists might gain control of Western European nations if their economies did not recover. This argument persuaded many officials. Congress eventually approved $6 billion for Marshall Plan aid. Congress later increased funding for the plan after it went into effect.

The United States offered to assist the Soviet Union under the Marshall Plan, but the Soviets refused the offer. The Soviet foreign minister called the plan a plot to enslave Europe by making it dependent on U.S. aid. Marshall insisted that his plan was not directed "against any country or doctrine but against hunger, poverty, desperation, and chaos." Soviet leaders ignored such statements. They prevented their Eastern European satellites from participating in the Marshall Plan and accepting U.S. aid.

The Marshall Plan helped Western Europe recover from the war. "We grabbed the lifeline with both hands," remembered a British minister. The plan also created a market for American exports. However, the Marshall Plan widened the division between the Soviet Union and the United States.

The Berlin Airlift

In the late 1940s a crisis in occupied Germany tested the containment policy. England, France, and the United States wanted an independent German nation. In June 1948 they proposed merging their areas of control to create the country of West Germany. The divided city of Berlin, however, would still be located in Soviet-controlled eastern Germany. Angered by this proposal, the Soviets blocked off all highway and rail traffic between West Berlin and Western Europe.

West Berlin could not survive without food and other necessities from the West. To solve the crisis without a direct military confrontation, U.S. officials decided to fly supplies into the city. In June 1948, U.S. and British planes began the **Berlin Airlift**. They brought food and supplies to the more than 2 million people in West Berlin. The effort was massive. Planes landed in Berlin every minute for weeks.

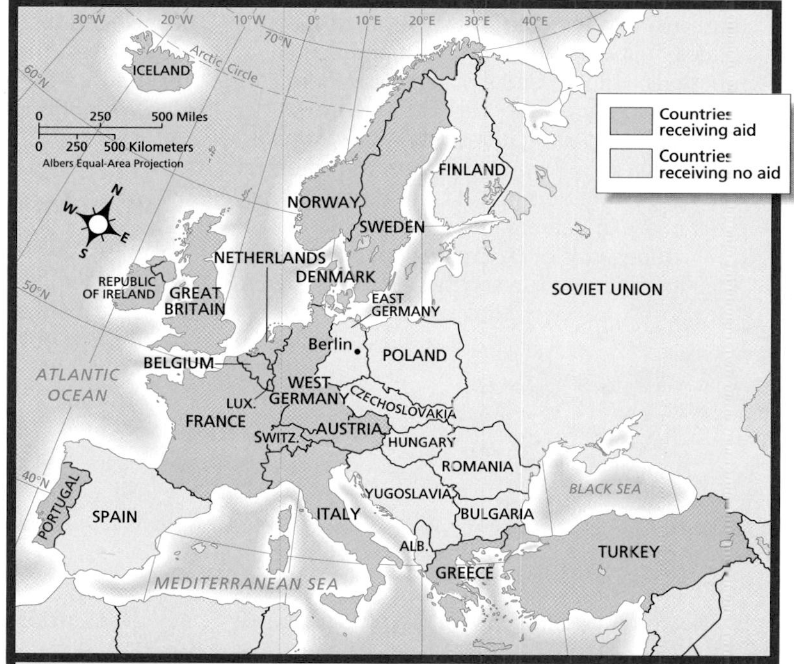

The Marshall Plan, 1948–1951

Learning from Maps The Marshall Plan lasted from 1948 until 1951, during which time the United States sent about $13 billion in aid to European countries recovering from World War II.

Location Which country in Western Europe did not receive aid under the Marshall Plan?

Containment

As the Cold War continued, the United States adopted a new foreign policy. This foreign policy, called **containment**, sought to contain the spread of communism by reacting quickly to any Soviet-backed aggression. U.S. officials saw containment as a defensive strategy. Soviet leaders , however, regarded the policy as an offensive strategy.

Global Relations

Supplying Berlin. President Truman was in the midst of an election campaign when the Soviets blockaded West Berlin. Some advisors and U.S. military leaders proposed using armored military convoys to send in supplies by force. They reasoned that the Soviets would not dare risk war by attacking the supply trucks. Opponents of the plan believed Stalin would not hesitate to use force against a ground convoy. Based on pilots who had flown supplies over Burma in World War II, this group thought it possible to fly enough supplies into West Berlin. This method had the advantage of not directly challenging Soviet military forces. Truman thought the idea less risky and thus ordered the Berlin airlift.

Critical Thinking: Why might it be more difficult for a president to respond to an international crisis in an election year?

ANSWER: Answers will vary but students should point out that during these times presidents often are concerned with winning voters' support and may not want to do anything that might lose the public's favor.

MAP ANSWER
Spain

Doctrine and the policy of containment. Call on volunteers to present their briefs to the class. Finally, have the class, acting as the committee, vote on whether to continue funding the Marshall Plan.

CLOSE

Linguistic, Logical-Mathematical. Have each student write two editorials about the growing Cold War. Ask students to write the first from an American perspective and the second from a Soviet perspective. Call on volunteers to read their editorials to the class. Encourage feedback and discussion.

CHALLENGE AND EXTEND

TEACHER TO TEACHER

Linguistic, Logical-Mathematical. Anne Edwards of Denver, Colorado, suggested the following activity: Ask students to imagine that they live in West Berlin during the Soviet blockade. Have them write letters to friends in the United States evaluating the Berlin Airlift's success in achieving the U.S. policy of containment. Ask volunteers to read their letters to the class. Encourage discussion.

Across the Curriculum

GEOGRAPHY

Military Bases. Overseas military bases were an important component of U.S. postwar foreign strategy. Overseas bases served two purposes. First, in the age of strategic bombing, analysts hoped that U.S. military forces stationed overseas could stop any attack before it reached the U.S. mainland. Second, the bases would enable the United States to respond quickly to any crises that developed in Europe or Asia.

Critical Thinking: Why might another nation agree to allow the United States to establish military bases in its territory?

ANSWER: Answers will vary but students might mention that such a country would receive assistance from U.S. forces if it ever were attacked.

LINKING PAST TO PRESENT ANSWERS

1. to provide protection against Soviet aggression; during the Cold War

2. With East Germany as its neighbor, West Germany seemed particularly vulnerable to attack.

Linking Past to Present

American Military Bases Abroad

The United States has maintained overseas military bases since the mid-1800s. In the 1860s and 1870s, the U.S. Navy gained the use of Pacific islands as refueling stations. Victory in the Spanish-American War brought bases in Cuba and the Philippines under U.S. control.

After World War II, U.S. presidents believed that Soviet aggression required a near-global U.S. military presence. As a result, the United States built many more bases in foreign countries. With Soviet-dominated East Germany as a neighbor, West Germany was particularly vulnerable. Therefore, the United States built multiple army command headquarters, airfields, and smaller bases there. The United States also built bases in other Western European nations, as well as in Japan, South Korea, and the Philippines. To protect its interests in the Persian Gulf, the United States built bases in Bahrain and Saudi Arabia.

Thousands of U.S. military personnel and their families have lived on these overseas bases. Their experiences have been both rewarding and challenging. One air force colonel's son fondly remembers the years he lived in Italy. "We went to festivals where there were big floats and people threw confetti." Others, however, did not experience the local culture. An army sergeant's daughter recalls, "We were pretty much isolated. We lived in this compound, and for all we figured, that was the way everybody lived."

Camp Foster on the Japanese island of Okinawa

In the post–Cold War era, the Department of Defense re-examined strategic needs and foreign-policy goals. It concluded that there was less need for overseas bases. The United States has thus closed or reduced the size of many overseas bases, mostly in Europe.

Understanding What You Read

1. Why and when were most U.S. overseas military bases established?
2. Why were so many U.S. military bases located in West Germany?

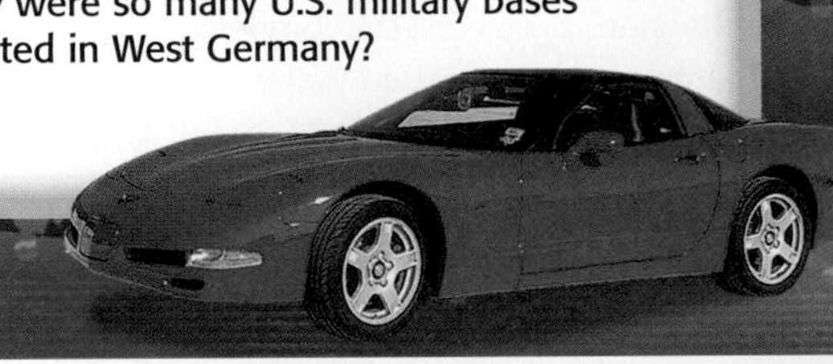

In September 1948 Ernst Reuter, the mayor of West Berlin, declared:

> **"We cannot be bartered [traded], we cannot be negotiated, we cannot be sold. . . . Whoever would surrender the people of Berlin, would surrender a world. . . . People of the world, look upon this city! You cannot, you must not, forsake us!"**

The so-called Operation Vittles lasted 321 days. During this time, planes brought more than 2 million tons of food and supplies into West Berlin. The Soviets did not want to risk a war by stopping the airlift. On May 12, 1949, the Soviet Union lifted its blockade. That same year, Germany became two nations—the Federal Republic of Germany (West Germany) and the German Democratic Republic (East Germany).

REVIEW

Linguistic, Logical-Mathematical. Have students complete the Section Review questions. Then have students compose a paragraph using all the section's key terms to describe U.S. policy toward the Soviet Union after World War II and the events that took place as a result. Call on volunteers to read their paragraphs to the class.

ASSESS

Have students complete Daily Quiz 17.2.

RETEACH

Logical-Mathematical, Interpersonal. Have students complete Main Idea Activities for Reteaching and Sheltered English 17.2. Then organize students into pairs. Have each pair identify and list five major events from the section. Then have each partner separately determine whether each event served to ease or increase tensions between the United States and the Soviet Union. Finally, have partners discuss how they classified each event.
SHELTERED ENGLISH

Defensive Moves

Concern over the growing military strength of the Soviet Union led the United States, Canada, Iceland, and nine Western European nations to form a military alliance in April 1949. Each member of this **North Atlantic Treaty Organization** (NATO) pledged to defend the others. The treaty then went to the U.S. Senate to be ratified. Some senators worried that NATO might require the United States to go to war without congressional approval. Similar concerns had stopped the United States from joining the League of Nations after World War I. Yet the threat of Soviet expansion convinced the Senate to approve NATO. In 1955 the Soviet Union created its own military alliance, the Warsaw Pact, with the Eastern European nations it controlled.

Another concern for U.S. leaders was the rise of a Soviet nuclear threat. In August 1949 the Soviets shocked U.S. military experts by detonating their own atomic bomb. The Cold War grew more intense. In 1950 the U.S. National Security Council issued NSC-68, a foreign-policy paper. This paper argued that the Soviet Union sought to control not just Europe but the entire world. According to NSC-68, U.S. leaders had to be prepared to oppose Soviet-backed Communists worldwide. The United States might have to use force in small or remote countries to protect its interests.

This NATO badge bears the Latin inscription "Vigilance is the price of liberty."

Not all Americans agreed with this viewpoint. Some critics argued that the resources of the United States would be stretched too thin if it tried to fight communism everywhere. They also worried that the United States would be tempted to support even undemocratic governments that were anticommunist. Despite such criticisms, global containment had strong support among many American politicians and military leaders.

To support containment, the United States strengthened its international alliances. It also quadrupled defense spending. President Truman authorized the development of even more powerful nuclear weapons for national defense. Just a few years after the end of World War II, the Cold War between the United States and the Soviet Union was spreading around the world.

SECTION 2 REVIEW

Identify and explain the significance of the following:
- **Cold War**
- **Truman Doctrine**
- **George C. Marshall**
- **Marshall Plan**
- **containment**
- **Berlin Airlift**
- **North Atlantic Treaty Organization**

Locate and explain the importance of the following:
- **Berlin**
- **West Germany**
- **East Germany**

Reading for Content Understanding

1. **Main Idea** What major foreign policies did the United States develop at the start of the Cold War?
2. **Main Idea** Create a graphic organizer listing the major events of the Cold War between 1946 and 1950. Include the year that each event occurred and its outcome.
3. **Economic Development** Why did the United States create the Marshall Plan, and what were its results?
4. **Writing** *Persuading* Imagine that you are a member of Congress in 1949. Write a short speech persuading other members to support or oppose the North Atlantic Treaty Organization.
5. **Critical Thinking** *Drawing Conclusions* Why do you think the Western Allies put so much effort and money into keeping the Soviets from controlling West Berlin?

Section 2 Review ANSWERS

Identify
For significance, see the following pages:
- Cold War, p. 513
- Truman Doctrine, p. 514
- George C. Marshall, p. 514
- Marshall Plan, p. 514
- containment, p. 515
- Berlin Airlift, p. 515
- North Atlantic Treaty Organization, p. 517

Locate
For locations, see the map on page 515.

Reading for Content Understanding

1. Truman Doctrine—economic aid to help nations fight communism; Marshall Plan—aid to help Europe rebuild; containment—policy to stop Soviet-backed aggression and communist expansion

2. Organizers will vary but may include the Greek revolt (1946), Truman Doctrine (1947), Marshall Plan (1947; began 1948), Berlin Airlift (1948), creation of NATO (1949), Soviet atomic bomb test (1949), and the NSC-68 report (1950).

3. to help Europe rebuild so that nations might not turn to communism; helped Western Europe recover, created more markets for American goods, increased U.S.-Soviet tensions

4. Supporters might state the need to oppose Soviet aggression through a united effort; those opposed might cite the danger of becoming entangled in foreign alliances.

5. They feared that if they let the Soviets take West Berlin, they might move to take all of Western Europe.

OBJECTIVES

- Explain how the U.S. government tried to ease the transition to peacetime.
- Describe the issues and the outcome of the 1948 presidential election.
- Describe what President Truman hoped to accomplish with his Fair Deal.

FOCUS

Motivate Before Reading

Ask students to describe how U.S. civilians adjusted during World War II. Have students consider the following: How did production change during the war? How did the war affect unemployment? Who filled soldiers' old jobs? Write students' responses on the chalkboard. Then tell students that in this section they will learn how Truman dealt with postwar domestic problems.

Section 3 RESOURCES

PRINT

★ Guided Reading Strategies 17.3

★ Section 3 Review, p. 521

★ Daily Quiz 17.3

MULTIMEDIA

★ *Teaching Resources CD–ROM,* Lesson 17.3

★ HRW Web site

SHELTERED ENGLISH

★ Main Idea Activities for Reteaching and Sheltered English 17.3

The Truman Era

Reading Focus

How did the U.S. government try to ease the transition to peacetime?

What were the major issues and the outcome of the 1948 presidential election?

What did President Truman hope to accomplish with his Fair Deal?

Key Terms

GI Bill of Rights
United Mine Workers
Taft-Hartley Act
Dixiecrats
Fair Deal

AS A YOUNG MAN, Chesterfield Smith just wanted to have a good time. He entered the University of Florida in 1935. By 1940 he had completed only three and a half years of school. "I'd go to school a semester and then drop out a semester," Smith explained. "I chose the easy life in college." Then World War II came, and Smith served in France. In 1946 he returned to college and quickly finished the classes he needed to graduate. Smith's wife explained: "Something happened to Chesterfield's attitude in the war, I don't know just what, but he was a serious man when he returned." Smith was one of many Americans who became serious about the future after the war.

Like many Americans, these people were overjoyed by the victory in World War II.

 Returning to Peace

After World War II, President Truman wanted the United States to return to a peacetime economy. He considered loosening wartime price controls and canceling defense contracts. Yet he worried that too much spending by consumers would cause inflation. Truman also feared that canceling defense contracts might cause a recession. This had taken place following World War I. Truman believed that the United States needed a strong economy to compete in the Cold War.

Postwar Jobs

More than 16 million men and women had served in the armed forces. Most of them needed jobs when they returned to civilian life. To provide more positions for these veterans, the government encouraged the millions of women who had gone to work during wartime to give up their jobs.

Many women resented the loss of the income and independence that their jobs had provided. "They say a woman doesn't belong behind a factory machine or in any business organization," one female worker remarked. "But . . . who will give

Introduce Key Terms

Linguistic, Logical-Mathematical. Review this section's key terms with students. Have volunteers write sentences using the terms. Have students still unfamiliar with a term look up its correct meaning in their textbooks. **SHELTERED ENGLISH**

TEACH

Have students read Section 3 and complete Guided Reading Strategies 17.3. Choose one or more of the following activities to explore the section content with students. For further suggestions on block scheduling or team teaching, see the *Block Scheduling Handbook.*

LEVEL 1: Linguistic. (Suggested time: 15 min.) As a class, go over students' Guided Reading Strategies. Then use the Reading Focus questions to highlight the main ideas of the section. **SHELTERED ENGLISH**

ALL LEVELS: Logical-Mathematical, Visual-Spatial. (Suggested time: 35 min.) Ask students to imagine that World War II recently has ended and that they work for the government. Have students create flyers depicting actions the government has taken to help ease the transition to peacetime.

Harry S Truman

Harry S Truman was born in May 1884 in Lamar, Missouri. From an early age he was a good student. "I don't know anybody in the world ever read as much or as constantly as he did," a friend remembered. Truman also studied human nature, a skill that helped him in his political career. "When I was growing up," Truman said, "it occurred to me to watch the people around me to find out what they thought and what pleased them the most."

After the United States entered World War I, Truman felt a deep obligation to serve his country. A number of personal factors—his age and poor eyesight, for example—would have allowed him to avoid military service. He enlisted nonetheless, saying it was "a job somebody had to do." After serving in a command position, Truman returned to Missouri and soon began his political career. He became a U.S. senator in 1934. Ten years later he was elected vice president.

my family the help they have been getting from me? No one has thought to ask me whether or not I need my job."

New laws provided veterans with benefits that eased the transition to civilian life. Government officials had feared that 8 million people would be unemployed by the spring of 1946. The figure never rose above 2.7 million.

The GI Bill

The Servicemen's Readjustment Act, also called the **GI Bill of Rights**, helped keep unemployment low. Congress passed the GI Bill in 1944. It offered veterans educational benefits to attend colleges and technical schools. The bill also provided veterans with affordable home and business loans.

Guy Owen was a veteran from North Carolina who became a novelist and a professor. He explained how the GI Bill changed his life:

> **"The GI Bill, I can't emphasize enough, really saved me. [Without it] I don't think I would have been able to go on for the doctorate [graduate degree]. . . . The GI Bill took me . . . to places . . . where I had different experiences from what I would have ever seen in Carolina."**

Nearly 9 million veterans took advantage of the GI Bill's educational benefits.

These veterans are entering Austin College in Sherman, Texas.

Labor Unrest

Despite President Truman's efforts, there were some postwar economic troubles. When Truman ended rationing and price controls on goods, consumers rushed to buy products. As a result, prices skyrocketed. Food prices rose by more than 25 percent between 1945 and 1947. The inflation rate for 1946 rose to just over 18 percent.

Presidential Profiles

Harry S Truman. Harry Truman carried out the ceremonial and constitutional duties of the vice presidency after he took office in January 1945. Although he presided over the Senate and attended numerous state dinners and receptions, he was not informed about important matters of state. For example, he did not know about the program to build an atomic bomb. Nor did he learn about the Yalta Conference agreements until he became president in April 1945.

Activity: Have students use the library and search the Internet through the HRW Web site to find more information on Harry Truman's career. Have students write a biography of Truman that describes his accomplishments.

go.hrw.com
SB1 Truman

ALL LEVELS: Logical-Mathematical, Visual-Spatial, Interpersonal. (Suggested time: 35 min.) Have students re-enact the 1948 presidential campaign. Organize the class into groups and have each act as the campaign committee for one candidate. Ask each group to create signs that give the major issues of the election and their candidate's stance on them. Have each group explain its signs. Finally, discuss the election results. **SHELTERED ENGLISH**

LEVEL 3: Linguistic, Logical-Mathematical, Intrapersonal. (Suggested time: 30 min. plus homework) Ask students to imagine that they are President Truman's speechwriter. Have them write a speech to win congressional support for his Fair Deal. The speech should explain the major programs and the impact each will have and employ persuasive language to convince listeners of the reforms' importance. Ask volunteers to read their speeches. Then discuss which Fair Deal reforms passed, which did not, and why.

CLOSE

Logical-Mathematical, Visual-Spatial. Organize students into groups of three. Have each group member create a political cartoon addressing a different Reading Focus question. Then have groups discuss their cartoons and, finally, answer each question.

Across the Curriculum

MATH

Union Membership. A growing number of Americans joined unions during the Great Depression and World War II. Union membership in 1932 stood at 3.2 million. Ten years later, 8.9 million Americans belonged to unions. Five years later, at the end of World War II, 14.8 million Americans—nearly 22 percent of the total workforce—were union members.

Activity: Have students determine the number of Americans who joined unions from 1932 to 1942 *(about 5.7 million)* and between 1942 and 1945 *(about 5.9 million)*. Then have students determine the size of the nation's workforce in 1945 *(take 14.8 million and divide by .22 to get about 67.3 million).*

MAP ANSWER

the Northeast and the Great Plains states

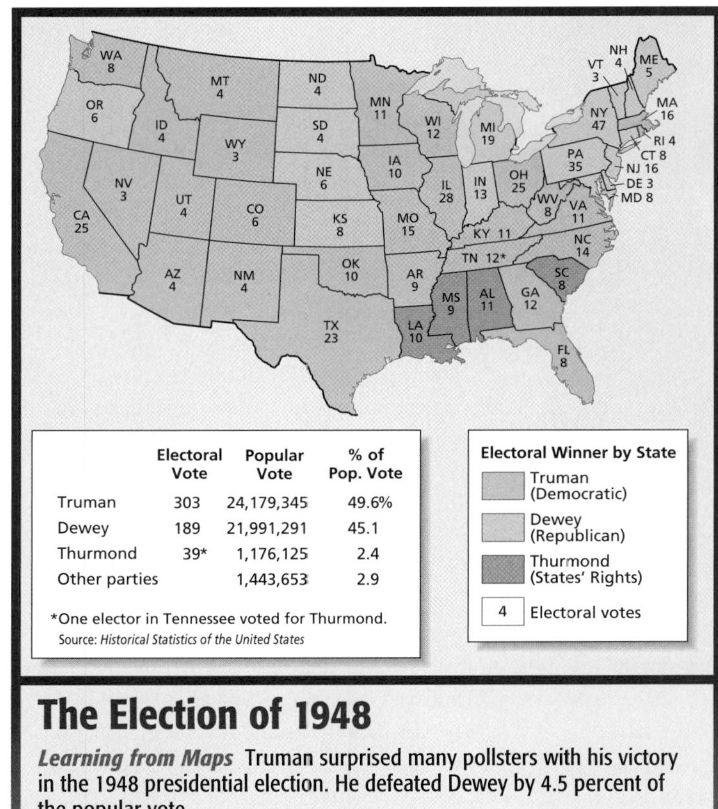

	Electoral Vote	Popular Vote	% of Pop. Vote
Truman	303	24,179,345	49.6%
Dewey	189	21,991,291	45.1
Thurmond	39*	1,176,125	2.4
Other parties		1,443,653	2.9

*One elector in Tennessee voted for Thurmond.
Source: *Historical Statistics of the United States*

The Election of 1948

Learning from Maps **Truman surprised many pollsters with his victory in the 1948 presidential election. He defeated Dewey by 4.5 percent of the popular vote.**

Region **What parts of the country voted primarily for Dewey in 1948?**

As inflation soared, unions went on strike to demand higher wages. In 1946 alone, some 4.5 million workers took part in nearly 5,000 strikes across the country. In April of that year some 400,000 members of the **United Mine Workers** (UMW) went on strike. When President Truman could not negotiate a settlement, he placed the mines under government control.

In November, UMW president John Lewis called a second strike even though the mines were still under federal control. This time, Truman said, it would be a "fight to the finish." He ordered U.S. troops to take control of the mines. The government ordered Lewis to stand trial for contempt, or disobeying an official order. "You can't dig coal with bayonets," replied Lewis. He refused to send the miners back to work. After a federal court fined the UMW $3.5 million, however, he finally halted the strike.

Republicans in Congress wanted to weaken labor unions. They were particularly concerned with the closed shop. A closed shop is a workplace in which job applicants have to join a union before they can be hired. In 1947 Senator Robert Taft of Ohio led the drive to pass the **Taft-Hartley Act**. This act outlawed closed shops. It also required union leaders to take an oath saying that they were not Communists. The act gave the president the authority to obtain court orders forcing striking unions to call off their strikes for an 80-day "cooling off" period. Despite his conflicts with the UMW, Truman thought that the Taft-Hartley Act placed too many restrictions on unions. He vetoed it, but Congress overrode his veto.

The 1948 Election

The labor unrest caused many Americans to question Truman's presidential skills. The Republicans had gained control of Congress in 1946. They believed they could win the White House in 1948. Republicans nominated New York governor Thomas Dewey for president and California governor Earl Warren for vice president.

Even leaders of the Democratic Party did not think that Truman could win re-election in 1948. Many wanted to dump him in favor of another candidate. At the 1948 national convention, the Democrats were sharply divided. Nonetheless, Truman managed to win the nomination.

Stunning the experts and forcing newspapers to rewrite headlines, President Truman won the 1948 election.

CHALLENGE AND EXTEND

Linguistic. Have students use the library and other resources to research the GI Bill of Rights. Encourage students to analyze the law's provisions, examine ways veterans and their families took advantage of the law, and how it changed people's lives or shaped their experiences. Have students present their findings in a report.

REVIEW

Linguistic, Logical-Mathematical. Have students complete the Section Review questions. Then ask students to list the major events of the Truman years and explain the impact of each.

ASSESS

Have students complete Daily Quiz 17.3.

RETEACH

Linguistic, Logical-Mathematical, Visual-Spatial. Have students complete Main Idea Activities for Reteaching and Sheltered English 17.3. Then have them outline the major points of this section. Ask students to color-code the outline by highlighting the points of the Fair Deal in one color, those of the 1948 presidential election in a second color, and issues relating to the nation's peacetime transition in a third color. **SHELTERED ENGLISH**

Some southern Democrats were upset with Truman's actions on civil rights issues. They walked out of the convention. Many of them joined the newly formed States' Rights Party, known as the **Dixiecrats**. The Dixiecrats favored racial segregation and wanted to restrict African American voting rights. The party nominated South Carolina governor Strom Thurmond for president. A second group of Democrats disliked the way Truman had dealt with the labor strikes. These politicians formed a new Progressive Party. They nominated Henry Wallace for president. Wallace had previously served as vice president in Franklin D. Roosevelt's third administration.

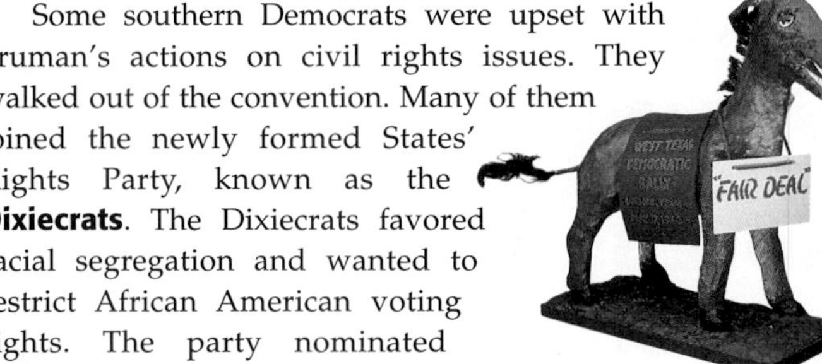

A donkey made for President Truman by a supporter

Truman campaigned with tremendous energy. He traveled more than 30,000 miles by train and delivered hundreds of speeches. He attacked Congress as the "do-nothing, good-for-nothing, worst Congress." Nonetheless, public opinion polls predicted a landslide victory for Dewey, right up to election night.

When the results were in, Truman had won a surprising victory. He later declared:

> **"It seemed to have been a terrific political upset. It was not—it was merely a continuation of the policies . . . that the people wanted."**

Truman's success was based on several factors. His veto of the Taft-Hartley Act had won back union support. He also gained a large number of African American votes. In addition, many Wallace supporters switched to Truman when it looked as if Dewey would win.

The recovering economy was another reason for Truman's victory. By 1948 American industries had successfully shifted back to peacetime production. Personal income began to increase. Cold War spending also created new jobs. As one Truman supporter explained, "I own a nice house, I have a new car. . . . Why change?"

Truman was confident that the American public supported his policies. He proposed a series of reform programs that became known as the **Fair Deal**. The Fair Deal was intended to provide full employment, a higher minimum wage, and a national health insurance plan. Truman also called for more affordable housing, expanded Social Security benefits, and aid for farmers.

Congress approved a few key Fair Deal reforms. It extended Social Security and raised the minimum wage. Congress rejected some civil rights legislation, federal aid to education, and national health insurance. The government also spent billions on domestic improvements and the GI Bill. This government spending helped to sustain the postwar boom.

SECTION 3 REVIEW

Identify and explain the significance of the following:
- **GI Bill of Rights**
- **United Mine Workers**
- **John Lewis**
- **Taft-Hartley Act**
- **Dixiecrats**
- **Fair Deal**

Reading for Content Understanding

1. **Main Idea** What public concerns affected the outcome of the 1948 presidential election?
2. **Main Idea** What were the main goals of the Fair Deal?
3. **Economic Development** What steps did the U.S. government take to avoid a recession after World War II?
4. **Writing** *Describing* Imagine that you are a reporter observing the labor unrest of 1946. Write an article describing President Truman's efforts to end the labor strikes.
5. **Critical Thinking** *Identifying Cause and Effect* How did the GI Bill help promote long-term economic growth?

Section 3 Review ANSWERS

Identify

For significance, see the following pages:
- GI Bill of Rights, p. 519
- United Mine Workers, p. 520
- John Lewis, p. 520
- Taft-Hartley Act, p. 520
- Dixiecrats, p. 521
- Fair Deal, p. 521

Reading for Content Understanding

1. concerns over labor unrest lost support for Truman; concerns over civil rights actions both lost and gained support for Truman; concerns over Republican opposition to labor and Wallace's chances to win gained support for Truman

2. full employment, higher minimum wage, national health insurance plan, more affordable housing, expanded Social Security benefits, aid for farmers

3. encouraged women to give up their jobs to veterans; passed the GI Bill of Rights, which provided veterans with educational benefits and affordable loans; did not cancel defense contracts or immediately loosen price controls

4. Articles will vary but should mention Truman's attempts at negotiation and his use of government control and military force to end strikes in mines.

5. Answers will vary but might mention that accessible education and training resulted in more effective workers who could then better help expand production and would likely have more money to buy goods. In addition, affordable loans meant that many GIs bought houses, farms, and businesses.

SECTION 4 LESSON PLAN

OBJECTIVES

- **Identify events that led to China becoming a communist nation.**
- **Explain why the United States was involved in Korea and how the war ended.**
- **Describe how the Korean War affected the 1952 presidential election.**

FOCUS

Motivate Before Reading

Create a chart on the chalkboard. Label the columns *World War I* and *World War II* and the rows *Reasons for U.S. Involvement* and *Results of the War.* Have the class complete it. Then add a column labeled *Korean War.* Tell students that in this section they will learn about this war, reasons for U.S. involvement, and the results. Have students copy the chart and finish it as they read the section.

Section 4 RESOURCES

PRINT

- ★ Guided Reading Strategies 17.4
- ★ Literature Reading 17: Fighting in Korea
- ★ Section 4 Review, p. 526
- ★ Daily Quiz 17.4

MULTIMEDIA

- ★ *Teaching Resources CD–ROM,* Lesson 17.4
- ★ HRW Web site

SHELTERED ENGLISH

- ★ Main Idea Activities for Reteaching and Sheltered English 17.4

The Korean War

Reading Focus

What events led China to become a communist nation?

Why was the United States involved in Korea and how did the Korean War end?

How did the Korean War affect the 1952 presidential election?

Key Terms

Long March

38th parallel

IN 1911 A GROUP OF YOUNG Chinese army officers revolted against the 2,000-year-old Chinese empire. Early the next year, China's 400 million people learned that China had become a republic. The emperor, Pu Yi, was only six years old when he received the news that he would no longer rule the nation. Pu Yi was confined in the Imperial Palace with his servants. "It was in this tiny world that I was to spend the most absurd childhood possible . . . ," he later wrote. "When China was called a republic . . . I was still living the life of an emperor, breathing the dust of the nineteenth century."

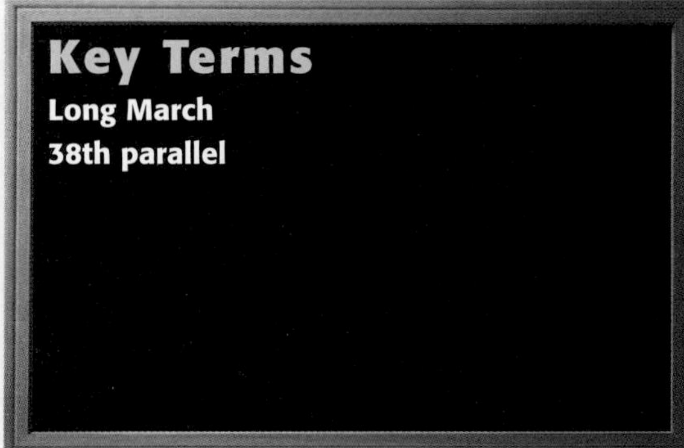

The Granger Collection, New York

The Imperial Palace in Beijing

 Communist China

When China's monarchy fell in 1912, it caused great political unrest. During the 1920s the Chinese Nationalist Party and the Chinese Communists struggled for power. This struggle turned into a bitter civil war. In 1934 about 100,000 Communists had to flee from a Nationalist army attack. Led by Mao Zedong (MOW DZUH-DOOHNG), the Communists began a 6,000-mile, 12-month retreat to northwestern China. This escape became known as the **Long March**.

During the mid-1930s the Nationalists joined with the Communists to fight against the invading Japanese. After World War II, however, the civil war resumed. Suspicious of any communist government, the United States backed the Nationalists led by Chiang Kaishek (chang-ky-SHEK). However, his government lacked popular support. U.S. Army general Joseph Stilwell wrote that he saw "corruption, neglect, chaos" in the Nationalist government and military.

Nevertheless, the United States gave millions of dollars in aid to the Nationalists to fight the

Introduce Key Terms

Linguistic, Visual-Spatial. Review this section's key terms with students. Then ask students to draw a picture for each term. Have students write definitions to accompany their drawings. Finally, call on volunteers to explain their work to the class.
SHELTERED ENGLISH

TEACH

Have students read Section 4 and complete Guided Reading Strategies 17.4. Choose one or more of the following activities to explore the section content with students. For further suggestions on block scheduling or team teaching, see the *Block Scheduling Handbook.*

LEVEL 1: Linguistic. (Suggested time: 15 min.) As a class, go over students' Guided Reading Strategies. Then use the Reading Focus questions to highlight the main ideas of the section.
SHELTERED ENGLISH

ALL LEVELS: Linguistic, Visual-Spatial. (Suggested time: 35 min.) Have half the class prepare a time line of events related to the creation of communist China. The time line should span from 1911 to 1949. Have the rest of the class prepare a time line of events related to the Korean War. The time line should span

Communists. This U.S. support was not enough to defeat the Communists. In 1949 they drove the Nationalists off the Chinese mainland to the island of Taiwan. Mao then founded the communist People's Republic of China.

Relations between the United States and China were poor. The United States refused to formally recognize Mao's new government. Instead, the United States continued diplomatic relations with Taiwan. Many Americans were concerned that the People's Republic of China would join forces with the Soviet Union. Such an alliance would threaten U.S. security.

The Granger Collection, New York

The Chinese government made posters celebrating the Communists' victory in 1949.

U.S. secretary of state Dean Acheson wrote that the takeover of China by the Communist Party "was beyond the control of the government of the United States." Despite such claims, many U.S. leaders thought that the United States had "lost" China to the Communists because of foreign-policy mistakes. Some U.S. politicians vowed never to lose another nation in Asia to communism.

The Cold War in Asia

The postwar period also brought new governments to other Asian nations. After World War II, U.S. forces occupied Japan and began rebuilding Japan's devastated economy. Military leaders such as General Douglas MacArthur also helped create a U.S.-style constitution. The new government placed more power in the hands of the Japanese people. It also granted women the right to vote. In addition, the Japanese constitution prohibited Japan from waging war.

Japan had controlled Korea from 1910 until the end of World War II. In 1945 the Allies divided Korea. U.S. forces occupied the southern half of the Korean Peninsula. Soviet troops occupied the north. The United States then asked the United Nations to allow national elections in Korea to reunite the country. The Soviet Union vetoed this proposal in the UN Security Council. As a result, the United States and the Soviet Union each established a government in its area of occupation.

The Soviets backed the communist Democratic People's Republic of Korea in the northern half of the peninsula. The United States supported the Republic of Korea in the southern half. U.S. officials realized that this compromise was awkward. They hoped that the division would keep the peace and prevent further communist expansion in Asia.

The U.S. and Soviet troops finally pulled out in 1949. Both the North and South Korean governments then claimed the entire country. The Soviets had left behind a well-equipped and well-trained North Korean army. On June 25, 1950, North Korean forces crossed the **38th parallel**, the line of latitude dividing the two countries. The South Korean army was no match for the invaders. North Korean forces quickly advanced. The UN Security Council immediately called for a cease-fire. The North Koreans, however, continued their attack. Top U.S. advisers were determined not to allow another Asian nation such as South Korea to become communist.

General Douglas MacArthur directed the demobilization of Japan.

Biography

Mao Zedong. Communist leader Mao Zedong governed China from 1949 until his death in 1976. Mao was born in 1893 to a moderately wealthy family. He hated working on the family farm, and at age 13 ran away from home to live with an uncle. There, Mao continued his schooling. After serving as a soldier, Mao spent six months studying on his own in a library. Although he studied to become a teacher, Mao instead became a vocal critic of government policies. By 1920 he was a committed Marxist. It was in that role that he would rise to power over the world's most populous nation.

Activity: Have students use the library or search the Internet through the HRW Web site to find information on Mao Zedong (alternate spelling Mao Tse-tung). Ask students to write a summary on how he promoted communism in China and his influence on the Chinese people.

go.hrw.com
SB1 Mao

from 1945 to 1953. Have all students write brief annotations explaining the significance of each event they include. Call on volunteers to explain their time lines. Encourage other students to suggest additions or refinements for classmates' time lines. **SHELTERED ENGLISH**

LEVEL 3: Linguistic, Logical-Mathematical. (Suggested time: 30 min.) Direct students' attention to Eisenhower's promise to "go to Korea" if elected president in 1952. Have students imagine that they are advisers to Adlai Stevenson. Have each student prepare a campaign memorandum advising the Democratic candidate on how to respond to Eisenhower's promise. The memo should be designed to limit the influence of Eisenhower's pledge. The memo also should propose a better alternative course of action for dealing with the Korean War. Finally, discuss with students the overall effects of the Korean War on the 1952 presidential election.

LEVEL 3: Linguistic, Logical-Mathematical. (Suggested time: 25 min. plus homework) Ask students to imagine that they are military strategists who have been assigned to write evaluations of U.S. involvement in Korea. Ask students to analyze the reasons for U.S. involvement and the effectiveness of U.S. strategy during the war. Finally, have students determine whether by the war's end, the United States had achieved its objectives. Call on volunteers to read their reports to the class.

Historical Sidelight

The Surprise Chinese Attack. The Chinese attack during the Korean War caught U.S. forces by surprise, as Private Doug Michaud's recollection of the event reveals. In *The Korean War: Pusan to Chosin* Michaud said, "The bugles were the fir7st thing I remember. Then the chaos. There didn't seem to be any sense of order. I was in my sleeping bag snoozing. . . . A guy who'd been on watch grabbed the bottom of the bag and began dragging me down the hill. He kept hollering, 'They're here! They're here!' A lot of guys must have been caught with their boots off. I saw them running in their stockings. It all happened so fast."

Critical Thinking: What impact might a successful surprise attack have?

ANSWER: Students might mention that a surprise attack can prevent defending forces from organizing and thus often results in confusion, high numbers of casualties, and in some cases, retreat.

MAP ANSWER
South Korea

War in Korea

On June 27, 1950, the UN Security Council called on UN members to support South Korea. The Soviet ambassador was not present to veto this proposal. That same day President Truman announced to Americans, "I have ordered United States air and sea forces to give the Korean government troops cover and support."

General Douglas MacArthur flew to Korea to review the situation. He reported that South Korea needed ground troops immediately. In response, the United States and 15 other nations offered troops to the UN effort. It was the first time that UN forces had fought in a major conflict. In July, MacArthur was named commander of the UN forces. These troops consisted largely of U.S. and South Korean soldiers.

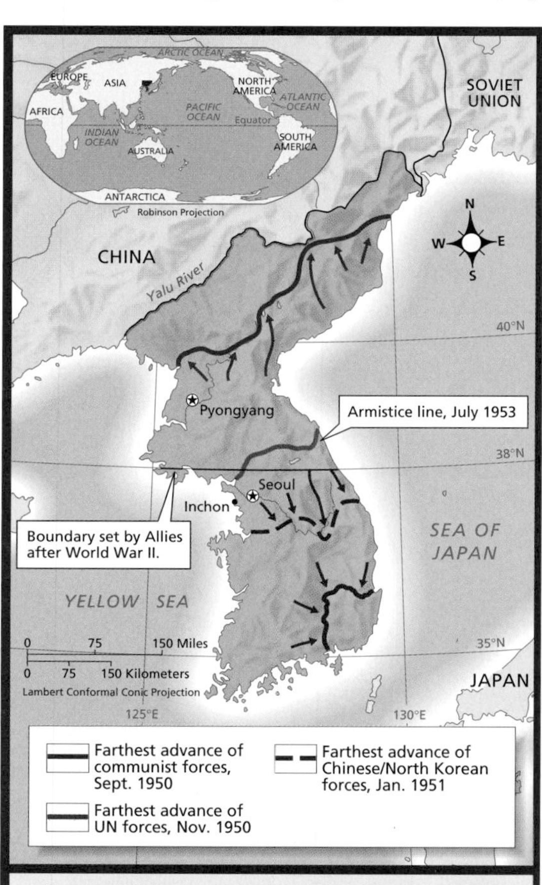

The Korean War, 1950–1953

Learning from Maps After three years of fighting, the boundary between North and South Korea remained roughly the same.

Movement Which country increased in size after the armistice line of 1953 was established?

Changes of Fortune

By late July the North Korean army had driven UN forces to the southeastern tip of the peninsula, into a small area near the port city of Pusan. General Walton "Bulldog" Walker told his men, "There will be no more retreating. . . . We must fight to the end. We must fight as a team. If some of us die, we will die fighting together."

For six weeks, fierce fighting raged along the Pusan front. The situation seemed desperate at times. MacArthur and other military leaders developed a daring plan to turn the tide of the war—a surprise attack behind enemy lines. On September 15, UN forces landed near the port city of Inchon. There they attacked the North Korean troops from behind. The UN forces quickly drove the invading army out of South Korea.

MacArthur's forces pursued. Just over a month later, they captured Pyongyang (pyuhng-YANG), North Korea's capital. Eventually, they reached the Yalu River, the border between China and North Korea. U.S. soldiers looked forward to a quick end of the war. MacArthur boasted that he would "have the boys [the soldiers] home by Christmas."

China Enters the War

During the fighting, it had become clear that some Chinese troops were fighting alongside the North Koreans. Hundreds of thousands more Chinese troops joined the North Koreans in launching a counteroffensive. They drove the UN forces back below the 38th parallel in brutal fighting. One platoon leader in the U.S. 24th Infantry described a battle that took place in a rice paddy:

> **"The medics could scarcely keep up with the men who had been hit. . . . How we managed to survive I don't know, but when we reached the top of the hill, the enemy had cut and run, and we collapsed on the ground, not bothering to dig in."**

CLOSE

Logical-Mathematical, Visual-Spatial. Call on volunteers to identify significant events related to Korean history and the Korean War. As they identify events, have students add them to a time line on the chalkboard. (If you used the All Levels strategy in which students created a Korean War time line, you can skip this step.) For each event, call on volunteers to state whether the incident pulled the United States further into or out of the war.

CHALLENGE AND EXTEND

Linguistic, Visual-Spatial, Intrapersonal. Have students use the library and other resources to research the Korean War Veterans Memorial in Washington, D.C. Ask students to write narratives about soldiers' experiences in the Korean War based on the depictions in the memorial. Ask volunteers to share their narratives with the class. Encourage feedback and discussion.

Fighting during the Korean winters was uncomfortable and difficult.

General MacArthur knew President Truman did not want the war to expand beyond Korea. Nonetheless, MacArthur publicly called for air strikes on Chinese cities and a ground attack on the Chinese coast. Truman refused. MacArthur then criticized the president openly. He wrote that "there is no substitute for victory." In response, Truman relieved MacArthur of his command in April 1951. Truman's decision was not a popular one. MacArthur returned home to parades and celebrations in his honor.

In early 1951 a UN offensive pushed the Chinese and North Koreans back across the 38th parallel. The fighting then settled into a standstill. Groups of diplomats from both sides attempted unsuccessfully to hammer out a peace treaty.

The Election of 1952

By the spring of 1951 it had become clear that neither side in Korea was going to defeat the other on the battlefield. As one British soldier stated, "Everybody could see that we had reached stalemate, unless someone started chucking atom bombs." Peace negotiations began in July but saw little progress. As the negotiations and the war dragged on, the American public grew increasingly frustrated.

The Korean War became the major issue in the presidential election of 1952. Knowing that many voters blamed him for the war, President Truman chose not to seek re-election. The Democrats nominated Adlai Stevenson, the governor of Illinois, for president. Stevenson was intelligent and quick-witted. However, his speaking style made him seem out of touch with the "real world" to many voters.

Hoping to win the White House for the first time since the election of 1928, the Republicans nominated General Dwight D. Eisenhower. Ike, as he was often called, was a respected war hero. He was also charming and popular with the American public. For vice president, the Republicans nominated Senator Richard Nixon of California. Nixon was a strong anticommunist.

The Eisenhower-Nixon campaign faced a potential problem. Nixon was accused of receiving illegal gifts and money from a number of wealthy donors. Eisenhower considered replacing Nixon with a new candidate. Nixon then went on television to offer an explanation to the American people. He said that one of the gifts was a small puppy named Checkers. Nixon declared that he could not return it because his children loved the dog. The Checkers speech, as it became known, saved Nixon's place on the ticket.

A 1952 Eisenhower campaign sign

Already leading the polls, Eisenhower probably secured the election when he said in October:

> **"The first task of a new administration will be to . . . bring the Korean War to an early and honorable end. That is my pledge to the American people. For this task a wholly new administration is necessary. The reason for this is simple. The old administration cannot be expected to repair what it failed to prevent. . . . That job requires a personal trip to Korea. . . . I shall go to Korea."**

Eisenhower easily won, gaining 442 electoral votes to Stevenson's 89 electoral votes.

Cultural Diversity

Integration of the Armed Forces. The Korean War had a great effect on the rights of African Americans. For the first time in combat, U. S. military personnel were assigned to integrated, or racially mixed, units. This action was the result of an executive order that President Truman issued in 1948 banning segregation in the armed forces. The Eighth Army was the first combat force in American history to assign soldiers without regard to race. That same year, Truman also issued an executive order ending racial discrimination in the hiring of civil service employees.

Critical Thinking: How might desegregation of the military have helped decrease segregation in civilian life?

ANSWER: Answers will vary but students might mention that black veterans might have wanted the same equality in civilian life that they experienced in the military, and that white soldiers' interactions with other races may have made them less inclined to practice discrimination.

REVIEW

Linguistic, Logical-Mathematical, Visual-Spatial. Have students complete the Section Review questions. Then have each student create a crossword puzzle based on the Section Review. Have students use the Identify and Locate terms as the puzzle's answers, and the explanations of these terms as the clues. Then have students exchange their crossword puzzles, complete them, and return them to their authors for grading.

ASSESS

Have students complete Daily Quiz 17.4.

RETEACH

Logical-Mathematical. Have students complete the Main Idea Activities for Reteaching and Sheltered English 17.4. Then list the following in random order on the chalkboard: *Communist China, Division of Korea, Korean War, Outcome of the Election of 1952, Eisenhower in Korea,* and *cease-fire.* Have each student arrange the terms in a sequence that shows their relationship. Call on volunteers to explain their sequences and have the class comment on their accuracy. **SHELTERED ENGLISH**

Section 4 Review ANSWERS

Identify

For significance, see the following pages:

- Mao Zedong, p. 522
- Long March, p. 522
- Chiang Kaishek, p. 522
- Douglas MacArthur, p. 523
- 38th parallel, p. 523
- Adlai Stevenson, p. 525
- Dwight D. Eisenhower, p. 525

Locate

For locations, see the map on page 524.

Reading for Content Understanding

1. Organizers will vary but students may include the Chinese revolt against the emperor, the power struggle between the Nationalists and Communists, the Long March, World War II cooperation, resumption of the civil war, and the eventual victory of the Communists and the Nationalists' retreat to Taiwan.

2. Eisenhower may have won the election because of his promise to go to Korea and bring the war to an end.

3. The United States did not want South Korea to become a communist nation.

4. Journal entries will vary but should mention the use of UN troops, advances and retreats, fighting along the Pusan front, China's entry into the war, Truman's removal of MacArthur, Eisenhower's trip to Korea, and the terms of the cease-fire agreement.

5. Answers will vary but supporters might back Truman because he was commander in chief. Opponents might cite a need to expand the war to win it and contain communism.

On his trip to Korea, Eisenhower joined his old army unit for a meal.

The End of the War

President-elect Eisenhower made good on his promise to go to Korea. He flew to Korea and met with U.S. commanders in early December 1952. Despite his visit, the peace negotiations remained stalled. Eisenhower was desperate for a solution. He let the Chinese and North Koreans know that the United States might use atomic weapons if the conflict continued.

After the death of Soviet leader Joseph Stalin on March 5, 1953, the new Soviet leadership also pushed both sides to end the war. As the peace talks slowly progressed, fighting flared up again. Thousands more soldiers were killed or wounded.

The war remained at a stalemate while the negotiations continued. On July 27, 1953, the two sides signed a cease-fire that effectively ended the Korean War. After three years of fighting that devastated both sides, the two countries were once again divided roughly along the 38th parallel. The U.S. forces suffered more than 155,000 casualties. The South Korean army suffered about 845,000 casualties. North Korean and Chinese military casualties totaled more than 1.5 million. Some 3 million North and South Korean civilians had also died. Many thousands more Koreans were left homeless as a result of the war.

The Korean War was over so far as the United Nations and the United States were concerned. However, North and South Korea had signed a truce rather than a peace treaty. Tensions remained high between both governments. A narrow demilitarized zone (DMZ) was established between the two nations along the 38th parallel. On each side, thousands of soldiers continue to face each other across a no-man's-land. Thousands of U.S. troops are still stationed along the DMZ to help defend South Korea against an invasion from the North.

SECTION 4 REVIEW

Identify and explain the significance of the following:

- **Mao Zedong**
- **Long March**
- **Chiang Kaishek**
- **Douglas MacArthur**
- **38th parallel**
- **Adlai Stevenson**
- **Dwight D. Eisenhower**

Locate and explain the importance of the following:

- **North Korea**
- **South Korea**
- **Inchon**

Reading for Content Understanding

1. **Main Idea** Create a graphic organizer to show the events that resulted in China becoming a communist nation.
2. **Main Idea** How were the results of the 1952 presidential election influenced by the Korean War?
3. **Global Relations** Why did the United States become involved in the Korean War?
4. **Writing** *Describing* Imagine that you are a U.S. soldier who has been stationed in South Korea since the start of the war. In a series of short journal entries, describe the main events of the conflict, including its conclusion.
5. **Critical Thinking** *Supporting a Point of View* Do you agree with President Truman's decision to remove General MacArthur? Explain your answer.

OBJECTIVES

- **Analyze the causes of the new Red Scare.**
- **Identify the role Senator Joseph McCarthy played in the new Red Scare.**
- **Describe how post–World War II popular culture reflected Cold War fears.**

FOCUS

Motivate Before Reading

Write the word *Communist* on the chalkboard. Have students identify ways they might prove that someone is a Communist. As students provide answers, discuss whether each one indeed proves communist affiliation. Write those that do on the chalkboard. Then tell students that in this section they will learn about Americans' rising fears of communism during the 1940s and 1950s.

Cold War Fears

Reading Focus

What caused the new Red Scare?

What role did Senator Joseph McCarthy play in the new Red Scare?

How did popular culture after World War II reflect Cold War fears?

Key Terms

House Un-American Activities Committee
blacklisting
Internal Security Act
McCarthyism
Army-McCarthy hearings

TO ATTORNEY GENERAL J. Howard McGrath and many other Americans, the signs were everywhere. The Soviet Union controlled Eastern Europe. Communists governed in China as well, and they had fought fiercely in Korea. Were there Communists in the United States, too? McGrath answered the question by saying, "There are today many Communists in America. They are everywhere—in factories, offices, butcher shops, on street corners." He warned that every Communist "carries . . . the germs of death for society." Soon some Americans were caught up in a hunt for Communists.

Anticommunist images were common during the Cold War.

A New Red Scare

The Cold War shaped American life at home, where intense fears of Communists and communism led to a new Red Scare. The first Red Scare had begun just after World War I, following the communist revolution in Russia. It took place amid postwar social unrest in the United States.

The new Red Scare started in the late 1930s. The scare reached its full strength during the late 1940s and early 1950s. Several factors help explain this new scare. The growth of domestic communism during the 1930s worried many Americans. The growth of the U.S. Communist Party was a particular concern. Fears intensified after World War II, when the Soviet Union expanded its influence across Eastern Europe. The Communists' takeover of China and communist aggression in Korea further increased anticommunist feelings in the United States.

In May 1938 Congress had established the **House Un-American Activities Committee** (HUAC) to investigate disloyalty and harmful foreign influences in the United States. In 1947 the

Section 5 RESOURCES

PRINT

- ★ Guided Reading Strategies 17.5
- ★ Biography Reading 17: Margaret Chase Smith
- ★ Graphic Organizer 17: The United States Fights Communism
- ★ Section 5 Review, p. 531
- ★ Daily Quiz 17.5

MULTIMEDIA

- ★ *Teaching Resources CD–ROM,* Lesson 17.5
- ★ *American History Interactive Maps CD–ROM:* Living in the Cold War

SHELTERED ENGLISH

- ★ Main Idea Activities for Reteaching and Sheltered English 17.5

Introduce Key Terms

Linguistic, Logical-Mathematical. Review this section's key terms with students. Have them use context cues from the text to write a definition for each term. Then have students explain how each term relates to the U.S. struggle against communism.
SHELTERED ENGLISH

TEACH

Have students read Section 5 and complete Guided Reading Strategies 17.5. Choose one or more of the following activities to explore the section content with students. For further suggestions on block scheduling or team teaching, see the *Block Scheduling Handbook.*

LEVEL 1: Linguistic. (Suggested time: 15 min.) As a class, go over students' Guided Reading Strategies. Then use the Reading Focus questions to highlight the main ideas of the section.
SHELTERED ENGLISH

ALL LEVELS: Linguistic, Logical-Mathematical, Visual-Spatial. (Suggested time: 30 min.) Ask students to imagine that it is 1952 and they have been asked to create a cover for the first issue of *Red Scare Magazine.* Have each student provide an illustration and previews of stories. The cover should depict the

Constitutional Heritage

HUAC. Critics of the House Un-American Activities Committee (HUAC) maintained that its investigations weakened Americans' constitutional rights to freedom of speech, association, and due process. The 1957 U.S. Supreme Court decision in *Watkins* v. *United States* placed limitations on congressional investigations. The Court ruled that Congress did not have the authority to expose individuals' private affairs unless performing a valid legislative function. The Court stated that in the HUAC investigations Congress had overstepped its legislative bounds. The decision set aside Watkin's conviction for contempt of Congress. In the early to mid-1960s almost all of HUAC's contempt convictions were overturned.

Critical Thinking: What does the Court's ruling in *Watkins* v. *United States* say about the importance of constitutional guarantees?

ANSWER: Answers will vary but students should point out that the Court's decision shows that the threat of communism was insufficient reason to violate the constitutional rights of U.S. citizens.

Multimedia Resources

American History Interactive Maps CD–ROM: Living in the Cold War

HUAC launched a series of widely publicized hearings. Their purpose was to prove the presence of Communists both in the Hollywood movie industry and in the U.S. State Department.

The committee often disregarded citizens' rights in its rush to expose Communists. In the tense climate of the late 1940s, being questioned by the HUAC could ruin people's lives. Having a past association with a communist organization was often seen as proof of disloyalty. One writer called before the committee charged that the HUAC "has conducted an illegal and indecent trial of American citizens." He added:

> **"I . . . appear here as a representative of 130 million Americans because the illegal conduct of this committee has linked me with every citizen. If I can be destroyed, no American is safe. . . . Forces are trying to introduce fascism in this country. They know that the only way to trick the American people into abandoning their rights and liberties is to manufacture an imaginary danger."**

The HUAC investigations revealed that some people in the motion picture industry had communist sympathies. They did not, however, uncover widespread communist activity. Nonetheless, executives in film, radio, television, and theater began **blacklisting**, or refusing to hire, suspected Communists. The most famous blacklisted individuals were called the Hollywood Ten. This group of writers refused to cooperate with the HUAC.

Some magazines claimed that Communists controlled the media.

In response to HUAC investigations, actor Lauren Bacall helped create and lead the Committee for the Fifth Amendment. The committee protested the anticommunist tactics of some members of Congress.

Paul Robeson, an African American singer and actor, was also affected by the new Red Scare. After the HUAC accused Robeson of being a Communist, promoters canceled many of his shows. Mob attacks disrupted his two remaining concerts. Concerned by Robeson's support of a close U.S.-Soviet friendship, the State Department took away his passport in 1950. An interviewer later asked Robeson why he did not move to the Soviet Union. "My father was a slave, and my people died to build this country," Robeson said. "No . . . people will drive me from it."

Actors Lauren Bacall and Humphrey Bogart lead members of the Committee for the Fifth Amendment on their way to Congress.

Spies in Government

After World War II, many Republicans accused President Truman of having let Communists sneak into the government. In response, Truman created the Loyalty Review Board in March 1947. Its purpose was to investigate the background of some 16,000 federal workers. The board's reviews failed to discover any Communists. However, about 100 people lost their jobs because of "reasonable grounds" to suspect their loyalty. Many other organizations soon began requiring loyalty oaths. These groups included the FBI, the Justice Department, state and local governments, and schools and universities. Thousands more people lost their jobs because of suspected communist ties.

In 1950 Congress passed the **Internal Security Act**. The act required suspected communist organizations to register with the government. The law also gave the government the right during times of national emergency to arrest people suspected of treasonous activities.

causes of the new Red Scare and its effects on post–World War II popular culture. **SHELTERED ENGLISH**

LEVEL 2: Linguistic, Logical-Mathematical, Intrapersonal. (Suggested time: 20 min. plus homework) Have each student write a letter to Senator Joseph McCarthy either defending his attempts to purge government of Communists or condemning him for his goals, his methods, or both. Call on a volunteer defending McCarthy to read his or her letter to the class. Ask other students who side with the volunteer to offer additional arguments they would include. Then call on a volunteer who opposes McCarthy to read his or her letter. Ask other students who side with the volunteer to offer additional arguments they would include in their letters.

LEVEL 3: Logical-Mathematical, Visual-Spatial, Interpersonal. (Suggested time: 45 min. plus presentation) Organize the class into groups. Assign each the task of creating a script for a documentary on the new Red Scare. Documentaries should discuss the causes of the new Red Scare, McCarthy's role, and how the Red Scare affected American society and popular culture. Have each group present its work to the class.

In the late 1940s, explosive spy cases deepened Cold War fears. In 1948 journalist Whittaker Chambers confessed that he had spied for the Soviet Union. Testifying before the HUAC, Chambers claimed that Alger Hiss, a former State Department officer, was also a communist spy. Hiss denied the charges. Chambers later produced secret government papers that he claimed Hiss had passed to the Soviets. Although Hiss maintained his innocence, he was tried and found guilty of perjury. He was sentenced to five years in prison.

The Rosenberg case shocked the nation.

The spy cases continued into the 1950s. In 1951 Julius and Ethel Rosenberg were convicted of passing secret atomic weapons information to the Soviet Union. The case divided Americans. Many people claimed that the Rosenbergs were innocent victims of the Red Scare. Others argued that the Rosenbergs were part of a communist spy ring that threatened national security. Despite protests from their supporters, the Rosenbergs were executed in June 1953 for spying.

McCarthyism

More than anyone else, Senator Joseph McCarthy helped stir up Cold War fears. In 1950 McCarthy, a Republican from Wisconsin, began a campaign to expose Communists in the U.S. government.

McCarthy's Rise to Power

In February 1950 McCarthy told a West Virginia audience, "This is the time for the show-down between the democratic . . . world and the Communist." McCarthy blamed the spread of communism on

> **"the traitorous actions of those . . . individuals who have been helping to shape our foreign policy. . . . The State Department . . . is thoroughly infested with Communists. I have in my hand fifty-seven cases of individuals who would appear to be either card-carrying members or certainly loyal to the Communist Party, but who nevertheless are still helping to shape our foreign policy."**

McCarthy's charges stunned many people. Members of Congress challenged him to reveal the names on his list. McCarthy refused. When an early investigation labeled McCarthy's claims a fraud, however, he responded by making new charges. He even accused the head of the investigation of being pro-communist. His practice of making serious accusations without providing proof became known as **McCarthyism**.

Few Americans challenged McCarthy. Some accepted his charges because they were not used to questioning their public officials. Others were afraid of being labeled "soft on communism." In addition, many Americans wanted an explanation for the spread of communism in Eastern Europe and Asia. McCarthy gave them one.

The Truth Revealed

A few people attempted to stop Senator McCarthy. Journalist Edward R. Murrow tried to expose McCarthy's unfair methods on the television show *See It Now.* Murrow was not congratulated for his courage. Instead, he received bundles of hate mail from McCarthy supporters.

Senator McCarthy charged that there were Communists plotting to overthrow the U.S. government.

Citizenship and Democracy

Internal Security Act. President Truman vetoed the Internal Security Act of 1950 after being asked to do so by the CIA and the Departments of Defense, Justice, and State. Truman stated that the proposed law actually might help Communists by hurting the intelligence operations responsible for monitoring communist threats. He stated that the law appeared to be the greatest threat to First Amendment rights since the Alien and Sedition Acts of 1798. He warned that the law would put the government in the "thought control business" and destroy the liberties it sought to preserve. Congress overrode the veto the following day.

Critical Thinking: Why do you think Congress overrode President Truman's veto?

ANSWER: Answers will vary but students might mention that Congress supported the bill because of the new Red Scare in America.

AMERICAN LITERATURE ANSWERS

(page 530)

1. He had no proof of their guilt and did not want to accuse anyone wrongly.

2. Answers will vary but students might say that the court wanted to use Proctor's fear of execution to get the proof it needed to condemn others.

CLOSE

Logical-Mathematical, Intrapersonal. Ask students to imagine that they are members of the Senate in 1954. They must decide to either support or condemn Senator Joseph McCarthy's recent actions. Encourage students in making their decisions to consider the causes of the new Red Scare and its effects on American politics and popular culture. Have students write paragraphs explaining their decision and the reasoning behind it. Call on volunteers to read their paragraphs.

CHALLENGE AND EXTEND

Linguistic, Visual-Spatial, Interpersonal. Have students work in groups to prepare illustrated articles for *Red Scare Magazine*. The articles should reflect the Cold War's effects on popular American culture during the 1950s. Have groups investigate such areas as movies; television shows; atomic-bomb drills in schools; backyard bomb shelters; blacklisting of writers, directors, and actors; and any other logical topics. Then have students assemble the pieces of their articles. Students should provide captions for all illustrations.

Section 5 Review ANSWERS

Identify

For significance, see the following pages:

- House Un-American Activities Committee, p. 527
- blacklisting, p. 528
- Internal Security Act, p. 528
- Alger Hiss, p. 529
- Julius and Ethel Rosenberg, p. 529
- Joseph McCarthy, p. 529
- McCarthyism, p. 529
- Army-McCarthy hearings, p. 531

Reading for Content Understanding

1. growth of the U.S. Communist Party and domestic communism in the 1930s, Soviet takeover of Eastern Europe and test of the atomic bomb, Communist takeover of China, the Korean War

2. Magazines, movies, and news clips featured the evils of communism; science fiction movies became popular, reflecting Americans' fear of communism and new types of technologies.

3. These fears ultimately led to laws, loyalty oaths, and blacklisting that restricted Americans' rights to free speech, freedom of expression, and equal employment opportunities.

4. Scripts will vary but may mention McCarthy's use of fear and unsubstantiated charges to gain power and prestige.

5. Answers will vary but those in favor may mention that during certain times, such as war, people with certain political beliefs can pose threats to national security. Those opposed might mention that in a democracy, citizens should have the freedom to hold any political affiliation they want.

American Literature

The Crucible

Arthur Miller

In his 1953 play, The Crucible, *author Arthur Miller compared McCarthyism to the Salem witch trials of 1692. Miller suggested that in both cases individuals were accused without evidence of wrongdoing. He wrote that this treatment violated their civil liberties. In the excerpt that follows, John Proctor has confessed to witchcraft in an effort to save himself from being hanged. Deputy Governor Danforth wants Proctor to identify other witches—just as the HUAC asked its witnesses to identify other Communists.*

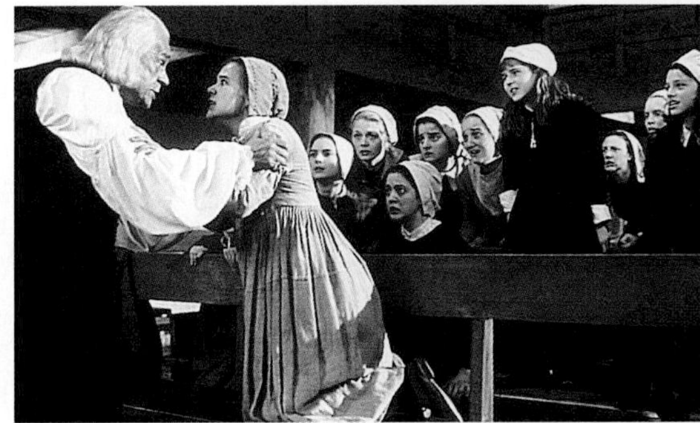

A film version of Arthur Miller's play The Crucible

[DEPUTY GOVERNOR] DANFORTH: Mr. Proctor. When the Devil came to you did you see Rebecca Nurse in his company? *Proctor is silent.* Come, man, take courage—did you ever see her with the Devil?

[JOHN] PROCTOR, *almost inaudibly:* No. *Danforth, now sensing trouble, glances at John and goes to the table, and picks up a sheet—the list of condemned.*

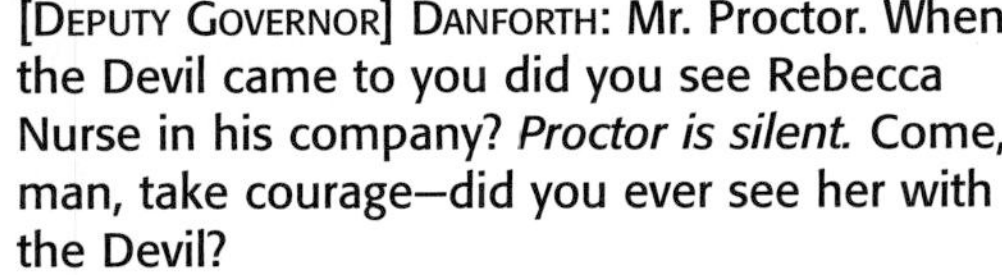

DANFORTH: Did you ever see her sister, Mary Easty, with the Devil?

PROCTOR: No, I did not.

DANFORTH, *his eyes narrow on Proctor:* Did you ever see Martha Corey with the Devil?

PROCTOR: I did not.

DANFORTH, *realizing, slowly putting the sheet down:* Did you ever see anyone with the Devil?

PROCTOR: I did not.

DANFORTH: Proctor, you mistake me. I am not empowered [allowed] to trade your life for a lie. You have most certainly seen some person with the Devil. *Proctor is silent.* Mr. Proctor, a score of people have already testified they saw this woman with the Devil.

PROCTOR: Then it is proved. Why must I say it?

DANFORTH: Why "must" you say it! Why, you should rejoice to say it if your soul is truly purged of any love for Hell!

PROCTOR: They [the accused] think to go [be executed] like saints. I like not to spoil their names [reputation].

DANFORTH, *inquiring, incredulous:* Mr. Proctor, do you think they go like saints?

PROCTOR, *evading:* This woman never thought she done the Devil's work.

DANFORTH: Look you, sir. I think you mistake your duty here. It matters nothing what she thought—she is convicted. . . . Your soul alone is the issue here, Mister, and you will prove its whiteness or you cannot live in a Christian country. Will you tell me now what persons conspired with you in the Devil's company? *Proctor is silent.* To your knowledge was Rebecca Nurse ever—

PROCTOR: I speak my own sins; I cannot judge another. *Crying out, with hatred:* I have no tongue for it.

Understanding Literature

1. Why does John Proctor refuse to accuse others of witchcraft?
2. Why do you think that the court insists that Proctor testify against others?

REVIEW

Linguistic, Logical-Mathematical. Have students complete the Section Review questions. Then have students pair terms in the Identify portion of the review. For each pair, ask students to write a sentence that highlights the terms' connection. Students may use each term more than once. Call on volunteers to read their sentences. Continue until all terms have been paired.

ASSESS

Have students complete Daily Quiz 17.5.

RETEACH

Linguistic, Logical-Mathematical. Have students complete Main Idea Activities for Reteaching and Sheltered English 17.5. Then ask students to create slogans related to the causes of the new Red Scare, the actions of Senator McCarthy, and the impact of Cold War fears on popular culture. Encourage students to consider how Cold War fears became exaggerated.
SHELTERED ENGLISH

In late 1953, however, the senator went too far. McCarthy charged that there were Communists in the military. He wanted to pressure the army to go easy on an assistant of his who had been drafted. A group of senators decided to hold televised hearings to investigate his charges. These **Army-McCarthy hearings** proved to be McCarthy's downfall.

During the hearings, Joseph Welch, the army's attorney, won the support of viewers with his charm and humor. At one point the desperate McCarthy revealed that Welch's law firm employed a former member of a pro-communist legal group. Welch was stunned by this statement, which had nothing to do with the hearings. He replied, "I think I never really gauged [understood] your cruelty. . . . Have you left no sense of decency, sir, at long last?" At this remark, the people watching burst into applause.

Viewers across the nation finally saw McCarthy for what he was—a bully. One commentator wrote that McCarthy "lied vividly and with bold imagination." In 1954 the Senate voted 67 to 22 to condemn McCarthy. For the people whose careers and lives had been destroyed by McCarthy's lies, however, it was a classic case of too little, too late.

Science fiction movies like Forbidden Planet *reflected Americans' concerns about Cold War technology.*

Fears at Home

During the Red Scare popular culture reflected many Americans' fear of communism. Magazines published articles like "How Communists Get That Way" and "Communists Are After Your Child." Between 1948 and 1954, Hollywood produced more than 40 anticommunist films. News-oriented trailers offered frightening details about international communist expansion.

Science fiction movies such as *Invasion of the Body Snatchers* and *Forbidden Planet* also revealed Americans' Cold War fears. Such movies were so popular that the 1950s became known as the Golden Age of Science Fiction. Science fiction films often combined anxiety over new forms of technology with the fear of communism. In the 1954 film *Gog*, for example, a Russian spy takes control of an important U.S. computer. Despite the postwar power of the United States, Americans were worried about the potential threat presented by the Soviet Union and other communist nations.

SECTION 5 REVIEW

Identify and explain the significance of the following:

- **House Un-American Activities Committee**
- **blacklisting**
- **Internal Security Act**
- **Alger Hiss**
- **Julius and Ethel Rosenberg**
- **Joseph McCarthy**
- **McCarthyism**
- **Army-McCarthy hearings**

Reading for Content Understanding

1. **Main Idea** What factors led to a Red Scare in the late 1940s and 1950s?
2. **Main Idea** How did the Cold War influence American popular culture?
3. **Citizenship and Democracy** In what ways did Cold War anxieties and fear of communism affect Americans' rights and freedoms?
4. **Writing** *Informing* Imagine that you are a radio broadcaster who has observed Joseph McCarthy's rise to power. Write the script to a radio editorial explaining McCarthy's role in the new Red Scare.
5. **Critical Thinking** *Evaluating* Review the material on the HUAC investigations and the Loyalty Review Board. Do you think the government has the right to investigate citizens' political beliefs? Explain your answer.

Chapter 17 Review ANSWERS

Identifying People and Ideas

1. conference held by the Big Three—outlined plans for a world peacekeeping organization, for free elections and democratic governments in nations freed from Axis control, and for the Soviet Union to join the war against Japan after Germany surrendered

2. trials of Nazis accused of war crimes

3. former World War II general who as Truman's secretary of state proposed an economic recovery plan for Europe

4. law that provided veterans with educational funding and low-cost loans for houses, farms, and businesses

5. Truman's program of economic and social reforms to improve civil rights, the economy, and social benefits

6. vice president who assumed the presidency upon Roosevelt's death; served from 1945 to 1953

7. line of latitude at which the Allies chose to divide North and South Korea

8. war hero who was elected president in 1952; served from 1953 to 1961

9. the refusal to hire suspected Communists

10. practice of making serious accusations without proof

Using the Time Line

1. c
2. d
3. a
4. b
5. e

Review and Assessment RESOURCES

PRINT
- ★ Chapter 17 Review, pp. 532–33
- ★ Vocabulary Activity 17
- ★ Chapter 17 Study Guide
- ★ Chapter 17 Test (Form A or B)

MULTIMEDIA
- ★ Audio Program, Ch. 17 (English and Spanish)
- ★ *Global Skill Builder CD–ROM*
- ★ Chapter 17 Test Generator
- ★ HRW Web site

SHELTERED ENGLISH
- ★ Spanish Glossary
- ★ Sheltered English Chapter 17 Test

ASSESS

Have students complete one of the Chapter 17 Tests. As an alternate assessment, assign the Chapter 17 Investigation.

Understanding Main Ideas

1. to prevent the expansion of communism

2. created the United Nations

3. Truman's reform program; called for full employment, higher minimum wage, national health insurance, more affordable housing, expanded Social Security benefits, and aid for farmers

4. Public opinion polls had predicted a landslide victory for his Republican opponent, Thomas Dewey.

5. causes—Allies divided Korea at 38th parallel, Soviet Union refused to approve national elections in Korea, Soviets and the United States each established governments in their areas of Korea, Soviet and U.S. forces pulled out of Korea, North Korea invaded South Korea; results—many UN, Chinese, North Korean, and South Korean soldiers killed along with many Korean civilians; cease-fire ended fighting; Korea remained divided roughly at the 38th parallel

6. Soviet test of an atomic bomb, Soviet aggression in Eastern Europe, China falling to the Communists, the Korean War, Senator Joseph McCarthy's accusations of Communists in government

Reviewing Themes

1. He believed the countries would become more stable, would be less likely to experience revolution, and would see Americans as allies.

2. Soviet refusal to remove occupation armies from Eastern Europe or to allow free elections in those countries, a communist revolt in Greece, the Marshall Plan, the creation of NATO, and the publication of NSC-68

CHAPTER 17 REVIEW

Chapter Summary

The postwar world was marked by the spread of communism and the creation of the United Nations. The U.S.-funded Marshall Plan helped European countries rebuild their economies. The United States issued the Truman Doctrine and fought the Korean War to prevent the spread of communism. At home, a postwar recession was followed by a new Red Scare. The Cold War between the United States and the Soviet Union deepened. ■

On a separate sheet of paper, complete the following activities.

Identifying People and Ideas

Describe the historical significance of the following:

1. Yalta Conference
2. Nuremberg Trials
3. George C. Marshall
4. GI Bill of Rights
5. Fair Deal
6. Harry S Truman
7. 38th parallel
8. Dwight D. Eisenhower
9. blacklisting
10. McCarthyism

Internet Activity 

go.hrw.com
SB1 Cold War

Search the Internet through the HRW Web site to find information about Cold War–era science fiction films. Use the information to outline a scene from a movie that reveals Cold War fears.

Understanding Main Ideas

1. What was the goal of containment?
2. What steps did the Allies take to prevent another world war?
3. What was the Fair Deal?
4. Why was President Truman's victory in the 1948 election a surprise?
5. What were the causes and the outcome of the Korean War?
6. What led to a new Red Scare in the United States?

Reviewing Themes

1. **Economic Development** Why did Secretary of State George C. Marshall think that aiding European economies would help prevent the spread of communism?
2. **Global Relations** What events led to the Cold War between the United States and the Soviet Union?
3. **Citizenship and Democracy** How did the Cold War affect Americans' freedoms?

Using the Time Line

Number your paper from 1 to 5. Match the letters on the time line below with the following events.

1. **The Soviets blockade West Berlin.**
2. **North Korea invades South Korea.**
3. **The Nuremberg Trials begin to try high-ranking Nazi officials.**
4. **Israel declares its independence.**
5. **The Rosenbergs are executed for passing secret atomic weapons information to the Soviets.**

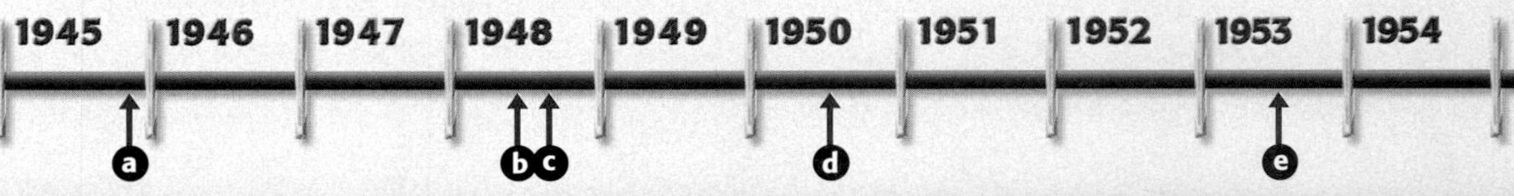

RETEACH

Logical-Mathematical, Interpersonal. Organize the class into five groups and assign each group one of the chapter sections. Have each group create a flowchart illustrating the main topics discussed in its section. Have groups include all their section's key terms and connect them to the appropriate topics.

SHELTERED ENGLISH

Using the Internet

Have students continue their research to find information about post-1950 movies that have plots based on the Cold War or American fears of communism. Ask students to choose one of the films and compare a scene in it to the scene they outlined in the Internet Activity. Have students list similarities and differences between the two scenes.

Portfolio Extensions

American History

1. Have students choose one of the strategic countries and research U.S. involvement with that country during the late 1940s, the 1950s, and 1960s. Have students write articles describing significant events between the United States and that country.

2. After students have completed their documents, have them compare their plans to what the United States actually did.

Thinking Critically

1. **Drawing Conclusions** Why do you think the United States offered economic aid to the Soviet Union? Why do you think the Soviet Union refused?
2. **Identifying Cause and Effect** How did Americans' fear of communism during the Cold War affect U.S. foreign policy?
3. **Making Comparisons** How did Americans' view of foreign involvement after World War II differ from their view following World War I?

Writing About History

1. **Persuading** Imagine that you are a Harry S Truman supporter in 1948. Write a letter to your friends persuading them to vote for Truman instead of Thomas Dewey.
2. **Creating** Imagine that you are a member of the Hollywood Ten. Write the opening two paragraphs to an autobiography describing your life after the blacklists.

Linking Geography and History

1. **Region** Why did the United States consider Greece and Korea strategically important in the fight against communism?
2. **Location** How did West Berlin's location make it difficult for the Western Allies to aid the city?

Building Your Portfolio

American History

Complete the following activities individually or in groups.

1. **The Cold War** Imagine that you are a U.S. government official assigned to evaluate the threat posed by Communists during the Cold War. Create a map of the world in the 1950s. Identify countries that are of strategic importance to the United States. When deciding what is strategically important, be sure to consider criteria such as a nation's location and its resources. You might consider dividing the countries you choose into the most and the least strategically vital. Include a brief caption for each strategic country explaining why it is important to the United States. Present your map to the class.
2. **Honoring the Veterans** The Korean War is often called the "Forgotten War." Imagine that you have been chosen to design a memorial to the soldiers of the Korean War. Consider the causes, major battles, and results of the war and decide what your memorial should look like. Create a sketch of the memorial and write a paragraph explaining what the memorial represents. Hold a ceremony to present the memorial to your class.

History Skills Workshop

Using Primary Sources Even before World War II ended, the Women's Advisory Committee (WAC) was concerned that returning veterans would displace female workers. WAC issued the following report urging government officials to protect women's jobs. After reading the excerpt to the right, answer the following questions: (a) What did WAC ask for in this excerpt? (b) Who did WAC appeal to for support? (c) Why do you think WAC referred to "democratic ideals"?

> "Prospects for job security and other new job opportunities after the war are as important to women as to men. The American people therefore must demand consideration of the status of women in all postwar plans. . . . No society can boast of democratic ideals if it utilizes womanpower in a crisis and neglects it in peace."

3. Cold War fears ultimately led to laws, loyalty oaths, and blacklisting that restricted Americans' freedoms and constitutional rights.

Thinking Critically

1. to show the Soviets the benefits of democracy and thus perhaps to lessen Soviet support for communism; the Soviet Union did not want its citizens to be influenced by U.S. policies.

2. Fear of further communist expansion led to the Truman Doctrine, the Marshall Plan, and the U.S. policy of containment.

3. After World War I, the United States retreated to isolationist policies; after World War II, it became more involved in world events.

Writing About History

1. Letters will vary but might mention economic prosperity, Truman's veto of the Taft-Hartley Act, and his role as an advocate of ordinary people.

2. Paragraphs will vary but might include feelings of hopelessness or anger over the loss of a Hollywood career.

Linking Geography and History

1. U.S. officials feared that communist successes in either nation would encourage more takeovers in Europe and Asia.

2. West Berlin lay deep within Soviet-occupied East Germany.

History Skills Workshop

(a) job security and new job opportunities for women;
(b) the American people;
(c) The United States prides itself on democratic ideals, had just fought a war for those ideals, yet was ignoring women's rights.

FOCUS

Ask students to imagine that they are advisers to the leader of a superpower. Have students make a list of three things they would advise the leader to do to protect the superpower and to gain an advantage over a rival superpower. At the end of the lesson, have students evaluate how their list compares to what they have learned about U.S. government actions in the Cold War.

TEACH

Have students read the Geography and History lesson. Choose one or more of the following activities to explore the Geography and History content with students.

ALL LEVELS: Logical-Mathematical, Visual-Spatial. (Suggested time: 45 min.) Have students use the information presented on pages 534–35 to create a graphic organizer identifying

Global Relations

Warsaw Pact. The Warsaw Pact was created in May 1955 when the Soviet Union and seven other nations in Eastern Europe signed the East European Mutual Assistance Treaty and the Treaty of Friendship, Cooperation, and Mutual Assistance. The Soviet Union formed the alliance in response to West Germany's entry into the North Atlantic Treaty Organization (NATO). Members of the Warsaw Pact coordinated their military strategies by sending officers to the Soviet General Staff Academy. The Warsaw Pact lasted until the breakup of the Soviet Union and the collapse of communist-led governments in Eastern Europe. Thirty-six years after its creation, the Warsaw Pact was officially terminated in May 1991.

Critical Thinking: Why might West Germany's entry into NATO have prompted the Soviet Union to form the Warsaw Pact?

ANSWER: The Soviets might have feared that NATO forces stationed in West Germany might stage an invasion of communist East Germany and Eastern Europe.

Geography & History

The Cold War

The end of World War II left much of Europe and parts of Asia in ruins. Great Britain and France, two traditional world powers, were greatly weakened. Much of Germany and Japan had been destroyed.

After the war only two great powers remained—the capitalist and democratic United States and the communist Soviet Union. For some 45 years, the two superpowers were locked in an ongoing struggle that became known as the Cold War.

The United States and the Soviet Union competed to establish alliances and spread their influence. The two superpowers never openly went to war with each other, but they supported opposing sides in many small wars and conflicts.

The superpower rivalry also created a new kind of arms race, as the United States and the Soviet Union competed to build huge arsenals of nuclear weapons. This nuclear arms race was one of the most frightening aspects of the Cold War. ■

A World Divided

YOU ARE NOW LEAVING BRITISH SECTOR

By the end of the 1950s, much of the world was divided into two camps. Many countries were allied with either the United States or the Soviet Union. In Europe, the U.S.-backed North Atlantic Treaty Organization (NATO) faced the Soviet-backed Warsaw Pact.

The Height of the Cold War, 1960

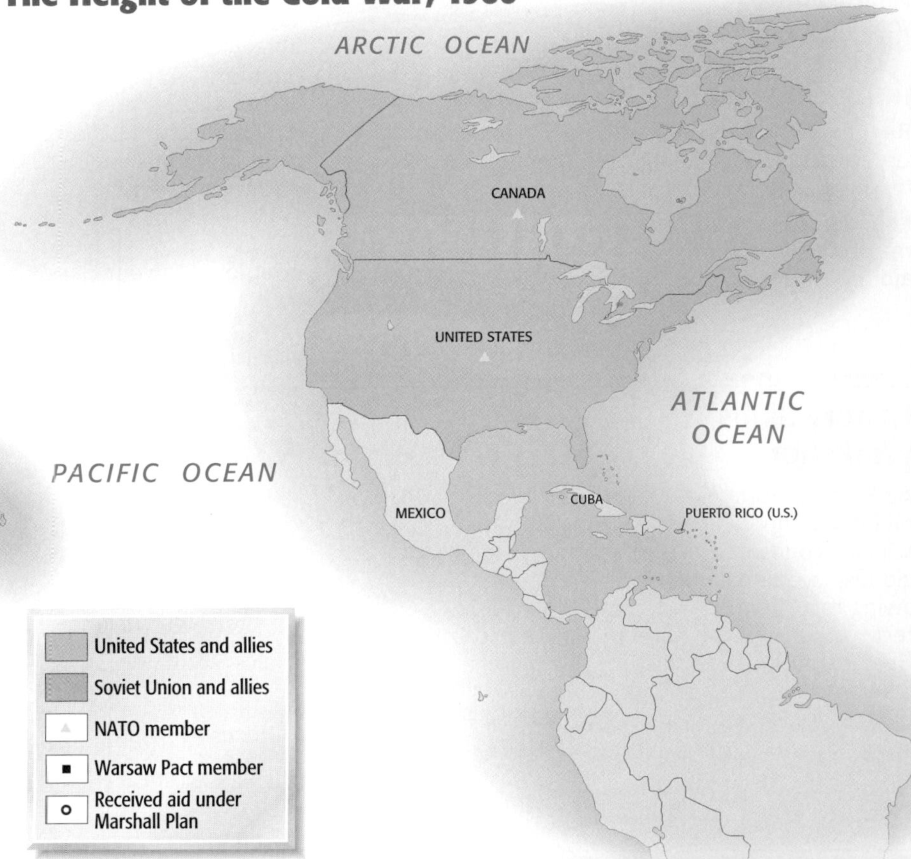

534

the United States and the Soviet Union and their respective allies in 1960. The organizer should have three circles, labeled *U.S. Allies, Soviet Allies,* and *Other Nations*. Students should list in the appropriate circle each nation labeled on the map. Encourage students to use color-coding to distinguish NATO and Warsaw Pact member nations. **SHELTERED ENGLISH**

LEVEL 3: Linguistic, Visual-Spatial. (Suggested time: 45 min.) Have students imagine that it is 1960 and they have just joined the U.S. armed forces. They have been told that after boot camp they will be stationed overseas. Instruct students to use information from the map on page 537 to write a letter to a friend from home describing the possible places they could be stationed. The letters should include the names of the military bases and the countries and continents in which they are located. Students should also note any conflicts that have occurred near each base and the location of those conflicts.

History Note 1

When the United States offered the Marshall Plan to aid countries weakened by World War II, the Soviet Union refused to participate. Instead the Soviets set up a similar plan for their own allies, the so-called Molotov Plan, named after Soviet foreign minister Vyacheslav Molotov.

The Marshall Plan created new opportunities through economic aid.

Geography Skills

Reading Special-Purpose Maps

1. Which countries in 1960 were members of NATO? Which were members of the Warsaw Pact?
2. Which non-NATO nations in Europe received aid under the Marshall Plan?
3. Which East Asian and Pacific countries were allies of the United States in 1960?

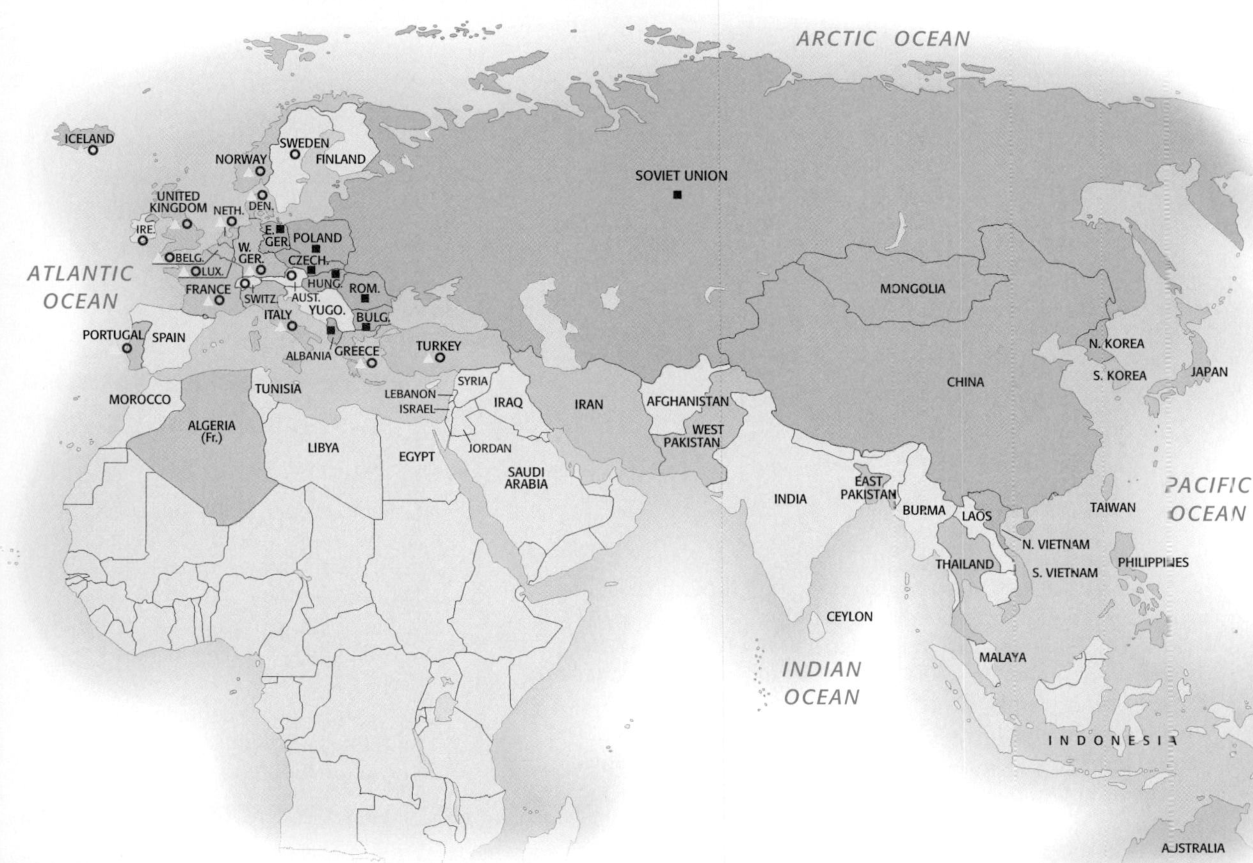

Economic Development

COMECON. In 1949 Bulgaria, Czechoslovakia, Hungary, Poland, Romania, and the Soviet Union formed the Council for Mutual Economic Assistance (COMECON). This organization was created to coordinate the activities of member states and promote economic growth. At first, COMECON was used to negotiate trade treaties, but later it tried to convince member nations to specialize their economies. However, less-developed nations rejected this approach. For example, Romania refused COMECON's suggestions that it focus on farming and raw-materials production.

Activity: Have students use the library or other resources to write a brief history of COMECON.

SKILLS ANSWERS

1. Belgium, Canada, Denmark, France, Greece, Iceland, Italy, Luxembourg, the Netherlands, Norway, Portugal, Turkey, the United Kingdom, the United States, West Germany; Albania, Bulgaria, Czechoslovakia, East Germany, Hungary, Poland, Romania, the Soviet Union
2. Austria, Ireland, Sweden, Switzerland
3. Australia, East Pakistan, Japan, the Philippines, South Korea, South Vietnam, Taiwan, Thailand

CLOSE

Logical-Mathematical, Visual-Spatial. Explain to students that they will be designing on paper a mock Web site based on the Cold War. Have each student design one or more Web pages illustrating the information from the graph or one of the maps in this lesson. Allow time in class for students to design their pages. Once students have finished, ask volunteers to share their work with the class. As a class, students should identify links among the various pages. Finally, combine select pages to create the Web site.

CHALLENGE AND EXTEND

Linguistic, Logical-Mathematical. Have students use the library or other resources to find more information about U.S. defense spending. Students should then use their research to write an essay describing the graph on page 536. The essays should identify on what defense funds were spent (e.g., personnel, nuclear weapons, etc.) and account for the variations in the percentage of the U.S. budget dedicated to defense. Encourage students to include graphs and charts with their essays.

Technology and Society

Eisenhower's Nuclear Arsenal. Under the Eisenhower administration's strategy of massive retaliation, the United States worked hard to develop its nuclear arsenal. In 1953 the U.S. government authorized the construction of the B-52, the first intercontinental jet bomber. The Eisenhower administration also called for the development of an intercontinental ballistic missile (ICBM). The first such missile, known as the Atlas, could travel more than 6,000 miles. The United States also built an intermediate range ballistic missile (IRBM) called the Thor, which could travel 1,500 miles. By 1960 the United States held 18,000 nuclear weapons, ranging from ICBMs to atomic land mines.

Critical Thinking: Why might the development of long-range missiles have increased tensions in the Cold War?

ANSWER: Long-range missiles enabled both the United States and the Soviet Union to attack each other's homelands, a threat that increased public fears.

SKILLS ANSWERS

1. 1945; 1955
2. 30 percentage points
3. 6 percentage points

A U.S. Air Force B-52 bomber

Defending America

U.S. military spending fell dramatically in the years just after World War II. However, after communist North Korea invaded South Korea in 1950, the United States increased its military spending in an attempt to contain communist expansion around the world. Over the next 40 years, the United States spent more than a trillion dollars on defense.

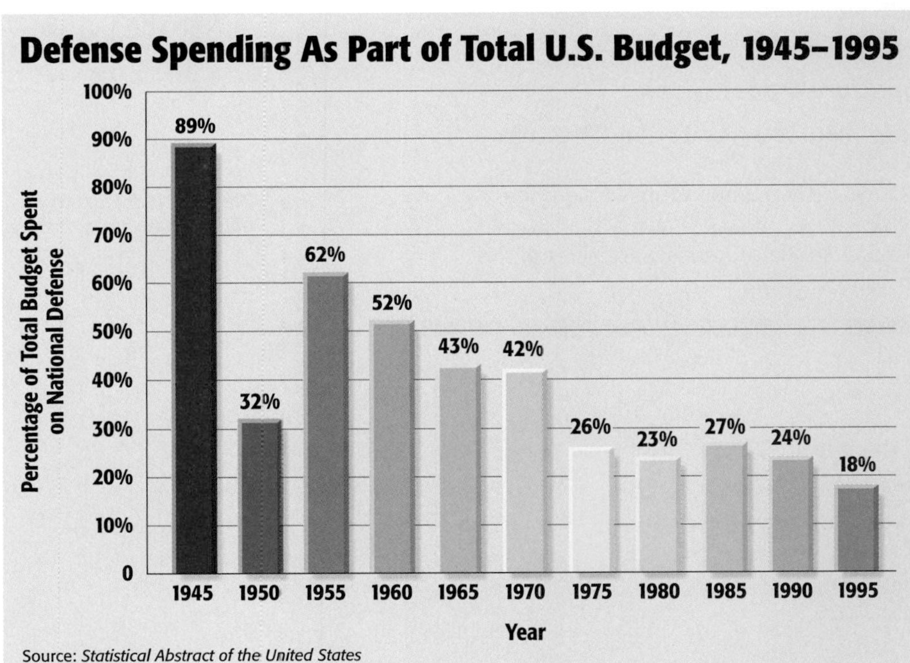

Geography Skills
Reading Bar Graphs

1. In which year did the United States spend the highest percentage of its national budget on defense? What was the next highest year?
2. By how many percentage points did defense spending increase from 1950 to 1955?
3. By how many percentage points did defense spending decrease between 1990 and 1995?

History Note 2

As part of its Cold War defense program, the United States put great effort into building a vast nuclear stockpile. At first the United States and the Soviet Union relied mainly on intercontinental bombers to carry nuclear weapons, but these were largely replaced by nuclear missiles by 1970. Most estimates made during the Cold War showed that the United States had more nuclear warheads than the Soviet Union until the late 1970s or early 1980s.

REVIEW

Linguistic, Musical-Rhythmic. Have students use the information from pages 534–37 to create a song or poem about the Cold War. In their work, students should mention members of the opposing sides, points of conflict, and U.S. defense strategies.

ASSESS

Have students complete Geography and History Quiz 6.

RETEACH

Logical-Mathematical, Interpersonal. Organize the class into two groups—one to cover the Cold War alliances and the other to cover Cold War defenses. Have each group look at the graph and maps in this lesson that deal with its assigned topic. Then have each group make 10 flashcards based on its topic that can be answered from the lesson. Finally, have the groups use the flashcards to play a quiz game reviewing the lesson material.

SHELTERED ENGLISH

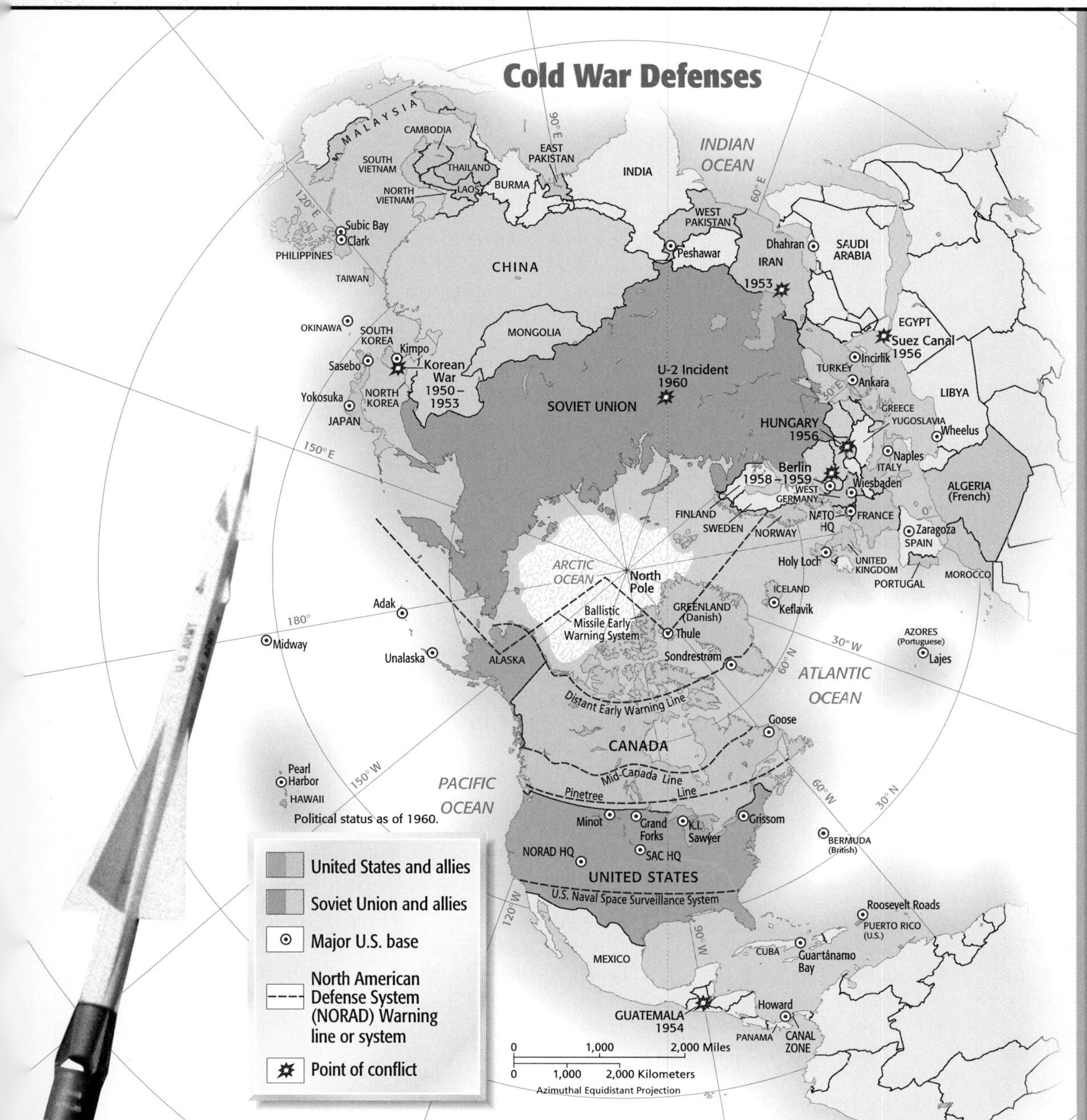

Cold War Defenses

Political status as of 1960.

- United States and allies
- Soviet Union and allies
- Major U.S. base
- North American Defense System (NORAD) Warning line or system
- Point of conflict

Azimuthal Equidistant Projection

Missiles were a major part of Cold War defenses.

Geography Skills

Reading Special-Purpose Maps

1. Where did conflicts occur in 1956?
2. How many major military bases did the United States have in Western Europe?
3. What system did the United States put into place to provide the first warning of a Soviet attack?

Geographic Diversity

Overseas Service. The U.S. Bureau of the Census counted 240,421 U.S. soldiers, sailors, marines, and airmen on active duty outside the United States in 1996. The largest contingent of these servicepeople—48,878 of them—was based in Germany. Some 42,962 U.S. military personnel were stationed in Japan, and another 36,539 were in the Republic of Korea (South Korea). Other nations with a substantial U.S. military presence included Bosnia and Herzegovina, with 15,003; Panama, with 6,435; and Kuwait, with 5,531.

Activity: Have students discuss the reasons for the U.S. military presence in each of the six countries mentioned above. Then have students make a special-purpose map illustrating the percentage of military personnel on active duty outside the United States that was stationed in each of these countries in 1996.

SKILLS ANSWERS

1. Hungary, the Suez Canal
2. seven
3. North American Defense System (NORAD)

CHAPTER PLANNING GUIDE
Peace and Prosperity

	SECTION LESSON OBJECTIVES	PRINT RESOURCES	MULTIMEDIA RESOURCES	SHELTERED ENGLISH RESOURCES
Section 1: Eisenhower's Foreign Policy (pp. 539–43)	★ Explain how the existence of nuclear weapons influenced President Eisenhower's foreign policy. ★ Identify the methods the United States used to fight communism abroad. ★ Describe the Cold War crises that occurred during Eisenhower's presidency.	★ Guided Reading Strategies 18.1 ★ American History Political Cartoon 26: Brinkmanship ★ Biography Reading 18: John Foster Dulles ★ Section 1 Review, p. 543 ★ Daily Quiz 18.1	★ *Teaching Resources CD–ROM*, Lesson 18.1 ★ Linking Geography and History Transparency 20: Cold War Defenses ★ HRW Web site	★ Main Idea Activities for Reteaching and Sheltered English 18.1
Section 2: A Prosperous Nation (pp. 544–49)	★ Describe how economic prosperity increased under President Eisenhower. ★ Evaluate the ways inventions helped change American industry and society in the 1950s. ★ Examine what life was like in the suburbs.	★ Guided Reading Strategies 18.2 ★ American History Political Cartoon 27: The Spread of Suburbia ★ Geography Activity 18: The Growth of Los Angeles ★ Section 2 Review, p. 549 ★ Daily Quiz 18.2	★ *Teaching Resources CD–ROM*, Lesson 18.2 ★ Linking Geography and History Transparency 21: America on the Move, 1950–1960	★ Main Idea Activities for Reteaching and Sheltered English 18.2
Section 3: A Changing Culture (pp. 550–53)	★ Evaluate how television affected American culture. ★ Describe the comments some writers made about American society. ★ Explain why certain films and music appealed to teenagers during the 1950s.	★ Guided Reading Strategies 18.3 ★ Literature Reading 18: *On the Road* ★ Section 3 Review, p. 553 ★ Daily Quiz 18.3	★ *Teaching Resources CD–ROM*, Lesson 18.3 ★ *American Music Audio CD Program:* "New Blues (Bop or Modern)" ★ Everyday Life in America Transparency 28: Queen of 1950s TV: Lucille Ball ★ *Exploring America's Past* Video Segment: Remember When; *Teacher's Guide,* pp. 33–34	★ Main Idea Activities for Reteaching and Sheltered English 18.3
Section 4: The Early Civil Rights Movement (pp. 554–59)	★ Examine ways in which African American World War II veterans influenced the early civil rights movement. ★ Describe some of the main events in the struggle for school desegregation. ★ Explain why the Montgomery bus boycott succeeded.	★ Guided Reading Strategies 18.4 ★ Graphic Organizer 18: Changing America ★ Primary Source Reading 18: Integrating Central High ★ Section 4 Review, p. 559 ★ Daily Quiz 18.4	★ *Teaching Resources CD–ROM*, Lesson 18.4 ★ *Exploring America's Past* Video Segment: More Than a Game; *Teacher's Guide*, pp. 31–32 ★ Linking Geography and History Transparency 17A: African American Population, 1950 ★ HRW Web site	★ Main Idea Activities for Reteaching and Sheltered English 18.4
Chapter Review and Assessment (pp. 560–61)		★ Chapter 18 Review, pp. 560–61 ★ Vocabulary Activity 18 ★ Chapter 18 Study Guide ★ Chapter 18 Test (Form A or B)	★ Audio Program, Ch. 18 (English and Spanish) ★ *Global Skill Builder CD–ROM* ★ Chapter 18 Test Generator ★ HRW Web site	★ Spanish Glossary ★ Sheltered English Chapter 18 Test

CHAPTER OVERVIEW

In 1952 and 1956, Americans elected Dwight D. Eisenhower president. His middle-of-the-road approach to politics promised peace and prosperity. However, some people felt increasingly insecure as a series of conflicts between the United States and the Soviet Union led to an arms race and fears of nuclear war. Eisenhower adopted the Cold War foreign policies of massive retaliation and brinkmanship.

During the 1950s the U.S. economy boomed and the income of many families rose, creating a larger middle class. Businesses hired more managers, and more women joined the workforce. At the same time, automation replaced some workers, and unions declined. Many people moved to the suburbs, where life tended to center on children. Technological advances improved life, and an interstate highway system improved transportation. New types of entertainment, including television and rock 'n' roll, became popular. Social critics, however, criticized suburban life for its conformity and materialism.

African American veterans returning from World War II pointed out the contradictions between American ideals and the reality of a segregated society. Many African Americans turned to the courts to challenge segregation. Desegregation of public schools led to violence in Little Rock, Arkansas. In some cities, African Americans challenged segregation on public transportation.

CHAPTER INVESTIGATION

The Chapter Investigation is an extended, multipart activity designed for students to work cooperatively and apply the chapter content in the creation of a project. You may choose to use the Chapter 18 Investigation, 1950s Living History Park, either as a substitute for teaching the section lessons or as an alternate assessment.

BLOCK SCHEDULING 

The teacher lesson plans for each section offer a variety of activity choices to help you present the material in a block scheduling format. For further suggestions on block scheduling, see the *Block Scheduling Handbook with Team Teaching Strategies,* pp. 103–08.

Meeting Individual Needs

ABILITY LEVELS

LEVEL 1 Basic level activities designed for all students encountering new material.

LEVEL 2 Intermediate level activities designed for average students.

LEVEL 3 Challenging activities designed for above-average students.

SHELTERED ENGLISH These activities address the needs of students with Limited English Proficiency.

Smithsonian Institution®

Internet Connections and Lesson 18
www.si.edu/hrw

CNN Presents America:
Yesterday and Today 1850 to the Present
Segment: A Few Views of the 1950s

Additional Resources

Books for Teachers

Branch, Taylor. *Parting the Waters: America in the King Years, 1954–1963.* Simon and Schuster, 1988. Describes the early years of the civil rights movement.

Halberstam, David. *The Fifties.* Random House, 1993. Highly acclaimed review of the 1950s.

May, Elaine Tyler. *Homeward Bound: American Families in the Cold War Era.* Basic Books, 1988. Analyzes the roles of women in suburban life.

Books for Students

Levine, Ellen. *Freedom's Children: Young Civil Rights Activists Tell Their Own Stories.* Putnam, 1993. A collection of firsthand accounts of segregation and the civil rights movement.

Oakley, J. Ronald. *God's Country: America in the Fifties.* Barricade Books, 1990. Entertaining and informative look at the 1950s.

Tames, Richard. *The 1950s: Picture History of the 20th Century.* Watts, 1990. Review of the major issues and events of the decade (for students reading below grade level).

Multimedia Materials

A Bigger Bang for the Buck. Video, 60 min. WGBH/Boston. Explores the Soviet Union's successful launch of *Sputnik* and the reaction of the American public and government.

Eisenhower and the Cold War. Video, 17 min. Encyclopaedia Britannica Education Corporation. Covers Eisenhower's Cold War diplomacy.

The Second American Revolution, Part II. Video, 58 min. PBS. Details the fight to end segregation.

Peace and Prosperity

CHAPTER MOTIVATOR

Play several selections of music from the 1950s. Try to give students a sense of the different types of music that were popular: from Elvis Presley, Little Richard, and Bill Haley, to Pat Boone, Perry Como, and Patti Page. In addition, discuss the jazz innovations introduced by Charlie Parker, Miles Davis, and John Coltrane, as well as the continued popularity of swing bands directed by Benny Goodman and Duke Ellington. Discuss the music with students. Then ask them to draw a scene illustrating one of the musical selections you played. Have volunteers explain their drawings. Then tell students that in this chapter they will learn about how the diversity of this music reflects the contrasts and variety that characterized American society in the 1950s.

Presenting Themes

- **Technology and Society** Students might mention that such weapons would assure that society a dominant place among nations. Students might also mention that the weapons' destructive power could make people anxious and fearful.
- **Economic Development** Students might mention that prosperity could enable people to create secure lives for themselves and their families. In addition, students might say that prosperity could encourage people to spend their money more freely.
- **Constitutional Heritage** Students might say that minority groups who are being discriminated against can use the courts as a way of protecting their constitutional rights.

Using the Time Line

Have students choose the three events on the time line that they think may have had the most influence on American society in the 1950s. Ask volunteers to explain their reasoning to the class. After students have finished the chapter, ask them to revise their lists. Call on volunteers to explain their revised lists.

CHAPTER 18

Peace and Prosperity

(1945–1960)

While on a family trip to Washington, D.C., Kemmons Wilson saw a special opportunity. Many of the nation's motels were dirty. Some charged extra for children to stay in the rooms. Wilson thought he could do better. He decided to go into the hotel business. His Holiday Inns proved very popular as people traveled the nation's new highways in their cars.

Technology and Society
In what ways might the existence of weapons of mass destruction affect a society?

Economic Development
How might economic prosperity affect people's daily lives?

Constitutional Heritage
Why might minority groups use the courts to fight for increased rights?

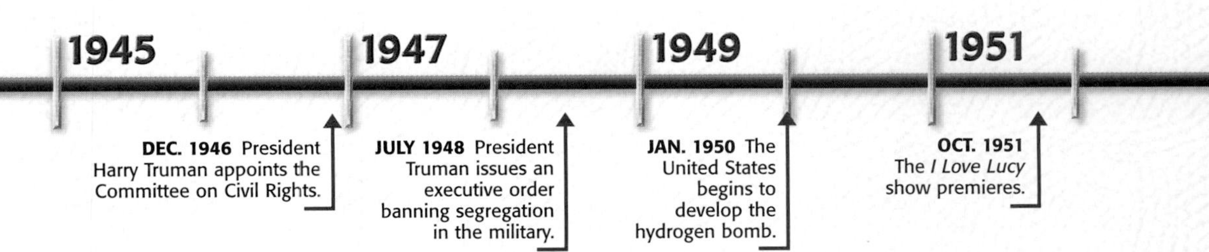

OBJECTIVES

- Explain how the existence of nuclear weapons influenced President Eisenhower's foreign policy.
- Identify the methods the United States used to fight communism abroad.
- Describe the Cold War crises that occurred during Eisenhower's presidency.

FOCUS

Motivate Before Reading

Describe the "duck-and-cover" drill and its purpose to students. Have them practice the drill by leaving their seats, crouching under their desks, and covering their heads with their hands. After they return to their desks, ask them to describe how they felt during the drill. Tell students that in this section they will learn why

Eisenhower's Foreign Policy

Reading Focus

- How did the existence of nuclear weapons influence President Eisenhower's foreign policy?
- What methods did the United States use to fight communism abroad?
- What Cold War crises occurred during Eisenhower's presidency?

Key Terms

- hydrogen bomb
- *Sputnik*
- National Aeronautics and Space Administration
- massive retaliation
- brinkmanship
- covert operations
- Central Intelligence Agency
- Suez Canal crisis
- Eisenhower Doctrine
- U-2 incident

SHERMAN ADAMS, the governor of New Hampshire, had a problem. He wanted to enter Dwight D. Eisenhower in the state's Republican presidential primary. However, he did not know for certain if the quiet World War II general was a Republican. Adams contacted the county clerk in Abilene, Kansas—Eisenhower's boyhood town—for more information. The letter Adams received in reply stated, "I don't think [Eisenhower] has any politics." Eisenhower, who was often called Ike, campaigned on his personal popularity with the American people. His approach was successful, and he won the 1952 presidential election.

General Dwight D. Eisenhower was a decorated war hero.

IMAGE ON LEFT PAGE: *A suburban family takes to the open road in the 1950s.*

1953 — **1955** — **1957** — **1959**

- **MAY 1954** The *Brown* v. *Board of Education* ruling declares segregation in public schools illegal.
- **DEC. 1955** Rosa Parks is arrested in Montgomery, Alabama.
- **NOV. 1956** The Soviet Union invades Hungary.
- **SEPT. 1957** Federal troops arrive in Little Rock, Arkansas, to enforce the desegregation of Central High School.
- **MAY 1960** The U-2 incident increases Cold War tensions.

Section 1 RESOURCES

PRINT

- ★ Guided Reading Strategies 18.1
- ★ American History Political Cartoon 26: Brinkmanship
- ★ Biography Reading 18: John Foster Dulles
- ★ Section 1 Review, p. 543
- ★ Daily Quiz 18.1

MULTIMEDIA

- ★ *Teaching Resources CD–ROM*, Lesson 18.1
- ★ Linking Geography and History Transparency 20: Cold War Defenses
- ★ HRW Web site

SHELTERED ENGLISH

- ★ Main Idea Activities for Reteaching and Sheltered English 18.1

Americans took seriously such drills and study the tension that existed during the Cold War.

Introduce Key Terms

Linguistic. Review this section's key terms with students. After students find the key terms in the section, ask them to use each word in a sentence describing the 1950s. Ask volunteers each to put a sentence on the chalkboard and explain how the key term is used. **SHELTERED ENGLISH**

TEACH

Have students read Section 1 and complete Guided Reading Strategies 18.1. Choose one or more of the following activities to explore the section content with students. For further suggestions on block scheduling or team teaching, see the *Block Scheduling Handbook.*

LEVEL 1: Linguistic. (Suggested time: 15 min.) As a class, go over students' Guided Reading Strategies. Then use the Reading Focus questions to highlight the main ideas of the section. **SHELTERED ENGLISH**

Across the Curriculum

MATH

Defense Budget. A goal of massive retaliation was to reduce the U.S. military budget. In 1952 the military budget was $40 billion, which amounted to approximately 70 percent of federal expenses. By 1953 Eisenhower had cut the defense budget to $34.5 billion.

Activity: Have students use these figures to estimate the total federal expenses in 1952. *($57 billion)*. Then have students search the Internet through the HRW Web site to find information about the current defense budget. Have students calculate the current percentage of the total budget that goes to defense.

go.hrw.com
SB1 Defense

The Nuclear Age

Shortly after Eisenhower was elected president, the U.S. military tested the first **hydrogen bomb**. The United States had begun developing this nuclear weapon in January 1950. It was far more powerful than the atomic bombs dropped on Japan in World War II. An observer recalled the test of the bomb, which was exploded on an island in the South Pacific:

> **"The fireball expanded to three miles in diameter. Observers, all evacuated to 40 miles or more away, saw . . . that the island . . . had vanished, vaporized also. In its place a crater 1/2 mile deep and two miles wide had been born."**

Less than a year later, the Soviet Union tested its own hydrogen bomb. "The United States no longer has a monopoly," one Soviet official bragged. Both the United States and the Soviet Union were afraid to let the other side gain nuclear superiority. As a result, each nation built more nuclear bombs.

The nuclear arms race frightened many Americans. Some families created underground bomb shelters to protect themselves in case of attack. Children practiced emergency "duck-and-cover" drills at school. They would duck under their desks and cover their heads in case of emergency. A few Americans formed antinuclear groups, such as the Committee for a Sane Nuclear Policy, to protest the arms race. They argued that nuclear weapons tests released radioactive particles that caused birth defects and disease.

The first test of the hydrogen bomb

Despite such protests, the arms race continued. In October 1957 the Soviet Union launched ***Sputnik***, the first artificial satellite, into orbit. Many Americans worried that the advanced technology used in *Sputnik* gave the Soviets a military advantage. One reporter asked President Eisenhower, "What are we going to do about it?"

The launch of Sputnik *started a space race between the United States and the Soviet Union.*

In January 1958 the United States launched its first satellite. Later that same year, Congress established the **National Aeronautics and Space Administration** (NASA) to conduct space research. Congress also created programs to improve math, science, and foreign language education in public schools. Officials hoped that better-educated students would help the nation win the arms and space races.

During the Truman years, the United States had tried to contain the spread of communism around the world. President Eisenhower and Secretary of State John Foster Dulles established a "New Look" in U.S. foreign policy. Eisenhower wanted the United States to actually "roll back" communism from certain regions.

The New Look relied on a strategy known as **massive retaliation**, or the threat to use nuclear weapons to halt communist aggression. Few diplomats supported the use of nuclear weapons. However, most accepted that the nation might have to go to the brink of war to oppose communism. This approach was known as **brinkmanship**. Dulles explained the strategy by saying, "The ability to get to the verge [brink, or edge] without getting into war is the necessary art." Brinkmanship was a difficult policy to pursue, however. In 1953 the Soviets crushed anticommunist protests in three East German cities. U.S. leaders sympathized with the protesters but were unwilling to become involved and risk a nuclear war.

ALL LEVELS: Visual-Spatial. (Suggested time: 30 min.) Have students create a political cartoon that might have appeared in an American newspaper during the 1950s. Cartoons should depict U.S. efforts to fight communism abroad. Have students describe their cartoons. Then have them create a cartoon on the same subject but that might have appeared in a foreign newspaper. Discuss reasons cartoons appearing abroad might differ from cartoons found in the United States. **SHELTERED ENGLISH**

LEVEL 2: Logical-Mathematical, Visual-Spatial. (Suggested time: 45 min.) Have students create a detailed time line of foreign-policy decisions made during the Eisenhower administration. Then have students create a second time line of the Cold War crises that occurred during the same period. Ask students to label each event on the time lines to indicate the date, the countries involved, and the outcome. Next, have students write a paragraph explaining how the events in the two time lines relate. Then discuss how Eisenhower's foreign policy was influenced by the existence of nuclear weapons

LEVEL 3: Linguistic, Intrapersonal. (Suggested time: 30 min. plus homework) During class, have students brainstorm ideas about what ordinary citizens and national leaders did to ease people's fears about the atomic bomb and the Cold War. For homework, ask students to use the ideas generated in class to write an article entitled "Easing Nuclear Fears" that might have

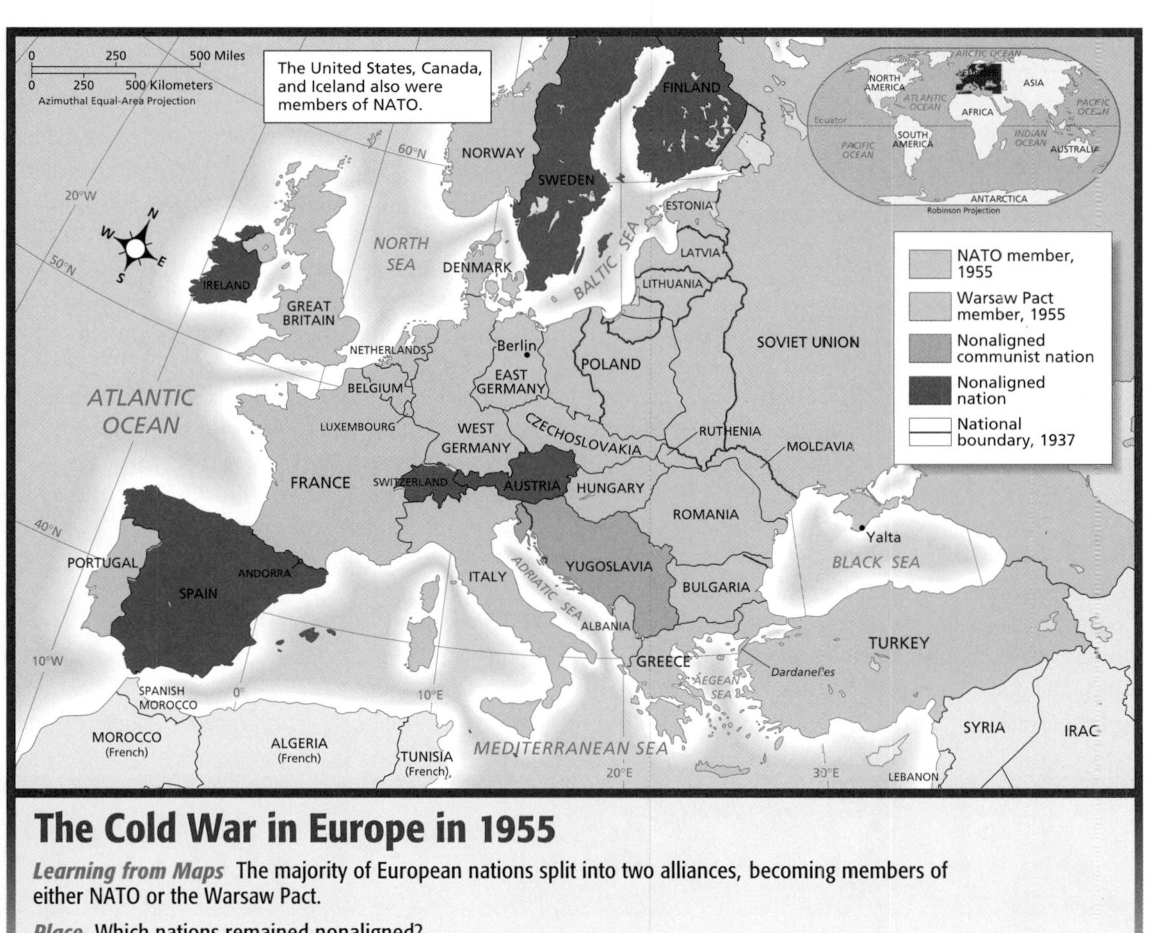

The Cold War in Europe in 1955

Learning from Maps The majority of European nations split into two alliances, becoming members of either NATO or the Warsaw Pact.

Place Which nations remained nonaligned?

Historical Sidelight

The Overthrow of Mosaddeq. The shah of Iran met several times with CIA agent Kermit Roosevelt, Teddy Roosevelt's grandson, to arrange aid from the United States and Britain in overthrowing Mosaddeq. Once Mosaddeq was ousted, the shah promised 40 percent of Iran's oil to a group of American oil companies and another 40 percent to the British Anglo-Iranian Company.

Critical Thinking: Why would the shah give up so much Iranian oil?

ANSWER: The shah knew that such oil concessions would help gain U.S. and British aid, which he needed to help him regain control of his country.

MAP ANSWER

Andorra, Austria, Finland, Ireland, Spain, Sweden, Switzerland, Yugoslavia

Covert Operations

Some Americans criticized brinkmanship. They argued that not every Cold War conflict required the threat of nuclear weapons. A single nuclear attack might lead to a nuclear war that could destroy the world. President Eisenhower sometimes used **covert operations**, or secret missions, to expand his foreign-policy options. The **Central Intelligence Agency** (CIA), a secretive intelligence organization established by the National Security Act in 1947, conducted these covert operations. During Eisenhower's presidency, the CIA's size and influence increased greatly.

The CIA's first major covert operation took place in the Middle Eastern nation of Iran. In 1951 Mohammad Mosaddeq (MAWS-ad-dek) became Iran's premier. He grew more powerful than the shah, Iran's ruler and a U.S. ally. Mosaddeq nationalized, or placed under government control, Iran's oil industry. His actions made U.S. diplomats fear that he was a Communist. In 1953 British and U.S. leaders organized "Operation Ajax." This mission overthrew Mosaddeq and returned sole power to the shah.

The CIA also became involved in the Central American nation of Guatemala. In 1951 Colonel Jacobo Arbenz Guzmán became president of Guatemala and began land and labor reforms. He nationalized the local fields and processing plants of the American-owned United Fruit Company.

After the takeover, Secretary of State Dulles went to the UN World Court to protest Arbenz's actions. He argued that Guatemala had turned to "international communism." In 1954 the CIA hired an army to invade Guatemala and overthrow

Multimedia Resources

Linking Geography and History Transparency 20: Cold War Defenses

appeared in a magazine in the 1950s. The article should contain descriptions of at least two events that heightened people's anxiety along with some solutions to nuclear fears. Encourage students to share their articles with the class. Then discuss whether fears of nuclear weapons exist today.

CLOSE

Linguistic. Have each student create a front-page newspaper headline for each of the major events in this section. Students should include a date in each headline. Then call on volunteers to describe their headlines to the class and explain each event's relation to the section as a whole.

CHALLENGE AND EXTEND

Logical-Mathematical, Visual-Spatial. Organize the class into three groups. Have one group research nuclear weapons, another early space exploration, and the last covert operations. Instruct students to focus on what Americans at the time might have known about these issues. Then ask students to prepare a 15-minute lesson that a teacher during the 1950s might have

Global Relations

Middle Eastern Aid. During the 1950s many Middle Eastern leaders turned to the United States for help to put down periodic uprisings. In 1957 King Hussein of Jordan asked the United States to help repel pro-Nasser rebels in his country who he claimed were Communists. President Eisenhower gave Hussein $10 million and sent U.S. naval forces to the area.

Critical Thinking: Why might Middle Eastern leaders claim that social unrest was instigated by Communists?

ANSWER: They may have feared a Communist takeover or they may have believed that the United States would be more likely to help if the goal was to stop communist-backed uprisings.

GLOBAL CONNECTIONS ANSWERS

1. He thought that without U.S. aid Middle Eastern countries almost certainly would be taken over by Soviet communism.
2. It lies close to the Soviet Union and adjacent to the Black Sea, a major water access to the Soviet Union. To provide a protective buffer against attack, the Soviet Union preferred neighboring countries to be communist and under its control. In addition, the Middle East contained much of the world's oil resources.

Arbenz. This army failed, but CIA pilots using Nicaraguan aircraft continued the fight. These CIA actions resulted in an anticommunist military government replacing Arbenz.

Cold War Crises

The Eisenhower administration used a variety of methods to oppose communism around the world. For example, in 1955 the United States agreed to help Egypt pay for the Aswan High Dam, a project on the Nile River. U.S. officials hoped Egypt would support the United States in the Cold War.

The Suez Canal Crisis

Just a year later, however, Egyptian leader Gamal Abdel Nasser was cooperating with communist nations. In response, the United States dropped out of the Aswan project. Nasser announced that Egypt would pay for the dam by nationalizing the Suez Canal, an important waterway connecting the Mediterranean and Red Seas. Nasser's decision upset Britain, France, and Israel. These nations invaded the areas around the Suez Canal in November 1956.

The **Suez Canal crisis** raised the possibility of a third world war. The Soviet Union threatened to fire missiles on Britain and France. To prevent a broader conflict, the United States joined the Soviet Union in condemning the invasion. The Suez Canal crisis ended peacefully. To show that the United States still opposed communism in the Middle East, Eisenhower announced the **Eisenhower Doctrine** in January 1957. He promised U.S. aid to any Middle Eastern country facing communist aggression.

Uprisings in Eastern Europe

Before the Suez Canal crisis erupted, Nikita Khrushchev (KROOSH-chawf) shocked the communist world. He had replaced Soviet premier

Global Connections

The Eisenhower Doctrine

After the Suez Canal crisis, President Eisenhower reconsidered his Middle Eastern policy. In 1957 he announced the Eisenhower Doctrine, in which he asked Congress for money to help Middle Eastern nations fight communism.

Many in Congress disliked Eisenhower's plan. One senator asked, "Why is it necessary to make this commitment here in such broad terms of permanent military and economic aid to these countries? It leaves us open now to be blackmailed." Secretary of State Dulles argued that if the United States did not aid the free nations of the Middle East, "then that critical area will almost certainly be taken over by Soviet communism."

President Eisenhower and Secretary of State John Foster Dulles

After a long debate, Congress adopted a revised version of the Eisenhower Doctrine. It stated that the United States would use armed force to help countries in the Middle East resist aggression.

Understanding What You Read

1. Why did Secretary of State Dulles support the Eisenhower Doctrine?
2. How might the geographic location of the Middle East encourage Soviet aggression?

presented about the topic. Encourage students to use visuals, posters, and handouts to highlight their presentations.

REVIEW

Linguistic, Interpersonal. Have students complete the Section Review questions. Next, have students write a paragraph that answers one of the Reading Focus questions. Then organize students into groups of three so that each group contains members who have answered each question. Finally, have students discuss their answers in their groups.

ASSESS

Have students complete Daily Quiz 18.1

RETEACH

Logical-Mathematical, Visual-Spatial. Have students complete Main Idea Activities for Reteaching and Sheltered English 18.1. Then have students label an outline map of the world to show the Cold War crises of the Eisenhower years. Students' labels should include the date and the outcome of each crisis. Finally, lead a discussion on the significance of each crisis.
SHELTERED ENGLISH

Joseph Stalin after his death in 1953. Khrushchev announced that Stalin had committed criminal acts, including mass murder, against the Soviet people. He argued that Stalin's policies should no longer be followed. Khrushchev also said that capitalism and communism could peacefully coexist in the world.

Stalin's death and Khrushchev's speech were followed by unrest in communist Eastern Europe. In Hungary, for example, new leaders argued for democratic reforms. The Soviet army invaded Hungary in November 1956 to stop this uprising. Hungarians fought back against the tanks with stones, rifles, and homemade bombs. The United States refused to intervene, and the Soviets easily crushed the revolt.

The U-2 Incident

In 1959 it appeared that the Cold War might be thawing. Vice President Richard Nixon visited the Soviet Union. Nikita Khrushchev then visited the United States. However, a new crisis erupted. On May 5, 1960, Khrushchev announced that the Soviets had shot down a U.S. spy plane. At first U.S. officials denied the charge. Khrushchev then revealed that the pilot, Francis Gary Powers, had survived. Powers admitted that he had been on a secret mission in a U-2 spy plane. The event was called the **U-2 incident**.

The U-2 was an advanced spy plane that flew at very high altitudes.

Eisenhower admitted that he had approved the U-2 flight. In a speech he explained:

> **"Our safety, and that of the free world, demand, of course, effective systems for gathering information about the military capabilities of other powerful nations . . . to guard ourselves and our allies against surprise attack."**

Despite the U-2 incident Eisenhower and Khrushchev attended a summit in Paris, France. The meeting was a disaster. The summit talks collapsed. The thaw in the Cold War was over.

SECTION 1 REVIEW

Identify and explain the significance of the following:

- **Dwight D. Eisenhower**
- **hydrogen bomb**
- ***Sputnik***
- **National Aeronautics and Space Administration**
- **John Foster Dulles**
- **massive retaliation**
- **brinkmanship**
- **covert operations**
- **Central Intelligence Agency**
- **Suez Canal crisis**
- **Eisenhower Doctrine**
- **Nikita Khrushchev**
- **U-2 incident**

Locate and explain the importance of the following:

- **Soviet Union**
- **Hungary**

Reading for Content Understanding

1. **Main Idea** How did the United States attempt to fight communism abroad?
2. **Main Idea** Make a graphic organizer showing major Cold War events that took place in East Germany, Egypt, Guatemala, Hungary, and Iran in the 1950s. Include the dates and outcomes of the events.
3. **Technology and Society** What role did nuclear weapons play in President Eisenhower's foreign policy?
4. **Writing** *Informing* Imagine that you are a member of the State Department under John Foster Dulles. Write a memo explaining the U.S. reaction to the Suez Canal crisis and the uprisings in Eastern Europe.
5. **Critical Thinking** *Making Comparisons* How are the policies of brinkmanship and covert operations similar? How are they different?

Section 1 Review ANSWERS

Identify

For significance, see the following pages:

- Dwight D. Eisenhower, p. 539
- hydrogen bomb, p. 540
- *Sputnik*, p. 540
- National Aeronautics and Space Administration, p. 540
- John Foster Dulles, p. 540
- massive retaliation, p. 540
- brinkmanship, p. 540
- covert operations, p. 541
- Central Intelligence Agency, p. 541
- Suez Canal crisis, p. 542
- Eisenhower Doctrine, p. 542
- Nikita Khrushchev, p. 542
- U-2 incident, p. 543

Locate

For locations, see the map on page 541.

Reading for Content Understanding

1. used brinkmanship and the threat of massive retaliation, covert operations, Eisenhower Doctrine, and foreign aid

2. Organizers should show that in Iran and Guatemala leaders with communist leanings were overthrown; that Egypt was invaded, but U.S. and Soviet actions helped end the invasion; and that in East Germany and Hungary the Soviets put down anticommunist protests.

3. Nuclear weapons were used to threaten communist countries and to maintain a balance of power with the Soviet Union.

4. Memos will vary but should state that the United States acted to avoid nuclear war.

5. similar—goal of each was to roll back communism; different—brinkmanship was a stated policy; covert operations were secret.

Section 2 Lesson Plan

OBJECTIVES

- **Describe how economic prosperity increased under President Eisenhower.**
- **Evaluate the ways inventions helped change American industry and society in the 1950s.**
- **Examine what life was like in the suburbs.**

FOCUS

Motivate Before Reading

Ask students to brainstorm a list of economic changes triggered by the invention of the Internet. For instance, students could mention how the Internet has changed the way people work and the way goods and services are bought and sold. Tell students that in this section they will study the factors leading to the economic

Section 2 RESOURCES

PRINT
- ★ Guided Reading Strategies 18.2
- ★ American History Political Cartoon 27: The Spread of Suburbia
- ★ Geography Activity 18: The Growth of Los Angeles
- ★ Section 2 Review, p. 549
- ★ Daily Quiz 18.2

MULTIMEDIA
- ★ *Teaching Resources CD–ROM*, Lesson 18.2
- ★ Linking Geography and History Transparency 21: America on the Move, 1950–1960

SHELTERED ENGLISH
- ★ Main Idea Activities for Reteaching and Sheltered English 18.2

A Prosperous Nation

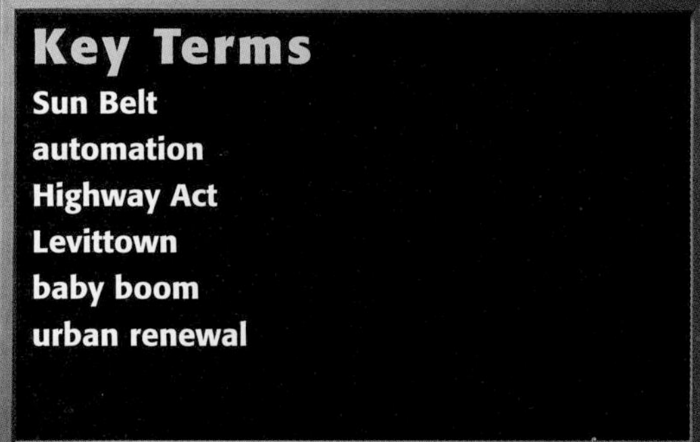

Reading Focus

How did economic prosperity increase under President Eisenhower?

In what ways did inventions help change American industry and society in the 1950s?

What was life like in the suburbs?

Key Terms

Sun Belt
automation
Highway Act
Levittown
baby boom
urban renewal

IN THE 1950S REVEREND Norman Vincent Peale was one of the best-selling authors in the United States. In The Power of Positive Thinking, *his most popular book, Peale told Americans that "happiness is achievable and the process for obtaining it is not complicated. Anyone who desires it, who wills it, and who learns and applies the right formula may become a happy person." Peale's books were very influential in the 1950s, a time when many Americans were confident that they could achieve wealth and happiness.*

The 1952 edition of Peale's book

America Under Eisenhower

The economy boomed during the 1950s. Undamaged by World War II, American industries were the strongest in the world. The federal government spent millions of dollars on Cold War defense, creating new jobs. President Dwight D. Eisenhower took a middle-of-the-road approach to managing the growing economy. He wanted to reduce the size of the federal government and give states and private companies control over some federal projects. However, during his presidency Congress increased the minimum wage and expanded Social Security.

During Eisenhower's administration, personal income soared for most Americans. By the mid-1950s nearly 60 percent of the population qualified as middle class, with annual incomes between $3,000 and $10,000. As a result, more Americans were able to buy luxuries such as large home appliances and TV sets. One woman proudly noted:

> **"When we were married my husband earned $30 a week. . . . Now we have . . . an income of over $25,000 a year. We own our own eight-room house—also a nice house on a lake. . . . Our oldest child goes to a prep school."**

boom of the Eisenhower years and some of the changes in society resulting from economic prosperity.

Introduce Key Terms

Linguistic. Review this section's key terms with students. Then have students write a paragraph describing suburban life in the 1950s. Have students incorporate as many of the key terms into the paragraph as possible. Ask volunteers to read their paragraphs to the class. **SHELTERED ENGLISH**

TEACH

Have students read Section 2 and complete Guided Reading Strategies 18.2. Choose one or more of the following activities to explore the section content with students. For further suggestions on block scheduling or team teaching, see the *Block Scheduling Handbook.*

LEVEL 1: Linguistic. (Suggested time: 15 min.) As a class, go over students' Guided Reading Strategies. Then use the Reading Focus questions to highlight the main ideas of the section. **SHELTERED ENGLISH**

Science and Technology

Television

Television, or TV, developed from radio broadcasting technology. In the late 1920s, researchers discovered how to add a video signal to radio broadcasts. The video signal carries information about the shape, brightness, and color of the images being filmed. This video signal is transmitted to the television set.

When a television receives this transmission, it turns the signal into beams of electrons. These electron beams scan rapidly back and forth in alternating lines across the TV screen. When the electron beams hit the screen, they activate tiny strips of material called phosphors. The phosphors then light up in the appropriate colors. Together all the phosphors on a screen create a picture.

TV sets typically show about 30 still images every second—a rate so fast that the viewer's eyes cannot see individual pictures. The eyes are also tricked into seeing a moving picture instead of a series of many still images.

Early televisions showed only black-and-white pictures on small screens about a foot wide. Much like early radio programs, the first TV shows were live broadcasts. Broadcasters also televised political speeches and debates.

TV changed how people saw the world. Televised congressional hearings were widely watched in the 1950s. Dwight D. Eisenhower's presidential campaign in 1952 was the first to rely heavily on TV ads. Eventually, the nightly news broadcast pictures from around the globe.

Television technology continued to change. In 1968 color TV sets outsold black-and-white TVs for the first time. Cable and satellite television provide many channels for a fee. A new technology known as high-definition television (HDTV) offers a sharper TV image.

Understanding What You Read

1. How do televisions work?
2. In what ways has TV changed daily life?

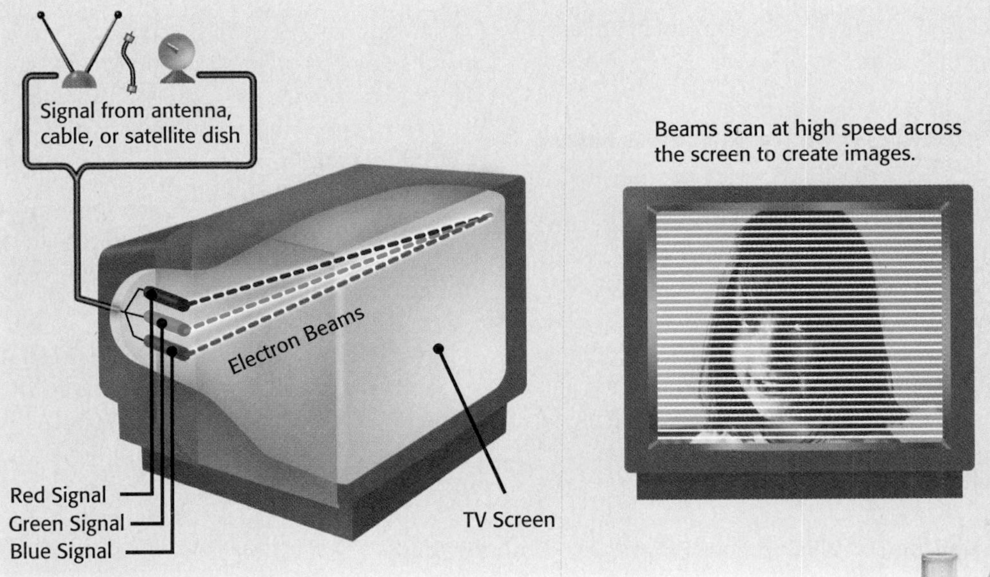

Signal from antenna, cable, or satellite dish

Electron Beams

Red Signal
Green Signal
Blue Signal

TV Screen

Beams scan at high speed across the screen to create images.

Technology and Society

Early Televisions. The first televisions were expensive. Most TVs came fixed in large cabinets that were more like furniture. Screens were small, and the sets often unreliable. Images frequently became greenish and blurry. Viewers had to use TV test patterns to adjust their sets. Nonetheless, television gained in popularity.

Critical Thinking. Why do you think early TV viewers were so excited about television even though sets were small and unreliable?

ANSWER. Television was a novelty and an alternative to movies and radio shows.

SCIENCE AND TECHNOLOGY ANSWERS

1. They convert video signals into beams of electrons, which move and activate phosphors to make a picture.

2. Answers will vary but may mention that television makes news immediate, provides a variety of entertainment and information, and affects what people buy.

ALL LEVELS: Logical-Mathematical, Visual-Spatial. (Suggested time: 45 min.) Have students create two cause-and-effect charts. One should explain how new inventions changed American industry; the second, how new inventions changed American society. Have students, when creating the second chart, pay special attention to changes related to family life and women's roles. Each chart should include positive and negative effects of changes in technology. After students have finished their charts, lead a discussion on how changes in American industry contributed to changes in American society.

ALL LEVELS: Logical-Mathematical, Visual-Spatial. (Suggested time: 45 min. plus homework) In class, have students discuss how economic prosperity increased under President Eisenhower. For homework, have students draw posters that show the factors as ingredients in a recipe for Prosperity Pie. Call on volunteers to explain their posters to the class. As they do, create a master circle graph on the chalkboard. Then lead a class discussion on who benefited from economic prosperity during the 1950s, and who did not. **SHELTERED ENGLISH**

Economic Development

Working Women. Three fourths of women who held jobs during World War II wanted to keep working. Many did, but at wages that averaged $13 a week less than those of men. Still, the number of working women tripled between 1940 and 1960.

Critical Thinking: How might working women have affected consumer culture?

ANSWER: With a second income, families could afford more goods and maintain a higher standard of living.

Across the Curriculum

SCIENCE

Jonas Salk. Polio is caused by a virus. Because this virus changes rapidly, Dr. Jonas Salk believed that a vaccine made from a dead virus, versus a live one, would be most effective. The vaccine would trigger patients' immune systems without actually infecting them. Salk's use of dead viruses and parts of viruses to make vaccines led to the development of others, such as one for hepatitis B.

Critical Thinking: How might the polio vaccine have affected public attitudes about epidemic diseases?

ANSWER: Students may say that people might have thought any disease could be prevented eventually.

Large cars such as this Dodge convertible were popular in the 1950s.

The healthy economy helped Eisenhower easily win re-election in 1956.

The new prosperity brought many changes. Millions of Americans moved to the **Sun Belt** states of the South and Southwest. They were attracted to the region by the warm winters, low taxes, and job opportunities. As a result, the population of the Sun Belt rose much faster than the national average. Families were on the move in other ways as well. They bought houses in the suburbs, took vacations, and sent their children to college. However, not everyone shared in the prosperity of the 1950s. In 1960 more than 20 percent of all families earned less than $3,000 a year.

A Changing Workforce

Many changes also occurred in the workforce in the 1950s. New corporate structures greatly increased the number of middle managers. The growth of the service sector created a greater need for clerical and sales workers. Women filled many of these typically low-paying positions. Such jobs offered little chance for advancement. Women who pursued careers often faced harsh criticism. One woman recalled:

> **"The only person who approved of me in those days was my father. He had encouraged me to be an accountant and whatever I did was all right with him."**

New technology also caused changes in the workforce. Many factories increased **automation**, or the use of machines in production. This change affected labor unions. Automation took jobs away from industrial workers, who often were strong union supporters. At the same time, few new managers, clerical workers, or sales staff joined unions.

In an effort to remain powerful, the nation's two largest unions—the American Federation of Labor (AFL) and the Congress of Industrial Organizations (CIO)—merged in 1955. They formed the AFL–CIO. Led by George Meany, the new union represented both skilled and unskilled workers. Despite such efforts, unions faced tough challenges. In the 1950s the Senate investigated the illegal use of union funds. Reports also surfaced that unions were pro-socialist or even Communist. As a result of such developments, the power of unions declined.

Technological Advances

Factories were not alone in being changed by technology in the 1950s. Advances in medical technology helped millions of Americans. Some devices, such as hearing aids and better contact lenses, improved the quality of life. Other advances were lifesaving breakthroughs, such as Dr. Jonas Salk's polio vaccine. Polio was a serious disease that had affected many Americans, including former president Franklin D. Roosevelt. The disease often caused paralysis or death.

During the late 1940s and early 1950s a polio epidemic swept across the United States, infecting thousands of children. In 1952 Dr. Salk developed a vaccine that

Dr. Jonas Salk on the cover of Time *magazine.*

LEVEL 3: Linguistic, Visual-Spatial. (Suggested time: 45 min.) Ask students to imagine that they are members of a Sun Belt suburb's chamber of commerce. Tell students that their task is to create an advertising campaign that encourages people to move to their town. Have students develop a campaign that focuses on the advantages of living in a Sun Belt suburb and points out shortcomings of living in large cities elsewhere. Ask volunteers to explain their campaigns to the class. Finally, discuss why so many people moved to the suburbs and the Sun Belt during the 1950s.

LEVEL 3: Linguistic, Interpersonal, Intrapersonal. (Suggested time: 20 min. plus homework) Have each student write a letter that someone living in the suburbs in the 1950s might write to an advice columnist. Letters should describe life in the suburbs and mention a problem related to an issue covered in this section. Then have students exchange letters and, for homework, write a response giving the type of advice they think a columnist of the 1950s might have given.

ended the epidemic and helped eliminate polio around the world. One reporter called this vaccine "one of the greatest triumphs in the history of medicine."

Many new technologies developed out of military research begun during World War II and the Cold War. The government spent millions of dollars on research projects for national defense. For example, researchers improved computer technology, which was first developed during World War II. Computers remained bulky and expensive. However, they were very useful for sorting large amounts of data.

Other advances included jet planes. In the 1950s Boeing introduced the first successful commercial jetliner, the 707. These large jet planes made long-distance travel cheaper because they could carry more passengers.

Some technologies affected home life. Engineers put nuclear technology to civilian use by building the first nuclear power plant. Nuclear power provided electricity to homes and businesses. The introduction of affordable home air conditioners helped residents of the Sun Belt endure hot summers.

Suburban America

Federal government programs also altered the countryside of the United States. In June 1956 Congress passed the **Highway Act**. This act funded

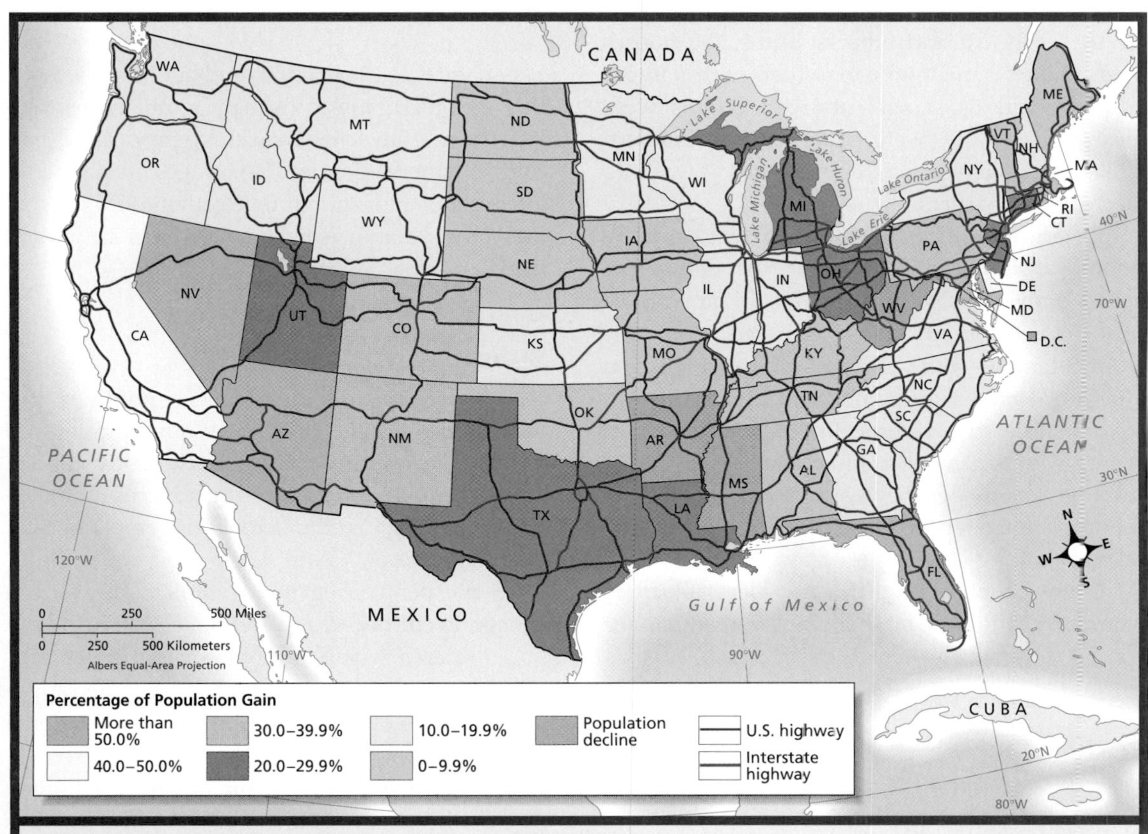

America on the Move, 1950–1960

Learning from Maps The national highway system crisscrossed the United States, allowing Americans to move easily from one region to another.

Place Which state populations increased by more than 50 percent after the expansion of the U.S. highway system? Which state populations declined?

Daily Life

The Automobile. During the 1950s, automobile companies began emphasizing styling details that made cars look sleeker and flashier. One designer, Harley Earl, set the tone for many cars of the era. Earl designed cars to look like jet planes—sleek with long, finlike attachments in the rear. He covered the cars with large, shiny chrome details. Flashy fins and chrome added little to cars' performance. Nonetheless, many Americans bought the larger, fancier cars during the 1950s, perhaps as a symbol of their increasing prosperity.

Activity: Have students research other popular products of the 1950s and write an essay describing how they reflected 1950s culture.

MAP ANSWER

increased by more than 50 percent—Arizona, Florida, Nevada; declined—Arkansas, Mississippi, West Virginia

Multimedia Resources

Linking Geography and History Transparency 21: America on the Move, 1950–1960

CLOSE

Linguistic, Intrapersonal. Ask students to imagine that it is the 1950s and their now economically prosperous family has moved from the city to the suburbs. Have students write a journal entry describing how economic prosperity, the changing workforce, the growth of highways, technological advances, and suburban living have changed their family's lives. Students should mention positive and negative aspects of change, where applicable.

CHALLENGE AND EXTEND

Linguistic, Kinesthetic. Have students use the library and other resources to find out more about the Eisenhower administration's domestic and economic policies. Then have students write and deliver a campaign speech that either a Republican or Democratic candidate for the 1960 election might have given on the practicality, appropriateness, and success of the Eisenhower administration's domestic policies.

Cultural Diversity

African Americans and Levittowns. African Americans could not purchase homes in any of the suburbs that William Levitt built. Levitt felt that he was justified in his racial exclusiveness. He claimed, "We can solve a housing problem or we can try to solve a racial problem, but we cannot combine the two." These types of racial restrictions created another growing difference between suburban life and life in inner-city neighborhoods.

Critical Thinking: How might Levitt's suburbs have benefited from racial integration?

Answer: Residents might have met, befriended, and learned from people with different backgrounds and experiences.

a new national system of interstate highways. This system greatly increased business and personal travel throughout the nation. The number of cars sold between 1946 and 1960 tripled. In addition, the highway system made it easier for many middle-class Americans to move to suburbs and commute to work. By 1960 more than one fifth of the entire U.S. population lived in suburbs.

Life in the Suburbs

As more Americans moved out of the cities, developers built new suburban neighborhoods. These sprawling subdivisions soon included their own parks, schools, and public services. William Levitt created **Levittown** on Long Island, New York. Levittown was an early example of a preplanned and mass-produced housing development.

In Levittown and other suburbs, the houses often looked similar to each other, with garages and large yards. Most suburban homes were inexpensive. Many were equipped with modern kitchens and labor-saving devices such as washing machines and dryers.

Americans welcomed these comforts. A **baby boom**—a significant increase in the number of babies born—took place after World War II. Most suburban neighborhoods centered activities around families and children. Suburban children often participated in organized activities, including music lessons, sports, Boy Scouts, and Girl Scouts. Mothers spent so much time driving their children from one activity to another that one commentator referred to the task as "motherhood on wheels."

Many people thought of the ideal suburban woman as a full-time mother who devoted most of her energies to her children and her home. Despite this image, many suburban mothers, particularly those with school-age children, worked part-time outside the home. Their wages often paid for after-school and summertime activities for the children. These activities included summer camps and dance or music lessons.

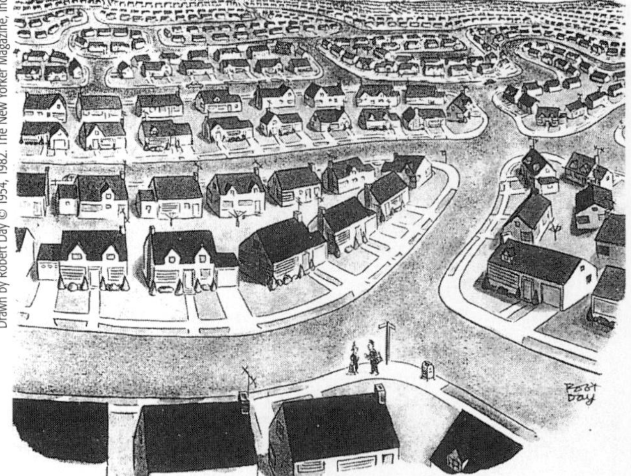

Drawn by Robert Day © 1954, 1982. The New Yorker Magazine, Inc.

"I'm Mrs. Edward M. Barnes. Where do I live?"

Some people made fun of the similar appearance of houses in the suburbs.

Suburban Culture

Suburban culture placed a strong emphasis on consumer goods. Many neighbors quietly competed to see which family could buy the latest clothes, gadgets, and cars. The growing advertising industry often encouraged much of this competition for material goods.

Some people began to complain that such a consumer culture was wasteful. Social critics wondered whether people really needed new cars every two years, or new kitchen appliances every three years. Others wondered whether material things could make people happy. One woman called suburban life "quite stale," despite her family's many possessions.

A few Americans disliked suburban life because they thought it encouraged conformity, or sameness. Most suburban residents were white and middle class. Some suburban communities tried to

Magazines promoted an idealized image of suburban life.

REVIEW

Linguistic. Have students complete the Section Review questions. Then have each student write a short story that contains all the section's key terms and summarizes the events described in the section. Ask volunteers to share their stories with the class.

ASSESS

Have students complete Daily Quiz 18.2

RETEACH

Visual-Spatial. Have students complete Main Idea Activities for Reteaching and Sheltered English 18.2. Then have students create a map of a typical 1950s suburb. Ask them to label on the map the types of businesses and facilities that might be found in a typical suburb, such as sports facilities and dance studios. Call on volunteers to explain their maps. Then have students discuss the economic and other changes that enabled more people to move to the suburbs during the 1950s and why people wanted to live in suburbs. **SHELTERED ENGLISH**

prevent people who did not fit their mold—whether because of race, ethnicity, or religion—from moving into their neighborhoods. Despite critics' complaints about the suburbs, residents often praised their communities. Many residents appreciated the strong social networks provided by suburban life.

Life in the City

As more white, middle-class Americans moved to the suburbs from the cities, they left behind many poor and nonwhite residents. Fewer tax dollars remained in the cities, leading to a decline in urban conditions and services.

As urban decay set in, the federal government launched an **urban renewal** program to improve life in the cities. The project began with a plan to improve public services and housing in the cities. The program called for replacing buildings in poor, run-down neighborhoods with large housing projects. Additional legislation in the 1950s provided further funds and a wide-ranging urban renewal plan.

Some city residents, however, felt that the plain-looking, multilevel housing projects destroyed the unique culture of older neighborhoods. Responding to these concerns, officials gradually altered the program to focus on restoring old buildings rather than demolishing them and building new ones. Despite the various efforts to improve living conditions, many city residents struggled to match the prosperity of the suburbs.

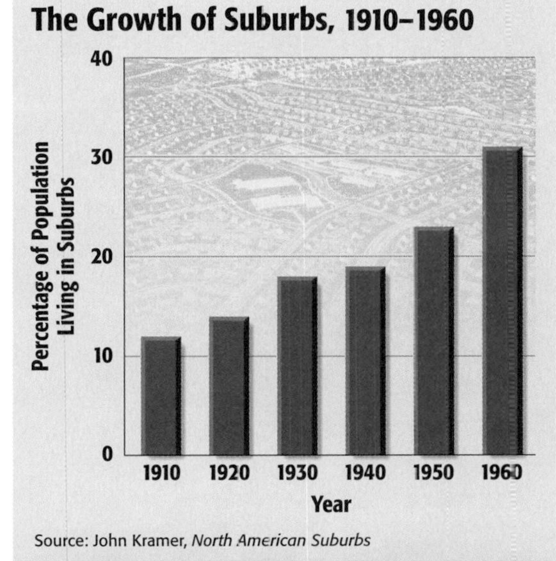

Suburban Life With improved roads, people increasingly moved to the suburbs and commuted to nearby cities for work. By about how much did the percentage of Americans living in suburbs increase between 1950 and 1960?

SECTION 2 REVIEW

Identify and explain the significance of the following:

- **Sun Belt**
- **automation**
- **Jonas Salk**
- **Highway Act**
- **William Levitt**
- **Levittown**
- **baby boom**
- **urban renewal**

Reading for Content Understanding

1. **Main Idea** How did inventions bring change to American life during the 1950s?
2. **Main Idea** What aspects of suburban life appealed to Americans in the 1950s? What aspects were criticized?
3. **Economic Development** In what ways did national prosperity increase during President Eisenhower's terms in office?
4. **Writing** *Describing* Imagine that you are a reporter living in a Sun Belt state after World War II. Write an article describing how the population has changed and explaining some of the reasons why this has happened.
5. **Critical Thinking** *Identifying Cause and Effect* What factors contributed to the economic prosperity of the 1950s? Consider the contributions of businesses and government programs in your answer.

Section 2 Review ANSWERS

Identify

For significance, see the following pages:

- Sun Belt, p. 546
- automation, p. 546
- Jonas Salk, p. 546
- Highway Act, p. 547
- William Levitt, p. 548
- Levittown, p. 548
- baby boom, p. 548
- urban renewal, p. 549

Reading for Content Understanding

1. Inventions improved the quality of life, eliminated polio, and made storage and transfer of information easier and faster.

2. appealing aspects—larger houses, planned communities, strong social networks; criticized aspects—conformity, emphasis on consumer goods

3. The minimum wage rose; social benefits expanded; industries grew stronger; defense spending increased, creating new jobs; and people's personal incomes soared.

4. Articles will vary but could include information on the growth in population because of the warm climate, air conditioning, low taxes, and job opportunities.

5. Answers will vary but may include increased defense spending and highway construction, a higher minimum wage, and expanded government benefits.

CHART ANSWER

about 9 percent

SECTION 3 LESSON PLAN

OBJECTIVES

- Evaluate how television affected American culture.
- Describe the comments some writers made about American society.
- Explain why certain films and music appealed to teenagers during the 1950s.

FOCUS

Motivate Before Reading

Have students write two sentences, one on the positive and one on the negative aspects of TV in present-day society. Then have students write two sentences on the positive and negative aspects of modern rock. Ask for volunteers to write their responses on the chalkboard and discuss them. Tell students that in this section they will learn about cultural change during the Eisenhower years.

Section 3 RESOURCES

PRINT

★ Guided Reading Strategies 18.3

★ Literature Reading 18: *On the Road*

★ Section 3 Review, p. 553

★ Daily Quiz 18.3

MULTIMEDIA

★ *Teaching Resources CD–ROM,* Lesson 18.3

★ *American Music Audio CD Program:* "New Blues (Bop or Modern)"

★ Everyday Life in America Transparency 28: Queen of 1950s TV: Lucille Ball

★ *Exploring America's Past* Video Segment: Remember When; *Teacher's Guide,* pp. 33–34

SHELTERED ENGLISH

★ Main Idea Activities for Reteaching and Sheltered English 18.3

A Changing Culture

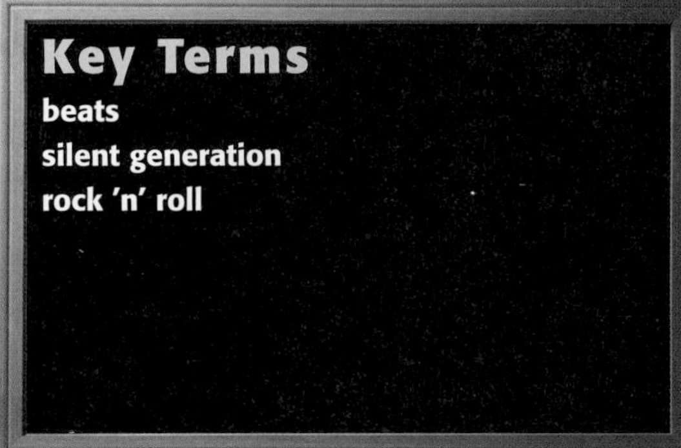

Reading Focus

How did television affect American culture?

What comments did some writers make about American society?

Why did certain films and music appeal to teenagers during the 1950s?

Key Terms

beats

silent generation

rock 'n' roll

SOON AFTER ITS DEBUT in 1951, I Love Lucy *became the most popular program on television. Millions of Americans tuned in to the 1953 episode in which actor Lucille Ball's character gave birth. In fact, more people watched that episode than tuned in the next day to see Dwight D. Eisenhower's inauguration. "It looks like Lucy is more popular than Ike," declared her co-star and husband, Desi Arnaz. "I wonder if we could run her for President in fifty-six?"*

Lucille Ball doll

Hake's Americana, York, PA

 The Golden Age of Television

The 1950s have been called television's golden years. In 1946 there were fewer than 10,000 television sets in the United States. Ten years later there were almost 35 million households with a TV set. Much like radio, television allowed many Americans to share the same experiences. Millions of viewers could watch a single program, whether a sports event or a news broadcast.

Milton Berle was one of television's earliest stars. As a boy he appeared in vaudeville shows—stage productions that combined singing, dancing, and comedy routines. When vaudeville became less popular Berle turned to television. He headlined *Texaco Star Theatre,* a popular variety show. He eventually appeared in so many TV shows that many people called him "Mr. Television."

Lucille Ball was another TV star of the 1950s. Her weekly series *I Love Lucy* started in October 1951. It co-starred her real-life husband, Cuban American bandleader Desi Arnaz. Week after week the couple found themselves in unusual situations. Ball's character was constantly trying to get herself into show business, while Arnaz always acted bewildered by her wild ideas. The result was a huge comedy hit. A TV producer

Introduce Key Terms

Linguistic, Visual-Spatial. Review this section's key terms with students. Then ask students to make a drawing representing one of the terms. Ask volunteers—one for each term—to share their drawings with the class and to explain how the images illustrate the chosen key terms. **SHELTERED ENGLISH**

TEACH

Have students read Section 3 and complete Guided Reading Strategies 18.3. Choose one or more of the following activities to explore the section content with students. For further suggestions on block scheduling or team teaching, see the *Block Scheduling Handbook.*

LEVEL 1: Linguistic. (Suggested time: 15 min.) As a class, go over students' Guided Reading Strategies. Then use the Reading Focus questions to highlight the main ideas of the section. **SHELTERED ENGLISH**

ALL LEVELS: Linguistic, Visual-Spatial. (Suggested time: 30 min.) Ask students to imagine that they are either a writer or artist living in the 1950s. Have them, based on the role chosen, either write a poem or draw a picture that expresses the type of comments some 1950s writers were making about American

later explained how Ball had appealed to her as a young girl:

> **"The main thing that Lucy did for me was that she acted. She was an active person who was having a grand adventure. . . . And I felt [when] watching Lucy that she wasn't afraid of anything."**

Frozen TV dinners became popular in the 1950s.

In addition to comedy shows, popular types of programs included dramas, game shows, soap operas, and westerns. Usually a TV show was sponsored by only one company. During the show the stars took short breaks to encourage viewers to buy the sponsor's product. Companies hoped that TV advertising would be even more successful than radio advertising. The success of this strategy led to the creation of more commercials and more elaborate advertising approaches. By 1955, advertisers were spending more than $1 billion a year on TV commercials. Television encouraged millions of American families to buy the latest products and participate in the expanding consumer culture.

Writers and Artists

For many Americans, the prosperity of the 1950s was an enjoyable relief from the strains of wartime. However, some writers criticized American society as being too focused on conformity. For example, in *The Lonely Crowd* writer David Riesman argued that social pressure to fit in discouraged people from being creative.

African American authors also served as powerful social critics during the 1950s. In his 1952 novel, *Invisible Man,* Ralph Ellison explores a young African American man's search for identity in the postwar world. James Baldwin also wrote about racism in his novel *Notes of a Native Son.* Baldwin viewed his work as an act of patriotism:

> **"I love America more than any other country in the world, and, exactly for this reason, I insist on the right to criticize her."**

A young group of writers called beatniks, or **beats**, used their unusual writing styles and rebellious behavior to criticize American life. In *On the Road,* beat author Jack Kerouac urged people to reject traditional society and choose their own path.

Some American artists also challenged traditional styles. Painter Jackson Pollock developed a bold new method called action painting. David Smith sculpted steel into unusual geometric shapes. Critics of such experimental writing and art claimed that the new styles did not have any real meaning. They accused the beats and other artists of being self-absorbed and immature.

Some people called teenagers and college students of the time the **silent generation** because young people appeared to conform to social expectations without protest. However, some teenagers rebelled by reading materials such as *Mad* magazine, which made fun of 1950s society.

Movies

Many young people also identified with and tried to imitate the young rebels that they saw in popular movies of the era. Actor James Dean was particularly popular. Dean starred in only three films

James Dean and Natalie Wood were the young stars of Rebel Without a Cause.

Cultural Diversity

Desi Arnaz. When Lucille Ball was approached by CBS executives to do a television show, she insisted they cast her husband, Desi Arnaz, as her TV husband. The network and advertisers objected because Arnaz was not well known in the United States and did not speak English well. One executive complained that no one would believe Ball was married to Arnaz. She is said to have replied, "What do you mean nobody'll believe? We *are* married." Arnaz became a critical element of *I Love Lucy's* success.

Critical Thinking: Why might viewers have appreciated that Arnaz was Ball's real husband?

ANSWER: People may have felt that *I Love Lucy* presented a real family and more accurately portrayed married life.

Multimedia Resources

Everyday Life in America Transparency 28: Queen of 1950s TV: Lucille Ball

Multimedia Resources

Exploring America's Past Video Segment: Remember When; *Teacher's Guide,* pp. 33–34

Search 34461, Play to 40639
Videodisc Blue Side A

Play

Pause

See *Teacher's Guide* for Spanish barcode.

society. Call on volunteers to share and explain their work to the class. Encourage feedback and discussion. **SHELTERED ENGLISH**

LEVEL 3: Linguistic, Musical-Rhythmic. (Suggested time: 30 min. plus homework) Ask students to imagine that they are a 1950s musician. Have each student write the lyrics for a rock 'n' roll song about the changes occurring in popular entertainment. Songs should address either television's effect on American culture or why certain films and music appeal to teenagers. Students might put their lyrics to the tune of a 1950s rock 'n' roll song. Call on volunteers to share their work with the class.

CLOSE

Linguistic. Assign each student one of four topics: television, writers and artists, movies, or rock 'n' roll. Have students write a brief paragraph explaining how the topic relates to 1950s society. Then have volunteers read their paragraphs to the class.

CHALLENGE AND EXTEND

Linguistic, Visual-Spatial, Interpersonal. Ask students to use the library or other resources to research television during the 1950s. Next, have them watch one or more 1950s TV shows

Across the Curriculum

MUSIC

Bebop. The beats enjoyed an unconventional new style of jazz called bebop. Earlier jazz was based on traditional, Western 7-note scales and maintained a fairly steady beat. Bebop musicians used all 12 notes and often changed tempo. The result was a more complex, less familiar sound. Although many young jazz musicians were excited by the new possibilities of bebop, many older jazz musicians and audiences did not like the new style.

Critical Thinking: Why might the beats in the 1950s have liked bebop?

ANSWER: Like beat poetry, bebop defied expected styles.

Multimedia Resources

American Music Audio CD
Program: "New Blues (Bop or Modern)"

AMERICAN ARTS ANSWERS

1. He felt more at ease and more a part of his painting.

2. He dripped and splashed paint to create wild, swirling, abstract compositions that seem to have lives of their own.

3. action painting

American Arts

Jackson Pollock

Paul Jackson Pollock was born in Cody, Wyoming, in 1912. He grew up in California and Arizona. When he was still a teenager, he began studying art with regionalist painter Thomas Hart Benton. During the Great Depression, Pollock worked on the Federal Arts Project.

At first, Pollock experimented with different styles and subjects. Around 1947, he began the work that would make his reputation—the so-called drip and splash paintings.

Pollock's method was bold and original. He spread a huge piece of canvas across the floor and then stood over it, dripping different types and colors of paint onto the canvas. Pollock argued that his new method helped his painting. "On the floor I am more at ease, I feel nearer, more a part of the painting, since this way I can walk around it, work from the four sides and internally be in the painting," he said.

Pollock's drip and splash paintings stunned the art world and the larger public. Unlike traditional paintings, Pollock's pieces did not feature identifiable subjects in standard places on the canvas. His paintings were wild combinations of color, shape, and texture. "The painting has a life of its own," Pollock commented. "I try to let it come through."

Jackson Pollock titled this 1948 drip and splash painting Silver over Black, White, Yellow, and Red.

Pollock's creations were leading examples of a new movement in art called action painting. During the 1950s, the action painters looked for freedom—the freedom to paint abstract images in a new style.

Understanding the Arts

1. Why did Jackson Pollock prefer to paint with his canvas on the floor?
2. How did Pollock use colors and shapes in new ways?
3. What 1950s art movement did Pollock represent?

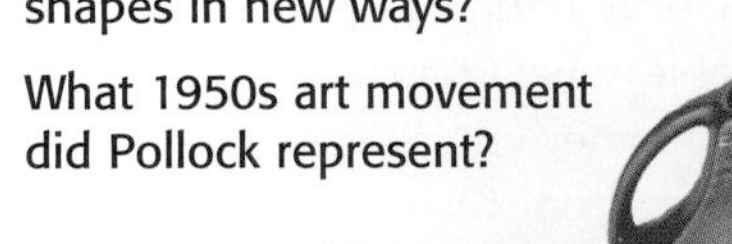

before dying in a car wreck at the age of 24. In *Rebel Without a Cause,* Dean plays a troubled middle-class teen. His character feels like an outcast and a failure because he cannot live up to other people's expectations of him.

Actor Marlon Brando also appealed to young audiences. In *The Wild One,* Brando plays a wild biker who challenges the rules of adult society—settle down, work hard, get ahead. When one character in the film asks, "What are you rebelling against?" Brando replies, "Whadda ya got?"

Music

Young people also rebelled by listening to new kinds of music. During the 1950s two important new styles of music became popular.

and write a summary of each. Then have students use their research and the shows they watched to compare and contrast 1950s TV shows to those of today.

REVIEW

Linguistic, Logical-Mathematical. Have students complete the Section Review questions. Then ask students to outline the following main ideas: how television affected American culture, what comments some writers made about American society, and why certain films and music appealed to teenagers during the 1950s.

ASSESS

Have students complete Daily Quiz 18.3

RETEACH

Linguistic, Logical-Mathematical, Visual-Spatial. Have students complete Main Idea Activities for Reteaching and Sheltered English 18.3. Ask students to create a comic strip that illustrates how American culture changed during the 1950s, and the type of criticisms some writers were making about American society. Call on volunteers to share their work with the class.
SHELTERED ENGLISH

Bebop

Bebop, or bop, got its start in the 1940s, when African American jazz musicians Charlie Parker and Dizzy Gillespie paired up. This complex type of jazz music, often played at a rapid pace, thrilled listeners. "It was new, and it was fresh, . . . it was so inventive," recalled bebop bandleader Lionel Hampton.

Elvis Presley

Rock 'n' Roll

Even more popular than bebop was the loud and enthusiastic sound of **rock 'n' roll**. This new musical style drew heavily from African American rhythm and blues. Rock 'n' roll musicians used new instruments such as electric guitars to create a fast-paced sound. Rock 'n' roll attracted many teenagers who wanted to challenge social restrictions.

The biggest rock star of the 1950s was Elvis Presley. Born in Tupelo, Mississippi, Presley was influenced by the blues and by country and western music. His silky voice, good looks, and energetic stage performances made him hugely popular with audiences, particularly teenage girls. During his career he sold millions of records. He also starred in more than 30 movies, mainly musicals.

Other rock 'n' roll stars included Chuck Berry, Fats Domino, Buddy Holly, Jerry Lee Lewis, and Little Richard. Berry and Holly were noted for their guitar playing, while Domino, Lewis, and Little Richard were piano players.

Critics argued that rock 'n' roll contributed to youth crime. Other adults simply thought it was bad music—too loud and filled with lyrics, such as "*do*-wop, *do*-wop," that meant nothing. Still others worried that rock 'n' roll cut across racial lines. Many teenagers were fans of white rock 'n' roll artists such as Presley, Lewis, and Holly as well as black artists such as Berry, Domino, and Little Richard. In spite of its critics, rock 'n' roll continued to grow in popularity. The new sound even attracted large audiences in other countries, particularly in Europe. Eventually, rock 'n' roll was seen by many people as a uniquely American contribution to music, similar to jazz or the blues.

SECTION 3 REVIEW

Identify and explain the significance of the following:

- **Lucille Ball**
- **Ralph Ellison**
- **James Baldwin**
- **beats**
- **Jack Kerouac**
- **Jackson Pollock**
- **silent generation**
- **rock 'n' roll**
- **Elvis Presley**

Reading for Content Understanding

1 **Main Idea** How did television change American culture in the 1950s?

2 **Main Idea** What attracted teenagers to rock 'n' roll and to movies such as *Rebel Without a Cause*?

3 **Cultural Diversity** What did authors such as James Baldwin, Ralph Ellison, David Riesman, and Jack Kerouac write about American life in the 1950s?

4 **Writing** *Persuading* Imagine that you are a student in the 1950s writing an article about bebop or rock 'n' roll for your school newspaper. Try to persuade your readers that these new forms of music are or are not exciting and worthwhile.

5 **Critical Thinking** *Evaluating* Did American teenagers in the 1950s deserve the label of "silent generation"? Explain your answer.

Section 3 Review ANSWERS

Identify

For significance, see the following pages:

- Lucille Ball, p. 550
- Ralph Ellison, p. 551
- James Baldwin, p. 551
- beats, p. 551
- Jack Kerouac, p. 551
- Jackson Pollock, p. 551
- silent generation, p. 551
- rock 'n' roll, p. 553
- Elvis Presley, p. 553

Reading for Content Understanding

1. Television became a major form of entertainment; TV ads increased, encouraging more people to buy products and influencing what they bought; TV shows began to define popular culture.

2. They challenged the rules of mainstream, adult society; youth identified with the musicians and movie characters.

3. They criticized traditional society as being materialistic, conformist, and racist and urged readers to find their own paths.

4. Articles will vary. Students who like the music may state that it is inventive, energetic, fun to dance to, and encourages listeners to examine new ideas. Those who dislike it may write that it is chaotic, loud, meaningless, and contributes to youth crime.

5. Answers will vary. Students who disagree may state that teenagers subtly challenged society by reading books and magazines, watching movies, and listening to music that rebelled against the mainstream. Students who agree may state that most youth conformed by doing the same rebellious acts as their peers.

Section 4 Lesson Plan

OBJECTIVES

- **Examine ways in which African American World War II veterans influenced the early civil rights movement.**
- **Describe some of the main events in the struggle for school desegregation.**
- **Explain why the Montgomery bus boycott succeeded.**

FOCUS

Motivate Before Reading

Write *poll taxes, literacy tests,* and *intimidation* on the chalkboard. Ask students what they think each term means. Then have students describe and discuss how each term might keep someone from voting. Finally, tell students that in this section they will learn how African Americans fought racial injustice during the 1950s.

Section 4 RESOURCES

PRINT

- ★ Guided Reading Strategies 18.4
- ★ Graphic Organizer 18: Changing America
- ★ Primary Source Reading 18: Integrating Central High
- ★ Section 4 Review, p. 559
- ★ Daily Quiz 18.4

MULTIMEDIA

- ★ *Teaching Resources CD–ROM,* Lesson 18.4
- ★ *Exploring America's Past* Video Segment: More Than a Game; *Teacher's Guide,* pp. 31–32
- ★ Linking Geography and History Transparency 17A: African American Population, 1950
- ★ HRW Web site

SHELTERED ENGLISH

- ★ Main Idea Activities for Reteaching and Sheltered English 18.4

Multimedia Resources

Linking Geography and History Transparency 17A: African American Population, 1950

SECTION 4

The Early Civil Rights Movement

Reading Focus

How did African American World War II veterans influence the early civil rights movement?

What were some of the main events in the struggle for school desegregation?

Why did the Montgomery bus boycott succeed?

Key Terms

Committee on Civil Rights
Brown* v. *Board of Education
Little Rock Nine
Montgomery bus boycott
Montgomery Improvement Association
Southern Christian Leadership Conference

MANY AFRICAN AMERICAN VETERANS came home from service in World War II filled with anger. Civil rights lawyer Constance Baker Motley explained their feelings. "Black servicemen were overseas dying for this country," she said, "and . . . they would be coming home to a situation that said, in effect, You're a second-class citizen. . . . You can't stay in a hotel or eat in a restaurant because you're black." James Hicks, an African American veteran, described the response of many fellow ex-soldiers: "I paid my dues over there and I'm not going to take this anymore over here." Black veterans prepared to take up another fight—this one against discrimination in the United States.

Civil rights picketer outside the 1948 Democratic National Convention

Segregation After World War II

Many returning African American veterans focused their efforts on voting discrimination. Fees, literacy tests, and threats of violence in some states—particularly those in the South—prevented African Americans from voting or even registering to vote. Some white politicians encouraged such discrimination when they ran for office.

The drive for African American voting rights brought intense conflict. As the violence grew, many black leaders asked President Truman for help. In the summer of 1946, a group of civil rights activists protested outside the White House. They held signs that read "SPEAK, SPEAK, MR. PRESIDENT." That same summer nearly 15,000 protesters marched to the Lincoln Memorial to demand an end to the threats and violence carried out by the Ku Klux Klan.

Introduce Key Terms

Linguistic. Review this section's key terms with students. Then have students use each of the terms to create a time line of events. Call on volunteers to share their time lines with the class. As they do, have other students define each key term and point out related terms. Finally, have students write a definition of each term in their notebooks. **SHELTERED ENGLISH**

TEACH

Have students read Section 4 and complete Guided Reading Strategies 18.4. Choose one or more of the following activities to explore the section content with students. For further suggestions on block scheduling or team teaching, see the *Block Scheduling Handbook.*

LEVEL 1: Linguistic. (Suggested time: 15 min.) As a class, go over students' Guided Reading Strategies. Then use the Reading Focus questions to highlight the main ideas of the section. **SHELTERED ENGLISH**

Even though the U.S. military had been desegregated, this airman still faced segregation at the Atlanta Terminal Station in 1956. Such segregation inspired many African Americans to work for civil rights.

President Truman responded to these requests in December 1946. He appointed the **Committee on Civil Rights** to investigate racial discrimination and suggest federal solutions to the problem. The committee's report, *To Secure These Rights*, noted the existence of racial discrimination throughout the country. The report also recommended a number of federal actions to help African Americans. The recommended actions included passing new laws to better protect all voters, desegregating the armed forces, and establishing a permanent Fair Employment Practices Commission. Truman pledged to support the committee's recommendations.

President Truman's verbal support for civil rights pleased African American leaders. They began, however, to express frustration as months dragged on with little real action by the president or Congress. Finally, African American labor leader A. Philip Randolph threatened to organize a massive protest if Truman did not at least desegregate the armed forces. In July 1948 Truman issued an executive order banning segregation in the military. That same year he also announced an executive order banning racial discrimination in the hiring of federal employees.

Brown v. Board of Education

Early civil rights leaders, particularly members of the National Association for the Advancement of Colored People (NAACP), had one main goal. They wanted to end the segregation of black and white Americans. They were particularly concerned with school segregation.

A Long Struggle

Many states, in both the North and the South, maintained separate schools for black and white students. Most officials argued that these institutions were "separate but equal." However, African American schools typically received far less money and supplies than did white schools.

The NAACP legal defense team won a series of court cases that challenged the practice of maintaining separate-but-equal educational facilities. In 1938 the U.S. Supreme Court had issued a ruling declaring that every state had to offer equal educational opportunities within its borders. In other words, a state that offered a law school or a medical school for white students had to provide a school for black students as well. Some states already had such separate facilities, and a few others established them after the ruling.

The NAACP then tried to show that separate schools did not provide equal educational opportunities for black students. In 1946 an African American named Heman Sweatt applied to the law school at the University of Texas. The law school did not accept black students, and school officials refused to admit Sweatt. Instead, they created a separate black law school. In 1950 the Supreme Court ruled in *Sweatt* v. *Painter* that the new school did not provide African Americans with access to equal academic prestige, facilities, or instructors. The Court ordered the university to admit Sweatt into its law school.

A Crucial Case

Starting around 1950, the NAACP focused on abolishing segregation in public schools in the United States. Thurgood Marshall, the NAACP attorney who had argued the *Sweatt* case, led the courtroom

Citizenship and Democracy

Segregation in World War II. Segregation in the army outraged many African Americans. At one base segregation was so pervasive that during shows put on for the soldiers' entertainment, African American soldiers had to sit behind German prisoners of war. Some entertainers, such as Lena Horne, refused to perform at segregated military bases.

Critical Thinking: What did segregation at bases show about the military?

ANSWER: That African American soldiers still faced discrimination.

Multimedia Resources

Exploring America's Past Video Segment: More Than a Game; *Teacher's Guide*, pp. 31–32

Search 27031, Play to 34453
Videodisc Blue Side A

Play

Pause

See *Teacher's Guide* for Spanish barcode.

ALL LEVELS: Linguistic. (Suggested time: 30 min.) Ask students to write newspaper headlines for the main events of the struggle for school desegregation, including the key Supreme Court decision in *Brown* v. *Board of Education* and the events as Little Rock attempted to desegregate its schools. Work with students to develop a list of details that might have been used to write articles to accompany the headlines.

ALL LEVELS: Linguistic, Visual-Spatial. (Suggested time: 20 min.). Have students create posters or flyers in support of boycotting the Montgomery bus system in 1955. Students should create a slogan and an image that will motivate people to stay off the buses and support desegregation. **SHELTERED ENGLISH**

LEVEL 2: Linguistic, Intrapersonal. (Suggested time: 30 min.) Have students reread the description of the Little Rock Nine. Then ask students to write essays describing the main events that occurred and expressing how they think the Little Rock Nine felt about these events.

LEVEL 2: Logical-Mathematical. (Suggested time: 45 min.) Ask students to imagine that they were one of the organizers of the Montgomery bus boycott. Leaders in another city have asked them for help in organizing a similar boycott. Have students list steps to organize a successful protest. Call on volunteers to explain their lists.

Constitutional Heritage

The Warren Court. Chief Justice Earl Warren, realizing that the Supreme Court must unite the nation behind the *Brown* decision, wanted all the justices to agree with the ruling. However, Justice Stanley Reed, a southerner and committed segregationist, asked one of his clerks to prepare a dissenting brief. The clerk argued with his boss, explaining that a dissenting brief would undermine the authority of the Court and U.S. efforts to fight communism in nonwhite countries. Under pressure from these arguments and from Warren himself, Reed agreed to make the ruling unanimous. Reed did ask that the desegregation of schools happen gradually, rather than quickly and perhaps violently.

Critical Thinking: Why do you think Chief Justice Warren felt that the Court needed to be united behind the *Brown* decision?

ANSWER: Racial segregation was such a volatile issue in the United States that Warren likely felt he needed total support to make some Americans accept the ruling.

battles. A number of school segregation cases came together under the title of ***Brown* v. *Board of Education***. The title case involved Linda Brown, a seven-year-old girl from Topeka, Kansas. Even though she lived very close to a school for white children, she had to travel across town to attend an all-black school. Her father sued to allow Linda to attend the nearby white school.

The NAACP team used studies by African American psychologist Kenneth Clark to oppose segregation. Clark argued that segregation led many black children to feel that they were less important than white children. "Segregation was, is, the way in which a society tells a group of human beings that they are inferior to other groups of human beings in the society," he explained.

The Court Ruling

In May 1954 the U.S. Supreme Court decided *Brown* v. *Board of Education*. The Court ruled that segregation in public schools is illegal. The majority opinion said:

> **"To separate [black students] from others of similar age and qualifications solely because of their race generates a feeling of inferiority as to their status in the community that may affect their hearts and minds in a way very unlikely ever to be undone. . . . In the field of public education the doctrine [belief] of 'separate but equal' has no place. Separate educational facilities are inherently [by their very nature] unequal."**

Many schools segregated students on the basis of race. Nearly 90 African American children crowd into this kindergarten class.

The Court's decision effectively overturned the 1896 *Plessy* v. *Ferguson* ruling that had established the "separate-but-equal" doctrine. In 1955 the Court strengthened its ruling by ordering public schools to desegregate "with all deliberate speed."

Public reaction to the *Sweatt* and *Brown* decisions was mixed. Some white leaders promised to follow the law. Others such as South Carolina governor James F. Byrnes predicted the very collapse of American culture. Byrnes argued that desegregation "would mark the beginning of the end of civilization in the South as we have known it." Some white citizens pledged to close their local public schools and open private, all-white academies.

Most African Americans were pleased with the Court decisions but wondered whether white leaders would really support desegregation. As one black lawyer explained years before the *Brown* v. *Board of Education* ruling, African Americans knew from experience that there was a "difference between the law in books and the law in action."

The Little Rock Nine

Despite the Court's "all deliberate speed" order, desegregation proceeded slowly in most places. Only three school districts in the entire South began desegregating in 1954. Most other school districts adopted gradual desegregation plans. The school board in Little Rock, Arkansas, decided to integrate one high school first, then slowly work down to the elementary level. The school board selected nine outstanding black students, nicknamed the **Little Rock Nine**, to attend Central High School in 1957.

At first, most African American leaders expected the Little Rock integration plan to go smoothly. Although Little Rock was highly segregated, it had a reputation for being moderate. As the start of the 1957 school year got closer, however, many white residents tried to stop the

LEVEL 3: Linguistic, Interpersonal, Intrapersonal. (Suggested time: 30 min. plus homework) For homework, have each student write a newspaper editorial from the perspective of an African American veteran who has just returned to the United States from World War II. Editorials should describe veterans' feelings about discrimination after fighting for their country, their decision to organize a group to protest discrimination, and their arguments about why people in the community should join the organization. In class, pair students and have them read their editorials to each other. Then have them critique each other's work and revise their editorials based on these suggestions.

CLOSE

Logical-Mathematical, Visual-Spatial. Draw a Venn diagram on the chalkboard. Label one circle *Court Decisions* and the other *Community Activism.* Ask students to copy the Venn diagram onto a piece of paper. Then have students write events from the section in the appropriate circle in the diagram. Tell students to place in the intersection of the two circles the court decisions and activism that produced combined results.

Elizabeth Eckford tries to make her way into Little Rock's Central High School.

integration plan. Arkansas governor Orval Faubus arranged for a group to appeal to a judge to halt integration. When the effort failed, he went on television the day before school started and declared that state National Guard units would prevent the Little Rock Nine from starting school. Faubus claimed that the reason for his action was to prevent violence over integration.

Daisy Bates, the president of the Arkansas NAACP, told the students to meet her on the morning of September 4 to get rides to school. Bates forgot to notify Elizabeth Eckford, a member of the Little Rock Nine. When Eckford went to school by herself, a mob greeted her at Central High. With the screaming crowd behind her, the National Guard soldiers refused her entrance to the school. She was alone and without protection, facing a large mob of enraged protesters. About that time, Eckford recalled, "Somebody started yelling, *'Lynch her! Lynch her!'*" Eckford ran to a nearby bus stop to escape, but the crowd followed. Finally, a white man and woman guided her to safety.

The tense situation continued for several weeks. President Eisenhower tried to persuade Faubus to follow the law, but he refused. In late September, Eisenhower sent federal troops to enforce desegregation at Central High. One of the Little Rock Nine, Melba Pattillo Beals, remembered the soldiers' presence at the school:

> **"I went in not through the side doors, but up the front stairs, and there was a feeling of pride and hope that yes, this is the United States; yes, there is a reason I salute the flag; and it's going to be okay."**

Problems resumed after the federal troops left, and Eisenhower asked that Arkansas National Guard units protect the students.

Despite these efforts, the Little Rock Nine continued to suffer insults and abuse from white students. Even so, eight of the nine remained. In May 1958 Ernest Green became the first African American student to graduate from Central High School. "When they called my name . . . there was eerie silence. Nobody clapped," Green remembered. "But I figured they didn't have to . . . because after I got that diploma, that was it. I had accomplished what I had come there for."

Governor Faubus continued to fight integration. He even closed the Little Rock public schools during the 1958–59 school year. The schools finally reopened under a court order in 1959 and began a process of slow integration.

The Montgomery Bus Boycott

Even before the Arkansas NAACP helped integrate Central High, the Alabama NAACP worked to desegregate public transportation in Montgomery, Alabama. In most southern cities all public facilities, including buses, were segregated. In Montgomery, white passengers rode in the front of the buses and black passengers rode in the back section. If the front section filled up, black passengers had to give up their back seats to white passengers. The Montgomery system also required that African American passengers enter through the front door to pay their fare, then get off the bus, walk to the back door, and board.

Using Visual Resources

Elizabeth Eckford. The image of Elizabeth Eckford standing alone in the midst of an angry white mob remains one of the most powerful of the civil rights movement. This image and others like it built sympathy across the United States for African Americans' struggle.

Activity: Have students use the library and the Internet through the HRW Web site to research the Little Rock Nine. Ask students to write a magazine article entitled "The Little Rock Nine: Where Are They Now?" and giving biographical information on each of the nine students.

go.hrw.com
SB1 Little Rock

Biography

Rosa Parks. In July 1999 Rosa Parks was awarded the Congressional Gold Medal. This medal is the highest U.S. civilian honor. The award was given for Parks's contribution as a "living icon for freedom in America." Other winners of the award include George Washington, the first recipient, and South African president Nelson Mandela.

Critical Thinking. How has Parks served as an icon for freedom in the United States?

ANSWER: Her refusal to give up her seat sparked the modern civil rights movement.

CHALLENGE AND EXTEND

1. **Linguistic, Logical-Mathematical, Visual-Spatial.** Ask students to research one of the individuals discussed in this section. Then have students write a brief biography of the person and obtain or draw a picture of him or her. Encourage students to focus their biographies on how the individual influenced one of the events or movements mentioned in the text. Remind students to use standard spelling, punctuation, and grammar in their writing. Have volunteers share their biographies and pictures with the class.

TEACHER TO TEACHER

2. **Linguistic, Logical-Mathematical, Interpersonal.** Dave Leckrone of Charlottesville, Virginia, suggested the following activity: Discuss the idea of a boycott with students. Then have them identify countries the United States is currently boycotting or has boycotted. In addition, ask students to search for examples of boycotts taking place in their community and, if possible, contact the organizers. Have students, either individually or in groups, make a presentation to the class about the

Section 4 Review ANSWERS

Identify

For significance, see the following pages:

- Committee on Civil Rights, p. 555
- Thurgood Marshall, p. 555
- *Brown* v. *Board of Education*, p. 556
- Little Rock Nine, p. 556
- Rosa Parks, p. 558
- Montgomery bus boycott, p. 558
- Montgomery Improvement Association, p. 558
- Martin Luther King Jr., p. 558
- Southern Christian Leadership Conference, p. 559

Reading for Content Understanding

1. Angered at being treated like second-class citizens after fighting overseas, they joined the civil rights movement. Their actions led President Truman to create the Committee on Civil Rights.

2. NAACP lawyers filed suits against segregated public schools and these cases were combined under *Brown* v. *Board of Education*. The Supreme Court ruled such segregation illegal.

3. They challenged segregated schools and Montgomery's segregated bus system in court.

4. Outlines will vary but should highlight massive community participation and organization.

5. Answers will vary but students might state that other African Americans might have thought that if these nine, young people can make a difference, then so can I.

Biography

Rosa Parks

Rosa Parks spent most of her early life in Montgomery, Alabama, and attended a high school run by Alabama State College. She worked as a seamstress after graduation.

Parks became involved with the local NAACP and served as the secretary of the Montgomery branch as well as its youth council adviser. In the summer of 1955, she attended a workshop on race relations at the Highlander Folk School in Tennessee. This integrated school taught people how to organize movements for social reform. As Parks recalled years later, "At Highlander I found out for the first time in my adult life that this could be a unified society." This lesson inspired her later actions and beliefs.

Parks lost her seamstress job after her arrest for refusing to give up her seat on the Montgomery bus. She and her husband later moved to Detroit, Michigan, where she continued to work for civil rights.

The Rosa Parks Case

In the mid-1950s the NAACP was prepared to challenge Montgomery's segregated bus system. On December 1, 1955, African American seamstress Rosa Parks refused to give up her bus seat to a white passenger, as required by law. She was quickly arrested.

Parks later explained that years of ill treatment had led to her bold act:

> **"Having to take a certain section [on a bus] because of your race was humiliating, but having to stand up because a particular driver wanted to keep a white person from having to stand was, to my mind, most inhumane."**

After Parks's arrest, former NAACP leader E. D. Nixon organized an effort to use her case to challenge Montgomery's bus segregation law. Jo Ann Robinson, a local professor, organized a campaign to get African Americans to boycott the city bus system. This effort became known as the **Montgomery bus boycott**.

Martin Luther King Jr., his wife, Coretta, and their children

To help strengthen the boycott and coordinate their efforts, local African American leaders formed an organization that they called the **Montgomery Improvement Association**. They chose 26-year-old Baptist minister Martin Luther King Jr. to lead the association. King had a reputation as an inspiring speaker who could motivate listeners. In addition, he was new to town. The other members of the association thought that he might have less to lose from his participation in the protest.

reasons behind the boycotts they identified and their likelihood of success.

REVIEW

Linguistic, Visual-Spatial. Have students complete the Section Review questions. Then organize the class into groups and have each group create a detailed time line of one of the major topics described in the section. When the groups have finished, have them show and explain their time lines. Discuss how the time lines overlap and how various events affected each other.

ASSESS

Have students complete Daily Quiz 18.4

RETEACH

Logical-Mathematical, Visual-Spatial. Have students complete Main Idea Activities for Reteaching and Sheltered English 18.4. Then have them work in groups to create two political cartoons—one that illustrates the effects of the U.S. Supreme Court's *Brown* decision on Central High School, and one that shows the Court's effects in Montgomery. **SHELTERED ENGLISH**

A Community Effort

The majority of the city's African Americans supported the Montgomery bus boycott. They refused to ride the buses, depriving the system of about 70 percent of its regular passengers. Some sympathetic white citizens also supported the boycott. City buses were practically empty.

African American leaders established a carpool system to replace the buses. The community pitched in to help with the cost of gas and other items. Jo Ann Robinson explained why so many people supported the boycott: "I think people were fed up, they had reached the point that they knew there was no return."

After a 1956 Supreme Court ruling, companies began removing separate seating signs on buses.

The city of Montgomery refused to integrate its public transit system. Some white residents resorted to violence in their attempt to break the boycott. The homes of King and Nixon were bombed by people who wanted to maintain segregation. The boycott continued, however. It inspired similar protests in cities such as Birmingham, Alabama, and Tallahassee, Florida.

In November 1956 the U.S. Supreme Court ruled that Montgomery's segregated bus system was illegal. The victory brought Martin Luther King Jr. to the forefront of the civil rights movement. In 1957 King helped found the **Southern Christian Leadership Conference**, a group of ministers that helped lead the struggle for civil rights. The boycott victory also energized the black community. "We had won self-respect," Robinson remembered. "It . . . makes you feel that America is a great country and we're going to do more to make it greater."

SECTION 4 REVIEW

Identify and explain the significance of the following:

- **Committee on Civil Rights**
- **Thurgood Marshall**
- ***Brown* v. *Board of Education***
- **Little Rock Nine**
- **Rosa Parks**
- **Montgomery bus boycott**
- **Montgomery Improvement Association**
- **Martin Luther King Jr.**
- **Southern Christian Leadership Conference**

Reading for Content Understanding

1 **Main Idea** What effect did African American war veterans have on the early civil rights movement?

2 **Main Idea** What events led to school desegregation?

3 **Constitutional Heritage** How did African Americans use the court system to try to gain equal rights?

4 **Writing** *Informing* Imagine that you have played an important role in the Montgomery bus boycott. Civil rights supporters in another state have asked you to give a speech explaining why the Montgomery protest worked. Write a detailed outline of your speech.

5 **Critical Thinking** *Drawing Conclusions* How do you think the example of the Little Rock Nine affected other African Americans?

Chapter 18 Review ANSWERS

Identifying People and Ideas

1. president elected in 1952, who served during most of the 1950s

2. President Eisenhower's secretary of state who helped clarify the meaning of brinkmanship

3. policy pursued by the United States that attempted to control the outcome of Cold War crises by moving to the very brink of war

4. world's first satellite, launched by the Soviet Union in October 1957

5. suburb created by William Levitt in Pennsylvania

6. the large increase in the birthrate following World War II

7. comedian who starred in the television series *I Love Lucy*

8. the first nine African American students to attend Central High School in Little Rock, Arkansas, in 1957

9. African American woman who refused to give up her seat on a bus, which led to the Montgomery bus boycott

10. African American refusal to ride city buses; organized protest of segregation policies in Montgomery, Alabama

Using the Time Line

1. c
2. d
3. e
4. b
5. a

Understanding Main Ideas

1. He supported programs to help business and the economy, as well as some programs to meet citizens' basic needs.

Review and Assessment RESOURCES

PRINT
★ Chapter 18 Review, pp. 560–61
★ Vocabulary Activity 18
★ Chapter 18 Study Guide
★ Chapter 18 Test (Form A or B)

MULTIMEDIA
★ Audio Program, Ch. 18 (English and Spanish)
★ *Global Skill Builder CD–ROM*
★ Chapter 18 Test Generator
★ HRW Web site

SHELTERED ENGLISH
★ Spanish Glossary
★ Sheltered English Chapter 18 Test

ASSESS

Have students complete one of the Chapter 18 tests. As an alternate assessment, assign the Chapter 18 Investigation.

2. Under Eisenhower the United States used massive retaliation as a threat to communist countries and engaged in covert operations to overthrow communist governments.

3. new corporate structures increased the number of middle managers; growing service sector led to more clerical and sales jobs; more women entered the workforce; increased automation replaced some industrial workers

4. Beat authors criticized society with their unconventional writing and defiant behavior. Other writers criticized the conformity and materialism of American society. African American writers spoke out against racism.

5. voting discrimination; segregation in the armed forces, in public colleges and schools, and on public transportation

6. The Supreme Court ruled that Montgomery's segregated bus system was illegal.

Reviewing Themes

1. U.S. foreign policy—Nuclear weapons led to an arms race with the Soviet Union and provided the means for the U.S. foreign policies of massive retaliation and brinkmanship. Threats of nuclear war influenced the United States's decisions in various Cold War crises; American society—Many Americans feared a nuclear attack and built bomb shelters to protect themselves and their families. Some people also formed antinuclear groups to protest the arms race.

2. They had more money to buy consumer goods, such as automobiles; more of them bought houses in planned suburbs; and millions of middle-class families moved to the Sun Belt.

CHAPTER 18 REVIEW

Chapter Summary

The 1950s were a decade full of contrasts. Americans enjoyed peace, while the shadow of the Cold War hung over the United States. Many Americans moved to new suburbs and enjoyed prosperity. Some people objected to the emphasis on material success in American society. African Americans battled discrimination in courtrooms and communities with some success.

On a separate sheet of paper, complete the following activities.

Identifying People and Ideas

Describe the historical significance of the following:

1. Dwight D. Eisenhower
2. John Foster Dulles
3. brinkmanship
4. *Sputnik*
5. Levittown
6. baby boom
7. Lucille Ball
8. Little Rock Nine
9. Rosa Parks
10. Montgomery bus boycott

Internet Activity 

go.hrw.com
SB1 Suez Canal

Search the Internet through the HRW Web site to find information about the Suez Canal today. Use the information to create a "then and now" chart with information on the canal and the region in both 1956 and the present.

Understanding Main Ideas

1. What were President Eisenhower's main domestic policies?
2. How did the United States attempt to fight communism overseas?
3. What business trends affected workers during the 1950s?
4. How did some writers criticize American society during the 1950s?
5. What areas did African American civil rights leaders focus their reform efforts on in the 1950s?
6. What happened as a result of the Montgomery bus boycott?

Reviewing Themes

1. **Technology and Society** How did nuclear weapons affect U.S. foreign policy and American society during the Cold War?
2. **Economic Development** How did postwar prosperity affect the daily lives of many middle-class Americans?

Using the Time Line

Number your paper from 1 to 5. Match the letters on the time line below with the following events.

1. **Rosa Parks's arrest leads to the Montgomery bus boycott.**
2. **Federal troops enforce school desegregation in Little Rock, Arkansas.**
3. **The Soviet Union shoots down a U.S. U-2 spy plane.**
4. ***I Love Lucy* first appears on television.**
5. **An executive order integrates the U.S. military.**

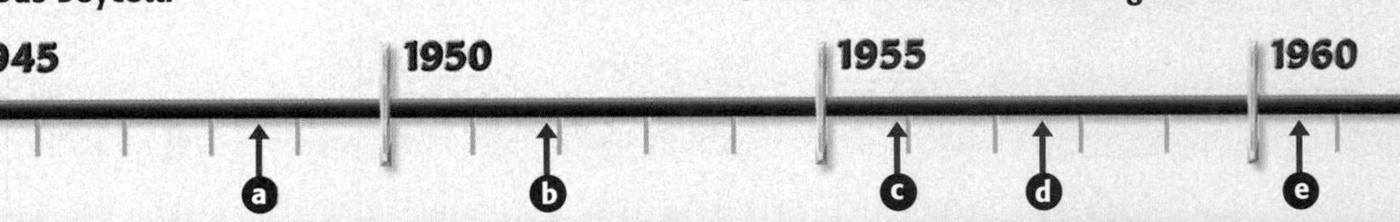

RETEACH

Visual-Spatial, Interpersonal. Organize students into groups and assign each group one of the chapter's sections. Have each group create a slide show of the main events in its section. Group members should find or create images for the slide show, decide the order in which to present them, and write a script to accompany them. Have each group present its show. **SHELTERED ENGLISH**

Using the Internet

Have students continue their research to examine how people's lives along the Suez Canal have changed. Then have each student write a short story about a person who has lived along the canal since 1956, and how that person's life has been affected by the changes.

Portfolio Extension

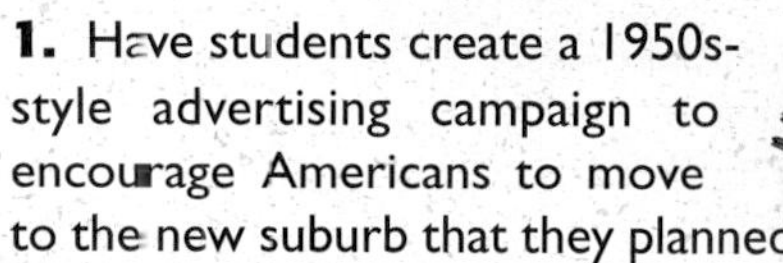

1. Have students create a 1950s-style advertising campaign to encourage Americans to move to the new suburb that they planned.

2. Have students write letters to their imaginary grandparents from the activity to explain how their actions have influenced civil rights.

3. **Constitutional Heritage** How did important court decisions affect African Americans' civil rights?

Thinking Critically

1. **Evaluating** What economic factors helped make the Montgomery bus boycott a success?
2. **Making Comparisons** How were the beats similar to and different from other writers who criticized society during the 1950s?
3. **Drawing Conclusions** Were U.S. efforts to halt the spread of communism in the 1950s successful? Explain your answer.

Writing About History

1. **Describing** Imagine that you are a newspaper reporter sent to Little Rock, Arkansas, in the fall of 1957. Write a feature story describing the events at Central High.
2. **Creating** Imagine that you work as a television editor in Hollywood during the late 1950s. Create a proposal for a comedy program set in a suburb.

Building Your Portfolio

Complete the following activities individually or in groups.

1. **Designing the Perfect Suburb** Imagine that you are an architect in a large downtown firm. Draw a plan or build a model for a new suburb just outside the city. Your plan should include designs for houses, streets, and community buildings. Include a brief paragraph explaining why people would want to live in your suburb.
2. **Fighting for Civil Rights** Imagine that you are the grandchild of a black World War II veteran who played an important role in the early civil rights movement. Create a scrapbook of the period to present to your grandparent at his or her birthday party. Your scrapbook might include photographs and captions, drawings, time lines, articles, interviews, and more.

Linking Geography and History

1. **Region** Why did many Americans move to the Sun Belt states?
2. **Human-Environment Interaction** How did the 1956 Highway Act change Americans' ability to travel?

History Skills Workshop

Reading Maps After petitioning for statehood for many years, the territories of Alaska and Hawaii became U.S. states in the late 1950s. Study the maps of Alaska and Hawaii below. Then answer the following questions: (a) On which dates did Alaska and Hawaii gain statehood? (b) Why was Alaska strategically important during the Cold War? (c) Approximately how far is Hawaii from the West Coast of the United States?

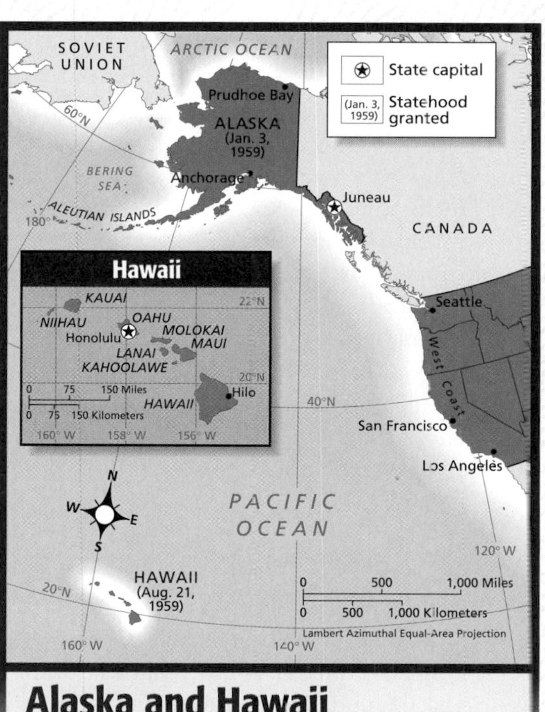

Alaska and Hawaii

3. Important court decisions, such as *Brown* v. *Board of Education*, denied that public schools could be both separate and equal, and made segregation illegal on some public transportation.

Thinking Critically

1. The loss of about 70 percent of its riders hurt the bus system, while people pitching in for gas helped the boycotters.

2. They were similar to other writers because they criticized American society; they were different in their unconventional writings, behavior, and lifestyle.

3. Answers will vary but students should consider the successful CIA covert operations as well as incidents where the United States took no action.

Writing About History

1. Stories will vary but students should describe the effect of the *Brown* decision, the efforts of the African American students, the response by white students, the need for the National Guard, and Eisenhower's decision to send in troops.

2. Proposals will vary but should refer to common elements of 1950s culture.

Linking Geography and History

1. The Sun Belt states offered new jobs, low taxes, and sunny and warm climates.

2. It enabled Americans to move to suburbs and increased business and personal travel.

History Skills Workshop

(a) Alaska—January 3, 1959; Hawaii—August 21, 1959; (b) It was close to the Soviet Union; (c) a little over 2,000 miles (4,000 kilometers)

TEACH

ALL LEVELS: Linguistic, Logical-Mathematical. (Suggested time: 45 min.) Ask students to reread the excerpt from the Truman Doctrine on page 514. Ask students to describe the historical background of the Truman Doctrine and to explain President Truman's purpose in issuing it. Then ask them to consider the audience that Truman was addressing. Next, ask students to identify words and phrases that show Truman's bias. Ask students to compare Truman's opinions with the textbook's coverage of the beginnings of the Cold War. Finally, have students write a paragraph showing how they would incorporate short quotations from the Truman Doctrine into a book on the beginnings of the Cold War.

SKILLS ANSWERS

1. They can illustrate the physical aspects of a culture, such as clothing or tools. The subject matter of paintings and photographs may also provide clues about what people, places, and events of the time that artists and photographers considered important to record.

2. both primary and secondary; consider whether the source is a firsthand account or a period illustration, photograph, or newspaper article.

3. Students' reports will vary depending on the topics they choose.

Understanding Primary Sources. For further practice, have students study the photograph of two soldiers on page 525. Ask them to look closely at the photograph and to write two questions about the Korean War that could be answered from the photograph. Then have students write two questions about the Korean War that could best be answered by a contemporary historian. Have volunteers discuss their questions with the class.

History Skills
WORKSHOP

Using Primary and Secondary Sources

There are many sources of firsthand historical information, including diaries, letters, editorials, and legal documents such as wills and titles. All of these are *primary sources.* Newspaper reports are also considered primary sources, even though they are generally written after an event has taken place. The same is true for personal memoirs and autobiographies, which are usually written late in a person's life. Paintings, photographs, and editorial cartoons that make up history's visual record are also primary sources. Because they provide an opportunity to learn how people felt and what they believed, primary sources are valuable historical tools.

Secondary sources are descriptions or interpretations of events written after the events have occurred, by persons who did not participate in or witness the events. History books, biographies, encyclopedias, and other reference works are examples of secondary sources. Writers of secondary sources have the advantage of knowing an event's long-term consequences. This knowledge helps shape writers' analyses.

How to Study Primary and Secondary Sources

1. **Study the material carefully** Consider the type of material. Is it verbal or visual? Is it based on firsthand information or on the accounts of others? Note the major ideas and supporting details.
2. **Consider the audience** Ask yourself: For whom was this message meant originally? Whether material was intended, for example, for the general public or for a specific, private audience may have influenced its style or content.
3. **Check for bias** Watch for words or phrases that signal a one-sided view of a person or event.
4. **When possible, compare sources** Study more than one source on a topic if you can. Comparing sources gives you a more complete, balanced account.

Practicing the Skill

1. How can you use paintings and photographs as primary sources?
2. What kinds of sources are available on the Internet? How can you distinguish between primary and secondary sources on Web sites?
3. Select a topic from Unit 6. Write a brief report using at least two primary sources and two secondary sources. Create a bibliography and explain why each source is considered a primary or a secondary source.

ALL LEVELS: Linguistic, Logical-Mathematical, Visual-Spatial. (Suggested time: 45 min.) Have each group create a time line to add to its scrapbook. The top half of the time line should include the date and a brief annotation for each item in the scrapbook. Students should then use their textbook to add at least 15 significant dates in the history of the Cold War to the bottom half of their time lines. Any connections between a scrapbook item and a historical event should be mentioned in the annotation for the item. Remind students to make their time lines visually appealing. Encourage students to color code the scrapbook items and historical events by categories such as Armed Conflicts, Politics, Popular Culture, or Technology. Have volunteers share their time lines with the class.

History in Action

UNIT 6 PORTFOLIO

American History

A Cold War Scrapbook

Complete the following activity in small, cooperative groups.

You and the members of your group will be researching and creating items to be included in a Cold War Scrapbook. Each group member will be responsible for five scrapbook items. All of these items must be primary sources. Each group member will then write a paragraph using the information from the primary sources. This paragraph must be an unbiased account of the Cold War events discussed in the primary source documents. As a group, you will need to decide on which aspects of the Cold War each group member should focus.

Materials To complete this activity, you will need butcher paper, posterboard, construction paper, and various art materials, such as pens, pencils, paper, twine, glue, paints, or cloth for creating scrapbook items.

Parts of the Project To create your scrapbook, complete the following tasks:

1. **Research** Conduct research to locate primary sources relating to the Cold War. These sources might include diaries, letters, newspaper articles, photographs, quotes, or speeches. Use your textbook and library resources to find your sources. Be sure to include sources from a variety of media.

2. **Writing** When you have finished with your research, each group member should use information from the sources to write a one-paragraph account of the events represented. However, your account must be factually accurate and unbiased. You may need to use your textbook for additional information and to help you identify bias. You also need to write captions for your scrapbook items. In addition, one or two members of the group will be responsible for writing (and typing, if possible) a table of contents and an introduction for the scrapbook.

3. **Presentation** One or two group members will be responsible for putting the scrapbook together. For the layout, students should consider the visual impact. Use a variety of shapes and colors on each page. The other group members will make a cover for the scrapbook.

Display your group's finished scrapbook for the class. Have one member of your group read his or her paragraph aloud. Ask the class to identify some differences in opinion and bias between the paragraph and the primary sources.

Students use a variety of materials and sources to create a scrapbook.

Research. Encourage groups to assign each member a time period, presidential administration, or category—such as Armed Conflicts or Popular Culture—in order to get a good variety of scrapbook items. Remind students to include both written and visual material.

Writing. As students are writing the captions for each scrapbook item, encourage them to point out any discrepancies between the primary and secondary sources. In their captions students can suggest reasons for the discrepancies.

Presentation. Encourage students to lay out each page using the colors, type styles, and design elements that were popular during the time period of each scrapbook item. Popular magazines from the appropriate time period can be a useful source for this information.

Introducing UNIT 7

CHAPTER 19
The Sixties

In 1960 John F. Kennedy became president of the United States and launched the New Frontier. He faced foreign-policy challenges, including the Cuban missile crisis. After Kennedy was assassinated, Lyndon B. Johnson became president. Johnson promoted civil rights and policies to help the poor. He also increased the U.S. military presence in South Vietnam. At home, many young people rebelled against traditional society.

CHAPTER 20
The Search for Equal Rights

African Americans struggled to achieve desegregation and voting rights through boycotts, protests, and sit-ins. Important leaders of the civil rights movement included Martin Luther King Jr. and Malcolm X. Hispanics in the United States also fought discrimination and worked to increase Hispanic cultural pride. Many women worked to achieve equal rights. Congress passed the Equal Rights Amendment, but opponents prevented it

Internet Activity

The Free-Speech Movement. Have students search the Internet through the HRW Web site to find more information about the free-speech movement at the University of California at Berkeley. Have each student create a sign that a demonstrator might have carried at a campus rally. The sign's message should either support or oppose the free-speech movement. Remind students that their signs should reflect the main issues of the movement.

go.hrw.com
SB1 Free Speech

UNIT 7 Searching for Solutions (1945–1978)

CHAPTER 19 **The Sixties** (1960–1969)

CHAPTER 20 **The Search for Equal Rights** (1960–1978)

CHAPTER 21 **War in Vietnam** (1945–1975)

from being ratified. American Indians challenged federal policies that affected them. Americans with disabilities organized to fight discrimination and increase their accessibility to public facilities.

CHAPTER 21
War in Vietnam

As the North Vietnamese fought to reunify their country, President Kennedy continued to support the corrupt, anticommunist government of South Vietnam. President Johnson increased U.S. participation in the war. As U.S. casualties rose and it became clear that U.S. leaders had been deceptive about the progress of the war, public support for the war eroded. Under President Richard Nixon, in 1973 the United States announced a cease-fire and withdrew its troops from Vietnam.

UNIT MOTIVATOR

Ask students to remember a time when they questioned, or witnessed someone else questioning, the traditional way of doing things. Have students write a brief description of the situation, along with the reaction to and the results of the challenge. Ask students how these types of challenges have affected American society. Tell students that in this unit they will learn about many Americans who demanded changes during the 1960s.

American Teens
IN HISTORY
Young Politicians

During the 1960s many American teenagers became interested in political issues. Some participated in civil rights protests and free-speech movements. Other teenagers became involved in the U.S. political process.

Some teenagers received experience as politicians at special programs in Washington, D.C. For example, the American Legion sponsored programs for teen leaders from each state. Participants visited sites in the nation's capital. Delegates met with U.S. senators and in some cases the president.

In the late 1960s high school student Susan Collins participated in the William Randolph Hearst Foundation's Senate Youth Program. She visited the office of Margaret Chase Smith, a Republican senator from Maine. According to Collins,

> *"I remember leaving her office thinking that women can do anything, and that women can get to the highest level of government and make a real difference."*

Bill Clinton, a Boys Nation delegate from Arkansas, shakes hands with President John F. Kennedy in July 1963.

Their experience in Washington inspired many teenagers to seek political office in later years. Teenagers participated in other educational programs designed to introduce them to politics and leadership roles.

Other teenagers became involved in local politics. Some participated on junior city councils. In the mid-1960s Bob Torricelli became the youngest person ever elected as junior mayor of Franklin Lakes, New Jersey. He was 14 years old. In 1996 Torricelli was elected a U.S. senator.

Many teenagers campaigned for local and national candidates even though they were too young to vote. High school student Hillary Rodham was a "Goldwater Girl." She campaigned for Senator Barry Goldwater, the Republican presidential candidate in 1964.

For many teenagers in the 1960s these activities represented just one of the many ways they became active in politics. In this unit you will learn more about how young Americans helped bring about great changes in society. You will also learn about U.S. involvement in Vietnam and the role of young people in the war.

LEFT PAGE: *U.S. astronaut Edwin "Buzz" Aldrin on the moon in July 1969*

Using Visual Resources

Walking on the Moon. On July 20, 1969, U.S. astronauts Neil Armstrong and Edwin "Buzz" Aldrin Jr. became the first people to walk on the surface of the moon. Aldrin and Armstrong planted an American flag on an area of the moon called the Sea of Tranquillity. They collected nearly 50 pounds of lunar samples to bring back to Earth for further study, set up a television camera, and installed scientific instruments. Armstrong and Aldrin were also able to describe their experiences to the millions of people listening on Earth.

Activity: Allow students time to study the photograph on the opposite page. Then have them make a list of questions about the photograph (e.g., *Who took the picture? Of what is the flag made?*). Instruct students to use the library or other resources to answer at least three of their questions.

TEACH

ALL LEVELS: Visual-Spatial, Interpersonal. (Suggested time: 40 min.) Read to students the time line entry about the capital of Brazil being moved to the planned city of Brasília in 1960. Then ask students to imagine that they have been chosen to design a new capital city for the United States. Organize the students into four groups. Each group will prepare and present a design for the new capital. Students should consider where to locate the new capital, decide what buildings and facilities will be needed, and include a theme or symbol that will be reflected in the design of the new capital.

ALL LEVELS: Kinesthetic, Visual-Spatial. (Suggested time: 45 min.) Discuss with students how the United States celebrated its bicentennial in 1976. Ask students to study U.S. events on the time line and to choose one that they would have wanted to have commemorated in a bicentennial parade. Have each student design a float to showcase his or her chosen event. Encourage the class to create a bulletin board that displays their floats in chronological order.

Cultural Diversity

Jackie Robinson and Happy Chandler. In 1947 Major League Baseball's commissioner was Albert B. "Happy" Chandler, a former governor of Kentucky. Baseball team owners had voted against Brooklyn Dodgers general manager Branch Rickey from signing Jackie Robinson. Commissioner Chandler, however, overrode their objections and supported integration. Chandler was fired in March 1951, partly because of his support for desegregation of the major league.

Critical Thinking: Why might Chandler and Rickey have wanted to integrate the major league?

Answer: Answers will vary but students may mention that the two men felt it was the right thing to do or that they believed the league would profit from the addition of new, skilled players.

Time Line: 1945–1978

UNIT 7 Searching for Solutions

UNITED STATES

1947 Jackie Robinson becomes the first African American to play in major league baseball.

Jackie Robinson

George Nelson's marshmallow sofa

1955 Americans Charles Eames, Florence Knoll, and George Nelson are among the pioneers of furniture design.

1958 Americans buy more than 25 million hula hoops, but the fad ends quickly.

Peace Corps logo

1961 President John F. Kennedy establishes the Peace Corps. Many Americans will volunteer to assist other countries in development projects.

1945 | 1948 | 1951 | 1954 | 1957 | 1960

WORLD

1945 George Orwell's novel *Animal Farm,* a political fable based on the story of the Russian Revolution, is published.

1948 The National Party gains control in South Africa and introduces its policy of apartheid.

Godzilla

1954 The Japanese movie *Gojira* (or *Godzilla* in the United States) features a dinosaur-like monster, created as a result of nuclear weapons testing.

1960 The capital of Brazil is moved from Rio de Janeiro to the planned city of Brasília. Architects designed the shape of the city to resemble an airplane or a bird.

Cathedral of Brasília

CHALLENGE AND EXTEND

1. **Linguistic, Logical-Mathematical.** Have students use the library or other resources to find more information about the Peace Corps. Have them research the agency's history and its current membership and major projects. Then have students use their research to write a public service announcement that highlights the major contributions of the Peace Corps and encourages Americans to join. Have volunteers read their announcements to the class.

2. **Linguistic, Logical-Mathematical.** Tell students about the Nobel Peace Prize. Have students use the library or other resources to find information about the winners of this award during the period the time line covers (1945–1978). Have students create a Nobel Peace Prize time line that names the person or people who won the prize each year. In addition, have students write brief annotations giving the reason for each award. As a class, discuss which award recipients students found to be the most interesting or the most important.

The Lincoln Memorial

Ms. magazine covers

A bicentennial pitcher

Beatles' harmonica box

South Vietnamese medal

USING THE TIME LINE

1. Which entries on the time line represent cultural or artistic events?
2. Which entries on the time line are related to civil rights?

Activity Using the entries listed on Unit 7 Time Line, create a new time line. Illustrate the time line with new images. These images should represent the entries without images on the Unit 7 Time Line. Use images from newspapers, magazines, or books or create drawings. Write captions for the new images, questions for the new time line and a new time-line activity.

Daily Life

Women's Magazines. In her book *The Feminine Mystique* Betty Friedan points out that many women's magazines of the late 1950s overwhelmingly focused on women as homemakers. In 1970 a group of feminists led by author Susan Brownmiller went into the offices of the *Ladies' Home Journal* to demand change. In 1972 Gloria Steinem launched *Ms.*, an independent feminist magazine. Steinem wrote for and edited the magazine for the next 15 years.

Critical Thinking: If you had been with the group who protested at the offices of the *Ladies' Home Journal*, what changes might you have demanded? If you had been the editor of the *Ladies' Home Journal*, how might you have responded?

ANSWER: Answers will vary but students might mention demanding articles about a wider range of women and responding by offering to do a special feature or issue on some of the topics proposed by the protesters.

USING THE TIME LINE ANSWERS

1. *Animal Farm;* Beatlemania; Brasília; Godzilla; hula hoops; pioneer furniture design
2. apartheid; Jackie Robinson; March on Washington; *Ms.* magazine

CHAPTER PLANNING GUIDE

The Sixties

	SECTION LESSON OBJECTIVES	PRINT RESOURCES	MULTIMEDIA RESOURCES	SHELTERED ENGLISH RESOURCES
Section 1: Kennedy and the Nation (pp. 569–72)	★ Identify important elements in the 1960 presidential campaign. ★ Explain how John F. Kennedy's presidency inspired young Americans. ★ Describe the advances and setbacks of Kennedy's domestic programs.	★ Guided Reading Strategies 19.1 ★ Literature Reading 19: First Lady Jacqueline Kennedy ★ Primary Source Reading 19: Kennedy's Inaugural Address ★ Section 1 Review, p. 572 ★ Daily Quiz 19.1	★ *Teaching Resources CD–ROM*, Lesson 19.1	★ Main Idea Activities for Reteaching and Sheltered English 19.1
Section 2: Kennedy's Foreign Policy (pp. 573–77)	★ Explain why President Kennedy developed a new Cold War strategy. ★ Evaluate the impact of the Bay of Pigs invasion and the Berlin Wall on Kennedy's administration. ★ Identify the causes of the Cuban missile crisis.	★ Guided Reading Strategies 19.2 ★ Section 2 Review, p. 577 ★ Daily Quiz 19.2	★ *Teaching Resources CD–ROM*, Lesson 19.2	★ Main Idea Activities for Reteaching and Sheltered English 19.2
Section 3: The Johnson Administration (pp. 578–82)	★ Discuss the public's reaction to President Kennedy's assassination. ★ Identify ways in which President Johnson's domestic programs helped many Americans. ★ Describe Johnson's approach to foreign policy.	★ Guided Reading Strategies 19.3 ★ Biography Reading 19: Henry B. Gonzales ★ Section 3 Review, p. 582 ★ Daily Quiz 19.3	★ *Teaching Resources CD–ROM*, Lesson 19.3 ★ HRW Web site	★ Main Idea Activities for Reteaching and Sheltered English 19.3
Section 4: New Movements in America (pp. 583–87)	★ Identify reasons students protested in the 1960s. ★ Describe some aspects of the counterculture. ★ Explain how art and music reflected changes in culture.	★ Guided Reading Strategies 19.4 ★ Section 4 Review, p. 587 ★ Daily Quiz 19.4	★ *Teaching Resources CD–ROM*, Lesson 19.4 ★ *American Music Audio CD Program:* "Blowin' in the Wind" ★ Art in American History Transparency 39: *Return of the Prodigal Son* and Transparency 46: *Moonwalk* ★ Everyday Life in America Transparency 29: The Woodstock Nation, 1960s ★ HRW Web site	★ Main Idea Activities for Reteaching and Sheltered English 19.4
Section 5: Science in the 1960s (pp. 588–91)	★ Identify President Kennedy's goal for the U.S. space program. ★ Explain the applications of space technology for daily life. ★ Describe how scientific advances raised environmental concerns.	★ Guided Reading Strategies 19.5 ★ Geography Activity 19: The Space Race ★ Graphic Organizer 19: Foreign Policy and Domestic Strife ★ Section 5 Review, p. 591 ★ Daily Quiz 19.5	★ *Teaching Resources CD–ROM*, Lesson 19.5 ★ *American History Simulations CD–ROM:* Race to the Moon	★ Main Idea Activities for Reteaching and Sheltered English 19.5
Chapter Review and Assessment (pp. 592–93)		★ Chapter 19 Review, pp. 592–93 ★ Vocabulary Activity 19 ★ Chapter 19 Study Guide ★ Chapter 19 Test (Form A or B)	★ Audio Program, Ch. 19 (English and Spanish) ★ *Global Skill Builder CD–ROM* ★ Chapter 19 Test Generator ★ HRW Web site	★ Spanish Glossary ★ Sheltered English Chapter 19 Test

CHAPTER OVERVIEW

The 1960s were years of social and political unrest in the United States. The Kennedy administration had to deal with several Cold War crises, such as the presence of nuclear missiles in Cuba and the construction of the Berlin Wall. Competition with the Soviet Union also prompted the space race, which led to the 1969 moon landing.

In 1963 President Kennedy was assassinated. Vice President Lyndon B. Johnson took command and tried to remain true to Kennedy's goals. Johnson initiated a War on Poverty and pushed many of his Great Society reforms through Congress. On the international front, Johnson escalated the U.S. military involvement in Vietnam and opposed communist aggression.

The 1960s led many young people to rebel. Some rebelled through the student movement, which protested government actions and rigid school policies. Others rebelled by becoming part of the counterculture, which separated itself from mainstream society by its use of new clothing, hair styles, and new forms of music and art.

The 1960s also was a period of scientific and technological advances. Space research led to advances in satellites, which improved communications, weather forecasts, and the ability to spy on other countries. Scientists also learned of new hazards, such as the dangers of DDT.

CHAPTER INVESTIGATION

The Chapter Investigation is an extended, multipart activity designed for students to work cooperatively and apply the chapter content in the creation of a project. You may choose to use the Chapter 19 Investigation, The Sixties, either as a substitute for teaching the section lessons or as an alternate assessment.

BLOCK SCHEDULING

The teacher lesson plans for each section offer a variety of activity choices to help you present the material in a block scheduling format. For further suggestions on block scheduling, see the *Block Scheduling Handbook with Team Teaching Strategies*, pp. 109–14.

Meeting Individual Needs

ABILITY LEVELS

LEVEL 1 Basic level activities designed for all students encountering new material.

LEVEL 2 Intermediate level activities designed for average students.

LEVEL 3 Challenging activities designed for above-average students.

SHELTERED ENGLISH These activities address the needs of students with Limited English Proficiency.

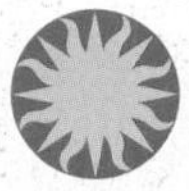

Smithsonian Institution®

Internet Connections and Lesson 19
www.si.edu/hrw

CNN Presents America:
Yesterday and Today 1850 to the Present
Segment: Reaching for the Moon

Additional Resources

Books for Teachers

Berman, Paul. *A Tale of Two Utopias: The Political Journey of the Generation of 1968*. Norton, 1996. Captures the idealism and confusion of the turbulent 1960s.

Califano, Joseph A. Jr. *The Triumph and Tragedy of Lyndon Johnson: The White House Years*. Simon & Schuster, 1991. A portrait of Johnson during his presidency, by one of his closest domestic advisors.

May, Ernest R., and Philip D. Zelikow, eds. *The Kennedy Tapes: Inside the White House During the Cuban Missile Crisis*. Belknap Press, 1997. Provides transcripts and analysis of the taped recordings made in the Oval Office during the Cuban missile crisis.

Books for Students

Archer, Jules. *The Incredible Sixties: The Stormy Years That Changed America*. Harcourt Brace, 1986. Begins with Kent State and moves backward to cover the Kennedy years, the civil rights movement, Vietnam, feminism, and other elements of the counterculture (for students reading below grade level).

Griffiths, John C. *The Cuban Missile Crisis*. Rourke, 1987. Chronicles events leading up to the Cuban missile crisis.

Haskins, James, and Kathleen Benson. *The Sixties Reader*. Viking, 1988. Uses primary sources to outline the 1960s.

Multimedia Materials

At the Brink. Video, 60 min. WGBH/Boston. Examines events leading up to the Cuban missile crisis and the confrontation between Kennedy and Khrushchev.

Making Sense of the Sixties: Breaking Boundaries, Testing Limits. Video, 60 min. PBS. Study of 1960s youth rebellion and counterculture.

The Sixties. Video, 15 min. Phoenix BFA Films & Video Inc. Brief review of the political and social movements of the 1960s.

The Sixties

CHAPTER MOTIVATOR

Locate and play a protest song from the 1960s. Then ask students to speculate on some social changes people sought during the decade. List students' replies on the chalkboard and give students ample time to explain their reasoning. Next, ask students to speculate on what barriers people might have had to overcome to make the changes listed.

Then tell students that in this chapter they will learn about changes that occurred in American society during the 1960s, and about the tensions and conflicts that arose in response to these changes. Finally, play the recording a second time and ask students to focus on the mood of the song. Tell them to keep this mood in mind as they read the chapter.

THEMES

Presenting Themes

- **Global Relations** Students might mention that one country's act of aggression or human rights abuses might bring two nations to the brink of war.
- **Economic Development** Students might mention that a government could provide job training and educational opportunities, create programs to aid the poor, and try to improve employment opportunities by adopting policies designed to spur growth in the nation's industries.
- **Citizenship and Democracy** Students might mention that groups can use protests, educational campaigns, and boycotts. They can submit petitions for new laws, initiate letter-writing campaigns, publish pamphlets, hold rallies, and participate in politics.

Using the Time Line

Have students discuss which events in the time line might have had positive or negative results on the lives of Americans. After students complete the chapter, have them write a brief description of the ways in which each of these events changed Americans' lives.

CHAPTER 19

The Sixties

(1960–1969)

For many people, Bob Dylan's song "The Times They Are A-Changin'" captured the spirit of the 1960s:

> "Come mothers and fathers
> Throughout the land
> And don't criticize
> What you can't understand
> Your sons and your daughters
> Are beyond your command
> Your old road is
> Rapidly agin'.
> Please get out of the new one
> If you can't lend your hand
> For the times they are a-changin'."

Global Relations
What events might bring countries close to waging a nuclear war?

Economic Development
How might a government increase citizens' economic opportunities?

Citizenship and Democracy
In what ways might a group work to change society?

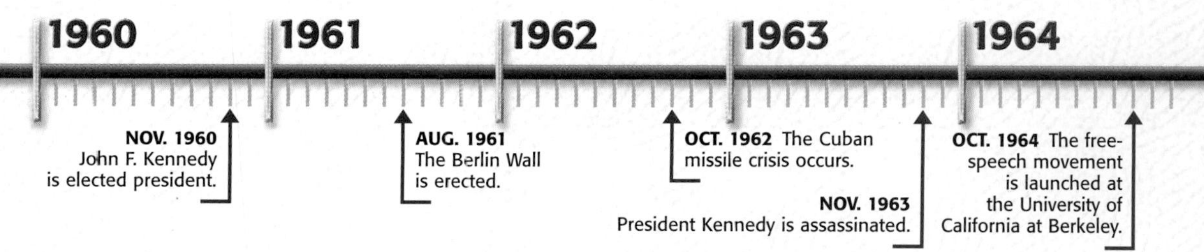

OBJECTIVES

- Identify important elements in the 1960 presidential campaign.
- Explain how John F. Kennedy's presidency inspired young Americans.
- Describe the advances and setbacks of Kennedy's domestic programs.

FOCUS

Motivate Before Reading

Have students read Primary Source Reading 19: Kennedy's Inaugural Address. Ask students to speculate on Kennedy's concept of the New Frontier. Follow up by asking them to predict the types of legislation Kennedy might sponsor and the domestic issues he might consider important. Make a list of these predictions and encourage students to explain their reasoning.

Kennedy and the Nation

Reading Focus

What were some of the important elements in the 1960 presidential campaign?

How did John F. Kennedy's presidency inspire young Americans?

What advances and setbacks did Kennedy's domestic programs face?

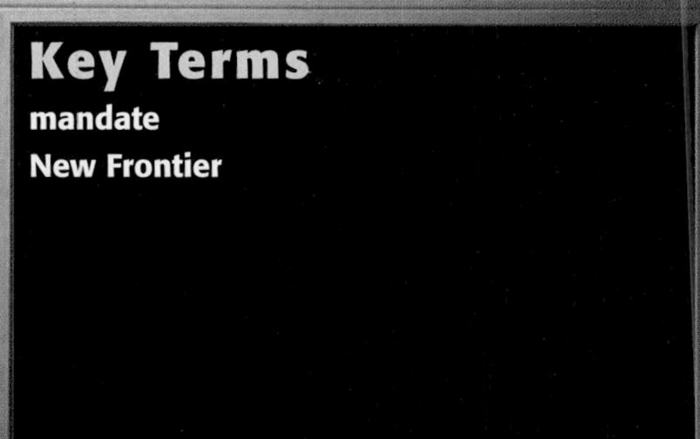

Key Terms

mandate

New Frontier

ON THE EVENING OF SEPTEMBER 26, 1960, American viewers watched the first-ever televised debate between presidential candidates. Looking at their television screens, most Americans saw John F. Kennedy as calm and confident. He seemed comfortable in front of the cameras. Richard Nixon appeared tense and sweaty, with a tight smile. "As the moderator signed off," one Kennedy adviser remembered, "our small band erupted in cheers. . . . It was over! We had won! Not just the debate. We had won the election!" Even Kennedy admitted, "We wouldn't have had a prayer without that gadget [television]." The prediction proved true in November, when Americans turned to Kennedy to lead the nation in the 1960s.

Campaign pins from the 1960 presidential election

IMAGE ON LEFT PAGE: *John F. Kennedy arrives in Los Angeles for the Democratic National Convention.*

1965 | **1966** | **1967** | **1968** | **1969**

JULY 1965 President Johnson signs Medicare into law.

SEPT. 1966 The National Traffic and Motor Vehicle Safety Act is signed into law.

JULY 1969 U.S. astronauts walk on the moon.

AUG. 1969 More than 400,000 people attend the Woodstock Music and Art Fair.

Section 1 RESOURCES

PRINT

- ★ Guided Reading Strategies 19.1
- ★ Literature Reading 19: First Lady Jacqueline Kennedy
- ★ Primary Source Reading 19: Kennedy's Inaugural Address
- ★ Section 1 Review, p. 572
- ★ Daily Quiz 19.1

MULTIMEDIA

- ★ *Teaching Resources CD–ROM,* Lesson 19.1

SHELTERED ENGLISH

- ★ Main Idea Activities for Reteaching and Sheltered English 19.1

Introduce Key Terms

Linguistic, Visual-Spatial. Review this section's key terms with students. Then have each student create drawings illustrating the terms' meanings. **SHELTERED ENGLISH**

TEACH

Have students read Section 1 and complete Guided Reading Strategies 19.1. Choose one or more of the following activities to explore the section content with students. For further suggestions on block scheduling or team teaching, see the *Block Scheduling Handbook*.

LEVEL 1: Linguistic. (Suggested time: 15 min.) As a class, go over students' Guided Reading Strategies. Then use the Reading Focus questions to highlight the main ideas of the section. **SHELTERED ENGLISH**

ALL LEVELS: Logical-Mathematical, Visual-Spatial. (Suggested time: 30 min.) Have students evaluate each issue in Kennedy's domestic policy as either a success or failure. Then have them draw a scale (balance) and place the successes on the left side and the failures on the right. Tell students to have the scale lean to one side to show whether they think his overall domestic policy was a success or a failure. **SHELTERED ENGLISH**

Across the Curriculum

MATH

The Electoral College. In the 1960 presidential election, both candidates focused on the seven states with the most electoral votes: California, Illinois, Michigan, New York, Ohio, Pennsylvania, and Texas. Kennedy added Massachusetts and New Jersey to his target list. He also chose a southern running mate to boost his support in the South, with its 166 electoral votes. Nixon chose a running mate from Kennedy's home state, Massachusetts, in hopes of winning its 16 electoral votes. After the election, Kennedy had won 101 of the southern votes and all his target states except California and Ohio.

Critical Thinking: Use the map to determine how many more electoral votes Kennedy needed beyond those he won in the South and in his target states to reach 269, the minimum number he needed to win the election.

ANSWER: 27 (IL) + 20 (MI) + 45 (NY) + 32 (PA) + 16 (MA) + 16 (NJ) + 101 (southern votes) = 257; 269 − 257 = 12

MAP ANSWER
New York

The Election of 1960

This carriage was part of a parade in Cookeville, Tennessee, in support of Kennedy's campaign.

Many Americans considered the presidential election of 1960 to be an opportunity for change. The Republican Party nominated Richard Nixon. During his service as vice president in the 1950s, Nixon made his reputation as a conservative anticommunist. In 1960 he declared himself to be a "new Nixon." He promised to focus on domestic and economic reforms if elected president. Nixon chose United Nations ambassador and former senator Henry Cabot Lodge of Massachusetts as his running mate.

The Democratic Party nominated Massachusetts senator John F. Kennedy, a moderate on most issues. He chose Texan Lyndon B. Johnson, the Senate majority leader, as his running mate. During the campaign, Kennedy argued that the economy had stalled. He promised to make changes and to "get the country moving again."

Kennedy and Nixon differed little on issues. However, Kennedy had the advantage of style, as demonstrated by his success in the televised debates. Kennedy was only four years younger than Nixon, but he appeared youthful and energetic on camera. In contrast, Nixon seemed tired and unsure of himself. Referring to Kennedy, one young voter said: "The idea that this guy, who looked like your cool older brother might be President . . . was . . . really exciting."

Early in the campaign, some people raised questions about Kennedy's religion. These critics argued that as a Catholic, Kennedy might allow the pope to influence his political decisions. Kennedy answered these charges in a speech:

> **"I am a Catholic, but . . . does that mean that I can't be president of the United States? I'm able to serve in Congress and my brother was able to give his life [in World War II], but we can't be president? . . . I will not allow any pope or church to dictate to the president of the United States."**

Kennedy's speech quieted many people's doubts about the role his religion would play in his presidency.

Another boost to Kennedy's campaign came from one short telephone call. Civil rights leader Martin Luther King Jr. was in a

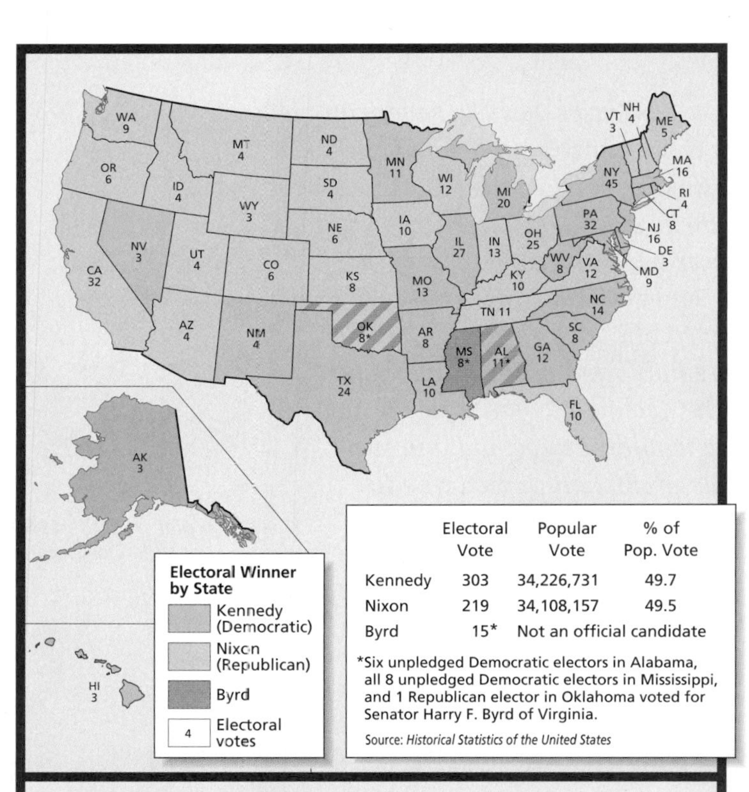

	Electoral Vote	Popular Vote	% of Pop. Vote
Kennedy	303	34,226,731	49.7
Nixon	219	34,108,157	49.5
Byrd	15*	Not an official candidate	

*Six unpledged Democratic electors in Alabama, all 8 unpledged Democratic electors in Mississippi, and 1 Republican elector in Oklahoma voted for Senator Harry F. Byrd of Virginia.

Source: *Historical Statistics of the United States*

The Election of 1960

Learning from Maps The election of 1960 was very close, but John F. Kennedy won the presidency.

Place Which state gave Kennedy the largest number of electoral votes?

LEVEL 3: Linguistic, Logical-Mathematical. (Suggested time: 45 min. plus homework) For homework, have students write an essay explaining why Kennedy won the 1960 presidential election and why his presidency inspired young people. In class, call on volunteers to read their essays. Encourage discussion.

CLOSE

Linguistic, Logical-Mathematical. Remind students of their predictions about the New Frontier, from the Motivate activity. Have each student write a summary indicating which predictions proved accurate and which proved inaccurate.

CHALLENGE AND EXTEND

TEACHER TO TEACHER

Visual-Spatial, Intrapersonal. Nancy Hammond of Montclair, Virginia, suggested the following activity: Have students use the library and other resources to research the results of the 1960 presidential election. Then ask students to create charts showing, for each state and the nation, the amount of support each candidate received from various age, income, racial, and special interest groups. Next, have students examine, for each state and the nation,

Georgia jail for participating in a protest. Kennedy, who had not met King or his wife, Coretta Scott King, called Mrs. King to offer support. King was released but never publicly endorsed Kennedy. One of his aides, however, told a crowd celebrating King's release to "take off your Nixon buttons." Kennedy won about 70 percent of the African American vote.

This support proved important in one of the closest elections of the 1900s. On election day in November 1960, Kennedy won the popular vote by less than 120,000 votes out of more than 68 million cast. This narrow victory did not give Kennedy a clear **mandate**, or public support, for his plans.

The Kennedy Era

At age 43, John F. Kennedy was the youngest person ever elected president. His youthful image helped to define a new era. The media focused attention on Kennedy's family, particularly his elegant wife, Jacqueline, and their two young children.

The Kennedys brought a sense of style and glamour to the White House. They invited many famous artists, musicians, and writers there. The first lady was an enthusiastic supporter of the arts. She believed, "Whoever lives in the White House must preserve its traditions, enhance it, and leave something of herself there." As a result of her efforts, Congress passed new legislation declaring the mansion's furnishings to be property of the White House. Presidents could no longer give away china, furniture, or other property as gifts.

First Lady Jacqueline Kennedy shows television viewers the White House. She called it "a showcase of American art and history."

President Kennedy saw his inauguration as "a celebration of freedom."

Scenes of President Kennedy playing sports contributed to his image of youth and strength. In reality, he suffered from many health problems. "At least one half of the days he spent on this earth were days of intense physical pain," his brother Robert recalled. In addition to serious back problems, Kennedy suffered from Addison's disease, an often fatal ailment. Few Americans knew of Kennedy's illnesses.

Kennedy's New Frontier

President Kennedy assembled a group of highly educated advisers who were active in a variety of causes. The press nicknamed this group "the best and the brightest." Many of Kennedy's advisers were admirers of the New Deal. They believed in using government to bring about positive reform.

In his inaugural address, Kennedy announced a set of domestic- and foreign-policy proposals he called the **New Frontier**. He asked Americans to work for freedom and justice throughout the world:

> **"And so, my fellow Americans—ask not what your country can do for you—ask what you can do for your country. My fellow citizens of the world—ask not what America will do for you but what together we can do for freedom of man."**

Kennedy's call inspired many young people to become involved in reform movements and to enter public service.

Historical Sidelight

A President's Public Image. President Kennedy, who had Addison's disease, was not the first president to hide a serious physical ailment from the public. Woodrow Wilson suffered a serious stroke in 1919 that left him close to death for some weeks. During this time, his wife and doctor hid the full extent of his illness from the public and even from many government officials. Franklin Roosevelt had limited use of the lower part of his body as a result of polio. The press cooperated in shielding the extent of his disability from the American people. His public appearances were arranged to show his vibrant personality and to highlight the upper part of his body.

Critical Thinking: Why might presidents hide physical illnesses or disabilities from the public?

ANSWER: Students might mention that the public could lose confidence in an unwell president, and that their knowledge of the condition could hurt the leader politically.

the number of popular and electoral votes each candidate received. Then have students discuss their findings and whether they support the electoral college system.

REVIEW

Linguistic, Logical-Mathematical. Have students complete the Section Review questions. Then ask students to write a summary of this section, but leave blanks for key names, terms, and events. Have students exchange summaries, fill in the blanks, and return them to their authors for grading.

ASSESS

Have students complete Daily Quiz 19.1.

RETEACH

Visual-Spatial. Have students complete Main Idea Activities for Reteaching and Sheltered English 19.1. Then ask students to create three political cartoons: one about the 1960 presidential election, one about the Kennedy Era, and one about Kennedy's domestic policies. Call on volunteers to explain their cartoons. SHELTERED ENGLISH

Section 1 Review ANSWERS

Identify
For significance, see the following pages:

- John F. Kennedy, p. 570
- Jacqueline Kennedy, p. 571
- mandate, p. 571
- New Frontier, p. 571

Reading for Content Understanding

1. the candidates' appearances on a televised presidential debate; Kennedy's youthful appearance and style; Kennedy's religion; the African American community's support of Kennedy

2. successes—increases in people entering public service; raise in the minimum wage; and federal funds for improving urban areas, education, and mental health facilities; failures—difficulties with business and congressional leaders; many proposed laws not passed

3. His youthfulness, style, and calls for action inspired many young people to become involved in reform movements and public service.

4. Columns will vary but could say that the candidate who appeared most youthful and at ease on television appealed more to many voters, particularly younger voters.

5. Answers will vary but students might mention that Kennedy's speech implied that he would be giving to his country, which inspired idealism and public service; students' responses will vary but should be explained and consistent with the facts.

Conflict with the Steel Industry

One goal of the New Frontier was to improve the economy. A slight economic decline in the late 1950s caused many Americans to worry that the prosperity of the postwar era was over. In 1961 the economy improved slightly—largely because of increased defense spending. However, the next year unemployment rose again, reaching about 7 percent. Kennedy took steps to lower inflation and reduce unemployment. He proposed a series of voluntary wage and price controls for businesses.

Initially, he focused his efforts on the steel industry, whose workers were preparing for new contract negotiations. Kennedy appealed to union members to accept smaller wage increases. He also asked business owners not to raise prices. Steelworkers agreed to smaller raises, which owners could pay without increasing prices.

However, U.S. Steel raised its prices significantly. Kennedy's secretary of labor called the act a "double cross." Several other steel companies joined in this price increase. Kennedy ordered the Federal Trade Commission to investigate whether the steel industry had violated antitrust laws when it raised prices. U.S. Steel soon backed down and lowered its prices. It took longer for Kennedy to repair his relationship with business leaders, who had objected to his involvement in the steel crisis.

Conflicts with Congress

President Kennedy looked for other ways to boost the economy. In August 1962 he proposed a major tax cut to stimulate investment and consumer spending. As part of his New Frontier policies, Kennedy had also proposed new programs to help the poor and expand the military and the space program. Worried about the cost of these programs, Republicans and conservative southern Democrats blocked much of the legislation.

Kennedy did help to pass laws that increased the minimum wage and funded improvements in urban areas and education. He also advanced the cause of mental health. In 1963 Congress approved new funding for local mental-health centers. The purpose of these centers was to reduce the number of people in psychiatric institutions.

Kennedy's proposal to expand health insurance for the elderly did not pass. In general, Kennedy focused his efforts more on foreign policy than on domestic issues. He once remarked to Nixon, "Foreign affairs is the only important issue for a President to handle, isn't it?"

The Defense Department was one of the leading buyers of steel.

SECTION 1 REVIEW

Identify and explain the significance of the following:

- **John F. Kennedy**
- **Jacqueline Kennedy**
- **mandate**
- **New Frontier**

Reading for Content Understanding

1. **Main Idea** What were some of the factors that influenced voters in the 1960 presidential campaign?
2. **Main Idea** What were some of President Kennedy's successes and failures with his domestic programs?
3. **Citizenship and Democracy** Why did many young people become interested in government during Kennedy's presidency?
4. **Writing** *Informing* Imagine that you are a political commentator. Write a newspaper column on the roles that television and style played in the 1960 presidential campaign.
5. **Critical Thinking** *Drawing Conclusions* Why do you think Kennedy's 1961 inaugural address inspired the nation? How do you think you would have responded?

OBJECTIVES

- **Explain why President Kennedy developed a new Cold War strategy.**
- **Evaluate the impact of the Bay of Pigs invasion and the Berlin Wall on Kennedy's administration.**
- **Identify the causes of the Cuban missile crisis.**

FOCUS

Motivate Before Reading

Ask students to imagine that the government has just found out that another nation has nuclear missiles aimed at major U.S. cities. The missiles can reach their targets in seconds. Ask students how such a situation might make them feel. Next, have students speculate on how the president might deal with such a crisis. Write their

Kennedy's Foreign Policy

Reading Focus

Why did President Kennedy develop a new Cold War strategy?

How did the Bay of Pigs invasion and the Berlin Wall reflect on Kennedy's administration?

What caused the Cuban missile crisis?

Key Terms

flexible response
Alliance for Progress
Peace Corps
Bay of Pigs
Berlin Wall
Cuban missile crisis
Limited Nuclear Test Ban Treaty

Section 2
RESOURCES

PRINT
- ★ Guided Reading Strategies 19.2
- ★ Section 2 Review, p. 577
- ★ Daily Quiz 19.2

MULTIMEDIA
- ★ *Teaching Resources CD–ROM*, Lesson 19.2

SHELTERED ENGLISH
- ★ Main Idea Activities for Reteaching and Sheltered English 19.2

*ON JANUARY 23, 1961—just days after President Kennedy's inauguration—*Newsweek *magazine published a special section on the foreign-policy issues facing the new president. The article began, "Around the restive [uneasy] globe from Berlin to Laos, the Communist threat seethed [raged], and nowhere more . . . than in Cuba." The special section concluded with a warning, "The greatest single problem that faces John Kennedy—and the key to most of his other problems—is how to meet the aggressive power of the Communist bloc."*

Newsweek *magazine published a special section on President Kennedy's New Frontier.*

Flexible Response

In foreign policy, President Kennedy continued the policies of Eisenhower's administration. Kennedy maintained a strong military and increased the nation's supply of nuclear weapons. However, he thought that Eisenhower had relied too heavily on the threat of nuclear weapons. Such weapons were not practical for use in regional conflicts.

Kennedy wanted to increase the number of military forces and conventional, or non-nuclear, weapons such as tanks. He hoped that this increase would give the United States more military options, an approach he called **flexible response**. Kennedy explained the policy in July 1961: "We intend to have a wider choice than humiliation or all-out war." Part of Kennedy's new flexible-response policy involved the use of "counter-insurgency" forces. These troops would lead secret operations to weaken communist movements in other countries.

Kennedy also pursued a nonmilitary approach to foreign policy. Under his leadership, the United States attempted to fight communism in Africa, Asia, and Latin America with economic assistance rather than military force.

replies on the chalkboard. Then tell students that in this section they will learn about President Kennedy's foreign policies and how he dealt with a similar situation involving Cuba, the Soviet Union, and the United States.

Introduce Key Terms

Linguistic. Review this section's key terms with students. Ask each student to write a sentence using each key term, but to leave a blank space where the term goes. Then have students exchange their sentences, fill in the blanks, and return the work to its author for grading. **SHELTERED ENGLISH**

TEACH

Have students read Section 2 and complete Guided Reading Strategies 19.2. Choose one or more of the following activities to explore the section content with students. For further suggestions on block scheduling or team teaching, see the *Block Scheduling Handbook.*

LEVEL 1: Linguistic. (Suggested time: 15 min.) As a class, go over students' Guided Reading Strategies. Then use the Reading Focus questions to highlight the main ideas of the section. **SHELTERED ENGLISH**

Geographic Diversity

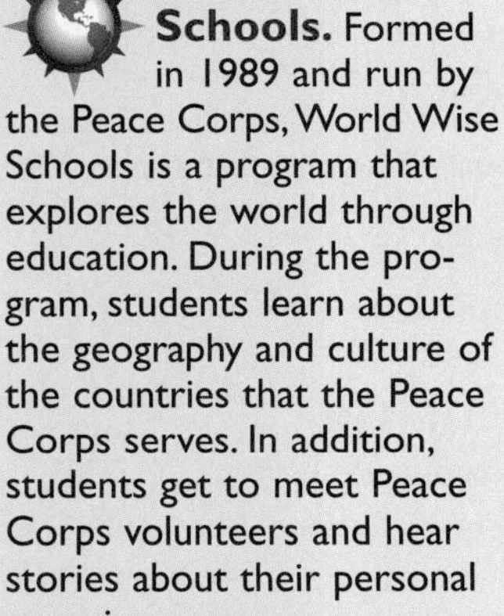

World Wise Schools. Formed in 1989 and run by the Peace Corps, World Wise Schools is a program that explores the world through education. During the program, students learn about the geography and culture of the countries that the Peace Corps serves. In addition, students get to meet Peace Corps volunteers and hear stories about their personal experiences.

Activity: Ask students to write to the following address to find out more information about World Wise Schools and how your school can participate. Have students present their findings in an oral report.

Peace Corps
World Wise Schools
1111 20th Street, N.W.
Washington, DC 20526

LINKING PAST TO PRESENT ANSWERS

1. The Peace Corps helps volunteers learn about other ways of life. It helps those being served to raise their standard of living.

2. Answers will vary but students should indicate that U.S. relations with the Soviet Union were strained during the 1960s because of the Cold War.

The Kennedy administration developed the **Alliance for Progress**. This aid program sought to encourage economic development and promote democracy in Latin America. The United States pledged $20 billion in aid. The assistance did little to improve conditions in Latin America or U.S. relations with the region, however. The Alliance, one scholar later wrote, "attempted to accomplish in a decade what could only be attained [reached] in several generations."

As part of his New Frontier, Kennedy created the **Peace Corps**. This program sends American volunteers to developing countries to work on a wide variety of improvement projects. Thousands of young people responded to Kennedy's call to "make a difference." In 1961 the Peace Corps began sending volunteers overseas. One early volunteer explained her decision to apply:

> **"The idea was to go there and help people to help themselves. . . . I felt that this was a way that I could give something back. I don't think any of us who joined the Peace Corps had an international view of the world. We just thought that . . . the Peace Corps was a way in which we could bring the best of our nation to these . . . countries."**

 The Bay of Pigs

President Kennedy was particularly interested in helping Latin America because of a new political situation in Cuba. In 1959 Fidel Castro had led a rebellion that overthrew an unpopular dictator. Castro organized a social and economic revolution, promising all Cubans "neither bread without liberty nor liberty without bread." However, by 1960 he had established a communist dictatorship in Cuba and formed an alliance with the Soviet Union. Cuba is located less than 90 miles from

Linking Past to Present

The Changing Peace Corps

In March 1961 President Kennedy established the Peace Corps to "promote world peace and friendship." Since then, more than 125,000 Americans have served in more than 100 countries.

In the early 1960s, Peace Corps volunteers were primarily young college graduates who served in Africa, Asia, and Latin America. They worked on agriculture, education, engineering, and health projects.

Today, however, the Peace Corps actively recruits retired people because of their broad experience and knowledge. In recent years, many countries have requested help in new areas, particularly economic development.

A Peace Corps volunteer in Honduras

The Peace Corps has expanded its program to include places such as Eastern Europe and the former Soviet Union.

Many Peace Corps veterans say that they learned a lot from their experiences. One volunteer explained: "I have come to appreciate not only the luxuries, but also the freedoms we, as Americans, take for granted."

Understanding What You Read

1. How has the Peace Corps helped both volunteers and those they serve?
2. Why do you think the Peace Corps did not send early volunteers to the Soviet Union?

LEVEL 2: Linguistic, Logical-Mathematical, Visual-Spatial. (Suggested time: 30 min. plus homework) Discuss with students why Kennedy developed his flexible response strategy. Then ask students to label Berlin, Cuba, the Soviet Union, and the United States on a blank outline map of the world. Next, have students create an annotated time line of the major events in this section. Ask a volunteer to share his or her time line with the class and have other students discuss relationships among the events. Finally, for homework, have students write a few paragraphs discussing how Kennedy's flexible response policy relates to the Cold War events on their time line and how the outcome of these events reflects on his presidency. **SHELTERED ENGLISH**

LEVEL 3: Linguistic, Logical-Mathematical, Intrapersonal. (Suggested time: 45 min. plus homework) Ask students to identify Cold War crises of the Kennedy administration, such as the creation of the Berlin Wall and the Cuban missile crisis. Have each student choose an event and write a memoir that President Kennedy might have written. The memoirs should explain the causes of the event and describe how Kennedy dealt with it. Ask volunteers to read their memoirs to the class. Encourage student feedback and discussion.

Florida. Many Americans were worried about having a communist nation so close. They feared that the Soviet Union might use Cuba as a base from which to attack the United States or spread communism in Latin America.

Before he left office, President Eisenhower approved a secret plan for the Central Intelligence Agency to train Cuban exiles and help them invade the island. When Kennedy took office, he approved the final plan. In April 1961 some 1,500 exiles waded ashore at the **Bay of Pigs** on the southwest coast of Cuba. Castro's forces quickly attacked them, and the invasion turned into a disaster. Kennedy decided not to send in U.S. military air support. After three days of fighting, about 300 of the invaders had been killed and the rest captured. Castro remained firmly in power.

Communist leaders Fidel Castro of Cuba and Nikita Khrushchev of the Soviet Union

At a news conference, Kennedy admitted that the U.S. government had sponsored the invasion. He accepted blame for its failure, saying, "I am the responsible officer of the government." The failed invasion reflected poorly on the administration.

The Berlin Wall

Soviet leader Nikita Khrushchev viewed the Bay of Pigs disaster as a sign of American weakness. He decided to test the determination of the U.S. government to continue the Cold War. He chose Berlin as the testing ground.

After World War II, the Soviet Union and the Western Allies had divided the city of Berlin. The western sections became West Berlin, while the Soviet section became East Berlin. For many people in East Berlin, West Berlin stood as a model of prosperity and freedom. Gradually, East Berliners began crossing into West Berlin. Their numbers soon increased. In the summer of 1961, more than 1,000 people a day were fleeing East Berlin.

On the morning of August 13, 1961, Berliners woke to find East German workers building the **Berlin Wall**. This wall between East and West Berlin was a 28-mile barrier of barbed wire and cement. The Berlin Wall was a desperate attempt to stop the border crossings. President Kennedy protested the "brutal border closing." He also sent 1,500 U.S. troops to West Berlin as a show of support for the city's residents. However, neither Kennedy nor Congress wanted to go to war with the Soviet Union.

On June 26, 1963, Kennedy restated his public support for West Berlin in a speech at the Berlin Wall. He assured thousands of West Berliners that the United States was prepared to "risk its cities to defend yours because we need your freedom to protect ours." Kennedy's symbolic support reassured Americans that he would not back down from communism. However, he had no intention of involving the United States in a military operation. The Berlin Wall would stand for decades as a symbol of the Cold War.

The Cuban Missile Crisis

After the Berlin Wall went up, Soviet premier Khrushchev continued to challenge President Kennedy. The most serious Cold War crisis occurred in Cuba in the fall of 1962.

Built in August 1961, the Berlin Wall became a visible symbol of the Cold War and of the Iron Curtain that separated Western and Eastern Europe.

Global Relations

The Bay of Pigs. The Cuban exiles who participated in the Bay of Pigs invasion expected the Cuban people to rise up and help them overthrow Castro. In addition, the CIA led them to believe that they would receive U.S. air and naval support. Although unmarked U.S. planes attacked Cuban air bases before the invasion, the United States provided no other military support. Moreover, when the exiles invaded, the Cuban people did not revolt. Without support, the invading exiles were forced to surrender within three days.

Activity: Have students write an article that might have appeared in an American newspaper after Kennedy admitted to the U.S. role in the failed Bay of Pigs invasion.

CLOSE

Logical-Mathematical, Interpersonal. Have students create a report card of Kennedy's major foreign-policy decisions. Students should describe Kennedy's actions and "grade" his performance. Have volunteers share their report cards with the class. Then have the class vote on an overall grade for Kennedy's handling of foreign-policy affairs.

CHALLENGE AND EXTEND

Linguistic, Interpersonal, Intrapersonal. Have students use the library and other sources to find additional information about the Cuban missile crisis. If possible, students might interview people who were adults during the crisis. Ask students to use their research to write a three-act play about the crisis. The first act should cover the causes of the crisis. The second act should address its impact on Americans, and the third act should relate students' own attitudes about the crisis. Choose the best play and have volunteers perform it for the class.

Technology and Society

America Under the Gun. Before ordering the naval blockade of Cuba in 1962, Kennedy announced his intentions in a televised address to the American public. In a 17-minute speech on October 22, he informed the public that medium-range missiles in Cuba were aimed at the United States. He stated that the missiles could reach several major U.S. cities. Moreover, long-range missiles that could reach as far as New York City were at that moment believed to be en route to Cuba from the Soviet Union. The news shocked and horrified Americans. After Kennedy peacefully resolved the crisis, many Americans felt extreme relief. As a result of his success in handling the crisis, Kennedy's approval rating soared.

Activity: Ask students to imagine that it is 1962 and they have just heard Kennedy's speech. Ask them to write a journal entry expressing their reactions and feelings.

MAP ANSWER

Guantánamo Bay

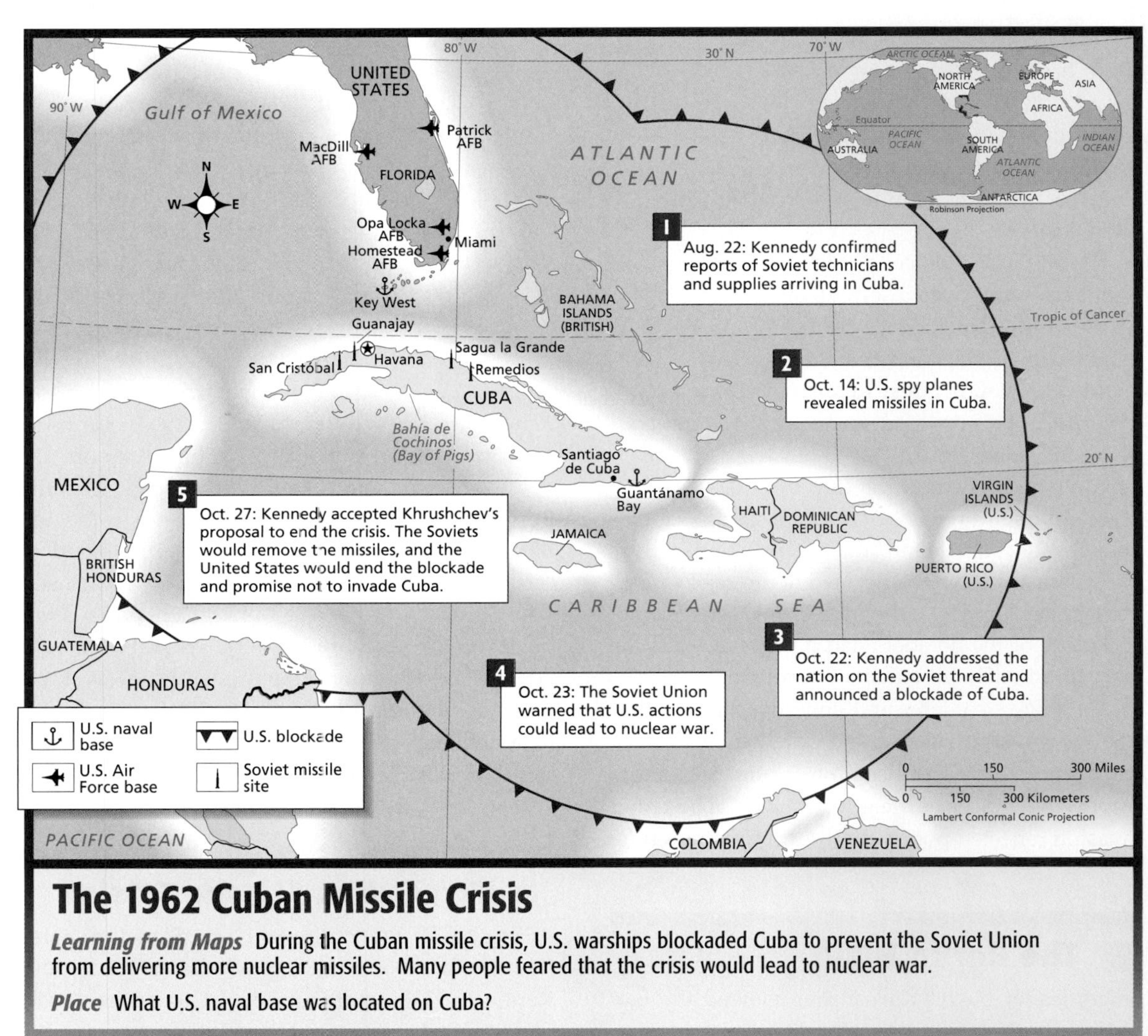

The 1962 Cuban Missile Crisis

Learning from Maps During the Cuban missile crisis, U.S. warships blockaded Cuba to prevent the Soviet Union from delivering more nuclear missiles. Many people feared that the crisis would lead to nuclear war.

Place What U.S. naval base was located on Cuba?

Missiles in Cuba

Beginning in 1961 the Soviet Union sent increasing numbers of military personnel to Cuba. The Soviets started arming Cuba with missiles during the summer of 1962. Cuban and Soviet officials claimed that these weapons were only to protect the country against another invasion like the Bay of Pigs. "We can now repel an American invasion," said Raul Castro, Fidel Castro's brother.

In September, Kennedy warned Soviet leader Khrushchev against putting on Cuban soil missiles that could attack U.S. targets. Khrushchev denied he was doing so. In mid-October, however, photographs from U.S. spy planes provided evidence that the Soviets were installing nuclear missiles. These missiles had enough range to hit major U.S. population centers, such as Miami, Florida, and Atlanta, Georgia. Over the next several days, while the Soviets prepared the missiles for operation, Kennedy met with his advisers to plan his response.

During a televised address on October 22, Kennedy demanded that Khrushchev withdraw the missiles. He also pledged that the United States would attack the Soviet Union if the Soviets fired any missile in the Western Hemisphere. Kennedy warned that he had ordered the U.S. Navy to surround Cuba and prevent Soviet ships from bringing in more missiles.

Kennedy's speech alarmed people worldwide. Many feared that the crisis would lead to nuclear war and global destruction. One American

REVIEW

Logical-Mathematical, Visual-Spatial. Have students complete the Section Review questions. Then have students create a graphic organizer identifying the causes and effects of the major Cold War events covered in this section. Ask volunteers to share their organizers with the class. As they do, create a master organizer on the chalkboard and have students copy it to use as a review of this section.

ASSESS

Have students complete Daily Quiz 19.2.

RETEACH

Linguistic, Visual-Spatial, Interpersonal. Have students complete Main Idea Activities for Reteaching and Sheltered English 19.2. In advance, write on blank index cards each term from the Identify portion of the Section Review. Organize students into two groups. Give one of the cards to a member of one group and tell him or her to draw pictures on the chalkboard as clues to the words that make up the term on the card. Give the rest of the group a certain amount of time to guess the term and define it. If the group fails, give the other group a chance. Each group receives one point for a correct response. Continue until all the terms have been identified. **SHELTERED ENGLISH**

newspaper reported that local high school students were breaking down in class and sobbing, "I don't want to die."

A Soviet nuclear missile on parade in Moscow

A Tense Standoff

Soviet ships loaded with missile parts continued toward Cuba. The world waited anxiously to see what would happen that October in the **Cuban missile crisis**. Attorney General Robert Kennedy later recalled the president's reaction as the superpowers came closer to a confrontation.

> **"I think those few minutes were the time of gravest concern for the President. Was the world on the brink [edge] of a holocaust [destruction]? Was it our error? . . . His face seemed drawn, his eyes pained. . . . He would have to wait."**

Soon word came that at the last moment the Soviet ships had turned back. One Kennedy adviser described the moment, "We're eyeball to eyeball, and the other fellow just blinked." Later, Kennedy and Khrushchev agreed to a compromise. "We and you ought not to pull on the ends of the rope in which you have tied the knot of war," the Soviet leader wrote him. "Let us take measures to untie that knot." The Soviets removed their missiles from Cuba in return for a U.S. promise not to invade the island. Kennedy also agreed to remove some U.S. missiles from Italy and Turkey. In 1963 Kennedy and Khrushchev established a teletype "hot line." The leaders of the two superpowers could use the hotline to communicate with each other at a moment's notice.

The two leaders also signed the **Limited Nuclear Test Ban Treaty** in August 1963. This treaty banned the testing of new nuclear weapons aboveground. More than 90 nations eventually signed the treaty.

The outcome of the Cuban missile crisis restored public confidence in Kennedy's foreign policy. Unlike his actions during the Bay of Pigs crisis, Kennedy had relied less heavily on his advisers and more on his instincts. He believed that the compromise agreement and the easing of tensions after the crisis showed the effectiveness of flexible response. "It was a combination of toughness and restraint [holding back], of will, nerve, and wisdom," observed Kennedy adviser Arthur Schlesinger Jr. "It dazzled the world." Although the Cold War continued, the United States and the Soviet Union made efforts to prevent future conflicts.

SECTION 2 REVIEW

Identify and explain the significance of the following:
- **flexible response**
- **Alliance for Progress**
- **Peace Corps**
- **Fidel Castro**
- **Bay of Pigs**
- **Berlin Wall**
- **Cuban missile crisis**
- **Limited Nuclear Test Ban Treaty**

Locate and explain the importance of the following:
- **Cuba**
- **Miami**

Reading for Content Understanding

1. **Main Idea** Why did President Kennedy develop the strategy of flexible response?
2. **Main Idea** How did the Bay of Pigs and the Berlin Wall affect Kennedy's presidency?
3. **Global Relations** Why did the United States and the Soviet Union come so close to nuclear war over the placing of offensive missiles in Cuba?
4. **Writing** *Classifying* Create a chart listing the foreign-policy crises during the Kennedy administration. Classify their outcomes as positive or negative.
5. **Critical Thinking** *Identifying Cause and Effect* How did the Bay of Pigs invasion contribute to the Cuban missile crisis?

Section 2 Review ANSWERS

Identify
For significance, see the following pages:

- flexible response, p. 573
- Alliance for Progress, p. 574
- Peace Corps, p. 574
- Fidel Castro, p. 574
- Bay of Pigs, p. 575
- Berlin Wall, p. 575
- Cuban missile crisis, p. 577
- Limited Nuclear Test Ban Treaty, p. 577

Locate
For locations, see the map on page 576.

Reading for Content Understanding

1. to give the United States more military options and to provide other nations with alternatives to humiliation or all-out nuclear war

2. The first reflected poorly on Kennedy's presidency and both events made the United States appear weak to some people. As a result, Kennedy's administration had to continue dealing with Soviet challenges.

3. Cuba was a communist nation and a Soviet ally located less than 90 miles off the coast of Florida, and the Cuban missiles had the range to strike some major U.S. cities.

4. Charts will vary but should include and classify the following: Bay of Pigs invasion, construction of the Berlin Wall, and the Cuban missile crisis.

5. Answers will vary but students might say that the failed invasion angered Cuba and made the United States appear weak, which contributed to the Soviet and Cuban decision to place nuclear missiles in Cuba.

Section 3 Lesson Plan

OBJECTIVES

- Discuss the public's reaction to President Kennedy's assassination.
- Identify ways in which President Johnson's domestic programs helped many Americans.
- Describe Johnson's approach to foreign policy.

FOCUS

Motivate Before Reading

At the start of class, tell students that in this section they will learn about the assassination of President Kennedy and public reaction to his death. Ask students to speculate on how American people might have reacted to news of the president's death. List the better answers on the chalkboard. Then have students write down some advice that might help Kennedy's replacement, Vice

Section 3
RESOURCES

PRINT
- ★ Guided Reading Strategies 19.3
- ★ Biography Reading 19: Henry B. Gonzales
- ★ Section 3 Review, p. 582
- ★ Daily Quiz 19.3

MULTIMEDIA
- ★ *Teaching Resources CD–ROM,* Lesson 19.3
- ★ HRW Web site

SHELTERED ENGLISH
- ★ Main Idea Activities for Reteaching and Sheltered English 19.3

The Johnson Administration

Reading Focus

How did people react to President Kennedy's assassination?

How did President Johnson's domestic programs help many Americans?

What was Johnson's approach to foreign policy?

Key Terms

Warren Commission
War on Poverty
Great Society
Medicare
Medicaid
Immigration and Nationality Act

IN NOVEMBER 1963 President Kennedy began a quick tour of Texas cities. On the morning of November 22, he polished a speech he planned to deliver that day in Dallas. "We ask therefore that we may be worthy of our power and responsibility," he planned to say, "and that we may achieve in our time and for all time the ancient vision of 'peace on earth, good will toward men.'" Kennedy never delivered that speech. By that afternoon, he had died from an assassin's bullet. That same day, Vice President Lyndon B. Johnson assumed the presidency.

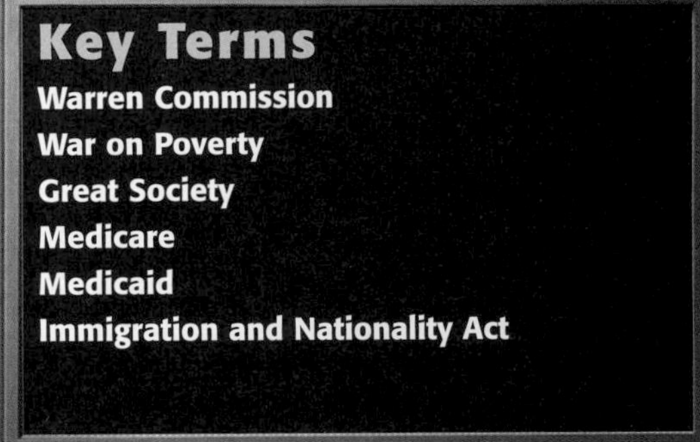
The Dallas Citizens Council
The Dallas Assembly
The Science Research Center
request the pleasure of
the company of
Mr. Carlos Hedstrom Jr.
at a luncheon in honor of
The President and Mrs. Kennedy
The Vice-President and Mrs. Johnson
The Governor and Mrs. Connally
Friday, the twenty-second of November
at twelve noon
The Trade Mart

An invitation to a luncheon in Dallas for Kennedy

 The Kennedy Assassination

On November 22, 1963, as President Kennedy's car traveled through Dallas, shots rang out. Kennedy slumped forward, severely wounded. He died soon afterward. Vice President Lyndon B. Johnson, traveling in another car, was unharmed. Just hours after the assassination, *Air Force One,* the presidential airplane, carried Kennedy's body back to Washington, D.C. Standing next to First Lady Jacqueline Kennedy, Johnson took the presidential oath of office.

The assassination shocked Americans. One Kennedy administration official remembered his reaction on hearing of the president's death:

> **"I was crying. It was unbelievable, stunning. An awful feeling of helplessness—nothing could be done, no recall. It—he—was over, done, finished. . . . John Kennedy was not the sixties. But he fueled the smoldering embers [fire], and, for a brief while, was the exemplar [prime example] who led**

President Lyndon Johnson, better assume his new office. Ask volunteers to share their suggestions with the class. Then tell students that in this section they also will learn about President Johnson's administration.

Introduce Key Terms

Linguistic. Review this section's key terms with students. Organize students into six groups, one for each key term. Have each group create a *positive* slogan for its assigned key term. Then have each group select a volunteer to present and explain its slogan to the rest of the class. **SHELTERED ENGLISH**

TEACH

Have students read Section 3 and complete Guided Reading Strategies 19.3. Choose one or more of the following activities to explore the section content with students. For further suggestions on block scheduling or team teaching, see the *Block Scheduling Handbook.*

LEVEL 1: Linguistic. (Suggested time: 15 min.) As a class, go over students' Guided Reading Strategies. Then use the Reading Focus questions to highlight the main ideas of the section. **SHELTERED ENGLISH**

Lyndon B. Johnson

Lyndon B. Johnson was born in 1908 in central Texas. His father was a local politician, and Johnson grew up with politics in his blood.

Johnson became known as the wonder kid of Texas politics for his early accomplishments. In 1935 President Franklin D. Roosevelt appointed Johnson director of the Texas National Youth Administration (NYA), a New Deal program. He was the youngest state NYA director. Under his leadership the NYA constructed highways, parks, and playgrounds throughout Texas. Johnson won election to the House of Representatives in 1937 at age 29.

Johnson continued his rise into the Senate, on to the vice presidency, and then the presidency. A former colleague described Johnson's ambitious pace: "Lyndon behaves as if there were no tomorrow coming and he had to do everything today."

others to discover their own strength and resurgent [renewed] energy."

People around the world also mourned Kennedy's death. More than 90 percent of American homes and millions of people worldwide watched Kennedy's funeral on television.

Within hours of the assassination, police arrested Soviet sympathizer and former U.S. Marine Lee Harvey Oswald. Two days later, officials prepared to transfer Oswald to another jail. Nightclub owner Jack Ruby pushed his way through a crowd and killed Oswald.

Oswald's death left many unanswered questions. To try to clear up the mystery surrounding Kennedy's assassination, President Johnson appointed a special commission headed by Chief Justice Earl Warren. The **Warren Commission** spent months studying the evidence. It concluded that Oswald was the assassin and that he had acted alone. Not everyone agreed with that conclusion, however. The controversy surrounding the Kennedy assassination continues to this day.

After Kennedy's death, the media created an idealized image of him. Jacqueline Kennedy also popularized this view of her late husband. Days after his funeral, she told a journalist of Kennedy's love of Camelot. This legendary court of King Arthur was featured in a popular Broadway musical in the early 1960s. The first lady referred to the Kennedy administration as

"a magic moment in American history, when gallant men danced with beautiful women, when great deeds were done, when artists, writers, and poets met at the White House. . . . There'll never be another Camelot again."

On his third birthday, John F. Kennedy Jr. saluted his father's coffin in the funeral procession.

Presidential Profiles

Lyndon B. Johnson. As a young man, Lyndon Johnson witnessed the effects of racism and poverty on the people of Texas. In 1928 he took a teaching position in Cotulla, a small, poor town in the southern part of the state. Most of his students were Mexican Americans and lived in run-down homes without electricity. Many children came to school hungry, and on occasion they would ask why people hated them for their skin color. Johnson later recalled, "I was determined to spark something inside them, to fill their souls with ambition and interest and belief in the future. I was determined to give them what they needed to make it in this world, to help them finish their education."

Activity: Have students use the library or search the Internet through the HRW Web site to research Lyndon B. Johnson's presidency. Ask students to use their research to create a collage or montage portraying the main domestic policies of Johnson's administration.

go.hrw.com
SB1 Johnson

ALL LEVELS: Linguistic, Musical-Rhythmic, Intrapersonal. (Suggested time: 45 min.) Have each student prepare a poem, song, or work of art that expresses people's reactions, and the student's own feelings, to President Kennedy's assassination. Call on volunteers to exhibit or perform their work for the class. **SHELTERED ENGLISH**

LEVEL 2: Linguistic, Intrapersonal. (Suggested time: 35 min.) Ask students to imagine that they are members of President Johnson's staff. Tell them that their assignment is to create a briefing for the official presidential biographer describing Johnson's domestic and foreign-policy achievements. Have students add to the end of the briefing a statement that Johnson might have written summarizing what he feels his best achievements were while in office. Ask volunteers to share their briefings with the class. Wrap up with a class discussion evaluating Johnson's presidency and comparing it to Kennedy's.

LEVEL 3: Linguistic, Logical-Mathematical, Visual-Spatial. (Suggested time: 20 min. plus homework) Have students review the previous section on President Kennedy's foreign policies. Then have each student prepare a chart comparing and contrasting the foreign-policy approaches of Presidents Johnson and Kennedy. For homework, have students write a lecture that uses the chart as

Cultural Diversity

The 1964 Election. The outcome of the 1964 presidential election signaled a significant shift in regional voting patterns. For decades southern voters had supported Democratic candidates. However, of the six states that Republican candidate Barry Goldwater won, five of them—Alabama, Georgia, Louisiana, Mississippi, and South Carolina—were in the South. (The sixth, Goldwater's home state of Arizona, was in the Southwest.) This change in voting patterns had a large impact on later presidential elections because it showed that Republican candidates could win southern support.

Critical Thinking: Why do you think many southerners decided not to vote for President Johnson?

ANSWER: Answers will vary but students might mention that southern voters might have disliked some of Johnson's reforms, particularly in the area of civil rights.

President Johnson

The new president tried to comfort the nation in its grief. Five days after the assassination, President Johnson addressed Congress and the American public: "All I have I would gladly have given not to be standing here today." He promised to push for New Frontier reforms.

The Head Start program helped many underprivileged children.

The Johnson Style

President Johnson differed from Kennedy in his personal background and leadership style. Johnson grew up in the rural Hill Country of central Texas. He worked his way through a local teacher's college. Kennedy had appeared athletic and poised, while Johnson was known for his physical clumsiness and use of crude language.

Johnson, however, had much more political experience than Kennedy. Johnson served in the House of Representatives for 12 years before moving to the Senate. After his first term as senator, he became majority leader. Johnson worked hard to get to know his fellow senators and to learn what it took to win their votes. He was extremely skilled in the art of compromise, even if his methods were sometimes sharp. One member of Congress recalled Johnson's forceful manner: "Lyndon got me by the lapels [collar] and put his face on top of mine and he talked and talked."

The Kennedy Legacy

As president, Johnson was determined to win the civil rights and education legislation that he had favored as a senator and that Kennedy had supported. Johnson also wanted to help poor Americans. In the 1962 book *The Other America,* journalist Michael Harrington had reported that about 50 million Americans were living in poverty. They earned less than $3,500 per year for a family of four. The news disturbed many people and created some support for government action.

Harrington explained that many Americans enjoyed one of the highest standards of living in the world. At the same time, however, many poor people in the United States were becoming poorer. "If the nation does not measure up to the challenge . . . ," he warned, "poverty in the 1960s might be on the increase." Groups that had limited political power and influence were more likely to be poor. About 50 percent of African Americans and female-headed households were living in poverty. An estimated one third of people over 65 years of age also lived at the poverty level.

To help poor Americans, Johnson launched what he called the **War on Poverty**. He created a new agency, the Office of Economic Opportunity (OEO), to develop programs to help poor people earn money. The OEO started a new Job Corps to teach young adults basic job skills. The agency funded Head Start, an educational program to prepare poor children for school. The OEO also created a domestic version of the Peace Corps—the Volunteers in Service to America (VISTA).

The 1964 Election

Johnson's popularity soared because of his success in establishing such programs. The Democrats nominated him as their candidate for president in 1964. Johnson's choice for vice president was Minnesota senator Hubert Humphrey. After Kennedy's assassination, Johnson had served without a vice president.

Barry Goldwater ran as the Republican presidential candidate. A conservative senator from Arizona, Goldwater wanted to reduce federal social programs and expand the U.S. military. The Democrats accused him of being an extreme anticommunist who might lead the nation into war. Many voters seemed to agree. Johnson won with more than 60 percent of the popular vote and with 486 electoral votes to Goldwater's 52.

A campaign pin for Lyndon B. Johnson, also known as LBJ

a visual aid. The lecture should address the foreign-policy approaches of both administrations and highlight continuities between the two presidents' policies.

CLOSE

Linguistic, Visual-Spatial. Have students create a print advertisement promoting Johnson's Great Society as a "new and improved" America. Encourage students to make their ads creative and fun. Display students' advertisements around the class and call on volunteers to explain their work.

CHALLENGE AND EXTEND

Linguistic, Interpersonal, Intrapersonal. Have students interview at least two adults born before 1950 to find out what each person was doing when he or she learned that President Kennedy had been assassinated and how the news affected them. Have students report the results of their interviews to the class. Then tell students to write an essay explaining why they think so many Americans who were alive when Kennedy died still vividly remember the moment when they first learned of his assassination. Call on volunteers to read their essays to the class.

The Great Society

President Johnson saw his election victory as a mandate for his policies. He set out to expand his domestic reforms. Johnson called his new program for reform and aid for Americans living in poverty the **Great Society**. In a speech before the 1964 election, Johnson had described his vision:

> **"The Great Society rests on abundance and liberty for all. It demands an end to poverty and racial injustice. . . . The Great Society is a place where every child can find knowledge to enrich his mind and to enlarge his talents. . . . It is a place where the city . . . serves not only the needs of the body and the demands of commerce but the desire for beauty and the hunger for community."**

Reprinted with permission from the *Atlanta Journal* and the *Atlanta Constitution*

President Johnson was a teacher before he turned to politics.

New Reforms

Johnson considered his Great Society to be an expansion of Roosevelt's New Deal of the 1930s. During Johnson's first 100 days in office in 1965, he introduced and won passage of his Great Society legislation. Some Great Society reforms focused on improving health care and education. These programs continue today. **Medicare** helps people over age 65 meet medical expenses by including them in a government health care plan. **Medicaid** provides health insurance for people with low incomes. President Harry S Truman had first proposed these reforms in 1945. Johnson signed the bill for Medicare in July 1965.

The Elementary and Secondary School Education Act supplied more than $1 billion in aid to assist students with special needs. To help improve housing for low-income families, Congress created the Department of Housing and Urban Development (HUD). Johnson appointed former New Deal reformer Robert Weaver as HUD's secretary. Weaver was the first African American appointed to a presidential cabinet.

Immigration Policy

Johnson's Great Society plan also included a revision of national immigration policy. In October 1965 Congress passed the **Immigration and Nationality Act**. The legislation set the quota for all immigrants from countries in the Western Hemisphere at 120,000. For other immigrants, the annual limit was 170,000, with no more than 20,000 from any one country. Close relatives of individuals already in the United States, however, would be admitted regardless of the quota. As a

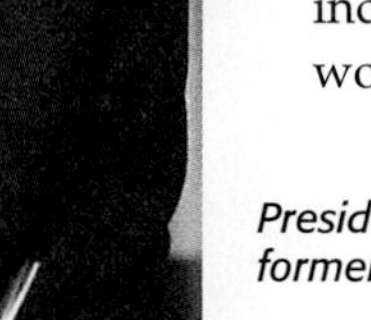

President Johnson signed the Medicare bill in former president Truman's hometown.

Historical Sidelight

The Great Society. During his campaign in 1964, President Johnson described his Great Society in a speech at the University of Michigan. He stated that the first place to focus on was the cities. "It is harder and harder to live the good life in American cities today. The catalogue of ills is long . . . the decay of the centers . . . the despoiling of the suburbs. . . . Our society will never be great until our cities are great." He next focused on the countryside. "We have always prided ourselves on being . . . America the beautiful. Today that beauty is in danger . . . threatened with pollution. . . . We must act to prevent an Ugly America." Last, he focused on America's classrooms. "Our society will not be great until every young mind is set free to scan the farthest reaches of thought and imagination. . . . Poverty must not be a bar to learning, and learning must offer an escape from poverty."

Critical Thinking: Do you think that the three areas of concern addressed by Johnson are still of concern today? Explain. If you had to choose three areas of American society to focus on improving today, what would you choose and why?

ANSWER: Answers will vary but students should support their opinions and explain their reasoning.

REVIEW

Linguistic, Interpersonal. Have students complete the Section Review questions. Then ask students to create study guides for the section. Have students write five true-or-false questions and five multiple-choice questions about the main events and people in this section. Then ask students to exchange their study guides, answer the questions, and return them to their authors for grading.

ASSESS

Have students complete Daily Quiz 19.3.

RETEACH

Kinesthetic, Interpersonal. Have students complete Main Idea Activities for Reteaching and Sheltered English 19.3. Prepare several questions of mid-level difficulty and several that are more difficult. Organize the class into two teams for a game of basketball review. Have teams take turns answering questions. Award two points for correct answers to mid-level questions and three points for correct answers to more difficult questions. For each correct answer, allow the team to select a student to attempt a one-point free throw by shooting a foam ball or wadded-up piece of paper into a wastebasket. The game ends when all questions have been answered correctly. **SHELTERED ENGLISH**

Section 3 Review ANSWERS

Identify

For significance, see the following pages:

- Lyndon B. Johnson p. 578
- Warren Commission, p. 579
- Michael Harrington, p. 580
- War on Poverty, p. 580
- Barry Goldwater, p. 580
- Great Society, p. 581
- Medicare, p. 581
- Medicaid, p. 581
- Robert Weaver, p. 581
- Immigration and Nationality Act, p. 581

Reading for Content Understanding

1. with despair, mourning, shock, and grief

2. He had a strong Cold War policy and worked to fight communist aggression in South Vietnam and the Dominican Republic.

3. Organizers should include the War on Poverty, which included the creation of the OEO and through it the Job Corps, Head Start, and VISTA programs; and the Great Society, which included Medicare, Medicaid, aid to education, HUD, and the Immigration and Nationality Act.

4. Scripts will vary but students might advise viewers to remain calm, that the situation is being investigated, that Vice President Johnson has assumed the presidency, and that many people are expressing shock, great sadness, and uncertainty about the nation's future.

5. Students may mention that the book's results may either have supported or gone against people's stereotypes as to who and how many people were living in poverty at a time widely considered to be prosperous.

result, many more newcomers immigrated than legislators had planned. In particular, the number of immigrants from Asia and Latin America rose.

Partly because of Johnson's Great Society, poverty in the United States declined. Overall unemployment levels stayed low in the second half of the 1960s. The percentage of Americans living below the poverty level dropped to about 12 percent by 1969. Americans' income levels rose more during the 1960s than during the prosperous years of the 1950s.

Some Dominican citizens resented the arrival of U.S troops in 1965.

Johnson and Foreign Policy

President Johnson devoted most of his attention to his Great Society programs. Unlike Kennedy, Johnson had little interest in international affairs. However, like former presidents Eisenhower and Kennedy, Johnson regarded communism as a major threat to democracy and world peace.

Johnson relied heavily on Kennedy's foreign-policy advisers as he tried to maintain a strong Cold War policy. During his presidency, Johnson increased the U.S. military presence in South Vietnam to help defend it from communist North Vietnam. (See Chapter 21 for more information.)

In April 1965 Johnson sent U.S. Marines to stop rioting in the Dominican Republic. He feared that Communists allied with Cuban leader Fidel Castro wanted to take over the nation's unstable government. Overall, Johnson sent some 22,000 soldiers and marines to the small country. Latin American and Caribbean leaders were angered by this use of U.S. force. They viewed U.S. involvement as an extreme reaction to an internal conflict. Eventually, a group of these leaders met with U.S. and Dominican officials. They created a plan for restoring local control to the country.

Most of Johnson's foreign-policy decisions were a response to his fear of communist aggression. However, some Americans wondered if military intervention was the best course to take.

SECTION 3 REVIEW

Identify and explain the significance of the following:

- **Lyndon B. Johnson**
- **Warren Commission**
- **Michael Harrington**
- **War on Poverty**
- **Barry Goldwater**
- **Great Society**
- **Medicare**
- **Medicaid**
- **Robert Weaver**
- **Immigration and Nationality Act**

Reading for Content Understanding

1. **Main Idea** How did Americans respond to the assassination of President Kennedy?
2. **Main Idea** What was President Johnson's foreign policy?
3. **Economic Development** Make a graphic organizer listing Johnson's domestic programs. Include the goals and results of these efforts.
4. **Writing** *Informing* Imagine that you are a TV newscaster in 1963. Write a script informing your audience of Kennedy's assassination and what his death might mean for the nation.
5. **Critical Thinking** *Identifying Generalizations and Stereotypes* How might Michael Harrington's *The Other America* have changed or reinforced people's ideas about poverty in the United States?

OBJECTIVES

- Identify reasons students protested in the 1960s.
- Describe some aspects of the counterculture.
- Explain how art and music reflected changes in culture.

FOCUS

Motivate Before Reading

Ask students to identify items, events, and expressions associated with the 1960s. List students' responses on the chalkboard. Then tell students that in this section they will learn about changes in society that took place during the 1960s.

New Movements in America

Reading Focus

- What did students protest in the 1960s?
- What were some aspects of the counterculture?
- How were cultural changes reflected in art and music?

Key Terms

- Students for a Democratic Society
- generation gap
- counterculture
- hippies
- pop art
- Motown Records
- Woodstock

IN THE FALL OF 1964, school administrators at the University of California at Berkeley took steps that stunned students. The administrators announced that students could no longer conduct political activity on campus. They could not even hand out pamphlets outside the main gate of the campus. The school's decision angered many students. They objected to their loss of the right to free speech as guaranteed in the First Amendment. They soon took action that captured the attention of the nation.

Student protests occurred on many college campuses.

Student Protests

Mario Savio led some 2,000 other Berkeley students in a free-speech movement in October 1964. Savio had gained much experience from his earlier work with the civil rights movement. He issued a document criticizing university officials.

When there was no response, the students began a strike. They also took over an administration building in an effort to shut down the university. Savio explained:

> **"There is a time when the operation of the machine [the university] becomes so odious [hated], . . . that . . . you've got to put your bodies upon the gears and upon the wheels, upon the levers, upon all the apparatus [parts] and you've got to make it stop. And you've got to indicate to the people who run it . . . that unless you're free, the machine will be prevented from running at all."**

Police arrested more than 770 protesters, but other students continued the strike. Eventually, university officials agreed to some reforms.

Student protests occurred across the nation. The civil rights movement greatly inspired some

Section 4
RESOURCES

PRINT

- ★ Guided Reading Strategies 19.4
- ★ Section 4 Review, p. 587
- ★ Daily Quiz 19.4

MULTIMEDIA

- ★ *Teaching Resources CD–ROM,* Lesson 19.4
- ★ *American Music Audio CD Program:* "Blowin' in the Wind"
- ★ Art in American History Transparency 39: *Return of the Prodigal Son* and Transparency 46: *Moonwalk*
- ★ Everyday Life in America Transparency 29: The Woodstock Nation, 1960s
- ★ HRW Web site

SHELTERED ENGLISH

- ★ Main Idea Activities for Reteaching and Sheltered English 19.4

Introduce Key Terms

Linguistic. Review this section's key terms with students. Ask students to speculate on the meaning of each term. Then call on volunteers to offer possible definitions. Next, have students use context cues from the section to write a definition for each term. Finally, have students use each of the terms in a paragraph describing what they think were some of the changes occurring in American culture during the 1960s. Call on volunteers to read their paragraphs to the class. **SHELTERED ENGLISH**

TEACH

Have students read Section 4 and complete Guided Reading Strategies 19.4. Choose one or more of the following activities to explore the section content with students. For further suggestions on block scheduling or team teaching, see the *Block Scheduling Handbook.*

LEVEL 1: Linguistic. (Suggested time: 15 min.) As a class, go over students' Guided Reading Strategies. Then use the Reading Focus questions to highlight the main ideas of the section. **SHELTERED ENGLISH**

Linking Past to Present

Utopian Communities. The communes that many hippies lived in during the 1960s were not a new idea. In 1663 a group of Dutch Mennonites established the first commune in North America. Historically, groups formed communes in an attempt to create a utopian, or perfect, society. Religious communes, such as that of the Shakers, tended to last longer than those based on secular ideals. The communes of the 1960s were more numerous and, on average, smaller than earlier ones. In addition, many emphasized collective living as a means to greater self-fulfillment rather than as a benefit for society. Communes began losing popularity in the early to mid-1970s. Today, cohousing, a variation on communes, is gaining popularity. This movement emphasizes community and cooperation. Families live in individual homes and maintain separate finances, but share resources and common areas, such as a communal dining hall.

Critical Thinking: Why might it be difficult for communes to exist within the larger American society for any lengthy period of time?

ANSWER: Answers will vary but students might mention that some Americans will distrust and try to close down the communes because they are different and go against mainstream society.

Mario Savio addresses students at the University of California at Berkeley.

students in the **Students for a Democratic Society** (SDS). This organization saw nuclear arms and racial discrimination as two great threats to American society. SDS activist Tom Hayden helped explain these issues of concern in the Port Huron Statement. SDS and other students launched protests against racial discrimination, rigid college rules, and the growing U.S. military presence in Vietnam. (See Chapters 20 and 21 for more information.)

The Youth Revolt

The student protests shocked many older Americans. For them, the protests showed a lack of respect for authority.

The Generation Gap

During the 1960s some children of the post–World War II baby boom were beginning to enter young adulthood. The number of people aged 15 through 24 increased almost 50 percent from 1960 to 1970. In 1964 the first wave of the baby-boom generation entered college. Columbia University president Grayson Kirk declared, "I know of no other time in our history when the gap between the generations has been wider or more potentially dangerous." This **generation gap**, or division between older and younger people, grew as more young people rejected their parents' values and beliefs.

In the early 1960s much of society and culture looked a lot like it had in the 1950s. The media celebrated white, middle-class suburban values and institutions. The optimism of the time could perhaps be summed up in the words one high school principal had written in a graduating senior's yearbook:

> **"As you in the class of 1959 go on to higher education, you are in full accord [agreement] with the times. . . . The signposts everywhere read, 'Opportunity Unlimited!'"**

The Counterculture

Some young people rejected traditional society and chose instead to "drop out." They created a **counterculture**—an alternative culture with values that ran counter to, or against, those of the main society. The counterculture emphasized individual freedom, nonviolence, and communal sharing. Members of the counterculture, who called themselves **hippies**, experimented with different lifestyles. They often wore their hair long and dressed in unconventional clothing. African, American Indian, and Indian clothing were popular with hippies. Many hippies dyed their own clothes in a process known as tie-dying. Some hippies experimented with drugs.

Some young leaders tried to bring together members of the student movement and the counterculture. In 1967, protesters in San Francisco organized the Human Be-In. This event attracted some 20,000 young people from both movements.

Hippies explored new styles of clothing and behavior.

ALL LEVELS: Linguistic, Logical-Mathematical. (Suggested time: 30 min.) Ask students to imagine that they are magazine editors during the 1960s. Have them create a table of contents for a special issue covering recent changes in art, music, and youth culture. Students should create titles for columns and articles that they think might appear in the special issue. Then have each student write one to three sentences to provide clues about the information in each article or column.

LEVEL 2: Linguistic, Musical-Rhythmic, Visual-Spatial. (Suggested time: 45 min. plus homework) Have students either create a work of art or write song lyrics that address the issues that youth, particularly student activists, protested during the 1960s. Encourage students to use art and music styles popular during the 1960s, such as pop art, folk music, or soul music. When students are through, call on volunteers to share their work or perform it for the class. **SHELTERED ENGLISH**

American Arts

Andy Warhol

Andy Warhol was born in Pittsburgh, Pennsylvania. His parents were immigrants from Czechoslovakia. After graduating from the Carnegie Institute of Technology in 1949, he worked as a commercial artist in New York City. Many of his commercial drawings were used in advertisements and greeting cards. In the late 1950s Warhol began to paint and create his own art.

In the 1960s Warhol exhibited his prints of Campbell's soup cans, a turning point in his career. His work was known as pop art—art that uses popular or common objects as subjects. Warhol often reproduced brightly colored copies of familiar everyday objects and celebrities. These images of mass culture were intended to question American materialism in the 1960s and the seriousness of traditional art. As one critic stated, Warhol turned products into art.

Warhol's prints of Marilyn Monroe and other celebrities became symbols of the 1960s. Warhol used a process known as silk-screen printing to mass-produce his art. With silk-screen printing, a person rubs or forces color through a patterned screen made of silk. The pattern will create the image on the material to be printed. This process allows many copies of one image to be made quickly and easily.

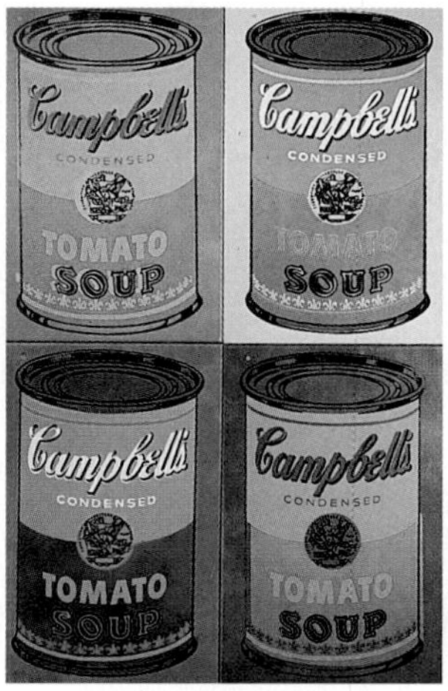

As the 1960s progressed, Warhol became more involved with filmmaking, producing, and writing. He established a studio in New York City called the Factory, which attracted well-known artists and celebrities. In 1968 Warhol made his often quoted prediction about the age of mass media: "In the future everyone will have 15 minutes of fame."

Andy Warhol turned soup cans into art and showed that art could be found in anything.

Understanding the Arts

1. What is pop art?
2. Why do you think pop art was so popular in the 1960s?

Many student leaders believed, however, that the aims of the counterculture were too different from their goals. Student activists wanted to challenge society in order to improve it. Hippies rejected society and tried to create an alternative culture. Many students believed the counterculture abandoned its responsibility to society by encouraging unhealthy behavior, such as drug abuse.

The counterculture and the student rights movement challenged the way many Americans viewed their world. The movements encouraged a greater tolerance for differences in dress, music, and personal relationships.

A Different Perspective

Changes in the art world reflected this new point of view. The **pop art** movement took its name from the popular, commonplace images and objects

Across the Curriculum

ART

Andy Warhol. Born Andrew Warhola to an impoverished coal miner, Andy Warhol began his art career as a commercial illustrator. He worked for a time in the art department of a New York City shoe store. This early work in commercial arts influenced the pop art he produced in the 1960s. His famous painting of Campbell's soup cans was first displayed in 1962.

Activity: Have students use the library or search the Internet through the HRW Web site to find examples of works by Andy Warhol. Then have students write a critique of one Warhol piece.

go.hrw.com
SB1 Warhol

AMERICAN ARTS ANSWERS

1. art that uses popular or commonplace objects as subjects

2. This type of art often was meant to question American materialism and tradition, values that many youth were questioning in a broader sense at the time.

Multimedia Resources

Art in American History Transparency 39: *Return of the Prodigal Son* and Transparency 46: *Moonwalk*

LEVEL 3: Linguistic, Logical-Mathematical, Visual-Spatial. (Suggested time: 30 min. plus homework) Have students refer to this section to create an encyclopedia entry on the youth movement of the 1960s. Entries should explain similarities and differences between two factions of the movement: the student activists and the advocates of the counterculture. The entry also should describe the issues each faction protested or addressed and explain cultural changes brought about by each movement. For homework, have students design a poster that symbolizes the overall youth culture of the 1960s. Encourage students to design their posters in a style that was popular at the time.

CLOSE

Linguistic, Intrapersonal. Ask students to write a paragraph explaining how art and music can be used to understand the values of a society and conflicts within that society. Have students point out how popular art and music of the 1960s reflected the values of the student movement and the counterculture.

CHALLENGE AND EXTEND

Musical-Rhythmic, Visual-Spatial, Interpersonal. Have students locate recordings of popular music from the 1960s. (You may wish to suggest songs with appropriate content for

Daily Life

Woodstock. During the 1960s, thousands of young people attended outdoor rock festivals in areas as diverse as California, Georgia, and Texas. While successful, none of these concerts compared with the Woodstock Music and Art Fair in 1969. Originally planned to be held in Woodstock, New York, the festival was moved to a farm in a neighboring county following protests from the townspeople. Despite the out-of-the-way location, more than 400,000 people attended the three-day event to hear performers such as Joan Baez; Crosby, Stills, Nash, and Young; Jefferson Airplaine; Jimi Hendrix; Sly and the Family Stone; and the Who.

Critical Thinking: Why do you think outdoor music festivals became so popular with youth of the 1960s?

ANSWER: Answers will vary but students should support their opinions and explain their reasoning.

Multimedia Resources

Everyday Life in America Transparency 29: The Woodstock Nation, 1960s

Multimedia Resources

American Music Audio CD Program: "Blowin' in the Wind"

shown in its works. Pop art challenged the values of traditional art and criticized it for a lack of humor and humanity.

Robert Rauschenberg was one of the first artists to use mass media images in his artwork. In the early 1960s he began to fill large canvases with images from the news and anonymous photographs of city scenes.

Andy Warhol was pop art's most famous artist. His best-known paintings are of brightly colored Campbell's soup cans and of 1950s movie star Marilyn Monroe's face. Art critics debated whether Warhol was criticizing consumer culture or celebrating it. Although some critics saw little merit in pop art, it forced people to discuss the question "What is Art?"

A Musical Revolution

Popular music also underwent many changes during the 1960s. Musical styles and song lyrics reflected the frequent experimentation and social changes of the era.

The "British Invasion"

The popularity of British performers increased in the United States during the mid-1960s. This "British Invasion" began with the Beatles, a foursome from Liverpool, England. Their early songs were upbeat, romantic tunes such as "I Want to Hold Your Hand" and "She Loves You."

The Beatles' 1964 American tour sparked a tremendous wave of excitement among their fans. Reporters labeled the reaction "Beatlemania." One journalist was puzzled by the screaming adoration of excited teenage girls. He concluded, "The Beatles themselves don't know how they do it."

The Beatles' popularity in the United States created opportunities for other British bands. The Rolling Stones, The Who, the Moody Blues, and many other British bands toured the United States and sold millions of records. The success of the Beatles and other rock 'n' roll bands made the growing generation gap in the United States more obvious. Most older Americans could not understand why young women screamed excitedly for the Beatles, or why young men copied their shaggy hairstyles.

Beatles fans react to the arrival of the "Fab Four."

Motown

Changes in the music business resulted in increased opportunities for African Americans. In 1959 businessman Berry Gordy founded **Motown Records** in Detroit, Michigan. The name Motown is a contraction of "Motortown" and refers to Detroit's main industry, automobile manufacturing. Motown Records was the first major record label owned by an African American. In 1960 the company produced the first of many gold records—records selling 500,000 or more copies.

The "Motown sound" was a form of soul music, the most popular black music in the 1960s.

Album covers from 1960s artists Jimi Hendrix, Aretha Franklin, and Bob Dylan

students to research.) Have students work in groups to prepare a design for a Web site on the musical changes that took place and how this music served as a form of protest and a means of change.

REVIEW

Logical-Mathematical, Intrapersonal. Have students complete the Section Review questions. Then direct students' attention to the lyrics of Bob Dylan's "The Times They Are A-Changin,'" located in the introduction to the chapter. Ask students to explain how the lyrics might have appealed to student activists and to advocates of the counterculture.

ASSESS

Have students complete Daily Quiz 19.4.

RETEACH

Logical-Mathematical. Have students complete Main Idea Activities for Reteaching and Sheltered English 19.4. Then ask students to list the terms in the Identify portion of the Section Review. Have students identify whether each term is associated with the student movement, the counterculture, or art and music. Then lead a discussion on how each term influenced American culture during the 1960s. **SHELTERED ENGLISH**

Soul music combined the strong beat of traditional rhythm and blues with smoother sounds and melodies. Some of the most successful soul artists included Aretha Franklin, Marvin Gaye, the Jackson Five, Diana Ross and the Supremes, and Stevie Wonder. Diana Ross gave Motown Records credit for the success of the Supremes: "Had it not been for Berry Gordy searching for talent in our black community we wouldn't have been discovered." Many Motown performers were popular with white listeners as well as black fans.

Folk Music

During the 1960s folk music also became popular. Musician Odetta Gordon performed a wide range of blues, folk, and gospel songs. Folk musicians such as Joan Baez performed songs that addressed political and social issues of the times. Inspired by 1930s folk singer Woody Guthrie, Bob Dylan wrote songs about the struggles of poor and powerless people to rise above their troubles. Although one critic complained that Dylan's voice sounded like "a dog with his leg caught in barbed wire," few critics denied that his lyrics reflected the spirit of the times.

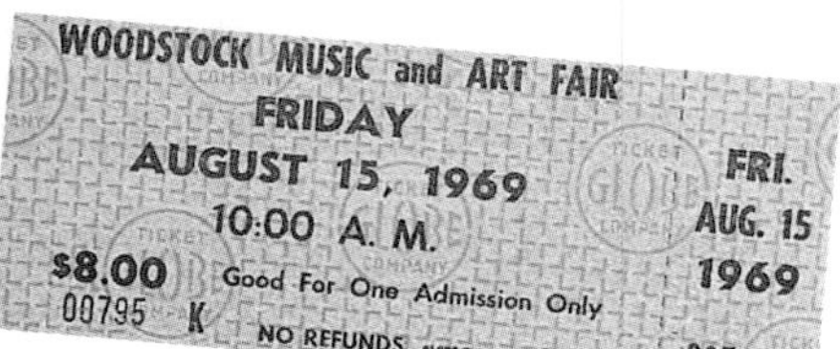

A ticket for Woodstock

Rock Music

In the 1960s rock 'n' roll became the most popular American music. Electrically amplified instruments, particularly the electric guitar, became the driving sound. Jimi Hendrix incorporated electronic distortions, called feedback, into his guitar playing. In his version of "The Star-Spangled Banner," Hendrix used his guitar to produce the screaming sound of the "rockets' red glare."

Blues singer Janis Joplin's instrument was her voice. With her loud vocals and enthusiastic performances, Joplin was a symbol of 1960s rebellious youth. A fan once asked Joplin if she worried that she might ruin her voice. She replied, "Why should I hold back now and sound mediocre [average] just so I can sound mediocre twenty years from now?" Joplin died in 1970 at the age of 27.

In August 1969 more than 400,000 people gathered in upstate New York for the Woodstock Music and Art Fair. In spite of rain, overcrowding, and food shortages, many fans considered it the cultural high point of the 1960s. **Woodstock** soon became a symbol of the counterculture's idealistic spirit. "I call it a cosmic event myself," said folk singer Richie Havens, who performed at Woodstock. "I felt . . . the vibration which was freedom."

SECTION 4 REVIEW

Identify and explain the significance of the following:

- **Mario Savio**
- **Students for a Democratic Society**
- **Tom Hayden**
- **generation gap**
- **counterculture**
- **hippies**
- **pop art**
- **Andy Warhol**
- **Beatles**
- **Berry Gordy**
- **Motown Records**
- **Bob Dylan**
- **Janis Joplin**
- **Woodstock**

Reading for Content Understanding

1 **Main Idea** What were some of the characteristics of the counterculture?

2 **Main Idea** How did art and music reflect social and cultural changes in the 1960s?

3 **Citizenship and Democracy** What issues motivated students to stage protests during the 1960s?

4 **Writing** *Describing* Imagine that you are a reporter. Write an article describing the differences between the student movement and the counterculture.

5 **Critical Thinking** *Making Comparisons* Compare the various musical styles of the 1960s. How do these styles reflect experimentation and social change?

Section 4 Review ANSWERS

Identify

For significance, see the following pages:

- Mario Savio, p. 583
- Students for a Democratic Society, p. 584
- Tom Hayden, p. 584
- generation gap, p. 584
- counterculture, p. 584
- hippies, p. 584
- pop art, p. 585
- Andy Warhol, p. 586
- Beatles, p. 586
- Berry Gordy, p. 586
- Motown Records, p. 586
- Bob Dylan, p. 587
- Janis Joplin, p. 587
- Woodstock, p. 587

Reading for Content Understanding

1. values that ran against mainstream society; emphasis on individual freedom, nonviolence, and communal sharing

2. They challenged traditional beliefs and institutions.

3. racial discrimination, rigid college rules, the growing U.S. military presence in Vietnam, and nuclear weapons

4. Articles will vary but students should state that student activists fought to support causes they believed would challenge and improve society; members of the counterculture rejected society, led alternative lifestyles, and encouraged some unhealthy behaviors.

5. Students should compare the music of the British invasion, Motown, folk music, and rock 'n' roll; answers will vary but students might mention that all the styles experimented with new sounds and that some addressed political and social issues of the day.

OBJECTIVES

- Identify President Kennedy's goal for the U.S. space program.
- Explain the applications of space technology for daily life.
- Describe how scientific advances raised environmental concerns.

FOCUS

Motivate Before Reading

Begin class by asking students to think of examples of space exploration from books, television, and movies. Ask volunteers to describe their examples. Then lead a discussion on reasons for exploring space. Ask students to speculate on how space exploration might improve society and lead to other scientific advances. Write the better suggestions on the chalkboard. Finally, tell

Section 5 RESOURCES

PRINT
- ★ Guided Reading Strategies 19.5
- ★ Geography Activity 19: The Space Race
- ★ Graphic Organizer 19: Foreign Policy and Domestic Strife
- ★ Section 5 Review, p. 591
- ★ Daily Quiz 19.5

MULTIMEDIA
- ★ *Teaching Resources CD–ROM*, Lesson 19.5
- ★ *American History Simulations CD–ROM*: Race to the Moon

SHELTERED ENGLISH
- ★ Main Idea Activities for Reteaching and Sheltered English 19.5

Science in the 1960s

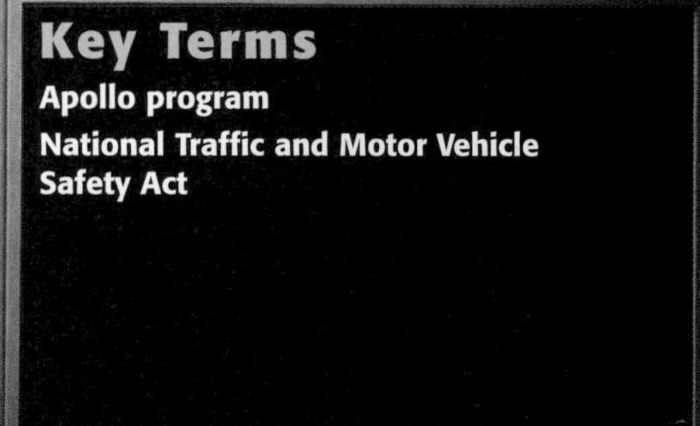

Reading Focus

What goal did President Kennedy set for the U.S. space program?

What applications did space technology have in daily life?

How did scientific advances raise environmental concerns?

Key Terms

Apollo program

National Traffic and Motor Vehicle Safety Act

IN MARCH 1961 "Ivan Ivanovich" was launched into space aboard the Soviet spacecraft Vostok. *He orbited for a while, then re-entered Earth's atmosphere and was ejected from the spacecraft. He parachuted into the snowy Ural Mountains. Since then he has remained in his spacesuit. Ivanovich appeared so lifelike that "model" was written on his forehead so that anyone who found him would not be confused. Model astronaut Ivan Ivanovich now hangs in the Smithsonian National Air and Space Museum in Washington, D.C.*

"Ivan Ivanovich" is the Russian-language equivalent of "John Doe."

 The Space Race

On April 12, 1961, the Soviets launched a real person into space. Soviet cosmonaut Yuri Gagarin became the first human space traveler. He orbited Earth once, a trip that took less than 90 minutes. With Gagarin's successful orbit, the Soviet Union had beaten the United States into space again. NASA, established after the Soviets launched *Sputnik,* was still trying to catch up. Project Mercury was NASA's attempt to put the first American in space.

The Astronauts

In early 1959 NASA had begun its selection process for the project, choosing from a group of military test pilots. NASA required that the astronaut "not be taller than five feet eleven inches, he must weigh less than one hundred eighty pounds, and must be under forty years of age." The 32 pilots who volunteered underwent a series of medical examinations, psychiatric interviews, and physical endurance tests. For example, doctors measured the pilots' ability to withstand extreme cold and heat.

students that in this section they will learn about the early history of America's space program and about how scientific advances raised environmental concerns during the 1960s.

Introduce Key Terms

Linguistic, Visual-Spatial. Review this section's key terms with students. Then display pictures of an *Apollo* rocket and a 1960s automobile. For each image, have students write a caption that uses one of the section's key terms. Call on volunteers to share their captions with the class. **SHELTERED ENGLISH**

TEACH

Have students read Section 5 and complete Guided Reading Strategies 19.5. Choose one or more of the following activities to explore the section content with students. For further suggestions on block scheduling or team teaching, see the *Block Scheduling Handbook.*

LEVEL 1: Linguistic. (Suggested time: 15 min.) As a class, go over students' Guided Reading Strategies. Then use the Reading Focus questions to highlight the main ideas of the section. **SHELTERED ENGLISH**

Photographers and camera crews pressed around the seven test pilots selected to be Project Mercury astronauts.

On April 9, 1959, NASA formally introduced the seven selected astronauts to the public. The media attention on the astronauts and their families was enormous.

Into Space

Despite the excitement of the astronaut selection, the successful Soviet spaceflight disappointed many Americans. Astronaut John Glenn told the press:

> **"[The Soviets] just beat the pants off us, that's all. There's no use kidding ourselves about that. But now that the space age has begun, there's going to be plenty of work for everybody."**

On May 5, 1961—23 days after Gagarin's flight—Alan Shepard Jr. became the first American to enter space. His *Mercury* space capsule reached a maximum altitude of 116 miles above Earth's surface but did not orbit Earth. Later that month, President Kennedy committed the nation to "landing a man on the moon and returning him safely to the earth" before the end of the decade. Kennedy wanted the United States to win the space race because he believed it would be an important symbol of national strength during the Cold War.

In February 1962 John Glenn became the first American to orbit Earth. As the space program advanced, NASA launched the **Apollo program** to prepare for a moon landing. NASA soon pushed far ahead of the Soviets. On July 20, 1969—beating Kennedy's target date by nearly six months—U.S. astronauts reached the moon. As their *Apollo 11* spacecraft settled into lunar orbit, Neil Armstrong and Edwin "Buzz" Aldrin launched themselves in a lunar lander toward the moon's surface. Some 500 million people around the world watched on television as Armstrong took the first steps on the moon.

Most viewers were amazed to see a human on the moon. However, some critics complained that the space program cost a great deal while contributing little to daily life. The Apollo program cost between $25 and $35 billion. Each moon trip cost about half a billion dollars. Nevertheless, the majority of Americans saw the moon landing as a human triumph. *New York Times* reporter James Reston wrote:

> **"The great achievement of the men on the moon is not only that they made history, but that they expanded man's vision of what history might be."**

Technology in Daily Life

The live television broadcast of Armstrong's historic moon walk was an example of a practical application of space research. In the late 1950s the U.S. government began developing satellites to gather scientific data and to send and receive messages. NASA launched its first communications satellite, *Echo I*, in 1960. Once in place, radio waves could be bounced off *Echo I* and redirected to another location.

Private companies began using the technology to improve communications. American Telephone and Telegraph (AT&T), the country's largest communications company, sponsored the building of a satellite. In 1962 *Telstar* was launched. *Telstar* was the first satellite to transmit live television signals and telephone conversations across the Atlantic.

The United States joined with several countries to develop Intelsat, a worldwide commercial

Global Relations

The Space Race. The United States and the Soviet Union each wanted to win the space race as a matter of national security and pride. Lyndon Johnson noted in 1963, "I do not think this generation of Americans is willing to go to bed each night by the light of a Communist moon." Both superpowers saw winning the space race as not only a technological victory but also as a symbolic victory of national supremacy.

Critical Thinking: Do you think the $25 to $35 billion that the U.S. government spent on the space race was a good investment? Explain.

ANSWER: Answers will vary. Students who agree may note the technological advances that resulted from the space race, such as satellites. Those who disagree may argue that these advances could have been developed through other research and that space travel has not benefited society enough to justify the high cost.

Multimedia Resources

American History Simulations CD–ROM: Race to the Moon

ALL LEVELS: Linguistic, Visual-Spatial. (Suggested time: 30 minutes) Ask students to imagine that it is the 1960s and their job is to promote funding for NASA. Have students design a poster that shows the goal and importance of the space race or the benefits of space technology spin-offs. **SHELTERED ENGLISH**

LEVEL 3: Linguistic, Logical-Mathematical. (Suggested time: 25 min. plus homework) For homework, have students create a script for a public service announcement informing Americans about one of the consumer or environmental dangers discussed in this section. In class, call on volunteers to share their scripts. Then lead a discussion on how scientific advances raised environmental concerns during the 1960s.

CLOSE

Logical-Mathematical, Intrapersonal. Have the class rank in order of importance the scientific and technological advances mentioned in this section. Then lead students in a discussion on the importance of each advance they listed.

CHALLENGE AND EXTEND

Linguistic, Visual-Spatial. Have students use the library and other resources to research the history of the environmental movement from the 1960s to the present. Have students use their research to make an annotated time line of the movement.

SCIENCE AND TECHNOLOGY ANSWERS

1. Neil Armstrong; July 20, 1969

2. new technologies, or "spin-offs"

Section 5 Review ANSWERS

Identify

For significance, see the following pages:

- Alan Shepard Jr., p. 589
- John Glenn, p. 589
- Apollo program, p. 589
- Neil Armstrong, p. 589
- Edwin "Buzz" Aldrin, p. 589
- Rachel Carson, p. 591
- Ralph Nader, p. 591
- National Traffic and Motor Vehicle Safety Act, p. 591

Reading for Content Understanding

1. to beat the Soviets in putting a person on the moon

2. led to the development of satellites, which improved communications, weather forecasts, and military spy techniques

3. Scientific advances produced DDT; its harmful effects made people aware of dangers some products posed to the environment, wildlife, and people.

4. Statements will vary but should point out dangers related to a consumer issue mentioned in the section.

5. Answers will vary but students might mention that putting the first person in space would prove that U.S. technology was equal to or better than that of the Soviets and would make the United States appear strong.

Science and Technology

The Apollo Program

On July 20, 1969, two *Apollo 11* astronauts landed on the moon. As Mission Commander Neil Armstrong first touched the surface of the moon, he said, "That's one small step for [a] man, one giant leap for mankind." The people who made this leap possible were the astronauts, engineers, and scientists of the Apollo program.

The Apollo program was created to fulfill the long-range goal of landing an American on the moon. By the time of the first Apollo flight, NASA engineers had built all the equipment as light and small as possible to save fuel for the long trip. Even with careful planning, the Apollo astronauts faced great danger. Three astronauts had died in a fire during a prelaunch test for *Apollo 1,* the first planned flight. Later, on *Apollo 13,* a malfunction left the crew dangerously low on oxygen while in space. Quick thinking and technical skill brought the astronauts safely back to Earth.

Despite its difficulties, the Apollo program was very successful. Altogether, there were eight missions to the moon, six of which landed on the surface. The final Apollo moon mission took place in 1972.

Along with increasing our scientific knowledge of the moon and space, the Apollo program contributed to the development of new technologies. These "spin-offs" included improved computers, satellites, medical equipment, and high-tech construction materials.

After the Apollo program ended, space exploration changed. Today, astronauts work mainly in space stations that orbit Earth or on new types of spacecraft, such as the space shuttle. NASA uses robots, not humans, to explore space. For now, at least, history remembers the 12 Apollo astronauts who landed on the moon as the only human beings to set foot on another world.

Understanding What You Read

1. Who was the first person on the moon? What year did he land?
2. What were some of the benefits of the Apollo program?

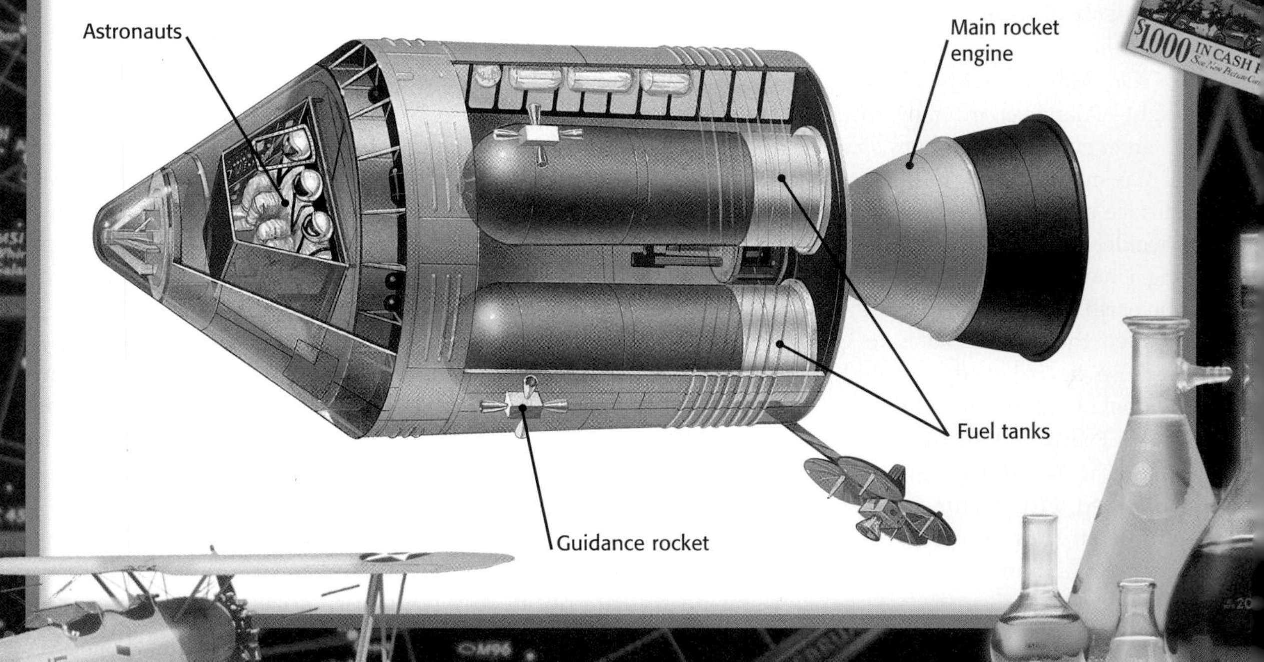

REVIEW

Logical-Mathematical. Have students complete the Section Review questions. Then organize students into groups and assign each part of the section. Have groups outline their section. Photocopy the outlines and distribute them for use as review aids.

ASSESS

Have students complete Daily Quiz 19.5.

RETEACH

Logical-Mathematical, Visual-Spatial. Have students complete Main Idea Activities for Reteaching and Sheltered English 19.5. Organize students into pairs. Ask each pair to create a chart listing the main topics in this section and identifying any advantages or disadvantages associated with each. Then have pairs use their chart to quiz each other on the section. **SHELTERED ENGLISH**

satellite system. Intelsat provided the global television coverage of the *Apollo* moon landing. Satellites soon became the most common way of transmitting telephone messages and TV images.

The U.S. military also launched spy satellites, which could provide detailed pictures of the Soviet Union. Perhaps the most useful technology to come out of the space program was the development of weather satellites. During the 1960s the United States launched many weather satellites. The information they relayed allowed for the early detection of hurricanes. Warnings could then be delivered to areas in danger.

Science and the Environment

While NASA pioneered space exploration, scientists discovered new dangers on Earth. Some problems were created by scientific advances. Biologist Rachel Carson, for example, studied an outbreak of bird deaths in Massachusetts. In her 1962 book, *Silent Spring,* she examines why "the voices of spring in countless towns in America" have been silenced. Carson concluded that DDT—a widely used insect poison, or pesticide—had caused the bird deaths. The birds were poisoned by bugs that had eaten leaves on trees sprayed with DDT. Carson feared that DDT would harm humans. Additional studies confirmed her findings. In 1972 the United States restricted the use of DDT.

Biologist and author Rachel Carson in the woods near her home

In the mid-1960s lawyer Ralph Nader raised concerns about other dangers to consumers. In his 1965 book, *Unsafe at Any Speed,* he criticized the auto industry for unsafe car designs. According to Nader, car bumpers could not withstand an impact of three miles per hour. Head-on collisions, even at 25 miles per hour, were often fatal. Nader's efforts led to the passage of the **National Traffic and Motor Vehicle Safety Act** in September 1966. This law required the federal government to enact safety standards for all cars sold in the United States.

Nader then turned his attention to other consumer issues. He called for new government regulation to protect citizens. His associates, known as Nader's Raiders, investigated baby food, gas pipelines, land use, and the meat industry. For many Americans, Nader's efforts were an example of the reform spirit of the 1960s.

SECTION 5 REVIEW

Identify and explain the significance of the following:

- **Alan Shepard Jr.**
- **John Glenn**
- **Apollo program**
- **Neil Armstrong**
- **Edwin "Buzz" Aldrin**
- **Rachel Carson**
- **Ralph Nader**
- **National Traffic and Motor Vehicle Safety Act**

Reading for Content Understanding

1. **Main Idea** What was the goal of the U.S. space program in the 1960s?
2. **Main Idea** How did space technology improve daily life?
3. **Geographic Diversity** *Human-Environment Interaction* Why did scientific advances increase environmental awareness?
4. **Writing** *Describing* Imagine that you are one of Nader's Raiders in the 1960s. Write a press statement about a consumer issue you are investigating.
5. **Critical Thinking** *Synthesizing Information* Why do you think sending an American to the moon was such an important symbolic goal during the Cold War?

Chapter 19 Review ANSWERS

Identifying People and Ideas

1. U.S. president elected in 1960; represented youthful idealism; assassinated in 1963

2. succeeded to the presidency following Kennedy's death; elected in 1964; expanded aid and reform programs, civil rights, and the war in Vietnam

3. 1962 conflict that resulted when Kennedy demanded the Soviets remove missiles they had placed in Cuba

4. failed 1961 invasion of Cuba by U.S.-trained Cuban exiles

5. Johnson's social reform program that focused on improving health care, education, civil rights, and aid for the poor

6. student leader of the 1964 free-speech movement at the University of California at Berkeley

7. members of the 1960s counterculture

8. NASA's program to put a person on the moon

9. the first human to step onto the moon

10. environmental biologist who wrote *Silent Spring,* warning that the use of DDT could harm humans and wildlife

Using the Time Line

1. f **4.** d

2. e **5.** b

3. a **6.** c

Review and Assessment RESOURCES

PRINT
- ★ Chapter 19 Review, pp. 592–93
- ★ Vocabulary Activity 19
- ★ Chapter 19 Study Guide
- ★ Chapter 19 Test (Form A or B)

MULTIMEDIA
- ★ Audio Program, Ch. 19 (English and Spanish)
- ★ *Global Skill Builder CD–ROM*
- ★ Chapter 19 Test Generator
- ★ HRW Web site

SHELTERED ENGLISH
- ★ Spanish Glossary
- ★ Sheltered English Chapter 19 Test

ASSESS

Have students complete one of the Chapter 19 tests. As an alternate assessment, assign the Chapter 19 Investigation.

Understanding Main Ideas

1. Bay of Pigs, Berlin Wall, Cuban missile crisis

2. Medicare, Medicaid, Elementary and Secondary School Education Act, Immigration and Nationality Act

3. It was a large, organized movement of students who wanted to improve society and believed that they could.

4. alternative lifestyles; long hair and unconventional clothes; communal living; tolerant and peaceful attitudes

5. In both, the United States and the Soviet Union competed for global supremacy. Also, space research led to technological advances in espionage and weapons systems used in the Cold War.

6. improved communications, weather information, and military knowledge through the development of satellites

Reviewing Themes

1. After the Soviet Union installed missiles in Cuba that could reach some U.S. cities, Kennedy demanded the missiles be removed, threatened to attack the Soviet Union if any of the missiles were fired, and had the U.S. Navy blockade Cuba. The possibility of nuclear war loomed, but the Soviet Union finally backed down and removed the missiles.

2. Job training, improved educational opportunities, and housing for low-income Americans opened doors previously closed to many. Programs such as Medicare and Medicaid helped some Americans afford health care, and poverty in the United States declined.

CHAPTER 19 REVIEW

Chapter Summary

In 1961 President John F. Kennedy brought a sense of energy and hope to the White House. He successfully guided the United States through the Cuban missile crisis. After Kennedy's assassination, President Lyndon B. Johnson tried to create a Great Society with many social reform programs. At the same time, many American youths rebelled against society and began a student movement. The moon landing of U.S. astronauts inspired great national pride.

On a separate sheet of paper, complete the following activities.

Identifying People and Ideas

Describe the historical significance of the following:

1. John F. Kennedy
2. Lyndon B. Johnson
3. Cuban missile crisis
4. Bay of Pigs
5. Great Society
6. Mario Savio
7. hippies
8. Apollo program
9. Neil Armstrong
10. Rachel Carson

Internet Activity 

go.hrw.com **SB1 Apollo Program**

Search the Internet through the HRW Web site to find information about the Apollo program. Use the information to create a multimedia display of the astronauts' experience during the Apollo missions.

Understanding Main Ideas

1. What major Cold War crises took place during President Kennedy's administration?
2. What major legislation was passed while President Johnson was in office?
3. What made the student movement of the 1960s new and different?
4. What were some of the characteristics of the counterculture?
5. How was the space race related to the Cold War?
6. What contributions did space technology make to everyday life?

Reviewing Themes

1. **Global Relations** Why did the United States and the Soviet Union almost fight a nuclear war in the 1960s?
2. **Economic Development** How did President Johnson's War on Poverty and Great Society programs improve many citizens' economic situations?

Using the Time Line

Number your paper from 1 to 6. Match the letters on the time line below with the following events.

1. **The Woodstock Music and Art Fair attracts thousands of people.**
2. **U.S. astronauts make the first moon landing.**
3. **People fear the Cuban missile crisis may lead to nuclear war.**
4. **Medicare legislation is signed into law.**
5. **John F. Kennedy is assassinated.**
6. **The free-speech movement begins.**

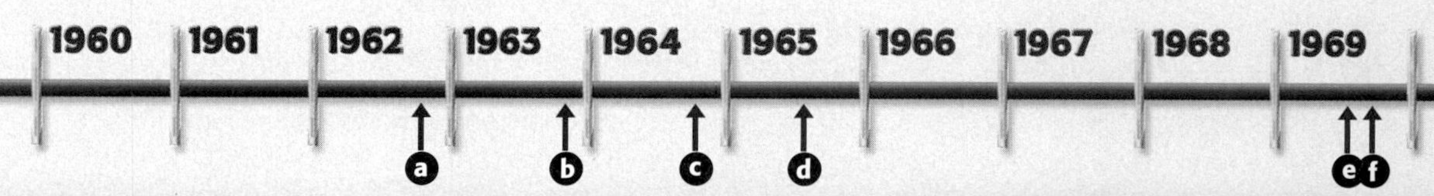

RETEACH

Logical-Mathematical, Interpersonal. Organize the class into five teams and assign each one a section. Have each team make two sets of cards, one listing important people, events, or dates; the other giving the significance of each item. Have teams trade cards and compete to match them up correctly. Award points based on which team finishes first. Continue until each team has seen all the cards.

SHELTERED ENGLISH

Using the Internet

Have students continue their research to find information about the U.S. space program today: its size, funding, activities, and goals. Then have students write a newspaper article describing the current space program.

Portfolio Extensions

1. Ask students to imagine that they participated in the project they described. Have them write one or more journal entries describing their experiences.

2. Have students plan and hold a student rally to raise awareness of the issue they chose. Students should schedule speakers to describe the issue and to present a plan of action for change or improvement.

3. **Citizenship and Democracy** How did hippies and student groups attempt to change society?

Thinking Critically

1. **Identifying Cause and Effect** How did the Bay of Pigs invasion contribute to increased Cold War tensions in the 1960s?
2. **Making Comparisons** How did the interests and leadership styles of Presidents Kennedy and Johnson contribute to their administrations?
3. **Drawing Conclusions** Why do you think the civil rights movement was important to Students for a Democratic Society and the free-speech movement?

Writing About History

1. **Persuading** Write a television commercial persuading people to vote for either John F. Kennedy or Richard Nixon for president.
2. **Expressing** Imagine that it is 1969 and the Soviet Union has made the first moon landing instead of the United States. Write a science-fiction short story expressing the consequences.

Linking Geography and History

1. **Location** Why did the Kennedy administration view the Soviet missiles in Cuba as a serious threat?
2. **Movement** Why did the Communists build a wall in Berlin?

Building Your Portfolio

Complete the following activities individually or in groups.

1. **Peace Corps Recruitment** Imagine that you are a Peace Corps volunteer who is recruiting Americans to work on a specific project in a foreign country. Design a recruitment program that offers information about what the project is, where it is, what it will accomplish, and what kinds of skills volunteers will need. Create a poster and a recruiting brochure to advertise your program.
2. **Community Activist** Pick an issue in your community that is important to you and that you think needs attention. Start a campaign to get your local government to take action. Your campaign should include a petition for signatures and a speech to present your position at the next city government meeting.

History Skills Workshop

Using Visual Resources Study the image below, which is Robert Rauschenberg's 1963 painting *Estate.* Then answer the following questions: (a) What media does Rauschenberg appear to use? (b) How does this picture represent the pop art movement? (c) What can you learn about 1960s culture from this painting? Explain your answer.

Robert Rauschenberg, *Estate*, 1963, Philadelphia Museum of Art: Gift of the Friends of the Philadelphia Museum of Art

3. They protested in strikes and demonstrations, expressed their beliefs through music and art, and held festivals and rallies.

Thinking Critically

1. The invasion increased Soviet leaders' feelings of distrust and animosity toward the United States.

2. Kennedy's charm and style made him extremely popular; Johnson's political experience enabled him to achieve some of his goals.

3. These movements relied on many of the same protest techniques and supported many similar causes.

Writing About History

1. Commercials will vary but should include some information about the candidate's background, qualifications, and political beliefs and goals.

2. Stories will vary but may include growing American fears of the Soviets, war and eventual Soviet domination of the United States, or a future that is not too different from the present.

Linking Geography and History

1. From their nearby location in Cuba, the missiles had the capacity to hit some major U.S. population centers.

2. to stop the growing flow of East Berliners to West Berlin

History Skills Workshop

(a) pastels and photographs; (b) many of its subjects are everyday objects; (c) Answers will vary but students might say that the painting symbolizes how some people at the time were stopping to reconsider and break free from traditional American values and institutions.

CHAPTER PLANNING GUIDE
The Search for Equal Rights

	SECTION LESSON OBJECTIVES	PRINT RESOURCES	MULTIMEDIA RESOURCES	SHELTERED ENGLISH RESOURCES
Section 1: The Civil Rights Movement (pp. 595–601)	★ Describe the events that led to new civil rights laws. ★ Explain how Freedom Summer and the marches in Selma brought about the Voting Rights Act of 1965. ★ Discuss how the civil rights movement changed in the late 1960s and the 1970s.	★ Guided Reading Strategies 20.1 ★ Geography Activity 20: The Civil Rights Movement ★ Literature Reading 20: *The Autobiography of Malcolm X* ★ Section 1 Review, p. 601 ★ Daily Quiz 20.1	★ *Teaching Resources CD–ROM*, Lesson 20.1 ★ *Exploring America's Past* Video Segment: Marching to Freedom: *Teacher's Guide*, pp. 35–36 ★ HRW Web site	★ Main Idea Activities for Reteaching and Sheltered English 20.1
Section 2: Rights for Hispanics (pp. 604–09)	★ Explain how César Chávez and the United Farm Workers helped migrant workers. ★ Describe how other Mexican Americans fought for civil rights. ★ Identify some of the goals of the Chicano movement.	★ Guided Reading Strategies 20.2 ★ Section 2 Review, p. 609 ★ Daily Quiz 20.2	★ *Teaching Resources CD–ROM*, Lesson 20.2 ★ Art in American History Transparency 47: *Tamalada*	★ Main Idea Activities for Reteaching and Sheltered English 20.2
Section 3: The Women's Rights Movement (pp. 610–15)	★ Explain the significance of the year 1963 for the women's rights movement. ★ Describe the goals and tactics of younger feminists. ★ Analyze the successes and failures of the women's rights movement.	★ Guided Reading Strategies 20.3 ★ Biography Reading 20: Betty Friedan ★ Section 3 Review, p. 615 ★ Daily Quiz 20.3	★ *Teaching Resources CD–ROM*, Lesson 20.3 ★ Art in American History Transparency 49: *Dream 2: King and the Sisterhood* ★ HRW Web site	★ Main Idea Activities for Reteaching and Sheltered English 20.3
Section 4: Rights for All (pp. 616–19)	★ Describe how American Indians protested their treatment by the federal government. ★ Explain the goals of the disability rights movement. ★ Identify how older Americans and young Americans were affected by the civil rights movement.	★ Guided Reading Strategies 20.4 ★ Graphic Organizer 20: Working for Equal Rights for All ★ Primary Source Reading 20: The Life of a Disabled Teenager ★ Section 4 Review, p. 619 ★ Daily Quiz 20.4	★ *Teaching Resources CD–ROM*, Lesson 20.4 ★ Linking Geography and History Transparency 12B: Native American Resistance, 1830–1980	★ Main Idea Activities for Reteaching and Sheltered English 20.4
Chapter Review and Assessment (pp. 620–21)		★ Chapter 20 Review, pp. 620–21 ★ Vocabulary Activity 20 ★ Chapter 20 Study Guide ★ Chapter 20 Test (Form A or B)	★ Audio Program, Ch. 20 (English and Spanish) ★ *Global Skill Builder CD–ROM* ★ Chapter 20 Test Generator ★ HRW Web site	★ Spanish Glossary ★ Sheltered English Chapter 20 Test

CHAPTER OVERVIEW

The 1960s marked an era of change in the United States. African Americans struggled to gain their civil rights. Leaders such as Martin Luther King Jr. supported the use of nonviolent protest to fight racial segregation and discrimination. The movement's refusal to resort to violence, even when confronted with it, helped gain public support. The movement later became divided, however, when advocates of Black Power began calling for separation from white society.

In turn, the African American civil rights movement inspired other minority groups to fight for equal rights under the law. César Chávez and the United Farm Workers pushed for better conditions and pay for migrant workers. Hispanics also struggled to overcome discrimination and increase cultural pride and political power.

Women worked to gain equal rights in society and in the workplace through groups such as the National Organization for Women. Younger feminists focused on "women's liberation," while feminists united to push for an Equal Rights Amendment.

American Indians fought for land claims and for equal rights, with mixed success. Americans with disabilities fought for better education, job opportunities, and access to public buildings. Civil rights activists also worked to protect the rights of young and older Americans.

CHAPTER INVESTIGATION

The Chapter Investigation is an extended, multipart activity designed for students to work cooperatively and apply the chapter content in the creation of a project. You may choose to use the Chapter 20 Investigation, Civil Rights Rally, either as a substitute for teaching the section lessons or as an alternate assessment.

BLOCK SCHEDULING 

The teacher lesson plans for each section offer a variety of activity choices to help you present the material in a block scheduling format. For further suggestions on block scheduling, see the *Block Scheduling Handbook with Team Teaching Strategies*, pp. 115–20.

Meeting Individual Needs

ABILITY LEVELS

LEVEL 1 Basic level activities designed for all students encountering new material.

LEVEL 2 Intermediate level activities designed for average students.

LEVEL 3 Challenging activities designed for above-average students.

SHELTERED ENGLISH These activities address the needs of students with Limited English Proficiency.

Smithsonian Institution®

Internet Connections and Lesson 20
www.si.edu/hrw

CNN Presents America:
Yesterday and Today 1850 to the Present
Segment: "I Have a Dream"

Additional Resources

Books for Teachers

Blum, John M. *Years of Discord: American Politics and Society, 1961–1974.* Norton, 1992. Highly readable narrative of the 1960s and early 1970s.

Friedan, Betty. *It Changed My Life: Writings on the Women's Movement.* Dell, 1991. Includes essays on women's struggle for equality in the 1960s.

Powledge, Fred. *Free at Last?* HarperCollins, 1992. Details the course of the civil rights movement through first-person accounts.

Books for Students

Archer, Jules. *The Incredible Sixties: The Stormy Years That Changed America.* Harcourt Brace, 1986. Begins with Kent State and moves backward to cover the Kennedy years, the civil rights movement, Vietnam, feminism, and elements of the counterculture movement (for students reading below grade level).

Carson, Clayborne, et al., eds. *Eyes on the Prize Civil Rights Reader.* Viking Penguin, 1991. Accounts of the African American struggle for equal rights.

Haskins, James, and Kathleen Benson. *The Sixties Reader.* Viking, 1988. Uses primary sources to outline the 1960s.

Multimedia Materials

The Second American Revolution, Part II. Video, 58 min. PBS. Details the assault on segregation.

The Sixties. Video, 15 min. Phoenix BFA Films & Video Inc. Brief review of politics and society in the 1960s.

Women in American Life: 1955–1977. Video, 25 min. National Women's History Project. Charts the dramatic changes in women's lives.

The Search for Equal Rights

CHAPTER MOTIVATOR

Have a volunteer read aloud the opening passage of this chapter. Draw students' attention to the quote by Diane Nash. Ask the class to identify areas of concern today that require action "to extend equal rights to all." List students' replies on the chalkboard. Then ask students to speculate on what they might do to accomplish change in the areas they listed. Conclude by having students write a short paragraph in response to Nash's question, "What can I do?" When students are finished, call on volunteers to read their paragraphs. Then tell students that in this chapter they will learn about civil rights movements between 1960 and 1978, and what these movements accomplished.

Presenting Themes

- **Citizenship and Democracy** Students might mention that groups could hold protests and demonstrations, submit petitions for laws in states that give citizens the initiative, initiate campaigns to inform the community, initiate lawsuits, support like-minded political candidates, and run for public office.
- **Constitutional Heritage** Students might mention that a government could pass laws to guarantee civil rights and use the police, national guard, and other groups to enforce compliance.
- **Geographic Diversity** Students might mention that discrimination and opposition to change may be greater in some regions than in others. In addition, groups facing discrimination can vary by region. Thus, activists may need to adjust the tactics they use to address the specific civil rights problems a particular region poses.

Using the Time Line

Have students identify which events were the result of government action and which were the result of civic action. After students complete the chapter, have them write a paragraph about the way civic action can change American society.

CHAPTER 20

The Search for Equal Rights

(1960–1978)

During the 1960s many American teenagers participated in movements to extend equal rights to all citizens. "Young people [today] should realize that it was people just like them, their age, that formulated goals and strategies," recalled activist Diane Nash. "When they look around now, and see things that need to be changed, they should say: 'What can I do?'" Nash and many others answered that question in their search for equal rights.

Citizenship and Democracy
How might groups work to change a society?

Constitutional Heritage
In what ways might a government help its citizens gain civil rights?

Geographic Diversity
How might civil rights efforts vary in different regions?

OBJECTIVES

- Describe the events that led to new civil rights laws.
- Explain how Freedom Summer and the marches in Selma brought about the Voting Rights Act of 1965.
- Discuss how the civil rights movement changed in the late 1960s and the 1970s.

FOCUS

Motivate Before Reading

Write Section 1 of the Fifteenth Amendment on the chalkboard and ask students to draft a short paragraph explaining what the text means to them. Ask volunteers to share their interpretations. Then explain to students that although this amendment was ratified in 1870, many African Americans were still being denied the right to vote during the 1960s. Tell students that in this section

The Civil Rights Movement

Reading Focus

What events led to new civil rights laws?

Why were Freedom Summer and the marches in Selma successful in bringing about the Voting Rights Act of 1965?

How did the civil rights movement change in the late 1960s and 1970s?

Key Terms

sit-in
Student Nonviolent Coordinating Committee
Freedom Rides
Civil Rights Act of 1964
Freedom Summer
Voting Rights Act of 1965
Black Power
affirmative action
University of California v. Bakke

On February 1, 1960, Joseph McNeil bought a tube of toothpaste at a Woolworth's department store in Greensboro, North Carolina. His friend Franklin McCain bought some school supplies. Then the two black college students sat down together at the lunch counter and ordered coffee. The waitress refused to serve them. McCain asked her, "Why is it that you serve me at one counter and deny me at another?" The two shoppers were joined by two other African American students. They sat at the counter without being served until the store closed for the day. They returned the next morning with about 20 more students. Soon other African American students throughout the South were staging similar protests that captured the nation's attention.

Restaurants throughout the South segregated white and black customers.

IMAGE ON LEFT PAGE: *More than 200,000 Americans participated in the March on Washington.*

Section 1 RESOURCES

PRINT

- ★ Guided Reading Strategies 20.1
- ★ Geography Activity 20: The Civil Rights Movement
- ★ Literature Reading 20: *The Autobiography of Malcolm X*
- ★ Section 1 Review, p. 601
- ★ Daily Quiz 20.1

MULTIMEDIA

- ★ *Teaching Resources CD–ROM,* Lesson 20.1
- ★ *Exploring America's Past* Video Segment: Marching to Freedom: *Teacher's Guide,* pp. 35–36
- ★ HRW Web site

SHELTERED ENGLISH

- ★ Main Idea Activities for Reteaching and Sheltered English 20.1

they will learn about the African American struggle for civil rights during the 1960s and 1970s, and its accomplishments.

Introduce Key Terms

Linguistic. Review this section's key terms with students. Have students use context cues to write a definition for each term. Ask students to share their definitions with the class. Then assist students in correcting any inaccuracies in their definitions. **SHELTERED ENGLISH**

TEACH

Have students read Section 1 and complete Guided Reading Strategies 20.1. Choose one or more of the following activities to explore the section content with students. For further suggestions on block scheduling or team teaching, see the *Block Scheduling Handbook.*

LEVEL 1: Linguistic. (Suggested time: 15 min.) As a class, go over students' Guided Reading Strategies. Then use the Reading Focus questions to highlight the main ideas of the section. **SHELTERED ENGLISH**

Citizenship and Democracy

The Sit-In Movement. Word of the Greensboro sit-in spread quickly among civil rights activists, and within days similar events were in the planning stages. Less than a month after the four students took their seats at the Greensboro lunch counter, students were conducting sit-ins in other southern cities, such as Richmond, Virginia, and Tallahassee, Florida. Within two months, more than 50,000 students—black and white—had participated in sit-ins protesting racial segregation.

Critical Thinking: Why do you think sit-ins became such a popular form of protest?

ANSWER: Answers will vary but students might mention that protesters wanted to remain true to the principle of nonviolence and that sit-ins were a simple and highly visible means of protest.

The Sit-Ins

The four young men who started the Greensboro protest—McCain, McNeil, Ezell Blair, and David Richmond—had become friends at college. They had spent hours discussing race relations in the United States. They hungered for action. However, as McCain recalled, "There were many words and few deeds." During one conversation, McNeil declared, "It's time that we take some action." The four students decided to start by protesting racial segregation in local businesses.

They targeted Woolworth's, a popular variety store with a racially segregated lunch counter. On February 1, 1960, the four students sat down at the "whites only" section of the local Woolworth's lunch counter. They were staging a **sit-in**—a demonstration in which protesters sit down in a location and refuse to leave. Newspapers throughout the country reported their protest. Their sit-in inspired other African American students to protest segregation.

To achieve their goals, the sit-in protesters practiced nonviolent resistance. This strategy of peaceful protest rejected the use of violence, even for self-defense. Remaining nonviolent was not always easy. Crowds of angry white citizens often shouted insults at the protesters, threw food on them, and even assaulted them. An African American named Anne Moody described her appearance after a sit-in that turned violent:

> **"[My hair] was stiff with dried mustard, ketchup and sugar. . . . I didn't have on any shoes because I had lost them when I was dragged across the floor at Woolworth's. My stockings were sticking to my legs from the mustard that had dried on them."**

Over time, Woolworth's began to integrate its lunch counters. Some other businesses in the South also integrated. This success encouraged African American student leaders to organize. Civil rights activist Ella Baker gathered student leaders together in the spring of 1960. They formed the **Student Nonviolent Coordinating Committee** (SNCC) to coordinate civil rights demonstrations and provide training for protesters.

Anne Moody (seated, far right) wrote about her experiences in the civil rights movement in Coming of Age in Mississippi.

Freedom Rides

Despite the move toward integration in some businesses, bus stations all over the South still required travelers to use segregated facilities. In December 1960 the Supreme Court had ruled this practice illegal, but it continued nonetheless. The Congress of Racial Equality (CORE), a civil rights organization, decided to pressure the federal government to enforce the Court ruling. CORE organized **Freedom Rides** to protest segregation. On these rides, black and white riders traveled in buses throughout the South. Black riders would use "whites only" facilities. White riders would use facilities reserved for African Americans.

The Freedom Rides started in May 1961, when 13 riders began a bus trip from Washington, D.C., to New Orleans, Louisiana. By the time the bus reached Anniston, Alabama, a white mob had gathered. The mob pounded the riders with clubs and threw a firebomb through the bus's back window. The riders narrowly escaped with their lives.

Another mob attacked a second bus with CORE riders in Birmingham, Alabama. CORE leaders called off the bus protests because of the threats to the riders' lives. In spite of the enormous danger, SNCC leaders stepped in and decided to

ALL LEVELS: Logical-Mathematical, Visual-Spatial. (Suggested time: 45 min.) Explain to students that legislation results from a series of events. Then ask students to create flowcharts describing the events that led to the Civil Rights Act of 1964 and the Voting Rights Act of 1965. For each event, have students list important dates, leaders, organizations, strategies, and goals. When students have finished, call on volunteers to explain the sequence of events they used. As they do, construct a class flowchart on the board. Finally, lead a discussion on the significance of the Civil Rights Act of 1964 and the Voting Rights Act of 1965. **SHELTERED ENGLISH**

LEVEL 2: Logical-Mathematical, Visual-Spatial. (Suggested time: 45 min.) Explain to students that a group problem-solving process requires several steps. First, a problem must be identified. Second, people need to organize to decide how to solve the problem. Third, the group has to take steps to solve the problem. Finally, the group evaluates the results to determine the effects of their actions and if they have achieved their goals. You may want to create a visual representation of this process on the chalkboard. Then have students apply this process to the African American civil rights movement of the 1960s and 1970s. First, have students point out the civil rights issues the movement addressed. Second, have students identify civil rights organizations linked to each issue.

continue the Freedom Rides. Nashville student leader Diane Nash said:

> **"These people faced the probability of their own deaths before they ever left Nashville. Several made out wills. A few more gave me sealed letters to be mailed if they were killed. Some told me frankly that they were afraid, but they knew this was something that they must do because freedom was worth it."**

In late May, SNCC riders arrived in Montgomery, Alabama. A mob immediately attacked them. The Kennedy administration feared more violence and wanted the Freedom Rides to end. Attorney General Robert Kennedy advised the riders to observe a "cooling-off period." Ride organizer James Farmer responded, "Please tell the attorney general that we have been cooling off for three hundred and fifty years."

The attorney general provided a police escort, and the rides continued. Many Freedom Riders were jailed in Jackson, Mississippi. Despite the arrests, new people volunteered to participate.

The Freedom Rides ended only after the Interstate Commerce Commission banned bus and railroad companies from using segregated facilities. The ban went into effect on November 1. One SNCC member recalled, "From that moment on, segregation was dead." Although segregation did not die then, the Freedom Riders had struck an important blow.

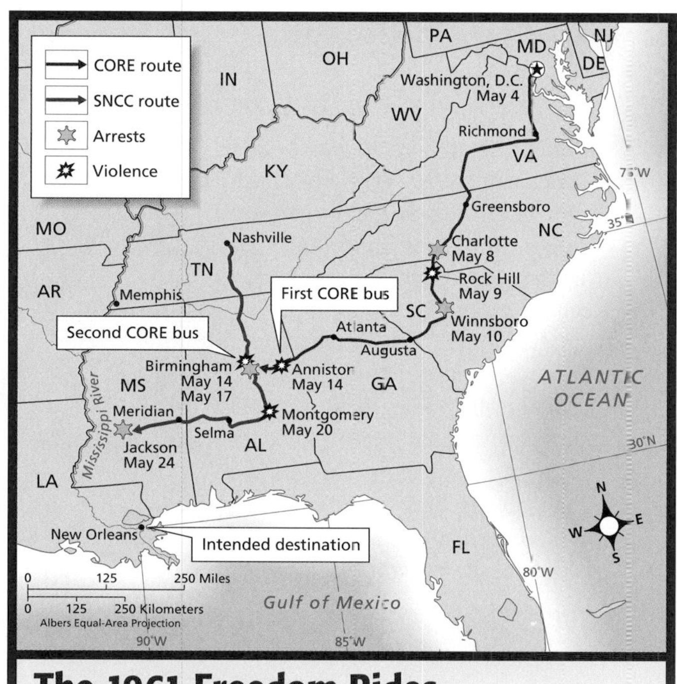

The 1961 Freedom Rides

Learning from Maps Civil rights workers staged Freedom Rides throughout the South to protest the region's segregated bus stations.

Location In which states did the Freedom Riders meet with violence?

Demonstrations in Birmingham

Following these incidents, Martin Luther King Jr. decided to force the end of Jim Crow laws that segregated the South. In 1963 the Southern Christian Leadership Conference (SCLC) chose Birmingham as the site for a campaign of boycotts, sit-ins, and demonstrations. Reverend Fred Shuttlesworth, a Birmingham civil rights leader, hoped to break down the city's segregation policies.

In April, King was arrested during one of the protests. While in custody, King wrote his now famous *Letter from Birmingham Jail.* This letter confirmed his commitment to nonviolence. Responding to a plea for patience made by white clergymen, King wrote:

> **"When you have to concoct [make up] an answer for a five-year-old son asking . . . 'Daddy, why do white people treat colored people so mean?' . . . then you will understand why we find it difficult to wait."**

Working for Freedom

In the fall of 1962 the fight for civil rights continued. Some 20,000 federal troops protected black student James Meredith as he registered at the all-white University of Mississippi. A few months later, Alabama governor George Wallace declared that he would fight for "segregation now, segregation tomorrow, segregation forever."

Global Relations

Kennedy and the Freedom Rides. President Kennedy was not pleased with the timing of the Freedom Rides. He was scheduled to meet with Nikita Khrushchev the next month. Kennedy worried that the Soviet leader would raise the issue of racial strife in the United States and point to the Freedom Rides as proof that American democracy did not work. Kennedy did not want to see the United States embarrassed before the rest of the world. He nonetheless approved police protection for the Freedom Riders when they insisted on continuing the protests.

Activity: Ask students to use the library and search the Internet through the HRW Web site to research the Freedom Rides. Then ask students to imagine that they are participants and have them write letters to President Kennedy explaining why they joined the Freedom Rides.

go.hrw.com
SB1 Freedom

MAP ANSWER
Alabama, South Carolina

Third, have students specify the protest strategies each group used, such as Freedom Summer and the marches in Selma. Finally, have students analyze the effectiveness of these strategies. You may want to have students create graphic organizers that show the processes they are identifying. **SHELTERED ENGLISH**

LEVEL 3: Linguistic, Intrapersonal. (Suggested time: 30 min. plus homework) Discuss with the class the changes in the civil rights movement in the late 1960s and the 1970s. Then have students write a dialogue for an imaginary discussion between Martin Luther King Jr. and Malcolm X. Dialogues should focus on the differences between the two leaders' political goals *(e.g., King's belief in integration of the races, and Malcolm X's belief that African Americans should work for social and economic independence)* and on their differing views on how to achieve these goals *(e.g., King's belief in nonviolent protest, and Malcolm X's belief that African Americans have the right to use violence to protect themselves)*. Ask two students to perform one of the dialogues for the class. Encourage feedback. Then lead a class discussion on why nonviolent protest has proved so effective in many situations.

Biography

Martin Luther King Jr.
Throughout his life, Martin Luther King Jr. remained committed to the philosophy of nonviolence. He believed that peace, love, and brotherhood were the paths to uniting humanity. King thought that if African Americans fought for their rights with endurance and intelligence instead of with violence, they would be more likely to win support for their cause. In 1964, shortly after passage of the Civil Rights Act, King was awarded the Nobel Peace Prize for his dedication to nonviolence to secure civil rights. At the time, he was the youngest person ever to receive the honor.

Critical Thinking: Why might more people support nonviolent protesters than those who use violence?

ANSWER: Answers will vary but students might mention that people would be more likely to respect, listen to, and feel sympathy for nonviolent protesters.

Multimedia Resources

Exploring America's Past Video Segment: Marching to Freedom; *Teacher's Guide*, pp. 35–36

Search 40651, Play to 47323
Videodisc Blue Side A

Play

Pause

See *Teacher's Guide* for Spanish barcode.

Biography

Martin Luther King Jr.

Martin Luther King Jr. was born in Atlanta, Georgia, in 1929. His family included many preachers and reformers who taught him the importance of fighting for justice. King entered college at age 15. After graduating, he studied at a seminary to become a minister. This seminary was the first integrated school King had attended. His experiences there greatly shaped his personal philosophies. King also studied the writings of Mohandas Gandhi, an Indian leader who used nonviolent resistance to help end British rule over India. These ideas helped shape King's later tactics in the civil rights movement.

While doing graduate work at Boston University, King met and married Coretta Scott. She would become one of his most important allies in his civil rights work. In 1954 the Kings moved to Montgomery, Alabama, where King became a minister at Dexter Avenue Baptist Church. He joined the local NAACP and began his lifelong participation in the civil rights movement.

The demonstrations continued after King's release from jail. In early May some 2,500 marchers walked through downtown Birmingham streets. Police Commissioner Eugene "Bull" Connor ordered the fire department to turn high-pressure hoses on the demonstrators. Connor then ordered his officers to release their attack dogs. TV camera crews captured the violence in shocking detail. The televised events gave many Americans their first real understanding that the civil rights movement in the South was a life-and-death struggle.

March on Washington

With public pressure mounting, President Kennedy announced his support for a new civil rights bill to end racial discrimination. African American leaders were hopeful but cautious. They decided to hold a nationwide demonstration—known as the March on Washington—to encourage support for the bill. A. Philip Randolph presided over the march, which was originally planned only for African Americans.

On August 28 more than 200,000 people—both black and white—filled the area around the Washington Monument. They marched to the Lincoln Memorial, where they listened to speakers. In his "I Have a Dream" speech, Martin Luther King Jr. filled the crowd with hope. According to one marcher, King's speech "just seemed to move you almost off the platform, off the earth."

Two weeks after the march, however, the hopeful mood crumbled in a wave of violence. A bomb exploded at an African American church in Birmingham and killed four young girls. A near riot followed. Two months later, President Kennedy was assassinated. After Kennedy's death, President Johnson took up the challenge of civil rights legislation. Johnson signed the **Civil Rights Act of 1964** in July 1964. The law banned segregation in public places, such as restaurants and transportation facilities. The law also prohibited employers, unions, or universities with federal government contracts from discriminating on the basis of color, sex, religion, and national origin.

Some participants in the March on Washington stood in front of the Lincoln Memorial as they listened to the speeches.

CLOSE

Linguistic, Logical-Mathematical, Intrapersonal. Ask students to list changes in the United States that resulted from the African American civil rights movement of the 1960s and 1970s. Call on volunteers to explain some of the items on their lists. As they do, make a master list on the chalkboard. Then lead a discussion on which efforts students think were most effective in African Americans' struggle for civil rights.

TEACHER TO TEACHER

CHALLENGE AND EXTEND

1. **Linguistic, Interpersonal.** Paul Lemmon of New Braunfels, Texas, suggested the following activity: Have students interview someone born before 1945 about examples of segregation and discrimination that he or she remembers seeing during the 1960s and earlier. Students might also ask what the person remembers about local events or reactions connected to the

Voting Rights

That same summer, SNCC leader Robert Moses organized hundreds of volunteers. Most of them were white students from northern colleges. They volunteered for **Freedom Summer**, a campaign in Mississippi to register African Americans to vote. In Mississippi and some other southern states, threats of job loss, unfair election rules, and violence kept most African Americans from voting.

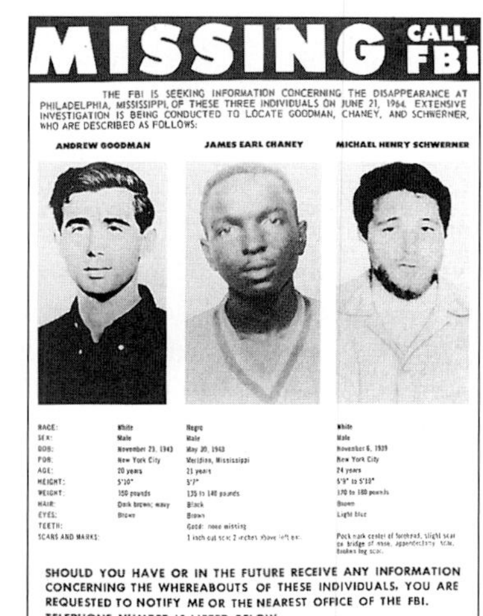

President Johnson ordered the Federal Bureau of Investigation to help locate the missing civil rights workers.

Murder in Mississippi

On June 21, 1964, three Freedom Summer volunteers disappeared. Andrew Goodman and Michael Schwerner, white activists from the North, and James Chaney, a black activist from Mississippi, remained missing for weeks. The search for them focused national attention on civil rights. Rita Schwerner, the wife of Michael Schwerner, noted:

> **"I personally suspect that if Mr. Chaney . . . had been alone at the time of the disappearance, that this case, like so many others, . . . would have gone completely unnoticed."**

Searchers found the men in early August. All three had been shot to death. Violence against other volunteers continued throughout the summer.

Selma

The brutal murders made voter registration a national issue. The Johnson administration prepared a new bill to protect black voters. To dramatize the need for the law, the SCLC organized a series of marches in Selma, Alabama. Martin Luther King Jr. chose Selma because, as in much of the state, only about 2 percent of African Americans of voting age were registered.

SCLC leaders had planned to march from Selma to Montgomery, the state capital, on March 7. Alabama state troopers ordered the civil rights marchers to stop. Then, as one marcher recalled, "they came upon us and started beating us with their nightsticks." More than 70 marchers were injured. The day became known as Bloody Sunday. Televised images of the violence shocked millions of Americans.

One week later President Johnson appealed to the nation to support a voting rights bill. On March 21, some 4,000 people completed a march from Selma to Montgomery. In August, Johnson signed the **Voting Rights Act of 1965**. The act gave the federal government the power to inspect voter registration procedures and to protect all citizens' right to vote. Within three years, more than half of all black voters in the South had registered to vote.

Black Leaders

While Martin Luther King Jr. had become the best-known civil rights leader, other African Americans also inspired action. Many young black activists, particularly in northern cities, supported Malcolm X, a leader of the Nation of Islam. The religious group, also known as Black Muslims, supported black separatism. They encouraged black people to form their own, all-black communities.

In the early 1960s Malcolm X argued that the African American community should work for social and economic independence rather than integration. Unlike Martin Luther King Jr., Malcolm X insisted that African Americans had the right to protect themselves from violence:

> **"You're getting a new generation . . . and they're beginning to think with their own minds and see that you can't negotiate up on freedom nowadays. If something is yours by right, then fight for it or shut up. If you can't fight for it, then forget it."**

Constitutional Heritage

The Right to Vote. Ratification of the Twenty-fourth Amendment in 1964 banned the use of poll taxes or any other type of tax as a requirement to vote in federal elections. Since the late 1800s, southern states had been using poll taxes as a means to prevent African Americans from voting. When the amendment was ratified, five states were still using poll taxes: Alabama, Arkansas, Mississippi, Texas, and Virginia. The Voting Rights Act of 1965 banned the use of poll taxes in state and local elections.

Activity: Have students create a poster or bumper sticker supporting the right of all adult American citizens to vote.

civil rights movement. Have students make a written transcript of their interviews. In addition, encourage students to tape record or videotape the interviews, if possible. Call on volunteers to share their interviews with the class.

2. **Logical-Mathematical, Visual-Spatial.** Have students use the library and other resources to research one of the major protest campaigns discussed in this section. Then ask students to prepare a photo essay on their topic. Students' photo essays should construct a narrative of what happened during the campaign, analyze key events or turning points in the campaign, and explain its outcome and long-term significance. Display students' work around the classroom.

3. **Linguistic, Logical-Mathematical.** Have students use the library and other resources to research the U.S. Supreme Court case *University of California v. Bakke*, 438 U.S. 265 (1978). Ask students to write a summary of the case. Finally, lead a discussion on the case. You might also discuss any similar cases that have occurred recently.

Across the Curriculum

LITERATURE

The Autobiography of Malcolm X. During the last years of his life, Malcolm X worked with writer Alex Haley on an autobiography. Haley was working as a freelance journalist—one of the few African Americans at the time doing such work—when he first was asked to interview Malcolm X. The assignment eventually led to Haley's work on the autobiography. Writing the book was a painstaking process. Malcolm X did not like being tape-recorded, so Haley had to type while Malcolm X spoke. The effort was worth it. Published in October 1965, the book was a huge success and gained international acclaim. It has since been translated into 15 languages and has sold more than 3 million copies.

Activity: Read passages from *The Autobiography of Malcolm X* that deal with Malcolm X's views on the civil rights movement. Then have students explain how his attitudes differed from those of other black leaders such as Martin Luther King Jr.

Malcolm X posed for this picture while visiting Egypt in 1964.

In the spring of 1964 Malcolm X split with the Nation of Islam and formed the Organization of Afro-American Unity. He then traveled to the Islamic holy city of Mecca in Saudi Arabia. There he met Muslims of many races and began to reconsider his antiwhite views. However, Malcolm X still remained committed to African Americans relying mainly on themselves. He still believed that the use of violence was sometimes justifiable. "There can be no revolution without bloodshed," he proclaimed. In February 1965, three members of the Nation of Islam assassinated Malcolm X in New York City.

Shortly after Malcolm X was killed, the civil rights movement reached a crossroads. King continued to support moderation and interracial participation. However, many young SNCC reformers became frustrated by the slow rate of change. They believed that the federal government had not done enough to stop violence against African Americans. Other critics believed that the movement should focus on improving the economic situation of African Americans.

In June 1966 SNCC leader Stokely Carmichael called for "black power." The **Black Power** movement wanted African Americans to have greater economic and political power. Carmichael explained its goals: "We determined to win political power, with the idea of moving on from there into activity that would have economic effects."

That same year Black Power supporters Huey Newton and Bobby Seale organized the Black Panther Party. Seale described the group's goals: "We want power to determine our own destiny in our own black community." The Panthers called for full employment and provided some community services. To reduce harassment against African Americans, the Panthers formed disciplined patrols to "police the police."

The Panthers' willingness to use violence to achieve their goals frightened many Americans. The Panthers engaged in gun fights with police, federal officers, and other black leaders. At least 19 Panthers were killed and many others jailed as a result of these various incidents. By 1969 the Black Panthers had virtually broken up.

Civil rights leaders Stokely Carmichael and Eldridge Cleaver helped spark the Black Power movement.

Racial Riots

In the mid- to late 1960s racial riots occurred in many urban areas. The first major riot took place in the Watts section of Los Angeles in August 1965. The immediate cause of the riot was the arrest of a black motorist. However, frustrations over discrimination and economic hardships kept many African Americans rioting for several days. Some 30,000 people rioted, looted, and set fires for five days. The riot ended only after some 14,000 National Guard troops came in to restore order. After the riot, more than 20 people lay dead.

Over the next three years, hundreds more riots broke out. President Johnson appointed the Kerner Commission to investigate the violence. In its 1968 report, the commission identified racial issues as a leading cause of the riots. The report also warned that "the nation is rapidly moving toward two increasingly separate Americas"—one white and wealthy, the other black and poor.

In early 1968 Martin Luther King Jr. announced plans for a march to begin the "Poor People's Campaign." He wanted poor people of all races to unite to address economic problems such as poverty and unemployment. Before the march began, King traveled to Memphis, Tennessee, to support striking garbage workers. On April 4, 1968, as he stood talking with supporters, a hidden gunman fired at him. King was hit and died instantly. Some two months later, ex-convict James Earl Ray was arrested for the murder.

REVIEW

Linguistic, Interpersonal. Have students complete the Section Review Questions. Organize the class into three groups. Have each group create a study guide based on one of the following topics dealing with the civil rights movement: leaders and organizations, events, or strategies. Have each group explain its study guide and encourage other students to give feedback. Then, have each group revise its study guide based on the feedback. Finally, make photocopies of the study guides and distribute them to the class.

ASSESS

Have students complete Daily Quiz 20.1.

RETEACH

Linguistic, Logical-Mathematical. Have students complete Main Idea Activities for Reteaching and Sheltered English 20.1. For each term in the Identify portion of the Section Review, call on volunteers to supply information about the term and its relationship to the civil rights movement. SHELTERED ENGLISH

King's assassination horrified many people worldwide. Riots erupted in more than 100 U.S. cities. The violence ended with nearly 50 people dead. The nonviolent part of the civil rights movement seemed in danger of dying with King. However, other leaders vowed to pursue his goal.

Educational opportunities for African Americans increased in the 1970s.

Reaction and Successes

In the 1970s, civil rights leaders focused on school desegregation. The Supreme Court had declared racial segregation in public schools illegal in 1954. Yet school segregation continued, particularly in the North. Most students went to local schools in their neighborhoods. However, most neighborhoods were segregated. To desegregate schools, some judges ordered forced busing. As a result, students were taken to schools outside their neighborhoods.

Many parents, particularly white parents, objected to forced busing. One mother said it violated "the basic right for a parent to choose how . . . and where the child should be educated." Extreme antibusing protests took place in Boston in 1974. A federal judge had ordered the busing of nearly half of all Boston students to schools outside their neighborhoods.

Some people also opposed **affirmative action**, the practice by some businesses and government agencies of giving special consideration to nonwhites or women to make up for past discrimination.

Some critics argued that any race- or gender-based preference was unfair. In June 1978 in ***University of California* v. *Bakke***, the Supreme Court ruled that white applicant Allan Bakke had been unfairly denied admission to medical school. The university had set a quota, or a specific number of spaces, for African Americans. The Court ruled that race could be a factor in admissions, but that setting quotas was illegal. Despite this ruling, affirmative action programs continued to offer new opportunities to many African Americans.

African Americans made gains in other areas. The number of African Americans enrolled in college in the 1970s increased significantly. More African Americans became involved in politics. Between 1966 and 1973, the number of African Americans serving in Congress more than doubled. The percentage of African American elected officials was still low, but African Americans hoped that progress would continue.

SECTION 1 REVIEW

Identify and explain the significance of the following:

- **sit-in**
- **Ella Baker**
- **Student Nonviolent Coordinating Committee**
- **Freedom Rides**
- **Martin Luther King Jr.**
- **Civil Rights Act of 1964**
- **Freedom Summer**
- **Voting Rights Act of 1965**
- **Malcolm X**
- **Black Power**
- **affirmative action**
- ***University of California* v. *Bakke***

Reading for Content Understanding

1. **Main Idea** What led to the passage of the Civil Rights Act of 1964?
2. **Main Idea** What changes occurred in the civil rights movement in the late 1960s and early 1970s?
3. **Geographic Diversity** Why did civil rights activists stage campaigns for voting rights in Mississippi and Alabama? Why was this strategy successful?
4. **Writing** *Expressing* Imagine that you are a participant in a civil rights sit-in. Write a poem expressing your reaction to the protest.
5. **Critical Thinking** *Making Comparisons* Compare and contrast the goals, strategies, and achievements of Malcolm X and Martin Luther King Jr.

Section 1 Review ANSWERS

Identify

For significance, see the following pages:

- sit-in, p. 596
- Ella Baker, p. 596
- Student Nonviolent Coordinating Committee, p. 596
- Freedom Rides, p. 596
- Martin Luther King Jr., p. 597
- Civil Rights Act of 1964, p. 598
- Freedom Summer, p. 599
- Voting Rights Act of 1965, p. 599
- Malcolm X, p. 599
- Black Power, p. 600
- affirmative action, p. 601
- *University of California* v. *Bakke*, p. 601

Reading for Content Understanding

1. sit-ins, Freedom Rides, the nationally televised use of violence against protesters, the March on Washington and King's "I Have a Dream" speech, public reaction to all these events, presidential support of civil rights

2. rise of the Black Power movement, growing support for use of violence, racial riots, emphasis on school desegregation through busing

3. because few African Americans could vote there; it met with violence, which focused national attention on voter registration.

4. Poems will vary but may include feelings of fear and outrage as well as feelings of pride, self-respect, and unity.

5. similar—both wanted to improve life for African Americans; different—King supported nonviolence and racial integration; Malcolm X supported self-defense and black independence

Historical Sidelight

Giving the Speech. Each speaker at the March on Washington was allowed only seven minutes to address the crowd. Martin Luther King Jr. worked all night on his speech. However, when he spoke the following day, he departed from his prepared text. The story goes that during the speech, singer Mahalia Jackson called out, "Tell 'em about the dream, Martin." At that point, King abandoned his written speech and launched into describing his dream for a better America. His "I Have a Dream" speech inspired many Americans to join the civil rights struggle.

Critical Thinking: Why might King have switched to an unprepared speech?

ANSWER: Answers will vary but students might suggest that he recognized that if Mahalia Jackson was impressed by his dream, others also were likely to be moved by it. In addition, as a preacher, King was experienced at giving unrehearsed speeches as opposed to using a scripted text.

Martin Luther King Jr.'s

I Have a Dream

On August 28, 1963, more than 200,000 people participated in the March on Washington in support of civil rights. The demonstrators marched from the Washington Monument to the Lincoln Memorial, where Martin Luther King Jr. delivered his "I Have a Dream" speech. His address is remembered as one of the most powerful and effective speeches of modern times. An excerpt appears here.

Five score [100] years ago, a great American, in whose symbolic shadow we stand, signed the Emancipation Proclamation. This momentous decree [important order] came as a great beacon [light of hope] to millions of Negro slaves who had been seared [burned] in the flames of withering injustice. It came as a joyous daybreak to end the long night of captivity.

But one hundred years later, we must face the tragic fact that the Negro is still not free. One hundred years later, the life of the Negro is still sadly crippled by the manacles [handcuffs] of segregation and the chains of discrimination. . . .

In a sense we have come to our nation's Capital to cash a check. When the architects of our republic wrote the magnificent words of the Constitution and the Declaration of Independence, they were signing a promissory note [note promising payment] to which every American was to fall heir [inherit]. This note was a promise that all men would be guaranteed the unalienable [permanent] rights of life, liberty, and the pursuit of happiness.

It is obvious today that America has defaulted [failed to pay] on this promissory note insofar as her citizens of color are concerned. Instead of honoring this sacred obligation, America has given the Negro people a bad check; a check which has come back marked "insufficient funds." But we refuse to believe that the bank of justice is bankrupt. . . .

But there is something that I must say to my people who stand on the warm threshold [entrance] which leads into the palace of justice. In the process of gaining our rightful place we must not be guilty of wrongful deeds. Let us not seek to satisfy our thirst for freedom by drinking from the cup of bitterness and hatred. We must forever conduct our struggle on the high plane of dignity and discipline. We must not allow our creative protest to degenerate [fall] into physical violence. Again and again we must rise to the majestic heights of meeting physical force with soul force. . . .

I say to you today, my friends, that in spite of the difficulties and frustrations of the moment I still have a dream. It is a dream deeply rooted in the American dream.

I have a dream that one day this nation will rise up and live out the true meaning of its creed [formal statement]: "We hold these truths to be self-evident; that all men are created equal."

I have a dream that one day on the red hills of Georgia the sons of former slaves and the sons of former slaveowners will be able to sit down together at the table of brotherhood.

I have a dream that one day even the state of Mississippi, a desert state sweltering with the heat of injustice and oppression [persecution], will be transformed into an oasis of freedom and justice.

I have a dream that my four little children will one day live in a nation where they will not be judged by the color of their skin but by the content of their character.

I have a dream today.

I have a dream that one day the state of Alabama, whose governor's lips are presently dripping with the words of interposition [interference] and nullification [refusal], will be transformed into a situation where little black boys and black girls will be able to join hands with little white boys and white girls and walk together as sisters and brothers.

I have a dream today.

I have a dream that one day every valley shall be exalted [glorified], every hill and mountain shall be made low, the rough places will be made plain, and the crooked places will be made straight, and the glory of the Lord shall be revealed, and all flesh shall see it together.

This is our hope. This is the faith with which I return to the South. With this faith we will be able to hew [carve] out of the mountain of despair a stone of hope. With this faith we will be able to transform the jangling discords [disagreements] of our nation into a beautiful symphony of brotherhood. . . .

This will be the day when all of God's children will be able to sing with new meaning, "My country 'tis of thee, sweet land of liberty, of thee I sing. Land where my fathers died, land of the Pilgrims' pride, from every mountainside, let freedom ring."

And if America is to be a great nation, this must become true. So let freedom ring from the prodigious [vast] hilltops of New Hampshire. Let freedom ring from the mighty mountains of New York. Let freedom ring from the heightening Alleghenies of Pennsylvania!

Let freedom ring from the snowcapped Rockies of Colorado! Let freedom ring from the curvaceous peaks of California! But not only that; let freedom ring from Stone Mountain of Georgia! Let freedom ring from Lookout Mountain of Tennessee!

Let freedom ring from every hill and molehill of Mississippi. From every mountainside, let freedom ring.

When we let freedom ring, when we let it ring from every village and every hamlet [community], from every state and every city, we will be able to speed up that day when all of God's children, black men and white men, Jews and Gentiles [non-Jews], Protestants and Catholics, will be able to join hands and sing in the words of the old Negro spiritual, "Free at last! Free at last! Thank God Almighty, we are free at last!"

Understanding Primary Sources

1. What did Martin Luther King Jr. mean when he said that the United States had given African Americans a "bad check"?
2. What did King caution African Americans against in their fight for freedom?

Originally intended to be a protest over African American unemployment, the March on Washington became a wider civil rights demonstration. Here Martin Luther King Jr. waves to the crowd.

Using Visual Resources

Capturing the Dream. The photograph on this page reveals much about Martin Luther King Jr. For one, the image depicts the strength of his following by showing a number of the 200,000 people who joined the March on Washington, many of whom were his supporters. The image also captures King's serene facial expression and his friendly wave to the crowd after his delivery of one of the most emotional and powerful speeches of modern times.

Critical Thinking: How might the contrast of King's emotional speech and his peaceful expression and gesture have helped his cause?

Answer: Students might mention that by remaining peaceful, King may have showed the crowd that people need not resort to violence during trying times and that their goals could be reached.

Historical Documents Answers

1. King meant that although the Constitution and the Declaration guaranteed Americans equality, African Americans were still being denied this right.

2. King cautioned African Americans against becoming bitter, hateful, or violent in their fight for freedom.

OBJECTIVES

- **Explain how César Chávez and the United Farm Workers helped migrant workers.**
- **Describe how other Mexican Americans fought for civil rights.**
- **Identify some of the goals of the Chicano movement.**

FOCUS

Motivate Before Reading

Ask students to imagine that they belong to a local intramural baseball team. Their team has noticed that the owners of some of the local ball parks give certain other teams preference in reserving playing fields. The team then reads about an intramural basketball team that successfully protested discriminatory practices by some gymnasiums. Ask students what their reaction would be to

Section 2 RESOURCES

PRINT
- ★ Guided Reading Strategies 20.2
- ★ Section 2 Review, p. 609
- ★ Daily Quiz 20.2

MULTIMEDIA
- ★ *Teaching Resources CD–ROM*, Lesson 20.2
- ★ Art in American History Transparency 47: *Tamalada*

SHELTERED ENGLISH
- ★ Main Idea Activities for Reteaching and Sheltered English 20.2

Rights for Hispanics

Reading Focus

How did César Chávez and the United Farm Workers help migrant workers?

In what ways did other Mexican Americans fight for civil rights?

What were some goals of the Chicano movement?

Key Terms

League of United Latin American Citizens
United Farm Workers
Chicano movement
Mexican American Youth Organization
La Raza Unida Party
Voting Rights Act of 1975

LIKE MANY OTHER AMERICANS, Félix Longoria answered the call to serve his country in World War II. After he was killed in action, his body was returned to his hometown in Texas for burial. The local funeral home director refused to hold services in the chapel for him because he was a Mexican American. Lyndon B. Johnson, a U.S. senator from Texas, stepped in to settle the dispute. He arranged for Longoria to be buried with full honors alongside other veterans at Arlington National Cemetery in Virginia.

World War II veteran Félix Longoria

Political Activism

Hispanics in the United States had faced discrimination for years. The mistreatment of World War II veterans pushed many Hispanics into action. "We have proven ourselves true and loyal Americans by every test that has confronted us," declared a Hispanic newspaper. The newspaper demanded "social, political and economic equality and the opportunity to practice that equality." The Longoria case inspired Héctor P. García, a highly decorated U.S. Army surgeon. He formed the American GI Forum to defend the rights of Mexican Americans.

One of the oldest Hispanic civil rights organizations also responded with greater action. In 1929, Mexican Americans had joined together to form the **League of United Latin American Citizens** (LULAC). LULAC's mission was to "make living conditions better for future generations of Mexican Americans." LULAC concentrated its efforts on civil rights, education, and employment.

In the 1940s LULAC won two important school desegregation cases—*Méndez* v. *Westminster School District* (1945) and *Delgado* v. *The Bastrop Independent School District* (1948). In these cases the federal courts established that segregating Mexican American children in public schools was this information. Encourage discussion. Finally, tell students that in this section they will learn how the African American civil rights movement influenced Hispanic movements for civil rights and ethnic pride, and the results of these movements.

Introduce Key Terms

Linguistic, Logical-Mathematical. Review this section's key terms with students. Ask them to write questions that have as their answers one of the key terms. Have students exchange questions, answer them, and return them to their authors for grading. **SHELTERED ENGLISH**

TEACH

Have students read Section 2 and complete Guided Reading Strategies 20.2. Choose one or more of the following activities to explore the section content with students. For further suggestions on block scheduling or team teaching, see the *Block Scheduling Handbook*.

LEVEL 1: Linguistic. (Suggested time: 15 min.) As a class, go over students' Guided Reading Strategies. Then use the Reading Focus questions to highlight the main ideas of the section. **SHELTERED ENGLISH**

illegal. The courts ordered the school districts to stop this practice, but discrimination continued.

The United Farm Workers

In the 1960s the Hispanic population in the United States continued to grow. Encouraged by the success of the African American civil rights movement, Hispanics launched a fight for their own rights. Some Hispanic rights activists focused on improving economic opportunities.

Migrant Workers

Mexican Americans and Mexicans formed the largest ethnic group of migrant workers. Most of these farm laborers earned low wages and worked in unhealthy conditions. Their employers frequently took advantage of them. One California farmer admitted that

> **"farmworkers . . . were considered just another item in producing . . . like fertilizers. . . . Most growers didn't treat their workers with any degree of respect or dignity."**

Mexican American César Chávez had worked in farm fields since childhood. In the early 1960s he began organizing other migrant farmworkers. Chávez shared Martin Luther King Jr.'s belief in nonviolent protest. Chávez explained:

> **"Naturally, nonviolence takes time. But poverty has been with us since the beginning of time. We just have to work for improvement. I despise exploitation [unfair gain] and I want change, but I'm willing to pay the price in terms of time. There's a Mexican saying, 'Hay más tiempo que vida'—there's more time than life. We've got all the time in the world."**

Migrant workers picked grapes for long hours for little pay.

Biography

César Chávez

César Chávez was born in Arizona in 1927. He lived in dozens of towns as his family moved in search of farmwork. His early experience led him to help form unions for migrant workers. Chávez viewed union work as a part of a larger fight for human rights—a goal he called *La Causa,* or "The Cause."

Frail and soft-spoken, Chávez seemed to be an unlikely protest movement leader. However, his patience and dedication to the cause of human rights inspired many people and won many supporters. He helped make migrant farmworkers' rights a national issue. Some of his followers called him a "twentieth-century saint." Before his death in 1993, Chávez insisted, "It's not me who counts, it's the Movement."

In 1962 Chávez and Mexican American political lobbyist Dolores Huerta organized the National Farm Workers Association (NFWA). In September 1965 Chávez decided that the NFWA should help Mexican American and Filipino grape workers. They were on strike for higher wages in Delano, California. According to Chávez, the grower kept saying, "I can't pay. I just haven't got the money." Nonetheless, Chávez noted, the grower managed to meet the strikers' demands: "He must have found the money somewhere, because we were asking for $1.40 and we got it."

Biography

César Chávez. Growing up, César Chávez worked with his family in the fields of California. He attended some 65 different schools before entering the navy during World War II. Following the war, he returned to migrant work. Then in 1952 he met Fred Ross, an organizer with the Community Service Organization (CSO). Ross convinced Chávez to join the group. There, he learned about labor organizing and within a few years became national director of the CSO. In 1962 he resigned his position and dedicated the rest of his life to improving conditions for migrant farmworkers.

Critical Thinking: Why might Chávez have believed that a labor union was necessary to improve conditions for migrant workers?

ANSWER: Answers will vary but students might mention that groups have more power than people acting alone.

ALL LEVELS: Linguistic, Logical-Mathematical. (Suggested time: 45 min.) Ask students to imagine that they are preparing to write a magazine article on the Hispanic civil rights movement of the 1960s and 1970s. To prepare, they have decided to create a fact sheet for each group or organization. Each fact sheet should list a group, its connection to any other groups, its leaders, goals, actions, and results. Call on volunteers to explain their work to the class.

ALL LEVELS: Visual-Spatial. (Suggested time: 30 minutes) Have students create a drawing that represents some of the goals of the Chicano movement. You might first show students some examples of Chicano art from the period and discuss the images employed. Display students' artwork around the classroom. Then call on volunteers to explain their drawings to the class.
SHELTERED ENGLISH

LEVEL 2: Linguistic, Musical-Rhythmic. (Suggested time: 45 min.) Ask a student to read on textbook page 608 the poem *"Yo Soy Joaquín"* by Rodolfo "Corky" Gonzales. Ask students to explain what the poem means. Then have them write a poem in response from the perspective of one of the other Hispanic civil rights leaders discussed in this section. Call on volunteers to read their poems and explain them.

Across the Curriculum

MATH

Hispanics in America. The 1980 U.S. census revealed that out of a total population of 226.5 million, 14.6 million Americans were Hispanics. Ten years later, the total U.S. population had risen to 248.7 million, and the Hispanic population had grown to 22.4 million.

Activity: Have students determine the percentage of the U.S. population that claimed Hispanic origin in 1980 *(6.4 percent)* and in 1990 *(9 percent).*

Geographic Diversity

Regional Differences. People of Cuban, Mexican, and Puerto Rican descent form the largest percentage of Hispanics in the United States. In 1990 most Americans of Cuban descent lived in the South, particularly in Florida. Most Mexican Americans lived in California and the Southwest. Most Americans of Puerto Rican descent lived in the Northeast, particularly in New York.

Activity: Have students make a chart showing the ethnic/racial breakdown for their region of the country.

Later that year, Chávez led a larger strike of table-grape workers in California's San Joaquin Valley. Growers brought in other workers to pick the grapes before they rotted. In early 1966 Chávez organized a 250-mile march from Delano to Sacramento, the state capital. He used the march to connect farmworker issues with those of the African American civil rights movement. Some 10,000 workers and supporters participated in the march. In August 1966 Chávez brought together NFWA members and Filipino workers to create what would become the **United Farm Workers** (UFW). Huerta served as its first vice president.

Dolores Huerta reports on union activities during a meeting in Delano, California.

Striking for Rights

Chávez also called for a consumer boycott of table grapes. By 1968 neither the boycott nor the continuing strike was succeeding. Chávez used an unusual tactic to encourage strikers. In March 1968 he began a hunger strike. Presidential candidate Robert F. Kennedy met with Chávez on the 24th day of his fast. Kennedy promised to commit himself to the farmworkers' cause. Televised images of a thin and weak Chávez revived the consumer boycott of grapes. At the peak of the boycott some 17 million Americans stopped buying grapes. The boycott cost growers millions of dollars. The strike was finally settled in 1970. Huerta led the negotiations. The union won a series of favorable three-year contracts with most table-grape growers.

A poster announcing a concert by the musical group Peter, Paul and Mary to benefit la huelga*, or the UFW strike*

Chávez and the UFW continued to fight for the rights of migrant workers. In 1975 California governor Jerry Brown introduced the Agricultural Labor Relations Act. This act officially provided migrant farmworkers the right to strike and to bargain collectively. Chávez's success in California inspired many farmworkers in Arizona, Florida, Texas, and the Midwest to organize.

Hispanic Civil Rights Leaders

During the 1960s the activities of Reies López Tijerina also gained public attention. Tijerina founded La Alianza Federal de Mercedes, or the Federal Alliance of Land Grants. He hoped to regain land for Mexican Americans in New Mexico.

According to Tijerina, Mexican Americans had been losing their land since the 1848 Treaty of Guadalupe Hidalgo. The treaty had guaranteed that Mexicans living in the Mexican Cession

LEVEL 3: Linguistic, Musical-Rhythmic. (Suggested time: 15 min. plus homework and presentation) Have students write a ballad describing either César Chávez and the United Farm Workers or the Chicano movement. Ballads should include the goals, actions, and results of the chosen topic as well as students' opinions on the subject. Students might choose to set their ballads to the tune of an existing song, such as a folk song, or to original music. Call on volunteers to read or perform their ballads for the class.

CLOSE

Linguistic, Visual-Spatial. Ask students to imagine that a local university is hosting a conference on the Hispanic civil rights movement of the 1960s and 1970s. Have students design a promotional poster for the conference. The poster should give the name, location, and date of the conference; list and describe the topics to be discussed; and encourage people to attend. Display students' posters around the classroom.

would still own their lands even after the area became U.S. territory. Tijerina charged that over time, state and local governments had been taking some of the Mexican Americans' land grants. Tijerina explained why he became involved in the issue:

> **"Our land was stolen, we wanted it back. Our towns were alive and now they're dead, they're frozen, and the common lands that belonged to the towns were taken away."**

After legal appeals failed, Tijerina turned to direct action. In October 1966 some Alianza members briefly occupied part of the Kit Carson National Forest. Tijerina claimed that the area was part of a disputed land grant. The following June, Tijerina and Alianza members raided a county courthouse. The incident ended in a shoot-out between Alianza members and local officials. A massive search for the raiders followed. Officials used helicopters, planes, and tanks. Tijerina was captured, arrested, and charged with numerous offenses. Before he was convicted, Tijerina led a group of Hispanics in the 1968 Poor People's March on Washington, D.C.

Rodolfo "Corky" Gonzales, a young Hispanic activist, participated in this march. In 1966 Gonzales had begun protesting city government policies toward Mexican Americans in Denver, Colorado. Gonzales declared that "a new crusade for justice had been born." His Crusade for Justice emphasized cultural nationalism, or Mexican American ethnic pride. Gonzales also encouraged greater Hispanic economic and political independence. He issued *"Demandas de la Raza,"* which called for reform in education, employment, housing, and land. Gonzales also helped organize a Crusade community center. It included classrooms, a library, a gymnasium, a meeting hall, and a social center.

American Literature

Poetry of Angela de Hoyos

Angela de Hoyos is a poet and graphic artist. Born in Mexico, de Hoyos was raised in San Antonio, Texas. Her first book of poetry was ARISE, CHICANO! and Other Poems.

Angela de Hoyos

BRINDIS*: FOR THE BARRIO
"Brothers, today we drink
the fresh milk of dawn
—for once, not tasting
of sourness.

For once,
the table is set
with plates full of hope,
and in our illiterate hands
some kind fate has placed
a promise of gold for tomorrow.

Not that the hollows
in your sad face of death
will ever be filled
—or the seedy, stale figure
of the poor
feel at ease in fine clothes—

but today we eat
to soothe a pain
—a pain of alien-hungers
Vallejo** never knew."

*a toast **Mariano G. Vallejo (1808–90); California leader born in Mexico

Understanding Literature

1. How does the poem express issues in the Mexican American community? Use specific words from the poem.
2. What do you think the phrase *a promise of gold for tomorrow* means?

Across the Curriculum

LITERATURE

Sandra Cisneros. A number of Hispanic women have achieved prominence as authors. Sandra Cisneros longed to be a writer but believed she did not have anything important to say. Then one day, while attending a writers workshop, she realized that her very life as a Hispanic woman provided her with original and meaningful material. In 1991 she became the first Chicana writer to obtain a major publishing contract, and her book *Woman Hollering Creek and Other Stories* won critical acclaim.

Critical Thinking: How might Cisneros's experiences inspire others to write?

ANSWER: Others might realize that their experiences are interesting enough to write about as well.

AMERICAN LITERATURE ANSWERS

1. The poem addresses problems within the Mexican American community by using descriptive words such as *sourness, illiterate, stale, poor,* and *pain* to describe the difficult conditions Mexican Americans were enduring.

2. Answers will vary but might state that the phrase refers to the fulfillment of improved living standards for Hispanics in America.

CHALLENGE AND EXTEND

1. **Logical-Mathematical, Visual-Spatial, Interpersonal.** Organize the class into several research teams. Ask each team to use the library and other resources to gather statistics on Hispanics in the United States today. Assign each team a region of the country and have them gather data on total population; total Hispanic population; Hispanic population by age, gender, national origin, and income bracket; number of Hispanics who hold public office, and so forth. Have each team create tables and other visuals to present their findings to the class.

2. **Linguistic, Visual-Spatial, Interpersonal.** Organize students into groups. Assign each group one of the major Hispanic civil rights issues of the 1960s and 1970s. Have each group use the library and other resources to prepare a protest campaign. Groups should prepare a clearly defined set of goals, a written summary of their proposed actions or strategies, and a written explanation of why they think these actions will achieve success. Groups also should prepare slogans, symbols, press releases, posters, and bumper stickers for their campaign. Have each group display its campaign plans in the classroom.

Cultural Diversity

***El Movimiento Artistico Chicano* (The Chicano Art Movement).** The Chicano movement led to a flowering of Hispanic art. Often taking the form of murals, this art both protests discrimination and celebrates Hispanic culture and ethnic pride. Many Chicano murals blend scenes of the Hispanic civil rights movement with pre-Columbian Indian subjects, which illustrate the Indian heritage of many Hispanics. Images of pyramids, Olmec heads, and Aztec figures are common as well as images of César Chávez, the huelga eagle (the UFW symbol), and Chicano protests.

Critical Thinking: Why might murals have been popular with Chicano artists?

ANSWER: Answers will vary but students might mention that murals can express multiple ideas and usually appear in public places, where many people can see them.

Multimedia Resources

Art in American History Transparency 47: *Tamalada*

The Chicano movement sought to end discrimination and increase Mexican American pride.

Gonzales influenced many young Hispanics with his poem *"Yo Soy Joaquín"* (I am Joaquín):

> **"I am Joaquín,**
> **lost in a world of confusion,**
> **caught up in the whirl of a**
> **gringo [white] society,**
> **. . .**
> **My fathers**
> **have lost the economic battle**
> **and won**
> **the struggle of cultural survival."**

The Chicano Movement

Gonzales inspired many younger Hispanic activists to join the struggle to end discrimination and increase Hispanic cultural pride. Their efforts became known as the **Chicano movement**, or *el movimiento.* Young Mexican Americans turned the word "Chicano" into a term of pride.

Student Protests

During the 1960s the number of Hispanics attending high school and college increased. Many of these students began to demand bilingual education, or instruction in two languages. They also wanted more Hispanic teachers. Some Mexican American students staged walkouts in protest. They remained out of school until administrators met some of their demands.

In March 1968 teacher Sal Castro led a student walkout in East Los Angeles. More than 15,000 students walked out as the protest spread to five Los Angeles area high schools. The sight of the students on picket lines prompted one reporter to call the walkouts "the Birth of Brown Power." School authorities called in the police. Officers broke up meetings and made mass arrests. Similar walkouts occurred throughout the Southwest the following school year.

In the Crystal City, Texas, school system, about 85 percent of the student body was Hispanic. However, most of the administrators and teachers were not. Severita Lara recalled life at school:

> **"In all of our activities, like for example, cheerleaders . . . there's always three Anglos and one mexicana. . . . We started questioning. Why should it be like that? . . . [We] started looking at other things."**

In the fall of 1969, students staged a massive walkout to end discrimination. The **Mexican American Youth Organization** (MAYO), formed in 1967 by José Angel Gutiérrez, supported the walkout. The students stayed out of school until January 1970, when the Crystal City school board agreed to a series of reforms.

La Raza Unida

Following the events in Texas, Gutiérrez and some 300 other Hispanic activists organized to increase Hispanic political power. They founded **La Raza Unida Party** (LRUP), or the "United People's Party," in January 1970. In elections that spring, Gutiérrez and two other LRUP members won seats on the school board in Crystal City.

REVIEW

Linguistic, Logical-Mathematical. Have students complete the Section Review questions. Ask students to write one true-false question for each of the terms in the Identify portion of the Section Review. Then have students exchange their questions, answer them, and return them to their authors for grading. Finally, have students use all the terms to write a paragraph summarizing the main points of this section.

ASSESS

Have students complete Daily Quiz 20.2.

RETEACH

Linguistic, Logical-Mathematical. Have students complete Main Idea Activities for Reteaching and Sheltered English 20.2. Ask students to pick out pairs of related terms in the Identify portion of the Section Review. Have students explain how the terms relate to each other. Encourage students to try to use each term in more than one pairing. Continue until students have used all the terms. **SHELTERED ENGLISH**

Two Mexican Americans were also elected to the city council.

One Hispanic reported, "Chicanos were in a state of jubilation [happiness]." Hispanic women played an important role in the elections. Party leader Marta Cotera recalled that women "were very much in evidence as . . . candidates, [and] as organizers in leadership positions." Organizers performed the crucial task of getting supporters registered to vote and attracting new members to the party.

Some Hispanics set up alternative schools when students boycotted the public schools.

New Laws

As a result of the Hispanic civil rights movement, new legislation was enacted. Congress passed the 1968 Elementary and Secondary Education Act. It required that children whose first language is not English be instructed in two languages until they mastered English. The Bilingual Education Act of 1974 provided further federal funding for such programs. From 1969 to 1978 federal funding of bilingual education increased from $7.5 million to $135 million.

Hispanic leaders also hoped to increase the turnout of voters who had limited understanding of English. The **Voting Rights Act of 1975** required areas with large immigrant populations to provide ballots in the voters' preferred language.

By 1970 the Hispanic population in the United States had increased to more than 10 million. People of Mexican descent made up the largest number. However, many people from Puerto Rico, Cuba, other Caribbean islands, and Latin America also moved to the United States. In 1992 one activist declared, "We are still building. . . . There are a lot of fights [left]."

SECTION 2 REVIEW

Identify and explain the significance of the following:

- **Héctor P. García**
- **League of United Latin American Citizens**
- **César Chávez**
- **Dolores Huerta**
- **United Farm Workers**
- **Reies López Tijerina**
- **Rodolfo "Corky" Gonzales**
- **Chicano movement**
- **Mexican American Youth Organization**
- **La Raza Unida Party**
- **Voting Rights Act of 1975**

Reading for Content Understanding

1 **Main Idea** How did César Chávez and the UFW expand the rights of migrant workers?

2 **Main Idea** What actions did other Mexican American civil rights leaders take to gain their rights?

3 **Cultural Diversity** What changes did the Chicano movement achieve?

4 **Writing** *Informing* Imagine that you are the historian for La Raza Unida Party. Write a paragraph informing party members of the role that women played in helping Hispanic Americans gain equal rights.

5 **Critical Thinking** *Identifying Cause and Effect* How did the treatment of Hispanic war veterans help inspire the movement for Hispanic rights?

Section 2 Review ANSWERS

Identify

For significance, see the following pages:

- Héctor P. García, p. 604
- League of United Latin American Citizens, p. 604
- César Chávez, p. 605
- Dolores Huerta, p. 605
- United Farm Workers, p. 606
- Reies López Tijerina, p. 606
- Rodolfo "Corky" Gonzales, p. 607
- Chicano movement, p. 608
- Mexican American Youth Organization, p. 608
- La Raza Unida Party, p. 608
- Voting Rights Act of 1975, p. 609

Reading for Content Understanding

1. They gave workers bargaining power to improve salaries and conditions and eventually helped many workers gain protection under the Agricultural Labor Relations Act.

2. organized politically; filed lawsuits and appeals; held raids, demonstrations, and walkouts; ran for and won public office

3. increased Hispanic cultural pride, ended some discrimination of Hispanics in public schools, and led to increased Hispanic educational and political representation

4. Answers will vary but students might mention that women served as candidates, leaders, and organizers.

5. Answers will vary but students might mention that the negative treatment of some Hispanic war veterans motivated Hispanic veterans and other Hispanics to organize and protest for their civil rights.

OBJECTIVES

- **Explain the significance of the year 1963 for the women's rights movement.**
- **Describe the goals and tactics of younger feminists.**
- **Analyze the successes and failures of the women's rights movement.**

FOCUS

Motivate Before Reading

Ask students to imagine that they and a friend have an after-school job at a local grocery store. Each of them performs the same tasks and does the job extremely well. Then ask students to imagine that they find out that their friend receives far more pay than they do. Ask students to write about how this situation would make them feel. Call on volunteers to share their responses with the class.

The Women's Rights Movement

Reading Focus

Why was the year 1963 significant to the women's rights movement?

What were the goals and tactics of younger feminists?

What were the successes and failures of the women's rights movement?

Key Terms

Commission on the Status of Women
Equal Pay Act
The Feminine Mystique
feminism
National Organization for Women
Equal Rights Amendment

ONE NIGHT IN FEBRUARY 1960, Jerrie Cobb checked into a motel in New Mexico. She was about to begin a week of astronaut qualification tests. A veteran pilot, Cobb had set three speed and altitude records. She had more flying hours than some of the men then training to be astronauts. Despite her qualifications and her exceptional performance on the tests, Cobb never flew into space. At that time women were banned from spaceflight. Cobb brought her case to Congress, where several people opposed having women in the space program. "The men go off and fight the wars and fly the airplanes. . . . The fact that women are not in this field is a fact of our social order," one astronaut testified. "It may be undesirable."

Jerrie Cobb in front of her jet plane in 1961

New Frontiers for Women

In the 1960s some women began to challenge this social order. By 1960 nearly 40 percent of women over the age of 16 held jobs. Those workers included almost 40 percent of women with school-age children. An increasing number of working women were college educated. Yet most women were wage laborers or in low-paying, traditionally female professions such as teaching and nursing. Women earned on average only 60 percent of what men with the same experience, responsibility, and skills earned. Women were paid less than men even when they performed the same job. They also had fewer opportunities for advancement. This situation led one magazine to wonder in 1960, "Wives with Brains: Babies, Yes—But What Else?"

In 1961 President Kennedy appointed Esther Peterson to lead the Women's Bureau in the Department of Labor. She persuaded the president to establish a **Commission on the Status of Women** to study workplace inequality. Former first lady Eleanor Roosevelt and Peterson headed the commission.

Section 3 RESOURCES

PRINT
- ★ Guided Reading Strategies 20.3
- ★ Biography Reading 20: Betty Friedan
- ★ Section 3 Review, p. 615
- ★ Daily Quiz 20.3

MULTIMEDIA
- ★ *Teaching Resources CD–ROM,* Lesson 20.3
- ★ Art in American History Transparency 49: *Dream 2: King and the Sisterhood*
- ★ HRW Web site

SHELTERED ENGLISH
- ★ Main Idea Activities for Reteaching and Sheltered English 20.3

Explain to students that this was the situation women faced in the 1960s and 1970s. Tell students that in this section they will learn how women addressed this and other women's rights issues during the 1960s and 1970s.

Introduce Key Terms

Linguistic. Review this section's key terms with students. Then have students use each of the terms to create a time line of events. Call on volunteers to share their time lines with the class. Then have students write in their notebooks a definition of each term.
SHELTERED ENGLISH

TEACH

Have students read Section 3 and complete Guided Reading Strategies 20.3. Choose one or more of the following activities to explore the section content with students. For further suggestions on block scheduling or team teaching, see the *Block Scheduling Handbook.*

LEVEL 1: Linguistic. (Suggested time: 15 min.) As a class, go over students' Guided Reading Strategies. Then use the Reading Focus questions to highlight the main ideas of the section.
SHELTERED ENGLISH

Its report, released in 1963, offered contradictory messages. The report declared that motherhood was the major role of American women. It also supported special training to prepare young women for marriage. However, the commission also brought attention to women's lower wages and fewer job opportunities. The commission declared, "Equality of rights under the law for all persons . . . must be reflected in the fundamental law of the land." The report recommended paid maternity leave and the expansion of public child-care facilities to help female workers.

Journalist Betty Friedan gave a name to "the problem with no name" that many women experienced. The Feminine Mystique *became a worldwide best-seller.*

W.W. Norton & Co., Inc.

In 1963 Kennedy issued an executive order banning gender discrimination in civil service jobs. That same year, Congress passed the **Equal Pay Act**. This act required employers to pay men and women the same wages for the same job. In the next 10 years, more than 170,000 female employees received about $84 million in back pay under the act.

Despite such legislation, the Kennedy administration had a mixed record on women in the workplace. Kennedy appointed fewer women to high-level federal posts than other presidents. He was the only president since Herbert Hoover not to have a female cabinet member.

The Movement Begins

For many women, the commission's report led to a re-evaluation of their roles in American society. In 1957 part-time journalist and full-time mother Betty Friedan attended a Smith College reunion. Like Friedan, some classmates had become dissatisfied with their lives after giving up their careers to become homemakers.

Friedan studied this situation further. She reported her findings in ***The Feminine Mystique***, published in 1963. Friedan challenged what she defined as the "feminine mystique." This myth said that all a woman needed to be happy and fulfilled was a husband and family. Friedan described the frustrations of some homemakers:

> **"As she made the beds, shopped for groceries, matched slipcover material, ate peanut butter sandwiches with her children, chauffeured Cub Scouts and Brownies, lay beside her husband at night—she was afraid to ask even of herself the silent question—'Is this all?'"**

Many white, college-educated women agreed with Friedan's argument.

NOW

The modern women's rights movement began when more Americans began to question the traditional role of women in society. The movement was based on **feminism**. This theory states that women are entitled to economic, political, and social equality with men. The Civil Rights Act of 1964 provided a legal basis for women's call for equal rights. It prohibited employers from discriminating on the basis of sex, among other categories. The act also established the Equal Employment Opportunity Commission (EEOC) to investigate and evaluate discrimination complaints.

In the mid-1960s many people began to think that the government was not doing enough to protect women's rights. In October 1966 Betty Friedan and other feminist leaders founded the **National Organization for Women** (NOW). NOW lobbied for political issues that affected women. "Now that we've organized," declared one supporter, "it must be apparent that feminism is no passing fad but indeed a profound, universal . . . revolution." NOW focused on an "equal partnership of the sexes" in education, government, household

Daily Life

The Feminine Mystique. Betty Friedan's book *The Feminine Mystique* describes what she terms "the problem with no name" that many women faced at the time. The book cites psychiatrists, the media, women's magazines, social scientists, advertisers, and society as a whole for fostering the "feminine mystique" that all women should be happy as homemakers and mothers. Although it received mixed reviews, *The Feminine Mystique* became an instant best-seller and helped spark the modern women's rights movement.

Critical Thinking: How do you think television shows and advertisements of the 1950s contributed to the "feminine mystique"?

ANSWER: They often portrayed women as mothers and homemakers, defined childrearing and domestic work as women's work, and portrayed women as happy and content in these roles.

Multimedia Resources

Art in American History Transparency 49: *Dream 2: King and the Sisterhood*

ALL LEVELS: Linguistic, Visual-Spatial. (Suggested time: 45 min.) Ask students to create a page titled *Women's Rights* for a new book that will be called *1963: The Year in Review.* Have students provide either a newspaper headline, an illustration, or a photograph for each significant event of 1963 that relates to women's rights. In addition, have students include captions describing the significance of the events. When students are finished, call on volunteers to share their work with the class. Finally, lead a discussion of other important events in the women's rights movement as covered in this section. You may want to create a time line on the chalkboard as you discuss each event. **SHELTERED ENGLISH**

ALL LEVELS: Logical-Mathematical, Visual-Spatial. (Suggested time: 30 min.) Draw a Venn diagram on the chalkboard. Label one circle *Older Feminist Movement* and the other *Younger Feminist Movement.* Ask students to copy the Venn diagram onto a piece of paper. Then have students list in the appropriate circle the goals, tactics, successes, and failures of each movement. Tell students to place items common to both movements in the intersection of the two circles. Call on volunteers to share their work with the class. As they do, complete the Venn diagram on the board.

Linking Past to Present

Abolitionists to Feminists. Female activists in the 1960s were not the first women to become feminists as a result of male activists treating them poorly. In 1840 female abolitionists who attended the World Anti-Slavery Convention in London were not allowed to participate and had to sit in a separate area behind a curtain. In response, Lucretia Mott and Elizabeth Cady Stanton, who had both attended the convention and become friends, turned their focus to women's rights. In 1848 they held the Seneca Falls Convention. This event launched the early women's rights movement in the United States.

Critical Thinking: Why might women seeking rights for African Americans in the 1960s have shifted their focus to seeking rights for women?

ANSWER: Answers will vary but students might mention that the female activists began to realize that they lacked some of the very rights they were seeking for others.

NOW was both the name of the organization and when women wanted their rights.

responsibilities, and job opportunities. The leaders of NOW sought to challenge

> “the traditional assumption that a woman has to choose between marriage and motherhood on the one hand and serious participation in industry or the professions on the other.”

NOW leaders launched a massive attack on gender discrimination. NOW filed lawsuits against newspapers that printed employment advertisements specifying "male only" or "female only" applicants. Other women's rights groups, such as the Women's Equity Action League (WEAL), joined NOW's fight. WEAL filed suit against more than 300 colleges and universities for paying female professors less than their male professors. WEAL ultimately won millions of dollars in salary raises for female faculty members. NOW and WEAL also achieved important legal and political changes for women.

Critics

As the women's rights movement grew, so did its critics. Some African American and Hispanic women criticized organizations like NOW for not addressing the needs of nonwhite women. Most feminists were middle-class, college-educated white women. As a result, some African American women viewed the women's movement as "basically a family quarrel between White women and White men."

Other African Americans argued that the movement needed to do more to help working-class women. They wanted higher wages and more benefits. White women wanted to receive wages equal to white men's wages. Black women wanted their wages to be at least the same as white women's. Hispanic and Asian women were more likely to participate in organizations such as the United Farm Workers. These organizations addressed concerns in their communities.

Younger Feminists

In the late 1960s a new group of feminists emerged. These women called for more radical change. Many of these women belonged to a "second wave" of younger activists. They had first worked in the student or civil rights movements. For some women, their experiences with these movements changed their outlook. SNCC activist Mary King noted:

> “If you are spending your time [doing] community organization, . . . opening people's awareness to their own power in themselves, it inevitably strengthens your own conceptions, your own ability.”

Many women were angry that male leaders in activist organizations did not treat them with respect. According to one male member of Students for a Democratic Society, women in SDS "made peanut butter, waited on tables, cleaned up. . . . That was their role." Feminist Shulasmith Firestone broke with a student protest movement after the men on an equal-rights panel refused to allow her to discuss women's rights. "Move on little girl," one man told her. "We have more important issues to talk about here than women's liberation."

Many feminists believed that beauty pageants presented women as objects, not as human beings.

LEVEL 3: Linguistic, Logical-Mathematical, Intrapersonal. (Suggested time: 20 min. plus homework) Ask students to imagine that they are writing an article on the women's rights movement to appear in a women's magazine of the early 1970s. The article should evaluate and assess the goals and tactics of both the older and younger feminist movements and discuss the successes and failures of each. Students should also state whether they support or oppose the Equal Rights Amendment and explain why.

CLOSE

Linguistic, Visual-Spatial. Ask students to imagine that they are a newspaper illustrator who supports the women's rights movement. Have students draw a political cartoon that illustrates some aspect of the movement as described in this section. Students should include a caption with their cartoon. Have volunteers share their cartoons with the class.

Linking Past to Present

Women in the Workplace Today

As a result of the women's rights movement, many women gained greater employment opportunities. Today, women make up almost half of the workforce in the United States. Gail Shaffer, executive director of an association of professional women, views the women's movement as a success. "One of the most significant developments of our century," according to Shaffer, is "the progress of women into nontraditional roles and their emergence as a major economic and political force."

In 1997 Madeleine Albright became the first female secretary of state and the highest-ranking woman in the U.S. government.

Women today hold more professional positions and political offices than in 1970. By 1997 more than 44 percent of executives and managers were women. Women have made progress in nearly all employment and educational areas. Women have served as U.S. Supreme Court justices, secretary of state, and astronauts. These changes led one mother to write in 1998:

> *"I know we feminists have made progress, because my 12-year-old daughter believes she can do, say and be anything, and go anywhere her male friends can. She not only believes it–she expects it to be that way."*

That same year, however, 30 percent of people who responded to a survey said that inequality in the workplace was still a problem. In fact, workplace inequality was the main problem that women, but not men, faced. Almost 40 years after Congress passed the Equal Pay Act, most women still earn less money than men. This inequality exists even when men and women have comparable positions. For example, in 1997 women in professional and managerial positions earned about 70 percent of men's salaries for similar positions.

Women in the United States are also more likely than men to be poor. About 45 percent of women earn too little money to support a family of three. One explanation for some women's low wages is their employment in traditionally female occupations. These jobs include sales clerks, cashiers, child care workers, home health care workers, cooks, and office cleaners. More than half of all American women are employed in these positions, which are poorly paid. The women's rights movement has made women's presence in the workplace standard. However, complete equality in the workplace has not yet been achieved.

Understanding What You Read

1. Compare and contrast jobs held by women today and in the 1960s.
2. Do you think that the women's movement has succeeded? Explain your answer.

Cultural Diversity

A Southern, Black Congresswoman. Barbara Jordan was the first southern black woman to serve in the U.S. Congress. Jordan graduated with honors from Texas Southern University, a historically black college. She then received a law degree from Boston University. In 1966 she became the first black woman to serve in the Texas legislature when she won a state Senate seat. Six years later, she was elected to the U.S. House of Representatives. She served for three terms and sat on the House Judiciary Committee during each one. Known for her eloquence and integrity, Jordan became professor of political ethics at the Lyndon B. Johnson School of Public Affairs at the University of Texas in 1979. She died in 1996.

Activity: Have students list societal changes that Barbara Jordan's career represents.

Linking Past to Present Answers

1. Answers will vary but students should mention that traditionally "male" jobs are often performed by women today.

2. Answers will vary but students might mention that while women have more opportunities than in the past, pay for women still often remains lower than that for men and some fields remain "closed" to women.

CHALLENGE AND EXTEND

1. **Linguistic, Logical-Mathematical, Interpersonal.** Have students use the library and other resources to research the Equal Rights Amendment. Have students investigate the origins of the proposal dating back to 1923, the reasons for its revival in 1972, arguments for and against the amendment's adoption, and which states ratified the amendment. Ask students to report on the information they find. Then have the class discuss and vote on whether they think the nation still needs an equal rights amendment.

2. **Logical-Mathematical, Visual-Spatial, Interpersonal.** Tell students that their class has been chosen to serve as a new Commission on the Status of Women. Have students use the library and other resources to research the status of women in America today. Assign students, individually or in groups, specific information to gather. Major topics might include women in politics, women in the workplace, women at home, women in sports, and women in poverty. Have the class use the information they find to create a bulletin board display. When students are finished, have them discuss the extent to which the status of women has improved since 1963.

Technology and Society

High-Tech Women. In the mid-1990s women made up 37 percent of chemists, 33 percent of mathematicians and computer scientists, 22 percent of physicians, and 14.5 percent of aerospace engineers in the United States.

Activity: Have students use the library and the Internet through the HRW Web site to research outstanding women in science, mathematics, and technology today. Then ask students to select one woman they read about and write a profile about her career and achievements.

go.hrw.com
SB1 Women

CHART ANSWER
by about 15 percent

In response, many young female activists focused more of their energies on women's rights. Firestone and other feminists began organizing "consciousness-raising" groups to increase awareness of discrimination that women faced. These female activists called not only for equal rights but also for "women's liberation." Rejecting NOW's politically oriented methods, these women launched dramatic protests. They pushed their way into all-male clubs and restaurants. They also held sit-ins at magazine offices to protest the media's portrayal of women.

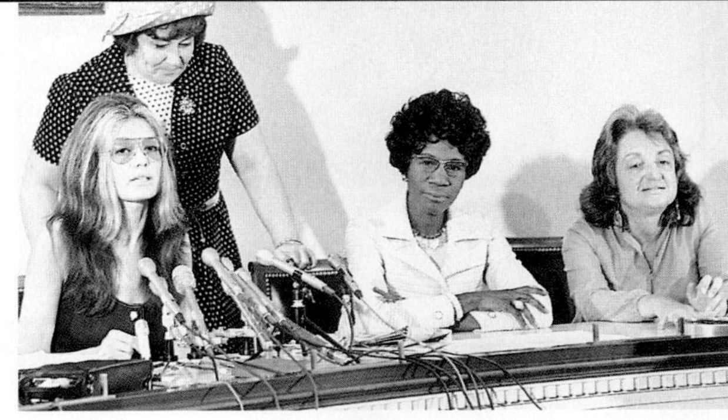
The leaders of the National Women's Political Caucus in 1971 (from left to right): Gloria Steinem, Bella Abzug, Shirley Chisholm, and Betty Friedan

 The ERA

Despite differences among feminists, the movement gained strength in the early 1970s. NOW called for a Women's Strike for Equality. In response, thousands of women marched in cities across the country on August 26, 1970. In 1971 Betty Friedan, political leaders Bella Abzug and Shirley Chisholm, and writer Gloria Steinem helped found the National Women's Political Caucus. The organization wanted to increase women's political participation.

According to Abzug, 1972 was "a watershed year." It was a turning point for women's rights. Congress approved the **Equal Rights Amendment** (ERA) and submitted it to the states for ratification. The amendment stated, "Equality of rights under the law shall not be denied or abridged [reduced] by the United States or by any State on account of sex." Many women's groups supported the constitutional amendment. By mid-1973, 28 of the necessary 34 states had ratified the ERA.

Many men and women began organizing to defeat the amendment. Opponents believed that feminism destroyed women's true nature. Connie Marshner, a leading antifeminist, wrote:

> **"The less time women spend thinking about themselves, the happier they are. . . . Women are ordained [appointed] by nature to spend themselves in meeting the needs of others."**

Political lobbyist Phyllis Schlafly was the most outspoken ERA critic. She founded STOP–ERA (Stop Taking Our Privileges) to block ratification. She also presented her objections to the ERA in the *Phyllis Schlafly Report.* Schlafly warned that if the ERA passed, women would be drafted into the military. She stated that husbands would no longer be required to provide for their wives. Schlafly also warned that separate rest rooms for men and women would become illegal.

A Widening Workforce Increasing numbers of women joined the workforce after 1950. By about how much did the percentage of women in the workforce increase between 1950 and 1980?

REVIEW

Linguistic, Logical-Mathematical. Have students complete the Section Review questions. Then have students answer the Reading Focus questions. Tell students to incorporate into their answers as many of the terms in the Identify portion of the Section Review as possible. Call on volunteers to read their answers to the class.

ASSESS

Have students complete Daily Quiz 20.3.

RETEACH

Visual-Spatial. Have students complete Main Idea Activities for Reteaching and Sheltered English 20.3. Ask students to create protest signs or slogans related to three aspects of the women's rights movement. Display students' work around the classroom and call on volunteers to explain their work.

SHELTERED ENGLISH

People on both sides of the ERA issue showed their position by wearing pins.

Anti-ERA groups strongly objected to the amendment because they believed that it would hurt the family. Gradually, such arguments weakened support for the amendment. The ERA never became law because it fell three states short of ratification by its June 30, 1982, deadline.

Achievements for Women

Despite the ERA's failure, other reform projects that started in 1972 met with greater success. Journalist Gloria Steinem began publishing *Ms.*, a magazine committed to covering the women's movement. New legislation included Title IX of the Education Amendments Act of 1972. This law prohibited any college or university that received federal aid from discriminating against women. Male-only schools began admitting women. With more education, women's career opportunities improved. More women entered traditionally male professions, such as business, law, and medicine.

Some women turned to politics. Between 1968 and 1972 the percentage of female delegates to the Democratic National Convention jumped from 13 to 40 percent. The percentage of women at the Republican National Convention rose from 17 to 30 percent. In addition, more women began to seek and win political office. In 1968 Shirley Chisholm became the first African American woman elected to Congress. She ran for the Democratic presidential nomination in 1972. Despite such political gains, only 14 of 435 U.S. Representatives in 1973 were women. No women served in the U.S. Senate between 1973 and 1978.

Many women in the 1970s continued to face economic challenges. Women's wages remained less than two thirds of the wages of men. The number of female-headed households rose. The number of those households living in poverty also increased.

The women's rights movement did change the roles and status of women in society. "The point of feminism . . . ," an activist once said, "is to win women a wider range of experience." The movement succeeded with that goal.

SECTION 3 REVIEW

Identify and explain the significance of the following:
- **Commission on the Status of Women**
- **Equal Pay Act**
- **Betty Friedan**
- ***The Feminine Mystique***
- **feminism**
- **National Organization for Women**
- **Bella Abzug**
- **Shirley Chisholm**
- **Gloria Steinem**
- **Equal Rights Amendment**
- **Phyllis Schlafly**

Reading for Content Understanding

1 **Main Idea** What did the "second wave" of feminists want, and what methods did they use to reach these goals?

2 **Main Idea** Create a graphic organizer that lists the successes and failures of the women's rights movement. Include the year that each event occurred.

3 **Constitutional Heritage** What was the debate over the Equal Rights Amendment?

4 **Writing** *Describing* Write a short newspaper editorial on the significant events in the women's rights movement that took place in 1963.

5 **Critical Thinking** *Determining the Strength of an Argument* Do you agree or disagree with Phyllis Schlafly's opposition to the Equal Rights Amendment? Explain your answer.

Section 3 Review ANSWERS

Identify

For significance, see the following pages:
- Commission on the Status of Women, p. 610
- Equal Pay Act, p. 611
- Betty Friedan, p. 611
- *The Feminine Mystique*, p. 611
- feminism, p. 611
- National Organization for Women, p. 611
- Bella Abzug, p. 614
- Shirley Chisholm, p. 614
- Gloria Steinem, p. 614
- Equal Rights Amendment, p. 614
- Phyllis Schlafly, p. 614

Reading for Content Understanding

1. women's liberation, rather than just equality; they held dramatic protests

2. Organizers will vary but should include dates and descriptions of legal, political, and business successes; failures include the Equal Rights Amendment and unequal job opportunities and pay for men and women.

3. Opponents feared that women would lose some protections and that the amendment would hurt the family; supporters believed the amendment was needed to help guarantee women full equality.

4. Editorials will vary but should include the release of the report by the Commission on the Status of Women, Kennedy's ban on gender discrimination in civil service jobs, the Equal Pay Act, and *The Feminine Mystique*.

5. Answers will vary but students should explain Schlafly's viewpoint and provide support for their opinions.

SECTION 4 LESSON PLAN

OBJECTIVES

- **Describe how American Indians protested their treatment by the federal government.**
- **Explain the goals of the disability rights movement.**
- **Identify how older Americans and young Americans were affected by the civil rights movement.**

FOCUS

Motivate Before Reading

Ask students to identify other Americans who might have fought discrimination during the 1960s and 1970s. Write the responses on the chalkboard. Then ask what rights may have been at issue. After some discussion tell students that in this section they will learn how the civil rights movements they studied in previous sections led other groups to demand equal rights.

Section 4
RESOURCES

PRINT

★ Guided Reading Strategies 20.4

★ Graphic Organizer 20: Working for Equal Rights for All

★ Primary Source Reading 20: The Life of a Disabled Teenager

★ Section 4 Review, p. 619

★ Daily Quiz 20.4

MULTIMEDIA

★ *Teaching Resources CD–ROM,* Lesson 20.4

★ Linking Geography and History Transparency 12B: Native American Resistance, 1830–1980

SHELTERED ENGLISH

★ Main Idea Activities for Reteaching and Sheltered English 20.4

SECTION 4

Rights for All

Reading Focus

How did American Indians protest their treatment by the federal government?

What were the goals of the disability rights movement?

How were older Americans and young Americans affected by the civil rights movement?

Key Terms

American Indian Movement
Disabled in Action
Education for All Handicapped Children Act
Children's Defense Fund
Gray Panthers
ageism

IN 1947 AN ALASKAN TLINGIT woman wrote a letter to Ruth Muskrat Bronson. Bronson had played an important role in achieving New Deal legislation for American Indians. The Tlingit woman complained that the U.S. government was trying to take away Indian lands. Noting that the government protected endangered animals, the woman wrote, "Perhaps if we were wolves or bears we could have . . . protection. But we are only human beings."

An Alaskan Tlingit headdress

American Indian Rights

In the 1950s the U.S. government reversed some of its policies protecting American Indian tribes. The Termination Resolution began a plan to end federal control over tribes and reservations. From 1954 to 1960, federal support to more than 60 tribes was ended. Some tribes sank deeper into poverty without the assistance of federally supported educational, health, and social services. Other Indian tribes lost land to private groups seeking control of natural resources such as oil and timber. Within a few years some tribes ceased to exist as organized groups.

In 1961 some 420 American Indians from 67 tribes gathered in Chicago to find solutions to these problems. They wanted Indians from all tribes to unite. The conference's declaration of purpose called for changes in how the federal government treated the tribes. The statement began, "We, the Indian People, must be governed . . . in a democratic manner, with a right to choose our own way of life." Some reformers worked with the National Congress of American Indians (NCAI) to win passage of the Indian Civil Rights Act in 1964. This law protected the constitutional rights of American Indians. It also affirmed their right to self-government on reservations.

Introduce Key Terms

Linguistic. Review this section's key terms with students. Ask students to use the key terms to identify the groups they will be studying. Then have them define each term. **SHELTERED ENGLISH**

TEACH

Have students read Section 4 and complete Guided Reading Strategies 20.4. Choose one or more of the following activities to explore the section content with students. For further suggestions on block scheduling or team teaching, see the *Block Scheduling Handbook*.

LEVEL 1: Linguistic. (Suggested time: 15 min.) As a class, go over students' Guided Reading Strategies. Then use the Reading Focus questions to highlight the main ideas of the section. **SHELTERED ENGLISH**

ALL LEVELS: Logical-Mathematical, Visual-Spatial. (Suggested time: 30 min.) On the chalkboard, draw a two-column chart with four rows. Label the columns *Goals* and *Achievements*, and the rows *American Indians, Americans with Disabilities, Young Americans*, and *Older Americans*. Have students refer to this section to complete the chart. Call on volunteers to share their answers. **SHELTERED ENGLISH**

Red Power

Some Indians rejected the NCAI's efforts as too slow and started the "Red Power" movement. In 1968, Indian activists formed the **American Indian Movement** (AIM). This group fought for the rights and properties that had been guaranteed in earlier treaties. AIM leader Russell Means expressed the group's goal: "We don't want civil rights in the white man's society—we want our own sovereign [self-governing] rights." AIM inspired cultural and racial pride among Indians.

American Indian Movement leader Russell Means

AIM organized a number of protests to bring attention to its cause. In 1969 some members seized the deserted federal prison on Alcatraz Island in San Francisco Bay. They stayed there for 19 months. In 1972, AIM organized thousands of Indians in the "Trail of Broken Treaties." This group traveled to Washington, D.C., to demand the return of 110 million acres of land. The group ended its protest by temporarily occupying some federal offices.

AIM members made their most dramatic protest in February 1973. They seized a trading post and church at Wounded Knee, South Dakota. In 1890 the U.S. Army had massacred many Sioux at that location. After a 71-day standoff, a gun battle broke out. Two protesters died. One federal marshal suffered serious injuries. AIM's protests increased awareness of American Indian issues. However, AIM's tactics frightened many non-Indian supporters. The organization achieved few of its long-term goals.

Fights in the Courts

Some Indians fought more successfully through the legal system. In 1971 many Alaskan Indian tribes settled their land claims with the federal government. They received more than $962 million and some 44 million acres of land. Other American Indian tribes won more than $800 million in damages.

The Indian movement achieved more success when the federal government officially replaced its termination policy with a policy of Indian self-determination. This approach gave the Indians the right to govern themselves on reservations.

The Disability Rights Movement

In the 1960s, Americans with disabilities also began fighting for their rights. In particular, they wanted better educational and job opportunities and better access to buildings. Ed Roberts, a quadriplegic paralyzed by polio, was denied admission to the University of California at Berkeley. The university refused to admit students with disabilities because its facilities could not accommodate wheelchairs. After Roberts challenged this policy, the school admitted him in 1962.

By 1967 Roberts was working on a graduate degree. Eleven other students with serious disabilities had joined him on campus. They called themselves the "Rolling Quads." These students protested university efforts to restrict their use of student facilities. They demanded that public areas be made wheelchair accessible.

In the fall of 1970 the Rolling Quads received federal funds for the Physically Disabled Students'

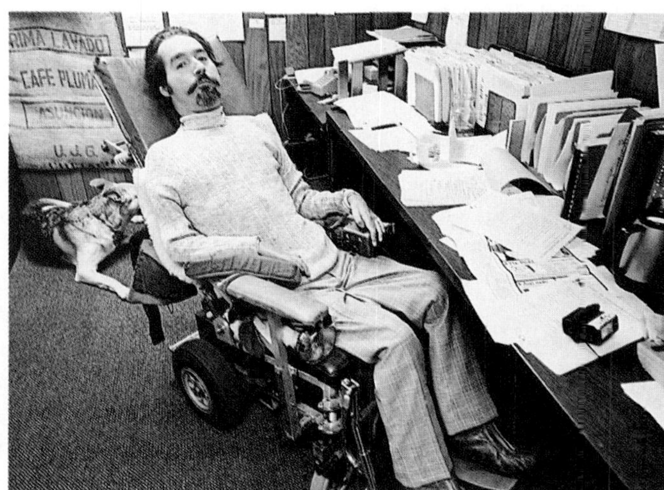

Ed Roberts became director of the California Department of Rehabilitation in 1975.

Citizenship and Democracy

American Indians and the Courts. Before the 1970s, American Indians had limited success in fighting treaty violations in the courts. One reason was the limited number of American Indian lawyers or legal assistance groups for Indians. Beginning in 1970, however, several organizations were created to improve this situation. The Native American Rights Fund was formed to provide free legal aid to Indians. The American Indian Law Center at the University of New Mexico was created to provide aid to Indian law students. The Institute for the Development of Indian Law and the Indian Law Resource Center was established to aid tribes legally fighting treaty violations. The result was greater success for American Indians in the nation's courts.

Critical Thinking: Why might some minority groups have trouble fighting for their civil rights in the courts?

ANSWER: They might face discrimination or be unable to find or afford experienced legal aid.

Multimedia Resources

Linking Geography and History Transparency 12B: Native American Resistance, 1830–1980

LEVEL 3: Linguistic, Logical-Mathematical, Visual-Spatial. (Suggested time: 30 min. plus homework) Ask students to create graphic organizers showing the causes and effects of the various actions American Indians took to protest their treatment by the federal government. For homework, ask students to write an essay analyzing why some actions succeeded and others did not and suggesting how the protesters might have achieved more success. Call on volunteers to discuss their organizers and read their essays to the class.

CLOSE

Linguistic, Musical-Rhythmic. Organize the class into four groups and assign each group one of the four movements in this section. Have each student compose a poem or song lyrics about the assigned movement. Have volunteers read their poems or songs lyrics to the class.

CHALLENGE AND EXTEND

Visual-Spatial, Interpersonal. Assign students, individually or in groups, various sites within your community. Have students visit the sites and determine to what extent each accommodates for

Section 4 Review ANSWERS

Identify

For significance, see the following pages:

- American Indian Movement, p. 617
- Russell Means, p. 617
- Ed Roberts, p. 617
- Disabled in Action, p. 618
- Education for All Handicapped Children Act, p. 618
- Marian Wright Edelman, p. 618
- Children's Defense Fund, p. 618
- Gray Panthers, p. 618
- ageism, p. 618

Reading for Content Understanding

1. worked for new legislation, seized government property, held a violent stand-off, sued in court

2. better educational and job opportunities and better access to public buildings

3. young Americans—led to the legal requirement of a quality public education for children with disabilities and to the formation of the Children's Defense Fund; older Americans—led to the founding of the Gray Panthers to defend and promote the rights of elderly Americans

4. Paragraphs will vary but students should mention at least two of the Warren Court rulings discussed on page 619.

5. Answers will vary but students might mention that the protests were not that effective because some American Indians used extreme tactics, which did not encourage public support for their cause.

Program. Two years later, Roberts set up the Center for Independent Living. People with disabilities ran both organizations. Program counselors helped people find accessible apartments and set up workshops to fix broken wheelchairs. The goal was to help people with disabilities function in the community.

Leaders of the disability rights movement also insisted on equal job opportunities. In 1970 the New York City Board of Education refused to give Judy Heumann a teaching certificate because she was a quadriplegic. Heumann, who had studied for the certificate for years, sued for discrimination. She took her campaign to the newspapers. One headline read, "You Can Be President, Not Teacher, with Polio." The newspaper was referring to former president Franklin D. Roosevelt.

Heumann's campaign introduced her to other people facing similar discrimination. In 1970 she founded the group **Disabled in Action** (DIA) to coordinate reform efforts. DIA brought together people with many different disabilities. One member said, "We all felt powerful. . . . Everybody who came out felt, We are beautiful, we are powerful, we are strong, we are important."

Attorney Marian Wright Edelman worked for the civil rights movement in Mississippi before founding the Children's Defense Fund.

Protests by DIA achieved some legislative successes. The Rehabilitation Act of 1973 made it illegal for any federal agency to discriminate against persons with disabilities. Passed in November 1975, the **Education for All Handicapped Children Act** required public schools to provide a quality education for children with disabilities.

Rights of Young and Old Americans

Attorney Marian Wright Edelman had provided some of the information that helped lead to the passage of the 1975 education act. In 1973 she had learned that about 750,000 American children between the ages of 7 and 13 did not attend school. Edelman founded the **Children's Defense Fund** (CDF) in part to discover why. She learned that the majority of children not enrolled in school were children with disabilities.

Through the CDF, Edelman expanded her focus to include issues affecting all children. She found that politicians were not doing enough to help children. Edelman observed:

> **"Everybody loves children. Everybody is for them in general. Everybody kisses them in elections. . . . But when they get into the budget rooms, or behind closed doors—to really decide how they're going to carve up money—children get lost in the process because they are not powerful."**

The CDF wanted to expand the Head Start program, reform the system of foster parent care, and improve children's health care.

Older Americans also struggled to protect their rights. In 1970 Margaret Kuhn was forced to retire at age 65. In response, she and other retired Americans founded the **Gray Panthers** to defend the interests of the elderly. The Gray Panthers fought **ageism**, discrimination against an age group, particularly the elderly. The Panthers opposed forced retirement. They also fought to improve health care treatment in nursing homes. Believing that older Americans were often being ignored, Kuhn reminded anyone younger than she that "every one of us is growing old."

persons with disabilities. Ask students to report their findings and make a class list of observed accommodations. Then have students discuss accommodations still needed.

REVIEW

Linguistic, Visual-Spatial. Have students complete the Section Review questions. Ask students to create political cartoons showing the gains made by each of the groups discussed in this section. Students should include captions with their cartoons. Have volunteers explain their cartoons to the class.

ASSESS

Have students complete Daily Quiz 20.4.

RETEACH

Linguistic, Visual-Spatial. Have students complete Main Idea Activities for Reteaching and Sheltered English 20.4. Ask students to create bumper stickers describing the issues addressed by each group discussed in this section. Then lead a discussion on the goals and accomplishments of each of these groups.
SHELTERED ENGLISH

The Warren Court

During the 1960s Chief Justice Earl Warren led the U.S. Supreme Court in many rulings that affected equal rights. In a series of cases about state legislative districts, the Court ruled that the number of districts must be based on the state's population. In some states the legislative districts had not changed with the state's population. For example, in Alabama, one state senator represented more than 600,000 people. Another senator had only about 15,000 voters in his district. As a result, political power was not evenly distributed. In *Reynolds v. Sims* (1964), the Court required states to create districts of nearly equal population.

Warren also led the Court in rulings that expanded the legal rights of Americans accused of crimes. In 1963 in *Gideon v. Wainwright*, a poor Florida man accused of burglary appealed to the U.S. Supreme Court. In a petition he wrote himself, Clarence Earl Gideon argued that the trial judge's refusal to provide him with a lawyer was unconstitutional. The Court agreed and ruled that people accused of a crime had a constitutional right to free legal counsel. The ruling required states to provide an attorney for people unable to afford one.

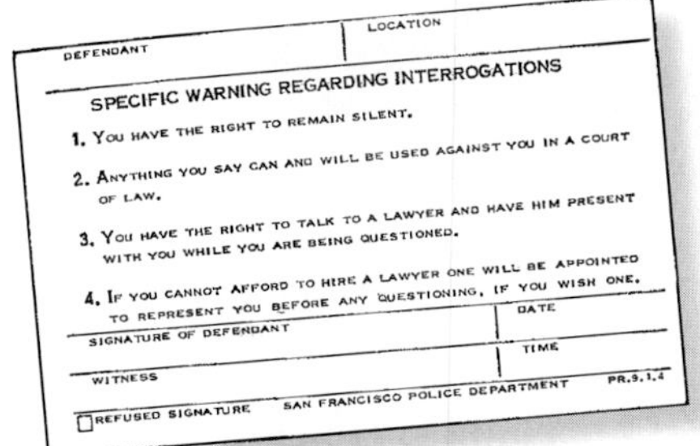

DEFENDANT | LOCATION

SPECIFIC WARNING REGARDING INTERROGATIONS

1. YOU HAVE THE RIGHT TO REMAIN SILENT.
2. ANYTHING YOU SAY CAN AND WILL BE USED AGAINST YOU IN A COURT OF LAW.
3. YOU HAVE THE RIGHT TO TALK TO A LAWYER AND HAVE HIM PRESENT WITH YOU WHILE YOU ARE BEING QUESTIONED.
4. IF YOU CANNOT AFFORD TO HIRE A LAWYER ONE WILL BE APPOINTED TO REPRESENT YOU BEFORE ANY QUESTIONING, IF YOU WISH ONE.

SIGNATURE OF DEFENDANT | DATE

WITNESS | TIME

REFUSED SIGNATURE — SAN FRANCISCO POLICE DEPARTMENT — PR.9.1.4

After the Miranda *ruling, police officers began asking suspects to sign a form acknowledging their rights.*

In *Escobedo* v. *Illinois* (1964) and *Miranda* v. *Arizona* (1966), the Court expanded the protections for the accused. *Escobedo* established that suspects have a right to have their attorney present during police questioning. *Miranda* ordered police to notify suspects of their rights prior to any questioning. Justice Warren wrote that an accused

> **"person must be warned that he has a right to remain silent, that any statement he does make may be used in evidence against him, and that he has a right to the presence of an attorney, either retained [hired] or appointed."**

The *Miranda* decision was controversial. Some critics complained that the *Escobedo* and *Miranda* rulings hurt the police's ability to investigate crimes.

Throughout the 1960s and the early 1970s, many Americans became more aware of inequalities in society. As a result, many different groups worked to gain their equal civil and political rights during these years.

SECTION 4 REVIEW

Identify and explain the significance of the following:

- **American Indian Movement**
- **Russell Means**
- **Ed Roberts**
- **Disabled in Action**
- **Education for All Handicapped Children Act**
- **Marian Wright Edelman**
- **Children's Defense Fund**
- **Gray Panthers**
- **ageism**

Reading for Content Understanding

1 **Main Idea** What did American Indians do to protest government policies?

2 **Main Idea** What did the disability rights movement want to achieve?

3 **Citizenship and Democracy** How did the civil rights movement affect the rights of young and old Americans?

4 **Writing** *Informing* Write a short paragraph that provides information about some of the rulings of the Supreme Court during the 1960s.

5 **Critical Thinking** *Drawing Conclusions* Do you think the protests by American Indians in the late 1960s and early 1970s were effective? Explain your answer.

Chapter 20 Review ANSWERS

Identifying People and Ideas

1. protest strategy that African Americans and other groups used to fight segregation and other forms of discrimination

2. African American civil rights leader who advocated use of nonviolent protest to achieve equal rights; assassinated in April 1968

3. law banning segregation in public places and prohibiting discrimination by employers, unions, or universities with federal government contracts

4. Hispanic labor leader for migrant workers; helped found the United Farm Workers

5. labor union for migrant farmworkers

6. feminist and author whose book *The Feminine Mystique* helped spark the women's rights movement

7. lobby group that advocated economic, political, and social equality for women

8. activist and leader of the American Indian Movement

9. American Indian political group formed to fight for rights and land promised in former U.S. treaties

10. African American leader of the Nation of Islam, or Black Muslims; supported black nationalism and the use of violence for self-protection; assassinated in 1965

Using the Time Line

1. e
2. c
3. b
4. d
5. a

Review and Assessment RESOURCES

PRINT
- ★ Chapter 20 Review, pp. 620–21
- ★ Vocabulary Activity 20
- ★ Chapter 20 Study Guide
- ★ Chapter 20 Test (Form A or B)

MULTIMEDIA
- ★ Audio Program, Ch. 20 (English and Spanish)
- ★ *Global Skill Builder CD–ROM*
- ★ Chapter 20 Test Generator
- ★ HRW Web site

SHELTERED ENGLISH
- ★ Spanish Glossary
- ★ Sheltered English Chapter 20 Test

ASSESS

Have students complete one of the Chapter 20 tests. As an alternate assessment, assign the Chapter 20 Investigation.

Understanding Main Ideas

1. The protests and the violent responses to some of them helped change public perceptions about the need for civil rights protection, united African Americans, and gained the federal government's attention and response.

2. Events included the murder of black and white voter registration workers and the violence against the Selma marchers.

3. He organized migrant farmworkers to form a union and went on a hunger strike to gain support for them.

4. It pushed for economic, political, and social equality with men.

5. Conditions included poverty, loss of federal support services, loss of tribal lands, and loss of tribal identity.

6. Groups included African Americans, Hispanics, women, American Indians, Americans with disabilities, children's rights advocates, older Americans.

Reviewing Themes

1. Tactics include sit-ins, marches, Freedom Rides, boycotts, demonstrations, lawsuits, street patrols, unionizing, strikes, occupying federal sites, and walkouts; groups that used each tactic vary.

2. It passed the Indian Civil Rights Act of 1964.

3. The South, because of its past dependence on slavery, had many remaining laws and attitudes that discriminated against African Americans.

CHAPTER 20 REVIEW

Chapter Summary

The 1960s was an era of change. African Americans struggled to gain civil rights. In turn, the civil rights movement inspired other groups, including Mexican Americans, women, and American Indians, to fight for their rights. These groups used sit-ins, boycotts, marches, and other efforts to demand equal rights. By the 1970s these movements had affected the lives of nearly all Americans.

On a separate sheet of paper, complete the following activities.

Identifying People and Ideas

Describe the historical significance of the following:

1. sit-in
2. Martin Luther King Jr.
3. Civil Rights Act of 1964
4. César Chávez
5. United Farm Workers
6. Betty Friedan
7. National Organization for Women
8. Russell Means
9. American Indian Movement
10. Malcolm X

Internet Activity

go.hrw.com
SB1 Civil Rights

Search the Internet through the HRW Web site to find quotations and images for an exhibit on the 1960s civil rights movement. Use this information to make a collage reflecting the goals and important figures of the movement.

Understanding Main Ideas

1. How did the sit-ins, the Freedom Rides, and the March on Washington help bring about new civil rights laws?
2. What events helped lead to the passage of the Voting Rights Act of 1965?
3. What role did César Chávez play in helping Mexican Americans gain equal opportunities?
4. What were the goals of the women's rights movement?
5. What were the economic and political conditions that led to protests by some American Indian groups?
6. List some of the groups that became involved in civil rights efforts in the 1960s and early 1970s. Explain their roles.

Reviewing Themes

1. **Citizenship and Democracy** List four tactics used by different groups in the United States to gain equal rights. Give a specific example of each tactic and a group that used it.

Using the Time Line

Number your paper from 1 to 5. Match the letters on the time line below with the following events.

1. **Congress passes the Education for All Handicapped Children Act.**
2. **Hispanics form La Raza Unida Party.**
3. **The National Organization for Women is founded.**
4. **Members of the American Indian Movement seize federal property at Wounded Knee.**
5. **Four African American students stage a sit-in in North Carolina.**

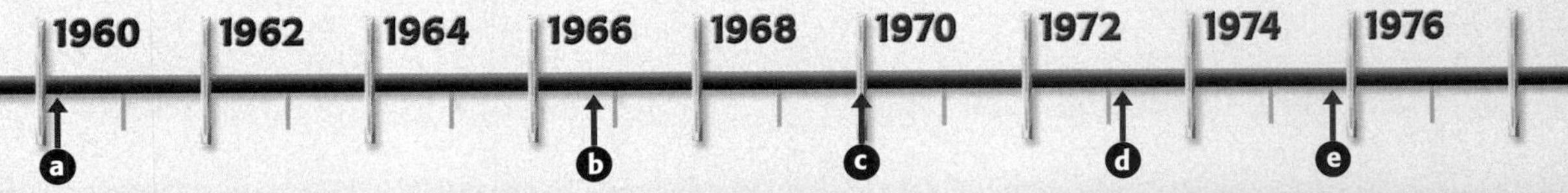

RETEACH

Logical-Mathematical, Interpersonal. Ask students to list and discuss the more successful strategies that groups used to achieve civil rights during the 1960s and early 1970s. Then remind students of the current issues that they listed in the Chapter Motivator activity. Ask students how they would now answer the question, "What can I do?" Encourage class discussion. **SHELTERED ENGLISH**

Using the Internet

HRW Have students continue their research by learning more about one of the important figures they included in their collage. Tell students to use their research to write a biography of the person's life, career, and achievements.

Portfolio Extension

1. Have students continue their interviews by asking about areas in which Americans aged 50 and older face discrimination. Have students add their findings to their reports.

2. Have students write a second chapter on another of the groups listed.

2. **Constitutional Heritage** What legislation did the U.S. government pass to help American Indians gain their constitutional rights?
3. **Geographic Diversity** Why did leaders of the civil rights movement focus most of their efforts in the South?

Thinking Critically

1. **Evaluating** Do you think requiring workers to retire at a certain age is good or bad for society? Explain your answer.
2. **Synthesizing Information** How did women respond to the feminist movement?
3. **Identifying Cause and Effect** Why do you think that the African American civil rights movement inspired other groups to fight for their civil rights?

Writing About History

1. **Creating** Imagine that you are a migrant worker striking against grape growers. Create a brochure to hand out in support of the strike.
2. **Expressing** Imagine that you have just heard Martin Luther King Jr.'s "I Have A Dream" speech. Write a journal entry expressing what the speech and the march mean to American society.

Building Your Portfolio

Complete the following activities individually or in groups.

1. **Then and Now** Prepare a list of questions to ask of someone who is at least 50 years old. At least five questions should ask the person about his or her life today and at least five questions should be about when he or she was a teenager. Interview this person and write a short report of how that person's life has changed with age.
2. **Civil Rights Movements** Imagine that you are the author of a children's book titled *The 1960s Civil Rights Movements.* Write a chapter on one of the following groups: African Americans, Mexican Americans, American Indians, women, or people with disabilities. Use images and maps to illustrate your chapter.

Linking Geography and History

1. **Region** What was the importance of the particular route the Freedom Riders selected for their demonstration?
2. **Location** Why do you think that the American Indian Movement chose Wounded Knee, South Dakota, as the site for a dramatic protest?

History Skills Workshop

Reading Maps Study the map below, which shows African American voter registration after the passage of the Voting Rights Act of 1965. Then answer the following questions: (a) Which states show the smallest increase in African American voter registration? (b) Which states show the greatest increase in voter registration? (c) What reasons can you give for the different levels of increase in voter registration?

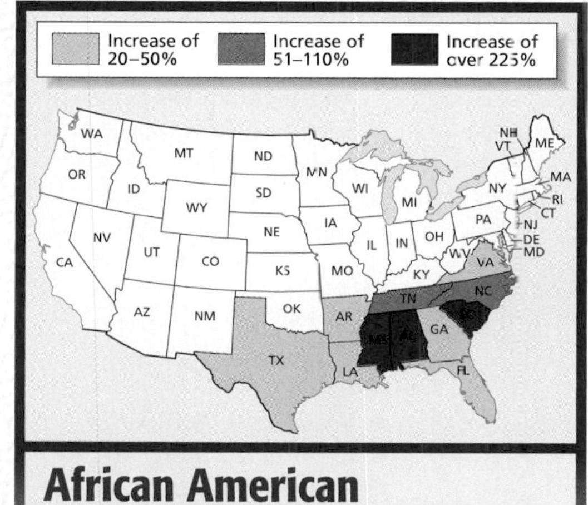

African American Voter Registration, 1965

Thinking Critically

1. Answers will vary but students might mention that forced retirement opens up jobs for younger people; on the other hand, it deprives society of older workers' expertise and experience.

2. Answers will vary but students should mention that some women actively supported the movement, while others actively opposed it.

3. Answers will vary but students might mention that the success of the movement gave other groups hope that they too could achieve change by using similar tactics.

Writing About History

1. Brochures will vary but should use persuasive text and images to show the goals of the strike.

2. Journal entries will vary but may include feelings that the event shows that society is moving closer to King's dream and could one day resemble that dream.

Linking Geography and History

1. The route crossed the most segregated region of the United States.

2. The location was the site where the U.S. Army had massacred Sioux Indians.

History Skills Workshop

(a) Arkansas, Florida, Georgia, Louisiana, Texas, Virginia; (b) Alabama, Mississippi, South Carolina; (c) Answers will vary but students might mention that the states where the most voter activists went are those that had the greatest increase in voter registration.

CHAPTER PLANNING GUIDE
War in Vietnam

	SECTION LESSON OBJECTIVES	PRINT RESOURCES	MULTIMEDIA RESOURCES	SHELTERED ENGLISH RESOURCES
Section 1: Early Conflicts in Vietnam (pp. 623–26)	★ Explain how French colonization affected Vietnam. ★ Examine the reasons why Vietnam was divided into two countries in 1954. ★ Identify why many South Vietnamese opposed their government and how they expressed their disapproval.	★ Guided Reading Strategies 21.1 ★ Section 1 Review, p. 626 ★ Daily Quiz 21.1	★ *Teaching Resources CD–ROM*, Lesson 21.1 ★ HRW Web site	★ Main Idea Activities for Reteaching and Sheltered English 21.1
Section 2: The Escalation of the War (pp. 627–30)	★ Examine President Johnson's decision to continue supporting the war in Vietnam. ★ Describe the tactics the U.S. military used to fight the Communists in Vietnam. ★ Analyze the effect of the Vietnam War on U.S. soldiers.	★ Guided Reading Strategies 21.2 ★ Primary Source Reading 21: American Indians and the Vietnam War ★ Literature Reading 21: Women in Vietnam ★ Graphic Organizer 21: Tracing the Path into Vietnam ★ Section 2 Review, p. 630 ★ Daily Quiz 21.2	★ *Teaching Resources CD–ROM*, Lesson 21.2 ★ HRW Web site	★ Main Idea Activities for Reteaching and Sheltered English 21.2
Section 3: A Divided Nation (pp. 631–35)	★ Describe how the Tet Offensive changed public opinion on the Vietnam War. ★ Analyze the effects of the Vietnam War on the Democratic Party. ★ Identify factors that led to Richard Nixon's victory in the 1968 presidential election.	★ Guided Reading Strategies 21.3 ★ Biography Reading 21: Benjamin Spock ★ Geography Activity 21: Geography and the Vietnam War ★ Section 3 Review, p. 635 ★ Daily Quiz 21.3	★ *Teaching Resources CD–ROM*, Lesson 21.3 ★ Everyday Life in America Transparency 30: Protest During the Vietnam War	★ Main Idea Activities for Reteaching and Sheltered English 21.3
Section 4: The War Under Nixon (pp. 636–41)	★ Explain President Nixon's Vietnam policy. ★ Identify the outcome of the 1972 presidential election. ★ Describe some of the war's legacies.	★ Guided Reading Strategies 21.4 ★ American History Political Cartoon 28: The Vietnam War ★ Section 4 Review, p. 641 ★ Daily Quiz 21.4	★ *Teaching Resources CD–ROM*, Lesson 21.4 ★ Art in American History Transparency 45: Vietnam Veterans Memorial ★ *Exploring America's Past* Video Segment: The Wall; *Teacher's Guide*, pp. 37–39	★ Main Idea Activities for Reteaching and Sheltered English 21.4
Chapter Review and Assessment (pp. 642–43)		★ Chapter 21 Review, pp. 642–43 ★ Vocabulary Activity 21 ★ Chapter 21 Study Guide ★ Chapter 21 Test (Form A or B)	★ Audio Program, Ch. 21 (English and Spanish) ★ *Global Skill Builder CD–ROM* ★ Chapter 21 Test Generator ★ HRW Web site	★ Spanish Glossary ★ Sheltered English Chapter 21 Test

CHAPTER OVERVIEW

Fear over the spread of communism in Southeast Asia led to U.S. involvement in the Vietnam War. By 1963 President Kennedy had sent more than 16,000 U.S. personnel to Vietnam.

President Johnson escalated U.S. involvement in the war by sending more troops and by beginning bombing campaigns and search-and-destroy missions. People in the United States became increasingly divided over whether America should be involved in the fighting in Vietnam. Official reports of the war made victory seem near, but the Tet Offensive caused many Americans to realize that they had been deceived about the war's progress. This realization helped lead to Richard Nixon's victory in the 1968 presidential election.

The public believed that Nixon was trying to end the war, but news spread that he had actually expanded fighting into Laos and Cambodia. This led to even more war protests back home and made Nixon rethink his Vietnam policy. The United States began peace negotiations in 1972. The outcome was the 1973 Paris Peace Accords, which called for the gradual removal of U.S. troops from Vietnam. By 1975 the South Vietnamese capital of Saigon had fallen to North Vietnamese forces, leaving the United States and Southeast Asian countries to deal with the aftermath of the war.

CHAPTER INVESTIGATION

The Chapter Investigation is an extended, multipart activity designed for students to work cooperatively and apply the chapter content in the creation of a project. You may choose to use the Chapter 21 Investigation, Newsmagazine: Remembering Vietnam, either as a substitute for teaching the section lessons or as an alternate assessment.

BLOCK SCHEDULING 

The teacher lesson plans for each section offer a variety of activity choices to help you present the material in a block scheduling format. For further suggestions on block scheduling, see the *Block Scheduling Handbook with Team Teaching Strategies*, pp. 121–26.

Meeting Individual Needs

ABILITY LEVELS

LEVEL 1 Basic level activities designed for all students encountering new material.

LEVEL 2 Intermediate level activities designed for average students.

LEVEL 3 Challenging activities designed for above-average students.

SHELTERED ENGLISH These activities address the needs of students with Limited English Proficiency.

Smithsonian Institution®

Internet Connections and Lesson 21

www.si.edu/hrw

CNN Presents America:

Yesterday and Today 1850 to Present

Segment: America Honors the Vets

Additional Resources

Books for Teachers

Herring, George. *America's Longest War: The United States and Vietnam, 1950–1975.* Temple University Press, 1986. A critical examination of U.S. policy in Vietnam.

Hunt, Michael. *Lyndon Johnson's War: America's Cold War Crusade in Vietnam, 1945–1965.* Doubleday, 1996. Explores and analyzes the origins of the Vietnam War.

Moser, Richard R. *The New Winter Soldiers: GI and Veteran Dissent During the Vietnam Era.* Rutgers University Press, 1996. Chronicles actions of Vietnam veterans who opposed the war, both at home and in combat.

Books for Students

Edelman, Bernard. *Dear America: Letters Home from Vietnam.* Pocket Books, 1989. Shows the war through the eyes of U.S. personnel.

Hoobler, Dorothy, and Thomas Hoobler. *Vietnam, Why We Fought: An Illustrated History.* Alfred A. Knopf, 1990. Uses photographs and text to tell the story of U.S. involvement in the Vietnam War. Includes an examination of Vietnam's history. (for students reading below grade level).

Kent, Deborah. *The Vietnam War: "What are We Fighting For?"* Enslow Publishers, 1994. An introduction to U.S. involvement in the Vietnam War. Examines the antiwar movement and problems faced by veterans.

Multimedia Materials

How Far from Home: Veterans After Vietnam. Video, 30 min. Northern Light Productions. Portrays the many problems veterans faced upon returning home from Vietnam.

Passage to Vietnam. CD–ROM Windows/MAC. Against All Odds Productions, 1995. Essays by 70 of the world's leading photojournalists. Contains over 400 photographs, an hour of full-motion video, interactive photo-editing sessions, and an interactive map of Vietnam.

Vietnam—Chronicle of War. Video, 88 min. University of Illinois. Chronicles the Vietnam War through the eyes of news correspondents Dan Rather and Walter Cronkite.

War in Vietnam

CHAPTER MOTIVATOR

Remind students that after World War II, U.S. foreign policy was based on the desire to contain communism. Display a world map to the class and ask students to identify Asian countries that were communist by the 1950s. Students will probably identify the Soviet Union and China. Then ask them to write a few sentences explaining why stopping the spread of communism into Southeast Asia was important to the United States in the late 1950s. Explain to students that in this chapter they will learn about events preceding the outbreak of war in Vietnam, U.S. involvement in the war, and consequences for the countries involved. As students read the chapter, ask them how their reasons for the United States's efforts to stop communism compare to the reasons discussed in the chapter.

Presenting Themes

- **Global Relations**
  Students might mention the desire to protect economic interests such as natural resources or trade, to protect a country from an aggressor, or to gain more territory.
- **Geographic Diversity**
  Students might note that familiarity with the land can serve as an advantage to the nation fighting on its own soil. They might also mention the difficulties of moving supplies in some environments and of waging war in extreme climates such as deserts, jungles, or mountains.
- **Citizenship and Democracy**
  Students might mention that legislation can increase or decrease a branch's power or alter interactions among the branches.

Using the Time Line

Have students identify each event as either political or military in nature. After completing the chapter, have them discuss the ways in which political considerations influenced military decisions during the Vietnam War.

CHAPTER 21

War in Vietnam

(1945–1975)

In Vietnam, U.S. soldiers faced uncertainty with every step. As they marched through rice paddies and dense jungles, they tried to avoid land mines and other hidden traps. According to one GI, soldiers asked themselves: "Should you put your foot to that flat rock or the clump of weeds to its rear?" The wrong answer could have deadly consequences. The war in Vietnam raised troubling questions for everyone involved in the conflict.

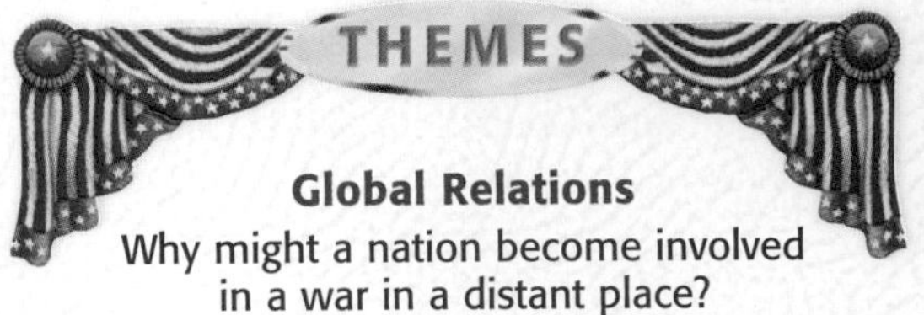

Global Relations
Why might a nation become involved in a war in a distant place?

Geographic Diversity
How might geography affect the outcome of a war?

Citizenship and Democracy
How might legislation change the roles of the different branches of a government?

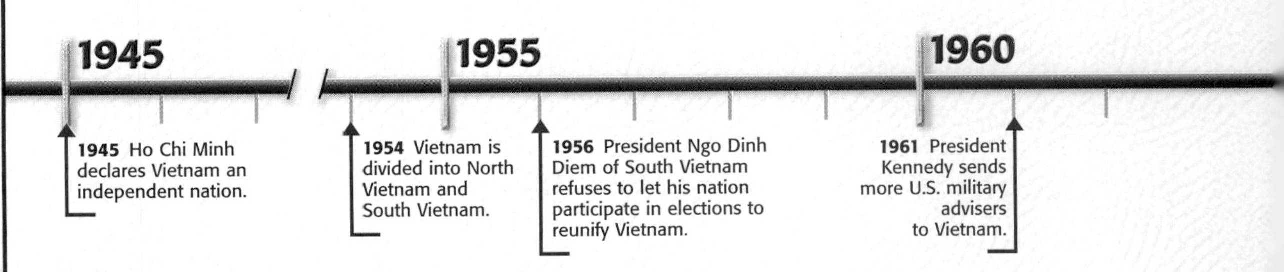

OBJECTIVES

- **Explain how French colonization affected Vietnam.**
- **Examine the reasons why Vietnam was divided into two countries in 1954.**
- **Identify why many South Vietnamese opposed their government and how they expressed their disapproval.**

FOCUS

Motivate Before Reading

Prior to class, set up a series of dominoes. Arrange them so that by knocking over one domino, you cause the entire series to fall. Then ask students to imagine that each domino is a country. Tap the first domino and watch the series fall. Tell students that in this section they will see how a political belief known as the domino theory led to U.S. involvement in Vietnam.

Early Conflicts in Vietnam

Reading Focus

How did French colonization affect Vietnam?

Why was Vietnam divided into two countries in 1954?

Why did many South Vietnamese oppose their government, and how did they express their disapproval?

Key Terms

Vietminh

domino theory

Geneva Accords

National Liberation Front

Vietcong

Section 1 RESOURCES

PRINT

★ Guided Reading Strategies 21.1

★ Section 1 Review, p. 626

★ Daily Quiz 21.1

MULTIMEDIA

★ *Teaching Resources CD–ROM,* Lesson 21.1

★ HRW Web site

SHELTERED ENGLISH

★ Main Idea Activities for Reteaching and Sheltered English 21.1

IN 1873 FRENCH EXPLORER Francis Garnier published Voyages of Exploration, *a description of his expedition to Southeast Asia. Garnier encouraged the French to colonize this area for trade and to bring Western culture to its people. However, one of Garnier's associates believed that it was a mistake for France to impose its culture on the peoples of the region. "The extraordinary resistance, sometimes violent, sometimes passive [inactive] in nature, day by day more hateful . . . by all classes of the people, is stronger now than at any time since the conquest," he warned. "We must open our eyes."*

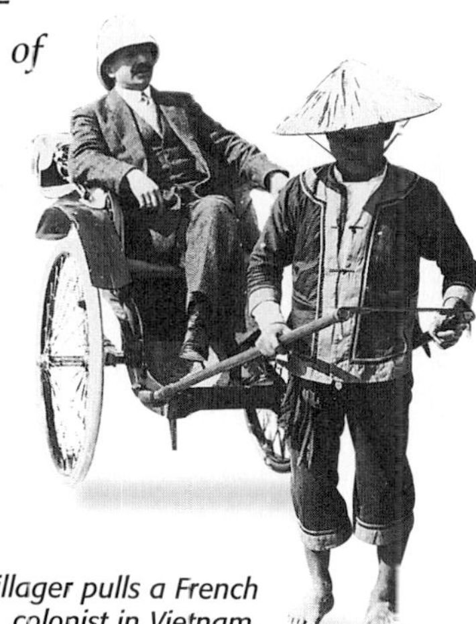

A villager pulls a French colonist in Vietnam.

IMAGE ON LEFT PAGE: *The Vietnam Veterans Memorial in Washington, D.C., honors the dead and missing in action from the Vietnam War.*

1965 — **1970** — **1975**

- **1964** Congress passes the Tonkin Gulf Resolution.
- **1965** The first U.S. combat troops arrive in Vietnam.
- **1968** Communist forces attack throughout South Vietnam in the Tet Offensive.
- **1970** U.S. troops invade Cambodia.
- **1973** The Paris Peace Accords are signed.
- **1975** Saigon falls to North Vietnamese forces.

Introduce Key Terms

Linguistic, Interpersonal. Review this section's key terms with students. Have them write each term on one side of a note card and clues about the term on the other side. Ask students to use the note cards to take turns quizzing each other.
SHELTERED ENGLISH

TEACH

Have students read Section 1 and complete Guided Reading Strategies 21.1. Choose one or more of the following activities to explore the section content with students. For further suggestions on block scheduling or team teaching, see the *Block Scheduling Handbook.*

LEVEL 1: Linguistic. (Suggested time: 15 min.) As a class, go over students' Guided Reading Strategies. Then use the Reading Focus questions to highlight the main ideas of the section.
SHELTERED ENGLISH

ALL LEVELS: Linguistic, Interpersonal. (Suggested time: 25 min.) Discuss note-taking techniques with the class and tell them that good notes should enable a person to explain the topic being discussed to someone who did not hear the presentation. Read students the segment of this section entitled "The Division

Economic Development

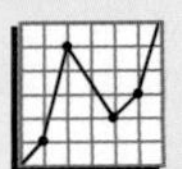

Motives for Colonization. Francis Garnier set out in 1866 to explore the Mekong River, which the French hoped would provide a trade route to China. Garnier and his comrades spent two years exploring the Mekong and southern China. In Garnier's *Voyage d'Exploration* he announced that the Mekong had many rapids and sandbars, making it difficult to travel and unsuitable as a trade route. Garnier declared that the Red River, which stretched from China to northern Vietnam, could serve as a supply route for silk, tea, and other Chinese goods that the French desired. His conclusions gave France the incentive to colonize the area not only for trade, but to secure the route into China.

Activity: Have students use the library or search the Internet through the HRW Web site to find information about the geography of Southeast Asia. Have students create a map depicting the area's various geographic features.

go.hrw.com
SB1 Southeast Asia

MAP ANSWER
Hanoi, Pnompenh, Vientiane

French Vietnam

Vietnam is a small country in Southeast Asia. It has endured many foreign invasions and occupations. The Vietnamese fiercely opposed the invading powers. In the late 1700s the French became interested in Vietnam after Catholic missionaries journeyed there. By 1883, French forces had conquered Vietnam. France soon combined it with neighboring Laos and Cambodia to create a new colony called French Indochina. The French imposed harsh taxes and limited political freedoms. Many of the people in Indochina, particularly the Vietnamese, fought French colonization for years.

Starting about 1900, Vietnamese nationalists began to renew the fight for independence. The most successful nationalist was born as Nguyen That Thanh (NY-en TAHT TAHN) in central Vietnam in 1890. Later he adopted the name Ho Chi Minh (HOH CHEE MIN), meaning "He who enlightens." Ho spent years studying in France. Over time, he came to believe that the best way to fight colonial imperialism was through a communist revolution.

Ho Chi Minh led his people through wars with Japan, France, South Vietnam, and the United States.

During World War II Japanese troops and local nationalists drove French soldiers out of Indochina. Ho then refused to accept Japanese rule. To fight the Japanese, Ho organized the League for the Independence of Vietnam, also called the **Vietminh** (vee-ET-MIN). After Japan surrendered to the Allies, he declared the independence of the Democratic Republic of Vietnam in a great celebration in Hanoi on September 2, 1945.

French Indochina

Learning from Maps French Indochina consisted of Vietnam, Laos, and Cambodia. At the end of World War II, Vietnam sought independence from French control.

Place What were the capitals of the three countries that made up French Indochina?

War Breaks Out

Vietnam was not yet free, however. The French insisted that Vietnam was still part of Indochina. Ho tried to make peace with the French, but he warned:

> **"If they [the French] force us into war, we will fight. The struggle will be atrocious [extremely bad], but the Vietnamese people will suffer anything rather than renounce [give up] their freedom."**

The French refused Ho's offers and moved to retake Vietnam. President Eisenhower's administration funded and supplied the French fight based on the belief in the **domino theory**. Like others, the president argued that if Vietnam fell to the Communists—as

Grows." Ask students to take notes as you read. Then have students discuss growing opposition in South Vietnam and the forms of protest used.

LEVEL 3: Linguistic, Logical-Mathematical. (Suggested time: 20 min. plus homework) Tell students to imagine that they are news correspondents who have covered Southeast Asia since World War II and have recently been assigned the Geneva Conference. Have them write articles describing the effects of French colonization on Vietnam, the situation in Vietnam that led up to the Geneva Accords, and the actual terms of the accords. Then lead a class discussion on the background of the Vietnam War. Have students use their articles to guide the discussion.

CLOSE

Logical-Mathematical, Visual-Spatial. Have students create an annotated time line that describes events surrounding the conflict in Vietnam. Have students begin with the French conquering Vietnam by 1883, and end with Kennedy's actions regarding Vietnam.

CHALLENGE AND EXTEND

Linguistic, Intrapersonal. Remind students that U.S. policy regarding communism in Asia was based on the domino theory. Ask students to write an essay in which they take a stand on whether the domino theory justified U.S. intervention in Vietnam.

China and North Korea had done—all of Southeast Asia would fall as well, like dominoes in a row.

The Vietminh slowly weakened the better-equipped French forces with hit-and-run guerrilla attacks and ambushes. In 1954 the Vietminh trapped and surrounded 12,000 French troops at the village of Dien Bien Phu (DYEN BYEN FOO). The fighting was fierce, and the French suffered more than 7,000 casualties in the battle. Finally, on May 7, the French surrendered.

Just weeks before the French defeat, representatives from the major world powers and delegates from Southeast Asia had met in Geneva, Switzerland. The day after the battle in Dien Bien Phu, the leaders discussed the future of Indochina. In July the parties worked out a compromise known as the **Geneva Accords**. This agreement temporarily divided Vietnam into two separate nations—North Vietnam and South Vietnam. North Vietnam was a communist state led by Ho Chi Minh and the Vietminh. South Vietnam was a Western-style government led by Ngo Dinh Diem (en-GOHDIN de-EM), a committed anticommunist. The Geneva Accords also called for free elections in July 1956 to reunite North and South Vietnam under one government.

Michigan State University Archives & Historical Collections

President Diem, on the left, ruled South Vietnam with the help of his family. Together, they worked to reduce opposition to his government.

A Divided Country

U.S. officials fully supported Diem and South Vietnam. They hoped the anticommunists would win control of the entire country in the 1956 elections.

U.S. troops trained South Vietnamese soldiers and supplied them with the latest weapons.

Rival Governments

The new government in South Vietnam was dishonest and brutal. President Diem put family members in top positions and used a secret police force to silence his enemies. His methods raised some concerns, but the Eisenhower administration saw his government as the only alternative to a communist state. The United States began sending supplies and providing military training to Diem's forces.

Many North Vietnamese favored the widespread social reforms and land redistribution policies carried out by Ho Chi Minh's communist government. One North Vietnamese man recalled:

> **"The living conditions of the people were getting better and better every day. The people were well off. They had enough to eat. . . . They had land to work and buffaloes to help them plow the land."**

Not everyone benefited in Ho's new nation, however. Ho blamed landlords for North Vietnam's poverty. Communist government officials searched out landowners, imprisoning and killing thousands of them.

Historical Sidelight

Discussing Vietnam. On January 19, 1961, the day before he took office, John F. Kennedy met with President Eisenhower at the White House to discuss problems facing the United States. Eisenhower identified Laos, a country neighboring Vietnam, as the most serious trouble spot in Southeast Asia. He told Kennedy that Laos was "the cork in the bottle of the Far East. If Laos is lost to the free world, in the long run we will lose all of Southeast Asia. . . . You are going to have to put troops in Laos." Vietnam, however, was hardly mentioned in the discussion between the two leaders.

Critical Thinking: How do Eisenhower's remarks reveal his belief in the domino theory?

ANSWER: He stated that the fall of one country, Laos, would cause all the other countries in the region to become communist.

REVIEW

Linguistic, Logical-Mathematical, Interpersonal. Have students complete the Section Review questions. Ask each student to create a 10-question quiz based on this section. Then organize the class into pairs. Have each partner quiz the other. Ask them to provide feedback for each incorrect response.

ASSESS

Have students complete Daily Quiz 21.1.

RETEACH

Logical-Mathematical, Visual-Spatial, Interpersonal. Have students complete Main Idea Activities for Reteaching and Sheltered English 21.1. Then organize students into small groups. Give each group a piece of butcher paper. Ask each group to create a drawing that provides information on the history of Vietnam in the 1940s and 1950s, or reasons why the United States sent troops to Vietnam. **SHELTERED ENGLISH**

Section 1 Review ANSWERS

Identify
For significance, see the following pages:

- Ho Chi Minh, p. 624
- Vietminh, p. 624
- domino theory, p. 624
- Geneva Accords, p. 625
- Ngo Dinh Diem, p. 625
- National Liberation Front, p. 626
- Vietcong, p. 626

Locate
For locations, see the map on page 624.

Reading for Content Understanding

1. The Vietnamese paid high taxes and had their political freedoms restricted. These hardships eventually led to war against France and the division of Vietnam.

2. The country was divided in half—North Vietnam and South Vietnam—until free elections could be held in 1956; all sides agreed because they could arrive at no other solution to the problems in Vietnam.

3. The United States wanted to stop the spread of communism and feared that if Vietnam fell to communism, the rest of Southeast Asia would fall along with it.

4. Reports will vary but students should refer to Diem's troops firing on Buddhist demonstrators and that some of the monks set themselves on fire.

5. Answers will vary but students should offer their opinions and use material from the section to support them.

The Vietcong

As the planned 1956 reunification elections approached, Diem refused to allow South Vietnam to participate. He feared that the northern communist government would win. U.S. officials backed his decision. To stamp out growing support for Ho and the Vietminh in South Vietnam, Diem began arresting thousands of citizens.

As discontent mounted in South Vietnam, many nationalists there joined the **National Liberation Front** (NLF), an organization dedicated to fighting Diem's government. The NLF largely relied on the **Vietcong**, communist guerrilla forces, as its army. North Vietnam supplied and funded the Vietcong as its soldiers began a civil war against Diem's government in the late 1950s.

The Division Grows

As fighting between the Vietcong and Diem's Army of the Republic of Vietnam (ARVN) increased, President Eisenhower sent more aid and advisers to South Vietnam. By the end of 1960, about 800 U.S. military advisers were stationed in Vietnam.

As senator, John F. Kennedy had called Vietnam a "test of American responsibility and determination in Asia." As president, he sent more military advisers and 400 special forces soldiers there in May 1961. By 1963 some 16,000 U.S. military personnel were serving in Vietnam.

Diem's forces arrest Buddhist monks after an antigovernment protest.

Despite U.S. support, Diem's government steadily lost power. Diem became more unpopular when his troops fired on Buddhist demonstrators. Some Buddhist monks set themselves on fire in protest. Media images of these protests helped turn U.S. public opinion against Diem.

Over time, some of Diem's military leaders had come to believe that his unpopularity hurt the war effort. In November 1963 a group of South Vietnamese generals took over the government and killed Diem and his brother. After the takeover, the political situation in South Vietnam grew worse.

SECTION 1 REVIEW

Identify and explain the significance of the following:

- **Ho Chi Minh**
- **Vietminh**
- **domino theory**
- **Geneva Accords**
- **Ngo Dinh Diem**
- **National Liberation Front**
- **Vietcong**

Locate and explain the importance of the following:

- **Vietnam**
- **Laos**
- **Cambodia**
- **Dien Bien Phu**

Reading for Content Understanding

1. **Main Idea** What were the long-term effects of French colonization in Vietnam?
2. **Main Idea** What were the terms of the Geneva Accords? Why do you think all sides agreed to the compromise?
3. **Global Relations** Why was the United States involved in Vietnamese affairs?
4. **Writing** *Informing* Imagine that you are a State Department officer. Write a report explaining why many South Vietnamese oppose Diem's government. Explain how they are expressing their disapproval.
5. **Critical Thinking** *Determining the Strength of an Argument* Do you think Americans had good reason to believe in the domino theory during the 1950s? Explain your answer.

OBJECTIVES

- **Examine President Johnson's decision to continue supporting the war in Vietnam.**
- **Describe the tactics the U.S. military used to fight the Communists in Vietnam.**
- **Analyze the effect of the Vietnam War on U.S. soldiers.**

FOCUS

Motivate Before Reading

Ask students to identify strategies that were used during World War I and II, and ask them to identify how geography influenced these tactics. Discuss students' responses. Then explain that in this section they will learn about some tactics the U.S. military used in Vietnam and how geography influenced these strategies.

The Escalation of the War

Reading Focus

Why did President Johnson continue supporting the war in Vietnam?

What tactics did the U.S. military use to fight the Communists in Vietnam?

How did the Vietnam War affect U.S. soldiers?

Key Terms

Tonkin Gulf Resolution
Operation Rolling Thunder
Ho Chi Minh Trail
escalation
search-and-destroy missions
pacification

TWO DAYS AFTER President Kennedy's assassination on November 22, 1963, President Lyndon B. Johnson met with his foreign-policy advisers to decide how to proceed in Vietnam. One aide recalled Johnson's worry that the Communists would think that the new president was weak—that "with Kennedy dead [the Americans] have lost heart." Johnson decided to increase U.S. military support for the new government in South Vietnam. The message went out to South Vietnamese officials "that Lyndon Johnson intends to stand by [the United States's] word."

President Johnson expanded U.S. support of South Vietnam.

Johnson's Vietnam Policy

The new president, Lyndon B. Johnson, faced a complicated situation in Vietnam. Some of the new South Vietnamese leaders wanted to negotiate with the Communists. Johnson and his advisers, however, refused to accept the possibility of a communist South Vietnam.

The Tonkin Gulf Resolution

In the summer of 1964, a naval incident between U.S. and North Vietnamese ships led to a further increase in U.S. involvement in Vietnam. On August 2, a navy vessel exchanged gunfire with North Vietnamese vessels in the Gulf of Tonkin, a body of water off the North Vietnamese coast. Two days later, during bad weather, U.S. ships reported that their radar showed torpedo attacks. Although the ships were not damaged, Johnson branded the reported attack an act of war. He ordered air strikes against bases in the North.

On August 7, Congress passed the **Tonkin Gulf Resolution**. It gave President Johnson the authority "to take all necessary measures to repel any armed attack against the forces of the United

Section 2 RESOURCES

PRINT

- ★ Guided Reading Strategies 21.2
- ★ Primary Source Reading 21: American Indians and the Vietnam War
- ★ Literature Reading 21: Women in Vietnam
- ★ Graphic Organizer 21: Tracing the Path into Vietnam
- ★ Section 2 Review, p. 630
- ★ Daily Quiz 21.2

MULTIMEDIA

- ★ *Teaching Resources CD–ROM*, Lesson 21.2
- ★ HRW Web site

SHELTERED ENGLISH

- ★ Main Idea Activities for Reteaching and Sheltered English 21.2

Introduce Key Terms

Linguistic, Logical-Mathematical. Review this section's key terms with students. Have them write newspaper headlines using the terms. Each headline should use at least one key term and should reflect events in Vietnam. Ask volunteers to share their headlines with the class. **SHELTERED ENGLISH**

TEACH

Have students read Section 2 and complete Guided Reading Strategies 21.2. Choose one or more of the following activities to explore the section content with students. For further suggestions on block scheduling or team teaching, see the *Block Scheduling Handbook.*

LEVEL 1: Linguistic. (Suggested time: 15 min.) As a class, go over students' Guided Reading Strategies. Then use the Reading Focus questions to highlight the main ideas of the section. **SHELTERED ENGLISH**

ALL LEVELS: Linguistic, Intrapersonal. (Suggested time: 20 min. plus homework) Have students imagine that they are U.S. soldiers being interviewed by reporters. Encourage students to discuss tactics used in Operation Rolling Thunder and those that were used in search-and-destroy missions, as well as the war's

Cultural Diversity

Vietnamese Attitudes Toward the Land. One hardship that Vietnamese civilians faced during the war was their removal from their ancestral homelands. In Vietnamese culture, the land of one's ancestors is considered sacred, and the members of a family protect their land so that it can be passed on to their children and grandchildren. Frances FitzGerald's account, *Fire in the Lake: The Vietnamese and the Americans in Vietnam,* contains an elderly Vietnamese man's account of the importance of the land. As soldiers attempted to evacuate the man from his land, he said, "I have to stay behind to look after this piece of garden. Of all the property handed down to me by my ancestors, only this garden now remains. I have to guard it for my grandson." The soldiers left the man, who later was killed while guarding his land.

Critical Thinking: What does the importance of the land in Vietnamese culture suggest about the difficulty of winning the war?

ANSWER: Answers will vary but students might suggest that it would be difficult to defeat an enemy with such strong ties to the land.

MAP ANSWER

Cambodia, Laos, and South Vietnam

States." The resolution shifted the power to determine the course of the Vietnam War from Congress to the president. Johnson would use his increased powers to expand U.S. involvement in the conflict.

Operation Rolling Thunder

With the authority given to him by the Tonkin Gulf Resolution, Johnson dramatically increased U.S. military involvement in Vietnam. In March 1965 the first U.S. combat troops arrived in South Vietnam. At the same time, Johnson ordered **Operation Rolling Thunder**, a series of air strikes to destroy war industries in North Vietnam. Johnson also saw the operation as a way to destroy the **Ho Chi Minh Trail**. This network of paths, small roads, and tunnels led from North Vietnam through neighboring Laos and Cambodia and into South Vietnam. The Vietcong used the Ho Chi Minh Trail as their major supply route. Johnson and his advisers believed that if they destroyed North Vietnam's ability to supply the Vietcong, the United States could end the war.

Dense jungle covered much of the trail and hid the movement of the supplies. To burn off the forests, U.S. airplanes dropped napalm, or jellied gasoline. The planes also released chemical poisons, such as Agent Orange, that killed vegetation and tree leaves. These chemicals were later blamed for environmental damage in the area and serious health problems among Vietnamese civilians and U.S. veterans alike.

The bombing raids lasted until late 1968. During the operation, U.S. planes dropped more than a million tons of explosives, much of it on South Vietnam. Operation Rolling Thunder killed many Vietnamese soldiers and civilians, but the effort did not stop the Communists' ability to wage war.

The Vietnam War

Learning from Maps North Vietnam used the Ho Chi Minh Trail to supply communist forces in the South.

Movement Through which countries did the Ho Chi Minh Trail pass?

The Ground War

In the mid-1960s, President Johnson authorized an increase in the use of ground forces. The number of U.S. soldiers grew rapidly from 1965 to 1967 as Johnson pursued a policy of **escalation**, or increased U.S. involvement in the war. North Vietnam also escalated its involvement, sending more of its regular army units, the North Vietnamese Army (NVA), to fight alongside the Vietcong.

General William Westmoreland, who commanded the U.S. ground forces effects on U.S. soldiers. Students can either work in pairs and perform the interview for the class or work alone and write a transcript of the interview. **SHELTERED ENGLISH**

LEVEL 3: Logical-Mathematical, Interpersonal, Intrapersonal. (Suggested time: 45 min.) Assign students the roles of President Johnson and several U.S. senators. Have students role-play a congressional meeting in which President Johnson states his reasons for continuing U.S. involvement in Vietnam and asks the Senate to pass the Gulf of Tonkin Resolution. Students acting as President Johnson should outline the reasons he felt the Senate should pass the resolution. Students acting as senators should explain how they are going to vote on the resolution and why.

CLOSE

Linguistic, Interpersonal. Ask students to create study guides that discuss how the following groups were affected by the escalation of the Vietnam War: North Vietnamese, South Vietnamese, and U.S. soldiers in Vietnam. When students finish creating their study guides, have them exchange them and discuss the similarities and differences between them.

CHALLENGE AND EXTEND

Linguistic, Visual-Spatial. Ask students to use the library or other resources to research what soldiers carried with them

The Vietcong placed sharpened bamboo sticks, called punji *stakes, in covered holes to injure enemy soldiers.*

in Vietnam, developed a new fighting strategy. With his **search-and-destroy missions**, U.S. patrols searched for enemy camps and supplies hidden in the jungle, then destroyed them with massive firepower and air raids. Officials expected the missions, backed as they were by superior U.S. military technology, to quickly defeat the Vietcong and the NVA. One U.S. general said, "The solution in Vietnam is more bombs, more shells, more napalm." However, U.S. generals underestimated the North Vietnamese, who proved difficult to defeat.

The Vietcong and the NVA offset their inferior firepower with effective guerrilla tactics and a better knowledge of the local geography. Moving secretly, they set traps and land mines to kill and injure Americans. When the Vietcong and the NVA attacked, they usually did so in quick surprise assaults. U.S. Marine Philip Caputo recalled the effects of this kind of fighting:

> **"The discovery that the men we had scorned [disregarded] as peasant guerrillas were, in fact, a lethal [deadly], determined enemy . . . broke our early confidence."**

South Vietnamese villagers were caught in the middle of the fighting with no safe place to go. U.S. and South Vietnamese officials tried to win the support of villagers through a policy of **pacification**. Under this program, they created civilian areas guarded by government troops.

Across the Curriculum

LITERATURE

Soldiers' Memoirs. After returning home from Vietnam, some U.S. soldiers wrote books about their experiences. Philip Caputo published his memoirs, *A Rumor of War*, in 1977. Others, such as Tim O'Brien, the author of *Going After Cacciato*, turned to fiction to help Americans understand the war.

Activity: Have students use the library and search the Internet through the HRW Web site to research soldiers' experiences during the Vietnam War. Then ask students to write an interview with a fictional soldier.

go.hrw.com
SB1 Vietnam

Linking Past to Present

The United States and Vietnam Today

After the war, hostility between the United States and Vietnam continued. Recently, however, the countries have established closer ties. The United States lifted its trade embargo against Vietnam in 1994. In May 1997 a new U.S. embassy opened there.

The U.S. ambassador to Vietnam, Douglas "Pete" Peterson, symbolized the new relationship. A pilot during the war, Peterson was shot down and spent nearly seven years in a North Vietnamese prison. Yet he returned to Vietnam with an eager, forgiving spirit.

Sign in Vietnam for an American corporation

Like Peterson, Vietnam seems focused on the future. Leaders have encouraged American businesses to open operations in Vietnam. Today, signs for well-known American products can be seen all over the streets of Hanoi and Ho Chi Minh City, formerly Saigon.

Understanding What You Read

1. Give examples of the new relationship between Vietnam and the United States.
2. How did Ambassador Peterson symbolize the new relationship?

LINKING PAST TO PRESENT ANSWERS

1. The trade embargo was lifted in 1994, and a U.S. embassy opened in Vietnam in 1997. Signs for American products can now be seen in Vietnam.
2. He had once been a prisoner of war in Vietnam, so his appointment signified U.S. attempts to move past issues surrounding the Vietnam War.

into battle during the Vietnam War. Then have students create a diagram of a soldier's pack and identify items that were typical of what they carried. Next to each item, have students write an explanation of why it was included.

REVIEW

Linguistic, Logical-Mathematical. Have students complete the Section Review questions. Then have students take the study guides they created in the Close activity and replace the key words and phrases with blank spaces. Have students exchange guides and fill in the missing information.

ASSESS

Have students complete Daily Quiz 21.2.

RETEACH

Logical-Mathematical, Visual-Spatial. Have students complete Main Idea Activities for Reteaching and Sheltered English 21.2. Then provide students with a blank map of Indochina. Ask them to draw the Ho Chi Minh Trail in the appropriate location on the map. Below the map have students describe the Ho Chi Minh Trail's importance and list some of the significant events that took place along it. **SHELTERED ENGLISH**

Section 2 Review ANSWERS

Identify

For significance, see the following pages:

- Tonkin Gulf Resolution, p. 627
- Operation Rolling Thunder, p. 628
- Ho Chi Minh Trail, p. 628
- escalation, p. 628
- William Westmoreland, p. 628
- search-and-destroy missions, p. 629
- pacification, p. 629

Reading for Content Understanding

1. He thought that after Kennedy's assassination the Communists would view the new president as weak, and he wanted to prove to them that he stood by his word.

2. They used bombing and search-and-destroy missions; these tactics failed to stop the enemy and made Vietnamese civilians turn against the Americans.

3. Dense jungles covered much of the Ho Chi Minh Trail, making it difficult to spot troop movements and stop the Vietcong from delivering supplies; the dense jungle also enabled the Vietcong, familiar with the local geography, to launch deadly surprise attacks.

4. Letters will vary but students should use information from the section to describe the conditions faced in Vietnam and the possible effects on soldiers.

5. Answers will vary but students' evaluations should consider the high civilian casualty rate and the damage to buildings and farmland.

Even in areas protected by soldiers, however, the Vietcong attacked. At night, while the government forces remained in their camps, the Vietcong came out of hiding. They assaulted or killed the people they believed had cooperated with the South Vietnamese government.

South Vietnamese civilians also suffered at the hands of their own government and U.S. forces. Sometimes U.S. troops destroyed the villages and crops of innocent civilians in the mistaken belief that they belonged to Vietcong. Soldier Kenneth Campbell recalled how an officer justified the destruction of two seemingly peaceful farming villages: "He said they were probably feeding the NVA with rice anyway, so therefore they are the enemy." Such reasoning contributed to high civilian casualty rates and lessened any chance the Americans had of winning local support or loyalty.

U.S. troops grew weary from the fighting and from trying to avoid traps and ambushes.

The Soldiers' Stories

The war in Vietnam greatly affected the more than 2 million U.S. soldiers who served in it. Many soldiers were very young. Their average age was 19, about six years younger than in previous wars. Most of the soldiers had been drafted into service. They tended to be from minority groups and poor families. College students—most of whom were white and from the middle and upper classes—could earn draft releases called deferments.

Many young men who served in Vietnam supported the war in the beginning. However, as the war dragged on, support among soldiers declined as casualty rates increased. By mid-1967 more than 300 U.S. soldiers a week were dying in combat.

More than 7,500 women also served in the military during the war. One nurse recalled watching a soldier die:

> **"When you are sitting there working on . . . a 19-year-old kid who's 10,000 miles from home, and you know that he's going to die before dawn . . . and you're the only one that he's got . . . well it [gets] into your soul."**

Like the nurse, many of those who served in Vietnam found that the experience "got into their souls" and left them forever changed.

SECTION 2 REVIEW

Identify and explain the significance of the following:

- **Tonkin Gulf Resolution**
- **Operation Rolling Thunder**
- **Ho Chi Minh Trail**
- **escalation**
- **William Westmoreland**
- **search-and-destroy missions**
- **pacification**

Reading for Content Understanding

1 **Main Idea** Why did President Johnson think it was important to fight the Communists in South Vietnam?

2 **Main Idea** How did U.S. troops try to defeat the Communists in Vietnam, and what were the results?

3 **Geographic Diversity** *Place* How did Vietnam's landscape affect the war?

4 **Writing** *Describing* Imagine that you are a U.S. soldier stationed in Vietnam. In a letter home, describe how the war has affected you. You might also describe the difficulties of fighting in Vietnam.

5 **Critical Thinking** *Identifying Cause and Effect* How did the Vietnam War affect South Vietnamese civilians?

OBJECTIVES

- Describe how the Tet Offensive changed public opinion on the Vietnam War.
- Analyze the effects of the Vietnam War on the Democratic Party.
- Identify factors that led to Richard Nixon's victory in the 1968 presidential election.

FOCUS

Motivate Before Reading

Show the class a photograph of an antiwar protest during the Vietnam War, such as the one on page 635, but do not tell them what is pictured. Have students write a few sentences explaining the following information about the photograph: What is the average age of the people in the crowd? What are their signs demanding? What are the people in the crowd doing? Once students have

A Divided Nation

Reading Focus

How did the Tet Offensive change public opinion on the Vietnam War?

How did the Vietnam War affect the Democratic Party?

What factors led to Richard Nixon's victory in the 1968 presidential election?

Key Terms

doves
hawks
Tet Offensive

THE WOMEN GATHERED ABOUT 6:00 A.M. outside the military office. Soon the new recruits would arrive, ready to go to boot camp—and then to Vietnam. The women shouldered signs reading "I Support Draft Refusal" and began to walk up and down the sidewalk. Some of the women sat down in the street, preventing the recruits' buses from moving. When the police arrived, an officer told an older woman, "Missus, you don't want to get arrested." She said, "I have to, my grandson's in Vietnam." As more U.S. soldiers went off to fight—and to die—in Vietnam, the antiwar movement gained strength.

Sara Matthews/Swarthmore College Peace Collection
Peace button

Divided Opinions

Journalists, particularly television reporters, played an important role in shaping public opinion about the war. Through television, civilians saw real images of the war's brutality right in their own homes. As journalists continued to cover stories about the war, some began to report their growing suspicions that the fighting was not going as well as the military claimed. Gradually, some people who had originally supported the Vietnam War began to call for U.S. withdrawal from the conflict. They were called **doves**—named after the birds that symbolize peace.

Arkansas senator J. William Fulbright became a leading dove. As the chairman of the Senate Foreign Relations Committee, Fulbright had strongly supported the Tonkin Gulf Resolution. Later, Fulbright came to believe that the Johnson administration had exaggerated the communist threat and that it was unwilling to allow a peaceful settlement in the region. He accused a group of Johnson's advisers with the words: "You don't want to negotiate. . . . You're bombing that little . . .

Section 3 RESOURCES

PRINT

★ Guided Reading Strategies 21.3

★ Biography Reading 21: Benjamin Spock

★ Geography Activity 21: Geography and the Vietnam War

★ Section 3 Review, p. 635

★ Daily Quiz 21.3

MULTIMEDIA

★ *Teaching Resources CD–ROM*, Lesson 21.3

★ Everyday Life in America Transparency 30: Protest During the Vietnam War

SHELTERED ENGLISH

★ Main Idea Activities for Reteaching and Sheltered English 21.3

finished writing, explain to them that the photo depicts a protest against American involvement in Vietnam. Tell students that in this section they will learn how the nation became divided over the war in Vietnam.

Introduce Key Terms

Linguistic, Logical-Mathematical. Review this section's key terms with students. Then ask them to use each term in a sentence. Call on volunteers—one for each term—to write their sentences on the chalkboard. Have each volunteer explain how the sentence properly uses the term. **SHELTERED ENGLISH**

TEACH

Have students read Section 3 and complete Guided Reading Strategies 21.3. Choose one or more of the following activities to explore the section content with students. For further suggestions on block scheduling or team teaching, see the *Block Scheduling Handbook.*

LEVEL 1: Linguistic. (Suggested time: 15 min.) As a class, go over students' Guided Reading Strategies. Then use the Reading Focus questions to highlight the main ideas of the section. **SHELTERED ENGLISH**

Citizenship and Democracy

SDS Protests. Members of Students for a Democratic Society (SDS) related their protests against the Vietnam War to other aspects of life in the United States. At an antiwar protest, SDS president Paul Potter told the crowd, "It is only when that system [of power in the United States] is changed and brought under control that there can be any hope for stopping the forces that create a war in Vietnam today." He then went on to link these forces to those that create racism. Potter's words urged listeners to create a movement that would alter the institutions that were forcing the United States to remain in the war.

Critical Thinking: How did the SDS link events in Vietnam to problems in American society?

ANSWER: They claimed that the war and the problems in the United States stemmed from the same source—the system of power in the United States.

Multimedia Resources

Everyday Life in America Transparency 30: Protest During the Vietnam War

Television reporters, like Morley Safer, brought the horror of the war into Americans' homes. Vietnam was the first "televised" war.

country up there, and you think you can blow them up."

Other doves, such as Martin Luther King Jr., warned that the war effort was preventing the growth of important social programs. President Johnson, with congressional approval, tried to provide funding for both his Great Society programs and the Vietnam War. However, he believed that communism in Southeast Asia posed a more serious threat because it affected world peace.

A majority in Congress agreed with Johnson. They believed that winning the Cold War against communism in Vietnam took priority over domestic reform. Called **hawks** for their warlike opinions, these leaders pushed for increased military spending in order to send more forces to Vietnam.

 Protest Groups

Many citizens opposed the hawks' point of view. They organized protests to pressure the government to change its war policy. College students—many of whom had already been activists in the student rights and civil rights movements—often led the protests against the Vietnam War. The Students for a Democratic Society (SDS) became one of the most active antiwar groups. SDS protested the draft system and the companies that manufactured weapons used in the war. In 1965, SDS led a 20,000-person protest march to Washington, D.C.

As the war continued, the student movement grew more aggressive and sometimes even violent. These violent demonstrations were very different from earlier civil rights protests, which were almost entirely nonviolent. At Columbia University in New York City, students took over several campus buildings in March 1968 to protest the school's research ties to the defense industry. Violent clashes erupted between the protesters and police. A strike by students shut down the campus. School administrators eventually yielded to the students' demands. The Columbia strike inspired other student actions. By the end of 1968, students had protested the war on almost 75 percent of the country's college campuses.

Students were not the only protesters. Many other Americans voiced their concerns as well. Charlotte Keyes helped organize a group called Women Strike for Peace. She described the different types of people in the antiwar movement:

> **"The peaceniks [war protesters] these days are legion [many]—they are ninety years old and fifteen, heads of families and housewives with babies, students, (and) young people."**

The Tet Offensive

Despite the growth of the antiwar movement, a majority of Americans continued to support the Vietnam War until early 1968. On January 30, during Tet—the Vietnamese New Year—enemy forces

SDS organized this early antiwar march in 1965. As the war escalated, marches grew larger and were sometimes violent.

ALL LEVELS: Logical-Mathematical. (Suggested time: 30 min.) Write the following events on the chalkboard: *Eugene McCarthy and Robert Kennedy challenge Lyndon Johnson for the Democratic nomination; Lyndon Johnson announces he will not seek office in 1968; Robert Kennedy is assassinated; violence erupts at the 1968 Democratic National Convention; George Wallace runs as an independent;* and *Republican nominee Richard Nixon campaigns as the candidate who can restore order to America.* Have students discuss the events and determine which of them played the most significant role in Richard Nixon's 1968 presidential election; have students number the events from 1 to 6 in the order of most significant to least significant and write a few sentences explaining their reasoning. Then explain to students how public sentiment over Vietnam, along with the events listed, hurt the Democratic Party and led to Richard Nixon's election. **SHELTERED ENGLISH**

LEVEL 2: Logical-Mathematical, Visual-Spatial. (Suggested time: 45 min.) Explain to students that the Tet Offensive convinced many Americans that the government had been deceiving them about the progress of the war and that after Tet, public support for the war dropped significantly. Have each student create a political cartoon that depicts either the government's deceptive reporting of the war or the decreasing public confidence in the war effort. Have students write captions to clarify their political cartoons.

launched the **Tet Offensive**. In previous years, a cease-fire had halted all fighting during Tet, so the attack came as a complete surprise. North Vietnamese and Vietcong soldiers attacked U.S. forces throughout the South and even invaded the U.S. Embassy in the heart of Saigon. In most places, the U.S. and South Vietnamese troops overcame the communist forces quickly.

Nonetheless, the extent of the Tet Offensive shocked Americans and changed many people's opinions about the war. A short time earlier, General Westmoreland had said that the war would soon be over. There is "a light at the end of the tunnel," he promised. The Tet Offensive showed the opposite—that the enemy forces still had the strength and the will to fight.

The Tet Offensive convinced many Americans that officials could not be trusted to tell the truth about the war. Several well-known journalists, including television news anchor Walter Cronkite, expressed doubts about claims of success. "To say that we are closer to victory today is to believe, in the face of the evidence, the optimists [people who hope for the best] who have been wrong in the past," Cronkite declared in late February 1968. That same month, Westmoreland requested 206,000 more troops for service in Vietnam. With about 510,000 U.S. troops already there, many people questioned whether such an increase was necessary if the United States was really winning the war. President Johnson denied Westmoreland's request.

 The Democrats in 1968

The Tet Offensive weakened public confidence in the government's conduct of the war. One poll showed that after the offensive, only 33 percent of Americans believed that the United States was winning the Vietnam War. About 49 percent said that the United States should never have gotten involved in the conflict. During this time of increasing doubts, the 1968 presidential primary elections began.

The Primaries

Initially, President Johnson's main opponent in the Democratic primaries was Eugene McCarthy, a senator from Minnesota. McCarthy was a major antiwar critic who ran largely on this issue. "The

Historical Sidelight

Assessing Tet. Ironically, while U.S. Army leaders contended it was a failure for the North Vietnamese, most Americans considered the Tet Offensive to be a defeat for the United States and South Vietnam. However, the North Vietnamese who planned and carried out the attack regarded it as a defeat. A 1982 military history published in North Vietnam claimed that the Tet Offensive had been poorly planned and resulted in a loss of soldiers and supplies from which it took years for the North to recover. Provoking a negative public reaction in the United States was not a North Vietnamese goal in the offensive; instead, the Communists had hoped that it would spark a popular rebellion in South Vietnam, an outcome that never occurred.

Critical Thinking: How did the failed offensive ultimately benefit the North Vietnamese?

ANSWER: It weakened Americans' support for continuing the war.

CHART ANSWER
1968

U.S. Troops in Vietnam, 1964–1972

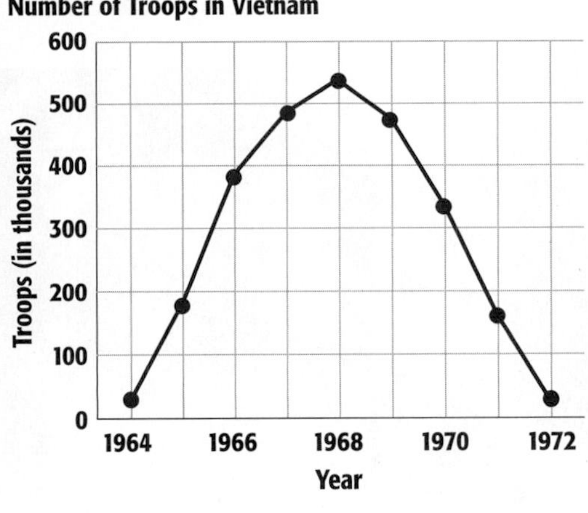

Soldiers Killed in Battle

Number Killed (in thousands): 0, 2, 4, 6, 8, 10, 12, 14, 16

Year: 1964, 1966, 1968, 1970, 1972

Source: National Archives and Records Administration

A Costly War The number of U.S. troops sent to Vietnam escalated as the United States became more involved in the conflict. In what year did the number of U.S. troops in Vietnam peak?

TEACHER TO TEACHER

LEVEL 3: Linguistic, Logical-Mathematical, Interpersonal. (Suggested time: 45 min. plus homework) Dwane Martinson of Seattle, Washington, suggested the following activity: Organize the class into two groups—one to act as supporters of U.S. involvement in Vietnam, and the other to act as opposition. Allow each group time to prepare arguments supporting its position. Then have the groups debate whether the United States should have remained involved in Vietnam during the late 1960s.

CLOSE

Linguistic, Logical-Mathematical. Have students imagine that they are columnists for a local paper. The date is December 31, 1968, and the year's final edition is about to go to print. Ask students to write headlines summarizing events in the United States during 1968. Ask volunteers to share their headlines with the class.

CHALLENGE AND EXTEND

Linguistic, Musical-Rhythmic, Intrapersonal. Have students locate examples of songs that protested the Vietnam War. Ask

Using Visual Resources

Dealing with Vietnam. The pictures on this page reveal much about the emotions surrounding U.S. involvement in the Vietnam War. The picture in the upper left-hand corner depicts the frustrations that Lyndon Johnson faced after his decision to continue U.S. involvement in Vietnam. His body language suggests a feeling of personal defeat. This frustration contributed to his withdrawal as a candidate in the 1968 election. The picture in the bottom right-hand corner of the page seems to suggest that Robert Kennedy was confident in his decision to negotiate a peaceful ending to the war if elected president. Kennedy was assassinated shortly after this picture was taken. Americans were left to wonder if he would have been able to bring a peaceful end to the war.

Activity: Have students use the library and other resources to find information about public support for the war effort. Ask students to create bar graphs depicting the changes in public support that occurred throughout the course of the war.

President Johnson was troubled by the course of the war but felt obligated to support South Vietnam.

Democratic Party in 1964 promised 'no wider war,'" he reminded voters. "Yet the war is getting wider every month."

Johnson, who had won the presidency by a landslide in 1964, was expected to win the 1968 Democratic primaries easily. However, the Tet Offensive and the war situation in general had produced a massive shift in voter sympathies. In the New Hampshire primary, Johnson narrowly beat McCarthy—48 percent to 42 percent. His slim victory in this first primary of the year showed how unpopular Johnson's Vietnam policies were and how much his political support had declined. On March 31 Johnson withdrew from the election entirely, promising to spend the last months of his presidency trying to end the war.

After McCarthy's strong showing in New Hampshire, Senator Robert F. Kennedy of New York, the former attorney general, entered the race for the Democratic nomination. He believed that the United States should do everything it could to negotiate a peaceful end to the war as soon as possible. During the Tet Offensive, he said:

> **"Unable to defeat our enemy or break his will—at least without a huge, long, and ever more costly effort—we must actively seek a peaceful settlement. . . . We must be willing to foresee a settlement which will give the Vietcong and the National Liberation Front a chance to participate in the political life of the country. Not because we want them to but because that is the only way in which this struggle can be settled."**

Like his brother, the late president John F. Kennedy, Robert Kennedy believed in civil rights reform and assistance to the poor. These beliefs, along with his position on the war, drew many idealists and reformers to his campaign.

Johnson threw his support for the Democratic nomination behind yet another candidate—his vice president, Hubert Humphrey. Voters tended to dislike Humphrey for his long-standing support of the war. Kennedy soon began to gain ground on Humphrey. On June 5, 1968, Kennedy won the California primary, a major step before the upcoming Democratic National Convention in Chicago. That night, Kennedy declared to his supporters, "On to Chicago and let's win there." Moments later, as he departed, a gunman named Sirhan Sirhan assassinated him.

The Convention

Robert Kennedy's death almost guaranteed that Humphrey would win the nomination. However, the party was still bitterly divided. Many delegates wanted a candidate who was not associated with Johnson and the war. Angry debates soon flared inside the convention hall.

Robert Kennedy won the California Democratic primary on a platform opposing the Vietnam War. Yet some doves criticized him for not entering the presidential race earlier.

each student to choose a protest song and write a summary analyzing the lyrics to determine what was being protested.

REVIEW

Linguistic, Logical-Mathematical. Have students complete the Section Review questions. Then have them outline the following main ideas: how the Tet Offensive changed the public's opinions toward the Vietnam War, how the war affected the Democratic Party, and what events affected the outcome of the 1968 presidential election.

ASSESS

Have students complete Daily Quiz 21.3.

RETEACH

Linguistic, Logical-Mathematical, Visual-Spatial. Have students complete Main Idea Activities for Reteaching and Sheltered English 21.3. Then ask each student to choose four important events discussed in this section and create a series of commemorative stamps depicting the events. Encourage students to provide a brief caption next to each stamp that describes what is portrayed. **SHELTERED ENGLISH**

Some distance outside the convention hall, hundreds of antiwar protesters joined together. They marched in the city streets, shouting, "Peace now! Peace now!" Under orders from Chicago mayor Richard J. Daley, police officers moved in to stop the demonstration.

A riot broke out. TV cameras broadcasted live images of the event. "Instead of nice young people ringing doorbells," one protester said, "the public saw the image of mobs shouting obscenities and disrupting the city." To the millions of Americans watching, the events in Chicago illustrated the loss of law and order in society and politics. Many voters blamed the Democrats.

More people, including returned veterans, protested the war as it escalated.

A Republican Victory

Although divisions marked the convention, Humphrey won the Democratic nomination for president. Humphrey was a long-time supporter of civil rights. He chose Maine senator Edmund Muskie as his running mate.

The conservative governor of Alabama, George Wallace, entered the race as the candidate of the American Independent Party. He wanted to overturn civil rights legislation and most federal social programs. Wallace also criticized what he called the "overeducated, ivory-tower folks with pointed heads" who advised President Johnson.

The Republican candidate, former vice president Richard Nixon, claimed that he could restore order to American society. He also hinted that he had a "secret plan" for ending the Vietnam War.

The election of 1968 was quite close. Nixon received only 43.4 percent of the popular vote but won the presidency with 302 electoral votes. Humphrey received 191 electoral votes. Wallace won 45 votes, all from southern states. As President-elect Nixon prepared to take office, Americans watched developments in Vietnam closely.

SECTION 3 REVIEW

Identify and explain the significance of the following:

- **doves**
- **hawks**
- **Tet Offensive**
- **Eugene McCarthy**
- **Robert F. Kennedy**
- **Hubert Humphrey**
- **George Wallace**
- **Richard Nixon**

Reading for Content Understanding

1 **Main Idea** What effect did the Tet Offensive have on Americans' attitudes?

2 **Main Idea** How did disagreements about the Vietnam War affect the Democratic Party?

3 **Citizenship and Democracy** Why did Richard Nixon win the presidency in 1968? What might the Democrats have done differently to try to beat him?

4 **Writing** *Persuading* Imagine that you are either a hawk or a dove during the Vietnam War. Write a letter to the editor trying to persuade others to agree with your position toward the war, whether for or against it.

5 **Critical Thinking** *Evaluating* Can people disagree with the policies and actions of their government and still be loyal citizens? Explain your answer.

Section 3 Review ANSWERS

Identify

For significance, see the following pages:

- doves, p. 631
- hawks, p. 632
- Tet Offensive, p. 633
- Eugene McCarthy, p. 633
- Robert F. Kennedy, p. 634
- Hubert Humphrey, p. 634
- George Wallace, p. 635
- Richard Nixon, p. 635

Reading for Content Understanding

1. Tet convinced many Americans that they could not trust the government's reports about the progress of the war; it also decreased support for the war.

2. Disagreements led to divisions within the party and less overall support of the party, all of which contributed to a Republican victory in the 1968 presidential election.

3. Nixon took advantage of divisions within the Democratic Party and the ultraconservatism of the Wallace campaign; answers will vary but students should suggest alternate strategies and explain how these strategies might have influenced the election.

4. Letters will vary but should discuss U.S. goals in Vietnam and present arguments consistent with and supporting the chosen position.

5. Answers will vary but students should state their opinions and offer arguments to support them.

OBJECTIVES

- **Explain President Nixon's Vietnam policy.**
- **Identify the outcome of the 1972 presidential election.**
- **Describe some of the war's legacies.**

FOCUS

Motivate Before Reading

Remind students that one of Richard Nixon's campaign promises was to restore peace to Vietnam and order to American society. Ask students to suggest ways in which Nixon might end the war. *(Answers will vary but might include the use of nuclear weapons, an increase in the number of U.S. troops in Vietnam, or negotiations with North Vietnam and the Vietcong.)* Lead a discussion on these various

Section 4 RESOURCES

PRINT

★ Guided Reading Strategies 21.4

★ American History Political Cartoon 28: The Vietnam War

★ Section 4 Review, p. 641

★ Daily Quiz 21.4

MULTIMEDIA

★ *Teaching Resources CD–ROM,* Lesson 21.4

★ Art in American History Transparency 45: Vietnam Veterans Memorial

★ *Exploring America's Past* Video Segment: The Wall; *Teacher's Guide,* pp. 37–39

SHELTERED ENGLISH

★ Main Idea Activities for Reteaching and Sheltered English 21.4

The War Under Nixon

Reading Focus

What was President Nixon's Vietnam policy?

What was the outcome of the presidential election of 1972?

What were some of the war's lasting effects?

Key Terms

Vietnamization
Khmer Rouge
Twenty-sixth Amendment
Paris Peace Accords
MIAs
War Powers Act
Vietnam Veterans Memorial

ON JANUARY 20, 1969—the day of President Nixon's inauguration—a top aide distributed a detailed questionnaire about Vietnam to high-level military and diplomatic personnel. One question was implied but not directly asked: Could the United States win the war, even at that late date? The responses came back with a concrete answer. "The differences . . . were largely ones of degree," remembered one army general who participated in the study. "Nobody believed the war could be won in the foreseeable future." That left the new president with another pressing issue: How to end the Vietnam War.

U.S. combat troops arriving in Vietnam

 Peace with Honor

Although President Nixon said that he wanted to "end the war as quickly as was honorably possible," he also wanted to avoid the appearance of defeat. "I will not be the first President of the United States to lose a war," he told Republican leaders.

Nixon and his national security adviser, Henry Kissinger, created a policy to bring about "peace with honor." They planned to gradually turn over all of the fighting to the South Vietnamese army, a process they called **Vietnamization**. Under the new policy, the United States would continue to provide supplies and training to South Vietnam even as U.S. troops left the country.

Nixon also believed that he could bluff the North Vietnamese into thinking that he would use nuclear weapons as a last resort to end the war. In a private talk with an aide, he said:

> **"I call it the madman theory. . . . I want the North Vietnamese to believe I've reached the point where I might do**

methods and have students come up with possible problems that could arise from them. Tell students that in this section they will learn about how the war came to an end under President Nixon, along with some of the long-term effects the war had on American society and Vietnam.

Introduce Key Terms

Linguistic, Logical-Mathematical. Review this section's key terms with students. Then have them use context cues from the section to write a definition for each key term. Ask students to apply their definitions to create a crossword puzzle that uses the key terms as answers. Have students exchange their crossword puzzles, complete them, and return them for grading. **SHELTERED ENGLISH**

TEACH

Have students read Section 4 and complete Guided Reading Strategies 2 .4. Choose one or more of the following activities to explore the section content with students. For further suggestions on block scheduling or team teaching, see the *Block Scheduling Handbook.*

Richard Nixon

Richard Nixon was born in 1913 and grew up in and around Whittier, California. Even as a young man, Nixon demonstrated the opposites in his nature that would drive him throughout his life. Shy and socially awkward, he nevertheless pushed himself to meet people and win their backing and support. Gradually, through his own determination and will to succeed, he became a leader. He was twice elected student-body president, first at Whittier College and later at Duke Law School.

Nixon's desire to win political office continued after he graduated. After practicing law and then serving in World War II, he ran as a Republican for Congress in 1946. He won against the odds, and as writer David Halberstam described it, "Once he started in politics, he could never stop: there would always be one more office to run for."

anything to stop the war. We'll just slip the word to them that, . . . 'Nixon is obsessed [crazed] about Communists. We can't restrain [control] him when he's angry—and he has his hand on the nuclear button,'—and Ho Chi Minh himself will be in Paris in two days begging for peace."

Yet, like other U.S. officials before them, Nixon and Kissinger underestimated the determination of the North Vietnamese and the Vietcong. Even after Ho Chi Minh died in September 1969, his followers vowed to continue the fight to reunite Vietnam and rid it of foreign troops. To achieve this, the North Vietnamese leaders refused to consider any peace agreement that did not include the immediate withdrawal of all U.S. troops.

The Attack on Cambodia

After he took office, President Nixon did begin withdrawing U.S. ground troops from Vietnam. At the same time, however, he secretly expanded the war by increasing air attacks in Laos and Cambodia.

A Wider War

Laos and Cambodia were officially neutral countries in the Vietnam War. Yet the use of the Ho Chi Minh Trail and other Vietcong supply lines drew these countries into the war. Nixon ordered bombing raids on Cambodia in 1969 to cut the supply routes. He did so without the knowledge of the American public or Congress.

In reaction to the bombings, the North Vietnamese increased their support of the **Khmer Rouge** (kuh-MER ROOZH), the Cambodian communist army. The Khmer Rouge increased its attacks in Cambodia, and Nixon sent U.S. troops in May 1970 to protect the country's pro-U.S. government. When he announced the invasion of Cambodia, many Americans were outraged. Instead of working for peace, the United States was expanding the war even further.

U.S. troops hoped that NVA papers captured in Cambodia would reveal military secrets.

Presidential Profiles

Nixon and Vietnam. Throughout his career, Richard Nixon had supported the fight against communism in Vietnam. As vice president, he traveled to Vietnam in 1953, visiting with French troops who were then battling communist forces. In a 1964 *Reader's Digest* article dealing with the U.S. battle against communism, Nixon argued, "All that is needed, in short, is the will to win—and the courage to use our power—now." Three years later he pointed to the importance of the war in Vietnam when he wrote, "Whatever one may think of the 'domino theory,' it is beyond question that without the American commitment in Vietnam, Asia would be a far different place today."

Critical Thinking: How did Nixon's position on the Vietnam War change?

ANSWER: He saw an honorable ending to the war as more important than victory.

Multimedia Resources

Exploring America's Past Video Segment: The Wall; *Teacher's Guide*, pp. 37–39

Search 14471, Play to 21291
Videodisc Blue Side B

Play

Pause

See *Teacher's Guide* for Spanish barcode.

LEVEL 1: Linguistic. (Suggested time: 15 min.) As a class, go over students' Guided Reading Strategies. Then use the Reading Focus questions to highlight the main ideas of the section.
SHELTERED ENGLISH

ALL LEVELS: Linguistic, Logical-Mathematical, Visual-Spatial. (Suggested time: 45 min. plus homework) Remind students that in order for a conflict to be resolved amicably, all parties must usually compromise. Have students create a pamphlet describing the necessary steps for resolving a conflict between countries. Have students list the steps necessary to reach a peaceful resolution. (An example of a step might include leaders of each nation sitting down to discuss political and social reforms.) For homework have students review their pamphlets to see how the terms of the Paris Peace Accords accomplished the necessary steps for resolving the conflict in Vietnam.
SHELTERED ENGLISH

LEVEL 2: Kinesthetic, Visual-Spatial, Interpersonal. (Suggested time: 45 min. plus homework and presentation) Organize the class into two groups—one to serve as the campaign staff for Richard Nixon, and the other to work for George McGovern. Have each group develop a campaign platform complete with banners, signs, and commercials. The focus of each campaign should be the candidate's stance regarding U.S. involvement in Vietnam. Give students time to prepare the campaigns.

Using Visual Resources

Kent State. The photograph on this page depicts the results of four days of student protests at Kent State University. What had started as a protest march on May 1, 1970, quickly turned into a riot. On May 2, the intensity of the rioting increased as protesters set fire to the ROTC facilities. As a result, Ohio governor James Rhodes called in the National Guard and prohibited the assembly of student groups until the incident had ended. On May 4, students gathered to protest, and were asked to disperse. Students threw objects at the guardsmen, who in return shot tear gas into the crowd. During the confusion a guardsman fired into the crowd. Soon other shots followed. The guardsmen eventually were tried for the incident, but none were convicted.

Critical Thinking: Why might students have ignored the governor's ban on the assembly of student groups?

ANSWER: They may have felt their cause was important enough to break the order; they also may have disagreed with the constitutionality of the order.

The killings of antiwar protesters by National Guardsmen at Kent State in 1970 hardened many people's attitudes against the war.

New Protests

After the announcement, students demonstrated at hundreds of college campuses. When students at Kent State University in Ohio attacked a military training building to protest the war, the governor called in the National Guard to restore order. On May 4, 1970, Kent State students started to demonstrate again. Campus police ordered them to leave, but the students refused. National Guard troops then advanced on the protesters and tried to break up the demonstration with tear gas. As the students threw rocks at the soldiers, some of the guardsmen opened fire. When the smoke cleared, 4 students were dead and 14 others were wounded.

The Kent State killings horrified the public. Outraged antiwar activists increased their protests. Some of these new demonstrations also ended in violence. In one such instance in May, police killed two student protesters at Mississippi's Jackson State University.

A Shift in Policy

As the year progressed, political and public opinion continued to turn against the war. In December 1970 Congress acted by repealing the Tonkin Gulf Resolution.

Public opinion became further divided with the publication in the *New York Times* of secret U.S. government documents known as the Pentagon Papers. Daniel Ellsberg, a former Pentagon official, leaked the papers to the newspaper. The papers revealed that U.S. government officials had been lying about the progress of the Vietnam War for years. "This is a system . . . that lies automatically from top to bottom," claimed Ellsberg.

After the publication of the Pentagon Papers, some members of Congress threatened to cut off funds for the Vietnam War altogether. As his 1972 re-election campaign approached and as public opinion hardened against the war, President Nixon began to revise his strategy. He ordered an end to the invasion of Cambodia and became more open to compromise. In 1972 Henry Kissinger began secret peace negotiations with North Vietnamese officials.

The Election of 1972

The presidential election of 1972 offered voters a choice of candidates with very different positions on ending the war. The Democratic candidate was South Dakota senator George McGovern, an outspoken and long-standing opponent of the war. McGovern promised that he would immediately withdraw all U.S. troops from Vietnam. "The doors of government will be opened, and that brutal war will be closed," he pledged.

McGovern tried to appeal to young voters. In 1971 the **Twenty-sixth Amendment** had lowered the federal voting age from 21 to 18. Many Americans saw this change as fair, because men from this age group were being drafted to serve in Vietnam. Some politicians expected this amendment to lead to a "youth rebellion" in the election.

Although McGovern won the support of a majority of younger voters, most older voters from both parties supported Nixon. Most Americans were tired of the war, but they feared continued disorder and protests. Nixon also promised to end the war soon if re-elected. "Help him finish the job," his campaign advertisements said. The public re-elected Nixon by a huge margin—520 electoral votes compared to 17 for McGovern.

 The End of the War

President Nixon kept his promise to end the war, although the peace process was rocky. Negotiations stalled after the election. The United

Then have each group present its materials to the class. Finally, discuss the results of the 1972 presidential election with the class.

LEVEL 3: Linguistic, Logical-Mathematical. (Suggested time: 45 min.) Ask students to write an essay on the legacy of the Vietnam War. Encourage them to consider the gains and losses the United States and Vietnam experienced as a result of the war. Ask volunteers to read their essays to the class or have students read one another's work. If time permits, lead a discussion on the pros and cons of U.S. involvement in Vietnam.

CLOSE

Linguistic, Logical-Mathematical, Interpersonal. Organize the class into small groups. Assign each group one of the following topics: Vietnamization, Kent State, the Paris Peace Accords, MIAs, the Twenty-sixth Amendment, the War Powers Act, or the Vietnam Veterans Memorial. Have groups list the date each occurred, was established, or was recognized; what it was; and why it is considered significant. Ask groups to elect a spokesperson to share their information with the rest of the class.

States began large-scale bombings of North Vietnam in December 1972—the so-called Christmas bombing. Finally, the peace talks resumed. On January 27, 1973, representatives of the National Liberation Front, North Vietnam, South Vietnam, and the United States signed a cease-fire and a series of peace agreements in Paris.

The agreement, known as the **Paris Peace Accords**, called for the removal of all U.S. troops and the return of all American prisoners of war (POWs). To maintain peace between South and North Vietnamese troops, the Paris Peace Accords established a demilitarized buffer zone in the South to separate the two sides. Under the agreement, the Communists in South Vietnam could take part in politics. Further decisions about unification of the country were put off until later.

Many South Vietnamese tried to flee before the North Vietnamese army arrived in 1975.

Late in 1974, however, fighting broke out again between North and South Vietnam. The United States made it clear that it would not send troops back to South Vietnam. The following year, North Vietnam invaded the South in large numbers. South Vietnamese resistance collapsed rapidly. By the end of April 1975, the North Vietnamese had captured the southern capital of Saigon.

Panic gripped the city in the final days of the war. South Vietnamese citizens who had helped the United States during the war swarmed the U.S. Embassy. They hoped to escape before the communist takeover. They feared imprisonment or death in the unified Vietnam. U.S. helicopters managed to carry many people to safety, but more were left behind. Watching the frightened people, one U.S. official wondered, "What will happen to them?"

The Consequences of War

The Vietnam War left long-lasting problems in both Southeast Asia and the United States. Many have yet to be resolved.

Southeast Asia

In Vietnam, life was extremely difficult after the war. The fighting had killed a huge number of citizens. About 1 million North Vietnamese and Vietcong soldiers, more than 185,000 South Vietnamese soldiers, and some 500,000 civilians had died. Almost 1 million Vietnamese children were orphans. Cities and villages lay in ruins. Forests and farmlands lay bare. One Vietnamese editor noted, "The war lasted thirty years, but it will take another twenty years before we will be

Causes and Effects of the Vietnam War

Long-Term Causes
Fear of communist expansion
U.S. support of South Vietnam's government

Immediate Causes
Gulf of Tonkin incident
Communist attacks against South Vietnam

Vietnam War

Effects
Many thousands of Americans and Vietnamese killed and injured
Vietnam united as a communist nation
Political divisions created in the United States
Ailments suffered by U.S. veterans

Across the Curriculum

ART

The Vietnam Veterans Memorial. Maya Ying Lin's proposed Vietnam Veterans Memorial met with opposition. Some observers condemned her design as the "black wall of shame." Other Americans supported the memorial as an acknowledgment solely of U.S. soldiers who fought in Vietnam, because it did not touch on controversial issues that surrounded the war.

Activity: Have students discuss the role that war memorials play as people remember America's past. Then have students prepare their own sketches of a Vietnam War memorial.

AMERICAN ARTS ANSWERS

(page 640)

1. It is a black granite wall containing the names of Americans who died in the war or are missing.

2. The memorial reveals the tragedy of war by spelling out the names of the U.S. soldiers who died.

Multimedia Resources

Art in American History Transparency 45: Vietnam Veterans Memorial

CHALLENGE AND EXTEND

1. **Linguistic, Logical-Mathematical.** Ask students to use the library or other resources to find information about the Paris Peace Accords. Have students write a one-page paper summarizing the main points outlined in the agreement. Students should include expectations for each of the involved parties: the United States, South Vietnam, North Vietnam, and the National Liberation Front. Lead a discussion on the effectiveness of this agreement and whether each of the expectations it outlines was kept by the parties involved.

2. **Linguistic, Visual-Spatial.** Explain to students that organizations such as the Veterans' Administration or Veterans of Foreign Wars have been established for veterans. Have students use the library or other resources to find information on groups designed to assist or promote veterans. Have students develop a pamphlet describing an organization's activities and how it serves veterans of the Vietnam War. Encourage volunteers to share their information with the class.

Section 4 Review ANSWERS

Identify

For significance, see the following pages:

- Henry Kissinger, p. 636
- Vietnamization, p. 636
- Khmer Rouge, p. 637
- George McGovern, p. 638
- Twenty-sixth Amendment, p. 638
- Paris Peace Accords, p. 639
- MIAs, p. 640
- War Powers Act, p. 641
- Vietnam Veterans Memorial, p. 641

Reading for Content Understanding

1. At first he pursued the policy of Vietnamization, then he expanded the war by sending troops into Laos and Cambodia.

2. It did not change the outcome of the election. While McGovern did win the support of a majority of younger voters, Nixon carried the support of most older voters and won the election.

3. Organizers will vary but should include information regarding the war's human, political, and economic effects.

4. Letters will vary but students should identify actions such as the secret bombing of Cambodia during the Vietnam War as one reason for passing the War Powers Act.

5. Answers will vary but students may identify a lack of public support for the war.

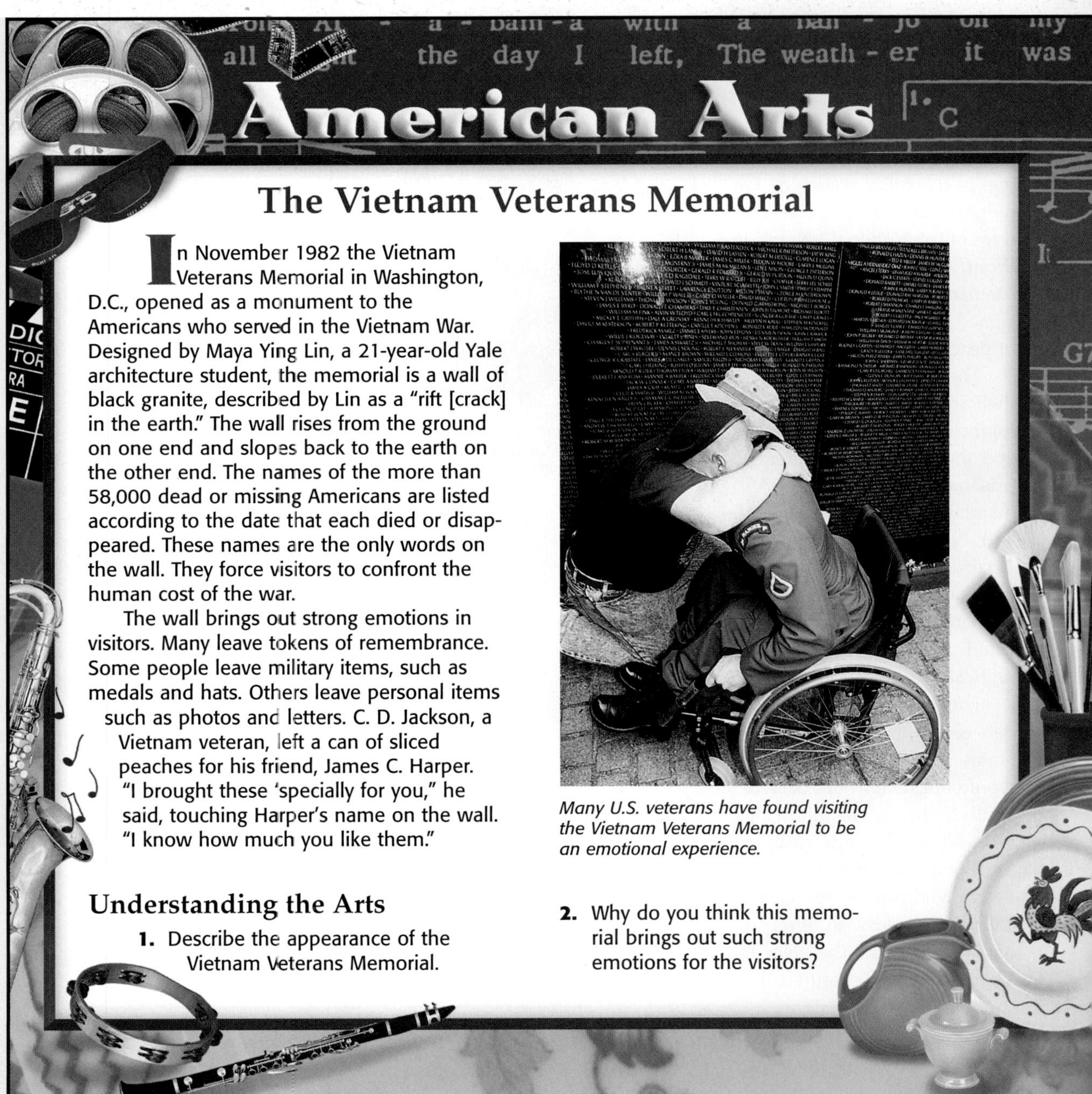

American Arts

The Vietnam Veterans Memorial

In November 1982 the Vietnam Veterans Memorial in Washington, D.C., opened as a monument to the Americans who served in the Vietnam War. Designed by Maya Ying Lin, a 21-year-old Yale architecture student, the memorial is a wall of black granite, described by Lin as a "rift [crack] in the earth." The wall rises from the ground on one end and slopes back to the earth on the other end. The names of the more than 58,000 dead or missing Americans are listed according to the date that each died or disappeared. These names are the only words on the wall. They force visitors to confront the human cost of the war.

The wall brings out strong emotions in visitors. Many leave tokens of remembrance. Some people leave military items, such as medals and hats. Others leave personal items such as photos and letters. C. D. Jackson, a Vietnam veteran, left a can of sliced peaches for his friend, James C. Harper. "I brought these 'specially for you," he said, touching Harper's name on the wall. "I know how much you like them."

Many U.S. veterans have found visiting the Vietnam Veterans Memorial to be an emotional experience.

Understanding the Arts

1. Describe the appearance of the Vietnam Veterans Memorial.
2. Why do you think this memorial brings out such strong emotions for the visitors?

able to overcome the legacy [history] of the problems it has left."

Laos and Cambodia also had difficulties after the war. Both countries fell to communist dictatorships in 1975. In Cambodia the Khmer Rouge killed an estimated 2 million people in a massive campaign to destroy supposed enemies of communism. Eventually, the Vietnamese and Cambodian Communists clashed. In 1979 Vietnam invaded Cambodia to drive out the Khmer Rouge. Since then, Cambodia and its people have experienced ongoing conflict and little peace.

The United States

The war also carried huge costs for the United States. About 58,000 Americans died in the fighting. More than 2,000 remain **MIAs**, which stands for missing in action. The conflict also left the nation deeply divided.

REVIEW

Logical-Mathematical, Visual-Spatial. Have students complete the Section Review questions. Then ask them to create an album cover depicting information from this section. The back of the cover should have liner notes and image captions that answer the section's Focus Questions. Have volunteers explain the information their covers depict to the class.

ASSESS

Have students complete Daily Quiz 21.4.

RETEACH

Logical-Mathematical, Visual-Spatial, Interpersonal. Have students complete Main Idea Activities for Reteaching and Sheltered English 21.4. Organize the class into pairs. Have each pair create an annotated time line for the years 1968 through 1982, and include significant events related to the Vietnam War and its aftermath. Ask students to include a title for the time line, as well as brief annotations summarizing the events.

SHELTERED ENGLISH

The discoveries of government deception had weakened many Americans' trust in officials, including the president. In 1973 Congress passed the **War Powers Act**. It required the president to get congressional approval before committing U.S. troops to an armed struggle. The act did not apply to Vietnam, but was written to prevent undeclared wars. President Nixon vetoed the measure, but Congress overrode the veto. Passage of the War Powers Act gave Congress increased responsibility for setting U.S. war policy. Since then, presidents have had to exercise more caution in sending troops into war zones and to consult with Congress more fully when they did.

Many Southeast Asians fled their homelands after the war, hoping to escape instability and brutal communist governments. Between 1975 and 1985, more than 1.5 million people left the region. Many of them died while trying to escape. About half of the Southeast Asian refugees immigrated to the United States. Le Ly Hayslip, for example, was a former Vietcong supporter who fled Vietnam and later became a successful businesswoman in California. In her memoirs she addressed the U.S. soldiers who had fought in the war, saying:

> **"Most of you did not know, or fully understand, the different wars my people were fighting when you got [to Vietnam]. . . . The least you did—the least any of us did—was our duty. For that we must be proud."**

Air Force captain Ronald Bliss runs to greet his wife after spending seven years as a POW in Vietnam.

American Veterans

Hayslip's words reflected the difficulties that some American veterans experienced after the war. Instead of a warm welcome, some veterans faced insults from antiwar protesters. Most readjusted well to civilian life, but some veterans suffered from depression and a condition known as post-traumatic stress disorder.

On Veterans Day in 1982, officials dedicated the **Vietnam Veterans Memorial** to honor those who died in the war. Designed by Maya Ying Lin, the memorial is a black granite wall that displays the names of the dead and the missing. Bruce Weigl explained why he and other veterans have visited the wall: "We came to find the names of those we lost in the war, as if by tracing the letters cut into the granite we could find what was left of ourselves."

SECTION 4 REVIEW

Identify and explain the significance of the following:

- **Henry Kissinger**
- **Vietnamization**
- **Khmer Rouge**
- **George McGovern**
- **Twenty-sixth Amendment**
- **Paris Peace Accords**
- **MIAs**
- **War Powers Act**
- **Vietnam Veterans Memorial**

Reading for Content Understanding

1 **Main Idea** What policy did President Nixon pursue in Vietnam?

2 **Main Idea** How did the Twenty-sixth Amendment affect the outcome of the 1972 presidential election? Who won?

3 **Global Relations** Make a graphic organizer listing the consequences of the Vietnam War, both in Southeast Asia and in the United States.

4 **Writing** *Persuading* Imagine that you are a member of Congress in 1973. Respond to a letter that criticizes your support of the War Powers Act. Note the specific events that led you to support the act and why you think it is necessary.

5 **Critical Thinking** *Drawing Conclusions* Why do you think the United States did not send troops back to South Vietnam in 1974 to protect it from invasion by North Vietnam?

Chapter 21 Review ANSWERS

Identifying People and Ideas

1. Vietnamese communist leader who founded the Vietminh

2. American belief that if Vietnam fell to communism, the other Southeast Asian nations would also become communist

3. communist guerrilla army fighting in South Vietnam

4. prime minister of South Vietnam who was killed in a 1963 coup

5. President Johnson's policy of increased U.S. involvement in Vietnam

6. congressmembers who agreed that communism needed to be fought and who supported both increased military spending and more forces in Vietnam

7. U.S. strategy of gradually turning over all fighting to the South Vietnamese Army

8. North Vietnamese attack launched in 1968 throughout South Vietnam; its results convinced many Americans not to trust information the government gave about the progress of the war

9. became U.S. president because he claimed to have a secret plan for ending the Vietnam War, among other reasons

10. final agreement that called for the removal of all U.S. troops and the return of American POWs

Using the Time Line

1. c
2. b
3. e
4. a
5. d

Review and Assessment RESOURCES

PRINT
- ★ Chapter 21 Review, pp. 642–43
- ★ Vocabulary Activity 21
- ★ Chapter 21 Study Guide
- ★ Chapter 21 Test (Form A or B)

MULTIMEDIA
- ★ Audio Program, Ch. 21 (English and Spanish)
- ★ *Global Skill Builder CD–ROM*
- ★ Chapter 21 Test Generator
- ★ HRW Web site

SHELTERED ENGLISH
- ★ Spanish Glossary
- ★ Sheltered English Chapter 21 Test

ASSESS

Have students complete one of the Chapter 21 Tests. As an alternate assessment, assign the Chapter 21 Investigation.

Understanding Main Ideas

1. Harsh French policies provoked an armed rebellion, which France lost in 1954. To prevent the Communists from controlling all of Vietnam, it was split into two nations by the Geneva Conference.

2. Kennedy supported South Vietnam's anticommunist efforts by sending military personnel. Johnson believed that the United States had to abide by its commitments if it were to avoid appearing weak to the rest of the world.

3. Americans used bombing and search-and-destroy missions. The prolonged war and the civilian casualties caused some soldiers to stop supporting the war. In time, it was revealed that some soldiers suffered from depression and post-traumatic stress disorder as a result of the war.

4. As a result of the Tet Offensive, many Americans began to oppose the war and question government reports about the war's progress.

5. It split the Democratic Party so that Johnson did not seek a second term, and it helped Republican Richard Nixon win the presidency.

6. The Paris Peace Accords called for the removal of U.S. forces from Vietnam, which marked the beginning of the end of the war. The final significant event in the war occurred when the North Vietnamese captured Saigon in 1975. Vietnam and several neighboring countries suffered economic and political turmoil as a result of the war. Americans debated the meaning of the war long after it was over, and veterans were left to deal with various psychological problems linked to fighting in Vietnam.

CHAPTER 21 REVIEW

Chapter Summary

In the 1950s the United States began sending aid, and in the 1960s troops, to help anticommunist South Vietnam fight against a takeover by communist North Vietnam. Many Americans protested U.S. involvement in the Vietnam War. In 1973 the United States signed a cease-fire agreement and withdrew its troops. The many years of war left deep scars, both in Southeast Asia and the United States.

On a separate sheet of paper, complete the following activities.

Identifying People and Ideas

Describe the historical significance of the following:

1. Ho Chi Minh
2. domino theory
3. Vietcong
4. Ngo Dinh Diem
5. escalation
6. hawks
7. Vietnamization
8. Tet Offensive
9. Richard Nixon
10. Paris Peace Accords

Internet Activity

go.hrw.com
SB1 South Vietnam

Search the Internet through the HRW Web site to find information about the Republic of Vietnam (South Vietnam). Make a graphic organizer showing the leaders of that country from 1954 to 1973, how they came to power, and what difficulties they faced while in office.

Understanding Main Ideas

1. How did French colonization affect Vietnam?
2. What was President Kennedy's policy in South Vietnam, and why did President Johnson continue it?
3. How did U.S. troops fight the Communists in Vietnam, and what were the effects on U.S. soldiers?
4. How did Americans react to the Tet Offensive?
5. How did the Vietnam War affect the presidential election of 1968?
6. How did the war end, and what were its long-term effects?

Reviewing Themes

1. **Global Relations** Why did the United States fight in Vietnam?
2. **Geographic Diversity** How did Vietnam's geography make the U.S. military effort there difficult?

Using the Time Line

Number your paper from 1 to 5. Match the letters on the time line below with the following events.

1. **The first U.S. combat troops arrive in Vietnam.**
2. **U.S. ships exchange fire with North Vietnamese forces in the Gulf of Tonkin.**
3. **By signing the Paris Peace Accords, the United States agrees to withdraw from Vietnam.**
4. **Ho Chi Minh announces the independent nation of Vietnam.**
5. **President Nixon sends U.S. troops into Cambodia.**

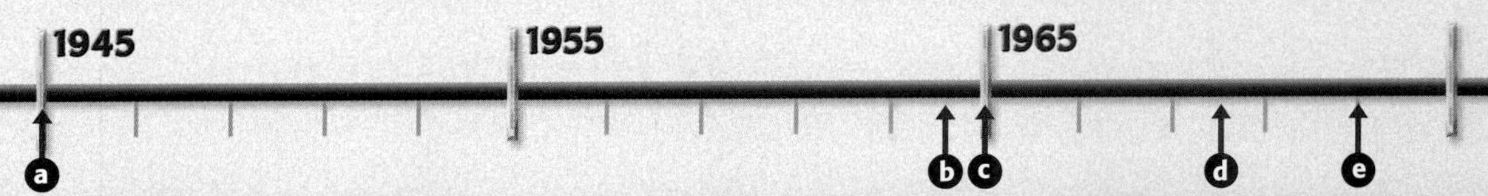

RETEACH

Visual-Spatial, Interpersonal. Organize the class into four groups and assign each group a section from this chapter. Ask each group to use the information in its section to create an act of a play. Give groups time to prepare. Then have each group present its act to the rest of the class. Finally, have students discuss events depicted in the plays.

Using the Internet

Have students continue their research to find information on the leaders of the Democratic Republic of Vietnam (North Vietnam) from 1954 to 1973. Ask students to make graphic organizers similar to the ones they made in the Internet Activity. Then have students compare information on the different leaders they researched.

Portfolio Extensions

1. Have students create a list of ways that the area depicted in the map has changed from 1954 to 1975. For each change they identify, have students explain what caused that change.

2. Have each student choose an item from his or her collage and write a journal entry describing its importance.

3. **Citizenship and Democracy** How did the Gulf of Tonkin Resolution and the War Powers Act affect the relationship between the legislative and executive branches of the government?

Thinking Critically

1. **Evaluating** What could President Diem of South Vietnam have done differently to try to win the support of people in his country?
2. **Drawing Conclusions** Why did Americans' attitudes toward the war change?
3. **Identifying Cause and Effect** How did U.S. military strategies affect the outcome of the Vietnam War?

Writing About History

1. **Describing** Imagine that you are a European reporter visiting the United States in 1970. Write a magazine article describing the different opinions on the Vietnam War.
2. **Classifying** Imagine that you are a U.S. official just returning from a trip to Vietnam in 1965. Write a memo to President Johnson noting the pros and cons of sending combat troops to South Vietnam.

Building Your Portfolio

Complete the following activities individually or in groups.

1. **Southeast Asia Map** Imagine that you work in the map bureau of the State Department. A new U.S. diplomat to Southeast Asia has asked for a historical map of the region spanning the years 1954 to 1975. Create a detailed map for the diplomat. Make sure that your map explains important historical events in the region.
2. **Vietnam War Veteran** Imagine that you are a Vietnam War veteran who is proud of serving the United States but has mixed emotions about the war. Create a collage for your children and grandchildren to show them what you did and how you feel. Your collage could include artifacts, drawings, news accounts, photographs, and poems. Write a paragraph explaining the parts of your collage.

Linking Geography and History

1. **Location** How did Cambodia and Laos become part of the war in Vietnam?
2. **Movement** What different kinds of passages did the Ho Chi Minh Trail allow?

History Skills Workshop

Using Primary Sources Presidents John F. Kennedy and Lyndon B. Johnson committed U.S. forces to Vietnam without congressional approval. The Tonkin Gulf Resolution gave Johnson some authority to send troops. However, Congress never declared war on Vietnam. In November 1973, Congress passed the War Powers Act over President Nixon's veto. This law outlined the authority of the president and Congress in relation to war. Read the excerpt below and then answer the following questions: (a) How does this act clarify the executive office's military powers? Refer to the Constitution, p. 44. (b) Why do you think that Congress passed this law after U.S. troops pulled out of Vietnam?

> "Whenever United States Armed Forces are introduced into hostilities . . . the President shall . . . report to the Congress . . . on the status of such hostilities. . . . Within sixty calendar days after a report is submitted . . . the President shall terminate any use of the United States Armed Forces . . . unless the Congress (1) has declared war . . . (2) has extended by law such sixty-day period, or (3) is physically unable to meet as a result of an armed attack upon the United States."

Reviewing Themes

1. to fight the spread of communism

2. It made it difficult to stop troop movements and the flow of supplies.

3. The Tonkin Gulf Resolution shifted the power of determining the war's course to the president, while the War Powers Act shifted this power back to Congress.

Thinking Critically

1. Answers will vary but students might suggest that he could have supported economic changes to improve the lives of the Vietnamese.

2. Attitudes changed because of the length of the war, the growing number of American casualties, and the suspicion that politicians were deceiving the public about the war.

3. By failing to continue increasing military involvement, then gradually decreasing it, the United States failed to win.

Writing About History

1. Articles will vary but students should discuss the hawks and doves, as well as the protests that occurred.

2. Memos will vary but students should identify U.S. goals in Vietnam and discuss the role that troops could play in achieving these goals.

Linking Geography and History

1. because the Ho Chi Minh Trail ran through them

2. it had paths, small roads, and tunnels

History Skills Workshop

(a) It states exactly what the president may do and the powers Congress has over the use of U.S. armed forces; (b) to restrict the president from sending in more troops

FOCUS

Write the term *communism* on one side of the chalkboard and the word *democracy* on the other side. Have students brainstorm what both words mean and how they might impact people's lives. Lead a brief discussion about why the United States wanted to prevent the spread of communism to South Vietnam. Tell students that in this activity they will learn about U.S. involvement in Vietnam.

TEACH

Have students read the Geography and History lesson. Choose one or more of the following activities to explore the Geography and History content with students.

ALL LEVELS: Visual-Spatial, Intrapersonal. (Suggested time: 30 min.) Organize students into two groups. Assign one group the year 1965 and the other group the year 1972. Provide

Geographic Diversity

The Ho Chi Minh Trail. The Ho Chi Minh Trail was bombed many times by the U.S. Air Force, requiring the North Vietnamese to constantly repair it. The trail was maintained and expanded by some 300,000 people working full-time. As many as 200,000 farmers also helped in their spare time. Some additional aid was provided by engineers from China and earth-moving equipment from Russia, but the majority of the work was done by hand, using bicycles, shovels, and carrying-poles to move dirt. By the end of the war, the trail was some 9,600 miles long, including detours around sections damaged by U.S. bombing. When the North Vietnamese maximized the use of the trail at various times in the mid-1960s, they could move up to 5,000 people per month and about 400 tons of supplies per week into South Vietnam.

Critical Thinking: Why do you think the North Vietnamese chose not to use a sea route to South Vietnam?

ANSWER: They might lose a costly shipload of supplies to a U.S. Navy attack.

SKILLS ANSWERS

1. Cambodia, Laos, North Vietnam, South Vietnam

2. Annamese

3. Dak To

Geography & History

The Struggle for Vietnam

In 1954 a peace agreement divided Vietnam into two countries. North Vietnam had a communist government, while South Vietnam struggled to establish a democracy. Soon the Communists began to support rebels in South Vietnam. U.S. leaders wanted to prevent the spread of communism in Asia. By 1964, the United States and South Vietnam were fighting a war against North Vietnam and the Communist-backed Vietcong rebels.

The inland mountains and dense jungles of Vietnam provided excellent cover for communist guerrilla forces and made it difficult for the U.S. military to wage war. The United States finally withdrew its troops from Vietnam in 1973. ■

A Foreign Battlefield

Most communist troops and their supplies entered South Vietnam along the Ho Chi Minh Trail or the Sihanouk Trail. U.S. bombing was unable to stop the flow of enemy troops and weapons along these jungle and mountain roads.

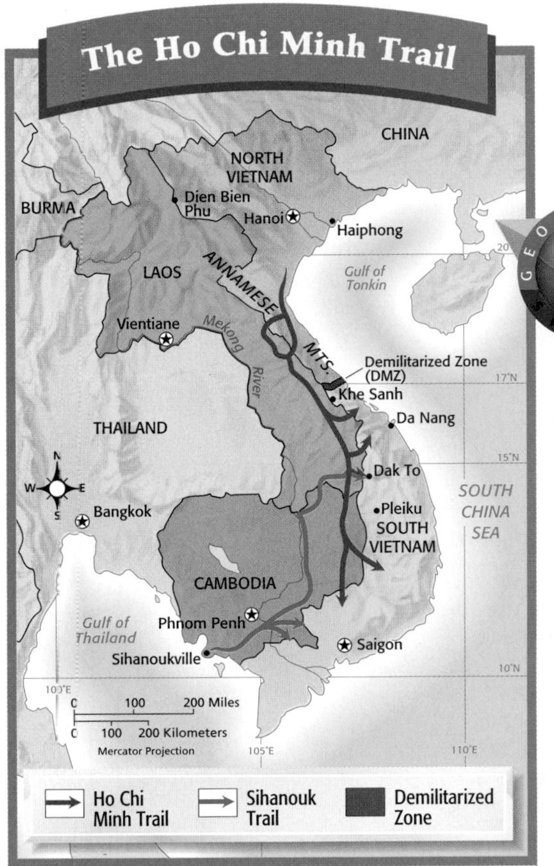

Geography Skills
Reading Special-Purpose Maps

1. What countries did the Ho Chi Minh Trail pass through?
2. What mountain range did the Ho Chi Minh Trail cross?
3. What South Vietnamese city lay at the end of the Sihanouk Trail?

644

students with poster board and art supplies and ask them to create a sign that might have been carried during a Vietnam War rally or demonstration in their assigned year. Encourage students to use pictures or slogans that would have reflected public opinion about the war at those times. **SHELTERED ENGLISH**

LEVEL 3: Linguistic. (Suggested time: 40 min.) Ask students to imagine that they are U.S. soldiers who have discovered an abandoned Vietcong tunnel complex similar to the one on page 645. Have students write a brief for their commanding officer describing the complex. Students should speculate as to what other types of chambers they would find farther along the tunnels leading off the diagram (hospital, equipment-repair workrooms, weapons-production areas, etc.).

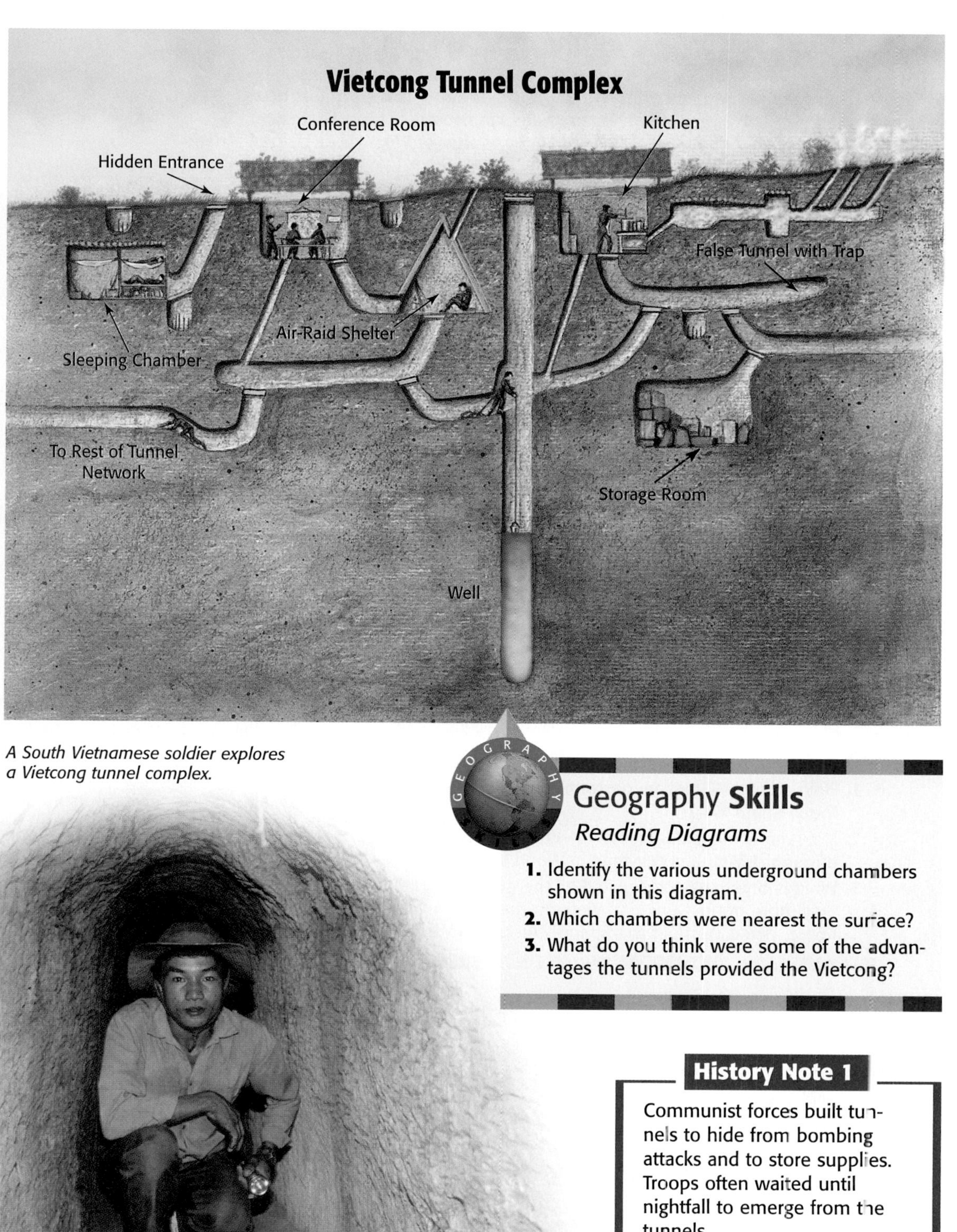

A South Vietnamese soldier explores a Vietcong tunnel complex.

Geography Skills
Reading Diagrams

1. Identify the various underground chambers shown in this diagram.
2. Which chambers were nearest the surface?
3. What do you think were some of the advantages the tunnels provided the Vietcong?

History Note 1

Communist forces built tunnels to hide from bombing attacks and to store supplies. Troops often waited until nightfall to emerge from the tunnels.

Daily Life

The Bombing of North Vietnam. To try to save as much of the population as they thought possible from the U.S. bombing campaigns, the government of North Vietnam sent children and the elderly out of the larger cities to live in the countryside. In rural areas, people built deep air-raid shelters and set up facilities to stockpile food. The North Vietnamese also took advantage of the country's geography to protect their economy. The government moved textile mills, machine shops, and small factories to new locations in the forested mountains. In the area closest to the demilitarized zone, where the bombing was most intense, the North Vietnamese dug a series of deep tunnels. Much of the population lived in these tunnels.

Critical Thinking: Why would moving a factory to the mountains help protect it?

ANSWER: The forest would make it harder to see the buildings from the air.

SKILLS ANSWERS

1. sleeping chamber, air-raid shelter, storage room, conference room, kitchen
2. conference room, kitchen
3. protection from bombing; allowed them to move without being seen

CLOSE

Logical-Mathematical, Visual-Spatial. Have students transfer the data from the bar graph on page 646 to a pie graph. The total number of troops that served during the five wars is 35.5 million. Students can calculate the percentage of the pie to allocate to each war by taking the number (in millions) of troops who served, multiplying it by 100, and then dividing it by 35.5.

CHALLENGE AND EXTEND

Linguistic, Visual-Spatial. Have students use the library or other resources to locate a site near the Ho Chi Minh Trail where a battle was fought during the Vietnam War and research the battle. Students' reports should include which side won the battle, how many soldiers fought on each side, and the number of casualties for each side. Encourage students to include graphs with their reports.

Cultural Diversity

The Vietnam Women's Memorial. The original Vietnam Veterans Memorial, a black granite wall inscribed with the names of the war's casualties, was built in 1982 on the National Mall in Washington, D.C. A statue of three worn and tired servicemen who appear to be waiting and looking at the Wall was added soon after. However, the statue did not represent the contributions of the approximately 11,000 military women who were stationed in Vietnam during the war. Former army nurse Diane Carlson Evans, founder of the Vietnam Women's Memorial Project, helped lead the effort that resulted in the addition of the Vietnam Women's Memorial to the site in 1993. The bronze statue of three women is surrounded by eight trees, one for each of the eight military women who died in Vietnam.

Activity: Have students use the library or other resources to make a list of the various jobs that U.S. servicewomen performed in Vietnam.

Americans and the War

The Vietnam War lasted more than eight years, making it the longest continuous conflict in U.S. history. Thousands of Americans died in Vietnam. The economic cost of the war was second only to that of World War II.

U.S. Armed Forces Serving During Wartime

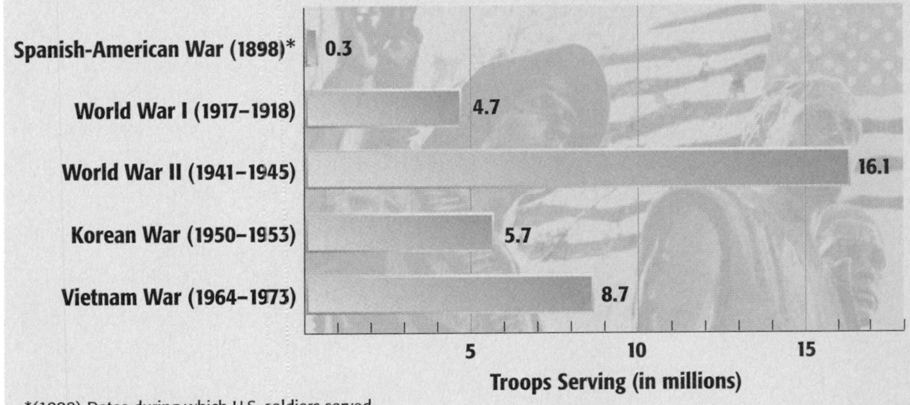

*(1898) Dates during which U.S. soldiers served

Source: *Statistical Abstract of the United States*

Geography **Skills**
Reading Bar Graphs

1. How many U.S. military personnel served during the Vietnam War?
2. How many more U.S. military personnel served during the Vietnam War than in World War I?
3. What is one reason suggested by the graph for why more troops served in Vietnam than in Korea, World War I, or the Spanish-American War?

Skills Answers

1. 8.7 million
2. 4 million
3. U.S. involvement lasted much longer in Vietnam.

History Note 2

Millions of Americans served in the U.S. armed forces during the Vietnam War. However, not all of these service personnel were stationed in Vietnam during the war. Many served in the United States or in European nations. The majority of those serving during the Vietnam War were not combat personnel. An estimated five noncombat personnel—such as drivers, mechanics, medical staff, and instructors—were required to support each combat soldier.

Helicopters were widely used by the U.S. military for the first time in the Vietnam War.

REVIEW

Logical-Mathematical, Interpersonal. Refer students to History Note 2, which mentions that there were approximately five noncombat personnel for every combat soldier. Organize students into groups and ask each group to brainstorm as many types of noncombat personnel as they can. When time expires, write each group's list on the chalkboard. Finally, hold a class discussion on the importance of noncombat personnel.
SHELTERED ENGLISH

ASSESS

Have students complete Geography and History Quiz 7.

RETEACH

Interpersonal. Organize students into four groups and assign each group one page of the lesson. Have each group create five questions based on their assigned page. Read each question to the class and have students write their answers on a sheet of paper. Review the answers with the class. **SHELTERED ENGLISH**

American Opinions on the Vietnam War, 1965–1971

Percentage of People Who Believed the Vietnam War Was a Mistake: 0, 10, 20, 30, 40, 50, 60, 70

Year: 1965, 1966, 1967, 1968, 1969, 1970, 1971

Source: *Trends in Public Opinion: A Compendium of Survey Data*

Geography **Skills**

Reading Bar Graphs

1. What percentage of respondents opposed the Vietnam War in 1967?
2. Which year's poll had the highest percentage of respondents who opposed the war?

The Vietnam Service Medal was awarded to members of the U.S. armed forces who served in Vietnam between 1965 and 1973.

History Note 3

As troop levels and casualties increased, more Americans began to challenge U.S. military involvement in Vietnam. In 1968 the number of U.S. troops serving in Vietnam peaked. That same year more than 14,000 Americans were killed in action—the highest total for any year during the war. By 1969, polls showed that a majority of Americans across the country believed that it was a mistake for the United States to be fighting in Vietnam.

A squad of U.S. soldiers returning to its base from a jungle patrol

Citizenship and Democracy

Vietnam Veterans Against the War. College students were not the only antiwar activists. The group Vietnam Veterans Against the War (VVAW) was founded in 1967. In early 1971 the VVAW organized the "Winter Soldier Investigation" of the U.S. military's actions in Vietnam. A "winter soldier" is someone who does not avoid difficult duty. The VVAW's investigation involved more than 100 veterans and 16 civilians who testified to war crimes they had either witnessed or committed. The VVAW took additional action. In April 1971 the group organized a five-day demonstration that included veterans throwing away their medals and a sit-in at the Supreme Court. VVAW leader and future U.S. senator John Kerry addressed the Senate Foreign Relations Committee about the need to end the war.

Critical Thinking: Why might a veteran protest a war after returning home?

ANSWER: Students answers will vary but might mention that veterans might place a higher value on life after having been so close to death.

SKILLS ANSWERS

1. 40 percent
2. 1971

TEACH

ALL LEVELS: Linguistic, Logical-Mathematical. (Suggested time: 45 min.) Organize students into teams for a scavenger hunt that uses topics from the subsection in Chapter 19 titled "A Musical Revolution." Have groups use the library or other resources to find as many sources as possible that could be used to research each topic. Encourage students to look at sources such as encyclopedias, the Internet, maps, nonfiction books, periodical indexes, and specialized dictionaries. Have each group turn in their results in the form of a bibliography, listing each source alphabetically by author's last name and giving the title and subject topic.

SKILLS ANSWERS

1. They are listed by title, author's last name, and subject topic—all arranged in alphabetical order.
2. Outlines will vary slightly but should basically be organized with the following headings as roman numerals I–IV: The "British Invasion," Motown, Folk Music, and Rock Music.

Writing and Using Outlines. For further practice, have students bring an article from a newsmagazine to class. Students should create an outline of the article and then use their outline to write a brief report summarizing the article. Ask volunteers to share their outlines and reports with the class.

History Skills WORKSHOP

Doing Research and Making an Outline

To complete a paper or a special project, you may need to do some research at a library or on the Internet. An outline will help you organize your research and plan your project.

Gathering Information A catalog, which may be in the form of cards or computer listings, notes the locations of all the library's books. Catalogs list each nonfiction book by title, author's last name, and subject topic—all arranged in alphabetical order.

A library's reference section contains other sources for research, such as encyclopedias, maps, specialized dictionaries, and periodical indexes. Encyclopedias contain information about people, places, events, and general subject topics. Specialized dictionaries, such as geographical dictionaries, contain definitions of terms and important information in a specific subject area.

Making an Outline An outline is a way to organize the information you collected in your research. An outline summarizes your main points. Note only your main ideas in an outline, saving the facts and details for your paper or project. If your outline is thorough and well thought-out, it helps you organize your ideas and makes writing the paper or project much easier.

How to Find Information

1. **Search the library catalog** Use the catalog to find a specific book or author, or find books on certain topics.
2. **Search reference works** Use reference works to find more information. Encyclopedias include information on many topics. In periodical indexes, you can find which magazine and newspaper articles cover your subject.

How to Create an Outline

1. **Order your material** Decide what to emphasize, then organize your material. Decide what information belongs in your paper's introduction, body, and conclusion.
2. **Identify main ideas** Identify the main ideas, then make these your outline's main headings.
3. **List supporting details** List the details that support each main heading as subheadings. Subheadings must come in pairs, at the least: no *A*'s without *B*'s, no *1*'s without *2*'s.

Example:

4. **Put your outline to use** Structure your report according to your outline. Each main heading might form the basis for a topic sentence of a paragraph. Subheadings would then make up the content of the paragraph.

Practicing the Skill

1. How are nonfiction library books listed in the catalog?
2. Read the subsection in Chapter 19 titled "A Musical Revolution" (pages 586–87) and create an outline of the material.

LEVEL 3: Linguistic, Logical-Mathematical. (Suggested time: 45 min. plus homework and presentation) Offer students a choice of two different images for a proposed postage stamp to commemorate the Vietnam War. The first image is the photograph of the Vietnam Veterans Memorial on page 622. The second image is the photograph of the soldier on page 630. Ask students to outline a brief speech in favor of one of the images. For homework, students should write the speech. Then ask volunteers to deliver speeches for each image. Finally, have the class vote on the image students prefer for the proposed stamp.

History in Action

UNIT 7 PORTFOLIO

Vietnam War Documentary

Complete the following activity in small, cooperative groups.

You and the members of your group are trying to create a documentary on the Vietnam War. Your first step is to present your idea to ATW video production company. If ATW likes your idea, they will make your documentary. Your presentation will consist of a series of storyboards—images that show what each scene in the video will look like. To go along with the images, each storyboard should also have a written text that a narrator will read during each scene.

Materials To complete this activity, you will need a tape recorder, posterboard, glue, and various art supplies.

Parts of the Project To create your storyboards, complete the following tasks:

1. **Planning** Meet as a group and assign one of the following topics to each group member: The history of Vietnam, the major battles of the war, U.S. soldiers, the antiwar movement, news coverage of the war, and the effects of the war on U.S. politics. Create an outline for your documentary. In it, note the order in which these topics will be covered and the kinds of images to use for each topic.

2. **Research** Each group member will conduct research to find news articles, quotations, maps, images, and any other information available about their topic.

3. **Creating the Storyboards** Using several pieces of posterboard, draw or paste together the images you want to use for each scene in your portion of the documentary. Under each image, write a short description of the scene.

4. **Writing the Narration** Organize the information you gathered into an outline. Use the outline to write the narrator's script. The script should tell the story in words that the images tell visually. While the text should relate to the images, it does not have to describe them exactly. For example, you could show a picture of an antiwar demonstration in Chicago while the narrator describes the whole antiwar movement.

5. **Editing and Recording** Meet as a group and organize your storyboards in the order they will be presented. Choose one group member to be the narrator. Record the narrator reading the script. You may also want to include sound effects, news reports, or music from the Vietnam War era.

6. **Presentation** Meet with the executives at ATW (the class) and make your presentation. Display the storyboards one at a time while playing the tape of the narrator.

You may want to continue this project by creating your proposed documentary.

Students use computers and a video camera to complete an assignment.

Searching the Internet.
If students will be doing some of their research on the Internet, you may want to familiarize them with several suitable search engines. Students may also need guidance in determining the level of reliability of the Web sites they find.

Evaluate Sources.
Encourage students to evaluate the quality of their research materials. Students should apply what they previously have learned about using visual resources (History Skills Workshop Unit 4), distinguishing fact from opinion and identifying bias (History Skills Workshop Unit 5), and using primary and secondary sources (History Skills Workshop Unit 6).

Organize Research.
Students may find it useful to record the results of their research on note cards. They should write one fact or quotation on each card. This will make it easier to organize their research into a logical sequence. Students should also note the source of the fact or quotation on each card.

Introducing UNIT 8

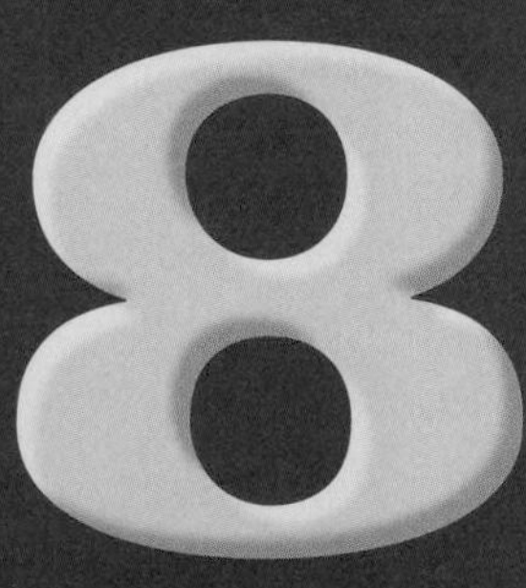

CHAPTER 22
A Search for Order

During the 1970s Americans struggled with a sluggish economy and an energy crisis. President Richard Nixon tried to resolve these issues and to appease the nation's Silent Majority. Nixon's foreign policy focused on advancing U.S. interests. As his second term began, however, Nixon was faced with the Watergate scandal and forced to resign. Vice President Gerald Ford replaced him. In 1976 Jimmy Carter became president. Carter had little success in improving the economy. Abroad, he focused foreign policy on human rights. In the 1970s new immigration patterns emerged, and Americans began to focus on the environment and health and fitness.

CHAPTER 23
The Republican Years

President Ronald Reagan believed that using supply-side economics would improve the U.S. economy. After a brief recession, the economy

Internet Activity

The Persian Gulf War. In August 1990 Iraq invaded its neighbor Kuwait. Iraq quickly seized the nation and then began amassing its forces along the border of Saudi Arabia. Many nations around the world depend on oil from Kuwait and Saudi Arabia. Fearing that Iraq would gain control of both nations and consequently of much of the world's oil, UN troops—many of whom were U.S. soldiers—launched an attack on Iraq in early 1991. By late February, they had liberated Kuwait. Have students search the Internet through the HRW Web site to find out more about the Persian Gulf War. Then ask them to imagine that they were a soldier in the war. Have them use their research to write a letter home describing their experiences in the Middle East.

go.hrw.com
SB1 Gulf War

UNIT 8 Modern America (1968–Present)

CHAPTER 22 **A Search for Order** (1968–1980)

CHAPTER 23 **The Republican Years** (1980–1992)

CHAPTER 24 **The United States Looks to the Future** (1992–PRESENT) boomed. Reagan worked to limit the size and role of government. He cut taxes but also greatly increased deficit spending. Abroad, Reagan focused on fighting communism. During George Bush's presidency, the Cold War came to an end, and the United States led the UN victory in the Persian Gulf War. Unemployment remained high, however, and the federal deficit continued to grow. The 1980s also saw AIDS emerge as an epidemic and many technological advances.

CHAPTER 24
The United States Looks to the Future

In 1992 the nation elected Democrat Bill Clinton president. Clinton worked to improve the economy and to decrease crime. His foreign policy placed the United States in the role of world protector of peace and democracy. Republicans won majorities in both houses of Congress in 1994, but Clinton won re-election in 1996. He and Congress balanced the federal budget and reformed welfare. However, scandal and his impeachment took up much of his second term. In the 1990s, immigration increased and technology made continued advances.

UNIT MOTIVATOR

Share the chapter overviews with students. Then have them use the information to create a "Coming Attractions" poster for each chapter. When the class finishes the unit, have students examine the accuracy of their posters.

American Teens IN HISTORY
Young Volunteers

"I think everybody should volunteer," says high school student Beth Kungel. "You don't need to get paid to help somebody else. It's fun, and it makes you feel good." Many children and teenagers from across the nation share Kungel's feelings. Through their volunteer work, these active young people have improved the world around them. They have saved animals, protected the environment, tutored classmates, fed the homeless, and built homes—among many other projects.

Young people have volunteered to protect the environment in different ways. Some young volunteers raise money to buy and preserve acres of tropical rain forest. Others focus their efforts closer to home. Some junior high school students from the Chicago area took part in the Spring into Action campaign. The project cleaned up local parks, planted trees, and restored sports fields in the community. In 1998 the Rouge River Rescue Cleanup in Michigan received assistance from MTV. The cable music channel held a cleanup party for volunteers to encourage more young people to join the effort.

Young people at work on a community garden project

Other young people have chosen to help fellow citizens and community members. Many have joined Habitat for Humanity, a nonprofit organization that relies on volunteers to build homes for poor people. When asked why she chose to spend her vacations working for free, teenager Regan Beard answered, "Because it's awesome. It's definitely worth it. . . . We start with a concrete base and end with walls." Some volunteers have even met former president Jimmy Carter, a longtime Habitat worker who makes time to visit with the young volunteers.

Other young volunteers like to help their friends and classmates. Peer-tutoring programs match students who want to teach with students who need extra help. Many schools have also begun "cross-age" tutoring programs in which older students work with younger students.

In this unit you will learn more about recent American history. You will learn about political and economic challenges, advances in science and technology, and the spirit with which Americans start the new century.

LEFT PAGE: *Fireworks brighten the sky over the Statue of Liberty during a bicentennial celebration.*

Using Visual Resources

July 4. The photograph opposite shows the fireworks at the bicentennial, or 200th anniversary, celebration at the Statue of Liberty in New York Harbor on July 4, 1976. At the time, the United States was facing many economic and other problems. Still, many people took part in the bicentennial of the founding of the United States. The bicentennial celebrations provided Americans with a time to remember their patriotism. The July 4 holiday commemorates the date in 1776 that the Continental Congress approved the final version of the Declaration of Independence. Although July 4 has been celebrated for more than 200 years, it has been a federal legal holiday only since 1941.

Critical Thinking: Why do you think the Statue of Liberty was chosen as a site for a bicentennial celebration?

ANSWER: Answers will vary but students might mention that the Statue of Liberty is a symbol of American democracy, freedom, and patriotism.

TEACH

ALL LEVELS: Visual-Spatial, Interpersonal. (Suggested time: 45 min.) Write each event from the time line on a separate slip of paper. Divide the class into six groups and give each group three slips. (You may want to remove any events involving violence, such as the assassination of Robert Kennedy.) Ask students to prepare a stamp commemorating one of their events. When groups have finished preparing their stamps, have them share them with the class. Have students vote on the stamp they like most. **SHELTERED ENGLISH**

ALL LEVELS: Linguistic, Logical-Mathematical. (Suggested time: 35 min.) Ask students to imagine that they can travel back in time. Have them choose three events from the time line that they would like to experience or witness firsthand. Then have students create a journal that describes their time travels and their experiences witnessing each event. Call on volunteers to read aloud their journal entries to the class. Then have the class vote on the two or three events at which they would most like to have been present.

Daily Life

The Muppet Show. During the 1970s Muppets entertained both children and adults alike on *The Muppet Show*, a television show. Jim Henson created the show and its Muppet stars. After finishing high school, Henson had worked as a puppeteer. As he progressed in his career, he invented "Muppets," puppet-like figures that combined the features of traditional puppets with the movable limbs of marionettes. In the 1960s Henson's Muppets began appearing on TV commercials and shows. The Muppets got their big break, however, in 1969 when they were featured on a new educational program called *Sesame Street.* Soon Kermit the Frog and the other Muppet characters were household names. In 1976 *The Muppet Show* began airing weekly during prime time. The program was a family variety show featuring a cast of Muppets, one human guest star, and both silly and sophisticated humor and antics. During its five-year run, the highly popular show won three Emmy awards.

Critical Thinking: Why do you think *The Muppet Show* was so popular with both children and adults?

ANSWER: Adults enjoyed the more sophisticated humor of the show, while children enjoyed watching the cute and silly puppet-like characters.

Time Line: 1968–Present

UNIT 8

Modern America

President Reagan

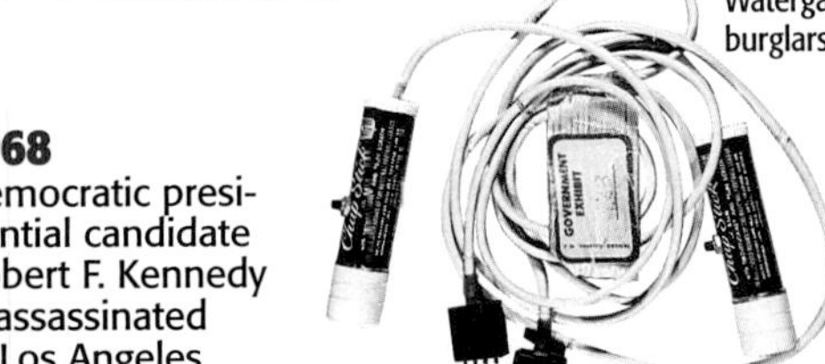

Microphones used by the Watergate burglars

UNITED STATES

1968 Democratic presidential candidate Robert F. Kennedy is assassinated in Los Angeles after winning the California primary.

1972 A burglary at the Watergate building will lead to the resignation of President Richard Nixon.

1976 *The Muppet Show* begins. The TV show features animal-like puppets.

1979 The worst nuclear accident in U.S. history occurs at the Three Mile Island power plant in Pennsylvania.

Nuclear reactors at Three Mile Island

1981 53 Americans return to the United States after being held hostage in Tehran, Iran, for 444 days.

1984 Republican Ronald Reagan is elected to a second term as president.

1968 | 1971 | 1974 | 1977 | 1980 | 1983

WORLD

1969 Golda Meir, a former teacher in the United States, is elected as Israel's first female prime minister.

Golda Meir

1974 Chinese farmers working near the city of Xi'an accidentally discover the tomb of emperor Shi Huangdi. It contains an army of more than 6,000 life-sized terra-cotta soldiers.

1979 Nicaraguan dictator General Anastasio Somoza flees from Sandinista rebels, who take over the government.

1981 Great Britain's Prince Charles weds Lady Diana Spencer. The televised ceremony is watched by an estimated 700 million people worldwide.

The terra-cotta soldiers in military formation

Prince Charles and Princess Diana

CHALLENGE AND EXTEND

1. Linguistic, Logical-Mathematical. Have students use the library and other resources to research the accident at the Three Mile Island nuclear power plant in Pennsylvania. Have students use their research to write a report on the advantages and risks of using nuclear power. The report should include the 1979 nuclear accident and its aftermath and discuss the current safety procedures at American nuclear power plants.

2. Linguistic, Visual-Spatial. Have students use the library and other resources to research the 1994 elections in South Africa. Ask students to imagine that they are a magazine writer covering the event. Have students gather photographs and other visuals of the event as well as firsthand accounts of people's thoughts and feelings about the elections. Then have students use their research to prepare a two-page magazine spread about the elections. Display students' work around the classroom.

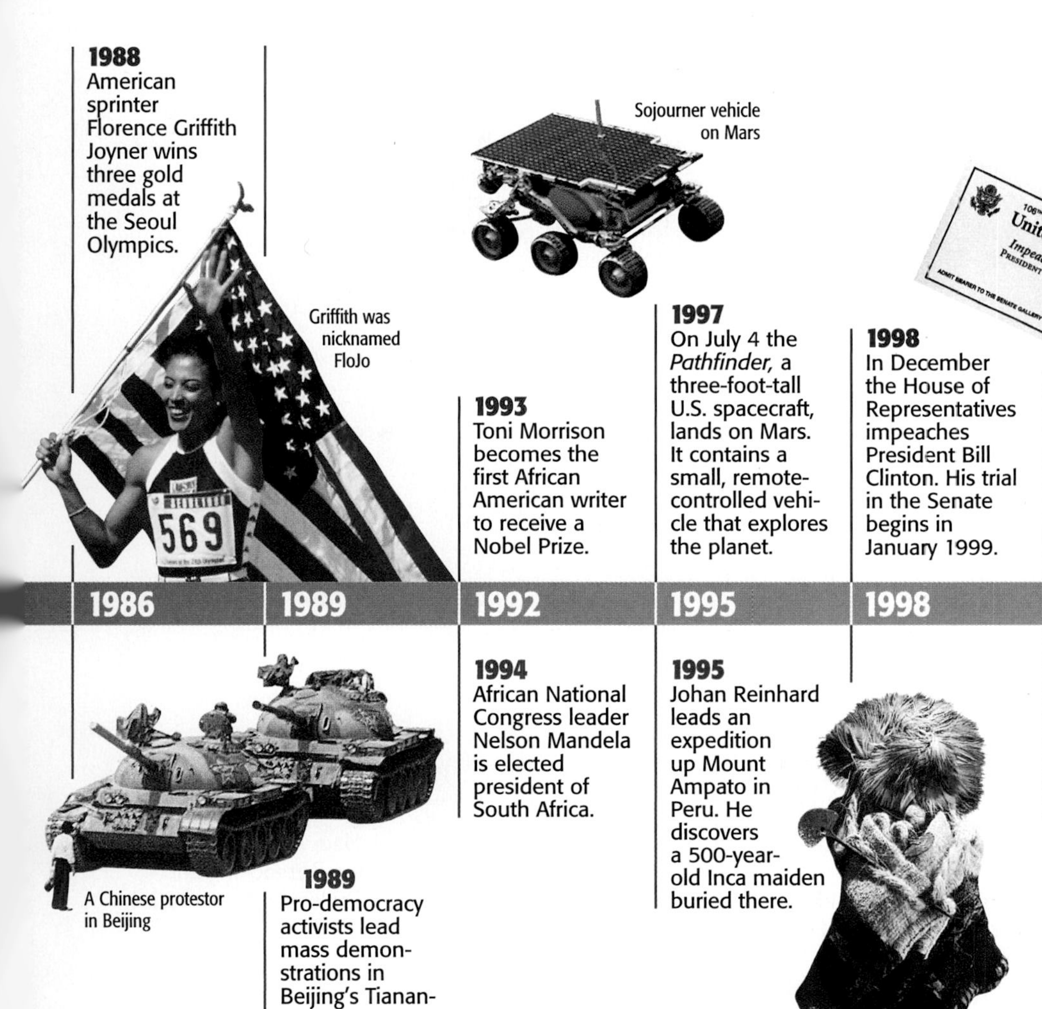

1988 American sprinter Florence Griffith Joyner wins three gold medals at the Seoul Olympics.

Griffith was nicknamed FloJo

Sojourner vehicle on Mars

1993 Toni Morrison becomes the first African American writer to receive a Nobel Prize.

1997 On July 4 the *Pathfinder,* a three-foot-tall U.S. spacecraft, lands on Mars. It contains a small, remote-controlled vehicle that explores the planet.

1998 In December the House of Representatives impeaches President Bill Clinton. His trial in the Senate begins in January 1999.

Ticket for President Clinton's impeachment trial

A Chinese protestor in Beijing

1989 Pro-democracy activists lead mass demonstrations in Beijing's Tiananmen Square. The protestors demand freedom of speech and other rights.

1994 African National Congress leader Nelson Mandela is elected president of South Africa.

1995 Johan Reinhard leads an expedition up Mount Ampato in Peru. He discovers a 500-year-old Inca maiden buried there.

Figurine found with the Inca maiden

1999 Yugoslav troops attack Kosovo residents. NATO forces bomb Serbia in response.

USING THE TIME LINE

1. What information do the time line entries provide about U.S. presidents from 1968 to the present?
2. What information do the entries provide about world leaders?

Activity Select one of the following topics: culture, economy, politics, social issues, or technology. Using the information on the time line, write a brief history of one of these topics from 1968 to the present. Use the Internet, the library, your textbook, or other sources to find additional information to complete the history.

Biography

An Olympic Hero. Sprinter Florence Griffith Joyner emerged as a new American star during the 1988 Summer Olympics held in Seoul, South Korea. Nicknamed FloJo, Joyner won three gold medals and one silver medal. In the process, she set a world record in the 200 meters. Joyner won her other gold medals in the 100 meters and the 4 x 100-meter relay. Adding to the victory, Joyner's sister-in-law, Jackie Joyner-Kersee, won two gold medals and also set a world record. The two women accounted for five of the six gold medals U.S. women won in track and field. On September 21, 1998, at age 38, FloJo died suddenly.

Critical Thinking: What is the importance of having positive role models, such as Florence Griffith Joyner?

ANSWER: Answers will vary but students should mention what role models mean to them.

USING THE TIME LINE ANSWERS

1. Nixon resigned; Reagan was re-elected in 1984; Clinton was impeached.

2. Golda Meir was elected as Israel's prime minister; Nicaraguan dictator General Anastasio Somoza was ousted; Prince Charles wed; Nelson Mandela was elected president of South Africa.

CHAPTER PLANNING GUIDE
A Search for Order

	SECTION LESSON OBJECTIVES	PRINT RESOURCES	MULTIMEDIA RESOURCES	SHELTERED ENGLISH RESOURCES
Section 1: The Nixon Presidency (pp. 655–59)	★ Explain how President Nixon addressed the Silent Majority's concerns. ★ Describe the effect of the poor economy and the energy crisis on Americans. ★ Evaluate how realpolitik affected U.S. relations with other countries.	★ Guided Reading Strategies 22.1 ★ Biography Reading 22: Henry Kissinger ★ Literature Reading 22: Nixon's Visit to China ★ Section 1 Review, p. 659 ★ Daily Quiz 22.1	★ *Teaching Resources CD–ROM*, Lesson 22.1	★ Main Idea Activities for Reteaching and Sheltered English 22.1
Section 2: Watergate and Beyond (pp. 660–65)	★ Explain how the events of Watergate led to President Nixon's resignation. ★ Identify constitutional issues addressed during the Watergate scandal. ★ Describe the challenges President Ford faced while in office.	★ Guided Reading Strategies 22.2 ★ American History Political Cartoon 29: Watergate ★ Section 2 Review, p. 665 ★ Daily Quiz 22.2	★ *Teaching Resources CD–ROM*, Lesson 22.2 ★ *Exploring America's Past* Video Segment: The Dark Side of Politics; *Teacher's Guide*, pp. 40–42 ★ HRW Web site	★ Main Idea Activities for Reteaching and Sheltered English 22.2
Section 3: The Carter Administration (pp. 666–71)	★ Explain how President Carter differed from other politicians and why he lost public support. ★ Evaluate how Carter handled economic problems during his presidency. ★ Describe Carter's approach to foreign policy.	★ Guided Reading Strategies 22.3 ★ Geography Activity 22: Southern Africa in the 1970s ★ Graphic Organizer 22: Foreign Events Affecting Domestic Events ★ Section 3 Review, p. 671 ★ Daily Quiz 22.3	★ *Teaching Resources CD–ROM*, Lesson 22.3 ★ HRW Web site	★ Main Idea Activities for Reteaching and Sheltered English 22.3
Section 4: American Society in the 1970s (pp. 672–77)	★ Describe how the U.S. population changed during the 1970s. ★ Identify environmental concerns that drew attention and explain how Americans reacted. ★ Describe how health care and popular entertainment changed in the 1970s.	★ Guided Reading Strategies 22.4 ★ Primary Source Reading 22: Defending the Equal Rights Amendment ★ Section 4 Review, p. 677 ★ Daily Quiz 22.4	★ *Teaching Resources CD–ROM*, Lesson 22.4 ★ Everyday Life in America Transparency 31: *Star Wars:* Sign of the Seventies and Transparency 33: Teens Today: Caring for Earth's Creatures ★ Linking Geography and History Transparency 17B: African American Population, 1970	★ Main Idea Activities for Reteaching and Sheltered English 22.4
Chapter Review and Assessment (pp. 678–79)		★ Chapter 22 Review, pp. 678–79 ★ Vocabulary Activity 22 ★ Chapter 22 Study Guide ★ Chapter 22 Test (Form A or B)	★ Audio Program, Ch. 22 (English and Spanish) ★ *Global Skill Builder CD–ROM* ★ Chapter 22 Test Generator ★ HRW Web site	★ Spanish Glossary ★ Sheltered English Chapter 22 Test

CHAPTER OVERVIEW

The 1970s began with President Nixon seeking to appease the nation's Silent Majority. He did so by giving states more control and opposing new civil rights legislation. During his presidency the nation faced economic problems caused by stagflation and an energy crisis brought on by an overdependence on foreign oil. Nixon's foreign policy emphasized working with other nations, even communist ones, to advance U.S. interests.

Nixon may best be remembered for the Watergate scandal. As evidence began to mount linking him to the scandal, he was forced to turn over White House audiotapes, which further implicated him. As a result, Nixon resigned. He was replaced by his newly appointed vice president, Gerald Ford.

In 1976 Jimmy Carter defeated Ford in the presidential election. Carter's administration saw mixed success. At home, he worked to end the energy crisis, improve the economy, and protect the environment. Carter based U.S. foreign policy on fairness rather than force. Perhaps his greatest achievement was his role in ending long-standing hostilities between Israel and Egypt. Although he was popular early on, the Iran hostage crisis and the troubled economy caused Carter to lose public confidence and the 1980 election.

The 1970s also saw changes in American society, particularly in immigration and population patterns, health and safety, and popular culture.

CHAPTER INVESTIGATION

The Chapter Investigation is an extended, multipart activity designed for students to work cooperatively and apply the chapter content in the creation of a project. You may choose to use the Chapter 22 Investigation, Former U.S. Presidents Tour, either as a substitute for teaching the section lessons or as an alternate assessment.

BLOCK SCHEDULING 

The teacher lesson plans for each section offer a variety of activity choices to help you present the material in a block scheduling format. For further suggestions on block scheduling, see the *Block Scheduling Handbook with Team Teaching Strategies,* pp. 127–32.

Meeting Individual Needs

ABILITY LEVELS

LEVEL 1 Basic level activities designed for all students encountering new material.

LEVEL 2 Intermediate level activities designed for average students.

LEVEL 3 Challenging activities designed for above-average students.

SHELTERED ENGLISH These activities address the needs of students with Limited English Proficiency.

Smithsonian Institution®

Internet Connections and Lesson 22
www.si.edu/hrw

CNN Presents America:
Yesterday and Today 1850 to the Present
Segment: Congresswoman Barbara Jordan

Additional Resources

Books for Teachers

Greene, John Robert. *The Presidency of Gerald R. Ford.* University Press of Kansas, 1995. Covers Gerald Ford's term as president, from his pardon of Richard Nixon to his loss to Jimmy Carter in the 1976 election.

Kutler, Stanley. *The Wars of Watergate: The Last Crisis of Richard Nixon.* Knopf, 1990. A comprehensive look at Watergate.

Smith, Gaddis. *Morality, Reason, and Power: American Diplomacy in the Carter Years.* Hill and Wang, 1986. An account of foreign policy during the Carter administration.

Books for Students

Feinberg, Barbara Silberdic. *Watergate: Scandal in the White House.* Watts, 1990. An in-depth report on the events following the Watergate break-in. Includes an examination of President Nixon's resignation (for students reading below grade level).

Larsen, Rebecca. *Richard Nixon: Rise and Fall of a President.* Watts, 1991. Traces President Nixon's career from his student days through the Watergate scandal.

Woodward, Bob, and Carl Bernstein. *All the President's Men.* Simon and Schuster, 1987. The Watergate scandal told by the journalists who uncovered it.

Multimedia Materials

Carter's New World. Video, 60 min. WGBH/Boston. Carter envisioned a world without nuclear weapons. To this end, he attempted improved relations with the Soviet Union. The video analyzes events that contributed to Carter's failure to eliminate nuclear weapons.

Modern U.S. History, Unit 3: 1969–1981. Video, 46 min. Guidance Associates/SSSS. Focuses on important events of the Nixon, Ford, and Carter presidencies.

One Step Forward. Video, 60 min. WGBH/Boston. Chronicles the Nixon-Kissinger era of détente.

A Search for Order

CHAPTER MOTIVATOR

Draw students' attention to the chapter title, "A Search for Order," and to the time period covered in this chapter. Remind students of the turmoil in American society during the 1960s and the Vietnam War. Ask students to speculate on circumstances that may have provoked a desire for order. List students' replies on the chalkboard and ask them to explain their reasoning. Then tell students that in this chapter they will learn about the Nixon, Ford, and Carter presidencies; the Watergate scandal; and the major cultural and social issues and trends of the 1970s.

Presenting Themes

- **Economic Development** Students might mention that abundant energy resources help an economy grow. If energy resources become expensive, prices for other goods will rise. If energy becomes scarce, severe problems might result for the economy and society.
- **Citizenship and Democracy** Students might mention that a scandal could cause Americans to lose faith in the office of the presidency. If the scandal is serious, it might lead to impeachment or the president's resignation, either of which would disrupt the governmental operations of the nation.
- **Global Relations** Students might mention that presidents may use different principles, such as national interest or the promotion of democracy, to guide foreign policy. They may also take different approaches to resolving foreign-policy conflicts; some relying on diplomacy, others on military force.

Using the Time Line

Have students create a chart listing the time line events as either domestic or foreign-policy issues. After students have completed the chapter, have them explain how each event affected Americans.

CHAPTER 22

A Search for Order

(1968–1980)

In February 1972 President Richard Nixon boarded the presidential airplane for his trip to communist China. In good spirits, he waved and shook hands as thousands cheered him. Speaking to the crowd, Nixon compared his journey to China with a recent moon landing. The U.S. astronauts had left a plaque on the moon that read, "We came in peace for all mankind." Nixon said he was going to China for the same reason.

Economic Development
What role might energy resources play in a nation's economy?

Citizenship and Democracy
How might the office of the U.S. presidency be affected by scandals?

Global Relations
How might U.S. foreign policy change depending on the president in office?

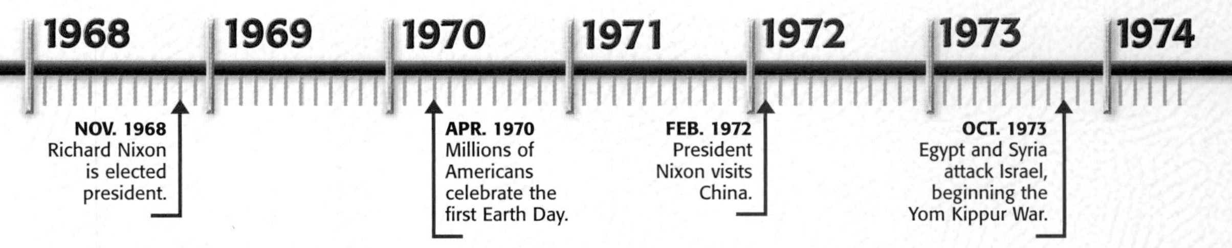

OBJECTIVES

- **Explain how President Nixon addressed the Silent Majority's concerns.**
- **Describe the effect of the poor economy and the energy crisis on Americans.**
- **Evaluate how realpolitik affected U.S. relations with other countries.**

FOCUS

Motivate Before Reading

Ask students to speculate on why they might befriend their enemies and list the steps they might take to do so. Have students consider how befriending one enemy might affect their ability to befriend others. Tell students that in this section they will learn how and why the United States changed its policy toward some of its enemies, how U.S. relations with other nations affected the lives

The Nixon Presidency

Reading Focus

How did President Nixon try to address the concerns of the Silent Majority?

What effect did the poor economy and the energy crisis have on Americans?

How did realpolitik affect U.S. relations with other countries?

Key Terms

Silent Majority
southern strategy
stagflation
New Federalism
Organization of Petroleum Exporting Countries
energy crisis
realpolitik
Strategic Arms Limitation Talks
détente

SOME 100,000 WORKERS—most of them construction workers—jammed shoulder to shoulder on already crowded New York City streets. "All the way with the U.S.A.," they yelled. They were determined to show their support for President Richard Nixon. Many of these workers considered themselves the backbone of the nation and saw student protesters as dangerous and anti-American. A few days later, one worker presented the president with a hard hat, calling it "a symbol, along with our great flag, for freedom and patriotism to our beloved country."

Demonstrators fill the streets of New York City to show their support for Richard Nixon.

IMAGE ON LEFT PAGE: *President Nixon at the Great Wall of China*

1975 | 1976 | 1977 | 1978 | 1979 | 1980

AUG. 1974 Nixon resigns the presidency, and Gerald Ford is sworn in as president.

NOV. 1976 Jimmy Carter is elected president.

SEPT. 1978 The Camp David Accords are signed.

MAR. 1979 A nuclear accident occurs at Three Mile Island, Pennsylvania.

NOV. 1980 Ronald Reagan wins the presidency.

Section 1 RESOURCES

PRINT

★ Guided Reading Strategies 22.1

★ Biography Reading 22: Henry Kissinger

★ Literature Reading 22: Nixon's Visit to China

★ Section 1 Review, p. 659

★ Daily Quiz 22.1

MULTIMEDIA

★ *Teaching Resources CD–ROM,* Lesson 22.1

SHELTERED ENGLISH

★ Main Idea Activities for Reteaching and Sheltered English 22.1

of Americans at home, and how President Richard Nixon dealt with both foreign and domestic issues.

Introduce Key Terms

Linguistic, Logical-Mathematical. Review this section's key terms with students. Make a list of the terms and a list of definitions. Have students scan the section to match each term with its definition. Call on students to identify the definition for each term. Finally, have students write the definitions in their notebooks.
SHELTERED ENGLISH

TEACH

Have students read Section 1 and complete Guided Reading Strategies 22.1. Choose one or more of the following activities to explore the section content with students. For further suggestions on block scheduling or team teaching, see the *Block Scheduling Handbook.*

LEVEL 1: Linguistic. (Suggested time: 15 min.) As a class, go over students' Guided Reading Strategies. Then use the Reading Focus questions to highlight the main ideas of the section.
SHELTERED ENGLISH

Cultural Diversity

A Divided People. Just weeks before construction workers marched in support of President Nixon, fighting broke out on the streets of New York City. Mayor John Lindsay had ordered the flags at City Hall lowered to half-staff in memory of some university students killed in Ohio as they protested the U.S. bombing of Cambodia. Lindsay's decision angered some construction workers, many of whom were veterans. A group of workers rushed to New York's City Hall, raised the flag to full-staff, and attacked students who were there protesting the war. Fearing more violence, President Nixon held a news conference in which he declared that he wanted the war to end just as much as the students did.

Critical Thinking: What divisions in American society did the incident in New York City reveal?

ANSWER: It showed the continued split over U.S. involvement in the Vietnam War, particularly between students and laborers, such as the construction workers.

The Silent Majority

Many Americans voted for Richard Nixon in November 1968 because they disliked the changes taking place in the 1960s. President Nixon called these voters the **Silent Majority**. One Nixon supporter expressed some views of this group:

> **"I want my children to live and grow up in an America as I knew it, where we were proud to be citizens of this country. I'm . . . sick and tired of listening to all this nonsense about how awful America is."**

A cartoon dollar showing American concerns over inflation

The Silent Majority blamed the federal government for high taxes and social unrest. Nixon promised to restore law and order. He called antiwar protesters criminals and supported policies that increased the power of the police and the courts. He also tried to reduce the size of the government.

In addition, Nixon wanted to limit further civil rights legislation. He said, "The laws have caught up with our consciences." This position was part of the Republicans' so-called **southern strategy**. Nixon hoped this strategy would win the support of white southern Democrats and other opponents of civil rights reforms.

The U.S. Supreme Court blocked some of Nixon's efforts. For example, the Court supported busing programs to desegregate public schools. Nixon opposed such programs. In 1969 he replaced retiring Chief Justice Earl Warren with Warren E. Burger, a more conservative judge. Nixon eventually appointed three additional conservative justices. Following these changes, the Court began to alter some of its earlier civil rights decisions.

The Economy

One critical problem facing President Nixon was the U.S. economy. In the early 1970s the country suffered from **stagflation**, a period of high inflation and high unemployment.

Several factors caused stagflation. The cost of social programs and the Vietnam War had increased the national debt. Paying the interest on this debt cost the federal government billions of dollars a year. These payments contributed to inflation. In addition, American manufacturers faced stronger foreign competition. As a result, some major industries downsized to cut costs. Many Americans lost their jobs. Even those who kept working were hurt by rising prices caused by inflation. From 1967 to 1974, the buying power of the U.S. dollar dropped by 30 percent. "I used to keep a budget," said one San Francisco woman, "but it got so discouraging, I gave it up."

Nixon hoped the economy would correct itself. He believed the federal government should avoid interfering with businesses and state governments. Instead, he proposed a system of revenue sharing called the **New Federalism**. Under this system, the federal government gave grants to the states. Local leaders then decided how to use this money. However, when inflation hit 6 percent in 1971, Nixon placed limits on wage and price increases. These controls temporarily slowed inflation.

The Energy Crisis

Scarce energy resources and rising oil prices also contributed to U.S. economic problems. By 1974

Long lines at the gas pump during the energy crisis

ALL LEVELS: Logical-Mathematical, Visual-Spatial. (Suggested time: 30 min.) Have each student create a poster to show how stagflation and the energy crisis affected life in the United States. Ask volunteers to explain their posters to the class. Then discuss the steps the Nixon administration took to deal with these problems. **SHELTERED ENGLISH**

ALL LEVELS: Logical-Mathematical, Visual-Spatial. (Suggested time: 30 min.) Have each student create a flowchart showing the causes of the Nixon administration's policy of realpolitik toward China and the effects of that policy, particularly on U.S. relations with the Soviet Union. Call on volunteers to explain their work to the class.

LEVEL 3: Linguistic, Kinesthetic, Interpersonal. (Suggested time: 30 min. plus homework) Tell half the class to imagine that they are members of the Silent Majority and the other half that they are citizens who oppose Nixon. They are all attending a state dinner at the White House during the early years of the Nixon presidency. Have volunteers stand and say a few words explaining how Nixon's views and actions do or do not address their concerns. Then ask volunteers to suggest policies they would like to see President Nixon support. For homework, have students write an essay describing how Nixon's domestic and foreign policies addressed the concerns of the Silent Majority. During the next class, call on volunteers to read their essays.

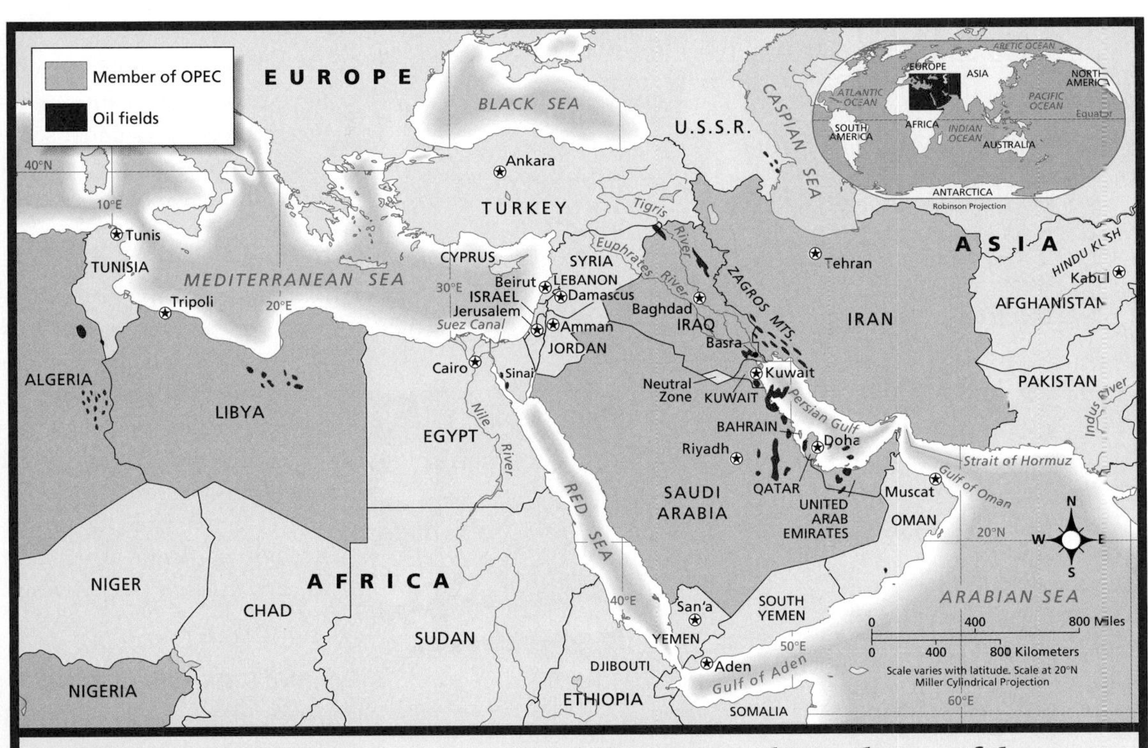

OPEC Member Nations in the Middle East and Northern Africa

Learning from Maps OPEC member countries produce much of the world's oil and work together to try to control its price.

Location Which OPEC members are located along the Persian Gulf?

the United States was importing more than a third of its oil. Much of it came from Middle Eastern nations. In 1960, five major oil-producing nations had formed the **Organization of Petroleum Exporting Countries** (OPEC). The membership of OPEC later expanded to include 13 countries. OPEC hoped to maintain a high price for oil by controlling its production and sale.

In the early 1970s OPEC controlled much of the world's oil supply. It used this power to influence international politics. Most OPEC members were Arab countries opposed to Israel, an ally of the United States. In October 1973 Egypt and Syria attacked Israel on Yom Kippur, a Jewish holy day. The United States sent military supplies to Israel during this Yom Kippur War. This act upset Egypt and Syria's OPEC allies.

OPEC declared an embargo, or a ban, on the sale of oil to the United States and some other countries. The oil embargo caused a worldwide **energy crisis** that was marked by high fuel prices and fuel shortages. Many gasoline stations remained open only part of the day. Customers waited in long lines to buy gas. The high cost of gasoline hurt sales of American-made cars, most of which got poor gas mileage.

Some schools and businesses had to shut down because they lacked fuel for heat and transportation. One Detroit hospital told its patients to stay in bed to keep warm. A hospital official explained, "We had so little oil left that we just had to cut back the thermostats."

President Nixon encouraged people to use less fuel by lowering their thermostats and limiting air travel. He asked Congress to lower speed limits so that cars would use less gas. Nixon also supported research into nuclear power. In addition, the president announced Project Independence, a plan to end the use of foreign oil by 1980. Under Project Independence, the United States

Economic Development

Wage and Price Controls. Officials in the Nixon administration hoped that freezing wages and prices would stop the inflation spiral. The American public, anxious about inflation, responded favorably to Nixon's announcement of a 90-day freeze. After the freeze, Nixon started a second phase in which the federal government developed schedules for moderately increasing wages and prices. However, the administration could not control the rise in oil prices, which foreign producers had set. In addition, many people feared that as soon as wage and price limits were lifted, prices would rise dramatically.

Critical Thinking: Should the government have the power to freeze wages to solve economic problems?

ANSWER: Answers will vary but some students might argue that freezing wages can interfere with a free market economy. Others might argue that freezing wages can be a necessary and proper function of government.

MAP ANSWER

Iran, Iraq, Kuwait, Qatar, Saudi Arabia, and United Arab Emirates

CLOSE

Linguistic, Logical-Mathematical, Intrapersonal. Ask students to imagine that it is 1973 and Nixon is president. Have students write letters to the editor of a local newspaper describing Nixon's main domestic and foreign policies, based on the information in this section. Students should state whether they agree with Nixon's policies and explain their position. When students are finished, call on volunteers to read their letters to the class. Finally, discuss the main events of Nixon's presidency.

CHALLENGE AND EXTEND

Visual-Spatial, Intrapersonal, Interpersonal. Have students investigate ways their community was affected by stagflation, the oil embargo, and the fuel shortage of the early 1970s. Students should interview local residents, businesspeople, and government officials and read newspapers and other media resources, if available, for firsthand accounts. Have students use their research to design a few pages of a local 1970s newspaper dealing with these issues and conditions.

Across the Curriculum

MATH

Rising Oil Prices. Oil prices rose steadily during the early 1970s. The price for a barrel of oil in 1970 was $1.80. The following year it reached $2.18. By the middle of 1973 it had risen to $2.90. Then prices began rising sharply. In October 1973 oil sold for $5.12 a barrel. Two months later, when OPEC oil ministers met, Saudi Arabia wanted the price per barrel raised to $8. Other ministers suggested prices as high as $23. The shah of Iran, who was considered an ally of the United States, recommended $11.65 per barrel. This price was based on a study that claimed any higher price would cause importing nations to turn to alternative energy sources. The ministers agreed, and the price of oil in December 1973 was set at $11.65 per barrel.

Activity: Have students create charts showing the rise in oil prices from 1970 through 1973.

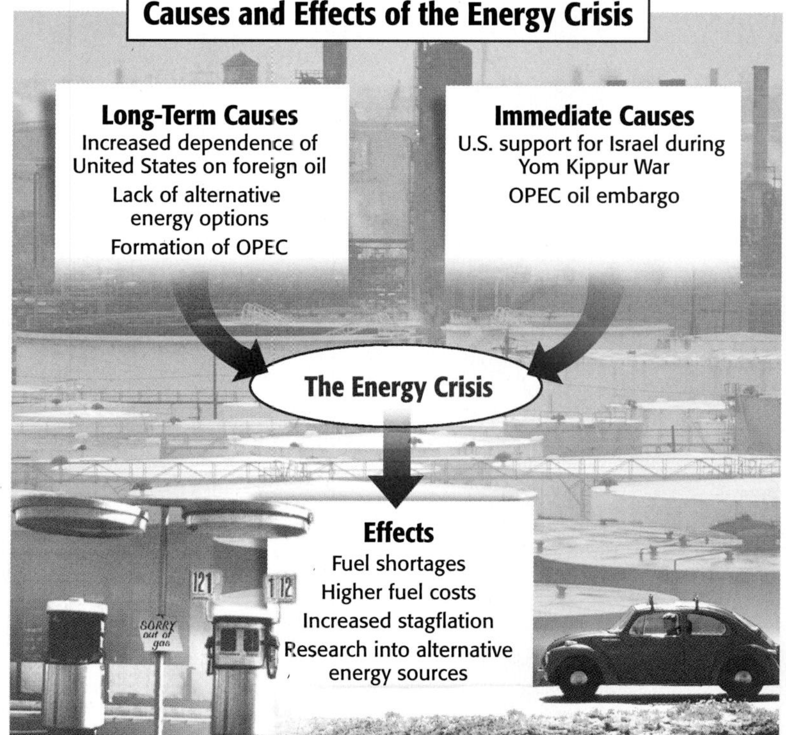

built a pipeline to connect the Alaskan oil fields to the lower 48 states.

Foreign Diplomacy

The energy crisis showed how complicated foreign policy had become. President Nixon had already begun developing a new foreign-policy approach to deal with such issues.

Realpolitik

Henry Kissinger served as Nixon's senior foreign-policy adviser. Kissinger was a respected German American professor of political science at Harvard University. He served as national security adviser during Nixon's first term. He became secretary of state during Nixon's second term.

Kissinger based his foreign policy on the idea of **realpolitik**. This German word means "practical politics." Kissinger argued that protecting U.S. interests was more important than defending political or moral ideals overseas. For example, Kissinger believed that the United States should be willing to cooperate with nondemocratic countries under some circumstances. Nixon agreed with most of Kissinger's policy views.

Some observers complained that realpolitik encouraged U.S. support for dictators who violated human rights. In Latin America, for example, the United States gave military and economic aid to several harsh military dictatorships. These governments were strongly anticommunist and were friendly to U.S. interests.

Relations with China

Realpolitik greatly affected U.S. relations with communist China. In 1949, communist rebels had defeated the U.S.-backed Chinese Nationalists. Since that time the United States had refused to officially recognize the government of communist China.

Many U.S. officials had long assumed that China and the Soviet Union were close allies. In early 1969, however, the two communist nations had argued over their shared border. This dispute almost caused a war. By 1970 China and the Soviet Union had become bitter rivals.

Hoping to widen this split, Nixon administration officials began secret talks with the Chinese. In February 1972 President Nixon and his wife, Pat, visited China. Journalists and television news teams covered the Nixons' trip extensively. Americans saw images of the Great Wall and the Imperial Palace. They also saw pictures of the Nixons at state banquets with Chinese leader Mao Zedong and his wife, Jiang Qing.

Although some people criticized Nixon for establishing closer ties with Communists, many Americans supported him. One observer said:

> **"I applaud [Nixon's] timely acceptance of the changing conditions in the world**

REVIEW

Linguistic, Logical-Mathematical. Have students complete the Section Review questions. Then ask each student to prepare a memorandum from Secretary of State Henry Kissinger to President Nixon. The memo should summarize key international developments discussed in this section, explain their impact on Americans, and advise the president to continue realpolitik in U.S. foreign policy.

ASSESS

Have students complete Daily Quiz 22.1.

RETEACH

Linguistic, Interpersonal. Have students complete Main Idea Activities for Reteaching and Sheltered English 22.1. Then ask students to pair terms from the Identify portion of the Section Review and write historically accurate sentences linking the terms in each pair. Students may use terms more than once. Call on volunteers to read their sentences to the class, but tell students to replace each term with the word *blank*. Then ask other students to identify the correct terms. Review any concepts that students are having difficulty understanding. **SHELTERED ENGLISH**

today. . . . If pragmatism [practicality] is indeed to be the byword [guiding principle] for U.S. policy, then all the better for the American people.”

Henry Kissinger (center) played a key role in U.S. negotiations with foreign governments.

Negotiating with the Soviet Union

The Soviets wanted to prevent the United States from allying with China. This concern encouraged them to negotiate with U.S. officials. In May 1972 Nixon became the first U.S. president to visit Moscow. He met with Soviet leader Leonid Brezhnev (BREZH-nef). The two leaders focused their talks on the nuclear arms race. The nuclear buildup was costing both nations billions of dollars. The risk of nuclear war also worried many observers.

To slow the arms buildup, the two leaders signed the **Strategic Arms Limitation Talks** (SALT) treaty. The treaty limited the numbers and types of long-range nuclear missiles each country could have. The SALT treaty began a period of **détente** (day-TAHNT), or an easing of tensions, between the United States and the Soviet Union. U.S. and Soviet officials continued to meet for diplomatic talks.

Détente also improved U.S.-Soviet economic relations. Trade between the United States and the Soviet Union tripled in 1972. The Soviets bought millions of tons of grain from American farmers. Many Americans were pleased that realpolitik had opened up new markets in the Soviet Union. Business leaders hoped this market expansion would improve the U.S. economy.

SECTION 1 REVIEW

Identify and explain the significance of the following:

- **Silent Majority**
- **southern strategy**
- **stagflation**
- **New Federalism**
- **Organization of Petroleum Exporting Countries**
- **energy crisis**
- **Henry Kissinger**
- **realpolitik**
- **Leonid Brezhnev**
- **Strategic Arms Limitation Talks**
- **détente**

Locate and explain the importance of the following:

- **Egypt**
- **Israel**
- **Syria**

Reading for Content Understanding

1. **Main Idea** How did President Nixon appeal to the Silent Majority?
2. **Main Idea** How did stagflation and the energy crisis affect Americans?
3. **Global Relations** What effect did realpolitik have on U.S. foreign relations?
4. **Writing** *Informing* Imagine that you work in Nixon's public affairs office. Write a brief brochure on his plans to ease the energy crisis.
5. **Critical Thinking** *Drawing Conclusions* Why do you think some people supported détente with China and the Soviet Union?

Section 1 Review ANSWERS

Identify

For significance, see the following pages:

- Silent Majority, p. 656
- southern strategy, p. 656
- stagflation, p. 656
- New Federalism, p. 656
- Organization of Petroleum Exporting Countries, p. 657
- energy crisis, p. 657
- Henry Kissinger, p. 658
- realpolitik, p. 658
- Leonid Brezhnev, p. 659
- Strategic Arms Limitation Talks p. 659
- détente, p. 659

Locate

For locations, see the map on page 657.

Reading for Content Understanding

1. Nixon proposed the New Federalism policy, under which the states received federal money through grants; pushed for "law and order"; opposed new civil rights legislation; and appointed conservative justices to the Supreme Court.

2. Stagflation and the energy crisis led to a rise in unemployment and inflation, energy conservation and research, and a decrease in Americans' confidence in the future.

3. It led to increased cooperation with China and the Soviet Union and to policies to protect U.S. interests abroad.

4. Brochures will vary but should mention efforts to conserve energy and to explore alternative energy sources.

5. Answers will vary but students might mention that many Americans thought détente would lessen the threat of war, slow the arms race, and improve the U.S. economy.

OBJECTIVES

- Explain how the events of Watergate led to President Nixon's resignation.
- Identify constitutional issues addressed during the Watergate scandal.
- Describe the challenges President Ford faced while in office.

FOCUS

Motivate Before Reading

Review with students the U.S. constitutional procedure for impeachment and the removal of the president from office (see the chart on textbook page 662). Make certain students understand the difference between impeachment and conviction. Explain to students that in this section they will learn about the Watergate scandal, President Nixon's involvement, and the results of these events.

Section 2 RESOURCES

PRINT

- ★ Guided Reading Strategies 22.2
- ★ American History Political Cartoon 29: Watergate
- ★ Section 2 Review, p. 665
- ★ Daily Quiz 22.2

MULTIMEDIA

- ★ *Teaching Resources CD–ROM,* Lesson 22.2
- ★ *Exploring America's Past* Video Segment: The Dark Side of Politics; *Teacher's Guide,* pp. 40–42
- ★ HRW Web site

SHELTERED ENGLISH

- ★ Main Idea Activities for Reteaching and Sheltered English 22.2

Watergate and Beyond

Reading Focus

How did the events of Watergate lead to President Nixon's resignation?

What constitutional issues were addressed during the Watergate scandal?

What challenges did President Ford face while in office?

Key Terms

Watergate
executive privilege
Saturday Night Massacre
trade deficit

AROUND 2:00 A.M. ON JUNE 17, 1972, a security guard at the Watergate apartment and office complex in Washington, D.C., conducted a routine inspection. At first, everything seemed quiet. Then he discovered that the doors to the Democratic National Committee headquarters were open. He called the police, who soon arrested five men. These were no ordinary burglars—they carried camera equipment, big rolls of cash, and secret electronic recording devices. Bob Woodward, a reporter for the Washington Post, *was convinced there was more to the story than simple burglary.*

Reporters Bob Woodward (top) and Carl Bernstein (bottom)

The Beginning of a Scandal

The police discovered that some of the Watergate burglars had ties to President Richard Nixon's administration. One worked for the Committee to Re-elect the President (CRP). Other people associated with the crime had been White House aides. The incident developed into **Watergate**, a political scandal named after the burglarized building.

President Nixon quickly denied that anyone in his administration was involved. The story had little effect on the presidential election of 1972. Nixon won in a landslide over the Democratic challenger, Senator George McGovern of South Dakota. However, Bob Woodward and Carl Bernstein, two reporters for the *Washington Post,* continued to investigate the break-in.

At first, all the key figures refused to talk. Then a secret White House informant contacted Woodward. This source, whom Woodward called Deep Throat, gave the reporter valuable inside information about Watergate. Like secret agents in a spy movie, the two men met in quiet places such as dark parking garages.

Students also will learn about the presidency of Gerald Ford and how he dealt with the economy and foreign policy.

Introduce Key Terms

Linguistic. Review this section's key terms with students. Have them use context cues in the section to define the terms. Call on volunteers to read just their definitions to the class. Then ask other students to identify the term described by each definition. Finally, have students write the definitions in their notebooks.
SHELTERED ENGLISH

TEACH

Have students read Section 2 and complete Guided Reading Strategies 22.2. Choose one or more of the following activities to explore the section content with students. For further suggestions on block scheduling or team teaching, see the *Block Scheduling Handbook.*

LEVEL 1: Linguistic. (Suggested time: 15 min.) As a class, go over students' Guided Reading Strategies. Then use the Reading Focus questions to highlight the main ideas of the section.
SHELTERED ENGLISH

Deep Throat's information led Woodward and Bernstein to a startling discovery. The CRP had used "dirty tricks" to help Nixon and other Republicans win the election. The CRP had hidden illegal campaign contributions and spread false rumors concerning Democratic candidates. The reporters began publishing articles about the CRP's activities in the *Washington Post.*

Nixon adviser John Ehrlichman testifying before the Senate

Evidence also began to build of a Watergate cover-up. Convicted Watergate burglar James McCord spoke out in January 1973. He claimed that he had been pressured to plead guilty and keep silent. In addition, McCord stated that there had been more people involved in the break-in than just the five who had been arrested.

The Investigation

Many members of Congress believed James McCord's claim of a Watergate cover-up. Some people even suspected that President Nixon was involved in the Watergate scandal. In the summer of 1973 the Senate launched its own investigation of the Watergate break-in.

The Senate Hearings

Nixon tried to shift blame to others in his administration. He forced H. R. Haldeman, his chief of staff, and John Ehrlichman, a chief adviser, to resign. He also fired White House attorney John Dean. Nixon agreed to Senate demands to appoint an independent special prosecutor to investigate the Watergate scandal. Attorney General Elliot Richardson chose Harvard law professor Archibald Cox. Professor Cox had a reputation for honesty and legal skill. The Senate approved Cox's appointment.

Senator Sam Ervin of North Carolina led the Senate Select Committee that investigated Watergate. Millions of Americans watched the Senate hearings on television. Accusations against the president and his closest advisers soon unfolded. The most damaging witness was former White House attorney John Dean. In his testimony Dean claimed that Nixon was directly involved in the cover-up. Dean also said that he had warned Nixon that the cover-up was "a cancer eating away at his presidency." As the investigations continued, a newspaper columnist wrote that Watergate was "a political bomb that could blow the Nixon administration apart."

Dean had no proof of his claims. However, another witness revealed that Nixon had recorded most of the conversations in his office. When the Senate committee asked Nixon to turn over the tapes, he refused. Nixon based his refusal on **executive privilege**, the president's right to keep information secret to protect national security.

The Battle over the Tapes

The tapes were the key to determining the truth of Dean's claims. Special Prosecutor Cox asked for a court order to get them. President Nixon and his attorneys believed that Cox's demand violated the special rights of the office of the president. Cox responded, "There is no exception for the President. . . . Even the highest executive officials are subject to the rule of law." The federal judge presiding over the case ordered Nixon to hand over the tapes.

The Senate hearings on the Watergate break-in were filled with reporters and cameras.

Historical Sidelight

Woodward's Source. For years after the Watergate scandal, Americans wondered about the identity of Deep Throat, Bob Woodward's secret informer. Some observers argued that the informer was Nixon's chief of staff, Alexander Haig. Others contended that the individual was Leonard Garment, Nixon's counsel—a claim Garment later denied. Some people even suggested that First Lady Pat Nixon was Deep Throat. Still others asserted that Deep Throat did not even exist. They claimed Woodward had several informers and that the character was a composite. Despite the public's interest, Woodward has refused to reveal the identity of Deep Throat.

Activity: Have students use the library or search the Internet through the HRW Web site to find information on the Watergate scandal. Have them write a paragraph on whether they think Deep Throat was one individual or a fictional character based on many informants.

go.hrw.com
SB1 Watergate

ALL LEVELS: Linguistic, Logical-Mathematical, Visual-Spatial. (Suggested time: 45 min. plus homework) Have students create a flowchart of the Watergate scandal, from the burglary through Nixon's resignation. Tell students to focus on key events and turning points. For homework, have each student draw a political cartoon summarizing how the events of Watergate led to Nixon's resignation. In class, call on volunteers to explain their flowcharts and cartoons. **SHELTERED ENGLISH**

LEVEL 2: Linguistic, Logical-Mathematical. (Suggested time: 30 min. plus homework) Ask students to imagine that they are members of the House Judiciary Committee examining Watergate. Tell them to use the U.S. Constitution in Chapter 2 of the textbook to determine the constitutional issues that the Watergate scandal addressed. Have students identify portions of the Constitution that apply. Then have each student write a short report to the committee on whether Nixon should be impeached; why or why not; and, if so, on what grounds. Call on volunteers to read their reports and encourage other students to discuss them.

LEVEL 2: Linguistic, Logical-Mathematical. (Suggested time: 30 min.) Have each student write a letter to President Ford advising him on whether to pardon Richard Nixon. The letter also should suggest how that course of action would likely affect Ford's presidency. Students should consider public opinion and pressing domestic and foreign issues, as well as the general mood of the

Linking Past to Present

The Nixon Tapes. Less than 40 hours of White House audiotapes were publicly released in 1974. In the years after Nixon's resignation, many historians and the public hoped to hear more of the remaining 3,700 hours of taped conversations. However, the former president did not want the tapes released. After five years of litigation that ended two years after Nixon died, the National Archives agreed to begin releasing some of the tapes. In November 1996 the first 201 hours of tapes were released.

Critical Thinking: Why would historians want to hear the unreleased White House tapes?

ANSWER: They might contain useful information about the Watergate scandal and other events that occurred during Nixon's presidency.

Nixon asked if he could provide summaries of the tapes rather than the originals. Cox refused. On Saturday evening, October 20, 1973, Nixon instructed Attorney General Richardson to fire the special prosecutor. Nixon claimed that Cox had to be replaced to protect the national interest. Richardson replied, "Mr. President, it would appear that we have a different assessment [view] of the national interest." He resigned rather than fire Cox. So did the next-highest officer in the Justice Department.

As the Watergate investigations continued, Nixon claimed that his opponents were plotting against him.

Nixon then named Robert H. Bork acting attorney general. Bork fired Cox. One senator called the firing "a reckless act of desperation." The resignations and firing became known as the **Saturday Night Massacre**. Nixon's approval rating dropped to 22 percent in some polls. Many government officials began discussing the possibility of impeaching the president.

Nixon's troubles were made worse by a scandal involving Vice President Spiro Agnew. Agnew faced charges that he had failed to pay his taxes and that he had taken bribes as a public official. He resigned just a few days before the Saturday Night Massacre, receiving a fine and probation. His resignation led *Time* magazine to declare that the White House was filled with "an atmosphere of immorality [corruption]." Nixon selected Michigan representative and House minority leader Gerald Ford as his new vice president.

The Impeachment Process

Grounds	Officials establish grounds for impeachment, which could include treason, bribery, and other offenses.
Phase 1	The House of Representatives announces articles of impeachment, thus formally accusing an official.
Phase 2	The Senate holds a trial for the accused, with a two-thirds vote needed for a conviction.
Penalty	A convicted official is removed from his or her post and cannot hold any public office in the future.

The Granger Collection, New York

Nixon's Resignation

Following the Saturday Night Massacre, some members of Congress began the formal process of requesting President Nixon's impeachment. The president then handed over a few of the tapes. He provided a heavily edited transcript of the rest. Investigators found that a large portion of one of the tapes had been erased.

The new special prosecutor, Leon Jaworski, demanded the release of all the tapes. In July 1974 the U.S. Supreme Court ordered the president to turn over the complete set. This time Nixon obeyed the court order. Conversations on the tapes proved that Nixon had ordered the Watergate cover-up. The president had also lied to Congress and the American people about his involvement.

The truth shocked many Americans who had until then believed the president. The evidence on the tapes moved Congress to act. The House nation. Call on volunteers to read their letters. Encourage students to provide feedback. Then lead a discussion on the challenges President Ford faced while in office.

LEVEL 3: Linguistic, Logical-Mathematical, Interpersonal. (Suggested time: 30 min. plus homework) Organize a debate on the impact of Watergate. Have students debate whether, as a result of the scandal, Americans justifiably can "assume that politicians are without honor," as Adrienne Rich believed, or conclude that "Watergate . . . proved our Constitution works," as Senator Sam Ervin stated. At the conclusion of the debate, have each student write an essay analyzing the effects of Watergate on Americans.

TEACHER TO TEACHER

CLOSE

Linguistic, Logical-Mathematical. James Pyne of Flossmoor, Illinois, suggested the following activity: Remind students of the principle derived from Magna Carta that no one, not even a king, is above the law. Review Nixon's actions during the Watergate scandal. Ask students to list any instances in which his actions may have contradicted this principle. Have volunteers share their answers with the class.

Judiciary Committee soon made a bipartisan recommendation. It asked the full House of Representatives to vote to impeach the president on three articles. The committee accused Nixon of abusing his authority, obstructing justice, and "violating the constitutional rights of citizens."

Texas congresswoman Barbara Jordan was a committee member. Like others, she believed that Nixon had violated his oath to uphold the nation's laws. She explained why she favored Nixon's impeachment:

> **"My faith in the Constitution is whole, it is complete, it is total, and I am not going to sit here and be an idle spectator to the . . . destruction of the Constitution."**

After resigning and making a farewell speech, Richard Nixon left the White House.

After the release of the tapes, there was little support for Nixon in Congress. If the House voted to impeach him, it was very possible that the Senate would then find him guilty. Yet Nixon refused to believe that he would be impeached. It was not until former supporters began asking for his resignation that he realized he was defeated.

In a televised announcement on August 8, 1974, Nixon became the first U.S. president to resign from office. In a shaky voice, he admitted only to "a few mistakes in judgment." The next day, Vice President Gerald Ford was sworn in as president. He was the first person to become president without being elected as either vice president or president.

The Watergate scandal damaged many Americans' faith in the government. "We [now] assume that politicians are without honor," wrote poet and journalist Adrienne Rich. Others, however, disagreed. They viewed the hearings and Nixon's resignation as evidence that the U.S. government had successfully fought against corruption. Senator Sam Ervin later wrote:

> **"Watergate . . . proved our Constitution works. That instrument commands the President to 'take care that the laws be faithfully executed.' When President Nixon was untrue to his constitutional obligation, Congress and the federal judiciary remained true to theirs. As a consequence, the United States weathered a great national crisis without turmoil [disturbance] and with all its institutions intact."**

The Ford Presidency

President Gerald Ford had established a reputation in Congress for honesty and cooperation. Many Americans hoped that Ford would restore confidence in the government.

The Pardons

Ford referred to Watergate as a "long national nightmare," which he declared was over. He granted a pardon to Richard Nixon soon after taking office. This pardon meant that Nixon would never face trial for any illegal activities committed during his presidency.

Many Americans received the news of the pardon with relief. They believed the pardon was a way to finally move beyond the Watergate scandal. Others, however, questioned why Nixon was allowed to escape punishment. Other Watergate figures had gone to jail. Ford's approval rating dropped from more than 70 to less than 50 percent.

Constitutional Heritage

Presidential Pardons. Article II of the U.S. Constitution gives the nation's president almost unlimited power to grant reprieves and pardons. This power has its origin in the right of English monarchs to grant pardons and has been used throughout U.S. history. George Washington granted a pardon to people who had participated in the Whiskey Rebellion. After the Civil War, some 200,000 former Confederate soldiers were granted amnesty. In 1946, following World War II, President Harry Truman granted pardons to more than 1,500 people in prison for having avoided the draft.

Critical Thinking: Why might presidents grant pardons to large groups after wars have ended?

ANSWER: perhaps to begin healing the country's wounds from the war

Multimedia Resources

Exploring America's Past Video Segment: The Dark Side of Politics; *Teacher's Guide,* pp. 40–42

Search 21301, Play to 26623
Videodisc Blue Side B

Play

Pause

See *Teacher's Guide* for Spanish barcode.

CHALLENGE AND EXTEND

1. Linguistic, Visual-Spatial, Interpersonal. Organize the class into three groups. Have the first group investigate the concept of executive privilege and review the Supreme Court's decision in *United States* v. *Nixon*. Ask the second group to look at the origins and meaning of the phrase "high crimes and misdemeanors" and judge whether Nixon's conduct falls under the standard definition. Have the third group research the restrictions on the U.S. president's power to grant pardons and decide whether President Ford should have pardoned Nixon. Have each group prepare a presentation of its findings.

2. Logical-Mathematical, Visual-Spatial. Remind students that one of the economic difficulties Gerald Ford had to deal with during his presidency was the growing U.S. trade deficit. Ask students to choose one of the nations that served as a major trading partner with the United States during the mid-1970s. *(A list may include France, Great Britain, Italy, and Japan.)* Have students research the annual amounts of imports and exports between the United States and that country from 1970 to 1980, and for the most recent year for which data are available. Ask students to create a balance sheet showing their findings. Tell students to list annual U.S. trade deficits in red.

Global Relations

Ford and Vietnam. In April 1975 President Ford ordered the evacuation of U.S. personnel as North Vietnamese forces approached Saigon. Some 6,000 Americans and South Vietnamese fled by climbing up a 16-foot ladder to the roof of the U.S. Embassy, where rescue helicopters picked them up. After Saigon's fall, some 130,000 other Vietnamese left and came to America. Ford requested $400 million to help these refugees resettle in the United States. He faced stiff opposition from some members of Congress, but prevailed. By late 1975 all the Vietnamese in U.S. refugee camps had been released to begin their new lives in the United States. When the U.S. Embassy in Vietnam was torn down in 1998, the ladder used in the evacuation was placed in the Gerald R. Ford Presidential Library.

Critical Thinking: Why might some Congress-members have objected to funding the resettlement of Vietnamese refugees in the United States?

ANSWER: Answers will vary but students might mention that some members of Congress may have thought the U.S. government already had spent too much money on the war and that the refugees, many of whom were poor, would be a drain on U.S. social programs.

Ford also offered a conditional pardon to young men who had illegally avoided the draft during the Vietnam War. Under Ford's plan, these people could avoid criminal charges by performing community service. Many veterans argued that the plan was too easy on those who had avoided military service. Antiwar activists thought it punished them unfairly for doing what they believed was morally right.

Ford faced another controversy in the mid-1970s. Congressional investigations revealed that both the CIA and the FBI had abused their power. The FBI, for example, had spied on radical groups without proper cause. Ford tried to reorganize and reform the agencies. He hoped these efforts would further restore Americans' faith in government.

The Economy

Within months of taking office, Ford admitted that the nation's economy was nearing the point of recession. Business had slowed because of high oil prices and continuing stagflation. The United States also had a growing **trade deficit**—a trade imbalance that occurs when a nation imports more goods than it exports. Japan and Western European nations were selling large amounts of manufactured products to the United States. These products included automobiles and electronics. For example, many American automakers struggled to compete with popular new import cars such as the Volkswagen Beetle. The trade deficit made inflation and unemployment even worse.

President Gerald Ford and First Lady Betty Ford

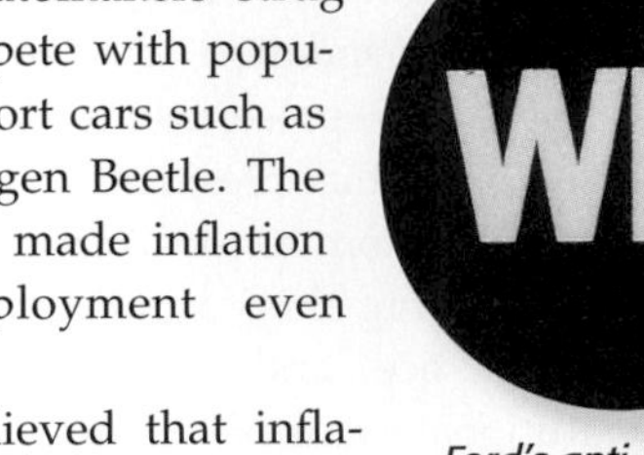

Ford's anti-inflation campaign was unsuccessful.

Ford believed that inflation was "public enemy Number 1." If the United States could control inflation, it could reduce prices for its products. Lower prices would make it easier for American companies to compete against inexpensive foreign imports. Reduced prices would also make American exports more affordable overseas. In addition, American consumers would benefit from lowered prices. Ford hoped that all these factors would combine to improve the economy.

To fight inflation, Ford launched a campaign called Whip Inflation Now (WIN). He asked Americans to save their money and businesses to voluntarily keep wages and prices down to reduce inflation. With no way to enforce these requests, however, the WIN campaign had little effect.

Ford also wanted to reduce government spending to reduce inflation. However, the Democrat-controlled Congress wanted to increase spending to help the poor and unemployed. As a result of this disagreement, little legislation was approved. Ford vetoed more than 30 Democrat-sponsored spending bills during his first year in office. It was not until 1975, when unemployment topped 9 percent, that the president and Congress finally compromised. They agreed to expand unemployment benefits and to cut some taxes. The economy recovered slightly. However, inflation and unemployment remained high, and the national deficit increased.

Ford's Foreign Policy

In foreign affairs, President Ford tried to continue Nixon's policy of détente. He achieved some success when he and Soviet leader Brezhnev agreed to limit underground nuclear testing. The two leaders also discussed a second SALT treaty to further limit nuclear arms.

REVIEW

Linguistic, Logical-Mathematical. Have students complete the Section Review questions. Ask students to write a summary of this section and leave blanks for several of the key names, terms, and events. Have students exchange summaries, fill in the blanks, and return them to their authors for grading.

ASSESS

Have students complete Daily Quiz 22.2.

RETEACH

Linguistic, Interpersonal. Have students complete Main Idea Activities for Reteaching and Sheltered English 22.2. Assign each student one of the five subsections in this section. Ask students to select a major issue from their assigned subsection and prepare a set of clues that, when taken together, describe the issue. When students are done, ask each one to present his or her clues and have the other students try to identify the issue. Review any concepts that students still are having difficulty understanding.
SHELTERED ENGLISH

There were also some gestures of friendship between the United States and the Soviet Union. One of the most dramatic events took place in outer space. In July 1975 the U.S. *Apollo 18* spacecraft linked up with the Soviet *Soyuz 19* spacecraft in orbit around Earth. The U.S. astronauts and Soviet cosmonauts then performed a series of joint experiments. The effort showed the benefits of international cooperation.

An artist's drawing of the historic meeting of the U.S. Apollo 18 *(left) and the Soviet* Soyuz 19 *spacecraft (right)*

Despite such events, détente was increasingly unpopular with conservative politicians. Critics of détente had several concerns. They worried that other NATO members might disapprove of U.S. cooperation with the Soviet Union. If NATO nations did not trust the United States as an ally, U.S. foreign policy in Western Europe would be damaged. Some conservatives also believed that the Soviet Union might interpret détente as a sign of American weakness.

President Ford shared these concerns. In the spring of 1975, communist Cambodians captured the American cargo ship *Mayaguez*. Ford was determined to show that the United States would not be bullied. He authorized a military operation to rescue the 40 crew members. The rescue attempt failed, resulting in the deaths of 41 U.S. Marines. It was later discovered that the hostages had already been released. Some observers charged that Ford had acted too hastily. His supporters, however, called the rescue attempt "a daring show of nerve and steel."

Support for détente decreased even further. Conservatives in Congress took a firm position against communism and opposed future compromises with the Soviet Union. The Soviets also became less cooperative. Further SALT discussions stalled, and Congress blocked several proposed economic agreements. By 1976 little remained of the cooperation between the Soviet Union and the United States.

SECTION 2 REVIEW

Identify and explain the significance of the following:

- **Richard Nixon**
- **Watergate**
- **Bob Woodward and Carl Bernstein**
- **executive privilege**
- **Saturday Night Massacre**
- **Gerald Ford**
- **Barbara Jordan**
- **trade deficit**

Reading for Content Understanding

1. **Main Idea** Create a time line describing the events of Watergate up to President Nixon's resignation.

2. **Main Idea** How did President Ford address domestic and foreign challenges?

3. **Constitutional Heritage** Why did Barbara Jordan and many other Americans believe that President Nixon deserved to be impeached?

4. **Writing** *Expressing* Imagine that it is 1974 and President Ford has just granted Nixon a full pardon. Write a letter to a friend explaining why you do or do not agree with Ford's action.

5. **Critical Thinking** *Supporting a Point of View* Do you agree or disagree with the House Judiciary Committee's conclusion that Nixon's role in Watergate was a serious violation of the Constitution? Explain your answer.

Section 2 Review ANSWERS

Identify

For significance, see the following pages:

- Richard Nixon, p. 660
- Watergate, p. 660
- Bob Woodward and Carl Bernstein, p. 660
- executive privilege, p. 661
- Saturday Night Massacre, p. 662
- Gerald Ford, p. 662
- Barbara Jordan, p. 663
- trade deficit, p. 664

Reading for Content Understanding

1. Time lines will vary but should include the Watergate break-in, Bob Woodward and Carl Bernstein's investigation, the Senate hearings, the Saturday Night Massacre, and the Supreme Court's ruling regarding the handing over of the White House tapes.

2. domestic—pardoned Nixon and Vietnam draft dodgers, reorganized and reformed the CIA and FBI, promoted WIN campaign to lower inflation and boost economy; foreign—tried to continue policy of détente with Soviet Union, took action to show U.S. strength to Communists

3. They argued that he had broken the law. Therefore, he should face the consequences of his actions.

4. Letters will vary but should reflect an understanding of Nixon's alleged criminal actions and the reason President Ford pardoned Nixon.

5. Answers will vary but students should state their opinions regarding Nixon's role in Watergate and use examples to explain their reasoning.

SECTION 3 LESSON PLAN

OBJECTIVES

- **Explain how President Carter differed from other politicians and why he lost public support.**
- **Evaluate how Carter handled economic problems during his presidency.**
- **Describe Carter's approach to foreign policy.**

FOCUS

Motivate Before Reading

Review with students the meaning of the word *boycott.* Then ask them to identify reasons why governments and groups might use boycotts. Tell students that in this section they will learn about Jimmy Carter's presidency, his handling of domestic issues, ways that he rejected Nixon and Kissinger's realpolitik in his handling of

Section 3
RESOURCES

PRINT

★ Guided Reading Strategies 22.3

★ Geography Activity 22: Southern Africa in the 1970s

★ Graphic Organizer 22: Foreign Events Affecting Domestic Events

★ Section 3 Review, p. 671

★ Daily Quiz 22.3

MULTIMEDIA

★ *Teaching Resources CD–ROM,* Lesson 22.3

★ HRW Web site

SHELTERED ENGLISH

★ Main Idea Activities for Reteaching and Sheltered English 22.3

The Carter Administration

Reading Focus

How did President Carter differ from other politicians, and why did he lose public support?

How did Carter handle economic problems during his presidency?

What was Carter's approach to foreign policy?

Key Terms

Panama Canal treaties
Camp David Accords
apartheid
sanctions
Iran hostage crisis

THE MORNING OF JULY 4, 1976, dawned clear and cool over New York Harbor. A steady wind filled the sails of 225 tall ships as they silently made their way past the Statue of Liberty. For a few days most Americans set aside their worries about the economy and foreign policy to celebrate the country's bicentennial, or 200th birthday. Citizens across the country gathered to ring in the event and honor the nation. One person declared that the bicentennial had "become a way of clearing the American soul in a very positive way."

The bicentennial celebration in New York Harbor

The Election of 1976

Democratic Party leaders hoped that the bicentennial would also mark a Democratic presidential victory. Democrats thought they had a good chance to win the White House in 1976. Many Americans associated the Republicans with the Watergate scandal. In addition, a large number of voters were disappointed with President Gerald Ford's handling of economic and diplomatic issues. Other Americans were upset that he had pardoned former president Nixon.

Despite these challenges, Ford won a tough battle for the Republican presidential nomination. He defeated former California governor Ronald Reagan. Ford chose Kansas senator Bob Dole as his running mate. The Democrats wanted a candidate free from political scandals. At first there was no clear front-runner. During the primaries, however, an unexpected candidate emerged. This individual was Jimmy Carter, a little-known former governor of Georgia.

The two most important factors in Carter's life were his family and his religion. These personal foreign-policy issues, and why he decided to have the United States boycott the 1980 Summer Olympics in Moscow.

Introduce Key Terms

Linguistic, Logical-Mathematical. Review this section's key terms with students. Have students use context cues to define each term. Then ask students to determine a common theme that links the terms. Make a list of the replies and let the class decide which one is the clearest and the most inclusive.
SHELTERED ENGLISH

TEACH

Have students read Section 3 and complete Guided Reading Strategies 22.3. Choose one or more of the following activities to explore the section content with students. For further suggestions on block scheduling or team teaching, see the *Block Scheduling Handbook.*

LEVEL 1: Linguistic. (Suggested time: 15 min.) As a class, go over students' Guided Reading Strategies. Then use the Reading Focus questions to highlight the main ideas of the section.
SHELTERED ENGLISH

Jimmy Carter

James Earl Carter Jr. was born in Plains, Georgia, in 1924. Carter attended the U.S. Naval Academy. After graduation he served as an engineer in the nuclear submarine program. He planned to make the navy his career. After his father died, however, he returned to Georgia to help his family rebuild their peanut warehouse. He became active in local politics, serving on the local school board and later in the state senate. In 1970 he was elected governor of Georgia.

When he began campaigning in January 1975, few politicians thought that Carter could win the Democratic nomination for the presidency. He stunned political pollsters by winning the New Hampshire primary. By the time of the Democratic National Convention in New York City, he had won 18 state primary elections. Convention delegates nominated him for president.

values strongly shaped Carter's political career. His mother, "Miss Lillian," had taught him the value of community service. She told him that "sharing yourself with others . . . is the most precious gift of all." Carter's religious faith played a key role in his political beliefs. He thought that political decisions should be based on moral ideals such as equality and justice.

Carter's campaign focused more on his personal character than on his political platform. His background and his open, straightforward approach impressed many people. "I will never lie to you," he told voters. He promised a "new era of honest, compassionate, responsive government." His words struck a deep chord with Americans still troubled by the Watergate incident. Carter won a narrow victory over Ford in the November 1976 election. Carter's overwhelming support among African American and Hispanic voters helped secure his victory.

As president, Carter wanted to show a new spirit of openness and modesty in the White House. On Inauguration Day, he and his family walked down Pennsylvania Avenue instead of riding in a limousine. Carter also tried to make the presidency more personal. He had few politicians from Washington in his cabinet. He also reduced the size of the presidential staff. Early in his administration, the public seemed to approve of Carter's approach.

Jimmy Carter chose to walk to his inauguration to show that he would be accessible to the American public.

Domestic Challenges

President Carter faced two major domestic problems—the economy and the energy crisis. The economy was still sluggish. Carter proposed a tax cut and increases in government spending. He also tried to get management and organized labor to cooperate. Carter hoped they would hold down prices and wages. His efforts met with little

Presidential Profiles

Jimmy Carter. After graduating from the U.S. Naval Academy, Jimmy Carter served as an instructor and engineer on the nuclear submarine *Sea Wolf.* When his father died in 1953, he left the navy to take over the family peanut business. He expanded operations and became quite wealthy. Entering politics, he ran for the Georgia Senate in 1962. He won and was re-elected in 1964. After an unsuccessful bid for the governorship of Georgia in 1966, Carter was elected to the office in 1970. Because Georgia law did not let individuals hold the office for two consecutive terms, he could not seek re-election. Only one month after he left the governorship, Carter announced his intention to run for president.

Activity: Have students use the library or search the Internet through the HRW Web site to find information on the life of Jimmy Carter. Ask each student to write a short biography based on their research.

go.hrw.com
SB1 Carter

ALL LEVELS: Logical-Mathematical, Musical-Rhythmic, Visual-Spatial. (Suggested time: 30 min.) Have each student create a campaign bumper sticker and slogan that explains how President Carter differed from other politicians. Then have students create a political cartoon or song that explains why he lost public support. Call on volunteers to explain or perform their work. Ask other students to comment on the accuracy and effectiveness of each piece. **SHELTERED ENGLISH**

LEVEL 2: Linguistic, Logical-Mathematical, Visual-Spatial. (Suggested time: 45 min.) Have each student make a cause-and-effect graphic organizer showing how emphasis on human rights affected U.S. foreign policy in Latin America, the Middle East, South Africa, and the Soviet Union during the Carter administration. Organizers should illustrate specific policy issues, their causes, and their consequences. Call on volunteers to explain their organizers to the class. Encourage feedback.

LEVEL 2: Logical-Mathematical, Visual-Spatial, Interpersonal. (Suggested time: 30 min.) Ask students to create a report card for Carter's handling of domestic issues, particularly economic problems, during his presidency. Students should list each domestic challenge, describe how Carter addressed it, explain the results, and then grade Carter's performance. In addition, have

Citizenship and Democracy

Saving Energy. When Jimmy Carter became president, the United States was importing about half of its oil. Cold weather during the early months of 1977 caused energy shortages that led to the closing of schools and factories. As a result, Carter declared 11 states disaster areas. He recognized that U.S. dependence on foreign oil was a serious problem. His National Energy Plan proposed several measures to force Americans to limit energy consumption. The bill included higher taxes on cars with poor gas mileage, an extra gas tax whenever American consumption reached a certain level, and tax breaks for groups that conserved energy.

Critical Thinking: How did Carter hope to end U.S. overdependence on foreign oil?

ANSWER: He hoped that by making energy consumption more expensive, Americans would start conserving.

LINKING PAST TO PRESENT ANSWERS

1. They began making smaller, more fuel-efficient cars.
2. electric, electric-gas "hybrid," and hydrogen cars that use less fuel and create less pollution

Linking Past to Present

The Changing Automobile

The energy crisis of the 1970s led car companies to make smaller, more fuel-efficient cars. Since then, however, the price of oil has generally dropped. Americans have bought record numbers of large vehicles. Big trucks, sport utility vehicles (SUVs), and vans are very popular, but not very fuel-efficient.

Automakers are also developing cars that use less fuel and cause less pollution. Some designs use alternative energy sources. These electric, electric-gas "hybrid," and hydrogen cars create less pollution than autos with conventional engines. However, early models of these new vehicles are also more expensive than traditional cars.

Electric cars run on powerful batteries instead of gasoline. They are quiet and produce no pollution. However, early electric cars could only travel about 100 miles before the batteries had to be recharged. Engineers have tried to increase this driving range. Hybrid cars combine electric batteries with small gasoline engines. This design extends battery life and provides high fuel efficiency. In the late 1990s, engineers developed hybrid cars capable of traveling up to 70 miles per gallon of gasoline. These early hybrid cars are quite small, however.

An advanced fuel-efficient concept car

Hydrogen-powered cars were still in the early design stages in the 1990s. These cars use devices called fuel cells to turn hydrogen and oxygen into electricity. Fuel cells that use pure hydrogen produce no pollution. The major drawbacks of these cars are that pure hydrogen is highly flammable and there are few places where it can be purchased.

Understanding What You Read

1. How did the energy crisis of the 1970s affect automobile manufacturers?
2. What are some of the new technologies being developed for cars?

success, however. Inflation soared again. It reached more than 13 percent in 1980.

The energy crisis continued to hurt the economy. Oil prices remained high, and the United States was still largely dependent on foreign oil. Nuclear energy was not a popular alternative. Many Americans began to fear nuclear power after an accident on Three Mile Island, Pennsylvania. In March 1979 a nuclear power plant's reactor core overheated, almost releasing deadly radiation into the air. The accident raised new questions about the safety of nuclear power.

Carter created a detailed energy policy and asked Americans to use less fuel. He also supported the development of alternative energy sources such as solar power. However, Carter had difficulty gaining public support for energy conservation.

As an inexperienced political "outsider," Carter also had trouble winning support in students give Carter an overall performance grade. Call on volunteers to share their work. Then have the class vote on an overall grade for Carter's handling of domestic challenges.

LEVEL 3: Linguistic, Logical-Mathematical, Kinesthetic. (Suggested time: 30 min. plus homework) Ask students to imagine that it is 1980 and they are running against Carter for president. Have them write a campaign speech evaluating Carter's performance in office, describing what they would do differently if elected, and explaining why voters should choose them over Carter. Students can choose to be either Democrats, Republicans, or independents. Call on volunteers to deliver their speeches to the class. Then have students vote for the candidate whose speech they like best.

CLOSE

Linguistic, Visual-Spatial, Interpersonal. Have each student prepare a sketch for a plaque to President Carter. The plaque should include a visual and an inscription that provides insight into Carter's presidency and its impact or legacy. Call on volunteers to explain their sketches and inscriptions to the class. Encourage students to provide feedback.

Congress. For example, Carter did not want Congress to make any changes to his complex energy proposal. As a result, only some of the plan was passed. One historian has said that Carter had a tendency

> **"to equate [make equal] his political goals with the just and the right, and to view his opponents as representative of some selfish or immoral [not moral] interest."**

Carter's inexperience and rigid approach hurt his effectiveness. Although his own party controlled Congress, few of his proposals were passed.

Carter's Foreign Policy

President Carter rejected the strategy of realpolitik. Instead, he used his own strict moral standards as guidelines for U.S. foreign policy. Carter declared that "fairness, not force, should lie at the heart of our dealings with the nations of the world." Carter condemned foreign governments that tortured or unlawfully jailed their citizens. He insisted that other governments protect citizens' human rights—the basic rights and freedoms owed to all human beings. Carter reduced U.S. aid to some former allies, such as Argentina and Ethiopia, for violations of these basic rights.

Latin America

President Carter soon applied his new foreign-policy approach to U.S. relations with Latin America. Many Latin Americans resented previous U.S. interference in their countries. In particular, they saw the Panama Canal, built and controlled by the United States, as a major symbol of U.S. influence in Latin America. In 1977 Carter signed the **Panama Canal treaties**, which would transfer control of the canal to Panama by the year 2000.

Many Americans opposed the treaties because of the canal's economic value. However, the Senate ratified them in 1978. Like Carter, the Senate hoped that the treaties would encourage friendship and cooperation between the United States and Latin America. U.S. leaders also thought that such treaties would reduce communist influence in Latin America. Panamanian leader Omar Torrijos Herrera assured a U.S. senator:

> **"I believe we have entered on an entirely new era, one in which our two countries are partners, are friends, [and] are going to work together."**

The Middle East

President Carter also became involved in Middle Eastern diplomacy. In September 1978 he brought Egyptian president Anwar Sadat and Israeli prime minister Menachem Begin (BAY-gin) together for peace talks. The leaders met at Camp David, the U.S. presidential retreat.

In two weeks of meetings they crafted a set of peace agreements known as the **Camp David Accords**. The accords marked the first time that an Arab nation had established peaceful relations with Israel. Afterward, Sadat announced: "The barrier of distrust that has been between us [Egypt and Israel] during the last 30 years has been broken down." Many historians consider the Camp David Accords to be President Carter's greatest achievement.

Anwar Sadat of Egypt (left) and Menachem Begin of Israel (right) signed the first peace treaty between Israel and an Arab nation.

Historical Sidelight

An Historic Peace. In June 1967 tensions between Israel and neighboring Arab countries led to the so-called Six-Day War. Israel won the war and captured Arab territory in the process. UN negotiations to return this territory yielded few results. In 1973 Egypt and Syria, which had both lost land in the 1967 war, launched a surprise attack on Israel. The Yom Kippur War (also known as the October or Ramadan War) resulted in little territorial change. Egyptian president Anwar Sadat then surprised the world in 1977 by asking to meet directly with Israel for peace talks. These talks led to the Camp David Accords and finally a peace treaty between Egypt and Israel in 1979. For their efforts, Sadat and Israeli prime minister Menachem Begin each received the Nobel Peace Prize in 1978.

Activity: Have students use the library or other resources to research other recipients of the Nobel Peace Prize. Have students write a report on one recipient and why he or she was awarded the international honor.

CHALLENGE AND EXTEND

1. **Linguistic, Logical-Mathematical, Visual-Spatial.** Have students prepare a voter profile of their community for the presidential elections of 1976 and 1980. Ask students to use the library and other resources to locate official vote totals by precinct. Students also should interview local residents on how they voted and why, and use this information to formulate conclusions about whether Carter's popularity rose or fell in their community between 1976 and 1980. Have students assemble their findings to create a segment of a local television show. Encourage students to include graphs and charts illustrating local voter behavior and attitudes.

2. **Linguistic, Visual-Spatial, Interpersonal.** Have students use the library and other available resources to prepare a multimedia exhibit on the Carter presidency for display at a local public library. Ask students to find images, quotations, video clips, and memorabilia to include in the exhibit. In addition, students should create descriptive labels for each item and prepare a banner and display booth for the exhibit. When students are through, have them set up the display.

Across the Curriculum

GEOGRAPHY

Iran. The location of Iran made it an area of critical concern for the United States during and after World War II. During the war, Iran provided an important route for sending supplies from the United States and other Allies to the Soviet Union. After the war, the United States feared an expanding Soviet influence in Iran. At the same time, the United States wanted to maintain its access to Iran's oil reserves. As a result, the U.S. government supplied economic and military aid to Iran from the 1950s until the late 1970s. The Islamic revolution in 1979, which led to the rise of Ayatollah Khomeini, ended all political ties between Iran and the United States.

Activity: Give each student an outline map of southwest Asia. Have them label the names of the countries on the map. Then have students discuss the importance of Iran's geographic location.

South Africa

In Africa, Carter tried to encourage respect for human rights and win allies. He provided economic assistance to developing nations, many of which had new governments. These countries were struggling to establish economic independence after years of colonial rule by European nations. At the same time, Carter tried to preserve U.S. trade interests in the region.

Carter's administration also addressed the issue of **apartheid**, the system of laws requiring racial segregation in South Africa. Andrew Young, the U.S. ambassador to the United Nations, was a strong critic of apartheid. Young supported **sanctions**, or economic penalties, to persuade South Africa to desegregate. The United States began applying sanctions against South Africa in 1985.

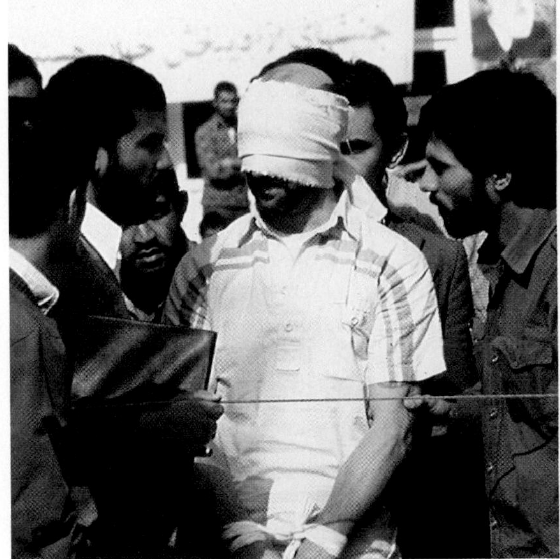

Iranian revolutionaries parade some of the U.S. hostages through the streets of Tehran.

The Soviet Union

U.S. relations with the Soviet Union grew worse during Carter's administration. Carter was very critical of the Soviet government's many human rights abuses. This criticism upset Soviet leaders. The situation became even more serious in 1979 when the Soviets invaded the central Asian country of Afghanistan. Carter reacted by postponing talks on SALT II—a new arms-control treaty. He also placed an embargo on U.S. grain shipments to the Soviet Union. Finally, Carter declared a U.S. boycott of the 1980 Summer Olympics in Moscow.

The Olympic boycott and the grain embargo upset many U.S. athletes and farmers. Some Americans believed that beating the Soviets in competition was a better way to show U.S. strength than the boycott. Other Americans were concerned about the economic impact of the grain embargo. "We think of ourselves as patriotic," said one Kansas farmer. "But we shouldn't have to go broke being patriotic."

The Iran Hostage Crisis

Another crisis soon drew Americans' attention. In the 1950s the United States had helped bring the shah of Iran, Mohammad Reza Pahlavi (RAY-zah pah-HLAHV-ee), to power. Over the next two decades, the shah had supported U.S. interests in the region. In the late 1970s, however, Islamic fundamentalists began to challenge the shah's power. They called for a strict return to Islamic teachings and an end to cooperation with the United States.

By February 1979, followers of religious leader Ayatollah Khomeini (eye-uh-TOH-luh koh-MAY-nee) had overthrown the shah. In his place they established a fundamentalist dictatorship. This new government was hostile to the United States. In October U.S. officials allowed the shah into the United States for medical treatment. In response, angry Iranian revolutionaries staged massive protests. They also attacked the U.S. Embassy in Tehran, the capital of Iran. On November 4 they seized 54 American hostages, whom they abused and tortured. One hostage was released, but the other 53 were still held captive.

The **Iran hostage crisis** dragged on for months. There was no solution in sight. The crisis horrified Americans. Many saw the hostage situation as evidence of America's declining strength. In April 1980 a rescue attempt by the U.S. military went terribly wrong. Confusion and mechanical problems caused several of the rescue helicopters to crash in the desert. The rescuers never reached Tehran. News of this failure decreased many

REVIEW

Linguistic, Logical-Mathematical. Have students complete the Section Review questions. Then ask students to write a letter to President Carter explaining whether they think his presidency was successful or unsuccessful. Call on volunteers to read their letters to the class.

ASSESS

Have students complete Daily Quiz 22.3.

RETEACH

Logical-Mathematical, Visual-Spatial, Interpersonal. Have students complete Main Idea Activities for Reteaching and Sheltered English 22.3. On each of three large pieces of butcher paper, write one of the Reading Focus questions. Then organize the class into three groups. Have each group draw visuals to answer its assigned question. Ask representatives to display and explain their group's work to the class. **SHELTERED ENGLISH**

Americans' confidence in Carter's ability to end the crisis. One American said bluntly:

> **"America today needs a tough-talking and tough-acting leader. America's strength was built on national pride and morale [positive feeling], and both of these have dropped under the weight of the defeat in Vietnam, the scandal of Watergate, and the catastrophic [disastrous] policies of Jimmy Carter."**

As the crisis continued, some of the hostages began to lose hope. One hostage later said, "I think there were times when all of us felt like we'd been left there and forgotten."

The Election of 1980

While President Carter prepared to run for re-election in 1980, his popularity was falling. Many people blamed him for the hostage crisis and the country's economic problems. He had also lost the support of many Democratic leaders in Congress. One southern Democratic senator said privately, "He hasn't a single friend up here [on Capitol Hill]."

Now it was the Republicans' turn to challenge an unpopular president. They chose Ronald Reagan, the former governor of California, to run against Carter. In his campaign ads, Reagan claimed that the country needed new leadership:

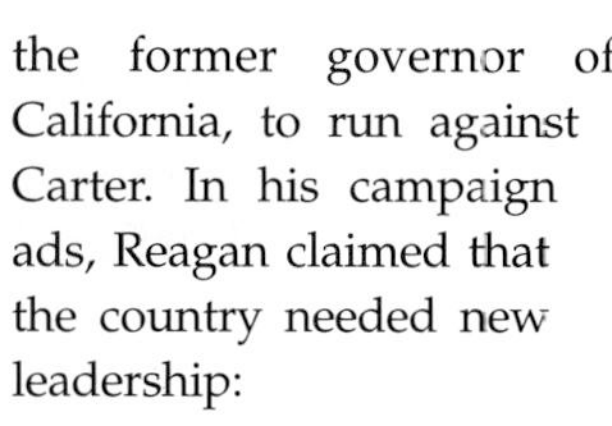

Carter was unable to generate wide-spread support in 1980.

> **"I will not stand by and watch this great country destroy itself under mediocre [average] leadership. . . . This is the greatest country in the world. We have the talent, we have the drive, we have the imagination. Now all we need is the leadership."**

When Reagan asked voters, "Are you better off than you were four years ago?" many of them answered "No."

In the November 1980 election Reagan defeated Carter in a landslide, 489 electoral votes to 49. Republicans also gained control of the Senate for the first time in 28 years. On January 20, 1981—the day of Reagan's inauguration—Iran finally released the hostages after 444 days of imprisonment. When they returned home, people all over the nation welcomed them with banners and parades.

SECTION 3 REVIEW

Identify and explain the significance of the following:

- **Jimmy Carter**
- **Panama Canal treaties**
- **Anwar Sadat**
- **Menachem Begin**
- **Camp David Accords**
- **apartheid**
- **sanctions**
- **Ayatollah Khomeini**
- **Iran hostage crisis**

Reading for Content Understanding

1 **Main Idea** What made many Americans see President Carter as a unique leader? Why did he lose public support?

2 **Main Idea** What ideas shaped Carter's foreign policy?

3 **Economic Development** What economic problems faced the nation during Carter's presidency? How did Carter address these problems?

4 **Writing** *Expressing* Imagine that you are an Olympic athlete in 1980. Write a letter to President Carter sharing your opinions on the boycott of the 1980 Summer Games in Moscow.

5 **Critical Thinking** *Evaluating* Do you think Jimmy Carter was a successful president? Use at least two examples from this section to support your answer.

Section 3 Review ANSWERS

Identify

For significance, see the following pages:

- Jimmy Carter, p. 666
- Panama Canal treaties, p. 669
- Anwar Sadat, p. 669
- Menachem Begin, p. 669
- Camp David Accords, p. 669
- apartheid, p. 670
- sanctions, p. 670
- Ayatollah Khomeini, p. 670
- Iran hostage crisis, p. 670

Reading for Content Understanding

1. Carter projected an open, honest image that seemed to reassure many Americans; his inability to resolve problems such as inflation and the hostage crisis lost him public support.

2. Carter sought to use fairness and morality as foreign-policy guides.

3. The nation was faced with inflation, particularly in rising energy prices. Carter proposed tax cuts and an energy bill, neither of which solved the problems.

4. Letters will vary but students should point to the Soviet invasion of Afghanistan and human rights abuses as reasons for Carter's decision. Students should also express the frustration that an athlete might feel at not being able to compete in the Olympics after years of preparation.

5. Answers will vary but students should state their opinions and offer at least two examples to support them.

SECTION 4 LESSON PLAN

OBJECTIVES

- Describe how the U.S. population changed during the 1970s.
- Identify environmental concerns that drew attention and explain how Americans reacted.
- Describe how health care and popular entertainment changed in the 1970s.

FOCUS

Motivate Before Reading

Ask students to describe what they think was the popular culture and style of the 1970s. Write students' responses on the chalkboard. Tell students that in this section they will learn about changes in American society during the 1970s, specifically changes related to population, the environment, safety and health, technology, and popular culture.

Section 4 RESOURCES

PRINT

★ Guided Reading Strategies 22.4

★ Primary Source Reading 22: Defending the Equal Rights Amendment

★ Section 4 Review, p. 677

★ Daily Quiz 22.4

MULTIMEDIA

★ *Teaching Resources CD–ROM,* Lesson 22.4

★ Everyday Life in America Transparency 31: *Star Wars:* Sign of the Seventies and Transparency 33: Teens Today: Caring for Earth's Creatures

★ Linking Geography and History Transparency 17B: African American Population, 1970

SHELTERED ENGLISH

★ Main Idea Activities for Reteaching and Sheltered English 22.4

SECTION 4

American Society in the 1970s

Reading Focus

How did the U.S. population change during the 1970s?

What environmental concerns drew Americans' attention, and how did they react?

In what ways did health care and popular entertainment change in the 1970s?

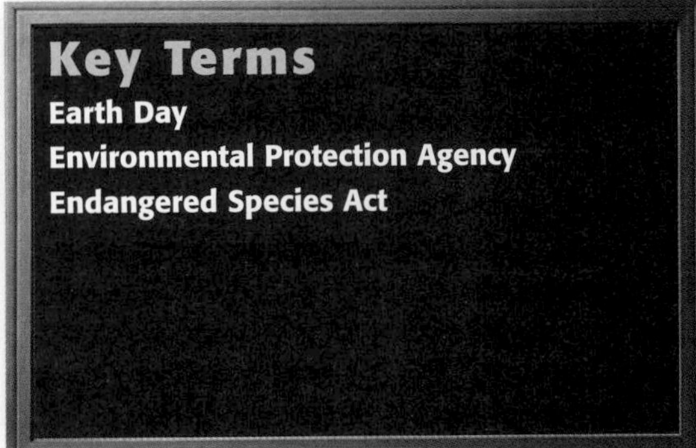

Key Terms

Earth Day

Environmental Protection Agency

Endangered Species Act

DESPITE THE PROBLEMS the United States faced in the 1970s, it was still a land of opportunity for many immigrants. Many were like Erasmo and Eloina Ortega, who emigrated from the Dominican Republic in the 1970s. Although their family struggled to earn a living in the troubled U.S. economy, they were happy to be in the United States. "The political situation [in the Dominican Republic] was bad," recalled Eloina. "We're very glad that our children have a future that our country could never provide them."

The flag of the Dominican Republic

Population Changes

The Ortegas were part of a changing pattern of immigration in the United States. Until the mid-1960s most people who immigrated to the United States came from Europe. By the 1970s, however, the majority of immigrants were coming from Latin America and Asia.

In Search of Opportunity

These immigrants were often political refugees. For example, thousands of people fled communist Cuba and came to the United States. Many of these Cuban immigrants were educated professionals. They helped create a powerful Cuban American political movement in southern Florida. Some Asian immigrants were also refugees from communist nations, such as Vietnam.

Thousands of other immigrants came to the United States seeking economic opportunities. Mexican immigrants looking for jobs made up the majority of Latin American immigrants during the 1970s. Although the U.S. economy was struggling, for many immigrants it provided better opportunities than the economies of their homelands.

Introduce Key Terms

Linguistic, Logical-Mathematical. Review this section's key terms with students. Have them use context cues to determine the meaning of each term. Then ask students to write a question about each term. Tell students to write answers to their questions as they read this section. **SHELTERED ENGLISH**

TEACH

Have students read Section 4 and complete Guided Reading Strategies 22.4. Choose one or more of the following activities to explore the section content with students. For further suggestions on block scheduling or team teaching, see the *Block Scheduling Handbook*.

Immigrants also sought educational opportunities. A large number of Asians came to the United States to attend college. After graduating, these students often decided to stay and work in technical industries. Sometimes they brought their families over to join them. Chinese immigrant Subi Lin Felipe recalled how her brother-in-law "brought in a sister and his wife, who brought over one of her brothers and me." Immigrants from many countries shared the outlook of Korean Kim Ta Tai. Kim explained:

> **"The fascination of America . . . is to come to a free and abundant country, and breathe the air of freedom, and make plans for a new life."**

Many older Americans enjoyed active lifestyles in the warm climate of the Sun Belt.

Growth in the Sun Belt

Thousands of immigrants settled in the Sun Belt states of the South and the West. Migrants from the Northeast and the Midwest also moved to the Sun Belt. By 1970 California had become the most populous state in the Union. The populations of other Sun Belt states such as Arizona and Florida also increased dramatically during the 1970s. By comparison, the population of the Midwest and Northeast grew slowly or even shrank.

Many people moved to the Sun Belt states to take new jobs in growing high-tech industries. These industries included aerospace and electronics. A large number of companies got their start in these industries by filling federal defense contracts during the Cold War military buildup. California, Florida, North Carolina, and Texas experienced the most growth in these defense fields.

Many older Americans moved to the Sun Belt for its warm climate. They were part of a major change in the U.S. population. More Americans were living longer because of improvements in health care. At the same time, the birthrate was declining. More adults were waiting longer to have children and were having smaller families. As a result of these trends, the percentage of the U.S. population aged 65 and older grew rapidly. These senior citizens gained financially from the expansion of Social Security benefits in the 1960s. These improved benefits made retirement easier for many older Americans.

Environmental Issues

Some Americans worried about the effect of rapid growth on the environment of the Sun Belt and northwestern states. The worldwide energy crisis also led to growing concern about the consumption of natural resources.

American activists tried to raise environmental awareness by sponsoring the first **Earth Day** on April 22, 1970. They declared that:

> **"Earth Day is to remind each person of his [or her] equal responsibility . . . to preserve and improve the Earth and the quality of life thereon."**

Many thousands of people have observed Earth Day since the first celebration was held in 1970.

Across the Curriculum

MATH

Population Changes. Between 1960 and 1990 the population of the northeastern United States increased from 45 million to 51 million. During the same period, the midwestern states grew in population from 52 million to 60 million. The South showed far greater gains. In 1960 some 55 million people lived in southern states. By 1990 some 85 million people called the South home. Western states also grew rapidly, with the population rising from 28 million in 1960, to 53 million in 1990.

Activity: Have students make bar graphs comparing population growth between 1960 and 1990 in the four regions listed above. Ask students to determine which region had the greatest population increase *(the South with 30 million)* and which had the smallest *(the Northeast with 6 million)*.

Multimedia Resources

Linking Geography and History Transparency 17B: African American Population, 1970

LEVEL 1: Linguistic. (Suggested time: 15 min.) As a class, go over students' Guided Reading Strategies. Then use the Reading Focus questions to highlight the main ideas of the section. **SHELTERED ENGLISH**

LEVEL 1: Visual-Spatial. (Suggested time: 30 min.) Explain to students that in the 1970s new patterns of immigration and migration changed the population makeup of the United States. Provide each student with a blank outline map of the world. Have students use colored markers to draw arrows on the map showing the global regions that served as the major sources of immigration to the United States in the 1970s. Then ask students to draw arrows showing the shift in American population to the Sun Belt states. In addition, have students write a caption summarizing their map. **SHELTERED ENGLISH**

ALL LEVELS: Linguistic, Logical-Mathematical, Visual-Spatial. (Suggested time: 30 min. plus homework) Have each student list the concerns of environmentalists during the 1970s. Then have students prepare agendas for the first Earth Day celebration. Call on volunteers to explain their agendas and have the class discuss the threat of each environmental issue. For homework, have students create posters promoting the first Earth Day celebration.

Historical Sidelight

The Bald Eagle. The bald eagle, native only to North America, became the national bird in 1782. At the time, tens of thousands of the regal birds existed. Over time, however, hunting and other activities greatly decreased their numbers. In 1940 Congress passed a law making it illegal to kill bald eagles in the United States (excluding Alaska). The use of DDT, a pesticide, continued to reduce the eagles' numbers, though. By 1960 fewer than 450 nesting pairs existed in the lower 48 states. Taking action, the government banned the use of DDT in 1972, and declared the bald eagle an endangered species in 1978. Since that time, the bald eagle population has risen steadily. Over 5,000 nesting pairs were counted in 1999. As a result of government protection, today bald eagles are off the endangered list.

Critical Thinking: Do you think it is important for the federal government to protect the national bird from extinction? Why?

ANSWER: Answers will vary but students might mention that the bald eagle is a symbol of the nation's strength and its extinction may make other nations see the United States as weaker.

Multimedia Resources

Everyday Life in America Transparency 33: Teens Today: Caring for Earth's Creatures

Since then, people around the world have held similar celebrations. Organizations also provide information on practices such as conserving energy, picking up litter, and recycling.

Protecting the Environment

Congress addressed concerns about the environment in the late 1960s and early 1970s. It passed laws to improve air and water quality and to limit pollution. In 1970 Congress established the **Environmental Protection Agency** (EPA) to enforce these laws. The EPA had a challenging task. It had to work with companies that opposed some of the new regulations. Many environmentalists, however, thought the new antipollution laws were not strict enough.

The EPA also inherited problems that had been created before there was great public concern about pollution. Years of unregulated or illegal dumping of industrial waste had created pollution problems across the country. One of the most shocking cases occurred in 1978. Some residents of Niagara Falls, New York, discovered that their homes had been built over an old toxic waste dump.

The dump was known as Love Canal, because it was located in an abandoned canal system. It was leaking dangerous levels of toxic chemicals into the water and soil. Scientists linked this toxic waste to health problems in the community, particularly among young children. "Do I let my three-year-old stay?" asked one concerned resident. Many people chose to move rather than risk exposure to dangerous chemicals.

In 1980 the government established a "Superfund" to pay for cleaning up toxic-waste dump sites such as Love Canal. These clean-up projects can cost millions of dollars and take years to complete.

Many places in Love Canal, such as this school, were still considered unsafe in the 1990s.

Endangered Animals

Some environmentalists also asked for better protection of another natural resource—wildlife. As the human population expanded throughout the United States, new housing and suburban development pushed wildlife species into smaller habitats. In 1966 Congress had passed one of the earliest environmental measures, the **Endangered Species Act**. This act protects animals threatened with extinction.

The Department of the Interior maintains a list of species that are in danger. Federal law forbids hunting these species or destroying their natural habitats. The Endangered Species Act directs the government to "halt and reverse the trend toward species extinction, whatever the cost."

Some activists have used the Endangered Species Act to stop building projects. Critics have responded by claiming that the law goes too far. Many critics agree that wildlife should be protected but argue that people need the jobs that new development brings. As the debate continues, some developers search for ways to both protect the environment and make a profit.

Safety and Health

Environmental concerns played a part in the consumer activist movement of the 1970s. This movement showed that concern for public health could change business practices and safety regulations.

Led by consumer advocate Ralph Nader, activists pushed for improved safety and environmental standards for a wide range of consumer goods. These activities led to stricter rules for product safety and tougher pollution standards

LEVEL 3: Linguistic, Intrapersonal. (Suggested time: 30 min. plus homework) For homework, ask students to imagine that they are young adults living in 1969. One day they wake up to discover that they mysteriously have transported in time to 1977. Have students use this section to write two to three journal entries describing how American health care and entertainment have changed. Students should also give their impressions of these changes. For the next class, ask volunteers to give an oral presentation based on their journal entries on what they think about living in the 1970s.

CLOSE

Linguistic, Interpersonal. Have students revise the list of 1970s popular culture that they made in the Motivate activity. Then ask students to imagine that they are preparing a 1970s time capsule. Have them suggest items to put in the time capsule. Write their suggestions on the chalkboard. When you have 15 or more suggestions, have the class discuss them and select the top-10 items to include. Have students explain why they chose each item and how it represents the 1970s.

for automobiles. In 1977 the federal government also banned the use of chemicals that were believed to weaken Earth's atmospheric ozone layer. The ozone layer helps shield Earth's surface from solar radiation. As a result of new laws, appliance and automobile manufacturers designed products that were safer, more efficient, and produced less air pollution.

The smiley face became a symbol of positive thinking and mental health in the 1970s.

Concern for public health also led to many advances in medical technology in the 1970s. The MRI machine was patented in 1972. This machine could detect tumors and other problems with greater accuracy than X-ray machines. The following year, researchers created a system known as the CAT scan, which can detect tumors and brain injuries.

Treatment of illnesses and injuries also improved. In 1977 a German doctor invented angioplasty, a surgical method for clearing clogged arteries to prevent heart attacks. In addition, doctors improved the success rate of organ transplants. This breakthrough prolonged the lives of those who received vital organs such as a heart, kidney, or liver.

Possibly the best medical news of the decade was how many Americans were taking responsibility for their own health. Research showed that people could significantly lower their risk of certain diseases by exercising and improving their diets.

These studies encouraged many Americans to adopt a healthier lifestyle during the 1970s. "There is no question that we are in the midst of a fitness explosion," declared one expert in 1977. Jogging, dance, and other aerobic activities became popular. Scientists credited improvements in diet and exercise with a 20 percent decline in the death rate from heart disease between 1969 and 1977.

American Arts

Twyla Tharp

Born in 1941, Twyla Tharp studied every kind of dance available as a child, including ballet, jazz, and tap. After beginning her own dance company in 1965, she described her goal: "I had to become the greatest choreographer of my time. That was my mission." Tharp's 1971 piece, *The Fugue* (FYOOG), named after a type of music composition, was a huge success. Tharp went on to choreograph many theater productions.

Tharp's unique style stretches the boundaries between classical and modern dance. It combines traditional ballet techniques with natural movements like running, walking, and skipping.

Twyla Tharp and dancers

Some of her dance pieces use no music at all. One critic wrote,

> "*Whether sashaying [gliding] across the stage to the music of Jelly Roll Morton, Frank Sinatra or the Beach Boys, Twyla Tharp can razzle-dazzle her way into the hearts of the most reluctant modern dance goer.*"

Understanding the Arts

1. What was Twyla Tharp's goal?
2. What is original about Tharp's style of choreography?

Technology and Society

Development of the Microchip. Computers once used hundreds of thousands of transistors. A need to fit these devices into smaller spaces led to the invention of the integrated circuit. Also called a microchip, this device was developed in 1958–59 by Jack Kilby and the team Jean Hoerni and Robert Noyce. Microchips use silicon, a common element in sand, to conduct electricity through millions of tiny components. By the 1970s the number of components on a 3-millimeter-square chip rose from 10 to more than 1,000. Besides being smaller, microchips were far faster than transistors. Chips soon were combined to produce microprocessors, the "brains" of modern computers. Today, microchips can be found in products from automobiles to musical greeting cards.

Activity: Have students research ways microchips affect Americans today. Have students report their findings to the class.

American Arts Answers

1. to become the greatest choreographer of her time

2. Her choreography combines classical ballet with natural movements.

CHALLENGE AND EXTEND

1. **Linguistic, Logical-Mathematical, Visual-Spatial.** Have students use the library and other resources to produce a public service announcement explaining the function of the Environmental Protection Agency and the Superfund. The announcement should mention when the EPA was formed, who the current director is, and at least three Superfund sites and what is being done at them.
2. **Linguistic, Visual-Spatial.** Have students use the library and other sources to research popular culture of the 1970s. Ask students to use their research to create a cultural scrapbook of the decade. Students' scrapbooks might include advertisements, articles, charts, headlines, illustrations, poems, photographs, song lyrics, and small artifacts. Tell students to write captions describing each item. When students are finished, have them display their scrapbooks and call on volunteers to explain their scrapbooks to the class.

REVIEW

Linguistic, Logical-Mathematical, Visual-Spatial. Have students complete the Section Review questions. Then ask students to use each term listed in the Identify portion of the Section

Section 4 Review ANSWERS

Identify
For significance, see the following pages:
- Earth Day, p. 673
- Environmental Protection Agency, p. 674
- Endangered Species Act, p. 674
- George Lucas, p. 676
- Donna Summer, p. 677

Reading for Content Understanding

1. effects of rapid growth on the environment, consumption of natural resources, pollution, waste disposal, threatened wildlife; Congress formed the EPA and passed the Endangered Species Act, and activists established an annual Earth Day.

2. Blockbuster, special-effects movies with family themes and dance-oriented music such as disco became popular.

3. The majority of immigrants came from Asia and Latin America rather than from Europe, and many Americans and immigrants settled in the Sun Belt states.

4. Speeches will vary but should include the development of MRIs and CAT scans as well as increased emphasis on physical fitness and exercise.

5. The species might serve an important role in the ecosystem; passing laws to protect threatened species

Multimedia Resources

Everyday Life in America Transparency 31: *Star Wars:* Sign of the Seventies

Advances in Computers

Computer technology also advanced during the 1970s. Computer designers began making wide use of the microchip, invented in 1958. A microchip is a tiny piece of silicon that contains many miniaturized electronic parts. Placing all of these parts on a single chip allowed computers to become smaller and faster.

The Apple II was the first fully assembled home computer.

As computers became more powerful and less expensive, their use increased. The most powerful machines, known as "supercomputers," were used mainly for advanced scientific research. The military also used computers in many of its new defense and weapons systems. In addition, scientists created the first computer networks for military research. These networks allowed computer users in different locations to share data.

For the first time small personal computers became practical. In 1977 Steven Jobs and Stephen Wozniak founded the Apple computer company. Their first successful home computer had crude graphics and could run only a few programs. Despite these limitations, Apple had sold thousands of computers by 1980.

Although computer designers made many improvements during the 1970s, few Americans owned a computer. For most people, the new machines were still too expensive and not practical enough.

Popular Culture

New technology found its way into the entertainment industry. Technology had a large effect on moviemaking.

Blockbuster Films

Directors such as Francis Ford Coppola and Robert Altman achieved success among adult audiences. The biggest hits of the 1970s, however, were aimed at younger moviegoers. The most successful film of the decade was George Lucas's 1977 classic, *Star Wars*. The movie tells the story of a battle between good and evil in a distant galaxy. It used familiar themes from traditional action films, such as westerns.

Lucas said that he felt the story appealed to young audiences because it dealt with "universal themes like friendship, loyalty, [and] morality [right and wrong]." The film also used new filmmaking and sound-recording techniques to create amazing special effects that fascinated audiences.

Star Wars earned more than $100 million during its initial release, a record at that time. Its success led to a new era of "blockbuster" films—big-budget, special-effects movies that targeted younger audiences. Director Steven Spielberg, who made hits such as *Close Encounters of the Third Kind,* praised this change:

> **"*Star Wars* was a seminal [creative and original] moment when the entire industry instantly changed. For me, personally, it's when the world recognized the value of childhood."**

Star Wars *dazzled audiences with its images of alien worlds.*

Review to design the cover of a special magazine issue entitled *The 1970s in Review.* The cover should include one or more images and a list of article titles relating to population changes, environmental issues, safety and health, advances in computers, and popular culture. Display students' work around the classroom.

ASSESS

Have students complete Daily Quiz 22.4.

RETEACH

Linguistic, Logical-Mathematical. Have students complete Main Idea Activities for Reteaching and Sheltered English 22.4. Make five columns on the chalkboard and label them *Population, Environment, Safety and Health, Computers,* and *Popular Culture.* Organize students into five groups. Have the members of each group use this section to list information about its assigned topic in the appropriate column on the chalkboard.

SHELTERED ENGLISH

Movie studios also benefited from making blockbusters because these action movies were popular in foreign countries. As a result, films became an increasingly valuable U.S. export. Audiences all around the world watched American movies and movie stars. The trend toward expensive movies filled with special effects also posed risks for movie studios, however. Big-budget films cost so much to make that if one failed it could ruin a studio. In addition, some viewers began to complain that blockbuster movie plots were too simple and violent.

Flashing lights and mirrored balls were common features of disco clubs.

The Disco Craze

Music also changed during the 1970s. Americans began to turn to dance-oriented styles such as disco. Millions of Americans crowded dance clubs called discotheques, or discos. New Yorker Gus Rodriguez described the appeal of disco music:

> **"Dancing to disco provided me with this incredible release. The music had this fast beat with a great melody behind it. When I danced, I wasn't just moving my legs up and down, I was flowing with the music."**

The disco craze inspired outrageous fashions, such as glittering sequined outfits that reflected the colorful strobe lights used in dance clubs. Dances like "The Hustle" were popular, and musicians such as the Bee Gees and Donna Summer made best-selling records. In addition to her many hit records, Summer won both a Grammy and an Academy Award for her song "Last Dance" in 1979.

As with big-budget movies, the new music had its critics. Some argued that disco lyrics encouraged irresponsible behavior. Other opponents thought that disco dances and fashions were foolish. Despite such criticisms, disco music remained popular with young fans in the 1970s in much the same way as rock 'n' roll had appealed to youth in the 1950s.

SECTION 4 REVIEW

Identify and explain the significance of the following:
- **Earth Day**
- **Environmental Protection Agency**
- **Endangered Species Act**
- **George Lucas**
- **Donna Summer**

Reading for Content Understanding

1. **Main Idea** What environmental issues concerned Americans in the 1970s? How were these concerns addressed?
2. **Main Idea** How did popular films and music change during the 1970s?
3. **Geography** *Region* How was the population of the United States affected by changes in immigration and migration during the 1970s?
4. **Writing** *Describing* Imagine that you are a doctor attending a medical conference in the late 1970s. Write a short speech describing the latest medical breakthroughs and noting how the health habits of Americans have changed during this decade.
5. **Critical Thinking** *Evaluating* Why might it be important to protect an endangered species from extinction? What steps might help make this possible?

Chapter 22 Review ANSWERS

Identifying People and Ideas

1. 37th president (1969–74), promoted New Federalism, opened relations with the People's Republic of China, resigned as a result of Watergate scandal

2. economic condition characterized by high inflation and high unemployment

3. a treaty between the Soviet Union and United States limiting the numbers and types of long-range nuclear missiles each country could have; began a period of détente between the two nations

4. political scandal that led President Nixon to resign

5. Texas congresswoman who served on the House Judiciary Committee investigating Watergate

6. 39th president (1977–81), attempted to restore American confidence in the government by enacting polices guided by fairness and honesty; lost public support

7. system of racial segregation in South Africa; opposed by the Carter administration

8. crisis that involved the capture of some 50 Americans after a fundamentalist Muslim political takeover in Iran; hurt Carter's presidency

9. day designated to increase environmental awareness

10. governmental agency established to enforce environmental laws

Using the Time Line

1. e
2. b
3. f
4. d
5. c
6. a

Review and Assessment RESOURCES

PRINT
★ Chapter 22 Review, pp. 678–79
★ Vocabulary Activity 22
★ Chapter 22 Study Guide
★ Chapter 22 Test (Form A or B)

MULTIMEDIA
★ Audio Program, Ch. 22 (English and Spanish)
★ *Global Skill Builder CD–ROM*
★ Chapter 22 Test Generator
★ HRW Web site

SHELTERED ENGLISH
★ Spanish Glossary
★ Sheltered English Chapter 22 Test

ASSESS

Have students complete one of the Chapter 22 Tests. As an alternate assessment, assign the Chapter 22 Investigation.

Understanding Main Ideas

1. proposed New Federalism to shift control of federal grants to states, supported giving police and courts more power, opposed new civil rights legislation, appointed more conservative judges to courts

2. through newspaper reports based on inside information and through Oval Office tapes

3. He had held no national office prior to becoming president, and he chose many people from outside of Washington circles as his advisers.

4. He brought together Egyptian president Anwar Sadat and Israeli prime minister Menachem Begin at Camp David to negotiate a peace agreement.

5. Blockbuster movies with special effects and family themes, and dance-oriented music such as disco became popular.

6. It passed clean air and water laws and established the EPA.

Reviewing Themes

1. The rise in the price of foreign oil contributed to high inflation, and the OPEC oil embargo created an energy crisis.

2. Watergate decreased many Americans' faith and confidence in the office of the presidency.

3. Nixon's foreign policy was guided by national interest and force, whereas Carter's was guided by moral beliefs and human rights issues.

CHAPTER 22 REVIEW

Chapter Summary

Many Americans hoped that the 1970s would be a time of stability and order after the social protests of the 1960s. Instead, the 1970s brought an economic downturn, an energy crisis, and the Watergate scandal. Presidents Ford and Carter struggled with domestic issues during their terms. They also faced new foreign-policy challenges. Americans witnessed technological breakthroughs in computers and medicine. Environmental concerns also increased.

On a separate sheet of paper, complete the following activities.

Identifying People and Ideas

Describe the historical significance of the following:

1. Richard Nixon
2. stagflation
3. Strategic Arms Limitation Talks
4. Watergate
5. Barbara Jordan
6. Jimmy Carter
7. apartheid
8. Iran hostage crisis
9. Earth Day
10. Environmental Protection Agency

Internet Activity

go.hrw.com
SB1 Wildlife Preserves

Search the Internet through the HRW Web site to locate wildlife preserves in the United States. Create a map with shaded areas indicating the different kinds of wildlife preserves.

Understanding Main Ideas

1. How did President Nixon try to address the concerns of the Silent Majority?
2. How was Nixon's role in Watergate gradually revealed?
3. Why did many people consider Jimmy Carter to be an "outsider" to Washington politics?
4. How did President Carter help bring peace to the Middle East?
5. In what ways did popular films and music change during the 1970s?
6. What actions did the federal government take to improve the environment in the 1970s?

Reviewing Themes

1. **Economic Development** How did U.S. dependence on foreign oil affect the economy during the mid-1970s?
2. **Citizenship and Democracy** How did Watergate affect the presidency?
3. **Global Relations** How did President Carter's foreign-policy approach differ from that of President Nixon?

Using the Time Line

Number your paper from 1 to 6. Match the letters on the time line below with the following events.

1. **Begin, Carter, and Sadat sign the Camp David Accords.**
2. **The Yom Kippur War begins.**
3. **An accident takes place at a nuclear power plant on Three Mile Island, Pennsylvania.**
4. **Jimmy Carter wins the presidency.**
5. **President Nixon announces his resignation.**
6. **The first Earth Day is celebrated.**

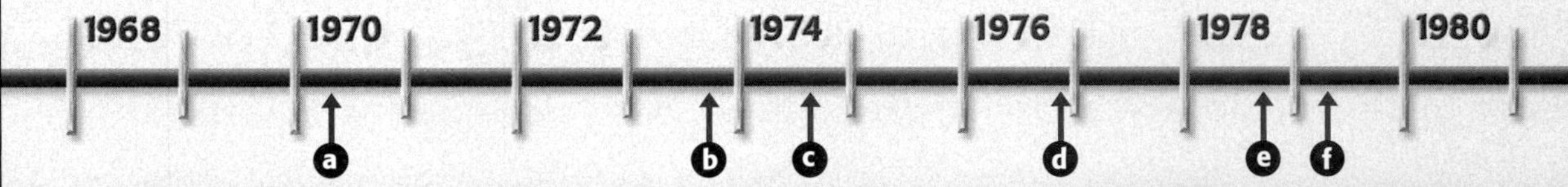

RETEACH

Logical-Mathematical, Visual-Spatial. Organize students into four groups. Assign each group one of the chapter sections. Have each group create a 6-column chart with columns labeled *Event, Who, What, Where, When,* and *Why.* Students should complete their charts, as much as possible, for each of the main events in their assigned sections.

SHELTERED ENGLISH

Using the Internet

Have students continue their research to find more information on one specific wildlife preserve. Ask students to use their research to create a brochure about the preserve. Have volunteers share their brochures with the class.

Portfolio Extensions

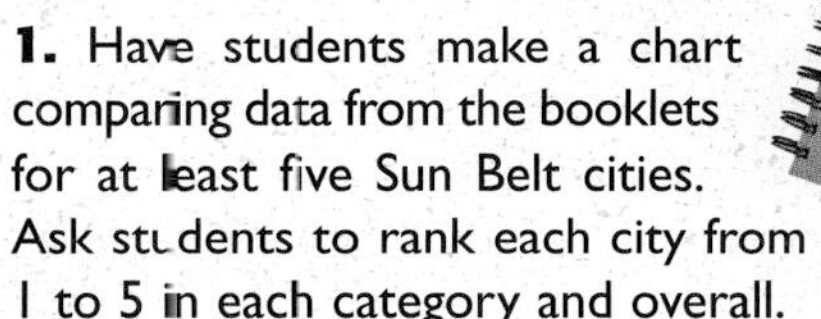

1. Have students make a chart comparing data from the booklets for at least five Sun Belt cities. Ask students to rank each city from 1 to 5 in each category and overall.

2. Have students create a T-shirt design, a bumper sticker, and a slogan to accompany their leaflets and poster.

Thinking Critically

1. **Supporting a Point of View** Which do you think would have been better for the nation—pardoning President Nixon for Watergate or trying him in a court of law? Explain your answer.
2. **Synthesizing Information** How did Presidents Nixon, Ford, and Carter try to improve economic conditions during the 1970s?
3. **Identifying Cause and Effect** How did President Nixon's opening of relations with China affect U.S. relations with the Soviet Union?

Writing About History

1. **Expressing** Imagine that you are a citizen writing a letter to the editor after Nixon's resignation. Express how the Watergate scandal has affected your view of the federal government and why.
2. **Persuading** Imagine that you are a U.S. State Department official. Write a memo to your superior explaining which foreign-policy approach—Nixon's or Carter's—would be the most successful and why.

Linking Geography and History

1. **Human-Environment Interaction** Why do some environmental activists attempt to stop building projects?
2. **Movement** What effects did migration to the Sun Belt have on the region and the rest of the United States?

Building Your Portfolio

American History

Complete the following activities individually or in groups.

1. **Recruiting Residents** Imagine that you are an official of a Sun Belt city hoping to attract new residents. Design a booklet advertising your city and region. Determine what advantages your city offers and include information about subjects such as business and industry, housing costs, taxes, cultural resources, recreation, and the crime rate. As part of your sales pitch, draw a general map of the city, highlighting places you think will be attractive to new residents.
2. **Celebrating Earth Day** Create a poster and leaflets that might be used for the next Earth Day celebration. On your poster, use art or photographs to show why Earth Day is important. In the leaflets, persuade people to work to preserve the environment and explain how to accomplish that goal.

History Skills Workshop

Using Visual Resources Study the cartoon below, which shows President Ford and a snake. Then answer the following questions: (a) What does the snake represent? (b) What is President Ford doing and why? (c) What do you think the cartoon's message is?

"You've got to admit we're getting Watergate behind us."

Draper Hill/© 1974 The Commercial Appeal, Memphis

Thinking Critically

1. Answers will vary but some students may think that pardoning Nixon was the best way to help the nation heal and move forward; others may think that trying him would have been better for the nation because other politicians would see that no American is above the law.

2. through forced and voluntary wage-price controls to slow inflation; by trying to reduce American dependence upon imported oil; by reducing spending and making tax cuts

3. Soviet leaders became more willing to work with U.S. leaders because they did not want the United States to ally itself too closely with China.

Writing About History

1. Letters will vary but students may express either dismay over government corruption or increased belief in the constitutional system.

2. Memos will vary but should either favor Nixon's practical approach or Carter's moral and fair approach.

Linking Geography and History

1. to preserve the habitat of endangered wildlife

2. increased population, industrial production, and increased concern for the environment

History Skills Workshop

(a) the problems associated with Watergate; (b) he is trying to break free of the problems left over from Watergate; (c) that problems related to Watergate continued to trouble President Ford and the nation even after President Nixon resigned.

CHAPTER PLANNING GUIDE
The Republican Years

	SECTION LESSON OBJECTIVES	PRINT RESOURCES	MULTIMEDIA RESOURCES	SHELTERED ENGLISH RESOURCES
Section 1: The Reagan Years (pp. 681–86)	★ Explain President Reagan's appeal to American voters. ★ Describe how Reagan hoped to balance the budget and improve the nation's economy. ★ Evaluate how Reagan's economic policies affected Americans.	★ Guided Reading Strategies 23.1 ★ Literature Reading 23: *The Bonfire of the Vanities* ★ Section 1 Review, p. 686 ★ Daily Quiz 23.1	★ *Teaching Resources CD–ROM*, Lesson 23.1 ★ *Exploring America's Past* Video Segment: Name That Court; *Teacher's Guide*, pp. 43–44 ★ HRW Web site	★ Main Idea Activities for Reteaching and Sheltered English 23.1
Section 2: Reagan's Foreign Policy (pp. 687–91)	★ Analyze ways the Reagan administration tried to stop the spread of communism in Central America. ★ Identify the actions that led to the Iran-contra affair. ★ Explain how changes within the Soviet Union affected the Cold War.	★ Guided Reading Strategies 23.2 ★ Section 2 Review, p. 691 ★ Daily Quiz 23.2	★ *Teaching Resources CD–ROM*, Lesson 23.2 ★ Linking Geography and History Transparency 22: Central America and the Caribbean, 1980s ★ HRW Web site	★ Main Idea Activities for Reteaching and Sheltered English 23.2
Section 3: George Bush's Presidency (pp. 692–98)	★ Describe some of President Bush's major domestic actions. ★ Identify events that led to the final breakup of the Soviet Union. ★ Explain what caused the Persian Gulf War and how the conflict ended.	★ Guided Reading Strategies 23.3 ★ Biography Reading 23: Colin Powell ★ Geography Activity 23: The International Drug Trade ★ Graphic Organizer 23: Issues of the Republican Years ★ Section 3 Review, p. 698 ★ Daily Quiz 23.3	★ *Teaching Resources CD–ROM*, Lesson 23.3 ★ Linking Geography and History Transparency 24: The Breakup of the Soviet Sphere	★ Main Idea Activities for Reteaching and Sheltered English 23.3
Section 4: Technology and Culture (pp. 699–703)	★ Describe important advances in medical research and space exploration in the 1980s. ★ Identify technological advances of the 1980s. ★ Explain how music and movies changed in the 1980s.	★ Guided Reading Strategies 23.4 ★ Primary Source Reading 23: President Reagan Remembers the *Challenger* Crew ★ Section 4 Review, p. 703 ★ Daily Quiz 23.4	★ *Teaching Resources CD–ROM*, Lesson 23.4 ★ Everyday Life in America Transparency 32: The AIDS Quilt Project, 1980s	★ Main Idea Activities for Reteaching and Sheltered English 23.4
Chapter Review and Assessment (pp. 704–05)		★ Chapter 23 Review, pp. 704–05 ★ Vocabulary Activity 23 ★ Chapter 23 Study Guide ★ Chapter 23 Test (Form A or B)	★ Audio Program, Ch. 23 (English and Spanish) ★ *Global Skill Builder CD–ROM* ★ Chapter 23 Test Generator ★ HRW Web site	★ Spanish Glossary ★ Sheltered English Chapter 23 Test

CHAPTER OVERVIEW

President Ronald Reagan served two terms. He worked to limit the size and role of government and to improve the economy. Using supply-side economics, he cut taxes and some social funding in an attempt to increase tax revenues and balance the federal budget. After a brief recession, the economy boomed. However, lower-than-expected tax revenues and a more than $100 billion increase in defense spending created large federal deficits.

Abroad, Reagan focused on fighting communism. He used financial aid, covert operations, and military force to support anticommunist rebels and oust communist regimes in the Caribbean and Central America. However, the Iran-contra scandal marked a low point during his administration.

Reagan's vice president, George Bush, was elected president in 1988. Bush dealt with a savings and loan crisis and launched a War on Drugs. He also saw the Cold War end as reforms made by Soviet leader Mikhail Gorbachev led to the breakup of the Soviet Union. In the Persian Gulf War, the United States helped liberate Kuwait from Iraqi occupation.

The 1980s saw scientific and technological changes as well. AIDS emerged as a growing epidemic. Scientists began focusing on genetic research, and NASA developed the space shuttle. In addition, cable TV, CDs, personal computers, and VCRs changed many aspects of daily life.

CHAPTER INVESTIGATION

The Chapter Investigation is an extended, multipart activity designed for students to work cooperatively and apply the chapter content in the creation of a project. You may choose to use the Chapter 23 Investigation, Lobbyists and Legislators, either as a substitute for teaching the section lessons or as an alternate assessment.

BLOCK SCHEDULING 

The teacher lesson plans for each section offer a variety of activity choices to help you present the material in a block scheduling format. For further suggestions on block scheduling, see the *Block Scheduling Handbook with Team Teaching Strategies*, pp. 133–38.

Meeting Individual Needs

ABILITY LEVELS

LEVEL 1 Basic level activities designed for all students encountering new material.

LEVEL 2 Intermediate level activities designed for average students.

LEVEL 3 Challenging activities designed for above-average students.

SHELTERED ENGLISH These activities address the needs of students with Limited English Proficiency.

Smithsonian Institution®

Internet Connections and Lesson 23
www.si.edu/hrw

CNN Presents America:
Yesterday and Today 1850 to the Present
Segment: The Wall Comes Down

Additional Resources

Books for Teachers

Campbell, Colin et al., eds. *The Bush Presidency.* Chatham House, 1991. A thoughtful collection of early assessments of the Bush administration.

Schaller, Michael. *Reckoning with Reagan: America and Its President in the 1980s.* Oxford University Press, 1992. An account of the Reagan administration.

Wills, Garry. *Reagan's America.* Viking Penguin, 1988. Biography focusing on how Reagan's political philosophy took shape and influenced America.

Books for Students

Bratman, Fred. *War in the Persian Gulf.* Millbrook Press, 1991. Chronicles the Persian Gulf War (for students reading below grade level).

Bullock, John, and Harvey Morris. *The Gulf War: Its Origins, History and Consequences.* Trafalgar Square, 1991. Offers a British perspective on the Persian Gulf War.

Kort, Michael. *Mikhail Gorbachev.* Watts, 1990. Looks at Mikhail Gorbachev's contributions.

Multimedia Materials

America in Search of Itself. Video, 43 min. Films Inc. Newsman John Chancellor and author Theodore H. White discuss the 1980 presidential election.

History of the 80s. 10 videos, 60 min. each. ABC News/SSSS. Each video documents a different year in the decade and focuses both on foreign and domestic issues.

A Line in the Sand. Video, 50 min. ABC News/SSSS. Presents the background of the Iraqi invasion of Kuwait and looks at the role of oil in Middle East politics.

The Republican Years

CHAPTER MOTIVATOR

Write on the chalkboard *Grenada, Iraq, Kuwait,* and *Lebanon.* Instruct students to turn to the North America: Political map on page xxvi and the Asia: Political map on page xxix and locate these countries. Call on volunteers to describe the locations. Next, ask students what they think these nations have in common. After they give some ideas, explain that these are all nations to which the United States sent troops during the presidencies of Ronald Reagan and George Bush. The reasons for sending troops varied, as did the troops' missions. Tell students that in this chapter they will learn about the end of the Cold War and how the United States redefined its role as the one remaining superpower in the world.

Presenting Themes

- **Economic Development** Students might mention that new policies could affect Americans' job opportunities, incomes, savings, investments, living conditions, and political leanings.
- **Global Relations** Students might mention that the events could lead people in other nations to protest government policies or the current political situation, could cause dissenters in other nations to rise up against their governments, or could lead governments in other nations to enforce stricter controls.
- **Technology and Society** Students might mention that scientific advances could lead to more cures for diseases, new time-saving inventions, and new types of foods or other products. Students also might mention that some advances can create controversy, problems, or fear.

Using the Time Line

Have students determine which events in the time line might have led to changes in U.S. economic policy and which might have led to changes in U.S. foreign policy. After students have completed the chapter, have them discuss how each event might have affected Americans.

CHAPTER 23

The Republican Years

(1980–1992)

In 1983 President Ronald Reagan called the Soviet Union the "focus of evil in the modern world." Yet when he met Soviet leader Mikhail Gorbachev (gawr-buh-CHAWF) in 1985, he liked him. Afterward Reagan said, "We've seen what the new Russian looks like. Now maybe we can figure out how to deal with him." At the time neither leader could have guessed that democratic reforms would soon sweep the Soviet Union.

Economic Development

How might new U.S. economic policies affect Americans?

Global Relations

How might events in one nation lead to political changes in other nations?

Technology and Society

How might scientific advances lead to changes in daily life?

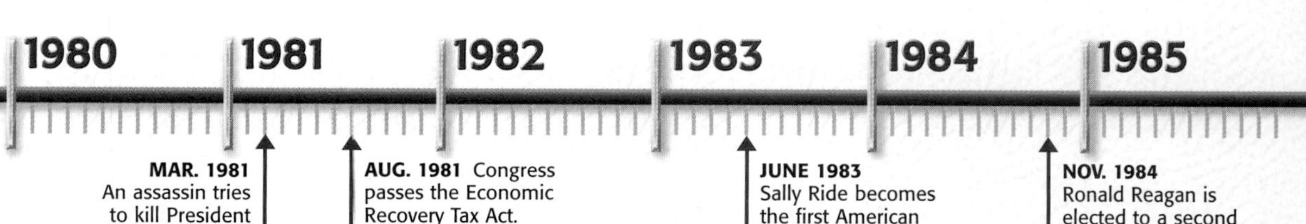

OBJECTIVES

- **Explain President Reagan's appeal to American voters.**
- **Describe how Reagan hoped to balance the budget and improve the nation's economy.**
- **Evaluate how Reagan's economic policies affected Americans.**

FOCUS

Motivate Before Reading

Tell students that President Ronald Reagan said, "Government is not the solution to our problems; government is the problem." As a class, have students list ways in which government can help citizens and reasons people might sometimes see government as a problem. Tell students that in this section they will learn about the domestic policies of President Reagan.

SECTION 1

The Reagan Years

Reading Focus

Why was President Reagan popular with American voters?

How did Reagan hope to balance the budget and improve the nation's economy?

In what ways did Reagan's economic policies affect Americans?

Key Terms

New Right
supply-side economics
Economic Recovery Tax Act
Gramm-Rudman-Hollings Act
Black Monday

DURING RONALD REAGAN'S first week as president, he was eager to explore his new home, the White House. He flipped light switches, explored closets, and even paid a sudden visit to the kitchen, startling the cooks. One morning, to President Reagan's delight, the Marine Band played "Hail to the Chief" as he ate breakfast. Despite his joy in the moment, he joked with the musicians that he would not expect the performance every day. A Reagan aide explained that although the president was "impressed with the history of it all, . . . he's not overwhelmed." Reagan's obvious ease in his all-important position reassured many Americans.

Ronald Reagan at his ranch in Santa Barbara, California

IMAGE ON LEFT PAGE: *President Reagan and Soviet leader Gorbachev in Moscow in 1988*

1986 | 1987 | 1988 | 1989 | 1990 | 1991 | 1992

JAN. 1986 The space shuttle *Challenger* explodes.

OCT. 1987 The U.S. stock market crashes.

NOV. 1989 Germans tear down the Berlin Wall.

FEB. 1991 The UN launches a ground attack in the Persian Gulf War.

DEC. 1991 The Commonwealth of Independent States is formed.

Section 1 RESOURCES

PRINT

- ★ Guided Reading Strategies 23.1
- ★ Literature Reading 23: *The Bonfire of the Vanities*
- ★ Section 1 Review, p. 686
- ★ Daily Quiz 23.1

MULTIMEDIA

- ★ *Teaching Resources CD–ROM*, Lesson 23.1
- ★ *Exploring America's Past* Video Segment: Name That Court; *Teacher's Guide*, pp. 43–44
- ★ HRW Web site

SHELTERED ENGLISH

- ★ Main Idea Activities for Reteaching and Sheltered English 23.1

Introduce Key Terms

Linguistic. Review this section's key terms with students. Have students use context cues to determine the meaning of each term. Then have students write sentences that link two or more of the terms in a historically correct way. Call on volunteers to read their sentences. Continue until all the key terms have been used in at least two sentences. Finally, have students write the terms' definitions in their notebooks. **SHELTERED ENGLISH**

TEACH

Have students read Section 1 and complete Guided Reading Strategies 23.1. Choose one or more of the following activities to explore the section content with students. For further suggestions on block scheduling or team teaching, see the Block Scheduling Handbook.

LEVEL 1: Linguistic. (Suggested time: 15 min.) As a class, go over students' Guided Reading Strategies. Then use the Reading Focus questions to highlight the main ideas of the section. **SHELTERED ENGLISH**

Economic Development

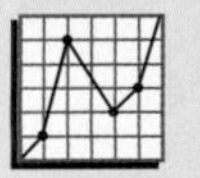

Reagan's Economics. Some economists claimed that supply-side economics would not work. They argued that for the government to receive an increase in tax revenues, the amount of revenues generated through economic growth would have to be three times the size of the original tax cut, which seemed highly unlikely. However, President Reagan also called for large cuts in government spending. He predicted that the combined spending and tax cuts would produce a balanced federal budget.

Critical Thinking: What other actions might Reagan have taken to improve the U.S. economy and increase federal tax revenues?

ANSWER: Possible answers include raising the minimum wage, using trade restrictions to protect American products, or working to lower inflation.

Multimedia Resources

Exploring America's Past Video Segment: Name That Court; *Teacher's Guide*, pp. 43–44

Search 26631, Play to 33693
Videodisc Blue Side B

Play Pause

See *Teacher's Guide* for Spanish barcode.

Reagan's Style

At age 69, Ronald Reagan was the oldest person ever elected president. His age and experience seemed to provide comfort for some Americans. One woman described the Reagan effect: "He made people feel good about being American." Reagan reassured Americans that better days were ahead for the United States. He was highly skilled at presenting this simple, yet effective message. After the Watergate scandal and the Iran hostage crisis, many Americans welcomed Reagan's message. His ability to motivate people through his speeches earned Reagan the nickname "The Great Communicator."

Nancy Reagan selected new White House china in red, her favorite color.

First Lady Nancy Reagan also paid attention to the image of the United States. In one of her first efforts, she decided to redecorate the White House. She believed that the residence needed to be updated to better entertain world leaders. She also decided to replace the official White House china set, which had many cracked and missing pieces. The White House "should be something very special," she explained.

Early in his first term Reagan showed how he used humor to put Americans at ease. In March 1981 John Hinckley Jr. tried to assassinate the president as he left a hotel after giving a speech. Hinckley fired several shots and hit Reagan, Press Secretary James Brady, a Secret Service agent, and a local police officer. Brady suffered permanent injury from the shooting. At the hospital, Reagan, although severely injured, reassured people around him with his humor. "Honey, I forgot to duck," he told his wife, Nancy.

Reagan recovered quickly from his injuries, and his popularity soared. One member of Congress remarked, "This [assassination attempt] is a long-term plus for Reagan. He has been through the fire and escaped."

The Rise of the Republicans

President Reagan received support from a conservative coalition, or alliance, of voters known as the **New Right**. This coalition included traditionally Republican voters, fundamentalist Christians, and so-called Reagan Democrats, who opposed some federal social programs. These conservatives wanted to limit the size of government and create a strong anticommunist foreign policy. Reagan supporters also wanted to decrease government regulation of business. Many members of the New Right opposed the Equal Rights Amendment and busing to achieve school integration. Most of them also supported capital punishment—the death penalty—and mandatory time for prayer in public schools.

Many conservative evangelicals joined the Moral Majority, a group led by minister Jerry Falwell. The Moral Majority wanted to organize people to achieve conservative Christian political goals. In describing the group's purpose, Falwell expressed the beliefs of many conservatives in the New Right:

> **"Right living must be re-established as an American way of life. We as American citizens must recommit ourselves to the faith of our fathers. . . . We must be willing to live by the moral convictions we claim to believe."**

Critics of the New Right complained that Falwell and his supporters defined "right living" in a narrow way. Throughout much of the 1980s, however, the New Right was an important influence on the Reagan presidency.

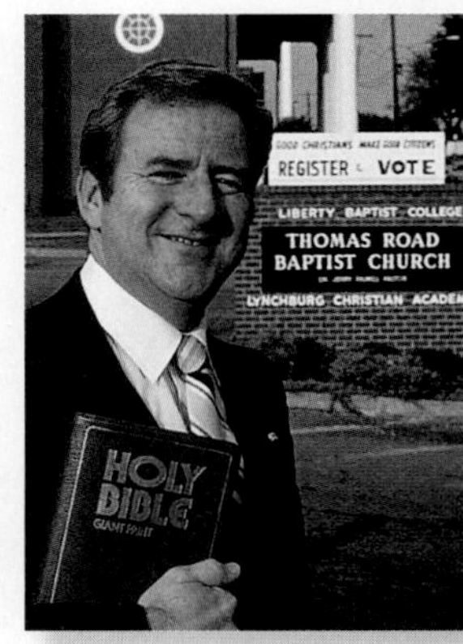

Jerry Falwell led a conservative religious group called the Moral Majority.

Like President Richard Nixon, Reagan wanted to appoint conservatives to the U.S. Supreme Court. In 1981 he appointed Sandra Day O'Connor, a conservative judge, as the first female Supreme Court justice. In the mid-1980s Reagan appointed Antonin Scalia and Anthony M. Kennedy. These appointments shifted the Court toward a more conservative outlook.

ALL LEVELS: Linguistic, Visual-Spatial, Interpersonal. (Suggested time: 45 min.) Organize the class into groups. Have each group develop a campaign platform complete with posters, slogans, and bumper stickers to support Ronald Reagan in the 1980 presidential election. Groups' campaigns should represent the views of the New Right, indicate why members of the New Right supported Reagan, and mention his economic and other domestic plans. Give students time to prepare the campaigns. Then have each group present its materials to the class. Finally, discuss Reagan's popularity with American voters. **SHELTERED ENGLISH**

LEVEL 2: Logical-Mathematical, Visual-Spatial. (Suggested time: 45 min.) Discuss how Reagan hoped to balance the budget and improve the nation's economy. During the discussion, have students create on the chalkboard a flowchart showing how supply-side economics was supposed to achieve these goals. Have students make a copy of the flowchart and, using a pen in a contrasting color, modify it to show the policy's actual results. Call on volunteers to explain their flowcharts. Finally, have students discuss the positive and negative effects of supply-side economics.

Ronald Reagan

Ronald Reagan was born in Tampico, Illinois, in 1911. He took a Hollywood screen test in 1937 and later became a popular actor. Reagan's experience in front of the camera would help him in politics.

Reagan twice served as president of his union, the Screen Actors Guild. At first, he was a Democrat. However, he became convinced that the party placed too much emphasis on social reform. Reagan switched to the Republican Party.

Reagan became involved in national politics in 1964, when he gave campaign speeches for Republican presidential candidate Barry Goldwater. Two years later, Reagan's combination of wit, positive thinking, and conservative politics helped him win election as governor of California. Reagan told voters, "It is time we ended our obsession with what is wrong, and realized how much is right." He carried this message with him to the White House.

Reagan also appointed several women to cabinet-level positions. Elizabeth Dole served as the secretary of transportation and Margaret Heckler served as secretary of health and human services. The decade marked a new trend as increasing numbers of conservative women entered politics.

Reagan's First Term

In his 1981 inaugural address President Reagan had expressed his views on the proper role of government:

> **"Government is not the solution to our problems; government is the problem. . . . It is not my intention to do away with government. It is, rather, to make it work—work with us, not over us."**

Reagan's main goals were to balance the federal budget, cut taxes, reduce regulations on business, and expand the military. He also wanted to scale back the size and role of the federal government. According to Republican senator Howard Baker, the Reagan administration had three immediate priorities: "economic recovery, economic recovery, and economic recovery."

To reduce the deficit, Americans needed to buy goods made in the United States.

Reagan's economic policies, which became known as Reaganomics, rested on an idea called **supply-side economics**. According to this economic theory, the government could eventually balance the budget by cutting taxes. A tax cut would increase personal income and business profits. People would then save or invest this extra income, thus expanding the economy and creating new jobs. Over time this increase in business activity would produce greater tax revenues. With more money coming in to the federal government, Congress would be able to balance the budget.

Tax Cuts and a New Budget

Congress passed the **Economic Recovery Tax Act** (ERTA) in August 1981. The act reduced personal income taxes by 25 percent. The ERTA also cut some other taxes. In total, the tax reduction amounted to some $750 billion. The wealthiest Americans received the greatest tax relief.

To help offset short-term reductions in tax revenues, Congress agreed to cut $500 billion from social programs over a five-year period. These programs included school lunches, unemployment

Presidential Profiles

Ronald Reagan. The son of a shoe salesman, Ronald Reagan worked as a lifeguard during his teens. In 1932 he took a job as a radio sportscaster. A few years later, while in California to cover baseball spring training, he took a movie screen test. Reagan's Hollywood career had begun. He went on to appear in 55 movies. During World War II, he made training films for the U.S. Army Air Corps. A long-time Democrat, Reagan switched to the Republican Party when he cast his vote for Eisenhower in the 1952 presidential election. From 1954 to 1962 he hosted a television show sponsored by General Electric. As a GE company spokesman, he often visited factories to talk to workers about the benefits of capitalism.

Activity: Have students use the library or search the Internet through the HRW Web site to find information on the life and presidency of Ronald Reagan. Ask students to use the information to write a biography on Reagan.

go.hrw.com
SB1 Reagan

LEVEL 3: Linguistic, Logical-Mathematical, Interpersonal. (Suggested time: 30 min. plus homework) Have students, individually or in pairs, write the script for a discussion between two friends, one who supports Reagan and one who does not. The script should touch on all the major topics of this section and address each Reading Focus question. When students are done, call on volunteers to act out one or more of the scripts. Follow-up with a class discussion of Reagan's economic policies and their effects on Americans.

LEVEL 3: Linguistic, Kinesthetic, Visual-Spatial. (Suggested time: 30 min. plus homework) Ask students to imagine that they are either a Reagan or a Mondale supporter in the 1984 presidential election. Have students write a speech supporting or opposing supply-side economics and Reagan's other economic policies. Encourage students to create charts or other visuals to accompany their speeches. In class, call on volunteers to deliver their speeches. Then have students discuss who they would have supported in the 1984 election and why.

Across the Curriculum

MATH

The Distribution of Wealth. From 1945 to 1965, the richest 1 percent of Americans owned about 33 percent of the total U.S. marketable wealth (sellable assets and goods). By 1992 this figure had risen to 42 percent. One reason for this increase was the economic policies of the 1980s. One historian has estimated that one third of the national wealth created between 1983 and 1989 went to the richest 1 percent of Americans.

Critical Thinking: How much did the total marketable wealth of the richest 1 percent of Americans increase from 1965 to 1992? How much of the nation's marketable wealth did 99 percent of Americans own in 1992?

ANSWER: 9 percent; 58 percent

CHART ANSWER
1980 to 1985

U.S. Defense Spending, 1945–1995

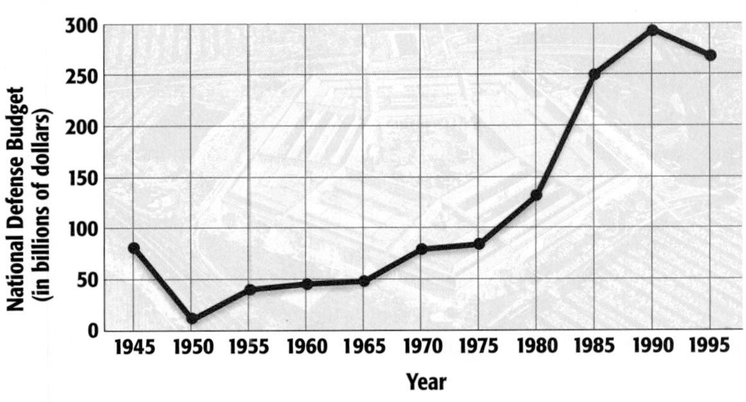

Source: *Statistical Abstract of the United States*

The Price of the Cold War The United States spent billions of dollars on national defense during the Cold War. During what five-year period did defense spending increase the most?

compensation, low-income housing, and the National Endowments for the Arts and Humanities. Congress did not, however, reduce overall spending on some of the most significant social welfare programs. For example, spending for Social Security rose significantly during Reagan's presidency.

The Reagan administration and Congress also spent more money to increase U.S. military capabilities. From 1981 to 1985, defense spending increased from about $134 billion to some $250 billion. Over time, defense and other federal spending greatly exceeded new tax revenues and budget cuts. As a result, the deficit—the amount by which a government's borrowing and expenditures exceed its revenues—increased dramatically. During Reagan's presidency, the national debt grew from less than $1 trillion to more than $2.6 trillion.

Recession

Early in Reagan's presidency, the nation experienced an economic recession. Heavy industries like steel and automobiles were losing sales to foreign competitors. For example, in 1982, Japanese cars accounted for more than 20 percent of all auto sales in the United States. This figure was 4 percent in 1970. In 1982 the United States imported almost $25 billion more in goods and services than it exported. By 1988 this trade deficit grew to about $150 billion.

As a result, companies began laying off thousands of workers. For example, in 1981 the American automobile industry laid off more than 200,000 workers, about 25 percent of its workforce. In 1982 and 1983, about 10 percent of American workers were out of a job.

The PATCO Strike

Some federal workers took action in response to the bad economic news. Members of the Professional Air Traffic Controllers Organization (PATCO) were dissatisfied with a new contract offer. In August 1981 they went on strike. Union members were violating a ban that prohibited federal employees from striking.

In response, President Reagan fired some 12,000 striking controllers. He told his aides, "The law says they can't strike. By striking they've quit their jobs." He also prohibited the Federal Aviation

Air traffic controllers at the John F. Kennedy Airport in New York walked the picket line as part of a larger strike of air traffic controllers.

CLOSE

Linguistic, Interpersonal. Tell students that they have been chosen to work on a new movie screenplay, *Reagan's America.* The movie is to focus on Reagan's domestic policies. Have the class suggest events and themes that the movie should include. Write the suggestions on the chalkboard. Then have students use the suggestions to create outlines for the screenplay.

CHALLENGE AND EXTEND

Linguistic, Logical-Mathematical, Visual-Spatial. Lotty Repp of Dallas, Texas, suggested the following activity: Show students clips from Ronald Reagan's films and political speeches. Have students list the qualities that Reagan exhibited in both. Then have students write an essay explaining why Reagan was called the "Great Communicator" and analyzing how his film career helped his political career.

Administration (FAA) from ever rehiring these controllers. The training of new, nonunion controllers ended up costing more money than asked for by PATCO. Nevertheless, the president had won an important symbolic victory.

The 1984 Election

By the time of the 1984 election, the economy had begun to turn around. The gross national product increased by almost 7 percent in 1984—its largest increase since 1951. Unemployment and inflation also dropped significantly. Many Americans gave President Reagan credit for the prosperous economy. The Republican Party nominated him for re-election. His campaign focused on the economic recovery with the slogan "It's Morning Again in America."

The Democratic Party chose Walter Mondale, Jimmy Carter's vice president, as its presidential candidate. Mondale selected Geraldine Ferraro as his running mate. She became the first woman to run for vice president on a major-party ticket. Ferraro told voters:

> **"By choosing an American woman to run for our nation's second-highest office, you send a powerful signal to all Americans. . . . We will place no limits on achievement. If we can do this, we can do *anything*."**

Mondale's campaign claimed that Reagan's economic policies greatly favored the rich. In one advertisement, Mondale said, "I refuse to let your family pay more while millionaires pay less." In November 1984 Reagan won the election in a landslide, capturing 515 electoral votes to Mondale's 13. He became the first president since Dwight D. Eisenhower to serve two complete terms.

The Financial World

After the election, the federal deficit continued to rise. To control future deficits, Congress passed the **Gramm-Rudman-Hollings Act** in December 1985. The law required the government to cut spending when the deficit grew above a certain level. Yet the nation's total debt continued to grow. A 1986 tax cut contributed to its growth. The tax cut further reduced the tax rate for the wealthiest Americans and lowered corporate taxes.

The tax cut helped some businesspeople make fortunes in the 1980s. Real-estate developer Donald Trump was one of them. Yuppies, or young urban professionals, were also part of this newly rich group. Many became wealthy by buying "junk" bonds, or bonds for companies that were risky investments. Financier Michael Milken pioneered the selling of these bonds. People could receive a large return on their investment if the companies succeeded. However, investors could lose their money if these risky businesses failed.

Milken and his associates raised almost $100 billion selling these bonds. They loaned this capital, or money, to investors who wanted to take over, or buy a controlling interest in, companies. One of the largest corporate transactions in financial history took place in 1988 when an investment firm purchased RJR Nabisco for $25 billion.

Ivan Boesky managed many corporate takeovers. He also summed up the attitude that many people had in the 1980s: "Greed is all right. . . . Everybody should be a little bit greedy." Boesky, however, proved to be a little too greedy. He paid for advance knowledge of mergers and takeovers. He used that information to buy and sell stocks, an illegal practice known as insider trading. Boesky and Milken both ended up in jail, convicted of illegal business activities.

Geraldine Ferraro was a U.S. representative from New York when she ran for vice president in 1984.

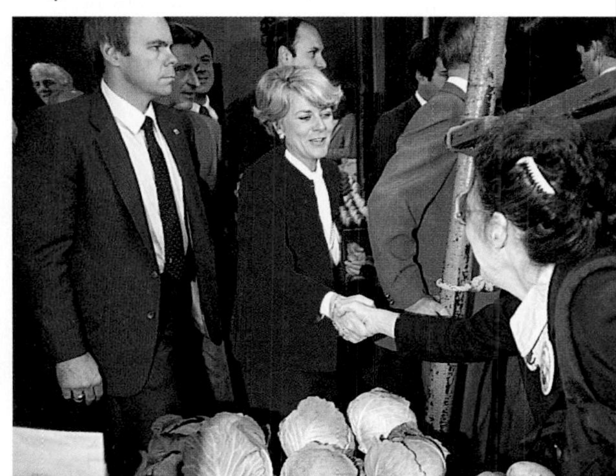

Citizenship and Democracy

The 1984 Election. The 1984 presidential election reflected the popularity of President Ronald Reagan and his policies. A 1983 poll showed that 44 percent of Americans approved of Reagan's job performance. As the nation's economy improved, so did Reagan's approval rating. Polls in 1984 showed support for Democrat presidential candidate Walter Mondale lagging at least 10 percentage points behind support for Reagan. On election day, Reagan received almost 59 percent of the popular vote. Mondale received less than 41 percent. Reagan won all but one state in the election. Mondale won his home state of Minnesota by less than 1 percent.

Critical Thinking: Which groups do you think supported Mondale in the 1984 election?

ANSWER: those not benefiting from Reagan's policies and the economic improvements of the mid-1980s, such as farmers and union members

REVIEW

Linguistic, Visual-Spatial. Have students complete the Section Review questions. Then make a three-column chart on the chalkboard. Label the columns *Reagan's Domestic Policies, Positive Effects,* and *Negative Effects.* Have students make a copy of the chart and use the information in this section to complete it. Call on volunteers to list items in their charts. As they do, complete the chart on the chalkboard.

ASSESS

Have students complete Daily Quiz 23.1.

RETEACH

Linguistic, Logical-Mathematical, Interpersonal. Have students complete Main Idea Activities for Reteaching and Sheltered English 23.1. Ask each student to link related terms in the Identify portion of the Section Review. Students should use each term at least once. Then organize students into pairs. Have one partner list a linked set of terms, and the other identify how they are linked. Partners should switch roles until they have gone through all their sets of links. **SHELTERED ENGLISH**

Section 1 Review ANSWERS

Identify

For significance, see the following pages:

- Ronald Reagan, p. 681
- New Right, p. 682
- Jerry Falwell, p. 682
- supply-side economics, p. 683
- Economic Recovery Tax Act, p 683
- Walter Mondale, p. 685
- Geraldine Ferraro, p. 685
- Gramm-Rudman-Hollings Act, p. 685
- Black Monday, p. 686

Reading for Content Understanding

1. his communication skills, his age and experience, and the way he made people feel good about being Americans

2. by cutting taxes and social programs, reducing business regulations, and increasing defense spending

3. Wealthier Americans tended to benefit; many businesspeople and yuppies grew rich; poorer Americans and minorities tended to lose jobs and government support.

4. Speeches will vary but should explain that cutting taxes will give Americans more money to invest or save, which will expand the economy, create more jobs, and eventually lead to increased tax revenues and a balanced budget.

5. Answers will vary but students might mention that Reagan's conservative stance, his promise to make America great again, the Iran hostage crisis, and the improved economy by 1984 led many Americans to vote for him in 1980 and 1984.

In the fall of 1987 even prosperous groups suffered. After reaching an all-time high in August, the stock market dropped more than 20 percent on October 19. The day became known as **Black Monday**. The market continued to drop, eventually losing some 40 percent of its value. Most economists had no clear explanation for the crash. Some blamed the crash on the rising federal deficit. Unlike the Panic of 1929, this stock market crash did not devastate the economy. The Federal Reserve helped stabilize the economy. One Wall Street broker remembered:

> **"It was bad the day the market crashed, but it wasn't as bad as most people think it was. . . . Good news, bad news, as long as there was news, we would make money."**

Reagan's Critics

Some of President Reagan's critics noted that the prosperity of the mid- to late 1980s did not include everyone. Reagan's budget director, David Stockman, promised that all Americans would eventually benefit from the effects of supply-side economics. However, he also admitted that the plan required "short-run pain in the name of long-run gain."

On Black Monday, traders on the floor of the New York Stock Exchange tried to sell shares and cut losses.

Farmers suffered both short- and long-term pain. They faced low prices for their products as well as falling land values. Many farmers had borrowed heavily. Some lost their land when they could not pay their debts.

Critics also pointed to the high unemployment rate among African Americans and Hispanics. The working poor—people who work, usually at unskilled positions, but do not earn enough to live above poverty level—also faced difficulties. The reductions in federal social welfare programs deeply affected these citizens. Nonetheless, many Americans believed that they were better off during the 1980s.

SECTION 1 REVIEW

Identify and explain the significance of the following:

- **Ronald Reagan**
- **New Right**
- **Jerry Falwell**
- **supply-side economics**
- **Economic Recovery Tax Act**
- **Walter Mondale**
- **Geraldine Ferraro**
- **Gramm-Rudman-Hollings Act**
- **Black Monday**

Reading for Content Understanding

1 **Main Idea** What qualities made President Reagan popular with many voters?

2 **Main Idea** In what ways did Reagan try to balance the budget and improve the economy?

3 **Economic Development** How were different groups in American society affected by Reagan's economic policies?

4 **Writing** *Describing* Imagine that you are Reagan's budget director. Write a two-paragraph speech describing supply-side economics for the president to present to Congress.

5 **Critical Thinking** *Synthesizing Information* How did political and economic events influence Reagan's election victories?

OBJECTIVES

- **Analyze ways the Reagan administration tried to stop the spread of communism in Central America.**
- **Identify the actions that led to the Iran-contra affair.**
- **Explain how changes within the Soviet Union affected the Cold War.**

FOCUS

Motivate Before Reading

Tell students that President Reagan once referred to the Soviet Union as the "focus of evil in the modern world." Ask students to speculate on why he might have held that opinion and how it may have affected his foreign policy. After some discussion, tell students that in this section they will learn about President Reagan's foreign-policy decisions and their results.

SECTION 2

Reagan's Foreign Policy

Reading Focus

In what ways did the Reagan administration try to stop the spread of communism in Central America?

What actions led to the Iran-contra affair?

How did changes within the Soviet Union affect the Cold War?

Key Terms

Sandinistas
contras
Iran-contra affair
Strategic Defense Initiative
perestroika
glasnost
Intermediate-Range Nuclear Forces Treaty

ONE MORNING IN JANUARY 1981, an Iranian guard told American hostage Barry Rosen, "Pack your bags. You're leaving." After 444 days in captivity, Rosen was blindfolded and marched onto a bus. When the bus stopped, he ripped off his blindfold and ran toward the airplane he saw. The plane carried the hostages home. In the United States, Rosen and the other hostages were greeted as heroes. According to Rosen, "In some ways, I think the people were celebrating what they believed was American power." For many Americans, President Ronald Reagan was the symbol of that power.

In Washington, D.C., Americans celebrate the release of the hostages in Iran.

Foreign-Policy Challenges

Many Americans believed that the prolonged Iranian hostage crisis had damaged the international reputation of the United States. President Reagan was determined to restore the public's sense of confidence and security. To demonstrate U.S. strength, he supported increased defense spending and military intervention.

Reagan also vigorously opposed communism. He saw the Cold War as a fight of "good versus evil, right versus wrong." The president and his advisers placed a priority on stopping the spread of communism. Jeane Kirkpatrick, U.S. ambassador to the United Nations (UN), explained Reagan's policy. The Reagan administration refused to support governments it saw as totalitarian, or controlling every aspect of its citizens' lives. However, the administration was willing to support governments with questionable human rights practices if those governments strongly opposed communism.

In October 1983 Reagan sent U.S. troops to overthrow the pro-communist government of

Section 2 RESOURCES

PRINT

★ Guided Reading Strategies 23.2

★ Section 2 Review, p. 691

★ Daily Quiz 23.2

MULTIMEDIA

★ *Teaching Resources CD–ROM*, Lesson 23.2

★ Linking Geography and History Transparency 22: Central America and the Caribbean, 1980s

★ HRW Web site

SHELTERED ENGLISH

★ Main Idea Activities for Reteaching and Sheltered English 23.2

Introduce Key Terms

Linguistic. Review this section's key terms with students. Have them use context cues to determine the meaning of each term. Then have students examine a map of the world and link each term to a region on the map. Ask volunteers to explain their links. Finally, have students write a definition for each term.
SHELTERED ENGLISH

TEACH

Have students read Section 2 and complete Guided Reading Strategies 23.2. Choose one or more of the following activities to explore the section content with students. For further suggestions on block scheduling or team teaching, see the *Block Scheduling Handbook.*

LEVEL 1: Linguistic. (Suggested time: 15 min.) As a class, go over students' Guided Reading Strategies. Then use the Reading Focus questions to highlight the main ideas of the section.
SHELTERED ENGLISH

Global Relations

Grenada. In 1979 Maurice Bishop became prime minister of Grenada. A marxist, Bishop had close ties to communist Cuban leader Fidel Castro. The United States opposed the new regime and stopped all aid to Grenada. In mid-1983, however, Bishop ceased his support of Castro and began making friendly overtures to the United States. The change was short-lived. That October, militant members of Bishop's own party killed him and took control. Citing the need to protect American students in Grenada, the United States invaded the nation. Some 1,900 U.S. troops defeated a mixed Grenadan and Cuban force in three days.

Activity: Use the library and other resources to create a fact sheet on the nation of Grenada today. Describe its geography, population, government, and economy.

MAP ANSWER

El Salvador, Grenada, Honduras, and Panama

Multimedia Resources

Linking Geography and History Transparency 22: Central America and the Caribbean, 1980s

Grenada, a tiny island in the Caribbean Sea. The U.S. mission was short and successful. Reagan hoped that it would encourage Americans to support anticommunist efforts in Central America. The Reagan administration considered stopping the spread of communism in Central America important to U.S. national security.

The U.S. position on El Salvador was particularly complicated. During President Carter's administration, the U.S. government had supported the Salvadoran government in a civil war against communist revolutionaries. The Salvadoran government allowed "death squads" to kill anyone who opposed its cause. In 1980 some 10,000 people were killed. Three American nuns and another American volunteer were among those killed. In response, Carter halted all U.S. aid to El Salvador. In one of his last actions as president, however, Carter renewed aid to El Salvador. He feared that the guerrilla forces would overthrow the government.

Soon after taking office, President Reagan approved $20 million in aid for El Salvador's government. The U.S. government shipped arms and supplies to El Salvador. Some Salvadoran soldiers came to the United States for training. In addition, U.S. military advisers went to El Salvador. During the 1980s the United States provided some $4 billion in aid to El Salvador's government.

U.S. Policy in Nicaragua

The United States was also involved in Nicaraguan affairs. In 1979 a revolutionary Nicaraguan political party known as the **Sandinistas** had overthrown its country's pro-American dictator. Sandinista Daniel Ortega became the country's new leader.

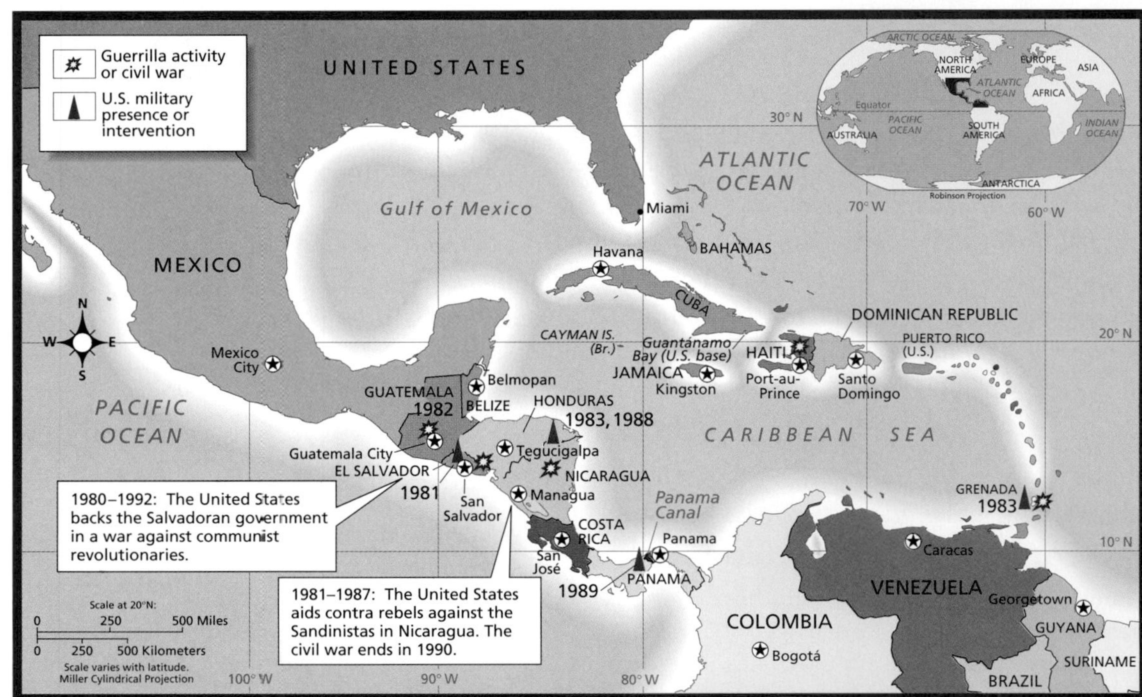

Central America and the Caribbean in the 1980s

Learning from Maps The United States played an active role in the political and military affairs of several countries in Central America and the Caribbean.

Place In which Central American and Caribbean countries did the U.S. military maintain a presence or intervene during the 1980s?

ALL LEVELS: Linguistic, Visual-Spatial. (Suggested time: 35 min.) On the chalkboard, draw a chart with four columns. Title it *Foreign Policy During the Reagan Administration* and label the columns *Nations Involved, Actions Taken, Reasons for Actions,* and *Results.* Have students copy the chart and, using this section, list the foreign-policy events of the Reagan administration. Call on volunteers to explain items in their charts. Then discuss with the class the main goals of Reagan's foreign policy and how well he achieved those goals.

LEVEL 2: Logical-Mathematical, Visual-Spatial. (Suggested time: 30 min.) Give students blank outline maps of the world and have them each create an annotated map that shows the main events in the Iran-contra affair. In addition to illustrating the events of the affair, the map should show the flow of money and arms that occurred. Call on volunteers to explain their maps to the class. Then discuss how the system of checks and balances helps prevent illegal actions in the U.S. government. **SHELTERED ENGLISH**

LEVEL 3: Linguistic, Visual-Spatial. (Suggested time: 25 min. plus homework) Ask students to design a dust jacket for a book on President Reagan's foreign policy. Students should choose a title, create the cover illustration or describe it in writing, and write the text to appear on the inside front and back covers. The text summary should describe the main topics of the book and be

Stopping Communism

The Reagan administration became convinced that the Sandinistas wanted to set up a communist dictatorship. President Reagan worried that if this happened, Central American nations would fall to communism.

In early 1981 the U.S. government demanded that the Nicaraguans stop helping "their revolutionary brothers" in El Salvador. The United States suspended some $15 million in economic aid and millions of dollars of wheat shipments to Nicaragua. Reagan also decided to support anti-Sandinista Nicaraguan rebels known as **contras**. He signed a national security order that provided the Central Intelligence Agency (CIA) with nearly $20 million. The CIA used this money to secretly recruit, train, arm, and pay the contras. By 1985 the contras' fighting force numbered some 20,000.

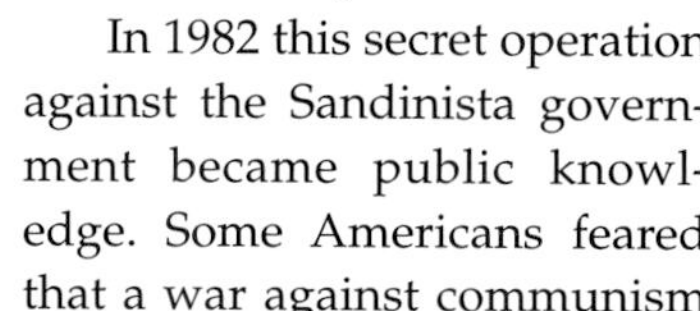

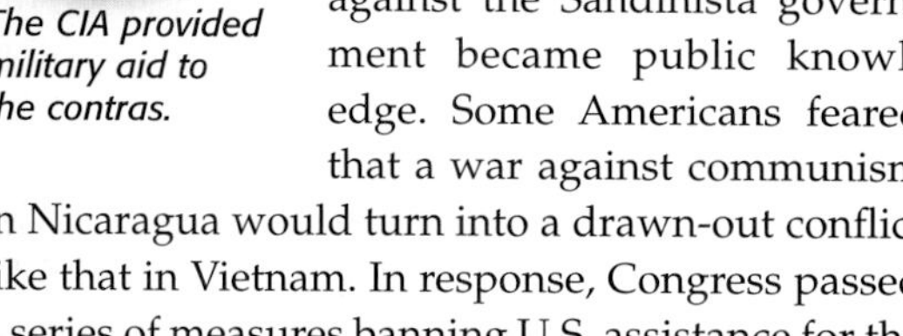

The CIA provided military aid to the contras.

In 1982 this secret operation against the Sandinista government became public knowledge. Some Americans feared that a war against communism in Nicaragua would turn into a drawn-out conflict like that in Vietnam. In response, Congress passed a series of measures banning U.S. assistance for the overthrow of the Sandinista government. The Boland Amendment of 1984 prohibited any U.S. government agency, including the CIA, from providing military aid to the contras.

The Iran-Contra Affair

In the mid-1980s, issues surrounding contra aid became a wider controversy. Pro-Iranian terrorists in Lebanon had taken some Americans hostage. In secret dealings, the terrorists offered to free the hostages. In return, they demanded that the United States sell arms—including ammunition and missiles—to Iran. A trade of arms for hostages would violate U.S. policy against dealing with terrorists. Therefore, the plan called for Israel to pass the weapons to Iran. The United States would then resupply Israel's weapons.

Oliver North, a U.S. Marine lieutenant colonel who served as a national security aide, arranged

Contra rebels train for their military effort against the Sandinistas.

the secret deal. In 1986 North passed some of the profits from the weapon sales to the contras. His actions violated the Boland Amendment. One man who assisted North explained why he helped:

> **"They [the contras] looked to the United States for guidance and for help. We had been supplying them with beans and bullets and blankets and Band-Aids and boots. . . . With the signing of the Boland Amendment, the U.S. Congress was about to walk away. . . . I didn't believe that the United States could just let this happen."**

In the fall of 1986 the **Iran-contra affair**—the name given to the arms deal and resulting scandal—became public. After the story broke, Reagan said:

> **"We did not—repeat—did not trade weapons or anything else for hostages nor will we. We . . . have had nothing to do with other countries or their shipment of arms."**

Many Americans doubted his denials. The Senate held hearings to investigate the Iran-contra affair. Members of Reagan's administration initially blamed North. Other people saw North as unfairly taking the blame for the incident.

The Senate hearings turned up no proof of illegal activity by the president. However, North and other White House officials were convicted of crimes associated with the Iran-contra affair. A court later overturned many of the convictions on technical grounds.

Constitutional Heritage

The Iran-contra Affair. Three different groups investigated the Iran-contra affair and President Reagan's role in it. A special review board criticized Reagan for not providing oversight of the activities of White House officials. Congressional committees concluded that Reagan supported the sale of arms to Iran, aided the contras, and failed to fulfill his responsibilities as president. Independent Counsel Lawrence Walsh, who directed a third investigation, argued that White House officials had attempted to cover up their activities and had previously withheld important information. However, there was never any serious discussion of impeaching President Reagan for his involvement in the Iran-contra affair.

Activity: Have students use the library and search the Internet through the HRW Web site to research the independent counsel's investigation of the Iran-contra affair. Ask students to write a position paper explaining whether they agree or disagree with the investigation's conclusions.

go.hrw.com
SB1 Iran-contra

at least four paragraphs in length. Encourage students to include events in the Soviet Union that affected the United States. Have volunteers share their work with the class.

CLOSE

Linguistic, Logical-Mathematical. Ask students to explain the goals of Reagan's foreign policy *(to show U.S. strength, stop communism, and oppose totalitarian governments)*. Then ask students how Reagan saw the Cold War *(a fight between good and evil, with the Soviet Union as the main force of evil)*. Finally, have students write a paragraph explaining how changes in the Soviet Union affected the Cold War and Reagan's foreign policy.

CHALLENGE AND EXTEND

Linguistic, Logical-Mathematical. Have students use the library and other resources to research Mikhail Gorbachev's leadership of the Soviet Union and his perestroika and glasnost policies. Students should examine what Gorbachev did during his administration and analyze the results of his actions. Have students use their findings to write an American newspaper editorial on Gorbachev's success as a Soviet leader.

Economic Development

Perestroika, Pepsi, and Pizza Hut. Under perestroika, the Soviet government gradually began letting state agencies and enterprises enter directly into joint ventures with companies in the West. In 1986 PepsiCo, a U.S.-based conglomerate, entered into a partnership to open Pizza Hut restaurants across the Soviet Union. The company had been selling its soft drink Pepsi-Cola in the communist nation since 1974. The drink was the first foreign product widely marketed there. In 1989 PepsiCo also became the first non-Soviet company to buy advertising airtime on Soviet television.

Critical Thinking: What effect might an American restaurant have on other eating establishments in the Soviet Union?

Answer: Students might mention that competition might improve food service or cause some establishments to go out of business.

U.S. Marines in Lebanon dig through the remains of their barracks after they were bombed by terrorists.

U.S. Troops in Lebanon

Other foreign-policy actions taken by the Reagan administration included sending U.S. Marines to Lebanon. The U.S. troops were part of a multinational force. They arrived in 1982 to keep the peace between Lebanon and Israel. However, not everyone wanted the troops there. In April 1983, explosions tore apart the U.S. Embassy in Beirut, Lebanon's capital. The explosions killed 63 people, including 17 Americans. In October some Muslim fundamentalists drove a truck loaded with dynamite into the U.S. Marine headquarters compound. The resulting blast killed 241 marines.

In a televised address, President Reagan told the story of a marine wounded in Lebanon. Unable to speak, the soldier wrote the Marine Corps motto, "*Semper fi* [always faithful]," on a piece of paper. Reagan tried to tell the story numerous times before he was able to complete it without becoming too emotional. He used the story to celebrate the courage of the troops.

Yet problems in Lebanon continued. In February 1984 Reagan ordered the U.S. Marines out of Lebanon. Later that year terrorists bombed the newly rebuilt U.S. Embassy in Beirut. The terrorists wanted the United States out of Beirut completely.

U.S.-Soviet Relations

In addition to these problems in the Middle East, the United States faced continuing Cold War pressures. During his first term, President Reagan saw the Soviet Union as an "evil empire." Therefore, he greatly expanded the U.S. defense budget. In addition, he supported the development of the **Strategic Defense Initiative** (SDI). This defense system was designed to shoot down Soviet missiles in space with laser weapons. Critics referred to the SDI as Star Wars. Congress approved $26 billion to develop the SDI, but scientists never produced a workable version of the system.

Political changes in the Soviet Union eventually softened Reagan's hard-line stand in the Cold War. In the early 1980s, three consecutive Soviet leaders died. When Mikhail Gorbachev became the Soviet leader in 1985, a new era of U.S.-Soviet relations began. Gorbachev realized that the Soviet Union was in desperate economic trouble. The country's economy suffered as it tried to keep up with the United States in the nuclear arms race. Gorbachev said, "We cannot remain a major power

The Strategic Defense Initiative was designed to work as a shield protecting the United States from Soviet missiles.

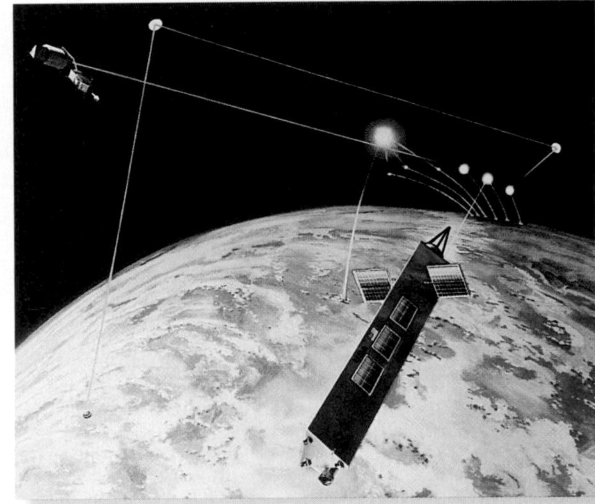

REVIEW

Linguistic, Interpersonal. Have students complete the Section Review questions. Organize students into groups. Assign each group member some portion of this section and have each student write one newspaper headline for a major event in the assigned text. Next, have students give their work to another group member. Tell students to write the first sentence for the article that might follow the headline they received. Then have students pass the work on again and add one sentence to the article they receive. Tell students to continue until all the articles are complete. Call on group members to read some of the articles.

ASSESS

Have students complete Daily Quiz 23.2.

RETEACH

Visual-Spatial, Interpersonal. Have students complete Main Idea Activities for Reteaching and Sheltered English 23.2. Then organize students into four groups and assign each group two of the terms from the Identify portion of the Section Review. Have the groups create illustrations for their terms. Call on each group to explain its work. **SHELTERED ENGLISH**

Many Soviets welcomed Mikhail Gorbachev's reforms.

in world affairs unless we put our domestic house in order." He began a series of political and economic reforms, known as **perestroika**, to restructure the economy. He also started a policy called **glasnost**, or freedom of expression.

To achieve these goals, Gorbachev needed to stabilize international relations. He also had to reduce defense spending and attract Western investment. He decided to reduce Soviet support for communist nations and to dismantle the Soviet "empire" in Eastern Europe. He also worked to reach new arms agreements with the United States.

For the first time since the earliest days of the Soviet state, the Soviet Union held free elections. These changes excited many Soviet citizens. Soviet writer Chengiz Aitmatov described Gorbachev, the new Soviet hero:

> **"Now comes a man who has stirred up the sleeping kingdom. He . . . arose from within this very system, possibly as our last chance of survival. . . . He dared, it would seem, the impossible—a revolution of minds."**

In November 1985 Reagan met with Gorbachev. The leaders held four different summit meetings to discuss nuclear arms reductions. In Iceland the men discussed cutting strategic nuclear forces in half.

In December 1987 the two leaders signed the **Intermediate-Range Nuclear Forces (INF) Treaty**. This treaty eliminated all medium-range nuclear weapons from Europe. The INF Treaty was the first to require the destruction of nuclear missiles. Cold War tensions between the United States and the Soviet Union appeared to be lessening. When asked if he still considered the Soviet Union to be an evil empire, Reagan responded, "No, I was talking about another time, another era."

Pershing II missiles were removed from Europe.

SECTION 2 REVIEW

Identify and explain the significance of the following:
- **Sandinistas**
- **contras**
- **Iran-contra affair**
- **Strategic Defense Initiative**
- **Mikhail Gorbachev**
- **perestroika**
- **glasnost**
- **Intermediate-Range Nuclear Forces Treaty**

Reading for Content Understanding

1 **Main Idea** How did the United States attempt to prevent communism from spreading in Central America?

2 **Main Idea** Make a graphic organizer of the events that led to the Iran-contra affair.

3 **Global Relations** What political changes took place in the Soviet Union in the 1980s?

4 **Writing** *Informing* Imagine that you are a U.S. State Department official. Write a memorandum explaining how Mikhail Gorbachev's reforms have led to a decrease in Cold War tensions.

5 **Critical Thinking** *Determining the Strength of an Argument* Why do you think President Reagan argued that Central America was an important national security concern?

Section 2 Review ANSWERS

Identify
For significance, see the following pages:
- Sandinistas, p. 688
- contras, p. 689
- Iran-contra affair, p. 689
- Strategic Defense Initiative, p. 690
- Mikhail Gorbachev, p. 690
- perestroika, p. 691
- glasnost, p. 691
- Intermediate-Range Nuclear Forces Treaty, p. 691

Reading for Content Understanding

1. by supporting anti-communist forces in Central America and by trying to oust pro-communist governments in the Caribbean

2. Organizers should include the Sandinistas' overthrow of the Nicaraguan government, covert CIA actions to aid the contras, the Boland Amendment, the taking of American hostages in Lebanon, Oliver North's secret deal to sell arms for hostages to fund the contras, discovery of the deal, Reagan's denial of knowledge, the Iran-contra Senate hearings, and the convictions and later reversals.

3. Changes included Gorbachev's policies of perestroika and glasnost.

4. Memorandums will vary but should cite specific examples of Gorbachev's reforms and how they changed U.S. relations with the Soviet Union.

5. Answers will vary but students might mention that Central America is close to the United States.

SECTION 3 LESSON PLAN

OBJECTIVES

- **Describe some of President Bush's major domestic actions.**
- **Identify events that led to the final breakup of the Soviet Union.**
- **Explain what caused the Persian Gulf War and how the conflict ended.**

FOCUS

Motivate Before Reading

Ask students to imagine that a barrier has divided their town. They have not been allowed to cross it, even to see family. Then, after 30 years, the wall is finally taken down. Ask students how it would feel to be able to go anywhere they wanted, visit their family again, and see how much the other side of town has changed. Tell students

Section 3 RESOURCES

PRINT

★ Guided Reading Strategies 23.3

★ Biography Reading 23: Colin Powell

★ Geography Activity 23: The International Drug Trade

★ Graphic Organizer 23: Issues of the Republican Years

★ Section 3 Review, p. 698

★ Daily Quiz 23.3

MULTIMEDIA

★ *Teaching Resources CD–ROM*, Lesson 23.3

★ Linking Geography and History Transparency 24: The Breakup of the Soviet Sphere

SHELTERED ENGLISH

★ Main Idea Activities for Reteaching and Sheltered English 23.3

SECTION 3

George Bush's Presidency

Reading Focus

What were some of President Bush's major domestic actions?

What events led to the final breakup of the Soviet Union?

What caused the Persian Gulf War, and how did the conflict end?

Key Terms

War on Drugs

Americans with Disabilities Act

Commonwealth of Independent States

Operation Desert Storm

THE BRANDENBURG GATE was originally built in the late 1700s as an entrance to the city of Berlin. Since 1961 the Berlin Wall had surrounded the gate. Instead of being an opening, the gate helped to close off Soviet-supported East Berlin. Standing at the gate in 1987, President Reagan asked Mikhail Gorbachev to show his commitment to democratizing efforts in Eastern Europe. Reagan shouted, "If you seek liberalization, come here to this gate. Mr. Gorbachev, open this gate! Mr. Gorbachev, tear down this wall!"

The Brandenburg Gate

The Election of 1988

As President Reagan's vice president, George Bush benefited from Reagan's popular tough stance on communism. In 1988 the Republican Party nominated Bush for president. Republicans hoped that he would appeal to Reagan supporters. However, some Americans did not think Bush was as effective a communicator as Reagan.

The Democrats had a difficult time selecting a candidate. Many challengers entered the presidential primaries, including African American civil rights leader Jesse Jackson. No one, though, clearly led the field. By the end of the primary season, Massachusetts governor Michael Dukakis had won the most presidential delegates. He became the Democratic nominee for president. Dukakis chose Senator Lloyd Bentsen of Texas as his running mate.

Bush selected Dan Quayle, a young, little-known senator from Indiana, as his running mate. During the campaign, Bush vowed to support no new taxes. He told American voters, "Read my lips: no new taxes." He also promised a "kinder, gentler America." The election battle itself, however, was bitter and hard fought. In November, that in this section they will learn about the fall of the Berlin Wall, the end of the Cold War, and the presidency of George Bush.

Introduce Key Terms

Linguistic. Review this section's key terms with students. Have them use context cues to determine each term's meaning and then write a definition for each. Next, tell students to modify some of the definitions to make them incorrect. Have students exchange papers, determine which definitions are incorrect, correct them, and return the papers to their authors for grading.
SHELTERED ENGLISH

TEACH

Have students read Section 3 and complete Guided Reading Strategies 23.3. Choose one or more of the following activities to explore the section content with students. For further suggestions on block scheduling or team teaching, see the *Block Scheduling Handbook.*

LEVEL 1: Linguistic. (Suggested time: 15 min.) As a class, go over students' Guided Reading Strategies. Then use the Reading Focus questions to highlight the main ideas of the section.
SHELTERED ENGLISH

The Republican team in 1988 (from left to right): Marilyn Quayle, Dan Quayle, George Bush, and Barbara Bush

Bush won the presidency with 426 electoral votes to Dukakis's 111.

The Savings and Loan Crisis

Public awareness of a savings and loan (S&L) crisis was one of the first issues that President Bush faced. Traditionally, S&L financial institutions accepted savings from individuals and invested their deposits in mortgages. During the Reagan years, the government had lifted restrictions on the types of investments S&Ls could make. As a result, some S&Ls rapidly expanded their lending. Many S&L owners invested recklessly in the stock market, commercial real estate, and "junk" bonds.

In some cases, bank officials acted fraudulently. They used their clients' deposits to buy themselves yachts, mansions, and corporate jets. When the stock market crashed in 1987, many S&Ls went bankrupt. Reagan's last economic report to the nation concluded, "The irony is that Federal Government policies have led to this debacle [general collapse]."

Many of these failing S&Ls were in Texas and other Sun Belt states. Texas financial institutions had made bad loans to real estate and oil entrepreneurs. As the price of oil dropped, these people were unable to repay their loans. The S&Ls then did not have the money to pay their depositors. However, the federal government insured depositors' savings in S&Ls up to $100,000 per account.

In August 1989 President Bush authorized $166 billion to close or merge many S&Ls. The S&L crisis, the federal deficit, and the need to balance the federal budget forced Bush to break his campaign pledge. In 1990 he agreed to a significant tax increase.

Bush's Domestic Policies

President Bush also responded to other domestic issues. In 1989 he launched a **War on Drugs**—an organized effort at home and abroad to end the trade and use of illegal drugs. As part of the War on Drugs, the Bush administration supported drug treatment centers and education programs. The effort also used law enforcement to end the drug trade. U.S. officials offered legal assistance and financial aid to help foreign nations arrest major drug smugglers. In December 1989 Bush authorized a military invasion of Panama to capture the country's dictator, Manuel Noriega. He was charged with drug smuggling. In 1992 a U.S. federal court convicted Noriega and sent him to prison.

Other domestic programs included an update of the Clean Air Act. This 1990 law required a reduction in the emission, or release, of ozone-destroying chemicals.

The ADA helps many Americans gain greater access to educational facilities.

That same year the president approved the **Americans with Disabilities Act** (ADA). The ADA guaranteed people with disabilities equal access to public accommodations, transportation, and employment opportunities. Congress estimated that the act would affect many millions of Americans.

Bush had more difficulty with one of his nominations to the U.S. Supreme Court. In 1990 the Senate

Citizenship and Democracy

ADA. Signed into law by President Bush in 1990, the Americans with Disabilities Act (ADA) guaranteed people with disabilities equal access to employment opportunities, public accommodations, state and local government services, telecommunications, and transportation. Changes ensuring access to public facilities, such as day-care centers, government offices, hotels, parks, restaurants, and theaters, were to be completed by 1992. By the fall of 1994 all businesses employing 15 or more people had to provide "reasonable accommodation" for all disabled employees who could handle their job's "essential functions." However, businesses did not have to provide accommodations if doing so would cause them "undue hardship."

Critical Thinking: What difficulties might arise in enforcing this law?

ANSWER: Answers will vary but students might mention that the phrases "reasonable accommodation," "essential functions," and "undue hardship" are vague and thus open to interpretation.

ALL LEVELS: Linguistic, Visual-Spatial. (Suggested time: 30 min. plus homework) Ask students to imagine that they have been hired to design the menu for a new upscale restaurant called the George Bush Bistro. Students should list and describe "dishes" that represent the main events and issues of the Bush administration. The menu should separate domestic and international "dishes," and include appetizers, entrees, desserts, and beverages. Encourage students to be creative in their menu design and descriptions. For example, a student might name the dessert section Operation Dessert Storm and focus it on the Persian Gulf War. Display students' menus around the class.

LEVEL 2: Linguistic, Visual-Spatial. (Suggested time: 45 min.) Tell students that they have been hired to make a documentary on the events that led to the end of the Cold War and the formation of the Commonwealth of Independent States. Ask students to create a storyboard for the documentary. The storyboard should use images and descriptive captions to show the main events the documentary will cover and the order in which it will present them. Call on volunteers to share their storyboards with the class. **SHELTERED ENGLISH**

Across the Curriculum

GEOGRAPHY

Berlin. The city of Berlin was a powerful symbol of the Cold War and of the differences between democracy and communism. During the 1980s the East German government showed little interest in reform. However, events in nearby countries forced East Germany to act. In 1989 nearby Hungary relaxed its border restrictions with Austria. As a result, East Germans could bypass the Berlin Wall and leave their country, and many began doing so. East Germans also began peacefully protesting for democratic reform. These protests led a number of government officials to resign. The Berlin Wall came down less than a week later.

Activity: Have students create maps of Europe in 1985 that highlight the locations of East Berlin, West Berlin, the Federal Republic of Germany (West Germany), the German Democratic Republic (East Germany), Austria, and Hungary.

GLOBAL CONNECTIONS ANSWERS

1. Celebrants tore it down when the East German government lifted restrictions on crossing to the West.
2. Answers will vary but students might say that it is easier to construct a physical wall than to restrain the human spirit.

Global Connections

The Fall of the Berlin Wall

Encouraged by new freedoms in the Soviet Union, many East Germans began to demand similar rights for themselves. These demands eventually led to the destruction of the Berlin Wall. East Germans filled the streets of East Berlin in 1989 to protest rules that restricted free movement. Eventually, the East German government withdrew its restrictions on crossing into the West.

Thousands of people gathered for the opening of the gates. At the designated hour of midnight, they streamed into the western side. Celebrators began to dismantle the wall piece by piece. A woman striking blows against the crumbling wall said, "This one's for my mother, [and] this one's for Aunt Frieda." She claimed that the wall had destroyed her family. Other people danced on top of the wall. Some chanted, "The Wall is gone, the Wall is gone." Members of the West German Green Party suggested that the process of breaking down the wall be halted until a waste management program could be administered. Most Germans, however, felt that the wall had stood too long. They did not wait for a trash system to be designed.

Removing the Berlin Wall

The fall of the Berlin Wall—perhaps the most fearsome symbol of communist rule in Eastern Europe—inspired people in many parts of the world. Hundreds of South Koreans living in West Berlin witnessed the emotional celebration at the wall. The event recalled bittersweet memories of their own still-divided country. One American observer was so moved by the wall's destruction that he declared, "It [removal of the wall] shows the indomitability [strength] of the human spirit."

Understanding What You Read

1. How and why was the Berlin Wall torn down?
2. Do you think that the fall of the Berlin Wall demonstrates "the indomitability of the human spirit"? Explain your answer.

easily confirmed David Souter's appointment. The next year Justice Thurgood Marshall, the first African American appointed to the Court, retired. Bush nominated Clarence Thomas, an African American federal judge, to fill Marshall's seat. During the confirmation process, law professor Anita Hill accused Thomas of sexual harassment, or unwanted sexual language or behavior in the workplace. Hill had worked with Thomas at the Equal Employment Opportunity Commission.

Thomas and Hill testified before the Senate in the televised confirmation hearings. The Senate narrowly confirmed Thomas by a vote of 52 to 48. The hearings ignited a national debate. Many women were angry that there were no female senators on the Senate committee. Senate Judiciary Committee chairman Joe Biden summed up the Senate's handling of the hearings, "The judge was wronged, Anita Hill was wronged, the process was wronged."

LEVEL 3: Linguistic, Logical-Mathematical, Intrapersonal. (Suggested time: 30 min. plus homework) Review with students the events leading to the final breakup of the Soviet Union and the formation of the Commonwealth of Independent States. Then ask students to write an essay analyzing how much of an effect U.S. actions had on the end of the Cold War and the Soviet Union's breakup. Have students use information in this section and in previous sections and chapters to support their positions. Call on volunteers to read their essays. Encourage feedback and discussion.

LEVEL 3: Kinesthetic, Linguistic, Intrapersonal. (Suggested time: 30 min. plus homework) Ask students to imagine that they are a speechwriter for President Bush. Have them write two speeches: one that Bush might have delivered to the American public to announce the launch of Operation Desert Storm and to explain the reasons for the war, and one that he might have delivered at the war's end to describe how the conflict concluded and what the effects for the United States will be. Call on volunteers to deliver their speeches as they think Bush would have done.

The End of the Cold War

Meanwhile, dramatic changes continued to sweep the Soviet Union. Soviet leader Mikhail Gorbachev pushed for even greater reforms. President Bush quietly encouraged these changes, and the country moved closer toward democracy.

Independence

Gradually, some Soviet republics—Estonia, Latvia, and Lithuania—declared their independence. In 1989 changes in the countries of Eastern Europe—Bulgaria, Czechoslovakia, East Germany, Hungary, Poland, and Romania—also began to occur more rapidly. Political and civil freedoms increased. East Germans found it easier to leave their country. By the fall, nearly 250,000 people—almost 300 an hour—had left. Faced with this emigration explosion, East Germany's government officially opened its borders.

A piece of the Berlin Wall

In November 1989 pro-democracy activists began tearing down the Berlin Wall. An American student living in West Berlin at the time described the historic moment:

> **"For . . . [East Germans] this was a day of newfound freedom. . . . There was also a feeling that the rules had changed—that people did not need police or armies or government, even if just for one day."**

In October 1990 West Germany and East Germany officially reunited. After the Berlin Wall fell, anticommunist revolutions continued throughout Eastern Europe.

The Collapse of the Soviet Union

Demands for democracy also intensified in the Soviet Union. In November 1990 the United States, the Soviet Union, and many European nations signed a treaty of security and cooperation. The Cold War was over.

Many Soviet republics declared independence. As hard-line Communists watched their nation dissolve, one military group made a desperate move to stop the reforms. In August 1991 the group took Gorbachev hostage. Military leaders ordered troops into the streets of Moscow to put down protests. Instead, crowds of people filled the streets. Pro-democracy leader Boris Yeltsin encouraged the people to stand strong and resist. Many soldiers joined the crowd and promised to fight for democracy. The hard-line Communists recognized their defeat and recalled the troops. Soon after, the Soviet Union disbanded. In December 1991 many of the former Soviet republics formed an alliance, the **Commonwealth of Independent States**.

Many people believed that the buildup of the U.S. military under President Reagan had played a decisive role in winning the Cold War. These observers argued that the Soviet Union's

Breakup of the Soviet Sphere, 1989–1992

Learning from Maps By 1992 largely peaceful revolutions had caused the collapse of many communist governments in Eastern Europe.

Place What countries shown above were part of the former Soviet Union?

Historical Sidelight

Pro-democracy Protests in China. Around the time that people across Eastern Europe and the Soviet Union were calling for greater freedoms, citizens in the People's Republic of China began protesting as well. In 1989 demonstrators, most of them students, began holding pro-democracy protests in Beijing's Tiananmen Square. At the height of the protests, some 1 million people gathered in the square. Unable to break up the demonstration peacefully, China's leaders had tanks and armed troops remove the protesters by force in June. Hundreds of the demonstrators were killed, and thousands more were injured and arrested. The democracy movement achieved no political reforms.

Activity: Have students write a letter to the Chinese government explaining the benefits of democracy and the importance of freedom of speech and assembly.

MAP ANSWER

Belarus, Estonia, Latvia, Lithuania, Moldova, Russia, Ukraine

Multimedia Resources

Linking Geography and History Transparency 24: The Breakup of the Soviet Sphere

CLOSE

Linguistic, Visual-Spatial. Have each student draw a political cartoon to express his or her understanding of a key event, idea, or development associated with George Bush's presidency. Ask students to include captions with their cartoons. Display students' work around the room and call on volunteers to explain their cartoons to the class.

CHALLENGE AND EXTEND

1. **Linguistic, Visual-Spatial, Interpersonal.** Have students use the library and other resources to research the weapons and military strategies of the Persian Gulf War. Ask students to examine how they differed from those used in the Korean and Vietnam Wars. Have students use the information to create a U.S. Military Factbook describing and illustrating the weapons and strategies of modern warfare and how they have changed since Korea. When students are finished, combine their work to compile the class book.

Global Relations

Allied Against Iraq. The Iraqi invasion of Kuwait prompted nations throughout the world to ally against the invading country. Iraq's positioning of its military forces to invade Saudi Arabia, which held 28 percent of the world's oil reserves, strengthened this alliance. Arab states, including Algeria, Egypt, and Syria, saw Saddam Hussein's actions as an attempt to grab more power in the Middle East. Japan and many western and central European countries saw his actions as a threat to their economies. The Soviet Union supported the United Nations and the United States. During the Persian Gulf War, a number of nations, including Great Britain, France, Pakistan, and the United Arab Emirates, contributed troops and weapons to the cause.

Critical Thinking: What did international cooperation in liberating Kuwait reveal about the world's economy?

Answer: It is heavily dependent on oil imported from the Persian Gulf region of the Middle East.

Standing on top of a tank, Boris Yeltsin (center, with papers) asks the Russian people to resist the military leaders who took Mikhail Gorbachev hostage.

attempt to keep up with increased U.S. defense spending had destroyed the Soviet economy. With the government unable to provide its citizens with jobs and food, the Soviet people had demanded democratic reforms.

The breakup of the Soviet Union transformed international relations. President Bush voiced his hope for newfound peace and stability. He declared, "We have before us the opportunity to forge [build] for ourselves and for future generations a new world order."

 Conflict in the Persian Gulf

A conflict in the Middle East soon raised concerns about this "new world order." Saddam Hussein (sah-DAHM hoo-SAYN), the leader of Iraq, had long claimed that neighboring Kuwait was actually a province of Iraq. On August 2, 1990, Iraqi tanks and ground troops poured across the border into Kuwait.

The Beginnings of War

Many nations depend on oil from Kuwait and Saudi Arabia, which borders both Iraq and Kuwait. Iraq's invasion threatened to limit the world's access to Kuwait's oil and to raise oil and gasoline prices. Some countries also feared that Iraq would next invade Saudi Arabia.

The United Nations (UN) quickly condemned the invasion and called on Iraq to withdraw. The UN also declared economic sanctions banning trade with Iraq. On August 7, U.S. troops began arriving in Saudi Arabia to protect the country. The next day President Bush explained to the American public why he was involving the United States in a faraway conflict:

> **"In the life of a nation, we're called upon to define who we are and what we believe. Sometimes these choices are not easy. But today as President, I ask for your support in a decision I've made to stand up for what's right and condemn what's wrong."**

Troops from 27 other nations eventually joined the U.S. forces in a UN military coalition.

While fighting in Kuwait and Saudi Arabia, U.S. and UN troops wore uniforms designed to help them blend in with the desert sand.

2. **Linguistic, Logical-Mathematical, Visual-Spatial.** Have students use the library and other resources to gather images related to the destruction of the Berlin Wall. Have students use the photos to illustrate an annotated time line of the events leading up to and resulting from the destruction of the wall. Call on volunteers to share their work with the class.

3. **Linguistic, Visual-Spatial, Interpersonal.** Have students use the library and other resources to research the results of President Bush's War on Drugs. Students should examine changes in the use and trade of illegal drugs in the United States before and after Bush's administration. Then have the class use the statistics they gathered to help them create an antidrug campaign. Students should discuss and select ways to prevent illegal drug use and then create materials for their campaign. Have students set up their display in a public area of the school, such as the cafeteria.

The UN gave Iraq until January 15, 1991, to remove its troops from Kuwait. Bush warned Saddam Hussein, "A line has been drawn in the sand. . . . Withdraw from Kuwait unconditionally and immediately, or face the terrible consequences." Many Americans supported this policy. One journalist wrote, "Like all bullies [Saddam Hussein] will in the end be deterred [stopped] only by superior force."

Operation Desert Storm

When the Iraqi forces did not withdraw from Kuwait by the deadline, the UN coalition launched **Operation Desert Storm**. During this offensive, airplanes dropped bombs and missiles on Iraq for six weeks. On February 23, the UN coalition launched a massive ground invasion into Kuwait and Iraq. U.S. Army general Norman Schwarzkopf (SHWAWRTS-kawf) commanded the UN troops. UN forces soon freed Kuwait from Iraqi control. Just four days after the invasion, Bush ordered a cease-fire. The United States had lost some 150 soldiers in battle. An estimated 100,000 Iraqi soldiers and civilians had died.

The Persian Gulf War made heroes out of both Schwarzkopf and Colin Powell, chairman of the Joint Chiefs of Staff of the U.S. armed forces.

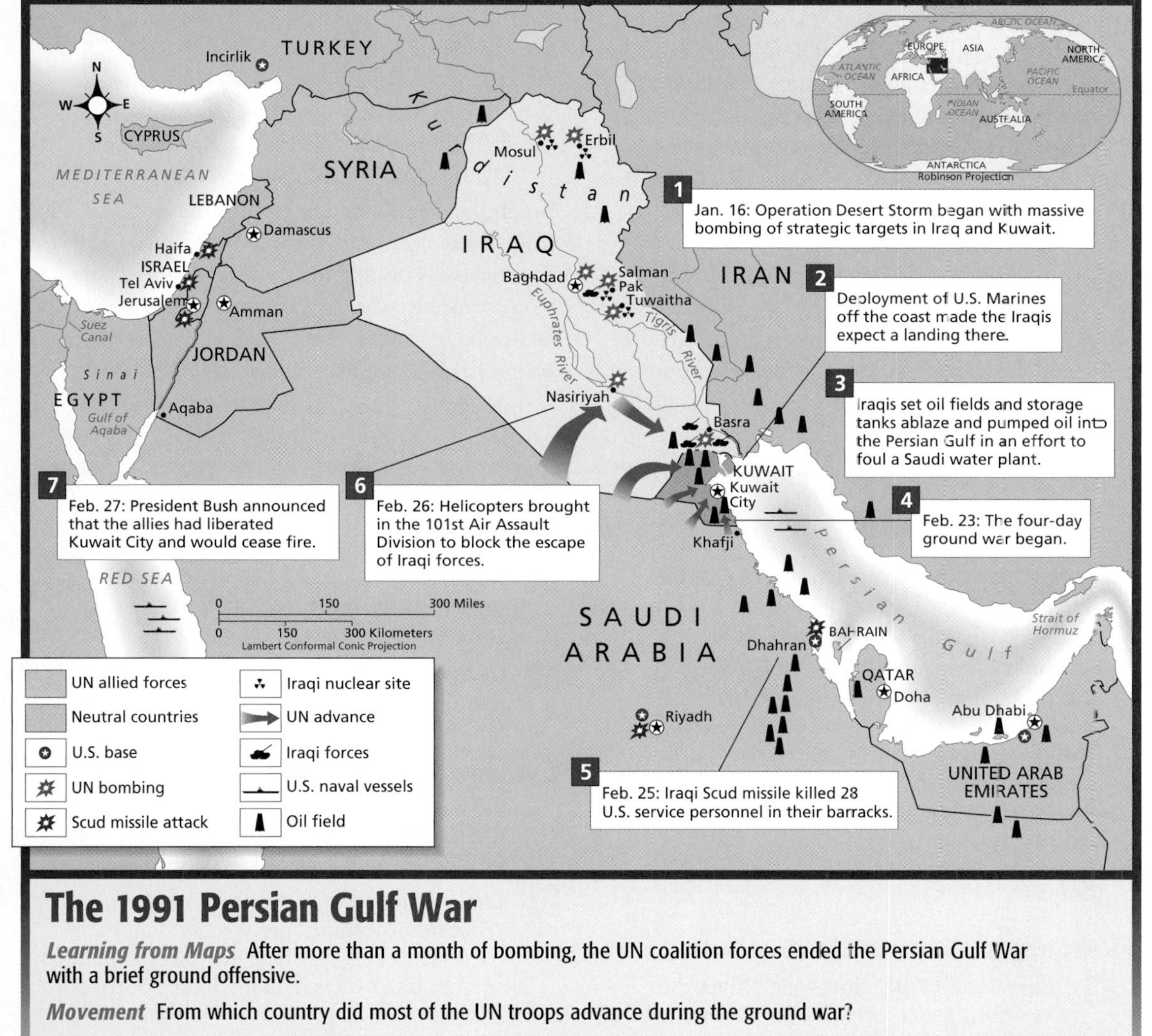

The 1991 Persian Gulf War

Learning from Maps After more than a month of bombing, the UN coalition forces ended the Persian Gulf War with a brief ground offensive.

Movement From which country did most of the UN troops advance during the ground war?

Cultural Diversity

Women in Combat. Women began officially serving in the U.S. military in World War II. They were restricted from combat, however; and the positions open to them were limited. Over time, women's military options have expanded. In the 1980s women flew cargo planes in the invasion of Grenada and tankers during the air strike on Libya. In the 1989 U.S. invasion of Panama, two female pilots flew Black Hawk helicopters carrying troops into what turned out to be battle zones. All pilots, including the two women, received Air Medals for their participation in the assault. These events and the contributions of servicewomen in the Persian Gulf War led Congress to end the restriction on female combat pilots. Female ground soldiers remained restricted to combat support roles, however.

Critical Thinking: What roles do you think women should serve in the U.S. military? Why?

ANSWER: Answers will vary but students should provide support for their opinions and explain their reasoning.

MAP ANSWER
Saudi Arabia

REVIEW

Linguistic, Logical-Mathematical, Interpersonal. Have students complete the Section Review questions. Organize students into four groups and assign each group two of the terms in the Identify portion of the Section Review (one term will be left over). Have each group write two multiple-choice questions related to its assigned terms. Combine the questions into a practice test. Have students take the test. Discuss the answers as a class.

ASSESS

Have students complete Daily Quiz 23.3.

RETEACH

Linguistic, Logical-Mathematical, Interpersonal. Have students complete Main Idea Activities for Reteaching and Sheltered English 23.3. Organize students into pairs. Have each pair list answers to each Reading Focus question. Call on pairs to share their answers with the class. **SHELTERED ENGLISH**

Section 3 Review ANSWERS

Identify

For significance, see the following pages:

- George Bush, p. 692
- Michael Dukakis, p. 692
- War on Drugs, p. 693
- Americans with Disabilities Act, p. 693
- Commonwealth of Independent States, p. 695
- Saddam Hussein, p. 696
- Operation Desert Storm, p. 697
- Norman Schwarzkopf, p. 697
- Colin Powell, p. 697

Reading for Content Understanding

1. S&L crisis, federal deficit, drug trade, air pollution, equal access for Americans with disabilities, U.S. Supreme Court vacancies

2. Flowcharts should include Gorbachev's push for reforms, independence of some Soviet republics, efforts for anticommunist reforms in Eastern Europe, Gorbachev being taken hostage, and the defeat of the hard-line Soviet Communists.

3. Iraq and Saudi Arabia; oil

4. Accounts will vary but should include Iraq's invasion of Kuwait, nations' fears of rising oil prices, UN economic sanctions against Iraq, U.S. troops in Saudi Arabia, the UN's launch of Operation Desert Storm, the success of UN troops in liberating Kuwait, and Bush's call for a cease-fire.

5. Answers will vary but students might say that Iraq may have gained control of much of the Middle East, which could have led to a global oil crisis.

General Powell was the highest-ranking African American to have served in the U.S. military. Even before the cease-fire, Powell had confidence in the coalition forces:

> **"I had no doubt that we would be successful. We had the troops, the weapons, and the plan. What I did not know was how long it would take, and how many of our troops would not be coming home."**

The U.S. government prohibited women from taking part in combat as fighter pilots or ground soldiers. However, more than 35,000 American women served in the Gulf War. One female soldier, a medical officer assigned to a combat unit, recalled, "I wasn't afraid that I would panic in combat or fail to do my job; I knew I could do it." After the Persian Gulf War, the debate over whether to expand the role of women in combat intensified. In December 1991 Congress voted to allow women to serve as combat pilots.

For many Americans, the victory in the Persian Gulf War eased some of the painful memories from the Vietnam War. However, the war did not completely resolve the situation in Iraq. Hussein reaffirmed his authority despite heavy economic sanctions following Iraq's military defeat. The Iraqi leader also failed to keep some of the cease-fire terms. For example, he prevented the UN from finding and destroying Iraq's remaining weapons of mass destruction. The situation in Iraq remained unstable throughout the 1990s.

In the Persian Gulf War, female soldiers were not allowed in combat positions.

SECTION 3 REVIEW

Identify and explain the significance of the following:

- **George Bush**
- **Michael Dukakis**
- **War on Drugs**
- **Americans with Disabilities Act**
- **Commonwealth of Independent States**
- **Saddam Hussein**
- **Operation Desert Storm**
- **Norman Schwarzkopf**
- **Colin Powell**

Reading for Content Understanding

1. **Main Idea** What domestic issues did President Bush tackle?
2. **Main Idea** Create a flowchart that describes the events leading to the collapse of the Soviet Union.
3. **Geographic Diversity** *Region* Which nations border Kuwait, and what important natural resource do they have?
4. **Writing** *Expressing* Imagine that you are a historian who is writing a brief account of the Persian Gulf War. Write two paragraphs on the war's causes and outcomes.
5. **Critical Thinking** *Drawing Conclusions* What do you think might have happened if the United States had not taken a stand against Iraq? Give reasons to support your answer.

OBJECTIVES

- Describe important advances in medical research and space exploration in the 1980s.
- Identify technological advances of the 1980s.
- Explain how music and movies changed in the 1980s.

FOCUS

Motivate Before Reading

Ask students to name and describe some major advances, developments, or trends in medical research, movies, music, space research, technology, television, and sports of the last five years. Write students' responses on the chalkboard and group the responses by category. Give students time to explain and discuss their responses. Then tell students that in this section they will

Technology and Culture

Reading Focus

What important advances were made in medical research and space exploration in the 1980s?

What new technological advances occurred in the 1980s?

How did music and movies change in the 1980s?

Key Terms

Acquired Immune Deficiency Syndrome
genetic engineering
Challenger
compact discs

In the early 1980s scientists inserted the gene that produces human insulin into E. coli. *This bacterial microorganism lives in humans' intestines. The scientists then manipulated the genes of the* E. coli. *The bacteria became capable of producing human insulin for diabetics. In 1982 scientist Robert Sinsheimer encouraged others to examine the possible effects of this ability to manipulate genes, the basic building blocks of human life. He worried that people were interfering with nature. He asked three crucial questions: "Is it safe? Is it wise? Is it moral?"*

Colored electron micrograph of E. coli

Medical Research

In 1981, scientists first reported the disease known as **Acquired Immune Deficiency Syndrome** (AIDS). Caused by the human immunodeficiency virus (HIV), AIDS forces the body's immune system to shut down. The probability increases that victims will contract other illnesses, such as pneumonia, and die.

In the early 1980s, AIDS spread quickly and threatened to become an epidemic. By the end of the decade an estimated 1 to 1.5 million Americans were infected with the virus. By 1997 the number of deaths from AIDS in the United States had reached more than 385,000. Scientists tried to find a cure or drug therapies to stop the disease.

By the end of the 1980s, medical researchers had also determined the causes of other diseases, including cystic fibrosis, muscular dystrophy, and some cancers. Some scientists thought that **genetic engineering**, the deliberate altering of genes, could prevent many diseases from developing in individuals. The biological office of the U.S. Department of Energy created the Human Genome Project to advance such research. The goal of the project is to "map" the human genome,

Section 4 RESOURCES

PRINT

- ★ Guided Reading Strategies 23.4
- ★ Primary Source Reading 23: President Reagan Remembers the *Challenger* Crew
- ★ Section 4 Review, p. 703
- ★ Daily Quiz 23.4

MULTIMEDIA

- ★ *Teaching Resources CD–ROM*, Lesson 23.4
- ★ Everyday Life in America Transparency 32: The AIDS Quilt Project, 1980s

SHELTERED ENGLISH

- ★ Main Idea Activities for Reteaching and Sheltered English 23.4

Multimedia Resources

Everyday Life in America Transparency 32: The AIDS Quilt Project, 1980s

learn about advances, developments, and trends in these same areas during the 1980s and how these changes affected American society.

Introduce Key Terms

Linguistic. Review this section's key terms with students. Then ask them to divide the terms into two pairs. Call on volunteers to explain the pairings they made. Then have students write in their notebooks the definition for each term. **SHELTERED ENGLISH**

TEACH

Have students read Section 4 and complete Guided Reading Strategies 23.4. Choose one or more of the following activities to explore the section content with students. For further suggestions on block scheduling or team teaching, see the *Block Scheduling Handbook.*

LEVEL 1: Linguistic. (Suggested time: 15 min.) As a class, go over students' Guided Reading Strategies. Then use the Reading Focus questions to highlight the main ideas of the section. **SHELTERED ENGLISH**

Across the Curriculum

SCIENCE

Genetic Engineering. Americans expressed mixed feelings about genetic engineering. A presidential commission declared that scientists had a responsibility to conduct research that could alleviate human suffering. The commission also called for the creation of a council to oversee genetic engineering studies. In response, Congress formed the biomedical Ethics Advisory Commission. The Human Genome Project, founded to study human genes, devoted some of its budget to studying the ethical and legal issues associated with its research.

Critical Thinking: What do you think were some of the aspects of genetic engineering that alarmed some people?

ANSWER: Students might mention unanticipated biological disasters or efforts to clone humans.

the complete set of genetic material. The genome is made up of about 60,000 to 100,000 genes. The project has sparked worldwide interest and involves an international network of genetic researchers.

The Space Shuttle

New scientific advances also occurred in space exploration. In 1981 NASA launched the world's first space shuttle, a cost-saving reusable spacecraft. The shuttle is launched as a rocket. While in orbit, it operates like a typical spacecraft. When the shuttle returns to Earth, however, it lands like an airplane on a runway. During the 1980s NASA sent several different space shuttles into orbit.

On a space shuttle mission in June 1983, scientist and astronaut Sally Ride became the first American woman to fly into outer space. After the voyage she noted that what she would "remember most about the flight was that it was fun. In fact, I'm sure it was the most fun that I'll ever have in my life."

In 1984 NASA opened the space program to include selected civilians on its missions. Social studies teacher Christa McAuliffe was the first person chosen for this honor. She explained her interest in the space program:

> **"I remember the excitement in my home when the first satellites were launched. . . . I watched the Space Age being born and I would like to participate."**

Seconds after the flight carrying McAuliffe lifted off in January 1986, a small cloud of smoke escaped from the space shuttle ***Challenger***. A little over a minute into the flight, the shuttle exploded and fell toward Earth. The NASA announcer reported that there was "obviously, a major malfunction." All seven crew members aboard *Challenger* were killed. Millions of people watched the horrifying event on live television. An investigation later concluded that the explosion had begun in the fuel tank. An O-ring, a tiny sealing ring, had failed. NASA worked for more than two years to improve the shuttle. In September 1988 NASA successfully launched the space shuttle *Discovery*.

Technological Developments

Technological advances during the 1980s affected many areas of society. New inventions changed the way people lived, worked, and played.

Personal Computers

In the 1980s the personal computer (PC) became a popular household item. The market for PCs began to grow after IBM produced its first PC in 1981. With aggressive marketing, IBM's PC sales climbed in three years from 25,000 to 3 million. Most of these PCs used a basic operating system called MS-DOS. This software was created by American programmer Bill Gates. The company Gates founded, Microsoft, was the world's first personal computer software business. It soon became the largest software company in the world.

An early computer mouse from the late 1960s

In 1984 Apple Computer introduced the Macintosh personal computer. These computers had an operating system that allowed people to use icons, or pictures, to perform many computer commands. The Macintosh also popularized the use of the "mouse," a device used to move a cursor across the computer screen. These

American artist George Segal created realistic, life-size sculptures for the cover of Time *magazine.*

ALL LEVELS: Linguistic, Logical-Mathematical, Visual-Spatial. (Suggested time: 30 min. plus homework) Ask students to plan a museum exhibit on change in American culture and society in the 1980s. The exhibit should include advances in medicine, space research, and technology; music, movies, and television; and sports. Have students choose a name for the exhibit, list artifacts and displays that they would like to include, and design a floorplan that shows where certain displays will be. Call on volunteers to share their work with the class.

SHELTERED ENGLISH

LEVEL 2: Linguistic, Musical-Rhythmic, Visual-Spatial. (Suggested time: 45 min. plus homework) Divide the class in half. Have half the class write song lyrics about advances in medicine, space research, or technology during the 1980s. Have the other half write song lyrics describing music, movies, television, or sports during the 1980s. Encourage students to put their lyrics to the tune of a song popular during the 1980s. For homework, have students write a description of a music video to accompany their song. Call on volunteers to present their work to the class.

American Literature

"Mother Tongue"

Amy Tan

Amy Tan became famous in 1989 with her best-selling novel The Joy Luck Club. *She often writes about the lives and concerns of Asian American women. In this essay excerpt Tan explores what it meant to grow up hearing different patterns of language.*

Chinese American author Amy Tan

I am a writer. And by that definition, I am someone who has always loved language. I am fascinated by language in daily life. . . .

Lately, I've been giving more thought to the kind of English my mother speaks. Like others, I have described it to people as "broken" or "fractured" English. . . .

. . . I was ashamed of her English. I believed that her English reflected the quality of what she had to say.

. . . It wasn't until 1985 that I finally began to write fiction. . . .

I later decided I should envision a reader for the stories I would write. And the reader I decided upon was my mother, because these were stories about mothers. So with this in mind . . .

I began to write stories using all the Englishes I grew up with: the English I spoke to my mother, which for lack of a better term might be described as "simple"; . . . my translation of her Chinese, which could certainly be described as "watered down"; and what I imagined to be her translation of her Chinese if she could speak in perfect English. . . . I wanted to capture . . . her intent, her passion, her imagery, the rhythms of her speech and the nature of her thoughts.

. . . I knew I had succeeded where it counted when my mother finished reading my book and gave me her verdict: "So easy to read."

Understanding Literature

1. What were the different ways that language was used in Amy Tan's household?
2. Do you think that hearing different languages when growing up would be an advantage or a disadvantage? Explain your answer.

Daily Life

A Puzzling Craze. During the early 1980s a colorful puzzle called a Rubik's Cube took the United States by storm. The puzzle was a cube consisting of 26 smaller cubes that could be rotated. When sold, each side of the cube was a single, different color. The challenge was to mix up the smaller cubes and then rearrange them to make each side a single color again. Although it seemed simple, the cube could theoretically be arranged in 43 quintillion combinations, and only one was correct. People of all ages played with Rubik's Cubes. Numerous books on solving the puzzle appeared and sold in the millions. At speed contests, people raced to solve the puzzle. Many people never could solve it, though.

Critical Thinking: Why do you think the Rubik's Cube became so popular?

ANSWER: Students might say that it was challenging for people of all ages, yet could be solved by children.

AMERICAN LITERATURE ANSWERS

1. the simple English Tan spoke to her mother, her mother's broken English, and Tan's translation of her mother's Chinese

2. Answers will vary but students might say that children can easily learn many languages if they hear them spoken every day.

"user-friendly" features were soon widely copied by other computer makers.

The potential influence of the personal computer was so great that in 1982 *Time* magazine chose a computer as Machine of the Year instead of the magazine's typical Man of the Year. By 1988 the sales of personal computers had reached 10 million. PCs had become an important part of many people's daily lives.

New Recording Inventions

The 1980s also saw the growth of the videocassette recorder (VCR). These machines allowed owners to program them to record TV shows. Most VCR owners, however, used them to play movie videotapes.

In the mid-1980s **compact discs**, or CDs, offered a new way

An early CD, or compact disc

LEVEL 3: Linguistic, Logical-Mathematical, Intrapersonal. (Suggested time: 45 min.) Ask students to review this section and choose the advance or trend that they think had the greatest impact on American society. Have them write an essay stating their choice, explaining why they chose it, and describing what they see as its short- and long-term effects on society. Call on volunteers to read their essays. Encourage feedback.

CLOSE

Linguistic, Interpersonal. Ask students to name some ways that the advances discussed in this section have changed American society. Encourage students to think of both positive and negative changes. Then have students write a paragraph describing how life today might be different if one of these advances had never been made. Call on volunteers to read their paragraphs.

CHALLENGE AND EXTEND

Linguistic, Visual-Spatial, Interpersonal. Organize students into groups and assign each group one of the major topics in this section. Have groups use the library and other resources to research their topics. Then tell the groups that they are making a film related to that topic. Have each group outline the plot of the

Section 4 Review ANSWERS

Identify

For significance, see the following pages:

- Acquired Immune Deficiency Syndrome, p. 699
- genetic engineering, p. 699
- Sally Ride, p. 700
- Christa McAuliffe, p. 700
- *Challenger*, p. 700
- Bill Gates, p. 700
- compact discs, p. 701
- Meryl Streep, p. 702
- Steven Spielberg, p.702
- Carl Lewis, p. 703

Reading for Content Understanding

1. discovered AIDS and the causes of some diseases; made advances in genetic research; developed the space shuttle

2. music on CDs; Bruce Springsteen and similar musicians; fund-raising concerts; movies about farmers' lives; science fiction, adventure, and fantasy movies with new, spectacular special effects

3. PCs, VCRs, CD players and CD–ROM drives; answers will vary but students might mention that these inventions provided more entertainment options and affected the way Americans played and worked.

4. Descriptions will vary but should include cable television, VCRs, CDs, computers, and special effects in movies.

5. Answers will vary but students might mention that many people attended or watched these events because they included many popular performers and raised money for worthy causes.

to record and play music. This new technology created a clearer sound than possible on record albums or cassette tapes.

CDs were also used for storing huge quantities of data, such as the contents of an encyclopedia, on a single disc. These discs were usually "read-only memory," or CD–ROM. Beginning in 1985, CD–ROM drives were built into some personal computers. By the early 1990s the CD had almost made the long-playing record album, or LP, extinct.

Music and Movies

The invention of compact discs helped rock music to continue its popularity. Bruce Springsteen was among the most popular performers of the 1980s. His 1984 recording *Born in the U.S.A.* sold more than 13 million copies in its first year and a half.

Springsteen also participated in some of the fund-raising musical events that became popular in the 1980s. Numerous musicians performed at Live Aid, a televised show of simultaneous concerts in London and Philadelphia. Live Aid was a fund-raiser for African famine relief. Some 1.5 billion people watched the show and pledged more than $40 million to help with relief efforts. One Live Aid organizer saw its appeal as a way for rock fans to participate in a good cause. The volunteer said, "The point is not problems. The point is, we can become winners."

Other musicians in the United States sponsored similar fund-raising concerts, called Farm Aid, to benefit American farmers. One concert supporter explained: "The main point of Farm Aid is to bring the plight [problems] of the American farmer to the attention of the nation."

Some movies in the mid-1980s also brought attention to the situation affecting farmers. These movies included *Places in the Heart*, *Country*, and *The River*. One of the most popular movie actors in the 1980s was Meryl Streep. She took on a different look, nationality, or accent in almost every one of her movie roles. Streep played a British woman, a Nazi concentration camp

Bruce Springsteen's Born in the U.S.A. *tour lasted 18 months. "The Boss" often performed for four hours.*

survivor, and a Danish writer. Responding to a question about her use of accents, Streep responded, "I'm always baffled by this question. How could I play that part and talk like me?" Streep received six Academy Award nominations for Best Actress.

Science fiction, adventure, and fantasy movies also gained popularity. George Lucas and Steven Spielberg, working separately or together, made some of the most popular movies of the 1980s. Following the success of *Star Wars* in 1977, Lucas released two sequels—*The Empire Strikes Back,* in 1980, and *Return of the Jedi,* in 1983. Spielberg's movie *E.T.—The Extraterrestrial* told the story of friendship between a lonely boy on Earth and an alien from space. *E.T.* introduced the phrase "Phone home" to many Americans. Lucas and Spielberg worked together on an action-adventure series of movies with archaeologist Indiana Jones as the hero. These movies contained spectacular special effects made possible by the technical advances of the 1980s.

Trends in Television

The television industry was also experiencing change. Cable television first began in the late 1960s, but grew rapidly during the 1980s. With

In the movie E.T., *Elliott helps an alien find his way home, which is 3 million light-years away.*

movie, choose a title, cast the major characters, select 1980s music for the soundtrack, and design a poster promoting the movie. Have each group present its project to the class. Then display each group's work in the classroom.

REVIEW

Linguistic, Interpersonal. Have students complete the Section Review questions. Then divide the class into pairs. Have each pair create flash cards for the main people and events in this section. Then have partners take turns using the cards to quiz each other on the section.

ASSESS

Have students complete Daily Quiz 23.4.

RETEACH

Visual-Spatial, Interpersonal. Have students complete Main Idea Activities for Reteaching and Sheltered English 23.4. On the chalkboard, make the first part of a graphic organizer covering the material in this section. You may want to use the section subheads as the top level of your organizer. Then have the class help you complete the organizer. **SHELTERED ENGLISH**

cable television, television signals are sent to an antenna and then relayed by cable to paying customers. By the end of the 1980s, nearly 60 percent of American homes had cable service. The average number of cable channels had risen to nearly 30. Many channels focused on one type of programming. For example, Cable News Network (CNN), an all-news channel, debuted in 1980. Owner Ted Turner said he created CNN to "offer those who want it a choice." All-sports and all-movie channels also began broadcasting.

In the early 1980s MTV, a rock music cable channel, went on the air. This channel showed music videos, which were first made in the late 1970s to promote bands. MTV videos featured experimental editing styles that became popular in movies and television.

Sports in the 1980s

Television was also important to one of the biggest sporting events of the decade—the 1984 Summer Olympics held in Los Angeles, California. The American Broadcasting Company (ABC) paid some $225 million to broadcast the Games in the United States. An estimated 2 billion viewers worldwide watched the Games. One writer described the Summer Games as

> **"ceremony and celebration, anticipation and achievement. For those who were there as participants and witnesses, the feeling and the images of that summer's fortnight [two weeks] will forever tarry [stay awhile] in memory."**

One of the most memorable competitors was American sprinter and long jumper Carl Lewis. Lewis won four gold medals, matching Jesse Owens's accomplishments in the 1936 Olympics. At age 16, U.S. gymnast Mary Lou Retton won five medals, including a gold in individual all-around gymnastics. Speaking of the Olympics, Retton said, "It was just like I dreamt it, the excitement, the tension, the crowd."

The competition, however, did not include all nations. The Soviet Union and some other communist nations boycotted the 1984 Summer Olympics. The 1988 Olympics in Seoul, South Korea, reflected the easing of Cold War tensions. The United States and the Soviet Union both participated for the first time since 1976.

Mary Lou Retton received perfect scores in her last two events to win a gold medal.

SECTION 4 REVIEW

Identify and explain the significance of the following:

- **Acquired Immune Deficiency Syndrome**
- **genetic engineering**
- **Sally Ride**
- **Christa McAuliffe**
- ***Challenger***
- **Bill Gates**
- **compact discs**
- **Meryl Streep**
- **Steven Spielberg**
- **Carl Lewis**

Reading for Content Understanding

1 **Main Idea** What new advances in medical research and space exploration were made in the 1980s?

2 **Main Idea** What were some of the trends in movies and music in the 1980s?

3 **Technology and Society** What new technological inventions became popular in the 1980s? How did they affect Americans?

4 **Writing** *Describing* Imagine that you are preparing a time capsule to be opened in 100 years. Write a description of the new entertainment technologies that were developed in the 1980s.

5 **Critical Thinking** *Drawing Conclusions* Why do you think an event like Live Aid was successful?

Chapter 23 Review ANSWERS

Identifying People and Ideas

1. conservative coalition that supported Reagan's call for smaller government and a stronger anticommunist foreign policy

2. economic theory, which Reagan supported, arguing that cutting taxes will spur economic growth and lead to increased tax revenues and a balanced federal budget

3. deal in which the United States sold arms to Iran via Israel in exchange for the freedom of American hostages in Lebanon, and used the money from the arms sale to fund the contras in Nicaragua; violated the Boland Amendment

4. Soviet leader whose glasnost and perestroika reform policies led to the breakup of the Soviet Union and helped end the Cold War

5. President Bush's organized effort at home and abroad to end the production, trade, and use of illegal drugs

6. law guaranteeing people with disabilities equal access to public accommodations, transportation, and employment opportunities

7. chairman of the U.S. military's Joint Chiefs of Staff during the Persian Gulf War; highest-ranking African American to have served in the U.S. military

8. Texan who served as U.S. president from 1989 to 1993; declared War on Drugs and oversaw Persian Gulf War

9. U.S. space shuttle that exploded moments into its flight when a faulty O-ring failed; the entire crew died

10. the altering of genes

Review and Assessment RESOURCES

PRINT
- ★ Chapter 23 Review, pp. 704–05
- ★ Vocabulary Activity 23
- ★ Chapter 23 Study Guide
- ★ Chapter 23 Test (Form A or B)

MULTIMEDIA
- ★ Audio Program, Ch. 23 (English and Spanish)
- ★ *Global Skill Builder CD–ROM*
- ★ Chapter 23 Test Generator
- ★ HRW Web site

SHELTERED ENGLISH
- ★ Spanish Glossary
- ★ Sheltered English Chapter 23 Test

ASSESS

Have students complete one of the Chapter 23 tests. As an alternate assessment, assign the Chapter 23 Investigation.

Using the Time Line
1. a **4.** c
2. e **5.** f
3. b **6.** d

Understanding Main Ideas
1. It demonstrated the desire of Americans to reduce the size of the government and to feel pride in being part of a great and strong nation again.

2. gains—lower taxes, fewer regulations, booming economy in the mid- to late 1980s; setbacks—recession in the early 1980s; increased layoffs and unemployment; hardships for farmers, minorities, and the working poor; failure of "junk" bonds; 1987 stock market crash; S&L crisis

3. It is close to the United States and several of the nations there had communist governments or ties, or were experiencing communist-backed rebellions.

4. The Soviet Union could no longer afford the arms race, Gorbachev instituted political and economic reforms, and people in Eastern Europe and the Soviet Union began demanding more freedoms. These events led to the breakup of the Soviet Union and the end of the Cold War.

5. economic sanctions and then military force to liberate Kuwait; Iraq withdrew from Kuwait.

6. PCs, VCRs, CD players and CD–ROM drives

Reviewing Themes
1. initially, caused a recession and layoffs; then led to an economic boom that made many people richer but also created hardships for farmers, minorities, and the working poor; increased the deficit and the national debt

CHAPTER 23 REVIEW

Chapter Summary

During the 1980s President Reagan tried to improve the U.S. economy. He also fought against communism in Central America. He increased military spending, which encouraged political changes in the Soviet Union. President Bush presided over the end of the Cold War and the victory in the Persian Gulf War. New scientific and technological advances in the 1980s included the space shuttle, personal computers, and CDs.

On a separate sheet of paper, complete the following activities.

Identifying People and Ideas

Describe the historical significance of the following:

1. New Right
2. supply-side economics
3. Iran-contra affair
4. Mikhail Gorbachev
5. War on Drugs
6. Americans with Disabilities Act
7. Colin Powell
8. George Bush
9. *Challenger*
10. genetic engineering

Internet Activity

go.hrw.com
SB1 End of the Cold War

Search the Internet through the HRW Web site to find sites on the fall of the Berlin Wall. Write down five quotations that describe how people on both sides of the wall felt about its destruction. Use the quotations as part of a news broadcast about the event.

Understanding Main Ideas

1. How did Ronald Reagan's presidency represent a new era in the United States?
2. What were some of the business gains and setbacks in the 1980s?
3. Why was Central America an important foreign-policy concern for Reagan?
4. Why did the Cold War end?
5. How did the United States respond to Iraq's invasion of Kuwait? What were the results?
6. What were some of the technological advances of the 1980s?

Reviewing Themes

1. **Economic Development** How did Reagan's use of supply-side economics affect Americans?
2. **Global Relations** How did reforms in the Soviet Union lead to changes in Europe?
3. **Technology and Society** In what ways did the scientific and technological advances of the 1980s change the lives of Americans?

Using the Time Line

Number your paper from 1 to 6. Match the letters on the time line below with the following events.

1. **The Economic Recovery Tax Act reduces personal income taxes.**
2. **The Berlin Wall is torn down.**
3. **Sally Ride becomes the first American woman to fly on a space shuttle.**
4. **American voters re-elect Ronald Reagan.**
5. **UN forces stage a massive ground invasion of Kuwait.**
6. **The stock market experiences Black Monday.**

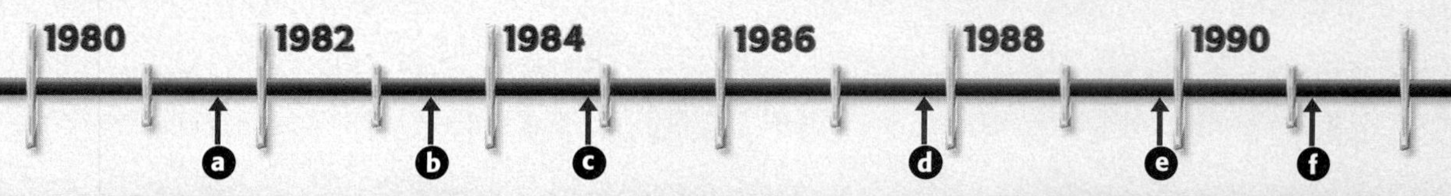

RETEACH

Linguistic, Visual-Spatial. Organize students into four groups and assign each group one section of the chapter. Ask the groups to create a time line of the significant events in the assigned section. Have the groups draw their time lines on the chalkboard or on sheets of butcher paper. Then have each group explain to the class the significance of each event.
SHELTERED ENGLISH

Using the Internet

HRW Have students continue their Internet research through the HRW Web site. Ask students to imagine that they are in Berlin at the time the wall is being taken down. Instruct them to write a postcard to a friend in the United States describing the events surrounding the destruction of the Berlin Wall.

Portfolio Extension

1. Have students continue by creating a brochure to describe the science museum exhibit they designed.

2. Have students design a marker to indicate the location of their time capsule. The marker should explain what the capsule is and its value to the future.

Thinking Critically

1. **Making Comparisons** Compare and contrast the foreign-policy actions of Presidents Reagan and Bush.
2. **Identifying Cause and Effect** How might women's participation in the Persian Gulf War have changed some people's opinions about women's role in the military?
3. **Drawing Conclusions** Why do you think most Americans supported U.S. involvement in the Persian Gulf War?

Writing About History

1. **Persuading** Imagine that you are an organizer for Farm Aid. Write a brochure persuading musicians to perform at the event. Be sure to explain how their participation will help American farmers.
2. **Expressing** Write a letter to the head of NASA expressing your opinion concerning the role the United States should play in space exploration over the next 20 years. Base your opinion on previous space missions. Be sure to explain your point of view.

Linking Geography and History

1. **Location** Why was Kuwait's fate seen as important to U.S. national interests?
2. **Region** Why did Reagan see communism in Nicaragua as such a threat?

Building Your Portfolio

Complete the following activities individually or in groups.

1. **Technology in Action** Design a science museum exhibit to show the medical and technological advances made in the 1980s. Be sure to include as much information as possible on how these different inventions or techniques work. You will need to include diagrams and photographs of the inventions as well as items related to them. Write a paragraph to accompany the images. Explain how each invention or advance was something new in the 1980s. Discuss the role the invention or advance plays in society today.
2. **A Modern Time Capsule** Imagine that a special government commission has asked you to create a time capsule from the 1980s. Design a storage plan and a box for your time capsule. Then create a "time capsule must have" document that lists the included items and explains their importance. Finally, write a speech to deliver to the American public when you bury your time capsule.

History Skills Workshop

Using Visual Resources Study the image to the right, which is a political cartoon from the 1980s. Briefly describe what the cartoon means and what the artist probably thinks of President Reagan's Strategic Defense Initiative. Then draw your own political cartoon showing one of the Reagan administration's accomplishments.

2. helped to undermine the Communist Party in the Soviet Union and to bring the Cold War to an end

3. They provided some medical advances and more entertainment options.

Thinking Critically

1. Reagan was more outspoken in his opposition of communism; both were willing to use military force, but Reagan used it more often to fight communism, while Bush used it more to protect U.S. interests.

2. Answers will vary but students might mention that it convinced more people to support women in combat because the women in the Gulf War proved they could handle wartime conditions.

3. Answers will vary but students might mention the need for oil and that many Americans opposed Iraq's invasion of Kuwait.

Writing About History

1. Brochures will vary but should point out the hardships farmers faced in the 1980s.

2. Letters will vary. Students' letters should support either expanding or limiting the U.S. space program.

Linking Geography and History

1. The United States wanted to protect its access to Kuwaiti and Saudi Arabian oil.

2. Nicaragua is located close to the United States.

History Skills Workshop

The cartoon seems to suggest that President Reagan was overreacting to the Soviet threat and that SDI was a piece of science fiction. Students' cartoons will vary.

CHAPTER PLANNING GUIDE
The United States Looks to the Future

	SECTION LESSON OBJECTIVES	PRINT RESOURCES	MULTIMEDIA RESOURCES	SHELTERED ENGLISH RESOURCES
Section 1: The Clinton Administration (pp. 707–12)	★ Describe the domestic issues of Clinton's administration. ★ Explain why Republicans gained majorities in Congress in 1994. ★ Analyze the issue that troubled the Clinton presidency in his second term.	★ Guided Reading Strategies 24.1 ★ Geography Activity 24: Capital Punishment ★ Primary Source Reading 24: It Takes a Village ★ Section 1 Review, p. 712 ★ Daily Quiz 24.1	★ *Teaching Resources CD–ROM,* Lesson 24.1 ★ HRW Web site	★ Main Idea Activities for Reteaching and Sheltered English 24.1
Section 2: Clinton's Foreign Policy (pp. 713–17)	★ Describe the role the United States played in the post–Cold War era. ★ Explain how the United States responded to problems with Iraq after the Persian Gulf War. ★ Analyze the U.S. reaction to events in the Balkans in the 1990s.	★ Guided Reading Strategies 24.2 ★ Biography Reading 24: Madeleine Albright ★ Section 2 Review, p. 717 ★ Daily Quiz 24.2	★ *Teaching Resources CD–ROM,* Lesson 24.2 ★ HRW Web site	★ Main Idea Activities for Reteaching and Sheltered English 24.2
Section 3: Americans in the 1990s (pp. 718–22)	★ Describe the changes Congress made to immigration laws in the 1980s and 1990s ★ Explain how professional sports have changed in recent years. ★ Analyze the effect of computers on people's access to information.	★ Guided Reading Strategies 24.3 ★ Literature Reading 24: Corridos: Songs of Exodus ★ Section 3 Review, p. 722 ★ Daily Quiz 24.3	★ *Teaching Resources CD–ROM,* Lesson 24.3 ★ *American History Simulations CD–ROM:* City Planning ★ Linking Geography and History Transparency 13B: Sources of Immigration, 1971–1990	★ Main Idea Activities for Reteaching and Sheltered English 24.3
Section 4: Preparing for the Twenty-first Century (pp. 723–27)	★ Analyze environmental issues that gained attention in the 1990s. ★ Describe the accomplishments of the space program in the 1990s. ★ Explain how the global economy changed in the 1990s.	★ Guided Reading Strategies 24.4 ★ American History Political Cartoon 30: Multinational Corporations ★ Graphic Organizer 24: The 1990s ★ Section 4 Review, p. 727 ★ Daily Quiz 24.4	★ *Teaching Resources CD–ROM,* Lesson 24.4 ★ *American History Interactive Maps CD–ROM:* Preserving the Wetlands ★ *Exploring America's Past* Video Segment; Toward the Future: *Teacher's Guide,* pp. 45–47 ★ Linking Geography and History Transparency 23: The Global Environment	★ Main Idea Activities for Reteaching and Sheltered English 24.4
Chapter Review and Assessment (pp. 728–29)		★ Chapter 24 Review, pp. 728–29 ★ Vocabulary Activity 24 ★ Chapter 24 Study Guide ★ Chapter 24 Test (Form A or B)	★ Audio Program, Ch. 24 (English and Spanish) ★ *Global Skill Builder CD–ROM* ★ Chapter 24 Test Generator ★ HRW Web site	★ Spanish Glossary ★ Sheltered English Chapter 24 Test

CHAPTER OVERVIEW

Voters elected Democrat Bill Clinton president in 1992 and again in 1996. Clinton worked to improve U.S. trade and the economy, increase crime prevention, and guard against domestic terrorism—with moderate success. In the 1994 elections, the Republicans won majorities in both houses of Congress. Clinton and Congress worked to balance the federal budget and reform welfare. However, Clinton spent much of his second term fighting impeachment.

Clinton's foreign policy gave the United States a greater role in preserving peace and democracy around the world. The United States used, with varying degrees of success, diplomacy, political pressure, economic sanctions, and military intervention to achieve its goals in the Balkans, Haiti, Iraq, and Somalia.

American society saw many changes in the 1990s. Immigration from Asia and Latin America increased greatly. The United States addressed this influx of people by reducing the number of immigrants let in and cracking down on illegal immigrants. Professional sports emerged as a major industry. Space research saw the creation of an international space station and the exploration of Mars. Advances in computer technology created an Information Revolution and changed the way Americans communicated, lived, and worked. The decade also saw growing environmental problems and effects of an increasingly global economy.

CHAPTER INVESTIGATION

The Chapter Investigation is an extended, multipart activity designed for students to work cooperatively and apply the chapter content in the creation of a project. You may choose to use the Chapter 24 Investigation, Informational CD–ROM for *Voyager III,* either as a substitute for teaching the section lessons or as an alternate assessment.

BLOCK SCHEDULING 

The teacher lesson plans for each section offer a variety of activity choices to help you present the material in a block scheduling format. For further suggestions on block scheduling, see the *Block Scheduling Handbook with Team Teaching Strategies,* pp. 139–44.

Meeting Individual Needs

ABILITY LEVELS

LEVEL 1 Basic level activities designed for all students encountering new material.

LEVEL 2 Intermediate level activities designed for average students.

LEVEL 3 Challenging activities designed for above-average students.

SHELTERED ENGLISH These activities address the needs of students with Limited English Proficiency.

Smithsonian Institution®

Internet Connections and Lesson 24
www.si.edu/hrw

CNN Presents America:
Yesterday and Today 1850 to the Present
Segment: Robots of the Future

Additional Resources

Books for Teachers

Duton, Robert E., Jr. and Rachael L. Holloway. *The Clinton Presidency: Images, Issues, and Communication Strategies.* Praeger, 1996. Examines President Clinton's first term.

McRae, Hamish. *The World in 2020: Power, Culture, and Prosperity.* Harvard Business School Press, 1996. Analyzes the consequences of current trends on the future.

Rogel, Carole. *The Breakup of Yugoslavia and the War in Bosnia.* Greenwood, 1998. Covers the breakup of Yugoslavia in 1991, the war in Bosnia, and the peace settlement.

Books for Students

Bentley, P. F. *Clinton: Portrait of Victory.* Warner Books, 1993. Pictorial history of the 1992 presidential election (for students reading below grade level).

Guernsey, JoAnn Bren. *Hillary Rodham Clinton: A New Kind of First Lady.* Lerner, 1993. Examines the life of Hillary Rodham Clinton and argues that she has changed the way the American people view the first lady.

Storm, Yale. *Quilted Landscape: Conversations with Young Immigrants.* Simon & Schuster, 1996. Includes interviews with 26 young immigrants. Provides facts about their countries of origin along with poetry and artwork they produced.

Multimedia Materials

Crisis in Kosovo (Newsmatters series). Video, 14 min. Knowledge Unlimited/SSSS. Covers Yugoslavia's breakup in 1991 and the resulting conflicts in Kosovo.

The Environment—New Global Concerns. Video, 16 min. American School Publishers. Examines current global environmental problems and the potential for further damage.

Immigration: Maintaining the Open Door. CD–ROM for Mac/Windows. Tom Snyder Productions. Explores issues related to immigration and refugees.

The United States Looks to the Future

CHAPTER MOTIVATOR

Ask students to participate in a brainstorming session about the 1990s. Have them name significant people, places, and events associated with the decade. Write their responses on the chalkboard. Have students determine whether each item on the board had a positive or negative impact on the United States. Depending on the class consensus, place a minus (−) or plus (+) sign next to each item. Point out to students that most decades are filled with events that both strengthen and weaken society. Tell students that in this chapter they will learn about people and events in the 1990s and how they helped shape the world of today.

Presenting Themes

- **Constitutional Heritage** Students might mention that a president might be impeached if found to have broken the law or violated his oath of office.
- **Global Relations** Students might mention that a nation could negotiate treaties with other nations, stockpile arms and use the threat of force, form alliances with other nations, create or join global peacekeeping organizations, or send diplomats to help resolve foreign conflicts that threaten peace.
- **Technology and Society** Students might mention that technology could provide faster, cheaper, and easier ways for people to communicate. For example, advances such as satellite links and video conferencing can enable people around the world to communicate quickly.

Using the Time Line

Ask students to select the three time line events that they think have had the greatest impact on the United States today. Have students discuss their choices. After completing the chapter, have students review their lists, revise them if needed, and briefly describe the importance of each event they chose.

CHAPTER 24

The United States Looks to the Future

(1992–Present)

One high school student expressed his view of the twenty-first century:

> “I have a good feeling about the future. The people of my generation are . . . more in tune with what's going on, and I'd like to think that when my generation are in [power], they're gonna be more sensitive and more representative of the people of our country. I think a lot of progress has been made . . . But more . . . needs to be done.”

Constitutional Heritage
Why might the House of Representatives impeach a president?

Global Relations
How might a nation try to keep world peace and encourage the spread of democracy?

Technology and Society
How might technology improve international communication?

1992 | **1993** | **1994** | **1995**

- **APR. 1992** Riots erupt in Los Angeles, California.
- **NOV. 1992** Democrat Bill Clinton is elected president.
- **NOV. 1993** The Senate ratifies the North American Free Trade Agreement.
- **DEC. 1995** The Dayton peace accords are signed.

SECTION 1 LESSON PLAN

OBJECTIVES

- **Describe the domestic issues of Clinton's administration.**
- **Explain why Republicans gained majorities in Congress in 1994.**
- **Analyze the issue that troubled the Clinton presidency in his second term.**

FOCUS

Motivate Before Reading

Tell students that in his teens Bill Clinton met President John F. Kennedy and resolved to pursue a career in politics. Ask students to imagine what it would be like to meet the president. Have them list questions they would ask if they were thinking of pursuing a political career. Call on volunteers to share their questions. Then

The Clinton Administration

Reading Focus

What domestic issues were addressed during President Clinton's administration?

Why were Republicans able to gain majorities in Congress in 1994?

What issue troubled the Clinton presidency in his second term?

Key Terms

Family and Medical Leave Act
North American Free Trade Agreement
Brady Bill
terrorism
independent counsel
Contract with America

IN AN INTERVIEW, a young man in Dallas, Texas, proudly displayed photos of his military service during Operation Desert Storm. Crowds had cheered as his ship left San Diego, California, for the Middle East. Parades had greeted the soldiers when they returned home. Life got tougher after the young man left the army, though. He answered help-wanted advertisements and made the rounds of employment agencies, but he could not find a job. The recession that had begun in 1990 was in full swing. Many companies were laying off people. Many Americans who had praised President Bush for his leadership in the Persian Gulf War now blamed him for the hard times.

American workers protest losing jobs to Japan

IMAGE ON LEFT PAGE: *A restaurant at the Los Angeles airport reflects space-age design.*

1996 — 1997 — 1998 — 1999

JULY 1997 The *Pathfinder* spacecraft lands on Mars.

NOV. 1998 John Glenn becomes the oldest space traveler.

DEC. 1998 The House of Representatives impeaches President Clinton.

FEB. 1999 The Senate finds Clinton not guilty.

MAR. 1999 NATO launches air attacks on Serbia.

Section 1 RESOURCES

PRINT

- ★ Guided Reading Strategies 24.1
- ★ Geography Activity 24: Capital Punishment
- ★ Primary Source Reading 24: It Takes a Village
- ★ Section 1 Review, p. 712
- ★ Daily Quiz 24.1

MULTIMEDIA

- ★ *Teaching Resources CD–ROM,* Lesson 24.1
- ★ HRW Web site

SHELTERED ENGLISH

- ★ Main Idea Activities for Reteaching and Sheltered English 24.1

tell students that in this section they will learn about the Clinton administration and its handling of domestic issues.

Introduce Key Terms

Linguistic, Interpersonal. Review this section's key terms with students. Have them use context cues to determine each term's meaning and then write the definitions in their notebooks. Next, organize students into pairs. Have one partner read a definition and the other guess the term. Partners then should reverse roles. Have partners continue reversing roles until each has had a chance to guess each term. **SHELTERED ENGLISH**

TEACH

Have students read Section 1 and complete Guided Reading Strategies 24.1. Choose one or more of the following activities to explore the section content with students. For further suggestions on block scheduling or team teaching, see the *Block Scheduling Handbook.*

LEVEL 1: Linguistic. (Suggested time: 15 min.) As a class, go over students' Guided Reading Strategies. Then use the Reading Focus questions to highlight the main ideas of the section. **SHELTERED ENGLISH**

Cultural Diversity

The Congressional Elections of 1992. The congressional elections of 1992 saw several changes in voter support. In the Senate races, voters nominated 11 women and elected 5, including Carol Moseley Braun (D-IL), the first African American woman to win a Senate seat. Ben Nighthorse Campbell (D-CO) became only the second American Indian elected to the Senate. Likewise, in the House races voters elected African Americans, Hispanics, and women in record numbers. Moreover, 19 incumbents failed to win their primaries, and others lost their elections. These results reflected changing voter attitudes as well as widespread dissatisfaction with Congress. Nonetheless, after the election Democrats retained a majority in both houses of Congress. The Senate had 57 Democrats and 43 Republicans. The House had 258 Democrats, 176 Republicans, and 1 Independent.

Activity: Ask students to research the most recent national congressional elections. Have students create a chart showing the gender, ethnic and racial, and party breakdown for the winners.

The Election of 1992

Business had boomed during much of the late 1980s. However, the overall economy had weakened as the federal deficit grew. By 1991 the United States was in a recession. President George Bush downplayed the severity of the recession. He reminded Americans of his leadership during the Persian Gulf War:

> **"We can bring the same . . . sense of common purpose to the economy that we brought to Desert Storm. And we can defeat hard times together."**

The Republican Party nominated Bush for re-election. Bill Clinton, governor of Arkansas, won the Democratic nomination. He chose Tennessee senator Al Gore as his running mate. Clinton called himself a New Democrat—a Democrat who favors some traditionally Republican policies. These policies included balancing the budget, limiting government spending, and encouraging private enterprise. Clinton also wanted an "end to welfare as we know it." He pledged to introduce an extensive job training program. In addition, he suggested a $200 billion, four-year program of domestic investments. He criticized Bush for raising taxes and failing to end the recession.

Texas billionaire Ross Perot (per-OH) entered the race as an independent candidate. He pledged to balance the budget and run the government like a business. Perot said his lack of experience in government was an asset: "I don't have any experience in running up a $4 trillion debt. I don't have any experience in gridlock [stalled] government."

Born after World War II, the Clintons and the Gores are members of the baby-boom generation.

Perot's campaign as an independent candidate, along with the nation's significant economic problems, contributed to increased voter interest and participation. Some 55 percent of registered voters turned out in November 1992. This turnout was a greater percentage than for any presidential election since 1972. Clinton won the election with 370 electoral votes to Bush's 168. Perot did not win any electoral votes, but he received 19 percent of the popular vote.

Clinton's First Term

At age 46, Bill Clinton was the youngest president elected since John F. Kennedy. Vice President Al Gore was about one year younger. They were the youngest team ever in the White House. After 12 years of Republican leadership, President Clinton promised in his inaugural address to bring an end to gridlock. He announced:

> **"A new season of American renewal has begun. To renew America, we must be bold. We must do what no generation has had to do before. We must invest more in our own people, in their jobs, in their future, and at the same time cut our massive debt. . . . We must do what America does best: offer more opportunity to all and demand responsibility from all."**

He called for "bold, persistent [continuing] experimentation" to help solve the nation's problems.

Clinton was determined to improve the economy. The budget he submitted to Congress called for a large reduction of the federal deficit and a tax increase. The House of Representatives passed a revised version of the budget by two votes. Vice President Gore cast a tie-breaking vote in the Senate, and the budget was approved.

Health Care

In February 1993 Clinton signed the **Family and Medical Leave Act**.

ALL LEVELS: Linguistic, Logical-Mathematical, Visual-Spatial. (Suggested time: 35 min.) Remind students that although presidential elections are held every four years, congressional elections occur every two years. Ask students to imagine that it is 1994. Have them create a flyer persuading Americans to vote either for their local Democratic or Republican candidates in the upcoming congressional elections. Encourage students to focus on the achievements of the party they selected as well as on reasons not to vote for the other party. Call on volunteers to explain their fliers. Then discuss with students why the Republicans gained majorities in Congress in 1994. **SHELTERED ENGLISH**

LEVEL 2: Linguistic, Interpersonal. (Suggested time: 45 min.) Ask students to imagine that they work for the campaign committee for one of the candidates in the 2000 presidential election. The candidate would like to find out what voters liked and disliked about President Clinton's domestic policies. Have students create a questionnaire to gather the desired information. Questionnaires should include at least 10 questions and address each of the important domestic issues of Clinton's administration. Call on volunteers to share some of their questions with the class. Encourage the class to discuss the questions and decide which ones would generate the best information.

Bill Clinton

William Jefferson Blythe IV was born in 1946 in Hope, Arkansas. His father had died before he was born. Blythe later changed his last name to that of his stepfather, Roger Clinton. Bill Clinton grew up in Hot Springs, Arkansas. As a young man, he was determined to succeed. He frequently earned academic honors. At age 16, he was selected as a delegate to a high school program in Washington, D.C. On the trip Clinton met President John F. Kennedy. Clinton would later say that the encounter inspired him to enter a life of public service.

After graduating from Georgetown University, Clinton studied at Oxford University as a Rhodes Scholar. In 1973 he received a law degree from Yale University. He then returned to Arkansas to teach law and to prepare himself for a career in politics. In 1978 Clinton was elected governor of Arkansas. He was the nation's youngest governor. Clinton suffered his biggest political loss when he was defeated for re-election in 1980. Clinton revised his political strategy and won the governorship again in 1982. He held that position until he was elected president in 1992.

The law provided many workers with up to 12 weeks of unpaid leave for family or medical purposes. Under this law, employees could take time off to care for themselves or sick family members, or to have or adopt a child. The law guaranteed that these workers would have a job when they returned to work.

In September, Clinton announced a plan to reform the health care system. He had appointed First Lady Hillary Rodham Clinton, a Yale-educated lawyer, to lead the President's Task Force on National Health Care Reform. The task force made several recommendations. Its main priority was to provide universal medical coverage to all Americans. At the time, nearly 40 million Americans lacked health insurance. Many Americans, small business owners, in particular, opposed the plan. The plan failed to pass in Congress and was a major defeat for the Clinton administration.

In 1996 the president achieved some success in health care reform. He signed legislation to allow workers who changed or lost their jobs to pay to keep their health insurance coverage. At the signing ceremony, Clinton called the bill "a long step toward the kind of health-care reform our nation needs."

Trade

Clinton also persuaded the Senate to pass a trade agreement initiated by the Bush administration. In November 1993 the Senate ratified the **North American Free Trade Agreement** (NAFTA). NAFTA eliminated trade barriers between the United States, Canada, and Mexico. Supporters saw NAFTA as a way to increase international trade and business profits. Opponents feared that it would shift production and jobs out of the United States.

Some labor leaders feared that NAFTA would eliminate many jobs in the United States.

Presidential Profiles

Bill Clinton. At only 30 years of age, Bill Clinton won the race for attorney general of Arkansas in 1976. Two years later he became governor of the state. His decision to raise taxes angered voters, however; and he was not re-elected in 1980. In the 1982 race, he publicly apologized for raising taxes. Apparently satisfied, voters returned him to office. Clinton then won re-election in 1984, 1986 (when the term of office changed from two to four years), and 1990. The next year, he announced his intention to run for president.

Activity: Have students use the library or search the Internet through the HRW Web site to find information on the life and presidency of Bill Clinton. Tell students to use their research to write a biography of Clinton.

go.hrw.com
SB1 Clinton

LEVEL 3: Linguistic. (Suggested time: 30 min. plus homework) Briefly discuss with students the issue that troubled the Clinton presidency in its second term. Then describe the impeachment process and discuss how it incorporates checks and balances by involving both Congress and the Supreme Court. For homework, have students write an essay about how the impeachment process and its use of checks and balances ensures that no powerful elected official or governmental branch can gain control or break the law without fear of punishment. Call on volunteers to read their essays to the class.

CLOSE

Logical-Mathematical. Tell students that they have been chosen to set up the Clinton presidential library. Have students suggest ways to categorize the papers and materials related to the domestic issues of Clinton's administration. Encourage students to group related domestic issues.

CHALLENGE AND EXTEND

1. **Linguistic, Visual-Spatial, Interpersonal.** Give each student a copy of the Republican Party's Contract with America. After discussing its origins and components, organize the class

Constitutional Heritage

Strengthening States' Rights. The 1990s saw increased power returned to the states. The U.S. Supreme Court ruled in favor of states in health care spending, welfare, school desegregation, prisoner lawsuits, and parole policy. The Court also ruled unconstitutional the Gun-Free School Zone Act of 1990 on the grounds that it infringed upon powers reserved for the states. In 1995 the U.S. Congress passed a law forbidding unfunded mandates, or federally required laws that states have to enforce out of their own budgets. Congress also repealed the federal law restricting the speed limit to 55 miles per hour and banned states from taxing former residents' pension incomes.

Critical Thinking: Why do you think Congress repealed the national speed limit law?

ANSWER: Students might mention that the energy crisis was over and that states have the right to determine speed limits within their own borders.

Fighting Crime

President Clinton also pushed for new anticrime laws. In November 1993 Congress approved the Handgun Violence Prevention Act, or the **Brady Bill**. This legislation was named after President Reagan's press secretary, James Brady. He had been wounded during an assassination attempt on the president in 1981. The Brady Bill established a five-day waiting period for handgun purchases. In 1998 a computerized system that provides immediate background checks on potential gun buyers replaced the waiting period.

In 1994 Clinton supported a bill to provide funding for 100,000 new police officers and for new prisons and crime-prevention programs. The legislation also prohibited the sale and possession of some assault weapons. Clinton hoped these measures would reduce violent crime. For a variety of reasons, the rate of violent crime fell during the mid-1990s.

Although crime decreased, many Americans were shocked by an increase in **terrorism**. This type of violence is used by individuals or small groups to advance political goals. In February 1993 a bomb exploded in New York City's World Trade Center. The explosion killed 6 people and injured more than 1,000. Several members of an Arab terrorist group were later arrested and sentenced to life imprisonment for the bombing.

Sarah Brady lobbied for a gun control law after her husband, James Brady, was wounded.

In April 1995, terrorists bombed the Alfred P. Murrah Federal Building in Oklahoma City, Oklahoma. The explosion killed 169 people, including many children, and injured many others. One army veteran who was an eyewitness said it was "as bad as anything I'd ever witnessed in Vietnam." The federal government tried and convicted two Americans—Timothy McVeigh and Terry Nichols—for the crime. The government also took measures, such as increasing airport security, to reduce the risk of terrorism at home and abroad.

Republicans Gain Strength

The Clinton administration faced setbacks in 1994. Attorney General Janet Reno appointed Kenneth Starr as **independent counsel**—a special prosecutor to investigate accusations against government officials. After the Watergate scandal, Congress had questioned whether the executive branch could investigate itself adequately. In 1978 Congress established the office of independent counsel to look into charges of wrongdoing by high-ranking government officials. Starr's initial assignment was to investigate the role of the president and the first lady in the so-called Whitewater affair. Whitewater was a failed Arkansas real estate development. The investigation was a significant issue during Clinton's first term.

Contract with America

As the 1994 congressional elections approached, Republican representative Newt Gingrich of Georgia helped create the **Contract with America**. Many Republican candidates signed this campaign pledge. The Contract included promises for smaller government, a balanced budget amendment, tax reforms, and term limits for members of Congress. Republicans proposed to introduce this legislation in 100 days.

into research teams and assign each team several components. Have teams use the library and other resources to research the adoption or rejection of their components. Have teams present their findings in oral reports. Encourage students to use visual aids in their reports.

2. **Logical-Mathematical, Visual-Spatial, Interpersonal.** Have students use the library and other resources to research the Brady Bill and gun control. Have the class use the information to create a school display on the issue of gun control. The display should address reasons people support and oppose gun control. It also should provide information to help people make informed decisions on this important and controversial topic.

3. **Linguistic, Logical-Mathematical.** Ask students to imagine that they have been assigned to serve on an antiterrorism task force. Have them research recent terrorist acts in the United States. Then have students use the information to write a report proposing measures the U.S. government might take to reduce domestic terrorism. Remind students to consider Americans' constitutional rights when formulating their suggestions. Call on volunteers to share some of their ideas and have the class discuss the positive and negative aspects of each one.

Newt Gingrich became Speaker of the House after the Contract with America helped Republicans gain majorities in Congress.

Many voters responded favorably to the Contract. Republicans gained majorities in both houses of Congress for the first time since the 1952 elections. The House passed all items in the Contract, except one to limit the number of terms in office for members of Congress. By the end of 1995, five items in the Contract had become law.

Budget and Welfare Reform

According to Gingrich, the Republicans in Congress "changed the whole debate in American politics. There is now a universal agreement [that] you've got to balance the budget." The Republicans lost some public support, however, when they tried to force the president to accept their proposed budget.

After President Clinton refused to sign the budget, the federal government shut down twice in late 1995 and early 1996. Only necessary federal government agencies were open. Nonessential federal government employees did not work because there was no money to pay them. Federal museums and national parks were closed. After a public outcry, the Republicans and Democrats compromised on a budget. The government began to operate again.

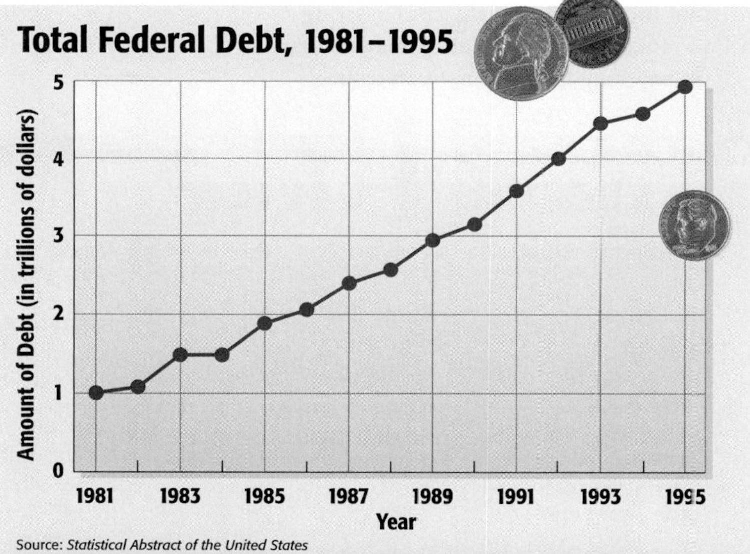

The Growing Debt Despite efforts to reduce the rate of growth of the federal debt, it continued to rise throughout the 1980s and the 1990s. How much was the federal debt in 1992?

Congress also passed a major revision of the federal welfare system. In 1996 Clinton signed a bill that ended the Aid to Families with Dependent Children (AFDC). This federally funded program had provided cash assistance to poor families. The welfare reform bill replaced AFDC with direct grants to states. Each state became responsible for designing and operating its own welfare program.

The 1996 Election

In 1996, Americans turned their attention to the presidential election. Republicans chose Senator Bob Dole of Kansas as their candidate for president. Dole was a World War II veteran and longtime congressional leader. Based on their success in the midterm elections, Republicans thought they might be able to win back the presidency. The Democrats nominated the Clinton-Gore ticket for re-election.

During the campaign, Dole noted that President Clinton seemed to be supporting conservative Republican measures. Dole joked, "If this keeps up, Bill Clinton won't have to make speeches anymore. All he'll have to do is find out my stand on an issue and say 'Me too.'"

Economic Development

The 1998 Budget Surplus. In October 1998 the U.S. government announced that it had achieved its first budget surplus since 1969. Democrats and Republicans alike claimed credit for the approximately $70 billion of excess revenue over projected spending. President Clinton praised the achievement at a White House celebration, where an electronic billboard displayed the deficit falling and then the surplus rising. In response, the Republican majority in Congress claimed that they had made balancing the budget an important goal, without which the surplus could not have been achieved. Almost from the moment Democrats and Republicans ceased arguing over who deserved credit for the surplus, they began arguing over what to do with the excess money.

Activity: Have students use the library and other resources to find out the current estimated U.S. budget deficit or surplus for the present fiscal year.

CHART ANSWER
$4 trillion

REVIEW

Linguistic, Logical-Mathematical, Interpersonal. Have students complete the Section Review questions. Then assign each student one of the terms from the Identify portion of the Section Review. Have students create lists of clues for their terms. Finally, have students take turns reading their clues to the class and have the other students identify each term.

ASSESS

Have students complete Daily Quiz 24.1.

RETEACH

Linguistic, Logical-Mathematical, Visual-Spatial. Have students complete Main Idea Activities for Reteaching and Sheltered English 24.1. Ask students to place the heading, *The Clinton Presidency*, at the top of a piece of paper. Then have them create two columns, one labeled *Successes*, and the other labeled *Failures*. Have students use the material in this section to list in the appropriate column the successes and the failures of the Clinton administration. When students have finished, review their lists with them. **SHELTERED ENGLISH**

Section 1 Review ANSWERS

Identify

For significance, see the following pages:

- Bill Clinton, p. 708
- Ross Perot, p. 708
- Family and Medical Leave Act, p. 708
- Hillary Rodham Clinton, p. 709
- North American Free Trade
- Agreement, p. 709
- Brady Bill, p. 710
- terrorism, p. 710
- independent counsel, p. 710
- Newt Gingrich, p. 710
- Contract with America, p. 710

Reading for Content Understanding

1. the economy and the federal deficit, family and medical leave for workers, health care, North American trade, crime, and gun control

2. voter dissatisfaction over Clinton's alleged involvement in the Whitewater affair; Republicans' Contract with America, which promised to limit the size of the government and to balance the budget

3. It proved the president had lied under oath, the president became involved in scandal, his personal conduct came under review, and he was impeached but not removed from office.

4. Letters will vary but should be persuasive, mention problems resulting from the shutdown of the federal government, and address the correct congressmember.

5. Answers will vary but might mention that both Clinton and the Republicans tried to limit the size of the government and balance the budget, but that they used different approaches and held different positions on health care and other issues.

Clinton made a campaign pledge to "build a bridge to the twenty-first century." In particular, he wanted to improve public education. Many voters credited Clinton with the booming economy. He won 379 electoral votes to Dole's 159. Republicans maintained majorities in both houses of Congress.

Clinton's Second Term

Following the election, the president and Congress worked on the federal budget. In 1997 they reached an agreement to balance the budget by the year 2002. The deal included tax cuts and reductions in domestic spending, including a $75 billion decrease in defense spending. Funding would be increased for education, health insurance, and welfare.

Questions about President Clinton's personal conduct dominated much of his second term. During the mid-1990s, Independent Counsel Kenneth Starr had widened the scope of his investigation. In 1998 he released a lengthy report charging that, among other things, the president had lied under oath before a grand jury. Clinton denied lying under oath, but he did apologize for other actions cited in the report.

> **"I let you down. I let my family down. I let this country down. But I'm trying to make it right. I'm determined to never let anything like that happen again."**

Chief Justice William Rehnquist presided over the impeachment trial.

As a result of Starr's report, the House Judiciary Committee began an impeachment inquiry.

Despite the investigation, Democrats gained five new seats in the House in the November 1998 congressional elections. Many people interpreted these results as a sign that the public opposed impeachment. Some people questioned whether the investigation had gone beyond its original assignment.

Nonetheless, the House continued its inquiry. It approved two of four articles of impeachment against the president. In December, Clinton became the second U.S. president to be impeached. According to the articles of impeachment, Clinton

> **"has undermined [weakened] the integrity of his office, has brought disrepute [dishonor] on the Presidency, has betrayed his trust as President, and has acted in a manner subversive of [doing harm to] the rule of law and justice, to the . . . injury of the people of the United States."**

On February 12, 1999, the Senate acquitted Clinton of both charges. He therefore remained in office.

SECTION 1 REVIEW

Identify and explain the significance of the following:

- **Bill Clinton**
- **Ross Perot**
- **Family and Medical Leave Act**
- **Hillary Rodham Clinton**
- **North American Free Trade Agreement**
- **Brady Bill**
- **terrorism**
- **independent counsel**
- **Newt Gingrich**
- **Contract with America**

Reading for Content Understanding

1 **Main Idea** On what domestic issues did President Clinton focus while in office?

2 **Main Idea** Why did the Republicans win majorities in Congress in 1994?

3 **Constitutional Heritage** What was the result of Kenneth Starr's investigation of the president?

4 **Writing** *Persuading* Write a letter to your congressmember to persuade him or her to reach a budget agreement in late 1995. Be sure to include why re-opening the federal government is important.

5 **Critical Thinking** *Making Comparisons* Compare Clinton's domestic policies with those of the Republicans in Congress.

OBJECTIVES

- Describe the role the United States played in the post–Cold War era.
- Explain how the United States responded to problems with Iraq after the Persian Gulf War.
- Analyze the U.S. reaction to events in the Balkans in the 1990s.

FOCUS

Motivate Before Reading

Ask students to list pressing foreign affairs issues of the Bush administration *(e.g., the Persian Gulf War with Iraq, the breakup of the Soviet Union).* Then ask students to speculate on Clinton's foreign policy. Ask them on which foreign nations they think he would have focused and why he might have decided to intervene in some foreign conflicts. Tell students that in this section they will learn

Clinton's Foreign Policy

Reading Focus

What role did the United States play in the post–Cold War era?

How did the United States respond to problems with Iraq after the Persian Gulf War?

How did the United States react to events in the Balkans in the 1990s?

Key Terms

Operation Restore Hope

Operation Desert Fox

Dayton peace accords

During the 1992 presidential campaign, Bill Clinton had promised that if elected he would support a more aggressive role for the United States in Bosnia. A bitter civil war had erupted in the Balkan nation. Clinton charged: "The [Bush] administration is turning its back on violations of basic human rights and our own democratic values." During the 1990s, many Americans debated the role the United States should play in helping other nations maintain peace.

UN troops in Bosnia tried to maintain peace.

New Challenges Abroad

The end of the Cold War and the collapse of the Soviet Union changed the goals of U.S. foreign policy. The United States became the world's only superpower. One White House official noted, "No other nation has the muscle . . . or the trust to mediate [settle] disputes . . . or . . . help enforce the terms of an agreement." In the 1990s the United States played a greater role in trying to strengthen democracy, protect human rights, and negotiate peace in different parts of the world.

Haiti

For example, the United States tried to support democracy in Haiti. Haitian military leaders had overthrown the country's democratically elected president, Jean-Bertrand Aristide (ah-ree-steed), in 1991. These military leaders led a campaign of violence against their political opponents. Tens of thousands of Haitians left their country between 1991 and 1994. Most of them headed to the United States.

Concerned about the flood of refugees, the U.S. government pressured the Haitian military

Section 2 RESOURCES

PRINT

- ★ Guided Reading Strategies 24.2
- ★ Biography Reading 24: Madeleine Albright
- ★ Section 2 Review, p. 717
- ★ Daily Quiz 24.2

MULTIMEDIA

- ★ *Teaching Resources CD–ROM,* Lesson 24.2
- ★ HRW Web site

SHELTERED ENGLISH

- ★ Main Idea Activities for Reteaching and Sheltered English 24.2

about conflicts the United States faced abroad and about U.S. involvement in Iraq, the Balkans, and other "hot spots" around the world.

Introduce Key Terms

Linguistic, Visual-Spatial. Review this section's key terms with students. Then have them link each term to one or more foreign nations and locate those nations on a world map. Finally, have students write in their notebooks the definition for each term and the locations of the nations related to each term.
SHELTERED ENGLISH

TEACH

Have students read Section 2 and complete Guided Reading Strategies 24.2. Choose one or more of the following activities to explore the section content with students. For further suggestions on block scheduling or team teaching, see the *Block Scheduling Handbook.*

LEVEL 1: Linguistic. (Suggested time: 15 min.) As a class, go over students' Guided Reading Strategies. Then use the Reading Focus questions to highlight the main ideas of the section.
SHELTERED ENGLISH

Historical Sidelight

Jimmy Carter as Diplomat. Following his presidency, Jimmy Carter continued working in the area of human rights by serving unofficially as a U.S. diplomat. In Nicaragua, he helped the local Miskito Indians regain the right to live on their tribal homelands. In 1994 in Panama, he helped monitor election procedures to prevent corruption. That same year, he also helped convince North Korean leaders to cease developing nuclear weapons, assisted in returning the Aristide government to power in Haiti, and participated in negotiations to achieve a brief cease-fire in Bosnia.

Activity: Have students use the library and other resources to research Carter's continuing role as a public servant since his presidency. Have students write a speech for a banquet recognizing Carter's public service.

AMERICAN ARTS ANSWERS

1. music that combines many cultural sounds
2. Answers will vary but students might mention that advances in technology, such as the Internet, have made it easier for people to explore and gain interest in the music of other cultures.

government to resign. The Clinton administration also called for the return of Aristide, who was in exile in the United States. In September 1994 President Clinton sent a peace mission to Haiti. Former president Jimmy Carter, former chairman of the Joint Chiefs of Staff Colin Powell, and Senator Sam Nunn negotiated a compromise. Some 20,000 U.S. troops soon arrived in Haiti to help restore order and the Aristide government. The military rulers quickly withdrew. One month later President Aristide returned to Haiti. He urged Haitians to say "no to violence, no to vengeance, yes to reconciliation [coming to peaceful agreement]."

Peace Accords

The United States also supported peace efforts in the Middle East. After years of conflict, Israel and the Palestine Liberation Organization (PLO), an Arab political group, reached a peace agreement. At the White House in 1993 Israeli prime minister Yitzhak Rabin and PLO leader Yasir Arafat signed the historic agreement in which Israel and the PLO officially recognized each other. The agreement also set guidelines for Palestinian self-rule in occupied areas of Israel.

In 1994 Israel and Jordan also agreed to peace. They signed the Washington Declaration at the White House. This peace agreement formally ended the 46-year-long state of war between Israel and Jordan.

Terrorist actions by both Israelis and Palestinians slowed the Israeli-PLO peace process. In 1995 an Israeli opposed to Palestinian self-rule assassinated Rabin. The Palestinians gained self-rule in some occupied areas in 1997. However, no final agreements were reached about the creation of an independent Palestinian state.

American Arts

Worldbeat Music

As barriers between nations were removed in the post–Cold War era, musicians turned to many countries for inspiration. Worldbeat music is one example of this new global music. Unlike traditional Western music, which has its roots in Europe, worldbeat music combines many cultural sounds, including Caribbean, calypso, African, and funk.

Reggae, a type of Jamaican music, combines African and European styles. It comes in different forms including raggamuffin, hip-hop, and dancehall. Musicians such as Bob Marley and Shabba Ranks have popularized reggae.

In Japan, worldbeat music may combine Brazilian and Caribbean beats and West African dance music with rhythms of the island of Okinawa. For example, Japanese musician Kikusuimaru blends story-telling music and reggae sounds. As more people worldwide draw inspiration from a variety of cultures, new styles of music are developed.

The Brazilian percussion group, Olodum

Understanding the Arts

1. What is worldbeat music?
2. Why do you think worldbeat music is becoming more popular?

ALL LEVELS: Logical-Mathematical, Visual-Spatial. (Suggested time: 30 min.) On the chalkboard, create a chart with four columns labeled *Foreign Hot Spot, Situation, U.S. Actions,* and *Results.* Ask students to copy the chart and then complete it for each of the foreign nations discussed in this section. When students are finished, call on volunteers to share some of their entries with the class. As they do, fill in the correct answers in the chart on the chalkboard.

ALL LEVELS: Linguistic, Visual-Spatial. (Suggested time: 30 min.) Ask students to imagine that it is 1999 and they are part of a CIA team assigned to decrease the Iraqi people's support of Saddam Hussein. Have students create posters for U.S. pilots to drop over Iraq. The posters should show why the United States and Great Britain launched air strikes on Iraq in 1998, why the air strikes might resume soon, and what part Hussein has played in causing these actions and their damaging results. Display students' posters around the class. **SHELTERED ENGLISH**

LEVEL 3: Kinesthetic, Linguistic. (Suggested time: 30 min. plus homework) Ask students to imagine that it is late 1998 and President Clinton has sent them to urge the International Tribunal for the Prosecution of War Crimes to indict Slobodan Milosevic. Have students write a speech to present. The speech should describe the nature and severity of Milosevic's crimes, explain why the international community should condemn his actions, and

Changes in Africa

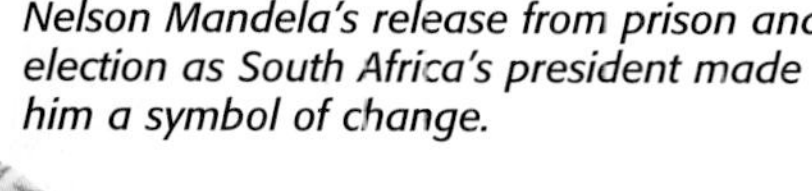

Nelson Mandela's release from prison and election as South Africa's president made him a symbol of change.

Meanwhile, significant political changes were also occurring in Africa. The United States played a variety of roles in events in Africa.

South Africa

One of the greatest changes occurred in South Africa, which had practiced apartheid and denied black citizens many basic rights. Within South Africa, political groups like the African National Congress (ANC) had fought to end apartheid. In the 1980s many countries had applied political and economic pressure to the South African government to end apartheid. The U.S. Congress approved economic sanctions against South Africa and overrode President Reagan's veto of them. Many American college students encouraged divestment, or removal, of funds invested in South African businesses.

Combined with protest in South Africa, international pressure helped lead to reform. ANC founder Nelson Mandela, who had been held as a political prisoner since 1964, was released in 1990. The next year South Africa's white government repealed the basic apartheid laws. In 1994 the nation held its first elections in which adult South Africans of all races could vote. Mandela became the nation's first black president.

Somalia and Rwanda

In other African countries, the United States took military action and operated as part of a larger United Nations force. In late 1992 President Bush had sent U.S. troops to the African country of Somalia, which was in the midst of a civil war. U.S. soldiers joined **Operation Restore Hope**, a UN relief effort to help Somalia. UN forces opened roads and distributed food to starving Somalis. However, the civil war continued.

In 1993, 18 U.S. soldiers were killed in a gun battle. A number of others were captured. The United States began to re-evaluate its involvement in Somalia. President Clinton removed most of the U.S. troops in 1994. Although problems in Somalia continued, the remaining UN troops left in 1995.

The events in Somalia affected the U.S. response to a bloody ethnic war in the African nation of Rwanda. In 1994 the UN sent a peacekeeping force to Rwanda, but Clinton refused to send U.S. troops. The fighting there was particularly brutal. The UN established a war-crimes tribunal to investigate the murder of some 500,000 Tutsi, a minority ethnic group in Rwanda. The situation in Rwanda demonstrated some of the difficult foreign-policy choices the United States faced in the 1990s.

Tensions in Iraq

As part of a UN delegation, the United States continued to play a role in Iraq. After the Persian Gulf War, Iraq had agreed in the cease-fire agreement to destroy its weapons of mass destruction. UN officials were to inspect Iraq's industrial, chemical, and biological facilities to make sure the weapons were destroyed. However, Iraqi leader Saddam Hussein hindered the efforts of the UN inspectors.

An Iraqi soldier watches as UN inspectors prepare to leave the country.

Economic Development

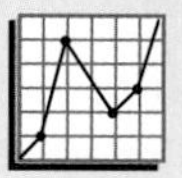

Sanctions as a Diplomatic Tool. Many nations use economic sanctions to penalize other nations, in hopes of convincing their leaders to change certain policies or cease certain actions. In 1986, in an attempt to end apartheid, the U.S. Congress imposed sanctions on South Africa. The sanctions halted air travel and limited trade between the United States and South Africa. They also banned U.S. investments in and loans to the nation. In 1992 the United States joined the United Nations in placing sanctions on Serbia to force a peace agreement ending the war in Bosnia. The UN also imposed sanctions on Iraq in the early 1990s.

Activity: Have students search the Internet through the HRW Web site to research any economic sanctions the United States or United Nations currently have in place. Ask students to report on what they find and the reasons for any current sanctions.

go.hrw.com
SB1 Sanctions

propose the extent to which nations should go to ensure that Milosevic is prosecuted, if he is indicted. Call on volunteers to deliver their speeches to the class. Encourage feedback.

CLOSE

Linguistic, Logical-Mathematical. Using a map of the world, review with students the different countries with which the United States was involved during the 1990s. Then ask students to suggest common characteristics among the situations that led to U.S. involvement. Finally, have students come up with a list of "Foreign-Policy Guidelines" that they think best represents the Clinton administration's foreign policy.

CHALLENGE AND EXTEND

Linguistic, Logical-Mathematical. Ask students to create a profile of one of the foreign leaders discussed in this section. Have them research the individual's past, early career, and leadership career. Encourage students to present the information in a creative way, such as in a resume, obituary, or character sketch. Select the better projects and have the authors present their work to the class.

Global Relations

Letters from Kosovo. In January 1999 Finnegan Hamill, a California high school student, began corresponding by e-mail with a 16-year-old Albanian girl in Kosovo. Hamill had received her e-mail address from a Kosovo peace worker who had visited his church. Hamill shared the e-mail letters he received with Youth Radio in Berkeley, California. In the letters, the Kosovar teen is known only as "Adona" to protect her safety. Adona wrote about what it was like living in the middle of a war zone. In one letter, she describes the scene from her balcony. "I can see people running with suitcases and I can hear some gunshots. A village just a few hundred meters from my home is all surrounded. I have prepared my bag with necessary things: clothes, documents, and money . . . in case of emergency." People such as Adona helped inform others around the world about events happening in Kosovo.

Critical Thinking: Describe what you think Adona might have felt as she saw the scene she described.

ANSWER: Answers will vary but students might mention that Adona felt scared for herself and her family, and worried for her friends' safety.

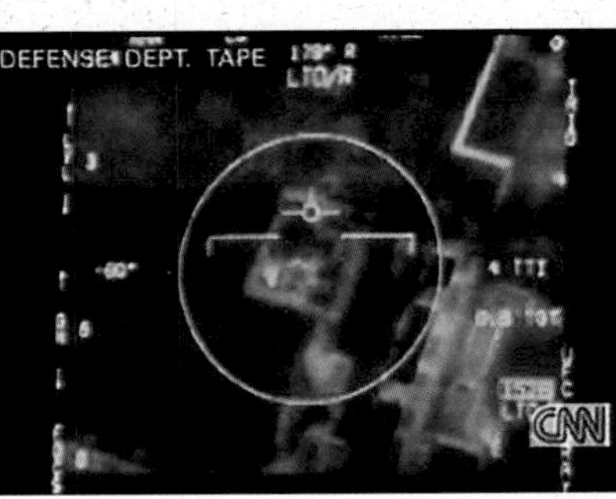

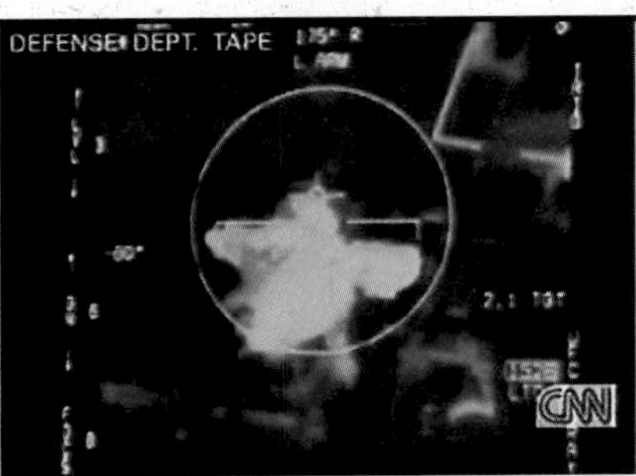

The radar in U.S. fighter planes could target specific locations in Iraq.

In 1998 Hussein's actions pushed the UN coalition to act. Secretary of State Madeleine Albright explained the U.S. position:

> **"Our fundamental goal . . . is to contain or end the threat posed by Saddam Hussein to Iraq's neighbors and the world. . . . We retain the authority, the responsibility, the means and the will to use military force if that is required."**

By the fall, all diplomatic efforts to convince Iraq to allow UN inspection teams to do their job had failed. The inspectors left the country. In December 1998 President Clinton launched **Operation Desert Fox**. This military operation included a series of joint U.S. and British air strikes against military and strategic targets in Iraq.

Even after the air strikes, problems with Iraq continued. In 1999 more air attacks were launched on Iraq. The United Nations continued to watch the area for more cease-fire violations.

 War in the Balkans

The United States also tried to help resolve conflicts in the Balkans, a region in southeastern Europe. Following World War II, the nation of Yugoslavia was created. This communist country was a federation of six republics. Each republic had several ethnic populations. Differences had divided these ethnic groups for centuries. In the early 1990s, four republics—Bosnia and Herzegovina (often referred to as Bosnia), Croatia, Macedonia, and Slovenia—declared their independence. The republics of Serbia and Montenegro remained as the nation of Yugoslavia.

Fighting in Bosnia

Tension among the Balkans' three main ethnic groups—Serbs, Croats, and Muslims—soon led to war. Fighting erupted in the new nations of Croatia and Bosnia. Some of the worst violence was between Serbs and Muslims in Bosnia. Serb president Slobodan Milosevic (sloh-buh-DAHN mi-LOH-suh-vitch) supported Bosnian Serbs who did not want to separate from Yugoslavia.

The Bosnian Serbs practiced ethnic cleansing—the violent removal of ethnic minority groups by a dominant ethnic group. The Serbs used threats, destroyed homes and villages, and killed many Muslims to "cleanse" parts of Bosnia. In November 1994 the International Tribunal for the Prosecution of War Crimes announced that it would prosecute some Serbs for actions related to ethnic cleansing. The trials were the first war crimes trials to be held since World War II.

Fighting in Croatia stopped in 1994. UN efforts to stop the violence in Bosnia were unsuccessful. During President Clinton's first term, U.S. diplomats hosted a peace conference at Wright Patterson Air Force base in Dayton, Ohio. The presidents of Bosnia, Croatia, and Serbia participated in the negotiations. The plan was to reach a permanent peace agreement and a settlement on the boundaries of Bosnia. Richard Holbrooke was

Thousands of Kosovar Albanians fled their homes. Many children ended up in refugee camps separated from their parents.

REVIEW

Linguistic, Visual-Spatial. Have students complete the Section Review questions. Then have students create two political cartoons, each related to one of the terms in the Identify portion of the Section Review. Each cartoon should address a different nation discussed in this section. Each cartoon also should include a caption. Call on volunteers to explain their cartoons to the class.

ASSESS

Have students complete Daily Quiz 24.2.

RETEACH

Linguistic, Logical-Mathematical, Visual-Spatial. Have students complete Main Idea Activities for Reteaching and Sheltered English 24.2. Then give students maps of the world. Ask students to create annotated maps showing the foreign countries with which the United States was involved during the 1990s. The maps should also explain the reasons for U.S. involvement and the outcomes. Call on volunteers to share their maps with the class.
SHELTERED ENGLISH

the chief U.S. negotiator. The warring sides signed the **Dayton peace accords** in December 1995. NATO and Russia sent thousands of peacekeeping troops to the area. Many were from the United States. For a short while the accords were successful, but unrest in Bosnia continued.

Conflict in Kosovo

In early 1998 President Milosevic extended his campaign of ethnic cleansing to the Serbian province of Kosovo. Serbian nationalists regard Kosovo as the birthplace of Serbian culture. The Serbs in Kosovo were the largest of several minorities. However, of the province's approximately 2 million inhabitants, more than 90 percent were of Albanian heritage.

Some of these Kosovars, or residents of Kosovo, began to demand independence. In response, Milosevic's troops killed thousands of Kosovar Albanians and forced thousands more to leave their homes. Serbian military forces increased their attacks on the Kosovars in March 1999. NATO responded by launching air strikes on Serbia.

Retired U.S. diplomat James Hooper, head of the Balkan Action Council, explained the significance of the problem. He wrote,

> **"The Kosovo problem is as much about the resolve of American leadership and the credibility of NATO as it is about the complexities of Balkan politics."**

NATO celebrated its 50th anniversary in April 1999.

Russia also played a role in the peace process. In June 1999 NATO and Yugoslavia reached an agreement that required Serbian troops to leave Kosovo. NATO agreed to send a security force of more than 50,000 to the area.

NATO's actions in the Balkans represented its first effort as an expanded organization. After the breakup of the Soviet Union, several Eastern European nations had established democratic governments. As communist nations, they had belonged to the Warsaw Pact. In the post–Cold War era, some of these countries became members of NATO.

SECTION 2 REVIEW

Identify and explain the significance of the following:
- **Jean-Bertrand Aristide**
- **Nelson Mandela**
- **Operation Restore Hope**
- **Madeleine Albright**
- **Operation Desert Fox**
- **Dayton peace accords**

Reading for Content Understanding

1 **Main Idea** How did U.S. foreign policy change after the end of the Cold War?

2 **Main Idea** What actions did the United States and the United Nations take against Iraq in the 1990s?

3 **Global Relations** Make a graphic organizer showing the actions the United States took in Haiti, Iraq, Bosnia, and Kosovo. Indicate the kind of action and the results.

4 **Writing** *Describing* Write two paragraphs describing the role of NATO in the post–Cold War era.

5 **Critical Thinking** *Determining the Strength of an Argument* Do you believe that as the world's only superpower the United States has a responsibility to promote peace and democracy? Use specific examples to support your argument.

Section 2 Review ANSWERS

Identify

For significance, see the following pages:
- Jean-Bertrand Aristide, p. 713
- Nelson Mandela, p. 715
- Operation Restore Hope, p. 715
- Madeleine Albright, p. 716
- Operation Desert Fox, p. 716
- Dayton peace accords, p. 717

Reading for Content Understanding

1. As the world's only remaining superpower, the United States played a greater role in trying to strengthen democracy, protect human rights, and keep peace around the world.

2. attempted monitoring of weapons facilities, diplomacy, air strikes

3. Haiti—political pressure and peace negotiations led to the return of the Aristide government; Iraq—diplomacy and air strikes led to some resumption of weapons inspections; Bosnia—peace negotiations led to Dayton peace accords; Kosovo—air strikes led to Serb withdrawal from Kosovo

4. Paragraphs will vary but should include NATO's expansion and its involvement in Iraq and Kosovo as a global human-rights guardian and peacekeeping force.

5. Arguments will vary but students should state their opinions and use specific examples to support them.

OBJECTIVES

- **Describe the changes Congress made to immigration laws in the 1980s and 1990s.**
- **Explain how professional sports have changed in recent years.**
- **Analyze the effect of computers on people's access to information.**

FOCUS

Motivate Before Reading

Write the terms *computers, immigrants,* and *professional sports* on the chalkboard. Ask students to describe ways in which each subject affects their daily lives. Then have students discuss shifting attitudes toward these subjects in the 1980s and 1990s. After a period of discussion, tell students that in this section they will learn about changes in computer technology, immigration laws,

Section 3 RESOURCES

PRINT

★ Guided Reading Strategies 24.3

★ Literature Reading 24: Corridos: Songs of Exodus

★ Section 3 Review, p. 722

★ Daily Quiz 24.3

MULTIMEDIA

★ *Teaching Resources CD–ROM,* Lesson 24.3

★ *American History Simulations CD–ROM:* City Planning

★ Linking Geography and History Transparency 13B: Sources of Immigration, 1971–1990

SHELTERED ENGLISH

★ Main Idea Activities for Reteaching and Sheltered English 24.3

Multimedia Resources

Linking Geography and History Transparency 13B: Sources of Immigration, 1971–1990

Multimedia Resources

American History Simulations CD–ROM: City Planning

SECTION 3

Americans in the 1990s

Reading Focus

What changes did Congress make to immigration laws in the 1980s and 1990s?

How have professional sports changed in recent years?

What effect have computers had on people's access to information?

Key Terms

Immigration Reform and Control Act

Los Angeles riots

Information Revolution

Internet

In September 1978 Juan Chanax set out from the Guatemalan highlands of Totonicapán. The United States was his destination. He left his village because he thought he had no choice. "With little land and little education and little money, I had no chance to sobresalir *[excel]." Chanax ended up in Houston, Texas, where he found work in a supermarket. He sent home as much as $100 a week—twice as much money as most people earned in Guatemala. He was the first person from his hometown to immigrate. Within 15 years about half of the village's population had immigrated to the United States.*

A Guatemalan weaving

Immigrants in the 1990s

Juan Chanax and his Guatemalan neighbors were part of an enormous increase in the number of immigrants to the United States in the 1980s and 1990s. This increase in immigration was the largest since the 1910s. The populations of California, Florida, and Texas grew in part as a result of this immigration. Many of these recent immigrants came from Latin America and Asia. Like previous immigrants, they often settled in large cities with other people from their native countries.

In response to this increased immigration, Congress passed the **Immigration Reform and Control Act** in 1986. This act granted legal status to illegal aliens, or noncitizens, who could prove they had lived continuously in the United States since before January 1, 1982. The act also called for employers who knowingly hired illegal aliens to receive large fines. Illegal aliens had until May 1988 to register with the Immigration and Naturalization Service. By the deadline, more than 1 million illegal aliens had sought legal status. More than 70 percent of these aliens were from Mexico.

and professional sports that occurred during the 1990s, and how these changes affected American society.

Introduce Key Terms

Linguistic, Visual-Spatial. Review this section's key terms with students. Next, have them create a three-column chart with the headings *Key Term, Description,* and *Impact on Society.* Ask students to use context cues to complete the first two columns. Then tell students that they will finish the chart in a later activity.
SHELTERED ENGLISH

TEACH

Have students read Section 3 and complete Guided Reading Strategies 24.3. Choose one or more of the following activities to explore the section content with students. For further suggestions on block scheduling or team teaching, see the *Block Scheduling Handbook.*

LEVEL 1: Linguistic. (Suggested time: 15 min.) As a class, go over students' Guided Reading Strategies. Then use the Reading Focus questions to highlight the main ideas of the section.
SHELTERED ENGLISH

The Immigration Act of 1990 set a permanent limit of 675,000 immigrants per year after 1994. Of these immigrants, 80,000 were to be aliens with special skills. The law also increased the number of visas for immigrants with families already living in the United States.

The Los Angeles Riots

Other changes in the 1990s included increased tensions among some citizens. Many Americans were shocked by a videotape that showed four white police officers beating black motorist Rodney King. In April 1992 a jury found the Los Angeles officers not guilty of assault. The verdict triggered the **Los Angeles riots**. During four days of rioting, more than 50 people died and hundreds of businesses were destroyed. On the second day of rioting, King asked the people of Los Angeles to stop their rampage. At a news conference, he asked, "People, I just want to say, . . . can we all get along? Can we stop making it horrible for the older people and the kids?"

Many illegal aliens had to wait in long lines to submit their request to become legal immigrants.

Most of the riot damage occurred in South Central Los Angeles. Frustration over rising poverty in the area contributed to the violence. In many cases, immigrant businesses were the target of the attacks. The riots were one of the most violent episodes of urban unrest in the United States in the 1900s.

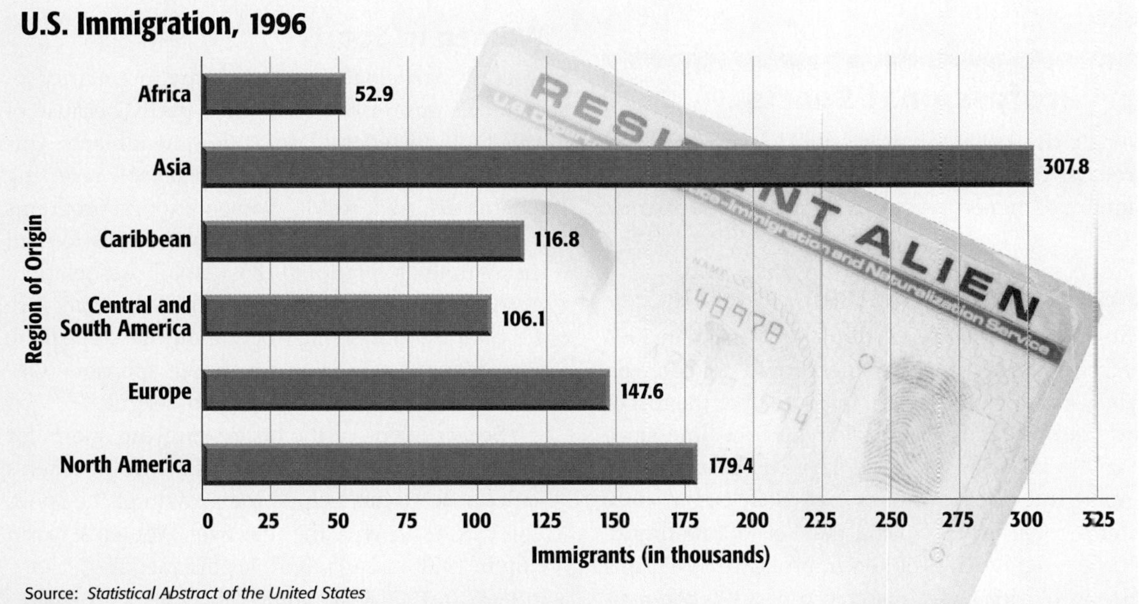

Changes in Immigration In the 1990s an increasing number of immigrants came to the United States from Asia and Latin America. More than one third of all immigrants to the United States in 1996 came from five countries: China, India, Mexico, the Philippines, and Vietnam. According to the chart above, how many immigrants came to the United States from other countries in the Americas in 1996?

Across the Curriculum

GOVERNMENT

Proposition 187. In 1994 California's voters passed a controversial initiative called Proposition 187. The law denied public education and social services, such as public health care, to illegal immigrants in the state. It also required people in certain jobs to report suspected illegal aliens to authorities. Supporters of the proposition pointed out that California spent more than $2.5 billion a year on social services for illegal aliens. Opponents argued that the law could prevent children from getting needed medical care and other services. Proposition 187 never went into effect. A U.S. district judge, declaring that only the federal government may regulate immigration, ruled key parts of it unconstitutional. California's government fought the ruling until 1999, when the governor gave up the legal battle. By that time, new federal laws provided many of the same restrictions as Proposition 187.

Activity: Have students use the library and other resources to research Proposition 187. Then ask students to write a position paper either supporting or opposing the proposition.

CHART ANSWER
285.5 million

ALL LEVELS: Linguistic. (Suggested time: 30 min.) Ask students to imagine that they work for a TV news show and that their job is to cover new pieces of legislation. Assign half the class the Immigration Reform and Control Act of 1986, and the other half the Immigration Act of 1990. Have students write two news briefs on their assigned law. In the first, they should report that the law has just passed and describe it. In the second, they should imagine that time has passed and describe the effects of the law.

ALL LEVELS: Linguistic, Visual-Spatial. (Suggested time: 30 min. plus homework) Ask students to list as many activities involving computers as they can think of in five minutes. When time is up, call on students to name some of the activities on their lists. Help students to think of some additional activities, if necessary. Then discuss how various activities were done before computers, and how the Information Revolution and the Internet have affected society. For homework, have students create a collage showing the effect computers have had on information access. **SHELTERED ENGLISH**

LEVEL 3: Linguistic, Logical-Mathematical, Intrapersonal. (Suggested time: 30 min. plus homework) Ask students to imagine that they write for a sports magazine. Have them write an article describing the impact of professional sports on American society and the U.S. economy in the 1990s. Students should examine positive and negative aspects of the growth of

Economic Development

The Sports Industry. In the 1990s professional sports emerged as one of the fastest-growing industries in the United States. From 1988 to 1993, the amount television networks paid for the air rights to pro baseball, basketball, football, and hockey games more than doubled, increasing from $700 million to $1.5 billion. During that same time span, cable TV coverage of golf, soccer, auto racing, and figure skating also increased. Another sign of the growing financial importance of sports was the trend for corporate sponsors to pay to have their names become part of the titles of sporting events or the names of sports arenas.

Critical Thinking: Why might corporations pay to have their names made part of the title of a sporting event or sports arena?

ANSWER: Students might mention that these companies can gain a lot of advertising by having their names attached to sports events and displayed on sports arenas.

Michael Jordan of the Chicago Bulls

Professional Sports

During the 1990s the professional sports industry grew. As professional sports involved an increasing amount of money, several labor disputes broke out.

Baseball and Basketball

The Major League Baseball players' strike in 1994 began after players and owners could not agree on salary and revenue issues. In September the rest of the season was canceled. For the first time since 1905, no World Series was played. The strike continued into the next season, which began only after a court order. During that season, Baltimore Oriole infielder Cal Ripken Jr. broke Lou Gehrig's 56-year-old major league record of 2,130 consecutive games played. In September 1998 Ripken sat out one game and ended his streak at 2,632 games.

Angered by the strike, many baseball fans did not return to the games until the summer of 1998. Mark McGwire of the St. Louis Cardinals and Sammy Sosa of the Chicago Cubs were trying to break Roger Maris's 37-year-old record for the most home runs—61—in a single season. One fan saw the race as "what we need." Referring to the Clinton investigation, the fan noted,

> **"This is what the country needs to help with the healing process and all the trouble that's going on in Washington. This will help cure the ills of the country."**

On September 8, 1998, McGwire broke Maris's record. Sosa also broke the record later in the season.

In professional basketball several spectacular players, including Larry Bird, Julius "Dr. J" Erving, Earvin "Magic" Johnson, and Michael Jordan, helped attract fans. During the 1990s, Jordan led the Chicago Bulls to six world championships. He also contributed to the growth of professional basketball as a business. According to what one magazine called the "Jordan Effect," his presence in the NBA added an estimated $10 billion to the economy. This figure included ticket sales, television revenue, and merchandise.

Women in Sports

Overall participation in and the popularity of women's sports also increased, partly because of Title IX of the federal Education Amendments. This act banned sex discrimination in schools receiving federal aid. As a result, women's sports programs received more funding. In 1997, 10 teams formed the Women's National Basketball Association. According to league president Val Ackerman, "we are building a first-class operation that appeals to fans, players, television, corporate sponsors. Our dream is to become the fifth major league."

Soccer is one of the fastest-growing sports for girls and women. The success of the U.S. women's national team has helped the growth of the sport. The U.S. team won the first ever Women's World Cup in 1991 and an Olympic gold medal in 1996. In 1999 Mia Hamm, Michelle Akers, and Brandi Chastain led the U.S team to its second World Cup.

The largest crowd ever for a women's sporting event watched the 1999 cup final.

professional sports as a business, rising salaries for sports stars, increases in labor disputes in the sports industry, and the growth of women's professional sports. When students meet again, have volunteers read their articles.

CLOSE

Logical-Mathematical, Visual-Spatial. Draw a three-column chart on the chalkboard and label the columns *Computer Technology, Immigration,* and *Professional Sports.* Have the class list ways in which each category has affected American society in the 1990s.

CHALLENGE AND EXTEND

Linguistic, Logical-Mathematical, Visual-Spatial. Ask students to use the library and other resources to research the development of computer technology. Have students use the information to create an illustrated, annotated time line that spans from the development of the first computers to the present. Display students' time lines around the class and then have students discuss how computers affect their lives today.

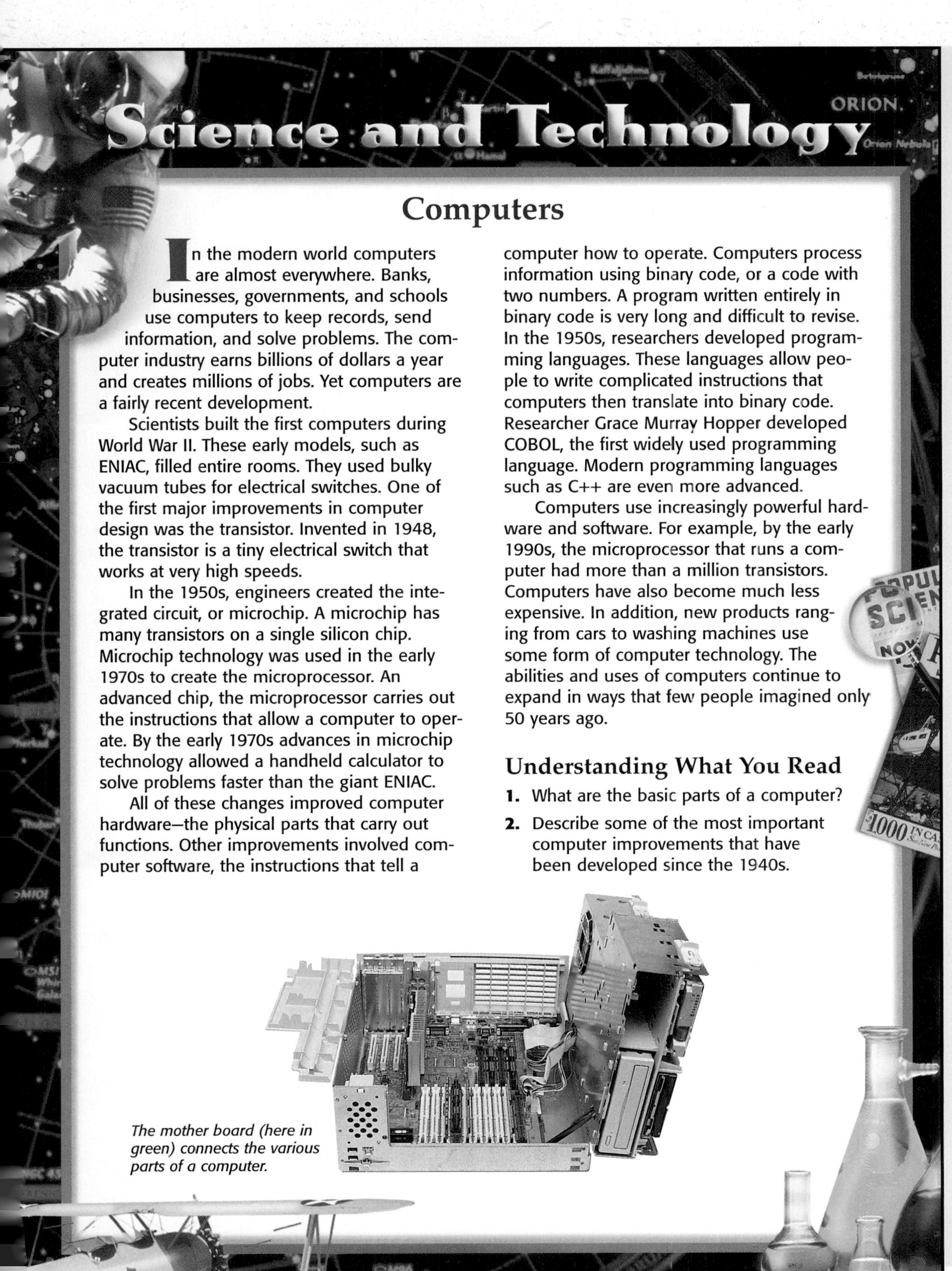

Science and Technology

Computers

In the modern world computers are almost everywhere. Banks, businesses, governments, and schools use computers to keep records, send information, and solve problems. The computer industry earns billions of dollars a year and creates millions of jobs. Yet computers are a fairly recent development.

Scientists built the first computers during World War II. These early models, such as ENIAC, filled entire rooms. They used bulky vacuum tubes for electrical switches. One of the first major improvements in computer design was the transistor. Invented in 1948, the transistor is a tiny electrical switch that works at very high speeds.

In the 1950s, engineers created the integrated circuit, or microchip. A microchip has many transistors on a single silicon chip. Microchip technology was used in the early 1970s to create the microprocessor. An advanced chip, the microprocessor carries out the instructions that allow a computer to operate. By the early 1970s advances in microchip technology allowed a handheld calculator to solve problems faster than the giant ENIAC.

All of these changes improved computer hardware—the physical parts that carry out functions. Other improvements involved computer software, the instructions that tell a computer how to operate. Computers process information using binary code, or a code with two numbers. A program written entirely in binary code is very long and difficult to revise. In the 1950s, researchers developed programming languages. These languages allow people to write complicated instructions that computers then translate into binary code. Researcher Grace Murray Hopper developed COBOL, the first widely used programming language. Modern programming languages such as C++ are even more advanced.

Computers use increasingly powerful hardware and software. For example, by the early 1990s, the microprocessor that runs a computer had more than a million transistors. Computers have also become much less expensive. In addition, new products ranging from cars to washing machines use some form of computer technology. The abilities and uses of computers continue to expand in ways that few people imagined only 50 years ago.

Understanding What You Read

1. What are the basic parts of a computer?
2. Describe some of the most important computer improvements that have been developed since the 1940s.

The mother board (here in green) connects the various parts of a computer.

Biography

Bill Gates. William H. Gates, born in 1955, wrote his first computer software program at age 13. While in high school, he helped form a programming group, which among other things computerized his school's payroll system. After graduating, Gates attended Harvard University. During his sophomore year, he and longtime friend Paul Allen developed a modified form of BASIC, a programming language used on mainframe computers. Their new version was designed for use on microcomputers, or personal computers. The project was a success. The next year Gates left school, and he and Allen formed the software company Microsoft.

Activity: Have students use the library and other resources to research and write a biography about Bill Gates's life and career.

Science and Technology Answers

1. hardware and software

2. development of the transistor, microchip, microprocessor, and programming languages

REVIEW

Logical-Mathematical, Visual-Spatial. Have students complete the Section Review questions. Then tell students to get out the chart they made in the Introduce Key Terms activity. Have students use this section to review the charts' columns that they already completed, make any necessary revisions, and then complete the final column by explaining the impact each subject has had on society. Call on volunteers to share their answers with the class. As they do, create a master chart on the chalkboard.

ASSESS

Have students complete Daily Quiz 24.3.

RETEACH

Linguistic, Logical-Mathematical. Have students complete Main Idea Activities for Reteaching and Sheltered English 24.3. Ask students to write newspaper headlines for imaginary articles about each subject and person listed in the Identify portion of the Section Review. Call on volunteers to share their headlines with the class. **SHELTERED ENGLISH**

Section 3 Review ANSWERS

Identify

For significance, see the following pages:

- Immigration Reform and Control Act, p. 718
- Los Angeles riots, p. 719
- Mark McGwire, p. 720
- Michael Jordan, p. 720
- Information Revolution, p. 722
- Internet, p. 722

Reading for Content Understanding

1. by passing laws to decrease the number of illegal immigrants in the United States and to limit the number and type of immigrants legally allowed into the country each year

2. Changes included increases in salaries and economic importance, labor disputes, and women's pro sports.

3. They have increased and simplified the transfer of information across computer networks, such as the World Wide Web.

4. Journal entries will vary but might describe the difficulties of adapting to a new country and the advantages of living in this country.

5. Answers will vary but students might mention that advances in both the Internet and the Industrial Revolution dramatically changed the way people worked and lived, and the speed at which products were made and information was distributed.

Computer Technology

Many people worldwide began keeping up with sporting events and other news on their computers. In the 1990s, computers increased and simplified the transfer of information—a development called the **Information Revolution**. Computers became essential to business, education, and every activity that requires the organization and processing of information.

In the 1980s, new technologies linked computers into networks. These networks allowed different computers to communicate and work together. With computers linked to one network, whole systems have been networked to create a worldwide link. This link is the **Internet**—a system of computer networks in which people anywhere in the world can communicate and share information. Some people have referred to the system as the information superhighway.

The Internet had its roots in a 1960s Defense Department project. However, the Internet's growth exploded in the 1990s with the creation of the World Wide Web. By 1998 as many as 60 million Americans, and more than 100 million people globally, were using the World Wide Web.

Some cafes and restaurants provide their customers with access to the Internet.

Microsoft chairman Bill Gates saw the growth of the Internet as a major step in the Information Revolution. Gates predicted some of the changes that would result:

> **"The information highway is going to break down boundaries. . . . We are watching something historic happen, and it will affect the world . . . the same way the scientific method, the invention of printing, and the arrival of the Industrial Age did."**

SECTION 3 REVIEW

Identify and explain the significance of the following:

- **Immigration Reform and Control Act**
- **Los Angeles riots**
- **Mark McGwire**
- **Michael Jordan**
- **Information Revolution**
- **Internet**

Reading for Content Understanding

1. **Main Idea** How did Congress try to change immigration in the 1980s and 1990s?
2. **Main Idea** In what ways did professional sports change in the 1980s and 1990s?
3. **Technology and Society** How have advances in computer technology changed the way information is shared?
4. **Writing** *Describing* Imagine that you have just immigrated to the United States. Write a brief journal entry describing life in your new country.
5. **Critical Thinking** *Synthesizing Information* Why do you think Bill Gates compared the information highway to the Industrial Revolution?

OBJECTIVES

- **Analyze environmental issues that gained attention in the 1990s.**
- **Describe the accomplishments of the space program in the 1990s.**
- **Explain how the global economy changed in the 1990s.**

FOCUS

Motivate Before Reading

Ask students to discuss some changes or advances that they think the future holds for them and the nation. List some of the replies on the chalkboard and group them into categories as you go. After a period of discussion, tell students that in this section they will learn about environmental issues, space exploration, and the world

Preparing for the Twenty-first Century

Reading Focus

What environmental issues gained attention in the 1990s?

What did the space program accomplish in the 1990s?

How has the global economy changed?

Key Terms

global warming

El Niño

European Union

TEENAGERS MARIA PEREZ, Fabiola Tostado, and Nevada Dove spent hours studying test results, chemical analyses, and groundwater-safety studies. Sometimes they read the reports aloud and made note of anything that sounded odd to them. The girls were not preparing for a school test. These environmental activists were preparing for a meeting. They lobbied for the temporary closing of a middle school so that potentially hazardous materials could be cleaned up at the site. Dove explained why the teenagers took action: "We're the new generation. One day you're going to have to stand up on your own two feet for something you believe in. Why not get an early start?"

The disposal of harmful materials has become a major concern.

The Environment

During the 1980s and 1990s more Americans began to share such concerns about the environment. In 1990 Congress took steps to limit industrial and auto pollution. Congress hoped that reducing pollution would limit urban smog and acid rain. Toxins from air pollution combine with water vapor to form acid rain. This rain can damage forests, lakes, and rivers.

Global Concerns

Increasingly, Americans became aware that environmental problems required worldwide cooperation. Many people were concerned that a thinning of the ozone layer would increase cases of skin cancer. This thin layer of gas in the upper atmosphere prevents harmful solar rays from reaching Earth's surface. To protect the ozone layer, many countries, including the United States, agreed to limit the release of certain chemicals into the air.

Section 4
RESOURCES

PRINT

- ★ Guided Reading Strategies 24.4
- ★ American History Political Cartoon 30: Multinational Corporations
- ★ Graphic Organizer 24: The 1990s
- ★ Section 4 Review, p. 727
- ★ Daily Quiz 24.4

MULTIMEDIA

- ★ *Teaching Resources CD–ROM,* Lesson 24.4
- ★ *American History Interactive Maps CD–ROM:* Preserving the Wetlands
- ★ *Exploring America's Past* Video Segment: Toward the Future; *Teacher's Guide,* pp. 45–47
- ★ Linking Geography and History Transparency 23: The Global Environment

SHELTERED ENGLISH

- ★ Main Idea Activities for Reteaching and Sheltered English 24.4

economy in the 1990s, all of which affected American society as it moved into the twenty-first century.

Introduce Key Terms

Linguistic, Logical-Mathematical. Review this section's key terms with students. Ask students to use each term in a sentence and leave a blank in place of the term. When students are finished, have them exchange their sentences, fill in the blanks, and return them to their authors for grading. **SHELTERED ENGLISH**

TEACH

Have students read Section 4 and complete Guided Reading Strategies 24.4. Choose one or more of the following activities to explore the section content with students. For further suggestions on block scheduling or team teaching, see the *Block Scheduling Handbook.*

LEVEL 1: Linguistic. (Suggested time: 15 min.) As a class, go over students' Guided Reading Strategies. Then use the Reading Focus questions to highlight the main ideas of the section. **SHELTERED ENGLISH**

Across the Curriculum

SCIENCE

Deforestation and Desertification. Two areas of concern at the end of the 1990s were deforestation and desertification. Deforestation occurs when woodlands are cleared for pasture, crops, lumber, or firewood. The effects of such clearing have been particularly devastating in the Amazon River Basin, an area which some scientists believe has a large impact on the world's climate. Desertification occurs when climatic changes and human actions, such as the excessive cultivation of crops, turn an area into a desert region. Desertification is characterized by declining water tables, salinization of topsoil and water, and erosion.

Critical Thinking: How might deforestation lead to desertification?

ANSWER: Land may be deforested for use as farmland, at which point overcultivation may result, leading to desertification.

Multimedia Resources

American History Interactive Maps CD–ROM: Preserving the Wetlands

Multimedia Resources

Linking Geography and History Transparency 23: The Global Environment

Environmental hazards include smog, a type of air pollution (as shown above in Los Angeles), and holes in the ozone layer (shown in the satellite image).

Another issue of concern was **global warming**. Some scientists argue that excessive heat is being trapped in Earth's atmosphere. Thus, temperatures around the globe are rising. Scientists blame this "greenhouse effect" on the buildup of carbon dioxide in the atmosphere. This buildup is caused in part by the burning of fossil fuels and the destruction of forests. Environmentalists warn that this climate change could have dangerous consequences. Other scientists disagree about the extent of the problem, however.

In 1992 the United States participated in the Earth Summit, a large gathering of world leaders, to discuss Earth's environment. Most of the 178 nations represented made a commitment to protect Earth's environment and resources.

Senator Al Gore played an active role in the summit. He had written a book on the environment, *Earth in the Balance.* As vice president, he continued to play an active role in environmental issues. In 1997 Gore spoke about the need to continue research on global warming. He said,

> **"We don't have all the answers today. But we know we must reverse the trend of global warming. We must safeguard our precious natural resources, and put a premium on public health and safety."**

Weather Extremes

Some people blamed global warming for a series of weather-related disasters in the 1990s. In 1993 some of the worst flooding in U.S. history occurred in the Midwest. From North Dakota to Missouri, heavy rains forced rivers out of their banks.

During 1996 parts of the Great Plains and the Southwest experienced a drought almost as bad as the Dust Bowl of the 1930s. Parts of Arizona, Colorado, Kansas, New Mexico, Oklahoma, Texas, and Utah suffered extremely dry conditions. According to a New Mexico state official, parts of his state had received "more rain during the Dust Bowl." The drought ruined wheat and corn crops. Having learned from the Dust Bowl problems, many farmers had crop insurance for such natural disasters.

Later that same year scientists noticed the first indications of a particularly strong **El Niño** weather system. El Niño, Spanish for "the boy child," is an irregularly occurring flow of warm surface water along the Pacific coast of South America. It is often accompanied by weather extremes. In 1998 El Niño was blamed for one of the worst heat waves of the century. Record heat and drought occurred throughout the Great Plains and Texas. Scientists also saw El Niño as the cause of severe flooding and tornadoes. In 1999 the mid-Atlantic states were hurt by record heat and drought.

Space 2000

While some scientists studied conditions on Earth, others were looking into space. In the 1990s the United States entered into many new space ventures. Some of these projects resulted from a new relationship between the United States and the former Soviet Union.

U.S. astronaut Shannon Lucid had to stay longer than expected on Mir, the Russian space station, because of mechanical problems.

ALL LEVELS: Logical-Mathematical, Visual-Spatial. (Suggested time: 35 min.) Organize students into three groups. Assign each group one of the three main environmental issues discussed in this section. Then have students, working independently, use butcher paper or posterboard to create a public service announcement designed to raise awareness about the impact of the environmental issue. Call on volunteers to share their work with the class. **SHELTERED ENGLISH**

ALL LEVELS: Linguistic, Visual-Spatial. (Suggested time: 30 min. plus homework) Ask students to create a scrapbook about the space program in the 1990s. Students might find or create headlines, drawings, charts, maps, or other items and artifacts to represent major advances. Have students share their scrapbooks with the class. **SHELTERED ENGLISH**

LEVEL 3: Linguistic, Logical-Mathematical. (Suggested time: 45 min.) Ask students to write an article for a special 1999 issue of *Financial Review* magazine devoted to the growth of the global economy during the 1990s. Articles should discuss factors that contributed to the growth of the global economy, how increased globalization has affected some nations, and positive and negative effects of a growing global economy. Call on volunteers to read their articles to the class.

The United States and Russia agreed in 1993 to jointly design and build an international space station. Two years later the U.S. space shuttle *Atlantis* linked up in orbit with the Russian space station, *Mir,* for five days. The mission was the first in preparation for the construction of the new space station. In 1996 U.S. astronaut Shannon Lucid spent 188 days stationed aboard *Mir.* Her stay was the longest by any American.

In November 1998, 77-year-old John Glenn, who had been the first American to orbit Earth, became the oldest space traveler. He flew on a shuttle mission and performed medical tests on the effects of weightlessness.

The U.S. space program began a new phase of exploration in the 1990s. This program used smaller spacecraft to explore other planets. NASA launched *Pathfinder,* a three-foot-tall spacecraft, toward Mars. On July 4, 1997, *Pathfinder* landed on Mars. *Sojourner,* a small robotic car known as a rover, emerged from the spacecraft. It traveled over the planet collecting information and sending back images. Rover engineer Henry Moore remarked, "Nobody has ever driven a car on Mars before." The Pathfinder project cost an estimated $250 million.

In 1999 NASA launched another spacecraft headed for Mars. For the first time in NASA's history, three female scientists were in charge of the project. According to manager Sarah Gavit, the age and gender of the team gave it a new outlook:

> **"[NASA] didn't want people with the old ways of thinking because they knew it was a really challenging mission."**

 A Global Economy

NASA's decision to establish an international space station reflected a trend toward globalization. Increased international trade has made economies of different countries more closely

Global Relations

GATT and WTO. After World War II, several of the world's major economic powers began working to establish new rules for reducing trade barriers and for settling international trade disputes. These rules, known as the General Agreement on Tariffs and Trade (GATT), were worked out over several decades. In 1993 in Uruguay, 117 countries met and completed an international trade agreement. Part of the agreement was the decision to replace GATT with the World Trade Organization (WTO). The WTO officially came into existence in 1995, and has since expanded to include the European Union as well as some 125 nations.

Activity: Have students research and write an essay on some positive and negative effects of reducing international trade barriers.

CHART ANSWER
jobs related to health care

U.S. Employment

Distribution of Employment by Industry, March 1998

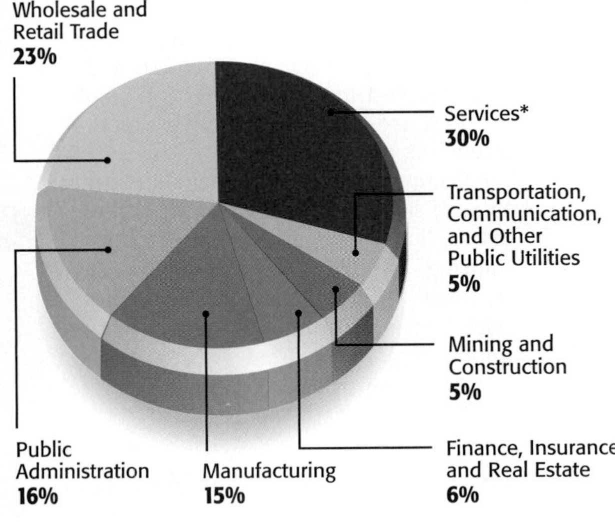

Predicted Fastest-Growing Jobs, 1996–2006

1. Database administrators and computer specialists
2. Computer engineers
3. Systems analysts
4. Personal and home care aides
5. Physical and corrective therapy assistants and aides
6. Home health aides
7. Medical assistants
8. Desktop-publishing specialists
9. Physical therapists
10. Occupational therapy assistants and aides

*Includes business, computer education, entertainment, health, legal, and repair services, among others.
Sources: Bureau of Labor Statistics; *1998–99 Occupational Outlook Handbook*

Concerns for the Future Due to the widespread use of computers, jobs related to the computer industry are expected to skyrocket in the coming years. According to the list above, what other industry is expected to expand significantly by the year 2006?

Multimedia Resources

Exploring America's Past Video Segment: Toward the Future; *Teacher's Guide,* pp. 45–47

Search 33701, Play to 39972
Videodisc Blue Side B

Play

Pause

See *Teacher's Guide* for Spanish barcode.

CLOSE

Logical-Mathematical, Interpersonal. Ask students to list positive and negative events related to the environment, space exploration, and the global economy during the 1990s. Call on volunteers to explain some of the items on their lists. Then have students discuss current issues related to these three topics.

CHALLENGE AND EXTEND

TEACHER TO TEACHER

Linguistic, Interpersonal. Rudy Martinez of San Antonio, Texas, suggested the following activity: Organize the class into two groups to debate whether the United States should spend large amounts of money on space exploration when there are many Americans living below the poverty line. Organize students into two teams to research and then debate the issue.

LINKING PAST TO PRESENT ANSWERS

1. Employers need people who are skilled when they start their jobs, who work well with others, and who manage their time well; fast-paced technological changes and work environments

2. high-tech, engineering, accounting, finance, and health care skills

Section 4 Review ANSWERS

Identify

For significance, see the following pages:

- global warming, p. 724
- El Niño, p. 724
- Shannon Lucid, p. 725
- European Union, p. 727

Reading for Content Understanding

1. air and water pollution, depletion of the ozone layer, global warming, weather extremes

2. cooperative efforts with Russia to build a space station, the exploration of Mars

3. Current ties involve increased international trade and economic dependence.

4. Paragraphs will vary but should include an explanation of the possible causes and effects of global warming.

5. Answers will vary but may mention that trade would be easier among EU countries and that as a group they would have more power in world trade.

Linking Past to Present

Careers in the Twenty-first Century

In the twenty-first century, many careers will require people to have computer or technological knowledge. The job market for college students graduating in the late 1990s was typical of this change. Some of the biggest growth was in computer-related fields. Workers in these areas include computer engineers, computer support specialists, database administrators, and systems analysts. Many of these positions require a good deal of computer knowledge. According to one writer, "If you can work a computer by the time you stroll to the podium [at graduation], you can, it seems, get a great job."

High-tech workers, like this one inspecting a computer microchip, will be in demand in the twenty-first century.

The industries that need more workers than they have been able to hire include high-tech, engineering, accounting, finance, and health care. The growth in health care positions such as home health aides and physical therapists is largely a result of the aging of the U.S. population. High growth is also expected in jobs for cashiers, retail salespersons, receptionists, and information clerks. The increase in these positions reflects the fact that the U.S. economy is becoming more service-oriented. American companies are producing fewer goods or products but are offering more services.

Even though many companies desperately need technical workers, some of these same companies are making their hiring practices more strict. According to one career placement adviser, "Companies are more concerned with organizational fit." To achieve a proper fit between employer and employee, some employers are requiring three to four sets of interviews. For example, one young job seeker had an interview and took a written test analyzing charts and graphs. He then had to perform another round of interviews and tests.

Companies want their new employees to have skills such as team work, organization, time management, and analytical thinking. The director of an employment research institute explained why the fast-paced environment made these skills so important. He said, "Things are moving so fast that companies can't take the time to teach [these skills]."

Understanding What You Read

1. How have employment needs in the United States changed in the 1990s? What may have contributed to these changes?
2. What skills are in demand for careers in the twenty-first century?

REVIEW

Linguistic, Logical-Mathematical, Interpersonal. Have students complete the Section Review questions. Give students index cards and ask them to prepare a review question for the section's material. Have them write the question on the front of the card and provide the answer on the back. Then collect the cards and organize the class into small groups. Hold a review session, using students' questions as the review material. The group that answers the most questions correctly is the winner.

ASSESS

Have students complete Daily Quiz 24.4.

RETEACH

Logical-Mathematical. Have students complete Main Idea Activities for Reteaching and Sheltered English 24.4. Ask students to create a "Top 5" list of significant environmental, space-exploration, and economic events in the 1990s. Encourage students to choose those events that they think had the greatest impact (good or bad) on American society. Call on students to explain the items on their lists to the class. **SHELTERED ENGLISH**

connected and dependent on each other. The rise of multinational corporations—corporations that operate in more than one country at a time—has also shaped the global economy.

Some nations have even joined together to increase their global economic power. In 1991, 11 nations of Western Europe joined together to form the **European Union** (EU). The EU wanted to join its members' economies into one single market with a common currency and a common central bank. In 1999 the EU introduced the "euro," its common currency. One European proudly announced, "There are now two economic superpowers [the EU and the United States]."

The European Union created 11 different versions of the euro. Each version has an image or symbol of the member nation that designed it.

In 1995, 125 nations joined together in the World Trade Organization (WTO), which supervises international trade. The WTO replaced the General Agreement on Tariffs and Trade (GATT). GATT was a series of trade agreements reached since World War II to reduce quotas and limit tariffs.

As global markets become more integrated, there is more risk that difficult times in one nation will hurt the economies of other countries. In 1994 and 1995, for example, Mexico suffered a serious economic crisis. The value of its currency, the peso, dropped significantly. The crisis threatened the financial situations of international investors. President Clinton and the United Nations' World Bank supported a $50 billion package to get Mexico's economy back on track.

The World Bank helps its member nations establish international economic cooperation. The International Monetary Fund (IMF) of the World Bank lends money to countries in need. The number of loans and the amount of money loaned by the IMF has increased as international trade has expanded. After the Cold War ended, the IMF loaned money to Russia and a number of Eastern European nations. Russia has had difficulty making the transition from communism to a free-market economy.

In 1997 the IMF also provided more than $100 billion in financial assistance to several Asian countries experiencing economic crisis. A downturn in their economies threatened to cause currency problems throughout the world. Russia was one of the nations affected. The IMF agreed to loan the country more than $17 billion.

The IMF is just one way that nations can work together to keep the global economy strong. The United States continues to look for new ways to support economic stability with its trading partners throughout the world.

SECTION 4 REVIEW

Identify and explain the significance of the following:
- **global warming**
- **El Niño**
- **Shannon Lucid**
- **European Union**

Reading for Content Understanding

1. **Main Idea** What environmental issues and weather-related events were important in the late 1980s and the 1990s?
2. **Main Idea** What did NASA achieve in its space programs in the 1990s?
3. **Economic Development** How have economic ties among nations changed?
4. **Writing** *Informing* Imagine that you are a scientist who thinks that global warming is a serious problem. Write a paragraph explaining the situation.
5. **Critical Thinking** *Drawing Conclusions* What advantages might European nations gain by forming the European Union?

Chapter 24 Review ANSWERS

Identifying People and Ideas

1. U.S. president who served from 1993 to 2001; impeached but not removed from office
2. law that established a five-day waiting period for handgun purchases
3. special U.S. prosecutor appointed to investigate allegations against high-ranking government officials
4. Republican House member who helped create the Contract with America; became Speaker of the House
5. 1994 Republican campaign pledge to reduce the size of government and balance the federal budget
6. secretary of state during Clinton's administration
7. 1986 law granting legal status to some illegal aliens and imposing fines on employers of illegal aliens
8. advances in computer technology that increased, simplified, and sped up the transfer and gathering of information
9. increased global temperatures caused by the trapping of carbon dioxide and other gases within Earth's atmosphere
10. astronaut whose 188-day stay on the *Mir* space station was the longest American stay in space

Using the Time Line

1. d
2. e
3. b
4. a
5. c

Review and Assessment RESOURCES

PRINT
- ★ Chapter 24 Review, pp. 728–29
- ★ Vocabulary Activity 24
- ★ Chapter 24 Study Guide
- ★ Chapter 24 Test (Form A or B)

MULTIMEDIA
- ★ Audio Program, Ch. 24 (English and Spanish)
- ★ *Global Skill Builder CD–ROM*
- ★ Chapter 24 Test Generator
- ★ HRW Web site

SHELTERED ENGLISH
- ★ Spanish Glossary
- ★ Sheltered English Chapter 24 Test

ASSESS

Have students complete one of the Chapter 24 tests. As an alternate assessment, assign the Chapter 24 Investigation.

Understanding Main Ideas

1. successful—family and medical leave act, transfer of medical insurance coverage, reform of welfare system; unsuccessful—universal medical coverage

2. reduce the size of the government and balance the federal budget

3. forced it to increase security measures, particularly at airports

4. to restore to power the democratically elected Aristide government

5. granted legal status to illegal immigrants residing in the United States since before 1982, imposed fines on employers of illegal immigrants, set annual immigration limits, opened up immigration for family members of immigrants in the United States

6. joined with Russia to build an international space station and used small spacecraft and robotics to explore Mars

Reviewing Themes

1. for lying under oath before a grand jury; the Senate did not convict him and he remained in office with little loss to his popularity

2. a greater role in helping to preserve peace and democracy around the world

3. It has made international communication easier and more instantaneous.

CHAPTER 24 REVIEW

Chapter Summary

Voters elected Bill Clinton president in 1992 and 1996. The Clinton administration and Congress balanced the federal budget and reformed welfare. However, President Clinton faced many challenges. In the post–Cold War world, the United States tried to help some nations achieve peace. Countries have become more connected through computer technologies and the global economy.

On a separate sheet of paper, complete the following activities.

Identifying People and Ideas

Describe the historical significance of the following:

1. Bill Clinton
2. Brady Bill
3. independent counsel
4. Newt Gingrich
5. Contract with America
6. Madeleine Albright
7. Immigration Reform and Control Act
8. Information Revolution
9. global warming
10. Shannon Lucid

Internet Activity 

go.hrw.com
SB1 Environment

Search the Internet through the HRW Web site to find sites related to environmental issues in the United States. In particular, find out how students are involved in environmental projects. Use the information to create an action guide listing possible issues and projects in which students might want to participate.

Understanding Main Ideas

1. What health care and welfare reforms did President Clinton support? Which were successful?
2. What did many Republicans running for Congress promise to do after the 1994 elections?
3. How did acts of terrorism affect the United States during the 1990s?
4. Why did President Clinton send U.S. troops to Haiti?
5. What immigration reforms did Congress approve in the 1980s and 1990s?
6. What are some of NASA's recent efforts in space?

Reviewing Themes

1. **Constitutional Heritage** Why did the House of Representatives impeach President Clinton? What was the outcome?

Using the Time Line

Number your paper from 1 to 5. Match the letters on the time line below with the following events.

1. **President Clinton is impeached.**
2. **The United States and NATO launch air strikes on Serbia.**
3. **The North American Free Trade Agreement is ratified.**
4. **Bill Clinton is the first Democrat elected president since 1976.**
5. **NASA lands the *Pathfinder* spacecraft on Mars.**

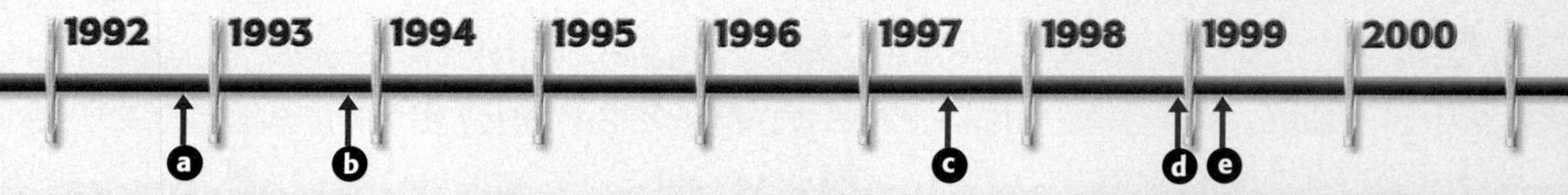

RETEACH

Linguistic, Visual-Spatial, Interpersonal. Organize students into four groups and assign each group one section of the chapter. Have the groups create a time line showing the significant events in their assigned section. Have each group present its time line to the class and explain the significance of each event included. SHELTERED ENGLISH

Using the Internet

Have students continue their research on environmental projects in which students can participate. Then ask each student to develop a plan for an environmental club at their school. Have students create brochures that describe their club, its focus, and some possible future projects.

Portfolio Extensions

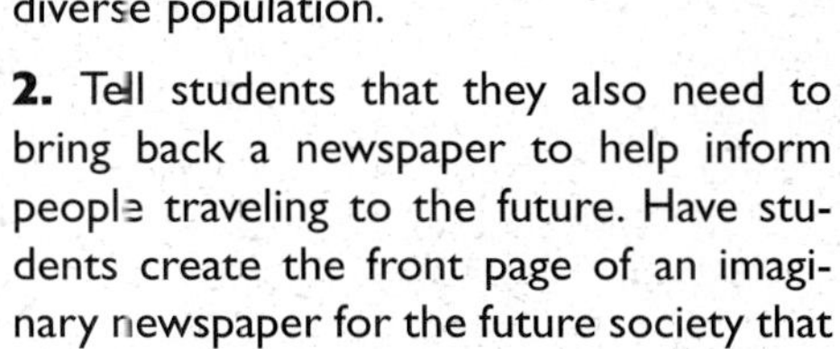

1. Have students write an essay explaining how a nation benefits by having a culturally rich and diverse population.

2. Tell students that they also need to bring back a newspaper to help inform people traveling to the future. Have students create the front page of an imaginary newspaper for the future society that they predicted.

2. **Global Relations** What international role has the United States assumed in the 1990s?
3. **Technology and Society** How has the Information Revolution changed international communication?

Thinking Critically

1. **Identifying Cause and Effect** How did the 1994 congressional elections affect Clinton's presidency?
2. **Drawing Conclusions** What historical reasons might the United States have for being concerned about events in the Balkans?
3. **Evaluating** How do you think the women's rights movement in the 1960s and 1970s contributed to the growth of women's sports in the 1990s?

Writing About History

1. **Creating** Imagine that you are a campaign adviser during the 1992 presidential campaign. Select one of the candidates mentioned in the chapter. Create a flyer explaining why U.S. voters should support your candidate.
2. **Persuading** Write a letter to the head of the World Bank urging the bank to help other countries that are experiencing financial problems. Be sure to include reasons why the World Bank should offer aid to these nations.

Building Your Portfolio

Complete the following activities individually or in groups.

1. **A Nation of Many** Create a collage on the theme that the United States is a nation of many people with different cultural and ethnic backgrounds. Use as many newspaper and magazine clippings as you can find, and write captions for them.
2. **Journey into the Future** Imagine that you have been transported 50 years into the future. You will stay there just long enough to write a guide to life at that time for the next person to be transported into your future. Your guide should explain how people live, what kinds of careers they have, and how technology affects their daily lives. Your guide should also include information about food, clothing, and transportation. Be sure to include illustrations.

Linking Geography and History

1. **Location** How did the breakup of Yugoslavia lead to conflict in the Balkans?
2. **Movement** Why did many Haitians leave their country in the early 1990s?

History Skills Workshop

Using Primary Sources Maya Angelou is an African American writer, poet, and civil rights activist. She is best known for her autobiographical novels. Bill Clinton asked her to compose and read a poem for his 1993 inauguration. When she read "On the Pulse of Morning," she became the second poet to read his or her work at a presidential inauguration. Robert Frost had presented a poem at John F. Kennedy's inauguration in 1961. Read the following excerpt from "On the Pulse of Morning." Then answer the following questions: (a) What does Maya Angelou mean by "the pulse of this new day"? (b) What message is Angelou offering? (c) Why do you think Bill Clinton selected Angelou to participate in his inauguration?

"Here on the pulse of this new day
You may have the grace to look up
and out
And into your sister's eyes, and into
Your brother's face, your country
And say simply
Very simply
With hope
Good morning."

Thinking Critically

1. the elections resulted in a Republican majority in both houses of Congress, which made it more difficult for Clinton to achieve his goals

2. World War I began there; ethnic cleansing reminded people of the Holocaust.

3. Answers will vary but students might mention that the women's rights movement helped women achieve more equality and move into more traditionally male fields, such as sports.

Writing About History

1. Flyers will vary but should accurately reflect the positions of the chosen candidate.

2. Letters will vary but should mention how with the growth of the global economy, economic problems in one nation can lead to economic problems around the world.

Linking Geography and History

1. It divided the country across ethnic and cultural lines, and some groups opposed the breakup.

2. because of violence against opponents of the new military dictatorship

History Skills Workshop

(a) the start of a new presidential administration; (b) that unity across racial and gender lines can lead to hope for a better world; (c) because of her message for hope and unity and because she was a black woman who had been politically active in civil rights and had achieved great success in her later writing career

FOCUS

Have students write answers to the following questions on a sheet of paper: What country do you think uses the most energy? What country might be the world's top oil producer? Do you think the United States imports or exports more energy? After the lesson, ask students to compare their answers to what they have learned about the production and consumption of energy.

TEACH

Have students read the Geography and History lesson. Choose one or more of the following activities to explore the Geography and History content with students.

ALL LEVELS: Linguistic, Visual-Spatial. (Suggested time: 30 min.) Assign each student a state that has at least one source of energy. Instruct students to use the information from the map

Across the Curriculum

SCIENCE

British Thermal Units. The British thermal unit (Btu) is a standard way of measuring energy. Until 1929 the 60° Btu was defined as the amount of heat energy it took to increase the temperature of one pound of water from 59.5° to 60.5°F. However, this method of calculating a Btu was difficult, so the definition was changed at an international conference held in London. Today, the Btu is defined in terms of other units of energy. For example, one Btu is equal to one third of a watt-hour.

Activity: Have students make a list of items around their home that might have heat output measured in Btu.

SKILLS ANSWERS

1. more than twice as much

2. Asia—China, India, Japan, Russia (also partly in Europe); Europe—France, Germany, Italy, the United Kingdom; North America—Canada, the United States

3. North America

Geography & History

The World's Energy

The United States is the world's largest consumer of energy, using about one fourth of the world's commercial power. The United States, as well as other nations with industrial economies, consumes much of that energy in running factories and in powering homes, businesses, and public facilities. Less industrialized nations, called developing countries, consume much less energy. Energy sources for heating buildings and cooking food in developing countries often are wood, charcoal, and manure.

Much of the world's energy resources consist of fossil fuels. These fuels include oil, natural gas, and coal. Fossil fuels were formed from the remains of prehistoric plants and animals. These fuels are limited and cannot be replaced, leading some people to fear energy depletion. Leaders from the United States and other nations are working to protect Earth's limited resources. ■

Energy Resources

Many wealthy countries, such as the United States and Canada, are among the biggest consumers and producers of energy.

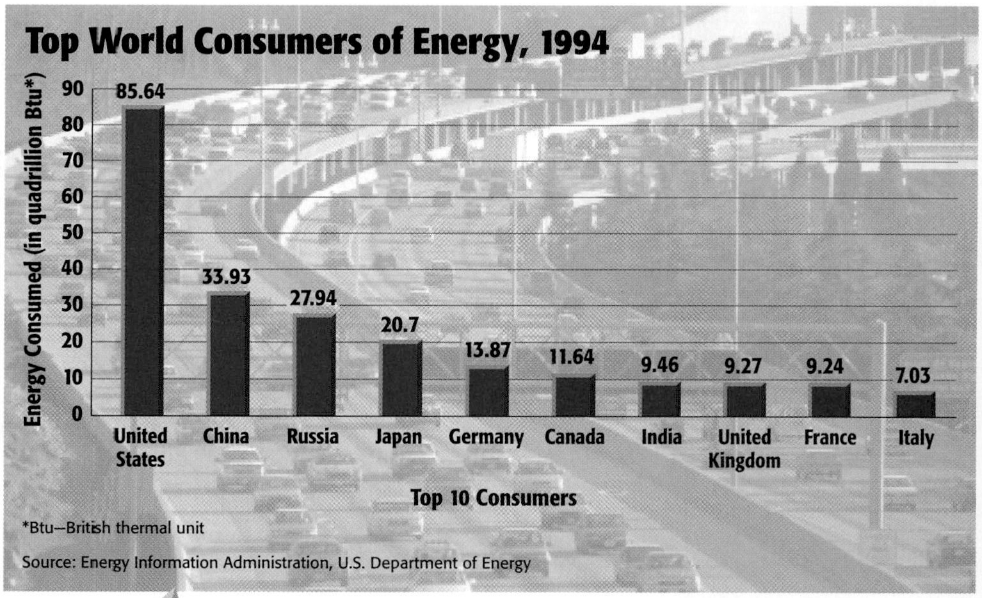

Top World Consumers of Energy, 1994

Top 10 Consumers	Energy Consumed (in quadrillion Btu*)
United States	85.64
China	33.93
Russia	27.94
Japan	20.7
Germany	13.87
Canada	11.64
India	9.46
United Kingdom	9.27
France	9.24
Italy	7.03

*Btu—British thermal unit

Source: Energy Information Administration, U.S. Department of Energy

Geography Skills

Reading Bar Graphs

1. About how much energy did the United States consume compared to the second-largest energy consumer in 1994?

2. Use the world map on page xxvi to check the location of the countries listed in this bar graph. On which continent is each country located?

3. Which continent consumes the most energy?

730

on page 732 to design a poster illustrating the source or sources of energy that are available in their assigned state. Posters should also include a state slogan that identifies the energy source or sources the state has to offer. **SHELTERED ENGLISH**

LEVEL 3: Logical-Mathematical, Visual-Spatial. (Suggested time: 45 min.) Have students calculate the total amount of energy used by the top 10 consumer nations in 1994. Then instruct students to calculate the percentage of the total that was consumed by each nation. *(Students should divide the amount a nation used by the total amount used by all 10 nations and multiply the result by 100.)* Tell students to use this information to create a pie graph illustrating the percentage of energy each of the top 10 consumers used in 1994. When students are finished, call on a volunteer to draw the final pie graph on the chalkboard.

Leading Energy Producers, 1990–1992

Oil Producers

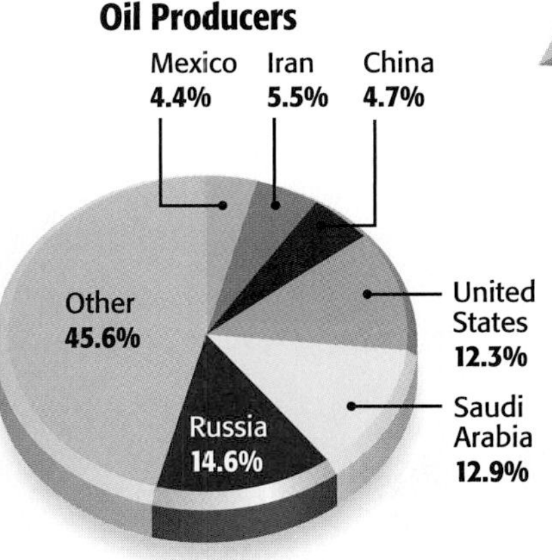

Coal Producers

India 5%
Russia 7.7%
Germany 8.2%
Other 35.3%
United States 20%
China 23.8%

Natural Gas Producers

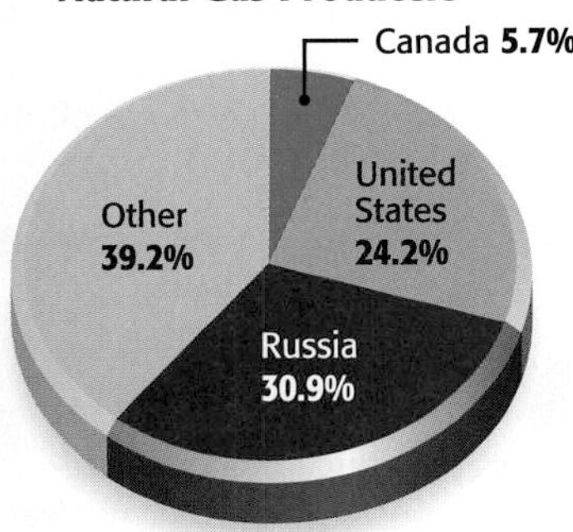

Source: *Rand McNally Goode's World Atlas*

Geography Skills

Reading Pie Graphs

1. What nation ranked in the top three in all areas of energy production?
2. What percentage of the world's coal was produced by China, Russia, and the United States combined?
3. What energy source owes more than half of its production to two nations?

Natural gas, oil, and coal provide most of the world's energy.

History Note 1

These pie graphs show the three major sources of energy in the world today. These fossil fuels—oil, coal, and gas—made up about 90 percent of the world's total commercial energy production at the beginning of the 1990s.

Technology and Society

Alternate Energy Sources. People have explored using energy sources other than oil, gas, and coal. However, alternate energy sources can also pose problems. Nuclear power plants produce radioactive waste and create plutonium that could conceivably be used to build weapons. Solar energy can be used to heat small buildings, but may not be practical for large-scale industrial projects. Hydroelectric power requires the construction of dams, which can have negative environmental impacts. Wind can be used to generate electricity, but requires the construction of huge windmills that some people find unattractive. These windmills can also interfere with radar and communications devices.

Activity: Have students use the library and other resources to examine the advantages and disadvantages of using oil, coal, natural gas, and one alternate energy source. Instruct students to present the information in a chart.

SKILLS ANSWERS

1. the United States
2. 51.5 percent
3. natural gas

CLOSE

Logical-Mathematical, Visual-Spatial. Have students create a Venn diagram with three overlapping circles labeled *Leading Oil Producers, Leading Coal Producers,* and *Leading Natural Gas Producers.* Have students write in the appropriate circle the name of each country listed on the pie graphs on page 731. Tell students to place countries that are multiple producers into the appropriate intersection of the circles. For example, because the United States is a leading producer of oil, coal, and natural gas, students should write its name in the area where all three circles overlap.

CHALLENGE AND EXTEND

Logical-Mathematical, Visual-Spatial. Have students use the library or other resources to create an annotated time line showing five-year intervals from 1970 to 1995. Above the line, tell students to note the figures for U.S. energy consumption, production, imports, and exports from the graph on page 733. Below the line, students should write a brief annotation at each five-year mark that describes U.S. or global events that may help explain the trends in the figures above the line. Have volunteers share their time lines with the class.

Economic Development

Coal. In 1977 the United States had an estimated 283 billion tons of coal in reserve, enough to last for over 400 years at then-current production levels. Despite this fact, the United States has become increasingly dependent on oil, both domestic and foreign. One reason for this result is that coal has many drawbacks. Underground mining is dangerous work and can cause water pollution. Surface mining leaves ugly scars on the land and pollutes water. Burning coal releases chemical compounds into the air, many of which can harm humans and animals.

Critical Thinking: How might some of the problems of using coal be solved?

ANSWER: Students might mention that laws on mining and burning coal might limit the negative impact.

SKILLS ANSWERS

1. Alabama, Arkansas, California, Colorado, Illinois, Indiana, Iowa, Kansas, Kentucky, Maryland, Michigan, Missouri, Nebraska, New Mexico, Ohio, Oklahoma, Pennsylvania, Tennessee, Texas, Utah, Virginia, Washington, West Virginia, Wyoming

2. Alaska, Arkansas, California, Colorado, Kansas, Louisiana, Mississippi, New Mexico, North Dakota, Oklahoma, Texas

3. oil and natural gas

Energy at Home

Most of the United States's energy is produced at home. The United States does buy large amounts of oil, as well as certain other fuels, from other countries. Foreign fuel is important because of high U.S. consumption.

Energy Sources in the United States

- Major oil-producing field
- Minor oil-producing field
- Major natural gas field
- Major coal deposit
- Minor coal deposit
- Uranium deposits
- Nuclear power plants

Geography Skills

Reading Special-Purpose Maps

1. Where are major U.S. coal deposits located?
2. Where are major U.S. oil fields found?
3. What energy sources can be found off the coast in the Gulf of Mexico?

Miners tunnel deep into the ground to reach coal deposits.

History Note 2

About 80 percent of U.S. energy production in the mid-1990s came from fossil fuels. Power generated by nuclear plants accounted for another 10 percent of the country's energy production. Coal has been the largest single source of U.S. energy production since the mid-1970s and is the country's largest energy-resource export.

REVIEW

Linguistic. Have each student create a transcript of a mock interview with the U.S. secretary of energy. Transcripts should include questions about both global and U.S. production and consumption of energy. Instruct students to include at least four questions. The secretary's answers should be based on the information presented on each page of the lesson.

ASSESS

Have students complete Geography and History Quiz 8.

RETEACH

Kinesthetic, Logical-Mathematical. Have each student create a collage illustrating energy consumption. For example, students could include a newspaper headline about the price of gasoline, or magazine pictures of a car or a lightbulb. Instruct students to write a caption for their collage that includes some facts from the lesson about energy consumption and production.
SHELTERED ENGLISH

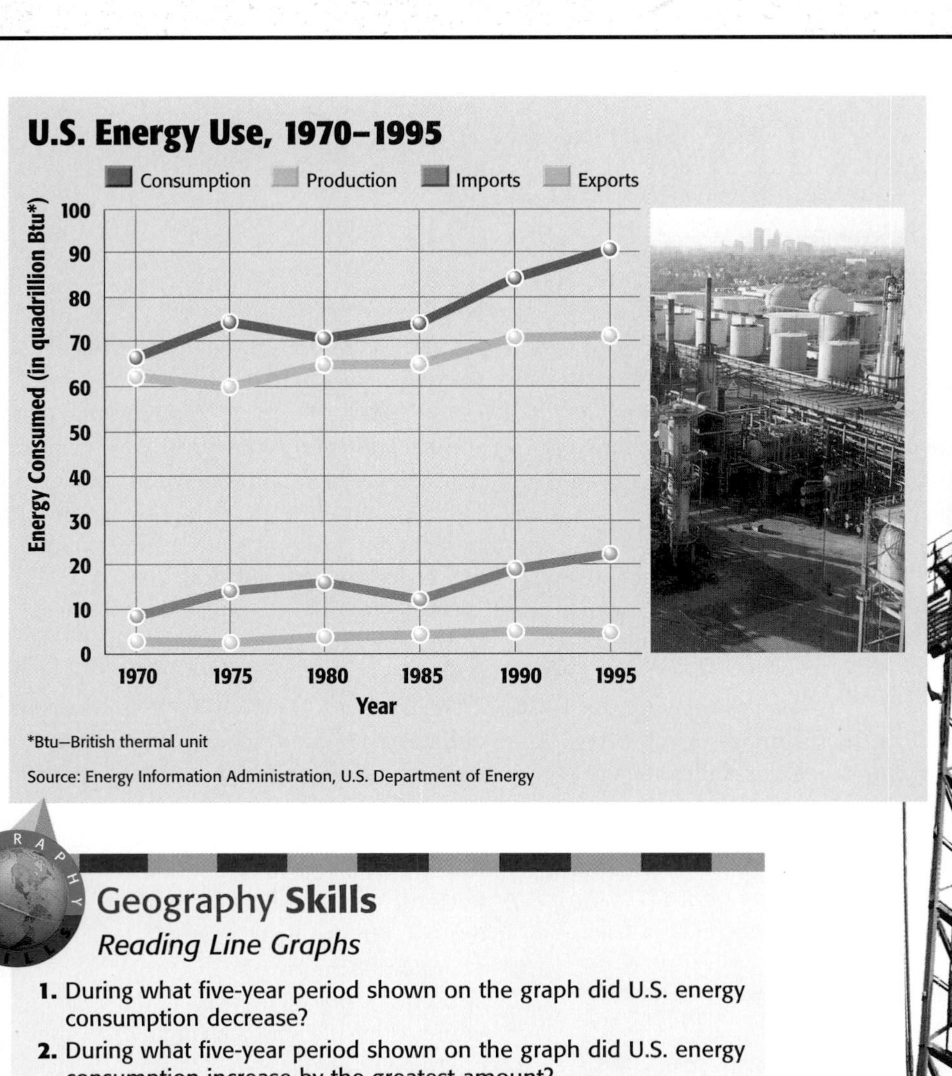

Geography Skills
Reading Line Graphs

1. During what five-year period shown on the graph did U.S. energy consumption decrease?
2. During what five-year period shown on the graph did U.S. energy consumption increase by the greatest amount?
3. In what year shown on the graph did the United States import the most energy? How much energy was imported in that year?
4. How much more energy did the United States import in 1990 than it exported in that year?

History Note 3

Texas and California, the nation's two most populous states, rank first and second among the 50 states in the amount of energy consumed. However, Alaska—where winters are long and extremely cold—consumes more energy per person than any other state. The typical New York resident on average consumes less energy than residents of any other state.

Derricks like this one pump oil from beneath Earth's surface.

Citizenship and Democracy

The U.S. Department of Energy. Concern over the increasing price of foreign oil during the 1970s led U.S. government officials to design a national energy policy. To achieve this goal, President Jimmy Carter signed a bill in 1977 that created the Department of Energy (DOE), the first new cabinet office in 11 years. The DOE brought the widespread agencies involved with energy issues together into one department. When oil prices dropped during the 1980s, many conservatives argued that the DOE was unnecessary and should be abolished. However, Congress refused to eliminate the DOE. When the Persian Gulf War began in 1991, DOE officials took the lead in drafting a comprehensive energy plan to lessen the nation's dependence on foreign oil.

Activity: Have students use the library or other resources to create a public service announcement that encourages Americans to conserve energy and explains at least three methods of conservation.

SKILLS ANSWERS

1. 1975 to 1980
2. 1985 to 1990
3. 1995; more than 20 quadrillion Btu
4. about 15 quadrillion Btu

TEACH

ALL LEVELS: Linguistic, Logical-Mathematical. (Suggested time: 45 min.) Organize the class into three groups. Instruct all students to write short papers on the topic "The Importance of Homework." Each group, however, will aim their papers at a different audience: a kindergarten class, a peer group, or a PTA meeting. Have students turn in their papers. Read aloud several papers from each group without telling students which paper is from which group. As a class, have students select for which audience they think each paper is intended. Note on the chalkboard the clues they used to make their selections. To conclude, see how many papers the class identified correctly.

SKILLS ANSWERS

1. so that you will be able to best communicate your message by addressing your audience in a way that they can readily understand
2. Read it, reorganize it if necessary for clarity, add appropriate adjectives and adverbs, rewrite awkward sentences, and check for proper spelling, punctuation, and grammar.
3. Papers will vary based on the individual chosen. Students should provide all the requested materials to show that they did the necessary research, made an outline, and wrote both a first and final draft.

Proofreading. For further practice, have students reread the text under "The Pardons" heading on pages 663–64 of Chapter 22. Ask students to decide for themselves whether they agree with President Ford's decision to pardon Richard Nixon. Ask students to write the first draft of a brief paper defending their decision. Then have students exchange the first drafts of their papers and edit each other's work. Ask students to return the papers to their authors. Finally, have students use the peer comments to revise their papers and write the final versions.

History Skills
WORKSHOP

Writing a Paper

When writing a paper, you should keep a particular focus in mind. You may want to analyze some information, inform your audience about a particular topic, or persuade someone on an important issue.

Stages of Writing a Paper When you are writing a paper, divide your work into steps. Focus on completing each before you begin the next.

Writing with a Purpose Always keep your purpose for writing the paper in mind—it will determine the best approach to take. Different types of writing require their own tone and content. For example, you would use a different tone in writing a paper analyzing the causes of the oil embargo than you would in trying to persuade readers to recycle.

Research is an important part of writing a paper.

How to Write a Paper

Regardless of what you are writing, you should follow certain basic steps.

1. **Choose a topic** If possible, choose a topic that interests you. Keep the subject of your topic specific so that your research and writing is focused and clear.
2. **Identify your purpose in writing** Understand the directions for your assignment so that you can plan your paper.
3. **Consider your audience** When writing for a specific audience, choose the tone and style that will best communicate your message.
4. **Collect information** Use your library and/or Internet and take notes of the information you collect on your subject.
5. **Create an outline** Organize your themes, main ideas, and supporting details into an outline.
6. **Write a first draft and evaluate it** Use your outline as a guide. Each paragraph should express one main idea and contain details to support it. Use transitions—sentences that build connections between paragraphs—to show the relationships between ideas.
7. **Review, revise, and proofread** Read your draft and reorganize it as needed to make your points. Improve sentences by adding appropriate adjectives and adverbs. Make your writing clearer by changing the length or structure of awkward sentences. Check for proper spelling, punctuation, and grammar.
8. **Write your final version** Prepare a neat, clean final version. Appearance is important. It can affect the way people understand your writing.

Practicing the Skill

1. Why is it important to consider the audience for whom you are writing?
2. What steps should you take to edit a first draft?
3. Choose one of the presidents in this unit and write a three-paragraph paper about his administration. Along with the paper's final version, turn in your research notes, outline, first draft, and revisions.

ALL LEVELS: Linguistic, Logical-Mathematical. (Suggested time: 30 min. plus homework) Ask students to imagine that the Committee for the Future has asked them each to submit one item that best represents the current year, for possible inclusion in a time capsule. Ask students to suggest memorable events of the past year and list them on the chalkboard. Then have each student write a short paper describing the item they think should be chosen and persuading the committee to include it in the time capsule. Students can start their papers in class and finish them for homework.

History in Action

UNIT 8 PORTFOLIO

Textbook Final Chapter

Complete the following activity in small, cooperative groups.

History is more than just what happened long ago. Events taking place today are also part of the continuing story of history. Your editor has asked you to add a chapter to this textbook. This chapter will cover the important events in U.S. history that have occurred since the end of Chapter 24. Your class will be divided into four teams and each team will create one section of the chapter.

Materials To complete this activity, you will need posterboard, construction paper, or typing paper. You may wish to use a computer to write your chapter. In addition, you will need markers, pens, pencils, and glue, tape, or rubber cement.

Parts of the Project Complete the following tasks to create your chapter:

1. **Planning and Outlining** Each group will take one of the following topics—American Culture; The Election of 2000; Major World Events; or Science and Technology—as the subject for its section. Meet as a group and create an outline for your section. Review the last few chapters of this book for ideas on how to organize your section. Further divide your section's main topic into smaller, more specific topics. Use these topics to divide your sections into subsections. Assign each person a subsection.

2. **Researching and Writing** Use recent newspapers and magazines, the library, and other sources to gather information on your topic. Compare what you find with what you have already learned and take note of any new developments or changes that have occurred. Also gather any images, maps, or charts you think will be useful. Then, write your subsection.

These students are selecting photographs for their project.

3. **Editing** When you have finished writing, meet as a group again. Have each group member exchange his or her subsection with another group member. Read and edit the subsection you have received, checking spelling and grammar. Ask questions about anything that seems unclear and offer constructive suggestions to improve the work. Get back your original subsection, revise it, and write a final draft.

4. **Laying out the Chapter** Meet as a group and decide how to arrange the images and text of your section. Paste the subsections with images onto posterboard to create the pages of your section. Combine it with the other groups' sections to create a chapter.

Have the class vote on a title for the chapter. Display the chapter in your classroom or another area of the school and use it to answer questions about recent history.

Primary Sources. Remind students that they can make use of a variety of primary sources when writing about recent history. Students should consider using editorials, interviews, photographs, and other types of primary sources in their work.

Literature and Art. Encourage students to add segments on current literature or art to their chapter. They may be able to incorporate an introductory piece called "American Teens in History: Young Artists" or "American Teens in History: Young Writers" at the beginning of the chapter or in the "American Culture" section.

Opening Image. After the entire chapter has been put together, ask volunteers to submit images from their research for the chapter's title page. Select several of the most appropriate images and submit them to the class for a vote.

American flag
I LIKE IKE
Dwight Eisenhower campaign item
Cotton, an important southern product
Space shuttle
Streetcar
Saxophone and jukebox
Iwo Jima memorial

Call to FREEDOM

1865 to the Present

REFERENCE

Presidents of the United States 738
Facts About the States 743
Important Supreme Court Cases 744
Gazetteer 748
Glossary 757
Index 772
Acknowledgments........... 796

737

Presidents of the United States

The Official Portraits

1 George Washington
Born: 1732 **Died:** 1799
Years in Office: 1789–97
Political Party: None
Home State: Virginia
Vice President: John Adams

2 John Adams
Born: 1735 **Died:** 1826
Years in Office: 1797–1801
Political Party: Federalist
Home State: Massachusetts
Vice President: Thomas Jefferson

3 Thomas Jefferson
Born: 1743 **Died:** 1826
Years in Office: 1801–09
Political Party: Republican*
Home State: Virginia
Vice Presidents: Aaron Burr, George Clinton

4 James Madison
Born: 1751 **Died:** 1836
Years in Office: 1809–17
Political Party: Republican
Home State: Virginia
Vice Presidents: George Clinton, Elbridge Gerry

5 James Monroe
Born: 1758 **Died:** 1831
Years in Office: 1817–25
Political Party: Republican
Home State: Virginia
Vice President: Daniel D. Tompkins

6 John Quincy Adams
Born: 1767 **Died:** 1848
Years in Office: 1825–29
Political Party: Republican
Home State: Massachusetts
Vice President: John C. Calhoun

7 Andrew Jackson
Born: 1767 **Died:** 1845
Years in Office: 1829–37
Political Party: Democratic
Home State: Tennessee
Vice Presidents: John C. Calhoun, Martin Van Buren

* The Republican Party of the third through sixth presidents is not the party of Abraham Lincoln, which was founded in 1854.

8 Martin Van Buren
Born: 1782 **Died:** 1862
Years in Office: 1837–41
Political Party: Democratic
Home State: New York
Vice President: Richard M. Johnson

9 William Henry Harrison
Born: 1773 **Died:** 1841
Years in Office: 1841
Political Party: Whig
Home State: Ohio
Vice President: John Tyler

10 John Tyler
Born: 1790 **Died:** 1862
Years in Office: 1841–45
Political Party: Whig
Home State: Virginia
Vice President: None

11 James K. Polk
Born: 1795 **Died:** 1849
Years in Office: 1845–49
Political Party: Democratic
Home State: Tennessee
Vice President: George M. Dallas

12 Zachary Taylor
Born: 1784 **Died:** 1850
Years in Office: 1849–50
Political Party: Whig
Home State: Louisiana
Vice President: Millard Fillmore

13 Millard Fillmore
Born: 1800 **Died:** 1874
Years in Office: 1850–53
Political Party: Whig
Home State: New York
Vice President: None

14 Franklin Pierce
Born: 1804 **Died:** 1869
Years in Office: 1853–57
Political Party: Democratic
Home State: New Hampshire
Vice President: William R. King

15 James Buchanan
Born: 1791 **Died:** 1868
Years in Office: 1857–61
Political Party: Democratic
Home State: Pennsylvania
Vice President: John C. Breckinridge

16 Abraham Lincoln
Born: 1809 **Died:** 1865
Years in Office: 1861–65
Political Party: Republican
Home State: Illinois
Vice Presidents: Hannibal Hamlin, Andrew Johnson

739

PRESIDENTS OF THE UNITED STATES

17 Andrew Johnson
Born: 1808 **Died:** 1875
Years in Office: 1865–69
Political Party: Republican
Home State: Tennessee
Vice President: None

18 Ulysses S. Grant
Born: 1822 **Died:** 1885
Years in Office: 1869–77
Political Party: Republican
Home State: Illinois
Vice Presidents: Schuyler Colfax, Henry Wilson

19 Rutherford B. Hayes
Born: 1822 **Died:** 1893
Years in Office: 1877–81
Political Party: Republican
Home State: Ohio
Vice President: William A. Wheeler

20 James A. Garfield
Born: 1831 **Died:** 1881
Years in Office: 1881
Political Party: Republican
Home State: Ohio
Vice President: Chester A. Arthur

21 Chester A. Arthur
Born: 1829 **Died:** 1886
Years in Office: 1881–85
Political Party: Republican
Home State: New York
Vice President: None

22 Grover Cleveland
Born: 1837 **Died:** 1908
Years in Office: 1885–89
Political Party: Democratic
Home State: New York
Vice President: Thomas A. Hendricks

23 Benjamin Harrison
Born: 1833 **Died:** 1901
Years in Office: 1889–93
Political Party: Republican
Home State: Indiana
Vice President: Levi P. Morton

24 Grover Cleveland
Born: 1837 **Died:** 1908
Years in Office: 1893–97
Political Party: Democratic
Home State: New York
Vice President: Adlai E. Stevenson

25 William McKinley
Born: 1843 **Died:** 1901
Years in Office: 1897–1901
Political Party: Republican
Home State: Ohio
Vice Presidents: Garret A. Hobart, Theodore Roosevelt

26 THEODORE ROOSEVELT
Born: 1858 **Died:** 1919
Years in Office: 1901–09
Political Party: Republican
Home State: New York
Vice President: Charles W. Fairbanks

27 WILLIAM HOWARD TAFT
Born: 1857 **Died:** 1930
Years in Office: 1909–13
Political Party: Republican
Home State: Ohio
Vice President: James S. Sherman

28 WOODROW WILSON
Born: 1856 **Died:** 1924
Years in Office: 1913–21
Political Party: Democratic
Home State: New Jersey
Vice President: Thomas R. Marshall

29 WARREN G. HARDING
Born: 1865 **Died:** 1923
Years in Office: 1921–23
Political Party: Republican
Home State: Ohio
Vice President: Calvin Coolidge

30 CALVIN COOLIDGE
Born: 1872 **Died:** 1933
Years in Office: 1923–29
Political Party: Republican
Home State: Massachusetts
Vice President: Charles G. Dawes

31 HERBERT HOOVER
Born: 1874 **Died:** 1964
Years in Office: 1929–33
Political Party: Republican
Home State: California
Vice President: Charles Curtis

32 FRANKLIN D. ROOSEVELT
Born: 1882 **Died:** 1945
Years in Office: 1933–45
Political Party: Democratic
Home State: New York
Vice Presidents: John Nance Garner, Henry Wallace, Harry S Truman

33 HARRY S TRUMAN
Born: 1884 **Died:** 1972
Years in Office: 1945–53
Political Party: Democratic
Home State: Missouri
Vice President: Alben W. Barkley

34 DWIGHT D. EISENHOWER
Born: 1890 **Died:** 1969
Years in Office: 1953–61
Political Party: Republican
Home State: Kansas
Vice President: Richard M. Nixon

35 John F. Kennedy
Born: 1917 **Died:** 1963
Years in Office: 1961–63
Political Party: Democratic
Home State: Massachusetts
Vice President: Lyndon B. Johnson

36 Lyndon B. Johnson
Born: 1908 **Died:** 1973
Years in Office: 1963–69
Political Party: Democratic
Home State: Texas
Vice President: Hubert H. Humphrey

37 Richard M. Nixon
Born: 1913 **Died:** 1994
Years in Office: 1969–74
Political Party: Republican
Home State: California
Vice Presidents: Spiro T. Agnew, Gerald R. Ford

38 Gerald R. Ford
Born: 1913
Years in Office: 1974–77
Political Party: Republican
Home State: Michigan
Vice President: Nelson A. Rockefeller

39 Jimmy Carter
Born: 1924
Years in Office: 1977–81
Political Party: Democratic
Home State: Georgia
Vice President: Walter F. Mondale

40 Ronald Reagan
Born: 1911
Years in Office: 1981–89
Political Party: Republican
Home State: California
Vice President: George Bush

41 George Bush
Born: 1924
Years in Office: 1989–93
Political Party: Republican
Home State: Texas
Vice President: J. Danforth Quayle

42 Bill Clinton
Born: 1946
Years in Office: 1993–
Political Party: Democratic
Home State: Arkansas
Vice President: Albert Gore Jr.

742

Facts About the States

STATE	YEAR OF STATEHOOD	1997 POPULATION	REPS. IN CONGRESS	AREA (SQ. MI.)	POPULATION DENSITY (SQ. MI.)	CAPITAL
Alabama	1819	4,319,154	7	51,705	83.5	Montgomery
Alaska	1959	609,311	1	591,004	1.0	Juneau
Arizona	1912	4,554,966	6	114,000	40.0	Phoenix
Arkansas	1836	2,522,819	4	53,187	47.4	Little Rock
California	1850	32,268,301	52	158,706	203.3	Sacramento
Colorado	1876	3,892,644	6	104,091	37.4	Denver
Connecticut	1788	3,269,858	6	5,018	651.6	Hartford
Delaware	1787	731,581	1	2,045	357.7	Dover
District of Columbia	–	528,964	–	69	7,666.1	–
Florida	1845	14,653,945	23	58,664	249.8	Tallahassee
Georgia	1788	7,486,242	11	58,910	127.1	Atlanta
Hawaii	1959	1,186,602	2	6,471	183.4	Honolulu
Idaho	1890	1,210,232	2	83,564	14.5	Boise
Illinois	1818	11,895,849	20	56,345	211.1	Springfield
Indiana	1816	5,864,108	10	36,185	162.1	Indianapolis
Iowa	1846	2,852,423	5	56,275	50.7	Des Moines
Kansas	1861	2,594,840	4	82,277	31.5	Topeka
Kentucky	1792	3,908,124	6	40,410	96.7	Frankfort
Louisiana	1812	4,351,769	7	42,752	101.8	Baton Rouge
Maine	1820	1,242,051	2	33,265	37.3	Augusta
Maryland	1788	5,094,289	8	10,460	487.0	Annapolis
Massachusetts	1788	6,117,520	10	8,284	738.5	Boston
Michigan	1837	9,773,892	16	58,527	167.0	Lansing
Minnesota	1858	4,685,549	8	84,402	55.5	St. Paul
Mississippi	1817	2,730,501	5	47,689	57.3	Jackson
Missouri	1821	5,402,058	9	69,697	77.5	Jefferson City
Montana	1889	878,810	1	147,046	6.0	Helena
Nebraska	1867	1,656,870	3	77,355	21.4	Lincoln
Nevada	1864	1,676,809	2	110,561	15.2	Carson City
New Hampshire	1788	1,172,709	2	9,279	126.4	Concord
New Jersey	1787	8,052,849	13	7,787	1,034.1	Trenton
New Mexico	1912	1,729,751	3	121,593	14.2	Santa Fe
New York	1788	18,137,226	31	49,108	369.3	Albany
North Carolina	1789	7,425,183	12	52,669	141.0	Raleigh
North Dakota	1889	640,883	1	70,702	9.1	Bismarck
Ohio	1803	11,186,331	19	41,330	270.7	Columbus
Oklahoma	1907	3,317,091	6	69,956	47.4	Oklahoma City
Oregon	1859	3,243,487	5	97,073	33.4	Salem
Pennsylvania	1787	12,019,661	21	45,038	266.9	Harrisburg
Rhode Island	1790	987,429	2	1,212	814.7	Providence
South Carolina	1788	3,760,181	6	31,113	120.9	Columbia
South Dakota	1889	737,973	1	77,116	9.6	Pierre
Tennessee	1796	5,368,198	9	42,144	127.4	Nashville
Texas	1845	19,439,337	30	266,807	72.9	Austin
Utah	1896	2,059,148	3	84,899	24.3	Salt Lake City
Vermont	1791	588,978	1	9,614	61.3	Montpelier
Virginia	1788	6,733,996	11	40,767	165.2	Richmond
Washington	1889	5,610,362	9	68,139	82.3	Olympia
West Virginia	1863	1,815,787	3	24,232	74.9	Charleston
Wisconsin	1848	5,169,677	9	56,153	92.1	Madison
Wyoming	1890	479,743	1	97,809	4.9	Cheyenne

743

Important Supreme Court Cases

IMPORTANT SUPREME COURT CASES

MARBURY v. MADISON, 1 CRANCH (5 U.S.) 137 (1803)

Significance: This ruling established the Supreme Court's power of judicial review, giving the Court the power to decide whether laws passed by Congress are constitutional. This decision greatly increased the prestige of the Court and gave the judiciary branch a powerful check against the legislative and executive branches.

Background: William Marbury and several others were commissioned as judges by Federalist president John Adams during his last days in office. This act angered the new Democratic-Republican president, Thomas Jefferson. Jefferson ordered his secretary of state, James Madison, not to deliver the commissions. Marbury took advantage of a section in the Judiciary Act of 1789 that allowed him to take his case directly to the Supreme Court. He sued Madison, demanding the commission and the judgeship.

Decision: This case was decided on February 24, 1803, by a vote of 5 to 0. Chief Justice John Marshall spoke for the Court, which decided against Marbury. The court ruled that although Marbury's commission had been unfairly withheld, he could not lawfully take his case to the Court without first trying it in a lesser court. Marshall said that the section of the Judiciary Act that Marbury had used was actually unconstitutional, and that the Constitution must take priority over laws passed by Congress.

MCCULLOCH v. MARYLAND, 4 WHEAT. (17 U.S.) 316 (1819)

Significance: This ruling established that Congress had the constitutional right to charter a national bank. The case also established the principle of national supremacy, which stated that the Constitution and other laws of the federal government take priority over state laws. In addition, the ruling reinforced the loose construction interpretation of the Constitution favored by many Federalists.

Background: In 1816 the federal government set up the Second Bank of the United States to stabilize the economy following the War of 1812. Many states were opposed to the competition provided by the new national bank. Some of these states passed heavy taxes on the Bank. The national bank refused to pay the taxes. This led the state of Maryland to sue James McCulloch, the cashier of the Baltimore, Maryland, branch of the national bank.

Decision: This case was decided on March 6, 1819, by a vote of 7 to 0. Chief Justice John Marshall spoke for the unanimous Court, which ruled that the national bank was constitutional because it helped the federal government carry out the other powers granted to it by the Constitution. The Court declared that any attempt by the states to interfere with the duties of the federal government could not be permitted.

GIBBONS v. OGDEN, 9 WHEAT. (22 U.S.) 1 (1824)

Significance: This ruling was the first case to deal with the clause of the Constitution that allows Congress to regulate interstate and foreign commerce. This case was important because it reinforced both the authority of the federal government over the states and the division of powers between the federal government and the state governments.

Background: Steamboat operators who wanted to travel on New York waters had to obtain a state license. Thomas Gibbons had a federal license to travel along the coast, but not a state license for New York. He wanted the freedom to compete with state-licensed Aaron Ogden for steam travel between New Jersey and the New York island of Manhattan.

Decision: This case was decided on March 2, 1824, by a vote of 6 to 0. Chief Justice John Marshall spoke for the Court, which ruled in favor of Gibbons. The Court stated that the congressional statute (Gibbons's federal license) took priority over the state statute (Ogden's state-monopoly license). The ruling also defined commerce as more than simply the exchange of goods, broadening it to include the transportation of people and the use of new inventions (such as the steamboat).

WORCESTER v. GEORGIA, 6 PET. (31 U.S.) 515 (1832)

Significance: This ruling made Georgia's removal of the Cherokee illegal. However, Georgia, with President Andrew Jackson's support, defied the Court's decision. By not enforcing the Court's ruling, Jackson violated his constitutional oath as president. As a result, the Cherokee and other American Indian tribes continued to be forced off of lands protected by treaties.

Background: The state of Georgia wanted to remove Cherokee Indians from lands they held by treaty. Samuel Worcester, a missionary who worked with the Cherokee Nation, was arrested for failing to take an oath of allegiance to the state and to obey a Georgia militia order to leave the Cherokee's lands. Worcester sued, charging that Georgia had no legal authority on Cherokee lands.

Decision: This case was decided on March 3, 1832, by a vote of 5 to 1 in favor of Worcester. Chief Justice John Marshall spoke for the Supreme Court, which ruled that the Cherokee were an independent political community. The Court decided that only the federal government, not the state of Georgia, had authority over legal matters involving the Cherokee people.

SCOTT v. SANDFORD, 19 HOW. (60 U.S.) 393 (1857)

Significance: This ruling denied enslaved African Americans U.S. citizenship and the right to sue in federal court. The decision also contradicted the Missouri Compromise, which had prevented slavery in territories north of the 36° 30' line of latitude. The ruling increased the controversy over the expansion of slavery in new states and territories.

Background: John Emerson, an army doctor, took his slave Dred Scott with him to live in Illinois and then Wisconsin Territory, both of which had banned slavery. In 1842 the two moved to Missouri, a slave state. Four years later, Scott sued for his freedom according to a Missouri legal principle of "once free, always free." The principle meant that a slave was entitled to freedom if he or she had once lived in a free state or territory.

Decision: This case was decided March 6–7, 1857, by a vote of 7 to 2. Chief Justice Roger B. Taney spoke for the Court, which ruled that slaves did not have the right to sue in federal courts because they were considered property, not citizens. In addition, the Court ruled that Congress did not have the power to abolish slavery in territories because that power was not strictly defined in the Constitution. Furthermore, the Court overturned the once-free, always-free principle.

PLESSY v. FERGUSON, 163 U.S. 537 (1896)

Significance: This case upheld the constitutionality of racial segregation by ruling that separate facilities for different races were legal as long as those facilities were equal to one another. This case provided a legal justification for racial segregation for more than 50 years until it was overturned by *Brown* v. *Board of Education* in 1954.

Background: An 1890 Louisiana law required that all railway companies in the state use "separate-but-equal" railcars for white and

African American passengers. A group of citizens in New Orleans banded together to challenge the law and chose Homer Plessy to test the law in 1892. Plessy took a seat in a whites-only coach, and when he refused to move, he was arrested. Plessy eventually sought review by the U.S. Supreme Court, claiming that the Louisiana law violated his Fourteenth Amendment right to equal protection.

Decision: This case was decided on May 18, 1896, by a vote of 7 to 1. Justice Henry Billings Brown spoke for the Court, which upheld the constitutionality of the Louisiana law that segregated railcars. Justice John M. Harlan dissented, arguing that the Constitution should not be interpreted in ways that recognize class or racial distinctions.

LOCHNER v. *NEW YORK*, 198 U.S. 45 (1905)

Significance: This decision established the Supreme Court's role in overseeing state regulations. For more than 30 years *Lochner* was often used as a precedent in striking down state laws, minimum-wage laws, child labor laws, and regulations placed on the banking and transportation industries.

Background: In 1895 the state of New York passed a labor law limiting bakers to working no more than 10 hours per day or 60 hours per week. The purpose of the law was to protect the health of bakers, who worked in hot and damp conditions and breathed in large quantities of flour dust. In 1902 Joseph Lochner, the owner of a small bakery in New York, claimed that this law violated his Fourteenth Amendment rights by unfairly depriving him of the liberty to make contracts with employees. This case went to the U.S. Supreme Court.

Decision: This case was decided on April 17, 1905, by a vote of 5 to 4 in favor of Lochner. The Supreme Court judged that the Fourteenth Amendment protected the right to sell and buy labor, and that any state law restricting that right was unconstitutional. The Court rejected the argument that the limited workday and workweek were necessary to protect the health of bakery workers.

MULLER v. *OREGON*, 208 U.S. 412 (1908)

Significance: A landmark for cases involving social reform, this decision established the Court's recognition of social and economic conditions (in this case, women's health) as a factor in making laws.

Background: In 1903 Oregon passed a law limiting workdays to 10 hours for female workers in laundries and factories. In 1905 Curt Muller's Grand Laundry was found guilty of breaking this law. Muller appealed, claiming that the state law violated his freedom of contract (the Supreme Court had upheld a similar claim that year in *Lochner* v. *New York*). When this case came to the Court, the National Consumers' League hired lawyer Louis D. Brandeis to present Oregon's argument. Brandeis argued that the Court had already defended the state's police power to protect its citizens' health, safety, and welfare.

Decision: This case was decided on February 24, 1908, by a vote of 9 to 0 upholding the Oregon law. The Court agreed that women's well-being was in the state's public interest and that the 10-hour law was a valid way to protect their well-being.

BROWN v. *BOARD OF EDUCATION*, 347 U.S. 483 (1954)

Significance: This ruling reversed the Supreme Court's earlier position on segregation set by *Plessy* v. *Ferguson* (1896). The decision also inspired Congress and the federal courts to help carry out further civil rights reforms for African Americans.

Background: When the Browns, an African American family, moved into an all-white neighborhood in Topeka, Kansas, they were told that their daughter would have to attend a distant all-black school that was supposedly "separate but equal." Oliver Brown sued the school board, saying that school segregation violated the equal protection clause of the Fourteenth Amendment.

Decision: This case was decided on May 17, 1954, by a vote of 9 to 0. Chief Justice Earl Warren spoke for the unanimous Court, which ruled that segregation in public education created inequality. The Court held that racial segregation in public schools was by nature unequal, even if the school facilities were equal. The Court noted that such segregation created feelings of inferiority that could not be undone. Therefore, enforced separation of the races in public education is unconstitutional.

GIDEON v. WAINWRIGHT, 372 U.S. 335 (1963)

Significance: This ruling was one of several key Supreme Court decisions establishing free legal help for those who cannot otherwise afford representation in court.

Background: Clarence Earl Gideon was accused of robbery in Florida. Gideon could not afford a lawyer for the trial, and the judge refused to supply him with one for free. Gideon tried to defend himself and was found guilty. He eventually appealed to the U.S. Supreme Court, claiming that the lower court's denial of a court-appointed lawyer violated his Sixth and Fourteenth Amendment rights.

Decision: This case was decided on March 18, 1963, by a vote of 9 to 0 in favor of Gideon. The Court agreed that the Sixth Amendment (which protects a citizen's right to have a lawyer for his or her defense) applied to the states because it fell under the due process clause of the Fourteenth Amendment. Thus, the states are required to provide legal aid to those defendants in criminal cases who cannot afford to pay for legal aid.

MIRANDA v. ARIZONA, 384 U.S. 436 (1966)

Significance: This decision ruled that an accused person's Fifth Amendment rights begin at the time of arrest. The ruling caused controversy because it made questioning suspects and collecting evidence more difficult for law enforcement officers.

Background: In 1963 Ernesto Miranda was arrested in Arizona for a kidnapping. Miranda signed a confession and was later found guilty of the crime. The arresting police officers, however, admitted that they had not told Miranda of his right to talk with an attorney before his confession. Miranda appealed his conviction on the grounds that by not informing him of his legal rights the police had violated his Fifth Amendment right against self-incrimination.

Decision: This case was decided on June 13, 1966, by a vote of 5 to 4. Chief Justice Earl Warren spoke for the Court, which ruled in Miranda's favor. The Court decided that an accused person must be given four warnings after being taken into police custody: (1) the suspect has the right to remain silent, (2) anything the suspect says can and will be used against him or her, (3) the suspect has the right to consult with an attorney and to have an attorney present during questioning, and (4) if the suspect cannot afford a lawyer, one will be provided before questioning begins.

REED v. REED, 404 U.S. 71 (1971)

Significance: This ruling was the first in a century of Fourteenth Amendment decisions to say that gender discrimination violated the equal protection clause. This case was later used to strike down several other statutes that violated women's rights.

Background: Cecil and Sally Reed were separated. When their son died without a will, the law gave preference to Cecil to be appointed the administrator of the son's estate. Sally sued Cecil for the right to administer the estate, challenging the gender preference in the law.

Decision: This case was decided on November 22, 1971, by a vote of 7 to 0. Chief Justice Warren Burger spoke for the unanimous Supreme Court. Although the Court had upheld laws based on gender preference in the past, in this case it reversed its position. The Court declared that gender discrimination violated the equal protection clause of the Constitution and therefore could not be the basis for a law.

Gazetteer

Abilene Cattle town in east-central Kansas. (39°N 97°W) **168**

Africa Second-largest continent. Lies in both the Northern and the Southern Hemispheres. **xxx**

Aisne River River in northern France. **340**

Akron City in northeast Ohio. (41°N 81°W) **448**

Alabama (AL) State in the southern United States. Admitted as a state in 1819. Capital: Montgomery. (33°N 87°W) **xx**

Alamogordo City in southern New Mexico. (33°N 106°W) **496**

Alaska (AK) U.S. state in northwestern North America. Admitted as a state in 1959. Capital: Juneau. (64°N 150°W) **xx**

Albany Capital of New York State. (42°N 74°W) **16**

Alcatraz Island Island in San Francisco Bay once used as a federal prison. **617**

Aleutian Islands Chain of islands off the coast of Alaska. (52°N 176°W) **493**

Alsace-Lorraine Region between Belgium, France, Germany, and Switzerland. Part of the German Empire from 1871 to 1918; returned to France by the Treaty of Versailles in 1919. Held by Germany during World War II from 1940 to 1944. **347**

Anniston City in northeastern Alabama. (34°N 86°W) **597**

Antietam Creek Creek in northern Maryland. **109**

Antwerp City in northern Belgium. (51°N 5°E) **487**

Anzio Town in central Italy. (41°N 12°E) **487**

Appalachian Mountains Mountain system in eastern North America that extends from Canada to central Alabama. **xxii**

Appomattox Courthouse Town in central Virginia. (37°N 79°W) **109**

Arctic Circle Line of latitude that encircles the northern frigid zone of Earth. **7**

Ardennes Forest in southern Belgium and northwestern France. **489**

Argentina Republic located in the south-central and southern part of South America. Capital: Buenos Aires. (34°S 64°W) **xxvii**

Argonne Forest Wooded plateau in northeastern France. **342**

Arizona (AZ) State in the southwestern United States. Became a territory in 1863. Admitted as a state in 1912. Capital: Phoenix. (34°N 113°W) **xx**

Arkansas (AR) State in the south-central United States. Admitted as a state in 1836. Capital: Little Rock. (35°N 93°W) **xx**

Asia Largest continent. Occupies the same land mass as Europe. **xxix**

Atlanta Capital of Georgia. (33°N 84°W) **109**

Atlantic Ocean Vast body of water separating North and South America from Europe and Africa. **xxiv**

Attu Island located off the coast of southwestern Alaska. (53°N 173°E) **491**

Australia Island-continent and country located between the Indian and Pacific Oceans. Capital: Canberra. (25°S 135°E) **xxxi**

Austria Republic in central Europe. Capital: Vienna. (48°N 16°E) **xxviii**

Austria-Hungary Monarchy in central Europe from 1867 to 1918. Consisted of Austria, Bohemia, Hungary, and parts of Italy, Poland, Romania, and Yugoslavia. **332**

Bahamas Country in the Atlantic Ocean consisting of a chain of islands. Capital: Nassau. (26°N 76°W) **xxvi**

Bahrain Nation made up of islands located in the Persian Gulf off the coast of the Arabian Peninsula. Capital: Manama. (26°N 50°E) **xxix**

Balkans Region that occupies the Balkan Peninsula and includes Albania, Bulgaria, Greece, Romania, Yugoslavia, and northwestern Turkey. **332**

Baltic Sea Arm of the Atlantic Ocean in northern Europe. **xxviii**

Baltimore Maryland city northeast of Washington, D.C., on the Chesapeake Bay. (39°N 76°W) **xx**

Bataan Peninsula Peninsula in the western Philippines. (14°N 120°E) **491**

Baton Rouge Capital of Louisiana. (30°N 91°W) **109**

Bay of Pigs Bay on the western coast of Cuba. Also called Bahía de Cochinos. **576**

Beirut Capital of Lebanon. (34°N 35°E) **xxix**

Belgium Kingdom in northwestern Europe. Capital: Brussels. (51°N 13°E) **xxviii**

Belgrade Capital of Yugoslavia and of Serbia. (45°N 20°W) **xxviii**

Belleau Wood Forest in northern France. **341**

Beringia Land bridge that once connected present-day Alaska with Siberia. **6**

Berkeley City on California's San Francisco Bay. (38°N 122°W) **xx**

Berlin Capital of Germany. Divided into East Berlin and West Berlin in 1945. Reunited in 1990. (52°N 13°E) **477**

Birmingham City in north-central Alabama. (33°N 86°W) **xx**

Black Hills Mountains in western South Dakota and northeastern Wyoming. **153**

Black Sea Sea between Europe and Asia. **xxviii**

Bonin Islands Group of islands in the western Pacific Ocean. (27°N 142°E) **492**

Bosnia and Herzegovina Country annexed to Austria-Hungary in 1908; after World War I became part of what would become Yugoslavia; declared independence in 1992. Capital: Sarajevo. (44°N 17°E) **xxviii**

Bosque Redondo Location of a former Navajo reservation in New Mexico. **155**

Boston Capital of Massachusetts. (42°N 71°W) **16**

Boston Harbor Massachusetts port that was the scene of the Boston Tea Party in 1773. **22**

Brandywine Creek Creek in Pennsylvania and Delaware that was the site of the Revolutionary War's Battle of Brandywine Creek in 1777. **24**

Brazil Republic in eastern South America. Largest country on the continent. Ruled by Portugal from 1500 to 1822. Capital: Brasília. (9°S 53°W) **xxix**

Breed's Hill Hill in Boston, Massachusetts, that was one site of the Revolutionary War's Battle of Bunker Hill in 1775. **23**

Brooklyn Borough that is part of New York City. **218**

Buffalo City in western New York. (43°N 79°W) **xx**

Bulgaria Republic in southeastern Europe. Capital: Sofia. (42°N 23°E) **xxviii**

Bull Run Creek in northeastern Virginia where the Confederates won two major battles during the Civil War. **109**

Bunker Hill Hill in Boston, Massachusetts, that was one site of the Revolutionary War's Battle of Bunker Hill in 1775. **23**

Burma Country in southeast Asia. Now called Myanmar. Capital: Rangoon. (16°N 96°E) **xxix**

California (CA) State in the western United States. Admitted as a state in 1850. Capital: Sacramento. (38°N 121°W) **xx**

Cambodia Republic in southeastern Asia. Capital: Phnom Penh. (11°N 105°E) **xxix**

Canada Country in northern North America. Capital: Ottawa. (50°N 100°W) **xxvi**

Cape of Good Hope Southern tip of Africa. **10**

Caribbean Sea Arm of the Atlantic Ocean bounded by the West Indies, Central America, and South America. **xxvi**

Central America Region of land connecting North and South America. **xxvi**

Chagres River River in Panama that is dammed to form Gatún Lake. **303**

Chancellorsville Town in northeastern Virginia where Confederate forces won a major victory during the Civil War. Now called Chancellor. **109**

Charleston Port city in southeastern South Carolina. (33°N 80°W) **16**

Château-Thierry Town in northern France. (49°N 3°E) **342**

Chesapeake Bay Inlet of the Atlantic Ocean in Virginia and Maryland. **xxii**

Chicago City in northeastern Illinois on Lake Michigan. (41°N 87°W) **xx**

Chile Country in southwestern South America. Capital: Santiago. (35°S 72°W) **xxvii**

China Vast country in Asia. Capital: Beijing. (36°N 93°E) **xxix**

Ciudad Juárez City in the Chihuahua state of northern Mexico. (31°N 106°W) **308**

Colombia Republic in northwestern South America. Capital: Bogotá. (3°N 72°W) **xxvii**

Colón City in north-central Panama. (9°N 80°W) **302**

Colorado (CO) State in the western-central United States. Admitted as a state in 1876. Capital: Denver. (39°N 107°W) **xx**

Colorado River River located in the southwestern United States. **xxii**

Columbia Capital of South Carolina. (34°N 81°W) **123**

Columbia River River that flows from southeastern British Columbia, Canada, through Washington and Oregon, where it empties into the Pacific Ocean. **89**

Columbus Town in southwestern New Mexico. (32°N 107°W) **305**

Compiègne Town in northern France. (49°N 3°E) **343**

Concord Town in northeastern Massachusetts. (42°N 71°W) **22**

Coney Island Section of southern Brooklyn in New York City that has been home to several amusement parks. **223**

Confederacy (Confederate States of America) Nation made up of 11 southern states during their secession from the United States from 1860 to 1865. **107**

Connecticut (CT) State in the northeastern United States. One of the original thirteen colonies. Capital: Hartford. (41°N 73°W) **xx**

Coral Sea Part of the southwestern Pacific Ocean. **xxxi**

Corregidor Island located in Manila Bay off of the Bataan Peninsula. (14°N 120°E) **491**

Croatia Country in southeastern Europe; was part of the republic of Yugoslavia until 1991. Capital: Zagreb. (45°N 15°E) **xxviii**

Crystal City City in southern Texas. (28°N 100°W) **608**

Cuba Nation south of Florida in the Caribbean Sea made up of the large island of Cuba and other surrounding small islands. Capital: Havana. (22°N 79°W) **xxvi**

Cumberland Road First U.S. federal road; began in Cumberland, Maryland, and ended in St. Louis, Missouri. **91**

Czechoslovakia Former republic in central Europe made up of present-day Czech Republic and Slovakia. **xxviii**

Czech Republic Country in central Europe. Capital: Prague. (50°N 14°E) **xxviii**

Dakota Territory Former territory in the northwestern United States made up of much of the region on both sides of the Missouri River and west of the Red River of the North. Admitted to the Union as North Dakota and South Dakota in 1889. **153**

Dallas City in northeastern Texas. (32°N 96°W) **xx**

Danzig Seaport on the Gulf of Gdańsk. Polish name: Gdańsk. (54°N 18°E) **477**

Dayton City in southwestern Ohio. (40°N 84°W) **xx**

Delaware (DE) State in the eastern United States. One of the original thirteen colonies. Capital: Dover. (38°N 75°W) **xx**

Delaware River River that forms the boundary between Pennsylvania and New Jersey. **23**

Denmark Kingdom in northwestern Europe. Capital: Copenhagen. (56°N 10°E) **xxviii**

Denver Capital of Colorado. (39°N 105°W) **xx**

Detroit City in southeastern Michigan. (42°N 83°W) **xx**

Dien Bien Phu Village in northwestern Vietnam. (21°N 102°E) **624**

Dodge City Town in southern Kansas. (38°N 100°W) **168**

Dominican Republic Country in the Caribbean Sea. Located on the eastern part of the island of Hispaniola. Capital: Santo Domingo. (19°N 70°W) **xxvi**

Dresden City in east-central Germany that was destroyed by Allied bombing during World War II. (51°N 13°E) **495**

Dunkirk Seaport in northern France. (51°N 2°E) **477**

East Germany *See* Germany.

East Prussia Former province of Prussia located in central Europe. Divided between Poland and the Soviet Union in 1945. **347**

Egypt Country in northeastern Africa on the Mediterranean Sea. Capital: Cairo. (27°N 27°E) **xxx**

Elbe River River that flows through Germany and the Czech Republic. **513**

El Caney Community in eastern Cuba. **297**

Ellis Island Island in New York Bay where the Statue of Liberty is located. (40°N 74°W) **211**

El Paso City in western Texas. (32°N 106°W) **261**

El Salvador Country in Central America. Capital: San Salvador. (14°N 89°W) **xxvi**

England Region of the United Kingdom that makes up of most of the southern part of the island of Great Britain. Capital: London. (51°N 1°W) **xxviii**

English Channel Strait between southern England and northern France that connects the Atlantic Ocean with the North Sea. **xxviii**

Erie Canal Canal that extends from Buffalo, New York, to Albany, New York. **91**

Estonia Country in northeastern Europe. Annexed to the Soviet Union in 1940. Became an independent republic in 1991. Capital: Tallinn. (55°N 23°E) **xxviii**

Ethiopia Country in eastern Africa. Capital: Addis Ababa. (7°N 38°E) **xxx**

Europe Continent occupying the same land mass as Asia. **xxviii**

Finland Country in northeastern Europe. Capital: Helsinki. (62°N 26°E) **xxviii**

Flint City in southeast-central Michigan. (43°N 83°W) **449**

Florida (FL) State in the southeastern United States. Admitted as a state in 1845. Capital: Tallahassee. (30°N 84°W) **xx**

Fort McHenry U.S. fort that guarded Baltimore, Maryland, during the War of 1812. **91**

Fort Mims Site in Alabama where Creek Indians massacred settlers in 1813. **91**

Fort Sumter Fort in Charleston Harbor, South Carolina. Attack by Confederate forces there started the Civil War. **107**

Fort Ticonderoga Strategic fort in northern New York that Patriots secured from the British in 1775 during the Revolutionary War. **23**

Fort Worth City in northern Texas. (33°N 97°W) **172**

France Country in Western Europe. Capital: Paris. (46°N 0°E) **xxviii**

French Indochina Former colony in southeastern Asia that France held from 1887 to 1940 and from 1946 to 1955. **493**

Gatún Lake Lake in Panama that forms part of the system of the Panama Canal. **303**

Geneva City in southwestern Switzerland. (46°N 6°E) **625**

Genoa Port city in northwestern Italy. (44°N 10°E) **11**

Georgia (GA) State in the southeastern United States. One of the original thirteen colonies. Capital: Atlanta. (32°N 84°W) **xx**

Germany Country in central Europe. Divided into German Democratic Republic (East Germany) and Federal Republic of Germany (West Germany) after World War II. Reunified in 1990. Capital: Berlin. (51°N 8°E) **xxviii**

Gettysburg Town in southern Pennsylvania. (40°N 77°W) **109**

Gilbert Islands Group of islands in the western Pacific Ocean. (0°S 174°E) **493**

Gleiwitz City in southwestern Poland. Polish name: Gliwice. (50°N 18°E) **475**

Gonzales Town in south-central Texas. (30°N 97°W) **101**

Grand Canyon Gorge in the Colorado River, located in northwestern Arizona, that is now a national park. **270**

Great Basin Elevated region made up of parts of California, Idaho, Nevada, Oregon, Utah, and Wyoming that was home to many American Indian groups. **7**

Great Britain Kingdom in Western Europe. Consists of England, Scotland, and Wales. Capital: London. (54°N 4°W) **xxviii**

Great Lakes Chain of lakes located in central North America and extending across the U.S.-Canada border. Includes Lake Erie, Lake Huron, Lake Michigan, Lake Ontario, and Lake Superior. **xxii**

Great Plains Region of central North America that lies between the Mississippi River and the Rocky Mountains and stretches north into Canada and south into Texas. **7**

Great Salt Lake Saltwater lake in northern Utah. **103**

Greece Southeastern European country on the Balkan Peninsula that includes numerous surrounding islands. Capital: Athens. (39°N 21°E) **xxviii**

Greenland Island located in northeastern North America. Capital: Godthåb. (71°N 40°W) **xxvi**

Greensboro City in north-central North Carolina. (36°N 80°W) **597**

Grenada Country in the Caribbean Sea made up of the island of Grenada and the southern Grenadines. Capital: St. George's. (12°N 61°W) **xxvi**

Guadalcanal One of the Solomon Islands in the western Pacific Ocean. (9°S 160°E) **493**

Guam Pacific island that became a U.S. territory after the Spanish-American War. Capital: Agana. (14°N 143°E) **xxxi**

Guatemala Republic in Central America. Capital: Guatemala City. (15°N 91°W) **xxvi**

Hague, The City in the southwestern Netherlands that serves as the seat of the Dutch government. (52°N 4°E) **xxviii**

Haiti Country in the Caribbean Sea located on the western part of the island of Hispaniola. Capital: Port-au-Prince. (19°N 72°W) **xxix**

Hamburg City in northern Germany. (53°N 10°E) **xxviii**

Hanoi Capital of Vietnam. (21°N 106°E) **624**

Harlem Area of northern Manhattan in New York City. **401**

Harpers Ferry Town in present-day northeastern West Virginia where John Brown attempted to start a slave revolt in 1859. (39°N 78°W) **107**

Havana Capital and seaport of Cuba located on the northwest coast. (23°N 82°W) **297**

Hawaii (HI) State in the central Pacific Ocean that is made up of the Hawaiian Islands. Organized as a U.S. territory in 1900. Admitted as a state in 1959. Capital: Honolulu. (20°N 157°W) **xx**

Hillsboro City in southern Ohio. (39°N 83°W) **255**

Hiroshima Japanese city bombed by a U.S. atomic weapon in August 1945. (34°N 132°E) **493**

Ho Chi Minh Trail Former system of trails running from North Vietnam to South Vietnam. **628**

Hollywood District in Los Angeles, California, known for its association with the motion picture industry. **396**

Homestead Town in southwestern Pennsylvania. (40°N 80°W) **198**

Honduras Republic in Central America. Capital: Tegucigalpa. (15°N 86°W) **xxvi**

Hong Kong British colony from 1842 to 1997 located off the coast of China. Returned to China in 1997. Capital: Victoria. (21°N 115°E) **xxix**

Honolulu Capital of Hawaii. **292**

Houston City located in southeastern Texas. (30°N 95°W) **xx**

Hudson Bay Inland sea in east-central Canada. **xxvi**

Hudson River River flowing from northeastern to southern New York. **xxii**

Hungary Republic in central Europe. Capital: Budapest. (47°N 19°E) **xxviii**

Iceland Island republic located between the Arctic and North Atlantic Oceans. Capital: Reykjavík. (65°N 18°W) **xxviii**

Idaho (ID) State in the northwestern United States. Admitted as a state in 1890. Capital: Boise. (44°N 15°W) **xx**

Illinois (IL) State in the north-central United States. Admitted as a state in 1818. Capital: Springfield. (40°N 90°W) **xx**

Independence City in western Missouri that was the starting point of the Santa Fe and Oregon Trails. (39°N 94°W) **103**

India Large republic in southern Asia. Capital: New Delhi. (28°N 77°E) **xxix**

Indiana (IN) State in the north-central United States. Admitted as a state in 1816. Capital: Indianapolis. (40°N 86°W) **xx**

Indiana Territory Former territory created from the division of the Northwest Territory in 1800 that included present-day Illinois, Indiana, Wisconsin, much of Michigan, and part of Minnesota. **89**

Indian Ocean Vast body of water east of Africa, south of Asia, west of Australia, and north of Antarctica. **xxiv**

Indian Territory Former territory that included most of present-day Oklahoma. **103**

Indonesia Country in southeastern Asia. Capital: Jakarta. (7°S 106°E) **xxix**

Iowa (IA) State in the north-central United States. Admitted as a state in 1846. Capital: Des Moines. (42°N 94°W) **xx**

Iran Country in southwestern Asia. Capital: Tehran. (31°N 53°E) **xxix**

Iraq Country in southwestern Asia. Capital: Baghdad. (32°N 43°E) **xxix**

Ireland Island in the British Isles. Divided into Northern Ireland (Capital: Belfast), which is part of the United Kingdom, and the independent republic of Ireland (Capital: Dublin). (54°N 6°W and 54°N 8°W) **xxviii**

Israel Country in southwestern Asia on the eastern Mediterranean coast. Established by Jews after the United Nations divided Palestine in 1948. Capital: Jerusalem. (32°N 34°E) **511**

Isthmus of Panama Landmass that links North America to South America and separates the Atlantic and the Pacific Oceans. Forms the Republic of Panama. **305**

Italy Country in southern Europe. Capital: Rome. (44°N 11°E) **xxviii**

Jackson Capital of Mississippi. (32°N 90°W) **597**

Jamaica Island-nation in the Caribbean Sea. Capital: Kingston. (18°N 78°W) **xxvi**

Jamestown First permanent English colony in America. Established in eastern Virginia in 1607. **16**

Japan Country made up of a chain of islands in the western Pacific Ocean. Capital: Tokyo. (37°N 134°E) **xxix**

Kansas (KS) State in the central United States. Admitted as a state in 1861. Capital: Topeka. (38°N 99°W) **xx**

Kentucky (KY) State in the east-central United States. Admitted as a state in 1792. Capital: Frankfort. (37°N 87°W) **xx**

Kiel Seaport city in northern Germany. (54°N 10°E) **342**

Kiska Island located off the coast of southwestern Alaska. (52°N 177°E) **490**

Kitty Hawk Town in eastern North Carolina. (36°N 76°N) **188**

Korea Peninsula and former country of eastern Asia located between the Yellow Sea and the Sea of Japan. Officially divided into two independent nations, North Korea (40°N 127°E) and South Korea (36°N 128°E), in 1948. **xxix**

Kosovo Province in southwestern Serbia, in southern Yugoslavia. (42°N 21°E) **717**

Kuwait Country on the northeast Arabian Peninsula at the northern end of the Persian Gulf. Capital: Kuwait City. (29°N 48°E) **xxix**

Labrador Mainland section of the Newfoundland province in eastern Canada. **8**

Lake Erie One of the Great Lakes, located in the United States and Canada. **89**

Laos Country in southeastern Asia. Capital: Vientiane. (18°N 102°E) **xxix**

Latin America Spanish-speaking countries of North and South America that once belonged to the Spanish empire and Portugal. **xxiv**

Latvia Country in northern Europe on the Baltic Sea. Former republic of the Soviet Union. Capital: Riga. (57°N 24°E) **xxviii**

Lawrence (KS) City in eastern Kansas. (39°N 95°W) **107**

Lawrence (MA) City in northeastern Massachusetts. (42°N 71°W) **251**

Lebanon Country at the eastern end of the Mediterranean Sea. Capital: Beirut. (34°N 36°E) **xxix**

Leipzig City in eastern-central Germany. (51°N 12°E) **495**

Lexington Town in northeastern Massachusetts. (42°N 71°W) **22**

Leyte Gulf Inlet of the Pacific Ocean in the eastern Philippines. **493**

Libya Republic in northern Africa on the Mediterranean Sea. Capital: Tripoli. (27°N 17°E) **xxx**

Lithuania Country in northern Europe on the Baltic Sea. Declared independence from the Soviet Union in 1990. Capital: Vilnius. (59°N 25°E) **xxviii**

Little Bighorn River River in southern Montana. **153**

Little Rock Capital of Arkansas. (34°N 92°W) **xx**

London Capital of the United Kingdom. Located in England. (51°N 0°W) **xxviii**

Long Island Island in southeastern New York that is located between the Atlantic Ocean and Long Island Sound. (41°N 73°W) **398**

Los Angeles Large city in southwestern California. (34°N 118°W) **xx**

Louisiana (LA) State in the southeastern United States carved out of the Louisiana Territory. Admitted as a state in 1812. Capital: Baton Rouge. (31°N 93°W) **xx**

Louisiana Territory Huge region of land stretching from the Mississippi River to the Rocky Mountains and from the Gulf of Mexico to present-day Canada. Acquired by the U.S. government from France through the Louisiana Purchase of 1803. **89**

Low Countries Name given to the region made up of the countries of the Netherlands, Belgium, and Luxembourg. **498**

Lowell Massachusetts city on the Merrimack River northwest of Boston. (42°N 71°W) **94**

Macedonia Republic in southeastern Europe. Declared independence from Yugoslavia in September 1991. Capital: Skopje. (41°N 23°E) **xxviii**

Maine (ME) State in the northeastern United States. Admitted as a state in 1820. Capital: Augusta. (45°N 70°W) **xx**

Manchuria Region in northeastern China. (47°N 125°E) **493**

Manhattan Island Island at north end of New York Bay; one of the five boroughs that make up New York City. **401**

Manila Capital of the Philippines. (15°N 121°E) **297**

Manila Bay Large inlet of the South China Sea located in western Luzon, an island in the Philippines. **297**

Marianas Islands in the western Pacific Ocean. (16°N 145°E) **493**

Marne River River in northeastern France. **342**

Marshall Islands Group of islands in the western Pacific Ocean. Capital: Majuro. (9°S 152°E) **493**

Maryland (MD) State in the east-central United States. One of the original thirteen colonies. Capital: Annapolis. (39°N 76°W) **xx**

Massachusetts (MA) State in the northeastern United States. One of the original thirteen colonies. Capital: Boston. (42°N 72°W) **xx**

Mediterranean Sea Large sea bordered by southern Europe, southwestern Asia, and northern Africa. **xxviii**

Memphis City in southwestern Tennessee. (35°N 90°W) **126**

Menlo Park Community in central New Jersey. (40°N 74°W) **185**

Mesoamerica Extremely fertile region made up of present-day Mexico and parts of Central America that was the home to the first major Native American cultures. Also known as Middle America. **7**

Meuse River River in western Europe that flows from northeastern France to the North Sea. **342**

Mexico Country in southern North America. Capital: Mexico City. (23°N 104°W) **xxvi**

Mexico City Capital of Mexico. (19°N 99°W) **xxvi**

Miami City in southeastern Florida. (26°N 80°W) **xx**

Michigan (MI) State in the north-central United States. Admitted as a state in 1837. Capital: Lansing. (46°N 87°W) **xx**

Middle East Vast region made up of countries in southwestern Asia and northeastern Africa. **657**

Midway Islands Two islands northwest of Hawaii that have been under U.S. administration since 1867. (28°N 177°W) **493**

Milwaukee City in southeastern Wisconsin. (43°N 88°W) **276**

Minnesota (MN) State in the north-central United States. Admitted as a state in 1858. Capital: St. Paul. (46°N 90°W) **xx**

Mississippi (MS) State in the southeastern United States. Admitted as a state in 1817. Capital: Jackson. (32°N 89°W) **xx**

Mississippi River River that flows from Minnesota to the Gulf of Mexico. **xxii**

Mississippi River valley Vast area of land drained by the Mississippi River. **6**

Missouri (MO) State in the central United States. Admitted as a state in 1821. Capital: Jefferson City. (38°N 93°W) **xx**

Missouri River River located in the central and northwest-central United States. **xxii**

Missouri River valley Vast area of land drained by the Missouri River. **6**

Monongahela River River in northern West Virginia and southwestern Pennsylvania that merges with the Allegheny River at Pittsburgh to form the Ohio River. **198**

Montana (MT) State in the northwestern United States. Admitted as a state in 1889. Capital: Helena. (47°N 112°W) **xx**

Monterey City in western California that was the province's capital when the region was held by Mexico. (36°N 122°W) **103**

Montgomery Capital of Alabama. (32°N 86°W) **xx**

Montreal City in southeastern Canada that was founded by the French in 1642. (46°N 74°W) **23**

Moscow Capital of Russia. (61°N 60°E) **xxviii**

Munich City in southern Germany. (48°N 11°E) **xxviii**

Nagasaki Second Japanese city bombed by a U.S. atomic weapon in August 1945. (32°N 130°E) **493**

Nashville Capital of Tennessee. (36°N 87°W) **126**

Natchez City in southwestern Mississippi. (31°N 91°W) **110**

Nebraska (NE) State in the central United States. Admitted as a state in 1867. Capital: Lincoln. (41°N 101°W) **xx**

Netherlands Kingdom located in northwestern Europe. Capital: Amsterdam. (52°N 5°E) **xxviii**

Nevada (NV) State in the western United States. Admitted as a state in 1864. Capital: Carson City. (39°N 117°W) **xx**

New Amsterdam Dutch settlement on Manhattan Island founded c. 1625. **18**

New England Northeastern section of the United States made up of Connecticut, Maine, Massachusetts, New Hampshire, Rhode Island, and Vermont. **16**

Newfoundland Island off the eastern coast of Canada. (48°N 56°W) **xxvi**

New France Former French territory in North America that included eastern Canada and the Mississippi Valley. France lost all North American territory to Britain in 1763. **16**

New Guinea Island in the western Pacific Ocean. Western half is part of Indonesia, and eastern half is part of Papua New Guinea. (5°S 140°E) **xxxi**

New Hampshire (NH) State in the northeastern United States. One of the original thirteen colonies. Capital: Concord. (44°N 71°W) **xx**

New Jersey (NJ) State in the eastern United States. One of the original thirteen colonies. Capital: Trenton. (40°N 75°W) **xx**

New Mexico (NM) State in the southwestern United States. Organized as a U.S. territory that included Arizona and part of Colorado in 1850. Capital: Santa Fe. (34°N 107°W) **xx**

New Netherland Former Dutch colony in North America from c. 1613 to 1664 that included parts of present-day New Jersey and New York. **13**

New Orleans Port city in southeastern Louisiana, located between the Mississippi River and Lake Pontchartrain. (30°N 90°W) **89**

New Sweden Swedish colony that was located in eastern North America on the Delaware River. **13**

New York (NY) State in the northeastern United States. One of the original thirteen colonies. Capital: Albany. (42°N 78°W) **xx**

New York Bay Atlantic Ocean inlet located at the mouth of the Hudson River in southeastern New York State. **24**

New York City Largest city in the United States. First capital of the United States. (41°N 74°W) **xx**

Niagara Falls City in New York State on the Niagara River on the border of the United States and Canada. (43°N 79°W) **259**

Nicaragua Central American country on the Caribbean Sea and the Pacific Ocean. Capital: Managua. (12°N 86°W) **xxviii**

Nicodemus Town in Kansas settled by African Americans in the late 1800s. **171**

Nile River River that flows through east and northeast Africa. **xxx**

Norfolk City in southeast Virginia. (38°N 76°W) **221**

Normandy Historic region in northern France that was the site of the D-Day invasion during World War II. (49°N 0°W) **487**

North America Continent in the northern Western Hemisphere. **xxvi**

North Carolina (NC) State in the southeastern United States. One of the original thirteen colonies. Capital: Raleigh. (35°N 81°W) **xx**

North Dakota (ND) State in the north-central United States. Admitted as a state in 1889. Capital: Bismarck. (47°N 102°W) **xx**

North Sea Arm of the Atlantic Ocean that separates the British Isles from the European continent. **xxviii**

Northwest Territory Region of the north-central United States that extended from the Ohio and Missouri Rivers to the Great Lakes. Awarded to the United States by the Treaty of Paris of 1783 and organized as a U.S. territory in 1787. Later divided into the present-day states of Illinois, Indiana, Michigan, Ohio, Wisconsin, and part of Minnesota. **31**

Norway Kingdom in northwestern Europe. Capital: Oslo. (62°N 10°E) **xxviii**

Nuremberg City in southern Germany where the Nuremberg Trials were held from 1945 to 1946. (49°N 11°E) **511**

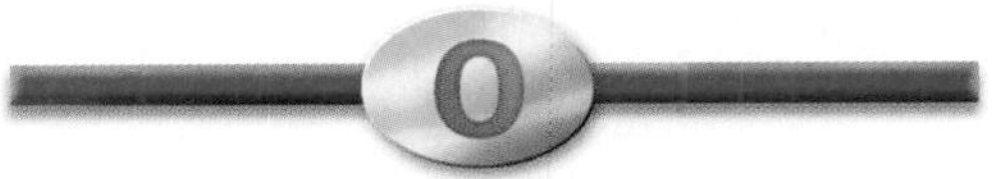

Oahu Third-largest Hawaiian island. (21°N 158°W) **xx**

Ohio (OH) State in the north-central United States. Admitted as a state in 1803. Capital: Columbus. (40°N 83°W) **xx**

Ohio River valley Region of land drained by the Ohio River. **6**

Okinawa Japanese island captured by U.S. forces after tremendous resistance during World War II. (26°N 128°E) **493**

Oklahoma (OK) State in the southwest-central United States. Organized as a territory in 1890. Admitted as a state in 1907. Capital: Oklahoma City. (36°N 98°W) **xx**

Oklahoma City Capital of Oklahoma. (36°N 98°W) **xx**

Omaha City in eastern Nebraska. (41°N 96°W) **168**

Oregon (OR) State in the northwestern United States. Admitted as a state in 1859. Capital: Salem. (43°N 122°W) **xx**

Oregon Country Region in western North America that extended from the Pacific coast to the Rocky Mountains and from the northern border of California to Alaska. So called from 1818 until it became Oregon Territory in 1848. **103**

Ottoman Empire Former empire in Europe, Asia, and Africa whose remaining territory was proclaimed Republic of Turkey in 1923. Capital: Constantinople. (42°N 28°E) **332**

Pacific Ocean Body of water extending from the Arctic Circle to Antarctica and from western North America and South America to Australia, the Malay Archipelago, and eastern Asia. **xxiv**

Palestine Historic region in southwestern Asia that is now present-day Israel and part of Jordan. **511**
Panama Country in southern Central America that occupies the Isthmus of Panama. Location of the Panama Canal. Capital: Panama City. (8°N 81°W) **xxvi**
Paris Capital of France. (49°N 2°E) **xxviii**
Paterson City in northern New Jersey. (41°N 74°W) **251**
Pearl Harbor Harbor on the Hawaiian island of Oahu where the Japanese launched a surprise attack against the U.S. Pacific Fleet in 1941. (21°N 158°W) **493**
Pennsylvania (PA) State in the eastern United States. One of the original thirteen colonies. Capital: Harrisburg. (41°N 78°W) **xx**
Persian Gulf Arm of the Arabian Sea between the Arabian Peninsula and southwestern Iran in southwestern Asia. **xxix**
Philadelphia City in southeastern Pennsylvania. Capital of the United States from 1790 to 1800. (40°N 75°W) **xx**
Philippines Archipelago of about 7,100 islands lying approximately 500 miles off the southeast coast of Asia. Gained full independence from the United States in 1946. Capital: Manila. (14°N 125°E) **xxix**
Pikes Peak Mountain in east-central Colorado that was part of an important mining region in the mid- to late 1800s. **153**
Pittsburgh City in southwestern Pennsylvania. (40°N 80°W) **xx**
Plymouth Town in Massachusetts that is the site where the Pilgrims first landed in North America in 1620. (42°N 70°W) **16**
Poland Country in central Europe bordering on the Baltic Sea. Capital: Warsaw. (52°N 17°E) **xxviii**
Portugal Country in southwestern Europe on the western Iberian Peninsula. Includes the island groups of Madeira and the Azores in the Atlantic Ocean. Capital: Lisbon. (38°N 8°W) **xxviii**
Princeton Town in west-central New Jersey. (40°N 75°W) **23**
Promontory Location in northwestern Utah where the Central and Union Pacific Railroads were joined in 1869. **168**
Providence Settlement established by Roger Williams in 1636 that later became Rhode Island. Present-day capital of Rhode Island. (42°N 71°W) **16**
Puerto Rico Island east of Cuba and southeast of Florida that is a U.S. commonwealth. Capital: San Juan. (18°N 67°W) **xxvi**
Puget Sound Arm of the Pacific Ocean located in western Washington State. **301**
Pullman Town established near Chicago, Illinois, in 1880 by the Pullman Palace Car Company for its workers. **198**
P'yŏngyang Capital of North Korea. (39°N 126°E) **524**

Quebec City in eastern Canada on the St. Lawrence River. (47°N 71°W) **xxvi**

Red Sea Inland sea between the Arabian Peninsula and northeastern Africa. **xxix**
Rhine River River in western Europe that flows from Switzerland to the North Sea. **342**
Rhineland Region west of the Rhine River in western Germany. **347**
Rhode Island (RI) State in the northeastern United States. One of the original thirteen colonies. Capital: Providence. (41°N 71°W) **xx**
Richmond Capital of Virginia. (37°N 77°W) **109**
Rio Grande "Great River" that forms the border between Texas and Mexico. **xxii**
Roanoke Island Island off the coast of North Carolina. **13**
Rocky Mountains Mountain range in western North America that extends from Mexico to the Arctic. **xxii**
Romania Republic in southeastern Europe. Capital: Bucharest. (46°N 25°E) **xxviii**
Rome Capital of Italy. (42°N 12°E) **487**
Russia Country in Eastern Europe and northwestern Asia. Formerly part of the Soviet Union. Capital: Moscow. (61°N 60°E) **xxviii**
Rwanda Republic in east-central Africa. Capital: Kigali. (2°S 30°E) **xxx**

Saar Valley Region around the Saar River near the western German border. **347**
Sacramento Capital of California. (38°N 121°W) **168**
Sacramento River River in northwestern California. **102**
Sahara Vast desert in northern Africa. **9**
Saigon City in South Vietnam that is now known as Ho Chi Minh City. (11°N 106°E) **624**
Saint-Mihiel Community in northeastern France. (49°N 5°E) **341**
Saipan One of the Mariana Islands, located in the western Pacific Ocean. (15°N 146°E) **492**
Samoa Group of volcanic islands in the southwestern-central Pacific Ocean. Divided into American Samoa and Western Samoa. (14°S 171°W) **292**
San Antonio City in south-central Texas. (29°N 99°W) **89**
San Carlos Location of an Apache reservation in Arizona. **156**
Sand Creek Site in southeastern Colorado of the Sand Creek Massacre in 1864. **153**
San Diego City in southwestern California on San Diego Bay, an inlet of the Pacific Ocean near the Mexican border. (33°N 117°W) **xx**
San Francisco City in western California on a peninsula between the Pacific Ocean and San Francisco Bay. (37°N 122°W) **168**
San Francisco Bay Inlet of the Pacific Ocean in western-central California. **xx**
San Gabriel City in southwestern California. **104**
San Jacinto River River in southeastern Texas that flows into Galveston Bay. Site of the Mexican surrender to the Texans in 1836 that ended the Texas Revolution. **102**
Santa Fe Capital of New Mexico. (35°N 106°W) **103**
Santiago de Cuba Seaport located on the southern part of Cuba. Captured by U.S. forces during the Spanish-American War. (20°N 76°W) **297**
Sarajevo Capital of Bosnia and Herzegovina. (44°N 17°E) **xxviii**
Saratoga Site in eastern New York of the Revolutionary War's Battle of Saratoga in 1777. **23**

Saudi Arabia Kingdom on the Arabian Peninsula in southwest Asia. Capital: Riyadh. (22°N 46°E) **xxix**

Savannah Port city in southeastern Georgia. (32°N 81°W) **16**

Scandinavia Region of northern Europe that includes Denmark, Norway, and Sweden. **xxviii**

Scotland Northern part of the island of Great Britain. Capital: Edinburgh. (57°N 4°W) **xxviii**

Seattle City in west-central Washington. (47°N 122°W) **xx**

Selma City in southwest-central Alabama. (32°N 87°W) **597**

Seneca Falls Town in west-central New York State. (43°N 77°W) **99**

Seoul Capital of South Korea. (37°N 127°E) **xxix**

Serbia Part of Yugoslavia, located in southeastern Europe. Capital: Belgrade. (45°N 20°E) **xxviii**

Shandong Province Coastal province in northeastern China. **292**

Shenandoah Valley Valley in Virginia that is located between the Allegheny and the Blue Ridge Mountains and is drained by the Shenandoah River. **124**

Sicily Italian island in the Mediterranean Sea. (37°N 14°E) **xxviii**

Sierra Nevada Large mountain range in eastern California. **xxii**

Singapore Southeastern Asian republic made up of Singapore Island and several smaller islands. Capital: Singapore. (1°N 104°E) **xxix**

Slovakia Country in central Europe. Capital: Bratislava. (48°N 17°E) **xxviii**

Slovenia Country in southern Europe. Declared independence from Yugoslavia in June 1991. Capital: Ljubljana. (46°N 15°E) **xxviii**

Solomon Islands Island group in the southwestern Pacific Ocean. (8°S 159°E) **493**

Somalia Country in eastern Africa. Capital: Mogadishu. (3°N 44°E) **xxx**

Somme River River in northern France. **332**

South Africa Country in southern Africa. Pretoria is the administrative capital, Cape Town is the legislative capital, and Bloemfontein is the judicial capital. (30°S 26°E) **xxx**

South America Continent in the southern Western Hemisphere. **xxvii**

South Carolina (SC) State in the southeastern United States. One of the original thirteen colonies. Capital: Columbia. (34°N 81°W) **xx**

South Dakota (SD) State in the north-central United States. Organized as part of the Dakota Territory in 1861. Admitted as a state in 1889. Capital: Pierre. (44°N 102°W) **xx**

South Korea Country in southeastern Asia. Established in 1948. Capital: Seoul. (40°N 127°E) **xxix**

Soviet Union Former communist country in Eastern Europe and Asia. **515**

Spain Kingdom in southwestern Europe occupying the greater part of the Iberian Peninsula and including the Balearic and Canary Islands. Capital: Madrid. (40°N 4°W) **xxviii**

Springfield Capital of Illinois. (40°N 89°W) **129**

Sri Lanka Independent island state in the Indian Ocean. Capital: Colombo. (7°N 81°E) **xxix**

Stalingrad Present-day Volgograd. City in southwestern Russia. (48°N 42°E) **487**

St. Louis City in Missouri on the Mississippi River. (38°N 90°W) **89**

St. Petersburg City in northwestern Russia that was formerly called Leningrad. (60°N 30°E) **487**

Stockholm Capital of Sweden. (59°N 18°E) **397**

Stone Mountain Large rocky mass near Atlanta, Georgia. **388**

Sudan Republic in northeast Africa. Capital: Khartoum. (15°N 30°E) **xxx**

Sudetenland Region in the northwestern Czech Republic along the Polish border. Ceded to Germany in 1938 and restored to Czechoslovakia in 1945. **476**

Suez Canal International waterway in the Middle East that connects the Red Sea and the Mediterranean Sea. **487**

Sumatra Island in the western part of Indonesia. (0°S 102°E) **9**

Sutter's Fort Colony established in 1839 in northern California. **103**

Sweden Kingdom in northwestern Europe. Capital: Stockholm. (62°N 15°E) **xxviii**

Switzerland Federal republic in central Europe. Capital: Bern. (47°N 7°E) **xxviii**

Syria Country in southwestern Asia on the eastern Mediterranean coast. Capital: Damascus. (35°N 37°E) **xxix**

Taiwan Island-nation off the southeastern coast of China. Capital: Taipei. (23°N 121°E) **xxix**

Tallahassee Capital of Florida. (30°N 84°W) **xx**

Tampico Seaport in eastern Mexico. Arrest of U.S. solders there in 1914 led to the sending of troops to Mexico. (22°N 98°W) **305**

Tarawa Pacific island captured by the Allies in 1943. (1°N 173°E) **xxxi**

Tehran Capital of Iran. (31°N 53°E) **xxix**

Tennessee (TN) State in the south-central United States. Admitted as a state in 1796. Capital: Nashville. (36°N 88°W) **xx**

Texas (TX) State in the southwest-central United States. Admitted as a state in 1845. Capital: Austin. (31°N 101°W) **xx**

Thames River River that flows from southeastern Ontario, Canada, and empties into Lake St. Clair. **91**

Three Mile Island Island in the Susquehanna River in Pennsylvania. **668**

Tinian One of the Mariana Islands, located in the western Pacific Ocean. (15°N 145°E) **493**

Tippecanoe River River that flows from northern Indiana to join the Wabash River in west-central Indiana. **90**

Tonkin, Gulf of Arm extending from the South China Sea, east of North Vietnam. **624**

Topeka Capital of Kansas. (39°N 95°W) **xx**

Trenton Capital of New Jersey. (40°N 75°W) **23**

Tulsa City in northeast Oklahoma. (36°N 96°W) **xx**

Turkey Country in southwestern Asia and southeastern Europe between the Mediterranean and the Black Seas. Capital: Ankara. (38°N 32°W) **xxix**

United States of America Federal republic in central North America. Capital: Washington, D.C. (39°N 77°W) **xx**

Utah (UT) State in the western United States. Admitted as a state in 1896. Capital: Salt Lake City. (39°N 112°W) **xx**

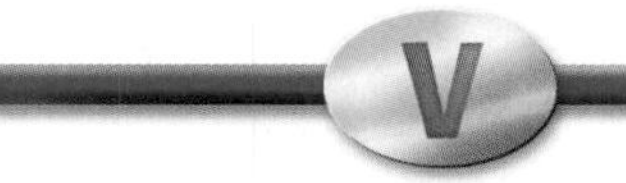

Valley Forge Site in southeastern Pennsylvania where General George Washington and his troops spent the harsh winter of 1777–78 during the Revolutionary War. **23**

Venezuela Country in northern South America on the Caribbean Sea. Capital: Caracas. (8°N 65°W) **xxvii**

Venice City and trading center in northeastern Italy that was particularly important during the Renaissance. (45°N 12°E) **10**

Veracruz Seaport in eastern Mexico. (19°N 96°W) **305**

Verdun City in northeastern France. (44°N 1°E) **332**

Vermont (VT) State in the northeastern United States. Capital: Montpelier. (44°N 73°W) **xx**

Vicksburg City in western Mississippi on the bluffs above the Mississippi River. (42°N 85°W) **109**

Vietnam Country in southeastern Asia that was divided into North Vietnam and South Vietnam between 1954 and 1975. Capital: Hanoi. (18°N 107°E) **xxix**

Virginia (VA) State in the eastern United States. One of the original thirteen colonies. Capital: Richmond. (37°N 80°W) **xx**

Virginia City Town in western Nevada that was established in 1859 when people came to mine the Comstock Lode. (39°N 119°W) **158**

Volcano Islands Small group of islands in the western Pacific Ocean. (25°N 141°E) **492**

Wake Island Island in the northern Pacific Ocean. A U.S. territory since the 1890s. (19°N 166°E) **493**

Waltham City in northeastern Massachusetts. (43°N 71°W) **94**

Warsaw Capital of Poland. (52°N 21°E) **xxviii**

Washington (WA) State in northwestern United States, bounded by British Columbia, Canada, to the north and by the Pacific Ocean to the west. Admitted as a state in 1889. Capital: Olympia. (47°N 121°W) **xx**

Washington, D.C. Capital of the United States, located on the Potomac River between Virginia and Maryland. (39°N 77°W) **xx**

Watts Neighborhood in southwestern Los Angeles. (34°N 118°W) **600**

Western Ghats Mountain range in southern India. **161**

West Germany *See* Germany.

West Indies Islands between North and South America enclosing the Caribbean Sea. **xxvi**

West Virginia (WV) State in the east-central United States. Admitted as a state in 1863. Capital: Charleston. (39°N 81°W) **xx**

Wisconsin (WI) State in the north-central United States. Admitted as a state in 1848. Capital: Madison. (44°N 91°W) **xx**

Woodstock Town in southeastern New York. (42°N 74°W) **587**

Wounded Knee Site in southwestern South Dakota of the Massacre at Wounded Knee in 1890. **153**

Wyoming (WY) State in the northwestern United States. Admitted as a state in 1890. Capital: Cheyenne. (43°N 108°W) **xx**

Yalta Town in the Ukraine. (44°N 34°E) **510**

Yalu River River that flows between northeastern China and North Korea. **524**

Yorktown Town in southeastern Virginia. (41°N 74°W) **23**

Yugoslavia Country in southeastern Europe that was formed as the Kingdom of the Serbs, Croats, and Slovenes after the collapse of Austria-Hungary in 1918; renamed Yugoslavia in 1929; Serbia and Montenegro formed new Republic of Yugoslavia in 1992. Capital: Belgrade. **xxviii**

Yukon Territory Territory in northwestern Canada. **288**

Zion Canyon in southwestern Utah that is now a national park. **270**

Glossary

This Glossary contains terms you need to understand as you study American history. After each key term there is a brief definition or explanation of the meaning of the term as it is used in *Call to Freedom.* The page number refers to the page on which the term is introduced in the textbook.

Phonetic Respelling and Pronunciation Guide

Many of the key terms in this textbook have been respelled to help you pronounce them. The letter combinations used in the respelling throughout the narrative are explained in the following phonetic respelling and pronunciation guide. The guide is adapted from *Webster's Tenth New College Dictionary, Merriam-Webster's New Geographical Dictionary,* and *Merriam-Webster's New Biographical Dictionary.*

MARK	AS IN	RESPELLING	EXAMPLE
a	alphabet	a	*AL-fuh-bet
ā	Asia	ay	AY-zhuh
ä	cart, top	ah	KAHRT, TAHP
e	let, ten	e	LET, TEN
ē	even, leaf	ee	EE-vuhn, LEEF
i	it, tip, British	i	IT, TIP, BRIT-ish
ī	site, buy, Ohio	y	SYT, BY, oh-HY-oh
	iris	eye	EYE-ris
k	card	k	KAHRD
ō	over, rainbow	oh	OH-vuhr, RAYN-boh
u̇	book, wood	ooh	BOOHK, WOOHD
ȯ	all, orchid	aw	AWL, AWR-kid
ȯi	foil, coin	oy	FOYL, KOYN
au̇	out	ow	OWT
ə	cup, butter	uh	KUHP, BUHT-uhr
ü	rule, food	oo	ROOL, FOOD
yü	few	yoo	FYOO
zh	vision	zh	VIZH-uhn

*A syllable printed in small capital letters receives heavier emphasis than the other syllable(s) in a word

ABC Powers Argentina, Brazil, and Chile. **310**

abolition An end to slavery. **98**

Acquired Immune Deficiency Syndrome (AIDS) Disease caused by the human immunodeficiency virus (HIV) that forces the body's immune system to shut down, making it easier for a person to contract other illnesses. **699**

Adamson Act Reform legislation passed during President Woodrow Wilson's administration that limited the workday on the nation's railroads to eight hours. **283**

affirmative action Practice by some businesses and government agencies of giving special consideration to nonwhites or women to make up for past discrimination. **601**

ageism Discrimination against an age group, particularly the elderly. **618**

Agricultural Marketing Act (1929) Legislation that ended some farm subsidies and established the Federal Farm Board. **429**

Alien and Sedition Acts (1798) Laws passed by a Federalist-dominated Congress that made it illegal to print or speak words hostile to the government; used against Republicans. **87**

Alliance for Progress Aid programs developed by President John F. Kennedy's administration that sought to encourage economic development and promote democracy in Latin America. **574**

Allied Powers World War I alliance that included Britain, France, Russia, and later the United States; also the World War II alliance between Britain and France, and later the United States and other countries, that fought against the Axis Powers. **328, 476**

amendments Official changes, corrections, or additions to a constitution. **33**

American Civil Liberties Union (ACLU) Organization formed in 1920 to protect civil rights. **360**

American Expeditionary Force (AEF) U.S. troops that served overseas in World War I. **339**

American Federation of Labor (AFL) One of the first large labor unions in the United States; organized in the

1880s by Samuel Gompers as an association of individual skilled craft unions. **197**

American Indian Movement (AIM) Organization formed in 1968 to fight for the rights of American Indians. **617**

American Liberty League Group formed by business leaders to oppose the New Deal. **437**

American Plan Campaign launched by business leaders in the early 1900s to create open shops, or businesses where union membership was not required and was sometimes forbidden. **376**

Americans with Disabilities Act (ADA) (1990) Law that guarantees people with disabilities equal access to public accommodations, transportation, and employment opportunities. **693**

amnesty An official pardon issued by the government for an illegal act. **125**

anarchists People who want to abolish all forms of government. **359**

Anti-Imperialist League Group of Americans who opposed the treaty ending the Spanish-American War because they believed that the sections of the treaty acquiring former Spanish territories was the beginning of a U.S. colonial empire. **299**

Anti-Saloon League Organization founded in 1893 to fight alcohol abuse; particularly active during the early 1900s. **255**

apartheid System of laws in South Africa that required racial segregation. **670**

Apollo program The National Aeronautics and Space Administration's program to land astronauts on the Moon. **589**

appeasement The act of giving in to an aggressor to preserve peace. **476**

Appomattox Courthouse Town in which Union general Ulysses S. Grant accepted the surrender of Confederate general Robert E. Lee, ending the Civil War. **111**

apportionment The use of population to determine how many legislative representatives an area will have. **38**

arbitration Formal meetings to discuss and settle disagreements. **266**

armistice A truce between warring groups or countries. **343**

Armory Show An art exhibition held in New York City in 1913. **403**

Army-McCarthy hearings Televised hearings in the 1950s of the U.S. Senate's investigations into Senator Joseph McCarthy's charges that Communists were in the U.S. military. **531**

Articles of Confederation (1777) Document that created the first permanent national government for the United States; was replaced by the U.S. Constitution in 1789. **30**

artifacts Remains of objects that have been made by humans. **6**

assembly line A system that moves parts and partly assembled products among factory workers to reduce production time. **368**

Atlanta Compromise (1895) Speech given by Booker T. Washington stating that African Americans should focus on improving their education and economic situation instead of fighting discrimination and segregation. **259**

Atlantic Charter (1941) Pledge signed by U.S. president Franklin D. Roosevelt and British prime minister Winston Churchill not to acquire new territory as a result of World War II and to work for peace after the war. **478**

atomic bomb A nuclear weapon that produced an explosion by splitting atoms; the United States dropped two atomic bombs on Japan during World War II. **496**

automation The use of machines in production. **546**

Axis Powers Military alliance formed by Italy and Germany in 1936; later joined by other countries. Fought against the Allied Powers in World War II. **465**

baby boom A significant increase in the number of children being born; one took place in the United States after World War II. **548**

Bacon's Rebellion (1676) Attack led by Nathaniel Bacon against American Indians and the colonial government in Virginia. **15**

balance of power A situation in which the strength of rival nations is nearly equal. **326**

Bataan Death March (1942) Forced march of tens of thousands of American and Filipino prisoners during World War II up the Bataan Peninsula to internment camps. **491**

Battle of Antietam (1862) Union victory in Maryland during the Civil War that marked the bloodiest single-day battle in U.S. military history. **108**

Battle of Britain (1940–41) Series of bombing raids launched against British cities by the German air force. **477**

Battle of Bunker Hill (1775) Revolutionary War battle in Boston that demonstrated that the colonists could fight well against the British army. **23**

Battle of El Alamein (1942) British victory in World War II that stopped Axis forces from advancing in North Africa. **485**

Battle of Gettysburg (1863) Union victory at Gettysburg, Pennsylvania, during the Civil War that turned the tide against the Confederates; resulted in the loss of more than 50,000 soldiers. **110**

Battle of Leyte Gulf (1944) World War II battle in the Philippines that was the largest naval battle in history. **493**

Battle of Midway (1942) World War II battle in which U.S. warplanes crippled Japan's navy. **491**

Battle of New Orleans (1815) Greatest U.S. victory in the War of 1812; actually took place two weeks after the signing of a peace treaty that ended the war. **91**

Battle of Saratoga (1777) Revolutionary War battle in New York that resulted in a major defeat of British troops; marked the Patriots' greatest victory up to that point in the war. **24**

Battle of Stalingrad (1942–43) Allied victory by the Soviet Union in World War II in which the Axis Powers lost many soldiers. **486**

Battle of the Atlantic Long-lasting World War II naval war to control Atlantic Ocean trade routes. **478**

Battle of the Bulge (1944–45) World War II battle in which Allied forces ended Germany's ability to wage an offensive war. **489**

Battle of the Coral Sea (1942) World War II battle in which the Allies stopped the Japanese advance to New Guinea. **491**

Battle of the Little Bighorn (1876) "Custer's Last Stand"; battle between U.S. soldiers led by George Armstrong Custer and Sioux warriors led by Crazy Horse; resulted in the worst defeat of the U.S. Army in the West. **154**

Battle of Yorktown (1781) Last major battle of the Revolutionary War; site of British general Charles Cornwallis's surrender to the Patriots in Virginia. **25**

Bay of Pigs Bay on the coast of Cuba that Cuban exiles, secretly trained by the United States, tried to invade; the exiles were quickly defeated. **575**

bear market A stock market with declining stock prices. **420**

beats Young writers who criticized American life in the 1950s through their writings and behavior; also called beatniks. **551**

benevolent societies Organizations that helped immigrants in cases of sickness, unemployment, and death. **212**

Berlin Airlift (1948) Joint effort by the United States and Britain to fly food and supplies into West Berlin after the Soviets blocked off all ground routes to the city. **515**

Berlin Wall Wall constructed in 1961 between East and West Berlin to prevent East Berliners from crossing into the West. **575**

Bessemer process Less expensive, easier way to make steel; developed by British inventor Henry Bessemer in the 1850s. **184**

bicameral legislature A lawmaking body made up of two houses. **19**

Big Four Collective name given to U.S. president Woodrow Wilson, British prime minister David Lloyd George, French premier Georges Clemenceau, and Italian prime minister Vittorio Orlando during the post–World War I peace conference at Versailles. **346**

Bill of Rights First 10 amendments to the U.S. Constitution; ratified in 1791. **33**

Black Cabinet Group of African Americans who were appointed to significant government positions by President Franklin D. Roosevelt. **456**

Black Codes Laws passed in the southern states during Reconstruction that greatly limited the freedom and rights of African Americans. **130**

blacklisting Refusing to hire a person; common action toward suspected Communists during the 1950s. **528**

Black Monday October 19, 1987; the day the stock market dropped more than 20 percent after reaching an all-time high in August. The market continued to drop following this day, eventually losing some 40 percent of its value. **686**

Black Power Social and political movement in the 1960s that called for greater African American economic and political power. **600**

Blackshirts Group of Italians led by Benito Mussolini that gained power in the early 1920s. **464**

Black Tuesday October 29, 1929; the day the stock market collapsed. Led to the Panic of 1929. **420**

Blitzkrieg "Lightning war"; type of fast-moving warfare used by German forces against Poland in 1939. **476**

bonanza A large find of precious ore. **158**

Bonus Army Group of World War I veterans that marched on Washington, D.C., in 1932 to demand the immediate payment of their government war bonuses in cash. **430**

boom towns Western communities that grew quickly because of mining booms and often disappeared soon after. **159**

bootleggers People who smuggled liquor into the United States from Canada and Mexico during prohibition. **384**

bosses Corrupt political leaders who used bribery and payoffs to win elections. **238**

Boston Massacre (1770) Incident in which British soldiers fired into a group of colonists, killing five people. **22**

Boxer Rebellion (1900) Revolt in which Chinese nationalists known as the Boxers attacked foreigners in order to end outside involvement in China's affairs; put down by U.S. Marines and other forces after two months. **293**

Bozeman Trail Trail used by miners, named after pioneer John M. Bozeman; ran from Wyoming to Montana. **153**

braceros Mexican workers authorized by the U.S. government to enter and work in the United States during World War II. **482**

Brady Bill (1993) Handgun Violence Prevention Act; legislation that established a five-day waiting period for handgun purchases. **710**

Brain Trust Group of expert policy advisers who worked with President Franklin D. Roosevelt in the 1930s to end the Great Depression. **432**

brinkmanship The Eisenhower administration's policy of being willing to go to the very brink of war to oppose communist expansion. **540**

Brown* v. *Board of Education (1954) Supreme Court ruling that declared that segregation in public schools is illegal; overturned the separate-but-equal doctrine established in 1896 case *Plessy* v. *Ferguson*. **556**

bull market A stock market with rising stock prices. **420**

Bull Moose Party Nickname for the Progressive Party, which was formed by Theodore Roosevelt and his supporters in 1912. **276**

business cycle Economic pattern in which business goes through periods of prosperity and depression. **422**

buying on margin Purchasing stocks on credit. **420**

cabinet Group made up of the heads of the executive departments that advises the U.S. president. **41**

California Gold Rush (1849) Migration of thousands of people to California after gold was first discovered there. **105**

Camp David Accords (1978) Peace agreements between Israel and Egypt, negotiated by President Jimmy Carter. **669**

capitalism Economic system in which private businesses own and operate most industries; competition determines the cost of goods as well as workers' pay. **251**

carpetbaggers Republicans from the North who moved to the South during Reconstruction. **136**

cattle drive Long journeys on which cowboys herded cattle to northern markets or better grazing lands. **167**

Cattle Kingdom Area of the Great Plains, stretching from Texas to Canada, on which many ranchers raised cattle during the late 1800s. **165**

Central Intelligence Agency (CIA) An organization established by the federal government in 1947 to conduct covert operations. **541**

Central Powers World War I alliance led by Austria-Hungary and Germany and later joined by Bulgaria and the Ottoman Empire. **327**

Challenger U.S. space shuttle that exploded in 1986 after takeoff, killing all seven crew members. **700**

charter Official English document that gave a person or group the right to establish a colony. **13**

checks and balances A system established by the Constitution that shares power between branches of government and prevents any one branch from becoming too powerful. **32**

Chicano movement Effort of young Hispanic activists to end discrimination and increase cultural pride. **608**

Children's Defense Fund Program founded in the 1970s by Marian Wright Edelman to protect the rights of children. **618**

Chinese Exclusion Act (1882) Law prohibiting Chinese people from immigrating to the United States for a period of 10 years; was extended into the early 1900s. **214**

Chisholm Trail Trail from San Antonio, Texas, to Abilene, Kansas, established by Jesse Chisholm in 1867 for cattle drives. **167**

Civil Rights Act of 1866 Law that gave African Americans legal rights equal to those of white Americans. **132**

Civil Rights Act of 1875 Law allowing African Americans to sue private businesses for racial discrimination. **139**

Civil Rights Act of 1964 Law banning segregation in public places and prohibiting employers, unions, and universities from discriminating on the basis of color, sex, religion, and national origin. **598**

Clayton Antitrust Act (1914) Act that strengthened federal laws against monopolies. **281**

Cold War Power struggle between the United States and the Soviet Union that lasted from 1945 to 1991. **513**

collective bargaining Process in which union leaders negotiate with factory owners on behalf of workers in a particular business or industry for better wages and working conditions. **196**

Columbian Exchange Transfer of plants, animals, and diseases between the Americas and Africa, Asia, and Europe. **12**

Commercial Revolution Period of economic development that took place in Europe in the 1400s and greatly expanded trade. **10**

Commission on the Status of Women Commission formed by President John F. Kennedy in 1961 to study workplace inequality; headed by Esther Peterson and former first lady Eleanor Roosevelt. **610**

Committee on Civil Rights (1946) Committee appointed by President Harry S Truman to investigate racial discrimination and to suggest federal solutions to the problem. **555**

Committee on Public Information (CPI) Agency created by President Woodrow Wilson in 1917 to increase public support for World War I. **335**

Commonwealth of Independent States (CIS) An alliance formed by many of the former Soviet republics in December 1991. **695**

Communists People who favor the equal distribution of wealth and the end of all forms of private property. **340**

compact discs (CDs) Devices on which to record music or sounds; also capable of storing huge quantities of data. **701**

Compromise of 1850 Agreement proposed by Henry Clay that allowed California to enter the Union as a free state and divided the rest of the Mexican Cession into two territories where slavery would be decided by popular sovereignty; also settled land claims between Texas and New Mexico, abolished the slave trade in Washington, and introduced the Fugitive Slave Act. **106**

Compromise of 1877 Agreement to settle the disputed presidential elections of 1876; Democrats agreed to accept Republican Rutherford B. Hayes as president in return for the removal of federal troops from the South. **140**

Comstock Lode (1859) Nevada gold and silver mine that Henry Comstock claimed to have discovered. **158**

concurrent powers Powers that are shared by the federal and state governments. **38**

Confederate States of America Nation formed by the southern states on February 4, 1861; also known as the Confederacy. **107**

Congress of Industrial Organizations (CIO) Labor group formed in 1938 that joined together industrial unions. **448**

conservation Preservation of nature and its resources. **270**

Constitutional Convention (1787) Meeting in Philadelphia at which delegates from the states wrote the U.S. Constitution. **31**

containment U.S. foreign policy followed during the Cold War that sought to prevent the expansion of Soviet communism. **515**

Contract with America Ten-point Republican reform plan created in the mid-1990s. **710**

contras A group of anti-Sandinista rebels in Nicaragua. **689**

corporations Companies that sell shares of ownership, called stocks, to investors in order to raise money. **189**

cotton gin Device refined by Eli Whitney in the 1790s to separate the seeds from the fibers in cotton plants; revolutionized the cotton industry. **97**

counterculture An alternative culture with values that run counter to, or against, those in the main society. **584**

covert operations Secret missions. **541**

Crusades (1096–1221) Series of five wars launched by European Christians to gain possession of the Holy Land. **9**

Cuban missile crisis (1962) Military crisis that almost led to nuclear war when U.S. naval ships blockaded Cuba until the Soviet Union agreed to remove its nuclear missiles from the island; in return, the United States promised not to invade Cuba and to remove certain missiles from Europe. **577**

culture Common values and traditions of a society, such as language, government, and family relationships. **6**

Dawes General Allotment Act (1887) Legislation passed by Congress that split up Indian reservation lands among individual Indians and promised them citizenship; goal was to lessen tribal influence. **157**

Dayton peace accords (1995) Peace agreements signed in Dayton, Ohio, by the presidents of Bosnia, Croatia, and Serbia; unrest in Bosnia continued in spite of the accords. **717**

D-Day June 6, 1944; date of Allied invasion of France during World War II. **487**

Declaration of Independence (1776) Statement of the Second Continental Congress that defined the colonists' rights and explained their complaints against Britain; declared the colonies independent. **23**

deficit spending Government spending that exceeds the amount received in revenue. **443**

delegated powers Powers that are granted to the federal government. **38**

demobilization The process of returning to a peacetime economy. **356**

Democratic Party Political party formed by supporters of Andrew Jackson after the presidential election of 1824. **92**

department stores Large retail shops that first appeared in cities in the late 1800s. **217**

deport To send an immigrant back to his or her country of origin. **71**

détente Period in the 1970s when relations between the United States and the Soviet Union were less hostile than in the past. **659**

direct primary Method of allowing voters to choose their own candidates for office. **243**

Disabled in Action (DIA) Group formed in 1970 to coordinate reform efforts for people with disabilities. **618**

disarmament The act of limiting military weapons. **365**

Dixiecrats Members of the States' Rights Party; formed in the 1940s by southern Democrats who were upset with President Harry S Truman's support for civil rights. **521**

dollar diplomacy President William Howard Taft's policy of influencing Latin American governments through economic, not military, intervention. **306**

Dominion of New England (1686–89) Unpopular union of some northeastern American colonies under one government organized by King James II. **19**

domino theory Belief common during President Dwight D. Eisenhower's administration and beyond; stated that if one nation in Southeast Asia fell to communism, the rest of Southeast Asia would also fall. **624**

double jeopardy Act of trying a person twice for the same crime. **67**

doves Americans who called for U.S. withdrawal from the Vietnam War. **631**

draft A system of required service in the armed services. **72**

***Dred Scott* decision** (1857) Supreme Court ruling that declared African Americans were not U.S. citizens, that the Missouri Compromise's restriction on slavery was unconstitutional, and that Congress did not have the right to ban slavery in any federal territory. **107**

dry farming Hardy Campbell's farming method taught to Great Plains farmers in the 1890s; allowed farmers to grow certain crops with less water. **173**

due process Fair application of the law. **67**

Dust Bowl Name given to parts of the Great Plains in the 1930s after a severe drought dried out the region. **450**

Earth Day Day celebrated annually on April 22 to increase environmental awareness; first celebrated in 1970. **673**

Economic Recovery Tax Act (ERTA) (1981) Federal legislation that reduced personal income taxes by 25 percent and cut some other taxes, amounting to some $750 billion in tax reduction. **683**

Education for All Handicapped Children Act (1975) Legislation that required public schools to provide a quality education for children with disabilities. **618**

Eighteenth Amendment (1919) Constitutional amendment that outlawed the production, sale, and transportation of alcoholic beverages in the United States; repealed in 1933. **255**

Eisenhower Doctrine (1957) President Dwight D. Eisenhower's promise of U.S. aid to any Middle Eastern nation fighting communist aggression. **542**

elastic clause Article I, Section 8, of the U.S. Constitution that has been interpreted as giving Congress authority to stretch its delegated powers to address issues not otherwise specified in the document. **38**

El Niño Weather system marked by an irregularly occurring flow of warm surface water along the Pacific coast of South America; often accompanied by weather extremes. **724**

emancipation Freedom from slavery. **98**

Emancipation Proclamation (1863) Order announced by President Abraham Lincoln in 1862 that freed the slaves in nonoccupied areas rebelling against the Union; took effect January 1, 1863. **109**

Emergency Quota Act (1921) Law that limited the number of immigrants to the United States to 357000 per year. **388**

Emergency Relief Appropriation Act (1935) Second New Deal legislation that provided close to $4.9 billion to help the unemployed. **439**

eminent domain The government's right to take personal property to further the public's interest. **68**

Endangered Species Act (1966) Legislation that protects animals threatened with extinction. **674**

energy crisis Situation in the 1970s marked by high fuel prices and fuel shortages. **657**

entrepreneurs People who organize new businesses. **189**

Environmental Protection Agency (EPA) Agency established by Congress in 1970 to enforce environmental laws. **674**

Equal Pay Act (1963) Legislation that required employers to pay men and women the same wages for the same job. **611**

Equal Rights Amendment Proposed constitutional amendment that would guarantee women's rights by prohibiting discrimination based on sex; passed by Congress in 1972 but never ratified by enough states to become a constitutional amendment. **614**

escalation President Lyndon B. Johnson's policy of increasing U.S. involvement in the Vietnam War. **628**

European Union (EU) Group of 11 European nations that joined together in 1991 to form a single market with a common currency and a common bank in order to increase their global economic power. **727**

executive branch Division of the federal government that includes the president and the administrative departments; enforces the nation's laws. **32**

executive orders Nonlegislative directives issued by the U.S. president in certain circumstances; executive orders have the force of congressional law. **41**

executive privilege Right of the president to keep information secret to protect national security. **661**

Exodusters Some 20,000 to 40,000 southern African Americans who settled in western lands in the late 1800s. **171**

expatriates People who leave their native country to live elsewhere. **402**

exports Items that a country sells to other countries. **19**

fads Interests followed for a short time with great enthusiasm. **393**

Fair Deal Series of reform programs proposed by President Harry S Truman. **521**

Fair Employment Practices Committee (FEPC) Committee created during World War II to prevent discrimination in war industries and government jobs. **482**

Fair Labor Standards Act (1938) Legislation that established a minimum wage of 40 cents an hour by 1940. **448**

Family and Medical Leave Act (1993) Legislation that provides workers with up to 12 weeks of unpaid leave for family or medical purposes. **709**

Farmers' Alliances Political groups formed by farmers in the late 1800s that worked to elect candidates favorable to farmers. **203**

Farm Security Administration Federal agency created in the 1930s to increase farm ownership by issuing long-term loans at low interest rates. **452**

fascism Political theory that calls for a strong government headed by one individual and in which the state is more important than the individual. **464**

Federal Deposit Insurance Corporation (FDIC) Organization created by Congress during the Hundred Days to protect bank accounts by insuring deposits. **433**

Federal Emergency Relief Administration (FERA) Organization authorized by Congress in 1933 to provide money directly to families in need. **433**

Federal Farm Loan Act Legislation passed during President Woodrow Wilson's administration that made it easier for farmers to obtain credit. **283**

Federal Home Loan Bank Act (1932) Legislation that provided money to banks, financial institutions, and insurance companies so they could offer low-interest mortgages. **429**

federalism U.S. system of government in which power is distributed between a central authority and the individual states. **32**

Federal Reserve Act (1913) Act that created a national banking system to help the government control the economy. **280**

Federal Trade Commission (FTC) (1914) Commission established to investigate corporations to try to keep them from conducting unfair trade practices. **281**

Feminine Mystique, The Book published by Betty Friedan in 1963 that drew national attention to the lives of female homemakers. **611**

feminism Theory that states that women are entitled to economic, political, and social equality with men. **611**

feudalism System of government that arose during the Middle Ages in which people pledge their loyalty to a lord in exchange for protection. **8**

Fifteenth Amendment (1870) Constitutional amendment that gave African American men the right to vote. **135**

fireside chats President Franklin D. Roosevelt's radio addresses to the American people. **433**

First Battle of the Marne (1914) World War I battle in which French forces stopped a German advance near Paris. **328**

Five-Power Naval Treaty Treaty following the Washington Conference that called for reductions in naval strength and imposed a limit on the maximum size of each nation's navy. **365**

flappers Young women in the 1920s who challenged social traditions with their dress and behavior. **382**

flexible response President John F. Kennedy's policy of increasing the number of military forces and conventional weapons, thus providing more military options. **573**

Food Administration Agency created during World War I to increase the food supply for the war by expanding agricultural production and decreasing domestic consumption. **337**

Fordney-McCumber Tariff Act Legislation passed in the 1920s that placed high taxes on imported farm products. **377**

Fort Laramie Treaty (1851) Agreement with the northern Plains Indians that allowed the U.S. government to build forts and roads in Indian homelands while promising to pay for any damage to Indian land. **152**

forty-niners Gold-seekers who traveled to California during the gold rush. **105**

Fourteen Points (1918) President Woodrow Wilson's plan for organizing post–World War I Europe and for avoiding future wars. **345**

Fourteenth Amendment (1868) Constitutional amendment passed by Congress in 1866 giving full rights of citizenship to all people born or naturalized in the United States, except for American Indians. **132**

free coinage Type of monetary system in which both gold and silver were coined; the value of paper money was worth a specific amount of gold or silver. **202**

Freedmen's Bureau Agency established by Congress in 1865 to help poor people in the South. **126**

Freedom Rides (1961) Bus trips by civil rights workers through several southern states in which protesters challenged illegal bus segregation. **596**

Freedom Summer (1964) A campaign in Mississippi to register African Americans to vote. **599**

free enterprise System in which businesses operate free from government involvement. **189**

Fundamentalism Protestant religious movement that teaches that the Bible is literally true. **385**

Gadsden Purchase (1853) United States's purchase of land from Mexico that included the southern parts of present-day New Mexico and Arizona. **104**

General Amnesty Act of 1872 Law that repealed the section of the Fourteenth Amendment that forbade former Confederates from holding public office. **139**

generation gap Division between older and younger people. **584**

genetic engineering The deliberate altering of genes by scientists. **699**

Geneva Accords (1954) Agreement that temporarily divided Vietnam into North and South Vietnam and called for free elections in 1956 to reunite the country. **625**

genocide Deliberate murder of an entire people. **499**

Gettysburg Address (1863) Speech given by Abraham Lincoln in which he praised Union soldiers' bravery and renewed his commitment to winning the Civil War. **110**

Ghost Dance A religious movement among American Indians that spread across the Great Plains in the 1880s. **156**

GI Bill of Rights (1944) Servicemen's Readjustment Act, which offered World War II veterans education benefits and loans for houses, farms, and businesses. **519**

glasnost Soviet policy established in the 1980s that promoted political openness and freedom of expression. **691**

global warming Potential environmental threat caused by the rising temperature on Earth from heat trapped in the planet's atmosphere. **724**

gold standard Type of monetary system in which money is worth a specific amount in gold. **202**

Good Neighbor policy President Franklin D. Roosevelt's foreign policy of promoting better relations with Latin America by using economic influence rather than military force in the region. **462**

Gramm-Rudman-Hollings Act (1985) Law that required the government to cut spending when the deficit grew above a certain level. **685**

Gray Panthers Group formed by Margaret Kuhn to defend the rights of the elderly. **618**

Great Awakening A Christian evangelical movement that became widespread in the American colonies in the 1730s and 1740s. **20**

Great Compromise (1787) Agreement worked out at the Constitutional Convention; established that a state's population would determine representation in the lower house of the legislature, while each state would have equal representation in the upper house of the legislature. **31**

Great Depression Serious, global economic decline that began with the crash of the U.S. stock market in 1929. **421**

Great Migration Mass migration of some 500,000 African Americans to midwestern and northern U.S. cities during and after World War I. **389**

Great Society Legislation introduced by President Lyndon B. Johnson to create government programs to end poverty and racism. **581**

Harlem Renaissance Period of great African American artistic achievement in the 1920s; named for the Harlem neighborhood of New York City. **400**

hawks Americans who pushed for increased military spending and involvement in the Vietnam War. **632**

Hay–Bunau-Varilla Treaty (1903) Agreement between the United States and Panama that gave the United States a 99-year lease to build a canal on a 10-mile-wide strip of land across the Isthmus of Panama. **302**

Hay-Herrán Treaty (1903) Agreement with Colombia that would have given the United States a 99-year lease on a five-mile-wide strip of land across the Isthmus of Panama; rejected by the Colombian senate. **302**

Haymarket Riot (1886) Incident in which a bomb exploded during a labor protest held in Haymarket Square in Chicago, killing several police officers. **197**

Highway Act (1956) An act that provided money to create a national interstate highway system. **547**

hippies Members of the 1960s counterculture who experimented with different ways of living and behaving. **584**

Ho Chi Minh Trail A network of paths, small roads, and tunnels that led from North Vietnam, through Laos and Cambodia, to South Vietnam; the major supply route of the Vietcong. **628**

Holocaust Adolf Hitler's carefully planned extermination of about 6 million European Jews. **498**

Homestead Act (1862) Law passed by Congress to encourage settlement in the West by giving government-owned land to small farmers. **170**

Homestead Strike (1892) Strike at Andrew Carnegie's Homestead Steel factory in Pennsylvania that erupted in violence between strikers and private detectives. **198**

Hoovervilles Camps built outside of major cities by people who had lost their homes during the Great Depression; called Hoovervilles because the people blamed President Herbert Hoover for their situation. **426**

horizontal integration Ownership of all businesses in a particular field. **191**

House of Burgesses Colonial Virginia's elected assembly. **19**

House Un-American Activities Committee (HUAC) Congressional committee created in 1938 to investigate U.S. citizens accused of communist activities. **527**

Hull House Settlement house founded by Jane Addams and Ellen Gates Starr in Chicago in 1889. **221**

Hundred Days Special session of Congress in 1933 during which the bulk of New Deal programs was passed. **432**

hydrogen bomb A type of nuclear bomb. **540**

Immigration and Nationality Act (1965) Legislation that established new quotas for immigrants; limits did not apply to those who had relatives in the United States. **581**

Immigration Reform and Control Act (1986) Legislation that granted legal status to illegal aliens, or noncitizens, who could prove they had lived continuously in the United States since before January 1, 1982. **718**

Immigration Restriction League Organization formed in 1894 by nativists who wanted to reduce immigration; called for a new law requiring immigrants to prove that they were able to read and write before they could enter the United States. **214**

impeach To bring charges against. **40**

imperialism The practice of extending a nation's power by gaining territories for a colonial empire. **288**

imports Items that a country purchases from other countries. **19**

independent counsel Special prosecutor appointed to investigate claims against government officials. **710**

Indian Citizenship Act (1924) Legislation that granted all American Indians the legal protections and voting privileges of U.S. citizenship. **391**

Indian Removal Act (1830) Congressional act that authorized the removal of American Indians from east of the Mississippi River to Indian Territory. **93**

Indian Reorganization Act (IRA) (1934) Legislation that ended land allotment to individual American Indians and allowed some land to be returned to tribal ownership. **455**

indict To formally accuse a person of a crime. **67**

Industrial Revolution Period of rapid growth in the use of machines in manufacturing and production that began in Britain in the mid-1700s and later spread to the United States. **94**

Industrial Workers of the World (IWW) Socialist organization formed in 1905 to bring all workers into one large union. **251**

Information Revolution Rapid growth in the availability and transfer of information that took place in the 1990s; made possible by the increased use of computers. **722**

initiative Law enabling voters to propose a new law by collecting signatures on a petition. **243**

installment plan A program for purchasing goods in which the customer makes a small initial payment and then continues to make monthly payments with interest until the item is paid for. **371**

Intermediate-Range Nuclear Forces Treaty (INF) (1987) Treaty signed by President Ronald Reagan and Soviet leader Mikhail Gorbachev that eliminated all medium-range nuclear weapons from Europe. **691**

Internal Security Act (1950) Law that required suspected communist organizations to register with the federal government and that gave the government the right to arrest people suspected of treasonous activities. **528**

Internet Worldwide system of computer networks. **722**

internment Forced relocation and imprisonment of people. **483**

Interstate Commerce Act (1887) Law that provided uniform national regulations for trade between the states. **201**

Interstate Commerce Commission (ICC) (1887) Commission created by the Interstate Commerce Act to ensure that railroads charged fair rates and treated all shipping customers fairly. **201**

Intolerable Acts (1774) Four laws passed by Parliament to punish colonists for the Boston Tea Party; closed Boston Harbor and canceled the Massachusetts colony's charter. **22**

Iran-contra affair Name given to the 1986 scandal in which the U.S. government secretly sold weapons to Iran and then used the profits to fund the contras in Nicaragua. **689**

Iran hostage crisis Situation that began in 1979 in which 53 Americans taken hostage in the U.S. Embassy in Tehran, Iran, and were held for 444 days. **670**

Iroquois League A political confederation of five northeastern tribes—the Cayuga, Mohawk, Oneida, Onondaga, and Seneca—developed by the Iroquois. **8**

island-hopping World War II strategy of conquering only certain Pacific islands that were important to the Allied advance toward Japan. **492**

isolationism National policy of avoiding involvement in other nations' affairs. **288**

Jazz Age A term for the 1920s; so called because of jazz music's popularity during the decade. **400**

Jim Crow laws Laws that enforced segregation in the southern states. **140**

judicial branch Division of the federal government that is made up of the national courts; interprets laws, punishes criminals, and settles disputes between states. **32**

judicial review Principle that gives the Supreme Court the right to declare an act of Congress unconstitutional. **88**

Judiciary Act (1789) Legislation passed by Congress that created a federal court system. **84**

kamikaze World War II tactic used by Japanese pilots of crashing planes filled with explosives into Allied ships. **494**

Kansas-Nebraska Act (1854) Law that created the territories of Kansas and Nebraska and allowed voters there to choose whether to allow slavery. **106**

Keating-Owen Child Labor Act (1916) Legislation that prohibited companies from shipping their products across state lines if they employed children under 14; was overturned by the Supreme Court in 1918. **283**

Kellogg-Briand Pact (1928) Pact signed by the United States and 14 other nations that outlawed war. **366**

Khmer Rouge Cambodian communist army. **637**

Knights of Labor The first national labor union in the United States; organized in 1869 and included workers of different races, gender, and skills. **196**

Kristallnacht "Night of broken glass," November 9, 1938; night when Nazis killed or injured many Jews and destroyed many Jewish properties. **465**

Ku Klux Klan Secret society created by white southerners in 1866 that used terror and violence to keep African Americans from obtaining their civil rights. **138**

La Raza Unida Party (LRUP) The "United People's Party"; organized in 1970 to increase Hispanic political power. **608**

League of Nations International congress of nations formed in 1919 that was designed to settle disputes and protect democracy. **345**

League of United Latin American Citizens Hispanic civil rights organization formed in 1929. **604**

legislative branch Division of the government that proposes bills and passes them into laws. **32**

Lend-Lease Act (1941) Law that allowed the United States to loan weapons and other war supplies to Britain, and later to the Soviet Union, to fight against the Axis Powers in World War II. **478**

Levittown Early example of a preplanned and mass-produced housing development; created by William Levitt on Long Island in New York. **548**

Liberty bonds U.S. bonds sold during World War I to raise money for loans to the Allies. **337**

Limited Nuclear Test Ban Treaty (1963) Agreement signed by U.S. president John F. Kennedy and Soviet leader Nikita Khrushchev to ban above-ground testing of new nuclear weapons. **577**

Little Rock Nine African American students who first integrated Central High School in Little Rock, Arkansas, in 1957. **556**

Long March (1934) Year-long retreat of Chinese Communists to escape a Chinese Nationalist army attack. **522**

Long Walk (1864) Three-hundred-mile march made by Navajo captives to a reservation in Bosque Redondo, New Mexico, that led to the deaths of hundreds of Navajo. **155**

loose construction Way of interpreting the Constitution that allows the federal government to take reasonable actions that the Constitution does not specifically forbid it from taking. **84**

Los Angeles Riots (1992) Riots that erupted after the verdict in the Rodney King case, in which police officers were found not guilty of using excessive force against an African American motorist. **719**

Lost Generation A group of writers who reacted to the death and destruction of World War I by criticizing post-war society. **402**

Louisiana Purchase (1803) Purchase of French land between the Mississippi River and the Rocky Mountains that doubled the size of the United States. **89**

Lusitania British passenger liner sunk by a German U-boat in May 1915; the deaths of 128 Americans on board contributed to U.S. entry into World War I. **333**

Maginot Line Fortified wall that France built along its border with Germany after World War I. **476**

mandate Public support. **571**

Manhattan Project Secret Allied project begun in 1942 to develop an atomic bomb. **496**

manifest destiny Belief shared by many Americans in the mid-1800s that the United States should expand across the continent to the Pacific Ocean. **103**

Marshall Plan U.S. program of giving aid to European countries to help them rebuild their economies after World War II. **514**

Massacre at Wounded Knee (1890) U.S. Army's killing of approximately 150 Sioux at Wounded Knee Creek in South Dakota; ended U.S.-Indian wars on the Great Plains. **157**

mass culture Leisure and cultural activities shared by large numbers of people. **222**

massive retaliation The strategy of threatening to use nuclear weapons in order to stop communist aggression. **540**

mass transit Public transportation. **217**

Mayflower Compact (1620) Legal contract written by the Pilgrims to specify basic laws and social rules for their colony. **15**

McCarthyism Method of making vicious accusations without offering proof; named after Senator Joseph McCarthy. **529**

McKinley Tariff (1890) Law that allowed all countries to ship sugar duty-free to the United States; a serious blow to Hawaiian sugar producers. **289**

Medicaid (1965) Federal health insurance program for people with low incomes. **581**

Medicare (1965) Federal health care program for people over the age of 65. **581**

Mexican American Youth Organization (MAYO) Group formed in 1967 by José Angel Gutiérrez to help fight discrimination. **608**

Mexican Cession Land that Mexico ceded to the United States after the Mexican War through the Treaty of Guadalupe Hidalgo; included present-day California, Nevada, and Utah, most of Arizona and New Mexico, and parts of Colorado, Texas, and Wyoming. **104**

Mexican Revolution Revolution begun in 1910 by Francisco Madero against Mexican dictator Porfirio Díaz. **308**

MIAs Soldiers who are missing in action. **640**

Middle Ages Period of European history that lasted from the late 400s until around 1350. **8**

Middle Passage Voyage that brought enslaved Africans across the Atlantic Ocean to North America and the West Indies. **19**

migration Movement of people from one region to another. **6**

militarism Policy of aggressive military preparedness. **326**

Missouri Compromise (1820) Agreement proposed by Henry Clay that allowed Missouri to enter the Union as a slave state, Maine to enter as a free state, and outlawed slavery in any territories or states formed north of the 36°30′ line. **91**

mobilize Prepare a military force for war. **327**

Model T Car created by Henry Ford in 1908 that was priced low enough that many Americans could afford to buy it; also known as the Tin Lizzie. **367**

monopoly Sole economic control of a business or product. **10**

Monroe Doctrine (1823) President James Monroe's statement warning European nations not to colonize or interfere in the Americas. **91**

Montgomery bus boycott (1955–56) African American boycott of the city buses in Montgomery, Alabama, that led to the changing of discriminatory bus rules. **558**

Montgomery Improvement Association Organization formed by African Americans in Montgomery, Alabama, in 1956 to strengthen the bus boycott and to coordinate the protest efforts of African Americans; led by Martin Luther King Jr. **558**

Morrill Act (1862) Federal law that gave land to western states to encourage them to build colleges. **170**

Motown Records First major record label owned by an African American; founded by businessman Berry Gordy in 1959. **586**

muckrakers Journalists who wrote about corruption in business and politics in order to bring about reform. **242**

mugwumps Algonquian word for "big chiefs"; referred to Republican reformers in the 1880s who supported Democrat Grover Cleveland in the presidential election of 1884. **239**

Munich Conference (1938) Meeting between British, French, and German leaders in which Germany was given control of the Sudetenland in exchange for German leader Adolf Hitler's promise to make no more claims on European territory. **476**

National Aeronautics and Space Administration (NASA) Agency established by Congress in 1958 to conduct space research. **540**

National American Woman Suffrage Association (NAWSA) Group formed in 1890 by Elizabeth Cady Stanton and Susan B. Anthony to win the vote for women. **256**

National Association for the Advancement of Colored People (NAACP) Group formed by W. E. B. Du Bois and others in 1909 to pursue the goals of economic, educational, and social equality for African Americans; inspired by the Niagara Movement. **259**

National Association of Colored Women Group led by Mary Church Terrell that supported political reforms for African Americans, including women's suffrage and protecting the voting rights of black men in the South. **260**

National Grange Social and educational organization founded in 1867 to gain more political representation for farmers and to improve their living standards. **201**

National Industrial Recovery Act (NIRA) (1933) Federal law to encourage economic growth by suspending antitrust laws and eliminating unfair competition among employers; declared unconstitutional in 1935. **434**

nationalism The feeling that a specific nation, language, or culture is superior to others. **326**

National Labor Relations Act (NLRA) (1935) Federal law that made unions and collective bargaining legal; also known as the Wagner-Connery Act. **448**

National Liberation Front (NLF) Organization formed to fight Ngo Dinh Diem's government in South Vietnam. **626**

National Organization for Women (NOW) Group formed in 1966 by Betty Friedan and other feminists to increase women's political power. **611**

National Origins Act (1924) Law that reduced immigration, gave preference to northern and western European immigrants, and banned Japanese immigrants. **388**

National Park Service Federal organization created in 1916 to supervise U.S. parks and monuments. **271**

National Traffic and Motor Vehicle Safety Act (1966) Law that required the federal government to enact safety standards for all cars sold in the United States. **591**

National War Labor Board Agency created by President Woodrow Wilson in 1918 to settle disputes between workers and management. **338**

National Woman's Party (NWP) Organization founded by Alice Paul in 1913 that used controversial methods to help women win the vote. **257**

nativists U.S. citizens who opposed immigration because they were suspicious of immigrants and feared losing jobs to them. **95**

Nat Turner's Rebellion (1831) Rebellion in which Nat Turner and a group of Virginia slaves killed local planter families in an unsuccessful attempt to overthrow slavery. **98**

naturalization Legal process by which a foreign-born person becomes a U.S. citizen. **70**

Navigation Acts (1650–96) A series of English laws that regulated trade in the American colonies in order to increase England's profits. **19**

Nazis National Socialist Party; political group led by Adolf Hitler that rose to power in Germany during the 1930s. **464**

Neutrality Acts Four laws passed in the late 1930s that were designed to keep the United States out of international incidents. **467**

New Deal President Franklin D. Roosevelt's programs for helping the U.S. economy during the Great Depression. **431**

New Federalism A system of revenue sharing proposed by President Richard Nixon that had the federal government give money to the states to use as they saw fit. **656**

New Freedom Woodrow Wilson's program during the presidential campaign of 1912 that called for government action against monopolies to ensure free competition. **276**

New Frontier A set of domestic and foreign-policy proposals announced by President John F. Kennedy in his 1961 inaugural address. **571**

new immigrants Immigrants who came to the United States during and after the 1880s; most were from southern and eastern Europe. **210**

New Nationalism Theodore Roosevelt's plan for government that called for a strong executive, more active business regulation, and additional social welfare measures; Roosevelt ran on this platform in the 1912 presidential election. **275**

New Right Conservative voters' groups that grew in strength during the 1980s. **682**

Niagara Movement Group of African Americans, including W. E. B. Du Bois, formed in 1905 that demanded economic and educational equality, as well as an end to segregation and discrimination. **259**

nickelodeons Early motion picture theaters; so called because admission was usually a nickel. **396**

Nineteenth Amendment (1920) Constitutional amendment that gave women the vote. **257**

no-man's-land Strip of land between the trenches of opposing armies along the western front during World War I. **330**

nonaggression pact (1939) Secret agreement between German leader Adolf Hitler and Soviet leader Joseph Stalin not to attack one another and to divide Poland. **476**

North American Free Trade Agreement (NAFTA) (1993) Trade agreement between the United States, Canada, and Mexico. **709**

North Atlantic Treaty Organization (NATO) Military alliance formed in 1949 by the United States, Britain, and 10 other countries to help defend each other in case of attack. **517**

Northwest Passage A waterway in North America that would allow ships to sail from the Atlantic to the Pacific Oceans; early explorers searched for but never found it. **12**

Nuremberg Trials (1945) War crimes trials of high-ranking Nazi officials held by the International Military Tribunal in Nuremberg, Germany. **511**

Ohio Gang Group of President Warren Harding's friends from Ohio, many of whom were involved in a series of government scandals. **363**

old immigrants Immigrants who came to the United States before the 1880s; most were from northern Europe. **210**

Open Door Policy (1899) Declaration made by Secretary of State John Hay that all nations should have equal access to trade with China. **293**

open range Public land used by ranchers to graze herds. **165**

Operation Desert Fox (1998) A series of joint U.S. and British air strikes against Iraq after the nation refused to allow United Nations weapons inspectors to perform their job. **716**

Operation Desert Storm (1991) United Nations invasion led by the United States to make Iraq withdraw from Kuwait. **697**

Operation Restore Hope A United Nations relief effort in the early to mid-1990s to help provide food to starving people in Somalia, where a civil war was taking place. **714**

Operation Rolling Thunder A series of air strikes launched by the United States during the Vietnam War to destroy North Vietnam's war industries. **628**

Oregon Trail A 2,000-mile trail stretching from western Missouri to Oregon Territory. **102**

Organization of Petroleum Exporting Countries (OPEC) Alliance formed by five major oil-producing nations in 1960 to maintain high prices by controlling the production and sale of oil. **657**

pacification Policy followed by U.S. and South Vietnamese officials of trying to protect villagers by creating civilian areas guarded by government troops. **629**

Pacific Railway Acts (1862, 1864) Two laws passed by the federal government that gave loans and land grants to railroad companies to encourage them to build a transcontinental railroad. **160**

Paleo-Indians The first Americans who crossed from Asia into North America sometime between 50,000 and 10,000 B.C. **6**

Palmer raids (1920) Raids ordered by Attorney General A. Mitchell Palmer on suspected radical organizations. **360**

Panama Canal Canal built across the Isthmus of Panama to link the Atlantic and Pacific Oceans; opened in 1914. **304**

Panama Canal treaties (1977) Agreement made between U.S. and Panamanian leaders to transfer control of the Panama Canal to Panama by the year 2000. **669**

Panic of 1873 A U.S. financial crisis; beginning of an economic downturn that weakened the Republican Party. **139**

Panic of 1929 Continued drop in stock prices following Black Tuesday. **421**

pardons Freedom from punishment. **41**

Paris Peace Accords (1973) Agreement made by leaders of the National Liberation Front, North Vietnam, South Vietnam, and the United States to end the Vietnam War; called for the removal of all U.S. troops from Vietnam, the return of American prisoners of war, and the establishment of a demilitarized buffer zone to separate North Vietnam and South Vietnam. **639**

Parliament The British legislature. **19**

patent Exclusive right to manufacture or sell an invention. **185**

Payne-Aldrich Tariff Act passed in 1909 that reduced some tariffs but raised others. **274**

Peace Corps President John F. Kennedy's program that sends American volunteers to assist developing nations with improvement projects. **574**

Pendleton Civil Service Act (1883) Act that established a merit system for awarding federal jobs. **240**

perestroika Soviet policy established in the 1980s that initiated political and economic reforms. **691**

petition A formal request. **66**

Platt Amendment (1902) Amendment to the Cuban constitution that gave the United States the right to become involved in Cuba's foreign and domestic affairs; was in effect until 1934. **300**

Plessy* v. *Ferguson (1896) Supreme Court case that established the separate-but-equal doctrine for public facilities. **141**

political action committees (PACs) Organizations that collect money to contribute to candidates who support the same issues as the contributors. **73**

political machines Political organizations that used legal and illegal methods to ensure that their candidates won elections. **238**

political parties Groups of people who organize to help elect government officials and influence government policies. **86**

poll tax A special tax that a person had to pay in order to vote. **140**

Pontiac's Rebellion (1763) Unsuccessful attack by Ottawa chief Pontiac and his allies against British forts on the northwestern frontier in an attempt to drive out European settlers. **21**

Pony Express A system of messengers on horseback established in 1860 to carry mail across the United States. **160**

pop art Art movement that challenged the values of traditional art by using popular, commonplace images and objects. **585**

Populist Party National political party formed in 1891 that supported free coinage of silver, labor reforms, immigration restrictions, and government ownership of railroads and the telegraph and telephone systems. **203**

Potsdam Conference (1945) Meeting of U.S. president Harry S Truman, British prime minister Winston Churchill, and Soviet leader Joseph Stalin after Germany's surrender in World War II, at which they divided Germany and Austria into four zones of occupation. **510**

progressives Group of reformers who worked to improve social and political problems, beginning in the late 1800s. **241**

prohibition The banning of the manufacture, sale, and transportation of alcohol. **383**

Protestant Reformation Religious movement begun by Martin Luther and others in 1517 to reform the Catholic Church. **13**

public works Building projects such as hospitals, roads, and schools funded by federal money. **429**

Pullman Strike (1894) Railroad strike by workers at Pullman's Palace Car Company that stopped traffic on many railroad lines until federal courts ordered the workers to return to their jobs. **199**

Pure Food and Drug Act (1906) Legislation that prohibited the manufacture, sale, or transportation of mislabeled or contaminated food and drugs through interstate commerce. **268**

Radical Republicans Members of Congress who felt that southern states needed to make great social changes before they could be readmitted into the Union. **131**

range rights Rights to water sources on the Great Plains; ranchers bought these rights to give them exclusive control of both the water and the land around it. **165**

range wars Battles among large ranchers, small ranchers, and farmers on the Great Plains for use of the open range. **168**

realism A writing style that became popular during the late 1800s that concentrates on presenting accurate images of American society. **225**

realpolitik German word meaning "practical politics"; policy developed by Henry Kissinger and implemented by President Richard Nixon that put American interests, rather than political or moral ideals, first in foreign-policy decisions. **658**

recall Measure allowing voters to remove an official from office before his or her term is over. **243**

Reconstruction (1865–77) Period following the Civil War during which the U.S. government worked to rebuild the southern states and reunite the nation. **125**

Reconstruction Acts (1867–68) Laws that put the southern states under military control and required them to draft new constitutions upholding the Fourteenth Amendment. **133**

Reconstruction Finance Corporation (RFC) (1932) Organization established by President Herbert Hoover to loan money to businesses and banks to help them keep operating. **429**

Redeemers Group of southern Democrats that helped return the Democratic Party to political power in the South during Reconstruction and tried to limit the civil rights of African Americans. **140**

Red Scare A wave of anticommunist fear that swept the United States after World War I. **359**

referendum Measure allowing citizens to vote on proposed laws. **243**

regionalists Painters during the 1930s who sought inspiration from regional customs and folk themes. **458**

relief Food, clothing, shelter, and money provided to people in need. **427**

reparations Payments for damages and expenses brought on by war. **346**

representative democracy Government by elected representatives of the people. 38

Republican Party Political party formed in 1854 to stop the spread of slavery to the West. 106

Republic of Texas Independent nation of Texas that existed from 1836 to 1845, when Texas was annexed by the United States. 102

reservations Federal lands set aside for American Indians. 152

reserved powers Powers retained by the state governments or by citizens. 38

rock 'n' roll Musical style developed in the 1950s that drew heavily from African American rhythm and blues and used new instruments such as electric guitars. 553

Roosevelt Corollary (1904) President Theodore Roosevelt's addition to the Monroe Doctrine; declared that the United States would police affairs in the Western Hemisphere to keep Europeans from intervening in the region. 306

roundup Act of driving cattle together and collecting them in a herd. 166

Rural Electrification Administration Organization established during the Second New Deal that extended electrical power lines into isolated rural areas. 439

sanctions Economic penalties. 670

Sand Creek Massacre (1864) Surprise attack led by Colonel John M. Chivington in which some 200 peaceful Cheyenne in southeastern Colorado were killed. 153

Sandinistas Revolutionary political party in Nicaragua that overthrew a pro-American dictator in 1979. 688

Saturday Night Massacre Name given to the series of events that included the firing of a special prosecutor investigating Watergate and the resignations of the U.S. attorney general and his next in command for refusing to fire the prosecutor. 662

scalawags Name that southern Democrats gave to white southern Republicans during Reconstruction; means "liars and cheats." 136

Scopes trial (1925) Trial of John T. Scopes, a high school science teacher who was arrested in Dayton, Tennessee, and tried for teaching Darwin's theory of evolution. 386

search-and-destroy missions U.S. strategy in the Vietnam War in which U.S. patrols searched for hidden enemy camps and supplies and destroyed them with massive firepower and air raids. 629

search warrant A judge's order authorizing the search of a person's home or property to look for evidence relating to a crime. 67

Second Battle of the Marne (1918) Last offensive launched by the Germans during World War I and a turning point of the war for the Allies. 341

Second Great Awakening A period of religious evangelism that began in the 1790s and became widespread in the United States by the 1830s. 98

Second Industrial Revolution A period of explosive growth in manufacturing and industry in the late 1800s. 184

Second New Deal New program of reforms proposed by President Franklin D. Roosevelt's administration in 1935. 438

segregation Forced separation of people of different races in public places. 140

Selective Service Act (1917) Law that required men between the ages of 21 and 30 to register for the draft into the armed forces. 336

Selective Training and Service Act (1940) First peacetime draft in U.S. history. 481

self-determination Right of people to decide their own political status. 345

Seneca Falls Convention (1848) National women's rights convention; site at which the Declaration of Sentiments was written. 99

settlement houses Neighborhood centers that arose in the late 1800s to offer education, recreation, and social activities to immigrants and poor people. 221

Seventeenth Amendment (1913) Constitutional amendment allowing American voters to directly elect U.S. senators. 243

sharecropping System used on southern farms after the Civil War in which sharecroppers worked land owned by someone else in return for a small share of the crops. 142

Share-Our-Wealth Plan organized in 1934 by U.S. senator Huey Long that called for the federal government to limit the size of all personal fortunes so that every family would be guaranteed a minimum income of $2,500 a year. 438

Sherman Antitrust Act (1890) Law that made it illegal to create monopolies or trusts that restrained trade. 194

Sherman Silver Purchase Act (1890) Law that increased the amount of silver purchased by the U.S. government for coinage. 203

silent generation Name given to teenagers and college students in the 1950s because many of them seemed to conform to social expectations without protest. 551

Silent Majority President Richard Nixon's term for a large group of conservative voters who disliked the changes that took place in the 1960s. 656

Silk Road Overland trade route from China as far west as the Black Sea. 9

sit-down strike Type of strike in which striking workers refuse to work or to leave the factories so that owners cannot replace them. 448

sit-in Demonstration in which protesters sit down in a location and refuse to leave. 596

Sixteenth Amendment (1913) Constitutional amendment that allowed the federal government to pass direct taxes, such as an income tax. 279

Smoot-Hawley Tariff (1930) Legislation that raised U.S. duties on imports to all-time highs; caused foreign governments to raise their own trade restrictions. 424

socialism Economic system in which the government or the workers own and operate the means of production. 251

Social Security Act (1935) Law that created Social Security, which provides retirement pensions and unemployment insurance to U.S. workers. 438

societies Groups of people who live together and share a culture. 6

Society of American Indians Group founded in 1911 by several American Indians to assist Indians living on reservations. 260

sodbusters Name given to both the Plains farmers and the plows they used to break up the region's tough sod. 173

Southern Christian Leadership Conference Group founded by Martin Luther King Jr. and other ministers that helped lead the struggle for civil rights. **559**

southern strategy The Republican Party's attempt to win the support of southern Democrats and others who opposed civil rights reform by limiting further civil rights legislation. **656**

Southern Tenant Farmers' Union (STFU) Group formed by tenants, sharecroppers, and farm laborers in 1934 to bring attention to the problems these groups faced. **449**

Spanish Armada Large Spanish naval fleet defeated by England in 1588. **13**

speakeasies Secret, illegal clubs that served alcohol during prohibition. **384**

speculation The investing of money in a high-risk venture in hopes of making a profit. **420**

spheres of influence Areas of a country, particularly in China during the late 1800s, where foreign nations control much of the trade and natural resources. **292**

Sputnik (1957) The world's first artificial satellite; launched by the Soviet Union. **540**

Square Deal Political program designed by President Theodore Roosevelt to treat every citizen fairly; approach was applied to resolving disputes between labor and management in business. **267**

stagflation Economic situation characterized by both high inflation and high unemployment. **656**

stalemate Situation in which neither side of a conflict can win a decisive victory. **330**

Stamp Act (1765) Law passed by Parliament that raised tax money by requiring colonists to pay for an official stamp whenever they bought paper items, such as newspapers, licenses, and legal documents. **22**

states' rights Belief that the power of the states should be greater than the power of the federal government. **92**

steerage Area in a ship's lower levels; many immigrants who came to the United States traveled in this less-expensive space. **210**

Strategic Arms Limitation Talks (SALT) (1972) Talks between U.S. president Richard Nixon and Soviet leader Leonid Brezhnev that led to a treaty limiting the numbers and types of long-range nuclear missiles each country could have. **659**

Strategic Defense Initiative (SDI) A plan for a space-based defense system to protect the United States from Soviet missiles. **690**

strict construction Way of interpreting the Constitution that allows the federal government to take only the actions the Constitution specifically says it can take. **84**

Student Nonviolent Coordinating Committee (SNCC) Student organization formed in 1960 to coordinate civil rights demonstrations and provide training for protesters. **596**

Students for a Democratic Society (SDS) Student group that actively protested discrimination, rigid college rules, and the growing U.S. presence in Vietnam. **584**

subsidy Bonus payment. **290**

suburbs Residential neighborhoods outside a city. **217**

Suez Canal crisis International crisis that began in 1956 when Britain, France, and Israel invaded the Suez Canal region in Egypt. **542**

Sun Belt States in the South and Southwest that attracted many new people and businesses in the 1950s because of low tax rates, a warm climate, and job opportunities. **546**

supply-side economics Economic theory stating that government tax cuts would lead to increased economic activity, increased tax revenues, and a balanced budget. **683**

***Sussex* pledge** (1916) Promise issued by German leaders during World War I not to sink merchant vessels without warning. **333**

swing New style of jazz developed by big-band leaders during the 1930s. **459**

synthetic Artificial. **374**

Taft-Hartley Act (1947) Law that gave the federal government greater authority to end strikes and required union leaders to take an oath stating that they were not Communists. **520**

talkies Movies with sound or dialogue. **396**

Teapot Dome scandal Scandal during President Warren Harding's administration involving Secretary of the Interior Albert Fall's leasing of oil reserves in return for personal gifts and loans. **364**

Teller Amendment (1898) Amendment to a U.S. resolution declaring that the United States did not intend to take over and annex an independent Cuba. **296**

temperance movement A social reform effort begun in the mid-1800s to encourage people to limit their alcohol consumption. **100**

tenements Poorly built, overcrowded housing where many immigrants lived. **211**

Tennessee Valley Authority (TVA) (1933) New Deal program that built dams to provide hydroelectric power and flood control to the Tennessee River valley. **436**

terrorism Use of violent attacks by individuals or small groups to advance political goals. **710**

Tet Offensive (1968) Attack by North Vietnamese and Vietcong troops against South Vietnam during the Vietnam War; took place during Tet (the Vietnamese New Year) and demonstrated that the North Vietnamese were still militarily strong. **633**

Texas longhorn Hardy breed of cow raised by ranchers throughout western Texas. **164**

Thirteenth Amendment (1865) Constitutional amendment that outlawed slavery. **126**

38th parallel Line of latitude that divides North Korea and South Korea. **523**

Three-Fifths Compromise (1787) Agreement worked out at the Constitutional Convention stating that three fifths of the slaves in each state would be counted as part of the state's population for determining representation in the lower house of Congress. **32**

Tonkin Gulf Resolution (1964) Congressional measure that gave President Lyndon B. Johnson the authority to wage war in Vietnam. **627**

totalitarianism Political system in which the government controls every aspect of citizens' lives. **463**

town meetings Political meetings, first started in New England, at which people make decisions on local issues. **16**

Townshend Acts (1767) Laws passed by Parliament placing duties on certain items imported by the colonists. **22**

trade deficit An imbalance in which a nation imports more than it exports. **664**

769

transcontinental railroad A railroad that crossed the continental United States, connecting the East to the West. **160**

Transportation Revolution Rapid growth in the speed and convenience of transportation; began in the United States in the early 1800s. **95**

Treaty of Brest-Litovsk (1918) Peace agreement between the Central Powers and Russia that removed Russia from World War I. **340**

Treaty of Ghent (1814) Treaty between the United States and Britain that ended the War of 1812. **91**

Treaty of Guadalupe Hidalgo (1848) Treaty that ended the Mexican War and ceded much of Mexico's northern territory to the United States. **104**

Treaty of Medicine Lodge (1867) Agreement between the U.S. government and southern Plains Indians in which most of the tribes agreed to live on reservations. **154**

Treaty of Paris of 1783 Peace agreement that officially ended the Revolutionary War and established British recognition of the United States. **25**

Treaty of Versailles (1919) Treaty ending World War I that required Germany to pay billions of dollars of war costs and established the League of Nations. **347**

trench warfare World War I military strategy of defending a position by fighting from the protection of deep ditches. **329**

Triangle Shirtwaist Factory Fire Accident at a New York City factory in which 146 workers died after a fire broke out in the building; helped spur legislation to improve factory safety standards. **248**

Triple Alliance Military alliance formed by Austria-Hungary, Germany, and Italy in the late 1800s. **326**

Triple Entente Military alliance formed by Britain, France, and Russia in 1907. **326**

Truman Doctrine (1947) President Harry S Truman's policy stating that the United States would provide economic aid to any country fighting against communism. **514**

trust Legal arrangement grouping several companies under one board of directors to eliminate competition and to regulate production. **191**

Twelfth Amendment (1804) Constitutional amendment that created a separate ballot for president and vice president. **87**

Twenty-first Amendment (1933) Constitutional amendment that ended national prohibition by repealing the Eighteenth Amendment. **385**

Twenty-sixth Amendment (1971) Constitutional amendment that lowered the federal voting age from 21 to 18. **638**

U-boats German submarines. **330**

Underwood Tariff Act (1913) Act that significantly lowered U.S. tariff rates and introduced the first modern personal income tax. **279**

United Farm Workers (UFW) Union formed by César Chávez to improve pay and working conditions for migrant farm-workers. **606**

United Mine Workers (UMW) Union of coal mine workers that went on strike in 1946. **520**

United Nations (UN) International organization chartered in 1945 to promote world peace and resolve conflicts between nations. **510**

Universal Negro Improvement Association (UNIA) Association founded by Marcus Garvey in 1914 to end imperialism in Africa and discrimination in the United States. **389**

University of California* v. *Bakke (1978) Supreme Court case that ruled that a white applicant had been unfairly denied admission to medical school because the university followed a quota system based on race. **601**

urban renewal Program launched by the federal government to improve life in U.S. cities through better public services and new housing projects. **549**

U-2 incident (1960) Event in which the Soviets shot down a U.S. U-2 spy plane over the Soviet Union. **543**

vaqueros Mexican cowboys in the West who tended cattle and horses. **166**

vertical integration Ownership of businesses involved in each step of a manufacturing process. **191**

veto To cancel legislation. **40**

Vietcong Communist guerrilla force that functioned as the National Liberation Front's army and began fighting against Ngo Dinh Diem's government in South Vietnam in the 1950s. **626**

Vietminh Group of Vietnamese nationalists organized in the 1940s by Ho Chi Minh to drive the Japanese out of Vietnam; also known as the League for the Independence of Vietnam. **624**

Vietnamization Policy followed by the Nixon administration of gradually turning over all the fighting in the Vietnam War to the South Vietnamese Army. **636**

Vietnam Veterans Memorial Memorial in Washington, D.C., dedicated in 1982 to honor Americans who died in or went missing in the Vietnam War. **641**

Volstead Act (1919) Legislation that established federal penalties for the manufacture and sale of alcohol during prohibition. **383**

Voting Rights Act of 1965 Law that protected all citizens' right to vote. **599**

Voting Rights Act of 1975 Legislation that required areas with large immigrant populations to provide ballots in the voters' preferred language. **609**

War Industries Board (WIB) Agency created by President Woodrow Wilson during World War I to oversee the production and distribution of goods manufactured by the nation's war industries. **337**

War on Drugs President George Bush's organized effort to end the trade and use of illegal drugs both in the United States and abroad. **693**

War on Poverty President Lyndon B. Johnson's programs to help poor Americans. **580**

War Powers Act (1973) Legislation that required the president to get congressional approval before committing U.S. troops to an armed struggle. **641**

War Production Board (WPB) World War II agency that oversaw the conversion of factories to war production. **481**

Warren Commission Special group appointed by President Lyndon B. Johnson to investigate the assassination of President John F. Kennedy. **579**

Washington Conference (1921) Meeting among the United States and the world's major nations to discuss disarmament. **365**

Watergate Scandal in which President Richard Nixon authorized a cover-up of a break-in at the Democratic National Committee headquarters; led to Nixon's resignation in 1974. **660**

welfare state System of government institutions that provides for basic needs of citizens. **443**

Whiskey Rebellion (1794) Protest by small farmers in Pennsylvania against new taxes on whiskey and other alcohol. **85**

Wisconsin Idea Governor Robert La Follette's program of reforms for Wisconsin in the early 1900s; became a model for other state governments. **244**

Woman's Christian Temperance Union Women's reform organization founded in 1874 to fight alcohol abuse. **255**

Woodstock (1969) Concert that took place near Woodstock, New York; became a symbol of the counterculture's idealistic spirit. **587**

Works Progress Administration (WPA) (1935) New Deal agency created to put American men and women to work repairing bridges, roads, buildings, and parks. **439**

xenophobia Fear and hatred of foreigners. **360**

XYZ affair (1797) Incident in which French agents attempted to get a bribe from U.S. diplomats in exchange for discussions on French-U.S. relations; led to an undeclared naval war between the United States and France. **87**

Yalta Conference (1945) Meeting of U.S. president Franklin D. Roosevelt, British prime minister Winston Churchill, and Soviet leader Joseph Stalin during World War II to plan for the postwar world. **510**

yellow journalism The use of sensational, often exaggerated stories in newspapers or other publications to attract readers. **295**

Zimmerman Note Telegram sent by Germany's foreign minister to Mexico during World War I proposing an alliance between the two countries. **334**

zoot-suit riots (1943) Attacks by U.S. sailors against Mexican Americans in Los Angeles. **483**

771

Index

Key to Index

c = *chart* m = *map*
f = *feature* p = *photo*

A&P (grocery chain), 371
ABC Powers, 310
abolition, 98, 107
Absalom, Absalom! (William Faulkner), 458
Abzug, Bella, 614, *p614*
Acquired Immune Deficiency Syndrome (AIDS), 699, *p699*
Adams, Ansel, 403, *p403,* 405
Adams, John, 84, 86, 87, *p87, p738*
Adams, John Quincy, 92, *p738*
Adams, Samuel, 21
Adamson Act, 283
Adams-Onís Treaty, 91
Addams, Jane, *f220,* 221, 259, 276, 338
Adena (culture), 6
Adventures of Tom Sawyer (Mark Twain), 145
advertising, 224; consumerism and, in 1920s, 372, *p372;* on radio, 394; on television, 551
affirmative action, 601
AFL–CIO, 545. *See also* American Federation of Labor, Congress of Industrial Organizations, unions (labor)
Africa, *mxxx;* ancient kingdoms in, 9; black nationalism and, 359–60; Columbian Exchange and, 12; international trade and, 9–10, *m317;* Middle Passage, 19; Peace Corps and, *f574;* political changes in 1990s, 715, *p715;* U.S. foreign policy and, 573, 669–70; World War II and, *m477,* 484–86, *m487. See also* individual African nations
African Americans: abolition movement, 98–99; armed forces and, 109, 297, 336, 342, *p343,* 481, *p481,* 555; artists, 403, 458; blues and, 399–400, *p400;* Black Cabinet, 456, *p456;* Black Codes and, 130–31, *p131;* black nationalism and, 389–90; Black Panther Party, 600; Black Power, 600, *p600;* boycotts and, 558–59; business efforts and, 258–59, 374, *p374,* 389–90; Civil Rights Act of 1866, 132; Civil Rights Act of 1875, 139; civil rights movement, 554–59, *p554, p557, p558, f558, p559,* 595–601, *p596, m597, f598, p599, p600;* in Civil War, 109; desegregation and 555–57, *p557, p559,* 598, 601; *Dred Scott* decision, 107; early colleges and universities, *f127;* education and, 100, 126–28, *f127,* 555–57, *p556,* 601, *p601;* election of 1936 and, 441; Emancipation Proclamation, 109, *f112–13;* Exodusters, 171, *p171;* farmers' alliances in late 1800s and, 203, *p204;* Fifteenth Amendment and, 135, *p135;* Ford Motor Company and, 369; Fourteenth Amendment and, 132; freepeople in South, 124–25, *p125, m126;* Great Depression and, 425, 454–56, *p456,* 458; the Great Migration and, 389, 410–11, *c410, m411;* Harlem Renaissance, 400–02, *m401, p402,* 403; jazz and, 399–400, *p400,* 459, *p459;* Ku Klux Klan and, 138–39, 389; literature of, 145, *f146,* 401, 458, 551; lynchings, 259, 361, 456; March on Washington, *p594,* 598, *p598, f602;* migration to northern cities in 1890s, 215; music of, 146–47, *p147,* 399–400, *p400,* 402, 459, *p459,* 553; NAACP and, 259–60, *p282,* 389, 555–58; New Deal programs for, 455–56, *p456;* in politics, 40, 137, *f137,* 581, 601, 615; progressive reform and, 258–60, *p258, p259;* as property owners, *c143;* race riots, 133, *p133,* 361, *p361,* 600, 601, 719; racial discrimination, 410–11, *m411,* 482; during Reagan years, 686; Reconstruction and, 130–31, *p131,* 133, *p133,* 135, *p135,* 137, *p137;* religion and, 98, 220, *p220;* in Franklin D. Roosevelt's administration, 456; segregation and, 140–41, *p140,* 397, 554–56, *p555, p556,* 595–97, *p595,* 598, 601; settlement houses and, 221; slavery in the South, 97–98, *p98;* in Spanish-American War, 297; sports and, 244, 397, 461, 720, *p720;* support of Harry S Truman, 521, 555; as Supreme Court justices, 43, 694; theater and, 402, *p402;* Thirteenth Amendment and, 126; union membership and, *p196,* 448; voting rights, 135, 140, 554, 599; in the West, *p152,* 166, *p166;* women's rights movement and, 612; Woodrow Wilson and, 281–82; in World War I, 336, 342, *p343;* in World War II, 481–82, *p481;* writers, 145, *f146,* 401, 458, 551
African National Congress (ANC), 714
Agee, James, 458
ageism, 618
Agent Orange, 628
Agnew, Spiro, 662
Agricultural Adjustment Act (AAA) of 1933, 435–36, *c441,* 449
Agricultural Adjustment Act (AAA) of 1938, 452
Agricultural Labor Relations Act, 606
Agricultural Marketing Act, 429
agriculture: colonial, 17, 19–20; during 1920s, 376–77, *c377;* 423; Great Depression and, 449–50, *p449, p450, m450, f451;* Hoover's aid policies and, 429; New Deal programs and, 435–36, 452; Populism and, 202–05, *m202;* in the South, 97, *c97,* 142–43, *c144. See also* farmers, farming, migrant workers
Aguinaldo, Emilio, 296
AIDS. *See* Acquired Immune Deficiency Syndrome
Aid to Families with Dependent Children (AFDC): 1990s reform of, 711
airplane, 188, *p188,* 330, *f331*
air traffic controllers, 684–85, *p684*
Alabama, *mxx, c743;* civil rights movement and, 596–98, *m597,* 599; Reconstruction and, 134, *m134;* secession and, 107
Alamogordo, New Mexico, 496
Alaska, *mxx, p289, c743;* gold rush in, 288; purchase of, from Russia, 288
Albanians: war in the Balkans and, 717
Albright, Madeleine, 71, *p613,* 715
Alcatraz Island, 617
alcohol. *See* prohibition
Alcott, Louisa May, 225
Aldrich, Nelson, *p274*
Aldrin, Edwin "Buzz," 589
Aleut, 6, *m7*
Aleutian Islands, 490–91, *m493*
Algeria: OPEC member nation, *m657*
Algonquian, *m7,* 8, 14
Alien and Sedition Acts, 87
Allen, Florence, 454
Allen, Frederick Lewis, 373
Alliance for Progress, 574
Allied Powers: World War I and, 328–30, 332–34, *m332,* 339–47, *p340, m342, p343, p344, m347;* World War II and, 476–79, *m477,* 484–89, *p486, m487, f488, p489,* 491–94, *p491, p492, m493,* 495–96, *p496*
Altman, Robert, 676
amendments, 33. *See also* individual amendments
American Anti-Slavery Society, 98
American Civil Liberties Union (ACLU), 386; Sacco and Vanzetti trial and, 360
American Expeditionary Force, 339
American Farm Bureau Federation, 73
American Federation of Labor (AFL), 197, 250–51, *c251,* 546; strikes and, 356–58, *p358. See also* strikes, unions (labor)
American GI Forum, 604
American Gothic (Grant Wood), *p458*
American Independent Party, 635
American Indian Movement (AIM), 617, *p617*
American Indians, *m7, m153;* Aleut, 6; Algonquian, 8, 14; American Indian Movement (AIM), 617, *p617;* Apache, 8, 152, 156; Arapaho, 152; Aztec, 12; Battle of Fallen Timbers, 85; Battle of the Little Bighorn, *m153,* 154, *p154;* Battle of Tippecanoe, 90; Black Kettle, 152–53; buffalo and, 151–52; Bureau of Indian Affairs, 93, 152, 455; Cherokee, 93; Cheyenne, 152; Chickasaw, 93; Chief Joseph, 155–56, *f155;* Choctaw, 93; civil rights movement and, 616–17; Columbian Exchange and, 12; Comanche, 152, 154; conflict with settlers and U.S. government, 85, 90–91, 152–54, *m153, p154;* Crazy Horse, 153, 154; Creek, 91, 93; Dawes General Allotment Act, 157, 260, 390; and European colonists, 12, 14–15; Fort Laramie Treaty, 152; Geronimo, 156, *f156;* Ghost Dance, 156; Great Depression and, 454–55, *p455;* Inca, 12; Indian Citizenship Act, 391; Indian Removal Act, 93; Indian Reorganization Act, 455, *p455;* Inuit, 7; Iroquois, 8; land

claims and protests, 157, 260, 390–91, *p390,* 617; Little Turtle, 85; Long Walk, 155; Miami, 85; Navajo, 8, 155; Nez Percé, 155, *f155;* Parker, Quanah, 154; Pawnee, 152; Pontiac's Rebellion, 21; Pueblo, 8, *m153, p390,* 391; Red Cloud, 153; reservations and, 152, *m153,* 157, 390–91, 455; Sacajawea, 89; Sand Creek Massacre, 152–53, *m153;* Seminole, 93; Shawnee, 90; Shoshoni, 89; Sioux, 152–54, 156; Sitting Bull, 154, 156; Society of American Indians, 260, *p260;* in Spanish-American War, 297; Tecumseh, 90–91; Trail of Tears, 93; Treaty of Greenville, 85; Treaty of Medicine Lodge, 153, *m153;* tribal ownership of lands, 93, 391, 455, *p455;* Wampanoag, 16; Winnemucca, Sarah, 157, *p157; Worcester* v. *Georgia* and, 93; in World War I, 391; Wounded Knee Massacre, *m153,* 156. *See also* names of individual tribes
American Liberty League, 437
American Medical Association (AMA), 246, 268
American Missionary Society, 127
American Plan, 376
American Railway Union, 199
American Red Cross, 75, 110, 427–28
Americans with Disabilities Act (ADA), 693, *p693*
American System, 91
American Telephone and Telegraph (AT&T), 187, 589
amnesty, 125
amusement parks, 223, *p223*
anarchists, 359
Anasazi, 6
Anderson, Marian, 456
Anderson, Robert, 107
Andros, Edmund, 19
Anniston, Alabama, 596, *m597*
Anthony, Susan B., 99, 256, *f256*
Antifederalists, 33, 38, 64
Anti-Imperialist League, 299
Anti-Saloon League, 255, 383. *See also* temperance movement
antitrust laws, 194, 199; Theodore Roosevelt and, 267–68, *p268;* Taft administration and, 273–74; Wilson and, 281, *p281*
Apache, 8, 152, *m153*
apartheid, 670
Apollo program, 589, *f590,* 665, *p665*
appeasement, 476
Apple (computer company), 676, *p676,* 700
Appomattox Courthouse, 111, *p111*
apportionment, 38
Arafat, Yasir, 714
Arapaho, 152, *m153*
Arbella (ship), 16
arbitration, 266
architecture: in the late 1800s, 216–17, *f218;* in the 1920s, 405, *p405;* in the 1950s, 548–49, *p549;* modern, *p706;* Vietnam Veterans Memorial, *f640,* 641
Argentina, *mxxvii,* 310
Aristide, Jean-Bertrand, 713–14
Aristotle, 36
Arizona, *mxx, c743;* Mexican Cession and, 104
Arkansas, *mxx, c743;* Reconstruction and, 134, *m134;* secession and, 108
armed forces, *f516;* in Balkans, 713, *p713,* 716–17; Berlin Airlift and, 515–16; Bonus Army and, 429–30, *p430;* during Civil War, 107–11, *m109, p110, p111;* Cold War and, *m534,* 536, *c536, p536, p572,* 573, 576–77, *m576, c684,* 690–91, *p705;* desegregation of, 554–55; during Korean War, 523–26, *p523, m524, p525, p526;* and Latin America, 304, *m305,* 306–07, *m307,* 310–11, *p311, m698,* 714; McCarthyism and, 531; during Mexican War, 104; in Middle East, 690, *p690,* 696–98, *p696, m697, p698;* during Persian Gulf War, 696–98, *p696, m697, p698;* in Somalia, 714; during Spanish-American War, 296–99, *m297, f298, p299;* during Vietnam War, 626–30, *m628, p630,* 632–33, *c633,* 637, *c639, p646,* 647, *p647;* during War of 1812, 90–91; and Washington Conference, 365; in the West, 152–57, *p152, m153, p154;* during World War I, *f331,* 336, *p336, p337,* 339–44, *m342, p343, c348, m353;* during World War II, 479, 481, *p481,* 485–96, *f485, p486, m487, p490, p492, m493, p494, c498, m501*
armistice, 343
Armory Show, 403
Armstrong, Louis, 400, *p400*
Armstrong, Louise, 426
Armstrong, Neil, 589
Army, U.S., *See* U.S. Armed Forces
Army-McCarthy hearings, 531
Arnaz, Desi, 550
art: Ansel Adams, 403–04; *p403;* Armory Show, 403, Thomas Hart Benton, 458; Mary Cassatt, 226, *f253, p253;* cubism, 403; John Steuart Curry, 458; Aaron Douglas, 403; Winslow Homer, 226, *p226;* Alexander Hogue, *p446;* Edward Hopper, 403, *p403;* Hudson River School, 226; impressionism, 226; Jacob Lawrence, *p407;* Anna "Grandma" Moses, 458; Georgia O'Keeffe, 403, *f404, p404;* Jackson Pollock, 551, *f552, p552;* pop, 586; Robert Rauschenburg, 586, *p593;* regionalists, 458; Diego Rivera, *p369;* David Smith, 551; Alfred Stieglitz, 227, 403; Andy Warhol, *f585, p585,* 586; James McNeil Whistler, 226, *p226;* Grant Wood, 458, *p458;* the WPA and, 440, *p440,* 458
Arthur, Chester, 239, 240, *c740*
Articles of Confederation, 30, 31, *c32*
artifacts, 6
Art Institute of Chicago, 217
artists: *See* art, names of individual artists
Asia, *mxxix;* Cold War in, 523, *m535, 537,* 626, 627; immigrants from, 71, *p71,* 105, 159, 161–62, *p162, p209, c210,* 211, 213–14, *f291,* 672–73, 718; impact of Great Depression on, 466–67, *m466;* immigration from, *p71, c210,* 581–82, 718; international trade and, 9–10, 290–93, *p292, c315, m316,* 656; railroads and, *f161, p161;* and settlement of North America, 6; World War II and, 479, 490–94, *p490, m493,* 496–98. *See also* individual Asian nations
assembly line, 368–69, *p369*
Astaire, Fred, 459, *p459*
astronauts, 588–89, *p588, p589, f590,* 665, 700, 724–25, *p724*
Aswan High Dam, 542
athletes. *See* sports
Atlanta, Georgia: in the Civil War, 111
Atlanta Compromise, 259
Atlantic Charter, 479
Atlantic Ocean: age of exploration and, 10–13, *m11;* Middle Passage and, 19; Panama Canal and, 301, *f303;* World War I and, 333, *p333;* World War II and, 478, *p479*
atomic bomb: bombing of Japan, 496, *p496,* 510; Harry S Truman and the, 496; testing of, 496, 510. *See also* nuclear weapons
Attlee, Clement, *p510*
Auschwitz, Germany, 499
Austin, Moses, 101
Austin, Stephen F., 101
Austria, *mxxviii,* 476; violence against Jews in 1930s, 465; in World War II, *m477, m487*
Austria-Hungary: World War I and, 324, 326–27, *m332,* 344, *m347, c348, f351*
auto industry, 367, 370, 664, 684; imports and, 684; strikes in, 448–49, *p448*
automation, 546
automobiles, 188, *p367,* 546, *f668;* impact of, 370, *m547,* 547–48; imports and, 664, 684; Model T, 367–68, *p368;* production of, 368–69, *p369;* safety standards and, 591; sales of, 370, *c371,* 548
aviation, 188, 398, *p398;* in World War I, *f331*
Axis Powers: formation of military alliance, 465; World War II and, 476–79, *m477,* 484–99, *p485, m487, f488, m493, p496*
Aztec, 6, *m7,* 12

Babbitt (Sinclair Lewis), 402
baby boom, 548; generation gap and, 584
Bacall, Lauren, 528, *p528*
Bacon, Nathaniel, 15
Bacon's Rebellion, 15
Bahrain, *mxxix;* OPEC member nation, *m657*
bail, 68
Baker, Ella, 596
Baker, Howard, 683
Baker, Josephine, 402
Bakke, Allan, 601
balance of power, 326
Balboa, Vasco Núñez de, 12
Baldwin, James, 551
Balkans, 326; war in the 1990s, 716–17, *p716. See also* World War I
Ball, Lucille, 550–51
Ballinger, Richard, 274
Ballinger-Pinchot controversy, 274–75, *p275*
banking, 84, 93; crisis during the Great Depression, 422; reform and, 279–81, *p279,* 432–33; savings and loan crisis, 693; stock market crash of 1929 and, 420–21, *p422*
Bank of the United States, 84
barbed wire, 168, *p169*
Barnum, P. T., 222
Barrett, Janie Porter, 221
Barton, Clara, 110
Baruch, Bernard, 337

baseball, 223, *p223,* 397, *p397,* 720
Basie, Count, 459
basketball, 720, *p720*
Bataan Death March, 491, *p491*
Bataan Peninsula, 491, *m493*
Bates, Daisy, 557
Battle of Antietam, 108, *m109*
Battle of Britain, 477
Battle of Bunker Hill, 23
Battle of El Alamein, 485, *m487*
Battle of Fallen Timbers, 85
Battle of Gettysburg, *m109,* 110, *p110*
Battle of Leyte Gulf, *m493,* 493
Battle of Midway, 491–92, *m493*
Battle of New Orleans, 91
Battle of Okinawa, 494
Battle of Saratoga, *m23,* 24
Battle of Shiloh, 109, *m109*
Battle of Stalingrad, 486, *m487*
Battle of the Atlantic, 478
Battle of the Bulge, *m487,* 489
Battle of the Coral Sea, 491, *m493*
Battle of the Little Bighorn, *m153,* 154, *p154*
Battle of Tippecanoe, 90
Battle of Yorktown, *m23,* 25
Bay of Pigs, 574–75
Beals, Melba Pattiool, 557
Bear Flag Revolt, 104
bear market, 420, *p421*
Beatles, 586, *p586*
beatniks. *See* beats
beats, 551
bebop, 553
Begin, Menachem, 669, *p669*
Belgium, *mxxviii;* Cold War and, *m515, m535;* World War I and, 328, *m432,* World War II and, 477
Bell, Alexander Graham, 187, *p187*
Bell, "Cool Papa," 397
Bell Telephone Company, 187
benevolent societies, 212
Benton, Thomas Hart, 458
Bentsen, Lloyd, 692
Berkeley, John, 18
Berle, Milton, 550
Berlin, Germany: division of, 510, 515; site of 1936 Olympics, 464–65. *See also* Berlin Airlift, Berlin Wall, Cold War, East Germany
Berlin Airlift, 515–16
Berlin Wall: construction of, 575, *p575;* fall of the, *f694, p694,* 695, *m695, p695*
Bernstein, Carl, 660–61, *p660*
Berry, Chuck, 553
Bessemer, Henry, 184
Bessemer process, 184
Bethune, Mary McLeod, 456, *p456*
bicameral legislature, 19
bicycles, 224, *p224*
Bierstadt, Albert, 226
big band music. *See* swing music
big business. *See* corporations
Big Four, 346
Big Three, *p508,* 510, *p510*
Bilingual Education Act of 1974, 608
Bill of Rights, 33, *f56–57,* 64–69, *f67*
Birmingham, Alabama: civil rights movement and, 596–98, *m597*
Black Boy (Richard Wright), 458
Black Cabinet, 456
Black Codes, 130–31, *p131*
Black Kettle, 152–53
blacklisting, 528. *See also* Red Scare
Black Monday, 686, *p686*
Black Muslims. *See* Nation of Islam
black nationalism, 389–90
Black Panther Party, 600
Black Power, 600, *p600*
Blackshirts, 464
Black Star (steamship line), 390
Black Tuesday, 420–21
Blair, Ezell, 596
Bland-Allison Act, 203
Blatch, Harriot Stanton, 392
Blitzkrieg, 476
Bleeding Kansas, 107
Bloomer, Amelia, 224
Blue Boat, The (Winslow Homer), *p226*
blues, 399–400, *p400*
Boesky, Ivan, 685
Bogart, Humphrey, *p528*
Boland Agreement, 689
bonanza, 158
Bonin, Gertrude S., *p260*
Bonus Army, 429–30, *p430*
boom towns, 159–60
Booth, John Wilkes, 128
bootleggers, 384
bop. *See* bebop
Bork, Robert, 662
Born in the U.S.A. (Bruce Springsteen), 702, *p702*
Bosnia, *mxxviii;* war in the Balkans, 713, *p713,* 716–17; World War I and, 326
Bosnia and Herzegovina. *See* Bosnia
bosses, 238
Boston, Massachusetts, 15, *m16,* 20, 22, *m23,* 217; antibusing protests in, 601; first subway in, 217; police strikes in, 359
Boston Massacre, 22, *p22*
Boston Museum of Fine Arts, 217
Boston Tea Party, 22
Bourke-White, Margaret, 452
Bow, Clara, 397
Bowie, Jim, 101
Boxer Rebellion, 293, *p293*
boycotts: Chicano movement and, 608; civil rights movement and, 558; colonial, 22; consumer, 606; workers' rights and the NLRA, 448
Boy Scouts, 75
Bozeman, John M., 153
Bozeman Trail, 153
braceros, 483
Bradford, William, 15
Bradley, Omar, 489
Bradstreet, Anne, *f17*
Brady, James, 682, 710, *p710*
Brady, Sarah, *p710*
Brady Bill, 710
Brain Trust, 432
Brandeis, Louis, 282, 437
Brando, Marlon, 552
Brazil, 310, *m315*
Brezhnev, Leonid, 659, 664
Briande, Aristide, 366
brinkmanship, 540–41
Brown, Jerry, 606
Brown, John, 107
Brown, Linda, 556
Brown v. ***Board of Education,*** 555–56, *f746*
Bruce, Blanche K., 137, 139
Bryan, William Jennings, 202–03, 205, *p205,* 273, 279, 307, 386
Buchanan, James, *c739*
buffalo, 151–52
"Buffalo Bill." *See* "Buffalo Bill" Cody
Buffalo Soldiers, *p152*
Bulgaria, *mxxviii,* and Cold War, *m515, m535, m695;* Marshall Plan and, *m515;* and World War I, *m332, m347;* and World War II, *m477, m487*
bull market, 420
Bull Moose Party, 275–76, *p275*
Bunau-Varilla, Philippe, 302
Bunche, Ralph, 455
Bureau of Indian Affairs, 93, 152, 391; John Collier and, 455, *p455*
Burgoyne, John, 24
Burma, (Myanmar), *mxxix,* 490
Burr, Aaron, 86
Bush, George, *p742;* domestic policies of, 693–94, *p493;* election of 1988, 692–93, *p693;* election of 1992, 708; Persian Gulf War and, 696–98, *m697, p696, p698;* savings and loan crisis, 693; Supreme Court nominations, 693–94; War on Drugs and, 693
business cycle, 422–23, *c423*
busing, 601
buying on margin, 420
Byrnes, James F., 556

cabinet, 41–42
Cable, George Washington, 145, 225
Cable News Network (CNN), 703
cable television, 702–03
Cabot, John, 12
Cabrillo, Juan Rodríguez, 12
Cagney, James, 459
Calhoun, John, 92
California, *mxx, c743;* Bear Flag Revolt, 104; Compromise of 1850, 106; exploration of, 12; gold rush, 105, 158; manifest destiny and, 103; Mexican War and, 104; migrant workers in, 605–06, *f605, p605, m606;* west-ward expansion and, 102, *m103*
California Gold Rush, 105
California Trail, 102, *m103*
Calvert, Cecilius, 17
Cambodia, *mxxix,* 624, *m624,* 637, *p637, m628,* 640
Campbell, Hardy, 173
Campbell's Soup, 372
Camp David Accords, 669, *p669*
Canada, *mxxvi;* establishment of border with U.S., 103; exploration of, 13; NAFTA and, 709, *p709;* NATO and, 517, *m535;* Underground Railroad and, 98; War of 1812, 91
canals, 91; Panama Canal, 302, *p302, f303,* 304, *p304*
canned goods, 371
Cape of Good Hope, 10
capitalism, 251; Andrew Carnegie on, *f192*
Capone, Al "Scarface," 384–85
Cárdenas, Lázaro, 463
Caribbean, *mxxvi,* 294–95, *c295, c314, c315, m316;* Spanish-American War

and, 296–97, *m297;* U.S. foreign policy in, 299–300, 304–07, *m305, p307,* 687–88, *m688,* 713–14. *See also* individual Caribbean nations
Carmichael, Stokely, 600
Carnegie, Andrew, 191–93, *f191, p191, f192,* 217
Carnegie Steel Company, 198
carpetbaggers, 136
Carranza, Venustiano, 309, 311
Carson, Kit, 155
Carson, Rachel, 591, *p591*
Carter, Jimmy, *f667, p667, p742;* aid to El Salvador and, 688; Camp David Accords and, 669, *p669;* domestic challenges, 667–69; election of 1976, 666–67, *p667;* election of 1980, 671, *p671;* foreign policy, 669–70, *p669;* Iran hostage crisis, 670–71, *p670;* peace mission to Haiti, 714
Carteret, George, 18
Cartier, Jacques, 13
Carver, George Washington, 258
Casement, Jack, 161
Cassatt, Mary, 226–27, *f253*
Castro, Cipriano, 305
Castro, Fidel, *p575;* Bay of Pigs, 574–75; Cuban missile crisis and, 575–77, *m576*
Castro, Sal, 608
Catholic Church: in Middle Ages, 8; Protestant Reformation and, 13
Catt, Carrie Chapman, 256, *p256*
cattle drive, 167
cattle industry, 165–71, *p165, m168, p169, m180, m181*
Cattle Kingdom, definition of, 165
Cayuga, 8
CD-ROM, 702
Centennial Exhibition, *p182,* 183–84
Center for Independent Living, 618
Central America, *mxxvi, c310,* immigration and, *c210,* 581–82; Monroe Doctrine and, 91; Panama Canal and, 301–02, *f303,* 304, 669; U.S. foreign policy and, 304–07, *m305,* 688–89, *m688,* 669
Central Intelligence Agency (CIA), 541; abuse of power, 664; Central America and, 689
Central Pacific Railroad, 160–62, *m168*
Central Park: design of, 217, *f218*
Central Powers, 327–28, *m332,* 334, *m342,* 344–48
Century of Dishonor, A (Helen Hunt Jackson), 157
Challenger (space shuttle), 700
Chambers, Whittaker, 529
Champlain, Samuel de, 13
Chaney, James, 599, *p599*
Chaplin, Charlie, 397
Charles I (England), 16
Charles II (England), 18
Charleston (South Carolina): establishment of town, 18
charter, 13
Chávez, César, 605–06, *f605, p605*
Checkers speech, 525
checks and balances, 32, *c63*
Cherokee, 93, *m153*
Chesnutt, Charles W., 145, *f146*
Cheyenne, 152
Chiang Kaishek, 522
Chicago, Illinois: elevated railroads in, 217; Haymarket Riot in, 197, *p197;* Hull House in, 221; jazz and, 400; in late 1800s, 215, 217, *p217;* race riots in, 361; railroads and, 184
Chicago Exposition (1893), 222–23
Chicano movement, 608–09, *p608, p609*
Chickasaw, 93, *m153*
Chief Joseph, 155–56, *f155, p155*
child labor, 94, 145, 233, 247–49, *p248;* reforms, 283, *p283,* 435, 438
children: disabilities and, 618; education and, 16, 100, 127, *p211,* 212, 245–46, *p300,* 382, 540, 618; Fair Labor Standards Act and, 448; foster parent care and, 618; health care and, 546–47, 618; immigration and, 119; industry and, 233; life during the Great Depression, 415, 426–27, *p447,* 453; movie industry and, *f396,* 460, *p460;* musicians, 505; politicians, 565; suburban life and, 548, volunteers, 651; and the West, 1; and World War I, 321
Children's Defense Fund, 618
Chile, *mxxvii,* 310, *m315*
China, *mxxix,* 292–93, *m315, p522;* ancient civilization in, 9; Boxer Rebellion, 293, *p293;* Communist victory in, 522, *p523;* détente and, 654, *p654,* 658; Japanese invasion of, 466–67, *m466;* Korea War and, 524–25, *m524,* 526; Nationalists in, 522–23; Nine-Power Treaty and, 365; Open Door Policy, 293; Silk Road and, 9; World War II and, 484, 492, *m493,* 497
Chinese Americans: 260, *p260;* literature and, *f701*
Chinese Exclusion Act, 214
Chinese immigrants: 209, *p209,* 214, 260; and California Gold Rush, 105; and railroad construction, 161
Chisholm, Jesse, 167
Chisholm, Shirley, 40, 614, *p614,* 615
Chisholm Trail, 167, *m168*
Choctaw, *m7,* 93, *m153*
Chrysler Building, 405, *p405*
Churchill, Winston: Atlantic Charter and, 478; on Great Britain's appeasement of Germany, 476; Iron Curtain speech, 512; at Potsdam Conference, 510; World War II and, 477–78, 484; at Yalta Conference, *p508,* 510
Church of England, 15
citizenship: *Dred Scott* decision and, 107; Fourteenth Amendment and, *f57–58,* 132; Indian Citizenship Act, 391; rights and responsibilities, 70–75, *p71, p72, p74. See also* Constitution
Citizens on Patrol, 75
Civilian Conservation Corps (CCC), 434, *p434, c441;* African Americans and, 455
civil rights: Alien and Sedition Acts, 87; Palmer raids and, 360; during Franklin D. Roosevelt's administration, 456; during Reconstruction, 132, 134, 139. *See also* civil rights movement
Civil Rights Act of 1866, 132
Civil Rights Act of 1875, 139
Civil Rights Act of 1964, 598, 611
civil rights movement, 554–59, *p554, p555, p556, p557, p558, f558, p559,* 594–601, *p594, p595, p596, m597, f598, p598, p599, p600;* American Indians and, 391, 616–17, *p617; Brown* v. *Board of Education,* 555–56; Freedom Rides, 596–97, *m597;* Freedom Summer, 599; Hispanics and, 604–09, *f605, p605, p606, f607, p608, p609;* John F. Kennedy and, 598; legislation in support of, 598, 599; Lyndon Johnson and, 598; Malcolm X and, 599–600, *p600, p603;* March on Washington, *p594,* 598, *p598;* Martin Luther King Jr. and, 558–59, *p558,* 597–99, *f598,* 600–01, *f602–03, p603;* nonviolent resistance and, 596; public school desegregation and, 555–57, *p556, p557,* 601, 604–05; race riots and, 600, 601; reactions and successes, 601; sit-ins during, 595, 596; violence during, 596, 597, 598, 599, 600; voting rights and, 599. *See also* disability rights movement, women's rights movement
civil service: gender discrimination in, 454, 611; reforms in, 240
Civil War, 106–11, *m109;* African Americans in, 109; antidraft riots, 110; Battle of Gettysburg, 110; division of Union, 107, *c107;* Emancipation Proclamation, 109, *f112–13;* end of war, 111, *p111;* Gettysburg Address, 110, *f113;* life during wartime, 110; major battles of, *m109, p110;* Northern opposition to, 110; strategies in, 108; war in the East, 108–09; war in the West, 109–10; women in, 110
Civil Works Administration (CWA), 434, *c441*
Clark, Kenneth, 556
Clark, William, 89, *m89, p89*
Clay, Henry, 91, 106
Clayton Antitrust Act, 231, *c282*
Clayton-Bulwer Treaty, 301–02
Clean Air Act, 693
Clemenceau, Georges, 346
Clemens, Samuel. *See* Mark Twain
Clermont (steamboat), 95
Cleveland, Grover, 203, *p203,* 204, 239, *c740;* Hawaii and, 290; on immigration, 214; Pullman Strike and, 199; relations with Cuba and, 296
Clinton, Bill, 40, 708, *f709, p742;* budget and welfare reform, 708, 710–12; election of 1992, 708, *p708;* election of 1996, 711; foreign policy of, 713–17, *p713, p714, p716, p717;* health care reform and, 708–09; impeachment of, 712, *p712;* independent counsel and, 710, 712; NAFTA and, 709; new crime laws and, 710; second term of, 712
Clinton, Hillary Rodham, *p708,* 709
coal industry, *p248,* 265–67, 374, *c731,* 732, *m732*
Cobb, Jerri, 610, *p610*
Coca-Cola, 372
Cody, "Buffalo Bill," 162
Coinage Act of 1873, 202
Cold War, 513–14, *f534–37, m534–35, c535, m537;* arms race, 540; in Asia, 523; Carter and, 669–70; containment in, 515; Eastern Europe and, 512; Eisenhower and, 540–43, *p540, m541, f542, p542, p543;* end of, 695–96, *f694, p694, m695, p695;* in Europe, 511–12, 513–17, *m541;* Ford and, 664–65, *p665;* Korean War and, 523–25, *m524, p525,* 526, *p526;* literature and, *f530;* and McCarthyism, 529, *p529,* 531; new Red Scare and, 527–29, *p527, p528, p529,* 531, *p531;* Nixon and, 654, *p654,* 658–59; roots of, 513–17, *f514, m515, f516, p517;*

popular culture influenced by, 531, *p531;* Reagan and, 687–91, *m688, p689, p690;* Vietnam War and, 625–41, *p625, p627, m628, p630, p632, c639*
collective bargaining, 196
Collier, John: Bureau of Indian Affairs and, 455
Collins, Elizabeth, 165, *p165*
Colombia, *mxxvii,* and Panama Canal, 302
colonial America, 13–20, *m16, m35;* economy of, 19–20; Jamestown, 14, *p14;* life in, 19–20, *p19;* Middle colonies, 18, *p18;* New England colonies, 16–17; Southern colonies, 17–18; Pilgrims, 15–16; Puritans, 15, 16, *f17;* Revolutionary War against England, 22–25, *m23, c25;* slavery in, 19–20, *p19;* taxes imposed on, 21–22; trade in, 19
Colorado, *mxx, c743;* gold mining in, 158; Mexican Cession and, 104
Colored Farmers' Alliance, 203, *p203*
Columbia Broadcasting System (CBS), 394
Columbian Exchange, 12
Columbus, Christopher, 11–12, *m11*
Columbus, New Mexico: invasion by Pancho Villa, 311
Comanche, *m7,* 152, 154
comic books, 457, *p457*
Coming of Age in Mississippi (Anne Moody), *p596*
Commercial Revolution, 10
Commission on the Status of Women, 610–11
Committee for the Fifth Amendment, 528, *p528*
Committee on Civil Rights, 555
Committee on Public Information (CPI), 335–36
Committee to Re-elect the President (CRP), 660, 661
Common Sense (Thomas Paine), 23
Commonwealth of Independent States, 695, *m695*
communications: Internet, 722, *p722;* satellites, 589, 591; telegraph, 97, 185, 187; telephone, *f186,* 187, *p187,* 371
communism: blacklisting and, 528; in China, 522–23, *p523;* beginning of Cold War and, 513–15, *f514;* end of Cold War and, 695–96, *m695;* Eisenhower Doctrine and, *f542;* in Korea, 523; McCarthyism and, 529, *p529,* 531; Red Scare, 359–60, *p359;* new Red Scare and, 527–29, *p527, p528, p529,* 531, *p531;* in Russia, 340, 462, *p462;* in Southeast Asia, 624–25. Truman Doctrine and, *f514. See also* Cold War, Soviet Union
Communist Party, 359, 527–29
compact discs (CDs), 701–02, *p701*
Compromise of 1850, 106
Compromise of 1877, 139–40
computers, 547, 676, *p676,* 700–02, *p700, f721,* 722, *p722, c725,* 726, *p726;* Information Revolution, 722; Internet, 722, *p722*
Comstock, Henry, 158
Comstock Lode, 158, *p159*
concentration camps, 498–99, *p498, p499*
Concord, Massachusetts: in Revolutionary War, 22–23
concurrent powers, 38
Coney Island (New York City), 223, *p223*
Confederate States of America, 107
Congress, U.S., 32–33, *c32,* 38–40, *p38, c63;* first African Americans in, 137, *p137;* first women in, 391; judicial review and, 88; Reconstruction and, 125–26, 129, 133–34, *p133;* terms of office, *c80. See also* individual acts, amendments, individual Congress members
Congress of Industrial Organizations (CIO), 448, 546
Congress of Racial Equality (CORE), 596, *m597*
Conjure Woman, The (Charles W. Chesnutt), 145
Connecticut, *mxx, c743;* establishment of colony, 16, *m16*
conservation: Taft and, 274–75, *p275;* Theodore Roosevelt and, 270–71, *m270. See also* energy conservation, environmentalism
Constitution, U.S., 31–33, *c32, p33,* 37–43, *f39, f44–54, c63, f65, f78–81;* amendments to, *f55–63, c68;* Articles of Confederation, 30, 31, *c32;* Bill of Rights and, 64–69; citizenship under, 70–75; federalism in, 32; Federalists vs. Anti-federalists, 33; Great Compromise and, 31; separation of powers, *c63;* Three-Fifths Compromise, 32; voting and, *c81*
Constitutional Convention, 31–32
consumers: activist movement in 1970s, 674–75
consumer society: advertising and, 372, *p372,* 373; rise of, 371–72, *c371;* safety and, 591, 674–75; in suburbs, 548, *p548*
containment, 515
Contract with America, 710, *p711*
contras, 689, *p689*
Convention of 1818, 91
Cook, James, 289
Coolidge, Calvin, 364–65, *p364, p365, p741;* election of 1920, 362; election of 1924, 364; election of 1928, 366; foreign policy of, 365–66; as governor of Massachusetts, 359
Cooper, James Fenimore, 225
cooperatives, 201
Copperheads, 110
Coppola, Francis Ford, 676
Cornwallis, Charles, 25
Coronado, Francisco Vásquez de, 12
corporations, 189, *f192;* and antitrust movement, 194, 273; growth of, 189–92, *c190,* 194. *See also* names of individual corporations
Cortés, Hernan, 12
cosmonauts, 588–89, *p588,* 665, 724–25
Cotera, Marta, 608
cotton, 97, *c97;* daily life in cotton mill, 145; prices of, *c144;* production of, *c144;* in the South, 143–44, *p143, c144;* setbacks in 1920s, 374, *p374*
Cotton Club, 400
cotton gin, 97
Coué, Emile, 394
Coughlin, Charles E., 437–38, 441
Council of the Indies, 12
counterculture, 584–85, *p584*
covert operations: definition of, 541
cowboys, 166, *p166*
Cow Skull: Red, White, and Blue (Georgia O'Keeffe), *f404*
Cox, Archibald, 661, 662
Cox, James M., 363
craft unions, 448
Crane, Stephen, 225, *f298*
Crazy Horse, 153, 154
Crédit Mobilier, 239
Creek, 91, 93, *m153*
Creek War, 91
Creel, George, 335
Crisis, The (NAACP magazine), 259, *p282*
Croatia, *mxxviii, m487;* war in the Balkans and, 716–17
Crockett, Davy, 101
Cronkite, Walter, 633
Crucible, The (Arthur Miller), *f530*
cruel and unusual punishment, 68–69
Crusade for Justice, 607
Crusades, 9
Crystal City, Texas: Mexican American student protests in, 608
Cuba, *mxxvi, m305;* Bay of Pigs and, 574–75; Cuban missile crisis, 575–77, *m576;* immigrants from, 672; independence and, 294–95; Platt Amendment and, 300; Spanish-American War, 295–97, *p296,* 298–300, *m297, f298, p298;* Teller Amendment, 296; trade with, *c295;* U.S. expansion and, *c314*
cubism, 403
Cullen, Countee, 401
culture: definition of, 6. *See also* architecture, art, literature, motion pictures, music, television
Cumberland Road, 91
Curry, John Steuart, 458
Custer, George Armstrong, 154
Czechoslovakia, *mxxviii;* Cold War and, *m535, m541, m695;* during Great Depression, *c470;* immigrants from, 210; Iron Curtain and, *p512;* Marshall Plan and, *m515;* World War I and, 347, *m347;* World War II and, 476, *m477, m487*
Czolgosz, Leon: assassin of McKinley, 265, *p265*

Dachau, Germany, 498
dance, modern, *f675*
"Dancin' Party at Harrison's Cove, The" (Mary Noailles Murfree), 146
Danzig, Germany, 476
Darrow, Clarence, 386, *p386*
Darwin, Charles, 192, 385
Daughters of the American Revolution (DAR), 456
Daugherty, Harry, 374
Davis, Henry, 126
Davis, Jefferson, 107, *p107*
Dawes, William, 22
Dawes General Allotment Act, 157, 260, 391, 455
Dayton peace accords, 717
D-Day, *p486,* 487–89, *m487*
Debs, Eugene V., 199, 276, *p276,* 336, 363
Dean, Dizzy, 461
Dean, James, 551–52, *p551*
Dean, John, 661
Declaration of Independence, 23, *f26–29*
Declaration of Sentiments (Elizabeth Cady Stanton and Lucretia Mott), *f99*

Deep Throat, 660–61
Deere, John, 173
defense spending, 481, 536, *c536,* 684, *c684*
deficit spending: defined, 443
Delaware, *mxx, c743;* establishment of colony, 18; first state to ratify the Constitution, 33
delegated powers, 38
Delgado* v. *The Bastrop Independent School District, 604
"Demandas de la Raza" (Rodolfo Gonzales), 607
demilitarized zone (DMZ), 526
demobilization, 356
Democratic National Convention: female delegates and, 615; origins of, 92. *See also* individual presidential elections
Democratic Party, 92
Democratic-Republican Party, 86
Denmark, *mxxviii;* Cold War and, *m535;* immigrants from, 192; Marshall Plan and, *m515;* World War I and, *m332; m347;* World War II and, 476, *m477, m487*
Department of Housing and Urban Development (HUD), 581
department stores, 217, 219, 371
deport, 71
Description of New England, A (John Smith), *f15*
desegregation: armed forces and, 555; Mexican Americans and, 604; public schools and, 555–57, *p556, p557,* 601; stores and, 596, *p596,* 598; transportation and, 557–59, *p559,* 596–98, *m597. See also* civil rights movement
Desert Storm. *See* Operation Desert Storm, Persian Gulf War
detective stories, 457, *p457*
détente, 659, 664–65
Dewey, George, 296
Dewey, John, 246, 259
Dewey, Thomas, 520
Dewson, Mary, 454
Dias, Bartolomeu, 10, 12
Díaz, Porfirio, 308, *p308*
Dien Bien Phu, 625, *m628*
Dietrich, Marlene, 459
direct primary, 243
disability rights movement, 617–18, *p617*
Disabled in Action (DIA), 618
disarmament: defined, 365
disco, 677, *p677*
Discovery (space shuttle), 700
District of Columbia, *mxx, c743*
Dix, Dorothea, 100, 110
Dixiecrats, 521
Dodge City, 167
Dole, Bob, 666; election of 1996, 711
Dole, Elizabeth, 682
Dole, Sanford P., 290
dollar diplomacy, 306
Dominican Republic, *mxxvi,* 305, *m305,* 307, 582, *p582*
Dominion of New England, 19
Domino, Fats, 553
domino theory, 624–25
Dos Passos, John, 402, 458
double jeopardy, 67
Douglas, Aaron, 403
Douglass, Frederick, 98, *p98,* 109, 126, 143, 390
doves, 631
draft, 72
Drake, Edwin L., 185
"Drake's Folly," 185
***Dred Scott* decision,** 107
Dreiser, Theodore, 225
Dresden, Germany, 495
Drought Stricken Area (Alexandre Hogue), *p446*
dry farming, 173
Du Bois, W. E. B., 258, *p258,* 259, 282, 389, 401
due process, 67
Dukakis, Michael: presidential candidate in 1988, 692–93; Sacco and Vanzetti proclamation, 360
Dulles, John Foster, 540–41, *f542, p542*
Dunkirk, France, 476, *m477*
Duryea, Charles, 188
Duryea, J. Frank, 188
Dust Bowl, 449–50, *m450, p450*
Dutch East India Company, 290
Dylan, Bob, 568, 587

Earhart, Amelia, 398
Earp, Wyatt, 167
Earth Day, 673, *p673*
Earth in the Balance (Al Gore), 724
Earth Summit, 724
East Berlin. *See* East Germany
Eastern Europe: Berlin Airlift and, 515–16; Berlin Wall and, 575, *p575,* 692, *p692, f694, p694, p695;* Cold War and, 510, 513, *f516, m535, m541,* 542–43; dismantling of Soviet "empire" in, 691, *p691;* end of Cold War, 695–96, *m695;* Iron Curtain and, 512, *p512;* Marshall Plan and, 515, *m515;* war in the Balkans, 716–17, *p716;* Warsaw Pact and, 517; World War I and, 326–28, *p326, p327, m332,* 342–43, *m347;* World War II and, 476, *m477,* 484, 486–87, *m487, f488. See also* individual nations
East Germany, *m515,* 516, *f516, m535, m541;* Berlin Airlift and, 515–16; Berlin Wall and, 575, *p575,* 692, *p692, f694, p694, p695;* creation of, 515–16; reunited with West Germany, 695. *See also* Cold War, Europe, West Germany
Eastman, George, 227
Echo I (satellite), 589
Eckford, Elizabeth, 557, *p557*
Economic Recovery Tax Act (ERTA), 683
economy: American System and, 91; under the Articles of Confederation, 31; during Bush presidency, 693, 708; business cycle and the, 422–23, *c423;* during Clinton years, 708–09, 711–12, *c711;* colonial, 19–20; Commercial Revolution, 10, *p10;* corporations and, 184–92, 194; demobilization and, 356, 387, 518–19; energy crisis and, 656–58, *p656, c658,* 668–69, *f669;* farming and, 94, 124, 143, *c144,* 173, *c179,* 200–01, *m202,* 376–77, *p376, c377,* 423, 449–50, *p450,* 452; Federal Reserve and, *p279,* 280–81; free coinage, 202–03; free enterprise, 189; global, 462–63, *c470, m471,* 725, 727; Great Depression and, 421–24, *p421, p422, c425,* 427, 472–73, *c472, c473;* imperialism and, 288–89; income taxes and, *f280;* Industrial Revolution and, 94–95, *p95;* manufacturing and, 94–95, 144, 163, 184, 368–70, 480, 546, 572, 664; New Deal programs and the, 434–35; during the 1920s, 370–74, *p373, p374,* 376–77, *c377;* during the 1950s, 544, 546–48; during the 1970s, 656–58, *p656, c658,* 664, *p664,* 667–68; Panic of 1893, 204–05, 240; railroads and, 162–63, *p162, m168;* during Reagan years, 683–86, *p683, c684, p686;* Second Industrial Revolution and, 184–85, 187, *f193,* 195; of the South, 97, *c97,* 124, 137, 143–44, *c144;* stock market crash of 1929, 420–22; trade deficit and, 664; of the West, 105, 159, 165, 167–69, 173, *c174, m180, m181;* mobilization of in World War I, 336–38, *p337;* mobilization of in World War II, 480–81, *p480, p481;* post–World War II, 514–15, *m515,* 518–20. *See also* computers, corporations, trade
Edelman, Marian Wright, 618, *p618*
Ederle, Gertrude, 397
Edison, Thomas Alva, 135, *p185, f186, p186,* 187, *f395*
education, 69; opportunities for African Americans, 172–28, *f127, m149,* 258; affirmative action and, 601; Americans with Disabilities Act and, 693, *p693;* bilingual, 608; colonial, 16; common school movement and, 100; desegregation and, 555–57, *p556, p557,* 601; gender discrimination banned in, 720; GI Bill and, 519, *p519;* Great Society reforms and, 580–81, *p580;* immigrants and, 212, *p212;* legislative reform and, 581, 608, 618; Mexican Americans and, 604, 608, *p608;* changes in 1920s, 382; changes in 1950s, 540, 546; progressive reform and 245–46, *p246;* during Reconstruction, 137, *m138;* Scopes trial and, 385–86; settlement houses and, 221; students with special needs and, 100, 618, *p618;* technology and, 711, 722; in the West, 175, *p175;* women's colleges and, 252, 254
Education for All Handicapped Children Act, 618
Edwards, Jonathan, 20
Egypt, *mxxx;* Camp David Accords and, 669, *p669;* Suez Canal crisis, 542, *f542;* in World War II, 485, *m487;* Yom Kippur War and, 657
Ehrlichman, John, 661, *p661*
Eighteenth Amendment, *f59,* 255, *m255,* 383. *See also* prohibition, Twenty-first Amendment
Eighth Amendment, *f56,* 68–69
Einstein, Albert, 71
Einstein, Isadore "Izzy," 384
Eisenhower, Dwight D., *p539, p741;* CIA and, 541; desegregation in Little Rock and, 557; domestic policy of, 544–45; Eisenhower Doctrine, 542, *f542, p542;* election of 1952, 525, *p525;* election of 1956, 545; foreign policy of, 540–43, *f542;* Korean War and 526, *p526;* Suez

Canal crisis, 542; U-2 incident and, 543; Vietnam policy and, 624–25; World War II and, 485
Eisenhower Doctrine, 542, *f542*
elastic clause, 38
Elcano, Juan Sebastián de, 12
election(s) presidential: of 1789, 84; of 1796, 86; of 1800, 87; of 1812, 90, of 1816, 91; of 1824, 92; of 1828, 92; of 1836, 93; of 1844, 103; of 1860, 104; of 1864, 111; of 1868, 134–35, 238; of 1872, 139, 238; of 1876, 139–40, *p140;* of 1880, 203, 239; of 1884, 239; of 1888, 203, 239; of 1892, 203–04, 240; of 1896, 205, *p205,* 240; of 1900, 240; of 1904, 268; of 1908, 272–73; of 1912, 275–77, *p275, p276, m277;* of 1916, 282–83, 333–34; of 1920, 362–63, *p362;* of 1924, 364–65, *p365;* of 1928, 366; of 1932, 431–32, *p431;* of 1936, 440–41; of 1940, 478; of 1948, 520–21, *m520, p521;* of 1952, 525, *p525,* 539; of 1956, 546; of 1960, 569–71, *p569, m570, p570;* of 1964, 580, *p580;* 1968, 633–35, *p634;* of 1972, 638; of 1976, 666–67; of 1980, 671, *p671;* of 1984, 685, *p685;* of 1988, 692–93, *p693;* of 1992, 708; of 1996, 711; reforms of, 243
electorate, 81, *c81*
electricity, 185, *p185, f186,* 187, *p370,* 371, *c371;* Rural Electrification Administration, 439; Tennessee Valley Authority and, 436, *m436*
Elementary and Secondary School Education Act, 581, 609
Elizabeth I (England), 13, *p13*
Ellington, Edward "Duke," 400, 459, *p459*
Ellis Island, 211, *p211*
Ellison, Ralph, 458, 551
Ellsberg, Daniel, 638
El Niño, 724
El Salvador, *xxvii, m305,* 462, 688, *m688*
emancipation, 98
Emancipation Proclamation, 109, *f112–13*
Embargo Act, 90
Emergency Banking Act, 433, *c441*
Emergency Relief Appropriation Act, 439
Emergency Quota Act, 388
eminent domain, 68
Empire State Building, 405
employment: Americans with Disabilities Act and, 693; careers in the twenty-first century, *c725, f726;* discrimination and, 392, 410, 425–26, 482, 600–01, 604, 611, 612; during the 1970s, 656, 664; Fair Labor Standards Act, *c441,* 448; Great Depression and, 420–21, 425, *p425,* 434–35, *p434,* 439–40, 472, *c472;* opportunities for women, 337–38, 392, *c392,* 481–82, 546, 611, *f613, c614,* 615; in World War I, 337–38; in World War II, 481–83; post-World War II, 518–19, 546. *See also* unemployment
Endangered Species Act, 674
energy crisis, 656–57, *p656, c658,* 668–69, *f668*
energy resources: global consumers and producers of, *m657,* 730–31, *c730, c731;* U.S. resources, 732, *m732, c733. See also* energy crisis
England, *mxxviii;* American colonies, 14–20, *p14, m16, p18, p19, p20;* defeat of the Spanish Armada, 13; early interest in exploration, 13; Revolutionary War against, 22–25, *m23, c25;* taxes imposed on American colonies, 21–22. *See also* Colonial America, Great Britain
Enola Gay (airplane), 496
entrepreneurs, 189
environmentalism, Clean Air Act, 693; conservation and, 270–71, *m270,* 274–75, *c282;* Earth Day, 673, *p673;* Earth Summit, 724; Endangered Species Act, 674; Environmental Protection Agency and, 674–75; global warming, 724; legislation and, 674, 693, 723; pollution and, 674, *p674, p723,* 724, *p724;* Rachel Carson and, 591
Environmental Protection Agency (EPA), 674
Equal Employment Opportunity Commission (EEOC), 611
Equal Pay Act, 611
Equal Rights Amendment (ERA), 391, 614, *p615;* critics of, 391, 614–15, *p615*
Equiano, Olaudah, 19
Erie Canal, 91
Eriksson, Leif, 8
Ervin, Sam, 661
escalation, 628
Escobedo* v. *Illinois, 619
Espionage Act (1917), 335–36
Ethiopia, *mxxx,* Italian invasion of, 464
ethnic cleansing, 716
E.T.–The Extraterrestrial (motion picture), 702
euro, 727, *p727*
Europe, *mxxviii;* Cold War in, 510–17, *p510, p512, f516, m535, m537, m541,* 542–43; end of Cold War and, 695–96, *m695;* Commercial Revolution in, 10; European Union, 727; global expansion and, 287–88, *p287,* 292–93, 316–17, *m316, m317;* immigration from, 95, 105, 172, 210–11, *c210, f212, p212,* 214, *p214;* impact of Great Depression on, 463–66, *f465,* 470–71, *c470, m471;* interest in exploration, 10–13; Marshall Plan and, 514–15, *m515;* Middle Ages in, 8–9, *p8;* Monroe Doctrine and, 304; NATO and, 517, *m535;* post–World War II, 497–98; Protestant Reformation in, 13; rise of dictators in, 463–66, *p463;* Spanish-American War, 296–97, 299; Truman Doctrine and, 514, *f514;* Washington Conference and, 365; World War I and, 326–34, *p326, p327, p328, p329, p330, m332,* 339–48, *p341, m342, p345, f346, p346, m347, c348, m353, f357;* World War II and, 476–77, 478, 479, 485, 486–89, *f487, m488,* 495–96. *See also* names of individual nations
European Union (EU), 727
Evans, Oliver, *f96*
Evans, Walker, 458
evolution: theory of, and Scopes trial, 386
executive branch, 32, *c32,* 40–42, *c41, f50–52, c63*
executive orders, 41
executive privilege, 661
Exodusters, 171
expansion. *See* imperialism
expatriates, 402
exports, 19; Asia and, 290–93; Cuba and, *c295;* Embargo Act and, 90; global, 315–16, *c315, m316, m317, m471;* during Great Depression, 425, *m471;* NAFTA and, 709; to Soviet Union, 659, 670; World War I and, 376. *See also* imports, trade

factories: assembly line and, 368–69; Industrial Revolution and, 94–95; reform and, 248–49; scientific management and, 196, *p196;* war production and, 481
fads: during 1920s, 393–94
Fairbanks, Douglas, 397
Fair Deal, 521
Fair Employment Practices Committee (FEPC), 482
Fair Labor Standards Act, *c441,* 448
Fall, Albert, 364
Falwell, Jerry, 682, *p682*
Family and Medical Leave Act, 708–09
Farewell to Arms, A (Ernest Hemingway), 402
Farm Aid, 702
Farm Credit Administration (FCA), 433, *c441*
Farmer, James, 597
farmers: alliances of, 203, *p203;* coining silver, 202–03; economic setbacks after World War I, 376–77, *p376, c377;* Federal Farm Loan Act and, 283; Hoover's aid policies and, 429; impact of Great Depression on, 423, 426, 449–50, *p449, p450, f451,* 452; in late 1800s, 200–05; migrant workers, 450, 452, 605–06, *p605;* National Grange and, 201; New Deal programs and, 433, 435–36, *p435,* 452; popular culture and, 702; Populist Party and, 202–05; during Reagan years, 686; recession of 1920–21, 423. *See also* agriculture
Farmers' Alliances, 203, *p203*
farming: life on farms, 174–75; migrant workers and, 450, 452, 605–06, *p605;* new ways of, 173–74; on the Plains, 172–74, *p173, c174;* in the South, 142–43, *c144;* water usage in the West, *f104;* in the West, 179, *c179, m180, m181. See also* agriculture
Farm Security Administration (FSA), *c441,* 452; African Americans and, 455
Farragut, David G., 110
Farrell, Frank J., *p196*
Farrell, James T., 458
fascism, 464
Faubus, Orval, 557
Faulkner, William, 457–58, *p458*
Federal Alliance of Land Grants, 606–07
Federal Arts Project, 440
Federal Aviation Administration (FAA), 684–85
Ferraro, Geraldine, 40; election of 1984, 685, *p685*
Federal Bureau of Investigation (FBI): abuse of power, 664
federal court system, 42–43; creation of, 84; first female judge on, 454
federal debt, *c711*
federal deficit, 684

Federal Deposit Insurance Corporation (FDIC), 433, *c441*
Federal Emergency Relief Administration (FERA), 433, *c441;* African Americans and, 455
Federal Farm Loan Act, 283
Federal Home Loan Bank Act, 429
Federal Housing Administration (FHA), *c441*
federalism, 32
***Federalist Paper* "No. 51"** (James Madison), *f39*
Federalist Papers, 33
Federalist Party, 86–87
Federalists, 33
Federal Music Project, 440
Federal Project One, 440, 458
Federal Reserve Act, 280–81, *c282*
Federal Reserve Building, *p279*
Federal Securities Act, 433
federal system, 38–43; separation of powers, *c63*
Federal Theater Project, 440
Federal Trade Commission, 281, *c282*
Federal Writers' Project (FWP), 440, 458
Feminine Mystique, The (Betty Friedan), 611, *p611*
feminism, 611, 612, *p612,* 614; anti-feminists, 614–15, *p615*
Ferdinand (Spain), 11
Ferdinand, Franz, 327, *p327*
Ferguson, Miriam "Ma" Wallace, 391
feudalism, 8
Fifteenth Amendment, 81, 135, *p135*
Fifth Amendment, *f55,* 67–68; blacklisting and, 528, *p528*
Fillmore, Millard, 291, *p739*
film industry. *See* motion pictures
fine arts. *See* art
Finland, *mxxviii,* 476
Finney, Charles Grandison, 98
fireside chats, 433, *p443*
Firestone, Shulasmith, 612, 614
First Amendment, *f55,* 64–66, *f67*
First Battle of Bull Run, 108
First Battle of the Marne, 328
First Continental Congress, 22
Fischer, Irving, 374
Fisk Jubilee Singers, 147, *p147*
Fitzgerald, F. Scott, *f375,* 402
Five-Power Naval Treaty, 365
flappers, 382
Fleming, Alexander, *f497, p497*
flexible response, 573
Florida, *mxx, c743;* Adams-Onís Treaty, 91; Cuban immigrants in, 672; secession and, 107; Spanish exploration of, 12
flu epidemic (of 1918–19), *f357*
Foch, Ferdinand, 340
folk music, 459, 587
Food Administration, 337
food-processing plants, 268, 371
football, 223, 397
Foraker Act, 300
Forbes, Charles, 364
Ford, Betty, *p664*
Ford, Gerald, 662, *p664, p742;* assuming the presidency, 663; domestic policy of, 663–64; election of 1976 and, 666–67; foreign policy of, 664–65
Ford, Henry, 367–69, *f368,* 374
Fordism, 369
Ford Motor Company, 367, 372, *p424*
Fordney-McCumber Tariff Act, 377
Ford's Theater, 128
Fort Donelson, 109
Fort Henry, 109
Fort Laramie Treaty, 152
Fort Sumter, 107
Fort Ticonderoga, 24
forty-niners, 105
For Whom the Bell Tolls (Ernest Hemingway), 466
Foster, William Z., 358
Four-Power Treaty, 365
Fourteen Points, 345, *f350–51*
Fourteenth Amendment, *f57,* 132
Fourth Amendment, *f55,* 66–67
Fox, William, 396
France, *mxviii;* appeasement of Germany, 476; early settlements, 13; Four-Power Treaty with U.S., 365; German occupation of, 477–78; imperialism and, 292; interest in exploration, 13; liberation of, in World War II, 487–89, *p489;* Louisiana Purchase, 89; Panama Canal and, 302; Potsdam Conference and, 510; Suez Canal crisis and, 542; United Nations and, 511; Vietnam and, 624–25, *m624;* World War I and, 326, 327, 328, 330, *p330, m332,* 339–43, *m342;* World War II and, 476, 477, *m477,* 478, 486–89, *m487;* XYZ affair, 87
Franco, Francisco, 465–66
free coinage, 202–03
Freedmen's Bureau, 126–28, *m126, f127*
freedom of assembly and petition, 65–66, *f67. See also* First Amendment
freedom of religion, 65. *See also* First Amendment
freedom of speech, 65. *See also* First Amendment
freedom of the press, 65. *See also* First Amendment
Freedom Rides, 596, *m597*
Freedom Summer, 599
free enterprise, 189
free-speech movement: college student protests and, 583–84, *p584*
French Canal Company, 302
French Indochina, 624, *m624;* Japanese occupation of, 479
Frick, Henry, 198
Friedan, Betty, 611, *p611,* 614, *p614*
Frost, Robert, 458
Fugitive Slave Act, 106
Fulbright, J. William, 631
Fuller, Alvan T., 360
Fulton, Robert, 95
Fundamentalism, 385; Scopes trial and, 385–86
fur trade, 102, *p102*

Gadsden Purchase, 104
Gagarin, Yuri, 588, 589
Gage, Thomas, 22
Gama, Vasco da, 12
Garbo, Greta, 397, 459
García, Héctor P., 604
Garfield, James, 239, *p740*
Garnet, Henry Highland, 98
Garrison, William Lloyd, 98, 135
Garvey, Marcus, 389–90, *p389*
Gaulle, Charles de, 477
gasoline, 187; energy crisis and, 656–67, *p656, c658, f668*
Gates, Bill, 700, 722
Gehrig, Lou "The Iron Horse," 461, *p461*
gender discrimination, 454, 611, 612, 720
General Agreement on Tariffs and Trade (GATT), 727
General Amnesty Act of 1872, 139
General Federation of Women's Clubs (GFWC), 391
Generall Historie of Virginia, The (John Smith), *f15*
General Motors (GM), 372; labor union strikes and, 449
generation gap, 584
genetic engineering, 699
Geneva Accords, 625
genocide, 499
George, David Lloyd, 346, *p351*
George II (England), 18
George III (England), *p21,* 22
Georgia, *mxx, c743;* establishment of colony, 18; secession and, 107
Germany, *mxxviii;* Berlin Airlift, 515–16; Berlin Wall and, 575, *p575, f694,* 695, *p695;* Blitzkrieg, 476; divided into two nations, 516; Hitler and, 464–65, 476–77, 478, 485, 487, 489, 496, 498–99; Holocaust in, 498–99, *p498, p499;* impact of Great Depression on, 464–65, *p464; f470–71;* imperialism and, 289, 292, 326 invasion of Czechoslovakia, 476; Jews during 1930s in, 464–65; *Kristallnacht* in, 465; military alliance with Italy and Japan, 465; Munich Conference and, 476; Nazi Party in, 464–65, *p464,* 498–99; nonaggression pact with Soviet Union, 476; post–World War I, 464; post–World War II, 510–11; Roosevelt's response to German aggression, 467; Soviet-controlled, 515–16; submarine warfare and, 333, 478, 484; war crimes trials and, 511; World War I and, 326–28, 329, 330, 332–34, *m332,* 339–43, *m342;* World War II and, 476–77, 479, 485, 486–89, *m487, f488,* 495–96, p496, 497–99; Zimmerman Note and, 334
Geronimo, 156, *f156*
Gershwin, George, 400
Gettysburg Address, 110, *f113*
Ghost Dance, 156
***Gibbons* v. *Ogden*:** summary of case, *f744*
GI Bill of Rights, 519, *p519*
Gibson, Josh, 397
***Gideon* v. *Wainwright*,** 619, *f747*
Gilded Age, 238–240
Gilded Age, The (Mark Twain and Charles Dudley Warner), 233
Gillespie, Dizzy, 553
Gilpin, Charles, 402
Gingrich, Newt, *p38,* 710, 711, *p711*
Ginsburg, Ruth Bader, 43, *p43*
Girl Scouts, 75
glasnost, 691
Gleiwitz, Germany, 475
Glenn, John, 589, 725
Glidden, Joseph, 168, *p169*
global warming, 724

Goethals, George W., 304, *p304*
gold, 105, 158, 288
Golden Age of Science Fiction, 531
Golden Hour of the Little Flower, The (radio show), 437
Goldmark, Josephine, 249, *p250*
gold rush, 105, 158
gold standard, 202
Goldwater, Barry: 1964 election and, 580
Goldwyn, Samuel, 396
golf, 224, 461
Goliad, Texas: Texas Revolution and, 102
Gompers, Samuel, 197, 250–51, 281
Gonzales, Rodolfo "Corky," 607
Gonzales, Texas: Texas Revolution and, 101
Goodman, Andrew, 599, *p599*
Goodman, Benny "King of Swing," 400, 459
Good Neighbor Policy, 462–63
Goodnight, Charles, 165, 167
Goodnight-Loving Trail, 167, *m168*
Goodyear Tire Factory: sit-down strike held at, 448–49
Gone With the Wind (Margaret Mitchell), 457
Gone With the Wind (motion picture), 460, *p460*
Gorbachev, Mikhail, *p680,* 690–91, *p691,* 695
Gordy, Berry, 586–87
Gore, Al, 708, *p708;* Earth Summit and, 724
Gorgas, William C., 304, *p304*
gospel music, 459
"Gospel of Wealth, The" (Andrew Carnegie), *f192*
Grady, Henry, 144
Gramm-Rudman-Hollings Act, 685
Grand Canyon, 12, *m270,* 271
Grand State Alliance, 203
Grange, Harold "Red" (the "Galloping Ghost"), 397
Grant, Ulysses S., 109–10, 111, *p111, p134,* 238–39, *p239, p740;* election of 1868, 134–35
Grapes of Wrath, The (John Steinbeck), *f451,* 458
Gray Panthers, 618
Great Awakening, 20
Great Britain: appeasement of Germany, 476; Atlantic Charter, 479; Five-Power imperialism and, 365; impact of Great Depression on, 463, *f470-71;* Jay's Treaty, 85; Lend-Lease Act and, 478; Operation Desert Fox and, 716; Panama Canal and, 301–02; Suez Canal crisis and, 542; Treaty of Ghent, 91; Treaty of Versailles, 344–45, 348; War of 1812, 90–91, *p91;* World War I and, 326–28, 330, 332, *m332,* 339–43; World War II and, 476–77, *m477,* 478, *p478,* 486–89, *m487,* 495–96. *See also* colonial America, England
Great Compromise, 31
Great Depression: African Americans in, 425, *f427,* 449, 455–56, *p456;* agriculture and, 423, 449–50, *p449, p450, f451;* American Indians during, 454–55, *p455;* arts and, 440, 457–58, *p458;* banking crisis, 422; business failures, 421–22; causes, 422–24, *c423;* documenting, 452, *p452;* Dust Bowl and, 449–50, *m450, p450;* entertainment culture during, 457–61; family life during, 453, *p453;* farmers during, 435–36, *p435;* 449–50, *p449, p450, f451,* 452; global impact of, 462–67, *p463, p464, f465, m466, f470–71;* Hoover's handling of, 428–40; Hoovervilles, 426; immigrants during, 425; international events during, 462–67, *p463, p464, f465, m466;* literature and, 457–58, *p457;* Mexican Americans during, 425; migrant workers and, *f427,* 450, 452; motion pictures and, 459–60, *p459, p460;* music and, 459, *p459;* New Deal policies and programs, 431–36, *c441,* 448–49, 452, 454–56, 458; painting and, 458, *p458;* photography and, 452, *p452;* radio during, 460; Second New Deal programs, 438–40; spectator sports during, 461, *p461;* stock market crash, 420–21; unemployment in, 425–26, *p425, c426,* 439–40, 442, 458; women during, 426, *p439,* 454, 456
Great Gatsby, The (F. Scott Fitzgerald), *f375,* 402
Great Lakes, 13
Great Migration: of African Americans, 389, *f410–11;* Harlem Renaissance and, 400
Great Plains, 152; communities, 175; Dust Bowl, 449, *p450;* farming on the, 172–74, *p173, c174;* Great Depression and, 449, *m450, p450;* life on the, 174–75; negotiations and conflicts with Indians, 152–53; pioneer schools, 175, *p175;* settlement on, 170–71, *m172*
Great Train Robbery, The (motion picture), *f395*
Great Society, 581
Greece, *mxxviii,* Axis occupation of, 484; civil war, 514
Green, Ernest, 557
Greenback Party, 203
Greenland, first settlement of, 8
Green Party, *f204*
Greenwich Village (New York City): cultural center for Lost Generation, 402
Grenada, *mxxviii,* U.S. invasion of, 688, *m688*
Grenville, George, 22
Grimké, Angelina, 98, 99
Grimké, Sarah, 98, 99
grocery stores, 371
gross national product (GNP), 421–22, *c470*
Guadalcanal, 492, *m493*
Guam, *mxxxi, m292,* 299, 479, 490, *m493*
Guatemala, *mxxvi,* CIA operations in, 541
Guernica (Pablo Picasso), *f465*
Guiding Light, The (radio show), 460
Guinn v. United States, 260
Guiteau, Charles, 239, *p239*
Gulf of Tonkin incident, 627, *m628*
Guthrie, Woody, 459
Gutiérrez, José Angel, 608
Guzmán, Jacobo Arbenz, 541

habeas corpus, 110
Habitat for Humanity, 75
Haiti, *mxxvi, m305,* 307, 713–14
Haldeman, H. R., 661
Hamilton, Alexander, 84, *p84,* 86; *Federalist Papers* and, 33
Hammerstein, Oscar II, *f482*
Hampton, Lionel, 553
Handgun Violence Prevention Act. *See* Brady Bill
Handy, W. C. "Father of the Blues," 399
Harding, Warren G., *p362, p741;* administration of, 363, *p363;* in election of 1920, 362–63, *p362;* political scandals and, 363–64; Teapot Dome scandal and, 364, *p364*
Harlan, John Marshall, 141
Harlem Renaissance, 400–02, *m401, p402*
Harpers Ferry, Virginia, 107
Harrington, Michael, 580
Harris, Joel Chandler, 145
Harris, Townsend, 291
Harrison, Benjamin, 203, 204, 239–40, *p740*
Harrison, William Henry, 90, 91, 93, *p739*
Harvard College, 16
Hawaii, *mxx, c743;* acquisition of, 289–90, *m292*; Japanese immigrants in, *f291;* Pearl Harbor attack, 479; U.S. expansion and, *c314,* 315
Hawkins, Hamilton, 299
hawks, 632
Hawthorne, Nathaniel, 225
Hay, John, 293, 302
Hay–Bunau-Varilla Treaty, 302
Hayden, Tom, 584
Hayes, John W., 194
Hayes, Rutherford B., 139–40, 157, 239
Hay-Herrán Treaty, 302
Haymarket Riot, 197, *p197*
Haymarket Square, 197, *p197*
Haywood, William D. "Big Bill," 251, 336
Head Start, 580, *p580, p581*
health care: Clinton and reform, 708–09; Great Society reforms and, 581
Hearst, William Randolph, 224, 295–96
Heckler, Margaret, 682
Hemingway, Ernest, 402; Spanish Civil War and, 466
Henderson, Fletcher, 459
Hendrix, Jimi, *p586,* 587
Henry, Patrick, 70
Henry (Prince of Portugal), 10
Herrán, Thomas, 302
Hidalgo y Costilla, Miguel, 101
Highway Act, 547, *m547*
highways: construction of, 370, 547, *m547*
hiking, 224
Hill, Anita, 694
Hinckley, John, Jr., 682
hippies, 584, *p584*
Hiroshima, Japan, 496, *p496*
Hispanics: civil rights and, 604–09, *p609;* during Reagan years, 686; women's rights movement and, 612. *See also* Mexican Americans, migrant workers
Hiss, Alger, 529
Hitler, Adolf, 464–65; death of, 496; German expansionism and, 476; Nazis and, 464–65, 498–99; nonaggression pact with Soviet Union and, 476; World War II and, 476–77, 487–89, 496, 498–99
HIV. *See* human immunodeficiency virus
Ho Chi Minh, 624–25, *p624*
Ho Chi Minh Trail, 628, *m628, m644*
Holbrooke, Richard, 717
Holly, Buddy, 553
Hollywood, California, 396
Hollywood. *See* motion pictures
Hollywood Ten, 528
Holmes, Oliver Wendell, 65

Holocaust, 498–99, *p498, p499*
home computers, 676, *p676*
Home Owners Loan Corporation (HOLC), 433, *c441*
Homer, Winslow, 226, *p226*
Homestead, Pennsylvania, 198
Homestead Act, 170, 180
Homestead Strike, 198, *m198, p199*
Honduras, *mxxvi; m305,* 306
Hong Kong, 490
Hooker, Thomas, 16
Hoover, Herbert, 337, 457, *p741;* Bonus Army and, 429–30, *p430;* domestic aid policies, 429; election of 1928, 366, *p366,* 419, *p419;* election of 1932, 431–32, *p432;* Great Depression and, 426–30; philosophy of, 428
Hoovervilles, 426
Hopewell (culture), 6
Hopkins, Harry L., 433, 440
Hopper, Edward, 403, *p403,* 458
horizontal integration, *c190,* 191
household appliances, *p370,* 371
House of Burgesses, 19
House of Mirth, The (Edith Wharton), *f193*
House of Representatives, U.S., 32, 38–40; terms of office, *c80*
House Un-American Activities Committee (HUAC), 527–28
Houston, Sam, 102, *p102*
Howard, Oliver O., 127
Howe, William, 23, 24
Howells, William Dean, 225
How the Other Half Lives (Jacob Riis), 219
Hoyos, Angela de, *f607*
Hudson, Henry, 13
Huerta, Dolores, 605–06, *p606*
Huerta, Victoriano, 308, 309, 310
Hughes, Charles Evans, 333, 363, 365
Hughes, Langston, 401, 455
Hull House, *f220,* 221, *p241*
Human Be-In, 585
Human Genome Project, 699–700
human immunodeficiency virus (HIV), 699
Humphrey, Hubert, 580, 634, 635
Hundred Days, 432
Hungary, *mxxviii;* invasion by Soviet Union, 543
Hurston, Zora Neale, *f427*
Hussein, Saddam, 696, 697, 698, 716
Hutchinson, Anne, 17
hydrogen bomb, 540

IBM, 700
Iceland, *mxxviii;* first settlement of, 8
Ickes, Harold, 432, 435
"I Have a Dream" (Martin Luther King Jr.), 598, *f602–03*
Illinois Central Railroad, *p185*
I Love Lucy (television show), 550–51, *p550*
immigrants: Asian, *p209,* 582, 672–73; Chinese, 161, 214, 260–61, *p260;* definition of, 70; European, 95, 105, 172, 210–11, *c210, f212, p212,* 214, *p214;* Great Society reforms and, 581; Industrial Revolution and, 95; Irish, 160–61; Japanese, *f291;* in late 1800s, 210–14, *c210, p211, p212, f212, p213;* Latin American, 582, 672–73; Mexican American, 261, *p261,* 311, 390; in 1990s, 718–19; migration patterns and, 408, 409, *m409;* new, 210, *c210;* old, 210, *c210;* progressive reform and, 258–61; transcontinental railroad and, 160–61; unemployment during Great Depression, 425; union membership and, 448; voting rights, 608; Western settlement and, 172; xenophobia and, 360; young, *f119*
immigration: Great Society reforms and, 581–82; in late 1800s, 210–11; migration patterns and, 408, 409, *m409;* nativists' response to, 387–88; in 1990s, 718–19, *c719;* opposition to, 213–14, *p214,* 387–88, *p388;* patterns of, *c210;* restricting, 388
Immigration Act of 1990, 719
Immigration and Nationality Act, 581–82
Immigration and Naturalization Service, U.S. (INS), 70–71
Immigration Reform and Control Act, 718
Immigration Restriction League, 214
impeach, 40
impeachment, *c662;* Clinton and, 40, 712, *p712;* Johnson and, 40, 133–34, *p133;* Nixon and, 40, 662
imperialism, 288, *m292, m305, f314–17,* 326
imports, 19, *c315, m316;* in the 1980s, 684; trade deficit and, 664
Inca, *m7,* 12
Inchon, South Korea, 524, *m524*
income tax, 279, *f280, p280*
independent counsel, 710, 712
India, *mxxix;* railroads of, *f161*
Indian Citizenship Act, 391
Indian Civil Rights Act, 616
Indian Removal Act, 93
Indian Reorganization Act (IRA), 455, *p455*
Indian Territory, 93
indict, 67
Indonesia, *mxxxi,* 490
Industrial Revolution, 94–95
industrial unions: creation of, 448
Industrial Workers of the World (IWW), 251
industry: "New South" movement and, 144, *p144;* in the 1920s, 370–71, 374; World War II and, 480
inflation, 664
Influence of Sea Power upon History (Alfred T. Mahan), 288
influenza. *See* flu epidemic
Information Revolution, 722
initiative, 243
Inness, George, 226
installment plan, 371
Intelsat, 589, 591
interchangeable parts, 95
Intermediate-Range Nuclear Forces (INF) Treaty, 691, *p691*
Internal Security Act, 528
International Ladies' Garment Workers Union, 448
International Military Tribunal, 511
International Military Tribunal for the Far East, 511
International Monetary Fund (IMF), 727
International Tribunal for the Prosecution of War Crimes: ethnic cleansing in Bosnia and, 716
Internet, 722, *p722*
internment, 483, *p483*
Interstate Commerce Act, 201
Interstate Commerce Commission (ICC), 201
Intolerable Acts, 22
Inuit, 6
Invisible Man (Ralph Ellison), 551
Iran, *mxxix;* American hostage crisis and, 670–71, *p670,* 687, *p687;* CIA operations in, 541; Iran-contra affair, 689; OPEC member nation, *m657*
Iran-contra affair, 689
Iran hostage crisis, 670–71, *p670,* 687, *p687*
Iraq, *mxxix;* OPEC member nation, *m657;* Persian Gulf War and, 696–98, *m697;* post–Persian Gulf War, 715–16, *p715*
Irish immigrants: railroad construction and, 160–61
Iron Curtain, 512, *p512*
Iroquois League, 8
irrigation, *f104*
Isabella (Spain), 11
Islam, 9
island-hopping, 492–93, *m493*
isolationism, 288; during 1930s, 467
Israel, *mxxix;* Camp David Accords and, 669; creation of, 511, *p511;* Iran-contra affair and, 698; peace accords and, 714–15; Suez Canal crisis and, 542; Yom Kippur War and, 657
Italy, *mxxviii;* impact of Great Depression on, 463–64, *p463, f470–71;* invasion of Ethiopia, 464; League of Nations and, 351; military alliance with Germany, 465; post–World War I, 346, 348; Franklin D. Roosevelt's response to Italian aggression, 467; World War I and, 326, 328; World War II and, 485–86
"Ivan Ivanovich," 588, *p588*
"I Will Fight No More Forever" (Chief Joseph), *f155*
Iwo Jima, 494, *p494*

Jack Benny Show, The (radio show), 460
Jackson, Andrew, 91, 92–93, *p93, p738*
Jackson, Helen Hunt, 157
Jackson, Jesse, 40, 692
Jackson, Mahalia, 459
Jackson, "Stonewall," 108
Jackson State University, 638
James, Henry, 226
James II (England), 19
Jamestown, Virginia, 14
Japan, *mxxix;* auto exports to U.S., 684; bombing of Pearl Harbor, 479; control of Korea, 523; expansionism, 466–67, *m466;* impact of Great Depression on, 466–67, *m466, p467;* imperialism and, 291–92; International Military Tribunal and, 511; military alliance with Germany, 465; occupation of Vietnam, 624; opening of trade with, 290–91; in World War II, 479, 490–94, *m493,* 496
Japanese Americans: during World War II, 483, *p483, f485*
Japanese immigrants: in Hawaii, *f291*
Jaworski, Leon, 662

Jay, John, 84, 85; *Federalist Papers* and, 33
Jay's Treaty, 85
jazz, 400; bebop, 553; during Great Depression, 459, *p459*
Jazz Age, 399–400, *p400*
Jazz Singer, The (motion picture), 396
Jefferson, Thomas, 23, *f26,* 36, 84, *p84,* 86, 87, 88, *p738;* Declaration of Independence and, 23, *f26;* and Louisiana Purchase, 89; as president, 88–90
Jewett, Sarah Orne, 225
Jews: in Germany during 1930s, 464–65, *p465;* Holocaust and, 498–99, *p498, p499*
Jim Crow laws, 140–41, *p140,* 597
jitterbugs, 459
Job Corps, 580
Jobs, Steven, 676
John (England), 8
Johnson, Andrew, 40, *f128, p740;* congressional opposition to, 131–32; critics of, 131; election of 1866, 132, *p132;* impeachment of, 133–34, *p133;* Reconstruction plan of, 128–29
Johnson, James Weldon, 401
Johnson, Lyndon B., 40, *p40, f579, p742;* assuming the presidency, 578, 580; civil rights movement and, 598–99; Cold War policy, 582; domestic policy, 581–82; election of 1964, 580, *p580;* foreign policy, 582; Great Society and, 581; as Kennedy's running mate, 570; legislation on civil rights and, 598, 599; Mexican Americans and, 604; Vietnam War and, 627–30, *p627, p634;* withdrawal from 1968 election, 634
Jolson, Al, 396
Jones, Mary Harris "Mother," 196–97, *p197*
Jones Act, 300
Joplin, Janis, 587
Joplin, Scott, 400
Jordan, *mxxix;* peace accords and, 714–15
Jordan, Barbara, 663
Jordan, Michael, 720, *p720*
Joseph, Chief, 155–56, *f155*
judicial branch, 32, *c32,* 42–43, *c63*
judicial review, 88
Judiciary Act (1789), 84
Jungle, The (Upton Sinclair), 268, *f269*
junk bonds, 685
Jurassic Park (motion picture), *f395*
jury duty, 72–73

Kalakaua, 289
Kamehameha, 289
kamikaze, 494
Kansas, *mxx,* 106, 107, 171, *c743*
Kansas-Nebraska Act, 106
Kearny, Stephen, 104
Keating-Owen Child Labor Act, 283
Kelley, Florence, *p221,* 248
Kelley, Oliver, 201
Kellogg, Frank, 366
Kellogg-Briand Pact, 366
Kelly, Alvin "Shipwreck," 393, *p393*
Kennedy, Anthony M., 682
Kennedy, Jacqueline, 571, *p571,* 579, *p579*
Kennedy, John F., 40, 569, 580, *p742;* assassination of, 578–79; Bay of Pigs, 574–75; Berlin Wall and, 575; Camelot and, 579; civil rights legislation and, 598; Cuban missile crisis, 575–77, *m576;* domestic policy of, 571–72; election of 1960 and, 570–71, *m570, p570, p571;* foreign policy of, 573–77; the Kennedy Era, 571; New Frontier and, 571–72; Peace Corps and, 574, *f574;* space exploration and, 589; steel industry and, 572; Vietnam War and, 626; women's rights movement and, 610–11
Kennedy, Robert, 577, 634, *p634;* civil rights movement and, 597; migrant workers and, 606
Kent State University, 638, *p638*
Kerner Commission, 600
kerosene, 185
Kerouac, Jack, 551
Key, Francis Scott, *f90*
Keyes, Charlotte, 632
Khan, Genghis, 9
Khan, Kublai, 9
Khmer Rouge, 637
Khomeini, Ayatollah, 670
Khrushchev, Nikita, 575, *p575;* Cold War and, 542–43, Cuban missile crisis and, 575–77, *m576;* on Joseph Stalin, 542–43; U-2 incident and, 543
kinetoscope, *f395*
King, Coretta Scott, *p558,* 571
King, Martin Luther, Jr., 558, *p558,* 559, 570–71, *f598,* 632; assassination of, 600–01; Birmingham letter, 597; civil rights movement and, 597–99, *f598,* 600–01; "I Have a Dream" speech, 598, *f602–03*
King, Rodney, 719
Kirkpatrick, Jeane, 687
Kissinger, Henry, 636, 638, 658, *p659*
Kit Carson National Forest: Hispanic land grant rights and, 607
Kitty Hawk, North Carolina, 188
Knights of Labor, 196–97, *p196*
Know-Nothing Party, 95
Knox, Henry, 84, *p84*
Kodak, 227, *p227*
Korea, *mxxix;* U.S./Soviet division of, 523
Korean War, 524–25, *m524, p525,* 526, *p526;* China enters the war, 524; demilitarized zone (DMZ), 526; election of 1952 and, 525; end of, 526
Kosovo: war in the Balkans and, *p716,* 717
Kristallnacht, 465
Kuhn, Margaret, 618
Ku Klux Klan, 138–39, 388–89, *p389*
Kuwait, *mxxix;* OPEC member nation, *m657;* Persian Gulf War and, 696–98, *m697*

La Alianza Federal de Mercedes, 606–07
labor movement, 356–59, 448–49, 519–20, 546
labor reform, 247–51, *c248, c251,* 448–49, 519–20; global, *f250*
labor unions. *See* unions
Lafayette, Marquis de, 24
La Follette, Robert, 244, *p244,* 273, 364
laissez-faire, 189
Lake Champlain, 24
La Navidad (colony), 11
Landon, Alfred M., 440
Land Ordinance of 1785, 31
Lange, Dorothea, 452, *p452*
Laos, *mxxix,* 624, *m624, m628,* 637, 640
La Raza Unida Party (LRUP), 608
La Salle, René-Robert de, 13
Latin America: dollar diplomacy, 306; Good Neighbor policy and, 462–63; immigrants from 672, 718; impact of Great Depression on, 462–63; Monroe Doctrine, 304; Panama Canal treaties and, 669; Roosevelt Corollary, 305–06; U.S. imperialism in, 301–07, *m305, c314*
Latvia, *mxxviii,* 476
Lawrence, Jacob, 458
Lawrence, Kansas, 107
League of Nations, 345, *f346,* 347–48, 349, 363
League of United Latin American Citizens (LULAC), 604
League of Women Voters: resistance to the Equal Rights Amendment, 391
Lease, Mary, 204, *p204*
Lebanon, *mxxix;* Iran-contra affair and, 689; U.S. Marines in, 690, *p690*
Lee, Robert E., 108, *p108,* 110–11, *p111*
legislative branch, 32, *c32,* 38–40, *c63*
Lend-Lease Act, 478
Lenin, Vladimir, 340
Letter from Birmingham Jail (Martin Luther King Jr.), 597
Let Us Now Praise Famous Men (Agee and Evans), 458
Lever Food and Fuel Control Act (1917), 337
Levitt, William, 548
Levittown, 548
Lewis, Carl, 703
Lewis, Jerry Lee, 553
Lewis, John L., 448, 520
Lewis, Meriwether, 89, *m89*
Lewis, Sinclair, 402
Lexington (battleship), 491
Lexington, Massachusetts: in Revolutionary War, 22
Liberator (antislavery newspaper), 98
Liberia, *mxxx;* OPEC member nation, *m657*
Liberty bonds, 337
Libya, *mxxx,* 485
light bulb, 185, *p185, f186*
Liliuokalani, 290, *f290*
Limited Nuclear Test Ban Treaty, 577
Lincoln, Abraham, *p106,* 107, 110, *p739;* assassination of, 128; during Civil War, 107–11; election of, 107; Emancipation Proclamation and, 109, *f112–13;* funeral of, *p129;* Gettysburg Address and, 110, *f113;* second inaugural address of, *f125;* as president, 107–11; Reconstruction plan of, 125; Ten-Percent Plan of, 125, 129
Lindbergh, Charles, 398, *p398,* 478
linotype, 224
liquor trade. *See* prohibition
literature, *f17, f146, f155, f193, f375, f451,* 457–58, *f530, f607, f701;* African Americans and, 145, 401, *f427,* 551; the beats and, 551; Great Depression and,

457–58, *p457;* Harlem Renaissance and, 401; of the late 1800s, 225–26; Lost Generation and, 402; muckraking, 269, *f269;* of New South, 145, *f146;* of the 1920s, 401–02; in 1950s, 551
Lithuania, *mxxviii,* 476
Little House in the Big Woods (Laura Ingalls Wilder), 458
Little House on the Prairie (Laura Ingalls Wilder), 458
Little Orphan Annie (radio show), 460
Little Richard, 553
Little Rock, Arkansas, 556
Little Rock Nine, 556–57, *p557*
Little Turtle, 85
Little Women (Louisa May Alcott), 225
Live Aid, 702
Lochner* v. *New York, 249, *f746*
Locke, Alain, 401
Lodge, Henry Cabot, 348–49, *p349*
Lôme, Dupuy de, 296
London Company, 14, 15
Lonely Crowd, The (David Riesman), 551
Lone Ranger, The (radio show), 460
Long, Huey (the Kingfish), 438, *p438,* 440
Long March, 522
Longoria, Félix, 604, *p604*
Long Walk, 155
Long Winter, The (Laura Ingalls Wilder), 174–75
loose construction, 84
Lorentz, Pare, 452
Los Angeles, California: Mexican American student protests in, 608; race riots in, 600, 719; zoot-suit riots and, 483
Los Angeles riots, 719
Lost Generation, 402
Lost World, The (motion picture), *f395*
Louisiana, *mxx, c743;* Huey Long and, 438, *p438;* secession and, 107; in the Civil War, 110
Louisiana Purchase, 89, *m89*
Love, Nat, 166, *p166*
Love Canal, 674, *p674*
Lowell, Francis Cabot, 94
Lowell girls, 94–95
Lowell system, 94
Loyalists, 24
Loyalty Review Board, 528
Lucas, George, 676, 702
Lucid, Shannon, *p724,* 725
Luftwaffe (German air force), 477
Luna Park (Coney Island), 223, *p223*
Lusitania (ship), 333, *p333*
Luther, Martin, 13
Luxembourg, 477
lynching, 361, 456

MacArthur, Douglas, 491, 493; Bonus Army riot and, 430; demobilization in Japan and, 523, *p523;* in Korean War, 524–25; relations with Truman, 525
Mad (magazine), 551
Madero, Francisco, 308
Madison, James, *p31,* 33, 64, *f65,* 86, 87, 90, *p738; Federalist Paper* "No. 51," *f39; Federalist Papers,* 33; War of 1812 and, 90
magazines, 224–25; advertising in 1920s and, 372; during Great Depression, 457; Red Scare popular culture and, *p528,* 531
Magellan, Ferdinand, 12
Maginot Line, 476
Magna Carta, 8
Mahan, Alfred T., 288, 302
mah jongg, 393, *p393*
***Maine,* USS** (battleship), 296
Malcolm X, 599–600, *p600*
Manchuria, 490; Japanese invasion of, 466, *m466*
mandate, 571
Mandela, Nelson, 715, *p715*
Manhattan Bridge Loop (Edward Hopper), *p403*
Manhattan Project, 496
manifest destiny, 103
Manila Bay, Philippines, 491; in Spanish-American War, 296, *m297*
Mann, Horace, 100
manufacturing, 94; assembly line and, 368–69; business boom in 1920s and, 370–71, *c371;* in the late 1800s, 189
Mao Zedong, 522–23
Marbury, William, 88
Marbury* v. *Madison, 88, *f744*
March on Washington, *p594,* 598, *p598*
Marines, U.S.: in Dominican Republic, 582, *p582;* in Lebanon, 690, *p690;* U.S. imperialism, 306–07, *p307,* 310
Marshall, George C., 487, 514
Marshall, John, 88
Marshall, Thurgood, 43, 555–56, 694
Marshall Plan, 514–15, *m515,* 535
Marshner, Connie, 614
Martí, José, 294, *p294*
Marx Brothers, 459
Maryland, *mxx, c743;* establishment of colony, 17
Massachusetts, *mxx, c743*
Massachusetts Bay Colony, 16
Massacre at Wounded Knee, *m153,* 156–57
mass culture, 222–23
massive retaliation, 540
mass production, 95; assembly line and, 368–69; Fordism and, 369; impact on auto industry, 370
mass transit, 217
Maya, 6, *m7*
Mayer, Louis B., 396
Mayflower (ship), 15
Mayflower Compact, 15
McAuliffe, Christa, 700
McCain, Franklin, 595, 596
McCarthy, Eugene, 633–34
McCarthy, Joseph, 529, *p529,* 531
McCarthyism, 529, 531
McClellan, George B., 108
McClendon, Rose, 402
McClure's Magazine, 242. *See also* muckrakers
McCord, James, 661
McCormack, Joseph, 246
McCormick, Cyrus, 173
McCulloch* v. *Maryland, 93, *f744*
McDowell, Irvin, 108
McGovern, George, 638, 660
McGwire, Mark, 720
McKay, Claude, 401
McKinley, William, 240, 265, *p265,* 266, *p740;* in election of 1896, 205; Spanish-American War and, 296, *p296,* 299
McKinley Tariff, 289
McLaughlin, Patrick, 153
McNeil, Joseph, 595–95
McPherson, Aimee Semple, 385, *p385*
McVeigh, Timothy, 710
Meade, George, 110
Means, Russell, 617, *p617*
meatpacking industry, 268, *f269*
Medicaid, 581
Medicare, 581, *p581*
medicine: advances in technology, 546–47, 675, 699–700; progressive reform and, 245, *p245;* World War II and, *f497;*
Meiji Restoration, 291
Mein Kampf (Adolf Hitler), 464
Méliès, George, *f395*
Mellon, Andrew, 363, 421, 423
Méndez* v. *Westminster School District, 604
Menlo Park, New Jersey: Thomas Alva Edison and, 185, *f186*
mercantilism, 19
Mercury (spacecraft), 589
Meredith, James, 597
Metal Workers Union, 357–58
Metropolitan Museum of Art, 217
Mexican Americans, 261, *p261;* Chicano movement, 607–09; civil rights movement and, 604–09; desegregation and, 604; discrimination and, 604–05, 608–09; during Great Depression, 425, 450, 454; education and, 604, 608, *p608;* employment 604; immigrants, 390, *p390;* land grant rights and, 606–07; La Raza Unida Party, 608; legislation in support of, 608–09; migration patterns and, 409, *m409;* migrant workers, *p409,* 605–06; in the 1920s, 390, *p390;* voting rights legislation and, 609; World War II and, 482–83; zoot-suit riots, 483. *See also* Hispanics, migrant workers
Mexican American Youth Organization (MAYO), 608
Mexican Cession, 104, 606
Mexican Revolution, 308–11, *p309*
Mexico, *mxxvi;* border dispute with U.S., 103; Good Neighbor policy, 463; impact of Great Depression on, 463; independence from Spain, 101; NAFTA and, 709; Treaty of Guadalupe Hidalgo, 104; U.S. investments in, *c310;* war with Texas, 101–02; war with U.S., 103–04; Woodrow Wilson and, 309–11; Zimmerman Note and, 334
Miami, 85
MIAs, 640
Mickey Mouse (cartoon character), 396, *p396*
Microsoft, 700
Middle Ages, 8–9, *p9*
middle colonies, 18
middle-class: rise of, in 1950s, 544
Middle East: Camp David Accords and, 669; CIA operations in, 541; Eisenhower Doctrine and the, *f542;* OPEC member nations in, *m657;* peace accords, 714–15; Suez Canal crisis, 542
Middle Passage, 19
Midway Islands: annexation of, 288–89, *m292*
Migrant Mother (Dorothea Lange), 452, *p452*

migrant workers: civil rights movement and, 605–06, *p605;* during Great Depression, 450, *f451;* New Deal and, 452
migration, 6; during 1865–1930, *f408–11*
Miles, Nelson, 299
militarism, 326
military bases: overseas, *f516*
military spending, 684, *c684*
militias: and the Second Amendment, 66
Milken, Michael, 685
Millay, Edna St. Vincent, 402; opposition to Sacco and Vanzetti trial, *p360*
Miller, Arthur, *f530*
Milosevic, Slobodan, 716, 717
miners, 105, 159, *p159, p160*
Ming dynasty, 9
minimum wage: establishment of, 448; increase in 1950s, 544
mining, 105, 158–60, *c178*
mining companies, 159–60
mining towns, 159–60
Mir (space station), *p724,* 725
Miranda* v. *Arizona, 619, *f747*
missionaries: in Hawaii, 289
Mississippi, *mxx, c743;* civil rights movement in, 599; secession and, 107
Mississippi (culture), 6
Mississippi Delta (region): birthplace of the blues, 399
Mississippi River: French exploration of, 13
Missouri Compromise, 91, 106, 107
Mitchell, Margaret, 457
mobilize, 327
Model A, *p424*
Model T, 367–68, *p368*
Mohawk, 8
Molotov Plan, *f535*
Mondale, Walter: election of 1984, 685
money: free coinage of silver, 202–05; gold standard, 202; U.S. Mint, 84
Mongol Empire, 9
monopolies. *See* antitrust laws, progressives, Theodore Roosevelt, William Howard Taft, Woodrow Wilson
monopoly, 10. *See also* antitrust laws
Monroe, James, 91, *f92,* 304, *p738*
Monroe Doctrine, 91, *f92,* 316; Roosevelt Corollary and, 306
Montenegro, *mxxviii,* 717
Montgomery, Alabama, 557–59; Freedom Rides and, 597, *m597*
Montgomery, Bernard, 485
Montgomery bus boycott, 557–59
Moody, Anne, 596, *p596*
Moody, Helen Wills, 461
Moore, Henry, 725
Moral Majority, 682
Morgan, J. P., 194, 267, 268
Mormons, 102
Mormon Trail, 102, *m103*
Morrill Act, 170
Morse, Samuel, 97
Morton, Ferdinand "Jelly Roll," 400
Mosaddeq, Mohammad, 541
Moses, Anna "Grandma," 458
Mother Jones. *See* Mary Harris Jones
Mothers Against Drunk Driving (MADD), 73–74
"Mother Tongue" (Amy Tan), *f701*
motion picture industry: blacklisting and, 528, *p528*
motion pictures, *f395,* 702, *p702;* blockbuster films and, 676–77, *p676;* during Great Depression, 459–60, *p459, p460;* impact on American society in 1920s, 394, 396–97; in 1950s, 551–52, *p551;* movie stars, 396–97; Red Scare popular culture and, 531
motorcar, 188
motor hotels: growth of in 1920s, 370
Motown Records, 586–87
Mott, Lucretia, 99, *f99*
movie stars: in the 1920s, 396–97
Ms. (magazine), 615
MS-DOS, 700
MTV, 703
muckrakers, 242–43, *p242,* 268–69, *f269*
mugwumps, 239
Muir, John, 270–71, *p271*
Muller* v. *Oregon, 250
Munich, Germany, 476
Munich Conference, 476
Munn* v. *Illinois, 201
Murfree, Mary Noailles, 145, *p145*
Murrow, Edward R., 529
music: of African Americans, 146–47; bebop, 552–53; blues, 399–400, *p400;* British invasion, 586, *p586;* disco, 677, *p677;* during Great Depression: 459, *p459;* folk, 459, 587; fund-raising concerts, 702; gospel, 459; jazz, 400, 459; Motown and, 586–87; of New South, 146–47; in 1920s, 399–400; in 1950s, 552–53; in 1960s, 586–87; in 1980s, 702, *p702;* ragtime, 400; rock 'n' roll, 553, 587; southern, 146–47; spirituals, 98; swing, 459; worldbeat, *f714;* young musicians and, *f505*
Muskie, Edmund, 635
Muslims: and the Crusades, 9
Mussolini, Benito, 463–64, *p463;* overthrow of, 485

NAACP. *See* National Association for the Advancement of Colored People
Nader, Ralph, *f204,* 591, 674–75
Nader's Raiders, 591
NAFTA. *See* North American Free Trade Agreement
Nagasaki, Japan, 486; atomic bombing of, 510
Narváez, Panfilo de, 12
NASA. *See* National Aeronautics and Space Administration
Nasser, Gamal Abdel, 542
Nation, Carry, 255, *p255*
National Aeronautics and Space Administration (NASA), 540, 588–89, *f590,* 700
National American Woman Suffrage Association (NAWSA), 256
national anthem, *f90*
National Association for the Advancement of Colored People (NAACP), 259–60, 336, 361, 389; civil rights movement and, 555–59; during Great Depression, *f411;* magazine of, 282, *p282*
National Association of Colored Women, 260
national borders, expansion of, 89, *m89,* 101–02, 103, *m103,* 104
National Broadcasting Company (NBC), 394
National Child Labor Committee, 248
National Congress of American Indians (NCAI), 616
National Consumers' League, 248
national debt, 84, 85, *c711*
National Farm Workers Association (NFWA), 605. *See also* César Chávez, United Farm Workers
National Grange, 201, *p201*
National Guard, U.S., 66 *p66;* labor strikes and, 199; role in Little Rock Nine, 557
National Industrial Recovery Act (NIRA), 434; African Americans and, 455; declared unconstitutional, 435
nationalism, 326
National Labor Relations Act (NLRA), *c441,* 448; migrant workers and, 606
National Liberation Front, 626
National Organization for Women (NOW), 611–12, *p612*
National Origins Act, 388
national parks: creation of, *m270,* 271. *See also* conservation
National Recovery Administration (NRA), 435, *p435, c441*
National Republicans, 92
National Socialist Party. *See* Nazis
National Traffic and Motor Vehicle Safety Act, 591
National Union for Social Justice, 438
National Urban League, 260
National War Labor Board, 338
National Woman's Party (NWP), 257, 391
National Women's Political Caucus, 614
National Youth Administration (NYA), 440, *c441, f415*
Nation of Islam, 599
Native Americans, 6, *m7,* 8; creation story, 5, culture areas, 6, *m7,* 8, of the East, *m7,* 8; of the Far North, 6, *m7;* of the Great Plains, *m7,* 150, 152, 153–54, *m153;* 156–57; of Mesoamerica, 6; migration to the Americas, 6; of North America, *6, m7, 8;* of the Pacific Coast, 6, *m7, m153,* 155–56, *f155, p155;* of South America, 6; of the West and Southwest, 6, *m7,* 8, *m153,* 155, 156, *f156, p155. See also* American Indians, names of individual tribes
nativism, 387–88, *p388;* Ku Klux Klan and, 388–89, *p389*
nativists, 38–88, 95, 213–14, *p214*
NATO. *See* North Atlantic Treaty Organization
Nat Turner's Rebellion, 98
natural gas, *f728–721, p729, c731;* U.S. production of, *c729, m730*
naturalization, 70–71, *p71*
natural resources, *m316. See also* conservation, natural gas, oil
natural rights, *f26*
Navajo, *m7,* 8, *m153,* 155, 455
Navigation Acts, 19
Navy, U.S.: in Mexican War, 104; in War of 1812, 91; in World War II, *p474,* 479, *p479, p486,* 487–88, 491–94, *p492, m493*
Nazis: Holocaust and, 498–99, *c498, p498, p499;* Nuremberg Trials and, 511,

p511; rise to power in Germany, 464–65, *p464. See also* World War II
Nebraska, *mxx,* 376, *c743;* American Indians in, 152; cattle towns and, 165; date of admission to Union, *m79;* railroads and, 160, *c163;* pioneers in, 171; territory of, 106
Negro National League, 397
Neighborhood Watch, 75
Netherlands, 477; early interest in exploration, 13; global possessions in 1914, *m316*
Neutrality Acts, 467
Neutrality Proclamation, 85
Nevada, *mxx, c743;* American Indian reservations in, *m153;* Comstock Lode and, 158; date of admission to Union, *m79;* Mexican Cession and, 104
New Amsterdam, 18, *m35*
New Deal: African Americans and, 455–56, *p456;* agricultural reforms of, 452; aid to farmers, 435–36; American Indians and, 454–55, *p455;* arts programs of the, 440, *p440,* 458; criticisms of, 437–38, 443; Eisenhower and, 544; end of, 442; evaluation of, 443, *f473;* federal spending during, *f473, m473;* labor programs, 434, 439–40, 448; recovery programs, 434–35; relief programs, 429, 434–35, 439–40, *c441;* Second New Deal, 438–40; Social Security and, 438, *f439;* supporters of, 443; U.S. Supreme Court and, 435, 436, 441–42; unemployment and, 434–35, *p434,* 436, 438–40, *f439, p439, c441,* 442, 443, *f473;* women and, *p439,* 454; work relief and, 429, *p434,* 435, 436, 439–40, *p439, p440, c441,*458. *See also* Franklin D. Roosevelt
New Democrat, 708
New England: colonial, 16–17, *m16;* colonial economy in, 20; Dominion of, 19; Great Awakening in, 20; textile mills in, 94–95; town meetings in, 16
New Federalism, 656. *See also* Richard Nixon
New France, 13
New Freedom, 276. *See also* Woodrow Wilson
New Frontier, 571–72. *See also* John F. Kennedy
New Hampshire, *mxx, c743;* date ratified U.S. constitution, *m79;* establishment of colony, 16, *m16*
new immigrants, 210–14, *c210, p210;* Ellis Island and, 211, *p211;* daily life of, 211–12, *p211, p212, f212;* labor and, 212–13, *p213;* opposition to, 213–14, *p214. See also* old immigrants
New Jersey, *mxx, c743;* date ratified U.S. constitution, *m79;* Edison's research laboratory in, 185, *f186, p186;* establishment of colony, *m16,* 18; labor strike in, *p358;* motion picture industry in, 396; Revolutionary War and, 24; *War of the Worlds* broadcast and, 460
New Mexico, *mxx, c743;* American Indian reservations in, *m153;* Compromise of 1850 and, 106; date of admission to Union, *m79;* Gadsden Purchase, 104; land grant rights for Mexican Americans and, 606; Mexican Cession and, 104; Mexican War and, 104; Santa Fe Trail in, 102, *m103;* territory of, *m103, m153;* testing of atomic bomb in, 510
New Nationalism, 275, 276. *See also* Theodore Roosevelt
New Netherland, 13, 18. *See also* New York
New Orleans, Louisiana: Battle of, 91; birthplace of jazz, 400; Civil War and, 110; 1866 riot in, 133; Freedom Rides and, 596, *m597;* jazz in, 400; Louisiana Purchase and, 89; Pinckney's Treaty and, 8; southern literature about, 145; "The Star-Spangled Banner" and, *f90;* War of 1812 and, 91
New Right, 682, *p682. See also* Moral Majority, Ronald Reagan
newspapers, 224–25; advertising in 1920s and, 372; African American, 390; antislavery, 98; muckracker articles in, 268; yellow journalism and, 295, *p296. See also* names of individual newspapers
New South movement, 144, *p144*
New Sweden, 13
Newton, Huey, 600
New York, *mxx, c743;* colonial boycott of British goods, 22; colonial economy of, 20; Erie Canal in, 91; establishment of colony, *m16,* 18; energy consumption in, *f731;* late 1800s high society in, 193; motion picture industry in, 396; Revolutionary War and, 24; stock market and, 190, 373, 420, *p420*
New York City, New York: Armory Show in, 403; bombing of World Trade Center, 710; colonial economy of, 20; Coney Island in, 223, *p223;* date ratified U.S. constitution, *m79;* design of Central Park, 217, *f218, m218;* Edison's power plant in, *f186,* 187; Harlem, 400–01, *m401;* immigrants in, 211, *p211;* jazz and, 400; Mormon Church founding in, 102; Panic of 1929 and, *p422;* philanthropy and, 217; Seneca Falls Convention in, 99; skyline of, *p374;* skyscrapers in, 216, 405; stock market in, 190, 373, 420, *p420;* subways in, 217; Tammany Hall in, 238, *p238;* tenement housing in, 263; Triangle Shirtwaist Factory Fire, 248, *p249*
New York Journal, 295, *p296*
New York State Tenement House Law, 243
New York Stock Exchange, 190, 373, 420, *p420*
New York World, 295
Nez Percé, *m7, m153,* 155–56; Chief Joseph and, 155–56, *f155, p155*
Ngo Dinh Diem, 625–26
Niagara Movement, 259
Nicaragua, *mxxvi, m305,* 306, 688–89, *m688, p689*
Nicholas II (Russia), 327
Nichols, Terry, 710
nickelodeons, 396. *See also* motion pictures
Nimitz, Chester, 491, 492
Niña (ship), 11
Nine-Power Treaty, 365
Nineteenth Amendment, *f59, f81,* 257, 391
Ninth Amendment, *f56,* 69
Nixon, E. D., 558
Nixon, Pat, 658
Nixon, Richard, 40, 543, 635, *f637, p742:* Checkers speech, 525; and civil rights, 656; and the economy, 656–57, *p656;* as Eisenhower's running mate (1952), 525; election of 1960, 570–71, *m570;* election of 1968, 656; election of 1972, 638; energy crisis and, 657, *c658;* foreign policy of, 658–59, *p659;* New Federalism and, 656; pardoning of, 663; resignation of, 662–63, *p663;* SALT treaty and, 659; Silent Majority and, 656; U.S. Supreme Court and, 656; Vietnam War and, 636–41; visit to China, 654, *p654,* 658; Watergate scandal and, 660–63, *p660, p661, p662*
no-man's-land, 330
nominating conventions, 92
nonaggression pact, 476
Non-Intercourse Act, 90
nonviolent resistance: César Chávez and, 605; civil rights and, 595–99, *p596, m597, f598, p598;* Martin Luther King Jr. and, *f598;* student movement and, 583–85, *p583, p584;* Student Nonviolent Coordinating Committee (SNCC), 596–97, 599, 612
Noriega, Manuel, 693
Normandy, France, 487–89
Norris, Frank, 200, 225
North, Oliver, 689
North, the: African Americans in, 389, *c410, f410–11;* American Indians in, 390–91; Civil War and, 107–11; Great Migration and, 389, *c410;* growth of transportation in 95, *f96,* 96, 184–85, *p185;* industry in, 94–95, 184, *c184,* 185; manufacturing and, 94–95; Mexican Americans in, *f409, m409;* migration to, *c410; f408–11, p410*
North Africa: OPEC member nation, *m657;* World War II and, 484, 485
North America, *mxxvi;* Columbian Exchange and, 12, Dutch colonies in, 13; early cultures of, 6, *m7,* 8; early European colonization in, 12–13, *m12;* English colonies in, 13, 14–20; first migration to, 6; French colonies in, 13; naming of, 12; Native American culture areas of, 6, *m7,* 8; major resources in, *m316;* political map of, *mxxvi;* Swedish colonies in, 13
North American Defense System (NORAD), *m537*
North American Free Trade Agreement (NAFTA), 709, *p709*
North Atlantic Treaty Organization (NATO), 517, *p517, p717;* air strikes on Serbia, 717; Cold War and, *f534–35, m534–35;* 50th anniversary of, *p717;* war in Balkans and, 716–17; war in Kosovo and, 717
North Carolina, *mxx, c743;* Civil War and, 108; date ratified U.S. constitution, *m79;* establishment of colony, *m16,* 18; proposed state of Franklin and, *f79;* readmission to Union, 134; Reconstruction and, *m134;* secession and, 108; Wright brothers' flight tests in, 188, *p188*
North Dakota, *mxx, c743;* American Indian reservations in, *m153;* date of admission to Union, *m79;* farming in, 173–74
North Korea: Korean War and 524–25, 526, *f536, m537;* 38th parallel and, 523. *See also* Korea, Korean War
North Vietnam, *f644, m644;* Ho Chi Minh Trail and, *m644;* support for Vietcong, *f644. See also* South Vietnam, Vietnam War
Northwest Ordinance of 1787, 31, *f78–79, c78, m78, m79*
Northwest Passage, 12–13

INDEX

Northwest Territory, 31, *m78,* 85, 90
Norway, *mxxviii,* 477
Notes of a Native Son (James Baldwin), 551
nuclear energy, 657, 668; percentage of U.S. energy production in mid-1990s, *f730;* U.S. power plants, *m730*
nuclear weapons, *f536;* atomic bomb, 496, 510; brinkmanship and, 540; as Cold War threats, 540; Cuban missile crisis, 575–77, *m576;* hydrogen bomb, 540, *p540;* Intermediate-Range Nuclear Forces (INF) Treaty, 691; limiting number of, 659, 691; massive retaliation and, 540; nuclear missiles, *f536, p536–37;* SALT treaty and, 659, 664; "Star Wars," 690; Strategic Defense Initiative (SDI), 690, *p690;* treaty to ban testing, 577; in World War II. *See also* Strategic Arms Limitation Talks (SALT)
nullification crisis, 92–93
Nunn, Sam: peace mission to Haiti, 714
Nuremberg, Germany, 511
Nuremberg Trials, 511, *p511*

O'Connor, Sandra Day, *f42,* 43, 682
Octopus, The (Frank Norris), 220, 225
Office of Economic Opportunity (OEO), 580
Oglethorpe, James, 18
Ohio, *mxx, c743;* date of admission to Union, *m79;* Dayton peace accords and, 716–17; oil production in, 185; site of Oberlin College, 100; Treaty of Greenville and, 85
Ohio Gang, 363
Ohio Valley: early Native American cultures in, 6
oil, 185, *c190,* 191, *m316;* American investments in Mexican oil, *c310;* energy crisis and, 656–57, *p656, c658;* as energy producer, *f728–731, p729;* impact of automobiles on, 370; U.S. production of, *c729, m730, p731;* prospectors, 185; Standard Oil Company, *c190,* 191–92; Teapot Dome scandal and, 364, *p364*
Ojibway, *m7, m103*
O'Keeffe, Georgia, 403, *f404*
Okinawa, Japan, 494
Oklahoma, *mxx, c743;* American Indians in, 152, 170; American Indian reservations in, *m153,* 155; date of admission to Union, *m79;* Dust Bowl in, 449, *m450;* land rush in, 170; territory of, *m153. See also* Indian Territory
***Oklahoma,* USS** (battleship), 479
Oklahoma! (musical), *f482*
Oklahoma City, Oklahoma; bombing of federal building in, 710
Old Age Revolving Pension (OARP), 437
old immigrants, 210. *See also* new immigrants
Oliver, Joseph "King," 400
Olmec, 6
Olmsted, Frederick Law, 208, 217, *f218*
Olympic Games, 397, 703
Omaha, Nebraska: railroads' effect on population, *c163*
Oneida, *m7,* 8
O'Neill, Eugene, 402
Onondaga, *m7,* 8
On the Road (Jack Kerouac), 551
"Open Boat, The" (Stephen Crane), 225
Open Door Policy, 293, 365
"Open Letter To Woodrow Wilson, An" (W. E. B. Du Bois), 282
open range (ranching), 165–66, 167–69. *See also* ranching
open shop (labor), 376. *See also* labor unions
Operation Ajax, 541. *See also* Iran
Operation Desert Fox, 716, *p716. See also* Iraq
Operation Desert Storm, 697, 707. *See also* Persian Gulf War
Operation Overlord, 487. *See also* D-Day
Operation Restore Hope, 714. *See also* Somalia
Operation Rolling Thunder, 628, *m628. See also* Vietnam War
Operation Vittles, 516. *See also* Berlin Airlift
Oregon, *mxx, c743;* American Indian reservations in, *m153;* British-U.S. joint occupation of, 91; date of admission to Union, *m79;* Nez Percé in, 155–56, *f155, p155;* territory of, 102, 103, *m103;* westward expansion and, 102, *m103*
***Oregon,* USS** (battleship): Mexican War and, 301
Oregon Country, 103; early settlements in, 102; manifest destiny and, 103; missionaries in, 102; as territory of United States, *m103*
Oregon Trail, 102, *m103*
Organization of Petroleum Exporting Countries (OPEC), 657, *m657*
organized crime. *See* crime, Al Capone
O'Riley, Peter, 158
Ortega, Daniel, 688
Osceola, 93
Osgood, Samuel, 84
O'Sullivan, John
Oswald, Lee Harvey, 579
Other American, The (Michael Harrington), 580
Otis, Elisha, 216
Otto, Nikolaus A., 187
Ottoman Empire: global possessions in 1914, *m316;* World War I and, 327
Ovington, Mary White, 259
Owen, Ruth Bryan, 454
Owens, Jesse, 461
ozone layer, 675, 723–24, *p724. See also* global warming

pacification, 629
Pacific Northwest: American Indians in, *m7, m153,* 155–56, 155, *p155;* exploration of, 89; Native American cultures in, 6, *m7;* settlement of, 102, *m103*
Pacific Ocean: Balboa and, 12; European discovery of, 12; U.S. expansion in, 287, *p287,* 288–90, *m292,* 299–300, *p313, f314–15, c314;* Lewis and Clark and, 89; Spanish-American War in, 296, *m297;* World War II and, 490–94, *m493,* 496
Pacific Railway Acts, 160, *f180, m180, m181*
Paige, Satchel, 397, 461
Paine, Thomas, 23
painting. *See* art
Paiute, *m7, m153;* Ghost Dance and, 156; Sarah Winnemucca and Indian reform, 157, *p157*
Paleo-Indians, 6
Palestine: division of, 511; Israeli peace accords and, 714–15
Palmer, A. Mitchell, 360
Palmer raids, 359–60
Panama, *mxxvi,* 301, 302, *p302, m305, m688;* early Spanish exploration of, 12; illegal drug trade and, 693; Manuel Noriega and, 693; Panama Canal and, 301–04; Panama Canal treaties, 669; U.S. invasion of, 693
Panama Canal, 301–04, *p302, f303, p304, m305;* disease and, 302, 304
Panama Canal treaties, 669
Panay (U.S. gunboat), 467
Panic of 1837, 93
Panic of 1873, 139, 163, 190
Panic of 1893, 204–05
Panic of 1929, 421
pardon, 41, 51
Paris, France: German occupation of, 477; liberation of (World War II), 488–89, *p489*
Paris Peace Accords, 639
Parker, Charlie, 553
Parker, Quanah, 154
Parks, Gordon, 452
Parks, Rosa, 558, *f558*
Parliament, 19, *f250;* taxes on English colonies, 21–22
patent, 185
Patriots, 24
Patton, George, 488
Paul, Alice, 257, 391
Pawnee, *m7,* 152
Payne-Aldrich Tariff, 274, *p274, c282*
Peace Corps, 574, *f574;* VISTA and, 580
Peace Democrats, 110
Peale, Norman Vincent, 544
Pearl Harbor: attack on, 479. *See also* World War II
Pemberton, John C., 110
Pendleton, George, *p240*
Pendleton Civil Service Act, 240
penicillin, *f497*
Penn, William, 18
Pennsylvania, *mxx, c743;* coal miners strike in, 266–67; colonial economy in, 20; date ratified U.S. constitution, *m79;* Homestead strike in, 198, *p199,* establishment of colony, *m16,* 18; oil industry in, 185; Revolutionary War and, 24–25; Whiskey Rebellion, 85, *p85*
Pentagon Papers, 638
perestroika, 691. *See also* Mikhail Gorbachev
Perkins, Frances, 432, 435, 454, *f454*
Perot, Ross, *f204;* election of 1992, 708
Perry, Matthew, 291
Perry, Oliver Hazard, 91
Pershing, John J. "Black Jack": attempt to capture Pancho Villa, 311, *p311;* leadership in World War I, 339–40
Persian Gulf, *mxxix;* conflict in, 696–98
Persian Gulf War, 696–98, *p696, m697;* female soldiers in, 698, *p698;* Iraq and terms of cease-fire, 715; military leaders in, 697–98. *See also* Operation Desert Storm

personal computer (PC), 700–01. *See also* computers
Petersburg, Virginia: Civil War siege of, *m109,* 111
Peterson, Esther, 610
petroleum. *See* oil
Philadelphia, Pennsylvania: Centennial Exhibition of 1876, 182, *p182,* 183, 222; colonial economy in, 20; Constitutional Convention at, 31; First Continental Congress, 22; founding of city, 18; Revolutionary War and, 24; Second Continental Congress, 22
philanthropy, 192, 217, 274
Philip II (Spain), 12, 13; rivalry with Elizabeth I, 13; Spanish Armada and, 13
Philippine Government Act, 299
Philippine Islands (Philippines), *mxxix;* flag of commonwealth, *p315;* political status of, 299; Spanish-American War and, 296, *m297,* 299, *f314;* U.S. overseas expansion and, *m292, c314, f314–15;* World War II and, 491
phonograph, *f186*
photography: during Great Depression, 452, *p452;* in the late 1800s, 227, *p227;* in the 1920s, 403–05, *p403*
Picasso, Pablo, 403, *f465*
Pickett, George, 110, *p110*
Pickett's Charge (Battle of Gettysburg), 110
Pickford, Mary, *f396,* 397
Pierce, Franklin, *p739*
Pike's Peak, 158
Pilgrims, 15–16
Pinchot, Gifford, 271, 274, *p274*
Pinckney, Thomas: Pinckney's Treaty and, 85; XYZ affair and, 86
Pinckney's Treaty, 85
Pinkerton detectives, 198, 199, *p199*
Pinta (ship), 11
pioneers, 102, *m103, m172, c174;* African American, *p171;* California Trail and, 102, *m103;* daily life of, 174–75, *p175;* immigrant, 172; Mormon, 102, *m103, f104;* Oregon Trail and, 102, *m103,* 170; Santa Fe Trail and, 102, *m103;* young, *f1;* westward settlement and, 102, *m103,* 152, 153, 170–71, *p171, m172, c174, p174, f178;* in Texas, 101
Pittsburgh, Pennsylvania: steel strike in, 358–59
Pizarro, Francisco, 12
Plains. *See* Great Plains
Plains Indians, *m7,* 152, *p152, m153;* Ghost Dance and, 156; Plains wars, 153–54, *m153,* 156–57; reservations and, 152, *m153,* 156, 157; treaties negotiated with the, 152, 154. See *also* American Indians; names of individual battles, treaties, and tribes
plantations: after the Civil War, 124, 142–43; and cotton, 97, 143, *p143;* in the English colonies, 18, 20; in Hawaii, 289, 291, *p291;* in the pre–Civil War South, 97; slavery on, 97. *See also* planters, slavery, sharecropping
planters, 97; after the Civil War, 142; in Hawaii
Platt Amendment, 300, 463
Plessy, Homer, 141
Plessy* v. *Ferguson, 141, 556, *f745–46*
Plow That Broke the Plains, The (documentary by Pare Lorentz), 452
Plymouth, Massachusetts, 15–16, *m16, m35*
Poland: German invasion of in World War II, 476; immigration to United States from, *f212;* impact of global depression on, *m471;* post–World War II, 497; Stalin and, 510; Warsaw ghetto, 49
polio epidemic, 547
political action committees (PACs), 73
political machines, 238, 244, 382
political parties, 86; effect on presidential elections, *f56–57;* George Washington on, *f86;* nominating conventions and, 92; role in 1796 presidential election, 39; third (independent), *f204. See also* individual parties
political reform. *See* reform
Polk, James K., 103, *p739;* Mexican War and, 103–04; U.S. expansion and, 103–04
Pollock, Jackson, 551, *f552*
poll tax, *f61,* 140
pollution, 674–75, 723; Environmental Protection Agency (EPA) and, 674
Ponce de León, Juan, 12
Pontiac, 21
Pontiac's Rebellion, 21
Pony Express, 160, *p160*
"Poor People's Campaign," 600
Poor People's March, 606
pop art. *See* art
Pope, John, 108
population: African Americans, *c410, f410;* Chinese Americans, 260; growth of after the Civil War, 150; growth of in late 1800s, 200, 215–16, *c216,* 219, 222; Harlem, 399; impact of migration from rural to urban areas, 382–83, *c408, c410, f408–11;* Mexican Americans in 1930, *m409;* Mexican immigration and, 261, 311; in the 1990s, 718–19; in the 1970s, 672–73; of states, *c743;* urban, 215, 216–17, *c216,* 219, 222, 382, 592–93, *m592;* urban problems and, 219; in the West, *c163, m172*
Populist Party, 203–04, *f204;* in election of 1892, 204; in election of 1896, 205
Porter, Edwin S., *f395*
Portrait of a Lady (Henry James), 226
Portugal, *mxxviii;* early exploration and colonization, 10, 12; global possessions in 1914, *m316;* slave trade and, 10
Potsdam Conference, 510, *p510*
Powderly, Terence V., 196–97, *p196*
Powell, Colin, 75, *p75,* 697–98; peace mission to Haiti, 714
Power of Positive Thinking, The (Norman Vincent Peale), 544
Powers, Francis Gary, 543
Powhatan Confederacy, 14–15
POWs, 639, *p641*
preservationists, 270, 271
presidency, 40–41, 50–52, *c63;* checks and balances, 32–33; duties of, 40–41, 42; electoral college and, *f50, f56–57;* executive departments, *c41;* executive orders, 41; filling vacancy of, *f50–51, f60, f62;* impeachment of, 40, *f46, f52,* 133–34, *c662,* 712, *p712;* powers of, 32, *c32,* 33, *c63;* requirements for, 40; separation of powers, 32–33, *c63;* State of the Union address, *f51;* terms of office, 40, *f59–60, f61, f80, c80;* U.S. Supreme Court and, 42; veto power and, 40, *f47. See also* individual presidents
presidio, 12
Presley, Elvis, 553, *p553*
Principles of Scientific Management, The (Frederick W. Taylor), 196, 369
Privy Council, 19
Proclamation of 1763, 21
Progressive Era, 241–46; presidents of, 264–83
Progressive Party, 264, 275–76, *m277,* 364; election of 1904, 268; election of 1912, 276–77, *m277;* election of 1916, 283. *See also* Bull Moose Party
progressives, 241–42, *c242, c282;* antitrust laws and, 267–68, 273–74, 281, *p281, c282;* conservation, 270–71, *m270;* education reform, 245–46, *p246;* federal income tax and, 279; immigrants and, *p243,* 260–61; journalism and, 243, *p243,* 245; labor reform, 247–51, 248–49, *c248, p248, p249, c251,* 283, *p283;* muckrakers, 243, *p243,* 268–69, *f269;* political reform, 244; poverty and, *p243,* 245; presidents as, 264–83; presidential reform, *c292; f280;* public health and, 246; settlement houses and, 245; social reform, 245–46; tariffs, 274, *c282;* temperance and, 254–55, *f254, m255, p255;* urban reform, 244–45; women right's and, 252, 255–57, *p252, f253,* 254, *f254, f256, p256, m257. See also* individual progressives
prohibition, *f59, f60,* 383–85, *p383, c384;* organized crime and, 384–85. *See also* crime, Al Capone, temperance
Promontory, Utah: transcontinental railroad and, 162, *p162*
prospectors: mining, 158, 159–60, *f178, p178;* oil, 185. *See also* oil, miners
protective tariff, 92, 189
Protestant, 13; election of 1928 and, 366; Ku Klux Klan and, 389; missionaries, 288. *See also* Fundamentalism, Pilgrims, Puritans, Quakers, religion
Protestant Reformation, 13
Providence, Rhode Island, *mxx, c743;* establishment of colony, *m16,* 17; role of Roger Williams in, 16–17
public education: affirmative action and, 601; American with Disabilities Act and, 693; bilingual education and, 608; desegregation and, 555–57, *p556, p557,* 601, 604–05; Bill Clinton and, 711; gender discrimination banned in, 720; in Reconstruction South, 137; Mexican Americans and, 604–05, 608, *p608;* reform of, 245–46; right to, 69, *p69*
public health: American Medical Association (AMA) and, 246, *p246,* 675; drinking hazards during prohibition, 384; flu epidemic of 1918–19, *f357;* polio epidemic, 547
public interest groups, 73–74
Public Works Administration (PWA), 435, *c441*
publishing, 224
Pueblo, *m7,* 8, *m153, p390,* 391
pueblos (Indian dwellings), 6
pueblos (towns in Spanish America), 12
Puerto Rico, *mxxvi,* citizenship in, 70; flag of commonwealth, *p315;* U.S. Spanish-American War and, *m297,* 299, 300, *p300;* under Spanish rule, 294; U.S. expansion and, *m305, c314, f314–15*

Pulitzer, Joseph, 224, 295
Pullman, George, 184, 199
Pullman Strike, *m198,* 199
Pure Food and Drug Act, 268–69, *c282*
Puritans: causes of migration, 15, 16; dissent in society, 16–17; economy, 20; educational institutions, 16; and founding of Massachusetts, 16; importance of family in society, 16; literature and, *f17;* religious beliefs, 16; and Salem witch trials, 17; system of government, 16; John Winthrop as leader, 16

Quakers (The Society of Friends), 18, *p18,* 336
Quayle, Dan, 692, *p693*
Quebec, 13, *m35;* in Revolutionary War, 24

Rabin, Yitzhak, 714
race riots, 361, *p361,* 600, 601, 719
racial discrimination, 243, 258–60, 391, 397, 410–11, *m411,* 483, 598, 604–05, 608; Ku Klux Klan and, 388–89, *p389;* violence and, 361, *p361,* 389. *See also* segregation
radar, 478
Radical Republicans, 131
radio: blacklisting and, 528; during the Great Depression, 460, 461; households with (1922–30), *c379;* impact on American society (1920s), 380, 382, 394
ragtime, 400
railroads, 95, *f96,* 97, 201, 204, 238–39, *p215;* Adamson Act and, 283; cattle industry and, 165, *p165, m168;* Civil War and, 111; economic impact of in late 1800s, 162–63, *c163, f181,* 204; farming and, *f181, m181,* 200, 201; global, *f161;* growth of in the late 1800s, 163, *c163, f180, m180,* 184–85, *p185;* immigrant labor and, 160–62, *p162,* 210; industry and, 163, *f181,* 184–85, *p185, c190,* 191, 194; labor strikes and, *m198,* 199, 376; land grants and, 160, 189; Pacific Railway Acts, 160, *f180;* regulation of, 201, 267; transcontinental lines, 160–62, *p162, p163,* 170, *p171, m181;* westward expansion of, 160, *m168;* western settlement and, 150, 160, 162–63, 170, *p170,* 171, *p171, f178, m180, f181, m181*
Rainey, Gertrude "Ma," 400
Raleigh, Walter, 13
ranching, 150, 164–69, *p164, m168, f178, f180, m180, m181;* cattle drives and towns, 167, *m168;* cowboys and, 166–67, *p166, p167;* decline of Cattle Kingdom, 169, *f178, m181;* open-range, 165–69, *p169;* railroads and, 163, 165, 167, *m168, f181, m181;* ranches and, 165–66, *p165;* range rights and, 165; range wars and, 168–69
Randolph, A. Philip, 483, 555, 598
Randolph, Edmund, 84, *p84*
range rights, 165–66
range wars, 168
Rankin, Jeannette, 338
ratification: of U.S. Constitution, 33
Rauschenberg, Robert, 586; art by, 593
Ravenel, William Henry, 136, *p136*
Ray, James Earl, 601
Reagan, Nancy, 682
Reagan, Ronald, 666, *p680, p681,* 682, *f683,* 710, *p742;* anticommunism and, 680, 687–88; assassination attempt on, 710; critics of, 686; defense spending and, 684, *c684;* economic policy of, 683–84; election of 1980, 671; election of 1984, 685; foreign policy of, 687–91; Gorbachev and, 691; inaugural address, 683; Iran-contra affair, 689; Reaganomics, 683; "Star Wars" and, 690–91; U.S.-Soviet relations and, 690–91; U.S. Supreme Court appointments, *f42,* 43, 682
Reaganomics, 683
realism, 225–26
realpolitik, 658
recall, 273
reconcentrados, 294–95
Reconstruction, 125–44, *m134, m138;* African Americans and, 125–28, *m126,* 130–35, *p130, p131, p133, p135,* 137, *p137, p139;* Black Codes, 130–31, *p131;* congressional legislation, 132–34, *m134,* 139; debate over, 130–35; definition of, 125; education and, 127–28; 137; Freedmen's Bureau, 126–28, *m126, f128,* 131–32; internal improvements during, 137–38; under Johnson, 128–29, 131–32; Ku Klux Klan and, 138–39; Lincoln's plan for, 125, *f125;* opposition to, 138–39; planning of, 125–26, 128–29; Radical Republicans and, 131, *p131,* 133, *m134,* 135; Redeemers and, 140; reforms under, 137–38; state governments under, *m134,* 136–37, *p137;* Wade-Davis Bill, 125–26
Reconstruction Acts, 133, *m134*
Reconstruction Finance Corporation (RFC), 429
Red Badge of Courage, The (Stephen Crane), *f298*
Red Cloud, 153
Red Cross. *See* American Red Cross
Red Eagle, 91
Redeemers, 140
"Red Power" movement, 617
Red Record (Ida B. Wells-Barnett), 259
Reds. *See* Communist Party, Red Scare
Red Scare, 359–60, *p359,* 387; post–World War II, 527–29, 531
Reed, Walter, 300, 304
Reed* v. *Reed: summary of case, *f747*
referendum, 243
reform: agricultural, 452; abolition movement, 98–99; business, *c242,* 267–68, *p268,* 273–74, *p274,* 281, *p281, c282;* budget, 710–11; civil service, 240; education, 581, 608; election, 243; health care, 709; mental illness, 100; labor, 243–44, *p244,* 247–51, *c248, p249, c251;* late 1800s and, 99–100, *f99, p100;* political, 243–44; prison, 100; settlement houses, 220, 221, *p221,* 241, *p241,* 245; social, 100, 219–20, *f220, c242,* 245–46; temperance, 100, 254–55, *f254, m255, p255,* 383; urban, 100, *c242,* 243, 244–45, *f280;* welfare, 710–11; women's rights, 99, *f99,* 252, *p252,* 254, *f254,* 255–57, *f256, p256, m257,* 391. *See also* civil rights, progressives, names of individual reformers
reggae, *f715*
regionalists, 458
regressive tax, 72
Rehnquist, William: chief justice of the United States, *p712;* role in Clinton's impeachment trial, *p712*
religion: African Americans and, 98, 124–25, 220, *p220;* Catholic, 8, 13, 17; Croats in Bosnia and, 716; in colonial America, 16–18, 20; English colonization and, 15–16; First Amendment on, *f55,* 65; freedom of, *f55,* 64, 65; Fundamentalism, 385–86, *p385;* Great Awakening, 20; immigration and, 210, 211; Ku Klux Klan and, 389; Mormon, 102; persecution of, 15–16, 102; Pilgrims, 15–16; prohibition debate and, 383; Protestant Reformation, 13; Protestant, 13, 17; Puritans, 15, 16, 17; Quakers, 18, *p18;* Salem witch trials, 17; Scopes trial and, 385–86; Second Great Awakening, 98; in slave culture, 98; temperance movement and, 100; in Texas, 101; Toleration Act of 1649, 17
Remington, Frederic, 295
Reno, Janet, 710
representative democracy, 38, 73, 74
Republican government, *f53*
Republican Party, 106; African Americans and, 137, *p137;* Contract with America and, 710, *p711;* effect of scandal on, 364; election of 1994, 710; formation of, 106; free coinage of silver and, 203; New Democrats and, 708; New Right and, 682, *p682;* progressives and, 269, 273, 274; in Reconstruction, 126, 128, 129, 131–33, 135–37; split of, 276; women in, 615; on women's suffrage, 257. *See also* Democratic-Republican Party, elections, individual presidents
Republic of Texas, 102. *See also* Texas
reservations (American Indian), 152, 156, 157, 164; Bureau of Indian Affairs, 152, 157; effect of Dawes General Allotment Act (1887) on, 157; Indian Reorganization Act, 455; policy of, 157; protest and reform of, 157, *p157,* 390–91, 455, 616–17. *See also* American Indians, individual tribes
reserved powers, 38, *f56*
Retton, Mary Lou, 703, *p703*
Revels, Hiram, 137, *p137*
Revenue Act of 1935, 438
Revere, Paul, 22
Revolutionary War, 22–25, *m23;* advantages and disadvantages, 24; battles of, 22–25, *m23;* causes and effects of, *c25;* Continental Congresses and, 22; Declaration of Independence, 23, *f26–29;* economic impact of the, 31, 84; foreign allies in, 24–25; militias in, 66; Thomas Paine and, 23; Patriots and Loyalists, 24; Treaty of Paris of 1783, 25. *See also* individual battles
Reynolds* v. *Sims, 619

Reza Pahlavi, Mohammad, 670
"Rhapsody in Blue" (jazz symphony), 400
Rhineland, 476; German invasion of, 464
Rhode Island, *mxx, c743;* constitutional convention and, 31; date ratified U.S. constitution, *m79;* textile mills in, 94
Rhode Island system, 94
Richardson, Elliot, 661, 662
Richmond, David, 596
Richmond, Virginia, *mxx, c743,* 108, *m109;* as capital of Confederacy, 108
Ride, Sally, 700
Riesman, David, 551
Riis, Jacob, 219, *p219,* 227, 263
Rio Grande River, 103, *m103,* 104
riots, 361, *p361;* race, 600, 601; Kerner Commission and, 600; Los Angeles of 1992, 719
Risen from the Ranks (Horatio Alger Jr.), 225
River, The (documentary by Pare Lorentz), 452
Rivera, Diego: mural by, 369
roads, 91; building of national, *m547,* 548; impact of automobiles on, 370; improvement of in late 1800s, 188; Public Works Administration and construction of, 435. *See also* Highway Act
Roanoke, Virginia: first English settlement in, 13
Roberts, Ed, 617–18, *p617*
Robeson, Paul, 402, *p402,* 528
Robinson, Jo Ann, 558
Rochambeau, Comte de, 25
Rockefeller, John D., 191–92, *p192,* 193, 242, *f280;* philanthropy of, 192
rock 'n' roll, 553, 587, 702
Rocky Mountains: fur trade in, 102; Lewis and Clark and, 89, *m89;* westward expansion, 102, *m103*
Rodgers, Richard, *f482*
Rogers, Ginger, 459, *p459*
Rogers, Will, 432
Romantics, 226
Rommel, Erwin "the Desert Fox," 485
Roosevelt, Eleanor, 40, 432, *p432,* 456, 610
Roosevelt, Franklin D., 40, 80, *p80, f434, p741;* African Americans and, 455–56, *p456;* American Indians and, 454–55, *p455;* antilynching bill and, 456; Atlantic Charter and, 479; "Black Cabinet" of, 456; court-packing debate and, 442; death of, 496, 509, *p509,* 510; election of 1920, 363; election of 1932, 431–32; election of 1936, 440–41; election of 1940, 478–79; federal appointments of women, 454, 456, *p456;* fireside chats of, 433, *p443;* first inaugural address, *f433;* Good Neighbor policy, 462–63; Hundred Days, 432; labor programs and 448; Latin American policy, 462–63; New Deal, 431–36, 448, 454, 458, *f473;* response to aggression in 1930s, 467; Second New Deal, 438–40; U.S. neutrality and, 467, 478; U.S. Supreme Court and, 441–42; World War II and, 478–79, 483, 484; at Yalta Conference, *p508,* 510
Roosevelt, Theodore, *p266, f267,* 272, 273, *p741;* attempted assassination of, 276, *p276;* big business and, 274; Bull Moose Party and, 275–77, *p275;* coal miners strike and, 266–67; conservation and, 270–71, *m270, p271;* election of 1904, 268; election of 1912, *p264,* 276–77, *m277, p285;* foreign policy and, 305–06; Latin America and, 304–06; muckrackers and, 268–69; New Nationalism, 275, 276; Panama Canal and, 302, *p302;* as president, 266–71, 272; Progressive Party and, 276; Square Deal, 267, 268, 272; reform and, *c282;* in Rough Riders, 297, 299; Russo-Japanese War and, 292; Spanish-American War and, 297, 299; Taft and, 272–75; trusts and, 267–68, *p268*
Roosevelt Corollary, 305–306
Rosenberg, Ethel, 529, *p529*
Rosenberg, Julius, 529, *p529*
Ross, Nellie Tayloe, 391
Roughing It (Mark Twain), 159–60
Rough Riders, 297, 299
roundup, 166
Ruby, Jack, 579
rural areas: African Americans in, *c410, f410;* electricity to, 439; Great Migration and, *c410, f410;* impact of industrial growth on, 382–83; Mexican immigrants in, *f408–09;* migration from, *c408, f408–11;* New Deal programs for, 435–36, 439; prohibition supporters in, 383
Rural Electrification Administration (REA), 439, *c441*
rural life: as criticized by 1920s writers, 383; documentation of, during Great Depression, 452, *p452*
Russia, *mxx;* communist revolution in, 359; Cuban missile crisis and, 575–77, *m576;* energy consumption of, *c728;* energy production of, *c729;* global possessions in 1914, *m316;* imperialism and, 292; purchase of Alaska from, 288; Balkans peace agreement and, 717; war with Japan, 292; World War I and, 326–28. *See also* Soviet Union
Russo-Japanese War, 292
Ruth, George "Babe," 397, *p397*
Rwanda, *mxxx,* 715

Sabin, Florence R., 392
Sacagawea, 89
Sacco, Nicola, 360, *p360*
Sadat, Anwar, 669, *p669*
Safer, Morley, *p632*
Saint Domingue. *See* Haiti
Salem, Massachusetts: witch trials in, 17
Salem witch trials, 17. *See also* Puritans
Salk, Jonas, 546–47, *p546*
Salt Lake City, Utah, *mxx, c743*
Sam, Guillaume, 307
Samoa Islands: 288, acquisition of, 287, *p287,* 289, *m292, c314*
Samoset, 15
San Antonio, Texas: Mexican immigrants in, 261; Texas Revolution and, 101–02
sanctions, 670
Sand Creek Massacre, 152–53, *m153*
San Diego, California, *mxx,* 707
Sandinistas, 688, *p689*
San Francisco, California, *mxx, m103, c743;* Chinese Americans in, 260, *p260;* counterculture and, 584–85, *p584;* gold rush and, 105; student activists and, 585
San Jacinto, Texas: battle at, 102, *p102*
San Juan Hill, *m297,* 299
Santa Anna, Antonio López de, 101–02, *p102*
Santa María (ship), 11
Sante Fe, New Mexico, 102, *m103;* in Mexican War, 104
Santa Fe Trail, 102, *m103*
Sarajevo, Bosnia: World War I and, 324
Sargent, Charles, 270
Sargent, John Singer, 226
satellites: communications, 589, 591; spy, 591
Saturday Night Massacre, 662
Saudi Arabia, *mxxix;* OPEC member nation, *m657;* Persian Gulf War and, 696, *m697*
Sauk, *m7,* 397
Savannah, Georgia, *mxx;* establishment of colony, *m16,* 18; in Civil War, 111
savings and loan crisis, 693
Savio, Mario, 583, *p584*
scalawags, 136
Scalia, Antonin, 682,
Schlafly, Phyllis, 614
Schneiderman, Rose, 249
Schwarzkopf, Norman, 697
Schwerner, Michael, 599, *p599*
science fiction: 1950s popular culture and, 531, *p531*
Scopes, John T., 386
Scopes trial, 385–86
Scott, Dred, 107
Scott, Winfield, 104, 108
Scott* v. *Sandford: summary of case, *f745*
Seale, Bobby, 600
search-and-destroy missions, 629
search and seizure: Fourth Amendment and, 66–67
search warrant, *f55,* 67, *p67*
Seattle, Washington, *mxx;* and general labor strike of 1919, 356–58, *p358*
secession (of southern states), 107
Second Amendment, *f55,* 66
Second Bank of the United States, 93
Second Battle of Bull Run, 108, *m109*
Second Battle of the Marne, 341
Second Continental Congress, 22
Second Great Awakening, 98. *See also* Great Awakening
Second Industrial Revolution, 184–85, 187–88, 267; influence on American literature, 225; workers during, 195–99
Second New Deal, 438–40. *See also* Franklin D. Roosevelt; New Deal
Securities and Exchange Commission (SEC), 433, *c441*
Sedition Act (1918), 336
segregation: of African Americans, 258, 259, 339, 554–56, *p555, p556;* armed forces and, 555; challenges to, 389–90; civil rights legislation and, 598; definition of, 140; during Wilson administration, 282; Freedom Rides and, 596–97, *m597;* Jim Crow laws and, 140–41, *p140;* in 1930, *m411; Plessy* v. *Ferguson,* 556; public schools and, 555–57, *p556, p557,* 601, 604–05;

public transportation and, 557–59, *p559;* sit-ins and, 595, 596; Supreme Court rulings, 555, 556; post–World War II, 554–55, *p554, p555*
Seguín, Juan, 102
Selassie, Haile, 464
Selective Service Act, 336
Selective Training and Service Act, 481
self-determination, 345
Selma, Alabama: civil rights movement and, 599
Seminole, *m7,* 93, *m153*
Senate, U.S., 32, 38–40, *f45,* 709; powers of, 40, *f46–49, f53;* checks and balances, 32–33; elections for, *f46;* filling vacancies in, *f59;* impeachment cases and, 40, *f46, p133,* 133–34, *c662,* 663, 712; role of vice president in, 39, *f46;* separations of powers, 32–33, *c63;* standing committees in, 39–40; terms of office, 38, *f45, f46, f59–60, c80;* U.S. Constitution on, *f45–49;* Watergate hearings, 661–62, *p661. See also* Congress
Seneca, 8
Seneca Falls Convention, 99, *f99*
separation of powers, 38, *c63*
Separatists, 15
Serbia: war in the Balkans and, 716–17, *p716*; Dayton peace accords and, 717; NATO air strikes on, 717
Servicemen's Readjustment Act. *See* GI Bill of Rights
settlement houses, *f220,* 221, 241, *p241,* 245
Seven Days Battles, 108
Seventeenth Amendment, *f59,* 243
Seventh Amendment, *f56,* 67, 68
7th Calvary, U.S. Army, 154, *p154*
Seward, William, 288
Seward's Folly, 288
Seymour, Horatio, 134
shah of Iran. *See* Mohammad Reza Pahlavi
Shame of the Cities, The (Lincoln Steffens), 242
sharecropping, 142–43
Share-Our-Wealth, 438. *See also* Huey Long
Shawnee, 90
Shays, Daniel, 31
Shays's Rebellion, 31
Shepard, Alan, Jr., 589
Sherman, John, 194
Sherman, William Tecumseh, 111, 125, *m126,* 153
Sherman Antitrust Act, 194, 199, 249, 267–68, 281
Sherman Silver Purchase Act, 203
Shoshoni, *m7,* 89, *m153*
Shuttlesworth, Fred, 597
Siberia, 463
silent generation, 551
Silent Majority, 656
Silent Spring (Rachel Carson), 591
Silk Road, 9
Silliman, Benjamin, Jr., 185
silver, 158; free coinage of, 202–03, 204–05; mining of, 158, 159–60, *f178, m178*
Simmons, William J., 388
Sinclair, Upton, 268, *f269*
Singapore, *mxxix,* 490
Singleton, Benjamin, 171
Sioux, *m7, m103,* 150, 152, *p152,* 153–54, *m153, p154,* 260; Ghost Dance and, 156–57; Massacre at Wounded Knee and, 156–57. *See also* names of individual Sioux
Sirhan, Sirhan, 634
Sister Carrie (Theodore Dreiser), 225–26
sit-down strike, 448–49, *p448*
sit-in, 596
Sitting Bull, 154, 156; on American Indian culture, 260
Sixteenth Amendment, *f58,* 279
Sixth Amendment, *f55–56,* 67, 68, 72
skyscrapers, 216, 219; design in the 1920s, 405, *p405*
Slater, Samuel, 94
slavery: abolishment of, *f57,* 126; abolition movement and, 98–99; in colonial America, 15, 18, 19, 20; Compromise of 1850, 106; culture of, 97–98, *p97;* as divisive issue, 106; *Dred Scott* decision, 107; Emancipation Proclamation, 109, *f112–13;* free African Americans and, 97, 98, *p98;* Fugitive Slave Act, 106; global, 10, 12; Kansas-Nebraska Act, 106, 107; labor of, 97; Lincoln on, 107; Mexican Cession and, 106; Missouri Compromise and, 91, 106, 107; opposition to, 98–99; revolts of, 98; slave codes, 20, 97, 98; slave trade, 10, 19, 20, 98; in the South, 97; in Spanish America, 12; in Texas, 101; Three-Fifths Compromise and, 31–32; Underground Railroad and, 98–99; westward expansion of, 101, 106. *See also* African Americans, freedpeople, slaves
slaves: aid for freedpeople, *m126;* apportionment and, 31–32; culture of, 97–98, *p97;* in early America, 15; early trade of, 10, 19, 20; emancipation of, 109, *f112–13;* Fugitive Slave Act, 106; Middle Passage and, 19; religion and, 98; revolts of, 98; Underground Railroad, 98–99. *See also* African Americans, freedpeople, indentured servants, slavery
Sloat, John Drake, 104
Slovenia: war in the Balkans and, 716–17
Smith, Alfred E., 366
Smith, Bessie, 400, *p400*
Smith, John, 14, *f15, p15*
Smith, Joseph, 102
Smith, Mamie, 400
Smith, Moe, 384
Smith, Sophia, 252
Smoot-Hawley Tariff, 424
Social Darwinism, 192
socialism, 251
Socialist Party, 276, *p276, m277,* 359, 363; Palmer raids and, 360
social reform. *See* progressives, reform
Social Security Act, 438, *f439, c441,* 544
societies, 6
Society of American Indians, 260, *p260*
Society of Friends, The. *See* Quakers
sodbusters, 173
Soil Conservation Act of 1935, 1952
Sojourner (space rover), 725
Somalia, *mxxx,* 714–715
Somme River (France): battle at the, 330
sonar technology, 484
Songhay Empire, 9
Sons of Liberty, 22
Sosa, Sammy, 720
Soto, de Hernando, 12
soul music, 586–87
Souls of Black Folk, The (W. E. B. Du Bois), 259
Sound and the Fury, The (William Faulkner), 457
Souter, David, 694
South, the: abolition and, 98–99; agriculture of, 142–43, *c144;* balance of power and, 91, 106, 107, *c107;* Black Codes, 130–31, *p131;* canals in, *m138;* in the Civil War, 107–11; Confederate States of America, 107; congressional representation, *c107;* cotton in, 97, *c97,* 143, *p143, c144;* education in, *f127,* 137, *m138,* 140, *m149;* farming in, 97, 142–43, *p142;* free African Americans in, 97, 124–25, *m126;* Great Depression and, *f472;* Great Migration and, *f410;* impact of Civil War on, 123, 124–25; industrial growth in, 140, 144–45; Jim Crow laws, 140; Ku Klux Klan in, 138–39, 388–89, *p389;* literature of, 145, *p145, f146;* migration out of, *f408–11;* mill life in, 145; music of, 98, *p145,* 146–47, *p147,* 399–400; New South, 144, *p144;* post–Civil War, 123, 124–25, *p124, m138;* Reconstruction and, 125–44, *m134, m138, c143, c144;* secession of, 107; sharecropping, 142–43; slavery in, 97–98, *p98,* 106
South Africa, *mxxx;* apartheid and, 670, 714, *p714;* Nelson Mandela and, 714
South America, *mxxvii;* early civilizations in, 6; European exploration of, 12; major resources in, *m316;* political map of, *mxxvii;* impact of global depression on, *m471*
South Carolina, *mxx, c743;* after Civil War, 123; in Civil War, 107; date ratified U.S. constitution, *m79;* establishment of colony, *m16,* 18; freedpeople in, 125, *m126;* labor in, *f472;* nullification crisis and, 92–93; readmitted to Union, 134; during Reconstruction, *m134;* secession and, 107
South Dakota, *mxx, c743;* American Indian reservations in, *m153;* date of admission to Union, *m79*
Southeast Asia: and consequences of Vietnam War, 639–40; imperialism in, 288
Southern Christian Leadership Conference (SCLC), 597, 599
southern colonies (English), *m16,* 17–18; economy in, 19–20
southern strategy, 656
Southern Tenant Farmers' Union (STFU), 449, *p449*
South Korea: Korean War and 524–25, 526; 38th parallel and, 523. *See also* Korea, Korean War
South Vietnam, *f644, m644;* Ho Chi Minh Trail and, *m644;* soldiers, *p645;* Vietcong, *c645, p645. See also* North Vietnam, Vietnam War
Southwest: American Indians and reservations in, 6, *m7,* 8, *m153,* 155, *f155, p155,* 156, *p156;* Gadsden Purchase and, 104; Mexican cession and, 104; Mexican immigration to, *f408–09;* Mexican Americans in, *m409;* migrant farming in, *p409;* migration out of, *f408–09;* Native American cultures in, 6, *m7;* ranching in, 164–66, *p166;*

Sante Fe Trail, 102, *m103;* settlement of in 1800s, 101, 102, *m103;* Treaty of Guadalupe Hildago, 104. *See also* individual states
Soviet Union: Berlin blockade and, *m537;* Berlin Airlift and, 515–16; breakup of, 695–96, *m695, p696;* Carter administration and, 670; Cold War and, 513–17, *f534–37, m534–35, m537, m541,* 542–43; Cuban missile crisis and, 575–77, *m576, p577;* defeat of Germany at Stalingrad, 486, *m488;* détente and, 659; during Reagan years, 690–91, *p691;* impact of Great Depression on, 463, *p463, m471;* invasion of Hungary, *m537,* 543; invasion of Poland, 476; Korea and, *m537,* 523; Nixon and, 659; nonaggression pact with Germany and, 476; nuclear weapons and 690–91, *p690;* occupation of Eastern Europe, 512; post–World War II, 497; SALT treaty and, 659; space exploration and, 588–89, *p588;* Sputnik, 540, *p540;* Suez Canal crisis and, *m537,* 542; U-2 incident, *m537,* 543; Warsaw Pact and, 517, *m534–35;* in World War II, 484, 486, *f487, m488. See also* individual leaders, Russia
space exploration, 540, 588–89, *p589, f590,* 665, *p665,* 700, 724–25, *p724;* women and, 610, *p610,* 700, *p724,* 725; National Aeronautics and Space Administration (NASA), 540, 588–89, *f590,* 700
Spain: Adams-Onís Treaty, 91; American empire, 12, 164, 294; American Revolution and, 24; civil war in, 465–66, *f465;* conquests of, 12; Council of the Indies, 12; Cuba and, 294–96, *c314;* early exploration of, 12; England and, 13; Florida and, 21; global possessions in 1914, *m316;* impact of Great Depression on, 465–66, *f465;* Mexican Revolution and, 101; Philippines and, *c314;* Pinkney's Treaty, 85; Protestant Reformation and, 13; Puerto Rico and, *c314;* quest for gold, 12; Spanish-American War, 294–300, *m297, c314, f314–15;* Spanish Armada, 13; support for Columbus's explorations 11–12; U.S. trade disadvantages with, 31
Spanish America, 12
Spanish-American War, 294–300, *m297;* African American soldiers in, 297, 299, *p299;* battles of, 296, *m297,* 299; causes of, 295, *c295,* 296; cease-fire, 299; Cuba and, 296, 297, *m297,* 299–300, *p299;* diseases during, 297, 299–300; Philippines and, 296, *m297,* 299; Puerto Rico and, *m297,* 299, 300, *p300;* Rough Riders and, 297, 299, *p299;* Theodore Roosevelt in, 297, 299; terms of peace treaty, 299–300; U.S. armed forces serving in, 297, *c646;* war dispatches and, *f298*
Spanish Armada, 13
Spanish Civil War, 465–66, *f465*
speakeasies, 384, *p384*
speculation, 420
Spencer, Herbert, 192
spheres of influence, 292–93
Spielberg, Steven, *f395,* 676, 702
Spirit of St. Louis (airplane), 398, *p398*
spirituals, 98, 147, *p147*
spoils system, 92
Spokane (American Indian tribe), *m7, m103*
sports, *p461,* 703, *p703,* 720, *p720,* 722; rise of in the late 1800s, 223–24; African Americans and, 224, 397; American Indians and, 397; National Football League (NFL), 397; in the 1920s, 382, 397, *p397;* in the 1990s, 720, 722. See also names of individual athletes, individual sports, individual teams
Springsteen, Bruce, 702, *p702*
Sputnik (spacecraft), 540, *p540,* 588
Squanto, 15–16
Square Deal, 267. *See also* Theodore Roosevelt
stagflation, 656
stalemate, 330
Stalin, Joseph: death of, 526; Krushchev on, 543; nonaggression pact with Hitler, 476; post–World War II plans, 512; at Potsdam Conference, 510, *p510;* at Yalta Conference, *p508,* 510
Stamp Act, 22
Standard Oil Company, *c190,* 191, 242, 273
Standing Bear, 151
Stanford, Leland, 161
Stanton, Elizabeth Cady, 99, *f99,* 256
Starr, Ellen Gates, 221
Starr, Kenneth, 710, 712
"Star-Spangled Banner, The," *f90*
Star Wars (motion picture), 676, *p676*
"Star Wars." *See* nuclear weapons, Ronald Reagan
state constitutions, 30
statehood, 78–79, *c78, m79;* steps to, *c78, f78, m78;* year of, by state, *c743*
State of the Union address, *f51*
states: area of, *c743;* capitals of, *c743;* denied powers, *f49;* populations of (1997), *c743;* powers of, 33, *f56, f57,* 69; representatives in Congress, *c743;* year of statehood, *c743*
states' rights, 92
steam, 95, *f96,* 97
steamboat, 95, *f96*
steel, 184, *c184, c190,* 191; Andrew Carnegie and, 191; impact of automobiles on, 370; impact on building design, 216; Kennedy and, 572; labor strikes and, 198, *m198, p199,* 358–59
steerage, 210
Steffens, Lincoln, 237, 242, *f267*
Stein, Gertrude, 402
Steinbeck, John, *f451,* 458
Steinem, Gloria, 614, *p614,* 615
Stephens, Alexander, 107
Stephens, Uriah, 196
Steuben, Friedrich von, 25
Stevens, John L., 290
Stevens, Thaddeus, 131, *p131,* 132, 133
Stevenson, Adlai, 525
Stewart, James, 460
Stieglitz, Alfred, 227, 403, *f404*
stock market, 189–90, *p190,* 374, 420, 685–86; Black Monday, 686; Black Tuesday, 420, *p420;* crash of 1929, 420–21, *p420;* effects of 1929 crash, 421–24, *p422, p424, c445;* investment in the 1920s, 373–74, 420; "junk" bonds and, 685; Panic of 1893, 204
Stockton, Robert, 104
Stone, Lucy, 99
Stowe, Harriet Beecher, 106
Strategic Arms Limitation Talks (SALT), 659, 664
Strategic Defense Initiative (SDI), 690, *p690*
Streep, Mery, 702
streetcar, *p217,* 219
strikes (labor), 95; air traffic controllers', 684–85, *p684;* coal miners', 266–67; global, *f250;* Homestead, *m198,* 199; migrant workers and 605–06; in the late 1800s, 197, 198–99, *m198, p199,* 205; in the 1920s, 356–59, *p358;* police, *p358,* 359; post–World War I, 356; post–World War II, 520; Pullman, *m198,* 199; railroads and, *m198,* 199, 376; Seattle general, 356–58, *p358;* silkworkers', 251; sit-down, 448–49, *p448;* steelworkers', 358; workers' rights and the NLRA, 448; violent confrontations in, 358. *See also* labor unions, individual labor leaders
Student Nonviolent Coordinating Committee (SNCC) 596–97, 599, 612. *See also* civil rights
student protests: Chicano movement and, 608–09, *p609;* civil rights and, *p594,* 596–97, *p596,* 599 disability rights movement and, 617–18; "Rolling Quads," 617–18; women's movement and, 612, *p612;* student movement and, 583–84, *p583, p584;* Students for a Democratic Society (SDS), 584, 612, 632, *p632;* Student Nonviolent Coordinating Committee (SNCC), 596–97, 599, 612
Students Against Drunk Driving (SADD), 73, 74, *p74*
Students for a Democratic Society (SDS), 584, 612, 632, *p632*
subsidy, 290, 377
suburbs, 217; impact of automobiles on, 370; impact of Great Depression on, 426; growth of, 548–49, *p548, c549*
Sudetanland, 476
Suez Canal crisis, 542
suffrage: African Americans and, *f58,* 134–35, *p135,* 140, 260; expansion of in constitution, *f81;* poll taxes and, *f61–62,* 140; restrictions on, *f61–62,* 140; age and, *f63;* Washington, D.C., and, *f61;* women and, *f59,* 134–35, *p135,* 140, 252, *p252,* 255–57, *f255, p255, m257,* 259, *p259,* 260, 391, *p391;* white men and, 92
sugar, *m316;* in Cuba, 294; in Hawaii, 289–90, *f314*
Sugar Act, 21
Sullivan, Louis H., 216 405
Summer, Donna, 677
Sumner, Charles, 131
Sun Belt, 546, 673, *p673*
Sunday, Billy, 385
supply-side economics, 683
Supreme Court, U.S., *c32,* 33, 42–43, *f42, p43, f52, c63, f80,* 93; affirmative action and, 601; African Americans on, 43; Agricultural Adjustment Act (AAA), 436; checks and balances, 32–33; citizenship and, *f57,* 107; court-packing debate, 442; equal rights issues and, 93, 141, 260, 619; federal income tax, 279; impeachment role of, *f46, c662, p712;* judicial review, 88; Judiciary Act of 1789,

84, 88; labor and, 249–50; 1960s reform and, 619; Nixon and, 656; right to bear arms and, 66; Reagan appointments to, 682, 693–94; Franklin D. Roosevelt and, 441–42; separation of powers, 32–33, *c63;* Sherman Antitrust Act, 268; summary of important cases, *f744–47;* terms of office, *c80;* Watergate tapes and, 662; women on, *f42,* 43. *See also* individual justices and cases
***Sussex* pledge,** 334
Sutter, John, 102
Sutter's Fort, 102, *m103,* 104–05
sweatshops, 212, *p212,* 435
Sweatt, Heman, 555
Sweatt* v. *Painter, 555
Sweden, *mxxviii;* colonization in North America, 13; global depression in, *c470*
Swift, Gustavus, 167
"Swing Low Sweet Chariot" (spiritual), 146–47
swing music, 459
synthetic, 374, *p374*
Syria, *mxxix;* Yom Kippur War and, 657

Taft, Robert, 520
Taft, William Howard, 43, 272–75, *p272, p273,* 306, *p741;* and antitrust lawsuits, 273–74; and conservation controversy, 274–75, *p275;* reforms under, 273–74; and tariffs, 274; and Theodore Roosevelt, 272–73, 275
Taft-Hartley Act, 520, 521
Taino: and Columbus, 11
talkies, 396. *See also* motion pictures
Tammany Hall, 238, *p238*
Tampico, Mexico, 309–10
Tan, Amy, *f701*
Tarbell, Ida, 242, *p242*
tariffs: the American System and, 91; in the early nation, 90; Fordney-McCumber Tariff Act, 377; on imported goods, 424; increases in, 708; and international trade, 727; McKinley Tariff, 289; Payne-Aldrich Tariff, 274; protective, 92–93, 189; Smoot-Hawley Tariff, 424; and Taft administration, 274; Underwood Tariff Act, 279; Wilson-Gorman Tariff, 294; and World Trade Organization (WTO), 727
taxes: and Bush, 692–93; and citizenship, 72; Economic Recovery Tax Act, 683–84; impact on social programs, 684–86; income, 72, 279, *f280,* 683; poll, 140; power to create and collect, 72; property, 72; Revenue Act of 1935, 438; sales, 72; and Shays's Rebellion, 31; Social Security, 438, *f439;* Stamp Act, 22; Sugar Act, 21; Tea Act, 22; Townshend Acts, 22; and Whiskey Rebellion, 85, *p85;* and World War II mobilization, 481. *See also* tariffs
Taylor, Frederick W., 195–96, 369
Taylor, Zachary, 103, 104, *p739*
Tea Act, 22
Teapot Dome scandal, 364
technology: automation and, 546; aviation, *f331;* canal building, 91, 302–04, *f303;* communications, 97, 186–87, *p187, f581;* communications satellites, 589, 591; computers, 547, 676, *p676,* 700–01, *f721,* 722, *p722;* cultural impact, 394, *f395,* 396, 702; and industrial growth in 1920s, 368–69, 370–71; in the Industrial Revolution, 94–97, *f96;* jet planes, 547; manufacturing, 195–96; medicine and, *f497, p546,* 546–47, 675, 699–700; mining, 159; in the 1950s, 546–47; nuclear, 547; recording inventions in the 1980s, 701–02; in the Second Industrial Revolution, *c184,* 184–88, *p185, f186, p187, p188;* and space exploration, 540, *p540,* 588–89, *f590,* 700, *p724,* 724–25; special effects in motion pictures, *f395,* 702; spy satellites, 591; steam, *f96;* television, *f545,* 702–03; and Thomas Edison, 185, *p185, f186,* 187; transportation, 184, 216–17, *p217,* 370; warfare, 330, 484, 496; weather satellites, 591. *See also* Industrial Revolution, individual inventions and inventors, Second Industrial Revolution, transportation
Tecumseh, 90, 91
telegraph, 97, 187
telephone, *f186,* 187, *p187*
television: *f545;* and advertising, 551; and blacklisting, 528; cable, 702–03; Golden Age of, 550–51; and space exploration, 589
Teller Amendment, 296
Telstar (satellite), 589
temperance, 100, *p100,* 254–55, *m255. See also* temperance movement
temperance movement, 100, *p100,* 254–55, *f254, m255, p255*
Temple, Shirley, 460, *p460*
Ten Bears, 154
tenements, 211, 263. *See also* urban areas
Tennessee, *mxxi, c743;* Scopes trial, 385–86; and secession, 108
Tennessee Valley Authority (TVA), 436, *m436, c441*
tennis, 224, 397, *p397,* 461
Ten-Percent Plan, 125, 129
Tenth Amendment, *f56,* 69
Termination Resolution, 616
Terrell, Mary Church, 260
terrorism, 689, 690, *p690,* 710
Tesla, Nikolas, 187
Tet Offensive, *m628,* 632–33
Texaco Star Theatre, 550
Texas, *mxx, c743;* Alamo, 101; annexation of, 103; and the Cattle Kingdom, 164–69; and manifest destiny, 103; and the Mexican Cession, 104; and the Mexican War, 103, 104; ranching in, 164–66, *m168;* and Rio Grande border dispute with Mexico, 103; and the S&L crisis, 693; and secession, 107; settlement in, 101; slavery in, 101; and Sunbelt growth, 673; war for independence, *p101,* 101–02, *p102*
Texas longhorn, 164
Texas Rangers, 154
Texas Revolution, *p101,* 101–12, *p102*
textile mills, 94, 95, *p95;* in the South 144–45
Thailand, *mxxix,* 490
Thanksgiving, 16
Tharp, Twyla, *f675*
Tharpe, Sister Rosetta, 459
theater: blacklisting in, 528; influence of the Harlem Renaissance in, 402, *p402*
Their Eyes Were Watching God (Zora Neale Hurston), *f427*
Third Amendment, *f55,* 66
third political parties, *f204. See also* individual elections
Third Reich, 464
Thirteenth Amendment, *f57,* 126
38th parallel, 523, 526
This Side of Paradise (F. Scott Fitzgerald), 402
Thomas, Clarence, 43, 694
Thorpe, Jim, 397
Three-Fifths Compromise, 32
Three Mile Island, Pennsylvania, 668
Thurmond, Strom, 521
Tijerina, Reies López, 606–07
Tilden, Samuel J., 139, 239
Tin Lizzie. *See* Model T
Tojo, Hideki, 511
Toleration Act of 1649, 17
Toltec, 6
"To My Dear and Loving Husband" (Anne Bradstreet), *f17*
Tonkin Gulf Resolution, 627–28
Topeka, Kansas, 556
To Secure These Rights, 555
town meetings, 16
Townsend, Francis, 437
Townshend Acts, 22
trade: in African kingdoms, 8; in Asia, 8; in colonial America, 19; and Columbian Exchange, 12; with Cuba in late 1800s, *c295;* deficit, 664, 684; early slave, 19; and expansion in the late 1800s, 288, *f314–17, c315;* in the Great Depression, 424; globalization of, 725, 727; international, 725, 727; interstate, 201; with Japan in the 1800s, 290–91; in the Middle Ages, 8, 10; and NAFTA, 709, *p709;* Navigation Acts, 19; Open Door Policy and China, 292–93; under the Articles of Confederation, 31; World Trade Organization (WTO), 727; in World War I, 332. *See also* economy, industry, tariffs
trade deficit, 664
"Trail of Broken Treaties," 617
Trail of Tears, 93
transcontinental railroad, 160–63, *p162, m168*
transportation: airplane, 187–88, *p188, f331,* 547; and Americans with Disabilities Act, 693; automobiles, 188, 370, 367–69, *p368, p369, c371,* 421, *p424, f668;* bridges, 370; canals, 91, 302–04, *f303;* desegregation of public, 557–59, *p559;* highways, 370; railroads, 95, 97, 160–63, *f161, p162, c163,* 184–85, *p185;* roads, 91, *m547,* 547–48; steam power, 95, *f96;* urban, 216–17, *p217*
Transportation Revolution: in early the 1800s, 95, *f96,* 97. *See also* transportation
Travis, William, 101–02
Treaty of Brest-Litovsk, 340
Treaty of Ghent, 91
Treaty of Greenville, 85
Treaty of Guadalupe Hidalgo, 104, 606
Treaty of Medicine Lodge, *m153,* 154
Treaty of Paris of 1783, 25
Treaty of Versailles, 347–49, *m349;* Hitler's violation of, 464–65

trench warfare, 329–30, *p330*
Triangle Shirtwaist Factory fire, 248–49, *p249*
Trinity Site, New Mexico, 510
Triple Alliance, 326
Triple Entente, 326
Trip to the Moon, A (motion picture), *f395*
Truman, Harry S, 581, *p741;* assuming the presidency, 496, 510; and the atomic bomb, 496, 510; Berlin Airlift, 515–16; civil rights and, 555; domestic policy of, 518–21; in election of 1948, 520–21, *m520, p520;* in election of 1952, 525; Fair Deal and, 521; foreign policy of, 513–17, *f514, m515, f516;* Korean War, 522–25, *m524,* 526; labor relations and, 519–20; at Potsdam Conference, 510, *p510;* Presidential Profile, *f519;* Red Scare and, 528; relations with MacArthur, 525; role in World War II, 496, and United Nations, 510
Truman Doctrine, 514, *f514*
Trump, Donald, 685
trust, 191–92; and Roosevelt, 267–68; and Taft, 273–74; and Wilson, 281, *p281*
Truth, Sojourner, 98, 99
Tubman, Harriet, 98–99
Turner, Nat, 98
Tuskegee Institute, 258
Twain, Mark, 145, 160, 225, 238
Tweed, William Marcy, 238
Twelfth Amendment, *f56–57,* 87
Twentieth Amendment, *f59–60*
Twenty-fifth Amendment, *f62*
Twenty-first Amendment, *f60–61,* 385
Twenty-fourth Amendment, *f61–62*
Twenty-second Amendment, 40, *f61,* 80
Twenty-seventh Amendment, *f63*
Twenty-sixth Amendment, *f63,* 81, 638
Twenty-third Amendment, *f61*
Tyler, John, *p739*

u-boats, 330, 332–34. *See also* World War I
Uncle Tom's Cabin (Harriet Beecher Stowe), 106
Underground Railroad, 98
Underwood Tariff Act, 279
unemployment: artists during the Great Depression and, 440, 458; in the 1980s, 684–86; in Europe during the Great Depression, 464, *m471;* GI Bill of Rights and, 519; in the Great Depression, 422, 425–26, *p425, c426,* 428, 434, 439–40, 442, *f472;* and Great Society reforms, 582; and New Deal work programs, 434, *p434, p439,* 439–40, 455, 458; in the 1990s, 707; post–World War I, 356; post–World War II, 518–19, in the 1970s, 656
Union Pacific Railroad, 160–61, *m168,* 238–39
Union Party, 438; in election of 1936, 441
unions, (labor), 95; American Federation of Labor (AFL), 197; AFL-CIO, 546; Clayton Antitrust Act and, 281, *c282;* coal miners strike, 266–67; collective bargaining, 196, 435; creation of industrial, 448; Fordism and, 369; in the Great Depression, 448–50, *p449;* impact of the American Plan on, 376; IWW, 251; Knights of Labor, 196–97, *p196;* in the late 1800s, 196–99, *p196, p197, m198,* 247–51, *c248, f250, c251;* and migrant workers, *f605,* 605–06; and National Recovery Administration, 435; and New Deal programs, 434–35, 448; in the 1920s, 376; in 1950s, 546; opposition to immigration, 213–14; political influence of, 448; post–World War II, 519–20; and progressive reform, 247–51, *c248, f250, c251;* sit-down strikes, 448–49, *p448;* and Square Deal, 267; strikes, 198–99, *m198,* 266–67, 356–59, *p358,* 448–50, 520, 605–6, 684–85, *p684;* Taft-Hartley Act, 520; and women, 196–97, 356, 448; workers' rights and the NLRA, 448. *See also* labor movement
United Auto Workers, 448, 449
United Farm Workers (UFW), 606, *p606,* 612
United Fruit Company, 541
United Mine Workers (UMW), 266, 448, 520
United Nations (UN), 510–11, *p510*
Universal Negro Improvement Association (UNIA), 389
University of California: student protests in 1960s, 583–84, *p584*
University of California* v. *Bakke, 601
University of Mississippi: civil rights movement and, 597
University of Texas: *Sweatt* v. *Painter* and, 555
Unsafe at Any Speed (Ralph Nader), 591
Up from Slavery (Booker T. Washington), 258
urban areas: in the Great Depression, 426; growth of, 208, *p208,* 215–16, *c216;* impact of industrial growth on, 382–83; impact of technology on, 216–17; mass migration to, *c408, f408–11;* and muckrakers, 237, 242–43; in 1950s, 549; organizations formed in, *f220, p220,* 220–21; prohibition opponents in, 383; problems in, 100, 219–20, *p219,* 263; public spaces in, 217, *f218,* 219; reform in, 100, 244–45, *p245;* riots in, 361, *p361,* 600, 601, 719; settlement houses, *f220,* 221, 245; and skyscrapers, 216; and transportation, 216–17, *p217*
urban renewal, 549
Urban II, Pope, 9
U.S. Steel, *c190,* 273, 358, 572
Utah, *mxx, c743;* and Mexican Cession, 104; settlement of Mormons, 102
Ute, *m153*
U-2 incident, 543, *p543*

Valentino, Rudolph, 397
Van Buren, Martin, 93, *p739;* labor unions and, 95
Vanderbilt, Cornelius, 184
Van Der Zee, James, 403
Vanzetti, Bartolomeo, 360, *p360*
vaqueros, 166
V-E Day (Victory in Europe), 496
Veracruz, Mexico, 310–11
Verdun, France: Battle of, 330, *m332*
Vermont, *mxx, c743*
vertical integration, *c190,* 191
Vespucci, Amerigo, 12
veto, 40
vice presidency: duties of 39–40; terms of office, *c80*
Vicksburg, Mississippi, in Civil War, *m109,* 110
video-cassette recorder (VCR), 701
Vietcong, 626, *p629;* tunnel complex of, *c645. See also* Vietnam War
Vietminh, 624–25. *See also* Vietnam War
Vietnam, *m624, m628, f629;* French occupation of, 624–25; Japanese occupation of, 624; and Ngo Dinh Diem, *p625,* 625–26. *See also* Vietnam War
Vietnamization, 636
Vietnam Veterans Memorial, *p622, f640,* 641
Vietnam War, *mxxix,* 628–30, 637–41, *m628, c633, m644, f644–47;* bombing campaigns, 628–29, 637, 639; casualties, *c633,* 639–40 647; congressional debate over, 631–32; consequences of, *c639,* 639–41; Diem government and, *p625,* 625–26; effect on postwar economy, 656; election of 1968, 633–35, *p634;* election of 1972, 638; end of, 638–39; escalation of, 626, 628–30; events leading to, 624–26, *m624, c639;* expansion of war into Cambodia and Laos, 637–38; ground war in, 628–30; Johnson administration and, 582, 627–33; Kennedy administration and, 626; media coverage of, 631, *p632;* Nixon administration and, 636–41; opposition to, 632, *p632, p635,* 638, *p638;* peace negotiations, 637–39; public opinion, 631–32, 647, *c647;* Tet offensive, 632–33; Tonkin Gulf Resolution, 627–28; U.S. forces in, 630, *p630, c633, p636, p637, c646;* U.S. withdrawal, 636–37, 639; veterans of, 641, *p634, p640, p641*
Vikings, 8
Villa, Francisco "Pancho," 309, *p309,* 311
Virginia, *mxxi, c743;* in American Revolution, *m24,* 25; in Civil War, 108, *m109,* 111; and ratification of Constitution, 64; and secession, 108; settlement of, 14–15
Virginia and Kentucky Resolutions, 87
Volstead Act, 383
volunteerism, 74–75, *p74, p77, f651*
Volunteers in Service to America (VISTA), 580
Vostok (spacecraft), 588
voting: and citizenship, 73, 81, *c81;* election reforms, 243, requirements for, 73. *See also* individual civil rights movements
voting rights: and African Americans, 134–35, 140, 554–55, 599; and American Indians, 391; and immigrants, 609, Kennedy on, 77; Nineteenth Amendment and, 257, 391; Twenty-sixth Amendment and, 638; women and, 255–57, *m257,* 391. See also individual civil rights movements, suffrage
Voting Rights Act of 1965, 599
Voting Rights Act of 1975, 609

793

***Wabash* v. *Illinois*,** 201
Wade, Benjamin, 126
Wade-Davis Bill, 125–26
Wagner, Robert, 448
Wagner-Connery Act. *See* National Labor Relations Act
Wake Island, 479, 490, *m493*
Walker, Madame C. J., 374, *p374*
Wallace, George, 635; civil rights movement and, 597
Wall Street, 420–21, *p420*
Walt Disney (film studio), 396
Wampanoag, 16
War Dispatches of Stephen Crane, The, *f298*
War Hawks, 90
Warhol, Andy, *f585,* 586
War Industries Board (WIB), 337
Warner, Albert, 396
Warner, Charles Dudley, 238
Warner, Harry, 396
Warner, Sam, 396
Warner Brothers (film studios), 396
War of 1812, *f90,* 90–91, *p91*
War of the Worlds (Orson Welles), 460
War on Drugs, 693
War on Poverty, 580
War Powers Act, 641, 643
War Production Board (WPB), 481
Warren, Earl, 579, 619
Warren Commission, 579
Warsaw, Poland, 498, *m541*
Warsaw Pact, 517, *f534–35*
Washington, *mxx, c743*
Washington, Booker T., 258–59, *p259*
Washington, George: in American Revolution, 22–25, *p24;* at Constitutional Convention, *p31;* domestic policy of, 85; farewell address, *f86;* foreign policy of, 85; as president, *p83,* 83–84, *p84, f85, p738*
Washington Conference, 365
Washington, D.C.: Bonus Army in, 429–30, *p430;* as site of nation's capital, 84; and Freedom Rides, 596, *m597;* March on, 598, *p598*
Washington Post (newspaper): Watergate and, 660–61
water: and the West, *f104*
Watergate scandal, 660–63; break-in, 661; Deep Throat, 660–61; effect on public's faith in government, 663; Nixon's pardon, 663; resignation of Nixon, 663; Saturday Night Massacre, 662; Senate hearings, 661–62; tape controversy, 661–62; *Washington Post* and, 660–61
waterpower, 94–96
Watt, James, *f96*
Wayne, Anthony, 85
Wayne, John, 459
Wealth Tax Act. *See* Revenue Act of 1935
weapons, *m537;* atomic bomb, 496, 510, 517; Brady Bill, 710, *p710;* hydrogen bomb, 540, *p540;* Strategic Defense Initiative (SDI), 691, *p691;* in World War I, 330; in World War II, 478, 484, 496. *See also* nuclear weapons, Strategic Arms Limitation Talks (SALT)
weather extremes: global warming and, 724
weather satellites, 591
Weaver, James B., 203, 204
Weaver, Robert, 456, 581
Welch, Joseph, 531
welfare: reform, 711
welfare state, 443
Welles, Orson, 460
Wells-Barnett, Ida B., 259, *p259,* 361
West, the, *f178–81;* American Indians in, 150–57, *m153, f155, p155, f156, p156, p157;* African Americans in, 166, *p166,* 171, *p171;* bison in, *c177;* California Gold Rush, 105; cattle industry in, 164–69, *p165, m168;* cowboys, 166–67, *p166;* economy of, *m180,* 181; Exodusters, 171, *p171;* expansion of, 101–05, *m103;* exploration of Louisiana Purchase, 88, *m88, p88;* farming in, 173–74, *p174,* 179, *c179;* Gadsden Purchase, 104; immigrants in, 172; life on the Great Plains, 170–75, *p171, m172, c174;* life on the trail, 102; major overland routes to, *m103;* and manifest destiny, 103; and Mexican Cession, 104; Mexican War and, 103, 104; mining in, 158–60, *p159, p160, c178;* railroads in, 160–63, *p162, p163, m168;* settlement of, 101, 102, 105, 171–72, *m172;* water rights, *f104. See also* American Indians, California Gold Rush, slavery, Texas
West Berlin: Berlin Airlift, 515–16; and construction of Berlin Wall, 575, *p575;* and fall of Berlin Wall, *f694*
West Germany, *mxxviii,* 515–16, *f516;* and fall of Berlin Wall, *f694;* and reunification with East Germany, 695
Westinghouse, George, 184, 187
Westmoreland, William, 628–29, 633
West Virginia, *mxxi, c743;* creation of, 108
We, Too, Are the People (Louise Armstrong), 426
Weyler, Valeriano, 294–95, 296
Wharton, Edith, *f193,* 226
Whip Inflation Now (WIN), 664, *p664*
Whiskey Rebellion, 85, *p85*
Whiskey Ring, 238
Whistler, James McNeill, *p226,* 227
White, John, 13
Whitefield, George, 20
Whiteman, Paul, 400
Whitewater affair, 710
Whitman, Marcus, 102
Whitman, Narcissa, 102
Whitney, Eli, 95, 97
"Wife of His Youth, The," (Charles W. Chesnutt), *f146*
wildcatters. *See* oil prospectors
Wilder, Laura Ingalls, 174–75, 458
wildlife: Endangered Species Act and, 674
Wild One, The, (movie) 552
Wilhelm I (Germany), 326
Wilhelm II (Germany), 328
Willard, Frances, *f254, p254,* 255
Williams, Eugene, 361
Williams, Roger, 16–17
Willkie, Wendell, 478
Wills, Helen, 397, *p397,* 461
Wilson, Edith, 337–38
Wilson, Woodrow, 278–79, *p278, p279, f333, p741;* and African Americans, 281–82; and antitrusts, 281, *p281, c282;* domestic policies of, 279–83, *c282;* economic reforms of, 279–81, *c282;* election of 1912 and, 276–77, *m277;* Fourteen Points of, 345, *f350–51, p351;* on imperialism, 307; and Latin America, 306–07; and the League of Nations, 348; and Mexico, 308–11; New Freedom campaign of, 276–77; at Paris Peace conference, 345–47; on strikes, 359; U.S. neutrality and, 332–34; and the Treaty of Versailles, 347–49; on women's rights, 281; World War I and, 332–34
Wilson-Gorman Tariff, 294
Winnemucca, Sarah, 157, *p157*
Winthrop, John, 16
Wisconsin, *mxx, c743*
Wisconsin Idea, 245
Wizard of Oz (motion picture), 460, *p640*
Woman's Christian Temperance Union (WCTU), 255
women, advertising in 1920s and, 372; African American, 98–99, 220, 374, p374, 400, *p400,* 454, 456, *p456,* 557, 558, 663; and antislavery, 98–99; and aviation, 398; in Civil War, 110; discrimination of, in civil service, 454; displacement after World War I, 356; employment post–World War II, 518–19; and education, 100, 615; and the Equal Rights Amendment (ERA), 614–15; feminists, 611–12, *p612,* 614; first female federal court judge, 454; first female governors, 391; flappers, 382, *p382;* and gender discrimination, 454, 610–15; and jobs in factories, 94, *p95;* and the Great Depression, 426, 453, 454; immigrants, 213; and labor reform, 249–50; and labor unions, 196–97, *p197,* 250, 356, 448; in 1950s, 548, *p548;* and New Deal programs, 454; Nineteenth Amendment and, 257, 391; in Persian Gulf War, 698, *p698;* pioneer life and, 174–75; in politics, 391, *p391,* 614–15, 694; as presidential candidates, 40, 685, *p685;* and Progressive Era, 252–57; in Reagan's cabinet, 682; in Franklin D. Roosevelt's administration, 432, 454, *f454,* 456, *p456;* Seneca Falls Convention and, 99, *f99;* and settlement houses, *f220,* 221, *p221,* 245; and space exploration, 610, *p610,* 700, *p724,* 725; and sports, 224, 397, *p397,* 461, 720; suffrage, 255–57, *f256, p256, m257,* 391; support of American Indians' civil rights, 391; as Supreme Court justices, *f42,* 43, *p43,* 682; and the temperance movement, 254–55, *f254, m255, p255;* and union membership, 448; in the Vietnam War, 630, 632; in the West, 152, 160, 167; and Woodrow Wilson, 281; in the workforce, 145, 392, *c392,* 546, 610–12, *f613, c614,* 615; workers in the South, 145; in World War I, 337–38, *p338, p356;* in World War II, 482. *See also* women's rights movement, women's suffrage
Women's Airforce Service Pilots (WASP), 482
Women's Auxiliary Army Corps (WAAC), 482
Women's Bureau (Department of Labor), 610
Women's Division of the Democratic National Committee, 454
Women's Equity Action League (WEAL), 612

"women's liberation." *See* women's rights movement
Women's National Basketball Association, 720
women's rights movement, 99, *f99,* 610–12, *f613,* 614–15; achievements of, 615; and African Americans, 612; critics of, 612, 614–15, *p615;* and the Equal Rights Amendment (ERA), 614–15; feminists, 611, 612, *p612,* 614; and Hispanics, 612; and legislation, 615
Women's Right to the Suffrage (Susan B. Anthony), *f256*
Women's Strike for Equality, 614
Women Strike for Peace, 632
women's suffrage, 255–57, *f256, p256, m257*
Women's Trade Union League (WTUL), 250; resistance to the Equal Rights Amendment, 391
Wood, Grant, 458, *p458*
Wood, Leonard, 299
Wood, Natalie, *p551*
Woods, Granville T., 184
Woodstock, 587, *p587*
Woodward, Bob, 660–61, *p660*
Woolworth's: civil rights movement and, 595, 596
Worcester* v. *Georgia, 93, *f745*
Work and Win (Horatio Alger Jr.), 225
workforce: children in, *f233;* gender discrimination in the, 454, 611, 612; impact of automation on, 546; women in 1960s in the, 610–11, *f613, c614,* 615. *See also* unions
work hours, 95, 247–48, *c248,* 435. *See also* unions
workplace: early reforms in, 95; progressive reform and the, 248–50; safety in the, 248–49; Second Industrial Revolution and the, 195–99, *p196;* in the South, 144–45. *See also* unions
Works Progress Administration (WPA),439–40, *p440, c441;* and African Americans, 455; employment of women, 454; and unemployed artists, 458
workweek: establishment of maximum hours, 95, 448. *See also* unions
World Bank, 727
worldbeat music, *f714*
world's fairs, 222–23, *p223*
World Trade Center: bombing of, 710;
World Trade Organization (WTO), 727
World War I: African Americans in, 336, *p336,* 342, *p343;* airplanes in, 330, *f331;* alliances in, 327–28; American Indians in, 391; armistice, 342–43; in the Atlantic, 330, 332; and aviation, *f331;* battles of, 328, 330, *m332,* 340–42, *m353;* casualities in, 344; causes of, 325–27, *c348;* draft 336; economic effects of, 344–45; effect on trade, 315; end of, 342–43; Europe after, 344–45; fighting in, 328–30, 332, 339–42; homefront in, 335–38; and labor, 335; mobilizing for, 336; peace negotiations, 345–49; and postwar problems, 356; and prohibition, 383; and Russia, 340; start of, 327; trench warfare, 329–30; U.S. armed forces serving during, *c646;* U.S. entrance into, 334; U.S. neutrality in, 332–34; veterans during Great Depression, 429–30, *p430;* and weapons, 330; women in, 337–38, *p338;* youth participation in war effort, *f321. See also Lusitania,* names of individual battles, Treaty of Versailles, Zimmerman Note
World War II, *m487, f488, m493, f497;* African Americans in, 481, *p481,* 482; alliances in, 476, 479; in the Atlantic, 478; atomic bomb in, 496, *p496;* battles in, 476–79, *m477,* 485–89, *m487, f488,* 491–94, *m493,* Blitzkrieg, 476; bombing of Germany, 485, 495; casualties in, 494, 497–99; costs of, 497–99, *c498;* draft, 481; early German aggression in, 476; the eastern front, 486–87, *f487;* economic involvement, 480–81; and Europe, 476–78, 485–89, *m487, f488,* 495–97; European recovery from 514–15, *m515;* events leading to, 463–67, *p463, p464, f465, m466, c498;* in France, 476–77, 487–89, *m487;* German invasion of Western Europe, 476–77; German surrender, 496; Holocaust, 498–99, *p498, p499;* on the homefront, 480–83; invasion of Czechoslovakia, 476; in Italy, 485–86; invasion of Poland, 475, *p475,* 476; and Japan, 479, 490–94, *m493,* 496; Japanese American internment in, *p483,* 483; Japanese Americans in, 483, *f485;* Japanese surrender, 496; Mexican Americans in, 481–83; military strategies, 484, 492–93; mobilizing for, 480–83; neutrality, 478; Normandy invasion, 487–89; in North Africa, 485; in the Pacific, 490–94, *m493;* and Pearl Harbor, 474, *p474,* 479; postwar economy, 518–20; post–World War II plans, 478, 510; preparations for, 478, 480–81; public support of, 481; in the Soviet Union, 484, 486–87, *m487, f488;* submarine warfare, 478; U.S. armed forces serving during, 481, 483, *c646;* U.S. declaration of war in, 479; victory in Europe, 495–96; victory in Pacific, 496; war crimes trials, 511, *p511;* women in, 481–82. *See also* Manhattan Project, names of individual battles
Wounded Knee, South Dakota, 156–57, 617
Wozniak, Stephen, 676
Wright, Frank Lloyd, 405
Wright, Orville, 188
Wright, Richard, 458
Wright, Wilbur, 188
Wyoming, *mxx, c743;* and Mexican Cession, 104

xenophobia, 360
XYZ affair, 87

Yalta Conference, *p508,* 510
Yamamoto, Isoroku, 479
yellow journalism, 295–96
Yeltsin, Boris, 695, *p696*
Yom Kippur War, 657
Yorktown (battleship), 491
Yosemite Valley, California, *p271, p403*
"Yo Soy Joaquín" (I am Joaquín) (Rodolfo "Corky" Gonzales), 608
Young, Brigham, 102
youth: civil rights movement and, 594–97, *p596,* 599; in the 1800s, *f1, f119, f233;* and the future, 706; New Deal programs for, *f415,* 440; in the 1950s, 551–52; in the 1960s, 571, 583–85, *p584;* in politics, *f565;* and public education in 1920s, 382, *p382,* and volunteerism, 651; and the war effort in World War I, 321. *See also* individual civil rights movements
Yugoslavia, *mxxviii;* Axis occupation of, 484; divided into four republics, 716; Greek civil war and, 514; war in the Balkans, *p716,* 716–17
yuppies (young urban professionals), 685

Zaharias, Mildred "Babe" Didrikson, 461
Zapata, Emiliano, 309, *p309,* 311
Zenger, John Peter, 65
Zimmermann, Arthur, 334
Zimmerman Note, 334
zoot-suit riots, 483

Acknowledgments

For permission to reprint copyrighted material, grateful acknowledgment is made to the following sources:

American Heritage Publishing Company: From "Abandon Ship! Abandon Ship!" by Stephen Bower Young from *World War II: The Best of American Heritage,* edited by Stephen W. Sears. Copyright © 1991 by American Heritage Publishing Company.

Arte Público Press: "Brindis: For the Barrio" from *Arise, Chicano! and Other Poems* by Angela de Hoyos. Copyright © 1975 by Angela de Hoyos and Mireya Robles. Published by M & A Editions, San Antonio.

Bantam, a division of Bantam Doubleday Dell Publishing Group, Inc.: Quote by Alexander Taffel from *The Sixties: Years of Hope, Days of Rage* by Todd Gitlin. Copyright © 1987 by Todd Gitlin.

Rodolfo Gonzales: From *I Am Joaquín/Yo Soy Joaquín: An Epic Poem* by Rodolfo Gonzales. Copyright © 1967 by Rodolfo Gonzales.

HarperCollins Publishers Ltd.: From "Stalingrad: December 1942, A German Infantryman's View" from *In Their Shallow Graves* by Benno Zieser, translated by Alec Brown. Copyright © 1956 by Elek Books.

Henry Holt and Company, Inc.: From *A Rumor of War* by Philip Caputo. Copyright © 1977, 1997 by Philip Caputo.

The Heirs to the Estate of Martin Luther King, Jr., c/o Writers House, Inc. as agent for the proprietor: From "I Have a Dream" by Martin Luther King, Jr. Copyright © 1963 by Martin Luther King, Jr.; copyright renewed © 1991 by Coretta Scott King. From *Stride Towards Freedom* by Martin Luther King, Jr. Copyright 1958 by Martin Luther King, Jr.; copyright renewed © 1986 by Coretta Scott King.

Alfred A. Knopf, Inc.: "I Too Sing America" from *Collected Poems* by Langston Hughes. Copyright © 1994 by the Estate of Langston Hughes.

G. P. Putnam's Sons, a division of Penguin Putnam Inc.: Quote by Winona Espinosa from *The Homefront: America During World War II* by Mark Jonathan Harris, Franklin D. Mitchell, and Steven J. Schechter. Copyright © 1984 by Putnam Publishing Group.

Random House, Inc.: From "On the Pulse of Morning" from *On the Pulse of Morning* by Maya Angelou. Copyright © 1993 by Maya Angelou.

Scribner, a division of Simon & Schuster, Inc.: From *The Great Gatsby* (Authorized Text) by F. Scott Fitzgerald. Copyright 1925 by Charles Scribner's Sons; copyright renewed 1953 by Frances Scott Fitzgerald Lanahan. Copyright © 1991, 1992 by Eleanor Lanahan, Matthew J. Bruccoli, and Samuel J. Lanahan as Trustees under Agreement dated 7/3/75 created by Frances Scott Fitzgerald Smith.

Special Rider Music: From lyrics from "Blowin' in the Wind" by Bob Dylan. Copyright © 1962 by Warner Bros. Music; copyright renewed © 1990 by Special Rider Music. All rights reserved. International copyright secured. From lyrics from "The Times They Are A-Changin'" by Bob Dylan. Copyright © 1963, 1964 by Warner Bros. Music; copyright renewed © 1991 by Special Rider Music. All rights reserved. International copyright secured.

Amy Tan and Sandra Dijkstra Literary Agency: From "Mother Tongue" by Amy Tan. Copyright © 1990 by Amy Tan. First published in *The Threepenny Review.*

Texas A&M University Press: From *With a Black Platoon in Combat: A Year in Korea* by Lyle Rishell. Copyright © 1993 by Lyle Rishell.

Time, Inc.: From letter by Tammy Scheuermann from "Is Feminism Dead?" Letters to the Editor section from *Time,* July 20, 1998. Copyright © 1998 by Time, Inc.

Viking Penguin, a division of Penguin Putnam Inc.: From *The Crucible* by Arthur Miller. Copyright 1952, 1953, 1954 and renewed © 1980, 1981, 1982 by Arthur Miller. From *The Grapes of Wrath* by John Steinbeck. Copyright 1939 and renewed © 1967 by John Steinbeck.

Sources Cited

From *A Kid on the Comstock: Reminiscences of a Virginia City Childhood* by John Taylor Waldorf. Published by American West Publishing Company, Palo Alto, 1970.

From Severita Lara interview by Jesús Treviño, January 31, 1992; from Lionel Steinberg interview by Sylvia Morales, December 7, 1994; and from Reies López Tijerina interview by Luis Torres, December 29, 1989, from *Chicano!* by F. Arturo Rosales. Published by Arte Público Press, Houston, TX, 1996.

Quote by Gale Kaplan from "Just a Housewife" from *A History of Women in America* by Carol Hymowitz and Michaele Weissman. Published by Bantam Books, 1978.

Quote by Diane Nash from "Inside the Sit-ins and Freedom Rides: Testimony of a Southern Student" from *The New Negro,* edited by Mathew H. Ahmann. Published by Biblo and Tannen, New York, 1969.

Quote by Sgt. Dave Richardson from "Battle above the Solomons" from *Yank: The Story of World War II as Written by the Soldiers* by the Staff of *Yank,* the Army Weekly. Published by Brassey's, Inc., McLean, VA, 1984.

From "A Preliminary New York to Buffalo Tour" by S. W. Rushmore from *Motoring in America: The Early Years,* edited by Frank Oppel. Published by Castle Books, New Jersey, 1989.

Quote by John Cash from "Howard University Becomes 'Hot Pick'" by Jonathan P. Decker from *Christian Science Monitor,* June 2, 1997, Philadelphia.

From "That Everyone's American Dream Would Come True" by Dan Helfrich from *Ordinary Americans,* edited by Linda R. Monk. Published by Close Up Publishing, 1994.

From *If I Die in a Combat Zone, Box Me Up and Ship Me Home* by Tim O'Brien. Copyright © 1973 by Tim O'Brien. Published by Delacorte Press/Seymour Lawrence, New York, 1973.

Quote by a Pittsburgh man from *America's History,* edited by James A. Henretta et al. Published by The Dorsey Press, Chicago, 1987.

Quotes by an assistant to Oliver North, an English visitor to the Berlin Olympic Games, a German woman, a Peace Corps volunteer, Gus Rodriguez, Barry Rosen, and a Wall street broker from *The Century* by Peter Jennings and Todd Brewster. Published by Doubleday, New York, 1998.

From *When Heaven and Earth Changed Places: A Vietnamese Woman's Journey from War to Peace* by Le Ly Hayslip. Published by Doubleday, 1989.

Quote by Christa McAuliffe from *No Downlink: A Dramatic Narrative about the Challenger Accident and Our Time* by Claus Jensen, translated by Barbara Haveland. Published by Farrar, Straus & Giroux, New York, 1996.

Quotes by Harvey Frommer and Michael Mitchell from *American Decades, 1980–1989,* edited by Victor Bondi. Published by Gale Research Inc., Detroit, 1996.

From "The Mexican Problem" from *North from Mexico: The Spanish-Speaking People of the United States* by Carey McWilliams. Published by Greenwood Press, New York, 1948.

Quotes by Dan Carpenter, Elton Fax, Selma Hannish, and Richard Nugent from *You Must Remember This: An Oral History of Manhattan from the 1890s to World War II* by Jeff Kisseloff. Published by Harcourt Brace & Company, San Diego, 1989.

Quote by Guy Owen from *The Private Side of American History: Readings in Everyday Life,* edited by Thomas R. Frazier. Published by Harcourt Brace, Orlando, FL, 1983.

Quotes by an Air Force colonel's son and an Army sergeant's daughter from *Military Brats: Legacies of Childhood Inside the Fortress* by Mary Edwards Wertsch. Copyright © 1991 by Mary Edwards Wertsch. Published by Harmony Books, New York, 1991.

From *Their Eyes Were Watching God* by Zora Neale Hurston. Published by HarperCollins Publishers, Inc., New York, 1937.

From *Georgia O'Keeffe* by Roxanna Robinson. Published by HarperCollins Publishers, Inc., New York.

From *The Long Winter* by Laura Ingalls Wilder. Published by HarperCollins Publishers, Inc., New York, 1940.

From *Yesterday: A Memoir of a Russian Jewish Family* by Miriam Shomer Zunser, edited by Emily Wortis Leider. Published by HarperCollins Publishers, New York, 1978.

Quote by a Hungarian immigrant from *This Was America* by Oscar Handlin. Published by Harvard University Press, Cambridge, Mass., 1949.

From "Fighting to Survive, A History of Survival" by Alison Ligon from the *Herald-Sun.* Available on the World Wide Web at http://www.herald-sun.com/hbcu/docs/history.html, February 10, 1998.

Quote by Ten Bears of the Vamparika Comanche from *Bury My Heart at Wounded Knee: An Indian History of the American West* by Dee Brown. Published by Henry Holt and Company, New York, 1971.

Quotes by a draft resister, Dr. Harold Bloomfield, John Osborne, and Claude Summers from *It Seemed Like Nothing Happened: The Tragedy and Promise of America in the 1970s* by Peter N. Carroll. Published by Henry Holt and Company, Inc., New York, 1982.

Quotes from "The Final Armistice" and from "The Collapse of the Central Powers" from *The First World War: A Complete History* by Martin Gilbert. Published by Henry Holt and Company, New York, 1994.

Quotes from *My People the Sioux* by Luther Standing Bear. Published by Houghton Mifflin Company, Boston, 1928.

From *A Place Called Chinese America* by Diane Mei Lin Mark and Ginger Chih. Published by Hunt Publishing Company, Dubuque, IA, 1985.

Quote by Mitsuo Fuchida from "Five Fatal Minutes: Japanese Carriers Crippled, Battle of Midway, 4 June 1942" from *Midway: The Battle That Doomed Japan* by Mitsuo Fuchida with Masataka Okumiya. Published by Hutchinson, 1957.

Quote by Mary Smith from "The Woman Worker Speaks" by Ruth Young and Catherine Filene Shouse from *Independent Woman,* vol. 24, October 1945.

Quote by C. D. Jackson from "Tokens Left at the Wall" by Arnold Abrams, May 24, 1996, from *Newsday.com: The Vietnam Memorial.*

From "Interview with Nguyen Huu Tho" by Christine Pelzer White from *Journal of Contemporary Asia,* vol. 11, no. 1, 1981.

Quote by a Garden City, Kansas, woman from *Kansas City Times,* March 1935.

Quote by Juan Chanax from *Strangers among Us* by Roberto Suro. Published by Alfred A. Knopf, Inc., New York, 1998.

From *Remembering America: A Voice from the Sixties* by Richard N. Goodwin. Published by Little, Brown and Company, Boston, 1988.

Quotes by Jerome Franks, Virginia Lewis MacInnes, and Sylvia Van Hazinga from *Ticket to Paradise: American Movie Theaters and How We Had Fun* by John Margolies and Emily Gwathmey. Published by Little, Brown and Company, Boston, 1991.

Quote by Gordon Parks from *The Great Depression: America in the 1930s* by T. H. Watkins. Published by Little, Brown and Company, Boston, 1993.

From "About Women" from *Los Angeles Times,* May 12, 1974.

Quote from *LULAC News,* Houston, TX, 1946.

Quote by Sam Rayburn from *Sam Johnson's Boy: A Close-up of the President from Texas* by Alfred Steinberg. Published by Macmillan, New York, 1968.

Quote by Jessie Lee Brown Foveaux from *The Manhattan (Kansas) Mercury,* March 1, 1998.

From quotes by Meryl Streep from *MAQ.* Available on the World Wide Web at http://www.geocities.com/Hollywood/Hills/2844/MSQ.html.

Quote by a rancher from Cut Bank, Montana, to David Houston and Florence Harrison from *America Enters the World: A People's History of the Progressive Era and World War I* by Page Smith. Published by McGraw-Hill Book Company, 1985.

From the "Memories of Max Mannheimer: Theresienstadt-Auschwitz-Warsah-Dachau, 10 November 1938" from "Night of Broken Glass." Published online at http://www.hagalil.com. English translation by Holt, Rinehart and Winston.

Quote by Juanita "Skeeter" Maxey from *America Goes to the Movies: 100 Years of Motion Picture Exhibition* by Barbara Stones. Published by the National Association of Theatre Owners, North Hollywood, 1993.

Quote by Sarah Gavit from "Tribe in Utah Fights for Nuclear Waste Dump" by Matthew L. Wald from *The New York Times,* April 18, 1999.

Quotes by a Reagan supporter and Earl B. Dunckel from *Sleepwalking through History: America in the Reagan Years* by Haynes Johnson. Published by W. W. Norton & Company, Inc., New York, 1991.
From "Vaudeville at Angelus Temple" by Sheldon Bissell from *The Outlook,* CXLIX, May 23, 1928.
Quotes by Stella Boone and Ethel Stringer from *From Ballots to Breadlines: American Women, 1920–1940* by Sarah Jane Deutsch. Published by Oxford University Press, New York , 1994.
From "The Reagan Years" from *The Unfinished Journey: America since World War II* by William H. Chafe. Published by Oxford University Press, New York, 1991.
Quote about Kermit Johnson and by an assembly-line worker from *Who Built America?* vol. 2, *From the Gilded Age to the Present,* edited by Joshua Freeman et al. Published by Pantheon Books, 1992.
Quote from *By Any Means Necessary: Speeches, Interviews, and a Letter* by Malcolm X. Published by Pathfinder, New York, 1970.
Quotes by Charles Houston on segregation and by Joseph McNeil from "Down Freedom's Main Line: The Movement's Next Generation" from *Eyes on the Prize: America's Civil Rights Years, 1954–1965* by Juan Williams. Published by Penguin Books, 1987.
Quote by Malcolm Cowley from *Poetry,* LII, July 1938.
Quotes by Florence Ausburn and George Robinson from *Listening to Radio, 1920–1950* by Ray Barfield. Published by Praeger Publishers, Westport, CT, 1996.
From letter by Mary McLeod Bethune to Charles H. Houston, April 10, 1939, from *Farewell to the Party of Lincoln* by Nancy J. Weiss. Published by Princeton University Press, Princeton, NJ, 1983.
Quote by Mary Jane Owen from *No Pity: People with Disabilities Forging a New Civil Rights Movement* by Joseph P. Shapiro. Published by Random House, Inc., New York, 1993.
Quote by Gutzon Borglum from *F.D.R., My Boss* by Grace Tully. Published by Scribner, New York, 1949.
From *The Spirit of St. Louis* by Charles Lindbergh. Published by Scribner's Sons, New York, 1953.
From *A Farewell to Arms* by Ernest Hemingway. Published by Scribner's Sons, New York, 1957.
Quote by Ethel Noland, friend of Harry Truman, from Oral History Transcripts from *Truman* by David McCullough. Published by Simon & Schuster, New York, 1992.
Quotes by Esther Clark, Mary Lyon, and Mary Roberts from *Pioneer Women: Voices from the Kansas Frontier* by Joanna L. Stratton. Published by Simon & Schuster, Inc., New York, 1981.
From "An Emigrant's Farewell" from "Songs of the Mexican Migration" from *Puro Mexicano,* edited by J. Frank Dobie. Published by Southern Methodist University Press, Dallas, 1969.
Quote by a baseball fan from "Record Smasher" by Tom Verducci from *Sports Illustrated,* April 22, 1999. Available on the World Wide Web at http://www.cnnsi.com/features/1998/weekly/980914/record.html.
Quote by Linda Bloodworth-Thomason from *A Century of Women,* based on a documentary script by Jacoba Atlas with Heidi Schulman and Kyra Thompson. Published by TBS Books, Atlanta, GA, 1994.
From *Over There: A Marine in the Great War* by Carl Andrew Brannen. Published by Texas A&M University Press, College Station, TX, 1996.
From interview with Barbara Baisley from "Man and Woman of the Year: Middle Americans" from *Time,* January 5, 1970. Published by Time, Inc., New York.
Quote by Nevada Dove from "Don't Mess Around with The Toxic Crusaders" by Deborah Elder Brown" from *Time,* May 3, 1999. Available on the World Wide Web at http://cgi.pathfinder.com/time/reports/environment/heroes/heroesgallery/.
Quote by Barbara Langsam from "Letters to the Editor" from *Time,* March 27, 1992. Published by Time, Inc., New York.
Quote by Eloina Ortega from "The Nation" section from *Time,* July 5, 1976. Published by Time, Inc., New York.
Quote by Gail S. Shaffer from "Letters to the Editor" from *Time,* July 20, 1998. Published by Time, Inc., New York.
Quote by Russell Baker's Aunt Pat from *The Great Depression: America, 1929–1941* by Robert S. McElvaine. Published by Times Books, New York, 1984.
Quote by a Victorio follower from *In the Days of Victorio: Recollections of a Warm Springs Apache* by Eve Ball. Published by University of Arizona Press, Tucson, 1970.
Quote by Chester Copeland and from an interview with Paul and Pauline Griffith from *Like a Family: The Making of a Southern Cotton Mill World* by Jacquelyn Dowd Hall et al. Published by the University of North Carolina Press, 1987.
From interview with Madge Alford from Indian-Pioneer Papers, University of Oklahoma, Norman.
Quote by Josia Reams from *Class and Tennessee's Confederate Generation* by Fred Arthur Bailey. Published by University of South Carolina Press, Chapel Hill, 1987.
From the film *The Plow That Broke the Plains* by Pare Lorentz. Published by the U.S. Resettlement Administration, 1936.
From "Students and the Movement: An Interview with Diane Nash" from *Eyes on the Prize: America's Civil Rights Years* by Juan Williams. Published by Viking Penguin, New York, 1987.
Quote by John Howard Lawson from *Thirty Years of Treason: Excerpts from Hearing Before the House Committee on Un-American Activities,* edited by Eric Bentley. Published by Viking Press, New York, 1971.
Quote about Richard Nixon and quote by Leona Marshall Libby from *The Fifties* by David Halberstam. Published by Villard Books, 1993.
Quote by Michiko Yamaoka, interviewed by Mitsuru Ohba, from "Voices of A-Bomb Survivors" Web site, October 13, 1998. Available on the World Wide Web at http://www.csi.ad.jp/ABOMB/Hibakusha/h03.html.
Quote by Moritz Vegh from *The Boys* by Martin Gilbert. Published by Weidenfeld & Nicolson, London, 1996.
From "Marian Wright Edelman" from *Current Biography Yearbook, 1992.* Published by H. W. Wilson Company, New York, 1992.
From *Fifty Years on the Old Frontier* by James H. Cook. Published by Yale University Press, 1994.

Photography Credits

Table of Contents and Front Matter: Page iv, Independence National Historical Park Collection; v (t) From The Civil War: Forward to Richmond. Photograph by Al Freni, © 1983 Time-Life Books, Inc. Courtesy, Troiani Collection; v (b) North Wind Picture Archives; vi (t) Frank Driggs Collection; vi (b) The Granger Collection, New York; vii (t) Corbis-Bettmann, vii (b) Culver Pictures, Inc.; viii (b) SuperStock; viii (t) The Granger Collection, New York; ix Library of Congress, FSA/OWI Collection; x (t) Ewing Galloway; x (b) Woodfin Camp & Associates, Inc.; xi (t) AP/Wide World Photos; xi (b) Novosti/SIPA Press; xii AP/Wide World Photos; xiv (b) Image copyright © 2000 PhotoDisc, Inc./HRW; xiv (t) Image copyright © 2000 PhotoDisc, Inc./HRW; xiv (c) National Portrait Gallery, Smithsonian Institution/Art Resource, NY; xv (tl) Image copyright © 2000 PhotoDisc, Inc./HRW; xv (extreme l coin) Sam Dudgeon/HRW Photo; xv (b) Sam Dudgeon/HRW Photo/The Nokia phone is a registered trademark of Nokia Corporation and/or one of its affiliates.; xv (tr) Image copyright © 2000 PhotoDisc, Inc./HRW; xv (br) The Granger Collection, New York; xv (cl coin) Sam Dudgeon/HRW Photo; xv (extreme r coin) Sam Dudgeon/HRW Photo.
Themes in American History: Page xvi-xvii (border), National Archives; xvi (t) Image copyright © 2000 PhotoDisc, Inc./HRW; (tl-poster) Peter Newark's Western Americana; (tl-rider/horse) The Granger Collection, New York; (cl) Michael Holford; (cr) Paul S. Conklin; (b) FSA/OWI Collection, photo by Alfred Palmer, May 1942, Library of Congress/HRW Photo Research Library; xvii (t) Courtesy Charlotte Luongo/HRW Photo by Victoria Smith; (tr) Sam Dudgeon/HRW Photo/The Nokia phone is a registered trademark of Nokia Corporation and/or one of its affiliates.; (c) The Granger Collection, New York; (r) © Catherine Karnow/Woodfin Camp/PNI; (b) Sam Dudgeon/HRW Photo.
Critical Thinking: Page xviii-xix (border), National Archives; xviii (cl) Corbis/Dave Bartruff; (crt) Victoria Smith/HRW Photo; (crb) Archive Photos; (t) Image copyright © 2000 PhotoDisc, Inc./HRW; (tl-poster) Peter Newark's Western Americana; (tl-rider/horse) The Granger Collection, New York; (b) FSA/OWI Collection, photo by Alfred Palmer, May 1942, Library of Congress/HRW Photo Research Library; xix (t) Courtesy Charlotte Luongo/HRW Photo by Victoria Smith; (c) The Granger Collection, New York; (tr) Sam Dudgeon/HRW Photo/The Nokia phone is a registered trademark of Nokia Corporation and/or one of its affiliates.; (r) © Catherine Karnow/Woodfin Camp/PNI; (b) Sam Dudgeon/HRW Photo.
Unit One: Page 0, Washington University Gallery of Art, St. Louis, MO/SuperStock; 1 (c) Culver Pictures, Inc.; 2 (tl & tr) The Granger Collection, New York; (bl) J. Brain/Peabody Museum, Harvard/Anthro-Photo File; (b) © Bill Bachmann/PhotoEdit; (c) Sistine Chapel, Vatican, Rome, Italy/SuperStock; (tr) The Granger Collection, New York; 3 (tc) Independence National Historical Park Collection; (tl) Corbis/Burnstein Collection; (bl) Corbis/copyright Werner Forman; (bc) Altar Cross from Peter I's Turning Shop, St. Petersburg, c.1720/Hermitage, St. Petersburg, Russia/Bridgeman Art Library; (br) D. Donne Bryant. **Chapter One:** Page 4, The Granger Collection, New York; 5 George Lepp/Tony Stone Images; 6 (t) Michael Holford; 5 (b) Rich Buzzelli/Tom Stack & Associates; 8 Musee Conde, Chantilly/Giraudon; 9 E.T. Archive; 10 British Library/E.T. Archive; 11 The Metropolitan Museum of Art, Gift of J. Pierpont Morgan, 1900. (00.18.2) Photograph copyright 1979 The Metropolitan Museum of Art; 12 Henry E. Huntington Library & Art Gallery/SuperStock; 13 Corbis-Bettmann; 14 Rare Books and Manuscripts Division, The New York Public Library, Astor, Lenox and Tilden Foundations; 15 The Granger Collection, New York; 16 Peabody Essex Museum, Salem, Massachusetts; 17 Culver Pictures, Inc.; 18 The Granger Collection, New York; 19 (t) State Capitol, Commonwealth of Virginia, Courtesy Library of Virginia, image altered; 19 (b) The Granger Collection, New York; 20 Courtesy of the Free Library Of Philadelphia; 21 The Granger Collection, New York; 22 Peter Newark's American Pictures; 23 Collection of the New-York Historical Society; 24 Art Resource, NY; 26 (b) Image copyright © 2000 PhotoDisc, Inc./HRW; 26 (tl) HRW Photo Research Library; 26–29 (border) Sam Dudgeon/HRW photo; 30 Independence National Historical Park Collection; 31 Detail of "Washington Addressing the Constitutional Convention." Virginia Museum of Fine Arts, Richmond, VA. Gift of Edgar William and Bernice Chrysler Garbisch. Photo: Ron Jennings, © 2000 Virginia Museum of Fine Arts.; 33 Library of Congress. **Chapter Two:** Page 36, Paul S. Conklin; 37 The Granger Collection, New York; 38 (l) Paul S. Conklin; 38 (r) Jay Mallin Photos; 40 from THE HERBLOCK GALLERY (Simon & Schuster, 1968); 42 Collection, the Supreme Court of the United States, courtesy The Supreme Court Historical Society; 43 Paul Conklin; 44 Independence National Historical Park Collection; 44–63 (border) HRW Photo by Sam Dudgeon; 64 Independence National Historical Park Collection; 65 The Granger Collection, New York; 66 (t) AP/Wide World Photos; 66 (b) Jeffrey Brown/Liaison Agency; 67 (t) Bob Daemmrich Photo, Inc.; 69 Louie Psihoyos/Woodfin Camp & Associates, Inc.; 70 Sandra Baker/Liaison Agency; 71 Paul Sakuma/AP/Wide World Photos; 72 (l) David Young Wolff/PhotoEdit; 72 (r) Spencer Grant/PhotoEdit; 73 Jeff Greenberg/PhotoEdit; 74 (t) Joe Marquette/AP/Wide World Photos; 74 (b) Bob Daemmrich/Stock, Boston; 75 Chris Gardner/AP/Wide World Photos; 78 (t, c, & b) Image copyright © 2000 PhotoDisc, Inc./HRW; 79 H. Abernathy/H. Armstrong Roberts; 80 (t) Image copyright © 2000 PhotoDisc, Inc./HRW; 80 (b) Corbis-Bettmann; 81 (br, tr, cr, & bl) HRW Photo by Lance Schriner; 81 (c) Image copyright © 1998 PhotoDisc, Inc./HRW; 81 (tl) Peter Van Steen/HRW Photo. **Chapter Three:** Page 82, Albert Bierstadt, "Emigrants Crossing the Plains," 1867, Oil on Canvas, A.011.1T: National Cowboy Hall of Fame, Oklahoma City, OK.; 83 Courtesy of the John Carter Brown Library at Brown University; 84 (b) Corbis-Bettmann; 84 (t) Larry Stevens/Nawrocki Stock Photo; 85 (b) The Granger Collection, New York; 85 (t) © Laurie Platt Winfrey Inc./Woodfin Camp & Associates, Inc.; 86 (border) Sam Dudgeon/HRW photo; 86 (t) HRW Photo Research Library; 87 Sally Anderson-Bruce/The Museum of American Political Life, University of Hartford, West Hartford,CT; 88 Collection of the American Numismatic Society, New York; 89 North Wind Picture Archives; 90 (c) & 91 The Granger Collection, New York; 92 (border) Sam Dudgeon/HRW photo; 92 (t) HRW Photo Research Library; 93 National Portrait Gallery, Smithsonian Institution, Gift of the Swedish Colonial Society through Mrs. William Hacker/Art Resource, NY; 94 Archive Photos; 95 Corbis-Bettmann; 97 (t) Smithsonian Institution neg. #75-2984; 97 (b) Image copyright © 1997 PhotoDisc, Inc./HRW; 98 (t) Kennedy Galleries; 98 (b) UPI/Corbis-Bettmann; 99 (border) Sam Dudgeon/HRW photo; 99 (t) HRW Photo Research Library; 100 Archive Photos; 101 Alamo Collection, photograph courtesy the Daughters of the Republic of Texas Library, CT97.23; 102 (b) Archives Division-Texas State Library, Photographer, Eric Beggs; 102 (t) Harcourt Brace Photo; 105 Colorado Historical Society; 106 & 107 The Granger Collection, New York; 108 (b) Virginia Historical Society; 108 (t) from THE CIVIL WAR: FORWARD TO RICHMOND, Photograph

by Al Freni, © 1983 Time-Life Books, Inc. Courtesy, Troiani Collection; 110 State Museum of Pennsylvania; 111 National Geographic Image Collection; 112–113 (border) Sam Dudgeon/HRW photo; 112, 113 (t) HRW Photo Research Library; 117 © Frank Siteman/Stock Boston.

Unit Two: Page 118 & 119 (c), The Granger Collection, New York; 120 (tl, & bl) The Granger Collection, New York; (tr) Corbis; (bc) National Maritime Museum, Greenwich, London; (br) Giraudon/Art Resource, NY; 121 (tl, & tc) The Granger Collection, New York; (tr) Photography by Karen Yamauchi for Chermayeff & Geismar Inc./Metaform Inc.; (bl) Corbis/Craig Aurness; (cbl & cbr) IOC/Olympic Museum Collections; (br) Spode three handled cup commemorating the South African War, 19th century/Spode Cotehele House, Cornwall, UK/Bridgeman Art Library. **Chapter Four:** Page 122, North Wind Picture Archives; 123 The Museum of the Confederacy Richmond, Virginia, Katherine Wetzel Photographer; 124 The Valentine Museum; 125 Library of Congress; 125 (r & bc) HRW Photo by Sam Dudgeon; 127 (c) The Stock Market/© William Taufic; 127 (trb) Sam Dudgeon/HRW Photo; 128 SuperStock; 129 Corbis-Bettmann: 130 Stock Montage, Inc.; 131 (b) Corbis-Bettmann; 131 (t), 132, & 133 (b) The Granger Collection, New York; 133 (t) Louisiana Collection, Howard Tilton Memorial Library, New Orleans, LA 70118; 134 The Granger Collection, New York; 135 Library of Congress: 136 Courtesy of South Caroliniana Library, University of South Carolina, Columbia.; 137 The Granger Collection, New York; 139 North Wind Picture Archives; 140 (t) U.S. Senate Collection; 140 (b) The Granger Collection, New York; 141 H. Armstrong Roberts; 142 Corbis-Bettmann; 143 & 144 The Granger Collection, New York; 145 (t) Archive Photos; 145 (b) North Wind Picture Archives; 146 (c) The Granger Collection, New York; 147 Courtesy of Fisk University Library, Special Collections. **Chapter Five:** Page 150, Peter Newark's Western Americana; 151 The Granger Collection, New York; 152 (t) Werner Forman Archive, Pohrt Collection, Plains Indian Museum, BBHC, Cody Wyoming, USA/Art Resource, NY; 152 (b) Corbis-Bettmann; 154 The Granger Collection, New York; 155 (c) & 156 Corbis-Bettmann; 157 The Granger Collection, New York; 158 E.R. Degginger/Color-Pic, Inc.; 159 National Archives (NARA); 160 (l) Colorado Historical Society; 160 (r) Peter Newark's Western Americana; 161 (c) Hulton Deutsch Collection/Tony Stone Images; 162 (t) Peter Newark's Western Americana; 162 (b) Peter Newark's American Pictures; 163 (l) Peter Newark's Western Americana; 163 (r) Union Pacific Museum Collection; 164 Boltin Picture Library; 165 (t) Peter Newark's Western Americana; 165 (b) Montana Historical Society, Helena; 166 (t) Peter Newark's Western Americana; 166 (b) Solomon D. Butcher Collection, Library of Congress; 167 (l) Buffalo Bill Historic Center, Cody, Wyoming; 167 (r) Peter Newark's Western Americana; 169 The Granger Collection, New York; 170 Peter Newark's Western Americana; 171 (t) AKG London; 171 (b) S.D. Butcher/Denver Public Library, Western History Collection; 173 Courtesy of the California History Room, California State Library, Sacramento, California; 174 (b) Peter Newark's Western Americana; 174 (bkgd) © PI/Photo © David Hardwood/Panoramic Images, Chicago 1998; 174 (tl) Peter Newark's Western Americana; 174 (tr) The Granger Collection, New York; 175 Library of Congress; 178 (tl, tr, & b) & 179 Image copyright © 2000 PhotoDisc, Inc./HRW; 178 (c) Colorado Historical Society; 180 National Archives (NARA); 181 Image copyright © 2000 PhotoDisc, Inc./HRW. **Chapter Six:** Page 182, The Granger Collection, New York; 183 Archive Photos; 185 (tl & br) The Granger Collection, New York; 185 (bl) Science Museum, London, UK/Bridgeman Art Library, London/New York; 186 (c) & 187 The Granger Collection, New York; 188 Stock Montage, Inc.; 189 From the Conwellana-Templana Collection of the Temple University Libraries; 190 (t) Culver Pictures, Inc.; 191 Carnegie Library of Pittsburg; 192 Courtesy of the Rockefeller Archive Center, photograph by Charles Uht. John D. Rockefeller, painted by Eastman Johnson, 1895; 192 (bl) Sam Dudgeon/HRW photo; 192 HRW Photo Research Library; 193 (c) The Granger Collection, New York; 194 & 195 Corbis-Bettmann; 196 The Granger Collection, New York; 197 Corbis-Bettmann; 199 The Granger Collection, New York; 200 Corbis-Bettmann; 201 The Granger Collection, New York; 202 J.R. Holland/Stock, Boston; 203 (t) The Granger Collection, New York; 203 (b) Library of Congress; 204 The Granger Collection, New York; 205 Corbis-Bettmann; 207 The Granger Collection, New York. **Chapter Seven:** Page 208, Library of Congress #LCUSZC4-4637 DLC Detroit Publishing Co. Photo Collection; 209 The Granger Collection, New York; 210 Photography by Karen Yamauchi for Chermayeff & Geismar Inc./Metaform Inc.; 211 (t) Frank Driggs Collection; 211 (b) FPG International; 212 Culver Pictures, Inc.; 213 & 214 The Granger Collection, New York; 215 Photography by Karen Yamauchi for Chermayeff & Geismar Inc./Metaform Inc.; 217 (t) The Granger Collection, New York; 217 (b) Photo courtesy of Illinois Railway Museum; 218 (c) The Granger Collection, New York; 219 (b) Corbis/Hulton-Deutsch Collection; 219 (t) 1901 Autumn Announcement reprinted courtesy of the Marshall Field's Archive, Chicago, IL; 220 (b) The Granger Collection, New York; 220 (t) National Gallery of Art, Washington, D.C./SuperStock; 221 Corbis; 222 David Spindel/SuperStock; 223 (l) Everett Collection; 223 (r) National Baseball Hall of Fame Library & Archive, Milo Stewart, Jr., Cooperstown, N.Y.; 224 (tr) Corbis; 224 (bl) Corbis-Bettmann; 225 KJA Dime Novels, Rare Books and Manuscripts Division, The New York Public Library, Astor, Lenox and Tilden Foundations; 226 (b) Museum of Fine Arts, Boston, Massachusetts/SuperStock; 226 (t) Giraudon/Art Resource, NY; 227 (r) Corbis/Paul Almasy; 227 (l) The Granger Collection, New York; 231 © Jonathan Nourok/PhotoEdit.

Unit Three: Page 232, SuperStock; 233 (c) Corbis-Bettmann; 234 (tl) The Granger Collection, New York; (c) Christie's Images; (tc) Sam Dudgeon/HRW Photo/Courtesy The European Influence, Austin, Texas.; (b & tr) SuperStock; 235 (tl & tr) The Granger Collection, New York; (bl) Stock Montage/SuperStock; (br) Archive Photos; (tc) Barbara Puorro Galasso/Courtesy George Eastman House; (bc) SuperStock. **Chapter Eight:** Page 236, (t) The Granger Collection, New York; 237 Stock Montage, Inc.; 238-240 The Granger Collection, New York; 241 Brown Brothers; 242 (bl) Corbis-Bettmann; 242 (tr) Culver Pictures, Inc.; 242 (l) Everett/CSU Archives; 242 (tr) SuperStock; 242 (l) Richard Berenholtz/The Stock Market; 243 Corbis-Bettmann; 244 (tr) Courtesy of the Rosenberg Library, Galveston, Texas; 244 (b) Library of Congress; 245 The Granger Collection, New York; 246 (tl) Corbis-Bettmann; 246 (r) Brown Brothers; 247 The Granger Collection, New York; 248 Corbis-Bettmann; 249 (tr) UPI/Corbis-Bettmann; 249 (tl) The Granger Collection, New York; 250 AP/Wide World Photos; 251 Library of Congress; 252 Library of Congress; 253 (c) © Mary Cassatt/Wood River Gallery/PNI; 254 & 255 Corbis-Bettmann; 256 National Portrait Gallery, Smithsonian Institution/Art Resource, NY; 258 Library of Congress; 259 (b) The Granger Collection, New York; 259 (t) Corbis-Bettmann; 260 (t) Courtesy of Rio Grande Press; 260 (b) Corbis; 261 Keystone-Mast Collection, UCR/CALIFORNIA MUSUEM OF PHOTOGRAPHY, University of California, Riverside.

Chapter Nine: Page 264, The Granger Collection, New York; 265 Library of Congress; 266 (b) The Granger Collection, New York; 266 (t) The National Museum of American History by Shirley Abbott. Published by Harry N. Abrams, Inc., New York; 267 Theodore Roosevelt Collection, Harvard College Library; 268 Corbis-Bettmann; 269 (c) © Laurie Platt Winfrey, Inc./Woodfin Camp & Associates, Inc.; 271 Corbis-Bettmann; 272 The Granger Collection, New York; 273 Archive Photos; 274 (t) Stock Montage, Inc.; 274 (b) The Granger Collection, New York; 275 (b) Corbis-Bettmann; 275 (t) Tacoma Tribune/Forest History Society; 276 (b) Theodore Roosevelt Collection, Harvard College Library; 276 (t) The Granger Collection, New York; 278 Bridgeman Art Library, London/New York; 279 (t) Corbis-Bettmann; 279 (b) © Spencer Grant/Stock, Boston/PNI; 280 (c) Bob Daemmrich Photography; 281 Stock Montage, Inc.; 282 Courtesy of the Crisis Publishing Co., the publisher of the magazine of the National Association for the Advancement of Colored People. General Research and Reference Division; Schomburg Center for Research in Black Culture; The New York Public Library; Astor, Lenox and Tilden Foundations; 283 The Granger Collection, New York; 285 Stock Montage, Inc. **Chapter Ten:** Page 286, Library of Congress; 287 Stock Montage, Inc.; 288 The Granger Collection, New York; 289 (t) Anchorage Museum of History and Art, Gift of Mr. and Mrs. John M. Sorenson; 289 (b) Library of Congress; 290 UPI/Corbis-Bettmann; 291 (c) Bishop Museum, The State Museum of Natural and Cultural History; 292 Peabody Essex Museum, Salem, Massachusetts; 293 Snark International/Art Resource, NY; 294 Brown Brothers; 296 (b) © Laurie Platt Winfrey Inc./Woodfin Camp & Associates, Inc.; 296 (t) & 298 (c) The Granger Collection, New York; 299 Library of Congress; 300 Keystone-Mast Collection #X6637, UCR/University of California at Riverside/California Museum of Photography ; 301 U.S. Naval Institute Photo Archives; 302 & 304 (t) The Granger Collection, New York; 304 (b) Brown Brothers; 306 The Granger Collection, New York; 307 Corbis-Bettmann; 308 & 309 (b) The Granger Collection, New York; 309 (t) Library of Congress; 311 & 313 The Granger Collection, New York; 314 (br) Davies & Starr Inc./Tony Stone Images; 314 (c) © Burke; Triolo/FoodPix/PNI; 314 (t) Stock Montage/SuperStock; 314 (bl) Image copyright © 1998 PhotoDisc, Inc./HRW; 315 National Archives/HRW Photo Library; 316 Courtesy of © The Mariners' Museum, Newport News, Virginia; 317 (t) SuperStock; 317 (b) Image copyright © 1998 PhotoDisc, Inc./HRW; 319 Michelle Bridwell/Frontera Fotos.

Unit Four: Page 320, National Archives (NARA); 321 (c) The Granger Collection, New York; 322 (tl) The Granger Collection, New York; (tc & tr) Photo by Sam Dudgeon/Courtesy The Neon Radio, Lockhart, Texas, www.neonradio.com; (br) SuperStock; (bl) Sam Dudgeon/HRW Photo/The Detroit News; 323 (tc) Corbis/Bettmann; (bc) Mary Evans Photo Library, England; (br) The Granger Collection, New York; (bl) AKG Photo, London; (tl) © Tribune Media Services, Inc. All Rights Reserved. Reprinted with permission.; (tr) SuperStock. **Chapter Eleven:** Page 324, Culver Pictures, Inc.; 325 Liaison Agency; 326 Nawrocki Stock Photo; 327 (t) The Granger Collection, New York; 327 (b) Archive Photos; 328 Corbis-Bettmann; 329 Lunch at Chatillon camp for the 8th Battalion, August 1918 (oil on canvas) by Joseph Felix Bouchor (1853–1937), Musee Franco-Americaine, Blerancourt, Chauny, France/Roger-Viollet, Paris/Bridgeman Art Library, London/New York; 330 (l) Trustees of the Imperial War Museum, London; 330 (r) Culver Pictures, Inc.; 333 (b) Woodfin Camp & Associates, Inc.; 333 (br) Stock Montage, Inc.; 333 (t) & 334 The Granger Collection, New York; 335 Sam Dudgeon/HRW photo; 336 © Archive Photos/PNI; 337 The Granger Collection, New York; 338 Archive Photos; 339 The Granger Collection, New York; 340 Eric Beggs/HRW Photo; 341 (t) Liaison Agency; 341 (b) Corbis-Bettmann; 343 (l) Archive Photos; 343 (r) © Dorling Kindersley Ltd./Courtesy of Spink & Son Ltd., London.; 344 UPI/Corbis-Bettmann; 345 Corbis-Bettmann; 346 (t) Trustees of the Imperial War Museum, London; 346 (b) © Laurent Van Der Stockt/Liaison Agency; 348 (bkgd) Corbis-Bettmann; 348 (r, & l) HRW Photo by Eric E. Beggs; 349 Corbis-Bettmann; 350 (c) HRW Photo Research Library; 350 (t & b) HRW Photo by Sam Dudgeon; 351 (c) The Granger Collection, New York; 351 (t & b) HRW Photo by Sam Dudgeon. **Chapter Twelve:** Page 354, Laurie Platt Winfrey Inc./Woodfin Camp & Associates, Inc.; 355 National Archives (NARA); 356 The Granger Collection, New York; 357 (c) Brown Brothers; 358 (t) Corbis/Pemco-Webster & Stevens Collection; Museum of History & Industry, Seattle; 358 (b) Corbis-Bettmann; 359 Stock Montage, Inc.; 360 (b) The Museum of Modern Art, New York. Gift of Abby Aldrich Rockefeller. Photograph © 1997 The Museum of Modern Art, New York. © 1997 Estate of Ben Shahn/Licensed by VAGA, New York, NY; 360 (t) & 361 UPI/Corbis-Bettmann; 362 HRW Photo by Lance Schriner; 363 Corbis-Bettmann; 364 The Granger Collection, New York; 365 (b) The Granger Collection, New York; 365 (t) Steven Laschever/The Museum of American Political Life, University of Hartford, West Hartford,CT; 366 Herbert Hoover Presidential Library/Corbis; 367 Archive Photos; 368 (b) The Granger Collection, New York; 368 (t) From the Collections of Henry Ford Museum and Greenfield Village; 369 Detail, Mural: Detroit Industry, South Wall, by Diego M. Rivera, Gift of Edsel B. Ford, Photograph © 1994, The Detroit Institute of Arts; 370 (t) Stock Montage, Inc.; 370 (b) & 371 (b) The Granger Collection, New York; 371 (t) Sam Dudgeon/HRW photo; 372 Culver Pictures, Inc.; 373 & 374 (bl) The Granger Collection, New York; 374 (tl) Christie's Images; 374 (b) ©Lionel Green/Archive Photos/PNI; 375 (c) Christie's Images; 376 Corbis/Pemco-Webster & Stevens Collection; Museum of History & Industry, Seattle; 379 Image copyright © 2000 PhotoDisc, Inc./HRW. **Chapter Thirteen:** Page 380, (l) The Granger Collection, New York; 380 (r) John Held Jr., LIFE Magazine, © TIME Inc./Courtesy of the general libraries, The University of Texas at Austin/HRW photo by Victoria Smith; 381 SuperStock; 382 (b) Brown Brothers; 382 (t) SuperStock; 383 ED Archive, London/SuperStock; 384 © Collection of the New-York Historical Society; 385 (l) Woodfin Camp & Associates, Inc.; 385 Culver Pictures, Inc.; 386 The Granger Collection, New York; 387 & 388 (t) Photography by Karen Yamauchi for Chermayeff & Geismar Inc./Metaform Inc.; 388 (b) The Granger Collection, New York; 389 (t) Photography by Karen Yamauchi for Chermayeff & Geismar Inc./Metaform Inc.; 389 (b) Archive Photos; 390 (t) Arte Publico Press, University of Houston, 1991; 390 (b) Corbis-Bettmann; 390 (cl) Courtesy of Rosie & Henry Montalvo/HRW Photo by Victoria Smith; 391 APA/Archive Photos; 393 (t) AP/Wide World Photos; 393 (b) Courtesy of Karen Sherrod, Austin, TX/HRW Photo by Victoria Smith; 394 Courtesy of Texas Highways Magazine; 395 (c) Walt Disney Pict./Shooting Star International; 396 (l) SuperStock; 396 (r) Walt Disney Pict./Shooting Star International; 397 (b) Corbis-Bettmann; 397 (t) & 398 The Granger Collection, New York; 399 & 400 Archive Photos; 400 (b) Ed Carlin/Archive Photos; 400 (tr) © Hulton Getty/Woodfin Camp & Associates, Inc.; 402 National Portrait Gallery, Smithsonian Institution/Art Resource, NY; 403 (t) Addison Gallery of American

Art, Phillips Academy; 403 (b) Corbis/Ansel Adams Publishing Rights Trust; 404 (c) © 1999 The Georgia O'Keeffe Foundation/Artists Rights Society (ARS), New York. The Metropolitan Museum of Art, Alfred Stieglitz Collection, 1952. (52.203) Photograph © 1994 The Metropolitan Museum of Art; 405 © Catherine Karnow/Woodfin Camp/PNI; 407 (b) The Phillips Collection, Washington, D.C.; 408 (t, c, bl, & br) Image copyright © 2000 PhotoDisc, Inc./HRW; 408 (br) Digital Stock Corp./HRW; 409 Library of Congress/Corbis; 410 (b) Photographs & Prints Division, Schomburg Center for Research in Black Culture, The New York Public Library, Astor, Lenox and Tilden Foundations; 410 (t) & 411 (r) Image copyright © 2000 PhotoDisc, Inc./HRW; 411 (l) Brown Brothers; 412 The Granger Collection, New York; 413 © William Hart/PhotoEdit.
Unit Five: Page 414, American Red Cross; 415 (c) The Granger Collection, New York; 416 (tl) O. J. Jordan/Time Magazine; (tc) Texas Ranger Hall of Fame and Museum, Waco, Texas. Sam Dudgeon/HRW Photo ; (cl) SIPA Press; (cr) Wood River Gallery/PNI; (b) National Maritime Museum, Greenwich, London; (tr) Corbis/Richard A. Cooke; 417 (tc) Courtesy Charlotte Luongo/Victoria Smith/HRW Photo; (bc) Courtesy of Jed Collectibles, Pemberton, New Jersey/© 1943 renewed 1971 by Harcourt Inc. /HRW Photo by Sam Dudgeon; (bl) Smithsonian Institute; (tr) Archive Photos; (br) Jodi Cobb/National Geographic Society Image Collection; (tl) Culver Pictures, Inc. **Chapter Fourteen:** Page 418, The Granger Collection, New York; 419 HRW Photo by Sam Dudgeon; 420 (br) Archive Photos; 420 (cr) FPG International; 420 (tl) John Held Jr., LIFE Magazine, © TIME Inc./Courtesy of the general libraries, The University of Texas at Austin/HRW photo by Victoria Smith; 421 & 422 (t) The Granger Collection, New York; 422 (b) Brown Brothers; 423 AP/Wide World Photos; 424 © Cindy Lewis 1997; 425 AP/Wide World Photos; 426 (br) National Museum of American Art, Smithsonian Institution, Washington, D.C./Art Resource, NY; 426 (t) Brown Brothers; 427 (c) Harry Ransom Humanities Research Center The University of Texas at Austin; 428 The Granger Collection, New York; 429 Brown Brothers; 430 Archive Photos; 431 The Granger Collection, New York; 432 (t) Franklin D. Roosevelt Library; 432 (b) FPG International; 434 (tl) National Portrait Gallery, Smithsonian Institution/Art Resource, NY; 434 (br) Corbis-Bettmann; 435 (tc) Culver Pictures, Inc.; 435 (br) AP/Wide World Photos; 437 Library of Congress; 438 UPI/Corbis-Bettmann; 439 (c) Lawrence Migdale/Stock Boston; 440 (tc) The Granger Collection, New York; 440 (b) Albro, Maxine: California Agriculture (detail). Coit Tower, San Francisco, 1934. Photo by Lito, courtesy Masha Zakheim; 440 (t) Franklin D. Roosevelt Library; 442 & 443 The Granger Collection, New York. **Chapter Fifteen:** Page 446, Dallas Museum of Art, Dallas Art Association Purchase; 447 Lambert/Archive Photos; 448 (cl, cr, & t) Sam Dudgeon/HRW Photo; 448 (b) Corbis-Bettmann; 449 Southern Historical Collection, University of North Carolina, Photo by Louise Boyle; 450 Franklin D. Roosevelt Library; 451 (c) The Granger Collection, New York. From THE GRAPES OF WRATH by John Steinbeck. Copyright 1939 renewed © 1967 by John Steinbeck. Used by permission of Viking Penguin, a division of Penguin Putnam, Inc.; 452 Library of Congress; 453 & 454 Brown Brothers; 455 UPI/Corbis-Bettmann; 456 National Archives (NARA); 457 Archive Photos; 458 (b) Art Institute of Chicago/SuperStock; 458 (tl) & 459 (b) The Granger Collection, New York; 459 (t) Archive Photos; 460 (tc) Courtesy of Ruth Sugeno from the Kerbey Lane Doll Shoppe, Austin, TX. Sam Dudgeon/HRW Photo; 460 (l) Jay Mallin Photos; 460 (b) Everett Collection; 461 Corbis/Bettman; 462 HRW Photo by Sam Dudgeon; 463 (tl & tc) David King Collection; 463 (b) Culver Pictures, Inc; 464 Nawrocki Stock Photo; 465 Arnold Kramer, United States Holocaust Memorial Museum; 467 The Granger Collection, New York; 470 (t) Classic PIO Partners; 470 (c, br, & bl) Image copyright © 2000 PhotoDisc, Inc./HRW; 471 Hulton-Deutsch Collection/Corbis; 472 (b) FPG International; 472 (t & c) Image copyright © 2000 PhotoDisc, Inc./HRW; 472 (t) Charles Apple; 473 (bl) Brown Brothers; 473 (br) Image copyright © 1998 PhotoDisc, Inc./HRW.
Chapter Sixteen: Page 474, The Granger Collection, New York; 475 Library of Congress/Corbis; 476 (t) Archive Photos; 476 (b) National Gallery of Canada, Ottawa, Gift of the Massey Collection of English Painting, 1946.; 478 Brown Brothers; 479 Archive Photos; 480 HRW Photo by Sam Dudgeon, stamps courtesy Kristen Darby; 481 (b) UPI/Corbis-Bettmann; 481 (t) The Granger Collection, New York; 482 (c) Archive Photos; 483 Library of Congress, FSA/OWI Collection; 484 Hulton-Deutsch Collection/Corbis; 485 (bl) AKG Photo; 485 (tr) Courtesy Sen. Daniel Inouye; 486 (b) Ria-Novosti/Sovfoto; 486 (t) Archive Photos; 488 (c) AKG Photo; 489 Library of Congress, FSA/OWI Collection; 490 Archive Photos; 491 (t) Nawrocki Stock Photo; 491 (b) United States Marine Corps; 492 AKG Photo; 494 AP Photo/Joe Rosenthal/Wide World Photos; 495 Photri; 496 (t) AKG Photo; 496 (bl) AP/Wide World Photos; 496 (br) Phillip Jones-Griffiths/Magnum Photos; 497 (c) Archive Photos; 498 Nawrocki Stock Photo; 499 Corbis-Bettmann; 502 Sam Dudgeon/HRW photo/Courtesy Victoria Smith and Blas Cantú; 503 © Robin L. Sachs/PhotoEdit.
Unit Six: Page 504, © Willinger/FPG International; 505 (c) Photofest; 506 (cl) Everett Collection; (tc) 1999 Jay Mallin; (tr) Ken Eward/Science Source/Photo Researchers, Inc.; (tl) Classic PIO Partners; (b) SuperStock; 507 (tl & br) SuperStock; (bc) © Colorsport; (tc) Everett Collection; (tr) J. David Andrews/Masterfile; (bl) Royal Geographic Society.
Chapter Seventeen: Page 508, Franklin D. Roosevelt Library; 509 Copyright © 1945 by The New York Times Co. Reprinted by Permission; 510 (t) UPI/Corbis-Bettmann; 510 (b) SuperStock; 511 (b) Archive Photos; 511 (t) UPI/Corbis-Bettmann; 512 Editorial cartoon by Tom Little, 1948; courtesy of the Nashville Tennessean.; 513 HRW Photo by Sam Dudgeon/U.S. Postal Service; 514 (border) Sam Dudgeon/HRW photo; 514 (c) HRW Photo Research Library; 515 Woodfin Camp & Associates, Inc.; 516 (c) © Andres Hernandez/Liaison Agency; 517 Victoria Smith/HRW Photo; 518 Alfred Eisenstaedt, LIFE Magazine, © TIME Inc.; 519 (t) The White House, Courtesy Harry S. Truman Library; 519 (b) Veterans Administration Photo; 520 Corbis-Bettmann; 521 The White House Collection, copyright White House Historical Association and The National Archives and Records Administration; 522 & 523 (t) The Granger Collection, New York; 523 (b) Corbis-Bettmann; 525 (l) Archive Photos; 525 (r) Corbis-Bettmann; 526 AP/Wide World Photos; 527 Michael Barson/Archive Photos; 528 (r) Corbis-Bettmann; 528 (l) Syracuse University Library Department of Special Collections. Syracuse, New York; 529 (l) Archive Photos; 529 (r) UPI/Corbis-Bettmann; 530 (c) Everett Collection; 531 Archive Photos; 534 (t & b) Image copyright © 2000 PhotoDisc, Inc./HRW; 534 (c) UPI/Corbis-Bettmann; 535 Library of Congress/Corbis; 536 (l) Archive Photos; 536 (r) Image copyright © 2000 PhotoDisc, Inc./HRW; 537 (l) © N/A/Chicago Historical Society/PNI; 537 (r) Image copyright © 1998 PhotoDisc, Inc./HRW. **Chapter Eighteen:** Page 538, Ewing Galloway; 539 Corbis-Bettmann; 540 (r) © Sovfoto/Eastfoto; 540 (l) Reuters/HO/Archive Photos; 542 (c) FPG International; 543 Lockheed Martin Corporation; 544 The Power of Positive Thinking © 1952, 1978 by Prentice-Hall, Inc. Courtesy the Norman Vincent Peale Center for Christian Living. HRW photo by Sam Dudgeon.; 546 (t) © Cindy Lewis; 546 (b) © 1954/TIME Inc. Reprinted by Permission; 548 (t) © The New Yorker Collection 1954 Robert Day from cartoonbank.com. All Rights Reserved; 548 (b) Archive Photos; 550 Hake's Americana, York, PA; 551 (t) © L.P. Winfrey/Woodfin Camp & Associates, Inc.; 551 (b) Everett Collection; 552 (c) © 1999 Pollock-Krasner Foundation/Artists Rights Society (ARS) New York. Musee National d'Art Moderne, Paris, France/Giraudon/Art Resource, NY; 553 Corbis; 554 Corbis-Bettmann; 555 UPI/Bettmann Newsphotos; 556 Black Star; 557 UPI/Corbis-Bettmann Newsphotos; 558 (t) AP/Wide World Photos; 558 (b) Brown Brothers; 559 UPI/Corbis-Bettmann Newsphoto; 562 Victoria Smith/HRW Photo, Courtesy Cynthia H. Luongo; 563 Sam Dudgeon/HRW Photo.
Unit Seven: Page 564, NASA/HRW Photo Research Library; 565 (c) Arnie Sachs, © 1994 Consolidated News Pictures; 566 (c & tl) Everett Collection; (tr) Courtesy of VISTA/Peace Corps; (tc) Christie's Images; (b) Corbis/Jeremy Horner; 567 (tcr & tcl) Reprinted by permission of Ms. Magazine © 1972/Courtesy of the general libraries, The University of Texas at Austin/Sam Dudgeon/HRW Photo; (tl) SuperStock; (br) Lyle Leduc/Liaison Agency; (bl) Corbis/Christopher Cormack; (tr) © 1999 Jay Mallin All rights reserved. **Chapter Nineteen:** Page 568, AP/Wide World Photos; 569 (t) HRW Photo by Victoria Smith; 569 (b) Victoria Smith/HRW Photo; 570 Corbis; 571 (l) AP/Wide World Photos; 571 (r) Owen/Black Star; 572 Photri; 573 ©1961 Newsweek, Inc. All rights reserved. Reprinted by permission. Courtesy of the general libraries, The University of Texas at Austin/HRW Photo by Victoria Smith.; 574 (c) © Bob Daemmrich/The Image Works; 575 UPI/Corbis-Bettmann; 577 Sovfoto; 578 Carlos A. Hedstrom, Jr. Collection/The Sixth Floor Museum at Dealey Plaza; 579 (t) Arnold Newman/Lyndon Baines Johnson Library Collection; 579 (b) AP/Wide World Photos; 580 (b) Lyndon Baines Johnson Library Collection/Photo by Victoria Smith; 580 (t) Ralph Morse LIFE Magazine, © TIME Inc.; 581 (b) Lyndon Baines Johnson Library Collection; 581 (t) Reprinted with permission from the Atlanta Journal and the Atlanta Constitution/Lyndon Baines Johnson Library Collection; 582 Charles Moore/Black Star; 583 Ted Cowell/Black Star; 584 (t) AP/Wide World Photos; 584 (b) Henry Diltz/Corbis; 585 (c) © 1999 The Andy Warhol Foundation for the Visual Arts /ARS, New York, Corbis-Bettmann; 586 (t) AP/Wide World Photos; 586 (bl, bc, & br) Archive Photos; 587 Jacques Chenet/Woodfin Camp & Associates, Inc.; 588 Smithsonian Institute; 589 L. P. Winfrey/Woodfin Camp & Associates, Inc.; 591 Alfred Eisenstaedt/Life Magazine © Time Inc.; 593 Rauschenberg, Robert, Estate, 1963, Philadelphia Museum of Art: Gift of the Friends of the Philadelphia Museum of Art. **Chapter Twenty:** Page 594, UPI/Corbis-Bettmann; 595 © 1976 Bill Pogue c/o MIRA; 596 AP/Wide World Photos; 598 UPI/Corbis-Bettmann; 599 UPI/Corbis-Bettmann; 600 (bl) AP/Wide World Photos; 600 (t) © 1998 John Launois/Black Star; 600 (br), 601, 602 & 603 (border) Sam Dudgeon/HRW Photo; 603 (c) Woodfin Camp & Associates, Inc.; 604 Dr. Hector P. Garcia Papers, Special Collections & Archives, Texas A&M University-Corpus Christi Bell Library; 605 (tc) Archive Photos; 605 (bl & br) Image copyright © 2001 PhotoDisc, Inc.; 606 (t) J.R. Eyerman/Time Magazine; 606 (b) Sally Andersen-Bruce. Museum of American Political Life; 607 (c) From Mexican American Literature; 608 Woodfin Camp & Associates, Inc.; 609 Courtesy of Elizabeth Martinez; 610 Associated Press AP/Wide World Photos; 611 (r) The Schlesinger Library, Radcliffe College/From THE FEMININE MYSTIQUE by Betty Friedan. Copyright ©1983, 1974, 1973, 1963 by Betty Friedan. Reprinted by permission of W. W. Norton & Company, Inc.; 611 (l) Corbis-Bettmann; 612 (t) Corbis/Reuters; 612 (b) AP/Wide World Photos; 613 (c) Corbis/AFP; 614 (t) AP/Wide World Photos; 614 (b) Richard Pasely/Stock Boston; 615 (r) © Martin A. Levick; 615 (l) Victoria Smith/HRW Photo; 616 © Chris Arend/AllStock/PNI; 617 (t) Dennis Brack/Black Star; 617 (b) AP/Wide World Photos; 618 © David Burnett/Contact Press Images/PNI; 619 Corbis-Bettmann. **Chapter Twenty-One:** Page 622, Arthur Grace/Sygma; 623 © Harlingue-Viollet/Liaison Agency; 624 Woodfin Camp & Associates, Inc.; 625 (t) Michigan State University Archives & Historical Collections; 625 (b) UPI/Corbis-Bettmann; 626 AP/Wide World Photos; 627 Max Scheler/Black Star; 629 (t) Archive Photos; 629 (bc) AP/Jeff Widener/Wide World Photos; 630 Larry Burrows, LIFE Magazine © TIME Warner Inc.; 631 Sara Matthews/Swathmore College Peace Collection; 632 (t) CBS News; 632 (b) AP/Wide World Photos; 634 (t) Jack Kightlinger/Lyndon Baines Johnson Library Collection; 634 (b) Archive Photos; 635 Roger Lubin/Jerobam 1972; 636 AP/Wide World Photos; 637 (t) Corbis-Bettmann; 637 (b) & 638 UPI/Corbis-Bettmann; 639 Jean Claude Fracolon/Liaison Agency; 639 (b) Sam Dudgeon/HRW Photo, Courtesy Gene Rumann; 640 (c) AP/Wide World Photos; 641 UPI/Corbis-Bettmann; 644 (c) Corbis/Tim Page; 644 (t) Corbis/Nik Wheeler; 644 (b) Image copyright © 1998 PhotoDisc, Inc./HRW; 645 Corbis/Wolfgang Kaehler; 646 (b) Photri; 646 (t) Lyle Leduc/Liaison Agency; 646 (c) Digital Stock Corp./HRW; 647 (bl) © Charles Bonnay/Black Star/PNI; 647 (t) Victoria Smith/HRW Photo; 647 (c) Law/The Image Works; 647 (br) Image copyright © 1998 PhotoDisc, Inc./HRW; 649 Andy Sacks/Tony Stone Images.
Unit Eight: Page 650, R. Krubner/H. Armstrong Roberts; 651 (c) Stephen Frisch/Stock Boston; 652 (tl) National Archives/HRW Photo Research Library; (tc) Bill Pierce/Woodfin Camp & Associates, Inc.; (c) Corbis/Wally McNamee; (tr) Dennis Brack/Black Star/PNI; (bl) SuperStock; (br) Copyright T.S.M./Woodfin Camp & Associates, Inc.; 653 (tr) © 1999 Jay Mallin; (bl) AP/Wide World Photos; (br) Stephen Alvarez/National Geographic Society Image Collection; (tl) Wally McNamee/Woodfin Camp & Associates, Inc.; (tc) JPL/NASA.
Chapter Twenty-Two: Page 654 & 655, AP/Wide World Photos; 656 (t) Archive Photos; 656 (b) © John Barr/Liaison Agency; 658 (bkgd) Image copyright © 2000 PhotoDisc, Inc./HRW; 658 (r-car) Digital Stock Corp./HRW; 658 (l-gas pumps) Richard Haynes/HRW Photo; 659 Liaison Agency; 660 ©1999 Dennis Brack/Black Star; 661 AP/Wide World Photos; 662 (t) Margulies/Rothco; 662 (b) The Granger Collection, New York; 663 UPI/Corbis-Bettmann; 664 (b) © 1976 Dirck Halstead/Liaison Agency; 664 (t) Corbis-Bettmann; 665 Photri; 666 Ted Hardin/Black Star; 667 (b) Wally McNamee/Woodfin Camp & Associates, Inc.; 667 (t) Corbis-Bettmann; 668 (c) Jeff Greenberg/PhotoEdit; 669 UPI/Corbis-Bettmann; 670 © Alain Mingam/Liaison Agency; 671 Sam Dudgeon/HRW Photo; 673 (t) Paul Barton/The Stock Market; 673 (b) Jason Laure/Woodfin Camp & Associates, Inc.; 674 Corbis/Galen Rowell; 675 (t) Image copyright © 2000 PhotoDisc, Inc./HRW; 675 (c) Jim Pozarik/Liaison Agency; 676 (t) Photo courtesy of Apple Computer, Inc.; 676 (b) © 1997 Lucasfilm Ltd./Photofest; 677 © Ned Matura/Liaison Agency; 679 Draper Hill/© 1974 The Commercial Appeal, Memphis.
Chapter Twenty-Three: Page 680, Novosti/SIPA Press; 681 © Michael Evans/Sygma; 682 (t) Sygma; 682 (b) Wally McNamee/Woodfin Camp & Associates, Inc.; 683 (t) Corbis-Bettmann; 683 (b) Michael J. Okonlewski/Liaison Agency; 684 Charles

Steiner/Sygma; 685 © Bilyk/Liaison Agency; 686 Alex Quesada/Woodfin Camp & Associates, Inc.; 687 O. Franken/Sygma; 689 (r) AP/Wide World Photos; 689 (l) Corbis/Roger Ressmeyer; 690 (t) © Keler/Sygma; 690 (b) Sygma; 691 (l) Sovfoto; 691 (r) © 1984 Department of Defense from Black Star; 692 Rohan/Tony Stone Images; 693 (tl) © 1999 Rick Friedman/Black Star; 693 (b) Amy Etra/PhotoEdit; 693 (tr) Sam Dudgeon/HRW Photo; 694 (c) AP/Wide World Photos; 695 Corbis/Dave Bartruff; 696 (t) AP/Wide World Photos; 696 (b) Bill Gentile/SIPA Press; 698 Woodfin Camp & Associates, Inc.; 699 Photo Researchers, Inc.; 700 (b) ©1983 Time Inc./Sculpture by George Segal Computer by Richardson/Smith Design; 700 (t) AP/Wide World Photos/LOGITECH/Julie Stupsker; 701 (b) Scott Sutton Archive Photos; 701 (c) Reuters/Corbis-Bettmann; 702 (t) © Armando Gallo/Retna, Ltd.; 702 (b) Everett Collection; 703 UPI/Corbis-Bettmann; 705 Ben Sargent. **Chapter Twenty-Four:** Page 706, Corbis/Chris Daniels; 707 AP/Wide World Photos; 708 © Ira Wyman; 709 (bc) © Reinstein/The Image Works; 709 (br) ETTA HULME reprinted by permission of Newspaper Enterprise Association, Inc.; 709 (t) SuperStock; 710 © Ron Sachs/Archive Photos/PNI; 711 (t) © Brad Markel/Liaison Agency; 711 (chart all) Image Club Graphics ©1998 Adobe Systems Inc./HRW; 712 AP/Wide World Photos; 713 © Mangino/The Image Works; 714 (c) © J. Maier, Jr./The Image Works; 715 (b) Corbis/AFP; 715 (t) Corbis-Reuters/Bettmann; 716 (tc) Associated Press, Department of Defense/Wide World Photos; 716 (b) Photo © 3054/Liaison Agency; 716 (tl & tc) Associated Press, Department of Defense/Wide World Photos; 717 AP/Wide World Photos; 718 Dave Bartruff/Corbis; 719 © 1988 /Zigy Kaluzny/Liaison Agency; 720 (t) Mark J. Terrill/AP/Wide World Photos; 720 (b) Ross M. Horowitz/The Image Bank/PNI; 721 (c) Sam Dudgeon/HRW Photo; 722 Corbis/Kevin Fleming; 723 SuperStock; 724 (tc) AP/Wide World Photos; 724 (t) © A. Ramey/Woodfin Camp & Associates, Inc.; 726 (c) © Mark & Audrey Gibson/Stock Connection/PNI; 727 (tl & tr) Corbis/AFP; 727 (tr & br) © Christian Vioujard/Liaison Agency; 730 (tl, tr & bl) Image copyright © 2000 PhotoDisc, Inc./HRW; 730 (c) © 1996 Chuck Pefley c/o MIRA; 731 (l) Jim Sugar Photography/Corbis; 731 (c) © Bob Strauss/Woodfin Camp & Associates, Inc.; 731 (r) Vince Streano/Corbis; 732 (b) © Phil Schofield/AllStock/PNI; 732 (t) Michael Howell/Photonica; 733 (c) Bob Daemmrich/Uniphoto Picture Agency; 733 (t) Mark Godfrey/The Image Works; 733 (b) Image copyright © 2000 PhotoDisc, Inc./HRW; 734 HRW Photo by John Langford; 735 HRW Photo by Michelle Bridwell.

Reference Section: Pages 736–737, (bkgd) Maps Division, The New York Public Library, Astor, Lenox and Tilden Foundations; 736 (tl) Image copyright © 2000 PhotoDisc, Inc./HRW; (tc) Corbis-Bettmann; 736 (l) NASA; 736 (bl-sax) Image Club Graphics © 2000 Adobe Systems Inc./HRW; 736 (c-jukebox) Classic PIO Partners; 736 (c-trolly car) Photo courtesy of Illinois Railway Museum; 736 (br) Archive Photos; 737 (t) Image copyright © 2000 PhotoDisc, Inc./HRW; 737 (bl-blue magazine & c) The Granger Collection, New York; 737 (bl-red magazine) John Held Jr., LIFE Magazine, © TIME Inc./Courtesy of the general libraries, The University of Texas at Austin/HRW photo by Victoria Smith; 737 (bc-box) Barbara Puorro Galasso/Courtesy George Eastman House; 737 (bc-Nixon pin) Victoria Smith/HRW Photo; 737 (bc-LB. pin) Lyndon Baines Johnson Library Collection/Photo by Victoria Smith; 737 (r) Sandra Baker/Liaison Agency; 738–741 (all) White House Collection, copyright White House Historical Association; 742 (all except br) White House Collection, copyright White House Historical Association; 742 (br) The White House; 744-747 (border) Jay Mallin Photos.

Feature Borders (full page):

American Arts: Pages 218, 253, & 404, (tl-film, glasses, & lc-board) Classic PIO Partners; (bl-saxophone, tambourine, & blc) Image Club Graphics © 2000 Adobe Systems Inc./HRW; (brc) Sam Dudgeon/HRW Photo/Courtesy Andy Christiansen; (br-sugar) Sam Dudgeon/HRW Photo/Courtesy Tim Taylor; (br-rooster plate & peach plate) Sam Dudgeon/HRW Photo; (r) Image copyright © 2000 PhotoDisc, Inc./HRW; (bkgd-b) Sam Dudgeon/HRW Photo/Courtesy Candace Moore; (bkgd-t) Richard Haynes/HRW Photo.

American Literature: Pages 193, 298, 375, 451, & 530, (tl) Sam Dudgeon/HRW Photo/Courtesy Darren Peterson; (bl-dictionary, pen, br-pencils & r) Image copyright © 2000 PhotoDisc, Inc./HRW; (bl-glasses) Sam Dudgeon/HRW Photo/Courtesy Rosa C. Moreno; (br-paper) Sam Dudgeon/HRW Photo.

Linking Past to Present: Pages 395, 613, & 726, (tl) NASA; (bl) Sam Dudgeon/HRW Photo/Courtesy Jane Dixon; (br) Sam Dudgeon/HRW Photo; (cr-cell phone) Sam Dudgeon/HRW Photo/The Nokia phone is a registered trademark of Nokia Corporation and/or one of its affiliates.; (cr-telephone) Image copyright © 2000 PhotoDisc, Inc./HRW; (tr-diskman) Sam Dudgeon/HRW Photo; (tr-radio) HRW Photo Research Library.

Science and Technology: Pages 96, 186, 302, 331, 545, 590, & 721, (tl) NASA; (bl) FSA/OWI Collection, photo by Alfred Palmer, May 1942, Library of Congress/HRW Photo Research Library; (br) Image copyright © 2000 PhotoDisc, Inc./HRW; (crb) Los Angeles Times Syndicate, October 1930 Popular Science Issue/Courtesy of the general libraries, The University of Texas at Austin/Eric Beggs/HRW Photo; (crt) Los Angeles Times Syndicate, May 1940 Popular Science Issue/Courtesy of the general libraries, The University of Texas at Austin/Eric Beggs/HRW Photo; (cr) Image copyright © 2000 PhotoDisc, Inc./HRW; (border) The Heavens Map © 1998, National Geographic Maps/National Geographic Society Image Collection.

Young People in History: Pages 1, 119, 233, 321, 415, 505, 565, & 651, (tl, bl, tr, r-paddles/ball, & robot) Image copyright © 2000 PhotoDisc, Inc./HRW; (tlc & bc) Sam Dudgeon/HRW Photo; (br) Classic PIO Partners; (crb) Eyewire, Inc./Image Club Graphics © 2000 Adobe Systems Inc./HRW.

Feature Borders (3/4 Page):

American Arts: Pages 552, 585, 640, & 714, (tl-film, glasses, & lc-board) Classic PIO Partners; (bl-saxophone, tambourine, & blc) Image Club Graphics © 2000 Adobe Systems Inc./HRW; (brc) Sam Dudgeon/HRW Photo/Courtesy Andy Christiansen; (br-sugar) Sam Dudgeon/HRW Photo/Courtesy Tim Taylor; (br-rooster plate & peach plate) Sam Dudgeon/HRW Photo; (r) Image copyright © 2000 PhotoDisc, Inc./HRW; (bkgd-b) Sam Dudgeon/HRW Photo/Courtesy Candace Moore; (bkgd-t) Richard Haynes/HRW Photo.

American Literature: Pages 39, 146, 269, 427, & 701, (tl) Sam Dudgeon/HRW Photo/Courtesy Darren Peterson; (bl-dictionary, pen, br-pencils & r) Image copyright © 2000 PhotoDisc, Inc./HRW; (bl-glasses) Sam Dudgeon/HRW Photo/Courtesy Rosa C. Moreno; (br-paper) Sam Dudgeon/HRW Photo.

Global Connections: Pages 161, 357, & 488, (bl) Sam Dudgeon/HRW Photo/Courtesy Bob McClellan; (bcl, bc, & bcr) Sam Dudgeon/HRW Photo; (brb) Image copyright © 2000 PhotoDisc, Inc./HRW; (brt) Image copyright © 2000 PhotoDisc, Inc./HRW; (cr-stamps) Sam Dudgeon/HRW Photo; (cr-letters) Sam Dudgeon/HRW Photo/Courtesy Charlotte Luongo; (tr) Sam Dudgeon/HRW Photo/Courtesy Elinor Strot/City of Sails Postcards; (tl) © Kenneth Jarecke/Contact Press Images/PNI; (cl) Courtesy Jie Sun; (border) National Geographic Society Image Collection/National Geographic Maps.

Linking Past to Present: Pages 127, 280, 346, 516, & 668, (tl) NASA; (bl) Sam Dudgeon/HRW Photo/Courtesy Jane Dixon; (br & tr-diskman) Sam Dudgeon/HRW Photo; (cr-cell phone) Sam Dudgeon/HRW Photo/The Nokia phone is a registered trademark of Nokia Corporation and/or one of its affiliates.; (cr-telephone) Image copyright © 2000 PhotoDisc, Inc./HRW; (tr-radio) HRW Photo Research Library.

Science and Technology: Page 497, (tl) NASA; (bl) FSA/OWI Collection, photo by Alfred Palmer, May 1942, Library of Congress/HRW Photo Research Library; (br) Image copyright © 2000 PhotoDisc, Inc./HRW; (crb) Los Angeles Times Syndicate, October 1930 Popular Science Issue/Courtesy of the general libraries, The University of Texas at Austin/Eric Beggs/HRW Photo; (crt) Los Angeles Times Syndicate, May 1940 Popular Science Issue/Courtesy of the general libraries, The University of Texas at Austin/Eric Beggs/HRW Photo; (cr) Image copyright © 2000 PhotoDisc, Inc./HRW; (border) The Heavens Map ©1998, National Geographic Maps/National Geographic Society Image Collection.

Feature Borders (1/2 page):

American Arts: Pages 90, 341, 482, & 674, (tl-film, glasses, & lc-board) Classic PIO Partners; (bl-saxophone, tambourine, & blc) Image Club Graphics © 2000 Adobe Systems Inc./HRW; (brc) Sam Dudgeon/HRW Photo/Courtesy Andy Christiansen; (br) Sam Dudgeon/HRW Photo/Courtesy Tim Taylor; (br-rooster plate & peach plate) Sam Dudgeon/HRW Photo; (r) Image copyright © 2000 PhotoDisc, Inc./HRW; (bkgd-b) Sam Dudgeon/HRW Photo/Courtesy Candace Moore; (bkgd-t) Richard Haynes/HRW Photo.

American Literature: Pages 17, 155, & 607, (tl) Sam Dudgeon/HRW Photo/Courtesy Darren Peterson; (bl-dictionary, pen, r & br-pencils) Image copyright © 2000 PhotoDisc, Inc./HRW; (bl-glasses) Sam Dudgeon/HRW Photo/Courtesy Rosa C. Moreno; (br-paper) Sam Dudgeon/HRW Photo.

Global Connections: Pages 212, 250, 290, 465, 542, & 694, (bl) Sam Dudgeon/HRW Photo/Courtesy Bob McClellan; (bc, bcl, bcr, cr-stamps) Sam Dudgeon/HRW Photo; (brt, brb) Image copyright © 2000 PhotoDisc, Inc./HRW; (tr) Sam Dudgeon/HRW Photo/Courtesy Elinor Strot/City of Sails Postcards; (tl) © Kenneth Jarecke/Contact Press Images/PNI; (cl) Courtesy Jie Sun; (border) National Geographic Society Image Collection/National Geographic Maps.

Linking Past to Present: Pages 67, 104, .204, 346, 439, .574, & 629, (tl) NASA; (bl) Sam Dudgeon/HRW Photo/Courtesy Jane Dixon; (br & tr-diskman) Sam Dudgeon/HRW Photo; (tr-radio) HRW Photo Research Library.

Art

All art, unless otherwise noted, by Holt, Rinehart & Winston

Chapter 1: Page 7, MapQuest.com, Inc.; 11, MapQuest.com, Inc.; 23, MapQuest.com, Inc.; 25, Karen Minot; 32, Leslie Kell; 35, MapQuest.com, Inc. **Unit 1:** Page 78, MapQuest.com, Inc.; 79, MapQuest.com, Inc.; 80, Karen Minot. **Chapter 3:** Page 89, MapQuest.com, Inc.; 96, Nenad Jakesevic; 97, Dave Merrill/Steven Edsey & Sons; 103, MapQuest.com, Inc.; 107, Leslie Kell; 109, MapQuest.com, Inc.; 115, MapQuest.com, Inc.; 116, MapQuest.com, Inc. **Unit 2:** Page 178, MapQuest.com, Inc.; 179, Dave Merrill; 180, MapQuest.com, Inc.; 181, MapQuest.com, Inc. **Chapter 6:** Page 190, Uhl Studio Incorporated; 198, MapQuest.com, Inc.; 202, MapQuest.com, Inc. **Chapter 7:** Page 210, Dave Merrill/Steven Edsey & Sons; 216, MapQuest.com, Inc.; 229, Charles Apple; 230, Charles Apple. **Chapter 8:** Page 242, MapQuest.com, Inc.; 248, Saul Rosenbaum/Deborah Wolfe Ltd.; 251, Charles Apple; 255, MapQuest.com, Inc.; 257, MapQuest.com, Inc. **Chapter 9:** Page 270, MapQuest.com, Inc.; 277, MapQuest.com, Inc.; 282, Leslie Kell. **Chapter 10:** Page 292, MapQuest.com, Inc.; 295, Charles Apple; 297, MapQuest.com, Inc.; 303, Nenad Jakesevic; 305, MapQuest.com, Inc.; 310, Charles Apple. **Unit 3:** Page 315, MapQuest.com, Inc.; (tl), (tl), (t); 316, MapQuest.com, Inc. **Chapter 12:** Page 371, Charles Apple; 377, Charles Apple. **Chapter 13:** Page 384, MapQuest.com, Inc.; 401, MapQuest.com, Inc. **Unit 4:** Page 408, Ken Mowrey; 409, MapQuest.com, Inc.; 410, Ken Mowrey; 411, MapQuest.com, Inc. **Chapter 14:** Page 426, Charles Apple; 436, MapQuest.com, Inc.; 441, Leslie Kell. **Chapter 15:** Page, 450, MapQuest.com, Inc.; 466, MapQuest.com, Inc. **Unit 5:** Page 470, Charles Apple; 471, MapQuest.com, Inc. ; 473, Charles Apple. **Chapter 17:** Page 515, MapQuest.com, Inc.; 520, MapQuest.com, Inc.; 524, MapQuest.com, Inc. **Unit 6:** Page 534, MapQuest.com, Inc.; 535, MapQuest.com, Inc.; 536, Charles Apple; 537, MapQuest.com, Inc. **Chapter 18:** Page 541, MapQuest.com, Inc.; 544, Nenad Jakesevic; 547, MapQuest.com, Inc.; 549, Charles Apple; 561, MapQuest.com, Inc. **Chapter 19:** Page 570, MapQuest.com, Inc.; 576, MapQuest.com, Inc.; 590, Craig Attebery/Jeff Lavaty Artist Agent. **Chapter 20:** Page 597, MapQuest.com, Inc.; 614, Charles Apple; 621, MapQuest.com, Inc. **Chapter 21:** Page 624, MapQuest.com, Inc.; 628, MapQuest.com, Inc.; 633, Dave Merrill/Steven Edsey & Sons; 639, Charles Apple. **Unit 7:** Page 644, MapQuest.com, Inc.; 645, Nenad Jakesevic; 647, Charles Apple. **Chapter 22:** Page 657, MapQuest.com, Inc.; 662, Leslie Kell; 672, MapQuest.com, Inc. **Chapter 23:** Page 684, Charles Apple; 688, MapQuest.com, Inc.; 695, MapQuest.com, Inc. **Chapter 24:** Page 711, Saul Rosenbaum; 725, Charles Apple. **Unit 8:** Page 730, Charles Apple; 731, Charles Apple; 732, MapQuest.com, Inc.; 733, Charles Apple.